ISBN 978-0-282-92455-3
PIBN 10873445

1 MONTH OF
FREE
READING

at
www.ForgottenBooks.com

By purchasing this book you are eligible for one month membership to ForgottenBooks.com, giving you unlimited access to our entire collection of over 1,000,000 titles via our web site and mobile apps.

To claim your free month visit:
www.forgottenbooks.com/free873445

DR. WILLIAM SMITH'S

DICTIONARY OF THE BIBLE;

COMPRISING ITS

ANTIQUITIES, BIOGRAPHY, GEOGRAPHY, AND NATURAL HISTORY.

REVISED AND EDITED BY

PROFESSOR H. B. HACKETT, D. D.

WITH THE COÖPERATION OF

EZRA ABBOT, LL. D.

ASSISTANT LIBRARIAN OF HARVARD COLLEGE.

VOLUME III.

MARRIAGE to REGEM.

Jerusalem.

NEW YORK:
PUBLISHED BY HURD AND HOUGHTON.

Cambridge: Riverside Press

1873.

RIVERSIDE, CAMBRIDGE:
STEREOTYPED AND PRINTED BY
H. O. HOUGHTON AND COMPANY.

WRITERS IN THE ENGLISH EDITION.

INITIALS.	NAMES.
H. A.	Very Rev. HENRY ALFORD, D. D., Dean of Canterbury.
H. B.	Rev. HENRY BAILEY, B. D., Warden of St. Augustine's College, Canterbury; late Fellow of St. John's College, Cambridge.
H. B.	Rev. HORATIUS BONAR, D. D., Kelso, N. B.; Author of "The Land of Promise." [The geographical articles, signed H. B., are written by Dr. Bonar: those on other subjects, signed H. B., are written by Mr. Bailey.]
A. B.	Rev. ALFRED BARRY, B. D., Principal of Cheltenham College; late Fellow of Trinity College, Cambridge.
W. L. B.	Rev. WILLIAM LATHAM BEVAN, M. A., Vicar of Hay, Brecknockshire.
J. W. B.	Rev. JOSEPH WILLIAMS BLAKESLEY, B. D., Canon of Canterbury; late Fellow and Tutor of Trinity College, Cambridge.
T. E. B.	Rev. THOMAS EDWARD BROWN, M. A., Vice-Principal of King William's College, Isle of Man; late Fellow of Oriel College, Oxford.
R. W. B.	Ven. ROBERT WILLIAM BROWNE, M. A., Archdeacon of Bath, and Canon of Wells.
E. H. B.	Right Rev. EDWARD HAROLD BROWNE, D. D., Lord Bishop of Ely.
W. T. B.	Rev. WILLIAM THOMAS BULLOCK, M. A., Assistant Secretary of the Society for the Propagation of the Gospel in Foreign Parts.
S. C.	Rev. SAMUEL CLARK, M. A., Vicar of Bredwardine with Brobury, Herefordshire.
F. C. C.	Rev. FREDERIC CHARLES COOK, M. A., Chaplain in Ordinary to the Queen.
G. E. L. C.	Right Rev. GEORGE EDWARD LYNCH COTTON, D. D., late Lord Bishop of Calcutta and Metropolitan of India.
J. Ll. D.	Rev. JOHN LLEWELYN DAVIES, M. A., Rector of Christ Church, Marylebone; late Fellow of Trinity College, Cambridge.
G. E. D.	Prof. GEORGE EDWARD DAY, D. D., Yale College, New Haven, Conn.
E. D.	EMANUEL DEUTSCH, M. R. A. S., British Museum.
W. D.	Rev. WILLIAM DRAKE, M. A., Chaplain in Ordinary to the Queen.
E. P. E.	Rev. EDWARD PAROISSIEN EDDRUP, M. A., Principal of the Theological College, Salisbury.
C. J. E.	Right Rev. CHARLES JOHN ELLICOTT, D. D., Lord Bishop of Gloucester and Bristol.
F. W. F.	Rev. FREDERICK WILLIAM FARRAR, M. A., Assistant Master of Harrow School; late Fellow of Trinity College, Cambridge.
J. F.	JAMES FERGUSSON, F. R. S., F. R. A. S., Fellow of the Royal Institute of British Architects.
E. S. Ff.	EDWARD SALUSBURY FFOULKES, M. A., late Fellow of Jesus College, Oxford.
W. F.	Right Rev. WILLIAM FITZGERALD, D. D., Lord Bishop of Killaloe

(iii)

| INITIALS. | NAMES. |

F. G.   Rev. Francis Garden, M. A., Subdean of Her Majesty's Chapels Royal.

F. W. G.   Rev. F. William Gotch, LL. D., President of the Baptist College, Bristol; late Hebrew Examiner in the University of London.

G.   George Grove, Crystal Palace, Sydenham.

H. B. H.   Prof. Horatio Balch Hackett, D. D., LL. D., Theological Institution, Newton, Mass.

E. H—s.   Rev. Ernest Hawkins, B. D., Secretary of the Society for the Propagation of the Gospel in Foreign Parts.

H. H.   Rev. Henry Hayman, B. D., Head Master of the Grammar School, Cheltenham; late Fellow of St. John's College, Oxford.

A. C. H.   Ven. Lord Arthur Charles Hervey, M. A., Archdeacon of Sudbury, and Rector of Ickworth.

J. A. H.   Rev. James Augustus Hessey, D. C. L., Head Master of Merchant Taylors' School.

J. D. H.   Joseph Dalton Hooker, M. D., F. R. S., Royal Botanic Gardens, Kew.

J. J. H.   Rev. James John Hornby, M. A., Fellow of Brasenose College, Oxford; Principal of Bishop Cosin's Hall.

W. H.   Rev. William Houghton, M. A., F. L. S., Rector of Preston on the Weald Moors, Salop.

J. S. H.   Rev. John Saul Howson, D. D., Principal of the Collegiate Institution, Liverpool.

E. H.   Rev. Edgar Huxtable, M. A., Subdean of Wells.

W. B. J.   Rev. William Basil Jones, M. A., Prebendary of York and of St. David's; late Fellow and Tutor of University College, Oxford.

A. H. L.   Austen Henry Layard, D. C. L., M. P.

S. L.   Rev. Stanley Leathes, M. A., M. R. S. L., Hebrew Lecturer in King's College, London.

J. B. L.   Rev. Joseph Barber Lightfoot, D. D., Hulsean Professor of Divinity, and Fellow of Trinity College, Cambridge.

D. W. M.   Rev. D. W. Marks, Professor of Hebrew in University College, London.

F. M.   Rev. Frederick Meyrick, M. A., late Fellow and Tutor of Trinity College, Oxford.

Oppert.   Prof. Jules Oppert, of Paris.

E. R. O.   Rev. Edward Redman Orger, M. A., Fellow and Tutor of St. Augustine's College, Canterbury.

T. J. O.   Ven. Thomas Johnson Ormerod, M. A., Archdeacon of Suffolk; late Fellow of Brasenose College, Oxford.

J. J. S. P   Rev. John James Stewart Perowne, B. D., Vice-Principal of St. David's College, Lampeter.

T. T. P.   Rev. Thomas Thomason Perowne, B. D., Fellow and Tutor of Corpus Christi College, Cambridge.

H. W. P.   Rev. Henry Wright Phillott, M. A., Rector of Staunton-on-Wye, Herefordshire; late Student of Christ Church, Oxford.

E. H. P.   Rev. Edward Hayes Plumptre, M. A., Professor of Divinity in King's College, London.

E. S. P.   Edward Stanley Poole, M. R. A. S., South Kensington Museum.

R. S. P.   Reginald Stuart Poole, British Museum.

J. L. P.   Rev. J. Leslie Porter, M. A., Professor of Sacred Literature, Assem-

LIST OF WRITERS.

INITIALS.	NAMES.
	bly's College, Belfast; Author of "Handbook of Syria and Palestine," and "Five Years in Damascus."
C. P.	Rev. CHARLES PRITCHARD, M. A., F. R. S., Hon. Secretary of the Royal Astronomical Society; late Fellow of St. John's College, Cambridge.
G. R.	Rev. GEORGE RAWLINSON, M. A., Camden Professor of Ancient History, Oxford.
H. J. R.	Rev. HENRY JOHN ROSE, B. D., Rural Dean, and Rector of Houghton Conquest, Bedfordshire.
W. S.	Rev. WILLIAM SELWYN, D. D., Chaplain in Ordinary to the Queen; Lady Margaret's Professor of Divinity, Cambridge; Canon of Ely.
A. P. S.	Rev. ARTHUR PENRHYN STANLEY, D. D., Regius Professor of Ecclesiastical History, and Canon of Christ Church, Oxford; Chaplain to His Royal Highness the Prince of Wales.
C. E. S.	Prof. CALVIN ELLIS STOWE, D. D., Hartford, Conn.
J. P. T.	Rev. JOSEPH PARRISH THOMPSON, D. D., New York.
W. T.	Most Rev. WILLIAM THOMSON, D. D., Lord Archbishop of York.
S. P. T.	SAMUEL PRIDEAUX TREGELLES, LL. D., Author of "An Introduction to the Textual Criticism of the New Testament," &c.
H. B. T.	Rev. HENRY BAKER TRISTRAM, M. A., F. L. S., Master of Greatham Hospital.
J. F. T.	Rev. JOSEPH FRANCIS THRUPP, M. A., Vicar of Barrington; late Fellow of Trinity College, Cambridge.
E. T.	Hon. EDWARD T. B. TWISLETON, M. A., late Fellow of Balliol College, Oxford.
E. V.	Rev. EDMUND VENABLES, M. A., Bonchurch, Isle of Wight.
B. F. W.	Rev. BROOKE FOSS WESTCOTT, M. A., Assistant Master of Harrow School; late Fellow of Trinity College, Cambridge.
C. W.	Rev. CHRISTOPHER WORDSWORTH, D. D., Canon of Westminster.
W. A. W.	WILLIAM ALDIS WRIGHT, M. A., Librarian of Trinity College, Cambridge.

WRITERS IN THE AMERICAN EDITION.

A.	EZRA ABBOT, LL. D., Assistant Librarian of Harvard College, Cambridge, Mass.
S. C. B.	Prof. SAMUEL COLCORD BARTLETT, D. D., Theol. Sem., Chicago, Ill.
T. J. C.	Rev. THOMAS JEFFERSON CONANT, D. D., Brooklyn, N. Y.
G. E. D.	Prof. GEORGE EDWARD DAY, D. D., Yale College, New Haven, Conn.
G. P. F.	Prof. GEORGE PARK FISHER, D. D., Yale College, New Haven, Conn.
F. G.	Prof. FREDERIC GARDINER, D. D., Middletown, Conn.
D. R. G.	Rev. DANIEL RAYNES GOODWIN, D. D., Provost of the University of Pennsylvania, Philadelphia.
H.	Prof. HORATIO BALCH HACKETT, D. D., LL. D., Theological Institution, Newton, Mass.
J. H.	Prof. JAMES HADLEY, LL. D., Yale College, New Haven, Conn.
F. W. H.	Rev. FREDERICK WHITMORE HOLLAND, F. R. G. S., London.
A. H.	Prof. ALVAH HOVEY, D. D., Theological Institution, Newton, Mass.

LIST OF WRITERS.

INITIALS.	NAMES.
A. C. K.	Prof. ASAHEL CLARK KENDRICK, D. D., University of Rochester, N. Y.
C. M. M.	Prof. CHARLES MARSH MEAD, Ph. D., Theol. Sem., Andover, Mass.
E. A. P.	Prof. EDWARDS AMASA PARK, D. D., Theol. Seminary, Andover, Mass.
W. E. P.	Rev. WILLIAM EDWARDS PARK, Lawrence, Mass.
A. P. P.	Prof. ANDREW PRESTON PEABODY, D. D., LL. D., Harvard College, Cambridge, Mass.
G. E. P.	Rev. GEORGE E. POST, M. D., Tripoli, Syria.
R. D. C. R.	Prof. RENSSELAER DAVID CHANCEFORD ROBBINS, Middlebury College, Vt.
P. S.	Rev. PHILIP SCHAFF, D. D., New York.
H. B. S.	Prof. HENRY BOYNTON SMITH, D. D., LL. D., Union Theological Seminary, New York.
C. E. S.	Rev. CALVIN ELLIS STOWE, D. D., Hartford, Conn.
D. S. T.	Prof. DANIEL SMITH TALCOTT, D. D., Theol. Seminary, Bangor, Me.
J. H. T.	Prof. JOSEPH HENRY THAYER, M. A., Theol. Seminary, Andover, Mass.
J. P. T.	Rev. JOSEPH PARRISH THOMPSON, D. D., New York.
C. V. A. V.	Rev. CORNELIUS V. A. VAN DYCK, D. D., Beirût, Syria.
W. H. W.	Rev. WILLIAM HAYES WARD, M. A., New York.
W. F. W.	Prof. WILLIAM FAIRFIELD WARREN, D. D., Boston Theological Seminary, Boston, Mass.
S. W.	Rev. SAMUEL WOLCOTT, D. D., Cleveland, Ohio.
T. D. W.	President THEODORE DWIGHT WOOLSEY, D. D., LL. D., Yale College, New Haven, Conn.

*** The new portions in the present edition are indicated by a *star* (*), the editorial additions being distinguished by the initials H. and A. Whatever is enclosed in *brackets* is also, with unimportant exceptions, editorial. This remark, however, does not apply to the *cross-references* in brackets, most of which belong to the original work, though a large number have been added to this edition.

ABBREVIATIONS.

Ald.	The Aldine edition of the Septuagint, 1518.
Alex.	The Codex Alexandrinus (5th cent.), edited by Baber, 1816–28.
A. V.	The authorized (common) English version of the Bible.
Comp.	The Septuagint as printed in the Complutensian Polyglott, 1514–17, published 1522.
FA.	The Codex Friderico-Augustanus (4th cent.), published by Tischendorf in 1846.
Rom.	The Roman edition of the Septuagint, 1587. The readings of the Septuagint for which no authority is specified are also from this source.
Sin.	The Codex Sinaiticus (4th cent.), published by Tischendorf in 1862. This and FA. are parts of the same manuscript.
Vat.	The Codex Vaticanus 1209 (4th cent.), according to Mai's edition, published by Vercellone in 1857. "Vat. H." denotes readings of the MS. (differing from Mai), given in Holmes and Parsons's edition of the Septuagint, 1798–1827. "Vat.¹" distinguishes the primary reading of the MS. from "Vat.²" or "2. m.," the alteration of a later reviser.

DICTIONARY

OF

BIBLICAL ANTIQUITIES, BIOGRAPHY, GEOGRAPHY, AND NATURAL HISTORY.

MARRIAGE. The topics which this subject presents to our consideration in connection with Biblical literature may be most conveniently arranged under the following five heads: —

I. Its origin and history.
II. The conditions under which it could be legally effected.
III. The modes by which it was effected.
IV. The social and domestic relations of married life.
V. The typical and allegorical references to marriage.

I. The institution of marriage is founded on the requirements of man's nature, and dates from the time of his original creation. It may be said to have been ordained by God, in as far as man's nature was ordained by Him; but its formal appointment was the work of man, and it has ever been in its essence a natural and civil institution, though admitting of the infusion of a religious element into it. This view of marriage is exhibited in the historical account of its origin in the of Genesis: the peculiar formation of man's ... is assigned to the Creator, who, seeing it ... good for man to be alone," determined to form an "help meet for him" (ii. 18), and accordingly completed the work by the addition of the female to the male (i. 27). The necessity for this step appears from the words used in the declaration of the Divine counsel. Man, as an intellectual and spiritual being, would not have been a worthy representative of the Deity on earth, so long as he lived in solitude, or in communion only with beings either high above him in the scale of creation, as angels, or far beneath him, as the beasts of the field. It was absolutely necessary, not only for his comfort and happiness, but still more for the per-

fection of the Divine work, that he should have a "help *meet* for him," [a] or, as the words more properly mean, "the exact counterpart of himself" — a being capable of receiving and reflecting his thoughts and affections. No sooner was the formation of woman effected, than Adam recognized in that act the will of the Creator as to man's social condition, and immediately enunciated the important statement, to which his posterity might refer as the charter of marriage in all succeeding ages, "Therefore shall a man leave his father and his mother, and shall cleave unto his wife: and they shall be one flesh" (ii. 24). From these words, coupled with the circumstances attendant on the formation of the first woman, we may evolve the following principles: (1) The unity of man and wife, as implied in her being formed out of man, and as expressed in the words "one flesh;" (2) the indissolubleness of the marriage bond, except on the strongest grounds (comp. Matt. xix. 9); (3) monogamy, as the original law of marriage, resulting from there having been but one original couple,[b] as is forcibly expressed in the subsequent references to this passage by our Lord ("they *twain*," Matt. xix. 5), and St. Paul ("*two* shall be one flesh," 1 Cor. vi. 16); (4) the social equality of man and wife, as implied in the terms *ish* and *ish-shah*,[c] the one being the exact correlative of the other, as well as in the words "help meet for him;" (5) the subordination of the wife to the husband, consequent upon her subsequent formation (1 Cor. xi. 8, 9; 1 Tim. ii. 13); and (6) the respective duties of man and wife, as implied in the words "help meet for him."

The introduction of sin into the world modified to a certain extent the mutual relations of man and wife. As the blame of seduction to sin lay on the latter, the condition of subordination was turned

---

[a] כְּנֶגְדּוֹ, literally, "as over against," and so "corresponding to." The renderings, in the A. V. "meet for him," in the LXX. κατ' αὐτόν, ὅμοιος αὐτῷ, and in the Vulg. *simile sibi*, are inadequate.

[b] The LXX. introduces δύο into the text in Gen. ii. 24, and is followed by the Vulgate.

[c] אִישׁ and אִשָּׁה. We are unable to express the verbal correspondence of these words in our language. The Vulgate retains the etymological identity at the expense of the sense: "*Virago quoniam de viro.*" The

old Latin term *vira* would have been better. Luther is more successful with *mann* and *männin*; but even this fails to convey the double sense of *ishshah* as — "woman" and "wife," both of which should be preserved, as in the German *weib*, in order to convey the full force of the original. We may here observe that *ishshah* was the only term in ordinary use among the Hebrews for "wife." They occasionally used גְּבֶרֶת, as we use "consort," for the wives of kings (Ps. xiv 9; Neh. ii. 6; Dan. v. 2).

into subjection, and it was said to her of her husband, " he shall rule over thee " (Gen. iii. 16.) — a sentence which, regarded as a prediction, has been strikingly fulfilled in the position assigned to women in Oriental countries,[a] but which, regarded as a rule of life, is fully sustained by the voice of nature and by the teaching of Christianity (1 Cor. xiv. 34; Eph. v. 22, 23; 1 Tim. ii. 12). The evil effects of the fall were soon apparent in the corrupt usages of marriage; the unity of the bond was impaired by polygamy, which appears to have originated among the Cainites (Gen. iv. 19); and its purity was deteriorated by the promiscuous intermarriage of the "sons of God " with the "daughters of men," i. e. of the Sethites with the Cainites, in the days preceding the flood (Gen. vi. 2).

In the post-diluvial age the usages of marriage were marked with the simplicity that characterizes a patriarchal state of society. The rule of monogamy was reëstablished by the example of Noah and his sons (Gen. vii. 13). The early patriarchs selected their wives from their own family (Gen. xi. 29, xxiv. 4, xxviii. 2), and the necessity for doing this on religious grounds superseded the prohibitions that afterwards held good against such marriages on the score of kindred (Gen. xx. 12; Ex. vi. 20; comp. Lev. xviii. 9, 12). Polygamy prevailed (Gen. xvi. 4, xxv. 1, 6, xxviii. 9, xxix. 23, 28; 1 Chr. vii. 14), but to a great extent divested of the degradation which in modern times attaches to that practice. In judging of it we must take into regard the following considerations: (1) that the principle of monogamy was retained, even in the practice of polygamy, by the distinction made between the chief or original wife and the secondary wives, or, as the A. V. terms them, "concubines " — a term which is objectionable, inasmuch as it conveys to us the notion of an illicit and unrecognized position, whereas the secondary wife was regarded by the Hebrews as a wife, and her rights were secured by law;[b] (2) that the motive which led to polygamy was that absorbing desire of progeny which is prevalent throughout eastern countries, and was especially powerful among the Hebrews; and (3) that the power of a parent over his child, and of a master over his slave (the potestas patria and dominica of the Romans), was paramount even in matters of marriage, and led in many cases to phases of polygamy that are otherwise quite unintelligible, as, for instance, to the cases where it was adopted by the husband at the request of his wife, under the idea that children born to a slave were in the eye of the law the

children of the mistress[c] (Gen. xvi. 3, xxx. 4, 9); or, again, to cases where it was adopted at the instance of the father (Gen. xxix. 23, 28; Ex. xxi. 9, 10). It must be allowed that polygamy, thus legalized and systematized, justified to a certain extent by the motive, and entered into, not only without offense to, but actually at the suggestion of, those who, according to our notions, would feel most deeply injured by it, is a very different thing from what polygamy would be in our own state of society.

Divorce also prevailed in the patriarchal age, though but one instance of it is recorded (Gen. xxi. 14). Of this, again, we must not judge by our own standard. Wherever marriages are effected by the violent exercise of the patria potestas, or without any bond of affection between the parties concerned, ill-assorted matches must be of frequent occurrence, and without the remedy of divorce, in such a state of society, we can understand the truth of the Apostles' remark, that "it is not good to marry " (Matt. xix. 10). Hence divorce prevails to a great extent in all countries where marriage is the result of arbitrary appointment or of purchase: we may instance the Arabians (Burckhardt's Notes, i. 111; Layard's Nineveh, i. 357) and the Egyptians (Lane, i. 235 ff.). From the enactments of the Mosaic law we may infer that divorce was effected by a mere verbal declaration, as it still is in the countries referred to, and great injustice was thus committed towards the wives.

The Mosaic law aimed at mitigating rather than removing evils which were inseparable from the state of society in that day. Its enactments were directed (1) to the discouragement of polygamy; (2) to obviate the injustice frequently consequent upon the exercise of the rights of a father or a master; (3) to bring divorce under some restriction; and (4) to enforce purity of life during the maintenance of the matrimonial bond. The first of these objects was forwarded by the following enactments: the prohibition imposed upon kings against multiplying[d] wives (Deut. xvii. 17); the prohibition against marrying two sisters together (Lev. xviii. 18); the assertion of the matrimonial rights of each wife (Ex. xxi. 10, 11); the slur cast upon the eunuch state, which has been ever regarded as indispensable to a system of polygamy (Deut. xxiii. 1); and the ritual observances entailed on a man by the duty of marriage (Lev. xv. 18). The second object was attained by the humane regulations relative to a captive whom a man might wish to marry (Deut. xxi. 10–14), to a purchased wife[e]

---

[a] The relation of the husband to the wife is expressed in the Hebrew term baal (בָּעַל), literally lord, for husband (Ex. xxi. 3, 22; Deut. xxi. 13; 2 Sam. xi. 26, etc., etc). The respectful term used by Sarah to Abraham (אֲדֹנִי, "my lord," Gen. xviii. 12; comp. 1 K. i. 17, 18, Ps. xlv. 11) furnishes St. Peter with an illustration of the wife's proper position (1 Pet. iii. 6).

[b] The position of the Hebrew concubine may be compared with that of the concubine of the early Christian Church, the sole distinction between her and the wife consisting in this, that the marriage was not in accordance with the civil law: in the eye of the Church the marriage was perfectly valid (Bingham, Ant. xi. 5, § 11). It is worthy of notice that the term pillegesh פִּלֶגֶשׁ ; A. V. "concubine ") nowhere occurs in the Mosaic law. The terms used are either "wife" (Deut.

xxi. 15) or "maid-servant" (Ex. xxi. 7); the latter applying to a purchased wife.

[c] The language in 1 Chr. ii. 18, " these are her sons," following on the mention of his two wives, admits of an interpretation on this ground.

[d] The Talmudists practically set aside this prohibition, (1) by explaining the word "multiply" of an inordinate number; and (2) by treating the motive for it, "that his heart turn not away," as a matter of discretion. They considered eighteen the maximum to be allowed a king (Selden, Ux. Ebr. i. 8). It is noteworthy that the high-priest himself authorizes bigamy in the case of king Joash (2 Chr. xxiv. 3).

[e] The regulations in Ex. xxi. 7–11 deserve a detailed notice, as exhibiting the extent to which the power of the head of a family might be carried. It must be premised that the maiden was born of Hebrew parents, was under age at the time of her sale (otherwise her father would have no power to sell), and that the

(Ex. xxi. 7–11), and to a slave who either was married at the time of their purchase, or who, having since received a wife [a] at the hands of his master, was unwilling to be parted from her (Ex. xxi. 2–6), and, lastly, by the law relating to the legal distribution of property among the children of the different wives (Deut. xxi. 15–17). The third object was effected by rendering divorce a formal proceeding, not to be done by word of mouth as heretofore, but by a "bill of divorcement" (Deut. xxiv. 1), which would generally demand time and the intervention of a third party, thus rendering divorce a less easy process, and furnishing the wife, in the event of its being carried out, with a legal evidence of her marriageability: we may also notice that Moses wholly prohibited divorce in case the wife had been seduced prior to marriage (Deut. xxii. 29), or her chastity had been groundlessly impugned (Deut. xxii. 19). The fourth object forms the subject of one of the ten commandments (Ex. xx. 14), any violation of which was punishable with death (Lev. xx. 10; Deut. xxii. 22), even in the case of a betrothed person (Deut. xxii. 23, 24).

The practical results of these regulations may have been very salutary, but on this point we have but small opportunities of judging. The usages themselves, to which we have referred, remained in full force to a late period. We have instances of the arbitrary exercise of the paternal authority in the cases of Achsah (Judg. i. 12), Ibzan (Judg. xii. 9), Samson (Judg. xiv. 20, xv. 2), and Michal (1 Sam. xvii. 25). The case of Abishag, and the language of Adonijah in reference to her (1 K. i. 2, ii. 17), prove that a servant was still completely at the disposal of his or her master. Polygamy also prevailed, as we are expressly informed in reference to Gideon (Judg. viii. 30), Elkanah (1 Sam. i. 2), Saul (2 Sam. xii. 8), David (2 Sam. v. 13), Solomon (1 K. xi. 3), the sons of Issachar (1 Chr. vii. 4), Shaharaim (1 Chr. viii. 8, 9), Rehoboam (2 Chr. xi. 21), Abijah (2 Chr. xiii. 21), and Joash (2 Chr. xxiv. 3); and as we may also infer from the number of children in the cases of Jair, Ibzan, and Abdon (Judg. x. 4, xii. 9, 14). It does not, however, follow that it was the general practice of the country: the inconveniences attendant on polygamy in small houses or with scanty incomes are

so great as to put a serious bar to its general adoption,[b] and hence in modern countries where it is fully established the practice is restricted to comparatively few (Niebuhr, Voyage, p. 65; Lane, i. 239). The same rule holds good with regard to ancient times: the discomforts of polygamy are exhibited in the jealousies between the wives of Abraham (Gen. xvi. 6), and of Elkanah (1 Sam. i. 6); and the cases cited above rather lead to the inference that it was confined to the wealthy. Meanwhile it may be noted that the theory of monogamy was retained and comes prominently forward in the pictures of domestic bliss portrayed in the poetical writings of this period (Ps. cxxviii. 3; Prov. v. 18, xviii. 22, xix. 14, xxxi. 10–29; Eccl. ix. 9). The sanctity of the marriage-bond was but too frequently violated, as appears from the frequent allusions to the "strange woman" in the book of Proverbs (ii. 16, v. 20, &c.), and in the denunciations of the prophets against the prevalence of adultery (Jer. v. 8; Ez. xviii. 11, xxii 11).

In the post-Babylonian period monogamy appears to have become more prevalent than at any previous time: indeed we have no instance of polygamy during this period on record in the Bible, all the marriages noticed being with single wives (Tob. i. 9, ii. 11; Susan. vv. 29, 63; Matt. xviii. 25; Luke i. 5; Acts v. 1). During the same period the theory of monogamy is set forth in Ecclus. xxvi. 1–27. The practice of polygamy nevertheless still existed; [c] Herod the Great had no less than nine wives at one time (Joseph. Ant. xvii. 1, § 3); the Talmudists frequently assume it as a well-known fact (e. g. Ketub. 10, § 1; Yebam. 1, § 1); and the early Christian writers, in their comments on 1 Tim. iii. 2, explain it of polygamy in terms which leave no doubt as to the fact of its prevalence in the Apostolic age. The abuse of divorce continued unabated (Joseph. Vit. § 76); and under the Asmonæan dynasty the right was assumed by the wife as against her husband, an innovation which is attributed to Salome by Josephus (Ant. xv. 7, § 10); but which appears to have been prevalent in the Apostolic age, if we may judge from passages where the language implies that the act emanated from the wife (Mark x. 12; 1 Cor. vii. 11), as well as

---

object of the purchase was that when arrived at puberty she should become the wife of her master, as is implied in the difference in the law relating to her (Ex. xxi. 7), and to a slave purchased for ordinary work (Deut. xv. 12–17), as well as in the term *âmâh*, "maid-servant," which is elsewhere used convertibly with "concubine" (Judg. ix. 18; comp. viii. 31). With regard to such it is enacted (1) that she is not to "go out as the men-servants " (*i. e.* be freed after six years' service, or in the year of jubilee), on the understanding that her master either already has made, or intends to make her his wife (ver. 7); (2) but, if he has no such intention, he is not entitled to retain her in the event of any other person of the Israelites being willing to purchase her of him for the same purpose (ver. 8); (3) he might, however, assign her to his son, and in this case she was to be treated as a daughter and not as a slave (ver. 9); (4) if either he or his son, having married her, took another wife, she was still to be treated as a wife in all respects (ver. 10); and, lastly, if neither of the three contingencies took place, *i. e.* if he neither married her himself, nor gave her to his son, nor had her redeemed, then the maiden was to become absolutely free without waiting for the expiration of the six years or for the year of jubilee (ver. 11).

a In this case we must assume that the wife assigned was a non-Israelitish slave ; otherwise, the wife would, as a matter of course, be freed along with her husband in the year of jubilee. In this case the wife and children would be the absolute property of the master, and the position of the wife would be analogous to that of the Roman *contubernalis*, who was not supposed capable of any *connubium*. The issue of such a marriage would remain slaves in accordance with the maxim of the Talmudists, that the child is liable to its mother's disqualification (*Kiddush.* 3, § 12). Josephus (*Ant.* iv. 8, § 28) states that in the year of jubilee the slave, having married during service, carried off his wife and children with him: this, however, may refer to an Israelite maid-servant.

b The Talmudists limited polygamists to four wives. The same number was adopted by Mohammed in the Koran, and still forms the rule among his followers (Niebuhr, Voyage, p. 62).

c Michaelis (*Laws of Moses*, iii. 5, § 95) asserts that polygamy ceased entirely after the return from the Captivity ; Selden, on the other hand, that polygamy prevailed among the Jews until the time of Honorius and Arcadius (circ. A. D. 400), when it was prohibited by an imperial edict (*Ux. Ebr.* i. 9).

from some of the comments of the early writers on 1 Tim. v. 9. Our Lord and his Apostles reëstablished the integrity and sanctity of the marriage bond by the following measures: (1) by the confirmation of the original charter of marriage as the basis on which all regulations were to be framed (Matt. xix. 4, 5); (2) by the restriction of divorce to the case of fornication, and the prohibition of re-marriage in all persons divorced on improper grounds (Matt. v. 32, xix. 9; Rom. vii. 3; 1 Cor. vii. 10, 11); and (3) by the enforcement of moral purity generally (Heb. xiii. 4, &c.), and especially by the formal condemnation of fornication,[a] which appears to have been classed among acts morally indifferent (ἀδιάφορα) by a certain party in the Church (Acts xv. 20).

Shortly before the Christian era an important change took place in the views entertained on the question of marriage as affecting the spiritual and intellectual parts of man's nature. Throughout the Old Testament period marriage was regarded as the indispensable duty of every man, nor was it surmised that there existed in it any drawback to the attainment of the highest degree of holiness. In the interval that elapsed between the Old and New Testament periods, a spirit of asceticism had been evolved, probably in antagonism to the foreign notions with which the Jews were brought into close and painful contact. The Essenes were the first to propound any doubts as to the propriety of marriage: some of them avoided it altogether, others availed themselves of it under restrictions (Joseph. B. J. ii. 8, §§ 2, 13). Similar views were adopted by the Therapeutæ, and at a later period by the Gnostics (Burton's *Lectures*, i. 214); thence they passed into the Christian Church, forming one of the distinctive tenets of the Encratites (Burton, ii. 161), and finally developing into the system of monachism. The philosophical tenets on which the prohibition of marriage was based are generally condemned in Col. ii. 16–23, and specifically in 1 Tim. iv. 3. The general propriety of marriage is enforced on numerous occasions, and abstinence from it is commended only in cases where it was rendered expedient by the calls of duty (Matt. xix. 12; 1 Cor. vii. 8, 26). With regard to re-marriage after the death of one of the parties, the Jews, in common with other nations, regarded abstinence from it, particularly in the case of a widow, laudable, and a sign of holiness (Luke ii. 36, 37; Joseph. *Ant.* xvii. 13, § 4, xviii. 6, § 6); but it is clear from the example of Josephus (*Vit.* § 76) that there was no prohibition even in the case of a priest. In the Apostolic Church re-marriage was regarded as occasionally undesirable (1 Cor. vii. 40), and as an absolute disqualification for holy functions, whether in a man or woman (1 Tim. iii. 2, 12, v. 9): at the same time it is recommended in the case of young widows (1 Tim. v. 14). .

II. The conditions of legal marriage are decided by the prohibitions which the law of any country imposes upon its citizens. In the Hebrew commonwealth these prohibitions were of two kinds, according as they regulated. marriage, (i.) between an Israelite and a non-Israelite, and (ii.) between an Israelite and one of his own community.

i. The prohibitions relating to foreigners were based on that instinctive feeling of exclusiveness, which forms one of the bonds of every social body, and which prevails with peculiar strength in a rude state of society. In all political bodies the right of marriage (*jus connubii*) becomes in some form or other a constituent element of citizenship, and, even where its nature and limits are not defined by legal enactment, it is supported with rigor by the force of public opinion. The feeling of aversion against intermarriage with foreigners becomes more intense, when distinctions of religious creed supervene on those of blood and language; and hence we should naturally expect to find it more than usually strong in the Hebrews, who were endowed with a peculiar position, and were separated from surrounding nations by a sharp line of demarcation. The warnings of past history and the examples of the patriarchs came in support of natural feeling: on the one hand, the evil effects of intermarriage with aliens were exhibited in the overwhelming sinfulness of the generation destroyed by the flood (Gen. vi. 2–13): on the other hand, there were the examples of the patriarchs Abraham, Isaac, and Jacob, marrying from among their own kindred (Gen. xx. 12, xxiv. 3, &c., xxviii. 2), and in each of the two latter cases there is a contrast between these carefully-sought unions and those of the rejected sons Ishmael, who married an Egyptian (Gen. xxi. 21), and Esau, whose marriages with Hittite women were "a grief of mind" to his parents (Gen. xxvi. 34, 35). The marriages of Joseph with an Egyptian (Gen. xli. 45), of Manasseh with a Syrian secondary wife (1 Chr. vii. 14; comp. Gen. xlvi. 20, LXX.), and of Moses with a Midianitish woman in the first instance (Ex. ii. 21), and afterwards with a Cushite or Ethiopian woman (Num. xii. 1), were of an exceptional nature, and yet the last was the cause of great dissatisfaction. A far greater objection was entertained against the marriage of an Israelitish woman with a man of another tribe, as illustrated by the narrative of Shechem's proposals for Dinah, the ostensible ground of their rejection being the difference in religious observances, that Shechem and his countrymen were uncircumcised (Gen. xxxiv. 14).

The only distinct prohibition in the Mosaic law refers to the Canaanites, with whom the Israelites were not to marry[b] on the ground that it would lead them into idolatry (Ex. xxxiv. 16; Deut. vii. 3, 4) — a result which actually occurred shortly after their settlement in the Promised Land (Judg. iii. 6, 7). But beyond this, the legal disabilities to which the Ammonites and Moabites were subjected (Deut. xxiii. 3) acted as a virtual bar to intermarriage with them, totally preventing (according to the interpretation which the Jews themselves put upon that passage) the marriage of

---

[a] The term πορνεία is occasionally used in a broad sense to include both adultery (Matt. v. 32) and incest (1 Cor. v. 1). In the decree of the Council of Jerusalem it must be regarded in its usual and restricted sense.

[b] The act of marriage with a foreigner is described in the Hebrew by a special term, chátan (חָתַן), expressive of the affinity thus produced, as appears

from the cognate terms, châtân, chotên, and chotênch, for "son-in-law," "father-in-law," and "mother-in-law." It is used in Gen. xxxiv. 9; Deut. vii. 3; Josh. xxiii. 12; 1 K. iii. 1; Ezr. ix. 14; and metaphorically in 2 Chr. xviii. 1. The same idea comes prominently forward in the term chátân in Ex. iv. 26, where it is used of the affinity produced by the rite of circumcision between Jehovah and the child.

Israelitish women with Moabites, but permitting that of Israelites with Moabite women, such as that of Mahlon with Ruth. The prohibition against marriages with the Edomites or Egyptians was less stringent, as a male of those nations received the right of marriage on his admission to the full citizenship in the third generation of proselytism (Deut. xxiii. 7, 8). There were thus three grades of prohibition — total in regard to the Canaanites on either side; total on the side of the males in regard to the Ammonites and Moabites; and temporary on the side of the males in regard of the Edomites and Egyptians, marriages with females in the two latter instances being regarded as legal (Selden, *de Jur. Nat.* cap. 14). Marriages between Israelite women and proselyted foreigners were at all times of rare occurrence, and are noticed in the Bible, as though they were of an exceptional nature, such as that of an Egyptian and an Israelitish woman (Lev. xxiv. 10), of Abigail and Jether the Ishmeelite, contracted probably when Jesse's family was sojourning in Moab (1 Chr. ii. 17), of Sheshan's daughter and an Egyptian, who was staying in his house (1 Chr. ii. 35), and of a Naphthalite woman and a Tyrian, living in adjacent districts (1 K. vii. 14). In the reverse case, namely, the marriage of Israelites with foreign women, it is, of course, highly probable that the wives became proselytes after their marriage, as instanced in the case of Ruth (i. 16); but this was by no means invariably the case. On the contrary we find that the Egyptian wife of Solomon (1 K. xi. 4), and the Phoenician wife of Ahab (1 K. xvi. .31), retained their idolatrous practices and introduced them into their adopted countries. Proselytism does not therefore appear to have been a *sine quâ non* in the case of a wife, though it was so in the case of a husband: the total silence of the Law as to any such condition in regard to a captive, whom an Israelite might wish to marry, must be regarded as evidence of the reverse (Deut. xxi. 10–14), nor have the refinements of Rabbinical writers on that passage succeeded in establishing the necessity of proselytism. The opposition of Samson's parents to his marriage with a Philistine woman (Judg. xiv. 3) lends to the same conclusion. So long as such unions were of merely occasional occurrence no veto was placed upon them by public authority; but, when after the return from the Babylonish Captivity the Jews contracted marriages with the heathen inhabitants of Palestine

in so wholesale a manner as to endanger their national existence, the practice was severely condemned (Ezr. ix. 2, x. 2), and the law of positive prohibition originally pronounced only against the Canaanites was extended to the Moabites, Ammonites, and Philistines (Neh. xiii. 23–25). Public feeling was thenceforth strongly opposed to foreign marriages, and the union of Manasseh with a Cuthaean led to such animosity as to produce the great national schism, which had its focus in the temple on Mount Gerizim (Joseph. *Ant.* xi. 8, § 2). A no less signal instance of the same feeling is exhibited in the cases of Joseph (*Ant.* xii. 4, § 6) and Anileus (*Ant.* xviii. 9, § 5), and is noticed by Tacitus (*Hist.* v. 5) as one of the characteristics of the Jewish nation in his day. In the N. T. no special directions are given on this head, but the general precepts of separation between believers and unbelievers (2 Cor. vi. 14, 17)[a] would apply with special force to the case of marriage; and the permission to dissolve mixed marriages, contracted previously to the conversion of one party, at the instance of the unconverted one, cannot but be regarded as implying the impropriety of such unions subsequently to conversion (1 Cor. vii. 12).

The progeny of illegal marriages between Israelites and non-Israelites was described under a peculiar term, *mamzer*[b] (A. V. "bastard"; Deut. xxiii. 2), the etymological meaning of which is uncertain,[c] but which clearly involves the notion of "foreigner," as in Zech. ix. 6, where the LXX. has ἀλλογενεῖς, "strangers." Persons born in this way were excluded from full rights of citizenship until the tenth generation (Deut. xxiii. 2). It follows hence that intermarriage with such persons was prohibited in the same manner as with an Ammonite or Moabite (comp. Mishna, *Kiddush* 4, § 1).

ii. The regulations relative to marriage between Israelites and Israelites may be divided into two classes: (1) general, and (2) special — the former applying to the whole population, the latter to particular cases.

1. The general regulations are based on considerations of relationship. The most important passage relating to these is contained in Lev. xviii. 6–18, wherein we have in the first place a general prohibition against marriages between a man and the "flesh of his flesh,"[d] and in the second place special prohibitions[e] against marriage with a

---

[a] The term ἑτεροζυγοῦντες (A. V. "unequally yoked with"), has no special reference to marriage : its meaning is shown in the cognate term ἑτερόζυγος (Lev. xix. 19; A. V. "of a diverse kind "). It is, however, correctly connected in the A. V. with the notion of a "yoke," as explained by Hesychius, οἱ μὴ συζυγοῦντες, and not with that of a "balance," as Theophylact.

[b] מַמְזֵר.

[c] Cognate words appear in Rabbinical writers, signifying (1) to *spin* or *weave*; (2) to be *corrupt*, as an addled egg ; (3) to *ripen*. The important point to be observed is that the word does not betoken *bastardy* in our sense of the term, but simply the progeny of a mixed marriage of a Jew and a foreigner. It may be with a special reference to this word that the Jews boasted that they were not born "of fornication" (ἐκ πορνείας, John viii. 41), implying that there was no admixture of foreign blood, or consequently of foreign idolatries, in themselves.

[d] The Hebrew expression שְׁאֵר בְּשָׂרוֹ (A. V. "near of kin ") is generally regarded as applying to

blood-relationship alone. The etymological sense of the term *sheer* is not decided. By some it is connected with *shadr*, "to remain," as by Michaelis (*Laws of Moses*, iii. 7, § 2), and in the marginal translation of the A. V. "remainder ; " but its ordinary sense of "flesh" is more applicable. Whichever of these two we adopt, the idea of blood-relationship evidently attaches to the term from the cases in which it is used (vv. 12, 13, 17 ; A. V. "near-kinswoman "), as well as from its use in Lev. xx. 19 ; Num. xxvii. 11. The term *basar*, literally "flesh " or "body," is also peculiarly used of blood-relationship (Gen. xxix. 14, xxxvii. 27 ; Judg ix. 2 ; 2 Sam. v. 1 ; 1 Chr. xi. 1). The two terms, *sheer basar*, are used conjointly in Lev. xxv. 49 as equivalent to *mishpachah*, "family." The term is applicable to relationship by affinity, in as far as it regards the blood-relations of a wife. The relationships specified may be classed under three heads: (1) blood-relationships proper in vv. 7–13 ; (2) the wives of blood-relations in vv. 14–16 ; (3) the blood relations of the wife in vv. 17, 18.

[e] The daughter is omitted ; whether as being pre-

mother, stepmother, sister, or half-sister, whether "born at home or abroad," [a] grand-daughter, aunt, whether by consanguinity on either side, or by marriage on the father's side, daughter-in-law, brother's wife, step-daughter, wife's mother, step-grand-daughter, or wife's sister during the lifetime of the wife.[b] An exception is subsequently made (Deut. xxv. 5) in favor of marriage with a brother's wife in the event of his having died childless: to this we shall have occasion to refer at length. Different degrees of guiltiness attached to the infringement of these prohibitions, as implied both in the different terms [c] applied to the various offenses, and in the punishments affixed to them, the general penalty being death (Lev. xx. 11–17), but in the case of the aunt and the brother's wife childlessness (19–21), involving probably the stain of illegitimacy in cases where there was an issue, while in the case of the two sisters no penalty is stated.

The moral effect of the prohibitions extended beyond cases of formal marriage to those of illicit intercourse, and gave a deeper dye of guilt to such conduct as that of Lot's daughters (Gen. xix. 33), of Reuben in his intercourse with his father's concubine (Gen. xxxv. 22), and of Absalom in the same act (2 Sam. xvi. 22); and it rendered such crimes tokens of the greatest national disgrace (Ez. xxii. 11). The Rabbinical writers considered that the prohibitions were abrogated in the case of proselytes, inasmuch as their change of religion was deemed equivalent to a new natural birth, and consequently involved the severing of all ties of

previous relationship: it was necessary, however, in such a case that the wife as well as the husband, should have adopted the Jewish faith.

The grounds on which these prohibitions were enacted are reducible to the following three heads: (1) moral propriety; (2) the practices of heathen nations; and (3) social convenience. The first of these grounds comes prominently forward in the expressions by which the various offenses are characterized, as well as in the general prohibition against approaching "the flesh of his flesh." The use of such expressions undoubtedly contains an appeal to the *horror naturalis*, or that repugnance with which man instinctively shrinks from matrimonial union with one with whom he is connected by the closest ties both of blood and of family affection. On this subject we need say no more than that there is a difference in kind between the affection that binds the members of a family together, and that which lies at the bottom of the matrimonial bond, and that the amalgamation of these affections cannot take place without a serious shock to one or the other of the two; hence the desirability of drawing a distinct line between the provinces of each, by stating definitely where the matrimonial affection may legitimately take root. The second motive to laying down these prohibitions was that the Hebrews might be preserved as a peculiar people, with institutions distinct from those of the Egyptians and Canaanites (Lev. xviii. 3), as well as of other heathen nations with whom they might come in contact. Marriages within the proscribed degrees prevailed in many civilized coun-

---

eminently the "flesh of a man's flesh," or because it was thought unnecessary to mention such a connection.

[a] The expression "born at home or abroad" has been generally understood as equivalent to "in or out of wedlock," *i. e.* the daughter of a father's concubine; but it may also be regarded as a re-statement of the preceding words, and as meaning "one born to the father, or mother, in a former marriage" (comp. Keil, *Archæol.* ii. 55). The distinction between the cases specified in vv. 9 and 11 is not very evident: it probably consists in this, that ver. 9 prohibits the union of a son of the first marriage with a daughter of the second, and ver. 11 that of a son of the second with a daughter of the first (Keil). On the other hand, Knobel (*Comm. in loc.*) finds the distinction in the words "wife of thy father" (ver. 11), which according to him includes the *mother* as well as the stepmother, and thus specifically states the *full* sister, while ver. 9 is reserved for the half-sister.

[b] The sense of this verse has been much canvassed, in connection with the question of marriage with a deceased wife's sister. It has been urged that the marginal translation, "one wife to another," is the correct one, and that the prohibition is really directed against polygamy. The following considerations, however, support the rendering of the text. (1.) The writer would hardly use the terms rendered "wife" and "sister" in a different sense in ver. 18 from that which he assigned to them in the previous verses. (2.) The usage of the Hebrew language and indeed of every language, requires that the expression "one to another" should be preceded by a plural noun. The cases in which the expression אִשָּׁה אֶל־אֲחֹתָהּ is equivalent to "one to another," as in Ex. xxvi. 3, 5, 6, 17, Ez. i. 9, 23, iii. 13, instead of favoring, as has generally been supposed, the marginal translation, exhibit the peculiarity above noted. (3.) The consent of the ancient versions is unanimous, including the LXX. (γυναῖκα ἐπ' ἀδελφῇ αὐτῆς), the Vulgate (*sororem*

uxoris tuæ), the Chaldee, Syriac, etc. (4.) The Jews themselves, as shown in the Mishna, and in the works of Philo, permitted the marriage. (5.) Polygamy was recognized by the Mosaic law, and cannot consequently be forbidden in this passage. Another interpretation, by which the sense of the verse is again altered, is effected by attaching the words "in her life-time" exclusively to the verb "vex." The objections to this are patent: (1) it is but reasonable to suppose that this clause, like the others, would depend on the principal verb; and (2), if this were denied, it would be but reasonable to attach it to the *nearest* ("uncover"), rather than the more remote secondary verb; which would be fatal to the sense of the passage.

[c] These terms are — (1.) *Zimmah* (זִמָּה; A. V. "wickedness"), applied to marriage with mother or daughter (Lev. xx. 14), with mother-in-law, step-daughter, or grand-step-daughter (xviii. 17). The term is elsewhere applied to gross violations of decency or principle (Lev. xix. 29; Job xxxi. 11; Ez. xvi. 43, xxii. 11). (2.) *Tebel* (תֶּבֶל; A. V. "confusion"), applied to marriage with a daughter-in-law (Lev. xx. 12): it signifies *pollution*, and is applied to the worst kind of defilement (Lev. xviii. 23). (3.) *Chesed* (חֶסֶד; A. V. "wicked thing"), applied to marriage with a sister (Lev. xx. 17): its proper meaning appears to be *disgrace*. (4.) *Niddah* (נִדָּה; A. V. "an unclean thing"), applied to marriage with a brother's wife (Lev. xx. 21): it conveys the notion of *impurity*. Michaelis (*Laws of Moses*, iii. 7, § 2) asserts that these terms have a forensic force; but there appears to be no ground for this. The view which the same authority propounds (§ 4) as to the reason for the prohibitions, namely, to prevent seduction under the promise of marriage among near relations, is singularly inadequate both to the occasion and to the terms employed.

tries in historical times, and were not unusual among the Hebrews themselves in the pre-Mosaic age. For instance, marriages with half-sisters by the same father were allowed at Athens (Plutarch *Cim.* p. 4, *Themistocl.* p. 32), with half-sisters by the same mother at Sparta (Philo, *de Spec. Leg.* p. 779), and with full sisters in Egypt (Diod. i. 27) and Persia, as illustrated in the well-known instances of Ptolemy Philadelphus in the former (Paus. i. 7, § 1), and Cambyses in the latter country (Herod. iii. 31). It was even believed that in some nations marriages between a son and his mother were not unusual (Ov. *Met.* x. 331; Eurip. *Androm.* p. 174). Among the Hebrews we have instances of marriage with a half-sister in the case of Abraham (Gen. xx. 12), with an aunt in the case of Amram (Ex. vi. 20), and with two sisters at the same time in the case of Jacob (Gen. xxix. 26). Such cases were justifiable previous to the enactments of Moses: subsequently to them we have no case in the O. T. of actual marriage within the degrees, though the language of Tamar towards her half-brother Amnon (2 Sam. xiii. 13) implies the possibility of their union with the consent of their father.[a] The Herods committed some violent breaches of the marriage law. Herod the Great married his half-sister (*Ant.* xvii. 1, § 3); Archelaus his brother's widow, who had children (xvii. 13, § 1); Herod Antipas his brother's wife (xviii. 5, § 1; Matt. xiv. 3). In the Christian Church we have an instance of marriage with a father's wife (1 Cor. v. 1), which St. Paul characterizes as "fornication" (πορνεία), and visits with the severest condemnation. The third ground of the prohibitions, social convenience, comes forward solely in the case of marriage with two sisters simultaneously, the effect of which would be to "vex" or *irritate* the first wife, and produce domestic jars.[b]

A remarkable exception to these prohibitions existed in favor of marriage with a deceased brother's wife, in the event of his having died childless.

The law which regulates this has been named the "Levirate," [c] from the Latin *levir*, "brother-in-law." The custom is supposed to have originated in that desire of perpetuating a name,[d] which prevails all over the world, but with more than ordinary force in eastern countries, and preëminently among Israelites, who each wished to bear part in the promise made to Abraham that "in his *seed* should all nations of the earth be blessed" (Gen. xxvi. 4). The first instance of it occurs in the patriarchal period, where Onan is called upon to marry his brother Er's widow (Gen. xxxviii. 8). The custom was confirmed by the Mosaic law, which decreed that "if brethren (*i. e.* sons of the same father) dwell together (either in one family, in one house, or, as the Rabbins explained it, in contiguous properties: the first of the three senses is probably correct), and one of them die and leave no child (*ben*, here used in its broad sense, and not specifically *son*; compare Matt. xxii. 25, μὴ ἔχων σπέρμα; Mark xii. 19; Luke xx. 28, ἄτεκνος), the wife of the dead shall not marry without (*i. e.* out of the family) unto a stranger (one unconnected by ties of relationship); her husband's brother shall go in unto her and take her to him to wife;" not, however, without having gone through the usual preliminaries of a regular marriage. The first-born of this second marriage then succeeded in the name of the deceased brother,[e] *i. e.* became his legal heir, receiving his name (according to Josephus, *Ant.* iv. 8, § 23; but compare Ruth i. 2, iv. 17), and his property (Deut. xxv. 5, 6). Should the brother object to marrying his sister-in-law, he was publicly to signify his dissent in the presence of the authorities of the town, to which the widow responded by the significant act of loosing his shoe and spitting in his face, or (as the Talmudists explained it) on the ground before him (*Yebam.* 12, § 6) — the former signifying the transfer of property from one person to another[f] (as usual among

---

[a] Various attempts have been made to reconcile this language with the Levitical law. The Rabbinical explanation was that Tamar's mother was a heathen at the time of her birth, and that the law did not apply to such a case. Josephus (*Ant.* vii. 8, § 1) regarded it as a mere *ruse* on the part of Tamar to evade Amnon's importunity: but, if the marriage were out of the question, she would hardly have tried such a poor device. Thenius (*Comm. in loc.*) considers that the Levitical prohibitions applied only to cases where a disruption of family bonds was likely to result, or where the motives were of a gross character; an argument which would utterly abrogate the authority of this and every other absolute law.

[b] The expression לִצְרֹר admits of another explanation, "to pack together," or combine the two in one marriage, and thus confound the nature of their relationship to one another. This is in one respect a preferable meaning, inasmuch as it is not clear why two sisters should be more particularly irritated than any two not so related. The usage, however, of the cognate word צָרַח, in 1 Sam. i. 6, favors the sense usually given; and in the Mishna צָרוֹת is the usual term for the wives of a polygamist (Mishna, *Yebam.* i. § 1).

[c] The Talmudical term for the obligation was *yibbûm* (יִבֻּם), from *yabem* (יָבֵם), "husband's brother;" hence the title *yebamoth* of the treatise in the Mishna for the regulation of such marriages. From the same

root comes the term *yibbem* (יְבֵּם), to contract such a marriage (Gen. xxxviii. 8).

[d] The reason here assigned is hardly a satisfactory one. May it not rather have been connected with the *purchase* system, which would reduce a wife into the position of a chattel or *mancipium*, and give the survivors a reversionary interest in her? This view derives some support from the statement in Haxthausen's *Transcaucasia*, p. 404, that among the Ossetes, who have a Levirate law of their own, in the event of none of the family marrying the widow, they are entitled to a certain sum from any other husband whom she may marry.

[e] The position of the issue of a Levirate marriage, as compared with other branches of the family, is exhibited in the case of Tamar, whose son by her father-in-law, Judah, became the head of the family, and the channel through whom the Messiah was born (Gen. xxxviii. 29; Matt. i. 3).

[f] The technical term for this act was *khalitzah* (חֲלִיצָה), from *khalatz* (חָלַץ), "to draw off." It is of frequent occurrence in the treatise *Yebamoth*, where minute directions are given as to the manner in which the act was to be performed; e. g. that the shoe was to be of leather, or a sandal furnished with a heel-strap; a felt shoe or a sandal without a strap would not do (*Yebam.* 12, §§ 1, 2). The *khalitzah* was not valid when the person performing it was deaf and dumb (§ 4), as he could not learn the precise formula which accompanied the act. The custom is retained by the modern Jews, and is minutely described by Picart (*Cérémonies Religieuses*, i. 243). It receives

the Indians and old Germans, Keil, *Archäol.* ii. 66), the latter the contempt due to a man who refused to perform his just obligations (Deut. xxv. 7–9; Ruth iv. 6–11). In this case it was permitted to the next of kin to come forward and to claim both the wife and the inheritance.

The Levirate marriage was not peculiar to the Jews; it has been found to exist in many eastern countries,[a] particularly in Arabia (Burckhardt's *Notes,* i. 112; Niebuhr's *Voyage,* p. 61), and among the tribes of the Caucasus (Haxthausen's *Transcaucasia,* p. 403). The Mosaic law brings the custom into harmony with the general prohibition against marrying a brother's wife by restricting it to cases of childlessness; and it further secures the marriage bond as founded on affection by relieving the brother of the obligation whenever he was averse to the union, instead of making it compulsory, as in the case of Onan (Gen. xxxviii. 9). One of the results of the Levirate marriage would be in certain cases the consolidation of two properties in the same family; but this does not appear to have been the object contemplated.[b]

The Levirate law offered numerous opportunities for the exercise of that spirit of casuistry, for which the Jewish teachers are so conspicuous. One such case is brought forward by the Sadducees for the sake of entangling our Lord, and turns upon the complications which would arise in the world to come (the existence of which the Sadducees sought to invalidate) from the circumstance of the same woman having been married to several brothers (Matt. xxii. 23–30). The Rabbinical solution of this difficulty was that the wife would revert to the first husband: our Lord on the other hand subverts the hypothesis on which the difficulty was based, namely, that the material conditions of the present life were to be carried on in the world to come; and thus He asserts the true character of marriage as a temporary and merely human institution. Numerous difficulties are suggested, and minute regulations laid down by the Talmudical writers, the chief authority on the subject being the book of the Mishna, entitled *Yebamoth.* From this we gather the following particulars, as illustrating the working of the law. If a man stood within the proscribed degrees of relationship in reference to his brother's widow, he was exempt from the operation of the law (2, § 3), and if he were on this or any other account exempt from the

obligation to marry one of the widows, he was also from the obligation to marry any of them (1, § 1); it is also implied that it was only necessary for one brother to marry one of the widows, in cases where there were several widows left. The marriage was not to take place within three months of the husband's death (4, § 10). The eldest brother ought to perform the duty of marriage; but, on his declining it, a younger brother might also do it (2, § 8, 4, § 5). The *khalitzah* was regarded as involving future relationship; so that a man who had received it could not marry the widow's relations within the prohibited degrees (4, § 7). Special rules are laid down for cases where a woman married under a false impression as to her husband's death (10, § 1), or where a mistake took place as to whether her son or her husband died first (10, § 3), for in the latter case the Levirate law would not apply; and again as to the evidence of the husband's death to be produced in certain cases (caps. 15, 16). ·

From the prohibitions expressed in the Bible, others have been deduced by a process of inferential reasoning. Thus the Talmudists added to the Levitical relationships several remoter ones, which they termed *secondary,* such as grandmother and great-grandmother, great-grandchild, etc.: the only points in which they at all touched the Levitical degrees were, that they added (1) the wife of the father's *uterine* brother under the idea that in the text the brother described was only by the same father, and (2) the mother's brother's wife, for which they had no authority (Selden, *Ux. Ebr.* i. 2). Considerable differences of opinion have arisen as to the extent to which this process of reasoning should be carried, and conflicting laws have been made in different countries, professedly based on the same original authority. It does not fall within our province to do more than endeavor to point out in what respects and to what extent the Biblical statements bear upon the subject. In the first place we must observe that the design of the legislator apparently was to give an exhaustive list of prohibitions; for he not only gives examples of *degrees* of relationship, but he specifies the prohibitions in cases which are strictly parallel to each other, *e. g.,* son's daughter and daughter's daughter (Lev. xviii. 10), wife's son's daughter and wife's daughter's daughter (ver. 17): whereas, had he wished only to exhibit the prohibited degree, one of these instances would have been sufficient. In

---

Illustration from the expression used by the modern Arabs, in speaking of a repudiated wife, "She was my slipper: I have cast her off" (Burckhardt, *Notes,* i. 113).

[a] The variations in the usages of the Levirate marriage are worthy of notice. Among the Ossetes in Georgia the marriage of the widow takes place if there are children, and may be contracted by the father as well as the brother of the deceased husband. If the widow has no children, the widow is purchaseable by another husband, as already noticed (Haxthausen, pp. 408, 404). In Arabia, the right of marriage is extended from the brother's widow to the cousin. Neither in this nor in the case of the brother's widow is the marriage compulsory on the part of the woman, though in the former the man can put a veto upon any other marriage (Burckhardt, *Notes,* i. 112, 113). Another development of the Levirate principle may perhaps be noticed in the privilege which the king enjoyed of succeeding to the wives as well as the throne of his predecessor (2 Sam. xii. 8). Hence Absalom's public seizure of his father's wives was not only a

breach of morality, but betokened his usurpation of the throne (2 Sam. xvi. 22). And so, again, Adonijah's request for the hand of Abishag was regarded by Solomon as almost equivalent to demanding the throne (1 K. ii. 22).

[b] The history of Ruth's marriage has led to some misconception on this point. Boaz stood to Ruth in the position, not of a Levir (for he was only her husband's cousin), but of a *Goel,* or redeemer in the second degree (A. V. "near kinsman," iii. 9): as such, he redeemed the inheritance of Naomi, after the refusal of the redeemer in the nearest degree, in conformity with Lev. xxv. 25. It appears to have been customary for the redeemer at the same time to marry the heiress, but this custom is not founded on any written law. The writer of the book of Ruth, according to Selden (*De Success.* cap. 15), *confuses* the laws relating to the *Goel* and the *Levir,* as Josephus (*Ant.* v. 9, § 4) has undoubtedly done; but this is an unnecessary assumption: the custom is one that may well have existed in conformity with the *spirit* of the law of the Levirate marriage.

the second place it appears certain that he did not regard the degree as the text of the prohibition; for he establishes a different rule in regard to a brother's widow and a deceased wife's sister, though the degree of relationship is in each case strictly parallel. It cannot, therefore, in the face of this express enactment be argued that Moses designed his countrymen to infer that marriage with a niece was illegal because that with the aunt was, nor yet that marriage with a mother's brother's wife was included in the prohibition of that with the father's brother's wife. For, though no explicit statement is made as to the legality of these two latter, the rule of interpretation casually given to us in the first must be held to apply to them also. In the third place, it must be assumed that there were some tangible and even strong grounds for the distinctions noted in the degrees of equal distance; and it then becomes a matter of importance to ascertain whether these grounds are of *perpetual* force, or arise out of a peculiar state of society or legislation; if the latter, then it seems justifiable to suppose that on the alteration of that state we may recur to the spirit rather than the letter of the enactment, and may infer prohibitions which, though not existing in the Levitical law, may yet be regarded as based upon it.

The cases to which these remarks would most pointedly apply are marriage with a deceased wife's sister, a niece, whether by blood or by marriage, and a maternal uncle's widow. With regard to the first and third of these, we may observe that the Hebrews regarded the relationship existing between the wife and her husband's family, as of a closer nature than that between the husband and his wife's family. To what extent this difference was supposed to hold good we have no means of judging; but as illustrations of the difference we may note (1) that the husband's brother stood in the special relation of *levir* to his brother's wife, and was subject to the law of Levirate marriage in consequence; (2) that the nearest relation on the husband's side, whether brother, nephew, or cousin, stood in the special relation of *goël*, or avenger of blood to his widow; and (3) that an heiress was restricted to a marriage with a relation on her father's side. As no corresponding obligations existed in reference to the wife's or the mother's family, it follows almost as a matter of course that the degree of relationship must have been regarded as different in the two cases, and that prohibitions might on this account be applied to the one, from which the other was exempt. When, however, we transplant the Levitical regulations from the Hebrew to any other commonwealth, we are fully warranted in taking into account the temporary and local conditions of relationship in each, and in extending the prohibitions to cases where alterations in the social or legal condition have taken place. The question to be fairly argued, then, is not simply whether marriage within a certain degree is or is not permitted by the Levitical law, but whether, allowing for the altered state of society, *mutatis mutandis*, it appears in conformity with the general spirit of that law. The ideas of different nations as to relationship differ widely; and, should it happen that in the social system of a certain country a relationship is, as a matter of fact, regarded as an intimate one, then it is clearly permissible

for the rulers of that country to prohibit marriage in reference to it, not on the ground of any expressed or implied prohibition in reference to it in particular in the book of Leviticus, but on the general ground that Moses intended to prohibit marriage among near relations. The application of such a rule in some cases is clear enough; no one could hesitate for a moment to pronounce marriage with a brother's widow, even in cases where the Mosaic law would permit it, as absolutely illegal in the present day: inasmuch as the peculiar obligation of the *levir* has been abolished. As little could we hesitate to extend the prohibition from the paternal to the maternal uncle's widow, now that the peculiar differences between relationships on the father's and the mother's side are abolished. With regard to the vexed question of the deceased wife's sister we refrain from expressing an opinion, inasmuch as the case is still *in lite ;* under the rule of interpretation we have already laid down, the case stands thus: such a marriage is not only not prohibited, but actually permitted by the letter of the Mosaic Law; but it remains to be argued (1) whether the permission was granted under peculiar circumstances; (2) whether those or strictly parallel circumstances exist in the present day; and (3) whether, if they do not exist, the general tenor of the Mosaic prohibitions would, or would not, justify a community in extending the prohibition to such a relationship on the authority of the Levitical law. In what has been said on this point, it must be borne in mind that we are viewing the question simply in its relation to the Levitical law: with the other arguments *pro* and *con* bearing on it, we have at present nothing to do. With regard to the marriage with the niece, we have some difficulty in suggesting any sufficient ground on which it was permitted by the Mosaic law. The Rabbinical explanation, that the distinction between the aunt and the niece was based upon the *respectus parentela*, which would not permit the aunt to be reduced from her natural seniority, but at the same time would not object to the elevation of the niece, cannot be regarded as satisfactory; for, though it explains to a certain extent the difference between the two, it places the prohibition of marriage with the aunt, and consequently the permission of that with the niece, on a wrong basis; for in Lev. xx. 19 consanguinity, and not *respectus parentela*, is stated as the ground of the prohibition. The Jews appear to have availed themselves of the privilege without scruple : in the Bible itself, indeed, we have but one instance, and that not an undoubted one, in the case of Othniel, who was probably the brother of Caleb (Josh. xv. 17), and, if so, then the uncle of Achsah his wife. Several such marriages are noticed by Josephus, as in the case of Joseph, the nephew of Onias (*Ant.* xii. 4, § 6), Herod the Great (*Ant.* xvii. 1, § 3), and Herod Philip (*Ant.* xviii. 5, § 1). But on whatever ground they were formerly permitted, there can be no question as to the propriety of prohibiting them in the present day.

2. Among the special prohibitions we have to notice the following. (1.) The high-priest was forbidden to marry any except a virgin selected from his own people, i. e. an Israelite (Lev. xxi. 13, 14). He was thus exempt from the action of the Levirate law. (2.) The priests were less restricted in their choice[a]; they were only prohibited from marrying

---

[a] From Ex. xliv. 22 it appears that the law relative to the marriage of priests was afterwards made more rigid : they could marry only maidens of Israelitish origin or the widows of priests.

prostitutes and divorced women (Lev. xxi. 7). (3.) Heiresses were prohibited from marrying out of their own tribe,[a] with the view of keeping the possessions of the several tribes intact (Num. xxxvi. 6–9; comp. Tob. vii. 10). (4.) Persons defective in physical powers were not to intermarry with Israelites by virtue of the regulations in Deut. xxiii. 1. (5.) In the Christian Church, bishops and deacons were prohibited from having more than one wife (1 Tim. iii. 2, 12), a prohibition of an ambiguous nature, inasmuch as it may refer (1) to polygamy in the ordinary sense of the term, as explained by Theodoret (in loc.), and most of the Fathers; (2) to marriage after the decease of the first wife; or (3) to marriage after divorce during the lifetime of the first wife. The probable sense is second marriage of any kind whatever, including all the three cases alluded to, but with a special reference to the two last, which were allowable in the case of the laity, while the first was equally forbidden to all. The early Church generally regarded second marriage as a disqualification for the ministry, though on this point there was not absolute unanimity (see Bingham, Ant. iv. 5, § 1–3). (6.) A similar prohibition applied to those who were candidates for admission into the ecclesiastical order of widows, whatever that order may have been (1 Tim. v. 9); in this case the words "wife of one man" can be applied but to two cases, (a) to re-marriage after the decease of the husband, or (b) after divorce. That divorce was obtained sometimes at the instance of the wife, is implied in Mark x. 12, and 1 Cor. vii. 11, and is alluded to by several classical writers (see Whitby, in loc.). But St. Paul probably refers to the general question of re-marriage. (7.) With regard to the general question of the re-marriage of divorced persons, there is some difficulty in ascertaining the sense of Scripture. According to the Mosaic Law, a wife divorced at the instance of the husband might marry whom she liked; but if her second husband died or divorced her she could not revert to her first husband, on the ground that, as far as be was concerned, she was "defiled" (Deut. xxiv. 2–4); we may infer, from the statement of the ground, that there was no objection to the re-marriage of the original parties, if the divorced wife had remained unmarried in the interval. If the wife was divorced on the ground of adultery, her re-marriage was impossible, inasmuch as the punishment for such a crime was death. In the N. T. there are no direct precepts on the subject of the re-marriage of divorced persons. All the remarks bearing upon the point had a primary reference to an entirely different subject, namely, the abuse of divorce. For instance, our Lord's declarations in Matt. v. 32, xix. 9, applying as they expressly do to the case of a wife divorced on other grounds than that of unfaithfulness, and again St. Paul's, in 1 Cor. vii. 11, pre-supposing a contingency which he himself had prohibited as being improper, cannot be regarded as directed to the general question of re-marriage. In applying these passages to our own circumstances, due regard must be had to the peculiar nature of the Jewish divorce, which was not, as with us, a judicial proceeding based on evidence and pronounced by authority, but the arbitrary, and sometimes capricious act of an in-

dividual. The assertion that a woman divorced on improper and trivial grounds is made to commit adultery, does not therefore bear upon the question of a person divorced by judicial authority; no such case as our Lord supposes can now take place; at all events it would take place only in connection with the question of what form adequate grounds for divorce. The early Church was divided in its opinion on this subject (Bingham, Ant. xxii. 2, § 12). [DIVORCE, Amer. ed.]

With regard to age, no restriction is pronounced in the Bible. Early marriage is spoken of with approval in several passages (Prov. ii. 17, v. 18; Is. lxii. 5), and in reducing this general statement to the more definite one of years, we must take into account the very early age at which persons arrive at puberty in oriental countries. In modern Egypt marriage takes place in general before the bride has attained the age of 16, frequently when she is 12 or 13, and occasionally when she is only 10 (Lane, i. 208). The Talmudists forbade marriage in the case of a man under 13 years and a day, and in the case of a woman under 12 years and a day (Buxtorf, Synagog. cap. 7, p. 143). The usual age appears to have been higher, about 18 years.

Certain days were fixed for the ceremonies of betrothal and marriage — the fourth day for virgins, and the fifth for widows (Mishna, Ketub. 1, § 1). The more modern Jews similarly appoint different days for virgins and widows, Wednesday and Friday for the former, Thursday for the latter (Picart, i. 240).

III. The customs of the Hebrews and of oriental nations generally, in regard to the preliminaries of marriage as well as the ceremonies attending the rite itself, differ in many respects from those with which we are familiar. In the first place, the choice of the bride devolved not on the bridegroom himself, but on his relations or on a friend deputed by the bridegroom for this purpose. Thus Abraham sends Eliezer to find a suitable bride for his son Isaac, and the narrative of his mission affords one of the most charming pictures of patriarchal life (Gen. xxiv.); Hagar chooses a wife for Ishmael (Gen. xxi. 21); Isaac directs Jacob in his choice (Gen. xxviii. 1); and Judah selects a wife for Er (Gen. xxxviii. 6). It does not follow that the bridegroom's wishes were not consulted in this arrangement; on the contrary, the parents made proposals at the instigation of their sons in the instances of Shechem (Gen. xxxiv. 4, 8) and Samson (Judg. xiv. 1–10). A marriage contracted without the parents' interference was likely to turn out, as in Esau's case, "a grief of mind" to them (Gen. xxvi. 35, xxvii. 46). As a general rule the proposal originated with the family of the bridegroom: occasionally, when there was a difference of rank, this rule was reversed, and the bride was offered by her father, as by Jethro to Moses (Ex. ii. 21), by Caleb to Othniel (Josh. xv. 17), and by Saul to David (1 Sam. xviii. 27). The imaginary case of women soliciting husbands (Is. iv. 1) was designed to convey to the mind a picture of the ravages of war, by which the greater part of the males had fallen. The consent of the maiden was sometimes asked (Gen. xxiv. 58); but this appears to have been subordinate to the previous consent of the father and the adult brothers (Gen. xxiv. 51, xxxiv. 11). Occasionally the whole business of selecting the wife was left in the hands of a friend, and hence the case might arise which is supposed by the Tal-

---

[a] The close analogy of this regulation to the Athenian law respecting the ἐπίκληροι has been already noticed in the article on HEIR.

sundists (*Yebam.* 2, §§ 6, 7), that a man might not be aware to which of two sisters he was betrothed. So in Egypt at the present day the choice of a wife is sometimes entrusted to a professional woman styled a *khát'beh*: and it is seldom that the bridegroom sees the features of his bride before the marriage has taken place (Lane, i. 209–211).

The selection of the bride was followed by the espousal, which was not altogether like our "engagement," but was a formal proceeding, undertaken by a friend or legal representative on the part of the bridegroom, and by the parents on the part of the bride; it was confirmed by oaths, and accompanied with presents to the bride. Thus Eliezer, on behalf of Isaac, propitiates the favor of Rebekah by presenting her in anticipation with a massive golden nose-ring and two bracelets; he then proceeds to treat with the parents, and, having obtained their consent, he brings forth the more costly and formal presents, "jewels of silver, and jewels of gold, and raiment," for the bride, and presents of less value for the mother and brothers (Gen. xxiv. 22, 53). These presents were described by different terms, that to the bride by *mohar* [a] (A. V. " dowry "), and that to the relations by *mattan.* [b] Thus Shechem offers "never so much dowry and gift " (Gen. xxxiv. 12), the former for the bride, the latter for the relations. It has been supposed indeed that the *mohar* was a price paid down to the father for the sale of his daughter. Such a custom undoubtedly prevails in certain parts of the East at the present day, but it does not appear to have been the case with free women in patriarchal times; for the daughters of Laban make it a matter of complaint that their father had bargained for the services of Jacob in exchange for their hands, just as if they were "strangers " (Gen. xxxi. 15); and the permission to sell a daughter was restricted to the case of a "servant" or secondary wife (Ex. xxi. 7): nor does David, when complaining of the non-completion of Saul's bargain with him, use the expression "I *bought* for," but "I *espoused* to me for an hundred foreskins of the Philistines " (2 Sam. iii. 14). The expressions in Hos. iii. 2, "So I bought her to me," and in Ruth iv. 10, "Ruth have I *purchased* to be my wife," certainly appear to favor the opposite view; it should be observed, however, that in the former passage great doubt exists as to the correctness of the translation [c]; and that in the latter the case

---

[a] The term *mohar* (מֹהַר) occurs only thrice in the Bible (Gen. xxxiv. 12; Ex. xxii. 17; 1 Sam. xviii. 25). From the second of the three passages, compared with Deut. xxii. 29, it has been inferred that the sum was in all cases paid to the father; but this inference is unfounded, because the sum to be paid according to that passage was not the proper *mohar*, but a sum " according to," i. e. equivalent to the *mohar*, and this, not as a price for the bride, but as a penalty for the offense committed. The origin of the term, and consequently its specific sense, is uncertain. Gesenius (*Thes.* p. 773) has evolved the sense of " purchase-money " by connecting it with מָכַר, " to sell." It has also been connected with מָהַר, " to hasten," as though it signified a present *hastily produced* for the bride when her consent was obtained; and again with מָחָר, " morrow," as though it were the gift presented to the bride on the *morning* after the wedding, like the German *Morgen-gabe* (Saalschütz, *Archäol.* ii. 193).

[e] Gussett (*Commentarii Ling. Hebr.* ed. 2d, p. 875) has well said: " Significationes dotandi et accelerandi quomodo coinciderint in unum verbum. quidque commune habeant, vix dixeris." The writer of the preceding paragraph, in speaking of " the origin of the term and its specific sense," neglects to notice Fürst's phonetic combinations, and the Arabic usage, by which he very naturally connects the different senses of מָהַר with the ground meaning *to flow*; namely, *to flow onward, to hasten on,* and *to flow away to,* in the sense of passing over from one to another in exchange, and " hence *to take in exchange* (through a gift, מֹהַר) a wife, i. e. *to marry,* Ex. xxii. 15." He defines מֹהַר, " *a gift, a marriage gift* or *price,* paid to the parents of the wife."

In Ex. xxii. 15, 16 (A. V. 16, 17) the offender, in the case supposed, is required to pay the usual purchase-money to the parent, the latter being allowed to give the daughter in marriage or not, at his own option. " According to the purchase-money of virgins " means the sum usually paid for a virgin received in marriage. The expression, " he shall pay money," in its immediate connection with the preceding clause, " if her father utterly refuse to give her unto him," certainly implies that it shall be paid to the "father."

The point now at issue is stated too strongly in the text, by saying, " it has been supposed that the *mohar* was a price paid down to the father for the sale of his daughter." The customary present to the father, in return for the gift of his daughter in marriage, originating in such a custom, continued to be expressed by this word, though only an honorary acknowledgment of the favor shown by him in bestowing his daughter's hand. This view of the case disposes, substantially, of the objections urged in the text. But it may be added, that the statement there made of the ground of complaint, on the part of Laban's daughters, is an unnecessary and forced construction of the language in ch. xxxi. 15. Laban's right to require Jacob's service, in return for giving them in marriage, was not questioned by Jacob, nor, so far as appears, by them. (See Gen. xxix. 15, 18, 20.) The natural construction of their complaint is, that they are treated, in all respects, as aliens, and not as of his own flesh and blood. Similar to this, in effect, is Jacob's complaint in ch. xxxi. 42, " Surely thou wouldst now have sent me away empty." In the case of David and Saul, the *mohar* is expressly declined by the latter (1 Sam. xviii. 25); and in place of it, he accepts the proofs that a hundred Philistines have been slain, " to be avenged of the king's enemies." Evidently, this requirement was made by the king on his own behalf, and in place of the usual present to the father. For this reason, as well as on the general ground above stated, that the *mohar* had become only an honorary present to the father, David could say (2 Sam. iii 14) " I espoused," etc., instead of " I bought."

T. J. C.

[b] מַתָּן. The importance of presents at the time of betrothal appears from the application of the term *áras* (אָרַשׂ), literally, " to make a present," in the special sense of " to betroth."

[c] The term used (כָּרָה) has a general sense " to make an agreement." The meaning of the verse appears to be this: the Prophet had previously married a wife, named Gomer, who had turned out unfaithful to him. He had separated from her; but he was ordered to renew his intimacy with her, and previous to doing this he places her on her probation, setting her apart for a time, and for her maintenance agreeing to give her fifteen pieces of silver, in addition to a certain amount of food.

would not be conclusive, as Ruth might well be considered as included in the purchase of her property. It would undoubtedly be expected that the *mohar* should be proportioned to the position of the bride, and that a poor man could not on that account afford to marry a rich wife (1 Sam. xviii. 23). Occasionally the bride received a dowry [a] from her father, as instanced in the cases of Caleb's (Judg. i. 15) and Pharaoh's (1 K. ix. 16) daughters. A "settlement," in the modern sense of the term, i. e. a written document securing property to the wife, did not come into use until the post-Babylonian period: the only instance we have of one is in Tob. vii. 14, where it is described as an "instrument" (συγγραφή). The Talmudists styled it a *ketubah*,[b] and have laid down minute directions as to the disposal of the sum secured, in a treatise of the Mishna expressly on that subject, from which we extract the following particulars. The peculiarity of the Jewish *ketubah* consisted in this, that it was a definite sum, varying not according to the circumstances of the parties, but according to the state of the bride, [c] whether she be a spinster, a widow, or a divorced woman[d] (1, § 2); and further, that the dowry could not be claimed until the termination of the marriage by the death of the husband or by divorce (5, § 1), though advances might be made to the wife previously (9, § 8). Subsequently to betrothal a woman lost all power over her property, and it became vested in the husband, unless he had previously to marriage renounced his right to it (8, § 1; 9, § 1). Stipulations were entered into for the increase of the *ketubah*, when the bride had a handsome allowance (6, § 3). The act of betrothal[e] was celebrated by a feast (1, § 5), and among the more modern Jews it is the custom in some parts for the bridegroom to place a ring on the bride's finger (Picart, i. 239) — a custom which also prevailed among the Romans (*Dict. of Ant.* p. 604). Some writers have endeavored to prove that the rings noticed in the O. T. (Ex. xxxv. 22; Is. iii. 21) were nuptial rings, but there is not the slightest evidence of this. The ring was nevertheless regarded among the Hebrews as a token of fidelity (Gen. xli. 42), and of adoption into a family (Luke xv. 22). According to Selden it was originally given as an equivalent for dowry-money (*Uxor Ebraic.* ii. 14). Between the betrothal and the marriage an interval elapsed, varying from a few days in the patriarchal age (Gen.

xxiv. 55), to a full year for virgins and a month for widows in later times. During this period the bride-elect lived with her friends, and all communication between herself and her future husband was carried on through the medium of a friend deputed for the purpose, termed the "friend of the bridegroom" (John iii. 29). She was now virtually regarded as the wife of her future husband; for it was a maxim of the Jewish law that betrothal was of equal force with marriage (Phil. *De spec. leg.* p. 788). Hence faithlessness on her part was punishable with death (Deut. xxii. 23, 24), the husband having, however, the option of "putting her away" (Matt. i. 19) by giving her a bill of divorcement, in case he did not wish to proceed to such an extreme punishment (Deut. xxiv. 1). False accusations on this ground were punished by a severe fine and the forfeiture of the right of divorce (Deut. xxii. 13–19). The betrothed woman could not part with her property after betrothal, except in certain cases (*Ketub.* 8, § 1): and, in short, the bond of matrimony was as fully entered into by betrothal, as with us by marriage. In this respect we may compare the practice of the Athenians, who regarded the formal betrothal as indispensable to the validity of a marriage contract (*Dict. of Ant.* p. 598). The customs of the Nestorians afford several points of similarity in respect both to the mode of effecting the betrothal and the importance attached to it (Grant's *Nestorians*, pp. 197, 198).

We now come to the wedding itself; and in this the most observable point is, that there were no definite religious ceremonies connected with it.[f] It is probable, indeed, that some formal ratification of the espousal with an oath took place, as implied in some allusions to marriage (Ex. xvi. 8; Mal. ii. 14), particularly in the expression, " the covenant of her God " (Prov. ii. 17), as applied to the marriage bond, and that a blessing was pronounced (Gen. xxiv. 60; Ruth iv. 11, 12) sometimes by the parents (Tob. vii. 13). But the essence of the marriage ceremony consisted in the removal of the bride from her father's house to that of the bridegroom or his father.[g]

The bridegroom prepared himself for the occasion by putting on a festive dress, and especially by placing on his head the handsome turban described by the term *peēr* (Is. lxi. 10; A. V. "ornaments"), and a nuptial crown or garland[h] (Cant. iii. 11): he was redolent of myrrh and frankincense and " all

a The technical term of the Talmudist for the dowry which the wife brought to her husband, answering to the *dos* of the Latins, was נְדוּנְיָא.

b כְּתֻבָּה, literally "a writing." The term was also specifically applied to the sum settled on the wife by the husband, answering to the Latin *donatio propter nuptias*.

c The practice of the modern Egyptians illustrates this : for with them the dowry, though its amount differs according to the wealth of the suitor, is still graduated according to the state of the bride. A certain portion only of the dowry is paid down, the rest being held in reserve (Lane, i. 211). Among the modern Jews also the amount of the dowry varies with the state of the bride, according to a fixed scale (Picart, i. 240).

d The amount of the dowry, according to the Mosaic law, appears to have been fifty shekels (Ex. xxii. 17, compared with Deut. xxii. 29).

e The technical term used by the Talmudists for betrothing was *kiddūshīn* (קִדּוּשִׁין), derived from

קָדַשׁ, "to set apart." There is a treatise in the Mishna so entitled, in which various questions of casuistry of slight interest to us are discussed.

f It is worthy of observation that there is no term in the Hebrew language to express the ceremony of marriage. The substantive *chatunnah* (חֲתֻנָּה) occurs but once, and then in connection with the day (Cant. iii. 11). The word " wedding " does not occur at all in the A. V. of the Old Testament.

g There seems indeed to be a literal truth in the Hebrew expression " to take " a wife (Num. xii. 1 ; 1 Chr. ii. 21); for the ceremony appears to have mainly consisted in the taking. Among the modern Arabs the same custom prevails, the capture and removal of the bride being effected with a considerable show of violence (Burckhardt's *Notes*, i. 108).

h The bridegroom's crown was made of various materials (gold or silver, roses, myrtle, or olive), according to his circumstances (Selden, *Ux. Ebr.* ii. 15). The use of the crown at marriages was familiar both to the Greeks and Romans (*Dict. of Ant.*, CORONA).

powders of the merchant" (Cant. iii. 6). The bride prepared herself for the ceremony by taking a bath, generally on the day preceding the wedding. This was probably in ancient as in modern times a formal proceeding, accompanied with considerable pomp (Picart, i. 240; Lane, i. 217). The notices of it in the Bible are so few as to have escaped general observation (Ruth iii. 3; Ez. xxiii. 40; Eph. v. 26, 27); but the passages cited establish the antiquity of the custom, and the expressions in the last ("having purified her by the laver of water," "not having spot") have evident reference to it. A similar custom prevailed among the Greeks (*Dict. of Ant.* s. v. *Balnea,* p. 185). The distinctive feature of the bride's attire was the *tsā'iph,*[a] or "veil" — a light robe of ample dimensions, which covered not only the face but the whole person (Gen. xxiv. 65; comp. xxxviii. 14, 15). This was regarded as the symbol of her submission to her husband, and hence in 1 Cor. xi. 10, the veil is apparently described under the term ἐξουσία, "authority." She also wore a peculiar girdle, named *kishshūrīm,*[b] the "attire" (A. V.), which no bride could forget (Jer. ii. 32); and her head was crowned with a chaplet, which was again so distinctive of the bride, that the Hebrew term *callah,*[c] "bride," originated from it. If the bride were a virgin, she wore her hair flowing (*Ketub.* 2, § 1). Her robes were white (Rev. xix. 8), and sometimes embroidered with gold thread (Ps. xlv. 13, 14), and covered with perfumes (Ps. xlv. 8): she was further decked out with jewels (Is. xlix. 18, lxi. 10; Rev. xxi. 2). When the fixed hour arrived, which was generally late in the evening, the bridegroom set forth from his house, attended by his groomsmen, termed in Hebrew *mēri'īm*[d] (A. V. "companions; Judg. xiv. 11), and in Greek υἱοὶ τοῦ νυμφῶνος (A. V. "children of the bride-chamber;" Matt. ix. 15), preceded by a band of musicians or singers

(Gen. xxxi. 27; Jer. vii. 34, xvi. 9; 1 Macc. ix. 39), and accompanied by persons bearing flambeaux[e] (2 Esdr. x. 2; Matt. xxv. 7; compare Jer. xxv. 10; Rev. xviii. 23, "the light of a candle") Having reached the house of the bride, who with her maidens anxiously expected his arrival (Matt. xxv. 6), he conducted the whole party back to his own or his father's[f] house, with every demonstration of gladness[g] (Ps. xlv. 15). On their way back they were joined by a party of maidens, friends of the bride and bridegroom, who were in waiting to catch the procession as it passed (Matt. xxv. 6; comp. Trench on *Parables,* p. 244 *note*). The inhabitants of the place pressed out into the streets to watch the procession (Cant. iii. 11). At the house a feast[h] was prepared, to which all the friends and neighbors were invited (Gen. xxix. 22, Matt. xxii. 1–10; Luke xiv. 8; John ii. 2), and the festivities were protracted for seven, or even fourteen days (Judg. xiv. 12; Tob. viii. 19). The guests were provided by the host with fitting robes (Matt. xxii. 11; comp. Trench, *Parables,* p. 230), and the feast was enlivened with riddles (Judg. xiv. 12) and other amusements. The bridegroom now entered into direct communication with the bride, and the joy of the friend was "fulfilled" at hearing the voice of the bridegroom (John iii. 29) conversing with her, which he regarded as a satisfactory testimony of the success of his share in the work. In the case of a virgin, parched corn was distributed among the guests (*Ketub.* 2, § 1), the significance of which is not apparent; the custom bears some resemblance to the distribution of the *mustaceum* (Juv. vi. 202) among the guests at a Roman wedding. The modern Jews have a custom of shattering glasses or vessels, by dashing them to the ground (Picart, i. 240). The last act in the ceremonial was the conducting of the bride to the bridal chamber, *cheder*[i] (Judg. xv. 1; Joel

---

[a] צָעִיף. See article on Dress. The use of the veil was not peculiar to the Hebrews. It was customary among the Greeks and Romans; and among the latter it gave rise to the expression *nubo,* literally "to veil," and hence to our word "nuptial." It is still used by the Jews (Picart, i. 241). The modern Egyptians envelope the bride in an ample shawl, which perhaps more than anything else resembles the Hebrew *tzaiph* (Lane, i. 220).

[b] קִשּׁוּרִים. Some difference of opinion exists as to this term. [GIRDLE.] The girdle was an important article of the bride's dress among the Romans, and gave rise to the expression *solvere zonam.*

[c] כַּלָּה. The bride's crown was either of gold or gilded. The use of it was interdicted after the destruction of the second Temple, as a token of humiliation (Selden, *Ux. Ebr.* ii. 15).

[d] מֵרֵעִים. Winer (*Rwb.* s. v. "Hochzeit") identifies the "children of the bridechamber" with the *shoshbenim* (שׁוֹשְׁבְּכִים) of the Talmudists. But the former were the attendants on the bridegroom alone, while the *shoshbenim* were two persons selected on the day of the marriage to represent the interests of bride and bridegroom, apparently with a special view to any possible litigation that might subsequently arise on the subject noticed in Deut. xxii. 15–21 (Selden, *Ux. Ebr.* ii. 16).

[e] Compare the λόγος νυμφικοί of the Greeks (Aristoph. *Pax,* 1317). The lamps described in Matt. xxv. 7

would be small hand-lamps. Without them none could join the procession (Trench's *Parables,* p. 257 note).

[f] The bride was said to "go to" (בּוֹא אֶל) the house of her husband (Josh. xv. 18; Judg. i. 14); an expression which is worthy of notice, inasmuch as it has not been rightly understood in Dan. xi. 6, where "they that brought her" is an expression for *husband.* The bringing home of the bride was regarded in the later days of the Roman empire as one of the most important parts of the marriage ceremony (Bingham, *Ant.* xxii. 4, § 7).

[g] From the joyous sounds used on these occasions the term *hālal* (הָלַל) is applied in the sense of marrying in Ps. lxxviii. 63; A. V. "their maidens were not given to marriage," literally, "were not praised," as in the margin. This sense appears preferable to that of the LXX., οὐκ ἐπένθησαν, which is adopted by Gesenius (*Thes.* p. 596). The noise in the streets, attendant on an oriental wedding, is excessive, and enables us to understand the allusions in Jeremiah to the "voice of the bridegroom and the voice of the bride."

[h] The feast was regarded as so essential a part of the marriage ceremony, that ποιεῖν γάμον acquired the specific meaning "to celebrate the marriage-feast" (Gen. xxix. 22; Esth. ii. 18; Tob. viii. 19; 1 Macc. ix. 37, x. 58, LXX.; Matt. xxii. 4, xxv. 10; Luke xiv. 8), and sometimes to celebrate any feast (Esth. ix. 22)

[i] חֶדֶר.

ii. 16), where a canopy, named *chuppâh* [a] was prepared (Ps. xix. 5; Joel ii. 16). The bride was still completely veiled, so that the deception practiced on Jacob (Gen. xxix. 25) was very possible. If proof could be subsequently adduced that the bride had not preserved her maiden purity, the case was investigated; and, if she was convicted,

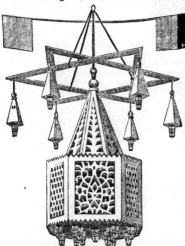

Lamp suspended at a modern Egyptian wedding. (Lane.)

she was stoned to death before her father's house (Deut. xxii. 13–21). A newly married man was exempt from military service, or from any public business which might draw him away from his home, for the space of a year (Deut. xxiv. 5): a similar privilege was granted to him who was betrothed (Deut. xx. 7).

Hitherto we have described the usages of marriage as well as they can be ascertained from the Bible itself. The Talmudists specify three modes by which marriage might be effected, namely, money, marriage-contract, and consummation (*Kiddush*. i. § 1). The first was by the presentation of a sum of money, or its equivalent, in the presence of witnesses, accompanied by a mutual declaration of betrothal. The second was by a *written*, instead of a verbal agreement, either with or without a sum of money. The third, though valid in point of law, was discouraged to the greatest extent, as being contrary to the laws of morality (Selden, *Ux. Ebr.* ii. 1, 2).

IV. In considering the social and domestic conditions of married life among the Hebrews, we must in the first place take into account the position assigned to women generally in their social scale. The seclusion of the *harem* and the habits consequent upon it were utterly unknown in early times, and the condition of the oriental woman, as pictured to us in the Bible, contrasts most favorably with that of her modern representative. There is abundant evidence that women, whether married or unmarried, went about with their faces unveiled

(Gen. xii. 14, xxiv. 16, 65, xxix. 11; 1 Sam. i. 13). An unmarried woman might meet and converse with men, even strangers, in a public place (Gen. xxiv. 24, 45–47, xxix. 9–12; 1 Sam. ix. 11): she might be found alone in the country without any reflection on her character (Deut. xxii. 25–27): or she might appear in a court of justice (Num. xxvii. 2). Women not unfrequently held important offices; some were prophetesses, as Miriam, Deborah, Huldah, Noadiah, and Anna: of others advice was sought in emergencies (2 Sam. xiv. 2, xx. 16–22). They took their part in matters of public interest (Ex. xv. 20; 1 Sam. xviii. 6, 7): in short, they enjoyed as much freedom in ordinary life as the women of our own country.

If such was her general position, it is certain that the wife must have exercised an important influence in her own home. She appears to have taken her part in family affairs, and even to have enjoyed a considerable amount of independence. For instance, she entertains guests at her own desire (2 K. iv. 8) in the absence of her husband (Judg. iv. 18), and sometimes even in defiance of his wishes (1 Sam. xxv. 14, &c.): she disposes of her child by a vow without any reference to her husband (1 Sam. i. 24): she consults with him as to the marriage of her children (Gen. xxvii. 46): her suggestions as to any domestic arrangements meet with due attention (2 K. iv. 9): and occasionally she criticizes the conduct of her husband in terms of great severity (1 Sam. xxv. 25; 2 Sam. vi. 20).

The relations of husband and wife appear to have been characterized by affection and tenderness. He is occasionally described as the "friend" of his wife (Jer. iii. 20; Hos. iii. 1), and his love for her is frequently noticed (Gen. xxiv. 67, xxix. 18). On the other hand, the wife was the consolation of the husband in time of trouble (Gen. xxiv. 67), and her grief at his loss presented a picture of the most abject woe (Joel i. 8). No stronger testimony, however, can be afforded as to the ardent affection of husband and wife, than that which we derive from the general tenor of the book of Canticles. At the same time we cannot but think that the exceptions to this state of affairs were more numerous than is consistent with our ideas of matrimonial happiness. One of the evils inseparable from polygamy is the discomfort arising from the jealousies and quarrels of the several wives, as instanced in the households of Abraham and Elkanah (Gen. xxi. 11; 1 Sam. i. 6). The purchase of wives, and the small amount of liberty allowed to daughters in the choice of husbands, must inevitably have led to unhappy unions. The allusions to the misery of a contentious and brawling wife in the Proverbs (xix. 13, xxi. 9, 19, xxvii. 15) convey the impression that the infliction was of frequent occurrence in Hebrew households, and in the Mishna (*Ketub.* 7, § 6) the fact of a woman being noisy is laid down as an adequate ground for divorce. In the N. T. the mutual relations of husband and wife are a subject of frequent exhortation (Eph. v. 22–33; Col. iii. 18, 19; Tit. ii. 4, 5; 1 Pet. iii. 1–7): it is certainly a noticeable coincidence that these exhortations should be found exclusively in the epistles addressed to Asiatics, nor is it improbable that they

---

[a] חֻפָּה. The term occurs in the Mishna (*Ketub.* i, § 5), and is explained by some of the Jewish commentators to have been a bower of roses and myrtles. The term was also applied to the canopy under which the nuptial benediction was pronounced, or to the robe spread over the heads of the bride and bridegroom (Selden, ii. 15).

were more particularly needed for them than for Europeans.

The duties of the wife in the Hebrew household were multifarious: in addition to the general super-intendence of the domestic arrangements, such as cooking, from which even women of rank were not exempted (Gen. xviii. 6; 2 Sam. xiii. 8), and the distribution of food at meal-times (Prov. xxxi. 15), the manufacture of the clothing and the various textures required in an eastern establishment de-volved upon her (Prov. xxxi. 13, 21, 22), and if she were a model of activity and skill, she produced a surplus of fine linen shirts and girdles, which she sold, and so, like a well-freighted merchant-ship, brought in wealth to her husband from afar (Prov. xxxi. 14, 24). The poetical description of a good housewife drawn in the last chapter of the Proverbs is both filled up and in some measure illustrated by the following minute description of a wife's duties towards her husband, as laid down in the Mishna: "She must grind corn, and bake, and wash, and cook, and suckle his child, make his bed, and work in wool. If she brought her husband one bondwoman, she need not grind, bake, or wash: if two, she need not cook nor suckle his child: if three, she need not make his bed nor work in wool: if four, she may sit in her chair of state" (Ketub. 5, § 5). Whatever money she earned by her labor belonged to her husband (ib. 6, § 1). The qualifi-cation not only of working, but of working at home (Tit. ii. 5, where οἰκουργούς is preferable to οἰκουρούς), was insisted on in the wife, and to spin in the street was regarded as a violation of Jewish customs (Ketub. 7, § 6).

The legal rights of the wife are noticed in Ex. xxi. 10, under the three heads of food, raiment, and duty of marriage or conjugal right. These were defined with great precision by the Jewish doctors; for thus only could one of the most cruel effects of polygamy be averted, namely, the sacrifice of the rights of the many in favor of the one whom the lord of the modern harem selects for his special attention. The regulations of the Talmudists founded on Ex. xxi. 10 may be found in the Mishna (Ketub. 5, § 6-9).

V. The allegorical and typical allusions to mar-riage have exclusive reference to one subject, namely, to exhibit the spiritual relationship between God and his people. The earliest form, in which the image is implied, is in the expression "to go a whoring," and "whoredom," as descriptive of the rupture of that relationship by acts of idolatry. These expressions have by some writers been taken in their primary and literal sense, as pointing to the licentious practices of idolaters. But this de-stroys the whole point of the comparison, and is opposed to the plain language of Scripture: for (1) Israel is described as the false wife [a] "playing the harlot" (Is. i. 21; Jer. iii. 1, 6, 8); (2) Je-hovah is the injured husband, who therefore divorces her (Ps. lxxiii. 27; Jer. ii. 20; Hos. iv. 12, ix. 1); and (3) the other party in the adultery is specified, sometimes generally, as idols or false gods (Deut. xxxi. 16; Judg. ii. 17; 1 Chr. v. 25; Ez. xx. 30, xxiii. 30), and sometimes particularly, as in the case of the worship of goats (A. V.

"devils," Lev. xvii. 7), Molech (Lev. xx. 5), wizards (Lev. xx. 6), an ephod (Judg. viii. 27), Baalim (Judg. viii. 33), and even the heart and eyes (Num. xv. 39) — the last of these objects being such as wholly to exclude the idea of actual adultery. The image is drawn out more at length by Ezekiel (xxiii.), who compares the kingdoms of Samaria and Judah to the harlots Aholah and Aholibah; and again by Hosea (i.-iii.), whose marriage with an adulterous wife, his separation from her, and subsequent reunion with her, were designed to be a visible lesson to the Israelites of their dealings with Jehovah.

The direct comparison with marriage is confined in the O. T. to the prophetic writings, unless we regard the Canticles as an allegorical work. [CAN-TICLES.] The actual relation between Jehovah and his people is generally the point of comparison (Is. liv. 5, lxii. 4; Jer. iii. 14; Hos. ii. 19; Mal. ii. 11); but sometimes the graces consequent thereon are described under the image of bridal attire (Is. xlix. 18, lxi. 10), and the joy of Jehovah in his Church under that of the joy of a bridegroom (Is. lxii. 5).

In the N. T. the image of the bridegroom is transferred from Jehovah to Christ (Matt. ix. 15; John iii. 29), and that of the bride to the Church (2 Cor. xi. 2; Rev. xix. 7, xxi. 2, 9, xxii. 17), and the comparison thus established is converted by St. Paul into an illustration of the position and mutual duties of man and wife (Eph. v. 23-32). The suddenness of the Messiah's appearing, particularly at the last day, and the necessity of watchfulness, are inculcated in the parable of the Ten Virgins, the imagery of which is borrowed from the customs of the marriage ceremony (Matt. xxv. 1-13). The Father prepares the marriage feast for his Son, the joys that result from the union being thus repre-sented (Matt. xxii. 1-14, xxv. 10; Rev. xix. 9; comp. Matt. viii. 11), while the qualifications requisite for admission into that union are prefigured by the marriage garment (Matt. xxii. 11). The breach of the union is, as before, described as fornication or whoredom in reference to the mystical Babylon (Rev. xvii. 1, 2, 5).

The chief authorities on this subject are Selden's *Uxor Ebraica*; Michaelis' *Commentaries*; the Mishna, particularly the books *Yebamoth, Ketuboth, Gittin,* and *Kiddushin*; Buxtorf's *Sponsal. et Divort.* Among the writers on special points we may notice Benary, *de Hebr. Leviratu,* Berlin, 1835; Redslob's *Leviratsehe,* Leipzig, 1836; and Kurtz's *Ehe des Hosea,* Dorpat, 1859.

W. L. B.

* **MARS' HILL,** another name in the A. V., Acts xvii. 22, for Areopagus, ver. 19. The name is the same in Greek (ὁ Ἄρειος πάγος), and should be the same in English. The variation seems to be without design, or certainly without any dis-tinction of meaning; for the translators remark in the margin against both passages that Areopagus was "the highest court in Athens." The older versions of Tyndale, Cranmer, and the Genevan ren-der "Mars strete" in both places, while Wycliffe writes "Areopage." Against the view that Paul was arraigned and tried before the court,[b] as well

---

[a] The term זָנָה (זָנָה), in its ordinary applica-tion, is almost without exception applied to the act of the woman. We may here notice the only exceptions to the ordinary sense of this term, namely, Is. xxiii. 17,

where it means "commerce," and Nah. iii. 4, where it is equivalent to "crafty policy," just as in 2 K. ix. 22 the parallel word is "witchcrafts."

[b] * The modern Greeks in their disposition to re-

as on the topography of the subject, see AREOPAGUS. It is proposed here to give some account of the speech itself, which Paul delivered on this hill, and which has given to it a celebrity "above all Greek, above all Roman fame."

Scholars vie with each other in their commendation of this discourse. In its suggestiveness, depth of thought, cogent reasonings, eloquence, and remarkable adaptation to all the congruities of time and place,[a] although not the longest it is beyond question the first of all the recorded speeches of the great Apostle. De Wette pronounces it "a model of the apologetic style of discourse." "The address of Paul before this assembly," says Neander, "is a living proof of his apostolic wisdom and eloquence. We perceive here how the Apostle, according to his own expression, could become also a heathen to the heathen, that he might win the heathen to a reception of the gospel." "The skill," says Hemsen, "with which he was able to bring the truth near to the Athenians, deserves admiration. We find in this discourse of Paul nothing of an ill-timed zeal, nothing like declamatory pomp. It is distinguished for clearness, brevity, coherence, and simplicity of representation." Some object that the speech has been overpraised because Paul was not enabled to bring it to a formal close. But in truth our astonishment is not that he was interrupted at length when he came to announce to them the Christian doctrine of a resurrection of the body, but that he held their attention so long while he exposed their errors and convicted them of the absurdity and sinfulness of their conduct.

The following is an outline of the general course of thought. The Apostle begins by declaring that the Athenians were more than ordinarily religious, and commends them for that trait of character. He had read on one of their altars an inscription[b] to "an unknown God." He recognizes in that acknowledgment the heart's testimony among the heathen themselves, that all men feel the limitations of their religious knowledge and their need of a more perfect revelation. It was saying to them in effect: "You are correct in acknowledging a divine existence beyond any which the ordinary rites of your worship recognize; there is such an existence. You are correct in confessing that this Being is unknown to you; you have no just conception of his nature and perfections." With this introduction he passes to his theme. "Whom therefore not knowing, ye worship, this one I announce unto you." He thus proposes to guide their religious instincts and aspirations to their proper object, i. e. to teach them what God is, his nature and attributes, and men's relations to Him, in opposition to their false views and practices as idolaters (ver. 23). In pursuance of this purpose he announces to them, first, that God is the Creator of the outward, material universe, and therefore not to be confounded with idols (ver. 24); secondly, that He is independent of his creatures, possessed of all sufficiency in Himself, and in no need of costly gifts or offer-

ings of food and drink (ver. 25); thirdly, that He is the Creator of all mankind, notwithstanding their separation into so many nations, and their wide dispersion on the earth (ver. 26); and fourthly, that he has placed men, as individuals and nations, in such relations of dependence on Himself as render it easy for them to see that He is their Creator and Disposer; and that it is their duty to seek and serve Him (vv. 27, 28). The ground has thus been won for a direct application of the truth to his auditors. At this point of the discourse, as we may well suppose, stretching forth his hand towards the gorgeous images within sight, he exclaims: "We ought not, therefore, to suppose that the Deity is like unto gold, or silver, or stone, sculptured by the art and device of man" (ver. 29). Nor is this all. That which men ought not to do, they may not with impunity any longer do. It was owing to the forbearance of God that the heathen had been left hitherto to disown the true God, and transfer to idols the worship which belongs to Him. He had borne with them as if he had not seen their willful ignorance, and would not call them to account for it; but now, with a knowledge of the gospel, they were required to repent of their idolatry and forsake it (ver. 30), because a day of righteous retribution awaited them, of which they had assurance in the resurrection of Christ from the dead (ver. 31).

Here their clamors interrupted him; but it is not difficult to conjecture what was left unsaid. The recorded examples of his preaching show that he would have held up to them more distinctly the character of Christ as the Saviour of men, and have urged them to call on his name and be saved. It is impossible to say just in what sense the Apostle adduced the resurrection of Christ as proof of a general judgment. His resurrection from the dead confirmed the truth of all his claims, and one of these was that He was to be the judge of men (John v. 28, 29). His resurrection also established the possibility of such a resurrection of all men as was implied in the Apostle's doctrine, that all men are to be raised from the dead and stand before the judgment-seat of Christ. The Apostle may have had these and similar connections of the fact in his mind; but whether he had developed them so far, when he was silenced, that the Athenians perceived them all or any of them, is uncertain. It was enough to excite their scorn to hear of a single instance of resurrection. The Apostle's reference in his last words to a great day of assize for all mankind would no doubt recall to the hearers the judicial character of the place where they were assembled, but it was too essential a part of his train of thought to have been accidentally suggested by the place.

We are to recognize the predominant anti-polytheistic aim of the discourse in the prominence which Paul here gives to his doctrine with respect to the common parentage of the human race, while at the same time he thereby rebuked the Athenians for

store the ancient names of their history now call their highest appellate court the Ἄρεος πάγος (Areopagus). It consists of a πρόεδρος, or Chief Justice, and several σύνεδροι or Associates, and holds its sessions at Athens.   H.

a * The speech if genuine must exhibit these correspondences; but with a strange perversity Baur (Der Apost. Paulus, p. 167 f.) admits their existence, and argues from them that the speech must be ficti-

tious, on account of this remarkable fitness to the occasion.   H.

b * The Apostle's use of δεισιδαιμονεστέρους, at the opening of the speech, Dean Howson very justly points out as one of the proofs of his tact and versatility. (See Lectures on the Character of St. Paul, p. 45, i. 194, note a, Amer. ed.) Rev. T. Kenrick's vindication of the rendering of the A. V. (Biblical Essays, pp. 108–129, Lond. 1864) shows only that the word admits of that sense.   H.

their contempt of the other nations, especially of the Jews. If all are the children of a common parent, then the idea of a multiplicity of gods from whom the various nations have derived their origin, or whose protection they specially enjoy, must be false. The doctrine of the unity of the race is closely interwoven with that of the unity of the divine existence. But if all nations have the same Creator, it would at once occur that nothing can be more absurd than the feeling of superiority and contempt with which one affects to look down upon another. As the Apostle had to encounter the prejudice which was entertained against him as a foreigner and a Jew, his course of remark was doubly pertinent, if adapted at the same time to remove this kindrance to a candid reception of his meaning.

It will be seen from the foregoing sketch that it has been proposed, not without some justification, to arrange the contents of the discourse under the three heads of *theology*, *anthropology*, and *Christology*. At all events it will be seen, by casting the eye back, that we have here all the parts of a perfect discourse, namely, the exordium, the proposition or theme, the proof or exposition, and the application. It is a beautiful specimen of the manner in which a powerful and well-trained mind, practiced in public speaking, conforms spontaneously to the rules of the severest logic. One can readily believe, looking at this feature of the discourse, that it was pronounced by the man who wrote the epistles to the Romans and Galatians, where we see the same mental characteristics so strongly reflected. As we must suppose, on any view of the case, that

Mars' Hill, on the south side, and west from the Acropolis. (Photograph.)

the general scheme of thought, the *nexus* of the argument, has been preserved, it does not affect our critical judgment whether we maintain that the discourse has been reported in full, or that a synopsis only has been given.

It might have seemed to the credit of Christianity if Luke had represented the preaching of Paul as signally effective here at Athens, the centre of Grecian arts and refinement: on the contrary, he records no such triumphs.[a] The philosophers who heard him mocked: the people at large derided him as "a babbler." At the close of that day on which Paul delivered the speech it might seem as if he had spoken almost to no purpose. But the end is not yet. Our proper rule for judging here is that which makes "a thousand years with God as one day, and one day as a thousand years." We place ourselves again on the rock where Paul stood, and look around us, and how different a spectacle presents itself from that which met the Apostle's eye.

The monuments of idolatry on which he looked have disappeared. The gorgeous image of Minerva which towered aloft on the Acropolis, has been broken to pieces, and scattered to the winds. The temples at that time there so magnificent and full of idols,[b] remain only as splendid ruins, literally inhabited by the owls and the bats. Churches and chapels dedicated to Christian worship appear on every side, surmounted with the sign of that cross, which was "to the Jews a stumbling-block, and to the Greeks foolishness." This cross itself has become the national emblem, and gilds the future of these descendants of Paul's hearers with its brightest hopes. These and such results may indeed fall short of the highest spiritual effects of Christianity; but they show nevertheless the mighty change which has taken place in the religious ideas and civilization of pagan Greece, and bear witness to the power of St. Paul's seemingly ineffective speech on Mars' Hill. One must read the discourse on the spot, amid the

---

a * It is worthy of notice, that although Paul spent the next two years at Corinth, so near Athens that the Acropolis of the one city may be seen from the other, he did not during that time turn his steps again to Athens. On his third missionary tour, he came once more into this part of Greece, and on the way passed

Athens twice at least, and yet he did not revisit that city.   H.

b * Zeune (*ad Vig.* p. 638 *a*) points out the mistranslation of κατειδωλον by "given to idolatry," instead of "full of idols." It conceals from the reader a striking mark of Luke's accuracy. No ancient city was so famous for its images as Athens.   H.

objects and associations which bring the past and present as it were into visible contact with each other, in order to understand and feel the impression of the contrast in its full extent.

Paul spoke of course in the open air. For a description of the scene under the Apostle's eye at the time, see Wordsworth's *Views of Greece, Pictorial, Descriptive, and Historical*, p. 85, also his *Athens* and *Attica*, ch. xi.; Robinson's *Bibl. Researches*, i. 10 f. (where the bearing of Mars' Hill from the Acropolis should be west, instead of north). For a view of the Acropolis restored, as seen from the Areopagus, see Conybeare and Howson's *Life and Letters of St. Paul*, i. 442. Stier treats at length of the discourse, exegetically and homiletically, in his *Reden der Apostel*, ii. 121-169. The events at Athens form an interesting sketch in Howson's *Scenes from the Life of St. Paul*, ch. vi. (Lond. 1866), and reprint by the American Tract Society (1868). Bentley's famous Sermons on Atheism and Deism (first of the series of Boyle Lectures, 1692) connect themselves almost historically with this address. Seven of the eight texts on which he founds the sermons are taken from Paul's Athenian speech. The topics on which the Apostle touched as the preacher enumerates them are "such as the existence, the spirituality, and all-sufficiency of God; the creation of the world; the origination of mankind from one common stock, according to the history of Moses; the divine Providence in overruling all nations and people; the new doctrine of repentance by the preaching of the gospel; the resurrection of the dead; and the appointed day of an universal judgment" (see his *Works*, iii. 33 f., Lond. 1838). We find here the germs of the best arguments employed in later times in controversies of the nature alluded to. Another later work furnishes a similar testimony. Mr. Merivale has recourse to Paul's sententious words for the principal text-mottoes prefixed to his Lectures on the *Conversion of the Roman Empire* (Boyle Lectures for 1864). It is one of those speeches of the Apostle, "from all the ideas of which" (as Schneckenburger remarks of the one at Antioch, Acts xiii.) "may be drawn lines which terminate in his peculiar doctrinal teachings in the epistles" (*Stud. u. Krit.* 1855, p. 550). "Nothing can be more genuinely Pauline," says Lechler, "than the division here of history into its two great epochs, the pre-Messianic and post-Messianic, and the union of God's manifestations in creation, conscience, and redemption. It gives us in outline the fuller discussion in Rom. i. and ii." (*Das Apost. u. Nach. apost. Zeitalter*, p. 155). Ch. J. Trip refutes some of Baur's hypercritical objections to the genuineness of the speech (*Paulus nach der Apostelgesch.* p. 200 ff.). Other writers who may be consulted are F. W. Laufs, *Ueber die areopagische Rede des Apostels Paulus* (Stud. u. Krit., 1850, pp. 583-595); Williger's *Apostelgesch. in Bibelstunden*, pp. 500-526 (2te Aufl.); Lange's *Kirchengesch.* ii. 222 ff., Gademann's "Theologische Studien," *Zeitschrift für luther. Theologie*, 1854, p. 648 ff.; Tholuck, *Glaubwürdigkeit*, p. 380 f.; Baumgarten, *Apostelgesch.* in loc.; and Pressensé, *Histoire de l'Église Chrétienne*, ii. 17-22. See also an article on "Paul at Athens" by Prof. A. C. Kendrick, *Christian Review*, xv. 95-110, and one on "Paul's Discourse at Athens: A Commentary on Acts xvii. 16-34," *Bibl. Sacra*, vi. 338-356.   H.

MAR'SENA (מַרְסְנָא [*worthy*, Pers., Fürst]:

Μαλισεάρ: [Vat. FA.] Alex. Μαλησεαν: *Marsana*), one of the seven princes of Persia, "wise men which knew the times," which saw the king's face and sat first in the kingdom (Esth. i. 14). According to Josephus they had the office of interpreters of the laws (*Ant.* xi. 6, § 1).

MAR'THA (Μάρθα: *Martha*). This name, which does not appear in the O. T., belongs to the later Aramaic, and is the feminine form of מָרָא = Lord. We first meet with it towards the close of the 2d century B. C. Marius, the Roman dictator, was attended by a Syrian or Jewish prophetess Martha during the Numidian war and in his campaign against the Cimbri (Plutarch, *Marius*, xvii.). Of the Martha of the N. T. there is comparatively little to be said. What is known or conjectured as to the history of the family of which she was a member may be seen under LAZARUS. The facts recorded in Luke x. and John xi. indicate a character devout after the customary Jewish type of devotion, sharing in Messianic hopes and accepting Jesus as the Christ; sharing also in the popular belief in a resurrection (John xi. 24), but not rising, as her sister did, to the belief that Christ was making the eternal life to belong, not to the future only, but to the present. When she first comes before us in Luke x. 38, as receiving her Lord into her house (it is uncertain whether at Bethany or elsewhere), she loses the calmness of her spirit, is "cumbered with much serving," is "careful and troubled about many things." She is indignant that her sister and her Lord care so little for that for which she cares so much. She needs the reproof "one thing is needful;" but her love, though imperfect in its form, is yet recognized as true, and she too, no less than Lazarus and Mary, has the distinction of being one whom Jesus loved (John xi. 3). Her position here, it may be noticed, is obviously that of the elder sister, the head and manager of the household. It has been conjectured that she was the wife or widow of "Simon the leper" of Matt. xxvi. 6 and Mark xiv. 3 (Schulthess, in Winer, *Rwb.*; Paulus, in Meyer, *in loc.*; Greswell, *Diss. on Village of Martha and Mary*). The same character shows itself in the history of John xi. She goes to meet Jesus as soon as she hears that He is coming, turning away from all the Pharisees and rulers who had come with their topics of consolation (vv. 19, 20). The same spirit of complaint that she had shown before finds utterance again (ver. 21), but there is now, what there was not before, a fuller faith at once in his wisdom and his power (ver. 22). And there is in that sorrow an education for her as well as for others. She rises from the formula of the Pharisee's creed to the confession which no "flesh and blood," no human traditions, could have revealed to her (vv. 24-27). It was an immense step upward from the dull stupor of a grief which refused to be comforted, that without any definite assurance of an *immediate* resurrection, she should now think of her brother as living still, never dying, because he had believed in Christ. The transition from vain fruitless regrets to this assured faith, accounts it may be for the words spoken by her at the sepulchre (ver. 39). We judge wrongly of her if we see in them the utterance of an impatient or desponding unbelief. The thought of that true victory over death has comforted her, and she is no longer expecting that the power of the eternal life will show itself in the renewal of the earthly The wonder that followed, no less than the tears which preceded, taught her how deeply her Lord sympathized with the passionate human sorrows of which He had seemed to her so unmindful. It taught her, as it teaches us, that the eternal life in which she had learnt to believe was no absorption of the individual being in that of the spirit of the universe — that it recognized and embraced all true and pure affections.

Her name appears once again in the N. T. She is present at the supper at Bethany as "serving" (John xii. 2). The old character shows itself still, but it has been freed from evil. She is no longer "cumbered," no longer impatient. Activity has been calmed by trust. When other voices are raised against her sister's overflowing love, hers is not heard among them.

The traditions connected with Martha have been already mentioned. [LAZARUS.] She goes with her brother and other disciples to Marseilles, gathers round her a society of devout women, and, true to her former character, leads them to a life of active ministration. The wilder Provençal legends make her victorious over a dragon that laid waste the country. The town of Tarascon boasted of possessing her remains, and claimed her as its patron saint (*Acta Sanctorum*, and *Brev. Rom.* in Jul. 29; Fabricii *Lux Evangel.* p. 388).

E. H. P.

* MARTYR occurs only in Acts xxii. 15 as the translation of μάρτυς, the proper sense of which is simply "witness," without the necessary idea of sealing one's testimony by his death as understood by our stricter use of "martyr." All the older English versions (from Wycliffe, 1380, to the Rheims, 1582) have "witness" in this passage. It was not till after the age of the Apostles that the Greek word (μάρτυρ or μάρτυς) signified "martyr," though we see it in its transition to that meaning in Acts xxii. 20 and Rev. xvii. 6. Near the close of the second century it had become so honorable a title, that the Christians at Lyons, exposed to torture and death, and fearful that they might waver in the moment of extremity, refused to be called "martyrs" (μάρτυρες). "This name," said they, "properly belongs only to the true and faithful witness, the Prince of Life; or, at least, only to those whose testimony Christ has sealed by their constancy to the end. We are but poor, humble confessors, *i. e.* ὁμόλογοι." (Euseb. *Hist. Eccles.* v. 2.) On μάρτυς see Cremer's *Wörterb. der Neutest. Gräcität*, p. 371 f.   H.

MA'RY OF CLE'OPHAS. So in A. V., but accurately "of CLOPAS" (Μαρία ἡ τοῦ Κλωπᾶ). In St. John's Gospel we read that "there stood by the cross of Jesus his mother, and his mother's sister, Mary of Clopas, and Mary Magdalene" (John xix. 25). The same group of women is described by St. Matthew as consisting of Mary Magdalene, and Mary of James and Joses, and the mother of Zebedee's children" (Matt. xxvii. 56); and by St. Mark, as "Mary Magdalene, and Mary of James the Little and of Joses, and Salome " [a] (Mark xv. 40). From a comparison of these passages, it appears that Mary of Clopas, and Mary

of James the Little and of Joses, are the same person, and that she was the sister of St. Mary the Virgin. The arguments, preponderating on the affirmative side, for this Mary being (according to the A. V. translation) the *wife* of Clopas or Alphæus, and the *mother* of James the Little, Joses, Jude, Simon, and their sisters, have been given under the heading JAMES. There is an apparent difficulty in the fact of two sisters seeming to bear the name of Mary. To escape this difficulty, it has been suggested (1) that the two clauses "his mother's sister" and "Mary of Clopas," are not in apposition, and that St. John meant to designate four persons as present — namely, the mother of Jesus; her sister, to whom he does not assign any name; Mary of Clopas; and Mary Magdalene (Lange). And it has been further suggested that this sister's name was Salome, wife of Zebedee (Wieseler). This is avoiding, not solving a difficulty. St. John could not have expressed himself as he does had he meant more than three persons. It has been suggested (2) that the word ἀδελφή is not here to be taken in its strict sense, but rather in the laxer acceptation, which it clearly does bear in other places. Mary, wife of Clopas, it has been said, was not the sister, but the cousin of St. Mary the Virgin (see Wordsworth, *Gk. Test.*, Preface to the Epistle of St. James). There is nothing in this suggestion which is objectionable, or which can be disproved. But it appears unnecessary and unlikely: unnecessary, because the fact of two sisters having the same name, though unusual, is not singular; and unlikely, because we find the two families so closely united — living together in the same house, and moving about together from place to place — that we are disposed rather to consider them connected by the nearer than the more distant tie. That it is far from impossible for two sisters to have the same name, may be seen by any one who will cast his eye over Betham's Genealogical Tables. To name no others, his eye will at once light on a pair of Antonias and a pair of Octavias, the daughters of the same father, and in one case of different mothers, in the other of the same mother. If it be objected that these are merely gentilic names, another table will give two Cleopatras. It is quite possible too that the same cause which operates at present in Spain, may have been at work formerly in Judæa. MIRIAM, the sister of Moses, may have been the holy woman after whom Jewish mothers called their daughters, just as Spanish mothers not unfrequently give the name of Mary to their children, male and female alike, in honor of St. Mary the Virgin.[b] This is on the hypothesis that the two names are identical, but on a close examination of the Greek text, we find that it is possible that this was not the case. St. Mary the Virgin is Μαριάμ; her sister is Μαρία. It is more than possible that these names are the Greek representatives of two forms which the antique מִרְיָם had then taken; and as in pronunciation the emphasis would have been thrown on the last syllable in Μαριάμ, while the final letter in Μαρία would have been almost unheard, there

---

[a] The form of the expression "Mary of Clopas," "Mary of James," in its more colloquial form "Clopas' Mary," "James' Mary," is familiar to every one acquainted with English village life. It is still a common thing for the unmarried, and sometimes for the married women of the laboring classes in a country town or village, to be distinguished from their namesakes, not

by their surnames, but by the name of their father or husband, or son, *e. g.* "William's Mary," "John's Mary," etc.

[b] Maria, Maria-Pia, and Maria-Immacolata, are the first names of three of the sisters of the late king of the Two Sicilies.

would, upon this hypothesis, have been a greater difference in the sisters' names than there is between Mary and Maria among ourselves.[a]

Mary of Clopas was probably the elder sister of the Lord's mother. It would seem that she had married Clopas or Alphæus while her sister was still a girl. She had four sons, and at least three daughters. The names of the daughters are unknown to us: those of the sons are James, Joses, Jude, Simon, two of whom became enrolled among the twelve Apostles [JAMES], and a third (Simon) may have succeeded his brother in the charge of the Church of Jerusalem. Of Joses and the daughters we know nothing. Mary herself is brought before us for the first time on the day of the Crucifixion — in the parallel passages already quoted from St. Matthew, St. Mark, and St. John. In the evening of the same day we find her sitting desolately at the tomb with Mary Magdalene (Matt. xxvii. 61; Mark xv. 47), and at the dawn of Easter morning she was again there with sweet spices, which she had prepared on the Friday night (Matt. xxviii. 1; Mark xiv. 1; Luke xxiii. 50), and was one of those who had "a vision of angels, which said that He was alive" (Luke xxiv. 23). These are all the glimpses that we have of her. Clopas or Alphæus is not mentioned at all, except as designating Mary and James. It is probable that he was dead before the ministry of our Lord commenced. Joseph, the husband of St. Mary the Virgin, was likewise dead; and the two widowed sisters, as was natural both for comfort and for protection, were in the custom of living together in one house. Thus the two families came to be regarded as one, and the children of Mary and Clopas were called the brothers and sisters of Jesus. How soon the two sisters commenced living together cannot be known. It is possible that her sister's house at Nazareth was St. Mary's home at the time of her marriage, for we never hear of the Virgin's parents. Or it may have been on their return from Egypt to Nazareth that Joseph and Mary took up their residence with Mary and Clopas. It is more likely that the union of the two households took place after the death of Joseph and of Clopas. In the second year of our Lord's ministry, we find that they had been so long united as to be considered one by their fellow-townsmen (Matt. xiii. 55) and other Galileans (Matt. xii. 47). At whatever period it was that this joint housekeeping commenced, it would seem to have continued at Nazareth (Matt. xiii. 55) and at Capernaum (John ii. 12), and elsewhere, till St. John took St. Mary the Virgin to his own home in Jerusalem, A. D. 30. After this time Mary of Clopas would probably have continued living with St. James the Little and her other children at Jerusalem until her death. The fact of her name being omitted on all occasions on which her children and her sister are mentioned, save only on the days of the Crucifixion and the Resurrection, would indicate a retiring disposition, or perhaps an advanced

age. That his cousins were older than Jesus, and consequently that their mother was the elder sister of the Virgin, may be gathered as likely from Mark iii. 21, as it is not probable that if they had been younger than Jesus, they would have ventured to have attempted to interfere by force with Him for over-exerting himself, as they thought, in the prosecution of his ministry. We may note that the Gnostic legends of the early ages, and the mediæval fables and revelations alike refuse to acknowledge the existence of a sister of St. Mary, as interfering with the miraculous conception and birth of the latter.   F. M.

MARY MAGDALENE (Μαρία ἡ Μαγδαληνή: *Maria Magdalene*). Four different explanations have been given of this name. (1.) That which at first suggests itself as the most natural, that she came from the town of Magdala. The statement that the women with whom she journeyed, followed Jesus in Galilee (Mark xv. 41) agrees with this notion. (2.) Another explanation has been found in the fact that the Talmudic writers in their calumnies against the Nazarenes make mention of a Miriam Megaddela (מגדלא), and deriving that word from the Piel of גָּדַל, to twine, explain it as meaning "the twiner or plaiter of hair." They connect with this name a story which will be mentioned later; but the derivation has been accepted by Lightfoot (*Hor. Heb.* on Matt. xxvii. 56; *Harm. Evang.* on Luke viii. 2), as satisfactory, and pointing to the previous worldliness of "Miriam with the braided locks," as identical with "the woman that was a sinner" of Luke vii. 37. It has been urged in favor of this, that the ἡ καλουμένη of Luke viii. 2 implies something peculiar, and is not used where the word that follows points only to origin or residence. (3.) Either seriously, or with the patristic fondness for *paronomasia*, Jerome sees in her name, and in that of her town, the old Migdol (= a watch-tower), and dwells on the coincidence accordingly. The name denotes the steadfastness of her faith. She is "vere συργίτης, vere turris candoris et Libani, quæ prospicit in faciem Damasci" (*Epist. ad Principiam*).[b] He is followed in this by later Latin writers, and the pun forms the theme of a panegyric sermon by Odo of Clugni (*Acta Sanctorum*, Antwerp, 1727, July 12). (4.) Origen, lastly, looking to the more common meaning of גָּדַל (*gâdal*, to be great), sees in her name a prophecy of her spiritual greatness as having ministered to the Lord, and been the first witness of his resurrection (*Tract. in Matt.* xxxv.). It will be well to get a firm standing-ground in the facts that are definitely connected in the N. T. with Mary Magdalene before entering on the perplexed and bewildering conjectures that gather round her name.

I. She comes before us for the first time in Luke viii. 2. It was the custom of Jewish women

---

a The ordinary explanation that Μαριάμ is the Hebraic form, and Μαρία the Greek form, and that the difference is in the use of the Evangelists, not in the name itself, seems scarcely adequate: for why should the Evangelists invariably employ the Hebraic form when writing of St. Mary the Virgin, and the Greek form when writing about all the other Maries in the Gospel history? It is true that this distinction is not constantly observed in the readings of the Codex Vaticanus, the Codex Ephraemi, and a few other MSS.;

but there is sufficient agreement in the majority of the Codices to determine the usage. That it is possible for a name to develop into several kindred forms, and for these forms to be considered sufficiently distinct appellations for two or more brothers or sisters, is evidenced by our daily experience.

b The writer is indebted for this quotation, and for one or two references in the course of the article, to the kindness of Mr. W. A. Wright.

(Jerome on 1 Cor. ix. 5) to contribute to the support of Rabbis whom they reverenced, and in conformity with that custom, there were among the disciples of Jesus, women who "ministered unto Him of their substance." All appear to have occupied a position of comparative wealth. With all the chief motive was that of gratitude for their deliverance from "evil spirits and infirmities." Of Mary it is said specially that "seven devils (δαιμόνια) went out of her," and the number indicates, as in Matt. xii. 45, and the "Legion" of the Gadarene demoniac (Mark v. 9), a possession of more than ordinary malignity. We must think of her, accordingly, as having had, in their most aggravated forms, some of the phenomena of mental and spiritual disease which we meet with in other demoniacs, the wretchedness of despair, the divided consciousness, the preternatural frenzy, the long-continued fits of silence. The appearance of the same description in Mark xvi. 9 (whatever opinion we may form as to the authorship of the closing section of that Gospel) indicates that this was the fact most intimately connected with her name in the minds of the early disciples. From that state of misery she had been set free by the presence of the Healer, and, in the absence, as we may infer, of other ties and duties, she found her safety and her blessedness in following Him. The silence of the Gospels as to the presence of these women at other periods of the Lord's ministry, makes it probable that they attended on Him chiefly in his more solemn progresses through the towns and villages of Galilee, while at other times he journeyed to and fro without any other attendants than the Twelve, and sometimes without even them. In the last journey to Jerusalem, to which so many had been looking with eager expectation, they again accompanied Him (Matt. xxvii. 55; Mark xv. 41; Luke xxiii. 55, xxiv. 10). It will explain much that follows if we remember that this life of ministration must have brought Mary Magdalene into companionship of the closest nature with Salome the mother of James and John (Mark xv. 40), and even also with Mary the mother of the Lord (John xix. 25). The women who thus devoted themselves are not prominent in the history: we have no record of their mode of life, or abode, or hopes or fears during the few momentous days that preceded the crucifixion. From that hour, they come forth for a brief two days' space into marvelous distinctness. They "stood afar off, beholding these things" (Luke xxiii. 49) during the closing hours of the Agony on the Cross. Mary Magdalene, Mary the mother of the Lord, and the beloved disciple were at one time not afar off, but close to the cross, within hearing. The same close association which drew them together there is seen afterwards. She remains by the cross till all is over, waits till the body is taken down, and wrapped in the linen cloth and placed in the garden-sepulchre of Joseph of Arimathea. She remains there in the dusk of the evening watching what she must have looked on as the final resting-place of the Prophet and Teacher whom she had honored (Matt. xxvii. 61; Mark xv. 47; Luke xxiii. 55). Not to her had there been given the hope of the Resurrection. The disciples to whom the words that

spoke of it had been addressed had failed to understand them, and were not likely to have reported them to her. The Sabbath that followed brought an enforced rest, but no sooner is the sunset over than she, with Salome and Mary the mother of James, "brought sweet spices that they might come and anoint" the body, the interment of which on the night of the crucifixion they looked on as hasty and provisional (Mark xvi. 1).

The next morning accordingly, in the earliest dawn (Matt. xxviii. 1; Mark xvi. 2), they come with Mary the mother of James, to the sepulchre. It would be out of place to enter here into the harmonistic discussions which gather round the history of the Resurrection. As far as they connect themselves with the name of Mary Magdalene, the one fact which St. John records is that of the chiefest interest. She had been to the tomb and had found it empty, had seen the "vision of angels" (Matt. xxviii. 5; Mark xvi. 5). To her, however, after the first moment of joy, it had seemed to be but a vision. She went with her cry of sorrow to Peter and John (let us remember that Salome had been with her), "they have taken away the Lord out of the sepulchre, and we know not where they have laid Him" (John xx. 1, 2). But she returns there. She follows Peter and John, and remains when they go back. The one thought that fills her mind is still that the body is not there. She has been robbed of that task of reverential love on which she had set her heart. The words of the angels can call out no other answer than that — "They have taken away my Lord, and I know not where they have laid Him" (John xx. 13). This intense brooding over one fixed thought was, we may venture to say, to one who had suffered as she had suffered, full of special danger, and called for a special discipline. The spirit must be raised out of its blank despair, or else the "seven devils" might come in once again, and the last state be worse than the first. The utter stupor of grief is shown in her want of power to recognize at first either the voice or the form of the Lord to whom she had ministered (John xx. 14, 15). At last her own name uttered by that voice as she had heard it uttered, it may be, in the hour of her deepest misery, recalls her to consciousness; and then follows the cry of recognition, with the strongest word of reverence which a woman of Israel could use, "Rabboni," and the rush forward to cling to his feet. That, however, is not the discipline she needs. Her love had been too dependent on the visible presence of her Master. She had the same lesson to learn as the other disciples. Though they had "known Christ after the flesh," they were "henceforth to know Him so no more." She was to hear that truth in its highest and sharpest form. "Touch me not, for I am not yet ascended to my Father." For a time, till the earthly affection had been raised to a heavenly one, she was to hold back. When He had finished his work and had ascended to the Father, there should be no barrier then to the fullest communion that the most devoted love could crave for. Those who sought, might draw near and touch Him then. He would be one with them, and they one with him.[a] — It was fit that

---

a • The passage referred to is one of acknowledged difficulty. It is certainly an objection to the view proposed above that it represents our Lord as forbidding Mary to touch him, though he permitted the other women to whom he showed himself on their

return to the city, not only to approach him, but to hold him by the feet and worship him (Matt. xxviii. 9). It is to be noted that the verb which describes the act of the others (ἐκράτησαν) is a different one from that which describes the act denied to Mary (μή

this should be the last mention of Mary. The Evangelist, whose position, as the son of Salome, must have given him the fullest knowledge at once of the facts of her after-history, and of her inmost thoughts, bore witness by his silence, in this case as in that of Lazarus, to the truth that lives, such as theirs, were thenceforth "hid with Christ in God."

II. What follows will show how great a contrast there is between the spirit in which he wrote and that which shows itself in the later traditions. Out of these few facts there rise a multitude of wild conjectures; and with these there has been constructed a whole romance of hagiology.

The questions which meet us connect themselves with the narratives in the four Gospels of women who came with precious ointment to anoint the feet or the head of Jesus. Each Gospel contains an account of one such anointing; and men have asked, in endeavoring to construct a harmony, "Do they tell us of four distinct acts, or of three, or of two, or of one only? On any supposition but the last, are the distinct acts performed by the same or by different persons; and if by different, then by how many? Further, have we any grounds for identifying Mary Magdalene with the woman or with any one of the women whose acts are thus brought before us?" This opens a wide range of possible combinations, but the limits of the inquiry may, without much difficulty, be narrowed. Although the opinion seems to have been at one time maintained (Origen, *Tract. in Matt.* xxxv.), few would now hold that Matt. xxvi. and Mark xiv. are reports of two distinct events. Few, except critics bent, like Schleiermacher and Strauss, on getting up a case against the historical veracity of the Evangelists, could persuade themselves that the narrative of Luke vii., differing as it does in well-nigh every circumstance, is but a misplaced and embellished version of the incident which the first two Gospels connect with the last week of our Lord's ministry. The supposition that there were three anointings has found favor with Origen (*l. c.*) and Lightfoot (*Harm. Evang.* in loc., and *Hor. Heb.* in Matt. xxvi.); but while, on the one hand, it removed some harmonistic difficulties, there is, on the other,

something improbable to the verge of being inconceivable, in the repetition within three days of the same scene, at the same place, with precisely the same murmur and the same reproof. We are left to the conclusion adopted by the great majority of interpreters, that the Gospels record two anointings, one in some city unnamed (Capernaum or Nain have been suggested), during our Lord's Galilean ministry (Luke vii.), the other at Bethany, before the last entry into Jerusalem (Matt. xxvi.; Mark xiv.; John xii.). We come, then, to the question whether in these two narratives we meet with one woman or with two. The one passage adduced for the former conclusion is John xi. 2. It has been urged (Maldonatus *in Matt.* xxvi. and *Joan.* xi. 2, *Acta Sanctorum*, July 22d) that the words which we find there (" It was that Mary which anointed the Lord with ointment . . . . . whose brother Lazarus was sick ") could not possibly refer by anticipation to the history which was about to follow in ch. xii., and must therefore presuppose some fact known through the other Gospels to the Church at large, and that fact, it is inferred, is found in the history of Luke vii. Against this it has been said on the other side, that the assumption thus made is entirely an arbitrary one, and that there is not the slightest trace of the life of Mary of Bethany ever having been one of open and flagrant impurity.[a]

There is, therefore, but slender evidence for the assumption that the two anointings were the acts of one and the same woman, and that woman the sister of Lazarus. There is, if possible, still less for the identification of Mary Magdalene with the chief actor in either history. (1.) When her name appears in Luke viii. 3 there is not one word to connect it with the history that immediately precedes. Though possible, it is at least unlikely that such an one as the "sinner" would at once have been received as the chosen companion of Joanna and Salome, and have gone from town to town with them and the disciples. Lastly, the description that *is* given — "Out of whom went seven devils" — points, as has been stated, to a form of suffering all but absolutely incompatible with the life implied in ἁμαρτωλός, and to a very

---

μου ἅπτου). This variation is of itself suggestive of a different purpose on the part of Mary in offering to touch him, and on the Saviour's part in interrupting the act.

Meyer on the basis of this difference in the language suggests another explanation, which deserves to be mentioned. It will be found in his remarks on John xx. 17 (*Comm.* pp. 499-502, 3te Aufl.). He adopted a different view in his earlier studies. It should be observed that this imperative present form (μὴ ἅπτου) implies an incipient act either actually begun, or one on the point of being done, as indicated by some look or gesture.

Mary, it may well be supposed, was in the same perplexed state of mind on the appearance of Christ to her, which was evinced in so many different ways by the other disciples after the resurrection. She had already, it is true, exclaimed in the ecstasy of her joy, " Rabboni," but she may not yet have been certain as to the precise form or nature of the body in which she beheld her Lord. It is He, the Great Master, verily, she is assured; but is He corporeal, having really come forth out of the grave? Or is it his glorified spirit, having already gone up to God, but now having descended to her in its spiritual investiture? In this state of uncertainty she extends her hand to assure herself of the truth. She would procure for herself

by the criterion of the sense of touch the conviction which the eye is unable to give her. The Saviour knows her thoughts, and arrests the act. The act is unnecessary: his words are a sufficient proof of what she would know. He "had not yet ascended to the Father," as she half believed, and consequently has not the spiritual body which she supposed he might possibly have. He gives her by this declaration the assurance respecting his bodily state which she had proposed to gain for herself through the medium of sense. Her case was that of Thomas, and yet unlike his; she wished, like him, to touch the object of her vision, but, unlike him, was not prompted by unbelief.

With this exegesis the confirmatory οὔπω γὰρ ἀναβέβηκα which follows has its logical justification. No explanation can be correct which fails to satisfy that condition.   H.

[a] The difficulty is hardly met by the portentous conjecture of one commentator, that the word ἁμαρτωλός does not mean what it is commonly supposed to mean, and that the "many sins" consisted chiefly (as the name Magdalene, according to the etymology noticed above, implies) in her giving too large a portion of the Sabbath to the braiding or plaiting of her hair (?) Lamy in Lampe on John xii. 2.

different work of healing from that of the divine words of pardon — "Thy sins be forgiven thee." To say, as has been said, that the "seven devils" are the "many sins" (Greg. Mag. *Hom. in Evang.* 25 and 53', is to identify two things which are separated in the whole tenor of the N. T. by the clearest line of demarcation. The argument that because Mary Magdalene is mentioned so soon afterwards she must be the same as the woman of Luke vii. (Butler's *Lives of the Saints,* July 22), is simply puerile. It would be just as reasonable to identify "the sinner" with Susanna. Never, perhaps, has a figment so utterly baseless obtained so wide an acceptance as that which we connect with the name of the "penitent Magdalene." It is to be regretted that the chapter-heading of the A. V. of Luke vii. should seem to give a quasi-authoritative sanction to a tradition so utterly uncertain, and that it should have been perpetuated in connection with a great work of mercy. (2.) The belief that Mary of Bethany and Mary Magdalene are identical is yet more startling. Not one single circumstance, except that of love and reverence for their Master, is common. The epithet Magdalene, whatever may be its meaning, seems chosen for the express purpose of distinguishing her from all other Maries. No one Evangelist gives the slightest hint of identity. St. Luke mentions Martha and her sister Mary in x. 38, 39, as though neither had been named before. St. John, who gives the fullest account of both, keeps their distinct individuality most prominent. The only *simulacrum* of an argument on behalf of the identity is that, if we do not admit it, we have no record of the sister of Lazarus having been a witness of the resurrection.

Nor is this lack of evidence in the N. T. itself compensated by any such weight of authority as would indicate a really trustworthy tradition. Two of the earliest writers who allude to the histories of the anointing — Clement of Alexandria (*Paedag.* ii. 8) and Tertullian (*de Pudic.* ch. 8) — say nothing that would imply that they accepted it. The language of Irenæus (iii. 4) is against it. Origen (*l. c.*) discusses the question fully, and rejects it. He is followed by the whole succession of the expositors of the Eastern Church: Theophilus of Antioch, Macarius, Chrysostom, Theophylact. The traditions of that Church, when they wandered into the regions of conjecture, took another direction, and suggested the identity of Mary Magdalene with the daughter of the Syro-Phœnician woman of Mark vii. 26 (Nicephorus, *H. E.* i. 33). In the Western Church, however, the other belief began to spread. At first it is mentioned hesitatingly, as by Ambrose (*de Virg. Vel.* and in *Luc.* lib. vi.), Jerome (in *Matt.* xxvi. 2; *contr. Jovin.* c. 16). Augustine at one time inclines to it (*de Consens. Evang.* c. 69), at another speaks very doubtingly (*Tract. in Joann.* 49). At the close of the first great period of Church history, Gregory the Great takes up both notions, embodies them in his Homilies (in *Ev.* 25, 53) and stamps them with his authority. The reverence felt for him, and the constant use of his works as a text-book of theology during the whole mediæval period, secured for the hypothesis a currency which it never would have gained on its own merits. The services of the feast of St. Mary Magdalene were constructed on the assumption of its truth (*Brev. Rom. in Jul.* p. 22). Hymns and paintings and sculptures fixed it deep in the minds of the Western nations, France

and England being foremost in their reverence for the saint whose history appealed to their sympathies. (See below.) Well-nigh all ecclesiastical writers, after the time of Gregory the Great (Albert the Great and Thomas Aquinas are exceptions), take it for granted. When it was first questioned by Fèvre d'Étaples (Faber Stapulensis) in the early Biblical criticism of the 16th century, the new opinion was formally condemned by the Sorbonne (*Acta Sanctorum,* l. c.), and denounced by Bishop Fisher of Rochester. The Prayer-book of 1549 follows in the wake of the Breviary; but in that of 1552, either on account of the uncertainty or for other reasons, the feast disappears. The Book of Homilies gives a doubtful testimony. In one passage the "sinful woman" is mentioned without any notice of her being the same as the Magdalene (*Serm. on Repentance,* Part ii.); in another it depends upon a comma whether the two are distinguished or identified (*ibid.* Part ii.). The translators under James I., as has been stated, adopted the received tradition. Since that period there has been a gradually accumulating *consensus* against it. Calvin, Grotius, Hammond, Casaubon, among older critics, Bengel, Lampe, Greswell, Alford, Wordsworth, Stier, Meyer, Ellicott, Olshausen, among later, agree in rejecting it. Romanist writers even (Tillemont, Dupin, Estius) have borne their protest against it in whole or in part; and books that represent the present teaching of the Gallican Church reject entirely the identification of the two Maries as an unhappy mistake (Migne, *Dict. de la Bible*). The mediæval tradition has, however, found defenders in Baronius, the writers of the *Acta Sanctorum,* Maldonatus, Bishop Andrewes, Lightfoot, Isaac Williams, and Dr. Pusey.

It remains to give the substance of the legend formed out of these combinations. At some time before the commencement of our Lord's ministry, a great sorrow fell upon the household of Bethany. The younger of the two sisters fell from her purity and sank into the depths of shame. Her life was that of one possessed by the "seven devils" of uncleanness. From the city to which she then went, or from her harlot-like adornments, she was known by the new name of Magdalene. Then she hears of the Deliverer, and repents and loves and is forgiven. Then she is received at once into the fellowship of the holy women and ministers to the Lord, and is received back again by her sister and dwells with her, and shows that she has chosen the good part. The death of Lazarus and his return to life are new motives to her gratitude and love; and she shows them, as she had shown them before, anointing no longer the feet only, but the head also of her Lord. She watches by the cross, and is present at the sepulchre and witnesses the resurrection. Then (the legend goes on, when the work of fantastic combination is completed), after some years of waiting, she goes with Lazarus and Martha and Maximin (one of the Seventy) to Marseilles [comp. LAZARUS]. They land there; and she, leaving Martha to more active work, retires to a cave in the neighborhood of Arles, and there leads a life of penitence for thirty years. When she dies a church is built in her honor, and miracles are wrought at her tomb. Clovis the Frank is healed by her intercession, and his new faith is strengthened; and the chivalry of France does homage to her name as to that of the greater Mary.

Such was the full-grown form of the Western story. In the East there was a different tradition.

Nicephorus (*H. E.* ii. 10) states that she went to Rome to accuse Pilate for his unrighteous judgment; Modestus, patriarch of Constantinople (*Hom. in Marias*), that she came to Ephesus with the Virgin and St. John, and died and was buried there. The Emperor Leo the Philosopher (circ. 890) brought her body from that city to Constantinople (*Acta Sanctorum*, l. c.).

The name appears to have been conspicuous enough, either among the living members of the Church of Jerusalem or in their written records, to attract the notice of their Jewish opponents. The Talmudists record a tradition, confused enough, that Stada or Satda, whom they represent as the mother of the Prophet of Nazareth, was known by this name as a "plaiter or twiner of hair;" that she was the wife of Paphus Ben-Jehudah, a contemporary of Gamaliel, Joshua, and Akiba; and that she grieved and angered him by her wantonness (Lightfoot, *Hor. Heb.* on Matt. xxvi., *Harm. Evang.* on Luke viii. 3). It seems, however, from the fuller report given by Eisenmenger, that there were two women to whom the Talmudists gave this name, and the wife of Paphus is not the one whom they identified with the Mary Magdalene of the Gospels (*Entdeckt. Judenth.* i. 277).

There is lastly the strange supposition (rising out of an attempt to evade some of the harmonistic difficulties of the resurrection history), that there were two women both known by this name, and both among those who went early to the sepulchre (Lampe, *Comm. in Joann.*; Ambrose, *Comm. in Luc.* x. 24).   E. H. P.

MARY, MOTHER OF MARK. The woman known by this description must have been among the earliest disciples. We learn from Col. iv. 10 that she was sister to Barnabas, and it would appear from Acts iv. 37, xii. 12, that, while the brother gave up his land and brought the proceeds of the sale into the common treasury of the Church, the sister gave up her house to be used as one of its chief places of meeting. The fact that Peter goes to that house on his release from prison indicates that there was some special intimacy (Acts xii. 12) between them, and this is confirmed by the language which he uses towards Mark as being his "son" (1 Pet. v. 13). She, it may be added, must have been, like Barnabas, of the tribe of Levi, and may have been connected, as he was, with Cyprus (Acts iv. 36). It has been surmised that filial anxiety about her welfare during the persecutions and the famine which harassed the Church at Jerusalem, was the chief cause of Mark's withdrawal from the missionary labors of Paul and Barnabas. The tradition of a later age represented the place of meeting for the disciples, and therefore probably the house of Mary, as having stood on the upper slope of Zion, and affirmed that it had been the scene of the wonder of the day of Pentecost, had escaped the general destruction of the city by Titus, and was still used as a church in the 4th century (Epiphan. *de Pond. et Mens.* xiv.: Cyril. Hierosol. *Catech.* xvi.).   E. H. P.

MARY, SISTER OF LAZARUS. For much of the information connected with this name, comp. LAZARUS and MARY MAGDALENE. The facts strictly personal to her are but few. She and her sister Martha appear in Luke x. 40, as receiving Christ in their house. The contrasted temperaments of the two sisters have been already in part discussed [MARTHA]. Mary sat listening eagerly

for every word that fell from the Divine Teacher. She had chosen the good part, the life that has found its unity, the "one thing needful," in rising from the earthly to the heavenly, no longer distracted by the "many things" of earth. The same character shows itself in the history of John xi. Her grief is deeper but less active. She sits still in the house. She will not go to meet the friends who come on the formal visit of consolation. But when her sister tells her secretly "The Master is come and calleth for thee," she rises quickly and goes forth at once (John xi. 20, 28). Those who have watched the depth of her grief have but one explanation for the sudden change: "She goeth to the grave to weep there!" Her first thought when she sees the Teacher in whose power and love she had trusted, is one of complaint. "She fell down at his feet, saying, Lord, if thou hadst been here, my brother had not died." Up to this point, her relation to the Divine Friend had been one of reverence, receiving rather than giving, blessed in the consciousness of his favor. But the great joy and love which her brother's return to life calls up in her, pour themselves out in larger measure than had been seen before. The treasured alabaster-box of ointment is brought forth at the final feast of Bethany, John xii. 3. St. Matthew and St. Mark keep back her name. St. John records it as though the reason for the silence held good no longer. Of her he had nothing more to tell. The education of her spirit was completed. The love which had been recipient and contemplative shows itself in action.

Of her after-history we know nothing. The ecclesiastical traditions about her are based on the unfounded hypothesis of her identity with Mary Magdalene.   E. H. P.

MARY THE VIRGIN (Μαριάμ: on the form of the name see p. 1811). There is no person perhaps in sacred or in profane literature, around whom so many legends have been grouped as the Virgin Mary; and there are few whose authentic history is more concise. The very simplicity of the evangelical record has no doubt been one cause of the abundance of the legendary matter of which she forms the central figure. Imagination had to be called in to supply a craving which authentic narrative did not satisfy. We shall divide her life into three periods. I. The period of her childhood, up to the time of the birth of our Lord. II. The period of her middle age, contemporary with the Bible Record. III. The period subsequent to the Ascension. The first and last of these are wholly legendary, except in regard to one fact mentioned in the Acts of the Apostles; the second will contain her real history. For the first period we shall have to rely on the early apocryphal gospels; for the second on the Bible; for the third on the traditions and tales which had an origin external to the Church, but after a time were transplanted within her boundaries, and there flourished and increased both by the force of natural growth, and by the accretions which from time to time resulted from supposed visions and revelations.

I. *The childhood of Mary, wholly legendary.* — Joachim and Anna were both of the race of David. The abode of the former was Nazareth; the latter passed her early years at Bethlehem. They lived piously in the sight of God, and faultlessly before man, dividing their substance into three portions, one of which they devoted to the service of the

Temple, another to the poor, and the third to their own wants. And so twenty years of their lives passed silently away. But at the end of this period Joachim went to Jerusalem with some others of his tribe, to make his usual offering at the Feast of the Dedication. And it chanced that Issachar was high-priest (Gospel of Birth of Mary); that Reuben was high-priest (Protevangelion). And the high-priest scorned Joachim, and drove him roughly away, asking how he dared to present himself in company with those who had children, while he had none; and he refused to accept his offerings until he should have begotten a child, for the Scripture said, "Cursed is every one who does not beget a man-child in Israel." And Joachim was shamed before his friends and neighbors, and he retired into the wilderness and fixed his tent there, and fasted forty days and forty nights. And at the end of this period an angel appeared to him, and told him that his wife should conceive, and should bring forth a daughter, and he should call her name Mary. Anna meantime was much distressed at her husband's absence, and being reproached by her maid Judith with her barrenness, she was overcome with grief of spirit. And in her sadness she went into her garden to walk, dressed in her wedding-dress. And she sat down under a laurel-tree, and looked up and spied among the branches a sparrow's nest, and she bemoaned herself as more miserable than the very birds, for they were fruitful and she was barren; and she prayed that she might have a child even as Sarai was blessed with Isaac. And two angels appeared to her, and promised her that she should have a child who should be spoken of in all the world. And Joachim returned joyfully to his home, and when the time was accomplished, Anna brought forth a daughter, and they called her name Mary. Now the child Mary increased in strength day by day, and at nine months of age she walked nine steps. And when she was three years old her parents brought her to the Temple, to dedicate her to the Lord. And there were fifteen stairs up to the Temple, and while Joseph and Mary were changing their dress, she walked up them without help; and the high-priest placed her upon the third step of the altar, and she danced with her feet, and all the house of Israel loved her. Then Mary remained at the Temple until she was twelve (Prot.) fourteen (G. B. M.) years old, ministered to by the angels, and advancing in perfection as in years. At this time the high-priest commanded all the virgins that were in the Temple to return to their homes and to be married. But Mary refused, for she said that she had vowed virginity to the Lord. Thus the high-priest was brought into a perplexity, and he had recourse to God to inquire what he should do. Then a voice from the ark answered him (G. B. M.), an angel spake unto him (Prot.); and they gathered together all the widowers in Israel (Prot.), all the marriageable men of the house of David (G. B. M.), and desired them to bring each man his rod. And amongst them came Joseph and brought his rod, but he shunned to present it, because he was an old man and had children. There-

fore the other rods were presented and no sign occurred. Then it was found that Joseph had not presented his rod; and behold, as soon as he had presented it, a dove came forth from the rod and flew upon the head of Joseph (Prot.); a dove came from heaven and pitched on the rod (G. B. M.). And Joseph, in spite of his reluctance, was compelled to betroth himself to Mary, and he returned to Bethlehem to make preparations for his marriage (G. B. M.); he betook himself to his occupation of building houses (Prot.); while Mary went back to her parents' house in Galilee. Then it chanced that the priests needed a new veil for the Temple, and seven virgins cast lots to make different parts of it; and the lot to spin the true purple fell to Mary. And she went out with a pitcher to draw water. And she heard a voice, saying unto her, "Hail, thou that art highly favored, the Lord is with thee. Blessed art thou among women!" and she looked round with trembling to see whence the voice came, and she laid down the pitcher and went into the house and took the purple and sat down to work at it. And behold the angel Gabriel stood by her and filled the chamber with prodigious light, and said, "Fear not," etc. And when Mary had finished the purple, she took it to the high-priest; and having received his blessing, went to visit her cousin Elizabeth, and returned back again.[a] Then Joseph returned to his home from building houses (Prot.); came into Galilee, to marry the Virgin to whom he was betrothed (G. B. M.), and finding her with child, he resolved to put her away privily; but being warned in a dream, he relinquished his purpose, and took her to his house. Then came Annas the scribe to visit Joseph, and he went back and told the priest that Joseph had committed a great crime, for he had privately married the Virgin whom he had received out of the Temple, and had not made it known to the children of Israel. And the priest sent his servants, and they found that she was with child; and he called them to him, and Joseph denied that the child was his, and the priest made Joseph drink the bitter water of trial (Num. v. 18), and sent him to a mountainous place to see what would follow. But Joseph returned in perfect health, so the priest sent them away to their home. Then after three months Joseph put Mary on an ass to go to Bethlehem to be taxed; and as they were going, Mary besought him to take her down, and Joseph took her down and carried her into a cave, and leaving her there with his sons, he went to seek a midwife. And as he went he looked up, and he saw the clouds astonished and all creatures amazed. The fowls stopped in their flight; the working people sat at their food, but did not eat; the sheep stood still; the shepherds' lifted hands became fixed; the kids were touching the water with their mouths, but did not drink. And a midwife came down from the mountains, and Joseph took her with him to the cave, and a bright cloud overshadowed the cave, and the cloud became a bright light, and when the bright light faded, there appeared an infant at the breast of Mary. Then the midwife went out and told

---

[a] Three spots lay claim to be the scene of the Annunciation. Two of these are, as was to be expected, in Nazareth, and one, as every one knows, is in Italy. The Greeks and Latins each claim to be the guardians of the true spot in Palestine; the third claimant is the holy house of Loretto. The Greeks point out the spring of water mentioned in the Protevangelion as

confirmatory of their claim. The Latins have engraved on a marble slab in the grotto of their convent in Nazareth the words *Verbum hic caro factum est*, and point out the pillar which marks the spot where the angel stood; whilst the Head of their Church is irretrievably committed to the wild legend of Loretto. (See Stanley, *S. & P.* ch. xiv.)

Salome that a Virgin had brought forth, and Salome would not believe; and they came back again into the cave, and Salome received satisfaction, but her hand withered away, nor was it restored, until, by the command of an angel, she touched the child, whereupon she was straightway cured. (Giles, *Codex Apocryphus Novi Testamenti*, pp. 33–47 and 66–81, Lond. 1852; Jones, *On the New Testament*, ii. c. xiii. and xv., Oxf. 1827; Thilo, *Codex Apocryphus*. See also *Vita glorississimæ Matris Annæ per F. Petrum Dorlando*, appended to Ludolph of Saxony's *Vita Christi*, Lyons, 1642; and a most audacious *Historia Christi*, written in Persian by the Jesuit P. Jerome Xavier, and exposed by Louis de Dieu, Lugd. Bat. 1639.)

II. *The real history of Mary.* — We now pass from legend to that period of St. Mary's life which is made known to us by Holy Scripture. In order to give a single view of all that we know of her who was chosen to be the mother of the Saviour, we shall in the present section put together the whole of her authentic history, supplementing it afterwards by the more prominent legendary circumstances which are handed down.

We are wholly ignorant of the name and occupation of St. Mary's parents. If the genealogy given by St. Luke is that of St. Mary (Greswell, *etc.*), her father's name was Heli, which is another form of the name given to her legendary father, Jehoiakim or Joachim. If Jacob and Heli were the two sons of Matthan or Matthat, and if Joseph, being the son of the younger brother, married his cousin, the daughter of the elder brother (Hervey, *Genealogies of our Lord Jesus Christ*), her father was Jacob. The Evangelist does not tell us, and we cannot know. She was, like Joseph, of the tribe of Judah, and of the lineage of David (Ps. cxxxii. 11; Luke i. 32; Rom. i. 3). She had a sister, named probably like herself, Mary (John xix. 25) [MARY OF CLEOPHAS], and she was connected by marriage (συγγενής, Luke i. 36) with Elisabeth, who was of the tribe of Levi and of the lineage of Aaron. This is all that we know of her antecedents.

In the summer of the year which is known as B. C. 5, Mary was living at Nazareth, probably at her parents' — possibly at her elder sister's — house, not having yet been taken by Joseph to his home. She was at this time betrothed to Joseph and was therefore regarded by the Jewish law and custom as his wife, though he had not yet a husband's rights over her. [MARRIAGE, p. 1804.] At this time the angel Gabriel came to her with a message from God, and announced to her that she was to be the mother of the long expected Messiah. He probably bore the form of an ordinary man, like the angels who manifested themselves to Gideon and to Manoah (Judg. vi., xiii.). This would appear both from the expression εἰσελθών, "he came in;" and also from the fact of her being troubled, not at his presence, but at the meaning of his words. The scene as well as the salutation is very similar to that recounted in the Book of Daniel, "Then there came again and touched me one like the appearance of a man, and he strengthened me, and said, O man greatly beloved, fear not: peace be unto thee, be strong, yea, be strong!" (Dan. x. 18, 19). The exact meaning of κεχαριτωμένη is "thou that hast bestowed upon thee a free gift of grace." The A. V. rendering of "highly favored" is therefore very exact and much nearer to the original than the "*gratia plena*" of the

Vulgate, on which a huge and wholly unsubstantial edifice has been built by Romanist devotional writers. The next part of the salutation, "The Lord is with thee," would probably have been better translated, "The Lord be with thee." It is the same salutation as that with which the angel accosts Gideon (Judg. vi. 12). "Blessed art thou among women" is nearly the same expression as that used by Ozias to Judith (Jud. xiii. 18). Gabriel proceeds to instruct Mary that by the operation of the Holy Ghost the everlasting Son of the Father should be born of her; that in Him the prophecies relative to David's throne and kingdom should be accomplished; and that his name was to be called Jesus. He further informs her, perhaps as a sign by which she might convince herself that his prediction with regard to herself would come true, that her relative Elisabeth was within three months of being delivered of a child.

The angel left Mary, and she set off to visit Elisabeth either at Hebron or JUTTAH (whichever way we understand the εἰς τὴν ὀρεινὴν εἰς πόλιν Ἰούδα, Luke i. 39), where the latter lived with her husband Zacharias, about 20 miles to the south of Jerusalem, and therefore at a very considerable distance from Nazareth. Immediately on her entrance into the house she was saluted by Elisabeth as the mother of her Lord, and had evidence of the truth of the angel's saying with regard to her cousin. She embodied her feelings of exultation and thankfulness in the hymn known under the name of the *Magnificat*. Whether this was uttered by immediate inspiration, in reply to Elisabeth's salutation, or composed during her journey from Nazareth, or was written at a later period of her three months' visit at Hebron, does not appear for certain. The hymn is founded on Hannah's song of thankfulness (1 Sam. ii. 1–10), and exhibits an intimate knowledge of the Psalms, prophetical writings, and books of Moses, from which sources almost every expression in it is drawn. The most remarkable clause, "From henceforth all generations shall call me blessed," is borrowed from Leah's exclamation on the birth of Asher (Gen. xxx. 13). The same sentiment and expression are also found in Prov. xxxi. 28; Mal. iii. 12; Jas. v. 11. In the latter place the word μακαρίζω is rendered with great exactness "count happy." The notion that there is conveyed in the word any anticipation of her bearing the title of "Blessed" arises solely from ignorance.

Mary returned to Nazareth shortly before the birth of John the Baptist, and continued living at her own home. In the course of a few months Joseph became aware that she was with child, and determined on giving her a bill of divorcement, instead of yielding her up to the law to suffer the penalty which he supposed that she had incurred. Being, however, warned and satisfied by an angel who appeared to him in a dream, he took her to his own house. It was soon after this, as it would seem, that Augustus' decree was promulgated, and Joseph and Mary travelled to Bethlehem to have their names enrolled in the registers (B. C. 4) by way of preparation for the taxing, which however was not completed till ten years afterwards (A. D. 6), in the governorship of Quirinus. They reached Bethlehem, and there Mary brought forth the Saviour of the world, and humbly laid him in a manger.

The visit of the shepherds, the circumcision, the adoration of the wise men, and the presentation in the Temple, are rather scenes in the life of Christ than in that of his mother. The presentation in the Temple might not take place till forty days after the birth of the child. During this period the mother, according to the law of Moses, was unclean (Lev. xii.). In the present case there could be no necessity for offering the sacrifice and making atonement beyond that of obedience to the Mosaic precept; but already He, and his mother for Him, were acting upon the principle of fulfilling all righteousness. The poverty of St. Mary and Joseph, it may be noted, is shown by their making the offering of the poor. The song of Simeon and the thanksgiving of Anna, like the wonder of the shepherds and the adoration of the magi, only incidentally refer to Mary. One passage alone in Simeon's address is specially directed to her, "Yea a sword shall pierce through thy own soul also." The exact purport of these words is doubtful. A common patristic explanation refers them to the pang of unbelief which shot through her bosom on seeing her Son expire on the cross (Tertullian, Origen, Basil, Cyril, etc.). By modern interpreters it is more commonly referred to the pangs of grief which she experienced on witnessing the sufferings of her Son.

In the flight into Egypt, Mary and the babe had the support and protection of Joseph, as well as in their return from thence, in the following year, on the death of Herod the Great (B. C. 3).[a] It appears to have been the intention of Joseph to have settled at Bethlehem at this time, as his home at Nazareth had been broken up for more than a year; but on finding how Herod's dominions had been disposed of, he changed his mind and returned to his old place of abode, thinking that the child's life would be safer in the tetrarchy of Antipas than in that of Archelaus. It is possible that Joseph might have been himself a native of Bethlehem, and that before this time he had been only a visitor at Nazareth, drawn thither by his betrothal and marriage. In that case, his fear of Archelaus would make him exchange his own native town for that of Mary. It may be that the holy family at this time took up their residence in the house of Mary's sister, the wife of Clopas.

Henceforward, until the beginning of our Lord's ministry — i. e. from B. C. 3 to A. D. 26 — we may picture St. Mary to ourselves as living in that light, in a humble sphere of life, the wife of Joseph the carpenter, pondering over the sayings of the angels, of the shepherds, of Simeon, and those of her Son, as the latter "increased in wisdom and stature and in favor with God and man" (Luke ii. 52). Two circumstances alone, so far as we know, broke in on the otherwise even flow of the still waters of her life. One of these was the temporary loss of her Son when he remained behind in Jerusalem, A. D. 8. The other was the death of Joseph. The exact date of this last event we cannot determine. But it was probably not long after the other.

From the time at which our Lord's ministry commenced, St. Mary is withdrawn almost wholly from sight. Four times only is the veil removed, which, not surely without a reason, is thrown over her. These four occasions are — 1. The marriage at Cana of Galilee (John ii.). 2. The attempt which she and his brethren made "to speak with him" (Matt. xii. 46; Mark iii. 21 and 31; Luke viii. 19). 3. The Crucifixion. 4. The days succeeding the Ascension (Acts i. 14). If to these we add two references to her, the first by her Nazarene fellow-citizens (Matt. xiii. 54, 55; Mark vi. 1-3), the second by a woman in the multitude (Luke xi. 27), we have specified every event known to us in her life. It is noticeable that, on every occasion of our Lord's addressing her, or speaking of her, there is a sound of reproof in his words, with the exception of the last words spoken to her from the cross.

1. The marriage at Cana in Galilee took place in the three months which intervened between the baptism of Christ and the passover of the year 27. When Jesus was found by his mother and Joseph in the Temple in the year 8, we find him repudiating the name of "father" as applied to Joseph. "*Thy father* and I have sought thee sorrowing" — "How is it that ye sought me? Wist ye not that I must be about" (not Joseph's and yours, but) "*my Father's* business?" (Luke-ii. 48, 49). Now, in like manner, at his first miracle which inaugurates his ministry, He solemnly withdraws himself from the authority of his earthly mother. This is St. Augustine's explanation of the "What have I to do with thee? my hour is not yet come." It was his humanity, not his divinity, which came from Mary. While therefore He was acting in his divine character He could not acknowledge her, nor does He acknowledge her again until He was hanging on the cross, when, in that nature which He took from her, He was about to submit to death (St. Aug. *Comm. in Joan. Evang.* tract viii., vol. iii. p. 1455, ed. Migne, Paris, 1845). That the words Τί ἐμοὶ καὶ σοί; = מַה־לִּי וָלָךְ, imply reproof, is certain (cf. Matt. viii. 29; Mark i. 24; and LXX., Judg. xi. 12; 1 K. xvii. 18; 2 K. iii. 13), and such is the patristic explanation of them (see Iren. *Adv. Hær.* iii. 18; *Apud Bibl. Patr. Max.* tom. ii. pt. ii. 293; S. Chrys. *Hom. in Joan.* xxi.). But the reproof is of a gentle kind (Trench, *on the Miracles*, p. 102, Lond. 1856; Alford, *Comm.* in loc.; Wordsworth, *Comm.* in loc.). Mary seems to have understood it, and accordingly to have drawn back desiring the servants to pay attention to her divine Son (Olshausen, *Comm.* in loc.). The modern Romanist translation, "What is that to me and to thee?" is not a mistake, because it is a willful misrepresentation (Douay version; Oraini, *Life of Mary*, etc.; see *The Catholic Layman*, p. 117, Dublin, 1852).

2. Capernaum (John ii. 12), and Nazareth (Matt. iv. 13, xiii. 54; Mark vi. 1), appear to have been

---

[a] In the Gospel of the Infancy, which seems to date from the 2d century, innumerable miracles are made to attend on St. Mary and her Son during their sojourn in Egypt: e. g., Mary looked with pity on a woman who was possessed, and immediately Satan came out of her in the form of a young man, saying, "Woe is me because of thee, Mary, and thy Son!" On another occasion they fall in with two thieves, named Titus and Dumachus; and Titus was gentle, and Dumachus was harsh; the Lady Mary therefore promised Titus that God should receive him on his right hand. And accordingly, thirty-three years afterwards, Titus was the penitent thief who was crucified on the right hand, and Dumachus was crucified on the left. These are sufficient as samples. Throughout the book we find St. Mary associated with her Son, in the strange freaks of power attributed to them, in a way which shows us whence the *cultus* of St. Mary took its origin. (See Jones, *On the New Test.*, vol. ii. Oxf. 1827; Giles, *Codex Apocryphus*; Thilo, *Codex Apocryphus*.)

the residence of St. Mary for a considerable period. The next time that she is brought before us we find her at Capernaum. It is the autumn of the year 28, more than a year and a half after the miracle wrought at the marriage feast in Cana. The Lord had in the mean time attended two feasts of the passover, and had twice made a circuit throughout Galilee, teaching and working miracles. His fame had spread, and crowds came pressing round him, so that he had not-even time "to eat bread." Mary was still living with her sister, and her nephews and nieces, James, Joses, Simon, Jude, and their three sisters (Matt. xiii. 55); and she and they heard of the toils which He was undergoing, and they understood that He was denying himself every relaxation from his labors. Their human affection conquered their faith. They thought that He was killing himself, and with an indignation arising from love, they exclaimed that He was beside himself, and set off to bring Him home either by entreaty or compulsion.[a] He was surrounded by eager crowds, and they could not reach Him. They therefore sent a message, begging Him to allow them to speak to Him. This message was handed on from one person in the crowd to another, till at length it was reported aloud to Him. Again He reproves. Again He refuses to admit any authority on the part of his relatives, or any privilege on account of their relationship. "Who is my mother, and who are my brethren? and He stretched forth his hand toward his disciples, and said, Behold my mother and my brethren! For whosoever shall do the will of my Father which is in heaven, the same is my brother, and sister, and mother" (Matt. xii. 48, 49). Comp. Theoph. in Marc. iii. 32; S. Chrys. Hom. xliv. in Matt.; S. Aug. in Joan. tract x., who all of them point out that the blessedness of St. Mary consists, not so much in having borne Christ, as in believing on Him and in obeying his words (see also Quæst. et Resp. ad Orthod. cxxxvi., ap. S. Just. Mart. in Bibl. Max. Patr. tom. ii. pt. ii. p. 138). This indeed is the lesson taught directly by our Lord himself on the next occasion on which reference is made to St. Mary. It is now the spring of the year 30, and only about a month before the time of his crucifixion. Christ had set out on his last journey from Galilee, which was to end at Jerusalem. As He passes along, He, as usual, healed the sick, and preached the glad tidings of salvation. In the midst, or at the completion, of one of his addresses, a woman of the multitude, whose soul had been stirred by his words, cried out, "Blessed is the womb that bare thee, and the paps which thou hast sucked!" Immediately the Lord replied, "Yea rather, blessed are they that hear the word of God, and keep it" (Luke xi. 28). He does not either affirm or deny anything with regard to the direct bearing of the woman's exclamation, but passes that by as a thing indifferent, in order to point out in what alone the true blessedness of his mother and of all consists. This is the full force of the μενοῦνγε, with which He commences his reply.

3. The next scene in St. Mary's life brings us to the foot of the cross. She was standing there with her sister Mary and Mary Magdalene, and Salome, and other women, having no doubt followed her Son as she was able throughout the terrible morn-

ing of Good Friday. It was about 3 o'clock in the afternoon, and He was about to give up his spirit. His divine mission was now, as it were, accomplished. While his ministry was in progress He had withdrawn himself from her that He might do his Father's work. But now the hour was come when his human relationship might be again recognized. "Tunc enim agnovit," says St. Augustine, "quando illud quod peperit moriebatur" (S. Aug. In Joan. ix.). Standing near the company of the women was St. John; and, with almost his last words, Christ commended his mother to the care of him who had borne the name of the Disciple whom Jesus loved. "Woman, behold thy son." "Commendat homo homini hominem," says St. Augustine. And from that hour St. John assures us that he took her to his own abode. If by "that hour" the Evangelist means immediately after the words were spoken, Mary was not present at the last scene of all. The sword had sufficiently pierced her soul, and she was spared the hearing of the last loud cry, and the sight of the bowed head. St. Ambrose considers the chief purpose of our Lord's words to have been a desire to make manifest the truth that the Redemption was his work alone, while He gave human affection to his mother. "Non egebat adjutore ad omnium redemptionem. Suscepit quidem matris affectum, sed non quæsivit hominis auxilium" (S. Amb. Exp. Evang. Luc. x. 132).

4. A veil is drawn over her sorrow and over her joy which succeeded that sorrow. Mediæval imagination has supposed, but Scripture does not state, that her Son appeared to Mary after his resurrection from the dead. (See, for example, Ludolph of Saxony, Vita Christi, p. 666, Lyons, 1642; and Ruperti, De Divinis Officiis, vii. 25, tom. iv. p. 92, Venice, 1751.) St. Ambrose is considered to be the first writer who suggested the idea, and reference is made to his treatise, De Virginitate, i. 3; but it is quite certain that the text has been corrupted, and that it is of Mary Magdalene that he is there speaking. (Comp. his Exposition of St. Luke, x. 156. See note of the Benedictine edition, tom. ii. p. 217, Paris, 1790.) Another reference is usually given to St. Anselm. The treatise quoted is not St. Anselm's, but Eadmer's. (See Eadmer, De Excellentia Mariæ, ch. v., appended to Anselm's Works, p. 138, Paris, 1721.) Ten appearances are related by the Evangelists as having occurred in the 40 days intervening between Easter and Ascension Day, but none to Mary. She was doubtless living at Jerusalem with John, cherished with the tenderness which her tender soul would have especially needed, and which undoubtedly she found preëminently in St. John. We have no record of her presence at the Ascension. Arator, a writer of the 6th century, describes her as being at the time not on the spot, but in Jerusalem (Arat. De Act. Apost. l. 50, apud Migne, tom. lxviii. p. 95, Paris, 1848, quoted by Wordsworth, Gk. Test. Com. on the Acts, i. 14). We have no account of her being present at the descent of the Holy Spirit on the day of Pentecost. What we do read of her is, that she remained steadfast in prayer in the upper room at Jerusalem with Mary Magdalene and Salome, and those known as the Lord's brothers and the Apostles. This is the last view that we have of her. Holy Scripture leaves her engaged in prayer (see Wordsworth as cited above). From this point forwards we know nothing of her. It is probable that the rest of her life was spent in

---

[a] It is a mere subterfuge to refer the words ἔλεγον γάρ, etc., to the people, instead of to Mary and his brethren (Calmet and Migne, Dict of the Bible)

Jerusalem with St. John (see Epiph. *Hær.* p. 78). According to one tradition the beloved disciple would not leave Palestine until she had expired in his arms (see Tholuck, *Light from the Cross*, ii. *Serm.* x. p. 234, Edinb., 1857); and it is added that she lived and died in the Coenaculum in what is now the Mosque of the Tomb of David, the traditional chamber of the Last Supper (Stanley, *S. & P.* ch. xiv. p. 456). Other traditions make her journey with St. John to Ephesus, and there die in extreme old age. It was believed by some in the 5th century that she was buried at Ephesus (see *Conc. Ephes.*, *Conc. Labb.* tom. iii. p. 574 a); by others, in the same century, that she was buried at Gethsemane, and this appears to have been the information given to Marcian and Pulcheria by Juvenal of Jerusalem. As soon as we lose the guidance of Scripture, we have nothing from which we can derive any sure knowledge about her. The darkness in which we are left is in itself most instructive.

5. The *character* of St. Mary is not drawn by any of the Evangelists, but some of its lineaments are incidentally manifested in the fragmentary record which is given of her. They are to be found for the most part in St. Luke's Gospel, whence an attempt has been made, by a curious mixture of the imaginative and rationalistic methods of interpretation, to explain the old legend which tells us that St. Luke painted the Virgin's portrait (Calmet, Kitto, Migne, Mrs. Jameson). We might have expected greater details from St. John than from the other Evangelists; but in his Gospel we learn nothing of her except what may be gathered from the scene at Cana and at the cross. It is clear from St. Luke's account, though without any such intimation we might rest assured of the fact, that her youth had been spent in the study of the Holy Scriptures, and that she had set before her the example of the holy women of the Old Testament as her model. This would appear from the *Magnificat* (Luke i. 46). The same hymn, so far as it emanated from herself, would show no little power of mind as well as warmth of spirit. Her faith and humility exhibit themselves in her immediate surrender of herself to the Divine will, though ignorant how that will should be accomplished (Luke i. 38); her energy and earnestness, in her journey from Nazareth to Hebron (Luke i. 39); her happy thankfulness, in her song of joy (Luke i. 48); her silent musing thoughtfulness, in her pondering over the shepherds' visit (Luke ii. 19), and in her keeping her Son's words in her heart (Luke ii. 51) though she could not fully understand their import. Again, her humility is seen in her drawing back, yet without anger, after receiving reproof at Cana in Galilee (John ii. 5), and in the remarkable manner in which she shuns putting herself forward throughout the whole of her Son's ministry, or after his removal from earth. Once only does she attempt to interfere with her Divine Son's freedom of action (Matt. xii. 46; Mark iii. 31; Luke viii. 19); and even here we can hardly blame, for she seems to have been roused, not by arrogance and by a desire to show her authority and relationship, as St. Chrysostom supposes (*Hom.* xliv. *in Matt.*); but by a woman's and a mother's feelings of affection and fear for him whom she loved. It was part of that exquisite tenderness which appears throughout to have belonged to her. In a word, so far as St. Mary is portrayed to us in Scripture, she is, as we should

have expected, the most tender, the most faithful, humble, patient, and loving of women, but a woman still.

III. *Her after life, wholly legendary.* — We pass again into the region of free and joyous legend which we quitted for that of true history at the period of the Annunciation. The Gospel record confined the play of imagination, and as soon as this check is withdrawn the legend bursts out afresh. The legends of St. Mary's childhood may be traced back as far as the third or even the second century. Those of her death are probably of a later date. The chief legend was for a length of time considered to be a veritable history, written by Melito, Bishop of Sardis, in the 2d century. It is to be found in the *Bibliotheca Maxima* (tom. ii. pt. ii. p. 212), entitled *Sancti Melitonis Episcopi Sardensis de Transitu Virginis Mariæ Liber*; and there certainly existed a book with this title at the end of the 5th century, which was condemned by Pope Gelasius as apocryphal (Op. Gelas. apud Migne, tom. 59, p 152). Another form of the same legend has been published at Elberfeld in 1854 by Maximilian Enger in Arabic. He supposes that it is an Arabic translation from a Syriac original. It was found in the library at Bonn, and is entitled *Joannis Apostoli de Transitu Beatæ Mariæ Virginis Liber*. It is perhaps the same as that referred to in Assemani (*Biblioth. Orient.* tom. iii. p. 287, Rome, 1725), under the name of *Historia Dormitionis et Assumptionis B. Mariæ Virginis Joanni Evangelistæ falso inscripta*. We give the substance of the legend with its main variations.

When the Apostles separated in order to evangelize the world, Mary continued to live with St. John's parents in their house near the Mount of Olives, and every day she went out to pray at the tomb of Christ, and at Golgotha. But the Jews had placed a watch to prevent prayers being offered at these spots, and the watch went into the city and told the chief priests that Mary came daily to pray. Then the priests commanded the watch to stone her. But at this time king Abgarus wrote to Tiberius to desire him to take vengeance on the Jews for slaying Christ. They feared therefore to add to his wrath by slaying Mary also, and yet they could not allow her to continue her prayers at Golgotha, because an excitement and tumult was thereby made. They therefore went and spoke softly to her, and she consented to go and dwell in Bethlehem; and thither she took with her three holy virgins who should attend upon her. And in the twenty-second year after the ascension of the Lord, Mary felt her heart burn with an inexpressible longing to be with her Son; and behold an angel appeared to her, and announced to her that her soul should be taken up from her body on the third day, and he placed a palm-branch from paradise in her hands, and desired that it should be carried before her bier. And Mary besought that the Apostles might be gathered round her before she died, and the angel replied that they should come. Then the Holy Spirit caught up John as he was preaching at Ephesus, and Peter as he was offering sacrifice at Rome, and Paul as he was disputing with the Jews near Rome, and Thomas in the extremity of India, and Matthew and James: these were all of the Apostles who were still living: then the Holy Spirit awakened the dead, Philip and Andrew, and Luke and Simon, and Mark and Bartholomew; and all of them were snatched away in a bright cloud and found themselves at Bethlehem. And angels and powers without number descended from heaven and stood round about the house; Gabriel stood at blessed Mary's head, and Michael at her feet, and they fanned her with their wings; and Peter and John wiped away her tears; and there was a great cry, and they all said "Hail blessed one! blessed is the fruit of thy womb!" And the people of Bethlehem brought their sick to the house, and they were all healed. Then news of these things was carried to Jerusalem, and the king sent and commanded that they should bring Mary and the disciples to Jerusalem. And horsemen came to Bethlehem to seize Mary, but they did not find her, for the Holy Spirit had taken her and the disciples in a cloud over the heads of the horsemen to Jerusalem. Then the men of Jerusalem saw angels ascending and descending at the spot where Mary's house was. And the high-priests went to the governor, and craved permission to burn her and the house with fire, and the governor gave them permission, and they brought wood and fire; but as soon as they came near to the house, behold there burst forth a fire upon them which consumed them utterly. And the governor saw these things afar off, and in the evening he brought his son, who was sick, to Mary, and she healed him.

Then, on the sixth day of the week, the Holy Spirit commanded the Apostles to take up Mary, and to carry her from Jerusalem to Gethsemane, and as they went the Jews saw them. Then drew near Juphia, one of the high-priests, and attempted to overthrow the litter on which she was being carried, for the other priests had conspired with him, and they hoped to cast her down into the valley, and to throw wood upon her, and to burn her body with fire. But as soon as Juphia had touched the litter the angel smote off his arms with a fiery sword, and the arms remained fastened to the litter. Then he cried to the disciples and Peter for help, and they said, "Ask it of the Lady Mary;" and he cried, "O Lady, O Mother of Salvation, have mercy on me!" Then she said to Peter, "Give him back his arms;" and they were restored whole. But the disciples proceeded onwards, and they laid down the litter in a cave, as they were commanded, and gave themselves to prayer.

And the angel Gabriel announced that on the first day of the week Mary's soul should be removed from this world. And on the morning of that day there came Eve and Anne and Elisabeth, and they kissed Mary and told her who they were: came Adam, Seth, Shem, Noah, Abraham, Isaac, Jacob, David, and the rest of the old fathers: came Enoch and Elias and Moses: came twelve chariots of angels innumerable: and then appeared the Lord Christ in his humanity, and Mary bowed before him and said, "O my Lord and my God, place thy hand upon me;" and he stretched out his hand and blessed her; and she took his hand and kissed it, and placed it to her forehead and said, "I bow before this right hand, which has made heaven and earth and all that in them is, and I thank thee and praise thee that thou hast thought me worthy of this hour." Then she said, "O Lord, take me to thyself!" And he said to her, "Now shall thy body be in paradise to the day of the resurrection, and angels shall serve thee; but thy pure spirit

shall shine in the kingdom, in the dwelling-place of my Father's fullness." Then the disciples drew near and besought her to pray for the world which she was about to leave. And Mary prayed. And after her prayer was finished her face shone with marvelous brightness, and she stretched out her hands and blessed them all; and her Son put forth his hands and received her pure soul, and bore it into his Father's treasure-house. And there was a light and a sweet smell, sweeter than anything on earth; and a voice from heaven saying, "Hail, blessed one! blessed and celebrated art thou among women!" [a]

And the Apostles carried her body to the Valley of Jehoshaphat, to a place which the Lord had told them of, and John went before and carried the palm-branch. And they placed her in a new tomb, and sat at the mouth of the sepulchre, as the Lord commanded them; and suddenly there appeared the Lord Christ, surrounded by a multitude of angels, and said to the Apostles, "What will ye that I should do with her whom my Father's command selected out of all the tribes of Israel that I should dwell in her?" And Peter and the Apostles besought him that he would raise the body of Mary and take it with him in glory to heaven. And the Saviour said, "Be it according to your word." And he commanded Michael the archangel to bring down the soul of Mary. And Gabriel rolled away the stone, and the Lord said, "Rise up, my beloved, thy body shall not suffer corruption in the tomb." And immediately Mary arose and bowed herself at his feet and worshipped; and the Lord kissed her and gave her to the angels to carry her to paradise.

But Thomas was not present with the rest, for at the moment that he was summoned to come he was baptizing Polodius, who was the son of the sister of the king. And he arrived just after all these things were accomplished, and he demanded to see the sepulchre in which they had laid his Lady: "For ye know," said he, "that I am Thomas, and unless I see I will not believe." Then Peter arose in haste and wrath, and the other disciples with him, and they opened the sepulchre and went in; but they found nothing therein save that in which her body had been wrapped. Then Thomas confessed that he too, as he was being borne in the cloud from India, had seen her holy body being carried by the angels with great triumph into heaven; and that on his crying to her for her blessing, she had bestowed upon him her precious Girdle, which when the Apostles saw they were glad.[b] Then the Apostles were carried back each to his own place.

Joannis Apostoli de Transitu Beatæ Mariæ Virginis Liber, Elberfeldæ, 1854; *S. Melitonis Episc. Sard. de Transitu V. M. Liber*, apud Bibl. Max. Patr. tom. ii. pt. ii. p. 212, Lugd. 1677; Jacobi a Voragine *Legenda Aurea*, ed. Græsse, ch. cxix. p. 504, Dresd. 1846; John Damasc. *Serm. de Dormit. Deiparæ*, Op. tom. ii. p. 857 ff., Venice, 1743; Andrew of Crete, *In Dormit. Deiparæ Serm.* iii. p. 115, Paris, 1644; Mrs. Jameson, *Legends of the Madonna*, Lond. 1852; Butler, *Lives of the Saints in Aug.* 15; Dressel, *Edita et inedita Epiphanii Monachi et Presbyteri*, p. 105, Paris, 1843. [Tischendorf, *Apocalypses Apoc.* Lips. 1866.]

---

[a] The legend ascribed to Melito makes her soul to be carried to paradise by Gabriel while her Son returns to heaven

[b] For the story of this *Sacratissimo Cintolo*, still preserved at Prato, see Mrs. Jameson's *Legends of the Madonna*, p. 344, Lond. 1852.

IV. *Jewish traditions respecting her.* — These are of a very different nature from the light-hearted fairy-tale-like stories which we have recounted above. We should expect that the miraculous birth of our Lord would be an occasion of scoffing to the unbelieving Jews, and we find this to be the case. To the Christian believer the Jewish slander becomes in the present case only a confirmation of his faith. The most definite and outspoken of these slanders is that which is contained in the book called תוֹלְדוֹת יֵשׁוּעַ, or *Toldoth Jesu.* It was grasped at with avidity by Voltaire, and declared by him to be the most ancient Jewish writing directed against Christianity, and apparently of the first century. It was written, he says, before the Gospels, and is altogether contrary to them (*Lettre sur les Juifs*). It is proved by Ammon (*Biblisch. Theologie*, p. 263, Erlang. 1801) to be a composition of the 13th century, and by Wagenseil (*Tela ignea Satanæ; Confut. Libr. Toldos Jeschu*, p. 12, Altorf, 1681) to be irreconcilable with the earlier Jewish tales. In the Gospel of Nicodemus, otherwise called the Acts of Pilate, we find the Jews represented as charging our Lord with illegitimate birth (c. 2). The date of this Gospel is about the end of the third century. The origin of the charge is referred with great probability by Thilo (*Codex Apocr.* p. 527, Lips. 1832) to the circular letters of the Jews mentioned by Grotius (*ad Matt.* xxvii. 63, *et ad Act. Apost.* xxviii. 22; *Op.* ii. 278 and 666, Basil. 1732), which were sent from Palestine to all the Jewish synagogues after the death of Christ, with the view of attacking " the lawless and atheistic sect which had taken its origin from the deceiver Jesus of Galilee " (*Justin. adv. Tryph.*). The first time that we find it openly proclaimed is in an extract made by Origen from the work of Celsus, which he is refuting. Celsus introduces a Jew declaring that the mother of Jesus ὑπὸ τοῦ γήμαντος, τέκτονος τὴν τέχνην ὄντος, ἐξεῶσθαι, ἐλεγχθεῖσαν ὡς μεμοιχευμένην (*Contra Celsum*, c. 28, Origenis *Opera*, xviii. 59, Berlin, 1845). And again, ἡ τοῦ Ἰησοῦ μήτηρ κύουσα, ἐξωσθεῖσα ὑπὸ τοῦ μνηστευσαμένου αὐτὴν τέκτονος, ἐλεγχθεῖσα ἐπὶ μοιχείᾳ καὶ τίκτουσα ἀπό τινος στρατιώτου Πανθήρα τοὔνομα (*ibid.* 33). Stories to the same effect may be found in the Talmud — not in the Mishna, which dates from the second century; but in the Gemara, which is of the fifth or sixth (see *Tract. Sanhedrin*, cap. vii. fol. 67, col. 1; *Shabbath*, cap. xii. fol. 104, col. 2; and the *Midrash Koheleth*, cap. x. 5). Rabanus Maurus, in the ninth century, refers to the same story: " Jesum filium Ethnici cujusdam Pandera adulteri, more latronum punitum esse." We then come to the *Toldoth Jesu*, in which these calumnies were intended to be summed up and harmonised. In the year 4671, the story runs, in the reign of King Jannæus, there was one Joseph Pandera who lived at Bethlehem. In the same village there was a widow who had a daughter named Miriam, who was betrothed to a God-fearing man named Johanan. And it came to pass that Joseph Pandera meeting with Miriam when it was dark, deceived her into the belief that he was Johanan her husband. And after three months Johanan consulted Rabbi Simeon Shetachides what he should do with Miriam, and the rabbi advised him to bring her before the great council. But Johanan was ashamed to do so, and instead he left his home and went and lived at Babylon; and there

Miriam brought forth a son and gave him the name of Jehoshua. The rest of the work, which has no merit in a literary aspect or otherwise, contains an account of how this Jehoshua gained the art of working miracles by stealing the knowledge of the unmentionable name from the Temple; how he was defeated by the superior magical arts of one Juda; and how at last he was crucified, and his body hidden under a watercourse. It is offensive to make use of sacred names in connection with such tales; but in Wagenseil's quaint words we may recollect, " hæc nomina non attinere ad Servatorem Nostrum aut beatissimam illius matrem cœterosque quos significare videntur, sed designari iis a Diabolo supposita Spectra, Larvas, Lemures, Lamias, Stryges, aut si quid turpius istis " (*Tela Ignea Satanæ, Liber Toldos Jeschu*, p. 2, Altorf, 1681). It is a curious thing that a Pandera or Panther has been introduced into the genealogy of our Lord by Epiphanius (*Hæres.* lxxviii.) who makes him grandfather of Joseph, and by John of Damascus (*De Fide orthodoxa*, iv. 15), who makes him the father of Barpanther and grandfather of St. Mary.

V. *Mohammedan Traditions.* — These are again cast in a totally different mould from those of the Jews. The Mohammedans had no purpose to serve in spreading calumnious stories as to the birth of Jesus, and accordingly we find none of the Jewish malignity about their traditions. Mohammed and his followers appear to have gathered up the floating oriental traditions which originated in the legends of St. Mary's early years, given above, and to have drawn from them and from the Bible indifferently. It has been suggested that the Koran had an object in magnifying St. Mary, and that this was to insinuate that the Son was of no other nature than the mother. But this does not appear to be the case. Mohammed seems merely to have written down what had come to his ears about her, without definite theological purpose or inquiry.

Mary was, according to the Koran, the daughter of Amram (sur. iii.) and the sister of Aaron (sur. xix.). Mohammed can hardly be absolved from having here confounded Miriam the sister of Moses with Mary the mother of our Lord. It is possible indeed that he may have meant different persons, and such is the opinion of Sale (*Koran*, pp. 38 and 251), and of D'Herbelot (*Bibl. Orient.* in voc. " Miriam "); but the opposite view is more likely (see Guadagnoli, *Apol. pro rel. Christ.* ch. viii. p. 277, Rom. 1631). Indeed, some of the Mohammedan commentators have been driven to account for the chronological difficulty, by saying that Miriam was miraculously kept alive from the days of Moses in order that she might be the mother of Jesus. Her mother Hannah dedicated her to the Lord while still in the womb, and at her birth "commended her and her future issue to the protection of God against Satan." And Hannah brought the child to the Temple to be educated by the priests, and the priests disputed among themselves who should take charge of her. Zacharias maintained that it was his office, because he had married her aunt. But when the others would not give up their claims, it was determined that the matter should be decided by lot. So they went to the river Jordan, twenty-seven of them, each man with his rod; and they threw their rods into the river, and none of them floated save that of Zacharias, whereupon the care of the child was committed to him (Al Beidawi; Jallalo'ddin). Then Zacharias placed her in an inner chamber by herself·

and though he kept seven doors ever locked upon her,[a] he always found her abundantly supplied with provisions which God sent her from paradise, winter fruits in summer, and summer fruits in winter. And the angels said unto her, " O Mary, verily God hath chosen thee, and hath purified thee, and hath chosen thee above all the women of the world " (*Koran*, sur. iii.). And she retired to a place towards the East, and Gabriel appeared unto her and said, " Verily I am the messenger of thy Lord, and am sent to give thee a holy Son " (sur. xix.). And the angels said, " O Mary, verily God sendeth thee good tidings that thou shalt bear the Word proceeding from Himself: His name shall be Christ Jesus, the son of Mary, honorable in this world and in the world to come, and one of them who approach near to the presence of God: and he shall speak unto men in his cradle and when he is grown up; and he shall be one of the righteous." And she said, " How shall I have a son, seeing I know not a man ? " The angel said, " So God createth that which He pleaseth: when He decreeth a thing, He only saith unto it, ' Be,' and it is. God shall teach him the scripture and wisdom, and the law and the gospel, and shall appoint him his apostle to the children of Israel " (sur. iii.). So God breathed of his Spirit into the womb of Mary;[b] and she preserved her chastity (sur. lxvi.); for the Jews have spoken against her a grievous calumny (sur. iv.). And she conceived a son, and retired with him apart to a distant place; and the pains of childbirth came upon her near the trunk of a palm-tree; and God provided a rivulet for her, and she shook the palm-tree, and it let fall ripe dates, and she ate and drank, and was calm. Then she carried the child in her arms to her people; but they said that it was a strange thing she had done. Then she made signs to the child to answer them; and he said, " Verily I am the servant of God: He hath given me the book of the gospel, and hath appointed me a prophet; and He hath made me blessed, wheresoever I shall be; and hath commanded me to observe prayer and to give alms so long as I shall live; and He hath made me dutiful towards my mother, and hath not made me proud or unhappy: and peace be on me the day whereon I was born, and the day whereon I shall die, and the day whereon I shall be raised to life." This was Jesus the Son of Mary, the Word of Truth concerning whom they doubt (sur. xix.).

Mohammed is reported to have said that many men have arrived at perfection, but only four women; and that these are, Asia the wife of Pharaoh, Mary the daughter of Amram, his first wife Khadijah, and his daughter Fâtima.

The commentators on the Koran tell us that every person who comes into the world is touched at his birth by the Devil, and therefore cries out; out that God placed a veil between Mary and her Son and the Evil Spirit, so that he could not reach them. For which reason they were neither of them guilty of sin, like the rest of the children of Adam. This privilege they had in answer to Hannah's prayer

for their protection from Satan. (Jallalo'ddin; Al Beidawi; Kitada.) The Immaculate Conception therefore, we may note, was a Mohammedan doctrine six centuries before any Christian theologians or schoolmen maintained it.

Sale, *Koran*, pp. 39, 79, 250, 458, Lond. 1734; Warner, *Compendium Historicum eorum quæ Muhammedani de Christo tradiderunt*, Lugd. Bat. 1643; Guadagnoli, *Apologia pro Christiana Religione*, Rom. 1631; D'Herbelot, *Bibliothèque Orientale*, p. 583, Paris, 1697; Weil, *Biblische Legenden der Muselmänner*, p. 230, Frankf. 1845.

VI. *Emblems.*—There was a time in the history of the Church when all the expressions used in the book of Canticles were applied at once to St. Mary. Consequently all the eastern metaphors of king Solomon have been hardened into symbols, and represented in pictures or sculpture, and attached to her in popular litanies. The same method of interpretation was applied to certain parts of the book of the Revelation. Her chief emblems are the sun, moon, and stars (Rev. xii. 1; Cant. vi. 10). The name of Star of the Sea is also given her, from a fanciful interpretation of the meaning of her name. She is the Rose of Sharon (Cant. ii. 1), and the Lily (ii. 2), the Tower of David (iv. 4), the Mountain of Myrrh and the Hill of Frankincense (iv. 6), the Garden enclosed, the Spring shut up, the Fountain sealed (iv. 12), the Tower of Ivory (vii. 4), the Palm-tree (vii. 7), the Closed Gate (Ez. xliv. 2). There is no end to these metaphorical titles. See Mrs. Jameson's *Legends of the Madonna*, and the ordinary Litanies of the B. Virgin.

VII. *Cultus of the Blessed Virgin.* — We do not enter into the theological bearings of the worship of St. Mary; but we shall have left our task incomplete if we do not add a short historical sketch of the origin, progress, and present state of the devotion to her. What was its origin? Certainly not the Bible. There is not a word there from which it could be inferred; nor in the Creeds; nor in the Fathers of the first five centuries. We may scan each page that they have left us, and we shall find nothing of the kind. There is nothing of the sort in the supposed works of Hermas and Barnabas, nor in the real works of Clement, Ignatius, and Polycarp: that is, the doctrine is not to be found in the 1st century. There is nothing of the sort in Justin Martyr, Tatian, Athenagoras, Theophilus, Clement of Alexandria, Tertullian: that is, in the 2d century. There is nothing of the sort in Origen, Gregory Thaumaturgus, Cyprian, Methodius, Lactantius: that is, in the 3d century. There is nothing of the sort in Eusebius, Athanasius, Cyril of Jerusalem, Hilary, Macarius, Epiphanius, Basil, Gregory Nazianzen, Ephrem Syrus, Gregory of Nyssa, Ambrose: that is, in the 4th century. There is nothing of the sort in Chrysostom, Augustine, Jerome, Basil of Seleucia, Orosius, Sedulius, Isidore, Theodoret, Prosper, Vincentius Lirinensis, Cyril of Alexandria, Popes Leo, Hilarius, Simplicius, Felix, Gelasius, Anastasius, Symmachus: that is, in the 5th century.[c] Whence, then, did it

---

c. Other stories make the only entrance to be by a adder and a door always kept locked.

b The commentators have explained this expression as signifying the breath of Gabriel (Yahya; Jallalo'ddin). But this does not seem to have been Mohammed's meaning.

c " Origen's Lament," the " Three Discourses " published by Vossius as the work of Gregory Thauma-

turgus, the Homily attributed to St. Athanasius containing an invocation of St. Mary, the Panegyric attributed to St. Epiphanius, the " Christ Suffering," and the Oration containing the story of Justina and St. Cyprian, attributed to Gregory Nazianzen; the Eulogy of the Holy Virgin, and the Prayer attributed to Ephrem Syrus; the Book of Meditations attributed to St. Augustine; the Two Sermons supposed to have

arise? There is not a shadow of doubt that the origin of the worship of St. Mary is to be found in the apocryphal legends of her birth and of her death which we have given above. There we find the germ of what afterwards expanded into its present portentous proportions. Some of the legends of her birth are as early as the 2d or 3d century. They were the production of the Gnostics, and were unanimously and firmly rejected by the Church of the first five centuries as fabulous and heretical. The Gnostic tradition seems to have been handed on to the Collyridians, whom we find denounced by Epiphanius for worshipping the Virgin Mary. They were regarded as distinctly heretical. The words which this Father uses respecting them were probably expressive of the sentiments of the entire Church in the 4th century. "The whole thing," he says, "is foolish and strange, and is a device and deceit of the Devil. Let Mary be in honor. Let the Lord be worshipped. Let no one worship Mary" (Epiph. *Hær.* lxxxix., Op. p. 1066, Paris, 1622). Down to the time of the Nestorian controversy, the *cultus* of the Blessed Virgin would appear to have been wholly external to the Church, and to have been regarded as heretical. But the Nestorian controversies produced a great change of sentiment in men's minds. Nestorius had maintained, or at least it was the tendency of Nestorianism to maintain, not only that our Lord had two natures, the divine and the human (which was right), but also that He was two persons, in such sort that the child born of Mary was not divine, but merely an ordinary human being, until the divinity subsequently united itself to Him. This was condemned by the Council of Ephesus in the year 431; and the title Θεοτόκος, loosely translated "Mother of God," was sanctioned. The object of the Council and of the Anti-Nestorians was in no sense to add honor to the mother, but to maintain the true doctrine with respect to the Son. Nevertheless the result was to magnify the mother, and, after a time, at the expense of the son. For now the title Θεοτόκος became a shibboleth; and in art the representation of the Madonna and Child became the expression of orthodox belief. Very soon the ·purpose for which the title and the picture were first sanctioned became forgotten, and the veneration of St. Mary began to spread within the Church, as it had previously existed external to it. The legends too were no longer treated so roughly as before. The Gnostics were not now objects of dread. Nestorians, and afterwards Iconoclasts, were objects of hatred. The old fables were winked at, and thus they "became the mythology of Christianity, universally credited among the Southern nations of Europe, while many of the dogmas, which they are grounded upon, have, as a natural consequence, crept into the faith" (Lord Lindsay, *Christian Art*, i. p. xl. Lond. 1847). From this time the worship of St. Mary grew apace. It agreed well with many natural aspirations of the heart. To paint the mother of the Saviour an ideal woman,

with all the grace and tenderness of womanhood, and yet with none of its weaknesses, and then to fall down and worship the image which the imagination had set up, was what might easily happen, and what did happen. Evidence was not asked for. Perfection "was becoming" to the mother of the Lord; therefore she was perfect. Adoration "was befitting" on the part of Christians; therefore they gave it. Any tales attributed to antiquity were received as genuine; any revelations supposed to be made to favored saints were accepted as true: and the Madonna reigned as queen in heaven, in earth, in purgatory, and over hell. We learn the present state of the religious regard in which she is held throughout the south of Europe from St. Alfonso de Liguori, whose every word is vouched for by the whole weight of his Church's authority. From the *Glories of Mary*, translated from the original, and published in London in 1852, we find that St. Mary is Queen of Mercy (p. 13) and Mother of all mankind (p. 23), our Life (p. 52), our Protectress in death (p. 71), the Hope of all (p. 79), our only Refuge, Help, and Asylum (p 81); the Propitiatory of the whole world (p. 81); the one City of Refuge (p. 89); the Comfortress of the world, the Refuge of the Unfortunate (p. 100); our Patroness (p. 106); Queen of Heaven and Hell (p. 110); our Protectress from the Divine Justice and from the Devil (p. 115); the Ladder of Paradise, the Gate of Heaven (p. 121); the Mediatrix of grace (p. 124); the Dispenser of all graces (p. 128); the Helper of the Redemption (p. 133); the Coöperator in our Justification (p. 133); a tender Advocate (p. 145); Omnipotent (p. 146); the singular Refuge of the lost (p. 156); the great Peacemaker (p. 165); the Throne prepared in mercy (p. 165); the Way of Salvation (p. 200); the Mediatrix of Angels (p. 278). In short, she is the Way (p. 200), the Door (p. 583), the Mediator (p. 295), the Intercessor (p. 129), the Advocate (p. 144), the Redeemer (p. 275), the Saviour (p. 343).

Thus, then, in the worship of the Blessed Virgin there are two distinctly marked periods. The first is that which commences with the apostolic times, and brings us down to the close of the century in which the Council of Ephesus was held, during which time the worship of St. Mary was wholly external to the Church, and was regarded by the Church as heretical, and confined to Gnostic and Collyridian heretics. The second period commences with the 6th century, when it began to spread within the Church; and, in spite of the shock given it by the Reformation, has continued to spread, as shown by Liguori's teaching; and is spreading still, as shown by the manner in which the papal decree of December 8, 1854, has been, not universally indeed, but yet generally, received. Even before that decree was issued, the sound of the word "deification" had been heard with reference to St. Mary (Newman, *Essay on Development*, p. 409, Lond. 1846); and she had been placed in "a throne far above all created powers, mediatorial, intercessory;" she had been invested with "a title archetypal; with a crown

---

been delivered by Pope Leo on the Feast of the Annunciation, — are all spurious. See *Moral and Devotional Theology of the Church of Rome* (Mosley, Lond. 1857). The Oration of Gregory, containing the story of Justina and Cyprian, is retained by the Benedictine editors as genuine; and they pronounce that nowhere else is the protection of the Blessed Virgin Mary so clearly and explicitly commended in the 4th century.

The words are: "Justina . . . meditating on these instances (and beseeching the Virgin Mary to assist a virgin in peril), throws before her the charm of fasting." It is shown to be spurious by Tyler (*Worship of the Blessed Virgin*, p. 378, Lond. 1844). Even suppose it were genuine, the contrast between the strongest passage of the 4th century and the ordinary language of the 19th would be sufficiently striking.

bright as the morning star; a glory issuing from the Eternal Throne; robes pure as the heavens; and a sceptre over all *(ibid.* p. 406).

VIII. *Her Assumption.* — Not only religious sentiments, but facts grew up in exactly the same way. The Assumption of St. Mary is a fact, or an alleged fact. How has it come to be accepted! At the end of the 5th century we find that there existed a book, *De Transitu Virginis Mariæ,* which was condemned by Pope Gelasius as apocryphal. This book is without doubt the oldest form of the legend, of which the books ascribed to St. Melito and St. John are variations. Down to the end of the 5th century, then, the story of the Assumption was external to the Church, and distinctly looked upon by the Church as belonging to the heretics and not to her. But then came the change of sentiment already referred to, consequent on the Nestorian controversy. The desire to protest against the early fables which had been spread abroad by the heretics was now passed away, and had been succeeded by the desire to magnify her who had brought forth Him who was God. Accordingly a writer, whose date Baronius fixes at about this time (*Ann. Eccl.* i. 347, Lucca, 1738), suggested the possibility of the Assumption, but declared his inability to decide the question. The letter in which this possibility or probability is thrown out came to be attributed to St. Jerome, and may be still found among his works, entitled *Ad Paulam et Eustochium de Assumptione B. Virginis* (v. 82, Paris, 1706). About the same time, probably, or rather later, an insertion (now recognized on all hands to be a forgery) was made in Eusebius' Chronicle, to the effect that "in the year A. D. 48 Mary the Virgin was taken up into heaven, as some wrote that they had it revealed to them." Another tract was written to prove that the Assumption was not a thing in itself unlikely; and this came to be attributed to St. Augustine, and may be found in the appendix to his works; and a sermon, with a similar purport, was ascribed to St. Athanasius. Thus the names of Eusebius, Jerome, Augustine, Athanasius, and others, came to be quoted as maintaining the truth of the Assumption. The first writers within the Church in whose extant writings we find the Assumption asserted, are Gregory of Tours in the 6th century, who has merely copied Melito's book, *De Transitu* (*De Glor. Mart.* lib. i. c. 4; Migne, 71, p. 708); Andrew of Crete, who probably lived in the 7th century; and John of Damascus, who lived at the beginning of the 8th century. The last of these authors refers to the Euthymiac history as stating that Marcian and Pulcheria being in search of the body of St. Mary, sent to Juvenal of Jerusalem to inquire for it. Juvenal replied, "In the holy and divinely inspired Scriptures, indeed, nothing is recorded of the departure of the holy Mary, Mother of God. But from an ancient and most true tradition we have received, that at the time of her glorious falling asleep all the holy Apostles, who were going through the world for the salvation of the nations, borne aloft in a moment of time, came together to Jerusalem; and when they were near her they had a vision of angels, and divine melody was heard; and then with divine and more than heavenly melody she delivered her holy soul into the hands of God in an unspeakable manner. But

that which had borne God, being carried with angelic and apostolic psalmody, with funeral rites was deposited in a coffin at Gethsemane. In this place the chorus and singing of the angels continued three whole days. But after three days, on the angelic music ceasing, those of the Apostles who were present opened the tomb, as one of them, Thomas, had been absent, and on his arrival wished to adore the body which had borne God. But her all glorious body they could not find; but they found the linen clothes lying, and they were filled with an ineffable odor of sweetness which proceeded from them. Then they closed the coffin. And they were astonished at the mysterious wonder; and they came to no other conclusion than that He who had chosen to take flesh of the Virgin Mary, and to become a man, and to be born of her — God the Word, the Lord of Glory — and had preserved her virginity after birth, was also pleased, after her departure, to honor her immaculate and unpolluted body with incorruption, and to translate her before the common resurrection of all men" (St. Joan. Damasc. *Op.* ii. 880, Venice, 1748). It is quite clear that this is the same legend as that which we have before given. Here, then, we see it brought over the borders and planted within the Church, if this "Euthymiac history" is to be accepted as veritable, by Juvenal of Jerusalem in the 5th century, or else by Gregory of Tours in the 6th century, or by Andrew of Crete in the 7th century, or finally, by John of Damascus in the 8th century (see his three *Homilies on the Sleep of the Blessed Virgin Mary,* Op. ii. 857-886).[a] The same legend is given in a slightly different form as veritable history by Nicephorus Callistus in the 13th century (Niceph. i. 171, Paris, 1630); and the fact of the Assumption is stereotyped in the Breviary Services for August 15th (*Brev. Rom. pars æst.* p. 551, Milan, 1851). Here again, then, we see a legend originated by heretics, and remaining external to the Church till the close of the 5th century, creeping into the Church during the 6th and 7th centuries, and finally ratified by the authority both of Rome and Constantinople. See Baronius, *Ann. Eccl.* (i. 344, Lucca, 1738), and *Martyrologium* (p. 314, Paris, 1607).

IX. *Her Immaculate Conception.* — Similarly with regard to the sinlessness of St. Mary, which has issued in the dogma of the Immaculate Conception. Down to the close of the 5th century the sentiment with respect to her was identical with that which is expressed by theologians of the Church of England (see Pearson, *On the Creed*). She was regarded as "highly favored;" as a woman arriving as near the perfection of womanhood as it was possible for human nature to arrive, but yet liable to the infirmities of human nature, and sometimes led away by them. Thus, in the 2d century, Tertullian represents her as guilty of unbelief (*De carne Christi,* vii. 315, and *Adv. Marcion.* iv. 19, p. 433, Paris, 1695). In the 3d century, Origen interprets the sword which was to pierce her bosom as being her unbelief, which caused her to be offended (*Hom. in Luc.* xvii. iii. 952, Paris, 1733). In the 4th century St. Basil gives the same interpretation of Simeon's words (*Ep.* 260, iii. 400, Paris, 1721); and St. Hilary speaks of her as having to come into the severity of the final

---

a This "Euthymiac History" is involved in the utmost confusion. Cave considers the Homily proved spurious by its reference to it. See *Historia Literar* i. 582, 625. Oxf. 1740.

judgment (*In Ps. cxix.* p. 262, Paris, 1693). In the 5th century St. Chrysostom speaks of the "excessive ambition," "foolish arrogancy," and "vain-glory," which made her stand and desire to speak with Him (vii. 467, Paris, 1718); and St. Cyril of Alexandria (so entirely is he misrepresented by popular writers) speaks of her as failing in faith when present at the Passion — as being weaker in the spiritual life than St. Peter — as being entrusted to St. John, because he was capable of explaining to her the mystery of the Cross — as inferior to the Apostles in knowledge and belief of the Resurrection (iv. 1064, vi. 391, Paris, 1638). It is plain from these and other passages, which might be quoted, that the idea of St. Mary's exemption from even actual sins of infirmity and imperfection, if it existed at all, was external to the Church. Nevertheless there grew up, as was most natural, a practice of looking upon St. Mary as an example to other women, and investing her with an ideal character of beauty and sweetness. A very beautiful picture of what a girl ought to be is drawn by St. Ambrose (*De Virgin.* ii. 2, p. 164, Paris, 1690), and attached to St. Mary. It is drawn wholly from the imagination (as may be seen by his making one of her characteristics to be that she never went out of doors except when she accompanied her parents to church), but there is nothing in it which is in any way superhuman. Similarly we find St. Jerome speaking of the clear light of Mary hiding the little fires of other women, such as Anna and Elisabeth (vi. 671; Verona, 1734). St. Augustine takes us a step further. He again and again speaks of her as under *original* sin (iv. 241, x. 654, &c., Paris, 1700); but with respect to her *actual* sin he says that he would rather not enter on the question, for it was possible (how could we tell ?) that God had given her sufficient grace to keep her free from actual sin (x. 144). At this time the change of mind before referred to, as originated by the Nestorian controversies, was spreading within the Church; and it became more and more the general belief that St. Mary was preserved from actual sin by the grace of God. This opinion had become almost universal in the 12th century. And now a further step was taken. It was maintained by St. Bernard that St. Mary was conceived in original sin, but that before her birth she was cleansed from it, like John the Baptist and Jeremiah. This was the sentiment of the 13th century, as shown by the works of Peter Lombard (*Sentent.* lib. iii. dist. 3), Alexander of Hales (*Sum. Theol.* num. ii. art. 2), Albertus Magnus (*Sentent.* lib. iii. dist. 3), and Thomas Aquinas (*Sum. Theol.* quaest. xxvii. art. 1, and *Comm.* in *Lib. Sentent.* dist. 3, quaest. 1). Early in the 14th century died J. Duns Scotus, and he is the first theologian or schoolman who threw out as a possibility the idea of an Immaculate Conception, which would exempt St. Mary from original as well as actual sin. This opinion had been growing up for the two previous centuries, having originated apparently in France, and having been adopted, to St. Bernard's indignation, by the canons of Lyons. From this time forward there was a struggle between the maculate and immaculate conceptionists, which has led at length to the decree of December 8, 1854, but which has not ceased with that decree. Here, then, we may mark four distinct theories with respect to the sinlessness of St. Mary. The first is that of the early Church to the close of the 5th century. It taught that St. Mary was born in original sin, was liable to actual sin, and

that she fell into sins of infirmity. The second extends from the close of the 5th to the 13th century. It taught that St. Mary was born in original sin, but by God's grace was saved from falling into actual sins. The third is *par excellence* that of the 13th century. It taught that St. Mary was conceived in original sin, but was sanctified in the womb before birth. The fourth may be found obscurely existing, but only existing to be condemned, in the 12th and 13th centuries; brought into the light by the speculations of Scotus and his followers in the 14th century; thenceforward running parallel with and struggling with the *sanctificata in utero* theory, till it obtained its apparently final victory, so far as the Roman Church is concerned, in the 19th century, and in the lifetime of ourselves. It teaches that St. Mary was not conceived or born in original sin, but has been wholly exempt from all sin, original and actual, in her conception and birth, throughout her life, and in her death.

See Laborde, *La Croyance à l'Immaculée Conception ne peut devenir Dogme de Foi*, Paris, 1855; Perrone, *De Immaculato B. V. M. Conceptu*, Avenione, 1848; *Christian Remembrancer*, vols. xxiii. and xxxvii.; Bp. Wilberforce, *Rome — her New Dogma, and our Duties*, Oxf. 1855; *Observateur Catholique*, Paris, 1855–60; Fray Morgaez, *Examen Bullæ Ineffabilis*, Paris, 1858.   F. M.

MARY (Rec. Text, with [Sin.] D, Μαριάμ; Lachmann, with A B C, Μαρία: *Maria*), a Roman Christian who is greeted by St. Paul in his Epistle to the Romans (xvi. 6) as having toiled hard for him — or according to some MSS. for them. Nothing more is known of her. But Professor Jowett (*The Epistles of St. Paul*, etc. *ad loc.*) has called attention to the fact that hers is the only Jewish name in the list.   G.

* **MAS'ADA** (Μασάδα) a remarkable Jewish fortress on the western shore of the Dead Sea, a few hours south of Engedi. It is mentioned by Pliny and Strabo, but is not named in the Bible nor in the Books of the Maccabees, although it was first built by Jonathan Maccabæus and was, probably, one of the "strongholds in Judea," (1 Macc. xii. 35), which he consulted with the elders about building. Josephus has given a full description of it, and of the terrible tragedy of which it was the theatre. (*B. J.* vii. 8.) It was an isolated rock, several hundred feet high, and inaccessible except by two paths hewn in its face. The summit was a plain, about three fourths of a mile in length, and a third of a mile in breadth. Herod the Great chose this spot for a retreat in case of danger, built a wall around the top, strengthened the original fortifications, and added a palace, with armories and ample store-houses and cisterns.

After the destruction of Jerusalem and the reduction of the other fortresses, this almost impregnable post was held by a garrison (which included many families) of Jewish zealots under the command of Eleazar, and here was made the last stand against the power of Rome. The Roman general, Flavius Silbon, gathered his forces to this fortress and laid siege to it, building a wall around the entire rock. He then raised his banks against the single narrow promontory by which it can now be climbed, and when, at length, he became evident that he would subdue it, the besieged, under the impassioned harangue of their leader, devoted themselves to self-destruction. Each man, after tenderly embracing his wife and children, put them to death with his own hand; ten men were then selected by lot to massacre the rest; and one of the survivors, in the same way, to despatch the others and then himself. This frantic resolve was executed, and 960 persons — men, women, and children — lay in their blood. The conqueror, pressing the siege, the next morning, encountered the silence of death, and entering the fortress, met the appalling spectacle. Two women and five children, who had been concealed in a cavern, alone survived.

The spot, thus signalized, was lost to history until the publication of Robinson and Smith's researches. At *'Ain Jidy*, their attention had been attracted to this singular rock with ruins on its summit, now called *Sebbeh* (سبّة), but it was not until they reached Germany, that it occurred to them it must be the ancient Masada (*Bibl. Res.* ii. 240 f.). The writer, in company with an English painter, under the protection of a Bedawy chief, visited the spot in the spring of 1842. Crossing from Hebron the territory which lies between the highlands of Judæa and the Dead Sea — the hills being first succeeded by an undulating country, at that season verdant and forming the principal pasture-ground of the Bedawin, this by a range of white, naked, conical hills, mostly barren, and the latter by a rugged, rocky strip, bordering the sea, and out through by deep wadies — we reached, across a scorched and desolate tract, the lofty cliffs of Sebbeh with its ruins, fronted on the west by precipices of a rich, reddish-brown color, the motionless sea lying far below on the east, and the mountains of Moab towering beyond — the whole region wearing an aspect of lonely and stern grandeur. The identification was complete — the lower part of the entire wall which Herod built around the top, and the entire Roman wall of circumvallation below, with the walls of the Roman camps connected with it, undisturbed for eighteen centuries, remaining as they were left, except as partially wasted by the elements. As we looked down on those lines, they vividly recalled the siege and the day when the crimsoned rock on which we stood bore witness to the fulfillment of the fearful imprecation : — "His blood be on us and on our children ! " (*Bibl. Sacra*, 1843, pp. 61-67).[a]   S. W.

MAS'ALOTH (Μασσαλώθ [so Sin.]; Alex. Μεσσαλωθ: *Masaloth*), a place in Arbela, which Bacchides and Alcimus, the two generals of Demetrius, besieged and took with great slaughter on their way from the north to Gilgal (1 Macc. ix. 2). Arbela is probably the modern *Irbid*, on the south side of the *Wady el-Hamâm*, about 3 miles N. W. of Tiberias, and half that distance from the Lake. The name Mesaloth is omitted by Josephus (*Ant.* xii. 11, § 1), nor has any trace of it been since discovered; but the word may, as Robinson (*Bibl. Res.* ii. 398) suggests, have originally signified the "steps" or "terraces" (as if מְסִלּוֹת). In that case it was probably a name given to the remarkable caverns still existing on the northern side of the same wady, and now called *Kula'at Ibn Ma'an*,

the "fortress of the son of Maan" — caverns which actually stood a remarkable siege of some length, by the forces of Herod (Joseph. *B. J.* i. 16, § 4).

A town with the similar name of MISHAL, or MASHAL, occurs in the list of the tribe of Asher, but whether its position was near that assumed above for Masaloth, we have no means of judging.   G.

MAS'CHIL (מַשְׂכִּיל: σύνεσις: *intellectus*, but in Ps. liii. *intelligentia*). The title of thirteen psalms; xxxii., xlii., xliv., xlv., lii.-lv., lxxiv., lxxviii., lxxxviii., lxxxix., cxlii. Jerome in his version from the Hebrew renders it uniformly *eruditio*, "instruction," except in Pss. xlii., lxxxix., where he has *intellectus*, "understanding." The margin of our A. V. has in Pss. lxxiv., lxxviii., lxxxix., "to give instruction; " and in Ps. lxxxviii., cxlii., "giving instruction." In other passages in which the word occurs, it is rendered "wise" (Job xxii. 2; Prov. x. 5, 19, &c.), "prudent" (Prov. xix. 14; Am. v. 13), "expert" (Jer. l. 9), and "skillful" (Dan. i. 4). In the Psalm in which it first occurs as a title, the root of the word is found in another form (Ps. xxxii. 8), "I will *instruct* thee," from which circumstance, it has been inferred, the title was applied to the whole psalm as "didactic." But since "Maschil " is affixed to many psalms which would scarcely be classed as didactic, Gesenius (or rather Roediger) explains it as denoting "any sacred song, relating to divine things, whose end it was to promote wisdom and piety " (*Thes.* p. 1330). Ewald (*Dichter d. alt. B.* i. 25) regards Ps. xlvii. 7 (A. V. "sing ye praises *with understanding*; " Heb. *maschil*), as the key to the meaning of Maschil, which in his opinion is a musical term, denoting a melody requiring great skill in its execution. The objection to the explanation of Roediger is, that it is wanting in precision, and would allow the term "Maschil " to be applied to every psalm in the Psalter. That it is employed to indicate to the conductor of the Temple choir the manner in which the psalm was to be sung, or the melody to which it was adapted, rather than as descriptive of its contents, seems to be implied in the title of Ps. xlv., where, after "Maschil," is added "a song of loves " to denote the special character of the psalm. Again, with few exceptions, it is associated with directions for the choir, "to the chief musician," etc., and occupies the same position in the titles as *Michtam* (Ps. xvi., lvi.-lx.), *Mizmor* (A. V. "Psalm; " Ps. iv.-vi., etc.), and *Shiggaion* (Ps. vii.). If, therefore, we regard it as originally used, in the sense of "didactic," to indicate the character of one particular psalm, it might have been applied to others as being set to the melody of the original Maschil-psalm. But the suggestion of Ewald, given above, has most to commend it. Comparing "Maschil " with the musical terms already alluded to, and observing the different manner in which the character of a psalm is indicated in other instances (1 Chr. xvi. 7; Pss. xxxviii., lxx., titles), it seems probable that it was used to convey a direction to the singers as to the mode in which they were to sing. There appear to have been Maschils of different kinds, for in addition to those of David which form the greater

---

a   * This place was visited in 1848 by Lieut. Lynch's party, who describes it, yet without alluding to the previous explorations. We record with pleasure M. de Saulcy's acknowledgment that, " the honor of having been the first to visit the ruins of Masada belongs unquestionably to Messrs. Wolcott and Tipping " (*Narrative of a Journey round the Dead Sea*, i. 191 f.). Von Raumer also refers to Dr. Wolcott's discoveries as settling the question of the identification of Masada with the present *Sebbeh* (see *Palästina*, p. 212, 4te Aufl.). H.

number, there are others of Asaph (Pss. lxxiv., txxviii.), Heman the Ezrahite (lxxxviii.), and Ethan (lxxxix.).   W. A. W.

MASH (מַשׁ : Μοσόχ: *Mes*), one of the sons of Aram, and the brother of Uz, Hul, and Gether (Gen. x. 23). In 1 Chr. i. 17 the name appears as Meshech, and the rendering of the LXX., as above given, leads to the inference that a similar form also existed in some of the copies of Genesis. It may further be noticed that in the Chronicles, Mash and his brothers are described as sons of Shem to the omission of Aram; this discrepancy is easily explained: the links to connect the names are omitted in other instances (comp. ver. 4), the ethnologist evidently assuming that they were familiar to his readers. As to the geographical position of Mash, Josephus (*Ant.* i. 6, § 4) connects the name with *Mesene* in lower Babylonia, on the shores of the Persian Gulf — a locality too remote, however, from the other branches of the Aramaic race. The more probable opinion is that which has been adopted by Bochart (*Phal.* ii. 11), Winer (*Rwb.* s. v.), and Knobel (*Völkert.* p. 237) — namely, that the name Mash is represented by the *Mons Masius* of classical writers, a range which forms the northern boundary of Mesopotamia, between the Tigris and Euphrates (Strab. xi. pp. 506, 527). Knobel reconciles this view with that of Josephus by the supposition of a migration from the north of Mesopotamia to the south of Babylonia, where the race may have been known in later times under the name of Meshech: the progress of the population in these parts was, however, in an opposite direction, from south to north. Kalisch (*Comm. on Gen.* p. 286) connects the names of Mash and Mysia: this is, to say the least, extremely doubtful; both the Mysians themselves and their name (= *Mœsia*) were probably of European origin.
              W. L. B.

MA′SHAL (מָשָׁל [*comparison, proverb*: Vat.] Μαασα; [Rom. Μαασὰλ; Alex.² Μασαλ:] *Masal*), the contracted or provincial (Galilean) form in which, in the later list of Levitical cities (1 Chr. vi. 74), the name of the town appears, which in the earlier records is given as MISHEAL and MISHAL. It suggests the MASALOTH of the Maccabean history.   G.

MASI′AS (Μισαίας [Vat. Μει-]; Alex. Μασιας: *Malsith*), one of the servants of Solomon, whose descendants returned with Zorobabel (1 Esdr. v. 34).

MAS′MAN (Μασμάν, [Vat.]; Alex. Μαασμαν: *Masman*). This name occurs for SHEMAIAH in 1 Esdr. viii. 43 (comp. Ezr. viii. 16). The Greek text is evidently corrupt, Σαμαίας (A. V. *Samaias*), which is the true reading, being misplaced in ver. 44 after Alnathan.

* **MASONS.** [HANDICRAFT, 3.]

MASORA. [OLD TESTAMENT.]

MAS′PHA. 1. (Μασσφά: *Maspha.*) A place opposite to (κατέναντι) Jerusalem, at which Judas Maccabæus and his followers assembled themselves to bewail the desolation of the city and the sanctuary, and to inflame their resentment before the battle of Emmaus, by the sight, not only of the distant city, which was probably visible from the eminence, but also of the Book of the Law mutilated and profaned, and of other objects of peculiar preciousness and sanctity (1 Macc. iii. 46).

There is no doubt that it is identical with MIZPEH of Benjamin, the ancient sanctuary at which Samuel had convened the people on an occasion of equal emergency. In fact, Maspha, or more accurately Massêpha, is merely the form in which the LXX. uniformly render the Hebrew name Mizpeh.

2. (Μασφά; [Sin. Μαφα; Alex. Μαασφα;] but Josephus Μάλλην· *Maspha.*) One of the cities which were taken from the Ammonites by Judas Maccabæus in his campaign on the east of Jordan (1 Macc. v. 35). It is probably the ancient city of Mizpeh of Gilead. The Syriac has the curious variation of *Olim*, ܡܠܚ, "salt." Perhaps Josephus also reads מֶלַח, "salt."   G

MAS′REKAH (מַשְׂרֵקָה [*place of vines*]: Μασσεκκᾶς, in Chron. Μασεκκᾶς, and so Alex. in both: *Masreca*), an ancient place, the native spot of Samlah, one of the old kings of the Edomites (Gen. xxxvi. 36; 1 Chr. i. 47). Interpreted as Hebrew, the name refers to vineyards — as if from *Sarak*, a root with which we are familiar in the " vine of Sorek," that is, the choice vine; and led by this, Knobel (*Genesis*, p. 257) proposes to place Masrekah in the district of the Idumæan mountains north of Petra, and along the Hadj route, where Burckhardt found "extensive vineyards," and "great quantities of dried grapes," made by the tribe of the *Refaya* for the supply of Gaza and for the Mecca pilgrims (Burckhardt, *Syria*, Aug. 21). But this is mere conjecture, as no name at all corresponding with Masrekah has been yet discovered in that locality. Schwarz (215) mentions a site called *En-Masrak*, a few miles south of Petra. He probably refers to the place marked *Ain Mafrak* in Palmer's Map, and *Ain el-Usdaka* in Kiepert's (Robinson, *Bibl. Res.* 1856). The versions are unanimous in adhering more or less closely to the Hebrew.   G.

MAS′SA (מַשָּׂא [*present, tribute*] : Μασσῆ; [in 1 Chron., Vat. Μανασση:] *Massa*), a son of Ishmael (Gen. xxv. 14; 1 Chr. i. 30). His descendants were not improbably the *Masani*, who are placed by Ptolemy (v. 19, § 2) in the east of Arabia, near the borders of Babylonia.
              W. L. B.

* According to some the proper rendering in Prov. xxx. 1 is "Agur the Massite." It is inferred, therefore, that the above Massa was the name also of the place where the wise Agur lived and where Lemuel reigned as king (Prov. xxxi. 1). In support of this conclusion see Bertheau, *Die Sprüche Salomo's*, p. 15 f. Prof. Stuart adopts this opinion in his notes on the above passages (*Comm. on Proverbs*, pp. 401, 421). That view, says Fürst (*Handc.* s. v.), is a doubtful one. The ordinary signification of הַמַּשָּׂא, *the utterance, proverb* (in the A. V. "the prophecy"), is entirely appropriate, and is more generally preferred by commentators. See Umbreit's *Sprüche Solomo's*, p. 392. [Further, see AGUR, LEMUEL, UCAL.]
              H.

MAS′SAH (מַסָּה : πειρασμός; [in Deut. xxxiii., πεῖρα: *Tentatio*]), i. e. *temptation*, a name given to the spot, also called MERIBAH, where the Israelites "tempted Jehovah, saying, Is Jehovah among us or not?" (Ex. xvii. 7). [See also Deut. vi. 16, ix. 22, xxxiii. 8.] The name also occurs, with mention of the circumstances which occasioned it, in Ps. xcv. 8, 9, and its Greek equivalent in Heb. iii. 8.   H. H.

MASSI'AS (Μασσίας: [Vat. Ασσειας:] *Hismœnis*) = MAASEIAH 3 (1 Esdr. ix. 22; comp. Ezr. x. 22).

* MAST. [SHIP.]

* MASTER stands in the A. V. as the representation of several different Hebrew and Greek words, but the principal use of the term which demands notice here is that in which, as in Matt. viii. 19 (διδάσκαλος, given in John i. 38, xx. 16, as equivalent to the Hebrew words Rabbi and Rabboni), it is often applied to our Lord as a title of respect. [RABBI.] It is by a reference to the common application of this term among the Jews, that we must probably explain our Lord's reproof of the person spoken of in Mark x. 17 and Luke xviii. 18 (designated in the latter account as a ruler; the reading of the received text, Matt. xix. 16, is apparently corrupt), for addressing him as "Good Master." The expression, in itself appropriate, was employed improperly by the speaker, who designed nothing more in the use of it than to recognize our Saviour as one who, although perhaps distinguished by preëminent attainments and character, was not essentially different from the ordinary Rabbis. Our Lord applies the term so rendered to Nicodemus (John iii. 10), with special emphasis: "Art thou the master (teacher) of Israel," as expressive probably of the high authority Nicodemus enjoyed among his countrymen as a teacher of religion. This title of "master," as the translation of διδάσκαλος, is given to our Lord about forty times in the Gospels. The sense would often be clearer to the English reader if "teacher" were substituted for it. By "master of the ship" (Acts xxvii. 11), the man at the rudder or the helmsman (κυβερνήτης) is meant. [GOVERNOR, 15.] For the interchange of "master of the house," and "good man of the house," see vol. i. p. 939.

The expression "master and scholar," Mal. ii. 12 (Heb. עֵר וְעֹנֶה), which suggests a usage somewhat like that so common in the N. T., is probably a mistranslation. The literal meaning seems to be *caller* (or *watcher*) *and answerer*, apparently a proverbial expression for every living person, referring perhaps originally to watchmen calling to and answering one another (comp. Ps. cxxxiv. 1; Is. lxii. 6).

The very obscure phrase בַּעֲלֵי אֲסֻפּוֹת (Eccl. xii. 11), translated in A. V. "masters of assemblies," is variously explained, as, *e. g.* referring (1) to the *nails driven in*, just spoken of, represented here as *instruments of fastening* (Rosenmüller); (2) to the gathered "words of the wise." *contents of collections* (Ewald, Heiligstedt, Hitzig); (3) to the collectors themselves, either as the masters, authors of the collections (De Wette), or as members of an assembly (Gesenius, Fürst, and Hengstenberg, comp. Jerome in Vulgate). The last view is

perhaps, on the whole, the most probable, especially if we are at liberty, with Kimchi, to supply דִּבְרֵי before בַּעֲלֵי אֲסֻפּוֹת.   D. S. T.

* MASTERIES is the rendering of ἀθλῇ in 2 Tim. ii. 5, which is literally "if any one strive," *i. e.* for preëminence as an athlete. The A. V. follows the earlier English versions from Tyndale onward, except the change of "mastery" to "masteries." Further, see GAMES, vol. i. p. 464 a.
                                        H.

MASTICH-TREE (σχῖνος, *lentiscus*) occurs only in the Apocrypha (Susan. ver. 54[a]), where the margin of the A. V. has *lentisk*. There is no doubt that the Greek word is correctly rendered, as is evident from the description of it by Theophrastus (*Hist. Plant.* ix. i. §§ 2, 4, § 7, &c.); Pliny (*H. N.* iii. 36, xxiv. 28); Dioscorides (i. 90), and other writers. Herodotus (iv. 177) compares the fruit of the lotus (the *Rhamnus lotus*, Linn., not the Egyptian *Nelumbium speciosum*) in size with the mastich berry, and Babrius (3, 5) says its leaves are browsed by goats. The fragrant resin known in the arts as "mastick," and which is obtained by incisions made in the trunk in the month of August, is the produce of this tree, whose scientific name is *Pistacia lentiscus*. It is used with us to strengthen the teeth and gums, and was so applied by the ancients, by whom it was much prized on this account, and for its many supposed medicinal virtues. Lucian (*Lexiph.* p. 12) uses the term σχινοτρώκτης of one who chews mastich wood in order to whiten his teeth. Martial (*Ep.* xiv. 22) recommends a mastich toothpick (*dentiscalpium*). Pliny (xxiv. 7) speaks of the leaves of this tree being rubbed on the teeth for toothache. Dioscorides (i. 90) says the resin is often mixed with other materials and used as tooth-powder, and that, if chewed,[b] it imparts a sweet odor to the breath. Both Pliny and Dioscorides state that the best mastich comes from Chios, and to this day the Arabs prefer that which is imported from that island (comp. Niebuhr, *Beschr. von Arab.* p. 144: Galen, *de fac. Simpl.* 7, p. 69). Tournefort (*Voyages*, ii. 58-61, transl. 1741) has given a full and very interesting account of the lentisks or mastich plants of Scio (Chios): he says that "the towns of the island are distinguished into three classes, those *del Campo*, those of *Apanomeria*, and those where they plant *lentisk-trees*, from whence the mastick in tears is produced." Tournefort enumerates several lentisk-tree villages. Of the trees he says, "these trees are very wide spread and circular, ten or twelve feet tall, consisting of several branchy stalks which in time grow crooked. The biggest trunks are a foot in diameter, covered with a bark, grayish, rugged, chapt . . . . . the leaves are disposed in three or four couples on each side, about an inch long, narrow at the beginning, pointed at their extremity, half an inch broad about the middle. From the junctures of the leaves grow flowers in bunches like grapes (see woodcut); the fruit too grows like bunches of grapes, in each berry whereof is contained a white

---

[a] This verse contains a happy play upon the word. "Under what tree sawest thou them? . . . under a mastich-tree (ὑπὸ σχῖνον). And Daniel said . . . the angel of God hath received the sentence of God to cut thee in two (σχίσει σε μέσον). This is unfortunately lost in our version; but it is preserved by the Vulgate, "sub schino scindet te;" and by

Luther, "Linde . . . finden." A similar play occurs in vv. 58, 59, between πρῖνον, and πρίσαι σε. For the bearing of these and similar characteristics on the date and origin of the book, see SUSANNA.

[b] Whence the derivation of *mastich*, from μαστίχη, the gum of the σχῖνος, from μάσταξ, μαστιχάω, μασάομαι, "to chew," "to masticate."

kernel. These trees blow in May, the fruit does not ripen but in autumn and winter." This writer gives the following description of the mode in which the mastich gum is procured. "They begin to make incisions in these trees in Scio the first of August, cutting the bark crossways with huge knives, without touching the younger branches; next day the nutritious juice distils in small tears, which by little and little form the mastick grains;

Mastich (*Pistacia lentiscus*).

they harden on the ground, and are carefully swept up from under the trees. The height of the crop is about the middle of August if it be dry serene weather, but if it be rainy, the tears are all lost. Likewise towards the end of September the same incisions furnish mastick, but in lesser quantities." Besides the uses to which reference has been made above, the people of Scio put grains of this resin in perfumes, and in their bread before it goes to the oven.

Mastick is one of the most important products of the East, being extensively used in the preparation of spirits, as juniper berries are with us, as a sweetmeat, as a masticatory for preserving the gums and teeth, as an antispasmodic in medicine, and as an ingredient in varnishes. The Greek writers occasionally use the word σχῖνος for an entirely different plant, namely, the Squill (*Scilla maritima*) (see Aristoph. *Plut.* p. 715; Sprengel, *Flor. Hippoc.* p. 41: Theophr. *Hist. Plant.* v. 6, § 10). The *Pistacia lentiscus* is common on the shores of the Mediterranean. According to Strand (*Flor. Palæst.* No. 559) it has been observed at Joppa, both by Rauwolf and Pococke. The mastich-tree belongs to the natural order *Anacardiaceæ*.

W. H.

* The *Pistacia lentiscus* is found in Syria, on Mt. Lebanon. I am not aware that the gum is extracted from it for purposes of commerce.

G. E. P.

MATHANI'AS (Μανθανίας; [Vat. Βεσκασπανς:] *Mathathias*) = MATTANIAH, a de-

scendant of Pahath-Moab (1 Esdr. ix. 31; comp. Ezr. x. 30).

MATHU'SALA (Μαθουσάλα: *Mathusale*) = METHUSELAH, the son of Enoch (Luke iii. 37).

MAT'RED (מַטְרֵד [*thrusting forth, repelling*]: Ματραίθ; Alex. Ματρασιθ; [in 1 Chr., Rom. Vat. omit, Alex. Ματραδ:] *Matred*), a daughter of Mezahab, and mother of Mehetabel, who was wife of Hadar (or Hadad) of Pau, king of Edom (Gen. xxxvi. 39; 1 Chr. i. 50). Respecting the kings of Edom, whose records are contained in the chapters referred to, see HADAD, IRAM, etc.

E. S. P.

MAT'RI (הַמַּטְרִי, with the art., properly *the Matri*: Ματταρί; [Vat. Ματταρει: Alex. Ματταρει and Ματταρειτ: *Metri*), a family of the tribe of Benjamin, to which Saul the king of Israel belonged (1 Sam. x. 21).

MAT'TAN (מַתָּן [*gift*]: Μαθάν, [Vat. Μαγθαν,] Alex. Μαχαν in Kings; Μαθθάν in Chron.: *Mathan*). 1. The priest of Baal slain before his altars in the idol temple at Jerusalem, at the time when Jehoiada swept away idolatry from Judah (2 K. xi. 18; 2 Chr. xxiii. 17). He probably accompanied Athaliah from Samaria, and would thus be the first priest of the Baal-worship which Jehoram king of Judah, following in the steps of his father-in-law Ahab, established at Jerusalem (2 Chr. xxi. 6, 13); Josephus (*Ant.* ix. 7, § 3) calls him Μααθάν.

2. (Ναθάν.) The father of Shephatiah. (Jer. xxxviii. 1). W. A. W.

MAT'TANAH (מַתָּנָה [*gift*]: Μανθαναείν; Alex. [Μανθανιν,] Μανθανειν: *Matthana*), a station in the latter part of the wanderings of the Israelites (Num. xxi. 18, 19). It lay next beyond the well, or Beer, and between it and Nahaliel: Nahaliel again being but one day's journey from the Bamoth or heights of Moab. Mattanah was therefore probably situated to the S. E. of the Dead Sea, but no name like it appears to have been yet discovered. The meaning at the root of the word (if taken as Hebrew) is a "gift," and accordingly the Targumists — Onkelos as well as Pseudojonathan and the Jerusalem — treat Mattanah as if a synonym for BEER, the well which was "given" to the people (ver. 16). In the same vein they further translate the names in verse 20; and treat them as denoting the valleys (Nahaliel) and the heights (Bamoth), to which the miraculous well followed the camp in its journeyings. The legend is noticed under BEER.[a] By Le Clerc it is suggested that Mattanah may be the same with the mysterious word *Vaheb* (ver. 14; A. V. "what he did") — since the meaning of that word in Arabic is the same as that of Mattanah in Hebrew. G.

MATTANI'AH (מַתַּנְיָה [*gift of Jehovah*]: Βατθανίας; [Vat. Μαθθαν:] Alex. Μεθθανιας: *Matthanias*). 1. The original name of Zedekiah king of Judah, which was changed when Nebuchadnezzar placed him on the throne instead of his nephew Jehoiachin (2 K. xxiv. 17). In like manner Pharaoh had changed the name of his brother Eliakim to Jehoiakim on a similar occa-

a Vol. i. p. 264 b. In addition to the authorities there cited, the curious reader who may desire to investigate this remarkable tradition will find it ex-

hausted in Buxtorf's *Exercitationes* (No. v. *Hist. Petræ in Deserto*).

sion (2 K. xxiii. 34), when he restored the succession to the elder branch of the royal family (comp. 2 K. xxiii. 31, 36).

2. (Ματθανίας in Chr., and Neh. xi. 17; Ματθανία, Neh. xii. 8, 35; Alex. Μαθθανιας, Neh. xi. 17, Μαθανια, Neh. xii. 8, Μαθθανια, Neh. xii. 35; [Vat. in Chr., Μανθανιας; in Neh. xi. 17, xii. 35, xiii. 13, Μαθανια; Neh. xii. 8, Μαχανια; 35, Ναθανια; Neh. xi. 22, xii. 25, Rom. Vat. Alex. FA.[1] omit:] Mathanias, exc. Neh. xii. 8, 35, Maththanias.) A Levite singer of the sons of Asaph (1 Chr. ix. 15). He is described as the son of Micah, Micha (Neh. xi. 17), or Michaiah (Neh. xii. 35), and after the return from Babylon lived in the villages of the Netophathites (1 Chr. ix. 16) or Netophathi (Neh. xii. 28), which the singers had built in the neighborhood of Jerusalem (Neh. xii. 29). As leader of the Temple choir after its restoration (Neh. xi. 17, xii. 8) in the time of Nehemiah, he took part in the musical service which accompanied the dedication of the wall of Jerusalem (Neh. xii. 25, 35). We find him among the Levites of the second rank, "keepers of the thresholds," an office which fell to the singers (comp. 1 Chr. xv. 18, 21). In Neh. xii. 35, there is a difficulty, for "Mattaniah, the son of Michaiah, the son of Zaccur, the son of Asaph," is apparently the same with "Mattaniah, the son of Micha, the son of Zabdi the son of Asaph" (Neh. xi. 17), and with the Mattaniah of Neh. xii. 8, 25, who, as in xi. 17, is associated with Bakbukiah, and is expressly mentioned as living in the days of Nehemiah and Ezra (Neh. xii. 26). But, if the reading in Neh. xii. 35 be correct, Zechariah, the great-grandson of Mattaniah (further described as one of "the priests' sons," a whereas Mattaniah was a Levite), blew the trumpet at the head of the procession led by Ezra, which marched round the city wall. From a comparison of Neh. xii. 35 with xii. 41, 42, it seems probable that the former is corrupt, that Zechariah in verses 35 and 41 is the same priest, and that the clause in which the name of Mattaniah is found is to be connected with ver. 36, in which are enumerated his "brethren" alluded to in ver. 8.

3. (Ματθανίας; [Vat. Μανθανιας:] Mathanias.) A descendant of Asaph, and ancestor of Jahaziel the Levite in the reign of Jehoshaphat (2 Chron. xx. 14).

4. (Ματθανία; [Vat. FA. Μαθανια;] Alex. Μαθθανια: Mathania.) One of the sons of Elam who had married a foreign wife in the time of Ezra (Ezr. x. 26). In 1 Esdr. ix. 27 he is called MATTHANIAS.

5. (Ματθαναί; [Vat. Αθανια:] Alex. Μαθθαναι.) One of the sons of Zattu in the time of Ezra who put away his foreign wife (Ezr. x. 27). He is called OTHONIAS in 1 Esdr. ix. 28.

6. (Ματθανία; [Vat. Αμαθανια:] Alex. Μαθθανια: Mathanias.) A descendant of Pahath-Moab who lived at the same time, and is mentioned under the same circumstances as the two preceding (Ezr. x. 30). In 1 Esdr. ix. 31, he is called MATHANIAS.

7. [Ματθανία; Vat. FA. Μαθανια; Alex. Μαθθανια: Mathanius.] One of the sons of Bani, who like the three above mentioned, put away his foreign wife at Ezra's command (Ezr. x. 37). In the

parallel list of Esdr. ix. 34, the names "Mattaniah, Mattenai," are corrupted into MAMNITANAIMUS.

8. (Ματθαναίας; [Vat. Ναθανια; FA.* Μαθανια;] Alex. Μαθθανιας.) A Levite, father of Zaccur, and ancestor of Hanan the under-treasurer who had charge of the offerings for the Levites in the time of Nehemiah (Neh. xiii. 13).

9. (מַתַּנְיָהוּ [gift of Jehovah]: Ματθανίας; [Vat. Μανθανιας:] Mathaniau, 1 Chr. xxv. 4; Mathanias, 1 Chr. xxv. 16), one of the fourteen sons of Heman the singer, whose office it was to blow the horns in the Temple service as appointed by David. He was the chief of the 9th division of twelve Levites who were "instructed in the songs of Jehovah."

10. [Ματθανίας: Mathanias.] A descendant of Asaph, the Levite minstrel, who assisted in the purification of the Temple in the reign of Hezekiah (2 Chr. xxix. 13).   W. A. W.

MATTATHA (Ματταθά: Mathatha), the son of Nathan, and grandson of David in the genealogy of our Lord (Luke iii. 31).

MATTATHAH (מַתָּתָה [gift of Jehovah, contracted from the above]: Ματθαθά; Alex. Μαθθαθα: Mathatha), a descendant of Hashum, who had married a foreign wife in the time of Ezra, and was separated from her (Ezr. x. 33). He is called MATTHIAS in 1 Esdr. ix. 33.

MATTATHI'AS (Ματταθίας: Mathathias). 1. = MATTITHIAH, who stood at Ezra's right hand when he read the Law to the people (1 Esdr. ix. 43; comp. Neh. viii. 4).

2. (Mathathias.) The father of the Maccabees (1 Macc. ii. 1, 14, 16, 17, 19, 24, 27, 39, 45, 49, xiv. 29). [MACCABEES, vol. ii. p. 1710 a.]

3. (Mathathias.) The son of Absalom, and brother of JONATHAN 14 (1 Macc. xi. 70, xiii. 11). In the battle fought by Jonathan with the high-priest with the forces of Demetrius on the plain of Nasor (the old Hazor), his two generals Mattathias and Judas alone stood by him, when his army was seized with a panic and fled, and with their assistance the fortunes of the day were restored.

4. (Mathathias.) The son of Simon Maccabeus, who was treacherously murdered, together with his father and brother, in the fortress of Docus, by Ptolemeus the son of Abubus (1 Macc. xvi. 14).

5. (Matthias.) One of the three envoys sent by Nicanor to treat with Judas Maccabeus (2 Macc. xiv. 19).

6. (Mathathias.) Son of Amos, in the genealogy of Jesus Christ (Luke iii. 25).

7. (Mathathias.) Son of Semei, in the same catalogue (Luke iii. 26).   W. A. W.

MATTENAI [3 syl.] (מַתְּנַי [gift of Jehovah, see above]: Ματθανία; [Vat. FA. Μαθανια;] Alex. Μαθθαναι: Mathanai). 1. One of the family of Hashum, who in the time of Ezra had married a foreign wife (Ezr. x. 33). In 1 Esdr. ix. 33 he is called ALTANEUS.

2. (Ματθαναί; [Vat. Μαθαναυ; FA. Μαθανα:] Alex. Μαθθαναί: Mathanai.) A descendant of Bani, who put away his foreign wife at Ezra's command (Ezr. x. 37). The place of this name and of Mattaniah which precedes it is occupied in 1 Esdr. ix. 34 by MAMNITANAIMUS.

---

* The word "priest" is apparently applied in a less restricted sense in later times, for we find in Ezr. viii. 24 Sherebiah and Hashabiah described as among the "chief of the priests," whereas, in vv. 18, 19, they are Merarite Levites; if, as is probable, the same persons are alluded to in both instances. Comp. also Josh. iii. 3 with Num. vii. 9.

3. [Vat. Alex. FA. omit; Rom. Μαρθαναί.] A priest in the days of Joiakim the son of Jeshua (Neh. xii. 19). He represented the house of Joiarib.

MATTHAN (Rec. Text, Ματθάν; Lachm. [Tisch. Treg.] with B, Μαθθάν: *Matthan, Matthan*). The son of Eleazar, and grandfather of Joseph "the husband of Mary" (Matt. i. 15). He occupies the same place in the genealogy as MATTHAT in Luke iii. 24, with whom indeed he is probably identical (Hervey, *Genealogies of Christ,* 129, 134, &c.). "He seems to have been himself descended from Joseph the son of Judah, of Luke iii. 26, but to have become the heir of the elder branch of the house of Abiud on the failure of Eleazar's issue (*ib.* 134).

MATTHANI'AS (Ματθανίας; [Vat. Ματταν]) =MATTANIAH, one of the descendants of Elam (1 Esdr. ix. 27; comp. Ezr. x. 26). In the Vulgate, "Eia, Mathanias," are corrupted into "Jolaman, Chamas," which is evidently a transcriber's error.

MATTHAT (Ματθάτ; but Tisch. [7th ed.] Μαθθάτ [8th edition, Μαθθάθ]: *Mathat, Mattat, Matthad,* etc.). 1. Son of Levi and grandfather of Joseph, according to the genealogy of Luke (iii. 24). He is maintained by Lord A. Hervey to have been the same person as the MATTHAN of Matt. i. 15 (see *Genealogies of Christ,* 137, 138, &c.).

2. [Tisch. Μαθθάθ.] Also the son of a Levi, and a progenitor of Joseph, but much higher up in the line, namely, eleven generations from David (Luke iii. 29). Nothing is known of him.

It should be remarked that no fewer than five names in this list are derived from the same Hebrew root as that of their ancestor NATHAN the son of David (see Hervey, *Genealogies,* etc., p. 150).

MATTHE'LAS (Μαθήλας; [Vat. Μαενλας:] *Maseas*) =MAASEIAH 1 (1 Esdr. ix. 19; comp. Ezr. x. 18). The reading of the LXX. which is followed in the A. V. might easily arise from a mistake betwen the uncial Θ and Σ (C).

MATTHEW (Lachm. [Tisch. Treg.] with [Sin.] BD, Μαθθαῖος; AC and Rec. Text, Ματθαῖος: *Matthæus*). Matthew the Apostle and Evangelist is the same as LEVI (Luke v. 27–29), the son of a certain Alphæus (Mark ii. 14). His call to be an Apostle is related by all three Evangelists in the same words, except that Matthew (ix. 9) gives the former, and Mark (ii. 14) and Luke (v. 27) the latter name. If there were two publicans, both called solemnly in the same form at the same place, Capernaum, then one of them became an Apostle, and the other was heard of no more; for Levi is not mentioned again after the feast which he made in our Lord's honor (Luke v. 29). This is most unlikely. Euthymius and many other commentators of note identify Alphæus the father of Matthew with Alphæus the father of James the Less. Against this is to be set the fact that in the lists of Apostles (Matt. x. 3; Mark iii. 18; Luke vi. 15; Acts i. 13), Matthew and James the Less are never named together, like other pairs of brothers in the apostolic body. [See addition to ALPHÆUS, Amer. ed.] It may be, as in other cases, that the name Levi was replaced by the name Matthew at the time of the call. According to Gesenius, the names Matthæus and Matthias are both contractions of Mattathias (= מַתִּתְיָה, "gift of Jehovah;" Θεόδωρος, Θεόδοτος), a common

Jewish name after the exile; but the true derivation is not certain (see Winer, Lange). The publicans, properly so called (*publicani*), were persons who farmed the Roman taxes, and they were usually, in later times, Roman knights, and persons of wealth and credit. They employed under them inferior officers, natives of the province where the taxes were collected, called properly *portitores,* to which class Matthew no doubt belonged. These latter were notorious for impudent exactions everywhere (Plautus, *Menæch.* i. 2, 5; Cic. *ad Quint. Fr.* i. 1; Plut. *De Curios.* p. 518 *e*); but to the Jews they were especially odious, for they were the very spot where the Roman chain galled them, the visible proof of the degraded state of their nation. As a rule, none but the lowest would accept such an unpopular office, and thus the class became more worthy of the hatred with which in any case the Jews would have regarded it. The readiness, however, with which Matthew obeyed the call of Jesus seems to show that his heart was still open to religious impressions. His conversion was attended by a great awakening of the outcast classes of the Jews (Matt. ix. 9, 10). Matthew in his Gospel does not omit the title of infamy which had belonged to him (x. 3); but neither of the other Evangelists speaks of "Matthew *the publican.*" Of the exact share which fell to him in preaching the Gospel we have nothing whatever in the N. T., and other sources of information we cannot trust.

Eusebius (*H. E.* iii. 24) mentions that after our Lord's ascension Matthew preached in Judæa (some add for fifteen years; Clem. *Strom.* vi.), and then went to foreign nations. To the lot of Matthew it fell to visit Æthiopia, says Socrates Scholasticus (*H. E.* i. 19; Ruff. *H. E.* x. 9). But Ambrose says that God opened to him the country of the Persians (*In Ps.* 45); Isidore the Macedonians (Isidore Hisp. *de Sanct.* 77); and others the Parthians, the Medes, the Persians of the Euphrates. Nothing whatever is really known. Heracleon, the disciple of Valentinus (cited by Clemens Alex. *Strom.* iv. 9), describes him as dying a natural death, which Clement, Origen, and Tertullian seem to accept: the tradition that he died a martyr, be it true or false, came in afterwards (Niceph. *H. E.* ii. 41).

If the first feeling on reading these meagre particulars be disappointment, the second will be admiration for those who, doing their part under God in the great work of founding the Church on earth, have passed away to meet their Master in heaven without so much as an effort to redeem their names from silence and oblivion. (For authorities see the works on the Gospels referred to under LUKE and GOSPELS; also Fritzsche, *In Matthæum,* Leipzig, 1826; Lange, *Bibelwerk,* part i.)   W. T.

MATTHEW. GOSPEL OF. The Gospel which bears the name of St. Matthew was written by the Apostle, according to the testimony of all antiquity.

I. *Language in which it was first written.* — We are told on the authority of Papias, Irenæus, Pantænus, Origen, Eusebius, Epiphanius, Jerome, and many other Fathers, that the Gospel was first written in Hebrew, *i. e.* in the vernacular language of Palestine, the Aramaic. (*a.*) Papias of Hierapolis (who flourished in the first half of the 2d century) says, "Matthew wrote the divine oracles (τὰ λόγια) in the Hebrew dialect; and each interpreted them as he was able" (Eusebius, *H. E.* iii. 39). It has been held that τὰ λόγια is to be understood as a collection of *discourses*, and that therefore the book here alluded to, contained not the acts of our Lord but his speeches; but this falls through, for Papias applies the same word to the Gospel of St. Mark, and he uses the expression λόγια κυριακά in the title of his own work, which we know from fragments to have contained facts as well as discourses (*Studien und Kritiken*, 1832, p. 735; Meyer, *Einleitung*; De Wette, *Einleitung*, § 97 a; Alford's *Prolegomena to Gr. Test.* p. 25). Eusebius, indeed, in the same place pronounces Papias to be "a man of very feeble understanding," in reference to some false opinions which he held; but it requires little critical power to bear witness to the fact that a certain Hebrew book was in use. (*b.*) Irenæus says (iii. 1), that "whilst Peter and Paul were preaching at Rome and founding the Church, Matthew put forth his written Gospel amongst the Hebrews in their own dialect." It is objected to this testimony that Irenæus probably drew from the same source as Papias, for whom he had great respect; this assertion can neither be proved nor refuted, but the testimony of Irenæus is in itself no mere copy of that of Papias. (*c.*) According to Eusebius (*H. E.* v. 10), Pantænus (who flourished in the latter part of the 2d century) "is reported to have gone to the Indians" (*i. e.* to the south of Arabia?), "where it is said that he found the Gospel of Matthew already among some who had the knowledge of Christ there, to whom Bartholomew, one of the Apostles, had preached, and left them the Gospel of Matthew written in Hebrew, which was preserved till the time referred to." We have no writings of Pantænus, and Eusebius recites the story with a kind of doubt. It reappears in two different forms: Jerome and Ruffinus say that Pantænus *brought back* with him this Hebrew Gospel, and Nicephorus asserts that Bartholomew *dictated* the Gospel of Matthew to the inhabitants of that country. Upon the whole, Pantænus contributes but little to the weight of the argument. (*d.*) Origen says (*Comment. on Matt.* i. in Eusebius, *H. E.* vi. 25), " As I have learnt by tradition concerning the four Gospels, which alone are received without dispute by the Church of God under heaven: the first was written by St. Matthew, once a tax-gatherer, afterwards an Apostle of Jesus Christ, who published it for the benefit of the Jewish converts, composed in the Hebrew language." The objections to this passage brought by Masch, are disposed of by Michaelis iii. part i. p. 127; the "tradition" does not imply a doubt, and there is no reason for tracing this witness also to Papias. (*e.*) Eusebius (*H. E.* iii. 24) gives as his own opinion the following: " Matthew having first preached to the Hebrews, delivered to them, when he was preparing to depart to other countries, his Gospel, composed in their native language." Other passages to the same effect occur in Cyril (*Catech.* p. 14), Epiphanius (*Hær.* li. 2, 1), Hieronymus (*de Vir. ill.* ch. 3), who mentions the Hebrew original in seven places at least of his works, and from Gregory of Nazianzus, Chrysostom, Augustine, and other later writers. From all these there is no doubt that the old opinion was that Matthew wrote in the Hebrew language. To whom we are to attribute the Greek translation, is not shown; but the quotation of Papias proves that in the time of John the Presbyter, and probably in that of Papias, there was no translation of great authority, and Jerome (*de Vir. ill.* ch. 3) ex-

pressly says that the translator's name was uncertain.

So far all the testimony is for a Hebrew original. But there are arguments of no mean weight in favor of the Greek, a very brief account of which may be given here. 1. The quotations from the O. T. in this Gospel, which are very numerous (see below), are of two kinds: those introduced into the narrative to point out the fulfillment of prophecies, etc., and those where in the course of the narrative the persons introduced, and especially our Lord Himself, make use of O. T. quotations. Between these two classes a difference of treatment is observable. In the latter class, where the citations occur in discourses, the Septuagint version is followed, even where it deviates somewhat from the original (as iii. 3, xiii. 14), or where it ceases to follow the very words, the deviations do not come from a closer adherence to the Hebrew O. T.; except in two cases, xi. 10 and xxvi. 31. The quotations in the narrative, however, do not follow the Septuagint, but appear to be a translation from the Hebrew text. Thus we have the remarkable phenomenon that, whereas the Gospels agree most exactly in the speeches of persons, and most of all in those of our Lord, the quotations in these speeches are reproduced not by the closest rendering of the Hebrew, but from the Septuagint version, although many or most of them must have been spoken in the vernacular Hebrew, and could have had nothing to do with the Septuagint. A mere translator could not have done this. But an independent writer, using the Greek tongue, and wishing to conform his narrative to the oral teaching of the Apostles (see vol. ii. p. 948 *b*), might have used for the quotations the well-known Greek O. T. used by his colleagues. There is an independence in the mode of dealing with citations throughout, which is inconsistent with the function of a mere translator. 2. But this difficulty is to be got over by assuming a high authority for this translation, as though made by an inspired writer; and it has been suggested that this writer was Matthew himself (Bengel, Olshausen, Lee, and others), or at least that he directed it (Guericke), or that it was some other Apostle (Gerhard), or James the brother of the Lord, or John, or the general body of the Apostles, or that two disciples of St. Matthew wrote, from him, the one in Aramaic and the other in Greek! We are further invited to admit, with Dr. Lee, that the Hebrew book "belonged to that class of writings which, although composed by inspired men, were never designed to form part of the Canon" (*On Inspiration*, p. 571). But supposing that there were any good ground for considering these suggestions as facts, it is clear that in the attempt to preserve the letter of the tradition, they have quite altered the spirit of it. Papias and Jerome make a Hebrew original, and dependent translations; the moderns make a Greek original, which is a translation only in name, and a Hebrew original never intended to be preserved. The modern view is not what Papias thought or uttered; and the question would be one of mere names, for the only point worthy of a struggle is this, whether the Gospel in our hands is or is not of apostolic authority, and authentic. 4. Olshausen remarks, "While all the fathers of the church relate that Matthew has written in Hebrew, yet they universally make use of the Greek text, as a genuine apostolic composition, without remarking what relation the Hebrew Matthew bears to our Greek

Gospel. For that the earlier ecclesiastical teachers did not possess the Gospel of St. Matthew in any other form than we now have it, is established" (*Echtheit*, p. 35). The original Hebrew of which so many speak, no one of the witnesses ever saw (Jerome, *de Vir. ill.* p. 3, is no exception). And so little store has the church set upon it, that it has utterly perished. 5. Were there no explanation of this inconsistency between assertion and fact, it would be hard to doubt the concurrent testimony of so many old writers, whose belief in it is shown by the tenacity with which they held it in spite of their own experience. But it is certain that a Gospel, not the same as our canonical Matthew, sometimes usurped the Apostle's name; and some of the witnesses we have quoted appear to have referred to this in one or other of its various forms or names. The Christians in Palestine still held that the Mosaic ritual was binding on them, even after the destruction of Jerusalem. At the close of the first century one party existed who held that the Mosaic law was only binding on Jewish converts — this was the Nazarenes. Another, the Ebionites, held that it was of universal obligation on Christians, and rejected St. Paul's Epistles as teaching the opposite doctrine. These two sects, who differed also in the most important tenets as to our Lord's person, possessed each a modification of the same Gospel, which no doubt each altered more and more, as their tenets diverged, and which bore various names — the Gospel of the Twelve Apostles, the Gospel according to the Hebrews, the Gospel of Peter. or the Gospel according to Matthew. Enough is known to decide that the Gospel according to the Hebrews was not identical with our Gospel of Matthew But it had many points of resemblance to the synoptical gospels, and especially to Matthew. What was its origin it is impossible to say: it may have been a description of the oral teaching of the Apostles, corrupted by degrees; it may have come in its early and pure form from the hand of Matthew, or it may have been a version of the Greek Gospel of St. Matthew, as the Evangelist who wrote especially for Hebrews. Now this Gospel, "the Proteus of criticism" (Thiersch), did exist; is it impossible that when the Hebrew Matthew is spoken of, this questionable document, the Gospel of the Hebrews, was really referred to? Observe that all accounts of it are at second hand (with a notable exception); no one quotes it; in cases of doubt about the text, Origen even does not appeal from the Greek to the Hebrew. All that is certain is, that Nazarenes or Ebionites, or both, boasted that they possessed the original Gospel of Matthew. Jerome is the exception; and him we can convict of the very mistake of confounding the two, and almost on his own confession. "At first he thought," says an anonymous writer (*Edinburgh Review*, 1851, July, p 39), "that it was the authentic Matthew, and translated it into both Greek and Latin from a copy which he obtained at Beroea, in Syria. This appears from his *De Vir. ill.*, written in the year 392. Six years later, in his Commentary on Matthew, he spoke more doubtfully about it, — 'quod vocatur a plerisque Matthæi authenticum.' Later still, in his book on the Pelagian heresy, written in the year 415, he modifies his account still further, describing the work as the 'Evangelium juxta Hebræos, quod Chaldaico quidem Syroque sermone, sed Hebraicis literis conscriptum est, quo utuntur usque hodie Nazareni secundum Apostolos, sive ut

plerique autumant juxta Matthæum, quod et in Cæsariensi habetur Bibliotheca.'" 5. Dr. Lee in his work on Inspiration asserts, by an oversight unusual with such a writer, that the theory of a Hebrew original is "generally received by critics as the only legitimate conclusion." Yet there have pronounced for a Greek original — Erasmus, Calvin, Le Clerc, Fabricius, Lightfoot, Wetstein, Paulus, Lardner, Hey, Hales, Hug, Schott, De Wette, Moses Stuart, Fritzsche, Credner, Thiersch, and many others. Great names are ranged also on the other side: as Simon, Mill, Michaelis, Marsh, Eichhorn, Storr, Olshausen, and others.

With these arguments we leave a great question unsettled still, feeling convinced of the early acceptance and the Apostolic authority of our "Gospel according to St. Matthew;" and far from convinced that it is a reproduction of another Gospel from St. Matthew's hand. May not the truth be that Papias, knowing of more than one Aramaic Gospel in use among the Judaic sects, may have assumed the existence of a Hebrew original from which these were supposed to be taken, and knowing also the genuine Greek Gospel, may have looked on all these, in the loose uncritical way which earned for him Eusebius' description, as the various "interpretations" to which he alludes?

The independence of the style and diction of the Greek Evangelist, will appear from the remarks in the next section.

BIBLIOGRAPHY. — Hug's *Einleitung*, with the Notes of Professor M. Stuart, Andover, 1836. Meyer, *Komm. Einleitung*, and the Commentaries of Kuinöl, Fritzsche, Alford, and others. The passages from the Fathers are discussed in Michaelis (ed. Marsh, vol. iii. part i.); and they will be found for the most part in Kirchhofer, *Quellensammlung;* where will also be found the passages referring to the Gospel of the Hebrews, p. 448. Credner's *Einleitung*, and his *Beiträge;* and the often cited works on the Gospels, of Gieseler, Baur, Norton, Olshausen, Weisse, and Hilgenfeld. Also Cureton's *Syriac Gospels;* but the views in the preface must not be regarded as established. Dr. Lee on *Inspiration*, Appendix P., London, 1857.

II. *Style and Diction.* — The following remarks on the style of St. Matthew are founded on those of Credner.

1. Matthew uses the expression "that it might be fulfilled which was spoken of the Lord by the prophet" (i. 22, ii. 15). In ii. 5, and in later passages of Matt. it is abbreviated (ii. 17, iii. 3, iv. 14, viii. 17, xii. 17, xiii. 14, 35, xxi. 4, xxvi. 56, xxvii. 9). The variation ὑπὸ τοῦ Θεοῦ in xxii. 31 is notable; and also the τοῦτο δὲ ὅλον γέγονεν of i. 22, not found in other Evangelists; but compare Mark xiv. 49; Luke xxiv. 44.

2. The reference to the Messiah under the name "Son of David," occurs in Matthew eight times; and three times each in Mark and Luke.

3. Jerusalem is called "the holy city," "the holy place" (iv. 5, xxiv. 15, xxvii. 53).

4. The expression συντέλεια τοῦ αἰῶνος is used five times; in the rest of the N. T. only once, in Ep. to Hebrews.

5. The phrase "kingdom of heaven," about thirty-three times ; other writers use "kingdom of God," which is found also in Matthew.

6. "Heavenly Father," used about six times; and "Father in heaven" about sixteen, and without explanation, point to the Jewish mode of speaking in this Gospel.

7. Matthew alone of the Evangelists uses τὸ ῥηθέν, ἐῤῥέθη as the form of quotation from O. T. The apparent exception in Mark xiii. 14 is rejected by Tischendorf, etc., as a wrong reading. In Matt. about twenty times.

8. Ἀναχωρεῖν is a frequent word for to retire. Once in Mark.

9. Κατ' ὄναρ used six times; and here only.

10. The use of προσέρχεσθαι preceding an interview, as in iv. 3, is much more frequent with Matt. than Mark and Luke; once only in John. Compare the same use of πορεύεσθαι, as in ii. 8, also more frequent in Matt.

11. Σφόδρα after a verb, or participle, six times; the same word used once each by Mark and Luke, but after adjectives.

12. With St. Matthew the particle of transition is usually the indefinite τότε; he uses it ninety times, against six times in Mark and fourteen in Luke.

13. Καὶ ἐγένετο ὅτε, vii. 28, xi. 1, xiii. 53, xix. 1, xxvi. 1; to be compared with the ὅτε ἐγένετο of Luke.

14. Ποιεῖν ὡς, ὥσπερ, etc., is characteristic of Matthew: i. 24, vi. 2, xx. 5, xxi. 6, xxvi. 19, xxviii. 15.

15. Τάφος six times in this Gospel, not in the others. They use μνημεῖον frequently, which is also found seven times in Matt.

16. Συμβούλιον λαμβάνειν, peculiar to Matt. Συμ. ποιεῖν twice in Mark; nowhere else.

17. Μαλακία, μαθητεύειν, σεληνιάζεσθαι, peculiar to Matt. The following words are either used by this Evangelist alone, or by him more frequently than by the others: φρόνιμος οἰκιακός, ὕστερον, ἐκεῖθεν, διστάζειν, καταποντίζεσθαι, μεταίρειν, ῥαπίζειν, φράζειν, συναίρειν λόγον.

18. The frequent use of ἰδού after a genitive absolute (as i. 20), and of καὶ ἰδού when introducing anything new, is also peculiar to St. Matt.

19. Adverbs usually stand after the imperative, not before it; except οὕτως, which stands first. Ch. x. 11 is an exception.

20. Προσκυνεῖν takes the dative in St. Matt., and elsewhere more rarely. With Luke and John it takes the accusative. There is one apparent exception in Matt. (iv. 10), but it is a quotation from O. T.

21. The participle λέγων is used frequently without the dative of the person, as in i. 20, ii. 2. Ch. vii. 21 is an exception.

22. The expression ὀμνύω ἐν or εἰς is a Hebraism, frequent in Matt., and unknown to the other Evangelists.

23. Ἱεροσόλυμα is the name of the holy city with Matt. always, except xxiii. 37. It is the same in Mark, with one (doubtful) exception (xi. 1). Luke uses this form rarely; Ἱερουσαλήμ frequently.

III. *Citations from O. T.* — The following list is nearly complete: —

Matt.		Matt.	
i. 23.	Is. vii. 14.	xvii. 2.	Ex. xxxiv. 29.
ii. 6.	Mic. v. 2.	11.	Mal. iii. 1, iv. 5.
15.	Hos. xi. 1.	xviii. 15.	Lev. xix. 17 (?)
18.	Jer. xxxi. 15.	xix. 4.	Gen. i. 27.
iii. 3.	Is. xl. 3.	5.	Gen. ii. 24.
iv. 4.	Deut. viii. 3.	7.	Deut. xxiv. 1.
6.	Ps. xci. 11, 12.	18.	Ex. xx. 12.
7.	Deut. vi. 16.	19.	Lev. xix. 18.
10.	Deut. vi. 13.	xxi. 5.	Zech. ix. 9.
15.	Is. ix. 1, 2.	9	Ps. cxviii. 25.

Matt.		Matt.	
v. 5.	Ps. xxxvii. 11.	13.	Is. lvi. 7, Jer vii. 11.
21.	Ex. xx. 13.		
27.	Ex. xx. 14.	16.	Ps. viii. 2.
31.	Deut. xxiv. 1.	42.	Ps. cxviii 22.
33.	Lev. xix. 12, Deut. xxiii. 23.	44.	Is. viii. 14.
		xxii. 24.	Deut. xxv. 5.
38.	Ex. xxi. 24.	32.	Ex. iii. 6.
43.	Lev. xix. 18.	37.	Deut. vi. 5.
viii. 4.	Lev. xiv. 2.	39.	Lev. xix. 18.
17.	Is. liii. 4.	44.	Ps. cx. 1.
ix. 13.	Hos vi. 6.	xxiii. 35.	Gen. iv. 8, Chr. xxiv. 21.
x. 35.	Mic. vii. 6.		
xi. 5.	Is. xxxv. 5, xxix. 18.		
		38.	Ps. lxix. 25 (?). Jer. xii. 7, xxii 5 (?).
10.	Mal iii. 1.		
14.	Mal. iv. 5		
xii. 3.	1 Sam. xxi. 6.	39.	Ps. cxviii. 26.
5.	Num. xxviii. 9 (?)	xxiv. 15.	Dan. ix. 27.
7.	Hos. vi. 6.	29.	Is. xiii. 10.
18.	Is. xlii. 1.	37.	Gen. vi. 11.
40.	Jon. i. 17.	xxvi. 31.	Zech. xiii. 7.
42.	1 K. x. 1.	52.	Gen. ix. 6 (?).
xiii. 14.	Is. vi. 9.	64.	Dan. vii. 13.
35.	Ps. lxxviii. 2.	xxvii. 9.	Zech. xi. 13.
xv. 4.	Ex. xx. 12, xxi. 17.	35.	Ps. xxii. 18.
		43.	Ps. xxii. 8.
xv. 8.	Is. xxix. 13.	46.	Ps. xxii. 1.

The number of passages in this Gospel which refer to the O. T. is about 65. In St. Luke they are 43. But in St. Matthew there are 43 *verbal citations* of O. T.; the number of these direct appeals to its authority in St. Luke is only about 19. This fact is very significant of the character and original purpose of the two narratives.

IV. *Genuineness of the Gospel.* — Some critics, admitting the apostolic antiquity of a part of the Gospel, apply to St. Matthew as they do to St. Luke (see vol. ii. p. 1695) the gratuitous supposition of a later editor or compiler, who by augmenting and altering the earlier document produced our present Gospel. Hilgenfeld (p. 106) endeavors to separate the older from the newer work, and includes much historical matter in the former: since Schleiermacher, several critics, misinterpreting the λόγια of Papias, consider the older document to have been a collection of "discourses" only. We are asked to believe that in the second century for two or more of the Gospels, new works, differing from them both in matter and compass, were substituted for the old, and that about the end of the second century our present Gospels were adopted by authority to the exclusion of all others, and that henceforth the copies of the older works entirely disappeared, and have escaped the keenest research ever since. Eichhorn's notion is that "the Church" sanctioned the four canonical books, and by its authority gave them exclusive currency; but there existed at that time no means for convening a Council; and if such a body could have met and decided, it would not have been able to force on the Churches books discrepant from the older copies to which they had long been accustomed, without discussion, protest, and resistance (see Norton, *Genuineness*, Chap. I.). That there was no such resistance or protest we have ample evidence. Irenæus knows the four Gospels only (*Hær.* iii. ch. i.). Tatian, who died A. D. 170, composed a harmony of the Gospels, lost to us, under the name of Diatessaron (Eus. *H. E.* iv. 29). Theophilus, bishop of Antioch, about 168, wrote a commentary on the Gospels (Hieron. *ad Algasiam* and *de Virill.*). Clement of Alexandria (flourished about 189) knew the four Gospels, and distinguished between them and the uncanonical Gospel according to the Egyptians. Tertullian (born about 160) knew the four Gospels, and was called on to vindicate the text of one of them against the corruptions of Marcion (see above, LUKE). Origen (born 185) calls the four Gospels the four elements of the Christian faith; and it appears that his copy of Matthew contained the genealogy (*Comm. in Joan.*). Passages from St. Matthew are quoted by Justin Martyr, by the author of the letter to Diognetus (see in Otto's *Justin Martyr*, vol. ii.), by Hegesippus, Irenæus, Tatian, Athenagoras, Theophilus, Clement, Tertullian, and Origen. It is not merely from the matter but the manner of the quotations, from the calm appeal as to a settled authority, from the absence of all hints of doubt, that we regard it as proved that the book we possess had not been the subject of any sudden change. Was there no heretic to throw back with double force against Tertullian the charge of alteration which he brings against Marcion? Was there no orthodox church or member of a church to complain, that instead of the Matthew and the Luke that had been taught to them and their fathers, other and different writings were now imposed on them? Neither the one nor the other appears.

The citations of Justin Martyr, very important for this subject, have been thought to indicate a source different from the Gospels which we now possess: and by the word ἀπομνημονεύματα (memoirs), he has been supposed to indicate that lost work. Space is not given here to show that the remains referred to are the Gospels which we possess, and not any one book; and that though Justin quotes the Gospels very loosely, so that his words often bear but a slight resemblance to the original, the same is true of his quotations from the Septuagint. He transposes words, brings separate passages together, attributes the words of one prophet to another, and even quotes the Pentateuch for facts not recorded in it. Many of the quotations from the Septuagint are indeed precise, but these are chiefly in the Dialogue with Trypho, where, reasoning with a Jew on the O. T., he does not trust his memory, but consults the text. This question is disposed of in Norton's *Genuineness*, vol. i., and in Hug's *Einleitung*. [See also Westcott's *Canon of the N. T.*, 2d ed., p. 85 ff.]

The genuineness of the two first chapters of the Gospel has been questioned; but is established on satisfactory grounds (see Fritzsche, on *Matt.*, Excursus iii.; Meyer, on *Matt.* p. 65). (i.) All the old MSS. and versions contain them; and they are quoted by the Fathers of the 2d and 3d centuries (Irenæus, Clement Alex., and others). Celsus also knew ch. ii. (see Origen cont. Cels. i. 38). (ii.) Their contents would naturally form part of a Gospel intended primarily for the Jews. (iii.) The commencement of ch. iii. is dependent on ii. 23; and in iv. 13 there is a reference to ii. 23. (iv.) In constructions and expressions they are similar to the rest of the Gospel (see examples above, in II. *Style and diction*). Professor Norton disputes the genuineness of these chapters upon the ground of the difficulty of harmonizing them with St. Luke's narrative, and upon the ground that a large number of the Jewish Christians did not possess them in their version of the Gospel. The former objection is discussed in all the commentaries; the answer would require much space. But, (1.) Such questions are by no means confined to these chapters, but are found in places of which the Apostolic origin is

admitted. (2.) The treatment of St. Luke's Gospel by Marcion (vol. ii. pp. 1694, 1695) suggests how the Jewish Christians dropped out of their version an account which they would not accept. (3.) Prof. N. stands alone, among those who object to the two chapters, in assigning the genealogy to the same author as the rest of the chapters (Hilgenfeld, pp. 46, 47). (4.) The difficulties in the harmony are all reconcilable, and the day has passed, it may be hoped, when a passage can be struck out, against all the MSS. and the testimony of early writers, for subjective impressions about its contents.

On the whole, it may be said that we have for the genuineness and Apostolic origin of our Greek Gospel of Matthew, the best testimony that can be given for any book whatever.

V. *Time when the Gospel was written.* — Nothing can be said on this point with certainty. Some of the ancients think that it was written in the eighth year after the Ascension (Theophylact and Euthymius); others in the fifteenth (Nicephorus, *H. E.* ii. 45); whilst Irenæus says (iii. 1) that it was written "when Peter and Paul were preaching in Rome," and Eusebius (*H. E.* iii. 24), at the time when Matthew was about to leave Palestine. From two passages, xxvii. 7, 8, xxviii. 15, some time must have elapsed between the events and the description of them, and so the eighth year seems out of the question; but a term of fifteen or twenty years would satisfy these passages. The testimony of old writers that Matthew's Gospel is the earliest must be taken into account (Origen in Eus. *H. E.* vi. 25; Irenæus, iii. 1; comp. Muratorian fragment, as far as it remains, in Credner's *Kanon*); this would bring it before A. D. 58–60 (vol. ii. p. 1696), the supposed date of St. Luke. The most probable supposition is that it was written between 50 and 60; the exact year cannot even be guessed at.

VI. *Place where it was written.* — There is not much doubt that the Gospel was written in Palestine. Hug has shown elaborately, from the diffusion of the Greek element over and about Palestine, that there is no inconsistency between the assertions that it was written for Jews in Palestine, and that it was written in Greek (*Einleitung*, ii. ch. i. § 10); the facts he has collected are worth study. [LANGUAGE OF THE N. T., Amer. ed.]

VII. *Purpose of the Gospel.* — The Gospel itself tells us by plain internal evidence that it was written for Jewish converts, to show them in Jesus of Nazareth the Messiah of the O. T. whom they expected. Jewish converts over all the world seem to have been intended, and not merely Jews in Palestine (Irenæus, Origen, and Jerome say simply that it was written "for the Hebrews"). Jesus is the Messiah of the O. T., recognizable by Jews from his acts as such (i. 22, ii. 5, 15, 17, iv. 14, viii. 17, xii. 17–21, xiii. 35, xxi. 4, xxvii. 9). Knowledge of Jewish customs and of the country is presupposed in the readers (Matt. xv. 1, 2 with Mark vii. 1–4; Matt. xxvii. 62 with Mark xv. 42; Luke xxiii. 54; John xix. 14, 31, 42, and other places). Jerusalem is the holy city (see above, *Style and Diction*). Jesus is the son of David, of the seed of Abraham (i. 1, ix. 27, xii. 23, xv. 22, xx. 30, xxi. 9, 15); is to be born of a virgin in David's place, Bethlehem (i. 22, ii. 6); must flee into Egypt and be recalled thence (ii. 15, 19); must have a forerunner, John the Baptist (iii. 3, xi. 10); was to labor in the outcast Galilee that sat in darkness (iv. 14–16); his healing was a promised mark of his office (viii. 17, xii. 17); and so was his mode of teaching in parables (xiii. 14); He entered the holy city as Messiah (xxi. 5–16); was rejected by the people, in fulfillment of a prophecy (xxi. 42); and deserted by his disciples in the same way (xxvi. 31, 56). The Gospel is pervaded by one principle, the fulfillment of the Law and of the Messianic prophecies in the person of Jesus. This at once sets it in opposition to the Judaism of the time; for it rebuked the Pharisaic interpretations of the Law (v., xxiii.), and proclaimed Jesus as the Son of God and the Saviour of the world through his blood, ideas which were strange to the cramped and limited Judaism of the Christian era.

VIII. *Contents of the Gospel.* — There are traces in this Gospel of an occasional superseding of the chronological order. Its principal divisions are — I. The Introduction to the Ministry, i.–iv. II. The laying down of the new Law for the Church in the Sermon on the Mount, v.–vii. III. Events in historical order, showing Him as the worker of Miracles, viii. and ix. IV. The appointment of Apostles to preach the kingdom, x. V. The doubts and opposition excited by his activity in divers minds — in John's disciples, in sundry cities, in the Pharisees, xi. and xii. VI. A series of parables on the nature of the Kingdom, xiii. VII. Similar to V. The effects of his ministry on his countrymen, on Herod, the people of Gennesaret, Scribes and Pharisees, and on multitudes, whom He feeds, xiii. 53 – xvi. 12. VIII. Revelation to his disciples of his sufferings. His instructions to them thereupon, xvi. 13 – xviii. 35. IX. Events of a journey to Jerusalem, xix., xx. X. Entrance into Jerusalem and resistance to Him there, and denunciation of the Pharisees, xxi.–xxiii. XI. Last discourses; Jesus as Lord and Judge of Jerusalem, and also of the world, xxiv., xxv. XII. Passion and Resurrection, xxvi.-xxviii.

Sources. — The works quoted under LUKE, pp. 1698, 1699; and Norton, *Genuineness of the Gospels*; Fritzsche, *on Matthew*; Lange. *Bibelwerk*; Credner, *Einleitung* and *Beiträge.*   W. T.

---

* *Additional Literature.* — Many of the more important recent works relating to the Gospel of Matthew have been already enumerated in the addition to the article GOSPELS, vol. ii. p. 959 ff. For the sake of brevity we may also pass over the older treatises on the critical questions respecting this gospel; they are referred to with sufficient fullness in such works as the Introductions to the N. T. by Credner, De Wette, Bleek, Reuss, and Guericke, in Meyer's Introduction to his Commentary on the Gospel, and in the bibliographical works of Winer, Danz, and Darling. The following may however be noted, as either comparatively recent, or easily accessible to the English reader : M. Stuart, *Inquiry into the Orig. Language of Matthew's Gospel, and the Genuineness of the first two Chapters of the same*, in the *Amer. Bibl. Repos.* for July and Oct. 1838, xii. 133–179, 315–356, in opposition to Mr. Norton's view (see his *Genuineness of the Gospels*, 2d ed. 1846, vol. i. Addit. Notes, pp. xlv. – lxiv.). G. C. A. Harless, *Fabula de Matthæo Syro-Chaldaice conscripto*, Erlang. 1841, and *De Compositionis Evang. quod Matthæo tribuitur*, ibid. 1842, the latter trans. by H. B. Smith in the *Bibl. Sacra* for Feb. 1844, i. 86–99. S. P. Tregelles, *The Original Language of St. Matthew's Gospel*, in Kitto's *Journ. of Sacred Lit.* for Jan. 1850, v. 151–186, maintaining the Hebrew original; comp. Dr. W. L. Alexander on

the other side, *ibid.* April, 1850, pp. 499–510. Dr. Tregelles's essay was also published separately. C. E. Luthardt, *De Compositione Ev. Matthæi*, Lips. 1861. R. Anger, *Ratio, qua loci V. T. in Ev. Matth. laudantur, quid valeat ad illustr. hujus Ev. Originem, quæritur*, 3 pt. Lips. 1861–62. A. Réville, *Études crit. sur l'Évangile selon St. Matthieu*, Leyde et Paris, 1862. Alex. Roberts, *On the Original Language of Matthew's Gospel*, in his *Discussions on the Gospels*, 2d ed. 1864, pp. 319–448, strongly contending for the Greek. T. Wizenmann, *Die Gesch. Jesu nach Matthäus als Selbstbeweis ihrer Zuverlässigkeit betrachtet, herausg. von Auberlen*, Basel, 1864 (1st ed. 1789). Hilgenfeld, *Ueber Particularismus u. Universalismus in dem Leben Jesu nach Matthäus, zur Vertheidigung gegen Hrn. Dr. Keim*, in his *Zeitschr. f. wiss. Theol.* 1865, viii. 43–61, and *Das Matthäus-Evangelium auf's Neue untersucht*, ibid. 1866 and 1867, x. 303–323, 366–447, xi. 22–76. J. H. Scholten, *Het oudste evangelie. Critisch onderzoek naar de zamenstelling . . . de hist. waarde en den oorsprong der evangeliën naar Mattheus en Marcus*, Leiden, 1868. Davidson, *Introd. to the Study of the N.T.*, Lond. 1868, i. 465–520; comp. his earlier *Introduction*, Lond. 1848, i. 1–197, where the subject is treated with 'greater fullness, from a more conservative " standpoint."

Among the *exegetical works* on the Gospel, we can only glance at the older literature, as the commentaries of Origen, Chrysostom (*Homilies*, best ed. by Field, 3 vols. Cantab. 1839, and Eng. trans. 3 vols. Oxford, 1843–51, in the Oxford Libr. of the Fathers), the author of the *Opus Imperfectum* published with Chrysostom's works (vol. vi. of the Benedictine edition), Theophylact, and Euthymius Zigabenus, among the Greek fathers, and of Hilary of Poictiers, Jerome, Augustine (*Quæstiones*), Bede, Thomas Aquinas (*Comm.* and *Catena aurea*), and others, among the Latin; Cramer's *Catena Græc. Patrum in Evv. Matthæi et Marci*, Oxon. 1840, and the Greek Scholia published by Card. Mai in his *Class. Auct. e Vaticanis Codd. edit.*, vol. vi. pp. 379–494. These patristic commentaries are generally of little critical value, but are of some interest in their bearing on the history of interpretation and of Christian theology. We must content ourselves with referring to the bibliographical works of Walch, Winer, Danz, and Darling for the older commentaries by Christian divines since the Reformation; those of Calvin and Grotius are the most important. See also the addition to the art. GOSPELS, vol. ii. pp. 960, 961, for the more recent expositions of the Gospels collectively. A few special works on the Gospel of Matthew may be mentioned here by way of supplement, namely: Sir John Cheke, *Translation from the Greek of the Gospel of St. Matthew*, etc. *with Notes*, etc. *edited by J. Goodwin*, Lond. (Pickering), 1843. Daniel Scott (author of the *Appendix ad Stephani Thesaurum Græcum*), *New Version of St. Matthew's Gospel, with Select Notes*, Lond. 1741, 4to, of some value for its illustrations of the language from Greek authors. Jac. Elsner, *Comm. crit.-philol. in Evang. Matthæi*, 2 vols. Zwollae, 1767–69, 4to. Gilb. Wakefield, *New Translation of the Gospel of Matthew, with Notes*, Lond. 1782, 4to. A. Gratz (Cath.), *Hist.-krit. Comm. üb. d. Ev. Matth.*, 2 Theile, Tübing. 1821–23. The elaborate commentary of Fritzsche, publ in 1826, followed by his equally or more thorough works on the Gospel of Mark and the Epistle to the Romans, marks an epoch in the history of the interpretation of the New Testament. In connection with Winer, over whom he exerted a great influence, as may be seen by a comparison of the third edition of his N. T. Grammar with the two preceding, he may be regarded as the pioneer of the strict grammatical method of interpretation, in opposition to the loose philology prevalent at the time, as illustrated by Schleusner's Lexicon and the commentary of Kuinoel. This grammatical rigor is sometimes, indeed, carried to an excess, sufficient allowance not being made for the looseness of popular phraseology, and especially for the difference between the classical and the later Greek; but Fritzsche's commentaries will always claim the attention of the critical student. We may further note: James Ford, *The Gospel of St. Matthew illustrated from Ancient and Modern Authors,* Lond. 1848. H. Goodwin, *Commentary on the Gospel of St. Matthew,* Cambr. (Eng.), 1857. T. J. Conant, *The Gospel by Matthew, with a Revised Version and Critical and Philological Notes, prepared for the Amer. Bible Union,* N. Y. 1860, 4to. J. H. Morison, *Disquisitions and Notes on the Gospels — Matthew,* 2d ed. Boston, 1861, one of the best of the more popular commentaries, both in plan and execution. J. A. Alexander, *The Gospel of Matthew explained,* N. Y. 1861, posthumous, and embracing only chaps. i.–xvi. with an analysis of the remainder. Lutteroth, *Essai d'interprétation de quelques parties de l'Ev. selon Saint Matthieu,* 3 pt. (ch. i.–xiii.) Paris, 1860–67. The recent commentaries of Nast (1864) and Lange, translated by Dr. Schaff (N. Y. 1865), are referred to under the art. GOSPELS. The latter has reached a third edition (4th impression) in Germany (1868). Among the later Roman Catholic commentaries, those of Bucher (2 vol. 1855–56), Arnoldi (1856), and Schegg (3 vol. 1856–58), may be mentioned On the Sermon on the Mount we have the masterly commentary of Tholuck, *Die Bergpredigt ausgelegt,* 4° Aufl. Gotha, 1856, translated by R. L. Brown, Phila. 1860; a translation of an earlier edition was published in Edinburgh in 1834–37 as a part of the *Biblical Cabinet.*   A.

MATTHI'AS (Ματθίας; [Tisch. Treg. Ματθίας:] *Matthias*), the Apostle elected to fill the place of the traitor Judas (Acts i. 26). All beyond this that we know for certainty is that he had been a constant attendant upon the Lord Jesus during the whole course of his ministry; for such was declared by St. Peter to be the necessary qualification of one who was to be a witness of the resurrection. The name of Matthias occurs in no other place in the N. T. We may accept as probable the opinion which is shared by Eusebius (*H. E.* lib. i. 12) and Epiphanius (i. 20) that he was one of the seventy disciples. It is said that he preached the Gospel and suffered martyrdom in Ethiopia (Nicephor. ii. 60). Cave believes that it was rather in Cappadocia. An apocryphal gospel was published under his name (Euseb. *H. E.* iii. 23), and Clement of Alexandria quotes from the Traditions of Matthias (*Strom.* ii. 163, &c.).

Different opinions have prevailed as to the manner of the election of Matthias. The most natural construction of the words of Scripture seems to be this:

After the address of St. Peter, the whole assembled body of the brethren, amounting in number to about 120 (Acts i. 15), proceeded to nominate two, namely, Joseph surnamed Barsabas, and Matthias, who answered the requirements of the Apostle: the subsequent selection between the two was referred in prayer to Him who, knowing the hearts of men, knew which of them was the fitter to be his witness and apostle. The brethren then, under the heavenly guidance which they had invoked, proceeded to give forth their lots, probably by each writing the name of one of the candidates on a tablet, and casting it into the urn. The urn was then shaken, and the name that first came out decided the election. Lightfoot (*Hor. Heb. Luc.* i. 9) describes another way of casting lots which was used in assigning to the priests their several parts in the service of the Temple. The Apostles, it will be remembered, had not yet received the gift of the Holy Ghost, and this solemn mode of casting the lots, in accordance with a practice enjoined in the Levitical law (Lev. xvi. 8), is to be regarded as a way of referring the decision to God (comp. Prov. xvi. 33). St. Chrysostom remarks that it was never repeated after the descent of the Holy Spirit. The election of Matthias is discussed by Bishop Beveridge, *Works,* vol. i. serm. 2.   E. H—s.

MATTHI'AS (Ματταθίας: *Mathathias*)= MATTATHAH, of the descendants of Hashum (1 Esdr. ix. 33; comp. Ezr. x. 33).

MATTITHI'AH (מַתִּתְיָה [*gift of Jehovah*]: Ματθαθίας; [Vat. Sin.] Alex. Ματταθίας: *Mathathias*). 1. A Levite, the first-born of Shallum the Korhite, who presided over the offerings made in the pans (1 Chr. ix. 31; comp. Lev. vi. 20 [12], &c.).

2. (Ματταθίας.) One of the Levites of the second rank under Asaph, appointed by David to minister before the ark in the musical service (1 Chr. xvi. 5), "with harps upon Sheminith" (comp. 1 Chr. xv. 21), to lead the choir. See below. 5.

3. (Ματθανίας; [Vat. FA. Θαμαθια;] Alex Ματθαθιας.) One of the family of Nebo, who had married a foreign wife in the days of Ezra (Ezr. x. 43). He is called MAZITIAS in 1 Esdr. ix. 35.

4. (Ματθαθίας; [Vat. FA.²] Alex. Ματταθιας.) Probably a priest, who stood at the right hand of Ezra when he read the Law to the people (Neh. viii. 4). In 1 Esdr. ix. 43, he appears as MATTATHIAS.

5. (מַתִּתְיָהוּ): 1 Chr. xv. 18, Ματθαθια, [Vat. Ιματταθια, FA. Alex. Ματταθια; 21, Ματταθιας, [Vat. FA.] Μετταθιας;] xxv. 3, 21, Ματθαθιας, [Vat. FA. Ματταθιας;] Alex. Ματταθιας, 1 Chr. xxv. 3; Ματθιας; 1 Chr. xxv. 21). The same as 2, the Hebrew being in the lengthened form. He was a Levite of the second rank, and a doorkeeper of the ark (1 Chr. xv. 18, 21.) As one of the six sons of Jeduthun, he was appointed to preside over the 14th division of twelve Levites into which the Temple choir was distributed (1 Chr. xxv. 3, 21).

MATTOCK.ᵃ The tool used in Arabia for loosening the ground, described by Niebuhr, answers generally to our mattock or grubbing-axe, *i. e.* a single-headed pickaxe, the *sarculus simplex,* as op-

━━━━━━━━━━━━━━━━━━

ᵃ 1. מַעְדֵּר; *sarculum,* Is. vii. 25. 2. מַחֲרֵשָׁה, *ploughshare, sarculum,* and מַחֲרֶשֶׁת, θεριστήριον, re-

mer, both from חָרַשׁ, "carve," "engrave," 1 Sam. xiii. 20. Which of these is the ploughshare and which the mattock cannot be ascertained. See Ges. p. 539.

posed to *bicornis*, of Palladius. The ancient Egyptian hoe was of wood, and answered for hoe, spade, and pick. The blade was inserted in the handle, and the two were attached about the centre by a twisted rope. (Palladius, *de Re rust.* i. 43; Niebuhr, *Descr. de l'Ar.* p. 137; Loudon, *Encycl. of Gardening*, p. 517; Wilkinson, *Anc. Eg.* ii. 16, 18, abridgm.; comp. Her. ii. 14; Hasselquist, *Trav.* p. 100.) [HANDICRAFT.]　　　　　　　H. W. P.

Egyptian hoes. (From Wilkinson.)

MAUL (*i. e.* a hammer; a variation of mall, from *malleus*), a word employed by our translators to render the Hebrew term מֵפִיץ. The Hebrew and English alike occur in Prov. xxv. 18 only. But a derivative from the same root, and differing but slightly in form, namely מַפֵּץ, is found in Jer. li. 20, and is there translated by "battle-axe" — how incorrectly is shown by the constant repetition of the verb derived from the same root in the next three verses, and there uniformly rendered "break in pieces." The root נָפַץ or פּוּץ, has the force of dispersing or smashing, and there is no doubt that some heavy warlike instrument, a mace or club, is alluded to. Probably such as that which is said to have suggested the name of Charles Martel.

The mace is frequently mentioned in the accounts of the wars of the Europeans with Saracens, Turks, and other Orientals, and several kinds are still in use among the Bedouin Arabs of remoter parts (Burckhardt, *Notes on Bedouins*, i. 55). In their European wars the Turks were notorious for the use they made of the mace (Knollys's *Hist. of the Turks*).

A similar word is found once again in the original of Ez. ix. 2. כְּלִי מַפָּץ = weapon of smashing (A. V. "slaughter-weapon"). The sequel shows how terrible was the destruction such weapons could effect.　　　　　　　　　　　　　　　　　G.

MAUZ'ZIM (מָעֻזִּים [see below]: [Theodot.] Μαωζείμ; Alex. Μαωζει: *Maozim*). The marginal note to the A. V. of Dan. xi. 38, "the God of *forces*," gives, as the equivalent of the last word, "Mauzzim, or gods protectors, or munitions." The Geneva version renders the Hebrew as a proper name both in Dan. xi. 38 and 39, where the word

occurs again (marg. of A. V. "munitions"). In the Greek version of Theodotion, given above, it is treated as a proper name, as well as in the Vulgate. The LXX. as at present printed is evidently corrupt in this passage, but ἰσχυρά (ver. 37) appears to represent the word in question. In Jerome's time the reading was different, and he gives "Deum fortissimum" for the Latin translation of it, and "Deum fortitudinum" for that of Aquila. He ridicules the interpretation of Porphyry, who, ignorant of Hebrew, understood by "the god of *Mauzzim*" the statue of Jupiter set up in *Modin*, the city of Mattathias and his sons, by the generals of Antiochus, who compelled the Jews to sacrifice to it, "the god of Modin." Theodoret retains the reading of Theodotion (Μαωζείμ being evidently for Μαωζείμ), and explains it of Antichrist, "a god strong and powerful." The Peshito-Syriac has ܐܠܗܐ ܕܥܘܫܢܐ, "the strong god," and Junius and Tremellius render it "Deum summi roboris," considering the Hebrew plural as intensive, and interpreting it of the God of Israel. There can be little doubt that "Mauzzim" is to be taken in its literal sense of "fortresses," just as in Dan. xi. 19, 39, "the god of fortresses" being then the deity who presided over strongholds. But beyond this it is scarcely possible to connect an appellation so general with any special object of idolatrous worship. Grotius conjectured that Mauzzim was a modification of the name Ἄζιζος, the war-god of the Phœnicians, mentioned in Julian's hymn to the sun. Calvin suggested that it denoted "money," the strongest of all powers. By others it has been supposed to be Mars, the tutelary deity of Antiochus Epiphanes, who is the subject of allusion. The only authority for this supposition exists in two coins struck at Laodicea, which are believed to have on the obverse the head of Antiochus with a radiated crown, and on the reverse the figure of Mars with a spear. But it is asserted on the contrary that all known coins of Antiochus Epiphanes bear his name, and that it is mere conjecture which attributes these to him; and further, that there is no ancient authority to show that a temple to Mars was built by Antiochus at Laodicea. The opinion of Gesenius is more probable, that "the god of fortresses" was Jupiter Capitolinus, for whom Antiochus built a temple at Antioch (Liv. xli. 20). By others it is referred to Jupiter Olympius, to whom Antiochus dedicated the Temple at Jerusalem (2 Macc. vi. 2). But all these are simply conjectures. Fürst (*Handw.* s. v.), comparing Is. xxiii. 4, where the reference is to Tyre, "the fortress of the sea," makes מָעֻזִּים equivalent to מָעוֹז יָם, or even proposes to read for the former מָעוֹז יָם; the god of the "stronghold of the sea" would thus be Melkart, the Tyrian Hercules. A suggestion made by Mr. Layard (*Nin.* ii. 456, *note*) is worthy of being recorded, as being at least as well founded as any already mentioned. After describing Hera, the Assyrian Venus, as "standing erect on a lion, and crowned with a tower or mural coronet, which, we learn from Lucian, was peculiar to the Semitic figure of the goddess," he adds in a note, "May she be connected with the 'El Maozem,' the deity presiding over bulwarks and fortresses, the 'god of forces' of Dan. xi. 38?" Pfeiffer (*Dub. Vex.* cent. 4, loc. 79) will only see in it "the idol of the *Mass* !'"

　　　　　　　　　　　　　　　　　W. A. W.

MAZITI'AS (Μαζιτίας; [Vat. Ζειτιας:] *Mathathias*) = MATTITHIAH 3 (1 Esdr. ix. 35; comp. Ezr. x. 43).

MAZZAROTH (מַזָּרוֹת: Μαζουρώθ: *Lucifer*). The margin of the A. V. of Job xxxviii. 32 gives "the twelve signs" as the equivalent of "Mazzaroth," and this is in all probability its true meaning. The Peshito-Syriac renders it by ܥܓܠܬܐ, 'ogalto, "the wain" or "Great Bear;" and J. D. Michaelis (*Suppl. ad Lex. Heb.* No. 1391) is followed by Ewald in applying it to the stars of "the northern crown" (Ewald adds "the southern"), deriving the word from בֵּזֶר, *nézer*, "a crown." Fürst (*Handw.* s. v.) understands by Mazzaroth the planet Jupiter, the same as the "star" of Amos v. 26.[a] But the interpretation given in the margin of our version is supported by the authority of Gesenius (*Thes.* p. 869). On referring to 2 K. xxiii. 5, we find the word מַזָּלוֹת, *mazzálôth* (A. V. "the planets"), differing only from Mazzaroth in having the liquid *l* for *r*, and rendered in the margin "the twelve signs," as in the Vulgate. The LXX. there also have μαζουρώθ, which points to the same reading in both passages, and is by Suidas explained as "the Zodiac," but by Procopius of Gaza as probably "Lucifer, the morning star," following the Vulgate of Job xxxviii. 32. In later Jewish writings *mazzálôth* are the signs of the Zodiac, and the singular, *mazzál*, is used to denote the single signs, as well as the planets, and also the influence which they were believed to exercise upon human destiny (Selden, *De Dis Syr.* Synt. i. c. 1). In consequence of this, Jarchi, and the Hebrew commentators generally, identify *mazzároth* and *mazzáloth*, though their interpretations vary. Aben Ezra understands "stars" generally; but R. Levi ben Gershon, "a northern constellation." Gesenius himself is in favor of regarding *mazzáróth* as the older form, signifying strictly "premonitions," and in the concrete sense, " stars that give warnings or presages," from the usage of the root בֵּזֶר, *nézar*, in Arabic. He deciphered, as he believed, the same word on some Cilician coins in the inscription מָזָרָךְ דָּךְ עַל, which he renders as a prayer, "may thy pure star (shine) over (us)" (*Mon. Phœn.* p. 279, tab. 36).   W. A. W.

  * Both Mazzaroth and Arcturus disappear from Job xxxviii. 32 in a more accurate translation. Dr. Conant (*Book of Job*, p. 143) renders the passage thus: "Dost thou lead forth the Signs in their season; and the Bear with her young, dost thou guide them?" He remarks on the words "that the circuit of the year is meant: first, as marked by the succession of the celestial signs; and, second, by the varying position of the great northern constellation, in its annual circuit of the Pole." He defends the view of Gesenius against that of Ewald.   H.

MEADOW. This word, so peculiarly English, is used in the A. V. to translate two words which are entirely distinct and independent of each other.

1. Gen. xli. 2 and 18. Here the word in the original is הָאָחוּ (with the definite article), *ha-Achú*. It appears to be an Egyptian term, literally transferred into the Hebrew text, as it is also into that of the Alexandrian translators, who give it as τῷ "Αχει.[b] The same form is retained by the Coptic version. Its use in Job viii. 11 (A. V. "flag")—where it occurs as a parallel to *gômé* (A. V. "rush"), a word used in Ex. ii. 3 for the "bulrushes" of which Moses' ark was composed —seems to show that it is not a "meadow," but some kind of reed or water-plant. This the LXX. support, both by rendering in the latter passage βούτομον, and also by introducing "Αχι as the equivalent of the word rendered "paper-reeds" in Is. xix. 7. St. Jerome, in his commentary on the passage, also confirms this meaning. He states that he was informed by learned Egyptians that the word *achi* denoted in their tongue any green thing that grew in a marsh— *omne quod in palude virens nascitur*. But as during high inundations of the Nile — such inundations as are the cause of fruitful years — the whole of the land on either side is a marsh, and as the cultivation extends up to the very lip of the river, is it not possible that *Achu* may denote the herbage of the growing crops? The fact that the cows of Pharaoh's vision were feeding there would seem to be as strong a figure as could be presented to an Egyptian of the extreme fruitfulness of the season: so luxuriant was the growth on either side of the stream, that the very cows fed amongst it unmolested. The lean kine, on the other hand, merely stand on the dry brink. [NILE.] No one appears yet to have attempted to discover on the spot what the signification of the term is. [FLAG, vol. i. p. 830 *a* and *b*, Amer. ed.]

2. Judg. xx. 33 only: "the meadows of Gibeah." Here the word is מַעֲרֵה, *Maareh*, which occurs nowhere else with the same vowels attached to it. The sense is thus doubly uncertain. "Meadows" around Gibeah can certainly never have existed: the nearest approach to that sense would be to take *maareh* as meaning an open plain. This is the dictum of Gesenius (*Thes.* p. 1069), on the authority of the Targum. It is also adopted by De Wette (*die Pläne von G.*). But if an open plain, where could the ambush have concealed itself?

The LXX., according to the Alex. MS.,[c] read a different Hebrew word — מַעֲרָב — "from the west of Gibeah." Tremellius, taking the root of the word in a figurative sense, reads "after Gibeah had been left open," i. e. by the quitting of its inhabitants — *post denudationem Gibha*. This is adopted by Bertheau (*Kurzgef. Handb.* ad loc.). But the most plausible interpretation is that of the Peshito-

---

  * A note to the Hexaplar Syriac version of Job (ed. Middeldorpf, 1835) has the following: "Some say it is the dog of the giant (Orion, i. e. Canis major), others that it is the Zodiac."

  b This is the reading of Codex A. Codex B, if we may accept the edition of Mai, has ὄλος; so also the rendering of Aquila and Symmachus, and of Josephus (*Ant.* ii. 5, § 5). Another version, quoted in the

fragments of the Hexapla, attempts to reconcile sound and sense by ὄχθη. The Veneto-Greek has λειμών.

  c Codex B, or the Vat. MS., wants Gen. i.-xlvi. 28 inclusive; this portion is supplied in Mai's edition from a later MS.   A.

  c The Vatican Codex transfers the word literally — Μαρααγαβά.

Syriac, which by a slight difference in the vowel-points makes the word מְעָרָה, "the cave;" a suggestion quite in keeping with the locality, which is very suitable for caves, and also with the requirements of the ambush. The only thing that can be said against this is that the liers-in-wait were "set round about" Gibeah, as if not in one spot, but several. [GIBEAH, vol. i. p. 914, note b.]

G.

ME'AH, THE TOWER OF (מִגְדָּל

הַמֵּאָה [see below]: πύργος τῶν ἑκατόν: turris centum cubitorum, turrim Emeth), one of the towers of the wall of Jerusalem when rebuilt by Nehemiah (iii. 1, xii. 39). It stood between the tower of Hananeel and the Sheep Gate, and appears to have been situated somewhere at the northeast part of the city, outside of the walls of Zion (see the diagram, vol. ii. p. 1322). The name in Hebrew means "the tower of the hundred," but whether a hundred cubits of distance from some other point, or a hundred in height (Syriac of xii. 39), or a hundred heroes commemorated by it, we are not told or enabled to infer. In the Arabic version it is rendered Bab-el-bostân, the Gate of the Garden, which suggests its identity with the "Gate Gennath 'a of Josephus. But the Gate Gennath appears to have lain further round towards the west, nearer the spot where the ruin known as the Kasr Jalûd now stands. G.

MEALS. Our information on this subject is but scanty: the early Hebrews do not seem to have given special names to their several meals, for the terms rendered "dine" and "dinner" in the A. V. (Gen. xliii. 16; Prov. xv. 17) are in reality general expressions, which might more correctly be rendered "eat" and "portion of food." In the N. T. we have the Greek terms ἄριστον and δεῖπνον, which the A. V. renders respectively "dinner" and "supper" b (Luke xiv. 12; John xxi. 12), but which are more properly "breakfast" and "dinner." There is some uncertainty as to the hours at which the meals were taken: the Egyptians undoubtedly took their principal meal at noon (Gen. xliii. 16): laborers took a light meal at that time (Ruth ii. 14; comp. verse 17); and occasionally that early hour was devoted to excess and reveling (1 K. xx. 16). It has been inferred from those passages (somewhat too hastily, we think) that the principal meal generally took place at noon: the Egyptians do indeed still make a substantial meal at that time (Lane's Mod. Egypt. i. 189), but there are indications that the Jews rather followed the custom that prevails among the Bedouins, and made their principal meal after sunset, and a lighter meal at about 9 or 10 A. M. (Burckhardt's Notes, i. 64). For instance, Lot prepared a feast for the two angels "at even" (Gen. xix. 1-3): Boaz evidently took his meal late in the evening (Ruth iii. 7): the Israelites ate flesh in the evening, and bread only, or manna, in the morning (Ex. xvi. 12): the context seems to imply that Jethro's feast was in the evening (Ex. xviii. 12, 14). But, above all, the institution of

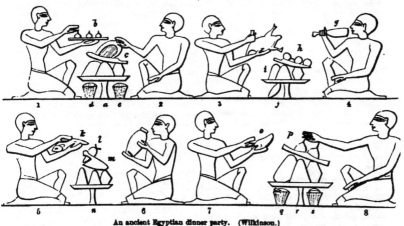

An ancient Egyptian dinner party. (Wilkinson.)

a, j, a, r. Tables with various dishes. b, p. Figs. d, e, q, and s. Baskets of grapes. Fig. 3 is taking a wing from a goose. Fig. 4 holds a joint of meat. Figs. 5 and 7 are eating fish. Fig. 6 is about to drink water from an earthen vessel.

the Paschal feast in the evening seems to imply that the principal meal was usually taken then; it appears highly improbable that the Jews would have been ordered to eat meat at an unusual time. In the later Biblical period we have clearer notices to the same effect: breakfast took place in the morning (John xxi. 4, 12), on ordinary days not before 9 o'clock, which was the first hour of prayer (Acts ii. 15), and on the Sabbath not before 12, when the service of the synagogue was completed (Joseph. Vit. § 54): the more prolonged and substantial meal took place in the evening (Joseph.

the Homeric age for the early or the late meal, the special meaning being the principal meal. In later times, however, the term was applied exclusively to the late meal — the δόρπον of the Homeric age.

Fit. § 44; *B. J.* i. 17, § 4). The general tenor of the parable of the great supper certainly implies that the feast took place in the working hours of the day (Luke xiv. 15–24): but we may regard this perhaps as part of the imagery of the parable, rather than as a picture of real life.

The posture at meals varied at various periods: there is sufficient evidence that the old Hebrews were in the habit of *sitting* (Gen. xxvii. 19; Judg. xix. 6; 1 Sam. xx. 5, 24; 1 K. xiii. 20); but it does not hence follow that they sat on chairs; they may have squatted on the ground, as was the occasional, though not perhaps the general, custom of the ancient Egyptians (Wilkinson, *Anc. Eg.* i. 58, 181). The table was in this case but slightly elevated above the ground, as is still the case in

Reclining at Table. (Montfaucon.)

Egypt. At the same time the chair *a* was not unknown to the Hebrews, but seems to have been regarded as a token of dignity. As luxury increased, the practice of sitting was exchanged for that of reclining: the first intimation of this occurs in the prophecies of Amos, who reprobates those " that lie upon beds of ivory, and stretch themselves upon their couches " (vi. 4), and it appears that the couches themselves were of a costly character — the " corners " *b* or *edges* (iii. 12) being finished with ivory, and the seat covered with silk or damask coverlets.*c* Ezekiel, again, inveighs against one who sat " on a stately bed with a table prepared before it " (xxiii. 41). The custom may have been borrowed in the first instance from the Babylonians and Syrians, among whom it prevailed at an early period (Esth. i. 6, vii. 8). A similar change took place in the habits of the Greeks, who are represented in the Heroic age as *sitting d* (*Il.* x. 578; *Od.* i. 145), but who afterwards adopted the habit of reclining, women and children excepted. In the time of our Saviour reclining was the universal custom, as is implied in the terms *e* used for *sitting* at meat," as the A. V. incorrectly has it. The couch itself (κλίνη) is only once mentioned (Mark vii. 4; A. V. " tables "), but there can be little doubt that the Roman *triclinium* had been introduced, and that the arrangements of the table resembled those described by classical writers. Generally speaking, only three persons reclined on each couch, but occasionally four or even five. The couches were provided with cushions on which the left elbow rested in support of the upper part of the body, while the right arm remained free: a room provided with these was described as ἐστρωμένον, lit. " spread " (Mark xiv. 15; A. V. " furnished "). As several guests reclined on the same couch, each overlapped his neighbor, as it were, and rested his head on or near the breast of the one who lay behind him: he was then said to " lean on the bosom [strictly recline on the bosom] " of his neighbor (ἀνακεῖσθαι ἐν τῷ κόλπῳ, John xiii. 23, xxi. 20, comp. Plin. *Epist.* iv. 22). The close proximity into which persons were thus brought rendered it more than usually agreeable that friend should be next to friend, and it gave the opportunity of making confidential communications (John xiii. 25). The ordinary arrangement of the couches was in three sides of a square, the fourth being left open for the servants to bring up the dishes. The couches were denominated respectively the highest, the middle, and the lowest couch: the three guests on each couch were also denominated highest, middle, and lowest — the terms being suggested by the circumstance of the guest who reclined on another's bosom always appearing to be *below* him. The *protoklisia* (πρωτοκλισία, Matt. xxiii. 6), which the Pharisees so much coveted, was not, as the A. V. represents it, " the uppermost *rooms* ['rooms,' A. V.]," but the highest seat in the highest couch — the seat numbered 1 in the annexed diagram.*f*

a The Hebrew term is *kisse!* (אָסֵּכ). There is only one instance of its being mentioned as an article of ordinary furniture, namely, in 2 K. iv. 10, where the A. V. incorrectly renders it " stool." Even there it seems probable that it was placed more as a mark of special honor to the prophet than for common use.

b The word is *peah* (הָאֵפ), which will apply to the edge as well as to the angle of a couch. That the seats and couches of the Assyrians were handsomely ornamented, appears from the specimens given by Layard (*Nineveh*, ii. 300–3).

c The A. V. has " in Damascus in a couch ; " but there can be no doubt that the name of the town was transferred to the silk stuffs manufactured there, which are still known by the name of " Damask."

d Sitting appears to have been the posture usual among the Assyrians on the occasion of great festivals. A bas-relief on the walls of Khorsabad represents the guests seated on high chairs (Layard, *Nineveh*, ii. 411).

e Ἀνακεῖσθαι, κατακεῖσθαι, ἀνακλίνεσθαι, κατακλίνεσθαι.

f * The difference between our own and the ancient

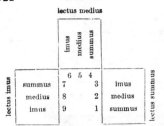

lectus medius

		imus	medius	summus		
		6	5	4		
lectus imus	summus	7		3	imus	lectus summus
	medius	8		2	medius	
	imus	9		1	summus	

Some doubt attends the question whether the females took their meals along with the males. The present state of society in the East throws no light upon this subject, as the customs of the Harem date from the time of Mohammed. The cases of Ruth amid the reapers (Ruth ii. 14), of Elkanah with his wives (1 Sam. i. 4), of Job's sons and daughters (Job i. 4), and the general intermixture of the sexes in daily life, make it more than probable that they did so join; at the same time, as the duty of attending upon the guests devolved upon them (Luke x. 40), they probably took a somewhat irregular and briefer repast.

Before commencing the meal, the guests washed their hands. This custom was founded on natural

Washing before or after a meal. (From Lane's *Modern Egyptians*.)

decorum; not only was the hand the substitute for our knife and fork, but the hands of all the guests were dipped into one and the same dish; uncleanliness in such a case would be intolerable. Hence not only the Jews, but the Greeks (*Od.* i. 136), the modern Egyptians (Lane, i. 190), and many other nations, have been distinguished by this practice; the Bedouins in particular are careful to wash their hands *before*, but are indifferent about doing so

custom at meals obscures the sense of several passages as rendered in the A. V. Thus the translation — "many shall come from the east and west and shall sit down with Abraham and Isaac and Jacob, in the kingdom of heaven" (Matt. viii. 11), instead of "shall recline," puts out of sight the figure of a banquet in Paradise of which the guests there partake. Still more perplexed from a similar inaccuracy is the meaning in Luke vii. 36; for if the Saviour "sat at meat" (A. V.) it is inconceivable how the woman who "washed and anointed his feet, and wiped them with the hairs of her head" could have "stood behind him" as she performed this office. Whether the expression in John i. 18 (ὁ ὢν εἰς τὸν κόλπον τοῦ πατρός) refers to the intimacy of the relation of the Father and

after their meals (Burckhardt's *Notes*, i. 63). The Pharisees transformed this conventional usage into a ritual observance, and overlaid it with burdensome regulations — a willful perversion which our Lord reprobates in the strongest terms (Mark vii. 1–13). Another preliminary step was the grace or blessing, of which we have but one instance in the O. T. (1 Sam. ix. 13), and more than one pronounced by our Lord himself in the N. T. (Matt. xv. 36; Luke ix. 16; John vi. 11); it consisted, as far as we may judge from the words applied to it, partly of a blessing upon the food, partly of thanks to the Giver of it. The Rabbinical writers have, as usual, laid down most minute regulations respecting it, which may be found in the treatise of the Mishna, entitled *Berachoth*, chaps. 6–8.

The mode of taking the food differed in no material point from the modern usages of the East; generally there was a single dish into which each guest dipped his hand (Matt. xxvi. 23); occasionally separate portions were served out to each (Gen. xliii. 34; Ruth ii. 14; 1 Sam. i. 4). A piece of bread was held between the thumb and two fingers of the right hand, and was dipped either into a bowl of melted grease (in which case it was termed ψωμίον, "a sop," John xiii. 26), or into the dish of meat, whence a piece was conveyed to the mouth between the layers of bread (Lane, i. 193, 194; Burckhardt's *Notes*, i. 63). It is esteemed an act of politeness to hand over to a friend a delicate morsel (John xiii. 26; Lane, i. 194). In allusion to the above method of eating, Solomon makes it a characteristic of the sluggard, that "he hideth his hand in his bosom and will not so much as bring it to his mouth again" (Prov. xix. 24, xxvi. 15). At the conclusion of the meal, grace was again said in conformity with Deut. viii. 10, and the hands were again washed.

Thus far we have described the ordinary meal: on state occasions more ceremony was used, and the meal was enlivened in various ways. Such occasions were numerous, in connection partly with public, partly with private events: in the first class we may place — the great festivals of the Jews (Deut. xvi.; Tob. ii. 1); public sacrifices (Deut. xii. 7, xxvii. 7; 1 Sam. ix. 13, 22; 1 K. i. 9, iii. 15; Zeph. i. 7); the ratification of treaties (Gen. xxvi. 30, xxxi. 54); the offering of the tithes (Deut. xiv. 26), particularly at the end of each third year (Deut. xiv. 28); in the second class — marriages (Gen. xxix. 22; Judg. xiv. 10; Esth. ii. 18; Tob. viii. 19; Matt. xxii. 2; John ii. 1), birth-days (Gen. xl. 20; Job i. 4; Matt. xiv. 6, 9), burials (2 Sam. iii. 35; Jer. xvi. 7; Hos. ix. 4; Tob. iv. 17), sheep-shearing (1 Sam. xxv. 2, 36; 2 Sam. xiii. 23), the vintage (Judg. ix. 27), laying the foundation stone of a house (Prov. ix. 1–5), the

the Son to each other, as symbolised in the relative position of guests at the table, may be uncertain. The archæology explains the occurrence between Peter and John at the Last Supper (John xiii. 23–26). John occupied the place of honor next to Jesus (ἐν τῷ κόλπῳ αὐτοῦ). Peter, reclining perhaps on the opposite side of the table, made signs to John to inquire who was to be the traitor; and John then throwing back his head (ἐπιπεσών) upon the breast of Jesus (στῆθος here and not κόλπος as before) could ask the question at once without being heard by the others. It is not correct to charge the A. V. with a mistranslation in Matt. xxiii. 6 (see the article above); for in the older English "rooms" often had the sense of "spaces" or "places."   H.

reception of visitors (Gen. xviii. 6 -8, xix. 3; 2 Sam.
iii. 20, xii. 4; 2 K. vi. 23; Tob. vii. 9; 1 Macc.
xvi. 15; 2 Macc. ii. 27; Luke v. 29, xv. 23; John
xii. 2), or any event connected with the sovereign
(Hos. vii. 5).[a] On each of these occasions a sumptuous repast was prepared; the guests were previously invited (Esth. v. 8; Matt. xxii. 3), and on
the day of the feast a second invitation was issued
to those that were bidden (Esth. vi. 14; Prov. ix.
3; Matt. xxii. 3). The visitors were received with
a kiss (Tob. vii. 6; Luke vii. 45); water was produced for them to wash their feet with (Luke vii.

A party at dinner or supper. (From Lane's *Modern
Egyptians.*)

44); the head, the beard, the feet, and sometimes
the clothes, were perfumed with ointment (Ps. xxiii.
5; Am. vi. 6; Luke vii. 38; John xii. 3); on
special occasions robes were provided (Matt. xxii.
11; comp. Trench *on Parables*, p. 230); and the
head was decorated with wreaths [b] (Is. xxviii. 1;
Wisd. ii. 7, 8; Joseph. *Ant.* xix. 9, § 1). The
regulation of the feast was under the superintendence of a special officer, named ἀρχιτρίκλινος [e]
(John ii. 8; A. V. "governor of the feast"), whose
business it was to taste the food and the liquors
before they were placed on the table, and to settle
about the toasts and amusements; he was generally
one of the guests (Ecclus. xxxii. 1, 2), and might
therefore take part in the conversation. The places
of the guests were settled according to their respective rank (Gen. xliii. 33; 1 Sam. ix. 22; Luke
xiv. 8; Mark xii. 39; John xiii. 23); portions of
food were placed before each (1 Sam. i. 4; 2 Sam.
vi. 19; 1 Chr. xvi. 3), the most honored guests
receiving either larger (Gen. xliii. 34; comp. Herod.
vi. 57) or more choice (1 Sam. ix. 24; comp. *Il.*

vii. 321) portions than the rest. The importance
of the feast was marked by the number of the guests
(Gen. xxix. 22; 1 Sam. ix. 22; 1 K. i. 9, 25;
Luke v. 29, xiv. 16), by the splendor of the vessels
(Esth. i. 7), and by the profusion or the excellence
of the viands (Gen. xviii. 6, xxvii. 9; Judg. vi. 19;
1 Sam. ix. 24; Is. xxv. 6; Am. vi. 4). The meal
was enlivened with music, singing, and dancing
(2 Sam. xix. 35; Ps. lxix. 12; Is. v. 12; Am. vi.
5; Ecclus. xxxii. 3-6; Matt. xlv. 6; Luke xv. 25),
or with riddles (Judg. xiv. 12); and amid these
entertainments the festival was prolonged for several
days (Esth. i. 3, 4). Entertainments designed
almost exclusively for drinking were known by the
special name of *mishteh*; [d] instances of such drink-
ing-bouts are noticed in 1 Sam. xxv. 36; 2 Sam.
xiii. 28; Esth. i. 7; Dan. v. 1; they are reprobated
by the prophets (Is. v. 11; Am. vi. 6). Somewhat
akin to the *mishteh* of the Hebrews was the *kômos* [e]
(κῶμος) of the apostolic age, in which gross licentiousness was added to drinking, and which is frequently made the subject of warning in the Epistles
(Rom. xiii. 13; Gal. v. 21; Eph. v. 18; 1 Pet
iv. 3).　　　　　　　　　　　　　　　　　W. L. B

* MEAN (Prov. xxii. 29; Is. ii. 9, v. 15,
xxxi. 8; Acts xxi. 39; Rom. xii. 16 m.) is repeatedly applied to persons in the sense of "ordinary,"
"obscure." As originally used it did not contain the
idea of baseness which now belongs to the word·
a "mean" man was one low in birth or rank.
　　　　　　　　　　　　　　　　　　　　　　　　H.

MEA'NI (Μανί; [Vat. Μανει; Ald. Μεανί;]
Alex. Μαανι: *Munei*). The same as MEHUNIM
(1 Esdr. v. 31; comp. Ezr. ii. 50). In the margin
of the A. V. it is given in the form "Meunim,"
as in Neh. vii. 52.

MEA'RAH (מְעָרָה [*a cave*]: LXX. omit,
both MSS.: *Maara*), a place named in Josh. xiii.
4 only, in specifying the boundaries of the land
which remained to be conquered after the subjugation of the southern portion of Palestine. Its description is "Mearah which is to the Zidonians "
(*i. e.* which belongs to — לְ: the "beside " of the
A. V. is an erroneous translation). The word
meârâh means in Hebrew a cave, and it is commonly assumed that the reference is to some remarkable cavern in the neighborhood of Zidon;
such as that which played a memorable part many
centuries afterwards in the history of the Crusades.
(See William of Tyre, xix. 11, quoted by Robinson, ii. 474 *note*.) But there is, as we have often
remarked, danger in interpreting these very ancient
names by the significations which they bore in later
Hebrew, and when pointed with the vowels of the
still later Masorets. Besides, if a cave were intended, and not a place called Mearah, the name
would surely have been preceded by the definite

---

a "The day of the king " in this passage has been
variously understood as his birthday or his coronation:
it may, however, be equally applied to any other event
of similar importance.

b This custom prevailed extensively among the
Greeks and Romans: not only were chaplets worn on
the head, but festoons of flowers were hung over the
neck and breast (Plut. *Symp.* iii. 1, § 3; Mart. x. 19;
Δν *Fast.* ii. 739). They were generally introduced
after the first part of the entertainment was completed.
They are noticed in several familiar passages of the

Latin poets (Hor. *Carm.* ii. 7, 24, *Sat.* ii. 3, 256;
Juv. v. 36).

c The classical designation of this officer among the
Greeks was συμποσίαρχος, among the Romans *magister*
or *rex convivii*. He was chosen by lot out of the
guests (*Dict. of Ant.* p. 925).

d מִשְׁתֶּה

e The κῶμος resembled the *comissatio* of the Romans.
It took place after the supper, and was a mere drinking reval, with only so much food as served to whet
the palate for wine (*Dict. of Ant.* p. 271).

article, and would have stood as הַמְּעָרָה, "the cave."

Reland (*Pal.* p. 896) suggests that Mearah may be the same with Meroth, a village named by Josephus (*Ant.* iii. 3, § 1) as forming the limit of Galilee on the west (see also *Ant.* ii. 20, § 6), and which again may possibly have been connected with the WATERS OF MEROM. The identification is not improbable, though there is no means of ascertaining the fact.

A village called *el Mughar* is found in the mountains of Naphtali, some ten miles W. of the northern extremity of the sea of Galilee, which may possibly represent an ancient Mearah (Rob. iii. 79, 80; Van de Velde's *map*).   G.

MEASURES. [WEIGHTS AND MEASURES.]

MEAT. It does not appear that the word "meat" is used in any one instance in the Authorized Version of either the Old or New Testament, in the sense which it now almost exclusively bears of animal food. The latter is denoted uniformly by "flesh."

1. The only possible exceptions to this assertion in the O. T. are: —

(*a.*) Gen. xxvii. 4, &c., "savory meat."

(*b.*) *Ib.* xlv. 23, "corn and bread and meat."

But (*a*) in the former of these two cases the Hebrew word, מַטְעַמִּים, which in this form appears in this chapter only, is derived from a root which has exactly the force of our word "taste," and is employed in reference to the manna. In the passage in question the word "dainties" would be perhaps more appropriate. (*b*) In the second case the original word is one of almost equal rarity, מָזוֹן; and if the Lexicons did not show that this had only the general force of food in all the other oriental tongues, that would be established in regard to Hebrew by its other occurrences, namely, 2 Chr. xi. 23, where it is rendered "victual:" and Dan. iv. 12, 21, where the "meat" spoken of is that to be furnished by a tree.

2. The only real and inconvenient ambiguity caused by the change which has taken place in the meaning of the word is in the case of the "meat-offering," the second of the three great divisions into which the sacrifices of the Law were divided — the burnt-offering, the meat-offering, and the peace-offering (Lev. ii. 1, &c.) — and which consisted solely of flour, or corn, and oil, sacrifices of flesh being confined to the other two. The word thus translated is מִנְחָה, elsewhere rendered "present" and "oblation," and derived from a root which has the force of "sending" or "offering" to a person. It is very desirable that some English term should be proposed which would avoid this ambiguity. "Food-offering" is hardly admissible, though it is perhaps preferable to "unbloody or bloodless sacrifice."

3. There are several other words, which, though entirely distinct in the original, are all translated in the A. V. by "meat;" but none of them present any special interest except מֶרַח. This word,

from a root signifying "to tear," would be perhaps more accurately rendered "prey" or "booty." Its use in Ps. cxi. 5, especially when taken in connection with the word rendered "good understanding" in ver. 10, which should rather be, as in the margin, "good success," throws a new and unexpected light over the familiar phrases of that beautiful psalm. It seems to show how inextinguishable was the warlike predatory spirit in the mind of the writer, good Israelite and devout worshipper of Jehovah as he was. Late as he lived in the history of his nation, he cannot forget the "power" of Jehovah's "works" by which his forefathers acquired the "heritage of the heathen:" and to him, as to his ancestors when conquering the country, it is still a firm article of belief that those who fear Jehovah shall obtain most of the spoil of his enemies — those who obey his commandments shall have the best success in the field.

4. In the N. T. the variety of the Greek words thus rendered is equally great; but dismissing such terms as ἀνακεῖσθαι or ἀνακλίνειν, which are rendered by "sit at meat — φαγεῖν, for which we occasionally find "meat" — τράπεζα (Acts xvi. 34), the same — εἰδωλοθύτα, "meat offered to idols" — κλάσματα, generally "fragments," but twice "broken meat" — dismissing these, we have left τροφή and βρῶμα (with its kindred words, βρῶσις, etc.), both words bearing the widest possible signification, and meaning everything that can be eaten, or can nourish the frame. The former is most used in the Gospels and Acts. The latter is found in St. John and in the epistles of St. Paul. It is the word employed in the famous sentences, "for meat destroy not the work of God," "if meat make my brother to offend," etc.   G.

MEAT-OFFERING (מִנְחָה: δῶρον θυσία, or θυσία: *oblatio sacrificii*, or *sacrificium*). The word *Minchah*[a] signifies originally a gift of any kind; and appears to be used generally of a gift from an inferior to a superior, whether God or man. Thus in Gen. xxxii. 13 it is used of the present from Jacob to Esau, in Gen. xliii. 11 of the present sent to Joseph in Egypt, in 2 Sam. viii. 2, 6 of the tribute from Moab and Syria to David, etc., etc.; and in Gen. iv. 3, 4, 5 it is applied to the sacrifices to God, offered by Cain and Abel, although Abel's was a whole burnt-offering. Afterwards this general sense became attached to the word "Corban (קָרְבָּן);" and the word *Minchah* restricted to an "unbloody offering" as opposed to זֶבַח, a "bloody" sacrifice. It is constantly spoken of in connection with the DRINK-OFFERING (נֶסֶךְ: σπονδή: *libamen*), which generally accompanied it, and which had the same meaning. The law or ceremonial of the meat-offering is described in Lev. ii. and vi. 14–23.[b] It was to be composed of fine flour, seasoned with salt, and mixed with oil and frankincense, but without leaven, and it was generally accompanied by a drink-offering of wine. A portion of it, including all the frankincense, was to be burnt on the altar as "a memorial;" the rest belonged to the priest;

---

[a] מִנְחָה, from the obsolete root מָנַח, "to distribute" or "to give."

[b] * "Food-offering" would be more correct at

present, since the rendering of מִנְחָה by "meat-offering" (A. V.) suggests as a part of the sacrifice precisely the part which the sacrifice excluded. [MEAT.]   H.

but the meat-offerings offered by the priests themselves were to be wholly burnt.

Its meaning (which is analogous to that of the offering of the tithes, the first-fruits, and the shew-bread) appears to be exactly expressed in the words of David (1 Chr. xxix. 10–14), "All that is in the heaven and in the earth is Thine . . . . . All things come of Thee, and of Thine own have we given Thee." It recognized the sovereignty of the Lord, and his bounty in giving them all earthly blessings, by dedicating to Him the best of his gifts: the flour, as the main support of life; oil, as the symbol of richness; and wine as the symbol of vigor and refreshment (see Ps. civ. 15). All these were unleavened, and seasoned with salt, in order to show their purity, and hallowed by the frankincense for God's special service. This recognition, implied in all cases, is expressed clearly in the form of offering the first-fruits prescribed in Deut. xxvi. 5–11.

It will be seen that this meaning involves neither of the main ideas of sacrifice — the atonement for sin and the self-dedication to God. It takes them for granted, and is based on them. Accordingly, the meat-offering, properly so called, seems always to have been a subsidiary offering, needing to be introduced by the sin-offering, which represented the one idea, and forming an appendage to the burnt-offering, which represented the other.

Thus, in the case of public sacrifices, a "meat-offering" was enjoined as a part of —

(1.) The daily morning and evening sacrifice (Ex. xxix. 40, 41).

(2.) The Sabbath-offering (Num. xxviii. 9, 10).

(3.) The offering at the new moon (Num. xxviii. 11–14).

(4.) The offerings at the great festivals (Num. xxviii. 20, 26, xxix. 3, 4, 14, 15, &c.).

(5.) The offerings on the great day of atonement (Num. xxix. 9, 10).

The same was the case with private sacrifices, as at —

(1.) The consecration of priests (Ex. xxix. 1, 2; Lev. vi. 20, viii. 2), and of Levites (Num. viii. 8).

(2.) The cleansing of the leper (Lev. xiv. 20).

(3.) The termination of the Nazaritic vow (Num. vi. 15).

The unbloody offerings offered alone did not properly belong to the regular meat-offering. They were usually substitutes for other offerings. Thus, for example, in Lev. v. 11, a tenth of an ephah of flour is allowed to be substituted by a poor man for the lamb or kid of a trespass-offering: in Num. v. 15 the same offering is ordained as the "offering of jealousy" for a suspected wife. The unusual character of the offering is marked in both cases by the absence of the oil, frankincense, and wine. We find also at certain times libations of water poured out before God; as by Samuel's command at Mizpeh during the fast (1 Sam. vii. 6), and by David at Bethlehem (2 Sam. xxiii. 16), and a libation of oil poured by Jacob on the pillar at Bethel (Gen. xxxv. 14). But these have clearly especial meanings, and are not to be included in the ordinary drink-offerings. The same remark will apply to the remarkable libation of water customary at the Feast of Tabernacles [TABERNACLES], but not mentioned in Scripture.   A. B.

* MEATS, UNCLEAN. [UNCLEAN MEATS.]

MEBUN'NAI [3 syl.] (מְבֻנַּי) [erected,

strong, Fürst]: ἐκ τῶν υἱῶν; [Comp. Μεβουναί; Ald. with 10 MSS. Ζαβουχαί; other MSS. Ζαβουχέ:] Mobonnaí). In this form appears, in one passage only (2 Sam. xxiii. 27), the name of one of David's guard, who is elsewhere called SIBBECHAI (2 Sam. xxi. 18; 1 Chr. xx. 4) or SIBBECAI (1 Chr. xi. 29, xxvii. 11) in the A. V. The reading "Sibbechai" (סִבְּכַי) is evidently the true one, of which "Mebunnai" was an easy and early corruption, for even the LXX. translators must have had the same consonants before them, though they pointed thus, מְבֻנַּי. It is curious, however, that the Aldine edition has Ζαβουχαί (Kennicott, Diss. i. p. 186).   W. A. W.

MECHER'ATHITE, THE (הַמְּכֵרָתִי: [Rom. Μεχωραθρί; Vat.] Μοχορ; [FA. ο φαρμοχορ;] Alex. φερομεχουραθι: Mecherathites), that is, the native or inhabitant of a place called Mecherah. Only one such is mentioned, namely, HEPHER, one of David's thirty-seven warriors (1 Chr. xi. 36). In the parallel list of 2 Sam. xxiii. the name appears, with other variations, as "the Maachathite" (ver. 34). It is the opinion of Kennicott, after a long examination of the passage, that the latter is the correcter of the two; and as no place named Mecherah is known to have existed, while the Maachathites had a certain connection with Israel, and especially with David, we may concur in his conclusion, more especially as his guard contained men of almost every nation round Palestine.   G.

MED'ABA (Μηδαβά: Madaba), the Greek form of the name MEDEBA. It occurs only in 1 Macc. ix. 36.   G.

ME'DAD. [ELDAD and MEDAD.]

ME'DAN (מְדָן, strife, contention, Ges.: Μαδάλ, Μαδάμ; [Alex. * Μαδαιμ, Μαδαν:] Madam), a son of Abraham and Keturah (Gen. xxv. 2; 1 Chr. i. 32), whose name and descendants have not been traced beyond this record. It has been supposed, from the similarity of the name, that the tribe descended from Medan was more closely allied to Midian than by mere blood relation, and that it was the same as, or a portion of, the latter. There is, however, no ground for this theory beyond its plausibility. — The traditional city Medyen of the Arab geographers (the classical Modiana), situate in Arabia on the eastern shore of the Gulf of Eyleh, must be held to have been Midianite, not Medanite (but Bunsen, Bibelwerk, suggests the latter identification). It has been elsewhere remarked [KETURAH] that many of the Keturahite tribes seem to have merged in early times into the Ishmaelite tribes. The mention of "Ishmaelite" as a convertible term with "Midianite," in Gen. xxxvii. 28, 36, is remarkable; but the Midianite of the A. V. in ver. 28 is Medanite in the Hebrew (by the LXX. rendered Μαδιηναῖοι and in the Vulgate Ismaelitæ and Madianitæ); and we may have here a trace of the subject of this article, though Midianite appears on the whole to be more likely the correct reading in the passages referred to. [MIDIAN.]   E. S. P.

MED'EBA (מֵידְבָא: Μαιδαβά and Μηδαβά[a]: Medaba), a town on the eastern side of Jor-

a It may be well to give a collation of the passages in the LXX. in which Medeba occurs in the Hebrew dan. Taken as a Hebrew word, Me-deba means "waters *a* of quiet," but except the tank (see below), what waters can there ever have been on that high plain? The Arabic name, though similar in sound, has a different signification.

Medeba is first alluded to in the fragment of a popular song of the time of the conquest, preserved in Num. xxi. (see ver. 30). Here it seems to denote the limit of the territory of Heshbon. It next occurs in the enumeration of the country divided amongst the Transjordanic tribes (Josh. xiii. 9), as giving its name to a district of level downs called "the Mishor of Medeba," or "the Mishor on Medeba." This district fell within the allotment of Reuben (ver. 16). At the time of the conquest Medeba belonged to the Amorites, apparently one of the towns taken from Moab by them. When we next encounter it, four centuries later, it is again in the hands of the Moabites, or which is nearly the same thing, of the Ammonites. It was before the gate of Medeba that Joab gained his victory over the Ammonites, and the horde of Aramites of Maachah, Mesopotamia, and Zobah, which they had gathered to their assistance after the insult perpetrated by Hanun on the messengers of David (1 Chr. xix. 7, compared with 2 Sam. x. 8, 14, &c.). In the time of Ahaz Medeba was a sanctuary of Moab (Is. xv. 2), but in the denunciation of Jeremiah (xlviii.), often parallel with that of Isaiah, it is not mentioned. In the Maccabæan times it had returned into the hands of the Amorites, who seem most probably intended by the obscure word JAMBRI in 1 Macc. ix. 36. (Here the name is given in the A. V. as Medaba, according to the Greek spelling.) It was the scene of the capture, and possibly the death, of John Maccabæus, and also of the revenge subsequently taken by Jonathan and Simon (Joseph. *Ant.* xiii. 1, § 4; the name is omitted in Macc. on the second occasion, see ver. 38). About 110 years B. C. it was taken after a long siege by John Hyrcanus (*Ant.* xiii. 9, § 1; *B. J.* i. 2, § 4), and then appears to have remained in the possession of the Jews for at least thirty years, till the time of Alexander Jannæus (xiii. 15, § 4); and it is mentioned as one of the twelve cities, by the promise of which Aretas, the king of Arabia, was induced to assist Hyrcanus II. to recover Jerusalem from his brother Aristobulus (*Ant.* xiv. 1, § 4).

Medeba has retained its name down to our own times. To Eusebius and Jerome (*Onomast.* "Medaba") it was evidently known. In Christian times it was a noted bishopric of the patriarchate of "Becerra, or Bitira Arabiæ," and is named in the Acts of the Council of Chalcedon (A. D. 451) and other Ecclesiastical Lists (Reland, pp. 217, 223, 226, 893. See also Le Quien, *Oriens Christ.*). Among modern travellers *Mâdeba* has been visited, recognized, and described by Burckhardt (*Syria*, July 13, 1812), Seetzen (i. 407, 408, iv. 223), and Irby (p. 145); see also Porter (*Handbook*, p. 303). It is in the pastoral district of the *Belka*, which probably answers to the Mishor of the Hebrews, 4 miles S. E. of *Heshbân*, and like it lying on a rounded but rocky hill (Burckh., Seetzen). A large tank,

columns, and extensive foundations are still to be seen; the remains of a Roman road exist near the town, which seems formerly to have connected it with Heshbon.   G.

MEDES (יָדַמ: Μῆδοι: *Medi*), one of the most powerful nations of Western Asia in the times anterior to the establishment of the kingdom of Cyrus, and one of the most important tribes composing that kingdom. Their geographical position is considered under the article MEDIA. The title by which they appear to have known themselves was *Mada*; which by the Semitic races was made into *Madai*, and by the Greeks and Romans into *Medi*, whence our "Medes."

1. *Primitive History.* — It may be gathered from the mention of the Medes, by Moses, among the races descended from Japhet [see MADAI], that they were a nation of very high antiquity; and it is in accordance with this view that we find a notice of them in the primitive Babylonian history of Berosus, who says that the Medes conquered Babylon at a very remote period (circ. B. C. 2458), and that eight Median monarchs reigned there consecutively, over a space of 224 years (Beros. ap. Euseb. *Chron. Can.* i. 4). Whatever difficulties may lie in the way of our accepting this statement as historical — from the silence of other authors, from the affectation of precision in respect of so remote a time, and from the subsequent disappearance of the Medes from these parts, and their reappearance, after 1300 years, in a different locality — it is too definite and precise a statement, and comes from too good an authority, to be safely set aside as unmeaning. There are independent grounds for thinking that an Aryan element existed in the population of the Mesopotamian Valley, side by side with the Cushite and Semitic elements, at a very early date.[b] It is therefore not at all impossible that the Medes may have been the predominant race there for a time, as Berosus states, and may afterwards have been overpowered and driven to the mountains, whence they may have spread themselves eastward, northward, and westward, so as to occupy a vast number of localities from the banks of the Indus to those of the middle Danube. The term Aryans, which was by the universal consent of their neighbors applied to the Medes in the time of Herodotus (*Herod.* vii. 62), connects them with the early Vedic settlers in western Hindustan; the *Mati*-eni of Mount Zagros, the Sauro-*Mata* of the steppe-country between the Caspian and the Euxine, and the *Mata* or *Mæota* of the Sea of Azov, mark their progress towards the north; while the *Mædi* or *Medi* of Thrace seem to indicate their spread westward into Europe, which was directly attested by the native traditions of the Sigynnæ (*Herod.* v. 9).

2. *Connection with Assyria.* — The deepest obscurity hangs, however, over these movements, and indeed over the whole history of the Medes from the time of their bearing sway in Babylonia (B. C. 2458–2234) to their first appearance in the cuneiform inscriptions among the enemies of Assyria, about B. C. 880. They then inhabit a portion of

text, which will show how frequently it is omitted: Num. xxi. 30, ἐπὶ Μωάβ; Josh. xiii. 9, [Rom. Μαιδαβάν, Vat.] Δαιδαβαν, Alex. Μαιδαβα; *ib.* 16. omit, both MSS. [but Comp. Μεδαβά]; 1 Chr. xix. 7, [Vat.] Μαιδαβα, [Rom.] Alex. Μηδαβά; Is. xv. 2, τῆς Μωαβίτιδος.

a To this Burckhardt seems to allude when he observes (*Syr.* p. 366), "this is the ancient Medeba; but there is no river near it."

b See the remarks of Sir H. Rawlinson ir Rawlinson's *Herodotus*, i. 621, note.

the region which bore their name down to the Mohammedan conquest of Persia; but whether they were recent immigrants into it, or had held it from a remote antiquity, is uncertain. On the one hand it is noted that their absence from earlier cuneiform monuments seems to suggest that their arrival was recent at the date above mentioned; on the other, that Ctesias asserts (ap. Diod. Sic. ii. 1, § 9), and Herodotus distinctly implies (i. 95), that they had been settled in this part of Asia at least from the time of the first formation of the Assyrian Empire (B. C. 1273). However this was, it is certain that at first, and for a long series of years, they were very inferior in power to the great empire established upon their flank. They were under no general or centralized government, but consisted of various petty tribes, each ruled by its chief, whose dominion was over a single small town and perhaps a few villages. The Assyrian monarchs ravaged their lands at pleasure, and took tribute from their chiefs; while the Medes could in no way retaliate upon their antagonists. Between them and Assyria lay the lofty chain of Zagros, inhabited by hardy mountaineers, at least as powerful as the Medes themselves, who would not tamely have suffered their passage through their territories. Media, however, was strong enough, and stubborn enough, to maintain her nationality throughout the whole period of the Assyrian sway, and was never absorbed into the empire. An attempt made by Sargon to hold the country in permanent subjection by means of a number of military colonies planted in cities of his building failed [SARGON]; and both his son Sennacherib, and his grandson Esarhaddon, were forced to lead into the territory hostile expeditions, which however seem to have left no more impression than previous invasions. Media was reckoned by the great Assyrian monarchs of this period as a part of their dominions; but its subjection seems to have been at no time much more than nominal, and it frequently threw off the yoke altogether.

3. *Median History of Herodotus.* — Herodotus represents the decadence of Assyria as greatly accelerated by a formal revolt of the Medes, following upon a period of contented subjection, and places this revolt more than 218 years before the battle of Marathon, or a little before B. C. 708. Ctesias placed the commencement of Median independence still earlier, declaring that the Medes had destroyed Nineveh and established themselves on the ruins of the Assyrian Empire, as far back as B. C. 875. No one now defends this latter statement, which alike contradicts the Hebrew records and the native documents. It is doubtful whether even the calculation of Herodotus does not throw back the independence to too early a date: his chronology of the period is clearly artificial; and the history, as he relates it, is fabulous. According to him the Medes, when they first shook off the yoke, established no government. For a time there was neither king nor prince in the land, and each man did what was right in his own eyes. Quarrels were settled by arbitration, and a certain Deïoces, having obtained a reputation in this way, contrived after a while to get himself elected sovereign. He then built the seven-walled Ecbatana [ECBATANA], established a court after the ordinary oriental model, and had a prosperous and peaceful reign of 53 years. Deïoces was succeeded by his son Phraortes, an ambitious prince, who directly after his accession began a career of conquest, first attacking and subduing

the Persians, then reducing nation after nation, and finally perishing in an expedition against Assyria, after he had reigned 22 years. Cyaxares, the son of Phraortes, then mounted the throne. Having first introduced a new military system, he proceeded to carry out his father's designs against Assyria, defeated the Assyrian army in the field, besieged their capital, and was only prevented from capturing it on this first attack by an invasion of Scythians, which recalled him to the defense of his own country. After a desperate struggle during eight-and-twenty years with these new enemies, Cyaxares succeeded in expelling them and recovering his former empire; whereupon he resumed the projects which their invasion had made him temporarily abandon, besieged and took Nineveh, conquered the Assyrians, and extended his dominion to the Halys. Nor did these successes content him. Bent on establishing his sway over the whole of Asia, he passed the Halys, and engaged in a war with Alyattes, king of Lydia, the father of Croesus, with whom he long maintained a stubborn contest. This war was terminated at length by an eclipse of the sun, which, occurring just as the two armies were engaged, furnished an occasion for negotiations, and eventually led to the conclusion of a peace and the formation of an alliance between the two powers. The independence of Lydia and the other kingdoms west of the Halys was recognized by the Medes, who withdrew within their own borders, having arranged a marriage between the eldest son of Cyaxares and a daughter of the Lydian king, which assured them of a friendly neighbor upon this frontier. Cyaxares, soon after this, died, having reigned in all 40 years. He was succeeded by his son Astyages, a pacific monarch, of whom nothing is related beyond the fact of his deposition by his own grandson Cyrus, 35 years after his accession — an event by which the Median Empire was brought to an end, and the Persian established upon its ruins.

4. *Its imperfections.* — Such is, in outline, the Median History of Herodotus. It has been accepted as authentic by most modern writers, not so much from a feeling that it is really trustworthy, as from the want of anything more satisfactory to put in its place. That the story of Deïoces is a romance, has been seen and acknowledged (Grote's *Greece*, iii. 307, 308). That the chronological dates are improbable, and even contradictory, has been a frequent subject of complaint. Recently it has been shown that the whole scheme of dates is artificial (Rawlinson's *Herodotus*, i. 421, 422); and that the very names of the kings, except in a single instance, are unhistorical. Though the cuneiform records do not at present supply the actual history of the time, they enable us in a great measure to test the narrative which has come down to us from the Greeks. We can separate in that narrative the authentic portions from those which are fabulous; we can account for the names used, and in most instances for the numbers given; and we can thus rid ourselves of a great deal that is fictitious, leaving a *residuum* which has a fair right to be regarded as truth.

The records of Sargon, Sennacherib, and Esarhaddon clearly show that the Median kingdom did not commence so early as Herodotus imagined. These three princes, whose reigns cover the space extending from B. C. 790 to B. C. 660, all carried their arms deep into Media, and found it, not under the dominion of a single powerful monarch, but under the rule of a vast number of petty chieftains. It cannot have been till near the middle of the 7th century B. C. that the Median kingdom was consolidated, and became formidable to its neighbors. How this change was accomplished is uncertain: the most probable supposition would seem to be, that about this time a fresh Aryan immigration took place from the countries east of the Caspian, and that the leader of the immigrants established his authority over the scattered tribes of his race, who had been settled previously in the district between the Caspian and Mount Zagros. There is good reason to believe that this leader was the great Cyaxares, whom Diodorus speaks of in one place as the first king (Diod. Sic. ii. 32), and whom Æschylus represents as the founder of the Medo-Persic empire (Pers. 761). The Deïoces and Phraortes of Herodotus are thus removed from the list of historical personages altogether, and must take rank with the early kings in the list of Ctesias,[a] who are now generally admitted to be inventions. In the case of Deïoces the very name is fictitious, being the Aryan dahák, "biter" or "snake," which was a title of honor assumed by all Median monarchs, but not a proper name of any individual. Phraortes, on the other hand, is a true name, but one which has been transferred to this period from a later passage of Median history, to which reference will be made in the sequel. (Rawlinson's Herod. i. 408.)

5. *Development of Median power, and formation of the Empire.* — It is evident that the development of Median power proceeded *pari passu* with the decline of Assyria, of which it was in part an effect, in part a cause. Cyaxares must have been contemporary with the later years of that Assyrian monarch who passed the greater portion of his time in hunting expeditions in Susiana. [ASSYRIA, § 11.] His first conquests were probably undertaken at this time, and were suffered tamely by a prince who was destitute of all military spirit. In order to consolidate a powerful kingdom in the district east of Assyria, it was necessary to bring into subjection a number of Scythic tribes, who disputed with the Aryans the possession of the mountain-country, and required to be incorporated before Media could be ready for great expeditions and distant conquests. The struggle with these tribes may be the real event represented in Herodotus by the Scythic war of Cyaxares, or possibly his narrative may contain a still larger amount of truth. The Scyths of Zagros may have called in the aid of their kindred tribes towards the north, who may have impeded for a while the progress of the Median arms, while at the same time they really prepared the way for their success by weakening the other nations of this region, especially the Assyrians. According to Herodotus, Cyaxares at last got the better of the Scyths by inviting their leaders to a banquet, and there treacherously murdering them. At any rate it is clear that at a tolerably early period of his reign they ceased to be formidable, and he was able to direct his efforts against other enemies. His capture of Nineveh and conquest of Assyria are facts which no skepticism can doubt; and the date of the capture may be fixed with tolerable certainty to the year B. C. 625. Abydenus (probably following Berosus) informs us that in his Assyrian war Cyaxares was assisted by the Babylonians under Nabopolassar, between whom and Cyaxares an intimate alliance was formed, cemented by a union of their children; and that a result of their success was the establishment of Nabopolassar as independent king on the throne of Babylon, an event which we know to belong to the above-mentioned year. It was undoubtedly after this that Cyaxares endeavored to conquer Lydia. His conquest of Assyria had made him master of the whole country lying between Mount Zagros and the river Halys, to which he now hoped to add the tract between the Halys and the Ægean Sea. It is surprising that he failed, more especially as he seems to have been accompanied by the forces of the Babylonians, who were perhaps commanded by Nebuchadnezzar on the occasion. [NEBUCHADNEZZAR.] After a war which lasted six years he desisted from his attempt, and concluded the treaty with the Lydian monarch, of which we have already spoken. The three great Oriental monarchies, Media, Lydia, and Babylon, were now united by mutual engagements and intermarriages, and continued at peace with one another during the remainder of the reign of Cyaxares, and during that of Astyages, his son and successor.

6. *Extent of the Empire.* — The limits of the Median Empire cannot be definitely fixed; but it is not difficult to give a general idea of its size and position. From north to south its extent was in no place great, since it was certainly confined between the Persian Gulf and the Euphrates on the one side, the Black and Caspian Seas on the other. From east to west it had, however, a wide expansion, since it reached from the Halys at least as far as the Caspian Gates, and possibly further. It comprised Persia, Media Magna, Northern Media, Matiene or Media Mattiana, Assyria, Armenia, Cappadocia, the tract between Armenia and the Caucasus, the low tract along the southwest and south of the Caspian, and possibly some portion of Hyrcania, Parthia, and Sagartia. It was separated from Babylonia either by the Tigris, or more probably by a line running about half way between that river and the Euphrates, and thus did not include Syria, Phœnicia, or Judæa, which fell to Babylon on the destruction of the Assyrian Empire. Its greatest length may be reckoned at 1500 miles from N. W. to S. E., and its average breadth at 400 or 450 miles. Its area would thus be about 600,000 square miles, or somewhat greater than that of modern Persia.

7. *Its character.* — With regard to the nature of the government established by the Medes over the conquered nations, we possess but little trustworthy evidence. Herodotus in one place compares, somewhat vaguely, the Median with the Persian system (i. 134), and Ctesias appears to have asserted the positive introduction of the satrapial organization into the empire at its first foundation by his Arbaces (Diod. Sic. ii. 28); but on the whole it is perhaps most probable that the As-

syrian organization was continued by the Medes, the subject-nations retaining their native monarchs, and merely acknowledging subjection by the payment of an annual tribute. This seems certainly to have been the case in Persia, where Cyrus and his father Cambyses were monarchs, holding their crown of the Median king, before the revolt of the former; and there is no reason to suppose that the remainder of the empire was organized in a different manner. The satrapial organization was apparently a Persian invention, begun by Cyrus, continued by Cambyses, his son, but first adopted as the regular governmental system by Darius Hystaspis.

8. *Its duration.* — Of all the ancient Oriental monarchies the Median was the shortest in duration. It commenced, as we have seen, after the middle of the 7th century B. C., and it terminated B. C. 558. The period of three quarters of a century, which Herodotus assigns to the reigns of Cyaxares and Astyages, may be taken as fairly indicating its probable length, though we cannot feel sure that the years are correctly apportioned between the monarchs. Two kings only occupied the throne during the period; for the Cyaxares II. of Xenophon is an invention of that amusing writer.

9. *Its final overthrow.* — The conquest of the Medes by a sister-Iranic race, the Persians, under their native monarch Cyrus, is another of those indisputable facts of remote history, which make the inquirer feel that he sometimes attains to solid ground in these difficult investigations. The details of the struggle, which are given partially by Herodotus (i. 127, 128), at greater length by Nicolaus of Damascus (*Fr. Hist. Gr.* iii. 404–406), probably following Ctesias, have not the same claim to acceptance. We may gather from them, however, that the contest was short, though severe. The Medes did not readily relinquish the position of superiority which they had enjoyed for 75 years; but their vigor had been sapped by the adoption of Assyrian manners, and they were now no match for the hardy mountaineers of Persia. After many partial engagements a great battle was fought between the two armies, and the result was the complete defeat of the Medes, and the capture of their king, Astyages, by Cyrus.

10. *Position of Media under Persia.* — The treatment of the Medes by the victorious Persians was not that of an ordinary conquered nation. According to some writers (as Herodotus and Xenophon) there was a close relationship between Cyrus and the last Median monarch, who was therefore naturally treated with more than common tenderness. The fact of the relationship is, however, denied by Ctesias; and whether it existed or no, at any rate the peculiar position of the Medes under Persia was not really owing to this accident. The two nations were closely akin; they had the same Aryan or Iranic origin, the same early traditions, the same language (Strab. xv. 2, § 8), nearly the same religion, and ultimately the same manners and customs, dress, and general mode of life. It is not surprising therefore that they were drawn together, and that, though never actually coalescing, they still formed to some extent a single privileged people. Medes were advanced to stations of high honor and importance under Cyrus and his successors, an advantage shared by no other conquered people. The Median capital was at first the chief royal residence, and always remained one of the places at which the court spent a portion of the

year; while among the provinces Media claimed and enjoyed a precedence, which appears equally in the Greek writers and in the native records. Still, it would seem that the nation, so lately sovereign, was not altogether content with its secondary position. On the first convenient opportunity Media rebelled, elevating to the throne a certain Phraortes (*Frawartish*), who called himself Xathrites, and claimed to be a descendant from Cyaxares Darius Hystaspis, in whose reign this rebellion took place, had great difficulty in suppressing it. After vainly endeavoring to put it down by his generals, he was compelled to take the field himself. He defeated Phraortes in a pitched battle, pursued, and captured him near Rhages, mutilated him, kept him for a time "chained at his door," and finally crucified him at Ecbatana, executing at the same time his chief followers (see the *Behistun Inscription*, in Rawlinson's *Herodotus*, ii. 601, 602). The Medes hereupon submitted, and quietly bore the yoke for another century, when they made a second attempt to free themselves, which was suppressed by Darius Nothus (Xen. *Hell.* i. 2, § 19). Henceforth they patiently acquiesced in their subordinate position, and followed through its various shifts and changes the fortune of Persia.

11. *Internal Divisions.* — According to Herodotus the Median nation was divided into six tribes (ἔθνη), called the Busæ, the Paretaceni, the Struchates, the Arizanti, the Budii, and the Magi. It is doubtful, however, in what sense these are to be considered as ethnic divisions. The Paretaceni appear to represent a geographical district, while the Magi were certainly a priest caste; of the rest we know little or nothing. The Arizanti, whose name would signify "of noble descent," or "of Aryan descent," must (one would think) have been the leading tribe, corresponding to the Pasargadæ in Persia; but it is remarkable that they have only the *fourth* place in the list of Herodotus. The Budii are fairly identified with the eastern *Phut* — the *Putiya* of the Persian inscriptions — whom Scripture joins with Persia in two places (Ez. xxvii. 10, xxxviii. 5). Of the Busæ and the Struchates nothing is known beyond the statement of Herodotus. We may perhaps assume, from the order of Herodotus's list, that the Busæ, Paretaceni, Struchates, and Arizanti were true Medes, of genuine Aryan descent, while the Budii and Magi were foreigners admitted into the nation.

12. *Religion.* — The original religion of the Medes must undoubtedly have been that simple creed which is placed before us in the earlier portions of the Zendavesta. Its peculiar characteristic was Dualism, the belief in the existence of two opposite principles of good and evil, nearly if not quite on a par with one another. Ormazd and Ahriman were both self-caused and self-existent, both indestructible, both potent to work their will — their warfare had been from all eternity, and would continue to all eternity, though on the whole the struggle was to the disadvantage of the Prince of Darkness. Ormazd was the God of the Aryans, the object of their worship and trust; Ahriman was their enemy, an object of fear and abhorrence, but not of any religious rite. Besides Ormazd, the Aryans worshipped the Sun and Moon, under the names of Mithra and Homa; and they believed in the existence of numerous spirits or genii, some good, some bad, the subjects and ministers respectively of the two powers of Good and Evil. Their cult was simple, consisting

In processions, religious chants and hymns, and a few simple offerings, expressions of devotion and thankfulness. Such was the worship and such the belief which the whole Aryan race brought with them from the remote east when they migrated westward. Their migration brought them into contact with the fire-worshippers of Armenia and Mount Zagros, among whom Magism had been established from a remote antiquity. The result was either a combination of the two religions, or in some cases an actual conversion of the conquerors to the faith and worship of the conquered. So far as can be gathered from the scanty materials in our possession, the latter was the case with the Medes. While in Persia the true Aryan creed maintained itself, at least to the time of Darius Hystaspis, in tolerable purity, in the neighboring kingdom of Media it was early swallowed up in Magism, which was probably established by Cyaxares or his successor as the religion of the state. The essence of Magism was the worship of the elements,

Median Dress. (From Monuments.)

fire, water, air, and earth, with a special preference of fire to the remainder. Temples were not allowed, but fire-altars were maintained on various sacred sites, generally mountain tops, where sacrifices were continually offered, and the flame was never suffered to go out. A hierarchy naturally followed, to perform these constant rites, and the Magi became recognized as a sacred caste entitled to the veneration of the faithful. They claimed in many cases a power of divining the future, and practiced largely those occult arts which are still called by their name in most of the languages of modern Europe. The fear of polluting the elements gave rise to a number of curious superstitions among the professors of the Magian religion (Herod. i. 138); among the rest to the strange practice of neither burying nor burning their dead, but exposing them to be devoured by beasts or birds of prey (Herod. i. 140; Strab. xv. 3, § 20). This custom is still observed by their representatives, the modern Parsees.

13. *Manners, customs, and national character.* — The customs of the Medes are said to have nearly resembled those of their neighbors, the Armenians and the Persians; but they were regarded as the inventors, their neighbors as the copyists (Strab. xi. 13, § 9). They were brave and warlike, excellent riders, and remarkably skillful with the bow. The flowing robe, so well known from the

Persepolitan sculptures, was their native dress, and was certainly among the points for which the Persians were beholden to them. Their whole costume was rich and splendid; they were fond of scarlet, and decorated themselves with a quantity of gold, in the shape of chains, collars, armlets, etc. As troops they were considered little inferior to the native Persians, next to whom they were usually ranged in the battle-field. They fought both on foot and on horseback, and carried, not bows and arrows only, but shields, short spears, and poniards. It is thought that they must have excelled in the manufacture of some kinds of stuffs.

14. *References to the Medes in Scripture.* — The references to the Medes in the canonical Scriptures are not very numerous, but they are striking. We first hear of certain "cities of the Medes," in which the captive Israelites were placed by "the king of Assyria" on the destruction of Samaria, B. C. 721 (2 K. xvii. 6, xviii. 11). This implies the subjection of Media to Assyria at the time of Shalmaneser, or of Sargon, his successor, and accords (as we have shown) very closely with the account given by the latter of certain military colonies which he planted in the Median country. Soon afterwards Isaiah prophesies the part which the Medes shall take in the destruction of Babylon (Is. xiii. 17, xxi. 2); which is again still more distinctly declared by Jeremiah (li. 11 and 28), who sufficiently indicates the independence of Media in his day (xxv. 25). Daniel relates, as a historian, the fact of the Medo-Persic conquest (v. 28, 31), giving an account of the reign of Darius the Mede, who appears to have been made viceroy by Cyrus (vi. 1-28). In Ezra we have a mention of Achmetha (Ecbatana), "the palace in the province of the Medes," where the decree of Cyrus was found (vi. 2-5) — a notice which accords with the known facts that the Median capital was the seat of government under Cyrus, but a royal residence only and not the seat of government under Darius Hystaspis. Finally, in Esther, the high rank of Media under the Persian kings, yet at the same time its subordinate position, are marked by the frequent combination of the two names in phrases of honor, the precedency being in every case assigned to the Persians.[a]

In the Apocryphal Scriptures the Medes occupy a more prominent place. The chief scene of one whole book (Tobit) is Media; and in another (Judith) a very striking portion of the narrative belongs to the same country. But the historical character of both these books is with reason doubted; and from neither can we derive any authentic or satisfactory information concerning the people. From the story of Tobias little could be gathered, even if we accepted it as true; while the history of Arphaxad (which seems to be merely a distorted account of the struggle between the rebel Phraortes and Darius Hystaspis) adds nothing to our knowledge of that contest. The mention of Rhages in both narratives as a Median town and region of importance is geographically correct; and it is historically true that Phraortes suffered his overthrow in the Rhagian district. But beyond these facts the narratives in question contain little

preceded the Persian, its chronicles came first in "the book." The precedency in Daniel (v. 28, and vi. 5, 12, &c.) is owing to the fact of a Median viceroy being established on the throne.

that even illustrates the true history of the Median nation. (See the articles on JUDITH and TOBIAS in Winer's *Realwörterbuch* ; and on the general subject compare Rawlinson's *Herodotus*, i. 401–422; Bosanquet's *Chronology of the Medes*, read before the Royal Asiatic Society, June 5, 1858; Brandis, *Rerum Assyriarum tempora emendata*, pp. 1–14; Grote's *History of Greece*, iii. pp. 301–312; and Hupfeld's *Exercitationum Herodotearum Specimina duo*, p. 56 ff.)   G. R.

MEʹDIA (‏מָדַי‎, *i. e.* Madai: Μηδία: *Media*), a country the general situation of which is abundantly clear, though its limits may not be capable of being precisely determined. Media lay northwest of Persia Proper, south and southwest of the Caspian, east of Armenia and Assyria, west and northwest of the great salt desert of Iram. Its greatest length was from north to south, and in this direction it extended from the 32d to the 40th parallel, a distance of 550 miles. In width it reached from about long. 45° to 53°; but its average breadth was not more than from 250 to 300 miles. Its area may be reckoned at about 150,000 square miles, or three-fourths of that of modern France. The natural boundary of Media on the north was the river *Aras ;* on the west Zagros and the mountain-chain which connects Zagros with Ararat; in the south Media was probably separated from Persia by the desert which now forms the boundary between *Farsistan* and *Irak Ajemi ;* on the east its natural limit was the desert and the Caspian Gates. West of the Gates, it was bounded, not (as is commonly said) by the Caspian Sea, but by the mountain range south of that sea, which separates the high and the low country. It thus comprised the modern provinces of *Irak Ajemi*, Persian *Kurdistan*, part of *Luristan*, *Azerbijan*, perhaps *Talish* and *Ghilan*, but not *Mazanderan* or *Asterabad.*

The division of Media commonly recognized by the Greeks and Romans was that into Media Magna, and Media Atropatene. (Strab. xi. 13, § 1; comp. Polyb. v. 44; Plin. *H. N.* vi. 13; Ptol. vi. 2, &c.) (1.) Media Atropatene, so named from the satrap Atropates, who became independent monarch of the province on the destruction of the Persian empire by Alexander (Strab. *ut. sup.*; Diod. Sic. xviii. 3), corresponded nearly to the modern *Azerbijan*, being the tract situated between the Caspian and the mountains which run north from Zagros, and consisting mainly of the rich and fertile basin of Lake *Urumiyeh*, with the valleys of the *Aras* and the *Sefid Rud*. This is chiefly a high tract, varied between mountains and plains, and lying mostly three or four thousand feet above the sea level. The basin of Lake *Urumiyeh* has a still greater elevation, the surface of the lake itself, into which all the rivers run, being as much as 4,200 feet above the ocean. The country is fairly fertile, well-watered in most places, and favorable to agriculture; its climate is temperate, though occasionally severe in winter; it produces rice, corn of all kinds, wine, silk, white wax, and all manner of delicious fruits. *Tabriz*, its modern capital, forms the summer residence of the Persian kings, and is a beautiful place, situated in a forest of orchards. The ancient Atropatene may have included also the countries of *Ghilan* and *Talish*, together with the plain of *Moghan* at the mouth of the combined *Kur* and *Aras* rivers. These tracts are low and flat; that of *Moghan* is sandy and sterile; *Talish*

is more productive; while *Ghilan* (like *Mazanderan*) is rich and fertile in the highest degree. The climate of *Ghilan*, however, is unhealthy, and at times pestilential; the streams perpetually overflow their banks; and the waters which escape stagnate in marshes, whose exhalations spread disease and death among the inhabitants. (2.) Media Magna lay south and east of Atropatene. Its northern boundary was the range of *Elburz* from the Caspian Gates to the *Rudbar* pass, through which the *Sefid Rud* reaches the low country of *Ghilan*. It then adjoined upon Atropatene, from which it may be regarded as separated by a line running about S. W. by W. from the bridge of *Menjil* to Zagros. Here it touched Assyria, from which it was probably divided by the last line of hills towards the west, before the mountains sink down upon the plain. On the south it was bounded by Susiana and Persia Proper, the former of which it met in the modern *Luristan*, probably about lat. 33° 30', while it struck the latter on the eastern side of the Zagros range, in lat. 32° or 32° 30'. Towards the east it was closed in by the great salt desert, which Herodotus reckons to Sagartia, and later writers to Parthia and Carmania. Media Magna thus contained great part of *Kurdistan* and *Luristan*, with all *Ardelan* and *Irak Ajemi*. The character of this tract is very varied. Towards the west, in *Ardelan*, *Kurdistan*, and *Luristan*, it is highly mountainous, but at the same time well watered and richly wooded, fertile and lovely; on the north, along the flank of *Elburz*, it is less charming, but still pleasant and tolerably productive; while towards the east and southeast it is bare, arid, rocky, and sandy, supporting with difficulty a spare and wretched population. The present productions of Zagros are cotton, tobacco, hemp, Indian corn, rice, wheat, wine, and fruits of every variety; every valley is a garden; and besides valleys, extensive plains are often found, furnishing the most excellent pasturage. Here were nurtured the valuable breed of horses called Nisæan, which the Persians cultivated with such especial care, and from which the horses of the monarch were always chosen. The pasture-grounds of *Khawah* and *Alishtar* between *Behistun* and *Khorram-abad*, probably represent the "Nisæan plain" of the ancients, which seems to have taken its name from a town Nisæa (*Nisaya*), mentioned in the cuneiform inscriptions.

Although the division of Media into these two provinces can only be distinctly proved to have existed from the time of Alexander the Great, yet there is reason to believe that it was more ancient, dating from the settlement of the Medes in the country, which did not take place all at once, but was first in the more northern and afterwards in the southern country. It is indicative of the division, that there were two Ecbatanas — one, the northern, at *Takht-i-Suleiman :* the other, the southern, at *Hamadan*, on the flanks of Mount Orontes (*Elwend*) — respectively the capitals of the two districts. [ECBATANA.]

Next to the two Ecbatanas, the chief town in Media was undoubtedly Rhages — the *Raga* of the inscriptions. Hither the rebel Phraortes fled on his defeat by Darius Hystaspis, and hither too came Darius Codomannus after the battle of Arbela, on his way to the eastern provinces (Arr. *Exp. Alex.* iii. 20). The only other place of much note was Bagistana, the modern *Behistun*, which guarded the chief pass connecting Media with the Mesopotamian plain.

No doubt both parts of Media were further subdivided into provinces; but no trustworthy account of these minor divisions has come down to us. The tract about Rhages was certainly called Rhagiana; and the mountain tract adjoining Persia seems to have been known as Paraetacene, or the country of the Paraetacae. Ptolemy gives as Median districts Elymais, Choromithrene, Sigrina, Daritis, and Syromedia; but these names are little known to other writers, and suspicions attach to some of them. On the whole it would seem that we do not possess materials for a minute account of the ancient geography of the country, which is very imperfectly described by Strabo, and almost omitted by Pliny.

(See Sir H. Rawlinson's Articles in the *Journal of the Geographical Society*, vol. ix. Art. 2, and vol. x. Articles 1 and 2; and compare Layard's *Nineveh and Babylon*, chap. xvii. and xviii.; Chesney's *Euphrates Expedition*, i. 122, &c.; Kinneir's *Persian Empire*; Ker Porter's *Travels*; and Rawlinson's *Herodotus*, vol. i. Appendix, Essay ix.) [On the geography, see also Ritter's *Erdkunde*, viii. and ix., and M. von Niebuhr's *Geschichte Assur's u. Babel's*, pp. 380–314.]　　G. R.

* We are now to add to the above sources Prof. Rawlinson's *Ancient Monarchies*, vol. iii., the first part of which (pp. 1–557) is occupied with the history of the Medes. This volume has appeared since the foregoing article was written. On some of the points of contact between Median history and the Bible, see Rawlinson's *Historical Evidences*, lect. v., and the Notes on the text (Bampton Lectures for 1859), and also Niebuhr's *Gesch. Assur's u. Babel's*, pp. 55 f., 144 f., 224, and elsewhere. Arnold comprises the history and the geography of the subject under the one head of "Medien," in Herzog's *Real-Encyk.* ix. 231–234. See in the *Dictionary* the articles on BABYLON, DANIEL, and DARIUS, THE MEDE.　　H.

ME'DIAN (מָדַי; *Keri*, מָדָאָה: ὁ Μῆδος: *Medus*). Darius, "the son of Ahasuerus, of the seed of the Medes" (Dan. ix. 1) or "the Mede" (xi. 1), is thus described in Dan. v. 31.

MEDICINE. I. Next to care for food, clothing, and shelter, the curing of hurts takes precedence even amongst savage nations. At a later period comes the treatment of sickness, and recognition of states of disease; and these mark a nascent civilization. Internal diseases, and all for which an obvious cause cannot be assigned, are in the most early period viewed as the visitation of God, or as the act of some malignant power, human — as the evil eye — or else superhuman, and to be dealt with by sorcery, or some other occult supposed agency. The Indian notion is that all diseases are the work of an evil spirit (Sprengel, *Gesch. der Arzeneikunde*, pt. ii. 48). But among a civilized race the preëminence of the medical art is confessed in proportion to the increased value set on human life, and the vastly greater amount of comfort and enjoyment of which civilized man is capable. It would be strange if their close connection historically with Egypt had not imbued

the Israelites with a strong appreciation of the value of this art, and with some considerable degree of medical culture. From the most ancient testimonies, sacred and secular, Egypt, from whatever cause, though perhaps from necessity, was foremost among the nations in this most human of studies purely physical. Again, as the active intelligence of Greece flowed in upon her, and mingled with the immense store of pathological records which must have accumulated under the system described by Herodotus, — Egypt, especially Alexandria, became the medical repertory and museum of the world. Thither all that was best worth preserving amid earlier civilizations, whether her own or foreign, had been attracted, and medicine and surgery flourished amidst political decadence and artistic decline. The attempt has been made by a French writer (Renouard, *Histoire de Médicine depuis son Origine*, etc.) to arrange in periods the growth of the medical art as follows: 1st. The Primitive or Instinctive Period, lasting from the earliest recorded treatment to the fall of Troy. 2d. The Sacred or Mystic Period, lasting till the dispersion of the Pythagorean Society, 500 B. C. 3d. The Philosophical Period, closing with the foundation of the Alexandrian Library, B. C. 320. 4th. The Anatomical Period, which continued until the death of Galen, A. D. 200. But these artificial lines do not strictly exhibit the truth of the matter. Egypt was the earliest home of medical and other skill for the region of the Mediterranean basin, and every Egyptian mummy of the more expensive and elaborate sort, involved a process of anatomy. This gave opportunities of inspecting a vast number of bodies, varying in every possible condition. Such opportunities were sure to be turned to account (Pliny, *N. H.* xix. 5) by the more diligent among the faculty — for "the physicians" embalmed (Gen. l. 2). The intestines had a separate receptacle assigned them, or were restored to the body through the ventral incision (Wilkinson, v. 468); and every such process which we can trace in the mummies discovered shows the most minute accuracy of manipulation. Notwithstanding these laborious efforts, we have no trace of any philosophical or rational system of Egyptian origin; and medicine in Egypt was a mere art or profession. Of science the Asclepiadae of Greece were the true originators. Hippocrates, who wrote a book on "Ancient Medicine," and who seems to have had many opportunities of access to foreign sources, gives no prominence to Egypt. It was no doubt owing to the repressive influences of her fixed institutions that this country did not attain to a vast and speedy proficiency in medical science, when *post mortem* examination was so general a rule instead of being a rare exception. Still it is impossible to believe that considerable advances in physiology could have failed to be made there from time to time, and similarly, though we cannot so well determine how far, in Assyria.[a] The best guarantee for the advance of medical science is, after all, the interest which every human being has in it; and this is most strongly felt in large grega-

---

[a] Recent researches at Kouyunjik have given proof, it is said, of the use of the microscope in minute service, and yielded up even specimens of magnifying lenses. A cone engraved with a table of cubes, so small as to be unintelligible without a lens, was brought home by Sir H Rawlinson, and is now in the British Museum. As to whether the invention was brought to bear on medical science, proof is wanting. Probably such science had not yet been pushed to the point at which the microscope becomes useful. Only those who have quick keen eyes for the nature-world feel the want of such spectacles.

rious masses of population. Compared with the
wild countries around them, at any rate, Egypt
must have seemed incalculably advanced. Hence
the awe, with which Homer's Greeks speak of her
wealth,[a] resources, and medi-
cal skill; and even the visit
of Abraham, though prior to
this period, found her no
doubt in advance of other
countries. Representations
of early Egyptian surgery
apparently occur on some of
the monuments of Beni-
Hassan. Flint knives used

Flint Knives. (Wilkinson.)

for embalming have been recovered — the "Ethiopic stone" of Herodotus (ii. 86; comp. Ex. iv.
25) was probably either black flint or agate; and
those who have assisted at the opening of a
mummy have noticed that the teeth exhibited a
dentistry not inferior in execution to the work of
the best modern experts. This confirms the statement of Herodotus that every part of the body was
studied by a distinct practitioner. Pliny (vii. 57)
asserts that the Egyptians claimed the invention
of the healing art, and (xxvi. 1) thinks
them subject to many diseases. Their
"many medicines" are mentioned (Jer.
xlvi. 11). Many valuable drugs may be
derived from the plants mentioned by
Wilkinson (iv. 621), and the senna of
the adjacent interior of Africa still excels all other. Athothmes II., king of
the country, is said to have written
on the subject of anatomy. Hermes
(who may perhaps be the same as
Athothmes, intellect personified, only
disguised as a deity instead of a
legendary king), was said to have written six books on medicine; in which an
entire chapter was devoted to diseases
of the eye (Rawlinson's *Herod.*, note to
ii. 84), and the first half of which related
to anatomy. The various recipes known to have
been beneficial were recorded, with their peculiar
cases, in the memoirs of physic, inscribed among
the laws, and deposited in the principal temples
of the place (Wilkinson, iii. 396, 397). The reputation of its practitioners in historical times was
such that both Cyrus and Darius sent to Egypt for
physicians or surgeons[b] (Herod. iii. 1, 129–132);
and by one of the same country, no doubt, Cambyses' wound was[c] tended, though not perhaps with
much zeal for his recovery.

Of midwifery we have a distinct notice (Ex. i.
15), and of women as its practitioners,[d] which fact
may also be verified from the sculptures (Rawlinson's note on Herod. ii. 84). The physicians

had salaries from the public treasury, and treated
always according to established precedents, or
deviated from these at their peril, in case of a
fatal termination ; if, however, the patient died
under accredited treatment no blame was attached.
They treated gratis patients when travelling or
on military service. Most diseases were by them
ascribed to indigestion and excessive eating (Diod.
Sicul.[e] i. 82), and when their science failed them
magic[f] was called in. On recovery it was also
customary to suspend in a temple an exvoto, which
was commonly a model of the part affected; and
such offerings doubtless, as in the Coan Temple of
Æsculapius, became valuable aids to the pathological

Doctors (or Barbers ?) and Patients. (Wilkinson.)

student. The Egyptians who lived in the corn-
growing region are said by Herodotus (ii. 77) to
have been specially attentive to health. The practice of circumcision is traceable on monuments
certainly anterior to the age of Joseph. Its antiquity is involved in obscurity; especially as all
we know of the Egyptians makes it unlikely
that they would have borrowed such a practice,
so late as the period of Abraham, from any
mere sojourner among them. Its beneficial effects
in the temperature of Egypt and Syria have
often been noticed, especially as a preservative of
cleanliness, etc. The scrupulous attention paid to
the dead was favorable to the health of the living.
Such powerful drugs as asphaltum, natron, resin,

*a Il. ix. 381; Od. iv. 229. See also Herod. ii. 84,
and i. 77. The simple heroes had reverence for the
healing skill which extended only to wounds. There
is hardly any recognition of disease in Homer. There
is sudden death, pestilence, and weary old age, but
hardly any fixed morbid condition, save in a simile
(Od. v. 396). See, however, a letter De rebus ex
Homero medicis, D. G. Wolf, Wittenberg, 1791.

*b Comp. the letter of Benhadad to Joram, 2 K. v.
6, to procure the cure of Naaman.

*c The words of Herod. (iii. 66), ὡς ἀσφακίλιοί τε τὸ
ἰσνέον καὶ ὁ μηρὸς τάχιστα ἰσσάτη, appear to indicate
medical treatment by the terms employed. It is not

unlikely the physician may have taken the opportunity
to avenge the wrongs of his nation.

*d The sex is clear from the Heb. grammatical forms.
The names of two, Shiphrah and Puah, are recorded.
The treatment of new-born Hebrew infants is mentioned (Ex. xvi. 4) as consisting in washing, salting,
and swaddling: this last was not used in Egypt (Wilkinson).

*e The same author adds that the most common
method of treatment was by κλυσμοῖς καὶ νηστείαις καὶ
ἐμέτοις.

*f Magicians and physicians both belonged to the
priestly caste, and perhaps united their professions in
one person.

pure bitumen, and various aromatic gums, suppressed or counteracted all noxious effluvia from [a] the corpse; even the saw-dust of the floor, on which the body had been cleansed, was collected in small linen bags, which, to the number of twenty or thirty, were deposited in vases near

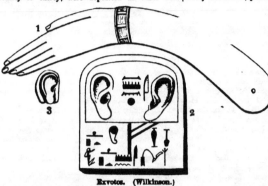

Exvotos. (Wilkinson.)

1. Ivory hand, in Mr. Salt's collection.
2. Stone tablet, dedicated to Amunre, for the recovery of a complaint in the ear; found at Thebes.
3. An ear, of terra cotta, from Thebes, in Sir J. Gardner Wilkinson's possession.

the tomb (Wilkinson,[b] v. 468, 469). For the extent to which these practices were imitated among the Jews, see EMBALMING; at any rate the uncleanness imputed to contact with a corpse was a powerful preservative [c] against the inoculation of the living frame with morbid humors. But, to pursue to later times this merely general question, it appears (Pliny, *N. H.* xix. 5 [d]) that the Ptolemies themselves practiced dissection, and that, at a period when Jewish intercourse with Egypt was complete and reciprocal,[e] there existed in Alexandria a great zeal for anatomical study. The only influence of

importance which would tend to check the Jews from sharing this was the ceremonial law, the special reverence of Jewish feeling towards human remains, and the abhorrence of "uncleanness." Yet those Jews — and there were at all times since the Captivity not a few, perhaps — who tended to foreign laxity, and affected Greek philosophy and culture, would assuredly, as we shall have further occasion to notice that they in fact did, enlarge their anatomical knowledge from sources which repelled their stricter brethren, and the result would be apparent in the general elevated standard of that profession, even as practiced in Jerusalem. The diffusion of Christianity in the 3d and 4th centuries exercised a similar but more universal restraint on the dissecting-room, until anatomy as a pursuit became extinct, and the notion of profaneness quelling everywhere such researches, surgical science became stagnant to a degree to which it had never previously sunk within the memory of human records.

In comparing the growth of medicine in the rest of the ancient world, the high rank of its practitioners — princes and heroes — settles at once the question as to the esteem in which it was held in the Homeric [f] and pre-Homeric [g] period. To descend to the historical, the story of Democedes [h] at the court of Darius illustrates the practice of Greek surgery before the period of Hippocrates; anticipating in its gentler waiting upon [i] nature, as compared (Herod. iii. 130) with that of the Per-

[a] "L'Égypte moderne n'en est plus là, et, comme M. Pariset l'a si bien signalé, les tombeaux des pères, infiltrés par les eaux du Nil, se convertissent en autant de foyers pestilentiels pour leurs enfants" (Michel Lévy, p. 12). This may perhaps be the true account of the production of the modern plague, which, however, disappears when the temperature rises above a given limit, excessive heat tending to dissipate the miasma.

[b] This author further refers to Pettigrew's *History of Egyptian Mummies.*

[c] Dr. Ferguson, in an article on pestilential infection, *Quarterly Review,* vol. xlvi., 1882, insists on actual contact with the diseased or dead as the condition of transmission of the disease. But compare a tract by Dr. Macmichael, *On the Progress of Opinion on the Subject of Contagion.* See also *Essays on State Medicine,* H. W. Rumsey, London, 1856, ess. iii. p 180, &c. For ancient opinions on the matter, see *Paulus Ægin.* ed. Sydenham Society, i. 284, &c. Thucydides, in his description of the Athenian plague, is the first who alludes to it, and that but inferentially. It seems on the whole most likely that contagiousness is a quality of morbid condition which may be present or absent. What the conditions are no one seems able to say. As an instance, elephantiasis was said by early writers (*e. g.* Aretæus and Rhazes) to be contagious, which some modern authorities deny. The assertion and denial are so clear and circumstantial in either case, that no other solution seems open to the question.

[d] "Regibus corpora mortuorum ad scrutandos morbos insecantibus."

[e] Cyrene, the well-known Greek African colony, had a high repute for physicians of excellence; and some of its coins bear the impress of the ὀπός, or *assafœtida,* a medical drug to which miraculous virtues were ascribed. Now the Cyrenaica was a home for the Jews of the dispersion (Acts ii. 10; *Paul. Ægin.* Sydenham Society, iii. 283).

[f] Galen himself wrote a book, περὶ τῆς 'Ομηρου ιατρικῆς, quoted by Alexander of Trallea, lib. ix. cap. 4.

[g] The indistinctness with which the medical, the magical, and the poisonous were confounded under the word φάρμακα by the early Greeks will escape no one. (So Ex. xxii. 18, the Heb. word for " witch " is in the LXX. rendered by φαρμακός.) The legend of the Argonauts and Medea illustrates this ; the Homeric Moly, and Nepenthes, and the whole story of Circe, confirm it.

[h] The fame which he had acquired in Samos had reached Sardis before Darius discovered his presence among the captives taken from Orœtes (Herod. iii. 129).

[i] The best known name amongst the pioneers of Greek medical science is Herodicus of Selymbria, " qui totam gymnasticam medicinæ adjunxit ; " for which he was censured by Hippocrates (*Biblioth. Script. Med. s. v.*). The alliance, however, of the ιατρική with the γυμναστική is familiar to us from the Dialogues of Plato.

sians and Egyptians, the method and maxims of that Father of physic, who wrote against the theories and speculations of the so-called philosophical school, and was a true Empiricist before that sect was formularized. The Dogmatic school was founded after his time by his disciples, who departed from his eminently practical and inductive method. It recognized hidden causes of health and sickness arising from certain supposed principles or elements, out of which bodies were composed, and by virtue of which all their parts and members were attempered together and became sympathetic. He has some curious remarks on the sympathy of men with climate, seasons, etc. Hippocrates himself rejected supernatural accounts of disease, and especially demoniacal possession. He refers, but with no mystical sense, to numbers [a] as furnishing a rule for cases. It is remarkable that he extols the discernment of Orientals above Westerns, and of Asiatics above Europeans, in medical diagnosis.[b] The empirical school, which arose in the third century B.C., under the guidance of Acron of Agrigentum, Serapion of Alexandria, and Philinus of Cos,[c] waited for the symptoms of every case, disregarding the rules of practice based on dogmatic principles. Among its votaries was a Zachalias (perhaps Zacharias, and possibly a Jew) of Babylon, who (Pliny, *N. H.* xxxvii. 10, comp. xxxvi. 10) dedicated a book on medicine to Mithridates the Great; its views were also supported [d] by Herodotus of Tarsus, a place which, next to Alexandria, became distinguished for its schools of philosophy and medicine; as also by a Jew named Theodas, or Theudas,[e] of Laodicea, but a student of Alexandria, and the last, or nearly so, of the Empiricists whom its schools produced. The remarks of Theudas on the right method of observing, and the value of experience, and his book on medicine, now lost, in which he arranged his subject under the heads of *indicatoria*, *curatoria*, and *salubria*, earned him high reputation as a champion of Empiricism against the reproaches of the dogmatists, though they were subsequently impugned by Galen and Theodosius of Tripoli. His period was that from Titus to Hadrian. "The empiricists held that observation and the application of known remedies in one case to others presumed to be similar constitute the whole art of cultivating medicine. Though their views were narrow, and their information scanty when compared with some of the chiefs of the other sects, and although they rejected as useless and unattainable all knowledge of the causes and recondite nature of diseases, it is undeniable that, besides personal experience, they freely availed themselves

of historical detail, and of a strict analogy founded upon observation and the resemblance of phenomena" (Dr. Adams, *Paul. Ægin.* ed. Sydenham Soc.).

This school, however, was opposed by another, known as the Methodic, which had arisen under the leading of Themison, also of Laodicea, about the period of Pompey the Great.[f] Asclepiades paved the way for the "method" in question, finding a theoretic [g] basis in the corpuscular or atomic theory of physics which he borrowed from Heraclides of Pontus. He had passed some early years in Alexandria, and thence came to Rome shortly before Cicero's time (comp. *quo nos medico amicoque usi sumus,* Crassus, ap. *Cic. de Orat.* i. 14). He was a transitional link between the Dogmatic and Empiric schools and this later or Methodic (Sprengel, *ub. sup.* pt. v. 16), which sought to rescue medicine from the bewildering mass of particulars in which empiricism had plunged it. He reduced diseases to two classes, chronic and acute, and endeavored likewise to simplify remedies. In the mean while the most judicious of medical theorists since Hippocrates, Celsus of the Augustan period, had reviewed medicine in the light which all these schools afforded, and not professing any distinct teaching, but borrowing from all, may be viewed as eclectic. He translated Hippocrates largely *verbatim*, quoting in a less degree Asclepiades and others. Antonius Musa, whose "cold-water cure," after its successful trial on Augustus himself, became generally popular, seems to have had little of scientific basis; but by the usual method, or the usual accidents, became merely the fashionable practitioner of his day in Rome.[h] Attalia, near Tarsus, furnished also, shortly after the period of Celsus, Athenæus, the leader of the last of the schools of medicine which divided the ancient world, under the name of the "Pneumatic," holding the tenet "of an etherial principle (πνεῦμα) residing in the microcosm, by means of which the mind performed the functions of the body." This is also traceable in Hippocrates, and was an established opinion of the Stoics. It was exemplified in the innate heat, θερμὴ ἔμφυτος (Aret. *de Caus. et Sign. Morb. Chron.* ii. 13), and the *calidum innatum* of modern physiologists, especially in the 17th century (Dr Adams, *Pref. Aretæus,* ed. Syd. Soc.). It is clear that all these schools may easily have contributed to form the medical opinions current at the period of the N. T., that the two earlier among them may have influenced rabbinical teaching on that subject at a much earlier period, and that especially at the time of Alexander's visit to Jerusa-

---

[a] Thus the product of seven and forty gives the term of the days of gestation; in his περὶ νούσων δ, why men died, ἐν τῇσι περισσῇσι τῶν ἡμερέων, is discussed; so the 4th, 8th, 11th, and 17th, are noted as the critical days in acute diseases.

[b] Sprengel, *ub. sup.* iv. 52-5, speaks of an Alexandrian school of medicine as having carried anatomy, especially under the guidance of Herophilus, to its highest pitch of ancient perfection. It seems not, however, to have claimed any distinctive principles, but stands chronologically between the Dogmatic and Empiric schools.

[c] The former of these wrote against Hippocrates, the latter was a commentator on him (Sprengel, *ub. sup.* iv. 81).

[d] It treats of a stone called *hæmatite*, to which the author ascribes great virtues, especially as regards the eye.

[e] The authorities for these statements about Theudas are given by Wunderbar, *Biblisch-Talmudische Medicin,* 1tes Heft, p. 26. He refers among others to Talmud, *Tr. Nasir,* 52 b; to *Tosiphta Ohloth,* § iv.; and to *Tr. Sankedrin,* 33 a, 93 d; *Bechoroth,* 28 b.

[f] "Alia est Hippocratis secta [the Dogmatic], alia Asclepiadis, alia Themisonis" (Seneca, *Epist.* 95; comp. Juv. *Sat.* x. 221).

[g] For his remains see *Asclepiadis Bithynici Fragmenta,* ed. Christ. Gottl. Gumpert, 8o. Vinar. 1794.

[h] Female medical aid appears to have been current at Rome, whether in midwifery only (the *obstetric*), or in general practice, as the titles *medica, iatpıvń,* would seem to imply (see Martial, *Epig.* xi. 72). The Greeks were not strangers to female study of medicine; *e. g.* some fragments of the famous Aspasia on women's disorders occur in Aëtius.

lem, the Jewish people, whom he favored and protected, had an opportunity of largely gathering from the medical lore of the West. It was necessary therefore to pass in brief review the growth of the latter, and especially to note the points at which it intersects the medical progress of the Jews. Greek Asiatic medicine culminated in Galen, who was, however, still but a commentator on his western predecessors, and who stands literally without rival, successor, or disciple of note, till the period when Greek learning was reawakened by the Arabian intellect. Galen himself [a] belongs to the period of the Antonines, but he appears to have been acquainted with the writings of Moses, and to have travelled in quest of medical experience over Egypt, Syria, and Palestine, as well as Greece, and a large part of the West, and, in particular, to have visited the banks of the Jordan in quest of opobalsamum, and the coasts of the Dead Sea to obtain samples of bitumen. He also mentions Palestine as producing a watery wine, suited for the drink of febrile patients.

II. Having thus described the external influences which, if any, were probably most influential in forming the medical practice of the Hebrews, we may trace next its internal growth. The cabalistic legends mix up the names of Shem and Heber in their fables about healing, and ascribe to those patriarchs a knowledge of simples and rare roots, with, of course, magic spells and occult powers, such as have clouded the history of medicine from the earliest times down to the 17th century.[b] So to Abraham is ascribed a talisman, the touch of which healed all disease. We know that such simple surgical skill as the operation for circumcision implies was Abraham's; but severer operations than this are constantly required in the flock and herd, and those who watch carefully the habits of animals can hardly fail to amass some guiding principles applicable to man and beast alike. Beyond this, there was probably nothing but such ordinary obstetrical craft as has always been traditional among the women of rude tribes, which could be classed as medical lore in the family of the patriarch, until his sojourn brought him among the more cultivated Philistines and Egyptians. The only notices which Scripture affords in connection with the subject are the cases of difficult midwifery in the successive households of Isaac,[c] Jacob, and Judah (Gen. xxv. 26, xxxv. 17, xxxviii. 27), and so, later, in that of Phinehas (1 Sam. iv. 19). The

traditional value ascribed to the mandrake, in regard to generative functions, relates to the same branch of natural medicine; but throughout this period occurs no trace of any attempt to study, digest, and systematize the subject. But, as Israel grew and multiplied in Egypt, they derived doubtless a large mental cultivation from their position, until cruel policy turned it into bondage; even then Moses was rescued from the lot of his brethren, and became learned in all the wisdom of the Egyptians, including, of course, medicine and cognate sciences (Clem. Alex. i. p. 413), and those attainments perhaps became suggestive of future laws. Some practical skill in metallurgy is evident from Ex. xxxii. 20. But, if we admit Egyptian learning as an ingredient, we should also notice how far exalted above it is the standard of the whole Jewish legislative fabric, in its exemption from the blemishes of sorcery and juggling pretenses. The priest, who had to pronounce on the cure, used no means to advance it, and the whole regulations prescribed exclude the notion of trafficking in popular superstition. We have no occult practices reserved in the hands of the sacred caste. It is God alone who doeth great things, working by the wand of Moses, or the brazen serpent; but the very mention of such instruments is such as to expel all pretense of mysterious virtues in the things themselves. Hence various allusions to God's "healing mercy," and the title "Jehovah that healeth" (Ex. xv. 26; Jer. xvii. 14, xxx. 17; Ps. ciii. 3, cxlvii. 3; Is. xxx. 26). Nor was the practice of physic a privilege of the Jewish priesthood. Any one might practice it, and this publicity must have kept it pure. Nay, there was no Scriptural bar to its practice by resident aliens. We read of "physicians," "healing," etc., in Ex. xxi. 19; 2 K. viii. 29; 2 Chr. xvi. 12; Jer. viii. 22. At the same time the greater leisure of the Levites and their other advantages would make them the students of the nation, as a rule, in all science, and their constant residence in cities would give them the opportunity, if carried out in fact, of a far wider field of observation. The reign of peace of Solomon's days must have opened, especially with renewed Egyptian intercourse, new facilities for the study. He himself seems to have included in his favorite natural history some knowledge of the medicinal uses of the creatures. His works show him conversant with the notion of remedial treatment (Prov. iii. 8, vi. 15, xii. 18, xvii. 22, xx. 30, xxix. 1; Eccl. iii. 3); and one passage

---

[a] The Arabs, however, continued to build wholly upon Hippocrates and Galen, save in so far as their advance in chemical science improved their pharmacopœia: this may be seen on reference to the works of Rhases, A. D. 920, and Haly Abbas, A. D. 980. The first mention of smallpox is ascribed to Rhases, who, however, quotes several earlier writers on the subject. Mohammed himself is said to have been versed in medicines and to have compiled some aphorisms upon it; and a herbalist literature was always extensively followed in the East from the days of Solomon downwards (Freind's *History of Medicine*, ii. 5, 27).

[b] See, in evidence of this, *Royal and Practical Chymistry, in three treatises*, London, 1670.

[c] Doubts have been raised as to the possibility of twins being born, one holding the other's heel; but there does not seem any such limit to the operations of nature as any objection on that score would imply. After all, it was perhaps only just such a relative position of the limbs of the infants at the mere moment

of birth as would suggest the "holding by the heel." The midwives, it seems, in case of twins, were called upon to distinguish the first-born, to whom important privileges appertained. The tying on a thread or ribbon was an easy way of preventing mistake, and the assistant in the case of Tamar seized the earliest possible moment for doing it. "When the hand or foot of a living child protrudes, it is to be pushed up . . and the head made to present" (*Paul. Ægin.* ed. Sydenh. Soc. i. 648, Hippocr. quoted by Dr. Adams). This probably the midwife did; at the same time marking him as first-born in virtue of being thus "presented" first. The precise meaning of the doubtful expression in Gen. xxxviii. 27 and marg. is discussed by Wunderbar, *ub. sup.* p. 50, in reference both to the children and to the mother. Of Rachel a Jewish commentator says, "Multis etiam ex itinere difficultatibus prægressis, viribusque post diu protractos dolores exhaustis, atonia uteri, forsan quidem hæmorrhagia in pariendo mortua est " (*ibid.*)

(see p. 1867 f.) indicates considerable knowledge of anatomy. His repute in magic is the universal [a] theme of eastern story. It has even been thought he had recourse to the shrine of Æsculapius at Sidon, and enriched his resources by its records or relics; but there seems some doubt whether this temple was of such high antiquity. Solomon, however, we cannot doubt, would have turned to the account, not only of wealth but of knowledge, his peaceful reign, wide dominion, and wider renown, and would have sought to traffic in learning, as well as in wheat and gold. To him the Talmudists ascribe a "volume of cures" (ספר רפואות), of which they make frequent mention (Fabricius, Cod. Pseudep. V. T. i. 1043 f.). Josephus (Ant. viii. 2) mentions his knowledge of medicine, and the use of spells by him to expel demons who cause sicknesses, "which is continued among us," he adds, "to this time." The dealings of various prophets with quasi-medical agency cannot be regarded as other than the mere accidental form which their miraculous gifts took (1 K. xiii. 6, xiv. 12, xvii. 17; 2 K. i. 4, xx. 7; Is. xxxviii. 21). Jewish tradition has invested Elisha, it would seem, with a function more largely medicinal than that of the other servants of God; but the Scriptural evidence on the point is scanty, save that he appears to have known at once the proper means to apply to heal the waters, and temper the noxious pottage (2 K. ii. 21, iv. 39–41). His healing the Shunammite's son has been discussed as a case of suspended animation, and of animal magnetism applied to resuscitate it; but the narrative clearly implies that the death was real. As regards the leprosy, had the Jordan commonly possessed the healing power which Naaman's faith and obedience found in it, would there have been "many lepers in Israel in the days of Eliseus the prophet," or in any other days? Further, if our Lord's words (Luke iv. 27) are to be taken literally, Elisha's reputation could not have been founded on any succession of lepers healed. The washing was a part of the enjoined lustration of the leper *after* his cure was complete; Naaman was to act as though clean, like the "ten men that were lepers," bidden to "go and show themselves to the priest" — in either case it was "as thou hast believed, so be it done unto thee."

---

[a] Josephus (Ant. viii. 2) mentions a cure of one possessed with a devil by the use of some root, the knowledge of which was referred by tradition to Solomon.

[b] Professor Newman remarks on the manner of Benhadad's recorded death, that "when a man is so near to death that this will kill him, we need good evidence to show that the story is not a vulgar scandal" (Hebrew Monarchy, p. 180, note). The remark seems to betray ignorance of what is meant by the crisis of a fever.

[c] Wunderbar, whom the writer has followed in a large portion of this general review of Jewish medicine, and to whom his obligations are great, has here set up a view which appears untenable. He regards the Babylonian Captivity as parallel in its effects to the Egyptian bondage, and seems to think that the people would return debased from its influence. On the contrary, those whom subjection had made ignoble and unpatriotic would remain. If any returned, it was a pledge that they were not so impaired; and, if not impaired, they would be certainly improved by the discipline they had undergone. He also thinks that sorcery had the largest share in any Babylonian or Persian system of medicine. This is assuming too

The sickness of Benhadad is certainly so described as to imply treachery on the part of Hazael (2 K. viii. 15). Yet the observation of Bruce, upon a "cold-water cure" practiced among the people near the Red Sea, has suggested a view somewhat different. The bed-clothes are soaked with cold water, and kept thoroughly wet, and the patient drinks cold water freely. But the crisis, it seems, occurs on the third day, and not till the fifth is it there usual to apply this treatment. If the chamberlain, through carelessness, ignorance, or treachery, precipitated the application, a fatal [b] issue may have suddenly resulted. The "brazen serpent," once the means of healing, and worshipped idolatrously in Hezekiah's reign, is supposed to have acquired those honors under its Æsculapian aspect. This notion is not inconsistent with the Scripture narrative, though not therein traceable. It is supposed that something in the "volume of cures," current under the authority of Solomon, may have conduced to the establishment of these rites, and drawn away the popular homage, especially in prayers during sickness, or thanksgiving after recovery, from Jehovah. The statement that King Asa (2 Chr. xvi. 12) "sought *not* to Jehovah, *but* to the physicians," may seem to countenance the notion that a rivalry of actual worship, based on some medical fancies, had been set up, and would so far support the Talmudical tradition.

The Captivity at Babylon brought the Jews in contact with a new sphere of thought. Their chief men rose to the highest honors, and an improved mental culture among a large section of the captives was no doubt the result which they imported on their return.[c] We know too little of the precise state of medicine in Babylon, Susa, and the "cities of the Medes," to determine the direction in which the impulse so derived would have led the exiles; but the confluence of streams of thought from opposite sources, which impregnate each other, would surely produce a tendency to sift established practice and accepted axioms, to set up a new standard by which to try the current rules of art, and to determine new lines of inquiry for any eager spirits disposed to search for truth. Thus the visit of Democedes to the court of Darius, though it

much: there were magicians in Egypt, but physicians also (see above) of high cultivation. Human nature has so great an interest in human life, that only in the savage rudimentary societies is its economy left thus involved in phantasms. The earliest steps of civilization include something of medicine. Of course superstitions are found copiously involved in such medical tenets, but this is not equivalent to abandoning the study to a class of professed magicians. Thus in the Uebersreste der altbabylonischen Literatur, p. 128, by D. Chwolson, St. Petersb. 1859 (the value of which is not however yet ascertained), a writer on poisons claims to have a magic antidote, but declines stating what it is, as it is not his business to mention such things, and he only does so in cases where the charm is in connection with medical treatment and resembles it; the magicians, adds the same writer on another occasion, use a particular means of cure, but he declines to impart it, having a repugnance to witchcraft. So (pp. 125, 126) we find traces of charms introduced into Babylonish treatises on medical science, but apologetically, and as if against sounder knowledge. Similarly, the opinion of fatalism is not without its influence on medicine; but it is chiefly resorted to where, as in pestilence often happens, all known aid seems useless.

seems to be an isolated fact, points to a general opening of oriental manners to Greek influence, which was not too late to leave its traces in some perhaps of the contemporaries of Ezra. That great reformer, with the leaders of national thought gathered about him, could not fail to recognize medicine among the salutary measures which distinguished his epoch. And whatever advantages the Levites had possessed in earlier days were now speedily lost even as regards the study of the divine Law, and much more therefore as regards that of medicine, into which competitors would crowd in proportion to its broader and more obvious human interest, and effectually demolish any narrowing barriers of established privilege, if such previously existed.

It may be observed that the priests in their ministrations, who performed at all seasons of the year barefoot on stone pavement, and without perhaps any variation of dress to meet that of temperature, were peculiarly liable to sickness.[a] Hence the permanent appointment of a Temple physician has been supposed by some, and a certain Ben-Ahijah is mentioned by Wunderbar as occurring in the Talmud in that capacity. But it rather appears as though such an officer's appointment were precarious, and varied with the demands of the ministrants.

The book of Ecclesiasticus shows the increased regard given to the distinct study of medicine, by the repeated mention of physicians, etc., which it contains, and which, as probably belonging to the period of the Ptolemies, it might be expected to show. The wisdom of prevention is recognized in Ecclus. xviii. 19, perhaps also in x. 10. Rank and honor are said to be the portion of the physician, and his office to be from the Lord (xxxviii. 1, 3, 12). The repeated allusions to sickness in vii. 35, xxx. 17, xxxi. 22, xxxvii. 30, xxxviii. 9, coupled with the former recognition of merit, have caused some to suppose that this author was himself a physician. If he was so, the power of mind and wide range of observation shown in his work would give a favorable impression of the standard of practitioners; if he was not, the great general popularity of the study and practice may be inferred from its thus becoming a common topic of general advice offered by a non-professional writer. In Wisd. xvi. 12, plaister is spoken of ; anointing, as a means of healing, in Tob. vi. 8.

To bring down the subject to the period of the N. T. St. Luke,[b] "the beloved physician," who practiced at Antioch whilst the body was his care,

could hardly have failed to be conversant with all the leading opinions current down to his own time. Situated between the great schools of Alexandria and Cilicia, within easy sea-transit of both, as well as of the western homes of science, Antioch enjoyed a more central position than any great city of the ancient world, and in it accordingly all the streams of contemporary medical learning may have probably found a point of confluence. The medicine of the N. T. is not solely, nor even chiefly, Jewish medicine; and even if it were, it is clear that the more mankind became mixed by intercourse, the more medical opinion and practice must have ceased to be exclusive. The great number of Jews resident in Rome and Greece about the Christian era, and the successive decrees by which their banishment from the former was proclaimed, must have imported, even into Palestine, whatever from the West was best worth knowing; and we may be as sure that its medicine and surgery expanded under these influences, as that, in the writings of the Talmudists, such obligations would be unacknowledged. But, beyond this, the growth of large mercantile communities such as existed in Rome, Alexandria, Antioch, and Ephesus, of itself involves a peculiar sanitary condition, from the mass of human elements gathered to a focus under new or abnormal circumstances. Nor are the words in which an eloquent modern writer describes the course of this action less applicable to the case of an ancient than to that of a modern metropolis. "Diseases once indigenous to a section of humanity are slowly but surely creeping up to commercial centres from whence they will be rapidly propagated. One form of Asiatic leprosy is approaching the Levant from Arabia. The history of every disease which is communicated from man to man establishes this melancholy truth, that ultimately such maladies overleap all obstacles of climate, and demonstrate a solidarity in evil as well as in good among the brotherhood of nations."[c] In proportion as this "melancholy truth" is perceived, would an intercommunication of medical science prevail also.

The medicine and surgery of St. Luke, then, was probably not inferior to that commonly in demand among educated Asiatic Greeks, and must have been, as regards its basis, Greek medicine, and not Jewish. Hence a standard Gentile medical writer, if any is to be found of that period, would best represent the profession to which the Evangelist belonged. Without absolute certainty as to date,[d] we seem to have such a writer in Aretæus, commonly called "the Cappadocian,"

---

a Thus we find Kall, *De Morbis Sacerdotum*, Hafn. 1745, referred to by Wunderbar, 1stes Heft, p. 60.

b This is not the place to introduce any discussion on the language of St. Luke; it may be observed, however, that it appears often tinctured by his early studies: *e. g.* v. 18, παραλελυμένος, the correct term, instead of the popular παραλυτικός of St. Matthew and St. Mark; so viii. 44, ἔστη ἡ ῥύσις, instead of the apparently Hebraistic phrase ἐξηράνθη ἡ πηγὴ of the latter; so vi. 19, ἰᾶτο πάντας, where διεσώθησαν and ἐσώζοντο are used by the others; and viii. 55, ἐπέστρεψε τὸ πνεῦμα (the breath?), as though a token of animation returning; and the list might easily be enlarged. St. Luke abounds in the narratives of demoniacs, while Hippocrates repudiates such influence, as producing maniacal and epileptic disorders. See this subject discussed in the Notes on the "Sacred Diseases" in the Sydenh. Soc. ed. of Hippocr. Aretæus, on the contrary, recognizes the opinion of

demoniac agency in disease. His words are: ἱερὴν κικλήσκουσι τὴν πάθην· ἀτὰρ καὶ δι' ἄλλας προφασίας, ἢ μέγεθος τοῦ κακοῦ, ἱερὸν γὰρ τὸ μέγα· ἢ ἰήσιος οὐκ ἀνθρωπίνης ἀλλὰ θείης· ἢ δαίμονος δόξῃς ἐς τὸν ἄνθρωπον εἰσόδου, ἢ ξυμπάντων ὁμοῦ, τήνδε ἐκικλήσκον ἱερήν. Περὶ ἐπιληψίης. (*De Caus. et Sign. Morb. Chron.* i. 4.) [See Wetstein's note on Matt. iv. 24.]

c Dr. Ferguson, *Pref. Essay to Gooch on Diseases of Women*, New Sydenham Society, London, 1859, p. xlvi. He adds, "Such has been the case with small-pox, measles, scarlatina, and the plague . . . The yellow fever has lately ravaged Lisbon under a temperature perfectly similar to that of London or Paris."

d The date here given is favored by the introductory review of Aretæus's life and writings prefixed to Boerhaave's edition of his works, and by Dr. Greenhill in Smith's *Dictionary of Biog. and Myth.* sub voc. *Aretæus*. A view that he was about a century later — a contemporary, in short, of Galen — is ad-

who wrote certainly after Nero's reign began, and probably flourished shortly before and after the decade in which St. Paul reached Rome and Jerusalem fell. If he were of St. Luke's age, it is striking that he should also be perhaps the only ancient medical authority in favor of demoniacal possession as a possible account of epilepsy (see p. 1860, note b). If his country be rightly indicated by his surname, we know that it gave him the means of intercourse with both the Jews and the Christians of the Apostolic period (Acts ii. 9; 1 Pet. i. 1). It is very likely that Tarsus, the nearest place of academic repute to that region, was the scene of at any rate the earlier studies of Aretæus, nor would any chronological difficulty prevent his having been a pupil in medicine there when Paul and also, perhaps, Barnabas were, as is probable, pursuing their early studies in other subjects at the same spot. Aretæus, then, assuming the date above indicated, may be taken as expounding the medical practice of the Asiatic Greeks in the latter half of the first century. There is, however, much of strongly marked individuality in his work, more especially in the minute verbal portraiture of disease. That of pulmonary consumption in particular is traced with the careful description of an eye-witness, and represents with a curious exactness the curved nails, shrunken fingers, slender sharpened nostrils, hollow glazy eye, cadaverous look and hue, the waste of muscle and startling prominence of bones, the scapula standing off like the wing of a bird: as also the habit of body marking youthful predisposition to the malady, the thin veneer-like frames, the limbs like pinions,[a] the prominent throat and shallow chest, with a remark that moist and cold climates are the haunts of it (Aret. περὶ φθίσεος). His work exhibits strong traits here and there of the Pneumatic school, as in his statement regarding lethargy, that it is frigidity implanted by nature; concerning elephantiasis even more emphatically, that it is a refrigeration of the innate heat, " or rather a congelation — as it were one great winter of the system." [b]　The same views betray themselves in his statement regarding the blood, that it is the warming principle of all the parts; that diabetes is a sort of dropsy, both exhibiting the watery principle; and that the effect of white hellebore is as that of fire: " so that whatever fire does by burning, hellebore effects still more by penetrating inwardly." The last remark shows that he gave some scope to his imagination, which indeed we might illustrate from some of his pathological descriptions, e. g. that of elephantiasis, where the resemblance of the beast to the afflicted human being is wrought to a fanciful parallel. Allowing for such overstrained touches here and there, we may say that he generally avoids extravagant crotchets, and rests chiefly on wide observation, and on the common sense which sobers theory and rationalizes facts. He hardly ever quotes an authority; and though much of what he states was taught before, it is dealt with as the common property of

science, or as become sui juris through being proved by his own experience. The freedom with which he follows or rejects earlier opinions, has occasioned him to be classed by some amongst the eclectic school. His work is divided into — I. the causes and signs of (1) acute, and (2) chronic diseases; and II. the curative treatment of (1) acute, and (2) chronic diseases. His boldness of treatment is exemplified in his selection of the vein to be opened in a wide range of parts, the arm, ankle, tongue, nose, etc. He first has a distinct mention of leeches, which Themison is said to have introduced; and in this respect his surgical resources appear to be in advance of Celsus. He was familiar with the operation for the stone in the bladder, and prescribes, as Celsus also does, the use of the catheter, where its insertion is not prevented by inflammation, then the incision [c] into the neck of the bladder, nearly as in modern lithotomy. His views of the internal economy were a strange mixture of truth and error, and the disuse of anatomy was no doubt the reason why this was the weak point of his teaching. He held that the work of producing the blood pertained to the liver, " which is the root of the veins; " that the bile was distributed from the gall bladder to the intestines; and, if this vesica became gorged, the bile was thrown back into the veins, and by them diffused over the system. He regarded the nerves as the source of sensation and motion; and had some notion of them as branching in pairs from the spine.[a] Thus he has a curious statement as regards paralysis, that in the case of any sensational point belina the head, e. g. from the membrane of the spinal marrow being affected injuriously, the parts on the right side will be paralyzed if the nerve toward the right side be hurt, and similarly, conversely, of the left side; but that if the head itself be so affected, the inverse law of consequence holds concerning the parts related, since each nerve passes over to the other side from that of its origin, decussating each other in the form of the letter X. The doctrine of the Pneuma, or ethereal principle existing in the microcosm by which the mind performs all the functions of the body, holds a more prominent position in the works of Aretæus than in those of any of the other authorities (Dr. Adams' pref. to Aret. pp. x., xl.). He was aware that the nervous function of sensation was distinct from the motive power; that either might cease and the other continue. His pharmacopœia is copious and reasonable, and the limits of the usefulness of this or that drug are laid down judiciously. He makes large use of wine,[e] and prescribing the kind and the number of cyathi to be taken; and some words of his on stomach disorders (περὶ καρδιαλγίης) forcibly recall those of St. Paul to Timothy (1 Tim. v. 23), and one might almost suppose them to have been suggested by the intenser spirituality of his Jewish or Christian patients. " Such disorders," he says, " are common to those who toil in teaching, whose yearning is after divine instruction, who de-

<hr />

vanced in the Syd. Soc. edition, and ably supported. Still the evidence, being purely negative, is slender, and the opposite arguments are not taken into account.

[a] Πτερυγώδεες.
[b] τῆξίς ἐστι τοῦ ἐμφύτου θερμοῦ οὐ μικρὰ τι, ἢ καὶ σάγος, ὡς ἐν τι μέγα χεῖμα (De Caus. et Sign. Morb. Chron. ii. 13).
[c] Τάμνειν τὴν τρίχαθα καὶ τὸν τῆς κύστιδος τράχηλον.

[d] Sprengel (ub. sup. iv. 52–5) thinks that an approximately right conception of the nervous system was attained by Hierophilus of the Alexandrian school of medicine.

[e] Galen (Hyg. v.) strenuously recommends the use of wine to the aged, stating the wines best adapted to them. Even Plato (Leg. ii.) allows old men thus to restore their youth, and correct the austerity of age

spise delicate and varied diet, whose nourishment is fasting, and whose drink is water." And as a purge of melancholy he prescribes "a little wine, and some other more liberal sustenance." In his essay on *Kausus*, or "brain" a fever, he describes the powers acquired by the soul before dissolution in the following remarkable words: " Every sense is pure, the intellect acute, the gnostic powers prophetic; for they prognosticate to themselves in the first place their own departure from life; then they foretell what will afterwards take place to those present, who fancy sometimes that they are delirious: but these persons wonder at the result of what has been said. Others, also, talk to certain of the dead, perchance they alone perceiving them to be present, in virtue of their acute and pure sense, or perchance from their soul seeing beforehand, and announcing the men with whom they are about to associate. For formerly they were immersed in humors, as if in mud and darkness; but when the disease has drained these off, and taken away the mist from their eyes, they perceive those things which are in the air, and through the soul being unencumbered become true prophets." b To those who wish further to pursue the study of medicine at this era, the edition of Aretæus by the Sydenham Society, and in a less degree that by Boerhaave (Lugd. Bat. 1735), to which the references have here been made, may be recommended.

As the general science of medicine and surgery of this period may be represented by Aretæus, so we have nearly a representation of its *Materia Medica* by Dioscorides. He too was of the same general region — a Cilician Greek, — and his first lessons were probably learnt at Tarsus. His period is tinged by the same uncertainty as that of Aretæus; but he has usually been assigned to the end of the 1st or beginning of the 2d century (see *Dict. of Biog. and Mythol.* s. v.). He was the first author of high mark who devoted his attention to *Materia Medica*. Indeed, this branch of ancient science remained as he left it till the times of the Arabians; and these, though they enlarged the supply of drugs and pharmacy, yet copy and repeat Dioscorides, as indeed Galen himself often does, on all common subject-matter. Above 90 minerals, 700 plants, and 168 animal substances, are said to be described in the researches of Dioscorides, displaying an industry and skill which has remained the marvel of all subsequent commentators. Pliny, copious, rare, and curious as he is, yet for want of scientific medical knowledge, is little esteemed in this particular branch, save when he follows Dios-

corides. The third volume of *Paulus Ægin.* (ed. Sydenham Soc.) contains a catalogue of medicines simple and compound, and the large proportion in which the authority of Dioscorides has contributed to form it, will be manifest at the most cursory inspection. To abridge such a subject is impossible, and to transcribe it in the most meagre form would be far beyond the limits of this article.

Before proceeding to the examination of diseases in detail, it may be well to observe that the question of identity between any ancient malady known by description, and any modern one known by experience, is often doubtful. Some diseases, just as some plants and some animals, will exist almost anywhere; others can only be produced within narrow limits depending on the conditions of climate, habit, etc.; and were only equal observation applied to the two, the *habitat* of a disease might be mapped as accurately as that of a plant. It is also possible that some diseases once extensively prevalent, may run their course and die out, or occur only casually; just as it seems certain that, since the Middle Ages, some maladies have been introduced into Europe which were previously unknown (*Biblioth. Script. Med.* Genev. 1731, s. v.; Hippocrates, Celsus, Galen; Leclerc's *History of Med.* Par. 1723, transl. Lond. 1699; Freind's *History of Med.*).

Eruptive diseases of the acute kind are more prevalent in the East than in colder climes. They also run their course more rapidly; e. g. common itch, which in Scotland remains for a longer time vesicular, becomes, in Syria, pustular as early sometimes as the third day. The origin of it is now supposed to be an acarus, but the parasite perishes when removed from the skin. Disease of various kinds is commonly regarded as a divine infliction, or denounced as a penalty for transgression; " the evil diseases of Egypt" (perhaps in reference to some of the ten plagues) are especially so characterized (Gen. xx. 18; Ex. xv. 26; Lev. xxvi. 16; Deut. vii. 15, xxviii. 60; 1 Cor. xi. 30); so the emerods (see EMERODS) c of the Philistines (1 Sam. v. 6); the severe dysentery d (2 Chr. xxi. 15, 19) of Jehoram, which was also epidemic [BLOOD, ISSUE OF; and FEVER], the peculiar symptom of which may perhaps have been *prolapsus ani* (Dr. Mason Good, i. 311–13, mentions a case of the entire colon exposed); or, perhaps, what is known as *diarrhœa tubularis*, formed by the coagulation of fibrine into a membrane discharged from the inner coat of the intestines, which takes the mould of the bowel, and is thus expelled (Kitto, s. v. " Diseases "); so the

a So Sir H. Halford renders it, *Essay* VI., in which occur some valuable comments on the subject treated by Aretæus.

b Aret. *de Sign. et Caus. Morb. Acut.* ii. 4.

c To the authorities there adduced may be added some remarks by Michel Lévy (*Traité d'Hygiène*, 206–7), who ascribes them to a plethoric state producing a congestion of the veins of the rectum, and followed by piles. Blood is discharged from them periodically or continuously; thus the plethora is relieved, and hence the ancient opinion that hemorrhoids were beneficial. Sanguineous flux of the part may, however, arise from other causes than these *varices* — e. g. ulceration, cancer, etc., of rectum. Wunderbar (*Bib.-Talm. Med.* iii. 17 d) mentions a bloodless kind, distinguished by the Talmudists as even more dangerous, and these he supposes meant in 1 Sam. v. To these is added (vi. 5, 11, 18) a mention of עֳפָלִים

(A. V. " mice "); but according to Lichtenstein (in Eichhorn's *Biblioth.* vi. 407–66) a venomous solpuga is with some plausibility intended, so large, and so similar in form to a mouse, as to admit of its being denominated by the same word. It is said to destroy and live upon scorpions, and to attack in the parts alluded to. The reference given is Pliny, *H. N.* xxix. 4; but Pliny gives merely the name, " solpuga : " the rest of the statement finds no foundation in him. See below, p. 1867. Wunderbar (3tes *Heft*, p. 19) has another interpretation of the " mice."

d See a singular quotation from the Talmud (*Shabbath*, 82), concerning the effect of tenesmus on the sphincter, Wunderbar, *Bib.-Tal. Med.* 3tes Heft, p. 17. The Talmudists say that those who die of such sickness as Jehoram's die painfully, but with full consciousness.

sudden deaths of Er, Onan (Gen. xxxviii. 7, 10), the Egyptian first-born (Ex. xi. 4, 5), Nabal, Bath-sheba's son, and Jeroboam's (1 Sam. xxv. 38; 2 Sam. xii. 15; 1 K. xiv. 1, 5), are ascribed to action of Jehovah immediately, or through a prophet. Pestilence (Hab. iii. 5) attends his path (comp. 2 Sam. xxiv. 15), and is innoxious to those whom He shelters (Ps. xci. 3–10). It is by Jeremiah, Ezekiel, and Amos associated (as historically in 2 Sam. xxiv. 13) with "the sword" and "famine" (Jer. xiv. 12, xv. 2, xxi. 7, 9, xxiv. 10, xxvii. 8, 13, xxviii. 8, xxix. 17, 18, xxxii. 24, 36, xxxiv. 17, xxxviii. 2, xlii. 17, 22, xliv. 13; Ez. v. 12, 17, vi. 11, 12, vii. 15, xii. 16, xiv. 21, xxxiii. 27; Am. iv. 6, 10). The sicknesses of the widow's son of Zarephath, of Ahaziah, Benhadad, the leprosy of Uzziah, the boil of Hezekiah, are also noticed as diseases sent by Jehovah, or in which He interposed, 1 K. xvii. 17, 20; 2 K. i. 4, xx. 1. In 2 Sam. iii. 29, disease is invoked as a curse, and in Solomon's prayer, 1 K. viii. 37 (comp. 2 Chr. xx. 9), antici-pated as a chastisement. Job and his friends agree in ascribing his disease to divine infliction; but the latter urge his sins as the cause. So, conversely, the healing character of God is invoked or promised, Ps. vi. 2, xli. 3, ciii. 3; Jer. xxx. 17. Satanic agency appears also as procuring disease, Job ii. 7; Luke xiii. 11, 16. Diseases are also mentioned as ordinary calamities, e. g. the sickness of old age, headache (perhaps by sunstroke), as that of the Shunammite's son, that of Elisha, and that of Ben-hadad, and that of Joram, Gen. xlviii. 1; 1 Sam. xxx. 13; 2 K. iv. 20, viii. 7, 29, xiii. 14; 2 Chr. xxii. 6.

Among special diseases named in the O. Test. is ophthalmia (Gen. xxix. 17, מְכֻלּוֹת עֵינַיִם), which is perhaps more common in Syria and Egypt than anywhere else in the world; especially in the fig season,[a] the juice of the newly-ripe fruit having the power of giving it. It may occasion partial or total blindness (2 K. vi. 18). The eye-salve (κολ-λύριον, Rev. iii. 18; Hor. Sat. i.) was a remedy common to Orientals, Greeks, and Romans (see Hippocr. κολλούριον; Celsus, vi. 8, de oculorum morbis, (2) de diversis collyriis). Other diseases are — barrenness of women, which mandrakes were

supposed to have the power of correcting (Gen. xx. 18; comp. xii. 17, xxx. 1, 2, 14–16) — "consump-tion,"[b] and several, the names of which are derived from various words, signifying to burn or to be hot (Lev. xxvi. 16; Deut. xxviii. 22; see FEVER); compare the kinds of fever distinguished by Hip-pocrates as καῦσος and πῦρ. The "burning boil," or "of a boil" (Lev. xiii. 23, צָרֶבֶת הַשְּׁחִין, LXX. οὐλὴ τοῦ ἕλκους), is again merely marked by the notion of an effect resembling that of fire, like the Greek φλεγμονή, or our "carbuncle;" it may possibly find an equivalent in the Damascus boil of the present time. The "botch (שְׁחִין) of Egypt" (Deut. xxviii. 27) is so vague a term as to yield a most uncertain sense; the plague, as known by its attendant bubo, has been suggested by Scheuchzer.[c] It is possible that the Elephantiasis Graecorum may be intended by שְׁחִין, understood in the widest sense of a continued ulceration until the whole body, or the portion affected, may be regarded as one שְׁחִין. Of this disease some further notice will be taken below; at present it is observable that the same word is used to express the "boil" of Hezekiah. This was certainly a single locally confined eruption, and was probably a carbuncle, one of which may well be fatal, though a single "boil" in our sense of the word seldom is so. Dr. Mead supposes it to have been a fever terminating in an abscess. The diseases rendered "scab"[d] and "scurvy" in Lev. xxi. 20, xxii. 22, Deut. xxviii. 27, may be almost any skin disease, such as those known under the names of lepra, psoriasis, pityriasis, icthyosis, favus, or common itch. Some of these may be said to approach the type of leprosy [LEPROSY] as laid down in Scrip-ture, although they do not appear to have involved ceremonial defilement, but only a blemish disquali-fying for the priestly office. The quality of being incurable is added as a special curse, for these dis-eases are not generally so, or at any rate are com-mon in milder forms. The "running of the reins" (Lev. xv. 2, 3, xxii. 4, marg.) may perhaps mean gonorrhoea.[e] If we compare Num. xxv. 1, xxxi. 7 with Josh. xxii. 17, there is ground for thinking

---

[a] Comp. Hippocr. περὶ ὄψιος. a. ὀφθαλμίης τῆς ἑσπε-ρίου καὶ ὀπωρίου ξυμφέρει κάθαρσις κεφαλῆς καὶ τῆς κάτω κοιλίης.

[b] Possibly the pulmonary tuberculation of the West, which is not unknown in Syria, and common enough in Smyrna and in Egypt. The word שַׁחֶפֶת is from a root meaning "to waste away." In Zech. xiv. 12 a plague is described answering to this meaning — an intense emaciation or atrophy; although no link of causation is hinted at, such sometimes results from severe internal abscesses.

[c] It should be noted that Hippocrates, in his Epidemics, makes mention of fevers attended with buboes, which affords presumption in favor of plague being not unknown. It is at any rate as old as the 1st century, A. D. See Littré's Hippocrates, tom. ii. p. 585, and iii. p. 5. The plague is referred to by writers of the 1st century, namely, Posaidonius and Rufus.

[d] Their terms in the respective versions are : —

גָּרָב   ψώρα ἀγρία,   scabies fugis.

יַלֶּפֶת   λειχήν,   impetigo.

[e] Or more probably blennorrhoea (mucous discharge).

The existence of gonorrhoea in early times — save in the mild form — has been much disputed. Michel Lévy (Traité d'Hygiène, p. 7) considers the affirmative as established by the above passage, and says of syphilis, "Que pour notre part, nous n'avons jamais pu considérer comme une nouveauté du xv.e siecle." He certainly gives some strong historical evidence against the view that it was introduced into France by Spanish troops under Gonsalvo de Cordova on their return from the New World, and so into the rest of Europe, where it was known as the morbus Gallicus. He adds, "La syphilis est perdue confusément dans la pathologie ancienne par la diversité de ses symp-tômes et de ses altérations; leur interprétation col-lective, et leur redaction en une seule unité morbide, a fait croire à l'introduction d'une maladie nouvelle." See also Freind's History of Med., Dr. Mead, Michaelis, Reinhart (Bibelkrankheiten), Schmidt (Biblischer Med.), and others. Wunderbar (Bib.-Talm. Med. iii. 20, com-menting on Lev. xv., and comparing Mishna, Zabim, ii. 2, and Maimon. ad loc.) thinks that gonorrhoea benigna was in the mind of the latter writers. Dr. Adams, the editor of Paul. Ægin. (Sydenh. Soc. ii. 14), considers syphilis a modified form of elephantiasis. For all ancient notices of the cognate diseases see that work, i. 598 foll.

that some disease of this class, derived from polluting sexual intercourse, remained among the people. The "issue" of Lev. xv. 19, may be [BLOOD, ISSUE OF] the *menorrhagia*, the duration of which in the East is sometimes, when not checked by remedies, for an indefinite period (Matt. ix. 20), or uterine hemorrhage from other causes. In Deut. xxviii. 35, is mentioned a disease attacking the "knees and legs," consisting in a "sore botch which cannot be healed," but extended, in the sequel of the verse, from the "sole of the foot to the top of the head." The latter part of the quotation would certainly accord with *Elephantiasis Græcorum* ; but this, if the whole verse be a mere continuation of one described malady, would be in contradiction to the fact that this disease commences in the face, not in the lower members. On the other hand, a disease which affects the knees and legs, or more commonly one of them only — its principal feature being intumescence, distorting and altering all the proportions — is by a mere accident of language known as Elephantiasis [a] *Arabum, Bucnemia Tropica* (Rayer, vol. iii. 820–841), or "Barbadoes leg," from being well known in that island. Supposing, however, that the affection of the knees and legs is something distinct, and that the latter part of the description applies to the *Elephantiasis Græcorum*,[b] the incurable and the all-pervading character of the malady are well expressed by it. This disease is what now passes under the name of "leprosy" (Michaelis, iii. 259) — the lepers, *e. g*, of the huts near the Zion gate of modern Jerusalem are elephantisiacs.[c] It has been asserted that there are two kinds, one painful, the other painless; but as regards Syria and the East this is contradicted. There the parts affected are quite benumbed and lose sensation. It is classed as a tubercular disease, not confined to the skin, but pervading the tissues and destroying the bones. It is not confined to any age or either sex. It first appears in general, but not always, about the face, as an indurated nodule (hence it is improperly called tubercular), which gradually enlarges, inflames, and ulcerates. Sometimes it commences in the neck or arms. The ulcers will heal spontaneously, but only after a long period, and after destroying a great deal of the neighboring parts. If a joint be attacked, the ulceration will go on till its destruction is complete, the joints of finger, toe, etc., dropping off one by one. Frightful dreams and fetid breath are symptoms mentioned by some pathologists. More nodules will develope them-

selves; and, if the face be the chief seat of the disease, it assumes a leonine [d] aspect, loathsome and hideous; the skin becomes thick, rugose, and livid; the eyes are fierce and staring, and the hair generally falls off from all the parts affected. When the throat is attacked the voice shares the affection, and sinks to a hoarse, husky whisper. These two symptoms are eminently characteristic. The patient will become bed-ridden, and, though a mass of bodily corruption, seem happy and contented with his sad condition, until sinking exhausted under the ravages of the disease, he is generally carried off, at least in Syria, by diarrhœa. It is hereditary, and may be inoculated, but does not propagate itself by the closest contact;[e] *e. g.* two women in the aforesaid leper-huts remained uncontaminated though their husbands were both affected, and yet the children born to them were, like the fathers, elephantisiac, and became so in early life. On the children of diseased parents a watch for the appearance of the malady is kept; but no one is afraid of infection, and the neighbors mix freely with them, though, like the lepers of the O. T., they live "in a several house." It became first prevalent in Europe during the crusades, and by their means was diffused, and the ambiguity of designating it leprosy then originated, and has been generally since retained. Pliny (*Nat. Hist.* xxvi. 5) asserts that it was unknown in Italy till the time of Pompey the Great, when it was imported from Egypt, but soon became extinct (*Paul. Ægin.* ed. Sydenh. Soc. ii. 6). It is, however, broadly distinguished from the λέπρα, λεύκη, etc. of the Greeks by name and symptoms, no less than by Roman medical and even popular writers; comp. Lucretius, whose mention of it is the earliest —

"Est elephas morbus, qui propter flumina Nili,
Gignitur Ægypto in mediâ, neque præterea usquam."

It is nearly extinct in Europe, save in Spain and Norway. A case was lately in the Crimea, but may have been produced elsewhere. It prevails in Turkey and the Greek Archipelago. One case, however, indigenous in England, is recorded amongst the medical fac-similes at Guy's Hospital. In Granada it was generally fatal after eight or ten years, whatever the treatment.

This favors the correspondence of this disease with one of those evil diseases of Egypt,[f] possibly its "botch," threatened Deut. xxviii. 27, 35. This "botch," however, seems more probably to mean the foul ulcer mentioned by Aretæus (*de Sign. et Caus. Morb. Acut.* i. 9), and called by him ἄφθα

---

[a] The Arabs call *Elephantiasis Græcorum* جذام, (*judhâm*) = mutilation, from the gradual dropping off of the joints of the extremities. They give to E. *Arabum* the name of الفيل ذاء, *Dà-ul-fîl* — *morbus elephas*, from the leg when swelled resembling that of the animal ; but the latter disease is quite distinct from the former.

[b] For its ancient description see Celsus, iii. 25, *de Elephantiasi.* Galen (*de Arte Curatoriâ ad Glauconn*, lib. ii. *de Cancro et Eleph.*) recommends viper's flesh, gives anecdotes of cases, and adds that the disorder was common in Alexandria. In Hippocr. (*Prorrhetic.* ii. *ap. fin.*) is mentioned ἡ νοῦσος ἡ Φοινικίη καλεομένη, but in the glossary of Galen is found, ἡ Φοινικίη νοῦσος· ἡ κατὰ Φοινίκην καὶ κατὰ τὰ ἀνατολικὰ μέρη πλεονάζουσα. Δηλοῦσθαι δὲ κἀνταῦθα δοκεῖ ἡ ἐλεφαντίασις.

[c] Schilling *de Lepra, Animadv. in Oussebium ad* § xix. says, "persuasum habeo lepram ab elephantiasi non differre nisi gradu ; ad § xxiii. he illustrates Num.

xii. 12, by his own experience, in dissecting a woman dead in childbed, as follows : "Corrupti fœtus dimidia pars in utero adhuc hærebat. Aperto utero tam immanis spargebatur fetor, ut non solum omnes adstantes aufugerent," etc. He thinks that the point of Moses' simile is the ill odor, which he ascribes to lepers, *i. e.* elephantisiacs.

[d] Hence called also *Leontiasis.* Many have attributed to these wretched creatures a *libido inexplebilis* (see *Proceedings of Med. and Chirurg. Soc. of London*, Jan. 1860, iii. 164, from which some of the above remarks are taken). This is denied by Dr. Robert Sim (from a close study of the disease in Jerusalem), save in so far as idleness and inactivity, with animal wants supplied, may conduce to it.

[e] Jahn (*Heb. Ant.* Upham's translation, p. 206) denies this.

[f] The editor of *Paul. Ægin.* (Sydenham Society, ii. 14) is convinced that the syphilis of modern times is a modified form of the elephantiasis

ἐσχάρη. He ascribes its frequency in Egypt to the mixed vegetable diet there followed, and to the use of the turbid water of the Nile, but adds that it is common in Cœlo-Syria. The Talmud speaks of the Elephantiasis (*Baba Kama*, 80 *b.*) as being " moist without and dry within " (Wunderbar, *Biblisch-Talmudische Med.* 3tes Heft, 10, 11). Advanced cases are said to have a cancerous aspect, and some [a] even class it as a form of cancer, a disease dependent on faults of nutrition. It has been asserted that this, which is perhaps the most dreadful disease of the East, was Job's malady. Origen, *Hexapla* on Job ii. 7, mentions, that one of the Greek versions gives it, *loc. cit.*, as the affliction which befell him. Wunderbar (*ut sup.* p. 10) supposes it to have been the Tyrian leprosy, resting chiefly on the itching [b] implied, as he supposes, by Job ii. 7, 8. Schmidt (*Biblischer Med.* iv. 4) thinks the " sore boil " may indicate some graver [c] disease, or concurrence of diseases. But there is no need to go beyond the statement of Scripture, which speaks not only of this " boil," but of " skin loathsome and broken," " covered with worms and clods of dust: " the second symptom is the result of the first, and the " worms " are probably the larvæ of some fly, known so to infest and make its *nidus* in any wound or sore exposed to the air, and to increase rapidly in size. The " clods of dust " would of course follow from his " sitting in ashes." The " breath strange to his wife," if it be not a figurative expression for her estrangement from him, may imply a fetor, which in such a state of body hardly requires explanation. The expression my " bowels boiled'" (xxx. 27) may refer to the burning sensation in the stomach and bowels, caused by acrid bile, which is common in ague. Aretæus (*de Cur. Morb. Acut.* ii. 3) has a similar expression, *θερμασίη τῶν σπλάγχνων οἷον ἀπὸ πυρός,* as attending syncope.

The " scaring dreams " and " terrifying visions " are perhaps a mere symptom [d] of the state of mind bewildered by unaccountable afflictions. The intense emaciation was (xxxiii. 21) perhaps the mere result of protracted sickness.

The disease of king Antiochus (2 Macc. ix. 5-10, &c.) is that of a boil breeding worms (*ulcus verminosum*). So Sulla, Pherecydes, and Alcman the poet, are mentioned (Plut. *vita Sullæ*) as similar cases. The examples of both the Herods (Jos. *Ant.* xvii. 6, § 5, *B. J.* i. 33, § 5) may also be adduced, as that of Pheretime (Herod. iv. 205). There is some doubt whether this disease be not allied to phthiriasis, in which lice are bred, and cause ulcers. This condition may originate either in a sore, or in a morbid habit of body brought on by uncleanliness, suppressed perspiration, or neglect; but the vermination, if it did not commence in a sore, would produce one. Dr. Mason Good (iv. 504–6), speaking of *μάλις, μαλιασμός* = cutaneous vermination, mentions a case in the Westminster Infirmary, and an opinion that universal phthiriasis was no unfrequent disease among the ancients; he also states (p. 500) that in gangrenous ulcers, especially in warm climates, innumerable grubs or maggots will appear almost every morning. The camel, and other creatures, are known to be the habitat of similar parasites. There are also cases of vermination without any wound or faulty outward state, such as the *Vena Medinensis*, known in Africa as the Guinea-worm,[e] of which Galen had heard only, breeding under the skin and needing to be drawn out carefully by a needle, lest it break, when great soreness and suppuration succeed (Freind, *Hist. of Med.* i. 49 ; De Mandelslo's *Travels*, p. 4; and *Paul. Ægin.* t. iv. Sydenh. Soc. ed.).

In Deut. xxviii. 65, it is possible that a palpitation of the heart is intended to be spoken of (comp. Gen. xlv. 96). In Mark ix. 17 (compare Luke ix. 38) we have an apparent case of epilepsy, shown especially in the foaming, falling, wallowing, and similar violent symptoms mentioned; this might easily be a form of demoniacal manifestation. The case of extreme hunger recorded 1 Sam. xiv. was merely the result of exhaustive fatigue; but it is remarkable that the Bulimia of which Xenophon speaks (*Anab.* iv. 5, 7) was remedied by an application in which " honey " (comp. 1 Sam. xiv. 27) was the chief ingredient.

Besides the common injuries of wounding, bruising, striking out eye, tooth, etc., we have in Ex. xxi. 22, the case of miscarriage produced by a blow, push, etc., damaging the fetus.

The plague of " boils and blains " is *not* said to have been fatal to man, as the murrain preceding was to cattle; this alone would seem to contradict the notion of Shapter (*Medic. Sacr.* p. 113), that the disorder in question was smallpox,[f] which, wherever it has appeared, until mitigated by vaccination, has been fatal to a great part, perhaps a majority of those seized. The smallpox also generally takes some days to pronounce and mature, which seems opposed to the Mosaic account. The expression of Ex. ix. 10, a " boil " [g] flourishing, or ebullient with blains, may perhaps be a disease analogous to phlegmonous erysipelas, or even common erysipelas, which is often accompanied by vesications such as the word " blains " might fitly describe.[h]

---

[a] Such is the opinion of Dr. R. Sim, expressed in a private letter to the writer. But see a letter of his to *Med. Times and Gazette*, April 14, 1860.

[b] The suppuration, etc., of ulcers, appears at least equally likely to be intended.

[c] He refers to Hippocr. *Lib. de Med.* tom. viii. *μαλίστον ἐστι νοσημάτων.*

[d] Hippocrates mentions, ii. 514, ed. Kühn, Lips. 1826, as a symptom of fever, that the patient *φοβέεται ἀπὸ ὁρυγμάτων.* See also i. 592, *περὶ ἱερῆς νόσου* . . . *δείματα νυκτὸς καὶ φόβοι.*

[e] Rayer, vol. iii. 808–819, gives a list of parasites, most of them in the skin. This " Guinea-worm," it appears, is also found in Arabia Petræa, on the coasts of the Caspian and Persian Gulf, on the Ganges, in Upper Egypt and Abyssinia (*ib.* 814). Dr. Mead refers Herod's disease to *ἐντερίζω,* or intestinal worms. Shapter, without due foundation, objects that the

word in that case should have been not *σκώληξ,* but *εὐλή* (*Medica Sacra,* p. 188).

[f] It has been much debated whether the smallpox be an ancient disease. On the whole, perhaps, the arguments in favor of its not being such predominate, chiefly on account of the strongly marked character of the symptoms, which makes the negative argument of unusual weight.

שְׁחִין אֲבַעְבֻּעֹת פֹּרֵחַ.

[h] This is Dr. Robert Sim's opinion. On comparing, however, the means used to produce the disorder (Ex. ix. 8), an analogy is perceptible to what is called " bricklayer's itch," and therefore to leprosy. [LÆROST.] A disease involving a white spot breaking forth from a boil related to leprosy, and clean or unclean according to symptoms specified, occurs under the general *locus* of leprosy (Lev. xiii. 18–23).

The "withered hand" of Jeroboam (1 K. xiii. 4-6), and of the man Matt. xii. 10-13 (comp. Luke vi. 10), is such an effect as is known to follow from the obliteration of the main artery of any member, or from paralysis of the principal nerve, either through disease or through injury. A case with a symptom exactly parallel to that of Jeroboam is mentioned in the life of Gabriel, an Arab physician. It was that of a woman whose hand had become rigid in the act of swinging,[a] and remained in the extended posture. The most remarkable feature in the case, as related, is the remedy, which consisted in alarm acting on the nerves, inducing a sudden and spontaneous effort to use the limb — an effort which, like that of the dumb son of Croesus (Herod. i. 85), was paradoxically successful. The case of the widow's son restored by Elisha (2 K. iv. 19) was probably one of sunstroke.

The disease of Asa "in his feet" (Schmidt, Biblischer Med. iii. 5, § 2), which attacked him in his old age (1 K. xv. 23; 2 Chr. xvi. 12) and became exceeding great, may have been either œdema, swelling, or podagra, gout. The former is common in aged persons, in whom, owing to the difficulty of the return upwards of the sluggish blood, its watery part stays in the feet. The latter, though rare in the East at present, is mentioned by the Talmudists (Sotah, 10 a, and Sanhedrin, 48 b), and there is no reason why it may not have been known in Asa's time. It occurs in Hippocr. Aphor. vi., Prognost. 15; Celsus, iv. 24; Aretæus, Morb. Chron. ii. 12, and other ancient writers.[b]

In 1 Macc. vi. 8, occurs a mention of "sickness of grief;" in Ecclus. xxxvii. 30, of sickness caused by excess, which require only a passing mention. The disease of Nebuchadnezzar has been viewed by Jahn as a mental and purely subjective malady. It is not easy to see how this satisfies the plain emphatic statement of Dan. iv. 33, which seems to include, it is true, mental derangement, but to assert a degraded bodily state[c] to some extent, and a corresponding change of habits. We may regard it as Mead (Med. Sacr. vii.), following Burton's Anatomy of Melancholy, does, as a species of the melancholy known as Lycanthropia[d] (Paulus Ægin. iii. 16; Avicenna, iii. 1, 5, 22). Persons so affected wander like wolves in sepulchres by night, and imitate the howling of a wolf or a dog. Further, there are well-attested accounts of wild or half-wild human creatures, of either sex, who have lived as beasts, losing human consciousness, and acquiring a superhuman ferocity, activity, and swiftness. Either the lycanthropic patients or these latter may furnish a partial analogy to Nebuchadnezzar, in regard to the various points of modified outward appearance and habits ascribed to him. Nor would

it seem impossible that a sustained lycanthropia might produce this latter condition.

Here should be noticed the mental malady of Saul.[e] His melancholy seems to have had its origin in his sin; it was therefore grounded in his moral nature, but extended its effects, as commonly, to the intellectual. The "evil spirit from God," whatever it mean, was no part of the medical features of his case, and may therefore be excluded from the present notice. Music, which soothed him for a while, has entered largely into the milder modern treatment of lunacy.

The palsy meets us in the N. T. only, and in features too familiar to need special remark. The words "grievously tormented" (Matt. viii. 6) have been commented on by Baier (de Paral. 39), to the effect that examples of acutely painful paralysis are not wanting in modern pathology, e. g. when paralysis is complicated with neuralgia. But if this statement be viewed with doubt, we might understand the Greek expression (βασανιζόμενος) as used of paralysis agitans, or even of chorea[f] (St. Vitus' dance), in both of which the patient, being never still for a moment save when asleep, might well be so described. The woman's case who was "bowed together" by "a spirit of infirmity," may probably have been paralytic (Luke xiii. 11). If the dorsal muscles were affected, those of the chest and abdomen, from want of resistance, would undergo contraction, and thus cause the patient to suffer as described.

Gangrene (γάγγραινα, Celsus, vii. 33, de gangrenâ), or mortification in its various forms, is a totally different disorder from the "canker" of the A. V. in 2 Tim. ii. 17. Both gangrene and cancer were common in all the countries familiar to the Scriptural writers, and neither differs from the modern disease of the same name (Dr. M. Good, ii. 669, &c., and 579, &c.).

In Is. xxvi. 18; Ps. vii. 14, there seems an allusion to false conception, in which, though attended by pains of quasi-labor and other ordinary symptoms, the womb has been found unimpregnated, and no delivery has followed. The medical term (Dr. M. Good, iv. 188) ἐμπνευμάτωσις, mola ventosa, suggests the Scriptural language, "we have as it were brought forth wind;" the whole passage is figurative for disappointment after great effort.[g]

Poison, as a means of destroying life, hardly occurs in the Bible, save as applied to arrows (Job vi. 4). In Zech. xii. 2, the marg. gives "poison" as an alternative rendering, which does not seem preferable; intoxication being probably meant. In the annals of the Herods poisons occur as the resource of stealthy murder.[h]

---

[a] "Inter jactandum se funibus ... remansit illa (manus) extensa, ita ut retrahere ipsam nequiret (Freind's Hist. Med. ii. Append. p. 2).

[b] Seneca mentions it (Epist. 95) as an extreme note of the female depravity current in his own time, that even the female sex has become liable to gout.

[c] The "eagles' feathers" and "birds' claws" are probably used only in illustration, not necessarily as describing a new type to which the hair, etc., approximated. Comp. the simile of Ps. ciii. 5, and that of 2 K. v. 14.

[d] Comp. Virg. Bucol. viii. 97: —

"Sæpe lupum fieri et se condere silvis."

[e] The Targ. of Jonathan renders the Heb. וַיִּתְהַלֵּל, 1 Sam. x. 10, by "he was mad or insane" (Jahn, Upham's transl. 212-13).

[f] Jahn (Upham's transl. 232) suggests that cramp, twisting the limb round as if in torture, may have been intended. This suits βασανιζόμενος, no doubt, but not παραλύτικος.

[g] For an account of the complaint, see Paul Ægin., ed. Syd. Soc. i. p. 632.

[h] In Chwolson's Ueberreste d. Altbab. Literatur, I 129, Ibn Wahschijjah's treatise on poisons contains references to several older writings by authors of other nations on that subject. His commentator, Jârbûqâ, treats of the existence and effects of poisons and antidotes, and in an independent work of his own thus classifies the subject: (1) of poisons which kill at sight (wenn sie man nur ansieht); (2) of those which kill through sound (Schall oder Laut); (3) of those which kill by smelling; (4) of those which kill by reaching the interior of the body; (5) of those which

The bite or sting of venomous beasts can hardly be treated as a disease; but in connection with the "fiery (i. e. venomous) serpents" of Num. xxi. 6, and the deliverance from death of those bitten, it deserves a notice. Even the Talmud acknowledges that the healing power lay not in the brazen serpent itself, but "as soon as they feared the Most High, and uplifted their hearts to their Heavenly Father, they were healed, and in default of this were brought to nought." Thus the brazen figure was symbolical only; or, according to the lovers of purely natural explanation, was the stage-trick to cover a false miracle. It was customary to consecrate the image of the affliction, either in its cause or in its effect, as in the golden emerods, golden mice, of 1 Sam. vi. 4, 8, and in the ex-votos common in Egypt even before the exodus; and these may be compared with this setting up of the brazen serpent. Thus we have in it only an instance of the current custom, fanciful or superstitious, being sublimed to a higher purpose.

The bite of a white she-mule, perhaps in the rutting season, is according to the Talmudists fatal; and they also mention that of a mad dog, with certain symptoms by which to discern his state (Wunderbar, ut sup. 21). The scorpion and centipede are natives of the Levant (Rev. ix. 5, 10), and, with a large variety of serpents, swarm there. To these, according to Lichtenstein, should be added a venomous solpuga,[a] or large spider, similar to the Calabrian Tarantula; but the passage in Pliny[b] adduced (H. N. xxix. 29), gives no satisfactory ground for the theory based upon it, that its bite was the cause of the emerods.[c] It is, however, remarkable that Pliny mentions with some fullness, a mus araneus — not a spider resembling a mouse, but a mouse resembling a spider — the shrew-mouse, and called araneus, Isidorus[d] says from this resemblance, or from its eating spiders. Its bite was venomous, caused mortification of the part, and a spreading ulcer attended with inward griping pains, and when crushed on the wound was its own best antidote.[e]

The disease of old age has acquired a place in Biblical nosology chiefly owing to the elegant allegory into which "The Preacher" throws the successive tokens of the ravage of time on man (Eccl. xii.). The symptoms enumerated have each their significance for the physician, for, though his art can do little to arrest them, they yet mark an altered condition calling for a treatment of its own. "The Preacher" divides the sum of human existence into that period which involves every mode of growth, and that which involves every mode of decline. The first reaches from the point of birth or even of generation, onwards to the attainment of the "grand climacteric," and the second from that epoch backwards through a corresponding period of decline till the point of dissolution is reached.[f] This latter course is marked in metaphor by the darkening of the great lights of nature, and the ensuing season of life is compared to the broken weather of the wet season, setting in when summer is gone, when after every shower fresh clouds are in the sky, as contrasted with the showers of other seasons, which pass away into clearness. Such he means are the ailments and troubles of declining age, as compared with those of advancing life. The "keepers of the house" are perhaps the ribs which support the frame, or the arms and shoulders which enwrap and protect it. Their "trembling," especially that of the arms, etc., is a sure sign of vigor past. The "strong men" are its supporters, the lower limbs "bowing themselves" under the weight they once so lightly bore. The "grinding" hardly needs to be explained of the teeth now become "few." The "lookers from the windows" are the pupils of the eyes, now "darkened," as Isaac's were, and Eli's; and Moses, though spared the dimness, was yet in that very exemption a marvel (Gen. xxvii., comp. xlviii. 10; 1 Sam. iv. 15; Deut. xxxiv. 7). The "doors shut" represent the dullness of those other senses which are the portals of knowledge; thus the taste and smell, as in the case of Barzillai, become impaired, and the ears stopped against sound. The "rising up at the voice of a bird" portrays the light, soon-fleeting, easily-broken slumber of the aged man; or possibly, and more literally, actual waking in the early morning, when first the cock crows, may be intended. The "daughters of music brought low," suggest the

——— "Big manly voice
Now turn'd again to childish treble;"

and also, as illustrated again by Barzillai, the failure in the discernment and the utterance of musical notes. The fears of old age are next noticed: "They shall be afraid of that which is high;[g] an

---

kill by contact, with special mention of the poisoning of garments.

[a] Comp. Lucan, Pharsalia, ix. 837-8: "Quis calcare teas timeat solpuga latebras," etc.

[b] His words are: "Est et formicarum genus venenatum, non fere in Italiâ: solpugas Cicero appellat."

[c] He says that the solpuga causes such swellings on the parts of the female camel, and that they are called by the same word in Arabic as the Heb. עֲפָלִים, which simply means "swellings." He supposes the men might have been "versetzt bei der Befriedigung natürlicher Bedürfnisse." He seems not to have given due weight to the expression of 1 Sam. vi. 5, "mice which mar the land," which seems to distinguish the "land" from the people in a way fatal to the ingenious notion he supports. For the multiplication of these and similar creatures to an extraordinary and fatal degree, comp. Varro, Fragm. ap. fin. "M. Varro auctor est, a cuniculis suffossum in Hispaniâ oppidum, a talpis in Thessaliâ, ab ranis civitatem in Galliâ pulsam, ab locustis in Africâ, ex Gyaro Cycladum insulâ incolas a muribus fugatos."

[d] His words are: "Mus araneus cujus morsu araneo

moritur est in Sardiniâ animal perexiguum araneae formâ quae solifuga dicitur, eo quod diem fugiat" (Orig. xii. 3).

[e] As regards the scorpion, this belief and practice still prevails in Palestine. Pliny says (H. N. xxix 27), after prescribing the ashes of a ram's hoof, young of a weasel, etc., "si jumenta momorderit mus (i. e. araneus) recens cum sale imponitur, aut fel vespertilionis ex aceto. Et ipse mus araneus contra se remedio est divulsus et impositus," etc. In cold climates, it seems, the venom of the shrew-mouse is not perceptible.

[f] These are respectively called the יְמֵי הָעֲלִיָּה and the יְמֵי הָעֲמִידָה of the Rabbins (Wunderbar. 2tes Heft). The same idea appears in Soph. Trachin.

[g] Or, even more simply, these words may be understood as meaning that old men have neither vigor nor breath for going up hills, mountains, or anything else that is "high;" nay, for them the plain, even road has its terrors — they walk timidly and cautiously even along that.

obscure expression, perhaps, for what are popularly called "nervous" terrors, exaggerating and magnifying every object of alarm, and "making," as the saying is, "mountains of molehills." "Fear in the way" [a] is at first less obvious; but we observe, that nothing unnerves and agitates an old person more than the prospect of a long journey. Thus regarded, it becomes a fine and subtile touch in the description of decrepitude. All readiness to haste is arrested, and a numb despondency succeeds. The "flourishing" of "the almond-tree" is still more obscure; but we observe this tree in Palestine blossoming when others show no sign of vegetation, and when it is dead winter all around — no ill type, perhaps, of the old man who has survived his own contemporaries and many of his juniors.[b] Youthful lusts die out, and their organs, of which "the grasshopper" [c] is perhaps a figure, are relaxed. The "silver cord" may be that of nervous sensation,[d] or motion, or even the spinal marrow itself. Perhaps some incapacity of retention may be signified by the "golden bowl broken;" the "pitcher broken at the well" suggests some vital supply stopping at the usual source — derangement perhaps of the digestion or of the respiration; the "wheel shivered at the cistern," conveys, through the image of the water-lifting process familiar in irrigation, the notion of the blood, pumped, as it were, through the vessels, and fertilizing the whole system; for "the blood is the life."

This careful register of the tokens of decline might lead us to expect great care for the preservation of health and strength; and this indeed is found to mark the Mosaic system, in the regulations concerning diet, [e] the "divers washings," and the pollution imputed to a corpse — nay, even in circumcision itself. These served not only the ceremonial purpose of imparting self-consciousness to the Hebrew, and keeping him distinct from alien admixture, but had a sanitary aspect of rare wisdom, when we regard the country, the climate, and the age. The laws of diet had the effect of tempering by a just admixture of the organic substances of the animal and vegetable kingdoms the regimen of Hebrew families, and thus providing for the vigor of future ages, as well as checking the stimulus which the predominant use of animal food gives to the passions. To these effects may be ascribed the immunity often enjoyed by the Hebrew race[f] amidst epidemics devastating the countries of their sojourn. The best and often the sole possible exercise of medicine is to prevent disease. Moses could not legislate for cure, but his rules did for the great mass of the people what no therapeutics however consummate could do, — they gave the best security for the public health by provisions incor-

porated in the public economy. Whether we regard the laws which secluded the leper, as designed to prevent infection or repress the dread of it, their wisdom is nearly equal, for of all terrors the imaginary are the most terrible. The laws restricting marriage have in general a similar tendency, degeneracy being the penalty of a departure from those which forbid commixture of near kin. Michel Lévy remarks on the salubrious tendency of the law of marital separation (Lev. xv.) imposed (Lévy, Traité d'Hygiène, p. 8). The precept also concerning purity on the necessary occasions in a desert encampment (Deut. xxiii. 12–14), enjoining the return of the elements of productiveness to the soil, would probably become the basis of the municipal regulations having for their object a similar purity in towns. The consequences of its neglect in such encampments is shown by an example quoted by Michel Lévy, as mentioned by M. de Lamartine (ib. 8, 9). Length of life was regarded as a mark of divine favor, and the divine legislator had pointed out the means of ordinarily insuring a fuller measure of it to the people at large than could, according to physical laws, otherwise be hoped for. Perhaps the extraordinary means taken to prolong vitality may be referred to this source (1 K. i. 2), and there is no reason why the case of David should be deemed a singular one. We may also compare the apparent influence of vital warmth enhanced to a miraculous degree, but having, perhaps, a physical law as its basis, in the cases of Elijah, Elisha, and the sons of the widow of Zarephath, and the Shunammite. Wunderbar [g] has collected several examples of such influence similarly exerted, which however he seems to exaggerate to an absurd pitch. Yet it would seem not against analogy to suppose, that, as pernicious exhalations, miasmata, etc., may pass from the sick and affect the healthy, so there should be a reciprocal action in favor of health. The climate of Palestine afforded a great range of temperature within a narrow compass, — e. g. a long sea-coast, a long deep valley (that of the Jordan), a broad flat plain (Esdraelon), a large portion of table-land (Judah and Ephraim), and the higher elevations of Carmel, Tabor, the lesser and greater Hermon, etc. Thus it partakes of nearly all supportable climates.[h] In October its rainy season begins with moist westerly winds. In November the trees are bare. In December snow and ice are often found, but never lie long, and only during the north wind's prevalence. The cold disappears at the end of February, and the "latter rain" sets in, lasting through March to the middle of April, when thunder-storms are common, torrents swell, and the heat rises in the low grounds. At the end of April the hot season begins, but preserves moderation till

---

[a] Compare also perhaps the dictum of the slothful man, Prov. xxii. 13, "There is a lion in the way."

[b] In the same strain Juvenal (Sat. x. 243-5) says :

"Hæc data pœna diu viventibus, ut renovatâ
Semper clade domus, multis in luctibus inque
Perpetuo mœrore et nigrâ veste senescant."

[c] Dr. Mead (Med. Sacr. vii.) thinks that the scrotum, swoln by a rupture, is perhaps meant to be typified by the shape of the grasshopper. He renders the Hebrew וְיִסְתַּבֵּל הֶחָגָב after the LXX. ἐπαχύνθη ἡ ἀκρίς, Vulg. impinguabitur locusta. Comp. Hor. Odes, ii. xi. 7, 8.

[d] We find hints of the nerves proceeding in pairs from the brain, both in the Talmudical writers and in Aretæus. See below in the text.

[e] Michel Lévy quotes Hallé as acknowledging the salutary character of the prohibition to eat pork, which he says is "sujet à une altération du tissu graisseux très analogue à la dégénérescence lépreuse."

[f] This was said of the Jews in London during the cholera attack of 1849.

[g] Biblisch-Talmud. Med. 2tes Heft, I. D. pp. 15-17. He speaks of the result ensuing from shaking hands with one's friends, etc.

[h] The possession of an abundance of salt tended to banish much disease (Ps. lx. (title) ; 2 Sam. viii. 13 ; 1 Chr. xviii. 12). Salt-pits (Zeph. ii. 9) are still dug by the Arabs on the shore of the Dead Sea. For the use of salt to a new-born infant, Ez. xvi. 4, comp. Galen de Sanit. lib. i. cap. 7.

June, thence till September becomes extreme; and during all this period rain seldom occurs, but often heavy dews prevail. In September it commences to be cool, first at night, and sometimes the rain begins to fall at the end of it. The migration with the season from an inland to a sea-coast position, from low to high ground, etc., was a point of social development never systematically reached during the Scriptural history of Palestine. But men inhabiting the same regions for centuries could hardly fail to notice the connection between the air and moisture of a place and human health, and those favored by circumstances would certainly turn their knowledge to account. The Talmudists speak of the north wind as preservative of life, and the south and east winds as exhaustive, but the south as the most insupportable of all, coming hot and dry from the deserts, producing abortion, tainting the babe yet unborn, and corroding the pearls in the sea. Further, they dissuade from performing circumcision or venesection during its prevalence (*Jebamoth*, 72 a, ap. Wunderbar, 2tes Heft, ii. A.). It is stated that " the marriage-bed placed between north and south will be blessed with male issue " (*Berachoth*, 14, ib.), which may, Wunderbar thinks, be interpreted of the temperature when moderate, and in neither extreme (which these winds respectively represent), as most favoring fecundity. If the fact be so, it is more probably related to the phenomena of magnetism, in connection with which the same theory has been lately revived. A number of precepts are given by the same authorities in reference to health, e. g. eating slowly, not contracting a sedentary habit, regularity in natural operations, cheerfulness of temperament, due sleep (especially early morning sleep is recommended, but not somnolence by day (Wunderbar, ut sup.).

The rite of circumcision, besides its special surgical operation, deserves some notice in connection with the general question of the health, longevity, and fecundity of the race with whose history it is identified. Besides being a mark of the covenant and a symbol of purity, it was perhaps also a protest against the phallus-worship, which has a remote antiquity in the corruption of mankind, and of which we have some trace in the Egyptian myth of Osiris. It has been asserted also (Wunderbar, 3tes Heft, p. 25), that it distinctly contributed to increase the fruitfulness of the race, and to check inordinate desires in the individual. Its beneficial effects in such a climate as that of Egypt and Syria, as tending to promote cleanliness, to prevent or reduce irritation, and thereby to stop the way against various disorders, have been the subject of comment to various writers on hygiene.[a] In particular a troublesome and sometimes fatal kind of boil (*phy-*

mosis and *paraphymosis*) is mentioned as occurring commonly in those regions, but only to the uncircumcised. It is stated by Josephus (*Cont. Ap.* ii. 13) that Apion, against whom he wrote, having at first derided circumcision, was circumcised of necessity by reason of such a boil, of which, after suffering great pain, he died. Philo also appears to speak of the same benefit when he speaks of the " anthrax " infesting those who retain the foreskin. Medical authorities have also stated that the capacity of imbibing syphilitic virus is less, and that this has been proved experimentally by comparing Jewish with other, e. g. Christian populations (Wunderbar, 3tes Heft, p. 27). The operation itself[b] consisted of originally a mere[c] incision; to which a further stripping[d] off the skin from the part, and a custom of sucking[e] the blood from the wound was in a later period added, owing to the attempts of Jews of the Maccabean period, and later (1 Macc. i. 15; Joseph. *Ant.* xii. 5, § 1: comp. 1 Cor. vii. 18) to cultivate heathen practices. [CIRCUMCISION.] The reduction of the remaining portion of the *præputium* after the more simple operation, so as to cover what it had exposed, known as *epispasmus*, accomplished by the elasticity of the skin itself, was what this anti-Judaic practice sought to effect, and what the later, more complicated and severe, operation frustrated. To these were subjoined the use of the warm-bath, before and after the operation, pounded cummin as a styptic, and a mixture of wine and oil to heal the wound. It is remarkable that the tightly swathed rollers which formed the first covering of the newborn child (Luke ii. 7) are still retained among modern Jews at the circumcision of a child, effectually preventing any movement of the body or limbs (Wunderbar,[f] p. 29). No surgical operation beyond this finds a place in Holy Scripture, unless indeed that adverted to under the article Eunuch. [EUNUCH.] The Talmudists speak of two operations to assist birth, one known as קריעה הדופן (*gastrotomia*), and intended to assist parturition, not necessarily fatal to the mother; the other known as קריעת הבמן (*hysterotomia*, *sectio cæsarea*), which was seldom practiced save in the case of death in the crisis of labor, or if attempted on the living, was either fatal, or at least destructive of the powers of maternity. An operation is also mentioned by the same authorities having for its object the extraction piecemeal of an otherwise inextricable fœtus (*ibid.* pp. 53, &c.). Wunderbar enumerates from the Mishna and Talmud fifty-six surgical instruments or pieces of apparatus; of these, however, the following only are at all alluded to in Scripture.[g] A cutting in-

---

[a] See some remarks in Michel Lévy, *Traité d'Hygiène*, Paris, 1850 : " Rien de plus rebutant que cette sorte de malpropreté, rien de plus favorable au développement des accidents syphilitiques." Circumcision is said to be also practiced among the natives of Madagascar, " qui ne paraissent avoir aucune notion du Judaïsme ni du Mahométisme " (p. 11, note).

[b] There is a good modern account of circumcision in the *Dublin Medical Press*, May 19, 1858, by Dr. Joseph Hirschfeld (from *Oestereich. Zeitschrift*).

[c] Known as the חָתָךְ, a word meaning " cut."

[d] Called the פְּרִיעַ, from פָּרַע, " to expose."

[e] Called *Mezize*, from מָצַץ, " to suck." This counteracted a tendency to inflammation.

[f] This writer gives a full account of the entire process as now in practice, with illustrations from the Turkish mode of operating, gathered, it seems, from a fragment of a rare work on the healing art by an anonymous Turkish author of the 16th century, in the public library at Leipsic. The Persians, Tartars, etc., have furnished him with further illustrations.

[g] Yet it by no means follows that the rest were not known in Scriptural times, " it being a well-known fact in the history of inventions that many useful discoveries have long been kept as family secrets." Thus an obstetrical forceps was found in a house excavated at Pompeii, though the Greeks and Romans, so far as their medical works show, were unacquainted with the instrument (*Paul. Æg.* i. 652, ed. Sydenham Soc.).

strument, called צוּר, supposed a "sharp stone" (Ex. iv. 25). Such was probably the Æthiopian stone" mentioned by Herodotus (ii. 86), and Pliny speaks of what he calls *Testa samia*, as a similar implement. Zipporah seems to have caught up the first instrument which came to hand in her apprehension for the life of her husband. The " knife " (מַאֲכֶלֶת) of Josh. v. 2 was probably a more refined instrument for the same purpose. An " awl " (מַרְצֵעַ) is mentioned (Ex. xxi. 6) as used to bore through the ear of the bondman who refused release, and is supposed to have been a surgical instrument.

A seat of delivery called in Scripture אָבְנָיִם, Ex. i. 16, by the Talmudists מַשְׁבֵּר (comp. 2 K. xix. 3), " the stools; " but some have doubted whether the word used by Moses does not mean rather the uterus itself as that which moulds [a] and shapes the infant. Delivery upon a seat or stool is, however, a common practice in France at this day, and also in Palestine.

The "roller to bind" of Ez. xxx. 21 was for a broken limb, as still used. Similar bands wound with the most precise accuracy involve the mummies.

A scraper (חֶרֶשׂ), for which the "potsherd" of Job was a substitute (Job ii. 8).

Ex. xxx. 23-5 is a prescription in form. It may be worth while also to enumerate the leading substances which, according to Wunderbar, composed the pharmacopœia of the Talmudists — a much more limited one — which will afford some insight into the distance which separates them from the leaders of Greek medicine. Besides such ordinary appliances as water, wine (Luke x. 34), beer, vinegar, honey, and milk, various oils are found; as opobalsamum[b] (" balm of Gilead "), the oil of olive,[c] myrrh, rose, palma christi, walnut, sesamum, colocynth, and fish; figs (2 K. xx. 7), dates, apples (Cant. ii. 5), pomegranates, pistachio-nuts,[d] and almonds (a produce of Syria, but not of Egypt, Gen. xliii. 11); wheat, barley, and various other grains; garlic, leeks, onions, and some other common herbs; mustard, pepper, coriander seed, ginger, preparations of beet, fish, etc., steeped in wine or vinegar; whey, eggs, salt, wax, and suet (in plaisters), gall of fish [e] (Tob. vi. 8, xi. 11), ashes, cowdung, etc.; fasting-saliva,[f] urine, bat's blood, and the following rarer herbs, etc.: *ammeisision, menta gentilis*, saffron, mandragora, *Lawsonia spinosa* (Arab. *alhenna*), juniper, broom, poppy, acacia, pine, lavender or rosemary, clover-root, jujub, hyssop, fern, *sampsuchum*, milk-thistle, laurel, *Eruca*

muralis, absynth, jasmine, narcissus, madder, curled mint, fennel, endive, oil of cotton, myrtle, myrrh, aloes, sweet cane (*Acorus calamus*), cinnamon, *cinella alba*, cassia, *ladanum, galbanum*, frankincense, *storax*, nard, gum of various trees, musk, *blatta byzantina*; and these minerals — bitumen, natrum, borax, alum, clay, aëtites,[g] quicksilver, litharge, yellow arsenic. The following preparations were also well known: *Theriacas*, an antidote prepared from serpents; various medicinal drinks, e. g. from the fruit-bearing rosemary; decoction of wine with vegetables; mixture of wine, honey, and pepper; of oil, wine, and water; of asparagus and other roots steeped in wine; emetics, purging draughts, soporifics, potions to produce abortion or fruitfulness; and various salves, some used cosmetically,[h] e. g. to remove hair; some for wounds, and other injuries.[i] The forms of medicaments were cataplasm, electuary, liniment, plaister (Is. i. 6; Jer. viii. 22, xlvi. 11, li. 8; Joseph. B. J. i. 33, § 5), powder, infusion, decoction, essence, syrup, mixture.

An occasional trace occurs of some chemical knowledge, e. g. the calcination of the gold by Moses; the effect of " vinegar upon nitre " [k] (Ex. xxxii. 20; Prov. xxv. 20; comp. Jer. ii. 22); the mention of " the apothecary " (Ex. xxx. 35; Eccl. x. 1), and of the merchant in " powders " (Cant. iii. 6), shows that a distinct and important branch of trade was set up in these wares, in which, as at a modern druggist's, articles of luxury, etc., are combined with the remedies of sickness; see further, Wunderbar, 1stes Heft, pp. 73, *ad fin.* Among the most favorite of external remedies has always been the bath. As a preventive of numerous disorders its virtues were known to the Egyptians, and the scrupulous levitical bathings prescribed by Moses would merely enjoin the continuance of a practice familiar to the Jews, from the example especially of the priests in that country. Besides the significance of moral purity which it carried, the use of the bath checked the tendency to become unclean by violent perspirations from within and effluvia from without; it kept the porous system in play, and stopped the outset of much disease. In order to make the sanction of health more solemn, most oriental nations have enforced purificatory rites by religious mandates — and so the Jews. A treatise collecting all the dicta of ancient medicine on the use of the bath has been current ever since the revival of learning, under the title *De Balneis*. According to it Hippocrates and Galen prescribe the bath medicinally in peripneumonia rather than in burning fever, as tending to allay the pain of the sides, chest, and back, promoting various secretions, removing lassitude, and suppling joints. A hot bath is recommended for those suffering

---

[a] In Jer. xviii. 3 the same word appears, rendered " wheels " in the A. V.; margin, " frames or seats; " that which gives shape to the work of the potter.

[b] See Tacit. *Hist.* v. 7, and Orelli's note *ad loc.*

[c] Tacitus, *ibid.* v. 6.

[d] Commended by Pliny as a specific for the bite of a serpent (Plin. *H. N.* xxiii. 78).

[e] Rhases speaks of a fish named *sabot*, the gall of which healed inflamed eyes (ix. 27); and Pliny says, " Callionymi fel cicatrices sanat et carnes oculorum supervacuas consumit " (N. H. xxxii. 24).

[f] Comp. Mark viii. 23, John. ix. 6; also the mention by Tacitus (*Hist.* iv. 81) of a request made of Vespasian at Alexandria. Galen (*De Simpl. Facult.*

[i]. 10) and Pliny (H. N. xxviii. 7) ascribe similar virtues to it.

[g] Said by Pliny to be a specific against abortion (N. H. xxx. 44).

[h] Antimony was and is used as a dye for the eyelids, the *kohol*. See Rosenmüller in the *Biblical Cabinet*, xxvii. 65.

[i] The Arabs suppose that a cornelian stone (the *Sardius lapis*, Ex. xxviii. 13, but in Joseph. *Ant.* iii. 7, § 5, *Sardonyx*), laid on a fresh wound, will stay hemorrhage.

[k] נֶתֶר meaning natron: the Egyptian kind was found in two lakes between Naukratis and Memphis (*Bibl. Cab.* xxvii. p. 7).

from aches (*De Baln.* 464). These, on the contrary, who have looseness of the bowels, who are languid, loathe their food, are troubled with nausea or bile, should not use it, as neither should the epileptic. After exhausting journeys in the sun the bath is commended as the restorative of moisture to the frame (456–458). The four objects which ancient authorities chiefly proposed to attain by bathing are — 1, to warm and distil the elements of the body throughout the whole frame, to equalize whatever is abnormal, to rarefy the skin, and promote evacuations through it; 2, to reduce a dry to a moister habit; 3 (the cold-bath), to cool the frame and brace it; 4 (the warm-bath), a sudorific to expel cold. Exercise before bathing is recommended, and in the season from April till November inclusive it is the most conducive to health; if it be kept up in the other months it should then be but once a week, and that fasting. Of natural waters some are nitrous, some saline, some aluminous,[a] some sulphureous, some bituminous, some copperish, some ferruginous, and some compounded of these. Of all the natural waters the power is, on the whole, desiccant and calefacient; and they are peculiarly fitted for those of a humid and cold habit. Pliny (*H. N.* xxxi.) gives the fullest extant account of the thermal springs of the ancients (*Paul. Ægin.* ed. Sydenh. Soc. i. 71). Avicenna gives precepts for salt and other mineral baths; the former he recommends in case of scurvy and itching, as rarefying the skin, and afterwards condensing it. Water medicated with alum, natron, sulphur, naphtha, iron, litharge, vitriol, and vinegar, are also specified by him. Friction and unction are prescribed, and a caution given against staying too long in the water (*ibid.* 338–340; comp. Aëtius, *de Baln.* iv. 484). A sick bather should lie quiet, and allow others to rub and anoint him, and use no strigil (the common instrument for scraping the skin), but a sponge (456). Maimonides chiefly following Galen, recommends the bath, especially for phthisis in the aged, as being a case of dryness with cold habit, and to a hectic fever patient as being a case of dryness with hot habit; also in cases of ephemeral and tertian fevers, under certain restrictions, and in putrid fevers, with the caution not to incur shivering. Bathing is dangerous to those who feel pain in the liver after eating. He adds cautions regarding the kind of water, but these relate chiefly to water for drinking (*De Baln.* 438, 439). The bath of oil was formed, according to Galen and Aëtius, by adding the fifth part of heated oil to a water-bath. Josephus speaks (*B. J.* i. 33, § 5) as though oil had, in Herod's case, been used pure.

There were special occasions on which the bath was ceremonially enjoined, after a leprous eruption healed, after the conjugal act, or an involuntary emission, or any gonorrhœal discharge, after menstruation, child-bed, or touching a corpse; so for the priests before and during their times of office such a duty was prescribed. [BATHS.] The Pharisees and Essenes aimed at scrupulous strictness of all such rules (Matt. xv. 2; Mark vii. 5;

Luke xi. 38). River-bathing[b] was common, but houses soon began to include a bath-room (Lev. xv. 13; 2 K. v. 10; 2 Sam. xi. 2; Susanna, p. 15). Vapor-baths, as among the Romans, were latterly included in these, as well as hot and cold-bath apparatus, and the use of perfumes and oils after quitting it was everywhere diffused (Wunderbar, 2tes Heft, ii. B.). The vapor was sometimes sought to be inhaled, though this was reputed mischievous to the teeth. It was deemed healthiest after a warm to take also a cold bath (*Paul. Ægin.* ed. Sydenh. Soc. i. 68). The Talmud has it — "Whoso takes a warm-bath, and does not also drink thereupon some warm water, is like a stove hot only from without, but not heated also from within. Whoso bathes and does not withal anoint is like the liquor outside a vat. Whoso having had a warm-bath does not also immediately pour cold water over him, is like an iron made to glow in the fire, but not thereafter hardened in the water." This succession of cold water to hot vapor is commonly practiced in Russian and Polish baths, and is said to contribute much to robust health (Wunderbar, *ibid.*).

Besides the usual authorities on Hebrew antiquities, Talmudical and modern, Wunderbar (1stes Heft, pp. 57–69) has compiled a collection of writers on the special subject of Scriptural etc. medicine, including its psychological and botanical aspects, as also its political relations: a distinct section of thirteen monographs treats of the leprosy; and every various disease mentioned in Scripture appears elaborated in one or more such short treatises. Those out of the whole number which appear most generally in esteem, to judge from references made to them, are the following: —

Rosenmüller's *Natural History of the Bible*, in the *Biblical Cabinet*, vol. xxvii. De Wette, *Hebräisch-jüdische Archäologie*, § 271 b. Calmet, Augustin, *La Médecine et les Médicins des anc. Hébreux*, in his *Comm. littéral*, Paris, 1724, vol. v. Idem, *Dissertation sur la Sueur du Sang*, Luke xxii. 43, 44. Pruner, *Krankheiten des Orients.* Sprengel, Kurt, *De medic. Ebræorum*, Halle, 1789, 8vo. Also, idem, *Beiträge zur Geschichte der Medicin*, Halle, 1794, 8vo. Idem, *Versuch einer pragm. Geschichte der Arzeneikunde*, Halle, 1792–1803, 1821. Also the last edition by Dr. Rosenbaum, Leipzig, 1846, 8vo. i. §§ 37–45. Idem, *Histor. Rei Herbar.* lib. i. cap. i. *Flora Biblica.* Bartholini, Thom., *De morbis biblicis, miscellanea medica*, in Ugolini, vol. xxx. p. 1521. Idem, *Paralytici novi Testamenti*, in Ugolini, vol. xxx. p. 1459. Schmidt, Joh. Jac., *Biblischer Medicus*, Züllichau, 1743, 8vo. p. 761. Kall, *De morbis sacerdot. V. T.* Hafn. 1745, 4to. Reinhard, Chr. Tob. Ephr., *Bibelkrankheiten, welche im Alten Testamente vorkommen*, books i. and ii. 1767, 8vo, p. 384; book v. 1768, 8vo, p. 244. Shapter, Thomas, *Medica Sacra, or Short Expositions of the more important Diseases mentioned in the Sacred Writings*, London, 1834. Wunderbar, R. J., *Biblisch-talmudische Medicin*, in 4 parts, Riga, 1850–53, 8vo. Also new series, 1857. Celsius, Ol., *Hierobotanicon s. de plantis*

---

[a] Dr. Adams (*Paul. Ægin.* ed. Syd. Soc. i. 72) says that the alum of the ancients found in mineral springs cannot have been the alum of modern commerce, since it is very rarely to be detected there; but the *alumen plumeum*, or hair alum, said to consist chiefly of the sulphate of magnesia and iron. The former exists, however, in great abundance in the aluminous spring of the Isle of Wight. The ancient nitre or natron was a native carbonate of soda (*ibid.*).

[b] The case of Naaman may be paralleled by Herod. iv. 90, where we read of the Tearus, a tributary of the Hebrus — λέγεται εἶναι ποταμῶν ἄριστος, τά τε ἄλλα ἐς ἄκεσιν φέροντα, καὶ δὴ καὶ ἀνδράσι καὶ ἵπποισι ψώρην ἀκέσασθαι.

Sacræ Scripturæ dissertationes breves, 2 parts, Upsal. 1745, 1747, 8vo; Amstelod. 1748. Bochart, Sam., Hierozoicon s. bipartitum opus de animalibus Sacræ Scripturæ, London, 1665, fol.; Francf. 1675, fol. Also edited by, and with the notes of, Ern. F. C. Rosenmüller, Lips. 1793, 3 vols. 4to. Spencer, De legibus Hebræorum ritualibus, Tübingen, 1732, fol. Reinhard, Mich. H., De cibis Hebræorum prohibitis; Diss. I. respon. Seb. Müller, Viteb. 1697, 4to; Diss. II. respon. Chr. Liske, ibid. 1697, 4to. Eschenbach, Chr. Ehrenfr., Progr. de lepra Judæorum, Rostock, 1774, 4to, in his Scripta medic. bibl. pp. 17–41. Schilling, G. G., De lepra commentationes, rec. J. D. Hahn, Lugd. Bat. 1788, 8vo. Chamseru, R., Recherches sur le véritable caractère de la lèpre des Hébreux, in Mém. de la Soc. médic. d'émulation de Paris, 1810, iii. 335. Rélation chirurgicale de l'Armée de l'Orient, Paris, 1804. Wedel,[a] Geo. W., De lepra in sacris, Jena, 1715, 4to, in his Exercitat. med. philolog. Cent. II. dec. 4, S. 93–107. Idem, De morb. Hiskia, Jena, 1692, 4to, in his Exercit. med. philol. Cent. I. Dec. 7. Idem, De morbo Jorami exercit. I., II. Jen. 1717, 4to, in his Exercit. med. philol. Cent. II. Dec. 5. Idem, De Saulo energumeno, Jena, 1685, in his Exercitat. med. philol. Cent. I. dec. II. Idem, De morbis senum Solomonæis, Jen. 1686, 4to, in his Exercit. med. phil. Cent. I. Dec. 3. Lichtensteiu, Versuch, etc., in Eichhorn's Allgem. Bibliothek, VI. 407–467. Mead, Dr. R., Medica Sacra, 4to, London. Gudius, G. F., Exercitatio philologica de Hebraica obstetricum origine, in Ugolini, vol. xxx. p. 1061. Kall, De obstetricibus matrum Hebræorum in Ægypto, Hamburg, 1746, 4to. Israels, Dr. A. H.,[b] Tentamen historico-medicum, exhibens collectanea Gynæcologica, quæ ex Talmude Babylonico depromsit, Groningen, 1845, 8vo.   H. H.[c]

MEEDA (Μεεδδά; [Vat. Δεδδα; Ald. Μεεδα:] Meedda) = MEHIDA (1 Esdr. v. 32).

MEGID'DO (מְגִדּוֹן; in Zech. xii. 11, מְגִדּוֹן; [perh. place of troops, Ges.]: in the LXX. [generally] Μαγεδδώ or Μαγεδδών, [but with a number of unimportant variations;] in 1 K. ix. 15 it is Μαγδό: [Mageddo]) was in a very marked position on the southern rim of the plain of ESDRAELON, on the frontier-line (speaking generally) of the territories of the tribes of ISSACHAR and MANASSEH, and commanding one of those passes from the north into the hill-country which were of such critical importance on various occasions in the history of Judæa (τὰς ἀναβάσεις τῆς ὀρεινῆς, ὅτι δι' αὐτῶν ἦν ἡ εἴσοδος εἰς τὴν Ἰουδαίαν, Judith iv. 7).

Megiddo is usually spoken of in connection with TAANACH, and frequently in connection with BETHSHAN and JEZREEL. This combination suggests a wide view alike over Jewish scenery and Jewish history. The first mention occurs in Josh. xii. 21, where Megiddo appears as the city of one of the "thirty and one kings," or petty chieftains, whom Joshua defeated on the west of the Jordan. This was one of the places within the limits of Issachar assigned to Manasseh (Josh. xvii. 11; 1 Chr. vii. 29). But the arrangement gave only an imperfect advantage to the latter tribe, for they did not drive out the Canaanites, and were only able to make them tributary (Josh. xvii. 12, 13; Judg. i. 27, 28). The song of Deborah brings the place vividly before us, as the scene of the great conflict between Sisera and Barak. The chariots of Sisera were gathered "unto the river ['torrent'] of KISHON" (Judg. iv. 13); Barak went down with his men "from Mount TABOR" into the plain (iv. 14); "then fought the kings of Canaan in Taanach by the waters of Megiddo" (v. 19). The course of the Kishon is immediately in front of this position; and the river seems to have been flooded by a storm: hence what follows: "The river ['torrent'] of Kishon swept them away, that ancient river, the river Kishon" (v. 21). Still we do not read of Megiddo being firmly in the occupation of the Israelites, and perhaps it was not really so till the time of Solomon. That monarch placed one of his twelve commissariat officers, named Baana, over "Taanach and Megiddo," with the neighborhood of Beth-shean and Jezreel (1 K. iv. 12). In this reign it appears that some costly works were constructed at Megiddo (ix. 15). These were probably fortifications, suggested by its important military position. All the subsequent notices of the place are connected with military transactions. To this place Ahaziah fled when his unfortunate visit to Joram had brought him into collision with Jehu; and here he died (2 K. ix. 27) within the confines of what is elsewhere called Samaria (2 Chr. xxii. 9).

But the chief historical interest of Megiddo is concentrated in Josiah's death. When Pharaoh-Necho came from Egypt against the King of Assyria, Josiah joined the latter, and was slain at Megiddo (2 K. xxiii. 29), and his body was carried from thence to Jerusalem (ib. 30). The story is told in the Chronicles in more detail (2 Chr. xxxv. 22–24). There the fatal action is said to have taken place "in the valley of Megiddo." The words in the LXX. are, ἐν τῷ πεδίῳ Μαγεδδών. This calamity made a deep and permanent impression on the Jews. It is recounted again in 1 Esdr. i. 25–31, where in the A. V. "the plain of Magiddo" represents the same Greek words. The lamentations for this good king became "an ordinance in Israel" (2 Chr. xxxv. 25). "In all Jewry" they mourned for him, and the lamentation was made perpetual "in all the nation of Israel" (1 Esdr. i. 32). "Their grief was no land-flood of present passion, but a constant channell of continued sorrow, streaming from an annuall fountain" (Fuller's Pisgah Sight of Palestine, p. 165). Thus, in the language of the prophets (Zech. xii. 11), "the mourning of Hadadrimmon in the valley

[a] This writer has several monographs of much interest on detached points, all to be found in his Dissertationes Acad. Medic. Jena, 17th and 18th centuries.

[b] This writer is remarkable for carefully abstaining from any reference to the O. T., even where such would be most apposite.

[c] The writer wishes to acknowledge his obligations to Dr. Rolleston, Linacre Professor of Physiology; Dr. Greenhill of Hastings; Dr. Adams, editor of several of the Sydenham Society's publications; Mr. H. Ramsey of Cheltenham, and Mr. J. Cooper Forster of Guy's Hospital, London, for their kindness in revising and correcting this article, and that on LEPROSY, in their passage through the press; at the same time that he does not wish to imply any responsibility on their part for the opinions or statements contained in them, save so far as they are referred to by name. Dr. Robert Sim has also greatly assisted him with the results of large actual experience in oriental pathology.

(πεδίῳ, LXX.) of Megiddon " becomes a poetical expression for the deepest and most despairing grief; as in the Apocalypse (Rev. xvi. 16) ARMA-GEDDON, in continuance of the same imagery, is presented as the scene of terrible and final conflict. For the Septuagintal version of this passage of Zechariah we may refer to Jerome's note on the passage. "Adadremmon, pro quo LXX. trans-takerunt 'Ροῶνος, urbs est juxta Jesraelem, quæ hoc olim vocabulo nuncupata est, et hodie vocatur Maximianopolis in Campo Mageddon." That the prophet's imagery is drawn from the occasion of Josiah's death there can be no doubt. In Stanley's S. & P. (p. 347) this calamitous event is made very vivid to us by an allusion to the "Egyptian archers, in their long array, so well known from their sculptured monuments." For the mistake in the account of Pharaoh-Necho's campaign in Herodotus, who has evidently put Migdol by mistake for Megiddo (ii. 149), it is enough to refer to Bähr's excursus on the passage. The Egyptian king may have landed his troops at Acre; but it is far more likely that he marched northwards along the coast-plain, and then turned round Carmel into the plain of Eadraelon, taking the left bank of the Kishon, and that there the Jewish king came upon him by the gorge of Megiddo.

The site thus associated with critical passages of Jewish history from Joshua to Josiah has been identified beyond any reasonable doubt. Robinson did not visit this corner of the plain on his first journey, but he was brought confidently to the conclusion that Megiddo was the modern el-Lejjún, which is undoubtedly the Legio of Eusebius and Jerome, an important and well-known place in their day, since they assume it as a central point from which to mark the position of several other places in this quarter (Bib. Res. ii. 328–330). Two of the distances are given thus: 15 miles from Nazareth and 4 from Taanach. There can be no doubt that the identification is substantially correct. The μέγα πεδίον Λεγεῶνος (Onomast. s. v. Γαβα-θῶν) evidently corresponds with the "plain (or valley) of Megiddo " of the O. T. Moreover el-Lejjún is on the caravan-route from Egypt to Damascus, and traces of a Roman road are found near the village. Van de Velde visited the spot in 1852, approaching it through the hills from the S. W.[a] He describes the view of the plain as seen from the highest point between it and the sea, and the huge tells which mark the positions of the "key-fortresses " of the hills and the plain, Taanuk and el-Lejjún, the latter being the most considerable, and having another called Tell Met-sellim, half an hour to the N. W. (Syr. & Pal. i. 350–356). About a month later in the same year Dr. Robinson was there, and convinced himself of the correctness of his former opinion. He too describes the view over the plain, northwards to the wooded hills of Galilee, eastwards to Jezreel, and southwards to Taanach, Tell Metzellim being also mentioned as on a projecting portion of the hills which are continuous with Carmel, the Kishon being just below (Bib. Res. ii. 116–119). Both writers mention a copious stream flowing down this gorge (March and April), and turning some mills before joining the Kishon. Here are probably the "waters of Megiddo" of Judg. v. 19,

though it should be added that by Professor Stanley (S. & P. p. 339) they are supposed rather to be "the pools in the bed of the Kishon " itself. The same author regards the "plain (or valley) of Megiddo " as denoting not the whole of the Esdraelon level, but that broadest part of it which is immediately opposite the place we are describing (pp. 335, 336).

The passage quoted above from Jerome suggests a further question, namely, whether Von Raumer is right in "identifying el-Lejjún also with Maximianopolis, which the Jerusalem Itinerary places at 20 miles from Cæsarea and 10 from Jezreel." Van de Velde (Memoir, p. 333) holds this view to be correct. He thinks he has found the true Hadadrimmon in a place called Rummaneh, "at the foot of the Megiddo-hills, in a notch or valley about an hour and a half S. of Tell Metzellim," and would place the old fortified Megiddo on this tell itself, suggesting further that its name, "the tell of the Governor," may possibly retain a reminiscence of Solomon's officer, Baana the son of Ahilud.

J. S. H.

MEGIDDON, THE VALLEY OF

(בִּקְעַת מְגִדּוֹן [plain of Megiddo rather than valley]: πεδίον ἐκκοπτομένου: campus Mageddon). The extended form of the preceding name. It occurs only in Zech. xii. 11. In two other cases the LXX. [Vat.] retain the n at the end of the name, namely, 2 K. ix. 27, and 2 Chr. xxxv. 22 [Vat. Μαγεδαων, Μαγεδων, but Rom. Alex. in both places Μαγεδδώ], though it is not their general custom. In this passage it will be observed that they have translated the word.

G.

MEHET'ABEEL [4 syl.] (מְהֵיטַבְאֵל [God (El) a benefactor, Fürst]: Μεταβεήλ; Alex. Μεν-ταβεηλ; [Vat. Μειταηλ; FA. Μιταηλ:] Metabeel). Another and less correct form of MEHET-ABEL. The ancestor of Shemaiah the prophet who was hired against Nehemiah by Tobiah and Sanballat (Neh. vi. 10). He was probably of priestly descent; and it is not unlikely that Delaiah, who is called his son, is the same as the head of the 23d course of priests in the reign of David (1 Chr. xxiv. 18).

MEHET'ABEL (מְהֵיטַבְאֵל [see above]: Samaritan Cod. מהיטבאל: Μετεβεήλ: Meetabel). The daughter of Matred, and wife of Hadad, or Hadar, the eighth and last-mentioned king of Edom, who had Pai or Pau for his birthplace or chief city, before royalty was established among the Israelites (Gen. xxxvi. 39). Jerome (de Nomin. Hebr.) writes the name in the form Mettabel, which he renders "quam bonus est Deus."

MEHI'DA (מְחִידָא [one famous, noble]: in Ezr., Μαουδδ, [Comp. Ald.] Alex. Μεϊδδ; in Neh., Μιδδ, [Vat. FA.] Alex. Μεειδα: Mahida), a family of Nethinim, the descendants of Mehida, returned from Babylon with Zerubbabel (Ezr. ii. 52; Neh. vii. 54). In 1 Esdr. the name occurs in the form MEEDA.

ME'HIR (מְחִיר [price, ransom]: Μαχιρ [Vat.]; Alex. Μαχειρ: Mahir), the son of Chelub, the brother of Shuah, or as he is described in .

---

a * The writer of this note had visited the spot ten years before (1842), and confirmed Robinson's conclusion — identifying "the waters of Megiddo," and
116

the modern remains of the ancient Legio (Bibl. Sac. 1843, p. 77; Ritter's Geography of Pal., Gage's translation, iv. 330).
S. W.

the LXX., "Caleb the father of Ascha" (1 Chr. iv. 11). In the Targum of R. Joseph, Mehir appears as "Perug," its Chaldee equivalent, both words signifying "price."

MEHO'LATHITE, THE (הַמְּחֹלָתִי) [patron.]: Alex. ο μοθυλαθειτης; [Rom.] Vat. omit; [Comp. Ald. Μολαθίτης:] *Molathita*), a word occurring once only (1 Sam. xviii. 19), as the description of Adriel, son of Barzillai, to whom Saul's daughter Merab was married. It no doubt denotes that he belonged to a place called Meholah, but whether that was Abel-Meholah afterwards the native place of Elisha, or another, is as uncertain as it is whether Adriel's father was the well-known Barzillai the Gileadite or not.   G.

MEHU'JAEL (מְחוּיָאֵל and מְחִיּיָאֵל) [prob. *smitten of God*]: Μαλελεήλ; [Comp. Ald.] Alex. Μαιήλ: *Mauiaël*), the son of Irad, and fourth in descent from Cain (Gen. iv. 18). Ewald, regarding the genealogies in Gen. iv. and v. as substantially the same, follows the Vat. LXX., considering Mahalaleel as the true reading, and the variation from it the result of careless transcription. It is scarcely necessary to say that this is a gratuitous assumption. The Targum of Onkelos follows the Hebrew even in the various forms which the name assumes in the same verse. The Peshito-Syriac, Vulgate, and a few MSS. retain the former of the two readings; while the Sam. text reads

מידאל, which appears to have been followed by the Aldine and Complutensian editions, and the Alex. MS.   W. A. W.

MEHU'MAN (מְהוּמָן) [perh. *true, faithful*]: 'Αμάν: *Maümam*), one of the seven eunuchs (A. V. "chamberlains,") who served before Ahasuerus (Esth. i. 10). The LXX. appear to have read לְמָהָן for לִמְהוּמָן.

MEHU'NIM (מְעוּנִים, without the article [*inhabitants, dwellers*: Vat.] Μανωεμείν; [Rom. Μοουνίμ:] Alex. Μοουνειμ: *Munim*), Ezr. ii. 50. Elsewhere called MEHUNIMS and MEUNIM; and in the parallel list of 1 Esdr. MEANI.

MEHU'NIMS, THE (הַמְּעוּנִים), i. e. the *Me'ûnim* [Vat.]: οι Μειναιοι [Rom.]; Alex. οι Μιναιοι: *Ammonitœ*), a people against whom king Uzziah waged a successful war (2 Chr. xxvi. 7). Although so different in its English [a] dress, yet the name is in the original merely the plural of MAON

(מָעוֹן), a nation named amongst those who in

the earlier days of their settlement in Palestine harassed and oppressed Israel. Maon, or the Maonites, probably inhabited the country at the back of the great range of Seir, the modern *esh-Sherah*, which forms the eastern side of the *Wady el Arabah*, where at the present day there is still a town of the same name [b] (Burckhardt, *Syria*, Aug. 24). And this is quite in accordance with the terms of 2 Chr. xxvi. 7, where the Mehunim are mentioned with "the Arabians of Gur-baal," or, as the LXX. render it, Petra.

Another notice of the Mehunims in the reign of Hezekiah (cir. B. C. 726–697) is found in 1 Chr. iv. 41.[c] Here they are spoken of as a pastoral people, either themselves Hamites or in alliance with Hamites, quiet and peaceable, dwelling in tents. They had been settled from "of old," i. e. aboriginally, at the east end of the Valley of Gedor or Gerar, in the wilderness south of Palestine. A connection with Mount Seir is hinted at, though obscurely (ver. 42). [See vol. i. p. 879 b.] Here, however, the A. V.—probably following the translations of Luther and Junius, which in their turns follow the Targum—treats the word as an ordinary noun, and renders it "habitations;" a reading now relinquished by scholars, who understand the word to refer to the people in question (Gesenius, *Thes.* 1002 a, and *Notes on Burckhardt*, 1069; Bertheau, *Chronik*).

A third notice of the Mehunim, corroborative of those already mentioned, is found in the narrative of 2 Chr. xx. There is every reason to believe that in ver. 1 "the Ammonites" should be read as "the [d] Maonites," who in that case are the "men of Mount Seir" mentioned later in the narrative (vv. 10, 22).

In all these passages, including the last, the LXX. render the name by οἱ Μειναῖοι, — the Minæans, — a nation of Arabia renowned for their traffic in spices, who are named by Strabo, Ptolemy, and other ancient geographers, and whose seat is now ascertained to have been the S. W. portion of the great Arabian peninsula, the western half of the modern Hadramaut (*Dict. of Geography*, "Minæi"). Bochart has pointed out (*Phaleg.* ii. cap. xxii.), with reason, that distance alone renders it impossible that these Minæans can be the Meunim of the Bible, and also that the people of the Arabian peninsula are Shemites, while the Meunim appear to have been descended from Ham (1 Chr. iv. 41). But with his usual turn for etymological speculation he endeavors nevertheless to establish an identity between the two, on the ground that *Carn al-Manasil*, a place two days' journey south of Mecca, one of the towns

a The instances of H being employed to render the strange Hebrew guttural *Ain* are not frequent in the A. V. "Hebrew" (עִבְרִי) — which in earlier versions was "Ebrew" (comp. Shakespeare, *Henry IV.* Part I. Act 2, Sc. 4) — is oftenest encountered.

b معان, *Ma'an*, all but identical with the Hebrew *Maon*.

c Here the *Cethib*, or original Hebrew text, has *Meïnim*, which is nearer the Greek equivalent than *Meunim* or *Maonim*.

d The text of this passage is accurately as follows: "The children of Moab and the children of Ammon, and with them of the Ammonites;" the words "other beside" being interpolated by our translators.

The change from "Ammonites" to "Mehunim" is

not so violent as it looks to an English reader. It is a simple transposition of two letters, מעונים for עמונים; and it is supported by the LXX., and by Josephus (*Ant.* ix. 1, § 2, "Αραβες); and by modern scholars, as De Wette (*Bibel*), Ewald (*Gesch.* iii. 474, note). A reverse transposition will be found in the Syriac version of Judg. x. 12, where "Ammon" is read for the "Maon" of the Hebrew. The LXX. make the change again in 2 Chr. xxvi. 8; but here there is no apparent occasion for it.

The Jewish gloss on 2 Chr. xx. 1 is curious. "By Ammonites Edomites are meant, who, out of respect for the fraternal relation between the two nations would not come against Israel in their own dress, but disguised themselves as Ammonites." (Jerome, *Quœst. Hebr.* ad loc.)

of the Minæans, signifies the "horn of habitations," and might therefore be equivalent to the Hebrew *Meonim.*

Josephus (*Ant.* ix. 10, § 3) calls them "the Arabs who adjoined Egypt," and speaks of a city built by Uzziah on the Red Sea to overawe them.

Ewald (*Geschichte*, i. 323, *note*) suggests that the southern Minæans were a colony from the Maonites and Mount Seir, who in their turn he appears to consider a remnant of the Amorites (see the text of the same page).

That the Minæans were familiar to the translators of the LXX. is evident from the fact that they not only introduce the name on the occasions already mentioned, but that they further use it as equivalent to NAAMATHITE. Zophar the Naamathite, one of the three friends of Job, is by them presented as "Sophar the Minæan," and "Sophar king of the Minæans." In this connection it is not unworthy of notice that as there was a town called Maon in the mountain-district of Judah, so there was one called Naamah in the lowland of the same tribe. *El-Minyây*, which is, or was, the first station south of Gaza, is probably identical with Minois, a place mentioned with distinction in the Christian records of Palestine in the 5th and 6th centuries (Reland, *Palæstina*, p. 899; Le Quien, *Oriens Christ.* iii. 669), and both may retain a trace of the Minæans. BAAL-MEON, a town on the east of Jordan, near Heshbon, still called *Ma'in*, probably also retains a trace of the presence of the Maonites or Mehunim north of their proper locality.

The latest appearance of the name MEHUNIMS in the Bible is in the lists of those who returned from the Captivity with Zerubbabel. Amongst the non-Israelites from whom the Nethinim — following the precedent of what seems to have been the foundation of the [a] order — were made up, we find their name (Ezr. ii. 50, A. V. "Mehunim;" Neh. vii. 52, A. V. "Meunim"). Here they are mentioned with the Nephishim, or descendants of Naphish, an Ishmaelite people whose seat appears to have been on the east of Palestine (1 Chr. v. 19), and therefore certainly not far distant from *Ma'an* the chief city of the Maonites.   G.

ME-JAR'KON (מֵי הַיַּרְקוֹן [see below]: θάλασσα Ἱεράκων: *Aquæ Jercon* [? Vulg. *Me-jarcon*]), a town in the territory of Dan (Josh. xix. 46 only); named next in order to Gath-rimmon, and in the neighborhood of Joppa or Japho. The lexicographers interpret the name as meaning "the yellow waters." No attempt has been made to identify it with any existing site. It is difficult not to suspect that the name following that of Me-hajjarkon, har-Rakon (A. V. Rakkon), is a mere corrupt repetition thereof, as the two bear a very

close similarity to each other, and occur nowhere else.   G.

MEKO'NAH (מְכֹנָה [b] [*place, base*]: LXX. [Rom. Vat. Alex. FA.[1] omits; [FA.[3] Μαχνα:] *Mochona*), one of the towns which were re-inhabited after the Captivity by the men of Judah (Neh. xi. 28). From its being coupled with Ziklag, we should infer that it was situated far to the south, while the mention of the "daughter towns" (בְּנוֹת, A. V. "villages") dependent on it seem to show that it was a place of some magnitude. Mekonah is not mentioned elsewhere, and it does not appear that any name corresponding with it has been yet discovered. The conjecture of Schwarz — that it is identical with the *Mechanum*, which Jerome [c] (*Onomasticon*, "Bethmacha") locates between Eleutheropolis and Jerusalem, at eight miles from the former — is entirely at variance with the above inference.   G.

MELATI'AH (מְלַטְיָה [*delivered by Jehovah* : Rom.] Μααλτίας; [Vat. Alex. FA. omit:] *Meltias*), a Gibeonite, who, with the men of Gibeon and Mizpah, assisted in rebuilding the wall of Jerusalem under Nehemiah (Neh. iii. 7).

MEL'CHI (Μελχεί in [Sin.] Vat. and Alex. MSS.; Μελχί, Tisch. [in 2d ed., but Μελχεί in 7th and 8th eds.]: *Melchi*). 1. The son of Janna, and ancestor of Joseph in the genealogy of Jesus Christ (Luke iii. 24). In the list given by Africanus, Melchi appears as the father of Heli, the intervening Levi and Matthat being omitted (Hervey, *Geneal.* p. 137).

2. The son of Addi in the same genealogy (Luke iii. 28).

MELCHI'AH (מַלְכִּיָּה [*Jehovah's king*]: Μελχίας: *Melchias*), a priest, the father of Pashur (Jer. xxi. 1). He is elsewhere called Malchiah and Malchijah. (See MALCHIAH 7, and MALCHIJAH 1.)

MELCHI'AS (Μελχίας: *Melchias*). 1. The same as MALCHIAH 2 (1 Esdr. ix. 26).

2. [Vat. Μελχειας.] = MALCHIAH 3 and MALCHIJAH 4 (1 Esdr. ix. 32).

3. ([Vat. Μελχειας:] *Malachias*.) The same as MALCHIAH 6 (1 Esdr. ix. 44).

MEL'CHIEL ([Vat.] Μελχειηλ; [Rom. Alex. Sin[c]. Μελχιήλ; Sin. Σελλημ]). Charmis, the son of Melchiel, was one of the three governors of Bethulia (Jud. vi. 15). The Vulgate has a different reading, and the Peshito gives the name *Manshajel*.

MELCHIS'EDEC (Μελχισεδέκ: [*Melchisedech*]), the form of the name MELCHIZEDEK adopted in the A. V. of the New Testament (Heb. v., vi., vii.).

---

[a] The institution of the Nethinim, *i. e.* "the given ones," seems to have originated in the Midianite war (Num. xxxi.), when a certain portion of the captives was "given" (the word in the original is the same) to the Levites who kept the charge of the Sacred Tent (vv. 30, 47). The Gibeonites were probably the next accession, and the invaluable lists of Ezra and Nehemiah alluded to above seem to show that the captives from many a foreign nation went to swell the numbers of the Order. See Mehunim, Nephusim, Harsha, Sisera, and other foreign names contained in these lists.

[b] Our translators have here represented the Hebrew

Caph by K, which they usually reserve for the Koph. Other instances are KITHLISH and KITTIM.

[c] This passage of Jerome is one of those which completely startle the reader, and incline him to mistrust altogether Jerome's knowledge of sacred topography. He actually places the Beth-maacha, in which Joab besieged Sheba the son of Bichri, and which was one of the first places taken by Tiglath-Pileser on his entrance into the north of Palestine, among the mountains of Judah, south of Jerusalem! A mistake of the same kind is found in Benjamin of Tudela and Hap-Parchi, who place the Maon of David's adventures in the neighborhood of *Mount Carmel.*

MEL'CHI-SHU'A (מַלְכִּי־שׁוּעַ), *i. e.* Mal-chishua: [Μελχισά; Vat.] Μελχεισα; Alex. Μελχισουε, [Μελχιρουε;] Joseph. Μέλχισος: *Melchisua*), a son of Saul (1 Sam. xiv. 49, xxxi. 2). An erroneous manner of representing the name, which is elsewhere correctly given MAL-CHISHUA.

MELCHIZ'EDEK (מַלְכִּי־צֶדֶק), *i. e.* Malchi-tzedek [*king of righteousness*]: Μελχισεδέκ: *Melchisedech*), king of Salem and priest of the Most High God, who met Abram in the Valley of Shaveh [or, the level valley], which is the king's valley, brought out bread and wine, blessed Abram, and received tithes from him (Gen. xiv. 18-20). The other places in which Melchizedek is mentioned are Ps. cx. 4, where Messiah is described as a priest for ever, "after the order of Melchizedek," and Heb. v., vi., vii., where these two passages of the O. T. are quoted, and the typical relation of Melchizedek to our Lord is stated at great length.

There is something surprising and mysterious in the first appearance of Melchizedek, and in the subsequent references to him. Bearing a title which Jews in after ages would recognize as designating their own sovereign, bearing gifts which recall to Christians the Lord's Supper, this Canaanite crosses for a moment the path of Abram, and is unhesitatingly recognized as a person of higher spiritual rank than the friend of God. Disappearing as suddenly as he came in, he is lost to the sacred writings for a thousand years; and then a few emphatic words for another moment bring him into sight as a type of the coming Lord of David. Once more, after another thousand years, the Hebrew Christians are taught to see in him a proof that it was the consistent purpose of God to abolish the Levitical priesthood. His person, his office, his relation to Christ, and the seat of his sovereignty, have given rise to innumerable discussions, which even now can scarcely be considered as settled.

The faith of early ages ventured to invest his person with superstitious awe. Perhaps it would be too much to ascribe to mere national jealousy the fact that Jewish tradition, as recorded in the Targums of Pseudo-Jonathan and Jerusalem, and in Rashi on Gen. xiv., in some cabalistic (*apud* Bochart, *Phaleg*, pt. 1, b. ii. 1, § 69) and rabbinical (*ap.* Schöttgen, *Hor. Heb.* ii. 645) writers, pronounces Melchizedek to be a survivor of the Deluge, the patriarch Shem, authorized by the superior dignity of old age to bless even the father of the faithful, and entitled, as the paramount lord of Canaan (Gen. ix. 26) to convey (xiv. 19) his right to Abram. Jerome in his *Ep.* lxxiii. *ad Evangelum* (*Opp.* i. 438), which is entirely devoted to a consideration of the person and dwelling-place of Melchizedek, states that this was the prevailing opinion of the Jews in his time; and it is ascribed to the Samaritans by Epiphanius, *Hær.* lv. 6, p. 472. It was afterwards embraced by Luther and Melanchthon, by our own countrymen, H. Broughton, Selden, Lightfoot (*Chor. Marco præm.* ch. x. 1, § 2), Jackson (*On the Creed*, b. ix. § 2), and by many others. It should be noted that this supposition does not appear in the Targum of Onkelos, — a presumption that it was not received by the Jews till after the Christian era — nor has it found favor with the Fathers. Equally old, per-haps, but less widely diffused, is the supposition not unknown to Augustine (*Quæst. in Gen.* lxxii. *Opp.* iii. 396), and ascribed by Jerome (*l. c.*) to Origen and Didymus, that Melchizedek was an angel. The Fathers of the fourth and fifth centuries record with reprobation the tenet of the Melchizedekians that he was a Power, Virtue, or Influence of God (August. *de Hæresibus*, § 34, *Opp.* viii. 11; Theodoret, *Hæret. fab.* ii. 6, p. 332; Epiphan. *Hær.* lv. 1, p. 468; compare Cyril Alex. *Glaph. in Gen.* ii. p. 57) superior to Christ (Chrysost. *Hom. in Melchiz. Opp.* vi. p. 269), and the not less daring conjecture of Hieracas and his followers that Melchizedek was the Holy Ghost (Epiphan. *Hær.* lxvii. 3, p. 711 and lv. 5, p. 472). Epiphanius also mentions (lv. 7, p. 474) some members of the church as holding the erroneous opinion that Melchizedek was the Son of God appearing in human form, an opinion which St. Ambrose (*De Abrah.* i. § 3, *Opp.* t. i. p. 288) seems willing to receive, and which has been adopted by many modern critics. Similar to this was a Jewish opinion that he was the Messiah (*apud* Deyling, *Obs. Sacr.* ii. 73, Schöttgen, *l. c.*; compare the Book Sohar *ap.* Wolf, *Curæ Phil.* in Heb. vii. 1). Modern writers have added to these conjectures that he may have been Ham (Jurieu), or a descendant of Japhet (Owen), or of Shem (*apud* Deyling, *l. c.*), or even Enoch (Hulse), or Job (Kohlreis). Other guesses may be found in Deyling (*l. c.*) and in Pfeiffer (*De personâ Melch.* — *Opp.* p. 51). All these opinions are unauthorized additions to Holy Scripture — many of them seem to be irreconcilable with it. It is an essential part of the Apostle's argument (Heb. vii. 6) that Melchizedek is "without father," and that his "pedigree is not counted from the sons of Levi;" so that neither their ancestor Shem, nor any other son of Noah can be identified with Melchizedek; and again, the statements that he fulfilled on earth the offices of Priest and King and that he was "made unlike unto the son of God" would hardly have been predicated of a Divine Person. The way in which he is mentioned in Genesis would rather lead to the immediate inference that Melchizedek was of one blood with the children of Ham, among whom he lived, chief (like the King of Sodom) of a settled Canaanitish tribe. Perhaps it is not too much to infer from the silence of Philo (*Abraham*, xl.) and Onkelos (*in Gen.*) as to any other opinion, that they held this. It certainly was the opinion of Josephus (*B. J.* vii. 18), of most of the early Fathers (*apud* Jerome, *l. c.*), of Theodoret (*in Gen.* lxiv. p. 77), and Epiphanius (*Hær.* lxvii. p. 716), and is now generally received (see Grotius *in Hebr.*; Patrick's *Commentary in Gen.*; Bleek, *Hebräer*, ii. 303; Ebrard, *Hebräer*; Fairbairn, *Typology*, ii. 313, ed. 1854). And as Balaam was a prophet, so Melchizedek was a priest among the corrupted heathen (Philo, *Abrah.* xxxix.; Euseb. *Præp. Evang.* i. 9), not self-appointed (as Chrysostom suggests, *Hom. in Gen.* xxxv. § 5, cf. Heb. v. 4), but constituted by a special gift from God, and recognized as such by Him.

Melchizedek combined the offices of priest and king, as was not uncommon in patriarchal times. Nothing is said to distinguish his kingship from that of the contemporary kings of Canaan; but the emphatic words in which he is described, by a title never given even to Abraham, as a "priest of the most High God," as blessing Abraham and receiving tithes from him, seem to imply that his priesthood was something more (see Hengstenberg, *Christol.*, Ps. cx.) than an ordinary patriarchal priesthood, such as Abram himself and other heads of families (Job i. 5) exercised. And although it has been observed (Pearson, *On the Creed*, p. 122, ed. 1843) that we read of no other sacerdotal act performed by Melchizedek, but only that of blessing [and receiving tithes, Pfeiffer], yet it may be assumed that he was accustomed to discharge all the ordinary duties of those who are "ordained to offer gifts and sacrifices," Heb. viii. 3; and we might concede (with Philo, Grotius, *l. c.* and others) that his regal hospitality to Abram was possibly preceded by an unrecorded sacerdotal act of oblation to God, without implying that his hospitality was in itself, as recorded in Genesis, a sacrifice.

The "order of Melchizedek," in Ps. cx. 4, is explained (by Gesenius and Rosenmüller to mean "manner"="likeness in official dignity "=a king and priest. The relation between Melchizedek and Christ as type and antitype is made in the Ep. to the Hebrews to consist in the following particulars. Each was a priest, (1) not of the Levitical tribe; (2) superior to Abraham ; (3) whose beginning and end are unknown; (4) who is not only a priest, but also a king of righteousness and peace. To these points of agreement, noted by the Apostle, human ingenuity has added others which, however, stand in need of the evidence of either an inspired writer or an eye-witness, before they can be received as facts and applied to establish any doctrine. Thus J. Johnson (*Unbloody Sacrifice*, i. 123, ed. 1847) asserts on very slender evidence, that the Fathers who refer to Gen. xiv. 18, understood that Melchizedek offered the bread and wine to God; and hence he infers that one great part of our Saviour's Melchizedekian priesthood consisted in offering bread and wine. And Bellarmine asks in what other respects is Christ a priest after the order of Melchizedek. Waterland, who does not lose sight of the deep significancy of Melchizedek's action, has replied to Johnson in his *Appendix* to "the Christian Sacrifice explained," ch. iii. § 2, *Works*, v. 165, ed. 1843. Bellarmine's question is sufficiently answered by Whitaker, *Disputation' on Scripture*, Quæst. ii. ch. x. 168, ed. 1849. And the sense of the Fathers, who sometimes expressed themselves in rhetorical language, is cleared from misinterpretation by Bp. Jewel, *Reply to Harding*, art. xvii. (*Works*, ii. 731, ed. 1847.) In Jackson *on the Creed*, bk. ix. § 2, ch. vi.-xi. 955 ff., there is a lengthy but valuable account of the priesthood of Melchizedek; and the views of two different theological schools are ably stated by Aquinas, *Summa* iii. 22, § 6, and Turretinus, *Theologia*, vol. ii. p. 443-453.

Another fruitful source of discussion has been found in the site of Salem and Shaveh, which certainly lay in Abram's road from Hobah to the plain of Mamre, and which are assumed to be near to each other. The various theories may be briefly enumerated as follows: (1) Salem is supposed to have occupied in Abraham's time the ground on which afterwards Jebus and then Jerusalem stood; and Shaveh to be the valley east of Jerusalem through which the Kidron flows. This opinion, abandoned by Reland, *Pal.* 833, but adopted by Winer, is supported by the facts that Jerusalem is called Salem in Ps. lxxvi. 2, and that Josephus (*Ant.* i. 10, § 2) and the Targums distinctly assert their identity: that the king's dale (2 Sam. xviii. 18), identified in Gen. xiv. 17 with Shaveh, is

placed by Josephus (*Ant.* vii. 10, § 3), and by mediæval and modern tradition (see Ewald, *Gesch.* iii. 239) in the immediate neighborhood of Jerusalem: that the name of a later king of Jerusalem, Adonizedec (Josh. x. 1), sounds like that of a legitimate successor of Melchizedek: and that Jewish writers (*ap.* Schöttgen, *Hor. Heb.* in Heb. vii. 2) claim Zedek = righteousness, as a name of Jerusalem. (2.) Jerome (*Opp.* i. 446) denies that Salem is Jerusalem, and asserts that it is identical with a town near Scythopolis or Bethshan, which in his time retained the name of Salem, and in which some extensive ruins were shown as the remains of Melchizedek's palace. He supports this view. by quoting Gen. xxxiii. 18, where, however, the translation is questioned (as instead of Salem the word may signify "safe"); compare the mention of Salem in Judith iv. 4, and in John iii. 23. (3.) Professor Stanley (*S. & P.* pp. 237, 238) is of opinion that there is every probability that Mount Gerizim is the place where Melchizedek, the priest of the Most High, met Abram. Eupolemus (ap. Euseb. *Præp. Evang.* ix. 17), in a confused version of this story, names Argerizim, the mount of the Most High, as the place in which Abram was hospitably entertained. (4.) Ewald (*Gesch.* iii. 239) denies positively that it is Jerusalem, and says that it must be north of Jerusalem on the other side of Jordan (i. 410): an opinion which Rödiger (Gesen. *Thesaurus*, 1422 *b*) condemns. There too Professor Stanley thinks that the king's dale was situate, near the spot where Absalom fell.

Some Jewish writers have held the opinion that Melchizedek was the writer and Abram the subject of Ps. cx. See Deyling, *Obs. Sacr.* iii. 137.

It may suffice to mention that there is a fabulous life of Melchizedek printed among the spurious works of Athanasius, vol. iv. p. 189.

Reference may be made to the following works in addition to those already mentioned: two tracts on Melchizedek by M. J. H. von Elswick, in the *Thesaurus Novus Theolog.-philologicus ;* L. Borgisius, *Historia Critica Melchisedeci*, 1706; Gaillard, *Melchisedecus Christus*, etc., 1686; M. C. Hoffman, *De Melchisedeco*, 1669; H. Broughton, *Treatise of Melchizedek*, 1591. See also J. A. Fabricius, *Cod. Pseudepig. V. T.*; P. Molinæus, *Vates*, etc., 1640, iv. 11; J. H. Heidegger, *Hist. Sacr. Patriarcharum*, 1671, ii. 288; Hottinger, *Ennead. Disput.*; and P. Cunæus, *De Republ. Heb.* iii. 3, apud *Crit. Sacr.* vol. v.

W. T. B.

MELEA (Μελεᾶ [Tisch. Μελεᾱ] : *Melea*). The son of Menan, and ancestor of Joseph in the genealogy of Jesus Christ (Luke iii. 31).

MELECH (מֶלֶךְ = *king*: in 1 Chr. viii. 35, Μελάχ, [Vat. Μελχηλ,] Alex. Μαλωθ; in 1 Chr. ix. 41, Μαλάχ, Alex. Μαλωχ: *Melech*). The second son of Micah, the son of Merib-baal or Mephibosheth, and therefore great-grandson of Jonathan the son of Saul.

MELICU (מְלִיכוּ ; *Keri*, מְלִיכִי, 'Αμαλούχ; [Vat.] Alex. Μαλουχ: *Milicho*). The same as MALLUCH 6 (Neh. xii. 14; comp. ver. 2).

MELITA (Μελίτη : [*Melita*]), Acts xxviii. 1, the modern *Malta*. This island has an illustrious place in Scripture, as the scene of that shipwreck of St. Paul which is described in such minute detail in the Acts of the Apostles. An attempt has been made, more than once, to connect this occurrence with another island, bearing the same name, in the Gulf of Venice; and our best course here seems to be to give briefly the points of evidence by which the true state of the case has been established.

(1.) We take St. Paul's ship in the condition in which we find her about a day after leaving FAIR HAVENS, i. e. when she was under the lee of CLAUDA (Acts xxvii. 16), laid-to on the starboard tack, and strengthened with "undergirders" [SHIP], the boat being just taken on board, and the gale blowing hard from the E. N. E. [EUROCLYDON.] (2.) Assuming (what every practiced sailor would allow) that the ship's direction of drift would be about W. by N., and her rate of drift about a mile and a half an hour, we come at once to the conclusion, by measuring the distance on the chart, that she would be brought to the coast of Malta on the thirteenth day (see ver. 27). (3.) A ship drifting in this direction to the place traditionally known as St. Paul's Bay would come to that spot on the coast without touching any other part of the island previously. The coast, in fact, trends from this bay to the S. E. This may be seen on consulting any map or chart of Malta. (4.) On *Koura Point*, which is the southeasterly extremity of the bay, there must infallibly have been breakers, with the wind blowing from the N. E. Now the alarm was certainly caused by breakers, for it took place in the night (ver. 27), and it does not appear that the passengers were at first aware of the danger which became sensible to the quick ear of the "sailors." (5.) Yet the vessel did not strike: and this corresponds with the position of the point, which would be some little distance on the port side, or to the left, of the vessel. (6.) Off this point of the coast the soundings are 20 fathoms (ver. 28), and a little further, *in the direction of the supposed drift*, they are 15 fathoms (*ib.*). (7.) Though the danger was imminent, we shall find from examining the chart that there would still be time to anchor (ver. 29) before striking on the rocks ahead. (8.) With bad holding ground there would have been great risk of the ship dragging her anchors. But the bottom of St. Paul's Bay is remarkably tenacious. In Purdy's *Sailing Directions* (p. 180) it is said of it that "while the cables hold there is no danger, as the anchors will never start." (9.) The other geological characteristics of the place are in harmony with the narrative, which describes the creek as having in one place a sandy or muddy beach (κόλπον ἔχοντα αἰγιαλόν, ver. 39), and which states that the bow of the ship was held fast in the shore, while the stern was exposed to the action of the waves (ver. 41). For particulars we must refer to the work (mentioned below) of Mr. Smith, an accomplished geologist. (10.) Another point of local detail is of considerable interest — namely, that as the ship took the ground, the place was observed to be διθάλασσος, i. e. a connection was noticed between two apparently separate pieces of water. We shall see, on looking at the chart, that this would be the case. The small island of Salmonetta would at first appear to be a part of Malta itself; but the passage would open on the right as the vessel passed to the place of shipwreck. (11.) Malta is in the track of ships between Alexandria and Puteoli; and this corresponds with the fact that the "Castor and Pollux," an Alexandrian vessel which ultimately conveyed St. Paul to Italy, had wintered in the island (Acts xxviii. 11). (12.)

Finally, the course pursued in this conclusion of the voyage, first to Syracuse and then to Rhegium, contributes a last link to the chain of arguments by which we prove that Melita is *Malta*.

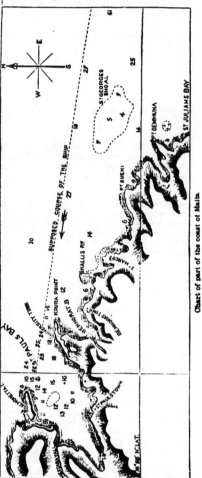

Chart of part of the coast of Malta.

The case is established to demonstration. Still it may be worth while to notice one or two objections. It is said, in reference to xxvii. 27, that the wreck took place in the Adriatic, or Gulf of Venice. It is urged that a well-known island like Malta could not have been unrecognized (xxvii. 39), nor its inhabitants called "barbarous" (xxviii. 2). [BARBAROUS, Amer. ed.] And as regards the occurrence recorded in xxviii. 3, stress is laid on the facts that Malta has no poisonous serpents, and hardly any wood. To these objections we reply at once that ADRIA, in the language of the period, denotes not the Gulf of Venice, but the open sea between Crete and Sicily; that it is no wonder if the sailors did not recognize a strange part of the coast on which they were thrown in stormy weather, and that they did recognize the place when they did leave the ship (xxviii. 1)^a; that the kindness recorded of the natives (xxviii. 2, 10) shows they were not "barbarians" in the sense of being savages, and that the word denotes simply that they did not speak Greek; and lastly, that the population of Malta has increased in an extraordinary manner in recent times, that probably there was abundant wood there formerly, and that with the destruction of the wood many indigenous animals would disappear.^b

In adducing positive arguments and answering objections, we have indirectly proved that Melita in the Gulf of Venice was not the scene of the shipwreck. But we may add that this island could not have been reached without a miracle under the circumstances of weather described in the narrative; that it is not in the track between Alexandria and Puteoli; that it would not be natural to proceed

from it to Rome by means of a voyage embracing Syracuse; and that the soundings on its shore do not agree with what is recorded in the Acts.

An amusing passage in Coleridge's *Table Talk* (p. 185) is worth noticing as the last echo of what is now an extinct controversy. The question has been set at rest forever by Mr. Smith of Jordan Hill, in his *Voyage and Shipwreck of St. Paul*, the first published work in which it was thoroughly investigated from a sailor's point of view. It had, however, been previously treated in the same manner, and with the same results, by Admiral Penrose, and copious notes from his MSS. are given in *The Life and Epistles of St. Paul.* In that work (2d ed. p. 426 *note*) are given the names of some of those who carried on the controversy in the last century. The ringleader on the Adriatic side of the question, not unnaturally was Padre Georgi, a

St. Paul's Bay.

Benedictine monk connected with the Venetian or Austrian *Meleda*, and his *Paulus Naufragus* is extremely curious. He was, however, not the first to suggest this untenable view. We find it, at a much earlier period, in a Byzantine writer, Const. Porphyrog. *De Adm. Imp.* (c. 36, v. iii. p. 164 of the Bonn ed.).

As regards the condition of the island of Melita, when St. Paul was there, it was a dependency of the Roman province of Sicily. Its chief officer

(under the governor of Sicily) appears from inscriptions to have had the title of πρῶτος Μελιταίων, or *Primus Melitensium*, and this is the very phrase which St. Luke uses (xxviii. 7). [PUBLIUS.] Mr. Smith could not find these inscriptions. There seems, however, no reason whatever to doubt their authenticity (see Bochart, *Opera*, i. 502; Abela, *Descr. Melitæ*, p. 146, appended to the last volume of the *Antiquities* of Graevius; and Boeckh, *Corp. Insc.* vol. iii. 5754). Melita, from its position in

---

^a * It may have been, as far as respects the verb (ἐπέγνωσαν or probably ἐπέγνωμεν), by recognition or by information that they learnt on what island they were cast. In this instance as what they learned was not that "the island is Melita" but "is called (καλεῖται) Melita," they were probably told this by the people whom the wreck of the ship had brought down to the coast. If "the sailors" as distinguished from the others "recognised the land" it would naturally have been the sea-view which was familiar to them, and yet they had failed to recognise the island from the sea, though they had seen it in full daylight (ver. 39) before landing.   H.

^b * There is a passage in another of Dean Howson's works respecting these verifications of Luke's accuracy which belongs also to this place. "Nothing is more certain than that the writer was on board that ship and that he tells the truth. It might be thought strange that so large a space, in a volume which we believe to be inspired, should contain so much circumstantial detail with so little of religious exhortation

and precept. The chapter might seem merely intended to give us information concerning the ships and sea-faring of the ancient world ; and certainly nothing in the whole range of Greek and Roman literature does teach us so much on these subjects. What if it was divinely ordained that there should be one large passage in the New Testament — one, and just one — that could be minutely tested in the accuracy of its mere circumstantial particulars — and that it *should* have been so tested and attested just at the time when such accuracy is most searchingly questioned? " (*Lectures on the Character of St. Paul*, Hulsean Lectures for 1864.)

The particulars in which this accuracy of the narrative shows itself are well enumerated in J. R. Oertel's *Paulus in der Apostelgeschichte*, pp. 107-110 (Halle, 1868). Klostermann (*Vindiciæ Lucana seu de itinerarii in libro Acto rum asservati auctore*, Gotting. 1866) argues from internal characteristics that the writer of this itinerary (Acts xxvii. and xxviii.) must have been an eye-witness, and was the Luke who wrote the other parts of the book.   H

the Mediterranean, and the excellence of its harbors, has always been important both in commerce and war. It was a settlement of the Phoenicians at an early period, and their language, in a corrupted form, continued to be spoken there in St. Paul's day. (Gesenius, *Versuch üb. die malt. Sprache.* Leipz. 1810.)[a] From the Carthaginians it passed to the Romans in the Second Punic War. It was famous for its honey and fruits, for its cotton fabrics, for excellent building-stone, and for a well-known breed of dogs. A few years before St. Paul's visit, corsairs from his native province of Cilicia made Melita a frequent resort; and through subsequent periods of its history, Vandal and Arabian, it was often associated with piracy. The Christianity, however, introduced by St. Paul was never extinct. This island had a brilliant period under the knights of St. John, and it is associated with the most exciting passages of the struggle between the French and English at the close of the last century and the beginning of the present. No island so small has so great a history, whether Biblical or political.   J. S. H.

MELONS (אֲבַטִּחִים,[b] *abattichim*: πέπονες: *pepones*) are mentioned only in the following verse: "We remember the fish, which we did eat in Egypt freely; the cucumbers, and the melons," etc. (Num. xi. 5); by the Hebrew word we are probably to understand both the melon (*Cucumis melo*) and the water-melon (*Cucurbita citrullus*), for the Arabic

Cucurbita citrullus.

noun singular, *batékh*, which is identical with the Hebrew word, is used generically, as we learn from Prosper Alpinus, who says (*Rerum Ægypt. Hist.* i. 17) of the Egyptians, "they often dine and sup on fruits alone, such as cucumbers, pumpkins, melons, which are known by the generic name *batech*." The Greek πέπων, and the Latin *pepo*, appear to be also occasionally used in a generic sense. According to Forskål (*Descr. plant.* p. 167) and Hasselquist (*Trav.* 255), the Arabs designated the water-

Melon. (*Cucumis melo.*)

melon *batech*, while the same word was used with some specific epithet to denote other plants belonging to the order *Cucurbitaceæ.* Though the watermelon is now quite common in Asia, Dr. Royle thinks it doubtful whether it was known to the ancient Egyptians, as no distinct mention of it is made in Greek writers; it is uncertain at what time the Greeks applied the term ἀγγούριον (*anguria*) to the water-melon, but it was probably at a comparatively recent date. The modern Greek word for this fruit is ἀγγούρι. Galen (*de Fac. Alim.* ii. 567) speaks of the common melon (*Cucumis melo*) under the name μηλοπέπων. Serapion, according to Sprengel (*Comment. in Dioscor.* ii. 162), restricts the Arabic *batikh* to the water-melon. The watermelon is by some considered to be indigenous to India, from which country it may have been introduced into Egypt in very early times; according to Prosper Alpinus, medical Arabic writers sometimes use the term *batikh-Indi*, or *anguria Indica*, to denote this fruit, whose common Arabic name is according to the same authority, *batikh el-Maooi* (water); but Hasselquist says (*Trav.* 256) that this name belongs to a softer variety, the juice of which, when very ripe, and almost putrid, is mixed with rose-water and sugar and given in fevers; he observes that the water-melon is cultivated on the banks of the Nile, on the rich clayey earth after the inundations, from the beginning of May to the end of July, and that it serves the Egyptians for meat, drink, and physic; the fruit, however, he says, should be eaten "with great circumspection, for if it be taken in the heat of the day when the body is warm, bad consequences often ensue." This observation

---

a * For the results of this investigation see also Brach and Gruber's *Encyklopadie*, art. "Arabien." The Maltese language approaches so nearly to the Arabic that the islanders are readily understood in all the ports of Africa and Syria. At the time of the Saracen irruption Malta was overrun by Arabs from whom the common people of the island derive their origin. Their dialect is a corrupt Arabic, interwoven at the same time with many words from the Italian, Spanish, and other European languages. Although the ancestral pride of the Maltese may dispose them to trace back

their language to the old Punic, yet it contains nothing which may not far more naturally be explained out of the modern Arabic. The Maltese Arabic is such that travellers in Arabia and Palestine often obtain their guides in Malta.   H.

b From root טָבַח, transp. for טָבַח (طبخ),

"to cook." Precisely similar is the derivation of πέπων, from πέττω. Gesenius compares the Spanish *budiecas,* the French *pastèques.*

no doubt applies only to persons before they have become acclimatized, for the native Egyptians eat the fruit with impunity. The common melon (*Cucumis melo*) is cultivated in the same places and ripens at the same time with the water-melon; but the fruit in Egypt is not so delicious as in this country (see Sonnini's *Travels*, ii. 328); the poor in Egypt do not eat this melon. "A traveller in the East," says Kitto (note on Num. xi. 5), "who recollects the intense gratitude which a gift of a slice of melon inspired while journeying over the hot and dry plains, will readily comprehend the regret with which the Hebrews in the Arabian desert looked back upon the melons of Egypt." The water-melon, which is now extensively cultivated all over India and the tropical parts of Africa and America, and indeed in hot countries generally, is a fruit not unlike the common melon, but the leaves are deeply lobed and gashed, the flesh is pink or white, and contains a large quantity of cold watery juice without much flavor; the seeds are black. The melon is too well known to need description. Both these plants belong to the order *Cucurbitaceæ*, the Cucumber family, which contains about sixty known genera and 300 species — *Cucurbita, Bryonia, Momordica, Cucumis*, are examples of the genera. [CUCUMBER; GOURD.]

W. H.

* Had the faith of the children of Israel been such as it ought to have been they needed not to have murmured at the loss of the Egyptian melons, inasmuch as Palestine and Syria are capable of producing the best species of them. Water-melons are now cultivated all through Palestine, and those of Jaffa are famous for their lusciousness. They are carried to all points on the coast, and transported to the inland towns on camels as far as Hums and Hamath and Aleppo, before the season when they ripen in those districts. They are among the cheapest and most widely diffused of all the fruits of the East. In most parts of Syria melons go by the generic name of بطيخ, *Bottikh*, while their specific names are *yellow Bottikh* for the musk-melon, *Jaffa Bottikh* for those from that city, *green Bottikh* for the water-melon. It is not, however, the custom to name other plants of the *cucurbitaceæ* "Bottikh." The cucumber, and the *Elaterium*, etc. have all their appropriate generic names.

G. E. P.

MEL'ZAR (מֶלְצַר [*overseer*]). The A. V. is wrong in regarding Melzar as a proper name; it is rather an official title, as is implied in the addition of the article in each case where the name occurs (Dan. i. 11, 16): the marginal reading, "the steward," is therefore more correct. The LXX. [*rather*, Theodotion] regards the article as a part of the name, and renders it Ἀμερσάρ [so Alex.; Rom. Vat. Ἀμελσάδ; the LXX. read Ἀβιεσδρί]; the Vulgate, however, has *Malasar*. The *melzar* was subordinate to the "master of the eunuchs;" his office was to superintend the nurture and education of the young; he thus combined the duties of the Greek παιδαγωγός and τροφεύς, and more nearly resembles our "tutor" than any other officer. As to the origin of the term, there is some doubt; it is generally regarded as of Persian origin, the words used as giving the sense of "head cup-bearer;"

Fürst (*Lex. s. v.*) suggests its connection with the Hebrew *nazar*, "to guard."

W. L. B.

MEM'MIUS, QUIN'TUS (Κόϊντος Μέμμιος), 2 Macc. xi. 34. [MANLIUS, T.]

MEM'PHIS, a city of ancient Egypt, situated on the western bank of the Nile, in latitude 30° 6 N. It is mentioned by Isaiah (xix. 13), Jeremiah (ii. 16, xlvi. 14, 19), and Ezekiel (xxx. 13, 16), under the name of NOPH; and by Hosea (ix. 6) under the name of MOPH in Hebrew, and MEMPHIS in our English version [LXX. Μέμφις, Vulg. *Memphis*]. The name is compounded of two hieroglyphics "*Men*" = foundation, station; and "*Nofre*" = good. It is variously interpreted; *e. g.* "haven of the good;" "tomb of the good man" — Osiris; "the abode of the good;" "the gate of the blessed." Gesenius remarks upon the two interpretations proposed by Plutarch (*De Isid. et Os.* 20) — namely, ὅρμος ἀγαθῶν, "haven of the good," and τάφος 'Οσίριδος, "the tomb of Osiris" — that "both are applicable to Memphis as the sepulchre of Osiris, the Necropolis of the Egyptians, and hence also the haven of the blessed, since the right of burial was conceded only to the good." Bunsen, however, prefers to trace in the name of the city a connection with Menes, its founder. The Greek coins have *Memphis*; the Coptic is *Memfi* or *Menfi* and *Memf*; Hebrew, sometimes *Moph* (Mph), and sometimes *Noph*; Arabic *Memf* or *Menf* (Bunsen, *Egypt's Place*, vol. ii. 53). There can be no question as to the identity of the *Noph* of the Hebrew prophets with *Memphis*, the capital of lower Egypt.

Though some regard Thebes as the more ancient city, the monuments of Memphis are of higher antiquity than those of Thebes. Herodotus dates its foundation from Menes, the first really historical king of Egypt. The era of Menes is not satisfactorily determined. Birch, Kenrick, Poole, Wilkinson, and the English school of Egyptologists generally, reduce the chronology of Manetho's lists, by making several of his dynasties contemporaneous instead of successive. Sir G. Wilkinson dates the era of Manes from B. C. 2690; Mr. Stuart Poole, B. C. 2717 (Rawlinson, *Herod.* ii. 342; Poole, *Horæ Ægypt.* p. 97). The German Egyptologists assign to Egypt a much longer chronology. Bunsen fixes the era of Menes at B. C. 3643 (*Egypt's Place*, vol. ii. 579); Brugsch at B. C. 4455 (*Histoire d' Egypte*, i. 287); and Lepsius at B. C. 3892 (*Königsbuch der alten Ægypter*). Lepsius also registers about 18,000 years of the dynasties of gods, demigods, and prehistoric kings, before the accession of Menes. But indeterminate and conjectural as the early chronology of Egypt yet is, all agree that the known history of the empire begins with Menes, who founded Memphis. The city belongs to the earliest periods of authentic history.

The building of Memphis is associated by tradition with a stupendous work of art which has permanently changed the course of the Nile and the face of the Delta. Before the time of Menes the river emerging from the upper valley into the neck of the Delta, bent its course westward toward the hills of the Libyan desert, or at least discharged a large portion of its waters through an arm in that direction. Here the generous flood whose yearly inundation gives life and fertility to Egypt, was largely absorbed in the sands of the desert, or wasted in stagnant morasses. It is even conjectured that up to the time of Menes the whole Delta was an uninhabitable marsh. The rivers of Damascus, the *Barada* and *'Awaj*, now lose themselves in the same way in the marshy lakes of the great desert plain southeast of the city. Herodotus informs us, upon the authority of the Egyptian priests of his time, that Menes "by banking up the river at the bend which it forms about a hundred furlongs south of Memphis, laid the ancient channel dry, while he dug a new course for the stream half-way between the two lines of hills. To this day," he continues, "the elbow which the Nile forms at the point where it is forced aside into the new channel is guarded with the greatest care by the Persians, and strengthened every year; for if the river were to burst out at this place, and pour over the mound, there would be danger of Memphis being completely overwhelmed by the flood. Měn, the first king, having thus, by turning the river, made the tract where it used to run, dry land, proceeded in the first place to build the city now called Memphis, which lies in the narrow part of Egypt; after which

be further excavated a lake outside the town, to the north and west, communicating with the river, which was itself the eastern boundary" (Herod. ii. 99). From this description it appears, that — like Amsterdam dyked in from the Zuyder Zee, or St. Petersburg defended by the mole at Cronstadt from the Gulf of Finland, or more nearly like New Orleans protected by its levee from the freshets of the Mississippi, and drained by Lake Pontchartrain, — Memphis was created upon a marsh reclaimed by the dyke of Menes and drained by his artificial lake. New Orleans is situated on the left bank of the Mississippi, about 90 miles from its mouth, and is protected against inundation by an embankment 15 feet wide and 4 feet high, which extends from 120 miles above the city to 40 miles below it. Lake Pontchartrain affords a natural drain for the marshes that form the margin of the city upon the east. The dyke of Menes began 12 miles south of Memphis, and deflected the main channel of the river about two miles to the eastward. Upon the

The Sphinx and Pyramids at Memphis.

rise of the Nile, a canal still conducted a portion of its waters westward through the old channel, thus irrigating the plain beyond the city in that direction, while an inundation was guarded against on that side by a large artificial lake or reservoir at Abousir. The skill in engineering which these works required, and which their remains still indicate, argues a high degree of material civilization, at least in the mechanic arts, in the earliest known period of Egyptian history.

The political sagacity of Menes appears in the location of his capital where it would at once command the Delta and hold the key of upper Egypt, controlling the commerce of the Nile, defended upon the west by the Libyan mountains and desert, and on the east by the river and its artificial embankments. The climate of Memphis may be inferred from that of the modern Cairo — about 10 miles to the north — which is the most equable that Egypt affords. The city is said to have had a circumference of about 19 miles (Diod. Sic. i. 50), and

the houses or inhabited quarters, as was usual in the great cities of antiquity, were interspersed with numerous gardens and public areas.

Herodotus states, on the authority of the priests, that Menes "built the temple of Hephæstus, which stands within the city, a vast edifice, well worthy of mention" (ii. 99). The divinity whom Herodotus thus identifies with Hephæstus was *Ptah*, "the creative power, the maker of all material things" (Wilkinson in Rawlinson's *Herod.* ii. 289; Bunsen, *Egypt's Place*, i. 367, 384). *Ptah* was worshipped in all Egypt, but under different representations in different Nomes: ordinarily "as a god holding before him with both hands the Nilometer, or emblem of stability, combined with the sign of life" (Bunsen, i. 382). But at Memphis his worship was so prominent that the primitive sanctuary of his temple was built by Menes; successive monarchs greatly enlarged and beautified the structure, by the addition of courts, porches, and colossal ornaments. Herodotus and Diodorus describe several of these additions and restorations, but nowhere give a complete description of the temple with measurements of its various dimensions (Herod. ii. 99, 101, 108-110, 121, 136, 153, 176; Diod. Sic. i. 45, 51, 62, 67). According to these authorities, Moeris built the northern gateway; Sesostris erected in front of the temple colossal statues (varying from 30 to 50 feet in height) of himself, his wife, and his four sons; Rhampsinitus built the western gateway, and erected before it the colossal statues of Summer and Winter; Asychis built the eastern gateway, which "in size and beauty far surpassed the other three;" Psammetichus built the southern gateway; and Amosis presented to this temple "a recumbent colossus 75 feet long, and two upright statues, each 20 feet high." The period between Menes and Amosis, according to Brugsch, was 3731 years; but according to Wilkinson only about 2100 years; but upon either calculation, the temple as it appeared to Strabo was the growth of many centuries. Strabo (xvii. 807) describes this temple as "built in a very sumptuous manner, both as regards the size of the Naos and in other respects." The Dromos, or grand avenue leading to the temple of Ptah, was used for the celebration of bull-fights, a sport pictured in the tombs. But these fights were probably between animals alone — no captive or gladiator being compelled to enter the arena. The bulls having been trained for the occasion, were brought face to face and goaded on by their masters; — the prize being awarded to the owner of the victor. But though the bull was thus used for the sport of the people, he was the sacred animal of Memphis.

Apis was believed to be an incarnation of Osiris. The sacred bull was selected by certain outward symbols of the indwelling divinity; his color being black, with the exception of white spots of a peculiar shape upon his forehead and right side. The temple of Apis was one of the most noted structures of Memphis. It stood opposite the southern portico of the temple of Ptah; and Psammetichus, who built that gateway, also erected in front of the sanctuary of Apis a magnificent colonnade, supported by colossal statues or Osiride pillars, such as may still be seen at the temple of Medeenet Habou at Thebes (Herod. ii. 153). Through this colonnade the Apis was led with great pomp upon state occasions. Two stables adjoined the sacred vestibule (Strab. xvii. 807). Diodorus (i. 85) describes the magnificence with which a deceased Apis was interred and his successor installed at Memphis. The place appropriated to the burial of the sacred bulls was a gallery some 2000 feet in length by 20 in height and width, hewn in the rock without the city. This gallery was divided into numerous recesses upon each side; and the embalmed bodies of the sacred bulls, each in its own sarcophagus of granite, were deposited in these "sepulchral stalls." A few years since, this burial-place of the sacred bulls was discovered by M. Mariette, and a large number of the sarcophagi have already been opened. These catacombs of mummied bulls were approached from Memphis by a paved road, having colossal lions upon either side.

At Memphis was the reputed burial-place of Isis (Diod. Sic. i. 22); it had also a temple to that "myriad-named" divinity, which Herodotus (ii. 176) describes as "a vast structure, well worthy of notice," but inferior to that consecrated to her in Busiris, a chief city of her worship (ii. 59). Memphis had also its Serapeium, which probably stood

in the western quarter of the city, toward the desert; since Strabo describes it as very much exposed to sand-drifts, and in his time partly buried by masses of sand heaped up by the wind (xvii. 807). The sacred cubit and other symbols used in measuring the rise of the Nile were deposited in the temple of Serapis.

Herodotus describes "a beautiful and richly ornamented inclosure," situated upon the south side of the temple of Ptah, which was sacred to Proteus, a native Memphite king. Within this inclosure there was a temple to "the foreign Venus" (Astarte?), concerning which the historian narrates a myth connected with the Grecian Helen. In this inclosure was "the Tyrian camp" (ii. 112). A temple of Ra or Phre, the Sun, and a temple of the Cabeiri, complete the enumeration of the sacred buildings of Memphis.

The mythological system of the time of Menes is ascribed by Bunsen to "the amalgamation of the religion of Upper and Lower Egypt;"—religion having "already united the two provinces before the power of the race of This in the Thebaid extended itself to Memphis, and before the giant work of Menes converted the Delta from a desert, checkered over with lakes and morasses, into a blooming garden." The political union of the two divisions of the country was effected by the builder of Memphis. "Menes founded the *Empire of Egypt*, by raising the people who inhabited the valley of the Nile from a little provincial station to that of an historical nation" (*Egypt's Place*, i. 441, ii. 409).

The Necropolis, adjacent to Memphis, was on a scale of grandeur corresponding with the city itself. The "city of the pyramids" is a title of Memphis in the hieroglyphics upon the monuments. The great field or plain of the Pyramids lies wholly upon the western bank of the Nile, and extends from *Aboo-Rodsh*, a little to the northwest of Cairo, to *Meydoom*, about 40 miles to the south, and thence in a southwesterly direction about 25 miles further, to the pyramids of *Howara* and of *Binhmu* in the *Fayoura*. Lepsius computes the number of pyramids in this district at sixty-seven; but in this he counts some that are quite small, and others of a doubtful character. Not more than half this number can be fairly identified upon the whole field. But the principal seat of the pyramids, the Memphite Necropolis, was in a range of about 15 miles from *Sakkara* to *Gizeh*, and in the groups here remaining nearly thirty are probably tombs of the imperial sovereigns of Memphis (Bunsen, *Egypt's Place*, ii. 88). Lepsius regards the "Pyramid fields of Memphis" as a most important testimony to the civilization of Egypt (*Letters*, Bohn, p. 25; also *Chronologie der Aegypter*, vol. i.). These royal pyramids, with the subterranean halls of Apis, and numerous tombs of public officers erected on the plain or excavated in the adjacent hills, gave to Memphis the preëminence which it enjoyed as "the haven of the blessed."

Memphis long held its place as a capital; and for centuries a Memphite dynasty ruled over all Egypt. Lepsius, Bunsen, and Brugsch, agree in regarding the 3d, 4th, 6th, 7th, and 8th dynasties of the Old Empire as Memphite, reaching through a period of about a thousand years. During a portion of this period, however, the chain was broken, or there were contemporaneous dynasties in other parts of Egypt.

The overthrow of Memphis was distinctly predicted by the Hebrew prophets. In his "burden of Egypt," Isaiah says, " The princes of Zoan are become fools. the princes of *Noph* are deceived" (Is. xix. 13). Jeremiah (xlvi. 19) declares that " *Noph* shall be waste and desolate without an inhabitant." Ezekiel predicts: " Thus saith the Lord God: I will also destroy the idols, and I will cause [their] images to cease out of *Noph*; and there shall be no more a prince of the land of Egypt." The latest of these predictions was uttered nearly 600 years before Christ, and half a century before the invasion of Egypt by Cambyses (cir. B. C. 525). Herodotus informs us that Cambyses, enraged at the opposition he encountered at Memphis, committed many outrages upon the city. He killed the sacred Apis, and caused his priests to be scourged. " He opened the ancient sepulchres, and examined the bodies that were buried in them. He likewise went into the temple of Hephæstus (Ptah) and made great sport of the image. . . . He went also into the temple of the Cabeiri, which it is unlawful for any one to enter except the priests, and not only made sport of the images but even burnt them " (Her. iii. 37). Memphis never recovered from the blow inflicted by Cambyses. The rise of Alexandria hastened its decline. The Caliph conquerors founded Fostát (Old Cairo) upon the opposite bank of the Nile, a few miles north of Memphis, and brought materials from the old city to build their new capital (A. D. 638). The Arabian physician, Abd-el-Latif, who visited Memphis in the 13th century, describes its ruins as then marvelous beyond description (see De Sacy's translation, cited by Brugsch, *Histoire d'Egypte*, p. 18). Abulfeda, in the 14th century, speaks of the remains of Memphis as immense; for the most part in a state of decay, though some sculptures of variegated stone still retained a remarkable freshness of color (*Descriptio Ægypti*, ed. Michaelis, 1776). At length so complete was the ruin of Memphis, that for a long time its very site was lost. Pococke could find no trace of it. Recent explorations, especially those of Messrs. Mariette and Linant, have brought to light many of its antiquities, which have been dispersed to the museums of Europe and America. Some specimens of sculpture from Memphis adorn the Egyptian hall of the British Museum; other monuments of this great city are in the Abbott Museum in New York. The dykes and canals of Menes still form the basis of the system of irrigation for Lower Egypt; the insignificant village of Meet Raheeneh occupies nearly the centre of the ancient capital. Thus the site and the general outlines of Memphis are nearly restored; but " the images have ceased out of Noph, and it is desolate, without inhabitant."

J. P. T.

* In the six years which have elapsed since the preceding article was written, much has been brought to light concerning the antiquities of Memphis, both by exploration and by discussion, and there is hardly a point in the topography or the history of the city which remains in obscurity. The illustrated work of Mariette-Bey, embodying the results of his excavations, when completed, will restore the first capital of Egypt, in great part, to its original grandeur.

Memphis appears upon the monuments under three distinct names: the first its name as the capital of the corresponding *Nome* or district; the second its profane, and the third its sacred name. The first, *Sebt-h'et*, is literally " the City of White Walls " — a name originally given to

the citadel (*Herodotus*, iii. c. 91), and especially to that part of the fortifications within which was inclosed the temple of the chief divinity of the city. Osiris is sometimes styled " the great king in the chief city of the Nome of the white walls.'

The second, which was the more common name of the city, *Men-nefr*, signifies literally *mansic bona*. Brugsch regards the commonly-received analogy of this with the *Moph* or *Noph* of the Hebrew Scriptures as of slight authority, and prefers to identify *Noph* with *Edfu*, which appears in the hieroglyphics under the form of " the city of *Nepu* or *Nup*" (*Geograph. Inschriften*, i. 166 and 235).

The sacred name of the city was *Ha-ptah* or *Pa-ptah*, " the House or City of *Ptah* " — *Hephaistopolis*.

Another name frequently given to Memphis on the monuments is *Tapanch*; this was particularly applied to the sacred quarter of the goddess *Basti*, and signifies " the World of Life." Brugsch traces here a resemblance to the second clause in the surname of Joseph given by Pharaoh (Gen. xli. 45), which the LXX. render by φαρὴχ. Brugsch reads this title as equivalent to *as pen-ta-panch*, which means " this is the Governor of *Tapanch*," Joseph being thus invested with authority over that sacred quarter of the capital, and bearing from it the title " Lord of the World of Life."

The royal grandeur of Memphis is attested by the groups of pyramids that mark the burial-place of her lines of kings; but a rich discovery has now brought to light a consecutive list of her sovereigns in almost unbroken continuity from Menes. This is the " New Table of Abydos " which Mariette-Bey came upon in 1865, in the course of his explorations at that primitive seat of monarchy, and which Dümichen has faithfully reproduced in his work. Inscriptions upon the great temple of Abydos show that this was erected by Sethos I. and further ornamented by his son, who is known in history as the second Rameses. Upon one lobby of the temple Sethos and Rameses are depicted as rendering homage to the Gods; and in the inscription appear 130 proper names of divinities, together with the names of the places where these divinities were particularly worshipped. Upon the opposite lobby the same persons, the king and his son, are represented in the act of homage to their royal predecessors, and an almost perfect list is given, embracing seventy-six kings from Menes to Sethos. This discovery has important bearings upon the chronology of the Egyptian Pharaonic dynasties. There are now four monumental lists of kings which serve for comparison with the lists of Manetho and the Turin Papyrus: (1.) The Tablet of Karnak, on which Tuthmosis III. appears sacrificing to his predecessors, sixty-one of whom are represented by their portraits and names. (2.) The Tablet of Abydos, now in the British Museum, which represents Rameses-Sesothis receiving congratulations from his royal predecessors, fifty in number. (3.) The Tablet of Saqqarah, discovered by Mariette in 1864, in a private tomb in the necropolis of Memphis, which represents a royal scribe in the act of adoration before a row of fifty-eight royal cartouches. (4.) The *new* Tablet of Abydos described above. When these four monumental lists are tabulated with one another, and with the lists of Manetho and the Turin Papyrus, the correspondences of names and dynasties are so many and so minute as to prove that they all stand related to some traditional series of kings which was of common authority. Their variations may be owing in part to diversities of reading, and in part to a preference for particular kings or lists of kings in contemporary dynasties; so that while, in some instances, contemporary dynasties have been drawn upon by different authorities, no Tablet incorporates contemporary dynasties into one. Now, since the date of Sethos I. falls within the fifteenth century, B. C., it is obvious that to allow for a succession of seventy-six Memphite kings from Menes to Sethos I., and for the growth of the mechanic arts and the national resources up to the point indicated at the consolidation of the empire under Menes, the received Biblical chronology between the Flood and the Exodus must be somewhat extended. We await some more definite determination of the Hyksos period, as a fixed point of calculation for the preceding dynasties. Bunsen (vol. v. pp. 58, 77, and 103) fixes the era of Menes at 3059 B. C. — "the beginning of chronological time in Egypt, by the settlement of the system of the vague solar year;" this is a reduction of about 600 years, for in vol. iv. p. 490, he placed Menes at 3623 B. C., and he also demanded at least 6000 years before Menes, for the settlement of Egypt and the development of a national life. This, however, is not history but conjecture; but the new Table of Abydos is a tangible scale of history. (For a comparison of these several tablets, see the *Revue Archéologique*, 1864 and 1865, Rougè, *Recherches sur les Monuments Historiques*, and Dümichen, *Zeitschrift für Ägypt. Sprache*, 1864.)   J. P. T.

MEMU'CAN (מְמוּכָן) [a Persian title]: Μουχαῖος: *Mamuchan*). One of the seven princes of Persia in the reign of Ahasuerus, who "saw the king's face," and sat first in the kingdom (Esth. i. 14). They were "wise men who knew the times" (skilled in the planets, according to Aben Ezra), and appear to have formed a council of state; Josephus says that one of their offices was that of interpreting the laws (*Ant.* xi. 6, § 1). This may also be inferred from the manner in which the royal question is put to them when assembled in council; "*According to law* what is to be done with the queen Vashti?" Memucan was either the president of the council on this occasion, or gave his opinion first in consequence of his acknowledged wisdom, or from the respect allowed to his advanced age. Whatever may have been the cause of this priority, his sentence for Vashti's disgrace was approved by the king and princes, and at once put into execution; "and the king did according to the word of Memucan" (Esth. i. 16, 21). The Targum of Esther identifies him with "Haman the grandson of Agag." The reading of the *Cethib*, or written text, in ver. 16 is מוּמְכָן.   W. A. W.

MEN'AHEM (מְנַחֵם [consoler, whence MANAEN, Acts xiii. 1]: Μαναήμ; [Alex. Μαναην, exc. in ver. 14:] *Manahem*), son of Gadi, who [a] slew the usurper Shallum and seized the vacant throne

of Israel, B. C. 772. His reign, which lasted ten years, is briefly recorded in 2 K. xv. 14-22. It has been inferred from the expression in verse 14, "from Tirzah," that Menahem was a general under Zechariah stationed at Tirzah, and that he brought up his troops to Samaria and avenged the murder of his master by Shallum (Joseph. *Ant.* ix. 11, § 1; Keil, Thenius).

In religion Menahem was a steadfast adherent of the form of idolatry established in Israel by Jeroboam. His general character is described by Josephus as rude and exceedingly cruel. The contemporary prophets, Hosea and Amos, have left a melancholy picture of the ungodliness, demoralization, and feebleness of Israel; and Ewald adds to their testimony some doubtful references to Isaiah and Zechariah.

In the brief history of Menahem, his ferocious treatment of Tiphsah occupies a conspicuous place. The time of the occurrence, and the site of the town have been doubted. Keil says that it can be no other place than the remote Thapsacus on the Euphrates, the northeast boundary (1 K. iv. 24) of Solomon's dominions; and certainly no other place bearing the name is mentioned in the Bible. Others suppose that it may have been some town which Menahem took in his way as he went from Tirzah to win a crown in Samaria (Ewald); or that it is a transcriber's error for Tappuah (Josh. xvii. 8), and that Menahem laid it waste when he returned from Samaria to Tirzah (Thenius). No sufficient reason appears for having recourse to such conjectures where the plain text presents no insuperable difficulty. The act, whether perpetrated at the beginning of Menahem's reign or somewhat later, was doubtless intended to strike terror into the hearts of reluctant subjects throughout the whole extent of dominion which he claimed. A precedent for such cruelty might be found in the border wars between Syria and Israel, 2 K. viii. 12. It is a striking sign of the increasing degradation of the land, that a king of Israel practices upon his subjects a brutality from the mere suggestion of which the unscrupulous Syrian usurper recoiled with indignation.

But the most remarkable event in Menahem's reign is the first appearance of a hostile force of Assyrians on the northeast frontier of Israel. King Pul, however, withdrew, having been converted from an enemy into an ally by a timely gift of 1000 talents of silver, which Menahem exacted by an assessment of 50 shekels a head on 60,000 Israelites. It seems perhaps too much to infer from 1 Chr. v. 26, that Pul also took away Israelite captives. The name of Pul (LXX. Phaloch or Phalos) appears according to Rawlinson (*Bampton Lectures* for 1859, Lect. iv. p. 133) in an Assyrian inscription of a Ninevite king, as Phallukha, who took tribute from Beth Khumri (= the house of Omri = Samaria) as well as from Tyre, Sidon, Damascus, Idumæa, and Philistia; the king of Damascus is set down as giving 2300 talents of silver besides gold and copper, but neither the name of Menahem, nor the

---

[a] Ewald (*Gesch. Isr.* iii. 598), following the LXX., would translate the latter part of 2 K. xv. 10, "And Kobolam (or Keblaam) smote him, and slew him, and reigned in his stead." Ewald considers the fact of such a king's existence a help to the interpretation of Zech. xi. 8; and he accounts for the silence of Scripture as to his end by saying that he may have thrown himself across the Jordan, and disappeared

among the subjects of king Uzziah. It does not appear, however, how such a translation can be made to agree with the subsequent mention (ver. 13) of Shallum, and with the express ascription of Shallum's death (ver. 14) to Menahem. Thenius excuses the translation of the LXX. by supposing that their MSS. may have been in a defective state, but ridicules the theory of Ewald.

amount of his tribute is stated in the inscription. Rawlinson also says that in another inscription the name of Menahem is given, probably by mistake of the stone-cutter, as a tributary of Tiglath-pileser.

Menahem died in peace, and was succeeded by his son Pekahiah.   W. T. B.

* ME'NAM, the reading of the A. V. ed. 1611 and other early eds. in Luke iii. 31 for MENAN, which see.   A.

ME'NAN (Μεννά; [Rec. Text, Μαϊνάν; Tisch. Treg. with Sin. BLX Μεννά; Lachm. Μεννά in brackets (A omits it); Erasmus, Ald., Gerbelius, Colinæus, Μεννά, whence the reading MENAM, A. V. ed. 1611: Bogardus (1543), Μεννά, like A. V. in later editions:] Menna). The son of Mattatha, one of the ancestors of Joseph in the genealogy of Jesus Christ (Luke iii. 31). This name and the following Melea are omitted in some Latin MSS., and are believed by Ld. A. Hervey to be corrupt (Genealogies, p. 88).

ME'NE (מְנֵא: Μανή, Theodot.: Mane). The first word of the mysterious inscription written upon the wall of Belshazzar's palace, in which Daniel read the doom of the king and his dynasty (Dan. v. 25, 26). It is the Peal past participle of the Chaldee מְנָה, menáh, "to number," and therefore signifies "numbered," as in Daniel's interpretation, "God hath numbered (מְנָה, menáh) thy kingdom and finished it."   W. A. W.

MENELA'US (Μενέλαος), a usurping high-priest who obtained the office from Antiochus Epiphanes (cir. B. C. 172) by a large bribe (2 Macc. iv. 23–25), and drove out Jason, who had obtained it not long before by similar means. When he neglected to pay the sum which he had promised, he was summoned to the king's presence, and by plundering the Temple gained the means of silencing the accusations which were brought against him. By a similar sacrilege he secured himself against the consequences of an insurrection which his tyranny had excited, and also procured the death of Onias (vv. 27–34). He was afterwards hard pressed by Jason, who, taking occasion from his unpopularity, attempted unsuccessfully to recover the high-priesthood (2 Macc. v. 5–10). For a time he then disappears from the history (yet comp. ver. 23), but at last he met with a violent death at the hands of Antiochus Eupator (cir. B. C. 163), which seemed in a peculiar manner a providential punishment of his sacrilege (xiii. 3, 4).

According to Josephus (Ant. xii. 5, § 1) he was a younger brother of Jason and Onias, and, like Jason, changed his proper name Onias for a Greek name. In 2 Maccabees, on the other hand, he is called a brother of Simon the Benjamite (2 Macc. iv. 23), whose treason led to the first attempt to plunder the Temple. If this account be correct, the profanation of the sacred office was the more marked by the fact that it was transferred from the family of Aaron.   B. F. W.

MENES'THEUS [3 syl.] (Μενεσθεύς; Alex. Μενεσθεσις: Mnestheus). The father of APOLLONIUS 3 (2 Macc. iv. 21).

ME'NI. The last clause of Is. lxv. 11 is rendered in the A. V. "and that furnish the drink-offering unto that number" (לַמְנִי), the marginal reading for the last word being "Meni." That the word so rendered is a proper name, and also the proper name of an object of idolatrous worship cultivated by the Jews in Babylon, is a supposition which there seems no reason to question, as it is in accordance with the context, and has every probability to recommend it. But the identification of Meni with any known heathen god is still uncertain. The versions are at variance. In the LXX the word is rendered ἡ τύχη, "fortune" or "luck." The old Latin version of the clause is "impletis dæmoni potionem;" while Symmachus (as quoted by Jerome) must have had a different reading, מְמִי: minni, "without me," which Jerome interprets as signifying that the act of worship implied in the drink-offering was not performed for God, but for the dæmon ("ut doceat non sibi fieri sed dæmoni"). The Targum of Jonathan is very vague — "and mingle cups for their idols;" and the Syriac translators either omit the word altogether, or had a different reading, perhaps לָמֹי, lámó, "for them." Some variation of the same kind apparently gave rise to the super eam of the Vulgate, referring to the "table" mentioned in the first clause of the verse. From the old versions we come to the commentators, and their judgments are equally conflicting. Jerome (Comm. in Is. lxv. 11) illustrates the passage by reference to an ancient idolatrous custom which prevailed in Egypt, and especially at Alexandria, on the last day of the last month of the year, of placing a table covered with dishes of various kinds, and a cup mixed with mead, in acknowledgment of the fertility of the past year, or as an omen of that which was to come (comp. Virg. Æn. ii. 763). But he gives no clew to the identification of Meni, and his explanation is evidently suggested by the renderings of the LXX. and the old Latin version; the former, as he quotes them, translating Gad by "fortune," and Meni by "dæmon," in which they are followed by the latter. In the later mythology of Egypt, as we learn from Macrobius (Saturn. i. 19), Δαίμων and Τύχη were two of the four deities who presided over birth, and represented respectively the Sun and Moon. A passage quoted by Selden (de Dis Syris, Synt. i. c. 1) from a MS. of Vettius Valens of Antioch, an ancient astrologer, goes also to prove that in the astrological language of his day the sun and moon were indicated by δαίμων and τύχη, as being the arbiters of human destiny.[a] This circumstance, coupled with the similarity between Meni and Μήν or Μήνη, the ancient name for the moon, has induced the majority of commentators to conclude that Meni is the Moon god or goddess, the Deus Lunus, or Dea Luna of the Romans; masculine as regards the earth which she illumines (terra maritus), feminine with respect to the sun (Solis uxor), from whom she receives her light. This twofold character of the moon is thought by David Millius to be indicated in the two names Gad and Meni, the former feminine, the latter masculine (Diss. v. § 23); but as both are mascu-

---

while the reading given by Jerome is supported by the fact that, in Gen. xxx. 11, גָד, gad, is rendered τύχη

ine in Hebrew, his speculation falls to the ground. Le Moyne, on the other hand, regarded both words as denoting the sun, and his double worship among the Egyptians: *Gad* is then the goat of Mendes, and *Meni* = Mnevis worshipped at Heliopolis. The opinion of Huetius that the *Meni* of Isaiah and the Μὴν of Strabo (xii. c. 31) both denoted the sun was refuted by Vitringa and others. Among those who have interpreted the word literally "number," may be reckoned Jarchi and Abarbanel, who understand by it the "number" of the priests who formed the company of revelers at the feast, and later Hoheisel (*Obs. ad diffic. Jes. loca*, p. 349) followed in the same track. Kimchi, in his note on Is. lxv. 11. says of Meni, "it is a star, and some interpret it of the stars which are *numbered*, and they are the seven stars of motion," i. e. the planets. Buxtorf (*Lex. Hebr.*) applies it to the "number" of the stars which were worshipped as gods; Schindler (*Lex. Pentagl.*) to "the number and multitude" of the idols, while according to others it refers to "Mercury the god of numbers;" all which are mere conjectures, *quot homines, tot sententiæ*, and take their origin from the play upon the word Meni, which is found in the verse next following that in which it occurs

("therefore will I *number* (וּמָנִיתִי, *âmânithí*) you to the sword"), and which is supposed to point to its derivation from the verb מָנָה, *mânâh*, to number. But the origin of the name of Noah, as given in Gen. v. 29,[a] shows that such plays upon words are not to be depended upon as the bases of etymology. On the supposition, however, that in this case the etymology of Meni is really indicated, its meaning is still uncertain. Those who understand by it the moon, derive an argument for their theory from the fact, that anciently years were *numbered* by the courses of the moon. But Gesenius (*Comm. üb. d. Jesaia*), with more probability, while admitting the same origin of the word, gives to the root *mânâh* the sense of assigning, or distributing,[b] and connects it with *manâh*,[c] one of the three idols worshipped by the Arabs before the time of Mohammed, to which reference is made in the Koran (Sura 53), "What think ye of Allat, and Al-Uzzah, and *Manah*, that other third goddess?" *Manah* was the object of worship of "the tribes of *Hudheyl* and *Khuzâ'oh*, who dwelt between Mekkeh and El-Medeeneh, and as some say, of the tribes of Ows, El-Khazraj, and Thakeek also. This idol was a large stone, demolished by one Saad, in the 8th year of the Flight, a year so fatal to the idols of Arabia" (Lane's *Sel. from the Kur ân*, pref. pp. 30, 31, from Pococke's *Spec. Hist. Ar.* p. 93, ed. White). But Al-Zamakhshari. the commentator on the Koran, derives *Manah* from the root مَنَى, "to flow," because of the blood which flowed at the sacrifices to this idol, or, as Millius

explains it, because the ancient idea of the moon was that it was a star full of moisture, with which it filled the sublunary regions.[d] The etymology given by Gesenius is more probable; and Meni would then be the personification of fate or destiny, under whatever form it was worshipped.[e] Whether this form, as Gesenius maintains, was the planet Venus, which was known to Arabic astrologers as "the lesser good fortune" (the planet Jupiter being the "greater"), it is impossible to say with certainty; nor is it safe to reason from the worship of *Manah* by the Arabs in the times before Mohammed to that of Meni by the Jews more than a thousand years earlier. But the coincidence is remarkable, though the identification may be incomplete.   W. A. W.

* **MEN-PLEASERS** (ἀνθρωπάρεσκοι) is a word which came into use with Tyndale's translation (Ep. vi. 6; Col. iii. 22). It is like "eye-service" in this respect, which occurs in the same passages   H.

* **MENU'CHAH** (מְנוּחָה: ἀπὸ Νουά: Alex. and Vulg. translate freely) in Judg. xx. 43 has been regarded by some critics as the name of a place, and is put as such in the margin of the A. V., but in the text is rendered "with ease." Fürst takes it to be the same as Manahath in 1 Chr. viii. 6, whence the patronymic Manahethites, 1 Chr. ii. 54. If a town be meant, it was in the tribe of Benjamin, and on the line of the retreat of the Benjamites before the other tribes at the siege of Gibeah (comp. Judg. xx. 41 ff.). It is held to be a proper name in Luther's version. But the word has more probably its ordinary signification: either "with ease" (literally "quiet" as the opposite of toil, trouble), with reference to the almost unresisted victory of the other tribes over the panic-stricken Benjamites; or "place of rest," i. e. in every such place where the men of Benjamin halted for a moment, their pursuers fell upon them and trampled them to pieces (וַיַּדְרִיכֻהוּ), like grapes in the wine-press.

It should be said that the name reappears in the margin of the A. V., Jer. li. 59: "Seraiah was a prince of Menucha, or chief chamberlain," where the text reads "was a quiet prince." The Bishops' Bible (connecting the word with the previous verb) translates "chased them diligently" or (margin) "from their rest." On the whole, it appears to the writer not easy to discover any better sense than that suggested in the A. V.   H.

MEON'ENIM, THE PLAIN OF (אֵלוֹן מְעוֹנְנִים [see below]: [Vat.] Ηλωνμαωνεμειν: [Rom. 'Ηλωνμαωνενίμ;] Alex. and Aquila, δρυὸς ἀποβλεπόντων: *qua respicit quercum*), an oak, or terebinth, or other great tree — for the translation of the Hebrew *Elon* by "plain" is most probably incorrect, as will be shown under the head of

---

a "And he called his name Noah (נֹחַ), saying, This one shall *comfort us*," etc. (יְנַחֲמֵנוּ, *yěnachă-mênû*). Yet no one would derive נֹחַ, *nâack*, from נָחַם, *nâcham*. The play on the word may be retained without detriment to the sense if we render Meni "destiny," and the following clause, "therefore will I *destine* you for the sword."

b Like the Arab. مَنَى, *mana*, whence مَنَا,

c مَنَاة

e "death," مَنِيّة, "fate," "destiny."

d   —— "The moist star Upon whose influence Neptune's empire stands."   SHAKESP. *Haml.* i. 1.

e The presence of the article seems to indicate that "Meni" was originally an appellative.

PLAIN — which formed a well-known object in central Palestine in the days of the Judges. It is mentioned — at least under this name — only in Judg. ix. 37, where Gaal ben-Ebed standing in the gateway of Shechem sees the ambushes of Abimelech coming towards the city, one by the middle [literally, "navel"] of the land, and another "by the way (מְדְרֶךְ) of Elon-Meonenim," that is, the road leading to it. In what direction it stood with regard to the town we are not told.

The meaning of Meonenim, if interpreted as a Hebrew word, is enchanters,[a] or "observers of times," as it is elsewhere rendered (Deut. xviii. 10, 14; in Mic. v. 12 it is "soothsayers"). This connection of the name with magical arts has led to the suggestion[b] that the tree in question is identical with that beneath which Jacob hid the foreign idols and amulets of his household, before going into the presence of God at the consecrated ground of Bethel (Gen. xxxv. 4). But the inference seems hardly a sound one, for meonenim does not mean "enchantments" but "enchanters," nor is there any ground for connecting it in any way with amulets or images; and there is the positive reason against the identification that while this tree seems to have been at a distance from the town of Shechem, that of Jacob was in it, or in very close proximity to it (the Hebrew particle used is עִם, which implies this).

Five trees are mentioned in connection with Shechem: —

1. The oak (not "plain" as in A. V.) of Moreh, where Abram made his first halt and built his first altar in the Promised Land (Gen. xii. 6).

2. That of Jacob, already spoken of.

3. "The oak which was in the holy place of Jehovah" (Josh. xxiv. 26), beneath which Joshua set up the stone which he assured the people had heard all his words, and would one day witness against them.

4. The Elon-Muttsab, or "oak [not 'plain,' as in A. V.) of the pillar in Shechem," beneath which Abimelech was made king (Judg. ix. 6).

5. The Elon-Meonenim.

The first two of these may, with great probability, be identical. The second, third, and fourth, agree in being all specified as in or close to the town. Joshua's is mentioned with the definite article — "the oak" — as if well known previously. It is therefore possible that it was Jacob's tree, or its successor. And it seems further possible that during the confusions which prevailed in the country after Joshua's death, the stone which he had erected beneath it, and which he invested, even though only in metaphor, with qualities so like those which the Canaanites attributed to the stones they worshipped — that during these confused times this famous block may have become sacred among the Canaanites, one of their "mattsebahs" [see IDOL, vol. ii. p. 1119 b], and thus the tree have acquired the name of "the oak of Muttsab" from the fetish below it.

That Jacob's oak and Joshua's oak were the same tree seems still more likely, when we observe the remarkable correspondence between the circumstances of each occurrence. The point of Joshua's address — his summary of the early history of the nation — is that they should "put away the foreign gods which were among them, and incline their hearts to Jehovah the God of Israel." Except in the mention of Jehovah, who had not revealed Himself till the Exodus, the words are all but identical with those in which Jacob had addressed his followers; and it seems almost impossible not to believe that the coincidence was intentional on Joshua's part, and that such an allusion to a well-known passage in the life of their forefather, and which had occurred on the very spot where they were standing, must have come home with peculiar force to his hearers.

But while four of these were thus probably one and the same tree, the oak of Meonenim for the reasons stated above seems to have been a distinct one.

It is perhaps possible that Meonenim may have originally been Maonim, that is Maonites or Mehunim; a tribe or nation of non-Israelites elsewhere mentioned. If so it furnishes an interesting trace of the presence at some early period of that tribe in Central Palestine, of which others have been noticed in the case of the Ammonites, Avites, Zemarites, etc. [See vol. i. p. 277, note b.] G.

MEON'OTHAI [4 syl.] (מְעוֹנֹתַי) [my dwellings, Ges.: see Fürst]: Μαναθί; [Vat. Μαναθει; Comp. Μαναθαεί:] Maonathi). One of the sons of Othniel, the younger brother of Caleb (1 Chr. iv. 14). In the text as it now stands there is probably an omission, and the true reading of vv. 13 and 14 should be, as the Vulgate and the Complutensian edition of the LXX. give it, "and the sons of Othniel, Hathath and Meonothai; and Meonothai begat Ophrah." It is not clear whether this last phrase implies that he founded the town of Ophrah or not: the usage of the word "father" in the sense of "founder" is not uncommon.

MEPHA'ATH (מֵיפָעַת) [height, Fürst; beauty, Ges.]: in Chron. and Jerem. מֵיפָעַת; in the latter the Cethib, or original text, has מוֹפְעַת: Μαιφαάθ; Alex.[c] Μηφααθ: Mephaath, Mephaat), a city of the Reubenites, one of the towns dependent on Heshbon (Josh. xiii. 18), lying in the district of the Mishor (comp. 17, and Jer. xlviii. 21, A. V. "plain"), which probably answered to the modern Belka. It was one of the cities allotted with their suburbs to the Merarite Levites (Josh. xxi. 37; 1 Chr. vi. 79; the former does not exist in the Rec. Hebr. Text). At the time of the conquest it was no doubt, like Heshbon, in the hands of the Amorites (Num. xxi. 26), but when Jeremiah delivered his denunciations it had been recovered by its original possessors, the Moabites (xlviii. 21).

Mephaath is named in the above passages with

---

a Gesenius (Thes. 51 b), incantatores and Zauberer; Michaelis and Fürst, Wahrsager. The root of the word is עָנֵן, probably connected with עַיִן, the eye, which bears so prominent a part in Eastern magic. Of this there is a trace in the respicit of the Vulgate. (See Gesen. Thes. 10 ? 2, 1063; also DIVINATION, vol. i. pp. 606, 607.)

b See Stanley, S. & P., p. 142.

c The name is given in the LXX. as follows: Josh. xiii. 18, Μαιφαάθ, Alex. Μηφααθ; xxi. 37, τὴν Μαφᾶ, Alex. τ. Μαοφα; 1 Chr. vi. 79, τὴν Μαεφλὰ, Alex. τ. Φααθ; Jer. xlviii. (xxxi.) 21, Μωφάτ, Alex. Νωφαθ [? Μωφαθ, according to Baber].

Dibon, Jahazah, Kirjathaim, and other towns, which have been identified with tolerable certainty on the north of the Arnon (*Wady Mojeb*); but no one appears yet to have discovered any name at all resembling it, and it must remain for the further investigation of those interesting and comparatively untrodden districts. In the time of Eusebius (*Onomast.* Μηφαάθ) it was used as a military post for keeping in check the wandering tribes of the desert, which surrounded, as it still surrounds, the cultivated land of this district.

The extended, and possibly later, form of the name which occurs in Chronicles and Jeremiah, as if *Mei Phaath*, "waters of Phaath," may be, as in other cases, an attempt to fix an intelligible meaning on an archaic or foreign word.   G.

MEPHIBO'SHETH (מְפִיבֹשֶׁת) [perh. *idol-exterminator*, Sim., Ges. ; but see Fürst] : Μεμφιβοσθέ; [Alex. Μεμφιβοσθαι, exc. 2 Sam. ix. 11, 13;] Joseph. Μεμφίβοσθος: *Miphibosheth*), the name borne by two members of the family of Saul — his son and his grandson.

The name itself is perhaps worth a brief consideration. Bosheth appears to have been a favorite appellation in Saul's family, for it forms a part of the names of no fewer than three members of it — Ish-bosheth and the two Mephi-bosheths. But in the genealogies preserved in 1 Chronicles these names are given in the different forms of Esh-baal and Merib-baal. The variation is identical with that of Jerub-baal and Jerub-besheth, and is in accordance with passages in Jeremiah (xi. 13) and Hosea (ix. 10), where Baal and Bosheth [a] appear to be convertible, or at least related, terms, the latter being used as a contemptuous or derisive synonym of the former. One inference from this would be that the persons in question were originally [b] named Baal; that this appears in the two fragments of the family records preserved in Chronicles; but that in Samuel the hateful heathen name has been uniformly erased, and the nickname Bosheth substituted for it. It is some support to this to find that Saul had an ancestor named BAAL, who appears in the lists of Chronicles only (1 Chr. viii. 30, ix. 36). But such a change in the record supposes an amount of editing and interpolation which would hardly have been accomplished without leaving more obvious traces, in reasons given

for the change, etc. How different it is, for example, from the case of Jerub-besheth, where the alteration is mentioned and commented on. Still the facts are as above stated, whatever explanation may be given of them.

1. Saul's son by Rizpah the daughter of Aiah, his concubine (2 Sam. xxi. 8). He and his brother Armoni were among the seven victims who were surrendered by David to the Gibeonites, and by them crucified [c] in sacrifice to Jehovah, to avert a famine from which the country was suffering. The seven corpses, protected by the tender care of the mother of Mephibosheth from the attacks of bird and beast, were exposed on their crosses to the fierce sun [d] of at least five of the midsummer months, on the sacred eminence of Gibeah. At the end of that time the attention of David was called to the circumstance, and also possibly to the fact that the sacrifice had failed in its purpose. A different method was tried: the bones of Saul and Jonathan were disinterred from their resting-place at the foot of the great tree at Jabesh-Gilead, the blanched and withered remains of Mephibosheth, his brother, and his five relatives, were taken down from the crosses, and father, son, and grandsons found at last a resting-place together in the ancestral cave of Kish at Zelah. When this had been done, "God was entreated for the land," and the famine ceased. [RIZPAH.]

2. The son of Jonathan, grandson of Saul, and nephew of the preceding.

1. His life seems to have been, from beginning to end, one of trial and discomfort. The name of his mother is unknown. There is reason to think that she died shortly after his birth, and that he was an only child. At any rate we know for certain that when his father and grandfather were slain on Gilboa he was an infant of but five years old. He was then living under the charge of his nurse, probably at Gibeah, the regular residence of Saul. The tidings that the army was destroyed, the king and his sons slain, and that the Philistines, spreading from hill to hill of the country, were sweeping all before them, reached the royal household. The nurse fled, carrying the child on her shoulder. [e] But in her panic and hurry she stumbled, and Mephibosheth was precipitated to the ground with such force as to deprive him for life of the use of both [f] feet (2 Sam. iv. 4). These early misfor-

[a] Translated in A. V. "shame."

[b] Some of the ancient Greek versions of the Hexapla give the name in Samuel as Memphi-baal (see Bahrdt's *Hexapla*, pp. 594, 599, 614). Also Procopius Gazzeus, *Scholia* on 2 Sam. xvi. No trace of this, however, appears in any MS. of the Hebrew text.

[c] There is no doubt about this being the real meaning of the word יָקַע, translated here and in Num. xxv. 4 "hanged up." (See Michaelis's *Supplement*, No. 1046; also Gesenius, *Thes.* 620; and Fürst, *Handwb.* 539 b.) Aquila has ἀνεπήγνυμι, understanding them to have been not crucified but impaled. The Vulgate rends *crucifixerunt* (ver. 9), and *qui affixi fuerant* (13).

The Hebrew term יָקַע is entirely distinct from תָּלָה, also rendered "to hang" in the A. V., which is its real signification. It is this latter word which is employed in the story of the five kings at Makkedah; in the account of the indignities practiced on Saul's body, 2 Sam. xxi. 12, on Baanah and Rechab by David, 2 Sam. iv. 12; and elsewhere.

[d] This follows from the statement that they hung from barley harvest (April) till the commencement of

the rains (October); but it is also worthy of notice that the LXX. have employed the word ἐξηλιάζειν, " to expose to the sun." It is also remarkable that on the only other occasion on which this Hebrew term is used — Num. xxv. 4 — an express command was given that the victims should be crucified "in front of the sun."

[e] This is the statement of Josephus — ἀπὸ τῶν ὤμων (*Ant.* vii. 5, § 5); but it is hardly necessary, for in the East children are always carried on the shoulder. See the woodcut in Lane's *Mod. Egyptians*, ch. i. p. 52.

[f] It is a remarkable thing, and very characteristic of the simplicity and unconsciousness of these ancient records, of which the late Professor Blunt has happily illustrated so many other instances, that this information concerning Mephibosheth's childhood, which contains the key to his whole history, is inserted, almost as if by accident, in the midst of the narrative of his uncle's death, with no apparent reason for the insertion, or connection between the two, further than that of their being relatives and having somewhat similar names.

tunes threw a shade over his whole life, and his personal deformity — as is often the case where it has been the result of accident — seems to have exercised a depressing and depreciatory influence on his character. He can never forget that he is a poor lame slave (2 Sam. xix. 26), and unable to walk; a dead dog (ix. 8); that all the house of his father were dead (xix. 28); that the king is an angel of God (ib. 27), and he his abject dependent (ix. 6, 8). He receives the slanders of Ziba and the harshness of David alike with a submissive equanimity which is quite touching, and which effectually wins our sympathy.

2. After the accident which thus embittered his whole existence, Mephibosheth was carried with the rest of his family beyond the Jordan to the mountains of Gilead, where he found a refuge in the house of Machir ben-Ammiel, a powerful Gadite or Manassite sheykh at Lo-debar, not far from Mahanaim, which during the reign of his uncle Ishbosheth was the head-quarters of his family. By Machir he was brought up (Jos. Ant. vii. 5, § 5), there he married, and there he was living at a later period, when David, having completed the subjugation of the adversaries of Israel on every side, had leisure to turn his attention to claims of other and hardly less pressing descriptions. The solemn oath which he had sworn to the father of Mephibosheth at their critical interview by the stone Ezel, that he "would not cut off his kindness from the house of Jonathan for ever: no! not when Jehovah had cut off the enemies of David each one from the face of the earth " (1 Sam. xx. 15); and again, that "Jehovah should be between Jonathan's seed and his seed for ever " (ver. 42), was naturally the first thing that occurred to him, and he eagerly inquired who was left of the house of Saul, that he might show kindness to him for Jonathan's sake (2 Sam. ix. 1). So completely had the family of the late king vanished from the western side of Jordan, that the only person to be met with in any way related to them was one ZIBA, formerly a slave of the royal house, but now a freed man, with a family of fifteen sons, who by arts which, from the glimpse we subsequently have of his character, are not difficult to understand, must have acquired considerable substance, since he was possessed of an establishment of twenty slaves of his own. [ZIBA.] From this man David learnt of the existence of Mephibosheth. Royal messengers were sent to the house of Machir at Lo-debar in the mountains of Gilead, and by them the prince and his infant son MICHA were brought to Jerusalem. The interview with David was marked by extreme kindness on the part of the king, and on that of Mephibosheth by the fear and humility which has been pointed out as characteristic of him. He leaves the royal presence with all the property of his grandfather restored to him, and with the whole family and establishment of Ziba as his slaves, to cultivate the land and harvest the produce. He himself is to be a daily guest at David's table. From this time forward he resided at Jerusalem.

3. An interval of about seventeen years now passes, and the crisis of David's life arrives. Of Mephibosheth's behavior on this occasion we possess two accounts — his own (2 Sam. xix. 24–30), and that of Ziba (xvi. 1–4). They are naturally at variance with each other. (1.) Ziba meets the king on his flight at the most opportune moment, just as David has undergone the most trying part of that trying day's journey, has taken the last look at the city so peculiarly his own, and completed the hot and toilsome ascent of the Mount of Olives. He is on foot, and is in want of relief and refreshment. The relief and refreshment are there. There stand a couple of strong he-asses ready saddled for the king or his household to make the descent upon; and there are bread, grapes, melons, and a skin of wine; and there — the donor of these welcome gifts — is Ziba, with respect in his look and sympathy on his tongue. Of course the whole, though offered as Ziba's, is the property of Mephibosheth: the asses are his, one of them his own a riding animal: the fruits are from his gardens and orchards. But why is not their owner here in person? Where is the "son of Saul " ? He, says Ziba, is in Jerusalem, waiting to receive from the nation the throne of his grandfather, that throne from which he has been so long unjustly excluded. It must be confessed that the tale at first sight is a most plausible one, and that the answer of David is no more than was to be expected. So the base ingratitude of Mephibosheth is requited with the ruin he deserves, while the loyalty and thoughtful courtesy of Ziba are rewarded by the possessions of his master, thus once more reinstating him in the position from which he had been so rudely thrust on Mephibosheth's arrival in Judah. (2.) Mephibosheth's story — which, however, he had not the opportunity of telling until several days later, when he met David returning to his kingdom at the western bank of Jordan — was very different to [from] Ziba's. He had been desirous to fly with his patron and benefactor, and had ordered Ziba to make ready his ass that he might join the cortége. But Ziba had deceived him, had left him, and not returned with the asses. In his helpless condition he had no alternative, when once the opportunity of accompanying David was lost, but to remain where he was. The swift pursuit which had been made after Ahimaaz and Jonathan (2 Sam. xvii.) had shown what risks even a strong and able man must run who would try to follow the king. But all that he could do under the circumstances he had done. He had gone into the deepest mourning possible b for his lost friend. From the very day that David left he had allowed his beard to grow ragged, his crippled feet were unwashed c and untended, his linen remained unchanged. That David did not disbelieve this story is shown by his revoking the judgment he had previously given. That he did not entirely reverse his decision, but allowed Ziba to retain possession of half the lands of Mephibosheth, is probably due partly to weariness at the whole

---

a The word used both in xvi. 1, 2, and xix. 26, is חֲמוֹר, i. e. the strong he-ass, a farm animal, as opposed to the she-ass, more commonly used for riding. For the first see ISSACHAR, vol. ii. p. 1180 a; for the second, ELISHA, vol. i. p. 717 a.

b The same mourning as David for his child (xii. 20).

c A singular Jewish tradition is preserved by Jerome

in his Quaest. Heb. on this passage, to the effect that the correct reading of the Hebrew is not " undressed," but rather " ill-made " — non illotis pedibus, sed pedibus infertis — alluding to false wooden feet which he was accustomed to wear. The Hebrew word — the same to both feet and beard, though rendered in A. V. "dressed " and "trimmed " — is עָשָׂה, answering to our word "done."

transaction, but mainly to the conciliatory frame of mind in which he was at that moment. "Shall then any man be put to death this day?" is the key-note of the whole proceeding. Ziba probably was a rascal, who had done his best to injure an innocent and helpless man: but the king had passed his word that no one was to be made unhappy on this joyful day; and so Mephibosheth, who believed himself ruined, has half his property restored to him, while Ziba is better off than he was before the king's flight, and far better off than he deserved to be.

4. The writer is aware that this is not the view generally taken of Mephibosheth's conduct, and in particular the opposite side has been maintained with much cogency and ingenuity by the late Professor Blunt in his *Undesigned Coincidences* (part ii. § 17). But when the circumstances on both sides are weighed, there seems to be no escape from the conclusion come to above. Mephibosheth could have had nothing to hope for from the revolution. It was not a mere anarchical scramble in which all had equal chances of coming to the top, but a civil war between two parties, led by two individuals, Absalom on one side, David on the other. From Absalom, who had made no vow to Jonathan, it is obvious that he had nothing to hope. Moreover, the struggle was entirely confined to the tribe of Judah, and, at the period with which alone we are concerned, to the chief city of Judah. What chance could a Benjamite have had there? — more especially one whose very claim was his descent from a man known only to the people of Judah as having for years hunted their darling David through the hills and woods of his native tribe; least of all when that Benjamite was a poor, nervous, timid cripple, as opposed to Absalom, the handsomest, readiest, and most popular man in the country. Again, Mephibosheth's story is throughout valid and consistent. Every tie, both of interest and of gratitude, combined to keep him faithful to David's cause. As not merely lame, but deprived of the use of both feet, he must have been entirely dependent on his ass and his servant: a position which Ziba showed that he completely appreciated by not only making off himself, but taking the asses and their equipments with him. Of the impossibility of flight, after the king and the troops had gone, we have already spoken. Lastly, we have, not his own statement, but that of the historian, to the fact that he commenced his mourning, not when his supposed designs on the throne proved futile, but on the very day of David's departure (xix. 24).

So much for Mephibosheth. Ziba, on the other hand, had everything to gain and nothing to lose by any turn affairs might take. As a Benjamite and an old adherent of Saul all his tendencies must have been hostile to David. It was David, moreover, who had thrust him down from his independent position, and brought himself and his fifteen sons back into the bondage from which they had before escaped, and from which they could now be delivered only by the fall of Mephibosheth. He had thus every reason to wish his master out of the way, and human nature must be different to what it is if we can believe that either his good offices to David or his accusation of Mephibosheth was the result of anything but calculation and interest.

With regard to the absence of the name of Mephibosheth from the dying words of David, which is the main occasion of Mr. Blunt's strictures, it is most natural — at any rate it is quite allow-able — to suppose that, in the interval of eight years which elapsed between David's return to Jerusalem and his death, Mephibosheth's painful life had come to an end. We may without difficulty believe that he did not long survive the anxieties and annoyances which Ziba's treachery had brought upon him.   G.

* The arguments which favor the side of Mephibosheth on this question of veracity between him and Ziba are somewhat fully stated above. It is due to an impartial view of the case to mention also some of the considerations on the other side, to which the reader's attention has not been called. Josephus supports this view, which was probably prevalent among the Jews of his day. Jerome names it as the early Christian tradition; and modern commentators (Henry, Jamieson, Kitto, and others) urge the same opinion. No tradition, of course, reaches back to the period, and any inference is legitimate which is fairly deducible from the record itself. We offer a few considerations to balance some of the preceding.

(1.) The relation of Ziba to Mephibosheth could not have been degrading and trying. It would have been a poor return for the information which enabled the king to reach the object of his favor, to inflict an injury on the informer. In delegating to an old servant of Saul the care of his late royal master's grandson with his restored estate — making him the steward of his property and (in his helplessness) the virtual guardian of his person, David conferred an honorable trust, and placed Ziba in a more important post than he occupied before. The novel suggestion that the king "*rudely* thrust" him from a better position, and that he harbored rancor as one who had been "thrust down" and "brought into bondage" from which he sought escape, has no apparent basis.

(2.) The open kindness which Ziba rendered king David was not only most opportune, but was also bestowed at an hour when there was no prospect of reward, if it did not even involve some risk. He could not have reasonably anticipated that the monarch, in his own extremity, would confiscate his master's estate (against whom he volunteered no charge) and announce its transfer to himself. If, withal, what was "offered as Ziba's" was "the property of Mephibosheth," would not the king know it? And would the servant be so presuming if the fact were so patent? And what is there in all his conduct to countenance the conjecture of "tendencies hostile to David"?

(3.) It would be natural for Mephibosheth (as David's ready credence shows) to imagine that dissension in the royal family and civil war might result in bringing him to the throne. As between David and Absalom, he had nothing to hope from the latter and much from the former; but this deadly breach between them may have awakened hopes of his own — and these failing, the countercharge against Ziba would be the natural cover and defense of his course, if the charge of the latter were true.

(4.) The proposal of Mephibosheth, when half the estate was restored to him, to allow Ziba to keep the whole — a token of his indifference to property, from genuine joy at his benefactor's safe return — will not, of itself, mislead any one who is familiar with eastern phrases and professions of friendship. The speech was purely oriental — as was Ziba's previous acknowledgment.

(5.) Aside from the charge of Mephibosheth,

made in self-exculpation, the character of Ziba is unimpeached, and there is no indication that David withdrew his confidence from him.

(6.) The final award of David is far more reconcilable with his belief of Mephibosheth's guilt, than of Ziba's. To pity the son of Jonathan, in his abject destitution, and permit him to retain half of his forfeited possessions, would accord with David's known magnanimity and befit his day of triumph. "The key-note of the whole proceeding," to which Mr. Grove properly refers, is certainly not less in harmony with this construction than with the other. It would be the reverse of magnanimous, and positively wrong, to reward the "treachery" of Ziba, and permit him to hold half of his master's estate as the fruit of falsehood and fraud of which he had been convicted. Nothing could justify or excuse this decision but the innocence of Ziba, or doubt in the king's mind between the conflicting stories — which is a possible supposition.

(7.) The argument of Prof. Blunt (see above) based on the omission of Mephibosheth's name from the dying messages of David, is not fully met by the suggestion that the former may have died " in the interval of eight years " — though known to be living some four years after (2 Sam. xxi. 1, 7) — for even if he were dead, he had left a son and grandsons (1 Chron. viii. 34, 35) and David's covenant with Jonathan pledged him to protect his offspring "for ever." If Mephibosheth proved faithful when rebellion was rife, whether he were now living or dead, it would be difficult to account for the omission of any allusion to this tender trust in the parting charge to Solomon. It is to be noted, moreover, that on his return to the capital David appears simply to have forgiven Mephibosheth and remitted half the penalty of confiscation. There is no evidence that from this time the latter was a guest at the royal table as he had been before.

In view of this difference of opinion between writers on the subject, and in the absence of all evidence in the premises except that of the unsupported testimony of the parties at variance, our conclusion is that we cannot safely pronounce either of them "a rascal " — though it is evident enough that there was rascality between them.   S. W.

MERAB (מֵרָב [increase, growth]: Μερόβ,[a] Alex. also Μερωβ; Joseph. Μερόβη: Merob), the eldest daughter, possibly the eldest child, of king Saul (1 Sam. xiv. 49). She first appears after the victory over Goliath and the Philistines, when David had become an inmate in Saul's house (1 Sam. xviii. 2), and immediately after the commencement of his friendship with Jonathan. In accordance with the promise which he made before the engagement with Goliath (xvii. 25), Saul betrothed Merab to David (xviii. 17), but it is evidently implied that one object of thus rewarding his valor was to incite him to further feats, which might at last lead to his death by the Philistines. David's hesitation looks as if he did not much value the honor — at any rate before the marriage Merab's younger sister Michal had displayed her attachment for David, and Merab was then married to Adriel the Me-

holathite, who seems to have been one of the wealthy sheikhs of the eastern part of Palestine, with whom the house of Saul always maintained an alliance. To Adriel she bore five sons, who formed five of the seven members of the house of Saul who were given up to the Gibeonites by David, and by them crucified to Jehovah on the sacred hill of Gibeah (2 Sam. xxi. 8). [RIZPAH.]

The Authorized Version of this last passage is an accommodation. The Hebrew text has "the five sons of Michal, daughter of Saul, which she bare to Adriel " [in the A. V. " whom she brought up for Adriel "], and this is followed in the LXX. and Vulgate. The Targum explains the discrepancy thus: "The five sons of Merab (which Michal, Saul's daughter, brought up) which she bare," etc. The Peshito substitutes Merab (in the present state of the text " Nadab ") for Michal. J. H. Michaelis, in his Hebrew Bible (2 Sam. xxi. 10), suggests that there were two daughters of Saul named Michal, as there were two Elishamas and two Eliphalets among David's sons. Probably the most feasible solution of the difficulty is that "Michal" is the mistake of a transcriber for "Merab."[b] But if so it is manifest from the agreement of the versions and of Josephus (Ant. vii. 4, § 30) with the present text, that the error is one of very ancient date.

Is it not possible that there is a connection between Merab's name and that of her nephew MERIB-BAAL, or Mephibosheth as he is ordinarily called?   G.

MERA'IAH [3 syl.] (מְרָיָה [rebellion, obstinacy, Ges.] : 'Αμαρία; [Vat. Μαρεα :] FA. Μαραια: Maraia). A priest in the days of Joiakim, the son of Jeshua. He was one of the "heads of the fathers," and representative of the priestly family of Seraiah, to which Ezra belonged (Neh. xii. 12). The reading of the LXX. — 'Αμαρία, is supported by the Peshito-Syriac.

MERA'IOTH [3 syl.] (מְרָיוֹת [rebellions, contumacies] : Μαριήλ, [Vat. Μαρεινλ,] in 1 Chr. vi. 6, 7, 52; Μαραιόθ, [Vat. Μαρμωθ,] 1 Chr. ix. 11; Μαρεόθ, [Vat. Μαρερωθ,] Ezr. vii. 3; Μαριόθ, Neh. xi. 11; Alex. Μαραιωθ, 1 Chr. vi. 6, 7, Ezr. vii. 3; Μεραωθ, 1 Chr. vi. 52; Μαριωθ, 1 Chr. 11, Neh. xi 11: Meraioth, except 1 Chr. ix. 11, Ezr. vii. 3, Maraioth). 1. A descendant of Eleazar the son of Aaron, and head of a priestly house. It was thought by Lightfoot that he was the immediate predecessor of Eli in the office of high-priest, and that at his death the high-priesthood changed from the line of Eleazar to the line of Ithamar (Temple Service, iv. § 1). Among his illustrious descendants were Zadok and Ezra. He is called elsewhere MEREMOTH (1 Esdr. vii. 2), and MARIMOTH (2 Esdr. i. 2). It is apparently another Meraioth who comes in between Zadok and Ahitub in the genealogy of Azariah (1 Chr. ix. 11, Neh. xi. 11), unless the names Ahitub and Meraioth are transposed, which is not improbable.

2. (Μαριόθ; [Vat. Alex. FA[1]. omit:] Maraioth.) The head of one of the houses of priests, which in the time of Joiakim the son of Jeshua was represented by Helkai (Neh. xii. 15). He is else-

[a] The omission of the name in the LXX. is remarkable. In the Vatican Codex it occurs in 1 Sam. xiv. 49 only. The Alexandrine MS. omits it there, and inserts it in xviii. 17 and 19.

[b] * Keil decides (Bibl. Comm. üb. das A. T. in loc.)

that Michal in the present text must be an error of memory or a copyist's mistake. 11. A. Perret-Gentil substitutes Merab for Michal in his version published by the Société Biblique Protestante de Paris (1866).   H.

where called MEREMOTH (Neh. xii. 3), a confusion being made between the letters ‏יו‎ and ‏ם‎. The Pshito-Syriac has *Marmuth* in both passages.

W. A. W.

ME'RAN (Μεῤῥάν: *Merrha*). The merchants of Meran and Theman are mentioned with the Hagarenes (Bar. iii. 23) as "searchers out of understanding." The name does not occur elsewhere, and is probably a corruption of "Medan" or "Midian." Junius and Tremellius give *Medanœi*, and their conjecture is supported by the appearance of the Midianites as nomade merchants in Gen. xxxvii. Both Medan and Midian are enumerated among the sons of Keturah in Gen. xxv. 2, and are closely connected with the Dedanim, whose "travelling companies," or caravans, are frequently alluded to (Is. xxi. 13; Ez. xxvii. 15). Fritzsche suggests that it is the *Marane* of Pliny (vi. 28, 32).

W. A. W.

MERA'RI (‏מְרָרִי‎ [*unhappy, sorrowful*, or, *my sorrow*, i. e. his mother's]: Μεραρί; [Vat. Μεραρει, Μεῤῥαρει, and once Μααραρει; Alex. sometimes Μεραρει: *Merari*]), third son of Levi,

and head of the third great division (‏מִשְׁפַּחַת‎) of the Levites, THE MERARITES, whose designation in Hebrew is the same as that of their progenitor, only with the article prefixed, namely, ‏הַמְּרָרִי‎.

Of Merari's personal history, beyond the fact of his birth before the descent of Jacob into Egypt, and of his being one of the seventy who accompanied Jacob thither, we know nothing whatever (Gen. xlvi. 8, 11). At the time of the Exodus, and the numbering in the wilderness, the Merarites consisted of two families, the Mahlites and the Mushites, Mahli and Mushi being either the two sons, or the son and grandson, of Merari (1 Chr. vi. 19, 47). Their chief at that time was Zuriel, and the whole number of the family, from a month old and upwards, was 6,200; those from 30 years old to 50 were 3,200. Their charge was the boards, bars, pillars, sockets, pins, and cords of the tabernacle and the court, and all the tools connected with setting them up. In the encampment their place was to the north of the tabernacle; and both they and the Gershonites were "under the hand" of Ithamar the son of Aaron. Owing to the heavy

TABLE OF THE MERARITES.

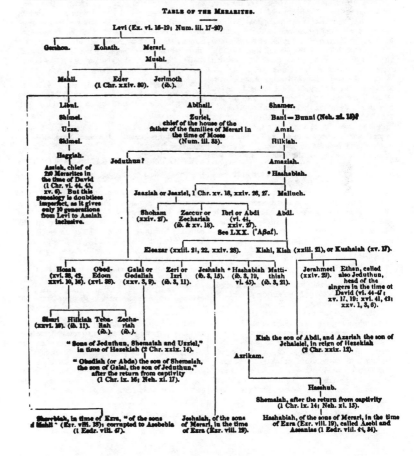

nature of the materials which they had to carry, four wagons and eight oxen were assigned to them; and in the march both they and the Gershonites followed immediately after the standard of Judah, and before that of Reuben, that they might set up the Tabernacle against the arrival of the Kohathites (Num. iii. 20, 33–37, iv. 29–33, 42–45, vii. 8, x. 17, 21). In the division of the land by Joshua, the Merarites had twelve cities assigned to them, out of Reuben, Gad, and Zebulun, of which one was Ramoth-Gilead, a city of refuge, and in later times a frequent subject of war between Israel and Syria (Josh. xxi. 7, 34-40:a 1 Chr. vi. 63, 77–81). In the time of David Asaiah was their chief, and assisted with 220 of his family in bringing up the ark (1 Chr. xv. 6). Afterwards we find the Merarites still sharing with the two other Levitical families the various functions of their caste (1 Chr. xxiii. 6, 21–23). Thus a third part of the singers and musicians were Merarites, and Ethan or Jeduthun was their chief in the time of David. [JEDUTHUN.] A third part of the door-keepers were Merarites (1 Chr. xxiii. 5, 6, xxvi. 10, 19), unless indeed we are to understand from ver. 19 that the doorkeepers were all either Kohathites or Merarites, to the exclusion of the Gershonites, which does not seem probable. In the days of Hezekiah the Merarites were still flourishing, and Kish the son of Abdi, and Azariah the son of Jehalelel, took their part with their brethren of the two other Levitical families in promoting the reformation, and purifying the house of the Lord (2 Chr. xxix. 12, 15). After the return from captivity Shemaiah represents the sons of Merari, in 1 Chr. ix. 14, Neh. xi. 15, and is said, with other chiefs of the Levites, to have " had the oversight of the outward business of the house of God." There were also at that time sons of Jeduthun under Obadiah or Abda, the son of Shemaiah (1 Chr. ix. 16; Neh. xi. 17). A little later again, in the time of Ezra, when he was in great want of Levites to accompany him on his journey from Babylon to Jerusalem, " a man of good understanding of the sons of Mahli " was found, whose name, if the text here and at ver. 24 is correct, is not given. " Jeshaiah also of the sons of Merari," with twenty of his sons and brethren, came with him at the same time (Exr. viii. 18, 19). But it seems pretty certain that Sherebiah, in ver. 18, is the name of the Mahlite, and that both he and Hashabiah, as well as Jeshaiah, in ver. 19, were Levites of the family of Merari, and not, as the actual text of ver. 24 indicates, priests. The copulative ו has fallen out before their names in ver. 24, as appears from ver. 30 (see also 1 Chr. ix. 14; Neh. xii. 24).

The preceding table gives the principal descents, as far as it is possible to ascertain them. But the true position of Jaaziah, Mahli, and Jeduthun is doubtful. Here too, as elsewhere, it is difficult to decide when a given name indicates an individual, and when the family called after him, or the head of that family. It is sometimes no less difficult to decide whether any name which occurs repeatedly designates the same person, or others of the family who bore the same name, as e. g. in the case of Mahli, Hilkiah, Shimri, Kishi or Kish, and others. As regards the confusion between Ethan and Jedu-

thun, it may perhaps be that Jeduthun was the patronymic title of the house of which Ethan was the head in the time of David. Jeduthun might have been the brother of one of Ethan's direct ancestors before Hashabiah, in which case Hashabiah in 1 Chr. xxv. 3, 19 might be the same as Hashabiah in vi. 45. Hosah and Obed-edom seem to have been other descendants or clansmen of Jeduthun, who lived in the time of David; and, if we may argue from the names of Hosah's sons, Simri and Hilkiah, that they were descendants of Shamer and Hilkiah, in the line of Ethan, the inference would be that Jeduthun was a son either of Hilkiah or Amaziah, since he lived after Hilkiah, but before Hashabiah. The great advantage of this supposition is, that while it leaves to Ethan the patronymic designation Jeduthun, it draws a wide distinction between the term " sons of Jeduthun " and " sons of Ethan," and explains how in David's time there could be sons of those who are called sons of Jeduthun above thirty years of age (since they filled offices, 1 Chr. xxvi. 10), at the same time that Jeduthun was said to be the chief of the singers. In like manner it is possible that Jaaziah may have been a brother of Malluch or of Abdi, and that if Abdi or Ibri had other descendants besides the lines of Kish and Eleazar, they may have been reckoned under the headship of Jaaziah. The families of Merari which were so reckoned were, according to 1 Chr. xxiv. 27, Shoham, Zaccur (apparently the same as Zechariah in 1 Chr. xv. 18, where we probably ought to read " Z. son of Jaaziah," and xxvi. 11), and Ibri, where the LXX. have 'Ωβδί, 'Αβαί, and 'Αβδί.   A. C. H.

2. (Μεραρί; [Vat. Μεραρει; Sin.] Alex. in Jud. viii. 1, Μεραρει; [Sin. in xvi. 7, Μεραρει:] Merari.)   The father of Judith (Jud. viii. 1, xvi. 7).

* MERA'RITES (מְרָרִי: Μεραρί, Vat. -ρει: Merarites), descendants of Merari, Num. xxvi. 57. [MERARI 1.]   A.

MERATHA'IM, THE LAND OF (אֶרֶץ מְרָתַיִם: terra dominantium), that is, of double rebellion (a dual form from the root מָרָה; Gesenius, Thes. p. 819 a; Fürst, Hdwb. p. 791 b), alluding to the country of the Chaldæans, and to the double captivity which it had inflicted on the nation of Israel (Jer. l. 21). This is the opinion of Gesenius, Fürst, Michaelis (Bibel für Ungelehrten), etc., and in this sense the word is taken by all the versions which the writer has consulted, excepting that of Junius and Tremellius, which the A. V.— as in other instances — has followed here. The LXX., ἐπὶ τῆς γῆς, λέγει κύριος, πικρῶς ἐπίβηθι, etc., take the root in its second sense of "bitter."   G.

MERCU'RIUS (Ἑρμῆς: Mercurius), [Acts xiv. 12,] properly Hermes, the Greek deity, whom the Romans identified with their Mercury the god of commerce and bargains. In the Greek mythology Hermes was the son of Zeus and Maia the daughter of Atlas, and is constantly represented as the companion of his father in his wanderings upon earth. On one of these occasions they were trav-

---

a Their cities were Jokneam, Kartah, Dimnah, Nahalal, in Zebulun; Bezer, Jahazah, Kedemoth, Mephaath, in Reuben; Ramoth, Mahanaim, Heshbon, and Jazer, in Gad. But in 1 Chr. vi., instead of the four in Zebulon, only Rimmon and Tabor are named though the total is given as twelve in ver. 63.

elling in Phrygia, and were refused hospitality by all save Baucis and Philemon, the two aged peasants of whom Ovid tells the charming episode in his *Metam.* viii. 620-724, which appears to have formed part of the folk-lore of Asia Minor, and strikingly illustrates the readiness with which the simple people of Lystra recognized in Barnabas and Paul the gods who, according to their wont, had come down in the likeness of men (Acts xiv. 11). They called Paul " Hermes, because he was the chief speaker," identifying in him as they supposed by this characteristic, the herald of the gods (Hom. *Od.* v. 28; *Hym. in Herm.* p. 3), and of Zeus (*Od.* i. 38, 84; *Il.* xxiv. 333, 461), the eloquent orator (*Od.* i. 86; Hor. *Od.* i. 10, 1), inventor of letters, music, and the arts. He was usually represented as a slender beardless youth, but in an older Pelasgic figure he was bearded. Whether St. Paul wore a beard or not is not to be inferred from this, for the men of Lystra identified him with their god Hermes, not from any accidental resemblance in figure or appearance to the statues of that deity, but because of the act of healing which had been done upon the man who was lame from his birth. [JUPITER, Amer. ed.]   W. A. W.

MERCY-SEAT (כַּפֹּרֶת): ἱλαστήριον: *propitiatorium*). This appears to have been merely the lid of the Ark of the Covenant, not another surface affixed thereto. It was that whereon the blood of the yearly atonement was sprinkled by the high-priest; and in this relation it is doubtful whether the sense of the word in the Hebrew is based on the material fact of its " covering " the Ark, or from this notion of its reference to the " covering " (*i. e.* atonement) of sin. But in any case the notion of a " seat," as conveyed by the name in English, seems superfluous and likely to mislead. Jehovah is indeed spoken of as " dwelling " and even as " sitting " (Ps. lxxx. 1, xcix. 1) between the cherubim, but undoubtedly his seat in this conception would not be on the same level as that on which they stood (Ex. xxv. 18), and an enthronement in the glory above it must be supposed. The idea with which it is connected is not merely that of " mercy," but of formal atonement made for the breach of the covenant (Lev. xvi. 14), which the Ark contained in its material vehicle — the two tables of stone. The communications made to Moses are represented as made " from off the Mercy-Seat that was upon the Ark of the Testimony " (Num. vii. 89; comp. Ex. xxv. 22, xxx. 6); a sublime illustration of the moral relation and responsibility into which the people were by covenant regarded as brought before God.   H. H.

MERED (מֶרֶד [*defection, rebellion*]: Μωρδδ [Vat. Μωραδ], 1 Chr. iv. 17; Μωρήδ, 1 Chr. iv. 18: *Mered*). This name occurs in a fragmentary genealogy in 1 Chr. iv. 17, 18, as that of one of the sons of Ezra. He is there said to have taken to wife BITHIAH the daughter of Pharaoh, who is enumerated by the Rabbins among the nine who entered Paradise (Hottinger, *Smegma Orientale,* p. 315), and in the Targum of R. Joseph on Chronicles is said to have been a proselyte. In the same Targum we find it stated that Caleb, the son of Jephunneh, was called Mered because he withstood or rebelled against (מָרַד) the counsel of the spies, a tradition also recorded by Jarchi. But another and very curious tradition is preserved

in the *Quæstiones in libr. Paral.,* attributed to Jerome. According to this, Ezra was Amram; his sons Jether and Mered were Aaron and Moses; Epher was Eldad, and Jalon Medad. The tradition goes on to say that Moses, after receiving the Law in the desert, enjoined his father to put away his mother because she was his aunt, being the daughter of Levi: that Amram did so, married again, and begat Eldad and Medad. Bithiah, the daughter of Pharaoh, is said, on the same authority, to have been " taken " by Moses, because she forsook idols, and was converted to the worship of the true God. The origin of all this seems to have been the occurrence of the name "Miriam " in 1 Chr. iv. 17, which was referred to Miriam the sister of Moses. Rabbi D. Kimchi would put the first clause of ver. 18 in a parenthesis. He makes Bithiah the daughter of Pharaoh the first wife of Mered, and mother of Miriam, Shammai, and Ishbah; Jehudijah, or " the Jewess," being his second wife. But the whole genealogy is so intricate that it is scarcely possible to unravel it.
     W. A. W

MEREMOTH (מְרֵמוֹת [*heights*]: Μεριμώθ, [Vat. Μερειμωθ;] Alex. Μαρμώθ, Ezr. viii. 33; Ραμώθ, Neh. iii. 4; Μεραμώθ, Neh. iii. 21: *Meremoth,* [*Marimuth, Merimuth*]). 1. Son of Uriah, or Urijah, the priest, of the family of Koz or Hakkoz, the head of the seventh course of priests as established by David. On the return from Babylon the children of Koz were among those priests who were unable to establish their pedigree, and in consequence were put from the priesthood as polluted (Ezr. ii. 61, 62). This probably applied to only one family of the descendants of Koz, for in Ezr. viii. 33, Meremoth is clearly recognized as a priest, and is appointed to weigh and register the gold and silver vessels belonging to the Temple, which Ezra had brought from Babylon, a function which priests and Levites alone were selected to discharge (Ezr. viii. 24-30). In the rebuilding of the wall of Jerusalem under Nehemiah we find Meremoth taking an active part, working between Meshullam and the sons of Hassenaah who restored the Fish Gate (Neh. iii. 4), and himself restoring the portion of the Temple wall on which abutted the house of the high-priest Eliashib (Neh. iii. 21). Burrington (*Genealogies,* ii. 154) is inclined to consider the two mentioned in Neh. iii. by the same name as distinct persons, but his reasons do not appear sufficient.

In I Esdr. viii. 62, he is called " MARMOTH the son of Iri."

* The A. V. ed. 1611 follows the Geneva version in reading Merimoth in Neh. iii. 4, 21; comp. MEREMOTH 3 The Bishops' Bible also reads Merimoth in Neh. iii. 21 and xii. 3.   A.

2. (Μαριμώθ; [Vat. Ιεραμωθ; FA. Χωιεραμωθ:] *Marimuth.*) A layman of the sons of Bani, who had married a foreign wife after the return from Babylon and put her away at Ezra's bidding (Ezr. x. 36).

3. (Μεραμώθ; [Vat. Αμεραμως; FA. Εραμωθ; in xii. 3, Rom. Vat. Alex. FA.[1] omit, FA.[3] Μαριμωθ:] *Merimuth.*) A priest, or more probably a family of priests, who sealed the covenant with Nehemiah (Neh. x. 5). The latter supposition is more probable, because in Neh. xii. 3 the name occurs, with many others of the same list, among those who went up with Zerubbabel a century

before. In the next generation, that is, in the days of Joiakim the son of Jeshua, the representative of the family of Meremoth was Helkai (Neh. xii. 15), the reading Meraioth in that passage being an error. [MERAIOTH 2.] The A. V. of 1611 had "Merimoth" in Neh. [x. 5 and] xii. 3, like the Geneva version. [MEREMOTH 1.]   W. A. W.

MERES (מֶרֶס: [Vat. Alex. FA. omit; Comp. Μέρες:] *Mares*). One of the seven counsellors of Ahasuerus king of Persia, "wise men which knew the times" (Esth. i. 14). His name is not traceable in the LXX., which in this passage is corrupt. Benfey (quoted by Gesenius, *Thes.* s. v.) suggests that it is derived from the Sanskrit *mârsha*, "worthy," which is the same as the Zend *meresh*, and is probably also the origin of *Marsena*, the name of another Persian counsellor.
W. A. W.

MER'IBAH (מְרִיבָה [*quarrel, strife*]: λοιδόρησις Ex. xvii. 7; ἀντιλογία Num. xx. 13, xxvii. 14; Deut. xxxii. 51; λοιδορία Num. xx. 24: *contradictio*). In Ex. xvii. 7 we read, "he called the name of the place Massah and Meribah,"[a] where the people murmured, and the rock was smitten. [For the situation see REPHIDIM.] The name is also given to Kadesh (Num. xx. 13, 24, xxvii. 14; Deut. xxii. 51 "Meribah-kadesh "), because there also the people, when in want of water, strove with God. There, however, Moses and Aaron incurred the Divine displeasure because they "believed not," because they "rebelled," and "sanctified not God in the midst" of the people. Impatience and self-willed assumption of plenary power are the prominent features of their behavior in Num. xx. 10; the "speaking to the rock" (which perhaps was to have been in Jehovah's name) was neglected, and another symbol, suggestive rather of themselves as the source of power, was substituted. In spite of these plain and distinctive features of difference between the event at Kadesh and that at Rephidim some commentators have regarded the one as a mere duplicate of the other, owing to a mixture of earlier and later legend.   H. H.

MERIB-BA'AL (מְרִיב בַּעַל, except on its fourth occurrence, and there less accurately מְרִי־בַעַל, i. e. Meri-baal [*strife against Baal*], though in many MSS. the fuller form is preserved: Μεριβάαλ; [in 1 Chr. ix. 40, Vat.] Μαρειβααλ, [Sin. Μαριβαλ, Μαρειβααλ;] Alex. Μεφριβααλ, Μεχριβααλ: *Meri-baal*), son of Jonathan the son of Saul (1 Chr. viii. 34, ix. 40), doubtless the same person who in the narrative of 2 Samuel is called MEPHI-BOSHETH. The reasons for the identification are, that in the history no other son but Meph ibosheth is ascribed to Jonathan; that Mephi bosheth, like Merib-baal, had a son named Micah; and that the terms "bosheth" and "baal" appear from other examples (e. g. Esh-Baal = Ish bosheth) to be convertible. What is the significance of the change in the former part of the name, and whether it is more than a clerical error between the two Hebrew letters ם and ר, does not appear to have been ascertained. It is perhaps in favor

_____

[a] Chiding, or strife, מַצָּה וּמְרִיבָה; παραπικρασμὸς καὶ λοιδόρησις, also ἀντιλογία; marg. "temptation," Deut. xxxiii. 8.

of the latter explanation that in some of the Greek versions of 1 Chr. viii. and ix. the name is given as Memphi-baal. A trace of the same thing is visible in the reading of the Alex. LXX. given above. If it is not a mere error, then there is perhaps some connection between the name of Merib-baal and that of his aunt Merab.

Neither is it clear why this name and that of Ishbosheth should be given in a different form in these genealogies to what they are in the historical narrative. But for this see ISH-BOSHETH and MKPHI-BOSHETH.   G.

* MER'IMOTH is the reading of the A. V. ed. 1611 in Neh. iii. 4, 21, x. 5, and xii. 3, for which the more correct form, "Meremoth," has been substituted in later editions. [MEREMOTH 1 and 3.]   A.

MERO'DACH (מְרֹדָךְ [see below]: Μαιρωδάχ; [Vat. Μαιωδαχ; Alex. FA. Μεωδαχ:] *Merodach*) is mentioned once only in Scripture, namely, in Jer. l. 2, where Bel and Merodach are coupled together, and threatened with destruction in the fall of Babylon. It has been commonly concluded from this passage that Bel and Merodach were separate gods; but from the Assyrian and Babylonian inscriptions it appears that this was not exactly the case. Merodach was really identical with the famous Babylonian Bel or Belus, the word being probably at first a mere epithet of the god, which by degrees superseded his proper appellation. Still a certain distinction appears to have been maintained between the names. The golden image in the great Temple at Babylon seems to have been worshipped distinctly as Bel rather than Merodach, while other idols of the god may have represented him as Merodach rather than Bel. It is not known what the word Merodach means, or what the special aspect of the god was, when worshipped under that title. In a general way Bel-Merodach may be said to correspond to the Greek Jupiter. He is "the old man of the gods," "the judge," and has the gates of heaven under his especial charge. Nebuchadnezzar calls him "the great lord, the senior of the gods, the most ancient," and Neriglissar "the first-born of the gods, the layer-up of treasures." In the earlier period of Babylonian history he seems to share with several other deities (as Nebo, Nergal, Bel-Nimrod, Anu, etc.) the worship of the people, but in the later times he is regarded as the source of all power and blessings, and thus concentrates in his own person the greater part of that homage and respect which had previously been divided among the various gods of the Pantheon. Astronomically he is identified with the planet Jupiter. His name forms a frequent element in the appellations of Babylonian kings, e. g. Merodach-Baladan, Evil-Merodach, Merodach-adin-akhi, etc.; and is found in this position as early as B. C. 1650. (See the *Essay* by Sir H. Rawlinson "*On the Religion of the Babylonians and Assyrians,*" in Rawlinson's *Herodotus*, i. 627-631.)   G. R.

MERO'DACH-BAL'ADAN (מְרֹאדַךְ בַּלְאָדָן: Μαρωδὰχ Βαλαδάν; [Vat. Μαιωδαχ; Vat. and Alex. omit Βαλαδάν:] *Merodach-Baladan*) is mentioned as king of Babylon in the days of Hezekiah, both in the second book of Kings (xx. 12) and in Isaiah (xxxix. 1). In the former place he is called BERODACH-BALADAN, by the ready interchange of the letters ב and מ, which was familiar to the Jews, as it has been to many other nations. The orthography "Merodach" is, however, to be preferred; since this element in the king's name is undoubtedly identical with the appellation of the famous Babylonian deity, who is always called "Merodach," both by the Hebrews and by the native writers. The name of Merodach-Baladan has been clearly recognized in the Assyrian inscriptions. It appears under the form of Marudachus-Baldanes, or Marudach-Baldan, in a fragment of Polyhistor, preserved by Eusebius (*Chron. Can.* pars i. v. 1); and under that of Mardoc-empad (or rather Mardoc-empal [a]) in the famous "Canon of Ptolemy." Josephus abbreviates it still more, and calls the monarch simply " Baladas " (*Ant. Jud.* x. 2, § 2).

The Canon gives Merodach-Baladan (*Mardoc-empal*) a reign of 12 years — from B. C. 721 to B. C. 709 — and makes him then succeeded by a certain Arceanus. Polyhistor assigns him a six months' reign, immediately before Elibus, or Belibus, who (according to the Canon) ascended the throne B. C. 702. It has commonly been seen that these must be two different reigns, and that Merodach-Baladan must therefore have been deposed in B. C. 709, and have recovered his throne in B. C. 702, when he had a second period of dominion lasting half a year. The inscriptions contain express mention of both reigns. Sargon states that in the twelfth year of his own reign he drove Merodach-Baladan out of Babylon, after he had ruled over it for twelve years; and Sennacherib tells us that in his first year he defeated and expelled the same monarch, setting up in his place " a man named Belib." Putting all our notices together, it becomes apparent that Merodach-Baladan was the head of the popular party, which resisted the Assyrian monarchs, and strove to maintain the independence of the country. It is uncertain whether he was self-raised or was the son of a former king. In the second Book of Kings he is styled " the son of Baladan; " but the inscriptions call him " the son of *Yagin*; " whence it is to be presumed that Baladan was a more remote ancestor. *Yagin*, the real father of Merodach-Baladan, is possibly represented in Ptolemy's Canon by the name Jugæus — which in some copies replaces the name Eluæus, as the appellation of the immediate predecessor of Merodach-Baladan. At any rate, from the time of Sargon, Merodach-Baladan and his family were the champions of Babylonian independence and fought with spirit the losing battle of their country. The king of whom we are here treating sustained two contests with the power of Assyria, was twice defeated, and twice compelled to fly his country. His sons, supported by the king of Elam, or Susiana, continued the struggle, and are found among the adversaries of Esar-Haddon, Sennacherib's son and successor. His grandsons contend against *Asshur-bani-pal*, the son of Esar-Haddon. It is not till the fourth generation that the family seems to become extinct, and the Babylonians, having no champion to maintain their cause, contentedly acquiesce in the yoke of the stranger.

There is some doubt as to the time at which Merodach-Baladan sent his ambassadors to Hezekiah, for the purpose of inquiring as to the astronomical marvel of which Judæa had been the scene (2 Chr. xxxii. 31). According to those commentators who connect the illness of Hezekiah with one or other of Sennacherib's expeditions against him, the embassy has to be ascribed to Merodach-Baladan's second or shorter reign, when alone he was contemporary with Sennacherib. If however we may be allowed to adopt the view that Hezekiah's illness preceded the first invasion of Sennacherib by several years (see above, *ad voc.* HEZEKIAH, and compare Rawlinson's *Herodotus*, i. 479, note 2), synchronizing really with an attack of Sargon, we must assign the embassy to Merodach-Baladan's earlier reign, and bring it within the period, B. C. 721-709, which the Canon assigns to him. Now the 14th year of Hezekiah, in which the embassy should fall (2 K. xx. 6; Is. xxxviii. 5), appears to have been B. C. 713. This was the year of Merodach-Baladan's first reign.

The increasing power of Assyria was at this period causing alarm to her neighbors, and the circumstances of the time were such as would tend to draw Judæa and Babylonia together, and to give rise to negotiations between them. The astronomical marvel, whatever it was, which accompanied the recovery of Hezekiah, would doubtless have attracted the attention of the Babylonians; but it was probably rather the pretext than the motive for the formal embassy which the Chaldæan king dispatched to Jerusalem on the occasion. The real object of the mission was most likely to effect a league between Babylon, Judæa, *and Egypt* (Is. xx. 5, 6), in order to check the growing power of the Assyrians.[b] Hezekiah's exhibition of " all his precious things " (2 K. xx. 13) would thus have been, not a mere display, but a mode of satisfying the Babylonian ambassadors of his ability to support the expenses of a war. The league, however, though designed, does not seem to have taken effect. Sargon, acquainted probably with the intentions of his adversaries, anticipated them. He sent expeditions both into Syria and Babylonia — seized the stronghold of Ashdod in the one, and completely defeated Merodach-Baladan in the other. That monarch sought safety in flight, and lived for eight years in exile. At last he found an opportunity to return. In B. C. 703 or 702, Babylonia was plunged in anarchy — the Assyrian yoke was thrown off, and various native leaders struggled for the mastery. Under these circumstances the exiled monarch seems to have returned, and recovered his throne. His adversary, Sargon, was dead or dying, and a new and untried prince was about to rule over the Assyrians. He might hope that the reins of government would be held by a weaker hand, and that he might stand his ground against the son, though he had been forced to yield to the father. In this hope, however, he was disappointed. Sennacherib had scarcely established himself on the throne, when he proceeded to engage his people in wars; and it seems that his very first step was to invade the kingdom of Babylon. Merodach-

---

[a] In the uncial writing A is very liable to be mistaken for Δ, and in the ordinary manuscript character λ is not unlike δ. M. Bunsen was (we believe) the first to suggest that there had been a substitution of the λ for the Λ in this instance. See his work, *Egypt's Place in Universal History*, vol. i. p. 726, E. T. The

abbreviation of the name has many parallels. (See Rawlinson's *Herodotus*, vol. i. p. 436, note 1.)

[b] Josephus expressly states that Merodach-Baladan sent the ambassadors in order to form an *alliance* with Hezekiah (*Ant. Jud.* x. 2, § 2).

Baladan had obtained a body of troops from his ally, the king of Susiana; but Sennacherib defeated the combined army in a pitched battle; after which he ravaged the entire country, destroying 79 walled cities and 820 towns and villages, and carrying vast numbers of the people into captivity. Merodach-Baladan fled to "the islands at the mouth of the Euphrates" (Fox Talbot's *Assyrian Texts*, p. 1) — tracts probably now joined to the continent — and succeeded in eluding the search which the Assyrians made for him. If we may believe Polyhistor however, this escape availed him little. That writer relates (*ap.* Euseb. *Chron. Can.* i. 5), that he was soon after put to death by Elibus, or Belibus, the viceroy whom Sennacherib appointed to represent him at Babylon. At any rate he lost his recovered crown after wearing it for about six months, and spent the remainder of his days in exile and obscurity.   G. R.

ME'ROM, THE WATERS OF (מֵי

מֵרוֹם [*waters of the height*, or *from above*]: τὸ ὕδωρ Μαρών [Vat. Μαρρων, and so Alex. ver. 7]; Alex. in ver. 5, Μεμρων: *aquæ Merom*), a place memorable in the history of the conquest of Palestine. Here, after Joshua had gained possession of the southern portions of the country, a confederacy of the northern chiefs assembled under the leadership of Jabin, king of Hazor (Josh. xi. 5), and here they were encountered by Joshua, and completely routed (ver. 7). The battle of Merom was to the north of Palestine what that of Bethhoron had been to the south, — indeed more, for there do not appear to have been the same number of important towns to be taken in detail after this victory that there had been in the former case.

The name of Merom occurs nowhere in the Bible but in the passage above[a] mentioned; nor is it found in Josephus. In his account of the battle (*Ant.* v. 1, § 18), the confederate kings encamp "near Beroth, a city of upper Galilee, not far from Kedes;" nor is there any mention of water. In the *Onomasticon* of Eusebius the name is given as "Merran," and it is stated to be "a village twelve miles distant from Sebaste (Samaria), and near Dothaim." It is a remarkable fact that though by common consent the "waters of Merom" are identified with the lake through which the Jordan runs between Banias and the Sea of Galilee — the Semechonitis[b] of Josephus, and *Bahr el-Hûleh* of the modern Arabs — yet that identity cannot be proved by any ancient record. The nearest approach to proof is an inference from[a] the statement

of Josephus (*Ant.* v. 5, § 1), that the second Jabin (Judg. iv., v.) "belonged to the city Asor (Hazor), which lay above the lake of Semechonitis." There is no reason to doubt that the Hazor of the first and the Hazor of the second Jabin were one and the same place; and as the waters of Merom are named in connection with the former it is allowable to infer that they are identical with the lake of Semechonitis. But it should be remembered that this inference is really all the proof we have, while against it we have to set the positive statements of Josephus and Eusebius just quoted; and also the fact that the Hebrew word *Me* is not that commonly used for a large piece of standing water, but rather *Yam*, "a sea," which was even employed for so small a body of water as the artificial pond or tank in Solomon's Temple. This remark would have still more force if, as was most probably the case, the lake was larger in the time of Joshua than it is at present. Another and greater objection, which should not be overlooked, is the difficulty attendant on a flight and pursuit across a country so mountainous and impassable to any large numbers, as the district which intervenes between the *Hûleh* and Sidon. The tremendous ravine of the *Litâny* and the height of *Kalat es-Shukîf* are only two of the obstacles which stand in the way of a passage in this direction. As, however, the lake in question is invariably taken to be the "waters of Merom," and as it is an interesting feature in the geography of the upper part of the Jordan, it may be well here to give some account of it.

The region to which the name of *Hûleh*[c] is attached — the *Ard el-Hûleh* — is a depressed plain or basin, commencing on the north of the foot of the slopes which lead up to the *Merj Ayûn* and *Tell el-Rady*, and extending southwards to the bottom of the lake which bears the same name — *Bahr el-Hûleh*. On the east and west it is inclosed between two parallel ranges of hills; on the west the highlands of Upper Galilee — the *Jebel Safat*; and on the east a broad ridge or table-land of basalt, thrown off by the southern base of Hermon, and extending downwards beyond the *Hûleh* till lost in the high ground east of the lake of Tiberias. The latter rises abruptly from the low ground, but the hills on the western side break down more gradually, and leave a tract of undulating table-land of varying breadth between them and the plain. This basin is in all about 15 miles long and 4 to 5 wide, and thus occupies an area about equal to that of the lake of Tiberias. It is the receptacle for the drainage of the highlands on each

---

[a] The mention of the name in the Vulgate of Judg. v. 18 — *in regione Merome* — is only apparent. It is a literal transference of the words עַל מְרוֹמֵי שָׂדֶה rightly rendered in the A. V. "in the high places of the field," and has no connection with Merom.

[b] 'Η Σεμεχωνῖτις, or Σεμεχωνιτῶν, λίμνη (*Ant.* v. 5, § 1; *B. J.* iii. 10, § 7, iv 1, § 1). This name does not occur in any part of the Bible; nor has it been discovered in any author except Josephus. For the possible derivations of it, see Reland (*Pal.* 262-264), and the summary of Stanley (*S. & P.* p. 391 *note*). To these it should be added that the name *Semakh* is not confined to this lake. A wady of that name is the principal torrent on the east of the Sea of Tiberias.

[c] *El-Hûleh*, الحولة, is probably a very ancient name derived from or connected with Hul, or more accurately Chul, who appears in the lists of Gen. x. as one of the sons of Aram (Syria, ver. 23). In the Arabic version of Saadiah of this passage, the name of Hul is given exactly in the form of the modern name — el-Hûleh. Josephus (*Ant.* i. 6, § 4), in his account of the descendants of Noah, gives Hul as Οὖλος, while he also calls the district in question Οὐλάθα (*Ant.* xv. 10, § 3). The word both in Hebrew and Arabic seems to have the force of depression — the low land (see Michaelis, *Suppl.* Nos. 687, 720); and Michaelis most ingeniously suggests that it is the root of the name Κοιλη χωρία, although in its present form it may have been sufficiently modified to transform it into an intelligible Greek word (Idem, *Spicilegium*, ii. 127 128).

side, but more especially for the waters of the *Merj Ayûn*, an elevated plateau which lies above it amongst the roots of the great northern mountains of Palestine. In fact the whole district is an enormous swamp, which, though partially solidified at its upper portion by the gradual deposit of detritus from the hills, becomes more swampy as its length is descended, and at last terminates in the lake or pool which occupies its southern extremity. It was probably at one time all covered with water, and even now in the rainy seasons it is mostly submerged. During the dry season, however, the upper portions, and those immediately at the foot of the western hills, are sufficiently firm to allow the Arabs to encamp and pasture their cattle, but the lower part, more immediately bordering on the lake, is absolutely impassable, not only on account of its increasing marshiness, but also from the very dense thicket of reeds which covers it. At this part it is difficult to say where the swamp terminates and the lake begins, but farther down on both sides the shores are perfectly well defined.

In form the lake is not far from a triangle, the base being at the north and the apex at the south. It measures about 3 miles in each direction. Its level is placed by Van de Velde at 190 feet above the Mediterranean. That of *Tell el-Kady*, 20 miles above, is 647 feet, and of the Lake Tiberias, 30 miles below, 653 feet, respectively above and below the same datum (Van de Velde, *Menuir*, 181). Thus the whole basin has a considerable slope southwards. The *Hasbâny* river, which falls almost due south from its source in the great *Wady et-Teim*, is joined at the northeast corner of the *Ard el-Hûleh* by the streams from *Banias* and *Tell el Kady*, and the united stream then flows on through the morass, rather nearer its eastern than its western side, until it enters the lake close to the eastern end of its upper side. From the apex of the triangle at the lower end the Jordan flows out. In addition to the *Hasbâny* and to the innumerable smaller watercourses which filter into it the waters of the swamp above, the lake is fed by independent springs on the slopes of its inclosing mountains. Of these the most considerable is the *Ain el-Melhhah,*[a] near the upper end of its western side, which sends down a stream of 40 or 50 feet in width. The water of the lake is clear and sweet; it is covered in parts by a broad-leaved plant, and abounds in water-fowl. Owing to its triangular form a considerable space is left between the lake and the mountains, at its lower end. This appears to be more the case on the west than on the east, and

the rolling plain thus formed is very fertile, and cultivated to the water's edge.[b] This cultivated district is called the *Ard el-Khait*, perhaps "the undulating land," *el-Khait*[c] being also the name which the Arabs call the lake (Thomson, *Bibl. Sacra*, 199; Rob. *Bibl. Res.* 1st ed. iii. App. 135, 136). In fact the name *Hûleh* appears to belong rather to the district, and only to the lake as occupying a portion thereof. It is not restricted to this spot, but is applied to another very fertile district in northern Syria lying below *Hamah*. A town of the same name is also found south of and close to the *Kasimiyeh* river a few miles from the castle of *Hunin*.

Supposing the lake to be identical with the "waters of Merom," the plain just spoken of on its southwestern margin is the only spot which could have been the site of Joshua's victory, though, as the Canaanites chose their own ground, it is difficult to imagine that they would have encamped in a position from which there was literally no escape. But this only strengthens the difficulty already expressed as to the identification. Still the district of the Huleh will always possess an interest for the Biblical student, from its connection with the Jordan, and from the cities of ancient fame which stand on its border — Kedesh, Hazor, Dan, Laish, Cæsarea, Philippi, etc.

The above account is compiled from the following sources: *The Sources of the Jordan*, etc. by Rev. W. M. Thomson, in *Bibl. Sacra*, Feb. 1846, pp. 198–201; Robinson's *Bibl. Res.* (1st ed. iii. 341–343, and App. 135), ii. 435, 436, iii. 395, 396; Wilson, *Lands*, etc., ii. 316; Van de Velde, *Syria and Pal.* ii. 416; Stanley, *S. & P.* chap. xi. [To these add Tristram's *Land of Israel*, 2d ed., pp 582–595.]

The situation of the Beroth, at which Josephus (as above) places Joshua's victory, is debated at some length by Michaelis (*Allg. Bibliothek*, etc., No. 84), with a strong desire to prove that it is Berytus, the modern *Beirût*, and that Kedesh is on the Lake of *Hums* (Emessa). His argument is grounded mainly on an addition of Josephus (*Ant.* v. 1, § 18) to the narrative as given both by the Hebrew and LXX., namely, that it occupied Joshua five days to march from Gilgal to the encampment of the kings. For this the reader must be referred to Michaelis himself. But Josephus elsewhere mentions a town called Meroth, which may possibly be the same as Beroth. This seems to have been a place naturally strong, and important as a military post (*Vita*, § 37; *B. J.* ii. 20, § 6), and moreover

---

[1] This name seems sometimes to have been applied to the lake itself. See the quotation from William of Tyre, — "lacum Meleha "— in Rob. ii. 435, note. Burckhardt did not visit it, but, possibly guided by the meaning of the Arabic word (salt), says that "the S. W. shore bears the name of Meleha from the ground being covered with a saline crust" (June 20, 1812). The same thing seems to be affirmed in the Talmud (Ahaloth, end of chap. iii. quoted by Schwarz, p 62 note); but nothing of the kind appears to have been observed by other travellers. See especially Wilson, *Lands*, etc., ii. 168. By Schwarz the name is given as "Ein al-Malcha, the King's spring." If this could be substantiated, it would be allowable to see in it a traditional reference to the encampment of the Kings. Schwarz also mentions (pp. 41, 42, note) the following names for the lake: "Sibehl," perhaps a mistake for "Somcho," i. e. Semechonitis: "Kalfayeh, ' the high,' identical with the Hebrew Merom ;"

"Yam Chavilah, יָם חֲוִילָה; " though this may merely be his translator's blunder for Chuileh, i. e. Hûleh.

[b] This undulating plain appears to be of volcanic origin. Van de Velde (*Syr. and Pal.* 415, 416), speaking of the part below the *Wady Feraîm*, a few miles only S. of the lake, calls it "a plain entirely composed of lava ; " and at the *Jisr-Benat-Yakôb* he speaks of the "black lava sides " of the Jordan. Wilson, however, (ii. 316), calls the soil of the same part the "débris of basaltic rocks and dykes."

[c] The writer has not succeeded in ascertaining the signification of this Arabic word. By Schwarz (p. 47) it is given as "Bachr Chît, ' wheat sea,' because much wheat is sown in its neighborhood." This is probably what Prof. Stanley alludes to when he reports the name as Bahr Hît or "sea of wheat" (*S. & P.* 391 note).

was the western limit of Upper Galilee (*B. J.* iii. 3, § 1). This would place it somewhere about the plain of *Akka*, much more suitable ground for the chariots of the Canaanites than any to be found near the *Hûleh*, while it also makes the account of the pursuit to Sidon more intelligible.   G.

MERON'OTHITE, THE (הַמֵּרֹנֹתִי) [gentilic]: *ὁ ἐκ Μεραθάν*, Alex. *Μαραθων*; in Neh. *ὁ Μηρωνωθίτης*, [Vat. -θειης, Alex. FA. omit:] *Meronathites*), that is, the native of a place called probably Meronoth, of which, however, no further traces have yet been discovered. Two Meronothites are named in the Bible: (1.) JEHDEIAH, who had the charge of the royal asses of King David (1 Chr. xxvii. 30); and (2.) JADON, one of those who assisted in the repair of the wall of Jerusalem after the return from the Captivity (Neh. iii. 7). In the latter case we are possibly afforded a clew to the situation of Meronoth by the fact that Jadon is mentioned between a Gibeonite and the men of Gibeon, who again are followed by the men of Mizpah: but no name like it is to be found among the towns of that district, either in the lists of Joshua (xviii. 11-28), of Nehemiah (xi. 31-35), or in the catalogue of modern towns given by Robinson (*Bibl. Res.* 1st ed. iii. Append. 121-125). For this circumstance compare MECHERATHITE.   G.

ME'ROZ (מָרוֹז) [prob. *refuge*, Ges.]: *Μηρώζ*; Alex. *Μαζωρ*: *terra Meroz*), a place mentioned only in the Song of Deborah and Barak in Judg. v. 23, and there denounced because its inhabitants had refused to take any part in the struggle with Sisera : —

"Curse ye Meroz, said the messenger of Jehovah,
Curse ye, curse ye, its inhabitants;
Because they came not to the help of Jehovah,
To the help of Jehovah against the mighty."

The denunciation of this faint-heartedness is made to form a pendant to the blessing proclaimed on the prompt action of Jael.

Meroz must have been in the neighborhood of the Kishon, but its real position is not known: possibly it was destroyed in obedience to the curse. A place named Merius (but Eusebius *Μεῤῥάν* is named by Jerome (*Onom.* "Merrom") as 12 miles north of Sebaste, near Dothain, but this is too far south to have been near the scene of the conflict. Far more feasible is the conjecture of Schwarz (168, and see 36), that Meroz is to be found at *Mernsas* — more correctly *el- Murússus* — a ruined site about 4 miles N. W. of *Beisan*, on the southern slopes of the hills, which are the continuation of the so-called "Little Hermon," and form the northern side of the valley (*Wudy Jalûd*) which leads directly from the plain of Jezreel to the Jordan. The town must have commanded the Pass, and if any of Sisera's people attempted, as the Midianites did when routed by Gideon, to escape in that direction, its inhabitants might no doubt have prevented their doing so, and have slaughtered them. *El-Murússus* is mentioned by Burckhardt (July 2: he calls it *Merauerass*), Robinson (ii. 356), and others.

Fürst (*Handwb.* 786 a) suggests the identity of Meroz with Merom, the place which may have given its name to the waters of Merom, in the neighborhood of which Kedesh, the residence of Jael, where Sisera took refuge, was situated. But putting aside the fact of the non-existence of any town named Merom there is against this suggestion the

consideration that Sisera left his army and fled alone in another direction.

In the Jewish traditions preserved in the Commentary on the Song of Deborah attributed to St. Jerome, Meroz, which may be interpreted as *secret*, is made to signify the evil angels who led on the Canaanites, who are cursed by Michael, the ange of Jehovah, the leader of the Israelites.   G.

* The scene of the battle was near the Kishon; but nothing in Deborah's ode or the narrative obliges us to find Meroz in just that neighborhood. The combatants were summoned from all parts of the land. Thomson raises the question whether Meroz may not be the present *Meirôn*, the place of the famous Jewish cemetery, about 6 miles west of Safed. It would be on the way between Kedesh (*Kûdes*), where Barak dwelt (Judg. iv. 12), and Tabor, so that as he marched thither from the north he would naturally summon the Meroxites to join his standard (*Land and Book*, i. 424). This argument may be better than that furnished by the slight resemblance of the names, but it does not prove much. Yet the Jews have given Deborah's name to a fountain near *Meirôn* (DEBORAH, vol. i. p. 576, *note*). Probably *Meirôn* is Meroth, a place mentioned by Josephus and fortified by him. See Raumer's *Palästina*, p. 133 (4te Aufl.).   H.

ME'RUTH ('Εμμηρούθ; [Vat. Ερμηρου; Ald. ἐκ Μηρούθ:] *Emerus*). A corruption of IMMER 1, in Ezr. ii. 37 (1 Esdr. v. 24).

ME'SECH [A. V. Ps. cxx. 5, for MESHECH, which see].

ME'SHA (מֵישָׁא, perhaps = מֵישָׁא, *retreat*, Ges.: *Μασσή*; [Alex. *Μασσηε*:] *Messa*), the name of one of the geographical limits of the Joktanites when they first settled in Arabia: " And their dwelling was from Mesha (מִמֵּשָׁא סְפָרָה הַר הַקֶּדֶם), [as thou goest] unto Sephar, a mount of the East" (Gen. x. 30). The position of the early Joktanite colonists is clearly made out from the traces they have left in the ethnology, language, and monuments of Southern Arabia; and without putting too precise a limitation on the possible situation of Mesha and Sephar, we may suppose that these places must have fallen within the southwestern quarter of the peninsula; including the modern Yemen on the west, and the districts of 'Omán, Mahreh, Shihr, etc., as far as Hadramäwt, on the east. These general boundaries are strengthened by the identification of Sephar with the port of *Zafári*, or *Dhafári*; though the site of Sephar may possibly be hereafter connected with the old Himyerite metropolis in the Yemen [see ARABIA, vol. i. p. 140, and SEPHAR], but this would not materially alter the question. In Sephar we believe we have the eastern limit of the early settlers, whether its site be the seaport or the inland city; and the correctness of this supposition appears from the Biblical record, in which the migration is apparently from west to east, from the probable course taken by the immigrants, and from the greater importance of the known western settlements of the Joktanites, or those of the Yemen.

If then Mesha was the western limit of the Joktanites, it must be sought for in northwestern Yemen. But the identifications that have been proposed are not satisfactory. The seaport called *Moûsa* or *Moúza*, mentioned by Ptolemy, Pliny Arrian, and others (see the *Dictionary of Geography*,

s. v. *Muza*) presents the most probable site. It was a town of note in classical times, but has since fallen into decay, if the modern *Moosà* be the same place. The latter is situate in about 13° 40′ N. lat., 43° 20′ E. long., and is near a mountain called the *Three Sisters*, or *Jebel Moosà*, in the Admiralty Chart of the Red Sea, drawn from the surveys of Captain Pullen, R. N. Gesenius thinks this identification probable, but he appears to have been unaware of the existence of a modern site called *Moosà*, saying that Muza was nearly where now is *Mawahid*. Bochart, also, holds the identification with Muza (*Phaleg*, xxx.) Mesha may possibly have lain inland, and more to the northwest of Sephar than the position of *Moosà* would indicate; but this is scarcely to be assumed. There is, however, a Mount Moosh,ᵃ situate in Nejd, in the territory of the tribe of Teiyi (*Marásid* and *Mushtarak*, s. v.). There have not been wanting writers among the late Jews to convert Mesha and Sephar into *Mekkah* and *El-Medeneh* (*Phaleg*, l. c.).

E. S. P.

MESHA (מֵישָׁע [*deliverance*]: Μωσά; Jos. Μισᾶν: *Mesa*). 1. The king of Moab in the reigns of Ahab and his sons Ahaziah and Jehoram, kings of Israel (2 K. iii. 4), and tributary to the first. Probably the allegiance of Moab, with that of the tribes east of Jordan, was transferred to the northern kingdom of Israel upon the division of the monarchy, for there is no account of any subjugation of the country subsequent to the war of extermination with which it was visited by David, when Benaiah displayed his prowess (2 Sam. xxiii. 20), and "the Moabites became David's servants, bearers of gifts" (2 Sam. viii. 2). When Ahab had fallen in battle at Ramoth Gilead, Mesha seized the opportunity afforded by the confusion consequent upon this disaster, and the feeble reign of Ahaziah, to shake off the yoke of Israel and free himself from the burdensome tribute of "a hundred thousand wethers and a hundred thousand rams with their wool." The country east of the Jordan was rich in pasture for cattle (Num. xxxii. 1), the chief wealth of the Moabites consisted in their large flocks of sheep, and the king of this pastoral people is described as *nôkêd* (נֹקֵד), "a sheep-master," or owner of herds.ᵇ About the signification of this word *nôkêd* there is not much doubt, but its origin is obscure. It occurs but once besides, in Am. i. 1, where the prophet Amos is described as "among the herdmen (נֹקְדִים, *nôkedîm*) of Tekoah." On this Kimchi remarks that a herdman was called *nôkêd*, because most cattle have black or white spots (comp. נָקֹד, *nâkôd*, Gen. xxx. 32, A. V. "speckled"), or, as Buxtorf explains it, because sheep are generally marked with certain signs so as

to be known. But it is highly improbable that any such etymology should be correct, and Fürst's conjecture that it is derived from an obsolete root, signifying to keep or feed cattle, is more likely to be true (*Concord.* s. v.).

When, upon the death of Ahaziah, his brother Jehoram succeeded to the throne of Israel, one of his first acts was to secure the assistance of Jehoshaphat, his father's ally, in reducing the Moabites to their former condition of tributaries. The united armies of the two kings marched by a circuitous route round the Dead Sea, and were joined by the forces of the king of Edom. [JEHORAM.] The disordered soldiers of Moab, eager only for spoil, were surprised by the warriors of Israel and their allies, and became an easy prey. In the panic which ensued they were slaughtered without mercy, their country was made a desert, and the king took refuge in his last stronghold and defended himself with the energy of despair. With 700 fighting men he made a vigorous attempt to cut his way through the beleaguering army, and when beaten back, he withdrew to the wall of his city, and there, in sight of the allied host, offered his first-born son, his successor in the kingdom, as a burnt-offering to Chemosh, the ruthless fire-god of Moab. His bloody sacrifice had so far the desired effect that the besiegers retired from him to their own land. There appears to be no reason for supposing that the son of the king of Edom was the victim on this occasion, whether, as R. Joseph Kimchi supposed, he was already in the power of the king of Moab, and was the cause of the Edomites joining the armies of Israel and Judah; or whether, as R. Moses Kimchi suggested, he was taken prisoner in the sally of the Moabites, and sacrificed out of revenge for its failure. These conjectures appear to have arisen from an attempt to find in this incident the event to which allusion is made in Am. ii. 1, where the Moabite is charged with burning the bones of the king of Edom into lime. It is more natural, and renders the narrative more vivid and consistent, to suppose that the king of Moab, finding his last resource fail him, endeavored to avert the wrath and obtain the aid of his god by the most costly sacrifice in his power. [MOAB.]

2. (מֵישָׁע: Μαρισά; [Vat. Μαρεισα;] Alex. Μαρισας; [Comp. Μωυσά; Ald. Μασά] *Mesa*.) The eldest son of Caleb the son of Hezron by his wife Azubah, as Kimchi conjectures (1 Chr. ii. 42). He is called the father, that is the prince or founder, of Ziph. Both the Syriac and Arabic versions have "Elishamai," apparently from the previous verse, while the LXX., unless they had a different reading, מרשע, seem to have repeated "Mareshah," which occurs immediately afterwards.

3. (מֵישָׁא [*retreat*, Ges., *firmness*, Fürst] Μισά; Alex. Μωσα: *Mosa*.) A Benjamite, son of

---

مُوش

ᵇ The LXX. leave it untranslated (νωκήδ, Alex. νακήδ), as does the Peshito Syriac; but Aquila renders it ποιμνιοτρόφος, and Symmachus τρέφων βοσκήματα, following the Targum and Arabic, and themselves followed in the margin of the Hexaplar Syriac. In Am. i. 1, Symmachus has simply ποιμήν. The Kamoos, as quoted by Bochart (*Hieroz.* l. c. 44), gives an Arabic word, نَقَّاد, *nakad*, not traced to any

origin, which denotes an inferior kind of sheep, ugly and little valued except for its wool. The keeper of such sheep is called نَقَّاد, *nakkâd*, which Bochart identifies with *nôkêd*. But if this be the case, it is a little remarkable that the Arabic translator should have passed over a word apparently so appropriate, and followed the version of the Targum, "an owner of flocks." Gesenius and Lee, however, accept this as the solution.

Shaharaim, by his wife Hodesh, who bare him in the land of Moab (1 Chr. viii. 9). The Vulgate and Alex. MS. must have had the reading מוֹרִישָׁא.

W. A. W.

ME'SHACH (מֵישַׁךְ [see below]: Μισάχ; Alex. Μισαχ: *Misach*). The name given to Mishael, one of the companions of Daniel, and like him of the blood-royal of Judah, who with three others was chosen from among the captives to be taught "the learning and the tongue *a* of the Chaldæans" (Dan. i. 4), so that they might be qualified to "stand before" king Nebuchadnezzar (Dan. i. 5) as his personal attendants and advisers (i. 20). During their three years of preparation they were maintained at the king's cost, under the charge of the chief of the eunuchs, who placed them with "the Melzar," or chief butler. The story of their simple diet is well known. When the time of their probation was ended, such was "the knowledge and skill in all learning and wisdom" which God had given them, that the king found them "ten times better than all the magicians and astrologers that were in all his realm" (i. 20). Upon Daniel's promotion to be "chief of the magicians," his three companions, by his influence, were set "over the affairs of the province of Babylon" (ii. 49). But, notwithstanding their Chaldæan education, these three young Hebrews were strongly attached to the religion of their fathers; and their refusal to join in the worship of the image on the plain of Dura gave a handle of accusation to the Chaldæans, who were jealous of their advancement, and eagerly reported to the king the heretical conduct of these "Jewish men" (iii. 12) who stood so high in his favor. The rage of the king, the swift sentence of condemnation passed upon the three offenders, their miraculous preservation from the fiery furnace heated seven times hotter than usual, the king's acknowledgment of the God of Shadrach, Meshach, and Abednego, with their restoration to office, are written in the 3d chapter of Daniel, and there the history leaves them. The name "Meshach" is rendered by Fürst (*Handw.*) "a ram," and derived from the Sanskrit *mêshah*. He goes on to say that it was the name of the Sun-god of the Chaldæans, without giving any authority, or stopping to explain the phenomenon presented by the name of a Chaldæan divinity with an Aryan etymology. That Meshach was the name of some god of the Chaldæans is extremely probable, from the fact that Daniel, who had the name of Belteshazzar, was so called after the god of Nebuchadnezzar (Dan. iv. 8), and that Abednego was named after Nego, or Nebo, the Chaldæan name for the planet Mercury.   W. A. W.

ME'SHECH (מֶשֶׁךְ [*drawing* or *sowing*, *possession*]: Μοσόχ, [Μεσόχ; Alex. Μοσοχ, once Μοσοχ: in Ps. cxx. 5, and Ez. xxvii. 13 LXX. translate]: *Mosoch*), [*Mesech*, A. V. Ps. cxx. 5,] a son of Japheth (Gen. x. 2; 1 Chr. i. 5), and the pro-

genitor of a race frequently noticed in Scripture in connection with Tubal, Magog, and other northern nations. They appear as allies of Gog (Ez. xxxviii 2, 3, xxxix. 1), and as supplying the Tyrians with copper and slaves (Ez. xxvii. 13); in Ps. cxx. 5,[b] they are noticed as one of the remotest, and at the same time rudest nations of the world. Both the name and the associations are in favor of the identification of Meshech with the *Moschi*: the form of the name adopted by the LXX. and the Vulg. approaches most nearly to the classical designation, while in Procopius (*B. G.* iv. 2) we meet with another form (Μέσχοι) which assimilates to the Hebrew. The position of the Moschi in the age of Ezekiel was probably the same as is described by Herodotus (iii. 94), namely, on the borders of Colchis and Armenia, where a mountain chain connecting Anti-Taurus with Caucasus was named after them the *Moschici Montes*, and where was also a district named by Strabo (xi. 497–499) *Moschice*. In the same neighborhood were the *Tibareni*, who have been generally identified with the Biblical Tubal. The Colchian tribes, the Chalybes more especially, were skilled in working metals, and hence arose the trade in the "vessels of brass" with Tyre; nor is it at all improbable that slaves were largely exported thence as now from the neighboring district of *Georgia*. Although the Moschi were a comparatively unimportant race in classical times, they had previously been one of the most powerful nations of Western Asia. The Assyrian monarchs were engaged in frequent wars with them, and it is not improbable that they had occupied the whole of the district afterwards named Cappadocia. In the Assyrian inscriptions the name appears under the form of *Muskri*: a somewhat similar name, *Mashoash*, appears in an Egyptian inscription, which commemorates the achievements of the third Rameses (Wilkinson, *Anc. Eg.* i. 398, Abridg.). The subsequent history of Meshech is unknown; Knobel's attempt to connect them with the Ligurians (*Völkertaf.* p. 119, &c.) is devoid of all solid ground. As far as the name and locality are concerned, *Muscovite* is a more probable hypothesis (Rawlinson, *Herod.* i. 652, 653).

W. L. B.

MESHELEMI'AH (מְשֶׁלֶמְיָה [*whom Jehovah recompenses*]: Μοσολλαμί: [Vat. Μοσαλαμι;] Alex. Μοσολλαμ: *Mosollamia*, 1 Chr. ix. 21; מְשֶׁלֶמְיָהוּ: Μοσολλεμία, [Μοσολλαμία; Vat. Μοσολαηλ, Μοσαληα, Μοσομαειδ;] Alex. Μοσολλαμ, Μασελλαμια, Μεσολλεμια: *Meselemia*, 1 Chr. xxvi. 1, 2, 9). A Korhite, son of Kore, of the sons of Asaph, who with his seven sons and his brethren, "sons of might," were porters or gate-keepers of the house of Jehovah in the reign of David. He is evidently the same as SHELEMIAH (1 Chr. xxvi. 14), to whose custody the East Gate, or principal entrance, was committed, and whose son Zechariah was a wise counsellor,

---

a The expression כָּל סֵפֶר וְלָשׁוֹן P includes the whole of the Chaldæan literature, written and spoken.

b Various explanations have been offered to account for the juxtaposition of two such remote nations as Mesech and Kedar in this passage. The LXX. does not recognise it as a proper name, but renders it μακρύνθη. Hitzig suggests the identity of *Mesech* with *Dammesech*, or Damascus. It is, however, quite pos-

sible that the Psalmist selects the two nations for the very reason which is regarded as an objection, namely, their *remoteness* from each other, though at the same time their wild and uncivilized character may have been the ground of the selection, as Hengstenberg (*Comm.* in loc.) suggests. We have already had to notice Knobel's idea, that the Mesech in this passage is the Meshech of 1 Chr. i. 5, and the Babylonian Mesech. [MASH.]

and had charge of the north gate. "SHALLUM the son of Kore, the son of Ebiasaph, the son of Korah" (1 Chr. ix. 19), who was chief of the porters (17), and who gave his name to a family which performed the same office, and returned from the Captivity with Zerubbabel (Ezr. ii. 42 ; Neh. vii. 45), is apparently identical with Shelemiah, Meshelemiah, and Meshullam (comp. 1 Chr. ix. 17, with Neh. xii. 25).   W. A. W.

MESHEZ'ABEEL [4 syl] (מְשֵׁיזַבְאֵל) [deliverer of God]: Μεζεβήλ; [Vat. omits;] Alex. Μασεζειηλ: FA. Μασεζεβηλ: Mesezebel).

1. Ancestor of Meshullam, who assisted Nehemiah in rebuilding the wall of Jerusalem (Neh. iii. 4). He was apparently a priest.

2. (Μεσωζεβήλ : Mesiznbel.) One of the "heads of the people," probably a family, who sealed the covenant with Nehemiah (Neh. x. 21).

3. (Βασηζά; FA. 3d hand, Βασηζαβεηλ: Mesezebel.) The father of Pethahiah, and descendant of Zerah the son of Judah (Neh. xi. 24).

* In Neh. xi. 24 the A. V. ed. 1611 has the more correct form, Meshezabel.   A.

MESHIL'LEMITH (מְשִׁלֵּמִית) [see next word]: Μασελμώθ; Alex. Μοσολλαμωθ: Mosollimith). The son of Immer, a priest, and ancestor of Amashai or Maasiai, according to Neh. xi. 13, and of Pashur and Adaiah, according to 1 Chr. ix. 12. In Neh. xi. 13 he is called MESHILLEMOTH.

MESHIL'LEMOTH (מְשִׁלֵּמוֹת) [retributions, requitals]: Μοσολαμώθ; [Vat. Μοσολαμωθ:] Alex. Μοσολλαμωθ: Mosollamoth). An Ephraimite, ancestor of Berechiah, one of the chiefs of the tribe in the reign of Pekah (2 Chr. xxviii. 12).

2. (Μεσαριμώθ; [Vat. Alex. FA.¹ omit; FA.³ Μασαλιμωθ.]) Neh. xi. 13. The same as MESHILLEMITH.

MESHUL'LAM (מְשֻׁלָּם) [friend, associate]). 1. (Μεσουλάμ; Alex. Μεσσαλην: Mesulam.) Ancestor of Shaphan the scribe (2 K. xxii. 3).

2. (Μοσολλάμ; [Vat. Μοσολοαμος;] Alex. Μοσολλαμος: Mosollam.) The son of Zerubbabel (1 Chr. iii. 19).

3. (Vat. [rather, Rom.] and Alex. Μοσολλαμ; [Vat. Μοσολαμ]) A Gadite, one of the chief men of the tribe, who dwelt in Bashan at the time the genealogies were recorded in the reign of Jotham king of Judah (1 Chr. v. 13).

4. (Μοσολλάμ) A Benjamite, of the sons of Elpaal (1 Chr. viii. 17).

5. ([In 1 Chr., Μοσολλάμ, Vat. Μοσλλαμ; in Neh.] Μεσουλάμ; FA. Αμεσσουλαμ.) A Benjamite, the son of Hodaviah or Joed, and father of Sallu, one of the chiefs of the tribe who settled at Jerusalem after the return from Babylon (1 Chr. ix. 7; Neh. xi. 7).

6. ([Μοσολλάμ; Vat. Μασεαλημ:] Alex. Μεσουλλαμ.) A Benjamite, son of Shephathiah, who lived at Jerusalem after the Captivity (1 Chr. ix. 8).

7. ([In 1 Chr. Μοσολλάμ, Vat. Μοσολλομι;] in Neh. Μεσουλάμ; [Vat. Μεσσουλαμ,] Alex. Μοσολλαμ.) The same as SHALLUM, who was high-priest probably in the reign of Amon, and father of Hilkiah (1 Chr. ix. 11; Neh. xi. 11).

His descent is traced through Zadok and Meraioth to Ahitub; or, as is more probable, the names Meraioth and Ahitub are transposed, and his descent is from Meraioth as the more remote ancestor (comp. 1 Chr. vi. 7).

8. [Μοσολλομ.] A priest, son of Meshillemith, or Meshillemoth, the son of Immer, and ancestor of Maasiai or Amashai (1 Chr. ix. 12; comp. Neh. xi. 13). His name does not occur in the parallel list of Nehemiah, and we may suppose it to have been omitted by a transcriber in consequence of the similarity of the name which follows; or in the passage in which it occurs it may have been added from the same cause.

9. [Μοσολλάμ.] A Kohathite, or family of Kohathite Levites, in the reign of Josiah, who were among the overseers of the work of restoration in the Temple (2 Chr. xxxiv. 12).

10. (Μεσολλάμ; [Vat. Μεσουαμ.]) One of the "heads" (A. V. "chief men") sent by Ezra to Iddo "the head," to gather together the Levites to join the caravan about to return to Jerusalem (Ezr. viii. 16). Called MOSOLLAMON in 1 Esdr. viii. 44.

11. (Alex. Μετασολλαμ; [Vat. FA. Μεσουγαμ:] Mesollam.) A chief man in the time of Ezra, probably a Levite, who assisted Jonathan and Jahaziah in abolishing the marriages which some of the people had contracted with foreign wives (Ezr. x. 15). Also called MOSOLLAM in 1 Esdr. ix. 14.

12. (Μοσολλάμ; [Vat. with following word, Μελονσαμαλουμ:] Mosollam.) One of the descendants of Bani, who had married a foreign wife and put her away (Ezr. x. 29). OLAMUS in 1 Esdr. ix. 30 is a fragment of this name.

13. ([Μοσολλάμ, Neh. iii. 3, but Vat. omits;] Μεσουλάμ, Neh. iii. 30, vi. 18.) The son of Berechiah, who assisted in rebuilding the wall of Jerusalem (Neh. iii. 4), as well as the Temple wall, adjoining which he had his "chamber" (Neh. iii. 30). He was probably a priest, and his daughter was married to Johanan the son of Tobiah the Ammonite (Neh. vi. 18).

14. (Μεσουλάμ.) The son of Besodeiah: he assisted Jehoiada the son of Paseah in restoring the old gate of Jerusalem (Neh. iii. 6).

15. (Μεσουλάμ; [Vat. FA.¹ omit; FA.³] Alex. Μοσολλαμ.) One of those who stood at the left hand of Ezra when he read the law to the people (Neh. viii. 4).

16. (Μεσουλάμ.) A priest, or family of priests, who sealed the covenant with Nehemiah (Neh. x. 7).

17. (Μεσουλάμ; [Vat. FA.] Alex. Μεσουλαμ.) One of the heads of the people who sealed the covenant with Nehemiah (Neh. x. 20).

18. (Μεσουλάμ.) A priest in the days of Joiakim the son of Jeshua, and representative of the house of Ezra (Neh. xii. 13).

19. (Μεσολάμ; [Vat. FA.¹ Alex. omit; FA.³ Μοσολλαμ]) Likewise a priest at the same time as the preceding, and head of the priestly family of Ginnethon (Neh. xii. 16).

20. (Omitted in LXX. [but FA.³ Μοσολλαμ.]) A family of porters, descendants of Meshullam (Neh. xii. 25), who is also called Meshelemiah (1 Chr. xxvi. 1), Shelemiah (1 Chr. xxvi. 14), and Shallum (Neh. vii. 45).

21. (Μεσολλάμ; [Vat. Μεσουλαμ: FA.¹ Μεσουλα, FA.³ Μεσουλλαμ;] Alex. Μοσολλαμ;

One of the princes of Judah who were in the right hand company of those who marched on the wall of Jerusalem upon the occasion of its solemn dedication (Neh. xii. 33).   W. A. W.

MESHUL'LEMETH (מְשֻׁלֶּמֶת [*a pious one*]: Μεσολλάμ; Alex. Μασσαλαμειθ: *Messelemeth*). The daughter of Haruz of Jotbah, wife of Manasseh king of Judah, and mother of his successor Amon (2 K. xxi. 19).

MESO'BAITE, THE (הַמְּצֹבָיָה, *i. e.* " the Metsobayah " [see below]: [Vat. FA.] ο Μειναβεια; [Rom.] Alex. Μεσωβία: *de Masobia*), a title which occurs only once, and then attached to the name of JASIEL, the last of David's guard in the extended list of 1 Chron. (xi. 47). The word retains strong traces of ZOBAH, one of the petty Aramite kingdoms, in which there would be nothing surprising, as David had a certain connection with these Aramite states, while this very catalogue contains the names of Moabites, Ammonites, and other foreigners. But on this it is impossible to pronounce with any certainty, as the original text of the passage is probably in confusion. Kennicott's conclusion (*Dissertation*, pp. 233, 234) is that originally the word was " the Metzobaites " (הַמְּצֹבָיִם), and applied to the three names preceding it.

It is an unusual thing in the A. V. to find צ (ts) rendered by s, as in the present case. Another instance is SIDON.   G.

* It cannot be " the Mesobaite " (A. V.), as this Hebrew ending is not strictly patronymic. (See Ges. *Lehrgebäude*, p. 504 f.) If we abide by the reading, it must be a compound name = Jasiel-Metsovajah. The latter may take the article in Hebrew from its appellative force. The name of the place is unknown. Fürst supposes it to mean " the gathering-place of Jehovah." Different readings have been suggested (see Bertheau, *Bücher der Chronik*).   H.

MESOPOTA'MIA (אֲרַם־נַהֲרַיִם [*high land of two rivers*]: Μεσοποταμία: *Mesopotamia*) is the ordinary Greek rendering of the Hebrew *Aram-Naharaim*, or "Syria of the two rivers," whereof we have frequent mention in the earlier books of Scripture (Gen. xxiv. 10; Deut. xxiii. 4; Judg. iii. 8, 10). It is also adopted by the LXX. to represent the פַּדַּן־אֲרָם (*Paddan-Aram*) of the Hebrew text, where our translators keep the term used in the original (Gen. xxv. 20, xxviii. 2, 5, etc.).

If we look to the signification of the name, we must regard Mesopotamia as the entire country between the two rivers — the Tigris and the Euphrates. This is a tract nearly 700 miles long, and from 20 to 250 miles broad, extending in a southeasterly direction from *Telek* (lat. 38° 23', long. 39° 18') to *Kurnah* (lat. 31°, long. 47° 30'). The Arabian geographers term it " the Island," a name which is almost literally correct, since a few miles only intervene between the source of the Tigris and the Euphrates at *Telek*. It is for the most part a vast plain, but is crossed about its centre by the range of the *Sinjar* hills, running nearly east and west from about Mosul to a little below *Rakkeh*; and in its northern portion it is even mountainous, the upper Tigris valley being separated from the Mesopotamian plain by an im-

portant range, the Mons Masius of Strabo (xi. 12, § 4; 14, § 2, &c.), which runs from *Birehjik* to *Jezireh*. This district is always charming; but the remainder of the region varies greatly according to circumstances. In early spring a tender and luxuriant herbage covers the whole plain, while flowers of the most brilliant hues spring up in rapid succession, imparting their color to the landscape, which changes from day to day. As the summer draws on, the verdure recedes towards the streams and mountains. Vast tracts of arid plain, yellow, parched, and sapless, fill the intermediate space, which ultimately becomes a bare and uninhabitable desert. In the *Sinjar*, and in the mountain-tract to the north, springs of water are tolerably abundant, and corn, vines, and figs, are cultivated by a stationary population; but the greater part of the region is only suited to the nomadic hordes, which in spring spread themselves far and wide over the vast flats, so utilizing the early verdure, and in summer and autumn gather along the banks of the two main streams and their affluents, where a delicious shade and a rich pasture may be found during the greatest heats. Such is the present character of the region. It is thought, however, that by a careful water-system, by deriving channels from the great streams or their affluents, by storing the superfluous spring-rains in tanks, by digging wells, and establishing *kanáts*, or subterraneous aqueducts, the whole territory might be brought under cultivation, and rendered capable of sustaining a permanent population. That some such system was established in early times by the Assyrian monarchs seems to be certain, from the fact that the whole level country on both sides of the *Sinjar* is covered with mounds marking the sites of cities, which, wherever opened, have presented appearances similar to those found on the site of Nineveh. [ASSYRIA.] If even the more northern portion of the Mesopotamian region is thus capable of being redeemed from its present character of a desert, still more easily might the southern division be reclaimed and converted into a garden. Between the 35th and 34th parallels, the character of the Mesopotamian plain suddenly alters. Above, it is a plain of a certain elevation above the courses of the Tigris and Euphrates, which are separated from it by low lime-stone ranges; below, it is a mere alluvium, almost level with the rivers, which frequently overflow large portions of it. Consequently, from the point indicated, canalization becomes easy. A skillful management of the two rivers would readily convey abundance of the life-giving fluid to every portion of the Mesopotamian tract below the 34th parallel. And the innumerable lines of embankment, marking the course of ancient canals, sufficiently indicate that in the flourishing period of Babylonia a network of artificial channels covered the country. [BABYLONIA.]

To this description of Mesopotamia in the most extended sense of the term, it seems proper to append a more particular account of that region, which bears the name *par excellence*, both in Scripture, and in the classical writers. This is the northwestern portion of the tract already described, or the country between the great bend of the Euphrates (lat. 35° to 37° 30') and the upper Tigris. (See particularly Ptolem. *Geograph.* v. 18; and compare Eratosth. ap. Strab. ii. 1, § 29; Arr. *Exp. Al.* iii. 7; *Dexipp. Fr.* p. 1, &c.) It consists of the mountain country extending from *Birehjik* to

Jesireh upon the north; and, upon the south, of the great undulating Mesopotamian plain, as far as the Sinjar hills, and the river *Khabour*. The northern range, called by the Arabs *Karajah Dagh* towards the west and *Jebel Tur* towards the east, does not attain to any great elevation. It is in places rocky and precipitous, but has abundant springs and streams which support a rich vegetation. Forests of chestnuts and pistachio-trees occasionally clothe the mountain sides; and about the towns and villages are luxuriant orchards and gardens, producing abundance of excellent fruit. The vine is cultivated with success; wheat and barley yield heavily; and rice is grown in some places. The streams from the north side of this range are short, and fall mostly into the Tigris. Those from the south are more important. They flow down at very moderate intervals along the whole course of the range, and gradually collect into two considerable rivers — the *Belik* (ancient *Bilichus*), and the *Khabour* (Habor or Chaboras) — which empty themselves into the Euphrates. [HABOR.] South of the mountains is the great plain already described, which between the *Khabour* and the Tigris is interrupted only by the *Sinjar* range, but west of the *Khabour* is broken by several spurs from the *Karajah Dagh*, having a general direction from north to south. In this district are the two towns of *Orfa* and *Harran*, the former of which is thought by many to be the native city of Abraham, while the latter is on good grounds identified with Haran, his resting-place between Chaldæa and Palestine. [HARAN.] Here we must fix the Padan-Aram of Scripture — the "plain Syria," or "district stretching away from the foot of the hills" (Stanley's *S. & P.* p. 129 *note*), without, however, determining the extent of country thus designated. Besides *Orfa* and *Harran*, the chief cities of modern Mesopotamia are *Mardin* and *Nisibin*, south of the *Jebel Tur*, and *Diarbekr*, north of that range, upon the Tigris. Of these places two, *Nisibin* and *Diarbekr*, were important from a remote antiquity, *Nisibin* being then Nisibis, and *Diarbekr* Amida.

We first hear of Mesopotamia in Scripture as the country where Nahor and his family settled after quitting Ur of the Chaldees (Gen. xxiv. 10). Here lived Bethuel and Laban; and hither Abraham sent his servant, to fetch Isaac a wife "of his own kindred" (*ib.* ver. 38). Hither too, a century later, came Jacob on the same errand; and hence he returned with his two wives after an absence of 21 years. After this we have no mention of Mesopotamia, till, at the close of the wanderings in the wilderness, Balak the king of Moab sends for Balaam "to Pethor of Mesopotamia" (Deut. xxiii. 4), which was situated among "the mountains of the east" (Num. xxiii. 7), by a river (*ib.* xxii. 5), probably the Euphrates. About half a century later, we find, for the first and last time, Mesopotamia the seat of a powerful monarchy. Chushan-Rishathaim, king of Mesopotamia, establishes his dominion over Israel shortly after the death of Joshua (Judg. iii. 8), and maintains his authority for the space of eight years, when his yoke is broken by Othniel, Caleb's nephew (*ib.* vv. 9, 10). Finally, the children of Ammon, having provoked a war with David, "sent a thousand talents of silver to hire them chariots and horsemen out of Mesopotamia, and out of Syria-Maachah, and out of Zobah" (1 Chr. xix. 6). It is uncertain whether the Mesopotamians were persuaded to

120

lend their aid at once. At any rate, after the first great victory of Joab over Ammon and the Syrians who took their part, these last "drew forth the Syrians that were beyond the river" (*ib.* ver. 16), who participated in the final defeat of their fellow-countrymen at the hands of David. The name of Mesopotamia then passes out of Scripture, the country to which it had applied becoming a part, first of Assyria, and afterwards of the Babylonian empire.

According to the Assyrian inscriptions, Mesopotamia was inhabited in the early times of the empire (B. C. 1200–1100) by a vast number of petty tribes, each under its own prince, and all quite independent of one another. The Assyrian monarchs contended with these chiefs at great advantage, and by the time of Jehu (B. C. 880) had fully established their dominion over them. The tribes were all called "tribes of the Naïri," a term which some compare with the *Naharaim* of the Jews, and translate "tribes of the *stream-lands*." But this identification is very uncertain. It appears, however, in close accordance with Scripture, first, that Mesopotamia was independent of Assyria till after the time of David; secondly, that the Mesopotamians were warlike and used chariots in battle; and thirdly, that not long after the time of David they lost their independence, their country being absorbed by Assyria, of which it was thenceforth commonly reckoned a part.

On the destruction of the Assyrian empire, Mesopotamia seems to have been divided between the Medes and the Babylonians. The conquests of Cyrus brought it wholly under the Persian yoke; and thus it continued to the time of Alexander, being comprised (probably) in the ninth, or Assyrian satrapy. At Alexander's death, it fell to Seleucus, and formed a part of the great Syrian kingdom till wrested from Antiochus V. by the Parthians, about B. C. 160. Trajan conquered it from Parthia in A. D. 115, and formed it into a Roman province; but in A. D. 117 Adrian relinquished it of his own accord. It was afterwards more than once reconquered by Rome, but never continued long under her sceptre, and finally reverted to the Persians in the reign of Jovian, A. D. 363.

(See Quint. Curt. v. 1; Dio Cass. lxviii. 22–26; Amm. Marc. xv. 8, &c.; and for the description of the district, compare C. Niebuhr's *Voyage en Arabie*, &c., vol. ii. pp. 300–334; Pococke's *Description of the East*, vol. ii. part i. ch. 17; and Layard's *Nineveh and Babylon*, chs. xi.–xv.).

G. R.

MESSI'AH. This word (מָשִׁיחַ, *Mâshiach*), which answers to the word Χριστός in the N. T., means *anointed*; and is applicable in its first sense to any one anointed with the holy oil. It is applied to the high priest in Lev. iv. 3, 5, 16; and possibly to the shield of Saul in a figurative sense in 2 Sam. i. 21. The kings of Israel were called *anointed*, from the mode of their consecration (1 Sam. ii. 10, 35, xii. 3, 5, xvi. 6, xxiv. 6, 10, xxvi. 9, 11, 23; 2 Sam. i. 14, 16, xix. 21, xxiii. 1).

This word also refers to the expected Prince of the chosen people who was to complete God's purposes for them, and to redeem them, and of whose coming the prophets of the old covenant in all time spoke. It is twice used in the N. T. of Jesus (John i. 41, iv. 25, A. V. "Messias"); but the Greek equivalent, *the Christ*, is constantly applied, at first with the article as a title, exactly *the Anointed One,* but later without the article, as a proper name, *Jesus Christ.*

Three points belong to this subject: 1. The expectation of a Messiah among the Jews; 2. The expectation of a suffering Messiah; 3. The nature and power of the expected Messiah. Of these the second will be discussed under SAVIOUR, and the third under SON OF GOD. The present article will contain a rapid survey of the first point only. The interpretation of particular passages must be left in a great measure to professed commentators.

The earliest gleam of the Gospel is found in the account of the fall, where it is said to the serpent " I will put enmity between thee and the woman, and between thy seed and her seed; it shall bruise thy head, and thou shalt bruise his heel" (Gen. iii. 15). The tempter came to the woman in the guise of a serpent, and the curse thus pronounced has a reference both to the serpent which was the instrument, and to the tempter that employed it; to the natural terror and enmity of man against the serpent, and to the conflict between mankind redeemed by Christ its Head, and Satan that deceived mankind. Many interpreters would understand by the seed of the woman, the Messiah only; but it is easier to think with Calvin that mankind, after they are gathered into one army by Jesus the Christ, the Head of the Church, are to achieve a victory over evil. The Messianic character of this prophecy has been much questioned by those who see in the history of the Fall nothing but a fable: to those who accept it as true, this passage is the primitive germ of the Gospel, the protevangelium.

The blessings in store for the children of Shem are remarkably indicated in the words of Noah, " Blessed be the Lord God of Shem," or (lit.) " Blessed be Jehovah the God of Shem" (Gen. ix. 26), where instead of blessing Shem, as he had cursed Canaan, he carries up the blessing to the great fountain of the blessings that shall follow Shem. Next follows the promise to Abraham, wherein the blessings to Shem are turned into the narrower channel of one family — " I will make of thee a great nation, and I will bless thee, and make thy name great; and thou shalt be a blessing; and I will bless them that bless thee and curse him that curseth thee; and in thee shall all families of the earth be blessed" (Gen. xii. 2, 3). The promise is still indefinite; but it tends to the undoing of the curse of Adam, by a blessing to all the earth through the seed of Abraham, as death had come on the whole earth through Adam. When our Lord says, " Your father Abraham rejoiced to see my day, and he saw it and was glad" (John viii. 56), we are to understand that this promise of a real blessing and restoration to come hereafter was understood in a spiritual sense, as a leading back to God, as a coming nearer to Him, from whom the promise came; and he desired with hope and rejoicing (" gestivit cum desiderio," *Bengel*) to behold the day of it.

A great step is made in Gen. xlix. 10, " The sceptre shall not depart from Judah, nor a lawgiver from between his feet, until Shiloh come; and unto him shall the gathering of the people be."

The derivation of the word Shiloh (שִׁילֹה) is probably from the root שָׁלָה; and if so, it means rest, or, as Hengstenberg argues, it is for Shilon,

and is a proper name, *the man of peace or rest, the peace-maker.* For other derivations and interpretations see Gesenius (*Thesaurus,* sub voc.) and Hengstenberg (*Christologie,* vol. i.). Whilst *man of peace* is far the most probable meaning of the name, those old versions which render it " He to whom the sceptre *belongs,*" see the Messianic application equally with ourselves. This then is the first case in which the promises distinctly centre in one person; and He is to be a man of peace; He is to wield and retain the government, and the nations shall look up to Him and obey Him. [For a different view, see the art. SHILOH in this Dictionary.]

The next passage usually quoted is the prophecy of Balaam (Num. xxiv. 17-19). The *star* points indeed to the glory, as the sceptre denotes the power, of a king. And Onkelos and Jonathan (Pseudo) see here the Messiah. But it is doubtful whether the prophecy is not fulfilled in David (2 Sam. viii. 2, 14); and though David is himself a type of Christ, the direct Messianic application of this place is by no means certain.

The prophecy of Moses (Deut. xviii. 18), " I will raise them up a prophet from among their brethren, like unto thee, and will put my words in his mouth; and he shall speak unto them all that I shall command him," claims attention. Does this refer to the Messiah? The reference to Moses in John v. 45-47 — " He wrote of me," seems to point to this passage; for it is a cold and forced interpretation to refer it to the whole types and symbols of the Mosaic Law. On the other hand, many critics would fain find here the divine institution of the whole prophetic order, which if not here, does not occur at all. Hengstenberg thinks that it does promise that an order of prophets should be sent, but that the singular is used in direct reference to the greatest of the prophets, Christ himself, without whom the words would not have been fulfilled. " The Spirit of Christ spoke in the prophets, and Christ is in a sense the only prophet." (1 Pet. i. 11.) Jews in earlier times might have been excused for referring the words to this or that present prophet; but the Jews whom the Lord rebukes (John v.) were inexcusable; for, having the words before them, and the works of Christ as well, they should have known that no prophet had so fulfilled the words as He had.

The passages in the Pentateuch which relate to " the Angel of the Lord " have been thought by many to bear reference to the Messiah.

The second period of Messianic prophecy would include the time of David. In the promises of a kingdom to David and his house " for ever " (2 Sam. vii. 13), there is more than could be fulfilled save by the eternal kingdom in which that of David merged; and David's last words dwell on this promise of an everlasting throne (2 Sam. xxiii.). Passages in the Psalms are numerous which are applied to the Messiah in the N. T.: such are Ps. ii., xvi., xxii., xl., cx. Other psalms quoted in the N. T. appear to refer to the actual history of another king; but only those who deny the existence of types and prophecy will consider this as an evidence against an ulterior allusion to Messiah: such psalms are xlv., lxviii., lxix., lxxii. The advance in clearness in this period is great. The name of Anointed, *i. e.* King, comes in, and the Messiah is to come of the lineage of David. He is described in his exaltation, with his great kingdom that shall be spiritual rather than temporal, Ps. ii., xxi., xl.,

ix. In other places he is seen in suffering and humiliation, Ps. xxii., xvi., xl.

After the time of David the predictions of the Messiah ceased for a time; until those prophets arose whose works we possess in the canon of Scripture. They nowhere give us an exact and complete account of the nature of Messiah; but different aspects of the truth are produced by the various needs of the people, and so they are led to speak of Him now as a Conqueror or a Judge, or a Redeemer from sin; it is from the study of the whole of them that we gain a clear and complete image of His Person and kingdom. This third period lasts from the reign of Uzziah to the Babylonish Captivity. The Messiah is a king and Ruler of David's house, who should come to reform and restore the Jewish nation and purify the church, as in Is. xi., xl.-lxvi. The blessings of the restoration, however, will not be confined to Jews; the heathen are made to share them fully (Is. ii., lxvi.). Whatever theories have been attempted about Isaiah liii., there can be no doubt that the most natural is the received interpretation that it refers to the suffering Redeemer; and so in the N. T. it is always considered to do. The passage of Micah v. 2 (comp. Matt. ii. 6) left no doubt in the mind of the Sanhedrim as to the birthplace of the Messiah. The lineage of David is again alluded to in Zechariah xii. 10-14. The time of the second Temple is fixed by Haggai ii. 9 for Messiah's coming; and the coming of the Forerunner and of the Anointed are clearly revealed in Mal. iii. 1, iv. 5, 6.

The fourth period after the close of the canon of the O. T. is known to us in a great measure from allusions in the N. T. to the expectation of the Jews. From such passages as Ps. ii. 2, 6, 8; Jer. xxiii. 5, 6; Zech. ix. 9, the Pharisees and those of the Jews who expected Messiah at all, looked for a temporal prince only. The Apostles themselves were infected with this opinion, till after the Resurrection, Matt. xx. 20, 21: Luke xxiv. 21; Acts i. 6. Gleams of a purer faith appear, Luke ii. 30, xxiii. 42; John iv. 25. On the other hand there was a skeptical school which had discarded the expectation altogether. No mention of Messiah appears in the Book of Wisdom, nor in the writings of Philo; and Josephus avoids the doctrine. Intercourse with heathens had made some Jews ashamed of their fathers' faith.

The expectation of a golden age that should return upon the earth, was common in heathen nations (Hesiod, Works and Days, 109; Ovid, Met. i. 89; Virg. Ecl. iv.; and passages in Euseb. Præp. Ev. i. 7, xii. 13). This hope the Jews also shared; but with them it was associated with the coming of a particular Person, the Messiah. It has been asserted that in Him the Jews looked for an earthly king, and that the existence of the hope of a Messiah may thus be accounted for on natural grounds and without a divine revelation. But the prophecies refute this: they hold out not a Prophet only, but a King and a Priest, whose business it should be to set the people free from sin, and to teach them the ways of God, as in Ps. xxii., xl., cx.; Is. ii., xi., liii. In these and other places too the power of the coming One reaches beyond the Jews and embraces all the Gentiles, which is contrary to the exclusive notions of Judaism. A fair consideration of all the passages will convince that the growth of the Messianic idea in the prophecies is owing to revelation from God. The witness of the

N. T. to the O. T. prophecies can bear no other meaning; it is summed up in the words of Peter; — "We have also a more sure word of prophecy; whereunto ye do well that ye take heed, as unto a light that shineth in a dark place, until the day dawn, and the day-star arise in your hearts: knowing this first, that no prophecy of the Scripture is of any private interpretation. For the prophecy came not in old time by the will of man: but holy men of God spake as they were moved by the Holy Ghost " (2 Pet. i. 19-21; compare the elaborate essay on this text in Knapp's Opuscula, vol. i.). Our Lord affirms that there are prophecies of the Messiah in O. T., and that they are fulfilled in Him, Matt. xxvi. 54; Mark ix. 12; Luke xviii. 31-33, xxii. 37, xxiv. 27; John v. 39, 46. The Apostles preach the same truth, Acts ii. 16, 25, viii. 28-35, x. 43, xiii. 23, 32, xxvi. 22, 23; 1 Pet. i. 11; and in many passages of St. Paul. Even if internal evidence did not prove that the prophecies were much more than vague longings after better times, the N. T. proclaims everywhere that although the Gospel was the sun, and O. T. prophecy the dim light of a candle, yet both were light, and both assisted those who heeded them, to see aright; and that the prophets interpreted, not the private longings of their own hearts but the will of God, in speaking as they did (see Knapp's Essay for this explanation) of the coming kingdom.

Our own theology is rich in prophetic literature; but the most complete view of this whole subject is found in Hengstenberg's Christologie, the second edition of which, greatly altered, is translated in Clark's Foreign Theological Library. See as already mentioned, SAVIOUR; SON OF God.

* A full critical history of the Jewish expectation of a Messiah, with particular reference to the opinions prevalent at the time of Christ, is a desideratum. The subject is attended with great difficulties. The date of some of the most important documents bearing upon it is still warmly debated by scholars. See, e. g., in this Dictionary, the articles DANIEL, BOOK OF; ENOCH, BOOK OF; MACCABEES (THE), vol. ii. pp. 1713, 1714, and note (on the so-called "Psalms of Solomon"); MOSES (addition in Amer. ed. on the recently discovered "Assumption of Moses"); and VERSIONS, ANCIENT (Targum). Most of the older works on the later opinions of the Jews (as those of Allix and Schöttgen) were written with a polemic aim, in an uncritical spirit, and depend largely upon untrustworthy authorities, making extensive use, for example, of the book Zohar, now proved to be a forgery of the thirteenth century. (See Ginsburg, The Kabbalah, etc. Lond. 1865.)

Besides the books of the Old and New Testament and the Greek Apocrypha, the principal original sources of information on the subject are the Septuagint Version; the Jewish portion of the Sibylline Oracles, particularly Lib. III. 97-817, about 140 B. C. (best editions by Friedlieb, Leipz. 1852, and Alexandre, 2 vols. in 4 parts, Paris, 1841-56; comp. the dissertations of Bleek, Lücke, Hilgenfeld, and Ewald): the book of Enoch; the Psalms of Solomon (see reference above); the Assumption of Moses (see above); the works of Philo and Josephus (which contain very little); the Book of Jubilees or Little Genesis (trans. from the Ethiopic by Dillmann in Ewald's Jahrb. f. Bibl. wiss. 1849, pp. 230-256, and 1850, pp. 1-96); the Second (Fourth) Book of Esdras (Ezra); the Apocalypse of Baruch (publ. in Syriac with a Latin translation by Ceriani in his *Monumenta sacra et profana ex Codd. Bibl. Ambrosiana*, tom. i. fasc. 1, 2, Mediolani, 1861-66); the Mishna (which does not contain much; ed. with Lat. version and the comm. of Maimonides and Bartenora by Surenhusius, 6 vols. fol. 1698-1703, Germ. trans. by Rabe, 1760-63, and by Jost, in Hebrew letters, Berl. 1832-34; eighteen treatises in English by De Sola and Raphall, Lond. 1845); the Targums (see reference above; the Targums of Onkelos and Pseudo-Jonathan on the Pentateuch trans. by Etheridge, 2 vols. Lond. 1862-65); the earliest Midrashim (*Mechilta*, *Siphra*, *Siphri*, on Exod., Levit., Numb,. and Deut., publ. with a Lat. version in Ugolini's *Thesaurus*, tom. xiv., xv.); the Jerusalem and Babylonian Gemara, and other Rabbinical writings. There is no complete translation of the Talmud; but 20 treatises out of the 39 in the Jerusalem Gemara are published with a Latin version in Ugolini's *Thesaurus* (tom. xvii., xviii., xx., xxx., xxx.), and three of the Babylonian (tom. xix., xxv.). Something on the opinions of the later Jews may be gathered from the Christian fathers, particularly Justin Martyr (*Dial. c. Tryph.*), Origen, and Jerome; and the early Christians appear to have transferred many of the Jewish expectations concerning the Messiah to their doctrine of the Second Advent of Christ, e. g. with reference to the appearance of ELIJAH as his precursor (see vol. i. p. 710, note, and add the full illustration of this point by Thilo, *Codex Apocr. N. T.* p. 761 ff.).

On the Messianic prophecies of the Old Testament the more important literature is referred to by Hase in his *Leben Jesu*, § 36 (4ª Aufl.). See also Knobel, *Prophetismus d. Hebr.*, Bresl. 1837, i. 311 note, 328 note, and Diestel, *Gesch. d. A. Test. in d. christl. Kirche*, Jena, 1869, p. 770 ff. With Hengstenberg's *Christology* should be compared his *Comm. on the Psalms*, in which his former views are considerably modified. See also Dr. Noyes's review of the first edition of the Christology, in the *Christ. Exam.* for July, 1834, xvi. 321-364, and the Introduction to his *New Trans. of the Heb. Prophets*, 3d ed. Bost. 1866. Hengstenberg's essay on the *Godhead of the Messiah in the Old Test.* was translated from his Christology in the *Bibl. Repos.* for 1833, iii. 653-683, and reviewed by Dr. Noyes in the *Christian Examiner* for January, May, and July, 1836, the last two articles relating to the "Angel of Jehovah." See, further, J. Pye Smith, *Script. Testimony to the Messiah*, 5th ed. 2 vols. Edin. 1859; J. J. Stähelin, *Die messian. Weissagungen des A. T.*, Berl. 1847; Rev. David Green, *The Knowledge and Faith of the O. T. Saints respecting the Promised Messiah*, in the *Bibl. Sacra* for Jan. 1857, xiv. 166-199; Prof. S. C. Bartlett, *Theories of Messianic Prophecy*, in the *Bibl. Sacra* for Oct. 1861, xviii. 724-770; and Ed. Riehm, *Zur Charakteristik d. messian. Weissagung*, in the *Theol. Stud. u. Krit.* 1865, pp. 3-71, 425-489, and 1869, pp. 209-284.

On the general subject of the Jewish opinions concerning the Messiah the following works may be referred to: Buxtorf, *Lex. Chald. Talm. et Rabbinicum*, Basil. 1640, fol., espec. coll. 1267 ff. and 221 ff.; also his *Synagoga Judaica*, c. 50, "De venturo Jud. Messia." Ant. Hulsius, *Theol. Judaica*, Bred., 1653, 4to. Ed. Pocock, *Porta Mosis*, etc. (of Maimonides), Oxon. 1654, see cap. vi. of the *Notæ Miscellaneæ*, "In quo variæ Judæorum de Resur. Mort. Sententiæ expenduntur;" also in his *Theol. Works*, i. 159-213. W. Schickard, *Jus Regium Hebr. cum Not's Carpzovii* (1674),

theor. xx. *ad fin.*, reprinted in Ugolini's *Thes.* xxiv. 792-824. Joh. a Lent, *Schediasma hist.-phil. de Judæorum Pseudo-Messiis*, in Ugolini's *Thes.* xxiii. 1019-90. Lightfoot's Works, particularly his *Horæ Hebraicæ*. The Dissertations of Witsius, Rhenferd, Dav'd Mill, and Schöttgen *De Seculo futuro*, partly reprinted in Meuschen (see below); comp. Koppe's Excursus I. to his notes on the Ep. to the Ephesians (*N. T. ed. Koppian.* vol. vi.). Eisenmenger, *Entdecktes Judenthum*. 2 Theile, Königsb. 1711, 4to, espec. ii. 647-889 (aims to collect everything that can bring discredit on the Jews, but gives the original of all the Rabbinical passages translated). Schöttgen, *Horæ Hebr. et Talmudicæ*, 2 vols. Dresd. 1733-42, 4to. His *Jesus der wahre Messias*, Leipz. 1748, is substantially a German translation of the treatise "De Messia," which occupies a large part of vol. ii. of the *Horæ*. ("Has accumulated a most valuable collection of Jewish traditions, but . . . exhibits no critical perception whatever of the relative value of the authorities which he quotes, and often seems to me to misinterpret the real tenor of their testimony." — Westcott.) Stehelin, *The Traditions of the Jews*, 2 vols. Lond. 1732-34; also 1748 with the title *Rabbinical Literature*. (A rare book; in the Astor Library.) Meuschen, *Nov. Test. ex Talmude illustratum*, Lips. 1736, 4to. Wetstein, *Nov. Test. Græcum*, 2 vols. Amst. 1751-52, fol. Imm. Schwarz, *Jesus Targumicus, Comm.* I., II. Torgav. 1758-59, 4to. G. B. De-Rossi, *Della vana aspettazione degli Ebrei del loro Re Messia*, Parma, 1773, 4to. Keil, *Hist. Dogmatis de Regno Messiæ Christi et Apost. Ætate*, Lips. 1781, enlarged in his *Opusc.* i. 22-83, i.-xxxi. Corrodi, *Krit. Gesch. des Chiliasmus*, Theil i., Zürich, 1781. Bertholdt, *Christologia Judæorum Jesu Apostolorumque Ætate*, Erlang. 1811, a convenient manual, but superficial and uncritical. F. F. Fleck, *De Regno Christi*, Lips. 1826, pp. 22-64; comp. his larger work, *De Regno Divino*, Lips. 1829. John Allen, *Modern Judaism*, 2d ed. Lond. 1830, pp. 253-289. D. G. C. von Coelln, *Bibl. Theol.* (Leipz. 1836), i. 487-511. Gfrörer, *Das Jahrhundert des Heils*, 2 Abth. Stuttg. 1838, espec. ii. 219-444 ("has given the best general view of the subject" — Westcott; but is too undiscriminating in the use of his authorities). F. Nork, *Rabbinische Quellen u. Parallelen zu neutest. Schriftstellen*, Leipz. 1839 ("has collected with fair accuracy the sum of Jewish tradition" — Westcott). Bruno Bauer, *Krit. d. ev. Gesch. d. Synoptiker* (1841), pp. 391-416, maintains that before the time of Christ there was no definite expectation among the Jews respecting the Messiah; see in opposition the remarks of Zeller, in his *Theol. Jahrb.* 1842, ii. 35-52, and Ebrard, *Wiss. Krit. d. ev. Geschichte*, 2ª Aufl. 1850, pp. 651-669. F. Böttcher, *De Inferis*, etc. Dresd. 1846, §§ 540-557, and elsewhere. Lücke, *Einl. in d. Offenb. d. Johannes*, 2ª Aufl. (1852), i. 7-342, valuable dissertations on the Apocalyptic literature, Jewish and Christian. Schumann, *Christus*, Hamb. 1852, i. 1-272. Robt. Young, *Christology of the Targums*, Edin. 1853. Hilgenfeld, *Die jüdische Apokalyptik in ihre geschichtl. Entwickelung*, Jena, 1857. Jost, *Gesch. d. Judenthums* (1857-59), i. 394-402, ii. 172-177, 283 f., 337 (Karaites). Michel Nicolas, *Des doctrines rel. des Juifs pendant les deux siècles antérieurs à l'ère chrétienne*, Paris, 1860, pp. 266-310. [James Martineau], *Early History of Messianic Ideas*, in the *National Rev.* Apr. 1863, xvi. 466-483 (Book of Daniel and

Sibylline Oracles), and Apr. 1864, xviii. 554–579 (Book of Enoch). Colani, *Jésus-Christ et les croyances messianiques de son temps*, 2e éd. Strasb. 1864. Langen (Cath.) *Das Judenthum in Palästina zur Zeit Christi*, Freib. im Br. 1866, pp. 391–461. Ewald, *Gesch. Christus' u. seiner Zeit*, 3e Ausg. Gött. 1867, pp. 135–170. Holtzmann, *Die Messiasidee zur Zeit Jesu*, in the *Jahrb. f. deutsche Theol.* 1867, xii. 389–411. Keim, *Gesch. Jesu von Nazara*, Zürich, 1867, i. 239–250. Hausrath, *Neutest. Zeitgeschichte*, Heidelb. 1868, i. 179–184, 420–432. C. A. Row, *The Jesus of the Evangelists*, Lond. 1868, pp. 145–198. Hamburger's *Real-Encycl. f. Bibel u. Talmud*, art. *Messias* (Heft iii. 1869; Abth. II., giving the Talmudic doctrine, is not yet published).

For a comprehensive view of the whole subject, see Oehler's art. *Messias* in Herzog's *Real-Encykl.* (1858) ix. 408–441, and B. F. Westcott's *Introd. to the Study of the Gospels*, pp. 110–173, Amer. ed. (1862). [ANTICHRIST.]   A.

MESSI'AS (Μεσσίας: *Messias*), the Greek form of MESSIAH (John i. 41; iv. 25).

METALS. The Hebrews, in common with other ancient nations, were acquainted with nearly all the metals known to modern metallurgy, whether as the products of their own soil or the results of intercourse with foreigners. One of the earliest geographical definitions is that which describes the country of Havilah as the land which abounded in gold, and the gold of which was good (Gen. ii. 11, 12). The first artist in metals was a Cainite, Tubal Cain, the son of Lamech, the forger or sharpener of every instrument of copper (A. V. "brass") and iron (Gen. iv. 22). "Abram was very rich in cattle, in silver, and in gold" (Gen. xiii. 2); silver, as will be shown hereafter, being the medium of commerce, while gold existed in the shape of ornaments, during the patriarchal ages. Tin is first mentioned among the spoils of the Midianites which were taken when Balaam was slain (Num. xxxi. 22), and lead is used to heighten the imagery of Moses' triumphal song (Ex. xv. 10). Whether the ancient Hebrews were acquainted with steel, properly so called, is uncertain; the words so rendered in the A. V. (2 Sam. xxii. 35; Job xx. 24; Ps. xviii. 34; Jer. xv. 12) are in all other passages translated brass, and would be more correctly copper. The "northern iron" of Jer. xv. 12 is believed by commentators to be iron hardened and tempered by some peculiar process, so as more nearly to correspond to what we call steel [STEEL]; and the "flaming torches" of Nah. ii. 3 are probably the flashing steel scythes of the war-chariots which should come against Nineveh. Besides the simple metals, it is supposed that the Hebrews used the mixture of copper and tin known as bronze, and probably in all cases in which copper is mentioned as in any way manufactured, bronze is to be understood as the metal indicated. But with regard to the chashmal (A. V. "amber") of Ez. i. 4, 27, viii. 2, rendered by the LXX. ἤλεκτρον, and the Vulg. *electrum*, by which our translators were misled, there is considerable difficulty. Whatever be the meaning of chashmal, for which no satisfactory etymology has been proposed, there can be but little doubt that by ἤλεκτρον the LXX. translators intended, not the fossil resin known by that name to the Greeks and to us as "amber," but the metal so called, which consisted of a mixture of four parts of gold with one of silver, described by

Pliny (xxxiii. 23) as more brilliant than silver by lamp-light. There is the same difficulty attending the χαλκολίβανον (Rev. i. 15, ii. 18, A. V. "fine brass"), which has hitherto been successfully resisted all the efforts of commentators, but which is explained by Suidas as a kind of *electron*, more precious than gold. That it was a mixed metal of great brilliancy is extremely probable, but it has hitherto been impossible to identify it. In addition to the metals actually mentioned in the Bible, it has been supposed that mercury is alluded to in Num. xxxi. 23, as "the water of separation," being "looked upon as the mother by which all the metals were fructified, purified, and brought forth," and on this account kept secret, and only mysteriously hinted at (Napier, *Metal. of the Bible*, Intr. p. 6). Mr. Napier adds, "there is not the slightest foundation for this supposition."

With the exception of iron, gold is the most widely diffused of all metals. Almost every country in the world has in its turn yielded a certain supply, and as it is found most frequently in alluvial soil among the débris of rocks washed down by the torrents, it was known at a very early period, and was procured with little difficulty. The existence of gold and the prevalence of gold ornaments in early times are no proof of a high state of civilization, but rather the reverse. Gold was undoubtedly used before the art of working copper or iron was discovered. We have no indications of gold streams or mines in Palestine. The Hebrews obtained their principal supply from the south of Arabia, and the commerce of the Persian Gulf. The ships of Hiram king of Tyre brought it for Solomon (1 K. ix. 11, x. 11), and at a later period, when the Hebrew monarch had equipped a fleet and manned it with Tyrian sailors, the chief of their freight was the gold of Ophir (1 K. ix. 27, 28). It was brought thence in the ships of Tarshish (1 K. xxii. 48), the Indiamen of the ancient world; and Parvaim (2 Chr. iii. 6), Raamah (Ez. xxvii. 22), Sheba (1 K. x. 2, 10; Ps. lxxii. 15; Is. lx. 6; Ez. xxvii. 22), and Uphaz (Jer. x. 9), were other sources of gold for the markets of Palestine and Tyre. It was probably brought in the form of ingots (Josh. vii. 21; A. V. "wedge," lit. "tongue"), and was rapidly converted into articles of ornament and use. Earrings, or rather nose-rings, were made of it, those given to Rebecca were half a shekel (½ oz.) in weight (Gen. xxiv. 22), bracelets (Gen. xxiv. 22), chains (Gen. xli. 42), signets (Ex. xxxv. 22), bullæ or spherical ornaments suspended from the neck (Ex. xxxv. 22), and chains for the legs (Num. xxxi. 50; comp. Is. iii. 18; Plin. xxxiii. 12). It was used in embroidery (Ex. xxxix. 3; 2 Sam. i. 24; Plin. viii. 74); the decorations and furniture of the tabernacle were enriched with the gold of the ornaments which the Hebrews willingly offered (Ex. xxxv.–xl.); the same precious metal was lavished upon the Temple (1 K. vi., vii.); Solomon's throne was overlaid with gold (1 K. x. 18), his drinking-cups and the vessels of the house of the forest of Lebanon were of pure gold (1 K. x. 21), and the neighboring princes brought him as presents vessels of gold and of silver (1 K. x. 25). So plentiful indeed was the supply of the precious metals during his reign that silver was esteemed of little worth (1 K. x. 21, 27). Gold and silver were devoted to the fashioning of idolatrous images (Ex. xx. 23, xxxii. 4; Deut. xxix. 17; 1 K. xii. 28). The crown on the head of Malcham (A. V. "their king"), the idol of the Ammonites at Rabbah, weighed a talent of gold, that is 125 lbs. troy, a weight so great that it could not have been worn by David among the ordinary insignia of royalty (2 Sam. xii. 30). The great abundance of gold in early times is indicated by its entering into the composition of every article of ornament and almost all of domestic use. Among the spoils of the Midianites taken by the Israelites, in their bloodless victory when Balaam was slain, were ear-rings and jewels to the amount of 16,750 shekels of gold (Num. xxxi. 48–54), equal in value to more than 30,000l. of our present money. 1700 shekels of gold (worth more than 3000l.) in nose jewels (A. V. "ear-rings") alone were taken by Gideon's army from the slaughtered Midianites (Judg. viii. 26). These numbers, though large, are not incredibly great, when we consider that the country of the Midianites was at that time rich in gold streams which have been since exhausted, and that like the Malays of the present day, and the Peruvians of the time of Pizarro, they carried most of their wealth about them. But the amount of treasure accumulated by David from spoils taken in war, is so enormous, that we are tempted to conclude the numbers exaggerated. From the gold shields of Hadadezer's army of Syrians and other sources he had collected, according to the chronicler (1 Chr. xxii. 14), 100,000 talents of gold, and 1,000,000 talents of silver; to these must be added his own contribution of 3,000 talents of gold and 7,000 of silver (1 Chr. xxix. 2–4), and the additional offerings of the people, the total value of which, estimating the weight of a talent to be 125 lbs. Troy, gold at 73s. per oz., and silver at 4s. 4½d. per oz., is reckoned by Mr. Napier to be 939,929,687l. Some idea of the largeness of this sum may be formed by considering that in 1855 the total amount of gold in use in the world was calculated to be about 820,000,000l. Undoubtedly the quantity of the precious metals possessed by the Israelites might be greater in consequence of their commercial intercourse with the Phœnicians, who were masters of the sea; but in the time of David they were a nation struggling for political existence, surrounded by powerful enemies, and without the leisure necessary for developing their commercial capabilities. The numbers given by Josephus (Ant. vii. 14, § 2) are only one tenth of those in the text, but the sum, even when thus reduced, is still enormous.[a] But though gold was thus common, silver appears to have been the ordinary medium of commerce. The first commercial transaction of which we possess the details was the purchase of Ephron's field by Abraham for 400 shekels of silver (Gen. xxiii. 16); slaves were bought with silver (Gen. xvii. 12); silver was the money paid by Abimelech as a compensation to Abraham (Gen. xx. 16); Joseph was sold to the Ishmaelite merchants for twenty pieces of silver (Gen. xxxvii. 28); and generally in the Old Testament, "money" in the A. V. is literally silver. The first payment in gold is mentioned in 1 Chr. xxi. 25, where David buys the threshing-floor of Ornan, or Araunah, the Jebusite, for six hundred shekels of gold by weight."[b] But in the parallel narrative of the transaction in 2 Sam. xxiv. 24, the price paid for the threshing-floor and the oxen is fifty shekels of silver. An attempt has been made

by Keil to reconcile these two passages by supposing that in the former the purchase referred to was that of the entire hill on which the threshing-floor stood, and in the latter that of the threshing-floor itself. But the close resemblance between the two narratives renders it difficult to accept this explanation, and to imagine that two different circumstances are described. That there is a discrepancy between the numbers in 2 Sam. xxiv. 9 and 1 Chr. xxi. 5 is admitted, and it seems impossible to avoid the conclusion that the present case is but another instance of the same kind. With this one exception there is no case in the O. T. in which gold is alluded to as a medium of commerce; the Hebrew coinage may have been partly gold, but we have no proof of it.

Silver was brought into Palestine in the form of plates from Tarshish, with gold and ivory (1 K. x. 22; 2 Chr. ix. 21; Jer. x. 9). The accumulation of wealth in the reign of Solomon was so great that silver was but little esteemed; "the king made silver to be in Jerusalem as stones" (1 K. x. 21, 27). With the treasures which were brought out of Egypt, not only the ornaments but the ordinary metal-work of the tabernacle were made. Silver was employed for the sockets of the boards (Ex. xxvi. 19, xxxvi. 24), and for the hooks of the pillars and their fillets (Ex. xxxviii. 10). The capitals of the pillars were overlaid with it (Ex. xxxviii. 17), the chargers and bowls offered by the princes at the dedication of the tabernacle (Num. vii. 13, &c.), the trumpets for marshalling the host (Num. x. 2), and some of the candlesticks and tables for the Temple were of silver (1 Chr. xxviii. 15, 16). It was used for the setting of gold ornaments (Prov. xxv. 11) and other decorations (Cant. i. 11), and for the pillars of Solomon's gorgeous chariot or palanquin (Cant. iii. 10).

From a comparison of the different amounts of gold and silver collected by David, it appears that the proportion of the former to the latter was 1 to 9 nearly. Three hundred talents of silver and thirty talents of gold were demanded of Hezekiah by Sennacherib (2 K. xviii. 14); but later, when Pharaohnechoh took Jehoahaz prisoner, he imposed upon the land a tribute of 100 talents of silver, and only one talent of gold (2 K. xxiii. 33). The difference in the proportion of gold to silver in these two cases is very remarkable, and does not appear to have been explained.

Brass, or more properly copper, was a native product of Palestine, "a land whose stones are iron, and out of whose hills thou mayest dig copper" (Deut. viii. 9; Job xxviii. 2). It was so plentiful in the days of Solomon that the quantity employed in the Temple could not be estimated, it was so great (1 K. vii. 47). Much of the copper which David had prepared for this work was taken from the Syrians after the defeat of Hadadezer (2 Sam. viii. 8), and more was presented by Toi, king of Hamath. The market of Tyre was supplied with vessels of the same metal by the merchants of Javan, Tubal, and Meshech (Ez. xxvii. 13). There is strong reason to believe that brass, a mixture of copper and zinc, was unknown to the ancients. To the latter metal no allusion is found. But tin was well known, and from the difficulty which attends

---

[a] As an illustration of the enormous wealth which it was possible for one man to collect, we may quote from Herodotus (vii. 28) the instance of Pythius the Lydian, who placed at the disposal of Xerxes, on his way to Greece, 2,000 talents of silver, and 3,993,000 gold darics; a sum which in these days would amount to about 5½ millions of pounds sterling.

[b] Literally, "shekels of gold, a weight of 600."

the toughening pure copper so as to render it fit for hammering, it is probable that the mode of deoxidizing copper by the admixture of small quantities of tin had been early discovered. "We are inclined to think," says Mr. Napier, "that Moses used no copper vessels for domestic purposes, but bronze, the use of which is less objectionable. Bronze, not being so subject to tarnish, takes on a finer polish, and, besides, [its] being much more easily melted and cast would make it to be more extensively used than copper alone. These practical considerations, and the fact of almost all the antique castings and other articles in metal that are preserved from these ancient times being composed of bronze, prove in our opinion that where the word 'brass' occurs in Scripture, except where it refers to an ore, such as Job xxviii. 2 and Deut. viii. 9, it should be translated bronze" (Metal. of the Bible, p. 66). Arms (2 Sam. xxi. 16; Job xx. 24; Ps. xviii. 34) and armor (1 Sam. xvii. 5, 6, 38) were made of this metal, which was capable of being so wrought as to admit of a keen and hard edge. The Egyptians employed it in cutting the hardest granite. The Mexicans, before the discovery of iron, "found a substitute in an alloy of tin and copper; and with tools made of this bronze could cut not only metals, but, with the aid of a siliceous dust, the hardest substances, as basalt, porphyry, amethysts, and emeralds" (Prescott, Conq. of Mexico, ch. 5). The great skill attained by the Egyptians in working metals at a very early period throws light upon the remarkable facility with which the Israelites, during their wanderings in the desert, elaborated the works of art connected with the structure of the Tabernacle, for which great acquaintance with metals was requisite. In the troublous times which followed their entrance into Palestine this knowledge seems to have been lost, for when the Temple was built the metal-workers employed were Phœnicians.

Iron, like copper, was found in the hills of Palestine. The "iron mountain" in the trans-Jordanic region is described by Josephus (B. J. iv. 8, § 2), and was remarkable for producing a particular kind of palm (Mishna, Succa, ed. Dachs, p. 182). Iron mines are still worked by the inhabitants of Kefr Hûneh in the S. of the valley Zaharâni; smelting works are found at Shemuster, 3 hours W. of Baalbek, and others in the oak-woods at Masbek (Ritter, Erdkunde, xvii. 73, 201); but the method employed is the simplest possible, like that of the old Samothracians, and the iron so obtained is chiefly used for horse-shoes.

Tin and lead were both known at a very early period, though there is no distinct trace of them in Palestine. The former was among the spoils of the Midianites (Num. xxxi. 22), who might have obtained it in their intercourse with the Phœnician merchants (comp. Gen. xxxvii. 25, 36), who themselves procured it from Tarshish (Ez. xxvii. 12) and the tin countries of the west. The allusions to it in the Old Testament principally point to its admixture with the ores of the precious metals (Is. i. 25; Ez. xxii. 18, 20). It must have occurred in the composition of bronze: the Assyrian bowls and dishes in the British Museum are found to contain one part of tin to ten of copper. "The tin was probably obtained from Phœnicia, and consequently that used in the bronzes in the British Museum may actually have been exported, nearly three thousand years ago, from the British Isles" (Layard, Nin. and Bab. p. 191).

Antimony (2 K. ix. 30; Jer. iv. 30, A. V. "painting"), in the form of powder, was used by the Hebrew women, like the kohl of the Arabs, for coloring their eyelids and eyebrows. [PAINT.]

Further information will be found in the articles upon the several metals, and whatever is known of the metallurgy of the Hebrews will be discussed under MINING.   W. A. W.

* **METAPHORS OF PAUL.** [GAMES; JAMES, EPISTLE OF.]

METE'RUS (Βαιτηρούς: [Ald. Μεττηρούς]). According to the list in 1 Esdr. v. 17, "the sons of Meterus" returned with Zorobabel. There is no corresponding name in the lists of Ezr. ii. and Neh. vii., nor is it traceable in the Vulgate.

ME'THEG-AM'MAH (מֶתֶג הָאַמָּה [see below]: τὴν ἀφωρισμένην: Frænum tributi), a place which David took from the Philistines, apparently in his last war with them (2 Sam. viii. 1). In the parallel passage of the Chronicles (1 Chr. xviii. 1), "Gath and her daughter-towns" is substituted for Metheg ha-Ammah.

The renderings are legion, almost each translator having his own;[a] but the interpretations may be reduced to two: 1. That adopted by Gesenius (Thesaur. 113) and Fürst (Handwb. 102 b), in which Ammah is taken as meaning "mother-city" or "metropolis" (comp. 2 Sam. xx. 19), and Metheg-ha-Ammah "the bridle of the mother-city" — namely of Gath, the chief town of the Philistines. If this is correct, the expression "daughter-towns" in the corresponding passage of Chronicles is a closer parallel, and more characteristic, than it appears at first sight to be.   2. That of Ewald (Gesch. iii. 190), who, taking Ammah as meaning the "forearm," treats the words as a metaphor to express the perfect manner in which David had smitten and humbled his foes, had torn the bridle from their arm, and thus broken forever the dominion with which they curbed Israel, as a rider manages his horse by the rein held fast on his arm.

The former of these two has the support of the parallel passage in Chronicles; and it is no valid objection to it to say, as Ewald in his note to the above passage does, that Gath cannot be referred to, because it had its own king still in the days of Solomon, for the king in Solomon's time may have been, and probably was, tributary to Israel, as the kings "on this side the Euphrates" (1 K. iv. 24) were.   On the other hand, it is an obvious objection to Ewald's interpretation that to control his horse a rider must hold the bridle not on his arm but fast in his hand.   G.

METHU'SAEL (מְתוּשָׁאֵל, man of God: Μαθουσάλα: Mathusaël), the son of Mehujael,

---

[a] A large collection of these will be found in Glassii Philologia Sacra (lib. iv. tr. 3, obs. 17), together with a singular Jewish tradition bearing upon the point. The most singular rendering, perhaps, is that of Aquila, χαλινὸν τοῦ ὑδραγωγίου, "the bridle of the aqueduct," perhaps with some reference to the irrigation of the rich district in which Gath was situated. Aqueduct is derived from the Chaldee version, אַמָּה, which has that signification amongst others. Aquila adopts a similar rendering in the case of the hill AMMAH.

fourth in descent from Cain, and father of Lamech (Gen. iv. 18).   A. B.

METHU′SELAH (מְתוּשֶׁלַח, *man of off-spring*, or possibly *man of a dart*:[a] Μαθουσάλα: *Mathusala*), the son of Enoch, sixth in descent from Seth, and father of Lamech. The resemblance of the name to the preceding, on which (with the coincidence of the name Lamech in the next generation in both lines) some theories have been formed, seems to be apparent rather than real. The life of Methuselah is fixed by Gen. v. 27 at 969 years, a period exceeding that of any other patriarch, and, according to the Hebrew chronology, bringing his death down to the very year of the Flood. The LXX. reckoning makes him die six years before it; and the Samaritan, although shortening his life to 720 years, gives the same result as the Hebrew. [CHRONOLOGY.] On the subject of Longevity, see PATRIARCHS.   A. B.

* **METE-YARD**, Lev. xix. 35. [MEASURE.]

MEU′NIM (מְעוּנִים [*habitation*]: [Rom. Μεἰνόν; Vat.] Μεσειναμ; [FA. Μεσσεἰναμ;] Alex. Μεεἰναμ: *Munim*), Neh. vii. 52. Elsewhere given in A. V. as MEHUNIM and MEHUNIMS.

MEZ′AHAB (מֵי זָהָב [see below]: Μαιζοόβ; Alex. Μεζοόβ in Gen., but omits in 1 Chr.; [in Chr., Comp. Μεζαδβ:] *Mezaab*). The father of Matred and grandfather of Mehetabel, who was wife of Hadar or Hadad, the last named king of Edom (Gen. xxxvi. 39; 1 Chr. i. 50). His name, which, if it be Hebrew, signifies "waters of gold," has given rise to much speculation. Jarchi renders it, "what is gold?" and explains it, "he was a rich man, and gold was not valued in his eyes at all." Abarbanel says he was "rich and great, so that on this account he was called Mezahab, for the gold was in his house as water." "Haggaon" (writes Aben Ezra) "said he was a refiner of gold, but others said that it pointed to those who make gold from brass." The Jerusalem Targum of course could not resist the temptation of punning upon the name, and combined the explanations given by Jarchi and Haggaon. The latter part of Gen. xxxvi. 39 is thus rendered: "the name of his wife was Mehetabel, daughter of Matred, the daughter of a refiner of gold, who was wearied with labor (מָטְרֵדָא, *matredâ*) all the days of his life; after he had eaten and was filled, he turned and said, what is gold? and what is silver?" A somewhat similar paraphrase is given in the Targum of the Pseudo-Jonathan, except that it is there referred to Matred, and not to Mezahab. The Arabic Version translates the name "water of gold," which must have been from the Hebrew, while in the Targum of Onkelos it is rendered "a refiner of gold," as in the *Quæstiones Hebraicæ in Paralip.*,

attributed to Jerome, and the traditions given above; which seems to indicate that originally there was something in the Hebrew text, now wanting, which gave rise to this rendering, and of which the present reading, מֵי, *mê*, is an abbreviation.
W. A. W.

MI′AMIN (מִיָּמִן [*on the right hand*, or perh. *son of the right hand*]: Μεαμίν; [Vat. FA. Αμαμείν;] Alex. Μεαμιμ: *Miamin*). 1. A layman of Israel of the sons of Parosh, who had married a foreign wife and put her away at the bidding of Ezra (Ezr. x. 25). He is called MAELUS in 1 Esdr. ix. 26.

2. (Omitted in Vat. MS., [also in Rom. Alex. FA.[1]; FA.[3]] Μεἰμιν: *Miamin*.) A priest or family of priests who went up from Babylon with Zerubbabel (Neh. xii. 5); probably the same as MIJAMIN in Neh. x. 7. In Neh. xii. 17 the name appears in the form MINIAMIN.

MIB′HAR (מִבְחָר [*choice*, and hence *chosen*, *best*]: Μεβαδλ; Alex. Μαβαρ: *Mibahar*). "Mibhar the son of Haggeri" is the name of one of David's heroes in the list given in 1 Chr. xi. The verse (38) in which it occurs appears to be corrupt, for in the corresponding catalogue of 2 Sam. xxiii. 36 we find, instead of "Mibhar the son of Haggeri," "of Zobah, Bani the Gadite." It is easy to see, if the latter be the true reading, how בְּנֵי הַגָּדִי, *Bani Haggadi*, could be corrupted into בֶּן־הַגְרִי, *ben-haggeri*; and הַגְרִי is actually the reading of three of Kennicott's MSS. in 1 Chr., as well as of the Syriac and Arab. versions, and the Targum of R. Joseph. But that "Mibhar" is a corruption of מִצֹּבָה (or מִצֹּבָא, acc. to some MSS.\, *mitstsôbâh*, "of Zobah," as Kennicott (*Dissert.* p. 215) and Cappellus (*Crit. Sacr.* i. c. 5) conclude, is not so clear, though not absolutely impossible. It would seem from the LXX. of 2 Sam., where, instead of "Zobah" we find πολυδυνάμεως, that both readings originally co-existed, and were read by the LXX. מִבְחַר הַיָּבָא, *mibchar hatstsâbâ*, "choice of the host." If this were the case, the verse in 1 Chr. would stand thus: "Igal the brother of Nathan, flower of the host; Bani the Gadite."
W. A. W.

MIB′SAM (מִבְשָׂם, *sweet odor*, Ges.: Μασσάμ; [in 1 Chr., Vat. Μασσα, Alex. Μαβσαν, Ald. Μαβσάμ:] *Mabsam*). 1. A son of Ishmael (Gen. xxv. 13; 1 Chr. i. 29), not elsewhere mentioned. The signification of his name has led some to propose an identification of the tribe sprung from him with some one of the Abrahamic tribes settled in Arabia aromatifera, and a connection with the balsam of Arabia is suggested (Bunsen, *Bibel-*

---

[a] There is some difficulty about the derivation of this name. The latter portion of the root is certainly שֶׁלַח (from שָׁלַח, "to send"), used for a "missile" in 2 Chr. xxxii. 5, Joel ii. 8, and for a "branch" in Cant. iv. 13, Is. xvi. 8. The former portion is derived by many of the older Hebraists from מוּת, "to die," and various interpretations given accordingly. See in Leusden's *Onomasticon*, "mortem suam misit," "mortis suæ arma," etc. Others make it "he dies, and it [i. e. the Flood] is sent," supposing it either a

name given afterwards from the event, or one given in prophetic foresight by Enoch. The later Hebraists (see Ges. *Lex.*) derive it from מְתוּ, the constructive form of מַת, "man," the obsolete singular, of which the plural מְתִים is found. This gives one or other of the interpretations in the text. We can only decide between them (if at all) by internal probability, which seems to incline to the former.

erk; Kalisch, *Gen.* 483). The situation of Mekkeh is well adapted for his settlements, surrounded as it is by traces of other Ishmaelite tribes; nevertheless the identification seems fanciful and far-fetched.

2. [Μαβασάμ; Alex. Μαβασαν: *Mapsam.*] A son of Simeon (1 Chr. iv. 25), perhaps named after the Ishmaelite Mibsam, for one of his brothers was named MISHMA, as was one of those of the older Mibsam.   E. S. P.

MIB'ZAR (מִבְצָר) [*fortress*]: in Gen. Μαζάρ; in 1 Chr., Βαβσάρ; [Vat. Μαζαρ;] Alex. Μαβσαρ: *Mabsar*). One of the phylarchs or "dukes" of Edom (1 Chr. i. 53) or Esau (Gen. xxxvi. 42) after the death of Hadad or Hadar. They are said to be enumerated " according to their settlements in the land of their possession; " and Knobel (*Genesis*), understanding Mibzar (lit. "fortress") as the name of a place, has attempted to identify it with the rocky fastness of Petra, "the strong city " (עִיר מִבְצָר, *'ir mibtsar*, Ps. cviii. 10; comp. Ps. lx. 9), "the cliff," the chasms of which were the chief stronghold of the Edomites (Jer. xlix. 16; Obad. 3).   W. A. W.

MI'CAH (מִיכָה), but in vv. 1 and 4, מִיכָיְהוּ, *i. e.* Micâyehu [*who is like Jehovah*]: Μιχαίας, but [Vat.] once [or more, Mai] Μειχαιας; Alex. Μειχα, but once [twice] Μιχα: *Michas, Micha*), an Israelite whose familiar story is preserved in the xviith and xviiith chapters of Judges. That it is so preserved would seem to be owing to Micah's accidental connection with the colony of Danites who left the original seat of their tribe to conquer and found a new Dan at Laish — a most happy accident, for it has been the means of furnishing us with a picture of the "interior " of a private Israelite family of the rural districts, which in many respects stands quite alone in the sacred records, and has probably no parallel in any literature of equal age.[a]

But apart from this the narrative has several points of special interest to students of Biblical history in the information which it affords as to the condition of the nation, of the members of which Micah was probably an average specimen.

We see (1.) how completely some of the most solemn and characteristic enactments of the Law had become a dead letter. Micah was evidently a devout believer in Jehovah. While the Danites in their communications use the general term *Elohim*, "God" ("ask counsel of God," xviii. 5; "God hath given it into your hands," ver. 10), with

Micah and his household the case is quite different. His one anxiety is to enjoy the favor of Jehovah[b] (xvii. 13); the formula of blessing used by his mother and his priest invokes the same awful name (xvii. 2, xviii. 6); and yet so completely ignorant is he of the Law of Jehovah, that the mode which he adopts of honoring Him is to make a molten and a graven image, teraphim or images of domestic gods, and to set up an unauthorized priesthood, first in his own family (xvii. 5), and then in the person of a Levite not of the priestly line (ver. 12) — thus disobeying, in the most flagrant manner, the second of the Ten Commandments, and the provisions for the priesthood — both laws which lay in a peculiar manner at the root of the religious existence of the nation. Gideon (viii. 27) had established an ephod; but here was a whole chapel of idols, a "house of gods" (xvii. 5), and all dedicated to Jehovah.

(2.) The story also throws a light on the condition of the Levites. They were indeed "divided in Jacob and scattered in Israel " in a more literal sense than that prediction is usually taken to contain. Here we have a Levite belonging to Bethlehem-judah, a town not allotted to the Levites, and with which they had, as far as we know, no connection; next wandering forth, with the world before him, to take up his abode wherever he could find a residence; then undertaking, without hesitation, and for a mere pittance, the charge of Micah's idol-chapel; and lastly, carrying off the property of his master and benefactor, and becoming the first priest to another system of false worship, one too in which Jehovah had no part, and which ultimately bore an important share in the disruption of the two kingdoms.[c]

But the transaction becomes still more remarkable when we consider (3.) that this was no obscure or ordinary Levite. He belonged to the chief family in the tribe, nay, we may say to the chief family of the nation, for though not himself a priest, he was closely allied to the priestly house, and was the grandson of no less a person than the great Moses himself. For the "Manasseh " in xviii. 30 is nothing else than an alteration of " Moses." to shield that venerable name from the discredit which such a descendant would cast upon it. [MANASSEH, vol. ii. p. 1776 *a*.] In this fact we possibly have the explanation of the much-debated passage, xviii. 3: " they knew the voice[d] of the young man the Levite." The grandson of the Lawgiver was not unlikely to be personally known to the Danites; when they heard his voice (whether in casual speech or in loud devotion we

---

a [*] For one of Stanley's finest sketches (drawn out of the incidents relating to this Micah), see his *Jewish Church*, i. 327–332. The fragment is invaluable as an illustration of the social and religious condition of the Hebrews in that rude age. Nothing so primitive in Greek or Roman literature reveals to us " such details of the private life " of those nations. For some of the practical teachings of this singular episode for all times, see Bishop Hall's *Contemplations*, bk. x. 6. H.

b One of a thousand cases in which the point of the sentence is lost by the translation of " Jehovah " by " the LORD."

c It does not seem at all clear that the words ' molten image " and " graven image " accurately express the original words *Pesel* and *Massecah*. [IDOL, vol. ii. p. 1121.] As the Hebrew text now stands, the ' graven image " only was carried off to Laish, and the ' molten " one remained behind with Micah (xviii. 20,

3); comp. 18). True the LXX. add the molten image in ver. 20, but in ver. 30 they agree with the Hebrew text.

d קוֹל — voice. The explanation of J. D. Michaelis (*Bibel für Ungelehrten*) is that they remarked that he did not speak with the accent of the Ephraimites. But Gesenius rejects this notion as repugnant alike to " the expression and the connection," and adopts the explanation given above (*Gesch. der hebr. Sprache*, § 15, 2, p. 55).

[*] Professor Cassel (*Richter und Ruth*, p. 161) offers another explanation of this " voice." He understands that it was the sound of the bells attached to the Levite's sacerdotal vestments, which notified the hearers of his entering the sanctuary for worship. See Ex. xxviii. 35. H.

are not told) they recognized it, and their inquiries as to who brought him hither, what he did there, and what he had there, were in this case the eager questions of old acquaintances long separated.

(4.) The narrative gives us a most vivid idea of the terrible anarchy in which the country was placed, when " there was no king in Israel, and every man did what was right in his own eyes," and shows how urgently necessary a central authority had become. A body of six hundred men completely armed, besides the train of their families and cattle, traverses the length and breadth of the land, not on any mission for the ruler or the nation, as on later occasions (2 Sam. ii. 12, &c., xx. 7, 14), but simply for their private ends. Entirely disregarding the rights of private property, they burst in wherever they please along their route, and plundering the valuables and carrying off persons, reply to all remonstrances by taunts and threats. The Turkish rule, to which the same district has now the misfortune to be subjected, can hardly be worse.

At the same time it is startling to our Western minds — accustomed to associate the blessings of order with religion — to observe how religious were these lawless freebooters : " Do ye know that in these houses there is an ephod, and teraphim, and a graven image, and a molten image ? Now therefore consider what ye have to do " (xviii. 14), " Hold thy peace, and go with us, and be to us a father and a priest " (ib. 19).

As to the date of these interesting events, the narrative gives us no direct information beyond the fact that it was before the beginning of the monarchy; but we may at least infer that it was also before the time of Samson, because in this narrative (xviii. 12) we meet with the origin of the name of Mahaneh-dan, a place which already bore that name in Samson's childhood (xiii. 25, where it is translated in the A. V. " the camp of Dan "). That the Danites had opponents to their establishment in their proper territory before the Philistines enter the field is evident from Judg. i. 34. Josephus entirely omits the story of Micah, but he places the narrative of the Levite and his concubine, and the destruction of Gibeah (chaps. xix., xx., xxi.) — a document generally recognized as part of the same [a] with the story of Micah, and that document by a different hand to the previous portions of the book — at the very beginning of his account of the period of the Judges, before Deborah or even Ehud. (See *Ant.* v. 2, § 8-12.) The writer is not aware that this arrangement has been found in any MS. of the Hebrew or LXX. text of the book of Judges; but the fact of its existence in Josephus has a certain weight, especially considering the accuracy of that writer when his interests or prejudices are not concerned; and it is supported by the mention of Phinehas the grandson of Aaron in xx. 28. An argument against the date being before the time of Deborah is drawn by Bertheau (p. 197) from the fact that at that time the north of Palestine was in the possession of the Canaanites — " Jabin king of Canaan, who reigned in Hazor," in the immediate

neighborhood of Laish. The records of the southern Dan are too scanty to permit of our fixing the date from the statement that the Danites had not yet entered on their [b] allotment — that is to say, the allotment specified in Josh. xix. 40-48. But that statement strengthens the conclusion arrived at from other passages, that these lists in Joshua contain the towns *allotted*, but not therefore necessarily *possessed* by the various tribes. " Divide the land first, in confidence, and then possess it afterwards," seems to be the principle implied in such passages as Josh. xiii. 7 (comp. 1); xix. 49, 51 (LXX. " so they went to take possession of the land ").

The date of the record itself may perhaps be more nearly arrived at. That, on the one hand, it was after the beginning of the monarchy is evident from the references to the ante-monarchical times (xviii. 1, xix. 1, xxi. 25); and, on the other hand, we may perhaps infer from the name of Bethlehem being given as " Bethlehem-Judah," — that it was before the fame of David had conferred on it a notoriety which would render any such affix unnecessary. The reference to the establishment of the house of God in Shiloh (xviii. 31) seems also to point to the early part of Saul's reign, before the incursions of the Philistines had made it necessary to remove the Tabernacle and Ephod to Nob, in the vicinity of Gibeah, Saul's head-quarters. G.

MI'CAH (מִיכָה, מִיכָיְה,[c] Cethib, Jer. xxvi. 18 [*who as Jehovah*]: Μιχαίας; [FA. in Jer. Μιχέας; Vat. in Mic. Μειχαιας:] *Michæas*). The sixth in order of the minor prophets, according to the arrangement in our present canon; in the LXX. he is placed third, after Hosea and Amos. To distinguish him from Micaiah the son of Imlah, the contemporary of Elijah, he is called the MORASTHITE, that is, a native of Moresheth, or some place of similar name, which Jerome and Eusebius call Morasthi and identify with a small village near Eleutheropolis to the east, where formerly the prophet's tomb was shown, but which in the days of Jerome had been succeeded by a church (*Epit. Paulæ*, c. 6). As little is known of the circumstances of Micah's life as of many of the other prophets. Pseudo-Epiphanius (*Op.* ii. p. 245) makes him, contrary to all probability, of the tribe of Ephraim; and besides confounding him with Micaiah the son of Imlah, who lived more than a century before, he betrays additional ignorance in describing Ahab as king of Judah. For rebuking this monarch's son and successor Jehoram for his impieties, Micah, according to the same authority, was thrown from a precipice, and buried at Morathi in his own country, hard by the cemetery of Enakim ('Εναχείμ, a place which apparently exists only in the LXX. of Mic. i. 10), where his sepulchre was still to be seen. The Chronicon Paschale (p. 148 c) tells the same tale. Another ecclesiastical tradition relates that the remains of Habakkuk and Micah were revealed in a vision to Zebennus bishop of Eleutheropolis, in the reign of Theodosius the Great, near a place called Berath-

---

a The proofs of this are given by Bertheau in his Commentary on the Book in the *Kurzgef. exeg Handb.* (lii. § 2; p. 192).

b xviii. 1. It will be observed that the words " all their " are interpolated by our translators.

c The full form of the name is מִיכָיְה, Micâyâhû, who is like Jehovah," which is found in 2 Chr.

xiii. 2, xvii. 7. This is abbreviated to מִיכָיְדָ, Micâyâhû, in Judg. xvii. 1, 4; still further to מְכָיְדָ, Micâyêhû (Jer. xxxvi. 11), מִיכָיְה, Micâyâh (1 K. xxii. 18); and finally to מִיכָה, Micâh, or מִיכָא Micâ (2 Sam. ix. 12).

atia, which is apparently a corruption of Morasthi (Sozomen, *H. E.* vii. 29; Nicephorus, *H. E.* xii. 46). The prophet's tomb was called by the inhabitants *Nephsameemana*, which Sozomen renders ἀνῆμα πιστόν.

The period during which Micah exercised the prophetical office is stated, in the superscription to his prophecies, to have extended over the reigns of Jotham, Ahaz, and Hezekiah, kings of Judah, giving thus a maximum limit of 59 years (B. C. 756–697), from the accession of Jotham to the death of Hezekiah, and a minimum limit of 16 years (B. C. 742–726), from the death of Jotham to the accession of Hezekiah. In either case he would be contemporary with Hosea and Amos during part of their ministry in Israel, and with Isaiah in Judah. According to Rabbinical tradition he transmitted to the prophets Joel, Nahum, and Habakkuk, and to Seraiah the priest, the mysteries of the Kabbala, which he had received from Isaiah (R. David Ganz, *Tsemach David*), and by Syncellus (*Chronogr.* p. 199 c) he is enumerated in the reign of Jotham as contemporary with Hosea, Joel, Isaiah, and Oded. With respect to one of his prophecies (iii. 12) it is distinctly assigned to the reign of Hezekiah (Jer. xxvi. 18), and was probably delivered before the great passover which inaugurated the reformation in Judah. The date of the others must be determined, if at all, by internal evidence, and the periods to which they are assigned are therefore necessarily conjectural. Reasons will be given hereafter for considering that none are later than the sixth year of Hezekiah. Bertholdt, indeed, positively denies that any of the prophecies can be referred to the reign of Hezekiah, and assigns the two earlier of the four portions into which he divides the book to the time of Ahaz, and the two later to that of Manasseh (*Einleitung*, § 411), because the idolatry which prevailed in their reigns is therein denounced. But in the face of the superscription, the genuineness of which there is no reason to question, and of the allusion in Jer xxvi. 18, Bertholdt's conjecture cannot be allowed to have much weight. The time assigned to the prophecies by the only direct evidence which we possess, agrees so well with their contents that it may fairly be accepted as correct. Why any discrepancy should be perceived between the statement in Jeremiah, that "Micah the Morasthite prophesied in the days of Hezekiah king of Judah," and the title of his book which tells us that the word of the Lord came to him "in the days of Jotham, Ahaz, and Hezekiah," it is difficult to imagine. The former does not limit the period of Micah's prophecy, and at most applies only to the passage to which direct allusion is made. A confusion appears to have existed in the minds of those who see in the prophecy in its present form a connected whole, between the actual delivery of the several portions of it, and their collection and transcription into one book. In the case of Jeremiah we know that he dictated to Baruch the prophecies which he had delivered in the interval between the 13th year of Josiah and the 4th of Jehoiakim, and that, when thus committed to writing, they were read before the people in the fast day (Jer. xxxvi. 2, 4, 6). There is reason to believe that a similar process took place

with the prophecies of Amos. It is, therefore, conceivable, to say the least, that certain portions of Micah's prophecy may have been uttered in the reigns of Jotham and Ahaz, and for the probability of this there is strong internal evidence, while they were collected as a whole in the reign of Hezekiah and committed to writing. Caspari (*Micha*, p. 78) suggests that the book thus written may have been read in the presence of the king and the whole people, on some great fast or festival day, and that this circumstance may have been in the minds of the elders of the land in the time of Jehoiakim, when they appealed to the impunity which Micah enjoyed under Hezekiah.[a] It is evident from Mic. i. 6, that the section of the prophecy in which that verse occurs must have been delivered before the destruction of Samaria by Shalmaneser, which took place in the 6th year of Hezekiah (cir. B. C. 722), and, connecting the "high-places" mentioned in i. 5 with those which existed in Judah in the reigns of Ahaz (2 K. xvi. 4; 2 Chr. xxviii. 4, 25) and Jotham (2 K. xv. 35), we may be justified in assigning ch. i. to the time of one of these monarchs, probably the latter; although, if ch. ii. be considered as part of the section to which ch. i. belongs, the utter corruption and demoralization of the people there depicted agree better with what history tells us of the times of Ahaz. Caspari maintains that of the two parallel passages, Mic. iv. 1–5, Is. ii. 2–5, the former is the original and the latter belongs to the times of Uzziah and Jotham.[b] The denunciation of the horses and chariots of Judah (v. 10) is appropriate to the state of the country under Jotham, after the long and prosperous reign of Uzziah, by whom the military strength of the people had been greatly developed (2 Chr. xxvi. 11–15, xxvii. 4–6). Compare Is. ii. 7, which belongs to the same period. Again, the forms in which idolatry manifested itself in the reign of Ahaz correspond with those which are threatened with destruction in Mic. v. 12–14, and the allusions in vi. 16 to the "statutes of Omri," and the "works of the house of Ahab" seem directly pointed at the king, of whom it is expressly said that "he walked in the way of the kings of Israel" (2 K. xvi. 3). It is impossible in dealing with internal evidence to assert positively that the inferences deduced from it are correct; but in the present instance they at least establish a probability, that in placing the period of Micah's prophetical activity between the times of Jotham and Hezekiah the superscription is correct. In the first years of Hezekiah's reign the idolatry which prevailed in the time of Ahaz was not eradicated, and in assigning the date of Micah's prophecy to this period there is no anachronism in the allusions to idolatrous practices. Maurer contends that ch. i. was written not long before the taking of Samaria, but the 3d and following chapters he places in the interval between the destruction of Samaria and the time that Jerusalem was menaced by the army of Sennacherib in the 14th year of Hezekiah. But the passages which he quotes in support of his conclusion (iii. 12, iv. 9, &c., v. 5, &c., vi. 9, &c., vii. 4, 12, &c.) do not appear to be more suitable to that period than to the first years of Hezekiah, while the context in many cases requires a still

---

[a] Knobel (*Prophetismus*, ii. § 20) imagines that the prophecies which remain belong to the time of Hezekiah, and that those delivered under Jotham and Ahaz have perished.

[b] Mic. iv. 1–4 may possibly, as Ewald and others have suggested, be a portion of an older prophecy current at the time, which was adopted both by Micah and Isaiah (Is. ii. 2–4).

earlier date. In the arrangement adopted by Wells (pref. to Micah, § iv.–vi.) ch. i. was delivered in the contemporary reigns of Jotham king of Judah and of Pekah king of Israel; ii. 1 – iv. 8 in those of Ahaz, Pekah, and Hosea; iii. 12 being assigned to the last year of Ahaz, and the remainder of the book to the reign of Hezekiah.

But, at whatever time the several prophecies were first delivered, they appear in their present form as an organic whole, marked by a certain regularity of development. Three sections, omitting the superscription, are introduced by the same phrase, שִׁמְעוּ, "hear ye," and represent three natural divisions of the prophecy — i., ii., iii. – v., vi. – vii. — each commencing with rebukes and threatenings and closing with a promise. The first section opens with a magnificent description of the coming of Jehovah to judgment for the sins and idolatries of Israel and Judah (i. 2–4), and the sentence pronounced upon Samaria (5–9) by the Judge Himself. The prophet, whose sympathies are strong with Judah, and especially with the lowlands which gave him birth, sees the danger which threatens his country, and traces in imagination the devastating march of the Assyrian conquerors from Samaria onward to Jerusalem and the south (i. 9–16). The impending punishment suggests its cause, and the prophet denounces a woe upon the people generally for the corruption and violence which were rife among them, and upon the false prophets who led them astray by pandering to their appetites and luxury (ii. 1–11). The sentence of captivity is passed upon them (10) but is followed instantly by a promise of restoration and triumphant return (ii. 12, 13). The second section is addressed especially to the princes and heads of the people, their avarice and rapacity are rebuked in strong terms, and as they have been deaf to the cry of the suppliants for justice, they too "shall cry unto Jehovah, but He will not hear them" (iii. 1–4). The false prophets who had deceived others should themselves · be deceived : "the sun shall go down over the prophets, and the day shall be dark over them" (iii. 6). For this perversion of justice and right, and the covetousness of the heads of the people who judged for reward, of the priests who taught for hire, and of the prophets who divined for money, Zion should "be ploughed as a field," and the mountain of the Temple become like the uncultivated woodland heights (iii. 9–12). But the threatening is again succeeded by a promise of restoration, and in the glories of the Messianic kingdom the prophet loses sight of the desolation which should befall his country. Instead of the temple mountain covered with the wild growth of the forest, he sees the mountain of the house of Jehovah established on the top of the mountains, and nations flowing like rivers unto it. The reign of peace is inaugurated by the recall from Captivity, and Jehovah sits as king in Zion, having destroyed the nations who had rejoiced in her overthrow. The predictions in this section form the climax of the book, and Ewald arranges them in four strophes, consisting of from seven to eight verses each (iv. 1–8, iv. 9–v. 2, v. 3–9, v. 10–15), with the exception of the last, which is shorter, and in which the prophet reverts to the point whence he started: all objects

of politic and idolatrous confidence must be removed before the grand consummation. In the last section (vi., vii.) Jehovah, by a bold poetical figure, is represented as holding a controversy with his people, pleading with them in justification of his conduct towards them and the reasonableness of his requirements. The dialogue form in which chap. vi. is cast renders the picture very dramatic and striking. In vi. 3–5 Jehovah speaks; the inquiry of the people follows in ver. 6, indicating their entire ignorance of what was required of them; their inquiry is met by the almost impatient rejoinder, "Will Jehovah be pleased with thousands of rams, with myriads of torrents of oil?" The still greater sacrifice suggested by the people, "Shall I give my firstborn for my transgression?" calls forth the definition of their true duty, "to do justly, and to love mercy, and to walk humbly with their God." How far they had fallen short of this requirement is shown in what follows (9–12), and judgment is pronounced upon them (13–16). The prophet acknowledges and bewails the justice of the sentence (vii. 1–6), the people in repentance patiently look to God, confident that their prayer will be heard (7–10), and are reassured by the promise of deliverance announced, as following their punishment (11–13), by the prophet, who in his turn presents his petition to Jehovah for the restoration of his people (14, 15). The whole concludes with a triumphal song of joy at the great deliverance, like that from Egypt, which Jehovah will achieve, and a full acknowledgment of his mercy and faithfulness to his promises (16–20). The last verse is reproduced in the song of Zacharias (Luke i. 72, 73).[a]

The predictions uttered by Micah relate to the invasions of Shalmaneser (i. 6–8; 2 K. xvii. 4, 6) and Sennacherib (i. 9–16; 2 K. xviii. 13), the destruction of Jerusalem (iii. 12, vii. 13), the Captivity in Babylon (iv. 10), the return (iv. 1–8, vii. 11), the establishment of a theocratic kingdom in Jerusalem (iv. 8), and the Ruler who should spring from Bethlehem (v. 2). The destruction of Assyria and Babylon is supposed to be referred to in v. 5, 6, vii. 8, 10. It is remarkable that the prophecies commence with the last words recorded of the prophet's namesake, Micaiah the son of Imlah, "Hearken, O people, every one of you" (1 K. xxii. 28). From this, Bleek (Einleitung, p. 539) concludes that the author of the history, like the ecclesiastical historians, confounded Micah the Morasthite with Micaiah; while Hengstenberg (Christology, i. 409, Eng. tr.) infers that the coincidence was intentional on the part of the later prophet, and that "by this very circumstance he gives intimation of what may be expected from him, shows that his activity is to be considered as a continuation of that of his predecessor, who was so jealous for God, and that he had more in common with him than the mere name." Either conclusion rests on the extremely slight foundation of the occurrence of a formula which was at once the most simple and most natural commencement of a prophetic discourse.

The style of Micah has been compared with that of Hosea and Isaiah. The similarity of their subject may account for many resemblances in language with the latter prophet, which were almost unavoidable (comp. Mic. i. 2 with Is. i. 2; Mic. ii

---

[a] Ewald now maintains that Mic. vi., vii. is by another hand; probably written in the course of the 7th cent. B. C., and that v. 9–14 is the original conclusion of Micah's prophecy (Jahrb. xi. p. 29).

2 with Is. v. 8; Mic. ii. 6, 11 with Is. xxx. 10;
Mic. ii. 12 with Is. x. 20–22; Mic. vi. 6–8 with Is.
i. 11–17). The diction of Micah is vigorous and
forcible, sometimes obscure from the abruptness of
its transitions, but varied and rich in figures derived from the pastoral (i. 8, ii. 12, v. 4, 5, 7, 8,
vii. 14) and rural life of the lowland country (i. 6,
iii. 12, iv. 3, 12, 13, vi. 15), whose vines and olives
and fig-trees were celebrated (1 Chr. xxvii. 27, 28),
and supply the prophet with so many striking allusions (i. 6, iv. 3, 4, vi. 15, vii. 1, 4) as to suggest
that, like Amos, he may have been either a herdsman or a vine-dresser, who had heard the howling
of the jackals (i. 8, A. V. "dragons") as he
watched his flocks or his vines by night, and had
seen the lions slaughtering the sheep (v. 8). One
peculiarity which he has in common with Isaiah is
the frequent use of paronomasia; in i. 10–15 there
is a succession of instances of this figure in the
plays upon words suggested by the various places
enumerated (comp. also ii. 4) which it is impossible
to transfer to English, though Ewald has attempted
to render them into German (*Propheten des A. B.*
i. 329, 330). The poetic vigor of the opening scene
and of the dramatic dialogue sustained throughout
the last two chapters has already been noticed.

The language of Micah is quoted in Matt. ii. 5,
6, and his prophecies alluded to in Matt. x. 35, 36;
Mark xiii. 12; Luke xii. 53; John vii. 42.

* The more important older writers on Micah are Chytræus (1565), Calvin (1671), Pocock
(1677), Schnurrer (1783), Justi (1799), Hartmann
(1800). The later writers are Theiner, Hitzig,
Maurer, Umbreit, Ewald, Keil, Henderson, Pusey,
Noyes, Cowles. (For the titles of their works
see AMOS; JOEL; MALACHI.) Add to these
Caspari, *Ueber Micha den Morasthiten u. seine
Schrift* (1852), and the articles of Nägelsbach in
Herzog's *Real-Encyk.* ix. 517 ff., and of Wunderlich
in Zeller's *Bibl. Wörterb.* ii. 122. The best introduction to Micah in the English language is
that of Dr. Pusey, prefixed to his Commentary.
Part xiv. of Lange's *Bibelwerk des A. Test.*, by
Dr. Paul Kleinert (1868), comprises Obadiah,
Jonah, Micah, Nahum, and Habakkuk. It contains a well classified list of the principal commentators of all periods on all the minor prophets.
For the Messianic passages in Micah see the writers
on Christology (Hengstenberg, Hävernick, Tholuck, Stähelin, Hofmann, J. Pye Smith). [MALA-
CHI.] On the prophet's personal appearance, and
the general scope of his predictions, see especially
Stanley (*Lectures on the Jewish Church*, ii. 492–
494). Micah's "last words are those which, centuries afterwards, were caught up by the aged
priest, whose song unites the Old and New Testaments together. 'Thou wilt perform the truth to
Jacob, and the mercy to Abraham, which thou
hast sworn;' to send forth a second David, the
mighty child, whose unknown mother is already
travailing for his birth (Mic. vii. 18–20; Luke i. 72,
73).''

A certain minuteness characterizes some of
Micah's predictions, not always found or to be
expected in the fulfillment of prophecy. It is he
who mentioned beforehand the name of the place
where the Messiah was to be born; and, accordingly, on Herod's proposing his question as to this
point to the Jewish scribes and priests, they were
ready at once with the answer that Micah had
declared that Bethlehem was to be made memorable by that event (Matt. ii. 3–6). He foretold

"that Zion should be ploughed as a field and
Jerusalem become heaps;" and the traveller at the
present day sees oxen ploughing and fields or grain
ripening on the slopes of the sacred mount. Of
the doom of Samaria he said in the glory and
pride of that city: "I will make Samaria as an heap
of the field, and as plantings of a vineyard: and
I will pour down the stones thereof into the valley, and I will discover the foundations thereof" (i
6). The site of Samaria has now been ploughed for
centuries. Its terraces are covered with grain and
fruit trees. The stones which belonged to the
town and walls have rolled down the sides of the
hill, or have been cast over the brow of it, and lie
scattered along the edge of the valley. Yet we
are not to insist on such circumstantiality (as in
the last two cases) as essential to the truth of
prophecy. It is a law of prophetic representation
that it often avails itself of specific traits and incidents as the drapery only of the general occurrence
or truth contemplated by the sacred writer. What
is peculiar in the above instances is that the form
and the reality of the predictions so strikingly
agree. Many of the popular treatises on prophecy
(that of Dr. Keith is not exempt from this fault)
carry this idea of a *literal* fulfillment too far.   H.

2. (Μιχά; [Vat. Ηχα:] *Micha.*) A descendant of Joel the Reubenite [JOEL, 5], and ancestor
of Beerah, who was prince of his tribe at the time
of the captivity of the northern kingdom (1 Chr.
v. 5).

3. [In 1 Chr. viii., Vat. Μιχια; ix., Vat. FA.
Μειχα.] The son of Merib-baal, or Mephibosheth,
the son of Jonathan (1 Chr. viii. 34, 35, ix. 40, 41).
In 2 Sam. ix. 12 he is called MICHA.

4. [Μιχα; Vat. Μειχας.] A Kohathite Levite,
eldest son of Uzziel the brother of Amram, and
therefore cousin to Moses and Aaron (1 Chr. xxiii.
20). In Ex. vi. 22 neither Micah nor his brother
Jesiah, or Isshiah, appears among the sons of Uzziel,
who are there said to be Mishael, Elzaphan, and
Zithri. In the A. V. of 1 Chr. xxiv. 24, 25, the
names of the two brothers are written MICHAH
and ISSHIAH, though the Hebrew forms are the
same as in the preceding chapter. This would
seem to indicate that cc. xxiii., xxiv., were translated by different hands.

5. (Μιχαίας; [Vat. Μειχαιας.]) The father
of Abdon, a man of high station in the reign of
Josiah. In 2 K. xxii. 12 he is called "MICHAIAH
the father of Achbor."   W. A. W.

MICA'IAH [3 syl.] (מִיכָיְהוּ [*who as Jehovah*]: Μιχαίας; [Vat. Μειχαιας:] *Michæas*).
There are seven persons of this name in the O. T.
besides Micah the Levite, to whom the name is
twice given in the Hebrew (Judg. xvii. 1, 4);
Micah and Micaiah meaning the same thing, "Who
like Jehovah?" In the A. V. however, with the
one exception following, the name is given as
MICHAIAH.

The son of Imlah, a prophet of Samaria, who,
in the last year of the reign of Ahab, king of
Israel, predicted his defeat and death, B. C. 897.
The circumstances were as follows: Three years
after the great battle with Benhadad, king of Syria,
in which the extraordinary number of 100,000
Syrian soldiers is said to have been slain without
reckoning the 27,000 who, it is asserted, were killed
by the falling of the wall at Aphek, Ahab proposed
to Jehoshaphat king of Judah that they should
jointly go up to battle against Ramoth Gilead;

which Benhadad was, apparently, bound by treaty to restore to Ahab. Jehoshaphat, whose son Jehoram had married Athaliah, Ahab's daughter, assented in cordial words to the proposal; but suggested that they should first "inquire at the word of Jehovah." Accordingly, Ahab assembled 400 prophets, while, in an open space at the gate of the city of Samaria, he and Jehoshaphat sat in royal robes to meet and consult them. The prophets unanimously gave a favorable response; and among them, Zedekiah, the son of Chenaanah, made horns of iron as a symbol, and announced, from Jehovah, that with those horns Ahab would push the Syrians till he consumed them. For some reason which is unexplained, and can now only be conjectured, Jehoshaphat was dissatisfied with the answer, and asked if there was no other prophet of Jehovah at Samaria. Ahab replied that there was yet one — Micaiah, the son of Imlah; but, in words which obviously call to mind a passage in the *Iliad* (i. 106), he added, "I hate him, for he does not prophecy good concerning me, but evil." Micaiah was, nevertheless, sent for; and after an attempt had in vain been made to tamper with him, he first expressed an ironical concurrence with the 400 prophets, and then openly foretold the defeat of Ahab's army and the death of Ahab himself. And in opposition to the other prophets, he said, that he had seen Jehovah sitting on his throne, and all the host of Heaven standing by Him, on his right hand and on his left: that Jehovah said, Who shall persuade Ahab to go up and fall at Ramoth Gilead? that a Spirit*c* came forth and said that he would do so; and on being asked, Wherewith? he answered, that he would go forth and be a lying spirit in the mouth of all the prophets. Irritated by the account of this vision, Zedekiah struck Micaiah on the cheek, and Ahab ordered Micaiah to be taken to prison, and fed on bread and water, till his return to Samaria. Ahab then went up with his army to Ramoth Gilead; and in the battle which ensued, Benhadad, who could not have failed to become acquainted with Micaiah's prophecy, uttered so publicly, which had even led to an act of public, personal violence on the part of Zedekiah, gave special orders to direct the attack against Ahab, individually. Ahab, on the other hand, requested Jehoshaphat to wear his royal robes, which we know that the king of Judah had brought with him to Samaria (1 K. xxii. 10); and then he put himself into disguise for the battle; hoping thus, probably, to baffle the designs of Benhadad, and the prediction of Micaiah — but he was, nevertheless, struck and mortally wounded in the combat by a random arrow. See 1 K. xxii. 1–35; and 2 Chr. xviii. — the two accounts in which are nearly word for word the same.

Josephus dwells emphatically on the death of Ahab, as showing the utility of prophecy, and the impossibility of escaping destiny, even when it is revealed beforehand (*Ant.* viii. 15, § 6). He says that it steals on human souls, flattering them with cheerful hopes, till it leads them round to the point whence it will gain the mastery over them. This was a theme familiar to the Greeks in many

tragic tales, and Josephus uses words in unison with their ideas. (See Euripides, *Hippolyt.* 1256, and compare Herodot. vii. 17, viii. 77, i. 91.) From his interest in the story, Josephus relates several details not contained in the Bible, some of which are probable, while others are very unlikely; but for none of which does he give any authority. Thus, he says, Micaiah was already in prison, when sent for to prophesy before Ahab and Jehoshaphat, and that it was Micaiah who had predicted death by a lion to the son of a prophet, under the circumstances mentioned in 1 K. xx. 35, 36; and had rebuked Ahab after his brilliant victory over the Syrians for not putting Benhadad to death. And there is no doubt that these facts would be not only consistent with the narrative in the Bible, but would throw additional light upon it; for the rebuke of Ahab in his hour of triumph, on account of his forbearance, was calculated to excite in him the intensest feelings of displeasure and mortification; and it would at once explain Ahab's hatred of Micaiah, if Micaiah was the prophet by whom the rebuke was given. And it is not unlikely that Ahab in his resentment might have caused Micaiah to be thrown into prison, just as the prince of Judah, about 300 years later, maltreated Jeremiah in the same way (Jer. xxxvii. 15). But some other statements of Josephus cannot so readily be regarded as probable. Thus he relates that when Ahab disguised himself, he gave his own royal robes to be worn by Jehoshaphat, in the battle of Ramoth Gilead — an act, which would have been so unreasonable and cowardly in Ahab, and would have shown such singular complaisance in Jehoshaphat, that, although supported by the translation in the Septuagint, it cannot be received as true. The fact that some of the Syrian captains mistook Jehoshaphat for Ahab is fully explained by Jehoshaphat's being the only person, in the army of Israel, who wore royal robes. Again, Josephus informs us that Zedekiah alleged, as a reason for disregarding Micaiah's prediction, that it was directly at variance with the prophecy of Elijah, that dogs should lick the blood of Ahab, where dogs had licked the blood of Naboth, in the city of Samaria: inasmuch as Ramoth Gilead, where, according to Micaiah, Ahab was to meet his doom, was distant from Samaria a journey of three days. It is unlikely, however, that Zedekiah would have founded an argument on Elijah's insulting prophecy, even to the meekest of kings who might have been the subject of it; but that, in order to prove himself in the right as against Micaiah, he should have ventured on such an allusion to a person of Ahab's character, is absolutely incredible.

It only remains to add, that, besides what is dwelt on by Josephus, the history of Micaiah offers several points of interest, among which the two following may be specified: 1st. Micaiah's vision presents what may be regarded as transitional ideas of one origin of evil actions. In Exodus, Jehovah Himself is represented as directly hardening Pharaoh's heart (vii. 3, 13, xiv. 4, 17, x. 20, 27). In the Book of Job, the name of Satan is mentioned; but he is admitted without rebuke, among the sons of God, into the presence of Jehovah (Job

---

c As the definite article is prefixed in Hebrew, Thenius, Bertheau, and Bunsen translate *the* Spirit, and understand a personification of the Spirit of Prophecy. But the original words seem to be merely an extreme instance of the Hebrews conceiving as definite what

would be indefinite in English. (See Gesen. *Gram.* § 107, and 1 K. iii. 24.) The Spirit is conceived as definite from its corresponding to the requirements in the preceding question of Jehovah.

ι. 6-12). After the Captivity, the idea of Satan, as an independent principle of evil, in direct opposition to goodness, becomes fully established (1 Chr. xxi. 1; and compare Wisd. ii. 24). [SATAN.] Now the ideas presented in the vision of Micaiah are different from each of these three, and occupy a place of their own. They do not go so far as the Book of Job—much less so far as the ideas current after the Captivity; but they go farther than Exodus. See Ewald, *Poet. Bücher*, 3ter Theil, 65. 2dly. The history of Micaiah is an exemplification in practice, of contradictory predictions being made by different prophets. Other striking instances occur in the time of Jeremiah (xiv. 13, 14; xxviii. 15, 16; xxiii. 16, 25, 26). The only rule bearing on the judgment to be formed under such circumstances seems to have been a negative one, which would be mainly useful after the event. It is laid down in Deut. xviii. 21, 22, where the question is asked, how the children of Israel *were to know* the word which Jehovah had not spoken. And the solution is, that "if *the thing follow not, nor come to pass, that* is the thing which Jehovah has not spoken." E. T.

MI'CHA (מִיכָא [*who is like God*, Fürst]; Μιχά: [Vat. Μειχα:] *Micha*). 1. The son of Mephibosheth (2 Sam. ix. 12); elsewhere (1 Chr. ix. 40) called MICAH.

2. [Vat. FA.¹ omits.] A Levite, or family of Levites, who signed the covenant with Nehemiah (Neh. x. 11).

3. ([Neh. xi. 17, Vat. FA. Μαχα; 22, Vat. FA.² Μειχα, FA.¹ Αμειχα.]) The father of Mattaniah, a Gershonite Levite and descendant of Asaph (Neh. xi. 17, 22). He is elsewhere called MICAH (1 Chr. ix. 15) and MICHAIAH (Neh. xii. 35).

4. [Μιχά; [Vat. Sin. Μειχα:] Alex. Χειμα: *Micha*.) A Simeonite, father of Ozias, one of the three governors of the city of Bethulia in the time of Judith (Jud. vi. 15). His name is remarkable as being connected with one of the few specific allusions to the ten tribes after the Captivity.

MI'CHAEL (מִיכָאֵל [as above]: [Vat. Μειχαηλ:] *Michaël*). 1. Μιχαήλ; an Asherite, father of Sethur, one of the twelve spies (Num. xiii. 13).

2. [Μιχαήλ.] The son of Abihail, one of the Gadites who settled in the land of Bashan (1 Chr. v. 13).

3. [Vat. Μειχαηλ.] Another Gadite, ancestor of Abihail (1 Chr. v. 14).

4. [Vat. Μειχαηλ.] A Gershonite Levite, ancestor of Asaph (1 Chr. vi. 40).

5. [Vat. Μειχαηλ.] One of the five sons of Izrahiah of the tribe of Issachar, "all of them chiefs," who with their "troops of the battle-host" mustered to the number of 36,000 in the days of David (1 Chr. vii. 3).

6. [Vat. Μειχαηλ.] A Benjamite of the sons of Beriah (1 Chr. viii. 16).

7. [Vat. Μειχαηλ.] One of the captains of the "thousands" of Manasseh who joined the fortunes of David at Ziklag (1 Chr. xii. 20).

8. [Vat. Μεισαηλ.] The father, or ancestor of Omri, chief of the tribe of Issachar in the reign of David (1 Chr. xxvii. 18); possibly the same as No. 5.

9. [Vat. Μεισαηλ, Alex. Μισαηλ.] One of the sons of Jehoshaphat who were murdered by their elder brother Jehoram (2 Chr. xxi. 2, 4).

10. [In Esr., Vat. Μειχαηλ, Alex. Μαχαηλ; in 1 Esdr., Μιχαήλος, Vat. Μειχαηλος: *Michaël, Michelus*.] The father or ancestor of Zebadiah of the sons of Shephatiah who returned with Ezra (Ezr. viii. 8; 1 Esdr. viii. 34). W. A. W.

11. "One," or "the first of the chief princes or archangels (Dan. x. 13; comp. ὁ ἀρχάγγελος in Jude 9), described in Dan. x. 21 as the "prince" of Israel, and in xii. 1 as "the great prince which standeth" in time of conflict "for the children of thy people." All these passages in the O. T. belong to that late period of its Revelation when, to the general declaration of the angelic office, was added the division of that office into parts, and the assignment of them to individual angels. [See ANGELS, vol. i. p. 97 α.] This assignment served, not only to give that vividness to man's faith in God's supernatural agents, which was so much needed at a time of captivity, during the abeyance of his local manifestations and regular agencies, but also to mark the finite and ministerial nature of the angels, lest they should be worshipped in themselves. Accordingly, as Gabriel represents the ministration of the angels towards man, so Michael is the type and leader of their strife, in God's name and his strength, against the power of Satan. In the O. T. therefore he is the guardian of the Jewish people in their antagonism to godless power and heathenism. In the N. T. (see Rev. xii. 7) he fights in heaven against the dragon — "that old serpent called the Devil and Satan, which deceiveth *the whole world*:" and so takes part in that struggle, which is the work of the Church on earth. The nature and method of his war against Satan are not explained, because the knowledge would be unnecessary and perhaps impossible to us: the fact itself is revealed rarely, and with that mysterious vagueness which hangs over all angelic ministration, but yet with plainness and certainty.

There remains still one passage (Jude 9; comp. 2 Pet ii. 11) in which we are told that "Michael the archangel, when, contending with the Devil, he disputed about the body of Moses, durst not bring against him a railing accusation, but said, The Lord rebuke thee." The allusion seems to be to a Jewish legend attached to Deut. xxxiv. 6. The Targum of Jonathan attributes the burial of Moses to the hands of the angels of God, and particularly of the archangel Michael, as the guardian of Israel. Later traditions (see Œcumen. *in Jud.* cap. i.) set forth how Satan disputed the burial, claiming for himself the dead body because of the blood of the Egyptian (Ex. ii. 12) which was on Moses' hands. The reply of Michael is evidently taken from Zech. iii. 1, where, on Satan's "resisting" Joshua the high-priest, because of the filthy garments of his iniquity, Jehovah, or "the angel of Jehovah" (see vol. i. p. 95 *b*), said unto Satan, "Jehovah rebuke thee, O Satan! Is not this a brand plucked from the fire?" The spirit of the answer is the reference to God's mercy alone for our justification, and the leaving of all vengeance and rebuke to Him; and in this spirit it is quoted by the Apostle.ᵃ

ᵃ From unwillingness to acknowledge a reference to a mere Jewish tradition (in spite of vv. 14, 15), some have supposed St. Jude's reference to be to Zech. iii.

1, and explained the "body of Moses" to be the Jewish, as the "body of Christ" is the Christian, Church. The whole explanation is forced; but the

The Rabbinical traditions about Michael are very numerous. They oppose him constantly to Sammael, the accuser and enemy of Israel, as disputing for the *soul* of Moses; as bringing the ram the substitute for Isaac, which Sammael sought to keep back, etc., etc.: they give him the title of the "great high-priest in heaven," as well as that of the "great prince and conqueror;" and finally lay it down that "wherever Michael is said to have appeared, there the glory of the Shechinah is intended." It is clear that the sounder among them, in making such use of the name, intended to personify the Divine Power, and typify the Messiah (see Schoettgen, *Hor. Hebr.* i. 1079, 1119, ii. 8, 15, ed. Dresd. 1742). But these traditions, as usual, are erected on very slender Scriptural foundation.   A. B.

MI'CHAH (מִיכָה [as above]: Μιχά; [Vat. Μειχα:] *Micha*), eldest son of Uzziel, the son of Kohath (1 Chr. xxiv. 24, 25), elsewhere (1 Chr. xxiii. 20) called MICAH.

MICHA'IAH [3 syl.] (מִיכָיָה [*who as Jehovah*]: Μιχαίας: [Vat. Μειχαιας:] *Micha*). The name is identical with that elsewhere rendered Micaiah. 1. The father of Achbor, a man of high rank in the reign of Josiah (2 K. xxii. 12). He is the same as MICAH the father of Abdon (2 Chr. xxxiv. 20).

2. (Μιχαία; Alex. Μιχαια; [Vat. FA. Μειχαια:] *Michaia*.) The son of Zaccur, a descendant of Asaph (Neh. xii. 35). He is the same as MICAH the son of Zichri (1 Chr. ix. 15) and MICHA the son of Zabdi (Neh. xi. 17).

3. (Omitted in Vat. MS. [also Rom. Alex. FA.¹]; Alex. [rather, FA.⁸] Μιχαίας: *Michea*.) One of the priests who blew the trumpets at the dedication of the wall of Jerusalem by Nehemiah (Neh. xii. 41).

4. (מִיכָיְהוּ: Μααχά [*who like Jehovah*]: *Michaia*.) The daughter of Uriel of Gibeah, wife of Rehoboam, and mother of Abijah king of Judah (2 Chr. xiii. 2). She is elsewhere called " Maachah the daughter of Abishalom " (1 K. xv. 2), or " Absalom " (2 Chr. xi. 20), being, in all probability, his granddaughter, and daughter of Tamar according to Josephus. [MAACHAH, 3.] The reading " Maachah " is probably the true one, and is supported by the LXX. and Peshito-Syriac.

5. (Μιχαία; [Vat. Μειχαια:] *Michœa*.) One of the princes of Jehoshaphat whom he sent with certain priests and Levites to teach the law of Jehovah in the cities of Judah (2 Chr. xvii. 7).   W. A. W.

6. (מִיכָיְהוּ [as above]: Μιχαίας; [Vat. Μειχαιας;] FA. Μιχεας: *Michœas*.) The son of Gemariah. He is only mentioned on one occasion. After Baruch had read, in public, prophecies of Jeremiah announcing imminent calamities, Michaiah went and declared them to all the princes assembled in king Zedekiah's house; and the princes forthwith sent for Baruch to read the prophecies to them (Jer. xxxvi. 11-14). Michaiah was the third in descent of a princely family, whose names are recorded in connection with important religious transactions. His grandfather Shaphan was the scribe, or secretary of king Josiah, to whom Hilkiah the high priest first delivered the book of the law which he said he had found in the House of Jehovah — Shaphan first perusing the book himself, and then reading it aloud to the youthful king (2 K. xxii. 10). And it was from his father Gemariah's chamber in the Temple, that Baruch read the prophecies of Jeremiah, in the ears of all the people. Moreover, Gemariah was one of the three who made intercession to king Zedekiah, although in vain, that he would not burn the roll containing Jeremiah's prophecies.   E. T.

MI'CHAL (מִיכַל [*who like God*]: Μελχόλ; [2 Sam. xxi. 8, Rom. Vat. Μιχόλ;] Joseph. Μιχόλα: *Michol*), the younger of Saul's two daughters (1 Sam. xiv. 49). The king had proposed to bestow on David his eldest daughter MERAB; but before the marriage could be arranged an unexpected turn was given to the matter by the behavior of Michal, who fell violently in love with the young hero. The marriage with her elder sister was at once put aside. Saul eagerly caught at the opportunity which the change afforded him of exposing his rival to the risk of death. The price fixed on Michal's hand was no less than the slaughter of a hundred Philistines.ᵃ For these the usual " dowry " by which, according to the custom of the East, from the time of Jacob down to the present day, the father is paid for his daughter, was relinquished. David by a brilliant feat doubled the tale of victims, and Michal became his wife. What her age was we do not know — her husband cannot have been more than sixteen.

It was not long before the strength of her affection was put to the proof. They seem to have been living at Gibeah, then the head-quarters of the king and the army. After one of Saul's attacks of frenzy, in which David had barely escaped being transfixed by the king's great spear, Michal learned that the house was being watched by the myrmidons of Saul, and that it was intended on the next morning to attack her husband as he left his door (xix. 11). That the intention was real was evident from the behavior of the king's soldiers, who paraded round and round the town, and " returning " to the house " in the evening," with loud cries, more like the yells of the savage dogs of the East than the utterances of human beings, " belched out " curses and lies against the young warrior who had so lately shamed them all (Ps. lix.ᵇ 3, 6, 7, 12). Michal seems to have known too well the vacillating and ferocious disposition of her father when in these demoniacal moods. The attack was ordered for the morning; but before the morning arrives the king will probably have changed his mind and hastened his stroke. So, like a true soldier's wife, she meets stratagem by stratagem.

---

analogy on which the last part is based is absolutely unwarrantable ; and the very attempt to draw it shows a forgetfulness of the true meaning of that communion with Christ, which is implied by the latter expression.

ᵃ Perhaps nothing in the whole Bible gives so complete an example of the gap which exists between Eastern and Western ideas, as the manner in which the tale of these uncircumcised enemies of Israel was to be counted. Josephus softens it by substituting heads for foreskins, but it is obvious that heads would not have answered the same purpose. The LXX., who often alter obnoxious expressions, adhere to the Hebrew text.

ᵇ This Psalm, by its title in the Hebrew, LXX., Vulgate, and Targum, is referred to the event in question, a view strenuously supported by Hengstenberg.

She first provided for David's safety by lowering him out of the window: to gain time for him to reach the residence of Samuel she next dressed up the bed as if still occupied by him: the teraphim. or household god, was laid in the bed, its head enveloped, like that of a sleeper, in the usual net [a] of goat's hair for protection from gnats, the rest of the figure covered with the wide *beged* or plaid. [DAVID, vol. i. p. 567 a.] It happened as she had feared; Saul could not delay his vengeance till David appeared out of doors, but sent his people into the house. The reply of Michal is that her husband is ill and cannot be disturbed. At last Saul will be baulked no longer: his messengers force their way into the inmost apartment and there discover the deception which has been played off upon them with such success. Saul's rage may be imagined: his fury was such that Michal was obliged to fabricate a story of David's having attempted to kill her.

This was the last time she saw her husband for many years; and when the rupture between Saul and David had become open and incurable, Michal was married to another man, Phalti or Phaltiel of Gallim (1 Sam. xxv. 44; 2 Sam. iii. 15), a village probably not far from Gibeah. After the death of her father and brothers at Gilboa, Michal and her new husband appear to have betaken themselves with the rest of the family of Saul to the eastern side of the Jordan. If the old Jewish tradition inserted by the Targum in 2 Sam. xxi. may be followed, she was occupied in bringing up the sons of her sister Merab and Adriel of Meholah. At any rate, it is on the road leading up from the Jordan Valley to the Mount of Olives that we first encounter her with her husband — Michal under the joint escort of David's messengers and Abner's twenty men, *en route* to David at Hebron, the submissive Phaltiel behind, bewailing the wife thus torn from him. It was at least fourteen years since David and she had parted at Gibeah, since she had watched him disappear down the cord into the darkness and had perilled her own life for his against the rage of her insane father. That David's love for his absent wife had undergone no change in the interval seems certain from the eagerness with which he reclaims her as soon as the opportunity is afforded him. Important as it was to him to make an alliance with Ishbosheth and the great tribe of Benjamin, and much as he respected Abner, he will not listen for a moment to any overtures till his wife is restored. Every circumstance is fresh in his memory. " I will not see thy face except thou first bring Saul's daughter . . . . my wife Michal whom I espoused to me for a hundred foreskins of the Philistines " (2 Sam. iii. 13, 14). The meeting took place at Hebron. How Michal comported herself in the altered circumstances of

David's household, how she received or was received by Abigail and Ahinoam, we are not told; but it is plain from the subsequent occurrences that something had happened to alter the relations of herself and David. They were no longer what they had been to each other. The alienation was probably mutual. On her side must have been the recollection of the long contests which had taken place in the interval between her father and David; the strong anti-Saulite and anti-Benjamite feeling prevalent in the camp at Hebron, where every word she heard must have contained some distasteful allusion, and where at every turn she must have encountered men like Abiathar the priest, or Ismaiah the Gibeonite (1 Chr. xii. 4; comp. 2 Sam. xxi. 2), who had lost the whole or the greater part of their relatives in some sudden burst of her father's fury. Add to this the connection between her husband and the Philistines who had killed her father and brothers; and, more than all perhaps, the inevitable difference between the boy-husband of her recollections and the matured and occupied warrior who now received her. The whole must have come upon her as a strong contrast to the affectionate husband whose tears had followed her along the road over Olivet [2 Sam. iii. 16], and to the home over which we cannot doubt she ruled supreme. On the side of David it is natural to put her advanced years, in a climate where women are old at thirty, and probably a petulant and jealous temper inherited from her father, one outburst of which certainly produced the rupture between them which closes our knowledge of Michal.

It was the day of David's greatest triumph, when he brought the Ark of Jehovah from its temporary resting-place to its home in the newly-acquired city. It was a triumph in every respect peculiarly his own. The procession consisted of priests, Levites, the captains of the . host, the elders of the nation; and conspicuous in front, " in the midst of the damsels playing on the timbrels," [b] was the king dancing and leaping. Michal watched this procession approach from the window of her apartments in the royal harem; the motions of her husband [c] shocked her as undignified and indecent — " she despised him in her heart." It would have been well if her contempt had rested there; but it was not in her nature to conceal it, and when, after the exertions of the long day were over, the last burnt-offering and the last peace-offering offered, the last portion distributed to the crowd of worshippers, the king entered his house to bless his family, he was received by his wife not with the congratulations which he had a right to expect and which would have been so grateful to him, but with a bitter taunt which showed how incapable she was of appreciating either her husband's temper or the service in which he had been engaged. David's

[a] כְּבִיר עִזִּים. This is Ewald's explanation of a term which has puzzled all other commentators (*Gesch* iii. 101). For כְּבִיר, the LXX. seem to have read כָּבֵד, a liver; since they state that Michal "put the liver of a goat at David's head." For an ingenious suggestion founded on this, see MAGIC, vol. ii. p. 1745 a.

[b] No doubt a similar procession to that alluded to in Ps. lxviii. 25. where it will be observed that the words interpolated by our translators — " among *them* were the damsels " — alter the sense. The presence

of the women as stated above is implied in the words of Michal in 2 Sam. vi. 20, when compared with the statement of Ps. lxviii.

[c] It seems from the words of Michal (vi. 20), which must be taken in their literal sense, coupled with the statement of 1 Chr. xv. 27, that David was clad in nothing but the ephod of thin linen. So it is understood by Procopius of Gaza (*in* 1 Chr. xv.). The ephod seems to have been a kind of tippet which went over the shoulders (ἐπωμίς), and cannot have afforded much protection to the person, especially of a man in violent action.

121

retort was a tremendous one, conveyed in words which once spoken could never be recalled. It gathered up all the differences between them which made sympathy no longer possible, and we do not need the assurance of the sacred writer that "Michal had no child unto the day of her death," to feel quite certain that all intercourse between her and David must have ceased from that date. Josephus (*Ant.* vii. 4, § 3) intimates that she returned to Phaltiel, but of this there is no mention in the records of the Bible; and, however much we may hesitate at doubting a writer so accurate as Josephus when his own interests are not concerned, yet it would be difficult to reconcile such a thing with the known ideas of the Jews as to women who had once shared the king's bed.[a] See RIZPAH, ABISHAG, ADONIJAH.

Her name appears but once again (2 Sam. xxi. 8) as the bringer-up, or more accurately the mother, of five of the grandchildren of Saul who were sacrificed to Jehovah by the Gibeonites on the hill of Gibeah. But it is probably more correct to substitute Merab for Michal in this place, for which see p. 1892.   G.

MICHE'AS (*Michœas*), the prophet Micah the Morasthite (2 Esdr. i. 39).

MICH'MAS (מִכְמָס: [in Ezr.,] Μαχμάς; Alex. Χαμμας: [in Neh., Μαχεμάς:] *Machmas*), a variation, probably a later[b] form, of the name MICHMASH (Ezr. ii. 27; Neh. vii. 31). In the parallel passage of 1 Esdras it is given as MACALON. See the following article.   G.

MICH'MASH (מִכְמָשׁ [*something hidden, treasure*, Ges.; *place of Chemosh*, Fürst]: Μαχμάς; [Vat. in 1 Sam. xiii. 11, 22, 23, xiv. 31, Μαχεμας:] *Machmas*), a town which is known to us almost solely by its connection with the Philistine war of Saul and Jonathan (1 Sam. xiii., xiv.). It has been identified with great probability in a village which still bears the name of *Mûkhmas*, and stands at about 7 miles north of Jerusalem, on the northern edge of the great *Wady Suweinit* — in some Maps *W. Fuwar* — which forms the main pass of communication between the central highlands on which the village stands, and the Jordan valley at Jericho. Immediately facing *Mukhmas*, on the opposite side of the ravine, is the modern representative of Geba; and behind this again are Ramah and Gibeah — all memorable names in the long struggle which has immortalized Michmash. Bethel is about 4 miles to the north of Michmash, and the interval is filled up by the heights of *Burka*, *Deir Diwan*, *Tell el-Hajar*, etc., which appear to have constituted the "Mount Bethel" of the nar-

rative (xiii. 2). So much is necessary to make the notices of Michmash contained in the Bible intelligible.

The place was thus situated in the very middle of the tribe of Benjamin. If the name be, as some scholars assert (Fürst, *Handwb.* 600 *b*, 732 *b*), compounded from that of Chemosh, the Moabite deity, it is not improbably a relic of some incursion or invasion of the Moabites, just as *Chephar-haammonai*, in this very neighborhood, is of the Ammonites. But though in the heart of Benjamin, it is not named in the list of the towns of that tribe (comp. Josh. xviii.), but first appears as one of the chief points of Saul's position at the outbreak of the war. He was occupying the range of heights just mentioned, one end of his line resting on Bethel, the other at Michmash (1 Sam. xiii. 2). In Geba, close to him, but separated by the wide and intricate valley, the Philistines had a garrison, with a chief[c] officer. The taking of the garrison or the killing of the officer by Saul's son Jonathan was the first move. The next was for the Philistines to swarm up from their sea-side plain in such numbers, that no alternative was left for Saul but to retire down the wady to Gilgal, near Jericho, that from that ancient sanctuary he might collect and reassure the Israelites. Michmash was then occupied by the Philistines, and was their furthest post to the East.[d] But it was destined to witness their sudden overthrow. While he was in Geba, and his father in Michmash, Jonathan must have crossed the intervening valley too often not to know it thoroughly; and the intricate paths which render it impossible for a stranger to find his way through the mounds and hummocks which crowd the bottom of the ravine — with these he was so familiar — the "passages" here, the "sharp rocks" there — as to be able to traverse them even in the dark. It was just as the day dawned (Joseph. *Ant.* vi. 6, § 2) that the watchers in the garrison at Michmash descried the two Hebrews clambering up the steeps beneath. We learn from the details furnished by Josephus, who must have had an opportunity of examining the spot when he passed it with Titus on their way to the siege of Jerusalem (see *B. J.* v. 2, § 1), that the part of Michmash in which the Philistines had established themselves consisted of three summits, surrounded by a line of rocks like a natural entrenchment, and ending in a long and sharp precipice believed to be impregnable. Finding himself observed from above, and taking the invitation as an omen in his favor, Jonathan turned from the course which he was at first pursuing, and crept up in the direction of the point reputed impregnable. And it was there, according to Jose-

---

paus, that he and his armor-bearer made their entrance to the camp (Joseph. *Ant.* vi. 6, § 2). [GIBEAH, vol. ii. p. 915; JONATHAN.]

Unless MAKAZ be Michmash — an identification for which we have only the authority of the LXX. — we hear nothing of the place from this time till the invasion of Judah by Sennacherib in the reign of Hezekiah, when it is mentioned by Isaiah (x. 28). He is advancing by the northern road, and has passed Ai and Migron. At Michmash, on the further side of the almost impassable ravine, the heavy baggage (A. V. " carriages," see vol. i. p. 392 a) is deposited, but the great king himself crosses the pass, and takes up his quarters for the night at Geba. All this is in exact accordance with the indications of the narrative of 1 Samuel, and with the present localities.

After the Captivity, the men of the place returned, 122 in number (Ezr. ii. 27; Neh. vii. 31; in both these the name is slightly altered to MICH-MAS), and reoccupied their former home (Neh. xi. 31).

At a later date it became the residence of Jonathan Maccabæus, and the seat of his government (1 Macc. ix. 73, "Machmas;" Joseph. *Ant.* xiii. 1, § 6). In the time of Eusebius and Jerome (*Onomasticon*, "Machmas") it was "a very large village retaining its ancient name, and lying near Ramah in the district of Ælia (Jerusalem), at 9 miles distance therefrom."

Later still it was famed for the excellence of its corn. See the quotation from the Mishna (*Menachoth*) in Reland (*Palæstina*, p. 897), and Schwarz (p. 131). Whether this excellence is still maintained we do not know. There is a good deal of cultivation in and amongst groves of old olives in the broad shallow wady which slopes down to the north and east of the village; but *Mukhmas* itself is a very poor place, and the country close to it has truly "a most forbidding aspect." "Huge gray rocks raise up their bald crowns, completely hiding every patch of soil, and the gray huts of the village, and the gray ruins that encompass them can hardly be distinguished from the rocks themselves." There are considerable remains of massive foundations, columns, cisterns, etc., testifying to former prosperity, greater than that of either Anathoth or Geba (Porter, *Hndbk.* 215, 216).

Immediately below the village, the great wady spreads out to a considerable width — perhaps half a mile; and its bed is broken up into an intricate mass of hummocks and mounds, some two of which, before the torrents of 3,000 winters had reduced and rounded their forms, were probably the two " teeth of cliff " — the Bozez and Seneh of Jonathan's adventure. Right opposite is *Jeba*, on a curiously terraced hill. To the left the wady contracts again, and shows a narrow black gorge of almost vertical limestone rocks pierced with mysterious caverns and fissures, the resort, so the writer was assured, of hyenas, porcupines, and eagles. In the wet season the stream is said to be often deeper than a man's neck, very strong, and of a bright yellow color.

In the Middle Ages *el-Bireh* was believed to be Michmash (see Maundrell, March 25; and the copious details in Quaresmius, *Elucidatio*, ii. 786, 787). But *el-Bireh* is now ascertained on good grounds to be identical with BEEROTH. G.

MICHMETHAH (הַמִּכְמְתָה, *i. e.* the Micmethath: 'Ικασμών, Δηλανάθ; Alex. Μαχθωθ,

in both cases: *Machmethath*), a place which formed one of the landmarks of the boundary of the territories of Ephraim and Manasseh on the western side of Jordan. (1.) It lay "facing (עַל פְּנֵי) Shechem;" it also was the next place on the boundary west of ASHER[a] (Josh. xvii. 7), if indeed the two are not one and the same place — ham-Micmethath a distinguishing affix to the commoner name of Asher. The latter view is taken by Reland (*Palæstina*, p. 596) — no mean authority — and also by Schwarz (p. 147), but it is not supported by the Masoretic accents of the passage. The former is that of the Targum of Jonathan, as well as our own A. V. Whichever may ultimately be found correct, the position of the place must be somewhere on the east of and not far distant from Shechem. But then (2.) this appears quite inconsistent with the mention of the same name in the specification of a former boundary (Josh. xvi. 6). Here the whole description seems to relate to the boundary between Benjamin and Ephraim (*i. e.* Ephraim's southern boundary), and Michmethath follows Beth-horon the upper, and is stated to be on its west or seaward side. Now Beth-horon is at least 20 miles, as the crow flies, from Shechem, and more than 30 from Asher. The only escape from such hopeless contradictions is the belief that the statements of chap. xvi. have suffered very great mutilation, and that a gap exists between verses 5 and 6, which if supplied would give the landmarks which connected the two remote points of Beth-horon and Michmethath. The place has not been met with nor the name discovered by travellers, ancient or modern. G.

MICH'RI (מִכְרִי [perh. *purchased, valuable*, Ges.] : Μαχίρ; [Vat. Μαχειρ;] Alex. Μοχορε· *Mochori*). Ancestor of Elah, one of the heads of the fathers of Benjamin (1 Chr. ix. 8) after the Captivity.

MICHTAM (מִכְתָּם: στηλογραφία: *tituli inscriptio*). This word occurs in the titles of six Psalms (xvi., lvi.-lx.), all of which are ascribed to David. The marginal reading of our A. V. is " *a golden* psalm," while in the Geneva version it is described as " a certain tune." From the position which it occupies in the title, compared with that of *Mizmor* (A. V. " Psalm," Ps. iv.-vi., etc.), *Maschil* (Ps. xxxii., etc.), and *Shiggaion* (Ps. vii.), the first of which certainly denotes a song with an instrumental accompaniment (as distinguished from *shir*, a song for the voice alone), we may infer that *michtam* is a term applied to these psalms to denote their musical character, but beyond this everything is obscure. The very etymology of the word is uncertain. 1. Kimchi and Aben Ezra, among Rabbinical writers, trace it to the root כֶּתֶם, *cétham*, as it appears in כֶּתֶם, *cethem*, which is rendered in the A. V. " gold " (Job xxviii. 16), " pure gold " (Job xxviii. 19), " fine gold " (Job xxxi. 24); because the psalm was to David precious as fine gold. They have been followed by the translators in the margin of our version, and the *Michtam* Psalms have been compared with the " Golden Sayings " of Pythagoras and the Proverbs of Ali. Others have thought the epithet " golden " was applied to these psalms, because they were

---

[a] For the situation of the town of AS HER see note to MANASSEH, vol. ii. p. 1170.

written in letters of gold and suspended in the Sanctuary or elsewhere, like the *Moallakát*, or suspended poems of Mecca, which were called *Mod-hahabát*, or "golden," because they were written in gold characters upon Egyptian linen. There is, however, no trace among the Hebrews of a practice analogous to this. Another interpretation, based upon the same etymology of the word, is given to *Michtam* by an unknown writer quoted by Jarchi (Ps. xvi. 1). According to this, it signifies "a crown," because David asked God for his protection, and He was as a crown to him (Ps. v. 12).

2. In Syriac the root in conj. *Pael*, ܟܬܡ, *cathem*, signifies "to stain," hence "to defile," the primary meaning in *Peal* being probably "to spot, mark with spots," whence the substantive is in common use in Rabbinical Hebrew in the sense of "spot" or "mark" (comp. Kimchi, *on Am.* i. 1). In this sense the Niphal participle occurs in Jer. ii. 22, "thine iniquity is *spotted* before me," which makes the parallelism more striking than the "marked" of our A. V. From this etymology the meanings have been given to *Michtam* of "a *noted* song" (Junius and Tremellius, *insignis*), or a song which was *graven* or carved upon stone, a monumental inscription; the latter of which has the merit of antiquity in its favor, being supported by the renderings of the LXX., Theodotion, the Chaldee Targum, and the Vulgate. (See Michaelis, *Suppl. ad Lex. Heb.* No. 1242.) There is nothing in the character of the psalms so designated to render the title appropriate; had the Hebrews been acquainted with musical notes, it would be as reasonable to compare the word *Michtam* with the old English "prick-song,"[a] a song *pricked* or *noted*. In the utter darkness which envelopes it, any conjecture is worthy of consideration; many are valueless as involving the transference to one language of the metaphors of another.

3. The corresponding Arab. كتم, *catama*, "to conceal, repress," is also resorted to for the explanation of *Michtam*, which was a title given to certain psalms, according to Hezel, because they were written while David was in concealment. This, however, could not be appropriate to Ps. lviii., lx. From the same root Hengstenberg attributes to them a *hidden*, mystical import, and renders Michtam by *Geheimniss*, which he explains as "ein Lied tiefen Sinnes." Apparently referring the word to the same origin, Ewald (*Jahrb.* viii. p. 68) suggests that it may designate a song accompanied by bass instruments, like "the cymbals of trumpet-sound" of Ps. cl. 5, which would be adapted to the plaintive character of Ps. xvi. and others of the series to which it is applied. The same mournful tone is also believed to be indicated in *Michtam* as derived

from a root analogous to the Arab. كتم, *cathama*, which in conj. vii. signifies "to be sad," in which case it would denote "an elegy."

4. But the explanation which is most approved by Rosenmüller and Gesenius is that which finds in Michtam the equivalent of מִכְתָּב, *mictâb*; a word which occurs in Is. xxxviii. 9 (A. V. "writing"), and which is believed by Capellus (*Crit. Sacr.* iv. 2, § 11) to have been the reading followed by the LXX. and Targum. Gesenius supports his decision by instances of similar interchanges of ב and מ in roots of cognate meaning. In accordance with this De Wette renders "Schrift."

5. For the sake of completeness another theory may be noticed, which is quite untenable in itself, but is curious as being maintained in the versions of Aquila[b] and Symmachus,[c] and of Jerome[d] according to the Hebrew, and was derived from the Rabbinical interpreters. According to these, מִכְתָּם is an enigmatic word equivalent to מָךְ (and תָּם), "humble and perfect," epithets applied to David himself.

It is evident from what has been said, that nothing has been really done to throw light upon the meaning of this obscure word, and there seems little likelihood that the difficulty will be cleared away. Beyond the general probability that it is a musical term, the origin of which is uncertain and the application lost, nothing is known. The subject will be found discussed in Rosenmüller's *Scholia* (*Psalm.* vol. i. *explic. titul.* xlii.-xlvi.), and by Hupfeld (*Die Psalmen*, i. 308-311), who has collected all the evidence bearing upon it, and adheres to the rendering *kleinod* (jewel, treasure), which Luther also gives, and which is adopted by Hitzig and Mendelssohn.   W. A. W.

MID'DIN (מִדִּין [*reach, extension*]: Αἰνών [Alex.] Μαδων; [Comp. Μαδδίν:] *Meddin*), a city of Judah (Josh. xv. 61), one of the six specified as situated in the district of "the midbar" (A. V. "wilderness"). This midbar, as it contained Beth ha-Arabah, the city of Salt, and Engedi, must have embraced not only the waste lands on the upper level, but also the cliffs themselves and the strip of shore at their feet, on the edge of the lake itself. Middin is not mentioned by Eusebius or Jerome, nor has it been identified or perhaps sought for by later travellers. By Van de Velde (*Memoir*, 256, and *Map*) mention is made of a valley on the southwestern side of the Dead Sea, below Masada, called *Um el-Bedun*, which may contain a trace of the ancient name.   G.

* **MIDDLE-WALL.** [PARTITION, WALL OF, Amer. ed.]

MID'IAN (מִדְיָן, *strife, contention*, Ges.: Μαδιάμ [occasionally Μαδιάν]: *Madian*), a son of Abraham and Keturah (Gen. xxv. 2; 1 Chr. i. 32); progenitor of the Midianites, or Arabians dwelling principally in the desert north of the peninsula of Arabia.[c] Southwards they extended along the eastern shore of the Gulf of Eyleh (*Sinus*

---

a Shakespeare, *Rom. and Jul.* ii. 4: "He fights as you sing *pricksong*, keeps time, distance, and proportion."

b Τοῦ ταπεινόφρονος καὶ ἀπλοῦ τοῦ Δαυίδ.

c Ταπεινόφρονος καὶ ἀμώμου.

d "Humilis et simplicis David."

e The notion that there were two peoples called Midian, founded on the supposed shortness of the interval

for any considerable multiplication from Abraham to Moses, and on the mention of Moses' Cushite wife, the writer thinks to be untenable. Even conceding the former objection, which is unnecessary, one tribe has often become merged into another, and older one, and only the name of the later retained. See below and Moses.

Ælaniticus); and northwards they stretched along .he eastern frontier of Palestine; while the oases in the peninsula of Sinai seem to have afforded them pasture grounds, and caused it to be included in the "land of Midian" (but see below on this point). The *people* is always spoken of, in the Hebrew, as

"Midian," מִדְיָן, except in Gen. xxxvii. 36; Num. xxv. 17, xxxi. 2, where we find the pl. מִדְיָנִים.

In Gen. xxxvii. 28, the form מִדְיָנִים occurs, rendered in the A. V. as well as in the Vulg.[a] "Midianites;" and this is *probably* the correct rendering, since it occurs in ver. 36 of the same chap.; though the people here mentioned may be descendants of MEDAN (which see). The gentilic form מִדְיָנִי, "Midianite," occurs once, Num. x. 29.

After the chronological record of Midian's birth, with the names of his sons, in the xxvth chapter of Genesis, the name disappears from the Biblical history until the time of Moses; Midian is first mentioned, as a people, when Moses fled, having killed the Egyptian, to the "land of Midian" (Ex. ii. 15), and married a daughter of a priest of Midian (21). The "land of Midian," or the portion of it specially referred to, was probably the peninsula of Sinai, for we read in the next chapter (ver. 1) that Moses led the flock of Jethro his father-in-law, the priest of Midian, " to the backside of the desert, and came to the mountain of God, even Horeb," and this agrees with a natural supposition that he did not flee far beyond the frontier of Egypt (compare Ex. xviii. 1-27, where it is recorded that Jethro came to Moses to the mount of God after the Exodus from Egypt; but in v. 27 "he went his way into his own land:" see also Num. x. 29, 30). It should, however, be remembered that the name of Midian (and hence the "land of Midian") was perhaps often applied, as that of the most powerful of the northern Arab tribes, to the northern Arabs generally, *i. e.* those of Abrahamic descent (comp. Gen. xxxvii. 28, but see respecting this passage above; and Judg. viii. 24); just as BENE-KEDEM embraced all those peoples, and, with a wider signification, other Eastern tribes. If this reading of the name be correct, "Midian" would correspond very nearly with our modern word "Arab;" limiting, however, the modern word to the Arabs of the northern and Egyptian deserts: all the Ishmaelite tribes of those deserts would thus be Midianites, as we call them Arabs, the desert being their "land." At least, it cannot be doubted that the descendants of Hagar and Keturah intermarried; and thus the Midianites are apparently called Ishmaelites, in Judg. viii. 24, being connected, both by blood and national customs, with the father of the Arabs. The wandering habits of nomadic tribes must also preclude our arguing from the fact of Moses' leading his father's flock to Horeb, that Sinai was necessarily more than a station of Midian: those tribes annually traverse a great extent of country in search of pasturage, and have their established summer and winter pastures. The Midianites were mostly (not always) dwellers in tents, not towns; and Sinai has not sufficient pasture to support more than a small, or a moving people. But it must be remembered that perhaps

---

a The LXX. have here Μαδιηναῖοι, which seems to be an unusual mode of writing the name of the people descended from Μαδιάμ. The Samaritan has מדינים.

(or we may say *probably*) the peninsula of Sinai has considerably changed in its physical character since the time of Moses; for the adjacent isthmus has, since that period, risen many feet, so that "the tongue of the Egyptian Sea" has "dried up:" and this supposition would much diminish the difficulty of accounting for the means of subsistence found by the Israelites in their wanderings in the wilderness, when not miraculously supplied. Apart from this consideration, we knew that the Egyptians afterwards worked mines at *Sardbet el-Khâdim* and a small mining population may have found sufficient sustenance, at least in some seasons of the year, in the few watered valleys, and wherever ground could be reclaimed: rock-inscriptions (though of later date) testify to the number of at least passersby; and the remains of villages of a mining population have been recently discovered. Whatever may have been the position of Midian in the Sinaitic peninsula, if we may believe the Arabian historians and geographers, backed as their testimony is by the Greek geographers, the city of Midian was situate on the opposite, or Arabian, shore of the Arabian gulf, and thence northwards and spreading east and west we have the true country of the wandering Midianites. See further in SINAI.

The next occurrence of the name of this people in the sacred history marks their northern settlements on the border of the Promised Land, "on this side Jordan [by] Jericho" in the plains of Moab (Num. xxii. 1-4), when Balak said, of Israel, to the elders (זְקֵנִים, or "old men," the same as the Arab "sheykhs") of Midian, "Now shall this company lick up all [that are] round about us, as the ox licketh up the grass of the field." In the subsequent transaction with Balaam, the elders of Midian went with those of Moab, "with the rewards of divination in their hand" (7); but in the remarkable words of Balaam, the Midianites are not mentioned. This might be explained by the supposition that Midian was a wandering tribe, whose pasture-lands reached wherever, in the Arabian desert and frontier of Palestine, pasture was to be found, and who would not feel, in the same degree as Moab, Amalek, or the other more settled and agricultural inhabitants of the land allotted to the tribes of Israel, the arrival of the latter. But the spoil taken in the war that soon followed, and more especially the mention of the dwellings of Midian, render this suggestion very doubtful, and point rather to a considerable pastoral settlement of Midian in the trans-Jordanic country. Such settlements of Arabs have, however, been very common. In this case the Midianites were evidently *tributary* to the Amorites, being "dukes of Sihon, dwelling in the country" (יֹשְׁבֵי הָאָרֶץ): this inferior position explains their omission from Balaam's prophecy. It was here, "on this side Jordan," that the chief doings of the Midianites with the Israelites took place. The latter, while they abode in Shittim, "joined themselves unto Baal-Peor" (Num. xxv. 1, &c.) — apparently a Midianite as well as a Moabitish deity — the result of the sin of whoredom with the Moabitish women; and when " the anger of the Lord was kindled against Israel . . . and the congregation of the children of Israel [were] weeping [before] the door of the tabernacle of the congregation," an Israelite brought a Midianitish woman openly into the camp. The

rank of this woman COZBI, that of a daughter of
Zur, who was "head over a people, of a chief house
in Midian," [a] throws a strange light over the obscure page of that people's history. The vices of
the Canaanites, idolatry and whoredom, had infected the descendants of Abraham, doubtless connected by successive intermarriages with those
tribes: and the prostitution of this chief's daughter,
caught as it was from the customs of the Canaanites, is evidence of the ethnological type of the latter tribes. Some African nations have a similar
custom: they offer their unmarried daughters to
show hospitality to their guests. Zur was one of
the five "kings" (מַלְכֵי), slain in the war with
Midian, recorded in ch. xxxi.

The influence of the Midianites on the Israelites
was clearly most evil, and directly tended to lead
them from the injunctions of Moses. Much of the
dangerous character of their influence may probably
be ascribed to the common descent from Abraham.
While the Canaanitish tribes were abhorred, Midian
might claim consanguinity, and more readily seduce
Israel from their allegiance. The events at Shittim
occasioned the injunction to vex Midian and smite
them — "for they vex you with their wiles, wherewith they have beguiled you in the matter of Peor
and in the matter of Cozbi, the daughter of a prince
of Midian, their sister, which was slain in the day
of the plague for Peor's sake" (Num. xxv. 18);
and further on, Moses is enjoined, "Avenge the
children of Israel of the Midianites: afterward shalt
thou be gathered unto thy people" (xxxi. 2).
Twelve thousand men, a thousand from each tribe,
went up to this war, a war in which all the males
of the enemy were slain, and the five kings of
Midian — Evi, Rekem, Zur, Hur, and Reba, together with Balaam; and afterwards, by the express
command of Moses, only the virgins and female
infants, of the captives brought into the camp, were
spared alive. The cities and castles of the vanquished, and the spoil taken, afford facts to which
we shall recur. After a lapse of some years (the
number is very doubtful, see CHRONOLOGY), the
Midianites appear again as the enemies of the
Israelites. They had recovered from the devastation of the former war, probably by the arrival of
fresh colonists from the desert tracts over which
their tribes wandered; and they now were sufficiently powerful to become the oppressors of the
children of Israel. The advocates of a short chronology must, however unwillingly, concede a considerable time for Midian thus to recover from the
severe blow inflicted by Moses. Allied with the
Amalekites, and the Bene-Kedem, they drove them
to make dens in the mountains and caves and
strongholds. and wasted their crops even to Gaza,
on the Mediterranean coast, in the land of Simeon.
The judgeship of Gideon was the immediate consequence of these calamities; and with the battle he
fought in the valley of Jezreel, and his pursuit of
'he flying enemy over Jordan to Karkor, the power

of Midian seems to have been broken. It is written.
"Thus was Midian subdued before the children of
Israel, so that they lifted up their heads no more"
(Judg. viii. 28). The part taken by Gideon in this
memorable event has been treated of elsewhere, but
the Midianite side of the story is pregnant with
interest. [GIDEON.]

Midian had oppressed Israel for seven years. As
a numberless eastern horde they entered the land
with their cattle and their camels. The imagination shows us the green plains of Palestine sprinkled
with the black goat's-hair tents of this great Arab
tribe, their flocks and herds and camels let loose in
the standing corn, and foraging parties of horsemen
driving before them the possessions of the Israelites;
for "they came like locusts (A. V. 'grasshoppers,'
(אַרְבֶּה) for multitude" (Judg. vi. 5), and when
the "angel of the Lord" came to Gideon, so severe
was the oppression that he was threshing wheat by
the wine-press to hide it from the Midianites (11).
When Gideon had received the Divine command
to deliver Israel, and had thrown down the altar
of Baal, we read, "Then all the Midianites and the
Amalekites and the Bene-Kedem were gathered together, and went over," descended from the desert
hills and crossed Jordan, "and pitched in the Valley
of Jezreel" (33) — part of the Plain of Esdraelon,
the battle-field of Palestine — and there, from "the
gray, bleak crowns of Gilboa," where Saul and
Jonathan perished, did Gideon, with the host that
he had gathered together of Israel, look down on
the Midianites, who "were on the north side of
them, by the hill of Moreh, in the valley" (vii. 1).
The scene over that fertile plain, dotted with the
enemies of Israel, "the Midianites and the Amalekites and all the Bene-Kedem, [who] lay along [c]
in the valley like locusts for multitude, and their
camels were without number, as the sand by the
sea-side for multitude" (vii. 12), has been pic-
turesquely painted by Professor Stanley (S. & P.).
The descent of Gideon and his servant into the
camp, and the conversation of the Midianite watch
forms a vivid picture of Arab life. It does more;
it proves that as Gideon, or Phurah, his servant,
or both, understood the language of Midian, the
Semitic languages differed much less in the 14th
or 13th century B. C. than they did in after times
[see ARABIA, vol. i. p. 142]; and we besides obtain
a remarkable proof of the consanguinity of the
Midianites, and learn that, though the name was
probably applied to all or most of the northern
Abrahamic Arabs, it was not applied to the Canaanites, who certainly did not then speak a Semitic
language that Gideon could understand.

The stratagem of Gideon receives an illustration
from modern oriental life. Until lately the police
in Cairo were accustomed to go their rounds with
a lighted torch thrust into a pitcher, and the
pitcher was suddenly withdrawn when light was
required (Lane's Mod. Eg. 5th ed. p. 120) — a
custom affording an exact parallel to the ancient

[a] רֹאשׁ אֻמּוֹת בֵּית־אָב, "head of families of
a patriarchal house;" afterwards in ver. 18, called
prince, נָשִׂיא. (See next note.)

[b] These are afterwards (Josh. xiii. 21) called
princes " (נְשִׂיאֵי), which may also be rendered
the leader or captain of a tribe, or even of a family
(Ges.), and "dukes" (נְסִיכֵי), not the word rendered

duke in the enumeration of the "dukes of Edom "),
"one anointed, a prince consecrated by anointing "
(Ges.) of Sihon king of the Amorites; apparently lieu
tenants of the Amorite, or princes of his appointing.
[HUR ; IRAM.]

[c] Prof. Stanley reads here "wrapt in sleep." Though
the Heb. will bear this interpretation, Gesenius has
"encamped."

expedient adopted by Gideon. The consequent panic of the great multitude in the valley, if it has no parallels in modern European history, is consistent with oriental character. Of all peoples, the nations of the East are most liable to sudden and violent emotions ; and a panic in one of their heterogeneous, undisciplined, and excitable hosts has always proved disastrous. In the case of Gideon, however, the result of his attack was directed by God, the Divine hand being especially shown in the small number of Israel, 300 men, against 135,000 of the enemy. At the sight of the 300 torches, suddenly blazing round about the camp in the beginning of the middle-watch (which the Midianites had newly set), with the confused din of the trumpets, " for the three companies blew the trumpets, and brake the pitchers, and held the lamps in their left hands, and the trumpets in their right hands to blow [withal], and they cried, [The sword] of the Lord and of Gideon " (vii. 20), " all the host ran, and cried, and fled " (21). The panic-stricken multitude knew not enemy from friend, for " the Lord set every man's sword against his fellow even throughout all the host " (22). The rout was complete, the first places made for being Beth-shittah (" the house of the acacia ") in Zere-rath, and the "border" [שְׂפָת] of Abel-me-holah, " the meadow of the dance," both being probably down the Jordan Valley, unto Tabbath, shaping their flight to the ford of Beth-barah, where probably they had crossed the river as invaders. The flight of so great a host, encumbered with slow-moving camels, baggage, and cattle, was calamitous. All the men of Israel, out of Naphtali, and Asher, and Manasseh, joined in the pursuit; and Gideon roused the men of Mount Ephraim to " take before " the Midianites " the waters unto Beth-barah and Jordan " (23, 24). Thus cut off, two princes, Oreb and Zeeb (the " raven," or, more correctly " crow," and the " wolf "), fell into the hands of Ephraim, and Oreb they slew at the rock Oreb, and Zeeb they slew at the wine-press of Zeeb (vii. 25; comp. Is. x. 26, where the " slaughter of Midian at the rock Oreb " is referred to).[a] But though we have seen that many joined in a desultory pursuit of the rabble of the Midianites, only the 300 men who had blown the trumpets in the Valley of Jezreel crossed Jordan with Gideon, " faint yet pursuing " (viii. 4). With this force it remained for the liberator to attack the enemy on his own ground, for Midian had dwelt on the other side Jordan since the days of Moses. Fifteen thousand men, under the " kings " [מַלְכֵי] of Midian, Zebah and Zalmunna, were at Karkor, the sole remains of 135,-000, " for there fell an hundred and twenty thousand men that drew sword " (viii. 10). The assurance of God's help encouraged the weary three hundred, and they ascended from the plain (or ghôr) to the higher country by a ravine or torrent-bed in the hills, " by the way of them that dwelt in tents [that is, the pastoral or wandering people as distinguished from towns people], on the east of Nobah and Jogbehah, and smote the host, for the host was secure " (viii. 11) — secure in that wild country,

on their own ground, and away from the frequent haunts of man. A sharp pursuit seems to have followed this fresh victory, ending in the capture of the kings and the final discomfiture of the Midianites. The overthrow of Midian in its encampment, when it was " secure," by the exhausted companies of Gideon (they were " faint," and had been refused bread both at Succoth and at Penuel, viii. 5–9), sets the seal to God's manifest hand in the deliverance of his people from the oppression of Midian. Zebah and Zalmunna were slain, and with them the name itself of Midian almost disappears from sacred history. That people never afterwards took up arms against Israel, though they may have been allied with the nameless hordes who under the common designation of " the people of the East," Bene-Kedem, harassed the eastern border of Palestine.

Having traced the history of Midian, it remains to show what is known of their condition and customs, etc., besides what has already been incidentally mentioned. The whole account of their doings with Israel — and it is only thus that they find a place in the sacred writings, plainly marks them as characteristically Arab. We have already stated our opinion that they had intermarried with Ishmael's descendants, and become nationally one people, so that they are apparently called Ishmaelites; and that, conversely, it is most probable their power and numbers, with such intermarriages, had caused the name of Midian to be applied to the northern Abrahamic Arabs generally. They are described as true Arabs — now Bedawees, or " people of the desert; " anon pastoral, or settled Arabs — the flock " of Jethro; the cattle and flocks of Midian, in the later days of Moses; their camels without number, as the sand of the sea-side for multitude when they oppressed Israel in the days of the Judges — all agree with such a description. Like Arabs, who are predominantly a nomadic people, they seem to have partially settled in the land of Moab, under the rule of Sihon the Amorite, and to have adapted themselves readily to the " cities " (עָרֵיהֶם), and forts? (A. V. " goodly castles," טִירֹתָם), which they did not build, but occupied, retaining even then their flocks and herds (Num. xxxi. 9, 10), but not their camels, which are not common among settled Arabs, because they are not required, and are never, in that state, healthy.[b] Israel seems to have devastated that settlement, and when next Midian appears in history it is as a desert-horde, pouring into Palestine with innumerable camels ; and, when routed and broken by Gideon, fleeing " by the way of them that dwelt in tents " to the east of Jordan. The character of Midian we think is thus unmistakably marked. The only glimpse of their habits is found in the vigorous picture of the camp in the Valley of Jezreel when the men talked together in the camp, and one told how he had dreamt that " a cake of barley-bread tumbled into the host of Midian, and came into a tent, and smote it that it fell, and overturned it, that the tent lay along " (Judg. vii. 13).

We can scarcely doubt, notwithstanding the dis-

---

[a] It is added, in the same verse, that they pursued Midian, and brought the heads of the princes to Gideon ' on the other side Jordan." This anticipates the account of his crossing Jordan (viii. 4), but such transpositions are frequent, and the Hebrew may be read ' on this side Jordan."

[b] Thus an Arab, believing in contagious diseases, asked Mohammed why camels in the desert are like gazelles, and become mangy as soon as they mix with camels in towns. The prophet answered, " Who made the first camel mangy ? "

putes of antiquaries, that the more ancient of the remarkable stone buildings in the *Lejdh*, and stretching far away over the land of Moab, are at least as old as the days of Sihon; and reading Mr. Porter's descriptions of the wild old-world character of the scenery, the "cities," and the "goodly castles," one may almost fancy himself in presence of the hosts of Midian. (See *Handbook*, 501, 508, 523, &c.)

The spoil taken in both the war of Moses and that of Gideon is remarkable. On the former occasion, the spoil of 575,000 sheep, 72,000 beeves, and 61,000 asses, seems to confirm the other indications of the then pastoral character of the Midianites; the omission of any mention of camels has been already explained. But the gold, silver, brass, iron, tin, and lead (Num. xxxi. 22), the "jewels of gold, chains, and bracelets, rings, earrings, and tablets" (50) — the offering to the Lord being 16,750 shekels (52) — taken by Moses, is especially noteworthy; and it is confirmed by the booty taken by Gideon; for when he slew Zebah and Zalmunna he "took away the ornaments that [were] on their camels' necks" (Judg. viii. 21), and (24-26) he asked of every man the earrings of his prey, "for they had golden earrings, because they [were] Ishmaelites." "And the weight of the golden earrings that he requested was a thousand and seven hundred [shekels] of gold; besides ornaments and collars, and purple raiment that [was] on the kings of Midian, and beside the chains that [were] about their camels' necks." (The rendering of A. V. is sufficiently accurate for our purpose here, and any examination into the form or character of these ornaments, tempting though it is, belongs more properly to other articles.) We have here a wealthy Arab nation, living by plunder, delighting in finery (especially their women, for we may here read "nose-ring"); and, where forays were impossible, carrying on the traffic southwards into Arabia, the land of gold — if not naturally, by trade — and across to Chaldæa; or into the rich plains of Egypt.[a]

Midian is named authentically only in the Bible. It has no history elsewhere. The names of places and tribes occasionally throw a feeble light on its past dwellings; but the stories of Arabian writers, borrowed, in the case of the northern Arabs, too frequently from late and untrustworthy Jewish writers, cannot be seriously treated. For reliable facts we must rest on the Biblical narrative. The city of "Medyen [say the Arabs] is the city of the people of Shu'eyb, and is opposite Tabook, on the shore of Bahr el-Kulzum [the Red Sea]: between these is six days' journey. It [Medyen] is larger than Tabook; and in it is the well from which Moses watered the flock of Shu'eyb" (*Mardsid*, s. v.). El-Makreezee (in his *Khitat*) enters into

considerable detail respecting this city and people. The substance of his account, which is full of incredible fables, is as follows: Medyen are the people of Shu'eyb, and are the offspring of Medyán[b] [Midian], son of Abraham, and their mother was Kantoorà,.the daughter of Yuktán [Joktan] the Canaanite: she bare him eight children, from whom descended peoples. He here quotes the passage above cited from the *Mardsid* almost *verbatim*, and adds, that the Arabs dispute whether the name be foreign or Arabic, and whether Medyen spoke Arabic, so-called. Some say that they had a number of kings, who were respectively named Abjad, Hawwez, Huttee, Kelemen, Saafas, and Karashet. This absurd enumeration forms a sentence common in Arabic grammars, which gives the order of the Hebrew and ancient Arabic alphabets, and the numerical order of the letters. It is only curious as possibly containing some vague reference to the *language* of Midian, and it is therefore inserted here. These kings are said to have ruled at Mekkeh, Western Nejd, the Yemen, Medyen, and Egypt, etc., contemporaneously. That Midian penetrated into the Yemen is, it must be observed. extremely improbable, as the writer of this article has remarked in ARABIA, notwithstanding the hints of Arab authors to the contrary, Yákoot, in the *Moajam* (cited in the *Journal of the Deutsch. Morgenl. Gesellschaft*), saying that a southern Arabian dialect is of Midian; and El-Mes'oodee (*ap.* Schultens, pp. 158, 159) inserting a Midianite king among the rulers of the Yemen: the latter being, however, more possible than the former, as an accidental and individual, not a national occurrence. The story of Shu'eyb is found in the Kur-án. He was sent as a prophet to warn the people of Midian, and being rejected by them, they were destroyed by a storm from heaven (Sale's *Kur-án*, vii. and xi.). He is generally supposed to be the same as Jethro, the father-in-law of Moses; but some, as Sale informs us, deny this; and one of these says "that he was first called Buyoon, and afterwards Shu'eyb, that he was a comely person. but spare and lean, very thoughtful, and of few words." The whole Arab story of Medyen and Shu'eyb, even if it contain any truth, is encumbered by a mass of late Rabbinical myths.

El-Makreezee tells us that in the land of Midian were many cities, of which the people had disappeared, and the cities themselves had fallen to ruin; that when he wrote (in the year 825 of the Flight) forty cities remained, the names of some being known, and of others lost. Of the former, he says, there were, between the Hijáz and Palestine and Egypt, sixteen cities; and ten of these in the direction of Palestine. They were El-Khalasah, Es-Saneetah, El-Medereh, El-Minyeh, El-Aawaj, El-Khuweyrak, El-Beereyn, El-Má-eyn, El-Seba, and El-Mu'allak.[c] The most important of these cities

---

a • Modern travellers confirm this Biblical account of the fertility and wealth of Midian. "We succeeded," says Tristram, "in reaching *Et Taiyibeh* just as the sun went down. We had magnificent views over the east as far as Jebel Hauran. Great was our astonishment to find, as we turned our glasses on Bozrah, that all the vast blank space on the map which lies between Gilead and Bozrah, instead of being a desert, was one boundless corn or grass plain, covered with crops. It is, in fact, the granary of North Arabia. Here was the wealth of Roman Syria, and the source of its population; and here the swarming Midianites, like the Beni Sakk'r of to-day, pastured their thousands of camels." (*Land of Israel*, 2d ed., p. 486.)　H.

.مديان[b]

الخُلَصَة,[c]

المِنْيَة, المَدَرَة, السُنَيطَة,

البِثْرَيْن, الخُوَيْرَق, الأَعْوَج,

المُعَلّق, السَبْع, المَاءَيْن.

were El-Khalasah [a] and El-Saneetah; the stones of many of them had been removed to El-Ghazzah (Gaza) to build with them. This list, however, must be taken with caution.

In the A. V. of Apocr. and N. T. the name is given as MADIAN.   E. S. P.

* MIDIANITE. [MIDIAN.]

MIDWIFE.[b] Parturition in the East is usually easy.[c] The office of a midwife is thus, in many eastern countries, in little use, but is performed, when necessary, by relatives (Chardin, *Voy.* vii. 23; Harmer, *Obs.* iv. 425). [CHILDREN.] It may be for this reason that the number of persons employed for this purpose among the Hebrews was so small, as the passage Ex. i. 19 seems to show; unless, as Knobel and others suggest, the two named were the principal persons of their class.

In the description of the transaction mentioned in Ex. i., one expression, " upon the [d] stools," receives remarkable illustration from modern usage. Gesenius doubts the existence of any custom such as the direct meaning of the passage implies, and suggests a wooden or stone trough for washing the new-born child. But the modern Egyptian practice, as described by Mr. Lane, exactly answers to that indicated in the book of Exodus. " Two or three days before the expected time of delivery, the *Layeh* (midwife) conveys to the house the *kursee elwiladeh*, a chair of a peculiar form, upon which the patient is to be seated during the birth " (Lane, *Mod. Egypt.* iii. 142).

The moral question arising from the conduct of the midwives does not fall within the scope of the present article. The reader, however, may refer to St. Augustine, *Contr. mendacium*, ch. xv. 32, and *Quæst. in Hept.* ii. 1; also Corn. a Lap. *Com. on Ex.* i.

When it is said, " God dealt well with the midwives, and built them houses," we are probably to understand that their families were blessed either in point of numbers or of substance. Other explanations of inferior value have been offered by Kimchi, Calvin, and others (Calmet, *Com. on Ex.* i.; Patrick; Corn. a Lap.; Knobel; Schleusner, *Lex. V. T. οἰκία*; Ges. p. 193; *Crit. Sacr.*).

It is worth while to notice only to refute on its own ground the Jewish tradition which identified Shiphrah and Puah with Jochebed and Miriam, and interpreted the " houses " built for them as the so-called royal and sacerdotal families of Caleb and Moses (Joseph. *Ant.* iii. 2, § 4; Corn. a Lap. and

Crit. Sacr. l. c.; Schöttgen, *Hor. Hebr.* ii. 450 *De Mess.* c. iv.).   H. W. P.

MIGDAL–EL' (מִגְדַּל־אֵל [*tower of God*: Rom. Μεγαλααρίμ; Vat.] Μεγαλααρειμ; Alex. Μαγδαλιηωραμ — both including the succeeding name: *Magdal-El*), one of the fortified towns of the possession of Naphtali (Josh. xix. 38 only), named between IRON and HOREM, possibly deriving its name from some ancient tower — the " tower of El, or God." In the present unexplored condition of the part of Palestine allotted to Naphtali, it is dangerous to hazard conjectures as to the situations of the towns: but if it be possible that *Hurah* is Horem and *Yarûn* Iron, the possibility is strengthened by finding a *Mujeidel*, at no great distance from them, namely, on the left bank of the *Wady Kerkerah*, 8 miles due east of the *Ras en-Nakurah*, 6 miles west of *Hurah* and 8 of *Yarûn* (see Van de Velde's Map, 1858). At any rate the point is worth investigation.

By Eusebius (*Onomasticon*, Μαγδιήλ) it is spoken of as a large village lying between Dora (*Tantura*) and Ptolemais (*Akka*) at 9 miles from the former. that is just about *Athlit*, the ancient " Castellum peregrinorum." No doubt the Castellum was anciently a migdol [e] or tower: but it is hard to locate a town of Naphtali below Carmel, and at least 25 miles from the boundaries of the tribe. For a similar reason *Mejdel* by Tiberias, on the shore of the Lake of Gennesaret, is not likely to be Migdal-el (Rob. *Bibl. Res.* ii. 397), since it must be outside the ancient limits of Naphtali and within those of Zebulun. In this case, however, the distance is not so great.

Schwarz (184), reading Migdal-el and Horem as one word, proposes to identify it with *Mejdel el-Kerûm*, a place about 12 miles east of *Akka*.

A *Mejdel* is mentioned by Van de Velde (*Syr. and Pal.* ii. 307) in the central mountains of Palestine, near the edge of the *Ghor*, at the upper end of the *Wady Fusail*, and not far from *Daumeh*, the ancient Edumia. This very possibly represents an ancient Migdal, of which no trace has yet been found in the Bible. It was also visited by Dr. Robinson (*Bibl. Res.* iii. 295), who gives good reasons for accepting it as the Magdal-senna mentioned by Jerome (*Onomast.* " Senna ") as seven miles north of Jericho, on the border of Judæa. Another Migdal probably lay about two miles south of Jerusalem, near the Bethlehem road, where the cluster of ruins called *Kirbet Um-Meghdala* is now situated (Tobler, *Dritte Wanderung*, p. 81).

---

[a] El-Khalasah (sometimes written El-Khulusah, and El-Khulsah), or Dhu-l-Khalasah, possessed an idol-temple, destroyed by order of Mohammad; the idol being named El-Khalasah, or the place, or " growing-place " of El-Khalasah. The place is said to be four days' journey from Mekkeh, in the 'Ablà, and called " the southern Kaabeh," El-Kaabeh el-Yemáneeyeh (*Marásd*, s. v., and El-Bekree, and the *Kámoos* there cited). El-Madereh seems also to be the same as Dhu-l-Madereh (*Marásid*, s. v.), and therefore (from the same) probably the site of an idol temple also.

[b] מְיַלְּדֹת, part in P. of יָלַד, " to bring forth :"

maia: *obstetrix*. It must be remarked that חָיוֹת, ᴸ. V., Ex. i. 19, " lively," is also in Rabbinical Hebrew " midwives," an explanation which appears to have been had in view by the Vulg., which interprets *chayoth* by " ipsæ obstetricandi habent scientiam." It is also rendered " living creatures," implying that

the Hebrew women were, like animals, quick in parturition. Gesenius renders " vividæ, robustæ," p. 468. In any case the general sense of the passage Ex. i. 19 is the same, namely, that the Hebrew women stood in little or no need of the midwives' assistance.

[c] See an illustration of Cant. viii. 5, suggested in Mishna, *Pesach.* x. 3.

[d] עַל־הָאָבְנָיִם, rendered in the LXX. ὅταν ὦσι πρὸς τῷ τίκτειν; Vulg. *quum partus tempus advenerit*.

[e] May this not be the Magdôlus named by Herodotus, ii. 159, as the site of Pharaoh Necho's victory over Josiah? (See Rawlinson's *Herod.* ii. 246, note.) But this was not the only Migdol along this coast. The Στράτωνος πύργος, or " Strato's tower," must have been another, and a third possibly stood near Ashkelon. [MEGIDDO; MIGDAL-GAD.]

The Migdal-Euer, at which Jacob halted on his way from Bethlehem to Hebron, was a short distance south of the former. [EDAR, TOWER OF.]

G.

MIGDAL-GAD (מִגְדַּל־גָּד) [*tower of Gad*]: [Rom. Μαγαδαλγαδ; Vat.] Μαγαδαγαδ; Alex. Μαγδαλγαδ: *Maydal-Gad*), a city of Judah (Josh. xv. 37); in the district of the *Shefelah*, or maritime lowland; a member of the second group of cities, which contained amongst others LACHISH, EGLON, and MAKKEDAM. By Eusebius and Jerome in the *Onomasticon*, it appears to be mentioned as "Magdala," but without any sign of its being actually known to them. A village called *el Medjdel* lies in the maritime plain, a couple of miles inland from Ascalon, 9 from *Um Lakhis*, and 11 from *Ajlun*. So far this is in support of Van de Velde's identification (*Syr. & Pal.* ii. 237, 238; *Memoir*, p. 334; Rob. 1st ed. vol. iii. Appendix, p. 118 *b*) of the place with Migdal-gad, and it would be quite satisfactory if we were not uncertain whether the other two places are Lachish and Eglon. Makkedah at any rate must have been much farther north. But to appreciate these conditions, we ought to know the principles on which the groups of towns in these catalogues are arranged, which as yet we do not. Migdal-gad was probably dedicated to or associated with the worship of the ancient deity Gad, another of whose sanctuaries lay. at the opposite extremity of the country at BAAL-GAD under Mount Hermon.

G.

MIGDOL (מִגְדֹּל, מִגְדּוֹל) [*tower, castle*]: Μάγδωλον, or Μαγδωλόν: *Magdalum*), proper name of one or two places on the eastern frontier of Egypt, cognate to מִגְדָּל, which appears properly to signify a military watch-tower, as of a town (2 K. ix. 17), or isolated (xvii. 9), and the look-out of a vineyard (Is. v. 2: comp. Matt. xxi. 33, Mark xii. 1), or a shepherd's look-out, if we may judge from the proper name, מִגְדַּל עֵדֶר, "the tower of the flock," in which, however, it is possible that the second word is a proper name (Gen. xxxv. 21; and comp. Mic. iv. 8, where the military signification seems to be implied, though perhaps rhetorically only). This form occurs only in Egyptian geography, and it has therefore been supposed by Champollion to be substituted for an Egyptian name of similar sound, the Coptic equivalent in the Bible, ⲙⲉϣⲧⲱⲗ, ⲙⲉϫⲧⲱⲗ (Sah.), being, according to him, of Egyptian origin (*L'Egypte sous les Pharaons*, ii. 79, 80; comp. 69). A native etymology has been suggested, giving the signification "multitude of hills"[a] (*Thes. s. v.*). The ancient Egyptian form of Migdol having, however, been found, written in a manner rendering it not improbable that it was a foreign word,[b] MAKTUR or MAKTeRU, as well as so used that it must be of similar meaning to the Hebrew מִגְדָּל, and the Coptic equivalent occur-

ring in a form, ⲙⲉϭⲧⲟⲗ (Sah.), slightly differing from that of the geographical name, with the significations "a circuit, citadels, towers, bulwarks," a point hitherto strangely overlooked, the idea of the Egyptian origin and etymology of the latter must be given up.

Another name on the frontier, Baal-zephon, appears also to be Hebrew or Semitic, and to have a similar signification. [BAAL-ZEPHON.] The ancient Egyptian name occurs in a sculpture on the outer side of the north wall of the great hypostyle hall of the Temple of El-Karnak at Thebes, where a fort, or possibly fortified town, is represented, with the name PA-MAKTUR EN RA-MA-MEN, "the tower of Pharaoh, establisher of justice;" the last four words being the prenomen of Sethes I. (B. C. cir. 1822). The sculpture represents the king's triumphal return to Egypt from an eastern expedition, and the place is represented as if on a main road, to the east of Leontopolis.

1. A Migdol is mentioned in the account of the Exodus. Before the passage of the Red Sea the Israelites were commanded "to turn and encamp before Pi-hahiroth, between Migdol and the sea, over against Baal-zephon" (Ex. xiv. 2). In Numbers we read, "And they removed from Etham, and turned again unto Pi-hahiroth, which [is] before Baal-zephon: and they pitched before Migdol. And they departed from before Pi-hahiroth, and passed through the midst of the sea into the wilderness" (xxxiii. 7, 8). We suppose that the position of the encampment was before or at Pi-hahiroth, behind which was Migdol, and on the other hand Baal-zephon and the sea, these places being near together. The place of the encampment and of the passage of the sea we believe to have been not far from the Persepolitan monument, which is made in Linant's map the site of the Serapeum. [EXODUS, THE.]

2. A Migdol is spoken of by Jeremiah and Ezekiel. The latter prophet mentions it as a boundary-town, evidently on the eastern border, corresponding to Seveneh, or Syene, on the southern. He prophesies the desolation of Egypt "from Migdol to Seveneh even unto the border of Cush," מִמִּגְדֹּל סְוֵנֵה וְעַד־גְּבוּל כּוּשׁ (xxix. 10), and predicts slaughter "from Migdol to Seveneh" (xxx. 6). That the eastern border is that on which Migdol was situate is shown not only by this being the border towards Palestine, and that which a conqueror from the east would pass, but also by the notices in the book of Jeremiah, where this town is spoken of with places in Lower Egypt. In the prophecy to the Jews in Egypt they are spoken of as dwelling at Migdol, Tahpanhes, and Noph, and in the country of Pathros (Jer. xliv. 1), and in that foretelling, apparently, an invasion of Egypt by Nebuchadnezzar, Migdol, Noph, and Tahpanhes are again mentioned together (xlvi. 14). It seems plain, from its being spoken of with Memphis, and from Jews dwelling there, that this Migdol was an important town, and not a mere fort, or even military

---

a The derivation is from ⲙⲏϣ, "multitude," and ⲑⲁⲗ, ⲧⲁⲗ (Sah.) "a hill," which is daring, notwithstanding the instability of the vowels in Coptic. The form ⲙⲉϣⲑⲁⲗ would better suit this etymology, were there not other reasons than its

rashness against it. Forster (J. R.) gives it, on what authority we know not: perhaps it is a misprint (*Epist. ad Michaelis*, p. 29).

b Foreign words are usually written with all of most of the vowels in ancient Egyptian: native words rarely.

settlement.[a] After this time there is no notice of any place of this name in Egypt, excepting of Magdolus, by Hecatæus of Miletus,[b] and in the *Itinerary of Antoninus*, in which *Magdolo* is placed twelve Roman miles to the southward of Pelusium, in the route from the Serapeum to that town.[c] This latter place most probably represents the Migdol mentioned by Jeremiah and Ezekiel. Its position on the route to Palestine would make it both strategetically important and populous, neither of which would be the case with a town in the position of the Migdol of the Pentateuch. Gesenius, however, holds that there is but one Migdol mentioned in the Bible (*Lex.* s. v.). Lepsius distinguishes two Migdols, and considers Magdolo to be the same as the Migdol of Jeremiah and Ezekiel. He supposes the name to be only the Semitic rendering of "the Camp," Στρατόπεδα, the settlement made by Psammetichus I. of Ionian and Carian mercenaries on the Pelusiac branch of the Nile.[d] He ingeniously argues that Migdol is mentioned in the Bible at the time of the existence — he rather loosely says foundation — of this settlement, but omitted by the Greek geographers — he should have said after Hecatæus of Miletus — the mercenaries having been removed by Amasis to Memphis (ii. 154), and not afterwards noticed excepting in the *Itinerary of Antoninus* (*Chronologie der Ægypter*, i. 340, and note 5). The Greek and Hebrew or Semitic words do not however offer a sufficient nearness of meaning, nor does the Egyptian usage appear to sanction any deviation in this case: so that we cannot accept this supposition, which, moreover, seems repugnant to the fact that Migdol was a town where Jews dwelt. Champollion (*L'Égypte sous les Pharaons*, ii. 69–71) and others (Ewald, *Geschichte*, 2d ed., ii. 7 *note*; Schleiden, *Die Landenge von Suêz*, pp. 140, 141) have noticed the occurrence of Arabic names which appear to represent the ancient name Migdol, and to be derived from its Coptic equivalent. These names, of which the most common form appears to be Mashtool,[e] are found in the Census of El-Melek en Násir (Mohammud Ibn Kalāoon), given by De Sacy in his translation of 'Abd el-Lateef's History of Egypt. Their frequency favors the opinion that Migdol was a name commonly given in Egypt to forts, especially on or near the eastern frontier. Dr. Schleiden (*l. c.*) objects that Mashtool has an Arabic derivation: but we reply that the modern geography of Egypt

offers examples that render this by no means a serious difficulty.

It has been conjectured that the Μάγδολον mentioned by Herodotus, in his reference to an expedition of Necho's (ii. 159), supposed to be that in which he slew Josiah, is the Migdol of the prophets (Mannert, *Afrika*, i. 489), and it has even been proposed to read in the Heb. text Migdol for Megiddo (Harenberg, *Bibl. Brem.* vi. 281, ff.; Rosenmüller, *Alterth.* ii. 99); but the latter idea is unworthy of modern scholarship.   R. S. P.

* Mons. Chabas finds traces of Migdol in the itinerary of an Egyptian grandee who visited Phœnicia, Palestine, and Syria, in the 14th century B. C. In crossing the eastern frontier of Egypt the traveller came to the house of *Ovati* erected by Rameses, to mark his victories. This *Ovati* was "the goddess of the North," answering to *Beel-Tsephon*, "the lord of the North." Rameses had probably appropriated by his own cartouche the fortress of *Ovati* already erected by Sethee I. Of this mention is made in one of the pictorial representations of the wars of Sethee I. — a sort of chart, indicating the last stations of this Pharaoh on his return from Asia to Egypt. These are, (1.) The *Ovati of Sethee I.* represented as a fortress near a reservoir of water: (2.) *The Miktal* of Sethee I., a fort with a well near by: (3.) *The House of the Lion*, a much larger fortress situated near a pond with trees upon either side: (4.) *The fortress of Djor*, consisting of several large buildings, separated by a canal, which connects with a lake filled with crocodiles, and which Brugsch identifies as lake Timsah.

From this sketch, the border of Egypt towards Palestine and Idumea appears to have been lined with forts, each of which, like the modern Suez, was furnished with a reservoir of sweet water (Chabas, *Voyage d'un Égyptien*, etc. p. 287).

The specification of a fortress of Sethee I. favors the opinion of Ewald that Migdol was a common name of frontier towers. Brugsch makes the *Maktir* or Migdol of Sethee I. identical with the *Magdolo* of the Itin. Anton., with the *Migdol-Magdalon* of Jeremiah and Ezekiel and the Migdol of the Books of Moses. (*Geog. Inschrift.* i. 261.)   J. P. T.

MIG'RON (מִגְרוֹן [*precipice*, or (Fürst) *land-slip*]: [Rom. Μαγδών, Vat.] Μαγων; in Isai. [Rom. Μαγγεδώ, Sin.[1] Μακεδω, Sin[ea], Vat.] Μαγεδω, and Alex. Μαγεδδω: *Magron*),[f] a town,

---

[a] We have no account of Jews in the Egyptian military service as early as this time; but it is not impossible that some of the fugitives who took Jeremiah with them may have become mercenaries in Pharaoh Hophra's army.

[b] Steph. Byz. *s. v.*, comp. *Fragmenta Historicorum Græcorum*, i. 20. If the latter part of the passage be from Hecatæus, the town was important in his time. Μαγδωλός, πόλις Αἰγύπτου. Ἑκαταῖος περιηγήσει· τὸ ἐθνικὸν Μαγδωλίτης, κ. τ. λ.

[c] The route is as follows: "a Serapiu Pelusio mpm ix Thaubasio viii Sile xxviii Magdolo xii Pelusio xii" (Ed. Parthey et Pinder, p. 76). These distances would place the Serapeum somewhat further southward than the site assigned to it in Linant's map [see EXODUS, THE], unless the route were very indirect, which in the desert might well be the case.

[d] Herodotus describes "the Camps" as two places, one on either side of the Nile, and puts them "near the sea, a little below the city Bubastis, on the mouth

of the Nile called the Pelusiac." Εἰσὶ δὲ οὗτοι οἱ χῶροι πρὸς θαλάσσης ὀλίγον ἔνερθε Βουβάστιος πόλιος, ἐπὶ τῷ Πηλουσίῳ καλευμένῳ στόματι τοῦ Νείλου (ii. 154). This statement is contradictory, as Bubastis is far from the Pelusiac mouth or the sea. Lepsius (*l. c.*) merely speaks of this settlement as near Pelusium, on the Pelusiac mouth below Bubastis, citing the last clause of the following passage of Diodorus Siculus, who gives but a loose repetition of Herodotus, and is not to be taken, here at least, as an independent authority, besides that he may fix the position of a territory only, and not of "the Camp." Τοῖς δὲ μισθοφόροις . . . . τὰ καλούμενα στρατόπεδα τόπον (γαρ. τοῖς καλουμένοις στρατοπέδοις τόπον) οἰκεῖν ἔδωκε, καὶ χώραν πολλὴν κατελήρουχησε μικρὸν ἐπάνω τοῦ Πηλουσιακοῦ στόματος (i. 67).

[e] مَشْتُول.

[f] Or in some MSS. *in agrum Gabaa*.

æ a spot — for there is nothing to indicate which — in the neighborhood of Saul's city, Gibeah, on the very edge of the district belonging to it (1 Sam. xiv 2), distinguished by a pomegranate-tree, under which, on the eve of a memorable event, we discover Saul and Ahiah surrounded by the poor remnants of their force. Josephus (*Ant.* vi. 6, § 2) presents it as a high hill (βουνὸς ὑψηλός), from which there was a wide prospect over the district devastated by the Philistines. But this gives no clew, for Palestine is full of elevated spots commanding wide prospects.

Migron is presented to our view only once again, namely, in the invaluable list of the places disturbed by Sennacherib's approach to Jerusalem (Is. x. 28). But here its position seems a little further north than that indicated in the former passage — supposing, that is, that Gibeah was at *Tuleil el-Ful.* It here occurs between Aiath — that is Ai — and Michmash, in other words was on the north of the great ravine of the *Wady-Suweinit,* while Gibeah was more than 2 miles to the south thereof. [GIBEAH, vol. ii. p. 916.] In Hebrew, *Migron* may mean a "precipice," a frequent feature of the part of the country in question, and it is not impossible therefore that two places of the same name are intended — a common occurrence in primitive countries and tongues where each rock or ravine has its appellation, and where no reluctance or inconvenience is found in having places of the same name in close proximity. As easily two Migrons, as two Gibeahs, or two Shochos.

The LXX. seem to have had MEGIDDO in their intentions, but this is quite inadmissible. (See Josephus, *Ant.* vi. 6, § 2.)　　　　G.

MI'JAMIN (מִיָּמִן [*on the right hand,* or = *Benjamin*]: Μειαμίν; [Vat. Βενιαμειν; Ald. Βενιαμίν;] Alex. Μεϊάμειν: *Maiman*). 1. The chief of the sixth of the 24 courses of priests established by David (1 Chr. xxiv. 9).

2. (Μιαμίν; [Vat.] Alex. Μιαμειν; FA. Μειαμων: *Miamin.*) A family of priests who signed the covenant with Nehemiah (Neh. x. 7); probably the descendants of the preceding, and the same as MIAMIN 2 and MINIAMIN 2.

MIK'LOTH (מִקְלוֹת [*staves,* Ges.; *branches* or *sticks,* Fürst: in 1 Chr. viii., Vat. Alex. Μακαλωθ, Rom.] Μακελώθ; in 1 Chr. ix., Alex. Μακεδωθ, [Vat. Sin. Μακελλωθ:] *Macelloth*). 1. One of the sons of Jehiel, the father or prince of Gibeon, by his wife Maachah (1 Chr. viii. 32, ix. 37, 38). His son is variously called Shimeah or Shimeam.

2. (Μακελλωθ; [Vat. omits.]) The leader (נָגִיד, *nãgid*) of the second division of David's army (1 Chr. xxvii. 4), of which Dodai the Ahohite was captain (שַׂר, *sar*). The *nãgid,* in a military sense, appears to have been an officer superior in rank to the captains of thousands and the captains of hundreds (1 Chr. xiii. 1).[a]

MIKNE'IAH (מִקְנֵיָהוּ [3 syl.] [*possession of Jehovah*]: Μακελλία, [Vat. Μακελλεια,] Alex. Μακενια, FA. Μακελλα, 1 Chr. xv. 18; Μακενία, Alex. Μακενιας, 1 Chr. xv. 21: *Macenias*). One of the Levites of the second rank, gatekeepers of

---

[a] This verse should be rendered, "And David consulted with the captains of thousands and hundreds, belonging to each leader" (*nãgid*).

---

the ark, appointed by David to play in the Temple band "with harps upon Sheminith."

MIL'ALAI [3 syl.] (מִלֲלָי [*eloquent*]: om in LXX.: *Malalai*). Probably a Gershonite Levite of the sons of Asaph, who, with Ezra at their head, played "the musical instruments of David the man of God" in the solemn procession round the walls of Jerusalem which accompanied their dedication (Neh. xii. 36). [MATTANIAH 2.]

MIL'CAH (מִלְכָּה [*counsel*]: Μελχά: *Melcha*). 1. Daughter of Haran and wife of her uncle Nahor, Abraham's brother, to whom she bare eight children: the youngest, Bethuel, was the father of Rebekah (Gen. xi. 29, xxii. 20, 23, xxiv. 15, 24, 47). She was the sister of Lot, and her son Bethuel is distinguished as "Nahor's son, whom Milcah bare unto him," apparently to indicate that he was of the purest blood of Abraham's ancestry, being descended both from Haran and Nahor.

2. The fourth daughter of Zelophehad (Num. xxvi. 33, xxvii. 1, xxxvi. 11; Josh. xvii. 3).

MIL'COM (מִלְכֹּם [*their king*]: ὁ βασιλεὺς αὐτῶν, [Comp. Μελχώμ,] *Moloch,* 1 K. xi. 5, 33; ὁ Μολόχ, [Vat. Ald. Μολχόλ,] Alex. Αμελχομ, *Melchom,* 2 K. xxiii. 13). The "abomination" of the children of Ammon, elsewhere called MOLECH (1 K. xi. 7, &c.) and MALCHAM (Zeph. i. 5, marg. "their king "), of the latter of which it is probably a dialectical variation. Movers (*Phönizier,* i. 358) calls it an Aramaic pronunciation.

MILE (Μίλιον, the Greek form of the Latin *milliarium*), a Roman measure of length equal to 1618 English yards. It is only once noticed in the Bible (Matt. v. 41), the usual method of reckoning both in it and in Josephus being by the stadium. The Roman system of measurement was fully introduced into Palestine, though probably at a later date; the Talmudists admitted the term "mile" (מִיל) into their vocabulary: both Jerome (in his *Onomasticon*) and the Itineraries compute the distances in Palestine by miles; and to this day the old milestones may be seen, here and there, in that country (Robinson's *Bib. Res.* ii. 161 *note,* iii. 306). The mile of the Jews is said to have been of two kinds, long or short, dependent on the length of the pace, which varied in different parts, the long pace being double the length of the short one (Carpzov's *Apparat.* p. 679). [DAY'S JOURNEY, Amer. ed.]　　　　W. L. B.

* **MILETUM,** 2 Tim. iv. 20, for Miletus. The A. V. follows here the older versions, except Wycliffe, who writes "Milete." The early English often inflected such names after the analogy of the Greek and Latin, though on this principle it would have been strictly *Mileto* in the above passage. See Trench, *Authorized Version,* p. 79 (ed. 1859).　　　　H.

MILE'TUS (Μίλητος: *Miletus*), Acts xx. 15, 17, less correctly called MILETUM in 2 Tim. iv. 20. The first of these passages brings before us the scene of the most pathetic occasion of St. Paul's life; the second is interesting and important in reference to the question of the Apostle's second imprisonment.

St. Paul, on the return voyage from his third missionary journey, having left Philippi after the passover (Acts xx. 6), and desirous, if possible, to be in Jerusalem at Pentecost (*ib.* 16), determined to pass by Ephesus. Wishing, however, to communicate with the church in which he had labored so long, he sent for the presbyters of Ephesus to meet him at Miletus. In the context we have the geographical relations of the latter city brought out as distinctly as if it were St. Luke's purpose to state them. In the first place it lay on the coast to the S. of Ephesus. Next, it was a day's sail from Trogyllium (ver. 15). Moreover, to those who are sailing from the north, it is in the direct line for Cos. We should also notice that it was near enough to Ephesus by land communication, for the message to be sent and the presbyters to come within a very narrow space of time. All these details correspond with the geographical facts of the case. As to the last point, Ephesus was by land only about 20 or 30 miles distant from Miletus. There is a further and more minute topographical coincidence, which may be seen in the phrase, "They accompanied him to the ship," implying as it does that the vessel lay at some distance from the town. The site of Miletus has now receded ten miles from the coast, and even in the Apostle's time it must have lost its strictly maritime position.

This point is noticed by Prof. Hackett in his *Comm. on the Acts* (2d ed. p. 344); compare Acts xxi. 5. In each case we have a low flat shore, as a marked and definite feature of the scene.

The passage in the second Epistle to Timothy, where Miletus is mentioned, presents a very serious difficulty to the theory that there was only one Roman imprisonment. When St. Paul visited the place on the occasion just described, Trophimus was indeed with him (Acts xx. 4); but he certainly did not " leave him sick at Miletus; " for at the conclusion of the voyage we find him with the Apostle at Jerusalem (Acts xxi. 29). Nor is it possible that he could have been so left on the voyage from Cæsarea to Rome: for in the first place there is no reason to believe that Trophimus was with the Apostle then at all; and in the second place the ship was never to the north of Cnidus (Acts xxvii. 7). But, on the hypothesis that St. Paul was liberated from Rome and revisited the neighborhood of Ephesus, all becomes easy, and consistent with the other notices of his movements in the Pastoral Epistles. Various combinations are possible. See *Life and Epistles of St. Paul*, ch. xxvii., and Birks, *Horæ Apostolicæ.*

Temple of Apollo at Miletus.

As to the history of Miletus itself, it was far more famous five hundred years before St. Paul's day, than it ever became afterwards. In early times it was the most flourishing city of the Ionian Greeks. The ships which sailed from it were celebrated for their distant voyages. Miletus suffered in the progress of the Lydian kingdom and became tributary to Croesus. In the natural order of events, it was absorbed in the Persian empire: and, revolting, it was stormed and sacked. After a brief period of spirited independence, it received a blow from which it never recovered, in the siege conducted by Alexander when on his Eastern campaign. But still it held, even through the Roman period, the rank of a second-rate trading town, and Strabo mentions its four harbors. At this time it was politically in the province of ASIA, though

CARIA was the old ethnological name of the district in which it was situated. Its preëminence on this coast had now long been yielded up to EPHESUS. These changes can be vividly traced by comparing the whole series of coins of the two places. In the case of Miletus, those of the autonomous period are numerous and beautiful, those of the imperial period very scanty. Still Miletus was for some time an episcopal city of Western Asia. Its final decay was doubtless promoted by that silting up of the Mæander, to which we have alluded. No remains worth describing are now found in the swamps which conceal the site of the city of Thales and Hecatæus.   J. S. H.

MILK. As an article of diet, milk holds a more important position in Eastern countries than with us. It is not a mere adjunct in cookery, or restricted to the use of the young, although it is naturally the characteristic food of childhood, both from its simple and nutritive qualities (1 Pet. ii. 2), and particularly as contrasted with meat (1 Cor. iii. 2; Heb. v. 12); but beyond this it is regarded as substantial food adapted alike to all ages and classes. Hence it is enumerated among "the principal things for the whole use of a man's life" (Ecclus. xxxix. 26), and it appears as the very emblem of abundance[a] and wealth, either in conjunction with honey (Ex. iii. 8; Deut. vi. 3, xi. 9) or wine (Is. lv. 1), or even by itself (Job xxi. 24[b]): hence also to "suck the milk" of an enemy's land was an expression betokening its complete subjection (Is. lx. 16; Ez. xxv. 4). Not only the milk of cows, but of sheep (Deut. xxxii. 14), of camels (Gen. xxxii. 15), and of goats (Prov. xxvii. 27) was used; the latter appears to have been most highly prized. The use of camel's milk still prevails among the Arabs (Burckhardt's *Notes*, i. 44).

Milk was used sometimes in its natural state, and sometimes in a sour, coagulated state: the former was named *khâlâb*,[c] and the latter *khemah*.[d] In the A. V. the latter is rendered "butter," but there can be no question that in every case (except perhaps Prov. xxx. 33) the term refers to a preparation of milk well known in Eastern countries under the name of *leben*. [BUTTER, Amer. ed.] The method now pursued in its preparation is to boil the milk over a slow fire, adding to it a small piece of old *leben* or some other acid, in order to make it coagulate (Russell, *Aleppo*, i. 118, 370; Burckhart, *Arabia*, i. 60). The refreshing draught which Jael offered "in a lordly dish" to Sisera (Judg. v. 25) was *leben*, as Josephus particularly notes (γάλα διαφθορὸς ἤδη, *Ant.* v. 5, § 4): it was produced from one of the goatskin bottles which are still used for the purpose by the Bedouins (Judg. iv. 19; comp. Burckhardt's *Notes*, i. 45). As it would keep for a considerable time, it was particularly adapted to the use of travellers (2 Sam. xvii. 29). The amount of milk required for its production was of course considerable; and hence in Is. vii. 22 the use of *leben* is predicted as a consequence of the depopulation of the land, when all agriculture had ceased, and the fields were covered with grass. In Job xx. 17, xxix. 6, the term is used as an emblem of abundance in the same sense as milk. *Leben* is still extensively used in the East; at certain seasons of the year the poor almost live upon it, while the upper classes eat it with salad or meat (Russell, i. 18). It is still offered in hospitality to the passing stranger, exactly as of old in Abraham's tent (Gen. xviii. 8; comp. Robinson, *Bibl. Res.* i. 571, ii. 70, 211), so freely indeed that in some parts of Arabia it would be regarded as a scandal if money were received in return (Burckhardt's *Arabia*, i. 120, ii. 106). Whether milk was used instead of water for the purpose of boiling meat, as is at present not unusual among the Bedouins, is uncertain. [COOKING.] The prohibition against seething a kid in its mother's milk (occurring as it does amid the regulations of the harvest festival, Ex. xxiii. 19, xxxiv. 26; Deut. xiv. 21) was probably directed against some heathen usage practiced at the time of harvest. W. L. B.

MILL. The mills (רֵחַיִם, *rechaim*)[e] of the ancient Hebrews probably differed but little from those at present in use in the East. These consist of two circular stones, about 18 in. or two feet in diameter, the lower of which (Lat. *meta*) is fixed, and has its upper surface slightly convex, fitting into a corresponding concavity in the upper stone (Lat. *catillus*). The latter, called by the Hebrews *receb* (רֶכֶב), "chariot," and by the Arabs *rekkab*, "rider," has a hole in it through which the grain passes, immediately above a pivot or shaft which rises from the centre of the lower stone, and about which the upper stone is turned by means of an upright handle fixed near the edge. It is worked by women, sometimes singly and sometimes two together, who are usually seated on the bare ground (Is. xlvii. 1, 2) "facing each other; both have hold of the handle by which the upper is turned

Women grinding corn with the hand-mill of modern Syria.

round on the 'nether' millstone. The one whose right hand is disengaged throws in the grain as occasion requires through the hole in the upper stone. It is not correct to say that one pushes it half round, and then the other seizes the handle. This would be slow work, and would give a spasmodic motion to the stone. Both retain their hold, and pull *to*, or push *from*, as men do with the whip or cross-cut saw. The proverb of our Saviour (Matt. xxiv. 41) is true to life, for *women* only grind. I cannot recall an instance in which men were at the mill" (Thomson, *Land and Book*, ch. 34). The labor is very hard, and the task of grinding in consequence performed only by the lowest servants (Ex. xi. 5; comp. Plaut. *Merc.* ii. 3), and

---

[a] This is expressed in the Hebrew term for milk, *shalab*, the etymological force of which is "fatness." We may compare with the Scriptural expression, "a and flowing with milk and honey," the following passages from the classical writers: —

'Peῖ δὲ γάλακτι πέδον,
'Peῖ δ' οἴνῳ, ῥεῖ δὲ μελισσᾶν
Νέκταρι. — EURIP. *Bacch.* 142.

[a] Flumina jam lactis, jam flumina nectaris ibant:
Flavaque de viridi stillabant ilice mella."
Ov. *Met.* i. 111.

[b] In this passage the marginal reading, "milk pails," is preferable to the text, "breasts." The Hebrew word

does not occur elsewhere, and hence its meaning is doubtful. Perhaps its true sense is "farm-yard" or "fold."

[c] חָלָב. 　　　[d] חֶמְאָה.

[e] Compare Arabic رَحَيَان, *rahayân*, the dual of رَحَى, *raha*, a mill. The dual form of course refers to the pair of stones composing the mill.

captives (Judg. xvi. 21; Job xxxi. 10; Is. xlvii. 1, 2; Lam. v. 13; comp. Hom. *Od.* vii. 103; Suet. *Tib.* c. 51).[a] So essential were mill-stones for daily domestic use, that they were forbidden to be taken in pledge (Deut. xxiv. 6; Jos. *Ant.* iv. 8, § 26), in order that a man's family might not be deprived of the means of preparing their food. Among the Fellahs of the Hauran one of the chief articles of furniture described by Burckhardt (*Syria*, p. 292) is the "*h·nd-mill* which is used in summer when there is no water in the wadies to drive the mills." The sound of the mill is the indication of peaceful household life, and the absence of it is a sign of desolation and abandonment, " When the sound of the mill is low " (Eccl. xii. 4). No more affecting picture of utter destruction could be imagined than that conveyed in the threat denounced against Judah by the mouth of the prophet Jeremiah (xxv. 10), " I will take from them the voice of mirth, and the voice of gladness, the voice of the bridegroom and the voice of the bride, *the sound of the mill-stones*, and the light of the candle " (comp. Rev. xviii. 22). The song of the women grinding is supposed by some to be alluded to in Eccl. xii. 4, and it was evidently so understood by the LXX.[b]; but Dr. Robinson says (i. 485), " we heard no song as an accompaniment to the work," and Dr. Hackett (*Bibl. Illust.* p. 49, Amer. ed.) describes it rather as shrieking than singing. It is alluded to in Homer (*Od.* xx. 105–119); and Athenæus (xiv. p. 619 a) refers to a peculiar chant which was sung by women winnowing corn and mentioned by Aristophanes in the *Thesmophoriazusæ*.

The hand-mills of the ancient Egyptians appear to have been of the same character as those of their descendants, and like them were worked by women (Wilkinson, *Anc. Eg.* ii. p. 118, &c.). " They had also a large mill on a very similar principle; but the stones were of far greater power and dimensions; and this could only have been turned by cattle or asses, like those of the ancient Romans, and of the modern Cairenes." It was the mill-stone of a mill of this kind, driven by an ass,[c] which is alluded to in Matt. xviii. 6 (μύλος ὀνικός), to distinguish it, says Lightfoot (*Hor. Hebr.* in loc.), from those small mills which were used to grind spices for the wound of circumcision, or for the delights of the Sabbath, and to which both Kimchi and Jarchi find a reference in Jer. xxv. 10. Of a married man with slender means it is said in the Talmud (*Kiddushin*, p. 29 b), "with a millstone on his neck he studies the law," and the expression is still proverbial (Tendlau, *Sprichwörter*, p. 181).

It was the movable upper millstone of the hand-mill with which the woman of Thebez broke Abimelech's skull (Judg. ix. 53). It is now generally made, according to Dr. Thomson, of a porous lava brought from the Hauran, both stones being of the same material, but, says the same traveller. " I have seen the *nether* made of a compact sand-stone, and quite thick, while the *upper* was of this lava, probably because from its lightness it is the more easily driven round with the hand " (*Land and Book*, ch. 34). The porous lava to which he refers is probably the same as the black tufa mentioned by Burckhardt (*Syria*, p. 57), the blocks of which are brought from the Lejah, and are fashioned into millstones by the inhabitants of Ezra, a village in the Hauran. " They vary in price according to their size, from 15 to 60 piastres, and are preferred to all others on account of the hardness of the stone."

The Israelites, in their passage through the desert, had with them hand-mills, as well as mortars [MORTAR], in which they ground the manna (Num. xi. 8). One passage (Lam. v. 13) is deserving of notice, which Hoheisel (*de Molis Manual. Vet.* in Ugolini, vol. xxix) explains in a manner which gives it a point which is lost in our A. V. It may be rendered, " the choice (men) bore the mill (מחון, *techón*),[d] and the youths stumbled beneath the wood ; " the wood being the woodwork or shaft of the mill, which the captives were compelled to carry. There are, besides, allusions to other apparatus connected with the operation of grinding, the sieve, or bolter (נָפָה, *náphâh*, Is. xxx. 28; or כְּבָרָה, *cĕbârâh*, Am. ix. 9), and the hopper, though the latter is only found in the Mishna (*Zabim*, iv. 3), and was a late invention. We also find in the Mishna (*Demai*, iii. 4) that mention is made of a miller (טוֹחֵן, *tóchén*), indicating that grinding corn was recognized as a distinct occupation. Wind-mills and water-mills are of more recent date.   W. A. W.

* Some other allusions to the mill and its uses deserve explanation. The common millstone rarely exceeds two feet in diameter, and hence its size fitted it to be used as an instrument of punishment. It was sometimes fastened to the necks of criminals who were to be drowned. The Saviour refers to this practice in Mark ix. 42, where he says: Sooner than " offend one of these little ones, it were better for a man that a millstone were hanged about his neck, and he were cast into the sea." See also Matt. xviii. 6; and Luke xvii. 2. It is stated that this mode of execution is not unknown in the East at the present day. As those who grind, in whatever order they may sit, have the mill before them, it becomes natural, in describing their position with reference to the mill, to speak of their being behind it. Hence it is said in Ex. xi. 5 that the pestilence which was to be sent on the Egyptians should " destroy from the first-born of Pharaoh that sitteth upon his throne, even unto the first-born of the maid-servant that is behind the mill."

The fact that grinding at the mill was looked upon as so ignoble (see above), shows how extreme was the degradation to which the Philistines subjected Samson. It is said (Judg. xvi. 21) that the Philistines " put out " (strictly," dug out " in the Hebrew)

---

[a] Grinding is reckoned in the Mishna (*Shabbath*, vii. 2) among the chief household duties, to be performed by the wife unless she brought with her one servant (*Sethuboth*, v. 5) ; in which case she was relieved from grinding, baking, and washing, but was still obliged to suckle her child, make her husband's bed, and work in wool.

[b] Ἐν ἀσθενείᾳ φωνῆς τῆς ἀληθούσης, reading מחנה,

τόchenâh, " a woman grinding," for הַמַּחֲנֶה, *tachânâh*, " a mill."

[c] Comp. Ovid, *Fast.* vi. 318, " et quæ pumiceas versat asella molas."

[d] Compare the Arabic طَاحُون, *tahoon*, a mill.

"the eyes of Samson, and made him grind in the prison-house;" that is, he was confined in prison, and required to grind there, by turning a hand-mill, such as has been described above. It was the great humiliation of his captivity. He who had been the hero of Israel, who had possessed the strength of a giant, was compelled to sit on the ground and work at the mill, like a woman or a slave The blinding was sometimes inflicted to prevent the giddiness liable to arise from the circular motion (Herod. iv. 2). At the same time it was a frequent barbarity of ancient warfare (Jer. lii. 11).

Possibly the woman of Thebez who threw the upper stone of the mill, the "rider" or "runner," on the head of Abimelech (see above) was occupied in grinding at the moment. She had only to lift the upper stone from its pedestal, and would then have at once an effectual weapon for her purpose. The A. V. erroneously suggests that it was "a piece" or fragment of the stone which she hurled at Abimelech. See the allusion to this incident in 2 Sam. xii. 21. The permanent or lower stone was called פֶּלַח תַּחְתִּים, Job xli. 16. Some of the larger mills in Syria at the present day are turned by mules and asses, as in ancient times (Matt. xviii. 6). The time of grinding would be regulated by the wants of the family, but from the nature of the case as a rule it would be one of the daily occupations. At Jerusalem one may see at night-fall the open ground on Bezetha alive with women performing this labor. The water-mills at present at *Nábulus* (Shechem) are somewhat noted.   H.

MILLET (דֹּחַן,[a] *dóchan:* κέγχρος· *milium*). In all probability the grains of *Panicum miliaceum* and *italicum*, and of the *Holcus sorghum*, Linn. (the *Sorghum vulgare* of modern writers), may all be comprehended by the Hebrew word. Mention of millet occurs only in Ez. iv. 9, where it is enumerated together with wheat, barley, beans. lentils, and fitches, which the prophet was ordered to make into bread. Celsius (*Hierob.* i. 454) has given the names of numerous old writers who are in favor of the interpretation adopted by the LXX. and Vulg.; the Chaldee, Syriac, and Arabic versions have a word identical with the Hebrew. That "millet" is the correct rendering of the original word there can be no doubt; the only question that remains for consideration is, what is the particular species of millet intended: is it the *Panicum miliaceum*, or the *Sorghum vulgare*, or may both kinds be denoted? The Arabs to this day apply the term *dukhan* to the *Panicum miliaceum*, but Forskål (*Descr. Plant.* p. 174) uses the name of the *Holcus dochna*, "a plant," says Dr. Royle (Kitto's *Cyc.* art. "Dokhan"), "as yet unknown to botanists." The *Holcus durrha* of Forskål, which he says the Arabs call *táam*, and which he distinguishes from the *H. dochna*, appears to be identical with the *dourrha*, *Sorghum vulgare*, of modern botanists. It is impossible, in the case of these and many other cereal grains, to say to what countries they are indigenous. Sir G. Wilkinson enumerates wheat, beans, lentiles, and *dourrha*, as being preserved by seeds, or by representation on the ancient tombs of Egypt, and has no doubt that the *Holcus sorghum* was known to the ancient inhabitants of

that country. Dr. Royle maintains that the true *dukhun* of Arab authors is the *Panicum miliaceum*.

Sorghum vulgare.

which is universally cultivated in the East. Celsius (*Hierob.* l. c.) and Hiller (*Hierophyt.* ii. 124) give *Panicum* as the rendering of *Dochan;* the

Panicum miliaceum.

LXX. word κέγχρος in all probability is the *Panicum italicum*, a grass cultivated in Europe as an article of diet. There is, however, some difficulty

---

[a] From root דָּחַן, "to be dusky," in allusion to the color of the seeds.

in identifying the precise plants spoken of by the Greeks and Romans under the names of κέγχρος, ἔλυμος, panicum, milium, etc.

The *Panicum miliaceum* is cultivated in Europe and in tropical countries, and, like the *dourrha*, is often used as an ingredient in making bread; in India it is cultivated in the cold weather with wheat and barley. Tournefort (*Voyage*, ii. 95) says that the poor people of Samos make bread by mixing half wheat and half barley and white millet. The seeds of millet in this country are, as is well known, extensively used as food for birds. It is probable that both the *Sorghum vulgare* and the *Panicum miliaceum* were used by the ancient Hebrews and Egyptians, and that the Heb. *Dochan* may denote either of these plants. Two cultivated species of *Panicum* are named as occurring in Palestine, namely, *P. miliaceum* and *P. italicum* (Strand's *Flor. Palæst.* Nos. 35, 37). The genera *Sorghum* and *Panicum* belong to the natural order *Gramineæ*, perhaps the most important order in the vegetable kingdom.   W. H.

MILLO (הַמִּלּוֹא: always with the definite article [see below] ἡ ἄκρα, once τὸ ἀνάλημμα; Alex. in 1 K. ix. [24] only, η μελω: *Mello*), a place in ancient Jerusalem. Both name and thing seem to have been already in existence when the city was taken from the Jebusites by David. His first occupation after getting possession was to build "round about, from the Millo and to the house" (A. V. "inward; "2 Sam. v. 9): or as the parallel passage has it, "he built the city round about, and from the Millo round about" (1 Chr. xi. 8). Its repair or restoration was one of the great works for which Solomon raised his "levy" (1 K. ix. 15, 24, xi. 27); and it formed a prominent part of the fortifications by which Hezekiah prepared for the approach of the Assyrians (2 Chr. xxxii. 5). The last passage seems to show that "the Millo" was part of the "city of David," that is of Zion, a conclusion which is certainly supported by the singular passage, 2 K. xii. 20, where, whichever view we take of Silla, the "house of Millo" must be in the neighborhood of the Tyropœon valley which lay at the foot of Zion. More than this it seems impossible to gather from the notices quoted above — all the passages in which the name is found in the O. T.

If "Millo" be taken as a Hebrew word, it would be derived from a root which has the force of "filling" (see Gesenius, *Thes.* pp. 787, 789). This notion has been applied by the interpreters after their custom in the most various and opposite ways: a rampart (*agger*); a mound; an open space used for assemblies, and therefore often filled with people; a ditch or valley; even a trench filled with water. It has led the writers of the Targums to render Millo by מְלֵירָא, *i. e. Millêtha*, the term by which in other passages they express the Hebrew, כֹּלְלָה, *sol'lah*, the mound which in ancient warfare was used to besiege a town. But unfortunately none of these guesses enable us to ascertain what Millo really was, and it would prob-

ably be nearer the truth — it is certainly safer — to look on the name as an ancient or archaic term, Jebusite, or possibly even still older, adopted by the Israelites when they took the town, and incorporated into their own nomenclature.[a] That it was an ante-Hebraic term is supported by its occurrence in connection with Shechem, so eminently a Canaanite place. (See the next article.) The only ray of light which we can obtain is from the LXX. Their rendering in every case (excepting[b] only 2 Chr. xxxii. 5) is ἡ ἄκρα, a word which they employ nowhere else in the O. T. Now ἡ ἄκρα means "the citadel," and it is remarkable that it is the word used with unvarying persistence throughout the Books of Maccabees for the fortress on Mount Zion, which was occupied throughout the struggle by the adherents of Antiochus, and was at last razed and the very hill leveled by Simon.[c] [JERUSALEM, vol. ii. pp. 1293 f. 1295, &c.] It is therefore perhaps not too much to assume that the word *millo* was employed in the Hebrew original of 1 Maccabees. The point is exceedingly obscure, and the above is at the best little more than mere conjecture, though it agrees so far with the slight indications of 2 Chr. xxxii. 5, as noticed already.   G.

MILLO, THE HOUSE OF. 1. (בֵּית מִלֹּא: οἶκος Βηθμααλό [Vat.-αλων and αλλων]; Alex. οικος Μααλλων: *urbs Mello; oppidum Mello.*) Apparently a family or clan, mentioned in Judg. ix. 6, 20 only, in connection with the men or lords of Shechem, and concerned with them in the affair of Abimelech. No clew is given by the original or any of the versions as to the meaning of the name.

2. (בֵּ מִלֹּא: οἶκος Μαλλό; [Vat. Alex. Μααλω:] *domus Mello.*) The "house of Millo that goeth down to Silla" was the spot at which king Joash was murdered by his slaves (2 K. xii. 20). There is nothing to lead us to suppose that the murder was not committed in Jerusalem, and in that case the spot must be connected with the ancient Millo (see preceding article). Two explanations have been suggested of the name SILLA. These will be discussed more fully under that head, but whichever is adopted would equally place Beth Millo in or near the Tyropœon, taking that to be where it is shown in the plan of Jerusalem, at vol. ii. p. 1312. More than this can hardly be said on the subject in the present state of our knowledge.   G.

MINES, MINING. "Surely there is a source for the *silver*, and a place for the *gold* which they refine. *Iron* is taken out of the soil, and stone man melts (for) copper. He hath put an end to darkness, and to all perfection (*i. e.*, most thoroughly) he searcheth the stone of thick darkness and of the shadow of death. He hath sunk a shaft far from the wanderer; they that are forgotten of the foot are suspended, away from man they waver to and fro. (As for) the earth, from her cometh forth bread, yet her nethermost parts are upturned as (by) fire. The place of sapphire (are) her stones, and dust of gold is his. A track which the bird of prey hath not known, nor the

---

eye of the falcon glared upon; which the sons of pride (i. e. wild beasts) have not trodden, nor the roaring lion gone over; in the flint man hath thrust his hand, he hath overturned mountains from the root; in the rocks he hath cleft channels,[a] and every rare thing hath his eye seen: the streams hath he bound that they weep not, and that which is hid he bringeth forth to light" (Job xxviii. 1–11). Such is the highly poetical description given by the author of the book of Job of the operations of mining as known in his day, the only record of the kind which we inherit from the ancient Hebrews. The question of the date of the book cannot be much influenced by it; for indications of a very advanced state of metallurgical knowledge are found in the monuments of the Egyptians at a period at least as early as any which would be claimed for the author. Leaving this point to be settled independently, therefore, it remains to be seen what is implied in the words of the poem.

It may be fairly inferred from the description that a distinction is made between gold obtained in the manner indicated, and that which is found in the natural state in the alluvial soil, among the débris washed down by the torrents. This appears to be implied in the expression "the gold they refine," which presupposes a process by which the pure gold is extracted from the ore, and separated from the silver or copper with which it may have been mixed. What is said of gold may be equally applied to silver, for in almost every allusion to the process of refining the two metals are associated. In the passage of Job which has been quoted, so far as can be made out from the obscurities with which it is beset, the natural order of mining operations is observed in the description. The whole point is obviously contained in the contrast, "Surely there is a source for the silver, and a place for the gold which men refine, — but where shall wisdom be found, and where is the place of understanding?" No labor is too great for extorting from the earth its treasures. The shaft is sunk, and the adventurous miner, far from the haunts of men, hangs in mid-air (v. 4): the bowels of the earth — which in the course of nature grows but corn — are overthrown as though wasted by fire. The path which the miner pursues in his underground course is unseen by the keen eye of the falcon, nor have the boldest beasts of prey traversed it, but man wins his way through every obstacle, hews out tunnels in the rock, stops the water from flooding his mine, and brings to light the precious metals as the reward of his adventure. No description could be more complete. The poet might have had before him the copper mines of the Sinaitic peninsula. In the Wady Maghârah, "the valley of the Cave," are still traces of the Egyptian colony of miners who settled there for the purpose of extracting copper from the freestone rocks, and left their hieroglyphic inscriptions upon the face of the cliff. That these inscriptions are of great antiquity there can be little doubt, though Lepsius may not be justified in placing them at a date B. C. 4000. "Already, under the fourth dynasty of Manetho," he says, "the same which erected the great pyramids of Gizeh, 4000 B. C., copper mines had been discovered in this desert, which were worked by a colony. The peninsula was then

inhabited by Asiatic, probably Semitic races; therefore do we often see in those rock sculptures the triumphs of Pharaoh over the enemies of Egypt. Almost all the inscriptions belong to the Old Empire, only one was found of the co-regency of Tuthmosis III. and his sister" (Letters from Egypt, p. 346, Eng. tr.). In the Maghârah tablets Mr. Drew (Scripture Lands, p. 50, note) "saw the cartouche of Suphis, the builder of the Great Pyramid, and on the stones at Sûrâbit el Khâdim there are those of kings of the eighteenth and nineteenth dynasties." But the most interesting description of this mining colony is to be found in a letter to the Athenæum (June 4, 1859, No. 1649, p. 747), signed M. Δ. and dated from "Sarabut el Khadem, in the Desert of Sinai, May, 1859." The writer discovered on the mountain exactly opposite the caves of Maghârah, traces of an ancient fortress intended, as he conjectures, for the protection of the miners. The hill on which it stands is about 1000 feet high, nearly insulated, and formed of a series of precipitous terraces, one above the other, like the steps of the pyramids. The uppermost of these was entirely surrounded by a strong wall within which were found remains of 140 houses, each about ten feet square. There were, besides, the remains of ancient hammers of green porphyry, and reservoirs "so disposed that when one was full the surplus ran into the other, and so in succession, so that they must have had water enough to last for years." The ancient furnaces are still to be seen, and on the coast of the Red Sea are found the piers and wharves whence the miners shipped their metal in the harbor of Abu Zelimeh. Five miles from Sarabut el Khadem the same traveller found the ruins of a much greater number of houses, indicating the existence of a large mining population, and, besides, five immense reservoirs formed by damming up various wadies. Other mines appear to have been discovered by Dr. Wilson in the granite mountains east of the Wady Mokatteb. In the Wady Nasb the German traveller Rüppell, who was commissioned by Mohammed Ali, the Viceroy of Egypt, to examine the state of the mines there, met with remains of several large smelting furnaces, surrounded by heaps of slag. The ancient inhabitants had sunk shafts in several directions, leaving here and there columns to prevent the whole from falling in. In one of the mines he saw huge masses of stone rich in copper (Ritter, Erdkunde, xiii. 786). The copper mines of Phæno in Idumæa, according to Jerome, were between Zoar and Petra: in the persecution of Diocletian the Christians were condemned to work them.

The gold mines of Egypt in the Bishâree desert, the principal station of which was Eshuranib, about three days' journey beyond Wady Allaga, have been discovered within the last few years by M. Linant and Mr. Bonomi, the latter of whom supplied Sir G. Wilkinson with a description of them, which he quotes (Anc. Eg. iii. 229, 230). Ruins of the miners' huts still remain as at Surâbit el-Khâdim. "In those nearest the mines lived the workmen who were employed to break the quartz into small fragments, the size of a bean, from whose hands the pounded stone passed to the persons who ground it in hand-mills, similar to those

---

been a technical term among the Egyptian miners of the Sinaitic peninsula.

now used for corn in the valley of the Nile made of granitic stone; one of which is to be found in almost every house at these mines, either entire or broken. The quartz thus reduced to powder was washed on inclined tables, furnished with two cisterns, all built of fragments of stone collected there; and near these inclined planes are generally found little white mounds, the residue of the operation." According to the account given by Diodorus Siculus (iii. 12-14), the mines were worked by gangs of convicts and captives in fetters, who were kept day and night to their task by the soldiers set to guard them. The work was superintended by an engineer, who selected the stone and pointed it out to the miners. The harder rock was split by the application of fire, but the softer was broken up with picks and chisels. The miners were quite naked, their bodies being painted according to the color of the rock they were working, and in order to see in the dark passages of the mine they carried lamps upon their heads. The stone as it fell was carried off by boys, it was then pounded in stone mortars with iron pestles by those who were over 30 years of age till it was reduced to the size of a lentil. The women and old men afterwards ground it in mills to a fine powder. The final process of separating the gold from the pounded stone was entrusted to the engineers who superintended the work. They spread this powder upon a broad slightly inclined table, and rubbed it gently with the hand, pouring water upon it from time to time so as to carry away all the earthy matter, leaving the heavier particles upon the board. This was repeated several times; at first with the hand and afterwards with fine sponges gently pressed upon the earthy substance, till nothing but the gold was left. It was then collected by other workmen, and placed in earthen crucibles with a mixture of lead and salt in certain proportions, together with a little tin and some barley bran. The crucibles were covered and carefully closed with clay, and in this condition baked in a furnace for five days and nights without intermission. Of the three methods which have been employed for refining gold and silver, 1, by exposing the fused metal to a current of air; 2, by keeping the alloy in a state of fusion and throwing nitre upon it; and 3, by mixing the alloy with lead, exposing the whole to fusion upon a vessel of bone-ashes or earth, and blowing upon it with bellows or other blast; the latter appears most nearly to coincide with the description of Diodorus. To this process, known as the cupelling process [LEAD], there seems to be a reference in Ps. xii. 6; Jer. vi. 28-30; Ez. xxii. 18-22, and from it Mr. Napier (Met. of the Bible, p. 24) deduces a striking illustration of Mal. iii. 2, 3, " he shall sit as a refiner and purifier of silver," etc. " When the alloy is melted . . . upon a cupell, and the air blown upon it, the surface of the melted metals has a deep orange-red color, with a kind of flickering wave constantly passing over the surface . . . As the process proceeds the heat is increased . . . and in a little the color of the fused metal becomes lighter. . . . At this stage the refiner watches the operation, either standing or sitting, with the greatest earnestness, until all the orange color and shading disappears, and the metal has the appearance of a highly-polished mirror, reflecting every object around it; even the refiner, as he looks upon the mass of metal, may see himself as in a looking-glass, and thus he can form a very correct judgment respecting the purity of the metal. If he is satisfied, the fire is withdrawn, and the metal removed from the furnace; but if not considered pure more lead is added and the process repeated."

Silver mines are mentioned by Diodorus (i. 33) with those of gold, iron, and copper, in the island of Meroe, at the mouth of the Nile. But the chief supply of silver in the ancient world appears to have been brought from Spain. The mines of that country were celebrated (1 Macc. viii. 3). Mt. Orospeda, from which the Guadalquivir, the ancient Baltes, takes its rise, was formerly called " the silver mountain," from the silver-mines which were in it (Strabo, iii. p. 148). Tartessus, according to Strabo, was an ancient name of the river, which gave its name to the town which was built between its two mouths. But the largest silver-mines in Spain were in the neighborhood of Carthago Nova, from which, in the time of Polybius, the Roman government received 25,000 drachmæ daily. These, when Strabo wrote, had fallen into private hands, though most of the gold-mines were public property (iii. p. 148). Near Castulo there were lead-mines containing silver, but in quantities so small as not to repay the cost of working. The process of separating the silver from the lead is abridged by Strabo from Polybius. The lumps of ore were first pounded, and then sifted through sieves into water. The sediment was again pounded, and again filtered, and after this process had been repeated five times the water was drawn off, the remainder of the ore melted, the lead poured away and the silver left pure. If Tartessus be the Tarshish of Scripture, the metal workers of Spain in those days must have possessed the art of hammering silver into sheets, for we find in Jer. x. 9, " silver spread into plates is brought from Tarshish, and gold from Uphas."

We have no means of knowing whether the gold of Ophir was obtained from mines or from the washing of gold-streams.[a] Pliny (vi. 32), from Juba, describes the litlus Hammæum on the Persian Gulf as a place where gold-mines existed, and in the same chapter alludes to the gold-mines of the Sabæans. But in all probability the greater part of the gold which came into the hands of the Phœnicians and Hebrews was obtained from streams; its great abundance seems to indicate this. At a very early period Jericho was a centre of commerce with the East, and in the narrative of its capture we meet with gold in the form of ingots (Josh. vii. 21, A. V. " wedge," lit. " tongue "),[b] in which it was probably cast for the convenience of traffic. That which Achan took weighed 25 oz.

As gold is seldom if ever found entirely free from silver, the quantity of the latter varying from 2 per cent. to 30 per cent., it has been supposed that the ancient metallurgists were acquainted with some means of parting them, an operation performed in modern times by boiling the metal in nitric or

---

a The Hebrew בֶּצֶר, betser (Job xxii. 24, 25), or בְּצַר btsâr (Job xxxvi. 19), which is rendered gold " in the A. V., and is mentioned in the first-

quoted passage in connection with Ophir, is believed to signify gold and silver ore.
b Compare the Fr. lingot, which is from Lat. lingua, and is said to be the origin of ingot.

sulphuric acid. To some process of this kind it has been imagined that reference is made in Prov. xvii. 3, " The *fining-pot* is for silver, and the *furnace* for gold; " and again in xxvii. 21. " If, for example," says Mr. Napier, " the term *fining-pot* could refer to the vessel or pot in which the silver is dissolved from the gold in parting, as it may be called with propriety, then these passages have a meaning in our modern practice " (*Met. of the Bible*, p. 28); but he admits this is at best but plausible, and considers that " the constant reference to certain qualities and kinds of gold in Scripture is a kind of presumptive proof that they were not in the habit of perfectly purifying or separating the gold from the silver."

A strong proof of the acquaintance possessed by the ancient Hebrews with the manipulation of metals is found by some in the destruction of the golden calf in the desert by Moses. " And he took the calf which they had made, and burnt it in fire, and ground it to powder, and strawed it upon the water, and made the children of Israel drink " (Ex. xxxii. 20). As the highly malleable character of gold would render an operation like that which is described in the text almost impossible, an explanation has been sought in the supposition that we have here an indication that Moses was a proficient in the process known in modern times as calcination. The object of calcination being to oxidize the metal subjected to the process, and gold not being affected by this treatment, the explanation cannot be admitted. M. Goguet (quoted in Wilkinson's *Anc. Eg.* iii. 221) confidently asserts that the problem has been solved by the discovery of an experienced chemist that " in the place of tartaric acid, which we employ, the Hebrew legislator used natron, which is common in the East." The gold so reduced and made into a draught is further said to have a most detestable taste. Goguet's solution appears to have been adopted without examination by more modern writers, but Mr. Napier ventured to question its correctness, and endeavored to trace it to its source. The only clew which he found was in a discovery by Stahl, a chemist of the 17th century, " that if 1 part gold, 3 parts potash, and 3 parts sulphur are heated together, a compound is formed which is partly soluble in water. If," he adds, " this be the discovery referred to, which I think very probable,[a] it certainly has been made the most of by Biblical critics " (*Met. of the Bible*, p. 49). The whole difficulty appears to have arisen from a desire to find too much in the text. The main object of the destruction of the calf was to prove its worthlessness and to throw contempt upon idolatry, and all this might have been done without any refined chemical process like that referred to. The calf was first heated in the fire to destroy its shape, then beaten and broken up by hammering or filing into small pieces, which were thrown into the water, of which the people were made to drink as a symbolical act. " Moses threw the atoms into the water as an emblem of the perfect annihilation of the calf, and he gave the Israelites that water to drink, not only to impress upon them the abomination and despicable character of the image which they had made. but as a symbol of purification, to remove the object of the transgression by those

very persons who had committed it " (Dr. Kalisch, *Comm. on Ex.* xxxii. 20).

How far the ancient Hebrews were acquainted with the processes at present in use for extracting copper from the ore it is impossible to assert, as there are no references in Scripture to anything of the kind, except in the passage of Job already quoted. Copper smelting, however, is in some cases attended with comparatively small difficulties. which the ancients had evidently the skill to overcome. Ore composed of copper and oxygen, mixed with coal and burnt to a bright red heat, leaves the copper in the metallic state, and the same result will follow if the process be applied to the carbonates and sulphurets of copper. Some means of toughening the metal so as to render it fit for manufacture must have been known to the Hebrews as to other ancient nations. The Egyptians evidently possessed the art of working bronze in great perfection at a very early time, and much of the knowledge of metals which the Israelites had must have been acquired during their residence among them.

Of tin there appears to have been no trace in Palestine. That the Phœnicians obtained their supplies from the mines of Spain and Cornwall there can be no doubt, and it is suggested that even the Egyptians may have procured it from the same source, either directly or through the medium of the former. It was found among the possessions of the Midianites, to whom it might have come in the course of traffic; but in other instances in which allusion is made to it, tin occurs in conjunction with other metals in the form of an alloy. The lead mines of Gebel e' Rossass, near the coast of the Red Sea, about half way between Berenice and Kossayr (Wilkinson, *Handb. for Egypt*, p. 403), may have supplied the Hebrews with that metal, of which there were no mines in their own country, or it may have been obtained from the rocks in the neighborhood of Sinai. The hills of Palestine are rich in iron, and the mines are still worked there [METALS] though in a very simple rude manner, like that of the ancient Samothracians: of the method employed by the Egyptians and Hebrews we have no certain information. It may have been similar to that in use throughout the whole of India from very early times, which is thus described by Dr. Ure (*Dict. of Arts*, etc., art. *Steel*). " The furnace or bloomery in which the ore is smelted is from four to five feet high; it is somewhat pear-shaped, being about five feet wide at bottom and one foot at top. It is built entirely of clay . . . . There is an opening in front about a foot or more in height, which is built up with clay at the commencement and broken down at the end of each smelting operation. The bellows are usually made of a goat's skin . . . . The bamboo nozzles of the bellows are inserted into tubes of clay, which pass into the furnace . . . . The furnace is filled with charcoal, and a lighted coal being introduced before the nozzles, the mass in the interior is soon kindled. As soon as this is accomplished, a small portion of the ore, previously molstened with water to prevent it from running through the charcoal, but without any flux whatever, is laid on the top of the coals and covered with charcoal to fill up the fur-

a This uncertainty might have been at once removed by a reference to Goguet's *Origine des Lois*, etc. (li. 1, 2, c. 4), where Stahl (*Vitulus aureus*; *Opusc.*

chym. phys. med. p. 585) is quoted as the authority for the statement.

ace. In this manner ore and fuel are supplied, and the bellows are urged for three or four hours. When the process is stopped and the temporary wall in front broken down, the bloom is removed with a pair of tongs from the bottom of the furnace."

It has seemed necessary to give this account of a very ancient method of iron smelting, because, from the difficulties which attend it, and the intense heat which is required to separate the metal from the ore, it has been asserted that the allusions to iron and iron manufacture in the Old Testament are anachronisms. But if it were possible among the ancient Indians in a very primitive state of civilization, it might have been known to the Hebrews, who may have acquired their knowledge by working as slaves in the iron furnaces of Egypt (comp. Deut. iv. 20).

The question of the early use of iron among the Egyptians, is fully disposed of in the following remarks of Sir Gardner Wilkinson (*Ancient Egyptians*, ii. pp. 154–156) : —

"In the infancy of the arts and sciences, the difficulty of working iron might long withhold the secret of its superiority over copper and bronze; but it cannot reasonably be supposed that a nation so advanced, and so eminently skilled in the art of working metals as the Egyptians and Sidonians, should have remained ignorant of its use, even if we had no evidence of its having been known to the Greeks and other people; and the constant employment of bronze arms and implements is not a sufficient argument against their knowledge of iron, since we find the Greeks and Romans made the same things of bronze long after the period when iron was universally known. . . . . To conclude, from the want of iron instruments, or arms, bearing the names of early monarchs of a Pharaonic age, that bronze was alone used is neither just nor satisfactory; since the decomposition of that metal, especially when buried for ages in the nitrous soil of Egypt, is so speedy as to preclude the possibility of its preservation. Until we know in what manner the Egyptians employed bronze tools for cutting stone, the discovery of them affords no additional light, nor even argument; since the Greeks and Romans continued to make bronze instruments of various kinds so long after iron was known to them; and Herodotus mentions the iron tools used by the builders of the Pyramids. Iron and copper mines are found in the Egyptian desert, which were worked in old times; and the monuments of Thebes, and even the tombs about Memphis, dating more than 4000 years ago, represent butchers sharpening their knives on a round bar of metal attached to their apron, which from its blue color can only be steel; and the distinction between the bronze and iron weapons in the tomb of Remeses III., one painted red, the other blue, leaves no doubt of *both* having been used (as in Rome) at the same periods. In Ethiopia iron was much more abundant than in Egypt, and Herodotus states that copper was a rare metal there; though we may doubt his assertion of prisoners in that country having been bound with fetters of gold. The speedy decomposition of iron

would be sufficient to prevent our finding implements of that metal of an early period, and the greater opportunities of obtaining copper ore, added to the facility of working it, might be a reason for preferring the latter whenever it answered the purpose instead of iron." [IRON, Amer. ed.]

W. A. W.

MINGLED PEOPLE. This phrase (עֶרֶב, *hā'ereb*), like that of "the mixed multitude," which the Hebrew closely resembles, is applied in Jer. xxv. 20, and Ez. xxx. 5, to denote the miscellaneous foreign population of Egypt and its frontier-tribes, including every one, says Jerome, who was not a native Egyptian, but was resident there. The Targum of Jonathan understands it in this passage as well as in Jer. l. 37, of the foreign mercenaries, though in Jer. xxv. 24, where the word again occurs, it is rendered "Arabs." It is difficult to attach to it any precise meaning, or to identify with the mingled people any race of which we have knowledge. "The kings of the mingled people that dwell in the desert" [a] are the same apparently as the tributary kings (A. V. "kings of Arabia") who brought presents to Solomon (1 K. x. 15); [b] the Hebrew in the two cases is identical. These have been explained (as in the Targum on 1 K. x. 15) as foreign mercenary chiefs who were in the pay of Solomon, but Thenius understands by them the sheykhs of the border tribes of Bedouins, living in Arabia Deserta, who were closely connected with the Israelites. The "mingled people" in the midst of Babylon (Jer. l. 37) were probably the foreign soldiers or mercenary troops, who lived among the native population, as the Targum takes it. Kimchi compares Ex. xii. 38, and explains *hā'ereb* of the foreign population of Babylon [c] generally, "foreigners who were in Babylon from several lands," or it may, he says, be intended to denote the merchants, *'ereb* being thus connected with the עֹרְבֵי מַעֲרָבֵךְ, *'ōrĕbê ma'ărābēc*, of Ez. xxvii. 27, rendered in the A. V. "the occupiers of thy merchandise." His first interpretation is based upon what appears to be the primary signification of the root עָרַב, *'ărab*, to mingle, while another meaning, "to pledge, guarantee," suggested the rendering of the Targum "mercenaries," [d] which Jarchi adopts in his explanation of "the kings of *hā'ereb*," in 1 K. x. 15, as the kings who were pledged to Solomon and dependent upon him. The equivalent which he gives is apparently intended to represent the Fr. *garantie*.

The rendering of the A. V. is supported by the LXX. σύμμικτος in Jer., and ἐπίμικτος in Ezekiel.

W. A. W.

MINIAMIN (מִנְיָמִין [*on the right*, or *son of the right hand*]: Βενιαμίν; [Vat.] Alex. Βαιαμειν: *Benjamin*). 1. One of the Levites in the reign of Hezekiah appointed to the charge of the freewill offerings of the people in the cities of the priests, and to distribute them to their brethren (2 Chr. xxxi. 15). The reading "Benjamin" of

---

a Kimchi observes that these are distinguished from the mingled people mentioned in ver. 20 by the addition, "that dwell in the desert."

b In the parallel passage of 2 Chr. ix. 14 the reading

c The same commentator refers the expression in Is. xiii. 14, "they shall every man turn to his own people," to the dispersion of the mixed population of Babylon at its capture.

e עֶרֶב, *'ereb*, or Arabia.

d גרנטיאה

the LXX. and Vulg. is followed by the Peshito Syriac.

2. (Μιαμίν; [Vat. Alex. FA.[1] omit; FA.[3] Βερ.αμειν:] *Mi.min.*) The same as MIAMIN 2 and MIJAMIN 2 (Neh. xii. 17).

3. ([Ald.] Βενιαμίν; [Rom. Vat. Alex. FA.[1] omit; FA.[3]] Βενιαμειν; [Comp. Μιαμίν.]) One of the priests who blew the trumpets at the dedication of the wall of Jerusalem (Neh. xii. 41).

* **MINISH** occurs (Ex. v. 19; Ps. cvii. 39) in the sense of our present "lessen " or "diminish." It comes from the Latin *minuere* through the old French *menuiser.* It now appears only as "diminish," which has taken its place. The old form is found in Wycliffe's translation of John iii. 30: "It behoveth him for to waxe, forsoth me to be *menusid,* or maad lesse."   H.

MIN'NI (מִנִּי: *Menni*), a country mentioned in connection with Ararat and Ashchenaz (Jer. li. 27). The LXX. erroneously renders it παρ' ἐμοῦ. It has been already noticed as a portion of Armenia. [ARMENIA.] The name may be connected with the *Minyas* noticed by Nicolaus of Damascus (Joseph. *Ant.* i. 3, § 6), with the *Minnai* of the Assyrian inscriptions, whom Rawlinson (*Herod.* i. 464) places about lake *Urumiyeh,* and with the *Minuas* who appears in the list of Armenian kings in the inscription at *Wan* (Layard's *Nin. and Bab.* p. 401). At the time when Jeremiah prophesied, Armenia had been subdued by the Median kings (*Herod.* i. 103, 177).   W. L. B.

MINISTER. This term is used in the A. V. to describe various officials of a religious and civil character. In the O. T. it answers to the Hebrew *meshâreth,*[a] which is applied (1), to an attendant upon a person of high rank, as to Joshua in relation to Moses (Ex. xxiv. 13; Josh. i. 1), and to the attendant on the prophet Elisha (2 K. iv. 43); (2) to the *attachés* of a royal court (1 K. x. 5, where, it may be observed, they are distinguished from the "servants " or officials of higher rank, answering to our *ministers,* by the different titles of the chambers assigned to their use, the "sitting " of the servants meaning rather their *abode,* and the "attendance " of the ministers the ante-room in which they were stationed); persons of high rank held this post in the Jewish kingdom (2 Chron. xxii. 8); and it may be in this sense, as the attendants of the King of Kings, that the term is applied to the angels (Ps. civ. 4); (3) to the Priests and Levites, who are thus described by the prophets and later historians (Is. lxi. 6; Ez. xliv. 11; Joel i. 9, 13; Ezr. viii. 17; Neh. x. 36), though the verb, whence *meshâreth* is derived, is not uncommonly used in reference to their services in the earlier books (Ex. xxviii. 43; Num. iii. 31; Deut. xviii. 5, *al.*). In the N. T. we have three terms each with its distinctive meaning — λειτουργός, ὑπηρέτης, and διάκονος. The first answers most nearly to the Hebrew *meshâreth* and is usually employed in the LXX. as its equivalent. It betokens a subordinate public administrator, whether civil or sacerdotal,

and is applied in the former sense to the magistrates in their relation to the Divine authority (Rom. xiii. 6), and in the latter sense to our Lord in relation to the Father (Heb. viii. 2), and to St. Paul in relation to Jesus Christ (Rom. xv. 16), where it occurs among other expressions of a sacerdotal character, "ministering " (ἱερουργοῦντα), "offering up " (προσφορά, etc.). In all these instances the original and special meaning of the word, as used by the Athenians,[b] is preserved, though this comes, perhaps, yet more distinctly forward in the cognate terms λειτουργία and λειτουργεῖν, applied to the sacerdotal office of the Jewish priest (Luke i. 23; Heb. ix. 21, x. 11), to the still higher priesthood of Christ (Heb viii. 6), and in a secondary sense to the Christian priest who offers up to God the faith of his converts (Phil. ii. 17, λειτουργία τῆς πίστεως), and to any act of public self devotion on the part of a Christian disciple (Rom. xv. 27; 2 Cor. ix. 12; Phil. ii. 30). The second term, ὑπηρέτης, differs from the two others in that it contains the idea of actual and personal attendance upon a superior. Thus it is used of the attendant in the synagogue, the *khazan*[c] of the Talmudists (Luke iv. 20), whose duty it was to open and close the building, to produce and replace the books employed in the service, and generally to wait on the officiating priest or teacher[d] (Carpzov, *Apparat.* p. 314). It is similarly applied to Mark, who, as the attendant on Barnabas and Saul (Acts xiii. 5), was probably charged with the administration of baptism and other assistant duties (De Wette, *in loc.*); and again to the subordinates of the high-priests (John vii. 32, 45, xviii. 3, *al.*), or of a jailer (Matt. v. 25 = πράκτωρ in Luke xii. 58; Acts v. 22). The idea of *personal attendance* comes prominently forward in Luke i. 2; Acts xxvi. 16, in both of which places it is alleged as a ground of trustworthy testimony (ipsi *viderunt,* et, quod plus est, *ministrarunt,* Bengel). Lastly, it is used interchangeably with διάκονος in 1 Cor. iv. 1 compared with iii. 5, but in this instance the term is designed to convey the notion of subordination and humility. In all these cases the etymological sense of the word (ὑπό, ἐρέτ,ς, literally a "*sub-rower,*" one who rows under command of the steersman) comes out. The term that most adequately represents it in our language is "attendant." The third term, διάκονος, is the one usually employed in relation to the ministry of the Gospel : its application is twofold, in a general sense to indicate ministers of any order, whether superior or inferior, and in a special sense to indicate an order of inferior ministers. In the former sense we have the cognate term διακονία applied in Acts vi. 1, 4, both to the ministration of tables and to the higher ministration of the word, and the term διάκονος itself applied, without defining the office, to Paul and Apollos (1 Cor. iii. 5), to Tychicus (Eph. vi. 21; Col. iv. 7), to Epaphras (Col. i. 7), to Timothy (1 Thes. iii. 2), and even to Christ himself (Rom. xv. 8; Gal. ii. 17). In the latter sense it is applied in the passages where the διάκονος is contradistinguished from the Bishop, as

---

[a] מְשָׁרֵת.

[b] The term is derived from λεῖτον ἔργον, "public work," and the *leitourgia* was the name of certain personal services which the citizens of Athens and some other states had to perform gratuitously for the public good. From the sacerdotal use of the word in the N. T., it obtained the special sense of a "public divine service," which is perpetuated in our word "liturgy."

[c] חָזָן.

[d] The ὑπηρέτης of ecclesiastical history occupied precisely the same position in the Christian Church that the *khazan* did in the synagogue: in Latin he was styled *sub-diaconus,* or sub-deacon (Bingham, *Ant.* iii. 2).

The verb λειτουργεῖν is used in this sense in Acts xiii. 2.

to Phil. i. 1; 1 Tim. iii. 8–13. It is, perhaps, worthy of observation that the word is of very rare occurrence in the LXX. (Esth. i. 10, ii. 2, vi. 3), and then only in a general sense: its special sense, as known to us in its derivative "deacon," seems to be of purely Christian growth. [DEACON.]   W. L. B.

MIN'NITH (מִנִּית [perh. given, allotted]: ἄχρις Ἀρνών; Alex. εἰς Σεμωειθ; [a] Joseph. πόλις Μαλιάθης: Pesh. Syriac, Machir: Vulg. Mennith), a place on the east of the Jordan, named as the point to which Jephthah's slaughter of the Ammonites extended (Judg. xi. 33). "From Aroer to the approach to Minnith" (עַד בּוֹאֲךָ מ) seems to have been a district containing twenty cities. Minnith was in the neighborhood of Abel-Ceramim, the "meadow of vineyards." Both places are mentioned in the Onomasticon — "Mennith" or "Maanith" as 4 miles from Heshbon, on the road to Philadelphia (Ammân), and Abel as 6 or 7 miles from the latter, but in what direction is not stated. A site bearing the name Menjah is marked in Van de Velde's Map, perhaps on the authority of Buckingham, at 7 Roman miles east of Heshbon on a road to Ammân, though not on the frequented track. But we must await further investigation of these interesting regions before we can pronounce for or against its identity with Minnith.

The variations of the ancient versions as given above are remarkable, but they have not suggested anything to the writer. Schwarz proposes to find Minnith in MAGED, a trans-Jordanic town named in the Maccabees, by the change of ג to ב. An episcopal city of "Palestina secunda," named Mennith, is quoted by Reland (Palæstina, p. 211), but with some question as to its being located in this direction (comp. 209).

The "wheat of Minnith " is mentioned in Ez. xxvii. 17, as being supplied by Judah and Israel to Tyre; but there is nothing to indicate that the same place is intended, and indeed the word is thought by some not to be a proper name. Philistia and Sharon were the great corn-growing districts of Palestine — but there were in these eastern regions also " fat of kidneys of wheat, and wine of the pure blood of the grape " (Deut. xxxii. 14). Of that cultivation Minnith and Abel-Ceramim may have been the chief seats.

In this neighborhood were possibly situated the vineyards in which Balaam encountered the angel on his road from Mesopotamia to Moab (Num. xxii. 24).   G.

MINSTREL. The Hebrew word in 2 K. iii. 15 (מְנַגֵּן, menaggén) properly signifies a player upon a stringed instrument like the harp or kinnor [HARP], whatever its precise character may have been, on which David played before Saul (1 Sam. xvi. 16, xviii. 10, xix. 9), and which the harlots of the great cities used to carry with them as they walked to attract notice (Is. xxiii. 16). The passage in which it occurs has given rise to much conjecture; Elisha, upon being consulted by Jehoram as to the issue of the war with Moab, at first indignantly refuses to answer, and is only induced to do so by the presence of Jehoshaphat. He calls for

a harper, apparently a camp follower (one of the Levites according to Procopius of Gaza),[b] " And now bring me a harper; and it came to pass as the harper harped that the hand of Jehovah was on him." Other instances of the same divine influence, or impulse connected with music, are seen in the case of Saul and the young prophets in 1 Sam. x. 5, 6, 10, 11. In the present passage the reason of Elisha's appeal is variously explained. Jarchi says that " on account of anger the Shechinah had departed from him; " Ephrem Syrus, that the object of the music was to attract a crowd to hear the prophecy; J. H. Michaelis, that the prophet's mind, disturbed by the impiety of the Israelites, might be soothed and prepared for divine things by a spiritual song. According to Keil (Comm. on Kings, i. 359, Eng. tr.), " Elisha calls for a minstrel, in order to gather in his thoughts by the soft tones of music from the impression of the outer world, and by repressing the life of self and of the world to be transferred into the state of internal vision by which his spirit would be prepared to receive the Divine revelation." This in effect is the view taken by Josephus (Ant. ix. 3, § 1), and the same is expressed by Maimonides in a passage which embodies the opinion of the Jews of the Middle Ages. " All the prophets were not able to prophesy at any time that they wished; but they prepared their minds, and sat joyful and glad of heart, and abstracted; for prophecy dwelleth not in the midst of melancholy nor in the midst of apathy, but in the midst of joy. Therefore the sons of the prophets had before them a psaltery, and a tabret, and a pipe, and a harp and (thus) sought after prophecy " (or prophetic inspiration), (Yad hachazakah, vii. 5, Bernard's Creed and Ethics of the Jews, p. 16; see also note to p. 114). Kimchi quotes a tradition to the effect that, after the ascension of his master Elijah, the spirit of prophecy had not dwelt upon Elisha because he was mourning, and the spirit of holiness does not dwell but in the midst of joy. In 1 Sam. xviii. 10, on the contrary, there is a remarkable instance of the employment of music to still the excitement consequent upon an attack of frenzy, which in its external manifestations at least so far resembled the rapture with which the old prophets were affected when delivering their prophecies, as to be described by the same term. " And it came to pass on the morrow, that the evil spirit from God came upon Saul, and he prophesied in the midst of the house: and David played with his hand as at other times." Weemse (Christ. Synagogue, ch. vi. § 3, par. 6, p. 143) supposes that the music appropriate to such occasions was " that which the Greeks called ἁρμονίαν, which was the greatest and the saddest, and settled the affections."

The " minstrels " in Matt. ix. 23 were the flute-players who were employed as professional mourners, to whom frequent allusion is made (Eccl. xii. 5; 2 Chr. xxxv. 25; Jer. ix. 17-20), and whose representatives exist in great numbers to this day in the cities of the East. [MOURNING.]

                        W. A. W.

MINT (ἡδύοσμον : mentha) occurs only in Matt. xxiii. 23 and Luke xi. 42, as one of those

---

[a] Ἔως τοῦ ἐλθεῖν εἰς σεμωειθ is the reading of the Alex. Codex, ingeniously corrected by Grabe to ἕως τοῦ ἐλθεῖν εἰς σεμ Μααειθ.

[b] The Targum translates, "and now bring me a

man who knows how to play upon the harp, and "came to pass as the harper harped there rested upon him the spirit of prophecy from before Jehovah."

herbs the tithe of which the Jews were most scrupulously exact in paying. Some commentators have supposed that such herbs as mint, anise (dill), and cummin, were not titheable by law, and that the Pharisees, solely from an overstrained zeal, paid tithes for them; but as dill was subject to tithe (*Maasroth*, cap. iv. § 5), it is most probable that the other herbs mentioned with it were also tithed, and this is fully corroborated by our Lord's own words: "these ought ye to have done." The Pharisees therefore are not censured for paying tithes of things untitheable by law, but for paying more regard to a scrupulous exactness in these minor duties than to important moral obligations.

There cannot be the slightest doubt that the A. V. is correct in the translation of the Greek word, and all the old versions are agreed in understanding some species of mint (*Mentha*) by it. Dioscorides (iii. 36, ed. Sprengel) speaks of ἡδύοσ-μον ἥμερον (*Mentha sativa*); the Greeks used the terms μίνθα, or μίνθη and μίνθος for mint, whence the derivation of the English word; the Romans have *mentha*, *menta*, *mentastrum*. According to Pliny (*H. N.* xix. 8) the old Greek word for mint was μίνθα, which was changed to ἡδύοσμον ("the sweet smelling"), on account of the fragrant prop-

Mentha sylvestris.

erties of this plant. Mint was used by the Greeks and Romans both as a carminative in medicine and a condiment in cookery. Apicius mentions the use of fresh (*viridis*) and dried (*arida*) mint. Compare also Pliny, *H. N.* xix. 8, xx. 14; Dioscor. iii. 36; the *Epityrum* of the Romans had mint as one of its ingredients (Cato, *de Re Rus.* § 120). Martial, Epig. x. 47, speaks of "ructatrix mentha," mint being an excellent carminative. "So amongst the Jews," says Celsius (*Hierob.* i. 547), "the Talmudical writers manifestly declare that mint was used with their food." (Tract. *Shem. Ve Jobel*, ch. vii. § 2, and Tr *Oketzin*, ch. i. § 2; *Sheb.* ch. 7, § 1. Lady Calcott, (*Script. Herb.* p. 280) makes the following ingenious remark : "I know not whether mint was originally one of the bitter herbs with which the Israelites eat the Paschal lamb, but

our use of it with roast lamb, particularly about Easter time, inclines me to suppose it was." The same writer also observes that the modern Jews eat horse-radish and chervil with lamb. The woodcut represents the horse-mint (*M. sylvestris*) which is common in Syria, and according to Russell (*Hist. of Aleppo*, p. 39) found in the gardens at Aleppo; *M. sativa* is generally supposed to be only a variety of *M. arvensis*, another species of mint: perhaps all these were known to the ancients.[a] The mints belong to the large natural order *Labiatæ*.

W. H.

MIPH'KAD, THE GATE (שַׁעַר הַמִּפְקָד) [*gate of the census*, or *of appointment*, Ges.] : πύλη τοῦ Μαφεκάδ: *porta judicialis*), one of the gates of Jerusalem at the time of the rebuilding of the wall after the return from Captivity (Neh. iii. 31). According to the view taken in this work of the topography of the city, this gate was probably not in the wall of Jerusalem proper, but in that of the city of David, or Zion, and somewhere near to the junction of the two on the north side (see vol. ii. p. 1322). The name may refer to some memorable census of the people, as for instance that of David, 2 Sam. xxiv. 9, and 1 Chr. xxi. 5 (in each of which the word used for "number" is *miphkad*), or to the superintendents of some portion of the worship (*Pekidim*, see 2 Chr. xxxi. 13).

G.

MIRACLES. The word "miracle" is the ordinary translation, in our authorized English version, of the Greek σημεῖον. Our translators did not borrow it from the Vulgate (in which *signum* is the customary rendering of σημεῖον), but, apparently, from their English predecessors, Tyndale, Coverdale, etc.; and it had, probably before their time, acquired a fixed technical import in theological language, which is not directly suggested by its etymology. The Latin *miraculum*, from which it is merely accommodated to an English termination, corresponds best with the Greek θαῦμα, and denotes any object of wonder, whether supernatural or not. Thus the "Seven Wonders of the World" were called *miracula*, though they were only miracles of art. It will perhaps be found that the habitual use of the term "miracle" has tended to fix attention too much on the physical *strangeness* of the facts thus described, and to divert attention from what may be called their *signality*. In reality, the practical importance of the *strangeness* of miraculous facts consists in this, that it is one of the circumstances which, taken together, make it reasonable to understand the phenomenon as a mark, seal, or attestation of the Divine sanction to something else. And if we suppose the Divine intention established that a given phenomenon is to be taken as a mark or sign of Divine attestation, theories concerning the *mode* in which that phenomenon was produced become of comparatively little practical value, and are only serviceable as helping our conceptions. In the case of such signs, when they vary from the ordinary course of nature, we may conceive of them as immediately wrought by the authorized intervention of some angelic being merely exerting invisibly his natural powers; or as the result of a provision made in the original scheme of the universe, by

---

a * "There are various species," says Tristram (*Nat. Hist. of the Bible*, p. 471), "wild and cultivated, in Palestine. The common wild mint of the country is

Mentha sylvestris, which grows on all the hills, and is much larger than our garden mint (*Mentha sativa*)."

H.

which such an occurrence was to take place at a given moment; [a] or as the result of the interference of some higher law with subordinate laws; or as a change in the ordinary working of God in that course of events which we call nature; or as a suspension by his immediate power of the action of certain forces which He had originally given to what we call natural agents. These may be hypotheses more or less probable of the mode in which a given phenomenon is to be conceived to have been produced; but if all the circumstances of the case taken together make it reasonable to understand that phenomenon as a Divine sign, it will be of comparatively little practical importance which of them we adopt. Indeed, in many cases, the phenomenon which constitutes a Divine sign may be one not, in itself, at all varying from the known course of nature. This is the common case of prophecy: in which the fulfillment of the prophecy, which constitutes the sign of the prophet's commission, may be the result of ordinary causes, and yet, from being incapable of having been anticipated by human sagacity, it may be an adequate mark or sign of the Divine sanction. In such cases, the miraculous or wonderful element is to be sought not in the fulfillment, but in the prediction. Thus, although we should suppose, for example, that the destruction of Sennacherib's army was accomplished by an ordinary simoom of the desert, called figuratively the Angel of the Lord, it would still be a SIGN of Isaiah's prophetic mission, and of God's care for Jerusalem. And so, in the case of the passage of the Red Sea by the Israelites under Moses, and many other instances. Our Lord's prediction of the destruction of Jerusalem is a clear example of an event brought about in the ordinary course of things, and yet being a sign of the Divine mission of Jesus, and of the just displeasure of God against the Jews.

It would appear, indeed, that in almost all cases of signs or evidential miracles something prophetic is involved. In the common case, for example, of healing sickness by a word or touch, the word or gesture may be regarded as a *prediction* of the cure: and then, if the whole circumstances be such as to exclude just suspicion of (1) a *natural* anticipation of the event, and (2) a casual coincidence, it will be indifferent to the signality of the cure whether we regard it as effected by the operation of ordinary causes, or by an immediate interposition of the Deity reversing the course of nature. Hypotheses by which such cures are attempted to be accounted for by ordinary causes are indeed generally wild, improbable, and arbitrary, and are (on that ground) justly open to objection; but, if the miraculous character of the predictive antecedent be admitted, they do not tend to deprive the phenomenon of its *signality:* and there are minds which, from particular associations, find it easier to conceive a miraculous agency operating in the region of mind, than one operating in the region of matter.

It may be further observed, in passing, that the proof of the actual occurrence of a sign, when in itself an ordinary event, and invested with signality only by a previous prediction, may be, in some respects, better circumstanced than the proof of the occurrence of a miraculous sign. For the prediction and the fulfillment may have occurred at a long distance of time the one from the other, and be attested by separate sets of independent witnesses, of whom the one was ignorant of the fulfillment, and the other ignorant, or incredulous, of the prediction. As each of these sets of witnesses are deposing to what is *to them* a mere ordinary fact, there is no room for suspecting, in the case of those witnesses, any coloring from religious prejudice, or excited feeling, or fraud, or that craving for the marvelous which has notoriously produced many legends. But it must be admitted that it is only *such* sources of suspicion that are excluded in such a case; and that whatever inherent improbability there may be in a fact considered as *miraculous* — or varying from the ordinary course of nature — remains still: so that it would be a mistake to say that the two facts *together* — the prediction and the fulfillment — required no stronger evidence to make them credible than *any two* ordinary facts. This will appear at once from a parallel case. That A B was seen walking in Bond Street, London, on a certain day, and at a certain hour, is a common ordinary fact, credible on very slight evidence. That A B was seen walking in Broadway, New York, on a certain day, and at a certain hour, is, when taken by itself, similarly circumstanced. But if the day and hour assigned in both reports be the same, the case is altered. We conclude, at once, that one or other of our informants was wrong, or both, until convinced of the correctness of their statements by evidence much stronger than would suffice to establish an ordinary fact. This brings us to consider the peculiar improbability supposed to attach to *miraculous* signs, as such.

The peculiar improbability of *Miracles* is resolved by Hume, in his famous Essay, into the circumstance that they are "contrary to experience." This expression is, as has often been pointed out, strictly speaking, incorrect. In strictness, that only can be said to be contrary to experience, which is contradicted by the immediate perceptions of persons present at the time when the fact is alleged to have occurred. Thus, if it be alleged that *all* metals are ponderous, this is an assertion contrary to experience; because daily actual observation shows that the metal potassium is not ponderous. But if any one were to assert that a particular piece of potassium, which we had never seen, was ponderous, our experiments on other pieces of the same metal would not prove his report to be, in the same sense, contrary to our experience, but only contrary to the *analogy* of our experience. In a looser sense, however, the terms "contrary to experience" are extended to this secondary application; and it must be admitted that, in this latter, less strict sense, miracles are contrary to general experience, *so far as their mere physical circumstances, visible to us, are concerned.* This should not only be admitted, but strongly insisted upon, by the maintainers of miracles, because it is an essential element of their *signal* character. It is only the analogy of general experience (necessarily

[a] This is said by Maimonides (*Moreh Nevochim*, part ii. c. 29) to have been the opinion of some of the older Rabbins: "Nam dicunt, quando Deus O. M. esse existentiam creavit, illum tum unicuique enti naturam suam ordinasse et determinasse, illisque na-

turis virtutem indidisse miracula illa producendi: et signum prophetæ nihil aliud esse, quam quod Deus significarit prophetis tempus quo dicere hoc vel illud debeant," etc.

narrow as all human experience is) that convinces us that a word or a touch has no efficacy to cure diseases or still a tempest. And, if it be held that the analogy of daily experience furnishes us with no measure of probability, then the so-called miracles of the Bible will lose the character of marks of the Divine Commission of the workers of them. They will not only become as probable as ordinary events, but they will assume the character of ordinary events. It will be just as credible that they were wrought by enthusiasts or impostors, as by the true Prophets of God, and we shall be compelled to own that the Apostles might as well have appealed to any ordinary event in proof of Christ's mission as to his resurrection from the dead. It is so far, therefore, from being true, that (as has been said with something of a sneer) "religion, *following in the wake of science*, has been *compelled* to acknowledge the government of the universe as being on the whole carried on by general laws, and not by special interpositions," that religion, considered as standing on miraculous evidence, necessarily presupposes a fixed order of nature, and is compelled to assume *that*, not by the discoveries of science, but by the exigency of its own position: and there are few books in which the general constancy of the order of nature is more distinctly recognized than the Bible. The witnesses who report to us miraculous facts are so far from testifying to the absence of general laws, or the instability of the order of nature, that, on the contrary, their whole testimony implies that the miracles which they record were at variance with their own general experience — with the general experience of their contemporaries — with what they believed to have been the general experience of their predecessors, and with what they anticipated would be the general experience of posterity. It is upon the very ground that the apparent *natural* causes, in the cases to which they testify, are known by uniform experience to be incapable of producing the effects said to have taken place, that *therefore* these witnesses refer those events to the intervention of a *supernatural* cause, and speak of these occurrences as Divine Miracles.

And this leads us to notice one grand difference between Divine Miracles and other alleged facts, that seem to vary from the ordinary course of nature. It is manifest that there is an essential difference between alleging a case in which, all the real antecedents or causes being similar to those which we have daily opportunities of observing, a consequence is said to have ensued quite different from that which general experience finds to be uniformly conjoined with them, and alleging a case in which there is supposed and *indicated by all the circumstances*, the intervention of an invisible antecedent, or cause, which we know to exist, and to be adequate to the production of such a result: for the special operation of which, in this case, we can assign probable reasons, and also for its not generally operating in a similar manner. This latter is the case of the Scripture miracles. They are wrought under a solemn appeal to God, in proof of a revelation worthy of Him, the scheme of which may be shown to bear a striking analogy to the constitution and order of nature; and it is manifest that, in order to make them fit *signs* for attesting a revelation, they *ought* to be phenomena capable of being shown by a full induction to vary from what is known to us as the ordinary course of nature.

To this it is sometimes replied that, as we collect the existence of God from the course of nature, we have no right to assign to Him powers and attributes in any higher degree than we find them in the course of nature; and consequently neither the power nor the will to alter it. But such persons must be understood *verbis ponere Deum, re tollere;* because it is impossible really to assign Power, Wisdom, Goodness, etc., to the first cause, as an inference from the course of nature, without attributing to Him the power of making it otherwise. There can be no design, for example, or anything analogous to design, in the Author of the Universe, unless out of other *possible* collocations of things, He *selected* those fit for a certain purpose. And it is, in truth, a violation of all analogy, and an utterly wild and arbitrary chimera, to infer, without the fullest evidence of such a *limitation*, the existence of a Being possessed of such power and intelligence as we see manifested in the course of nature, and yet unable to make one atom of matter move an inch in any other direction than that in which it actually does move.

And even if we do not regard the existence of God (in the proper sense of that term) as proved by the course of nature, still if we admit his existence to be in any degree probable, or even possible, the occurrence of miracles will not be incredible. For it is surely going too far to say, that, because the ordinary course of nature leaves us in doubt whether the author of it be able or unable to alter it, or of such a character as to be disposed to alter it for some great purpose, it is *therefore* incredible that He should ever have actually altered it. The true philosopher, when he considers the narrowness of human experience, will make allowance for the possible existence of many causes not yet observed by man, so as that their operation can be reduced to fixed laws understood by us; and the operation of which, therefore, when it reveals itself, must seem to vary from the ordinary course of things. Otherwise, there could be no new discoveries in physical science itself. It is quite true that such forces as magnetism and electricity are *now* to a great extent reduced to known laws: but it is equally true that no one would have taken the trouble to find out the laws, if he had not *first* believed in the facts. Our knowledge of the law was not the ground of our belief of the fact; but our belief of the fact was that which set us on investigating the law. And it is easy to conceive that there may be forces in nature, unknown to us, the regular periods of the recurrence of whose operations within the sphere of our knowledge (if they ever occur at all) may be immensely distant from each other in time — (as, *e. g.* the causes which produce the appearance or disappearance of stars) — so as that, when they occur, they may seem wholly different from all the rest of man's present or past experience. Upon such a supposition, the *rarity* of the phenomenon should not make it incredible, because such a rarity would be involved in the conditions of its existence. Now this is analogous to the case of miracles. Upon the supposition that there is a God, the immediate volition of the Deity, determined by Wisdom, Goodness, etc., is a VERA CAUSA; because all the phenomena of nature have, on that supposition, such volitions as at least their ultimate antecedents; and that physical effect, whatever it may be, that stands next the Divine volition, is a case of a physical effect having such a volition, so determined, for its immediate antecedent. And as for the unusualness of the way of acting, that is involved in the very conditions of the hypothesis, because this very *unusualness* would be necessary to fit the phenomenon for a miraculous *sign*.

In the foregoing remarks, we have endeavored to avoid all metaphysical discussions of questions concerning the nature of causation — the fundamental principle of induction, and the like; not because they are unimportant, but because they could not be treated of satisfactorily within the limits which the plan of this work prescribes. They are, for the most part, matters of an abstruse kind, and much difficulty; but (fortunately for mankind) questions of great practical moment may generally be settled, for practical purposes, without solving those higher problems — *i. e.* they may be settled on principles which will hold good, whatever solution we may adopt of those abstruse questions. It will be proper, however, to say a few words here upon some popular forms of expression which tend greatly to increase, in many minds, the natural prejudice against miracles. One of these is the usual description of a miracle, as, "a *violation* of the *laws of nature.*" This metaphorical expression suggests directly the idea of natural agents breaking, of their own accord, some rule which has the authority and sanctity of a law to them. Such a figure can only be applicable to the case of a supposed *causeless* and arbitrary variation from the uniform order of sequence in natural things, and is wholly inapplicable to a change in that order caused by God Himself. The word "law," when applied to material things, *ought* only to be understood as denoting a number of observed and anticipated sequences of phenomena, taking place with such a resemblance or analogy to each other *as if* a rule had been laid down, which those phenomena were constantly observing. But the *rule*, in this case, is nothing different from the actual order itself; and there is no cause of these sequences but the will of God choosing to produce those phenomena, and choosing to produce them in a certain order.

Again, the term "nature" suggests to many persons the idea of a great system of things endowed with powers and forces of its own — a sort of machine, set a-going originally by a first cause, but continuing its motions *of itself.* Hence we are apt to imagine that a change in the motion or operation of any part of it by God, would produce the same disturbance of the other parts, as such a change would be likely to produce in them, if made by us, or any other natural agent. But if the motions and operations of material things be produced really by the Divine will, then his choosing to change, for a special purpose, the ordinary motion of one part, does not necessarily, or probably, infer his choosing to change the ordinary motions of other parts in a way not at all requisite for the accomplishment of that special purpose. It is as easy for Him to continue the ordinary course of the rest, with the change of one part, as of all the phenomena without any change at all. Thus, though the stoppage of the motion of the earth in the ordinary course of nature, would be attended with terrible convulsions, the stoppage of the earth *miraculously*, for a special purpose to be served by *that only*, would not, of itself, be followed by any such consequences.

From the same conception of nature, as a machine, we are apt to think of interferences with the ordinary course of nature as implying some imperfection in it. Because machines are considered more and more perfect in proportion as they less and less need the interference of the workman. But it is manifest that this is a false analogy; for, the reason why machines are made is, to save us trouble: and, therefore, they are more perfect in proportion as they answer this purpose. But no one can seriously imagine that the universe is a machine for the purpose of saving trouble to the Almighty.

Again, when miracles are described as "interferences with the laws of nature," this description makes them appear improbable to many minds, from their not sufficiently considering that the laws of nature interfere with one another; that we cannot get rid of "interferences" upon any hypothesis consistent with experience. When organization is superinduced upon inorganic matter, the laws of inorganic matter are interfered with and controlled; when animal life comes in, there are new interferences; when reason and conscience are superadded to will, we have a new class of controlling and interfering powers, the *laws* of which are *moral* in their character. Intelligences of pure speculation, who could do nothing but observe and reason, surveying a portion of the universe — such as the greater part of the material universe may be — wholly destitute of living inhabitants, might have reasoned that such powers as active beings possess were incredible — that it was incredible that the Great Creator would suffer the majestic uniformity of laws which He was constantly maintaining through boundless space and innumerable worlds, to be controlled and interfered with at the caprice of such a creature as man. Yet we know by experience that God has enabled us to control and interfere with the laws of external nature for our own purposes: nor does this seem less improbable beforehand (but rather more), than that He should Himself interfere with those laws for our advantage. This, at least, is manifest — that the purposes for which man was made, whatever they are, involved the necessity of producing a power capable of controlling and interfering with the laws of external nature; and consequently that those purposes involve in some sense the necessity of interferences with the laws of nature external to man: and how far that necessity may reach — whether it extend only to interferences proceeding from man himself, or extend to interferences proceeding from other creatures, or immediately from God also, it is impossible for reason to determine beforehand.

Furthermore, whatever ends may be contemplated by the Deity for the laws of nature in reference to the rest of the universe — (in which question we have as little information as interest) — we know that, in respect of us, they answer discernible moral ends — that they place us, practically, under government, conducted in the way of rewards and punishment — a government of which the *tendency* is to encourage virtue and repress vice — and to form in us a certain character by discipline; which character our moral nature compels us to consider as the highest and worthiest object which we can pursue. Since, therefore, the laws of nature have, in reference to us, moral purposes to answer, which (as far as we can judge) they have not to serve in other respects, it seems not incredible that these peculiar purposes should occasionally require modifications of those laws in relation to us, which are not necessary in relation to other parts of the universe. For we see — as has been just observed —

that the power given to man of modifying the laws
of nature by which He is surrounded, is a power
directed by moral and rational influences, such as
we do not find directing the power of any other
creature that we know of. And how far, in the
nature of things, it would be possible or eligible,
to construct a system of material laws which should
at the same time, and by the same kind of operations, answer the other purposes of the Creator, and
also all his moral purposes with respect to a creature
endowed with such faculties as free-will, reason,
conscience, and the other peculiar attributes of man,
we cannot be supposed capable of judging. And
as the regularity of the laws of nature in themselves is the very thing which makes them capable
of being usefully controlled and interfered with by
man — (since, if their sequences were irregular and
capricious we could not know how or when to interfere with them) — so that same regularity is the
very thing which makes it possible to use Divine
interferences with them as attestations of a supernatural revelation from God to us; so that, in both
cases alike, the usual regularity of the laws, in themselves, is not superfluous, but necessary in order to
make the interferences with that regularity serviceable for their proper ends. In this point of view,
miracles are to be considered as cases in which a
higher law interferes with and controls a lower: of
which circumstance we see instances around us at
every turn.

It seems further that, in many disquisitions upon
this subject, some essentially distinct operations of
the human mind have been confused together in
such a manner as to spread unnecessary obscurity
over the discussion. It may be useful, therefore,
briefly to indicate the mental operations which are
chiefly concerned in this matter.

In the first place there seems to be a law of our
mind, in virtue of which, upon the experience of
any new external event, any phenomenon *limited* by
the circumstances of time and place, we refer it to
a *cause*, or powerful agent producing it as an *effect*.
The relative idea involved in this reference appears
to be a simple one, incapable of definition, and is
denoted by the term *efficiency*.

From this conception it has been supposed by
some that a scientific proof of the stability of the
laws of nature could be constructed; but the attempt has signally miscarried. Undoubtedly, while
we abide in the strict metaphysical conception of a
cause as such, the axiom that "similar causes produce similar effects" is intuitively evident; but it
is so because, in that point of view, it is merely a
barren truism. For my whole conception, within
these narrow limits, of the cause of the given
phenomenon B is that it is the cause or power producing B. I conceive of that cause merely as the
term of a certain relation to the phenomenon; and
therefore my conception of a cause similar to it,
precisely as a cause, can only be the conception of
a cause of a phenomenon similar to B.

But when the original conception is enlarged
into affording the wider maxim, that causes similar
as things, considered in themselves, and not barely
in relation to the effect, are similar in their effects
also, the case ceases to be not equally clear.

And, in applying even this to practice, we are
met with insuperable difficulties.

For, first, it may reasonably be demanded, on
what *scientific* ground we are justified in assuming
that any one material phenomenon or substance is,
in this proper sense, the cause of any given material

phenomenon? It does not appear at all self-evident,
à priori, that a material phenomenon must have a
material cause. Many have supposed the contrary;
and the phenomena of the apparent results of our
own volitions upon matter seem to indicate that
such a law should not be hastily assumed. Upon
the possible supposition, then, that the material
phenomena by which we are surrounded are the
effects of spiritual causes — such as the volitions of
the Author of Nature — it is plain that these are
causes of which we have no direct knowledge, and
the similarities of which to each other we can,
without the help of something more than the fundamental axiom of cause and effect, discover only
from the effects, and only so far as the effects carry
us in each particular.

But, even supposing it conceded that material
effects must have material causes, it yet remains to
be settled upon what ground we can assume that
we have ever yet found the true material cause of
any effect whatever, so as to justify us in predicting
that, wherever it recurs, a certain effect will follow.
All that our abstract axiom tells us is, that if we
have the true cause we have that which is always
attended with the effect: and all that experience
can tell us is that A has, so far as we can observe,
been always attended by B: and all that we can
infer from these premises, turn them how we will,
is merely this: that the case of A and B is, so far
as we have been able to observe, *like* a case of true
causal connection; and beyond this we cannot advance a step towards proving that the case of A
and B *is* a case of causal connection, without assuming further another principle (which would have
saved us much trouble if we had assumed it in the
beginning), that *likeness* or *verisimilitude* is a
ground of belief, gaining strength in proportion to
the closeness and constancy of the resemblance.

Indeed, physical analysis, in its continual advance, is daily teaching us that those things which
we once regarded as the true causes of certain material phenomena are only *marks* of the presence of
other things which we now regard as the true causes,
and which we may hereafter find to be only assem-
blages of adjacent appearances, more or less closely
connected with what may better claim that title.
It is quite possible, for example, that gravitation
may at some future time be demonstrated to be
the result of a complex system of forces, *residing*
(as some philosophers love to speak) in material
substances hitherto undiscovered, and as little suspected to exist as the gases were in the time of
Aristotle.

(2.) Nor can we derive much more practical
assistance from the maxim, that similar antecedents
have similar consequents. For this is really no
more than the former rule. It differs therefrom
only in dropping the idea of efficiency or causal
connection; and, however certain and universal it
may be supposed in the abstract, it fails in the
concrete just at the point where we most need
assistance. For it is plainly impossible to demonstrate that any two actual antecedents are precisely
similar in the sense of the maxim; or that any one
given apparent antecedent is the true unconditional
antecedent of any given apparently consequent
phenomenon. Unless, for example, we know the
whole nature of a given antecedent A, and also the
whole nature of another given antecedent B, we
cannot, by comparing them together, ascertain their
precise similarity. They may be similar in all
respects that we have hitherto observed, and yet in

the very essential quality which may make A the unconditional antecedent of a given effect C, in this respect A and B may be quite dissimilar.

It will be found, upon a close examination of all the logical canons of inductive reasoning that have been constructed for applying this principle, that such an assumption — of the real similarity of things apparently similar — pervades them all. Let us take, *e. g.*, what is called the first canon of the "Method of Agreement," which is this: "If two or more instances of the phenomenon under investigation have *only one* circumstance in common, the circumstance in *which alone* all the instances agree, is the cause (or effect) of the given phenomenon." Now, in applying this to any practical case, how can we be possibly certain that any two instances have *only one* circumstance in common? We can remove, indeed, by nicely varied experiments, all the different agents known to us from contact with the substances we are examining, except those which we choose to employ; but how is it possible that we can remove unknown agents, if such exist, or be sure that no agents do exist, the laws and periods of whose activity we have had hitherto no means of estimating, but which may reveal themselves at any moment, or upon any unlooked-for occasion? It is plain that, unless we can know the whole nature of all substances present at every moment and every place that we are concerned with in the universe, we cannot *know* that any two phenomena have *but one* circumstance in common. All we can say is, that unknown agencies count for nothing in practice; or (in other words) we must assume that things which appear to us similar *are* similar.

This being so, it becomes a serious question whether such intuitive principles as we have been discussing are of any real practical value whatever in mere physical inquiries. Because it would seem that they cannot be made use of without bringing in another principle, which seems quite sufficient without them, that the *likeness* of one thing to another in observable respects, is a ground for presuming likeness in other respects — a ground strong in proportion to the apparent closeness of the resemblances, and the number of times in which we have found ourselves right in acting upon such a presumption. Let us talk as we will of theorems deduced from intuitive axioms, about true causes or antecedents, still all that we can know in fact of any particular case is, that, *as far as we can observe*, it *resembles* what reason teaches us would be the case of a true cause or a true antecedent: and if this justifies us in drawing the inference that it is such a case, then certainly we must admit that *resemblance* is a just ground in itself of inference in practical reasoning.

And "therefore, even granting," it will be said, "the power of the Deity to work miracles, we can have no better grounds of determining how He is likely to exert that power, than by observing how He has actually exercised it. Now we find Him, by experience, by manifest traces and records, through countless ages, and in the most distant regions of space, continually — (if we do but set aside these comparatively few stories of miraculous interpositions) — working according to what we call, and rightly call, a settled order of nature, and we observe Him constantly preferring an adherence to this order before a departure from it, even in circumstances in which (apart from experience) we should suppose that his goodness would lead Him to vary from that order. In particular, we find that the greatest part of mankind have been left wholly in past ages, and even at present, without the benefit of that revelation which you suppose Him to have made. Yet it would appear that the multitudes who are ignorant of it needed it, and deserved it, just as much as the few who have been made acquainted with it. And thus it appears that experience refutes the inference in favor of the likelihood of a revelation, which we might be apt to draw from the mere consideration of his goodness, taken by itself." It cannot be denied that there seems to be much real weight in some of these considerations. But there are some things which diminish that weight: 1. With respect to remote ages, known to us only by physical traces, and distant regions of the universe, we have no record or evidence of the *moral* government carried on therein. We do not know of any. And, if there be or was any, we have no evidence to determine whether it was or was not, is or is not, connected with a system of miracles. There is no shadow of a presumption that, if it be or were, we should have records or traces of such a system. 2. With respect to the non-interruption of the course of nature, in a vast number of cases, where goodness would seem to require such interruptions, it must be considered that the very vastness of the number of such occasions would make such interruptions so frequent as to destroy the whole scheme of governing the universe by general laws altogether, and consequently also any scheme of attesting a revelation by miracles — *i. e.* facts varying from an established general law. This, therefore, is rather a presumption against God's interfering so often as to destroy the scheme of general laws, or make the sequences of things irregular and capricious, than against his interfering by miracles to attest a revelation, which, after that attestation, should be left to be propagated and maintained by ordinary means; and the very manner of the attestation of which (*i. e.* by miracles) implies that there *is* a regular and uniform course of nature, to which God is to be expected to adhere in all other cases. 3. It should be considered whether the just conclusion from the rest of the premises be (not so much this — that it is unlikely God would make a revelation — as) this — that it is likely that, if God made a revelation, He would make it subject to similar conditions to those under which He bestows his other *special* favors upon mankind — *i. e.* bestow it first directly upon some small part of the race, and impose upon them the responsibility of communicating its benefits to the rest. It is thus that He acts with respect to superior strength and intelligence, and in regard to the blessings of civilization and scientific knowledge, of which the greater part of mankind have always been left destitute.

Indeed, if by "the course of nature" we mean the whole course and series of God's government of the universe carried on by fixed laws, we cannot at all determine beforehand that miracles (*i. e.* occasional deviations, under certain moral circumstances, from the mere *physical* series of causes and effects) are not a part of the course of nature in that sense; so that, for aught we *know*, beings with a larger experience than ours of the history of the universe, might be able confidently to predict, from that experience, the occurrence of such miracles in a world circumstanced like ours. In this point of view, as Bishop Butler has truly said, nothing less than knowledge of another world.

placed in circumstances similar to our own, can furnish an argument from analogy against the credibility of miracles.

And, again, for aught we know, *personal* intercourse, or what Scripture seems to call "seeing God face to face," may be to myriads of beings the normal condition of God's intercourse with his intelligent and moral creatures; and to them the state of things in which we are, debarred from such direct perceptible intercourse, may be most contrary to their ordinary experience; so that what is to us miraculous in the history of our race may seem most accordant with the course of nature, or their customary experience, and what is to us most natural may appear to them most strange.

After all deductions and abatements have been made, however, it must be allowed that a certain antecedent improbability must always attach to miracles, considered as events varying from the ordinary experience of mankind as known to us: because likelihood, *verisimilitude*, or resemblance to what we know to have occurred, is, by the constitution of our minds, the very ground of probability; and, though we can perceive reasons, from the moral character of God, for thinking it likely that He may have wrought miracles, yet we know too little of his ultimate designs, and of the best mode of accomplishing them, to argue confidently from his character to his acts, except where the connection between the character and the acts is demonstrably indissoluble — as in the case of acts rendered necessary by the attributes of veracity and justice. Miracles are, indeed, in the notion of them, no breach of the high generalization that "similar antecedents have similar consequents;" nor, necessarily, of the maxim that "God works by general laws;" because we can see some laws of miracles (as *e. g.* that they are infrequent, and that they are used as attesting signs of, or in conjunction with, revelations), and may suppose more; but they do vary, when taken apart from their proper evidence, from this rule, that "what a general experience would lead us to regard as similar antecedents *are* similar antecedents;" because the only assignable specific difference observable by us in the antecedents in the case of miracles, and in the case of the experiments from the analogy of which they vary in their physical phenomena, consists in the moral antecedents; and these, in cases of physical phenomena, we generally throw out of the account; nor have we grounds *à priori* for concluding *with confidence* that these are not to be thrown out of the account here also, although we can see that the moral antecedents here (such as the fitness for attesting a revelation like the Christian) are, in many important respects, different from those which the analogy of experience teaches us to disregard in estimating the probability of physical events.

But, in order to form a fair judgment, we must take in all the circumstances of the case, and, amongst the rest, the *testimony* on which the miracle is reported to us.

Our belief, indeed, in human testimony seems to rest upon the same sort of instinct on which our belief in the testimony (as it may be called) of nature is built, and is to be checked, modified, and confirmed by a process of experience similar to that which is applied in the other case. As we learn, by extended observation of nature and the comparison of analogies, to distinguish the real laws of physical sequences from the casual conjunctions of phenomena, so are we taught in the same manner to distinguish the circumstances under which human testimony is certain or incredible, probable or suspicious. The circumstances of our condition force us daily to make continual observations upon the phenomena of human testimony; and it is a matter upon which we can make such experiments with peculiar advantage, because every man carries within his own breast the whole sum of the ultimate motives which can influence human testimony. Hence arises the aptitude of human testimony for overcoming, and more than overcoming, almost any antecedent improbability in the thing reported.

"The conviction produced by testimony," says Bishop Young, "is capable of being carried much higher than the conviction produced by experience: and the reason is this, because there may be concurrent testimonies to the truth of one individual fact; whereas there can be no concurrent experiments with regard to an individual experiment. There may, indeed, be *analogous* experiments, in the same manner as there may be analogous testimonies; but, in any course of nature, there is but one continued series of events: whereas in testimony, since the same event may be observed by different witnesses, their *concurrence* is capable of producing a conviction more cogent than any that is derived from any other species of events in the course of nature. In material phenomena the probability of an expected event arises solely from analogous experiments made previous to the event; and this probability admits of indefinite increase from the unlimited increase of the number of these previous experiments. The credibility of a witness likewise arises from our experience of the veracity of previous witnesses in similar cases, and admits of unlimited increase according to the number of the previous witnesses. But there is another source of the increase of testimony, likewise unlimited, derived from the number of *concurrent* witnesses. The evidence of testimony, therefore, admitting of unlimited increase on two different accounts, and the physical probability admitting only of one of them, the former is capable of indefinitely surpassing the latter."

It is to be observed also that, in the case of the Christian miracles, the truth of the facts, varying as they do from our ordinary experience, is far more credible than the falsehood of a testimony so circumstanced as that by which they are attested; because of the former strange phenomena — the miracles — a reasonable known cause may be assigned adequate to the effect — namely, the will of God producing them to accredit a revelation that seems not unworthy of Him; whereas of the latter — the falsehood of such testimony — no adequate cause whatever can be assigned, or reasonably conjectured.

So manifest, indeed, is this inherent power of testimony to overcome antecedent improbabilities, that Hume is obliged to allow that testimony may be so circumstanced as to require us to believe, in some cases, the occurrence of things quite at variance with general experience; but he pretends to show that testimony to such facts *when connected with religion* can never be so circumstanced. The reasons for this paradoxical exception are partly general remarks upon the proneness of men to believe in portents and prodigies; upon the temptations to the indulgence of pride, vanity, ambition, and such like passions which the human mind is subject to in religious matters, and the strange mixture of enthusiasm and knavery, sincerity and craft, that is to be found in fanatics, and partly particular instances of confessedly false miracles that seem to be supported by an astonishing weight of evidence — such as those alleged to have been wrought at the tomb of the Abbé Paris.

But (1) little weight can be attached to such general reflections, as discrediting any particular body of evidence, until it can be shown in detail that they apply to the special circumstances of that particular body of evidence. In reality, most of his general objections are, at bottom, objections to human testimony itself — i. e. objections to the medium by which alone we can know what is called the general experience of mankind, from which general experience it is that the only considerable objection to miracles arises. Thus, by general reflections upon the proverbial fallaciousness of "travellers' stories" we might discredit all antecedently improbable relations of the manners or physical peculiarities of foreign lands. By general reflections upon the illusions, and even temptations to fraud, under which scientific observers labor, we might discredit all scientific observations. By general reflections upon the way in which supine credulity, and passion, and party-interest have discolored civil history, we might discredit all antecedently improbable events in civil history — such as the conquests of Alexander, the adventures of the Buonaparte family, or the story of the late mutiny in India. (2) The same experience which informs us that credulity, enthusiasm, craft, and a mixture of these, have produced many false religions and false stories of miracles, informs us also what sort of religions, and what sort of legends, these causes have produced, and are likely to produce; and, if, upon a comparison of the Christian religion and miracles with these products of human weakness or cunning, there appear specific differences between the two, unaccountable on the hypothesis of a common origin, this not only diminishes the presumption of a common origin, but raises a distinct presumption the other way — a presumption strong in proportion to the extent and accuracy of our induction. Remarkable specific differences of this kind have been pointed out by Christian apologists in respect of the nature of the religion — the nature of the miracles — and the circumstances of the evidence by which they are attested.

Of the first kind are, for instance, those assigned by Warburton, in his Divine Legation; and by Archbp. Whately, in his Essays on the Peculiarities of the Christian Religion, and on Romanism. Differences of the second and third kind are largely assigned by almost every writer on Christian evidences. We refer, specially, for sample's sake, to Leslie's Short Method with the Deists — to Bishop Douglas's Criterion, in which he fully examines the pretended parallel of the cures at the tomb of Abbé Paris — and to Paley's Evidences, which may be most profitably consulted in the late edition by Archbp. Whately.

Over and above the direct testimony of human witnesses to the Bible-miracles, we have also what may be called the indirect testimony of events confirming the former, and raising a distinct presumption that some such miracles must have been wrought. Thus, for example, we know, by a copious induction, that, in no nation of the ancient world, and in no nation of the modern world

unacquainted with the Jewish or Christian revelation, has the knowledge of the one true God as the Creator and Governor of the world, and the public worship of Him, been kept up by the mere light of nature, or formed the groundwork of such religions as men have devised for themselves. Yet we do find that, in the Jewish people, though no way distinguished above others by mental power or high civilization, and with as strong natural tendencies to idolatry as others, this knowledge and worship was kept up from a very early period of their history, and, according to their uniform historical tradition, kept up by revelation attested by undeniable miracles.

Again, the existence of the Christian religion, as the belief of the most considerable and intelligent part of the world, is an undisputed fact; and it is also certain that this religion originated (as far as human means are concerned) with a handful of Jewish peasants, who went about preaching — on the very spot where Jesus was crucified — that He had risen from the dead, and had been seen by, and had conversed with them, and afterwards ascended into heaven. This miracle, attested by them as eye-witnesses, was the very ground and foundation of the religion which they preached, and it was plainly one so circumstanced that, if it had been false, it could easily have been proved to be false. Yet, though the preachers of it were everywhere persecuted, they had gathered, before they died, large churches in the country where the facts were best known, and through Asia Minor, Greece, Egypt, and Italy; and these churches, notwithstanding the severest persecutions, went on increasing till, in about 300 years after, this religion — i. e. a religion which taught the worship of a Jewish peasant who had been ignominiously executed as a malefactor — became the established religion of the Roman empire, and has ever since continued to be the prevailing religion of the civilized world.

It would plainly be impossible, in such an article as this, to enumerate all the various lines of confirmation — from the prophecies, from the morality, from the structure of the Bible, from the state of the world before and after Christ, etc. — which all converge to the same conclusion. But it will be manifest that almost all of them are drawn ultimately from the analogy of experience, and that the conclusion to which they tend cannot be rejected without holding something contrary to the analogies of experience from which they are drawn. For, it must be remembered, that disbelieving one thing necessarily involves believing its contradictory.

It is manifest that, if the miraculous facts of Christianity did not really occur, the stories about them must have originated either in fraud, or in fancy. The coarse explanation of them by the hypothesis of unlimited fraud, has been generally abandoned in modern times: but, in Germany especially, many persons of great acuteness have long labored to account for them by referring them to fancy. Of these there have been two principal schools — the Naturalistic, and the Mythic.

1. The Naturalists suppose the miracles to have been natural events, more or less unusual, that were mistaken for miracles, through ignorance or enthusiastic excitement. But the result of their labors in detail has been (as Strauss has shown in his Leben Jesu) to turn the New Testament, as interpreted by them, into a narrative far less credible than any narrative of miracles could be: just as a

novel, made up of a multitude of surprising natural events crowded into a few days, is less consistent with its own data than a tale of genii and enchanters. "Some infidels," says Archbishop Whately, "have labored to prove, concerning some one of our Lord's miracles that it might have been the result of an accidental conjuncture of natural circumstances; and they endeavor to prove the same concerning another, and so on; and thence infer that all of them, occurring as a series, might have been so. They might argue, in like manner, that, because it is not very improbable one may throw sixes in any one out of an hundred throws, therefore it is no more improbable that one may throw sixes a hundred times running." The truth is, that everything that is improbable in the mere *physical strangeness* of miracles applies to such a series of odd events as these explanations assume; while the hypothesis of their non-miraculous character deprives us of the means of *accounting for them* by the extraordinary interposition of the Deity. These and other objections to the thorough-going application of the naturalistic method, led to the substitution in its place of

2. The Mythic theory — which supposes the N. T. Scripture-narratives to have been legends, not stating the grounds of men's belief in Christianity, but springing out of that belief, and embodying the idea of what Jesus, if he were the Messiah, must have been conceived to have done in order to fulfill that character, and was therefore supposed to have done. But it is obvious that this leaves the origin of the belief, that a man who *did not fulfill* the idea of the Messiah in any one remarkable particular, *was* the Messiah — wholly unaccounted for. It begins with assuming that a person of mean condition, who was publicly executed as a malefactor, and who wrought no miracles, was so earnestly believed to be their Messiah by a great multitude of Jews, who expected a Messiah that *was* to work miracles, and was *not* to die, but to be a great conquering prince, that they modified their whole religion, in which they had been brought up, into accordance with that new belief, and imagined a whole cycle of legends to embody their idea, and brought the whole civilized world ultimately to accept their system. It is obvious, also, that all the arguments for the genuineness and authenticity of the writings of the N. T. bring them up to a date when the memory of Christ's real history was so recent, as to make the substitution of a set of mere legends in its place utterly incredible; and it is obvious, also, that the gravity, simplicity, historical decorum, and consistency with what we know of the circumstances of the times in which the events are said to have occurred, observable in the narratives of the N. T., make it impossible reasonably to accept them as mere *myths*. The same appears from a comparison of them with the style of writings really mythic — as the Gospels of the infancy, of Nicodemus, etc. — and with heathen or Mohammedan legends; and from the omission of matters which a mythic fancy would certainly have fastened on. Thus, though John Baptist was typified by Elijah, the great wonder-worker of the Old Testament, there are no miracles ascribed to John Baptist. There are no miracles ascribed to Jesus during his infancy and youth. There is no description of his personal appearance; no account of his adventures in the world of spirits; no miracles ascribed to the Virgin Mary, and very little said about her at all; no account of the

martyrdom of any Apostle, but of one, and that given in the driest manner, etc. — and so in a hundred other particulars.

It is observable that, in the early ages, the fact that extraordinary miracles were wrought by Jesus and his Apostles, does not seem to have been generally denied by the opponents of Christianity. They seem always to have preferred adopting the expedient of ascribing them to art, magic, and the power of evil spirits. This we learn from the N. T. itself; from such Jewish writings as the *Sepher Toldoth Jeshu;* from the Fragments of Celsus, Porphyry, Hierocles, Julian, etc., which have come down to us, and from the popular objections which the ancient Christian Apologists felt themselves concerned to grapple with. We are not to suppose, however, that this would have been a solution which, even in those days, would have been naturally preferred to a denial of the facts, if the facts could have been plausibly denied. On the contrary it was plainly, even then, a forced and improbable solution of *such* miracles. For man did not commonly ascribe to magic or evil demons an *unlimited* power, any more than we ascribe an unlimited power to mesmerism, imagination, and the occult and irregular forces of nature. We know that in two instances, in the Gospel narrative — the cure of the man born blind and the Resurrection — the Jewish priests were unable to pretend such a solution, and were driven to maintain unsuccessfully a charge of fraud; and the circumstances of the Christian miracles were, in almost all respects, so utterly unlike those of any pretended instances of magical wonders, that the Apologists have little difficulty in refuting this plea. This they do generally from the following considerations.

(1.) The greatness, number, completeness, and publicity of the miracles. (2.) The natural beneficial tendency of the doctrine they attested. (3.) The connection of them with a whole scheme of revelation extending from the first origin of the human race to the time of Christ.

It is also to be considered that the circumstance that the world was, in the times of the Apostles, full of Thaumaturgists, in the shape of exorcists, magicians, ghost-seers, etc., is a strong presumption that, in order to command any special attention and gain any large and permanent success, the Apostles and their followers must have exhibited works quite different from any wonders which people had been accustomed to see. This presumption is confirmed by what we read, in the Acts of the Apostles, concerning the effect produced upon the Samaritans by Philip the Evangelist in opposition to the prestiges of Simon Magus.

This evasion of the force of the Christian miracles, by referring them to the power of evil spirits, has seldom been seriously recurred to in modern times; but the English infidels of the last century employed it as a kind of *argumentum ad hominem*, to tease and embarrass their opponents — contending that, as the Bible speaks of "lying wonders" of Antichrist, and relates a long contest of apparent miracles between Moses and the Egyptian magicians, Christians could not *on their own principles*, have any certainty that miracles were not wrought by evil spirits.

In answer to this, some divines (as Bishop Fleetwood in his *Dialogues on Miracles*) have endeavored to establish a distinction in the nature of the works themselves, between the *seeming* miracles within the reach of intermediate spirits, — and the *true* miracles, which can only be wrought by God — and others (as Bekker, in his curious work *Le Monde Enchanté*, and Farmer, in his *Case of the Demoniacs*) have entirely denied the power of intermediate spirits to interfere with the course of nature. But, without entering into these questions, it is sufficient to observe —

(1.) That the light of nature gives us no reason to believe that there are any evil spirits having power to interfere with the course of nature at all.

(2.) That it shows us that, if there be, they are continually controlled from exercising any such power.

(3.) That the records we are supposed to have of such an exercise in the Bible, show us the power there spoken of, as exerted completely under the control of God, and in such a manner as to make it evident to all candid observers where the advantage lay, and to secure all well-disposed and reasonable persons from any mistake in the matter.

(4.) That the circumstances alleged by the early Christian Apologists — the number, greatness, beneficence, and variety of the Bible miracles — their connection with prophecy and a long scheme of things extending from the creation down — the character of Christ and his Apostles — and the manifest tendency of the Christian religion to serve the cause of truth and virtue — make it as incredible that the miracles attesting it should have been wrought by evil beings, as it is that the order of nature should proceed from such beings. For, as we gather the character of the Creator from his works, and the moral instincts which He has given us; so we gather the character of the author of revelation from his works, and from the drift and tendency of that revelation itself. This last point is sometimes shortly and unguardedly expressed by saying, that " the doctrine proves the miracles: " the meaning of which is *not* that the particular doctrines which miracles attest must first be proved to be *true aliunde*, before we can believe that any such works were wrought — (which would, manifestly, be making the miracles no *attestation* at all) — but the meaning *is* that the whole body of doctrine in connection with which the miracles are alleged, and its tendency, if it were divinely revealed, to answer visible good ends, makes it reasonable to think that the miracles by which it is attested were, if they were wrought at all, wrought by God.

Particular theories as to the manner in which miracles have been wrought are matters rather curious than practically useful. In all such cases we must bear in mind the great maxim SUBTILITAS NATURÆ LONGE SUPERAT SUBTILITATEM MENTIS HUMANÆ. Malebranche regarded the Deity as the sole agent in nature, acting always by *general laws*; but he conceived those general laws to contain the original provision that the manner of the Divine acting should modify itself, under certain conditions, according to the particular volitions of finite intelligences. Hence, he explained *man's* apparent power over external nature; and hence also he regarded miracles as the result of particular volitions of angels, employed by the Deity in the government of the world. This was called the system of *occasional causes*.

The system of Clarke allowed a proper real, though limited, efficiency to the wills of inferior intelligences, but denied any true *powers* to matter. Hence he referred the phenomena of the course of material nature immediately to the will of God as

their cause; making the distinction between natural events and miracles to consist in this, that the former happen according to what is, relatively to us, God's *usual* way of working, and the latter according to his *unusual* way of working.

Some find it easier to conceive of miracles as not really taking place in the external order of nature, but in the impressions made by it upon our minds. Others deny that there is, in any miracle, the production of anything new or the alteration of any natural power; and maintain that miracles are produced solely by the *intensifying* of known natural powers already in existence.

It is plain that these various hypotheses are merely ways in which different minds find it more or less easy to conceive the mode in which miracles may have been wrought.

Another question more curious than practical, is that respecting the precise period when miracles ceased in the Christian Church. It is plain, that, whenever they ceased in point of fact, they ceased *relatively to us* wherever a sufficient attestation of them to our faith fails to be supplied.

It is quite true, indeed, that a real miracle, and one sufficiently marked out to the spectators as a real miracle, may be so imperfectly reported to us, as that, if we have only that imperfect report, there may be little to show conclusively its miraculous character; and that, therefore, in rejecting accounts of miracles so circumstanced, we *may possibly* be rejecting accounts of what were real miracles. But this is an inconvenience attending *probable* evidence from its very nature. In rejecting the improbable testimony of the most mendacious of witnesses, we *may*, almost always, be rejecting something which is really true. But this would be a poor reason for acting on the testimony of a notorious liar to a story antecedently improbable. The narrowness and imperfection of the human mind is such that our wisest and most prudent calculations are continually baffled by unexpected combinations of circumstances, upon which we *could not* have reasonably reckoned. But this is no good ground for not acting upon the calculations of wisdom and prudence; because, after all, such calculations are in the long run our surest guides.

It is quite true, also, that several of the Scripture miracles are so circumstanced, that if the reports we have of them stood alone, and came down to us only by the channel of ordinary history, we should be without adequate evidence of their miraculous character; and therefore those particular miracles are not *to us* (though they doubtless were to the original spectators, who could mark all the circumstances), by themselves and taken alone, *signal* or proper *evidences* of revelation. But, then, they may be very proper *objects* of faith, though not the grounds of it. For (1.) these incidents are really reported to us as parts of a course of things which we *have* good evidence for believing to have been miraculous; and, as Bishop Butler justly observes, " supposing it acknowledged, that our Saviour spent some years in a course of working miracles, there is no more peculiar presumption worth mentioning, against his having exerted his miraculous powers in a certain degree greater, than in a certain degree less; in one or two more instances, than in one or two fewer: in this, than in another manner." And (2.) these incidents are reported to us by writers whom we have good reasons for believing to have been, not ordinary historians, but persons specially assisted by the Divine Spirit, for the purpose of giving a correct account of the ministry of our Lord and his Apostles.

In the case of the Scripture miracles, we must be careful to distinguish the *particular occasions* upon which they were wrought, from their *general purpose* and design; yet not so as to overlook the connection between these two things.

There are but few miracles recorded in Scripture of which the whole character was merely evidential — few, that is, that were merely displays of a supernatural power made for the sole purpose of attesting a Divine Revelation. Of this character were the change of Moses' rod into a serpent at the burning bush, the burning bush itself, the going down of the shadow upon the sun-dial of Ahaz, and some others.

In general, however, the miracles recorded in Scripture have, besides the ultimate purpose of affording evidence of a Divine interposition, some immediate temporary purposes which they were apparently wrought to serve — such as the curing of diseases, the feeding of the hungry, the relief of innocent, or the punishment of guilty persons. These immediate temporary ends are not without value in reference to the ultimate and general design of miracles, as providing evidence of the truth of revelation; because they give a *moral character* to the works wrought, which enables them to display not only the power, but the other attributes of the agent performing them. And, in some cases, it would appear that miraculous works of a particular kind were selected as emblematic or typical of some characteristic of the revelation which they were intended to attest. Thus, *e. g.*, the cure of bodily diseases not only indicated the general benevolence of the Divine Agent, but seems sometimes to be referred to as an emblem of Christ's power to remove the disorders of the soul. The gift of tongues appears to have been intended to manifest the universality of the Christian dispensation, by which all languages were consecrated to the worship of God. The casting out of demons was a type and pledge of the presence of a Power that was ready to "destroy the works of the devil," in every sense.

In this point of view, Christian miracles may be fitly regarded as *specimens* of a Divine Power, alleged to be present — specimens so circumstanced as to make obvious, and bring under the notice of common understandings, the operations of a Power — the gift of the Holy Ghost — which was really supernatural, but did not, in its moral effects, reveal itself externally as supernatural. In this sense, they seem to be called the *manifestation* or *exhibition* of the Spirit — outward phenomena which manifested sensibly his presence and operation in the Church: and the record of these miracles becomes evidence to us of the invisible presence of Christ in his Church, and of his government of it through all ages; though that presence is of such a nature as not to be immediately distinguishable from the operation of known moral motives, and that government is carried on so as not to interrupt the ordinary course of things.

In the case of the Old Testament miracles, again, in order fully to understand their evidential character, we must consider the general nature and design of the dispensation with which they were connected. The general design of that dispensation appears to have been to keep up in one particular race a knowledge of the one true God, and of he promise of a Messiah in whom "all the families of the earth" should be "blessed." And in order to this end, it appears to have been necessary that, for some time, God should have assumed the character of the local Tutelary Deity and Prince of that particular people. And from this peculiar relation in which He stood to the Jewish people (aptly called by Josephus a THEOCRACY) resulted the necessity of frequent miracles, to manifest and make sensibly perceptible his actual presence among and government over them. The miracles, therefore, of the Old Testament are to be regarded as evidential of the theocratic government; and this again is to be conceived of as subordinate to the further purpose of preparing the way for Christianity, by keeping up in the world a knowledge of the true God and of his promise of a Redeemer. In this view, we can readily understand why the miraculous administration of the theocracy was withdrawn, as soon as the purpose of it had been answered by working deeply and permanently into the mind of the Jewish people the two great lessons which it was intended to teach them; so that they might be safely left to the ordinary means of instruction, until the publication of a fresh revelation by Christ and his Apostles rendered further miracles necessary to attest their mission. Upon this view also we can perceive that the miracles of the Old Testament, upon whatever immediate occasions they may have been wrought, were subordinate (and, in general, necessary) to the design of rendering possible the establishment in due time of such a religion as the Christian; and we can perceive further that, though the Jewish theocracy implied in it a continual series of miracles, yet — as it was only temporary and local — those miracles did not violate God's general purpose of carrying on the government of *the world* by the ordinary laws of nature; whereas if the Christian dispensation — which is *permanent* and *universal* — necessarily implied in it a series of constant miracles, *that* would be inconsistent with the general purpose of carrying on the government of the world by those ordinary laws.

With respect to the *character* of the Old Testament miracles, we must also remember that the whole structure of the Jewish economy had reference to the peculiar exigency of the circumstances of a people imperfectly civilized, and is so distinctly described in the New Testament, as dealing with men according to the "hardness of their hearts," and being a system of "weak and beggarly elements," and a rudimentary instruction for "children" who were in the condition of "slaves." We are not, therefore, to judge of the probability of the miracles wrought in support of that economy (so far as the *forms* under which they were wrought are concerned) as if those miracles were immediately intended for ourselves. We are not justified in arguing either that those miracles are incredible because wrought in such a manner as that, if addressed to us, they would lower our conceptions of the Divine Being; or, on the other hand, that because those miracles — wrought under the circumstances of the Jewish economy — are credible and ought to be believed, there is therefore no reason for objecting against stories of similar miracles alleged to have been wrought under the quite different circumstances of the Christian dispensation.

In dealing with human testimony, it may be further needful to notice (though very briefly) some refined subtilties that have been occasionally introduced into this discussion.

It has been sometimes alleged that the freedom of the human will is a circumstance which renders reliance upon the stability of laws in the case of human conduct utterly precarious. " In arguing," it is said, " that human beings cannot be supposed to have acted in a particular way, because *that* would involve a violation of the analogy of human conduct, so far as it has been observed in all ages, we tacitly assume that the human mind is unalterably determined by fixed laws, in the same way as material substances. But this is not the case on the hypothesis of the freedom of the will. The very notion of a free will is that of a faculty which determines *itself*; and which is capable of choosing a line of conduct quite repugnant to the influence of any motive, however strong. There is therefore no reason for expecting that the operations of human volition will be conformable throughout to any fixed rule or analogy whatever."

In reply to this far-sought and barren refinement, we may observe — 1. That, if it be worth anything, it is an objection not merely against the force of human testimony in religious matters, but against human testimony in general, and, indeed, against all calculations of probability in respect of human conduct whatsoever. 2. That we have already shown that, even in respect of material phenomena, our practical measure of probability is not derived from any scientific axioms about *cause* and *effect*, or antecedents and consequences, but simply from the likeness or unlikeness of one thing to another; and therefore, not being deduced from premises which assume *causality*, cannot be shaken by the denial of causality in a particular case. 3. That the thing to be accounted for, on the supposition of the falsity of the testimony for Christian miracles, is not accounted for by any such capricious principle as the arbitrary freedom of the human will; because the thing to be accounted for is *the agreement* of a number of witnesses in a falsehood, for the propagation of which they could have no intelligible inducement. Now, if we suppose a *number* of independent witnesses to have determined themselves by rational motives, then, under the circumstances of this particular instance, their *agreement* in a *true* story is sufficiently accounted for. But, if we suppose them to have each determined themselves by mere whim and caprice, then their *agreement* in the same false story is not accounted for at all. The concurrence of such a number of *chances* is utterly incredible. 4. And finally we remark that no sober maintainers of the freedom of the human will claim for it any such unlimited power of self-determination as this objection supposes. The freedom of the human will exhibits itself either in cases where there is no motive for selecting one rather than another among many possible courses of action that lie before us — in which cases it is to be observed that there is nothing *moral* in its elections whatsoever; — or in cases in which there is a conflict of motives, and, *e. g.*, passion and appetite, or custom or temporal interest, draw us one way, and reason or conscience another. In these latter cases the maintainers of the freedom of the will contend that, under certain limits, we can determine ourselves (not by no motive at all, but) by *either* of the motives actually operating upon our minds. Now it is manifest that if, in the case of the witnesses to Christianity, we can show that theirs was a case of a conflict of motives (as it clearly *was*), and can show, further, that their contact is inconsistent with one set of motives, the

reasonable inference is that they determined themselves, in point of fact, by the other. Thus, though in the case of a man strongly tried by a conflict of motives, we might not, even with the fullest knowledge of his character and circumstances, have been able to predict beforehand how he *would* act, that would be no reason for denying that, after we had come to know how he *did act*, we could tell by what motives he had determined himself in choosing that particular line of conduct.

It has been often made a topic of complaint against Hume that, in dealing with testimony as a medium for proving miracles, he has resolved its force entirely into our *experience* of its veracity, and omitted to notice that, antecedently to all experience, we are predisposed to give it credit by a kind of natural instinct. But, however metaphysically erroneous Hume's analysis of our belief in testimony may have been, it is doubtful whether, in this particular question, such a mistake is of any great practical importance. Our original predisposition is doubtless (whether *instinctive* or not) a predisposition to believe all testimony indiscriminately: but this is so completely checked, modified, and controlled, in after-life, by experience of the circumstances under which testimony can be safely relied upon, and of those in which it is apt to mislead us, that, practically, our experience in these respects may be taken as a not unfair measure of its value as rational evidence. It is also to be observed that, while Hume has omitted this original instinct of belief in testimony, as an element in his calculations, he has also omitted to take into account, on the other side, any original *instinctive* belief in the constancy of the laws of nature, or expectation that our future experiences will resemble our past ones. In reality, he seems to have resolved both these principles into the mere association of ideas. And, however theoretically erroneous he may have been in this, still it seems manifest that, by making the same mistake on both sides, he has made one error compensate another; and so — as far as this branch of the argument is concerned — brought out a practically correct result. As we can only learn by various and repeated experiences under what circumstances we can safely trust our expectation of the recurrence of apparently similar phenomena, that expectation, being thus continually checked and controlled, modifies itself into accordance with its rule, and ceases to spring at all where it would be manifestly at variance with its director. And the same would seem to be the case with our belief in testimony.

The argument, indeed, in Hume's celebrated *Essay on Miracles*, was very far from being a new one. It had, as Mr. Coleridge has pointed out, been distinctly indicated by South in his sermon on the incredulity of St. Thomas; and there is a remarkable statement of much the same argument put into the mouth of Woolston's Advocate, in Sherlock's *Trial of the Witnesses*. The restatement of it, however, by a person of Hume's abilities, was of service in putting men upon a more accurate examination of the true nature and measure of probability; and it cannot be denied that Hume's bold statement of his unbounded skepticism had, as he contended it would have, many useful results in stimulating inquiries that might not otherwise have been suggested to thoughtful men, or, at least, not prosecuted with sufficient zeal and patience.

Bishop Butler seems to have been very sensible of the imperfect state, in his own time, of the logic of Probability; and, though he appears to have formed a more accurate conception of it than the Scotch school of Philosophers who succeeded and undertook to refute Hume, yet there is one passage in which we may perhaps detect a misconception of the subject in the pages of even this great writer.

"There is," he observes, "a very strong presumption against common speculative truths, and *against the most ordinary facts*, before the proof of them, which yet is overcome by *almost any proof*. There is a presumption of millions to one against the story of Cæsar or *any other man*. For, suppose a number of common facts so and so circumstanced, of which one had no kind of proof, *should happen to come into* one's thoughts; every one would, without any possible doubt, conclude them to be false. And the like may be said *of a single common fact*. And from hence it appears that the question of importance, as to the matter before us, is, concerning the degree of the peculiar presumption against miracles: not, whether there be any peculiar presumption at all against them. For *if there be a presumption of millions to one against the most common facts*, what can a small presumption, additional to this, amount to, though it be peculiar? It cannot be estimated, *and is as nothing*." (*Analogy*, part 2, c. ii.)

It is plain that, in this passage, Butler lays no stress upon the *peculiarities* of the story of Cæsar, which he casually mentions. For he expressly adds "or of any other man;" and repeatedly explains that what he says applies equally to any ordinary facts, or to a single fact; so that, whatever be his drift (and it must be acknowledged to be somewhat obscure), he is not constructing an argument similar to that which has been pressed by Archbishop Whately, in his *Historic Doubts respecting Napoleon Bonaparte*. And this becomes still more evident, when we consider the extraordinary medium by which he endeavors to show that there is a presumption of millions to one against such "common ordinary facts" as he is speaking of. For the way in which he proposes to estimate the presumption against ordinary facts is, by considering the likelihood of their being anticipated beforehand by a person *guessing at random*. But, surely, this is not a measure of the likelihood of the facts considered in themselves, but of the likelihood of the *coincidence of the facts* with a rash and arbitrary anticipation. The case of a person guessing beforehand, and the case of a witness reporting what has occurred, are essentially different. In the common instance, for example, of an ordinary die, before the cast, there is nothing to determine my mind, with any probability of a correct judgment, to the selection of any one of the six faces rather than another; and, therefore, we rightly say that there are five chances to one against any one side, considered as thus arbitrarily selected. But when a person, who has had opportunities of observing the cast, reports to me the presentation of a particular face, there is evidently no such presumption against the coincidence of *his* statement and the actual fact; because he *has*, by the supposition, had ample means of ascertaining the real state of the occurrence. And it seems plain that, in the case of a credible witness, we should as readily believe his report of the cast of a die with a million of sides, as of one with only six; though in respect of a random guess beforehand, the chances against the correctness of the guess would be vastly greater in the former case, than in that of an ordinary cube.

Furthermore, if any common by-stander were to report a series of successive throws, as having taken place in the following order — 1, 6, 3, 5, 6, 2 — no one would feel any difficulty in receiving his testimony; but if we further become aware that he, or anybody else, had beforehand professed to guess or predict that precise series of throws upon that particular occasion, we should certainly no longer give his report the same ready and unhesitating acquiescence. We should at once suspect, either that the witness was deceiving us, or that the die was loaded, or tampered with in some way, to produce a conformity with the anticipated sequence. This places in a clear light the difference between the case of the *coincidence* of an ordinary event with a random predetermination, and the case of an ordinary event considered in itself.

The truth is, that *the chances* to which Butler seems to refer as a presumption against ordinary events, are not in ordinary cases overcome by testimony at all. The testimony has nothing to do with them; because they are chances against the event considered as the subject of a random vaticination, not as the subject of a report made by an actual observer. It is possible, however, that, throughout this obscure passage, Butler is arguing upon the principles of some objector unknown to us: and, indeed, it is certain that some writers upon the doctrine of chances (who were far from friendly to revealed religion) have utterly confounded together the questions of the chances against the coincidence of an ordinary event with a random guess, and of the probability of such an event considered by itself.

But it should be observed that what we commonly call the chances against an ordinary event are not *specific*, but *particular*. They are chances against *this* event, not against *this kind* of event. The chances, in the case of a die, are the chances against a particular face; not against the coming *up of some face*. The coming up of some face is not a thing subject to *random* anticipation, and, therefore, we say that there are no chances against it at all. But, as the presumption that some face will come up is a *specific* presumption, quite different from the presumption against any particular face; so the presumption against no face coming up (which is really the same thing, and equivalent to the presumption against a miracle, considered merely in its physical strangeness) must be *specific* also, and different from the presumption against any particular form of such a miracle selected beforehand by an arbitrary anticipation. For miraculous facts, it is evident, are subject to the doctrine of chances, each in particular, in the same way as ordinary facts. Thus, *e. g.* supposing a miracle to be wrought, the cube might be changed into *any* geometrical figure; and we can see no reason for selecting one rather than another, or the substance might be changed from ivory to metal, and then one metal would be as likely as another. But no one, probably, would say that he would believe the specific fact of *such a miracle* upon the same proof, or anything like the same proof, as that on which, *such a miracle being supposed*, he would believe the report of any particular form of it — such form being just as likely beforehand as any other.

Indeed, if "almost any proof" were capable of overcoming presumptions of millions to one against a fact, it is hard to see how we could reasonably reject any report of anything, on the ground of antecedent presumptions against its credibility.

The *Ecclesiastical Miracles* are not delivered to us by inspired historians; nor do they seem to form any part of the same series of events as the miracles of the New Testament.

The miracles of the New Testament (setting aside those wrought by Christ Himself) appear to have been worked by a power conferred upon particular persons according to a regular law, in virtue of which that power was ordinarily transmitted from one person to another, and the only persons privileged thus to *transmit* that power were the *Apostles.* The only exceptions to this rule were, (1) the Apostles themselves, and (2) the family of Cornelius, who were the first-fruits of the Gentiles. In all other cases, miraculous gifts were conferred only by the laying on of the *Apostles'* hands. By this arrangement, it is evident that a provision was made for the total ceasing of that miraculous dispensation within a limited period: because, on the death of the last of the Apostles, the ordinary channels would be all stopped through which such gifts were transmitted in the Church.

Thus, in Acts viii., though Philip is described as working many miracles among the Samaritans, he does not seem to have ever thought of imparting the same power to any of his converts. That is reserved for the Apostles Peter and John, who confer the miraculous gifts by the imposition of their hands: and this power, of imparting miraculous gifts to others, is clearly recognized by Simon Magus as a distinct privilege belonging to the Apostles, and quite beyond anything that He had seen exercised before. "When Simon saw that *through laying on of the Apostles' hands* the Holy Ghost was given, he offered them money, saying, Give me also this power, that on whomsoever I lay hands, he may receive the Holy Ghost."

This separation of the Rite by which miraculous gifts were conferred from Baptism, by which members were admitted into the Church, seems to have been wisely ordained for the purpose of keeping the two ideas, of ordinary and extraordinary gifts, distinct, and providing for the approaching cessation of the former without shaking the stability of an institution which was designed to be a permanent Sacrament in the kingdom of Christ.

And it may also be observed in passing, that this same separation of the effects of these two Rites, affords a presumption that the miraculous gifts, bestowed, as far as we can see, only in the former, were not merely the result of highly raised enthusiasm; because experience shows that violent symptoms of enthusiastic transport would have been much more likely to have shown themselves in the first ardor of conversion than at a later period — in the very crisis of a change, than after that change had been confirmed and settled.

One passage has, indeed, been appealed to as seeming to indicate the permanent residence of miraculous powers in the Christian Church through all ages, Mark xvi. 17, 18. But —

(1.) That passage itself is of doubtful authority, since we know that it was omitted in most of the Greek MSS. which Eusebius was able to examine a the 4th century: and it is still wanting in some of the most important that remain to us.

(2.) It does not necessarily imply more than a promise that such miraculous powers should exhibit themselves among the immediate converts of the Apostles.

And (3) this latter interpretation is supported by what follows — "And they went forth, and preached everywhere, the Lord working with them, and *confirming the word with the accompanying signs.*"

It is, indeed, confessed by the latest and ablest defenders of the ecclesiastical miracles that the great mass of them were essentially a new dispensation; but it is contended, that by those who believe in the Scripture miracles no strong antecedent improbability against such a dispensation can be reasonably entertained; because, for them, the Scripture miracles have already "borne the brunt" of the infidel objection, and "broken the ice."

But this is wholly to mistake the matter.

If the only objection antecedently to proof against the ecclesiastical miracles were a presumption of their *impossibility* or *incredibility* — simply *as miracles,* this allegation might be pertinent; because he that admits that a miracle has taken place, cannot consistently hold that a *miracle as such* is impossible or incredible. But the antecedent presumption against the ecclesiastical miracles rises upon four distinct grounds, no one of which can be properly called a ground of *infidel* objection.

(1.) It arises from the very nature of probability, and the constitution of the human mind, which compels us to take the analogy of general experience as a measure of likelihood. And this presumption it is manifest is neither religious nor irreligious, but antecedent to, and involved in, all probable reasoning.

A miracle may be said to take place when, under certain moral circumstances, a physical consequent follows upon an antecedent which general experience shows to have no natural aptitude for producing such a consequent; or, when a consequent fails to follow upon an antecedent which is always attended by that consequent in the ordinary course of nature. A blind man recovering sight upon his touching the bones of SS. Gervasius and Protasius, is an instance of the former. St. Alban, walking after his head was cut off, and carrying it in his hand, may be given as an example of the latter kind of miracle. Now, though such occurrences cannot be called impossible, because they involve no self-contradiction in the notion of them, and we know that there is a power in existence quite adequate to produce them, yet they must always remain antecedently improbable, unless we can see reasons for expecting that that power will produce them. The invincible original instinct of our nature — without reliance on which we could not set one foot before another — teaches as its first lesson to expect similar consequents upon what seem similar physical antecedents; and the results of this instinctive belief, checked, modified, and confirmed by the experience of mankind in countless times, places, and circumstances, constitutes what is called our knowledge of the laws of nature. Destroy, or even shake, this knowledge, as applied to practice in ordinary life, and all the uses and purposes of life are at an end. If the real sequences of things were liable, like those in a dream, to random and capricious variations, on which no one could calculate beforehand, there would be no measures of probability or improbability. If e. g. it were a measuring case whether, upon immersing a lighted candle in water, the candle should be extinguished, or the water ignited, — or, whether inhaling the common air should support life or produce death -

It is plain that the whole course of the world would be brought to a stand-still. There would be no order of nature at all; and all the rules that are built on the stability of that order, and all the measures of judgment that are derived from it, would be worth nothing. We should be living in fairy-land, not on earth.

(2.) This *general* antecedent presumption against miracles, as varying from the analogy of general experience, is (as we have said) neither religious nor irreligious — neither rational nor irrational — but springs from the very nature of probability: and it cannot be denied without shaking the basis of all probable evidence whether for or against religion.

Nor does the admission of the existence of the Deity, or the admission of the actual occurrence of the Christian miracles, tend to remove this antecedent improbability against miracles circumstanced as the ecclesiastical miracles generally are.

If, indeed, the *only* presumption against miracles were one against their *possibility* — this might be truly described as an atheistic presumption; and then the proof, from natural reason, of the existence of a God, or the proof of the actual occurrence of any one miracle would *wholly remove* that presumption; and, upon the removal of that presumption, there would remain none at all against miracles, however frequent or however strange; and miraculous occurrences would be as easily proved, *and also as likely beforehand*, as the most ordinary events; so that there would be no improbability of a miracle being wrought at any moment, or upon any conceivable occasion; and the slightest testimony would suffice to establish the truth of any story, however widely at variance with the analogy of ordinary experience.

But the true presumption against miracles is not against their *possibility*, but their *probability*. And this presumption cannot be wholly removed by showing an adequate cause; unless we hold that *all presumptions* drawn from the analogy of experience or the assumed stability of the order of nature are removed by showing the existence of a cause capable of changing the order of nature — i. e. unless we hold that the admission of God's existence involves the destruction of *all* measures of probability drawn from the analogy of experience. The ordinary sequences of nature are, doubtless, the result of the Divine will. But to suppose the Divine will to vary its mode of operation in conjunctures upon which it would be impossible to calculate, and under circumstances apparently similar to those which are perpetually recurring, would be to suppose that the course of things is (to all intents and purposes of human life) as mutable and capricious as if it were governed by mere chance.

Nor can the admission that God *has* actually wrought such miracles as attest the Christian religion, remove the general presumption against miracles as improbable occurrences. The evidence on which revelation stands has proved that the Almighty has, under special circumstances and for special ends, exerted his power of changing the ordinary course of nature. This may be fairly relied on as mitigating the presumption against miracles *under the same circumstances* as those which it has established: but miracles which cannot avail themselves of the benefit of that *law* (as it may be called) of miracles, which such conditions indicate, are plainly involved in all the antecedent difficulties which attach to miracles in general, as

varying from the *law of nature*, besides the special difficulties which belong to them as varying from the *law of miracles*, so far as we know anything of that law. And it is vain to allege that God *may* have other ends for miracles than those plain ones for which the Scripture miracles were wrought. Such a plea can be of no weight, unless we can change at pleasure the "*may*" into a "*must*" or "*has*." Until the design *appear*, we cannot use it as an element of probability; but we must, in the mean while, determine the question by the ordinary rules which regulate the proof of facts. A mere "may" is counterbalanced by a "may not." It cannot surely be meant that miracles have, by the proof of a revelation, ceased to be miracles — i. e. rare and wonderful occurrences — so as to make the chances equal of a miracle and an ordinary event. And if this be not held, then it must be admitted that the laws which regulate miracles are, in some way or other, laws which render them essentially *strange* or unusual events, and insure the *general stability* of the course of nature. Whatever other elements enter into the law of miracles, a necessary *infrequency* is one of them: and until we can see some of the positive elements of the law of miracles in operation (i. e. some of the elements which do not check, but require miracles) this negative element, which we do see, must act strongly against the probability of their recurrence.

It is indeed quite true that Christianity has revealed to us the permanent operation of a supernatural order of things actually going on around us. But there is nothing in the notion of *such* a supernatural system as the Christian dispensation is, to lead us to expect continual interferences with the common course of nature. Not the necessity of *proving* its supernatural character: for (1.) that has been sufficiently proved once for all, and the proof sufficiently attested to us, and (2.) it is not pretended that the mass of legendary miracles are, in this sense, evidential. Nor are such continual miracles involved in it by express promise, or by the very frame of its constitution. For they manifestly are not. "So is the kingdom of God, as if a man should cast seed into the ground, and should sleep and rise, night and day, and the seed should spring and grow up he knoweth not how," etc. — the parable manifestly indicating that the ordinary visible course of things is only interfered with by the Divine husbandman, in *planting* and *reaping* the great harvest. Nor do the answers given to prayer, or the influence of the Holy Spirit on our minds, interfere *discoverably* with any one law of outward nature, or of the inward economy of our mental frame. The system of grace is, indeed, *supernatural*, but, in no sense and in no case, *preternatural*. It disturbs in no way the regular sequences which all men's experience teaches them to anticipate as not improbable.

(3.) It is acknowledged by the ablest defenders of the ecclesiastical miracles that, for the most part, they belong to those classes of miracles which are described as *ambiguous* and *tentative* — i. e. they are cases in which the effect (if it occurred at all) *may* have been the result of natural causes, and where, upon the application of the same means, the desired effect was only sometimes produced. These characters are always highly suspicious marks. And though it is quite true — as has been remarked already — that real miracles, and such as were clearly discernible as such to the original spectators, may be so imperfectly reported to us as to wear an ambiguous appearance — it still remains a violation of all the laws of evidence to admit a narrative which leaves a miracle ambiguous as the *ground* of our belief that a miracle has really been wrought. If an *inspired* author declare a particular effect to have been wrought by the immediate interposition of God, we then admit the miraculous nature of that event *on his authority*, though his description of its outward circumstances may not be full enough to enable us to form such a judgment of it from the report of those circumstances alone: or if, amongst a series of indubitable miracles, some are but hastily and loosely reported to us, we may safely admit them as a part of that series, though if we met them in any other connection we should view them in a different light. Thus, if a skillful and experienced physician records his judgment of the nature of a particular disorder, well known to him, and in the diagnosis of which it was almost impossible for him to be mistaken, we may safely take his word for that, even though he may have mentioned only a few of the symptoms which marked a particular case: or, if we knew that the plague was raging at a particular spot and time, it would require much less evidence to convince us that a particular person had died of that distemper there and then, than if his death were attributed to that disease in a place which the plague had never visited for centuries before and after the alleged occurrence of his case.

(4.) Though it is not true that the Scripture miracles have so " borne the brunt " of the *à priori* objection to miracles as to remove all peculiar presumption against them as improbable events, there is a sense in which they may be truly said to have prepared the way for those of the ecclesiastical legends. But it is one which aggravates, instead of extenuating, their improbability. The narratives of the Scripture miracles may very probably have tended to raise an expectation of miracles in the minds of weak and credulous persons, and to encourage designing men to attempt an imitation of them. And this suspicion is confirmed when we observe that it is precisely those instances of Scripture miracles which are most easily imitable by fraud, or those which are most apt to strike a wild and mythical fancy, which seem to be the types which — with extravagant exaggeration and distortion — are principally copied in the ecclesiastical miracles. In this sense it may be said that the Scripture narratives " broke the ice," and prepared the way for a whole succession of legends; just as any great and striking character is followed by a host of imitators, who endeavor to reproduce him, not by copying what is really essential to his greatness, but by exaggerating and distorting some minor peculiarities in which his great qualities may sometimes have been exhibited.

But — apart from any leading preparation thus afforded — we know that the ignorance, fraud, and enthusiasm of mankind have in almost every age and country produced such a numerous spawn of spurious prodigies, as to make false stories of miracles, under certain circumstances, a thing to be naturally expected. Hence, unless it can be distinctly shown, from the nature of the case, that narratives of miracles are *not attributable* to such causes — that they are *not* the offspring of such a parentage — the reasonable rules of evidence seem to require that we should refer them to their usual and best known causes.

Nor can there be, as some weak persons are apt to imagine, any *impiety* in such a course. On the contrary, true piety, or religious reverence of God, requires us to abstain with scrupulous care from attributing to Him any works which we have not good reason for believing Him to have wrought. It is not piety, but profane audacity, which ventures to refer to God that which, according to the best rules of probability which He has Himself furnished us with, is most likely to have been the product of human ignorance, or fraud, or folly.

On the whole, therefore, we may conclude that the mass of the ecclesiastical miracles do not form any part of the same series as those related in Scripture, which latter are, therefore, unaffected by any decision we may come to with respect to the former; and that they are pressed by the weight of three distinct presumptions against them — being improbable (1) as varying from the analogy of nature; (2) as varying from the analogy of the Scripture-miracles; (3) as resembling those legendary stories which are the known product of the credulity or imposture of mankind.

The controversy respecting the possibility of miracles is as old as philosophic literature. There is a very clear view of it, as it stood in the Pagan world, given by Cicero in his books *de Divinatione* In the works of Josephus there are, occasionally, suggestions of naturalistic explanations of O. T. miracles: but these seem rather thrown out for the purpose of gratifying skeptical Pagan readers than as expressions of his own belief. The other chief authorities for Jewish opinion are, Maimonides, *Moreh Nebochim*, lib. 2, c. 35, and the *Pirke Aboth*, in Surenhusius's *Mishna*, tom. iv. p. 469, and Abarbanel, *Miphaloth Elohim*, p. 93. It is hardly worth while noticing the extravagant hypothesis of Cardan (*De contradictione Medicorum*, l. 2, tract. 2) and of some Italian atheists, who referred the Christian miracles to the influence of the stars. But a new era in the dispute began with Spinoza's *Tractatus Theologico-politicus*, which contained the germs of almost all the infidel theories which have since appeared. A list of the principal replies to it may be seen in Fabricius, *Delectus Argumentorum*, etc., c. 43, p. 697, Hamburg, 1725.

A full account of the controversy in England with the deists, during the last century, will be found in Leland's *View of the Deistical Writers*, reprinted at London, 1836.

The debate was renewed, about the middle of that century, by the publication of Hume's celebrated essay — the chief replies to which are: Principal Campbell's *Dissertation on Miracles*; Hey's *Norrisian Lectures*, vol. i. pp. 197-200 : Bp. Elrington's *Donnellan Lectures*, Dublin, 1796; Dr. Thomas Brown, *On Cause and Effect*; Paley's *Evidences* (Introduction); Archbp. Whately, *Logic* (Appendix), and his *Historic Doubts respecting Napoleon Bonaparte* (the argument of which the writer of this article has attempted to apply to the objections of Strauss in *Historic Certainties*, or the *Chronicles of Ecnarf*, Parker, London, 1862). See also an interesting work by the late Dean Lyall, *Propædia Prophetica*, reprinted 1854, Rivington, London. Compare also Bp. Douglas, *Criterion, or Miracles Examined*, etc., London, 1754.

Within the last few years the controversy has been reopened by the late Professor Baden Powell in *The Unity of Worlds*, and some remarks on the study of evidences published in the now celebrated volume of *Essays and Reviews*. It would be pre-nature, at present, to give a list of the replies to so recent a work.

The question of the ecclesiastical miracles was slightly touched by Spencer in his notes on Origen against Celsus, and more fully by Le Moine; but did not attract general attention till Middleton published his famous *Free Enquiry*, 1748. Several replies were written by Dodwell (junior), Chapman, Church, etc., which do not seem to have attracted much permanent attention. Some good remarks on the general subject occur in Jortin's *Remarks on Ecclesiastical History*, and in Warburton's *Julian*. This controversy also has of late years been reopened by Dr. Newman, in an essay on miracles originally prefixed to a translation of Fleury's *Ecclesiastical History*, and since republished in a separate form. Dr. Newman had previously, while a Protestant, examined the whole subject of miracles in an article upon Apollonius Tyanæus in the *Encyclopædia Metropolitana*.

W. F.

* The differences of opinion in regard to the *reality* of miracles arise often from differences of opinion in regard to the meaning of the *word*; and the differences in regard to the word "miracles," arise often from differences in regard to the meaning of the term "laws of nature." Therefore we inquire: —

A. What are the laws of nature?

One definition involving several others is this: the forces and tendencies essential to material substances and the finite minds of the world, and so adjusted to each other in a system as, in their established mode of operation, to necessitate uniform phenomena. We speak of these forces and tendencies not as accidental but as *essential;* not as essential to matter *as such,* but to the different species of matter; not to *all* finite minds, but to those of which we are informed by reason as distinct from revelation. When the angel is described (Bel, 36) as carrying Habbacuc by the hair of the head to Babylon, he is not described as complying with *the* laws of *nature*, although he may have complied with *a* law of the *angels*. On the preceding definition of the laws of nature both an atheist and a theist can unite in discussing the question of miracles. Still, from those laws a theist infers that there is a law-giver and a law-administrator; from the system of natural forces and tendencies he infers the existence of a mind who once created and now preserves them. Believing that they are only the instruments by which God uniformly causes or occasions the phenomena which take place, a theist is correct when he defines the laws of nature in their *ultimate* reference as "the established method of God's operation." It may *seem,* but it is far from *being,* needless to add, that the phrase, laws of nature, is a figure of speech, and gives rise to other figures. Derived from the Saxon *lagu, lag, lah,* the word law suggests that which is (1) laid, fixed, *settled* (Gesetz, something laid down); (2) *laid down* by a superior being; (3) *so fixed* as to make uniform sequences necessary. In its literal use it denotes such a command of a superior as is addressed to the conscience and will, and is accompanied with a threat making obedience necessary in relation to happiness. In its figurative use the command is the system of natural forces and tendencies; the obedience is the course of natural phenomena which are necessary not in the relative but in the absolute sense. God *said:* "Let the earth bring forth grass"; he *spake* to the animals

and said: "Be fruitful and multiply." The legal words which he spoke in the creation he continues to speak in the preservation of the natural forces and tendencies; and they being, as it were, mandatory words, are followed by events which are, as it were, obedient acts.

B. What is a miracle?

Of this term various definitions may be given, each of them correct, one of them more convenient for one use, another for a different use.

1. A *general* definition, comprehending many specific statements, and appropriate to a miracle considered *as an event, as a phenomenon,* is this: a manifest violation of laws of nature in reference to the results dependent upon them. It is objected to this definition that it supposes *all* the laws of nature to be violated, whereas in a miracle some of these laws are complied with (B. 5–8). But the definition teaches only that laws, not *all the laws,* of nature are prevented, by some other than natural force, from producing the effects which, when they are not interfered with, they produce uniformly. It is again objected, that the definition supposes the laws of nature to be violated *in all their relations.* Just the reverse; it does not suppose these laws to be violated in their reference to a supposed or imagined power on which they depend, but only in reference to the results which almost uniformly depend upon them; not in respect of any thing which is above and before them, but merely in respect of events which are beneath and after them. It is again objected, that there is no power above the laws of nature, and therefore these laws *cannot* be violated (*vis, violare*). But the objector has no right to assume that there is no *superior* force able to control the *physical* forces and tendencies. An objector adds: If the laws of nature be laws of God, they cannot be broken down by a created power, and will not be broken down by himself: he will not break through his own ordinances. But here again is a *Petitio Principii,* a mere assumption that while for *one* purpose the author of nature sustains its laws, he will not for *another* purpose interfere with their usual sequences. An objector says: The word *violation* is too figurative to be used in defining a miracle. But it is a mere drawing out of the figure involved in the phrase "nature's laws." It gives consistency and completeness to the metaphor which suggests it. (A.) When the customary sequences of physical laws are suspended by some force which is not one of those laws, then the laws are said to be rebuffed, as when the Saviour "rebuked" the fever, and "rebuked" the winds, and said to the sea: "Peace, be still" (Matt. viii. 26; Mark iv. 39; Luke viii. 24, iv. 39). It is again objected that a violation of natural laws is a miracle, whether the violation be *manifest* or not. "This alters not its nature and essence" (Hume). But we do not care to include in our definition such imaginary events as never occurred, and we do not believe that there have been violations of natural law unless they have been manifest. Besides, if secret violations of this law have occurred, they excite no theological interest, and are not within the pale of our theological discussion. In proportion as men fail to *see evidence* that a physical law was violated in the phenomenon described as Joshua's "stopping the sun," just in that proportion do men lose their special motives for proving that the narrative is fabulous, or poetical, or a true history. A secret miracle belongs to a secret revelation, but a the-

dogian, as such, does not care for things "done in a corner." A true miracle is proved to be such by its own nature, and not by the mere testimony of the person who works it. Usage and convenience permit our limiting the word to those supernatural phenomena which give in themselves proof of their contrariety to natural law. Mohammed and his prophets may affirm the Koran to be a miracle; but we cannot take their word for it: the book does not, more than the Iliad or the Æneid, present obvious signs of a power going beyond the human. It is further objected, that, as the phrase, violation of nature's laws, may imply something more than a miracle, even an impossibility, so it may denote something less than a miracle. Thus we say that a clumsy mechanic violates the laws of the screw, lever, etc, when he breaks them by a violent use for which they were never adapted; a student violates the laws of the eye; an orator violates the laws of the larynx; a debauchee violates the laws of his constitution. But in these and similar instances the laws of nature are regarded in reference to their uses; in a miracle, they are regarded in reference to the results which would ensue from them if they were not suspended by a foreign power.

2. The general definition may be explained by a specific one; a miracle is a phenomenon which, occurring without regularity of time and place, and in manifest violation of nature's laws as they commonly operate, could not have been definitely foreseen and calculated upon by the man who pretends that it was wrought in his behalf. If it did not occur without regularity of time and place, it could not occur in manifest violation of the laws of nature. Many writers (like an Edinburgh Reviewer in No. 254) describe miracles as "the arrangements by which, at crossing places in their orbits, man's world is met and illumined by phenomena belonging to another zone and moving in another plane"; but such phenomena, like the appearance of a comet once in six hundred years, are still regular, and therefore are not obvious counteractions of nature's laws, and of course do not baffle the precise calculations of men.

3. If there are laws which, as ordinarily preserved, necessitate uniform phenomena, and if they are in a miracle as forcibly suspended as the general definition indicates, then the suspension must be a striking prodigy (hence the words, miraculum miror; θαῦμα, θαυμάσιον, παράδοξον); must excite the emotion of wonder (Mark i. 27, ii. 12, iv. 41, vi. 51; Luke xxiv. 12, 41; Acts iii. 10, 11); and, arousing the minds of men, will lead them to anticipate some message connected with it. The kingdom of nature, as nature, "suffereth violence"; and why? John Foster describes the phenomenon as the ringing of the great bell of the universe calling the multitudes to hear the sermon. Therefore one specific definition of a miracle may be: a phenomenon which occurs in violation of the laws of nature as they commonly operate, and which is designed to attest the divine authority of the messenger in whose behalf it occurs. Indirectly the miracle indicates the truth of the message (1 K. xvii. 24; Coleridge's Works, i. p. 323); directly it is intended to indicate the divine sanction of the messenger (Ex. vii. 9, 10; 1 K. xiii. 3–6). If a man pretend to have received a new revelation from Heaven, we may say to him, as Talleyrand said to Lepaux: The Founder of the Christian system suffered himself to be crucified and He rose again:

you should try and do as much." This second definition is a decisive one; because the characteristics of a miracle are learned from the design of it. If the miracle be intended to signify the divine authority of the worker, it must be an event which, in and of itself, gives evidence of its not being the effect of natural causes. This intent or the miracle is not essential to its abstract nature but is always connected with its actual occurrence. Without such an intent an obvious violation of nature's laws would be a miracle; but without such an intent there never is such a violation. Therefore the Bible, as a practical volume, gives prominence to the end for which the miracle is wrought; see Exodus iii. 2 ff., iv. 1–9; 2 K. i. 10; Matt. xi. 3–5; Mark ii. 10, 11; John ii. 23, iii. 2, v. 36, 37, ix. 16, 30–33, x. 25, 38, xi. 4, 40, 42, xii. 30, xiv. 10, 11, xx. 30, 31; Acts ii. 22, x. 37–43; Heb. ii. 3, 4.

4. If the material and mental forces and tendencies receive so violent a shock as is implied in the general definition, the miracle will lead men to infer: "This is the finger of God" (Ex. viii. 19). Even if it be performed instrumentally by an angel or any superhuman creature, still it is God who sustains that creature, and gives him power and opportunity to perform the miracle. Preserving the laws of nature, God also compels them to produce their effects. No created power can counteract his compulsory working. If he choose to intermit that working, and allow an angel to prevent the sequences of the law which God preserves, then it is God who works the miracle by means of an angel who is divinely permitted to come through the opened gates of nature. "Qui facit per alium," etc. Therefore another specific definition of a miracle may be: a work wrought by God interposing and manifestly violating laws of nature as they are viewed in reference to their ordinary results. It is not a mere "event" or "phenomenon," it is a "work," a work wrought by God (the Spirit of God, Matt. xii. 28); a work wrought by God interposing (the finger of God, Luke xi. 20). If the laws of nature be obviously violated (B. 1) there is a miracle, whether they be violated by a created or an uncreated cause, or by no cause at all. Still, in point of fact they never have been violated except by the divine interposition; not even by demons unless God first interposed, and opened the door of the world, and let them pass through, and perform the lesser works in order that he may at once overpower them by the greater. Even if the laws of nature were violated without the divine interposition, the irregularity would not fulfil the main design of a miracle (B. 4), and therefore should be distinguished by the word prodigy, or by a synonym ("mirabile non miraculum"). Hence it is the prevailing style of the Bible, to connect the miraculous phenomenon with the interposed power of Jehovah; see Exodus iv. 11, 12; Ps. cxvi. 8; Matt. xii. 24, 28; John iii. 2, ix. 33, x. 21; Acts x. 38, 40, and passages under B. 2.

5. In order to make the truth more prominent that the forces and tendencies which our unaided reason reveals to us are not thwarted in all, but only in some of their relations; that they are not made (as Spinoza thinks them to be) inconsistent with themselves, and that their Preserver intercalates a new force preventing their usual sequences, another specific definition of a miracle is: A work wrought by the divine power interposed between certain natural laws and the results which they

must have produced if they had not been violated by that power. It is often said, that the creation of the world was a miracle; but before the creation no laws of nature had been established, and of course no power was interposed (as a sign B. 3) *between* non-existing laws and their normal results. So it is said that the creation of new species of plants and animals was a miracle; but it was not, unless the preüestablished laws of some *other* substances were violated by the creating act interposed (as a sign) between those laws and their legitimate results. It is said again, that the preservation of the world is a constant miracle; but what forces and tendencies are there which must be resisted by a preserving energy interposed (as a sign) *between* them and their otherwise uniform effects?

6. Since the phrase, "violation of nature's laws," is condemned sometimes as expressing too much, and sometimes as expressing too little, it may give place to a synonymous phrase, and a miracle may be defined: A work wrought by God interposing and producing what otherwise the laws of nature *must* (not merely *would*) have prevented, or preventing (Dan. iii. 27) what otherwise the laws of nature *must* (not merely *would*) have produced. Thus the non-occurrence as well as the occurrence of a phenomenon may be a miracle (see B. 7), and thus also a miraculous is distinguished from a supernatural event (C. 7).

7. As we sometimes overlook the truth that all the laws of nature are constantly upheld and controlled by God, and in this sense are his established method of operation (A), and as we accordingly imagine that when they are violently broken over his power is counteracted, and an event takes place arbitrarily and wildly, another of the specific definitions, harmonizing in fact though not in phrase with all the preceding, may be: A miracle is an effect which, unless it had been produced by an interposition of God, would have been a violation of the laws of nature as they are related to Him and to their established sequences. If we suppose that a human body is thrown into a furnace heated as Daniel iii. 21–30 describes it, the law of fire is to consume that body. If the forces and tendencies of the fire are preserved, and if no volition of God be intercalated to resist them, and if in these circumstances the body remains uninjured, then the law of the fire is violated. If, however, God intercalates his volition and thwarts the action of the fire, He does not violate its laws in their relation to him, for it *has* no laws which can produce or prevent any phenomena in opposition to his interposed will (Brown on *Cause and Effect*). A miracle is natural to the supernatural act of God choosing to produce it.

8. Since the laws of nature are often supposed to include all existing forces, and are thus confounded (even by Dr. Thomas Brown) with the laws of the universe (B. 4), still another of the specific definitions, illustrating each of the preceding, may be: A miracle is a phenomenon which, if not produced by the interposition of God, would be a violation of the laws of the *universe*. In the universe God himself is included; it is no violation of any law in his nature that He is perfectly benevolent; it is in unison with all the laws of his being that He perform all those outward acts which perfect benevolence requires, and consequently that He put forth a volition for a miracle when the general good demands it. As it is consonant with he laws of God to choose the occurrence of a

needed miracle, so it is consonant with the laws of matter and finite mind to obey his volitions It would be a violation of their laws if He should exert his omnipotence upon his creatures and they should effectually resist it. Since then it is his invariable method of action to do all which the well-being of his universe demands, and to make that effect necessary which He wills to make so; and since it is the invariable order of sequence that matter and finite mind yield to the fiat of their Maker. it follows that a miracle (even as defined in B. 1) may not only be in harmony with the laws of the *created* universe as they are related to the divine will, but may be actually required by the laws of the *entire* universe, and while abnormal in their lower, may be normal in their higher relations (D. 1, *c. d*).

C. What are the distinctions between a miracle and other real or imagined phenomena?

1. A miracle is not an event without an adequate cause. The atheist and pantheist, believing that there is no personal author of nature, and that a miracle has no cause in the forces of nature, are misled to believe that it can have no cause at all.

2. A miracle is not an interposition amending or rectifying the laws of nature. Some (Spinoza, Schleiermacher) have regarded the common definitions of a miracle as implying that the courses of nature are imperfect and need to be set right. M. Renan describes a miracle as a special intervention "like that of a clock-maker putting his fingers in to remedy the defects of his wheels;" and Alexandre Dumas, borrowing an Italian epigram, describes a miracle as "the *coup d' état* of the Deity." By no means, however, is it an afterthought of God; by no means the result of a discovery that the laws of nature are not fitted to fulfill their design. Those laws were planned for the miracle as much as the miracle was planned for them. It would not be of use, unless they were essentially what they are. It is performed not because the works of God need to be supplemented, but because men will not make the right use of his works. It is prompted not by a desire to improve what He has done, but by his condescending pity for men who willfully pervert what He has done. It does not imply that the uniformity of nature is a mistake, but that it is a wise arrangement — so wise that it enables him by a sudden deviation from it to give an emphatic proof of his grace. It does not imply that the constitution of the human mind in expecting this uniformity is wrong, but that it is right, and specially right as it prepares the mind to be impressed because startled by the miraculous sign of superhuman love.

3. A miracle is not a counteraction of *some* laws by *other* laws of nature. Dynamic forces counteract the mechanical; vital forces counteract the chemical; voluntary forces counteract the physical. This counteraction of one force by another is not even supernatural, still less miraculous (B. 6, C. 7). It would not take place unless natural laws were uniform; it is a compliance with the law counteracted, as well as with the law counteracting; not only is it produced by nature, but *must* be produced, unless a power be interposed thwarting nature. A chemist, like Prof. Faraday, cannot prove his divine commission by his novel experiments of one chemical law resisting another. In such resistance lies one secret of various magi-

al arts; of the feats, for example, which the
Egyptians performed "by their enchantments."
A miraculous is distinguished from a magical wonder partly by its being such a "mighty work"
(δύναμις) as transcends all created energy; such a
work as science in its progressive tendencies becomes less and less able to explain by natural
causes.

4. A miracle is not merely a sign of divine
authority. It is a "sign" (σημεῖον, τέρας; mon-
strum, monstrans), but it is more. If we could
make exact distinctions between the nearly synonymous words of the Bible, we might say that
miracles are signs, and wonderful signs, and such
wonderful signs as could not have been wrought
by finite power (Acts ii. 22; 2 Cor. xii. 12; 2 Thess.
ii. 9). Mr. Webster, in his eulogy on Adams and
Jefferson, speaks of their dying on the same fourth
day of July as a sign from heaven; many persons
regard many remarkable events as tokens of the
divine will; many divines regard the internal worth
of the Bible as an indication of its celestial origin;
controversialists may believe in all these phenomena
and yet not believe in them as signs; or may
believe in them as signs præter-natural and even
super-natural, but not miraculous. The convenience of scientific inquiry demands a distinction
between that which is aside from nature, that
which is above nature, and that which is against
nature as such.

5. A miracle is not precisely defined as "an
exception" to, or a "deviation" from "the laws
of nature," "from some of the laws of nature,"
"from the uniform manner in which God exercises
his power throughout the world;" "from the uniform method in which second causes produce their
effects." Some writers teach that if an event be
"simply inexplicable by any known laws of nature"
it is a miracle in the negative sense; if it be also a
"distinct sign by which the divine power is made
known" in favor of a religious system, it is a
miracle in the positive sense. But it is a common
belief of theologians that the divine process of
sanctifying the soul (Heb. xiii. 20, 21) is not miraculous, and yet is "an exception to, or deviation
from some laws of nature." It is common, moreover, to speak of physical events as præter-natural,
when the speaker does not imagine them to be even
supernatural. One of the chaplains to Archbishop
Sancroft was born with two tongues; but this
"deviation from ordinary phenomena" was not a
"sign" that his faith had or had not the divine
approval. True, in the large view of mere nature
(C. 3), such phenomena are not real but only apparent deviations from nature's laws, for they result
ormally from peculiar combinations of these laws.
till they are familiarly called "deviations from
nature," and for the sake of precision ought to be
distinguished from miracles. A miracle is indeed a
wonder (B. 3), but we may conceive of wonders
which are not miracles, and are on the whole
stranger than miracles (D. 2).

6. A miracle is not (as Schleiermacher supposes
t to be) a phenomenon produced by an occult law
of nature. The following beautiful illustration of
this theory is quoted by Dr. J. F. Clarke (Orthodoxy, etc., pp. 64, 65) from Dr. Ephraim Peabody:
"A story is told of a clock on one of the high
cathedral towers of the older world, so constructed
that at the close of a century it strikes the years
as it ordinarily strikes the hours. As a hundred
years come to a close, suddenly, in the immense

mass of complicated mechanism, a little wheel
turns, a pin slides into the appointed place, and in
the shadows of the night the bell tolls a requiem
over the generations which during a century have
lived and labored and been buried around it. One
of these generations might live and die, and witness
nothing peculiar. The clock would have what we
call an established order of its own; but what
should we say when, at the midnight which brought
the century to a close, it sounded over a sleeping
city, rousing all to listen to the world's age?
Would it be a violation of law? No; only a
variation of the accustomed order, produced by
the intervention of a force always existing, but
never appearing in this way until the appointed
moment had arrived. The tolling of the century
would be a variation from the observed order of
the clock; but to an artist, in constructing it, it
would have formed a part of that order. . So a
miracle is a variation of the order of nature as it
has appeared to us; but to the Author of nature it
was a part of that predestined order — a part of
that order of which he is at all times the immediate Author and Sustainer; miraculous to us, seen
from our human point of view, but no miracle to
God; to our circumscribed vision a violation of
law, but to God only a part in the great plan and
progress of the law of the universe." We reply:
If such a marvelous phenomenon be, like the
blooming of the century plant, a result of physical
laws as already defined (A.), we cannot be certain
that some philosophers have not detected these
laws, as some have proved the existence of a particular planet before that planet had been detected
by the eye. We cannot be certain that these
sagacious philosophers have not waited for the
foreseen phenomenon and delivered their message
in connection with it, as some deceitful navigators
have uttered their threats to a savage king a few
hours before a solar or lunar eclipse, and have
represented the eclipse as giving a divine authority
for those threats. If a miracle is wrought at all,
it is wrought for an end; if for an end, then for a
special sign of the divine will (B. 3); if for a sign
of the divine will, then probably not by an occult
law of nature; for if it be wrought by an occult law,
then it becomes the less decisive as a sign, less conducive to its end. Therefore the antecedent presumptions for a miracle (D. 1, c. d.) are presumptions for it as the result of a force other than a
natural law. · It may be rejoined, however, that
the Deity has at the creation inserted in matter or
spirit certain exceptional forces, having no uniform
activity, and becoming operative only at irregular
and exceptional emergencies, for no other purpose
than that of giving to certain teachers an exceptional divine authority. But forces like these are
not in the system of uniform agencies, but out of
it, consequently they are not laws of nature (A);
their existence is at least as difficult to prove as is
the occurrence of transient divine volitions; they,
as mediate, represent and are equivalent to the
immediate interpositions of God's will; no essential
advantage can be gained, and in some cases perhaps no essential (but only a rhetorical) advantage
is lost, by referring the miracle to these special
and abnormal forces, instead of referring it to the
bare and immediate ictus of the divine volition.

7. A miracle is not a merely supernatural phenomenon. The supernatural is the genus, including all events produced by a power above the
natural laws (B. 6). Of these events the merely

supernatural is *one* species including those only which are *not* violations, the miraculous is *another* species including those only which *are* violations, of the natural laws. The renewal of the soul as described in John i. 12, 13, iii. 3–8; Eph. ii. 4–10, is *merely* supernatural, and not (as Coleridge terms it) miraculous; for the *essential* tendencies of the soul, the laws *essential* to its being a soul (A) are not manifestly violated when they are rectified; neither is the occurrence so irregular as to defy all possibility of anticipating definite examples of it (B. 2). So it *might* be maintained, consistently with the *strict* meaning of the terms, that Jesus performed his first *miracle* at the wedding of Cana (John ii. 11), and his second *miracle* upon the son of the Capernaum nobleman (John iv. 47–54); and still before the *first* of these miracles he had given *supernatural* signs of his Messiahship (John i. 48), and before the *second* he had given many such signs, as in his calling of the Apostles, his conversation with the Samaritan woman, his predictions, etc.; and Nicodemus (in John iii. 2) referred not merely to the miraculous but also to other supernatural " signs " that Jesus had a divine authority.

D. What is the difference between the proof of the *Biblical* and the proof of *other* alleged miracles?

1. There is a difference between the antecedent presumptions in regard to the Biblical, and the antecedent presumptions in regard to other miracles.

a. There is a strong presumption against all miracles considered *merely as violations of physical law.* At the outset of our inquiries we presume that the course of events will be as it has been; that it has been in the past ages as it is in the present age; and of course that no event *viewed simply as an event* has occurred in contrariety to this uniform order. While the testimony for common events is to be credited at once without strong reasons for rejecting it, the testimony for miracles *as mere phenomena* is to be rejected at once without strong reasons for crediting it. When divines refuse to say that a miracle is a violation of physical laws (B. 1) because the term *violation* makes the miracle appear intrinsically improbable, they seem to forget that so far as a miracle in itself, *i. e.* viewed as a mere phenomenon, is improbable, just so far does it become useful in proving that God has interposed in behalf of his revealed word; and so far as a miracle, in itself, ahd apart from its relations to a special divine intention, is probable, just so far does it lose its usefulness as a sign of God's interest in that word. The Christian apologist contends against his own cause, when he contends against Hume's doctrine that a miracle as a mere event is contrary to experience; for if it were not contrary to experience it could be calculated on (B. 2), and would thus lose its power to surprise and convince. He injures his own cause when he asserts, in opposition to Hume, that a miracle as a mere event is conformed to experience; for if an event be conformed to experience, then it is conformed to the general truth learned from experience, that physical changes have physical or finite causes; and if it be conformed to this truth then it is no miracle (B. 4–8). Let us represent the number of alleged miracles by the figure 1,000; whether these have been actually wrought is the question: at the outset we cannot say that they have been, or have not been; we cannot beg the question in the affirmative or in the negative; we

can say, however, that leaving out of account the disputed number 1,000, we have never experienced, and no other men have experienced the phenomenon of a physical change without a physical or a finite cause. Thus the miracle is contrary to experience and to *all* experience (Mark i. 27, ii. 12; Luke v. 26; John ix. 32, xv. 24). It is therefore intrinsically improbable. Whether we suppose (with Reid, Stewart, Campbell) that we have a constitutional tendency to believe the course of events to be uniform; or (with Mill, McCosh) that this belief results from experience; or, that it is both intuitive and confirmed by experience, it is a firm belief of all men. Because it is deep-seated, the presumption against miracles as mere phenomena is strong, and therefore when miracles are wrought they become the more startling and convincing, and are regarded not as mere phenomena but as divine signals.

b. Against the great majority of alleged miracles the presumption remains unrebutted. Some of them are connected with no apparent design good or bad; some with a design to commend a system of morals or religion which is false and injurious. No amount of testimony is strong enough to give us rest in believing that God has interposed and checked the operation of his own laws without any design, without a good design, without a great and good design. The presumption *against* such miracles as are said to have been wrought at the tomb of the Abbé Paris, or upon the daughter of Pascal, cannot be invalidated by the witnesses *for* them. " I should not believe such a story were it told me by Cato." We need not deny that the witnesses were honest, that they actually saw wonderful and even inexplicable phenomena; but they drew a wrong inference; they did not refer the phenomena to the real, though concealed causes: they mistook a monstrosity for a miracle: the amazing operation of *some one* law, as of electricity, odyle, concealed mental forces, for the palpable violation of the *laws* of nature.

c. Against the Biblical miracles, however, the antecedent presumption does not remain unrebutted; for they are not mere physical phenomena; for, first, they were wrought by a Mind infinitely desirous of the spiritual and eternal welfare of men (see Dr. Channing, iii. p. 118); secondly, they were *needed* for attesting a revelation which was *imminently* and *deplorably* needed; thirdly, the revelation was grand enough to deserve such miracles (" Nec Deus intersit," etc.), and the miracles were noble enough to fit such a revelation. If, as Paley says, the one message recorded in John v. 28, 29, was " well worthy of that splendid apparatus " of miracles which accompanied it, how much more worthy was such a condensed treatise as our Lord's discourse to Nicodemus? That discourse is a gem; there is an antecedent presumption that it will have a costly setting. The inspired word is called by Locke a telescope for the mind; there is an antecedent presumption that it will be mounted on a strong frame-work. Miracles are the setting and the frame-work for the Gospel. There is an antecedent presumption that the Father who is " very pitiful " will interpose for the children whom He loves with infinite tenderness, will reveal to them the truth which is essential to their peace, and will confirm it by miracles which are needed for its appropriate influence. Our conclusion then is exactly opposite to that of Hume. He says (whatever he means) that a miracle may possibly be proved, but not "so as to be the foundation of a system of religion;" we say that we have heard of no miracle which can be proved *unless it be* the foundation of a system of religion. The presumption against miracles *as mere physical phenomena* is rebutted by the presumption in favor of miracles *as related to infinite Benevolence.* The antecedent improbability of their occurring *as violations of physical law* is counterbalanced by the antecedent probability of their occurring as *attestations of religious truth.* The favorable presumption offsetting the antagonistic one prepares us to examine the testimony for miracles with as little impulse to reject it as if the testimony related to an ordinary event. In the logical order our belief in their necessity, fitness, worthiness, may be either the *conditio præcedens* or the *conditio subsequens* of our belief in their actual occurrence, but in the chronological order the testimony for them may be so overwhelming as to convince us of their occurrence and their worthiness *at one and the same time.*

d. In favor of the Biblical miracles there is not only one presumption which equals and thus rebuts, but there is another presumption which more than equals, which overpowers the presumption against them, and thus not only prepares but also predisposes us to credit the testimony in their favor. The religious system in behalf of which they were wrought involves internal marks of its having been revealed by God, but from that system the Biblical miracles are inseparable. (1.) We may take a *particular* view of this argument. According to the belief of many divines, some of the most important parts of the Christian system are in themselves miraculous phenomena. "Miracles and prophecies are not adjuncts appended from without to a revelation in itself independent of them, but constitutive elements of the revelation itself" (Rothe). He who believes in the *general* resurrection of the dead believes in the certainty of a future miracle far more stupendous than the resurrection of the widow's only son; how, then, can he *a priori* hesitate to believe in that past miracle? He who accepts the doctrine of the Incarnation as revealed in John i. 1–14, assents to a miracle far *more* astonishing than the appearance of the angels to the shepherds, and of the star to the Magi; how then can he be reluctant to receive the narrative of the *less astonishing* miracles? For a man to believe that a child was born in whom dwelt "all the fulness of the Godhead bodily" (Col. ii. 9), and at the same time to demur at the statement that the child who was named "The Wonderful" performed wonders which were miraculous, is as illogical as for a man to believe in the possibility of a sun, but not in the possibility of planets revolving around it. "Revelation itself is miraculous, and miracles are the proof of it." (Bp. Butler.) (2.) We may take a *more general* view of this argument. The supernatural truths of the Bible prompt us to believe that miracles have been wrought in attestation of them. Miracles are to such truths what the polish is to the agate, what the aroma is to the flower, what music is to the march of a triumphant army. It would be strange if tax-gatherers and publicans recorded sublimer truths than were recorded by Plato and Aristotle, and did not also attest them by miracles; if men received a supernatural inspiration, and did not record such truths as imply a miraculous interposition. Why were they inspired if they were not to reveal doctrines which transcended the human power of discovery, and did not confirm

them by wonders which transcended the human power of performance? Should we hear a man like Jesus Christ announce for the first time that he would cause the spiritually blind and deaf and dead to see and hear and live spiritually, we should expect that He would accompany his announcement with the miraculous gift of sight, hearing, life, to the corporeally blind, deaf, and dead. If we should hear Him predict the *new creation* of souls "unto good works" we should expect that He would illustrate his prediction by some miraculous control over nature. *In themselves* the miracles are improbable; *in itself* the revelation of such truths is improbable; but if such truths are to be revealed for the first time, then the miracles are to be expected; if the one improbability become a reality, we are to presume that the other will. The supernatural truths of the Bible are efflorescent, and miracles have been happily called their "efflorescence." They are so fit an accompaniment and so important a part of the truths connected with them that Dr. Channing (Memoir, ii. 442) goes so far as to say: "They are so inwoven in all his [Christ's] teachings and acts, that in taking them away we have next to nothing left;" and he says also (Works, iii. 119; see also iv. 392) as Augustine and others have said before him, that, on the whole, the wonder is not that *any* but that *so few* miracles have been wrought. (3.) We may take a *still more* general view of this argument. The miracles of the Bible are so interwoven with its didactic system, that if it stands, they stand; if they fall, it does not utterly fall, but it loses one strong prop; the intrinsic evidence in its favor becomes then a positive evidence in their favor. For example: the resurrection of Christ is an appropriate appendage to his atoning work. It is probable that if He died as our sacrifice, He rose from the dead; and if He rose from the dead, He died as our sacrifice; if He ascended to the throne, He rose from the grave; and if He rose from the grave, He ascended to the throne. In various other methods is his resurrection interlocked with the main teachings as well as with the personal character of his Apostles. Now the resurrection of Christ was an actual event, or it was not. If it were not, the narratives of it are not true; and if these narratives are not true, then the general system with which they are interlaced becomes the less probable. But that system is true; it so commends itself to our religious nature as to prove its divine original. Then the narratives of Christ's resurrection which are so inextricably intertwined with the system are true. To strike out those narratives from the New Testament and to retain the remainder, is like blotting out the figure of the Virgin from the Sistine Madonna.

The old objection arises: You prove the miracles by the doctrine, but you profess to prove the doctrine by the miracles. We do both. Each of the arguments lends aid to the other. Our Saviour did not perform his miracles as an anatomist conducts his demonstrations, by appealing to the intellect alone; but he required faith, or a right moral state, as a condition for his miraculous works; and on the other hand his miraculous works corroborated the moral faith (Mark vi. 5; Matt. xiii. 58). M. Renan mistakes the logical characteristics of the Bible, when he supposes that the resurrection of Lazarus should have been inquired into by a college of physicians relying on their anatomical instruments and demonstrating their conclusions. This might have been done safely; but the Bible

MIRACLES

does not profess to be a treatise on naked science; it relies not on *demonstrative* but on *moral* reasoning, and makes our intellectual pursuits a means of moral probation. We are predisposed by our proper reverence for the doctrine to believe in the miracles, which, however, are commended to us by their own independent proof ˈ(John v. 36, x. 25, 38, xiv. 10, 11); and we are predisposed by the miracles to believe in the doctrine, which, in its turn, is commended to us by its own independent evidence. The doctrine is the title-deed, and is *essential* to the significance of the seal attached to it. The miracle is the seal and is *important* for the authority of the title-deed. The seal torn away from the parchment cannot fulfill its main design, and the parchment with the seal cut out is lessened in value (Gerhard). The doctrine is the soul and is *essential* to the life of the body; the miracle is the body and is *important* for the full development of the soul. "Miracles test doctrine, and doctrine tests miracles" (Pascal).

2. There is a difference between the testimony in favor of the Biblical, and that in favor of other alleged miracles. Under the following seven heads are classified *some* of the peculiar evidences from testimony for the miracles of the Old and New Testaments; and it is easy to see that *all* these evidences are *not combined* in support of Pagan, Mohammedan, post-apostolic, or any other than the Scriptural miracles.

1. The nature of the miracles. (*a.*) They were such as could be judged by the senses (John xi.; Luke xxiv. 39). (*b.*) Many of them are not ambiguous; for how can we explain the resurrection of the dead by any natural law? (*c.*) They were not tentative; for we hear of no one who *faithfully* attempted to perform any miracle which he was authorized to perform, and who failed in the attempt. All who applied to Jesus were healed by his word (Matt. iv. 23, 24, viii. 16, ix. 35, xii. 15, xiv. 14; Mark vi. 56; Luke iv. 40, vi. 19). (*d.*) The alleged miracles were obviously connected with the volition of the person who professed to perform them, and were not, like the tentative works performed at the tombs and altars of saints, apparently independent of any particular volition producing them. (*e.*) They were connected *immediately* with the volition to produce them; a distant sufferer is instantly relieved by the spoken word (Matt. xi. 19, 20; John iv. 47–53). (*f.*) Many of them were of such a nature as cannot be explained by the acting of the imagination. The miracles of Christ were not like the cures effected by the touch of a *king*, but were wrought by a Galilean peasant in whose personal appearance we do not know that there was anything remarkable. In such methods as the preceding are the Biblical miracles distinguished from mere wonders, and the testimony in their favor from simply marvelous tales.

2. The circumstances in which they were performed. (*a.*) They were wrought at such times and places as favored the thorough examination of them: in broad daylight; in close contiguity to the observers (Luke xxiv. 39; John xx. 27). (*b.*) They were performed not privately, not before packed companies, but before promiscuous multitudes who could not be induced to combine in a stratagem (John ix.; Acts iii. 7 ff.). (*c.*) They were not performed by a band of artists or experts who remained together, and might cover each other's failings, and who were superintended by a skillful manager; but the Apostles separated from each other, did not act in concert, manifested no solicitude for each other's proceedings, imparted the miraculous gifts to men of different characteristics, who were selected not for their dexterity but for their moral worth (Acts xviii. 14–23, xix. 6; 1 Cor. xii. 7–11).

3. The character of the men on whose testimony we accept the miracles. (*a.*) Some of them were personal observers, eye and ear witnesses; John xv. 27; Acts ii. 32, iii. 15, iv. 20, v. 29–32, x. 39–41, xiii. 31; 2 Peter i. 16–18; 1 John i. 1–3. (*b.*) Whether personal witnesses or not, they were *able* to know the truth: men of sound and stable sense; practical men, like Mark, and Luke the physician, not credulous, not fanciful, not easily excited and beguiled (Mark xvi. 14; John xx. 24–29). If they had been poetical instead of prosaic, scholars instead of business men, politicians instead of tax-gatherers, they would have wanted one sign of credibility. (*c.*) They were *disposed* to utter the exact truth. They have such an air of veracity as cannot be mistaken. This air is made up (1) sometimes of childlike statements, as in Isaiah xxxviii. 21; (2) sometimes of omissions to ascribe miracles to particular men, as to Abraham, to Jacob, to David, to Solomon, to the Baptist (John x. 41), who however were special favorites of the historians, and would have been celebrated for their miraculous achievements, if the historians had indulged in mythical or fanciful narratives; (3) sometimes of incidental allusions to the labor of scrutinizing the reported facts, Luke i. 1–4; (4) sometimes of confessions of incipient incredulity, as in Matt. xxviii. 17; Mark xvi. 11, 13, 14; Luke xxiv. 11, 25; (5) sometimes of obvious freedom from anxiety to make out a consistent narrative. The reporters, seeming to be entirely at their ease, have admitted into their records unimportant discrepancies, which are apparent; and unimportant coincidences, which are occult. If their narratives had been written with a dishonest aim, the discrepancies would have been carefully concealed, and the coincidences would have been openly paraded. (6.) Sometimes their constitutional faults give an air of truthfulness to the Biblical narrators. Such an open-hearted man as Simon Peter could never have held out in a conspiracy to deceive the public. Such a skeptic as Thomas could never have united with him in so bold an enterprise. (*d.*) The historians were sure that their statements were correct. They appealed to their *interested* contemporaries. They challenged investigation. John x. 37; Acts ii. 22. (*e.*) Although able and disposed to give a true record, they were not able, had they been disposed, to *fabricate* such a record as they have given. Some of them, as Matthew, were deficient in genius, and this is an argument *for* rather than *against* their exact truthfulness. How could these men have invented a record of Christ's miracles só consonant with the principles of the divine administration, with the character of Christ, with the spirit of his Gospel? The great forces which God employs, gravitation for example, are noiseless. Christ's miracles were in the solitudes of Palestine. Christ was meek and lowly; he was born not in Rome but in Bethlehem, and dwelt not in the palace but in the cottage; so he did not perform his miracles upon consuls and prætors, but upon the little daughter of Jairus and upon the woman who was "bowed together." The spirit of his Gospel is that of mercy and grace; his miracles were wrought for the hungry, the epileptic, the paralytic, beggars

and sick children. Whose exuberant imagination invented this series of apposite wonders?

4. The circumstances in which the original narrators gave their testimony. (a.) They gave it at the time when the miracles were performed, not as the original reporters of many Pagan and Romish wonders, after the lapse of centuries from the performance of the exploits. (b.) There is reason to believe (Douglas's *Criterion*, pp. 80, 286–294) that the testimony for the Biblical miracles was first given at the place where they were performed (the Gospel of Jesus risen from the dead was first preached at Jerusalem), and not like the testimony for the miracles of Loyola and Xavier, at distant localities where the local evidence against them could not be scrutinized.

5. The effect of the miracles. (a.) They were partly the means of overcoming the opposition of the original narrators. The disciples of Christ were expecting him to be a temporal king, were looking forward to their own princely honors, and were hostile to the lowly and spiritual character of his mission His miracles helped to break down their hostility They were changed from enemies to friends partly by the σημεῖα which they described (Heb. ii. 4), and which they would, if they could, have rejected. (b.) The miracles were partly the means of turning masses of the people from a decided anti-Christian to a Christian belief (John ii. 23, iii. 2, vii. 31). (c.) Their converting influence is the more decisive sign of their reality, because every believer in them knew that he would be called by his faith to a continuous course of hard, self-denying, and often self-sacrificing work. Not without the most rigid scrutiny will men assent to a proposition which requires them to go through toil not only arduous but persevering, not only attended with habitual self-denial, but liable to end in the utter sacrifice of earthly good (John xi. 47–57). The alleged miracles of Pagans and Romanists have been performed among persons previously favorable to them, or liable to be imposed upon by excited fancy and feeling, and have not been connected with rigorous and repulsive exactions. (d.) A *new* religion was founded on the first Christian miracles. Men have a strong presumption against a faith not only exacting but new, and will disbelieve, if they can, in any miracles corroborating it. In order that the alleged miracles at the tomb of the Abbé Paris might be compared with the Biblical wonders, some instrumental worker of the miracles should have *appeared*, and should have declared his design in working them, and that design should have been to attest before unbelievers a novel as well as humiliating system of religious truth. (e.) External institutions (as the Passover, the Eucharist, the Lord's Day) were founded on, or in intimate connection with the Biblical miracles, and were established at the time and place when and where the miracles were said to have been wrought. Men who are to pay the cost have an economical objection to the rearing of expensive monuments for commemorating scenes of recent occurrence in their own neighborhood, when there is not clear proof that the scenes did occur. (f.) Not only the nature, but the degree of the influence exerted by the Biblical miracles is a proof of their reality. Against the selfishness and the prejudices of men he Christian system, originating with a few persons who were despised in Galilee, which was itself despised throughout Judæa, which in its turn was inspired in other countries, fought its own way into

the favor of the most enlightened nations, and partly by the aid of pretended miracles which, if they had been merely pretended, might have been shown to be such.

6. The testimony of persistent enemies. Men who denied the Biblical truths admitted the reality of the Biblical miracles. True, they ascribed the phenomena to magic; but this proves that they could not ascribe them to the working of natural law. True, they admitted the miraculous agency of all other religionists; but they had not the same motive for admitting the Christian miracles which they had for admitting others. The Christian system was exclusive, and would thus impel them to disprove it if they could; almost every Pagan system was liberal, and was thereby saved from arraying objectors in personal hostility to it. Is it said, that the early *opponents* of the Gospel confessed its miraculous attestation, because they were weak and credulous? But is it not said by the same objectors, that the early *friends* of the Gospel were weak and credulous? Why then did the alleged friends of the Gospel deny the miracles, " lying wonders," of heathenism? " The more weak and credulous any man is, the harder it is to convince him of anything that is opposite to his habits of thought and his inclinations. He will readily receive without proof anything that falls in with his prejudices, and will be disposed to hold out against any evidence that goes against them " (Whately's *Introductory Lessons*, p. 219, Cam. ed.).

7. The general coincidences of the Biblical narratives. (a.) The witnesses who recorded the Christian miracles differed from each other in personal character and style, and still agree with each other in the substance of their narratives. Their substantial concurrence is a sign, additional to every *individual* mark, that their narratives are true. (b.) The coincidence of the miraculous attestations with the internal character of the Biblical system (which moreover is itself composed of harmonizing doctrines, all of them witnesses concurring to recommend it, D. 1, d) forms another comprehensive sign that the simple-hearted men who recorded the miracles uttered the truth. (c.) The coincidence of the Biblical narratives with many general facts of history makes these narratives the more plausible. Miracles were *expected* by the nations to whom the Biblical theology was preached. Such an expectation is a correlate to the presumption that a benevolent God will interpose in behalf of such a theology (D. 1, c. d.). It is natural to think that the expectation would be met by the original preachers (Mark xvi. 20; Acts xiv. 3; Rom. xv. 18, 19), or that the hearers would have complained of the preachers, and the preachers would have apologized for their failure to meet it. Where are the complaints? Where are the apologies? Again, the Jews were an ignorant nation, but they retained their belief in one infinite God, who was to be worshipped spiritually; why did they cling to this sublime faith, while more cultivated nations, Egyptians, Greeks, Romans, did not rise above polytheism and idolatry? Had they more refined intuitions, or more logical skill than the masters of the Lyceum and Academy?

We have, then, a constitutional tendency to believe that as the original narrators of the Christian miracles were plain, sound, apparently ingenuous but not ingenious men, their narratives are true. Our experience favors this belief. The falsehood ot this testimony, *as mere testimony*, would be a monstrous deviation from the ordinary course of phenomena. The *concurrence* of all the preceding marks of truth in such a falsehood would be a still more monstrous deviation from the course of nature. It would be a deviation more monstrous than are the Biblical miracles themselves. It would be not only a marvel, but a *mere* marvel, for which there is no good moral reason; therefore it would be a *mere* monstrosity; but the miracles are not mere marvels, there is a good *moral* reason for them. We can see no adequate *natural*, and of course no supernatural cause of the mere monstrosity, but we can see an efficient cause of the miracles and an adorable one. The mere monstrosity has nothing to recommend it in its agreement with the laws of the universe; the miracles have much (B. 7, 8). If now there be two contradictory hypotheses both of which are marvelous, but one of them more unaccountable, more unreasonable, and thus more monstrous than the other, we are bound to reject the greater monstrosity.

Christian apologists have often adopted the maxim of Hume: Of two miracles, reject the greater; and they have said that if testimony having the preceding signs of trustworthiness were false the falsehood would be more *miraculous* than the miracles attested. But no; the falsehood of testimony which appears credible may be more wonderful than a miracle, and yet be in itself no miracle at all. While it may be *difficult* to account for the falsehood, it is absolutely *impossible* to account for the miracle, on any known principle of human or physical nature (B). Except in a few disputed cases there has never been an approximation to the phenomenon of raising the dead, but in numerous cases there has been an approximation to the phenomenon of false testimony which had all the appearance of being true. The falsehood of such testimony, then, must be less contrary to experience than the miracle, the very nature of which requires that, except in the few disputed instances, it be contrary to all, *i. e.* to the analogy of all experience (D. 1, *a*). Experience, however, is not our only guide. Antecedently to experience we have two contrary presumptions, and of these two the stronger prompts us to believe in such miracles as are recorded in the Bible (B. 5–8, C. 5, D. 1, *c. d.*). The character of God and his relations to men make it more rational to suppose that a wonderful event has occurred for which we can see a moral reason and an efficient cause, than that a monstrous event has occurred for which we see no moral reason and no natural cause.

E. The proper time for discussing the Question of Miracles.

In some rare cases it may be needful to discuss the question with an atheist, pantheist, or skeptic. In these cases the definitions of a miracle under B. 1, 2, are appropriate. As at the outset we cannot require him to assert, and he cannot require us to deny the existence of God, so these definitions neither assert nor deny it. A more appropriate, as well as a more common time, however, for discussing the question of miracles is *after* we have proved the existence and attributes of God. The discussion is between the Christian and the Deist, oftener than between the Theist and the Atheist. But the *most* appropriate time for the discussion is after we have proved man's need of a revelation and the fitness of the Biblical revelation to supply that need. The internal evidence of the inspiration of the Bible removes the obstacles which obstruct the proof of miracles, and also lends additional force to that proof and forms a part of it.   E. A. P.

MIR'IAM (מִרְיָם, *their rebellion*: LXX. Μαριάμ; hence Joseph. Μαριάμνη: in the N. T. Μαριάμ or Μαρία, Μαριάμ being the form always employed for the nominative case of the name of the *Virgin Mary*, though it is declined Μαρίας, Μαρίᾳ; while Μαρία is employed in all cases for the three other Maries). The name in the O. T. is given to two persons only: the sister of Moses, and a descendant of Caleb. At the time of the Christian era it seems to have been common. Amongst others who bore it was Herod's celebrated wife and victim, Mariamne. And through the Virgin Mary, it has become the most frequent female name in Christendom.

1. MIRIAM, the sister of Moses, was the eldest of that sacred family; and she first appears, probably as a young girl, watching her infant brother's cradle in the Nile (Ex. ii. 4), and suggesting her mother as a nurse (*ib.* 7). The independent and high position given by her superiority of age she never lost. "The sister of Aaron" is her Biblical distinction (Ex. xv. 20). In Num. xii. 1 she is placed before Aaron; and in Mic. vi. 4 reckoned as amongst the Three Deliverers — "I sent before thee Moses and Aaron and Miriam." She is the first personage in that household to whom the prophetic gifts are directly ascribed — "Miriam the Prophetess" is her acknowledged title (Ex. xv. 20). The prophetic power showed itself in her under the same form as that which it assumed in the days of Samuel and David, — poetry, accompanied with music and processions. The only instance of this prophetic gift is when, after the passage of the Red Sea, she takes a cymbal in her hand, and goes forth, like the Hebrew maidens in later times after a victory (Judg. v. 1, xi. 34; 1 Sam. xviii. 6; Ps. lxviii. 11, 25), followed by the whole female population of Israel, also beating their cymbals and striking their guitars (מְחֹלֹת, mistranslated "dances"). It does not appear how far they joined in the whole of the song (Ex. xv. 1–19); but the opening words are repeated again by Miriam herself at the close, in the form of a command to the Hebrew women. "She answered them, saying, Sing ye to JEHOVAH, for He hath triumphed gloriously: the horse and his rider hath He thrown into the sea."

She took the lead, with Aaron, in the complaint against Moses for his marriage with a Cushite. [ZIPPORAH.] "Hath JEHOVAH spoken by Moses? Hath He not also spoken by us?" (Num. xii. 1, 2). The question implies that the prophetic gift was exercised by them; while the answer implies that it was communicated in a less direct form than to Moses. "If there be a prophet among you, I JEHOVAH will make myself known unto him in a vision, and will speak unto him in a dream. My servant Moses is not so. . . . . With him will I speak mouth to mouth, even apparently, and not in dark speeches" (Num. xii. 6–8). A stern rebuke was administered in front of the sacred Tent to both Aaron and 'Miriam. But the punishment fell on Miriam, as the chief offender. The hateful Egyptian leprosy, of which for a moment the sign had been seen on the hand of her younger brother, broke out over the whole person of the proud prophetess. How grand was her position, and how heavy the blow, is implied in the cry of anguish which goes up from both her brothers — "Alas, my lord! . . . Let her not be as one dead, of whom the flesh is half consumed when he cometh out of his mother's womb. . . . Heal her now, O God! I beseech thee." And it is not less evident in the silent grief of the nation: "The people journeyed not till Miriam was brought in again" (Num. xii. 10–15). The same feeling is reflected, though in a strange and distorted form, in the ancient tradition of the drying-up and reflowing of the marvelous well of the Wanderings [BEER, vol. i. p. 264 *a*.]

This stroke, and its removal, which took place at Hazeroth, form the last public event of Miriam's life. She died towards the close of the wanderings at Kadesh, and was buried there (Num. xx. 1). Her tomb was shown near Petra in the days of Jerome (*De Loc. Heb.* in voce "*Cades Barnea*"). According to the Jewish tradition (Joseph. *Ant.* iv. 4, § 6), her death took place on the new moon of the month Xanthicus (*i. e.* about the end of February); which seems to imply that the anniversary was still observed in the time of Josephus. The burial, he adds, took place with great pomp on a mountain called Zin (*i. e.* the wilderness of Zin); and the mourning — which lasted, as in the case of her brothers, for thirty days — was closed by the institution of the purification through the sacrifice of the heifer (Num. xix. 1–10), which in the Pentateuch immediately precedes the story of her death.

According to Josephus (*Ant.* iii. 2, § 4, and 6, § 1), she was married to the famous HUR, and, through him, was grandmother of the architect BEZALEEL.

In the Koran (ch. iii.) she is confounded with the Virgin Mary; and hence the Holy Family is called the Family of Amram, or Imran. (See also D'Herbelot, *Bibl. Orient.* "*Zakaria.*") In other Arabic traditions her name is given as *Kolthum* (see Weil's *Bibl. Legends*, p. 101).

2. (Both Vat. and Alex. τον Μαιων; [Rom. Μαρὼν; Comp. Μαριάμ:] *Mariam*). A person — whether man or woman does not appear — mentioned in the genealogies of the tribe of Judah and house of Caleb (1 Chr. iv. 17); but in the present state of the Hebrew text it is impossible to say more than that Miriam was sister or brother to the founder of the town of Eshtemoa. Out of the numerous conjectures of critics and translators the following may be noticed: (*a*) that of the LXX., "and Jether begat M.;" and (*b*) that of Bertheau (*Chronik*, ad loc), that Miriam, Shammai, and Ishbah are the children of Mered by his Egyptian wife Bithiah, the daughter of Pharaoh: the last clause of ver. 18 having been erroneously transposed from its proper place in ver. 17. A. P. S.

MIRMA (מִרְמָה [*fraud, falsehood*]: Μαρμά; [Vat. Ιμαμα :] *Marma*). A Benjamite, "chief of the fathers," son of Shaharaim by his wife Hodesh; born in the land of Moab (1 Chr. viii. 10).

MIRROR. The two words, מַרְאָה, *marāh* (Ex. xxxviii. 8; κάτοπτρον, *speculum*), and רְאִי, *rĕī* (Job xxxvii. 18), are rendered "looking-glass" in the A. V., but from the context evidently denote a mirror of polished metal. The mirrors of the women of the congregation, according to the former passage, furnished the bronze for the laver of the tabernacle, and in the latter the beauty of the figure is heightened by rendering "Wilt thou beat out with him the clouds, strong as a molten mirror?"; the word translated "spread out" in the A. V. being that which is properly applied to the hammering of metals into plates, and from which the Hebrew term for "firmament" is derived. [FIRMAMENT.] The metaphor in Deut. xxviii. 23, "Thy heaven that is over thy head shall be brass," derived its force from the same popular belief in the solidity of the sky.

The Hebrew women on coming out of Egypt probably brought with them mirrors like those which were used by the Egyptians, and were made of a mixed metal, chiefly copper, wrought with such admirable skill, says Sir G. Wilkinson (*Anc. Eg.* iii. 384), that they were "susceptible of a lustre, which has even been partially revived at the present day, in some of those discovered at Thebes, though

Egyptian Mirror. (From Mr. Salt's collection.)

buried in the earth for many centuries. The mirror itself was nearly round, inserted into a handle of wood, stone, or metal, whose form varied according to the taste of the owner. Some presented the figure of a female, a flower, a column, or a rod ornamented with the head of Athor, a bird, or a fancy device; and sometimes the face of a Typhonian monster was introduced to support the mirror, serving as a contrast to the features whose beauty was displayed within it." With regard to the metal of which the ancient mirrors were composed there is not much difference of opinion. Pliny mentions that anciently the best were made at Brundusium of a mixture of copper and tin (xxxiii. 45), or of tin alone (xxxiv. 48). Praxiteles, in the time of Pompey the Great, is said to have been the first who made them of silver, though these were afterwards so common as, in the time of Pliny, to be used by the ladies' maids.[a] They are mentioned by Chrysostom among the extravagances of fashion for which he rebuked the ladies of his time, and Seneca long before was loud in his denunciation of similar follies (*Natur. Quæst.* i. 17). Mirrors were

---

[a] Silver mirrors are alluded to in Plautus (*Mostell.* i. 4, ver. 101) and Philostratus (*Icon.* i. 6); and one

of steel is said to have been found. They were even made of gold (Eur. *Hec.* 925; Sen. *Nat. Quæst.* i. 17).

used by the Roman women in the worship of Juno (Seneca, *Ep.* 95; Apuleius, *Metam.* xi. c. 9, p. 770). In the Egyptian temples, says Cyril of Alexandria (*De ador. in Spir.* ix.; *Opera,* i. p. 814, ed. Paris, 1638), it was the custom for the women to worship in linen garments, holding a mirror in their left hands and a sistrum in their right, and the Israelites, having fallen into the idolatries of the country, had brought with them the mirrors which they used in their worship.[a]

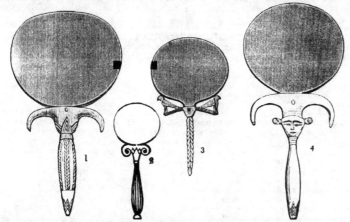

Egyptian Mirrors. 1, 3, 4, from Mr. Salt's collection; 2, from a painting at Thebes; 4 is about 11 inches high.

According to Beckmann (*Hist. of Inv.* ii. 64, Bohn), a mirror which was discovered near Naples was tested, and found to be made of a mixture of copper and regulus of antimony, with a little lead.

Egyptian Mirror. 2 and 3 show the bottom of the handle, to which something has been fastened. (Was in the possession of Dr. Hogg.)

Beckmann's editor (Mr. Francis) gives in a note the result of an analysis of an Etruscan mirror,

which he examined and found to consist of 67·12 copper, 24·93 tin, and 8·13 lead, or nearly 8 parts of copper to 3 of tin and 1 of lead, but neither in this, nor in one analyzed by Klaproth, was there any trace of antimony, which Beckmann asserts was unknown to the ancients. Modern experiments have shown that the mixture of copper and tin produces the best metal for specula (*Phil. Trans.* vol. 67, p. 296). Much curious information will be found in Beckmann upon the various substances employed by the ancients for mirrors, but which has no bearing upon the subject of this article. In his opinion it was not till the 13th century that glass, covered at the back with tin or lead, was used for this purpose, the doubtful allusion in Pliny (xxxvi. 66)[b] to the mirrors made in the glass-houses of Sidon having reference to experiments which were unsuccessful. Other allusions to bronze mirrors will be found in a fragment of Æschylus preserved in Stobæus (*Serm.* xviii. p. 164, ed. Gesner, 1608), and in Callimachus (*Hym. in Lav. Pall.* p. 21). Convex mirrors of polished steel are mentioned as common in the East, in a manuscript note of Chardin's upon Ecclus. xii. 11, quoted by Harmer (*Observ.* vol. iv. c. 11, obs. 55).

The metal of which the mirrors were composed being liable to rust and tarnish, required to be constantly kept bright (Wisd. vii. 26; Ecclus. xii. 11). This was done by means of pounded pumice-stone, rubbed on with a sponge, which was generally suspended from the mirror. The Persians used emery-powder for the same purpose, according to Chardin (quoted by Hartmann, *die Hebr. am Putztische,* ii. 245). The obscure image produced by a tarnished or imperfect mirror [δι' ἐσόπτρου, ἐν αἰνίγματι],

[a] Apparently in allusion to this custom Moore (*Epicurean,* c. 5), in describing the maidens who danced at the Island Temple of the Moon, says, " As they passed under the lamp, a gleam of light flashed from their bosoms, which, I could perceive, was the reflection of a small mirror, that in the manner of the women of the East each of the dancers wore beneath her left shoulder."

[b] " Sidone quondam iis officinis nobili: siquidem etiam specula excogitaverat."

appears to be alluded to in 1 Cor. xiii. 12. On the other hand a polished mirror is among the Arabs the emblem of a pure reputation. "More spotless than the mirror of a foreign woman" is with them a proverbial expression, which Meïdani explains of a woman who has married out of her country, and polishes her mirror incessantly that no part of her face may escape her observation (De Sacy, *Chrest. Arab.* iii. p. 236).

The obscure word גִּלְיוֹנִים, *gilyônim* (Is. iii. 23), rendered "glasses" in the A. V. after the Vulgate *specula*, and supported by the Targum, and the commentaries of Kimchi, Abarbanel, and Jarchi, is explained by Schroeder (*de Vest. Mul. Hebr.* ch. 18) to signify "transparent dresses" of fine linen, as the LXX. (τὰ διαφανῆ Λακωνικά) and even Kimchi in his Lexicon understand it (comp. *mollicia*, Juv. *Sat.* ii. 66, 76). In support of this view, it is urged that the terms which follow denote articles of female attire; but in Is. viii. 1, a word closely resembling it is used for a smooth writing tablet, and the rendering of the A. V. is approved by Gesenius (*Jesaia*, i. 215) and the best authorities.   W. A. W.

MIS'AEL (Μισαήλ; [Vat. Μεισαηλ:] *Misael*). **1.** The same as MISHAEL 2 (1 Esdr. ix. 44; comp. Neh. viii. 4).

2. = MISHAEL 3, the Hebrew name of Meshach (Song of the Three Child. 66).

MIS'GAB (הַמִּשְׂגָּב, with the def. article, [*the height, refuge:*] Ἀμάθ; [Ald. Μασιγάθ:] *fortis, sublimia*), a place in Moab named in company with NEBO and KIRIATHAIM in the denunciation of Jeremiah (xlviii. 1). It appears to be mentioned also in Is. xxv. 12,[a] though there rendered in the A. V. "high fort." [MOAB.] In neither passage is there any clew to its situation beyond the fact of its mention with the above two places; and even that is of little avail, as neither of them has been satisfactorily identified.

The name may be derived from a root signifying elevation (Gesenius, *Thes.* 1320), and in that case was probably attached to a town situated on a height. It is possibly identical with MIZPEH OF MOAB, named only in 1 Sam. xxii. 3. Fürst (*Handwb.* 794 *a*) understands "the Misgab" to mean the highland country of Moab generally, but its mention in company with other places which we know to have been definite spots, even though not yet identified with certainty, seems to forbid this.   G.

MISH'AEL (מִישָׁאֵל [*who (is) what God is*]: [Rom.] Μισαήλ in Ex., [Vat. Alex. omit;] Μισαδάι, [Vat. Alex. Μισαδαι in Lev.:] *Misaël, Misaele*). **1.** One of the sons of Uzziel, the uncle of Aaron and Moses (Ex. vi. 22). When Nadab and Abihu were struck dead for offering strange fire, Mishael and his brother Elzaphan, at the command of Moses, removed their bodies from the sanctuary, and buried them without the camp, their loose fitting tunics[b] (*cuttônôth*, A. V. "coats"), the sim-

plest of eastern dresses, serving for winding-sheets (Lev. x. 4, 5). The late Prof. Blunt (*Undes. Coincidences*, pt. i. § xiv.) conjectured that the two brothers were the "men who were defiled by the dead body of a man" (Num. ix. 6), and thus prevented from keeping the second passover.

2. (Μισαήλ; [Vat. FA.] Alex. Μεισαηλ: *Misael*). One of those who stood at Ezra's left hand on the tower of wood in the street of the water gate, when he read the Law to the people (Neh. viii. 4). Called MISAEL in 1 Esdr. ix. 44.

3. [Vat. (Theodot.) Μεισαηλ.] One of Daniel's three companions in captivity, and of the blood-royal of Judah (Dan. i. 6, 7, 11, 19, ii. 17). He received the Babylonian title of MESHACH, by which he is better known. In the Song of the Three Children he is called MISAEL.

MISH'AL and **MISH'EAL** (both מִשְׁאָל [*request*]: Μασσα, Alex. Μασαψ [Comp. Ald. Μασάλ;] τὴν Βασελλάν, Alex. Μασααλ: *Messal, Masil*), one of the towns in the territory of Asher (Josh. xix. 26), allotted to the Gershonite Levites (xxi. 30). It occurs between Amad and Carmel, but the former remains unknown, and this catalogue of Asher is so imperfect, that it is impossible to conclude with certainty that Mishal was near Carmel. True, Eusebius (*Onom.* "Masan") says that it was, but he is evidently merely quoting the list of Joshua, and not speaking from actual knowledge. In the catalogue of 1 Chr. vi. it is given as MASHAL, a form which suggests its identity with the MASALOTH of later history; but there is nothing to remark for or against this identification.   G.

MISH'AM (מִשְׁעָם [*purification, beauty*, Dietr.]: Μισαδλ: [Vat. Μεσααμ:] *Misaam*). A Benjamite, son of Elpaal, and descendant of Shaharaim (1 Chr. viii. 12).

MISH'MA (מִשְׁמָע [*hearing, report*]: Μασμά: *Masma*).

1. A son of Ishmael and brother of MIBSAM (Gen. xxv. 14; 1 Chr. i. 30). The Masamani of Ptolemy (vi. 7, § 21) may represent the tribe of Mishma; their modern descendants are not known to the writer, but the name (Misma')[c] exists in Arabia, and a tribe is called the Benee-Misma'. In the Mir-át ez-Zemán (MS.), Mishma is written Misma' — probably from Rabbinical sources; but it is added "and he is Mesmá'ah."[d] The Arabic word has the same signification as the Hebrew.

2. A son of Simeon (1 Chr. iv. 25), brother of MIBSAM. These brothers were perhaps named after the older brothers, Mishma and Mibsam.   E. S. P.

MISHMAN'NAH (מִשְׁמַנָּה [*fatness*]: Μασμανά; [Vat. Μασεμμαννη;] Alex. Μασμαν; FA. Μασεμαννη: *Masmana*). The fourth of the twelve lion-faced Gadites, men of the host for the battle, who "separated themselves unto David" in the hold of Ziklag (1 Chr. xii. 10).

---

[a] In this passage it is without the article. As a more appellative, the word *Misgab* is frequently used in the poetical parts of Scripture, in the sense of a safe place of refuge. Thus 2 Sam. xxii. 3; Ps. ix. 9, ix. 9; Is. xxxiii. 16; in which and other places it is variously rendered in the A. V. "high tower," "refuge," "defence," etc. See Stanley, *S. & P.* App. § 31.

[b] Their priestly frocks, or cassocks (Ex. xl. 14) which, as Jarchi remarks, were not burned.

[c] صَمِيعٌ.   [d] مَسْمَعَة.

* The A. V. ed. 1611 reads Mashmannah for Mishmannah, in accordance with six MSS. and printed editions noted by Michaelis (*Bibl. Hebr.*). This is also the marginal reading of the Geneva version; the Bishops' Bible has "Masmana."   A.

MISHRAITES, THE (הַמִּשְׁרָעִי [as appel., *slippery place*]: Ἡμασαραΐμ [Vat. -ειμ]; Alex. Ἡμασαραειν: *Maserei*), the fourth of the four "families of Kirjath-jearim," *i. e.* colonies proceeding therefrom and founding towns (1 Chr. ii. 53). Like the other three, Mishra is not elsewhere mentioned, nor does any trace of it appear to have been since discovered. But in its turn it founded — so the passage is doubtless to be understood — the towns of Zorah and Eshtaol, the former of which has been identified in our own times, while the latter is possibly to be found in the same neighborhood. [MAHANEH-DAN.]   G.

* MISPAR. So correctly A. V. ed. 1611 in Ezr. ii. 2, where later editions have MIZPAR. The Hebrew is מִסְפָּר.   A.

MISPE'RETH (מִסְפֶּרֶת [*number*]: Μασφαρθ; [Vat. Μασφεραν; Alex. Μαασφαραθ;] FA. Μασφαραδ: *Mespharath*). One of those who returned with Zerubbabel and Jeshua from Babylon (Neh. vii. 7). In Ezr. ii. 2 he is called MIZPAR, and in 1 Esdr. v. 8 ASPHARASUS.

MIS'REPHOTH-MA'IM (מִשְׂרְפוֹת מַיִם, and in xiii. 6, ם' מִשְׂרְפֹת [see below]: Μασερῶν, and Μασερὼθ Μεμφωμαΐμ; Alex. Μασρεφωθ μαειμ, and Μασερεφωθ μαιμ: *aqua Miserephoth*), a place in northern Palestine, in close connection with Zidon-rabbah, *i. e.* Sidon. From "the waters of Merom" Joshua chased the Canaanite kings to Zidon and Misrephoth-maim, and then eastward to the "plain of Mizpeh," probably the great plain of Baalbek — the *Bikah* of the Hebrews, the *Buka'a* of the modern Syrians (Josh. xi. 8). The name occurs once again in the enumeration of the districts remaining to be conquered (xiii. 6) — "all the inhabitants of the mountain from Lebanon unto M. Maim,[a] all the Zidonians." Taken as Hebrew, the literal meaning of the name is "burnings of waters," and accordingly it is taken by the old interpreters to mean "warm waters," whether natural, *i. e.* hot baths or springs — as by Kimchi and the interpolation in the Vulgate; or artificial, *i. e.* salt, glass, or smelting-works — as by Jarchi, and the others mentioned by Fürst (*Hdwb.* 803 b), Rödiger (in *Gesen. Thes.* 1341), and Keil (*Josua*, ad loc.).

Lord A. Hervey (*Genealogies*, etc., 228 note) considers the name as conferred in consequence of the "burning" of Jabin's chariots there. But were they burnt at that spot? and, if so, why is the name the "burning of *waters*?" The probability here, as in so many other cases, is, that a meaning has been forced on a name originally belonging to another language, and therefore unintelligible to the later occupiers of the country.

Dr. Thomson (*Land and Book*, ch. xv.), reviving the conjecture of himself and Schultz (*Bibl. Sacra*, 1855), treats Misrephoth-maim as identical with a collection of springs called *Ain-Musheirifeh*,

on the sea-shore, close under the *Ras en-Nakhura*; but this has the disadvantage of being very far from Sidon. May it not rather be the place with which we are familiar in the later history as Zarephath? In Hebrew, allowing for a change not unfrequent of S to Z (reversed in the form of the name current still later — Sarepta), the two are from roots almost identical, not only in sound, but also in meaning; while the close connection of Zarephath with Zidon — "Zarephath which belongeth to Zidon," — is another point of strong resemblance.   G.

MITE (λεπτόν), a coin current in Palestine in the time of our Lord. It took its name from a very small Greek copper coin, of which with the Athenians seven went to the χαλκοῦς. It seems in Palestine to have been the smallest piece of money, being the half of the farthing, which was a coin of very low value. The mite is famous from its being mentioned in the account of the poor widow's piety whom Christ saw casting two mites into the treasury (Mark xii. 41–44; Luke xxi. 1–4). From St. Mark's explanation, "two mites, which make a farthing" (λεπτὰ δύο, ὅ ἐστι κοδράντης, ver. 42), it may perhaps be inferred that the κοδράντης, or farthing, was the commoner coin, for it can scarcely be supposed to be there spoken of as a money of account, though this might be the case in another passage (Matt. v. 26). In the Græco-Roman coinage of Palestine, in which we include the money of the Herodian family, the two smallest coins, of which the assarion is the more common, seem to correspond to the farthing and the mite, the larger weighing about twice as much as the smaller. This correspondence is made more probable by the circumstance that the larger seems to be reduced from the earlier "quarter" of the Jewish coinage. It is noticeable, that although the supposed mites struck about the time referred to in the Gospels are rare, those of Alex. Jannæus's coinage are numerous, whose abundant money must have long continued in use. [MONEY; FARTHING.]   R. S. P.

MITH'CAH (מִתְקָה [*sweetness*]: Μαθεκκά; [Vat. Ματεκκά:] *Methca*), the name of an unknown desert encampment of the Israelites, meaning, perhaps, "place of sweetness"[b] (Num. xxxiii. 28, 29).   H. H.

MITH'NITE, THE (הַמִּתְנִי [appel. extension]: ὁ Βαιθανεί; Alex. ὁ Μαθθανί; [Vat. Βαιθανει; FA ὁ Βεθανει:] *Mathanites*), the designation of JOSHAPHAT, one of David's guard in the catalogue of 1 Chr. xi. (ver. 43). No doubt it signifies the native of a place or a tribe bearing the name of Methen; but no trace exists in the Bible of any such. It should be noticed that Joshaphat is both preceded and followed by a man from beyond Jordan, but it would not be safe to infer therefrom that Methen was also in that region.   G.

MITH'REDATH (מִתְרְדָת [see below]: Μιθραδάτης; [Alex. Vat.[2] Μιθριδατης:] *Mithridates*). 1. The treasurer (גִּזְבָּר, *gizbár*) of Cyrus king of Persia, to whom the king gave the vessels of the Temple, to be by him transferred to

---

[a] The "and" here inserted in the A. V. is quite gratuitous.

[b] Derived from מָתַק, "sweetness," with the suffix

ה of locality, which (or its plur. וֹת) is often found in names.

the hands of Sheshbazzar (Ezr. i. 8). The LXX. take *gizbâr* as a gentilic name, Γασβαρηνός, the Vulgate as a patronymic, *filius gazab ır*, but there is little doubt as to its meaning. The word occurs in a slightly different form in Dan. iii. 2, 3, and is there rendered "treasurer;" and in the parallel history of 1 Esdr. ii. 11, Mithredath is called MITH-RIDATES the treasurer (γαζοφύλαξ). The name Mithredath, " given by Mithra," is one of a class of compounds of frequent occurrence, formed from the name of Mithra, the Iranian sun-god.

2. A Persian officer stationed at Samaria, in the reign of Artaxerxes, or Smerdis the Magian (Ezr. iv. 7). He joined with his colleagues in prevailing upon the king to hinder the rebuilding of the Temple. In 1 Esdr. ii. 16 he is called MITHRIDATES.

MITHRIDATES ([*given by Mithra*]: Μιθραδάτης; [Vat.] Alex. Μιθριδάτης: *Mithridatus*).

1. (1 Esdr. ii. 11) = MITHREDATH 1.
2. (1 Esdr. ii. 16) = MITHREDATH 2.

MITRE. [CROWN; HEAD-DRESS.]

MITYLE'NE (Μιτυλήνη, in classical authors and on inscriptions frequently Μυτιλήνη: [*Mitylene*, Cod. Amiat. *Mytilene*]), the chief town of Lesbos, and situated on the east coast of the island. Its position is very accurately, though incidentally, marked (Acts xx. 14, 15) in the account of St. Paul's return-voyage from his third apostolical journey. Mitylene is the intermediate place where he stopped for the night between ASSOS and CHIOS. It may be gathered from the circumstances of this voyage that the wind was blowing from the N. W.; and it is worth while to notice that in the harbor or in the roadstead of Mitylene the ship would be sheltered from that wind. Moreover it appears that St. Paul was there at the time of dark moon: and this was a sufficient reason for passing the night there before going through the intricate passages to the southward. See *Life and Epistles of St. Paul*, ch. xx., where a view of the place is given, showing the fine forms of the mountains behind. The town itself was celebrated in Roman times for the beauty of its buildings (" Mitylene pulchra," Hor. *Epist.* I. xi. 17; see Cic. c. *Rull.* ii. 16). In St. Paul's day it had the privileges of a free city (Plin. *N. H.* v. 39). It is one of the few cities of the Ægean which have continued without intermission to flourish till the present day. It has given its name to the whole island, and is itself now called sometimes *Castro*, sometimes *Mitylen*. Tournefort gives a rude picture of the place as it appeared in 1700 (*Voyage du Levant*, i. 148, 149). It is more to our purpose to refer to our own Admiralty charts, Nos. 1665 and 1654. Mitylene concentrates in itself the chief interest of Lesbos, an island peculiarly famous in the history of poetry, and especially of poetry in connection with music. But for these points we must refer to the articles in the *Dict. of Geography*.   J. S. H.

MIXED MULTITUDE. With the Israelites who journeyed from Rameses to Succoth, the first stage of the Exodus from Egypt, there went up (Ex. xii. 38) " a mixed multitude " (עֵרֶב: ἐπίμικτος: *vulgus promiscuum*), who have not hitherto been identified. In the Targum the phrase is vaguely rendered "many foreigners," and Jarchi explains it as " a medley of outlandish people." Aben Ezra goes further and says it signifies " the Egyptians who were mixed with them, and they

are the ' mixed multitude ' (אֲסַפְסֻף, Num. xi. 4), who were gathered to them." Jarchi on the latter passage also identifies the " mixed multitude " of Num. and Exodus. During their residence in Egypt marriages were naturally contracted between the Israelites and the natives, and the son of such a marriage between an Israelitish woman and an Egyptian is especially mentioned as being stoned for blasphemy (Lev. xxiv. 11), the same law holding good for the resident or naturalized foreigner as for the native Israelite (Josh. viii. 35). This hybrid race is evidently alluded to by Jarchi and Aben Ezra, and is most probably that to which reference is made in Exodus. Knobel understands by the " mixed multitude " the remains of the Hyksos who left Egypt with the Hebrews. Dr. Kalisch (*Comm. on Ex.* xii. 38) interprets it of the native Egyptians who were involved in the same oppression with the Hebrews by the new dynasty, which invaded and subdued Lower Egypt; and Kurtz (*Hist. of Old Cov.* ii. 312. Eng. tr.), while he supposes the " mixed multitude " to have been Egyptians of the lower classes, attributes their emigration to their having " endured the same oppression as the Israelites from the proud spirit of caste which prevailed in Egypt," in consequence of which they attached themselves to the Hebrews, " and served henceforth as hewers of wood and drawers of water." That the " mixed multitude " is a general term including all those who were not of pure Israelite blood is evident; more than this cannot be positively asserted. In Exodus and Numbers it probably denoted the miscellaneous hangers-on of the Hebrew camp, whether they were the issue of spurious marriages with Egyptians, or were themselves Egyptians or belonging to other nations. The same happened on the return from Babylon, and in Neh. xiii. 3, a slight clew is given by which the meaning of the " mixed multitude " may be more definitely ascertained. Upon reading in the Law " that the Ammonite and the Moabite should not come into the congregation of God for ever," it is said, " they separated from Israel all the *mixed multitude*." The remainder of the chapter relates the expulsion of Tobiah the Ammonite from the Temple, of the merchants and men of Tyre from the city, and of the foreign wives of Ashdod, of Ammon, and of Moab, with whom the Jews had intermarried. All of these were included in the " mixed multitude," and Nehemiah adds, " thus cleansed I them from all *foreigners*." The Targ. Jon. on Num. xi. 4, explains the " mixed multitude " as proselytes, and this view is apparently adopted by Ewald, but there does not seem any foundation for it.   W. A. W.

MI'ZAR, THE HILL (הַר מִצְעָר) [*mountain small*]: ὄρος [μικρός, Vat.] μεικρος: *mons modicus*), a mountain — for the reader will observe that the word is *har* in the original (see vol. ii. p. 1077 *a*) — apparently in the northern part of trans-Jordanic Palestine, from which the author of Psalm xlii. utters his pathetic appeal (ver. 6). The name appears nowhere else, and the only clew we have to its situation is the mention of the "land of Jordan" and the "Hermons," combined with the general impression conveyed by the Psalm that it is the cry of an exile *a* from Je-

---

a In the Peshito-Syriac it bears the title, " The Psalm which David sang when he was in exile, and longing to return to Jerusalem."

rusalem, possibly on his road to Babylou (Ewald, *Dichter*, ii. 185). If taken as Hebrew, the word is derivable from a root signifying smallness — the same by which Zoar is explained in Gen. xix. 20–22. This is adopted by all the ancient versions, and in the Prayer-Book Psalms of the Church of England appears in the inaccurate form of "the little hill of Hermon." G.

MIZ'PAH and MIZ'PEH.

The name borne by several places in ancient Palestine. Although in the A. V. most frequently presented as MIZPEH, yet in the original, with but few exceptions, the name is Mizpah, and with equally few [a] exceptions is accompanied with the definite article — הַמִּצְפָּה, *ham-Mizpah*, [i. e. *the watch tower*].

1. MIZPAH (הַמִּצְפָּה; Samar. המצבה, i. e. the pillar: ἡ ὅρασις; Veneto-Gk. ὁ ἀτενισμός: Vulg. omits). The earliest of all, in order of the narrative, is the heap of stones piled up by Jacob and Laban (Gen. xxxi. 48) on Mount Gilead (ver. 25), to serve both as a witness to the covenant then entered into, and also as a landmark of the boundary between them (ver. 52). This heap received a name from each of the two chief actors in the transaction — GALEED and JEGAR SAHADUTHA. But it had also a third, namely, MIZPAH, which it seems from the terms of the narrative to have derived from neither party, but to have possessed already; which third name, in the address of Laban to Jacob, is seized and played upon after the manner of these ancient people: "Therefore he called the name of it Galeed, and the Mizpah; for he said, Jehovah watch (*itzeph*, יִצֶף) between me and thee," etc. It is remarkable that this Hebrew paronomasia is put into the mouth, not of Jacob the Hebrew, but of Laban the Syrian, the difference in whose language is just before marked by "Jegar-Sahadutha." Various attempts [b] have been made to reconcile this; but, whatever may be the result, we may rest satisfied that in Mizpah we possess a Hebraized form of the original name, whatever that may have been, bearing somewhat the same relation to it that the Arabic *Beit-ur* bears to the Hebrew Beth-horon, or — as we may afterwards see reason to suspect — as *Sufieh* and *Shafat* bear to ancient Mizpehs on the western side of Jordan. In its Hebraized form the word is derived from the root *tsápháh*, צָפָה, "to look out" (Gesen. *Lexicon*, ed. Robinson, *s. v.* צפה), and signifies a watch-tower. The root has also the signification of breadth — expansion. But that the original name had the same signification as it possesses in its Hebrew form is, to say the least, unlikely; because in such linguistic changes the meaning always appears to be secondary to the likeness in sound.

Of this early name, whatever it may have been, we find other traces on both sides of Jordan, not only in the various Mizpahs, but in such names as Zophim, which we know formed part of the lofty Pisgah; Zaphon, a town of Moab (Josh. xiii. 27); Zuph and Ramathaim-Zophim, in the neighborhood of Mizpeh of Benjamin; Zephathah in the

neighborhood of Mizpeh of Judah; possibly also in *Safed*, the well-known city of Galilee.

But, however this may be, the name remained attached to the ancient meeting-place of Jacob and Laban, and the spot where their conference had been held became a sanctuary of Jehovah, and a place for solemn conclave and deliberation in times of difficulty long after. On this natural "watch-tower" (LXX. σκοπιά [Alex. Ald. Μασσηφά]), when the last touch had been put to their "misery" by the threatened attack of the Bene-Ammon, did the children of Israel assemble for the choice of a leader (Judg. x. 17, comp. ver. 16); and when the outlawed Jephthah had been prevailed on to leave his exile and take the head of his people, his first act was to go to "the Mizpah," and on that consecrated ground utter all his words "before Jehovah." It was doubtless from Mizpah that he made his appeal to the king of the Ammonites (xi. 12), and invited, though fruitlessly, the aid of his kinsmen of Ephraim on the other side of Jordan (xii. 2). At Mizpah he seems to have henceforward resided; there the fatal meeting took place with his daughter on his return from the war (xi. 34), and we can hardly doubt that on the altar of that sanctuary the father's terrible vow was consummated. The topographical notices of Jephthah's course in his attack and pursuit (ver. 29) are extremely difficult to unravel; but it seems most probable that the "Mizpeh-Gilead" which is mentioned here, and here only, is the same as the ham-Mizpah of the other parts of the narrative; and both, as we shall see afterwards, are probably identical with the RAMATH-MIZPEH and RAMOTH-GILEAD, so famous in the later history.

It is still more difficult to determine whether this was not also the place at which the great assembly of the people was held to decide on the measures to be taken against Gibeah after the outrage on the Levite and his concubine (Judg. xx. 1, 3, xxi. 1, 5, 8). No doubt there seems a certain violence in removing the scene of any part of so local a story to so great a distance as the other side of Jordan. But, on the other hand, are the limits of the story so circumscribed? The event is represented as one affecting not a part only, but the whole of the nation, east of Jordan as well as west — "from Dan to Beer-sheba, and the land of Gilead" (xx. 1). The only part of the nation excluded from the assembly was the tribe of Benjamin, and that no communication on the subject was held with them, is implied in the statement that they only "heard" of its taking place (xx. 3); an expression which would be meaningless if the place of assembly were — as Mizpah of Benjamin was — within a mile or two of Gibeah, in the very heart of their own territory, though perfectly natural if it were at a distance from them. And had there not been some reason in the circumstances of the case, combined possibly with some special claim in Mizpah — and that claim doubtless its ancient sanctity and the reputation which Jephthah's success had conferred upon it — why was not either Bethel, where the ark was deposited (xx. 26, 27), or Shiloh,

---

only; 4. In every other case the Hebrew text presents the name as ham-Mizpah.

[b] See Ewald, *Komposition der Genesis*. Thus in the LXX. and Vulg. versions of ver. 49, the word *Mizpeh* is not treated as a proper name at all; and a different turn is given to the verse.

shown for the purpose? Suppose a Mizpah near Gibeah, and the subject is full of difficulty: remove it to the place of Jacob and Laban's meeting, and the difficulties disappear; and the allusions to Gilead (xx. 1), to Jabesh-Gilead (xxi. 8, &c.), and to Shiloh, as " in the land of Canaan," all fall naturally into their places and acquire a proper force.

Mizpah is probably the same as RAMATH-MIZ-PEH (רָ הַמִּצְפֶּה), mentioned Josh. xiii. 26 only. The prefix merely signifies that the spot was an elevated one, which we already believe it to have been; and if the two are not identical, then we have the anomaly of an enumeration of the chief places of Gilead with the omission of its most famous sanctuary. Ramath ham-Mizpeh was most probably identical also with Ramoth-Gilead; but this is a point which will be most advantageously discussed under the latter head.

Mizpah still retained its name in the days of the Maccabees, by whom it was besieged and taken with the other cities of Gilead (1 Macc. v. 35). From Eusebius and Jerome (Onomasticon, "Maspha") it receives a bare mention. It is probable, both from their notices (Onomasticon, "Rammoth") and from other considerations, that Ramoth-Gilead is the modern es-Salt; but it is not ascertained whether Mizpah is not rather the great mountain Jebel Osha, a short distance to the northwest. The name Safut appears in Van de Velde's map a few miles east of es-Salt.

A singular reference to Mizpah is found in the title of Ps. lx., as given in the Targum, which runs as follows: " For the ancient testimony of the sons of Jacob and Laban . . . . when David assembled his army and passed over the heap [a] of witness."

2. A second Mizpeh, on the east of Jordan, was the MIZPEH-MOAB (מִצְפֵּה מוֹאָב : Μασσηφὰθ [Vat. -φα, Alex. Μασηφα] τῆς Μωάβ: Maspha quæ est Moab), where the king of that nation was living when David committed his parents to his care (1 Sam. xxii. 3). The name does not occur again, nor is there any clew to the situation of the place. It may have been, as is commonly conjectured, the elevated and strong natural fortress afterwards known as KIR-MOAB, the modern Kerak. But is it not at least equally possible that it was the great Mount Pisgah, which was the most commanding eminence in the whole of Moab, which contained the sanctuary of Nebo, and of which one part was actually called Zophim (Num. xxiii. 14), a name derived from the same root with Mizpeh?

3. A third was THE LAND OF MIZPEH, or more accurately "OF MIZPEH" (אֶרֶץ הַמִּצְפָּה: γῆν Μασσύμα; [Comp. Ald. γῆν Μασσηφά: Vat. τὴν Μασσύμα; Alex. τὴν Μασσηφαθ:] [b] terra Maspha), the residence of the Hivites who joined the northern confederacy against Israel, headed by Jabin king of Hazor (Josh. xi. 3). No other mention is found of this district in the Bible, unless it be identical with

4. THE VALLEY OF MIZPEH (בִּקְעַת מִצְפֶּה):

τῶν πεδίων Μασσόχ [Alex. Ald. Μασσηφά]: campus Misphe), to which the discomfited hosts of the same confederacy were chased by Joshua (xi. 8). It lay eastward from MISREPHOTH-MAIM; but this affords us no assistance, as the situation of the latter place is by no means certain. If we may rely on the peculiar term here rendered " valley " — a term applied elsewhere in the records of Joshua only to the " valley of Lebanon," which is also said to have been " under Mount Hermon," and which contained the sanctuary of Baal-gad (Josh. xi. 17, xii. 7) — then we may accept the " land of Mizpah " or " the valley of Mizpeh " as identical with that enormous tract, the great country of Cœle-Syria, the Buka'a alike of the modern Arabs and of the ancient Hebrews (comp. Am. i. 5), which contains the great sanctuary of Baal-bek, and may be truly said to lie at the feet of Hermon (see Stanley, S. & P. p. 392 note). But this must not be taken for more than a probable inference, and it should not be overlooked that the name Mizpeh is here connected with a " valley " or " plain " — not, as in the other cases, with an eminence. Still the valley may have derived its appellation from an eminence of sanctity or repute situated therein; and it may be remarked that a name not impossibly derived from Mizpeh — Hawsh Tell-Safiyeh — is now attached to a hill a short distance north of Baalbek.

5. MIZPEH (הַמִּצְפָּה : Μασφά: Masepha), a city of Judah (Josh. xv. 38); in the district of the Shefelah or maritime lowland; a member of the same group with Dilean, Lachish, and Eglon, and apparently in their neighborhood. Van de Velde (Memoir, p. 335) suggests its identity with the present Tell es-Sâfiyeh — the Blanchegarde of the Crusaders; a conjecture which appears very feasible on the ground both of situation and of the likeness between the two names, which are nearly identical — certainly a more probable identification than those proposed with GATH and with LIBNAH. Tina, which is not improbably Dilean, is about 3 miles N. W., and Ajlun and um Lakis, respectively 10 and 12 to the S. W. of Tell es-Sâfieh, which itself stands on the slopes of the mountains of Judah, completely overlooking the maritime plain (Porter, Handbk. p. 252). It is remarkable too that, just as in the neighborhood of other Mizpahs we find Zophim, Zuph, or Zaphon, so in the neighborhood of Tell es-Sâfieh it is very probable that the valley of ZEPHATHAH was situated. (See Rob. Bibl. Res. ii. 31.)

6. MIZPEH, in Josh. and Samuel; elsewhere MIZPAH (הַמִּצְפָּה) in Joshua; elsewhere הַמִּצְפָּה: Μασσηφάθ; in Josh. Μασσημά [Alex. Μασφα]; Chron. and Neb. ἡ Μασφά, and ὁ Μασφέ; Kings and Hos. in both MSS. ἡ σκοπιά; Alex. Μασσηφα; [there are other variations not worth noting;] Mespha, Maspha, Masphath), a " city " of Benjamin, named in the list of the allotment between Beeroth and Chephirah, and in apparent proximity to Ramah and Gibeon (Josh. xviii. 26). Its connection with the two last-named towns is also

---

[a] The word here used — אֵינַר סַחֲדוּתָא — exhibits the transition from the "Jegar" of the ancient Aramaic of Laban to the Hajar of the modern Arabs — the word by which they designate the heaps which it is their custom, as it was Laban's, to erect as landmarks of a boundary.

[b] Here the LXX. (ed. Mai) omit "Hivites," and

perhaps read "Hermon" (חֶרמוֹן), as "Arabah" (עֲרָבָה) — the two words are more alike to the ear than the eye — and thus give the sentence, "they under the desert in the Maseuma." A somewhat similar substitution is found in the LXX version of Gen. xxxv. 27.

Implied in the later history (1 K. xv. 22; 2 Chr. xvi. 6; Neh. iii. 7). It was one of the places fortified by Asa against the incursions of the kings of the northern Israel (1 K. xv. 22; 2 Chr. xvi. 6; Jer. xli. 10); and after the destruction of Jerusalem it became the residence of the superintendent appointed by the king of Babylon (Jer. xl. 7, &c.), and the scene of his murder and of the romantic incidents connected with the name of Ishmael the son of Nethaniah.

But Mizpah was more than this. In the earlier periods of the history of Israel, at the first foundation of the monarchy, it was the great sanctuary of Jehovah, the special resort of the people in times of difficulty and solemn deliberation. In the Jewish traditions it was for some time the residence of the ark (see Jerome, *Qu. Hebr.* on 1 Sam. vii. 2; Reland, *Antiq.* i. § 6);[a] but this is possibly an inference from the expression "before Jehovah" in Judg. xx. 1. It is suddenly brought before us in the history. At Mizpah, when suffering the very extremities of Philistine bondage, the nation assembled at the call of the great Prophet, and with strange and significant rites confessed their sins, and were blessed with instant and signal deliverance (1 Sam. vii. 5-13). At Mizpah took place no less an act than the public selection and appointment of Saul as the first king of the nation (1 Sam. x. 17-25). It was one of the three holy cities (LXX. τοῖς ἡγιασμένοις τούτοις) which Samuel visited in turn as judge of the people (vii. 6, 16), the other two being Bethel and Gilgal. But, unlike Bethel and Gilgal, no record is preserved of the cause or origin of a sanctity so abruptly announced, and yet so fully asserted. We have seen that there is at least some ground for believing that the Mizpah spoken of in the transactions of the early part of the period of the judges, was the ancient sanctuary in the mountains of Gilead. There is, however, no reason for, or rather every reason against, such a supposition, as applied to the events last alluded to. In the interval between the destruction of Gibeah and the rule of Samuel, a very long period had elapsed, during which the ravages of Ammonites, Amalekites, Moabites, and Midianites (Judg. iii. 13, 14, vi. 1, 4, 33, x. 9) in the districts beyond Jordan, in the Jordan Valley itself at both its northern and southern ends — at Jericho no less than Jezreel — and along the passes of communication between the Jordan Valley and the western table-land, must have rendered communication between west and east almost, if not quite, impossible. Is it possible that as the old Mizpah became inaccessible, an eminence nearer at hand was chosen and invested with the sanctity of the original spot and used for the same purposes? Even if the name did not previously exist there in the exact shape of Mizpah, it may easily have existed in some shape sufficiently near to allow of its formation by a process both natural and frequent in Oriental speech. To a Hebrew it would require a very slight inflection to change Zophim or Zuph — both of which names were attached to places in the tribe of Benjamin — to Mizpah. This, however, must not be taken for more than a mere hypothesis. And against it

there is the serious objection that if it had been necessary to select a holy place in the territory of Ephraim or Benjamin, it would seem more natural that the choice should have fallen on Shiloh, or Bethel, than on one which had no previous claim but that of its name.

With the conquest of Jerusalem and the establishment there of the Ark, the sanctity of Mizpah, or at least its reputation, seems to have declined. The "men of Mizpah" (Neh. iii. 7), and the "ruler of Mizpah," and also of "part of Mizpah" (19 and 15) — assisted in the rebuilding of the wall of Jerusalem. The latter expressions perhaps point to a distinction between the sacred and the secular parts of the town. The allusion in ver. 7 to the "throne of the governor on this side the river" in connection with Mizpah is curious, and recalls the fact that Gedaliah, who was left in charge of Palestine by Nebuchadnezzar, had his abode there. But we hear of no religious act in connection with it till that affecting assembly called together thither, as to the ancient sanctuary of their forefathers, by Judas Maccabaeus, "when the Israelites assembled themselves together and came to Massepha over against Jerusalem: for in Maspha was there aforetime a place of prayer (τόπος προσευχῆς) for Israel" (1 Macc. iii. 46). The expression "over against" (κατέναντι), no less than the circumstances of the story, seems to require that from Mizpah the City or the Temple was visible: an indication of some importance, since, scanty as it is, it is the only information given us in the Bible as to the situation of the place. Josephus omits all mention of the circumstance, but on another occasion he names the place so as fully to corroborate the inference. It is in his account of the visit of Alexander the Great to Jerusalem (*Ant.* xi. 8, § 5), where he relates that Jaddua the high-priest went to meet the king "to a certain place called Sapha (Σαφά); which name, if interpreted in the Greek tongue, signifies a look-out place (σκοπήν), for from thence both Jerusalem and the sanctuary are visible." Sapha is doubtless a corruption of the old name Mizpah through its Greek form Maspha; and there can be no reasonable doubt that this is also the spot which Josephus on other occasions — adopting as he often does the Greek equivalent of the Hebrew name as if it were the original (witness the ἄνω ἀγορά, Ἄκρα, ἡ τῶν Τυροποιῶν φάραγξ, etc., etc.) — mentions as "appropriately named Scopus" (Σκοπός), because from it a clear view was obtained both of the city and of the great size of the Temple (*B. J.* v. 2, § 3). The position of this he gives minutely, at least twice (*B. J.* ii. 19, § 4, and v. 2, § 3), as on the north quarter of the city, and about 7 stadia therefrom; that is to say, as is now generally agreed, the broad [b] ridge which forms the continuation of the Mount of Olives to the north and east, from which the traveller gains, like Titus, his first view, and takes his last farewell, of the domes, walls, and towers of the Holy City.

Any one who will look at one of the numerous photographs of Jerusalem taken from this point, will satisfy himself of the excellent view of both city and temple which it commands; and it is the

a Rabbi Schwarz (127 *note*) very ingeniously finds a reference to Mizpeh in 1 Sam. iv. 13; where he would point the word מְצַפֶּה (A. V. "watching") as מִצְפָּה, and thus read "by the road to Mizpeh."

b The word used by Josephus in speaking of it (*B J.* v. 2, § 3) is χθαμαλός; and it will be observed that the root of the word Mizpah has the force of breadth as well as of elevation. See above.

only spot from which such a view is possible, which could answer the condition of the situation of Mizpah. *Neby Samweil*, for which Dr. Robinson argues (*B. R.* i. 460), is at least five miles, as the crow flies, from Jerusalem; and although from that lofty station the domes of the "Church of the Sepulchre," and even that of the Sakrah can be discerned, the distance is too great to allow us to accept it as a spot "over against Jerusalem," or from which either city or temple could with satisfaction be inspected.[a] Nor is the moderate height of Scopus, as compared with *Neby Samweil*, any argument against it, for we do not know how far the height of a "high place" contributed to its sanctity, or indeed what that sanctity exactly consisted in.[b] On the other hand, some corroboration is afforded to the identification of Scopus with Mizpah, in the fact that Mizpah is twice rendered by the LXX. σκοπιά.

Titus's approach through the villages of ancient Benjamin was, as far as we can judge, a close parallel to that of an earlier enemy of Jerusalem — Sennacherib. In his case, indeed, there is no mention of Mizpah. It was at NOB that the Assyrian king remained for a day feasting his eyes on "the house of Zion and the hill of Jerusalem," and menacing with "his hand" the fair booty before him. But so exact is the correspondence, that it is difficult not to suspect that Nob and Mizpah must have been identical, since that part of the rising ground north of Jerusalem which is crossed by the northern road is the only spot from which a view of both city and temple at once can be obtained, without making a long détour by way of the Mount of Olives. This, however, will be best discussed under NOB. Assuming that the hill in question is the Scopus of Josephus, and that that again was the Mizpah of the Hebrews, the σκοπιά (σκοπιά) and *Massephath* of the LXX. translators, it is certainly startling to find a village named *Shâfât*[c] lying on the north slope of the mountain a very short distance below the summit — if summit it can be called — from which the view of Jerusalem, and of Zion (now occupied by the Sakrah), is obtained. Can *Shâfat*, or *Safut*, be, as there is good reason to believe in the case of *Tell es-Sâfieh*, the remains of the ancient Semitic name? Our knowledge of the topography of the Holy Land, even of the city and environs of Jerusalem, is so very imperfect, that the above can only be taken as suggestions which may be not unworthy the notice of future explorers in their investigations.

Professor Stanley appears to have been the first to suggest the identity of Scopus with Mizpah (*S. & P.* 1st edit. 222). But since writing the above, the writer has become aware that the same view is taken by Dr. Bonar in his *Land of Promise* (Appendix, § viii.). This traveller has investigated

the subject with great ability and clearness; and he points out one circumstance in favor of Scopus being Mizpah, and against *Neby Samweil*, which had escaped the writer, namely, that the former lay directly in the road of the pilgrims from Samaria to Jerusalem who were murdered by Ishmael (Jer. xli. 7), while the latter is altogether away from it. Possibly the statement of Josephus (see vol. ii. p. 1173 *a*) that it was at Hebron, not Gibeon, that Ishmael was overtaken, coupled with Dr. B.'s own statement as to the pre-occupation of the districts east of Jerusalem — may remove the only scruple which he appears to entertain to the identification of Scopus with Mizpah.   G.

MIZ'PAR (מִסְפָּר [*number*]: Μασφάρ; [Vat. Μαλσαρ:] *Mesphar*). Properly MISPAR, as in the A. V. of 1611 and the Geneva version; the same as MISPERETH (Ezr. ii. 2).

MIZ'PEH. [MIZPAH.]

MIZRA'IM (מִצְרַיִם [see below]: Μεσραΐν: *Mesraim*), the usual name of Egypt in the O. T., the dual of Mazor, מָצוֹר, which is less frequently[d] employed: gent. noun, מִצְרִי.

If the etymology of Mazor be sought in Hebrew it might signify a "mound," "bulwark," or "citadel," or again "distress;" but no one of these meanings is apposite. We prefer, with Gesenius (*Thes.* s. v. מצור), to look to the Arabic, and we extract the article on the corresponding word from the *Kámoos*, "مِصْر, a partition between two things, as also مَاصِر: a limit between two lands: a receptacle: a city or a province [the explanation means both]: and red earth or mud. The well-known city [Memphis]." Gesenius accepts the meaning "limit" or the like, but it is hard to see its fitness with the Shemites, who had no idea that the Nile or Egypt was on the border of two continents, unless it be supposed to denote the divided land. We believe that the last meaning but one, "red earth or mud," is the true one, from its correspondence to the Egyptian name of the country, KEM, which signifies "black," and was given to it for the blackness of its alluvial soil. It must be recollected that the term "red" (أحمر) is not used in the *Kámoos*, or indeed in Semitic phraseology, in the limited sense to which Indo-European ideas have accustomed us; it embraces a wide range of tints, from what we call red

---

[a] * Dr. Valentiner, for several years a missionary at Jerusalem, and familiar with the topography of the region, agrees with Dr. Robinson that *Neby Samweil* is the ancient Mizpah. See *Zeitschr. der deutsch. M. Gesellsch.* xii. 164. Van de Velde thinks this to be the right opinion (*Syr. and Pal.* ii. 53). This *Neby Samweil* is so marked a feature of the landscape, that it may very justly be said to "confront" (κατέναντι, see above) the observer as he looks towards it from Jerusalem. The impression in such a case depends less on the distance than on the position and conspicuousness of the object. See wood-cut, vol. i. p. 917.   H.

[b] In the East, at the present time, a sanctity is

attached to the spot from which any holy place is visible. Such spots may be met with all through the hills a few miles north of Jerusalem, distinguished by the little heaps of stones erected by thoughtful or pious Mussulmans. (See Miss Beaufort's *Egypt. Sepulchres*, etc. ii. 88.)

[c] This is the spelling given by Van de Velde in his map. Robinson gives it as *Shâ'fat* (i. e. with the *Ain*), and Dr. Eli Smith, in the Arabic lists attached to Robinson's 1st edition (iii. App. 121), *Sa'fat*.

[d] It occurs only 2 K. xix. 24; Is. xix. 6, xxxvii. 25; Mic. vii. 12.

to a reddish brown. So, in like manner, in Egyptian the word "black" signifies dark in an equally wide sense. We have already shown that the Hebrew word Ham, the name of the ancestor of the Egyptians, is evidently the same as the native appellation of the country, the former signifying "warm" or "hot," and a cognate Arabic word,

لَحِمَ, meaning "black fetid mud" (Kamous), or "black mud" (Sihâh, MS.), and suggested that Ham and Mazor may be identical with the Egyptian KEM (or KHEM), which is virtually the same in both sound and sense as the former, and of the same sense as the latter. [EGYPT; HAM.] How then are we to explain this double naming of the country? A recent discovery throws light upon the question. We had already some reason for conjecturing that there were Semitic equivalents, with the same sense, for some of the Egyptian geographical names with which the Shemites were well acquainted. M. de Rougé has ascertained that Zoan is the famous Shepherd-stronghold Avaris, and that the Hebrew name צָעַן, from צָעַן, "he moved tents, went forward," is equivalent to the Egyptian one HA-WAR, "the place of departure" (Revue Archéologique, 1861, p. 250). This discovery, it should be noticed, gives remarkable significance to the passage, "Now Hebron was built seven years before Zoan in Egypt" (Num. xiii. 22). Perhaps a similar case may be found in Kush and Phut, both of which occur in Egyptian as well as Hebrew. In the Bible, African Cush is Ethiopia above Egypt, and Phut, an African people or land connected with Egypt. In the Egyptian inscriptions, the same Ethiopia is KEESH, and an Ethiopian people is called ANU-PET-MERU, "the Anu of the island of the bow," probably Meroë, where the Nile makes an extraordinary bend in its course. We have no Egyptian or Hebrew etymology for KEESH, or Cush, unless we may compare קֶשֶׁת, which would give the same connection with bow that we find in Phut or PET, for which our only derivation is from the Egyptian PET, "a bow." There need be no difficulty in thus supposing that Mizraim is merely the name of a country, and that Ham and Mazor may have been the same person, for the very form of Mizraim forbids any but the former idea, and the tenth chapter of Genesis is obviously not altogether a genealogical list. Egyptian etymologies have been sought in vain for Mizraim: ⲙⲉⲧⲟⲩⲣⲟ, "kingdom" (Gesen. Thes. s. v. מָצוֹר), is not an ancient form, and the old name, TO-MAR (Brugsch, Geog. Inschr. pl. x. nos. 367–370, p. 74), suggested as the source of Mizraim by Dr. Hincks, is too different to be accepted as a derivation.

MIZRAIM first occurs in the account of the Hamites in Gen. x., where we read, "And the sons of Ham; Cush, and Mizraim, and Phut, and Canaan" (ver. 6; comp. 1 Chr. i. 8). Here we have conjectured that instead of the dual, the original text had the gentile noun in the plural (suggesting מִצְרִים instead of the present מִצְרַיִם), since t seems strange that a dual form should occur in the first generation after Ham, and since the plural of the gentile noun would be consistent with the plural forms of the names of the Mizraite nations or tribes afterwards enumerated, as well as with

the like singular forms of the names of the Canaanites, excepting Sidon. [HAM.]

If the names be in an order of seniority, whether as indicating children of Ham, or older and younger branches, we can form no theory as to their settlements from their places; but if the arrangement be geographical, which is probable from the occurrence of the form Mizraim, which in no case can be a man's name, and the order of some of the Mizraites, the placing may afford a clew to the positions of the Hamite lands. Cush would stand first as the most widely spread of these peoples, extending from Babylon to the upper Nile, the territory of Mizraim would be the next to the north, embracing Egypt and its colonies on the northwest and northeast, Phut as dependent on Egypt might follow Mizraim, and Canaan as the northernmost would end the list. Egypt, the "land of Ham," may have been the primitive seat of these four stocks. In the enumeration of the Mizraites, though we have tribes extending far beyond Egypt, we may suppose that they all had their first seat in Mizraim, and spread thence, as is distinctly said of the Philistines. Here the order seems to be geographical, though the same is not so clear of the Canaanites. The list of the Mizraites is thus given in Gen. x.: "And Mizraim begat Ludim, and Anamim, and Lehabim, and Naphtuhim, and Pathrusim, and Casluhim (whence came forth the Philistines), and Caphtorim" (13, 14; comp. 1 Chr. i. 11, 12). Here it is certain that we have the names of nations or tribes, and it is probable that they are all derived from names of countries. We find elsewhere Pathros and Caphtor, probably Lud (for the Mizraite Ludim), and perhaps, Lub for the Lubim, which are almost certainly the same as the Lehabim. There is a difficulty in the Philistines being, according to the present text, traced to the Casluhim, whereas in other places they come from the land of Caphtor, and are even called Caphtorim. It seems probable that there has been a misplacement, and that the parenthetic clause originally followed the name of the Caphtorim. Of these names we have not yet identified the Anamim and the Casluhim; the Lehabim are, as already said, almost certainly the same as the Lubim, the REBU of the Egyptian monuments, and the primitive Libyans; the Naphtuhim we put immediately to the west of northern Egypt; and the Pathrusim and Caphtorim in that country, where the Casluhim may also be placed. There would therefore be a distinct order from west to east, and if the Philistines be transferred, this order would be perfectly preserved, though perhaps these last would necessarily be placed with their immediate parent among the tribes.

Mizraim therefore, like Cush, and perhaps Ham, geographically represents a centre whence colonies went forth in the remotest period of post-diluvian history. The Philistines were originally settled in the land of Mizraim, and there is reason to suppose the same of the Lehabim, if they be those Libyans who revolted, according to Manetho, from the Egyptians in a very early age. [LUBIM.] The list, however, probably arranges them according to the settlements they held at a later time, if we may judge from the notice of the Philistines' migration; but the mention of the spread of the Canaanites must be considered on the other side. We regard the distribution of the Mizraites as showing that their colonies were but a part of the great migration that gave the Cushites the command of the

Indian Ocean, and which explains the affinity the
Egyptian monuments show us between the pre-
Hellenic Cretans and Carians (the latter no doubt
the Leleges of the Greek writers) and the Philistines.

The history and ethnology of the Mizraite nations have been given under the article HAM, so
that here it is not needful to do more than draw
attention to some remarkable particulars which did
not fall under our notice in treating of the early
Egyptians. We find from the monuments of
Egypt that the white nations of western Africa
were of what we call the Semitic type, and we
must therefore be careful not to assume that they
formed part of the stream of Arab colonization
that has for full two thousand years steadily flowed
into northern Africa. The seafaring race that first
passed from Egypt to the west, though physically
like, was mentally different from, the true pastoral
Arab, and to this day the two elements have kept
apart, the townspeople of the coast being unable
to settle amongst the tribes of the interior, and
these tribes again being as unable to settle on the
coast.

The affinity of the Egyptians and their neighbors was long a safeguard of the empire of the
Pharaohs, and from the latter, whether Cretans,
Lubim, or people of Phut and Cush, the chief
mercenaries of the Egyptian armies were drawn;
facts which we mainly learn from the Bible, confirmed by the monuments. In the days of the
Persian dominion Libyan Inaros made a brave
stand for the liberty of Egypt. Probably the tie
was more one of religion than of common descent,
for the Egyptian belief appears to have mainly
prevailed in Africa as far as it was civilized, though
of course changed in its details. The Philistines
had a different religion, and seem to have been
identified in this matter with the Canaanites, and
thus they may have lost, as they seem to have done,
their attachment to their mother country.

In the use of the names Mazor and Mizraim for
Egypt there can be no doubt that the dual indicates
the two regions into which the country has always
been divided by nature as well as by its inhabitants.
Under the Greeks and Romans there was indeed
a third division, the Heptanomis, which has been
called Middle Egypt, as between Upper and Lower
Egypt, but we must rather regard it as forming,
with the Thebaïs, Upper Egypt. It has been supposed that Mazor, as distinct from Mizraim, signifies Lower Egypt; but this conjecture cannot be
maintained. For fuller details on the subject of
this article the reader is referred to HAM, EGYPT,
and the articles on the several Mizraite nations or
tribes.   R. S. P.

* According to Dr. Geo. Ebers, of Jena, who
has made this name the subject of a thorough
and learned discussion (*Aegypten und die Bücher
Mose's*), Mizraim was a Semitish term, which originated entirely outside of Egyptian forms of speech,
and was probably suggested by that feature of
Egypt which would most powerfully impress a
people living to the east of the Nile. In striking
contrast with the tribes of Northern Arabia which
roved from place to place, following the herbage
for their flocks, Egypt was an inclosed and secluded
country. At an early period the Pharaohs fortified themselves against the incursions of Asiatic
tribes, and for a long time they were extremely
jealous even of commerce with foreigners. Hence
the most secluded country known to the Semitic

peoples received the name of the Inclosed, the Fortified — the name Mizraim being derived from
מָצוֹר. Knobel, who gives the same derivation,
traces the idea of insulation (*Einschliessung*), to
the geographical configuration of the country, as
shut in within the hills and the desert — the double
chain of mountains suggesting the dual form — or
possibly this may have been intended to mark the
contrast between the Nile Valley and the Delta.
To this, however, it is objected by Ebers, that for
a long time, perhaps until the invasion of the
Hyksos, Egypt was known to the Phœnicians and
other nations of the East, only through its Delta.
Indeed Pliny and other classic writers speak of the
Thebaïd as a distinct country, and not as a part
of Egypt itself. Hence to account for the dual
form of Mizraim, Ebers falls back upon the double
line of fortifications that guarded the Isthmus of
Suez; the one terminating at Heliopolis, the other
at Klysma, at the head of the gulf, near the site
of the modern Suez. The dual would then signify
the doubly-fortified. If this hypothesis is not tenable, then the dual form may have been derived from
the twofold division which appeared very early in
the political constitution of the country, and under
the consolidated empire was still represented in the
colors and symbols of the double-crown. [EGYPT.]
The fundamental idea of the inclosed country
being retained, the term was adapted to this double
form. The Hebrews, already familiar with this
Semitic notion of Egypt, received their first impressions of the country from that doubly-fortified
section which was their allotted home, and they
naturally adhered to a descriptive name which is
not found in the hieroglyphics, nor explained by
the Coptic, and which probably the old Egyptians
never employed to designate their native land. In
Is. xi. 11 and Jer. xliv. 15 the plural Mizraim
appears to be used for the Delta alone.
                                        J. P. T.

MIZ'ZAH (מִזָּה [*fear*]: Μοζέ; Alex. Μοχε
[and Vat. Ομοζε] in 1 Chr.: *Meza*). Son of
Reuel and grandson of Esau; descended likewise
through Bashemath from Ishmael. He was one of
the "dukes" or chiefs of tribes in the land of
Edom (Gen. xxxvi. 13, 17; 1 Chr. i. 37). The
settlements of his descendants are believed by Mr.
Forster (*Hist. Geog. of Arab.* ii. 55) to be indicated in the μεσανίτης κόλπος, or Phrat-*Misan*,
at the head of the Persian Gulf.

MNA'SON (Μνάσων) is honorably mentioned
in Scripture, like Gaius, Lydia, and others, as one
of the hosts of the Apostle Paul (Acts xxi. 16).
One or two questions of some little interest, though
of no great importance, are raised by the context.
It is most likely, in the first place, that his residence at this time was not Cæsarea, but Jerusalem.
He was well known to the Christians of Cæsarea,
and they took St. Paul to his house at Jerusalem.
To translate the words ἄγοντες παρ᾽ ᾧ ξενισθῶμεν,
as in the A. V., removes no grammatical difficulty,
and introduces a slight improbability into the narrative. He was, however, a Cyprian by birth, and
may have been a friend of Barnabas (Acts iv. 36),
and possibly brought to the knowledge of Christianity by him. The Cyprians who are so prominently mentioned in Acts xi. 19, 20, may have
included Mnason. It is hardly likely that he could
have been converted during the journey of Paul
and Barnabas through Cyprus (Acts xiii. 4–13),

otherwise the Apostle would have been personally acquainted with him, which does not appear to have been the case. And the phrase ἀρχαῖος μαθητής points to an earlier period, possibly to the day of Pentecost (compare ἐν ἀρχῇ, Acts xi. 15), or to direct intercourse with our blessed Lord Himself. [CYPRUS.]   J. S. H.

MO'AB (מוֹאָב [see below]: Μωάβ; Josephus, Μόαβος: *Moab*), the name of the son of Lot's eldest daughter, the elder brother of Ben-Ammi, the progenitor of the Ammonites (Gen. xix. 37); also of the nation descended from him. though the name "Moabites" is in both the original and A. V. more frequently used for them.

No explanation of the name is given us in the original record, and it is not possible to throw an interpretation into it unless by some accommodation. Various explanations have however been proposed. (a.) The LXX. insert the words λέγουσα. ἐκ τοῦ πατρός μου, "saying 'from my father,'" as if מֵאָב. This is followed by the old interpreters; as Josephus (*Ant.* i. 11, § 5), Jerome's *Quæst. Hebr. in Genesim*, the gloss of the Pseudojon. Targum; and in modern times by De Wette (*Bibel*), Tuch (*Gen.* p. 370), and J. D. Michaelis (*B. für Ungelehrten*). (b.) By Hiller (*Onom.* p. 414), Simonis (*Onom.* p. 479), it is derived from מוֹבָא אָב, "ingressus, i. e. coitus, patris." (c.) Rosenmüller (see Schumann, *Genesis*, p. 302) proposes to treat מוֹ as equivalent for מַיִם, in accordance with the figure employed by Balaam in Num. xxiv. 7. This is countenanced by Jerome — "aqua paterna" (*Comm. in Mic.* vi. 8) — and has the great authority of Gesenius in its favor (*Thes.* p. 775 a); also of Fürst (*Handwb.* p. 707) and Bunsen (*Bibelwerk*). (d.) A derivation, probably more correct etymologically than either of the above, is that suggested by Maurer from the root אָבָה, "to desire" — "the desirable land" — with reference to the extreme fertility of the region occupied by Moab. (See also Fürst, *Handwb.* p. 707 b.) No hint, however, has yet been discovered in the Bible records of such an origin of the name.

Zoar was the cradle of the race of Lot.[a] The situation of this town appears to have been in the district east of the Jordan, and to the north or northeast of the Dead Sea. [ZOAR.] From this centre the brother-tribes spread themselves. AMMON, whose disposition seems throughout to have been more roving and unsettled, went to the northeast and took possession of the pastures and waste tracts which lay outside the district of the mountains; that which in earlier times seems to have been known as Ham, and inhabited by the Zuzim or Zamzummim (Gen. xiv. 5; Deut. ii. 20). MOAB, whose habits were more settled and peaceful, remained nearer their original seat. The rich highlands which crown the eastern side of the chasm of the Dead Sea, and extend northwards as far as the foot of the mountains of Gilead, appear at that early date to have borne a name, which in its Hebrew form is presented to us as Shaveh-Kiriathaim, and to have been inhabited by a branch of the great race of the Rephaim. Like

the Horim before the descendants of Esau, the Avim before the Philistines, or the indigenous races of the New World before the settlers from the West, this ancient people, the Emim, gradually became extinct before the Moabites, who thus obtained possession of the whole of the rich elevated tract referred to — a district forty or fifty miles in length by ten or twelve in width, the celebrated *Belka* and *Kerrak* of the modern Arabs, the most fertile on that side of Jordan, no less eminently fitted for pastoral pursuits than the maritime plans of Philistia and Sharon, on the west of Palestine, are for agriculture. With the highlands they occupied also the lowlands at their feet, the plain which intervenes between the slopes of the mountains and the one perennial stream of Palestine, and through which they were enabled to gain access at pleasure to the fords of the river, and thus to the country beyond it. Of the valuable district of the high lands they were not allowed to retain entire possession. The warlike Amorites — either forced from their original seats on the west, or perhaps lured over by the increasing prosperity of the young nation — crossed the Jordan and overran the richer portion of the territory on the north, driving Moab back to his original position behind the natural bulwark of the Arnon. The plain of the Jordan Valley, the hot and humid atmosphere of which had perhaps no attraction for the Amorite mountaineers, appears to have remained in the power of Moab. When Israel reached the boundary of the country, this contest had only very recently occurred. Sihon, the Amorite king under whose command Heshbon had been taken, was still reigning there — the ballads commemorating the event were still fresh in the popular mouth (Num. xxi. 27–30).[b]

Of these events, which extended over a period, according to the received Bible chronology, of not less than 500 years, from the destruction of Sodom to the arrival of Israel on the borders of the Promised Land, we obtain the above outline only from the fragments of ancient documents, which are found embedded in the records of Numbers and Deuteronomy (Num. xxi. 26–30; Deut. ii. 10, 11). The portion into which the Moabites were driven by the incursion of the Amorites was a very circumscribed one, in extent not so much as half that which they had lost. But on the other hand its position was much more secure, and it was well suited for the occupation of a people whose disposition was not so warlike as that of their neighbors. It occupied the southern half of the high tablelands which rise above the eastern side of the Dead Sea. On every side it was strongly fortified by nature. On the north was the tremendous chasm of the Arnon. On the west it was limited by the precipices, or more accurately the cliffs, which descend almost perpendicularly to the shore of the lake, and are intersected only by one or two steep and narrow passes. Lastly, on the south and east, it was protected by a half circle of hills which open only to allow the passage of a branch of the Arnon and another of the torrents which descend to the Dead Sea.

It will be seen from the foregoing description that the territory occupied by Moab at the period

---

[a] * This is an inadvertence. The "cradle of the race of Lot" was in the mountain above.   S. W.

[b] For an examination of this remarkable passage, in some respects without a parallel in the Old Testament, see NUMBERS.

of its greatest extent, before the invasion of the Amorites, divided itself naturally into three distinct and independent portions. Each of these portions appears to have had its name by which it is almost invariably designated. (1.) The enclosed corner [a] or canton south of the Arnon was the "field of Moab" (Ruth i. 1, 2, 6, &c.). (2.) The more open rolling country north of the Arnon, opposite Jericho, and up to the hills of Gilead, was the "land of Moab" (Deut. i. 5, xxxii. 49, &c.). (3.) The sunk district in the tropical depths of the Jordan Valley, taking its name from that of the great valley itself — the Arabah — was the Arboth-Moab, the dry regions — in the A. V. very incorrectly rendered the "plains of Moab" (Num. xxii. 1, &c.).

Outside of the hills, which inclosed the "field of Moab," or Moab proper, on the southeast, and which are at present called the Jebel Uru-Karaiyeh and Jebel el-Tarfuyeh, lay the vast pasture grounds of the waste uncultivated country or "Midbar," which is described as "facing Moab" on the east (Num. xxi. 11). Through this latter district Israel appears to have approached the Promised Land. Some communication had evidently taken place, though of what nature it is impossible clearly to ascertain. For while in Deut. ii. 28, 29, the attitude of the Moabites is mentioned as friendly, this seems to be contradicted by the statement of xxiii. 4, while in Judg. xi. 17, again, Israel is said to have sent from Kadesh asking permission to pass through Moab, a permission which, like Edom, Moab refused. At any rate the attitude perpetuated by the provision of Deut. xxiii. 3 — a provision maintained in full force by the latest of the Old Testament reformers (Neh. xiii. 1, 2, 23) — is one of hostility.

But whatever the communication may have been, the result was that Israel did not traverse Moab, but turning to the right passed outside the mountains through the "wilderness," by the east side of the territory above described (Deut. ii. 8; Judg. xi. 18), and finally took up their position in the country north of the Arnon, from which Moab had so lately been ejected. Here the headquarters of the nation remained for a considerable time while the conquest of Bashan was being effected. It was during this period that the visit of Balaam took place. The whole of the country east of the Jordan, with the exception of the one little corner occupied by Moab, was in possession of the invaders, and although at the period in question the main body had descended from the upper level to the plains of Shittim, the Arboth-Moab, in the Jordan Valley, yet a great number must have remained on the upper level, and the towns up to the very edge of the ravine of the Arnon were still occupied by their settlements (Num. xxi. 24; Judg. xi. 26). It was a situation full of alarm for a nation which had already suffered so severely. In his extremity the Moabite king, Balak — whose father Zippor was doubtless the chieftain who had lost his life in the encounter with Sihon (Num. xxi. 26) — appealed to the Midianites for aid (Num. xxii. 2–4). With a

metaphor highly appropriate both to his mouth and to the ear of the pastoral tribe he was addressing,[b] he exclaims that "this people will lick up all round about us as the ox licketh up the grass of the field." What relation existed between Moab and Midian we do not know, but there are various indications that it was a closer one than would arise merely from their common descent from Terah. The tradition of the Jews [c] is, that up to this time the two had been one nation, with kings taken alternately from each, and that Balak was a Midianite. This, however, is in contradiction to the statements of Genesis as to the origin of each people. The whole story of Balaam's visit and of the subsequent events, both in the original narrative of Numbers and in the remarkable statement of Jephthah — whose words as addressed to Ammonites must be accepted as literally accurate — bears out the inference already drawn from the earlier history as to the pacific character of Moab.

The account of the whole of these transactions in the Book of Numbers, familiar as we are with its phrases, perhaps hardly conveys an adequate idea of the extremity in which Balak found himself in his unexpected encounter with the new nation and their mighty Divinity. We may realize it better (and certainly with gratitude for the opportunity), if we consider what that last dreadful agony was in which a successor of Balak was placed, when, all hope of escape for himself and his people being cut off, the unhappy Mesha immolated his own son on the wall of Kir-haraseth, — and then remember that Balak in his distress actually proposed the same awful sacrifice — "his first-born for his transgression, the fruit of his body for the sin of his soul" (Mic. vi. 7), a sacrifice from which he was restrained only by the wise, the almost Christian [d] counsels, of Balaam. This catastrophe will be noticed in its proper place.

The connection of Moab with Midian, and the comparatively inoffensive character of the former, are shown in the narrative of the events which followed the departure of Balaam. The women of Moab are indeed said (Num. xxv. 1) to have commenced the idolatrous fornication which proved so destructive to Israel, but it is plain that their share in it was insignificant compared with that of Midian. It was a Midianitish woman whose shameless act brought down the plague on the camp, the Midianitish women were especially devoted to destruction by Moses (xxv. 16–18, xxxi. 16), and it was upon Midian that the vengeance was taken. Except in the passage already mentioned, Moab is not once named in the whole transaction.

The latest date at which the two names appear in conjunction, is found in the notice of the defeat of Midian "in the field of Moab" by the Edomite king Hadad-ben-Bedad, which occurred five generations before the establishment of the monarchy of Israel (Gen. xxxvi. 35; 1 Chr. i. 46). By the Jewish interpreters — e. g. Solomon Jarchi in his commentary on the passage — this is treated as implying not alliance, but war, between Moab and Midian (comp. 1 Chr. iv. 22).

---

[a] The word עָרֵי (A. V. "corners") is twice used with respect to Moab (Num. xxiv. 17; Jer. xlviii. 45). No one appears yet to have discovered its force in this relation. It can hardly have any connection with the shape of the territory as noticed in the text.

[b] Midian was eminently a pastoral people. See the

account of the spoil taken from them (Num. xxxi. 32–47). For the pastoral wealth of Moab, even at this early period, see the expressions in Mic. vi. 6, 7.

[c] See Targum Pseudojonathan on Num. xxii. 4.

[d] Balaam's words (Mic. vi. 8) are nearly identical with those quoted by our Lord Himself (Matt. ix. 13 and xii. 7).

It is remarkable that Moses should have taken his view of the Promised Land from a Moabite sanctuary, and been buried in the land of Moab. It is singular too that his resting-place is marked in the Hebrew Records only by its proximity to the sanctuary of that deity to whom in his lifetime he had been such an enemy. He lies in a ravine in the land of Moab, facing Beth-Peor, *i. e.* the abode of Baal-Peor (Deut. xxxiv. 6).

After the conquest of Canaan the relations of Moab with Israel were of a mixed character. With the tribe of Benjamin, whose possessions at their eastern end were separated from those of Moab only by the Jordan, they had at least one severe struggle, in union with their kindred the Ammonites, and also, for this time only, the wild Amalekites from the south (Judg. iii. 12–30). The Moabite king, Eglon, actually ruled and received tribute in Jericho for eighteen years, but at the end of that time he was killed by the Benjamite hero Ehud, and the return of the Moabites being intercepted at the fords, a large number were slaughtered, and a stop put to such incursions on their part for the future.[a] A trace of this invasion is visible in the name of Chephar-ha-Ammonai, the "hamlet of the Ammonites," one of the Benjamite towns; and another is possibly preserved even to the present day in the name of *Mukhmas*, the modern representative of Michmash, which is by some scholars believed to have received its name from Chemosh the Moabite deity.

The feud continued with true oriental pertinacity to the time of Saul. Of his slaughter of the Ammonites we have full details in 1 Sam. xi., and amongst his other conquests Moab is especially mentioned (1 Sam. xiv. 47). There is not, however, as we should expect, any record of it during Ishbosheth's residence at Mahanaim on the east of Jordan.

But while such were their relations to the tribe of Benjamin, the story of Ruth, on the other hand, testifies to the existence of a friendly intercourse between Moab and Bethlehem, one of the towns of Judah. The Jewish[b] tradition ascribes the death of Mahlon and Chilion to punishment for having broken the commandment of Deut. xxiii. 3, but no trace of any feeling of the kind is visible in the Book of Ruth itself — which not only seems to imply a considerable intercourse between the two nations, but also a complete ignorance or disregard of the precept in question, which was broken in the most flagrant manner when Ruth became the wife of Boaz. By his descent from Ruth, David may be said to have had Moabite blood in his veins. The relationship was sufficient, especially when combined with the blood-feud between Moab and Benjamin, already alluded to, to warrant his visiting the land of his ancestress, and committing his parents to the protection of the king of Moab, when hard pressed by Saul (1 Sam. xxii. 3, 4). But here all friendly relation stops for ever. The next time the name is mentioned is in the account of David's war, at least twenty years after the last-mentioned event (2 Sam. viii. 2; 1 Chr. xviii. 2).

The abrupt manner in which this war is intro-duced into the history is no less remarkable than the brief and passing terms in which its horrors are recorded. The account occupies but a few words in either Samuel or Chronicles, and yet it must have been for the time little short of a virtual extirpation of the nation. Two thirds of the people were put to death, and the remainder became bondmen, and were subjected to a regular tribute. An incident of this war is probably recorded in 2 Sam. xxiii. 20, and 1 Chr. xi. 22. The spoils taken from the Moabite cities and sanctuaries went to swell the treasures acquired from the enemies of Jehovah, which David was amassing for the future Temple (2 Sam. viii. 11, 12; 1 Chr. xviii. 11). It was the first time that the prophecy of Balaam had been fulfilled, — "Out of Jacob shall come he that shall have dominion, and shall destroy him that remaineth of Ar," that is of Moab.

So signal a vengeance can only have been occasioned by some act of perfidy or insult, like that which brought down a similar treatment on the Ammonites (2 Sam. x.). But as to any such act the narrative is absolutely silent. It has been conjectured that the king of Moab betrayed the trust which David reposed in him, and either himself killed Jesse and his wife, or surrendered them to Saul. But this, though not improbable, is nothing more than conjecture.

It must have been a considerable time before Moab recovered from so severe a blow. Of this we have evidence in the fact of their not being mentioned in the account of the campaign in which the Ammonites were subdued, when it is not probable they would have refrained from assisting their relatives had they been in a condition to do so. Throughout the reign of Solomon, they no doubt shared in the universal peace which surrounded Israel; and the only mention of the name occurs in the statement that there were Moabites amongst the foreign women in the royal harem, and, as a natural consequence, that the Moabite worship was tolerated, or perhaps encouraged (1 K. xi. 1, 7, 33). The high place for Chemosh, "the abomination of Moab," was consecrated "on the mount facing Jerusalem," where it remained till its "defilement" by Josiah (2 K. xxiii. 13), nearly four centuries afterwards.

At the disruption of the kingdom, Moab seems to have fallen to the northern realm, probably for the same reason that has been already remarked in the case of Eglon and Ehud — that the fords of Jordan lay within the territory of Benjamin, who for some time after the separation clung to its ancient ally the house of Ephraim. But be this as it may, at the death of Ahab, eighty years later, we find Moab paying him the enormous tribute, apparently annual, of 100,000 rams, and the same number of wethers with their fleeces; an amount which testifies at once to the severity of the terms imposed by Israel, and to the remarkable vigor of character, and wealth of natural resources, which could enable a little country, not so large as the county of Huntingdon, to raise year by year this enormous impost, and at the same time support its own people in prosperity and affluence.[c] It is not

<hr/>

[a] The account of Shaharaim, a man of Benjamin, who "begat children in the field of Moab," in 1 Chr. viii. 8, seems, from the mention of Ehud (ver. 6), to belong to this time; but the whole passage is very obscure.

[b] See Targum Jonathan on Ruth i. 4. The marriage of Boaz with the stranger is vindicated by making Ruth a proselyte in desire, if not by actual initiation.

[c] This affluence is shown by the treasures which they left on the field of Berachah (2 Chr. xx. 25), no less than by the general condition of the country, indicated in the narrative of Joram's invasion; and is

surprising that the Moabites should have seized the moment of Ahab's death to throw off so burdensome a yoke; but it is surprising, that, notwithstanding such a drain on their resources, they were ready to incur the risk and expense of a war with a state in every respect far their superior. Their first step, after asserting their independence, was to attack the kingdom of Judah in company with their kindred the Ammonites, and, as seems probable, the Mehunim, a roving semi-Edomite people from the mountains in the southeast of Palestine (2 Chr. xx.) The army was a huge heterogeneous horde of ill-assorted elements. The route chosen for the invasion was round the southern end of the Dead Sea, thence along the beach, and by the pass of En-gedi to the level of the upper country. But the expedition contained within itself the elements of its own destruction. Before they reached the enemy dissensions arose between the heathen strangers and the children of Lot; distrust followed, and finally panic; and when the army of Jehoshaphat came in sight of them they found that they had nothing to do but to watch the extermination of one half the huge host by the other half, and to seize the prodigious booty which was left on the field.

Disastrous as was this proceeding, that which followed it was even still more so. As a natural consequence of the late events, Israel, Judah, and Edom united in an attack on Moab. For reasons which are not stated, but one of which we may reasonably conjecture was to avoid the passage of the savage Edomites through Judah, the three confederate armies approached not as usual by the north, but round the southern end of the Dead Sea, through the parched valleys of upper Edom. As the host came near, the king of Moab, doubtless the same Mesha who threw off the yoke of Ahab, assembled the whole of his people, from the youngest who were of age to bear the sword-girdle,[a] on the boundary of his territory, probably on the outer slopes of the line of hills which encircles the lower portion of Moab, overlooking the waste which extended below them towards the east.[b] Here they remained all night on the watch. With the approach of morning the sun rose suddenly above the horizon of the rolling plain, and as his level beams burst through the night-mists they revealed no masses of the enemy, but shone with a blood-red glare on a multitude of pools in the bed of the wady at their feet. They did not know that these pools had been sunk during the night by the order of a mighty Prophet who was with the host of Israel, and that they had been filled by the sudden flow of water rushing from the distant highlands of Edom. To them the conclusion was inevitable. The army had, like their own on the late occasion, fallen out in the night; these red pools were the blood of the slain; those who were not killed had fled, and nothing stood between them and the pillage of the camp.

The cry "Moab to the spoil!" was raised. Down the slopes they rushed in headlong disorder, but not, as they expected, to empty tents; they found an enemy ready prepared to reap the result of his ingenious stratagem.[c] Then occurred one of those scenes of carnage which can happen but once or twice in the existence of a nation. The Moabites fled back in confusion, followed and cut down at every step by their enemies. Far inwards did the pursuit reach, among the cities and farms and orchards of that rich district: nor when the slaughter was over was the horrid work of destruction done. The towns both fortified and unfortified were demolished, and the stones strewed over the carefully tilled fields. The fountains of water, the life[d] of an eastern land, were choked, and all timber of any size or goodness felled. Nowhere else do we hear of such sweeping desolation; the very besom of destruction passed over the land. At last the struggle collected itself at KIR-HARESETH, apparently a newly constructed fortress, which, if the modern *Kerak* — and there is every probability that they are identical — may well have resisted all the efforts of the allied kings in its native impregnability. Here Mesha took refuge with his family and with the remnants of his army. The heights around, by which the town is entirely commanded, were covered with slingers, who, armed partly with the ancient weapon of David and of the Benjamites, partly perhaps with the newly-invented machines shortly to be famous in Jerusalem (2 Chr. xxvi. 15), discharged their volleys of stones on the town. At length the annoyance could be borne no longer. Then Mesha, collecting round him a forlorn hope of 700 of his best warriors, made a desperate sally, with the intention of cutting his way through to his special foe the king of Edom. But the enemy were too strong for him, and he was driven back. And then came a fitting crown to a tragedy already so terrible. An awful spectacle amazed and horrified the besiegers. The king and his eldest son, the heir to the throne, mounted the wall, and, in the sight of the thousands who covered the sides of that vast amphitheatre, the father killed and burnt his child as a propitiatory sacrifice to the cruel gods of his country. It was the same dreadful act to which, as we have seen, Balak had been so nearly tempted in his extremity.[e] But the danger, though perhaps not really greater than his, was more imminent; and Mesha had no one like Balaam at hand, to counsel patience and submission to a mightier Power than Chemosh or Baal-Peor.

Hitherto, though able and ready to fight when necessary, the Moabites do not appear to have been a fighting people; perhaps, as suggested elsewhere, the Ammonites were the warriors of the nation of Lot. But this disaster seems to have altered their disposition, at any rate for a time. Shortly after these events we hear of "bands" — that is pillaging marauding parties[f] — of the Moabites making

---

the passages of Isaiah and Jeremiah which are cited further on in this article.

[a] 2 K. iii. 21. This passage exhibits one of the most singular variations of the LXX. The Hebrew text is literally, "and all gathered themselves together that were girt with a girdle and upward." This the LXX. originally rendered ἀνεβόησαν ἐκ παντὸς περιεζωσμένου ζώνην καὶ ἐπάνω which the Alexandrine Codex still retains; but in the Vatican MS. the last words have actually been corrupted into καὶ εἶπον, ὦ — "and they said, Oh!"

[b] Compare Num. xxi. 11 — "towards the sun-rising."

[c] The lesson was not lost on king Joram, who proved himself more cautious on a similar occasion (2 K. vii 12, 13).

[d] Prius erat luxuria propter irriguos agros (Jerome, on Is. xv. 9).

[e] Jerome alone of all the commentators seems to have noticed this. See his *Comm. in Mich.* vi.

[f] גְּדוּדִים. The word "bands," by which this is

their incursions into Israel in the spring, as if to spoil the early corn before it was fit to cut (2 K. xiii. 20). With Edom there must have been many a contest. One of these, marked by savage vengeance — recalling in some degree the tragedy of Kir-haraseth — is alluded to by Amos (ii. 1), where a king of Edom seems to have been killed and burnt by Moab. This may have been one of the incidents of the battle of Kir-haraseth itself, occurring perhaps after the Edomites had parted from Israel, and were overtaken on their road home by the furious king of Moab (Gesenius, *Jesaia*, i. 504); or according to the Jewish tradition (Jerome, on Amos ii. 1), it was a vengeance still more savage because more protracted, and lasting even beyond the death of the king, whose remains were torn from his tomb and thus consumed : Non dico crudelitatem sed rabiem; ut incenderent ossa regis Idumææ, et non paterentur mortem esse omnium extremum malorum (*Ib.* ver. 4).

In the " Burden of Moab " pronounced by Isaiah (chaps. xv., xvi.), we possess a document full of interesting details as to the condition of the nation, at the time of the death of Ahaz king of Judah, B. C. 726. More than a century and a half had elapsed since the great calamity to which we have 'ust referred. In that interval, Moab has regained all, and more than all of his former prosperity, and has besides extended himself over the district which he originally occupied in the youth of the nation, and which was left vacant when the removal of Reuben to Assyria, which had been begun by Pul in 770, was completed by Tiglath-pileser about the year 740 (1 Chr. v. 25, 26).

This passage of Isaiah cannot be considered apart from that of Jeremiah, ch. xlviii. The latter was pronounced more than a century later, about the year 600, ten or twelve years before the invasion of Nebuchadnezzar, by which Jerusalem was destroyed. In many respects it is identical with that of Isaiah, and both are believed by the best modern scholars, on account of the archaisms and other peculiarities of language which they contain,

to be adopted from a common source — the work of some much more ancient prophet [a]

Isaiah ends his denunciation by a prediction — in his own words — that within three years Moab should be greatly reduced. This was probably with a view to Shalmaneser who destroyed Samaria, and no doubt overran the other side of the Jordan [b] in 725, and again in 723 (2 K. xvii. 3, xviii. 9). The only event of which we have a record to which it would seem possible that the passage, as originally uttered by the older prophet, applied, is the invasion of Pul, who about the year 770 appears to have commenced the deportation of Reuben (1 Chr. v. 26), and who very probably at the same time molested Moab.[c] The difficulty of so many of the towns of Reuben being mentioned, as at that early date already in the possession of Moab, may perhaps be explained by remembering that the idolatry of the neighboring nations — and therefore of Moab — had been adopted by the trans-Jordanic tribes for some time previously to the final deportation by Tiglath-pileser (see 1 Chr. v. 25), and that many of the sanctuaries were probably even at the date of the original delivery of the denunciation in the hands of the priests of Chemosh and Milcom. If, as Ewald (*Gesch.* iii. 588) with much probability infers, the Moabites, no less than the Ammonites, were under the protection of the powerful Uzziah [d] (2 Chr. xxvi. 8), then the obscure expressions of the ancient seer as given in Is. xvi. 1-5, referring to a tribute of lambs (comp. 2 K. iii. 4) sent from the wild pasture-grounds south of Moab to Zion, and to protection and relief from oppression afforded by the throne [e] of David to the fugitives and outcasts of Moab — acquire an intelligible sense.

On the other hand, the calamities which Jeremiah describes may have been inflicted in any one of the numerous visitations from the Assyrian army, under which these unhappy countries suffered at the period of his prophecy in rapid succession.

But the uncertainty of the exact dates referred to in these several denunciations does not in the least affect the interest or the value of the allusions they

---

commonly rendered with A. V. has not now the force of the original term. גְּדוּד is derived from גָּדַד, to rush together and fiercely, and signifies a troop of irregular marauders, as opposed to the regular soldiers of an army. It is employed to denote (1.) the bands of the Amalekites and other Bedouin tribes round Palestine : as 1 Sam. xxx. 8, 15, 23 (A. V. " troop " and "company "): 2 K. vi. 23, xiii. 20, 21, xxiv. 2 ; 1 Chr. xii. 21 ; 2 Chr. xxii. 1 (A. V. " band "). It is in this connection that it occurs in the elaborate play on the name of God, contained in Gen. xlix. 19 [see vol. i. p. 848 b], a passage strikingly corroborated by 1 Chr. xii. 18, where the Gadites who resorted to David in his difficulties — swift as roes on the mountains, with faces like the faces of lions — were formed by him into a " band." In 1 K. xi. 24 it denotes the roving troop collected by Rezon from the remnants of the army of Zobah, who took the city of Damascus by surprise, and by their forays molested — literally " played the Satan to " — Solomon (ver. 25). How formidable these bands were, may be gathered from 2 Sam. xxii. 30, where in a moment of most solemn exultation David speaks of breaking through one of them as among the most memorable exploits of his life.

(2.) The word is used in the general sense of hired soldiers — mercenaries ; as of the host of 100,000 Ephraimites hired by Amaziah in 2 Chr. xxv. 9, 10, 13 ; where the point is missed in the A. V. by the use of the word "army." No Bedouins could have shown a keener appetite for plunder than did these Israelites

(ver. 13). In this sense it is probably used in 2 Chr. xxvi. 11 for the irregular troops kept by Uzziah for purposes of plunder, and who are distinguished from his " army " (ver. 13) maintained for regular engagements.

(3.) In 2 Sam. iii. 22 (" troop ") and 2 K. v. 2 (" by companies ") it refers to marauding raids for the purpose of plunder.

[a] See Ewald (*Propheten*, 229-31). He seems to believe that Jeremiah has preserved the old prophecy more nearly in its original condition than Isaiah.

[b] Amos. B. c. cir. 780, prophesied that a nation should afflict Israel from the entering in of Hamath unto the " torrent of the desert " (probably one of the wadies on the S. E. extremity of the Dead Sea) ; that is, the whole of the country east of Jordan.

[c] Knobel refers the original of Is. xv., xvi. to the time of Jeroboam II., a great conqueror beyond Jordan.

[d] He died 758, i. e. 12 years after the invasion of Pul.

[e] The word used in this passage for the palace of David in Zion, namely " tent " (A. V. " tabernacle "), is remarkable as an instance of the persistence with which the memory of the original military foundation of Jerusalem by the warrior-king was preserved by the Prophets. Thus, in Ps. lxxvi. 2 and Lam. ii. 6 it is the " booth or bivouacking-hut of Jehovah ; " and in Is. xxix. 1 the city where David " pitched," or " encamped " (not " dwelt," as in A. V.).

contain to the condition of Moab. They bear the evident stamp of portraiture by artists who knew their subject thoroughly. The nation appears in them as high-spirited,[a] wealthy, populous, and even to a certain extent civilized, enjoying a wide reputation and popularity. With a metaphor which well expresses at once the pastoral wealth of the country and its commanding, almost regal, position, but which cannot be conveyed in a translation, Moab is depicted as the strong sceptre,[b] the beautiful staff,[c] whose fracture will be bewailed by all about him, and by all who know him. In his cities we discern a "great multitude" of people living in "glory," and in the enjoyment of great "treasure," crowding the public squares, the housetops, and the ascents and descents of the numerous high places and sanctuaries where the "priests and princes" of Chemosh or Baal-Peor minister to the anxious devotees. Outside the towns lie the "plentiful fields," luxuriant as the renowned Carmel [d] — the vineyards, and gardens of "summer fruits"; — the harvest is being reaped, and the "hay stored in its abundance," the vineyards and the presses are crowded with peasants, gathering and treading the grapes, the land resounds with the clamor [e] of the vintagers. These characteristics contrast very favorably with any traits recorded of Ammon, Edom, Midian, Amalek, the Philistines, or the Canaanite tribes. And since the descriptions we are considering are adopted by certainly two, and probably three prophets — Jeremiah, Isaiah, and the older seer — extending over a period of nearly 200 years, we may safely conclude that they are not merely temporary circumstances, but were the enduring characteristics of the people. In this case there can be no doubt that amongst the pastoral people of Syria, Moab stood next to Israel in all matters of material wealth and civilization.

It is very interesting to remark the feeling which actuates the prophets in these denunciations of a people who, though the enemies of Jehovah, were the blood-relations of Israel. Half the allusions of Isaiah and Jeremiah in the passages referred to, must forever remain obscure. We shall never know who the "lords of the heathen" were who, in that terrible [f] night, laid waste and brought to silence the prosperous Ar-moab and Kir-moab. Or the occasion of that flight over the Arnon, when the Moabite women were huddled together at the ford, like a flock of young birds, pressing to cross to the safe side of the stream, — when the dwellers in Aroer stood by the side of the high road which passed their town, and eagerly questioning the fugitives as they hurried up, "What is done?" —

received but one answer from all alike — "All is lost! Moab is confounded and broken down!"

Many expressions, also, such as the "weeping of Jazer," the "heifer of three years old," the "shadow of Heshbon," the "lions," must remain obscure. But nothing can obscure or render obsolete the tone [g] of tenderness and affection which makes itself felt in a hundred expressions throughout these precious documents. Ardently as the Prophet longs for the destruction of the enemy of his country and of Jehovah, and earnestly as he curses the man "that doeth the work of Jehovah deceitfully, that keepeth back his sword from blood," yet he is constrained to bemoan and lament such dreadful calamities to a people so near him both in blood and locality. His heart mourns — it sounds like pipes — for the men of Kir-heres; his heart cries out, it sounds like a harp for Moab.

Isaiah recurs to the subject in another passage of extraordinary force, and of fiercer character than before, namely, xxv. 10–12. Here the extermination, the utter annihilation, of Moab, is contemplated by the Prophet with triumph, as one of the first results of the reëstablishment of Jehovah on Mount Zion: "In this mountain shall the hand of Jehovah rest, and Moab shall be trodden down under Him, even as straw — the straw of his own threshing-floors at Madmenah — is trodden down for the dunghill. And He shall spread forth his hands in the midst of them — namely, of the Moabites — as one that swimmeth spreadeth forth his hands to swim, buffet following buffet, right and left, with terrible rapidity, as the strong swimmer urges his way forward: and He shall bring down their pride together with the spoils of their hands. And the fortress of Misgab [h] — thy walls shall He bring down, lay low, and bring to the ground, to the dust."

If, according to the custom of interpreters, this and the preceding chapter (xxiv.) are understood as referring to the destruction of Babylon, then this sudden burst of indignation towards Moab is extremely puzzling. But, if the passage is examined with that view, it will perhaps be found to contain some expressions which suggest the possibility of Moab having been at least within the ken of the Prophet, even though not in the foreground of his vision, during a great part of the passage. The Hebrew words rendered "city" in xxv. 2 — two entirely distinct terms — are positively, with a slight variation, the names of the two chief Moabite strongholds, the same which are mentioned in xv. 1, and one of which [i] is in the Pentateuch a synonym for the entire nation of

---

[a] Is. xvi. 6 ; Jer. xlviii. 29. The word *Gâôn* (גָּאוֹן), like our own word "pride," is susceptible of a good as well as a bad sense. It is the term used for the "majesty" and "excellency" of Jehovah (Is. ii. 10, &c., Ex. xv. 7), and is frequently in the A. V. rendered by "pomp."

[b] מַטֶּה ; the "rod" of Moses, and of Aaron, and of the heads of the tribes (Num. xvii. 2, &c.). The term also means a "tribe." No English word expresses all these meanings.

[c] מַקֵּל ; the word used for the "rods" of Jacob's stratagem ; also for the "staves" in the pastoral parable of Zechariah (xi. 7–14).

[d] *Carmel* is the word rendered "plentiful field" in Is. xvi. 10 and Jer. xlviii. 33.

[e] What the din of a vintage in Palestine was may

be inferred from Jer. xxv. 30: "Jehovah shall roar from on high. . . . He shall mightily roar. . . . He shall give a shout as those that tread the grapes."

[f] *La noche triste.*

[g] It is thus characterized by Ewald (*Propheten*, 230). "Eine so ganz von Trauer und Mitleid hingerissene, von Weichheit zerfliessende, mehr elegisch als prophetisch gestimmte Empfindung steht unter den ältern Propheten einzig da ; sogar bei Hosea ist nichts gans ähnliches."

[h] In the A. V. rendered "the high fort." But there is good reason to take it as the name of a place (Jer. xlviii. 1). [MISGAB.]

[i] Gesenius believes Ar, עָר, to be a Moabite form of Ir, עִיר, one of the two words spoken of above. Num. xxiv. 19 acquires a new force, if the word rendered "city" is interpreted as Ar, that is Moab. So

Moab. In this light, verse 2 may be read as follows: "For thou hast made of Ar a heap; of Kir the defenced a ruin; a palace[a] of strangers no longer is Ar, it shall never be rebuilt." The same words are found in verses 10 and 12 of the preceding chapter, in company with *hutsoth* (A. V. "streets") which we know from Num. xxii. 39 to have been the name of a Moabite town. [KIR-JATH-HUZOTH.] A distinct echo of them is again heard in xxv. 3, 4; and finally in xxvi. 1, 5, there seems to be yet another reference to the same two towns, acquiring new force from the denunciation which closes the preceding chapter: "Moab shall be brought down, the fortress and the walls of Misgab shall be laid low; but in the land of Judah this song shall be sung, 'Our Ar, our city, is strong . . . . . Trust in the Lord Jehovah who bringeth down those that dwell on high: the lofty Kir He layeth it low,'" etc.

It is perhaps an additional corroboration to this view to notice that the remarkable expressions in xxiv. 17, "Fear, and the pit, and the snare," etc., actually occur in Jeremiah (xlviii. 43), in his denunciation of Moab, embedded in the old prophecies out of which, like Is. xv., xvi., this passage is compiled, and the rest of which had certainly, as originally uttered, a direct and even exclusive reference to Moab.

Between the time of Isaiah's denunciation and the destruction of Jerusalem we have hardly a reference to Moab. Zephaniah, writing in the reign of Josiah, reproaches them (ii. 8-10) for their taunts against the people of Jehovah, but no acts of hostility are recorded either on the one side or the other. From one passage in Jeremiah (xxv. 9-21) delivered in the fourth year of Jehoiakim, just before the first appearance of Nebuchadnezzar, it is apparent that it was the belief of the Prophet that the nations surrounding Israel — and Moab among the rest — were on the eve of devastation by the Chaldæans and of a captivity for seventy years (see ver. 11), from which, however, they should eventually be restored to their own country (ver. 12, and xlviii. 47). From another record of the events of the same period or of one only just subsequent (2 K. xxiv. 2), it would appear, however, that Moab made terms with the Chaldæans, and for the time acted in concert with them in harassing and plundering the kingdom of Jehoiakim.

Four or five years later, in the first year of Zedekiah (Jer. xxvii. 1),[b] these hostilities must have ceased, for there was then a regular intercourse between Moab and the court at Jerusalem (ver. 3), possibly, as Bunsen suggests (*Bibelwerk, Propheten,* p. 536), negotiating a combined resistance to the common enemy. The brunt of the storm must have fallen on Judah and Jerusalem. The neighboring nations, including Moab, when the danger actually arrived probably adopted the advice of Jeremiah (xxvii. 11) and thus escaped, though not without much damage, yet without being carried away as the Jews were. That these nations did not suffer to the same extent as Judæa is evident from the fact that many of the Jews took refuge there when their own land was laid waste (Jer. xl. 11). Jeremiah expressly testifies that those who submitted themselves to the King of Babylon, though they would have to bear a severe yoke, — so severe that their very wild animals[c] would be enslaved, — yet by such submission should purchase the privilege of remaining in their own country. The removal from home, so dreadful to the Semitic mind,[d] was to be the fate only of those who resisted (Jer. xxvii. 10, 11, xxviii. 14). This is also supported by the allusion of Ezekiel, a few years later, to the cities of Moab, cities formerly belonging to the Israelites, which, at the time when the Prophet is speaking, were still flourishing, "the glory of the country," destined to become at a future day a prey to the Bene-Kedem, the "men of the East" — the Bedouins of the great desert of the Euphrates[e] (Ez. xxv. 8-11).

After the return from the Captivity it was a Moabite, Sanballat of Horonaim, who took the chief part in annoying and endeavoring to hinder the operations of the rebuilders of Jerusalem (Neh. ii. 19, iv. 1, vi. 1, &c.). He confines himself, however, to the same weapons of ridicule and scurrility which we have already noticed Zephaniah[f] resenting. From Sanballat's words (Neh. ii. 19) we should infer that he and his country were subject to "the king," that is, the King of Babylon. During the interval since the return of the first caravan from Babylon the illegal practice of marriages between the Jews and the other people around, Moab amongst the rest, had become frequent. So far had this gone, that the son of the high-priest was married to an Ammonite woman. Even among the families of Israel who returned from the Captivity was one bearing the name of PAHATH-MOAB (Ezr. ii. 6, viii. 4; Neh. iii. 11, &c.), a name which must certainly denote a Moabite connection,[g] though to the nature of the connection no clew seems to have been yet discovered. By Ezra and Nehemiah the practice of foreign marriages was strongly repressed, and we never hear of it again becoming prevalent.

In the book of Judith, the date of which is laid shortly after the return from Captivity (iv. 3), Moabites and Ammonites are represented as dwelling in their ancient seats and as obeying the call

---

also in Mic. vi. 9, at the close of the remarkable conversation between Balak and Balaam there preserved, the word עיר occurs again, in such a manner that it is difficult not to believe that the capital city of Moab is intended: "Jehovah's voice crieth unto Ar . . . . . . hear ye the rod, and who hath appointed it."

[a] *Armôn.* The same word is used by Amos (ii. 2) in his denunciation of Moab.

[b] There can be no doubt that "Jehoiakim" in this verse should be "Zedekiah." See ver. 3 of the same chap., and xxviii. 1.

[c] Jer. xxiii. 6.

[d] This feeling is brought out very strongly in Jer. xlviii. 11, where even the successive devastations from

which Moab had suffered are counted as nothing — as absolute immunity — since captivity had been escaped.

[e] To the incursions of these people, true Arabs, it is possibly due that the LXX. in Is. xv. 9 introduce Ἄραβας — "I will bring Arabs upon Dimon."

[f] The word חֶרְפָּה, rendered "reproach" in Zeph. ii. 8, occurs several times in Nehemiah in reference to the taunts of Sanballat and his companions. (See iv. 4, vi. 13, &c.)

[g] It will be observed that this name occurs in conjunction with Joab, who, if the well-known son of Zeruiah, would be a descendant of Ruth the Moabitess. But this is uncertain. [Vol. ii. p. 1397 a.]

of the Assyrian general. Their "princes" (ἄρχοντες) and "governors" (ἡγούμενοι) are mentioned (v. 2, vii. 8). The Maccabees, much as they ravaged the country of the Ammonites, do not appear to have molested Moab Proper, nor is the name either of Moab or of any of the towns south of the Arnon mentioned throughout those books. Josephus not only speaks of the district in which Heshbon was situated as "Moabitis" (Ant. xiii. 15, § 4; also B. J. iv. 8, § 2), but expressly says that even at the time he wrote they were a "very great nation" (Ant. i. 11, § 5). (See 5 Macc. xxix. 19.)

In the time of Eusebius (Onomast. Μωάβ), i. e. cir. A. D. 320, the name appears to have been attached to the district, as well as to the town of Rabbath — both of which were called Moab. It also lingered for some time in the name of the ancient Kir-Moab, which, as Charakmoba, is mentioned by Ptolemy [a] (Reland, Palaestina, p. 463), and as late as the Council of Jerusalem, A. D. 536, formed the see of a bishop under the same title (ib. p. 533). Since that time the modern name Kerak has superseded the older one, and no trace of Moab has been found either in records or in the country itself.

Like the other countries east of Jordan Moab has been very little visited by Europeans, and beyond its general characteristics hardly anything is known of it. The following travellers have passed through the district of Moab Proper, from Wady Mojeb on the N. to Kerak on the S.: —

Seetzen, March, 1306, and January, 1807. (U. I. Seetzen's Reisen, etc., von Prof. Kruse, etc., vol. i. p. 405-426 ; ii. 320-377. Also the editor's notes thereon, in vol. iv.)

Burckhardt, 1812, July 13, to Aug. 4. (Travels, London, 1822. See also the notes of Gesenius to the German translation, Weimar, 1824, vol. ii. p. 1061-1064.)

Irby and Mangles, 1818, June 5 to 8. (Travels in Egypt, etc., 1822, 8vo; 1847, 12mo. Chap. viii.)

De Sauley, 1851, January. (Voyage autour de la Mer Morte, Paris, 1853. Also translated into English.)

Of the character of the face of the country these travellers only give slight reports, and among these there is considerable variation even when the same district is referred to. Thus between Kerak and Rabba, Irby (141 a) found "a fine country," of great natural fertility, with "reapers at work and the corn luxuriant in all directions;" and the same district is described by Burckhardt as "very fertile, and large tracts cultivated " (Syr. July 15); while De Sauley, on the other hand, pronounces that "from Shihan (6 miles N. of Rabba) to the Wady Kerak the country is perfectly bare, not a tree or a bush to be seen" — "Toujours aussi nu . . . pas un arbre, pas un arbrisseau " (Voyage, i. 353); which again is contradicted by Seetzen, who not only found the soil very good, but encumbered with wormwood and other shrubs (Seetzen, i. 410). These discrepancies are no doubt partly due to difference in the time of year, and other temporary causes; but they also probably proceed from the disagreement which seems to be inherent in all descriptions of the same scene or spot by various describers, and which is enough to drive to despair those whose task it is to endeavor to combine them into a single account.

In one thing all agree, the extraordinary number of ruins which are scattered over the country, and which, whatever the present condition of the soil, are a sure token of its wealth in former ages. " Wie schrecklich," says Seetzen, "ist diese Residenz alter Könige und ihr Land verwüstet! " (i. 412).

The whole country is undulating, and, after the general level of the plateau is reached, without any serious inequalities; and in this and the absence of conspicuous vegetation has a certain resemblance to the downs of our own southern counties.

Of the language of the Moabites we know nothing or next to nothing. In the few communications recorded as taking place between them and Israelites no interpreter is mentioned (see Ruth; 1 Sam. xxii. 3, 4, &c.). And from the origin of the nation and other considerations we may perhaps conjecture that their language was more a dialect of Hebrew than a different tongue.[b] This indeed would follow from the connection of Lot, their founder, with Abraham. [WRITING, Amer. ed.]

The narrative of Num. xxii. - xxiv. must be founded on a Moabite chronicle, though in its present condition doubtless much altered from what it originally was before it came into the hands of the author of the Book of [c] Numbers. No attempt seems yet to have been made to execute the difficult but interesting task of examining the record, with the view of restoring it to its pristine form.

The following are the names of Moabite persons preserved in the Bible — probably Hebraized in their adoption into the Bible records. Of such a transition we seem to have a trace in Shomer and Shimrith (see below).

Zippor.
Balak.
Eglon.
Ruth.
Orpah (עָרְפָּה).
Mesha (מֵישַׁע).
Ithmah (1 Chr. xi. 46).
Shomer (2 K. xii. 21), or Shimrith (2 Chr. xxiv. 26).
Sanballat.

Add to these —

Emim, the name by which they called the Rephaim who originally inhabited their country and whom the Ammonites called Zamzummim or Zuzim.

Cemôsh, or Cemîsh (Jer. xlviii. 7), the deity of the nation.

Of names of places the following may be mentioned :—

Moab, with its compounds, Sedê-Moab, the fields

[a] From the order of the lists as they now stand, and the latitude affixed to Charakmoba, Ptolemy appears to refer to a place south of Petra.

[b] Some materials for an investigation of this subject may be found in the curious variations of some of the Moabite names — Chemosh, Chemish ; Kir-haraseth, Kir-heres, etc.; Shomer, Shimrith ; and — remembering the close connection of Ammon with

Moab — the names of the Ammonite god, Moloch, Milcom, Malcham.

[c] If this suggestion is correct — and there must be some truth in it — then this passage of Numbers becomes no less historically important than Gen xiv., which Ewald (Geschichte, i. 73, 151, &c.) with great reason maintains to be the work of a Canaanite chronicler.

of M. (A. V. "the country of M."); Arboth-Moab, the deserts (A. V. the "plains") of M., that is, the part of the Arabah occupied by the Moabites.

Ham-Mishor, the high undulating country of Moab Proper (A. V. "the plain ").

Ar, or Ar-Moab (עָר). This Gesenius conjectures to be a Moabite form of the word which in Hebrew appears as Ir (עִיר), a city.

Arnon, the river (אַרְנוֹן).
Bamoth Baal.
Beer Elim.
Beth-diblathaim.
Dibon, or Dimon.
Eglaim, or perhaps Eglath-Shelishiya (Is. xv. 8).
Horonaim.
Kiriathaim.
Kirjath-husoth (Num. xxii. 39; comp. Is. xxiv. 11).
Kir-haraseth, -haresh, -heres.
Kir-Moab.
Luhith.
Medeba.
Nimrim, or Nimrah.
Nobah or Nophah (Num. xxi. 30)
hap-Pisgah.
hap-Peor.
Shaveh-Kariathaim (?)
Zophim.
Zoar.

It should be noticed how large a proportion of these names end in im.[a]

For the religion of the Moabites see CHEMOSH, MOLECH, PEOR. [See especially BAAL-PEOR.]

Of their habits and customs we have hardly a trace. The gesture employed by Balak when he found that Balaam's interference was fruitless — "he smote his hands together" — is not mentioned again in the Bible, but it may not on that account have been peculiar to the Moabites. Their mode of mourning, namely, cutting off the hair at the back [b] of the head and cropping the beard (Jer. xlviii. 37), is one which they followed in common with the other non-Israelite nations, and which was forbidden to the Israelites (Lev. xxi. 5), who indeed seem to have been accustomed rather to leave their hair and beard disordered and untrimmed when in grief (see 2 Sam. xix. 24; xiv. 2).

For a singular endeavor to identify the Moabites with the Druses, see Sir G. H. Rose's pamphlet, The Afghans the Ten Tribes, etc. (London, 1852), especially the statement therein of Mr. Wood, late British consul at Damascus (p. 154–157).   G.

* MOAB, COUNTRY or FIELD OF (הַשָּׂדֵה מוֹאָב) denotes the cultivated ground in the upland (Gen. xxxvi. 35; Num. xxi. 20; Ruth, i. 1, 2, 6, 22, ii. 6, iv. 3; 1 Chr. i. 46, viii. 8). [MOAB.]   H.

* MOAB, PLAINS [A. V., but properly DESERTS) OF (עַרְבוֹת מוֹאָב), Num. xxii. 1, xxvi. 3, 63, xxxi. 12, xxxiii. 4–50, xxxv. 1, xxxvi. 13; Deut. xxxiv. 1, 8; Josh. viii. 32. [MOAB.] H.

* MO'ABITE (מוֹאָב, Μωάβ, Num. xxii. 4; Judg. iii. 28; 2 Sam. viii. 2; 1 K. xi. 33: 2 K. iii. 18, 21, 22, 24, xiii. 20, xxiii. 13, xxiv. 2; מוֹאָבִי, Μωαβί, Vat. Μωαβ, Ezr. ix. 1; מוֹאָבִי,

___
[a] So also does Shaharaim, a person who had a special connection with Moab (1 Chr. viii. 8).

[b] קָרַח, as distinguished from גָּבַח.

Μωαβίτης, Gen. xix. 37; ditto, Vat. -βει-, Deut. ii. 9, 11, 29, xxiii. 3; 1 Chr. xi. 46; Neh. xiii. 1: 1 Esdr. viii. 69; υἱοὶ Μωάβ, Jud. vi. 1 (Vat. and Vulg. omit); fem. מוֹאֲבִיָּה, Μωαβῖτις, Vat. -βει-, 1 K. xi. 1: Moab, Moabites, Moabitis), a descendant of Moab, or an inhabitant of the country so called. [MOAB.]   A.

* MO'ABITESS (מוֹאֲבִיָּה: Μωαβῖτις, Vat. -βει-: Moabitis), a Moabite woman, Ruth i. 22, ii. 2, 21, iv. 5, 10; 2 Chr. xxiv. 26.   A.

* MO'ABITISH (מוֹאֲבִיָּה: Μωαβῖτις, Vat. -βει-: Moabitis), belonging to MOAB (Ruth ii. 6).
    A.

MOADI'AH (מוֹעַדְיָה [festival of Jehovah]: Μααδαί; [Vat. Alex. FA.[1] omit;] FA.[2] ἐν καιροῖς: Moadia). A priest, or family of priests, who returned with Zerubbabel. The chief of the house in the time of Joiakim the son of Jeshua was Piltai (Neh. xii. 17). Elsewhere (Neh. xii. 5) called MAADIAH.

MOCHMUR, THE BROOK (ὁ χειμάρ-ρος Μοχμούρ; [Sin. Μουχμουρ;] Alex. omits Μοχ.: Vulg. omits; Syr. Nachal de Peor), a torrent, i. e. a small wady — the word "brook" conveys an entirely false impression — mentioned only in Jud. vii. 18; and there as specifying the position of Ekrebel — "near unto Chusi, and upon the brook Mochmur." EKREBEL has been identified, with great probability, by Mr. Van de Velde in Akrabeh, a ruined site in the mountains of Central Palestine, equidistant from Nabulus and Seilûn, S. E. of the former and N. E. of the latter; and the torrent Mochmour may be either the Wady Makfuriyeh, on the northern slopes of which Akrabeh stands, or the Wady Ahmar, which is the continuation of the former eastwards.

The reading of the Syriac possibly points to the existence of a sanctuary of Baal-Peor in this neighborhood, but is more probably a corruption of the original name, which was apparently מַחְמָר (Simonis, Onomasticon, N. T. etc. p. 111).   G.

MO'DIN (Μωδεΐν; Alex. Μωδεειμ, Μωδιειμ, Μωδαειμ, and in chap. ii. Μωδεειν; Joseph. Μωδειμ, and once Μωδεειν: Modin: the Jewish form is, in the Mishna, הַמּוֹדִיעִים, in Joseph ben-Gorion, ch. xx., הַמּוֹדָעִית; the Syriac version of Maccabees agrees with the Mishna, except in the absence of the article, and in the usual substitution of r for d, Mora'im), a place not mentioned in either Old or New Testament, though rendered immortal by its connection with the history of the Jews in the interval between the two. It was the native city of the Maccabean family (1 Macc. xiii. 25), and as a necessary consequence contained their ancestral sepulchre (τάφος) (ii. 70, ix. 19). Hither Mattathias removed from Jerusalem, where up to that time he seems to have been residing, at the commencement of the Antiochian persecution (ii. 1). It was here that he struck the first blow of resistance, by slaying on the heathen altar which had been erected in the place, both the commissioner of Antiochus and a recreant Jew whom he had induced to sacrifice, and then demolishing the altar. Mattathias himself, and subsequently his sons Judas and Jonathan, were buried in the family tomb, and over them Simon erected a structure which is minutely described in the book of Maccabees (xiii. 25–30), and, with less detail, by Josephus (*Ant.* xiii. 6, § 6), but the restoration of which has hitherto proved as difficult a puzzle as that of the mausoleum of Artemisia.

At Modin the Maccabæan armies encamped on the eves of two of their most memorable victories — that of Judas over Antiochus Eupator (2 Macc. xiii. 14), and that of Simon over Cendebæus (1 Macc. xvi. 4) — the last battle of the veteran chief before his assassination. The only indication of the position of the place to be gathered from the above notices is contained in the last, from which we may infer that it was near "the plain" (τὸ πεδίον), i. e. the great maritime lowland of Philistia (ver. 5). By Eusebius and Jerome (*Onom.* Μηδεείμ and "Modim") it is specified as near Diospolis, i. e. Lydda; while the notice in the Mishna (*Pesachim,* ix. 2), and the comments of Bartenora and Maimonides, state that it was 15 (Roman) miles from Jerusalem. At the same time the description of the monument seems to imply (though for this see below) that the spot was so lofty[a] as to be visible from the sea, and so near that even the details of the sculpture were discernible therefrom. All these conditions, excepting the last, are tolerably fulfilled in either of the two cites called *Latrûn* and *Kubâb.*[b] The former of these is, by the shortest road — that through *Wady Ali* — exactly 15 Roman miles from Jerusalem; it is about 8 English miles from *Lydd,* 15 from the Mediterranean, and 9 or 10 from the river *Rubin,* on which it is probable that Cedron — the position of Cendebæus in Simon's battle — stood. *Kubâb* is a couple of miles further from Jerusalem, and therefore nearer to *Lydd* and to the sea, on the most westerly spur of the hills of Benjamin. Both are lofty, and both apparently — *Latrûn* certainly — command a view of the Mediterranean. In favor of *Latrûn* are the extensive ancient remains with which the top of the hill is said to be covered (Rob. *Bibl. Res.* iii. 151; Tobler, *Dritte Wand.* 186), though of their age and particulars we have at present no accurate information. *Kubâb* appears to possess no ruins, but on the other hand its name may retain a trace of the monument.

The mediæval and modern tradition[c] places Modin at *Soba,* an eminence south of *Kuriet el-Enab;* but this being not more than 7 miles from Jerusalem, while it is as much as 25 from Lydd and 30 from the sea, and also far removed from the plain of Philistia, is at variance with every one of the conditions implied in the records. It has found advocates in our own day in M. de Saulcy (*l'Art Judïque,* etc., 377, 378) and M. Salzmann;[d] the latter of whom explored chambers there which may have been tombs, though he admits that there was nothing to prove it. A suggestive fact, which Dr. Robinson first pointed out, is the want of una-

nimity in the accounts of the mediæval travellers, some of whom, as William of Tyre (viii. 1), place Modin in a position near Emmaus-Nicopolis, Nob (*Annabeh*), and Lydda. M. Mislin also — usually so vehement in favor of the traditional sites — has recommended further investigation. If it should turn out that the expression of the book of Maccabees as to the monument being visible from the sea has been misinterpreted, then one impediment to the reception of *Soba* will be removed; but it is difficult to account for the origin of the tradition in the teeth of those which remain.

The descriptions of the tomb by the author of the book of Maccabees and Josephus, who had both apparently seen it, will be most conveniently compared by being printed together.

1 Macc. xiii. 27–30.	Josephus, *Ant.* xiii. 6, § 6
"And Simon made a building over the repulchre of his father and his brethren, and raised it aloft to view with polished stone behind and before. And he set up upon it seven pyramids, one against another, for his father and his mother and his four brethren. And on these he made engines of war, and set great pillars round about, and on the pillars he made suits of armour for a perpetual memory; and by the suits of armour ships carved, so that they might be seen by all that sail on the sea. This sepulchre he made at Modin, and it stands unto this day."	"And Simon built a very large monument to his father and his brethren of white and polished stone. And he raised it up to a great and conspicuous height, and threw cloisters around, and set up pillars of a single stone, a work wonderful to behold: and near to these he built seven pyramids to his parents and his brothers, one for each, terrible to behold both for size and beauty. And these things are preserved even to this day."

The monuments are said by Eusebius (*Onom.*) to have been still shown when he wrote — A. D. circa 320.

Any restoration of the structure from so imperfect an account as the above can never be anything more than conjecture. Something has been already attempted under MACCABEES (vol. ii. p. 1715). But in its absence one or two questions present themselves. [TOMB, Amer. ed.]

(1.) The "ships" (πλοῖα, *naves*). The sea and its pursuits were so alien to the ancient Jews, and the life of the Maccabæan heroes who preceded Simon was — if we except their casual relations with Joppa and Jamnia and the battle-field of the maritime plain — so unconnected therewith, that it is difficult not to suppose that the word is corrupted from what it originally was. This was the view of J. D. Michaelis, but he does not propose any satisfactory word in substitution for πλοῖα (see his suggestion in Grimm, *ad loc.*). True, Simon

---

[a] Thus the Vulg. of 1 Macc. ii. 1 has *Mons Modin.*

[b] Ewald (*Gesch.* iv. 350, *note*) suggests that the name Modin may be still surviving in *Deir Ma'in.* But is not this questionable on philological grounds? and the position of *Deir Ma'in* is less in accordance with the facts than that of the two named in the text.

[c] See the copious references given by Robinson (*Bibl. Res.* ii. 7. note).

[d] The lively account of M. Salzmann (*Jérusalem, Etude,* etc., pp. 37, 38), would be more satisfactory if it were less encumbered with mistakes. To name but two. The great obstacle which interposes itself in his quest of Modin is that Eusebius and Jerome state that it was "near Diospolis, on a mountain in the

tribe of Judah." This difficulty (which however is entirely imaginary, for they do not mention the name of Judah in connection with Modin) would have been "enough to deter him entirely from the task," if he had not "found in the book of Joshua that M'dim (from which Modim is derived) was a part of the territory allotted to the tribe of Judah." Now Middin (not M'dim) was certainly in the tribe of Judah, but not within many miles of the spot in question, since it was one of the six towns which lay in the district immediately bordering on the Dead Sea, probably in the depths of the *Ghor* itself (Josh. xv. 61).

[e] Λίθῳ ξεστῷ. This Ewald (iv. 388) renders "inscribed," or "graven" — *beschriebenen Steinen.*

appears to have been to a certain extent alive to the importance of commerce to his country,[a] and he is especially commemorated for having acquired the harbor of Joppa, and thus opened an inlet for the isles of the sea (1 Macc. xiv. 5). But it is difficult to see the connection between this and the placing of ships on a monument to his father and brothers, whose memorable deeds had been of a different description. It is perhaps more feasible to suppose that the sculptures were intended to be symbolical of the departed heroes. In this case it seems not improbable that during Simon's intercourse with the Romans he had seen and been struck with their war-galleys, no inapt symbols of the fierce and rapid career of Judas. How far such symbolical representation was likely to occur to a Jew of that period is another question.

(2.) The distance at which the "ships" were to be seen. Here again, when the necessary distance of Modin from the sea — Latrûn 15 miles, Kubâb 13, Lydda itself 10 — and the limited size of the sculptures are considered, the doubt inevitably arises whether the Greek text of the book of Maccabees accurately represents the original. De Saulcy (L'Art Judaïque, p. 377) ingeniously suggests that the true meaning is, not that the sculptures could be discerned from the vessels in the Mediterranean, but that they were worthy to be inspected by those who were sailors by profession. The consideration of this is recommended to scholars.   G.

MO'ETH (Μωέθ: *Medias*). In 1 Esdr. viii. 63, "NOADIAH the son of Binnui" (Ezr. viii. 33), a Levite, is called "Moeth the son of Sabban."

MOL'ADAH (מוֹלָדָה; but in Neh. מֹלָדָה [birth, lineage]: Μωλαδᾶ, Alex. Μωδαδα; [Καλαδᾶη, Vat.¹] Κωλαλαμ, Alex. Μωλαδα; [Vat.] Μωαλδα, [Rom.] Alex. Μωλαδα: *Molada*), a city of Judah, one of those which lay in the district of "the south," next to Edom. It is named in the original list between Shema and Hazar-gaddah, in the same group with Beer-sheba (Josh. xv. 26); and this is confirmed by another list in which it appears as one of the towns which, though in the allotment of Judah, were given to Simeon (xix. 2). In the latter tribe it remained at any rate till the reign of David (1 Chr. iv. 28), but by the time of the Captivity it seems to have come back into the hands of Judah, by whom it was reinhabited after the Captivity (Neh. xi. 26). It is, however, omitted from the catalogue of the places frequented by David during his wandering life (1 Sam. xxx. 27–31).

In the *Onomasticon* it receives a bare mention under the head of "Molada," but under "Ether" and "Iether" a place named Malatha is spoken of as in the interior of Daroma (a district which answered to the *Negeb* or "South" of the Hebrews); and further, under "Arath" or 'Αραμά (i. e. Arad) it is mentioned as 4 miles from the latter place and 20 from Hebron. Ptolemy also speaks of a Maliattha as near Elusa. And lastly, Josephus states that Herod Agrippa retired to a certain tower "in Malatha of Idumæa" (ἐν Μαλάθοις τῆς 'Ιδ.). The requirements of these notices are all very fairly answered by the position of the modern *el-Milh*, a site of ruins of some extent, and

two large wells, one of the regular stations on the road from Petra and *Ain el-Weibeh* to Hebron. *El-Milh* is about 4 English miles from *Tell Arad*, 17 or 18 from Hebron, and 9 or 10 due east of Beer-sheba. Five miles to the south is *Ararah*, the AROER of 1 Sam. xxx. 28. It is between 20 and 30 from Elusa, assuming *el-Khulasah* to be that place; and although Dr. Robinson is probably correct in saying that there is no verbal affinity, or only a slight one, between Molada or Malatha and *el-Milh*,[b] yet, taking that slight resemblance into account with the other considerations above named, it is very probable that this identification is correct (see *Bibl. Res.* ii. 201). It is accepted by Wilson (*Lands*, i. 347), Van de Velde (*Memoir*, p. 335), Bonar, and others.   G.

MOLE, the representative in the A. V. of the Hebrew words *Tinshemeth* and *Chephôr pêrôth*.

1. *Tinshemeth* (תִּנְשָׁמֶת: ἀσπάλαξ, Ald. σπάλαξ, in Lev. xi. 30; λάρος, Ald. λάρος: *cygnus, talpa, ibis*). This word occurs in the list of unclean birds in Lev. xi. 18; Deut. xiv. 16, where it is translated "swan" by the A. V.; in Lev. xi. 30, where the same word is found amongst the unclean "creeping things that creep upon the earth," it evidently no longer stands for the name of a bird, and is rendered "mole" by the A. V. adopting the interpretation of the LXX., Vulg., Onkelos, and some of the Jewish doctors. Bochart has, however, shown that the Hebrew *Choled*, the Arabic *Khuld* or *Khild*, denotes the "mole," and has argued with much force in behalf of the "chameleon" being the *tinshemeth*. The Syriac version and some Arabic MSS. understand "a centipede" by the original word, the Targum of Jonathan a "salamander," some Arabic versions read *sammábras*, which Golius renders "a kind of lizard." In Lev. xi. 30, the "chameleon" is given by the

The Chameleon. (*Chameleo vulgaris*.)

A. V. as the translation of the Hebrew כֹּחַ, *côach*, which in all probability denotes some larger kind of lizard. [CHAMELEON.] The only clew to an identification of *tinshemeth* is to be found in its etymology, and in the context in which the word occurs. Bochart conjectures that the root [c] from which the Hebrew name of this creature is derived, has reference to a vulgar opinion amongst the ancients that the chameleon lived on air (comp. Ov. *Met.* xv. 411, "Id quoque quod ventis animal nutritur et aura," and see numerous quotations from classical authors cited by Bochart (*Hieroz.* ii. 505). The lung of the chameleon is very large, and when filled with air it renders the body semitransparent; from the creature's power of abstinence, no doubt arose the fable that it lived on air.

---

b By Schwarz (100) the Aral[t]c name is quoted as

Muladah; by Stewart (*Tent and Khan*, p. 217) as *el-Melech*.

c כָּ֫שַׁם, "to breathe," whence נְשָׁמָה, "breath."

It is probable that the animals mentioned with the *tinshemeth* (Lev. xi. 30) denote different kinds of lizards; perhaps therefore, since the etymology of the word is favorable to that view, the chameleon may be the animal intended by *tinshemeth* in Lev. xi. 30. As to the change of color in the skin of this animal numerous theories have been proposed; but as this subject has no Scriptural bearing, it will be enough to refer to the explanation given by Milne-Edwards, whose paper is translated in vol. xvii. of the *Edinburgh New Philosophical Journal.* The chameleon belongs to the tribe *Dendrosaura,* order *Saura;* the family inhabits Asia and Africa, and the south of Europe; the *C. vulgaris* is the species mentioned in the Bible. As to the bird *tinshemeth,* see SWAN.

2. *Chéphôr pérôth* (חֲפֹר פֵּרוֹת: [a] τὰ μάταια: *talpæ*) is rendered "moles" by the A. V. in Is. ii. 20; three MSS. read these two Hebrew words as one, and so the LXX., Vulg., Aquila, Symmachus, and Theodotion, with the Syriac and Arabic versions, though they adopt different interpretations of the word (Bochart, *Hieroz.* ii. 449). It is difficult to see what Hebrew word the LXX. could have read; but compare Schleusner, *Nov. Thes.* in LXX. *s. v.* μάταιος. Gesenius follows Bochart in considering the Hebrew words to be the plural feminine of the noun *chapharpérôth,*[b] but does not limit the meaning of the word to "moles." Michaelis also (*Suppl. ad Lex. Heb.* p. 876 and 2042) believes the words should be read as one, but that "sepulchres," or "vaults" dug in the rocks are intended. The explanation of Oedmann (*Vermischt. Samm.* iii. 82, 83), that the Hebrew words signify "(a bird) that follows cows for the sake of their milk," and that the goat-sucker (*Caprimulgus Europæus*) is intended, is improbable. Perhaps no reference is made by the Hebrew words (which, as so few MSS. join them, it is better to consider distinct) to any particular animal, but to the holes and burrows of rats, mice, etc., which we know frequent ruins and deserted places. (Harmer's *Observ.* ii. 456.) "Remembering the extent to which we have seen," says Kitto (*Pict. Bib.* on Is. xx.), "the forsaken sites of the East perforated with the holes of various cave-digging animals, we are inclined to suppose that the words might generally denote *any* animals of this description." Rosenmüller's explanation, "*in effossionem,*" i. e. *foramen Murium,*" appears to be decidedly the best proposed; for not only is it the literal translation of the Hebrew, but it is more in accordance with the natural habits of rats and mice to occupy with bats deserted places than it is with the habits of moles, which for the most part certainly frequent cultivated lands, and this no doubt is true of the particular species, *Spalax typhlus,* the mole-rat of Syria and Mesopotamia, which by some has been supposed to represent the mole of the Scriptures; if, moreover, the prophet intended to speak exclusively of "moles," is it not probable that he would have used the term *Choled* (see above)? [WEASEL]   W. H.

MO'LECH (הַמֹּלֶךְ, with the article, except in 1 K. xi. 7 [*the king*]: ἄρχων, in Lev.; ὁ βασι-

---

[a] "Holes of rats."

[b] חֲפַרְפָּרָה, as if the Hebrew word was from פָּרָה, "a cow."

λεὺς αὐτῶν, 1 K. xi. 7; ὁ Μολόχ, 2 K. xxiii. 10. and ὁ Μολὸχ βασιλεύς, Jer. xxxii. 35: *Moloch*) The fire-god Molech was the tutelary deity of the children of Ammon, and essentially identical with the Moabitish Chemosh. Fire-gods appear to have been common to all the Canaanite, Syrian, and Arab tribes, who worshipped the destructive element under an outward symbol, with the most inhuman rites. Among these were human sacrifices, purifications and ordeals by fire, devoting of the first-born, mutilation, and vows of perpetual celibacy and virginity. To this class of divinities belonged the old Canaanitish Molech, against whose worship the Israelites were warned by threats of the severest punishment. The offender who devoted his offspring to Molech was to be put to death by stoning; and in case the people of the land refused to inflict upon him this judgment, Jehovah would Himself execute it, and cut him off from among his people (Lev. xviii. 21, xx. 2-5). The root of the word Molech is the same as that of

מֶלֶךְ, *melec,* or "king," and hence he is identified with Malcham ("their king"), in 2 Sam. xii. 30, Zeph. i. 5, the title by which he was known to the Israelites, as being invested with regal honors in his character as a tutelary deity, the lord and master of his people. Our translators have recognized this identity in their rendering of Am. v. 26 (where "your Moloch" is literally "your king," as it is given in the margin), following the Greek in the speech of Stephen, in Acts vii. 43. Dr. Geiger, in accordance with his theory that the worship of Molech was far more widely spread among the Israelites than appears at first sight from the Old Testament, and that many traces are obscured in the text, refers "the king," in Is. xxx. 33, to that deity: "for Tophet is ordained of old; yea for *the king* it is prepared." Again, of the Israelite nation, personified as an adulteress, it is said, "Thou wentest to *the king* with oil " (Is. lvii. 9); Amaziah the priest of Bethel forbade Amos to prophecy there, "for it is *the king's* chapel " (Am. vii. 13); and in both these instances Dr. Geiger would find a disguised reference to the worship of Molech (*Urschrift,* etc., pp. 299-308). But whether his theory be correct or not, the traces of Molech-worship in the Old Testament are sufficiently distinct to enable us to form a correct estimate of its character. The first direct historical allusion to it is in the description of Solomon's idolatry in his old age. He had in his harem many women of the Ammonite race, who "turned away his heart after other gods," and, as a consequence of their influence, high places to Molech, "the abomination of the children of Ammon," were built on "the mount that is facing Jerusalem " — one of the summits of Olivet (1 K. xi. 7). Two verses before, the same deity is called MILCOM, and from the circumstance of the two names being distinguished in 2 K. xxiii. 10, 13, it has been inferred by Movers, Ewald, and others, that the two deities were essentially distinct. There does not appear to be sufficient ground for this conclusion. It is true that in the later history of the Israelites the worship of Molech is connected with the Valley of Hinnom, while the high place of Milcom was on the Mount of Olives, and that no mention is made of human sacrifices to the latter. But it seems impossible to resist the conclusion that in 1 K. xi. "Milcom the abomination of the Ammonites," in ver. 5, is the same as "Molech the abomination of the children of Ammon," in ver. 7. To avoid this Movers contends, not very convincingly, that the latter verse is by a different hand. Be this as it may, in the reformation carried out by Josiah, the high place of Milcom, on the right hand of the Mount of Corruption, and Tophet in the valley of the children of Hinnom were defiled, that "no man might make his son or his daughter to pass through the fire to Molech" (2 K. xxiii. 10, 13). In the narrative of Chronicles these are included under the general term "Baalim," and the apostasy of Solomon is not once alluded to. Tophet soon appears to have been restored to its original uses, for we find it again alluded to, in the reign of Zedekiah, as the scene of child-slaughter and sacrifice to Molech (Jer. xxxii. 35).

Most of the Jewish interpreters, Jarchi (on Lev. xviii. 21), Kimchi, and Maimonides (Mor. Neb. iii. 38) among the number, say that in the worship of Molech the children were not burnt but made to pass between two burning pyres, as a purificatory rite. But the allusions to the actual slaughter are too plain to be mistaken, and Aben Ezra in his note on Lev. xviii. 21, says that "to cause to pass through" is the same as "to burn." "They sacrificed their sons and their daughters unto devils, and shed innocent blood, the blood of their sons and of their daughters, whom they sacrificed unto the idols of Canaan" (Ps. cvi. 37, 38). In Jer. vii. 31, the reference to the worship of Molech by human sacrifice is still more distinct: "they have built the high places of Tophet . . . to burn their sons and their daughters in the fire," as "burnt-offerings unto Baal," the sun-god of Tyre, with whom, or in whose character, Molech was worshipped (Jer. xix. 5). Compare also Deut. xii. 31; Ez. xvi. 20, 21, xxiii. 37. But the most remarkable passage is that in 2 Chr. xxviii. 3, in which the wickedness of Ahaz is described: "Moreover, he burnt incense in the valley of the son of Hinnom, and burnt (וַיַּבְעֵר) his children in the fire, after the abominations of the nations whom Jehovah had driven out before the children of Israel." Now, in the parallel narrative of 2 K. xvi. 3, instead of וַיַּבְעֵר, "and he burnt," the reading is הֶעֱבִיר, "he made to pass through," and Dr. Geiger suggests that the former may be the true reading, of which the latter is an easy modification, serving as a euphemistic expression to disguise the horrible nature of the sacrificial rites. But it is more natural to suppose that it is an exceptional instance, and that the true reading is וַיַּעֲבֵר, than to assume that the other passages have been intentionally altered.a The worship of Molech is evidently alluded to, though not expressly mentioned, in connection with star-worship and the worship of Baal in 2 K. xvii. 16, 17, xxi. 5, 6, which seems to show that Molech, the flame-god, and Baal, the sun-god, whatever their distinctive attributes, and whether or not the latter is a general appellation including the former, were worshipped with the same rites. The sacrifice of children is said by Movers to have been not so much an expiatory, as a purificatory rite, by which the victims were purged from the dross of the body and attained union with the

deity. In support of this he quotes the myth of Baaltis or Isis, whom Malcander, king of Byblus, employed as nurse for his child. Isis suckled the infant with her finger, and each night burnt whatever was mortal in its body. When Astarte the mother saw this she uttered a cry of terror, and the child was thus deprived of immortality (Plut. Is. & Os. ch. 16). But the sacrifice of Mesha king of Moab, when, in despair at failing to cut his way through the overwhelming forces of Judah, Israel, and Edom, he offered up his eldest son a burnt-offering, probably to Chemosh, his national divinity, has more of the character of an expiatory rite to appease an angry deity, than of a ceremonial purification. Besides, the passage from Plutarch bears evident traces of Egyptian, if not of Indian influence.

According to Jewish tradition, from what source we know not, the image of Molech was of brass, hollow within, and was situated without Jerusalem. Kimchi (on 2 K. xxiii. 10) describes it as "set within seven chapels, and whoso offered fine flour they open to him one of them, (whoso offered) turtle-doves or young pigeons they open to him two; a lamb, they open to him three; a ram, they open to him four: a calf, they open to him five: an ox, they open to him six, and so whoever offered his son they open to him seven. And his face was (that) of a calf, and his hands stretched forth like a man who opens his hands to receive (something) of his neighbor. And they kindled it with fire, and the priests took the babe and put it into the hands of Molech, and the babe gave up the ghost. And why was it called Tophet and Hinnom? Because they used to make a noise with drums (tophim), that the father might not hear the cry of his child and have pity upon him, and return to him. Hinnom, because the babe wailed (מְנַחֵם, menahem), and the noise of his wailing went up. Another opinion (is that it was called) Hinnom, because the priests used to say — "May it profit (יהנם) thee! may it be sweet to thee! may it be of sweet savor to thee!" All this detail is probably as fictitious as the etymologies are unsound, but we have nothing to supply its place. Selden conjectures that the idea of the seven chapels may have been borrowed from the worship of Mithra, who had seven gates corresponding to the seven planets, and to whom men and women were sacrificed (De Dis Syr. Synt. i. c. 6). Benjamin of Tudela describes the remains of an ancient Ammonite temple which he saw at Gebal, in which was a stone image richly gilt seated on a throne. On either side sat two female figures, and before it was an altar on which the Ammonites anciently burned incense and offered sacrifice (Early Travels in Palestine, p. 79, Bohn). By these chapels Lightfoot explains the allusion in Am. v. 26; Acts vii. 43, to "the tabernacle of Moloch;" "these seven chapels (if there be truth in the thing) help us to understand what is meant by Molech's tabernacle, and seem to give some reason why in the Prophet he is called Siccuth, or the Covert God, because he was retired within so many Cancelli (for that word Kimchi useth) before one could come at him" (Comm. on Acts vii. 43). It was

---

a We may infer from the expression, "after the abominations of the nations whom Jehovah had driven out before the children of Israel," that the

character of the Molech-worship of the time of Ahaz was essentially the same as that of the old Canaanites, although Movers maintains the contrary.

more probably a shrine or ark in which the figure of the god was carried in processions, or which contained, as Movers conjectures, the bones of children who had been sacrificed and were used for magical purposes. [AMMON, vol. i. p. 85 a.]

Many instances of human sacrifices are found in ancient writers, which may be compared with the descriptions in the Old Testament of the manner in which Molech was worshipped. The Carthaginians, according to Augustine (De Civit. Dei, vii. 19), offered children to Saturn, and by the Gauls even grown up persons were sacrificed, under the idea that of all seeds the best is the human kind. Eusebius (Præp. Ev. iv. 16) collected from Porphyry numerous examples to the same effect, from which the following are selected. Among the Rhodians a man was offered to Kronos on the 6th July; afterwards a criminal condemned to death was substituted. The same custom prevailed in Salamis, but was abrogated by Diiphilus king of Cyprus, who substituted an ox. According to Manetho, Amosis abolished the same practice in Egypt at Heliopolis sacred to Juno. Sanchoniatho relates that the Phœnicians, on the occasion of any great calamity, sacrificed to Saturn one of their relatives. Istrus says the same of the Curetes, but the custom was abolished, according to Pallas, in the reign of Hadrian. At Laodicea a virgin was sacrificed yearly to Athene, and the Dumatii, a people of Arabia, buried a boy alive beneath the altar each year. Diodorus Siculus (xx. 14) relates that the Carthaginians, when besieged by Agathocles tyrant of Sicily, offered in public sacrifice to Saturn 200 of their noblest children, while others voluntarily devoted themselves to the number of 300. His description of the statue of the god differs but slightly from that of Molech, which has been quoted. The image was of brass, with its hands outstretched towards the ground in such a manner that the child when placed upon them fell into a pit full of fire.

Molech, " the king," was the lord and master of the Ammonites; their country was his possession (Jer. xlix. 1), as Moab was the heritage of Chemosh; the princes of the land were the princes of Malcham (Jer. xlix. 3; Am. i. 15). His priests were men of rank (Jer. xlix. 3), taking precedence of the princes. So the priest of Hercules at Tyre was second to the king (Justin. xviii. 4, § 5), and like Molech, the god himself, Baal Chamman, is Melkart, " the king of the city." The priests of Molech, like those of other idols, were called Chemarim (2 K. xxiii. 5; Hos. x. 5; Zeph. i. 4).

Traces of the root from which Molech is derived are to be found in the Milichus, Malica, and Malcander of the Phœnicians; with the last mentioned may be compared Adrammelech, the fire-god of Sepharvaim. These, as well as Chemosh the fire-god of Moab, Urotal, Dusares, Sair, and Thyandrites, of the Edomites and neighboring Arab tribes, and the Greek Dionysus, were worshipped under the symbol of a rising flame of fire, which was imitated in the stone pillars erected in their honor (Movers, Phœn. i. c. 9). Tradition refers the origin of the fire-worship to Chaldæa. Abraham and his ancestors are said to have been fire-worshippers, and the Assyrian and Chaldæan armies took with them the sacred fire accompanied by the Magi.

There remains to be noticed one passage (2 Sam. xii. 31) in which the Hebrew written text has מַלְכֵּן, malkén, while the marginal reading is מַלְבֵּן, malbén, which is adopted by our translators in their rendering " brick-kiln." Kimchi explains malkén as " the place of Molech," where sacrifices were offered to him, and the children of Ammon made their sons to pass through the fire. And Milcom and Malken, he says, are one.a On the other hand Movers, rejecting the points, reads מַלְכָּן, malcân, " our king," which he explains as the title by which he was known to the Ammonites. Whatever may be thought of these interpretations, the reading followed by the A. V. is scarcely intelligible.   W. A. W.

MO'LI (Μοολί [Vat. -λει]: Moholi). MAHLI, the son of Merari (1 Esdr. viii. 47; comp. Ezr viii. 18).

MO'LID (מוֹלִיד [begetter]: Μωήλ; Alex. Μοδαδ: Molid). The son of Abishur by his wife Abihail, and descendant of Jerahmeel (1 Chr. ii. 29).

MO'LOCH. The Hebrew corresponding to " your Moloch " in the A. V. of Amos v. 26 is מַלְכְּכֶם, malkekem, " your king," as in the margin. In accordance with the Greek of Acts vii. 43 (ὁ Μολόχ: Moloch), which followed the LXX. of Amos, our translators have adopted a form of the name MOLECH which does not exist in Hebrew. Kimchi, following the Targum, takes the word as an appellative, and not as a proper name, while with regard to siccuth (סִכּוּת, A. V. "tabernacle ") he holds the opposite opinion. His note is as follows: " Siccuth is the name of an idol; and (as for) malkekem he spake of a star which was made an idol by its name, and he calls it ' king,' because they thought it a king over them, or because it was a great star in the host of heaven, which was as a king over his host; and so ' to burn incense to the queen of heaven,' as I have explained in the book of Jeremiah." Gesenius compares with the " tabernacle " of Moloch the sacred tent of the Carthaginians mentioned by Diodorus (xx. 65). Rosenmüller, and after him Ewald, understood by siccuth a pole or stake on which the figure of the idol was placed. It was more probably a kind of palanquin in which the image was carried in processions, a custom which is alluded to in Is. xlvi. 1; Epist. of Jer. 4 (Selden, De Dis Syr. Synt. i. c. 6).   W. A. W.

* **MOLTEN IMAGE.** [IDOL, 21.]

* **MOLTEN SEA.** [SEA, MOLTEN.]

MOM'DIS (Μομδίος; [Vat. Μομδειος;] Alex. Μομδεις: Mondias). The same as MAADAI, of the sons of Bani (1 Esdr. ix. 34; comp. Ezr. x. 34).

MONEY. This article treats of two principal matters, the uncoined money and the coined money mentioned in the Bible. Before entering upon the first subject of inquiry, it will be necessary to speak of uncoined money in general, and of the antiquity of coined money. An account of the principal monetary systems of ancient times is an equally need-

---

a The crown of Malcham, taken by David at Rabbah, is said to have had in it a precious stone (a magnet, according to Kimchi), which is described by Cyril on Amos as transparent and like the day-star, whence Molech has groundlessly been identified with the planet Venus (Vossius, De Orig. Idol., ii. c. 5, p. 331).

ful introduction to the second subject, which requires a special knowledge of the Greek coinages. A notice of the Jewish coins, and of the coins current in Judæa as late as the time of Hadrian, will be interwoven with the examination of the passages in the Bible and Apocrypha relating to them, instead of being separately given.

I. UNCOINED MONEY. 1. *Uncoined Money in general.* — It has been denied by some that there ever has been any money not coined, but this is merely a question of terms. It is well known that ancient nations that were without a coinage weighed the precious metals, a practice represented on the Egyptian monuments, on which gold and silver are shown to have been kept in the form of rings (see cut, p. 1995). The gold rings found in the Celtic countries have been held to have had the same use. It has indeed been argued that this could not have been the case with the latter, since they show no monetary system; yet it is evident from their weights that they all contain complete multiples or parts of a unit, so that we may fairly suppose that the Celts, before they used coins, had, like the ancient Egyptians, the practice of keeping money in rings, which they weighed when it was necessary to pay a fixed amount. We have no certain record of the use of ring-money or other uncoined money in antiquity excepting among the Egyptians. With them the practice mounts up to a remote age, and was probably as constant, and perhaps as regulated with respect to the weight of the rings, as a coinage. It can scarcely be doubted that the highly civilized rivals of the Egyptians, the Assyrians and Babylonians, adopted if they did not originate this custom, clay tablets having been found specifying grants of money by weight (Rawlinson, *Her.* vol. i. p. 684); and there is therefore every probability that it obtained also in Palestine, although seemingly unknown in Greece in the time before coinage was there introduced. There is no trace in Egypt, however, of any different size in the rings represented, so that there is no reason for supposing that this further step was taken towards the invention of coinage.

2. *The Antiquity of Coined Money.* — Respecting the origin of coinage, there are two accounts seemingly at variance: some saying that Phidon king of Argos first struck money, and according to Ephorus, in Ægina; but Herodotus ascribing its invention to the Lydians. The former statement probably refers to the origin of the coinage of European Greece, the latter to that of Asiatic Greece; for it seems, judging from the coins themselves, that the electrum staters of the cities of the coast of Asia Minor were first issued as early as the silver coins of Ægina, both classes appearing to comprise the most ancient pieces of money that are known to us. When Herodotus speaks of the Lydians, there can be no doubt that he refers not to the currency of Lydia as a kingdom, which seems to commence with the darics and similar silver pieces now found near Sardis, and probably of the time of Crœsus, being perhaps the same as the staters of Crœsus (Κροισεῖοι, Jul. Poll.), of the ancients; but that he intends the money of Greek cities at the time when the coins were issued or later under the authority of the Lydians. If we conclude that coinage commenced in European and Asiatic Greece about the same time, the next question is whether we can approximately determine the date. This is extremely difficult, since there are no coins of known period before the time of the

expedition of Xerxes. The pieces of that age are of so archaic a style, that it is hard, at first sight, to believe that there is any length of time between them and the rudest and therefore earliest of the coins of Ægina or the Asiatic coast. It must, however, be recollected that in some conditions of art its growth or change is extremely slow, and that this was the case in the early period of Greek art seems evident from the results of the excavations on what we may believe to be the oldest sites in Greece. The lower limit obtained from the evidence of the coins of known date, may perhaps be conjectured to be two, or at most three, centuries before their time; the higher limit is as vaguely determined by the negative evidence of the Homeric writings, of which we cannot guess the age, excepting as before the first Olympiad. On the whole it seems reasonable to carry up Greek coinage to the 8th century B. C. Purely Asiatic coinage cannot be taken up to so early a date. The more archaic Persian coins seem to be of the time of Darius Hystaspis, or possibly Cyrus, and certainly not much older, and there is no Asiatic money, not of Greek cities, that can be reasonably assigned to an early period. Crœsus and Cyrus probably originated this branch of the coinage, or else Darius Hystaspis followed the example of the Lydian king. Coined money may therefore have been known in Palestine as early as the fall of Samaria, but only through commerce with the Greeks, and we cannot suppose that it was then current there.

3. *Notices of Uncoined Money in the O. T.* — There is no distinct mention of coined money in the books of the O. T. written before the return from Babylon. The contrary was formerly supposed to be the case, partly because the word *shekel* has a vague sense in later times, being used for a coin as well as a weight. Since however there is some seeming ground for the older opinion, we may here examine the principal passages relating to money, and the principal terms employed, in the books of the Bible written before the date above mentioned.

In the history of Abraham we read that Abimelech gave the patriarch "a thousand [pieces] of silver," apparently to purchase veils for Sarah and her attendants; but the passage is extremely difficult (Gen. xx. 16). The LXX. understood shekels to be intended (χίλια δίδραχμα, *l. c.* also ver. 14), and there can be no doubt that they were right, though the rendering is accidentally an unfortunate one, their equivalent being the name of a coin. The narrative of the purchase of the burial place from Ephron gives us further insight into the use of money at that time. It is related that Abraham offered "full silver" for it, and that Ephron valued it at "four hundred shekels of silver," which accordingly the patriarch paid. We read, "And Abraham hearkened unto Ephron; and Abraham weighed (וַיִּשְׁקֹל) to Ephron the silver, which he had named in the audience of the sons of Heth, four hundred shekels of silver, current with the merchant" (עֹבֵר לַסֹּחֵר, xxiii. 3 *ad fin.* esp. 9, 16). Here a currency is clearly indicated like that which the monuments of Egypt show to have been there used in a very remote age; for the weighing proves that this currency, like the Egyptian, did not bear the stamp of authority, and was therefore weighed when employed in commerce. A similar purchase is recorded of Jacob, who bought a parcel of a field at Shalem for a hundred kesitahs (xxxiii.

18, 19). The occurrence of a name different from shekel, and, unlike it, not distinctly applied in any other passage to a weight, favors the idea of coined money. But what is the *kesitah* (קְשִׂיטָה)? The old interpreters supposed it to mean a lamb, and it has been imagined to have been a coin bearing the figure of a lamb. There is no known etymological ground for this meaning, the lost root, if we com-

pare the Arabic قَسَطَ, "he or it divided equally," being perhaps connected with the idea of division. Yet the sanction of the LXX., and the use of weights having the forms of lions, bulls, and geese, by the Egyptians, Assyrians, and probably Persians,

From Lepsius, *Denkmäler*, Abth. iii. Bl 39, No. 3. See also Wilkinson's *Anc. Eg.* ii. 10, for weights in the form of a crouching antelope: and comp. Layard's *Nin. and Bab.* pp. 600–602.

must make us hesitate before we abandon a rendering so singularly confirmed by the relation of the Latin *pecunia* and *pecus*. Throughout the history of Joseph we find evidence of the constant use of money in preference to barter. This is clearly shown in the case of the famine, when it is related that all the money of Egypt and Canaan was paid for corn, and that then the Egyptians had recourse to barter (xlvii. 13–26). It would thence appear that money was not very plentiful. In the narrative of the visits of Joseph's brethren to Egypt, we find that they purchased corn with money, which was, as in Abraham's time, weighed silver, for it is spoken of by them as having been restored to their sacks in "its [full] weight" (xliii. 21). At the time of the exodus, money seems to have been still weighed, for the ransom ordered in the Law is stated to be half a shekel for each man — "half a shekel after the shekel of the sanctuary [of] twenty gerahs the shekel " (Ex. xxx. 13). Here the shekel is evidently a weight, and of a special system of which the standard examples were probably kept by the priests. Throughout the Law, money is spoken of as in ordinary use: but only silver money, gold being mentioned as valuable, but not clearly as used in the same manner. This distinction appears at the time of the conquest of Canaan, when covetous Achan found in Jericho "a goodly Babylonish garment, and two hundred shekels of silver, and a tongue of gold of fifty shekels weight " (Josh. vii. 21). Throughout the period before the return from Babylon this distinction seems to obtain: whenever anything of the character of money is mentioned the usual metal is silver, and gold generally occurs

as the material of ornaments and costly works. A passage in Isaiah has indeed been supposed to show the use of gold coins in that prophet's time: speaking of the makers of idols, he says, "They lavish gold out of the bag, and weigh silver in the balance" (xlvi. 6). The mention of a bag is, however, a very insufficient reason for the supposition that the gold was coined money. Rings of gold may have been used for money in Palestine as early as this time, since they had been long previously so used in Egypt; but the passage probably refers to the people of Babylon, who may have had uncoined money in both metals like the Egyptians. A still more remarkable passage would be that in Ezekiel, which Gesenius supposes (*Lex.* s. v. נְחֹשֶׁת) to mention brass as money, were there any sound reason for following the Vulg. in the literal rendering of יַעַן הִשָּׁפֵךְ נְחֻשְׁתֵּךְ, *quia effusum est æs tuum*, instead of reading "because thy filthiness was poured out" with the A. V. (xvi. 36). The context does indeed admit the idea of money, but the sense of the passage does not seem to do so, whereas the other translation is quite in accordance with it, as well as philologically admissible (see Gesen. *Lex.* l. c.). The use of brass money at this period seems unlikely, as it was of later introduction in Greece than money of other metals, at least silver and electrum: it has, however, been supposed that that there was an independent copper coinage in further Asia before the introduction of silver money by the Seleucidæ and the Greek kings of Bactriana.

We may thus sum up our results respecting the money mentioned in the books of Scripture written before the return from Babylon. From the time of Abraham silver money appears to have been in general use in Egypt and Canaan. This money was weighed when its value had to be determined, and we may therefore conclude that it was not of a settled system of weights. Since the money of Egypt and that of Canaan are spoken of together in the account of Joseph's administration during the famine, we may reasonably suppose they were of the same kind; a supposition which is confirmed by our finding, from the monuments, that the Egyptians used uncoined money of gold and of silver. It is even probable that the form in both cases was similar or the same, since the ring-money of Egypt resembles the ordinary ring-money of the Celts, among whom it was probably first introduced by the Phœnician traders, so that it is likely that this form generally prevailed before the introduction of coinage. We find no evidence in the Bible of the use of coined money by the Jews before the time of Ezra, when other evidence equally shows that it was current in Palestine, its general use being probably a very recent change. This first notice of coinage, exactly when we should expect it, is not to be overlooked as a confirmation of the usual opinion as to the dates of the several books of Scripture founded on their internal evidence and the testimony of ancient writers; and it lends no support to those theorists who attempt to show that there have been great changes in the text. Minor confirmations of this nature will be found in the later part of this article.

II. COINED MONEY. 1. *The Principal Monetary Systems of Antiquity.* — Some notice of the principal monetary systems of antiquity, as determined by the joint evidence of the coins and of ancient writers, is necessary to render the next section comprehensible. We must here distinctly lay down what we mean by the different systems with which we shall compare the Hebrew coinage, as current works are generally very vague and discordant on this subject. The common opinions respecting the standards of antiquity have been formed from a study of the statements of writers of different age and authority, and without a due discrimination between weights and coins. The coins, instead of being taken as the basis of all hypotheses, have been cited to confirm or refute previous theories, and thus no legitimate induction has been formed from their study. If the contrary method is adopted, it has firstly the advantage of resting upon the indisputable authority of monuments which have not been tampered with; and, in the second place, it is of an essentially inductive character. The result simplifies the examination of the statements of ancient writers, by showing that they speak of the same thing by different names on account of a change which the coins at once explain, and by indicating that probably at least one talent was only a weight, not used for coined money unless weighed in a mass.

The earliest Greek coins, by which we here intend those struck in the age before the Persian War, are of three talents or standards: the Attic, the Æginetan, and the Macedonian or earlier Phœnician. The oldest coins of Athens, of Ægina, and of Macedon and Thrace, we should select as typical respectively of these standards; obtaining as the weight of the Attic drachm about 67·5 grains troy; of the Æginetan, about 96; and of the Macedonian, about 58 — or 116, if its drachm be what is now generally held to be the didrachm. The electrum coinage of Asia Minor probably affords examples of the use by the Greeks of a fourth talent, which may be called the later Phœnician, if we hold the staters to have been tetradrachms, for their full weight is about 248 grs.; but it is possible that the pure gold which they contain, about 186 grs., should alone be taken into account, in which case they would be didrachms on the Æginetan standard. Their division into sixths (hectæ) may be urged on either side. It may be supposed that the division into oboli was retained; but then the half hecta has its proper name, and is not called an obolus. However this may be, the gold and silver coins found at Sardis, which we may reasonably assign to Crœsus, are of this weight, and may be taken as its earliest examples, without of course proving it was a Greek system. They give a tetradrachm, or equivalent, of about 246 grains, and a drachm of 61·5: but neither of these coins is found of this early period. Among these systems the Attic and the Æginetan are easily recognized in the classical writers; and the Macedonian is probably their Alexandrian talent of gold and silver, to be distinguished from the Alexandrian talent of copper. Respecting the two Phœnician talents there is some difficulty. The Eubolc talent of the writers we recognize nowhere in the coinage. It is useless to search for isolated instances of Eubolc weight in Eubœa and elsewhere, when the coinage of the island and ancient coins generally afford no class on the stated Eubolc weight. It is still more unsound to force an agree-

ment between the Macedonian talent of the coins and the Eubolc of the writers. It may be supposed that the Eubolc talent was never used for money; and the statement of Herodotus, that the king of Persia received his gold tribute by this weight, may mean no more than that it was weighed in Eubolc talents. Or perhaps the nearness of the Eubolc talent to the Attic caused the coins struck on the two standards to approximate in their weights; as the Cretan coins on the Æginetan standard were evidently lowered in weight by the influence of the Asiatic ones on the later Phœnician standard.

We must now briefly trace the history of these talents.

(a.) The Attic talent was from a very early period the standard of Athens. If Solon really reduced the weight, we have no money of the city of the older currency. Corinth followed the same system; and its use was diffused by the great influence of these two leading cities. In Sicily and Italy, after, in the case of the former, a limited use of the Æginetan talent, the Attic weight became universal. In Greece Proper the Æginetan talent, to the north the Macedonian, and in Asia Minor and Africa the later Phœnician, were long its rivals, until Alexander made the Attic standard universal throughout his empire, and Carthage alone maintained an independent system. After Alexander's time the other talents were partly restored, but the Attic always remained the chief. From the earliest period of which we have specimens of money on this standard to the time of the Roman dominion it suffered a great depreciation, the drachm falling from 67·5 grains to about 65·5 under Alexander, and about 55 under the early Cæsars. Its later depreciation was rather by adulteration than by lessening of weight.

(b.) The Æginetan talent was mainly used in Greece Proper and the islands, and seems to have been annihilated by Alexander, unless indeed afterwards restored in one or two remote towns, as Leucas in Acarnania, or by the general issue of a coin equally assignable to it or the Attic standard as a hemidrachm or a *tetrobolon*.

(c.) The Macedonian talent, besides being used in Macedon and in some Thracian cities before Alexander, was the standard of the great Phœnician cities under Persian rule, and was afterwards restored in most of them. It was adopted in Egypt by the first Ptolemy, and also mainly used by the later Sicilian tyrants, whose money we believe imitates that of the Egyptian sovereigns. It might have been imagined that Ptolemy did not borrow the talent of Macedon, but struck money on the standard of Egypt, which the commerce of that country might have spread in the Mediterranean in a remote age, had not a recent discovery shown that the Egyptian standard of weight was much heavier, and even in excess of the Æginetan drachm, the unit being above 140 grs., the half of which, again, is greater than any of the drachms of the other three standards. It cannot therefore be compared with any of them.

(d.) The later Phœnician talent was always used for the official coinage of the Persian kings and commanders,[a] and after the earliest period was very

<hr/>

[a] Mr. Waddington has shown (*Mélanges de Numismatique*) that the so-called coins of the satraps were never issued excepting when these governors were in command of expeditions, and were therefore invested

with special powers. This discovery explains the putting to death of Aryandes, satrap of Egypt, for striking a coinage of his own.

general in the Persian empire. After Alexander, it was scarcely used excepting in coast-towns of Asia Minor, at Carthage, and in the Phœnician town of Aradus.

Respecting the Roman coinage it is only necessary here to state that the origin of the weights of its gold and silver money is undoubtedly Greek, and that the denarius, the chief coin of the latter metal, was under the early emperors equivalent to the Attic drachm, then greatly depreciated.

2. Coined Money mentioned in the Bible. — The earliest distinct mention of coins in the Bible is held to refer to the Persian money. In Ezra (ii. 69, viii. 27) and Nehemiah (vii. 70, 71, 72) current gold coins are spoken of under the name דַּרְכְּמוֹן,

אֲדַרְכּוֹן, which only occurs in the plural, and appears to correspond to the Greek στατὴρ Δαρεικός or Δαρεικός, the Daric of numismatists. The renderings of the LXX. and Vulg., χρυσοῦς, solidus, drachma, especially the first and second, lend weight to the idea that this was the standard gold coin at the time of Ezra and Nehemiah, and this would explain the use of the same name in the First Book of Chronicles (xxix. 7), in the account of the offerings of David's great men for the Temple, where it would be employed instead of shekel, as a Greek would use the term stater. [See Art. DARIC.]

Daric. Obv.: King of Persia to the right, kneeling, bearing bow and javelin. Rev.: Irregular incuse square. British Museum.

The Apocrypha contains the earliest distinct allusion to the coining of Jewish money, where it is narrated, in the First Book of Maccabees, that Antiochus VII. granted to Simon the Maccabee permission to coin money with his own stamp, as well as other privileges (Καὶ ἐπέτρεψά σοι ποιῆσαι κόμμα ἴδιον νόμισμα τῇ χώρᾳ σου. xv. 6). This was in the fourth year of Simon's pontificate, B. C. 140. It must be noted that Demetrius II. had in the first year of Simon, B. C. 143, made a most important decree granting freedom to the Jewish people, which gave occasion to the dating of their contracts and covenants, — "In the first year of Simon the great high-priest, the leader, and chief of the Jews" (xiii. 34–42), a form which Josephus gives differently, "In the first year of Simon, benefactor of the Jews, and ethnarch" (Ant. xiii. 6).

The earliest Jewish coins were until lately considered to have been struck by Simon on receiving the permission of Antiochus VII. They may be thus described, following M. de Saulcy's arrangement: —

SILVER.

1. שֶׁקֶל יִשְׂרָאֵל, "Shekel of Israel." Vase, above which א [Year] 1.

℞ יְרוּשָׁלֵם קְדֹשָׁה, "Jerusalem the holy." Branch bearing three flowers. Æ.

2. הֵצִי הַשֶּׁקֶל, "Half-shekel." Same type and date.

℞ יְרוּשָׁלֵם קְדֹשָׁה. Same type. Æ. (Cut.) B. M.

3. שֶׁקֶל יִשְׂרָאֵל, "Shekel of Israel." Same type, above which שב (שְׁנַת ב), "Year 2."

℞ יְרוּשָׁלֵים הַקְּדוֹשָׁה. Same type. Æ.

4. חֲצִי הַשֶּׁקֶל. "Half-shekel." Same type and date.

℞ יְרוּשָׁלֵים הַקְּדוֹשָׁה. Same type. Æ.

5. שֶׁקֶל יִשְׂרָאֵל, "Shekel of Israel." Same type, above which שג (שְׁנַת ג), "Year 3."

℞ יְרוּשָׁלֵים הַקְּדוֹשָׁה. Same type. Æ. (Cut) B. M.

COPPER.

1. שְׁנַת אַרְבַּע חֵצִי, "Year four: Half" A fruit, between two sheaves?

℞ לִגְאֻלַּת צִיּוֹן, "Of the redemption of Zion." Palm-tree between two baskets? Æ.

2. שְׁנַת אַרְבַּע רְבִיַע, "Year four: Quarter." Two sheaves?

℞ לִגְאֻלַּת צִיּוֹן, "Of the redemption of Zion." A fruit. Æ. (Cut) Mr. Wigan's collection.

3. שְׁנַת אַרְבַּע, "Year four." A leaf between two fruits?

לגאלת ציון Ry, "Of the redemption of Zion." Vase. Æ. (Cut) Wigan.

The average weight of the silver coins is about 220 grains troy for the shekel, and 110 for the half-shekel.[a] The name, from שֶׁקַל, shows that the shekel was the Jewish stater. The determination of the standard weight of the shekel, which, be it remembered, was a weight as well as a coin, and of its relation to the other weights used by the Hebrews, belongs to another article [WEIGHTS AND MEASURES]: here we have only to consider its relation to the different talents of antiquity. The shekel corresponds almost exactly to the tetradrachm or didrachm of the earlier Phœnician talent in use in the cities of Phœnicia under Persian rule, and after Alexander's time at Tyre, Sidon, and Berytus, as well as in Egypt. It is represented in the LXX. by didrachm, a rendering which has occasioned great difficulty to numismatists. Col. Leake suggested, but did not adopt, what we have no doubt is the true explanation. After speaking of the shekel as probably the Phœnician and Hebrew unit of weight, he adds: "This weight appears to have been the same as the Egyptian unit of weight, for we learn from Horapollo that the Movás, or unit, which they held to be the basis of all numeration, was equal to two drachmæ; and δίδραχμον is employed synonymously with σίκλος for the Hebrew word shekel by the Greek Septuagint; consequently, the shekel and the didrachmon were of the same weight. I am aware that some learned commentators are of opinion that the translators here meant a didrachmon of the Græco-Egyptian scale, which weighed about 110 grains; but it is hardly credible that δίδραχμον should have been thus employed without any distinguishing epithet, at a time when the Ptolemaic scale was yet of recent origin [in Egypt], the word didrachmon on the other hand, having for ages been applied to a silver money, of about 130 grains, in the currency of all cities which follow the Attic or Corinthian standard, as well as in the silver money of Alexander the Great and [most of] his successors. In all these currencies, as well as in those of Lydia and Persia, the stater was an Attic didrachmon, or, at least, with no greater difference of standard than occurs among modern nations using a denomination of weight or measure common to all; and hence the word δίδραχμον was at length employed as a measure of weight, without any reference to its origin in the Attic drachma. Thus we find the drachma of gold described as equivalent to ten didrachms, and the half-shekel of the Pentateuch, translated by the Septuagint τὸ ἥμισυ τοῦ διδράχμου. There can be no doubt, therefore, that the Attic, and not the Græco-Egyptian didrachmon, was intended by

them." He goes on to conjecture that Moses adopted the Egyptian unit, and to state the importance of distinguishing between the Mosaic weight and the extant Jewish shekel. "It appears," he continues, "that the half-shekel of ransom had, in the time of our Saviour, been converted into the payment of a didrachmon to the Temple; and two of these didrachma formed a stater of the Jewish currency. This stater was evidently the extant 'Shekel Israel,' which was a tetradrachm of the Ptolemaic scale, though generally below the standard weight, like most of the extant specimens of the Ptolemies; the didrachmon paid to the Temple was, therefore, of the same monetary scale. Thus the duty to the Temple was converted from the half of an Attic to the whole of a Ptolemaic didrachmon, and the tax was nominally raised in the proportion of about 105 to 65; but probably the value of silver had fallen as much in the two preceding centuries. It was natural that the Jews, when they began to strike money, should have revived the old name shekel, and applied it to their stater, or principal coin; and equally so, that they should have adopted the scale of the neighbouring opulent and powerful kingdom, the money of which they must have long been in the habit of employing. The inscription on the coin appears to have been expressly intended to distinguish the monetary shekel or stater from the Shekel ha-Kodesh, or Shekel of the Sanctuary." Appendix to Numismata Hellenica, pp. 2, 3.

The great point here gained is that the Egyptian unit was a didrachm, a conclusion confirmed by the discovery of an Egyptian weight not greatly exceeding the Attic didrachm. The conjecture, however, that the LXX. intend the Attic weight is forced, and leads to this double dilemma, the supposition that the didrachm of the LXX. is a shekel and that of the N. T. half a stater, which is the same as half a shekel, and that the tribute was greatly raised, whereas there is no evidence that in the N. T. the term didrachm is not used in exactly the same sense as in the LXX. The natural explanation seems to us to be that the Alexandrian Jews adopted for the shekel the term didrachm as the common name of the coin corresponding in weight to it, and that it thus became in Hebraistic Greek the equivalent of shekel. There is no ground for supposing a difference in use in the LXX. and N. T., more especially as there happen to have been few, if any, didrachms current in Palestine in the time of our Lord, a fact which gives great significance to the finding of the stater in the fish by St. Peter, showing the minute accuracy of the Evangelist. The Ptolemaic weight, not being Egyptian but Phœnician, chanced to agree with the Hebrew, which was probably derived from the same source, the primitive system of Palestine, and perhaps of Babylon also. — Respecting the weights of the copper coins we cannot as yet speak with any confidence.

The fabric of the silver coins above described is so different from that of any other ancient money, that it is extremely hard to base any argument on it alone, and the cases of other special classes, as the ancient money of Cyprus, show the danger of such reasoning. Some have been disposed to consider that it proves that these coins cannot be later than the time of Nehemiah, others will not admit

---

[a] Coins are not always exact in relative weight: in some modern coinages the smaller coins are intentionally heavier than they would be if exact divisions of the larger.

it to be later than Alexander's time, while some still hold that it is not too archaic for the Maccabean period. Against its being assigned to the earlier dates we may remark that the forms are too exact, and that apart from style, which we do not exclude in considering fabric, the mere mechanical work is like that of the coins of Phœnician towns struck under the Seleucidæ. The decisive evidence, however, is to be found by a comparison of the copper coins which cannot be doubted to complete the series. These, though in some cases of a similar style to the silver coins, are generally far more like the undoubted pieces of the Maccabees.

The inscriptions of these coins, and all the other Hebrew inscriptions of Jewish coins, are in a character of which there are few other examples. As Gesenius has observed (*Gram.* § 5), it bears a strong resemblance to the Samaritan and Phœnician, and we may add to the Aramæan of coins, which must be carefully distinguished from the Aramæan of the papyri found in Egypt.[a] The use of this character does not afford any positive evidence as to age; but it is important to notice that, although it is found upon the Maccabean coins, there is no palæographic reason why the pieces of doubtful time bearing it should not be as early as the Persian period.

The meaning of the inscriptions does not offer matter for controversy. Their nature would indicate a period of Jewish freedom from Greek influence as well as independence, and the use of an era dating from its commencement. The form used on the copper coins clearly shows the second and third points. It cannot be supposed that the dating is by the sabbatical or jubilee year, since the redemption of Zion is particularized. These are separated from the known Maccabean and later coins by the absence of Hellenism, and connected with them by the want of perfect uniformity in their inscriptions, a point indicative of a time of national decay like that which followed the dominion of the earlier Maccabees. Here it may be remarked that the idea of Cavedoni, that the form ירושלים, succeeding in the second year to ירושלם, is to be taken as a dual, because in that year (according to his view of the age of the coins) the fortress of Sion was taken from the Syrians (*Num. Bibl.* p. 23), notwithstanding its ingenuity must, as De Sauley has already said, be considered untenable.

The old explanation of the meaning of the types of the shekels and half-shekels, that they represent the pot of manna and Aaron's rod that budded, seems to us remarkably consistent with the inscriptions and with what we should expect. Cavedoni has suggested, however, that the one type is simply a vase of the Temple, and the other a lily, arguing against the old explanation of the former that the pot of manna had a cover, which this vase has not. But it may be replied, that perhaps this vase had a flat cover, that on later coins a vase is represented both with and without a cover, and that the different forms given to the vase which is so constant on the Jewish coins seem to indicate that it is a representation of something like the pot of manna lost when Nebuchadnezzar took Jerusalem, and of which there was therefore only a traditional recollection.

a See Mr. Waddington's paper on the so-called satrap coins (*Mélanges de Numismatique*).

Respecting the exact meaning of the types of the copper, save the vase, it is difficult to form a probable conjecture. They may reasonably be supposed to have a reference to the great festivals of the Jewish year, which were connected with thanksgiving for the fruits of the earth. But it may, on the other hand, be suggested that they merely indicate the products of the Holy Land, the fertility of which is so prominently brought forward in the Scriptures. With this idea the representation of the vine-leaf and bunch of grapes upon the later coins would seem to tally; but it must be recollected that the lower portion of a series generally shows a departure or divergence from the higher in the intention of its types, so as to be an unsafe guide in interpretation.

Upon the copper coins we have especially to observe, as already hinted, that they form an important guide in judging of the age of the silver. That they really belong to the same time is not to be doubted. Everything but the style proves this. Their issue in the 4th year, after the silver cease in the 3d year, their types and inscriptions, leave no room for doubt. The style is remarkably different, and we have selected two specimens for engraving, which afford examples of their diversity. We venture to think that the difference between the silver coins engraved, and the small copper coin, which most nearly resembles them in the form of the letters, is almost as great as that between the large copper one and the copper pieces of John Hyrcanus. The small copper coin, be it remembered, more nearly resembles the silver money than does the large one.

From this inquiry we may lay down the following particulars as a basis for the attribution of this class. 1. The shekels, half-shekels, and corresponding copper coins, may be on the evidence of fabric and inscriptions of any age from Alexander's time until the earlier period of the Maccabees. 2. They must belong to a time of independence, and one at which Greek influence was excluded. 3. They date from an era of Jewish independence.

M. de Sauley, struck by the ancient appearance of the silver coins, and disregarding the difference in style of the copper, has conjectured that the whole class was struck at some early period of prosperity. He fixes upon the pontificate of Jaddua, and supposes them to have been first issued when Alexander granted great privileges to the Jews. If it be admitted that this was an occasion from which an era might be reckoned, there is a serious difficulty in the style of the copper coins, and those who have practically studied the subject of the fabric of coins will admit that, though archaic style may be long preserved, there can be no mistake as to late style, the earlier limits of which are far more rigorously fixed than the later limits of archaic style. But there is another difficulty of even a graver nature. Alexander, who was essentially a practical genius, suppressed all the varying weights of money in his empire excepting the Attic, which he made the lawful standard. Philip had struck his gold on the Attic weight, his silver on the Macedonian. Alexander even changed his native currency in carrying out this great commercial reform, of which the importance has never been recognized. Is it likely that he would have allowed a new currency to have been issued by Jaddua on a system different from the Attic? If it be urged that this was a sacred coinage for the tribute, and that therefore an exception may have been made, it must be recollected that an excess of weight would not have been so serious a matter as a deficiency, and besides that it is by no means clear that the shekels follow a Jewish weight. On these grounds, therefore, we feel bound to reject M. de Saulcy's theory.

The basis we have laid down is in entire accordance with the old theory, that this class of coins was issued by Simon the Maccabee. M. de Saulcy would, however, urge against our conclusion the circumstance that he has attributed small copper coins, all of one and the same class, to Judas the Maccabee, Jonathan, and John Hyrcanus, and that the very dissimilar coins hitherto attributed to Simon must therefore be of another period. If these attributions be correct, his deduction is perfectly sound, but the circumstance that Simon alone is unrepresented in the series, whereas we have most reason to look for coins of him, is extremely suspicious. We shall, however, show in discussing this class, that we have discovered evidence which seems to us sufficient to induce us to abandon M. de Saulcy's classification of copper coins to Judas and Jonathan, and to commence the series with those of John Hyrcanus. For the present therefore we adhere to the old attribution of the shekels, half-shekels, and similar copper coins, to Simon the Maccabee.

We now give a list of all the principal copper coins of a later date than those of the class described above and anterior to Herod, according to M. de Saulcy's arrangement.

COPPER COINS.

1. *Judas Maccabæus.*

```
יהוד
הכהןגל
ולוחבר
היןהדים]
```
"Judah, the illustrious priest, and friend of the Jews."

Within a wreath of *olive !*

℞. Two cornua copiæ united, within which a pomegranate. Æ. W.

2. *Jonathan.*

```
יהוכ
תוהכה
בדולהב
```
"Jonathan the high-priest, friend of the Jews."

Within a wreath of *olive !*

℞. The same. Æ. W.

```
ינתן
הכהנה
חברי
```
℞. The same. Æ. W.

3. *Simon.*

(Wanting.)

4. *John Hyrcanus.*

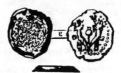

A   **A**

```
יהוחנן
הכהנהג
לוחברהי
הודים
```
" John the high-priest, and friend of the Jews "

Within a wreath of *olive !*

℞. Two cornua copiæ, within which a pomegranate. Æ. W.

```
יהוח
נוהכהו
הגדלוח
ברהיח
דים
```
℞. The same. Æ. W.

5. *Judas-Aristobulus and Antigonus.*

IOTΔΑ . .
ΒΑΞΙΛ ?
A ?

Within a crown.

℞. Two cornua copiæ, within which a pomegranate.

Similar coins.

7. *Alexander Jannæus.*

(A.) ΒΑΞΙΛΕΩ . . . . OT (ΒΑΞΙΛΕΩΞ ΑΛΕΞΑΝΔΡΟΤ). Anchor.

℞. יונתן המלך, "Jonathan the king;" within the spokes of a wheel. Æ. W.

(B.) ΑΣ . . . . . ΑΕΞΑΝΔΡΟ. Anchor.

℞. יְ ; . . . . כֹהֵן הַמֶּלֶךְ; within the spokes of a wheel. Æ. W.

(C.) ΒΑΣΙΛΕΩΣ ΑΛΕΞΑΝΔΡΟΥ. Anchor.

יְהוֹנָתָן הַמֶּלֶךְ, "Jonathan the king." Flower.

The types of this last coin resemble those of one of Antiochus VII.

(D.) ΒΑΣΙΛΕΩΣ ΑΛΕΞΑΝΔ . . . Anchor.
℞. Star.

Alexandra.

ΒΑΣΙΛΙΣ ΑΛΕΞΑΝΔ. Anchor.

℞. Star: within the rays nearly-effaced Hebrew inscription.

Hyrcanus (no coins).
Aristobulus (no coins).
Hyrcanus restored (no coins).
Oligarchy (no coins).
Aristobulus and *Alexander* (no coins).
Hyrcanus again restored (no coins).

Antigonus.

. . . . ΙΓΟΝΟΥ (ΒΑΣΙΛΕΩΣ ΑΝΤΙΓΟΝΟΥ) around a crown.

℞. . . . . מרתהי (? מרתיה הכהן הגדל)
" Mattathiah the high-priest "? Æ. W.

This arrangement is certainly the most satisfactory that has been yet proposed, but it presents serious difficulties. The most obvious of these is the absence of coins of Simon, for whose money we have more reason to look than for that of any other Jewish ruler. M. de Saulcy's suggestion that we may some day find his coins is a scarcely satisfactory answer, for this would imply that he struck very few coins, whereas all the other princes in the list, Judas only excepted, struck many, judging from those found. That Judas should have struck but few coins is extremely probable from the unsettled state of the country during his rule; but the prosperous government of Simon seems to require a large issue of money. A second difficulty is that the series of small copper coins, having the same, or essentially the same, reverse-type, commences with Judas, and should rather commence with Simon. A third difficulty is that Judas bears the title of priest, and probably of high-priest, for the word גלול is extremely doubtful, and the

extraordinary variations and blunders in the inscriptions of these copper coins make it more probable that גדול is the term, whereas it is extremely doubtful that he took the office of high-priest. It is, however, just possible that he may have taken an inferior title, while acting as high-priest during the lifetime of Alcimus. These objections are, however, all trifling in comparison with one that seems never to have struck any inquirer. These small copper coins have for the main part of their reverse-type a Greek symbol, the united cornua copiæ, and they therefore distinctly belong to a period of Greek influence. Is it possible that Judas the Maccabee, the restorer of the Jewish worship, and the sworn enemy of all heathen customs, could have struck money with a type derived from the heathen, and used by at least one of the hated family that then oppressed Israel, a type connected with idolatry, and to a Jew as forbidden as any other of the representations on the coins of the Gentiles? It seems to us that this is an impossibility, and that the use of such a type points to the time when prosperity had corrupted the ruling family and Greek usages once more were powerful in their influence. This period may be considered to commence in the rule of John Hyrcanus, whose adoption of foreign customs is evident in the naming of his sons far more than in the policy he followed. If we examine the whole series, the coins bearing the name of "John the high-priest" are the best in execution, and therefore have some claim to be considered the earliest.

It is important to endeavor to trace the origin of the type which we are discussing. The two cornua copiæ first occur on the Egyptian coins, and indicate two sovereigns. In the money of the Seleucidæ the type probably originated at a marriage with an Egyptian princess. The cornua copiæ, as represented on the Jewish coins, are first found, as far as we are aware, on a coin of Alexander II. Zebina (B. C. 128–122), who, be it recollected, was set up by Ptolemy Physcon. The type occurs, however, in a different form on the unique tetradrachm of Cleopatra, ruling alone, in the British Museum, but it may have been adopted on her marriage with Alexander I. Balas (B. C. 150). Yet even this earlier date is after the rule of Judas (B. C. 167–161), and in the midst of that of Jonathan; and Alexander Zebina was contemporary with John Hyrcanus. We have seen that Alexander Jannæus (B. C. 105–78) seems to have followed a type of Antiochus VII. Sidetes, of which there are coins dated B. C. 132–131.

Thus far there is high probability that M. de Saulcy's attributions before John Hyrcanus are extremely doubtful. This probability has been almost changed to certainty by a discovery the writer has recently had the good fortune to make. The acute Barthélemy mentions a coin of "Jonathan the high-priest," on which he perceived traces of the words ΒΑΣΙΛΕΩΣ ΑΛΕΞΑΝΔΡΟΥ, and he accordingly conjectures that these coins are of the same class as the bilingual ones of Alexander Jannæus, holding them both to be of Jonathan, and the latter to mark the close alliance between that ruler and Alexander I. Balas. An examination of the money of Jonathan the high-priest has led us to the discovery that many of his coins are restruck, that some of these restruck coins exhibit traces of Greek inscriptions, showing the original pieces to be probably of the class attributed to Alexander

Jannæus by M. de Saulcy, and that one of the latter distinctly bears the letters ΑΝΑΙ. Τ [ΑΛΕΞ-ΑΝΔΡΟΤ]. The two impressions of restruck coins are in general of closely consecutive dates, the object of restriking having usually been to destroy an obnoxious coinage. That this was the motive in the present instance appears from the large number of restruck coins among those with the name of Jonathan the high-priest, whereas we know of no other restruck Jewish coins, and from the change in the style from Jonathan the king to Jonathan the high-priest.

Under these circumstances but two attributions of the bilingual coins, upon which everything depends, can be entertained, either that they are of Jonathan the Maccabee in alliance with Alexander I. Balas, or that they are of Alexander Jannæus; the Jewish prince having, in either case, changed his coinage. We learn from the case of Antigonus that double names were not unknown in the family of the Maccabees. To the former attribution there are the following objections. 1. On the bilingual coins the title Jonathan the king corresponds to Alexander the king, implying that the same prince is intended, or two princes of equal rank. 2. Although Alexander I. Balas sent presents of a royal character to Jonathan, it is extremely unlikely that the Jewish prince would have taken the regal title, or that the king of Syria would have actually granted it. 3. The Greek coins of Jewish fabric with the inscription Alexander the king, would have to be assigned to the Syrian Alexander I., instead of the Jewish king of the same name. 4. It would be most strange if Jonathan should have first struck coins with Alexander I., and then cancelled that coinage and issued a fresh Hebrew coinage of his own and Greek of the Syrian king, the whole series moreover, excepting those with only the Hebrew inscription, having been issued within the years B. C. 153–146, eight out of the nineteen of Jonathan's rule. 5. The reign of Alexander Jannæus would be unrepresented in the coinage. To the second attribution there is this objection, that it is unlikely that Alexander Jannæus would have changed the title of king for that of high-priest; but to this it may be replied, that his quarrel with the Pharisees with reference to his performing the duties of the latter office, the turning-point of his reign, might have made him abandon the recent kingly title and recur to the sacerdotal, already used on his father's coins, for the Hebrew currency, while probably still issuing a Greek coinage with the regal title. On these grounds, therefore, we maintain Bayer's opinion that the Jewish coinage begins with Simon, we transfer the coins of Jonathan the high-priest to Alexander Jannæus, and propose the following arrangement of the known money of the princes of the period we have been just considering.

John Hyrcanus, B. C. 135–106.

Copper coins, with Hebrew inscription, "John the high-priest;" on some A, marking alliance with Antiochus VII. Sidetes.

Aristobulus and Antigonus, B. C. 106–105.
(Probable Attribution.)

Copper coins, with Hebrew inscription, "Judah the *high* (?) priest;" copper coins with Greek inscription, "Judah, the king," and A. for Antigonus? M. de Saulcy supposes that Aristobulus bore the Hebrew name Judah, and there is certainly some probability in the conjecture, though the classification

of these coins cannot be regarded as more than tentative.

Alexander Jannæus, B. C. 105–78.

First coinage: copper coins with bilingual inscriptions — Greek, "Alexander the king;" Hebrew, "Jonathan the king."

Second coinage: copper coins with Hebrew inscription, "Jonathan the high-priest;" and copper coins with Greek inscription, "Alexander the king." (The assigning of these latter two to the same ruler is confirmed by the occurrence of Hebrew coins of "Judah the high-priest," and Greek ones of "Judas the king," which there is good reason to attribute to one and the same person.)

Alexandra, B. C. 78–69.

The coin assigned to Alexandra by M. de Saulcy may be of this sovereign, but those of Alexander are so frequently blundered that we are not certain that it was not struck by him.

Hyrcanus, B. C. 69–66 (no coins).
Aristobulus, B. C. 66–63 (no coins).
Hyrcanus restored, B. C. 63–57 (no coins).
Oligarchy, B. C. 57–47 (no coins).
Aristobulus and *Alexander*, B. C. 49 (no coins).
Hyrcanus again B. C. 47–40 (no coins).
Antigonus, B. C. 40–37. Copper coins, with bilingual inscriptions.

It must be observed that the whole period unrepresented in our classification is no more than twenty-nine years, only two years in excess of the length of the reign of Alexander Jannæus, that it was a very troublous time, and that Hyrcanus, whose rule occupied more than half the period, was so weak a man that it is extremely likely that he would have neglected to issue a coinage. It is possible that some of the doubtful small pieces are of this unrepresented time, but at present we cannot even conjecturally attribute any.

It is not necessary to describe in detail the money of the time commencing with the reign of Herod and closing under Hadrian. We must, however, speak of the coinage generally, of the references to it in the N. T., and of two important classes — the money attributed to the revolt preceding the fall of Jerusalem, and that of the famous Barkokab.

The money of Herod is abundant, but of inferior interest to the earlier coinage, from its generally having a thoroughly Greek character. It is of copper only, and seems to be of three denominations, the smallest being apparently a piece of brass (χαλκοῦς), the next larger its double (δίχαλκος), and the largest its triple (τρίχαλκος), as M. de Saulcy has ingeniously suggested. The smallest is the commonest, and appears to be the farthing of the N. T. The coin engraved below is of the smallest denomination of these: it may be thus described :—

Η ΩΔ ΒΑΣΙ. Anchor.

℞ Two cornua copiæ, within which a caduceus (degraded from pomegranate). Æ. W.

We have chosen this specimen from its remarkable relation to the coinage of Alexander Jannæus, which makes it probable that the latter was still current money in Herod's time, having been abundantly issued, and so tends to explain the seeming neglect to coin in the period from Alexander or Alexandra to Antigonus.

The money of Herod Archelaus, and the similar coinage of the Greek Imperial class, of Roman rulers with Greek inscriptions, issued by the procurators of Judæa under the emperors from Augustus to Nero, present no remarkable peculiarities, nor do the coins attributed by M. de Saulcy to Agrippa I., but possibly of Agrippa II. We engrave a specimen of the money last mentioned to illustrate this class.

ΒΑΞΙΛΕ⍵C ΑΓΡΙΠΑ. State umbrella.

℞ Corn-stalk bearing three ears of bearded wheat. L S Year 6. Æ.

There are several passages in the Gospels which throw light upon the coinage of the time. When the twelve were sent forth our Lord thus commanded them, "Provide neither gold, nor silver, nor brass in your purses" (lit. "girdles"), Matt. x. 9. In the parallel passages in St. Mark (vi. 8), copper alone is mentioned for money, the Palestinian currency being mainly of this metal, although silver was coined by some cities of Phœnicia and Syria, and gold and silver Roman money was also in use. St. Luke, however, uses the term "money," ἀργύριον (ix. 3), which may be accounted for by his less Hebraistic style.

The coins mentioned by the Evangelists, and first those of silver, are the following: the *stater* is spoken of in the account of the miracle of the tribute money. The receivers of *didrachms* demanded the tribute, but St. Peter found in the fish a *stater*, which he paid for our Lord and himself (Matt. xvii. 24-27). This stater was therefore a tetradrachm, and it is very noteworthy that at this period almost the only Greek Imperial silver coin in the East was a tetradrachm, the didrachm being probably unknown, or very little coined.

The *didrachm* is mentioned as a money of account in the passage above cited, as the equivalent of the Hebrew shekel. [SHEKEL.]

The *denarius*, or Roman penny, as well as the Greek *drachm*, then of about the same weight, are spoken of as current coins. There can be little doubt that the latter is merely employed as another name for the former. In the famous passages respecting the tribute to Cæsar, the Roman denarius of the time is correctly described (Matt. xxii. 15-21; Luke xx. 19-25). It bears the head of Tiberius, who has the title Cæsar in the accompanying inscription, most later emperors having, after their accession, the title Augustus: here again therefore we have an evidence of the date of the Gospels. [DENARIUS; DRACHM.]

Of copper coins the farthing and its half, the mite, are spoken of, and these probably formed the chief native currency. [FARTHING; MITE.]

To the revolt of the Jews, which ended in the capture and destruction of Jerusalem, M. de Saulcy assigns some remarkable coins, one of which is represented in the cut beneath

חרת ציון, "The liberty of Zion." Vinestalk, with leaf and tendril.

℞ שנת שתים. "Year two." Vase. Æ.

There are other pieces of the year following, which slightly vary in their reverse-type, if indeed we be right in considering the side with the date to be the reverse.

Same obverse.

℞ שנת שלש. "Year three." Vase with cover.

M. de Saulcy remarks on these pieces: "De ces deux monnaies, celle de l'an III. est incomparablement plus rare que celle de l'an II. Cela tient probablement à ce que la liberté des Juifs était à son apogée dans la deuxième année de la guerre judaïque, et déjà à son déclin dans l'année troisième. Les pièces analogues des années I. et IV. manquent, et cela doit être. Dans la première année de la guerre judaïque, l'autonomie ne fut pas rétablie à Jérusalem; et dans la quatrième année l'anarchie et les divisions intestines avaient déjà préparé et facilité à Titus la conquête qu'il avait entreprise" (p. 154).

The subjugation of Judæa was not alone signalized by the issue of the famous Roman coins with the inscription IVDAEA CAPTA, but by that of similar Greek Imperial coins in Judæa of Titus, one of which may be thus described:—

ΑΥΤΟΚΡ ΤΙΤΟΣ ΚΑΙΣΑΡ. Head of Titus, laureate, to the right.

℞ ΙΟΥΔΑΙΑΣ ΕΑΛⱰΚΤΙΑΣ. Victory, to the right, writing upon a shield: before her a palmtree. Æ.

The proper Jewish series closes with the money of the famous Barkokab, who headed the revolt in the time of Hadrian. His most important coins are shekels, of which we here engrave one.

לחרות ירושלם. "Of the deliverance of Jerusalem." Bunch of fruits?

℞ שמעון. "Simeon." Tetrastyle temple: above which star. Æ. B. M. (Shekel.)

The half-shekel is not known, but the quarter, which is simply a restruck denarius, is common

The specimen represented below shows traces of the old types of a denarius of Trajan on both sides.

שמעון. "Simeon." Bunch of grapes.

℞ לחרותירושלם. "Of the deliverance of Jerusalem." Two trumpets. Æ. B. M.

The denarius of this time was so nearly a quarter of a shekel, that it could be used for it without occasioning any difficulty in the coinage. The copper coins of Barkokab are numerous, and like his silver pieces, have a clear reference to the money of Simon the Maccabee. It is indeed possible that the name Simon is not that of Barkokab, whom we know only by his surnames, but that of the earlier ruler, employed here to recall the foundation of Jewish autonomy. What high importance was attached to the issue of money by the Jews, is evident from the whole history of their coinage.

The money of Jerusalem, as the Roman Colonia Ælia Capitolina, has no interest here, and we conclude this article with the last coinage of an independent Jewish chief.

The chief works on Jewish coins are Bayer's treatise *De Numis Hebræo-Samaritanis*; De Saulcy's *Numismatique Judaïque*; Cavedoni's *Numismatica Biblica*, of which there is a translation under the title *Biblische Numismatik*, by A. von Werlhof, with large additions. Since writing this article we find that the translator had previously come to the conclusion that the coins attributed by M. de Saulcy to Judas Maccabæus are of Aristobulus, and that Jonathan the high-priest is Alexander Jannæus. We have to express our sincere obligations to Mr. Wigan for permission to examine his valuable collection, and have specimens drawn for this article.

R. S. P.

MONEY-CHANGERS (κολλυβιστής, Matt. xxi. 12; Mark xi. 15; John ii. 15). According to Ex. xxx. 13–15, every Israelite, whether rich or poor, who had reached or passed the age of twenty, must pay into the sacred treasury, whenever the nation was numbered, a half-shekel as an offering to Jehovah. Maimonides (*Shekal.* cap. 1) says that this was to be paid annually, and that even paupers were not exempt. The Talmud exempts priests and women. The tribute must in every case be paid in coin of the exact Hebrew half-shekel, about 15½d. sterling of English money. The premium for obtaining by exchange of other money the half-shekel of Hebrew coin, according to the Talmud, was a κόλλυβος (*collybus*), and hence the money-broker who made the exchange was called κολλυβιστής. The *collybus*, according to the same authority, was equal in value to a silver *obolus*, which has a weight of 12 grains, and its money value is about 1½d. sterling. The money-changers (κολλυβισταί) whom Christ, for their impiety, avarice, and fraudulent dealing, expelled from the Temple, were the dealers who supplied half-shekels, for such a premium as they might be able to exact, to the Jews from all parts of the world, who as-

sembled at Jerusalem during the great festivals, and were required to pay their tribute or ransom-money in the Hebrew coin; and also for other purposes of exchange, such as would be necessary in so great a resort of foreign residents to the ecclesiastical metropolis. The word τραπεζίτης (*trapezites*), which we find in Matt. xxv. 27, is a general term for banker or broker. Of this branch of business we find traces very early both in the oriental and classical literature (comp. Matt. xvii. 24–27: see Lightfoot, *Hor. Heb.* on Matt. xxi. 12; Buxtorf, *Lex. Rabbin.* 2032). C. E. S.

* The exchangers were called τραπεζίται from the tables (τράπεζαι, John ii. 15) at which they sat in the open air, with the coin before them (τὸ κέρμα collective, John ii. 15) which they were accustomed to pay out or receive in return. This is a very common sight at the present day in eastern cities, as well as in the south of Europe. H.

MONTH (חֹדֶשׁ; יֶרַח). The terms for "month" and "moon" have the same close connection in the Hebrew language, as in our own and in the Indo-European languages generally; we need only instance the familiar cases of the Greek μήν and μήνη, and the Latin *mensis*; the German *mond* and *monat*; and the Sanskrit *mâsa*, which answers to both month and moon. The Hebrew *chodesh* is perhaps more distinctive than the corresponding terms in other languages; for it expresses not simply the idea of a *lunation*, but the recurrence of a period commencing definitely with the *new moon*; it is derived from the word *châdâsh*, "new," which was transferred in the first instance to the "new moon," and in the second instance to the "month," or as it is sometimes more fully expressed, חֹדֶשׁ יָמִים, "a month of days" (Gen. xxix. 14; Num. xi. 20, 21; comp. Deut. xxi. 13; 2 K. xv. 13). The term *yerach* is derived from *yâreach*, "the moon;" it occurs occasionally in the historical (Ex. ii. 2; 1 K. vi. 37, 38, viii. 2; 2 K. xv. 13), but more frequently in the poetical portions of the Bible.

The most important point in connection with the month of the Hebrews is its length, and the mode by which it was calculated. The difficulties attending this inquiry are considerable in consequence of the scantiness of the data. Though it may fairly be presumed from the terms used that the month originally corresponded to a lunation, no reliance can be placed on the mere verbal argument to prove the exact length of the month in historical times. The word appears even in the earliest times to have passed into its secondary sense, as describing a period approaching to a lunation; for, in Gen. vii. 11, viii. 4, where we first meet with it, equal periods of 30 days are described, the interval between the 17th days of the second and the seventh months being equal to 150 days (Gen. vii. 11, viii. 3, 4). We have therefore in this instance an approximation to the solar month, and as, in addition to this, an indication of a double calculation by a solar and a lunar year has been detected in a subsequent date (for from viii. 14, compared with vii. 11, we find that the total duration of the flood exceeded the year by eleven days, in other words by the precise difference between the lunar year of 354 days and the solar one of 365 days), the passage has attracted considerable attention on the part of certain critics, who have endeavored to deduce from it arguments prejudicial to the originality of the Biblical narrative. It has been urged that the Hebrews themselves knew nothing of a solar month, that they must have derived their knowledge of it from more easterly nations (Ewald, *Jahrbüch.* 1854, p. 8), and consequently that the materials for the narrative, and the date of its composition, must be referred to .he period when close intercourse existed between the Hebrews and the Babylonians (Von Bohlen's *Introd. to Gen.* ii. 155 ff.). It is unnecessary for us to discuss in detail the arguments on which these conclusions are founded: we submit in answer to them that the *data* are insufficient to form any decided opinion at all on the matter, and that a more obvious explanation of the matter is to be found in the Egyptian system of months. To prove the first of these points, it will be only necessary to state the various calculations founded on this passage: it has been deduced from it (1) that there were 12 months of 30 days each [CHRONOLOGY]; (2) that there were 12 months of 30 days with 5 intercalated days at the end to make up the solar year (Ewald, *l. c.*); (3) that there were 7 months of 30 days, and 5 of 31 days (Von Bohlen); (4) that there were 5 months of 30 days, and 7 of 29 days (Knobel, *in Gen.* viii. 1–3): or, lastly, it is possible to cut away the foundation of any calculation whatever by assuming that a period might have elapsed between the termination of the 150 days and the 17th day of the 7th month (Ideler, *Chronol.* i. 70). But, assuming that the narrative implies equal months of 30 days, and that the date given in viii. 14, does involve the fact of a double calculation by a solar and a lunar year, it is unnecessary to refer to the Babylonians for a solution of the difficulty. The month of 30 days was in use among the Egyptians at a period long anterior to the period of the exodus, and formed the basis of their computation either by an unintercalated year of 360 days or an intercalated one of 365 (Rawlinson's *Herodotus,* ii. 283–286). Indeed, the Bible itself furnishes us with an indication of a double year, solar and lunar, in that it assigns the regulation of its length indifferently to both sun and moon (Gen. i. 14). [YEAR.]

From the time of the institution of the Mosaic Law downwards the month appears to have been a lunar one. The cycle of religious feasts, commencing with the Passover, depended not simply on the month, but on the moon (Joseph. *Ant.* iii. 10, § 5); the 14th of Abib was coincident with the full moon (Philo, *Vit. Mos.* iii. p. 686); and the new moons themselves were the occasions of regular festivals (Num. x. 10, xxviii. 11–14). The statements of the Talmudists (Mishna, *Rosh hash.* 1–3) are decisive as to the practice in their time, and the lunar month is observed by the modern Jews. The commencement of the month was generally decided by observation of the new moon, which may be detected about forty hours after the period of its conjunction with the sun: in the later times of Jewish history this was effected according to strict rule, the appearance of the new moon being reported by competent witnesses to the local authorities, who then officially announced the commence-

ment of the new month by the twice repeated word, "Mekûdash," i. e. *consecrated.*

According to the Rabbinical rule, however, there must at all times have been a little uncertainty beforehand as to the exact day on which the month would begin; for it depended not only on the appearance, but on the announcement: if the important word *Mekûdash* were not pronounced until after dark, the following day was the first of the month; if before dark, then that day (*Rosh hash,* 3, § 1). But we can hardly suppose that such a strict rule of observation prevailed in early times, nor was it in any way necessary; the recurrence of the new moon can be predicted with considerable accuracy by a calculation of the interval that would elapse either from the last new moon, from the full moon (which can be detected by a practiced eye), or from the disappearance of the waning moon. Hence, David announces definitely "To-morrow is the new moon," that being the first of the month (1 Sam. xx. 5, 24, 27) though the new moon could not have been as yet observed, and still less announced.[a] The length of the month by observation would be alternately 29 and 30 days, nor was it allowed by the Talmudists that a month should fall short of the former or exceed the latter number, whatever might be the state of the weather. The months containing only 29 days were termed in Talmudical language *châsar,* or "deficient," and those with 30 *mâlê,* or "full."

The usual number of months in a year was twelve, as implied in 1 K. iv. 7; 1 Chr. xxvii. 1–15; but inasmuch as the Hebrew months coincided, as we shall presently show, with the seasons, it follows as a matter of course that an additional month must have been inserted about every third year, which would bring the number up to thirteen. No notice, however, is taken of this month in the Bible. We have no reason to think that the intercalary month was inserted according to any exact rule; it was sufficient for practical purposes to add it whenever it was discovered that the barley harvest did not coincide with the ordinary return of the month of Abib. In the modern Jewish calendar the intercalary month is introduced seven times in every 19 years, according to the Metonic cycle, which was adopted by the Jews about A. D. 360 (Prideaux's *Connection,* i. 209 note). At the same time the length of the synodical month was fixed by R. Hillel at 29 days, 12 hours, 44 min., 3½ sec., which accords very nearly with the truth.

The usual method of designating the months was by their numerical order, *e. g.* "the second month" (Gen. vii. 11), "the fourth month" (2 K. xxv. 3); and this was generally retained even when the names were given, *e. g.* "in the month Zif, which is the second month" (1 K. vi. 1), "in the third month, that is, the month Sivan" (Esth. viii. 9). An exception occurs, however, in regard to Abib[b] in the early portion of the Bible (Ex. xiii. 4, xxiii. 15; Deut. xvi. 1), which is always mentioned by name alone, inasmuch as it was neces-

---

[a] Jahn (*Ant.* iii. 3, § 352) regards the discrepancy of the dates in 2 K. xxv. 27, and Jer. lii. 31, as originating in the different modes of computing, by astronomical calculation and by observation. It is more probable that it arises from a mistake of a copyist, substituting ז for ח, as a similar discrepancy exists in 2 K. xxv. 19 and Jer. lii. 25, without admitting of similar explanation.

[b] We doubt indeed whether Abib was really a proper name. In the first place it is always accompanied by the article, "*the* Abib;" in the second place, it appears almost impossible that it could have been superseded by Nisan, if it had been regarded as a proper name, considering the important associations connected with it.

arily coincident with a certain season, while the numerical order might have changed from year to year. The practice of the writers of the post-Babylonian period in this respect varied: Ezra, Esther, and Zechariah specify both the names and the numerical order; Nehemiah only the former; Daniel and Haggai only the latter. The names of the months belong to two distinct periods; in the first place we have those peculiar to the period of Jewish independence, of which four only, even including Abib, which we hardly regard as a proper name, are mentioned, namely, Abib, in which the Passover fell (Ex. xiii. 4, xxiii. 15, xxxiv. 18; Deut. xvi. 1), and which was established as the first month in commemoration of the exodus (Ex. xii. 2); Zif, the second month (1 K. vi. 1, 37); Bul, the eighth (1 K. vi. 38); and Ethanim, the seventh (1 K. viii. 2) — the three latter being noticed only in connection with the building and dedication of the Temple, so that we might almost infer that their use was restricted to the official documents of the day, and that they never attained the popular use which the later names had. Hence it is not difficult to account for their having been superseded. In the second place we have the names which prevailed subsequently to the Babylonish Captivity; of these the following seven appear in the Bible: Nisan, the first, in which the Passover was held (Neh. ii. 1; Esth. iii. 7); Sivan, the third (Esth. viii. 9; Bar. i. 8); Elul, the sixth (Neh. vi. 15; 1 Macc. xiv. 27); Chisleu, the ninth (Neh. i. 1; Zech. vii. 1; 1 Macc. i. 54); Tebeth, the tenth (Esth. ii. 16); Sebat, the eleventh (Zech. i. 7; 1 Macc. xvi. 14); and Adar, the twelfth (Esth. iii. 7, viii. 12; 2 Macc. xv. 36). The names of the remaining five occur in the Talmud and other works; they were Iyar, the second (Targum, 2 Chr. xxx. 2); Tammuz, the fourth (Mishn. Taan. 4, § 5); Ab, the fifth, and Tisri, the seventh (Rosh hash. 1, § 3); and Marcheshvan, the eighth (Taam. i. § 3; Joseph. Ant. i. 3, § 3). The name of the intercalary month was Veadar,[a] i. e. the additional Adar.

The first of these series of names is of Hebrew origin, and has reference to the characteristics of the seasons — a circumstance which clearly shows that the months returned at the same period of the year, in other words, that the Jewish year was a solar one. Thus Abib[b] was the month of "ears of corn," Zif[c] the month of "blossom," and Bul[d] the month of "rain." With regard to Ethanim[e] there may be some doubt, as the usual explanation, "the month of violent or, rather, incessant rain," is decidedly inappropriate to the seventh month. With regard to the second series, both the origin and the meaning of the name is controverted. It was the opinion of the Talmudists that the names were introduced by the Jews who returned from the Babylonish Captivity (Jerusalem Talmud, Rosh hash. 1, § 1), and they are certainly used exclusively by writers of the post-Babylonian period. It was therefore, perhaps natural to seek for their origin in the Persian language, and this was done some years since by Benfey (Monatsnamen) in a manner more ingenious than satisfactory. The view, though accepted to a certain extent by Gesenius in his Thesaurus, has been since abandoned, both on philological grounds and because it meets with no confirmation from the monumental documents of ancient Persia.[f] The names are probably borrowed from the Syrians,[g] in whose regular calendar we find names answering to Tisri, Sebat, Adar, Nisan, Iyar, Tammuz, Ab, and Elul (Ideler, Chronol. i. 430), while Chisleu and Tebeth[h] appear on the Palmyrene inscriptions (Gesen. Thesaur. pp. 702, 543). Sivan may be borrowed from the Assyrians, who appear to have had a month so named, sacred to Sin or the moon (Rawlinson, i. 615). Marcheshvan, coinciding as it did with the rainy season in Palestine, was probably a purely Hebrew[i] term. With regard to the meaning of the Syrian names we can only conjecture from the case of Tammuz, which undoubtedly refers to the festival of the deity of that name mentioned in Ez. viii. 14, that some of them may have been derived from the names of deities.[k] Hebrew roots are suggested by Gesenius for others, but without much confidence.[l]

---

[a] The name of the intercalary month originated in its position in the calendar after Adar and before Nisan. The opinion of Ideler (Chronol. i. 589), that the first Adar was regarded as the intercalary month, because the feast of Purim was held in Veadar in the intercalary year, has little foundation.

[b] אָבִיב [See CHRONOLOGY.]

[c] זִו or זִיו, or, more fully, as in the Targum, זִיו, נִצָּנָא, "the bloom of flowers." Another explanation is given in Rawlinson's Herodotus, i. 622; namely, that Ziv is the same as the Assyrian Giv, "bull," and answers to the zodiacal sign of Taurus.

[d] בּוּל. The name occurs in a recently discovered Phœnician inscription (Ewald, Jahrb. 1856, p. 135). A cognate term, מַבּוּל, is used for the "deluge" (Gen. vi. 17, &c.); but there is no ground for the inference drawn by Von Bohlen (Introd. to Gen. ii. 156), that there is any allusion to the month Bul.

[e] Thenius on 1 K. viii. 2, suggests that the true name was אֵרָנִים, as in the LXX. 'Αθανίμ, and that its meaning was the "month of gifts," i. e., of fruit, from תָּנַח "to give." There is the same peculiarity in this as in Abib, namely, the addition of the definite article.

[f] The names of the months, as read on the Behistun inscriptions, Garmapada, Bagayadish, Atriyata, etc.,

bear no resemblance to the Hebrew names (Rawlinson's Herodotus, ii. 593-596).

[g] The names of the months appear to have been in many instances of local use: for instance, the calendar of Heliopolis contains the names of Ag and Gelon (Ideler, i. 440), which do not appear in the regular Syrian calendar, while that of Palmyra, again, contains names unknown to either.

[h] The resemblance in sound between Tebeth and the Egyptian Tobi, as well as its correspondence in the order of the months, was noticed by Jerome, ad Ez xxxix. 1.

[i] Von Bohlen connects it with the root רֶחֶשׁ (רָחַשׁ), "to boil over" (Introd. to Gen. ii. 156). The modern Jews consider it a compound word, mar, "drop," and Cheshvan, the former betokening that it was wet, and the latter being the proper name of the month (De Sola's Mishna, p. 168 note).

[k] We draw notice to the similarity between Elul and the Arabic name of Venus Urania, Alil-at (Herod. iii. 8); and again between Adar, the Egyptian Athor, and the Syrian Atar-gatis.

[l] The Hebrew forms of the names are:— בִּיסָן, תִּשְׁרֵי, אֱלוּל, אָב, תַּמּוּז, סִינָן, אִיָר, אָדָר, שְׁבָט, טֵבֵת, כִּסְלוּ, מַרְ חֶשְׁוָן, and וְאֲדָר.

Subsequently to the establishment of the Syro-Macedonian empire, the use of the Macedonian calendar was gradually adopted for purposes of literature or intercommunication with other countries. Josephus, for instance, constantly uses the Macedonian months, even where he gives the Hebrew names (e. g. in *Ant.* i. 3, § 3, he identifies Marcheshvan with Dius, and Nisan with Xanthicus, and in xii. 7, § 6, Chisleu with Appellæus). The only instance in which the Macedonian names appear in the Bible is in 2 Macc. xi. 30, 33, 38, where we have notice of Xanthicus in combination with another named Dioscorinthius (ver. 21), which does not appear in the Macedonian calendar. Various explanations have been offered in respect to the latter. Any attempt to connect it with the Macedonian Dius fails on account of the interval being too long to suit the narrative, Dius being the first and Xanthicus the sixth month. The opinion of Scaliger (*Emend. Temp.* ii. 94), that it was the Macedonian intercalary month, rests on no foundation whatever, and Ideler's assumption that that intercalary month preceded Xanthicus must be rejected along with it (*Chronol.* i. 399). It is most probable that the author of 2 Macc. or a copyist was familiar with the Cretan calendar, which contained a month named Dioscurus, holding the same place in the calendar as the Macedonian Dystrus (Ideler, i. 426), i. e. immediately before Xanthicus, and that he substituted one for the other. This view derives some confirmation from the Vulgate rendering, *Dioscorus.* We have further to notice the reference to the Egyptian calendar in 3 Macc. vi. 38, Pachon and Epiphi in that passage answering to Pachons and Epep, the ninth and eleventh months (Wilkinson, *Anc. Egyp.* i. 14, 2d ser.).

The identification of the Jewish months with our own cannot be effected with precision on account of the variations that must inevitably exist between the lunar and the solar month, each of the former ranging over portions of two of the latter. It must, therefore, be understood that the following remarks apply to the general identity on an average of years. As the Jews still retain the names Nisan, etc., it may appear at first sight needless to do more than refer the reader to a modern almanac, and this would have been the case if it were not evident that the modern Nisan does not correspond to the ancient one. At present Nisan answers to March, but in early times it coincided with April; for the barley harvest — the first fruits of which were to be presented on the 15th of that month (Lev. xxiii. 10) — does not take place even in the warm district about Jericho until the middle of April, and in the upland districts not before the end of that month (Robinson's *Researches*, i. 551, iii. 102, 145). To the same effect Josephus (*Ant.* ii. 14, § 6) synchronizes Nisan with the Egyptian Pharmuth, which commenced on the 27th of March (Wilkinson, *l. c.*), and with the Macedonian Xanthicus, which answers generally to the early part of April, though considerable variation occurs in the local calendars as to its place (comp. Ideler, i. 435, 442). He further informs us (iii. 10, § 5) that the Passover

took place when the sun was in Aries, which it does not enter until near the end of March. Assuming from these data that Abib or Nisan answers to April, then Zif or Iyar would correspond with May, Sivan with June, Tammuz with July, Ab with August, Elul with September, Ethanim or Tisri with October, Bul or Marcheshvan with November, Chisleu with December, Tebeth with January, Sebat with February, and Adar with March.   W. L. B.

* **MONUMENTS** (נְצֻרִים, σπήλαια, Is. lxv. 4). The precise meaning of the Heb. word, as employed here (elsewhere rendered *preserved*, Is. xlix. 6, *hidden*, xlviii. 6, *besieged*, i. 8; Ezek. vi. 12, *subtil*, Prov. vii. 10) is somewhat obscure. It refers apparently to certain retired places, such perhaps as the *adyta* of heathen temples (Vulg. *delubra idolorum*) or (observe the parallelism) sepulchral caverns (less probably, *lune watch-towers*, see Fürst, *Lex.* s. v.), resorted to for necromantic purposes, or (as LXX. διὰ ἐνύπνια) in order to obtain prophetic dreams.   D. S. T.

MOON (לְבָנָה; יָרֵחַ). It is worthy of observation that neither of the terms by which the Hebrews designated the moon contains any reference to its office or essential character; they simply describe it by the accidental quality of color, *yârêach*, signifying "pale," or "yellow," *lebânâh*,[a] "white." The Indo-European languages recognized the moon as the measurer of time, and have expressed its office in this respect, all the terms applied to it, μήν, *moon*, etc., finding a common element with μετρεῖν, to measure, in the Sanscrit root *ma* (Pott's *Etym. Forsch.* i. 194). The nations with whom the Hebrews were brought into more immediate contact worshipped the moon under various designations expressive of its influence in the kingdom of nature. The exception which the Hebrew language thus presents would appear to be based on the repugnance to nature-worship, which runs through their whole system, and which induced the precautionary measure of giving it in reality no name at all, substituting the circuitous expressions "lesser light" (Gen. i. 16), the "pale," or the "white." The same tendency to avoid the notion of personality may perhaps be observed in the indifference to gender, *yârêach* being masculine, and *lebânâh* feminine.

The moon held an important place in the kingdom of nature, as known to the Hebrews. In the history of the creation (Gen. i. 14–16), it appears simultaneously with the sun, and is described in terms which imply its independence of that body as far as its light is concerned. Conjointly with the sun, it was appointed "for signs and for seasons, and for days and years;" though in this respect it exercised a more important influence, if by the "seasons" we understand the great religious festivals of the Jews, as is particularly stated in Ps. civ. 19 ("He appointed the moon for seasons"), and more at length in Ecclus. xliii. 6, 7. Besides this, it had its special office in the distribution of light; it was appointed "to rule over the night," as the sun over the day, and thus the appearance of the two founts of light served "to

---

[a] The term *lebânâh* occurs only three times in the Bible (Cant. vi. 10; Is. xxiv. 23, xxx. 26). Another explanation of the term is proposed in Rawlinson's *Herodotus*, i. 615, to the effect that it has reference to *libnâh*, "a brick," and embodies the Babylonian

notion of *Sin*, the moon, as being the god of architecture. The strictly parallel use of *yârêach* in Joel ii. 31 and Ez. xxxii. 7, as well as the analogy in the sense of the two words, seems a strong argument against the view.

divide between the day and between the night."
In order to enter fully into this idea, we must
remember both the greater brilliancy *a* of the moon-
light in eastern countries, and the larger amount
of work, particularly travelling, that is carried on
by its aid. The appeals to sun and moon conjointly are hence more frequent in the literature
of the Hebrews than they might otherwise have
been (Josh. x. 12; Ps. lxxii. 5, 7; Eccl. xii. 2;
Is. xxiv. 23, &c.); in some instances, indeed, the
moon receives a larger amount of attention than
the sun (e. g. Ps. viii. 3, lxxxix. 37 *b*). The inferiority of its light is occasionally noticed, as in
Gen. i. 16; in Cant. vi. 10, where the epithets
"fair," and "clear " (or rather *spotless*, and hence
extremely brilliant) are applied respectively to moon
and sun; and in Is. xxx. 26, where the equalizing
of its light to that of the sun conveys an image of
the highest glory. Its influence on vegetable or
animal life receives but little notice; the expression
in Deut. xxxiii. 14, which the A. V. refers to the
moon, signifies rather *months* as the period of
ripening fruits. The coldness of the night-dews is
prejudicial to the health, and particularly to the
eyes of those who are exposed to it, and the idea
expressed in Ps. cxxi. 6 (" The moon shall not smite
thee by night ") may have reference to the general or the particular evil effect: blindness is still
attributed to the influence of the moon's rays on
those who sleep under the open heaven, both by
the Arabs (Carne's *Letters*, i. 88), and by Europeans. The connection between the moon's phases
and certain forms of disease, whether madness or
epilepsy, is expressed in the Greek σελληνιάζεσθαι
(Matt. iv. 24, xvii. 15), in the Latin derivative
" lunatic," and in our " moon-struck."

The worship of the moon was extensively practiced by the nations of the East, and under a
variety of aspects. In Egypt it was honored under
the form of Isis, and was one of the only two
deities which commanded the reverence of all the
Egyptians (*Herod.* ii. 42, 47). In Syria it was
represented by that one of the Ashtaroth (i. e. of
the varieties which the goddess Astarte, or Ashtoreth, underwent) surnamed " Karnaim," from
the horns of the crescent moon by which she was
distinguished. [ASHTORETH.] In Babylonia, it
formed one of a triad in conjunction with Æther,
and the sun, and, under the name of Sin, received
the honored titles of " Lord of the month," "King
of the Gods," etc. (Rawlinson's *Herodotus*, i.
614.) There are indications of a very early introduction into the countries adjacent to Palestine of
a species of worship distinct from any that we have
hitherto noticed, namely, of the direct homage of
the heavenly bodies, sun, moon, and stars, which
is the characteristic of Sabianism. The first notice
we have of this is in Job (xxxi. 26, 27), and it is
observable that the warning of Moses (Deut. iv.
19) is directed against this nature worship, rather

than against the form of moon-worship, which the
Israelites must have witnessed in Egypt. At a
later period,*c* however, the worship of the moon in
its grosser form of idol-worship was introduced
from Syria: we have no evidence indeed that the
Ashtoreth of the Zidonians, whom Solomon introduced (1 K. xi. 5), was identified in the minds of
the Jews with the moon, but there can be no doubt
that the moon was worshipped under the form
of an image in Manasseh's reign, although
(*Phōniz.* i. 66, 164) has taken up the opposite
view; for we are distinctly told that the king
" made an *asherah* (A. V. "grove "), i. e. an *image*
of Ashtoreth, and worshipped all the host of
heaven " (2 K. xxi. 3), which *asherah* was destroyed by Josiah, and the priests that burned
incense to the moon were put down (xxiii. 4, 5).
At a somewhat later period the worship of the
" queen of heaven " was practiced in Palestine (Jer.
vii. 18, xliv. 17); the title has been generally supposed to belong to the moon, but we think it more
probable that the Oriental Venus is intended, for
the following reasons: (1) the title of *Urania* " of
heaven " was peculiarly appropriated to Venus,
whose worship was borrowed by the Persians from
the Arabians and Assyrians (*Herod.* i. 131, 199):
(2) the votaries of this goddess, whose chief function it was to preside over births, were women, and
we find that in Palestine the married women are
specially noticed as taking a prominent part: (3)
the peculiarity of the title, which occurs only in
the passages quoted, looks as if the worship was a
novel one; and this is corroborated by the term
cavvin *d* applied to the "cakes," which is again so
peculiar that the LXX. has retained it (χαυών),
deeming it to be, as it not improbably was, a foreign word. Whether the Jews derived their knowledge of the "queen of heaven " from the Philistines, who possessed a very ancient temple of Venus
Urania at Askalon (*Herod.* i. 105), or from the
Egyptians, whose god Athor was of the same character, is uncertain.

In the figurative language of Scripture the moon
is frequently noticed as presaging events of the
greatest importance through the temporary or permanent withdrawal of its light (Is. xiii. 10; Joel
ii. 31; Matt. xxiv. 29; Mark xiii. 24); in these
and similar passages we have an evident allusion to
the mysterious awe with which eclipses were viewed
by the Hebrews in common with other nations of
antiquity. With regard to the symbolic meaning
of the moon in Rev. xii. 1, we have only to observe
that the ordinary explanations, namely, the sublunary world, or the changeableness of its affairs,
seem to derive no authority from the language of
the O. T., or from the ideas of the Hebrews.

W. L. B.

MOON, NEW. [NEW MOON.]

* **MOONS** or **LUNETTES** as ornaments.
[BELLS, CAMELS, TIRES.]

---

a The Greek σελήνη, from σέλας, expresses this idea
of brilliancy more vividly than the Hebrew terms.

b In the former of these passages the sun may be
included in the general expression "heavens" in the
preceding verse. In the latter, " the faithful witness
in heaven " is undoubtedly the moon, and not the
rainbow, as some explain it. The regularity of the
moon's changes impressed the mind with a sense of
durability and certainty; and hence the moon was
specially qualified to be a witness to God's promise.

c The ambiguous expression of Hosea (ver. 7),

"Now shall a month devour them with their portions." is understood by Bunsen (*Bibelwerk*, in loc.)
as referring to an idolatrous worship of the new moon.
It is more generally understood of "a month " as a
short space of time. Hitzig (*Comment.* in loc.) explains it in a novel manner of the crescent moon, as
a symbol of destruction, from its resemblance to a
scimitar.

d כַּוָּן.

MOOSI'AS (Μοοσίας; [Vat. Μοοσυιας; Alex. Μοος Ξιας:] *Moosias*). Apparently the same as MAASEIAH 4 (1 Esdr. ix. 31; comp. Ezr. x. 30).

MO'RASTHITE, THE (הַמּרַשְׁתִּי; in Micah, הַמֹּרַשְׁתִּי: ὁ μωραθείτης, ὁ τοῦ Μωρασθεί; Alex. in Micah, Μωραθει; de Morasthi, *Morasthites*), that is, the native of a place named MORESHETH, such being the regular formation in Hebrew.

It occurs twice (Jer. xxvi. 18: Mic. i. 1), each time as the description of the prophet MICAH.

The Targum, on each occasion, renders the word " of Mareshah; " but the derivation from Mareshah would be Mareshathite, and not Morasthite, or more accurately Morashtite.   G.

MOR'DECAI [3 syl.] (מָרְדֳּכַי) [see below]: Μαρδοχαῖος: *Mardochaeus*), the deliverer, under Divine Providence, of the Jews from the destruction plotted against them by Haman [ESTHER], the chief minister of Xerxes: the institutor of the feast of Purim [PURIM], and probably the author as well as the hero of the Book of Esther, which is sometimes called the book of Mordecai.[a] The Scripture narrative tells us concerning him that he was a Benjamite, and one of the Captivity, residing in Shushan, whether or not in the king's service before Esther was queen, does not appear certainly. From the time, however, of Esther being queen he was one of those " who sat in the king's gate." In this situation he saved the king's life by discovering the conspiracy of two of the eunuchs to kill him. When the decree for the massacre of all the Jews in the empire was known, it was at his earnest advice and exhortation that Esther undertook the perilous task of interceding with the king on their behalf. He might feel the more impelled to exert himself to save them, as he was himself the cause of the meditated destruction of his countrymen. Whether, as some think, his refusal to bow before Haman arose from religious scruples, as if such salutation as was practiced in Persia (προσκύνησις) were akin to idolatry, or whether, as seems far more probable, he refused from a stern unwillingness as a Jew to bow before an Amalekite, in either case the affront put by him upon Haman was the immediate cause of the fatal decree. Anyhow, he and Esther were the instruments in the hand of God of averting the threatened ruin. The concurrence of Esther's favorable reception by the king with the Providential circumstance of the passage in the Medo-Persian chronicles, which detailed Mordecai's fidelity in disclosing the conspiracy, being read to the king that very night, before Haman came to ask leave to hang him; the striking incident of Haman being made the instrument of the exaltation and honor of his most hated adversary, which he rightly interpreted as the presage of his own downfall, and finally the hanging of Haman and his sons upon the very gallows which he had reared for Mordecai, while Mordecai occupied Haman's post as vizier of the Persian monarchy;

are incidents too well known to need to be further dwelt upon. It will be more useful, probably, to add such remarks as may tend to point out Mordecai's place in sacred, profane, and rabbinical history respectively. The first thing is to fix his date. This is pointed out with great particularity by the writer himself, not only by the years of the king's reign, but by his own genealogy in ch. ii. 5, 6. Some, however, have understood this passage as stating that Mordecai himself was taken captive with Jeconiah. But that any one who had been taken captive by Nebuchadnezzar in the 8th year of his reign should be vizier after the 12th year of any Persian king among the successors of Cyrus, is obviously impossible. Besides, too, the absurdity of supposing the ordinary laws of human life to be suspended in the case of any person mentioned in Scripture, when the sacred history gives no such intimation, there is a peculiar defiance of probability in the supposition that the cousin german of the youthful Esther, her father's brother's son should be of an age ranging from 90 to 170 years, at the time that she was chosen to be queen on account of her youth and beauty. But not only is this interpretation of Esth. ii. 5, 6, excluded by chronology, but the rules of grammatical propriety equally point out, not Mordecai, but Kish, as being the person who was taken captive by Nebuchadnezzar at the time when Jeconiah was carried away. Because, if it had been intended to speak of Mordecai as led captive, the ambiguity would easily have been avoided by either placing the clause אֲשֶׁר הָגְלָה, etc., immediately after בְּשׁוּשַׁן הַבִּירָה, and then adding his name and genealogy, וּשְׁמוֹ מ, or else by writing וְהוּא instead of אֲשֶׁר, at the beginning of verse 6. Again, as the sentence stands, the distribution of the copulative וְ distinctly connects the sentence וַיְהִי אֹמֵן in ver. 7, with הָיָה in ver. 5, showing that three things are predicated of Mordecai: (1) that he lived in Shushan; (2) that his name was Mordecai, son of Jair, son of Shimei, son of Kish the Benjamite who was taken captive with Jehoiachin; (3) that he brought up Esther. This genealogy does then fix with great certainty the age of Mordecai. He was great grandson of a contemporary of Jehoiachin. Now four generations cover 120 years — and 120 years from B. C. 599 bring us to B. C. 479, i. e. to the 6th year of the reign of Xerxes; thus confirming with singular force the arguments which led to the conclusion that Ahasuerus is Xerxes. [AHASUERUS.][b] The carrying back the genealogy of a captive to the time of the Captivity has an obvious propriety, as connecting the captives with the family record preserved in the public genealogies, before the Captivity, just as an American would be likely to carry up his pedigree to the ancestor who emigrated from England. And now it would seem both possible and probable (though it cannot be certainly

---

[a] De Wette thinks that " the opinion that Mordecai wrote the book does not deserve to be confuted," although the author " designed that the book should be considered as written by Mordecai." His translator adds, that " the greatest part of the Jewish and Christian scholars " refer it to him. But he adds, " more modern writers, with better judgment, affirm only their ignorance of the authorship " (*Introd.* ii. 345-

347). But the objections to Mordecai's authorship are only such as, if valid, would impugn the truth and authenticity of the book itself.

[b] Justin has the singular statement, " Primum Xerxes, rex Persarum, Judæos domuit " (lib. xxxvi. cap. iii.). May not this arise from a confused knowledge of the events recorded 'n Esther?

proved) that the Mordecai mentioned in the duplicate passage, Ezr. ii. 2; Neh. vii. 7, as one of the
leaders of the captives who returned from time to
time from Babylon to Judæa [EZRA], was the
same as Mordecai of the book of Esther. It is
very probable that on the death of Xerxes, or possibly during his lifetime, he may have obtained
leave to lead back such Jews as were willing to accompany him, and that he did so. His age need
not have exceeded 50 or 60 years, and his character
points him out as likely to lead his countrymen
back from exile, if he had the opportunity. The
name Mordecai not occurring elsewhere, makes this
supposition the more probable.

As regards his place in *profane* history, the domestic annals of the reign of Xerxes are so scanty,
that it would not surprise us to find no mention
of Mordecai. But there is a person named by
Ctesias, who probably saw the very chronicles of
the kings of Media and Persia referred to in Esth.
x. 2, whose name and character present some
points of resemblance with Mordecai, namely, Matacas, or Natacas (as the name is variously written),
whom he describes as Xerxes's chief favorite, and
the most powerful of them all. His brief notice
of him in these words, ἠμπαρρέντων δὲ μέγιστον
ἠδύνατο Ναταxᾶς, is in exact agreement with the
description of Mordecai, Esth. ix. 4, x. 2, 3. He
further relates of him, that when Xerxes after his
return from Greece had commissioned Megabyzus
to go and plunder the temple of Apollo at Delphi,[a]
upon his refusal, he sent Matacas the eunuch, to
insult the god, and to plunder his property, which
Matacas did, and returned to Xerxes. It is obvious how grateful to the feelings of a Jew, such
as Mordecai was, would be a commission to dese-
crate and spoil a heathen temple. There is also
much probability in the selection of a Jew to be
his prime minister by a monarch of such decided
iconoclastic propensities as Xerxes is known to have
had (Prideaux, *Connect.* i. 231-233). Xerxes
would doubtless see much analogy between the
Magian tenets of which he was such a zealous patron, and those of the Jews' religion; just as Pliny
actually reckons Moses (whom he couples with Jannes) among the leaders of the Magian sect, in the
very same passage in which he relates that Osthanes
the Magian author and heresiarch accompanied
Xerxes in his Greek expedition, and widely diffused
the Magian doctrines (lib. xxx. ch. i. § 2); and in
§ 4 seems to identify Christianity also with Magic.
From the context it seems highly probable that this
notice of Moses and of Jannes may be derived from
the work of Osthanes, and if so, the probable intercourse of Osthanes with Mordecai would readily
account for his mention of them. The point, however, here insisted upon is, that the known hatred
of Xerxes to idol-worship makes his selection of a
Jew for his prime minister very probable, and that
there are strong points of resemblance in what is
thus related of Matacas, and what we know from
Scripture of Mordecai. Again, that Mordecai was,
what Matacas is related to have been, a eunuch,
seems not improbable from his having neither wife
nor child, from his bringing up his cousin Esther

in his own house,[b] from his situation in the king's
gate, from his access to the court of the women,
and from his being raised to the highest post of
power by the king, which we know from Persian
history was so often the case with the king's
eunuchs. With these points of agreement between
them, there is sufficient resemblance in their names
to add additional probability to the supposition of
their identity. The most plausible etymology usually given for the name *Mordecai* is that favored
by Gesenius, who connects it with Merodach the
Babylonian idol (called Mardok in the cuneiform
inscriptions), and which appears in the names Mes-
esai Mordacus, Sisi-Mordachus, in nearly the same
form as in the Greek, Μαρδοχαῖος. But it is highly
improbable that the name of a Babylonian idol should
have been given to him under the Persian dynasty,[c]
and it is equally improbable that Mordecai should
have been taken into the king's service before the
commencement of the Persian dynasty. If then
we suppose the original form of the name to have
been Matacai, it would easily in the Chaldee orthography become Mordecai, just as פַּרְסָא is
for קְמָא, שֵׁרְבִים for שֵׁבְט, דַּרְמְשָׂה, דְּמֶשֶׂק for
דַּמֶּשֶׂק, etc. In the Targum of Esther he is said
to be called Mordecai, because he was like לְמֵירָא
דַּכְיָא, "to pure myrrh."

As regards his place in *Rabbinical* estimation,
Mordecai, as is natural, stands very high. The
interpolations in the Greek book of Esther are one
indication of his popularity with his countrymen.
The Targum (of late date) shows that this increased
rather than diminished with the lapse of centuries.
There Shimei in Mordecai's genealogy is identified
with Shimei the son of Gera who cursed David,
and it is said that the reason why David would not
permit him to be put to death then was, that it
was revealed to him that Mordecai and Esther
should descend from him; but that in his old age,
when this reason no longer applied, he was slain.
It is also said of Mordecai that he knew *the seventy
languages*, i. e. the languages of all the nations
mentioned in Gen. x., which the Jews count as
seventy nations, and that his age exceeded 400
years (*Juchasin* ap. Wolf, and Stehelin, *Rabb.
Liter.* i. 179). He is continually designated by the
appellation צַדִּיקָא, "the Just," and the amplifications of Esth. viii. 15 abound in the most glowing descriptions of the splendid robes, and Persian
buskins, and Median scimitars, and golden crowns,
and the profusion of precious stones and Macedonian
gold, on which was engraved a view of Jerusalem,
and of the phylactery over the crown, and the
streets strewed with myrtle, and the attendants,
and the heralds with trumpets, all proclaiming the
glory of Mordecai and the exaltation of the Jewish
people. Benjamin of Tudela mentions the ruins of
Shushan and the remains of the palace of Ahasuerus as still existing in his day, but places the
tomb of Mordecai and Esther at Hamadan, or Ecbatana (p. 128). Others, however, place the tomb

---

[a] It seems probable that some other temple, not
that at Delphi, was at this time ordered by Xerxes to
be spoiled, as no other writer mentions it. It might
be that of Apollo Didymæus, near Miletus, which was
destroyed by Xerxes after his return (Strab. xiv. cap.
i. § 5).

[b] To account for this, the Targum adds that he was
75 years old.

[c] Mr. Rawlinson (*Herod.* i. 270) points out Mr. Layard's conclusion (*Nin.* ii. 441), that the Persians
adopted generally the Assyrian religion, as "quite a
mistake."

of Mordecai in Susa, and that of Esther in or near Baram in Galilee (note to Asher's *Benj. of Tud.* p. 166). With reference to the above-named palace of Ahasuerus at Shushan, it may be added that considerable remains of it were discovered by Mr. Loftus's excavations in 1852, and that he thinks the plan of the great colonnade, of which he found the bases remaining, corresponds remarkably to the description of the palace of Ahasuerus in Esth. i. (Loftus, *Chaldæa,* ch. xxviii.). It was built or begun by Darius Hystaspis.   A. C. H.

MO'REH [מוֹרֶה, *archer* or *teacher*; perh. *fruitful*]. A local name of central Palestine, one of the very oldest that has come down to us. It occurs in two connections.

1. THE PLAIN, or PLAINS (or, as it should rather be rendered, the OAK or OAKS) OF MOREH (אֵלוֹן מוֹרֶה and אֵלוֹנֵי; Samar. in both cases, אֵלוֹן מֹרֶא: ἡ δρῦς ἡ ὑψηλή: convallis illustris, vallis tendens [et intrans procul]), the first of that long succession of sacred and venerable trees which dignified the chief places of Palestine, and formed not the least interesting link in the chain which so indissolubly united the land to the history of the nation.

The Oak of Moreh was the first recorded halting-place of Abram after his entrance into the land of Canaan (Gen. xii. 6). Here Jehovah "appeared" to him, and here he built the first of the series of altars[a] which marked the various spots of his residence in the Promised Land, and dedicated it "to Jehovah, who appeared[b] unto him" (ver. 7). It was at the "place of [c]Shechem" (xii. 6), close to (אֵצֶל) the mountains of Ebal and Gerizim (Deut. xi. 30), where the Samar. Cod. adds "over against Shechem."

There is reason for believing that this place, the scene of so important an occurrence in Abram's early residence in Canaan, may have been also that of one even more important, the crisis of his later life, the offering of Isaac, on a mountain in "the land of Moriah." [MORIAH.]

A trace of this ancient name, curiously reappearing after many centuries, is probably to be found in Morthia, which is given on some ancient coins as one of the titles of Neapolis, *i. e.* Shechem, and by Pliny and Josephus as Mamortha[d] or Mabortha (Reland, *Diss.* iii. § 8). The latter states (*B. J.* iv. 8, § 1), that "it was the name by which the place was called by the country-people" (ἐπιχώριοι), who thus kept alive the ancient appellation, just as the peasants of Hebron did that of Kirjath-arba down to the date of Sir John Maundeville's visit. [See vol. ii. p. 1565 *a*, and note.]

Whether the oaks of Moreh had any connection with

2. THE HILL OF MOREH (גִּבְעַת הַמּוֹרֶה: Γαβααθαμωραί [Vat. -μωρα]; Alex. απο του βωμου του αβωρ: collis excelsus), at the foot of which the Midianites and Amalekites were encamped before Gideon's attack upon them (Judg. vii. 1), seems, to say the least, most uncertain. Copious as are the details furnished of that great event of Jewish history, those which enable us to judge of its precise situation are very scanty. But a comparison of Judg. vi. 33 with vii. 1 makes it evident that it lay in the valley of Jezreel, rather on the north side of the valley, and north also of the eminence on which Gideon's little band of heroes was clustered. At the foot of this latter eminence was the spring of Ain-Charod (A. V. "the well of Harod"), and a sufficient sweep of the plain intervened between it and the hill Moreh to allow of the encampment of the Amalekites. No doubt — although the fact is not mentioned — they kept near the foot of Mount Moreh, for the sake of some spring or springs which issued from its base, as the Ain-Charod did from that on which Gideon was planted. These conditions are most accurately fulfilled if we assume *Jebel ed-Duhy,* the "Little Hermon" of the modern travellers, to be Moreh, the *Ain-Jalúd* to be the spring of Harod, and Gideon's position to have been on the northeast slope of *Jebel Fukúa* (Mount Gilboa), between the village of *Nuris* and the last-mentioned spring. Between *Ain Jalúd* and the foot of the "Little Hermon," a space of between 2 and 3 miles intervenes, ample in extent for the encampment even of the enormous horde of the Amalekites. In its general form this identification is due to Professor Stanley.[e] The desire to find Moreh nearer to Shechem, where the "oak of Moreh" was, seems to have induced Mr. Van de Velde to place the scene of Gideon's battle many miles to the south of the valley of Jezreel, "possibly on the plain of *Túbas* or of *Yásir*;" in which case the encampment of the Israelites may have been on the ridge between *Wadi Ferra'* and *Wadi Túbas,* near *Burj el-Ferra'* (*Syr. & Pal.* ii. 341-2). But this involves the supposition of a movement in the position of the Amalekites, for which there is no warrant either in the narrative or in the circumstances of the case; and at any rate, in the present state of our knowledge, we may rest tolerably certain that *Jebel ed-Duhy* is the HILL OF MOREH.
          G.

MORE'SHETH-GATH' (מוֹרֶשֶׁת גַּת: κληρονομία Γέθ: hæreditas Geth), a place named by the prophet Micah only (Mic. i. 14), in company with Lachish, Achzib, Mareshah, and other towns of the lowland district of Judah. His words, "therefore shalt thou give presents to Moresheth-gath," are explained by Ewald (*Propheten,* 330, 331) as referring to Jerusalem, and as containing an allusion

---

[a] It may be roughly said that Abraham built altars; Isaac dug wells; Jacob erected stones.

[b] הַפִּרְאֶה. This is a play upon the same word which, as we shall see afterwards, performs an important part in the name of MORIAH.

[c] Ecclus. l. 26 perhaps contains a play on the name Moreh — "that foolish people (ὁ λαὸς ὁ μωρός) who dwell in Sichem." If the pun existed in the Hebrew text it may have been between Sichem and Sichor (drunken).

[d] This form is possibly due to a confusion between Moreh and Mamre. (See Reland as above.)

[e] * This identification of Moreh and Harod (ascribed

above to Stanley) is suggested also in Bertheau's *Richter u. Ruth,* p. 119, and Bunsen's *Bibelwerk* on Judg. vii. 1. The reasons for this view are less obvious in the A. V., owing to the mistranslation of עַיִן by "well" (which would be strictly בְּאֵר), instead of "fountain," and of עַל by "beside," instead of "above." The identification of the places in question depends on these intimations. The position of Gideon "above the fountain of Harod" is evident from vii. 8, where it is said that the host of Midian were below him in the valley   H.

to the signification of the name Moresheth, which, though not so literal as the play on those of Achzib and Mareshah, is yet tolerably obvious: "Therefore shalt thou, O Jerusalem, give compensation to More-sheth-gath, itself only the possession of another city."

Micah was himself the native of a place called Moresheth, since he is designated, in the only two cases in which his name is mentioned, " Micah the Morashtite," which latter word is a regular deriva-tion from Moresheth; but whether Moresheth-gath was that place cannot be ascertained from any in-formation given us in the Bible.

Eusebius and Jerome, in the *Onomasticon*, and Jerome in his Commentary on Micah (*Prologus*), give Morasthi as the name, not of the person, but of the place; and describe it as " a moderate-sized village (*haud grandis viculus*) near Eleutheropolis, the city of Philistia (Palæstinæ), and to the east thereof."

Supposing *Beit-jibrin* to be Eleutheropolis, no traces of the name of Moresheth-gath have been yet discovered in this direction. The ruins of Maresha lie a mile or two due south of *Beit-jibrin;* but it is evident from Mic. i. 14, 15, that the two were distinct.

The affix " gath " may denote a connection with the famous Philistine city of that name — the site of which cannot, however, be taken as yet ascer-tained — or it may point to the existence of vine-yards and wine-presses, " gath " in Hebrew signi-fying a wine-press or vat.   G.

MORI'AH. A name which occurs twice in the Bible (Gen. xxii. 2; 2 Chr. iii. 1).

1. THE LAND OF *a* MORIÁH (אֶרֶץ הַמֹּרִיָּה

[see below]; Samar. א: הַמּוֹרָאָה *b* ὑψηλή: terra *b* visionis). On " one of the moun-tains " in this district took place the sacrifice of Isaac (Gen. xxii. 2). What the name of the moun-tain was we are not told; but it was a conspicuous one, visible from "afar off" (ver. 4). Nor does the narrative afford any data for ascertaining its position; for although it was more than two days' journey from the "land of the Philistines" — meaning no doubt the district of Gerar where Beer-sheba lay, the last place mentioned before and the first after the occurrence in question — yet it is not said how much more than two days it was. The mountain — the " place " — came into view in the course of the third day; but the time occupied in performing the remainder of the distance is not stated. After the deliverance of Isaac, Abraham, with a play on the name of Moriah impossible to convey in English, called the spot Jehovah-jireh, " Jehovah sees " (*i. e.* provides), and thus originated a proverb referring to the providential and op-portune interference of God. " In the mount of Jehovah, He will be seen."

It is most natural to take the "land of Moriah" as the same district with that in which the " Oak

---

a Michaelis (*Suppl.* No. 1458) suggests that the name may be more accurately Hammoriah, since it is not the practice in the early names of districts to add the article. Thus the land of Canaan is אֶרֶץ כְּנַעַן, not הַכְּנַעַן. [See LASHARON.]

b Following Aquila, τὴν γῆν τὴν καταφανῆ; and Symmachus, τὴν γῆν τῆς ὀπτασίας. The same ren-dering is adopted by the Samaritan version.

c Others take Moriah as Moreh-jah (i. e. Jehovah),

(A. V. 'plain') of Moreh" was situated, and not as that which contains Jerusalem, as the modern tradition, which would identify the Moriah of Gen. xxii. and that of 2 Chr. iii. 1, affirms. The former was well known to Abraham. It was the first spot on which he had pitched his tent in the Promised Land, and it was hallowed and endeared to him by the first manifestation of Jehovah with which he had been favored, and by the erection of his first altar. With Jerusalem on the other hand, except as possibly the residence of Melchizedek, he had not any connection whatever; it lay as entirely out of his path as it did out of that of Isaac and Jacob. The LXX. appear to have thus read or interpreted the original, since they render both Moreh and Moriah in Gen. by ὑψηλή, while in 2 Chr. iii. they have Ἀμωρία. The one name is but the feminine of the other *c* (Simonis, *Onom.* 414), and there is hardly more difference between them than between Maresha and Mareshah, and not so much as be-tween Jerushalem and Jerushalaim. The Jewish tradition, which first appears in Josephus — unless 2 Chr. iii. 1 be a still earlier hint of its existence — is fairly balanced by the rival tradition of the Samaritans, which affirms that Mount Gerizim was the scene of the sacrifice of Isaac, and which is at least as old as the 3d century after Christ. [GERIZIM.]

2. MOUNT MORIAH (הַר הַמּוֹרִיָּה: ὄρος τοῦ Ἀμωρία [Vat. -ρεια]; Alex. Ἀμορια: Mons Moria *d*). The name ascribed, in 2 Chr. iii. 1 only, to the eminence on which Solomon built the Tem-ple. " And Solomon began to build the house of Jehovah in Jerusalem on the Mount Moriah, where He appeared to David his father, in a place which David prepared in the threshing-floor of Araunah the Jebusite." From the mention of Araunah, the inference is natural that the " appearance " alluded to occurred at the time of the purchase of the threshing-floor by David, and his erection thereon of the altar (2 Sam. xxiv.; 1 Chr. xxi.). But it will be observed that nothing is said in the narra-tives of that event of any "appearance " of Jehovah. The earlier and simpler record of Samuel is abso-lutely silent on the point. And in the later and more elaborate account of 1 Chr. xxi. the only oc-currence which can be construed into such a mean-ing is that " Jehovah answered David by fire on the altar of burnt-offering."

A tradition which first appears in a definite shape in Josephus (*Ant.* i. 13, §§ 1, 2, vii. 13, § 4), and is now almost universally accepted, asserts that the " Mount Moriah " of the Chronicles is identical with the "mountain" in " the land of Moriah " of Genesis, and that the spot on which Jehovah appeared to David, and on which the Temple was built, was the very spot of the sacrifice of Isaac. In the early Targum of Onkelos on Gen. xxii., this belief is exhibited in a very mild form. The land of Moriah is called the "land of worship," *e* and

---

but this would be to anticipate the existence of the name of Jehovah, and, as Michaelis has pointed out (*Suppl.* No. 1458), the name would more probably be Moriel, El being the name by which God was known to Abraham. [But see JEHOVAH, Amer. ed.]

d For topographical notices of Mount Moriah see the articles on JERUSALEM; KIDRON; TEMPLE; TYRO-PŒON (Amer. ed.).   S. W.

e אַרְעָא פֻּלְחָנָא.

ver. 14 is given as follows: " And Abraham sacrificed and prayed in that place; and he said before Jehovah, In this place shall generations worship, because it shall be said in that day, In this mountain did Abraham worship before Jehovah." But in the Jerusalem Targum the latter passage is thus given, " Because in generations to come it shall be said, In the mount of the house of the sanctuary of Jehovah did Abraham offer up Isaac his son, and in this mountain which is the house of the sanctuary was the glory of Jehovah much manifest." And those who wish to see the tradition in its complete and detailed form, may consult the Targum of R. Joseph on 1 Chr. xxi. 15, and 2 Chr. iii. 1, and the passages collected by Beer (*Leben Abrahams nach jüdische Sage*, 57–71).[a] But the single occurrence of the name in this one passage of Chronicles is surely not enough to establish a coincidence, which if we consider it is little short of miraculous.[b] Had the fact been as the modern belief asserts, and had the belief existed in the minds of the people of the Old or New Testament, there could not fail to be frequent references to it, in the narrative — so detailed — of the original dedication of the spot by David; in the account of Solomon's building in the book of Kings; of Nehemiah's rebuilding (compare especially the reference to Abraham in ix. 7); or of the restorations and purifications of the Maccabees. It was a fact which must have found its way into the paronomastic addresses of the prophets, into the sermon of St. Stephen, so full of allusion to the Founders of the nation, or into the argument of the author of the Epistle to the Hebrews. But not so; on the contrary, except in the case of Salem, and that is by no means ascertained — the name of Abraham does not, as far as the writer is aware, appear once in connection with Jerusalem or the later royal or ecclesiastical glories of Israel. Jerusalem lies out of the path of the patriarchs, and has no part in the history of Israel till the establishment of the monarchy. The " high places of Isaac," as far as we can understand the allusion of Amos (vii. 9, 16) were in the northern kingdom. To connect Jerusalem in so vital a manner with the life of Abraham, is to antedate the whole of the later history of the nation and to commit a serious anachronism, warranted neither by the direct nor indirect statements of the sacred records.

But in addition to this, Jerusalem is incompatible with the circumstances of the narrative of Gen. xxii. To name only two instances — (1.) The Temple Mount cannot be spoken of as a conspicuous eminence. " The towers of Jerusalem," says Professor Stanley (*S. & P.* p. 251), "are indeed seen from the ridge of Mar Elias at the distance of three miles to the south, but there is no elevation; nothing corresponding to the 'place afar off'

to which Abraham 'lifted up his eyes.' And the special locality which Jewish tradition has assigned for the place, and whose name is the chief guarantee for the tradition — Mount Moriah, the hill of the Temple — is not visible till the traveller is close upon it at the southern edge of the Valley of Hinnom, from whence he looks down upon it as on a lower [c] eminence."

(2.) If Salem was Jerusalem, then the trial of Abraham's faith, instead of taking place in the lonely and desolate spot implied by the narrative, where not even fire was to be obtained, and where no help but that of the Almighty was nigh, actually took place under the very walls of the city of Melchizedek.

But, while there is no trace except in the single passage quoted of Moriah being attached to any part of Jerusalem — on the other hand in the slightly different form of MOREH it did exist attached to the town and the neighborhood of Shechem, the spot of Abram's first residence in Palestine. The arguments in favor of the identity of Mount Gerizim with the mountain in the land of Moriah of Gen. xxii., are stated under GERIZIM (vol. ii. pp. 901, 902). As far as they establish that identity, they of course destroy the claim of Jerusalem.   G.

* In another article, GERIZIM (Amer. ed.), we have given our reasons for rejecting the theory which would identify the Moriah of Genesis with Mount Gerizim, and which is again brought forward in the present article. This theory has the respectable authority of Dean Stanley (reviving the discredited Samaritan claim), and the weighty endorsement of Mr. Grove and Mr. Ffoulkes. On the other side, in corroboration of the view of its untenableness already given, may be cited the testimony of three most competent writers who have lately traversed the ground and examined this point. Prof..J. Leslie Porter, author of the valuable *Handbook*, etc., pronounces it "simply impossible" (Kitto's *Bibl. Cyc.* ii. 113); Dr. Thomson, the veteran American missionary, whose personal acquaintance with the country is unsurpassed, declares it "incredible" (*Land and Book*, ii. 212); and Mr. Tristram, the observant English traveller, who visited Gerizim two or three times, says: " I have traversed and timed these routes repeatedly, in a greater or less portion of their course, and feel satisfied that as long as the sacred text remains as it is, 'on the third day,' the claims of Gerizim are untenable" (*Land of Israel*, p. 153).

In disproving "that identity," we leave "the claim of Jerusalem" clear of a rival. But this claim is distinct, and, like the other, must rest on its own merits. Its principal proofs are the iden-

[a] The modern form of the belief is well expressed by the latest Jewish commentator (Kalisch, *Genesis*, 444, 445): " The place of the future temple, where it was promised the glory of God should dwell, and whence atonement and peace were to bless the hearts of the Hebrews, was hallowed by the most brilliant act of piety, and the deed of their ancestor was thus more prominently presented to the imitation of his descendants." The spot of the sacrifice of Isaac is actually shown in Jerusalem (Barclay, *City*, 109). Fürst likewise regards the mount of Abraham's sacrifice and that of Solomon's temple as the same (*Handw.* I. 726).—H.]

[b] There is in the East a natural tendency when a

place is established as a sanctuary to make it the scene of all the notable events, possible or impossible, which can by any play of words or other pretext be connected with it. Of this kind were the early Christian legends that Golgotha was the place of the burial of the first Adam as well as of the death of the Second (see Mislin, *Saints Lieux*, ii. 304, 305). Of this kind also are the Mohammedan legends which cluster round all the shrines and holy places, both of Palestine and Arabia. In the Targum of Chronicles (2 Chr. iii. 1) alluded to above, the Temple mount is made to be also the scene of the vision of Jacob.

[c] See JERUSALEM, vol. ii. p. 1277 a, and the plate in Bartlett's *Walks* there referred to.

tity of its name; the distance from Beer-sheba, which suits exactly the requirements of the narrative; and the tradition of the Jews, twice recorded by Josephus: "It was that mountain upon which King David afterwards built [purposed to build] the Temple" (*Ant.* i. 13, § 2). "Now it happened that Abraham came and offered his son Isaac for a burnt-offering at that very place, as we have before related. When King David saw that God had heard his prayer and graciously accepted his sacrifice, he resolved to call that entire place the altar of all the people, and to build a temple to God there" (*Ant.* vii. 13, § 4).

Without countervailing evidences these grounds would be accepted as sufficient. We will now examine the objections to this view which are brought forward in the present article.

(1.) "Although it was more than two days' journey from ' the land of the Philistines,' yet it is not said how much more than two days it was." This does not weigh against Jerusalem. It is merely a negative argument in behalf of the more distant locality, Gerizim, and has been answered under that head.

(2.) The Septuagint makes "Moreh and Moriah" etymologically the same; "the one name is but the feminine of the other." This argument, which belongs properly to the former article, we have already answered, and are sustained by a recent able author: "Moreh is strictly a proper name, and as such, both in Gen. xii. 6 and Deut. xxix. 30, though in the genitive after a definite noun, rejects the article; the ' hill of Moreh,' mentioned in Judg. vii. 1, where the name has the article, being a totally different place. On the other hand, the name Moriah, in the two places of its occurrence, namely, Gen. xxii. and 2 Chr. iii. 1, bears the article as an appellative, whether it denotes the same situation in both places or not. It is true the LXX. render the Moreh of Gen. xii. and the Moriah of Gen. xxii. alike by the adjective ὑψηλή, in one case translating by the words ' the lofty oak,' in the other, by ' the high land.' It is plain that, on whatever grounds they proceeded in thus translating, this gives no support to the supposition that the names, as names of places, are synonymous, inasmuch as they did not take the words for names of places at all, but as descriptive adjectives. Mr. Grove tells us that מוֹרִיָּה is only the feminine form of מוֹרֶה. According to no analogy of the construction of feminine forms can this be said; the masculine form should in his case have been מוֹרִי " (Quarry, *Genesis and its Authorship*, pp. 210, 211).

(3.) Abraham had little or no "connection" with Jerusalem. "It lay out of his path," while Gerizim was "well-known" to him, and "was hallowed and endeared to him." The obvious answer to this is, that the patriarch did not choose the spot; he went to the place which the Lord selected for him, and started apparently ignorant of his precise destination. This argument further assumes that he not only went to a place of his own selection, but also that he started on an agreeable excursion, which he would naturally wish to associate with the pleasant memories of his pilgrimage; the reverse of which we know to have been the fact.

(4.) "Had the fact been as the modern belief asserts, there could not fail to be frequent refer-

ence to it, by the writers both of the Old and New Testaments." The reply to this is strongly put by a learned writer whom we have already quoted: "This *argumentum ab silentio* is notoriously not to be relied on; the instances of unaccountable silence respecting undoubted facts, where we might have expected them to be mentioned, are too numerous among ancient writers to allow it any weight, except as tending to corroborate arguments that may have considerable weight in themselves. In the present case, the clause in 2 Chr. iii. 1, ' which was seen ' (נִרְאָה) or ' provided by David,' may fairly be taken as containing an obscure reference to the Jehovah-Jireh, and the saying, ' In the mount of the Lord it shall be seen,' of Gen. xxii. 14, so that the absence of all such reference is not so complete as is alleged " (Quarry, pp. 213, 214).

Still, if this site had been selected for the Temple by King David *because* it was the scene of the offering of Isaac (and another reason is assigned by the sacred writer, 1 Chr. xxi., xxii., without any intimation of this), the absence of some more distinct allusion to the fact, though not more unaccountable than other omissions in the Scriptures, must yet be admitted to be unaccountable.

(5.) "The Jewish tradition is fairly balanced by the rival tradition of the Samaritans." Surely not "balanced; " the latter is later and less reliable. Josephus and the rabbinical writers doubtless embodied the honest tradition of their countrymen supported by the identity of names; the Moriah of Genesis and the Moriah of Chronicles being not only the same word, but used in no other connection. The first tradition is natural; the second is suspicious — in keeping with other Samaritan claims, which we know to have been false.

(6.) "The temple-mount is not a conspicuous eminence, like the one to which Abraham ' lifted up his eyes.' " This objection we have already answered. The phrase simply indicates the direction of the eyes, whether up or down, and a further illustration is furnished in ver. 13 of this chapter.

(7.) "The eminence was seen "afar off," and "the hill of the Temple is not visible till the traveller is close upon it." The phrase, "afar off," is relative. It is modified by circumstances, as in Gen. xxxvii. 18, where it is limited to the distance at which a person would be seen and recognized on a plain. In most connections it would indicate a greater distance than is admissible here; but there is a circumstance which qualifies it in this passage. From the spot where the place became visible (as is conceded by Mr. Ffoulkes) Abraham and Isaac proceeded alone to the appointed spot, the latter bearing the wood. The distance to be traversed with this load from the point at which Moriah becomes visible to a traveller from the south to its summit is fully as great as any reader would naturally associate with this fact in the narrative.

(8.) "If Salem was Jerusalem, instead of the lonely and desolate spot implied by the narrative, it took place under the very walls of the city of Melchizedek." Mr. Grove, who suggests this, not being convinced of their identity — ("the arguments are almost equally balanced," ii. 1272) — while Dean Stanley is fully convinced that they are not identical, this argument is for other minds, for those who hold other and positive views on this point. We accept the identity, and we feel the force of the objection. Our only reply to it is, that the environs of an eastern walled town are often as free from observation, as secluded and still, as a solitude. The writer of this has passed hours together within a stone's throw of the walls of the modern Jerusalem at various points undisturbed by any sound, and as unobserved as though the city had been tenantless. This view is supported by a writer already quoted: "Even under the walls of the city of Melchizedek the whole may have taken place without attracting the notice of the inhabitants, and the desolate loneliness of the spot, supposed to be implied in the narrative, has no place in it whatever. It is not implied that Abraham could not obtain fire, but going to an unknown place, he took with him, by way of precaution, what would be needful for the intended sacrifice " (Quarry, p. 213).

This partially relieves the difficulty which Mr. Grove has raised for those of his readers who identify Salem and Jerusalem; but only in part, we think. It must be acknowledged that close proximity to a city is not a natural locality for such a scene. We should suppose that the patriarch would have been directed — we should naturally infer from the narrative itself that he was directed — to some spot remote from the dwellings of men, where, in the performance of this remarkable rite, which even his servants were not to witness, he would not be liable to interruption or intrusive observation.

It must also be admitted that the selection of this spot, with or without a design, for the two events associated with it, is a most unlikely occurrence. " It would take a vast amount of contrary evidence to force me to abandon this idea," says Dr. Thomson. It would require very little to lead us to relinquish it; for in itself it seems to us the height of improbability. That the altar of burnt-offering for the Hebrew worship should have been erected on the identical spot where centuries before the great progenitor of the nation had erected the altar for the sacrifice of his son, led thither for the purpose three days' journey from home — that this should have occurred without design, have been a mere " coincidence," — we must concur with Mr. Grove in pronouncing " little short of miraculous." Yet if it did occur, this is a somewhat less incredible supposition than that it was by design. That the locality became invested with any sanctity in the Divine mind — was divinely selected as the site of the Temple, the scene of the second manifestation, because it had been the scene of the first — is an assumption wholly uncountenanced by any fact or analogy within our knowledge. The "natural tendency" of the eastern mind, moreover, to cluster supernatural or sacred events around the supposed scene of a known miracle, is correctly stated by Mr. Grove. Nothing could be more natural than for the Jews, without any clear warrant, to connect if possible the scene of their sacrifices with the offering of Isaac, and associate the altars of their typical worship with the altar on which the son of promise was laid. This correspondence is thought by some to favor the identity; we cannot but regard a double claim, so peculiar, as in itself a suspicious circumstance.

We would say in conclusion that in favor of the identity of the two sites may be urged the identity of the name, used without explanation in these two passages of Scripture alone, and " in both places alike as an appellative bearing the article; " the possible allusion in a clause of the latter to a clause in the former; the correspondence of the distance with the specifications of the journey; the ancient and consistent Hebrew tradition, universally received in Christendom; the failure to establish a single presumption in favor of any other locality; and the absence of any fatal or decisive objection to this identification. On these grounds the traditional belief will probably abide. Nevertheless, for reasons above intimated, we cannot feel the absolute confidence in it which some express. And the most which we think can be safely affirmed is, that Mount Moriah in Jerusalem, on which the Temple of Solomon was built, was probably, also, the spot where Abraham offered up Isaac.   S. W.

* MORNING, SON OF THE. [LUCI-FER.]

MORTAR. The simplest and probably most ancient method of preparing corn for food was by pounding it between two stones (Virg. Æn. i. 179). Convenience suggested that the lower of the two stones should be hollowed, that the corn might not escape, and that the upper should be shaped so as to be convenient for holding. The pestle and mortar must have existed from a very early period. The Israelites in the desert appear to have possessed mortars and handmills among their necessary domestic utensils. When the manna fell they gathered it, and either ground it in the mill or pounded it in the mortar (מְדֹכָה, medôcâh) till it was fit for use (Num. xi. 8). So in the present day stone mortars are used by the Arabs to pound wheat for their national dish kibby (Thomson, The Land and the Book, ch. viii. p. 94). Niebuhr describes one of a very simple kind which was used on board the vessel in which he went from Jidda to Loheia. Every afternoon one of the sailors had to take the durra, or millet, necessary for the day's consumption and pound it "upon a stone, of which the surface was a little curved, with another stone which was long and rounded " (Descr. de l'Arab. p. 45). Among the inhabitants of Ezzehhoue, a Druse village, Burckhardt saw coffee-mortars made out of the trunks of oak-trees (Syria, pp. 87, 88). The spices for the incense are said to have been prepared by the house of Abtines, a family set apart for the purpose, and the mortar which they used was, with other spoils of the Temple, after the destruction of Jerusalem by Titus, carried to Rome, where it remained till the time of Hadrian (Reggio in Martinet's Hebr. Chrest. p. 35). Buxtorf mentions a kind of mortar (מַדְתַּשׁ, cûttûsh) in which olives were slightly bruised before they were taken to the olive-presses (Lex. Talm. s. v. כתש). From the same root as this last is derived mactésh (מַכְתֵּשׁ, Prov. xxvii. 22), which probably denotes a mortar of a larger kind in which corn was pounded. " Though thou bray the fool in the mortar among the bruised corn with the pestle, yet will not his folly depart from him." Corn may be separated from its husk and all its good properties preserved by such an operation, but the fool's folly is so essential a part of himself that no analogous process can remove it from him. Such seems the natural interpretation of this remarkable proverb. The language is intentionally exaggerated, and there is no necessity for supposing an allusion to a mode of punishment by which criminals were put to death, by being pounded in a mortar. A custom of this kind existed among the Turks, but there is no distinct trace of it among the Hebrews. The Ulemats, or body of lawyers, in Turkey had the distinguished privilege, according to De Tott (*Mem.* i. p. 28, Eng. tr.), of being put to death only by the pestle and the mortar. Such, however, is supposed to be the reference in the proverb by Mr. Roberts, who illustrates it from his Indian experience. "Large mortars are used in the East for the purpose of separating the rice from the husk. When a considerable quantity has to be prepared, the mortar is placed outside the door, and two women, each with a pestle of five feet long, begin the work. They strike in rotation, as blacksmiths do on the anvil. Cruel as it is, this is a punishment of the state: the poor victim is thrust into the mortar, and beaten with the pestle. The late king of Kandy compelled one of the wives of his rebellious chiefs thus to beat her own infant to death. Hence the saying, 'Though you beat that loose woman in a mortar, she will not leave her ways:' which means, Though you chastise her ever so much, she will never improve" (*Orient. Illustr.* p. 368).   W. A. W.

MORTER[a] (Gen. xi. 3; Ex. i. 14; Lev. xiv. 42, 45; Is. xli. 25; Ez. xiii. 10, 11, 14, 15, xxii. 28; Nah. iii. 14). Omitting iron cramps, lead [HANDICRAFT], and the instances in which large stones are found in close apposition without cement, the various compacting substances used in oriental buildings appear to be — 1, bitumen, as in the Babylonian structures; 2. common mud or moistened clay; 3, a very firm cement compounded of sand, ashes, and lime, in the proportions respectively of 1, 2, 3, well pounded, sometimes mixed and sometimes coated with oil, so as to form a surface almost impenetrable to wet or the weather. [PLASTER.] In Assyrian, and also Egyptian brick buildings stubble or straw, as hair or wool among ourselves, was added to increase the tenacity (Shaw, *Trav.* p. 206; Volney, *Trav.* ii. 436; Chardin, *Voy.* iv. 116). If the materials were bad in themselves, as mere mud would necessarily be, or insufficiently mixed, or, as the Vulgate seems to understand (Ez. xiii. 10), if straw were omitted, the mortar or cob-wall would be liable to crumble under the influence of wet weather. See Shaw, *Trav.* p. 136, and Ges. p. 1515, *s. v.* תָּפֵל: a word connected with the Arabic *Tafal*,[b] a substance resembling pipe-clay, believed by Burckhardt to be the detritus of the felspar of granite, and used for taking stains out of cloth (Burckhardt, *Syria*, p. 488; Mishn. *Pesach.* x. 3). Wheels for grinding chalk or lime for mortar, closely resembling our own machines for the same purpose, are in use in Egypt (Niebuhr, *Voy.* i. 122, pl. 17; Burckhardt, *Nubia*, pp. 82, 97, 102, 140; Hasselquist, *Trav.* p. 90). [HOUSE; CLAY.]   H. W. P.

• **MORTGAGE**, Neh. v. 3. [LOAN.]

• **MORTIFY** (from the late Latin *mortifico*) is used in its primitive sense, though metaphorically, in Rom. viii. 13 (A. V.): "If ye through the Spirit do *mortify* (θανατοῦτε, lit. "put to death," "make an end of," Noyes) the deeds of the body, ye shall live." So in Col. iii. 5, where it is the rendering of νεκρώσατε: "*Mortify* ('make dead,' Ellicott, Noyes; 'sle,' Wycliffe) therefore your members which are upon the earth;" comp. Gal. v. 24, "They that are Christ's have *crucified* the flesh with its affections and lusts."   A.

MOSE'RAH (מֹסֵרָה) [perh. *fetter*, *chastisement*]: Μισαδαί; Alex. Μεισαδαι; Comp. Μοσερά:] *Mosera*, Deut. x. 6, apparently the same as MOSEROTH, Num. xxxiii. 30, its plural form), the name of a place near Mount Hor. Hengstenberg (*Authent. der Pentat.*) thinks it lay in the Arabah, where that mountain overhangs it. Burckhardt suggests that possibly *Wady Mousa*, near Petra and Mount Hor, may contain a corruption of Mosera. This does not seem likely. Used as a common noun, the word means "bonds, fetters." In Deut. it is said that "there Aaron died." Probably the people encamped in this spot adjacent to the mount, which Aaron ascended, and where he died.   H. H.

• **MOSE'ROTH** (מֹסֵרוֹת: Μασουροίθ; Vat. in ver. 30, Μασουρωθ: *Moseroth*), Num. xxxiii. 30, 31. See MOSERAH.   A.

MO'SES (Heb. *Mōsheh*, מֹשֶׁה = *drawn*: LXX., Josephus, Philo, the most ancient MSS. of N. T., Μωϋσῆς, declined Μωϋσέως, Μωϋσεί or Μωϋσῇ, Μωϋσέα or Μωϋσῆν: Vulg. *Moyses*, declined *Moysi*, gen. and dat., *Moysen*, acc.: Rec. Text of N. T. and Protestant versions, *Moses*: Arabic, *Mûsa*: Numenius ap. Eus. *Præp. Ev.* ix. 8, 27, Μουσαῖος: Artapanus ap. Eus. *Ibid.* 27, Μώϋσος: Manetho ap. Joseph. *c. Ap.* i. 26, 28, 31, *Osarsiph*: Chæremon, ap. *ib.* 32, *Tisithen*: "the man of God," Ps. xc., title, 1 Chr. xxiii. 14; "the slave of Jehovah," Num. xii. 7, Deut. xxxiv. 5, Josh. i. 1, Ps. cv. 26; "the chosen," Ps. cvi. 23). The legislator of the Jewish people,[c] and in a certain sense the founder of the Jewish religion. No one else presented so imposing a figure to the external Gentile world; and although in the Jewish nation his fame is eclipsed by the larger details of the life of David, yet he was probably always regarded as their greatest hero.

The materials for his life are —

I. The details preserved in the four last books of the Pentateuch.

II. The allusions in the Prophets and Psalms, which in a few instances seem independent of the Pentateuch.

III. The Jewish traditions preserved in the N. T. (Acts vii. 20–38; 2 Tim. iii. 8, 9; Heb. xi. 23–28; Jude 9); and in Josephus (*Ant.* ii., iii., iv.), Philo (*Vita Moysis*), and Clemens. Alex. (*Strom.*).

IV. The heathen traditions of Manetho, Lysimachus, and Chæremon, preserved in Josephus (*c. Ap.* i. 26–32), of Artapanus and others in Euse-

---

[a] 1. חֹמֶר: πηλός: *cæmentum*, a word from the same root (חָמַר, "boil") as חֵמָר, "slime" or "bitumen," used in the same passage, Gen. xi. 3. Ghomœr is also rendered "clay," evidently plastic clay, Is. xxix. 16, and elsewhere. 2. עָפָר: χοῦς:

[b] طَفَل.

[c] Πρῶτος ἀπάντων ὁ θεσπιζόμενος θεολόγος τε καὶ νομοθέτης, Eus. *Præp. Ev.* vii. 8. Comp. Philo, *V. Mos.* i. 30.

lutum, also *limus, pulvis*, A. V. "dust," "powder," as in 2 K. xxiii. 6, and Gen. ii 7.

ums (*Præp. Ev.* ix. 8, 26, 27), and of Hecatæus in Diod. Sic. xl., Strabo xvi. 2.

V. The Mussulman traditions in the Koran (ii., vii., x., xviii., xx., xxviii., xl.), and the Arabian legends, as given in Weil's *Biblical Legends*, D'Herbelot ("Mousa"), and Lane's *Selections*, p. 182.

VL. Apocryphal Books of Moses (Fabricius, *Cod. Pseud. V. T.* i. 825): (1.) Prayers of Moses. (2.) Apocalypse of Moses. (3.) Ascension of Moses. (These are only known by fragments.)

VII. In modern times his career and legislation has been treated by Warburton, Michaelis, Ewald, and Bunsen.

His life, in the later period of the Jewish history, was divided into three equal portions of forty years each (Acts vii. 23, 30, 36). This agrees with the natural arrangement of his history into the three parts of his Egyptian education, his exile in Arabia, and his government of the Israelite nation in the Wilderness and on the confines of Palestine.

I. His birth and education. The immediate pedigree of Moses is as follows: —

In the Koran, by a strange confusion, the family of Moses is confounded with the Holy Family of Nazareth, chiefly through the identification of Mary and Miriam, and the 3d chapter, which describes the evangelical history, bears the name of the "Family of Amram." Although little is known of the family except through its connection with this its most illustrious member, yet it was not without influence on his after-life.

The fact that he was of the tribe of Levi no doubt contributed to the selection of that tribe as the sacred caste. The tie that bound them to Moses was one of kinship, and they thus naturally rallied round the religion which he had been the means of establishing (Ex. xxxii. 28) with an ardor which could not have been found elsewhere. His own eager devotion is also a quality, for good or evil, characteristic of the whole tribe.

The Levitical parentage and the Egyptian origin both appear in the family names. *Gershom, Eleazar,* are both repeated in the younger generations. *Moses* (*vide infra*) and *Phinehas* (see Brugsch, *Hist. de l'Égypte,* i. 173) are Egyptian. The name of his mother, Jochebed, implies the knowledge of the name of JEHOVAH in the bosom of the family. It is its first distinct appearance in the sacred history.

Miriam, who must have been considerably older than himself, and Aaron, who was three years older (Ex. vii. 7), afterwards occupy that independence of position which their superior age would naturally give them.

Moses was born, according to Manetho (Jos. *c. Ap.* i. 26, ii. 2), at Heliopolis, at the time of the deepest depression of his nation in the Egyptian servitude. Hence the Jewish proverb, "When the tale of bricks is doubled then comes Moses." His birth (according to Josephus, *Ant.* ii. 9, § 2, 3, 4) had been foretold to Pharaoh by the Egyptian magicians, and to his father Amram by a dream — as respectively the future destroyer and deliverer. The pangs of his mother's labor were alleviated so as to enable her to evade the Egyptian midwives. The story of his birth is thoroughly Egyptian in its scene. The beauty of the new-born babe — in the later versions of the story amplified into a beauty and size (Jos. *ib.* § 1, 5) almost divine (ἀστεῖος τῷ θεῷ, Acts vii. 20; the word ἀστεῖος is taken from the LXX. version of Ex. ii. 2, and is used again in Heb. xi. 23, and is applied to none but Moses in the N. T.) — induced the mother to make extraordinary efforts for its preservation from the general destruction of the male children of Israel. For three months the child was concealed in the house. Then his mother placed him in a small boat or basket of papyrus — perhaps from a current Egyptian belief that the plant is a protection from crocodiles (Plut. *Is. & Os.* 358) — closed against the water by bitumen. This was placed among the aquatic vegetation by the side of one of the canals of the Nile. [NILE.] The mother departed as if unable to bear the sight. The sister lingered to watch her brother's fate. The basket (Jos. *ib.* § 4) floated down the stream.

The Egyptian princess (to whom the Jewish traditions gave the name of *Thermuthis,* Jos. *Ant.* ii. 9, § 5; Artapanus, *Præp. Ev.* ix. 27, the name of *Merrhis,* and the Arabic traditions that of *Asiat,* Jalaladdin, 387) came down, after the Homeric simplicity of the age, to bathe in the sacred river,[a] or (Jos. *Ant.* ii. 9, § 5) to play by its side. Her attendant slaves followed her. She saw the basket in the flags, or (Jos. *ib.*) borne down the stream, and dispatched divers after it. The divers, or one of the female slaves, brought it. It was opened, and the cry of the child moved the princess to compassion. She determined to rear it as her own. The child (Jos. *ib.*) refused the milk of Egyptian nurses. The sister was then at hand to recommend a Hebrew nurse. The child was brought up as the princess's son, and the memory of the incident was long cherished in the name given to the foundling of the water's side — whether according to its Hebrew or Egyptian form. Its Hebrew form is מֹשֶׁה, *Mosheh,* from מָשָׁה, *Mâshâh,* "to draw out" — "because I have *drawn* him out of the water." But this (as in many other instances, *Babel,* etc.) is probably the Hebrew form given to a foreign word. In Coptic, *mo* = water, and *ushe* = saved. This is the explanation[b] given by Jo-

---

[a] She was, according to Artapanus, Eus. *Præp. Ev.* ix. 27) the daughter of Palmanothes, who was reigning at Heliopolis, and the wife of Chenephres, who was reigning at Memphis. In this tradition, and that of Philo (*V. M.* i. 4), she has no child, and hence her delight at finding one.

[b] Brugsch, however (*L'Histoire d'Égypte,* pp. 157, 173), renders the name *Mes* or *Messon* = child, borne by one of the princes of Ethiopia under Rameses II. In the Arabic traditions the name is derived from his discovery in the water and among the trees; "for in the Egyptian language *mo* is the name of water, and *se* is that of a tree" (Jalaladdin, 887).

sophus (*Ant.* ii. 9, § 6; *c. Apion.* i. 31[a]), and confirmed by the Greek form of the word adopted in the LXX., and thence in the Vulgate, Μωῦσῆς, *Moyses*, and by Artapanus Μώϋσος (Eus. *Præp. Ev.* ix. 27). His former Hebrew name is said to have been Joachim (Clem. Alex. *Strom.* i. p. 343). The child was adopted by the princess. Tradition describes its beauty as so great that passers-by stood fixed to look at it, and laborers left their work to steal a glance (Jos. *Ant.* ii. 9, § 6).

From this time for many years Moses must be considered as an Egyptian. In the Pentateuch this period is a blank, but in the N. T. he is represented as "educated (ἐπαιδεύθη) in all the wisdom of the Egyptians," and as "mighty in words and deeds" (Acts vii. 22). The following is a brief summary of the Jewish and Egyptian traditions which fill up the silence of the sacred writer. He was educated at Heliopolis (comp. Strabo, xvii. 1), and grew up there as a priest, under his Egyptian name of Osarsiph (Manetho, apud Jos. *c. Ap.* i. 26, 28, 31) or Tisithen (Chæremon, apud *ib.* 32). "Osarsiph" is derived by Manetho from Osiris, *i. e.* (Osiri-taf?) "saved by Osiris" (Osburn, *Monumental Egypt*). He was taught the whole range of Greek, Chaldee, and Assyrian literature. From the Egyptians, especially, he learned mathematics, to train his mind for the unprejudiced reception of truth (Philo, *V. M.* i. 5). "He invented boats and engines for building — instruments of war and of hydraulics — hieroglyphics — division of lands" (Artapanus, ap. Eus. *Præp. Ev.* ix. 27). He taught Orpheus, and was hence called by the Greeks Musæus (*ib.*), and by the Egyptians Hermes (*ib.*). He taught grammar to the Jews, whence it spread to Phœnicia and Greece (Eupolemus, ap. Clem. Alex. *Strom.* i. p. 343). He was sent on an expedition against the Ethiopians. He got rid of the serpents of the country to be traversed by turning baskets full of ibises upon them (Jos. *Ant.* ii. 10, § 2), and founded the city of Hermopolis to commemorate his victory (Artapanus, ap. Eus. ix. 27). He advanced to Saba, the capital of Ethiopia, and gave it the name of Meroë, from his adopted mother Merrhis, whom he buried there (*ib.*). Tharbis, the daughter of the king of Ethiopia, fell in love with him, and he returned in triumph to Egypt with her as his wife (Jos. *ibid.*).

II. The nurture of his mother is probably spoken of as the link which bound him to his own people, and the time had at last arrived when he was resolved to reclaim his nationality. Here again the N. T. preserves the tradition in a distincter form than the account in the Pentateuch. "Moses, when he was come to years, refused to be called the son of Pharaoh's daughter; choosing rather to suffer affliction with the people of God than to enjoy the pleasures of sin for a season; esteeming the reproach of Christ greater riches than the treasures" — the ancient accumulated treasure of Rhampsinitus and the old kings — "of Egypt" (Heb. xi. 24-26). In his earliest infancy he was reported to have refused the milk of Egyptian nurses (Jos. *Ant.* ii. 9, § 5), and when three years old to have trampled under his feet the crown which Pharaoh had playfully placed on his head (*ib.* 7). According to the Alexandrian representation of Philo (*V. M.* i. 6), he led an ascetic life, in order to pursue his high philosophic speculations. According to the Egyptian tradition, although a priest of Heliopolis, he always performed his prayers, according to the custom of his fathers, outside the walls of the city, in the open air, turning towards the sun-rising (Jos. *c. Apion.* ii. 2). The king was excited to hatred by the priests of Egypt, who foresaw their destroyer (*ib.*), or by his own envy (Artapanus, ap. Eus. *Præp. Ev.* ix. 27). Various plots of assassination were contrived against him, which failed. The last was after he had already escaped across the Nile from Memphis, warned by his brother Aaron, and when pursued by the assassin he killed him (*ib.*). The same general account of conspiracies against his life appears in Josephus (*Ant.* ii. 10). All that remains of these traditions in the sacred narrative is the simple and natural incident, that seeing an Israelite suffering the bastinado from an Egyptian, and thinking that they were alone, he slew the Egyptian (the later tradition, preserved by Clement of Alexandria, said, "with a word of his mouth"), and buried the corpse in the sand (the sand of the desert then, as now, running close up to the cultivated tract). The fire of patriotism which thus turned him into a deliverer from the oppressors, turns him in the same story into the peacemaker of the oppressed. It is characteristic of the faithfulness of the Jewish records that his flight is there occasioned rather by the malignity of his countrymen than by the enmity of the Egyptians. And in St. Stephen's speech it is this part of the story which is drawn out at greater length than in the original, evidently with the view of showing the identity of the narrow spirit which had thus displayed itself equally against their first and their last Deliverer (Acts vii. 25-35).

He fled into Midian. Beyond the fact that it was in or near the Peninsula of Sinai, its precise situation is unknown. Arabian tradition points to the country east of the Gulf of Akaba (see Laborde). Josephus (*Ant.* ii. 11, § 1) makes it "by the Red Sea." There was a famous well ("the well," Ex. ii. 15) surrounded by tanks for the watering of the flocks of the Bedouin herdsmen. By this well the fugitive seated himself "at noon" (Jos. *ibid.*), and watched the gathering of the sheep. There were the Arabian shepherds, and there were also seven maidens, whom the shepherds rudely drove away from the water. The chivalrous spirit (if we may so apply a modern phrase) which had already broken forth in behalf of his oppressed countrymen, broke forth again in behalf of the distressed maidens. They returned unusually soon to their father, and told him of their adventure. Their father was a person of whom we know little, but of whom that little shows how great an influence he exercised over the future career of Moses. It was JETHRO, or REUEL, or HOBAB, chief or priest ("Sheykh" exactly expresses the union of the religious and political influence) of the Midianite tribes.

Moses, who up to this time had been "an Egyptian" (Ex. ii. 19), now became for an unknown period, extended by the later tradition over forty years (Acts vii. 30), an Arabian. He married Zipporah, daughter of his host, to whom he also became the slave and shepherd (Ex. ii. 21, iii. 1).

The blank which during the stay in Egypt is filled up by Egyptian traditions, can here only be

a Philo (*V. M.* i. 4), *môs* = water: Clem. Alex. (*Strom.* i. p. 343), *môu* = water. Clement (*ib.*) derives *Moses* from "drawing breath." In an ancient Egyptian treatise on agriculture cited by Chwolson (*Ueberreste,* etc., 12 *note*) his name is given as *Mônies.*

supplied from indirect allusions in other parts of the O. T. The alliance between Israel and the Kenite branch of the Midianites, now first formed, was never broken. [KENITES.] Jethro became their guide through the desert. If from Egypt, as we have seen, was derived the secular and religious learning of Moses, and with this much of their outward ceremonial, so from Jethro was derived the organization of their judicial and social arrangements during their nomadic state (Ex. xviii. 21–23). Nor is the conjecture of Ewald (*Gesch.* ii. 59, 60) improbable, that in this pastoral and simple relation there is an indication of a wider concert than is directly stated between the rising of the Israelites in Egypt and the Arabian tribes, who, under the name of " the Shepherds," had been recently expelled. According to Artapanus (Eus. *Prœp. Ev.* ix. 27) Reuel actually urged Moses to make war upon Egypt. Something of a joint action is implied in the visit of Aaron to the desert (Ex. iv. 27; comp. Artapanus, *ut supra*); something also in the sacredness of Sinai, already recognized both by Israel and by the Arabs (Ex. viii. 27; Jos. *Ant.* ii. 12, § 1).

But the chief effect of this stay in Arabia is on Moses himself. It was in the seclusion and simplicity of his shepherd-life that he received his call as a prophet. The traditional scene of this great event is the valley of Shoayb, or Hobab, on the N. side of Jebel Mûsa. Its exact spot is marked by the convent of St. Catherine, of which the altar is said to stand on the site of the Burning Bush. The original indications are too slight to enable us to fix the spot with any certainty. It was at " the back " of " the wilderness " at Horeb (Ex. iii. 1): to which the Hebrew adds, whilst the LXX. omits, " the mountain of God." Josephus further particularizes that it was the loftiest of all the mountains in that region, and best for pasturage, from its good grass; and that, owing to a belief that it was inhabited by the Divinity, the shepherds feared to approach it (*Ant.* ii. 12, § 1). Philo (*V. M.* i. 12) adds " a grove " or " glade."

Upon the mountain was a well-known acacia [SHITTIM] (the definite article may indicate either " the particular celebrated tree," sacred perhaps already, or " the tree " or " vegetation peculiar to the spot "), the thorn-tree of the desert, spreading out its tangled branches, thick set with white thorns, over the rocky ground. It was this tree which became the symbol of the Divine Presence: a flame of fire in the midst of it, in which the dry branches would naturally have crackled and burnt in a moment, but which played round it without consuming it. In Philo (*V. M.* i. 12) " the angel " is described as a strange, but beautiful creature. Artapanus (Eus. *Prœp. Ev.* ix. 27) represents it as a fire suddenly bursting from the bare ground, and feeding itself without fuel. But this is far less expressive than the Biblical image. Like all the visions of the Divine Presence recorded in the O. T., as manifested at the outset of a prophetical career, this was exactly suited to the circumstances of the tribe. It was the true likeness of the condition of Israel, in the furnace of affliction, yet not destroyed (comp. Philo, *V. M.* i. 12). The place,

too, in the desert solitude, was equally appropriate, as a sign that the Divine protection was not confined either to the sanctuaries of Egypt, or to the Holy Land, but was to be found with any faithful worshipper, fugitive and solitary though he might be. The rocky ground at once became " holy," and the shepherd's sandal was to be taken off no less than on the threshold of a palace or a temple. It is this feature of the incident on which St. Stephen dwells, as a proof of the universality of the true religion (Acts vii. 29–33).

The call or revelation was twofold —

1. The declaration of the Sacred Name expresses the eternal self-existence of the One God. The name itself, as already mentioned, must have been known in the family of Aaron. But its grand significance was now first drawn out. [JEHOVAH.]

2. The mission was given to Moses to deliver his people. The two signs are characteristic — the one of his past Egyptian life — the other of his active shepherd life. In the rush of leprosy into his hand [a] is the link between him and the people whom the Egyptians called a nation of lepers. In the transformation of his shepherd's staff is the glorification of the simple pastoral life, of which that staff was the symbol, into the great career which lay before it. The humble yet wonder-working crook is, in the history of Moses, as Ewald finely observes, what the despised Cross is in the first history of Christianity.

In this call of Moses, as of the Apostles afterwards, the man is swallowed up in the cause. Yet this is the passage in his history which, more than any other, brings out his outward and domestic relations.

He returns to Egypt from his exile. His Arabian wife and her two infant sons are with him. She is seated with them on the ass — (the ass was known as the animal peculiar to the Jewish people from Jacob down to David). He apparently walks by their side with his shepherd's staff. (The LXX. substitute the general term τὰ ὑποζύγια.)

On the journey back to Egypt a mysterious incident occurred in the family, which can only be explained with difficulty. The most probable explanation seems to be, that at the caravanserai either Moses or Gershom (the context of the preceding verses, iv. 22, 23, rather points to the latter) was struck with what seemed to be a mortal illness. In some way, not apparent to us, this illness was connected by Zipporah with the fact that her son had not been circumcised — whether in the general neglect of that rite amongst the Israelites in Egypt, or in consequence of his birth in Midian. She instantly performed the rite. and threw the sharp instrument, stained with the fresh blood, at the feet of her husband, exclaiming in the agony of a mother's anxiety for the life of her child — " A bloody husband thou art, to cause the death of my son." Then, when the recovery from the illness took place (whether of Moses or Gershom), she exclaims again, " A bloody husband still thou art, but not so as to cause the child's death, but only to bring about his circumcision." [b]

---

[a] The Mussulman legends speak of his white shining hand as the instrument of his miracles (D'Herbelot). Hence " the white hand " is proverbial for the healing art.

[b] So Ewald (*Geschichte*, vol. ii. pt. 2, p. 105), taking

the sickness to have visited Moses. Rosenmüller makes Gershom the victim, and makes Zipporah address Jehovah, the Arabic word for " marriage " being a synonym for " circumcision." It is possible that on this story is founded the tradition of Artapanus (Eus

It would seem to have been in consequence of this event, whatever it was, that the wife and her children were sent back to Jethro, and remained with him till Moses joined them at Rephidim (Ex. xviii. 2–6), which is the last time that she is distinctly mentioned. In Num. xii. 1 we hear of a Cushite wife who gave umbrage to Miriam and Aaron. This may be — (1) an Ethiopian (Cushite) wife, taken after Zipporah's death (Ewald, *Gesch.* ii. 229). (2.) The Ethiopian princess of Josephus (*Ant.* i. 10, § 2): (but that whole story is probably only an inference from Num. xii. 1). (3.) Zipporah herself, which is rendered probable by the juxtaposition of Cushan with Midian in Hab. iii. 7.

The two sons also sink into obscurity. Their names, though of Levitical origin, relate to their foreign birthplace. Gershom, "stranger," and Eli-ezer, "God is my help," commemorate their father's exile and escape (Ex. xviii. 3, 4). Gershom was the father of the wandering Levite Jonathan (Judg. xviii. 30), and the ancestor of Shebuel, David's chief treasurer (1 Chr. xxiii. 16, xxiv. 20). Eliezer had an only son, Rehabiah (1 Chr. xxiii. 17), who was the ancestor of a numerous but obscure progeny, whose representative in David's time — the last descendant of Moses known to us — was Shelomith, guard of the consecrated treasures in the Temple (1 Chr. xxvi. 25–28).

After this parting he advanced into the desert, and at the same spot where he had had his vision encountered Aaron (Ex. iv. 27). From that meeting and coöperation we have the first distinct indication of his personal appearance and character. The traditional representations of him in some respects well agree with that which we derive from Michael Angelo's famous statue in the church of *S. Pietro in Vincoli* at Rome. Long shaggy hair and beard is described as his characteristic equally by Josephus, Diodorus (i. p. 424), and Artapanus (κομήτης, apud Eus. *Praep. Ev.* ix. 27). To this Artapanus adds the curious touch that it was of a reddish hue, tinged with gray (πυῤῥάκης, πολιός). The traditions of his beauty and size as a child have been already mentioned. They are continued to his manhood in the Gentile descriptions. "Tall and dignified," says Artapanus (μάκρος, ἀξιωματικός) — "Wise and beautiful as his father Joseph" (with a curious confusion of genealogies), says Justin (xxxvi. 2).

But beyond the slight glance at his infantine beauty, no hint of this grand personality is given in the Bible. What is described is rather the reverse. The only point there brought out is a singular and unlooked for infirmity. "O my Lord, I am not eloquent, neither heretofore nor since Thou hast spoken to Thy servant; but I am slow of speech and of a slow tongue. . . . How shall Pharaoh hear me, which am of uncircumcised lips?" (*i. e.* slow, without words, stammering, hesitating: ἰσχνόφωνος καὶ βαρύγλωσσος, LXX.), his "speech contemptible," like St. Paul's — like the English Cromwell (comp. Carlyle's *Cromwell*, ii. 219) — like the first efforts of the Greek Demosthenes. In the solution of this difficulty which Moses offers, we read both the disinterestedness, which is the most distinct trait of his personal character, and the future relation of the two brothers. "Send, I pray Thee, by the hand of him whom Thou wilt send" (*i. e.* "make any one Thy apostle rather than me").

Praep. Ev. ix. 27), that the Ethiopians derived circumcision from Moses

In outward appearance this prayer was granted. Aaron spoke and acted for Moses, and was the permanent inheritor of the sacred staff of power. But Moses was the inspiring soul behind; and so as time rolls on, Aaron, the prince and priest, has almost disappeared from view, and Moses, the dumb, backward, disinterested prophet, is in appearance, what he was in truth, the foremost leader of the chosen people.

III. The history of Moses henceforth is the history of Israel for forty years. But as the incidents of this history are related in other articles, under the heads of EGYPT, EXODUS, PLAGUES, SINAI, LAW, PASSOVER, WANDERINGS, WILDERNESS, it will be best to confine ourselves here to such indications of his personal character as transpire through the general framework of the narrative.

It is important to trace his relation to his immediate circle of followers. In the Exodus, he takes the decisive lead on the night of the flight. Up to that point he and Aaron appear almost on an equality. But after that, Moses is usually mentioned alone. Aaron still held the second place, but the character of interpreter to Moses which he had borne in speaking to Pharaoh withdrawn, and it would seem as if Moses henceforth became altogether, what hitherto he had only been in part, the prophet of the people. Another who occupies a place nearly equal to Aaron, though we know but little of him, is HUR, of the tribe of Judah, husband of Miriam, and grandfather of the artist Bezaleel (Joseph. *Ant.* iii. 2, § 4). He and Aaron are the chief supporters of Moses in moments of weariness or excitement. His adviser in regard to the route through the wilderness as well as in the judicial arrangements, was, as we have seen, JETHRO. His servant, occupying the same relation to him as Elisha to Elijah, or Gehazi to Elisha, was the youthful Hoshea (afterwards JOSHUA). MIRIAM always held the independent position to which her age entitled her. Her part was to supply the voice and song to her brother's prophetic power.

But Moses is incontestably the chief personage of the history, in a sense in which no one else is described before or since. In the narrative, the phrase is constantly recurring, "The Lord spake unto Moses," "Moses spake unto the children of Israel." In the traditions of the desert, whether late or early, his name predominates over that of every one else, "The Wells of Moses" — on the shores of the Red Sea. "The Mountain of Moses" (Jebel Mûsa) — near the convent of St. Catherine. The Ravine of Moses (Shuk Mûsa) — at Mount St. Catherine. The Valley of Moses (Wady Mûsa) — at Petra. "The Books of Moses" are so called (as afterwards the Books of Samuel), in all probability from his being the chief subject of them. The very word "Mosaic" has been in later times applied (as the proper name of no other saint of the O. T.) to the whole religion. Even as applied to tesselated pavement ("Mosaic," *Musivum*, μουσεῖον, μουσαϊκόν), there is some probability that the expression is derived from the variegated pavement of the later Temple, which had then become the representative of the religion of Moses (see an Essay of Redslob, *Zeitschrift der Deutsch. Morgenl. Gesells.* xiv. 663).

It has sometimes been attempted to reduce this great character into a mere passive instrument of the Divine Will, as though he had himself borne no conscious part in the actions in which he figures, or the messages which he delivers. This, however, is as incompatible with the general tenor of the Scriptural account, as it is with the common language in which he has been described by the Church in all ages. The frequent addresses of the Divinity to him no more contravene his personal activity and intelligence, than in the case of Elijah, Isaiah, or St. Paul. In the N. T. the Mosaic legislation is expressly ascribed to him: "*Moses* gave you circumcision" (John vii. 22). "*Moses*, because of the hardness of your hearts, suffered you" (Matt. xix. 8). "Did not *Moses* give you the law?" (John vii. 19). "*Moses* accuseth you" (John v. 45). St. Paul goes so far as to speak of him as the founder of the Jewish religion: "They were all baptized *unto Moses*" (1 Cor. x. 2). He is constantly called "a Prophet." In the poetical language of the O. T. (Num. xxi. 18; Deut. xxxiii. 21), and in the popular language both of Jews and Christians, he is known as "the Lawgiver." The terms in which his legislation is described by Philo (*V. M.* ii. 1–4) is decisive as to the ancient Jewish view. He must be considered, like all the saints and heroes of the Bible, as a man of marvelous gifts, raised up by Divine Providence for a special purpose; but as led, both by his own disposition and by the peculiarity of the Revelation which he received, into a closer communication with the invisible world than was vouchsafed to any other in the Old Testament.

There are two main characters in which he appears, as a Leader and a Prophet. The two are more frequently combined in the East than in the West. Several remarkable instances occur in the history of Mohammedanism: Mohammed himself, Abd-el-Kader in Algeria, Schamyl in Circassia.

(*a.*) As a Leader, his life divides itself into the three epochs — of the march to Sinai; the march from Sinai to Kadesh; and the conquest of the trans-Jordanic kingdoms. Of his natural gifts in this capacity, we have but few means of judging. The two main difficulties which he encountered were the reluctance of the people to submit to his guidance, and the impracticable nature of the country which they had to traverse. The patience with which he bore their murmurs is often described — at the Red Sea, at the apostasy of the golden calf, at the rebellion of Korah, at the complaints of Aaron and Miriam. The incidents with which his name was specially connected, both in the sacred narrative and in the Jewish, Arabian, and heathen traditions, were those of supplying water, when most wanted. This is the only point in his life noted by Tacitus, who describes him as guided to a spring of water by a herd of wild asses (*Hist.* v. 3). In the Pentateuch these supplies of water take place at Marah, at Horeb, at Kadesh, and in the land of Moab. That at Marah is produced by the sweetening of waters through a tree in the desert, those at Horeb and at Kadesh by the opening of a rift in the "rock" and in the "cliff;" that in Moab, by the united efforts, under his direction, of the chiefs and of the people (Num. xxi. 18).*a* (See Philo, *V. M.* i. 40.) Of the three first of these incidents, traditional sites, bearing his name, are shown in the desert at the present day, though most of them are rejected by modern travellers. One is *Ayûn Mûsa*, "the

wells of Moses," immediately south of Suez, which the tradition (probably from a confusion with Marah) ascribes to the rod of Moses. Of the water at Horeb, two memorials are shown. One is the *Shuk Mûsa*, or "cleft of Moses," in the side of Mount St. Catherine, and the other is the remarkable stone, first mentioned expressly in the Koran (ii. 57), which exhibits the 12 marks or mouths out of which the water is supposed to have issued for the 12 tribes.*b* The fourth is the celebrated "Sik," or ravine, by which Petra is approached from the east, and which, from the story of its being torn open by the rod of Moses, has given his name (the *Wady Mûsa*) to the whole valley. The quails and the manna are less directly ascribed to the intercession of Moses. The brazen serpent that was lifted up as a sign of the Divine protection against the snakes of the desert (Num. xxi. 8, 9) was directly connected with his name, down to the latest times of the nation (2 K. xviii. 4; John. iii. 14). Of all the relics of his time, with the exception of the Ark, it was the one longest preserved. [NEHUSHTAN.]

The route through the wilderness is described as having been made under his guidance. The particular spot of the encampment is fixed by the cloudy pillar. But the direction of the people first to the Red Sea, and then to Mount Sinai (where he had been before), is communicated through Moses, or given by him. According to the tradition of Memphis, the passage of the Red Sea was effected through Moses's knowledge of the movement of the tide (Eus. *Præp. Ev.* ix. 27). And in all the wanderings from Mount Sinai he is said to have had the assistance of Jethro. In the Mussulman legends, as if to avoid this appearance of human aid, the place of Jethro is taken by El Kuhdr, the mysterious benefactor of mankind (D'Herbelot, *Moussa*). On approaching Palestine the office of the leader becomes blended with that of the general or the conqueror. By Moses the spies were sent to explore the country. Against his advice took place the first disastrous battle at Hormah. To his guidance is ascribed the circuitous route by which the nation approached Palestine from the east, and to his generalship the two successful campaigns in which SIHON and OG were defeated, The narrative is told so shortly, that we are in danger of forgetting that at this last stage of his life Moses must have been as much a conqueror and victorious soldier as Joshua.

(*b.*) His character as a Prophet is, from the nature of the case, more distinctly brought out. He is the first as he is the greatest example of a prophet in the O. T. The name is indeed applied to Abraham before (Gen. xx. 7), but so casually as not to enforce our attention. But, in the case of Moses, it is given with peculiar emphasis. In a certain sense, he appears as the centre of a prophetic circle, now for the first time named. His brother and sister were both endowed with prophetic gifts. Aaron's fluent speech enabled him to act the part of Prophet for Moses in the first instance, and Miriam is expressly called "the Prophetess." The seventy elders, and Eldad and Medad also, all "prophesied" (Num. xi. 25–27).

But Moses (at least after the Exodus) rose high

---

a An illustration of these passages is to be found in one of the representations of Rameses II. (contemporary with Moses), in like manner calling out water

from the desert-rocks (see Brugsch, *Hist. de l'Eg.* vol. i. p. 158).

b See *S. & P.*, 46, 47, also Wolff's *Travels*, 2d ed p. 125

above all these. The others are spoken of as more or less inferior. Their communications were made to them in dreams and figures (Deut. xiii. 1-4; Num. xii. 6). But "Moses was not so." With him the Divine revelations were made—"mouth to mouth, even apparently, and not in dark speeches, and the similitude of JEHOVAH shall he behold" (Num. xii. 8). In the Mussulman legends his surname is "Kelim Allah," "the spoken to by God." Of the especial modes of this more direct communication, four great examples are given, corresponding to four critical epochs in his historical career, which help us in some degree to understand what is meant by these expressions in the sacred text. (1.) The appearance of the Divine Presence in the flaming acacia-tree has been already noticed. The usual pictorial representations of that scene — of a winged human form in the midst of the bush, belongs to Philo (*V. M.* i. 12), not to the Bible. No form is described. The "Angel," or "Messenger," is spoken of as being "in the flame." On this it was that Moses was afraid to look, and hid his face, in order to hear the Divine voice (Ex. iii. 2-6). (2.) In the giving the Law from Mount Sinai, the outward form of the revelation was a thick darkness as of a thunder-cloud, out of which proceeded a voice (Ex. xix. 19, xx. 21). The revelation on this occasion was especially of the Name of JEHOVAH. Outside this cloud Moses himself remained on the mountain (Ex. xxiv. 1, 2, 15), and received the voice, as from the cloud, which revealed the Ten Commandments, and a short code of laws in addition (Ex. xx.-xxiii.). On two occasions he is described as having penetrated within the darkness, and remained there, successively, for two periods of forty days, of which the second was spent in absolute seclusion and fasting (Ex. xxiv. 18, xxxiv. 28). On the first occasion he received instructions respecting the tabernacle, from a "pattern showed to him" (xxv. 9, 40; xxvi., xxvii.), and respecting the priesthood (xxviii.-xxxi.). Of the second occasion hardly anything is told us. But each of these periods was concluded by the production of the two slabs or tables of granite, containing the successive editions of the Ten Commandments (Ex. xxxii. 15, 16). On the first of these two occasions the ten moral commandments are those commonly so called (comp. Ex. xx. 1-17, xxxii. 15; Deut. v. 6-22). On the second occasion (if we take the literal sense of Ex. xxxiv. 27, 28), they are the ten (chiefly) ceremonial commandments of Ex. xxxiv. 14-26. The first are said to have been the writing of God (Ex. xxxi. 18, xxxii. 16; Deut. v. 22); the second, the writing of Moses (Ex. xxxiv. 28). (3.) It was nearly at the close of these communications in the mountains of Sinai that an especial revelation was made to him personally, answering in some degree to that which first called him to his mission. In the despondency produced by the apostasy of the molten calf, he besought JEHOVAH to show him "His glory." The wish was thoroughly Egyptian. The same is recorded of Amenoph, the Pharaoh preceding the Exodus. But the Divine answer is thoroughly Biblical. It announced that an actual vision of God was impossible. "Thou canst not see my face; for there shall no man see my face and live." He was commanded to hew two blocks of stone, like those which he had destroyed. He was to come absolutely alone. Even the flocks and herds which fed in the neigh-

boring valleys were to be removed out of the sight of the mountain (Ex. xxxiii. 18, 20; xxxiv. 1, 3). He took his place on a well-known or prominent rock ("the rock," xxxiii. 21). The cloud passed by (xxxiv. 5, xxxiii. 22). A voice proclaimed the two immutable attributes of God, Justice and Love — in words which became part of the religious creed of Israel and of the world (xxxiv. 6, 7). The importance of this incident in the life of Moses is attested not merely by the place which it holds in the sacred record, but by the deep hold that it has taken of the Mussulman traditions, and the local legends of Mount Sinai. It is told, with some characteristic variations, in the Koran (vii. 139), and is commemorated in the Mussulman chapel erected on the summit of the mountain which from this incident (rather than from any other) has taken the name of the Mountain of Moses (*Jebel Músa*). A cavity is shown in the rock, as produced by the pressure of the back of Moses, when he shrank from the Divine glory [a] (*S. & P.* p. 30).

(4.) The fourth mode of Divine manifestation was that which is described as commencing at this juncture, and which continued with more or less continuity through the rest of his career. Immediately after the catastrophe of the worship of the calf, and apparently in consequence of it, Moses removed the chief tent [b] outside the camp, and invested it with a sacred character under the name of "the Tent or Tabernacle of the Congregation" (xxxiii. 7). This tent became henceforth the chief scene of his communications with God. He left the camp, and it is described how, as in the expectation of some great event, all the people rose up and stood every man at his tent door, and looked — gazing after Moses until he disappeared within the tent. As he disappeared the entrance was closed behind him by the cloudy pillar, at the sight of which [c] the people prostrated themselves (xxxiii. 10). The communications within the tent were described as being still more intimate than those on the mountain. "JEHOVAH spake unto Moses face to face, as a man speaketh unto his friend" (xxxiii. 11). He was apparently accompanied on these mysterious visits by his attendant Hoshea (or Joshua), who remained in the tent after his master had left it (xxxiii. 11). All the revelations contained in the books of Leviticus and Numbers seem to have been made in this manner (Lev. i. 1; Num. i. 1).

It was during these communications that a peculiarity is mentioned which apparently had not been seen before. It was on his final descent from Mount Sinai, after his second long seclusion, that a splendor shone on his face, as if from the glory of the Divine Presence. It is from the Vulgate translation of "ray" (קָרַן), "*cornutam* habens faciem," that the conventional representation of the *horns* of Moses has arisen. The rest of the story is told so differently in the different versions that both must be given. (1.) In the A. V. and most Protestant versions, Moses is said to wear a veil in order to hide the splendor. In order to produce this sense, the A. V. of Ex. xxxiv. 33 reads, "and [till] Moses had done speaking with them" — and other versions, "he *had* put on the veil." (2.) In the LXX. and the Vulgate, on the other hand, he is said to put on the veil, not during, but after the conver-

---

a It is, this moment which is seized in the recent sculpture by Mr. Woolner in Llandaff Cathedral.

b According to the LXX. it was his own tent.

c Ewald, *Alterthümer*, p. 329.

sation with the people — in order to hide, not the splendor, but the vanishing away of the splendor; and to have worn it till the moment *a* of his return to the Divine Presence in order to rekindle the light there. With this reading agrees the obvious meaning of the Hebrew words, and it is this rendering of the sense which is followed by St. Paul in 2 Cor. iii. 13, 14, where he contrasts the fearlessness of the Apostolic teaching with the concealment of that of the O. T. "We have no fear, as Moses had, that our glory will pass away."

There is another form of the prophetic gift, in which Moses more nearly resembles the later prophets. We need not here determine (what is best considered under the several books which bear his name, PENTATEUCH, etc.) the extent of his authorship, or the period at which these books were put together in their present form. Eupolemus (Eus. *Praep. Ev.* ix. 26) makes him the author of letters. But of this the Hebrew narrative gives no indication. There are two portions of the Pentateuch, and two only, of which the actual *writing* is ascribed to Moses: (1.) The second Edition of the Ten Commandments (Ex. xxxiv. 28). (2.) The register of the Stations in the Wilderness (Num. xxxiii. 1). But it is clear that the prophetical office, as represented in the history of Moses, included the poetical form of composition which characterizes the Jewish prophecy generally. These poetical utterances, whether connected with Moses by ascription or by actual authorship, enter so largely into the full Biblical conception of his character, that they must be here mentioned.

1. "The song which Moses and the children of Israel sung" (after the passage of the Red Sea, Ex. xv. 1-19). It is, unquestionably, the earliest written account of that event; and, although it may have been in part, according to the conjectures of Ewald and Bunsen, adapted to the sanctuary of Gerizim or Shiloh, yet its framework and ideas are essentially Mosaic. It is probably this song to which allusion is made in Rev. xv. 2, 3: "They stand on the sea of glass mingled with fire . . . . and sing the song of Moses the servant of God."

2. A fragment of a war-song against Amalek —

"As the hand is on the throne of Jehovah,
So will Jehovah war with Amalek
From generation to generation."

(Ex. xvii. 16).

3. A fragment of a lyrical burst of indignation —

"Not the voice of them that shout for mastery,
Nor the voice of them that cry for being overcome,
But the noise of them that sing do I hear."

(Ex. xxxii. 18).

4. Probably, either from him or his immediate prophetic followers, the fragments of war-songs in Num. xxi. 14, 15, 27-30, preserved in the "book of the wars of Jehovah," Num. xxi. 14; and the address to the well, xxi. 16, 17, 18.

5. The song of Moses (Deut. xxxii. 1-43), setting forth the greatness and the failings of Israel. It is remarkable as bringing out with much force the idea of God as the Rock (xxxii. 4, 15, 18, 30, 31, 37). The special allusions to the pastoral riches

of Israel point to the trans-Jordanic territory as the scene of its composition (xxxii. 13, 14).

6. The blessing of Moses on the tribes (Deut. xxxiii. 1-29). If there are some allusions in this psalm to circumstances only belonging to a later time (such as the migration of Dan, xxxiii. 22), yet there is no one in whose mouth it could be so appropriately placed, as in that of the great leader on the eve of the final conquest of Palestine. This poem, combined with the similar blessing of Jacob (Gen. xlix.), embraces a complete collective view of the characteristics of the tribes.

7. The 90th Psalm, "A prayer of Moses, the man of God." The title, like all the titles of the Psalms, is of doubtful authority — and the psalm has often been referred to a later author. But Ewald (*Psalmen*, p. 91) thinks that, even though this be the case, it still breathes the spirit of the venerable Lawgiver. There is something extremely characteristic of Moses, in the view taken, as from the summit or base of Sinai, of the eternity of God, greater even than the eternity of mountains, in contrast with the fleeting generations of man.[b] One expression in the Psalm, as to the limit of human life (70, or at most 80 years) in ver. 10, would, if it be Mosaic, fix its date to the stay at Sinai. Jerome (*Adv. Ruffin.* i. § 13), on the authority of Origen, ascribes the next eleven Psalms to Moses. Cosmas (*Cosmogr.* v. 223) supposes that it is by a younger Moses of the time of David.

How far the gradual development of these revelations or prophetic utterances had any connection with his own character and history, the materials are not such as to justify any decisive judgment. His Egyptian education must, on the one hand, have supplied him with much of the ritual of the Israelite worship. The coincidences between the arrangements of the priesthood, the dress, the sacrifices, the ark, in the two countries, are decisive. On the other hand, the proclamation of the Unity of God not merely as a doctrine confined to the priestly order, but communicated to the whole nation, implies distinct antagonism, almost a conscious recoil against the Egyptian system. And the absence of the doctrine of a future state (without adopting to its full extent the paradox of Warburton) proves at least a remarkable independence of the Egyptian theology, in which that great doctrine held so prominent a place. Some modern critics have supposed that the Levitical ritual was an after-growth of the Mosaic system, necessitated or suggested by the incapacity of the Israelites to retain the higher and simpler doctrine of the Divine Unity — as proved by their return to the worship of the Heliopolitan calf under the sanction of the brother of Moses himself. There is no direct statement of this connection in the sacred narrative. But there are indirect indications of it, sufficient to give some color to such an explanation. The event itself is described as a crisis in the life of Moses, almost equal to that in which he received his first call. In an agony of rage and disappointment he destroyed the monument of his first revelation (Ex. xxxii. 19). He threw up his sacred

---

a In Ex. xxxiv. 34, 35, the Vulgate, apparently by following a different reading, דָּבָר, "with them," for אִתָּם, "with him," differs both from the LXX. and A. V.

b Lord Bacon has given a metrical version of this 90th Psalm, rising in some parts to a tone of grandeur which makes it one of the noblest hymns in our language. See his *Works*, xiv. 125-127 (N. Y. 1864).

      H.

mission (*ib.* 32). He craved and he received a new and special revelation of the attributes of God to console him (*ib.* xxxiii. 18). A fresh start was made in his career (*ib.* xxxiv. 29). His relation with his countrymen henceforth became more awful and mysterious (*ib.* 32–35). In point of fact, the greater part of the details of the Levitical system were subsequent to this catastrophe. The institution of the Levitical tribe grew directly out of it (xxxii. 26). And the inferiority of this part of the system to the rest is expressly stated in the Prophets, and expressly connected with the idolatrous tendencies of the nation. "Wherefore I gave them statutes that were not good, and judgments whereby they should not live" (Ez. xx. 25). "I spake not unto your fathers, nor commanded them in the day that I brought them out of the land of Egypt, concerning burnt-offerings or sacrifices" (Jer. vii. 22).

Other portions of the Law, such as the regulations of slavery, of blood-feud, of clean and unclean food, were probably taken, with the necessary modifications, from the customs of the desert tribes.

But the distinguishing features of the law of Israel, which have remained to a considerable extent in Christendom, are peculiarly Mosaic: the Ten Commandments; and the general spirit of justice, humanity, and liberty, that pervades even the more detailed and local observances.

The prophetic office of Moses, however, can only be fully considered in connection with his whole character and appearance. "By a prophet Jehovah brought Israel out of Egypt, and by a prophet was he preserved" (Hos. xii. 13). He was in a sense peculiar to himself the founder and representative of his people. And, in accordance with this complete identification of himself with his nation, is the only strong personal trait which we are able to gather from his history. "The man Moses was very meek, above all the men that were upon the face of the earth" (Num. xii. 3). The word "meek" is hardly an adequate reading of the Hebrew term עָנָו, which should be rather "much enduring;" and, in fact, his onslaught on the Egyptian, and his sudden dashing the tables on the ground, indicate rather the reverse of what we should call "meekness." It represents what we should now designate by the word "disinterested." All that is told of him indicates a withdrawal of himself, a preference of the cause of his nation to his own interests, which makes him the most complete example of Jewish patriotism. He joins his countrymen in their degrading servitude (Ex. ii. 11, v. 4). He forgets himself to avenge their wrongs (ii. 14). He desires that his brother may take the lead instead of himself (Ex. iv. 13). He wishes that not he only, but all the nation were gifted alike: "Enviest thou for my sake?" (Num. xi. 29). When the offer is made that the people should be destroyed, and that he should be made "a great nation" (Ex. xxxii. 10), he prays that they may be forgiven — if not, blot me, I pray Thee, out of Thy book which Thou hast written" (xxxii. 32). His sons were not raised to honor. The leadership of the people passed, after his death, to another tribe. In the books which bear his name, Abraham, and not himself, appears as the real father of the nation. In spite of his great preëminence, they are never "the children of Moses."

In exact conformity with his life is the account of his end. The Book of Deuteronomy describes, and is, the long last farewell of the prophet to his people. It takes place on the first day of the eleventh month of the fortieth year of the wanderings, in the plains of Moab (Deut. i. 3, 5), in the palm-groves of Abila (Joseph. *Ant.* iv. 8, § 1). [ABEL-SHITTIM.] He is described as 120 years of age, but with his sight and his freshness of strength unabated (Deut. xxxiv. 7). The address from ch. i. to ch. xxx. contains the recapitulation of the Law. Joshua is then appointed his successor. The Law is written out, and ordered to be deposited in the Ark (ch. xxxi). The song and the blessing of the tribes conclude the farewell (cc. xxxii., xxxiii.).

And then comes the mysterious close. As if to carry out to the last the idea that the prophet was to live not for himself, but for his people, he is told that he is to see the good land beyond the Jordan, but not to possess it himself. The sin for which this penalty was imposed on the prophet is difficult to ascertain clearly. It was because he and Aaron rebelled against Jehovah, and "believed Him not to sanctify him," in the murmurings at Kadesh (Num. xx. 12, xxvii. 14; Deut. xxxii. 51), or, as it is expressed in the Psalms (cvi. 33), because he spoke unadvisedly with his lips. It seems to have been a feeling of distrust. "*Can* we (not, as often rendered, can *we*) bring water out of the cliff?" (Num. xx. 10; LXX. μὴ ἐξάξομεν, "surely we cannot.") The Talmudic tradition, characteristically, makes the sin to be that he called the chosen people by the opprobrious name of "rebels." He ascends a mountain in the range which rises above the Jordan Valley. Its name is specified so particularly that it must have been well known in ancient times, though, owing to the difficulty of exploring the eastern side of the Jordan, it is unknown at present. The mountain tract was known by the general name of THE PISGAH. Its summits apparently were dedicated to different divinities (Num. xxiii. 14). On one of these, consecrated to Nebo, Moses took his stand, and surveyed the four great masses of Palestine west of the Jordan — so far as it could be discerned from that height. The view has passed into a proverb for all nations. In two remarkable respects it illustrates the office and character of Moses. First, it was a view, in its full extent, to be imagined rather than actually seen. The foreground alone could be clearly discernible; its distance had to be supplied by what was beyond, though suggested by what was within the actual prospect of the seer.

Secondly, it is the likeness of the great discoverer pointing out what he himself will never reach. To English readers this has been made familiar by the application of this passage to Lord Bacon, originally in the noble poem of Cowley, and then drawn out at length by Lord Macaulay.

"So Moses the servant of Jehovah died there in the land of Moab, according to the word of Jehovah, and He buried him in a 'ravine' in the land of Moab, 'before' Beth-peor — but no man knoweth of his sepulchre unto this day . . . . And the children of Israel wept for Moses in the plains of Moab thirty days" (Deut. xxxiv. 5–8). This is all that is said in the sacred record. Jewish, Arabian, and Christian traditions have labored to fill up the detail. "Amidst the tears of the people — the women beating their breasts, and the children giving way to uncontrolled wailing — he withdrew At a certain point in his ascent he made a sign to the weeping multitude to advance no further, taking with him only the elders, the high-priest Eliezer, and the general Joshua. At the top of the mountain he dismissed the elders — and then, as he was embracing Eliezer and Joshua, and still speaking to them, a cloud suddenly stood over him, and he vanished in a deep valley. He wrote the account of his own death [a] in the sacred books, fearing lest he should be deified" (Joseph. *Ant.* iv. 8, 48). "He died in the last month of the Jewish year." [b] After his death he is called "Melki" (Clem. Alex. *Strom.* i. 343).

His grave, though studiously concealed in the sacred narrative, in a manner which seems to point a warning against the excessive veneration of all sacred tombs, and though never acknowledged by the Jews, is shown by the Mussulmans on the *west* (and therefore the wrong) side of the Jordan, between the Dead Sea and St. Saba (*S. & P.* p. 302).

The Mussulman traditions are chiefly exaggerations of the O. T. accounts. But there are some stories independent of the Bible. One is the striking story (Koran, xviii. 65–80) on which is founded Parnell's *Hermit*. Another is the proof given by Moses of the existence of God to the atheist king (Chardin, x. 836, and in Fabricius, p. 836).

In the O. T. the name of Moses does not occur so frequently, after the close of the Pentateuch, as might be expected. In the Judges it occurs only once — in speaking of the wandering Levite Jonathan, his grandson. In the Hebrew copies, followed by the A. V., it has been superseded by "Manasseh," in order to avoid throwing discredit on the family of so great a man. [MANASSEH, vol. ii. p. 1776 a.] In the Psalms and the Prophets, however, he is frequently named as the chief of the prophets.

In the N. T. he is referred to partly as the representative of the Law — as in the numerous passages cited above — and in the vision of the Transfiguration, where he appears side by side with Elijah. It is possible that the peculiar word rendered "decease" (ἔξοδος) — used only in Luke ix. 31 and 2 Pet. i. 15, where it may have been drawn from the context of the Transfiguration — was suggested by the Exodus of Moses.

As the author of the Law he is contrasted with Christ, the Author of the Gospel: "The law was given by Moses" (John i. 17). The ambiguity and transitory nature of his glory is set against the permanence and clearness of Christianity (2 Cor. iii. 13–18), and his mediatorial character ("the law in the hand of a mediator ") against the unbroken communication of God in Christ (Gal. iii. 19). His "service " of God is contrasted with Christ's sonship (Heb. iii. 5, 6). But he is also spoken of as a likeness of Christ; and, as this is a point of view which has been almost lost in the Church, compared with the more familiar comparisons of Christ to Adam, David, Joshua, and yet has as firm a basis in fact as any of them, it may be well to draw it out in detail.

1. Moses is, as it would seem, the only character of the O. T. to whom Christ expressly likens Himself, "Moses wrote of me" (John v. 46). It is uncertain to what passage our Lord alludes, but the general opinion seems to be the true one — that

it is the remarkable prediction in Deut. xviii. 15, 18, 19 — "The Lord thy God will raise up unto thee a prophet from *the midst of thee*, from thy brethren, like unto me: unto him ye shall hearken . . . . I will raise them up a prophet from among their brethren, like unto thee, and will put my words in his mouth; and he shall speak unto their all that I shall command him. And it shall come to pass, that whosoever will not hearken unto my words which he shall speak in my name, I will require it of him." This passage is also expressly quoted by Stephen (Acts vii. 37, [and by Peter, Acts iii. 22]), and it is probably in allusion to it, that at the Transfiguration, in the presence of Moses and Elijah, the words were uttered, "Hear ye Him."

It suggests three main points of likeness: —

(*a.*) Christ was, like Moses, the great Prophet of the people — the last, as Moses was the first. In greatness of position, none came between them. Only Samuel and Elijah could by any possibility be thought to fill the place of Moses, and they only in a very secondary degree. Christ alone appears, like Moses, as the Revealer of a new name of God — of a new religious society on earth. The Israelites " were baptized unto Moses" (1 Cor. x. 2). The Christians were baptized unto Christ. There is no other name in the Bible that could be used in like manner.

(*b.*) Christ, like Moses, is a Lawgiver: "Him shall ye hear." His whole appearance as a Teacher, differing in much beside, has this in common with Moses, unlike the other prophets, that He lays down a code, a law, for his followers. The Sermon on the Mount almost inevitably suggests the parallel of Moses on Mount Sinai.

(*c.*) Christ, like Moses, was a Prophet out of the midst of the nation — "from their brethren." As Moses was the entire representative of his people, feeling for them more than for himself, absorbed in their interests, hopes, and fears, so, with reverence be it said, was Christ. The last and greatest of the Jewish prophets, He was not only a Jew by descent, but that Jewish descent is insisted upon as an integral part of his appearance. Two of the Gospels open with his genealogy. "Of the Israelites came Christ after the flesh" (Rom. ix. 5). He wept and lamented over his country. He confined himself during his life to their needs. He was not sent "but unto the lost sheep of the house of Israel " (Matt. xv. 24). It is true that his absorption into the Jewish nationality was but the symbol of his absorption into the far wider and deeper interests of all humanity. But it is only by understanding the one that we are able to understand the other; and the life of Moses is the best means of enabling us to understand them both.

2. In Heb. iii. 1–19, xii. 24–29, Acts vii. 37, Christ is described, though more obscurely, as the Moses of the new dispensation — as the Apostle, or Messenger, or Mediator, of God to the people — as the Controller and Leader of the flock or household of God. No other person in the O. T. could have furnished this parallel. In both, the revelation was communicated partly through the life, partly through the teaching; but in both the Prophet was incessantly united with the Guide, the Ruler, the Shepherd.

3. The details of their lives are sometimes, though not often, compared. Stephen (Acts vii.

<hr>

[a] According to the view also of Philo (*V. M.* iii. 39), Moses wrote the account of his death.

[b] In the Arabic traditions the 7th of Adar (Jalaladdin, p. 888).

24-28, 35) dwells, evidently with this view, on the likeness of Moses in striving to act as a peace-maker, and misunderstood and rejected on that very account. The death of Moses, especially as related by Josephus (*ut supra*), immediately sug-gests the Ascension of Christ; and the retardation of the rise of the Christian Church, till after its Founder was withdrawn, gives a moral as well as a material resemblance. But this, though dwelt upon in the services of the Church, has not been expressly laid down in the Bible.

In Jude 9 is an allusion to an altercation between Michael and Satan over the body of Moses. It has been endeavored (by reading 'Ιησοῦ for Μωϋσέως) to refer this to Zech. iii. 2. But it probably refers to a lost apocryphal book, mentioned by Origen, called the "Ascension, or Assumption, of Moses." All that is known of this book is given in Fabri-cius, *Cod. Pseudepigr. V. T.* i. 839–844. The "dispute of Michael and Satan" probably had reference to the concealment of the body to prevent idolatry. Gal. v. 6 is by several later writers said to be a quotation from the "Revelation of Moses" (Fabricius, *ib.* i. 838).[a]   A. P. S.

* If the birth of Moses fell within the period of the XVIIIth Dynasty, this surely cannot be styled an "age of Homeric simplicity." On the contrary, it was the most brilliant era of Egypt in arts and arms, and the monuments show that the manners of the people were highly luxurious. Women were allowed a freedom which is nowhere tolerated in the East at the present day, and which was exceptional among civilized nations of an-tiquity; hence the use of the Nile for bathing could not have been forbidden to their sex by any code of Egyptian propriety. Moreover, a princess would have been able to accomplish a degree of privacy in her ablutions, such, for instance, as could easily be secured to-day along the margin of the palace garden in the island of Koda in the Nile — where, indeed, the Mohammedan tradition locates the scene of the finding of Moses. This incident of the bathing, so contrary to the customs of other nations of antiquity with regard to women, gives veri-similitude to the story.

The entire absence of the marvelous in this Biblical narrative of the infancy of Moses is in striking contrast with the Rabbinical legends, and with the tendency of an inventor to exaggerate the early history of such a hero, and to multiply fables and wonders. The stories of Romulus and Remus, exposed on the bank of the Tiber, suckled by a wolf and fed by a wood-pecker, and of Semiramis preserved in infancy by pigeons that brought her food, bear no analogy to this account of the preser-vation of Moses. The whole air of the former is fabulous; while the latter gives a natural and suffi-cient explanation of the incident, without seeking to magnify the incident itself. It was natural, for the reason assigned, that the Egyptian king, jealous of the growing numbers of a foreign race, should seek to exterminate them by destroying their male

offspring. It was natural that the parents of Moses should seek to save him alive. When they could no longer hide him, the expedient of committing him to a floating cradle upon the reedy margin of the river that flowed by the door, was but the natural ingenuity of maternal affection. The find-ing of the child by the king's own daughter was a perfectly natural incident, and her immediate adoption of the child was but the natural prompting of a woman's sympathy. The addition of Philo that she afterwards used devices upon her own person with a view to represent Moses as her own child, is one of those fanciful legends which by con-trast enable one the better to appreciate the sim-plicity of the Bible story. (Phil. *Mos.* i. 5.) This narrative has nothing in common with the mythi-cal inventions of later times.

The incident which first brings Moses before us in the character of a deliverer illustrates the mag-nanimity of his nature, in openly espousing the cause of the injured, and identifying himself with his oppressed race, while at the same time it ex-hibits a rude impulsiveness of spirit which needed to be subdued before he could be fitted for his great work of leadership. Augustine condemns his kill-ing the Egyptian as a deed of unjustifiable violence. The Koran represents it as a work of Satan, of which Moses repented. Philo applauds it as a pious action. In his own code Moses makes a wide distinction between killing by guile, and killing through sudden heat, to avenge an injury or injus-tice. Certainly a quick sympathy with the suffer-ing and oppressed marks a noble nature; yet, from the subsequent narrative, it would appear that Moses in this act had mistaken the will of God as to the manner of delivering Israel, since this would be accomplished not by a violent insurrection, but by the manifestation of Divine power.

In the wilderness of Arabia Petræa Moses would find a secure retreat from the rage of Pharaoh — especially if at that time the Egyptians had been dispossessed of their dominion in the peninsula. Bunsen (*Egypt's Place*, bk. iv. pt. ii. sec. v.) argues that since the copper mines of Sarbût el Khadim were worked from the time of Tuthmosis II. down to that of Rameses the Great, the life of Moses could not have fallen within this period. Lepsius (*Briefe aus Ægypten*) traces the steles of Sarbût from the last dynasty of the old monarchy to the last king of the XIXth Dynasty. Yet the presence of an Egyptian garrison at Sarbût may have been no greater restraint upon the Nomads of that time, than are the garrisons of Nûkhl and Akaba upon the Alouins of to-day.

The scenes of the desert life of Moses, following so closely upon his life in Egypt, again verify the narrative by their fidelity to nature. The incident at the well could hardly have happened in Egypt, where water for almost all purposes was drawn from the river, and where the people were more agricultural than pastoral, — but it belongs to Arabian life.

---

[a] In later history, the name of Moses has not been forgotten. In the early Christian Church he appears in the Roman catacombs in the likeness of St. Peter, partly, doubtless, from his being the leader of the Jewish, as Peter of the Christian Church, partly from his connection with the Rock. It is as striking the Rock that he appears under Peter's name.

In the Jewish, as in the Arabian nation, his name has in later years been more common than in former ages, though never occurring again (perhaps, as in the case of David, and of Peter in the Papacy, from mo-tives of reverence) in the earlier annals, as recorded in the Bible. Moses Maimonides, Moses Mendelssohn. Músa the conqueror of Spain, are obvious instances. Of the first of these three a Jewish proverb testifies that "From Moses to Moses there was none like Moses."

It was in the desert, where the greatness and majesty of God are so strikingly contrasted with the littleness and nothingness of man, and where everything invites to religious contemplation, that Moses attained to that high spiritual development which qualified him to be "the spokesman and interpreter of the divine mysteries." As Ewald (*Geschichte des Volkes Israel*) has said, "It was necessary for Moses, before his prophetic work began, to be so imbued with the power of religion that from that moment he became a new man. This first seized on him in the calm and stillness of life; — the bush in the desolate waste suddenly became to the simple shepherd a burning shrine, out of whose brightness the angel of God spake to him. Thenceforth he thought and acted under the direct assurance of God. That there is no redemption from Egyptian bondage but in free obedience to the clearly perceived will of the Heavenly Father, no deliverance from idolatry and the whole superstition of Egypt but by the service of the purely spiritual God; these truths, and such as these, must have come before the eye of Moses in all the power of a divine illumination, while as yet they had never been recognized with equal certainty by any one. In Moses were present all the necessary conditions to make him the greatest prophet of high antiquity."

The influence of Egyptian thought, manners, and institutions has been considered in another place. [LAW OF MOSES.] But his conception of God as a pure spirit, infinitely holy, and his conception of love as the true basis of human society, are so remote from Egyptian influence, and so sublime in themselves, as almost to necessitate the theory of a divine inspiration to account for their existence.

As the incident of the burning bush rests solely upon the authority of Moses himself, some have treated it as a spiritual hallucination, and others have classed it with the pretended night-vision of Mohammed. But Mohammed never wrought a miracle openly; whereas Moses, using the staff given him at the burning-bush, wrought miracles upon the grandest scale in presence of two nations. Hence, to discredit his story of the burning bush and the serpent-rod, is either to set aside the whole history of the Exodus and of Israel in the desert, or to assume that by the miracles in Egypt Jehovah put his seal to a fantasy or an imposture. Moreover there is nothing in this story to magnify Moses as a hero; on the contrary, with a hesitancy that borders upon stubbornness, and a distrust that betrays a lurking unbelief, he appears quite at disadvantage. The story of the divine call of Moses is very unlike the mythical treatment of a hero. And the same is true of the whole narrative of his interviews with Pharaoh, and of the wonders performed in Egypt, at the Red Sea, and in the wilderness of Sinai. Never was there a great leader who obtruded himself so little, and was so careful to ascribe all his achievements to God — even putting upon record his own infirmities, whenever he was for a moment betrayed into petulance or presumption. The artlessness and honesty of the story in all that concerns Moses himself prepares us to receive as credible the supernatural events that are incorporated with it.

It is quite possible that some traces of Moses will yet be found in Egyptian literature, more definite and decisive than the brief allusions of Manetho which have come down to us through Josephus. Lauth (*Moses der Ebräer*) finds the Moses of the Hebrew books in the *Mesu* of the Papyri at Leyden, registered as Anastasi I. and Anastasy I. 350, and he has even attempted to identify him with the Mohar or hero whose travels in Syria and Phœnicia in the fourteenth century B. C. have lately been deciphered by Chabas (*Voyage d'un Égyptien*). As yet, however, this interpretation is simply tentative; but we may confidently hope to obtain from Egyptian sources some verification of the personality and the period of a man who figured so grandly in Egyptian and Arabian history.   J. P. T.

* A Latin version of a large portion of the work referred to by some of the Christian fathers as the "Ascension" or " Assumption ('Αναληψις) of Moses" is contained in a palimpsest manuscript of the sixth century belonging to the Ambrosian Library at Milan, and was first published by the Librarian, A. M. Ceriani, in his *Monumenta sacra et profana*, etc. Tom. I. Fasc. i., Mediolani, 1861. It was first *critically* edited by Hilgenfeld in his *Novum Testamentum extra Canonem receptum*, Fasc. i. pp. 93–115 (Lips. 1866), who, with the aid of Gutschmid, Lipsius, and others, corrected many of the errors of the manuscript, and brought the text, for the most part, into a readable condition. It was next edited with a German translation and copious notes by Volkmar, as the third volume of his *Handbuch zu den Apokryphen*, Leipz. 1867, and again by M. Schmidt and A. Merx in Merx's *Archiv für wissensch. Erforschung des alten Test.*, 1867, Heft 2. Still more recently it has been retranslated from Latin into Greek, with critical and explanatory notes, by Hilgenfeld, in his *Zeitschr. f. wiss. Theol.*, 1868, pp. 273–309, 356. Critical discussions of various points connected with the work will also be found in the same periodical for 1867, pp. 217 ff. (against Volkmar), 448 (by M. Haupt), 1868, pp. 76–108 (by H. Rönsch), 466 ff. (do.), and 1869, pp. 213–228 (do.). See also Ewald in the *Göttinger Gel. Anz.* for 1862, pp. 3–7; 1867, pp. 110–117; and *Gesch. Christus'*, 3e Aug. (1867), pp. 73–82; Langen (Cath.), *Das Judenthum*, etc. (1866), pp. 102–110; F. Philippi, *Das Buch Henoch*, etc. (1868), pp. 166–191; and an article by Wieseler. *Die jüngst aufgefundene Aufnahme Moses nach Ursprung und Inhalt untersucht*, in the *Jahrb. f. deutsche Theol.*, 1868, pp. 622–648.

The work may be divided into two principal parts. In the first, Moses, just before his death, is represented as giving to Joshua, as his appointed successor, a sketch of the future history of the chosen people, ending with their final triumph over the Roman power, here symbolized by the Eagle, as in the 2d book of Esdras. This is followed by a self-distrustful speech of Joshua, to which Moses makes an encouraging reply, broken off abruptly by the imperfection of the manuscript, which has, besides, a considerable number of illegible lines or words. Though the importance of this document is strangely exaggerated by Volkmar, it is of no little interest as illustrating the state of feeling and the theocratic or Messianic expectations of a portion, at least, of the Jews, at the time when it was written. The critics as yet differ pretty widely concerning the date. Ewald assigns its origin to the year 6 A. D. Wieseler supposes it to have been written by a Galilæan Zealot, about 2 years before Christ, soon after the troubles connected with the death of Herod. Hilgenfeld places it in the reign of Claudius, A. D. 44; Langen soon after the destruction of Jerusalem; Volkmar and Philippi about 1:17 A. D. The most important passage bearing on the date is unfortunately mutilated in the manuscript. To discuss here this or other questions connected with the work would lead us too far.

It should be added that a "Revelation of Moses" has recently been published from four Greek manuscripts by Tischendorf in his *Apocalypses apocryphae*, Lips. 1866. It is a fanciful amplification of the Biblical history of Adam and Eve and their immediate descendants, in the spirit of the Jewish Haggada, resembling the Book of Jubilees or Little Genesis.   A.

* MOSES, BOOKS OF. [PENTATEUCH.]
* MOSES, LAW OF. [LAW OF MOSES.]

MOSOL'LAM (Μοσόλλαμος: *Bosoramus*) = MESHULLAM 11 (1 Esdr. ix. 14; comp. Ezr. x. 15).

MOSOL'LAMON (Μοσόλλαμος; [Vat. Μεσολαβων:] *Mosolamus*) = MESHULLAM 10 (1 Esdr. viii. 44; comp. Ezr. viii. 16).

* MOTE (κάρφος: *festuca*), Matt. vii. 3–5; Luke vi. 41, 42. The original word here used properly denotes a small particle of something *dry*, as wood, chaff, or straw. The rendering "straw" or "splinter" is preferred by some as forming a more lively antithesis to "beam." For the proverb see the notes of Wetstein and Tholuck on Matt. vii. 3–5.   A.

MOTH (עָשׁ,[a] *'âsh:* σής, ἀράχνη, ταραχή, χρόνος; Sym. εὐρώς; Aq. βρῶσις: *tinea, aranea*). By the Hebrew word we are certainly to understand some species of clothes-moth (*tinea*); for the Greek σής, and the Latin *tinea*, are used by ancient authors to denote either the larva or the imago of this destructive insect, and the context of the several passages where the word occurs is sufficiently indicative of the animal. Reference to the destructive habits of the clothes-moth is made in Job iv. 19, xiii. 28; Ps. xxxix. 11; Is. l. 9, li. 8; Hos. v. 12; Matt. vi. 19, 20; Luke xii. 33, and in Ecclus. xix. 3, xlii. 13; indeed, in every instance but one where mention of this insect is made, it is in reference to its habit of destroying garments; in Job xxvii. 18, "He buildeth his house as a moth," it is clear that allusion is made either to the well-known case of the *Tinea pellionella* (see woodcut), or some allied species, or else to the leaf-building larvae of some other member of the *Lepidoptera*. "I will be to Ephraim as a moth," in Hos. v. 12, clearly means "I will consume him as a moth consumes garments." The expression of the A. V. in Job iv. 19, "are crushed before the moth," is certainly awkward and ambiguous; for the different interpretations of this passage see Rosenmüller's *Schol.* ad loc., where it is argued that the words rendered "before the moth" signify, "*as* a moth (destroys garments)." So the Vulg. "consumentur veluti a tinea" (for this use of the Hebrew phrase, see 1 Sam. i. 16. Similar is the Latin *ad faciem*, in Plaut. *Cistell.* i. 1, 73). Others take the passage thus — "who are crushed even as the frail moth is crushed." Either sense will suit the passage; but see the different explanation of Lee (*Comment. on Job*, ad loc.). Some writers understand the word βρῶσις of Matt. vi. 19, 20, to denote some species of moth (*tinea gra-*

nella?); others think that σής καὶ βρῶσις by hendiadys = σής βιβρώσκουσα (see Scultet. *Ex. Evang.* ii. c. 35). [RUST.] The Orientals were fond of forming repositories of rich apparel (Hammond, *Annot.* on Matt. vi. 19), whence the frequent allusion to the destructiveness of the clothes-moth.

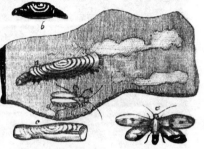

The Clothes-Moth.   (*Tinea pellionella.*)
a. Larva in a case constructed out of the substance on which it is feeding.
b. Case cut at the ends.
c. Case cut open by the larva for enlarging it.
d, e. The perfect insect.

The British tineae which are injurious to clothes, fur, etc., are the following: *tinea tapetzella*, a common species often found in carriages, the larva feeding under a gallery constructed from the lining; *t. pellionella*, the larva of which constructs a portable case out of the substance in which it feeds, and is very partial to feathers. This species, writes Mr. H. T. Stainton to the author of this article, "certainly occurs in Asia Minor, and I think you may safely conclude, that it and *bisellinta* (an abundant species often found in horse-hair linings of chairs) will be found in any old furniture warehouse at Jerusalem." For an interesting account of the habits and economy of the clothes-moths, see Rennie's *Insect Architecture*, p. 190, and for a systematic enumeration of the British species of the genus *Tinea*, see *Insecta Britannica*, vol. iii. The clothes-moths belong to the group *Tineina*, order *Lepidoptera*. For the Hebrew עָשׁ (*Sâs*) see WORM.   W. H.

MOTHER (אֵם: μήτηρ: *mater*). The superiority of the Hebrew over all contemporaneous systems of legislation and of morals is strongly shown in the higher estimation of the mother in the Jewish family, as contrasted with modern oriental, as well as ancient oriental and classical usage. The king's mother, as appears in the case of Bathsheba, was treated with especial honor (1 K. ii. 19; Ex. xx. 12; Lev. xix. 3; Deut. v. 16, xxi. 18, 21; Prov. x. 1, xv. 20, xvii. 25, xxix. 15, xxxi. 1, 30). [CHILDREN; FATHER; KINDRED; KING, vol. ii. p. 1540 b; WOMEN.]
                                H. W. P.

MOUNT, MOUNTAIN. In the O. T. our translators have employed this word to represent the following terms only of the original: (1) the Hebrew הַר, *har*, with its derivative or kindred הָרָר, *hârâr*, or הֶרֶר, *herer;* and (2) the Chaldee טוּר, *tûr:* this last occurs only in Dan. ii. 35, 45. In the New Testament it is confined almost exclusively to representing ὄρος. In the Apocrypha the same usage prevails as in the N. T., the only exception being in 1 Macc. xii. 36, where "mount" is put for ὄφος, probably a mound, as we should now say, or embankment, by which Simon cut off the communication between the citadel on the Temple mount and the town of Jerusalem. For this Josephus (*Ant.* xiii. 5, § 11) has τεῖχος, a wall.

But while they have employed "mount" and "mountain" for the above Hebrew and Greek terms only, the translators of the A. V. have also occasionally rendered the same terms by the English word "hill," thereby sometimes causing a confusion and disconnection between the different parts of the narrative which it would be desirable to avoid. Examples of this are given under HILLS (vol. ii. p. 1077). Others will be found in 1 Macc. xiii. 52, compared with xvi. 20; Jud. vi. 12, 13, comp. with x. 10, xiii. 10.

The Hebrew word *har*, like the English "mountain," is employed both for single eminences more or less isolated, such as Sinai, Gerizim, Ebal, Zion, and Olivet, and for ranges, such as Lebanon. It is also applied to a mountainous country or district, as in Josh. xi. 16, where "the mountain of Israel" is the highland of Palestine, as opposed to the "valley and the plain;" and in Josh. xi. 21, xx. 7, where "the mountain of Judah" (A. V. in the former case "mountains") is the same as "the hill-country" in xxi. 11. Similarly Mount Ephraim (Har Ephraim) is the mountainous district occupied by that tribe, which is evident from the fact that the Mount Gaash, Mount Zemaraim, and the hill of Phinehas, and the towns of Shechem, Shamir, Timnath-Serach, besides other cities (2 Chr. xv. 8), were all situated upon it.[c] So also the "mountain of the Amorites" is apparently the elevated country east of the Dead Sea and Jordan (Deut. i. 7, 19, 20), and "Mount Naphtali" the very elevated and hilly tract allotted to that tribe.

The various eminences or mountain-districts to which the word *har* is applied in the O. T. are as follow: —

ABARIM; AMANA; OF THE AMALEKITES; OF THE AMORITES; ARARAT; BAALAH; BAAL-HERMON; BASHAN; BETHEL; BETHER; CARMEL; EBAL; EPHRAIM; EPHRON; ESAU; GAASH; GERIZIM; GILBOA; GILEAD; HALAK; HERES; HERMON; HOR[b] (2); HOREB; OF ISRAEL; JEARIM; JUDAH; OLIVET, or OF OLIVES; MIZAR; MORIAH; NAPHTALI; NEBO; PARAN; PERAZIM; SAMARIA; SEIR; SEPHAR; SINAI; SION, SIRION, or SHENIR (all names for Hermon); SHAPHER; TABOR; ZALMON; ZEMARAIM; ZION.

THE MOUNT OF THE VALLEY (הַר הָעֵמֶק: ὁ ὄρος Ἐμέθ; Alex. ᵈ Ἐμακ: *mons convallis*) was a district on the East of Jordan, within the territory allotted to Reuben (Josh. xiii. 19), containing a number of towns. Its name recalls a similar juxtaposition of "mount" and "valley" in the name of "Langdale Pikes," a well-known mountain in our own country.

The word *har* became, at least in one instance, incorporated with the name which accompanied it, so as to form one word. Har Gerizzim, Mount Gerizim, appears in the writers of the first centuries of the Christian era as πόλις Ἀργαριζὶν (Eupolemius), ὄρος Ἀργαρίζον (Marinus), *mons Agazaren* (*Itin. Hierosolym.* p. 587). This is also, as has already been noticed (see vol. i. p. 156 b), the origin of the name of Armageddon; and it may possibly be that of Atabyrion or Itabyrion, the form under which the name of Mount Tabor is given by the LXX., Stephanus of Byzantium, and others, and which may have been a corruption, for the sake of euphony, from Ἀρταβύριον : — Ἀταβύριον, Ἰταβύριον.

The frequent occurrence throughout the Scriptures of personification of the natural features of the country is very remarkable. The following are, it is believed, all the words[e] used with this object in relation to mountains or hills: —

1. HEAD, רֹאשׁ, *Rôsh*, Gen. viii. 5; Ex. xix. 20; Deut. xxxiv. 1; 1 K. xviii. 42 (A. V "top").

2. EARS, אָזְנוֹת, *Aznôth*. Aznoth-Tabor, Josh xix. 34: possibly in allusion to some projection on the top of the mountain. The same word is perhaps found in UZZEN-SHERAH.

3. SHOULDER, כָּתֵף, *Cathéph*. Deut. xxxiii. 12; Josh. xv. 8, and xviii. 16 ("side"); all referring to the hills on or among which Jerusalem is placed. Josh. xv. 10, "the *side* of Mount Jearim."

4. SIDE, צַד, *Tsad*. (See the word for "side" of a man in 2 Sam. ii 16, Ez. iv. 4, &c.) Used in reference to a mountain in 1 Sam. xxiii. 26, 2 Sam. xiii. 34.

5. LOINS or FLANKS, כְּסָלֹת, *Cisloth*. Chisloth-Tabor, Josh. xix. 12. It occurs also in the name of a village, probably situated on this part of the mountain, Ha-Cesulloth, הַכְּסֻלּוֹת, *i. e.* the "loins" (Josh. xix. 18). [CHESULLOTH.]

6. RIB, צֵלָע, *Tséla*. Only used once, in speaking of the Mount of Olives, 2 Sam. xvi. 13, and there translated "side," ἐκ πλευρᾶς τοῦ ὄρους.

7. BACK, שְׁכֶם, *Shecem*. Possibly the root of the name of the town Shechem, which may be derived from its situation, as it were on the back of Gerizim.

8. THIGH, יָרְכָה, *Jarcah*. (See the word for the "thigh" of a man in Judg. iii. 16, 21.) Applied to Mount Ephraim, Judg. xix. 1, 18; and to Lebanon, 2 K. xix. 23; Is. xxxvii. 24. Used also for the "sides" of a cave, 1 Sam. xxiv. 3.

---

[a] In the same manner "The Peak," originally the name of the highest mountain of Derbyshire, has now been extended to the whole district.

[b] Mount Hor is probably the "great mountain" — the "mountain of mountains," according to the oriental custom of emphasizing an expression by doubling the word.

[c] 1 K. xvi. 24, "the hill Samaria;" accurately, "the mountain Shomeron."

[d] The same reading is found in the LXX. of Jer. xlvii. 5, xlix. 4.

[e] With perhaps four exceptions, all the above terms are used in our own language; but, in addition, we speak of the "crown," the "instep," the "foot," the "toe," and the "breast" or "bosom" of a mountain or hill. "Top" is perhaps only a corruption of *kopf*, "head." Similarly we speak of the "mouth," and the "gorge" (*i. e.* the "throat") of a ravine; and a "tongue" of land. Compare too the word *col*, "neck," in French.

v. The word translated "covert" in 1 Sam. xxv. 20 is סֵתֶר, *Séther*, from סָתַר, "to hide," and probably refers to the shrubbery or thicket through which Abigail's path lay. In this passage "hill" should be "mountain."

The Chaldee טוּר, *túr*, is the name still given to the Mount of Olives, the *Jebel et-Túr*.

The above is principally taken from the Appendix to Professor Stanley's *Sinai and Palestine*, § 23. See also 249, and 338 *note*, of that work. G.

MOUNT (Is. xxix. 3; Jer. vi. 6, &c.). [SIEGE.]

* MOUNT OF THE AM'ALEKITES (Judg. xii. 15, and comp. v. 14, A. V.), or MOUNT OF AM'ALEK. [AMALEKITES.]

* MOUNT E'PHRAIM. [EPHRAIM, MOUNT, Amer. ed.]

MOUNTAIN OF THE AM'ORITES

הַר הָאֱמֹרִי : ὄρος τοῦ Ἀμορραίου : *Mons Amorrhæi*), specifically mentioned Deut. i. 19, 20 (comp. 44), in reference to the wandering of the Israelites in the desert. It seems to be the range which rises abruptly from the plateau of *et-Tíh*, running from a little S. of W. to the N. of E., and of which the extremities are the *Jebel Araíf en-Nakah* westward, and *Jebel el-Mukrah* eastward, and from which line the country continues mountainous all the way to Hebron. [WILDERNESS OF WANDERING.] H. H.

MOURNING.*a* The numerous list of words employed in Scripture to express the various actions which are characteristic of mourning, show in a great degree the nature of the Jewish customs in this respect. They appear to have consisted chiefly in the following particulars:—

1. Beating the breast or other parts of the body.
2. Weeping and screaming in an excessive degree.
3. Wearing sad-colored garments.
4. Songs of lamentation.
5. Funeral feasts.
6. Employment of persons, especially women, to lament.

And we may remark that the same words, and in many points the same customs prevailed, not only in the case of death, but in cases of affliction or calamity in general.

(1.) Although in some respects a similarity exists between Eastern and Western usage, a similarity which in remote times and in particular nations was stronger than is now the case, the difference between each is on the whole very striking. One marked feature of oriental mourning is what may be called its studied publicity, and the careful observance of the prescribed ceremonies. Thus Abraham, after the death of Sarah, came, as it were in state, to mourn and weep for her, Gen. xxiii. 2. Job, after his misfortunes, "arose and rent his mantle (*meil*, DRESS, i. 621 *a*), and shaved his head, and fell down upon the ground, on the ashes," Job i. 20, ii. 8, and in like manner his friends "rent every one his mantle, and sprinkled dust upon their heads, and sat down with him on the ground seven days and seven nights" without speaking, ii. 12, 13. We read also of high places, streets, and house-tops, as places especially chosen for mourning, not only by Jews but by other nations, Is. xv. 3; Jer. iii. 21, xlviii. 38; 1 Sam. xi. 4, xxx. 4; 2 Sam. xv. 30.

(2.) Among the particular forms observed the following may be mentioned:—

a. Rending the clothes, Gen. xxxvii. 29, 34, xliv. 13; 2 Chr. xxxiv. 27; Is. xxxvi. 22; Jer. xxxvi. 24 (where the absence of the form is to be noted), xli. 5; 2 Sam. iii. 31, xv. 32; Josh. vii. 6; Joel ii. 13; Ezr. ix. 5; 2 K. v. 7, xi. 14; Matt. xxvi. 65, ἱμάτιον; Mark xiv. 63, χιτών.

b. Dressing in sackcloth [SACKCLOTH], Gen. xxxvii. 34; 2 Sam. iii. 31, xxi. 10; Ps. xxxv. 13; Is. xxxvii. 1; Joel i. 8, 13; Am. viii. 10; Jon. iii. 8, man and beast; Job xvi. 15; Esth. iv. 3, 4; Jer. vi. 26; Lam. ii. 10; 1 K. xxi. 27.

c. Ashes, dust, or earth sprinkled on the person, 2 Sam. xiii. 19, xv. 32; Josh. vii. 6; Esth. iv. 1, 3; Jer. vi. 26; Job ii. 12, xvi. 15, xlii. 6; Is. lxi. 3; Rev. xviii. 19.

d. Black or sad-colored garments, 2 Sam. xiv. 2; Jer. viii. 21; Ps. xxxviii. 6, xlii. 9, xliii. 2; Mal. iii. 14, marg.; Ges. p. 1195.

e. Removal of ornaments or neglect of person, Deut. xxi. 12, 13; Ex. xxxiii. 4; 2 Sam. xiv. 2, xix. 24; Ez. xxvi. 16; Dan. x. 3; Matt. vi. 16, 17. [NAIL.]

f. Shaving the head, plucking out the hair of the head or beard, Lev. x. 6; 2 Sam. xix. 24; Ezr. ix. 3; Job i. 20; Jer. vii. 29, xvi. 6.

g. Laying bare some part of the body. Isaiah himself naked and barefoot, Is. xx. 2. The Egyptian and Ethiopian captives, ib. ver. 4; Is. xlvii. 2, l. 6; Jer. xiii. 22, 26; Nah. iii. 5; Mic. i. 11; Am. viii. 10.

---

a 1. To mourn. אָבַל, πενθέω, *lugeo.*

2. (*a*) אָנַן, γογγύζω, and (*b*) אָנָה, πενθέω, *moereo.* From (*b*) אֲנִיָּה and תַּאֲנִיָּה, στεναγμός, *gemitus.* In Lam. ii. 5, ταπεινούμενος, *humiliatus*; A. V. "mourning," "lamentation."

3. בָּכוּת, πένθος, *fletus*; A. V. *Bachuth.* Also בְּכִית, and בָּכָא, *Baca*, from בָּכָה, κλαίω, *fleo.*

4. נְהִי, θρῆνος, *cantus.* In Ez. ii. 10, הִי, θρῆνος, *lamentatio.* In Ez. xxvii. 32, נִי, θρῆνος, *carmen lugubre*, from נָהָה, θρηνέω, *canto.*

5 סַפֵד, θρηνέω, *lugeo.*

6. מִסְפֵּד, κοπετός, *planctus*, from סָפַד, κόπτω, *plango.* See Eccl. xii. 5.

7. קָדַר, σκοτόομαι, *contristor*, i. e. to wear dark colored clothes. Jer. viii. 21.

8. אָוֶן, *dolor.* [BEN-ONI.]

9. הֶגֶה, μέλος, *carmen.* Ez. ii. 10.

10. מַרְזֵחַ, θίασος, *convivium*; A. V. marg. "mourning feast." Jer. xvi. 5.

11. קִין, or קִינָה, "to beat." Hence part. מְקוֹנְנוֹת, Jer. ix. 17; θρηνούσαι, *lamentatrices*, "mourning women."

In N. T. θρηνέω, ἀλαλάζω, ὀλολύζω, θορυβέομαι, πενθέω, κλαίω, κόπτομαι, κοπετός, πένθος, κλαυθμός, ὀδυρμός; *lugeo, fleo, ploro, plango, moereo, ejulo, luctus, fletus, moeror, planctus, ululatus.*

h. Fasting or abstinence in meat and drink, 2 Sam. i. 12, iii. 35, xii. 16, 22; 1 Sam. xxxi. 13; Ezr. x. 6; Neh. i. 4; Dan. x. 3, vi. 18; Joel i. 14, ii. 12; Ez. xxiv. 17; Zech. vii. 5, a periodical fast during captivity; 1 K. xxi. 9, 12; Is. lviii. 3, 4, 5, xxiv. 7, 9, 11; Mal. iii. 14; Jer. xxxvi. 9; Jon. iii. 5, 7 (of Nineveh); Judg. xx. 26; 2 Chr. xx. 3; Ezr. viii. 21; Matt. ix. 14, 15.

i. In the same direction may be mentioned diminution in offerings to God, and prohibition to partake in sacrificial food, Lev. vii. 20; Deut. xxvi. 14; Hos. ix. 4; Joel i. 9, 13, 16.

k. Covering the "upper lip," i. e. the lower part of the face, and sometimes the head, in token of silence; specially in the case of the leper, Lev. xiii. 45; 2 Sam. xv. 30, xix. 4; Jer. xiv. 4; Ez. xxiv. 17; Mic. iii. 7.

l. Cutting the flesh, Jer. xvi. 6, 7; xli. 5. [CUTTINGS in the FLESH.] Beating the body, Ez. xxi. 12; Jer. xxxi. 19.

m. Employment of persons hired for the purpose of mourning, women "skillful in lamentation," Eccl. xii. 5; Jer. ix. 17; Am. v. 16; Matt. ix. 23. Also flute-players, Matt. ix. 23 [MINSTREL]; 2 Chr. xxxv. 25.

n. Akin to this usage the custom for friends or passers-by to join in the lamentations of bereaved or afflicted persons, Gen. l. 3; Judg. xi. 40; Job ii. 11, xxx. 25, xxvii. 15; Ps. lxxviii. 64; Jer. ix. 1, xxii. 18; 1 K. xiv. 13, 18; 1 Chr. vii. 22; 2 Chr. xxxv. 24, 25; Zech. xii. 11; Luke vii. 12; John xi. 31; Acts viii. 2, ix. 39; Rom. xii. 15. So also in times of general sorrow we find large numbers of persons joining in passionate expressions of grief, Judg. ii. 4, xx. 26; 1 Sam. xxviii. 3, xxx. 4; 2 Sam. i. 12; Ezr. iii. 13; Ez. vii. 16, and the like is mentioned of the priests, Joel ii. 17; Mal. ii. 13; see below.

o. The sitting or lying posture in silence indicative of grief, Gen. xxiii. 3; Judg. xx. 26, 2 Sam. xii. 16, xiii. 31; Job i. 20, ii. 13; Ezr. ix. 3; Lam. ii. 10; Is. iii. 26.

p. Mourning feast and cup of consolation, Jer. xvi. 7, 8.

The period of mourning varied. In the case of Jacob it was seventy days, Gen. l. 3; of Aaron, Num. xx. 29, and Moses, Deut. xxxiv. 8, thirty. A further period of seven days in Jacob's case, Gen. l. 10. Seven days for Saul, which may have been an abridged period in time of national danger, 1 Sam. xxxi. 13.

Excessive grief in the case of an individual may be noticed in 2 Sam. iii. 16; Jer. xxxi. 15, and the same hypocritically, Jer. xli. 6.

(2.) Similar practices are noticed in the Apocryphal books.

a. Weeping, fasting, rending clothes, sackcloth, ashes, or earth on head, 1 Macc. ii. 14, iii. 47, iv. 39, v. 14, xi. 71, xiii. 45; 2 Macc. iii. 19, x. 25, xiv. 15; Jud. iv. 10. 11; viii. 6, ix. 1, xiv. 19 (Assyrians), x. 2, 3, viii. 5; 3 Macc. iv. 6; 2 Esdr. x. 4; Esth. xiv. 2.

b. Funeral feast with wailing, Bar. vi. 32 [or Epist. of Jer. 32]; also Tob. iv. 17; see in reproof of the practice, Aug. Civ. D. viii. 27.

c. Period of mourning, Jud. viii. 6; Ecclus. xxii. 12, seven days, so also perhaps 2 Esdr. v. 20. Bel and Dragon ver. 40.

d. Priests ministering in sackcloth and ashes, the altar dressed in sackcloth, Jud. iv. 11, 14, 15.

e. Idol priests with clothes rent, head and beard shorn, and head bare, Bar. vi. 31 [or Epist of Jer. 31 b].

(4.) In Jewish writings not Scriptural, these notices are in the main confirmed, and in some cases enlarged.

a. Tearing hair and beating breast, Joseph. Ant xvi. 7, § 5, xv. 3, § 9.

b. Sackcloth and ashes, Joseph. Ant. xx. 6, § 1, xix. 8, § 2, Bell. Jud. ii. 12, § 5; clothes rent, ii. 15, § 4.

c. Seven days' mourning for a father, Joseph. Ant. xvii. 8, § 4, Bell. Jud. ii. 1, § 1; for thirty days, B. J. iii. 9, § 5.

d. Those who met a funeral required to join it, Joseph. c. Ap. ii. 26; see Luke vii. 12, and Rom. xii. 15.

e. Flute-players at a funeral, Bell. Jud. iii. 9, § 5. [JAIRUS, Amer. ed.]

The Mishna prescribes seven days' mourning for a father, a mother, son, daughter, brother, sister, or wife (Bartenora, on Moed Katon, iii. 7).

Rending garments is regularly graduated according to the degree of relationship. For a father or mother the garment was to be rent, but not with an instrument, so as to show the breast; to be sewn up roughly after thirty days, but never closed. The same for one's own teacher in the Law, but for other relatives a palm breadth of the upper garment to suffice, to be sewn up roughly after seven days and fully closed after thirty days, Moed Kat. iii. 7; Shabb. xiii. 3; Carpzov, App. Bib. p. 650. Friendly mourners were to sit on the ground, not on the bed. On certain days the lamentation was to be only partial, Moed Kat. l. c. For a wife there was to be at least one hired mourner and two pipers, Cetuboth, iv. 4.

(5.) In the last place we may mention a, the idolatrous "mourning for Tammuz," Ez. viii. 14, as indicating identity of practice in certain cases among Jews and heathens; and the custom in later days of offerings of food at graves, Ecclus. xxx. 18. **b.** The prohibition both to the high-priest and to Nazarites against going into mourning even for a father or mother, Lev. xxi. 10, 11; Num. vi. 7; see Nezir, vii. 1. The inferior priests were limited to the cases of their near relatives, Lev. xxi. 1, 2, 4. **c.** The food eaten during the time of mourning was regarded as impure, Deut. xxvi. 14; Jer. xvi. 5, 7; Ez. xxiv. 17; Hos. ix. 4.

(6.) When we turn to heathen writers we find similar usages prevailing among various nations of antiquity. Herodotus, speaking of the Egyptians, says, "When a man of any account dies, all the womankind among his relatives proceed to smear their heads and faces with mud. They then leave the corpse in the house, and parade the city with their breasts exposed, beating themselves as they go, and in this they are joined by all the women belonging to the family. In like manner the men also meet them from opposite quarters, naked to the waist and beating themselves" (Her. ii. 85). He also mentions seventy days as the period of embalming (ii. 86). This doubtless includes the whole mourning period. Diodorus, speaking of a king's death, mentions rending of garments, suspension of sacrifices, heads smeared with clay, and breasts bared, and says men and women go about in companies of 200 of 300, making a wailing twice-a-day, εὐρύθμως μετ' ᾠδῆς. They abstain from flesh, wheat-bread, wine, the bath, dainties, and in general all pleasure; do not lie on beds, but lament as for an only child during seventy-two days. On the ast day a sort of trial was held of the merits of the deceased, and according to the verdict pronounced by the acclamations of the crowd, he was treated with funeral honors, or the contrary (Diod. Sic. i. 72). Similar usages prevailed in the case of private persons, ib. 91, 92.

The Egyptian paintings confirm these accounts as to the exposure of the person, the beating, and the throwing clay or mud upon the head; and women are represented who appear to be hired mourners (Long, Eg. Ant. ii. 154–159; Wilkinson, Eg. Ant. ii. pp. 358, 387). Herodotus also mentions the Persian custom of rending the garments with wailing, and also cutting off the hair on occasions of death or calamity. The last, he says, was also usual among the Scythians (Her. ii. 66, viii. 99, ix. 24, iv. 71).

Lucian, in his discourse concerning Greek mourning, speaks of tearing the hair and flesh, and wailing, and beating the breast to the sound of a flute, burial of slaves, horses, and ornaments as likely to be useful to the deceased, and the practice for relatives to endeavor to persuade the parents of the deceased to partake of the funeral-feast (περίδειπνον) by way of recruiting themselves after their three days' fast (De Luctu, vol. ii. p. 303, 305, 307, ed. Amsterdam). Plutarch mentions that the Greeks regarded all mourners as unclean, and that women in mourning cut their hair, but the men let it grow. Of the Romans, in carrying corpses of parents to the grave, the sons, he says, cover their heads, but the daughters uncover them, contrary to their custom in each case (Quæst. Rom. vol. vii. pp 74, 82, ed. Reiske).

Greeks and Romans both made use of hired mourners, præficæ, who accompanied the funeral procession with chants or songs. Flowers and perfumes were also thrown on the graves (Ov. Fast. vi. 660; Trist. v. 1, 47; Plato, Legg. vii. 9; Dict. of Antiq. art. Funus). The præficæ seem to be the predecessors of the "mutes" of modern funerals.

(7.) With the practices above mentioned, oriental and other customs, ancient and modern, in great measure agree. D'Arvieux says, Arab men are silent in grief, but the women scream, tear their hair, hands, and face, and throw earth or sand on their heads. The older women wear a blue veil and an old abba by way of mourning garments. They also sing the praises of the deceased (Trav. pp. 269, 270). Niebuhr says both Mohammedans and Christians in Egypt hire wailing women, and wail at stated times (Voy. i. 150). Burckhardt says the women of Atbara in Nubia shave their heads on the death of their nearest relatives, a custom prevalent also among several of the peasant tribes of Upper Egypt. In Berber on a death they usually kill a sheep, a cow, or a camel. He also mentions wailing women, and a man in distress besmearing his face with dirt and dust in token of grief (Nubia, pp. 176, 226, 374). And, speaking of the ancient Arab tribes of Upper Egypt, "I have seen the female relations of a deceased man dance before his house with sticks and lances in their hands and behaving like furious soldiers" (Notes on Bed. i. 280). Shaw says of the Arabs of Barbary, after a funeral the female relations during the space of two or three months go once a week to weep over the grave and offer eatables (see Ecclus. xxx. 18). He also mentions mourning women (Trav. pp. 220, 242). "In Oman," Wellsted says, "there are no hired mourning women, but the females from the neighborhood assemble after a funeral and continue for eight days, from sunrise to sunset, to utter loud lamentations" (Trav. i. 216). In the Arabian Nights are frequent allusions to similar practices, as rending clothes, throwing dust on the head, cutting off the hair, loud exclamation, visits to the tomb, plucking the hair and beard (i. 65, 263, 297, 358, 518, ii. 354, 237, 409). They also mention ten days and forty days as periods of mourning (i. 427, ii. 409). Sir J. Chardin, speaking of Persia, says the tombs are visited periodically by women (Voy. vi. 489). He speaks also of the tumult at a death (ib 482). Mourning lasts forty days: for eight days a fast is observed, and visits are paid by friends to the bereaved relatives; on the ninth day the men go to the bath, shave the head and beard, and return the visits, but the lamentation continues two or three times r week till the fortieth day. The mourning garments are dark-colored, but never black (ib. p. 481). Russell, speaking of the Turks at Aleppo, says, "the instant the death takes place, the women who are in the chamber give the alarm by shrieking as if distracted, and are joined by all the other females in the harem. This conclamation is termed the "wulwaly": a it is so shrill as to be heard, especially in the night, at a prodigious distance. The men disapprove of and take no share in it; they drop a few tears, assume a resigned silence, and retire in private. Some of the near female relations, when apprised of what has happened, repair to the house, and the wulwaly, which had paused for some time, is renewed upon the entrance of each visitant into the harem" (Aleppo, i. 306). He also mentions professional mourners, visits to the grave on the third, seventh, and fortieth days, prayers at the tomb, flowers strewn, and food distributed to the poor. At these visits the shriek of wailing is renewed: the chief mourner appeals to the deceased and reproaches him fondly for his departure. The men make no change in their dress; the women lay aside their jewels, dress in their plainest garments, and wear on the head a handkerchief of a dusky color. They usually mourn twelve months for a husband and six for a father (ib. 311, 312). Of the Jews he says, the conclamation is practiced by the women, but hired mourners are seldom called in to assist at the wulwaly. Both sexes make some alteration in dress by way of mourning. The women lay aside their jewels, the men make a small rent in their outer vestment (ii. 86, 87).

Lane, speaking of the modern Egyptians, says, "After death the women of the family raise cries of lamentation called 'welweléh ' or 'wilwál,' uttering the most piercing shrieks, and calling upon the name of the deceased, 'O, my master! O, my resource! O, my misfortune! O, my glory!' (see Jer. xxii. 18). The females of the neighborhood come to join with them in this conclamation; generally, also, the family send for two or more necklábehs, or public wailing women. Each brings a tambourine, and beating them they exclaim, 'Alas for him.'

---

a Arab. ولول, Heb. יָלַל, Gk. ὀλολύζω, ἀλαλάζω, Lat. ejulo, ululo, an onomatopoetic word common to many languages. See Ges. p. 596; Schœbel, Anal Constit. p. 54; and Russell, vol. i. note 82, chiefly from Schultens.

The female relatives, domestics, and friends, with their hair disheveled, and sometimes with rent clothes, beating their faces, cry in like manner, 'Alas, for him!' These make no alteration in dress, but women, in some cases, dye their shirts, head-veils, and handkerchiefs of a dark-blue color. They visit the tombs at stated periods" (*Mod. Eg.* iii. 152, 171, 195). Wealthy families in Cairo have in the burial-grounds regularly furnished houses of mourning, to which the females repair at stated periods to bewail their dead. The art of mourning is only to be acquired by long practice, and regular professors of it are usually hired, on the occasion of a death, by the wealthier classes (Mrs. Poole, *Englishw. in Egypt*, ii. 100). Dr. Wolff mentions the wailing over the dead in Abyssinia, *Autobiog.* ii. 273. Pietro della Valle mentions a practice among the Jews of burning perfumes at the site of Abraham's tomb at Hebron, for which see 2 Chr. xvi. 14, xxi. 19; Jer. xxxiv. 5; P. della Valle, *Viaggi*, i. 306. The customs of the N. American Indians also resemble those which have been described in many particulars, as the howling and wailing, and speeches to the dead: among some tribes the practice of piercing the flesh with arrows

or sharp stones, visits to the place of the dead (Carver, *Travels*, p. 401; Bancroft, *Hist. of U. States*, ii. 912; Catlin, *N. A. Indians*, i. 90).

The former and present customs of the Welsh, Irish, and Highlanders at funerals may also be cited as similar in several respects, *e. g.* wailing and howling, watching with the corpse, funeral entertainments ("funeral baked meats"), flowers on the grave, days of visiting the grave (Brand, *Pop. Antiq.* ii. 128, &c.; Harmer, *Obs.* iii. 40).

One of the most remarkable instances of traditional customary lamentation is found in the weekly wailing of the Jews at Jerusalem at a spot as near to the Temple as could be obtained. This custom, noticed by St. Jerome, is alluded to by Benjamin of Tudela, and exists to the present day. Jerome, *ad Sophon.* i. 15; *ad Paulam*, Ep. xxxix.; *Early Trav. in Pal.*, p. 83; Raumer, *Palästina*, p. 293; Martineau, *Eastern Life*, p. 471; Robinson, i. 237.

H. W. P.

* It is customary among the Christian men of the upper classes in Syria to make a change to black garments on occasion of a death in the family, or at least to wear black crape over the tarboosh.

G. E. P.

Copper Coins of Vespasian, representing the mourning of Judæa for her Captivity.

MOUSE (עַכְבָּר, *'akbâr:* μῦς: *mus*) occurs in Lev. xi. 29 as one of the unclean creeping things which were forbidden to be used as food. In 1 Sam. vi. 4, 5, five golden mice, "images of the mice that mar the land," are mentioned as part of the trespass offering which the Philistines were to send to the Israelites when they returned the ark. In Is. lxvi. 17, it is said, "They that sanctify themselves . . . . eating swine's flesh, and the abomination, and the mouse, shall be consumed together." The Hebrew word is in all probability generic, and is not intended to denote any particular species of mouse; although Bochart (*Hieroz.* ii. 427), following the Arabic version of Is. lxvi. 17, restricts its meaning to the jerboa (*Dipus jaculus*). The original word denotes a field-ravager,[a] and may therefore comprehend any destructive rodent. It is probable, however, that in 1 Sam. vi. 5, "the mice that mar the land" may include and more particularly refer to the short-tailed field-mice (*Arvicola agrestis*, Flem.), which Dr. Kitto says cause great destruction to the corn-lands of Syria. "Of all the smaller rodentia which are injurious, both in the fields and in the woods, there is not," says Prof. Bell (*Hist. Brit. Quad.* p. 325), "one

which produces such extensive destruction as this little animal, when its increase, as is sometimes the case, becomes multitudinous." The ancient writers frequently speak of the great ravages committed by mice. Herodotus (ii. 141) ascribes the loss of Sennacherib's army to mice, which in the night time gnawed through the bow-strings and shield-straps.

Col. Hamilton Smith (Kitto's *Cycl.* art. "Mouse") says that the hamster and the dormouse are still eaten in common with the jerboa by the Bedoueens; and Gesenius (*Thes. s. v.*) believes some esculent species of dormouse is referred to in Is. lxvi. 17.

W. H.

MOWING (גֵּז; *tonsio*, Am. vii. 1 — LXX. reads Γὼγ ὁ βασιλεύς, either from a various reading or a confusion of the letters ז and ג — a word signifying also a shorn fleece, and rendered in Ps. lxxii. 6 "mown grass"). As the great heat of the climate in Palestine and other similarly situated countries soon dries up the herbage itself, haymaking in our sense of the term is not in use. The term "hay," therefore, in P. B. version of Ps. ovi. 20, for עֵשֶׂב, is incorrect. A. V. "grass." So also Prov. xxvii. 25, and Is. xv. 6. The corn destined for forage is cut with a sickle. The term גֵּזֵר, A. V. "mower," Ps. cxxix. 7, is most com-

---

* Bochart derives it from עָכַל, "to devour," and בַּר, "corn."

monly in A. V. "reaper;" and once, Jer. ix. 22, "harvest-man."

The "king's mowings," Am. vii. 1, i. e. mown grass, Ps. lxxii. 6, may perhaps refer to some royal right of early pasturage for the use of the cavalry. See 1 K. xviii. 5. (Shaw, *Trav.* p. 138; Wilkinson, *Anc. Eg.* abridgm. ii. 43, 50; *Early Trav.*, p. 305. Pietro della Valle, *Viaggi*, ii. p. 237; Chardin, *Voy.*, iii. 370; Layard, *Nin. & Bab*, p. 330; Niebuhr, *Descr. de l'Ar.* p. 139; Harmer, *Obs.*, iv. 386; Burckhardt, *Notes on Bed.*, i. 210.)   H. W. P.

MO'ZA (מוֹצָא [*going forth, door, gate*:] Moσd; [Vat. Ιωσαν;] Alex. Ιωσα: *Mosa*). 1. Son of Caleb the son of Hezron by his concubine Ephah (1 Chr. ii. 46).

2. (Μαισδ, 1 Chr. viii. 36, 37; Μοασδ, Alex. [FA.] Μασα, 1 Chr. ix. 42, 43). Son of Zimri, and descendant of Saul through Micah the son of Mephibosheth.

MO'ZAH (הַמֹּצָה [perh. *the fountain*], with the definite article, ham-Motsah: 'Αμωκή; Alex. Αμωσα: *Amosa*), one of the cities in the allotment of Benjamin (Josh. xviii. 26 only), named between hac-Cephirah and Rekem. The former of these has probably been identified with *Kefir*, 2 miles east of *Yalo*, but no trace of any name resembling Motsah has hitherto been discovered. Interpreting the name according to its Hebrew derivation, it may signify "the spring-head" — the place at which the water of a spring gushes out (Stanley, *S. & P.* App. § 52). A place of this name is mentioned in the Mishna (*Succah*, iv. § 5) as follows: — "There was a place below Jerusalem named Motsa; thither they descended and gathered willow-branches," i. e. for the "Feast of Tabernacles" so called. To this the Gemara adds, "the place was a Colonia *a* (קוֹלְנִיא), that is, exempt from the king's tribute" (Buxtorf, *Lex. Talm.* 2043), which other Talmudists reconcile with the original name by observing that Motsah signifies an outlet or liberation, e. g. from tribute. Bartenora, who lived at Jerusalem, and now lies in the "valley of Jehoshaphat" there, says (in Surenhusius' *Mishna*, ii. 274) that Motsah was but a short distance from the city, and in his time retained the name of Colonia. On these grounds Schwarz (127) would identify Mozah with the present *Kulonieh*, a village about 4 miles west of Jerusalem on the Jaffa road, at the entrance of the great Wady *Beit Hannah*. The interpretations of the Rabbis, just quoted, are not inconsistent with the name being really derived from its having been the seat of a Roman *colonia*, as suggested by Robinson, (*Bibl. Res.* iii. 158). The only difficulty in the way of the identification is that *Kulonieh* can hardly be spoken of as " below Jerusalem " — an expression which is most naturally interpreted of the ravine beneath the city, where the *Bir-Eyub* is, and the royal gardens formerly were. Still there are vestiges of much vegetation about *Kulonieh*, and when the country was more

generally cultivated and wooded, and the climate less arid than at present, the dry river-bed *b* which the traveller now crosses may have flowed with water, and have formed a not unfavorable spot for the growth of willows.   G.

* MUFFLERS. [VEILS, (3.)]

MULBERRY-TREES (בְּכָאִים, *becâim:* κλαυθμών, ἄπιοι: *pyri*) occurs only in 2 Sam. v. 23 and 24, and in the parallel passage of 1 Chr. xiv. 14. The Philistines having spread themselves in the Valley of Rephaim, David was ordered to fetch a compass behind them and come upon them over against the mulberry-trees; and to attack them when he heard the "sound of a going in the tops of the mulberry-trees."

We are quite unable to determine what kind of tree is denoted by the Hebrew בָּכָא ; many attempts at identification have been made, but they are mere conjectures. The Jewish Rabbis, with several modern versions, understand the mulberry-tree; others retain the Hebrew word. Celsius (*Hierob.* i. 335) believes the Hebrew *bâcâ* is identical with a tree of similar name mentioned in a MS. work of the Arabic botanical writer Abu'l Fadli, namely, some species of *Amyris* or *Balsamodendron*. Most lexicographers are satisfied with this explanation. Some modern English authors have adopted the opinion of Dr. Royle, who (Kitto's *Cyc.* art. Baca) refers the Hebrew *bâcâ* to the Arabic *Shajrat-al-bak,c* "the gnat-tree," which he identifies with some species of poplar, several kinds of which are found in Palestine. Rosenmüller follows the LXX. of 1 Chr. xiv. 14, and believes "pear-trees" are signified. As to the claim of the mulberry-tree to represent the *becâim* of Scripture, it is difficult to see any foundation for such an interpretation — for, as Rosenmüller has observed (*Bib. Bot.* p. 256), it is neither "countenanced by the ancient versions nor by the occurrence of any similar term in the cognate languages " — unless we adopt the opinion of Ursinus, who (*Arbor. Bib.* iii. 75), having in view the root of the word *bacah,d* "to weep," identifies the name of the tree in question with the mulberry, "from the blood-like tears which the pressed berries pour forth." Equally unsatisfactory is the claim of the "pear-tree " to represent the *bâcâ ;* for the uncertainty of the LXX., in the absence of further evidence, is enough to show that little reliance is to be placed upon this rendering.

As to the tree of which Abu'l Fadli speaks, and which Sprengel (*Hist. Rei herb.* p. 12) identifies with *Amyris gileadensis*, Lin., it is impossible that it can denote the *bâcâ* of the Hebrew Bible, although there is an exact similarity in form between the Hebrew and Arabic terms: for the *Amyridaceæ* are tropical shrubs, and never could have grown in the Valley of Rephaim, the Scriptural locality for the *becâim*.

The explanation given by Royle, that some poplar

---

a Can this title be in any way connected with the Koulon (κούλον), which is one of the eleven names inserted by the LXX. in the catalogue of the cities of Judah, between verses 59 and 60 of Josh. xv.?

b * It depends on the season of the year whether this river-bed is "dry" or contains water. Several travellers, as Richardson, Otto von Richter, Prokesch, testify that it is quite a running stream, at certain periods of the year, of which indeed proof is seen in

the striking fertility of the valley which it irrigates. (See DECEITFULLY, vol. i. p. 577, Am. ed.)   H.

c شجرة البق, of which, however, Freytag says, " Arbor culicum, ulmus, quia ex succo in fali culis exsiccato culices gignuntur."

d בָּכָה: " to flow by drops," " to weep."

is signified, although in some respects it is well suited to the context of the Scriptural passages, is untenable; for the Hebrew *bàcà* and the Arabic *bukn* are clearly distinct both in form and signification, as is evident from the difference of the second radical letter in each word.[a]

As to the בָּכָא of Ps. lxxxiv. 6, which the A. V. retains as a proper name, we entirely agree with Hengstenberg (*Com. on Ps.* ad loc.), that the word denotes "weeping," and that the whole reference to Baca trees must be given up, but see BACA.

Though there is no evidence to show that the mulberry-tree occurs in the Hebrew Bible, yet the fruit of this tree is mentioned in 1 Macc. vi. 34, as having been, together with grape juice, shown to the elephants of Antiochus Eupator in order to irritate these animals and make them more formidable opponents to the army of the Jews. It is well known that many animals are enraged when they see blood or anything of the color of blood. For further remarks on the mulberry-trees of Palestine see SYCAMINE.   W. H.

MULE, the representative in the A. V. of the following Hebrew words, — *Pered or Pirddh, Recheh,* and *Yémim.*

1. *Pered, Pirddh* (פֶּרֶד, פִּרְדָּה:[b] ὁ ἡμίονος, ἡ ἡμίονος: *mulus, mula*), the common and feminine Hebrew nouns to express the "mule;" the first of which occurs in numerous passages of the Bible, the latter only in 1 K. i. 33, 38, 44. It is an interesting fact that we do not read of mules till the time of David (as to the *yémim,* A. V. "mules," of Gen. xxxvi. 24, see below), just at the time when the Israelites were becoming well acquainted with horses. After this time horses and mules are in Scripture often mentioned together. After the first half of David's reign, as Michaelis (*Comment. on Laws of Moses,* ii. 477) observes, they became all at once very common. In Ezr. ii. 66, Neh. vii. 68, we read of two hundred and forty-five mules; in 2 Sam. xiii. 29, "all the king's sons arose, and every man gat him up upon his mule." Absalom rode on a mule in the battle of the wood of Ephraim at the time when the animal went away from under him and so caused his death. Mules were amongst the presents which were brought year by year to Solomon (1 K. x. 25). The Levitical law forbade the coupling together of animals of different species (Lev. xix. 19), consequently we must suppose that the mules were imported, unless the Jews became subsequently less strict in their observance of the ceremonial injunctions, and bred their mules. We learn from Ezekiel (xxvii. 14) that the Tyrians, after the time of Solomon, were supplied with both horses and mules from Armenia (Togarmah), which country was celebrated for its good horses (see Strabo, xi. 13, § 7, ed. Kramer; comp. also Xenoph. *Anab.* iv. 5, 36; Herod. vii. 40). Michaelis conjectures that the Israelites first became acquainted with mules in the war which David carried on with the king of Nisibis

(Zobah), (2 Sam. viii. 3, 4). In Solomon's time it is possible that mules from Egypt occasionally accompanied the horses which we know the king of Israel obtained from that country; for though the mule is not of frequent occurrence in the monuments of Egypt (Wilkinson's *Anc. Egypt.* i. 386, Lond. 1854), yet it is not easy to believe that the Egyptians were not well acquainted with this animal. That a friendship existed between Solomon and Pharaoh is clear from 1 K. ix. 16, as well as from the fact of Solomon having married the daughter of the king of Egypt: but after Shishak came to the throne a very different spirit prevailed between the two kingdoms: perhaps, therefore, from this date mules were obtained from Armenia. It would appear that kings and great men only rode on mules. We do not read of mules at all in the N. T., perhaps therefore they had ceased to be imported.

2. *Recheh* (רֶכֶשׁ). See DROMEDARY.

3. *Yémim* (יֵמִם: [c] τὸν Ἰαμείν, Vat. and Alex.; τὸν ἐαμίν, Compl.; τοὺς ἰαμείν, Aq. and Sym.: *aquæ calidæ*) is found only in Gen. xxxvi. 24, where the A. V. has "mules" as the rendering of the word. The passage where the Hebrew name occurs is one concerning which various explanations have been attempted. Whatever may be the proper translation of the passage, it is quite certain that the A. V. is incorrect in its rendering — "This was that Anah that found the mules in the wilderness as he fed the asses of Zibeon his father." Michaelis has shown that at this time horses were unknown in Canaan; consequently mules could not have been bred there. The Talmudical writers believe that Anah was the first to find out the manner of breeding mules: but, besides the objection urged above, it may be stated that neither the Hebrew nor its cognates have any such a word to signify "mules." Bochart (*Hieroz.* i. 209, 10), following the reading of the Samaritan Version and Onkelos, renders *yémim* by "emims" or "giants" (Gen. xiv. 5); but this explanation has been generally abandoned by modern critics (see Rosenmüller, *Schol. in Gen.*; Geddes, *Crit. Rem.* xiv. 5). The most probable explanation is that which interprets *yémim* to mean "warm springs," as the Vulg. has it; and this is the interpretation adopted by Gesenius and modern scholars generally: the passage will then read, "this was that Anah who while he was feeding his father's asses in the desert discovered some hot springs." This would be considered an important discovery, and as such worthy of record by the historian; but if, with some writers, we are to understand merely that Anah discovered water, there is nothing very remarkable in the fact, for his father's asses could not have survived without it.[d]   W. H.

MUPPIM (מֻפִּים [perh. *darkness, sorrow,* Fürst]: Μαμφίμ; [Alex. Μαμφειμ:] *Mophim*), a Benjamite, and one of the fourteen descendants of Rachel who belonged to the original colony of the sons of Jacob in Egypt (Gen. xlvi. 21). In Num. xxvi. 39 the name is written Shupham, and the

---

[a] ב in the Hebrew, ﺝ in the Arabic; בכא, ﺑﻖ.

[b] A word of doubtful etymology. Gesenius refers it to the Syriac ܦܪܕ, "*scolavit.*" Comp. German *Pferd,* Lat. *burdo,* and see Michaelis' remarks.

[c] From unused root יֹם, "*quæ caloris potestatem habuisse videtur*" (Gesen. *Thes.*).

[d] The plural form of a noun (אֲחַשְׁתְּרָנִים) which is apparently of Persian origin, rendered "camel" by the A. V., occurs in Esth. viii. 10, 14, and seems to denote some fine breed of mules. See Bochart (*Hieroz.* i. 219). [On Gen. xxxvi. 24, see addition to ANAH, Amer. ed.]

family sprung from him are called Shuphamites. In 1 Chr. vii. 12, 15, it is Shuppim (the same as xxvi. 16), and viii. 5, Shephuphan. ·Hence it is probable that Muppim is a corruption of the text, and that Shupham is the true form. [BECHER.] According to 1 Chr. vii. 12, he and his brother Huppim were the sons of Ir, or Iri (ver. 7), the son of Bela, the son of Benjamin, and their sister Maachah appears to have married into the tribe of Manasseh (ib. 15, 16). But ver. 15 seems to be in a most corrupt state. 1 Chr. viii. 3, 5, assigns in like manner Shephuphan to the family of Bela, as do the LXX. in Gen. xlvi. 21. As it seems to be impossible that Benjamin could have had a great-grandson at the time of Jacob's going down into Egypt (comp. Gen. l. 23), and as Machir the husband of Maachah was Manasseh's son, perhaps the explanation of the matter may be that Shupham was Benjamin's son, as he is represented Num. xxvi. 39, but that his family were afterwards reckoned with that of which Ir the son of Bela was chief (comp. 1 Chr. xxv. 9–31, xxvi. 8, 9, 11).

A. C. H.

MURDER.[a] The principle on which the act of taking the life of a human being was regarded by the Almighty as a capital offense is stated on its highest ground, as an outrage, Philo calls it sacrilege, on the likeness of God in man, to be punished even when caused by an animal (Gen. ix. 5, 6, with Bertheau's note; see also John viii. 44; 1 John iii. 12, 15; Philo, *De Spec. Leg.* iii. 15, vol. ii. p. 313). Its secondary or social ground appears to be implied in the direction to replenish the earth which immediately follows (Gen. ix. 7). The exemption of Cain from capital punishment may thus be regarded by anticipation as founded on the social ground either of expediency or of example (Gen. iv. 12, 15). The postdiluvian command, enlarged and infringed by the practice of blood-revenge, which it seems to some extent to sanction, was limited by the Law of Moses, which, while it protected the accidental homicide, defined with additional strictness the crime of murder. It prohibited compensation or reprieve of the murderer, or his protection if he took refuge in the refuge-city, or even at the altar of Jehovah, a principle which finds an eminent illustration in the case of Joab (Ex. xxi. 12, 14; Lev. xxiv. 17, 21; Num. xxxv. 16, 18, 21, 31; Deut. xix. 11, 13; 2 Sam. xvii. 25, xx. 10; 1 K. ii. 5, 6, 31; Philo, *l. c.*; Michaelis, *On Laws of Moses*, § 132). Bloodshed even in warfare was held to involve pollution (Num. xxxv. 33, 34; Deut. xxi. 1, 9; 1 Chr. xxviii. 3). Philo says that the attempt to murder deserves punishment equally with actual perpetration; and the Mishna, that a mortal blow intended for another is punishable with death; but no express legislation on this subject is found in the Law (Philo, *l. c.*; Mishn. *Sanh.* ix. 2).

No special mention is made in the Law (a) of child-murder, (b) of parricide, nor (c) of taking life by poison, but its animus is sufficiently obvious in all these cases (Ex. xxi. 15, 17; 1 Tim. i. 9; Matt. xv. 4), and the 3d may perhaps be specially intended under the prohibition of witchcraft (Ex.

xxii. 18; Joseph. *Ant.* iv. 8, § 34; Philo, *De Spec. Leg.* iii. 17, vol. ii. p. 315).

It is not certain whether a master who killed his slave was punished with death (Ex. xxi. 20; Knobel, *ad loc.*). In Egypt the murder of a slave was punishable with death as an example à fortiori in the case of a freeman; and parricide was punished with burning; but child-murder, though treated as an odious crime, was not punished with death (Diod. Sic. i. 77). The Greeks also, or at least the Athenians, protected the life of the slave (*Dict. of Antiq.* art. *Servus*, p. 1036; Müller, *Dorians*, iii. 3, § 4; Wilkinson, *Anc. Eg.* ii. 208, 209).

No punishment is mentioned for suicide attempted, nor does any special restriction appear to have attached to the property of the suicide (2 Sam. xvii. 23).

Striking a pregnant woman so as to cause her death was punishable with death (Ex. xxi. 23; Joseph. *Ant.* iv. 8, § 33).

If an animal known to be vicious caused the death of any one, not only was the animal destroyed, but the owner also, if he had taken no steps to restrain it, was held guilty of murder (Ex. xxi. 29, 31; Michaelis, § 274, vol. iv. pp. 234, 235).

The duty of executing punishment on the murderer is in the Law expressly laid on the " revenger of blood;" but the question of guilt was to be previously decided by the Levitical tribunal. A strong bar against the license of private revenge was placed by the provision which required the concurrence of at least two witnesses in any capital question (Num. xxxv. 19–30; Deut. xvii. 6–12, xix. 12, 17). In regal times the duty of execution of justice on a murderer seems to have been assumed to some extent by the sovereign, as well as the privilege of pardon (2 Sam. xiii. 39, xiv. 7, 11; 1 K. ii. 34). During this period also the practice of assassination became frequent, especially in the kingdom of Israel. Among modes of effecting this object may be mentioned the murder of Benhadad of Damascus by Hazael by means of a wet cloth (1 K. xv. 27, xvi. 9; 2 K. viii. 15; Thenius, *ad loc.*; Jahn, *Hist.* i. 137; 2 K. x. 7, xi. 1, 16, xii. 20, xiv. 5, xv. 14, 25, 30).

It was lawful to kill a burglar taken at night in the act, but unlawful to do so after sunrise (Ex. xxii. 2, 3).

The Koran forbids child-murder, and allows blood-revenge, but permits money-compensation for bloodshed (ii. 21, iv. 72. xvii. 230, ed. Sale). [BLOOD, REVENGER OF; MANSLAYER.]

H. W. P.

* **MURRAIN.** [PLAGUES, THE TEN, 5]

MU'SHI (מוּשִׁי) [*withdrawing, forsaking*]: Ὀμουσί, Ex. vi. 19; ὁ Μουσί, 1 Chr. vi. 19, xxiii. 21, xxiv. 26, 30; Μουσί, Num. iii. 20; 1 Chr. vi. 47, xxiii. 23; [Vat. Ομουσει, o Μουσει, Μωσει, etc.;] Alex. Ομουσει, Ex. vi. 19; Ομουσι, Num. iii. 20; 1 Chr. vi. 47; o Μουσι, 1 Chr. vi. 19, xxiv. 30; Μουσι, 1 Chr. xxiii. 21, xxiv. 26: *Musi*). The son of Merari the son of Kohath.

* **MU'SHITES** (מוּשִׁי): Μουσί, Vat. Μου-

συι, Alex. Οφουσι: *Musitæ, Musi*), Num. iii. 33, xxvi. 58. Descendants of MUSHI.   A.

MUSIC. Of music as a science among the Hebrews we have no certain knowledge, and the traces of it are so slight as to afford no ground for reasonable conjecture. But with regard to its practice there is less uncertainty. The inventor of musical instruments, like the first poet and the first forger of metals, was a Cainite. According to the narrative of Gen. iv., Jubal the son of Lamech was "the father of all such as handle the harp and organ," that is of all players upon stringed and wind instruments.ᵃ It has been conjectured that Jubal's discovery may have been perpetuated by the pillars of the Sethites mentioned by Josephus (*Ant.* i. 2), and that in this way it was preserved till after the Flood; but such conjectures are worse than an honest confession of ignorance. The first mention of music in the times after the Deluge is in the narrative of Laban's interview with Jacob, when he reproached his son-in-law with having stolen away unawares, without allowing him to cheer his departure "with songs, with tabret, and with harp" (Gen. xxxi. 27). So that, in whatever way it was preserved, the practice of music existed in the upland country of Syria, and of the three possible kinds of musical instruments, two were known and employed to accompany the song. The three kinds are alluded to in Job xxi. 12. On the banks of the Red Sea sang Moses and the children of Israel their triumphal song of deliverance from the hosts of Egypt; and Miriam, in celebration of the same event, exercised one of her functions as a prophetess by leading a procession of the women of the camp, chanting in chorus the burden to the song of Moses, "Sing ye to Jehovah, for He hath triumphed gloriously; the horse and his rider hath He thrown into the sea." Their song was accompanied by timbrels and dances, or, as some take the latter word, by a musical instrument of which the shape is unknown but which is supposed to have resembled the modern tamborine (DANCE, vol. i. p. 536 *b*), and, like it, to have been used as an accompaniment to dancing. The expression in the A. V. of Ex. xv. 21, "and Miriam *answered* them," seems to indicate that the song was alternate, Miriam leading off with the solo while the women responded in full chorus. But it is probable that the Hebrew word, like the corresponding Arabic, has merely the sense of singing, which is retained in the A. V. of Ex. xxxii. 18; Num. xxi. 17; 1 Sam. xxix. 5; Ps. cxlvii. 7; Hos. ii. 15. The same word is used for the shouting of soldiers in battle (Jer. li. 14), and the cry of wild beasts (Is. xiii. 22), and in neither of these cases can the notion of response be appropriate. All that can be inferred is that Miriam led off the song, and this is confirmed by the rendering of the Vulg. *præcinebat.* The triumphal hymn of Moses had unquestionably a religious character about it, but the employment of music in religious service, though idolatrous, is more distinctly marked in the festivities which attended the erection of the golden calf.ᵇ The wild cries and shouts which reached the ears of Moses and Joshua as they came down from the mount, sounded to the latter as the din of battle, the voices of victor and vanquished blending in one harsh chorus. But the quicker sense of Moses discerned the rough music with which the people worshipped the visible representation of the God that brought them out of Egypt. Nothing could show more clearly than Joshua's mistake the rude character of the Hebrew music at this period (Ex. xxxii. 17, 18), as untrained and wild as the notes of their Syrian forefathers.ᶜ The silver trumpets made by the metal workers of the Tabernacle, which were used to direct the movements of the camp, point to music of a very simple kind (Num. x. 1–10), and the long blast of the jubilee horns, with which the priests brought down the walls of Jericho, had probably nothing very musical about it (Josh. vi.), any more than the rough concert with which the ears of the sleeping Midianites were saluted by Gideon's three hundred warriors (Judg. vii.). The song of Deborah and Barak is cast in a distinctly metrical form, and was probably intended to be sung with a musical accompaniment as one of the people's songs, like that with which Jephthah's daughter and her companions met her father on his victorious return (Judg. xi.).

The simpler impromptu with which the women from the cities of Israel greeted David after the slaughter of the Philistine, was apparently struck off on the spur of the moment, under the influence of the wild joy with which they welcomed their national champion, "the darling of the songs of Israel." The accompaniment of timbrels and instruments of music must have been equally simple, and such that all could take part in it (1 Sam. xviii. 6, 7). Up to this time we meet with nothing like a systematic cultivation of music among the Hebrews, but the establishment of the schools of the prophets appears to have supplied this want. Whatever the students of these schools may have been taught, music was an essential part of their practice. At Bethel (1 Sam. x. 5) was a school of this kind, as well as at Naioth in Ramah (1 Sam. xix. 19, 20), at Jericho (2 K. ii. 5, 7, 15), Gilgal (2 K. iv. 38), and perhaps at Jerusalem (2 K. xxii. 14). Professional musicians soon became attached to the court, and though Saul, a hardy warrior, had only at intervals recourse to the soothing influence of David's harp, yet David seems to have gathered round him "singing men and singing women," who could celebrate his victories and lend a charm to his hours of peace (2 Sam. xix. 35). Solomon did the same (Eccl. ii. 8), adding to the luxury of his court by his patronage of art, and obtaining a reputation himself as no mean composer (1 K. iv. 32).

But the Temple was the great school of music, and it was consecrated to its highest service in the worship of Jehovah. Before, however, the elaborate arrangements had been made by David for the

---

ᵃ From the occurrence of the name Mahalaleel, third in descent from Seth, which signifies "giving praise to God," Schneider concludes that vocal music is religious services must have been still earlier in use among the Sethites (*Bibl.-gesch. Darstellung der Hebr. Musik*, p. xl.).

ᵇ With this may be compared the musical service which accompanied the dedication of the golden image in the plains of Dura (Dan. iii.), the commencement of which was to be the signal for the multitude to prostrate themselves in worship.

ᶜ Compare Lam. ii. 7, where the war-cry of the enemy in the Temple is likened to the noise of the multitude on a solemn feast-day: "They have made a noise in the house of Jehovah as in the day of a solemn feast."

temple choir, there must have been a considerable body of musicians throughout the country (2 Sam. vi. 5), and in the procession which accompanied the ark from the house of Obededom, the Levites, with Chenaniah at their head, who had acquired skill from previous training, played on psalteries, harps, and cymbals, to the words of the psalm of thanksgiving which David had composed for the occasion (1 Chr. xv., xvi.). It is not improbable that the Levites all along had practiced music and that some musical service was part of the worship of the Tabernacle; for unless this supposition be made, it is inconceivable that a body of trained singers and musicians should be found ready for an occasion like that on which they make their first appearance. The position which the tribe of Levi occupied among the other tribes naturally favored the cultivation of an art which is essentially characteristic of a leisurely and peaceful life. They were free from the hardships attending the struggle for conquest and afterwards for existence, which the Hebrews maintained with the nations of Canaan and the surrounding countries, and their subsistence was provided for by a national tax. Consequently they had ample leisure for the various ecclesiastical duties devolving upon them, and among others for the service of song, for which some of their families appear to have possessed a remarkable genius. The three great divisions of the tribe had each a representative family in the choir: Heman and his sons represented the Kohathites, Asaph the Gershonites, and Ethan (or Jeduthun) the Merarites (1 Chr. xv. 17, xxiii. 6, xxv. 1-6). Of the 38,000 who composed the tribe in the reign of David, 4,000 are said to have been appointed to praise Jehovah with the instruments which David made (1 Chr. xxiii. 5) and for which he taught them a special chant. This chant for ages afterwards was known by his name, and was sung by the Levites before the army of Jehoshaphat, and on laying the foundation of the second Temple (comp. 1 Chr. xvi. 34, 41; 2 Chr. vii. 6, xx. 21; Ezr. iii. 10, 11); and again by the Maccabæan army after their great victory over Gorgias (1 Macc. iv. 24). Over this great body of musicians presided the sons of Asaph, Heman, and Jeduthun, twenty-four in number, as heads of the twenty-four courses of twelve into which the skilled minstrels were divided. These skilled or cunning (מֵבִין, 1 Chr. xxv. 6, 7) men were 288 in number, and under them appear to have been the scholars (תַּלְמִיד, 1 Chr. xxv. 8), whom, perhaps, they trained, and who made up the full number of 4,000. Supposing 4,000 to be merely a round number, each course would consist of a full band of 166 musicians presided over by a body of twelve skilled players, with one of the sons of Asaph, Heman, or Jeduthun as conductor. Asaph himself appears to have played on the cymbals (1 Chr. xvi. 5), and this was the case with the other leaders (1 Chr. xv. 19), perhaps to mark the time more distinctly, while the rest of the band played on psalteries and harps. The singers were distinct from both, as is evident in Ps. lxviii. 25, "the singers went before, the players on instruments followed after, in the midst of the damsels playing with timbrels;" unless the singers in this case were the cymbal-players, like Heman, Asaph, and Ethan, who, in 1 Chr. xv. 19, are called "singers," and perhaps while giving the time with their cym-

bals led the choir with their voices. The "players on instruments" (נֹגְנִים, nôgĕnîm), as the word denotes, were the performers upon stringed instruments, like the psaltery and harp, who have been alluded to. The "players on instruments" (חֹלְלִים, chôlĕlîm), in Ps. lxxxvii. 7, were different from these last, and were properly pipers or performers on perforated wind-instruments (see 1 K. i. 40). "The damsels playing with timbrels" (comp. 1 Chr. xiii. 8) seem to indicate that women took part in the temple choir, and among the family of Heman are specially mentioned three daughters, who, with his fourteen sons, were all "under the hands of their father for song in the house of Jehovah" (1 Chr. xxv. 5, 6). Besides, with those of the Captivity who returned with Zerubbabel were "200 singing men and singing women" (Ezr. ii. 65). Bartenora adds that children also were included.

The trumpets, which are mentioned among the instruments played before the ark (1 Chr. xiii. 8), appear to have been reserved for the priests alone (1 Chr. xv. 24, xvi. 6). As they were also used in royal proclamations (2 K. xi. 14), they were probably intended to set forth by way of symbol the royalty of Jehovah, the theocratic king of his people, as well as to sound the alarm against his enemies (2 Chr. xiii. 12). A hundred and twenty priests blew the trumpets in harmony with the choir of Levites at the dedication of Solomon's Temple (2 Chr. v. 12, 13, vii. 6), as in the restoration of the worship under Hezekiah, in the description of which we find an indication of one of the uses of the temple music. "And Hezekiah commanded to offer the burnt-offering upon the altar. And when the burnt-offering began, the song of Jehovah began also, with the trumpets and with the instruments of David king of Israel. And all the congregation worshipped, and the singers sang, and the trumpeters sounded; all until the burnt-offering was finished" (2 Chr. xxix. 27, 28). The altar was the table of Jehovah (Mal. i. 7), and the sacrifices were his feasts (Ex. xxiii. 18), so the solemn music of the Levites corresponded to the melody by which the banquets of earthly monarchs were accompanied. The Temple was his palace, and as the Levite sentries watched the gates by night they chanted the songs of Zion; one of these it has been conjectured with probability is Ps. cxxxiv.

The relative numbers of the instruments in the temple band have been determined in the traditions of Jewish writers. Of psalteries there were to be not less than two nor more than six; of flutes not less than two nor more than twelve; of trumpets not less than two but as many as were wished; of harps or citherns not less than nine but as many as were wished; while of cymbals there was only one pair (Forkel, Allg. Gesch. der Musik, c. iii. § 28). The enormous number of instruments and dresses for the Levites provided during the magnificent reign of Solomon would seem, if Josephus be correct (Ant. viii. 3, § 8), to have been intended for all time. A thousand dresses for the high-priest, linen garments and girdles of purple for the priests 10,000; trumpets 200,000; psalteries and harps of electrum 40,000; all these were stored up in the temple treasury. The costume of the Levite singers at the dedication of the Temple was of fine linen (2 Chr. v. 12).

In the private as well as in the religious life of the Hebrews music held a prominent place. The kings had their court musicians (Eccl. ii. 8) who bewailed their death (2 Chr. xxxv. 25), and in the luxurious times of the later monarchy the effeminate gallants of Israel, reeking with perfumes and stretched upon their couches of ivory, were wont at their banquets to accompany the song with the tinkling of the psaltery or guitar (Am. vi. 4-6), and amused themselves with devising musical instruments while their nation was perishing, as Nero fiddled when Rome was in flames. Isaiah denounces a woe against those who sat till the morning twilight over their wine, to the sound of "the harp and the viol, the tabret and pipe" (Is. v. 11, 12). But while music was thus made to minister to debauchery and excess, it was the legitimate expression of mirth and gladness, and the indication of peace and prosperity. It was only when a curse was upon the land that the prophet could say, "the mirth of tabrets ceaseth, the noise of them that rejoice endeth, the joy of the harp ceaseth, they shall not drink wine with a song" (Is. xxiv. 8, 9). In the sadness of captivity the harps hung upon the willows of Babylon, and the voices of the singers refused to sing the songs of Jehovah at their foreign captors' bidding (Ps. cxxxvii.). The bridal processions as they passed through the streets were accompanied with music and song (Jer. vii. 34), and these ceased only when the land was desolate (Ez. xxvi. 13). The high value attached to music at banquets is indicated in the description given in Ecclus. xxxii. of the duties of the master of a feast. "Pour not out words where there is a musician, and show not forth wisdom out of time. A concert of music in a banquet of wine is as a signet of carbuncle set in gold. As a signet of an emerald set in a work of gold, so is the melody of music with pleasant wine." And again, the memory of the good king Josiah was "as music at a banquet of wine" (Ecclus. xlix. 1). The music of the banquets was accompanied with songs and dancing (Luke xv. 25).[a] The triumphal processions which celebrated a victory were enlivened by minstrels and singers (Ex. xv. 1, 20; Judg. v. 1, xi. 34; 1 Sam. xviii. 6, xxi. 11; 2 Chr. xx. 28; Jud. xv. 12, 13), and on extraordinary occasions they even accompanied armies to battle. Thus the Levites sang the chant of David before the army of Jehoshaphat as he went forth against the hosts of Ammon, and Moab, and Mt. Seir (2 Chr. xx. 19, 21); and the victory of Abijah over Jeroboam is attributed to the encouragement given to Judah by the priests sounding their trumpets before the ark (2 Chr. xiii. 12, 14). It is clear from the narrative of Elisha and the minstrel who by his playing calmed the prophet's spirit till the hand of Jehovah was upon him, that among the camp followers of Jehoshaphat's army on that occasion there were to be reckoned musicians who were probably

Levites (2 K. iii. 15). Besides songs of triumph there were also religious songs (Is. xxx. 29; Am. v. 23; Jam. v. 13), "songs of the temple" (Am. viii. 3), and songs which were sung in idolatrous worship (Ex. xxxii. 18).[b] Love songs are alluded to in Ps. xlv. title, and Is. v. 1. There were also the doleful songs of the funeral procession, and the wailing chant of the mourners who went about the streets, the professional "keening" of those who were skillful in lamentation (2 Chr. xxxv. 25; Eccl. xii. 5; Jer. ix. 17-20; Am. v. 16). Lightfoot (Hor. Heb. on Matt. ix. 23) quotes from the Talmudists (Chetubh. cap. 4, hal. 6), to the effect that every Israelite on the death of his wife "will afford her not less than two pipers and one woman to make lamentation." The grape gatherers sang as they gathered in the vintage, and the wine-presses were trodden with the shout of a song (Is. xvi. 10; Jer. xlviii. 33); the women sang as they toiled at the mill, and on every occasion the land of the Hebrews during their national prosperity was a land of music and melody. There is one class of musicians to which allusion is casually made (Ecclus. ix. 4), and who were probably foreigners, the harlots who frequented the streets of great cities, and attracted notice by singing and playing the guitar (Is. xxiii. 15, 16).

There are two aspects in which music appears, and about which little satisfactory can be said: the mysterious influence which it had in driving out the evil spirit from Saul, and its intimate connection with prophecy and prophetical inspiration. Miriam "the prophetess" exercised her prophetical functions as the leader of the chorus of women who sang the song of triumph over the Egyptians (Ex. xv. 20). The company of prophets whom Saul met coming down from the hill of God had a psaltery, a tabret, a pipe, and a harp before them, and smitten with the same enthusiasm he "prophesied among them" (1 Sam. x. 5, 10). The priests of Baal, challenged by Elijah at Carmel, cried aloud, and cut themselves with knives, and prophesied till sunset (1 K. xviii. 29). The sons of Asaph, Heman, and Jeduthun, set apart by David for the temple choir, were to "prophesy with harps, with psalteries, and with cymbals" (1 Chr. xxv. 1); Jeduthun "prophesied with the harp" (1 Chr. xxv. 3), and in 2 Chr. xxxv. 15 is called "the king's seer," a term which is applied to Heman (1 Chr. xxv. 5) and Asaph (2 Chr. xxix. 30) as musicians, as well as to Gad the prophet (2 Sam. xxiv. 11; 1 Chr. xxix. 29). The spirit of Jehovah came upon Jahaziel, a Levite of the sons of Asaph, in the reign of Jehoshaphat, and he foretold the success of the royal army (2 Chr. xx. 14). From all these instances it is evident that the same Hebrew root (נבא) is used to denote the inspiration under which the prophets spoke and the minstrels sang: Gesenius assigns the latter as a secondary

---

[a] At the royal banquets of Babylon were sung hymns of praise in honor of the gods (Dan. v. 4, 23), and perhaps on some such occasion as the feast of Belshazzar the Hebrew captives might have been brought in to sing the songs of their native land (Ps. cxxxvii.).

[b] The use of music in the religious services of the Therapeutæ is described by Philo (De Vita contempl. p. 901, ed. Frankof.). At a certain period in the service one of the worshippers rose and sang a song of praise to God, either of his own composition, or one from the older poets. He was followed by others in a regular

order, the congregation remaining quiet till the concluding prayer, in which all joined. After a simple meal, the whole congregation arose and formed two choirs, one of men and one of women, with the most skillful singer of each for leader; and in this way sang hymns to God, sometimes with the full chorus, and sometimes with each choir alternately. In conclusion, both men and women joined in a single choir, in imitation of that on the shores of the Red Sea, which was led by Moses and Miriam.

meaning. In the case of Elisha, the minstrel and the prophet are distinct personages, but it is not till the minstrel has played that the hand of Jehovah comes upon the prophet (2 K. iii. 15). This influence of music has been explained as follows by a learned divine of the Platonist school: " These divine enthusiasts were commonly wont to compose their songs and hymns at the sounding of some one musical instrument or other, as we find it often suggested in the Psalms. So Plutarch . . . . describes the dictate of the oracle antiently . . . . ' how that it was uttered in verse, in pomp of words, similitudes, and metaphors, at the sound of a pipe.' Thus we have Asaph, Heman, and Jeduthun set forth in this prophetical preparation, 1 Chr. xxv. 1 . . . . Thus R. Sal. expounds the place . . . . ' when they played upon their musical instruments they prophesied after the manner of Elisha ' . . . . And this sense of this place, I think, is much more genuine than that which a late author of our own would fasten upon it, namely, that this prophesying was nothing but the singing of psalms. For it is manifest that these prophets were not mere singers but composers, and such as were truly called prophets or enthusiasts" (Smith, *Select Discourses*, vi. c. 7, pp. 238, 239, ed. 1660). All that can be safely concluded is that in their external manifestations the effect of music in exciting the emotions of the sensitive Hebrews, the frenzy of Saul's madness (1 Sam. xviii. 10), and the religious enthusiasm of the prophets, whether of Baal or Jehovah, were so nearly alike as to be described by the same word. The case of Saul is more difficult still. We cannot be admitted to the secret of his dark malady. Two turning points in his history are the two interviews with Samuel, the first and the last, if we except that dread encounter which the despairing monarch challenged before the fatal day of Gilboa. On the first of these, Samuel foretold his meeting with the company of prophets with their minstrelsy, the external means by which the Spirit of Jehovah should come upon him, and he should be changed into another man (1 Sam. x. 5). The last occasion of their meeting was the disobedience of Saul in sparing the Amalekites, for which he was rejected from being king (1 Sam. xv. 26). Immediately after this we are told the Spirit of Jehovah departed from Saul, and an " evil spirit from Jehovah troubled him " (1 Sam. xvi. 14); and his attendants, who had perhaps witnessed the strange transformation wrought upon him by the music of the prophets, suggested that the same means should be employed for his restoration. " Let our lord now command thy servants before thee, to seek out a man, a cunning player on an harp: and it shall come to pass, when the evil spirit from God is upon thee, that he shall play with his hand, and thou shalt be well. . . . And it came to pass when the spirit from God was upon Saul, that David took an harp and played with his hand. So Saul was refreshed, and was well, and the evil spirit departed from him " (1 Sam. xvi. 16, 23). But on two occasions, when anger and jealousy supervened, the remedy which had soothed the frenzy of insanity had lost its charm (1 Sam. xviii. 10, 11; xix. 9, 10). It seems therefore that the passage of Seneca, which has often been quoted ·in explanation of this phenomenon, " Pythagoras perturbationes lyra componebat " (*De Irâ*, iii. 9), is scarcely applicable, and we must be content to leave the narrative as it stands.　　　　　　　　　　　　　　· W. A. W.

MUSICAL INSTRUMENTS. In addition to the instruments of music which have been represented in our version by some modern word, and are treated under their respective titles, there are other terms which are vaguely or generally rendered. These are—

1. דַחֲוָן, *dachăvân*, Chald., rendered " instruments of musick " in Dan. vi. 18. The margin gives "or *table*, perhaps lit. *concubines*." The last-mentioned rendering is that approved by Gesenius, and seems most probable. The translation, " instruments of musick," seems to have originated with the Jewish commentators, R. Nathan, R. Levi, and Aben Ezra, among others, who represent the word by the Hebrew *neginoth*, that is, stringed instruments which were played by being struck with the hand or the plectrum.

2. מִנִּים, *minnim*, rendered with great probability " stringed-instruments " in Ps. cl. 4. It appears to be a general term, but beyond this nothing is known of it; and the word is chiefly interesting from its occurrence in a difficult passage in Ps. xlv. 8, which stands in the A. V. "out of the ivory palaces *whereby* (מִנִּי, *minni*) they have made thee glad," a rendering which is neither intelligible nor supported by the Hebrew idiom. Gesenius and most of the moderns follow Sebastian Schmid in translating, "out of the ivory palaces the stringed-instruments make thee glad."

3. עָשׂוֹר, *'âsôr*, "an instrument of ten strings,' Ps. xxxiii. 3. The full phrase is נֵבֶל עָשׂוֹר, *nebel 'âsôr*, "a ten-stringed psaltery," as in Ps. xxxiii. 2, cxliv. 9; and the true rendering of the first-mentioned passage would be "upon an instrument of ten strings, even upon the psaltery." [PSALTERY.]

4. שִׁדָּה, *shiddâh*, is found only in one very obscure passage, Eccl. ii. 8, " I gat me men-singers and women-singers, and the delights of the sons of men, *musical instruments, and that of all sorts* " (שִׁדָּה וְשִׁדּוֹת, *shiddâh veshiddôth*). The words thus rendered have received a great variety of meanings. They are translated "drinking-vessels" by Aquila and the Vulgate; "cup-bearers" by the LXX., Peshito-Syriac, Jerome, and the Arabic version ; "baths" by the Chaldee; and " musical instruments " by Dav. Kimchi, followed by Luther and the A. V., as well as by many commentators. By others they are supposed to refer to the women of the royal harem. But the most probable interpretation to be put upon them is that suggested by the usage of the Talmud, where שִׁידָה, *shiddâh*, denotes a "palanquin" or "litter" for women. The whole question is discussed in Gesenius' *Thesaurus*, p. 1365.

5. שָׁלִשִׁים, *shâlishîm*, rendered " instruments of musick " in the A. V. of 1 Sam. xviii. 6, and in the margin "three-stringed instruments," from the root *shâlôsh*, "three." Roediger (Gesen. *Thes.* p. 1429) translates "triangles," which are said to have been invented in Syria, from the same root. We have no means of deciding which is the more correct. The LXX. and Syriac give "cymbals," and the Vulgate "sistra; " while others render it "noble songs" (comp. Prov. xxii. 20).

　　　　　　　　　　　　　　　　W. A. W.

MUSTARD (σίναπι: *sinapis*) occurs in Matt. xiii. 31; Mark iv. 31; Luke xiii. 19, in which passages the kingdom of heaven is compared to a grain of mustard-seed which a man took and sowed in his garden; and in Matt. xvii. 20, Luke xvii. 6, where our Lord says to his Apostles, "if ye had faith as a grain of mustard-seed, ye might say to this mountain, remove hence to yonder place."

The subject of the mustard-tree of Scripture has of late years been a matter of considerable controversy, the common mustard-plant being supposed unable to fulfill the demands of the Biblical allusion. In a paper by the late Dr. Royle, read before the Royal Asiatic Society, and published in No. xv. of their Journal (1844), entitled, "On the Identification of the Mustard-tree of Scripture," the author concludes that the *Salvadora persica* is the tree in question. He supposes the *Salvadora persica* to be the same as the tree called *Khardal* (the Arabic for mustard), seeds of which are employed throughout Syria as a substitute for mustard, of which they have the taste and properties. This tree, according to the statement of Mr. Ameuny, a Syrian, quoted by Dr. Royle, is found all along the banks of the Jordan, near the lake of Tiberias, and near Damascus, and is said to be generally recognized in Syria as the mustard-tree of Scripture. It appears that Captains Irby and Mangles, who had observed this tree near the Dead Sea, were struck with the idea that it was the mustard-tree of the parable. As these travellers were advancing towards Kerek from the southern extremity of the Dead Sea, after leaving its borders they entered a wooded country with high rushes and marshes. "Occasionally," they say, "we met with specimens of trees, etc., such as none of our party had seen before. . . . Amongst the trees which we knew, were various species of Acacia, and in some instances we met with the dwarf Mimosa. . . . There was one curious tree which we observed in great numbers, and which bore a fruit in bunches, resembling in appearance the currant, with the color of the plum; it has a pleasant, though strong aromatic taste, resembling mustard, and if taken in any quantity, produces a similar irritability in the nose and eyes. The leaves of this tree have the same pungent flavor as the fruit, though not so strong. We think it probable that this is the tree our Saviour alluded to in the parable of the mustard-seed, and not the mustard-plant which is to be found in the north " (*Trav.* May 8). Dr. Royle thus sums up his arguments in favor of the *Salvadora persica* representing the mustard-tree of Scripture: "The *S. persica* appears better calculated than any other tree that has yet been adduced to answer to every thing that is required, especially if we take into account its name and the opinions held respecting it in Syria. We have in it a small seed, which sown in cultivated ground grows up and abounds in foliage. This being pungent, may like the seeds have been used as a condiment, as mustard-and-cress is with us. The nature of the plant is to become arboreous, and thus it will form a large shrub or a tree, twenty-five feet high, under which a horseman may stand when the soil and climate are favorable; it produces numerous branches and leaves, under which birds may and do take shelter, as well as build their nests; it has a name in Syria which may be considered as traditional from the earliest times, of which the Greek is a correct translation; its seeds are used for the same purposes as mustard; and in a country where trees are not plentiful, that is, the shores of the lake of Tiberias, this tree is said to abound, that is in the very locality where the parable was spoken " (*Treatise on the Mustard-tree*, etc., p. 24).

Notwithstanding all that has been adduced by Dr. Royle in support of his argument, we confess ourselves unable to believe that the subject of the mustard-tree of Scripture is thus finally settled. But, before the claims of the *Salvadora persica* are discussed, it will be well to consider whether some mustard-plant (*Sinapis*) may not after all be the mustard-tree of the parable: at any rate this opinion has been held by many writers, who appear never to have entertained any doubt upon the subject. Hiller, Celsius, Rosenmüller, who all studied the botany of the Bible, and older writers, such as Erasmus, Zegerus, Grotius, are content to believe that some common mustard-plant is the

Salvadora Persica.

plant of the parable; and more recently Mr. Lambert in his "Note on the Mustard-plant of Scripture" (see *Linnean Trans.* vol. xvii. p. 449), has argued in behalf of the *Sinapis nigra*.

The objection commonly made against any *Sinapis* being the plant of the parable is, that the seed grew into "a tree" (δένδρον), or as St. Luke has it, "a great tree" (δένδρον μέγα), in the branches of which the fowls of the air are said to come and lodge. Now in answer to the above objection it is urged with great truth, that the expression is figurative and oriental, and that in a proverbial simile no literal accuracy is to be expected; it is an error, for which the language of Scripture is not accountable, to assert, as Dr. Royle and some others have done, that the passage implies that birds "built their nests" in the tree, the Greek word κατασκηνόω has no such meaning, the word merely means "to settle or rest upon" any thing for a longer or shorter time; the birds came, "*insidendi et versandi causa*" as Hiller (*Hierophyt.* ii. 63) explains the phrase: nor is there any occasion to suppose that the expression "fowls of the air" denotes any other than the smaller *insessorial* kinds, linnets, finches, etc., and not the "aquatic fowls by the lake side, or partridges and pigeons hovering over the rich plain of Gennesareth," which Prof. Stanley (*S. & P.* p. 427) recognizes as "the birds that came and devoured the seed by the way-side" — for the larger birds are wild and avoid the way-side — or as those "which took refuge in the spreading branches of the mustard-tree." Hiller's explanation is probably the correct one; that the birds came and settled on the mustard-plant for the sake of the seed, of which they are very fond. Again, whatever the σίναπι may be, it is expressly said to be an herb, or more properly "a garden herb" (λάχανον, *olus*). As to the plant being called a "tree" or a "great tree," the expression is not only an oriental one, but it is clearly spoken with reference to some other thing; the σίναπι with respect to the other *herbs* of the garden may, considering the size to which it grows, justly be called "*a great tree*," though

Sinapis Nigra.

of course, with respect to trees properly so named, it could not be called one at all. This, or a somewhat similar explanation is given by Celsius and Hiller, and old commentators generally, and we confess we see no reason why we should not be satisfied with it. Irby and Mangles mention the large size which the mustard-plant attains in Palestine. In their journey from Bysan to Adjeloun, in the Jordan Valley, they crossed a small plain very thickly covered with herbage, particularly the mustard-plant, which reached as high as their horses' heads. (*Trav.* March 12.) Dr. Kitto says this plant was probably the *Sinapis orientalis*

(*nigra*), which attains under a favoring climate a statuse which it will not reach in our country. Dr. Thomson also (*The Land and the Book*, p. 414) says he has seen the Wild Mustard on the *rich plain* of Akkar as tall as the horse and the rider. Now, it is clear from Scripture that the σίναπι was cultivated in our Lord's time, the seed a "man took and sowed in his field;" St. Luke says, "cast into his garden:" if then, the wild plant on the *rich plain* of Akkar grows as high as a man on horseback, it might attain to the same or a greater height when in a cultivated garden; and if, as Lady Callcott has observed, we take into account the very low plants and shrubs upon which birds often roost, it will readily be seen that some common mustard-plant is able to fulfill all the Scriptural demands. As to the story of the Rabbi Simeon Ben Calaphtha having in his garden a mustard-plant, into which he was accustomed to climb as men climb into a fig-tree, it can only be taken for what Talmudical statements generally are worth, and must be quite insufficient to afford grounds for any argument. But it may be asked Why not accept the explanation that the *Salvadora persica* is the tree denoted? — a tree which will literally meet all the demands of the parable. Because, we answer, where the commonly received opinion can be shown to be in full accordance with the Scriptural allusions, there is no occasion to be dissatisfied with it; and again, because at present we know nothing certain of the occurrence of the *Salvadora persica* in Palestine, except that it occurs in the small, tropical, low valley of Engedi, near the Dead Sea, from whence Dr. Hooker saw specimens, but it is evidently of rare occurrence. Mr. Ameuny says he had seen it all along the banks of the Jordan, near the lake of Tiberias and Damascus; but this statement is certainly erroneous. We know from Pliny, Dioscorides, and other Greek and Roman writers, that mustard-seeds were much valued, and were used as a condiment; and it is more probable that the Jews of our Lord's time were in the habit of making a similar use of the seeds of some common mustard (*Sinapis*), than that they used to plant in their gardens the seed of a tree which certainly cannot fulfill the Scriptural demand of being called "a pot-herb."

The expression "which is indeed the least of all seeds," is in all probability hyperbolical, to denote a very small seed indeed, as there are many seeds which are smaller than mustard. "The Lord, in his popular teaching," says Trench (*Notes on Parables*, 108), "adhered to the popular language; " and the mustard-seed was used proverbially to denote anything very minute (see the quotations from the Talmud in Buxtorf, *Lex. Talm.* p. 322: also the Koran, *Sur.* 31).

The parable of the mustard-plant may be thus paraphrased : "The Gospel dispensation is like a grain of mustard-seed which a man sowed in his garden, which indeed is one of the least of all seeds; but which, when it springs up, becomes a tall, branched plant, on the branches of which the birds come and settle seeking their food." [a]

W. H.

satisfied that it is a very rare plant in Syria, and is probably confined to the hot, low, sub-tropical Engedi valley, where various other Indian and Arabian types appear at the *Ultima Thule* of their northern wanderings. Of the mustard-plants which I saw on the banks of the Jordan, one was 10 feet high, drawn

* The writer, in crossing the Plain of *Akka* from *Birweh*, on the north side, to Mount Carmel, on the south, met with a field — a little forest it might almost be called — of the common mustard-plant of the country. It was in blossom at the time, full grown; in some cases, as measured, six, seven, and nine feet high, with a stem or trunk more than an inch thick, throwing out branches on every side. It might well be called a tree, and certainly, in comparison with its tiny seed, "a great tree." But still the branches, or stems of the branches, were not very large, and to the eye did not appear very strong. Can the birds, I said to myself, rest upon them? Are they not too slight and flexible? Will they not bend or break beneath the superadded weight? At that very instant, as I stood and revolved the thought, lo! one of the fowls of heaven stopped in its flight through the air, alighted down on one of the branches, which hardly moved beneath the shock, and then began, perched there before my eyes, to warble forth a strain of the richest music.

In this occurrence every condition of the parable was fully met. As remarked above, the Greek expression does not say that the birds build their nests among such branches, but light upon them or make their abode among them. [NESTS, Amer. ed.] This plant is not only common in Palestine in a wild state, but is cultivated in gardens (comp. Matt. xiii. 31). This circumstance shows that the *Khardal* or mustard-tree of the Arabs (*Salvadora persica*) cannot be meant, for that grows wild only. Certain birds are fond of the seeds, and seek them as food. The associating of the birds and this plant as in the parable was the more natural on that account. Further, see Tristram, *Nat. Hist. of the Bible*, p. 472 f.   H.

MUTH-LABBEN. "To the chief musician upon Muth-Labben" (לַבֵּן מוּת עַל‎: ὑπὲρ τῶν κρυφίων τοῦ υἱοῦ: *pro occultis filii*) is the title of Ps. ix., which has given rise to infinite conjecture. Two difficulties in connection with it have to be resolved: first, to determine the true reading of the Hebrew, and then to ascertain its meaning. Neither of these points has been satisfactorily explained. It is evident that the LXX. and Vulgate must have read עֲלָמוֹת עַל‎, "concerning the mysteries," and so the Arabic and Ethiopic versions. The Targum, Symmachus,[a] and Jerome,[b] in his translation of the Hebrew, adhered to the received text, while Aquila,[c] retaining the consonants as they at present stand, read *al-muth* as one word, עֲלְמֻת‎, "youth," which would be the regular form of the abstract noun, though it does not occur in Biblical Hebrew. In support of the reading עלמות as one word, we have the authority of 28 of Kennicott's MSS., and the assertion of Jarchi that he had seen it so written, as in Ps. xlviii. 14, in the Great Masorah. If the reading of the Vulgate and LXX. be correct with regard to the consonants, the words might be pointed thus, עֲלָמוֹת יַעַל‎ *'al 'álámôth*, "upon Alamoth," as in the title of Ps. xlvi., and לֵב is

possibly a fragment of קֹרַח לִבְנֵי‎, *libné Korach*, "for the sons of Korah," which appears in the same title. At any rate, such a reading would have the merit of being intelligible, which is more than can be said of most explanations which have been given. But if the Masoretic reading be the true one, it is hard to attach any meaning to it. The Targum renders the title of the Psalm, — "on the death of the man who came forth from between (בֵּין‎) the camps," alluding to Goliath, the Philistine champion (הַבֵּינַיִם אִישׁ‎, 1 Sam. xvii. 4). That David composed the psalm as a triumphal song upon the slaughter of his gigantic adversary was a tradition which is mentioned by Kimchi merely as an *on dit*. Others render it "on the death of the son," and apply it to Absalom; but, as Jarchi remarks, there is nothing in the character of the psalm to warrant such an application. He mentions another interpretation, which appears to have commended itself to Grotius and Hengstenberg, by which *labben* is an anagram of *nabal*, and the psalm is referred to the death of Nabal, but the Rabbinical commentator had the good sense to reject it as untenable, though there is as little to be said in favor of his own view. His words are — "but I say that this song is of the future to come, when the childhood and youth of Israel shall be made white (ירתלבן‎), and their righteousness be revealed and their salvation draw nigh, when Esau and his seed shall be blotted out." He takes עַלְמוּת as one word, signifying "youth," and לַבֵּן = לְלַבֵּן "to whiten." Menahem, a commentator quoted by Jarchi, interprets the title as addressed "to the musician upon the stringed instruments called Alamoth, to instruct," taking לַבֵּן as if it were לְהָבִין or לְבוֹנֵן. Doneah supposes that *labben* was the name of a man who warred with David in those days, and to whom reference is made as "the wicked" in verse 5. Arama (quoted by Dr. Gill in his *Exposition*) identifies him with Saul. As a last resource Kimchi suggests that the title was intended to convey instructions to the Levite minstrel Ben, whose name occurs in 1 Chr. xv. 18, among the temple choir, and whose brethren played "with psalteries on Alamoth." There is reason, however, to suspect that the reading in this verse is corrupt, as the name is not repeated with the others in verse 20. There still remain to be noticed the conjectures of Delitzsch, that Muth-labben denotes the tone or melody with the words of the song associated with it, of others that it was a musical instrument, and of Hupfeld that it was the commencement of an old song, either signifying "die for the son," or "death to the son." Hitzig and others regard it as an abbreviation containing a reference to Ps. xlviii. 14. The difficulty of the question is sufficiently indicated by the explanation which Gesenius himself (*Thes.* p. 741, *a*) was driven to adopt, that the title of the psalm signified that it was "to be chanted by boys with virgins' voices."

The renderings of the LXX. and Vulgate induced the early Christian commentators to refer

---

a Περὶ θανάτου τοῦ υἱοῦ.   b *Super morte filii.*
c Νεανιότητος τοῦ υἱοῦ.

up among bushes, etc., and not thicker than whipcord. I was told it was a well-known condiment, and cultivated by the Arabs; it is the common wild *Sinapis Nigra*."

the psalm to the Messiah. Augustine understands "the son" as "the only begotten son of God." The Syriac version is quoted in support of this interpretation, but the titles of the Psalms in that version are generally constructed without any reference to the Hebrew, and therefore it cannot be appealed to as an authority.

On all accounts it seems extremely probable that the title in its present form is only a fragment of the original, which may have been in full what has been suggested above. But, in the words of the Assembly's Annotations, "when all hath been said that can be said, the conclusion must be the same as before; that these titles are very uncertain things, if not altogether unknown in these days."

W. A. W.

* MUZZLE. [OX.]

MYNDUS (Μύνδος), a town on the coast of CARIA, between MILETUS and HALICARNASSUS. The convenience of its position in regard to trade was probably the reason why we find in 1 Macc. xv. 23 that it was the residence of a Jewish population. Its ships were well known in very early times (Herod. v. 33), and its harbor is specially mentioned by Strabo (xiv. 658). The name still lingers in the modern *Mentesche*, though the remains of the city are probably at *Gumishlu*, where Admiral Beaufort found an ancient pier and other ruins.

J. S. H.

MYRA (τὰ Μύρα [ointments: Vulg. *Lystra*]), an important town in LYCIA, and interesting to us as the place where St. Paul, on his voyage to Rome (Acts xxvii. 5), was removed from the Adramyttian ship which had brought him from Cæsarea, and entered the Alexandrian ship in which he was wrecked on the coast of Malta. [ADRAMYTTIUM.] The travellers had availed themselves of the first of these vessels because their course to Italy necessarily took them past the coasts of the province of ASIA (ver. 2), expecting in some harbor on these coasts to find another vessel bound to the westward. This expectation was fulfilled (ver. 6).

It might be asked how it happened that an Alexandrian ship bound for Italy was so far out of her course as to be at Myra. This question is easily answered by those who have some acquaintance with the navigation of the Levant. Myra is nearly due north of Alexandria, the harbors in the neighborhood are numerous and good, the mountains high and easily seen, and the current sets along the coast to the westward (Smith's *Voyage and Shipwreck of St. Paul*). Moreover, to say nothing of the possibility of landing or taking in passengers or goods, the wind was blowing about this time continuously and violently from the N. W., and the same weather which impeded the Adramyttian ship (ver. 4) would be a hindrance to the Alexandrian (see ver. 7; *Life and Epistles of St. Paul*, ch. xxiii.).

Some unimportant MSS. having Λύστρα in this passage, Grotius conjectured that the true reading might be Λίμυρα (Bentleii *Critica Sacra*, ed. A. A. Ellis). This supposition, though ingenious, is quite unnecessary. Both Limyra and Myra were well known among the maritime cities of Lycia. The harbor of the latter was strictly Andriace, distant from it between two and three miles, but the river was navigable to the city (Appian, *B. C.* iv. 82).

Myra (called *Dembra* by the Greeks) is remarkable still for its remains of various periods of history. The tombs, enriched with ornament, and many of them having inscriptions in the ancient Lycian character, show that it must have been wealthy in early times. Its enormous theatre attests its considerable population in what may be called its Greek age. In the deep gorge which leads into the mountains is a large Byzantine church, a relic of the Christianity which may have begun with St. Paul's visit. It is reasonable to conjecture that this may have been a metropolitan church, inasmuch as we find that when Lycia was a province, in the later Roman empire, Myra was its capital (*Hierocl.* p. 684). In later times it was curiously called the port of the Adriatic, and visited by Anglo-Saxon travellers (*Early Travels in Palestine*, pp. 33, 138). Legend says that St. Nicholas, the patron saint of the modern Greek sailors, was born at PATARA, and buried at Myra, and his supposed relics were taken to St. Petersburg by a Russian frigate during the Greek revolution.

The remains of Myra have had the advantage of very full description by the following travellers: Leake, Beaufort, Fellows, Texier, and Spratt and Forbes.

J. S. H.

MYRRH, the representative in the A. V. of the Hebrew words *Môr* and *Lôt*.

1. *Môr* (מֹר[a]: σμύρνα, στακτή, μύρινος, κρόκος: *myrrha, myrrhinus, myrrha*) is mentioned in Ex. xxx. 23, as one of the ingredients of the "oil of holy ointment;" in Esth. ii. 12, as one of the substances used in the purification of women; in Ps. xlv. 8, Prov. vii. 17, and in several passages in Canticles, as a perfume. The Greek σμύρνα occurs in Matt. ii. 11 amongst the gifts brought by the wise men to the infant Jesus, and in Mark xv. 23, it is said that "wine mingled with myrrh" (οἶνος ἐσμυρισμένος) was offered to, but refused by, our Lord on the cross. Myrrh was also used for embalming (see John xix. 39, and Herod. ii. 86). Various conjectures have been made as to the real nature of the substance denoted by the Hebrew *môr* (see Celsius, *Hierob.* i. 522); and much doubt has existed as to the countries in which it is produced. According to the testimony of Herodotus (iii. 107), Dioscorides (i. 77), Theophrastus (ix. 4, § 1), Diodorus Siculus (ii. 49), Strabo, Pliny, etc.. the tree which produces myrrh grows in Arabia — Pliny (xii. 16) says, in different parts of Arabia, and asserts that there are several kinds of myrrh both wild and cultivated: it is probable that under the name of *myrrha* he is describing different resinous productions. Theophrastus, who is generally pretty accurate in his observations, remarks (ix. 4, § 1), that myrrh is produced in the middle of Arabia, around Saba and Adramytta. Some ancient writers, as Propertius (i. 2, 3) and Oppian (*Halieut* iii. 403), speak of myrrh as found in Syria (see also Belon, *Observ.* ii. ch. 80); others conjecture India and Æthiopia; Plutarch (*Is. et Osir.* p. 383) asserts that it is produced in Egypt, and is there called *Bal.* "The fact," observes Dr. Royle (s. v. *Môr*, Kitto's *Cycl.*), "of myrrh being called *bal* among the Egyptians is extremely curious, for *bol* is the Sanscrit *bola*, the name for myrrh throughout India."[b]

It would appear that the ancients generally are

---

[a] From root מָרַר, "to drop"

[b] Plutarch, however, was probably in error, and

has confounded the Coptic *sal*, "myrrh," with *ba*. "an eye." See Jablonski, *Opusc.* i. 49, ed. te Water.

correct in what they state of the localities where myrrh is produced, for Ehrenberg and Hemprich have proved that myrrh is found in Arabia Felix, thus confirming the statements of Theophrastus and Pliny; and Mr. Johnson (*Travels in Abyssinia,* i. 249) found myrrh exuding from cracks in the bark of a tree in *Koran-hedulaa* in Adal, and Forskål mentions two myrrh-producing trees, *Amyris Kataf* and *Amyris Kafal,* as occurring near Haes in Arabia Felix. The myrrh-tree which Ehrenberg and Hemprich found in the borders of Arabia Felix, and that which Mr. Johnson saw in Abyssinia, are believed to be identical; the tree is the *Balsamodendron myrrha,* " a low, thorny, ragged-looking tree, with bright trifoliate leaves: " it is probably the *Murr* of Abu 'l Fadli, of which he says " murr is the Arabic name of a thorny tree like an acacia, from which flows a white liquid, which thickens and becomes a gum."

Balsamodendron Myrrha.

That myrrh has been long exported from Africa we learn from Arrian, who mentions σμύρνα as one of the articles of export from the ancient district of Barbaria: the Egyptians perhaps obtained their myrrh from the country of the Troglodytes (Nubia), as the best wild myrrh-trees are said by Pliny (xii. 15) to come from that district. Pliny states also that " the Sabæi even cross the sea to procure it in the country of the Troglodytæ." From what Athenæus (xv. 689) says, it would appear that myrrh was imported into Egypt, and that the Greeks received it from thence. Dioscorides describes many kinds of myrrh under various names, for which see Sprengel's *Annotations,* i. 73, &c.

The *Balsamodendron myrrha,* which produces the myrrh of commerce, has a wood and bark which emit a strong odor; the gum which exudes from the bark is at first oily, but becomes hard by exposure to the air: it belongs to the natural order *Terebinthaceæ.* There can be little doubt that his tree is identical with the *Murr* of Abu'l Fadli, the σμύρνα of the Greek writers, the " stillata cortice myrrha " of Ovid and the Latin writers, and the *môr* of the Hebrew Scriptures.

The "wine mingled with myrrh," which the Roman soldiers presented to our Lord on the cross,

was given, according to the opinion of some commentators, in order to render him less sensitive to pain; but there are differences of opinion on this subject, for which see GALL.

2. *Lôt* (לֹט [a]: στακτή: *stacte*), erroneously translated "myrrh" in the A. V. in Gen. xxxvii. 25, xliii. 11, the only two passages where the word is found, is generally considered to denote the odorous resin which exudes from the branches of the *Cistus creticus,* known by the name of *ladanum* or *labdanum.* It is clear that *lôt* cannot signify " myrrh," which is not produced in Palestine, yet the Scriptural passages in Genesis speak of this substance as being exported from Gilead into Egypt.

Cistus Creticus.

Ladanum was known to the early Greeks, for Herodotus (iii. 107, 112) mentions λήδανον, or λάδανον, as a product of Arabia, and says it is found " sticking like gum to the beards of he-goats, which collect it from the wood; " similar is the testimony of Dioscorides (i. 128), who says that the best kind is " odorous, in color inclining to green, easy to soften, fat, free from particles of sand and dirt; such is that kind which is produced in Cyprus, but that of Arabia and Libya is inferior in quality." There are several species of *Cistus,* all of which are believed to yield the gum ladanum; but the species mentioned by Dioscorides is in all probability identical with the one which is found in Palestine, namely, the *Cistus creticus* (Strand, *Flor. Palæst.*

---

[a] From root לָלַט, " to cover; " the gum covering the plant.

No. 289). The *C. ladaniferus*, a native of Spain and Portugal, produces the greatest quantity of the ladanum; it has a white flower, while that of the *C. creticus* is rose-colored. Tournefort (*Voyage*, i. 79) has given an interesting account of the mode in which the gum ladanum is gathered, and has figured the instrument commonly employed by the people of Candia for the purpose of collecting it. There can be no doubt that the Hebrew *lôt*, the Arabic *ladan*, the Greek λήδανον, the Latin and English *ládanum*, are identical (see Rosenmüller, *Bib. Bot.* p. 158; Celsius, *Hierob.* i. 288). Ladanum was formerly much used as a stimulant in medicine, and is now of repute amongst the Turks as a perfume.

The Cistus belongs to the Natural order *Cistaceæ*, the Rock-rose family.   W. H.

MYRTLE (הֲדַס,[a] *hadas*: μυρσίνη, ὄρος:[b] *myrtus, myrtetum*). There is no doubt that the A. V. is correct in its translation of the Hebrew word, for all the old versions are agreed upon the point, and the identical noun occurs in Arabic — in the dialect of Yemen, S. Arabia — as the name of the "myrtle."[c]

Mention of the myrtle is made in Neh. viii. 15; Is. xli. 19, lv. 13; Zech. i. 8, 10, 11. When the Feast of Tabernacles was celebrated by the Jews on

Myrtus communis.

the return from Babylon, the people of Jerusalem were ordered to "go forth unto the mount and fetch olive-branches, and pine-branches, and myrtle-branches, and to make booths." The prophet Isaiah foretells the coming golden age of Israel, when the Lord shall plant in the wilderness "the shittah-tree and the myrtle-tree and the oil-tree." The modern Jews still adorn with myrtle the booths and sheds at the Feast of Tabernacles. Myrtles (*Myrtus communis*) will grow either on hills or in valleys, but it is in the latter locality where they

attain to their greatest perfection. Formerly, as we learn from Nehemiah (viii. 15), myrtles grew on the hills about Jerusalem. "On Olivet," says Prof. Stanley, "nothing is now to be seen but the olive and the fig tree:" on some of the hills, however, near Jerusalem, Hasselquist (*Trav.* 127, Lond. 1766) observed the myrtle. Dr. Hooker says it is not uncommon in Samaria and Galilee. Irby and Mangles (p. 222) describe the rivers from Tripoli towards Galilee as having their banks covered with myrtles (see also Kitto, *Phys. Hist. of Palest.* p. 268).

The myrtle (*hadas*) gave her name to Hadassah or Esther (Esth. ii. 7); the Greek names Myrtilus, Myrtoëssa, etc., have a similar origin. There are several species of the genus *Myrtus*, but the *Myrtus communis* is the only kind denoted by the Hebrew *hadas*: it belongs to the natural order *Myrtaceæ*, and is too well known to need description.   W. H.

* The myrtle is found very widely distributed through Mt. Lebanon, and on the whole sea-coast. I have collected it as far north as the plain of Lattakiyeh. The black berries are eaten in Syria.

The bush is known by the two names of *Âs*, آس, and *Rihân*, ريحان. The dried leaves of this plant are employed by the natives as a stuffing for the beds of children, with the idea that their odor is promotive of health, and that they keep off vermin.   G. E. P.

MY′SIA (Μυσία). If we were required to fix the exact limits of this northwestern district of Asia Minor, a long discussion might be necessary. But it is mentioned only once in the N. T. (Acts xvi. 7, 8), and that cursorily and in reference to a passing journey. St. Paul and his companions, on the second missionary circuit, were divinely prevented from staying to preach the Gospel either in ASIA or BITHYNIA. They had then come κατὰ τὴν Μυσίαν, and they were directed to Troas, παρελθόντες τὴν Μυσίαν; which means either that they skirted its border, or that they passed through the district without staying there. In fact the best description that can be given of Mysia at this time is that it was the region about the frontier of the provinces of Asia and Bithynia. The term is evidently used in an ethnological, not a political sense. Winer compares it, in this point of view, to such German terms as Suabia, Breisgau, etc. Illustrations nearer home might be found in such districts as Craven in Yorkshire or Appin in Argyllshire. Assos and ADRAMYTTIUM were both in Mysia. Immediately opposite was the island of Lesbos. [MITYLENE.] TROAS, though within the same range of country, had a small district of its own, which was viewed as politically separate.   J. S. H.

* MYSTERY (μυστήριον). The origin and etymological import of the Greek word (μυστήριον) are partially involved in doubt. Its claims to a Hebrew derivation, though plausible, are undoubtedly to be rejected. It evidently stands connected with μύστης, *one initiated*, namely, into the mys-

---

teries, and thus with μυέω, to *initiate*. This verb again is probably from μύω (μύζω) to *close*, to *shut*, but whether the *eye*, or the *mouth*, seems uncertain. If the former, the μύστης may either be one who voluntarily closes his bodily eyes that the eye of his spirit may be opened, or one who closes them as it were in *death*, the initiated being regarded as dead to the world of sense, and living only in the world of unseen realities. If the latter, he may be denominated either from whispering secrets with compressed lips, or from taking the vow of perpetual silence and secrecy, symbolized by the sealed mouth. Whichever be the precise explanation, the etymology of μυστήριον links it first naturally with religious doctrines and symbols, and secondly with truths hidden from the natural sense, and from the merely natural reason. It points to facts which need a *revelation* (ἀποκάλυψις), and which revelation may be made either by the sole internal influence of the Spirit, or by this conjointly with the progress of outward events. But while the μυστήριον thus implies something hidden, and inaccessible to the unaided reason, and usually also of weighty import, it by no means necessarily denotes anything strictly mysterious and incomprehensible. The fact or truth, though requiring to be *revealed*, may, when revealed, be of a very elementary character. It may be very adequately made known, and the sole condition of the reception of the knowledge is a spiritual mind; to the animal (ψυχικός) man the outward revelation is of course made in vain (1 Cor. ii. 14).

That such is the New Testament meaning of μυστήριον, namely, a hidden truth unveiled, but not unknowable, may be abundantly demonstrated. Thus Paul speaks of "knowing all mysteries " (1 Cor. xiii. 2), and prays that the Colossians may come into the " recognition of the mysteries of Christ " (Col. ii. 2). Our Lord declares to his disciples that to them it is given "to know the mysteries of the kingdom of God " (Matt. xiii. 11; Mark iv. 11); and even the person speaking with tongues, who " with the spirit speaketh mysteries " (1 Cor. xiv. 2), utters what is unintelligible indeed to others, but not to himself.

The word is applied in the New Testament to the doctrines and facts of the Gospel, as formerly hidden, but now unveiled both by outward facts and spiritual communications. The kingdom of heaven (Matt. xiii. 11), the doctrine of the cross (1 Cor. i. 18, ii. 7), the resurrection of the dead (1 Cor. xv. 51), are the great New Testament "mysteries." In fact the entire life of our Lord in its various cardinal features is the actual unveiled " great " mystery of godliness (1 Tim. iii. 16). Special mysteries are also the divine purpose in the partial hardening of Israel (Rom. xi. 25), and the admission of the Gentiles to co-heirship with the Jews (Eph. iii. 5, 6). In accordance too with the etymology of the word, it applies naturally to the hidden import of parables and symbols, which, as partly veiling the truths they set forth, demand a divine elucidation. Thus the hidden sense of the Saviour's parables (Matt. xiii. 11); the import of the seven stars and seven candlesticks (Rev. i. 20); and of the woman clothed in scarlet (Rev. xvii. 7); the deeper significance of marriage as symbolizing the union of Christ and his Church (Eph. v. 32), are illustrations of this use of the term.   A. C. K.

N.

NA'AM (נַעַם [*pleasantness, grace*]: Νοέμ; [Alex. Νααμ:] *Naham*). One of the sons of Caleb the son of Jephunneh (1 Chr. iv. 15).

NA'AMAH (נַעֲמָה [*pleasing, lovely*]). 1. (Νοεμά: *Noēma.*) One of the four women whose names are preserved in the records of the world before the Flood; all except Eve being Cainites. She was daughter of Lamech by his wife Zillah, and sister, as is expressly mentioned, to Tubal-cain (Gen. iv. 22 only). No reason is given us why these women should be singled out for mention in the genealogies; and in the absence of this most of the commentators have sought a clew in the significance of the names interpreted as Hebrew terms; endeavoring, in the characteristic words of one of the latest Jewish critics, by " due energy to strike the living water of thought even out of the rocky soil of dry names " (Kalisch, *Genesis*, p. 149). Thus Naamah, from *Na'am*, " sweet, pleasant," signifies, according to the same interpreter, " the lovely beautiful woman," and this and other names in the same genealogy of the Cainites are interpreted as tokens that the human race at this period was advancing in civilization and arts. But not only are such deductions at all times hazardous and unsatisfactory, but in this particular instance it is surely begging the question to assume that these early names are Hebrew; at any rate the *onus probandi* rests on those who make important deductions from such slight premises. In the Targum Pseudojonathan, Naamah is commemorated as the " mistress of lamenters and singers; " and in the Samaritan Version her name is given as Zalkipha.

2. ([Rom. Νααμά, Ναανἀ, Νοομμά; Vat. in 1 K. xiv. 21] Μααχαμ; Alex. Νααμα, Νοομμα; Joseph. Νοομᾶς: *Naama.*) Mother of king Rehoboam (1 K. xiv. 21, 31;[a] 2 Chr. xii. 13). On each occasion she is distinguished by the title " the (not ' an,' as in A. V.) Ammonite." She was therefore one of the foreign women whom Solomon took into his establishment (1 K. xi. 1). In the LXX. (1 K. xii. 24, answering to xiv. 31 of the Hebrew text) she is stated to have been the "daughter of Ana (*i. e.* Hanun) the son of Nahash." If this is a translation of a statement which once formed part of the Hebrew text, and may be taken as authentic history, it follows that the Ammonite war into which Hanun's insults had provoked David was terminated by a re-alliance; and, since Solomon reigned forty years, and Rehoboam was forty-one years old when he came to the throne, we can fix with tolerable certainty the date of the event. It took place before David's death, during that period of profound quiet which settled down on the nation, after the failure of Absalom's rebellion and of the subsequent attempt of Sheba the son of Bichri had strengthened more than ever the affection of the nation for the throne of David; and which was not destined to be again disturbed till put an end to by the shortsighted rashness of the son of Naamah.   G.

NA'AMAH (נַעֲמָה [*lovely*]: Νωμάν; Alex. Νωμα: *Naama*), one of the towns of Judah in the district of the lowland or *Shefelah*, belonging to the same group with Lachish, Eglon, and Makkedah (Josh. xv. 41). Nothing more is known of it, nor has any name corresponding with it been yet discovered in the proper direction. But it seems probable that Naamah should be connected with the Naamathites, who again were perhaps identical with the Mehunim or Minæans, traces of whom are found on the southwestern outskirts of Judah; one such at Minois or *el-Minyay*, a few miles below Gaza.   G.

NA'AMAN (נַעֲמָן [*pleasantness, grace*]: Ναιμάν; N. T. Rec. Text, Νεεμάν, but Lachm. [Tisch. Treg.] with [Sin.] A B D, Ναιμάν; Joseph. Ἀμανος: *Naaman*) — or to give him the title conferred on him by our Lord, "Naaman the Syrian." An Aramite warrior, a remarkable incident in whose life is preserved to us through his connection with the prophet Elisha. The narrative is given in 2 K. v.

The name is a Hebrew one, and that of ancient date (see the next article), but it is not improbable that in the present case it may have been slightly altered in its insertion in the Israelite records. Of Naaman the Syrian there is no mention in the Bible except in this connection. But a Jewish tradition, at least as old as the time of Josephus (*Ant.* viii. 15, § 5), and which may very well be a genuine one, identifies him with the archer whose arrow, whether at random or not, [a] struck Ahab with his mortal wound, and thus "gave deliverance to Syria." The expression is remarkable — "because that by him Jehovah had given deliverance to Syria." To suppose the intention to be that Jehovah was the universal ruler, and that therefore all deliverance, whether afforded to his servants or to those who, like the Syrians, acknowledged Him not, was wrought by Him, would be thrusting a too modern idea into the expression of the writer. Taking the tradition above-mentioned into account, the most natural explanation perhaps is that Naaman, in delivering his country, had killed one who was the enemy of Jehovah not less than he was of Syria. Whatever the particular exploit referred to was, it had given Naaman a great position at the court of Benhadad. In the first rank for personal prowess and achievements, he was commander-in-chief of the army, while in civil matters he was nearest to the person of the king, whom he accompanied officially, and supported, when the king went to worship in the Temple of Rimmon (ver. 18). He was afflicted with a leprosy of the white kind (ver. 27), which had hitherto defied cure. In Israel, according to the enactments of the Mosaic Law, this would have cut off even [b] Naaman from intercourse with every one; he would there have been compelled to dwell in a "several house." But not so in Syria; he maintained his access [c] to the king, and his contact with the members of his own household. The circumstances of his visit to Elisha have been drawn out under the latter head [vol. i. p. 718], and need not be repeated here. Naaman's appearance throughout the occurrence is most character-

istic and consistent. He is every inch a soldier ready at once to resent what he considers as a slight cast either on himself or the natural glories of his country, and blazing out in a moment into sudden "rage," but calmed as speedily by a few good-humored and sensible words from his dependants, and, after the cure has been effected, evincing a thankful and simple heart, whose gratitude knows no bounds and will listen to no refusal.

His request to be allowed to take away two mules' burden of earth is not easy to understand. The natural explanation is that, with a feeling akin to that which prompted the Pisan invaders to take away the earth of Aceldama for the Campo Santo at Pisa, and in obedience to which the pilgrims to Mecca are said to bring back stones from that sacred territory, the grateful convert to Jehovah wished to take away some of the earth of his country, to form an altar for the burnt-offering and sacrifice which henceforth he intended to dedicate to Jehovah only, and which would be inappropriate if offered on the profane earth of the country of Rimmon or Hadad. But it should be remembered that in the narrative there is no mention of an altar; [d] and although Jehovah had on one occasion ordered that the altars put up for offerings to Him should be of earth (Ex. xx. 24), yet Naaman could hardly have been aware of this enactment, unless indeed it was a custom of older date and wider existence than the Mosaic law, and adopted into that law as a significant and wise precept for some reason now lost to us.

How long Naaman lived to continue a worshipper of Jehovah while assisting officially at that of Rimmon, we are not told. When next we hear of Syria, another, Hazael, apparently holds the position which Naaman formerly filled. But, as has been elsewhere noticed, the reception which Elisha met with on this later occasion in Damascus probably implies that the fame of "the man of God," and of the mighty Jehovah in whose name he wrought, had not been forgotten in the city of Naaman.

It is singular that the narrative of Naaman's cure is not found in the present text of Josephus. Its absence makes the reference to him as the slayer of Ahab, already mentioned, still more remarkable.

It is quoted by our Lord (Luke iv. 27) as an instance of mercy exercised to one who was not of Israel, and it should not escape notice that the reference to this act of healing is recorded by none of the Evangelists but St. Luke the physician.

G.

NA'AMAN (נַעֲמָן [*amenity, pleasantness*]: Νοεμάν; [in Num., Alex. Νοεμα, Vat. omits; in 1 Chr., Νοαμά, Νοομά: Vat. Νοομα; Alex. in ver. 4, Μααμαν: *Naaman*, in Num. Νοëμαν]). One of the family of Benjamin who came down to Egypt with Jacob, as we read in Gen. xlvi. 21. According to the LXX. version of that passage he was the son of Bela, which is the parentage assigned to him in Num. xxvi. 40, where, in the

---

[a] LXX. εὔστοχως, *i. e.* "with good aim," possibly a transcriber's variation from εὐτυχώς.

[b] It did drive a king into strict seclusion (2 Chr. xxvi. 21).

[c] The A. V. of ver. 4 conveys a wrong impression. It is accurately not "one went in," but "he (*i. e.*

Naaman) went in and told his master" (*i. e.* the king). The word rendered "lord" is the same as is rendered "master" in ver. 1.

[d] The LXX. (Vat. MSS.) omits even the words "of earth," ver. 17

enumeration of the sons of Benjamin, he is said to be the son of Bela, and head of the family of the Naamites. He is also reckoned among the sons of Bela in 1 Chr. viii. 3, 4. Nothing is known of his personal history, or of that of the Naamites. For the account of the migrations, apparently compulsory, of some of the sons of Benjamin from Geba to Manahath, in 1 Chr. viii. 6, 7, is so confused, probably from the corruption of the text, that it is impossible to say whether the family of Naaman was or was not included in it. The repetition in ver. 7 of the three names Naaman, Ahiah, Gera, in a context to which they do not seem to belong, looks like the mere error of a copyist, inadvertently copying over again the same names which he had written in the same order in ver. 4, 5 — Naaman, Ahoah, Gera. If, however, the names are in their place in ver. 7, it would seem to indicate that the family of Naaman did migrate with the sons of Ehud (called *Abihud* in ver. 3) from Geba to Manahath.   A. C. H.

NA'AMATHITE (נַעֲמָתִי [patr. as below]:

Μιναίων [Vat. Sin. Μειναιων] βασιλεύς, ὁ Μιναίος [Vat. Μει-]: *Naamathites*), the gentilic name of one of Job's friends, Zophar the Naamathite (Job ii. 11, xi. 1, xx. 1, xlii. 9). There is no other trace of this name in the Bible, and the town,

נַעֲמָה, whence it is derived, is unknown. If we may judge from modern usage, several places so called probably existed on the Arabian borders of Syria. Thus in the Geographical Dictionary, *Marásid el-Ittáli*, are Noam, a castle in the Yemen, and a place on the Euphrates; Niameh, a place belonging to the Arabs; and Noamee, a valley in Tihameh. The name Naamán (of unlikely derivation however) is very common. Bochart (*Phaleg*, cap. xxii.), as might be expected, seizes the LXX. reading, and in the "king of the Minæi" sees a confirmation to his theory respecting a Syrian, or northern Arabian settlement of that well-known people of classical antiquity. It will be seen, in art. DIKLA, that the present writer identifies the Minæi with the people of Ma'een, in the Yemen; and there is nothing improbable in a northern colony of the tribe, besides the presence of a place so named in the Syro-Arabian desert. But we regard this point as apart from the subject of this article, thinking the LXX. reading, unsupported as it is, to be too hypothetical for acceptance.

        E. S. P.

NA'AMITES, THE (הַנַּעֲמִי: Samar.

דנעמי [*the lovely one*]: δῆμος ὁ Νοεμανί [Vat. -νει]. Alex. omits: *familia Naamitarum*, and *Noemanitarum*), the family descended from NAAMAN, the grandson of Benjamin (Num. xxvi. 40 only). [NAAMAN, p. 2048 b.] The name is a contraction, of a kind which does not often occur in Hebrew. Accordingly the Samaritan Codex, as will be seen above, presents it at length — "the Naamanites."

        G.

NA'ARAH (נַעֲרָה [*maiden*]: Θοαδά [rather

'Aαδά]; Alex. Noopá: *Naara*),the second wife of Ashur, a descendant of Judah (1 Chr. iv. 5, 6).

Nothing is known of the persons (or places) recorded as the children of Naarah. In the Vat. LXX. the children of the two wives are interchanged. [Rather, in ver. 5 the names of the two wives are transposed. A.]

NA'ARAI [3 syl] (נַעֲרַי [*Jehovah reveals?*].

Naapai; [Alex. Noopa:] *Naarai*). One of the valiant men of David's armies (1 Chr. xi. 37). In 1 Chr. he is called the son of Ezbai, but in 2 Sam. xxiii. 35 he appears as "Paarai the Arbite." Kennicott (*Diss.* pp. 209–211) decides that the former is correct.

NA'ARAN (נַעֲרָן [*boyish, juvenile*, Ges.]:

[Rom. Noapav; Vat.] *Naapvav*; Alex. *Naapav*: *Noran*), a city of Ephraim, which in a very ancient record (1 Chr. vii. 28) is mentioned as the eastern limit of the tribe. It is very probably identical with NAARATH, or more accurately Naarah, which seems to have been situated in one of the great valleys or torrent-beds which lead down from the highlands of Bethel to the depths of the Jordan valley.

In 1 Sam. vi. 21 the Peshito-Syriac and Arabic versions have respectively Naarin and Naaran for the Kirjath-jearim of the Hebrew and A. V. If this is anything more than an error, the Naaran to which it refers can hardly be that above spoken of, but must have been situated much nearer to Bethshemesh and the Philistine lowland.   G.

NA'ARATH (the Heb. is נַעֲרָתָה, = to

Naarah, נַעֲרָה, [*maiden:*] which is therefore the real form of the name: αἱ[a] κῶμαι αὐτῶν; Alex. Νααραθα και αι κωμαι αυτων: *Naratha*), a place named (Josh. xvi. 7, only) as one of the landmarks on the (southern) boundary of Ephraim. It appears to have lain between Ataroth and Jericho. If Ataroth be the present *Atára*, a mile and a half south of *el-Bireh* and close to the great natural boundary of the *Wady Suweinit*, then Naarah was probably somewhere lower down the wady. Eusebius and Jerome (*Onomast.*) speak of it as if well known to them — "Naorath,[b] a small village of the Jews five miles from Jericho." Schwarz (147) fixes it at "Neama," also "five miles from Jericho," meaning perhaps *Na'imeh*, the name of the lower part of the great *Wady Mutyah* or *el-Asas*, which runs from the foot of the hill of *Rûmmon* into the Jordan valley above Jericho, and in a direction generally parallel to the *Wady Suweinit* (Rob. *Bibl. Res.* iii. 290). A position in this direction is in agreement with 1 Chr. vii. 28, where NAARAN is probably the same name as that we are now considering.   G.

NAASH'ON, Ex. vi. 23. [NAHSHON.]

NAAS'SON (Ναασσών: *Naasson*). The

Greek form of the name NAHSHON (Matt. i. 4; Luke iii. 32 only).

NA'ATHUS (Νάαθος; [Vat. Λααθος:] *Naathus*). One of the family of Addi, according to the list of 1 Esdr. ix. 31. There is no name corresponding in Ezr. x. 30.

NA'BAL (נָבָל = *fool*: Ναβάλ), one of the

---

[a] Perhaps treating נַעֲרָה, "a damsel," as equivalent to בַּת, "a daughter," the term commonly used to express the hamlets dependent on a city.

[b] The 'Oopáð in the present text of Eusebius should obviously have prefixed to it the *v* from the ἐστιν which precedes it. [The edition of Larsow and Parthey reads Νοοράθ.] Compare NAБАЛ.

characters introduced to us in David's wanderings, apparently to give one detailed glimpse of his whole state of life at that time (1 Sam. xxv.). Nabal himself is remarkable as one of the few examples given to us of the private life of a Jewish citizen. He ranks in this respect with BOAZ, BARZILLAI, NABOTH. He was a sheep-master on the confines of Judæa and the desert, in that part of the country which bore from its great conqueror the name of CALEB (1 Sam. xxx. 14, xxv. 3; so Vulgate, A. V., and Ewald). He was himself, according to Josephus (*Ant.* vi. 13, § 6), a Ziphite, and his residence Emmaus, a place of that name not otherwise known, on the southern Carmel, in the pasture lands of Maon. (In the LXX. of xxv. 4 he is called "the Carmelite," and the LXX. read "Maon" for "Paran" in xxv. 1.) With a usage of the word, which reminds us of the like adaptation of similar words in modern times, he, like Barzillai, is styled "very great," evidently from his wealth. His wealth, as might be expected from his abode, consisted chiefly of sheep and goats, which, as in Palestine at the time of the Christian era (Matt. xxv.), and at the present day (Stanley, *S. & P.*), fed together. The tradition preserved in this case the exact number of each — 3000 of the former, 1000 of the latter. It was the custom of the shepherds to drive them into the wild downs on the slopes of Carmel; and it was whilst they were on one of these pastoral excursions, that they met a band of outlaws, who showed them unexpected kindness, protecting them by day and night, and never themselves committing any depredations (xxv. 7, 15, 16). Once a year there was a grand banquet, on Carmel, when they brought back their sheep from the wilderness for shearing — with eating and drinking "like the feast of a king" (xxv. 2, 4, 36).

It was on one of these occasions that Nabal came across the path of the man to whom he owes his place in history. Ten youths were seen approaching the hill; in them the shepherds recognized the slaves or attendants of the chief of the freebooters who had defended them in the wilderness. To Nabal they were unknown. They approached him with a triple salutation — enumerated the services of their master, and ended by claiming, with a mixture of courtesy and defiance, characteristic of the East, "whatever cometh into thy hand for thy servants (LXX. omit this — and have only the next words), and for *thy son* David." The great sheep-master was not disposed to recognize this unexpected parental relation. He was a man notorious for his obstinacy (such seems the meaning of the word translated "churlish") and for his general low conduct (xxv. 3, "evil in his doings;" xxv. 17, "a man of Belial"). Josephus and the LXX. taking the word *Caleb* not as a proper name, but as a quality (to which the context certainly lends itself) — add "of a disposition like a dog" — cynical — κυνικός. On hearing the demand of the ten petitioners, he sprang up (LXX. ἀνεπήδησε), and broke out into fury, "Who is David? and who is the son of Jesse?" — "What runaway slaves are these to interfere with my own domestic arrangements?" (xxv. 10, 11). The moment that the messengers were gone, the shepherds that stood by perceived the danger that their master and themselves would incur. To Nabal himself they durst not speak (xxv. 17). But the sacred writer, with a tinge of the sentiment which such a contrast always suggests, proceeds to describe that this brutal

ruffian was married to a wife as beautiful and as wise, as he was the reverse (xxv. 3). [ABIGAIL.] To her, as to the good angel of the household, one of the shepherds told the state of affairs. She, with the offerings usual on such occasions (xxv. 18, comp. xxx. 11, 2 Sam. xvi. 1, 1 Chr. xii. 40), loaded the asses of Nabal's large establishment — herself mounted one of them, and, with her attendants running before her, rode down the hill toward David's encampment. David had already made the fatal vow of extermination, couched in the usual terms of destroying the household of Nabal, so as not even to leave a dog behind (xxv. 22). At this moment, as it would seem, Abigail appeared, threw herself on her face before him, and poured forth her petition in language which both in form and expression almost assumes the tone of poetry: — "Let thine handmaid, I pray thee, speak in thine audience, and hear the words of thine handmaid." Her main argument rests on the description of her husband's character, which she draws with that mixture of playfulness and seriousness which above all things turns away wrath. His name here came in to his rescue. "As his name is, so is he: Nabal [*fool*] is his name, and folly is with him" (xxv. 25; see also ver. 26). She returns with the news of David's recantation of his vow. Nabal is then in, at the height of his orgies. Like the revellers of Palestine in the later times of the monarchy, he had drunk to excess, and his wife dared not communicate to him either his danger or his escape (xxv. 36). At break of day she told him both. The stupid reveller was suddenly roused to a sense of that which impended over him. "His heart died within him, and *he* became as a stone." It was as if a stroke of apoplexy or paralysis had fallen upon him. Ten days he lingered, "and the Lord smote Nabal, and he died" (xxv. 37, 38). The suspicions entertained by theologians of the last century, that there was a conspiracy between David and Abigail to make away with Nabal for their own alliance (see "Nabal" in Winer's *Renlw.* ii. 129), have entirely given place to the better spirit of modern criticism, and it is one of the many proofs of the reverential, as well as truthful appreciation of the Sacred Narrative now inaugurated in Germany, that Ewald enters fully into the feeling of the narrator, and closes his summary of Nabal's death, with the reflection that "it was not without justice regarded as 'a Divine judgment.'" According to the (not improbable) LXX. version of 2 Sam. iii. 33, the recollection of Nabal's death lived afterwards in David's memory to point the contrast of the death of Abner: "Died Abner as Nabal died?" A. P. S.

NABARI'AS (Ναβαρίας [Vat. -ρει-]: *Nabarias*). Apparently a corruption of Zechariah (1 Esdr. ix. 44; comp. Neh. viii. 4).

NABATHITES, THE (οἱ Ναβαρταῖοι, and Ναυαταῖοι; [Sin. in v. 25, οἱ αναβαρταιοι:] Alex. [in ix. 35] Ναβατεοι: *Nabuthæi*), 1 Macc. v. 25; ix. 35. [NABAIOTH.]

NABOTH (נָבוֹת [*fruits, productions*]: Ναβοθαί), victim of Ahab and Jezebel. He was a Jezreelite, and the owner of a small portion of ground (2 K. ix. 25, 26) that lay on the eastern slope of the hill of Jezreel. He had also a vineyard, of which the situation is not quite certain. According to the Hebrew text (1 K. xxi. 1) it was in Jezreel, but the LXX. render the whole clause differently, omitting the words "which was in

Jezreel," and reading instead of "the palace," the *threshing-floor* of Ahab king of Samaria." This points to the view, certainly most consistent with the subsequent narrative, that Naboth's vineyard was on the hill of Samaria, close to the "threshing-floor" (the word translated in A. V. "void place") which undoubtedly existed there, hard by the gate of the city (1 K. xxiv.). The royal palace of Ahab was close upon the city wall at Jezreel. According to both texts it immediately adjoined the vineyard (1 K. xxi. 1, 2, Heb.; 1 K. xx. 2, LXX.; 2 K. ix. 30, 36), and it thus became an object of desire to the king, who offered an equivalent in money, or another vineyard in exchange for this. Naboth, in the independent spirit of a Jewish landholder,[a] refused. Perhaps the turn of his expression implies that his objection was mingled with a religious scruple at forwarding the acquisitions of a half-heathen king: "Jehovah forbid it to me that I should give the inheritance of my fathers unto thee." Ahab was cowed by this reply; but the proud spirit of Jezebel was roused. She and her husband were apparently in the city of Samaria (1 K. xxi. 18). She took the matter into her own hands, and sent a warrant in Ahab's name and sealed with Ahab's seal, to the elders and nobles of Jezreel, suggesting the mode of destroying the man who had insulted the royal power. A solemn fast was proclaimed as on the announcement of some great calamity. Naboth was "set on high"[b] in the public place of Samaria; two men of worthless character accused him of having "cursed[c] God and the king." He and his children (2 K. ix. 26), who else might have succeeded to his father's inheritance, were dragged out of the city and despatched the same night.[d] The place of execution there, as at Hebron (2 Sam. iii.), was by the large tank or reservoir, which still remains on the slope of the hill of Samaria, immediately outside the walls. The usual punishment for blasphemy was enforced. Naboth and his sons were stoned; their mangled remains were devoured by the dogs (and swine, LXX.) that prowled under the walls; and the blood from their wounds ran down into the waters of the tank below, which was the common bathing-place of the prostitutes of the city (comp. 1 K. xxi. 19, xxii. 38, LXX.). Josephus (*Ant.* viii. 15, § 6) makes the execution to have been at Jezreel, where he also places the washing of Ahab's chariot.

For the signal retribution taken on this judicial murder — a remarkable proof of the high regard paid in the old dispensation to the claims of justice and independence — see AHAB, JEHU, JEZEBEL, JEZREEL.   A. P. S.

NABUCHODON'OSOR (Ναβουχοδονό-

σορ: *Nabuchodonosor*). Nebuchadnezzar king of Babylon (1 Esdr. i. 40, 41, 45, 48, [ii. 10, v. 7, vi. 15, 18, 26;] Tob. xiv. 15; Jud. i. 1, 5, 7, 11, 12, ii. 1, 4, 19, iii. 2, 8, iv. 1, vi. 2, 4, xi. [1, 4,] 7, 23, xii. 13, xiv. 18; [Bar. i. 9, 12; Esth. xi. 4].

NA'CHON'S THRESHING - FLOOR

(גֹּרֶן נָכוֹן: [Rom. ἅλως Ναχώρ; Vat.] αλως Ωδαβ; Alex. αλωμωνος Ναχων: *Area Nachon*), the place at which the ark had arrived in its progress from Kirjath-jearim to Jerusalem, when Uzzah lost his life in his too hasty zeal for its safety (2 Sam. vi. 6). In the parallel narrative of Chronicles the name is given as CHIDON, which is also found in Josephus. After the catastrophe it received the name of Perez-uzzah. There is nothing in the Bible narrative to guide us to a conclusion as to the situation of this threshing-floor, — whether nearer to Jerusalem or to Kirjath-jearim. The words of Josephus (*Ant.* vii. 4, § 2), however, imply that it was close to the former.[e] Neither is it certain whether the name is that of the place or of a person to whom the place belonged. The careful Aquila translates the words — ἕως ἅλωνος ἑτοίμης — "to the prepared[f] threshing-floor," which is also the rendering of the Targum Jonathan. G.

NA'CHOR. The form (slightly the more accurate) in which on two occasions the name elsewhere given as NAHOR is presented in the A. V.

1. (נָחוֹר) [*piercer, slayer*, Fürst; *snorting*, Ges.]: Ναχώρ: *Nachor*.) The brother of Abraham (Josh. xxiv. 2). [NAHOR 1.]

Ch is commonly used in the A. V. of the Old Testament to represent the Hebrew כ, and only very rarely for ח, as in Nachor. Charashim, Rachel, Marchesvan, are further examples of the latter usage.

2. (Ναχώρ: [*Nachor*].) The grandfather of Abraham (Luke iii. 34). [NAHOR, 2.]   G.

NA'DAB (נָדָב) [*noble, generous*: Ναδάβ: *Nadab*]). **1.** The eldest son of Aaron and Elisheba, Ex. vi. 23; Num. iii. 2. He, his father and brother, and seventy old men of Israel were led out from the midst of the assembled people (Ex. xxiv. 1), and were commanded to stay and worship God "afar off," below the lofty summit of Sinai, where Moses alone was to come near to the Lord. Subsequently (Lev. x. 1) Nadab and his brother [ABIHU] were struck dead before the sanctuary by fire from the Lord. Their offense was kindling the incense in their censers with "strange" fire, i. e., not taken from that which burned perpetually (Lev. vi. 13) on the altar. From the injunction given, Lev. x. 9, 10, immediately after their death, it has

---

[a] Compare the cases of David and Araunah (2 Sam. xxiv.), Omri and Shemer (1 K. xvi.).

[b] The Hebrew word which is rendered, here only, "on high," is more accurately "at the head of" or "in the chiefest place among" (1 Sam. ix. 22). The passage is obscured by our ignorance of the nature of the ceremonial in which Naboth was made to take part; but, in default of this knowledge, we may accept the explanation of Josephus, that an assembly (ἐκκλησία) was convened, at the head of which Naboth, in virtue of his position, was placed, in order that the charge of blasphemy and the subsequent catastrophe might be more telling.

[c] By the LXX. this is given εὐλόγησε, "blessed;" probably merely for the sake of euphemism.

[d] אֶמֶשׁ. The word rendered "yesterday" in 2 K. ix. 26 has really the meaning of *yesternight*, and thus bears testimony to the precipitate haste both of the execution and of Ahab's entrance on his new acquisition. [See ELIJAH, vol. i. p. 706 b.]

[e] His words are, "Having brought the ark *into Jerusalem*" (εἰς Ἱεροσόλυμα). In some of the Greek versions, or variations of the LXX., which fragments are preserved by Bahrdt, the name is given ἡ ἅλως Ἐρνά (Ornan) τοῦ Ιεβουσαίου, identifying it with the floor of Araunah.

[f] As if from כּוּן, to make ready. A similar rendering, אֲתַר מַהַקֵן is employed in the Targum Joseph, of 1 Chr. xiii. 9, for the floor of *Chidon*

been inferred (Rosenmüller, *in loco*) that the brothers were in a state of intoxication when they committed the offense. The spiritual meaning of the injunction is drawn out at great length by Origen, *Hom. vii. in Levitic.* On this occasion, as if to mark more decidedly the divine displeasure with the offenders, Aaron and his surviving son were forbidden to go through the ordinary outward ceremonial of mourning for the dead.

2. [Rom. Ναβάτ; Vat. Ναβαθ, Ναβατ; Alex. Ναβατ, Ναβαθ: *Nadab*.] King Jeroboam's son, who succeeded to the throne of Israel B. C. 954, and reigned two years, 1 K. xv. 25–31. Gibbethon in the territory of Dan (Josh. xix. 44), a Levitical town (Josh. xxi. 23), was at that time occupied by the Philistines, perhaps having been deserted by its lawful possessors in the general self-exile of the Levites from the polluted territory of Jeroboam. Nadab and all Israel went up and laid siege to this frontier-town. A conspiracy broke out in the midst of the army, and the king was slain by Baasha, a man of Issachar. Ahijah's prophecy (1 K. xiv. 10) was literally fulfilled by the murderer, who proceeded to destroy the whole house of Jeroboam. So perished the first Israelitish dynasty.

We are not told what events led to the siege of Gibbethon, or how it ended, or any other incident in Nadab's short reign. It does not appear what ground Ewald and Newman have for describing the war with the Philistines as unsuccessful. It is remarkable that, when a similar destruction fell upon the family of the murderer Baasha twenty-four years afterwards, the Israelitish army was again engaged in a siege of Gibbethon, 1 K. xvi. 15.

3. [Ναδάβ.] A son of Shammai, 1 Chr. ii. 28, 30, of the tribe of Judah.

4. [Vat. in 1 Chr. viii. 30, Αδαδ.] A son of Gibeon [rather, of Jehiel], 1 Chr. viii. 30, ix. 36, of the tribe of Benjamin.   W. T. B.

NADAB'ATHA [Sin. Γαβαδαν; Rom.] Alex. Ναδαβδθ: Syriac, ‏نَدَب‎, Nobot: *Madaba*), a place from which the bride was being conducted by the children of Jambri, when Jonathan and Simon attacked them (1 Macc. ix. 37). Josephus (*Ant.* xiii. 1, § 4) gives the name Γαβαθά· Jerome's conjecture (in the Vulgate) can hardly be admitted, because Medeba was the city of the Jambrites (see ver. 36) to which the bride was being brought, not that from which she came. That Nadabatha was on the east of Jordan is most probable; for though, even to the time of the Gospel narative, by "Chanaanites" — to which the bride in this case belonged — is signified Phœnicians, yet we have the authority (such as it is) of the Book of Judith (v. 3) for attaching that name especially to the people of Moab and Ammon; and it is not probable that when the whole country was in such disorder a wedding *cortége* would travel for so great a distance as from Phœnicia to Medeba.

On the east of Jordan the only two names that occur as possible are Nebo — by Eusebius and Jerome written Nabo and Nabau — and Nabathæa. Compare the lists of places round *es-Salt*, in Robinson, 1st ed. iii. 167–70.   G.

NAG'GE (Ναγγαί), or, as some MSS. read, Ναγαί), one of the ancestors of Christ (Luke iii. 25). It represents the Heb. נֹגַהּ, *Nogah* (Ναγαί, LXX.), which was the name of one of David's

sons, as we read in 1 Chr. iii. 7. Nagge must have lived about the time of Onias I. and the commencement of the Macedonian dynasty. It is interesting to notice the evidence afforded by this name, both as a name in the family of David, and from its meaning, that, amidst the revolutions and conquests which overthrew the kingdoms of the nations, the house of David still cherished the hope, founded upon promise, of the revival of the splendor (*nogah*) of their kingdom.   A. C. H.

NA'HALAL (נַהֲלָל [perh. *pasture*]: Σελλά; Alex. Νααλωλ: *Naalol*), one of the cities of Zebulun, given with its "suburbs" to the Merarite Levites (Josh. xxi. 35). It is the same which in the list of the allotment of Zebulun (Josh. xix. 15) is inaccurately given in the A. V. as NAHALLAL, the Hebrew being in both cases identical. Elsewhere it is called NAHALOL. It occurs in the list between Kattath and Shimron, but unfortunately neither of these places has yet been recognized. The Jerusalem Talmud, however (*Megillah*, ch. i ; *Maaser Sheni*, ch. v.), as quoted by Schwarz (172), and Reland (*Pal.* 717), asserts that Nahalal (or Mahalal, as it is in some copies) was in post-biblical times called Mahlul; and this Schwarz identifies with the modern *Malul*, a village in the plain of Esdraelon under the mountains which inclose the plain on the north, 4 miles west of Nazareth, and 2 of Japhia; an identification concurred in by Van de Velde (*Memoir*). One Hebrew MS. (30 K.) lends countenance to it by reading מהלל, *i. e.* Mahalal. in Josh. xxi. 35. If the town was in the great plain we can understand why the Israelites were unable to drive out the Canaanites from it, since their chariots must have been extremely formidable as long as they remained on level or smooth ground.

NA'HALLAL (נַהֲלָל [*pasture*]: Ναβαδλ; Alex. Νααλωλ: *Naalol*), an inaccurate mode of spelling, in Josh. xix. 15, the name which in Josh. xxi. 35, is accurately given as NAHALAL. The original is precisely the same in both.   G.

NAHA'LIEL (נַחֲלִיאֵל = *torrent* [or *valley*] *of God*; Samar. נחלאל: [Vat.] Μαναήλ; [Rom.] Alex. Νααλιήλ: *Nahaliel*), one of the halting-places of Israel in the latter part of their progress to Canaan (Num. xxi. 19). It lay "beyond," that is, north of the Arnon (ver. 13), and between Mattanah and Bamoth, the next after Bamoth being Pisgah. It does not occur in the catalogue of Num. xxxiii., nor anywhere besides the passage quoted above. By Eusebius and Jerome (*Onomast.* "Naaliel") it is mentioned as close to the Arnon. Its name seems to imply that it was a stream or wady, and it is not impossibly preserved in that of the *Wady Encheyle*, which runs into the *Mojeb*, the ancient Arnon, a short distance to the east of the place at which the road between Rabba and Aroer crosses the ravine of the latter river. The name *Encheyle*, when written in Hebrew letters (אנחילה), is little more than נחליאל, transposed. Burckhardt was perhaps the first to report this name, but he suggests the *Wady Wale* as the Nahliel (*Syria*, July 14). This, however, seems unnecessarily far to the north, and, in addition, it retains no likeness to the original name.

    G.

NA'HALOL (נַהֲלֹל) [*pasture*]: Δομανά; Alex. Εναμμαν; [Comp. Νααλωλ:] *Naalol*), a variation in the mode of giving the name (both in Hebrew and A. V.) of the place elsewhere called Nahalal. It occurs only in Judg. i. 30. The variation of the LXX. is remarkable.   G.

NA'HAM (נַחַם) [*consolation*]: Ναχαμ; [Vat. Ναχεθ; Alex. Ναχεμ:] *Naham*). The brother of Hodiah, or Jehudijah, wife of Ezra, and father of Keilah and Eshtemoa (1 Chr. iv. 19).

NAHAMA'NI (נַחֲמָנִי) [*compassionate*]: Ναεμανι; [Vat. Ναεμανει:] FA. Νααμμανει: *Nahamani*). A chief man among those who returned from Babylon with Zerubbabel and Jeshua (Neh. vii. 7.) His name is omitted in Ezr. ii. 2, and in the parallel list of 1 Esdr. v. 8, is written Enenius.

NA'HARAI (נַחֲרַי) [3 syl.] [*snorer*, Ges.]: Ναχορ; Alex. Νααραϊ: *Naarai*). The armor-bearer of Joab, called in the A. V. of 2 Sam. xxiii. 37, Nahari. [So in later editions, here and in 1 Chr. xi. 39, but not in the ed. of 1611 and other early editions.] He was a native of Beeroth (1 Chr. xi. 39).

NA'HARI (נַחֲרַי) [*snorer*]: Γελωρέ; Alex. Γεδωρε; [Comp. Ναχαραι:] *Naharai*). The same as Naharai, Joab's armor-bearer (2 Sam. xxiii. 37). In the A. V. of 1611 the name is printed " Naharai the Berothite."

NA'HASH (נָחָשׁ, *serpent*). 1. (Νάᾱς, but in 1 Chr. ix. 2 [Vat.] Αναϛ; [Rom.] Alex. in both Naas: *Naas*). " Nahash the Ammonite, king of the Bene-Ammon at the foundation of the monarchy in Israel, who dictated to the inhabitants of Jabesh-Gilead that cruel alternative of the loss of their right eyes or slavery, which roused the swift wrath of Saul, and caused the destruction of the whole of the Ammonite force (1 Sam. xi. 1, 2–11) According to Josephus (*Ant.* vi. 5, § 1) the siege of Jabesh was but the climax of a long career of similar [a] ferocity with which Nahash had oppressed the whole of the Hebrews on the east of Jordan, and his success in which had rendered him so self-confident that he despised the chance of relief which the men of Jabesh eagerly caught at. If, as Josephus (*Ib.* § 3) also states, Nahash himself was killed in the rout of his army, then the Nahash who was the father of the foolish young king Hanun (2 Sam. x. 2; 1 Chr. xix. 1, 2) must have been his son. In this case, like Pharaoh in Egypt, and also perhaps like Benhadad, Achish, and Agag, in the kingdoms of Syria, Philistia, and Amalek, " Nahash " would seem to have been the title of the king of the Ammonites rather than the name of an individual.

However this was, Nahash the father of Hanun had rendered David some special and valuable service, which David was anxious for an opportunity of requiting (2 Sam. x. 2). No doubt this had been during his wanderings, and when, as the victim of Saul, the Ammonite king would naturally sympathize with and assist him. The particulars of the service are not related in the Bible, but the Jewish traditions affirm that it consisted in his having afforded protection to one of David's brothers, who escaped alone when his family were massacred by the treacherous king of Moab, to whose care they had been entrusted by David (1 Sam. xxii. 3, 4), and who found an asylum with Nahash. (See the *Midrash* of R. Tanchum, as quoted by S. Jarchi on 2 Sam. x. 2.)

The retribution exacted by David for the annoying insults of Hanun is related elsewhere. [David, vol. i. 561 *b*; Joab, vol. ii. 1395 *b*; Uriah.] One casual notice remains which seems to imply that the ancient kindness which had existed between David and the family of Nahash had not been extinguished even by the horrors of the Ammonite war. When David was driven to Mahanaim, into the very neighborhood of Jabesh-Gilead, we find " Shobi the son of Nahash of Rabbah of the Bene-Ammon " (2 Sam. xvii. 27) among the great chiefs who were so forward to pour at the feet of the fallen monarch the abundance of their pastoral wealth, and that not with the grudging spirit of tributaries, but rather with the sympathy of friends, " for they said, the people is hungry and weary and thirsty in the wilderness " (ver. 29).

2. (*Nâas*.) A person mentioned once only (2 Sam. xvii. 25) in stating the parentage of Amasa, the commander-in-chief of Absalom's army. Amasa is there said to have been the son [b] of a certain Ithra, by Abigail, " daughter of Nahash, and sister [c] to Zeruiah." By the genealogy of 1 Chr. ii. 16 it appears that Zeruiah and Abigail were sisters of David and the other children of Jesse. The question then arises, How could Abigail have been at the same time daughter of Nahash and sister to the children of Jesse? To this three answers may be given: —

1. The universal tradition of the Rabbis that Nahash and Jesse were identical.[d] " Nahash," says Solomon Jarchi (in his commentary on 2 Sam. xvii. 25), " was Jesse the father of David, because he died without sin, by the counsel of the serpent " (*nachash*); *i. e.* by the infirmity of his fallen human nature only. It must be owned that it is easier to allow the identity of the two than to accept the reason thus assigned for it.

2. The explanation first put forth by Professor Stanley in this work (vol. i. 552 *a*), that Nahash was the king of the Ammonites, and that the same woman had first been his wife or concubine — in which capacity she had given birth to Abigail and Zeruiah — and afterwards wife to Jesse, and the mother of his children. In this manner Abigail and Zeruiah would be sisters to David, without being at the same time daughters of Jesse. This has in its favor the guarded statement of 1 Chr. ii. 16, that the two women were not themselves Jesse's children, but sisters of his children; and the improbability (otherwise extreme) of so close a connection between an Israelite and an Ammonite king is alleviated by Jesse's known descent from a Moabitess, and by the connection which has been shown above to have existed between David and Nahash of Ammon.

---

[a] The statement in 1 Sam. xii. 12 appears to be at variance with that of viii. 4, 5 ; but it bears a remarkable testimony to the dread entertained of this savage chief, in ascribing the adoption of monarchy by Israel to the panic caused by his approach.

[b] The whole expression seems to denote that he was an illegitimate son.

[c] The Alex. LXX. regards Nahash as *brother* of Zeruiah — θυγατερα Ναας αδελφον Ζαρουιας.

[d] See the extract from the Targum on Ruth iv. 22 given in the note to Jesse, vol. ii. p. 1346 *a*. Also the citations from the Talmud in Meyer, *Seder Olam*, 569 ; also Jerome, *Quæst. Hebr.* ad loc.

3. A third possible explanation is that Nahash was the name not of Jesse, nor of a former husband of his wife, but of his wife herself. There is nothing in the name to prevent its being borne equally by either sex, and other instances may be quoted of women who are given in the genealogies as the daughters, not of their fathers, but of their mothers: *e. g.* Mehetabel, daughter of Matred, daughter of Mezahab. Still it seems very improbable that Jesse's wife would be suddenly intruded into the narrative, as she is if this hypothesis be adopted.

G.

NA′HATH (נַחַת [*setting down, rest*]: Ναχόθ, Alex. Ναχομ, Gen. xxxvi. 13; Ναχώθ, Alex. Ναχοθ, Gen. xxxvi. 17; Ναχές, [Alex. Ναχεθ,] 1 Chr. i. 37: *Nahath*). **1.** One of the " dukes " or phylarchs in the land of Edom, eldest son of Reuel the son of Esau.

2. (Καιναθ; [Vat. Alex.² Καιναθ.]) A Kohathite Levite, son of Zophai and ancestor of Samuel the prophet (1 Chr. vi. 26).

3. (Ναέθ; [Vat. Μαεθ.]) A Levite in the reign of Hezekiah, who with others was overseer of the tithes and dedicated things under Cononiah and Shimei (2 Chr. xxxi. 13).

NAH′BI (נַחְבִּי [*hidden*, Ges.; *protection*, Fürst]: Ναβί; [Vat. Ναβει;] Alex. Ναβα: *Nahabi*). The son of Vophsi, a Naphtalite, and one of the twelve spies (Num. xiii. 14).

NA′HOR (נָחוֹר [see NACHOR]: Ναχώρ; Joseph. Ναχώρης: *a Nahor*, and *Nachor*), the name of two persons in the family of Abraham.

1. His grandfather: the son of Serug and father of Terah (Gen. xi. 22–25; [1 Chr. i. 26]). He is mentioned in the genealogy of our Lord, Luke iii. 34, though there the name is given in the A. V. in the Greek form of NACHOR.

2. Grandson of the preceding, son of Terah and brother of Abraham and Haran (Gen. xi. 26, 27). The members of the family are brought together in the following genealogy:—

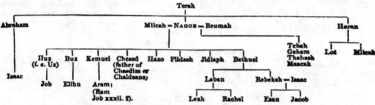

It has been already remarked, under LOT (vol. ii. p. 1685 *note*), that the order of the ages of the family of Terah is not improbably inverted in the narrative: in which case Nahor, instead of being younger than Abraham, was really older. He married Milcah, the daughter of his brother Haran; and when Abraham and Lot migrated to Canaan, Nahor remained behind in the land of his birth, on the eastern side of the Euphrates — the boundary between the Old and the New World of that early age — and gathered his family around him at the sepulchre of his father.[b] (Comp. 2 Sam. xix. 37.)

Like Jacob, and also like Ishmael, Nahor was the father of twelve sons, and further, as in the case of Jacob, eight of them were the children of his wife, and four of a concubine (Gen. xxii. 21–24). Special care is taken in speaking of the legitimate branch to specify its descent from Milcah — " the son of Milcah, which she bare unto Nahor." It was to this pure and unsullied race that Abraham and Rebekah in turn had recourse for wives for their sons. But with Jacob's flight from Haran the intercourse ceased. The heap of stones which he and " Laban the Syrian " erected on Mount Gilead (Gen. xxxi. 46) may be said to have formed at once the tomb of their past connection and the barrier against its continuance. Even at that time a wide variation had taken place in their language (ver. 47), and not only in their language, but, as it would seem, in the Object of their worship. The " God of Nahor " appears as a distinct divinity

from the " God of Abraham and the Fear of Isaac " (ver. 53). Doubtless this was one of the " other gods " which before the Call of Abraham were worshipped by the family of Terah; whose images were in Rachel's possession during the conference on Gilead; and which had to be discarded before Jacob could go into the Presence of the " God of Bethel " (Gen. xxxv. 2; comp. xxxi. 13). Henceforward the line of distinction between the two families is most sharply drawn (as in the allusion of Josh. xxiv. 2), and the descendants of Nahor confine their communications to their own immediate kindred, or to the members of other non-Israelite tribes, as in the case of Job the man of Uz, and his friends, Elihu the Buzite of the kindred of Ram, Eliphaz the Temanite, and Bildad the Shuhite. Many centuries later David appears to have come into collision — sometimes friendly, sometimes the reverse — with one or two of the more remote Nahorite tribes. Tibbath, probably identical with Tebah and Maacah, are mentioned in the relation of his wars on the eastern frontier of Israel (1 Chr. xviii. 8, xix. 6); and the mother of Absalom either belonged to or was connected with the latter of the above nations.

No certain traces of the name of Nahor have been recognized in Mesopotamia. Ewald (*Geschichte*, i. 359) proposes *Haditha*, a town on the Euphrates just above *Hit*, and bearing the additional name of *el-Naura;* also another place, likewise called *el-Na'ura*, mentioned by some Arabian geographers

---

a This is the form given in the Benedictine edition of Jerome's *Bibliotheca Divina*. The other is found in the ordinary copies of the Vulgate.

b The statements of Gen. xi. 27–32 appear to imply that Nahor did not advance from Ur to Haran at the same time with Terah, Abraham, and Lot, but remained there till a later date. Coupling this with the

statement of Judith v. 8, and the universal tradition of the East, that Terah's departure from Ur was a relinquishment of false worship, an additional force is given to the mention of " the god of Nahor " (Gen. xxxi. 53) as distinct from the God of Abraham's descendants. Two generations later Nahor's family were certainly living at Haran (Gen. xxviii. 10, xxix. 4).

as lying further north; and *Nachrein*, which, however, seems to lie out of Mesopotamia to the east. Others have mentioned Naarda, or Nehardea, a town or district in the neighborhood of the above, celebrated as the site of a college of the Jews (*Dict. of Geogr.* " Naarda ").

May not Aram-Naharaim have originally derived its name from Nahor? The fact that in its present form it has another signification in Hebrew is no argument against such a derivation.

In Josh. xxiv. 2 the name is given in the A. V. in the form (more nearly approaching the Hebrew than the other) of NACHOR.   G.

NAH'SHON, or **NAASH'ON** (נַחְשׁוֹן) [*enchanter*, Ges.]: Ναασσών, LXX. and N. T.: *Nahasson*, O. T.; *Naasson*, N. T.), son of Amminadab, and prince of the children of Judah (as he is styled in the genealogy of Judah, 1 Chr. ii. 10) at the time of the first numbering in the wilderness (Exod. vi. 23; Num. i. 7, &c.). His sister, Elisheba, was wife to Aaron, and his son, Salmon, was husband to Rahab after the taking of Jericho. From Elisheba being described as " sister of Naashon " we may infer that he was a person of considerable note and dignity, which his being appointed as one of the twelve princes who assisted Moses and Aaron in taking the census, and who were all " renowned of the congregation . . . . . heads of thousands in Israel," shows him to have been. No less conspicuous for high rank and position does he appear in Num. ii. 3, vii. 12, x. 14, where, in the encampment, in the offerings of the princes, and in the order of march, the first place is assigned to Nahshon the son of Amminadab as captain of the host of Judah. Indeed, on these three last-named occasions he appears as the first man in the state next to Moses and Aaron, whereas at the census he comes after the chiefs of the tribes of Reuben and Simeon.[a] Nahshon died in the wilderness according to Num. xxvi. 64, 65, but no further particulars of his life are given. In the N. T. he occurs twice, namely, in Matt. i. 4 and Luke iii. 32, in the genealogy of Christ, where his lineage in the preceding and following descents are exactly the same as in Ruth iv. 18-20; 1 Chr. ii. 10-12, which makes it quite certain that he was the sixth in descent from Judah, inclusive, and that David was the fifth generation after him. [AMMINADAB.]   A. C. H.

NA'HUM (נַחוּם [*consolation*]: Ναούμ: *Nahum*). " The book of the vision of Nahum the Elkoshite " stands seventh in order among the writings of the minor prophets in the present arrangement of the canon. Of the author himself we have no more knowledge than is afforded us by the scanty title of his book, which gives no indication whatever of his date, and leaves his origin obscure. The site of Elkosh, his native place, is disputed, some placing it in Galilee, with Jerome, who was shown the ruins by his guide; others in Assyria, where the tomb of the prophet is still visited as a sacred spot by Jews from all parts. Benjamin of Tudela (p. 53, Heb. text, ed. Asher) thus briefly

alludes to it: " And in the city of Asshur (Mosul) is the synagogue of Obadiah, and the synagogue of Jonah the son of Amittai, and the synagogue of Nahum the Elkoshite." [ELKOSH.] Those who maintain the latter view assume that the prophet's parents were carried into captivity by Tiglath pileser, and planted, with other exile colonists, in the province of Assyria, the modern Kurdistan, and that the prophet was born at the village of Alkush, on the east bank of the Tigris, two miles north of Mosul. Ewald is of opinion that the prophecy was written there at a time when Nineveh was threatened from without. Against this it may be urged that it does not appear that the exiles were carried into the province of Assyria Proper, but into the newly-conquered districts, such as Mesopotamia, Babylonia, or Media. The arguments in favor of an Assyrian locality for the prophet are supported by the occurrence of what are presumed to be Assyrian words: הֻצַּב, ii. 7 (Heb. 8), מִנְּזָרַיִךְ, טַפְסְרַיִךְ, iii. 17 ; and the strange form מַלְאָכֵה in ii. 13 (Heb. 14), which is supposed to indicate a foreign influence. In addition to this is the internal evidence supplied by the vivid description of Nineveh, of whose splendors it is contended Nahum must have been an eye-witness; but Hitzig justly observes that these descriptions display merely a lively imagination, and such knowledge of a renowned city as might be possessed by any one in Anterior Asia. The Assyrian warriors were no strangers in Palestine, and that there was sufficient intercourse between the two countries is rendered probable by the history of the prophet Jonah. There is nothing in the prophecy of Nahum to indicate that it was written in the immediate neighborhood of Nineveh, and in full view of the scenes which are depicted, nor is the language that of an exile in an enemy's country. No allusion is made to the Captivity; while, on the other hand, the imagery is such as would be natural to an inhabitant of Palestine (i. 4) to whom the rich pastures of Bashan, the vineyards of Carmel, and the blossom of Lebanon, were emblems of all that was luxuriant and fertile. The language employed in i. 15, ii. 2, is appropriate to one who wrote for his countrymen in their native land.[b] In fact, the sole origin of the theory that Nahum flourished in Assyria is the name of the village Alkush, which contains his supposed tomb, and from its similarity to Elkosh was apparently selected by mediæval tradition as a shrine for pilgrims, with as little probability to recommend it as exists in the case of Obadiah and Jephthah, whose burial-places are still shown in the same neighborhood. This supposition is more reasonable than another which has been adopted in order to account for the existence of Nahum's tomb at a place, the name of which so closely resembles that of his native town. Alkush, it is suggested, was founded by the Israelitish exiles, and so named by them in memory of Elkosh in their own country. Tradition, as usual, has usurped the province of history. According to Pseudo-Epiphanius (*De Vitis*

---

[a] It is curious to notice that, in the second numbering (Num. xxvi.), Reuben still comes first, and Judah fourth. So also 1 Chr. ii. 1.

[b] Capernaum, literally " village of Nahum," is supposed to have derived its name from the prophet. Schwarz (*Descr. of Pal.* p. 188) mentions a *Kefar Tan-*

chum or *Nachum*, close on Chinnereth, and 2½ English miles N. of Tiberias. " They point out there the graves of Nahum the prophet, of Rabbis Tanchum and Tanchuma, who all repose there, and through these the ancient position of the village is easily known."

Proph. Opp. ii. p. 247), Nahum was of the tribe of Simeon, "from Elcesei beyond the Jordan at Begabar (Βηγαβάρ; Chron. Pasch. 160 B. Βηταβαρή)," or Bethabara, where he died in peace and was buried. In the Roman martyrology the 1st of December is consecrated to his memory.

The date of Nahum's prophecy can be determined with as little precision as his birthplace. In the Seder Olam Rabba (p. 55, ed. Meyer) he is made contemporary with Joel and Habakkuk in the reign of Manasseh. Syncellus (*Chron.* p. 201 d) places him with Hosea, Amos, and Jonah in the reign of Joash king of Israel, more than a century earlier; while, according to Eutychius (*Ann.* p. 252), he was contemporary with Haggai, Zechariah, and Malachi, and prophesied in the fifth year after the destruction of Jerusalem. Josephus (*Ant.* ix. 11, § 3) mentions him as living in the latter part of the reign of Jotham; "about this time was a certain prophet, Nahum by name; who, prophesying concerning the downfall of Assyrians and of Nineveh, said thus," etc.; to which he adds, "and all that was foretold concerning Nineveh came to pass after 115 years." From this Carpzov concluded that Nahum prophesied in the beginning of the reign of Ahaz, about B. C. 742. Modern writers are divided in their suffrages. Bertholdt thinks it probable that the prophet escaped into Judah when the ten tribes were carried captive, and wrote in the reign of Hezekiah. Keil (*Lehrb. d. Einl. in d. A. T.*) places him in the latter half of Hezekiah's reign, after the invasion of Sennacherib. Vitringa (*Typ. Doctr. proph.* p. 37) was of the like opinion, and the same view is taken by De Wette (*Einl.* p. 328), who suggests that the rebellion of the Medes against the Assyrians (B. C. 710), and the election of their own king in the person of Deioces, may have been present in the prophet's mind. But the history of Deioces and his very existence are now generally believed to be mythical. This period also is adopted by Knobel (*Prophet.* ii. 207, &c.) as the date of the prophecy. He was guided to his conclusion by the same supposed facts, and the destruction of No Ammon, or Thebes of Upper Egypt, which he believed was effected by the Assyrian monarch Sargon (B. C. 717-715), and is referred to by Nahum (iii. 8) as a recent event. In this case the prophet would be a younger contemporary of Isaiah (comp. Is. xx. 1). Ewald, again, conceives that the siege of Nineveh by the Median king Phraortes (B. C. 630-625), may have suggested Nahum's prophecy of its destruction. The existence of Phraortes, at the period to which he is assigned, is now believed to be an anachronism. [MEDES.] Junius and Tremellius select the last years of Josiah as the period at which Nahum prophesied, but at this time not Nineveh but Babylon was the object of alarm to the Hebrews. The arguments by which Strauss (*Nahumi de Nino l'aticinium*, prol. c. 1, § 3) endeavors to prove that the prophecy belongs to the time at which Manasseh was in captivity at Babylon, that is between the years 680 and 667 B. C., are not convincing. Assuming that the position which Nahum occupies in the canon between Micah and Habakkuk supplies, as the limits of his prophetical career, the reigns of Hezekiah and Josiah, he endeavors to show from certain apparent resemblances to the writings of the older prophets, Joel, Jonah, and Isaiah, that Nahum must have been familiar with their writings, and consequently later in point of time than any of them. But a careful examina-

tion of the passages by which this argument is maintained, will show that the phrases and turns of expression upon which the resemblance is supposed to rest, are in no way remarkable or characteristic, and might have been freely used by any one familiar with oriental metaphor and imagery, without incurring the charge of plagiarism. Two exceptions are Nah. ii. 10, where a striking expression is used which only occurs besides in Joel ii. 6, and Nah. i. 15 (Heb. ii. 1), the first clause of which is nearly word for word the same as that of Is. lii. 7. But these passages, by themselves, would equally prove that Nahum was anterior both to Joel and Isaiah, and that his diction was copied by them. Other references which are supposed to indicate imitations of older writers, or, at least, familiarity with their writings, are Nah. i. 3 compared with Jon. iv. 2; Nah. i. 13 with Is. x. 27; Nah. iii. 10 with Is. xiii. 16; Nah. ii. 2 [1] with Is. xxiv. 1; Nah. iii. 5 with Is. xlvii. 2, 3; and Nah. iii. 7 with Is. li. 19. For the purpose of showing that Nahum preceded Jeremiah, Strauss quotes other passages in which the later prophet is believed to have had in his mind expressions of his predecessor with which he was familiar. The most striking of these are Jer. x. 19 compared with Nah. iii. 19; Jer. xiii. 26 with Nah. iii. 5; Jer. l. 37, li. 30 with Nah. iii. 13. Words, which are assumed by the same commentator to be peculiar to the times of Isaiah, are appealed to by him as evidences of the date of the prophecy. But the only examples which he quotes prove nothing: שֶׁטֶף, *sheteph* (Nah. i. 8, A. V. "flood"), occurs in Job, the Psalms, and in Proverbs, but not once in Isaiah; and מְצֻרָה, *metsúráh* (Nah. ii. 1 [2], A. V. "munition") is found only once in Isaiah, though it occurs frequently in the Chronicles, and is not a word likely to be uncommon or peculiar, so that nothing can be inferred from it. Besides, all this would be as appropriate to the times of Hezekiah as to those of Manasseh. That the prophecy was written before the final downfall of Nineveh, and its capture by the Medes and Chaldeans (cir. B. C. 625), will be admitted. The allusions to the Assyrian power imply that it was still unbroken (i. 12, ii. 13, 14 (E. V. 12, 13), iii. 15-17). The glory of the kingdom was at its brightest in the reign of Esarhaddon (B. C. 680-660), who for 13 years made Babylon the seat of empire, and this fact would incline us to fix the date of Nahum rather in the reign of his father Sennacherib, for Nineveh alone is contemplated in the destruction threatened to the Assyrian power, and no hint is given that its importance in the kingdom was diminished, as it necessarily would be, by the establishment of another capital. That Palestine was suffering from the effects of Assyrian invasion at the time of Nahum's writing seems probable from the allusions in i. 11, 12, 13, ii. 2; and the vivid description of the Assyrian armament in ii. 3, 4. At such a time the prophecy would be appropriate, and if i. 14 refers to the death of Sennacherib in the house of Nisroch, it must have been written before that event. The capture of No Ammon, or Thebes, has not been identified with anything like certainty. It is referred to as of recent occurrence, and it has been conjectured with probability that it was sacked by Sargon in the invasion of Egypt alluded to in Is. xx. 1. These circumstances seem to determine the 14th year of Hezekiah (B. C. 712, as the period before which the prophecy of Nahum could not have been written. The condition of Assyria in the reign of Sennacherib would correspond with the state of things implied in the prophecy, and it is on all accounts most probable that Nahum flourished in the latter half of the reign of Hezekiah, and wrote his prophecy soon after the date above mentioned, either in Jerusalem or its neighborhood, where the echo still lingered of "the rattling of the wheels, and of the prancing horses, and of the jumping chariots" of the Assyrian host, and "the flame of the sword and lightning of the spear" still flashed in the memory of the beleaguered citizens.

The subject of the prophecy is, in accordance with the superscription, "the burden of Nineveh." The three chapters into which it is divided form a consecutive whole. The first chapter is introductory. It commences with a declaration of the character of Jehovah, "a God jealous and avenging," as exhibited in his dealings with his enemies, and the swift and terrible vengeance with which He pursues them (i. 2–6), while to those that trust in Him He is "good, a stronghold in the day of trouble" (i. 7), in contrast with the overwhelming flood which shall sweep away his foes (i. 8). The language of the prophet now becomes more special, and points to the destruction which awaited the hosts of Assyria who had just gone up out of Judah (i. 9–11). In the verses that follow the intention of Jehovah is still more fully declared, and addressed first to Judah (i. 12, 13), and then to the monarch of Assyria (i. 14). And now the vision grows more distinct. The messenger of glad tidings, the news of Nineveh's downfall, trod the mountains that were round about Jerusalem (i. 15), and proclaimed to Judah the accomplishment of her vows. But round the doomed city gathered the destroying armies; "the breaker in pieces" had gone up, and Jehovah mustered his hosts to the battle to avenge his people (ii. 1, 2). The prophet's mind in vision sees the burnished bronze shields of the scarlet-clad warriors of the besieging army, the flashing steel scythes of their war-chariots as they are drawn up in battle-array, and the quivering cypress-shafts of their spears (ii. 3). The Assyrians hasten to the defense: their chariots rush madly through the streets, and run to and fro like the lightning in the broad ways, which glare with their bright armor like torches. But a panic has seized their mighty ones; their ranks are broken as they march, and they hurry to the wall only to see the covered battering-rams of the besiegers ready for the attack (ii. 4, 5). The crisis hastens on with terrible rapidity. The river-gates are broken in, and the royal palace is in the hands of the victors (ii. 6). And then comes the end; the city is taken and carried captive, and her maidens "moan as with the voice of doves," beating their breasts with sorrow (ii. 7). The flight becomes general, and the leaders in vain endeavor to stem the torrent of fugitives (ii. 8). The wealth of the city and its accumulated treasures become the spoil of the captors, and the conquered suffer all the horrors that follow the assault and storm (ii. 9, 10). Over the charred and blackened ruins the prophet, as the mouthpiece of Jehovah, exclaims in triumph, "Where is the lair of the lions, the feeding place of the young lions, where walked lion, lioness, lion's whelp, and none made (them) afraid?" (ii. 11, 12). But for all this the downfall of Nineveh was certain, for "behold! I am against thee, saith Jehovah of

Hosts" (ii. 13). The vision ends, and the prophet, recalled from the scenes of the future to the realities of the present, collects himself, as it were, for one final outburst of withering denunciation against the Assyrian city, not now threatened by her Median and Chaldean conquerors, but in the full tide of prosperity, the oppressor and corrupter of nations. Mingled with this woe there is no touch of sadness or compassion for her fate; she will fall unpitied and unlamented, and with terrible calmness the prophet pronounces her final doom: "all that hear the bruit of thee shall clap the hands over thee: for upon whom hath not thy wickedness passed continually?" (iii. 19).

As a poet, Nahum occupies a high place in the first rank of Hebrew literature. In proof of this it is only necessary to refer to the opening verses of his prophecy (i. 2–6), and to the magnificent description of the siege and destruction of Nineveh in ch. ii. His style is clear and uninvolved, though pregnant and forcible; his diction sonorous and rhythmical, the words reëchoing to the sense (comp. ii. 4, iii. 3). Some words and forms of words are almost peculiar to himself; as, for example, סְעָרָה for סְעָרָה, in i. 3, occurs only besides in Job ix. 17; קִפֹּא for קָפָא, in i. 2, is found only in Josh. xxiv. 19; תְּכוּנָה, ii. 9 [10], is found in Job xxiii. 3, and there not in the same sense; דֹּהַר, in iii. 2, is only found in Judg. v. 22; רָעַל and פְּלָדוֹת, ii. 3 [4], בָּהַב, ii. 7 [8], מִצְדִּים, iii. and מְבֻקָה and בּוּקָה, ii. 10 [11], פֻּהַק, iii. 17, and פֻּהַק, iii. 19, do not occur elsewhere. The unusual form of the pronominal suffix in מַלְאָכֵכֵה, ii. 13 [14], נְפֻשׁוּ for נָפֹצוּ, iii. 18, are peculiar to Nahum; סָעַר, iii. 5, is only found in 1 K. vii. 36; גֹּבַי, iii. 17, occurs besides only in Am. vii. 1; and the foreign word טִפְסָר, iii. 17, in the slightly different form טִפְסָר, is found only in Jer. li. 27.

For illustrations of Nahum's prophecy, see the article NINEVEH.   W. A. W.

* For the general writers on the Minor Prophets see the addition to MICAH (Amer. ed.). Part xix. of Lange's *Bibelwerk des A. Test.* by Dr. Paul Kleinert (1868) includes Nahum. It furnishes a new translation of the text, instead of adhering to that of Luther. Among the special writers on this prophet are Bibliander, *Propheta Nah. juxta veritatem Hebr.* (1534); Abarbanel, *Comm. in Nah. rabb. et Lat.* (1703); Kalinski, *Vaticinia (Hab. et) Nah.* etc. (1748); Kreenen, *Nah. vaticiniuns, phil. et crit. expositum* (1808); Justi, *Nah. neu übersetzt u. erläutert* (1820); Hoelemann, *Nah. oraculum illustravit* (1842); and O. Strauss, *Nahums de Nino vaticinium* (1853). There is a "Translation of the Prophecy of Nahum with Notes" by Prof. B. B. Edwards in the *Bibl. Sacra*, v. 551-576. It is a fine example of exact Biblical exegesis. Recent explorations in the East have given fresh interest to the study of Nahum. Among the works which illustrate the connections of the book with Assyrian and Babylonian history in addition to the commentaries, are M. von Niebuhr's *Geschichte Assur's u. Babel's* (1857); O. Strauss, *Nineve u. das Wort Gottes* (1855); Layard, *Nineveh and*

its Remains; Vance Smith, *The Prophecies relating to Nineveh and the Assyrians* (Lond. 1857); Rawlinson, *Ancient Monarchies,* vol. i. See the copious list of works in German, French, and English, relating to the fall of Nineveh in Lange's *Bibelwerk* (p. 100) as above. Nineveh, which disappeared so suddenly after its doom was pronounced by the prophet, may almost be said to stand before us again in the light of the remains restored to us by modern discoveries. The articles on Nahum by Winer in his *Bibl. Realw.,* by Nägelsbach in Herzog's *Real-Encyk.,* and by Wunderlich in Zeller's *Bibl. Wörterb.* should not be overlooked. In opposition to the view that Nahum lived in Assyria, Bleek (*Einl. in das A. Test.* p. 544) agrees with those who decide that the prophet was not only born in Palestine, but wrote the book which bears his name in Jerusalem or the vicinity (i. 12 f.). [ELKOSH, Amer. ed.]

The book of Nahum contains nothing strictly Messianic. It is important as a source of permanent instruction because it illustrates so signally the law of retribution according to which God deals with nations, and the fidelity with which He fulfils his promises and threatenings to the righteous or the wicked.   H.

NAÏDUS (Ναΐδος; Alex. Ναειδος: *Raanas*) = BENAIAH, of the sons of Pahath Moab (1 Esdr. ix. 31; comp. EZR. x. 30).

NAIL. I. (of finger).[a] — 1. A nail or claw of man or animal. 2. A point or style, *e. g.* for writing: see Jer. xvii. 1. *Tzippóren* occurs in Deut. xxi. 12, in connection with the verb עָשָׂה, *'âsâh,* "to make," here rendered περιονυχίζω, *circumcido,* A. V. "pare," but in marg. "dress," "suffer to grow." Gesenius explains "make neat."

Much controversy has arisen on the meaning of this passage: one set of interpreters, including Josephus and Philo, regarding the action as indicative of mourning, while others refer it to the deposition of mourning. Some, who would thus belong to the latter class, refer it to the practice of staining the nails with henneh.

The word *asah,* "make," is used both of "dressing," *i. e.* making clean the feet, and also of "trimming," *i. e.* combing and making neat the beard, in the case of Mephibosheth, 2 Sam. xix. 24. It seems, therefore, on the whole to mean "make suitable" to the particular purpose intended, whatever that may be: unless, as Gesenius thinks, the passage refers to the completion of the female captive's month of seclusion, that purpose is evidently one of mourning — a month's mourning interposed for the purpose of preventing on the one hand too hasty an approach on the part of the captor, and on the other too sudden a shock to natural feeling in the captive. Following this line of interpretation, the command will stand thus: The captive is to lay aside the "raiment of her captivity," namely, her ordinary dress in which she had been taken captive, and she is to remain in mourning retirement for a month with hair shortened and nails made suitable to the same purpose, thus presenting an appearance of woe to which the nails untrimmed and shortened hair would seem each in their way most suitable (see Job i. 20).

If, on the other hand, we suppose that the shaving the head, etc., indicate the time of retirement completed, we must suppose also a sort of Nazaritic initiation into her new condition, a supposition for which there is elsewhere no warrant in the Law, besides the fact that the "making," whether paring the nails or letting them grow, is nowhere mentioned as a Nazaritic ceremony, and also that the shaving the head at the end of the month would seem an altogether unsuitable introduction to the condition of a bride.

We conclude, therefore, that the captive's head was shaved at the commencement of the month, and that during that period her nails were to be allowed to grow in token of natural sorrow and consequent personal neglect. Joseph. *Ant.* iv. 8-23; Philo, περὶ φιλανθρ. c. 14, vol. ii. p. 394, ed. Mangey; Clem. Alex. *Strom.* ii. c. 18, iii. c. 11, vol. ii. pp. 475, 543, ed. Potter; Calmet, Patrick; *Crit. Sacr.* on Deut. xxi. 12; Schleusner, *Lex. V. T.* περιονυχίζω; Selden, *de Jur. Nat.* v. xiii. p. 644; Harmer, *Obs.* iv. 104; Wilkinson, *Anc. Eg.* ii. 345; Lane, *M. E.* i. 64; Gesenius, p. 1075; Michaelis, *Laws of Moses,* art. 88, vol. i. p. 464, ed. Smith; Num. vi. 2, 18.

II. — 1.[b] A nail (Is. xli. 7), a stake (Is. xxxiii. 20), also a tent-peg. Tent-pegs are usually of wood and of large size, but sometimes, as was the case with those used to fasten the curtains of the Tabernacle, of metal (Ex. xxvii. 19, xxxviii. 20; see Lightfoot, *Spicil.* in Ex. § 42; Joseph. *Ant.* v. 5, 4). [JAEL, TENT.]

2.[c] A nail, primarily a point.[d] We are told that David prepared iron for the nails to be used in the Temple; and as the holy of holies was plated with gold, the nails also for fastening the plates were probably of gold. Their weight is said to have been 50 shekels, = 25 ounces, a weight obviously so much too small, unless mere gilding be supposed, for the total weight required, that LXX. and Vulg. render it as expressing that of each nail, which is equally excessive. To remedy this difficulty Thenius suggests reading 500 for 50 shekels (1 Chr. xxii. 3; 2 Chr. iii. 9; Bertheau, *on Chronicles,* in *Kurzgef. Handb.*). [On "nails" in Eccl. xii. 11, see MASTER, Amer. ed.]

"Nail," Vulg. *palus,* is the rendering of πάσσαλος in Ecclus. xxvii. 2. In N. T. we have ἧλος and προσηλόω in speaking of the nails of the Cross (John xx. 25; Col. ii. 14). [See addition to CRUCIFIXION.]   H. W. P.

NAIN (Ναΐν [either from נָוָה, *pasture,* or נָעִים, *gracefulness: Naim*]). There are no materials for a long history or a detailed description of this village of Galilee, the gate of which is made illustrious by the raising of the widow's son (Luke

---

[a] צִפֹּרֶן, *t'phar,* a Chaldee form of the Heb. צִפֹּרֶן, *tzipporen,* from the root צָפַר, connected with סָפַר, *saphar,* "to scrape," or "pare:" ὄνυξ: *unguis.*

[b] יָתֵד, *jathêd:* πάσσαλος: *paxillus, clavus;* akin to Arab. وَتَد, *watada,* "to fix a peg."

[c] מַסְמֵר, *masmêr,*[1] only used in plur.: ἧλος: *clavus.*

[d] From סָמַר, "stand on end," as hair (Ges. p. 961).

[1] Closely allied to Arab. مِسْمَار, *mismâr,* "a nail."

vii. 12). But two points connected with it are of extreme interest to the Biblical student. The site of the village is certainly known: and there can be no doubt as to the approach by which our Saviour was coming when He met the funeral. The modern *Nein* is situated on the northwestern edge of the "Little Hermon," or *Jebel el-Duhy*, where the ground falls into the plain of Esdraelon. Nor has the name ever been forgotten. The crusaders knew it, and Eusebius and Jerome mention it in its right connection with the neighborhood of Endor. Again, the entrance to the place must probably always have been up the steep ascent from the plain; and here, on the west side of the village, the rock is full of sepulchral caves. It appears also that there are similar caves on the east side. (Robinson, *Bibl. Res.* ii. 361; Van de Velde, *Syria and Palestine*, ii. 382; Stanley, *Sinai and Palestine*, p. 357; Thomson, *Land and Book*, p. 445; Porter, *Handbook to Syria*, p. 358.)   J. S. H.

* Nain is distinctly visible from the top of Tabor across an intervening branch of the plain of Esdraelon. It is but a few miles distant from Nazareth. Shunem and Endor are in the neighborhood. The present name (though variously written by travellers) is the identical ancient name. Mr. Tristram (*Land of Israel*, p. 130) speaks of a fountain here, which explains why the place has been so long inhabited. Thomson states (*Land and Book*, ii. 158) that "the tombs are chiefly on the east of the village," and not on the west (see above). On the miracle of restoring to life the son of the widow at Nain (Luke vii. 11-15), see Trench on *Miracles*, p. 222. The custom of carrying the dead for interment outside of the cities and villages, is still, as on that occasion, almost universal in Palestine.

Whether we understand "bier" or "coffin" to be meant by σορός in the narrative, is immaterial to its accuracy. Present usages show that the body in either case was not so confined as to make it impossible for the "young man" to rise and sit up at the command of Christ. [COFFIN, Amer. ed.] The writer has witnessed funerals in Greece at which the upper side of the coffin was left entirely open, and the lid carried before the corpse until the procession reached the grave (see *Illustr. of Scripture*, p. 120).   H.

NAIOTH (נָוִיֹת,[a] according to the *Keri* or corrected text of the Masorets, which is followed by the A. V., but in the *Cethib* or original text נְוָיֹת,[a] i. e. Nevaioth [*habitations*]: [Rom. Ναυάθ; Vat.] Αυαθ: Alex. Ναυιωθ: *Naioth*), or more fully,[b] "Naioth in Ramah;" a place in which Samuel and David took refuge together, after the latter had made his escape from the jealous fury of Saul (1 Sam. xix. 18, 19, 22, 23, xx. 1). It is evident from ver. 18, that Naioth was not actually in Ramah, Samuel's habitual residence, though from the affix it must have been near it (Ewald, iii. 66). In its corrected form (*Keri*) the name signifies "habitations," and from an early date has been interpreted to mean the huts or dwellings of a

school or college of prophets over which Samuel presided, as Elisha did over those at Gilgal and Jericho.

This interpretation was unknown to Josephus who gives the name Γαλβάαθ, to the translators of the LXX. and the Peshito-Syriac (*Jonath*), and to Jerome.[c] It appears first in the Targum-Jonathan, where for Naioth we find throughout בֵּית אֻלְפָנָא, "the house of instruction," the term [d] which appears in later times to have been regularly applied to the schools of the Rabbis (Buxtorf, *Lex Talm.* 106) — and where ver. 20 is rendered, "and they saw the company of scribes singing praises, and Samuel teaching, standing over them," thus introducing the idea of Samuel as a teacher. This interpretation of Naioth is now generally accepted by the lexicographers and commentators.   G.

* **NAKED.** [DRESS, vol. i. p. 620 b.]

* **NAMES,** BIBLICAL; THEIR ORIGIN AND SIGNIFICANCE. — Names are archæological monuments. Especially is this true of those presented to us in the primitive languages of mankind. Originally given for the purpose of distinguishing different objects, or of indicating the significance which those objects possessed for the name-giver, they connate and perpetuate the conceptions, feelings, and modes of thought of their originators. It is on this account that their study is at once so fascinating and of such real utility. It is the study of the thought-fossils of mankind.

The two principal cautions to be given to the student of names, are, first, to guard against false etymologies, and secondly, to beware of mystical or merely fanciful interpretations. A recent English writer has wittily illustrated the first danger by saying, that the tyro must not think he has discovered a wonderful fitness in the denomination of the metropolitan residence of the English primate, Lambeth, because forsooth *Lama* is a Mongolian word for "Chief Priest," and *Beth* the Hebrew term for "house"; since, if the truth must be told, the term Lambeth is derived from an Anglo-Saxon compound, signifying "the muddy landing place"! An equally striking exemplification of the second liability is furnished us by a recent American writer in this department, Mr. W. Arthur. In his work on the "Derivation of Family Names" (N. Y. 1857) we find an old Christian-rabbinical idea thus rehabilitated: "The signification of the Hebrew names recorded in the fifth chapter of Genesis, when arranged in order, present an epitome of the ruin and recovery of man through a Redeemer, thus: —

Adam	'Man in the image of God'
Seth	'Substituted by.'
Enos	'Frail man.'
Canaan	'Lamenting.'
Mahalaleel	'The blessed God.'
Jered	'Shall come down'
Enoch	'Teaching.'
Methuselah	'His death shall send'
Lemech	'To the humble.'
Noah	'Consolation.'

---

[a] The plural of נָוֶה. The original form (*Cethib*) would be the plural of נְוָיָה (Simonis, *Onom.* 80), a word which does not appear to have existed.

[b] "Naioth" occurs both in Heb. and A. V. in 1 Sam. xix. 18, only. The LXX. supply ἐν Ῥαμά in that verse. The Vulgate adheres to the Hebrew.

[c] In his notice of this name in the *Onomasticon* ("Namoth"), Jerome refers to his observations thereon in the "libri Hebraicarum quæstionum." As, however, we at present possess those books, they contain no reference to Naioth.

[d] It occurs again in the Targum for the residence of Huldah the prophetess (2 K. xxii. 14).

"These names in the order in which they are recorded read thus: 'To man, once made in the image of God, now substituted by man, frail and full of sorrow, the blessed God shall come down himself to the earth teaching, and his death shall send to the humble consolation'" (!) The original author of this remarkable piece of interpretation seems to have been Ursinus, chief author of the Heidelberg Catechism. Dr. Alabaster repeated it in a sermon on 1 Chron. i. 1–4 delivered before the University of Cambridge, and Dr. Brown of Haddington introduces it with evident approbation into his "Dictionary of the Bible," art. Adam. (For analogous instances of exegetical trifling on the part of the cabalistic writers, see McClintock and Strong's *Cyclop. of Bib., Theol., and Ecclesiast. Literature*, art. *Cabala*.)

Notwithstanding such fanciful attempts to discover the whole system of Christian truth in a genealogical table, it must not be forgotten that the names of the Bible have in innumerable instances a real and profound significance. This is apparent from the fact, that on mentioning a name the sacred writers in almost countless cases pause to call our attention either to its etymological signification or to the reasons which led to its bestowment. In view of the special attention paid to etymology in the American edition of the present work, we shall restrict ourselves in this article to general facts and statements relative to names of places and persons. For information respecting particular names whose derivation or signification present especial problems, we may safely refer the reader to the appropriate articles in the Dictionary and to the literature given below.

I. NAMES OF PLACES. These may be divided into two general classes, descriptive and historical. The former are such as mark some peculiarity of the locality, usually a natural one, e. g., Sharon, "plain"; Gibeah, "hill"; Pisgah, "height"; Mizpah, "watchtower," *a* etc. The extraordinary richness and expressiveness of the Hebrew topographical vocabulary (see Stanley, *Appendix to S. and P.* pp. 471–519), rendered the construction of descriptive names in this way an exceedingly easy and natural process. How apt the designations were can yet be seen in hundreds of instances. See for example, Carmel, "the park," in volume first of this work.

Of the second class of local names, some were given in honor of individual men, e. g., the city Enoch, Gen. iv. 17; Dan, Judg. xviii. 29; Jebus, Cæsarea, Cæsarea Philippi, etc. More commonly, however, such names were given to perpetuate the memory of some important historic occurrence. Thus Babel, we are told, received its name "because the Lord did there confound the language of all the earth," Gen. xi. 9. (See, however, the native etymology. *sub voce*.) Bethel perpetuated through all Jewish history the early revelations of God to Jacob, Gen. xxviii. 19, xxxv. 15. See Jehovah-jireh, Gen. xxii. 14; Isaac's wells, Gen. xxvi. 20 ff.; Mahanaim, Gen. xxxii. 2; Peniel, Gen. xxxii. 30; Massah and Meribah, Ex. xvii. 7; Kibroth-hattaavah, Num. xi. 34; Hormah, Num. xxi. 3; Achor, Josh. vii. 26; Bochim, Jud. ii. 5; Cabul, 1 K. ix. 13, &c., &c. In some instances it may

---

a ° The Hebrew forms of the names in this article will be found in connection with the English forms in their respective places, and need not be repeated here.
             H.

be difficult to determine to which class a particular name belongs; thus Golgotha, or Calvary, is supposed by some to have been so called because in the form of "a skull," i. e. a well-marked hillock, others however, deny that the traditional conception of a "*Mount* Calvary" has any Scriptural warrant, and trace the name to the fact that it was the customary place for capital executions. The former class would make it a descriptive, the latter a historical, name. The importance of the question in a topographical point of view is self-evident.

In forming compounds to serve as names of towns or other localities, some of the most common terms employed by the Hebrews were *Kir*, a "wall" or "fortress" (Kir-haresh); *Kirjath*, "city" (Kirjath-arba; Kirjath-huzoth, "city of streets"; Kirjath-jearim, "city of woods" = Forestville; Kirjath-sepher, "city of books"; Kirjath-sannah, "city of learning"); *En*, "fountain" (En-eglaim, "fountain of the two calves"; En-gannim, "fountain of the gardens"; En-gedi, "fountain of the kid"; En-hakkore, "fountain of the cry or prayer," Judg. xv. 19; En-rogel, "fountain of the fuller," etc.); *Beer*, "a well" (Beer-elim, "well of the mighty ones" or "well of the terebinth"; Beer-lahai-roi, "*Puteus (Dei) viventis, aspicientis me*," Simonis; Beer-sheba, "well of the oath"); *Beth*, "house" (Beth-arabah, "house of the desert"; Beth-aven, "house of vanity" or of idols; Beth-emek, "house of the valley"; Beth-horon, "place of the great cavern"; Beth-lehem, "house of bread"; Beth-shan, "house of rest"; Beth-shemesh, "house of the sun" etc., etc.). The names of rivers and bodies of water were almost always of a descriptive character, e. g., Jordan, "descending"; Kishon, "tortuous"; Chebar, "abundant" or "vehement"; Kidron, "very black"; Merom, "a high place" (fully written *Mey-merom*, "waters of the heights"); *Jam-Suph*, "sea of weeds" (Red Sea); *Jam-Arabah*, "sea of the desert," or *Jam-Hammelach*, "salt sea" (Dead Sea); *Jam-chinnereth*, "sea of the Harp" (Sea of Galilee, said to have been so called from its shape). The names of countries and sections of country were almost universally derived from the name of their first settlers or earliest historic populations, e. g., Canaan; Misraim (Egypt); Edom; Asshur (Assyria); Tarshish; Havilah, etc. In the Geographical Appendix to Osborn's *Palestine, Past and Present*, Phila. 1858, may be found an exhaustive list of the names of all places and nations mentioned in the O. or N. Test., with references to all the passages where they occur and the latitude and longitude of each locality so far as ascertained. The Bible Atlas of Maps and Plans by the Rev. Samuel Clark, published by the Society for Promoting Christian Knowledge (Lond. 1868), has a "Complete Index to the Geographical Names in the English Bible," including the Apocrypha, by George Grove.

II. NAMES OF PERSONS. Unlike the Romans, but like the Greeks, the Hebrews were a mononymous people, that is, each person received but a single name. In the case of boys this was conferred upon the eighth day in connection with the rite of circumcision (Luke i. 59, ii. 21; comp. Gen. xvii. 5–14, xxi. 3, 4). To distinguish an individual from others of the same name it was customary, as among most, if not all primitive peoples, to add to his own proper name that of his father, or if that was insufficient, the names of several ancestors in ascending order (Jer. xxxvi. 14). Instead of the father's name that of the mother was sometimes used, possibly in cases where the mother was the more widely known of the two (1 Chr. ii. 16). In some instances the father is represented as conferring the name, in others the mother. Thus, to pass over the naming of the animals and of Eve by Adam, Seth named Enos, Lamech Noah, Jacob Benjamin, etc. On the other hand Eve named Cain and Seth, probably also Abel; Lot's daughters named Moab and Ammon; Leah gave names to Reuben, Simeon, Levi, Judah, Gad, Asher, Issachar, Zebulun, and Dinah; Rachel to Dan, Naphtali, Joseph, and her last born, which was however changed by Jacob. (See Moroni, *Dizionario*.)

Distinguishing with Ewald three classes of names, the simple, the derivative and the compound, we will briefly treat of each in order.

1. *Simple names.* These in Hebrew, as in all languages, were largely borrowed from nature, e. g., Deborah, "bee"; Arieh, "Leo" or "Lyon"; Tamar, "a palm-tree"; Jonah, "dove"; Rachel, "ewe"; Shual, "fox"; Caleb, "dog"; Hodesh, "new moon"; Cheran, "lamb"; Dishan, "gazelle," etc., etc. Others are of a descriptive character, e. g., Ashur, "black" (comp. however Simonis); Edom, "red"; Esau, "hairy"; Gareb, "scabbed"; Korah, "bald"; Chimcham, "pining" (can be understood, however, in the sense of *Desiderius*; so by Simonis); Paseah, "the lame"; Ikkesh, "crooked" (here too, Simonis has an interpretation of his own, understanding the term as relating to the hair, like the Latin name *Crispus*). Still other names were borrowed from human occupations and conditions, e. g., Dan, "a judge"; Sarah, "a princess"; Carmi, "vine-dresser," etc., etc. Whether diminutives are found in Hebrew may be doubted. Ewald and others have claimed that Zebulun and Jeduthun are such. This peculiarity of the Hebrew is the more remarkable from the fact, that its near cognate, the Arabic, abounds in diminutives.

2. *Derivative names.* Many names of women were derived from those of men by change of termination: Hammelech, "the king," Hammoleketh, "the queen," (like the German *König, Königin*); Meshullam, "*Pius*," Meshullameth, "*Pia*"; Haggi or Haggai, "exultation," and Haggith; Judah, Judith; Dan, Dinah, etc., etc. Such derivations, however, are limited to simple names, no instance occurring where a feminine name is derived from a compound masculine one. On this peculiarity Ewald remarks, that as the same compound names are sometimes used both for men and women, and as names are applied to women which could not originally have been applicable to any but men, as Abigail, and Ahinoam, we must assume that the plastic power of language had already exhausted itself in this remote province, and that for this reason, the distinction of the feminine was omitted; in the same way as Sanskrit and Greek adjectives of the form εὐδαίμων, εὐτυχής, are not able to distinguish the feminine in form.

The final syllable -*i*, or -*ai*, in such names as Amittai, Barzillai, is regarded by Ewald as a derivative particle, so that according to this grammarian the names mentioned would be equivalent to "Truman" and "Ironman." All other etymologists, however, whom we have consulted, regard the syllable in question as an imperfectly expressed *Jah*, and interpret the names "Truth of Jehovah," "Iron of Jehovah," etc. Of the use of the same

terminational syllable to form patronymics in Hebrew, see Wilkinson, pp. 29–42.

The most anomalous phenomenon observable in the derivation of Hebrew names is the fact, that in the employment of names derived from abstract nouns masculine ones are often applied to women, and feminine ones to men, while in other cases names identical in meaning and distinguished as to gender by their termination are applied to a single sex. In this respect Hebrew usage seems to have been subject to no rule. Thus Shelomi, "peaceable" or "my peace," and Shelomo, Hebrew for Solomon, are masculine forms and were used as masculine names, but Shelomith, the feminine form, was not only a name of women, but also of men, 1 Chr. xxvi. 25, 26, xxiii. 9. Shemer and Shimri, "watchful" or "guarded" (of God), are names of men both in form and fact. The feminine form, Shimrath, is nevertheless applied to a man, 1 Chr. viii. 21; while in 2 Chr. xxiv. 20 another feminine form, Shimrith, is the name of a woman. Analogous to this is the fact, that many titles of men were feminine and required to be construed with feminine adjectives, etc., as Pechah, "governor," Koheleth, "preacher," etc., while in other cases masculine nouns took feminine terminations in the plural, e. g. *Ab*, "father," plural *aboth* not *abim*; or feminine nouns the plural ending of the masculine, e. g., *Millah*, "word," *Millim*, "words." See the Grammars.

3. *Compound Names.* These constitute in all languages the most interesting and instructive class, since they reflect emotions and ideas, for whose expression a conscious exercise of the onomatopoetic faculty was requisite. In Hebrew we find some, which have no especial religious or social significance, as for example, Phinehas, "mouth of brass"; Ishod, "man of beauty"; Gemalli, "camel-owner." The majority, however, have such significance, being compounded either (1) with terms denoting relationship, as *Abi*, or *ab* (Abihud, "father of praise"; Abijam, "f. of the sea"; Abimelech, "f. of the king"; Abinoam, "f. of pleasantness"; Abitub, "f. of goodness" etc. etc.);—Achi (Eng. ver. *Ahi*), "brother" (Ahihud, Ahimelech, Ahinoam, Ahitub, etc., etc.); — *Ben* (Syriac *Bar*), "son" (Benoni, "son of my sorrow"; Benjamin, "s. of my right hand"; Ben-hail, "s. of the host"; Barabbas, Bar-jona, etc.,)— or *Bath*, "daughter" (Bathsheba, Bath-shua, "d. of an oath"); or (2) with nouns borrowed from the sphere of national life and aspiration, such as *Am* (עַם) "people," resembling the numerous Greek compounds with λαός; and δῆμος (Amminadab, q. v.; Ammizabad, "people of the Giver" i. e. God; Jeroboam, "whose people are countless," or "increaser of the people"; Jashobeam, "he will return among the people," Jones, "people's leader," Ewald. "habitabit in populo," Simonis; Jekameam, "gatherer of the people," etc.);— *Melech*, "king" (Abimelech, "father of the king"; Ahimelech, "brother of the king." On Nathan-melech, Ebed-melech, and Regem-melech, see Wilkinson, pp. 395–397); or (3) with names of God, as for instance, *Shaddai* (Ammishaddai, "people of the Almighty," and Zurishaddai, "my rock is the Almighty");— *El*, prefixed or suffixed (Elnathan or Nathaniel, equivalent to Theodotus or Dositheus; Eliezer, "God of help" or Ger. *Gotthilf*; Israel, "pugnator Dei," Winer; Eliphalet, "God of salvation"; Ariel, "lion of God"; Elishaphat, "God is judge;" Abdiel,

"servant of God ');—*Adoni*, "lord" (Adoniram, "lord of exaltation," Adonijah, "my lord is Jehovah"; Adonikam, "lord of the enemy," Gesenius, or "lord who assists," Fürst, "Dominus surrexit," Simonis and Jones);—*Jehovah*, when prefixed shortened to Jeho, or Jo, when suffixed to Jahn or jah or i (Jonathan and Nethaniah, parallel with Elnathan and Nathaniel, "Jehovah-given," comp. Jebonadah and Jehohanan; Jehoiada, "Jehovah knows"; Jehoiachin, "Jehovah will establish"; Joah, "whose father is Jehovah"; Elijah, "the strength of Jehovah"; Ishmerai, "whom Jehovah shall keep," etc.). It remains to be observed in this connection, that *Abi*, or *Ab*, is supposed by Gesenius and most etymologists to have originally designated in all instances a direct blood relationship, but in the process of time to have become a constituent part of proper names, which were used without reference to their strict etymological meanings. This view is opposed by Ewald, who thinks, however, that in later times the term "father" was often used to express a certain dignity, as "father" or lord of a town. So in 1 Chr. ii. 29, 42, 45, 50, &c., where *Ab* is compounded with names of places. On the possessive sense of *Ab* or *Abi* in composition, see Wilkinson, pp. 365–367.

The non-Hebrew names of the Old Testament are chiefly Egyptian, Canaanitish, and Persian. These are separately treated by Simonis, sec. xi., and Wilkinson, pp. 416–481.

Glancing a moment at the history of names and name-giving among the Hebrews, we readily distinguish many of those changes which characterize popular customs and habits in this particular among all peoples. In their first or ruder age their names are simple and "smell of nature." In the period of their highest national and religious development we find more compounds and more allusions to artificial refinements. In the period of their humiliation and conflicts under the judgments of God, whole passages of Scripture were appropriated as in modern times by the Puritans of Great Britain. Hence such names as Hodaiah, "praise-ye-the-Lord"; Elioënai, "mine-eyes-are-unto-Jehovah." Hazelelponi, "give-shade-thou-that-turnest-thy-face-to-me" (Oehler), or, "give-shadow-that-seest-me" (Ewald). As soon as the people grew weary of this unwieldly nomenclature a very natural reaction led to the repristination of the simple and hallowed names of early Hebrew history. Loss of independence and intermarriage with foreigners led to the introduction of foreign names, the use of the Greek language to a translation of many Hebrew ones and to the modification of others, so that in the New Testament we find almost as great a variety of names as among the modern nations of Europe. There are *pure Hebrew* names, such as, Joseph, Simeon or Simon, Levi, Gamaliel, Saul, etc.; Hebrew names which have become *grecized in form*, such as Lazarus from Eleazar, Matthæus from Mattathiah or Mattaniah, Anna from Hannah, Zebedæus from Zabdi or Zebadiah, Zacchæus from Zaccai, Ananias from Chananiah, Alcimus from Eliakim, Jason from Joshua, etc.; *Aramœan* names, such as Martha, Tabitha, Caiaphas, etc.; *Greek* names, such as Andreas, Andronicus, Euodia, Antipater, Philippos, etc.; *Latin* names: Marcus, Aquila, Priscilla, Justus, Paulus, etc., etc., and finally, even names which were *derived from those of the gods of Greece and Rome*, e. g., Apollonius, Phœbe, Nereus, Demetrius, Diotrephes,

Epaphroditus, Dionysius, Hermas, Olympiodorus, Hymenæus, Artemas, etc., etc. These last names were doubtless given by heathen parents. On the New Testament proper names see particularly Schirlitz's *Grundzüge der neutest. Gracität* (Giessen, 1861), pp. 140–161.

"Nomen est omen." Among no ancient people was this truer than among the Hebrews. Doubtless the more customary names became in time conventional, at least to some extent. Even an Ahab could give to sons borne him by Jezebel names compounded with Jehovah, as Ahaziah and Joram. Still, it cannot be denied that, in most instances, the choice of the name was understood as an act of religious profession and confession on the part of the parents. Even when the name must have grown perfectly familiar, we discover a tendency to seek for correspondences between its meaning and its bearer. See Abigail's allusion to the name of Nabal, 1 Sam. xxv. 25, Naomi's to her own, Ruth i. 20. Probably the perception of the significance of names was keener among ancient peoples, since their roots were almost universally of the vernacular language. Even Cicero cannot resist the temptation to play upon the name of the conspirators against Cæsar (the *Bruti*), and who can ever forget the cutting pasquinade on the Papal despoilers of the Pantheon: "*Quod non fecerunt Barbari, fecere Barberini!*" Among the Hebrews, this identification of name and person reached its climax. A tendency to it was characteristic of the nation, and under the supernatural tuition of Revelation it was fully developed. "In the spirit of that truthfulness, which desires to see all contradiction between name and nature done away, and every one called by his right name (comp. Is. v. 20, xxxii. 5; Rev. iii. 11), a series of names is here produced, which really express the personal significance and life-station of those who bear them, and which thus themselves become attestations of Revelation, abiding pledges of divine guidance and promise. These significant names are partly birth-names, partly and more commonly, new appellations. As outside the circle of Revelation, particularly among the oriental nations, it is customary to mark one's entrance into a new relation by a new name, in which case the acceptance of the new name involves the acknowledgment of the sovereignty of the name-giver, so the importance and new sphere assigned to the organs of Revelation in God's kingdom are frequently indicated by a change of name. Examples of this are Abraham, Gen. xvii. 5; Sarah, xvii. 15; Israel as designation of the spiritual character, in place of Jacob which designated the natural character, xxxii. 28; Joshua, Num. xiii. 16; comp. also Jerubbaal, Judg. vi. 32; in N. T. Cephas or Peter, John i. 42; Boanerges, Mar. iii. 17; Barnabas, Acts iv. 36. It is, however, remarkable, that in many instances where no particular reason is given, a striking correspondence is seen between the name and the character of the person; e. g. Saul, David, Solomon (comp. however 1 Chr. xxii. 9), Elijah (1 K. xviii. 36). What peculiar weight the prophets attached to names is well known. Nathan gives Solomon the name Jedidiah, "because of the Lord." Hosea (chap. i.) and Isaiah (viii. 3) express their prophecies in the names of their children. Isaiah comforts himself with the merciful pledge contained in the significance of his own name (viii. 18). The prophets frequently play upon the names of persons and places, and such instances of paronomasia are not to be regarded as mere rhetorical ornaments.

Compare Micah's play upon his own name, Mic. vii. 18 (Caspari, *Commentar*, p. 20 ff.); such passages as Is. xxv. 10; Micah i. 10 ff.; Jer. xx. 3, xxiii. 6. This intimate concrete relation betwixt name and person explains, finally, certain Biblical modes of speech. When God elects a man by virtue of personal qualification, he is said to call him by name (Ex. xxxi. 2; Is. xl. 3, 4). When Jehovah says to Moses, 'I know thee by name' (Ex. xxxiii. 12), he means, he has placed himself in a specifically personal relation to Moses, in a relation pertaining to Moses alone, and therefore connected with his name. This explains also Is. xliii. 1: 'I have called thee by thy name and thou art mine' (comp. xlix. 1). Receiving a 'new name' from God (Is. lxv. 15, lxii. 2; Rev. ii. 17, iii. 12) is the expression employed to denote a new personal relation to him established by an act of divine grace" (Oehler).

The attempt made by Strauss (*Leben Jesu*, passim), Bertholdt (*Einleitung ins A. T.* pp. 2337-2357), and others, to prove from the peculiar significance of names the mythical origin of different books of the canon is simply puerile. Even Theodore Parker ridicules the former, by showing in like manner the mythical character of the Declaration of Independence from the fact of its reputed promulgation at Philadelphia, "the city of brotherly love" (see his review of Strauss's *Leben Jesu*). He also styles Bertholdt's arguments "merely nugatory," adding that all B. says of the names in the book of Ruth "may be said of almost all Hebrew names" (*Translation of De Wette's Introduction to the Old Test.*, i. 319). What havoc some future myth-hunter may make even of the names and achievements of these brave destroyers themselves! Strauss means "ostrich," "dispute," "strife"; Hitzig, "hot-headed"; Bauer, a "peasant," "rude fellow"; Neander, "new man"; Schleiermacher, "veil-maker"; Hengstenberg, "stallion-mountain," comp. Ang. Sax. "mare's-nest," — Ergo the tale of the famous battle in the nineteenth century, in Germany, between belief and unbelief is all a myth! No such man as Strauss ever lived, no such men as his reputed opponents!

Literature. — Eusebius, *Onomasticon* (Ugolini's *Thesaurus*, vol. v.). Hieronymus, *Liber de nominibus Hebraicis*, *De Situ et Nominibus Locorum Hebraicorum*, etc. (Opera, Benedictine ed. vol. iii.). Hiller, *Onomasticon*, Hamb. 1706. J. Simonis, *Onomasticon Veteris Test.*, Halæ Magd. 1741; Ejusdem, *Onomasticon Novi Test. et Librorum V. T. Apocryphorum*, Halæ Magd. 1762 (the ablest writer of the last century in this field). Ewald, *Ausführ. Lehrbuch der hebr. Sprache*, § 271, *Die Eigennamen der Bibel*, bes. des A. T., pp. 578-593 (prepared for Kitto's *Cyclopædia*, where the Eng. version may be found). Redslob, *Die ältest. Namen der Bevölkerung des Israeliterstaats, etymol. betrachtet*, Hamb. 1846. Oehler, art. *Name*, in Herzog's *Real-Encykl.* Bd. x. (a translation by the present writer may be found in the *Theological Eclectic*, vol. iv. No. 5). Moroni, *Dizionario di erudizione storico-ecclesiastica*, art. *Nome*, vol. xlviii., Ven. 1847. (Of little value.) J. Farrar, *Proper Names of the Bible*, 2d ed. Lond. 1844. Alfred Jones, *The Proper Names of the Old Test. Scriptures expounded and illustrated*, Lond. 1856, 4to. (A valuable work, arranged in alphabetical order. Quite a number of the obscurer names, however, have been overlooked.) *Proper Names of the Old Testament with Hist. and Geog.*

Illustrations for the use of Hebrew Students and Teachers, Lond. 1860. W. F. Wilkinson, *Personal Names in the Bible interpreted and illustrated*, Lond. 1865. (Latest and most readable of English works upon this subject.)

On the general subject of names the following works may be consulted: A. F. Pott, *Die Personennamen, insbesondere die Familiennamen und ihre Entstehungsarten*, Leips 1853. Eusèbe Salverte, *Les noms d' Hommes de Peuples et de Lieux*, 2 tom. Paris, 1824; translated into Eng. by L. H. Mordacque, 2 vols. Lond. 1862-64. W. Pape, *Wörterbuch der Griechischen Eigennamen*, 2° Aufl., Braunschw. 1850. Articles *Nomen* and *Cognomen* in Pauly's *Real-Encyclopädie* and William Smith's *Dict. of Greek and Roman Antiquities*. Robt. Ferguson, *The Teutonic Name-System applied to the Family Names of France, England, and Germany*, Lond. 1864. Isaac Taylor, *Words and Places*, Lond. 1864. Miss C. M. Yonge, *History of Christian Names*, 2 vols. Lond. 1863. M. A. Lower, *English Surnames*, 3d ed., 2 vols. Lond. 1849; *Patronymica Britannica*, Lond. 1860. *De Cognominum origine dissertatio*, Muratori, *Antiq. Ital.*, vol. viii. Robt. Ferguson, *English Surnames and their Place in the Teutonic Family*, Lond. 1858. J. M. Kemble, *Names, Surnames, and Nicknames of the Anglo-Saxons*, Lond. 1846. Wiarda, *Ueber deutsche Vornamen und Geschlechtsnamen*, Berl. 1800. F. A. Pischon, *Die Taufnamen*, Berl. 1857. B. H. Dixon, *Surnames*, Bost. 1857. N. J. Bowditch, *Suffolk Surnames*, 3d ed. Bost. 1861 (very entertaining). C. E. Ferrari, *Vocabolario de' nomi proprii*, Bologna, 1827.

In conclusion, for literature of *the names of God*, see art. JEHOVAH, and the bibliographical manuals.   W. F. W.

NANE'A [more correctly NAN.E'A] (*Navala: Nanea*). The last act of Antiochus Epiphanes (vol. i. p. 116 *b*) was his attempt to plunder the temple of Nanæa at Elymais, which had been enriched by the gifts and trophies of Alexander the Great (1 Macc. vi. 1-4; 2 Macc. i. 13-16). The Persian goddess Nanæa, called also 'Αναῖτις by Strabo (xv. p. 733), is apparently the Moon goddess, of whom the Greek Artemis was the nearest representative in Polybius (quoted by Joseph. *Ant.* xii. 9, § 1). Beyer calls her the "Elymæan Venus" (*ad Joh. Seldeni*, etc., *addit.* p. 345), and Winer (*Realw.*) apparently identifies Nanæa with Meni, and both with the planet Venus, the star of luck, called by the Syrians ﻧﺎﻧﻲ, *Nani*, and in Zend *Nahid* or *Anahid.*

Elphinstone in 1811 found coins of the Sassanians with the inscription NANAIA, and on the reverse a figure with nimbus and lotus-flower (Movers, *Phæn.* i. 626). It is probable that Nanæa is identical with the deity named by Strabo (xi. p. 532) as the *numen patrum* of the Persians, who was also honored by the Medes, Armenians, and in many districts of Asia Minor. Other forms of the name are 'Αναλα, given by Strabo, Αἴνη by Polybius, 'Αναῖτις by Plutarch, and Ταναΐς by Clemens Alexandrinus, with which last the variations of some MSS. of Strabo correspond. In consequence of a confusion between the Greek and Eastern mythologies, Nanæa has been identified with Artemis and Aphrodite, the probability being that she corresponds with the Tauric or Ephesian Artemis, who was invested with the attributes of Aphrodite, and represented the productive power of nature.

In this case some weight may be allowed to the conjecture, that " the desire of women " mentioned in Dan. xi. 37 is the same as the goddess Nanæa.

In 2 Macc. ix. 1, 2, appears to be a different account of the same sacrilegious attempt of Antiochus; but the scene of the event is there placed at Persepolis, " the city of the Persians," where there might well have been a temple to the national deity. But Grimm considers it far more probable that it was an Elymæan temple which excited the cupidity of the king. See Gesenius, *Jesaia*, iii. 337, and Grimm's *Commentar* in the *Kurzgef. Handb.*   W. A. W.

NA'OMI (נָעֳמִי [*my delight, pleasure:* Rom. Νοεμίν: Vat.] Νωεμειν; Alex. Νοομμειν, Νοεμμειν, Νοομει, etc.: *Noemi*), the wife of Elimelech, and mother-in-law of Ruth (Ruth i. 2, &c., ii. 1, &c., iii. 1, iv. 3, &c.). The name is derived from a root signifying sweetness, or pleasantness, and this significance contributes to the point of the paronomasia in i. 20, 21, though the passage contains also a play on the mere sound of the name: — " Call me not Naomi (pleasant), call me Mara (bitter) . . . . why call ye me Naomi when Jehovah hath testified (*anah*, עָנָה) against me? "   G.

* The life of this Hebrew woman, one of the most checkered which is given in the sacred record, derives its chief general interest from her relation to Ruth, her daughter-in-law, and from the position of the latter in Jewish history. But Naomi is really the heroine of the Book of Ruth, and her character appears beautiful as presented in this charming narrative. Her tenderness and generosity, her devout trust in God and grateful recognition of his hand, serve to explain the strong confidence and affection which she inspired in the daughter of Moab who identified herself with her darkest fortunes. Her constant counsels guided her faithful daughter-in-law — and, spared to become the nurse of her son, not a little of the moral influence which distinguished the line thus founded may have been transmitted from her. [RUTH, BOOK OF, Amer. ed.]   S. W.

* The name is properly Noomi, and not Naomi as in the A. V., perhaps after the Latin translation of Tremellius and Junius (*Nahomi*). See Wright's *Book of Ruth*, p. 3. The orthography of the A. V. appears in the Bishops' Bible.   H.

NA'PHISH (נָפִישׁ, "according to the Syriac usage, 'refreshment,' " Ges.: Ναφές, Ναφισαίοι: *Naphis*), the last but one of the sons of Ishmael (Gen. xxv. 15; 1 Chr. i. 31). The tribe descended from Nodab was subdued by the Reubenites, the Gadites, and the half of the tribe of Manasseh, when "they made war with the Hagarites, with Jetur, and *Nephish* (Ναφισαίων, LXX.), and Nodab " (1 Chr. v. 19). The tribe is not again found

in the sacred records, nor is it mentioned by later writers. It has not been identified with any Arabian tribe; but identifications with Ishmaelite tribes are often difficult. The difficulty in question arises from intermarriages with Keturahites and Joktanites, from the influence of Mohammedan history, and from our ignorance respecting many of the tribes, and the towns and districts, of Arabia. The influence of Mohammedan history is here mentioned as the strongest instance of a class of influences very common among the Arabs, by which prominence has been given to certain tribes remarkable in the rise of the religion, or in the history of the country, its language, etc. But intermarriages exercise even a stronger influence on the names of tribes, causing in countless instances the adoption of an older name to the exclusion of the more recent, without altering the *pedigree*. Thus Mohammad claimed descent from the tribe of Mudád, although he gloried in being an Ishmaelite: Mudád took his name from the father of Ishmael's wife, and the name of Ishmael himself is merged in that of the older race. [ISHMAEL.]

If the Hagarenes went southwards, into the province of Hejer, after their defeat, Naphish may have gone with them, and traces of his name should in this case be looked for in that obscure province of Arabia. He is described in Chronicles, with the confederate tribes, as pastoral, and numerous in men and cattle. [NODAB.]

E. S. P.

NAPH'ISI ([Vat.] Ναφεισεί; [Rom.] Alex. Ναφισί: *Nasissim*), 1 Esdr. v. 31. [NEPHUSIM.]

NAPH'TALI (נַפְתָּלִי: Νεφθαλείμ, and so also Josephus; [Rom. Alex. Νεφθαλί, -λίμ, -λεί, -λείμ; Vat. -λει, -λειμ; Sin. in Ps. lxviii. 27, -λειμ, in Is. ix. 1, -λιμ: *Nephtali*,] *Nephthali*). The fifth son of Jacob; the second child borne to him by Bilhah, Rachel's slave. His birth and the bestowal of his name are recorded in Gen. xxx. 8: "and Rachel said ' wrestlings (or contortions — *naphtúle*) of God [a] have I wrestled (*niphtalti*) with my sister and have prevailed.' And she called his name [b] Naphtali."

By his birth Naphtali was thus allied to Dan (Gen. xxxv. 25); and he also belonged to the same portion of the family as Ephraim and Benjamin, the sons of Rachel; but, as we shall see, these connections appear to have been only imperfectly maintained by the tribe descended from him.

At the migration to Egypt four sons are attributed to Naphtali (Gen. xlvi. 24; Ex. i. 4; 1 Chr. vii. 13). Of the individual patriarch not a single trait is given in the Bible; but in the Jewish traditions he is celebrated for his powers as a swift runner, and he is named as one of the five who were chosen by Joseph to represent the family before Pharaoh (*Targ. Pseudojon.* on Gen. l. 13 and xlvii. 2).[c]

---

a That is, according to the Hebrew idiom, " immense wrestlings." Ἀμηχάνητος οἷον, " as if irresistible," is the explanation of the name given by Josephus (*Ant.* i. 19, § 8).

b An attempt has been made by Redslob, in his singular treatise *Die Alttest. Namen*, etc. (Hamb. 1846, pp. 88, 89), to show that " Naphtali " is nothing but a synonym for " Galilee," and that again for " Cabul," all three being opprobrious appellations. But if there were no other difficulties in the way, this has the disadvantage of being in direct contradiction to the high

estimation in which the tribe was held at the date of the composition of the Songs of Deborah and Jacob.

c In the " Testaments of the Twelve Patriarchs," Naphtali dies in his 132d year, in the 7th month, on the 4th day of the month. He explains his name as given " because Rachel had dealt deceitfully " (ἐν πανουργίᾳ ἐποίησε). He also gives the genealogy of his mother: Balla (Bilhah), the daughter of Routhaios, the brother of Deborah, Rebekah's nurse, was born the same day with Rachel. Routhaios was a Chaldæan of the kindred of Abraham, who, being taken

When the census was taken at Mount Sinai the tribe numbered no less than 53,400 fighting men (Num. i. 43, ii. 30). It thus held exactly the middle position in the nation, having five above it in numbers, and six below. But when the borders of the Promised Land were reached, its numbers were reduced to 45,400, with four only below it in the scale, one of the four being Ephraim (Num. xxvi. 48–50; comp. 37). The leader of the tribe at Sinai was Ahira ben-Enan (Num. ii. 29); and at Shiloh, Pedahel ben-Ammihud (xxxiv. 28). Amongst the spies its representative was Nahbi ben-Vophsi (xiii. 14).

During the march through the wilderness Naphtali occupied a position on the north of the Sacred Tent with Dan, and also with another tribe, which though not originally so intimately connected became afterwards his immediate neighbor — Asher (Num. ii. 25–31). The three formed the "Camp of Dan" and their common standard, according to the Jewish traditions, was a serpent or basilisk, with the motto, "Return, O Jehovah, unto the many thousands of Israel!" (*Targ. Pseudojon.* on Num. ii. 25).

In the apportionment of the land, the lot of Naphtali was not drawn till the last but one. The two portions then remaining unappropriated were the noble but remote district which lay between the strip of coast-land already allotted to Asher and the upper part of the Jordan, and the little canton or corner, more central, but in every other respect far inferior, which projected from the territory of Judah into the country of the Philistines, and formed the "marches" between those two never-tiring combatants. Naphtali chose the former of these, leaving the latter to the Danites, a large number of whom shortly followed their relatives to their home in the more remote but more undisturbed north, and thus testified to the wisdom of Naphtali's selection.

The territory thus appropriated was inclosed on three sides by those of other tribes. On the west, as already remarked, lay Asher; on the south Zebulun, and on the east the trans-Jordanic Manasseh. The north terminated with the ravine of the *Litany* or Leontes, and opened into the splendid valley which separates the two ranges of Lebanon. According to Josephus (*Ant.* v. 1, § 22) the eastern side of the tribe reached as far as Damascus; but of this — though not impossible in the early times of the nation and before the rise of the Syrian monarchy — there is no indication in the Bible. The south boundary was probably very much the same as that which at a later time separated Upper from Lower Galilee, and which ran from or about the town of *Akka* to the upper part of the Sea of Gennesaret. Thus Naphtali was cut off from the great plain of Esdraelon — the favorite resort of the hordes of plunderers from beyond the Jordan, and the great battlefield of the country — by the mass of the mountains of Nazareth; while on the east it had a communication with the Sea of Galilee, the rich district of the *Ard el-Huleh* and the *Merj Ayán*, and all the splendidly watered country about *Bániás* and *Hasbeya*, the springs of Jordan. "O Naphtali," thus accurately does the Song attributed to the dying lawgiver express itself with regard to this part of the territory of the tribe — "O Naphtali, satisfied with favor and full of Jehovah's blessing, the sea [a] and the south possess thou!" (Deut. xxxiii. 23). But the capabilities of these plains and of the access to the Lake, which at a later period raised GALILEE and GENNESARET to so high a pitch of crowded and busy prosperity, were not destined to be developed while they were in the keeping of the tribe of Naphtali. It was the mountainous country ("Mount Naphtali," Josh. xx. 7) which formed the chief part of their inheritance, that impressed or brought out the qualities for which Naphtali was remarkable at the one remarkable period of its history. This district, the modern *Belad-Besharah*, or "land of good tidings," comprises some of the most beautiful scenery. and some of the most fertile soil in Palestine (Porter, p. 363), forests surpassing those of the renowned Carmel itself (Van de Velde, i. 293); as rich in noble and ever-varying prospects as any country in the world (ii. 407). As it is thus described by one of the few travellers who have crossed its mountains and descended into its ravines, so it was at the time of the Christian era: "The soil," says Josephus (*B. J.* iii. 3, § 2), "universally rich and productive; full of plantations of trees of all sorts; so fertile as to invite the most slothful to cultivate it." But, except in the permanence of these natural advantages, the contrast between the present and that earlier time is complete; for whereas, in the time of Josephus, Galilee was one of the most populous and busy districts of Syria, now the population is in an inverse proportion to the luxuriance of the natural vegetation (Van de Velde, i. 170).

Three of the towns of Naphtali were allotted to the Gershonite Levites — Kedesh (already called Kedesh-in-Galilee), Hammoth-dor, and Kartan. Of these, the first was a city of refuge (Josh. xx. 7, xxi. 32). Naphtali was one of Solomon's commissariat districts, under the charge of his son-in-law Ahimaaz; who with his wife Basmath resided in his presidency, and doubtless enlivened that remote and rural locality by a miniature of the court of his august father-in-law, held at Safed or Kedesh, or wherever his residence may have been (1 K. iv. 15). Here he doubtless watched the progress of the unpromising new district presented to Solomon by Hiram — the twenty cities of Cabul, which seem to have been within the territory of Naphtali, perhaps the nucleus of the Galilee of later date. The ruler of the tribe (נָגִיד) — a different dignity altogether from that of Ahimaaz — was, in the reign of David, Jerimoth ben-Azriel (1 Chr. xxvii. 19).

Naphtali had its share in those incursions and molestations by the surrounding heathen, which were the common lot of all the tribes (Judah perhaps alone excepted) during the first centuries after the conquest. One of these, apparently the severest struggle of all, fell with special violence on the north of the country, and the leader by whom the invasion was repelled — BARAK of Kedesh-Naphtali — was the one great hero whom Naphtali is recorded to have produced. How gigantic were the efforts by which these heroic mountaineers

captive, was bought as a slave by Laban. Laban gave him his maid Aina or Eva to wife, by whom he had Satipha (Zilpah) — so called from the place in

which he had been captive — and Balla (Fabricius, *Cod. Pseudepigr. V. T.* i. 659, &c.).

[a] *Yam*, rendered "west" in the A. V., but obviously the "Sea" of Galilee.

saved their darling highlands from the swarms of Canaanites who followed Jabin and Sisera, and how grand the position which they achieved in the eyes of the whole nation, may be gathered from the narrative of the war in Judg. iv., and still more from the expressions of the triumphal song in which Deborah, the prophetess of Ephraim, immortalized the victors, and branded their reluctant countrymen with everlasting infamy. Gilead and Reuben lingered beyond the Jordan amongst their flocks: Dan and Asher preferred the luxurious calm of their hot lowlands to the free air and fierce strife of the mountains; Issachar with characteristic sluggishness seems to have moved slowly if he moved at all: but Zebulun and Naphtali on the summits of their native highlands devoted themselves to death, even to an extravagant pitch of heroism and self-devotion (Judg. v. 18):—

" Zebulun are a people that threw *a* away their lives
    even unto death —
And Naphtali, on the high places of the field."

The mention of Naphtali contained in the Song attributed to Jacob — whether it is predictive, or as some writers believe, retrospective — must have reference to this event: unless indeed, which is hardly to be believed, some other heroic occasion is referred to, which has passed unrecorded in the history. The translation of this difficult passage given by Ewald (*Geschichte*, ii. 380) has the merit of being more intelligible than the ordinary version, and also more in harmony with the expressions of Deborah's Song: —

    " Naphtali is a towering Terebinth ;
    He hath a goodly crest."

The allusion, at once to the situation of the tribe at the very apex of the country, to the heroes who towered at the head of the tribe, and to the lofty mountains on whose summits their castles, then as now, were perched — is very happy, and entirely in the vein of these ancient poems.

After this burst of heroism. the Naphtalites appear to have resigned themselves to the intercourse with the [b] heathen, which was the bane of the northern tribes in general, and of which there are already indications in Judg. i. 33. The location by Jeroboam within their territory of the great sanctuary for the northern part of his kingdom must have given an impulse to their nationality, and for a time have revived the connection with their brethren nearer the centre. But there was one circumstance fatal to the prosperity of the tribe, namely, that it lay in the very path of the northern invaders. Syrian and Assyrian, Benhadad and Tiglath-pileser, each had their first taste of the plunder of the Israelites from the goodly land of Naphtali. At length in the reign of Pekah king of Israel (cir. B. C. 730), Tiglath-pileser overran the whole of the north of Israel, swept off the population, and bore them away to Assyria.

But though the history of the tribe of Naphtali

ends here, and the name is not again mentioned except in the well-known citation of St. Matthew (iv. 15), and the mystical references of Ezekiel (xlviii. 3, 4, 34) and of the writer of the Apocalypse (Rev. vii. 6), yet under the title of GALILEE — apparently an ancient name, though not brought prominently forward till the Christian era — the district which they had formerly occupied was destined to become in every way far more important than it had ever before been. For it was the cradle of the Christian faith, the native place of most of the Apostles, and the " home " of our Lord. [GALILEE, vol. i. p. 860 *a*; CAPERNAUM, 381.]

It also became populous and prosperous to a degree far beyond anything of which we have any indications in the Old Testament; but this, as well as the account of its sufferings and heroic resistance during the campaign of Titus and Vespasian prior to the destruction of Jerusalem, must be given elsewhere. [GALILEE; PALESTINE.]   G.

NAPH'TALI, MOUNT (הַר נַפְתָּלִי: *ἐν τῷ ὄρει τῷ Νεφθαλεί* [Rom. -λί]: *Mons Nephtali*). The mountainous district which formed the main part of the inheritance of Naphtali (Josh. xx. 7), answering to " Mount Ephraim " in the centre and " Mount Judah " in the south of Palestine.

NAPH'THAR (*νέφθαρ: Nephthar*). The name given by Nehemiah to the substance [c] which after the return from Babylon was discovered in the dry pit in which at the destruction of the Temple the sacred Fire of the altar had been hidden (2 Macc. i. 36, comp. 19). The legend is a curious one; and it is plain, from the description of the substance — " thick water," [d] which, being poured over the sacrifice and the wood, was kindled by the great heat of the sun, and then burnt with an exceedingly bright and clear flame (ver. 32) — that it was either the same as or closely allied to the naphtha of modern commerce (*Petroleum*). The narrative is not at all extravagant in its terms, and is very probably grounded on some actual [e] occurrence. The only difficulty it presents is the explanation given of the name: " Naphthar, which is, being interpreted, cleansing " (*καθαρισμός*), and which has hitherto puzzled all the interpreters. It is perhaps due to some mistake in copying. A list of conjectures will be found in Grimm (*Kurzgef. Handb.* ad loc.), and another in Reland's *Diss. de vet. Ling. Pers.* lxviii.

The place from which this combustible water was taken was inclosed by the " king of Persia " (Artaxerxes Longimanus), and converted into a sanctuary (such seems the force of *ἱερὸν ποιεῖν*, ver. 34). In modern times it has been identified with the large well called by the Arabs *Bir-eyûb*, situated beneath Jerusalem, at the confluence of the valleys of Kidron and Hinnom with the *Wady en-Nar* (or " valley of the fire "), and from which the main water supply of the city is obtained.

This well, the Arab name of which may be the well of Joab or of Job, and which is usually identi-

---

a So Ewald, *wegwerfend* (*Dichter*, i. 180).

b This is implied in the name of Galilee, which, at an early date, is styled גְּלִיל הַגּוֹיִם, *gelil haggoyim*, Galilee of the Gentiles.

c Not to the *place*, as in the Vulgate, — *hunc locum*.

d The word " water " is here used merely for " liq-

uid," as in *aqua vitæ*. Native naphtha is sometimes obtained without color, and in appearance not unlike water.

e Grimm. (p. 50) notices a passage in the " Adam-book " of the Ethiopian Christians, in which Ezra is said to have discovered in the vaults of the Temple a censer full of the Sacred Fire which had formerly burnt in the Sanctuary.

fied with En-rogel, is also known to the Frank Christians as the "Well of Nehemiah." According to Dr. Robinson (*Bibl. Res.* i. 331, 2 *note*). the first trace of this name is in Quaresmius (*Elucidatio*, etc. ii. 270–4). who wrote in the early part of the 17th cent. (1616–25). He calls it "the well of Nehemiah and of fire," in words which seem to imply that such was at that time its recognized name: "Celebris ille et nominatus puteus, Nehemiae et ignis appellatus." The valley which runs from it to the Dead Sea is called *Wady en-Nar*, "Valley of the Fire; " but no stress can be laid on this, as the name may have originated the tradition. A description of the *Bir-eyûb* is given by Williams (*Holy City*, ii. 489–95), Barclay (*City*, etc., 513–16), and by the careful Tobler (*Umgebungen*, etc., p. 50). At present it would be an equally unsuitable spot either to store fire or to seek for naphtha. One thing is plain, that it cannot have been En-rogel (which was a living spring of water from the days of Joshua downwards), and a naphtha well also.   G.

NAPHTUHIM (נַפְתֻּחִים [Egyptian, see below]: Νεφθαλείμ; [in 1 Chr., Rom. Vat. omit, Comp. Ald. Νεφθωσεειμ; Alex. Νεφθαλεειμ, Νεφθαλιμ:] *Nephtuim, Nephthuim*), a Mizraite nation or tribe, mentioned only in the account of the descendants of Noah (Gen. x. 13; 1 Chr. i. 11). If we may judge from their position in the list of the Mizraites, according to the Masoretic text (in the LXX. in Gen. x. they follow the Ludim and precede the Anamim, 'Ενεμετιείμ), immediately after the Lehabim, who doubtless dwelt to the west of Egypt, and before the Pathrusim, who inhabited that country, the Naphtuhim were probably settled at first, or at the time when Gen. x. was written, either in Egypt or immediately to the west of it. In Coptic the city Marea and the neighboring territory, which probably corresponded to the older Mareotic nome, is called ⲚⲒⲪⲀⲒⲀⲦ or ⲚⲒⲪⲀⲒⲀⲀ, a name composed of the word ⲪⲀⲒⲀⲦ or ⲪⲀⲒⲀⲀ, of unknown meaning, with the plural definite article ⲚⲒ prefixed. In hieroglyphics mention is made of a nation or confederacy of tribes conquered by the Egyptians called "the Nine Bows," [a] a name which Champollion read Naphit, or, as we should write it, NA-PETU, "the bows," though he called them "the Nine Bows." [b] It seems, however, more reasonable to suppose that we should read (ix.) PETU "the Nine Bows" literally. It is also doubtful whether the Coptic name of Marea contains the word "bow," which is only found in the forms ⲠⲒⲦⲈ (S. masc.) and ⲪⲒϮ (M. fem. "a rainbow "); but it is possible that the second part of the former may have been originally the same as the latter. It is noteworthy that there should be two geographical names connected with the bow in hieroglyphics, the one of a country, MERU-PET, "the island of the bow," probably MEROË, and the other of a nation or confederacy, "the Nine Bows," and that in the list of the Hamites there should be two similar names, Phut and Naphtuhim, besides Cush, probably of like sense.

[a] Dr. Brugsch reads this name "the Nine Peoples" *Geographische Inschriften*, ii. p. 20).

[b] A bow in hieroglyphics is PET, PEET, or PETEE.

No important historical notice of the Nine Bows has been found in the Egyptian inscriptions: they are only spoken of in a general manner when the kings are said, in laudatory inscriptions, to have subdued great nations, such as the Negroes, or extensive countries, such as KEESH, or Cush. Perhaps therefore this name is that of a confederacy or of a widely-spread nation, of which the members or tribes are spoken of separately in records of a more particular character, treating of special conquests of the Pharaohs or enumerating their tributaries.
                                                R. S. P.

* NAPKIN (σουδάριον: *sudarium*), Luke xix. 20; John xi. 44, xx. 7. The original term is not so restricted in its meaning as our word *napkin*, but rather corresponds to HANDKERCHIEF, which see. "Napkin" was formerly used in this wider sense, as by Shakespeare.   A.

NARCISSUS (Νάρκισσος ["daffodil": *Narcissus*]). A dweller at Rome (Rom. xvi. 11), some members of whose household were known as Christians to St. Paul. Some persons have assumed the identity of this Narcissus with the secretary of the emperor Claudius (Suetonius, *Claudius*, § 28). But that wealthy and powerful freedman satisfied the revenge of Agrippina by a miserable death in prison (Tac. *Ann.* xiii. 1), in the first year of Nero's reign (A. D. 54–55), about three years before this Epistle was written. Dio Cassius, lxiv. 3, mentions another Narcissus, who probably was living in Rome at that time; he attained to some notoriety as an associate of Nero, and was put to an ignominious death with Helius, Patrobius, Locusta, and others, on the accession of Galba, A. D. 68. His name, however (see Reimar's note, *in loco*), was at that time too common in Rome to give any probability to the guess that he was the Narcissus mentioned by St. Paul. A late and improbable tradition (Pseudo-Hippolytus) makes Narcissus one of the seventy disciples, and bishop of Athens.   W. T. B.

NARD. [SPIKENARD.]

NASBAS (Ναοβάς; [Sin. Ναβαδ:] *Nabath*). The nephew of Tobit who came with Achiacharus to the wedding of Tobias (Tob. xi. 18). Grotius considers him the same with Achiacharus the son of Anael, but according to the Vulgate they were brothers. The margin of the A. V. gives "Junius" as the equivalent of Nasbas.

NASITH (Ναοί: [Vat. Ναοει;] Alex. Ναοιθ: *Nasit*) = NEZIAH (1 Esdr. v. 32: comp. Ezr. ii. 54).

NASOR, THE PLAIN OF (τὸ πεδίον Νασόρ [Sin. and 4 cursive MSS. Ασωρ, see below]: *Campus Asor*), the scene of an action between Jonathan the Maccabee and the forces of Demetrius (1 Macc. xi. 67, comp. 63). It was near Cades (Kadesh-Naphtali) on the one side, and the water of Gennesar (Lake of Gennesaret) on the other, and therefore may be safely identified with the Hazor which became so renowned in the history of the conquest for the victories of Joshua and Barak (vol. ii. p. 1015b). In fact the name is the same, except that through the error of a transcriber the N from the preceding Greek word has become attached to it. Josephus (*Ant.* xiii. 5, § 7) gives it correctly, 'Ασώρ. [Comp. NAARATH, p. 2049 *nota.*]
                                                G.

NATHAN (נָתָן [given i. e. of God]: Νάθαν: *Nathan*), an eminent Hebrew prophet in the reigns of David and Solomon. If the expression "first and last," in 2 Chr. ix. 29, is to be taken literally, he must have lived late into the life of Solomon, in which case he must have been considerably younger than David. At any rate he seems to have been the younger of the two prophets who accompanied him, and may be considered as the latest direct representative of the schools of Samuel.

A Jewish tradition mentioned by Jerome (*Qu. Heb.* on 1 Sam. xvii. 12) identifies him with the eighth son of Jesse. [DAVID, vol. i. p. 552 b.] But of this there is no proof.

He first appears in the consultation with David about the building of the Temple. He begins by advising it, and then, after a vision, withdraws his advice, on the ground that the time was not yet come (2 Sam. vii. 2, 3, 17). He next comes forward as the reprover of David for the sin with Bathsheba; and his famous apologue on the rich man and the ewe lamb, which is the only direct example of his prophetic power, shows it to have been of a very high order (2 Sam. xii. 1-12).

There is an indistinct trace of his appearing also at the time of the plague which fell on Jerusalem in accordance with the warning of Gad. "An angel," says Eupolemus (Euseb. *Præp. Ev.* ix. 30), "pointed him to the place where the Temple was to be, but forbade him to build it, as being stained with blood, and having fought many wars. His name was Dianathan." This was probably occasioned by some confusion of the Greek version, διὰ Νάθαν, with the parallel passage of 1 Chr. xxii. 8, where the bloodstained life of David is given as a reason against the building, but where Nathan is not named.

On the birth of Solomon he was either specially charged with giving him his name, JEDIDIAH, or else with his education, according as the words of 2 Sam. xii. 25, "He sent (or 'sent him') by (or 'into') the hand of Nathan," are understood. At any rate, in the last years of David, it is Nathan who, by taking the side of Solomon, turned the scale in his favor. He advised Bathsheba; he himself ventured to enter the royal presence with a remonstrance against the king's apathy; and at David's request he assisted in the inauguration of Solomon (1 K. i. 8, 10, 11, 22, 23, 24, 32, 34, 38, 45).

This is the last time that we hear directly of his intervention in the history. His son Zabud occupied the post of "King's Friend," perhaps succeeding Nathan (2 Sam. xv. 37; 1 Chr. xxvii. 33). His influence may be traced in the perpetuation of his manner of prophecy in the writings ascribed to Solomon (compare Eccl. ix. 14-16 with 2 Sam. xii. 1-4).

He left two works behind him — a Life of David (1 Chr. xxix. 29), and a Life of Solomon (2 Chr. ix. 29). The last of these may have been incomplete, as we cannot be sure that he outlived Solomon. But the biography of David by Nathan is, of all the losses which antiquity, sacred or profane, has sustained, the most deplorable.

The consideration in which he was held at the time is indicated by the solemn announcement of his approach — "Behold Nathan the prophet" (1 K. i. 23). The peculiar affix of "the prophet," as distinguished from "the seer," given to Samuel and Gad (1 Chr. xxix. 29), shows his identification with the later view of the prophetic office indicated in 1 Sam. ix. 9. His grave is shown at *Halhul* near Hebron (see Robinson, *Bibl. Res.* i. 216 *note*).

A. P. S.

2. A son of David; one of the four who were borne to him by Bathsheba (1 Chr. iii. 5; comp. xiv. 4, and 2 Sam. v. 14). He was thus own brother to Solomon — if the order of the lists is to be accepted, elder brother: though this is at variance with the natural inference from the narrative of 2 Sam. xii. 24, which implies that Solomon was Bathsheba's second son. The name was not unknown in David's family; Nethan-eel was one of his brothers, and Jo-nathan his nephew.

Nathan appears to have taken no part in the events of his father's or his brother's reigns. He is interesting to us from his appearing as one of the forefathers of Joseph in the genealogy of St. Luke (iii. 31) — "the private genealogy of Joseph, exhibiting his line as David's descendant, and thus showing how he was heir to Solomon's crown" (vol. i. p. 885). The hypothesis of Lord Arthur Hervey is that on the failure of Solomon's line in Jehoiachin or Jeconiah, who died without issue, Salathiel of Nathan's house became heir to David's throne, and then was entered in the genealogical tables as "son of Jeconiah" (i. 885 b). That the family of Nathan was, as this hypothesis requires, well known at the time of Jehoiachin's death, is implied by its mention in Zech. xii. 12, a prophecy the date of which is placed by Ewald (*Propheten*, i. 391) as fifteen years after Habbakuk, and shortly before the destruction of Jerusalem by Nebuchadnezzar — that is, a few years only after Jehoiachin's death.

3. [In 2 Sam., Rom. Vat. Ναθαν.] Son, or brother, of one of the members of David's guard (2 Sam. xxiii. 36: 1 Chr. xi. 38). In the former of these two parallel passages he is stated to be "of Zobah," *i. e.* Aram-Zobah, which Kennicott in his investigation (*Dissert.* 215, 216) decides to have been the original reading, though he also decides for "brother" against "son."

4. One of the head men who returned from Babylon with Ezra on his second expedition, and whom he despatched from his encampment at the river Ahava to the colony of Jews at Casiphia, to obtain thence some Levites and Nethinim for the Temple service (Ezr. viii. 16; 1 Esdr. viii. 44). That Nathan and those mentioned with him were laymen, appears evident from the concluding words of the preceding verse, and therefore it is not impossible that he may be the same with the "son of Bani" who was obliged to relinquish his foreign wife (Ezr. x. 39), though on the other hand these marriages seem rather to have been contracted by those who had been longer in Jerusalem than he, who had so lately arrived from Babylon, could be.

G.

NATHAN'AEL (Ναθαναηλ, *gift of God*: [*Nathanaël*]), a disciple of Jesus Christ concerning whom, under that name at least, we learn from Scripture little more than his birth-place, Cana of Galilee (John xxi. 2), and his simple truthful character (John i. 47). We have no particulars of his life. Indeed the name does not occur in the first three Gospels.

We learn, however, from St. John that Jesus, on the third or fourth day after his return from the scene of his temptation to that of his baptism, having been proclaimed by the Baptist as the Lamb of God, was minded to go into Galilee. He first then called Philip to follow Him, but Philip could not set forth on his journey without communicating to Nathanael the wonderful intelligence which he had received from his master the Baptist, namely, that the Messiah so long foretold by Moses and the Prophets had at last appeared. Nathanael, who seems to have heard the announcement at first with some distrust, as doubting whether anything good could come out of so small and inconsiderable a place as Nazareth — a place nowhere mentioned in the Old Testament — yet readily accepted Philip's invitation to go and satisfy himself by his own personal observation (John i. 46). What follows is a testimony to the humility, simplicity, and sincerity of his own character from One who could read his heart, such as is recorded of hardly any other person in the Bible. Nathanael, on his approach to Jesus, is saluted by Him as " an Israelite indeed, in whom is no guile " — a true child of Abraham, and not simply according to the flesh. So little, however, did he expect any such distinctive praise, that he could not refrain from asking how it was that he had become known to Jesus. The answer, " before that Philip called thee, when thou wast under the fig-tree, I saw thee," appears to have satisfied him that the speaker was more than man — that He must have read his secret thoughts, and heard his unuttered prayer at a time when he was studiously screening himself from public observation. The conclusion was inevitable. Nathanael at once confessed " Rabbi, thou art the Son of God; thou art the King of Israel " (John i. 49). The name of Nathanael occurs but once again in the Gospel narrative, and then simply as one of the small company of disciples to whom Jesus showed Himself at the Sea of Tiberias after his resurrection. On that occasion we may fairly suppose that he joined his brethren in their night's venture on the lake — that, having been a sharer of their fruitless toil, he was a witness with them of the miraculous draught of fishes the next morning — and that he afterwards partook of the meal, to which, without daring to ask, the disciples felt assured in their hearts, that He who had called them was the Lord (John xxi. 12). Once therefore at the beginning of our Saviour's ministry, and once after his resurrection, does the name of Nathanael occur in the Sacred Record.

This scanty notice of one who was intimately associated with the very chiefest Apostles, and was himself the object of our Lord's most emphatic commendation, has not unnaturally provoked the inquiry whether he may not be identified with another of the well-known disciples of Jesus. It is indeed very commonly believed that Nathanael and Bartholomew are the same person. The evidence for that belief is as follows: St. John, who twice mentions Nathanael, never introduces the name of Bartholomew at all. St. Matt. x. 3; St. Mark iii. 18, and St. Luke vi. 14, all speak of Bartholomew, but never of Nathanael. It may be, however, that Nathanael was the proper name, and Bartholomew (son of Tholmai) the surname of the same disciple, just as Simon was called Bar-Jona, and Joses, Barnabas.

It was Philip who first brought Nathanael to Jesus, just as Andrew had brought his brother Simon, and Bartholomew is named by each of the first three Evangelists immediately after Philip; while by St. Luke he is coupled with Philip precisely in the same way as Simon with his brother Andrew, and James with his brother John. It should be observed, too, that, as all the other disciples mentioned in the first chapter of St. John became Apostles of Christ, it is difficult to suppose that one who had been so singularly commended

by Jesus, and who in his turn had so promptly and so fully confessed Him to be the Son of God, should be excluded from the number. Again, that Nathanael was one of the original twelve, is inferred with much probability from his not being proposed as one of the candidates to fill the place of Judas. Still we must be careful to distinguish conjecture, however well founded, from proof.

To the argument based upon the fact, that in St. John's enumeration of the disciples to whom our Lord showed Himself at the Sea of Tiberias Nathanael stands before the sons of Zebedee, it is replied that this was to be expected, as the writer was himself a son of Zebedee; and further that Nathanael is placed after Thomas in this list, while Bartholomew comes before Thomas in St. Matthew, St. Mark, and St. Luke. But as in the Acts St. Luke reverses the order of the two names, putting Thomas first, and Bartholomew second, we cannot attach much weight to this argument.

St. Augustine not only denies the claim of Nathanael to be one of the Twelve, but assigns as a reason for his opinion, that whereas Nathanael was most likely a learned man in the Law of Moses, it was, as St. Paul tells us, 1 Cor. i. 26, the wisdom of Christ to make choice of rude and unlettered men to confound the wise (in Johan. Ev. c. i. § 17). St. Gregory adopts the same view (on John i. 33, c. 16. B). In a dissertation on John i. 46, to be found in Thes. Theo. philolog. ii. 370, the author, J. Kindler, maintains that Bartholomew and Nathanael are different persons.

There is a tradition that Nathanael was the bridegroom at the marriage of Cana (Calmet), and Epiphanius, Adc. Hær. i. § 223, implies his belief that of the two disciples whom Jesus overtook on the road to Emmaus Nathanael was one.

2. 1 Esdr. i. 9. [NETHANEEL.]

3. (Ναθαναῆλος: [Nathanee]) 1 Esdr. ix. 22. [NETHANEEL.]

4. (Nathanias.) Son of Samael; one of the ancestors of Judith (Jud. viii. 1), and therefore a Simeonite (ix. 2).   E. H. . . . s.

NATHANI'AS (Ναθανίας: om. in Vulg.)= NATHAN of the sons of Bani (1 Esdr. ix. 34; comp. Ezr. x. 39).

NA'THAN-ME'LECH (נְתַן־מֶלֶךְ [appointed of the king, Ges.]: Ναθὰν βασιλεύς: Nathan-melech). A eunuch (A. V. " chamberlain ") in the court of Josiah, by whose chamber at the entrance to the Temple were the horses which the kings of Judah had dedicated to the sun (2 K. xxiii. 11). The LXX. translate the latter part of the name as an appellative, " Nathan the king."

* NAUGHTINESS (1 Sam. xvii. 28; Prov. xi. 6; James i. 21), signified wickedness when our present version of the Scriptures was made. Recent translators (as Conant, Noyes) substitute "excess of wickedness " for " superfluity of naughtiness " (περισσείαν κακίας) in James as above. [NAUGHTY.]   H.

* NAUGHTY, formerly used in the sense of worthless, bad, as in Jer. xxiv. 2, " naughty figs ", and hence also morally corrupt, wicked, as Prov. vi. 12, " a naughty person, a wicked man," and Prov. xvii. 4, " a naughty tongue." It is now applied generally to the conduct of pert or mischievous children.   H.

NA'UM (Ναούμ: [Nahum], son of Esli, and father of Amos, in the genealogy of Christ (Luke

iii. 25), about contemporary with the high-priesthood of Jason and the reign of Antiochus Epiphanes. The only point to be remarked is the circumstance of the two consecutive names, Naum and Amos, being the same as those of the prophets N. and A. But whether this is accidental, or has any peculiar significance, it is difficult to say. Naum is also a Phœnician proper name (Gesen. *s. v.* and *Mon. Phœn.* p. 134). *Nehemiah* is formed from the same root, נָחַם, "to comfort."   A. C. H.

NAVE. The Heb. גַב, *gav*, conveys the notion of convexity or protuberance. It is rendered in A. V. boss of a shield, Job xv. 26; the eyebrow, Lev. xiv. 9; an eminent place, Ez. xvi. 31; once only in plur. naves, νῶτοι, radii, 1 K. vii. 33; but in Ez. i. 18 twice, νῶτοι, "rings," and marg. "strakes," an old word apparently used both for the nave of a wheel from which the spokes proceed, and also more probably the felloe or the tire, as making the streak or stroke upon the ground. (Halliwell, Phillips, Bailey, Ash, *Eng. Dictionaries*, "strake.") Gesenius, p. 256, renders *curvatura rotarum*. [CHARIOT; LAVER; GABBATHA.]
                           H. W. P.

NAVE (Ναυή: *Nave*). Joshua the son of Nun is always called in the LXX. "the son of Nave," and this form is retained in Ecclus. xlvi. 1.

NAZARENE (Ναζωραῖος, Ναζαρηνός: [*Nazaræus, Nazarenus*]), an inhabitant of Nazareth. This appellative is found in the N. T. applied to Jesus by the demons in the synagogue at Capernaum (Mark i. 24; Luke iv. 34); by the people, who so describe him to Bartimeus (Mark x. 47; Luke xviii. 37): by the soldiers who arrested Jesus (John xviii. 5, 7); by the servants at his trial (Matt. xxvi. 71; Mark xiv. 67); by Pilate in the inscription on the cross (John xix. 19); by the disciples on the way to Emmaus (Luke xxiv. 19); by Peter (Acts ii. 22, iii. 6, iv. 10); by Stephen, as reported by the false witness (Acts vi. 14); by the ascended Jesus (Acts xxii. 8); and by Paul (Acts xxvi. 9). This name, made striking in so many ways, and which, if first given in scorn, was adopted and gloried in by the disciples, we are told, in Matt. ii. 23, possesses a prophetic significance. Its application to Jesus, in consequence of the providential arrangements by which his parents were led to take up their abode in Nazareth, was the filling out of the predictions in which the promised Messiah is described as a *Nêtser* (נֵצֶר), *i. e.* a shoot, sprout, of Jesse, a humble and despised descendant of the decayed royal family. Whenever men spoke of Jesus as the Nazarene, they either consciously or unconsciously pronounced one of the names of the predicted Messiah, a name indicative both of his royal descent and his humble condition. This explanation, which Jerome mentions as that given by learned (Christian) Jews in his day, has been adopted by Surenhusius, Fritzsche, Gieseler, Krabbe (*Leben Jesu*), Drechsler (on Is. xi. 1), Schirlitz (*N. T. Wörterb.*), Robinson (*N. T. Lex.*), Hengstenberg (*Christol.*), De Wette, and Meyer. It is confirmed by the following considerations: (1.) *Nêtser*, as Hengstenberg, after de Dieu and others, has proved, was the proper Hebrew name of Nazareth. (2.) The reference to the etymological significance of the word is entirely in keeping with Matt. ii. 21-23. (3.) The Messiah is expressly called a *Nêtser* in Is. xi. 1. (4.) The same thought,

and under the same image, although expressed by a different word, is found in Jer. xxiii. 5, xxxiii. 15; Zech. iii. 8, vi. 12, which accounts for the statement of Matthew that this prediction was uttered "by the *prophets*" in the plural.

It is unnecessary therefore to resort to the hypothesis that the passage in Matt. ii. 23 is a quotation from some prophetical book now lost (Chrysost., Theophyl., Clericus), or from some apocryphal book (Ewald), or was a traditional prophecy (Calovius; Alexander, *Connection and Harmony of the Old and N. T.*), all which suppositions are refuted by the fact that the phrase "by the prophets," in the N. T., refers exclusively to the *canonical* books of the O. T. The explanation of others (Tert., Erasm., Calv., Bez., Grot., Wetstein), according to whom the declaration is that Jesus should be a *Nazarite* (נָזִיר), i. e. one specially *consecrated* or *devoted* to God (Judg. xiii. 5), is inconsistent, to say nothing of other objections, with the LXX. mode of spelling the word, which is generally Ναζιραῖος, and never Ναζωραῖος. Within the last century the interpretation which finds the key of the passage in the *contempt* in which Nazareth may be supposed to have been held has been widely received. So Paulus, Rosenm., Kuin., Van der Palm, Gersdorf, A. Barnes, Olsh., Davidson, Elsrard, Lange. According to this view the reference is to the *despised condition* of the Messiah, as predicted in Ps. xxii., Is. liii. That idea, however, is more surely expressed in the first explanation given, which has also the advantage of recognizing the apparent importance attached to the signification of the *name* ("He shall be *called*"). Recently a suggestion which Witsius borrowed from Socinus has been revived by Zuschlag and Riggenbach, that the true word is נֹצֵר or נֹצְרִי, *my Saviour*, with reference to Jesus as the Saviour of the world, but without much success. Once (Acts xxiv. 5) the term *Nazarenes* is applied to the followers of Jesus by way of contempt. The name still exists in Arabic as the ordinary designation of Christians, and the recent revolt in India was connected with a pretended ancient prophecy that the Nazarenes, after holding power for one hundred years, would be expelled. (Spanheim, *Dubia Evangelica*, ii. 583-648; Wolf, *Curæ Philologicæ*, i. 46-48; Hengstenberg, *Christology of the O. T.*, ii. 106-112; Zuschlag in the *Zeitschrift für die Lutherische Theologie*, 1854, 417-446; Riggenbach in the *Studien und Kritiken*, 1855, 588-612.)   G. E. D.

NAZARETH (written Ναζαρέτ and Ναζαρέθ; also Ναζαρά, Tisch. 8th ed., in Matt. iv. 13 and Luke iv. 16: *Nazareth*) is not mentioned in the Old Testament or in Josephus, but occurs first in Matt. ii. 23, though a town could hardly fail to have existed on so eligible a spot from much earlier times. It derives its celebrity almost entirely from its connection with the history of Christ, and in that respect has a hold on the imagination and feelings of men which it shares only with Jerusalem and Bethlehem. It is situated among the hills which constitute the south ridges of Lebanon, just before they sink down into the Plain of Esdraelon. Among those hills is a valley which runs in a waving line nearly east and west, about a mile long and, on the average, a quarter of a mile broad, but which at a certain point enlarges itself considerably so as to form a sort of basin. In this basin or inclosure, along the lower edge of

the hill-side, lies the quiet, secluded village in which the Saviour of men spent the greater part of his earthly existence. The surrounding heights vary in altitude, some of them rise to 400 or 500 feet. They have rounded tops, are composed of the glittering limestone which is so common in that country, and, though on the whole sterile and unattractive in appearance, present not an unpleasing aspect, diversified as they are with the foliage of fig-trees and wild shrubs and with the verdure of occasional fields of grain. Our familiar hollyhock is one of the gay flowers which grow wild there. The inclosed valley is peculiarly rich and well cultivated: it is filled with corn-fields, with gardens, hedges of cactus, and clusters of fruit-bearing trees. Being so sheltered by hills, Nazareth enjoys a mild atmosphere and climate. Hence all the fruits of the country, — as pomegranates, oranges, figs, olives, — ripen early and attain a rare perfection. No thoroughfare invaded the seclusion of Nazareth. The line of travel from the north through Cœle-Syria (the *Bâkâ'a*) to the south of Palestine passed it by different routes on the east and the

west, and that from East-Jordan to the Mediterranean passed it on the south.

Of the identification of the ancient site there can be no doubt. The name of the present village is *en-Nâzirah*, the same, therefore, as of old; it is situated among hills and on a hill-side (Luke iv. 29); it is within the limits of the province of Galilee (Mark i. 9); it is near Cana (whether we assume *Kana* on the east or *Kana* on the northeast as the scene of the first miracle), according to the implication in John ii. 1, 2, 11; a precipice exists in the neighborhood (Luke iv. 29); and, finally, a series of testimonies (Reland; *Pal.*, p. 905) reach back to Eusebius, the father of Church history, which represent the place as having occupied an invariable position.

The modern Nazareth belongs to the better class of eastern villages. It has a population variously estimated from 3000 to 5000. It consists of Mohammedans, Latin and Greek Christians, and a few Protestants. There are two mosques (one of them very small), a Franciscan convent of huge dimensions but displaying no great architectural

Nazareth.

beauty, a small Maronite church, a Greek church, and perhaps a church or chapel of some of the other confessions. Protestant missions have been attempted, but with no very marked success. Most of the houses are well built of stone, and have a neat and comfortable appearance. A few of the people dwell in recesses of the limestone cliffs, natural or excavated for that purpose. As streams in the rainy season are liable to pour down with violence from the hills, every "wise man," instead of building upon the loose soil on the surface, digs deep and lays his foundation upon the rock (ἐπὶ τὴν πέτραν) which is found so generally in that country at a certain depth in the earth. The streets or lanes are narrow and crooked, and after rain are so full of mud and mire as to be almost impassable.

A description of Nazareth would be incomplete

without mention of the remarkable view from the tomb of Neby Ismaïl on one of the hills behind the town. It must suffice to indicate merely the objects within sight. In the north are seen the ridges of Lebanon and, high above all, the white top of Hermon; in the west, Carmel, glimpses of the Mediterranean, the bay and the town of Akka; east and southeast are Gilead, Tabor, Gilboa; and south, the Plain of Esdraelon and the mountains of Samaria, with villages on every side, among which are Kana, Nein, Endor, Zerîn (Jezreel), and Tâannuk (Taanach). It is unquestionably one of the most beautiful and sublime spectacles (for it combines the two features) which earth has to show. Dr. Robinson's elaborate description of the scene (*Bibl. Res.*, ii. 336, 337) conveys no exaggerated idea of its magnificence or historical interest. It is easy to believe that the Saviour, during the days of his seclusion in the adjacent valley, came often to this very spot and looked forth thence upon those glorious works of the Creator which so lift the soul upward to Him. One of the grandest views of *Jebel esh-Sheik*, the ancient Hermon, is that which bursts on the traveller as he ascends from the valley eastward on the way to Cana and Tiberias.

The passages of Scripture which refer expressly to Nazareth, though not numerous, are suggestive and deserve to be recalled here.[a] It was the home of Joseph and Mary (Luke ii. 39). The angel announced to the Virgin there the birth of the Messiah (Luke i. 26–28). The holy family returned thither after the flight into Egypt (Matt. ii. 23). Nazareth is called the native country (ἡ πατρὶς αὐτοῦ) of Jesus: He grew up there from infancy to manhood (Luke iv. 16), and was known through life as "The Nazarene." He taught in the synagogue there (Matt. xiii. 54; Luke iv. 16), and was dragged by his fellow-townsmen to the precipice in order to be cast down thence and be killed (εἰς τὸ κατακρημνίσαι αὐτόν). "Jesus of Nazareth, king of the Jews" was written over his Cross (John xix. 19), and after his ascension He revealed Himself under that appellation to the persecuting Saul (Acts xxii. 8). The place has given name to his followers in all ages and all lands, a name which will never cease to be one of honor and reproach.

The origin of the disrepute in which Nazareth stood (John i. 46) is not certainly known. All the inhabitants of Galilee were looked upon with contempt by the people of Judæa because they spoke a ruder dialect, were less cultivated, and were more exposed by their position to contact with the heathen. But Nazareth labored under a special opprobrium, for it was a Galilæan and not a southern Jew who asked the reproachful question, whether "any good thing" could come from that source. As the term "good" (ἀγαθόν) has more commonly an ethical sense, it has been suggested that the inhabitants of Nazareth may have had a bad name among their neighbors for irreligion or some laxity of morals. The supposition receives support from the disposition which they manifested towards the person and ministry of our Lord. They attempted to kill Him; they expelled Him twice (for Luke iv. 16–29, and Matt. xiii. 54–58, relate probably to different occurrences) from their borders; they were so willful and unbelieving that He performed not many miracles among them (Matt. xiii. 58); and, finally, they compelled Him to turn his back upon them and reside at Capernaum (Matt. iv. 13).

It is impossible to speak of distances with much exactness. Nazareth is a moderate journey of three days from Jerusalem, seven hours, or about twenty miles, from Akka or Ptolemais (Acts xxi. 7), five or six hours, or eighteen miles, from the sea of Galilee, six miles west from Mount Tabor, two hours from Cana,[b] and two or three from Endor and Nain. The origin of the name is uncertain. For the conjectures on the subject, see NAZARENE.

We pass over, as foreign to the proper object of this notice, any particular account of the "holy places" which the legends have sought to connect with events in the life of Christ.[c] They are described in nearly all the books of modern tourists; but, having no sure connection with Biblical geography or exegesis, do not require attention here. Two localities, however, form an exception to this statement, inasmuch as they possess, though in different ways, a certain interest which no one will fail to recognize. One of these is the "Fountain of the Virgin," situated at the northeastern extremity of the town, where, according to one tradition, the mother of Jesus received the angel's salutation (Luke i. 28). Though we may attach no importance to this latter belief, we must, on other accounts, regard the spring with a feeling akin to that of religious veneration. It derives its name from the fact that Mary, during her life at Nazareth, no doubt accompanied often by "the child Jesus," must have been accustomed to repair to this fountain for water, as is the practice of the women of that village at the present day. Certainly, as Dr. Clarke observes (*Travels*, ii. 427), "if there be a spot throughout the holy land that was undoubtedly honored by her presence, we may consider this to have been the place: because the situation of a copious spring is not liable to change, and because the custom of repairing thither to draw water has been continued among the female inhabitants of Nazareth from the earliest period of its history." The well-worn path which leads thither from the town has been trodden by the feet of almost countless generations. It presents at all hours a busy scene, from the number of those, hurrying to and fro, engaged in the labor of water-carrying. See the engraving, i. 838 of this *Dictionary*.

The other place is that of the attempted Precipitation. We are directed to the true scene of this occurrence, not so much by any tradition as by internal indications in the Gospel history itself. A prevalent opinion of the country has transferred the event to a hill about two miles southeast of the town. But there is no evidence that Nazareth ever occupied a different site from the present one: and that a mob whose determination was to put to

---

a * The name of Nazareth occurs 27 times in the Greek text, and twice more in the A. V., namely, Luke xviii. 37 and xxiv. 19, where the Greek, however, is Ναζωραῖος.   H.

b * Yet, with this vicinity of Cana to Nazareth, Nathanael, who lived at Cana, appears never to have heard of Jesus until called to be one of his disciples at the beginning of his ministry (John i. 46–50). So strictly private, unofficial, was the Saviour's life at Nazareth until the time came for Him "to be made manifest to Israel" (John i. 31). This obscurity is irreconcilable with the idea that Christ wrought miracles before He entered on his public work. H.

c * For an enumeration of these "places" and the legends connected with them, one may see Sepp's (*Jerus. und das heil. Land*, ii. 73–91). They are described still more fully in the new work of Titus Tobler, *Nazareth in Palästina* (Berlin, 1868). This work is founded partly on the author's *third* journey to the Holy Land in 1846, but still more on communications from the missionary Zeller, who has resided at Nazareth since 1858. It forms a valuable contribution to our knowledge of the history, statistics, and topography of this sacred place. The plan of the little village, inserted at the end, representing the course of the valley, the market, streets, fountains, convents, churches, is a great help to the reader. It may be added that Dr. Tobler, though a Catholic, rejects the tradition of the Latin monks respecting the site of the precipice at Nazareth, and agrees with those who decide that it must be sought within the present village, probably near the Maronite Church.   H.

death the object of their rage, should repair to so distant a place for that purpose, is entirely incredible. The present village, as already stated, lies along the hill-side, but much nearer the base than the summit. Above the bulk of the town are several rocky ledges over which no person could be thrown without almost certain destruction. But there is one very remarkable precipice, almost perpendicular and forty or fifty feet high, near the Maronite Church, which may well be supposed to be the identical one over which his infuriated townsmen attempted to hurl Jesus. Not far from the town, on the northwest declivity of the hill, are a few excavated stone-sepulchres, almost the only Jewish monument which now remains to be seen there.

The singular precision with which the narrative relates the transaction deserves a remark or two. Casual readers would understand from the account that Nazareth was situated on the summit, and that the people brought Jesus down thence to the brow of the hill as if it was between the town and the valley. If these inferences were correct, the narrative and the locality would then be at variance with each other. The writer is free to say that he himself had these erroneous impressions, and was led to correct them by what he observed on the spot. Even Reland (*Pal.* p. 905) says: "Naζαρέθ — urbs aedificata *super rupem*, unde Christum praecipitare conati sunt." But the language of the Evangelist, when more closely examined, is found neither to require the inferences in question on the one hand, nor to exclude them on the other. What he asserts is, that the incensed crowd "rose up and cast Jesus out of the city, and brought him to the brow of the hill on which the city was built, that they might cast him down headlong." It will be remarked here, in the first place, that it is not said that the people either went up or descended in order to reach the precipice, but simply that they brought the Saviour to it, wherever it was; and in the second place, that it is not said that the city was built "on the brow of the hill" (ἕως τῆς ὀφρύος τοῦ ὄρους), but equally as well that the precipice was "on the brow," without deciding whether the cliff overlooked the town (as is the fact) or was below it.ᵃ It will be seen, therefore, how very nearly the terms of the history approach a mistake and yet avoid it. As Paley remarks in another case, none but a true account could advance thus to the very brink of contradiction without falling into it.

The fortunes of Nazareth have been various. Epiphanius states that no Christians dwelt there until the time of Constantine. Helena, the mother of that emperor, is related to have built the first Church of the Annunciation here. In the time of the Crusaders, the Episcopal See of Bethsean was transferred there. The birthplace of Christianity was lost to the Christians by their defeat at Hattin in 1183, and was laid utterly in ruins by Sultan Bibars in 1293. Ages passed away before it rose again from this prostration. In 1620 the Franciscans rebuilt the Church of the Annunciation

and connected a cloister with it. In 1799 the Turks assaulted the French General Junot at Nazareth; and shortly after, 2,100 French, under Kleber and Napoleon, defeated a Turkish army of 25,000 at the foot of Mount Tabor. Napoleon himself, after that battle, spent a few hours at Nazareth, and reached there the northern limit of his eastern expedition. The earthquake which destroyed Safed, in 1837, injured also Nazareth. No Jews reside there at present, which may be ascribed perhaps as much to the hostility of the Christian sects as to their own hatred of the prophet who was sent "to redeem Israel."　　　　H. B. H.

NAZ'ARITE, more properly NAZ'IRITE (נָזִיר and נְזִיר אֱלֹהִים: ἡγιμένος and εὐξάμενος, Num. vi.; ναζιραῖος, Judg. xiii. 7, Lam. iv. 7: *Nazaraeus*), one of either sex who was bound by a vow of a peculiar kind to be set apart from others for the service of God. The obligation was either for life or for a defined time. The Mishna names the two classes resulting from this distinction, נְזִירֵי עוֹלָם, "perpetual Nazarites" (*Nazarei nativi*), and נְזִירֵי יָמִים, "Nazarites of days" (*Nazarei votivi*).

I. There is no notice in the Pentateuch of Nazarites for life; but the regulations for the vow of a Nazarite of days are given Num. vi. 1–21.

The Nazarite, during the term of his consecration, was bound to abstain from wine, grapes, with every production of the vine, even to the stones and skin of the grape, and from every kind of intoxicating drink. He was forbidden to cut the hair of his head, or to approach any dead body, even that of his nearest relation. When the period of his vow was fulfilled, he was brought to the door of the Tabernacle and was required to offer a he-lamb for a burnt-offering, a ewe lamb for a sin-offering, and a ram for a peace-offering, with the usual accompaniments of peace-offerings (Lev. vii. 12, 13) and of the offering made at the consecration of priests (Ex. xxix. 2) "a basket of unleavened bread, cakes of fine flour mingled with oil, and wafers of unleavened bread anointed with oil" (Num. vi. 15). He brought also a meat-offering and drink-offering, which appear to have been presented by themselves as a distinct act of service (ver. 17). He was to cut off the hair of "the head of his separation" (that is, the hair which had grown during the period of his consecration) at the door of the Tabernacle, and to put it into the fire under the sacrifice on the altar. The priest then placed upon his hands the sodden left shoulder of the ram, with one of the unleavened cakes and one of the wafers, and then took them again and waved them for a wave-offering These, as well as the breast and the heave, or right shoulder (to which he was entitled in the case of ordinary peace-offerings, Lev. vii. 32–34), were the perquisite of the priest. The Nazarite also gave him a present proportioned to his circumstances (ver. 21).ᵇ

If a Nazarite incurred defilement by accidentally

ᵃ Mr. Tristram's view, that "the old Nazareth was on the brow of the hill" (*Land of Israel*, p. 122, 2d ed.), and not "on the steep slope" as at present, if not "a misinterpretation" (as Tobler characterizes it, *Nazareth*, p. 52), is certainly unnecessary.　　H.

ᵇ It is said that at the southeast corner of the court of the women, in Herod's temple, there was an apartment appropriated to the Nazarites, in which they used to boil their peace-offerings and cut off their hair. Lightfoot, *Prospect of the Temple*, c. xvii.; Reland, *A. S.* p. i. chap. 8, § 11.

touching a dead body, he had to undergo certain rites of purification and to recommence the full period of his consecration. On the seventh day of his uncleanness he was to cut off his hair, and on the following day he had to bring two turtle-doves or two young pigeons to the priest, who offered one for a sin-offering and the other for a burnt-offering. He then hallowed his head, offered a lamb of the first year as a trespass-offering, and renewed his vow under the same conditions as it had been at first made.

It has been conjectured that the Nazarite vow was at first taken with some formality, and that it was accompanied by an offering similar to that prescribed at its renewal in the case of pollution. But if any inference may be drawn from the early sections of the Mishnical treatise *Nazir*, it seems probable that the act of self-consecration was a private matter, not accompanied by any prescribed rite.

There is nothing whatever said in the Old Testament of the duration of the period of the vow of the Nazarite of days. According to *Nazir* (cap. i. § 3, p. 148) the usual time was thirty days, but double vows for sixty days, and treble vows for a hundred days, were sometimes made (cap. iii. 1–4). One instance is related of Helena, queen of Adiabene (of whom some particulars are given by Josephus, *Ant.* xx. 2), who, with the zeal of a new convert, took a vow for seven years in order to obtain the divine favor on a military expedition which her son was about to undertake. When her period of consecration had expired she visited Jerusalem, and was there informed by the doctors of the school of Hillel that a vow taken in another country must be repeated whenever the Nazarite might visit the Holy Land. She accordingly continued a Nazarite for a second seven years, and happening to touch a dead body just as the time was about to expire, she was obliged to renew her vow according to the law in Num. vi. 9, etc. She thus continued a Nazarite for twenty-one years.[a]

There are some other particulars given in the Mishna, which are curious as showing how the institution was regarded in later times. The vow was often undertaken by childless parents in the hope of obtaining children: this may, of course, have been easily suggested by the cases of Manoah's wife and Hannah. A female Nazarite whose vow was broken might be punished with forty stripes. — The Nazarite was permitted to smooth his hair with a brush, but not to comb it, lest a single hair might be torn out.

II. Of the Nazarites for life three are mentioned in the Scriptures : Samson, Samuel, and St. John the Baptist. The only one of these actually called a Nazarite is Samson. The Rabbis raised the question whether Samuel was in reality a Nazarite.[b] In Hannah's vow, it is expressly stated that no razor should come upon her son's head (1 Sam. i.

11); but no mention is made of abstinence from wine. It is, however, worthy of notice that Philo makes a particular point of this, and seems to refer the words of Hannah, 1 Sam. i. 15, to Samuel himself.[c] In reference to St. John the Baptist, the Angel makes mention of abstinence from wine and strong drink, but not of letting the hair grow (Luke i. 15).

We are but imperfectly informed of the difference between the observances of the Nazarite for life and those of the Nazarite for days. The later Rabbis slightly notice this point.[d] We do not know whether the vow for life was ever voluntarily taken by the individual. In all the cases mentioned in the sacred history, it was made by the parents before the birth of the Nazarite himself. According to the general law of vows (Num. xxx. 8), the mother could not take the vow without the father, and this is expressly applied to the Nazarite vow in the Mishna.[e] Hannah must therefore either have presumed on her husband's concurrence, or secured it beforehand.

The Mishna[f] makes a distinction between the ordinary Nazarite for life and the Samson-Nazarite (נזיר שמשון). The former made a strong point of his purity, and, if he was polluted, offered corban. But as regards his hair, when it became inconveniently long, he was allowed to trim it, if he was willing to offer the appointed victims (Num. vi. 14). The Samson-Nazarite, on the other hand, gave no corban if he touched a dead body, but he was not suffered to trim his hair under any conditions. This distinction, it is pretty evident, was suggested by the freedom with which Samson must have come in the way of the dead (Judg. xv. 16, etc.), and the terrible penalty which he paid for allowing his hair to be cut.

III. The consecration of the Nazarite bore a striking resemblance to that of the high-priest (Lev. xxi. 10–12). In one particular, this is brought out more plainly in the Hebrew text than it is in our version, in the LXX., or in the Vulgate.

One word (נזר),[g] derived from the same root as Nazarite, is used for the long hair of the Nazarite, Num. vi. 19, where the A. V. has "hair of his separation," and for the anointed head of the high-priest, Lev. xxi. 12, where it is rendered "crown." The Mishna points out the identity of the law for both the high-priest and the Nazarite in respect to pollution, in that neither was permitted to approach the corpse of even the nearest relation, while for an ordinary priest the law allowed more freedom (Lev. xxi. 2). And Maimonides (*More Nevochim*, iii. 48) speaks of the dignity of the Nazarite, in regard to his sanctity, as being equal to that of the high-priest. The abstinence from wine enjoined upon the high-priest on behalf of all the priests when they were about to enter upon their ministrations, is an obvious, but perhaps not such an important

---

a Nazir, cap. 3, § 6, p. 156.

b Nazir, cap. 9. § 5, with Bartenora's note, p. 178

c Διὰ τοῦτο ὁ καὶ βασιλέων καὶ προφητῶν μέγιστος Σαμουὴλ οἶνον καὶ μέθυσμα, ὡς ὁ ἱερὸς λόγος φησίν, ἄχρι τελευτῆς οὐ πίεται. — Phil. *de Ebrietate*, vol 1. p. 379, edit. Mangey.

d See *Pesikta*, quoted by Drusius on Num. vi.

e Nazir, cap. 4, § 6, p. 159.

f Nazir, cap. 1, § 2, p. 147.

g The primary meaning of this word is that of separation with a holy purpose. Hence it is used to ex-

press the consecration of the Nazarite (Num. vi. 4, 5, 9). But it appears to have been especially applied to a badge of consecration and distinction worn on the head, such as the crown of a king (2 Sam. i. 10 ; 2 K. xi. 12), the diadem (צִיץ) of the high-priest (Ex. xxix. 6, xxxix. 30), as well as his anointed hair, the long hair of the Nazarite, and, dropping the idea of consecration altogether, to long hair in a general sense (Jer. vii. 29). This may throw light on Gen. xlix. 26 and Deut. xxxiii. 16. See section VI. of this article.

point in the comparison. There is a passage in the account given by Hegesippus of St. James the Just (Eusebius, *Hist. Ecc.* ii. 23), which, if we may assume it to represent a genuine tradition, is worth a notice, and seems to show that Nazarites were permitted even to enter into the Holy of Holies. He says that St. James was consecrated from his birth neither to eat meat, to drink wine, to cut his hair, nor to indulge in the use of the bath, and that to him alone it was permitted (τούτῳ μόνῳ ἐξῆν) to enter the sanctuary. Perhaps it would not be unreasonable to suppose that the half sacerdotal character of Samuel might have been connected with his prerogative as a Nazarite. Many of the Fathers designate him as a priest, although St. Jerome, on the obvious ground of his descent, denies that he had any sacerdotal rank.[a]

IV. Of the two vows recorded of St. Paul, that in Acts xviii. 18,[b] certainly cannot be regarded as a regular Nazarite vow. All that we are told of it is that on his way from Corinth to Jerusalem, he "shaved his head in Cenchreæ, for he had a vow." It would seem that the cutting off the hair was at the commencement of the period over which the vow extended; at all events, the hair was not cut off at the door of the Temple when the sacrifices were offered, as was required by the law of the Nazarite. It is most likely that it was a sort of vow, modified from the proper Nazarite vow, which had come into use at this time amongst the religious Jews who had been visited by sickness, or any other calamity. In reference to a vow of this kind which was taken by Bernice, Josephus says that "they were accustomed to vow that they would refrain from wine, and that they would cut off their hair thirty days before the presentation of their offering." [c] No hint is given us of the purpose of St. Paul in this act of devotion. Spencer conjectures that it might have been performed with a view to obtain a good voyage; [d] Neander, with greater probability, that it was an expression of thanksgiving and humiliation on account of some recent illness or affliction of some kind.

The other reference to a vow taken by St. Paul is in Acts xxi. 24, where we find the brethren at Jerusalem exhorting him to take part with four Christians who had a vow on them, to sanctify (not *purify*, as in A. V.) himself with them, and to be at charges with them, that they might shave their heads. The reason alleged for this advice is that he might prove to those who misunderstood him, that he walked orderly and kept the law. Now it cannot be doubted that this was a strictly legal Nazarite vow. He joined the four men for the last seven days of their consecration, until the

offering was made for each one of them, and their hair was cut off in the usual form (ver. 26, 27). It appears to have been no uncommon thing for those charitable persons who could afford it to assist in paying for the offerings of poor Nazarites. Josephus relates that Herod Agrippa I., when he desired to show his zeal for the religion of his fathers, gave direction that many Nazarites should have their heads shorn:[e] and the Gemara (quoted by Reland, *Ant. Sac.*), that Alexander Jannæus contributed towards supplying nine hundred victims for three hundred Nazarites.

V. That the institution of Nazaritism existed and had become a matter of course amongst the Hebrews before the time of Moses is beyond a doubt. The legislator appears to have done no more than ordain such regulations for the vow of the Nazarite of days as brought it under the cognizance of the priest and into harmony with the general system of religious observance. It has been assumed, not unreasonably, that the consecration of the Nazarite for life was of at least equal antiquity.[f] It may not have needed any notice or modification in the Law, and hence, probably, the silence respecting it in the Pentateuch. But it is doubted in regard to Nazaritism in general, whether it was of native or foreign origin. Cyril of Alexandria considered that the letting the hair grow, the most characteristic feature in the vow, was taken from the Egyptians. This notion has been substantially adopted by Fagius,[g] Spencer,[h] Michaelis,[i] Hengstenberg,[k] and some other critics. Hengstenberg affirms that the Egyptians and the Hebrews were distinguished amongst ancient nations by cutting their hair as a matter of social propriety; and thus the marked significance of long hair must have been common to them both. The arguments of Bähr, however, to show that the wearing long hair in Egypt and all other heathen nations had a meaning opposed to the idea of the Nazarite vow, seem to be conclusive;[l] and Winer justly observes that the points of resemblance between the Nazarite vow and heathen customs are too fragmentary and indefinite to furnish a safe foundation for an argument in favor of a foreign origin for the former.

Ewald supposes that Nazarites for life were numerous in very early times, and that they multiplied in periods of great political and religious excitement. The only ones, however, expressly named in the Old Testament are Samson and Samuel. The rabbinical notion that Absalom was a Nazarite seems hardly worthy of notice, though Spencer and Lightfoot have adopted it.[m] When Amos wrote, the Nazarites, as well as the prophets, suffered from

[a] J. C. Ortlob, in an essay in the *Thesaurus Novus Theologico-Philologicus*, vol. i. p. 587, entitled "Samuel Judex et Propheta, non Pontifex aut sacerdos sacrificans," has brought forward a mass of testimony on this subject.

[b] Grotius, Meyer, Howson, and a few others, refer this vow to Aquila, not to St. Paul. The best arguments in favor of this view are given by Mr. Howson (*Life of St. Paul*, vol. i. p. 453). Dean Alford, in his note on Acts xviii. 18, has satisfactorily replied to them.

[c] Dr. Howson formerly held that opinion, but retracts it in his *Lectures on the Character of St. Paul*, p. 16 (2d ed. 1864), where he admits that the vow is more probably that of Paul than that of Aquila. Further, see addition to AQUILA, Amer. ed.   H.

[c] See Neander's *Planting and Training of the Church*, i. 206 (Ryland's translation). In the passage trans-

lated from Joseph. *B. J.* ii. 15, § 1, an emendation of Neander's is adopted. See also Kuinoel on Acts xviii. 18.

[d] *De Leg. Hebr.* lib. iii. chap. vi. § 1.

[e] *Antiq.* xix. 6, § 1.

[f] Ewald seems to think that it was the more ancient of the two (*Alterthümer*, p. 96).

[g] *Critici Sacri*, on Num. vi. 5.

[h] *De Leg. Hebr.* lib. iii. chap. vi. § 1.

[i] *Commentaries on the Law of Moses*, bk. iii. § 145.

[k] *Egypt and the Books of Moses*, p. 190 (English vers.).

[l] Bähr, *Symbolik*, vol. ii. p. 439.

[m] Spencer, *De Leg. Hebr.* lib. iii. c. vi. § 1. Lightfoot, *Exercit. in* 1 Cor. xi. 14. Some have imagined that Jephtha's daughter was consigned to a Nazarite vow by her father. See Carpzov, p. 156.

the persecution and contempt of the ungodly. The divine word respecting them was, "I raised up of your sons for prophets and of your young men for Nazarites. But ye gave the Nazarites wine to drink, and commanded the prophets, saying, Prophesy not" (Am. ii. 11, 12). In the time of Judas Maccabæus we find the devout Jews, when they were bringing their gifts to the priests, stirring up the Nazarites of days who had completed the time of their consecration, to make the accustomed offerings (1 Macc. iii. 49). From this incident, in connection with what has been related of the liberality of Alexander Jannæus and Herod Agrippa, we may infer that the number of Nazarites must have been very considerable during the two centuries and a half which preceded the destruction of Jerusalem. The instance of St. John the Baptist and that of St. James the Just (if we accept the traditional account) show that the Nazarite for life retained his original character till later times; and the act of St. Paul in joining himself with the four Nazarites at Jerusalem seems to prove that the vow of the Nazarite of days was as little altered in its important features.

VI. The word נָזִיר occurs in three passages of the Old Testament, in which it appears to mean one separated from others as a prince. Two of the passages refer to Joseph: one is in Jacob's benediction of his sons (Gen. xlix. 26), the other in Moses' benediction of the tribes (Deut. xxxiii. 16). As these texts stand in our version, the blessing is spoken of as falling "on the crown of the head of him who was separated from his brethren." The LXX. render the words in one place, ἐπὶ κορυφῆς ὧν ἡγήσατο ἀδελφῶν, and in the other ἐπὶ κορυφὴν δοξασθέντος ἐν ἀδελφοῖς. The Vulgate translates them in each place "in vertice Nazaræi inter fratres." The expression is strikingly like that used of the high-priest (Lev. xxi. 10–12), and seems to derive illustrations from the use of the word נֵזֶר.ᵃ

The third passage is that in which the prophet is mourning over the departed prosperity and beauty of Sion (Lam. iv. 7, 8). In the A. V. the words are "Her Nazarites were purer than snow, they were whiter than milk, they were more ruddy in body than rubies, their polishing was of sapphire, their visage is blacker than a coal, they are not known in the streets, their skin cleaveth to their bones, it is withered, it is become like a stick." In favor of the application of this passage to the Nazarites are the renderings of the LXX., the Vulg., and nearly all the versions. But Gesenius, de Wette, and other modern critics think that it refers to the young princes of Israel, and that the word נָזִיר is used in the same sense as it is in regard to Joseph, Gen. xlix. 26 and Deut. xxxiii. 16.

VII. The vow of the Nazarite of days must have been a self-imposed discipline, undertaken with a specific purpose. The Jewish writers mostly re-

garded it as a kind of penance, and hence accounted for the place which the law regulating it holds in Leviticus immediately after the law relating to adultery.ᵇ As the quantity of hair which grew within the ordinary period of a vow could not have been very considerable, and as a temporary abstinence from wine was probably not a more noticeable thing amongst the Hebrews than it is in modern society, the Nazarite of days might have fulfilled his vow without attracting much notice until the day came for him to make his offering in the Temple.

But the Nazarite for life, on the other hand, must have been, with his flowing hair and persistent refusal of strong drink, a marked man. Whether in any other particular his daily life was peculiar is uncertain.ᶜ He may have had some privileges (as we have seen) which gave him something of a priestly character, and (as it has been conjectured) he may have given up much of his time to sacred studies.ᵈ Though not necessarily cut off from social life, when the turn of his mind was devotional, consciousness of his peculiar dedication must have influenced his habits and manner, and in some cases probably led him to retire from the world.

But without our resting on anything that may be called in question, he must have been a public witness for the idea of legal strictness and of whatever else Nazaritism was intended to express: and as the vow of the Nazarite for life was taken by his parents before he was conscious of it, his observance of it was a sign of filial obedience, like the peculiarities of the Rechabites.

The meaning of the Nazarite vow has been regarded in different lights. Some consider it as a symbolical expression of the Divine nature working in man, and deny that it involved anything of a strictly ascetic character; others see in it the principle of stoicism, and imagine that it was intended to cultivate, and bear witness for, the sovereignty of the will over the lower tendencies of human nature: while some regard it wholly in the light of a sacrifice of the person to God.

(a.) Several of the Jewish writers have taken the first view more or less completely. Abarbanel imagined that the hair represents the intellectual power, the power belonging to the head, which the wise man was not to suffer to be diminished or to be interfered with, by drinking wine or by any other indulgence; and that the Nazarite was not to approach the dead because he was appointed to bear witness to the eternity of the divine nature.ᵉ Of modern critics, Bähr appears to have most completely trodden in the same track.ᶠ While he denies that the life of the Nazarite was, in the proper sense, ascetic, he contends that his abstinence from wine,ᵍ and his not being allowed to approach the dead, figured the separation from other men which characterizes the consecrated servant of the Lord; and that his long hair signified his holiness. The hair, according to his theory, as being the bloom

ᵃ See note g, p. 2074.

ᵇ Maimonides, *Mor. Nec.* ii 48.

ᶜ Nicolas Fuller has discussed the subject of the dress of the Nazarites (as well as of the prophets) in his *Miscellanea Sacra*. See *Critici Sacri*, vol. ix. p. 1023. Those who have imagined that the Nazarites wore a peculiar dress, doubt whether it was of royal purple, or rough hair-cloth (like St. John's), or of some white material.

ᵈ Vatablus on Num. vi. (*Critici Sacri*).

ᵉ Quoted by De Muis on Num. vi. (*Critici Sacri*).

ᶠ *Symbolik*, vol. ii. p. 416–430.

ᵍ He will not allow that this abstinence at all resembled in its meaning that of the priests, when engaged in their ministrations, which was intended only to secure strict propriety in the discharge of their duties.

of manhood, is the symbol of growth in the vegetable as well as the animal kingdom, and therefore of the operation of the Divine power.[a]

(b.) But the philosophical Jewish doctors, for the most part, seem to have preferred the second view. Thus Bechai speaks of the Nazarite as a conqueror who subdued his temptations, and who wore his long hair as a crown, " quod ipse rex sit cupiditatibus imperans præter morem reliquorum hominum, qui cupiditatum sunt servi." [b] He supposed that the hair was worn rough, as a protest against foppery.[c] But others, still taking it as a regal emblem, have imagined that it was kept elaborately dressed, and fancy that they see a proof of the existence of the custom in the seven locks of Samson (Judg. xvi. 13–19).[d]

(c.) Philo has taken the deeper view of the subject. In his work, On Animals fit for Sacrifice,[e] he gives an account of the Nazarite vow, and calls it ἡ εὐχὴ μεγάλη. According to him the Nazarite did not sacrifice merely his possessions but his person, and the act of sacrifice was to be performed in the completest manner. The outward observances enjoined upon him were to be the genuine expressions of his spiritual devotion. To represent spotless purity within, he was to shun defilement from the dead, at the expense even of the obligation of the closest family ties. As no spiritual state or act can be signified by any single symbol, he was to identify himself with each one of the three victims which he had to offer as often as he broke his vow by accidental pollution, or when the period of his vow came to an end. He was to realize in himself the ideas of the whole burnt-offering, the sin-offering, and the peace-offering. That no mistake might be made in regard to the three sacrifices being shadows of one and the same substance, it was ordained that the victims should be individuals of one and the same species of animal. The shorn hair was put on the fire of the altar in order that, although the divine law did not permit the offering of human blood, something might be offered up actually a portion of his own person. Ewald, following in the same line of thought, has treated the vow of the Nazarite as an act of self-sacrifice; but he looks on the preservation of the hair as signifying that the Nazarite is so set apart for God, that no change or diminution should be made in any part of his person, and as serving to himself and the world for a visible token of his peculiar consecration to Jehovah.[f]

That the Nazarite vow was essentially a sacrifice of the person to the Lord is obviously in accordance with the terms of the Law (Num. vi. 2). In the old dispensation it may have answered to that " living sacrifice, holy, acceptable unto God," which the believer is now called upon to make. As the

Nazarite was a witness for the straitness of the law, as distinguished from the freedom of the Gospel, his sacrifice of himself was a submission to the letter of a rule. Its outward manifestations were restraints and eccentricities. The man was separated from his brethren that he might be peculiarly devoted to the Lord. This was consistent with the purpose of divine wisdom for the time for which it was ordained. Wisdom, we are told, was justified of her child in the life of the great Nazarite who preached the baptism of repentance when the Law was about to give way to the Gospel. Amongst those born of women, no greater than he had arisen, " but he that is least in the kingdom of Heaven is greater than he." The sacrifice which the believer now makes of himself is not to cut him off from his brethren, but to unite him more closely with them; not to subject him to an outward bond, but to confirm him in the liberty with which Christ has made him free. It is not without significance that wine under the Law was strictly forbidden to the priest who was engaged in the service of the sanctuary, and to the few whom the Nazarite vow bound to the special service of the Lord; while in the Church of Christ it is consecrated for the use of every believer to whom the command has come, " drink ye all of this." [g]

Carpzov, Apparatus Criticus, p. 148; Reland, Ant. Sacræ, p. ii. c. 10; Meinhard, Pauli Naziræatus (Thesaurus Theologico-philologicus, ii. 473). The notes of De Muis and Drusius on Num. vi. (Critici Sacri); the notes of Grotius on Luke i. 15, and Kuinoel on Acts xviii. 18; Spencer, De Legibus Hebræorum, lib. iii. cap. vi. § 1; Michaelis, Commentaries on the Laws of Moses, book iii. § 145; the Mishnical treatise Nazir, with the notes in Surenhusius's Mishna, iii. 146, &c.; Bähr, Symbolik, ii. 416–430; Ewald, Alterthümer, p. 96; also Geschichte, ii. 43. Carpzov mentions with praise Naziræus, seu Commentarius literalis et mysticus in Legem Naziræorum, by Cremer. The essay of Meinhard contains a large amount of information on the subject, besides what bears immediately on St. Paul's vows. Spencer gives a full account of heathen customs in dedicating the hair. The Notes of De Muis contain a valuable collection of Jewish testimonies on the meaning of the Nazarite vow in general. Those of Grotius relate especially to the Nazarites' abstinence from wine. Hengstenberg (Egypt and the Books of Moses, p. 190, English translation) confutes Bähr's theory.   S. C.

NE'AH (הַנֵּעָה [the settlement, Fürst; perh. inclination, descent, Dietr.], with the def. article: Vat. omits; Alex. Αννουα: Anea[h]), a place which was one of the landmarks on the boundary of Zebulun (Josh. xix. 13 only). By Eusebius and

---

[a] Bähr defends this notion by several philological arguments, which do not seem to be much to the point. The nearest to the purpose is that derived from Lev. xxv. 5, where the unpruned vines of the sabbatical year are called Nazarites. But this, of course, can be well explained as a metaphor from unshorn hair.

[b] Carpzov, App. Crit. p. 152. Abenezra uses very similar language (Drusius, on Num. vi. 7).

[c] This was also the opinion of Lightfoot, Exercit. in 1 Cor. xi. 14, and Sermon on Judg. xi. 39.

[d] Spencer, De Leg. Hebr. iii. vi. § 1.

[e] Opera, vol. ii. p. 249 (ed. Mangey).

[f] Lightfoot is inclined to favor certain Jewish writers who identify the vine with the tree of knowledge of good and evil, and to connect the Nazarite law

with the condition of Adam before he fell (Exercit. in Luc. i. 15). This strange notion is made still more fanciful by Magee (Atonement and Sacrifice, Illustration xxxviii.).

[g] This consideration might surely have furnished St. Jerome with a better answer to the Tatianists, who alleged Amos ii. 12 in defense of their abstinence from wine, than his bitter taunt that they were bringing " Judaicas fabulas " into the church, and that they were bound, on their own ground, neither to eat their hair, to eat grapes or raisins, or to approach the corpse of a dead parent (in Amos ii. 12).

[h] This is the reading of the text of the Vulgate given in the Benedictine edition of Jerome. The ordinary copies have Nea.

Jerome (*Onomast.* "Anua") it is mentioned merely with a caution that there is a place of the same name, 10 miles S. of Neapolis. It has not yet been identified even by Schwarz. If *el-Meshhad*, about 2¼ miles E. of *Seffurieh*, be GATH-HEPHER, and *Rummaneh* about 4 miles N. E. of the same place, RIMMON, then Neah must probably be sought somewhere to the north of the last-named town.

G.

NEAP'OLIS (Νεάπολις, "new city": *Neapolis*) is the place in northern Greece where Paul and his associates first landed in Europe (Acts xvi. 11); where, no doubt, he landed also on his second visit to Macedonia (Acts xx. 1), and whence certainly he embarked on his last journey through that province to Troas and Jerusalem (Acts xx. 6). Philippi being an inland town, Neapolis was evidently the port; and hence it is accounted for, that Luke leaves the verb which describes the voyage from Troas to Neapolis (εὐθυδρομήσαμεν), to describe the continuance of the journey from Neapolis to Philippi. It has been made a question whether this harbor occupied the site of the present Kavalla, a Turkish town on the coast of Roumelia, or should be sought at some other place. Cousinéry (*Voyage dans la Macédoine*) and Tafel (*De Via Militari Romanorum Egnatia*, etc.) maintain, against the common opinion, that Luke's Neapolis was not at Kavalla, the inhabited town of that name, but at a deserted harbor ten or twelve miles further west, known as Eski or Old Kavalla. Most of those who contend for the other identification assume the point without much discussion, and the subject demands still the attention of the Biblical geographer. It may be well, therefore, to mention with some fullness the reasons which support the claim of Kavalla to be regarded as the ancient Neapolis, in opposition to those which are urged in favor of the other harbor.

First, the Roman and Greek ruins at Kavalla prove that a port existed there in ancient times. Neapolis, wherever it was, formed the point of contact between Northern Greece and Asia Minor, at a period of great commercial activity, and would be expected to have left vestiges of its former importance. The antiquities found still at Kavalla fulfill entirely that presumption. One of these is a massive aqueduct, which brings water into the town from a distance of ten or twelve miles north of Kavalla, along the slopes of Symbolum. It is built on two tiers of arches, a hundred feet long and eighty feet high, and is carried over the narrow valley between the promontory and the mainland. The upper part of the work is modern, but the substructions are evidently Roman, as is seen from the composite character of the material, the cement, and the style of the masonry. Just out of the western gate are two marble sarcophagi, used as watering-troughs, with Latin inscriptions, of the age of the emperor Claudius. Columns with chaplets of elegant Ionic workmanship, blocks of marble, fragments of hewn stone, evidently antique, are numerous both in the town and the suburbs. On some of these are inscriptions, mostly in Latin, but one at least in Greek. In digging for the foundation of new houses the walls of ancient ones are often brought to light, and sometimes tablets with sculptured figures, which would be deemed curious at Athens or Corinth. For fuller details, see *Bibl. Sacra*, xvii. 881 ff. (October, 1860). [COLONY, Amer. ed.] On the contrary, no ruins have been found at Eski Kavalla, or l'aleopoli, as it is also called, which can be pronounced unmistakably ancient. No remains of walls, no inscriptions, and no indications of any thoroughfare leading thence to Philippi, are reported to exist there. Cousinéry, it is true, speaks of certain ruins at the place which he deems worthy of notice: but according to the testimony of others these ruins are altogether inconsiderable, and, which is still more decisive, are modern in their character.[a] Cousinéry himself, in fact, corroborates this, when he says that on the isthmus which binds the peninsula to the main land, "*on trouve les ruines de l'ancienne Néapolis ou celles d'un château reconstruit dans le moyen âge.*"[b] It appears that a mediæval or Venetian fortress existed there; but as far as is yet ascertained, nothing else has been discovered which points to an earlier period.

Secondly, the advantages of the position render Kavalla the probable site of Neapolis. It is the first convenient harbor south of the Hellespont, on coming from the east. Thasos serves as a natural landmark. Tafel says, indeed, that Kavalla has no port, or one next to none; but that is incorrect. The fact that the place is now the seat of an active commerce proves the contrary. It lies open somewhat to the south and southwest, but is otherwise well sheltered. There is no danger in going into the harbor. Even a rock which lies off the point of the town has twelve fathoms alongside of it. The bottom affords good anchorage; and although the bay may not be so large as that of Eski Kavalla, it is ample for the accommodation of any number of vessels which the course of trade or travel between Asia Minor and Northern Greece would be likely to bring together there at any one time.

Thirdly, the facility of intercourse between this port and Philippi shows that Kavalla and Neapolis must be the same. The distance is nearly ten miles,[c] and hence not greater than Corinth was from Cenchreæ, and Ostia from Rome. Both places are in sight at once from the top of Symbolum. The distance between Philippi and Eski Kavalla must be nearly twice as great. Nature itself has opened a passage from the one place to the other. The mountains which guard the plain of Philippi on the coast-side fall apart just behind Kavalla, and render the construction of a road there entirely easy. No other such defile exists at any other point in this line of formidable hills. It is impossible to view the configuration of the country from the sea, and not feel at once that the only natural place for crossing into the interior is this breakdown in the vicinity of Kavalla.

---

a Colonel Leake did not visit either this Kavalla or the other, and his assertion that there are " the ruins of a Greek city " there (which he supposes, however, to have been Galepsus, and not Neapolis) appears to rest on Cousinéry's statement. But as involving this claim of Eski Kavalla in still greater doubt, it may be added that the situation of Galepsus itself is quite uncertain. Dr. Arnold (note on Thucyd. iv. 107) places it near the mouth of the Strymon, and hence much

further west than Leake supposes. According to Cousinéry, Galepsus is to be sought at Kavalla.

b On p. 119 he says again : " Les ruines de l'ancienne ville de Néapolis se composent principalement des restes d'un château du moyen âge entièrement abandonné et peu accessible."

c * The recent French explorers (*Mission Archéologique*) make the distance from 12 to 18 kilomètres, *i. e.* about 9 Roman miles.   H.

Fourthly, the notices of the ancient writers lead us to adopt the same view. Thus Dio Cassius says (*Hist. Rom.* xlvii. 35), that Neapolis was opposite Thasos (κατ' ἀντικέρας Θάσου), and that is the situation of Kavalla. It would be much less correct, if correct at all, to say that the other Kavalla was so situated, since no part of the island extends so far to the west. Appian says (*Bell. Civ.* iv. 106), that the camp of the Republicans near the Gangas, the river (ποταμός) at Philippi, was nine Roman miles from their triremes at Neapolis (it was considerably further to the other place), and that Thasos was twelve Roman miles from their naval station (so we should understand the text); the latter distance appropriate again to Kavalla, but not to the harbor further west.

Finally, the ancient Itineraries support entirely the identification in question. Both the Antonine and the Jerusalem Itineraries show that the Egnatian Way passed through Philippi. They mention Philippi and Neapolis as next to each other in the order of succession; and since the line of travel which these Itineraries sketch was the one which led from the west to Byzantium, or Constantinople, it is reasonable to suppose that the road, after leaving Philippi, would pursue the most convenient and direct course to the east which the nature of the country allows. If the road, therefore, was constructed on this obvious principle, it would follow the track of the present Turkish road, and the next station, consequently, would be Neapolis, or Kavalla, on the coast, at the termination of the only natural defile across the intervening mountains. The distance, as has been said, is about ten miles. The Jerusalem Itinerary gives the distance between Philippi and Neapolis as ten Roman miles, and the Antonine Itinerary as twelve miles. The difference in the latter case is unimportant, and not greater than in some other instances where the places in the two Itineraries are unquestionably the same. It must be several miles further than this from Philippi to Old Kavalla, and hence the Neapolis of the Itineraries could not be at that point. The theory of Tafel is, that Akontisma or Herkontroma (the same place, without doubt), which the Itineraries mention next to Neapolis, was at the present Kavalla, and Neapolis at Leutere or Faki Kavalla. This theory, it is true, arranges the places in the order of the Itineraries; but, as Leake objects, there would be a needless detour of nearly twenty miles, and that through a region much more difficult than the direct way. The more accredited view is that Akontisma was beyond Kavalla, further east.

Neapolis, therefore, like the present Kavalla, was on a high rocky promontory which juts out into the Ægean. The harbor, a mile and a half wide at the entrance, and half a mile broad, lies on the west side. The indifferent roadstead on the east should not be called a harbor. Symbolum, 1670 feet high, with a defile which leads into the plain of Philippi, comes down near to the coast a little to the west of the town. In winter the sun sinks behind Mount Athos in the southwest as early as 4 o'clock P. M. The land along the eastern shore is low, and otherwise unmarked by any peculiarity. The island of Thasos bears a little to the S. E., twelve or fifteen miles distant. Plane-trees just beyond the walls, not less than four or five hundred years old, cast their shadow over the road which Paul followed on his way to Philippi. Kavalla has a population of five or six thousand, nine-tenths of whom are Mussulmans, and the rest Greeks.

For Neapolis as the Greek name of Shechem, now *Nabulus*, see SHECHEM.   H. B. H.

* The region of Neapolis or Macedonia appears to have been the northern limit of Paul's travels. It may have been in this country and climate that the Apostle suffered some of the privations (among which were "cold" and "nakedness") of which he writes in 2 Cor. xi. 27. The winter, for example, of 1857 is said to have been one of great severity. Symbolum, over which the road passes to Philippi from the coast, was covered with deep snow, and the road thence onward to Thessalonica became for a time impassable. Shepherds and travellers were frozen to death, and the flocks were destroyed in a frightful manner. During a sojourn there of two weeks in December, 1858, the thermometer fell repeatedly below zero. Huge icicles hung from the arches of the old aqueduct. All the streams and pools were frozen, and Thasos in the distance appeared white with snow to the very shore. For successive days the streets of Kavalla were almost deserted. It is not at all improbable that the Apostle's first sojourn in Macedonia, and perhaps part of his second, fell in that season of the year. The Apostle arrived in Macedonia on his second visit early in the summer; for, remaining at Ephesus until Pentecost (as may be inferred from 1 Cor. xvi. 8), and tarrying for a short time at Troas (2 Cor. ii. 12, 13), he then proceeded directly to Macedonia. But as he went, at this time, westward as far as Illyricum (Rom. xv. 19), and as he spent but three months at Corinth before his return to Macedonia, at the time of the succeeding Pentecost (Acts xx. 6), he must have prolonged his stay in northern Greece into or through December.

Kavalla (*Cavallo*, so common in many of the books, is unknown on the ground) consists of an inner or upper part, inclosed by a crenelated mediæval wall, and an outer part or suburb, also surrounded by a wall, but of more recent construction. Even the outer wall does not include the entire promontory, but leaves the western slope outside, part of which is tilled, and the remainder is naked rock. The celebrated Mohammed Ali, Pasha of Egypt, was born here in 1769. He showed, through life, a warm attachment to his native place; and, among the proofs of this, was his munificent endowment of a *madreseh*, or college, in which at the present time three hundred scholars are taught and supported, without any expense to themselves. The funds are so ample, that doles of bread and rice are given out, daily, to hundreds of the inhabitants of Kavalla. Just before his death in 1848, the Pasha made a final visit to his birthplace. On landing he went to the house in which he was born; but remained there only a few hours, and having spent these in religious worship, under the roof which first sheltered him, hastened back to his ship, and the next day departed for Egypt. (For other information see *Bibl. Sacra* as above.)   H.

* NEAP'OLIS, a later name of Emmaus in the south of Palestine. [EMMAUS, 2.]

NEARI'AH (נְעַרְיָה [*servant of Jehovah*]: Νααβία; [Vat. Νωαδεια; Comp. Νεαρία:] *Naaria*). 1. One of the six sons of Shemaiah in the line of the royal family of Judah after the Captivity (1 Chr. iii. 22, 23).

2. [Comp. Νααρία.] A son of Ishi, and one of the captains of the 500 Simeonites who, in the

days of Hezekiah, drove out the Amalekites from Mount Seir (1 Chr. iv. 42).

NE'BAI [2 syl.] (נוֹבָי; Keri, נֵיבָי [perh. *fruitful*]: Ναβαί; [Vat. FA. Βωναι:] *Nebaï*). A family of the heads of the people who signed the covenant with Nehemiah (Neh. x. 19). The LXX. followed the written text, while the Vulgate adopted the reading of the margin.

NEBA'IOTH, [3 syl.] **NEBA'JOTH** (נְבָיוֹת) [*height:* in Gen. xxv. 13, Ναβαιώθ; xxviii. 9, Rom. Ναβεωθ:] Ναβαιώθ: *Nabajoth*). the "first-born of Ishmael" (Gen. xxv. 13; 1 Chr. i. 29), and father of a pastoral tribe named after him, the "rams of Nebaioth" being mentioned by the prophet Isaiah (lx. 7) with the flocks of Kedar. From the days of Jerome (*Comment. in Gen. xx. 13*), this people had been identified with the Nabathæans, until M. Quatremère first investigated the origin of the latter, their language, religion, and history; and by the light he threw on a very obscure subject enabled us to form a clearer judgment respecting this assumed identification than was, in the previous state of knowledge, possible. It will be convenient to recapitulate, briefly, the results of M. Quatremère's labors, with those of the later works of M. Chwolson and others on the same subject, before we consider the grounds for identifying the Nabathæans with Nebaioth.

From the works of Arab authors, M. Quatremère (*Mémoire sur les Nabatéens*, Paris, 1835, reprinted from the *Nouveau Journ. Asiat.* Jan.-Mar., 1835) proved the existence of a nation called Nabat

(نَبَط), or Nabeet (نَبِيط), pl. Anbát (أَنْبَاط), (*Sihâh* and *Kámoos*), reputed to be of ancient origin, of whom scattered remnants existed in Arab times, after the era of the Flight. The Nabat, in the days of their early prosperity, inhabited the country chiefly between the Euphrates and the Tigris, Beyn en Nahreyn and El-Irák (the Mesopotamia and Chaldæa of the classics). That this was their chief seat and that they were Aramæans, or more accurately Syro-Chaldæans, seems in the present state of the inquiry (for it will presently be seen that, by the publication of oriental texts, our knowledge may be very greatly enlarged) to be a safe conclusion. The Arabs loosely apply the name Nabat to the Syrians, or especially the eastern Syrians, to the Syro-Chaldæans, etc. Thus El-Mes'oodee (*ap.* Quatremère, *l. c.*) says, "The Syrians are the same as the Nabathæans (Nabat). . . . The Nimrods were the kings of the Syrians whom the Arabs call Nabathæans. . . . The Chaldæans are the same as the Syrians, otherwise called Nabat (*Kitáb et-Tenbeeh*). The Nabathæans . . . founded the city of Babylon. . . . The inhabitants of Nineveh were part of those whom we call Nabeet or Syrians, who form one nation and speak one language; that of the Nabeet differs only in a small number of letters; but the foundation of the language is identical " (*Kitáb Murooj-edh-Dhahab*). These, and many other fragmentary passages, prove sufficiently the existence of a great Aramæan people called Nabat, celebrated among the Arabs for their knowledge of agriculture, and of magic, astronomy, medicine, and science (so called) generally. But we have stronger evidence to this effect. Quatremère introduced to the notice of the learned world the most important relic of that people's literature, a

treatise on Nabat agriculture. A study of an imperfect copy of that work, which unfortunately was all he could gain access to, induced him to date it about the time of Nebuchadnezzar, or *cir.* B. C. 600. M. Chwolson, professor of oriental languages at St. Petersburg, who had shown himself fitted for the inquiry by his treatise on the Sabians and their religion (*Die Ssabier und der Ssabismus*), has since made that book a subject of special study; and in his *Remains of Ancient Babylonian Literature in Arabic Translations* (*Ueber die Ueberreste der Alt-Babylonischen Literatur in Arabischen Uebersetzungen*, St. Petersburg, 1859), he has published the results of his inquiry. Those results, while they establish all M. Quatremère had advanced respecting the existence of the Nabat, go far beyond him both in the antiquity and the importance M. Chwolson claims for that people. Ewald, however, in 1857, stated some grave causes for doubting this antiquity, and again in 1859 (both papers appeared in the *Goettingische gelehrte Anzeigen*) repeated moderately but decidedly his misgivings. M. Renan followed on the same side (*Journ. de l' Institut*, Ap.-May, 1860); and more recently, M. de Gutschmid (*Zeitschrift d. Deutsch. Morgenländ. Gesellschaft*, xv. 1-100) has attacked the whole theory in a lengthy essay. The limits of this Dictionary forbid us to do more than recapitulate, as shortly as possible, the bearings of this remarkable inquiry, as far as they relate to the subject of the article.

The remains of the literature of the Nabat consist of four works, one of them a fragment: the "Book of Nabat Agriculture" (already mentioned); the "Book of Poisons;" the "Book of Tenkeloosha the Babylonian;" and the "Book of the Secrets of the Sun and Moon" (Chwolson, *Ueberreste*, pp. 10, 11). They purport to have been translated, in the year 904, by Aboo-Bekr Ahmad Ibn-'Alee the Chaldean of Kisseen,[a] better known as *Ibn-Wahsheeyeh*. The "Book of Nabat Agriculture" was, according to the Arab translator, commenced by Daghreeth, continued by Yánbushádh, and completed by Kuthámee. Chwolson, disregarding the dates assigned to these authors by the translator, thinks that the earliest lived some 2500 years B. C., the second some 300 or 400 years later, and Kuthámee, to whom he ascribes the chief authorship (Ibn-Wahsheeyeh says he was little more than editor), at the earliest under the 6th king of a Cannanite dynasty mentioned in the book, which dynasty Chwolson — with Bunsen — makes the same as the 5th (or Arabian) dynasty of Berosus (Chwolson, *Ueberreste*, p. 68, &c.; Bunsen, *Egypt*, iii. 432, &c.; Cory's *Ancient Fragments*, 2d ed. p. 60), or of the 13th century B. C. It will thus be seen that he rejects most of M. Quatremère's reasons for placing the work in the time of Nebuchadnezzar. It is remarkable that that great king is not mentioned, and the author or authors were, it is argued by Chwolson, ignorant not only of the existence of Christianity, but of the kingdom and faith of Israel. While these and other reasons, if granted, strengthen M. Chwolson's case for the antiquity of the work, on the other hand it is urged that even neglecting the difficulties attending an Arab's translating so ancient a writing (and we reject altogether the supposition that it was modernized as being without a parallel, at least in *Arabic* literature), and conceding that

---

[a] Or Keysee. See Chwolson, *Ueberreste*, p. 8, note. De Lacy's *'Abd-el-Lateef*, p. 484.

he was of Chaldæan or Nabat race — we encounter
formidable intrinsic difficulties. The book contains mentions of personages bearing names closely
resembling those of Adam, Seth, Enoch, Noah,
Shem, Nimrod, and Abraham; and M. Chwolson
himself is forced to confess that the particulars
related of them are in some respects similar to those
recorded of the Biblical patriarchs. If this difficulty proves insurmountable, it shows that the
author borrowed from the Bible, or from late Jews,
and destroys the claim of an extreme antiquity.
Other apparent evidences of the same kind are
not wanting. Such are the mentions of Ermeeshá
(Hermes), Agáthádeemoon (Agathodæmon), Tammuz (Adonis), and Yoonán (Ionians). It is even
a question whether the work should not be dated
several centuries after the commencement of our
era. Anachronisms, it is asserted, abound; geographical, linguistic (the use of late words and
phrases), historical, and religious (such as the traces
of Hellenism, as shown in the mention of Hermes,
etc., and influences to be ascribed to Neoplatonism).
The whole style is said to be modern, wanting the
rugged vigor of antiquity (this, however, is a delicate issue, to be tried only by the ripest scholarship). And while Chwolson dates the oldest part
of the Book of Agriculture B. C. 2500, and the
Book of Tenkelooshá in the 1st century, A. D. at
the latest (p. 136), Renan asserts that the two are
so similar as to preclude the notion of their being
separated by any great interval of time (Journal
de l'Institut).

Although Quatremère recovered the broad outlines of the religion and language of the Nabat, a
more extended knowledge of these points hangs
mainly on the genuineness or spuriousness of the
work of Kuthámee. If M. Chwolson's theory is
correct, that people present to us one of the most
ancient forms of idolatry; and by their writings
we can trace the origin and rise of successive
phases of pantheism, and the roots of the complicated forms of idolatry, heresy, and philosophical
infidelity, which abound in the old seats of the
Aramæan race. At present, we may conclude that

they were Sabians (صَابِيُوف), a at least in late

times, as Sabeism succeeded the older religions;
and their doctrines seem to have approached (how
nearly a further knowledge of these obscure subjects will show) those of the Mendá'ees, Mendaites,
or Gnostics. Their language presents similar difficulties; according to M. Chwolson, it is the ancient
language of Babylonia. A cautious criticism would
(till we know more) assign it a place as a comparatively modern dialect of Syro-Chaldee (comp. Quatremère, Mém. 100–103).

Thus, if M. Chwolson's results are accepted,
the Book of Nabat Agriculture exhibits to us an
ancient civilization, before that of the Greeks, and
at least as old as that of the Egyptians, of a great
and powerful nation of remote antiquity; making us acquainted with sages hitherto unknown,
and with the religious and sciences they either
founded or advanced; and throwing a flood of
light on what has till now been one of the darkest
pages of the world's history. But until the original text of Kuthámee's treatise is published, we
must withhold our acceptance of facts so startling,

and regard the antiquity ascribed to it even by
Quatremère as extremely doubtful. It is sufficient for the present to know that the most important facts advanced by the latter — the most
important when regarded by sober criticism — are
supported by the results of the later inquiries of
M. Chwolson and others It remains for us to
state the grounds for connecting the Nabat with
the Nabathæans.

As the Arabs speak of the Nabat as Syrians, so
conversely the Greeks and Romans knew the Nabathæans (οἱ Ναβαταῖοι and Ναβαταῖοι, LXX.;
Alex. Ναβατεοι; Nabuthæi, Vulg.: 'Αναταῖοι, or
Ναναταῖοι, Pt. vi. 7, § 21; Ναβίται, Suid. s. v.:
Nabathæ) as Arabs. While the inhabitants of
the peninsula were comparative strangers to the
classical writers, and very little was known of the
further-removed peoples of Chaldæa and Mesopotamia, the Nabathæans bordered the well-known
Egyptian and Syrian provinces. The nation was
famous for its wealth and commerce. Even when,
by the decline of its trade (diverted through Egypt),
its prosperity waned, Petra is still mentioned as a
centre of the trade both of the Sabæans of Southern Arabia [SHEBA] and the Gerrhæans on the
Persian Gulf. It is this extension across the desert
that most clearly connects the Nabathæan colony
with the birthplace of the nation in Chaldæa.
The notorious trade of Petra across the well-
trodden desert-road to the Persian gulf is sufficient
to account for the presence of this colony; just as
traces of Abrahamic peoples [DEDAN, etc.] are
found, demonstrably, on the shores of that sea on
the east, and on the borders of Palestine on the
west, while along the northern limits of the Arabian peninsula remains of the caravan stations still
exist. Nothing is more certain than the existence
of this great stream of commerce, from remote
times, until the opening of the Egyptian route
gradually destroyed it. Josephus (Ant. i. 12, § 4)
speaks of Nabatæa (Ναβαταία, Strab.; Ναβατηνή,
Joseph.) as embracing the country from the Euphrates to the Red Sea — i. e. Petræa and all the
desert east of it. The Nabat of the Arabs, however, are described as famed for agriculture and
science; in these respects offering a contrast to the
Nabathæans of Petra, who were found by the
expedition sent by Antigonus (B. C. 312) to be
dwellers in tents, pastoral, and conducting the
trade of the desert; but in the Red Sea again they
were piratical, and by sea-faring qualities showed
a non-Semitic character.

We agree with M. Quatremère (Mém. p. 81),
while rejecting other of his reasons, that the civilization of the Nabathæans of Petra, far advanced
on that of the surrounding Arabs, is not easily explained except by supposing them to be a different
people from those Arabs. A remarkable confirmation of this supposition is found in the character
of the buildings of Petra, which are unlike anything constructed by a purely Semitic race. Architecture is a characteristic of Aryan or mixed
races. In Southern Arabia, Nigritians and Semites (Joktanites) together built huge edifices; so in
Babylonia and Assyria, and so too in Egypt, mixed
races left this unmistakable mark. [ARABIA.]
Petra, while it is wanting in the colossal features
of those more ancient remains, is yet unmistakably
foreign to an unmixed Semitic race. Further, the
subjects of the literature of the Nabat, which are
scientific and industrial, are not such as are found
in the writings of pure Semites or Aryans, as Renan

---

a Sabi-ees is commonly held by the Arabs to signify
originally "Apostates."

131

(*Hist. des Langues Sémitiques*, p. 227) has well observed; and he points, as we have above, to a foreign ("Couschite," or partly Nigritian) settlement in Babylonia. It is noteworthy that 'Abd-el-Lateef (at the end of the fourth section of his first book, or treatise, see De Lacy's ed.) likens the Copts in Egypt (a mixed race) to the Nabat in El-'Irâk.

From most of these, and other considerations,[a] we think there is no reasonable doubt that the Nabathæans of Arabia Petræa were the same people as the Nabat of Chaldæa; though at what ancient epoch the western settlement was formed remains unknown.[b] That it was not of any importance until after the Captivity appears from the notices of the inhabitants of Edom in the canonical books, and their absolute silence respecting the Nabathæans, except (if Nebaioth be identified with them) the passage in Isaiah (lx. 7).

The Nabathæans were allies of the Jews after the Captivity, and Judas the Maccabee, with Jonathan, while at war with the Edomites, came on them three days south of Jordan (1 Macc. v. 3, 24, &c.; Joseph. *Ant.* xii. 8, § 3), and afterwards "Jonathan had sent his brother John, a captain of the people, to pray his friends the Nabathites that they might leave with them their carriage, which was much " (ix. 35, 36). Diod. Sic. gives much information regarding them, and so too Strabo, from the expedition under Ælius Gallus, the object of which was defeated by the treachery of the Nabathæans (see the *Dict. of Geography*, to which the history of Nabatæa in classical times properly belongs).

Lastly, did the Nabathæans, or Nabat, derive their name, and were they in part descended, from Nebaioth, son of Ishmael? Josephus says that Nabatæa was inhabited by the twelve sons of Ishmael: and Jerome, " Nebaioth omnis regio ab Euphrate usque ad Mare Rubrum Nabathena usque hodie dicitur, quæ pars Arabiæ est " (*Comment. in* Gen. xxv. 13). Quatremère rejects the identification for an etymological reason — the change of ת to ط; but this change is not unusual; in words Arabicized from the Greek, the like change of τ generally occurs. Renan, on the other hand, accepts it; regarding Nebaioth, after his manner, merely as an ancient name unconnected with the Biblical history. The Arabs call Nebaioth, Nábit (نَابِت), and do not connect him with the Nabat, to whom they give a different descent; but all their Abrahamic genealogies come from late Jews, and are utterly untrustworthy. When we remember the darkness that enshrouds the early history of the " sons of the concubines " after they were sent into the east country, we hesitate to deny a relationship between peoples whose names are strikingly similar, dwelling in the same tract. It is possible that Nebaioth went to the far east, to the country of his grandfather Abraham, intermarried

with the Chaldæans, and gave birth to a mixed race, the Nabat. Instances of ancient tribes adopting the name of more modern ones, with which they have become fused, are frequent in the history of the Arabs (see MIDIAN, foot-note); but we think it is also admissible to hold that Nebaioth was so named by the sacred historian because he intermarried with the Nabat. It is, however, safest to leave unsettled the identification of Nebaioth and Nabat until another link be added to the chain that at present seems to connect them.   E. S. P.

NEBAL'LAT (נְבַלָּט [perh. *projection, spur*, Dietr.; *hard, firm soil*, Fürst]: Vat. [Rom. Alex.] omit; Alex. [rather, FA.⁸] Ναβαλλατ: *Neballat*), a town of Benjamin, one of those which the Benjamites reoccupied after the Captivity (Neh. xi. 34), but not mentioned in the original catalogue of allotment (comp. Josh. xviii. 11-28). It is here named with ZEBOIM, LOD, and ONO. Lod is Lydda, the modern *Lŭdd*, and Ono not impossibly *Kefr Aunu*, four miles to the north of it. East of these, and forming nearly an equilateral triangle with them,[c] is *Beit Nebâla* (Rob. ii. 232), which is possibly the *locum tenens* of the ancient village. Another place of very nearly the same name, *Bir Nebâla*, lies to the east of *el-Jib* (Gibeon), and within half a mile of it. This would also be within the territory of Benjamin, and although further removed from Lod and Ono, yet if ZEBOIM should on investigation prove (as is not impossible) to be in one of the wadies which penetrate the eastern side of this trict and lead down to the Jordan Valley (comp. 1 Sam. xiii. 18), then, in that case, this situation might not be unsuitable for Neballat.   G.

NE'BAT (נְבָט [*view, aspect*, Ges.: *cultivation?* Fürst]: Ναβάτ; [Vat. in 1 K. Ναβαθ and Ναβατ, elsewhere Ναβατ:] *Nabat*, but *Nabath* in 1 K. xi.). The father of Jeroboam, whose name is only preserved in connection with that of his distinguished son (1 K. xi. 26, xii. 2, 15, xv. 1, xvi. 3, 26, 31, xxi. 22, xxii. 52; 2 K. iii. 3, ix. 9, x. 29, xiii. 2, 11, xiv. 24, xv. 9, 18, 24, 28, xvii. 21, xxiii. 15; 2 Chr. ix. 29, x. 2, 15, xiii. 6). He is described as an Ephrathite, or Ephraimite, of Zereda in the Jordan Valley, and appears to have died while his son was young. The Jewish tradition preserved in Jerome (*Quæst. Hebr. in lib. Reg.*) identifies him with Shimei of Gera, who was a Benjamite. [JEROBOAM.]

NE'BO, MOUNT (הַר־נְבוֹ [*Mount Nebo*, i. e., a heathen god = Mercury]: ὄρος Ναβαῦ: means *Nebo*). The mountain from which Moses took his first and last view of the Promised Land (Deut. xxxii. 49, xxxiv. 1). It is so minutely described, that it would seem impossible not to recognise it: in the land of Moab; facing Jericho; the head or summit of a mountain called the Pisgah, which again seems to have formed a portion of the general range of the " mountains of Abarim." Its position is further denoted by the mention of the valley (or perhaps more correctly the ravine) in

---

[a] We have not entered into the subject of the language of the Nabathæans. The little that is known of it tends to strengthen the theory of the Chaldæan origin of that people. The Duc de Luynes, in a paper on the coins of the latter in the *Revue Numismatique* (nouv. série, III. 1858), adduces facts to show that they called themselves Nabat נ טב‎.

[b] It is remarkable that, while remnants of the Nabat

are mentioned by trustworthy Arab writers as existing in their own day, no Arab record connecting that people with Petra has been found. Caussin believes this to have arisen from the Chaldæan speech of the Nabathæans, and their corruption of Arabic (*Essai sur l'Hist. des Arabes avant l'Islamisme*, i. 38).

[c] Schwarz (p. 134), with less than usual accuracy, places " Beth-Naballa " at " five miles south of Ramleh." It is really about that distance N. E. of it.

which Moses was buried, and which was apparently one of the clefts of the mount itself (xxxii. 50) — "the ravine in the land of Moab facing Beth-Peor" (xxxiv. 6). And yet, notwithstanding the minuteness of this description, no one has yet succeeded in pointing out any spot which answers to Nebo. Viewed from the western side of Jordan (the nearest point at which most travellers are able to view them) the mountains of Moab present the appearance of a wall or cliff, the upper line of which is almost straight and horizontal. "There is no peak or point perceptibly higher than the rest; but all is one apparently level line of summit without peaks or gaps" (Rob. *Bibl. Res.* i. 570). "On ne distingue pas un sommet, pas la moindre cime; seulement on aperçoit, çà et là, de legères inflexions, *comme si la main du peintre qui a tracé cette ligne horizontale sur le ciel eût tremblé dans quelques endroits*" (Chateaubriand, *Itinéraire*, part 3). "Possibly," continues Robinson, "on travelling among these mountains, some isolated point or summit might be found answering to the position and character of Nebo." Two such points have been named. (1.) Seetzen (March 17, 1806; *Reise*, vol. i. 408) seems to have been the first to suggest the *Dschibbal Attarús* (between the *Wady Zerka-Main* and the Arnon, 3 miles below the former, and 10 or 12 south of Heshbon) as the Nebo of Moses. In this he is followed (though probably without any communication) by Burckhardt (July 14, 1812), who mentions it as the highest point in that locality, and therefore probably "Mount *Nebo* of the Scripture." This is adopted by Irby and Mangles, 'hough with hesitation (*Travels*, June 8, 1818).

(2.) The other elevation above the general summit level of these highlands is the *Jebel 'Osha*, or *Ausha'*, or *Jebel el-Jil'âd*, "the highest point in all the eastern mountains," "overtopping the whole of the *Belka*, and rising about 3000 feet above the *Ghôr*" (Burckhardt, July 2, 1812; Robinson, i. 537 *note*, 570).

But these eminences are alike wanting in one main essential of the Nebo of the Scripture, which is stated to have been "facing Jericho," words which in the widest interpretation must imply that it was "some elevation immediately over the last stage of the Jordan," while '*Osha* and *Attarús* are equally remote in opposite directions, the one 15 miles north, the other 15 miles south of a line drawn eastward from Jericho. Another requisite for the identification is, that a view should be obtainable from the summit, corresponding to that prospect over the whole land which Moses is said to have had from Mount Nebo: even though, as Professor Stanley has remarked (*S. & P.* 301), that was a view which in its full extent must have been imagined rather than actually seen.[a] The view from *Jebel Jil'ad* has been briefly described by Mr. Porter (*Handb.* 309), though without reference to the possibility of its being Nebo. Of that from *Jebel Attarús*, no description is extant, for, almost incredible as it seems, none of the travellers above named, although they believed it to be Nebo, appear to have made any attempt to deviate so far from their route as to ascend an eminence, which, if their conjectures be correct, must be the most interesting spot in the world.   G.

---

[a] This view was probably identical with that seen by Balaam (Num. xxiii. 14). It is beautifully drawn out in detail by Prof. Stanley (*S. & P.* 299).

* It is a pleasure to add, that since the date of the preceding article, the lost Nebo from which Moses beheld the land of promise, just before his death, has in all probability been identified. De Saulcy may have singled out the right summit, but he did not verify his conjecture, and we are mainly indebted to Mr. Tristram for the discovery. This traveller ascended one of the ridges or "brows" of the Abarim or Moab Mountains, on the east of the Jordan, which in its position and the wide prospect which it commands agrees remarkably with the Biblical account. It is about three miles southwest of *Heshbân* (Heshbon), and about a mile and a half due west of *Main* (Baal-Meon). It overlooks the mouth of the Jordan, "over against Jericho" (Deut. xxxiv. 1), and the gentle slope of its sides may well answer to "the field of Zophim" (Num. xxiii. 14). It is not an isolated peak, but one of "a succession of bare turf-clad eminences, so linked together that the depressions between them were mere hollows rather than valleys." It is "the highest" of these, which differ, however, so little that Mr. Tristram thought it impossible "to pitch upon the exact Pisgah with certainty."

It must be left to the traveller's own words to describe the magnificent panorama which lies spread out before the eye from this summit.

"The altitude of the brow cannot be less than 4,500 feet, so completely does it overlook the heights of Hebron and of Central Judæa. To the eastward, as we turned round, the ridge seemed gently to slope for two or three miles, when a few small ruin-clad 'tells' or hillocks (*Heshbân*, *Main*, and others) broke the monotony of the outline; and then, sweeping forth, rolled in one vast unbroken expanse the goodly *Belka* — one boundless plain, stretching far into Arabia, till lost in the horizon — one waving ocean of corn and grass. Well may the Arabs boast, 'Thou canst not find a country like the *Belka*.' . . . . As the eye turned southwards towards the line of the ridge on which we were clustered, the peak of *Jebel Shihân* just stood out behind *Jebel Attarús*, which opened to reveal to us the situation of *Kerak*, though not its walls. Beyond and behind these, sharply rose Mounts Hor and Seir, and the rosy granite peaks of Arabia faded away into the distance towards *Akabah*. Still turning westwards, in front of us, two or three lines of terraces reduced the height of the plateau as it descended to the Dead Sea, the western outline of which we could trace, in its full extent, from *Usdum* to *Feshkhah*. It lay like a long strip of molten metal, with the sun mirrored on its surface, waving and undulating on its further edge, unseen on its eastern limits, as though poured from some deep cavern beneath our feet. There, almost in the centre of the line, a break in the ridge and a green spot below marked Engedi, the nest once of the Kenite, now of the wild goat. The fortress of *Masada* and jagged *Shukif* rose above the mountain-line, but still far below us, and lower, too, than the ridge of Hebron, which we could trace, as it lifted gradually from the southwest, as far as Bethlehem and Jerusalem. The buildings of Jerusalem we could not see, though all the familiar points in the neighborhood were at once identified. *There* was the Mount of Olives, with the church at its top, the gap in the hills leading up from Jericho, and the rounded heights of Benjamin on its other side. Still turning northward, the eye was riveted by the deep *Ghôr*, with the rich green islets of *Ain Sultân* and *Ain Dûk* — the twin oases, nestling, as it were, under the wall of

Quarantania [the traditional scene of Christ's temptation] There — closer still, beneath us — had Israel's last camp extended, in front of the green fringe which peeped forth from under the terraces in our foreground. The dark sinuous bed of Jordan, clearly defined near its mouth, was soon lost in dim haze. Then, looking over it, the eye rested on Gerizim's rounded top; and, further still, opened the plain of Esdraelon, a shoulder of Carmel, or some other intervening height, just showing to the right of Gerizim; while the faint and distant bluish haze beyond it told us that there was the sea, the utmost sea. It seemed as if but a whiff were needed to brush off the haze and reveal it clearly. Northwards, again, rose the distinct outline of unmistakable Tabor, aided by which we could identify Gilboa and *Jebel Duhy.* Snowy Hermon's top was mantled with cloud, and Lebanon's highest range must have been exactly shut behind it; but in front, due north of us, stretched in long line the dark forests of *Ajlun,* bold and undulating, with the steep sides of mountains here and there whitened by cliffs; terminating in Mount Gilead, behind *es-Salt.* To the northeast the vast Hauran stretched beyond, filling in the horizon line to the *Belka,* between which and the Hauran (Bashan) there seems to be no natural line of separation. The tall range of *Jebel Hauran,* behind Bozrah, was distinctly visible." (*Land of Israel,* pp. 541-543, 2d ed.)

De Saulcy reports that he heard this mountain (it seems to have been this) called *Nebbeh* (Neb) by the Arabs; but the statement needs confirmation. Mr. Tristram states his own conclusion thus: " We were undoubtedly on the range of Nebo, among the highlands of Abarim, and in selecting this highest point, the crest just west of *Main,* we might reasonably flatter ourselves that we stood on Pisgah's top." [NEBO.] Mr. Grove, who in the above article rejects all previous claims to the identification of this Nebo, admits now (Clark's *Bible Atlas,* p. 104), that "probably " *Jebel Nebbah* is the mount in question. The difficulty in regard to the possibility of seeing so far has been exaggerated. An oriental atmosphere, as compared with our own, has a transparency which is marvelous. Dr. Thomson, who has dwelt more than a quarter of a century amid the scenery of Lebanon, says (*Land and Book,* i. p. 18) that he can show " many a Pisgah in Lebanon and Hermon from which the view is far more extensive " than that on which the eye of Moses rested as he looked abroad from Nebo. We are to remember, too, that, though the Hebrew lawgiver was a hundred and twenty years old when he died, we are expressly told that " his eye was not dim nor his natural force abated " (Deut. xxxiv. 7).   H.

NE'BO (נְבֹו [see above]). 1. (Ναβαῦ: *Nebo*

---

a The name is omitted in this passage in the Vatican LXX. The Alex. MSS. has τὴν βαμα.

b See MOAB, p. 1984 *a.*

c Selden (*De D's Syr. Synt.* ii. cap. 12) assumes on the authority of Hesychius' interpretation of Is. xv. 1, that Dibon contained a temple or sanctuary of Nebo. But it would appear that Nebo the place, and not Nebo the divinity, is referred to in that passage.

d In another passage (*ad Esaiam,* xv. 2), Jerome states that the " consecrated idol of Chemosh — that is, Belphegor " — Baal Peor, resided in Nebo.

e *Kenawat,* the representative of Kenath, is 100 Roman miles N. E. of Heshbon.

---

and *Nabo.*) A town on the eastern side of Jordan, situated in the pastoral country (Num. xxxii. 3), one of those which were taken possession of and rebuilt by the tribe of Reuben (ver. 38).*a* In these lists it is associated with Kirjathaim and Baalmeon or Beon; and in another record (1 Chr. v. 8) with Aroer, as marking one extremity, possibly the west, of a principal part of the tribe. In the remarkable prophecy adopted *b* by Isaiah (xv. 2) and Jeremiah (xlviii. 1, 22) concerning Moab, Nebo is mentioned in the same connection as before, though no longer an Israelite town, but in the hands of Moab. It does not occur in the catalogue of the towns of Reuben in Joshua (xiii. 15-23): but whether this is an accidental omission, or whether it appears under another name — according to the statement of Num. xxxii. 38, that the Israelites changed the names of the heathen cities they retained in this district — is uncertain. In the case of Nebo, which was doubtless called after the deity *c* of that name, there would be a double reason for such a change (see Josh. xxiii. 7).

Neither is there anything to show whether there was a connection between Nebo the town and Mount Nebo. The notices of Eusebius and Jerome (*Onomasticon*) are confused, but they at least denote that the two were distinct and distant from each other.*d* The town (Ναβώρ and " Nabo ") they identify with Nobah or Kenath, and locate it 8 miles south *e* of Heshbon, where the ruins of *el-Habis* appear to stand at present; while the mountain (Ναβαῦ and " Naban ") is stated to be 6 miles east (Jer.) or west (Eus.) from the same spot.

In the list of places south of *es-Salt* given by Dr. Robinson (*Bibl. Res.* 1st ed. vol. iii. App. 170) one occurs named *Neba,* which may possibly be identical with Nebo, but nothing is known of its situation or of the character of the spot.

2. (Ναβού, Alex. Ναβω; in Neh. [Rom. Alex. Ναβία, FA. Ναβεια, Vat.] Ναβιαα: *Nebo.*) The children of Nebo (*Bene-Nebo*) to the number of fifty-two, are mentioned in the catalogue of the men of Judah and Benjamin, who returned from Babylon with Zerubbabel (Ez. ii. 29; Neh. vii. 33)*f.* Seven of them had foreign wives, whom they were compelled to discard (Ezr. x. 43). The name occurs between Bethel and Ai, and Lydda, which, if we may trust the arrangement of the list, implies that it was situated in the territory of Benjamin to the N. W. of Jerusalem. This is possibly the modern *Beit-Nûbah,* about 12 miles N. W. by W. of Jerusalem, 8 from Lydda, and close to *Yalo,* which seems to be the place mentioned by Jerome (*Onom.* " Anab," and " Anob;" and *Epit. Paulæ,* § 8) as Nob the city of the priests (though that identification is hardly admissible), and both in his and later times known as Bethannaba or Bettenuble.*g*

It is possible that this Nebo was an offshoot of

---

f In Neh. the name is given as the " other Nebo," נְבֹו אַחֵר (comp. ELAM), as if two places of that name were mentioned, but this is not the case.

g The words of William of Tyre (xiv. 8) are well worth quoting. They are evidently those of an eye witness. " Nobe qui hodie vulgari appellatione dicitur Bettenuble, *in descensu montium, in primis auspiciis* (aspiciis ?) *campestrium,* via quâ itur Liddam . . . . ibi enim in faucibus montium inter angustias inevitabiles . . . . Ascalonitis subitas irruptiones illic facere consuetis." Just as the Philistines did in the time of Saul. — Can this be Gob or Nob, where they were so frequently encountered?

that on the east of Jordan; in which case we have another town added to those already noticed in the territory of Benjamin which retain the names of foreign and heathen settlers. [BENJAMIN, vol. i. p. 277, note; MICHMASH; OPHNI.]

A town named Nomba is mentioned by the LXX. (not in Heb.) amongst the places in the south of Judah frequented by David (1 Sam. xxx. 30), but its situation forbids any attempt to identify this with Nebo. G.

NE'BO (נְבוֹ [see above]: Ναβώ, [Ναβαῦ; in Is., Alex. Δαγων:] Nabo), which occurs both in Isaiah (xlvi. 1) and Jeremiah (xlviii. 1) as the name of a Chaldæan god, is a well-known deity of the Babylonians and Assyrians. The original native name was, in Hamitic Babylonian, Nabiu, in Semitic Babylonian and Assyrian, Nabu. It is reasonably conjectured to be connected with the Hebrew נבא, "to prophesy," whence the common word נָבִיא, "prophet" (Arab. Neby). Nebo was the god who presided over learning and letters.

" Nebo."

He is called "the far-hearing," "he who possesses intelligence," "he who teaches or instructs." The wedge or arrow-head — the essential element of cuneiform writing — appears to have been his emblem; and hence he bore the name of Tir, which signifies "a shaft or arrow." His general character corresponds to that of the Egyptian Thoth, the Greek Hermes, and the Latin Mercury. Astronomically he is identified with the planet nearest the sun, called Nebo also by the Mendæans, and Tir by the ancient Persians.

Nebo was of Babylonian rather than of Assyrian origin. In the early Assyrian Pantheon he occu-

plies a very inferior position, being either omitted from the lists altogether, or occurring as the last of the minor gods. The king supposed to be Pul first brings him prominently forward in Assyria and then apparently in consequence of some peculiar connection which he himself had with Babylon. A statue of Nebo was set up by this monarch at Calah (Nimrud), which is now in the British Museum. It has a long inscription, written across the body, and consisting chiefly of the god's various epithets. In Babylonia Nebo held a prominent place from an early time. The ancient town of Borsippa was especially under his protection, and the great temple there (the modern Birs-Nimrud) was dedicated to him from a very remote age. [BABEL, TOWER OF.] He was the tutelar god of the most important Babylonian kings, in whose names the word Nabu, or Nebo, appears as an element: e. g. Nabo-nassar, Nabo-polassar, Nebuchadnezzar, and Nabo-nadius or Labynetus; and appears to have been honored next to Bel-Merodach by the later kings. Nebuchadnezzar completely rebuilt his temple at Borsippa, and called after him his famous seaport upon the Persian Gulf, which became known to the Greeks as Teredon or Diridotis — "given to Tir," i. e. to Nebo. The worship of Nebo appears to have continued at Borsippa to the 3d or 4th century after Christ, and the Sabæans of Harran may have preserved it even to a later date. (See the Essay On the Religion of the Babylonians and Assyrians, by Sir H. Rawlinson, in the 1st vol. of Rawlinson's Herodotus, pp. 637–640; and compare Norberg's Onomasticon, s. v. Nebo, pp. 98, 99.) G. R.

NEBUCHADNEZ'ZAR, or NEBUCHAD-REZ'ZAR (נְבֻכַדְנֶצַּר, [נְבוּכַדְנֶאצַּר, נְבוּכַדְרֶאצַּר: Ναβουχοδονόσορ: Nabuchodonosor), was the greatest and most powerful of the Babylonian kings. His name, according to the native orthography, is read as Nabu-kuduri-utsur, and is explained to mean "Nebo is the protector against misfortune," kuduri being connected with the Hebrew כִּידוֹר, "trouble" or "attack," and utsur being a participle from the root נָצַר "to protect.' The rarer Hebrew form, used by Jeremiah and Ezekiel, — Nebuchadrezzar, is thus very close indeed to the original. The Persian form, Nabukudrachara (Beh. Inscr. col. i. par. 16), is less correct; while the Greek equivalents are sometimes very wide of the mark. Ναβουκοδρόσορος, which was used by Abydenus and Megasthenes, is the best of them: Ναβοκολάσαρος, which appears in the Canon of Ptolemy, the worst. Strabo's Ναβοκοδρόσορος (xv. 1, § 6) and Berosus's Ναβουχοδονόσορος lie between these extremes.

Nebuchadnezzar was the son and successor of Nabopolassar, the founder of the Babylonian Empire. He appears to have been of marriageable age at the time of his father's rebellion against Assyria, B. C. 625; for, according to Abydenus (ap. Euseb. Chron. Can. i. 9), the alliance between this prince and the Median king was cemented by the betrothal of Amuhia, the daughter of the latter, to Nebuchadnezzar, Nabopolassar's son. Little further is known of him during his father's lifetime. It is suspected, rather than proved, that he was the leader of a Babylonian contingent which accompanied Cyaxares in his Lydian war [MEDES], by whose interposition, on the occasion of an eclipse, that war was brought to a close,[a] B. C. 610. At any rate, a few years later, he was placed at the head of a Babylonian army, and sent by his father, who was now old and infirm, to chastise the insolence of Pharaoh-Necho, king of Egypt. This prince had recently invaded Syria, defeated Josiah, king of Judah, at Megiddo, and reduced the whole tract, from Egypt to Carchemish on the upper Euphrates [CARCHEMISH], which in the partition of the Assyrian territories on the destruction of Nineveh had been assigned to Babylon (2 K. xxiii. 29, 30; Beros. ap. Joseph. c. Ap. i. 19). Necho had held possession of these countries for about three years, when (B. C. 605) Nebuchadnezzar led an army against him, defeated him at Carchemish in a great battle (Jer. xlvi. 2–12), recovered Cœle-syria, Phœnicia, and Palestine, took Jerusalem (Dan. i. 1, 2), pressed forward to Egypt, and was engaged in that country or upon its borders when intelligence arrived which recalled him hastily to Babylon. Nabopolassar, after reigning 21 years, had died, and the throne was vacant: for there is no reason to think that Nebuchadnezzar, though he appeared to be the "king of Babylon" to the Jews, had really been associated by his father. In some alarm about the succession he hurried back to the capital, accompanied only by his light troops; and crossing the desert, probably by way of Tadmor or Palmyra, reached Babylon before any disturbance had arisen, and entered peaceably on his kingdom (B. C. 604). The bulk of the army, with the captives — Phœnicians, Syrians, Egyptians, and Jews — returned by the ordinary route, which skirted instead of crossing the desert. It was at this time that Daniel and his companions were brought to Babylon, where they presently grew into favor with Nebuchadnezzar, and became persons of very considerable influence (Dan. i. 3–20).

Within three years of Nebuchadnezzar's first expedition into Syria and Palestine, disaffection again showed itself in those countries. Jehoiakim — who, although threatened at first with captivity (2 Chr. xxxvi. 5), had been finally maintained on the throne as a Babylonian vassal — after three years of service "turned and rebelled" against his suzerain, probably trusting to be supported by Egypt (2 K. xxiv. 1). Not long afterwards Phœnicia seems to have broken into revolt; and the Chaldæan monarch, who had previously endeavored to subdue the disaffected by his generals (ib. ver. 2), once more took the field in person, and marched first of all against Tyre. Having invested that city in the seventh year of his reign (Joseph. c. Ap. i. 21), and left a portion of his army there to continue the siege, he proceeded against Jerusalem, which submitted without a struggle. According to Josephus, who is here our chief authority, Nebuchadnezzar punished Jehoiakim with death (Ant. x. 6, § 3; comp. Jer. xxii. 18, 19, and xxxvi. 30), but placed his son Jehoiachin upon the throne. Jehoiachin reigned only three months; for, on his showing symptoms of disaffection, Nebuchadnezzar came up against Jerusalem for the third time, deposed the young prince (whom he carried to Babylon, together with a large portion of the population of the city, and the chief of the Temple treasures), and made his uncle, Zedekiah, king in his room. Tyre still held out; and it was not

till the thirteenth year from the time of its first investment that the city of merchants fell (B. C 585). Ere this happened, Jerusalem had been totally destroyed. This consummation was owing to the folly of Zedekiah, who, despite the warnings of Jeremiah, made a treaty with Apries (Hophra), king of Egypt (Ez. xvii. 16), and on the strength of this alliance renounced his allegiance to the king of Babylon. Nebuchadnezzar commenced the final siege of Jerusalem in the ninth year of Zedekiah, his own seventeenth year (B. C. 588), and took it two years later (B. C. 586). One effort to carry out the treaty seems to have been made by Apries. An Egyptian army crossed the frontier, and began its march towards Jerusalem; upon which Nebuchadnezzar raised the siege, and set off to meet the new foe. According to Josephus (Ant. x. 7, § 3) a battle was fought, in which Apries was completely defeated; but the Scriptural account seems rather to imply that the Egyptians retired on the advance of Nebuchadnezzar, and recrossed the frontier without risking an engagement (Jer. xxxvii. 5–8). At any rate the attempt failed, and was not repeated; the "broken reed, Egypt," proved a treacherous support, and after an eighteen months' siege Jerusalem fell. Zedekiah escaped from the city, but was captured near Jericho (ib. xxxix. 5) and brought to Nebuchadnezzar at Riblah in the territory of Hamath, where his eyes were put out by the king's order, while his sons and his chief nobles were slain. Nebuchadnezzar then returned to Babylon with Zedekiah, whom he imprisoned for the remainder of his life; leaving Nebuzar-adan, the captain of his guard, to complete the destruction of the city and the pacification of Judæa. Gedaliah, a Jew, was appointed governor, but he was shortly murdered, and the rest of the Jews either fled to Egypt, or were carried by Nebuzar-adan to Babylon.

The military successes of Nebuchadnezzar cannot be traced minutely beyond this point. His own annals have not come down to us; and the historical allusions which we find in his extant inscriptions are of the most vague and general character. It may be gathered from the prophetical Scriptures and from Josephus, that the conquest of Jerusalem was rapidly followed by the fall of Tyre and the complete submission of Phœnicia (Ez. xxvi.–xxviii.; Joseph. c. Ap. i. 21); after which the Babylonians carried their arms into Egypt, and inflicted severe injuries on that fertile country (Jer. xlvi. 13–26; Ez. xxix. 2–20; Joseph. Ant. x. 9, § 7). But we have no account, on which we can depend, of these campaigns. Our remaining notices of Nebuchadnezzar present him to us as a magnificent prince and beneficent ruler, rather than a warrior; and the great fame which has always attached to his name among the eastern nations depends rather on his buildings and other grand constructions than on any victories or conquests ascribed to him.

We are told by Berosus that the first care of Nebuchadnezzar, on obtaining quiet possession of his kingdom after the first Syrian expedition, was to rebuild the Temple of Bel (Bel-Merodach) at Babylon out of the spoils of the Syrian war (ap. Joseph. Ant. x. 11, § 1). He next proceeded to strengthen and beautify the city, which he reno-

---

[a] Herodotus terms this leader Labynetus (I. 74); a word which does not rightly render the Babylonian *Nabu-kuduri-uzur*, but does render another Babylonian name, *Nabu-nahit*. Nabopolassar may have had a son of this name; or the Labynetus of Herod. I. 74 may be Nabopolassar himself.

tated throughout, and surrounded with several lines of fortification, himself adding one entirely new quarter. Having finished the walls and adorned the gates magnificently, he constructed a new palace, adjoining the old residence of his father — a superb edifice, which he completed in fifteen days! In the grounds of this palace he formed the celebrated "hanging garden," which was a pleasaunce, built up with huge stones to imitate the varied surface of mountains, and planted with trees and shrubs of every kind. Diodorus, probably following Ctesias, describes this marvel as a square, four *plethra* (400 feet) each way, and 50 cubits (75 feet) high, approached by sloping paths, and supported on a series of arched galleries increasing in height from the base to the summit. In these galleries were various pleasant chambers; and one of them contained the engines by which water was raised from the river to the surface of the mound. This curious construction, which the Greek writers reckoned among the seven wonders of the world, was said to have been built by Nebuchadnezzar for the gratification of his wife, Amuhis, who, having been brought up among the Median mountains, desired something to remind her of them. Possibly, however, one object was to obtain a pleasure-ground at a height above that to which the musquitoes are accustomed to rise.

This complete renovation of Babylon by Nebuchadnezzar, which Berosus asserts, is confirmed to us in every possible way. The Standard Inscription of the king relates at length the construction of the whole series of works, and appears to have been the authority from which Berosus drew. The ruins confirm this in the most positive way, for nine-tenths of the bricks *in situ* are stamped with Nebuchadnezzar's name. Scripture, also, adds an indirect but important testimony, in the exclamation of Nebuchadnezzar recorded by Daniel, "Is not this great Babylon *which I have built?*" (Dan. iv. 30).

But Nebuchadnezzar did not confine his efforts to the ornamentation and improvement of his capital. Throughout the empire, at Borsippa, Sippara, Cutha, Chilmad, Duraba, Teredon, and a multitude of other places, he built or rebuilt cities, repaired temples, constructed quays, reservoirs, canals, and aqueducts, on a scale of grandeur and magnificence surpassing everything of the kind recorded in history, unless it be the constructions of one or two of the greatest Egyptian monarchs. "I have examined," says Sir H. Rawlinson, "the bricks *in situ*, belonging perhaps to a hundred different towns and cities in the neighborhood of Baghdad, and I never found any other legend than that of Nebuchadnezzar, son of Nabopolassar, king of Babylon " (*Comm. on the Inscr. of Assyria and Babylonia*, pp. 76, 77). "Nebuchadnezzar," says Abydenus, "on succeeding to the throne, fortified Babylon with three lines of walls. He dug the *Nahr Malcha*, or Royal River, which was a branch stream derived from the Euphrates, and also the Acracanus. He likewise made the great reservoir above the city of Sippara, which was thirty parasangs (90 miles) in circumference, and twenty fathoms (120 feet) deep. Here he placed sluices or flood-gates, which enabled him to irrigate the low country. He also built a quay along the shore of the Red Sea (Persian Gulf), and founded the city of Teredon on the borders of Arabia." It is reasonably concluded from these statements, that an extensive system of irrigation was devised by this monarch, to whom the Babylonians were probably indebted for the greater portion of that vast net-work of canals which covered the whole alluvial tract between the two rivers, and extended on the right bank of the Euphrates to the extreme verge of the stony desert. On that side the principal work was a canal of the largest dimensions, still to be traced, which left the Euphrates at *Hit*, and skirting the desert ran southeast a distance of above 400 miles to the Persian Gulf, where it emptied itself into the Bay of *Grane*.

The wealth, greatness, and general prosperity of Nebuchadnezzar are strikingly placed before us in the book of Daniel. "The God of heaven" gave him, not a kingdom only, but "power, strength, and glory" (Dan. ii. 37). His wealth is evidenced by the image of gold, 60 cubits in height, which he set up in the plain of Dura (*ib.* iii. 1). The grandeur and careful organization of his kingdom appears from the long list of his officers, "princes, governors, captains, judges, treasurers, councillors, sheriffs, and rulers of provinces," of whom we have repeated mention (*ib.* vv. 2, 3, and 37). We see the existence of a species of hierarchy in the "magicians, astrologers, sorcerers," over whom Daniel was set (*ib.* ii. 48). The "tree, whose height was great, which grew and was strong, and the height thereof reached unto the heavens, and the sight thereof to the end of all the earth; the leaves whereof were fair, and the fruit much, and in which was food for all; under which the beasts of the field had shadow, and the fowls of heaven dwelt in the branches thereof, and all flesh was fed of it" (*ib.* iv. 10–12), is the fitting type of a kingdom at once so flourishing and so extensive.

It has been thought by some (De Wette, Th. Parker, etc.), that the book of Daniel represents the satrapial system of government (*Satrapen-Einrichtung*) as established throughout the whole empire; but this conclusion is not justified by a close examination of that document. Nebuchadnezzar, like his Assyrian predecessors (Is. x. 8), is represented as a "king of kings" (Dan. ii. 37); and the officers enumerated in ch. ii. are probably the authorities of Babylonia proper, rather than the governors of remoter regions, who could not be all spared at once from their employments. The instance of Gedaliah (Jer. xl. 5; 2 K. xxv. 22) is not that of a satrap. He was a Jew; and it may be doubted whether he stood really in any different relation to the Babylonians from Zedekiah or Jehoiachin; although as he was not of the seed of David, the Jews considered him to be "governor" rather than king.

Towards the close of his reign the glory of Nebuchadnezzar suffered a temporary eclipse. As a punishment for his pride and vanity, that strange form of madness was sent upon him which the Greeks called Lycanthropy (λυκανθρωπία); wherein the sufferer imagines himself a beast, and quitting the haunts of men, insists on leading the life of a beast (Dan. iv. 33).[a] Berosus, with the pardon-

---

1865). "This malady, which is not unknown to physicians, has been termed 'Lycanthropy.' It consists in the belief that one is not a man but a beast,

able tenderness of a native, anxious for the good fame of his country's greatest king, suppressed this fact; and it may be doubted whether Herodotus in his Babylonian travels, which fell only about a century after the time, obtained any knowledge of it. Nebuchadnezzar himself, however, in his great inscription appears to allude to it, although in a studied ambiguity of phrase which renders the passage very difficult of translation. After describing the construction of the most important of his great works, he appears to say — "For four years (?) . . . the seat of my kingdom . . . did not rejoice my heart. In all my dominions I did not build a high place of power, the precious treasures of my kingdom I did not lay up. In Babylon, buildings for myself and for the honor of my kingdom I did not lay out. In the worship of Merodach, my lord, the joy of my heart, in Babylon the city of his sovereignty, and the seat of my empire, I did not sing his praises, I did not furnish his altars with victims, nor did I clear out the canals " (Rawlinson's *Herod.* ii. 586). Other negative clauses follow. It is plain that we have here narrated a suspension — apparently for four years — of all those works and occupations on which the king especially prided himself — his temples, palaces, worship, offerings, and works of irrigation; and though the cause of the suspension is not stated, we can scarcely imagine anything that would account for it but some such extraordinary malady as that recorded in Daniel.

It has often been remarked that Herodotus ascribes to a queen, Nitocris, several of the important works, which other writers (Berosus, Abydenus) assign to Nebuchadnezzar. The conjecture naturally arises that Nitocris was Nebuchadnezzar's queen, and that, as she carried on his constructions during his incapacity, they were by some considered to be hers. It is no disproof of this to urge that Nebuchadnezzar's wife was a Median princess, not an Egyptian (as Nitocris must have been from her name), and that she was called, not Nitocris, but Amyitis or Amyhia; for Nebuchadnezzar, who married Amyitis in B. C. 625, and who lived after this marriage more than sixty years, may easily have married again after the decease of his first wife, and his second queen may have been an Egyptian. His latter relations with Egypt appear to have been friendly; and it is remarkable that the name Nitocris, which belonged to very primitive Egyptian history, had in fact been resuscitated about this time, and is found in the Egyptian monuments to have been borne by a princess belonging to the family of the Psammetiks.

After an interval of four, or perhaps *a* seven years (Dan. iv. 16), Nebuchadnezzar's malady left him. As we are told in Scripture that "his reason returned, and for the glory of his kingdom his honor and brightness returned;" and he "was estab-

lished in his kingdom, and excellent majesty was added to him "(Dan. iv. 36), so we find in the Standard Inscription that he resumed his great works after a period of suspension, and added fresh "wonders " in his old age to the marvelous constructions of his manhood. He died in the year B. C. 561, at an advanced age (83 or 84), having reigned 43 years. A son, EVIL-MERODACH, succeeded him.

The character of Nebuchadnezzar must be gathered principally from Scripture. There is a conventional formality in the cuneiform inscriptions, which deprives them of almost all value for the illustration of individual mind and temper. Ostentation and vainglory are characteristics of the entire series, each king seeking to magnify above all others his own exploits. We can only observe as peculiar to Nebuchadnezzar a disposition to rest his fame on his great works rather than on his military achievements, and a strong religious spirit, manifesting itself especially in a devotion, which is almost exclusive, to one particular god. Though his own tutelary deity and that of his father was Nebo (Mercury), yet his worship, his ascriptions of praise, his thanksgivings, have in almost every case for their object the god Merodach. Under his protection he placed his son, Evil-Merodach. Merodach is "his lord," "his great lord," "the joy of his heart," "the great lord who has appointed him to the empire of the world, and has confided to his care the far-spread people of the earth," "the great lord who has established him in strength," etc. One of the first of his own titles is, "he who pays homage to Merodach." Even when restoring the temples of other deities, he ascribes the work to the suggestions of Merodach, and places it under his protection. We may hence explain the appearance of a sort of monotheism (Dan. i. 2; iv. 24, 32, 34, 37), mixed with polytheism (*ib.* ii. 47; iii. 12, 18, 29; iv. 9), in the Scriptural notices of him. While admitting a qualified divinity in Nebo, Nana, and other deities of his country, Nebuchadnezzar maintained the real *monarchy* of Bel-Merodach. HE was to him "the supreme chief of the gods," "the most ancient," "the king of the heavens and the earth." [b] It was *his* image, or symbol, undoubtedly, which was "set up " to be worshipped in the "plain of Dura " (*ib.* iii. 1), and *his* "house " in which the sacred vessels from the Temple were treasured (*ib.* i. 2). Nebuchadnezzar seems at some times to have identified this, his supreme god, with the God of the Jews (*ib.* ch. iv.); at others, to have regarded the Jewish God as one of the local and inferior deities (ch. iii.) over whom Merodach ruled.

The genius and grandeur which characterized Nebuchadnezzar, and which have handed down his name among the few ancient personages known generally throughout the East, are very apparent in

in the disuse of language, the rejection of all ordinary human food, and sometimes in the loss of the erect posture and a preference for walking on all fours. Within a year of the time that he received the warning (Dan. iv. 29), Nebuchadnezzar was smitten. The great king became a wretched maniac. Allowed to indulge his distempered fancy, he eschewed human habitations, lived in the open air night and day, fed on herbs, disused clothing, and became covered with a rough coat of hair (ver. 33). His subjects generally, it is probable, were not allowed to know of his condition, though they could not but be aware that

he was suffering from some terrible malady. The queen most likely held the reins of power, and carried on the government in his name.

We must not suppose that the afflicted monarch was allowed to range freely through the country. He was no doubt strictly confined to the private gardens attached to the palace."   H.

a Daniel's expression is "seven *times.*" We cannot be sure that by a " time " is meant a year.

b These expressions are all applied to Merodach by Nebuchadnezzar in his Inscriptions.

Scripture, and indeed in all the accounts of his reign and actions. Without perhaps any strong military turn, he must have possessed a fair amount of such talent to have held his own in the east against the ambitious Medes, and in the west against the Egyptians. Necho and Apries were both princes of good warlike capacity, whom it is some credit to have defeated. The prolonged siege of Tyre is a proof of the determination with which he prosecuted his military enterprises. But his greatness lay especially in the arts of peace. He saw in the natural fertility of Babylonia, and its ample wealth of waters, the foundation of national prosperity, and so of power. Hence his vast canals and elaborate system of irrigation, which made the whole country a garden; and must have been a main cause of the full treasury, from which alone his palaces and temples can have received their magnificence. The forced labor of captives may have raised the fabrics; but the statues, the enameled bricks, the fine woodwork, the gold and silver plating, the hangings and curtains, had to be bought; and the enormous expenditure of this monarch, which does not appear to have exhausted the country, and which cannot have been very largely supported by tribute, must have been really supplied in the main from that agricultural wealth which he took so much pains to develop. We may gather from the productiveness of Babylonia under the Persians (Herod. i. 192, 193, iii. 92), after a conquest and two (three ?) revolts, some idea of its flourishing condition in the period of independence, for which (according to the consentient testimony of the monuments and the best authors) it was indebted to this king.

The moral character of Nebuchadnezzar is not such as entitles him to our approval. Besides the overweening pride which brought upon him so terrible a chastisement, we note a violence and fury (Dan. ii. 12, iii. 19) common enough among oriental monarchs of the weaker kind, but from which the greatest of them have usually been free; while at the same time we observe a cold and relentless cruelty which is particularly revolting. The blinding of Zedekiah may perhaps be justified as an ordinary eastern practice, though it is the earliest case of the kind on record; but the refinement of cruelty by which he was made to witness his sons' execution before his eyes were put out (2 K. xxv. 7) is worthier of a Dionysius or a Domitian than of a really great king. Again, the detention of Jehoiachin in prison for 36 years for an offense committed at the age of eighteen (2 K. xxiv. 8), is a severity surpassing oriental harshness. Against these grave faults we have nothing to set, unless it be a feeble trait of magnanimity in the pardon accorded to Shadrach, Meshach, and Abed-nego, when he found that he was without power to punish them (Dan. iii. 26).

It has been thought remarkable that to a man of this character, God should have vouchsafed a revelation of the future by means of visions (Dan. ii. 29, iv. 2). But the circumstance, however it may disturb our preconceived notions, is not really at variance with the general laws of God's providence as revealed to us in Scripture. As with his natural, so with his supernatural gifts, they are no confined to the worthy. Even under Christianity, miraculous powers were sometimes possessed by those who made an ill use of them (1 Cor. xiv. 2-33). And God, it is plain, did not leave the old heathen world without some supernatural aid, but made his presence felt from time to time in visions, through prophets, or even by a voice from Heaven. It is only necessary to refer to the histories of Pharaoh (Gen. xli. 1-7, and 28), Abimelech (ib. xx. 3), Job (Job iv. 13, xxxviii. 1, xl. 6; comp. Dan. iv. 31), and Balaam (Num. xxii.-xxiv.), in order to establish the parity of Nebuchadnezzar's visions with other facts recorded in the Bible. He was warned, and the nations over which he ruled were warned through him, God leaving not Himself "without witness" even in those dark times. In conclusion, we may notice that a heathen writer (Abydenus), who generally draws his inspirations from Berosus, ascribes to Nebuchadnezzar a miraculous speech just before his death, announcing to the Babylonians the speedy coming of "a Persian mule," who with the help of the Medes would enslave Babylon (Abyd. ap. Euseb. Præp. Ev. ix. 41).
                               G. R.

NEBUSHAS'BAN (נְבוּשַׁזְבָּן[a], i. e. Nebushazban: LXX. omits: Nabusezban), one of the officers of Nebuchadnezzar at the time of the capture of Jerusalem. He was Rab-saris, i. e. chief of the eunuchs (Jer. xxxix. 13), as Nebuzaradan was Rab-tabbachim (chief of the body-guard), and Nergal-sharezer, Rab-Mag (chief of the magicians), the three being the most important officers then present, probably the highest dignitaries of the Babylonian court.[b] Nebu-shasban's office and title were the same as those of Ashpenaz (Dan. i. 3), whom he probably succeeded. In the list given (ver. 3) of those who took possession of the city in the dead of the night of the 11th Tammuz, Nebushasban is not mentioned by name, but merely by his title Rab-saris. His name, like that of Nebuchadnezzar and Nebu-zaradan, is a compound of Nebo, the Babylonian deity, with some word which though not quite ascertained, probably signified adherence or attachment (see Gesen. Thes. 840 b; Fürst, Handwb. ii. 7 b).   G.

NEBUZAR'ADAN (נְבוּזַרְאֲדָן [see below]: Ναβουζαρδάν or Ναβουζαρδάν; Joseph. Ναβουζαρδάνης: Nebuzardan), the Rab-tabba-chim, i. e. chief of the slaughterers (A. V. "captain of the guard"), a high officer in the court of Nebuchadnezzar, apparently (like the Tartan in the Assyrian army) the next to the person of the monarch. He appears not to have been present during the siege of Jerusalem; probably he was occupied at the more important operations at Tyre, but as soon as the city was actually in the hands of the Babylonians he arrived, and from that moment everything was completely directed by him. It was he who decided, even to the minutest

---

In the usual copies of the Hebrew Bible this final ן is written small, and noted in the Masora accordingly. In several of Kennicott's MSS. ז (ז) is found instead of ן (ן), making the name Nebushasbas, with perhaps an intentional play of sound, baz meaning prey or spoil.

So at the Assyrian invasion in the time of Hezekiah Tartan, Rab-saris, and Rab-shakeh, as the three highest dignitaries, addressed the Jews from the head of their army (2 K. xviii. 17). Possibly these three officers in the Assyrian court answered to the three named above in the Babylonian.

details of fire-pans and bowls (2 K. xxv. 15), what should be carried off and what burnt, which persons should be taken away to Babylon and which left behind in the country. One act only is referred directly to Nebuchadnezzar, the appointment of the governor or superintendent of the conquered district. All this Nebuzaradan seems to have carried out with wisdom and moderation. His conduct to Jeremiah, to whom his attention had been directed by his master (Jer. xxxix. 11), is marked by even higher qualities than these, and the prophet has preserved (xl. 2–5) a speech of Nebuzaradan's to him on liberating him from his chains at Ramah, which contains expressions truly remarkable in a heathen. He seems to have left Judæa for this time when he took down the chief people of Jerusalem to his master at Riblah (2 K. xxv. 18–20). In four years he again appeared (Jer. lii. 30). Nebuchadnezzar in his twenty-third year made a descent on the regions east of Jordan, including the Ammonites and Moabites (Joseph. *Ant.* x. 9, § 7), who escaped when Jerusalem was destroyed. [MOAB, p. 1986 b.] Thence he proceeded to Egypt (Joseph. *ibid.*), and, either on the way thither or on the return, Nebuzaradan again passed through the country and carried off seven hundred and forty-five more captives (Jer. lii. 30).

The name, like Nebu-chadnezzar and Nebu-shasban, contains that of Nebo the Babylonian deity. The other portion of the word is less certain. Gesenius (*Thes.* p. 839 b) translates it by "Mercurii dux dominus," taking the זַר as = שַׂר, "prince," and אֲדָן as = אָדוֹן, "lord." Fürst, on the other hand (*Handwb.* ii. 6), treats it as equivalent in meaning to the Hebrew *rab-tabbachim*, which usually follows it, and sometimes occurs by itself (2 K. xxv. 18; Jer. xl. 2, 5). To obtain this meaning he compares the last member of the name to the Sanskr. *dána*, from *dó*, "to cut off." Gesenius also takes zaradan as identical with the first element in the name of Sardanapalus. But this latter name is now explained by Sir H. Rawlinson as Assur-dan-i-pal (Rawlinson's *Herod.* i. 460).   G.

NE′CHO (נְכוֹ: Νεχαώ: [*Nechao*]), 2 Chr. xxxv. 20, 22; xxxvi. 4. [PHARAOH-NECHO.]

NECO′DAN (Νεκωδάν: *Nechodaīcus*) = NE-KODA (1 Esdr. v. 37; comp. Ezr. ii. 60).

● **NECROMANCER** (Deut. xviii. 11). See MAGIC.

NEDABI′AH (נְדַבְיָה: Ναβαδίας; [Vat. Δενεθει:] *Nadabia*). Apparently one of the sons of Jeconiah, or Jehoiachin, king of Judah (1 Chr. iii. 18). Lord A. Hervey, however, contends that this list contains the order of succession and not of lineal descent, and that Nedabiah and his brothers were sons of Neri.

● **NEEDLEWORK.** See DRESS, 2.

NEEMI′AS (Νεεμίας; [in Ecclus., Vat. Νε-μουσιν, Sin. Νεμουσι; in 2 Macc. i. 18, 21, 23, 36, ii. 13, Alex. Νεεμειας:] *Nehemias*) = NEHE-MIAH the son of Hachaliah (Ecclus. xlix. 13; 2 Macc. i. 18, 20, 21, 23, 31, 36, ii. 13).

NEG′INAH (נְגִינָה), properly *Neginath*, as the text now stands, occurs in the title of Ps. lxi., "to the chief musician upon Neginath." If the present reading be correct, the form of the word may be compared with that of Mahalath (Ps. liii.) But the LXX. (ἐν ὕμνοις), and Vulg. (*in hymnis*), evidently read "Neginoth" in the plural, which occurs in the titles of five Psalms, and is perhaps the true reading. Whether the word be singular or plural, it is the general term by which all stringed instruments are described. In the singular it has the derived sense of "a song sung to the accompaniment of a stringed instrument," and generally of a taunting character (Job xxx. 9; Ps. lxix. 12; Lam. iii. 14). [NEGINOTH.]
W. A. W.

NEG′INOTH (נְגִינוֹת). This word is found in the titles of Ps. iv., vi., liv., lv., lxvii., lxxvi., and the margin of Hab. iii. 19, and there seems but little doubt that it is the general term denoting all stringed instruments whatsoever, whether played with the hand, like the harp and guitar, or with a plectrum.[a] It thus includes all those instruments which in the A. V. are denoted by the special terms "harp," "psaltery" or "viol," "sackbut," as well as by the general descriptions "stringed instruments" (Ps. cl. 4), "instruments of music" (1 Sam. xviii. 6), or, as the margin gives it, "three-stringed instruments," and the "instrument of ten strings" (Ps. xxxiii. 2, xcii. 3, cxliv. 9). "The chief musician on *Neginoth*" was therefore the conductor of that portion of the Temple-choir who played upon the stringed instruments, and who are mentioned in Ps. lxviii. 25 (נֹגְנִים, *nógnīm*).

The root (נָגַן = κρούειν) from which the word is derived occurs in 1 Sam. xvi. 16, 17, 18, 23, xviii. 10, xix. 9; Is. xxxviii. 20, and a comparison of these passages confirms what has been said with regard to its meaning. The author of the *Shilte Haggibborim*, quoted by Kircher (*Musurgia*, i. 4, p. 48), describes the Neginoth as instruments of wood, long and round, pierced with several apertures, and having three strings of gut stretched across them, which were played with a bow of horsehair. It is extremely doubtful, however, whether the Hebrews were acquainted with anything so closely resembling the modern violin.
W. A. W.

NEHEL′AMITE, THE (הַנֶּחֱלָמִי: ὁ Αἰλαμίτης [Vat. -ει; Alex. FA. Ελαμιτης:] *Nehelamites*). The designation of a man named Shemaiah, a false prophet, who went with the Captivity to Babylon (Jer. xxix. 24, 31, 32). The name is no doubt formed from that either of Shemaiah's native place, or the progenitor of his family: which of the two is uncertain. No place called Nehelam is mentioned in the Bible, or known to have existed in Palestine,[b] nor does it occur in any of the genealogical lists of families. It resembles the name which the LXX. have attached to Ahijah the Prophet, namely the Enlamite—ὁ Ἐνλαμεί; but by what authority they substitute that name for "the Shilonite" of the Hebrew text is doubtful. The word "Nehelamite" also probably contains a play on the "dreams" (*halam*) and "dreamers," whom Jeremiah is never wearied of denouncing (see cc. xxiii., xxvii., xxix.). This

---

[a] Hence Symmachus renders διὰ ψαλτηρίων.

[b] The Targum gives the name as *Halam*, חלם. A place of this name lay somewhere between the Jordan and the Euphrates. See vol. ii. p. 1085 f.

is hinted in the margin of the A. V. — from what source the writer has not been able to discover.

G.

NEHEMI'AH (נְחֶמְיָה [consoled by Jehovah: Νεεμία,] Νεεμίας: [Nehemias]). . **1.** Son of Hachaliah, and apparently of the tribe of Judah, since his fathers were buried at Jerusalem, and Hanani his kinsman seems to have been of that tribe (Neh. i. 2, ii. 3, vii. 2). He is called indeed "Nehemiah the Priest" (Neh. sacerdos) in the Vulgate of 2 Macc. i. 21; but the Greek has it, that "Nehemiah ordered the priests (ἱερεῖς) to pour the water," etc. Nor does the expression in ver. 18, that Nehemiah "offered sacrifice," imply any more than that he provided the sacrifices. Others again have inferred that he was a priest from Neh. x. 1–8; but the words "these were the priests" naturally apply to the names which follow Nehemiah's, who signed first as the head of the whole nation. The opinion that he was connected with the house of David is more feasible, though it cannot be proved. The name of Hanani his kinsman, as well as his own name, are found slightly varied in the house of David, in the case of Hananiah the son of Zerubbabel (1 Chr. iii. 19), and Naum (Luke iii. 25).[a] If he were of the house of David, there would be peculiar point in his allusion to his "fathers' sepulchres" at Jerusalem. Malalas of Antioch (*Chronogr.* vi. 160), as cited by Grimm, on 2 Macc. i. 21, singularly combines the two views, and calls him "Nehemiah the priest, of the seed of David."

All that we know certainly concerning this eminent man is contained in the book which bears his name. His autobiography first finds him at Shushan, the winter [b] residence of the kings of Persia, in high office as the cupbearer of king Artaxerxes Longimanus. In the 20th year of the king's reign, i. e. B. C. 445, certain Jews, one of whom was a near kinsman of Nehemiah's, arrived from Judæa, and gave Nehemiah a deplorable account of the state of Jerusalem, and of the residents in Judæa. He immediately conceived the idea of going to Jerusalem to endeavor to better their state. After three or four months (from Chisleu to Nisan), in which he earnestly sought God's blessing upon his undertaking by frequent prayer and fasting, an opportunity presented itself of obtaining the king's consent to his mission. Having received his appointment as governor [c] of Judæa, a troop of cavalry, and letters from the king to the different satraps through whose provinces he was to pass, as well as to Asaph the keeper of the king's forests, to supply him with timber, he started upon his journey: being under promise to return to Persia within a given time. Josephus says that he went in the first instance to Babylon, and gathered round him a band of exiled Jews, who returned with him. This is important as possibly indicating that the book which Josephus followed, understood the Nehemiah mentioned in Ezr. ii. 2; Neh. vii. 7, to be the son of Hachaliah.

Nehemiah's great work was rebuilding, for the first time since their destruction by Nebuzaradan, the walls of Jerusalem, and restoring that city to its former state and dignity, as a fortified town It is impossible to overestimate the importance to the future political and ecclesiastical prosperity of the Jewish nation of this great achievement of their patriotic governor. How low the community of the Palestine Jews had fallen, is apparent from the fact that from the 6th of Darius to the 7th of Artaxerxes, there is no history of them whatever; and that even after Ezra's commission, and the ample grants made by Artaxerxes in his 7th year, and the considerable reinforcements, both in wealth and numbers, which Ezra's government brought to them, they were in a state of abject "affliction and reproach" in the 20th of Artaxerxes; their country pillaged, their citizens kidnapped and made slaves of by their heathen neighbors, robbery and murder rife in their very capital, Jerusalem almost deserted, and the Temple falling again into decay. The one step which could resuscitate the nation, preserve the Mosaic institutions, and lay the foundation of future independence, was the restoration of the city walls. Jerusalem being once again secure from the attacks of the marauding heathen, civil government would become possible, the spirit of the people, and their attachment to the ancient capital of the monarchy would revive, the priests and Levites would be encouraged to come into residence, the tithes and first-fruits and other stores would be safe, and Judah, if not actually independent, would preserve the essentials of national and religious life. To this great object therefore Nehemiah directed his whole energies without an hour's unnecessary delay.[d] By word and example he induced the whole population, with the single exception of the Tekoite nobles, to commence building with the utmost vigor, even the lukewarm high-priest Eliashib performing his part. In a wonderfully short time the walls seemed to emerge from the heaps of burnt rubbish, and to encircle the city as in the days of old. The gateways also were rebuilt, and ready for the doors to be hung upon them. But it soon became apparent how wisely Nehemiah had acted in hastening on the work. On his very first arrival, as governor, Sanballat and Tobiah had given unequivocal proof of their mortification at his appointment; and, before the work was even commenced, had scornfully asked whether he intended to rebel against the king of Persia. But when the restoration was seen to be rapidly progressing, their indignation knew no bounds. They not only poured out a torrent of abuse and contempt upon all engaged in the work, but actually made a great conspiracy to fall upon the builders with an armed force and put a stop to the undertaking. The project was defeated by the vigilance and prudence of Nehemiah, who armed all the people after their families, and showed such a strong front that their enemies dared not attack them. This armed attitude was continued from

<hr>

[a] See *Genealog. of our Lord J. C.*, p. 145. [NEHEMIAH, SON OF AZBUK.]

[b] Ecbatana was the summer, Babylon the spring, and Persepolis the autumn residence of the kings of Persia (Pilkington). Susa was the principal palace (Strab. lib. xv. cap. iii. § 3).

[c] פֶּחָה, the term applied to himself and other satraps by Nehemiah. The meaning and etymology

of *Tirshatha*, which is applied only to Nehemiah, are doubtful. It is by most modern scholars thought to mean Governor (Gesen. *s. v.*); but the sense *cupbearer*, given by older commentators, seems more probable.

[d] The three days, mentioned Neh. ii. 11, and Ezr viii. 32, seems to point to some customary interval perhaps for purification after a journey. See in Cruden's *Concordance* "Third Day" and "Three Days."

that day forward. Various stratagems were then resorted to to get Nehemiah away from Jerusalem, and if possible to take his life. But that which most nearly succeeded was the attempt to bring him into suspicion with the king of Persia, as if he intended to set himself up for an independent king, as soon as the walls were completed. It was thought that the accusation of rebellion would also frighten the Jews themselves, and make them cease from building. Accordingly a double line of action was taken. On the one hand Sanballat wrote a letter to Nehemiah, in an apparently friendly tone, telling him, on the authority of Geshem, that it was reported among the heathen (i. e. the heathen nations settled in Samaria, and Galilee of the nations), that he was about to head a rebellion of the Jews, and that he had appointed prophets to aid in the design by prophesying of him, "thou art the king of Judah;" and that he was building the walls for this purpose. This was sure, he added, to come to the ears of the king of Persia, and he invited Nehemiah to confer with him as to what should be done. At the same time he had also bribed Noadiah the prophetess, and other prophets, to induce Nehemiah by representations of his being in danger, to take refuge in the fortress of the Temple, with a view to cause delay, and also to give an appearance of conscious guilt. While this portion of the plot was conducted by Sanballat and Tobiah, a yet more important line of action was pursued in concert with them by the chief officers of the king of Persia in Samaria. In a letter addressed to Artaxerxes they represented that the Jews had rebuilt the walls of Jerusalem, with the intent of rebelling against the king's authority and recovering their dominion on "this side the river." Referring to former instances of the seditious spirit of the Jewish people, they urged that if the king wished to maintain his power in the province he must immediately put a stop to the fortification. This artful letter so far wrought upon Artaxerxes, that he issued a decree stopping the work till further orders.[a] It is probable that at the same time he recalled Nehemiah, or perhaps Nehemiah's leave of absence had previously expired; in either case had the Tirshatha been less upright and less wise, and had he fallen into the trap laid for him, his life might have been in great danger. The sequel, however, shows that his perfect integrity was apparent to the king. For after a delay, perhaps of several years, he was permitted to return to Jerusalem, and to crown his work by repairing the Temple, and dedicating the walls. What, however, we have here to notice is, that owing to Nehemiah's wise haste, and his refusal to pause for a day in his work, in spite of threats, plots, and insinuations, the designs of his enemies were frustrated. The wall was actually finished and ready to receive the gates, before the king's decree for suspending the work arrived. A little delay, therefore, was all they were able to effect. Nehemiah does not indeed mention this adverse decree, which may have arrived during his absence, nor give us any clew to the time of his return; nor should we have suspected his absence at all from Jerusalem, but for the incidental allusion in ch. ii. 6, xiii. 6, coupled with the long

interval of years between the earlier and later chapters of the book. But the interval between the close of ch. vi. and the beginning of ch. vii. is the only place where we can suppose a considerable gap in time, either from the appearance of the text, or the nature of the events narrated. It seems to suit both well to suppose that Nehemiah returned to Persia, and the work stopped immediately after the events narrated in vi. 16-19, and that chapter vii. goes on to relate the measures adopted by him upon his return with fresh powers. These were, the setting up the doors in the various gates of the city, giving a special charge to Hanani and Hananiah, as to the time of opening and shutting the gates, and above all providing for the due peopling of the city, the numbers of which were miserably small, and the rebuilding of the numerous decayed houses within the walls. Then followed a census of the returned captives, a large collection of funds for the repair of the Temple, the public reading of the Law to the people by Ezra (who now appears again on the scene, perhaps having returned from Persia with Nehemiah), a celebration of the Feast of Tabernacles, such as had not been held since the days of Joshua: a no less solemn keeping of the Day of Atonement, when the opportunity was taken to enter into solemn covenant with God, to walk in the law of Moses and to keep God's commandments.

It may have been after another considerable interval of time, and not improbably after another absence of the Tirshatha from his government, that the next event of interest in Nehemiah's life occurred, namely, the dedication of the walls of Jerusalem, including, if we may believe the author of 2 Macc., supported by several indications in the Book of Nehemiah, that of the Temple after its repair by means of the funds collected from the whole population. This dedication was conducted with great solemnity, and appears to have been the model of the dedication by Judas Maccabæus, when the Temple was purified and the worship restored at the death of Antiochus Epiphanes, as related 1 Macc. iv. The author of 2 Macc. says that on this occasion Nehemiah obtained the sacred fire which had been hid in a pit by certain priests at the time of the Captivity, and was recovered by their descendants, who knew where it was concealed. When, however, these priests went to the place, they found only muddy water. By Nehemiah's command they drew this water, and sprinkled it upon the wood of the altar and upon the victims, and when the sun, which had been over-clouded, presently shone out, a great fire was immediately kindled; which consumed the sacrifices, to the great wonder of all present. The author also inserts the prayer, a simple and beautiful one, said to have been uttered by the priests, and responded to by Nehemiah, during the sacrifice; and adds, that the king of Persia inclosed the place where the fire was found, and that Nehemiah gave it the name of Naphthar, or cleansing. [NAPHTHAR.] He tells us further that an account of this dedication was contained in the "writings and commentaries of Nehemiah" (2 Macc. ii. 13), and that Nehemiah founded "a library, and gathered together the acts of the kings, and the prophets, and of David,

ments mentioned in Neh. vii. 70; Ezr. ii. 68; the allusion to the pollution of the Temple, xiii. 7-9 and the nature of the ceremonies described in ch. xii 26-43.

and the epistles of the kings (of Persia) concerning the holy gifts." How much of this has any historical foundation is difficult to determine. It should be added, however, that the son of Sirach, in celebrating Nehemiah's good deeds, mentions only that he "raised up for us the walls that were fallen, and set up the gates and the bars, and raised up our ruins again," Ecclus. xlix. 13. Returning to the sure ground of the sacred narrative, the other principal achievements of this great and good governor may be thus signalized. He firmly repressed the exactions of the nobles, and the usury of the rich, and rescued the poor Jews from spoliation and slavery. He refused to receive his lawful allowance as governor from the people, in consideration of their poverty, during the whole twelve years that he was in office, but kept at his own charge a table for 150 Jews, at which any who returned from captivity were welcome. He made most careful provision for the maintenance of the ministering priests and Levites, and for the due and constant celebration of Divine worship. He insisted upon the sanctity of the precincts of the Temple being preserved inviolable, and peremptorily ejected the powerful Tobias from one of the chambers which Eliashib had assigned to him. He then replaced the stores and vessels which had been removed to make room for him, and appointed proper Levitical officers to superintend and distribute them. With no less firmness and impartiality he expelled from all sacred functions those of the high priest's family who had contracted heathen marriages, and rebuked and punished those of the common people who had likewise intermarried with foreigners; and lastly, he provided for keeping holy the Sabbath day, which was shamefully profaned by both Jews and foreign merchants, and by his resolute conduct succeeded in repressing the lawless traffic on the day of rest.

Beyond the 32d year of Artaxerxes, to which Nehemiah's own narrative leads us, we have no account of him whatever. Neither had Josephus. For when he tells us that "when Nehemiah had done many other excellent things . . . he came to a great age and then died," he sufficiently indicates that he knew nothing more about him. The most probable inference from the close of his own memoir, and in the absence of any further tradition concerning him is, that he returned to Persia and died there. On reviewing the character of Nehemiah, we seem unable to find a single fault to counterbalance his many and great virtues. For pure and disinterested patriotism he stands unrivaled. The man whom the account of the misery and ruin of his native country, and the perils with which his countrymen were beset, prompted to leave his splendid banishment, and a post of wealth, power, and influence, in the first court in the world, that he might share and alleviate the sorrows of his native land, must have been preëminently a patriot. Every act of his during his government bespeaks one who had no selfishness in his nature. All he did was noble, generous, high-minded, courageous, and to the highest degree upright. But to stern integrity he united great humility and kindness, and a princely hospitality. As a statesman he combined forethought, prudence, and sagacity in counsel, with vigor, promptitude, and decision in action. In dealing with the enemies of his country he was wary, penetrating, and bold. In directing the internal economy of the state, he took a comprehensive view of the real welfare of the people, and adopted the measures best calculated to promote it. In dealing whether with friend or foe, he was utterly free from favor or fear, conspicuous for the simplicity with which he aimed only at doing what was right, without respect of persons. But in nothing was he more remarkable than for his piety, and the singleness of eye with which he walked before God. He seems to have undertaken everything in dependence upon God, with prayer for his blessing and guidance, and to have sought his reward only from God.

The principal authorities for the events of Nehemiah's life, after Josephus, are Carpzov's *Introduct. ad V. T.*; Eichhorn, *Einleitung*; Hävernick's *Einleit.*; Rambach *in Lib. Nehem*; Le Clerc *in Lib. histor. V. T.*, besides those referred to in the following article. Those who wish to see the questions discussed of the 20th Artaxerxes, as the *terminus a quo* Daniel's seventy weeks commence, and also the general chronology of the times, may refer to *Genealogy of our Lord Jesus Christ*, ch. xi.; and for a different view to Prideaux, *Connect.* i. 251, &c. The view of Scaliger, Hottinger, etc., adopted by Dr. Mill, *Vindic. of our Lord's Genealogy*, p. 165 *note*, that Artaxerxes Mnemon was Nehemiah's patron, is almost universally abandoned. The proof from the parallel genealogies of the kings of Persia and the high-priests, that he was Longimanus, is stated in a paper printed for the Chronolog. Institute by the writer of this article.

2. [Νεεμίας, Νεεμία; Vat. in Ezr., Νεεμιος: *Nehemia, Nehemias*.] One of the leaders of the first expedition from Babylon to Jerusalem under Zerubbabel (Ezr. ii. 2; Neh. vii. 7).

3. [Νεεμίας; FA. Νεεμειας: *Nehemias*.] Son of Azbuk, and ruler of the half part of Beth-zur, who helped to repair the wall of Jerusalem (Neh. iii. 16). Beth-zur was a city of Judah (Josh. xv. 58; 1 Chr. ii. 45), belonging to a branch of Caleb's descendants, whence it follows that this Nehemiah was also of the tribe of Judah.   A. C. H.

NEHEMIAH, BOOK OF. The latest of all the historical books of Scripture, both as to the time of its composition and the scope of its narrative in general, and as to the supplementary matter of ch. xii. in particular, which reaches down to the time of Alexander the Great. This book, like the preceding one of Ezra [EZRA, BOOK OF], is clearly and certainly not all by the same hand. By far the principal portion, indeed, is the work of Nehemiah, who gives, in the first person, a simple narrative of the events in which he himself was concerned; but other portions are either extracts from various chronicles and registers, or supplementary narratives and reflections, some apparently by Ezra, others, perhaps, the work of the same person who inserted the latest genealogical extracts from the public chronicles.

1. The main history contained in the book of Nehemiah covers about 12 years, namely, from the 20th to the 32d year of Artaxerxes Longimanus, *i. e.* from B. C. 445 to 433. For so we seem to learn distinctly from v. 14 compared with xiii. 6; nor does there seem to be *any historical ground whatever* for asserting with Prideaux and many others that the government of Nehemiah, after his return in the 32d of Artaxerxes, extended to the 15th year of Darius Nothus, and that the events of ch. xiii. belong to this later period (Prid. *Connect.* B. C. 409). The argument attempted to be derived from Neh. xiii. 28, that Eliashib was then dead and

Joiada his son high-priest, is utterly without weight. There is a precisely parallel phrase in 2 Chr. xxxv. 3, where we read " the house which Solomon the son of David king of Israel did build.'" But the doubt whether the title " king of Israel " applies to David or Solomon is removed by the following verse, where we read, " according to the writing of David king of Israel, and according to the writing of Solomon his son." The LXX. also in that passage have βασιλέως agreeing with David. There is, therefore, not the slightest pretense for asserting that Nehemiah was governor after the 32d of Artaxerxes (see below).

The whole narrative gives us a graphic and interesting account of the state of Jerusalem and the returned captives in the writer's times, and, incidentally, of the nature of the Persian government and the condition of its remote provinces. The documents appended to it also give some further information as to the times of Zerubbabel on the one hand, and as to the continuation of the genealogical registers and the succession of the high-priesthood to the close of the Persian empire on the other. The view given of the rise of two factions among the Jews — the one the strict religious party, adhering with uncompromising faithfulness to the Mosaic institutions, headed by Nehemiah; the other, the gentilizing party, ever imitating heathen customs, and making heathen connections, headed, or at least encouraged by the high-priest Eliashib and his family — sets before us the germ of much that we meet with in a more developed state in later Jewish history from the commencement of the Macedonian dynasty till the final destruction of Jerusalem.

Again, in this history as well as in the book of Ezra, we see the bitter enmity between the Jews and Samaritans acquiring strength and definitive form on both religious and political grounds. It would seem from iv. 1, 2, 8 (A. V.), and vi. 2, 6, &c., that the depression of Jerusalem was a fixed part of the policy of Sanballat, and that he had the design of raising Samaria as the head of Palestine, upon the ruin of Jerusalem, a design which seems to have been entertained by the Samaritans in later times.

The book also throws much light upon the domestic institutions of the Jews. We learn incidentally the prevalence of usury and of slavery as its consequence, the frequent and burdensome oppressions of the governors (v. 15), the judicial use of corporal punishment (xiii. 25), the continuance of false prophets as an engine of policy, as in the days of the kings of Judah (vi. 7, 12, 14), the restitution of the Mosaic provision for the maintenance of the priests and Levites and the due performance of the Temple service (xiii. 10-13), the much freer promulgation of the Holy Scriptures by the public reading of them (viii. 1, ix. 3, xiii. 1), and the more general acquaintance [a] with them arising from their collection into one volume and the multiplication of copies of them by the care of Ezra the scribe and Nehemiah himself (2 Macc. ii. 13), as well as from the stimulus given to the art of reading among the Jewish people during their residence in Babylon [HILKIAH]; the mixed form of political govern-

ment still surviving the ruin of their independence (v. 7, 13, x.), the reviving trade with Tyre (xiii. 16), the agricultural pursuits and wealth of the Jews (v. 11, xiii. 15), the tendency to take heathen wives, indicating, possibly, a disproportion in the number of Jewish males and females among the returned captives (x. 30, xiii. 3, 23), the danger the Jewish language was in of being corrupted [b] (xiii. 24), with other details which only the narrative of an eye-witness would have preserved to us.

Some of these details give us incidentally information of great historical importance.

(a.) The account of the building and dedication of the wall, iii., xii., contains the most valuable materials for settling the topography of Jerusalem to be found in Scripture. [JERUSALEM, vol. ii. pp. 1321-22.] (Thrupp's Ancient Jerusalem.)

(b.) The list of returned captives who came under different leaders from the time of Zerubbabel to that of Nehemiah (amounting in all to only 42,360 adult males, and 7,337 servants), which is given in ch. vii., conveys a faithful picture of the political weakness of the Jewish nation as compared with the times when Judah alone numbered 470,000 fighting men (1 Chr. xxi. 5). It justifies the description of the Palestine Jews as " the remnant that are left of the captivity " (Neh. i. 3), and as " these feeble Jews " (iv. 2), and explains the great difficulty felt by Nehemiah in peopling Jerusalem itself with a sufficient number of inhabitants to preserve it from assault (vii. 3, 4, xi. 1, 2). It is an important aid, too, in understanding the subsequent history, and in appreciating the patriotism and valor by which they attained their independence under the Maccabees.

(c.) The lists of leaders, priests, Levites, and of those who signed the covenant, reveal incidentally much of the national spirit as well as of the social habits of the captives, derived from older times. Thus the fact that twelve leaders are named in Neh. vii. 7, indicates the feeling of the captives that they represented the twelve tribes, a feeling further evidenced in the expression " the men of the people of Israel." The enumeration of 21 and and 22, or, if Zidkijah stands for the head of the house of Zadok, 23 chief priests in x. 1-8, xii. 1-7, of whom 9 bear the names of those who were heads of courses in David's time (1 Chr. xxiv.) [JEHOIARIB], shows how, even in their wasted and reduced numbers, they struggled to preserve these ancient institutions, and also supplies the reason of the mention of these particular 22 or 23 names. But it does more than this. Taken in conjunction with the list of those who sealed (x. 1-27), it proves the existence of a social custom, the knowledge of which is of absolute necessity to keep us from gross chronological error, that, namely, of calling chiefs by the name of the clan or house of which they were chiefs. One of the causes of the absurd confusion which has prevailed, as to the times of Zerubbabel and Nehemiah respectively, has been the mention, e. g. of Jeshua and Kadmiel (Ezr. iii. 9) as taking part with Zerubbabel in building the Temple, while the very same Levites take an active part in the reformation of Nehemiah (Neh. ix. 4, 5, x. 9, 10); and the statement that some

---

21 or 22 priests came up with Zerubbabel (xii. 1–7), coupled with the fact that these very same names were the names of those who sealed the covenant under Nehemiah (x. 1–8). But immediately [as soon as] we perceive that these were the names of the courses, and of great Levitical houses (as a comparison of 1 Chr. xxiv.; Ezr. ii. 40; Neh. vii. 43; and of Neh. x. 14–27 with vii. 8–38, proves that they were), the difficulty vanishes, and we have a useful piece of knowledge to apply to many other passages of Scripture. It would be very desirable, if possible, to ascertain accurately the rules, if any, under which this use of proper names was confined.

(d.) Other miscellaneous information contained in this book embraces the hereditary crafts practiced by certain priestly families, e. g. the apothecaries, or makers of the sacred ointments and incense (iii. 8), and the goldsmiths, whose business it probably was to repair the sacred vessels (iii. 8), and who may have been the ancestors, so to speak, of the money-changers in the Temple (John ii. 14, 15); the situation of the garden of the kings of Judah by which Zedekiah escaped (2 K. xxv. 4), as seen iii. 15; and statistics, reminding one of Domesday-Book, concerning not only the cities and families of the returned captives, but the number of their horses, mules, camels, and asses (ch. vii.): to which more might be added.

The chief, indeed the only real historical difficulty in the narrative, is to determine the time of the dedication of the wall, whether in the 32d year of Artaxerxes or before. The expression in Neh. xiii. 1, "On that day," seems to fix the reading of the law to the same day as the dedication (see xii. 43). But if so, the dedication must have been after Nehemiah's return from Babylon (mentioned xiii. 7); for Eliashib's misconduct, which occurred "before" the reading of the law, happened in Nehemiah's absence. But then, if the wall only took 52 days to complete (Neh. vi. 15), and was begun immediately [when] Nehemiah entered upon his government, how came the dedication to be deferred till 12 years afterwards? The answer to this probably is that, in the first place, the 52 days are not to be reckoned from the commencement of the building, seeing that it is incredible that it should be completed in so short a time by so feeble a community and with such frequent hindrances and interruptions; seeing, too, that the narrative itself indicates a much longer time. Such passages as Nehemiah iv. 7, 8, 12, v., and v. 16 in particular, vi. 4, 5, coupled with the indications of temporary cessation from the work which appear at iv. 6, 10, 15, seem quite irreconcilable with the notion of less than two months for the whole. The 52 days, therefore, if the text is sound, may be reckoned from the resumption of the work after iv. 15, and a time exceeding two years may have elapsed from the commencement of the building. But even then it would not be ready for dedication. There were the gates to be hung, perhaps much rubbish to be removed, and the ruined houses in the immediate vicinity of the walls to be repaired. Then, too, as we shall see below, there were repairs to be done to the Temple, and it is likely that the dedication of the walls would not take place till those repairs were completed. Still, even these causes would not be adequate to account for a delay of 12 years. Josephus, who is seldom in harmony with the book of Nehemiah, though he justifies our suspicion that a longer time must have elapsed, by assuming two years and four months to the rebuilding, and

placing the completion in the 28th year of the king's reign whom he calls Xerxes (thus interposing an interval of 8 years between Nehemiah's arrival at Jerusalem as governor and the completion), yet gives us no real help. He does not attempt to account for the length of time, he makes no allusion to the dedication, except as far as his statement that the wall was completed in the ninth month, Chisleu (instead of Elul, the sixth, as Neh. vi. 15), may seem to point to the dedication (1 Macc. iv. 59), and takes not the slightest notice of Nehemiah's return to the king of Persia. We are left, therefore, to inquire for ourselves whether the book itself suggests any further causes of delay. One cause immediately presents itself, namely, that Nehemiah's leave of absence from the Persian court, mentioned ii. 6, may have drawn to a close shortly after the completion of the wall, and before the other above-named works were complete. And this is rendered yet more probable by the circumstance, incidentally brought to light, that, in the 32d year of Artaxerxes, we know he was with the king (xiii. 6).

Other circumstances, too, may have occurred to make it imperative for him to return to Persia without delay. The last words of ch. vi. point to some new effort of Tobiah to interrupt his work, and the expression used seems to indicate that it was the threat of being considered as a rebel by the king. If he could make it appear that Artaxerxes was suspicious of his fidelity, then Nehemiah might feel it matter of necessity to go to the Persian court to clear himself of the charge. And this view both receives a remarkable confirmation from, and throws quite a new light upon the obscure passage in Ezr. iv. 7–23. We have there a detailed account of the opposition made by the Samaritan nations to the building of the WALLS of Jerusalem, in the reign of ARTAXERXES, and a copy of the letter they wrote to the king, accusing the Jews of an intention to rebel as soon as the wall should be finished; by which means they obtained a decree stopping the building till the king's further orders should be received. Now, if we compare Neh. vi. 6, 7, where mention is made of the report "among the heathen" as to the intended rebellion of Nehemiah, with the letter of the heathen nations mentioned in Ezr. iv., and also recollect that the only time when, as far as we know, the WALLS of Jerusalem were attempted to be rebuilt, was when Nehemiah was governor, it is difficult to resist the conclusion that Ezra iv. 7–23 relates to the time of Nehemiah's government, and explains the otherwise unaccountable circumstance that 12 years elapsed before the dedication of the walls was completed. Nehemiah may have started on his journey on receiving the letters from Persia (if such they were) sent him by Tobiah, leaving his lieutenants to carry on the works, and after his departure Rehum and Shimshai and their companions may have come up to Jerusalem with the king's decree and obliged them to desist. It should seem, however, that at Nehemiah's arrival in Persia, he was able to satisfy the king of his perfect integrity, and that he was permitted to return to his government in Judæa. His leave of absence may again have been of limited duration, and the business of the census, of repeopling Jerusalem, setting up the city gates, rebuilding the ruined houses, and repairing the Temple, may have occupied his whole time till his second return to the king. During this second absence another evil arose — the gentilizing party recovered strength, and the intrigues with Tobiah (vi. 17), which had already begun before his first departure, were more actively carried on, and led so far that Eliashib the high-priest actually assigned one of the store-chambers in the Temple to Tobiah's use. This we are not told of till xiii. 4–7, when Nehemiah relates the steps he took on his return. But this very circumstance suggests that Nehemiah does not relate the events which happened in his absence, and would account for his silence in regard to Rehum and Shimshai. We may thus, then, account for 10 or 11 years having elapsed before the dedication of the walls took place. In fact it did not take place till the last year of his government; and this lends to the right interpretation of xiii. 6 and brings it into perfect harmony with v. 14, a passage which obviously imports that Nehemiah's government of Judæa lasted only 12 years, namely, from the 20th to the 32d of Artaxerxes. For the literal and grammatical rendering of xiii. 6 is, "And in all this *time* was not I at Jerusalem: BUT in the two-and-thirtieth year of Artaxerxes king of Babylon, came I unto the king, and after certain days obtained I leave of the king,

and I came to Jerusalem " — the force of בִּי after a negative being *but* rather than *for* (Gesen. *Thes.* p. 680): the meaning of the passage being, therefore, not that he left Jerusalem to go to Persia in the 32d of Artaxerxes, but, on the contrary, that in that year he returned from Persia to Jerusalem. The dedication of the walls and the other reforms named in ch. xiii. were the closing acts of his administration.

It has been already mentioned that Josephus does not follow the authority of the Book of Nehemiah. He detaches Nehem. viii. from its context, and appends the narratives contained in it to the times of Ezra. He makes Ezra die before Nehemiah came to Jerusalem as governor, and consequently ignores any part taken by him in conjunction with Nehemiah. He makes no mention either whatever of Sanballat in the events of Nehemiah's government, but places him in the time of Jaddua and Alexander the Great. He also makes the daughter of Sanballat marry a son, not of Joiada, as Neh. xiii. 28, but of Jonathan, namely, Manasseh the brother of the High-priest Jaddua, thus entirely shifting the age of Sanballat from the reign of Artaxerxes Longimanus, to that of Darius Codomanus, and Alexander the Great. It is scarcely necessary to observe, that as Artaxerxes Longimanus died B. C. 424, and Alexander the Great was not master of Syria and Palestine till B. C. 332, all attempts to reconcile Josephus with Nehemiah must be lost labor. It is equally clear that on every ground the authority of Josephus must yield to that of Nehemiah. The only question therefore is what was the cause of Josephus' variations. Now, as regards the appending the history in Neh. viii. to the times of Ezra, we know that he was guided by the authority of the Apocryphal 1 Esdr. as he had been in the whole story of Zerubbabel and Darius. From the florid additions to his narrative of Nehemiah's first application to Artaxerxes, as well as from the passage below referred to in 2 Macc. i. 23, we may be sure that there were apocryphal versions

of the story of Nehemiah.[a] The account of Jaddua's interview with Alexander the Great savors strongly of the same origin. There can be little doubt, therefore, that in all the points in which Josephus differs from Nehemiah, he followed apocryphal Jewish writings, some of which have since perished. The causes which led to this were various. One doubtless was the mere desire for matter with which to fill up his pages where the narrative of the canonical Scriptures is meagre. In making Nehemiah succeed to the government after Ezra's death, he was probably influenced partly by the wish to give an orderly, dignified appearance to the succession of Jewish governors, approximating as nearly as possible to the old monarchy, and partly by the desire to spin out his matter into a *continuous* history. Then the difficulties of the books of Ezra and Nehemiah, which the compiler of 1 Esdr. had tried to get over by his arrangement of the order of events, coupled with Josephus' gross ignorance of the real order of the Persian kings, and his utter misconception as to what monarchs are spoken of in the books of Ezra, Nehemiah, and Esther, had also a large influence. The writer, however, who makes Darius Codomanus succeed Artaxerxes Longimanus, and confounds this last-named king with Artaxerxes Mnemon; who also thinks that Xerxes reigned above 52 years, and who falsifies his best authority, altering the names, as in the case of the substitution of Xerxes for Artaxerxes throughout the book of Nehemiah, and suppressing the facts, as in the case of the omission of all mention of Ezra, Tobias, and Sanballat during the government of Nehemiah, is not entitled to much deference on our part. What has been said shows clearly how little Josephus' unsupported authority is worth; and how entirely the authenticity and credibility of Nehemiah remains unshaken by his blunders and confusions, and that there is no occasion to resort to the improbable hypothesis of two Sanballats, or to attribute to Nehemiah a patriarchal longevity, in order to bring his narrative into harmony with that of the Jewish historian.

2. As regards the authorship of the book, it is admitted by all critics that it is, as to its main parts, the genuine work of Nehemiah. But it is no less certain that interpolations and additions have been made in it since his time;[b] and there is considerable diversity of opinion as to what are the portions which have been so added. From i. 1 to vii. 6, no doubt or difficulty occurs. The writer speaks throughout in the first person singular, and in his character of governor תִּרְשָׁתָא. Again, from xii. 31, to the end of the book (except xii. 44–47), the narrative is continuous, and the use of the first person singular constant (xii. 31, 38, 40, xiii. 6, 7, &c.). It is therefore only in the intermediate chapters, vii. 6 to xii. 26, and xii. 44–47), that we have to inquire into the question of authorship, and this we will do by sections: —

(a.) The first section begins at Neh. vii. 6, and ends in the first half of viii. 1, at the words "one man." It has already been asserted [EZRA, BOOK OF. vol. i. p. 805 b] that this section is identical with the paragraph beginning Ezr. ii. 1, and ending iii. 1; and it was there also asserted that the par-

---

a It is worth remarking, that the apocryphal book quoted in 2 Macc. i. 28 seems to have made Nehemiah contemporary with Jonathan, or Johana, the high-priest

b K. F. Keil, in his *Einleitung*, endeavors indeed to vindicate Nehemiah's authorship for the whole book, but without success.

agraph originally belonged to the book of Nehe-miah, and was afterwards inserted in the place it occupies in Ezra.[a] Both these assertions must now be made good: and first as to the identity of the two passages. They are actually identical word for word, and letter for letter, except in two points. One that the numbers repeatedly vary. The other that there is a difference in the account of the offerings made by the governor, the nobles, and the people. But it can be proved that these are merely variations (whether accidental or designed) of the same text. In the first place the two passages are one and the same. The heading, the contents, the narrative about the sons of Barzillai, the fact of the offerings, the dwelling in their cities, the coming of the seventh month, the gathering of all the people to Jerusalem as one man, are in words and in sense the very self-same passage. The idea that the very same words, extending to 70 verses, describe differ-ent events, is simply absurd and irrational. The numbers therefore must originally have been the same in both books. But next, when we examine the varying numbers, we see the following particu-lar proofs that the variations are corruptions of the original text. Though the items vary, the sum total, 42,360, is the same (Ezr. ii. 64; Neh. vii. 66). In like manner the totals of the servants, the singing men and women, the horses, mules, and asses are all the same, except that Ezra has two hundred, instead of two hundred and forty-five, singing men and women. The numbers of the Priests and of the Levites are the same in both, except that the singers, the sons of Asaph, are 128 in Ezra against 148 in Nehemiah, and the porters 139 against 138. Then in each particular case when the numbers differ, we see plainly how the difference might arise. In the statement of the number of the sons of Arah (the first case in which the lists differ), Ezr. ii. 5, we read, שְׁבַע מֵאוֹת

חֲמִשָּׁה וְשִׁבְעִים, "seven hundred five and seventy," whereas in Neh. vii. 10, we read, שְׁ

מֵאוֹת חֲמִשִּׁים וּשְׁנַיִם. But the order of the numerals in Ezr. ii. 5, where the units precede the tens, is the only case in which this order is found. Obviously, therefore, we ought to read חֲמִשִּׁים instead of חֲמִשָּׁה, fifty instead of five. No less obviously שִׁבְעִים may be a corruption of the almost identical שְׁנַיִם and probably caused the preceding change of חֲמִשָּׁה into חֲמִשִּׁים.[b] But the tens and units being identical, it is evi-dent that the variation in the hundreds is an error, arising from both six and seven beginning with the same letter שׁ. The very same interchange of six and seven takes place in the number of Adonikam, and Bigvai, only in the units (Neh. vii. 18, 19; Ezr. ii. 13, 14). In Pahath-Moab, the variation from 2812, Ezr. ii. 6, to 2818, Neh. vii. 11; in Zattu, from 945, Ezr. ii. 8, to 845, Neh. vii. 13; in Bin-nui, from 642 to 648; in Bebai, from 623 to 628;

in Hashum, from 223 to 328; in Senaah, from 3630 to 3930; the same cause has operated, name-ly, that in the numbers two and eight, three and eight, nine and six, the same initial שׁ is found; and the resemblance in these numbers may prob-ably have been greatly increased by abbreviations. In Azgad (1222 and 2322) as in Senaah, the mere circumstance of the tens and units being the same in both passages, while the thousands differ by the mere addition or omission of a final ם, is suf-ficient proof that the variation is a clerical one only. In Adin, Neh. vii. 20, six for four, in the hundreds, is probably caused by the six hundred of the just preceding Adonikans. In the four remaining cases the variations are equally easy of explanation, and the result is to leave not the slightest doubt that the enumeration was identical in the first instance in both passages. It may, however, be added, as completing the proof that these variations do not arise from Ezra giving the census in Zerubbabel's time, and Nehemiah that in his own time (as Ceillier, Prideaux, and other learned men have thought), that in the cases of Paroeh, Pahath-Moab, Elam, Shephatiah, Bebai, Azgad, and Adonikam, of which we are told in Ezr. viii. 3-14, that considerable numbers came up to Judæa in the reign of Artaxerxes — long sub-sequent therefore to the time of Zerubbabel — the numbers are either exactly the same in Ezr. ii. and Neh vii., or exhibit such variations as have no relation whatever to the numbers of those families respectively who were added to the Jewish resi-dents in Palestine under Artaxerxes.

To turn next to the offerings. The book of Ezra (ii. 68, 69) merely gives the sum total, as follows: 61,000[c] drachms of gold, 5,000 pounds of silver, and 100 priests' garments. The book of Nehemiah gives no sum total, but gives the following items (vii. 72): —

The Tirshatha gave 1000[c] drachms of gold, 50 basons, 530 priests' garments.

The chief of the fathers gave 20,000 drachms of gold, and 2,200 pounds of silver.

The rest of the people gave 20,000 drachms of gold, 2,000 pounds of silver, and 67 priests' garments.

Here then we learn that these offerings were made in three shares, by three distinct parties: the governor, the chief fathers, the people. The sum total of drachms of gold, we learn from Ezra, was 61,000. The shares, we learn from Nehemiah, were 20,000 in two out of the three donors, but 1,000 in the case of the third and chief donor! Is it not quite evident that in the case of Nehe-miah the 20 has slipped out of the text (as in 1 Esdr. v. 45, 60,000 has), and that his real con-tribution was 21,000? his generosity prompting him to give in excess of his fair third. Next, as regards the pounds of silver. The sum total was, according to Ezra, 5,000. The shares were, accord-ing to Nehemiah, 2,200 pounds from the chiefs, and 2,000 from the people. But the LXX. give 2,300 for the chiefs, and 2,200 for the people, making 4,500 in all, and so leaving a deficiency

stead of שִׁבְעִים), then the שְׁנַיִם of Neh. vii. 10 is easily accounted for by the fact that the two pre-ceding numbers of Paroeh and Shephatiah both end with the same number two.

[c] Observe the odd thousand in both cases

NEHEMIAH, BOOK OF

of 500 pounds as compared with Ezra's total of 5,000, and ascribing no silver offering to the Tirshatha. As regards the priests' garments. The sum total as given in both the Hebrew and Greek text of Ezra, and in 1 Esdr., is 100. The items as given in Neh. vii. 70, are 530 + 67 = 597. But the LXX. give 30 + 67 = 97, and that this is nearly correct is apparent from the numbers themselves. For the total being 100, 33 is the nearest whole number to 1 8 8 , and 67 is the nearest whole number to 8 ⁄ 8 × 100. So that we cannot doubt that the Tirshatha gave 33 priests' garments, and the rest of the people gave 67, probably in two gifts of 34 and 33, making in all 100. But how came the 500 to be added on to the Tirshatha's tale of garments? Clearly it is a fragment of the missing 500 pounds of silver, which, with the 50 bowls, made up the Tirshatha's donation of silver. So that Neh. vii. 70 ought to be read thus, " The Tirshatha gave to the treasure 21,000 drachms of gold, 50 basons, 500 pounds of silver, and 33 priests' garments." The offerings then, as well as the numbers in the lists, were once identical in both books, and we learn from Ezr. ii. 68, what the book of Nehemiah does not expressly tell us (though the *priests' garments* strongly indicate it), what was the purpose of this liberal contribution, namely, " to set up the House of God in his place " (לְהַעֲמִידוֹ עַל מְכוֹנוֹ). From this phrase occurring in Ezr. ii. just before the account of the building of the Temple by Zerubbabel, it has usually been understood as referring to the rebuilding. But it really means no such thing. The phrase properly implies restoration and preservation, as may be seen in the exactly similar case of the restoration of the Temple by Jehoiada, 2 Chr. xxiv. 13, after the injuries and neglect under Athalia, where we read, וַיַּעֲמִידוּ אֶת־בֵּית הָאֱלֹהִים עַל מַתְכֻּנְתּוֹ, " they set the House of God in its state " (comp. also 1 K. xv. 4). The fact then was that, when all the rulers and nobles and people were gathered together at Jerusalem to be registered in the seventh month, advantage was taken of the opportunity to collect their contributions to restore the Temple also (2 Macc. i. 18), which had naturally partaken of the general misery and affliction of Jerusalem, but which it would not have been wise to restore till the rebuilding of the wall placed the city in a state of safety. At the same time, and in the same spirit, they formed the resolutions recorded in Neh. x. 32–39, to keep up the Temple ritual.

It already follows, from what has been said, that the section under consideration is in its right place in the book of Nehemiah, and was inserted subsequently in the book of Ezra out of its chronological order. But one or two additional proofs of this must be mentioned. The most convincing and palpable of these is perhaps the mention of the Tirshatha in Ezr. ii. 63; Neh. vii. 65. That the Tirshatha, here and at Neh. vii. 70, means Nehemiah, we are expressly told (Neh. viii. 9, x. 1),[a] and therefore it is perfectly certain that what is related (Ezr. ii. 62; Neh. vii. 64) happened in Nehemiah's time, and not in Zerubbabel's. Consequently the

taking of the census, which gave rise to that incident, belongs to the same time. In other words, the section we are considering is in its original and right place in the book of Nehemiah, and was transferred from thence to the book of Ezra, where it stands out of its chronological order. And this is still further evident from the circumstance that the closing portion of this section is an abbreviation of the same portion as it stands in Nehemiah, proving that the passage existed in Nehemiah before it was inserted in Ezra. Another proof is the mention of Ezra as taking part in that assembly of the people at Jerusalem which is described in Ezr. iii. 1; Neh. viii. 1; for Ezra did not come to Jerusalem till the reign of Artaxerxes (Ezr. vii.). Another is the mention of Nehemiah as one of the leaders under whom the captives enumerated in the census came up, Ezr. ii. 2; Neh. vii. 7: in both which passages the juxtaposition of Nehemiah with Seraiah, when compared with Neh. x. 1, 2, greatly strengthens the conclusion that Nehemiah the Tirshatha is meant. Then again, that Nehemiah should summon all the families of Israel to Jerusalem to take their census, and that, having done so at great cost of time and trouble, he, or whoever was employed by him, should merely transcribe an old census taken nearly 100 years before, instead of recording the result of his own labors, is so improbable that nothing but the plainest necessity could make one believe it. The only difficulty in the way is that the words in Neh. vii. 5, 6, seem to describe the register which follows as " the register of the genealogy of them which came up at the first," and that the expression, " and found written therein," requires that the words which follow should be a quotation from that register (comp. vi. 6). To this difficulty (and it is a difficulty at first sight) it is a sufficient answer to say that the words quoted are only those (in Neh. vii. 6) which contain the title of the register found by Nehemiah. His own new register begins with the words at ver. 7: הַבָּאִים, etc., " The men who came with Zerubbabel," etc., which form the descriptive title of the following catalogue.[b] Nehemiah, or those employed by him to take the new census, doubtless made use of the old register (sanctioned as it had been by Haggai and Zechariah) as an authority by which to decide the genealogies of the present generation. And hence it was that when the sons of Barzillai claimed to be entered into the register of priestly families, but could not produce the entry of their house in that old register, Nehemiah refused to admit them to the priestly office (63–65), but made a note of their claim, that it might be decided whenever a competent authority should arise. From all which it is abundantly clear that the section under consideration belongs properly to the book of Nehemiah. It does not follow, however, that it was written in its present form by Nehemiah himself. Indeed the sudden change to the third person, in speaking of the Tirshatha, in vv. 65, 70 (a change which continues regularly till the section beginning xii. 31), is a strong indication of a change in the writer, as is also the use of the term Tirshatha instead of Pechah, which last is

---

[a] It is worth noticing that Nehemiah's name is mentioned as the Tirshatha in 1 Esdr. v. 40.
[b] Were it not for the mention of Nehemiah and

Mordecai in ver. 7, one might have thought Nehemiah's register began with the words, " The number of the men," in ver. 7.

the official designation by which Nehemiah speaks of himself and other governors (v. 14, 18, ii. 7, 9, iii. 7). It seems probable, therefore, that ch. vii., from ver. 7, contains the substance of what was found in this part of Nehemiah's narrative, but abridged, and in the form of an abstract, which may account for the difficulty of separating Nehemiah's register from Zerubbabel's, and also for the very abrupt mention of the gifts of the Tirshatha and the people at the end of the chapter. This abstract formed a transition from Nehemiah's narrative in the preceding chapters to the entirely new matter inserted in the following sections.

(b.) The next section commences Neh. viii., latter part of ver. 1, and ends Neh. xi. 3. Now throughout this section several things are observable. (1.) Nehemiah does not once speak in the first person (viii. 9, x. 1). (2.) Nehemiah is no longer the principal actor in what is done, but almost disappears from the scene, instead of being, as in the first six chapters, the centre of the whole action. (3.) Ezra for the first time is introduced, and throughout the whole section the most prominent place is assigned either to him personally, or to strictly ecclesiastical affairs. (4.) The prayer in ch. ix. is very different in its construction from Nehemiah's prayer in ch. i., and in its frequent references to the various books of the O. T. singularly suited to the character and acquirements of Ezra, "the ready scribe in the law of Moses." (5.) The section was written by an eye-witness and actor in the events described. This appears by the minute details, e. g. viii. 4, 5, 6, &c., and the use of the first person plural (x. 30–39). (6.) There is a strong resemblance to the style and manner of Ezra's narrative, and also an identity in the use of particular phrases (comp. Ezr. iv. 18, Neh. viii. 8; Ezr. vi. 22, Neh. viii. 17). This resemblance is admitted by critics of the most opposite opinions (see Keil's Einleitung, p. 461). Hence, as Ezra's manner is to speak of himself in the third as well as in the first person, there is great probability in the opinion advocated by Hävernick and Kleinert,[a] that this section is the work of Ezra. The fact, too, that 1 Esdr. ix. 38 sqq. annexes Neh. viii. 1–13 to Ezr. x., in which it is followed by Josephus (Ant. xi. 5, § 5), is perhaps an indication that it was known to be the work of Ezra. It is not necessary to suppose that Ezra himself inserted this or any other part of the present book of Nehemiah in the midst of the Tirshatha's history. But if there was extant an account of these transactions by Ezra, it may have been thus incorporated with Nehemiah's history by the last editor of Scripture. Nor is it impossible that the union of Ezra and Nehemiah as one book in the ancient Hebrew arrangement (as Jerome testifies), under the title of the Book of Ezra, may have had its origin in this circumstance.

(c.) The third section consists of ch. xi. 3–36. It contains a list of the families of Judah, Benjamin, and Levi (priests and Levites), who took up their abode at Jerusalem, in accordance with the resolution of the volunteers, and the decision of the lot, mentioned in xi. 1, 2. This list forms a kind of supplement to that in vii. 8–60, as

appears by the allusion in xi. 3 to that previous document. For ver. 3 distinguishes the following list of the "dwellers at Jerusalem" from the foregoing one of "Israel, priests, Levites, Nethinim, and children of Solomon's servants," who dwelt in the cities of Israel, as set forth in ch. vii. This list is an extract from the official roll preserved in the national archives, only somewhat abbreviated, as appears by a comparison with 1 Chr. ix., where an abstract of the same roll is also preserved in a fuller form, and in the latter part especially with considerable variations and additions: it seems also to be quite out of its place in Chronicles, and its insertion there probably caused the repetition of 1 Chr. viii. 29–40, which is found in duplicate ix. 35–44: in the latter place wholly unconnected with ix. 1–34, but connected with what follows (ch. x. ff.), as well as with what precedes ch. ix. Whence it appears clearly that 1 Chr. ix. 2–34 is a later insertion made after Nehemiah's census,[b] but proving by its very incoherence that the book of Chronicles existed previous to its insertion. But this by the way. The nature of the information in this section, and the parallel passage in 1 Chr., would rather indicate a Levitical hand. It might or might not have been the same which inserted the preceding section. If written later, it is perhaps the work of the same person who inserted xii. 1–30, 44–47. In conjunction with 1 Chr. ix. it gives us minute and interesting information concerning the families residing at Jerusalem,[c] and their genealogies, and especially concerning the provision for the Temple-service. The grant made by Artaxerxes (ver. 23) for the maintenance of the singers is exactly parallel to that made by Darius as set forth in Ezr. vi. 8, 9, 10. The statement in ver. 24 concerning Pethahiah the Zarhite, as "at the king's hand in all matters concerning the people," is somewhat obscure, unless perchance it alludes to the time of Nehemiah's absence in Babylon, when Pethahiah may have been a kind of deputy-governor ad interim.

(d.) From xii. 1 to 26 is clearly and certainly an abstract from the official lists made and inserted here long after Nehemiah's time, and after the destruction of the Persian dynasty by Alexander the Great, as is plainly indicated by the expression Darius the Persian, as well as by the mention of Jaddua. The allusion to Jeshua, and to Nehemiah and Ezra, in ver. 26, is also such as would be made long posterior to their lifetime, and contains a remarkable reference to the two censuses taken and written down, the one in Jeshua and Zerubbabel's time, the other in the time of Nehemiah; for it is evidently from these two censuses, the existence of which is borne witness to in Neh. vii. 5, that the writer of xii. 26 drew his information concerning the priestly families at those two epochs (compare also xii. 47).

The juxtaposition of the list of priests in Zerubbabel's time, with that of those who sealed the covenant in Nehemiah's time, as given below, both illustrates the use of proper names above referred to, and also the clerical fluctuations to which proper names are subject.

---

a Kleinert ascribes ch. viii. to an assistant, ix. and x. to Ezra himself. See De Wette's Einleitung, Parker's transl. ii. 332.

b Comp. 1 Chr. ix. 2 with Neh. vii. 73

c That these families were objects of especial interest appears from Neh. xi. 2.

Neh. x. 1-8.	Neh. xii. 1-7.
Seraiah	Seraiah
Azariah	Ezra
Jeremiah	Jeremiah
Pashur	—
Amariah	Amariah
Malchijah	Malluch
Hattush	Hattush
Shebaniah	Shecaniah
Malluch	*Malluch* (above)
Harim	Rehum
Meremoth	Meremoth
Obadiah	Iddo
Daniel	—
Ginnethon	Ginnetho
Baruch	—
Meshullam	
Abijah	Abijah
Mijamin	Miamin
Maaziah	Maadiah
Bilgai	Bilgah
Shemaiah	Shemaiah
	Joiarib
	Jedaiah
	Sallu
	Amok
	Hilkiah
	Jedaiah.

(e.) xii. 44–47 is an explanatory interpolation, made in later times, probably by the last reviser of the book, whoever he was. That it is so is evident not only from the sudden change from the first person to the third, and the dropping of the personal narrative (though the matter is one in which Nehemiah necessarily took the lead), but from the fact that it describes the identical transaction described in xiii. 10–13 by Nehemiah himself, where he speaks as we should expect him to speak: "And I made treasurers over the treasuries," etc. The language, too, of ver. 47 is manifestly that of one looking back upon the times of Zerubbabel and those of Nehemiah as alike past. In like manner xii. 27–30 is the account by the same annotator of what Nehemiah himself relates, xiii. 10–12.

Though, however, it is not difficult thus to point out those passages of the book which were not part of Nehemiah's own work, it is not easy, by cutting them out, to restore that work to its integrity. For Neh. xii. 31 does not fit on well to any part of ch. vii., or, in other words, the latter portion of Nehemiah's work does not join on to the former. Had the former part been merely a kind of diary entered day by day, one might have supposed that it was abruptly interrupted and as abruptly resumed. But as Neh. v. 14 distinctly shows that the whole history was either written or revised by the author after he had been governor twelve years, such a supposition cannot stand. It should seem, therefore, that we have only the first and last parts of Nehemiah's work, and that for some reason the intermediate portion has been displaced to make room for the narrative and documents from Neh. vii. 7 to xii. 27.

And we are greatly confirmed in this supposition by observing that in the very chapter where we first notice this abrupt change of person, we have another evidence that we have not the whole of what Nehemiah wrote. For at the close of chap. vii. we have an account of the offerings made by the governor, the chiefs, and the people; but we are not even told for what purpose these offerings were made. Only we are led to guess that it must have been for the Temple, as the parallel passage in Ezr. ii. tells us it was, by the mention of the priests' garments which formed a part of the offerings. Obviously, therefore, the original work must have contained an account of some transactions connected with repairing or beautifying the Temple, which led to these contributions being made. Now, it so happens that there is a passage in 2 Macc. ii. 13, in which "the writings and commentaries of Nehemiah" are referred to in a way which shows that they contained matter relative to the sacred fire having consumed the sacrifices offered by Nehemiah on some solemn occasion when he repaired and dedicated the Temple, which is not found in the present book of Nehemiah; and if any dependence can be placed upon the account there given, and in i. 18–36, we seem to have exactly the two facts that we want to justify our hypothesis. The one, that Nehemiah's narrative at this part contained some things which were not suited to form part of the Bible;[a] the other, that it formerly contained some account which would be the natural occasion for mentioning the offerings which come in so abruptly at present. If this were so, and the exceptional matter was consequently omitted, and an abridged notice of the offerings retained, we should have exactly the appearance which we actually have in chap. vii.

Nor is such an explanation less suited to connect the latter portion of Nehemiah's narrative with the former. Chap. xii. 31 goes on to describe the dedication of the wall and its ceremonial. How naturally this would be the sequel of that dedication of the restored Temple spoken of by the author of 2 Macc. it is needless to observe. So that if we suppose the missing portions of Nehemiah's history which described the dedication service of the Temple to have followed his description of the census in ch. vii., and to have been followed by the account of the offerings, and then to have been succeeded by the dedication of the wall, we have a perfectly natural and consistent narrative. In erasing what was irrelevant, and inserting the intervening matter, of course no pains were taken, because no desire existed, to disguise the operation, or to make the joints smooth; the object being simply to preserve an authentic record without reference to authorship or literary perfection.

Another circumstance which lends much probability to the statement in 2 Macc., is that the writer closely connects what Nehemiah did with what Solomon had done before him, in this, one may guess, following Nehemiah's narrative. But in the extant portion of our book, Neh. i. 6, we have a distinct allusion to Solomon's prayer (1 K. viii. 28, 29), as also in Neh. xiii. 26, we have to another part of Solomon's life. So that on the whole the passage in 2 Macc. lends considerable support to the theory that the middle portion of Nehemiah's work was cut out, and that there was substituted for it partly an abridged abstract, and partly Ezra's narrative and other appended documents.[b]

---

[a] It is not necessary to believe that Nehemiah wrote all that is attributed to him in 2 Macc. It is very probable that there was an apocryphal version of his book, with additions and embellishments. Still even the original work may have contained matter either not strictly authentic, or for some other reason not suited to have a place in the canon.

[b] Cellérier also supposes that part of Nehemiah's work may be now lost.

We may then affirm with tolerable certainty that all the middle part of the book of Nehemiah has been supplied by other hands, and that the first six chapters and part of the seventh, and the last chapter and half, were alone written by him, the intermediate portion being inserted by those who had authority to do so, in order to complete the history of the transactions of those times. The difference of authorship being marked especially by this, that, in the first and last portions, Nehemiah *invariably* speaks in the first person singular (except in the inserted verses vii. 44–47), but in the middle portion *never*. It is in this middle portion alone that matter unsuited to Nehemiah's times (as *e. g.* Neh. xii. 11, 22) is found, that obscurity of connection exists, and that the variety of style (as almost all critics admit) suggests a different authorship. But when it is remembered that the book of Nehemiah is in fact a continuation of the Chronicles,[a] being reckoned by the Hebrews, as Jerome testifies, as one with Ezra, which was confessedly so, and that, as we have seen under EZRA, CHRONICLES, and KINGS, the customary method of composing the national chronicles was to make use of contemporary writings, and work them up according to the requirements of the case, it will cease to surprise us in the least that Nehemiah's diary should have been so used: nor will the admixture of other contemporary documents with it, or the addition of any reflections by the latest editor of it, in any way detract from its authenticity or authority.

As regards the time when the book of Nehemiah was put into its present form, we have only the following data to guide us. The latest high-priest mentioned, Jaddua, was doubtless still alive when his name was added. The descriptive addition to the name of Darius (xii. 22) "the Persian," indicates that the Persian rule had ceased, and the Greek rule had begun. Jaddua's name, therefore, and the clause at the end of ver. 22, were inserted early in the reign of Alexander the Great. But it appears that the registers of the Levites, entered into the Chronicles, did not come down lower than the time of Johanan (ver. 23); and it even seems from the distribution of the conjunction "and" in ver. 22, that the name of Jaddua was not included when the sentence was first written, but stopped at *Johanan*, and that Jaddua and the clause about the priests were added later. So that the close of the Persian dominion, and the beginning of the Greek, is the time clearly indicated when the latest additions were made. But whether this addition was anything more than the insertion of the documents contained from ch. xi. 3 to xii. 26, or even much less; or whether at the same time, or at an earlier one, the great alteration was made of substituting the abridgment in ch. vii. in the contemporary narratives in ch. viii., ix., x., for what Nehemiah had written, there seems to be no means of deciding.[b] Nor is the decision of much consequence, except that it would be interesting to know exactly when the volume of Holy Scripture definitively assumed its present shape, and who were the persons who put the finishing hand to it.

3. In respect to language and style, this book is very similar to the Chronicles and Ezra. Nehemiah has, it is true, quite his own manner, and, as De Wette has observed, certain phrases and modes of expression peculiar to himself. He has also some few words and forms not found elsewhere in Scripture; but the general Hebrew style is exactly that of the books purporting to be of the same age. Some words, as מְצִלְתַּיִם, "cymbals," occur in Chron., Ezr., and Neh., but nowhere else. הִתְנַדֵּב occurs frequently in the same three books, but only twice (in Judg. v.) besides. אִגֶּרֶת or אִגְּרָא, "a letter," is common only to Neh., Esth., Ezr., and Chron. בִּירָה, and its Chaldee equivalent, בִּירְתָא, whether spoken of the palace at Susa, or of the Temple at Jerusalem, are common only to Neh., Ezr., Esth., Dan., and Chron. שֶׁגַל to Neh., and Dan., and Ps. xlv. The phrase אֱלֹהֵי הַשָּׁמַיִם, and its Chaldee equivalent, "the God of Heavens," are common to Ezr., Neh., and Dan. מְפֹרָשׁ, "distinctly," is common to Ezr. and Neh. Such words as פַּרְדֵּס, מְדִינָה, סָגָן, and such Aramaisms as the use of חֶבֶל, i. 7, יִמְלָךְ, v. 7, מִדָּה, v. 4, &c., are also evidences of the age when Nehemiah wrote. As examples of peculiar words or meanings, used in this book alone, the following may be mentioned: שָׁבַר, "to inspect," ii. 13, 15; מְאָה, in the sense of "interest," v. 11; נוּף (in Hiph.), "to shut," vii. 3; מוֹעֵל, "a lifting up," viii. 6; הִידוֹת, "praises," or "choirs," xii. 8; תַּהֲלוּכָה, "a procession," xii. 31; מִקְרָא, in sense of "reading," viii. 8; אֲצָרֶה, for אֲצָרָה, xiii. 13, where both form and sense are alike unusual.

The Aramean form, יְהוֹדָה, Hiph. of יָדָה for יוֹדָה, is very rare, only five[c] other analogous examples occurring in the Heb. Scriptures, though it is very common in Biblical Chaldee.

The phrase אִישׁ שָׁלְחוּ הַפַּיִם, iv. 17 (which is omitted by the LXX.) is incapable of explanation. One would have expected, instead of הַפַּיִם, בְּיָדוֹ, as in 2 Chr. xxiii. 10.

הַתִּרְשָׁתָא, "the Tirshatha," which only occurs in Ezr. ii. 63; Neh. vii. 65, 70, viii. 9, x. 1, is of uncertain etymology and meaning. It is a term applied only to Nehemiah, and seems to be more likely to mean "cupbearer" than "governor," though the latter interpretation is adopted by Gesenius (*Thes.* s. v.).

The text of Nehemiah is generally pure and free from corruption, except in the proper names, in which there is considerable fluctuation in the orthography, both as compared with other parts of the same book and with the same names in other parts of Scripture; and also in numerals.

---

[a] So Ewald also.

[b] If we knew the real history of the title Tirshatha, it might assist us in determining the date of the passage where it appears.

[c] Ps. xlv. 18, cxvi. 6; 1 Sam. xvii. 47; Is. lii. 5; Ez. xlvi. 2d (*Journ. of Sac Lit.* Jan. 1861, p. 382).

Of the latter we have seen several examples in the parallel passages Ezr. ii. and Neh. vii.; and the same lists will give variations in names of men. So will xii. 1-7, compared with xii. 12, and with x. 1-8.

A comparison of Neh. xi. 3, &c., with 1 Chr. ix. 2, &c., exhibits the following fluctuations: Neh. xi. 4, *Athaiah* of the children of Perez = 1 Chr. ix. 4, *Uthai* of the children of Perez; v. 5, *Maaseiah* the son of Shiloni = v. 5, of the Shilonites, *Asaiah*; v. 9, *Judah* the son of Senuah (Heb. Hasenuah) = v. 7, *Hodaviah* the son of Hasenuah; v. 10, Jedaiah the son of Joiarib, Jachin = v. 10, Jedaiah, Jehoiarib, Jachin; v. 13, *Amasai* son of Azareel = v. 12, *Maasai* son of Jahzerah; v. 17, Micah the son of *Zabdi* = v. 15, Micah the son of *Zichri* (comp. Neh. xii. 35). To which many others might be added.

Many various readings are also indicated by the LXX. version. For example, at ii. 13, for תַּנִּים, "dragon," they read תְּאֵנִים, "figs," and render it τῶν συκῶν. At ii. 20, for נָקוּם, "we will arise," they read נְקִיִּים, "pure," and render it καθαροί. At iii. 2, for בָּנוּ, "they built," they read twice בְּנֵי, υἱῶν; and so at ver. 13. At iii. 15, for בְּרֵכַת הַשֶּׁלַח לְגַן הַמֶּלֶךְ, "the pool of Siloah by the king's garden," they read בֵּ֑ ח֑ לְגַז ח֑ "the king's fleece," and render it κολυμβήθρας τῶν κωδίων τῇ κουρᾷ τοῦ βασιλέως· κουρά being the word by which גַּז is rendered in Deut. xviii. 4. הַשֶּׁלַח is rendered by κωδίων, "sheep-skins," in the Chaldee sense of שֶׁלַח or שַׁלְחָא, a fleece recently stripped from the animal (Castell. *Lex.*). At iii. 16, for נֶגֶד, "over against," they read גַּן, "the garden;" comp. ver. 26: in iii. 34, 35 (iv. 2, 3), they seem to have had a corrupt and unintelligible text. At v. 5, for אֲחֵרִים, "others," they read הֶחָרִים, "the nobles:" v. 11, for מְאָת, "the hundredth," they read מְנָת, "some of," rendering ἀπό: vi. 1, for בָּהּ פֶּרֶץ, there was left no "breach in it," namely, the wall, they read בָּם רוּחַ, "spirit in them," namely, Sanballat, etc., rendering ἐν αὐτοῖς πνοή· vi. 3, for אֶרְפֶּה, "I leave it," they read אֲרַפֶּאנָה, "I complete it," τελειώσω which gives a better sense. At vii. 68, ff., the number of asses is 2,700 instead of 6,720; of priests' garments, 30 instead of 530; of pounds of silver, 2,300 and 2,200, instead of 2,200 and 2,000, as has been noticed above; and ver. 70, τῷ Νεεμίᾳ, for "the Tirshatha." At xi. 11, for נָגִיד, "ruler," they read נֶגֶד, "over against," ἀπέναντι. At xii. 8, for הֻיְּדוֹת, "thanksgiving," הַיְּדוֹת, ἐπὶ τῶν χειρῶν: xii. 25, for אֲסֻפֵּי, "the treasuries," אֲסֻפֵּי, "my gathering together," ἐν τῷ συναγαγεῖν με· and at xii. 44, for שָׂדֵי, "the fields,"

they read שָׂרֵי, "the princes," ἄρχουσι τῶν πό λεων: with other minor variations. The principal additions are at viii. 8, 15, and ix. 6, where the name of Ezra is introduced, and in the first passage also the words ἐν ἐπιστήμην κυρίου. The omissions of words and whole verses are numerous: as at iii. 37, 38 (A. V. 5, 6); iv. 17 (23, A. V. and LXX.); vi. 4, 5, 6, 10, 11; vii. 68, 69; viii. 4, 7, 9, 10; ix. 3, 5, 23; xi. 13, 16-21, 23-26, 28-35; xii. 3-7, 9, 25, 28, 29, the whole of 38, 40, 41, and half 42; xiii. 13, 14, 16, 20, 24, 25.

The following discrepancies seem to have their origin in the Greek text itself: viii. 16, πλατείαις τῆς πόλεως, instead of πυλῆς, Heb. שַׁעַר הַמָּיִם: x. 2, ΥΙΟΣ ΑΡΑΙΑ for ΚΑΙ ΣΑΡΑΙΑ: xi. 4, Σαμαρία for Ἀμαρία, the final Σ of the preceding υἱός having stuck to the beginning of the name: xii. 31, ἀνήνεγκαν, instead of —κα· "I brought up:" xii. 39, ἰχθυρὰν, instead of ἰχθυρὰν, as in iii. 3. It is also worthy of remark that a number of Hebrew words are left untranslated in the Greek version of the LXX., which probably indicates a want of learning in the translator. The following are the chief instances: Chaps. i. 1, and vii. 2, ἀβιρά, and τῆς βιρά, for הַבִּירָה; ii. 13, τοῦ γωληλά for הַגַּיא לַיְלָה; ib. 14, τοῦ αἰν for הָעָיִן; iii. 5, οἱ Θεκωῒμ for הַתְּקוֹעִים; ib. ἀδωρίμ for אַדִּירֵיהֶם; ib. 6, Ιασαναῒ for הַיְשָׁנָה; ib. 8, ῥωκεῒμ for הָרַקָּחִים; ib. 11, τῶν θανουρίμ for הַתַּנּוּרִים; iii. 16, Βηθαγγαρίμ for בֵּית הַגַּבֹּרִים; ib. 20, 21, Βηθελιασσούβ for בֵּית אֶלְיָשִׁיב, cf. 24; ib. 22, Ἐκχεχάρ for הַכִּכָּר; ib. 31, τοῦ σαρεφὶ for הַצֹּרְפִי, and Βηθὰν Ναθινίμ for בֵּית הַנְּתִינִים; vii. 34, Ἠλαμαδρ for עֵילָם אַחֵר; ib. 65, ἀθερσασθά, and x. 1, ἀρτασασθά, for הַתִּרְשָׁתָא; vii. 70, 72, χωθωνώθ for כָּתְנוֹת; xii. 27, θωδαθά for תּוֹדֹת; xiii. 5, 9, τὴν μαναά for הַמִּנְחָה.

4. The book of Nehemiah has always had an undisputed place in the Canon, being included by the Hebrews under the general head of the Book of Ezra, and as Jerome tells us in the *Prolog. Gal.*, by the Greeks and Latins under the name of the Second Book of Ezra. [ESDRAS, FIRST BOOK OF.] There is no quotation from it in the N. T., and it has been comparatively neglected by both the Greek and Latin fathers, perhaps on account of its simple character, and the absence of anything supernatural, prophetical, or mystical in its contents. St. Jerome (*ad Paulinam*) does indeed suggest that the account of the building of the walls, and the return of the people, the description of the Priests, Levites, Israelites, and proselytes, and the division of the labor among the different families, have a hidden meaning: and also hints that Nehemiah's name, which he interprets *consolator a Domino*, points to a mystical sense. But the book does not easily lend itself to such applications, which are so manifestly forced and strained, that even Augustine says of the whole book of Ezra that it is simply historical rather than prophetical (*De Civit. Dei*, xviii. 36). Those, however,

who wish to see St. Jerome's hint elaborately carried out, may refer to the Ven. Bede's *Allegorica Expositio in Librum Nehemiæ, qui et Ezræ Secundus*, as well as to the preface to his exposition of Ezra; and, in another sense, to Bp. Pilkington's Exposition upon Nehemiah, and John Fox's Preface (*Park. Soc.*). It may be added that Bede describes both Ezra and Nehemiah as *prophets*, which is the head under which Josephus includes them in his description of the sacred books (*C. Ap.* i. 8).

Keil's *Einleitung*; Winer's *Realwört.*; De Wette's *Einleitung*, by Th. Parker; Prideaux's *Connection*; Caillier's *Auteurs Ecclésiast.*; Wolf, *Bibl. Hebraic*; Ewald, *Geschichte*, i. 225, iv. 144; Thrupp's *Ancient Jerusalem*; Bosanquet's *Times of Ezra and Nehemiah.*   A. C. H.

* The circle of inquiry relating to the authorship, structure, and contents of the book of Nehemiah, coincides very nearly with that of the same topics connected with EZRA. We are not to lay too much stress on the argument against the unity of the book, from the narrator's interchange of the first and third persons in different parts. That conclusion, as Prof. Rawlinson remarks, does not always follow from such premises. Daniel, for instance, uses the third person through his first six chapters and at the opening of the seventh, and then the first to the end of ch. ix. In the first verse of ch. x. he returns to the third person, but in the two remaining chapters employs again the first (*Historical Evidences*, lect. V.). Thucydides furnishes a similar example among Greek writers. Neh. xii. 10–22 appears to be the only part which it is necessary, on account of the subject of discourse, to ascribe to a later hand. As for the rest, Ezra and Nehemiah may have depended on each other, or have used common sources.

Among the commentators on Nehemiah are Jo. Clericus, *Comm. in Libros Historicos V. T.* (1708); Strigelius, *Scholia in Neham.* (1575); Rambach, *Annotatt. in Libr. Nehem.*; Bertheau, *Exeget. Handb.* xvii.; Wordsworth, *Holy Bible, with Notes and Introductions*, iii. 325–357. Other important writers are Hävernick, *Handb. der Einl. in das A. T.*, ii. 302–328; Herbst-Welte, *Einl. in das A. Test.*, ii. 231–249; Keil, *Lehrbuch der Einl. in das A. Test.*, pp. 460–468 (3te Aufl.); Bleek, *Einl. in das A. Test.*, pp. 373–391; G. Nägelsbach, *Ezra u. Nehemia* in Herzog's *Real-Encyk* iv. 165–174; Wunderlich in Zeller's *Bibl. Wörterb.* ii. 186–188. Davidson's *Hebrew Text of the O. T., revised from Critical Sources*, pp. 206–209, furnishes some material for textual emendation (Lond. 1855). The true orthography of several of the proper names is uncertain.   H.

NEHEMI'AS (Νεεμίας: *Nehemias*). 1. Nehemiah, the contemporary of Zerubbabel and Jeshua (1 Esdr. v. 8).

2. [Vat. Ναμμας.] Nehemiah the Tirshatha, son of Hachaliah (1 Esdr. v. 40).

NE'HILOTH. The title of Ps. v. in the A. V. is rendered "to the chief musician upon Nehiloth" (אֶל־הַנְּחִילוֹת); LXX., Aquila, Symmachus, and Theodotion translate the last 'wo words ὑπὲρ τῆς κληρονομούσης, and the Vulgate, "pro ea quæ hæreditatem consequitur." by which Augustine understands the Church. The origin of their error was a mistaken etymology, by which Nehiloth is derived from נָחַל, *nāchal*,

to inherit. Other etymologies have been proposed which are equally unsound. In Chaldee נָחִיל, *nāchīl*, signifies "a swarm of bees," and hence Jarchi attributes to Nehiloth the notion of multitude, the Psalm being sung by the whole people of Israel. R. Hai, quoted by Kimchi, adopting the same origin for the word, explains it as an instrument, the sound of which was like the hum of bees, a wind instrument, according to Sonntag (*de tit. Psal.* p. 430), which had a rough tone. Michaelis (*Suppl. ad Lex. Heb.* p. 1629) suggests, with not unreasonable timidity, that the root is to be found in the Arab. نَخَلَ, *nachala*, to winnow, and hence to separate and select the better part, indicating that the Psalm, in the title of which Nehiloth occurs, was "an ode to be chanted by the purified and better portion of the people." It is most likely, as Gesenius and others explain, that it is derived from the root חָלַל, *chālal*, to bore, perforate, whence חָלִיל *chālīl*, a flute or pipe (1 Sam. x. 5; 1 K. i. 40), so that Nehiloth is the general term for perforated wind instruments of all kinds, as Neginoth denotes all manner of stringed instruments. The title of Ps. v. is therefore addressed to the conductor of that portion of the Temple-choir who played upon flutes and the like, and are directly alluded to in Ps. lxxxvii. 7, where (חֹלְלִים, *chōlĕlīm*) "the players upon instruments" who are associated with the singers are properly "pipers" or "flute-players."

W. A. W.

NE'HUM (נָחוּם [*comfort*, Fürst]: 'Ιναούμ; [Vat. Alex. FA. Ναουμ:] *Nahum*). One of those who returned from Babylon with Zerubbabel (Neh. vii. 7). In Ezr. ii. 2 he is called REHUM, and in 1 Esdr. v. 8, ROIMUS.

NEHUSH'TA (נְחֻשְׁתָּא [*brass*]: Νέσθα; Alex. Ναισθα: *Nohesta*). The daughter of Elnathan of Jerusalem, wife of Jehoiakim, and mother of Jehoiachin, kings of Judah (2 K. xxiv. 8).

NEHUSH'TAN (נְחֻשְׁתָּן [*brazen*]: Νεεσθάν, but [Vat.] Mai's ed. Νεεσθαλεί; Alex. Νεεσθαν: *Nohestan*). One of the first acts of Hezekiah, upon coming to the throne of Judah, was to destroy all traces of the idolatrous rites which had gained such a fast hold upon the people during the reign of his father Ahaz. Among other objects of superstitious reverence and worship was the brazen serpent, made by Moses in the wilderness (Num. xxi. 9), which was preserved throughout the wanderings of the Israelites, probably as a memorial of their deliverance, and according to a late tradition was placed in the Temple. The lapse of nearly a thousand years had invested this ancient relic with a mysterious sanctity which easily degenerated into idolatrous reverence, and at the time of Hezekiah's accession it had evidently been long an object of worship, "for unto those days the children of Israel did burn incense to it," or as the Hebrew more fully implies, "had been in the habit of burning incense to it." The expression points to a settled practice. The name by which the brazen serpent was known at this time, and by which it was worshipped, was Nehushtan (2 K. xviii. 4). It is evident that our translators by their rendering, "and he called it Nehushtan," understood with many commentators that the subject of the sentence is Hezekiah, and that when he destroyed the brazen serpent he gave it the name Nehushtan, "a brazen thing," in token of his utter contempt, and to impress upon the people the idea of its worthlessness. This rendering has the support of the LXX. and Vulgate, Junius and Tremellius, Münster, Clericus, and others; but it is better to understand the Hebrew as referring to the name by which the serpent was generally known, the subject of the verb being indefinite — "and one called it 'Nehushtan.'" Such a construction is common, and instances of it may be found in Gen. xxv. 26, xxxviii. 29, 30, where our translators correctly render "his name was called," and in Gen. xlviii. 1, 2. This was the view taken in the Targ. Jon. and in the Peshito-Syriac, "and they called it Nehushtan," which Buxtorf approves (*Hist. Serp. Æn.* cap. vi.). It has the support of Luther, Pfeiffer (*Dub. Vex.* cent. 3, loc. 5), J. D. Michaelis (*Bibel für Ungel.*), and Bunsen (*Bibelwerk*), as well as of Ewald (*Gesch.* iii. 622), Keil, Thenius, and most modern commentators. [SERPENT.]   W. A. W.

NEIEL (נְעִיאֵל [perh. = יַעֲשִׂיאֵל, *treasure of God*, Ges.]: 'Ιναήλ; Alex. Aνιηλ: *Nehiel*), a place which formed one of the landmarks of the boundary of the tribe of Asher (Josh. xix. 27, only). It occurs betweeen JIPHTHAH-EL and CABUL. If the former of these be identified with *Jefât*, and the latter with *Kabûl*, 8 or 9 miles E. S. E. of *Akka*, then Neiel may possibly be represented by *Mi'ar*, a village conspicuously placed on a lofty mountain brow, just half-way between the two (Rob. iii. 87, 103; also Van de Velde's *Map*, 1858). The change of N into M, and L into R, is frequent, and Miar retains the *Ain* of Neiel.
    G.

NEKEB (הַנֶּקֶב with the def. article [*the cavern*]: καὶ Ναβόκ; [Vat. Ναβωκ·] Alex. Nακεβ: *qua est Neceb*), one of the towns on the boundary of Naphtali (Josh. xix. 33, only). It lay between ADAMI and JABNEEL.

A great number of commentators, from Jonathan the Targumist and Jerome (*Vulgate* as above) to Keil (*Josua*, ad loc.), have taken this name as being connected with the preceding — Adami-han-Nekeb (Junius and Tremellius, "Adamæi fossa"); and indeed this is the force of the accentuation of the present Hebrew text. But on the other hand the LXX. give the two as distinct, and in the Talmud the post-biblical names of each are given, that of han-Nekeb being *Tsiadathah* (*Gemara Hieros.* Cod. Megilla, in Reland, *Pal.* pp. 545, 717, 817; also Schwarz, p. 181).

Of this more modern name Schwarz suggests that a trace is to be found in "*Hazedhi*," 3 English miles N. from *al-Chatti*.   G.

NEKODA (נְקוֹדָא [*distinguished*]: Νεκωδά; in Ezr. ii. 48, [Vat. Νεχωδα,] Alex. Νεκωδαν; [in Neh., FA. Νεκωδαμ :] *Necoda*). 1. The descendants of Nekoda returned among the Nethinim after the Captivity (Ezr. ii. 48; Neh. vii. 50).

2. [Νεκωδά.] The sons of Nekoda were among 'hose who went up after the Captivity from Tel-melah, Tel-harsa and other places, but were unable to prove their descent from Israel (Ezr. ii. 60; Neh. vii. 62).

NEMUEL (נְמוּאֵל [*day of God*, Ges.]:

Ναμουήλ : *Namuel*). 1. A Reubenite, son of Eliab, and eldest brother of Dathan and Abiram (Num. xxvi. 9).

2. The eldest son of Simeon (Num. xxvi. 12; 1 Chr. iv. 24), from whom were descended the family of the Nemuelites. In Gen. xlvi. 10 he is called JEMUEL.

NEMUELITES, THE (הַנְּמוּאֵלִי [see above]: δῆμος ὁ Ναμουηλί: Alex. Ναμουηλει, and so [Vat.] Mai: *Namuelitæ*). The descendants of Nemuel the first-born of Simeon (Num. xxvi. 12).

NEPHEG (נֶפֶג [*sprout*]: Ναφέκ: *Nepheg*). 1. One of the sons of Izhar the son of Kohath, and therefore brother of Korah (Ex. vi. 21).

2. [Ναφέκ;] in 1 Chr. iii. 7, [Vat. Ναφαθ,] Alex. Ναφεγ; 1 Chr. xiv. 6, Ναφαθ, [Alex. Ναφαγ, FA. Ναφατ: *Nepheg, Napheg*.] One of David's sons born to him in Jerusalem after he was come from Hebron (2 Sam. v. 15 ; 1 Chr. iii. 7, xiv. 6).

* **NEPHEW.** This term wherever employed in the A. V., is used in the sense of *grandchild* or *descendant* generally. The corresponding Hebrew and Greek words are נֶכֶד, Job xviii. 19, Is. xiv. 22; בְּנֵי בָנִים, Judg. xii. 14; and ἔκγονα, 1 Tim. v. 4. For the old English usage of this word, see Richardson's *Eng. Dict.* s. v., and Trench's *Authorized Vers. of the N. T.* p. 446 (ed. 1859). [SISTER'S SON.]   D. S. T.

NEPHI (Νεφθαεί; Alex. Νεφθαρ: *Nephi*). The name by which the NAPHTHAR of Nehemiah was usually (παρὰ τοῖς πολλοῖς) called (2 Macc. i. 36). The A. V. [after the Bishops' Bible] has here followed the Vulgate.

NEPHIS (Νιφίς ; [Vat. Νειφεις; Alex. Φινεις ; Ald. Νηφίς:] *Liptis*). In the corrupt list of 1 Esdr. v. 21, "the sons of Nephis " apparently correspond with "the children of Nebo" in Ezr. ii. 29, or else the name is a corruption of MAGBISH.

NEPHISH (נָפִישׁ [*recreate* : Vat.] Ναφισαδαιοι; [Rom.] Alex. Ναφισαιοι: *Naphis*). An inaccurate variation (found in 1 Chr. v. 19 only [where the Bishops' Bible reads *Nephis*]) of the name elsewhere correctly given in the A. V. NAPHISH, the form always preserved in the original.

NEPHISHESIM (נְפוּשְׁסִים [*expansions*, Ges.]; Keri, נְפִישְׁסִים: Νεφωσασ [Vat. -σει]; Alex. Νεφωσαειμ; [FA. Νεφωσασειμ:] *Nephussim*). The children of Nephishesim were among the Nethinim who returned with Zerubbabel (Neh. vii. 52). The name elsewhere appears as NEPHUSIM and NAPHISI. Gesenius decides that it is a corruption of the former. (*Thes.* p. 899.)

NEPHTHALI ([Rom. Νεφθαλί ; Vat. Alex. FA.] Νεφθαλειμ: *Nephthali*). The Vulgate form of the name NAPHTALI (Tob. i. 1, 2, 4, 5).

NEPHTHALIM ([Νεφθαλί; Vat.] Νεφθαλει; [Sin.] Alex. Νεφθαλειμ and so N. T.: *Nephthali, Nephthalim*). Another form of the same name as the preceding (Tob. vii. 3; Matt. iv. 13, 15; Rev. vii. 6).

NEPHTO'AH, THE WATER OF (מֵ

נִפְתּוֹחַ [*waters of opening*]: ὕδωρ Ναφθώ; [Vat. in Josh. xv. 9,] Μαφθω: *aqua*, and *aqua, Nephtoa*). The spring or source (עַיִן, A. V. " fountain " and " well ") of the water or (inaccurately) waters of Nephtoah was one of the landmarks in the boundary-line which separated Judah from Benjamin (Josh. xv. 9, xviii. 15). It was situated between the " head," or the " end," of the mountain which faced the valley of Hinnom on the west, and the cities of Ephron, the next point beyond which was Kirjath-jearim. It lay therefore N. W. of Jerusalem, in which direction it seems to have been satisfactorily identified in *Ain Lifta*, a spring situated a little distance above the village of the same name, in a short valley which runs into the east side of the great *Wady Beit Hanina*, about 2½ miles from Jerusalem and 6 from *Kuriet el-Enab* (K.-jearim). The spring — of which a view is given by Dr. Barclay (*City*, etc., 544) — is very abundant, and the water escapes in a considerable stream into the valley below.

Nephtoah was formerly identified with various springs — the spring of St. Philip (*Ain Haniyeh*) in the *Wady el-Werd*; the *Ain Yalo* in the same valley, but nearer Jerusalem; the *Ain Karim*, or Fountain of the Virgin of mediæval times (Doubdan, *Voyage*, 187; see also the citations of Tobler, *Topographie*, 351; and Sandys, lib. iii. p. 184); and even the so-called well of Job at the western end of the *Wady Aly*[a] (*Mislin*, ii. 155); but these, especially the last, are unsuitable in their situation as respects Jerusalem and Kirjath-jearim, and have the additional drawback that the features of the country there are not such as to permit a boundary-line to be traced along it, while the line through *Ain Lifta* would, in Barclay's words, " pursue a course indicated by nature."

The name of *Lifta* is not less suitable to this identification than its situation, since T and L frequently take the place of each other, and the rest of the word is almost entirely unchanged. The earliest notice of it appears to be by Stewart[b] (*Tent and Khan*, 349), who speaks of it as at that time (Feb. 1854) " recognized." G.

NEPHU'SIM (נְפוּסִים; Keri: נְפוּשִׂים: Νεφουσίμ; [Vat. Ναφεισων;] Alex. Νεφουσειμ: *Nephusim*). The same as NEPHISHESIM, of which name according to Gesenius it is the proper form (Ezr. ii. 50).

NER (נֵר [*light, lamp*]: Νήρ [Vat. in 1 Sam. xiv. 50, Νηρει:] *Ner*), son of Jehiel, according to 1 Chr. viii. 33, father of Kish and Abner, and grandfather of King Saul. Abner was, therefore, uncle to Saul, as expressly stated 1 Sam. xiv. 50. But some confusion has arisen from the statement in 1 Chr. ix. 36, that Kish and Ner were both sons of Jehiel, whence it has been concluded that they were brothers, and consequently that Abner and Saul were first cousins. But, unless there was an elder Kish, uncle of Saul's father, which is not at all probable, it is obvious to explain the insertion of Kish's name (as that of the

numerous names by the side of it) in 1 Chr. ix. 36, by the common practice in the Chronicles of calling all the heads of houses of fathers, *sons* of the phylarch or demarch from whom they sprung, or under whom they were reckoned in the genealogies, whether they were sons or grandsons, or later descendants, or even descendants of collateral branches. [BECHER.]

The name Ner, combined with that of his son Abner, may be compared with Nadab in ver. 36, and Abinadab ver. 39; with Jesse, 1 Chr. ii. 13, and Abishai, ver. 16; and with Juda, Luke iii. 26, and Abiud, Matt. i. 13. The subjoined table shows Ner's family relations.

Benjamin
|
Becher, or Bechorath (1 Sam. ix. 1; 1 Chr. vii. 6, 8)
|
Abiah, or Aphiah (ib.)
|
Zeror, or Zur (1 Chr. viii. 30)
|
Abiel, or Jehiel (1 Chr. ix. 35)

Abdon Zur Kish Baal **Ner** Nadab Gedor Ahio
                                      |
                                Zechariah Mikloth
                             |
                          Kish   Abner
                          |
                        Saul[c]

The family seat of Ner was Gibeon, where 'his father Jehiel was probably the first to settle (1 Chr. ix. 35). From the pointed mention of his mother, Maachah, as the wife of Jehiel, she was perhaps the heiress of the estate in Gibeon. This inference receives some confirmation from the fact that " Maachah, Caleb's concubine," is said, in 1 Chr. ii. 59, to have borne " Sheva the father of Machbenah and the father of Gibea," where, though the text is in ruins, yet a connection of some sort between Maachah (whoever she was) and Gibeah, often called Gibeah of Saul, and the same as Gibeon, 1 Chr. xiv. 16, is apparent. It is a curious circumstance that, while the name (Jehiel) of the " father of Gibeon " is not given in the text of 1 Chr. viii. 29, the same is the case with " the father of Gibea " in 1 Chr. ii. 49, naturally suggesting, therefore, that in the latter passage the same name *Jehiel* ought to be supplied which is supplied for the former by the duplicate passage 1 Chr. ix. 35. If this inference is correct it would place the time of the settlement of Jehiel at Gibeon — where one would naturally expect to find it — near the time of the settlement of the tribes in their respective inheritances under Joshua. Maachah, his wife, would seem to be a daughter or descendant of Caleb by Ephah his concubine. That she was not " Caleb's concubine " seems pretty certain, both because Ephah is so described in ii. 46 and because the recurrence of the name Ephah in ver. 47, separated from the words פִּילֶגֶשׁ כָּלֵב only by the name Shaaph,[d] creates a strong presumption that Ephah, and not Maachah, is the name to which this description belongs in ver. 47, as in ver. 46. Moreover, *Maachah* cannot be the nom. case to the masculine verb יָלַד. Supposing,

---

[a] This must arise from a confusion between *Yalo* (*Ajalon*), near which the " well of Job " is situated, and the *Ain Yalo*.

[b] Stewart, while accusing Dr. Robinson of inaccuracy (p. 349), has himself fallen into a curious confusion between Nephtoah and Netophah. Dr. Robinson is in this instance perfectly right.

[c] There are doubtless some links missing in this genealogy, as at all events the head of the family of Matri.

[d] *Shaaph* has nearly the same letters as *Ephah*.

then, Maachah, the ancestress of Saul, to have been thus a daughter or granddaughter of Caleb, we have a curious coincidence in the occurrence of the name SAUL, as one of the Edomitish kings, 1 Chr. i. 48, and as the name of a descendant of the Edomitish Caleb. [CALEB.] The element *Baal* (1 Chr. ix. 36, &c.) in the names *Esh-Baal*, *Meribbaal*, the descendants of Saul the son of Kish, may also, then, be compared with *Baal-Hanan*, the successor of Saul of Rehoboth (1 Chr. i. 49), as also the name *Matred* (ib. 50) with *Matri* (1 Sam. x. 21).   A. C. H.

NE'REUS [2 syl.] (Νηρεύς: *Nereus*). A Christian at Rome, saluted by St. Paul, Rom. xvi. 15. Origen conjectures that he belonged to the household of Philologus and Julia. Estius suggests that he may be identified with a Nereus, who is said to have been baptized at Rome by St. Peter. A legendary account of him is given in Bolland, *Acta Sanctorum*, 12th May; from which, in the opinion of Tillemont, *H. E.* ii. 139, may be gathered the fact that he was beheaded at Terracina, probably in the reign of Nerva. His ashes are said to be deposited in the ancient church of SS. Nereo ed Archilleo at Rome.

There is a reference to his legendary history in Bp. Jeremy Taylor's Sermon, *The Marriage-ring*, Part i.   W. T. B.

NER'GAL (נֵרְגַל: 'Εργέλ: *Nergel*), one of the chief Assyrian and Babylonian deities, seems to have corresponded closely to the classical Mars. He was of Babylonian origin, and his name signifies, in the early Cushite dialect of that country, "the great man," or "the great hero." His monumental titles are — "the storm-ruler," "the king of battle," "the champion of the gods," "the male principle" (or "the strong begetter"), "the tutelar god of Babylonia," and "the god of the chase." Of this last he is the god preëminently; another deity, *Nin*, disputing with him the presidency over war and battles. It is conjectured that he may represent the deified Nimrod — "the mighty hunter before the Lord " — from whom the kings both of Babylon and Nineveh were likely to claim descent. The city peculiarly dedicated to his worship is found in the inscriptions to be Cutha or Tiggaba, which is in Arabian tradition the special city of Nimrod. The only express mention of Nergal contained in sacred Scripture is in 2 K. xvii. 30, where "the men of Cutha," placed in the city of Samaria by a king of Assyria (Esar-haddon?), are said to have "made Nergal their god " when transplanted to their new country — a fact in close accordance with the frequent notices in the inscriptions, which mark him as the tutelar god of that city. Nergal's name occurs as the initial element in *Nergal-shar-ezer* (Jer. xxxix. 3 and 13); and is also found, under a contracted form, in the name of a comparatively late king — the Abennerigus of Josephus (*Ant.* xx. 2, § 1).

Nergal appears to have been worshipped under the symbol of the "Man-Lion." The Semitic name for the god of Cutha was *Aria*, a word which signifies "lion " both in Hebrew and Syriac. *Nir*, the first element of the god's name, is capable of the same signification. Perhaps the habits of the lion as a hunter of beasts were known, and he was thus regarded as the most fitting symbol of the god who presided over the chase.

It is in connection with their hunting excursions that the Assyrian kings make most frequent mention of this deity. As early as b. c. 1150, Tiglath-pileser I. speaks of him as furnishing the arrows with which he slaughtered the wild animals *Assur-dani-pal* (Sardanapalus), the son and successor of Esar-haddon, never fails to invoke his aid, and ascribes all his hunting achievements to his influence. Pul sacrificed to him in Cutha, and Sennacherib built him a temple in the city of Tarbisa near Nineveh: but in general he was not much worshipped either by the earlier or the later kings (see the *Essay* of Sir H. Rawlinson in Rawlinson's *Herodotus*, i. 631–634).   G. R.

NER'GAL-SHARE'ZER (נֵרְגַל שַׂרְאֶצֶר) [see above]: [Rom. Vat. Μαργανασάρ; FA. Μαργανασαρ; Alex.] Νηργελ-Σαασάρ: *Neregel, Sereser*, [*Neregel et Sereser*]) occurs only in Jeremiah xxxix. 3 and 13. There appear to have been two persons of the name among the "princes of the king of Babylon," who accompanied Nebuchadnezzar on his last expedition against Jerusalem. One of these is not marked by any additional title; but the other has the honorable distinction of Rab-mag (רַב־מָג), and it is to him alone that any particular interest attaches. In sacred Scripture he appears among the persons, who, by command of Nebuchadnezzar, released Jeremiah from prison; profane history gives us reason to believe that he was a personage of great importance, who not long afterwards mounted the Babylonian throne. This identification depends in part upon the exact resemblance of name, which is found on Babylonian bricks in the form of *Nergal-shar-uzur ;* but mainly it rests upon the title of *Rubu-emga*, or Rab-Mag, which this king bears in his inscriptions, and on the improbability of there having been towards the close of the Babylonian period — when the monumental monarch must have lived — two persons of exactly the same name holding this office. [RAB-MAG.]

Assuming on these grounds the identity of the Scriptural "Nergal-sharezer, Rab-Mag," with the monumental "*Nergal-shar-uzur, Rubu-emga*," we may learn something of the history of the prince in question from profane authors. There cannot be a doubt that he was the monarch called Neriglissar or Neriglissoor by Berosus (Joseph. *c. Ap.* i. 20), who murdered Evil-Merodach, the son of Nebuchadnezzar, and succeeded him upon the throne. This prince was married to a daughter of Nebuchadnezzar, and was thus the brother-in-law of his predecessor, whom he put to death. His reign lasted between three and four years. He appears to have died a natural death. and certainly left his crown to a young son, Laborosoarchod, who was murdered after a reign of nine months. In the canon of Ptolemy he appears, under the designation of Nerigassolassar, as reigning four years between Illoarudamus (Evil-Merodach) and Nabonadius, his son's reign not obtaining any mention, because it fell short of a year.

A palace, built by Neriglissar, has been discovered at Babylon. It is the only building of any extent on the right bank of the Euphrates. (See plan of BABYLON.) The bricks bear the name of Nergal-shar-uzur, the title of Rab-Mag, and also a statement — which is somewhat surprising — that Nergal-shar-uzur was the son of a certain "Bel-sikkariskun, *king of Babylon*." The only explanation which has been offered of this statement is a conjecture (Rawlinson's *Herodotus*, vol. i. p. 518), that Bel-zikkar-iskun may possibly have been the "chief Chaldæan," who (according to Berosus) kept the royal authority for Nebuchadnezzar during the interval between his father's death and his own arrival at Babylon. [NEBUCHADNEZZAR.] Neriglissar could scarcely have given his father the title of king without some ground; and this is at any rate a possible ground, and one compatible with the non-appearance of the name in any extant list of the later Babylonian monarchs. Neriglissar's office of Rab-Mag will be further considered under that word. It is evident that he was a personage of importance before he mounted the throne. Some (as Larcher) have sought to identify him with Darius the Mede. But this view is quite untenable. There is abundant reason to believe from his name and his office that he was a native Babylonian — a grandee of high rank under Nebuchadnezzar, who regarded him as a fitting match for one of his daughters. He did not, like Darius Medus, gain Babylon by conquest, but acquired his dominion by an internal revolution. His reign preceded that of the Median Darius by 17 years. It lasted from B. C. 559 to B. C. 556, whereas Darius the Mede cannot have ascended the throne till B. C. 538, on the conquest of Babylon by Cyrus.   G. R.

NE'RI (Νηρί [Tisch. Νηρεί with Sin. A B etc.] representing the Heb. בֵּרִי, which would be a short form for בְּרָיָה, Neriah, "Jehovah is my lamp:" *Neri*),[a] son of Melchi, and father of Salathiel, in the genealogy of Christ, Luke iii. 27. Nothing is known of him, but his name is very important as indicating the principle on which the genealogies of our Lord are framed. He was of the line of Nathan; but his son Salathiel became Solomon's heir on the failure of Solomon's line in king Jeconiah, and was therefore reckoned in the royal genealogy among the sons of Jeconiah; to whose status and prerogatives he succeeded, 1 Chr. iii. 17; Matt. i. 12. The supposition that the son and heir of David and Solomon would be called the son of Neri, an obscure individual, because he had married Neri's daughter, as many pretend, is too absurd to need refutation. The information given us by St. Luke — that Neri, of the line of Nathan, was Salathiel's father — does, in point of fact, clear up and settle the whole question of the genealogies. [GENEALOGY OF JESUS CHRIST.]   A. C. H.

NERI'AH (בֵּרִיָה [and בְּרִיָּהוּ, *lamp of Jehovah*]: Νηρίας, but Νηρείας [Alex. Νηρίας] in Jer. li. 59; [Vat. also *-ρει-* in xliii. 3:] *Nerius*, but *Neri* in xxxii. 12). The son of Maaseiah, and father of Baruch (Jer. xxxii. 12, xxxvi. 4, xliii. 3, [also xxxii. 16, xxxvi. 8, 14, 32, xliii. 6, xlv. 1]), and Seraiah (Jer. li. 59).

NERI'AS (Νηρίας: *Nerias*). The father of Baruch and Seriah (Bar. i. 1).

• **NEST.** The Greek word κατασκήνωσις, rendered *nest* in Matt. viii. 20 and Luke ix. 58, means strictly *the pitching of a tent* and then a *tent* or *dwelling*, an *abode*. Coupled as it is in these passages with the holes of foxes, and contrasted with our Saviour's want of a home or lodging-place, it seems plainly not to have the specific meaning of *nests* but places of resort, lodging places, "haunts." So the corresponding verb in Matt. xiii. 32, Mark iv. 32, and Luke xiii. 19 is rendered *lodge*; in Acts ii. 26, *rest*. "Nest" is undoubtedly meant by "house" in Ps. civ. 17: "As for the stork the fir-trees are her house." This bird "in the East selects ruins wherever they are to be found, more especially or for the most part where there is water or neglected marsh in their neighborhood. But when neither houses nor ruins occur, it selects any trees tall and strong enough to provide a firm platform for its huge nest, and for this purpose none are more convenient than the fir-tree" (Tristram, *Nat. Hist. of the Bible*, p. 248). The eagle's stirring up of her nest, *i. e.* the young in the nest (Deut. xxxii. 12), refers to the efforts of the eagle to encourage her young ones to fly and coax them to leave their nest (Tristram, p. 176).   R. D. C. R.

NET. The various terms applied by the Hebrews to nets had reference either to the construction of the article, or to its use and objects. To the first of these we may assign the following terms: -*Macmôr*,[b] and its cognates, *micmâr*[c] and *miomôreth*,[d] all of which are derived from a root signifying "to weave;" and, again, *sĕbâcáh*[e] and *sĕbâc*,[f] derived from another root of similar signification. To the second head we may assign *chêrem*,[g] from a root signifying "to enclose;" *mâtzôd*,[h] with its cognates, *mĕtzôdáh*[i] and *mĕtzûdáh*,[k] from a root signifying "to lie in wait;" and *resheth*,[l] from a root signifying "to catch." Great uncertainty prevails in the equivalent terms in the A. V.: *mâtzôd* is rendered "snare" in Eccl. vii. 26, and "net" in Job xix. 6 and Prov. xii. 12, in the latter of which passages the true sense is "prey;" *sĕbâcáh* is rendered "snare" in Job xviii. 8; *mĕtzôdáh*

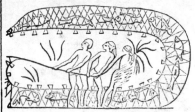

Egyptian landing-net.   (Wilkinson.)

"snare" in Ez. xli. 13, xvii. 20, and "net" in Ps. lxvi. 11; *micmôreth*, "drag" or "flue-net" in Hab. i. 15, 16. What distinction there may have been between the various nets described by the Hebrew terms, we are unable to decide. The etymology tells us nothing, and the equivalents in the LXX. vary. In the New Testament we meet with three terms, — σαγήνη (from σάττω, "to load "), whence our word *seine*, a large hauling or draw-net; it is the term used in the parable of the draw-net (Matt. xiii. 47): ἀμφίβληστρον (from ἀμφιβάλλω, "to cast around "), a casting-net (Matt. iv. 18; Mark i. 16): and δίκτυον (from δίκω, "to throw "), of the same description as the one just mentioned (Matt. iv. 20; John xxi.

---

*a See *Geneal. of Our Lord J. C.*, p. 159.

b מִכְמֹר.	c מִכְמָר.	d מִכְמֹרֶת.
e שְׂבָכָה.	f שְׂבָךְ.	g חֵרֶם.

h מָצוֹד.	i מְצוֹדָה.	k מְצוּדָה.
	l רֶשֶׁת.	

6, al.). The net was used for the purposes of fishing and hunting: the mode in which it was used
has been already described in the articles on those
subjects. [FISHING; HUNTING.] The Egyptians
constructed their nets of flax-string: the netting-
needle was made of wood, and in shape closely resembled our own (Wilkinson, ii. 95). The nets
varied in form according to their use; the landing-
net has been already represented; we here give a
sketch of the draw-net from the same source.

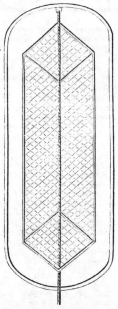

Egyptian draw-net (Wilkinson).

As the nets of Egypt were well known to the
early Jews (Is. xix. 8), it is not improbable that
the material and form was the same in each country. The nets used for birds in Egypt were of two
kinds, clap-nets and traps. The latter consisted
of network strained over a frame of wood, which
was so constructed that the sides would collapse by
pulling a string and catch any birds that might have
alighted on them while open. The former was
made on the same principle, consisting of a double
frame with the network strained over it, which
might be caused to collapse by pulling a string.[a]

The metaphorical references to the net are very
numerous: it was selected as an appropriate image
of the subtle devices of the enemies of God on the
one hand (e. g. Ps. ix. 15, xxv. 15, xxxi. 4), and
of the unavertable vengeance of God on the other
hand (Lam. i. 13; Ez. xii. 13; Hos. vii. 12).

We must still notice the use of the term *sĕbâc*,
in an architectural sense, applied to the open ornamental work about the capital of a pillar (1 K. vii.
17), and described in similar terms by Josephus,
δίκτυον ἐλάτῃ χαλκείᾳ περιπεπλεγμένον (Ant.
viii. 3, § 4).   W. L. B.

NETHAN'EEL (נְתַנְאֵל [given of God]:
Ναθαναήλ: Nathanael). 1. The son of Zuar, and
prince of the tribe of Issachar at the time of the
Exodus. With his 54,400 men his post in the
camp was on the east, next to the camp of Judah,
which they followed in the march. The same order
was observed in the offerings at the dedication of
the Tabernacle, when Nethaneel followed Nahshon
the prince of the tribe of Judah (Num. i. 8, ii. 5,
vii. 18, 23, x. 15).

2. The fourth son of Jesse and brother of David
(1 Chr. ii. 14).

3. A priest in the reign of David who blew the
trumpet before the ark, when it was brought from
the house of Obed-edom (1 Chr. xv. 24).

4. A Levite, father of Shemaiah the scribe in
the reign of David (1 Chr. xxiv. 6).

5. [Vat. Ναας Ιειηλ.] The fifth son of Obed-
edom the doorkeeper of the ark (1 Chr. xxvi. 4).

6. One of the princes of Judah, whom Jehoshaphat in the third year of his reign sent to teach in
the cities of his kingdom (2 Chr. xvii. 7).

7. A chief of the Levites in the reign of Josiah,
who took part in the solemn passover kept by that
king (2 Chr. xxxv. 9).

8. A priest of the family of Pashur, in the time
of Ezra, who had married a foreign wife (Ezr. x.
22). He is called NATHANAEL in 1 Esdr. ix. 22.

9. [Vat. Alex. FA.[1] omit.] The representative
of the priestly family of Jedaiah in the time of
Joiakim the son of Jeshua (Neh. xii. 21).

10. [Vat. Alex. FA.[1] omit.] A Levite, of the
sons of Asaph, who with his brethren played upon
the musical instruments of David, in the solemn
procession which accompanied the dedication of the
wall of Jerusalem under Ezra and Nehemiah (Neh.
xii. 36).   W. A. W.

NETHANI'AH (נְתַנְיָה [given of Je-
hovah]: and in the lengthened form נְתַנְיָהוּ,
Jer. xl. 8, xli. 9: Ναθανίας, exc. 2 K. xxv. 23, where
the Alex. MS. has Μαθθανίας: Nathania). 1. The
son of Elishama, and father of Ishmael who murdered Gedaliah (2 K. xxv. 23, 25; Jer. xl. 8, 14,
15, xli. 1, 2, 6, 7, 9, 10, 11, 12, 15, 16, 18). He
was of the royal family of Judah.

2. (נְתַנְיָהוּ, in 1 Chr. xxv. 12: [Ναθανίας,
Ναθὰν; Vat. in ver. 12 Ναθαλιας.]) One of the
four sons of Asaph the minstrel, and chief of the
5th of the 24 courses into which the Temple choir
was divided (1 Chr. xxv. 2, 12).

3. (נְתַנְיָהוּ: [Vat. Μαθθανιας.]) A Levite
in the reign of Jehoshaphat, who with eight others
of his tribe and two priests accompanied the princes
of Judah who were sent by the king through the
country to teach the law of Jehovah (2 Chr.
xvii. 8).

4. The father of Jehudi (Jer. xxxvi. 14).

NETH'INIM [A. V. "Nethinims"] (נְתִינִים
[see below]: [FA.[3]] Ναθιναῖοι, Neh. xi. 21, [Rom.
Vat. Alex. FA.[1] omit;] Ναθινίμ [Vat. Ναθειννμ,
Alex. Ναθιναιοι], Ezr. ii. 43: [there are many
variations in the MSS. in other places:] οἱ δε-
δομένοι [Comp. Ναθίνεοι], 1 Chr. ix. 2: Nathinæi).
As applied specifically to a distinct body of men
connected with the services of the Temple, this

[a] Prov. i. 17, is accurately as follows: "Surely
in the eyes of any bird the net is spread for nothing."
As it stands in the A. V. it is simply contrary to fact.

This is one of the admirable emendations of the late
Mr. Bernard. (See Mason and Bernard's *Hebrew
Grammar.*)

name first meets us in the later books of the O. T.; in 1 Chron., Ezra, and Nehemiah. The word, and the ideas embodied in it may, however, be traced to a much earlier period. As derived from the verb נָתַן, *nâthan* (= give, set apart, dedicate), it was applied to those who were specially appointed to the liturgical offices of the Tabernacle.[a] Like many other official titles it appears to have had at first a much higher value than that afterwards assigned to it. We must not forget that the Levites were *given* to Aaron and his sons, *i. e.* to the priests as an order, and were accordingly the first Nethinim (נְתוּנִם, Num. iii. 9, viii. 19). At first they were the only attendants, and their work must have been laborious enough. The first conquests, however, brought them their share of the captive slaves of the Midianites, and 320 were *given* to them as having charge of the Tabernacle (Num. xxxi. 47), while 32 only were assigned specially to the priests. This disposition to devolve the more laborious offices of their ritual upon slaves of another race showed itself again in the treatment of the Gibeonites. They, too, were "given" (A. V. "made") to be "hewers of wood and drawers of water" for the house of God (Josh. ix. 27), and the addition of so large a number (the population of five cities) must have relieved the Levites from much that had before been burdensome. We know little or nothing as to their treatment. It was a matter of necessity that they should be circumcised (Ex. xii. 48), and conform to the religion of their conquerors, and this might at first seem hard enough. On the other hand it must be remembered that they presented themselves as recognizing the supremacy of Jehovah (Josh. ix. 9), and that for many generations the remembrance of the solemn covenant entered into with them made men look with horror on the shedding of Gibeonite blood (2 Sam. xxi. 9), and protected them from much outrage. No addition to the number thus employed appears to have been made during the period of the Judges, and they continued to be known by their old name as the Gibeonites. The want of a further supply was however felt when the reorganization of worship commenced under David. Either the massacre at Nob had involved the Gibeonites as well as the priests (1 Sam. xxii. 19), or else they had fallen victims to some other outburst of Saul's fury, and, though there were survivors (2 Sam. xxi. 2), the number was likely to be quite inadequate for the greater stateliness of the new worship at Jerusalem. It is to this period accordingly that the origin of the class bearing this name may be traced. The Nethinim were those " whom David and the princes appointed (Heb. *gave*) for the service of the Levites " (Ezr. viii. 20). Analogy would lead us to conclude that, in this as in the former instances, these were either prisoners taken in war, or else some of the remnant of the Canaanites;[b] but the new name in which the old seems to have been merged leaves it uncertain. The foreign character of the names in Ezr. ii. 43–54 is

unmistakable, but was equally natural on either hypothesis.

From this time the Nethinim probably lived within the precincts of the Temple, doing its rougher work, and so enabling the Levites to take a higher position as the religious representatives and instructors of the people. [LEVITES.] They answered in some degree to the male Ιερόδουλοι, who were attached to Greek and Asiatic temples (Josephus, *Ant.* xi. 5, § 1, uses this word of them in his paraphrase of the decree of Darius), to the grave-diggers, gate-keepers, bell-ringers of the Christian Church. Ewald (*Alterthüm.* p. 299) refers to the custom of the more wealthy Arabs dedicating slaves to the special service of the Kaaba at Mecca, or the Sepulchre of the Prophet at Medina.

The example set by David was followed by his successor. In close union with the Nethinim in the statistics of the return from the Captivity, attached like them to the Priests and Levites, we find a body of men described as " Solomon's servants " (Ezr. ii. 55; Neh. vii. 60, xi. 3), and these we may identify, without much risk of error, with some of the " people that were left " of the earlier inhabitants whom he made " to pay tribute of bond-service " (1 K. ix. 20; 2 Chr. viii. 7). The order in which they are placed might even seem to indicate that they stood to the Nethinim in the same relation that the Nethinim did to the Levites. Assuming, as is probable, that the later Rabbinic teaching represents the traditions of an earlier period, the Nethinim appear never to have lost the stigma of their Canaanite origin. They had no *jus connubii* (Gemar. Babyl. *Jebam.* ii. 4; *Kiddush.* iv. 1, in Carpzov, *App. Crit. de Neth.*), and illicit intercourse with a woman of Israel was punished with scourging (Carpzov, *l. c.*); but their quasi-sacred position raised them in some measure above the level of their race, and in the Jewish order of precedence, while they stood below the Mamzerim (bastards, or children of mixed marriages), they were one step above the Proselytes fresh come from heathenism and emancipated slaves (Gemar. Hieros. *Horajoth*, fol. 482; in Lightfoot, *Hor. Heb. ad Matt.* xxiii. 14). They were thus all along a servile and subject caste. The only period at which they rise into anything like prominence is that of the return from the Captivity. In that return the priests were conspicuous and numerous, but the Levites, for some reason unknown to us, hung back. [LEVITES.] Under Zerubbabel there were but 341 to 4,289 priests (Ezr. ii. 36–42). Under Ezra none came up at all till after a special and solemn call (Ezr. viii. 15). The services of the Nethinim were consequently of more importance (Ezr. viii. 17), but in their case also, the small number of those that joined (392 under Zerubbabel, 220 under Ezra, including " Solomon's servants ") indicates that many preferred remaining in the land of their exile to returning to their old service. Those that did come were consequently thought worthy of special mention. The names of their families were registered with as much care as those of the priests

however, without adequate grounds, and at variance with facts. Comp. Pfeffinger *De Nathinais*, in Ugolini's *Thesaurus*, vol. xiii.

b The identity of the Gibeonites and Nethinim, excluding the idea of any addition, is however, maintained by Pfeffinger.

(Ezr. ii. 43–58). They were admitted, in strict conformity to the letter of the rule of Deut. xxix. 11, to join in the great covenant with which the restored people inaugurated its new life (Neh. x. 28). They, like the Priests and Levites, were exempted from taxation by the Persian Satraps (Ezr. vii. 24). They were under the control of a chief of their own body (Ezr. ii. 43; Neh. vii. 46). They took an active part in the work of rebuilding the city (Neh. iii. 26), and the tower of Ophel, convenient from its proximity to the Temple, was assigned to some of them as a residence (Neh. xi. 21), while others dwelt with the Levites in their cities (Ezr. ii. 70). They took their place in the chronicles of the time as next in order to the Levites (1 Chr. ix. 2).

Neither in the Apocrypha, nor in the N. T., nor yet in the works of the Jewish historian, do we find any additional information about the Nethinim. The latter, however, mentions incidentally a festival, that of the Xylophoria, or wood carrying, of which we may perhaps recognize the beginning in Neh. x. 34, and in which it was the custom for all the people to bring large supplies of firewood for the sacrifices of the year. This may have been designed to relieve them. They were at any rate likely to bear a conspicuous part in it (Joseph. B. J. ii. 17, § 6).

Two hypotheses connected with the Nethinim are mentioned by Pfeffinger in the exhaustive monograph already cited: (1), that of Förster (Dict. Hebr., Basil, 1564), that the first so called were sons of David, i. e., younger branches of the royal house to whom was given the defense of the city and the sanctuary; (2), that of Boulduc (referred to also by Selden, De Jure Nat. et Gent.), connected apparently with (1), that Joseph the husband of the Virgin was one of this class.[a]

E. H. P.

NETO'PHAH (נְטֹפָה [distillation, Ges.]: Νετωφά, 'Ατωφά; Alex. Νιφωτα; [Ανετωφα; in 1 Esdr. v. 18, Νετωφάς, Vat. Νετεβας, Alex. Νετωφαε:] Netupha, [in 1 Esdr. Nepopas]), a town the name of which occurs only in the catalogue of those who returned with Zerubbabel from the Captivity (Ezr. ii. 22; Neh. vii. 26; 1 Esdr. v. 18). But, though not directly mentioned till so late a period, Netophah was really a much older place. Two of David's guard, MAHARAI and HELEB or HELDAI, leaders also of two of the monthly courses (1 Chr. xxvii. 13, 15), were Netophathites, and it was the native place of at least one[b] of the captains who remained under arms near Jerusalem after its destruction by Nebuchadnezzar. The "villages of the Netophathites" were the residence of the Levites (1 Chr. ix. 16), a fact which shows that they did not confine themselves to the places named in the catalogues of Josh. xxi. and 1 Chr. vi. From another notice we learn that the particular Levites who inhabited these villages were singers (Neh. xii. 28).

That Netophah belonged to Judah appears from the fact that the two heroes above mentioned belonged, the one to the Zarbites — that is, the great family of Zerah, one of the chief houses of the tribe — and the other to Othniel, the son-in-law of Caleb. To judge from Neh. vii. 26 it was in the neighborhood of, or closely connected with, Bethlehem, which is also implied by 1 Chr. ii. 54, though the precise force of the latter statement cannot now be made out. The number of Netophathites who returned from Captivity is not exactly ascertainable, but it seems not to have been more than sixty — so that it was probably only a small village, which indeed may account for its having escaped mention in the lists of Joshua.

A remarkable tradition, of which there is no trace in the Bible, but which nevertheless is not improbably authentic, is preserved by the Jewish authors, to the effect that the Netophathites slew the guards which had been placed by Jeroboam on the roads leading to Jerusalem to stop the passage of the first-fruits from the country villages to the Temple (Targum on 1 Chr. ii. 54; on Ruth iv. 20, and Eccl. iii. 11). Jeroboam's obstruction, which is said to have remained in force till the reign of Hoshea (see the notes of Beck to Targum on 1 Chr. ii. 54), was commemorated by a fast on the 23d Sivan, which is still retained in the Jewish calendar (see the calendar given by Basnage, Hist. des Juifs, vi. ch. 29).

It is not mentioned by Eusebius and Jerome, and although in the Mishna reference is made to the "oil of Netophah" (Peah 7, §§ 1, 2), and to the "valley of Beth Netophah," in which artichokes flourished, whose growth determined the date of some ceremonial observance (Sheviith 9, § 7), nothing is said as to the situation of the place. The latter may well be the present village of Beit Nettif, which stands on the edge of the great valley of the Wady es-Sumt (Rob. Bibl. Res. ii. 16, 17; Porter, Handbk. 248); but can hardly be the Netophah of the Bible, since it is not near Bethlehem, but in quite another direction. The only name in the neighborhood of Bethlehem suggestive of Netophah is that which appears in Van de Velde's map (1858) as Antûbeh, and in Tobler (3tte Wand. 80) as Om Tûba (أم طوبا), attached to a village about 2 miles N. E. of Bethlehem and a wady which falls therefrom into the Wady en Nar, or Kidron.

G.

NETO'PHATHI (נְטֹפָתִי [patron. see above]: Vat. [Rom. Alex. FA.[1]] omit: Alex. [rather, FA.[3]] Νετωφαθι: Nethophathi), Neh. xii. 28. The same word which in other passages is accurately rendered "the Netophathite," except that here it is not accompanied by the article.

NETO'PHATHITE, THE (נְטֹפָתִי), in Chron. הַנְּטֹפָתִי [as above]: ὁ Ετωφατείτης, Νεφφαθιείτης, Νεθωφατεί, ὁ ἐκ Νετουφάτ; [these are readings of Vat. M.; Rom. Alex. FA. have many other variations:] Netophathites, [Netophati, Netophatites, de Netophati]), 2 Sam. xxiii. 28, 29; 2 K. xxv. 23; 1 Chr. xi. 30, xxvii. 13, 15; Jer. xl. 8. The plural form, THE NETOPHATHITES (the Hebrew word being the same as the above) occurs in 1 Chr. ii. 54, ix. 16.

G.

NETTLE. The representative in the A. V.

---

[a] The only trace of any tradition corresponding to this theory is the description in the Arabian History of Joseph (c. 2), according to which he is of the city of David and the tribe of Judah, and yet, on account of his wisdom and piety, "sacerdos factus est in Templo Domini" (Tischendorf, Evang. Apoc., p. 114).

[b] Comp. 2 K. xxv. 23, with Jer. xl. 8.

of the Hebrew words *chârûl* and *kimmôsh* or *kimôsh.*

1. *Chârûl* (חָרוּל: φρύγανα ἄγρια:^a *sentis, urien, spina*) occurs in Job xxx. 7 — the patriarch complains of the contempt in which he was held by the lowest of the people, who, from poverty, were obliged to live on the wild shrubs of the desert: "Among the bushes they brayed, under the *chârûl* they were gathered together," and in Prov. xxiv. 31, where of "the field of the slothful," it is said, "it was all grown over with thorns (*kimmêshônîm*), and *charullim* had covered the face thereof;" see also Zeph. ii. 9: the curse of Moab and Ammon is that they shall be "the breeding of *chârûl* and salt-pits."

There is very great uncertainty as to the meaning of the word *chârûl*, and numerous are the plants which commentators have sought to identify with it: brambles, sea-orache, butchers' broom, thistles, have all been proposed (see Celsius, *Hierob.* ii. 165). The generality of critics and some modern versions are in favor of the *nettle*. Some have objected to the nettle as not being of a sufficient size to suit the passage in Job (*l. c.*); but in our own country nettles grow to the height of six or even seven feet when drawn up under trees or hedges; and it is worthy of remark that, in the passage of Job quoted above, bushes and *chârûl* are associated. Not much better founded is Dr. Royle's objection (Kitto's *Cyc.* art. *Charul*) that both thorny plants and nettles must be excluded, "as no one would voluntarily resort to such a situation;" for the people of whom Job is speaking might readily be supposed to resort to such a shade, as in a sandy desert the thorn-bushes and tall nettles growing by their side would afford; or we may suppose that those who "for want and famine" were driven into the wilderness were gathered together under the nettles for the purpose of gathering them for food, together with the sea-orache and juniper-roots (Job xxx. 4). Celsius believes the *chârûl* is identical with the Christ-thorn (*Zizyphus Paliurus*)—the *Paliurus aculeatus* of modern botanists — but his opinion is by no means well founded. The passage in Proverbs (*l. c.*) appears to forbid us identifying the *chârûl* with the *Paliurus aculeatus;* for the context, "I went by, and lo it was all grown over with *kimshôn* and *charullim*," seems to point to some weed of quicker growth than the plant proposed by Celsius. Dr. Royle has argued in favor of some species of wild mustard, and refers the Hebrew word to one of somewhat similar form in Arabic, namely, *Khardal*, to which he traces the English *charlock* or *kedlock*, the well-known troublesome weed. The Scriptural passages would suit this interpretation, and it is quite possible that wild mustard may be intended by *chârûl*. The etymology^b too, we may add, is as much in favor of the wild mustard as of

the nettle, one or other of which plants appears to be denoted by the Hebrew word. We are inclined to adopt Dr. Royle's opinion, as the following word probably denotes the *nettle.*

2. *Kimmôsh* or *kimôsh* (קִמּוֹשׁ, קִמֹּשׁ: ἀκάνθινα ξύλα, ἄκανθα, ὄλεθρος: *urticœ*). "Very many interpreters," says Celsius (*Hierob.* ii. 207) "understand the *nettle* by this word. Of the older Jewish doctors, R. Ben Melech, on Prov. xxiv. 31, asserts that *kimmôsh* is a kind of thorn (*spina*), commonly called a nettle." The Vulgate, Arias Montanus, Luther, Deodatius,^c the Spanish and English versions, are all in favor of the nettle. The word occurs in Is. xxxiv. 13: of Edom it is said, that "there shall come up nettles and brambles in the fortresses thereof:" and in Hos. ix. 6. Another form of the same word, *kimmêshônîm*^d ("thorns," A. V.), occurs in Prov. xxiv. 31: the field of the slothful was all grown over with *kimmêshônîm*." Modern commentators are generally agreed upon the signification of this term, which, as it is admirably suited to all the Scriptural passages, may well be understood to denote some species of nettle (*Urtica*).   W. H.

NEW MOON (רֹאשׁ הַחֹדֶשׁ, חֹדֶשׁ: νεομηνία, νουμηνία: *calendœ, neomenia*). The first day of the lunar month was observed as a holy day. In addition to the daily sacrifice there were offered two young bullocks, a ram and seven lambs of the first year as a burnt offering, with the proper meat-offerings and drink-offerings, and a kid as a sin-offering (Num. xxviii. 11-15).^e It was not a day of holy convocation [FESTIVALS], and was not therefore of the same dignity as the Sabbath.^f But, as on the Sabbath, trade and handicraft-work were stopped (Am. viii. 5), the Temple was opened for public worship (Ez. xlvi. 3; Is. lxvi. 23), and, in the kingdom of Israel at least, the people seem to have resorted to the prophets for religious instruction.^g The trumpets were blown at the offering of the special sacrifices for the day, as on the solemn festivals (Num. x. 10; Ps. lxxxi. 3). That it was an occasion for state-banquets may be inferred from David's regarding himself as especially bound to sit at the king's table at the new moon (1 Sam. xx. 5-24). In later, if not in earlier times, fasting was intermitted at the new moons, as it was on the Sabbaths and the great feasts and their eves (Jud. viii. 6). [FASTS.]

The new moons are generally mentioned so as to show that they were regarded as a peculiar class of holy days, to be distinguished from the solemn feasts and the Sabbaths (Ez. xlv. 17; 1 Chr. xxiii. 31; 2 Chr. ii. 4, viii. 13, xxxi. 3; Ezr. iii. 5; Neh x. 33).

The seventh new moon of the religious year, being that of Tisri, commenced the civil year, and had

---

^a φρύγανα (from φρύγω, "to burn," "to roast," with reference to the derivation of the Hebrew word) properly signifies "dry sticks," "fagots."

^b חָרַד, from חָרַד (חָרַר), "to burn"), "addita terminatione hypochoristica *âl.*" See Fürst, *Heb. Cxec.;* cf. *urtica* ab *uro.*

^c *i. e.* the Italian version of Diodati. We have often obtained the Latin forms of writers, as being familiar to the readers of Celsius and Bochart.

^d הַמְּשׁוֹנִים, plur. from קִמָּשׁוֹן.

^e The day of the new moon is not mentioned in Exodus, Leviticus, or Deuteronomy.

^f It has been usual to understand "new moon days" as intended in Gal. iv. 10; but the term (μῆνας) may signify "months," *i. e.* certain of them regarded as specially sacred, in conformity with the stricter sense of the word and an ancient Jewish usage (see Meyer *in loc.*).   II.

^g 2 K. iv. 23. When the Shunammite is going to the prophet, her husband asks her, "Wherefore wilt thou go to him to-day? It is neither new moon nor sabbath." See the notes of Vatablus, Grotius, and Keil.

a significance and rites of its own. It was a day of holy convocation. [TRUMPETS, FEAST OF.]

By what method the commencement of the month was ascertained in the time of Moses is uncertain. The Mishna[a] describes the manner in which it was determined seven times in the year by observing the first appearance of the moon, which, according to Maimonides, derived its origin, by tradition, from Moses, and continued in use as long as the Sanhedrim existed. On the 30th day of the month watchmen were placed on commanding heights round Jerusalem to watch the sky. As soon as each of them detected the moon he hastened to a house in the city, which was kept for the purpose, and was there examined by the president of the Sanhedrim. When the evidence of the appearance was deemed satisfactory, the president rose up and formally announced it, uttering the words, "It is consecrated" (מְקֻדָּשׁ). The information was immediately sent throughout the land from the Mount of Olives, by beacon-fires on the tops of the hills. At one period the Samaritans are said to have deceived the Jews by false fires, and swift messengers were afterwards employed. When the moon was not visible on account of clouds, and in the five months when the watchmen were not sent out, the month was considered to commence on the morning of the day which followed the 30th. According to Maimonides the Rabbinists altered their method when the Sanhedrim ceased to exist, and have ever since determined the month by astronomical calculation, while the Caraites have retained the old custom of depending on the appearance of the moon.

The religious observance of the day of the new moon may plainly be regarded as the consecration of a natural division of time. Such a usage would so readily suggest itself to the human mind that it is not wonderful that we find traces of it amongst other nations. There seems to be but little ground for founding on these traces the notion that the Hebrews derived it from the Gentiles, as Spencer and Michaelis have done;[b] and still less for attaching to it any of those symbolical meanings which have been imagined by some other writers (see Carpzov, *App. Crit.* p. 425). Ewald thinks that it was at first a simple household festival, and that on this account the law does not take much notice of it. He also considers that there is some reason to suppose that the day of the full moon was similarly observed by the Hebrews in very remote times. (Carpzov, *Apparat. Hist. Crit.* p. 423; Spencer, *De Leg. Heb.* lib. iii. dissert. iv.; Selden, *De Ann. Civ. Heb.* iv., xi.; Mishna, *Rosh Hashanah*, vol. ii. p. 338, ed. Surenhus.; Buxtorf, *Synagoga Judaica,* cap. xxii.; Ewald, *Alterthümer,* p. 394; Cudworth on *the Lord's Supper,* c. iii.; Lightfoot, *Temple Service,* cap. xi.)   S. C.

NEW TESTAMENT. The origin, history, and characteristics of the constituent books and of the great versions of the N. T., the mutual relations of the Gospels, and the formation of the Canon, are discussed in other articles. It is proposed now to consider the Text of the N. T. The subject

naturally divides itself into the following heads, which will be examined in succession:—

I. THE HISTORY OF THE WRITTEN TEXT.
§§ 1-11. The earliest history of the text Autographs. Corruptions. The text of Clement and Origen.
§§ 12-15. Theories of recensions of the text.
§§ 16-25. External characteristics of MSS.
§§ 26-29. Enumeration of MSS. § 28. Uncial.   29. Cursive.
§§ 30-40. Classification of various readings.

II. THE HISTORY OF THE PRINTED TEXT.
§ 1. The great periods.
§§ 2-5. § 2. The Complutensian Polyglott.
§ 3. The editions of Erasmus. § 4. The editions of Stephens. § 5. Beza and Elzevir (English version).
§§ 6-10. § 6. Walton; Curcellæus; Mill. § 7. Bentley. § 8. G. v. Maestricht; [Bengel:] Wetstein. § 9. Griesbach; Matthæi. § 10. Scholz.
§§ 11-13. § 11. Lachmann. § 12. Tischendorf. § 13. Tregelles; Alford.

III. PRINCIPLES OF TEXTUAL CRITICISM.
§§ 1-9. External evidence.
§§ 10-13. Internal evidence.

IV. THE LANGUAGE OF THE NEW TESTAMENT.

I. THE HISTORY OF THE WRITTEN TEXT.

1. The early history of the Apostolic writings offers no points of distinguishing literary interest. Externally, as far as it can be traced, it is the same as that of other contemporary books. St. Paul, like Cicero or Pliny, often employed the services of an amanuensis, to whom he dictated his letters, affixing the salutation "with his own hand" (1 Cor. xvi. 21; 2 Thess. iii. 17; Col. iv. 18). In one case the scribe has added a clause in his own name (Rom. xvi. 22). Once, in writing to the Galatians, the Apostle appears to apologize for the rudeness of the autograph which he addressed to them, as if from defective sight (Gal. vi. 11). If we pass onwards one step, it does not appear that any special care was taken in the first age to preserve the books of the N. T. from the various injuries of time, or to insure perfect accuracy of transcription. They were given as a heritage to man, and it was some time before men felt the full value of the gift. The original copies seem to have soon perished; and we may perhaps see in this a providential provision against that spirit of superstition which in earlier times converted the symbols of God's redemption into objects of idolatry (2 K. xviii. 4). It is certainly remarkable that in the controversies at the close of the second century, which often turned upon disputed readings of Scripture, no appeal was made to the Apostolic originals. The few passages in which it has been supposed that they are referred to will not bear examination. Ignatius, so far from appealing to Christian archives, distinctly turns, as

[a] *Rosh Hashanah,* Surenhusius, ii. 338, sq.

[b] The three passages from ancient writers which seem most to the point of those which are quoted, are in Macrobius, Horace, and Tacitus. The first says, " Priscis temporibus pontifici minori hæc provincia delegata fuit, ut novæ lunæ primum observaret aspectum vi-

samque regi sacrificulo nuntiaret " (*Sat.* i. 15). In the second the day is referred to as a social festival (*Od.* iii. 23, 9); and in Tacitus we are informed that the ancient Germans assembled on the days of new and full moon, considering them to be auspicious for new undertakings (*Germ.* c. xi.).

the whole context shows, to the examples of the Jewish Church (τὰ ἀρχαῖα — ad Philad. 8). Tertullian again, when he speaks of "the authentic epistles" of the Apostles (De Praescr. Haer. xxxvi., "apud quas ipsae authenticae litterae eorum recitantur "), uses the term of the pure Greek text as contrasted with the current Latin version (comp. de Monog. xi., "sciamus plane non sic esse in Graeco authentico" a). The silence of the sub-Apostolic age is made more striking by the legends which were circulated after. It was said that when the grave of Barnabas in Cyprus was opened, in the fifth century, in obedience to a vision, the saint was found holding a (Greek) copy of St. Matthew written with his own hand. The copy was taken to Constantinople, and used as the standard of the sacred text (Credner, Einl. § 39; Assem. Bibl. Or. ii. 81). The autograph copy of St. John's Gospel (αὐτὸ τὸ ἰδιόχειρον τοῦ εὐαγγελιστοῦ) was said to be preserved at Ephesus "by the grace of God, and worshipped (προσκυνεῖται) by the faithful there," in the fourth century (?), ([Petr. Alex.] p. 518, ed. Migne, quoted from Chron. Pasch. p. 5); though according to another account it was found in the ruins of the Temple when Julian attempted to rebuild it (Philostorg. vii. 14). A similar belief was current even in the last century. It was said that parts of the (Latin) autograph of St. Mark were preserved at Venice and Prague; but on examination these were shown to be fragments of a MS. of the Vulgate of the sixth century (Dobrowsky, Fragmentum Pragense Ev. S. Marci, 1778).

2. In the natural course of things the Apostolic autographs would be likely to perish soon. The material which was commonly used for letters, the papyrus-paper to which St. John incidentally alludes (2 John 12, διὰ χάρτου καὶ μέλανος; comp. 3 John 13, διὰ μέλανος καὶ καλάμου), was singularly fragile, and even the stouter kinds, likely to be used for the historical books, were not fitted to bear constant use. The papyrus fragments which have come down to the present time have been preserved under peculiar circumstances, as at Herculaneum or in Egyptian tombs: and Jerome notices that the library of Pamphilus at Caesarea was already in part destroyed (ex parte corruptam) when, in less than a century after its formation, two presbyters of the Church endeavored to restore the papyrus MSS. (as the context implies) on parchment ("in membranis," Hieron. Ep. xxxiv. (141), quoted by Tischdf. in Herzog's Encykl., Bibeltext des N. T. p. 159). Parchment (2 Tim. iv. 13, μεμβράνα), which was more durable, was proportionately rarer and more costly. And yet more than this. In the first age the written word of the Apostles occupied no authoritative position above their spoken word, and the vivid memory of their personal teaching. And when the true value of the Apostolic writings was afterwards revealed by the progress of the Church, then collections of "the divine oracles" would be chiefly sought for among Christians. On all accounts it seems reasonable to conclude that the autographs perished during that solemn pause which followed the Apostolic age, in which the idea of a Christian Canon, parallel and supple-

mentary to the Jewish Canon, was first distinctly realized.

3. In the time of the Diocletian persecution (A. D. 303) copies of the Christian Scriptures were sufficiently numerous to furnish a special object for persecutors, and a characteristic name to renegades who saved themselves by surrendering the sacred books (traditores, August. Ep. lxxvi. 2). Partly, perhaps, owing to the destruction thus caused, but still more from the natural effects of time, no MS. of the N. T. of the first three centuries remains.b Some of the oldest extant were certainly copied from others which dated from within this period, but as yet no one can be placed further back than the time of Constantine. It is recorded of this monarch that one of his first acts after the foundation of Constantinople was to order the preparation of fifty MSS. of the Holy Scriptures, required for the use of the Church, " on fair skins (ἐν διφθέραις εὐκατασκεύοις) by skillful calligraphists " (Euseb. Vit. Const. iv. 36); and to the general use of this better material we probably owe our most venerable copies, which are written on vellum of singular excellence and fineness. But though no fragment of the N. T. of the first century still remains, the Italian and Egyptian papyri, which are of that date, give a clear notion of the calligraphy of the period. In these the text is written in columns, rudely divided, in somewhat awkward capital letters (uncials), without any punctuation or division of words. The iota, which was afterwards subscribed, is commonly, but not always, adscribed; and there is no trace of accents or breathings. The earliest MSS. of the N. T. bear a general resemblance to this primitive type, and we may reasonably believe that the Apostolic originals were thus written. (Plate i. fig. 1.)

4. In addition to the later MSS., the earliest versions and patristic quotations give very important testimony to the character and history of the ante-Nicene text. Express statements of readings which are found in some of the most ancient Christian writers are, indeed, the first direct evidence which we have, and are consequently of the highest importance. But till the last quarter of the second century this source of information fails us. Not only are the remains of Christian literature up to that time extremely scanty, but the practice of verbal quotation from the N. T. was not yet prevalent. The evangelic citations in the Apostolic Fathers and in Justin Martyr show that the oral tradition was still as widely current as the written Gospels (comp. Westcott's Canon of the N. T. pp. 125–195), and there is not in those writers one express verbal citation from the other Apostolic books.c This latter phenomenon is in a great measure to be explained by the nature of their writings. As soon as definite controversies arose among Christians, the text of the N. T. assumed its true importance. The earliest monuments of these remain in the works of Irenaeus, Hippolytus (Pseudo-Origen), and Tertullian, who quote many of the arguments of the leading adversaries of the Church. Charges of corrupting the sacred text are urged on both sides with great acrimony. Dio-

---

a Griesbach (Opuscula, ii. 69–76) endeavors to show that the word simply means pure, uncorrupted.

b Papyrus fragments of part of St. Matthew, dating from the first century (??), are announced (1861) for publication by Dr. Simonides. [It is hardly necessary to say that these are forgeries. A.]

c In the epistle of Polycarp some interesting various readings occur, which are found also in later copies. Acts ii. 24, τοῦ ᾅδου for τοῦ θανάτου; 1 Tim. vi. 7, ἀλλ' οὐδέ for δῆλον ὅτι οὐδέ; 1 John iv. 3, ἐν σαρκὶ ἐληλυθέναι. Comp. 1 Pet. i. 8 (Polyc. ad Phil. i 4).

nysius of Corinth († cir. A. D. 176, ap. Euseb. *H. E.* iv. 23), Irenæus (cir. A. D. 177; iv. 6, 1), Tertullian (cir. A. D. 210; *De Carne Christi*, 19, p. 385; *Adv. Marc.* iv., v. *passim*), Clement of Alexandria (cir. A. D. 200; *Strom.* iv. 6, § 41), and at a later time Ambrose (cir. A. D. 375; *De Spir. S.* iii. 10), accuse their opponents of this offense; but with one great exception the instances which are brought forward in support of the accusation generally resolve themselves into various readings, in which the decision cannot always be given in favor of the catholic disputant; and even where the unorthodox reading is certainly wrong it can be shown that it was widely spread among writers of different opinions (*e. g.* Matt. xi. 27, "nec Filium nisi Pater et cui voluerit Filius revelare:" John i. 13, ὃς — ἐγεννίθη). Willful interpolations or changes are extremely rare, if they exist at all (comp. Valent. ap. Iren. i. 4, 5, add. θεότητες, Col. i. 16), except in the case of Marcion. His mode of dealing with the writings of the N. T., in which he was followed by his school, was, as Tertullian says, to use the knife rather than subtlety of interpretation. There can be no reasonable doubt that he dealt in the most arbitrary manner with whole books, and that he removed from the Gospel of St. Luke many passages which were opposed to his peculiar views. But when these fundamental changes were once made he seems to have adhered scrupulously to the text which he found. In the isolated readings which he is said to have altered, it happens not unfrequently that he has retained the right reading, and that his opponents are in error (Luke v. 14 om. τὸ δῶρον; Gal. ii. 5, οἷς οὐδέ; 2 Cor. iv. 5?). In very many cases the alleged corruption is a various reading, more or less supported by other authorities (Luke xii. 38, ἑσπερινῇ; 1 Cor. x. 9, Χριστόν; 1 Thess. ii. 15, add. ἰδίους). And where the changes seem most arbitrary there is evidence to show that the interpolations were not wholly due to his school: Luke xviii. 19, ὁ πατήρ; xxiii. 2; 1 Cor. x. 19 (28), add. ἱερόθυτον. (Comp. Hahn, *Evangelium Marcionis;* Thilo, *Cod. Apocr.* i. 403-486; Ritschl, *Das Evang. Marc.* 1846; Volckmar, *Das Evang. Marc.*, Leipsic, 1852: but no examination of Marcion's text is completely satisfactory).

5. Several very important conclusions follow from this earliest appearance of textual criticism. It is in the first place evident that various readings existed in the books of the N. T. at a time prior to all extant authorities. History affords no trace of the pure Apostolic originals. Again, from the preservation of the first variations noticed, which are often extremely minute, in one or more of the primary documents still left, we may be certain that no important changes have been made in the sacred text which we cannot now detect. The materials for ascertaining the true reading are found to be complete when tested by the earliest witnesses. And yet further: from the minuteness of some of the variations which are urged in controversy, it is obvious that the words of the N. T. were watched with the most jealous care, and that the least differences of phrase were guarded with scrupulous

and faithful piety, to be used in after-time by that wide-reaching criticism which was foreign to the spirit of the first ages.[a]

6. Passing from these isolated quotations we find the first great witnesses to the Apostolic text in the early Syriac and Latin versions, and in the rich quotations of Clement of Alexandria († cir. A. D. 220) and Origen (A. D. 184–254). The versions will be treated of elsewhere, and with them the Latin quotations of the translator of Irenæus and of Tertullian. The Greek quotations in the remains of the original text of Irenæus and in Hippolytus are of great value, but yield in extent and importance to those of the two Alexandrine fathers. From the extant works of Origen alone no inconsiderable portion of the whole N. T., with the exception of St. James, 2 Peter, 2 and 3 John, and the Apocalypse, might be transcribed, and the recurrence of small variations in long passages proves that the quotations were accurately made and not simply from memory.

7. The evangelic text of Clement is far from pure. Two chief causes contributed especially to corrupt the text of the Gospels, the attempts to harmonize parallel narratives, and the influence of tradition. The former assumed a special importance from the *Diatessaron* of Tatian (cir. A. D. 170. Comp. *Hist. of N. T. Canon*, 358–362; Tischdf. on Matt. xxvii. 49)[b] and the latter, which was, as has been remarked, very great in the time of Justin M., still lingered.[c] The quotations of Clement suffer from both these disturbing forces (Matt. viii. 22, x. 30, xi. 27, xix. 24, xxiii. 27. xxv. 41, x. 26, omitted by Tischdf. [cf. Mark iv. 22 and the reading of Origen, *Opp.* iii. 235] Luke iii. 23), and he seems to have derived from his copies of the Gospels two sayings of the Lord which form no part of the canonical text. (Comp. Tischdf. on Matt. vi. 33; Luke xvi. 11.) Elsewhere his quotations are free, or a confused mixture of two narratives (Matt. v. 45, vi. 26, 32 f., xxii. 37; Mark xii. 43), but in innumerable places he has preserved the true reading (Matt. v. 4, 5, 42, 48. viii. 22, xi. 17, xiii. 25, xxiii. 26; Acts ii. 41, xvii. 26). His quotations from the Epistles are of the very highest value. In these tradition had no prevailing power, though Tatian is said to have altered in parts the language of the Epistles (Euseb. *H. E.* iv. 29); and the text was left comparatively free from corruptions. Against the few false readings which he supports (*e. g.* 1 Pet. ii. 3, Χριστός; Rom. iii. 26, Ἰησοῦν; viii. 11, διὰ τοῦ ἐνοικ. πν.) may be brought forward a long list of passages in which he combines with a few of the best authorities in upholding the true text (*e. g.* 1 Pet. ii. 2; Rom. ii. 17, x. 3, xv. 29; 1 Cor. ii. 13, vii. 3, 5, 35, 39, viii. 2, x. 24).

8. But Origen stands as far first of all the ante-Nicene fathers in critical authority as he does in commanding genius, and his writings are an almost inexhaustible storehouse for the history of the text. In many places it seems that the printed text of his works has been modernized; and till a new and thorough collation of the MSS. has been made, a doubt must remain whether his quotations have

---

[a] Irenæus notices two various readings of importance, in which he maintains the true text, Matt. i. 18, τοῦ δὲ χριστοῦ (iii. 16, 2), Apoc. xiii. 18 (v. 30, 1).

The letter of Ptolemæus (cir. A. D. 150) to Flora (Epiph. i. 216) contains some important early variations in the evangelic text.

[b] Jerome notices the result of this in his time in strong terms, *Pref. in Evang.*

[c] To what extent tradition might modify the current text is still clearly seen from the *Codex Bezæ* and some Latin copies, which probably give a text dating in essence from the close of the 2d century.

not suffered by the hands of scribes, as the MSS. of the N. T. have suffered, though in a less degree. The testimony which Origen bears as to the corruption of the text of the Gospels in his time differs from the general statements which have been already noticed as being the deliberate judgment of a scholar and not the plea of a controversialist. "As the case stands," he says, "it is obvious that the difference between the copies is considerable, partly from the. carelessness of individual scribes, partly from the wicked daring of some in correcting what is written, partly also from [the changes made by] those who add or remove what seems good to them in the process of correction " *a* (Orig. *In Matt.* t. xv. § 14). In the case of the LXX., he adds, he removed or at least indicated those corruptions by a comparison of "editions" (ἐκδόσεις), and we may believe that he took equal care to ascertain, at least for his own use, the true text of the N. T., though he did not venture to arouse the prejudice of his contemporaries by openly revising it, as the old translation adds (*In Matt.* xv. ret. int. "in exemplaribus autem Novi Testamenti hoc ipsum me posse facere sine periculo non putavi"). Even in the form in which they have come down to us, the writings of Origen, as a whole, contain the noblest early memorial of the apostolic text. And, though there is no evidence that he published any recension of the text, yet it is not unlikely that he wrote out copies of the N. T. with his own hand (Redepenning, *Origenes*, ii. 184), which were spread widely in after time. Thus Jerome appeals to "the copies of Adamantius," *i. e.* Origen (*In Matt.* xxiv. 36; *Gal.* iii. 1), and the copy of Pamphilus can hardly have been other than a copy of Origen's text (Cod. H₂ Subscription, Inf. § 26). From Pamphilus the text passed to Eusebius and Euthalius, and it is scarcely rash to believe that it can be traced, though imperfectly, in existing MSS. as C L. (Comp. Griesbach, *Symb. Crit.* i. lxxvi. ff.; cxxx. ff.)

9. In thirteen cases (Norton, *Genuineness of the Gospels*, i. 234–236 [Add. Notes, pp. xcviii.-ci., 2d Amer. ed.]) Origen has expressly noticed varieties of reading in the Gospels (Matt. viii. 28, xvi. 20, xviii. 1, xxi. 5, 9, 15, xxvii. 17; Mark iii. 18; Luke i. 46, ix. 48, xiv. 19, xxiii. 45; John i. 3, 4: 28).[b] In three of these passages the variations which he notices are no longer found in our Greek copies (Matt. xxi. 9 or 15, οἴκῳ for υἱῷ; Tregelles, *ad loc.*; Mark iii. 18 (ii. 14), Λεβὴν τὸν τοῦ 'Αλφ. (? [D with some Latin MSS. reads Λεββ αῖον])); Luke i. 46, 'Ελισάβετ for Μαριάμ; so in some Latin copies); in seven our copies are still divided (as two (Matt. viii. 28, Γαδαρηνῶν; John i. 28, Βηθαβαρᾷ) the reading which was only found in a few MSS. is now widely spread: in the remaining place (Matt. xxvii. 17, 'Ιησοῦν Βαραββᾶν) a few copies of no great age retain the interpolation which was found in his time " in very ancient copies." It is more remarkable that Origen asserts, in answer to Celsus, that our Lord is nowhere called "the carpenter" in the Gospels circulated in the churches, though this is undoubtedly the true reading in Mark vi. 3 (Orig. *c. Cels.* vi. 36).

10. The evangelic quotations of Origen are not wholly free from the admixture of traditional glosses

which have been noticed in Clement, and often present a confusion of parallel passages (Matt. v. 44, vi. (3-3), vii. 21 ff., xiii. 11, xxvi. 27 f.; 1 Tim. iv. 1); but there is little difficulty in separating his genuine text from these natural corruptions, and a few references are sufficient to indicate its extreme importance (Matt. iv. 10, vi. 13, xv. 8, 35; Mark i 2, x. 23; Luke xxi. 19; John vii. 39; Acts x. 10; Rom. viii. 28).

11. In the Epistles Origen once notices a striking variation in Heb. ii. 9, χωρὶς θεοῦ for χάριτι θεοῦ, which is still attested; but, apart from the specific reference to variations, it is evident that he himself used MSS. at different times which varied in many details (Mill, *Prolegg.* § 687). Griesbach, who has investigated this fact with the greatest care (*Meletema* i. appended to *Comm. Crit.* ii. ix.–xl.), seems to have exaggerated the extent of these differences while he establishes their existence satisfactorily. There can be no doubt that in Origen's time the variations in the N. T. MSS., which we have seen to have existed from the earliest attainable date, and which Origen describes as considerable and wide-spread, were beginning to lead to the formation of specific groups of copies.

Though materials for the history of the text during the first three centuries are abundant, nothing has been written in detail on the subject since the time of Mill (*Prolegg.* 240 ff) and R. Simon (*Histoire Critique*, 1685–93). What is wanted is nothing less than a complete collection at full length, from MS. authority, of all the ante-Nicene Greek quotations. These would form a centre round which the variations of the versions and Latin quotations might be grouped. A first step towards this has been made by Anger in his *Synopsis Ev.ˈ Matt. Marc., Luc.*, 1851. The *Latin* quotations are well given by Sabatier, *Bibliorum Sacrorum Latinae versiones antiquae*, 1751.

12. The most ancient MSS. and versions now extant exhibit the characteristic differences which have been found to exist in different parts of the works of Origen. These cannot have had their source later than the beginning of the third century, and probably were much earlier. In classical texts, where the MSS. are sufficiently numerous, it is generally possible to determine a very few primary sources, standing in definite relations to one another, from which the other copies can be shown to flow; and from these the scholar is able to discover one source of all. In the case of the N. T. the authorities for the text are infinitely more varied and extensive than elsewhere, and the question has been raised whether it may not be possible to distribute them in like manner and divine from later documents the earliest history of the text. Various answers have been made which are quite valueless as far as they profess to rest on historical evidence; and yet are all more or less interesting as explaining the true conditions of the problem. The chief facts, it must be noticed, are derived from later documents, but the question itself belongs to the last half of the second century.

Bengel was the first (1734) who pointed out the affinity of certain groups of MSS., which, as he remarks, must have arisen before the first versions were made (*Apparatus Criticus*, ed. Burk, p. 425).

---

a These words seem to refer to the professional corrector (διορθωτής).

b To these Mr. Hort (to whom the writer owes many

suggestions and corrections in this article) adds Matt. v. 22. from Cramer, *Cat. in* Eph. iv. 21, where Origen blames the insertion of εἰκῇ.

Originally he distinguished three families, of which the *Cod. Alex.* (A), the Græco-Latin MSS., and the mass of the more recent MSS. were respectively the types. At a later time (1737) he adopted the simpler division of "two nations," the Asiatic and the African. In the latter he included *Cod. Alex.*, the Græco-Latin MSS., the Æthiopic, Coptic [Memphitic], and Latin versions: the mass of the remaining authorities formed the Asiatic class. So far no attempt was made to trace the history of the groups, but the general agreement of the most ancient witnesses against the more recent, a fact which Bentley announced, was distinctly asserted, though Bengel was not prepared to accept the ancient reading as necessarily true. Semler contributed nothing of value to Bengel's theory, but made it more widely known (*Spicilegium Observationum*, etc., added to his edition of Wetstein's *Libelli ad Crisin atque Int. N. T.* 1766; *Apparatus, etc.*, 1767). The honor of carefully determining the relations of critical authorities for the N. T. text belongs to Griesbach. This great scholar gave a summary of his theory in his *Historia Text. Gr. Epist. Paul.* (1777, *Opusc.* ii. 1–135) and in the preface to his first edition of the Greek Test. His earlier essay, *Dissert. Crit. de Codd. quat. Evang. Origenianis* (1771, *Opusc.* i.), is incomplete. According to Griesbach (*Nov. Test.* Praef. pp. lxx. ff.) two distinct recensions of the Gospels existed at the beginning of the third century: the *Alexandrine*, represented by B C L, 1, 13, 33, 69, 106, the Coptic, Æthiop., Arm., and later Syrian versions, and the quotations of Clem. Alex., Origen, Eusebius, Cyril. Alex., Isid. Pelus.; and the *Western*, represented by D, and in part by 1, 13, 69, the ancient Latin version and Fathers, and sometimes by the Syriac and Arabic versions. *Cod. Alex.* was to be regarded as giving a more recent (Constantinopolitan) text in the Gospels. As to the origin of the variations in the text, Griesbach supposed that copies were at first derived from the separate autographs or imperfect collections of the apostolic books. These were gradually interpolated, especially as they were intended for private use, by glosses of various kinds, till at length authoritative editions of the collection of the Gospels and the letters (εὐαγγέλιον ὁ ἀπόστολος, τὸ ἀποστολικόν) were made. These gave in the main a pure text, and thus two classes of MSS. were afterwards current, those derived from the interpolated copies (*Western*), and those derived from the εὐαγγέλιον and ἀποστολικόν (Alexandrine, *Eastern; Opusc.* ii. 77–99; *Meletemata*, xliv.). At a later time Griesbach rejected these historical conjectures (*Nov. Test.* ed. 2, 1796; yet comp. *Meletem.* l. c.), and repeated with greater care and fullness, from his enlarged knowledge of the authorities, the threefold division which he had originally made (*N. T.* i. *Praef.* lxx.-lxxvii. ed. Schulz). At the same time he recognized the existence of mixed and transitional texts; and when he characterized by a happy epigram (*grammaticum egit Alexandrinus censor, interpretem occidentalis*) the difference of the two ancient families, he frankly admitted that no existing document exhibited either "recension" in a pure form. His great merit was independent of the details of

his system: he established the existence of a group of ancient MSS. distinct from those which could be accused of Latinizing (Tregelles, *Horne*, p. 105).

13. The chief object of Griesbach in propounding his theory of recensions was to destroy the weight of mere numbers.[a] The critical result with him had far more interest than the historical process; and, apart from all consideration as to the origin of the variations, the facts which he pointed out are of permanent value. Others carried on the investigation from the point where he left it. Hug endeavored, with much ingenuity, to place the theory on a historical basis (*Einleitung in N. T.* 1st ed. 1808; 3d, 1826). According to him, the text of the N. T. fell into a state of considerable corruption during the second century. To this form he applied the term κοινὴ ἔκδοσις (*common edition*), which had been applied by Alexandrine critics to the unrevised text of Homer, and in later times to the unrevised text of the LXX. (i. 144). In the course of the third century this text, he supposed, underwent a threefold revision, by Hesychius in Egypt, by Lucian at Antioch, and by Origen in Palestine. So that our existing documents represent four classes: (1.) The *unrevised*, D. 1, 13, 69 in the Gospels; D E$_2$ in the Acts; D$_2$ F$_2$ G$_2$ in the Pauline Epistles: the old Latin and Thebaic, and in part the Peshito Syriac; and the quotations of Clement and Origen. (2.) The Egyptian recension of Hesychius; B C L in Gospels; A B C 17 in the Pauline Epistles; A B C Acts and Catholic Epistles; A C in the Apocalypse: the Memphitic version; and the quotations of Cyril. Alex. and Athanasius. (3.) The Asiatic (Antioch-Constantinople) recension of Lucian; E F G H S V and the recent MSS. generally; the Gothic and Slavonic versions, and the quotations of Theophylact. (4.) The Palestinian recension of Origen (of the Gospels); A K M; the Philoxenian Syriac; the quotations of Theodoret and Chrysostom. But the slender external proof which Hug adduced in support of this system was, in the main, a mere misconception of what Jerome said of the labors of Hesychius and Lucian on the LXX. (*Praef. in Paralip.*; e. Ruff. ii. 27; and Ep. cvi. (135) § 2. The only other passages are *De Viris illustr.* cap. lxxvii. Lucianus; *Praef. in quat. Ev.*); the assumed recension of Origen rests on no historical evidence whatever. Yet the new analysis of the internal character of the documents was not without a valuable result. Hug showed that the line of demarcation between the Alexandrine and Western families of Griesbach was practically an imaginary one. Not only are the extreme types of the two classes connected by a series of intermediate links, but many of the quotations of Clement and Origen belong to the so-called Western text. Griesbach, in examining Hug's hypothesis, explained this phenomenon by showing that at various times Origen used MSS. of different types, and admitted that many Western readings are found in Alexandrine copies (*Meletem.* xlviii. comp. Laurence, *Remarks on the Systematic Classification of MSS.*, 1814).

14. Little remains to be said of later theories. Eichhorn accepted the classification of Hug (*Ein-*

---

a This he states distinctly (*Symb. Crit.* i. cxxii.): "Præcipuus vero recensionum in crisees sacræ exercitio usus hic est, ut eorum auctoritate lectiones bonas, ted in paucis libris superstites defendamus adversus juniorum et vulgarium codicum innumerabilem pæne

turbam." Comp. *id.* ii. 624 n. The necessity of destroying this grand source of error was supreme, as may be seen not only from such canons as G. v. Maestricht (II. § 8, n.), but also from Wetstein's Rule xviii. " Lectio plurium codicum cæteris paribus præferenda est."

leitung, 1818–27). Matthæi, the bitter adversary of Griesbach, contented himself with asserting the paramount claims of the later copies against the more ancient, allowing so far their general difference (*Ueber die sog. Recensionen*, 1804; *N. T.* 1783–88). Scholz returning to a simpler arrangement divided the authorities into two classes, Alexandrine and Constantinopolitan (*N. T.* i. p. xv. ff.), and maintained the superior purity of the latter on the ground of their assumed unanimity. In practice he failed to carry out his principles; and the unanimity of the later copies has now been shown to be quite imaginary. Since the time of Scholz theories of recensions have found little favor. Lachmann, who accepted only ancient authorities, simply divided them into Eastern (Alexandrine) and Western. Tischendorf, with some reserve, proposes two great classes, each consisting of two pairs, the Alexandrine and Latin, the Asiatic and Byzantine. Tregelles, discarding all theories of recension as historic facts, insists on the general accordance of ancient authorities as giving an ancient text in contrast with the recent text of the more modern copies. At the same time he points out what we may suppose to be the " genealogy of the text." This he exhibits in the following form:—

D   ℵ B Z
       C L ℵ 1 33
       P Q T R   A
       X (Δ) 69   K M H
                 E F G S U, etc.[a]

15. The fundamental error of the recension theories is the assumption either of an actual recension or of a pure text of one type, which was variously modified in later times, while the fact seems to be exactly the converse. Groups of copies spring not from the imperfect reproduction of the character of one typical exemplar, but from the multiplication of characteristic variations. They are the results of a tendency, and not of a fact. They advance *towards* and do not lead *from* that form of text which we regard as their standard. Individuals, as Origen, may have exercised an important influence at a particular time and place, but the silent and continual influence of circumstances was greater. A pure Alexandrine or Western text is simply a fiction. The tendency at Alexandria or Carthage was in a certain direction, and necessarily influenced the character of the current texts with accumulative force as far as it was unchecked by other influences. This is a general law, and the history of the apostolic books is no exception to it. The history of their text differs from that of other books chiefly in this, that, owing to the great multiplicity of testimony, typical copies are here represented by typical groups of copies, and the intermediate stages are occupied by mixed texts But if we look beneath this complication general lines of change may be detected. All experience shows that certain types of variation propagate and perpetuate themselves, and existing documents prove that it was so with the copies of the N. T. Many of the links

in the genealogical table of our MSS. may be wanting, but the specific relations between the groups, and their comparative antiquity of origin, are clear. This antiquity is determined, not by the demonstration of the immediate dependence of particular copies upon one another, but by reference to a common standard. The secondary uncials (E S U, etc.) are not derived from the earlier (B C A) by direct descent, but rather both are derived by different processes from one original. And here various considerations will assist the judgment of the critic. The accumulation of variations may be more or less rapid in certain directions. A disturbing force may act for a shorter time with greater intensity, or its effects may be slow and protracted. Corruptions may be obvious or subtle, the work of the ignorant copyist or of the rash scholar; they may lie upon the surface or they may penetrate into the fabric of the text. But on such points no general rules can be laid down. Here as elsewhere, there is an instinct or tact which discerns likenesses or relationships and refuses to be measured mechanically. It is enough to insist on the truth that the varieties in our documents are the result of slow and natural growth and not of violent change. They are due to the action of intelligible laws and rarely, if ever, to the caprice or imperfect judgment of individuals. They contain in themselves their history and their explanation.

16. From the consideration of the earliest history of the N. T. text we now pass to the æra of MSS. The quotations of DIONYSIUS ALEX. (†A. D. 264), PETRUS ALEX. (†c. A. D. 312), METHODIUS (†A. D. 311), and EUSEBIUS (†A. D. 340), confirm the prevalence of the ancient type of text; but the public establishment of Christianity in the Roman empire necessarily led to important changes. Not only were more copies of the N. T. required for public use (Comp. § 3). but the nominal or real adherence of the higher ranks to the Christian faith must have largely increased the demand for costly MSS. As a natural consequence the rude Hellenistic forms gave way before the current Greek, and at the same time it is reasonable to believe that smoother and fuller constructions were substituted for the rougher turns of the apostolic language. In this way the foundation of the Byzantine text was laid, and the same influence which thus began to work, continued uninterruptedly till the fall of the Eastern empire. Meanwhile the multiplication of copies in Africa and Syria was checked by Mohammedan conquests. The Greek language ceased to be current in the West. The progress of the Alexandrine and Occidental families of MSS. was thus checked; and the mass of recent copies necessarily represent the accumulated results of one tendency.

17. The appearance of the oldest MSS. has been already described. (§ 3.) The MSS. of the 4th century, of which *Cod. Vatican.* (B) may be taken as a type, present a close resemblance to these. The writing is in elegant continuous (capitals) uncials,[b] in three columns[c] without initial letters or *iota subscript*, or *ascript*. A small interval serves

---

[a] "Those codices are placed together which appear to demand such an arrangement; and those which stand below others are such as show still more and more of the intermixture of modernised readings" (Tregelles, *Horne*, [vol. iv.] p. 106).

[b] Jerome describes the false taste of many in his time (c. A. D. 400) with regard to MSS. of the Bible: "Habeant qui volunt veteres libros, vel in membranis

purpureis auro argentoque descriptos, vel *uncialibus*, ut vulgo aiunt, litteris onera magis exarata, quam codices; dummodo mihi meisque permittant pauperes habere schedulas, et non tam pulcros codices quam emendatos " (*Praef. in Jobum*, ix. 1004, ed. Migne).

[c] The Codex Sinaiticus (Cod. Frid. Aug.) has *four* columns; Cod. Alex. (A) two. Cf. Scrivener, *Introduction*, p. 26, n., for other examples.

as a simple punctuation; and there are no accents or breathings by the hand of the first writer, though these have been added subsequently. *Uncial* writing continued in general use till the middle of the 10th century.[a] One uncial MS. (S), the earliest dated copy, bears the date 949; and for service books the same style was retained a century later. From the 11th century downwards *cursive* writing prevailed, but this passed through several forms sufficiently distinct to fix the date of a MS. with tolerable certainty. The earliest cursive Biblical MS. is dated 964 A. D. (Gosp. 14, Scrivener, *Introduction*, p. 36 *note*), though cursive writing was used a century before (A. D. 888, Scrivener, *l. c.*). The MSS. of the 14th and 15th centuries abound in the contractions which afterwards passed into the early printed books. The material as well as the writing of MSS. underwent successive changes. The oldest MSS. are written on the thinnest and finest vellum: in later copies the parchment is thick and coarse. Sometimes, as in *Cod. Cotton.* (N = J), the vellum is stained. Papyrus was very rarely used after the 9th century. In the 10th century cotton paper (*charta bombycina* or *Damascena*) was generally employed in Europe; and one example at least occurs of its use in the 9th century (Tischdf. *Not. Cod. Sin.* p. 54, quoted by Scrivener, *Introduction*, p. 21). In the 12th century the common linen or rag paper came into use; but paper was "seldom used for Biblical MSS. earlier than the 13th century, and had not entirely displaced parchment at the æra of the invention of printing, c. A. D. 1450" (Scrivener, *Introduction*, p. 21). One other kind of material requires notice, redressed parchment (παλίμψηστος, *charta deleticia*). Even at a very early period the original text of a parchment MS. was often erased, that the material might be used afresh (Cic. *ad Fam.* vii. 18; Catull. xxii.).[b] In lapse of time the original writing frequently reappears in faint lines below the later text, and in this way many precious fragments of Biblical MSS. which had been once obliterated for the transcription of other works have been recovered. Of these palimpsest MSS. the most famous are those noticed below under the letters C R Z Ξ. The earliest Biblical palimpsest is not older than the 5th century (Plate i. fig. 3).

18. In uncial MSS. the contractions are usually limited to a few very common forms (ΘC, IC, [ΧC, ΚC, ΤC,] ΠΗΡ, ΔΑΔ, etc., *i. e.* θεός, Ἰησοῦς, [χριστός, κύριος, υἱός,] πατήρ, Δαυείδ;

comp. Scrivener, *Introduction*, p. 43). A few more occur in later uncial copies, in which there are also some examples of the ascript *iota*, which occurs rarely in the Codex Sinaiticus.[c] Accents are not found in MSS. older than the 8th century.[d] Breathings and the apostrophus (Tischdf. *Proleg.* cxxxi.) occur somewhat earlier. The oldest punctuation after the simple interval, is a stop like the modern Greek colon (in A C D), which is accompanied by an interval, proportioned in some cases to the length of the pause.[e] In E (Gospp.) and B[2] (Apoc.), which are MSS. of the 8th century, this point marks a full stop, a colon, or a comma, according as it is placed at the top, the middle, or the base of the letter (Scrivener, p. 42).[f] The present note of interrogation (;) came into use in the 9th century.

19. A very ingenious attempt was made to supply an effectual system of punctuation for public reading, by Euthalius, who published an arrangement of St. Paul's Epistles in clauses (στίχοι) in 458, and another of the Acts and Catholic Epistles in 490. The same arrangement was applied to the Gospels by some unknown hand, and probably at an earlier date. The method of subdivision was doubtless suggested by the mode in which the poetic books of the O. T. were written in the MSS. of the LXX. The great examples of this method of writing are D (Gospels), H₃ (Epp.), D₂ (Epp.). The *Cod. Laud.* (E₂ Acts) is not strictly stichometrical, but the parallel texts seem to be arranged to establish a verbal connection between the Latin and Greek (Tregelles, *Horne*, 187). The στίχοι vary considerably in length, and thus the amount of vellum consumed was far more than in an ordinary MS., so that the fashion of writing in "clauses" soon passed away; but the numeration of the στίχοι in the several books was still preserved, and many MSS. (*e. g.* Δ Ep., K Gosp.) bear traces of having been copied from older texts thus arranged.[g]

20. The earliest extant division of the N. T. into sections occurs in Cod. B. This division is elsewhere found only in the palimpsest fragment of St. Luke, Ξ. In the Acts and the Epistles there is a double division in B, one of which is by a later hand. The Epistles of St. Paul are treated as one unbroken book divided into 93 sections, in which the Epistle to the Hebrews originally stood between the Epistles to the Galatians and the Ephesians. This appears from the numbering of the sections, which the writer of the MS. preserved, though he

---

[a] A full and interesting account of the various changes in the uncial alphabet at different times is given by Scrivener, *Introduction*, pp. 27-36.

[b] This practice was condemned at the Quinisextine Council (A. D. 692), Can. 68; but the Commentary of Balsamon shows that in his time († A. D. 1204) the practice had not ceased: σημειοῦσαι ταῦτα διὰ τοὺς βιβλιοκαπήλους τοὺς ἀπαλείφοντας τὰς μεμβράνας τῶν θείων γραφῶν. A Biblical fragment in the British Museum has been erased, and used *twice* afterwards for Syrian writing (Add. 17, 136. Cod. Nb Tischdf.).

[c] As to the use of cursive MSS. in this respect of *iota ascript* or *subscript*, Mr. Scrivener found that "of forty-three MSS. now in England, twelve have no vestige of either fashion, fifteen represent the *ascript* use, nine the *subscript* exclusively, while the few that remain have both indifferently" (*Introduction*, p. 39). The earliest use of the subscript is in a MS. (71) dated 1160 (Scrivener, *l. c.*).

[d] Mr. Scrivener makes an exception in the case of the first four lines of each column of the Book of Gen-

esis " in Cod. A, which, he says, is furnished with accents and breathings by the *first* hand (*Introduction*, p. 40) Dr. Tregelles, to whose kindness I am indebted for several remarks on this article, expressed to me his strong doubts as to the correctness of this assertion: and a very careful examination of the MS. leaves no question but that the accents and breathings were the work of the later scribe who accentuated the whole of the first three columns. There is a perceptible difference in the shade of the red pigment, which is decisively shown in the initial Ε.

[e] The division in John i. 3, 4, ὃ γέγονεν ἐν αὐτῷ ζωὴ ἦν (cf. Tregelles, *ad loc.*), Rom. viii. 20 (Origen), ix. 5, shows the attention given to this question in the earliest times.

[f] Dr. Tregelles, whose acquaintance with ancient MSS. is not inferior to that of any scholar, expresses a doubt "whether this is at all uniformly the case."

[g] Comp. Tischd. *N. T.* ed. 1859, under the subscriptions to the several books. Wetstein *Prolegg.* pp. 100-102.

transposed the book to the place before the pastoral epistles.[a]

21. Two other divisions of the Gospels must be noticed. The first of these was a division into "chapters" (κεφάλαια, τίτλοι, breves), which correspond with distinct sections of the narrative, and are on an average a little more than twice as long as the sections in B. This division is found in A, C, R, Z, and must therefore have come into general use some time before the 5th century.[b] The other division was constructed with a view to a harmony of the Gospels. It owes its origin to Ammonius of Alexandria, a scholar of the 3d century, who constructed a Harmony of the Evangelists, taking St. Matthew as the basis round which he grouped the parallel passages from the other Gospels. Eusebius of Cæsarea completed his labor with great ingenuity, and constructed a notation and a series of tables, which indicate at a glance the parallels which exist to any passage in one or more of the other Gospels, and the passages which are peculiar to each. There seems every reason to believe that the sections as they stand at present, as well as the ten "Canons," which give a summary of the Harmony, are due to Eusebius, though the sections sometimes occur in MSS. without the corresponding Canons.[c] The Cod. Alex. (A), and the Cottonian fragments (N), are the oldest MSS. which contain both in the original hand. The sections occur in the palimpsests C, R, Z, P, Q, and it is possible that the Canons may have been there originally, for the vermilion (κιννάβαρις, Euseb. *Ep. ad Carp.*), or paint with which they were marked, would entirely disappear in the process of preparing the parchment afresh.[d]

22. The division of the Acts and Epistles into chapters came into use at a later time. It does not occur in A or C, which give the Ammonian sections, and is commonly referred to Euthalius (Comp. § 19), who, however, says that he borrowed the divisions of the Pauline Epistles from an earlier father; and there is reason to believe that the division of the Acts and Catholic Epistles which he published was originally the work of Pamphilus the Martyr (Montfaucon, *Bibl. Coislin.* p. 78). The Apocalypse was divided into sections by Andreas of Cæsarea about A. D. 500. This division consisted of 24 λόγοι, each of which was subdivided into three "chapters" (κεφάλαια).[e]

23. The titles of the sacred books are from their nature additions to the original text. The distinct names of the Gospels imply a collection, and the titles of the Epistles are notes by the possessors and not addresses by the writers ('Ιωάννου ά, β′, etc.). In their earliest form they are quite simple, *According to Matthew*, etc. (κατὰ Ματθαῖον κ.τ.λ.); *To the Romans*, etc. (πρὸς 'Ρωμαίους κ.τ.λ.); *First of Peter*, etc. (Πέτρου ά′); *Acts of Apostles*, (πράξεις ἀποστόλων): *Apocalypse*. These headings were gradually amplified till they

assumed such forms as *The holy Gospel according to John; The first Catholic Epistle of the holy and all-praiseworthy Peter; The Apocalypse of the holy and most glorious Apostle and Evangelist, the beloved virgin who rested on the bosom of Jesus, John the Divine.* In the same way the original subscriptions (ὑπογραφαί), which were merely repetitions of the titles, gave way to vague traditions as to the dates, etc., of the books. Those appended to the Epistles, which have been translated in the A. V., are attributed to Euthalius, and their singular inaccuracy (Paley, *Horæ Paulinæ,* ch. xv.) is a valuable proof of the utter absence of historical criticism at the time when they could find currency.

24. Very few MSS. contain the whole N. T., "twenty-seven in all out of the vast mass of extant documents" (Scrivener, *Introduction,* p. 61). The MSS. of the Apocalypse are rarest; and Chrysostom complained that in his time the Acts was very little known. Besides the MSS. of the N. T., or of parts of it, there are also Lectionaries, which contain extracts arranged for the Church-services. These were taken from the Gospels (εὐαγγελιστάρια), or from the Gospels and Acts (πραξαπόστολοι), or, rarely from the Gospels and Epistles (ἀποστολοευαγγέλια). The calendars of the lessons (συναξάρια), are appended to very many MSS. of the N. T.; those for the saints'-day lessons, which varied very considerably in different times and places, were called μηνολόγια (Scholz, *N. T.* i. 453–493; Scrivener, 68–75).

25. When a MS. was completed it was commonly submitted, at least in early times, to a careful revision. Two terms occur in describing this process, ὁ ἀντιβάλλων and διορθωτής. It has been suggested that the work of the former answered to that of "the corrector of the press," while that of the latter was more critical (Tregelles, *Horne,* pp. 85, 86). Possibly, however, the words only describe two parts of the same work. Several MSS. still preserve a subscription which attests a revision by comparison with famous copies, though this attestation must have referred to the earlier exemplar (comp. Tischdf. Jude *subscript.*); but the Coislinian fragment (H³) may have been itself compared, according to the subscription, "with the copy in the library at Cæsarea, written by the hand of the holy Pamphilus." (Comp. Scrivener, *Introduction,* p. 47.) Besides this official correction at the time of transcription, MSS. were often corrected by different hands in later times. Thus Tischendorf distinguishes the work of two correctors in C, and of three chief correctors in D₂. In later MSS. the corrections are often much more valuable than the original text, as in 67 (Epp.); and in the *Cod. Sinait.* the readings of one corrector (2 b) are frequently as valuable as those of the original text.[f]

(The work of Montfaucon still remains the classi-

---

[a] The oldest division is not found in 2 Pet. (ed. Vercell. p. 125). (Mr. Hort.) It is found in Jude ; 2, 3 John.

[b] The κεφάλαια do not begin with the beginning of the books (Griesbach, *Comm. Crit.* ii. 49) This is important in reference to the objections raised against Matt. i.

[c] These very useful canons and sections are printed in the Oxford Text (Lloyd) in Tischendorf (1859), and the notation is very easily mastered. A more complete arrangement of the canons, giving the order of the

sections in each Evangelist, originally drawn up by Dr. Tregelles, is found in Dr. Wordsworth's *Gk. Test.* vol. i.

[d] A comparative table of the ancient and modern divisions of the N. T. is given by Scrivener (*Introduction,* p. 58).

[e] For the later division of the Bible into our present chapters and verses, see BIBLE, i. 307, 308.

[f] Examples of the attestation and signature of MSS with a list of the names of scribes, are given by Montfaucon (*Palæographia,* pp. 39–108).

eal authority on Greek Palæography (*Palæographia Græca*, Paris, 1708), though much has been discovered since his time which modifies some of his statements. The plates in the magnificent work of Silvestre and Champollion (*Paléographie Universelle*, Paris, 1841, *Eng. Trans.* by Sir F. Madden, London, 1850) give a splendid and fairly accurate series of facsimiles of Greek MSS. (Plates, liv.–xciv.). Tischendorf announces a new work on Palæography (*N. T. Præf.* cxxxiii.), and this, if published, will probably leave nothing to be desired in the Biblical branch of the study.

26.[a] The number of uncial MSS. remaining, though great when compared with the ancient MSS. extant of other writings, is inconsiderable.[b] Tischendorf (*N. T. Præf.* cxxx.) reckons 40 in the Gospels, of which 5 are entire, B K M S U; 3 nearly entire, E L Δ; 10 contain very considerable portions, A C D F G H V X Γ Λ; of the remainder 14 contain very small fragments, 8 fragments more (I P Q R Z) or less considerable (N T Y). To these must be added ℵ (*Cod. Sinait.*), which is entire; Σ (?) [Π] a new MS. of Tischendorf (*Not. Cod. Sin.* pp. 51, 52), which is nearly entire; and Ξ (*Cod. Zacynth.*), which contains considerable fragments of St. Luke. Tischendorf has likewise obtained 6 [9] additional fragments (*l. c.*). In the Acts there are 9 (10 [12] with ℵ [G₂ P₂]), of which 4 contain the text entire (ℵ A B), or nearly (E₂) so; 4 [5] have large fragments, (C D H₂ G₂ = I₂ [P₂]); 2 [3] small fragments. In the Catholic Epistles 5 [7] of which 4 [5, ℵ] A B K₂ G₂ = L₂ are entire; 1 [2] (C [P₂]) nearly entire. In the Pauline Epistles there are 14 [18, ℵ entire;] 2 [3] nearly entire, D₂ L₂ [P₂]; 7 have very considerable portions, A B C E₃ F₂ G₃ K₂ (but E₃ should not be reckoned); the remaining 5 [7] some fragments. In the Apocalypse 3 [5], 2 [3] entire ([ℵ] A B₂), 2 nearly entire (C [P₂]).

27. According to date these MSS. are classed as follows:—

Fourth century. ℵ B.
Fifth century. A C, and some fragments including [I¹, ², ³, I^b] Q [Q₂] Tᵃ.
Sixth century. D P R Z, E₂, D₂ H₃, and 4 [9] smaller fragments.
Seventh century. Some fragments including Θ, [Fᵃ, and G₂.]
Eighth century. E L Λ [? 9th cent.] Ξ, B₂ and some fragments.
Ninth century. F K M X [V Γ Λ Π] Δ, H₂ G₂ = L₂ [P₂], F₂ G₃ K₂ M₂ and fragments.
Tenth century. G H S U, (E₃.)

28. A complete description of these MSS. is given in the great critical editions of the N. T.: here those only can be briefly noticed which are of primary importance, the first place being given to

the latest discovered and most complete *Codex Sinaiticus.*

A (i). Primary Uncials of the Gospels.

ℵ (*Codex Sinaiticus = Cod. Frid. Aug.* of LXX.), at St. Petersburg, obtained by Tischendorf from the convent of St. Catherine, Mount Sinai, in 1859. The fragments of LXX. published as *Cod. Frid. Aug.* (1846), were obtained at the same place by Tischendorf in 1844. The N. T. is entire, and the Epistle of Barnabas and parts of the Shepherd of Hermas are added. The whole MS. is to be published in 1862 by Tischendorf at the expense of the Emperor of Russia. It is probably the oldest of the MSS. of the N. T., and of the 4th century (Tischdf. *Not. Cod. Sin.* 1860).

* The MS. was published at St. Petersburg in 1862 in magnificent style, in 4 vols. folio, with the title: "*Bibliorum Codex Sinaiticus Petropolitanus . . . edidit C. Tischendorf,*" the edition being limited to about 300 copies. It was printed with type cast for the purpose so as to resemble the characters of the MS., which it represents line for line with the greatest attainable accuracy. The first vol. contains Prolegomena, notes on the alterations made at different times by many correctors, and 21 pages of facsimiles, the first 19 representing different parts of the MS., and the remaining 2 containing facsimiles of the writing of 36 MSS. of great palæographical interest, illustrating the changes in the style of writing from the first century (papyri) to the seventh. In 1863 a comparatively cheap edition of the N. T. part of the MS. was published by Tischendorf at Leipsic, in ordinary type, with enlarged Prolegomena and some corrections (*Novum Testamentum Sinaiticum*, etc., 4to). The Rev. F. H. Scrivener published in 1864 *A Full Collation of the Codex Sinaiticus with the Received Text of the N. T.* (rather, Stephens' ed. of 1550), *to which is prefixed a Critical Introduction*; the same collation also appeared in a new edition of Wordsworth's *Greek Testament*, for which it was originally made. In 1865 Tischendorf issued a new edition of the N. T. portion of the MS. (*N. T. Græce ex Sinaitico Codice*, 8vo), noting in the margin the alterations of later correctors, as also the various readings of the Vat. MS. (B) so far as they were then known, and of the Elzevir or Received Text, with a valuable Introduction of 83 pages, in which (pp. xliii.–xlix.) he gives a list of errata in Scrivener's generally accurate collation.   A.

A (*Codex Alexandrinus*, Brit. Mus.), a MS. of the entire Greek Bible, with the Epistles of Clement added. It was given by Cyril Lucar, patriarch of Constantinople, to Charles I. in 1628, and is now in the British Museum. It contains the whole of the N. T. with some chasms: Matt. i.–xxv. 6, ἐξέρχεσθε; John vi. 50, ἵνα–viii. 52, λέγει; 2 Cor. iv. 13, ἐπίστευσα–xii. 6, ἐξ ἐμοῦ. It was probably written in the first half of the 5th century. The N. T. has been published by Woide (fol. 1786), and with some corrections by Cowper

<hr>

a * In supplementing the account of the MSS. in this and the following sections much use has been made of Tischendorf's art. *Bibeltext des N. Testaments* in Herzog's *Real-Encykl.* xix. pp. 187–196 (1865).   A.

b Since the time of Wetstein the uncial MSS. have been marked by capital letters, the cursives by numbers.

bers (and later by small letters). In consequence of the confusion which arises from applying the same letter to different MSS., I have distinguished the different MSS. by the notation M, M₂, M₃, [H, H₂, H₃ — there is no M₃], retaining the asterisk (as originally used) to mark the first, etc., hands.

(8vo. 1860).[a] Comp. Wetstein, *Prolegg.* pp. 13–30 (ed. Lotze). (Plate i. fig. 2.)

B (*Codex Vaticanus*, 1209), a MS. of the entire Greek Bible, which seems to have been in the Vatican Library almost from its commencement (c. A. D. 1450). It contains the N. T. entire to Heb. ix. 14, καθα: the rest of the Epistle to the Hebrews, the Pastoral Epistles, and the Apocalypse were added in the 15th century. Various collations of the N. T. were made by Bartolocci (1669), by Mico for Bentley (c. 1720), whose collation was in part revised by Rulotta (1726), and by Birch (1788). An edition of the whole MS., on which Mai had been engaged for many years, was published three years after his death, in 1857 (5 voll. 4to, ed. Vercellone; N. T. reprinted Lond. and Leipsic). Mai had himself kept back the edition (printed 1828–1838), being fully conscious of its imperfections, and had prepared another edition of the N. T., which was published also by Vercellone in 1859 (8vo.). The errors in this are less numerous than in the former collation; but the literal text of B is still required by scholars. The MS. is assigned to the 4th century (Tischdf. *N. T.* cxxxvi.-cxlix.).

* In 1837 Tischendorf published at Leipsic *Test. Nov. Vaticanum, post Ang. Maii aliorumque imperfectos Labores,* etc., 4to, and also *Appendix Codd. Sin. Vat. Alex. cum Imitatione ipsorum antiqui Manu Scriptorum,* fol. Though allowed to examine the Vatican MS. but 42 hours, he spent the time so well that he was able to determine the true reading in all cases of discrepancy between different collators, and to correct the text as given by Card. Mai in more than 400 places. In 1868 a splendid edition of the N. T. portion of the Vat. MS. and also of Cod. B of the Apocalypse was published at Rome, by authority of the Pope, under the editorship of Vercellone and Cozza. This is printed with type cast from the same font that was made for the Codex Sinaiticus, and in the style of Tischendorf's edition of that MS.; the Old Testament is to follow in 4 vols., and a volume of Prolegomena and Notes will complete the long desired work. Though not immaculate, it appears to be executed with great care. Since its appearance, Tischendorf has published at Leipsic an *Appendix N. T. Vaticani,* containing the text of MS. B of the Apocalypse and corrections of his *N. T. Vat.* from the recent Roman edition, together with a criticism on that edition, in which he points out some defects and oversights. A.

C (*Codex Ephraemi rescriptus,* Paris, *Bibl. Imp.* 9), a palimpsest MS. which contains fragments of the LXX. and of every part of the N. T. In the 12th century the original writing was effaced

and some Greek writings of Ephraem Syrus were written over it. The MS. was brought to Florence from the East at the beginning of the 16th century, and came thence to Paris with Catherine de Médicis. Wetstein was engaged to collate it for Bentley (1716), but it was first fully examined by Tischendorf, who published the N. T. in 1843: the O. T. fragments in 1845. The only entire books which have perished are 2 Thess. and 2 John, but lacunæ of greater or less extent occur constantly. It is of about the same date as *Cod. Alex.*

D (*Codex Bezæ,* Univ. Libr. Cambridge), a Græco-Latin MS. of the Gospels and Acts, with a small fragment of 3 John, presented to the University of Cambridge by Beza in 1581. Some readings from it were obtained in Italy for Stephens' edition; but afterwards Beza found it at the sack of Lyons in 1562 in the monastery of St. Irenæus. The text is very remarkable, and, especially in the Acts, abounds in singular interpolations. The MS. has many lacunæ. It was edited in a splendid form by Kipling (1793, 2 vols. fol.), and no complete collation has been since made; but arrangements have lately been (1861) made for a new edition under the care of the Rev. F. H. Scrivener. The MS. is referred to the 6th century. Cf. Credner, *Beiträge,* i. 452–518; Bornemann, *Acta Apostolorum,* 1848; Schulz, *De Codice D, Cantab.* 1827.[b]

* Scrivener's edition of the *Codex Bezæ* was published at Cambridge in 1864, 4to. It appears to be executed with great care and thoroughness.   A.

L (*Paris. Cod. Imp.* p. 62), one of the most important of the late uncial MSS. It contains the four Gospels, with the exception of Matt. iv. 22–v. 14, xxviii. 17–20; Mark x. 16–20, xv. 2–20; John xxi. 15–25. The text agrees in a remarkable manner with B and Origen. It has been published by Tischendorf, *Monumenta Sacra Inedita,* 1846. Cf. Griesbach, *Symb. Crit.* i. pp. lxvi. - cxli. It is of the 8th century.

R (*Brit. Mus. Add.* 17,211), a very valuable palimpsest, brought to England in 1847 from the convent of St. Mary Deipara in the Nitrian desert. The original text is covered by Syrian writing of the 9th or 10th century. About 585 verses of St. Luke were deciphered by Tregelles in 1854, and by Tischendorf in 1855. The latter has published them in his *Mon. Sacra Inedita, Nova Coll.,* vol. i. 1857. It is assigned to the 6th century. (Plate i. fig. 3.)

X (*Codex Monacensis*), in the University Library at Munich. Collated by Tischendorf and Tregelles. Of the [9th or] 10th century.

Z (*Cod. Dublinensis rescriptus,* in the Library

Σαμαριτάνων, λέπρωσος, φλαγελλώσας (Wetstein, *Prolegg.* p 40): but the charge of more serious alterations from this source cannot be maintained.

* The work of Mr. Hansell, referred to above, was published at Oxford in 1864, in 3 vols. 8vo., with the title: *Nov. Test. Græce Antiquissimorum Codd. Textus in Ordine parallelo dispositi Accedit Collatio Cod. Sinaitici.* It gives, in such a manner that they can be compared at one view, the readings of A B C D Z, and also those of E_2 in the Acts and D_2 in the Epistles. But the editor does not seem to have been altogether competent for his task (see Tischendorf's *N. T. Gr. ex Sin. Cod.* p. li., note), and the readings of both B and D have since been published far more completely and accurately.   A.

NEW TESTAMENT

of Trin. Coll. Dublin), a palimpsest containing large portions of St. Matthew. It was edited by Barrett (1801); and Tregelles has since (1853) re-examined the MS. and deciphered all that was left undetermined before (*History of Printed Text*, pp. 166-169). It is assigned to the 6th century.

Δ (*Codex Sangallensis*), a MS. of the Gospels, with an interlinear Latin translation, in the Library of St. Gall. It once formed part of the same volume with G³. Published in lithographed fac-simile by Rettig (Zurich, 1836). [9th cent.]

Ξ (*Codex Zacynthius*), a palimpsest in posses-sion of the Bible Society, London, containing important fragments of St. Luke. It is probably of the 8th century, and is accompanied by a *Catena*. The later writing is a Greek Lectionary of the 13th century. It has been transcribed and published by Tregelles (London, 1861).

The following are important fragments: —

* Fᵃ (*Cod. Cislin.*, Paris). A few fragments of the Gospels, Acts, and Pauline Epistles. 7th cent. A.

I (Tischendorf), various fragments of the Gos-pels (Acts, Pauline Epistles), some of great value, published by Tischendorf, *Monum. Sacr. Nova Coll.* vol. i. 1855. [5th, 6th, and 7th cent.]

* Iᵇ is now used by Tischendorf to denote the MS. described below under Nᵇ. A.

N (*Cod. Cotton.*), (formerly J N), twelve leaves of purple vellum, the writing being in silver. Four leaves are in Brit. Mus. (Cotton. C. xv.). Pub-lished by Tischendorf, *Mon. Sacr. ined.*, 1846. Sæc. vi.

* 33 additional leaves of this MS., containing fragments of the Gospel of Mark, have been recently found at Patmos, and are used in Tischen-dorf's 8th critical edition of the N. T. A.

Nᵇ (Brit. Mus. *Add.* 17, 136), a palimpsest. Deciphered by Tregelles and Tischendorf, and pub-lished by the latter: *Mon. Sacr. ined. Nova Coll.*, vol. ii. Sæc. iv., v. [This MS. is now desig-nated by Tischendorf as Iᵇ. — A.]

* O denotes fragments of the Gospel of John at Moscow (Matthæi, No. 15). 9th cent. A.

* Oᵃᵇᶜᵈᵉᶠ denote the hymns in Luke i. as found in uncial MSS. of the Psalms in various libraries. Oᶜ, 6th cent.; Oᵈ, 7th; Oᵃᵇᵉᶠ, 9th. A.

P Q (*Codd. Guelpherbytani*, Wolfenbüttel), two palimpsests, respectively of the 6th and 5th cen-turies. Published by Knittel, 1762, and P [Q rather] again, more completely, by Tischendorf, *Mon. Sacr. ined.* iii. 1860, who has Q [P rather] ready for publication.

T (*Cod. Borgianus*, Propaganda at Rome), of the 5th century. The fragments of St. John, ed-ited by Giorgi (1789); those of St. Luke, collated by B. H. Alford (1859). Other fragments were pub-lished by Woide. (Tischd. *N. T. Proleg.* clxvii.).

* Tᵇ denotes fragments of John, and Tᶜ of Mat-thew, similar to the above, the former at St. Peters-burg (Imp. Lib.), the latter belonging to the Rus-sian bishop Porfiri. 6th cent. Tᵈ denotes frag-ments of Matt., Mark, and John, from Borgian MSS. of the 7th cent. A.

Y (*Cod. Barberini*, 225, Rome). Sæc. viii. Edited by Tischendorf, *Mon. Sacr. ined.* 1846.

Θᵃ (*Cod. Tischendorf.* i., Leipsic). Sæc. vii. Edited by Tischendorf in *Mon. Sacr. ined.* 1846.

* Θᵇᶜᵈᵉᶠᵍʰ are fragments at St. Pet----burg,

ranging from the 6th to the 9th cent. Of these Θᶜᵍ are the most valuable. A.

(ii.) The Secondary Uncials are in the Gos-pels: —

E (*Basileensis*, K. iv. 35, Basle). Collated by Tischendorf, Mueller, Tregelles. Sæc. viii.

F (*Rheno-Trajectinus*. Utrecht, formerly Bo-reeli). Coll. by Heringa, Traj. 1843. Sæc. ix.

G (Brit. Mus. Harl. 5684). Coll. by Tregelles and Tischendorf. Sæc. ix., x.

H (*Hamburgensis*, Seidelii). Coll. by Tregelles, 1850. Sæc. ix. [vel x.].

K (*Cod. Cyprius*, Paris, Bibl. Imp. 63). Coll. by Tregelles and Tischendorf. Sæc. ix.

M (*Cod. Campianus*, Paris, Bibl. Imp. 48). Coll. by Tregelles, and transcribed by Tischendorf. Sæc. x. [ix. Tisch.]

S (*Vaticanus*, 354). Coll. by Birch. Sæc. x.

U (*Cod. Nanianus*, Venice). Coll. by Tregelles and Tischendorf. Sæc. x.

V (*Mosquensis*). Coll. by Matthæi. Sæc. ix.

* Wᵃᵇᶜᵈ denote fragments of the 8th and 9th centuries at Paris, Naples, St. Gall, and the Library of Trinity College, Cambridge, respectively. A.

Γ (*Bodleianus*). Sæc. ix. Cf. Tischdf., *N. T.* p. clxxiii. Coll. by Tischendorf and Tregelles. Fresh portions of this MS. have lately been taken by Tischendorf to St. Petersburg.

Δ. Cod. Tischendorf iii. (*Bodleian*). Sæc. viii. ix. Coll. by Tischendorf and Tregelles. [9th cent., Tisch.]

[Π, *not*] Σ (St. Petersburg). Sæc. viii. ix. (?). A new MS. as yet uncollated.

* This MS., containing the Gospels nearly com-plete, was procured by Tischendorf at Smyrna. Its readings are given in his 8th ed. of the Greek N. T. A.

B (i.). Primary Uncials of the Acts and Cath-olic Epistles.

ℵ A B C D.

E₂ (*Codex Laudianus*, 35), a Græco-Latin MS. of the Acts, probably brought to England by Theo-dore of Tarsus, 668, and used by Bede. It was given to the University of Oxford by Archbishop Laud in 1636. Published by Hearne, 1715; but a new edition has been lately undertaken (1861) by Scrivener, and is certainly required. [Another edition is promised by Tischendorf.] Sæc. vi., vii.

* Fᵃ. A few fragments of the Acts, 7th cent. A.

* I (St. Petersburg). 3 fragments, one, Acts xxviii. 8-17, of the 5th cent.; the others 7th cent. A.

(ii.) The Secondary Uncials are —

G₂ = I₂ (*Cod. Angelicus* (Passionei) Rome). Coll. by Tischdf. and Treg. Sæc. ix.

* G₂ is now used by Tischendorf to denote a leaf of the 7th cent. brought by him in 1859 to St. Petersburg, containing Acts ii. 45 - iii. 8. A.

H₂ (*Cod. Mutinensis*, Modena), of the Acts. Coll. by Tischdf. and Treg. Sæc. ix.

K₂ (*Mosquensis*), of the Catholic Epistles. Coll. by Matthæi. Sæc. ix.

* I₂. Formerly G₂; see above. A.

* P₂, an important palimpsest of the 9th cent. belonging to the library of the bishop Porfiri Us-penski in St. Petersburg, containing the principal part of the Acts, the Catholic and Pauline Epistles, and the Apocalypse. In the Acts and 1 Peter its

text agrees with that of the later uncials, but in the remainder of the N. T., particularly in the Apocalypse, it is greatly superior to them. It was published in 1865 (Epistles) and 1869 (Acts and Rev.) in vols. v. and vi. of Tischendorf's *Monum. Sacra ined., Nova Collectio.*   A.

C (i.). Primary Uncials of the Pauline Epistles: —

א A B C.

D₂ (*Codex Clrromontınus*, i. e. from Clermont, near Beauvais, Paris, Bibl. Imp 107), a Græco-Latin MS. of the Pauline Epistles, once (like D) in the possession of Beza. It passed to the Royal Library at Paris in 1707, where it has since remained. Wetstein collated it carefully, and, in 1852, it was published by Tischendorf, who had been engaged on it as early as 1840. The MS. was independently examined by Tregelles, who communicated the results of his collation to Tischendorf, and by their combined labors the original text, which has been altered by numerous correctors, has been completely ascertained. The MS. is entire except Rom. i. 1-7. The passages Rom. i. 27-30 (in Latin, i. 24-27) were added at the close of the 6th century, and 1 Cor. xiv. 13-22 by another ancient hand. The MS. is of the middle of the 6th century. Cf. Griesbach, *Symb. Crit.* ii. 31-77.

F₂ (*Codex Augiensis*, Coll. SS. Trin. Cant. B, 17, 1), a Græco-Latin MS. of St. Paul's Epistles, bought by Bentley from the Monastery of Reichenau (Augia Major) in 1718, and left to Trin. Coll. by his nephew in 1786. This and the *Cod. Boernerianus* (G₃) were certainly derived from the same Greek original. The Greek of the Ep. to the Hebrews is wanting in both, and they have four common lacunæ in the Greek text: 1 Cor. iii. 8-16, vi. 7-14; Col. ii. 1-8; Philem. 21-25. Both likewise have a vacant space between 2 Tim. ii. 4 and 5. The Latin version is complete from the beginning of the MS. Rom. iii. 19, *μω λεγει, dicit.* The MS. has been admirably edited by F. H. Scrivener, Cambr. 1859. It is assigned to the 9th century. The Latin version is of singular interest; it is closer to the best Hieronymian text than that in G₃, especially where the Greek text is wanting (Scrivener, *Cod. Aug.* xxviii.), but has many peculiar readings and many in common with G₇.

G₃ (*Codex Boernerianus*, Dresden), a Græco-Latin MS., which originally formed a part of the same volume with Δ. It was derived from the same Greek original as F₃, which was written continuously, but the Latin version in the two MSS. is widely different.[a] Δ and G₂ seem to have been written by an Irish scribe in Switzerland (St. Gall) in the 9th century. The Greek with the *interlinear* Latin version was carefully edited by Matthæi, 1791. Scrivener has given the variations from F₂ in his edition of that MS.

* P₂. For this important palimpsest, see above under **B** (ii.)   A.

The following fragments are of great value: —

* Fᵃ. A few fragments of the 7th cent.   A.

* I (St. Petersburg), 2 leaves, 1 Cor. xv. 53 — xvi. 9, Tit. i. 1-13, 5th cent.   A.

---

a At the end of the lacuna after Philemon 20 G₃ adds,

ad laudicenses incipit epistola·
προς Λαουδακησας αρχεται επιστολη;

set the form of the Greek name shows almost con-

H₃ (*Codex Cvislinianus*, Paris, Bibl. Imp. 202), part of a stichometrical MS. of the 6th century, consisting of twelve leaves: two more are at St. Petersburg. Edited by Montfaucon, *Bibl. Coislin.* 251-61; and again transcribed and prepared for the press by Tischendorf. It was compared, according to the subscription (Tischdf. *N. T.* p. clxxxix.), with the autograph of Pamphilus at Cæsarea.

* Two more leaves at Moscow, marked Nᵒ by Tischendorf *N. T.* ed. vii., belong to this MS., and there is another in the possession of the Russian bishop Porfiri Uspenski at St. Petersburg.   A.

M₂ (Hamburg; London), containing Heb. i. 1-iv. 3; xii. 20-end, and 1 Cor. xv. 52-2 Cor. i. 15; 2 Cor. x. 13-xii. 5, written in bright red ink in the 10th [9th, Tisch.] century. The Hamburg fragments were collated by Tregelles: all were published by Tischendorf, *Anecdot. Sacr. et Prof* 1855 [new ed., with corrections, 1861].

* O₂ (St. Petersburg). Fragments of the 6th cent., containing 1 Cor. i. 20 - ii. 12.   A.

* Q₂ (St. Petersburg, Porfiri). Fragments of a papyrus MS. of the 5th century.   A.

(ii.). The Secondary Uncials are: —

K₂ L₂ [formerly J].

E₃ (*Cod. Sangermanensis*, St. Petersburg), a Græco-Latin MS., of which the Greek text was badly copied from D₂ after it had been thrice corrected, and is of no value. The Latin text is of some slight value, but has not been well examined. Griesbach, *Symb. Crit.* ii. 77-85.

* N₂ (St. Petersburg): Fragments of the 9th cent., from Heb. v., vi., and Gal. v., vi.   A.

D (i.) The Primary Uncials of the Apocalypse. א A C.

(ii.) The Secondary Uncial is —

B₂ (*Codex Vaticanus*) (Basilianus), 2066). Edited (rather imperfectly) by Tischendorf, *Mon. Sacr.* 1846, and by Mai in his edition of B. Tischendorf gives a collation of the differences, *N. T.* Præf. cxlii.-iii. [Tregelles proposes to call this MS. L.]

* This MS. was accurately published at Rome in 1868 by Vercellone and Cozza in connection with their edition of the N. T. portion of the Vat. MS., and from their edition by Tischendorf in his *Appendix N. T. Vaticani,* 1869.   A.

* P₂. See above under **B** (ii.) The text of this palimpsest in the Apocalypse is more valuable than that of B₂. It has just been published by Tischendorf (1869).   A.

23. The number of the cursive MSS. (*minuscules*) in existence cannot be accurately calculated. Tischendorf catalogues about 500 of the Gospels, 200 of the Acts and Catholic Epistles, 250 of the Pauline Epistles, and a little less than 100 of the Apocalypse (exclusive of lectionaries); but this enumeration can only be accepted as a rough approximation. Many of the MSS. quoted are only known by old references; still more have been " inspected " most cursorily; a few only have been thoroughly collated. In this last work the Rev.

clusively that the Greek words are only a translation of the Latin title which the scribe found in his Latin MS., in which, as in many others, the apocryphal epistle to the Laodiceans was found.

F. H. Scrivener (*Collation of about 20 MSS. of the Holy Gospels*, Camb. 1853: *Cod. Aug., etc.*, Camb. 1859) has labored with the greatest success, and removed many common errors as to the character of the later text [a] Among the MSS. which are well known and of great value the following are the most important: —

A. Primary Cursives of the Gospels.

1 (Act. i.; Paul. i.; *Basileensis*, K. iii. 3). Sæc. x. Very valuable in the Gospels. Coll. by Roth and Tregelles.

33 (Act. 13; Paul. 17; Paris, Bibl. Imp. 14). Sæc. xi. Coll. by Tregelles.

59 (Coll. Gonv. et Cai. Cambr.). Sæc. xii. Coll. by Scrivener, 1860, but as yet unpublished.

69 (Act. 31; Paul. 37; Apoc. 14; *Cod. Leicestrensis*). Sæc. xiv. The text of the Gospels is especially valuable. Coll. by Treg. 1852, and by Scriv. 1855, who published his collation in *Cod. Aug. etc.*, 1859.

118 (Bodleian. Miscell. 13: Marsh i. 24). Sæc. xiii. Coll. by Griesbach, *Symb. Crit.*, p. ccii. ff.

124 (Cæsar. Vindob. Nessel. 188). Sæc. xii. Coll. by Treschow, Alter, Birch.

127 (Cod. Vaticanus, 349). Sæc. xi. Coll. by Birch.

131 (Act. 70; Paul. 77; Apoc. 66; Cod. Vaticanus, 360). Sæc. xi. Formerly belonged to Aldus Manutius, and was probably used by him in his edition. Coll. by Birch.

157 (Cod. Urbino-Vat. 2). Sæc. xii. Coll. by Birch.

218 (Act. 65; Paul..57; Apoc. 33; Cæsar. Vindob. 23). Sæc. xiii. Coll. by Alter.

238, 259 (Moscow, S. Synod. 42, 45). Sæc. xi. Coll. by Matthæi.

262, 300 (Paris, *Bibl. Imp.* 53, 186). Sæc. x. xi. Coll. (?) by Scholz.

346 (Milan, *Ambros.* 23). Sæc. xii. Coll. (?) by Scholz.

2^{pe} (St. Petersburg. *Petropol.* vi. 470). Sæc. ix. Coll. by Muralt. (Transition cursive.)

o^{scr}, g^{scr}, (Lambeth, 1177, 528, Wetstein, 71). Sæc. xii. Coll. by Scrivener.

p^{scr} (Brit. Mus. Burney 20). Sæc. xiii. Coll. by Scrivener.

w^{scr} (Cambr. Coll. SS. Trin. B. x. 16). Sæc. xiv. Coll. by Scrivener.

To these must be added the Evangelistarium (B. M. Burney, 22), marked y^{scr}, collated by Scrivener.[b] Plate ii. fig. 4.)

[a] Mr. Scrivener has kindly furnished me with the following summary of his catalogue of N. T. MSS., which is by far the most complete and trustworthy enumeration yet made (*Plain Introduction*, p. 225): —

	Uncial.	Cursive.	Duplicates already deducted.
Gospels	34	601	32
Act. Cath. Epp. . .	10	229	12
Paul	14	283	14
Apoc.	4	102	..
Evangelistaria . .	58	183	6
Apostolos	7	65	..
Total . . .	127	1463	64

The following are valuable, but need careful collation: [c]

13 (Paris, Bib. Imp. 50). Coll. 1797. Sæc. xii. (Cf. Griesbach, *Symb. Crit.* i. pp. cliv.-clxvi.)

22 (Paris, Bibl. Imp. 72). Sæc. xi.

28 (Paris, Bibl. Imp. 379). Coll. Scholz.

72 (Brit. Mus. Harl. 5647). Sæc. xi.

106 (Cod. Winchelsea). Sæc. x. Coll. Jackson (used by Wetstein), 1748.

113, 114 (B. M. Harl. 1810, 5540).

126 (Cod. Guelpherbytanus, xvi. 16). Sæc. xi.

130 (Cod. Vaticanus, 359). Sæc. xiii.

209 (Act. 95; Paul. 138; Apoc. 46; Venice. Bibl. S. Marci 10). Sæc. xv. The text of the Gospels is especially valuable.

225 (Vienna, *Bibl. Imp.* Kollar. 9, Forlos. 31). Sæc. xii.

372, 382 (Rome, Vatican. 1161, 2070). Sæc. xv., xiii.

405, 408, 409 (Venice, S. Marci, i. 10, 14, 15). Sæc. xi., xii.

B. Primary Cursives of the Acts and Catholic Epistles.

13 = Gosp. 33, Paul. 17.

31 = Gosp. 69 (*Codex Leicestrensis*).

65 = Gosp. 218.

73 (Paul. 80. Vatican. 367). Sæc. xi. Coll. by Birch.

95, 96 (Venet. 10, 11). Sæc. xiv. xi. Coll. by Rinck.

180 (Argentor. Bibl. Sem. M.). Coll. by Arendt.

lo^{ti} = p^{scr} 61 (Tregelles), (Brit. Mus. *Add.* 20,003). Sæc. xi. Coll. by Scrivener.

a^{scr} (Lambeth, 1182). Sæc. xii. Coll. by Scrivener.

c^{scr} (Lambeth, 1184). Coll. Sanderson ap. Scrivener.

The following are valuable, but require more careful collation.

5 (Paris, *Bibl. Imp.* 106).

25, 27 (Paul. 31, Apoc. 7; Paul. 33. Brit. Mus. Harl. 5537, 5620). Cf. Griesbach, *Symb. Crit.* ii. 184, 185.

29 (Paul. 35, Genev. 20). Sæc. xi., xii.

36 (*Coll. Nov.* Oxon.).

40 (Paul. 46, Apoc. 12, Alex. Vatican. 179). Sæc. xi. Coll. by Zacagni.

66 (Paul. 67).

68 (Paul. 73, Upsal). Sæc. xii., xi.

69 (Paul. 74, Apoc. 30, Guelph. xvi. 7). Sæc. xiv., xiii.

81 (Barberini, 377). Sæc. xi.

137 (Milan, *Ambros.* 97). Sæc. xi., Coll. by Scholz.

142 (Mutinensis, 243). Sæc. xii.[d]

[b] The readings marked 102 (Matt. xxiv.-Mark viii 1) which were taken by Wetstein from the margin of a printed copy, and said to have been derived from a Medicean MS., cannot have been derived from any other source than an imperfect collation of B. I have noticed 85 places in which it is quoted in St. Mark, and in every one, except ii. 22, it agrees with B. In St. Matthew it is noticed as agreeing with B 70 times, while it differs from it 5 times. These few variations are not difficult of explanation.

[c] It is to be hoped that scholars may combine to accomplish complete collations of the MSS. given in these lists. One or two summer vacations, with proper coöperation, might accomplish the work.

[d] Three other MSS., containing the Catholic Epistles

Pl. I.

1. Brit. Mus.—Pap. 98.

ΔΡΟΥΚΔΜϕΝΟϹΜΕΝΔΕ
ΠΟΤΟΥΤΗΝΟΙΚΟΥΜΕΝΗΝΥΠΗΚΟ
ΟΝΔΠΔϹΔΝΕΙΝΔΙΝΔΙΙΩΙΔΕΤΩΙ
ΤΟΥΤΩΙΤΡΟΠΩΙΕΖΔΝΔΠΚΗϹΧΡΗϹ
ΘΔΙΤΗΝΕΛΛΔΔΔϹΥΝΕΛΟΝΤΔΙ

2. Brit. Mus.—Cod. Alex.—(St. John i. 1-5.)

ΕΝΔΡΧΗΗΝΟΛΟΓΟϹΚΔΙΟΛΟΓΟϹΗΝ
ΠΡΟϹΤΟΝΘΝ·ΚΔΙΘϹΗΝΟΛΟΓΟϹ·
ΟΥΤΟϹΗΝΕΝΔΡΧΗΠΡΟϹΤΟΝΘΝ
ΠΔΝΤΔΔΙΔΥΤΟΥΕΓΕΝΕΤΟΙΚΔΙΧω
ΡΕΙϹΔΥΤΟΥΕΓΕΝΕΤΟΟΥΔΕΕΝ
ΟΓΕΓΟΝΕΝΕΝΔΥΤωΖωΗΗΝ
ΚΔΙΗΖωΗΗΝΤΟΦωϹΤωΝΔΝωΝ
ΚΔΙΤΟΦωϹΕΝΤΗϹΚΟΤΙΔΦΔΙ
ΝΕΙΚΔΙΗϹΚΟΤΙΔΔΥΤΟΟΥΚΔΤΕ
ΛΔΒΕΝ·

3. Brit. Mus.—Add. 17, 211.—(St. Luke xx. 9, 10.)

SPECIMENS OF GREEK MSS. FROM THE Ist TO THE VIth CENTURY.

C. Primary Cursives in the Pauline Epistles.

17 = Gosp. 33.

37 = Gosp. 69 (*Cod. Leicestrensis*).

57 = Gosp. 218.

108, 109 = Act. 95, 96.

115, 116 (Act. 100, 101, Mosqu. Matt. d. f.).

137 (Gosp. 263, Act. 117. Paris, Bibl. Imp. 61).
The following are valuable, but require more careful collation.

5 = Act. 5.

23 (Paris, Coislin. 28). Saec. xi. Descr. by Montfaucon.

31 (Brit. Mus. *Harl.* 5,537) = l^scr. Apoc. Saec. xiii.

39 (Act. 33. Oxford, Coll. Lincoln. 2).

46 = Act. 40.

47 (Oxford, Bodleian. Roe 16). Saec. xi. [Collated by Tregelles for his ed. of the Greek Test. Griesb. *Symb. Crit.* i. 155 ff. A.]

55 (Act. 46. Monacensis).

67 (Act. 66. Vindob. Lambec. 34). The corrections are especially valuable.

70 (Act. 67. Vindob. Lambec. 37)

71 (Vindob. Forlos. 19). Saec. xii.

73 (Act. 68).

80 (Act. 73. Vatican. 367).

177–8–9 (Mutin.).

D. Primary Cursives of the Apocalypse.

7 = l^scr (Act. 25. Brit. Mus. *Harl.* 5,537). Saec. xi. Coll. by Scrivener.

14 = Gosp. 69 (*Cod. Leicestrensis*).

31 = e^scr (Brit. Mus. *Harl.* 5,678). Saec. xv. Coll. by Scrivener.

38 (Vatican. 579). Saec. xiii. Coll. by B. H. Alford.

47 (Cod. Dresdensis). Saec. xi. Coll. by Matthaei.

51 (Paris, *Bibl. Imp.*). Coll. by Reiche.

g^scr (Parham, 17). Saec. xi., xii. Coll. by Scrivener.

m^scr (Middlehill) = 87. Saec. xi., xii. Coll by Scrivener.

The following are valuable, but require more careful collation.

2 (Act. 10. Paul. 12. Paris. Bibl. Imp. 237).

6 (Act. 23. Paul. 28. Bodleian. Barocc. 3). Saec. xii., xiii.

11 (Act. 39. Paul. 45).

12 = Act. 40.

17, 19 (Ev. 35. Act. 14. Paul. 18; Act. 17 Paul. 21. Paris. Coislin. 199, 205).

28 (Bodleian, Barocc. 48).

36 (Vindob. Forlos. 29). Saec. xiv.

41 (Alex-Vatican. 68). Saec. xiv.

46 = Gosp.' 209.

82 (Act. 179. Paul. 128. Monac. 211).

30. Having surveyed in outline the history of the transmission of the written text, and the chief characteristics of the MSS.[a] in which it is preserved, we are in a position to consider the extent and nature of the variations which exist in different copies. It is impossible to estimate the number of these exactly, but they cannot be less than 120,000 in all (Scrivener, *Introduction*, 3), though of these a very large proportion consist of differences

require notice, not from their intrinsic worth, but from their connection with the controversy on 1 John v. 7, 8.

34 (Gosp. 61, Coll. 33. Trin. Dublin, *Codex Montfortianus*). Saec. xv., xvi. There is no doubt that this was the *Codex Britannicus*, on the authority of which Erasmus, according to his promise, inserted the interpolated words, ἐν τῷ οὐρανῷ, πατήρ, λόγος καὶ πνεῦμα ἅγιον, καὶ οὗτοι οἱ τ. ἑ. ἑ. καὶ τ. ἑ. οἱ μ. ἐν τ. γ.; but did not omit, on the same authority (which exactly follows the late Latin MSS.), the last clause of ver. 8, καὶ οἱ τρ. — εἰσίν. The page on which the verse stands is the only glazed page in the volume. A collation of the MS. has been published by Dr. Dobbin, London, 1854.

162 (Paul. 200. Vat. Ottob. 298.) Saec. xv. A Graeco-Latin MS. It reads, ἀπὸ τοῦ οὐρανοῦ, πατήρ, λόγος καὶ πνεῦμα ἅγιον καὶ οἱ τρεῖς εἰς τὸ ἕν εἰσι (Tregelles, Horne, p. 217). Scholz says that the MS. contains "innumerable transpositions," but gives no clear account of its character.

173 (Paul. 211. Naples, Bibl. Borbon.) Saec. xi. The interpolated words, with the articles, and the last clause of ver. 8, are given by a second hand (Saec. xvi.).

Codex Ravianus (110 Gosp.) is a mere transcript of the N. T. of the Complutensian Polyglot, with variations from Erasmus and Stephens. Comp. Griesbach, *Symb. Crit.* i. clxxxi-clxxxiii.

a The accompanying plates will give a good idea of the different forms of Biblical Gk. MSS. For permission to take the tracings, from which the engravings have been admirably made by Mr. Netherclift, my sincere thanks are due to Sir F. Madden, K. H.; and I am also much indebted to the other officers of the MSS. department of the British Museum, for the help which they gave me in making them.

Pl. i. fig. 1. A few lines from the Λόγος ἐπιτάφιος of Hyperides (col. 9, l. 4, of the edition of Rev. C. Babington), a papyrus of the first century, or not much later. In Mr. Babington's facsimile the ι

adscript after νομω is omitted wrongly. It is in fact partly hidden under a fibre of the papyrus, but easily seen from the side. Two characteristic transcriptural errors occur in the passage: τῷ τούτῳ τρόπῳ for τῷ τούτου τρόπῳ, and (by itacism, § 31) συνελόνται for συνελόντι.

Fig. 2. The opening verses of St. John's Gospel from the *Cod. Alex.* The two first lines are rubricated. The specimen exhibits the common contractions, ΘΟ, ΑΝΩΝ, and an example of itacism, χωρείς. The stop at the end of the fifth line, οὐδ ἕν, is only visible in a strong light, but certainly exists there, as in C D L, etc.

Fig. 3. A very legible specimen of the Nitrian palimpsest of St. Luke. The Greek letters in the original are less defined, and very variable in tint: the Syriac somewhat heavier than in the engraving, which is on the whole very faithful. The dark lines show where the vellum was folded to form the new book for the writings of Severus of Antioch. The same MSS. contained fragments of the *Iliad*, edited by Dr. Cureton, and a piece of Euclid.

Pl. ii. fig. 1. Part of the first column of the famous Harleian *Evangelistarium*, collated by Scrivener. It is dated A. D. 995 (Scrivener, *Cod. Aug.* p. xlviii.). The letters on this page are all in gold. The initial letter is illuminated with red and blue. The MS. is a magnificent example of a service-book.

Fig. 2. From Tischendorf's valuable MS. of the Acts (61 Tregelles). It was written A. D. 1044 (Scrivener, *Cod. Aug.* lxix.). The specimen contains the itacisms χρόνον (χρόνον) and πεντίκοντα.

Fig. 3. The beginning of St. John, from Cod. 114 of the Gospels (Griesbach, *Symb. Crit.* i. p. cxciii.), a MS. of the 13th cent.

Fig. 4. Part of the beginning of St. John, from the very valuable *Evangelistarium* y^scr (Scrivener, *Collation*, etc., pp. lxi. ff.). The initial letter of the Gospel is a rude illumination. The MS. bears a date 1819; but Mr. Scrivener justly doubts whether this is in the hand of the original scribe

of spelling and isolated aberrations of scribes,[a] and of the remainder comparatively few alterations are sufficiently well supported to create reasonable doubt as to the final judgment. Probably there are not more than 1600–2000 places in which the true reading is a matter of uncertainty, even if we include in this questions of order, inflexion, and orthography: the doubtful readings by which the sense is in any way affected are very much fewer, and those of dogmatic importance can be easily numbered.

31. Various readings are due to different causes: some arose from accidental, others from intentional alterations of the original text. (i.) Accidental variations or *errata*, are by far the most numerous class, and admit of being referred to several obvious sources. (*a*) Some are errors of *sound*. The most frequent form of this error is called *Itacism*, a confusion of different varieties of the I-sound, by which (οι, υ) η, ι, ει, ε, etc., are constantly interchanged.[b] Other vowel-changes, as of ο and ω, ου and ω, etc., occur, but less frequently. Very few MSS. are wholly free from mistakes of this kind, but some abound in them. As an illustration the following variants occur in F₂ in Rom. vi. 1–16: 1 ἐρεύμεν; 2 ὅτινες, εἴτει (ἔτι); 3 ἀγνοεῖται (-τε); 5 ἐσθμαιθα; 8 ἀποθάνομεν; 9 ἀποθνῇσκι, ἔτει; 11 ὑμῖς, λογίζεσθαι; 18 παραστήσαται; 14 ἔσται (-τε); 15 ὅτει; 16 οἴδαται, ὅτει, παρειστάνεται (παριστάνετε), ἔσται, ὑπακούεται. An instance of fair doubt as to the true nature of the reading occurs in ver. 2, where ζήσωμεν may be an error for ζήσομεν, or a real variant.[c] Other examples of disputed readings of considerable interest which involve this consideration of Itacism are found, Rom. xii. 2, συσχηματίζεσθαι -θε; xvi. 20, συντρίψει -αι. James iii. 3, εἰ δέ (ἴδε). Rom. v. 1, ἔχωμεν, ἔχομεν (cf. vi. 15). Luke iii. 12, 14; John xiv. 23; Hebr. vi. 3; James iv. 15 (ποιήσωμεν -ομεν). Matt. xxvii. 60, καινῷ, κενῷ. John xv. 4, μείνῃ, μένῃ (cf. 1 John ii. 27). Matt. xi. 16, ἑτέροις, ἑταίροις. Matt. xx. 15, ἤ, εἰ. 2 Cor. xii. 1, δεῖ, δή. 1 Tim. v. 21, πρόσκλησιν, πρόσκλισιν. 1 Pet. ii. 3, χρηστὸς ὁ κύριος, χριστὸς ὁ κύριος.

To these may be added such variations as Matt. xxvi. 29, &c. γένημα, γέννημα. 2 Pet. ii. 12, γεγεννημένα, γεγενημένα. Matt. i. 18; Luke i. 14, γέννησις, γένεσις. Matt. xxvii. 35, βάλλοντες, βαλόντες. 1 Pet. ii. 1, φθόνοις, φόνος.

32. (β) Other variations are due to errors of *sight*. These arise commonly from the confusion of similar letters, from the repetition or omission of the same letters, or from the recurrence of a similar ending in consecutive clauses which often causes one to be passed over when the eye mechanically returns to the copy (ὁμοιοτέλευτον). To these may be added the false division of words in transcribing the text from the continuous uncial

writing The uncial letters Θ, Ο, C, Ε, are peculiarly liable to confusion, and examples may easily be quoted to show how their similarity led to mistakes; 1 Tim. iii. 18, ΟⳞ. Θ̄Ⳟ; 2 Cor. ii. 3, ⲈΧΩ ⲤΧΩ; Mark iv. 22, ⲈΑΝ, ⲞⲈΑΝ, ⲞⳞΑΝ.

The repetition or omission of similar letters may be noticed in Matt. xxi. 18, ΕΠΑΝΑΓΑΓΩΝ, ΕΠΑΝΑΓΩΝ. Luke x. 27; Rom. xiii. 9; Tit. ii. 7; James i. 27, ⳞⲈΑΤΤΟΝ, ⲈΑΤΤΟΝ (cf. Tischdf. *ad Rom.* xiii. 9). Luke vii. 21, ΕΧΑΡΙⳞΑΤΟ ΒΛΕΠΕΙΝ, ΕΧΑΡΙⳞΑΤΟ ΤΟ ΒΛΕΠΕΙΝ. Mark viii. 17, ⳞΤΝΙΕΤΕ, ⳞΤΝΙΕΤΕ ΕΤΙ. Luke ii. 38, (ΑΤΤΗ) ΑΤΤΗ ΤΗ ΩΡΑ. Matt. xi. 23, ΚΑΦΑΡΝΑΟΤΜ ΜΗ, ΚΑΦΑΡΝΑΟΤΜ Η. 1 Thess. ii. 7, ΕΓΕΝΗΘΗΜΕΝ ΝΗΠΙΟΙ, ΕΓΕΝΗΘΗΜΕΝ ΗΠΙΟΙ. Luke ix. 49, ΕΚΒΑΛΛΟΝΤΑ ΔΑΙΜΟΝΙΑ, ΕΚΒΑΛΛΟΝΤΑ ΤΑ ΔΑΙΜ. Mark xiv. 35, ΠΡΟⳞΕΛΘΩΝ, ΠΡΟΕΛΘΩΝ. 2 Cor. iii. 10, ΟΤ ΔΕΔΟΞΑⳞΤΑΙ, ΟΤΔΕ ΔΕΔΟΞΑⳞΤΑΙ 1 Pet. iii. 20, ΑΠΑΞ ΕΔΕΧΕΤΟ, ΑΠΕΞΕΔΕΧΕΤΟ [the received text appears to be a mere conjecture of Erasmus. — A.]. Acts x. 36, ΤΟΝ ΛΟΓΟΝ ΑΠΕⳞΤΕΙΛΕ, ΤΟΝ ΛΟΓΟΝ ΟΝ ΑΠΕⳞΤΕΙΛΕ. Sometimes this cause of error leads to further change: 2 Cor. iii. 15, ΗΝΙΚΑ ΑΝ ΑΝΑΓΙΝΩⳞΚΗΤΑΙ, ΗΝΙΚΑ ΑΝΑΓΙΝΩⳞΚΕΤΑΙ.[d] Examples of omission from Homoioteleuton occur John vii. 7 (in T); 1 John ii. 23, iv. 3; Apoc. ix. 1, 2, xiv. 1; Matt. v. 20 (D). Cf. 1 Cor. xv. 25–27, 54 (F₂, G₃); xv. 15 (Origen). And some have sought to explain on this principle the absence from the best authorities of the disputed clause in Matt. x. 23, and the entire verses, Luke xvii. 36, Matt. xxiii. 14.

Instances of false division are found, Mark xv. 6, ὅνπερ ᾐτοῦντο, ὃν παρῃτοῦντο. Phil. i. 1, συνεπισκόποις, σὺν ἐπισκόποις. Matt. xx. 23, ἄλλοις, ἀλλ᾽ οἷς. Gal. i. 9, προειρήκαμεν, προείρηκα μέν. Acts xvii. 25, κατὰ πάντα, καὶ τὰ πάντα. In a more complicated example, σρα ιν (σωτῆρα Ἰησοῦν) is changed into σριαν (σωτηρίαν) in Acts xiii. 23; and the remarkable reading of Latin authorities in 1 Cor. vi. 20 *et portate* arose from confounding ἄρα τε and ἄρατε. In some places the true division of the words is still doubtful. 2 Cor. xii. 19, τάδε πάντα, τὰ δὲ παντα. Acts xvii. 26, προστεταγμένους καιρούς, πρὸς τεταγμένους καιρούς. In *Cod. Aug.* (F₂) the false divisions of the original scribe have been carefully corrected by a contemporary hand, and the frequency of their occurrence is an instructive illustration of the corruption to which the text was exposed from this source (e. g. in Gal. i. there are 15 such corrections, and four mistakes, vv. 13, 16, 18 are left uncorrected). Errors of breathing, though necessarily more rare, are closely connected with these: Matt. ix. 18, οἷς ἐλθών, εἰσελθών. John ix. 30, ὁ τούτῳ, ἐν τούτο. Luke vii. 12; Rom. vii. 10: 1 Cor. vii. 12, αὕτη, αὐτή. Mark xii. 31, αὕτη, αὑτή.

---

[a] The whole amount is considerably less in number than is found in the copies of other texts, if account be taken of the number of the MSS. existing. Comp. Norton, *Genuineness of the Gospels.* i. p. 191 n.

[b] * The perpetual interchange of αι and ε (which were pronounced alike) should be particularly noticed. "The spelling," says Tregelles, " has no authority at all between ἔσται and ἔστε, ἔχετε and ἔχεται, and similar words. Even if every MS. should agree in one spelling, there would be no liberty taken by any who read the other; since these vowels and diphthongs were used indiscriminately." — *Introd. to the Textual Crit. of the N. T.*, p. 51. A.

[c] The readings are taken from Mr. Scrivener's admirable transcript. In the same volume Mr. Scrivener has given valuable summaries of the frequency of the occurrence of the different forms of Itacism in other MSS. which he has collated.

[d] The remarkable reading in Matt. xxvii. 17, Ἰησοῦν Βαραββᾶν, seems to have originated in this way: YMINBAPABBAN being written YMININBAPAB BAN, and hence YMIKIΝ, i. e. ὑμῖν Ἰησοῦν (Tregelles, *ad loc.*).

1. Brit. Mus.—Harl. 5598.—(St. John. i. 1, 2)

2. Brit. Mus.—Add. 20,003.—(Acts xiii. 18-20.)

3. Brit. Mus.—Harl. 5540.—(St. John i. 1-3.)

4. Brit. Mus.—Burney 22.—(St. John i. 1-2.)

There are yet some other various readings which are errors of sight, which do not fall under any of the heads already noticed: e. g. 2 Pet. i. 3, ἰδίᾳ δόξῃ, διὰ δόξης. 2 Cor. v. 10, τὰ διὰ τοῦ σώματος, τὰ ἴδια τοῦ σώματος.[a] Rom. xii. 13, χρείαις, μνείαις. Hebr. ii. 9, χάρις, χάριτι (?). And the remarkable substitution of καιρῷ for κυρίῳ in Rom. xii. 11 seems to have been caused by a false rendering of an unusual contraction. The same explanation may also apply to the variants in 1 Cor. ii. 1, μαρτύριον, μυστήριον. 1 Tim. i. 4, οἰκονομίαν, οἰκοδομίαν, οἰκοδομήν.

33. Other variations may be described as errors of *impression* or *memory*. The copyist after reading a sentence from the text before him often failed to reproduce it exactly. He transposed the words, or substituted a synonym for some very common term, or gave a direct personal turn to what was objective before. Variations of order are the most frequent, and very commonly the most puzzling questions of textual criticism. Examples occur in every page, almost in every verse of the N. T. The exchange of synonyms is chiefly confined to a few words of constant use, to variations between simple and compound words, or to changes of tense or number: λέγειν, εἰπεῖν, φάναι, λαλεῖν, Matt. xii. 48, xv. 12, xix. 21; Mark xiv. 31; John xiv. 10, &c.; ἐγείρω, διεγείρω Matt. i. 24; ἐγερθῆναι, ἀναστῆναι, Matt. xvii. 9; Luke ix. 22; ἐλθεῖν, ἀπελθεῖν, ἐξελθεῖν, Matt. xiv. 25; Luke xxiii. 23; Acts xvi. 39; 'I. X., 'Ιησοῦς, Χριστός, ὁ κύριος, Hebr. iii. 1; 1 Pet. v. 10; Col. iii. 17; Acts xviii. 25, xxi. 13; ὑπό, ἀπό, ἐκ, Matt. vii. 4; Mark i. 26, viii. 31; Rom. xiii. 1, &c., ἔδωκα, δέδωκα, δίδωμι, Luke x. 19; John vii. 19, xii. 40, &c.; *sing.* and *plur.* Matt. iii. 8; 1 Pet. ii. 1; Matt. xxiv. 18. The third form of change to a more personal exhortation is seen constantly in the Epistles in the substitution of the pronoun of the first person (ἡμεῖς) for that of the second (ὑμεῖς): 1 Pet. i. 4, 10, 12, &c. To these changes may be added the insertion of pronouns of reference (αὐτός, etc.): Matt. vi. 4, xxv. 17, &c.; μαθηταί, μαθηταὶ αὐτοῦ, Matt. xxvi. 36, 45, 56, xxvii. 64, &c.; πατήρ, πατὴρ μου, John vi. 65, viii. 28, &c. And it may be doubtful whether the constant insertion of connecting particles καί, δέ, γάρ, οὖν, is not as much due to an unconscious instinct to supply natural links in the narrative or argument, as to an intentional effort to give greater clearness to the text. Sometimes the impression is more purely *mechanical*, as when the copyist repeats a termination incorrectly: Apoc. xi. 9 (C); 1 Thess. v. 4 (?); 2 Pet. iii. 7 (?).[b]

34. (ii.) Of intentional changes some affect the expression, others the substance of the passage. (a.) The intentional changes in language are partly changes of Hellenistic forms for those in common use, and partly modifications of harsh constructions. These may in many cases have been made unconsciously, just as might be the case if any one now were to transcribe rapidly one of the original MS. pages of Milton; but more commonly the later scribe would correct as mere blunders dialectic peculiarities which were wholly strange to him. Thus the forms τεσσεράκοντα, ἐραυνᾶν, ἐκαθερίσθη, λεγίων, etc., ἦλθα, ἔπεσα, etc., and the

irregular constructions of ἐάν, ὅταν, are removed almost without exception from all but a few MSS. Imperfect constructions are completed in different ways: Mark vii. 2, adil. ἐμέμψαντο, or κατέγνωσαν; Rom. i. 32, add. οὐκ ἐνόησαν, etc.; 2 Cor viii. 4, add. δέξασθαι; 1 Cor. x. 24, add. ἕκαστος. Apparent solecisms are corrected: Matt. v. 28, αὐτῆς for αὐτήν; xv. 32, ἡμέρας for ἡμέραι; Heb. iv. 2, συγκεκερασμένος for -μένους. The Apocalypse has suffered especially from this grammatical revision, owing to the extreme boldness of the rude Hebraizing dialect in which it is written: e. g. Apoc. iv. 1, 8, vi. 11, xi. 4, xxi. 14, &c. Variations in the orthography of proper names ought probably to be placed under this head, and in some cases it is perhaps impossible to determine the original form ('Ισκαριώτης, 'Ισκαριώθ, Σκαριώθ; Ναζαρά, -εθ, -αθ, -ατ, -ετ).

35. (β.) The changes introduced into the substance of the text are generally additions, borrowed either from parallel passages or from marginal glosses. The first kind of addition is particularly frequent in the Gospels, where, however, it is often very difficult to determine how far the parallelism of two passages may have been carried in the original text. Instances of unquestionable interpolation occur: Luke iv. 8, xi. 4; Matt. i. 25, v. 44, viii. 13, xxvii. 35 (49); Mark xv. 28; Matt. xix. 17 (compare Acts ix. 5, 6, xxii. 7, xxvi. 14). Similar interpolations occur also in other books: Col. i. 14; 1 Pet. i. 17; Jude 15 (Rom. xvi. 27); Apoc. xx. 2; and this is especially the case in quotations from the LXX., which are constantly brought into exact harmony with the original text: Luke iv. 18, 19, xix. 46; Matt. xii. 44, xv. 8; Heb. ii. 7, xii. 20.

Glosses are of more partial occurrence. Of all Greek MSS. *Cod. Bezæ* (D) is the most remarkable for the variety and singularity of the glosses which it contains. Examples of these may be seen: Matt. xx. 28; Luke v. 5, xxii. 26–28; Acts i. 5, xiv. 2. In ten verses of the Acts, taken at random, the following glosses occur: Acts xii. 1, ἐν τῇ 'Ιουδαίᾳ; 3, ἡ ἐπιχείρησις ἐπὶ τοὺς πιστούς; 5, πολλὴ δὲ προσευχὴ ἦν ἐν ἐκτενείᾳ περὶ αὐτοῦ; 7, ἐνέστη τῷ Πέτρῳ; 10, κατέβησαν τοὺς ζ βαθμούς. Some simple explanatory glosses have passed into the common text: Matt. vi. 1, ἐλεημοσύνην for δικαιοσύνην; Mark vii. 5, ἀνίπτοις for κοιναῖς; Matt. v. 11, ψευδόμενοι: comp. John v. 4 (Luke xxii. 43, 44).

36. (γ.) Many of the glosses which were introduced into the text spring from the ecclesiastical use of the N. T., just as in the Gospels of our own Prayer-book introductory clauses have been inserted here and there (e. g. 3d and 4th Sundays after Easter: "Jesus said to his disciples"). These additions are commonly notes of person or place: Matt. iv. 12, xii. 25, &c., ὁ 'Ιησοῦς inserted; John xiv. 1, καὶ εἶπεν τοῖς μαθηταῖς αὐτοῦ; Acts iii. 11, xxviii. 1 (cf. Mill, *Prolegg.* 1055–56). Sometimes an emphatic clause is added: Matt. xiii. 23, xxv. 29; Mark vii. 16; Luke viii. 15, xii. 21, ὁ ἔχων ὦτα κ. τ. λ.; Luke xiv. 24, πολλοὶ γάρ εἰσιν κλητοί κ. τ. λ. But the most remarkable liturgical insertion is the doxology in the Lord's Prayer, Matt. vi. 13; and it is probable that the

---

[a] By a similar change Athanasius (De Incarn. Verbi, 5) and others give in Wisd. ii. 23, καὶ εἰκόνα τῆς ἰδίας ἀϊδιότητος for the reading τῆς ἰδίας ἰδιότητος.

[b] It was apparently by a similar error (Tregelles,

Horne, iv. 227) that, in the A. V. of Hebr. x. 23, "the profession of our *faith*" stands for "the profession of our *hope*." The former is found in no document whatever.

interpolated verse (Acts viii. 37) is due to a similar cause. An instructive example of the growth of such an addition may be seen in the readings of Luke i. 55, as given in the text of the Gospel and in the collections of ecclesiastical hymns.

37. (δ.) Sometimes, though rarely, various readings noted on the margin are incorporated in the text, though this may be reckoned as the effect of ignorance rather than design. Signal examples of this confusion occur: Matt. xvii. 26, xxvi. 59, 60 (D); Rom. vi. 12. Other instances are found, Matt. v. 19; Rom. xiv. 9; 2 Cor. i. 10; 1 Pet. lii. 8.

38. (ε.) The number of readings which seem to have been altered for distinctly dogmatic reasons is extremely small. In spite of the great revolutions in thought, feeling, and practice through which the Christian Church passed in fifteen centuries, the copyists of the N. T. faithfully preserved, according to their ability, the sacred trust committed to them. There is not any trace of intentional revision designed to give support to current opinions (Matt. xvii. 21; Mark ix. 29; 1 Cor. vii. 5, need scarcely be noticed). The utmost that can be urged is that internal considerations may have decided the choice of readings: Acts xvi. 7, xx. 28; Rom. v. 14; 1 Cor. xv. 51; 2 Co. v. 7: 1 Tim. iii. 16; 1 John v. 7, in Latin copies; (Rom. viii. 11). And in some cases a feeling of reverence may have led to a change in expression, or to the introduction of a modifying clause: Luke ii. 33, 'Ιωσὴφ for ὁ πατὴρ αὐτοῦ; ii. 43, 'Ιωσὴφ καὶ ἡ μήτηρ αὐτοῦ for οἱ γονεῖς αὐτοῦ: John vii. 39, οὔπω γάρ ἦν πνεῦμα δεδομένον; Acts xix. 2 (D); Gal. ii. 5; Mark xiii. 32, om. οὐδὲ ὁ υἱός (cf. Matt. xxiv. 36); Matt. v. 22, add. εἰκῆ; 1 Cor. xi. 29, add. ἀναξίως (Luke xxii. 43, 44, om.).

But the general effect of these variations is scarcely appreciable; nor are the corrections of assumed historical and geographical errors much more numerous: Matt. i. 11, viii. 28, Γεργεσηνῶν; xxiii. 35, om. υἱοῦ Βαραχίου; xxvii. 9, om. 'Ιερεμίου, or Ζαχαρίου; Mark i. 2, ἐν τοῖς προφήταις for ἐν 'Ησ. τῷ πρ.; ii. 28, om. ἐπὶ 'ΑΒ. ἀρχιερέως; John i. 28, Βηθαβαρᾷ; v. 2, ἦν δέ for ἔστι δέ; vii. 8, οὔπω for οὐκ (?); viii. 57, τεσσεράκοντα for πεντήκοντα; xix. 14, ὥρα ἦν ὡς τρίτη for ἕκτη; Acts xiii. 33, τῷ δευτέρῳ for τῷ πρώτῳ.

39. It will be obvious from an examination of the instances quoted that the great mass of various readings are simply variations in form. There are, however, one or two greater variations of a different character. The most important of these are John vii. 53–viii. 12; Mark xvi. 9–end; Rom. xvi.

25–27. The first stands quite by itself; and there seems to be little doubt that it contains an authentic narrative, but not by the hand of St. John. The two others, taken in connection with the last chapter of St. John's Gospel, suggest the possibility that the apostolic writings may have undergone in some cases authoritative revision: a supposition which does not in any way affect their canonical claims: but it would be impossible to enter upon the details of such a question here.

40. Manuscripts, it must be remembered, are but one of the three sources of textual criticism. The versions and patristic quotations are scarcely less important in doubtful cases.[a] But the texts of the versions and the Fathers were themselves liable to corruption, and careful revision is necessary before they can be used with confidence. These considerations will sufficiently show how intricate a problem it is to determine the text of the N. T., where "there is a mystery in the very order of the words," and what a vast amount of materials the critic must have at his command before he can offer a satisfactory solution. It remains to inquire next whether the first editors of the printed text had such materials, or were competent to make use of them.

II. The History of the Printed Text.

1. The history of the printed text of the N. T. may be divided into three periods. The first of these extends from the labors of the Complutensian editors to those of Mill: the second from Mill to Scholz: the third from Lachmann to the present time. The criticism of the first period was necessarily tentative and partial: the materials available for the construction of the text were few, and imperfectly known: the relative value of various witnesses was as yet undetermined; and however highly we may rate the scholarship of Erasmus or Beza, this could not supersede the teaching of long experience in the sacred writings any more than in the writings of classical authors. The second period marks a great progress: the evidence of MSS., of versions, of Fathers, was collected with the greatest diligence and success: authorities were compared and classified: principles of observation and judgment were laid down. But the influence of the former period still lingered. The old "received" text was supposed to have some prescriptive right in virtue of its prior publication, and not on the ground of its merits: this was assumed as the copy which was to be corrected only so far as was absolutely necessary. The third period was introduced by the declaration of a new and sounder law. It was laid down that no right of posses-

---

a The history and characteristics of the Versions are discussed elsewhere. It may be useful to add a short table of the Fathers whose works are of the greatest importance for the history of the text. Those of the first rank are marked by [small] capitals; the Latin Fathers by *italics*.

Justinus M., c. 103–168.	Petrus Alex., † 313.
IRENÆUS, c. 120–190.	Methodius, † c. 311.
Irenæi Interpres. c. 180.	EUSEBIUS CÆSAR., 264–340.
TERTULLIANUS (Marcion), c. 160–240.	ATHANASIUS, 296–373.
CLEMENS ALEX., † c. 220.	Cyrillus Hierosol., 315–386.
ORIGENES, 186–253.	LUCIFER, † 370.
Hippolytus.	Ephraem Syrus, † 378.
CYPRIANUS, † 247.	BASILIUS MAGNUS, 329–379.
Dionysius Alex., † 265.	HIERONYMUS, 340–420.

Ambrosius, 340–397.	Euthalius, c. 450.
AMBROSIASTER, c. 380.	Cassiodorus, c. 468–566.
Victorinus, c. 360.	Victor Antiochenus.
CHRYSOSTOMUS, 347–407.	Theophylactus, † c. 628.a
DIDYMUS, † 396.	ANDREAS (Apoc.), c. 635–700.
EPIPHANIUS, † 402.	
Rufinus, c. 345–410.	Primasius (Apoc.). [c. 550.]
AUGUSTINUS, 354–430.	Johannes Damascenus, † c. 756.
Theodorus Mops., † 429.	Œcumenius, c. 950.
CYRILLUS ALEX., † 444.	Euthymius, c. 1100.
Hilarius, † 449.	
Theodoretus, 393–458.	

a • Mr. Westcott has here inadvertently confounded Theophylactus Simocatta, whose writings are of no importance in textual criticism, with the celebrated Greek commentator Theophylact, c. 1077.

A.

sion could be pleaded against evidence. The "received" text, as such, was allowed no weight whatever. Its authority, on this view, must depend solely on its critical worth. From first to last, in minute details of order and orthography, as well as in graver questions of substantial alteration, the text must be formed by a free and unfettered judgment. Variety of opinions may exist as to the true method and range of inquiry, as to the relative importance of different forms of testimony: all that is claimed is to rest the letter of the N. T. completely and avowedly on a critical and not on a conventional basis. This principle, which seems, indeed, to be an axiom, can only be called in question by supposing that in the first instance the printed text of the N. T. was guarded from the errors and imperfections which attended the early editions of every classical text; and next that the laws of evidence which hold good everywhere else fail in the very case where they might be expected to find their noblest and most fruitful application — suppositions which are refuted by the whole history of the Bible. Each of these periods will now require to be noticed more in detail.

(i.) *From the Complutensian Polyglott to Mill.*

2. *The Complutensian Polyglott.* — The Latin Vulgate and the Hebrew text of the O. T. had been published some time before any part of the original Greek of the N. T. The Hebrew text was called for by numerous and wealthy Jewish congregations (Soncino, 1482–88), the Vulgate satisfied ecclesiastical wants; and the few Greek scholars who lived at the close of the 15th century were hardly likely to hasten the printing of the Greek Testament. Yet the critical study of the Greek text had not been wholly neglected. Laurentius Valla, who was second to none of the scholars of his age (comp. Russell's *Life of Bp. Andrewes*, pp. 282–310, quoted by Scrivener), quotes in one place (Matt. xxvii. 12) three, and in another (John vii. 39), seven Greek MSS. in his commentaries on the N. T., which were published in 1505, nearly half a century after his death (Michaelis, *Introd.* ed. Marsh, ii. 339, 340). J. Faber (1512) made use of five Greek MSS. of St. Paul's Epistles (Michaelis, p. 420. Meanwhile the Greek Psalter had been published several times (first at Milan, 1481?), and the Hymns of Zacharias and the Virgin (Luke i. 42–56, 68–80) were appended to a Venetian edition of 1486, as frequently happens in MS. Psalters. This was the first part of the N. T. which was printed in Greek. Eighteen years afterwards (1504), the first six chapters of St. John's Gospel were added to an edition of the poems of Gregory of Nazianzus, published by Aldus (Guericke, *Einl.* § 41).

But the glory of printing the first Greek Testament is due to the princely Cardinal XIMENES. This great prelate as early as 1502 engaged the services of a number of scholars to superintend an edition of the whole Bible in the original Hebrew and Greek, with the addition of the Chaldee Targum of Onkelos, the LXX. version, and the Vulgate. The work was executed at Alcala (Complutum), where he had founded a university. The volume containing the N. T. was printed first, and was completed on January 10, 1514. The whole work was not finished till July 10, 1517, about four months before the death of the Cardinal. Various obstacles still delayed its publication, and it was not generally circulated till 1522, though Leo X. (to whom it was dedicated) authorized the publication March 22, 1520 (Tregelles, *Hist. of Printed Text of N T.*; Mill, *Prolegg.*).

The most celebrated men who were engaged on the N. T., which forms the fifth volume of the entire work, were Lebrixa (Nebrissensis) and Stunica. Considerable discussion has been raised as to the MSS. which they used. The editors describe these generally as "copies of the greatest accuracy and antiquity," sent from the Papal Library at Rome; and in the dedication to Leo acknowledgment is made of his generosity in sending MSS. of both "the Old and N. T." [a] Very little time, however, could have been given to the examination of the Roman MSS. of the N. T., as somewhat less than eleven months elapsed between the election of Leo and the completion of the Complutensian Testament; and it is remarkable that while an entry is preserved in the Vatican of the loan and return of two MSS. of parts of the LXX., there is no trace of the transmission of any N. T. MS. to Alcala (Tischd. *N.* 7 1859. p. lxxxii. n.). The whole question, however, is now rather of bibliographical than of critical interest. There can be no doubt that the copies, from whatever source they came, were of late date, and of the common type.[b] The preference which the editors avow for the Vulgate, placing it in the centre column in the O. T. "between the Synagogue and the Eastern Church, tanquam duos hinc et inde latrones," to quote the well-known and startling words of the preface, "medium autem Jesum hoc est, Romanam sive Latinam ecclesiam" (vol. i. f. iii. b.), has subjected them to the charge of altering the Greek text to suit the Vulgate. But except in the famous interpolation and omission in 1 John v. 7, 8, and some points of orthography (Βεελζεβούβ, Βελίαλ, Tischdf. p. lxxxiii.), the charge is unfounded (Marsh, on Michaelis ii. p. 851, gives the literature of the controversy). The impression was limited to six hundred copies, and as, owing to the delays

a "Testari possumus, Pater sanctissime [i. e. Leo X.], maximam laboris nostri partem in eo praecipue fuisse versatam ut . . . . castigatissima omni ex parte vetustissimaque exemplaria pro archetypis haberemus quorum quidem tam Hebraeorum quam Graecorum ac Latinorum multiplicem copiam variis ex locis non sine summo labore conquisivimus. Atque ex ipsis quidem Graeca Sanctitati tuae debemus: qui ex ista Apostolica Bibliotheca antiquissimos tam Veteris tum Novi Testamenti codices perquam humane ad nos misisti; qui nobis in hoc negocio maximo fuerunt adjumento" (*Prol.* ff. a). And again, tom. v. *Praef.*: "Illud lectorum non latest non quaevis exemplaria impressioni huic archetypa fuisse, sed antiquissima emendatissimaque ac tantae praeterea vetustatis ut fidem eis abrogare nefas videatur (πρὸς ὀυσούλον εἶναι τοταρώναν καὶ φαῦλον, sic) quam sanctissimus in Christo pater et

b One MS. is specially appealed to by Stunica in his controversy with Erasmus, the *Cod. Rhodiensis*, but nothing is known of it which can lead to its identification. The famous story of the destruction of MSS. by the fire-work maker, as useless parchments, has been fully and clearly refuted. All the MSS. of Ximenes which were used for the Polyglott are now at Madrid, but there is no MS. of any part of the Gk. Test. among them (Tregelles, *Hist. of Printed Text*, pp. 12–18). The edition has many readings in common with the Laudian MS. numbered 51 Gosp., 32 Acts, 38 Paul (Mill. *Proleg.* 1090, 1436–38). Many of the peculiar readings are collected by Mill (*Proleg.* 1092–1095)

dominus noster Leo X. pontifex maximus huic instituto favere cupiens ex Apostolica Bibliotheca educta misit."

which occurred between the printing and publication of the book, its appearance was forestalled by
that of the edition of Erasmus, the Complutensian
N. T. exercised comparatively small influence on
later texts, except in the Apocalypse (comp. § 3).
The chief editions which follow it in the main, are
those of Plantin, Antwerp, 1564–1612 ; Geneva,
1609–1632; Mainz, 1753 (Reuss, *Gesch. d. N. T.*
§ 401; Le Long, *Biblioth. Sacra*, ed. Masch. i. 191–
195); Mill regretted that it was not accepted as
the standard text (*Proleg.* 1115); and has given
a long list of passages in which it offers, in his
opinion, better readings than the Stephanic or Elzevirian texts (*Proleg.* 1098–1114).

3. *The editions of Erasmus.* — The history of
the edition of ERASMUS, which was the first *published* edition of the N. T., is happily free from all
obscurity. Erasmus had paid considerable attention
to the study of the N. T. when he received an application from Froben, a printer of Basle with whom
he was acquainted, to prepare a Greek text for the
press. Froben was anxious to anticipate the publication of the Complutensian edition, and the haste
with which the work of Erasmus was completed,
shows that little consideration was paid to the exigencies of textual criticism. The request was made
on April 17, 1515, while Erasmus was in England.
The details of the printing were not settled in September in the same year, and the whole work was
finished in February, 1516 (Tregelles, *Hist. of
Printed Text*, 19, 20). The work, as Erasmus
afterwards confessed, was done in reckless haste
("præcipitatum verius quam editum." Comp. *Epp.*
v. 26; xii. 19), and that too in the midst of other
heavy literary labors (*Ep.* i. 7. Comp. Wetstein,
Prolegg. pp. 166–67).[a] The MSS. which formed
the basis of his edition are still, with one exception,
preserved at Basle; and two which he used for the
press contain the corrections of Erasmus and the
printer's marks (Michaelis, ii. 220, 221). The one
is a MS. of the Gospels of the 16th century of the
ordinary late type (marked 2 Gosp. in the catalogues of MSS. since Wetstein); the other a MS.
of the Acts and the Epistles (2 Acts, Epp.), somewhat older, but of the same general character.[b]
Erasmus also made some use of two other Basle
MSS. (1 Gosp.; 4 Acts, Epp.); the former of these
is of great value, but the important variations from

the common text which it offers, made him suspect
that it had been altered from the Latin.[c] For the
Apocalypse he had only an imperfect MS. which
belonged to Reuchlin.[d] The last six verses were
wanting, and these he translated from the Latin,[e]
a process which he adopted in other places where it
was less excusable. The received text contains two
memorable instances of this bold interpolation.
The one is Acts viii. 37, which Erasmus, as he says,
found written in the margin of a Greek MS. though
it was wanting in that which he used: the other is
Acts ix. 5. 6, σκληρόν σοι — ἀνάστηθι for ἀλλὰ
ἀνάστηθι, which has been found as yet in no
Greek MS. whatsoever, though it is still perpetuated on the ground of Erasmus' conjecture. But
he did not insert the testimony of the heavenly witnesses (1 John v. 7), an act of critical faithfulness
which exposed him to the attacks of enemies. Among
these was Stunica — his rival editor — and when
argument failed to silence calumny, he promised to
insert the words in question on the authority of
any one Greek MS. The edition of Erasmus, like
the Complutensian, was dedicated to Leo X.; and
it is a noble trait of the generosity of Cardinal Ximenes, that when Stunica wished to disparage the
work of Erasmus which robbed him of his well-
earned honor, he checked him in the words of
Moses, " I would that all might thus prophesy,"
Num. xi. 29 (Tregelles, p. 19). After his first edition was published Erasmus continued his labors on
the N. T. (*Ep.* iii. 31); and in March, 1519, a second
edition appeared which was altered in about 400
places, of which Mill reckons that 330 were improvements (*Prolegg.* § 1134). But his chief labor
seems to have been spent upon the Latin version,
and in exposing the "solecisms" of the common
Vulgate, the value of which he completely misunderstood (comp. Mill, *Prolegg.* 1124–1133).[f] These
two editions consisted of 3,300 copies, and a third
edition was required in 1522, when the Complutensian Polyglott also came into circulation. In
this edition 1 John v. 7 was inserted for the first
time, according to the promise of Erasmus, on the
authority of the " Codex Britannicus " (*i. e.* Cod.
Montfortianus), in a form which obviously betrays
its origin as a clumsy translation from the Vulgate
(" ne cui foret causa calumniandi," *Apol. ad Stuni-
cam*, ad loc.).[g] The text was altered in about 118

---

[a] A marvelous proof of haste occurs on the title-
page, in which he quotes "Vulgarius " among the
chief fathers whose authority he followed. The name
was formed from the title of the see of Theophylact
(Bulgaria), and Theophylact was converted into an
epithet. This " Vulgarius " is quoted on Luke xi. 35,
and the name remained unchanged in subsequent
editions (Wetstein, *Proleg.* 169).

[b] According to Mill (*Proleg.* 1120), Erasmus altered
the text in a little more than fifty places in the Acts,
and in about two hundred places in the Epistles, of
which changes all but about forty were improvements.
Specimens of the corrections on the margin of the MS.
are given by Wetstein (*Proleg.* p 66, ed. Lotze). Of
these several were simply on the authority of the Vulgate, one of which (Matt. ii. 11, εὗρον for εἶδον) has
retained its place in the received text.

[c] The reading in the received text, Mark vi. 15, ἢ
ὡς εἷς τῶν προφητῶν, in place of ὡς εἷς τῶν προφητῶν,
is a change introduced by Erasmus on the authority
of this MS., which has been supported by some slight
additional evidence since. Mill (*Proleg.* §§ 1117, 18)
states that Erasmus used the uncial Basle MS. of the
Gospels (E), " correcting it rightly in about sixty-eight

places, wrongly in about fifty seven." This opinion
has been refuted by Wetstein (*Proleg.* p. 50). The
MSS. was not then at Basle: " Hicce codex Basileensi
Academiæ dono datus est anno 1559 " (Lotze ad Wetstein, *l. c.*).

[d] * This MS. has been recently discovered by F.
Delitzsch and carefully collated with the text of Erasmus, who, it appears, did not use the MS. itself for his
edition of the Apocalypse, but only an inaccurate transcript of it. See Delitzsch, *Handschriftliche Funde*, 2
Hefte, Leips. 1861–62.   A.

[e] Traces of this unauthorised retranslation remain
in the received text: Apoc. xxii. 16, ὀρθρινός. 17.
ἐλθέ (bis) ; ἐλθέτω ; λαμβανέτω τό. 18. συμμαρτυροῦμαι
γάρ, ἐπιτιθῇ πρὸς ταῦτα. 19. ἀφαιρῇ βίβλον, ἀπὸ βίβλου
τ. ζ. Some of these are obvious blunders in rendering
from the Latin, and yet they are consecrated by use.

[f] Luther's German version was made from this text
(Reuss, *Gesch. d. H. S.* § 400 [471, 3e Aug.]) One conjecture of Erasmus 1 Pet. iii. 20, ἅπαξ ἐξεδέχετο, supported by no MS., passed from this edition into the
received text.

[g] In the course of the controversy on this passage
the *Cod. Vatic.* B was appealed to (1521). Some years

places (Mill, *Prolegg.* 1138). Of these corrections 36 were borrowed from an edition published at Venice in the office of ALDUS, 1518, which was taken in the main from the first edition of Erasmus, even so as to preserve errors of the press, but yet differed from it in about 200 places, partly from error and partly on MS. authority (Mill, § 1122). This edition is further remarkable as giving a few (19) various readings. Three other early editions give a text formed from the second edition of Erasmus and the Aldine, those of [Gerbelius at] Hagenau, 1521, of Cephalæus at Strasburg, 1524, of Bebelius at Basle [1524], 1531. Erasmus at length obtained a copy of the Complutensian text, and in his fourth edition in 1527, gave some various readings from it in addition to those which he had already noted, and used it to correct his own text in the Apocalypse in 90 places, while elsewhere he introduced only 16 changes (Mill, § 1141). His fifth and last edition (1535) differs only in 4 places from the fourth, and the fourth edition afterwards became the basis of the received text. This, it will be seen, rested on scanty and late Greek evidence, without the help of any versions except the Latin, which was itself so deformed in common copies, as not to show its true character and weight.

4. *The editions of Stephens.* — The scene of our history now changes from Basle to Paris. In 1543, Simon de Colines (COLINÆUS) published a Greek text of the N. T., corrected in about 150 places on fresh MS. authority. He was charged by Beza with making changes by conjecture; but of the ten examples quoted by Mill, all but one (Matt. viii. 33, ἄπαντα for πάντα) are supported by MSS., and four by the Parisian MS. *Reg.* 85 (119 Gospp.).[a] The edition of Colinæus does not appear to have obtained any wide influence. Not long after it appeared, R. Estienne (STEPHANUS) published his first edition (1546), which was based on a collation

of MSS. in the Royal Library with the Complutensian text.[b] He gives no detailed description of the MSS. which he used, and their character can only be discovered by the quotation of their readings, which is given in the third edition. According to Mill, the text differs from the Complutensian in 581 places, and in 198 of these it follows the last edition of Erasmus. The former printed texts are abandoned in only 37 places in favor of the MSS., and the Erasmian reading is often preferred to that supported by all the other Greek authorities with which Stephens is known to have been acquainted : *e. g.* Matt. vi. 18, viii. 5, ix. 5, &c.[c] A second edition very closely resembling the first both in form and text, having the same preface and the same number of pages and lines, was published in 1549; but the great edition of Stephens is that known as the *Regia*, published in 1550.[d] In this a systematic collection of various readings, amounting, it is said, to 2194 (Mill, § 1227), is given for the first time; but still no consistent critical use was made of them. Of the authorities which he quoted most have been since identified. They were the Complutensian text, 10 MSS. of the Gospels, 8 of the Acta, 7 of the Catholic Epistles, 8 of the Pauline Epistles, 2 of the Apocalypse, in all 15 distinct MSS. One of these was the *Codex Bezæ* (D). Two have not yet been recognized (comp. Griesbach, N. T. ff. xxiv.–xxxvi.). The collations were made by his son Henry Stephens; but they fail entirely to satisfy the requirements of exact criticism. The various readings of D alone in the Gospels and Acts are more than the whole number given by Stephens; or, to take another example, while only 598 variants of the Complutensian are given, Mill calculates that 700 are omitted (*Prolegg.* § 1226).[e] Nor was the use made of the materials more satisfactory than their quality. Less than thirty changes were made on MS. authority (Mill,

---

later (1534) Sepulveda describes the MS. in a letter to Erasmus, giving a general description of its agreement with the Vulgate, and a selection of various readings. In reply to this Erasmus appeals to a supposed *fœdus cum Græcis*, made at the Council of Florence, 1439, in accordance with which Greek copies were to be altered to agree with the Latin; and argues that B may have been so altered. When Sepulveda answers that no such compact was made, Erasmus replies that he had heard from Cuthbert [Tonstall] of Durham that it was agreed that the Greek MSS. should be corrected to harmonise with the Latin, and took the statement for granted. Yet on this simple misunderstanding the credit of the oldest MSS. has been impugned. The influence of the idea in "*fœdus cum Græcis*" has survived all belief in the fact (Tregelles, *Horne,* iv. pp. xv.–xvii.)

[a] An examination of the readings quoted from Colinæus by Mill shows conclusively that he used Cod. 119 of the Gospels, 10 of the Pauline Epistles (8 of the Acta, the MS. marked *ι4* by Stephens), and probably 83 of the Gospels and 5 of the Catholic Epistles. The readings in 1 Cor. xiv. 2, 1 Pet. v. 2, 2 Pet. iii. 17, seem to be mere errors, and are apparently supported by no authority.

[b] This edition and its counterpart (1549) are known as the " *O mirificam* " edition, from the opening words of the preface : "O mirificam regis nostri optimi et præstantissimi principis liberalitatem," in allusion to the new font of small Greek type which the king had ordered to be cut, and which was now used for the first time.

[*] The Complutensian influence on these editions has been over-estimated. In the last verses of the

Apocalypse (§ 3) they follow what Erasmus supplied and not any Greek authority " (Tregelles).

[c] Stephens' own description of his edition cannot be received literally. " Codices nacti aliquot ipsa vetustatis specie pene adorandos, quorum copiam nobis bibliotheca regia facile suppeditabit, ex iis ita hunc nostrum recensuimus, *ut nullam omnino litteram secus esse pateremur, quam plures iique meliores libri, tanquam testes, comprobarent.* Adjuti præterea sumus cum aliis (*i. e.* Erasmi) tum vero Complutensi editione, quam ad vetustissimos bibliothecæ Leonis X. Pont. codices excudi jusserat Hispan. Card. Fr. Simenius : quos cum nostris miro consensu sæpissime convenire ex ipsa collatione deprehendimus " (Pref. edit. 1546–9). In the preface to the third edition, he says that he used the same 16 copies for these editions as for that

[d] " Novum Jesu Christi D. N. Testamentum. Ex Bibliotheca Regia. Lutetiæ. Ex officinâ Roberti Stephani typographi regii, regiis typis. MDL." In this edition Stephens simply says of his " 16 copies," that the first is the Complutensian edition, the second (*Codex Bezæ*) " a most ancient copy, collated by friends in Italy ; 3–8, 10, 15, copies from the Royal Library ; cætera sunt ea quæ undique corrogare licuit " (Pref.).

[e] According to Scrivener (*Introd.* p. 300), the Complutensian differs from Stephens' third edition in more than 2,300 places, in which it is cited correctly only 554 times, falsely 66 times, and in more than 1,690 places (not including itacisms and mere errata) the variation is not noted. Scrivener has given in the same work (pp. 349–368) a full collation of the Complutensian N. T. with the Elzevir edition of 1624. The text of the Complutensian has been carefully reprinted by Gratz, Tübing. 1821, new ed., Mentz, 1827. A.

1228); and except in the Apocalypse, which follows the Complutensian text most closely, "it hardly ever deserts the last edition of Erasmus" (Tregelles). Numerous instances occur in which Stephens deserts his former text and *all his MSS.* to restore an Erasmian reading. Mill quotes the following examples among others, which are the most interesting, because they have passed from the Stephanic text into our A. V.: Matt. ii. 11, εὗρον for εἶδον (without the authority of any Greek MS., as far as I know, though Scholz says "*cum codd. multis* "), iii. 8, καρποὺς ἀξίους for καρπὸν ἄξιον. Mark vi. 33 *add.* οἱ ὄχλοι: xvi. 8 *add.* ταχύ. Luke vii. 31 *add.* εἶπε δὲ ὁ κύριος. John xiv. 30 *add.* τούτου. Acts v. 23 *add.* ἔξω. Rom. ii. 5 *om.* καὶ before δικαιοκρισίας. James. v. 9, κατακριθῆτε for κριθῆτε. Prescription as yet occupied the place of evidence; and it was well that the work of the textual critic was reserved for a time when he could command trustworthy and complete collations. Stephens published a fourth edition in 1551 (Geneva), which is only remarkable as giving for the first time the present division into verses.

5. *The editions of Beza and Elzevir.* — Nothing can illustrate more clearly the deficiency among scholars of the first elements of the textual criticism of the N. T. than the annotations of BEZA (1556). This great divine obtained from H. Stephens a copy of the N. T. in which he had noted down various readings from about twenty-five MSS. and from the early editions (Cf. Marsh, on Michaelis, ii. 858-60), but he used the collection rather for exegetical than for critical purposes. Thus he pronounced in favor of the obvious interpolations in Matt. i. 11; John xviii. 13. which have consequently obtained a place in the margin of the A. V., and elsewhere maintained readings which, on crit-

ical grounds, are wholly indefensible: Matt. ii. 17 Mark iii. 16, xvi. 2. The interpolation in Apoc. xi. 11, καὶ ὁ ἄγγελος εἱστήκει has passed into the text of the A. V. The Greek text of Beza (dedicated to Queen Elizabeth) was printed by H. Stephens in 1565, and again in 1576; but his chief edition was the third, printed in 1582, which contained readings from the *Codices Bezæ and Claromontanus.* The reading followed by the text of A. V. in Rom. vii. 6 (ἀποθανόντος for ἀποθανόντες), which is supported by no Greek MS. or version whatever, is due to this edition. Other editions by Beza appeared in 1588-89, 1598, and his (third) text found a wide currency.[a] Among other editions which were wholly or in part based upon it, those of the ELZEVIRS alone require to be noticed. The first of these editions, famous for the beauty of their execution, was published at Leyden in 1624. It is not known who acted as editor, but the text is mainly that of the third edition of Stephens. Including every minute variation in orthography, it differs from this in 278 places (Scrivener, *N. T.* Cambr. 1860, p. vi.). In these cases it generally agrees with Beza, more rarely it differs from both, either by typographical errors (Matt. vi. 34, xv. 27; Luke x. 6 *add.* δ, xi. 12, xiii. 19; John iii. 6) or perhaps by manuscript authority (Matt. xxiv. 9, *om.* τῶν; Luke vii. 12, viii. 29; John xii. 17, ὅτι). In the second edition (Leyden, 1633) it was announced that the text was that which was universally received (*textum ergo habes nunc ab omnibus receptum*), and the declaration thus boldly made was practically fulfilled. From this time the Elzevirian text was generally reprinted on the continent, and that of the third edition of Stephens in England, till quite recent times. Yet it has been shown that these texts were substantially formed on late MS. authority, without the help of any complete collations or of any readings (except of D) of a first class MS., without a good text of the Vulgate, and without the assistance of oriental versions. Nothing short of a miracle could have produced a critically pure text from such materials and those treated without any definite system. Yet, to use Bentley's words, which are not too strong, "the text stood as if an apostle were R. Stephens' compositor." Habit hallowed what was commonly used, and the course of textual polemics contributed not a little to preserve without change the common field on which controversialists were prepared to engage.

(ii.) *From Mill to Scholz.* — 6. The second period of the history of the printed text may be treated with less detail. It was influenced, more or less, throughout by the *textus receptus*, though the authority of this provisional text was gradually shaken by the increase of critical materials and the bold enunciation of principles of revision. The first important collection of various readings — for that of Stephens was too imperfect to deserve the name — was given by WALTON in the 6th volume of his Polyglott. The Syriac, Arabic, Æthiopic, and Persian versions of the N. T., together with the readings of *Cod. Alex.*, were printed in the 5th volume together with the text of Stephens. To these were added in the 6th the readings collected by Stephens, others from an edition by Wechel at Frankfort (1597), the readings of the *Codices Bezæ* and *Claromont.*, and of fourteen other MSS. which had been collated under the care of Archbp. Usher. Some of these collations were extremely imperfect (Scrivener, *Cod. Aug.* p. lxvii.; *Introduction*, p. 148), as appears from later examination, yet it is not easy to overrate the importance of the exhibition of the testimony of the oriental versions side by side with the current Greek text. A few more MS. readings were given by CURCELLÆUS (de Courcelles) in an edition published at Amsterdam, 1658, &c., but the great names of this period continue to be those of Englishmen. The readings of the Coptic and Gothic versions were first given in the edition of (Bp. Fell) Oxford, 1675; ed. Gregory, 1703; but the greatest service which Fell rendered to the criticism of the N. T. was the liberal encouragement which he gave to Mill. The work of Mill (Oxon. 1707; Amstelod. [also Roterod.] ed. Küster, 1710; other copies have on the title-page 1723, 1746, &c.) marks an epoch in the history of the N. T. text. There is much in it which will not bear the test of historical inquiry, much that is imperfect in the materials, much that is crude and capricious in criticism, but when every drawback has been made, the edition remains a splendid monument of the labors of a life. The work occupied Mill about thirty years, and was finished only a fortnight before his death. One great merit of Mill was that he recognized the importance of each element of critical evidence, the testimony of MSS. versions and citations, as well as internal evidence. In particular he asserted the claims of the Latin version and maintained, against much opposition, even from his patron Bp. Fell, the great value of patristic quotations. He had also a clear view of the necessity of forming a general estimate of the character of each authority, and described in detail those of which he made use. At the same time he gave a careful analysis of the origin and history of previous texts, a labor which, even now, has in many parts not been superseded.

But while he pronounced decided judgments on various readings both in the notes and, without any reference or plan, in the Prolegomena, he did not venture to introduce any changes into the printed text. He repeated the Stephanic text of 1550 without any intentional change, and from his edition this has passed (as Mill's) into general use in England. His caution, however, could not save him from vehement attacks. The charge which was brought against Walton *a* of unsettling the sacred text, was renewed against Mill, and, unhappily, found an advocate in Whitby (*Examen variantium lectionum J. Millii S. T. P.* annexed to his Annotations), a man whose genius was worthy of better things. The 30,000 various readings which he was said to have collected formed a common-place with the assailants of the Bible (Bentley, *Remarks*, iii. 348–358, ed. Dyce). But the work of Mill silently produced fruit both in England and Germany. Men grew familiar with the problems of textual criticism and were thus prepared to meet them fairly.

7. Among those who had known and valued Mill was R. BENTLEY, the greatest of English scholars. In his earliest work (*Epist. ad J. Millium*, ii. 362, ed. Dyce), in 1691, Bentley had expressed generous admiration of the labors of Mill, and afterwards, in 1713, in his *Remarks*, triumphantly refuted the charges of impiety with which they were assailed. But Mill had only "accumulated various readings as a promptuary to the judicious and critical reader;" Bentley would "make use of that promptuary . . . . . and not leave the reader in doubt and suspense" (*Answer to Remarks*, iii. 503). With this view he announced, in 1716, his intention of publishing an edition of the Greek Testament on the authority of the oldest Greek and Latin MS., "exactly as it was in the best examples at the time of the Council of Nice, so that there shall not be twenty words nor even particles' difference" (iii. 477 to Archbp. Wake). Collations were shortly afterwards undertaken both at Paris (including C) and Rome (B), and Bentley himself spared neither labor nor money. In 1720 he published his Proposals and a Specimen (Apoc. xxii.). In this notice he announces his design of publishing " a new edition of the Greek and Latin . . . . as represented in the most ancient and venerable MSS. in Greek and Roman (?) capital letters." In this way " he believes that he has retrieved (except in a very few places) the true exemplar of Origen . . . . and is sure that the Greek and Latin MSS., by their mutual assistance, do so settle the original text to the smallest nicety as cannot be performed now in any *classic* author whatever." He purposed to add all the various readings of the first five centuries, " and what has crept into any copies since is of no value or authority." The proposals were immediately assailed by Middleton. A violent controversy followed, but Bentley continued his labors till 1729 (Dyce, iii. 483). After that time they seemed to have ceased. The troubles in which Bentley was involved render it unnecessary to seek for any other explanation of the suspension of his work. The one chapter which he published shows clearly enough that he was prepared to deal with variations in his copies, and

---

a Especially by the great Puritan Owen in his *Considerations*. Walton replied with severity in *The Considerator considered*.

there is no sufficient reason for concluding that the disagreement of his ancient codices caused him to abandon the plan which he had proclaimed with undoubting confidence (Scrivener, *Cod. Aug.* p. xix.). A complete account of Bentley's labors on the N. T. is prepared for publication (1861) by the Rev. A. A. Ellis, under the title *Bentleii Critica Sacra.* [Published in 1862. — A.]

8. The conception of Bentley was in advance both of the spirit of his age and of the materials at his command. Textual criticism was forced to undergo a long discipline before it was prepared to follow out his principles. During this time German scholars hold the first place. Foremost among these was BENGEL (1687–1752), who was led to study the variations of the N. T. from a devout sense of the infinite value of every divine word. His merit in discerning the existence of families of documents has been already noticed (i. § 12); but the evidence before him was not sufficient to show the paramount authority of the most ancient witnesses. His most important rule was, *Procliri scriptioni præstat ardua;* but except in the Revelation he did not venture to give any reading which had not been already adopted in some edition (*Prodromus N. T. Gr. recte cauteque adornandi,* 1725; *Nov. Testam. . . . . 1734; Apparatus criticus,* ed. 2da cura P. D. Burk, 1763). But even the partial revision which Bengel had made exposed him to the bitterest attacks; and Wetstein, when at length he published his great edition, reprinted the received text. The labors of WETSTEIN (1693–1754) formed an important epoch in the history of the N. T. While still very young (1716) he was engaged to collate for Bentley, and he afterwards continued the work for himself. In 1733 he was obliged to leave Basle, his native town, from theological differences, and his Greek Testament did not appear till 1751–52 at Amsterdam. A first edition of the *Prolegomena* had been published previously in 1730; but the principles which he then maintained were afterwards much modified by his opposition to Bengel (comp. Preface to *N. T. cura Gerardi de Trajecto,* ed. 2da, 1735).[a] The great service which Wetstein rendered to sacred criticism was by the collection of materials. He made nearly as great an advance on Mill as Mill had made on those who preceded him. But in the use of his materials he showed little critical tact; and his strange theory of the *Latinization* of the most ancient MSS. proved for a long time a serious drawback to the sound study of the Greek text (*Prolegomena,* ed. Semler, 1766, ed. Lotze, 1831).

9. It was the work of GRIESBACH (1745–1812) to place the comparative value of existing docu-

ments in a clearer light. The time was now come when the results of collected evidence might be set out; and Griesbach, with singular sagacity, courtesy, and zeal, devoted his life to the work. His first editions (*Synopsis,* 1774; *Nov. Test.* ed. 1, 1777–75) were based for the most part on the critical collections of Wetstein. Not long afterwards MATTHÆI published an edition based on the accurate collation of Moscow MSS. (*N. T. ex Codd. Mosquensibus . . . .* Riga, 1782–88, 12 vols.; ed. 2da, 1803–1807, 3 vols.). These new materials were further increased by the collections of Alter (1786–87), Birch, Adler, and Moldenhawer (1788–1801), as well as by the labors of Griesbach himself. And when Griesbach published his second edition (1796–1806, 3d ed. of vol. i. by D. Schulz, 1827) he made a noble use of the materials thus placed in his hands. His chief error was that he altered the received text instead of constructing the text afresh; but in acuteness, vigor, and candor he stands below no editor of the N. T., and his judgment will always retain a peculiar value. In 1805 he published a manual edition with a selection of readings which he judged to be more or less worthy of notice, and this has been often reprinted (comp. *Symbolæ Criticæ,* 1785–1793; *Opuscula,* ed. Gabler, 1824–25; *Commentarius Criticus,* 1798–1811; White's *Criseos Griesbachianæ . . . Synopsis,* 1811).

10. The edition of SCHOLZ contributed more in appearance than reality to the furtherance of criticism (*N. T. ad fidem test. crit. . . . .* 1830–1836). This laborious scholar collected a greater mass of various readings than had been brought together before, but his work is very inaccurate, and his own collations singularly superficial. Yet it was of service to call attention to the mass of unused MSS.; and, while depreciating the value of the more ancient MSS., Scholz himself showed the powerful influence of Griesbach's principles by accepting frequently the Alexandrine in preference to the Constantinopolitan reading (i. § 14. Comp. *Biblisch-Kritische Reise . . .* 1823; *Curæ Criticæ . . .* 1820–1845).[b]

(iii.) *From Lachmann to the present time.* — 11. In the year after the publication of the first volume of Scholz's N. T. a small edition appeared in a series of classical texts prepared by LACHMANN († 1851). In this the admitted principles of scholarship were for the first time applied throughout to the construction of the text of the N. T. The prescriptive right of the *textus receptus* was wholly set aside, and the text in every part was regulated by ancient authority. Before publishing his small edition (*N. T. Gr. ex recensione* C. Lachmanni, Berol. 1831) Lachmann had given a short

---

[a] Gerhard von Maestricht's *N. T.* first appeared in 1711, with a selection of various readings, and a series of canons composed to justify the received text. Some of these canons deserve to be quoted, as an illustration of the bold assertion of the claims of the *printed* text, as such.

CAN. ix "*Unus codex* non facit variantem lectionem . . . modo recepta lectio sit secundum analogiam fidei*" . . .

CAN. x "Neque *duo codices* faciunt variantem lectionem . . . contra receptam et editam et sani sensus lectionem . . maxime in omittendo " . . .

CAN. xiv. "*Versiones* etiam antiquissimæ *ab editis* et manuscriptis differenter . ostendunt oscitantiam interpretis"

CAN. xvii. "*Citationes Patrum* textus N. T. non facere debent variantem lectionem."

CAN. xxix. "*Efficacior lectio textus recepti.*"

As examples of Can. ix. we find, Matt. i. 16, χριστός for 'I. ὁ λεγ. χρ.; i. 25, om. τὸν πρωτότοκον: Rom. i. 31, om. ἀσπόνδους. On 1 John v. 7, 8, the editor refers to the Complutensian edition, and adds : " Ex hac editione, quæ ad fidem præstantissimorum MSS. edita est, indicium clarum habemus, quod in plurimis manuscriptis locus sic inventus et lectus sit " (p. 25).

[b] In a pamphlet published in 1845, Scholz says that if he should prepare another edition of the N. T., he should receive into the text *most* of those readings which he had designated in the inner margin of his Greek Testament as Alexandrine. See the quotation in Scrivener's *Introd.* p. 340.   A.

account of his design (*Stud. u. Krit.* 1830, iv.), to which he referred his readers in a brief postscript, but the book itself contained no Apparatus or Prolegomena, and was the subject of great and painful misrepresentations. When, however, the distinct assertion of the primary claims of evidence throughout the N. T. was more fairly appreciated, Lachmann felt himself encouraged to undertake a larger edition, with both Latin and Greek texts. The Greek authorities for this, limited to the primary uncial MSS. (A B C D P Q T Z E₂ G₂ D₂ H₃), and the quotations of Irenæus and Origen, were arranged by the younger Buttmann. Lachmann himself prepared the Latin evidence (Tregelles, *Hist. of Gr. Text*, p. 101), and revised both texts. The first volume appeared in 1842, the second was printed in 1845, but not published till 1850, owing in a great measure to the opposition which Lachmann found from his friend De Wette (*N. T.* ii. *Præf.* iv.; Tregelles, p. 111). The text of the new edition did not differ much from that of the former; but while in the former he had used Western (*Latin*) authority only to decide in cases where Eastern (*Greek*) authorities were divided; in the latter he used the two great sources of evidence together. Lachmann delighted to quote Bentley as his great precursor (§ 7); but there was an important difference in their immediate aims. Bentley believed that it would be possible to obtain the true text directly by a comparison of the oldest Greek authorities with the oldest MSS. of the Vulgate. Afterwards very important remains of the earlier Latin versions were discovered, and the whole question was complicated by the collection of fresh documents. Lachmann therefore wished in the first instance only to give the current text of the *fourth* century, which might then become the basis of further criticism. This at least was a great step towards the truth, though it must not be accepted as a final one. Griesbach had changed the current text of the 15th and 16th centuries in numberless isolated passages, but yet the late text was the foundation of his own; Lachmann admitted the authority of antiquity everywhere, in orthography, in construction, in the whole complexion and arrangement of his text. But Lachmann's edition, great as its merits are as a first appeal to ancient evidence, is not without serious faults. The materials on which it was based were imperfect. The range of patristic citations was limited arbitrarily. The exclusion of the oriental versions, however necessary at the time, left a wide margin for later change (t. i. *Præf.* p. xxiv.). The neglect of primary cursives often necessitated absolute confidence on slender MS. authority. Lachmann was able to use, but little fitted to collect, evidence (t. i. pp. xxv., xxxviii., xxxix.). It was, however, enough for him to have consecrated the highest scholarship by devoting it to the service of the N. T., and to have claimed for the Holy Scriptures as a field for reverent and searching criticism. (The best account of Lachmann's plan and edition is in Tregelles, *Hist. of Printed Text*, pp. 97–115. His most important critics are Fritzsche, *De Conformatione N. T. Critica* . . . 1841; Tischendorf, *Prolegg.* pp. cil. – cxii.)

12. The chief defects of Lachmann's edition aris from deficiency of authorities. Another German scholar, TISCHENDORF, has devoted twenty years to enlarging our accurate knowledge of ancient MSS. The first edition of Tischendorf (1841) has now no special claims for notice. In his second (Leipsic) edition (1849) he fully accepted the great principle of Lachmann (though he widened the range of ancient authorities), that the text " must be sought solely from ancient authorities, and not from the so-called received edition " (*Præf.* p. xii), and gave many of the results of his own laborious and valuable collations. The size of this manual edition necessarily excluded a full exhibition of evidence: the editor's own judgment was often arbitrary and inconsistent; but the general influence of the edition was of the very highest value, and the text, as a whole, probably better than any which had preceded it. During the next few years Tischendorf prosecuted his labors on MSS. with unwearied diligence, and in 1855–59 he published his third (seventh [a]) critical edition. In this he has given the authorities for and against each reading in considerable detail, and included the chief results of his later discoveries. The whole critical apparatus is extremely valuable, and absolutely indispensable to the student. The text, except in details of orthography, exhibits generally a retrograde movement from the most ancient testimony. The Prolegomena are copious and full of interest.

* In Oct. 1864 Tischendorf published the 1st *Lieferung* of his 8th critical edition of the N. T., of which 5 parts have now appeared, extending to John vi. 23, and the 6th part, completing the Gospels, has probably by this time (May, 1869) been issued in Germany. The critical apparatus is greatly enlarged, and in settling the text, Tischendorf attaches more importance to the most ancient authorities, and in particular, to the agreement of the oldest Greek and Latin MSS., than he did in the preceding edition.   A.

13. Meanwhile the sound study of sacred criticism had revived in England. In 1844 TREGELLES published an edition of the Apocalypse in Greek and English, and announced an edition of the N. T.[b] From this time he engaged in a systematic examination of all unpublished uncial MSS., going over much of the same ground as Tischendorf, and comparing results with him. In 1854 he gave a detailed account of his labors and principles (*An Account of the Printed Text of the Greek New Testament* . . . . London), and again in his new edition of Horne's *Introduction* (1856), [to which " additions " and a " Postscript " were published in 1860. On the remarkable reading μονογενὴς θεός, John i. 18, discussed in this Postscript, there is an article in the *Bibl. Sacra* for Oct. 1861, pp. 840–872. — A.] The first part of his Greek Testament, containing St. Matthew and St. Mark, appeared in 1857; the second, completing the Gospels, has just appeared (1861). [The third, Acts and Cath. Epistles, was published in 1865; the fourth, Romans to 2 Thess., in 1869. — A.] In this he gives at length the evidence of *all* uncial MSS., and of some peculiarly valuable cursives: of all versions up to the 7th century: of all Fathers to Eusebius inclusive. The

---

a The second and third editions were Græco-Latin editions, published at Paris in 1842, of no critical value (cf. *Prolegg.* cxxiv.–v.). [The 3d edition contained no Latin text. — A.] The fifth was a simple text, with the variations of Elzevir, chiefly a reprint of the

(fourth) edition of 1849. The sixth was a Triglott N. T. 1854–55 (Greek, Latin, German) ; 1858 (Greek and Latin).

b Dr. Tregelles' first specimen was published in 1824 (*Hist. of Printed Text*, p. 153).

Latin Vulgate is added, chiefly from the *Cod. Amiatinus* with the readings of the Clementine edition. This edition of Tregelles differs from that of Lachmann by the greater width of its critical foundation; and from that of Tischendorf by a more constant adherence to ancient evidence. Every possible precaution has been taken to insure perfect accuracy in the publication, and the work must be regarded as one of the most important contributions, as it is perhaps the most exact, which has been yet made to the cause of textual criticism. The editions of Knapp (1797, &c.), Vater (1824), Tittmann (1820, &c.), and Hahn (1840, &c.) [also Theile, 1844, &c.] have no peculiar critical value.[a] Meyer (1829, &c.) paid greater attention to the revision of the text which accompanies his great commentary; but his critical notes are often arbitrary and unsatisfactory. In the Greek Testament of Alford, as in that of Meyer, the text is subsidiary to the commentary; but it is impossible not to notice the important advance which has been made by the editor in true principles of criticism during the course of its publication. The fourth edition of the 1st vol. (1859) contains a clear enunciation of the authority of ancient evidence, as supported both by its external and internal claims, and corrects much that was vague and subjective in former editions. Other annotated editions of the Greek Testament, valuable for special merits, may be passed over as having little bearing on the history of the text. One simple text, however, deserves notice (Cambr. 1860, [ed. auctior et emend., 1862]), in which, by a peculiar arrangement of type, Scrivener has represented at a glance all the changes which have been made in the text of Stephens (1550), Elzevir (1624), and Beza (1565), by Lachmann, Tischendorf, and Tregelles.

14. Besides the critical editions of the text of the N. T., various collections of readings have been published separately, which cannot be wholly omitted. In addition to those already mentioned (§ 9), the most important are by Rinck, *Lucubratio Critica*, 1830; Reiche, *Codicum MSS. N. T. Gr. aliquot insigniorum in Bibl. Reg. Paris . . . . collatio* 1847; Scrivener, *A Collation of about Twenty Greek MSS. of the Holy Gospels* . . . . 1853; *A Transcript of the Cod. Aug., with a full Collation of Fifty MSS.* 1859; and E. de Muralt, of Russian MSS. (N. T. 1848). The chief contents of the splendid series of Tischendorf's works (*Codex Ephraemi Rescriptus*, 1843: *Codex Claromontanus*, 1852; *Monumenta sacra inedita*, 1846–1856: [*Mon. sacra ined. nova coll.*, vol. i. (1855). ii. (1857), iii. (1860), v. (1865), vi. (1869);] *Anecdota sacra et profana*, 1855, [new ed., enlarged, 1861;] *Notitia Cod. Sinaitici*, 1860; [*Codex Sinaiticus*, 1862, *N. T. Sinaiticum*, 1863, and *N. T. Gr. ex Sin. Cod.* 1865; *Appendix Codd. Sin. Vat. Alex.* 1867; *Nov. Test. Vat.* 1867, and *Appendix Nov. Test. Vaticani*, 1869]) are given in his own and other editions of the N. T. [His editions of important Latin MSS., *Evangelium Palatinum* (ante-Hieronymian), 1847, and *Cod. Amiatinus*, 1850. new ed. 1854, may also be mentioned here. — A.] (The chief works on the history of the printed text are those of Tregelles, *Hist. of Printed Text*, 1854; Reuss, *Geschichte d. H. Schrift.* §§ 395 ff., where are very complete bibliographical references; and

the Prolegomena of Mill, Wetstein, Griesbach, and Tischendorf. To these must be added the promised (1861) *Introduction* of Mr. Scrivener.

III. PRINCIPLES OF TEXTUAL CRITICISM.

The work of the critic can never be shaped by definite rules. The formal enunciation of principles is but the first step in the process of revision. Even Lachmann, who proposed to follow the most directly mechanical method, frequently allowed play to his own judgment. It could not, indeed, be otherwise with a true scholar; and if there is need anywhere for the most free and devout exercise of every faculty, it must be in tracing out the very words of the Apostles and of the Lord himself. The justification of a method of revision lies in the result. Canons of criticism are more frequently corollaries than laws of procedure. Yet such canons are not without use in marking the course to be followed, but they are intended only to guide, and not to dispense with the exercise of tact and scholarship. The student will judge for himself how far they are applicable in every particular case; and no exhibition of general principles can supersede the necessity of a careful examination of the characteristics of separate witnesses and of groups of witnesses. The text of Holy Scripture, like the text of all other books, depends on evidence. Rules may classify the evidence and facilitate the decision, but the final appeal must be to the evidence itself. What appears to be the only sound system of criticism will be seen from the rules which follow. The examples which are added can be worked out in any critical edition of the Greek Testament, and will explain better than any lengthened description the application of the rules.

1. *The text must throughout be determined by evidence without allowing any prescriptive right to printed editions.* In the infancy of criticism it was natural that early printed editions should possess a greater value than individual MSS. The language of the Complutensian editors, and of Erasmus and Stephens, was such as to command respect for their texts prior to examination. Comparatively few manuscripts were known, and none thoroughly; but at present the whole state of the question is altered. We are now accurately acquainted with the materials possessed by the two latter editors and with the use which they made of them. If there is as yet no such certainty with regard to the basis of the Complutensian text, it is at least clear that no high value can be assigned to it. On the other hand we have, in addition to the early apparatus, new sources of evidence of infinitely greater variety and value. To claim for the printed text any right of possession is, therefore, to be faithless to the principles of critical truth. The received text may or may not be correct in any particular case but this must be determined solely by an appeal to the original authorities. Nor is it right even to assume the received text as our basis. The question before us is not *What is to be changed?* but, *What is to be read?* It would be superfluous to insist on this if it were not that a natural infirmity makes every one unjustly conservative in criticism. It seems to be irreverent to disturb an old belief, when real irreverence lies in perpetuating an error, however slight it may appear to be. This holds good universally. In Holy Scripture nothing

---

[a] * The unwary student should be *warned* against the editions of Hahn and Buttmann (1856, &c.). See

Appendix to Norton's *Statement of Reasons*, 2d ed., p. 448 ff, and *Bibl. Sacra* for Oct. 1853, p. 877 ff. A

can be indifferent; and it is the supreme duty of the critic to apply to details of order and orthography the same care as he bestows on what may be judged weightier points. If, indeed, there were anything in the circumstances of the first publication of the N. T. which might seem to remove it from the ordinary fortunes of books, then it would be impossible not to respect the pious sentiment which accepts the early text as an immediate work of Providence. But the history shows too many marks of human frailty to admit of such a supposition. The text itself contains palpable and admitted errors (Matt. ii. 11, εὖρον; Acts viii. 37, ix. 5, 6; Apoc. v. 14, xxii. 11; not to mention 1 John v. 7), in every way analogous to those which occur in the first classical texts. The conclusion is obvious, and it is superstition rather than reverence which refuses to apply to the service of Scripture the laws which have restored so much of their native beauty to other ancient writings. It may not be possible to fix the reading in every case finally, but it is no less the duty of the scholar to advance as far as he can and mark the extreme range of uncertainty.

2. *Every element of evidence must be taken into account before a decision is made.* Some uncertainty must necessarily remain; for, when it is said that the text must rest upon evidence, it is implied that it must rest on an examination of the whole evidence. But it can never be said that the mines of criticism are exhausted. Yet even here the possible limits of variation are narrow. The available evidence is so full and manifold that it is difficult to conceive that any new authorities could do more than turn the scale in cases which are at present doubtful. But to exclude remote chances of error it is necessary to take account of every testimony. No arbitrary line can be drawn excluding MSS. versions or quotations below a certain date. The true text must (as a rule) explain all variations, and the most recent forms may illustrate the original one. In practice it will be found that certain documents may be neglected after examination, and that the value of others is variously affected by determinable conditions; but still, as no variation is inherently indifferent, no testimony can be absolutely disregarded.

3. *The relative weight of the several classes of evidence is modified by their generic character.* Manuscripts, versions, and citations, the three great classes of external authorities for the text, are obviously open to characteristic errors. The first are peculiarly liable to errors from transcription (comp. i. § 31 ff.). The two last are liable to this cause of corruption and also to others. The genius of the language into which the translation is made may require the introduction of connecting particles or words of reference, as can be seen from the italicised words in the A. V. Some uses of the article and of prepositions cannot be expressed or distinguished with certainty in translation. Glosses or marginal additions are more likely to pass into the text in the process of translation than in that of transcription. Quotations, on the other hand, are often partial or from memory, and long use may give a traditional fixity to a slight confusion or adaptation of passages of Scripture. These grounds of inaccuracy are, however, easily determined, and there is generally little difficulty in deciding whether the rendering of a version or the testimony of a Father can be fairly quoted. Moreover, the most important versions are so close to the Greek text

that they preserve the order of the original with scrupulous accuracy, and even in representing minute shades of expression, observe a constant uniformity which could not have been anticipated (comp. Lachmann, *N. T.* i. p. xlv. ff.). It is a far more serious obstacle to the critical use of these authorities that the texts of the versions and Fathers generally are in a very imperfect state. With the exception of the Latin Version there is not one in which a thoroughly satisfactory text is available; and the editions of Clement and Origen are little qualified to satisfy strict demands of scholarship. As a general rule the evidence of both may be trusted where they differ from the late text of the N. T., but where they agree with this against other early authorities, there is reason to entertain a suspicion of corruption. This is sufficiently clear on comparing the old printed text of Chrysostom with the text of the best MSS. But when full allowance has been made for all these drawbacks, the mutually corrective power of the three kinds of testimony is of the highest value. The evidence of versions may show at once that a MS reading is a transcriptural error: John i. 14, ὁ εἰκών (B C); Jude 12, ἀπάταις (A); 1 John i. 2, καὶ ὃ ἑορδκαμεν (B), ii. 8, σκία for σκοτία (A), iii. 21, ἔχει (B); 2 Pet. ii. 16, ἐν ἀνθρώποις: and the absence of their support throws doubt upon readings otherwise of the highest probability: 2 Pet. ii. 4, σειροῖς, ii. 6, ἀσεβέσιν. The testimony of an early Father is again sufficient to give preponderating weight to slight MS. authority: Matt. i. 18, τοῦ δὲ χριστοῦ ἡ γένεσις; and since versions and Fathers go back to a time anterior to any existing MSS., they furnish a standard by which we may measure the conformity of any MS. with the most ancient text. On questions of orthography MSS. alone have authority. The earliest Fathers, like our own writers, seem (if we may judge from printed texts) to have adopted the current spelling of their time, and not to have aimed at preserving in this respect the dialectic peculiarities of N. T. Greek. But MSS., again, are not free from special idiosyncrasies (if the phrase may be allowed) both in construction and orthography, and unless account be taken of these a wrong judgment may be made in isolated passages.

4. *The mere preponderance of numbers is in itself of no weight.* If the multiplication of copies of the N. T. had been uniform, it is evident that the number of later copies preserved from the accidents of time would have far exceeded that of the earlier, yet no one would have preferred the fuller testimony of the 13th to the scantier documents of the 4th century. Some changes are necessarily introduced in the most careful copying, and these are rapidly multiplied. A recent MS. may have been copied from one of great antiquity, but this must be a rare occurrence. If all MSS. were derived by successive reproduction from one source, the most ancient, though few, would claim supreme authority over the more recent ones. As it is, the case is still stronger. It has been shown that the body of later copies was made under one influence. They give the testimony of one church only, and not of all. For many generations Byzantine scribes must gradually, even though unconsciously, have assimilated the text to their current form of expression. Meanwhile the propagation of the Syrian and African types of text was left to the casual reproduction of an ancient exemplar. These were necessarily far rarer than later and modified copies, and at the same time likely to

be far less used. Representatives of one class were therefore multiplied rapidly, while those of other classes barely continued to exist. From this it follows that MSS. have no abstract numerical value. Variety of evidence, and not a crowd of witnesses, must decide on each doubtful point; and it happens by no means rarely that one or two MSS. alone support a reading which is unquestionably right (Matt. i. 25, v. 4, 5; Mark ii. 22, &c.).

5. *The more ancient reading is generally preferable.* This principle seems to be almost a truism. It can only be assailed by assuming that the recent reading is itself the representative of an authority still more ancient. But this carries the decision from the domain of evidence to that of conjecture, and the issue must be tried on individual passages.

6. *The more ancient reading is generally the reading of the more ancient MSS.* This proposition is fully established by a comparison of explicit early testimony with the text of the oldest copies. It would be strange, indeed, if it were otherwise. In this respect the discovery of the *Codex Sinaiticus* cannot but have a powerful influence upon Biblical criticism. Whatever may be its individual peculiarities, it preserves the ancient readings in characteristic passages (Luke ii. 14; John i. 4, 18; 1 Tim. iii. 16). If the secondary uncials (E F S U, etc.) are really the direct representatives of a text more ancient than that in א B C Z, it is at least remarkable that no unequivocal early authority presents their characteristic readings. This difficulty is greatly increased by internal considerations. The characteristic readings of the most ancient MSS. are those which preserve in their greatest integrity those subtle characteristics of style which are too minute to attract the attention of a transcriber, and yet too marked in their recurrence to be due to anything less than an unconscious law of composition. The laborious investigations of Gersdorf (*Beiträge zur Sprach-Charakteristik d. Schriftsteller d. N. T.* Leipzig, 1816) have placed many of these peculiarities in a clear light, and it seems impossible to study his collections without gaining the assurance that the earliest copies have preserved the truest image of the Apostolic texts. This conclusion from style is convincingly confirmed by the appearance of the genuine dialectic forms of Hellenistic Greek in those MSS., and those only, which preserve characteristic traits of construction and order. As long as it was supposed that these forms were Alexandrine, their occurrence was naturally held to be a mark of the Egyptian origin of the MSS., but now that it is certain that they were characteristic of a class and not of a locality, it is impossible to resist the inference that the documents which have preserved delicate and evanescent traits of apostolic language must have preserved its substance also with the greatest accuracy.

7. *The ancient text is often preserved substantially in recent copies.* But while the most ancient copies, as a whole, give the most ancient text, yet it is by no means confined exclusively to them. The text of D in the Gospels, however much it has been interpolated, preserves in several cases almost alone the true reading. Other MSS. exist of almost every date (8th cent. L H, 9th cent. X Δ F₂ G₃, 10th cent. 1,106, 11th cent. 33, 22, &c.), which contain in the main the oldest text, though

in these the orthography is modernized, and other changes appear which indicate a greater or less departure from the original copy. The importance of the best cursives has been most strangely neglected, and it is but recently that their true claims to authority have been known. In many cases where other ancient evidence is defective or divided they are of the highest value, and it seldom happens that any true reading is wholly unsupported by late evidence.

8. *The agreement of ancient MSS., or of MSS. containing an ancient text, with all the earliest versions and citations marks a certain reading.* The final argument in favor of the text of the most ancient copies lies in the combined support which they receive in characteristic passages from the most ancient versions and patristic citations. The reading of the oldest MSS. is, as a general rule, upheld by the true reading of Versions and the certain testimony of the Fathers, where this can be ascertained. The later reading, and this is not less worthy of notice, is with equal constancy repeated in the corrupted text of the Versions, and often in inferior MSS. of Fathers. The force of this combination of testimony can only be apprehended after a continuous examination of passages. A mere selection of texts conveys only a partial impression; and it is most important to observe the errors of the weightiest authorities when isolated, in order to appreciate rightly their independent value when combined. For this purpose the student is urged to note for himself the readings of a few selected authorities (A B C D L X 1, 33, 69, &c., the MSS. of the old Latin *a b c ff k*, etc., the best MSS. of the Vulgate, *am. for. harl.*, etc., the great oriental versions) through a few chapters; and it may certainly be predicted that the result will be a perfect confidence in the text, supported by the combined authority of the classes of witnesses, though frequently one or two Greek MSS. are to be followed against all the remainder.

9. *The disagreement of the most ancient authorities often marks the existence of a corruption anterior to them.* But it happens by no means rarely that the most ancient authorities are divided. In this case it is necessary to recognize an alternative reading; and the inconsistency of Tischendorf in his various editions would have been less glaring, if he had followed the example of Griesbach in noticing prominently those readings to which a slight change in the balance of evidence would give the preponderance. Absolute certainty is not in every case attainable, and the peremptory assertion of a critic cannot set aside the doubt which lies on the conflicting testimony of trustworthy witnesses. The differences are often in themselves (as may appear) of little moment, but the work of the scholar is to present clearly in its minutest details the whole result of his materials. Examples of legitimate doubt as to the true reading occur Matt. vii. 14, &c.; Luke x. 42, &c.; John i. 18, ii. 8, &c.; 1 John iii. 1, v. 10, &c.; Rom. iii. 26, iv. 1, &c. In rare cases this diversity appears to indicate a corruption which is earlier than any remaining documents: Matt. xi. 27; Mark i. 27; 2 Peter i. 21; James iii. 6, iv. 14; Rom. i. 32, v. 6 (17), xiii. 5, xvi. 25 ff. (One special form of variation in the most valuable authorities requires particular mention. An early difference of order frequently indicates the interpolation of a gloss; and when the best authorities are thus divided,

any ancient though slight evidence for the omission of the transferred clause deserves the greatest consideration: Matt. i. 18, v. 32, 39, xii. 38, &c.; Rom. iv. 1, &c.; Jam. i. 22. And generally serious variations in expression between the primary authorities point to an early corruption by addition: Matt. x. 29; Rom. i. 27, 29, iii. 22, 26.

10. *The argument from internal evidence is always precarious.* If a reading is in accordance with the general style of the writer, it may be said on the one side that this fact is in its favor, and on the other that an acute copyist probably changed the exceptional expression for the more usual one: *e. g.* Matt. i. 24, ii. 14, vii. 21, &c. If a reading is more emphatic, it may be urged that the sense is improved by its adoption: if less emphatic, that scribes were habitually inclined to prefer stronger terms: *e. g.* Matt. v. 13, vi. 4, &c. Even in the case of the supposed influence of parallel passages in the synoptic Evangelists, it is by no means easy to resist the weight of ancient testimony when it supports the parallel phrase, in favor of the natural canon which recommends the choice of variety in preference to uniformity: *e. g.* Matt. iii. 6, iv. 9, viii. 32, ix. 11, &c. But though internal evidence is commonly only of subjective value, there are some general rules which are of very wide, if not of universal application. These have force to decide or to confirm a judgment: but in every instance they must be used only in combination with direct testimony.

11. *The more difficult reading is preferable to the simpler* (proclivi lectioni præstat ardua, Bengel). Except in cases of obvious corruption this canon probably holds good without exception, in questions of language, construction, and sense. Rare or provincial forms, irregular usages of words, rough turns of expression, are universally to be taken in preference to the ordinary and idiomatic phrases. The bold and emphatic agglomeration of clauses, with the fewest connecting particles, is always likely to be nearest to the original text. The usage of the different apostolic writers varies in this respect, but there are very few, if any, instances where the mass of copyists have left out a genuine connection; and on the other hand there is hardly a chapter in St. Paul's Epistles where they have not introduced one. The same rule is true in questions of interpretation. The hardest reading is generally the true one: Matt. vi. 1, xix. 17, xxi. 31 (ὁ ὕστερος); Rom. viii. 28 (ὁ θεός): 2 Cor. v. 3; unless, indeed, the difficulty lies below the surface: as Rom. xii. 11 (καιρῷ for κυρίῳ), xii. 13 (μνείαις for χρείαις). The rule admits yet further of another modified application. The less definite reading is generally preferable to the more definite. Thus the future is constantly substituted for the pregnant present, Matt. vii. 3; Rom. xv. 18: compound for simple words, Matt. vii. 28, viii. 17, xi. 25; and pronouns of reference are frequently introduced to emphasize the statement, Matt. vi. 4. But caution must be used lest our own imperfect sense of the naturalness of an idiom may lead to the neglect of external evidence (Matt. xxv. 16, ἐποίησεν wrongly for ἐκέρδησεν).

12. *The shorter reading is generally preferable to the longer.* This canon is very often coincident to the former one; but it admits also of a wider application. Except in very rare cases copyists never omitted intentionally, while they constantly introduced into the text marginal glosses and even various readings (comp. § 13), either from igno-

rance or from a natural desire to leave out nothing which seemed to come with a claim to authority The extent to which this instinct influenced the character of the later text can be seen from an examination of the various readings in a few chapters. Thus in Matt. vi. the following interpolations occur: 4 (αὐτός), ἐν τῷ φανερῷ. 5 (ἄν) ὅτι ἀπ· 6 ἐν·τῷ φανερῷ. 10 ἐπὶ τῆς γ. 13 ὅτι σοῦ · · ἀμήν. 15 (τὰ παραπτ. αὐτῶν)· 16 ὅτι ἀπ· 19 ἐν τῷ φανερῷ. The synoptic Gospels were the most exposed to this kind of corruption, but it occurs in all parts of the N. T. Everywhere the fuller, rounder, more complete form of expression is open to the suspicion of change: and the pre-eminence of the ancient authorities is nowhere seen more plainly than in the constancy with which they combine in preserving the plain, rigorous, and abrupt phraseology of the apostolic writings. A few examples taken almost at random will illustrate the various cases to which the rule applies: Matt. ii. 15, iv. 6, xii. 25; James iii. 12; Rom. ii. 1, viii. 23, x. 15, xv. 29 (comp. § 13).

13. *That reading is preferable which explains the origin of the others.* This rule is chiefly of use in cases of great complication, and it would be impossible to find a better example than one which has been brought forward by Tischendorf for a different purpose (N. T. *Præf.* pp. xxxiii, xxxiv.). The common reading in Mark ii. 22 is ὁ οἶνος ἐκχεῖται καὶ οἱ ἀσκοὶ ἀπολοῦνται, which is perfectly simple in itself, and the undoubted reading in the parallel passage of St. Matthew. But here there are great variations. One important MS. (L) reads ὁ οἶνος ἐκχεῖται καὶ οἱ ἀσκοί: another (D with *it.*) ὁ οἶνος καὶ ἀσκοὶ ἀπολοῦνται: another (B) ὁ οἶνος ἀπόλλυται καὶ οἱ ἀσκοί. Here, if we bear in mind the reading in St. Matthew, it is morally certain that the text of B is correct. This may have been changed into the common text, but cannot have arisen out of it. Compare James iv. 4, 12; Matt. xxiv. 38; Jude 18; Rom. vii. 25; Mark i. 16, 27.

(For the principles of textual criticism compare Griesbach, *N. T. Prolegg.* § 3, pp. lviii. ff.; Tischendorf, *N. T. Prolegg.* pp. xxxii.–xliv.; Tregelles, *Printed Text,* pp. 132 ff.; (Horne's) *Introduction,* iv. pp. 342 ff. The *Crisis* of Wetstein (*Prolegy* pp. 206–240, Lotze) is very unsatisfactory.)

* On the application of these principles the student will find valuable hints in Griesbach's *Commentarius Criticus,* 2 pt. 1798–1811, and in T. S. Green's *Course of Developed Criticism,* etc., Lond. 1856. Reiche's *Commentarius Criticus,* 3 tom. Gött. 1853–62, 4to, is not very important.

A.

IV. THE LANGUAGE OF THE NEW TESTAMENT. ·

1. The eastern conquests of Alexander opened a new field for the development of the Greek language. It may be reasonably doubted whether a specific Macedonian dialect is not a mere fiction of grammarians; but increased freedom both in form and construction was a necessary consequence of the wide diffusion of Greek. Even in Aristotle there is a great declension from the classical standard of purity, though the Attic formed the basis of his language; and the rise of the *common* or *Grecian* dialect (διάλεκτος κοινή, or δ. Ἑλληνική) is dated from his time. In the writings of educated men who were familiar with ancient models, this "common" dialect always preserved a close resemblance to the normal Attic, but in the inter-

course of ordinary life the corruption must have been both great and rapid.

2. At no place could the corruption have been greater or more rapid than at Alexandria, where a motley population, engaged in active commerce, adopted Greek as their common medium of communication. [ALEXANDRIA, i. p. 63.] And it is in Alexandria that we must look for the origin of the language of the New Testament. Two distinct elements were combined in this marvelous dialect which was destined to preserve forever the fullest tidings of the Gospel. On the one side there was Hebrew conception, on the other Greek expression. The thoughts of the East were wedded to the words of the West. This was accomplished by the gradual translation of the Hebrew Scriptures into the vernacular Greek. The Greek had already lost the exquisite symmetry of its first form, so that it could take the clear impress of Hebrew ideas; and at the same time it had gained rather than lost in richness and capacity. In this manner what may be called the theocratic aspect of nature and history was embodied in Greek phrases, and the power and freedom of Greek quickened and defined Eastern speculation. The theories of the "purists" of the 17th century (comp. Winer, Grammatik, § 1; Reuss, Gesch. d. H. S. § 47) were based on a complete misconception of what we may, without presumption, feel to have been required for a universal Gospel. The message was not for one nation only, but for all; and the language in which it was promulgated — like its most successful preacher — united in one complementary attributes. [HELLENIST, ii. p. 1039 ff.]

3. The Greek of the LXX. — like the English of the A. V. or the German of Luther — naturally determined the Greek dialect of the mass of the Jews. It is quite possible that numerous provincialisms existed among the Greek-speaking Jews of Egypt, Palestine, and Asia Minor, but the dialect of their common Scriptures must have given a general unity to their language. It is, therefore, more correct to call the N. T. dialect Hellenistic than Alexandrine, though the form by which it is characterized may have been peculiarly Alexandrine at first. Its local character was lost when the LXX. was spread among the Greek Dispersion; and that which was originally confined to one city or one work was adopted by a whole nation. At the same time much of the extreme harshness of the LXX. dialect was softened down by intercourse with Greeks or grecising foreigners, and conversely the wide spread of proselytism familiarized the Greeks with Hebrew ideas.

4. The position of Palestine was peculiar. The Aramaic (Syro-Chaldaic), which was the national dialect after the Return, existed side by side with the Greek. Both languages seem to have been generally understood, though, if we may judge from other instances of bilingual countries, the Aramaic would be the chosen language for the common intercourse of Jews (2 Macc. vii. 8, 21, 27). It was in this language, we may believe, that our Lord was accustomed to teach the people; and it appears that He used the same in the more private acts of his life (Mark iii. 17, v. 41, vii. 34; Matt. xxvii. 46; John i. 42; cf. John xx. 16). But the habitual use of the LXX. is a sufficient proof of the familiarity of the Palestinian Jews with the Greek dialect; and the judicial proceedings before Pilate must have been conducted in

Greek. (Comp. Grinfield, Apology for the LXX., pp. 76 ff.) [LANGUAGE OF THE N. T.]

5. The Roman occupation of Syria was not altogether without influence upon the language. A considerable number of Latin words, chiefly referring to acts of government, occur in the N. T., and they are probably only a sample of larger innovations (κῆνσος, λεγιών, κουστωδία, ἀσσάριον, κοδράντης, δηνάριον, μίλιον, πραιτώριον, φραγελλοῦν, St. Matt., etc.; κεντυρίων, σπεκουλάτωρ, τὸ ἱκανὸν ποιῆσαι, St. Mark; λέντιον, σουδάριον, τίτλος, St. John, etc.; λιβερτῖνος, κολωνία, σιμικίνθιον, σικάριος, St. Luke; μάκελλον, μεμβράνα, St. Paul). Other words in common use were of Semitic (ἀρραβών, ζιζάνιον, κορβανᾶς, ῥαββεί), Persian (ἀγγαρεύω, μάγοι, τιάρα, παράδεισος), or Egyptian origin (βαίον).

6. The language which was moulded under these various influences presents many peculiarities, both philological and exegetical, which have not yet been placed in a clear light. For a long time it has been most strangely assumed that the linguistic forms preserved in the oldest MSS. are Alexandrine and not in the widest sense Hellenistic, and on the other hand that the Aramaic modifications of the N. T. phraseology remove it from the sphere of strict grammatical analysis. These errors are necessarily fatal to all real advance in the accurate study of the words or sense of the apostolic writings. In the case of St. Paul, no less than in the case of Herodotus, the evidence of the earliest witnesses must be decisive as to dialectic forms. Egyptian scribes preserved the characteristics of other books, and there is no reason to suppose that they altered those of the N. T. Nor is it reasonable to conclude that the later stages of a language are governed by no law or that the introduction of fresh elements destroys the symmetry which in reality it only changes. But if old misconceptions still linger, very much has been done lately to open the way to a sounder understanding both of the form and the substance of the N. T. by Tischendorf (as to the dialect, N. T. [ed. 7] Prolegg. pp. xlvi.–lxii.), by Winer (as to the grammatical laws, Gramm. d. N. T. Sprachid., 6th ed., 1855 [7th ed., 1867]; comp. Green's Grammar of N. T. dialect, 1842 [2d ed., 1862, and A. Buttmann, Gram. d. neutest. Sprachgebrauchs, 1859]), and by the later commentators (Fritzsche, Lücke, Bleek, Meyer, Alford, [Ellicott, Lightfoot, Bäumlein]). In detail comparatively little remains to be done, but a philosophical view of the N. T. language as a whole is yet to be desired. For this it would be necessary to take account of the commanding authority of the LXX. over the religious dialect, of the constant and living power of the spoken Aramaic and Greek, of the mutual influence of inflection and syntax, of the inherent vitality of words and forms, of the history of technical terms, and of the creative energy of Christian truth. Some of these points may be discussed in other articles; for the present it must be enough to notice a few of the most salient characteristics of the language as to form and expression.

7. The formal differences of the Greek of the N. T. from classical Greek are partly differences of vocabulary and partly differences of construction. Old words are changed in orthography (1) or in inflection (2); new words (3) and rare or novel constructions (4) are introduced. One or two examples of each of these classes may be noticed. But it must be again remarked that the language

of the N. T., both as to its lexicography and as to its grammar, is based on the language of the LXX. The two stages of the dialect cannot be examined satisfactorily apart. The usage of the earlier books often confirms and illustrates the usage of the later; and many characteristics of N. T. Greek have been neglected or set aside from ignorance of the fact that they are undoubtedly found in the LXX. With regard to the forms of words, the similarity between the two is perfect; with regard to construction, it must always be remembered that the LXX. is a translation, executed under the immediate influence of the Hebrew, while the books of the N. T. (with a partial exception in the case of St. Matthew) were written freely in the current Greek.

(1.) Among the most frequent peculiarities of orthography of Hellenistic Greek which are supported by conclusive authority, are — the preservation of the μ before ψ and φ in λαμβάνω and its derivations, λήμψεται, ἀντιλήμψεις; and of ν in compounds of σύν and ἐν, συνζῆν, συνμαθητής, ἐγγεγραμμένη. Other variations occur in τεσσεράκοντα, ἐραυνᾶν, etc., ἐκαθερίσθη, etc. It is more remarkable that the aspirate appears to have been introduced into some words, as ἐλπίς (Rom. viii. 20; Luke vi. 35). The ν ἐφελκυστικόν in verbs (but not in nouns) and the s of οὕτως are always preserved before consonants, and the hiatus (with ἀλλά especially) is constantly (perhaps always) disregarded. The forms in -ει-, -ι-, are more difficult of determination, and the question is not limited to later Greek.

(2.) Peculiarities of inflection are found in μαχαίρῃ, -ης, χεῖραν (?), συγγένην (?), βαθέως, etc. These peculiarities are much more common in verbs. The augment is sometimes doubled: ἀπεκατεστάθη, sometimes omitted: οἰκοδόμησεν, κατεισχύνθη. The doubling of ρ is commonly neglected: ἐράντισεν. Unusual forms of tenses are used: ἔπεσα, εἶπα, [ἦλθαν,] etc.; unusual moods: καυθήσωμαι (1 Cor. xiii. 3?); and unusual conjugations: νικοῦντι for νικῶντι, ἐλλόγα for ἐλλόγει, παρεισεδύησαν for παρεισέδυσαν (Jude 4).

• Note also ἀναπήσονται, Rev. xiv. 13, 2d fut. pass. of ἀναπαύω, strangely misunderstood by Robinson, *N. T. Lex.* p. 804 (Addenda); also such forms as εἴληφες, κεκοπίακες; ἔγνωκαν, εἴρηκαν, πέπωκαν, γέγοναν; εἴχοσαν, ἐδίδοσαν, παρελάβοσαν.   A.

(3.) The new words are generally formed according to old analogy — οἰκοδεσπότης, εὐκαιρεῖν, καθημερινός, ἀποκαραδοκεῖν; and in this respect the frequency of compound words is particularly worthy of notice. Other words receive new senses: χρηματίζειν, ὀψάριον, περισπᾶσθαι, συνίστημι; and some are slightly changed in form: ἀνάθεμα (-ημα), ἐξέπινα (-ης), βασίλισσα (comp. Winer, *Gramm.* § 2).

(4.) The most remarkable construction, which is well attested both in the LXX. and in the N. T., is that of the conjunctions ἵνα, ὅταν, with the present indicative: Gal. vi. 12 (?), ἵνα διώκονται, Luke xi. 2, ὅταν προσεύχεσθε, as well as with the future indicative (comp. Tischdf. Mark iii. 2). Ὅταν is even found with the imperfect and aor. indic., Mark iii. 11, ὅταν ἐθεώρουν; Apoc. viii. 1, ?ταν ἤνοιξεν. Other irregular constructions in the combination of moods (Apoc. iii. 9) and in defective concords (Mark ix. 26) can be paralleled

in classical Greek, though such constructions are more frequent and anomalous in the Apocalypse than elsewhere.

8. The peculiarities of the N. T. language which have been hitherto mentioned have only a rare and remote connection with interpretation. They illustrate more or less the general history of th decay of a language, and offer in some few instances curious problems as to the corresponding changes of modes of conception. Other peculiarities have a more important bearing on the sense. These are in part Hebraisms (Aramaisms) in (1) expression or (2) construction, and in part (3) modifications of language resulting from the substance of the Christian revelation.

(1.) The general characteristic of Hebraic expression is vividness, as simplicity is of Hebraic syntax. Hence there is found constantly in the N. T. a personality of language (if the phrase may be used) which is foreign to classical Greek. At one time this occurs in the substitution of a pregnant metaphor for a simple word: οἰκοδομεῖν (St. Paul), σπλαγχνίζομαι (Gospels), πλατύνειν τὴν καρδίαν (St. Paul), πρόσωπον λαμβάνειν, προσωποληψία, προσωπολημπτεῖν. At another time in the use of prepositions in place of cases: κράζειν ἐν μεγάλῃ φωνῇ, ἐν μαχαίρᾳ ἀπολέσθαι, ἀθῶος ἀπὸ τοῦ αἵματος. At another in the use of a vivid phrase for a preposition: διὰ χειρῶν τινος γενέσθαι, ἀποστέλλειν σὺν χειρὶ ἀγγέλου, ἐν χειρὶ μεσίτου, φεύγειν ἀπὸ προσώπου τινός. And sometimes the one personal act is used to describe the whole spirit and temper: πορεύεσθαι ὀπίσω τινός.

(2.) The chief peculiarities of the syntax of the N. T. lie in the reproduction of Hebrew forms. Two great features by which it is distinguished from classical syntax may be specially singled out. It is markedly deficient in the use of particles and of oblique and participial constructions. Sentences are more frequently coördinated than subordinated. One clause follows another rather in the way of constructive parallelism than by distinct logical sequence. Only the simplest words of connection are used in place of the subtle varieties of expression by which Attic writers exhibit the interdependence of numerous ideas. The repetition of a key-word (John i. 1, v. 31, 32, xi. 33) or of a leading thought (John x. 11 ff., xvii. 14–19) often serves in place of all other conjunctions. The words quoted from another are given in a direct objective shape (John vii. 40, 41). Illustrative details are commonly added in abrupt parenthesis (John iv. 6). Calm emphasis, solemn repetition, grave simplicity, the gradual accumulation of truths, give to the language of Holy Scripture a depth and permanence of effect found nowhere else. It is difficult to single out isolated phrases in illustration of this general statement, since the final impression is more due to the iteration of many small points than to the striking power of a few. Apart from the whole context the influence of details is almost inappreciable. Constructions which are most distinctly Hebraic (πληθύνων πληθυνῶ, θανάτῳ τελευτᾶν, εὐδοκεῖν ἔν τινι, σὰρξ ἁμαρτίας, etc.) are not those which give the deepest Hebrew coloring to the N. T. diction, but rather that pervading monotony of form which, though correct in individual clauses, is wholly foreign to the vigor and elasticity of classical Greek. If the student will carefully analyse a few chapters of St. John, in whom the Hebrew spirit is most constant and marked, inquiring at each step how a classical writer would have avoided repetition by the use of pronouns and particles, how he would have indicated dependence by the use of absolute cases and the optative, how he would have united the whole by establishing a clear relation between the parts, he will gain a true measure of the Hebraic style more or less pervading the whole N. T. which cannot be obtained from a mere catalogue of phrases. The character of the style lies in its total effect and not in separable elements: it is seen in the spirit which informs the entire text far more vividly than in the separate members (comp. [Westcott's] *Introduction to the Gospels*, pp. 241-252).

(3) The purely Christian element in the N. T. requires the most careful handling. Words and phrases already partially current were transfigured by embodying new truths and forever consecrated to their service. To trace the history of these is a delicate question of lexicography which has not yet been thoroughly examined. There is a danger of confounding the apostolic usage on the one side with earlier Jewish usage, and on the other with later ecclesiastical terminology. The steps by which the one served as a preparation for the apostolic sense and the latter naturally grew out of it require to be diligently observed. Even within the range of the N. T. itself it is possible to notice various phases of fundamental ideas and a consequent modification of terms. Language and thought are both living powers, mutually dependent and illustrative. Examples of words which show this progressive history are abundant and full of instruction. Among others may be quoted, πίστις, πιστός, πιστεύειν εἴς τινα; δίκαιος, δικαιόω; ἅγιος, ἁγιάζω; καλεῖν, κλῆσις, κλητός, ἐκλεκτός; ἀγάπη, ἐλπίς, χάρις; εὐαγγέλιον, εὐαγγελίζεσθαι, κηρύσσειν, κήρυγμα; ἀπόστολος, πρεσβύτερος, ἐπίσκοπος, διάκονος; ἄρτον κλάσαι, βαπτίζειν, κοινωνία; σάρξ, ψυχή, πνεῦμα; κόσμος, σωτηρία, σώζειν; λυτροῦσθαι, καταλλάσσειν. Nor is it too much to say that in the history of these and such like words lies the history of Christianity. The perfect truth of the apostolic phraseology, when examined by this most rigorous criticism, contains the fulfillment of earlier anticipations and the germ of later growth.

9. For the language of the N. T. calls for the exercise of the most rigorous criticism. The complexity of the elements which it involves makes the inquiry wider and deeper, but does not set it aside. The overwhelming importance, the manifold expression, the gradual development of the message which it conveys, call for more intense devotion in the use of every faculty trained in other schools, but do not suppress inquiry. The Gospel is for the whole nature of man, and is sufficient to satisfy the reason as well as the spirit. Words and idioms admit of investigation in all stages of a language. Decay itself is subject to law. A mixed and degenerate dialect is not less the living exponent of definite thought, than the most pure and vigorous. Rude and unlettered men may have characteristic modes of thought and speech, but even (naturally speaking) there is no reason to expect that they will be less exact than others in using their own idiom. The literal sense of the apostolic writings must be gained in the same way as the literal sense of any other writings, by the fullest use of every appliance of scholarship, and the most complete confidence in the necessary and absolute connection of words and thoughts. No variation of phrase, no peculiarity of idiom, no change of tense, no change of order can be neglected. The truth lies in the whole expression, and no one can presume to set aside any part as trivial or indifferent.

10. The importance of investigating most patiently and most faithfully the literal meaning of the sacred text must be felt with tenfold force, when it is remembered that the literal sense is the outward embodiment of a spiritual sense, which lies beneath and quickens every part of Holy Scripture [OLD TESTAMENT]. Something of the same kind of double sense is found in the greatest works of human genius, in the *Orestea* for example, or *Hamlet*; and the obscurity which hangs over the deepest utterances of a dramatist may teach humility to those who complain of the darkness of a prophet. The special circumstances of the several writers, their individual characteristics reflected in their books, the slightest details which add distinctness or emphasis to a statement, are thus charged with a divine force. A spiritual harmony rises out of an accurate interpretation. And exactly in proportion as the spiritual meaning of the Bible is felt to be truly its primary meaning, will the importance of a sound criticism of the text be recognized as the one necessary and sufficient foundation of the noble superstructure of higher truth which is afterwards found to rest upon it. Faith in words is the beginning, faith in the WORD is the completion of Biblical interpretation. Impatience may destroy the one and check the other; but the true student will find the simple text of Holy Scripture ever pregnant with lessons for the present and promises for ages to come. The literal meaning is one and fixed: the spiritual meaning is infinite and multiform. The unity of the literal meaning is not disturbed by the variety of the inherent spiritual applications. Truth is essentially infinite. There is thus one sense to the words, but countless relations. There is an absolute fitness in the parables and figures of Scripture, and hence an abiding pertinence. The spiritual meaning is, so to speak, the life of the whole, living on with unchanging power through every change of race and age. To this we can approach only (on the human side) by unwavering trust in the ordinary laws of scholarship, which finds in Scripture its final consecration.

For the study of the language of the N. T., Tischendorf's 7th edition (1859), Grinfield's *Editio Hellenistica* (with the *Scholia*, 1843–48), Bruder's *Concordantiae* (1842 [3d ed. 1867]), and Winer's *Grammatik* (6th edition, 1853, translated by Masson, Edinb. 1859), are indispensable. To these may be added Trommius's *Concordantiae . . . LXX. interpretum*, 1718, for the usage of the LXX., and Suicer's *Thesaurus*, 1682 [2d ed. 1728], for the later history of some words. The lexicons of Schleusner to the LXX. (1820–21), and N. T. (4th ed. 1819) contain a large mass of materials, but are most uncritical. Those of Wahl (N. T. 1822 [translated by E. Robinson, Andover, 1825: 3d ed. of the original, 1843]; Apocrypha, 1853) are much better in point of accuracy and scholarship. On questions of dialect and grammar there are important collections in Sturz, *De Dialecto Maced. et Alex.* (1786); Thiersch, *De Pent. vers. Alex.* (1841); Lobeck's *Phrynichus* (1820), *Paralipomena Gr. Gr.* (1837), *Pathol. Serm. Gr. Prolegg.* (1843), [Ῥηματικὸν s. Verbb. Gr. et Nominum verbal. *Technologia*, (1846),] *Pathol. Serm. Gr. Elem.* ([2 pt. 1853–62]). The Indices of Jacobson to the *Patres Apostolici* (1840) are very complete and useful. The parallels gathered by Ott and Krebs from Josephus, and by Loesner and Kühn from Philo have been fully used by most recent commentators. Further bibliographical references are given by Winer, *Gramm.* pp. 1–31; Reuss, *Gesch. d. Heil. Schriften*, pp. 28–37; Grinfield's *N. T. Editio Hellenistica*, Præf. xi., xii. [Schirlitz, *Grundzüge d. neutest. Grācitāt*, pp. 101–126.]   B. F. W.

* Among the more recent works on the language of the N. T. the following also deserve notice. K. G. Bretschneider, *Lex. man. Gr.-Lat. in Libros N. T.*, 1824, 3d ed., greatly improved, 1840, 4to. E. Robinson, *Gr. and Eng. Lex. of the N. T.*, Bost. 1836, new ed. N. Y. 1850, largely combining the best features of Wahl and Bretschneider. S. T. Bloomfield, *Gr. and Eng. Lex. to the N. T.*, Lond. 1840, 3d ed. 1860. C. G. Wilke, *Clavis N. T. philologica*, Dresd. et Lips. 1840–41, 2d ed. 1850, new ed. mostly rewritten by C. L. W. Grimm, under whose name it also appears with the title *Lex. Gr.-Lat. N. T.*, Lips. 1868 (a translation of this is promised by Professor Thayer of Andover). S. C. Schirlitz, *Griech.-Deutsches Wörterb. zum N. T.*, Giessen, 1851, 3e Aufl. 1858. Herm Cremer, *Bibl.-theol. Wörterb. der Neutest. Grācitāt*, Gotha, 1866, Engl. trans. 1869. *The Glossary of Later and Byzantine Greek* by E. A Sophocles, forming vol. vii. (New Ser.) of the *Memoirs of the Amer. Academy*, Cambr., 1860, 4to, has been for some time out of print, but a new edition greatly enlarged and improved, is now in press (1869). Of the works named above, those of Bloomfield and Schirlitz are the least important: Bretschneider is rich in illustrations from the LXX., Josephus, Philo, and the Pseudepigrapha of the O. and N. T.; Wahl is particularly full on the particles, and in grammatical references; and the new Lexicon of Grimm is characterized by good judgment, competent learning, and the exclusion of useless matter.

On the *synonyms* of the N. T. we have J. A. H. Tittmann, *De Syn. in N. T.* lib. I., II., Lips. 1829 –32, transl. by E. Craig, 2 vols. Edin. 1833–34; R. C. Trench, *Syn. of the N. T.*, 2 parts, reprinted N. Y. 1855–64, new ed. in 1 vol., Lond. 1865; and the work of Webster, referred to below.

On the *grammar* of the N. T., we may note also the works of Professor Stuart, Andover, 1834, 2d ed. 1841; W. Trollope, Lond. 1842; T. S. Green, *Treatise on the Gram. of the N. T.*, new ed. Lond. 1862 (first ed. 1842), containing some acute observations; Alex. Buttmann, *Gram. des neutest. Sprachidioms*, Berl. 1859 (valuable); S. C. Schirlitz, *Grundzüge der neutest. Grācitāt*, Giessen, 1861; K H. A. Lipsius, *Gram. Untersuchungen üb. d. bibl. Grācitāt* (only *über die Leseteichen*), Leipz. 1863; and William Webster, *Syntax and Synonyms of the Gr. Test.*, Lond. 1864, strangely extolling Schirlitz, and disparaging Winer. The 7th edition of Winer, superintended by Lünemann (Leipz. 1867), we have at last, thanks to Professor Thayer, in a really accurate translation (Andover, 1869). In the 3d ed. of Jelf's *Greek Grammar* (Oxf. 1861, 4th ed. 1868) particular attention is paid to the constructions of the Greek Testament. Professor W. W. Goodwin's *Syntax of the Moods and Tenses of the Greek Verb*, 2d ed. Cambr. 1865, though not often referring specially to the N. T., will be found of great value to the philological student. On the Greek article there is the well-known work of Bishop Middleton, Lond. 1808, reprinted N. Y. 1813, new ed. by Rose, Lond. 1855;

comp. Professor Stuart's *Hints and Cautions in the Bibl. Repos.* for April 1834, iv. 277–327, and C Winstanley, *Vindication of Certain Passages in the Com. Eng. Version of the N. T.*, addressed to *Granville Sharp, Esq.*, reprinted with additions, Cambr. 1819.

See further, on the language and style of the N. T., Planck, *De vera Natura et Indole Orat. Græcæ N. T.*, Gotting. 1810, 4to, transl. by Dr. Robinson in the *Bibl. Repos.* for Oct. 1831, i. 638–691. (In the same vol. of this periodical are other valuable articles bearing on the subject.) Also Klausen (*Danish* Clausen), *Hermeneutik d. N. T.*, Leipz. 1841, p. 337 ff.; Wilke, *Hermeneutik d. N. T.*, Leipz. 1843–44, and *Neutest. Rhetorik*, ibid. 1843; and Zezschwitz, *Profangrācitāt u. biblischer Sprachgeist* (1859).

Works on the style of particular writers of the N. T. might also be mentioned here; see, for example, the addition to JOHN, GOSPEL OF, vol. ii. p. 1439 *b*. See also J. D. Schulze, *Der schriftstellerische Werth u. Char. des Petrus, Judas u. Jacobus*, Weissenfels, 1802; ditto, *des Evang. Markus*, in Keil and Tzschirner's *Analekten*, Bde. ii., iii.; Gersdorf, *Beiträge zur Sprach-Charakteristik der Schriftsteller des N. T.*, Theil i. (Leipz. 1816; no more published); Holtzmann, *Die Synopt. Evangelien* (Leipz. 1863), pp. 271–358; and the various discussions on the genuineness of the Acts of the Apostles, the Pastoral Epistles of Paul, the authorship of the Epistle to the Hebrews, the 2d Epistle of Peter, and the Apocalypse, for which see the articles on the respective books.

The *Critical Greek and English Concordance to the N. T.*, by the late C. F. Hudson, which is announced for speedy publication (Boston, 1869), will be a valuable supplement to Bruder, giving the various readings of Griesbach, Lachmann, Tischendorf, and Tregelles, and at the same time preserving the best features of the *Englishman's Greek Concordance of the N. T.* It will be incomparably superior to Schmoller's recent work, which is very unsatisfactory.   A.

NEW YEAR. [TRUMPETS, FEAST OF.]

NEZI'AH (נְצִיחַ [*famous*, Fürst; *conquered*, Ges.]: Ναθιέ, [Vat. Ναcoυς,] Alex. Νεθιέ in Ezr.: Νιcια, [Vat. FA. Αcεια, Alex. Νειcεια,] in Neh.: *Nasia*). The descendants of Neziah were among the Nethinim who returned with Zerubbabel (Ezr. ii. 54; Neh. vii. 56). The name appears as NASITH in 1 Esdr. v. 32.

NE'ZIB (נְצִיב [*garrison, pillar*: Vat.]: Ναcειβ; [Rom. Ναcιβ:] Alex. Νεcιβ: *Nesib*), a city of Judah (Josh. xv. 43 only), in the district of the *Shefelah* or Lowland, one of the same group with Keilah and Mareshah. To Eusebius and Jerome it was evidently known. They place it on the road between Eleutheropolis and Hebron, 7 or 9 (Euseb.) miles from the former, and there it still stands under the almost identical name of *Beit Nāsib*, or *Chirbeh Nasib*, 2½ hours from *Beit Jibrin*, on a rising ground at the southern end of the *Wady es-Sūr*, and with Keilah and Mareshah within easy distance. It has been visited by Dr. Robinson (ii. 220, 221) and Tobler (*3te Wanderung*, 150). The former mentions the remains of ancient buildings, especially one of apparently remote age, 190 feet long by 30 broad. This, however — with the curious discrepancy which is so remarkable in Eastern explorers — is denied by the latter traveller, who states that " but for the ancient name no one would suspect this of being an ancient site."

Nezib[a] adds another to the number of places which, though enumerated as in the Lowland, have been found in the mountains. [JIPHTAH; KEI-LAH.]

G.

NIBHAZ (נִבְחָז, and in some MSS. נִבְחָן

and נִבְחָז [see below]: Νιβχάς [?] or [Alex.] Ναιβάς; for which there is substituted in some copies an entirely different name, 'Αβαα(ίρ, Ναβααζίρ, or 'Εβλαζίρ [Rom.], the latter being probably the more correct, answering to the Hebrew

נֶבֶּר־עֶצֶר, " grief of the ruler": Nebahaz), a deity of the Avites, introduced by them into Samaria in the time of Shalmaneser (2 K. xvi. 31). There is no certain information as to the character of the deity, or the form of the idol so named. The Rabbins derived the name from a Hebrew root nâbach (נָבַח), " to bark," and hence assigned to it the figure of a dog, or a dog-headed man. There is no a priori improbability in this; the Egyptians worshipped the dog (Plut. De Is. 44), and according to the opinion current among the Greeks and Romans they represented Anubis as a dog-headed man, though Wilkinson (Anc. Egypt. i. 440, Second Series) asserts that this was a mistake, the head being in reality that of a jackal. Some indications of the worship of the dog have been found in Syria, a colossal figure of a dog having formerly existed between Berytus and Tripolis (Winer, Reulx. s. v.). It is still more to the point to observe that on one of the slabs found at Khorsabad and represented by Botta (pl. 141), we have the front of a temple depicted with an animal near the entrance, which can be nothing else than a bitch suckling a puppy, the head of the animal having, however, disappeared. The worship of idols representing the human body surmounted by the head of an animal (as in the well-known case of Nisroch) was common among the Assyrians. According to another equally unsatisfactory theory, Nibhaz is identified with the god of the nether world of the Sabian worship (Gesen. Thesau. p. 842).   W. L. B.

NIBSHAN (with the definite article,

הַנִּבְשָׁן [the furnace, Fürst; soft soil, Ges.]: Ναφλαζών; Alex. Νεβσαν: Nebsan). One of the six cities of Judah (Josh. xv. 62) which were in the district of the Midbar (A. V. " wilderness "), which probably in this one case only designates the depressed region on the immediate shore of the Dead Sea, usually in the Hebrew Scriptures called the Arábâh. [Vol. ii. p. 1491 a.] Under the name of Nempsan or Nebsan it is mentioned by Eusebius and Jerome in the Onomasticon, but with no attempt to fix its position. Nor does any subsequent traveller appear to have either sought for or discovered any traces of the name.   G.

NICA'NOR (Νικάνωρ [conqueror]: Nicanor), the son of Patroclus (2 Macc. viii. 9), a general

who was engaged in the Jewish wars under Antiochus Epiphanes and Demetrius I. He took part in the first expedition of Lysias, B C. 166 (1 Macc. iii. 38), and was defeated with his fellow-commander at Emmaus (1 Macc. iv.; cf. 2 Macc. viii. 9 ff.). After the death of Antiochus Eupator and Lysias, he stood high in the favor of Demetrius (1 Macc. vii. 26), who appointed him governor of Judæa (2 Macc. xiv. 12), a command which he readily undertook as one " who bare deadly hate unto Israel" (1 Macc. vii. 26). At first he seems to have endeavored to win the confidence of Judas, but when his treacherous designs were discovered he had recourse to violence. A battle took place at Capharsalama, which was indecisive in its results; but shortly after Judas met him at Adasa (B. C. 161), and he fell " first in the battle." A general rout followed, and the 13th of Adar, on which the engagement took place, " the day before Mardocheus' day," was ordained to be kept forever as a festival (1 Macc. vii. 49; 2 Macc. xv. 36).

There are some discrepancies between the narratives in the two books of Maccabees as to Nicanor. In 1 Macc. he is represented as acting with deliberate treachery: in 2 Macc. he is said to have been won over to a sincere friendship with Judas, which was only interrupted by the intrigues of Alcimus, who induced Demetrius to repeat his orders for the capture of the Jewish hero (2 Macc. xiv. 23 ff.). Internal evidence is decidedly in favor of 1 Macc. According to Josephus (Ant. xii. 10, § 4), who does not, however, appear to have had any other authority than 1 Macc. before him, Judas was defeated at Capharsalama; and though his account is obviously inaccurate (ἀναγκάζει τὸν Ἰούδαν . . . ἐπὶ τὴν ἄκραν φεύγειν), the events which followed (1 Macc. vii. 33 ff.; comp. 2 Macc. xiv. 33 ff.) seem at least to indicate that Judas gained no advantage. In 2 Macc. this engagement is not noticed, but another is placed (2 Macc. xiv. 17) before the connection of Nicanor with Judas, while this was after it (1 Macc. vii. 27 ff.), in which " Simon Judas' brother " is said to have been " somewhat discomfited."

2. One of the first seven deacons (Acts vi. 5). According to the Pseudo-Hippolytus he was one of the seventy disciples, and " died at the time of the martyrdom of Stephen " (p. 953, ed. Migne).

B. F. W.

NICODE'MUS (Νικόδημος [conqueror of the people]: Nicodemus), a Pharisee, a ruler of the Jews, and c teacher of Israel (John iii. 1, 10), whose secret visit to our Lord was the occasion of the discourse recorded by St. John. The name was not uncommon among the Jews (Joseph. Ant. xiv. 3, § 2), and was no doubt borrowed from the Greeks. In the Talmud it appears under the form בקדימון, and some would derive it from בקי, innocent, דם, blood (i. e. " Sceleris purus "); Wetstein, N. T. i. 150. In the case of Nicodemus Ben Gorion, the name is derived by R. Nathan from a miracle which he is supposed to have performed (Otho, Lex. Rab. s. v.).

---

a The word netsib, identical with the above name, is several times employed for a garrison or an officer of the Philistines (see 1 Sam. x. 5. xiii. 3, 4; 1 Chr. xi. 16). This suggests the possibility of Nezib having been a Philistine place. But the application of the term t the Philistines, though frequent, is not exclusive.

b If originally a Hebrew name, probably from the same root as Bashan — a sandy soil.

c The article in John iii. 10 (ὁ διδάσκ.), is probably only generic, although Winer and Bp. Middleton suppose that it implies a rebuke.

Nicodemus is only mentioned by St. John, who narrates his nocturnal visit to Jesus, and the conversation which then took place, at which the Evangelist may himself have been present. The high station of Nicodemus as a member of the Jewish Sanhedrim, and the avowed scorn under which the rulers concealed their inward conviction (John iii. 2) that Jesus was a teacher sent from God, are sufficient to account for the secrecy of the interview. A constitutional timidity is discernible in the character of the inquiring Pharisee, which could not be overcome by his vacillating desire to befriend and acknowledge One whom he knew to be a Prophet, even if he did not at once recognize in him the promised Messiah. Thus the few words which he interposed against the rash injustice of his colleagues are cautiously rested on a general principle (John vii. 50), and betray no indication of his faith in the Galilean whom his sect despised. And even when the power of Christ's love, manifested on the cross, had made the most timid disciples bold, Nicodemus does not come forward with his splendid gifts of affection until the example had been set by one of his own rank, and wealth, and station in society (xix. 39).

In these three notices of Nicodemus a noble candor and a simple tone of truth shine out in the midst of hesitation and fear of man. We can therefore easily believe the tradition that after the resurrection (which would supply the last outward impulse necessary to confirm his faith and increase his courage) he became a professed disciple of Christ, and received baptism at the hands of Peter and John. All the rest that is recorded of him is highly uncertain. It is said, however, that the Jews, in revenge for his conversion, deprived him of his office, beat him cruelly, and drove him from Jerusalem; that Gamaliel, who was his kinsman, hospitably sheltered him until his death in a country house. and finally gave him honorable burial near the body of Stephen, where Gamaliel himself was afterwards interred. Finally, the three bodies are said to have been discovered on August 3, A. D. 415, which day was set apart by the Romish Church in honor of the event (Phot. *Biblioth. Cod.* 171; Lucian, *De S. Steph. inventione*).

The conversation of Christ with Nicodemus is appointed as the Gospel for Trinity Sunday. The choice at first sight may seem strange. There are in that discourse no mysterious numbers which might shadow forth truths in their simplest relations; no distinct and yet simultaneous actions of the divine persons; no separation of divine attributes. Yet the instinct[a] which dictated this choice was a right one. For it is in this conversation alone that we see how our Lord himself met the difficulties of a thoughtful man; how he checked, without noticing, the self-assumption of a teacher; how he lifted the half-believing mind to the light of nobler truth.

If the Nicodemus of St. John's Gospel be identical with the Nicodemus Ben Gorion of the Talmud, he must have lived till the fall of Jerusalem, which is not impossible, since the term γέρων, in John iii. 4, may not be intended to apply to Nicodemus himself. The arguments for their identification are that both are mentioned as Pharisees, wealthy, pious, and members of the Sanhedrim (*Taanith*,

f. 19, &c. See Otho, *Lex. Rab.* s. v.); and that in *Taanith* the original name (altered on the occasion of a miracle performed by Nicodemus in order to procure rain) is said to have been בוני, which is also the name of one of five Rabbinical disciples of Christ mentioned in *Sanhed.* f. 43, 1 (Otho, s. v. *Christus*). Finally, the family of this Nicodemus are said to have been reduced from great wealth to the most squalid and horrible poverty, which however may as well be accounted for by the fall of Jerusalem, as by the change of fortune resulting from an acceptance of Christianity.

On the Gospel of Nicodemus, see Fabricius, *Cod. Pseudepigr.* i. 213; Thilo, *Cod. Apocr.* i. 478. In some MSS. it is also called "The Acts of Pilate." It is undoubtedly spurious (as the conclusion of it sufficiently proves), and of very little value. F. W. F.

* Nicodemus is called a "ruler of the Jews" (ἄρχων τῶν Ἰουδαίων) in John iii. 1; and as that title (ἄρχων) is given in some passages (John vii. 26; Acts iii. 17, &c.) to members of the Sanhedrim, it has been inferred that he was one of that body. He was probably also a scribe or teacher of the Law (διδάσκαλος τοῦ Ἰσραήλ, John iii. 10 = νομοδιδάσκαλος); and hence belonged to that branch of the Council which represented the learned class of the nation. Of the three occurrences (see above) in which Nicodemus appears in the Gospel-history, the second occupies an intermediate position between the first and the third as to the phase of character which they severally exhibit; and in this respect, as Tholuck suggests, the narrative is seen to be "psychologically true" (*Evang. Johannis*, p. 205, 6te Aufl.). We have no means of deciding whether Nicodemus was present in the Sanhedrim at the time of the Saviour's arraignment and trial before that court. If he was present he may have been too undecided to interpose any remonstrance (none is recorded), or may have deemed it unavailing amid so much violence and passion. Stier would find in οἴδαμεν as plural a characteristic shrinking from anything like a direct personal avowal of his own belief (*Reden Jesu*, iv. 11, 4te Aufl.); but, more probably, he meant, in this way, to recognize more strongly the ample evidence furnished by Christ's miracles that He was a teacher sent from God. In this confession perhaps he associates with himself some of his own rank who were already known to him as secret believers (see xli. 42; xix. 38).

For a list of writers on the character of Nicodemus and his interview with Christ, see Hase's *Leben Jesu*, § 52 (4te Aufl.). On the apocryphal Gospel of Nicodemus see the articles on the Apocryphal Gospels generally by Hofmann in Herzog's *Real-Encyk.* xii. 325–327; by Bishop Ellicott in the *Cambridge Essays* for 1856, p. 161 ff.; and by C. E. Stowe, D. D., in the *Bibl. Sacra*, ix. p. 79 f.; and particularly Tischendorf, *Evangelia Apocrypha* (Lips. 1853), pp. liv. ff., 203 ff. H.

NICOLAITANS (Νικολαΐται: *Nicolaïta*). The question how far the sect that is mentioned by this name in Rev. ii. 6, 15, was connected with the Nicolas of Acts vi. 5, and the traditions that have gathered round his name, will be discussed below. [NICOLAS.] It will here be considered how far we can get at any distinct notion of what the sect itself was, and in what relation it stood to the life of the Apostolic age.

It has been suggested as one step towards this

---

[a] The writer is indebted for this remark to a MS. sermon by Mr. Westcott.

result that the name before us was symbolic rather than historical. The Greek Νικόλαος is, it has been said, an approximate equivalent to the Hebrew Balaam, the lord (Vitringa, deriving it from בַּעַל): or, according to another derivation, the devourer of the people (so Hengstenberg. as from בָּלַע).[a] If we accept this explanation we have to deal with one sect instead of two — we are able to compare with what we find in Rev. ii. the incidental notices of the characteristics of the followers of Balaam in Jude and 2 Peter, and our task is proportionately an easier one. It may be urged indeed that this theory rests upon a false or at least a doubtful etymology (Gesenius, s. v. בִּלְעָם, makes it = peregrinus), and that the message to the Church of Pergamos (Rev. ii. 14, 15) appears to recognize "those that hold the doctrine of Balaam," and "those that hold the doctrine of the Nicolaitans," as two distinct bodies. There is, however, a sufficient answer to both these objections. (1.) The whole analogy of the mode of teaching which lays stress on the significance of names would lead us to look, not for philological accuracy, but for a broad, strongly-marked paronomasia, such as men would recognize and accept. It would be enough for those who were to hear the message that they should perceive the meaning of the two words to be identical.[b] (2.) A closer inspection of Rev. ii. 15 would show that the οὗτος ἔχεις, κ. τ. λ. imply the resemblance of the teaching of the Nicolaitans with that of the historical Balaam mentioned in the preceding verse, rather than any kind of contrast.

We are now in a position to form a clearer judgment of the characteristics of the sect. It comes before us as presenting the ultimate phase of a great controversy, which threatened at one time to destroy the unity of the Church, and afterwards to taint its purity. The controversy itself was inevitable as soon as the Gentiles were admitted, in any large numbers, into the Church of Christ. Were the new converts to be brought into subjection to the whole Mosaic law? Were they to give up their old habits of life altogether — to withdraw entirely from the social gatherings of their friends and kinsmen? Was there not the risk, if they continued to join in them, of their eating, consciously or unconsciously, of that which had been slain in the sacrifices of a false worship, and of thus sharing in the idolatry? The apostles and elders at Jerusalem met the question calmly and wisely. The burden of the Law was not to be imposed on the Gentile disciples. They were to abstain, among other things, from "meats offered to idols" and from "fornication" (Acts xv. 20, 29), and this decree was welcomed as the great charter of the Church's freedom. Strange as the close union of the moral and the positive commands may seem to us, it did not seem so to the synod at Jerusalem. The two sins were very closely allied, often even in the closest proximity of time and place. The fathomless impurity which overspread the empire made the one almost as inseparable as the other from its daily social life.

The messages to the Churches of Asia and the later Apostolic Epistles (2 Peter and Jude) indicate that the two evils appeared at that period also in close alliance. The teachers of the Church branded them with a name which expressed their true character. The men who did and taught such things were followers of Balaam (2 Pet. ii. 15; Jude 11). They, like the false prophet of Pethor, united brave words with evil deeds. They made their "liberty" a cloak at once for cowardice and licentiousness. In a time of persecution, when the eating or not eating of things sacrificed to idols was more than ever a crucial test of faithfulness, they persuaded men more than ever that it was a thing indifferent (Rev. ii. 13, 14). This was bad enough, but there was a yet worse evil. Mingling themselves in the orgies of idolatrous feasts, they brought the impurities of those feasts into the meetings of the Christian Church. There was the most imminent risk that its Agapæ might become as full of abominations as the Bacchanalia of Italy had been (2 Pet. ii. 12, 13, 18; Jude 7, 8; comp. Liv. xxxix. 8–19). Their sins had already brought scandal and discredit on the "way of truth." And all this was done, it must be remembered, not simply as an indulgence of appetite, but as part of a system, supported by a "doctrine," accompanied by the boast of a prophetic illumination (2 Pet. ii. 1). The trance of the son of Beor and the sensual debasement into which he led the Israelites were strangely reproduced.

These were the characteristics of the followers of Balaam, and, worthless as most of the traditions about Nicolas may be, they point to the same distinctive evils. Even in the absence of any teacher of that name, it would be natural enough, as has been shown above, that the Hebrew name of ignominy should have its Greek equivalent. If there were such a teacher, whether the proselyte of Antioch or another,[c] the application of the name to his followers would be proportionately more pointed. It confirms the view which has been taken of their character to find that stress is laid in the first instance on the "deeds" of the Nicolaitans. To hate those deeds is a sign of life in a Church that otherwise is weak and faithless (Rev. ii. 6). To tolerate them is well nigh to forfeit the glory of having been faithful under persecution (Rev. ii. 14, 15). (Comp. Neander's Apostelgesch. p. 620; Gieseler's Eccl. Hist. § 29; Hengstenberg and Alford on Rev. ii. 6; Stier, Words of the Risen Saviour, x.)   E. H. P.

---

[a] Cocceius (Cogitat. in Rev. ii. 6) has the credit of being the first to suggest this identification of the Nicolaitans with the followers of Balaam. He has been followed by the elder Vitringa (Dissert. de Argum Epist. Petri poster. in Hase's Thesaurus, ii. 987), Hengstenberg (in loc.), Stier (Words of the Risen Lord, p. 125, Eng. transl), and others. Lightfoot (Hor. Heb. in Act. Apost. vi. 5) suggests another and more startling paronomasia. The word, in his view, was chosen, as identical in sound with נִיכוֹלָא, "let us eat," and as thus marking out the special characteristic of the sect.

[b] Vitringa (l. c.) finds another instance of this indirect expression of feeling in the peculiar form, "Balaam the son of Bosor," in 2 Pet. ii. 15. The substitution of the latter name for the Beor of the LXX. originated, according to his conjecture, in the wish to point to his antitype in the Christian Church as a true בֶּן־בָּשָׂר, a filius carnis.

[c] It is noticeable (though the documents themselves are not of much weight as evidence) that in two instances the Nicolaitans are said to be "falsely so called" (ψευδώνυμοι, Ignat. ad Trall. xi., Const Apost. vi. 8).

NIC'OLAS (Νικόλαος [*conqueror of the people*]: *Nicolaus*), Acts vi. 5 A native of Antioch, and a proselyte to the Jewish faith. When the church was still confined to Jerusalem he became a convert; and being a man of honest report, full of the Holy Ghost and of wisdom, he was chosen by the whole multitude of the disciples to be one of the first seven deacons, and he was ordained by the Apostles, A. D. 33.

A sect of Nicolaitans is mentioned in Rev. ii. 6, 15; and it has been questioned whether this Nicolas was connected with them, and if so, how closely.

The Nicolaitans themselves, at least as early as the time of Irenæus (*Contr. Hær.* i. 26, § 3), claimed him as their founder. Epiphanius, an inaccurate writer, relates (*Adv. Hær.* i. 2, § 25, p. 76) some details of the life of Nicolas the deacon, and describes him as gradually sinking into the grossest impurity, and becoming the originator of the Nicolaitans and other immoral sects. Stephen Gobar (Photii *Bib'ioth.* § 232, p. 291, ed. 1824) states — and the statement is corroborated by the recently discovered *Philosophumena*, bk. vii. § 36 — that Hippolytus agreed with Epiphanius in his unfavorable view of Nicolas. The same account is believed, at least to some extent, by Jerome (*Ep.* 147, t. i. p. 1032, ed. Vallars. etc.) and other writers in the 4th century. But it is irreconcilable with the traditionary account of the character of Nicolas, given by Clement of Alexandria (*Strom.* iii. 4, p. 187, Sylb. and *apud Euseb. H. E.* iii. 29; see also Hammond, *Annot.* on Rev. ii. 4), an earlier and more discriminating writer than Epiphanius. He states that Nicolas led a chaste life and brought up his children in purity, that on a certain occasion having been sharply reproved by the Apostles as a jealous husband, he repelled the charge by offering to allow his wife to become the wife of any other person, and that he was in the habit of repeating a saying which is ascribed to the Apostle Matthias also, — that it is our duty to fight against the flesh and to abuse (παραχρῆσθαι) it. His words were perversely interpreted by the Nicolaitans as an authority for their immoral practices. Theodoret (*Hæret. Fab.* iii. 1) in his account of the sect repeats the foregoing statement of Clement; and charges the Nicolaitans with false dealing in borrowing the name of the deacon. Ignatius,[a] who was contemporary with Nicolas, is said by Stephen Gobar to have given the same account as Clement, Eusebius, and Theodoret, touching the personal character of Nicolas. Among modern critics, Cotelerius in a note on *Constit. Apost.* vi. 8, after reciting the various authorities, seems to lean towards the favorable view of the character of Nicolas. Professor Burton (*Lectures on Ecclesiastical History*, Lect. xii. p. 364, ed. 1833) is of opinion that the origin of the term Nicolaitans is uncertain; and that, "though Nicolas the deacon has been mentioned as their founder, the evidence is extremely slight which would convict that person himself of any immoralities." Tillemont (*H. E.* ii. 47), possibly influenced by the fact that no honor is paid to the memory of Nicolas by any branch of the Church, allows perhaps too much weight to the testimony against him; rejects peremptorily Cassian's statement — to which Neander (*Planting of the Church*, bk. v. p. 390, ed. Bohn) gives his adhesion — that some other Nicolas was

the founder of the sect; and concludes that if not the actual founder, he was so unfortunate as to give occasion to the formation of the sect, by his indiscreet speaking. Grotius's view, as given in a note on Rev. ii. 6, is substantially the same as that of Tillemont.

The name Balaam is perhaps (but see Gesen. *Thes.* 210) capable of being interpreted as a Hebrew equivalent of the Greek Nicolas. Some commentators think that this is alluded to by St. John in Rev. ii. 14; and C. Vitringa (*Obs. Sacr.* iv. 9) argues forcibly in support of this opinion.

W. T. B.

NICOP'OLIS (Νικόπολις [*city of victory*]: *Nicopolis*) is mentioned in Tit. iii. 12, as the place where, at the time of writing the epistle, St. Paul was intending to pass the coming winter, and where he wished Titus to meet him. Whether either or both of these purposes were accomplished we cannot tell. Titus was at this time in Crete (Tit. i. 5). The subscription to the epistle assumes that the Apostle was at Nicopolis when he wrote; but we cannot conclude this from the form of expression. We should rather infer that he was elsewhere, possibly at Ephesus or Corinth. He urges that no time should be lost (σπούδασον ἐλθεῖν); hence we conclude that winter was near.

Nothing is to be found in the epistle itself to determine which Nicopolis is here intended. There were cities of this name in Asia, Africa, and Europe. If we were to include all the theories which have been respectably supported, we should be obliged to write at least three articles. One Nicopolis was in Thrace, near the borders of Macedonia. The subscription (which, however, is of no authority) fixes on this place, calling it the Macedonian Nicopolis: and such is the view of Chrysostom and Theodoret. De Wette's objection to this opinion (*Pastoral-Briefe*, p. 21), that the place did not exist till Trajan's reign, appears to be a mistake. Another Nicopolis was in Cilicia; and Schrader (*Der Apostel Paulus*, i. pp. 115–119) pronounces for this; but this opinion is connected with a peculiar theory regarding the Apostle's journeys. We have little doubt that Jerome's view is correct, and that the Pauline Nicopolis was the celebrated city of Epirus ("scribit Apostolus de Nicopoli, quæ in Actiaco littore sita," Hieron. *Proœm.* ix. 195). For arrangements of St. Paul's journeys, which will harmonize with this, and with the other facts of the Pastoral Epistles, see Birks, *Horæ Apostolicæ*, pp. 296–304; and Conybeare and Howson, *Life and Epp. of St. Paul* (2d ed.), ii. 564–573. It is very possible, as is observed there, that St. Paul was arrested at Nicopolis and taken thence to Rome for his final trial.

This city (the "City of Victory") was built by Augustus in memory of the battle of Actium, and on the ground which his army occupied before the engagement. It is a curious and interesting circumstance, when we look at the matter from a Biblical point of view, that many of the handsomest parts of the town were built by Herod the Great (Joseph. *Ant.* xvi. 5, § 3). It is likely enough that many Jews lived there. Moreover, it was conveniently situated for apostolic journeys in the eastern parts of Achaia and Macedonia, and also to the northwards, where churches perhaps were founded. St. Paul had long before preached the

---

a   Usher conjectures that this reference is to the interpolated copy of the Epistle to the Trallians, ch. xi.

(*De Ignatii Epistolis*, § 6, apud Coteler. *Patr. Apost.* ii. 195, ed. 1724.)

Gospel, at least on the confines of Illyricum (Rom. xv. 19), and soon after the very period under consideration Titus himself was sent on a mission to Dalmatia (2 Tim. iv. 10).

Nicopolis was on a peninsula to the west of the Bay of Actium, in a low and unhealthy situation, and it is now a very desolate place. The remains have been often described. We may refer to Leake's *Northern Greece*, i. 178, and iii. 491; Bowen's *Athos and Epirus*, 211; Wolfe in *Journ. of R. Geog. Soc.* iii. 92; Merivale's *Rome*, iii. 327, 328; Wordsworth's *Greece*, 229-232. In the last mentioned work, and in the *Dict. of Greek and Roman Geog.* maps of the place will be found.

J. S. H.

NI'GER (Νίγερ [*black*]: *Niger*) is the additional or distinctive name given to the Symeon (Συμεών), who was one of the teachers and prophets in the Church at Antioch (Acts xiii. 1). He is not known except in that passage. The name was a common one among the Romans; and the conjecture that he was an African proselyte, and was called Niger on account of his complexion, is unnecessary as well as destitute otherwise of any support. His name, Symeon, shows that he was a Jew by birth; and as in other similar cases (*e. g.* Saul, Paul — Silas, Silvanus) he may be supposed to have taken the other name as more convenient in his intercourse with foreigners. He is mentioned second among the five who officiated at Antioch, and perhaps we may infer that he had some preëminence among them in point of activity and influence. It is impossible to decide (though Meyer makes the attempt) who of the number were prophets (προφῆται), and who were teachers (διδάσκαλοι).

H. B. H.

NIGHT. The period of darkness, from sunset to sunrise, including the morning and evening twilight, was known to the Hebrews by the term לַיִל, *layil*, or לַיְלָה, *layēlâh*. It is opposed to "day," the period of light (Gen. i. 5). Following the oriental sunset is the brief evening twilight (נֶשֶׁף, *nesheph*, Job xxiv. 15, rendered "night" in Is. v. 11, xxi. 4, lix. 10), when the stars appeared (Job iii. 9). This is also called "evening" (עֶרֶב, *'ereb*, Prov. vii. 9, rendered "night" in Gen. xlix. 27, Job vii. 4), but the term which especially denotes the evening twilight is עֲלָטָה, *ŭlâtâh* (Gen xv. 17, A. V. "dark;" Ez. xii. 6, 7, 12). *'Ereb* also denotes the time just before sunset (Deut. xxiii. 11; Josh. viii. 29), when the women went to draw water (Gen. xxiv. 11), and the decline of the day is called "the turning of evening" (פְּנוֹת עֶרֶב, *pēnôth 'ereb*, Gen. xxiv. 63), the time of prayer. This period of the day must also be that which is described as "night" when Boaz winnowed his barley in the evening breeze (Ruth iii. 2), the cool of the day (Gen. iii. 8), when the shadows begin to fall (Jer. vi. 4), and the wolves prowl about (Hab. i. 8; Zeph. iii. 3). The time of midnight (חֲצִי הַלַּיְלָה, *châtsî hallayēlâh*, Ruth iii. 8, and חֲצוֹת הַלַּיְלָה, *châtsôth hallayēlâh*, Ex. xi. 4) or greatest darkness is called in

פַּתְרִיעָנֶה *

Prov. vii. 9 "the pupil of night" (אִישׁוֹן לַיְלָה, *ishôn laylâh*, A. V. "black night"). The period between midnight and the morning twilight was generally selected for attacking an enemy by surprise (Judg. vii. 19.) The morning twilight is denoted by the same term, *nesheph*, as the evening twilight, and is unmistakably intended in 1 Sam. xxxi. 12; Job vii. 4; Ps. cxix. 147; possibly also in Is. v. 11. With sunrise the night ended. In one passage, Job xxvi. 10, חֹשֶׁךְ, *chôshec*, "darkness," is rendered "night" in the A. V., but is correctly given in the margin.

For the artificial divisions of the night see the articles DAY and WATCHES.

W. A. W.

NIGHT-HAWK (תַּחְמָס, *tachmâs*: γλαύξ: *noctua*). Bochart (*Hieroz.* ii. 830) has endeavored to prove that the Hebrew word, which occurs only (Lev. xi. 16; Deut. xiv. 15) amongst the list of unclean birds, denotes the "male ostrich," the preceding term, *bath-yaǎnâh* [a] (*owl*, A. V.), signifying the female bird. The etymology of the word points to some bird of prey, though there is great uncertainty as to the particular species indicated. The LXX., Vulg., and perhaps Onkelos, understand some kind of "owl;" most of the Jewish doctors indefinitely render the word "a rapacious bird:" Gesenius (*Thes.* s. v.) and Rosenmüller (*Schol. ad Lev.* xi. 16) follow Bochart. Bochart's explanation is grounded on an overstrained interpretation of the etymology of the verb *châmas*, the root of *tachmâs;* he restricts the meaning of the root to the idea of acting "unjustly" or "deceitfully," and thus comes to the conclusion that the "unjust bird" is the male ostrich [OSTRICH]. Without stopping to consider the etymology of the word further than to refer the reader to Gesenius, who gives as the first meaning of *châmas* "he acted violently," and to the Arabic *chamash*, "to wound with claws," [b] it is not at all probable that Moses should have specified both the *male* and *female* ostrich in a list which was no doubt intended to be as comprehensive as possible. The not unfrequent occurrence of the expression "after their kind" is an argument in favor of this assertion. Michaelis believes some kind of swallow (*Hirundo*) is intended: the word used by the Targum of Jonathan is by Kitto (*Pict. Bib.* Lev. xi. 16) and by Oedmann (*Vermisch. Samm.* i. p. 3, c. iv.) referred to the swallow, though the last-named authority says, "it is uncertain, however, what Jonathan really meant." Buxtorf (*Lex. Rabbin.* s. v. חֲטִיפִיתָא) translates the word used by Jonathan, "a name of a rapacious bird, *harpyja*." It is not easy to see what claim the swallow can have to represent the *tachmâs*, neither is it at all probable that so small a bird should have been noticed in the Levitical law. The rendering of the A. V. rests on no authority, though from the absurd properties which, from the time of Aristotle, have been ascribed to the night-hawk or goat-sucker, and the superstitions connected with this bird, its claim is not so entirely destitute of every kind of evidence.

As the LXX. and Vulg. are agreed that *tachmas* denotes some kind of owl, we believe it is safer to follow these versions than modern commentators.

<hr>

[b] خمش‎ scalpsit, unguibus vulneravit faciem See Freytag s. v.

The Greek γλαύξ is used by Aristotle for some common species of owl, in all probability for the *Strix fl immea* (white owl), or the *Syrnium stridula* (tawny owl); [a]. the Veneto-Greek reads *νυκτικόραξ*. a synonym of ὦτος, Aristot., *i. e.* the *Otus vulgaris*, Flem. (long-eared owl): this is the species which Oedmann (see above) identifies with *tichmâs*. "The name," he says, "indicates a bird which exercises power, but the force of the power is in the Arabic root *chamash*, ' to tear a face with claws.' Now, it is well known in the East that there is a species of owl of which people believe that it glides into chambers by night and tears the flesh off the faces of sleeping children." Hasselquist (*Trav.* p. 196, Lond. 1766) alludes to this nightly terror, but he calls it the "Oriental owl" (*Strix Orientalis*), and clearly distinguishes it from the *Strix alus*, Lin. The Arabs in Egypt call this infant-killing owl *massuen*, the Syrians *bana*. It is believed to be identical with the *Syrnium stridula*, but what foundation there may be for the belief in its child-killing propensities we know not. It is probable that some common species of owl is denoted by *tachmâs*, perhaps the *Strix flammea* or the *Athene meridionalis*, which is extremely common in Palestine and Egypt. [OWL.]   W. H.

* NIGHT-MONSTER, Is. xxxiv. 14, marg. [OWL.]

NILE. 1. *Names of the Nile.* — The Hebrew names of the Nile, excepting one that is of ancient Egyptian origin, all distinguish it from other rivers. With the Hebrews the Euphrates, as the great stream of their primitive home, was always " the river," and even the long sojourn in Egypt could not put the Nile in its place. Most of their geographical terms and ideas are, however, evidently traceable to Canaan, the country of the Hebrew language. Thus the sea, as lying on the west, gave its name to the west water. It was only in such an exceptional case as that of the Euphrates, which had no rival in Palestine, that the Hebrews seem to have retained the ideas of their older country. These circumstances lend no support to the idea that the Shemites and their language came originally from Egypt. The Hebrew names of the Nile are *Shichôr*, " the black," a name perhaps of the same sense as Nile; *Yeôr*, "the river," a word originally Egyptian; "the river of Egypt;" "the Nachal of Egypt" (if this appellation designate the Nile, and Nachal be a proper name); and "the rivers of Cush," or "Ethiopia." It must be observed that the word Nile nowhere occurs in the A. V.

(*a.*) *Shichôr*, שִׁיחוֹר, שִׁחוֹר, שִׁחֹר, שִׁחֹר, " the black," from שָׁחַר, " he or it was or became black." The idea of blackness conveyed by this word has, as we should expect in Hebrew, a wide sense, applying not only to the color of the hair (Lev. xiii. 31, 37), but also to that of a face tanned by the sun (Cant. i. 5, 6), and that of a skin black through disease (Job xxx. 30). It seems, however, to be indicative of a very dark color; for it is said in the Lamentations, as to the famished Nazarites in the besieged city, "Their visage is darker than blackness" (iv. 8). That the Nile is meant by Shihor is evident from it mention as equivalent to *Yeôr*, "the river," and as a great river, where Isaiah says of Tyre, "And by great waters, the sowing of Shihor, the harvest of the river (יְאֹר) [is] her revenue" (xxiii. 3); from its being put as the western boundary of the Promised Land (Josh. xiii. 3; 1 Chr. xiii. 5), instead of "the river of Egypt" (Gen. xv. 18); and from its being spoken of as the great stream of Egypt, just as the Euphrates was of Assyria (Jer. ii. 18). If, but this is by no means certain, the name Nile, Νεῖλος, be really indicative of the color of the river, it must be compared with the Sanskrit नील, *nila*, " blue " especially, probably " dark blue," also even " black," as नीलपंक, *nilapanka*, " black mud," and must be considered to be the Indo-European equivalent of Shihor. The signification " blue " is noteworthy, especially as a great confluent, which most nearly corresponds to the Nile in Egypt, is called the Blue River, or, by Europeans, the Blue Nile.

(*b.*) *Yeôr*, יְאֹר, יְאוֹר, is the same as the ancient Egyptian ATUR, AUR, and the Coptic ⲉⲓⲉⲣⲟ, ⲓⲁⲣⲟ, ⲓⲁⲣⲱ (M), ⲓⲉⲣⲟ (S). It is important to notice that the second form of the ancient Egyptian name alone is preserved in the later language, the second radical of the first having been lost, as in the Hebrew form; so that, on this double evidence, it is probable that this commoner form was in use among the people from early times. *Yeôr*, in the singular, is used of the Nile alone, excepting in a passage in Daniel (xii. 5, 6, 7), where another river, perhaps the Tigris (comp. x. 4), is intended by it. In the plural, יְאֹרִים, this name is applied to the branches and canals of the Nile (Ps. lxxviii. 44; Ez. xxix. 3 ff., xxx. 12), and perhaps tributaries also, with, in some places, the addition of the names of the country, Mitsraim, Matsor, יְאֹרֵי מִצְרַיִם (Is. vii. 18, A. V. "rivers of Egypt"), יְאֹרֵי מָצוֹר (xix. 6, " brooks of defence;" xxxvii. 25,[b] " rivers of the besieged places "); but it is also used of streams or channels, in a general sense, when no particular ones are indicated (see Is. xxxiii. 21; Job xxviii. 10). It is thus evident that this name specially designates the Nile; and although properly meaning a river, and even used with that signification, it is probably to be regarded as a proper name when applied to the Egyptian river. The latter inference may perhaps be drawn from the constant mention of the Euphrates as " the river;" but it is to be observed that Shihor, or " the river of Egypt," is used when the Nile and the Euphrates are spoken of together, as though *Yeôr* could not be well employed for the former, with the ordinary term for river, *nâhâr*, for the latter.[c]

(*c.*) " The river of Egypt," נְהַר מִצְרַיִם, is mentioned with the Euphrates in the promise of

---

[a] Not to be confounded with the *Nycticorax* of modern ornithology, which is a genus of *Ardeidæ* (herons).

[b] In Is. xxxvii. 25 the reference seems to be to an Assyrian conquest of Egypt.

[c] The Nile was probably mentioned by this name in the original of Ecclesiasticus xxiv. 27, where the Greek text reads ὡς φῶς, יְאֹר having been misunderstood (Gesenius, *Thes. s. v.*).

the extent of the land to be given to Abraham's posterity, the two limits of which were to be " the river of Egypt " and " the great river, the river Euphrates " (Gen. xv. 18).

(d.) " The Nachal of Egypt," בַּחַל מִצְרַיִם, has generally been understood to mean " the torrent " or " brook of Egypt," and to designate a desert stream at Rhinocorura, now El-'Areesh, on the eastern border.   Certainly בַּחַל usually signifies a stream or torrent, not a river; and when a river, one of small size, and dependent upon mountain-rain or snow; but as it is also used for a valley, corresponding to the Arabic *wadee* (وَادِي), which is in like manner employed in both senses, it may apply like it, in the case of the Guadalquivir, etc., to great rivers.   This name must signify the Nile, for it occurs in cases parallel to those where Shihor is employed (Num. xxxiv. 5; Josh. xv. 4, 47; 1 K. viii. 65; 2 K. xxiv. 7; Is. xxvii. 12), both designating the easternmost or Pelusiac branch of the river as the border of the Philistine territory, where the Egyptians equally put the border of their country towards Kanaan or Kanana (Canaan).   It remains for us to decide whether the name signify the " brook of Egypt," or whether Nachal be a Hebrew form of Nile.   On the one side may be urged the unlikelihood that the middle radical should not be found in the Indo-European equivalents, although it is not one of the most permanent letters; on the other, that it is improbable that *nahar* " river " and *nachal* " brook " would be used for the same stream.   If the latter be here a proper name, Νεῖλος must be supposed to be the same word; and the meaning of the Greek as well as the Hebrew name would remain doubtful, for we could not then positively decide on an Indo-European signification.   The Hebrew word *nachal* might have been adopted as very similar in sound to an original proper name; and this idea is supported by the forms of various Egyptian words in the Bible, which are susceptible of Hebrew etymologies in consequence of a slight change.   It must, however, be remembered that there are traces of a Semitic language, apparently distinct from Hebrew, in geographical names in the east of Lower Egypt, probably dating from the Shepherd-period; and therefore we must not, if we take *nachal* to be here Semitic, restrict its meaning to that which it bears or could bear in Hebrew.

(e.) " The rivers of Cush," נַהֲרֵי כוּשׁ, are alone mentioned in the extremely difficult prophecy contained in Is. xviii.   From the use of the plural, a single stream cannot be meant, and we must suppose " the rivers of Ethiopia " to be the confluents or tributaries of the Nile.   Gesenius (*Lex.* s. v. נָהָר) makes them the Nile and the Astaborus.   Without attempting to explain this prophecy, it is interesting to remark that the expression, ' Whose land the rivers have spoiled " (vv. 2, 7), .f it apply to any Ethiopian nation, may refer to the ruin of great part of Ethiopia, for a long distance above the First Cataract, in consequence of the fall of the level of the river.   This change has been effected through the breaking down of a barrier at that cataract, or at Silsilis, by which the valley has been placed above the reach of the

fertilizing annual deposit.   The Nile is sometimes poetically called a sea, יָם (Is. xviii. 2; Nah. iii. 8; Job. xli. 31; but we cannot agree with Gesenius, *Thes.* s. v., that it is intended in Is. xix. 5): this, however, can scarcely be considered to be one of its names.

It will be instructive to mention the present appellations of the Nile in Arabic, which may illustrate the Scripture terms.   By the Arabs it is called Bahr en-Neel, " the river Nile," the word " bahr " being applied to seas and the greatest rivers.   The Egyptians call it Bahr, or " the river " alone; and call the inundation En-Neel, or " the Nile."   This latter use of what is properly a name of the river resembles the use of the plural of *Yeôr* in the Bible for the various channels or even streams of Nile-water.

With the ancient Egyptians, the river was sacred, and had, besides its ordinary name already given, a sacred name, under which it was worshipped, HAPEE, or HAPEE-MU, " the abyss," or " the abyss of waters," or " the hidden."   Corresponding to the two regions of Egypt, the Upper Country and the Lower, the Nile was called HAPEE-RES, " the Southern Nile," and HAPEE-MEHEET, " the Northern Nile," the former name applying to the river in Nubia as well as in Upper Egypt.   The god Nilus was one of the lesser divinities.   He is represented as a stout man having woman's breasts, and is sometimes painted red to denote the river during its rise and inundation, or High Nile, and sometimes blue, to denote it during the rest of the year, or Low Nile.   Two figures of HAPEE are frequently represented on each side of the throne of a royal statue, or in the same place in a bas-relief, binding it with water-plants, as though the prosperity of the kingdom depended upon the produce of the river.   The name HAPEE, perhaps, in these cases, HEPEE, was also applied to one of the four children of Osiris, called by Egyptologers the genii of AMENT or Hades, and to the bull Apis, the most revered of all the sacred animals.   The genius does not seem to have any connection with the river, excepting indeed that Apis was sacred to Osiris   Apis was worshipped with a reference to the inundation, perhaps because the myth of Osiris, the conflict of good and evil, was supposed to be represented by the struggle of the fertilizing river or inundation with the desert and the sea, the first threatening the whole valley, and the second wasting it along the northern coast.

2. *Description of the Nile.* — We cannot as yet determine the length of the Nile, although recent discoveries have narrowed the question.   There is scarcely a doubt that its largest confluent is fed by the great lakes on and south of the equator.   It has been traced upwards for about 2,700 miles, measured by its course, not in a direct line, and its extent is probably upwards of 1,000 miles more, making it longer than even the Mississippi, and the longest of rivers.   In Egypt and Nubia it flows through a bed of silt and slime, resting upon marine or nummulitic limestone, covered by a later formation, over which, without the valley, lie the sand and rocky *débris* of the desert.   Beneath the limestone is a sandstone formation, which rises and bounds the valley in its stead in the higher part of the Thebais.   Again beneath the sandstone is the breccia verde, which appears above it in the desert eastward of Thebes, and yet lower a group of azoic rocks, gneisses, quartzes, mica schists, and clay

slates, resting upon the red granite and syenite that rise through all the upper strata at the First Cataract.[a] The river's bed is cut through these layers of rock, which often approach it on either side, and sometimes confine it on both sides, and even obstruct its course, forming rapids and cataracts. To trace it downwards we must first go to equatorial Africa, the mysterious half-explored home of the negroes, where animal and vegetable life flourishes around and in the vast swamp-land that waters the chief part of the continent. Here are two great shallow lakes, one nearer to the coast than the other. From the more eastern (the Ukerewe, which is on the equator), a chief tributary of the White Nile probably takes its rise, and the more western (the Ujeejee), may feed another tributary. These lakes are filled, partly by the heavy rains of the equatorial region, partly by the melting of the snows of the lofty mountains discovered by the missionaries Krapf and Rebmann. Whether the lakes supply two tributaries or not, it is certain that from the great region of waters where they lie, several streams fall into the Bahr el-Abyad, or White Nile. Great, however, as is the body of water of this the longer of the two chief confluents, it is the shorter, the Bahr el-Azrak, or Blue River, which brings down the alluvial soil that makes the Nile the great fertilizer of Egypt and Nubia. The Bahr el-Azrak rises in the mountains of Abyssinia, and carries down from them a great quantity of decayed vegetable matter and alluvium. The two streams form a junction at Khartoom, now the seat of government of Soodán, or the Black Country under Egyptian rule. The Bahr el-Azrak is here a narrow river, with high steep mud-banks like those of the Nile in Egypt, and with water of the same color; and the Bahr el-Abyad is broad and shallow, with low banks and clear water. Further to the north another great river, the Atbara, rising, like the Bahr el-Azrak, in Abyssinia, falls into the main stream, which, for the remainder of its course, does not receive one tributary more. Throughout the rest of the valley the Nile does not greatly vary, excepting that in Lower Nubia, through the fall of its level by the giving way of a barrier in ancient times, it does not inundate the valley on either hand. From time to time its course is impeded by cataracts or rapids, sometimes extending many miles, until, at the First Cataract, the boundary of Egypt, it surmounts the last obstacle. After a course of about 550 miles, at a short distance below Cairo and the Pyramids, the river parts into two great branches, which water the Delta, nearly forming its boundaries to the east and west, and flowing into the shallow Mediterranean. The references in the Bible are mainly to the characteristics of the river in Egypt. There, above the Delta, its average breadth may be put at from half a mile to three-quarters, excepting where large islands increase the distance. In the Delta its branches are usually narrower. The water is extremely sweet, especially at the season when it is turbid. It is said by the people that those who have drunk of it and left the country must return to drink of it again.

The great annual phenomenon of the Nile is the

---

a The geology of the Nile-valley is excellently given by Hugh Miller (*Testimony of the Rocks*, p. 509 ff.).

inundation, the failure of which produces a famine, for Egypt is virtually without rain (see Zech. xiv. 17, 18). The country is therefore devoid of the constant changes which make the husbandmen of other lands look always for the providential care of God. " For the land, whither thou goest in to possess it, [is] not as the land of Egypt, from whence ye came out, where thou sowedst thy seed, and wateredst [it] with thy foot, as a garden of herbs: but the land, whither ye go to possess it, [is] a land of hills and valleys, [and] drinketh water of the rain of heaven: a land which the LORD thy God careth for: the eyes of the LORD thy God [are] always upon it, from the beginning of the year even unto the end of the year " (Deut. xi. 10-12). At Khartoom the increase of the river is observed early in April, but in Egypt the first signs of rising occur about the summer solstice, and generally the regular increase does not begin until some days after, the inundation commencing about two months after the solstice. The river then pours, through canals and cuttings in the banks, which are a little higher than the rest of the soil, over the valley, which it covers with sheets of water. It attains to its greatest height about, or not long after, the autumnal equinox, and then, falling more slowly than it had risen, sinks to its lowest point at the end of nine months, there remaining stationary for a few days before it again begins to rise. The inundations are very various, and when they are but a few feet deficient or excessive cause great damage and distress. The rise during a good inundation is about 40 feet at the First Cataract, about 36 at Thebes, and about 4 at the Rosetta and Damietta mouths. If the river at Cairo attain to no greater height than 18 or 20 feet, the rise is scanty; if only to 2 or 4 more, insufficient; if to 24 feet or more, up to 27, good; if to a greater height, it causes a flood. Sometimes the inundation has failed altogether, as for seven years in the reign of the Fátimee Khaleefeh El-Mustansir billáh, when there was a seven years' famine; and this must have been the case with the great famine of Joseph's time, to which this later one is a remarkable parallel [FAMINE]. Low inundations always cause dearths; excessive inundations produce or foster the plague and murrain, besides doing great injury to the crops. In ancient times, when every square foot of ground must have been cultivated, and a minute system of irrigation maintained, both for the natural inundation and to water the fields during the Low Nile, and when there were many fish-pools as well as canals for their supply, far greater ruin than now must have been caused by excessive inundations. It was probably to them that the priest referred, who told Solon, when he asked if the Egyptians had experienced a flood, that there had been many floods, instead of the one of which he had spoken, and not to the successive past destructions of the world by water, alternating with others by fire, in which some nations of antiquity believed (Plat. *Timæus*, 21 ff.).

The Nile in Egypt is always charged with alluvium, especially during the inundation; but the annual deposit, excepting under extraordinary circumstances, is very small in comparison with what would be conjectured by any one unacquainted with subjects of this nature. Inquiries have come to different results as to the rate, but the discrepancy does not generally exceed an inch in a century. The ordinary average increase of the soil in Egypt is about four inches and a half in a century. The cultivable soil of Egypt is wholly the deposit of the Nile, but it is obviously impossible to calculate, from its present depth, when the river first began to flow in the rocky bed now so deeply covered with the rich alluvium. An attempt has however been made to use geology as an aid to history, by first endeavoring to ascertain the rate of increase of the soil, then digging for indications of man's existence in the country, and lastly applying to the depth at which any such remains might be discovered the scale previously obtained. In this manner Mr. Horner (*Phil. Transactions*, vol. 148), when his laborers had found, or pretended to find, a piece of pottery at a great depth on the site of Memphis, argued that man must have lived there, and not in the lowest state of barbarism, about 13,000 years ago. He however entirely disregarded various causes by which an object could have been deposited at such a depth, as the existence of canals and wells, from the latter of which water could be anciently as now drawn up in earthen pots from a very low level, and the occurrence of fissures in the earth. He formed his scale on the supposition that the ancient Egyptians placed a great statue before the principal temple of Memphis in such a position that the inundation each year reached its base, whereas we know that they were very careful to put all their stone works where they thought they would be out of the reach of its injurious influence; and, what is still more serious, he laid stress upon the discovery of burnt brick even lower than the piece of pottery, being unaware that there is no evidence that the Egyptians in early times used any but crude brick, a burnt brick being as sure a record of the Roman dominion as an imperial coin. It is important to mention this extraordinary mistake, as it was accepted as a correct result by the late Baron Bunsen, and urged by him and others as a proof of the great antiquity of man in Egypt (*Quarterly Review*, Apr. 1859, No. ccx.; *Modern Egyptians*, 5th ed., note by Ed., p. 593 ff.).

In Upper Egypt the Nile is a very broad stream, flowing rapidly between high, steep mud-banks, which are scarped by the constant rush of the water, which from time to time washes portions away, and stratified by the regular deposit. On either side rise the bare yellow mountains, usually a few hundred feet high, rarely a thousand, looking from the river like cliffs, and often honeycombed with the entrances of the tombs which make Egypt one great city of the dead, so that we can understand the meaning of that murmur of the Israelites to Moses, "Because [there were] no graves in Egypt, hast thou taken us away to die in the wilderness?" (Ex. xiv. 11). Frequently the mountain on either side approaches the river in a rounded promontory, against whose base the restless stream washes, and then retreats and leaves a broad bay-like valley, bounded by a rocky curve. Rarely both mountains confine the river in a narrow bed, rising steeply on either side from a deep rock-cut channel through which the water pours with a rapid current. Perhaps there is a remote allusion to the rocky channels of the Nile, and especially to its primeval bed wholly of bare rock, in that passage of Job where the plural of Yeor is used. "He cutteth out rivers (יְאֹרִים) among the rocks, and his eye seeth every precious thing. He bindeth the floods from overflowing" (xxviii. 10, 11). It

must be recollected that there are allusions to Egypt, and especially to its animals and products in this book, so that the Nile may well be here referred to, if the passage do not distinctly mention it. In Lower Egypt the chief differences are that the view is spread out in one rich plain, only bounded on the east and west by the desert, of which the edge is low and sandy, unlike the mountains above, though essentially the same, and that the two branches of the river are narrower than the undivided stream. On either bank, during Low Nile, extend fields of corn and barley, and near the river-side stretch long groves of palm-trees. The villages rise from the level plain, standing upon mounds, often ancient sites, and surrounded by palm-groves, and yet higher dark-brown mounds mark where of old stood towns, with which often "their memorial is perished" (Ps. ix. 6). The villages are connected by dykes, along which pass the chief roads. During the inundation the whole valley and plain is covered with sheets of water, above which rise the villages like islands, only to be reached along the half-ruined dykes. The aspect of the country is as though it were overflowed by a destructive flood, while between its banks, here and there broken through and constantly giving way, rushes a vast turbid stream, against which no boat could make its way, excepting by tacking, were it not for the north wind that blows ceaselessly during the season of the inundation, making the river seem more powerful as it beats it into waves. The prophets more than once allude to this striking condition of the Nile. Jeremiah says of Pharaoh-Necho's army, "Who [is] this [that] cometh up as the Nile [Yeor], whose waters are moved as the rivers? Egypt riseth up like the Nile, and [his] waters are moved like the rivers; and he saith, I will go up, [and] will cover the land; I will destroy the city and the inhabitants thereof" (xlvi. 7, 8). Again, the prophecy "against the Philistines, before that Pharaoh smote Gaza," commences, "Thus saith the LORD; Behold, waters rise up out of the north, and shall be as an overflowing stream (*nachal*),[a] and shall overflow the land, and all that is therein; the city, and them that dwell therein" (xlvii. 1, 2). Amos, also, a prophet who especially refers to Egypt, uses the inundation of the Nile as a type of the utter desolation of his country. "The LORD hath sworn by the excellency of Jacob, Surely I will never forget any of their works. Shall not the land tremble for this, and every one mourn that dwelleth therein? and it shall rise up wholly as the Nile (פְּאֹר); and it shall be cast out and drowned, as [by] the Nile (כִּיאֹר מִצְרָיִם) of Egypt" (viii. 7, 8; see ix. 5).

The banks of the river are enlivened by the women who come down to draw water, and, like Pharaoh's daughter, to bathe, and the herds of kine and buffaloes which are driven down to drink and wash, or to graze on the grass of the swamps, like the good kine that Pharaoh saw in his dream as "he stood by the river," which were "coming up out of the river," and "fed in the marsh-grass" (Gen. xli. 1, 2).

The river itself abounds in fish, which anciently formed a chief means of sustenance to the inhabi-

---

a The use of "*nachal*" here affords a strong argument in favor of the opinion that it is applied to the Nile.

tants of the country. Perhaps, as has been acutely remarked in another article, Jacob, when blessing Ephraim and Manasseh, used for their multiplying the term דָּגָה (Gen. xlviii. 16), which is connected with דָּג, a fish, though it does not seem certain which is the primitive; as though he had been struck by the abundance of fish in the Nile or the canals and pools fed by it. [MANASSEH, vol. ii. p. 1769 a.] The Israelites in the desert looked back with regret to the fish of Egypt: "We remember the fish, which we did eat in Egypt freely" (Num. xi. 5). In the Thebais crocodiles are found, and during Low Nile they may be seen basking in the sun upon the sandbanks. The crocodile is constantly spoken of in the Bible as the emblem of Pharaoh, especially in the prophecies of Ezekiel. [EGYPT, vol. i. p. 674 a.]

The great difference between the Nile of Egypt in the present day and in ancient times is caused by the failure of some of its branches, and the ceasing of some of its chief vegetable products; and the chief change in the aspect of the cultivable land, as dependent on the Nile, is the result of the ruin of the fish-pools and their conduits, and the consequent decline of the fisheries. The river was famous for its seven branches, and under the Roman dominion eleven were counted, of which, however, there were but seven principal ones. Herodotus notices that there were seven, of which he says that two, the present Damietta and Rosetta branches, were originally artificial, and he therefore speaks of "the five mouths" (ii. 10). Now, as for a long period past, there are no navigable and unobstructed branches but these two that Herodotus distinguishes as in origin works of man. This change was prophesied by Isaiah: "And the waters shall fail from the sea, and the river shall be wasted and dried up" (xix. 5). Perhaps the same prophet, in yet more precise words, predicts this, where he says, "And the LORD shall utterly destroy the tongue of the Egyptian sea; and with his mighty wind shall he shake his hand over the river, and shall smite it in the [or 'into'] seven streams, and make [men] go over dryshod ['in shoes']" (xi. 15). However, from the context, and a parallel passage in Zechariah (x. 10, 11), it seems probable that the Euphrates is intended in this passage by "the river." Ezekiel also prophesies of Egypt that the Lord would "make the rivers drought" (xxx. 12), here evidently referring to either the branches or canals of the Nile. In exact fulfillment of these prophecies the bed of the highest part of the Gulf of Suez has dried, and all the streams of the Nile, excepting those which Herodotus says were originally artificial, have wasted, so that they can be crossed without fording.

The monuments and the narratives of ancient writers show us in the Nile of Egypt in old times, a stream bordered by flags and reeds, the covert of abundant wild fowl, and bearing on its waters the fragrant flowers of the various-colored lotus. Now, in Egypt, scarcely any reeds or water-plants — the famous papyrus being nearly if not quite extinct, and the lotus almost unknown — are to be seen, excepting in the marshes near the Mediterranean. This also was prophesied by Isaiah: "The papyrus-reeds (עָרוֹת?) in the river (יְאוֹר), on the edge of the river, and everything growing [lit. "sown"] in the river shall be dried up, driven away [by the wind], and [shall] not be" (xix. 7). When it

is recollected that the water-plants of Egypt were so abundant as to be a great source of revenue in the prophet's time, and much later, the exact fulfillment of his predictions is a valuable evidence of the truth of the old opinion as to "the sure word of prophecy." The failure of the fisheries is also foretold by Isaiah (xix. 8, 10), and although this was no doubt a natural result of the wasting of the river and streams, its cause could not have been anticipated by human wisdom. Having once been very productive, and a main source of revenue as well as of sustenance, the fisheries are now scarcely of any moment, excepting about Lake Menzeleh, and in some few places elsewhere, chiefly in the north of Egypt.

Of old the great river must have shown a more fair and busy scene than now. Boats of many kinds were ever passing along it, by the painted walls of temples, and the gardens that extended around the light summer pavilions, from the pleasure-galley, with one great square sail, white or with variegated pattern, and many oars, to the little papyrus skiff, dancing on the water, and carrying the seekers of pleasure where they could shoot with arrows, or knock down with the throw-stick, the wild-fowl that abounded among the reeds, or engage in the dangerous chase of the hippopotamus or the crocodile. In the Bible the papyrus-boats are mentioned; and they are shown to have been used for their swiftness to carry tidings to Ethiopia (Is. xviii. 2).

The great river is constantly before us in the history of Israel in Egypt. Into it the male children were cast; in it, or rather in some canal or pool, was the ark of Moses put, and found by Pharaoh's daughter when she went down to bathe. When the plagues were sent, the sacred river — a main support of the people — and its waters everywhere, were turned into blood. [PLAGUES OF EGYPT.]

The prophets not only tell us of the future of the Nile: they speak of it as it was in their days. Ezekiel likens Pharaoh to a crocodile, fearing no one in the midst of his river, yet dragged forth with the fish of his rivers, and left to perish in the wilderness (xxix. 1-5; comp. xxxiii. 1-6). Nahum thus speaks of the Nile, when he warns Nineveh by the ruin of Thebes: "Art thou better than No-Amon, that was situate among the rivers, [that had] the waters round about it, whose rampart [was] the sea, [and] her wall [was] from the sea?" (iii. 8). Here the river is spoken of as the rampart, and perhaps as the support of the capital, and the situation, most remarkable in Egypt, of the city on the two banks is indicated [NO-AMON]. But still more striking than this description is the use which we have already noticed of the inundation, as a figure of the Egyptian armies, and also of the coming of utter destruction, probably by an invading force.

In the New Testament there is no mention of the Nile. Tradition says that when Our Lord was brought into Egypt, his mother came to Heliopolis [ON.] If so, He may have dwelt in his childhood by the side of the ancient river which witnessed so many events of sacred history, perhaps the coming of Abraham, certainly the rule of Joseph, and the long oppression and deliverance of Israel their posterity. R. S. P.

* The problem of the sources of the Nile has been solved by the explorations of Captain J. H. Speke in 1860-63, and of Sir Samuel W. Baker in 1861-64. Already in 1858 Speke had discovered

the *Victoria Nyanza*, a vast sheet of water 3,308 feet above the ocean, lying approximately between 31° 30′ and 95° 30′ E. long. and lat. 3° S. and the equator. This lake Speke explored only along its western border, from *Muanza*, its extreme southern point, to a corresponding point at the extreme north. Information derived from Arabs who had traversed the country to the east, between the lake and the mountain region of *Kilimandjaro* and *Kenia*, satisfied him that upon that side the *Nyanza* receives no tributaries of any importance, the country being hilly, with salt lakes and salt plains chiefly between the first and second degrees of south latitude, and having only occasional runnels and rivulets along the margin of the lake. This opinion, however, does not coincide with the impressions of the missionaries Krapf and Rebmann, who travelled extensively in the countries of *Usambara*, *Jagga*, and *Ukambani*, and heard of rivers running westward from Mount *Kenia*, although from the more southern peak of *Kilimandjaro* the waters flow to the east.

Dr. Krapf penetrated as far as *Kitui*, from which point he distinctly saw the horns of the *Kenia* Mountain, in lat. 2° S., lon. 36° E. He did not attempt to reach the mountain, but he learned from the natives that a river ran from *Kenia* toward the Nile, and also that there was a large salt lake to the northeast of the *Victoria Nyanza*. Upon the western side of the lake the only feeder of any importance is the *Kitangulé* River, a broad, deep stream, — about eighty yards wide at the point where Speke crossed it — that issues from the great "Moon mountain" *Mfumbiro*, and enters the lake at about the first degree of south latitude. Just north of the equator, between 33° and 34° E. long., the White Nile emerges from the *Victoria Nyanza* by the plunge of *Ripon Falls*, a cataract between four and five hundred feet in width, and about twelve feet deep. From *Ripon Falls* to *Urondogani* the river is clear but boisterous; thence to *Karuma* it presents the sluggish appearance of a large pond. Between the head of the lake and *Gondokoro* are three principal cataracts — to *Urondogani* a fall of 507 feet, to *Paira* a second fall of 1072 feet, and the third to *Gondokoro*, of 561 feet. After following the course of the Nile from *Ripon Falls* to *Karuma Falls*, Captain Speke there crossed the river, and leaving it upon the west of him, continued his journey by land to *Goydokoro*, and so lost the opportunity of completing his great discovery.

At *Gondokoro* Speke met Baker, who was about starting for *Karuma Falls*, and communicated to him the results of his own explorations, together with a map of his route, and some valuable suggestions touching the westward bend of the Nile, and its probable connection with the *Little Lúta Nziyé*. Baker had already devoted much time to the exploration of the numerous tributaries of the White Nile. Of these one of the most important is the *Sobat*, coming from the southeast, which he estimated to be 120 yards wide and 25 feet deep. The *Bàhr Gazal*, farther to the south, flows so sluggishly that it seems like dead water, and the whole region between *Khartum* and *Gondokoro* abounds in desolate and fever-smitten marshes. The main river now received his attention. Following the course of the stream from the point where Speke had abandoned it, he found that from *Karuma Falls* the Nile runs almost due west; that its whole volume is precipitated through a

granite gap fifty yards wide over a perpendicular fall of 120 feet. To this stupendous cataract the explorer gave the name Murchison Falls, in honor of the President of the Royal Geographical Society. After passing these falls, the river enters into a vast lake, the *Albert Nyanza*, which stretches over a distance of 260 geographical miles, — from 2° south lat. to nearly 3° north, and mainly between 29° and 31° E. long. Emerging from this lake near its northern extremity, the Nile pursues its course toward *Gondokoro*. The *Albert Nyanza* lies in a vast rock basin, about 1,500 feet below the general level, and receives the drainage of a region of ten-months' rain. In the volume of water and the area of drainage the *Albert Nyanza* is probably the principal source of the Nile; but the southern extremity of the *Victoria Nyanza* marks the greatest distance yet measured, and gives a total length of 2,300 miles.

While the substantial fruits of the discoveries of Speke and Baker, as given above, cannot be affected by any future exploration, it is necessary for a complete knowledge of the sources of the Nile, that the *Victoria Nyanza* shall be circumnavigated, and the country to the east of it scientifically explored; and also, that the *Albert Nyanza* be followed up to its head, and explored for tributaries along its western shore.   J. P. T.

NIM′RAH (נִמְרָה [*panther*]: [Rom. Nαμρα; Vat.] Nαμβρα; Alex. Aμβραμ: *Nemra*), a place mentioned, by this name, in Num. xxxii. 3 only, among those which formed the districts of the "land of Jazer and the land of Gilead," on the east of Jordan, petitioned for by Reuben and Gad. It would appear from this passage to have been near Jazer and Heshbon, and therefore on the upper level of the country. If it is the same as BETH-NIMRAH (ver. 36), it belonged to the tribe of Gad. By Eusebius, however (*Onomast.* Nεβρά), it is cited as a "city of Reuben in Gilead," and said to have been in his day a very large place (κώμη μεγίστη) in ªBatanæa, bearing the name of Abara. This account is full of difficulties, for Reuben never possessed the country of Gilead, and Batanæa was situated several days' journey to the N. W. of the district of Heshbon, beyond not only the territory of Reuben, but even that of Gad. A wady and a town, both called *Nimreh*, have, however, been met with in *Betheniyeh*, east of the *Lejah*, and five miles N. W. of *Kunawât* (see the maps of Porter, Van de Velde, and Wetzstein). On the other hand the name of *Nimrin* is said to be attached to a watercourse and a site of ruins in the Jordan Valley, a couple of miles east of the river, at the embouchure of the *Wady Shoaib*. [BETH-NIMRAH.] But this again is too far from Heshbon in the other direction.

The name *Nimr* ("panther"), appears to be a common one on the east of Jordan, and it must be left to future explorers (when exploration in that region becomes possible) to ascertain which (if either) of the places so named is the Nimrah in question.   G.

NIM′RIM, THE WATERS OF (מֵי נִמְרִים: in Is. τὸ ὕδωρ τῆς Nεμηρείμ, [Sin. τῆς Nεβριμ,] Alex. τῆς Nεμρειμ; in Jer. τὸ ὕδωρ Nεββρείν, Alex. Nεβρειμ: *Aquæ Nemrim*), a stream

---

ª The present Greek text has Kαταναια; but the correction is obvious.

æ brook (not improbably a stream with pools) within the country of Moab, which is mentioned in the denunciations of that nation uttered, or quoted, by Isaiah (xv. 6) and Jeremiah (xlviii. 34). From the former of these passages it appears to have been famed for the abundance of its grass.

If the view taken of these denunciations under the head of MOAB (pp. 1984, 1985) be correct, we should look for the site of Nimrim in Moab proper, i. e. on the southeastern shoulder of the Dead Sea, a position which agrees well with the mention of the " brook of the willows " (perhaps *Wady Beni Hammed*) and the " borders of Moab," that is, the range of hills encircling Moab at the lower part of the territory.

A name resembling Nimrim still exists at the southeastern end of the Dead Sea, in the *Wady en-Nemeirah* and *Burj en-Nemeirah*, which are situated on the beach, about half-way between the southern extremity and the promontory of *el-Lissan* (De Saulcy, *Voyage*, i. 284, &c.; Seetzen, ii. 354). Eusebius (*Onom.* Νεκηρίμ) places it N. of Soora, i. e. Zoar. How far the situation of *en-Nemeirah* corresponds with the statement of Eusebius cannot be known until that of Zoar is ascertained. If the *Wady en-Nemeirah* really occupies the place of the waters of Nimrim, Zoar must have been considerably further south than is usually supposed. On the other hand the name *a* is a common one in the transjordanic localities, and other instances of its occurrence may yet be discovered more in accordance with the ancient statements.   G.

NIM′ROD (נִמְרֹד [*firm, strong,* Dietr.; *a hero,* Fürst]: Νεβρώδ, [in 1 Chr., Comp. Νεμρόδ:] *Nemrod*), a son of Cush and grandson of Ham. The events of his life are recorded in a passage (Gen. x. 8 ff.) which, from the conciseness of its language, is involved in considerable uncertainty. We may notice, in the first place, the terms in ver. 8, 9, rendered in the A. V. " mighty " and " mighty hunter before the Lord." The idea of any moral qualities being conveyed by these expressions may be at once rejected; for, on the one hand, the words " before the Lord " are a mere superlative adjunct (as in the parallel expression in Jon. iii. 3), and contain no notion of Divine approval; and, on the other hand, the ideas of violence and insolence with which tradition invested the character of the hero, as delineated by Josephus *b* (*Ant.* i. 4, § 2), are not necessarily involved in the Hebrew words,

though the term *gibbôr c* is occasionally taken in a bad sense (e. g. Ps. lii. 1). The term may be regarded as betokening personal prowess with the accessory notion of gigantic stature (as in the LXX. γίγας). It is somewhat doubtful whether the prowess of Nimrod rested on his achievements as a hunter or as a conqueror. The literal rendering of the Hebrew words would undoubtedly apply to the former, but they may be regarded as a translation of a proverbial expression originally current in the land of Nimrod, where the terms significant of " hunter " and " hunting " appear to have been applied to the forays of the sovereigns against the surrounding nations.*d* The two phases of prowess, hunting and conquering, may indeed well have been combined in the same person in a rude age, and the Assyrian monuments abound with scenes which exhibit the skill of the sovereigns in the chase. But the context certainly favors the special application of the term to the case of conquest, for otherwise the assertion in ver. 8, " he *began* to be a mighty one in the earth," is devoid of point — while, taken as introductory to what follows, it seems to indicate Nimrod as the first who, after the flood, established a powerful empire on the earth, the limits of which are afterwards defined. The next point to be noticed is the expression in ver. 10, " The beginning of his kingdom," taken in connection with the commencement of ver. 11, which admits of the double sense: " Out of that land went forth Asshur," as in the text of the A. V., and " out of that land he went forth to Assyria," as in the margin. These two passages mutually react on each other; for if the words " beginning of his kingdom " mean, as we believe to be the case, " his *first* kingdom," or, as Gesenius (*Thes.* p. 1252) renders it " the territory of which it was at first composed," then the expression implies a subsequent extension of his kingdom, in other words, that " he went forth to Assyria." If, however, the sense of ver. 11 be, " out of that land went forth Asshur," then no other sense can be given to ver. 10 than that " the capital of his kingdom was Babylon," though the expression must be equally applied to the towns subsequently mentioned. This rendering appears untenable in all respects, and the expression may therefore be cited in support of the marginal rendering of ver. 11. With regard to the latter passage, either sense is permissible in point of grammatical construction, for the omission of the local affix to the word As-

a A racy and characteristic passage, aimed at the *doctrina hæreticorum*, and playing on the name as signifying a leopard, will be found in Jerome's Commentary on Is. xv. 6.

b The view of Nimrod's character taken by this writer originated partly perhaps in a false etymology of the name, as though it were connected with the Hebrew root *mârad* (מָרַד), " to rebel," and partly from the supposed connection of the hero's history with the building of the tower of Babel. There is no ground for the first of these assumptions: the name is either Cushite or Assyrian. Nor, again, does the Bible connect Nimrod with the building of the tower; for it only states that Babel formed one of his capitals Indications have, indeed, been noticed by Bunsen (*Bibelwerk*, v. 74) of a connection between the two narratives; they have undoubtedly a common Jehovistic character; but the point on which he lays most stress (the expression in 1 2, " from the east," or " eastward ") is in reality worthless for the purpose. The influence of the view taken by Josephus is curiously developed

in the identification of Nimrod with the constellation Orion, the Hebrew name *cesil* (כְּסִיל), " foolish," being regarded as synonymous with Nimrod, and the giant form of Orion, together with its Arabic name, " the giant," supplying another connecting link. Josephus follows the LXX. In his form of the name, Νεβρώδης. The variation in the LXX. is of no real importance, as it may be paralleled by a similar exchange of β for מ in the case of Σεβλά (1 Chr. i. 47), and, in a measure, by the insertion of the β before the liquids in other cases, such as Μαμβρῆ (Gen. xiv. 18). The variation hardly deserves the attention it has received in Rawlinson's *Herod.* i. 596.

c נִבֹּר.

d Tiglath-pileser I., for instance, is described as he that " pursues after " or " hunts the people of Bilu-Nipru." So also of other kings (Rawlinson's *Herod.* i. 597).

shur, which forms the chief objection to the marginal rendering, is not peculiar to this passage (comp. 1 K. xi. 17; 2 K. xv. 14), nor is it necessary even to assume a *prolepsis* in the application of the term Asshur to the land of Assyria at the time of Nimrod's invasion, inasmuch as the historical date of this event may be considerably later than the genealogical statement would imply. Authorities both ancient and modern are divided on the subject, but the most weighty names of modern times support the marginal rendering, as it seems best to accord with historical truth. The unity of the passage is moreover supported by its peculiarities both of style and matter. It does not seem to have formed part of the original genealogical statement, but to be an interpolation of a later date; [a] it is the only instance in which personal characteristics are attributed to any of the names mentioned; the proverbial expression which it embodies bespeaks its traditional and fragmentary character, as there is nothing to connect the passage either with what precedes or with what follows it. Such a fragmentary record, though natural in reference to a single mighty hero, would hardly admit of the introduction of references to others. The only subsequent notice of the name Nimrod occurs in Mic. v. 6, where the " land of Nimrod " is a synonym either for Assyria, just before mentioned, or for Babylonia.

The chief events in the life of Nimrod, then, are (1) that he was a Cushite; (2) that he established an empire in Shinar (the classical Babylonia), the chief towns being Babel, Erech, Accad, and Calneh; and (3) that he extended this empire northwards along the course of the Tigris over Assyria, where he founded a second group of capitals, Nineveh, Rehoboth, Calah, and Resen. These events correspond to and may be held to represent the salient historical facts connected with the earliest stages of the great Babylonian empire. 1. In the first place, there is abundant evidence that the race that first held sway in the lower Babylonian plain was of Cushite or Hamitic extraction. Tradition assigned to Belus, the mythical founder of Babylon, an Egyptian origin, inasmuch as it described him as the son of Poseidon and Libya (Diod. Sicul. i. 28; Apollodor. ii. 1, § 4; Pausan. iv. 23, § 5); the astrological system of Babylon (Diod. Sicul. i. 81) and perhaps its religious rites (Hestiaeus [b] ap. Joseph. *Ant.* i. 4, § 3) were referred to the same quarter; and the legend of Oannes, the great teacher of Babylon, rising out of the Erythraean sea, preserved by Syncellus (*Chronogr.* p. 28), points in the same direction. The name Cush itself was preserved in Babylonia and the adjacent countries under the forms of Cossæi, Cissia, Cuthah, and Susiana or *Chuzistan.* The earliest written language of Babylonia, as known to us from existing inscriptions, bears a strong resemblance to that of Egypt and Ethiopia, and the same words have been found in each country, as in the case of *Mirikh,* the Meroë of Ethiopia, the Mars of Babylonia (Rawlinson, i. 442). Even the name

Nimrod appears in the list of the Egyptian kings of the 22d dynasty, but there are reasons for thinking that dynasty to have been of Assyrian extraction. Putting the above-mentioned considerations together, they leave no doubt as to the connection between the ancient Babylonians and the Ethiopian or Egyptian stock (respectively the Nimrod and the Cush of the Mosaic table). More than this cannot be fairly inferred from the data, and we must therefore withhold our assent from Bunsen's view (*Bibelwerk,* v. 69) that the Cushite origin of Nimrod betokens the westward progress of the Scythian or Turanian races from the countries eastward of Babylonia; for, though branches of the Cushite family (such as the Cossæi) had pressed forward to the east of the Tigris, and though the early language of Babylonia bears in its structure a Scythic or Turanian character, yet both these features are susceptible of explanation in connection with the original eastward progress of the Cushite race.

2. In the second place, the earliest seat of empire was in the south part of the Babylonian plain. The large mounds, which for a vast number of centuries have covered the ruins of ancient cities, have already yielded some evidences of the dates and names of their founders, and we can assign the highest antiquity to the towns represented by the mounds of *Niffer* (perhaps the early Babel, though also identified with Calneh), *Warka* (the Biblical Erech), *Mugheir* (Ur), and *Senkereh* (Ellasar), while the name of Accad is preserved in the title *Kinzi Akkad,* by which the founder or embellisher of those towns was distinguished (Rawlinson, i. 435). The date of their foundation may be placed at about B. C. 2200. We may remark the coincidence between the quadruple groups of capitals noticed in the Bible, and the title *Kiprat* or *Kiprat-arba,* assumed by the early kings of Babylon and supposed to mean " four races " (Rawlinson, i. 438, 447).

3. In the third place, the Babylonian empire extended its sway northwards along the course of the Tigris at a period long anterior to the rise of the Assyrian empire in the 13th century B. C. We have indications of this extension as early as about 1860 when Shamas-Iva, the son of Ismi-dagon king of Babylon, founded a Temple at *Kilek-shergat* (supposed to be the ancient Asshur). The existence of Nineveh itself can be traced up by the aid of Egyptian monuments to about the middle of the 15th century B. C., and though the historical name of its founder is lost to us, yet tradition mentions a Belus as king of Nineveh at a period anterior to that assigned to Ninus (Layard's *Nineveh,* ii. 231), thus rendering it probable that the dynasty represented by the latter name was preceded by one of Babylonian origin.

Our present information does not permit us to identify Nimrod with any personage known to us either from inscriptions or from classical writers. Ninus and Belus are representative titles rather

---

[a] The expressions וַיָּ֫חֶל, גִּבֹּר, and still more the use of the term יְהֹוָה, are regarded as indications of a Jehovistic original, while the genealogy itself is Elohistic. It should be further noticed that there is nothing to mark the connection or distinction between Nimrod and the other sons of Cush.

[b] The passage quoted by Josephus is of so fragmentary a character, that its original purport can hardly be guessed. He adduces it apparently to illustrate the name Shinar, but the context favors the supposition that the writer referred to the period subsequent to the flood, in which case we may infer the belief (1) that the population of Babylonia was not autochthonous, but immigrant; (2) that the point from which it immigrated was from the west, Belus being identified with Zeus Enyalius.

than personal names, and are but equivalent terms for "the lord," who was regarded as the founder of the empires of Nineveh and Babylon. We have no reason on this account to doubt the personal existence [a] of Nimrod, for the events with which he is connected fall within the shadows of a remote antiquity. But we may, nevertheless, consistently with this belief, assume that a large portion of the interest with which he was invested was the mere reflection of the sentiments with which the nations of western Asia looked back on the overshadowing greatness of the ancient Babylonian empire, the very monuments of which seemed to tell of days when "there were giants in the earth." The feeling which suggested the coloring of Nimrod as a representative hero still finds place in the land of his achievements, and to him the modern Arabs [b] ascribe all the great works of ancient times, such as the Birs-Nimrúd near Babylon, Tel Nimrúd near Baghdad, the dam of Suhr el-Nimrúd across the Tigris below Mosul, and the well-known mound of Nimrúd in the same neighborhood.   W. L. B.

NIM'SHI (נִמְשִׁי [drawn out, saved, Ges.]: Ναμεσσί; [Vat. Ναμεσθει, Ναμεσσει, Ναμεσσειου; Alex. Αμεσει, Ναμεσσει, Ναμεσιου; in 2 Chr Ναμεσσεί, [Alex. Ναμεσσι:] Namsi). The grandfather of Jehu, who is generally called "the son of Nimshi" (1 K. xix. 16; 2 K. ix. 2, 14, 20; 2 Chr. xxii. 7).

* NIN'EVE [3 syl.] (Apocr. Νινευή, Ninive; N. T. Νινευΐ, Rec. Text, but Lachm. Treg. Νινευῖrai, Tisch. 8th ed. -εῖται: Ninivitæ), only Luke xi. 32 in the N. T., but repeatedly in the O. T. Apocrypha (Tob. i. 3, 10, 17, &c.). It is the Greek form, instead of the Hebrew employed elsewhere [NINEVEH]. See Wahl's Clavis Libr. Vet. Test. Apocr. s. v.   H.

NIN'EVEH (נִינְוֵה [see below] · [Νινευή, in Gen., Rom.] Νινευΐ: the capital of the ancient kingdom and empire of Assyria; a city of great power, size, and renown, usually included amongst the most ancient cities of the world of which there is any historic record. The name appears to be compounded from that of an Assyrian deity, "Nin," corresponding, it is conjectured, with the Greek Hercules, and occurring in the names of several Assyrian kings, as in "Ninus," the mythic founder, according to Greek tradition, of the city. In the Assyrian inscriptions Nineveh is also supposed to be called "the city of Bel."

Nineveh is first mentioned in the O. T. in connection with the primitive dispersement and migrations of the human race. Asshur, or, according to the marginal reading, which is generally preferred. Nimrod, is there described (Gen. x. 11) as extending his kingdom from the land of Shinar, or Babylonia, in the south, to Assyria in the north, and founding four cities, of which the most famous was Nineveh. Hence Assyria was subsequently known to the Jews as "the land of Nimrod" (cf Mic. v. 6), and was believed to have been first peopled by a colony from Babylon. The kingdom of Assyria and of the Assyrians is referred to in the O. T. as connected with the Jews at a very early period; as in Num. xxiv. 22, 24, and Ps. lxxxiii. 8: but after the notice of the foundation of Nineveh in Genesis no further mention is made of the city until the time of the book of Jonah, or the 8th century B. C., supposing we accept the earliest date for that narrative [JONAH], which, however, according to some critics, must be brought down 300 years later, or to the 5th century B. C. In this book neither Assyria nor the Assyrians are mentioned, the king to whom the prophet was sent being termed the "king of Nineveh," and his subjects "the people of Nineveh." Assyria is first called a kingdom in the time of Menahem, about B. C. 770. Nahum (? B. C. 645) directs his prophecies against Nineveh; only once against the king of Assyria, ch. iii. 18. In 2 Kings (xix. 36) and Isaiah (xxxvii. 37) the city is first distinctly mentioned as the residence of the monarch. Sennacherib was slain there when worshipping in the temple of Nisroch his god. In 2 Chronicles (xxxii. 21), where the same event is described, the name of the place where it occurred is omitted. Zephaniah, about B. C. 630, couples the capital and the kingdom together (ii. 13); and this is the last mention of Nineveh as an existing city. He probably lived to witness its destruction, an event impending at the time of his prophecies. Although Assyria and the Assyrians are alluded to by Ezekiel and Jeremiah, by the former as a nation in whose miserable ruin prophecy had been fulfilled (xxxi.), yet they do not refer by name to the capital. Jeremiah, when enumerating "all the kingdoms of the world which are upon the face of the earth" (ch. xxv.), omits all mention of the nation and the city. Habakkuk only speaks of the Chaldæans, which may lead to the inference that the date of his prophecies is somewhat later than that usually assigned to them. [HABAKKUK] From a comparison of these data, it has been generally assumed that the destruction of Nineveh and the extinction of the empire took place between the time of Zephaniah and that of Ezekiel and Jeremiah. The exact period of these events has consequently been fixed, with a certain amount of concurrent evidence derived from classical history, at B. C. 606 (Clinton, Fasti Hellen. i. 269). It has been shown that it

---

[a] We must notice, without however adopting, the views lately propounded by M. D. Chwolson in his pamphlet, Ueber die Ueberreste der altbabylonischen Literatur. He has discovered the name Nemrod or Nemroda in the manuscript works of an Arabian writer named Ibn-Wa'hschijjah, who professes to give a translation of certain original literary works in the Nabathæan language, one of which, "on Nabathæan agriculture," is in part assigned by him to a writer named Qut'ami. This Qut'ami incidentally mentions that he lived in Babylon under a dynasty of Canaanites, which had been founded by a priest named Nemrod. M. Chwolson assigns Ibn-Wa'hschijjah to the 2nd of the 9th century of our new era, and Qut'ami to the early part of the 13th century B. C. He regards the term Nabathæan as meaning old Babylonian, and the works of Qut'ami as the remains of a Babylonian literature. He further identifies the Canaanite dynasty with the fifth or Arabian dynasty of Berosus, and adduces the legend of Cepheus, the king of Joppa, who reigned from the Mediterranean to the Erythræan sea, in confirmation of such a Canaanitish invasion. It would be beyond our province to follow the various questions raised by this curious discovery. The result, if established, would be to bring the date of Nimrod down to about B. C. 1500.

[b] The Arabs retain Josephus' view of the impiety of Nimrod, and have a collection of legends respecting his idolatry, his enmity against Abraham, etc (Layard's Nineveh, i. 24, note).

may have occurred 20 years earlier. [ASSYRIA.]
The city was then laid waste, its monuments destroyed, and its inhabitants scattered or carried away into captivity. It never rose again from its ruins. This total disappearance of Nineveh is fully confirmed by the records of profane history. There is no mention of it in the Persian cuneiform inscriptions of the Achæmenid dynasty. Herodotus (i. 193) speaks of the Tigris as "the river upon which the town of Nineveh formerly stood." He must have passed, in his journey to Babylon, very near the site of the city — perhaps actually over it. So accurate a recorder of what he saw would scarcely have omitted to mention, if not to describe, any ruins of importance that might have existed there. Not two centuries had then elapsed since the fall of the city. Equally conclusive proof of its condition is afforded by Xenophon, who with the ten thousand Greeks encamped during his retreat on, or very near, its site (B. C. 401). The very name had then been forgotten, or at least he does not appear to have been acquainted with it, for he calls one group of ruins "Larissa," and merely states that a second group was near the deserted town of Mespila (Anab. b. iii. 4, § 7). The ruins, as he describes them, correspond in many respects with those which exist at the present day, except that he assigns to the walls near Mespila a circuit of six parasangs, or nearly three times their actual dimensions. Ctesias placed the city on the Euphrates (Frag. i. 2), a proof either of his ignorance or of the entire disappearance of the place. He appears to have led Diodorus Siculus into the same error (ii. 27, 28).[a] The historians of Alexander, with the exception of Arrian (Ind. pp. 42, 43), do not even allude to the city, over the ruins of which the conqueror must have actually marched. His great victory of Arbela was won almost in sight of them. It is evident that the later Greek and Roman writers, such as Strabo, Ptolemy, and Pliny, could only have derived any independent knowledge they possessed of Nineveh from traditions of no authority. They concur, however, in placing it on the eastern bank of the Tigris. During the Roman period, a small castle or fortified town appears to have stood on some part of the site of the ancient city. It was probably built by the Persians (Ammian. Marcell. xxiii. 22); and subsequently occupied by the Romans, and erected by the Emperor Claudius into a colony. It appears to have borne the ancient traditional name of Nineve, as well as its corrupted form of Ninos and Ninus, and also at one time that of Hierapolis. Tacitus (Ann. xii. 13), mentioning its capture by Meherdates, calls it "Ninos:" on coins of Trajan it is "Ninus," on those of Maximinus "Niniva," in both instances the epithet Claudiopolis being added. Many Roman remains, such as sepulchral vases, bronze and other ornaments, sculptured figures in marble, terra-cottas, and coins, have been discovered in the rubbish covering the Assyrian ruins; besides wells and tombs, constructed long after the destruction of the Assyrian edifices. The Roman settlement appears to have been in its turn abandoned, for there is no mention of it when Heraclius gained the great victory over the Persians in the battle of Nineveh, fought on the very site of the ancient city, A. D. 627. After the Arab conquest, a fort on the east bank of the Tigris bore the name of "Ninawi" (Rawlinson, As. Soc. Journal, vol. xii. p. 418). Benjamin of Tudela, in the 12th century, mentions the site of Nineveh as occupied by numerous inhabited villages and small townships (ed. Asher, i. 91). The name remained attached to the ruins during the Middle Ages; and from them a bishop of the Chaldæan Church derived his title (Assemani, iv. 459); but it is doubtful whether any town or fort was so called. Early English travellers merely allude to the site (Purchas, ii. 1387). Niebuhr is the first modern traveller who speaks of "Nuniyah" as a village standing on one of the ruins which he describes as "a considerable hill" (ii. 353). This may be a corruption of "Nebbi Yunus," the Prophet Jonah, a name still given to a village containing his apocryphal tomb. Mr. Rich, who surveyed the site in 1820, does not mention Nuniyah, and no such place now exists. Tribes of Turcomans and sedentary Arabs, and Chaldæan and Syrian Christians, dwell in small mud-built villages, and cultivate the soil in the country around the ruins; and occasionally a tribe of wandering Kurds, or of Bedouins driven by hunger from the desert, will pitch their tents amongst them. After the Arab conquest of the west of Asia, Mosul, at one time the flourishing capital of an independent kingdom, rose on the opposite or western bank of the Tigris. Some similarity in the names has suggested its identification with the Mespila of Xenophon; but its first actual mention only occurs after the Arab conquest A. H. 16, and A. D. 637). It was sometimes known as Athur, and was united with Nineveh as an Episcopal see of the Chaldæan Church (Assemani, iii. 269). It has lost all its ancient prosperity, and the greater part of the town is now in ruins.

Traditions of the unrivaled size and magnificence of Nineveh were equally familiar to the Greek and Roman writers, and to the Arab geographers. But the city had fallen so completely into decay before the period of authentic history, that no description of it, or even of any of its monuments, is to be found in any ancient author of trust. Diodorus Siculus asserts (ii. 3) that the city formed a quadrangle of 150 stadia by 90, or altogether of 480 stadia (no less than 60 miles), and was surrounded by walls 100 feet high, broad enough for three chariots to drive abreast upon them, and defended by 1,500 towers, each 200 feet in height. According to Strabo (xvi. 737) it was larger than Babylon, which was 385 stadia in circuit. In the O. T. we find only vague allusions to the splendor and wealth of the city, and the very indefinite statement in the book of Jonah that it was "an exceeding great city," or "a great city to God," or "for God" (i. e. in the sight of God), "of three days' journey;" and that it contained "six score thousand persons who could not discern between their right hand and their left hand, and also much cattle" (iv. 11). It is obvious that the accounts of Diodorus are for the most part absurd exaggerations, founded upon fabulous traditions, for which existing remains afford no warrant. It may, however, be remarked that the dimensions he assigns to the area of the city would correspond to the three days' journey of Jonah — the Jewish day's journey being 20 miles — if that expression be applied to the circuit of the walls. "Persons not discerning between their right hand and their left" may either allude to children, or to the ignorance of the whole population. If the first be intended, the number of inhabitants, according to the usual calculation, would have amounted to about 600,000. But such expressions are probably mere eastern figures of speech to denote vastness, and far too vague to admit of exact interpretation.

The political history of Nineveh is that of Assyria, of which a sketch has already been given. [ASSYRIA.] It has been observed that the territory included within the boundaries of the kingdom of Assyria proper was comparatively limited in extent, and that almost within the immediate neighborhood of the capital petty kings appear to have ruled over semi-independent states, owning allegiance and paying tribute to the great Lord of the Empire, "the King of Kings," according to his oriental title, who dwelt at Nineveh. (Cf. Is. x. 8: "Are not my princes altogether kings?") These petty kings were in a constant state of rebellion, which usually shewed itself by their refusal to pay the apportioned tribute — the principal link between the sovereign and the dependent states — and repeated expeditions were undertaken against them to enforce this act of obedience. (Cf. 2 K. xvi. 7, xvii. 4, where it is stated that the war made by the Assyrians upon the Jews was for the purpose of enforcing the payment of tribute.) There was, consequently, no bond of sympathy arising out of common interests between the various populations which made up the empire. Its political condition was essentially weak. When an independent monarch was sufficiently powerful to carry on a successful war against the great king, or a dependent prince sufficiently strong to throw off his allegiance, the empire soon came to an end. The fall of the capital was the signal for universal disruption. Each petty state asserted its independence, until reconquered by some warlike chief who could found a new dynasty and a new empire to replace those which had fallen. Thus on the borders of the great rivers of Mesopotamia arose in turn the first Babylonian, the Assyrian, the Median, the second Babylonian, the Persian, and the Seleucid empires. The capital was however invariably changed, and generally transferred to the principal seat of the conquering race. In the East men have rarely rebuilt great cities which have once fallen into decay — never perhaps on exactly the same site. If the position of the old capital was deemed, from political or commercial reasons, more advantageous than any other, the population was settled in its neighborhood, as at Delhi, and not amidst its ruins. But Nineveh, having fallen with the empire, never rose again. It was abandoned at once, and suffered to perish utterly. It is probable that, in conformity with an eastern custom, of which we find such remarkable illustrations in the history of the Jews, the entire population was removed by the conquerors, and settled as colonists in some distant province.

The Ruins. — Previous to recent excavations and researches, the ruins which occupied the presumed site of Nineveh seemed to consist of mere shapeless heaps or mounds of earth and rubbish. Unlike the vast masses of brick masonry which mark the site of Babylon, they showed externally no signs of artificial construction, except perhaps here and there the traces of a rude wall of sun-dried bricks. Some of these mounds were of enormous dimensions — looking in the distance rather like natural elevations than the work of men's hands. Upon and around them, however, were scattered innumerable fragments of pottery — the unerring evidence of former habitations. Some had been chosen by the scattered population of the land as sites for villages, or for small mud-built forts, the mound itself affording means of refuge and defense against the marauding parties of Bedouins and Kurds which for generations have swept over the face of the country. The summits of others were sown with corn or barley. During the spring months they were covered with grass and flowers, bred by the winter rains. The Arabs call these mounds "Tel," the Turcomans and Turks "Teppeh," both words being equally applied to natural hills and elevations, and the first having been used in the same double sense by the most ancient Semitic races (cf. Hebrew תֵּל, "a hill," "a mound," "a heap of rubbish," Ez. iii. 15; Ezr. ii. 59; Neh. vii. 61; 2 K. xix. 12). They are found in vast numbers throughout the whole region watered by the Tigris and Euphrates and their confluents, from the Taurus to the Persian Gulf. They are seen, but are less numerous, in Syria, parts of Asia Minor, and in the plains of Armenia. Wherever they have been examined they appear to have furnished remains which identify the period of their construction with that of the alternate supremacy of the Assyrian, Babylonian, and Persian empires. They differ greatly in form, size, and height. Some are mere conical heaps, varying from 50 to 150 feet high; others have a broad, flat summit, and very precipitous cliff-like sides, furrowed by deep ravines worn by the winter rains. Such mounds are especially numerous in the region to the east of the Tigris, in which Nineveh stood, and some of them must mark the ruins of the Assyrian capital. There is no edifice mentioned by ancient authors as forming part of the city, which we are required, as in the case of Babylon, to identify with any existing remains, except the tomb, according to some, of Ninus, according to others of Sardanapalus, which is recorded to have stood at the entrance of Nineveh (Diod. Sic. ii. 7; Amynt. *Frag.* ed. Müller, p. 136). The only difficulty is to determine which ruins are to be comprised within the actual limits of the ancient city. The northern extremity of the principal collection of mounds on the eastern bank of the Tigris may be fixed at Shereef Khan, and the southern at Nimroud, about 6¼ miles from the junction of that river with the great Zab, the ancient Lycus. Eastward they extend to Khorsabad, about 10 miles N. by E. of Shereef Khan, and to Karamless, about 15 miles N. E. of Nimroud. Within the area of this irregular quadrangle are to be found, in every direction, traces of ancient edifices and of former population. It comprises various separate and distinct groups of ruins, four of which, if not more, are the remains of fortified inclosures or strongholds, defended by walls and ditches, towers and ramparts. The principal are — 1, the group immediately opposite Mosul, including the great mounds of Kouyunjik (also called by the Arabs, Armousheeyah) and Nebbi Yunus; 2, that near the junction of the Tigris and Zab, comprising the mounds of Nimroud and Athur; 3, Khorsabad, about 10 miles to the east of the former river; 4, Shereef Khan, about 5½ miles to the north of Kouyunjik; and 5, Selamiyah, 3 miles to the north of Nimroud. Other large mounds are Baaskeikhah, and Karamless, where the remains of fortified inclosures may perhaps be traced.

Baazani, Yarumjeh, and Bellawat. It is scarcely necessary to observe that all these names are comparatively modern, dating from after the Mohammedan conquest. The respective position of these ruins will be seen in the accompanying map. We will describe the most important.

The ruins opposite Mosul consist of an inclosure formed by a continuous line of mounds, resembling a vast embankment of earth, but marking the remains of a wall, the western face of which is interrupted by the two great mounds of Kouyunjik and Nebbi Yunus (p. 2161). To the east of this in-

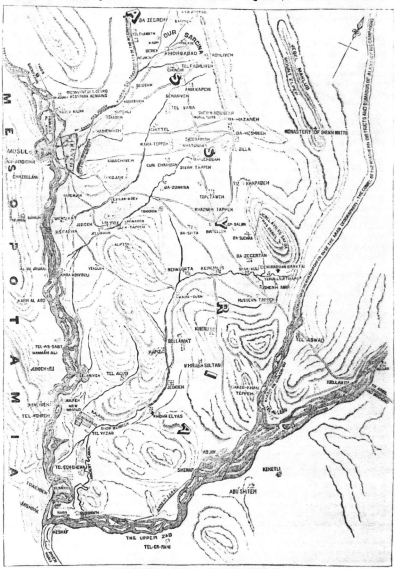

Plan of Ruins which comprise ancient Nineveh.

closure are the remains of an extensive line of defenses, consisting of moats and ramparts. The inner wall forms an irregular quadrangle with very unequal sides — the northern being 2,333 yards, the western, or the river-face, 4,533, the eastern (where the wall is almost the segment of a circle) 5,300 yards, and the southern but little more than 1,000; altogether 13,200 yards, or 7 English miles 4 furlongs. The present height of this earthen wall is between 40 and 50 feet. Here and there a mound more lofty than the rest covers the remains of a tower or a gateway. The walls appear to have been originally faced, at least to a certain height, with stone masonry, some remains of which have been discovered. The mound of Kouyunjik is of irregular form, being nearly square at the S. W. corner, and ending almost in a point at the N. E. It is about 1,300 yards in length, by 500 in its greatest width; its greatest height is 96 feet, and its sides are precipitous, with occasional deep ravines or watercourses. The summit is nearly flat, but falls from the W. to the E. A small village formerly stood upon it, but has of late years been abandoned. The Khosr, a narrow but deep and sluggish stream, sweeps round the southern side of the mound on its way to join the Tigris. Anciently dividing itself into two branches, it completely surrounded Kouyunjik. Nebbi Yunus is considerably smaller than Kouyunjik, being about 530 yards by 430, and occupying an area of about 40 acres. In height it is about the same. It is divided into two nearly equal parts by a depression in the surface. Upon it is a Turcoman village containing the apocryphal tomb of Jonah, and a burial-ground held in great sanctity by Mohammedans from its vicinity to this sacred edifice. Remains of entrances or gateways have been discovered in the N. and E. walls (b). The Tigris formerly ran beneath the W. wall, and at the foot of the two great mounds. It is now about a mile distant from them, but during very high spring floods it sometimes reaches its ancient bed. The W. face of the inclosure (a) was thus protected by the river. The N. and S. faces (b and d) were strengthened by deep and broad moats. The E. (c) being most accessible to an enemy, was most strongly fortified, and presents the remains of a very elaborate system of defenses. The Khosr, before entering the inclosure, which it divides into two nearly equal

parts, ran for some distance almost parallel to it (f), and supplied the place of an artificial ditch for about half the length of the E. wall. The remainder of the wall was protected by two wide moats (h), fed by the stream, the supply of water being regulated by dams, of which traces still exist In addition, one or more ramparts of earth were thrown up, and a moat excavated between the inner walls and the Khosr, the eastern bank of which was very considerably raised by artificial means. Below, or to the S. of the stream, a third ditch

Plan of Kouyunjik and Nebbi Yunus.

excavated in the compact conglomerate rock, and about 200 feet broad, extended almost the whole length of the E. face, joining the moat on the S. An enormous outer rampart of earth, still in some places above 80 feet in height (i), completed the defenses on this side. A few mounds outside this rampart probably mark the site of detached towers

The great mound of Nimroud.

or fortified posts. This elaborate system of fortifications was singularly well devised to resist the attacks of an enemy. It is remarkable that within the inclosure, with the exception of Kouyunjik and Nebbi Yunus, no mounds or irregularities in the surface of the soil denote ruins of any size. The

ground is, however, strewed in every direction with fragments of brick, pottery, and the usual signs of ancient population.

Nimroud consists of a similar inclosure of consecutive mounds — the remains of ancient walls. The system of defenses is however very inferior in importance and completeness to that of Kouyunjik. The indications of towers occur at regular intervals; 108 may still be traced on the N. and E. sides. The area forms an irregular square, about 2,331 yards by 2,095, containing about 1,000 acres. The N. and E. sides were defended by moats, the W. and S. walls by the river, which once flowed immediately beneath them. On the S. W. face is a great mound, 700 yards by 400, and covering about 60 acres, with a cone or pyramid of earth about 140 feet high rising in the N. W. corner of it. At the S. E. angle of the inclosure is a group of lofty mounds called by the Arabs, after Nimroud's lieutenant, Athur (cf. Gen. x. 11). According to the Arab geographers this name at one time applied to all the ruins of Nimroud (Layard. *Nin. and its Rem.* ii. 245, note). Within the inclosure a few slight irregularities in the soil mark the sites of ancient habitations, but there are no indications of ruins of buildings of any size. Fragments of brick and pottery abound. The Tigris is now 1½ mile distant from the mound, but sometimes reaches them during extraordinary floods.

The inclosure-walls of Khorsabad form a square of about 2,000 yards. They show the remains of towers and gateways. There are apparently no traces of moats or ditches. The mound which gives its name to this group of ruins rises on the N. W. face. It may be divided into two parts or stages, the upper about 650 feet square, and 30 feet high, and the lower adjoining it, about 1,350 by 300. Its summit was formerly occupied by an Arab village. In one corner there is a pyramid or cone, similar to that at Nimroud. but very inferior in height and size. Within the interior are a few mounds marking the sites of propylæa and similar detached monuments, but no traces of considerable buildings. These ruins were known to the early Arab geographers by the name of "Saraoun," probably a traditional corruption of the name of Sargon, the king who founded the palaces discovered there.

Shereef Khan, so called from a small village in the neighborhood, consists of a group of mounds of no great size when compared with other Assyrian ruins, and without traces of an outer-wall. Selamiyah is an inclosure of irregular form, situated upon a high bank overlooking the Tigris, about 5,000 yards in circuit, and containing an area of about 410 acres, apparently once surrounded by a ditch or moat. It contains no mound or ruin, and even the earthen rampart which marks the walls has in many places nearly disappeared. The name is derived from an Arab town once of some importance, but now reduced to a miserable village inhabited by Turcomans.

The greater part of the discoveries which, of late years, have thrown so much light upon the history and condition of the ancient inhabitants of Nineveh were made in the ruins of Nimroud, Kouyunjik, and Khorsabad. The first traveller who carefully examined the supposed site of the city was Mr. Rich, formerly political agent for the East India Company at Bagdad; but his investigations were almost entirely confined to Kouyunjik and the surrounding mounds, of which he made a survey in 1820. From them he obtained a few relics, such as inscribed pottery and bricks, cylinders, and gems. Some time before a bas-relief representing men and animals had been discovered, but had been destroyed by the Mohammedans. He subsequently visited the mound of Nimroud, of which, however, he was unable to make more than a hasty exami-

nation (*Narrative of a Residence in Kurdistan*, ii. 131). Several travellers described the ruins after Mr. Rich, but no attempt was made to explore them systematically until M. Botta was appointed French consul at Mosul in 1843. Whilst excavating in the mound of Khorsabad, to which he had been directed by a peasant, he discovered a row of upright alabaster slabs, forming the paneling or skirting of the lower part of the walls of a chamber. This chamber was found to communicate with others of similar construction, and it soon became evident that the remains of an edifice of considerable size were buried in the mound. The French government having given the necessary funds, the ruins were fully explored. They consisted of the lower part of a number of halls, rooms, and passages, for the most part wainscoted with slabs of coarse gray alabaster, sculptured with figures in relief, the principal entrances being formed by colossal human-headed winged bulls. No remains of exterior architecture of any great importance were discovered. The calcined limestone and the great accumulation of charred wood and charcoal showed that the building had been destroyed by fire. Its upper part had entirely disappeared, and its general plan could only be restored by the remains of the lower story. The collection of Assyrian sculptures in the Louvre came from these ruins.

The excavations subsequently carried on by MM. Place and Fresnel at Khorsabad led to the discovery, in the inclosure below the platform, of propylæa, flanked by colossal human-headed bulls, and of other detached buildings forming the approaches to the palace, and also of some of the gateways in the inclosure-walls, ornamented with similar mythic figures.

M. Botta's discoveries at Khorsabad were followed by those of Mr. Layard at Nimroud and Kouyunjik, made between the years 1845 and 1850. The mound of Nimroud was found to contain the ruins of several distinct edifices, erected at different periods — materials for the construction of the latest having been taken from an earlier building. The most ancient stood at the N. W. corner of the platform, the most recent at the S. E. In general plan and in construction they resembled the ruins at Khorsabad — consisting of a number of halls, chambers, and galleries, paneled with sculptured and inscribed alabaster slabs, and opening one into the other by doorways generally formed by pairs of colossal human-headed winged bulls or lions. The exterior architecture could not be traced. The lofty cone or pyramid of earth adjoining this edifice covered the ruins of a building the basement of which was a square of 165 feet, and consisted, to the height of 20 feet, of a solid mass of sundried bricks, faced on the four sides by blocks of stone carefully squared, beveled, and adjusted. This stone facing singularly enough coincides exactly with the height assigned by Xenophon to the stone plinth of the walls (*Anab* iii. 4). and is surmounted, as he describes the plinth to have been, by a superstructure of bricks, nearly every kiln-burnt brick bearing an inscription. Upon this solid substructure there probably rose, as in the Babylonian temples, a succession of platforms or stages, diminishing in size, the highest having a shrine or altar upon it (BABEL; Layard, *Nin. and Bab.* ch. v). A vaulted chamber or gallery, 100 feet long, 6 broad, and 12 high, crossed the centre of the mound on a level with the summit of the stone-masonry. It had evidently been broken into and rifled of its contents at some remote period, and may have been a royal sepulchre — the tomb of Ninus, or Sardanapalus, which stood at the entrance of Nineveh. It is the tower described by Xenophon at Larissa as being 1 plethron (100 feet) broad and 2 plethra high. It appears to have been raised by the son of the king who built the N. W. palace, and whose name in the cuneiform inscriptions is supposed to be identified with that of Sardanapalus. Shalmanubar or Shalmaneser,[a] the builder of this tomb or tower, also erected in the centre of the great mound a second palace, which appears to have been destroyed to furnish materials for later buildings. The black obelisk now in the British Museum was found amongst its ruins. On the W. face of the mound, and adjoining the centre palace, are the remains of a third edifice, built by the grandson of Shalmanubar, whose name is read Iva-Lush, and who is believed to be the Pul of the Hebrew Scriptures. It contained some important inscribed slabs, but no sculptures. Esarhaddon raised (about B. C. 680) at the S. W.

corner of the platform another royal abode of considerable extent, but constructed principally with materials brought from his predecessor's palaces. In the opposite or S. E. corner are the ruins of a still later palace, built by his grandson Ashur-emit-ili, very inferior in size and in splendor to other Assyrian edifices. Its rooms were small; it appears to have had no great halls, and the chambers were paneled with slabs of common stone without sculpture or inscriptions. Some important detached figures, believed to bear the name of the historical Semiramis, were, however, found in its ruins. At the S. W. corner of the mound of Kouyunjik stood a palace built by Sennacherib (about B. C. 700), exceeding in size and in magnificence of decoration all others hitherto explored. It occupied nearly 100 acres. Although much of the building yet remains to be examined, and much has altogether perished, about 60 courts, halls (some nearly 150 feet square), rooms, and passages (one 200 feet long), have been discovered, all paneled with sculptured slabs of alabaster. The entrances to the edifice and to the principal cham-

Khorsabad — View of the Mounds. — Botta's Ninivé.

bers were flanked by groups of winged human-headed lions and bulls of colossal proportions — some nearly 20 feet in height; 27 portals thus formed were excavated by Mr. Layard. A second palace was erected on the same platform by the son of Esarhaddon, the third king of the name of Sardanapalus. In it were discovered sculptures of great interest and beauty, amongst them the series representing the lion-hunt now in the British Museum. Owing to the sanctity attributed by Mohammedans to the supposed tomb of Jonah, great difficulties were experienced in examining the mound upon which it stands. A shaft sunk within the walls of a private house led to the discovery of sculptured slabs; and excavations subsequently carried on by agents of the Turkish Government proved that they formed part of a palace erected by Esarhaddon. Two entrances or gateways in the great inclosure-walls have been excavated — one (at *b* on plan) flanked by colossal

human-headed bulls and human figures. They, as well as the walls, appear, according to the inscriptions, to have been constructed by Sennacherib. No propylæa or detached buildings have as yet been discovered within the inclosure. At Shereeff Khan are the ruins of a temple, but no sculptured slabs have been dug up there. It was founded by Sennacherib, and added to by his grandson. At Selamiyah no remains of buildings nor any fragments of sculpture or inscriptions have been discovered.

The Assyrian edifices were so nearly alike in general plan, construction, and decoration, that one description will suffice for all. They were built upon artificial mounds or platforms, varying in height, but generally from 30 to 50 feet above the level of the surrounding country, and solidly constructed of regular layers of sun-dried bricks, as at Nimroud, or consisting merely of earth and rubbish heaped up, as at Kouyunjik. The mode of raising

---

a It must be observed, once for all, that whilst the Assyrian proper names are given in the text according

to the latest interpretations of the cuneiform inscriptions, they are very doubtful.

the latter kind of mound is represented in a series of bas-reliefs, in which captives and prisoners are seen amongst the workmen (Layard, *Mon. of Nin.* 2d series, pl. 14, 15). This platform was probably

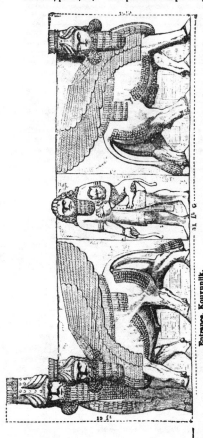

Entrance, Kouyunjik.

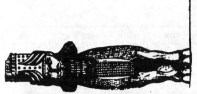

faced with stone-masonry, remains of which were discovered at Nimroud, and broad flights of steps (such as were found at Khorsabad) or inclined ways led up to its summit. Although only the

general plan of the ground-floor can now be traced, it is evident that the palaces had several stories built of wood and sun-dried bricks, which, when the building was deserted and allowed to fall to decay, gradually buried the lower chambers with their ruins, and protected the sculptured slabs from the effects of the weather. The depth of soil and rubbish above the alabaster slabs varied from a few inches to about 20 feet. It is to this accumu-lation of rubbish above them that the bas-reliefs owe their extraordinary preservation. The portions of the edifices still remaining consist of halls, chambers, and galleries, opening for the most part into large uncovered courts. The partition walls vary from 6 to 15 feet in thickness, and are solidly built of sun-dried bricks, against which are placed the paneling or skirting of alabaster slabs. No windows have hitherto been discovered, and it is probable that in most of the smaller chambers light was only admitted through the doors. The wall, above the wainscoting of alabaster, was plastered, and painted with figures and ornaments. The pavement was formed either of inscribed slabs of alabaster, or large, flat, kiln-burnt bricks. It rested upon layers of bitumen and fine sand. Of nearly similar construction are the modern houses of Mosul, the architecture of which has probably been preserved from the earliest times as that best suited to the climate and to the manners and wants of an oriental people. The rooms are grouped in the same manner round open courts or large halls. The same alabaster, usually carved with ornaments, is used for wainscoting the apartments, and the walls are constructed of sun-dried bricks. The upper part and the external architecture of the Assyrian palaces, both of which have entirely dis-appeared, can only be restored conjecturally, from a comparison of monuments represented in the bas-reliefs, and of edifices built by nations, such as the Persians, who took their arts from the Assyrians. By such means Mr. Fergusson has, with much ingenuity, attempted to reconstruct a palace of Nineveh (*The Palaces of Nineveh and Persepolis restored*). He presumes that the upper stories were built entirely of sun-dried bricks and wood — a supposition warranted by the absence of stone and marble columns, and of remains of stone and burnt-brick masonry in the rubbish and soil which cover and surround the ruins; that the exterior was richly sculptured and painted with figures and ornaments, or decorated with enameled bricks of bright colors, and that light was admitted to the principal chambers on the ground-floor through a kind of gallery which formed the upper part of them, and upon which rested the wooden pillars necessary for the support of the superstructure. The capitals and various details of these pillars, the friezes and architectural ornaments, he restores from the stone columns and other remains at Persepolis. He conjectures that curtains, sus-pended between the pillars, kept out the glaring light of the sun, and that the ceilings were of wood-work, elaborately painted with patterns sim-ilar to those represented in the sculptures, and probably ornamented with gold and ivory. The discovery at Khorsabad of an arched entrance of considerable size and depth, constructed of sun-dried and kiln-burnt bricks, the latter enameled with figures, leads to the inference that some of the smaller chambers may have been vaulted.

The sculptures, with the exception of the human-headed lions and bulls, were for the most part in tow relief. The colossal figures usually represent the king, his attendants, and the gods; the smaller sculptures, which either cover the whole face of the slab, or are divided into two compartments by bands of inscriptions, represent battles, sieges, the chase, single combats with wild beasts, religious ceremonies, etc., etc. All refer to public or national events; the hunting-scenes evidently recording the prowess and personal valor of the king as the head of the people — "the mighty hunter before the Lord." The sculptures appear to have been painted — remains of color having been found on most of them. Thus decorated, without and within, the Assyrian palaces must have displayed a barbaric magnificence, not, however, devoid of a certain grandeur and beauty, which no ancient or modern edifice has probably exceeded. Amongst the small objects, undoubtedly of the Assyrian period, found in the ruins, were copper-vessels (some embossed and incised with figures of men and animals and graceful ornaments), bells, various instruments and tools of copper and iron, arms (such as spear and arrow heads, swords, daggers, shields, helmets, and fragments of chain and plate armor), ivory ornaments, glass bowls and vases, alabaster urns, figures and other objects in terra-cotta, pottery, parts of a throne, inscribed cylinders and seals of agate and other precious materials, and a few detached statues. All these objects show great mechanical skill and a correct and refined taste, indicating considerable advance in civilization.

These great edifices, the depositories of the national records, appear to have been at the same time the abode of the king and the temple of the gods — thus corresponding, as in Egypt, with the character of the monarch, who was both the political and religious chief of the nation, the special favorite of the deities, and the interpreter of their decrees. No building has yet been discovered which possesses any distinguishing features to mark it specially as a temple. They are all precisely similar in general plan and construction. Most probably a part of the palace was set apart for religious worship and ceremonies. Altars of stone, resembling the Greek tripod in form, have been found in some of the chambers — in one instance before a figure of the king himself (Layard, *Nin. and Bab.* p. 351). According to the inscriptions, it would, however, appear that the Assyrian monarchs built temples of great magnificence at Nineveh, and in various parts of the empire, and profusely adorned them with gold, silver, and other precious materials.

Site of the City. — Much diversity of opinion exists as to the identification of the ruins which may be properly included within the site of ancient Nineveh. According to Sir H. Rawlinson and those who concur in his interpretation of the cuneiform characters, each group of mounds we have described represents a separate and distinct city. The name applied in the inscriptions to Nimroud is supposed to read "Kalkhu," and the ruins are consequently identified with those of the Calah of Genesis (x. 11); Khorsabad is Sargina, as founded by Sargon, the name having been retained in that of Sarghun, or Sarsoun, by which the ruins were known to the Arab geographers; Shereef Khan is Tarbisi. Selamiyah has not yet been identified, no inscription having been found in the ruins. The name of Nineveh is limited to the mounds opposite Mosul, including Kouyunjik and Nebbi Yunus. Sir H. Rawlinson was at one time inclined to exclude even the former mound from the precincts of the city (*Journ.*

of *As. Soc.* xii. 418). Furthermore, the ancient and primitive capital of Assyria is supposed to hav been not Nineveh, but a city named Asshur, whose ruins have been discovered at Kalah Sherghat, a mound on the right or W. bank of the Tigris, about 60 miles S. of Mosul. It need scarcely be observed that this theory rests entirely upon the presumed accuracy of the interpretation of the cuneiform inscriptions, and that it is totally at variance with the accounts and traditions preserved by sacred and classical history of the antiquity, size, and importance of Nineveh. The area of the inclosure of Kouyunjik, about 1,800 acres, is far too small to represent the site of the city, built as it must have been in accordance with eastern customs and manners, even after allowing for every exaggeration on the part of ancient writers. Captain Jones (*Topography of Nineveh, Journ. of R. Asiat. Soc.* xv. p. 324) computes that it would contain 174,000 inhabitants, 50 square yards being given to each person; but the basis of this calculation would scarcely apply to any modern eastern city. If Kouyunjik represents Nineveh, and Nimroud Calah, where are we to place Resen, "a great city" between the two? (Gen. x. 12.) Scarcely at Selamiyah, only three miles from Nimroud, and where no ruins of any importance exist. On the other hand, it has been conjectured that these groups of mounds are not ruins of separate cities, but of fortified royal residences, each combining palaces, temples, propylæa, gardens, and parks, and having its peculiar name; and that they all formed part of one great city built and added to at different periods, and consisting of distinct quarters scattered over a very large area, and frequently very distant one from the other. Nineveh might thus be compared with Damascus, Ispahan, or perhaps more appropriately with Delhi, a city rebuilt at various periods, but never on exactly the same site, and whose ruins consequently cover an area but little inferior to that assigned to the capital of Assyria. The primitive site, the one upon which Nineveh was originally founded, may possibly have been that occupied by the mound of Kouyunjik. It is thus alone that the ancient descriptions of Nineveh, if any value whatever is to be attached to them, can be reconciled with existing remains. The absence of all traces of buildings of any size within the inclosures of Nimroud, Kouyunjik, and Khorsabad, and the existence of propylæa forming part of the approaches to the palace, beneath and at a considerable distance from the great mound at Khorsabad, seem to add weight to this conjecture. Even Sir H. Rawlinson is compelled to admit that all the ruins may have formed part of "that group of cities, which in the time of the prophet Jonah, was known by the common name of Nineveh" (*On the Inscriptions of Babylonia and Assyria, Journ. As. Soc.*). But the existence of fortified palaces is consistent with oriental custom, and with authentic descriptions of ancient eastern cities. Such were the residences of the kings of Babylon, the walls of the largest of which were 60 stadia, or 7 miles in circuit, or little less than those of Kouyunjik, and considerably greater than those of Nimroud [BABYLON]. The Persians, who appear to have closely imitated the Assyrians in most things, constructed similar fortified parks, or paradises — as they were called — which included royal dwelling-places (Quint. Curt. l. 7, c. 8). Indeed, if the interpretation of the cuneiform inscriptions is to be trusted, the Assyrian palaces were of precisely the same character; for that built by Essarhaddon at Nebbi Yunus is stated to have been so large that horses and other animals were not only kept, but even bred within its walls (Fox Talbot, *Assyr. Texts translated*, p. 17,18). It is evident that this description cannot apply to a building occupying so confined an area as the summit of this mound, but to a vast inclosed space. This aggregation of strongholds may illustrate the allusion in Nahum (iii. 14), " Draw thee waters for the siege, fortify thy strongholds," and " repair thy fortified places." They were probably surrounded by the dwellings of the mass of the population, either collected in groups, or scattered singly in the midst of fields, orchards, and gardens. There are still sufficient indications in the country around of the sites of such habitations. The fortified inclosures, whilst including the residences of the king, his family or immediate tribe, his principal officers, and probably the chief priests, may also have served as places of refuge for the inhabitants of the city at large in times of danger or attack. According to Diodorus (ii. 9) and Quintus Curtius (v. 1), there was land enough within the precincts of Babylon, besides gardens and orchards, to furnish corn for the wants of the whole population in case of siege; and in the book of Jonah, Nineveh is said to contain, besides its population, " much cattle " (iv. 11). As at Babylon, no great consecutive wall of inclosure comprising all the ruins, such as that described by Diodorus, has been discovered at Nineveh, and no such wall ever existed, otherwise some traces of so vast and massive a structure must have remained to this day. The river Gomel, the modern Ghazir-Su, may have formed the eastern boundary or defense of the city. As to the claims of the mound of Kalah Sherghat to represent the site of the primitive capital of Assyria called Asshur, they must rest entirely on the interpretation of the inscriptions. This city was founded, or added to, they are supposed to declare, by one Shamas-Iva, the son and viceroy, or satrap, of Ismi-Dagon, king of Babylon, who reigned, it is conjectured, about B. C. 1840. Assyria and its capital remained subject to Babylonia until B. C. 1273, when an independent Assyrian dynasty was founded, of which fourteen kings, or more, reigned at Kalah Sherghat. About B. C. 930 the seat of government, it is asserted, was transferred by Sardanapalus (the second of the name, and the Sardanapalus of the Greeks) to the city of Kalkhu or Calah (Nimroud), which had been founded by an earlier monarch named Shalmanubar. There it continued about 250 years, when Sennacherib made Nineveh the capital of the empire [ASSYRIA]. These assumptions seem to rest upon very slender grounds; and Dr. Hincks altogether rejects the theory of the Babylonian character of these early kings, believing them to be Assyrian (*Report to Trustees of Brit. Mus. on Cylinders and Terra-Cottas*). It is believed that on an inscribed terra-cotta cylinder discovered at Kalah Sherghat, the foundation of a temple is attributed to this Shamas-Iva. A royal name similar to that of his father, Ismi-Dagon, is read on a brick from some ruins in southern Babylonia, and the two kings are presumed to be identical, although there is no other evidence of the fact (Rawl. *Herod.* i. p.

456, note 5); indeed the only son of this Babylonian king mentioned in the inscriptions is read Ibil-anu-duina, a name entirely different from that of the presumed viceroy of Asshur. It is by no means an uncommon occurrence that the same names should be found in royal dynasties of very different periods.[a] The Assyrian dynasties furnish more than one example. It may be further observed that no remains of sufficient antiquity and importance have been discovered at Kalah Sherghat to justify the opinion that it was the ancient capital. The only sculpture found in the ruins, the seated figure in black basalt now in the British Museum, belongs to a later period than the monuments from the N. W. palace at Nimroud. Upon the presumed identification above indicated, and upon no other evidence, as far as we can understand, an entirely new system of Assyrian history and chronology has been constructed, of which a sketch has been given under the title ASSYRIA (see also Rawlinson's *Herod.* vol. i. p. 489). It need only be pointed out here that this system is at variance with sacred, classical, and monumental history, and can scarcely be accepted as proven, until the Assyrian ruins have been examined with more completeness than has hitherto been possible, and until the decipherment of the cuneiform inscriptions has made far greater progress. It has been shown how continuously tradition points to Nineveh as the ancient capital of Assyria. There is no allusion to any other city which enjoyed this rank. Its name occurs in the statistical table of Karnak, in conjunction with Naharaina or Mesopotamia. and on a fragment recently discovered by M. Mariette, of the time of Thotmas III., or about B. C. 1490 (Birch, *Trans. R. Soc. of Lit.* ii. 345, second series), and no mention has been found on any Egyptian monument of such cities as Asshur and Calah. Sir H. Rawlinson, in a paper read before the R. S. of Lit., has, however, contended that the Naharayn, Saeukar, and Assuri of the Egyptian inscriptions are not Mesopotamia, Singar, and Assyria, and that Nin-i-lu is not Nineveh at all, but refers to a city in the chain of Taurus. But these conclusions are altogether rejected by Egyptian scholars. Further researches may show that Sennacherib's palace at Kouyunjik, and that of Sardanapalus at Nimroud, were built upon the site and above the remains of very much earlier edifices. According to the interpretation of the inscriptions, Sardanapalus himself founded a temple at " Nineveh " (Rawl. *Herod.* i. 462), yet no traces of this building have been discovered at Kouyunjik. Sargon *restored* the walls of Nineveh, and declares that he erected his palace " near to Nineveh " (*id.* 474), whilst Sennacherib only claims to have *rebuilt* the palaces, which were " rent and split from extreme old age " (*id.* 475), employing 360,000 men, captives from Chaldæa, Syria, Armenia, and Cilicia, in the undertaking, and speaks of Nineveh as founded of old, and governed by his forefathers, " kings of the old time " (Fox Talbot, on Bellino's cylinder, *Journ. of As. Soc.* vol. xviii.). Old palaces, a great tower, and ancient temples dedicated to Ishtar and Bar Muri, also stood there. Hitherto the remains of no other edifices than those attributed to Sennacherib and

---

[a] To support the theory of the ancient capital of Assyria being Asshur, a further identification is required of two kings whose names are read Tiglath-pilese. one found in a rock-cut inscription at Bavian in the mountains to the E of Mosul, the other occurring on the Kalah Sherghat cylinder. M. Oppert has questioned the identity of the two (Rawl. *Herod.* i. 456, and note.)

his successors have been discovered in the group of ruins opposite Mosul.

Prophecies relating to Nineveh, and Illustrations of the O. T. — These are exclusively contained in the books of Nahum and Zephaniah; for although Isaiah foretells the downfall of the Assyrian empire (chs x. and xiv.), he makes no mention of its capital. Nahum threatens the entire destruction of the city, so that it shall not rise again from its ruins: "With an overrunning flood he will make an utter end of the place thereof." "He will make an utter end; affliction shall not rise up the second time" (i. 8, 9). "Thy people is scattered upon the mountains, and no one gathereth them. There is no healing of thy bruise" (iii. 18, 19). The manner in which the city should be taken seems to be indicated. "The defence shall be prepared" (ii. 5) is rendered in the marginal reading "the covering or coverer shall be prepared," and by Mr. Vance Smith (*Prophecies on Assyria and the Assyrians*, p. 242), "the covering machine," the covered battering-ram or tower supposed to be represented in the bas-reliefs as being used in-sieges. Some commentators believe that "the overrunning flood" refers to the agency of water in the destruction of the walls by an extraordinary overflow of

the Tigris, and the consequent exposure of the city to assault through a breach; others, that it applies to a large and devastating army. An allusion to the overflow of the river may be contained in ii. 6, "The gates of the rivers shall be opened, and the palace shall be dissolved," a prophecy supposed to have been fulfilled when the Medo-Babylonian army captured the city. Diodorus (ii. 27) relates of that event, that "there was an old prophecy that Nineveh should not be taken till the river became an enemy to the city; and in the third year of the siege the river being swoln with continued rains, overflowed part of the city, and broke down the wall for twenty stadia; then the king thinking that the oracle was fulfilled and the river become an enemy to the city, built a large funeral pile in the palace, and collecting together all his wealth, and his concubines and eunuchs, burnt himself and the palace with them all: and the enemy entered the breach that the waters had made, and took the city." Most of the edifices discovered had been destroyed by fire, but no part of the walls of either Nimroud or Kouyunjik appears to have been washed away by the river. The Tigris is still subject to very high and dangerous floods during the winter and spring rains, and even now frequently reaches

King feasting. From Kouyunjik.

the ruins. When it flowed in its ancient bed at the foot of the walls a part of the city might have been overwhelmed by an extraordinary inundation. The likening of Nineveh to "a pool of water" (ii. 8) has been conjectured to refer to the moats and dams by which a portion of the country around Nineveh could be flooded. The city was to be partly destroyed by fire, "The fire shall devour thy bars," "then shall the fire devour thee" (iii. 13, 15). The gateway in the northern wall of the Kouyunjik inclosure had been destroyed by fire as well as the palaces. The population was to be surprised when unprepared, "while they are drunk as drunkards they shall be devoured as stubble fully dry" (i. 10). Diodorus states that the last and fatal assault was made when they were overcome with wine. In the bas-reliefs carousing scenes are represented, in which the king, his courtiers, and even the queen, reclining on couches or seated on thrones, and attended by musicians, appear to be pledging each other in bowls of wine (Botta, *Mon. de Nin.* pl. 63-67, 112, 113, and one very interesting slab in the Brit. Mus., figured above). The captivity of the inhabitants, and their removal to distant provinces, are predicted (iii. 18). Their dispersion, which occurred when the

city fell, was in accordance with the barbarous custom of the age. The palace-temples were to be plundered of their idols, "out of the house of thy gods will I cut off the graven image and the molten image" (i. 14), and the city sacked of its wealth: "Take ye the spoil of silver, take the spoil of gold" (ii. 9). For ages the Assyrian edifices have been despoiled of their sacred images; and enormous amounts of gold and silver were, according to tradition, taken to Ecbatana by the conquering Medes (Diod. Sic. ii.). Only one or two fragments of the precious metals were found in the ruins. Nineveh, after its fall, was to be "empty, and void, and waste" (ii. 10); "it shall come to pass, that all they that look upon thee shall flee from thee, and say, Nineveh is laid waste" (iii. 7). These epithets describe the present state of the site of the city. But the fullest and the most vivid and poetical picture of its ruined and deserted condition is that given by Zephaniah, who probably lived to see its fall. "He will make Nineveh a desolation, and dry like a wilderness. And flocks shall lie down in the midst of her, all the beasts of the nations: both the cormorant and the bittern shall lodge in the upper lintels of it! their voice shall sing in the windows: desolation shall be in the thresholds: for he shall uncover the cedar work . . . how is she become a desolation, a place for beasts to lie down in! every one that passeth by her shall hiss

Winged deity.

and wag his hand' (ii. 13, 14, 15.) The canals which once fertilized the soil are now dry. Except when the earth is green after the periodical rains the site of the city, as well as the surrounding country, is an arid yellow waste. Flocks of sheep and herds of camels may be seen seeking scanty pasture amongst the mounds. From the unwholesome swamp within the ruins of Khorsabad, and from the reedy banks of the little streams that flow by Kouyunjik and Nimroud may be heard the croak of the cormorant and the bittern. The cedar-wood which adorned the ceilings of the pal-

Winged globe.

aces has been uncovered by modern explorers (Layard, *Nin. and Bab.* p. 357), and in the deserted halls the hyena, the wolf, the fox, and the jackal, now lie down. Many allusions in the O. T. to the dress, arms, modes of warfare, and customs of the people of Nineveh, as well as of the Jews, are explained by the Nineveh monuments. Thus (Nah. ii. 3), "the shield of his mighty men is made red, the valiant men are in scarlet." The shields and the dresses of the warriors are generally painted red in the sculptures. The magnificent description of the assault upon the city (iii. 1, 2, 3) is illustrated in almost every particular (Layard, *Nin. and its Rem.* ii., part ii., ch. v.). The mounds built up against the walls of a besieged town (Is. xxxvii. 33; 2 K. xix. 32; Jer. xxxii. 24, &c.), the battering-ram (Ez. iv. 2), the various kinds of armor, helmets, shields, spears, and swords, used in battle and during a siege; the chariots and horses (Nah. iii. 3; CHARIOT), are all seen in various bas-reliefs (Layard, *Nin. and its Rem.* ii., part ii., chaps. iv. and v.). The custom of cutting off the heads of the slain and placing them in heaps (2 K. x. 8) is constantly represented (Layard, ii 184). The allusion in 2 K. xix. 29, "I will put my hook in thy nose and my bridle in thy lips," is illustrated in a bas-relief from Khorsabad (*id.* 376).

The interior decoration of the Assyrian palaces is described by Ezekiel, himself a captive in Assyria and an eye-witness of their magnificence

(xxiii. 14, 15). "She saw men of sculptured workmanship upon the walls; likenesses of the Chaldeans pictured in red, girded with girdles upon their loins, with colored flowing head-dresses upon their heads, with the aspect of princes all of them" (Lay. *Nin. and its Rem.* ii. 307); a description strikingly illustrated by the sculptured likenesses of the Assyrian kings and warriors (see especially Botta, *Mon. de Nin.* pl. 12). The mystic figures seen by the prophet in his vision (ch. i.), uniting the man, the lion, the ox, and the eagle, may have been suggested by the eagle-headed idols, and man-headed bulls and lions (by some identified with the cherubim of the Jews [CHERUB]), and the sacred emblem of the "wheel within wheel" by the winged circle or globe frequently represented in the bas-reliefs (Lay. *Nin. and its Rem.* ii. 465).

Arts. — The origin of Assyrian art is a subject at present involved in mystery, and one which offers a wide field for speculation and research. Those who derive the civilization and political system of the Assyrians from Babylonia would trace their arts to the same source. One of the principal features of their architecture, the artificial platform serving as a substructure for their national edifices, may have been taken from a people inhabiting plains perfectly flat, such as those of Shinar, rather than an undulating country in which natural elevations are not uncommon, such as Assyria proper. But it still remains to be proved that there are artificial mounds in Babylonia of an earlier date than mounds on or near the site of Nineveh. Whether other leading features and the details of Assyrian architecture came from the same source, is much more open to doubt. Such Babylonian edifices as have been hitherto explored are of a later date than those of Nineveh, to which they appear to bear but little resemblance. The only features in common seem to be the ascending stages of the temples or tombs, and the use of enameled bricks. The custom of paneling walls with alabaster or stone must have originated in a country in which such materials abound, as in Assyria, and not in the alluvial plains of southern Mesopotamia, where they cannot be obtained except at great cost or by great labor. The use of sun-dried and kiln-burnt bricks and of wooden columns would be common to both countries, as also such arrangements for the admission of light and exclusion of heat as the climate would naturally suggest.

In none of the arts of the Assyrians have any traces hitherto been found of progressive change. In the architecture of the most ancient known edifice all the characteristics of the style are already fully developed; no new features of any importance seem to have been introduced at a later period. The palace of Sennacherib only excels those of his remote predecessors in the vastness of its proportions, and in the elaborate magnificence of its details. In sculpture, as probably in painting also, if we possessed the means of comparison, the same thing is observable as in the remains of ancient Egypt. The earliest works hitherto discovered show the result of a lengthened period of gradual development, which, judging from the slow progress made by untutored men in the arts, must have extended over a vast number of years. They exhibit the arts of the Assyrians at the highest stage of excellence they probably ever attained. The only change we can trace, as in Egypt, is one of decline or "decadence." The latest monuments, such as those from the palaces of Essarhaddon and his son, show perhaps a closer imitation of nature, especially in the representation of animals, such as the lion, dog, wild ass, etc., and a more careful and minute execution of details than those from the earlier edifices; but they are wanting in the simplicity yet grandeur of conception, in the invention, and in the variety of treatment displayed in the most ancient sculptures. This will at once be perceived by a comparison of the ornamental details of the two periods. In the older sculptures there occur the most graceful and varied combinations of flowers, beasts, birds, and other natural objects, treated in a conventional and highly artistic manner; in the later there is only a constant and monotonous repetition of rosettes and commonplace forms, without much display of invention or imagination (compare Layard, *Mon. of Nineveh*, 1st series, especially plates 5, 8, 43–48, 50, with 2d series, *passim;* and with Botta, *Monumens de Ninive*). The same remark applies to animals. The lions of the earlier period are a grand, ideal, and, to a certain extent, conventional representation of the beast — not very different from that of the Greek sculptor in the noblest period of Greek art (Layard, *Mon. of Nin.*, 2d series, pl. 2). In the later bas-reliefs, such as those from the palace of Sardanapalus III., now in the British Museum, the lions are more closely imitated from nature without any conventional elevation; but what is gained in truth is lost in dignity.

The same may be observed in the treatment of the human form, though in its representation the Assyrians, like the Egyptians, would seem to have been, at all times, more or less shackled by religious prejudices or laws. For instance, the face is almost invariably in profile, not because the sculptor was unable to represent the full face, one or two examples of it occurring in the bas-reliefs, but probably because he was bound by a generally received custom, through which he would not break. No new forms or combinations appear to have been introduced into Assyrian art during the four or five centuries, if not longer period, with which we are acquainted with it. We trace throughout the same eagle-headed, lion-headed, and fish-headed figures, the same winged divinities, the same composite forms at the doorways. In the earliest works, an attempt at composition, that is at a pleasing and picturesque grouping of the figures, is perhaps more evident than in the later — as may be illustrated by the Lion-hunt from the N. W. Palace, now in the British Museum (Layard, *Mon. of Nin.*, pl. 10). A parallel may in many respects be drawn between the arts of the Assyrians from their earliest known period to their latest, and those of Greece from Phidias to the Roman epoch, and of Italy from the 15th to the 18th century.

The art of the Nineveh monuments must in the present state of our knowledge be accepted as an original and national art, peculiar, if not to the Assyrians alone, to the races who at various periods possessed the country watered by the Tigris and Euphrates. As it was undoubtedly brought to its highest perfection by the Assyrians, and is especially characteristic of them, it may well and conveniently bear their name. From whence it was originally derived there is nothing as yet to show.

If from Babylon, as some have conjectured, there are no remains to prove the fact. Analogies may perhaps be found between it and that of Egypt, but they are not sufficient to convince us that the one was the offspring of the other. These analogies, if not accidental, may have been derived, at some very remote period, from a common source. The two may have been offshoots from some common trunk which perished ages before either Nineveh or Thebes was founded; or the Phœnicians, as it has been suggested, may have introduced into the two countries, between which they were placed, and between which they may have formed a commercial link, the arts peculiar to each of them. Whatever the origin, the development of the arts of the two countries appears to have been affected and directed by very opposite conditions of national character, climate, geographical and geological position, politics, and religion. Thus, Egyptian architecture seems to have been derived from a stone prototype, Assyrian from a wooden one — in accordance with the physical nature of the two countries. Assyrian art is the type of power, vigor, and action; Egyptian that of calm dignity and repose. The one is the expression of an ambitious, conquering, and restless nature; the other of a race which seems to have worked for itself alone and for eternity. At a late period of Assyrian history, at the time of the building of the Khorsabad palace (about the 8th century B. C.), a more intimate intercourse with Egypt through war or dynastic alliances than had previously existed, appears to have led to the introduction of objects of Egyptian manufacture into Assyria, and may have influenced to a limited extent its arts. A precisely similar influence proceeding from Assyria has been remarked at the same period in Egypt, probably arising from the conquest and temporary occupation of the latter country by the Assyrians, under a king whose name is read Asshur-bani-pal, mentioned in the cuneiform inscriptions (Birch, *Trans. of R. Soc. of Lit.*, new series). To this age belong the ivories, bronzes, and nearly all the small objects of an Egyptian character, though not apparently of Egyptian workmanship, discovered in the Assyrian ruins. It has been asserted, on the authority of an inscription believed to contain the names of certain Hellenic artists from Idalium, Citium, Salamis, Paphos, and other Greek cities, that Greeks were employed by Essarhaddon and his son in executing the sculptured decorations of their palaces (Rawl. *Herod.* i. 483). But, passing over the extreme uncertainty attaching to the decipherment of proper names in the cuneiform character, it must be observed that no remains whatever of Greek art of so early a period are known, which can be compared in knowledge of principles and in beauty of execution and of design with the sculptures of Assyria. Niebuhr has remarked of Hellenic art, that "anything produced before the Persian war was altogether barbarous" (34th Lecture on *Ancient History*). If Greek artists could execute such monuments in Assyria, why, it may be asked, did they not display equal skill in their own country? The influence, indeed, seems to have been entirely in the opposite direction. The discoveries at Nineveh show almost beyond a doubt that the Ionic element in Greek art was derived from Assyria, as the Doric came from Egypt. There is scarcely a leading form or a detail in the Ionic order which cannot be traced to Assyria — the volute of the column, the frieze of griffins, the honeysuckle-border, the guilloche, the Caryatides, and many other ornaments peculiar to the style.

The arts of the Assyrians, especially their architecture, spread to surrounding nations, as is usually the case when one race is brought into contact with another in a lower state of civilization. They appear to have crossed the Euphrates, and to have had more or less influence on the countries between it and the Mediterranean. Monuments of an Assyrian character have been discovered in various parts of Syria, and further researches would probably disclose many more. The arts of the Phœnicians, judging from the few specimens preserved, show the same influence. In the absence of even the most insignificant remains, and of any implements which may with confidence be attributed to the Jews [ARMS], there are no materials for comparison between Jewish and Assyrian art. It is possible that the bronzes and ivories discovered at Nineveh were of Phœnician manufacture, like the vessels in Solomon's Temple. On the lion-weights, now in the British Museum, are inscriptions both in the cuneiform and Phœnician characters. The Assyrian inscriptions seem to indicate a direct dependence of Judæa upon Assyria from a very early period. From the descriptions of the Temple and "houses" of Solomon (cf. 1 K. vi., vii.; 2 Chr. iii., iv.; Joseph. viii. 2; Fergusson's *Palaces of Nineveh*; and Layard, *Nin. and Bab.* p. 642), it would appear that there was much similarity between them and the palaces of Nineveh, if not in the exterior architecture, certainly in the interior decorations, such as the walls paneled or wainscoted with sawn stones, the sculptures on the slabs representing trees and plants, the remainder of the walls above the skirting painted with various colors and pictures, the figures of the winged cherubim carved "all the house round," and especially on the doorways, the ornaments of open flowers, pomegranates, and lilies (apparently corresponding exactly with the rosettes, pomegranates, and honeysuckle ornaments of the Assyrian bas-reliefs, Botta, *Mon. de Nin.*, and Layard, *Mon. of Nin.*), and the ceiling, roof, and beams of cedar-wood. The Jewish edifices were however very much inferior in size to the Assyrian. Of objects of art (if we may use the term) contained in the Temple we have the description of the pillars, of the brazen sea, and of various bronze or copper vessels. They were the work of Hiram, the son of a Phœnician artist by a Jewish woman of the tribe of Naphtali (1 K. vii. 14), a fact which gives us some insight into Phœnician art, and seems to show that the Jews had no art of their own, as Hiram was fetched from Tyre by Solomon. The Assyrian character of these objects is very remarkable. The two pillars and "chapiters" of brass had ornaments of lilies and pomegranates; the brazen sea was supported on oxen, and its rim was ornamented with flowers of lilies, whilst the bases were graven with lilies, oxen, and cherubim on the borders, and the plates of the ledges with cherubim, ons, and palm-trees. The vail of the Temple, of different colors, had also cherubim wrought upon it. (Cf. Layard, *Nin. and Bab.* woodcut, p. 588, in which a large vessel, probably of bronze or copper, is represented supported upon oxen, and *Mon. of Nin.*, series 2, pl. 60, 65, 68, — in which vessels with embossed rims apparently similar to those in Solomon's Temple are figured. Also series 1, pl. 8, 44, 48, in which embroideries with cherubim occur.)

The influence of Assyria to the eastward was even more considerable, extending far into Asia. The Persians copied their architecture (with such modifications as the climate and the building-materials at hand suggested), their sculpture, probably their painting and their mode of writing, from the Assyrians. The ruined palaces of Persepolis show the same general plan of construction as those of Nineveh — the entrances formed by human-headed animals, the skirting of sculptured stone, and the inscribed slabs. The various religious emblems and the ornamentation have the same Assyrian character. In Persia, however, a stone architecture prevailed, and the columns in that material have resisted to this day the ravages of time.

The Persians made an advance in one respect upon Assyrian sculpture, and probably painting likewise, in an attempt at a natural representation of drapery by the introduction of folds, of which there is only the slightest indication on Assyrian monuments. It may have been partly through Persia that the influence of Assyrian art passed into Asia Minor and thence into Greece; but it had probably penetrated far into the former country long before the Persian domination. We find it strongly shown in the earliest monuments, as in those of Lycia and Phrygia, and in the archaic sculptures of Branchidæ. But the early art of Asia Minor still offers a most interesting field for investigation. Amongst the Assyrians, the arts were principally employed, as amongst all nations in their earlier stages of civilization, for religious and national purposes. The colossal figures at the doorways of the palaces were mythic combinations to denote the attributes of a deity. The "Man-Bull" and the "Man-Lion," are conjectured to be the gods "Nin" and "Nergal," presiding over war and the chase; the eagle-headed and fish-headed figures so constantly repeated in the sculptures, and as ornaments on vessels of metal, or in embroideries — Nisroch and Dagon. The bas-reliefs almost invariably record some deed of the king, as head of the nation, in war, and in combat with wild beasts, or his piety in erecting vast palace-temples to the gods. Hitherto no sculptures specially illustrating the private life of the Assyrians have been discovered, except one or two incidents, such as men baking bread or tending horses, introduced as mere accessories into the historical bas-reliefs. This may be partly owing to the fact that no traces whatever have yet been found of their burial-places, or even of their mode of dealing with the dead. It is chiefly upon the walls of tombs that the domestic life of the Egyptians has been so fully depicted. In the useful arts, as in the fine arts, the Assyrians had made a progress which denotes a very high state of civilization [ASSYRIA]. When the inscriptions have been fully examined and deciphered, it will probably be found that they had made no inconsiderable advance in the sciences, especially in astronomy, mathematics, numeration, and hydraulics. Although the site of Nineveh afforded no special advantages for commerce, and although she owed her greatness rather to her political position as the capital of the empire, yet, situated upon a navigable river communicating with the Euphrates and the Persian Gulf, she must have soon formed one of the great trading stations between that important inland sea, and Syria, and the Mediterranean, and must have become a depôt for the merchandise supplied to a great part of Asia Minor, Armenia, and Persia. Her merchants are described in Ezekiel (xxvii. 24) as trading in blue clothes and broidered work (such as is probably represented in the sculptures), and in Nahum (iii. 16) as "multiplied above the stars of heaven." The animals represented on the black obelisk in the British Museum and on other monuments, the rhinoceros, the elephant, the double-humped camel, and various kinds of apes and monkeys, show a communication direct or indirect with the remotest parts of Asia. This intercourse with foreign nations, and the practice of carrying to Assyria as captives the skilled artists and workmen of conquered countries, must have contributed greatly to the improvement of Assyrian manufactures.

Writing and Language. — The ruins of Nineveh have furnished a vast collection of inscriptions partly carved on marble or stone slabs, and partly impressed upon bricks, and upon clay cylinders, or six-sided and eight-sided prisms, barrels, and tablets, which, used for the purpose when still moist, were afterwards baked in a furnace or kiln. (Cf. Ezekiel, iv. 1, "Take thee a tile . . . and portray upon it the city, even Jerusalem.") The cylinders are hollow, and appear, from the hole pierced through them, to have been mounted so as to turn round, and to present their several sides to the reader. The character employed was the arrow-headed or cuneiform — so called from each letter being formed by marks or elements resembling an arrow-head or a wedge. This mode of writing, believed by some to be of Turanian or Scythic origin, prevailed throughout the provinces comprised in the Assyrian, Babylonian, and the eastern portion of the ancient Persian empires, from the earliest times to which any known record belongs, or at least twenty centuries before the Christian era, down to the period of the conquests of Alexander; after which epoch, although occasionally employed, it seems to have gradually fallen into disuse. It never extended into Syria, Arabia, or Asia Minor, although it was adopted in Armenia. A cursive writing resembling the ancient Syrian and Phœnician, and by some believed to be the original form of all other cursive writing used in Western Asia, including the Hebrew, appears to have also been occasionally employed in Assyria, probably for documents written on parchment or papyrus, or perhaps leather skins. The Assyrian cuneiform character was of the same class as the Babylonian, only differing from it in the less complicated nature of its forms. Although the primary elements in the later Persian and so-called Median cuneiform were the same, yet their combination and the value of the letters were quite distinct. The latter, indeed, is but a form of the Assyrian. Herodotus terms all cuneiform writing the "Assyrian writing" (Herod. iv. 87). This character may have been derived from some more ancient form of hieroglyphic writing; but if so, all traces of such origin have disappeared. The Assyrian and Babylonian alphabet (if the term may be applied to above 200 signs) is of the most complicated, imperfect, and arbitrary nature — some characters being phonetic, others syllabic, others deographic — the same character being frequently

used indifferently. This constitutes one of the principal difficulties in the process of decipherment. The investigation first commenced by Grotefend (Heeren, *Asiatic Nations*, vol. ii. App. 2) has since been carried on with much success by Sir H. Rawlinson, Dr Hincks; Mr. Norris, and Mr. Fox Talbot, in England, and by M. Oppert in France (see papers by those gentlemen in the *Journals of the Roy. As. Soc.*, in *Transactions of Royal Irish Academy*, in *Journal of Sacred Literature*, and in the *Athenæum*). Although considerable doubt may still reasonably prevail as to the interpretation of details, as to grammatical construction, and especially as to the rendering of proper names, sufficient progress has been made to enable the student to ascertain with some degree of confidence the general meaning and contents of an inscription. The people of Nineveh spoke a Semitic dialect, connected with the Hebrew and with the so-called Chaldee of the Books of Daniel and Ezra. This agrees with the testimony of the O. T. But it is asserted that there existed in Assyria, as well as in Babylonia, a more ancient tongue belonging to a

Specimen of the Arrow-headed or Cuneiform Writing

Turanian or Scythic race, which is supposed to have inhabited the plains watered by the Tigris and Euphrates long before the rise of the Assyrian empire, and from which the Assyrians derived their civilization and the greater part of their mythology. It was retained for sacred purposes by the conquering race, as the Latin was retained after the fall of the Roman Empire in the Catholic Church. In fragments of vocabularies discovered in the record-chamber at Kouyunjik words in the two languages are placed in parallel columns, whilst a centre column contains a monographic or ideographic sign representing both. A large number of Turanian words or roots are further supposed to have existed in the Assyrian tongue, and tablets apparently in that language have been discovered in the ruins. The monumental inscriptions occur on detached stelæ and obelisks, of which there are several specimens in the British Museum from the Assyrian ruins, and one in the Berlin Museum discovered in the island of Cyprus; on the colossal human-headed lions and bulls, upon parts not occupied by sculpture, as between the legs; on the sculptured slabs, generally in bands between two bas-reliefs, to which they seem to refer; and, as in Persia and Armenia, carved on the face of rocks in the hill-country. At Nimroud the same inscription is carved on nearly every slab in the N. W. palace, and generally repeated on the back, and even carried across the sculptured colossal figures. The Assyrian inscriptions usually contain the chronicles of the king who built or restored the edifice in which they are found, records of his wars and expeditions into distant countries, of the amount of tribute and spoil taken from conquered tribes, of the building of temples and palaces, and invocations to the gods of Assyria. Frequently every stone and kiln-burnt brick used in a building bears the name and titles of the king, and generally those of his father and grandfather are added. These inscribed bricks are of the greatest value in restoring the royal dynasties. The longest inscription on stone, that from the N. W. palace of Nineveh containing the records of Sardanapalus II., has 325 lines, that on the black obelisk has 210. The most important hitherto discovered in connection with Biblical history, is that upon a pair of colossal human-headed bulls from Kouyunjik, now in the British Museum, containing the records of Sennacherib, and describing, amongst other events, his wars with Hezekiah. It is accompanied by a series of bas-reliefs believed to represent the siege and capture of Lachish (LACHISH; Layard, *Nin. and Bab.* pp. 148–153)

Sennacherib on his Throne before Lachish.

Jewish Captives from Lachish (Kouyunjik).

A long list might be given of Biblical names occurring in the Assyrian inscriptions (*id.* 626). Those of three Jewish kings have been read, Jehu son of Khumri (Omri), on the black obelisk (JEHU;

Impressions of the Signets of the Kings of Assyria and Egypt. (Original size.)

Part of Cartouche of Sabaco, enlarged from the impression of his Signet.

Layard, *Nin. and Bab.* p. 613), Menahem on a slab from the S. W. palace, Nimroud, now in the British Museum (*id.* 617), and Hezekiah in the Kouyunjik records. The most important inscribed terracotta cylinders are — those from Kalah Sherghat, with the annals of a king, whose name is believed to read Tiglath Pileser, not the same mentioned in the 2d Book of Kings, but an earlier monarch, who is supposed to have reigned about B. C. 1110 (Rawl. *Herod.* i. 457); those from Khorsabad containing the annals of Sargon; those from Kouyunjik, especially one known as Bellino's cylinder, with the chronicles of Sennacherib; that from Nebbi Yunus with the records of Esarhaddon, and the fragments of three cylinders with those of his son. The longest inscription on a cylinder is of 820 lines. Such cylinders and inscribed slabs were generally buried beneath the foundations of great public buildings. Many fragments of cylinders and a vast collection of inscribed clay tablets, many in perfect preservation, and some bearing the impressions of seals, were discovered in a chamber at Kouyunjik, and are now deposited in the British Museum. They appear to include historical documents, vocabularies, astronomical and other calculations, calendars, directions for the performance of religious ceremonies, lists of the gods, their attributes, and the days appointed for their worship, descriptions of countries, lists of animals, grants of lands, etc., etc. In this chamber was also found the piece of clay bearing the seal of the Egyptian king, So or Sabaco, and that of an Assyrian monarch, either Sennacherib or his son, probably affixed to a treaty between the two, which having been written on parchment or papyrus, had entirely perished (Layard, *Nin. and Bab.* p. 156).

The most important results may be expected when inscriptions so numerous and so varied in character are deciphered. A list of nineteen or twenty kings can already be compiled, and the annals of the greater number of them will probably be restored to the lost history of one of the most powerful empires of the ancient world, and of one which appears to have exercised perhaps greater influence than any other upon the subsequent condition and development of civilized man. [ASSYRIA.]

The only race now found near the ruins of Nineveh or in Assyria which may have any claim to be considered descendants from the ancient inhabitants of the country are the so-called Chaldæan or Nestorian tribes, inhabiting the mountains of Kurdistan, the plains round the lake of Ooroomiyah in Persia, and a few villages in the neighborhood of Mosul. They still speak a Semitic dialect, almost identical with the Chaldee of the books of Daniel and Ezra. A resemblance, which may be but fanciful, has been traced between them and the representations of the Assyrians in the bas-reliefs. Their physical characteristics at any rate seem to mark them as of the same race. The inhabitants of this part of Asia have been exposed perhaps more than those of any other country in the world to the devastating inroads of stranger hordes. Conquering tribes of Arabs and of Tartars have more than once well-nigh exterminated the population which they found there, and have occupied their places. The few survivors from these terrible massacres have taken refuge in the mountain fastnesses, where they may still linger. A curse seems to hang over a land naturally rich and fertile, and capable of sustaining a vast number of human beings. Those who now inhabit it are yearly diminishing, and there seems no prospect that for generations to come this once-favored country should remain other than a wilderness.

(Layard's *Nineveh and its Remains; Nineveh and Babylon;* and *Monuments of Nineveh*, 1st and 2d series; Botta's *Monumens de Ninivé;* Fergusson, *Palaces of Nineveh and Persepolis Restored;* Vaux's *Nineveh and Persepolis.*)
A. H. L.

* We referred under NAHUM to some of the writers on the history and fall of Nineveh. We add here the names of a few others who treat of this subject, relying in part on Dr. Kleinert's catalogue mentioned under the above head. G. F. Grotefend, *Ueber Anlage u. Zerstörung der Gebäude Nimrud* (1851). J. Brandis, *Ueber den hist. Gewinn aus der Entzifferung der Assyr. Inschriften* (1853). Gumpach, *Abriss der Assyrisch-babyl. Geschichte.* J. Olshausen, *Prüfung des Characters der in den Assyr. Inschriften semit. Sprache.* F. A. and O. Strauss, *Länder u. Stätten der heil. Schrift,* § 861, p. 328 (1855). F. Spiegel, "Ninive" in Herzog's *Real-Encyk.* x. 361–381 (1858), and a supplementary article, under the same title, xx. 219–235 (1866). J. Oppert, *Chronologie des Assyriens et Babyloniens.* F.

Fresnel, *Expédition Scientifique en Mésopotamie,* publiée par J. Oppert (1858). Bonomi, *Nineveh and its Palaces* (1852), founded on Botta and Layard. W. K. Loftus, *Travels and Researches in Chaldæa and Susiana* (1858). Dr. Pusey on Jonah, *Minor Prophets, with a Commentary,* Part iii. (1861). Dr. Spiegel speaks in his second article in a much stronger tone of confidence with regard to the success of the efforts which have been made to read the Assyrian inscriptions. He declares his belief that the deciphering of the Assyrian alphabet has been pursued hitherto on systematic and scientific principles; that there is good reason to hope that future studies will overcome any still remaining obstacles to a more perfect interpretation, and, in the mean time, that we may confide in the results already gained. It would be premature to expect this view to be universally accepted at present.

The cabinet of Amherst College contains some interesting antiquities from the ruins of Nineveh and Babylon. They are such as several mystic figures of Assyrian deities sculptured on alabaster slabs, taken from the palace of Sardanapalus (one of them eagle-headed, and supposed to be the NISROCH of Scripture, 2 K. xix. 37); a representation of Sardanapalus, armed as a warrior, and in the act of giving thanks for victory, with inscriptions which record his exploits; a winged human-headed lion; Sennacherib at the siege of Lachish (2 Chr. xxxii. 9);[a] a fish-god, the head of the fish forming a mitre above the man; a sphinx, the body that of a lion, the face beardless, surmounted with a highly ornamented cap; a winged horse, the original type of the Greek Pegasus; a gryphon, the body that of a lion, with the wings and head of an eagle; and five bricks bearing inscriptions, among which are the names and titles of three successive kings. "All the slabs bear inscriptions, reading from left to right, which are precisely identical, and refer to the king who built the palace. They are written in the cuneiform character, which was the monumental writing of the Assyrians, while an entirely distinct form was used for private documents" (see *Guide to the Public Rooms and Cabinets of Amherst College,* Amh. 1868).   H.

NIN'EVITES (Νινευῖται; [Tisch. 8th ed. Νινευεῖται:] *Ninevitæ*). The inhabitants of Nineveh (Luke xi. 30).

NI'SAN. [MONTHS.]

NIS'ROCH (נִסְרֹךְ [see below]: Μεσεράχ, Mai's ed. 'Εσδράχ; Alex. Εσθραχ [Comp. Νεσράχ] in 2 K.; Νασαράχ [Alex. Ασαραχ] in Is.: *Nesroch*). The proper name of an idol of Nineveh, in whose temple Sennacherib was worshipping when assassinated by his sons, Adrammelech and Sharezer (2 K. xix. 37; Is. xxxvii. 38). Selden confesses his ignorance of the deity denoted by this name (*de Dis Syris,* synt. ii. c. 10); but Beyer, in his *Additamenta* (pp. 323–325) has collected several conjectures. Jarchi, in his note on Is. xxxvii. 38, explains Nisroch as "a beam, or plank, of Noah's ark," from the analysis which is given of the word by Rabbinical expositors (נסרא נודא = נסרא). What the true ety-

---

a * See the plate which probably represents the siege of Lachish as depicted on the monuments, vol ii. p. 1579.   H.

mology may be is extremely doubtful. If the origin of the word be Shemitic, it may be derived, as Gesenius suggests, from the Heb. נֶשֶׁר, which is in Arab. *nisr*, " an eagle," with the termination *óch* or *dch*, which is intensive in Persian,[a] so that Nisroch would signify " fhe great ·eagle " (comp. ARIOCH). But it must be confessed that this explanation is far from satisfactory. It is adopted, however, by Mr. Layard, who identifies with Nisroch the eagle-headed human figure, which is one of the most prominent on the earliest Assyrian monuments, and is always represented as contending with and conquering the lion or the bull (*Nineveh*, ii. 458, 459). In another passage he endeavors to reconcile the fact that Asshur was the supreme god of the Assyrians, as far as can be determined from the inscriptions, with the appearance of the name Nisroch as that of the chief god of Nineveh, by supposing that Sennacherib may have been slain in the temple of Asshur, and that the Hebrews, seeing everywhere the eagle-headed figure, " may have believed it to be that of the peculiar god of the Assyrians, to whom they consequently gave a name denoting an eagle " (*Nin. and Bab.* p: 637, note). Other explanations, based upon the same etymology, have been given; such as that suggested by Beyer (*Addit.* p. 324), that Nisroch denotes " Noah's eagle," that is " Noah's bird," that is " Noah's dove," the dove being an object of worship among the Assyrians (Lucian, *de Jov. trag.* c. 42); or that mentioned as more probable by Winer (*Realw.* s. v.), that it was the constellation Aquila, the eagle being in the Persian religion a symbol of Ormuzd. Parkhurst, deriving the word from the Chaldee root סְרַךְ, *serac* (which occurs in Dan. vi. in the form סָרְכַיָּא, *sârecayyâ*, and is rendered in the A. V. " presidents "), conjectures that Nisroch may be the impersonation of the solar fire, and substantially identical with Molech and Milcom, which are both derived from a root similar in meaning to *serac*. Nothing, however, is certain with regard to Nisroch, except that these conjectures, one and all, are very little to be depended on. Sir H. Rawlinson says that Asshur had no temple at Nineveh in which Sennacherib could have been worshipping (Rawlinson, *Herod.* i. p. 590). He conjectures that Nisroch is not a genuine reading. Josephus has a curious variation. He says (*Ant.* x. 1, § 5) that Sennacherib was buried in his own temple called *Araace* (ἐν τῷ ἰδίῳ ναῷ Ἀράσκῃ λεγομένῳ).   W. A. W.

NITRE (נֶתֶר, *nether*: ὕλκος, νίτρον: *nitrum*) occurs in Prov. xxv. 20, " As he that taketh away a garment in cold weather, and as vinegar upon *nether*, so is he that singeth songs to an heavy heart; " and in Jer. ii. 22, where it is said of sinful Judah, " though thou wash thee with *nether* and take thee much *borith* [SOAP], yet thine iniquity is marked before me." The substance denoted is not that which we now understand by the term *nitre*, i. e. nitrate of potassa — "saltpetre " — but the νίτρον or λίτρον of the Greeks, the *nitrum* of the Latins, and the *natron* or native carbonate of soda of modern chemistry. Much has been written on the subject of the nitrum

---

of the ancients; it will be enough to refer the reader to Beckmann, who (*History of Inventions*, ii. 482, Bohn's ed.) has devoted a chapter to this subject, and to the authorities mentioned in the notes. It is uncertain at what time the English term *nitre* first came to be used for *saltpetre*, but our translators no doubt understood thereby the carbonate of soda, for *nitre* is so used by Holland in his translation of Pliny (xxxi. 10) in contra-distinction to *saltpetre*, which he gives as the marginal explanation of *aphronitrum*.

The latter part of the passage in Proverbs is well explained by Shaw, who says (*Trav.* ii. 387), "the unsuitableness of the singing of songs to a heavy heart is very finely compared to the contrariety there is between vinegar and natron." This is far preferable to the explanation given by Michaelis (*De Nitro Hebraor.* in *Commentat. Societ. Reg. prælect.* i. 166; and *Suppl. Lex. Heb.* p. 1704), that the simile alludes to the unpleasant smell arising from the admixture of the acid and alkali; it points rather to the extreme mental agitation produced by ill-timed mirth, the *grating* against the feelings, to make use of another metaphor. Natron was and is still used by the Egyptians for washing linen; the value of soda in this respect is well known; this explains Jer. l. c., "though thou wash thee with soda," etc. Hasselquist (*Trav.* p. 275) says that natron is dug out of a pit or mine near Mantura in Egypt, and is mixed with limestone and is of a whitish-brown color. The Egyptians use it, (1) to put into bread instead of yeast, (2) instead of soap, (3) as a cure for the toothache, being mixed with vinegar. Compare also Forskål (*Flor. Ægypt. Arab.* p. xlvi.) who gives its Arabic names, *atrun* or *natrun*.

Natron is found abundantly in the well-known soda lakes of Egypt described by Pliny (xxxi. 10), and referred to by Strabo (xvii. A. 1155, ed. Kramer), which are situated in the barren valley of *Bakr-bela-ma* (the Waterless Sea), about 50 miles W. of Cairo; the natron occurs in whitish or yellowish efflorescent crusts, or in beds three or four feet thick, and very hard (Volney, *Trav.* i. 15), which in the winter are covered with water about two feet deep; during the other nine months of the year the lakes are dry, at which period the natron is procured. (See Andréossi, *Mémoire sur la Vallée des Lacs de Natron*, in *Mém. sur l'Égypte*, ii. 276, &c.; Berthollet, *Observat. sur le Natron*, *ibid.* 310; *Descript. de l'Égypte*, xxi. 205.)   W. H.

NO. [NO-AMON.]

NOADI'AH (נוֹעַדְיָה [*whom Jehovah meets*]: Νωαδία: [Vat. Νωαδεια; Alex. Νωαδα:] *Noadaia*). 1. A Levite, son of Binnui, who with Meremoth, Eleazar, and Jozabad, weighed the vessels of gold and silver belonging to the Temple which were brought back from Babylon (Ezr. viii. 33). In 1 Esdr. viii. 63, he is called " Moeth the son of Sabban."

2. ([Νωαδία; FA. Νοαδια:] *Noadia*.) The prophetess Noadiah joined Sanballat and Tobiah in their attempt to intimidate Nehemiah while rebuilding the wall of Jerusalem (Neh. vi. 14). She is only mentioned in Nehemiah's denunciation of his enemies, and is not prominent in the narrative.

NO'AH (נֹחַ [*rest*, Ges. ; or, *consolation*

First]: Nôe; Joseph. Nóeos: Noê), the tenth in descent from Adam, in the line of Seth, was the son of Lamech, and grandson of Methuselah. Of his father Lamech all that we know is comprised in the words that he uttered on the birth of his son, words the more significant when we contrast them with the saying of the other Lamech of the race of Cain, which have also been preserved. The one exults in the discovery of weapons by which he may defend himself in case of need. The other, a tiller of the soil, mourns over the curse which rests on the ground, seeing in it evidently the consequence of sin. It is impossible to mistake the religious feeling which speaks of "the ground which *Jehovah* hath cursed." Not less evident is the bitter sense of weary and fruitless labor, mingled with better hopes for the future. We read that on the birth of a son "he called his name Noah, saying, This shall comfort us, for our work and labor of our hands, because of (or from) the ground which Jehovah hath cursed." Nothing can be more exquisitely true and natural than the way in which the old man's saddened heart turns fondly to his son. His own lot had been cast in evil times; "but this," he says, "shall comfort us." One hardly knows whether the sorrow or the hope predominates. Clearly there is an almost prophetic feeling in the name which he gives his son, and hence some Christian writers have seen in the language a prophecy of the Messiah, and have supposed that as Eve was mistaken on the birth of Cain, so Lamech in like manner was deceived in his hope of Noah. But there is no reason to infer from the language of the narrative that the hopes of either were of so definite a nature. The knowledge of a personal Deliverer was not vouchsafed till a much later period.

In the reason which Lamech gives for calling his son Noah, there is a play upon the name which it is impossible to preserve in English. He called his name Noah (נֹחַ, Noach, *rest*), saying, "this same shall *comfort* us" (יְנַחֲמֵנוּ, yenachaménú). It is quite plain that the name "rest," and the verb "comfort," are of different roots; and we must not try to make a philologist of Lamech, and suppose that he was giving an accurate derivation of the name Noah. He merely plays upon the name, after a fashion common enough in all ages and countries.

Of Noah himself from this time we hear nothing more till he is 500 years old, when it is said he begat three sons, Shem, Ham, and Japhet.[a]

Very remarkable, however, is the glimpse which we get of the state of society in the antediluvian world. The narrative it is true is brief, and on many points obscure: a mystery hangs over it which we cannot penetrate. But some few facts are clear. The wickedness of the world is described

as having reached a desperate pitch, owing, it would seem, in a great measure to the fusion of two races which had hitherto been distinct. And further the marked features of the wickedness of the age were lust and brutal outrage. "They took them wives of all which they chose:" and, "the earth was filled with violence." "The earth was corrupt for all flesh had corrupted his way upon the earth." So far the picture is clear and vivid. But when we come to examine some of its details, we are left greatly at a loss. The narrative stands thus:

"And it came to pass when men (the Adam) began to multiply on the face of the ground and daughters were born unto them; then the sons of God (the Elohim) saw the daughters of men (the Adam) that they were fair, and they took to them wives of all that they chose. And Jehovah said, My spirit shall not for ever rule (or be humbled) in men, seeing that they are [or, in their error they are] but flesh, and their days shall be a hundred and twenty years. The Nephilim were in the earth in those days; and also afterwards when the sons of God (the Elohim) came in unto the daughters of men (the Adam), and children were born to them, these were the heroes which were of old, men of renown."

Here a number of perplexing questions present themselves: Who were the sons of God? Who the daughters of men? Who the Nephilim? What is the meaning of "My spirit shall not always rule, or dwell, or be humbled in men;" and of the words which follow, "But their days shall be an hundred and twenty years?"

We will briefly review the principal solutions which have been given of these difficulties.

a. Sons of God and daughters of men.

Three different interpretations have from very early times been given of this most singular passage.

1. The "sons of Elohim" were explained to mean sons of princes, or men of high rank (as in Ps. lxxxii. 6, *b'nê 'Elyón*, sons of the Most High) who degraded themselves by contracting marriages with "the daughters of men," *i. e.* with women of inferior position. This interpretation was defended by Ps. xlix. 2, where "sons of men," *b'nê ádám*, means "men of low degree," as opposed to *b'nê ish*, "men of high degree." Here, however, the opposition is with *b'nê ha-Elohim*, and not with *b'nê ish*, and therefore the passages are not parallel. This is the interpretation of the Targum of Onkelos, following the oldest Palestinian Kabbala, of the later Targum, and of the Samaritan Vers. So also Symmachus, Saadia, and the Arabic of Erpenius, Aben Ezra, and R. Sol. Isaaki. In recent times this view has been elaborated and put in the most favorable light by Schiller (*Werke*, x. 401, &c.): but it has been entirely abandoned by every modern commentator of any note.

---

[a] In marked contrast with the simplicity and soberness of the Biblical narrative, is the wonderful story told of Noah's birth in the Book of Enoch. Lamech's wife, it is said, "brought forth a child, the flesh of which was white as snow, and red as a rose; the hair of whose head was white like wool, and long; and whose eyes were beautiful. When he opened them he illuminated all the house like the sun. And when he was taken from the hand of the midwife, opening also his mouth, he spoke to the Lord of righteousness." Lamech is terrified at the prodigy, and goes to his father Mathusala, and tells him that he has begotten a son who is unlike other children. On hearing the story, Mathusala proceeds, at Lamech's entreaty, to consult Enoch, "whose residence is with the angels." Enoch explains that, in the days of his father Jared, "those who were from heaven disregarded the word of the Lord . . . laid aside their class and intermingled with women;" that consequently a deluge was to be sent upon the earth, whereby it should be "washed from all corruption;" that Noah and his children should be saved; and that his posterity should beget on the earth giants, not spiritual, but carnal (*Book of Enoch* ch. cv. p. 161-63).

2. A second interpretation, perhaps not less ancient, understands by the "sons of Elohim," angels. So some MSS. of the LXX., which according to Procopius and Augustine (De Civit. Dei, xv. 23), had the reading ἄγγελοι τοῦ Θεοῦ, whilst others had υἱοὶ τοῦ Θεοῦ, the last having been generally preferred since Cyril and Augustine; so Joseph. Ant. i. 3; Philo De Gigantibus (perhaps Aquila, who has υἱοὶ τοῦ Θεοῦ, of which, however, Jerome says, Deos intelligens angelos sive sanctos); the Book of Enoch as quoted by Georgius Syncellus in his Chronographia, where they are termed οἱ ἐγρήγοροι, "the watchers" (as in Daniel); the Book of Jubilees (translated by Dillmann from the Ethiopic); the later Jewish Hagada, whence we have the story of the fall of Shamchazai and Azazel,[a] given by Jellinek in the Midrash Abchir; and most of the older Fathers of the Church, finding probably in their Greek MSS. ἄγγελοι τοῦ Θεοῦ, as Justin, Tatian, Athenagoras, Clemens Alex., Tertullian, and Lactantius. This view, however, seemed in later times to be too monstrous to be entertained. R. Sim. b. Jochai anathematized it. Cyril calls it ἀτοπώτατον. Theodoret (Quaest. in Gen.) declares the maintainers of it to have lost their senses, ἐμβρόντητοι καὶ ἄγαν ἠλίθιοι; Philastrius numbers it among heresies, Chrysostom among blasphemies. Finally, Calvin says of it, "Vetus illud commentum de angelorum concubitu cum mulieribus sua absurditate aliunde refellitur, ac mirum est doctos viros tam crassis et prodigiosis deliriis fuisse olim fascinatos." Notwithstanding all which, however, many modern German commentators very strenuously assert this view. They rest their argument in favor of it mainly on these two particulars: first, that "sons of God" is everywhere else in the O. T. a name of the angels; and next, that St. Jude seems to lend the sanction of his authority to this interpretation. With regard to the first of these reasons, it is not even certain that in all other passages of Scripture where "the sons of God" are mentioned angels are meant. It is not absolutely necessary so to understand the designation either in Ps. xxix. 1 or lxxxix. 6, or even in Job i., ii. In any of these passages it might mean holy men. Job xxxviii. 7, and Dan. iii. 25, are the only places in which it certainly means angels. The argument from St. Jude is of more force; for he does compare the sin of the angels to that of Sodom and Gomorrha (τούτοις in ver. 7 must refer to the angels mentioned in ver. 6), as if it were of a like unnatural kind. And that this was the meaning of St. Jude is rendered the more probable when we recollect his quotation from the Book of Enoch where the same view is taken. Further, that the angels had the power of assuming a corporeal form seems clear from many parts of the O. T. All that can be urged in support of this view has been said by Delitzsch in his Die Genesis ausgelegt, and by Kurtz, Gesch. des Alten Bundes, and his treatise, Die Ehen der Söhne Gottes. And it must be confessed that their arguments are not without weight. The early existence of such an interpretation seems at any rate to indicate a starting-point for the heathen

mythologies. The fact, too, that from such an intercourse "the mighty men" were born, points in the same direction. The Greek "heroes" were sons of the gods; οὐκ οἶσθα, says Plato in the Cratylus, ὅτι ἡμίθεοι οἱ ἥρωες; πάντες δήπου γεγόνασιν ἐρασθέντες ἢ θεὸς θνητῆς ἢ θνητοὶ θεᾶς. Even Hesiod's account of the birth of the giants, monstrous and fantastic as it is, bears tokens of having originated in the same belief. In like manner it may be remarked that the stories of incubi and succubi, so commonly believed in the Middle Ages, and which even Heidegger (Hist. Sacr. i. 289) does not discredit, had reference to a commerce between demons and mortals of the same kind as that narrated in Genesis.[b]

Two modern poets, Byron (in his drama of Cain) and Moore (in his Loves of the Angels), have availed themselves of this last interpretation for the purpose of their poems.

3. The interpretation, however, which is now most generally received, is that which understands by "the sons of the Elohim" the family and descendants of Seth, and by "the daughters of man (Adam)," the women of the family of Cain. So the Clementine Recognitions interpret "the sons of the Elohim" as Homines justi qui angelorum vixerant vitam. So Ephrem, and the Christian Adam-Book of the East: so also, Theodoret, Chrysostom, Cyril of Alexandria, Jerome, Augustine, and others; and in later times Luther, Melancthon, Calvin, and a whole host of recent commentators. They all suppose that whereas the two lines of descent from Adam — the family of Seth who preserved their faith in God, and the family of Cain who lived only for this world — had hitherto kept distinct, now a mingling of the two races took place which resulted in the thorough corruption of the former, who falling away, plunged into the deepest abyss of wickedness, and that it was this universal corruption which provoked the judgment of the Flood.[c]

4. A fourth interpretation has recently been advanced and maintained with considerable ingenuity, by the author of the Genesis of the Earth and Man. He understands by "the sons of the Elohim" the "servants or worshippers of false gods" [taking Elohim to mean not God but gods], whom he supposes to have belonged to a distinct pre-Adamite race. "The daughters of men," he contends, should be rendered "the daughters of Adam, or the Adamites," women, that is, descended from Adam. These last had hitherto remained true in their faith and worship, but were now perverted by the idolaters who intermarried with them. But this hypothesis is opposed to the direct statements in the early chapters of Genesis, which plainly teach the descent of all mankind from one common source.

Whichever of these interpretations we adopt (the third perhaps is the most probable), one thing at least is clear, that the writer intends to describe a fusion of races hitherto distinct, and to connect with this two other facts: the one that the offspring of these mixed marriages were men remarkable for strength and prowess (which is only in accordance with what has often been observed since, namely, the superiority of the mixed race as compared with either of the parent stocks); the other,

---

[a] In Beresh. Rab. in Gen. vi. 2, this Azazel is declared to be the tutelary deity of women's ornaments and paint, and is identified with the Azazel in Lev. xvi. 8.

[b] Thomas Aquin. (pars 1. qu. 51, art. 3) argues that it was possible for angels to have children by mortal women

[c] Dr. Conant supports this explanation in a good note on Gen. vi. 2 (Book of Genesis, with a Revised Version, N. Y. 1868). H.

that the result of this intercourse was the thorough and hopeless corruption of both families alike.

b. But who were the Nephilim? It should be observed that they are not spoken of (as has sometimes been assumed) as the offspring of the "sons of the Elohim" and "the daughters of men." The sacred writer says, "the Nephilim were on the earth in those days," before he goes on to speak of the children of the mixed marriages. The name, which has been variously explained, only occurs once again in Num. xiii. 33, where the Nephilim are said to have been one of the Canaanitish tribes. They are there spoken of as "men of great stature," and hence probably the rendering γίγαντες of the LXX. and "the giants" of our A. V. But there is nothing in the word itself to justify this interpretation. If it is of Hebrew origin (which, however, may be doubted), it must mean either "fallen," *i. e.* apostate ones; or those who "fall upon" others, violent men, plunderers, freebooters, etc. It is of far more importance to observe that if the Nephilim of Canaan were descendants of the Nephilim in Gen. vi. 4, we have here a very strong argument for the non-universality of the Deluge. [GIANTS.]

c. In consequence of the grievous and hopeless wickedness of the world at this time, God resolves to destroy it. "My spirit," He says, "shall not always dwell" (LXX. Vulg. Saad.), or "bear sway," in man, inasmuch as he is but flesh. The meaning of which seems to be that whilst God had put his Spirit in man, *i. e.* not only the breath of life, but a spiritual part capable of recognizing, loving, and worshipping Him, man had so much sunk down into the lowest and most debasing of fleshly pleasures, as to have almost extinguished the higher light within him; as one of the Fathers says: *anima victa libidine fit caro:* the soul and spirit became transubstantiated into flesh. Then follows: "But his days shall be a hundred and twenty years," which has been interpreted by some to mean, that still a time of grace shall be given for repentance, namely, 120 years before the Flood shall come; and by others that the duration of human life should in future be limited to this term of years, instead of extending over centuries as before. This last seems the most natural interpretation of the Hebrew words. Of Noah's life during this age of almost universal apostasy we are told but little. It is merely said, that he was a righteous man and perfect in his generations (*i. e.* amongst his contemporaries), and that he, like Enoch, walked with God. This last expressive phrase is used of none other but these two only. To him God revealed his purpose to destroy the world, commanding him to prepare an ark for the saving of his house. And from that time till the day came for him to enter into the ark, we can hardly doubt that he was engaged in active, but as it proved unavailing efforts to win those about him from their wickedness and unbelief. Hence St. Peter calls him "a preacher of righteousness." Besides this we are merely told that he had three

sons, each of whom had married a wife: that he built the ark in accordance with Divine direction: and that he was 600 years old when the Flood came.

Both about the ark and the Flood so many questions have been raised, that we must consider each of these separately.

The Ark. — The precise meaning of the Hebrew word (תֵּבָה, *têbâh*) is uncertain. The word only occurs here and in the second chapter of Exodus, where it is used of the little papyrus boat in which the mother of Moses entrusted her child to the Nile. In all probability it is to the Old Egyptian that we are to look for its original form. Bunsen, in his vocabulary,[a] gives *tb ı*, "a chest," *tpt*, "a boat," and in the Copt. Vers. of Ex. ii. 3, 5, ΘΗΒΙ is the rendering of *tébâh*. The LXX. employ two different words. In the narrative of the Flood they use κιβωτός, and in that of Moses θίβις, or according to some MSS. θηβή. The Book of Wisdom has σχεδία; Berosus and Nicol. Damasc. quoted in Josephus, πλοῖον and λάρναξ. The last is also found in Lucian, *De Ded Syr.* c. 12. In the Sibylline Verses the ark is δουράτεον δῶμα, οἶκος and κιβωτός. The Targum and the Koran have each respectively given the Chaldee and the Arabic form of the Hebrew word.

This "chest," or "boat," was to be made of gopher (*i. e.* cypress) wood, a kind of timber which both for its lightness and its durability was employed by the Phœnicians for building their vessels. Alexander the Great, Arrian tells us (vii. 19), made use of it for the same purpose. The planks of the ark, after being put together, were to be protected by a coating of pitch, or rather bitumen (כֹּפֶר, LXX. ἄσφαλτος), which was to be laid on both inside and outside, as the most effectual means of making it water-tight, and perhaps also as a protection against the attacks of marine animals. Next to the material, the method of construction is described. The ark was to consist of a number of "nests" (קִנִּים), or small compartments, with a view no doubt to the convenient distribution of the different animals and their food. These were to be arranged in three tiers, one above another; "with lower, second, and third (stories) shalt thou make it." Means were also to be provided for letting light into the ark. In the A. V. we read, "A window shalt thou make to the ark, and in a cubit shalt thou finish it above: " — words which it must be confessed convey no very intelligible idea. The original, however, is obscure, and has been differently interpreted. What the "window," or "light-hole" (צֹהַר, *tsôhar*) was, is very puzzling. It was to be at the top of the ark apparently. If the words "unto a cubit (אֶל־אַמָּה) shalt thou finish it *above*," refer to the window and not to the ark itself, they seem to imply that this aperture, or skylight, extended to the breadth of a cubit the whole length of the roof.[b] But if

---

[a] *Egypt's Place,* etc., i. 482.

[b] Knobel's explanation is different. By the words, "to a cubit (or within a cubit) shalt thou finish it above," he understands that, the window being in the side of the ark, a space of a cubit was to be left between the top of the window and the overhanging roof of the ark which Noah removed after the flood had abated (viii. 13). There is, however, no reason to con-

clude, as he does, that there was only one light. The great objection to supposing that the window was in the side of the ark, is that then a great part of the interior must have been left in darkness. And again we are told (viii. 13), that when the Flood abated Noah removed the covering of the ark, to look about him to see if the earth were dry. This would have been unnecessary if the window had been in the side

NOAH

so, it could not have been merely an open slit, for that would have admitted the rain. Are we then to suppose that some transparent, or at least translucent, substance was employed? It would almost seem so [a] A different word is used in Gen. viii. 6, where it is said that Noah opened the window of the ark. There the word is חַלּוֹן (challôn), which frequently occurs elsewhere in the same sense. Certainly the story as there given does imply a transparent window as Saalschütz (Archäol. i. 311) has remarked.[b] For Noah could watch the motions of the birds outside, whilst at the same time he had to open the window in order to take them in. Supposing then the tsôhar to be, as we have said, a skylight, or series of skylights running the whole length of the ark (and the fem. form of the noun inclines one to regard it as a collective noun), the challôn [c] might very well be a single compartment of the larger window, which could be opened at will. But besides the window there was to be a door. This was to be placed in the side of the ark. "The door must have been of some size to admit the larger animals, for whose ingress it was mainly intended. It was no doubt above the highest draught mark of the ark, and the animals ascended to it probably by a sloping embankment. A door in the side is not more difficult to understand than the port holes in the sides of our vessels." [d]

Of the shape of the ark nothing is said; but its dimensions are given. It was to be 300 cubits in length, 50 in breadth, and 30 in height. Supposing the cubit here to be the cubit of natural measurement, reckoning from the elbow to the top of the middle finger, we may get a rough approximation as to the size of the ark. The cubit, so measured (called in Deut. iii. 11, "the cubit of a man"), must of course, at first, like all natural measurements, have been inexact and fluctuating. In later times no doubt the Jews had a standard common cubit, as well as the royal cubit and sacred cubit. We shall probably, however, be near enough to the mark if we take the cubit here to be the common cubit, which was reckoned (according to Mich.,

Jahn, Gesen. and others) as equal to six hand breadths, the hand-breadth being 3½ inches. This therefore gives 21 inches for the cubit.[e] Accordingly the ark would be 525 feet in length, 87 feet 6 inches in breadth, and 52 feet 6 inches in height. This is very considerably larger than the largest British man-of-war. The Great Eastern, however, is both longer and deeper than the ark, being 680 feet in length (691 on deck), 83 in breadth, and 58 in depth. Solomon's Temple, the proportions of which are given in 1 K. vi. 2, was the same height as the ark, but only one-fifth of the length, and less than half the width.

It should be remembered that this huge structure was only intended to float on the water, and was not in the proper sense of the word a ship. It had neither mast, sail, nor rudder; it was in fact nothing but an enormous floating house, or oblong box rather, "as it is very likely," says Sir W. Raleigh, "that the ark had fundum planum, a flat bottom, and not raysed in form of a ship, with a sharpness forward, to cut the waves for the better speed." The figure which is commonly given to it by painters, there can be no doubt is wrong. Two objects only were aimed at in its construction: the one was that it should have ample stowage, and the other that it should be able to keep steady upon the water. It was never intended to be carried to any great distance from the place where it was originally built. A curious proof of the suitability of the ark for the purpose for which it was intended was given by a Dutch merchant, Peter Jansen, the Mennonite, who in the year 1604 had a ship built at Hoorn of the same proportions (though of course not of the same size) as Noah's ark. It was 120 feet long, 20 broad, and 12 deep. This vessel, unsuitable as it was for quick voyages, was found remarkably well adapted for freightage.[f] It was calculated that it would hold a third more lading than other vessels without requiring more hands to work it. A similar experiment is also said to have been made in Denmark, where, according to Reyher, several vessels called "fleuten" or floats were built after the model of the ark.

" Unto a cubit shalt thou finish it above " can hardly mean, as some have supposed, that the roof of the ark was to have this pitch ; for, considering that the ark was to be 50 cubits in breadth, a roof of a cubit's pitch would have been almost flat.

a Symm. renders the word διαφανές. Theodoret has merely θύραν ; Gr. Venet. φωταγωγόν ; Vulg. fenestram. The LXX. translate, strangely enough, ἐπισυνάγων ποιήσεις τὴν κιβωτόν. The root of the word indicates that the tsôhar was something shining. Hence probably the Talmudic explanation, that God told Noah to fix precious stones in the ark, that they might give as much light as midday (Sanh. 108 b).

b The only serious objection to this explanation is the supposed improbability of any substance like glass having been discovered at that early period of the world's history. But we must not forget that even according to the Hebrew chronology the world had been in existence 1656 years at the time of the Flood, and according to the LXX., which is the more probable, 2,262. Vast strides must have been made in knowledge and civilization in such a lapse of time. Arts and sciences may have reached a ripeness, of which the record, from its scantiness, conveys no adequate conception. The destruction caused by the Flood must have obliterated a thousand discoveries, and left men to recover again by slow and patient steps the ground they had lost.

c A different word from either of these is used in vii. 11 of the windows of heaven, אֲרֻבָּה, 'arubbôth (from אָרַב, " to interweave "), lit. " net-works " or " gratings " (Ges. Thes. in v.).

d Kitto, Bible Illustrations, Antediluvians, etc., p. 142. The Jewish notion was that the ark was entered by means of a ladder. On the steps of this ladder, the story goes, Og, king of Bashan, was sitting when the Flood came ; and on his pledging himself to Noah and his sons to be their slave forever, he was suffered to remain there, and Noah gave him his food each day out of a hole in the ark (Pirke R. Eliezer).

e See Winer, Realw. " Elle." Sir Walter Raleigh, in his History of the World, reckons the cubit at 18 inches. Dr. Kitto calls this a safe way of estimating the cubit in Scripture, but gives it himself as = 21.888 inches. For this inconsistency he is taken to task by Hugh Miller, who adopts the measurement of Sir W Raleigh.

f Augustine (De Civ. D. lib. xv.) long ago discovered another excellence in the proportions of the ark ; and that is, that they were the same as the proportions of the perfect human figure, the length of which from the sole to the crown is six times the width across the chest, and ten times the depth of the recumbent figure measured in a right line from the ground.

After having given Noah the necessary instruc-tions for the building of the ark, God tells him the purpose for which it was designed. Now for the first time we hear how the threatened destruction was to be accomplished, as well as the provision which was to be made for the repeopling of the earth with its various tribes of animals. The earth is to be destroyed by water. " And I, behold I do bring the flood (הַמַּבּוּל) — waters upon the earth — to destroy all flesh wherein is the breath of life . . . but I will establish my covenant with thee, etc." (vi. 17, 18). The inmates of the ark are then specified. They are to be Noah and his wife, and his three sons with their wives: whence it is plain that he and his family had not yielded to the prevailing custom of polygamy. Noah is also to take a pair of each kind of animal into the ark with him that he may preserve them alive; birds, domestic animals (בְּהֵמָה),[a] and creeping things are particularly mentioned. He is to pro-vide for the wants of each of these stores " of every kind of food that is eaten." It is added, " Thus did Noah; according to all that God (Elohim) commanded him, so did he."

A remarkable addition to these directions occurs in the following chapter. The pairs of animals are now limited to one of unclean animals, whilst of clean animals and birds (ver. 2) Noah is to take to him seven pairs (or as others think, seven individ-uals, that is three pairs and one supernumerary male for sacrifice).[b] How is this addition to be accounted for? May we not suppose that we have here traces of a separate document interwoven by a later writer with the former history? The passage indeed has not, to all appearance, been incorporated intact, but there is a coloring about it which seems to indicate that Moses, or whoever put the Book of Genesis into its present shape, had here consulted a differ-ent narrative. The distinct use of the Divine names in the same phrase, vi. 22, and vii. 5 — in the former Elohim, in the latter Jehovah — sug-gests that this may have been the case.[c] It does not follow, however, from the mention of clean and unclean animals that this section reflects a Levitical or post-Mosaic mind and handling. There were sacrifices before Moses, and why may there not have been a distinction of clean and unclean animals? It may be true of many other things besides circumcision: Moses gave it you, not

because it was of Moses, but because it was of the fathers.

Are we then to understand that Noah literally conveyed a pair of all the animals of the world into the ark? This question virtually contains in it another, namely, whether the deluge was universal, or only partial? If it was only partial, then of course it was necessary to find room but for a comparatively small number of animals; and the dimensions of the ark are ample enough for the required purpose. The argument on this point has already been so well stated by Hugh Miller in his Testimony of the Rocks, that we need do little more than give an abstract of it here. After say-ing that it had for ages been a sort of stock problem to determine whether all the animals in the world by sevens, and by pairs, with food suffi-cient to serve them for a twelvemonth could have been accommodated in the given space, he quotes Sir W. Raleigh's calculation on the subject.[d] Sir Walter proposed to allow " for eighty-nine distinct species of beasts, or lest any should be omitted, for a hundred several kinds." He then by a curious sort of estimate, in which he considers " one ele-phant as equal to four beeves, one lion to two wolves," and so on, reckons that the space occupied by the different animals would be equivalent to the spaces required for 91 (or say 120) beeves, four score sheep, and three score and four wolves. " All these two hundred and eighty beasts[e] might be kept in one story, or room of the ark, in their several cabins; their meat in a second; the birds and their provision in a third, with space to spare for Noah and his family, and all their necessaries." " Such," says Hugh Miller, " was the calculation of the great voyager Raleigh, a man who had a more practical acquaintance with stowage than perhaps any of the other writers who have specu-lated on the capabilities of the ark, and his esti-mate seems sober and judicious." He then goes on to show how enormously these limits are ex-ceeded by our present knowledge of the extent of the animal kingdom. Buffon doubled Raleigh's number of distinct species. During the last thirty years so astonishing has been the progress of dis-covery, that of mammals alone there have been ascertained to exist more than eight times the number which Buffon gives. In the first edition of Johnston's Physical Atlas (1848), one thousand six hundred and twenty-six different species of

---

[a] Only tame animals of the larger kinds are ex-pressly mentioned (vi. 20) ; and if we could be sure that none others were taken, the difficulties connected with the necessary provision, stowage, etc., would be materially lessened. It may, however, be urged that in the first instance " every living thing of all flesh " (vi. 19) was to come into the ark, and that afterwards (vii. 14) " every living thing " is spoken of not as in-cluding, but as distinct from the tame cattle, and that consequently the inference is that wild animals were meant.

[b] Calv., Ges., Tuch, Baumg., and Delitzsch, under-stand seven individuals of each species. Del. argues that, if we take שִׁבְעָה here to mean seven pairs, we must also take the שְׁנַיִם before to mean two pairs (and Origen does so take it, cont. Cels. iv. 41). But without arguing, with Knobel, that the repetition of the numeral in this case, and not in the other, may perhaps be designed to denote that here pairs are to be understood, at any rate the addition " male and his female " renders this the more probable interpretation.

[c] It is remarkable, moreover, that whilst in ver. 2 it is said, " Of every clean beast thou shalt take to thee by sevens," in vv. 8, 9, it is said, " Of clean beasts, and of beasts that are not clean," etc., " there went in two and two unto Noah into the ark." This again looks like a compilation from different sources.

[d] The earliest statement on the subject I have met with is in the Pirke R. Eliezer, where it is said that Noah took 32 kinds of birds, and 365 species of beasts, with him into the ark.

[e] Heidegger in like manner (Hist. Sacr. i. 518) thinks he is very liberal in allowing 300 kinds of ani-mals to have been taken into the ark, and considers that this would give 50 cubits of solid contents for each kind of animal. He then subjoins the far more elaborate and really very curious computation of Joh. Temerarius in his Chronol. Demonstr., who reckons after Sir W. Raleigh's fashion, but enumerates all the different species of known animals (amongst which he mentions Pegasi, Sphinxes, and Satyrs), the kind and quantity of provision, the method of stowage, etc. See Heidegger, as above, pp. 506, 507, and 518-521.

mammals are enumerated; and in the second edition (1856) one thousand six hundred and fifty-eight species. To these we must add the six thousand two hundred and sixty-six birds of Lesson, and the six hundred and fifty-seven or (subtracting the sea-snakes, and perhaps the turtles) the six hundred and forty-two reptiles of Charles Bonaparte.

Take the case of the *clean* animals alone, of which there were to be seven introduced into the ark. Admitting, for argument sake, that only seven individuals, and not seven pairs, were introduced, the number of these alone, as now known, is sufficient to settle the question. Mr. Waterhouse, in the year 1856, estimated the oxen at twenty species; the sheep at twenty-seven species; the goats at twenty; and the deer at fifty-one. "In short, if, excluding the lamas and the musks as doubtfully *clean*, tried by the Mosaic test, we but add to the sheep, goats, deer, and cattle, the forty-eight species of unequivocally *clean* antelopes, and multiply the whole by seven, we shall have as the result a sum total of one thousand one hundred and sixty-two individuals, a number more than four times greater than that for which Raleigh made provision in the ark." It would be curious to ascertain what number of animals could possibly be stowed, together with sufficient food to last for a twelvemonth, on board the Great Eastern.

But it is not only the inadequate size of the ark to contain all, or anything like all, the progenitors of our existing species of animals, which is conclusive against a universal deluge.[a] Another fact points with still greater force, if possible, in the same direction, and that is the manner in which we now find these animals distributed over the earth's surface. "Linnæus held, early in the last century, that all creatures which now inhabit the globe had proceeded originally from some such common centre as the ark might have furnished; but no zoölogist acquainted with the distribution of species can acquiesce in any such conclusion now. We now know that every great continent has its own peculiar fauna; that the original centres of distribution must have been not one, but many; further, that the areas or circles around these centres must have been occupied by their pristine animals in ages long anterior to that of the Noachian Deluge; nay that in even the latter geologic ages they were preceded in them by animals of the same general type." Thus, for instance, the animals of South America, when the Spaniards first penetrated into it, were found to be totally distinct from those of Europe, Asia, or Africa. The puma, the jaguar, the tapir, the lama, the sloths, the armadilloes, the opossums, were animals which had never been seen elsewhere. So again Australia has a whole class of animals, the marsupials, quite unknown to other parts of the world. The various species of kangaroo, phascolomys, dasyurus, and perameles, the flying phalangers, and other no less singular creatures, were the astonishment of naturalists when this continent was first discovered. New Zealand likewise, "though singularly devoid of indigenous mammals and reptiles . . . has a scarcely less remarkable fauna than either of these great continents. It consists almost exclusively of birds, some of them so ill provided

with wings, that, like the *wika* of the natives, they can only run along the ground." And what is very remarkable, this law with regard to the distribution of animals does not date merely from the human period. We find the gigantic forms of those different species which during the later tertiary epochs preceded or accompanied the existing forms, occupying precisely the same habitats. In S. America, for instance, there lived then, side by side, the gigantic sloth (megatherium) to be seen in the British Museum, and the smaller animal of the same species which has survived the extinction of the larger. Australia in like manner had then its gigantic marsupials, the very counterpart in everything but in size of the existing species. And not only are the same mammals found in the same localities, but they are surrounded in every respect by the same circumstances, and exist in company with the same birds, the same insects, the same plants. In fact so stable is this law that, although prior to the pleistocene period we find a different distribution of animals, we still find each separate locality distinguished by its own species both of fauna and of flora, and we find these grouped together in the same manner as in the later periods. It is quite plain, then, that if all the animals of the world were literally gathered together in the ark and so saved from the waters of a universal deluge, this could only have been effected (even supposing there was space for them in the ark) by a most stupendous miracle. The sloth and the armadillo must have been brought across oceans and continents from their South American home, the kangaroo from his Australian forests and prairies, and the polar bear from his icebergs, to that part of Armenia, or the Euphrates Valley, where the ark was built. These and all the other animals must have been brought in perfect subjection to Noah, and many of them must have been taught to forget their native ferocity in order to prevent their attacking one another. They must then further, having been brought by supernatural means from the regions which they occupied, have likewise been carried back to the same spots by supernatural means, care having moreover been taken that no trace of their passage to and fro should be left.

But the narrative does not compel us to adopt so tremendous an hypothesis. We shall see more clearly when we come to consider the language used with regard to the Flood itself, that even that language, strong as it undoubtedly is, does not oblige us to suppose that the Deluge was universal. But neither does the language employed with regard to the animals lead to this conclusion. It is true that Noah is told to take two "of every living thing of all flesh," but that could only mean two of every animal *then known* to him, unless we suppose him to have had supernatural information in zoölogy imparted — a thing quite incredible. In fact, but for some misconceptions as to the meaning of certain expressions, no one would ever have suspected that Noah's knowledge, or the knowledge of the writer of the narrative, could have extended beyond a very limited portion of the globe.

Again, how were the carnivorous animals supplied with food during their twelve months' abode in the ark? This would have been difficult even

---

[a] * This argument against the universality of the Deluge is valid, of course, only against those who deny the propagation of "existing species" from their genera or types.   H.

for the very limited number of wild animals in Noah's immediate neighborhood. For the very large numbers which the theory of a universal Deluge supposes, it would have been quite impossible, unless again we have recourse to miracle, and either maintain that they were miraculously supplied with food, or that for the time being the nature of their teeth and stomach was changed, so that they were able to live on vegetables. But these hypotheses are so extravagant, and so utterly unsupported by the narrative itself, that they may be safely dismissed without further comment.

The Flood. — The ark was finished, and all its living freight was gathered into it as in a place of safety. Jehovah shut him in, says the chronicler, speaking of Noah. And then there ensued a solemn pause of seven days before the threatened destruction was let loose. At last the Flood came; the waters were upon the earth. The narrative is vivid and forcible, though entirely wanting in that sort of description which in a modern historian or poet would have occupied the largest space. We see nothing of the death-struggle; we hear not the cry of despair; we are not called upon to witness the frantic agony of husband and wife, and parent and child, as they fled in terror before the rising waters. Nor is a word said of the sadness of the one righteous man who, safe himself, looked upon the destruction which he could not avert. But one impression is left upon the mind with peculiar vividness, from the very simplicity of the narrative, and it is that of utter desolation. This is heightened by the contrast and repetition of two ideas. On the one hand we are reminded no less than six times in the narrative in cc. vi., vii., viii., who the tenants of the ark were (vi. 18-21, vii. 1-3, 7-9, 13-16, viii. 16, 17, 18, 19), the favored and rescued few; and on the other hand the total and absolute blotting out of everything else is not less emphatically dwelt upon (vi. 13, 17, vii. 4, 21-23). This evidently designed contrast may especially be traced in ch. vii. First, we read in ver. 6, "And Noah was six hundred years old when the flood came — waters upon the earth." Then follows an account of Noah and his family and the animals entering into the ark. Next, verses 10-12 resume the subject of ver. 7: "And it came to pass after seven days that the waters of the flood were upon the earth. In the six hundredth year of Noah's life, in the second month, on the seventeenth day of the month, on the self-same day were all the fountains of the great deep broken up, and the windows (or flood-gates) of heaven were opened. And the rain was upon the earth forty days and forty nights." Again the narrative returns to Noah and his companions and their safety in the ark (vv. 13-16). And then in ver. 17 the words of ver. 12 are resumed, and from thence to the end of the chapter a very simple but very powerful and impressive descrip-

tion is given of the appalling catastrophe: "And the flood was forty days upon the earth: and the waters increased and bare up the ark, and it was lift up from off the earth. And the waters prevailed and increased exceedingly upon the earth: and the ark went on the face of the waters. And the waters prevailed very exceedingly upon the earth, and all the high mountains which [were] under the whole heaven were covered. Fifteen cubits upwards did the waters prevail, and the mountains were covered. And all flesh died which moveth upon the earth, of fowl, and of cattle, and of wild beasts, and of every creeping thing which creepeth upon the earth, and every man. All in whose nostrils was the breath of life, of all that was in the dry land, died. And every substance which was on the face of the ground was blotted out, as well man as cattle and creeping thing and fowl of the heaven: they were blotted out from the earth, and Noah only was left, and they that were with him in the ark. And the waters prevailed on the earth a hundred and fifty days."

The waters of the Flood increased for a period of 190 days (40+150, comparing vii. 12 and 24). And then "God remembered Noah," and made a wind to pass over the earth, so that the waters were assuaged. The ark rested on the seventeenth day of the seventh month [a] on the mountains of Ararat. After this the waters gradually decreased till the first day of the tenth month, when the tops of the mountains were seen. It was then that Noah sent forth, first, the raven,[b] which flew hither and thither, resting probably on the mountain-tops, but not returning to the ark; and next, after an interval of seven days (cf. viii. 10) the dove, "to see if the waters were abated from the ground" (*i. e.* the lower plain country). "But the dove," it is beautifully said, "found no rest for the sole of her foot, and she returned unto him into the ark." After waiting for another seven days he again sent forth the dove, which returned this time with a fresh (טָרָף) olive-leaf in her mouth, a sign that the waters were still lower.[c] And once more, after another interval of seven days, he sent forth the dove, and she "returned not again unto him any more," having found a home for herself upon the earth. No picture in natural history was ever drawn with more exquisite beauty and fidelity than this: it is admirable alike for its poetry and its truth.

On reading this narrative it is difficult, it must be confessed, to reconcile the language employed with the hypothesis of a partial deluge. The difficulty does not lie in the largeness of most of the terms used, but rather in the precision of one single expression. It is natural to suppose that the writer, when he speaks of "all flesh," "all in whose nostrils was the breath of life," refers

---

a It is impossible to say how this reckoning of time was made, and whether a lunar or solar year is meant. Much ingenuity has been expended on this question (see Delitzsch's *Comment.*), but with no satisfactory results.

b The raven was supposed to foretell changes in the weather both by its flight and its cry (Ælian, *H. A.* vii. 7; Virg. *Georg.* i. 382, 410). According to Jewish tradition, the raven was preserved in the ark in order to be the progenitor of the birds which afterwards fed Elijah by the brook Cherith.

c The olive-tree is an evergreen, and seems to have the power of living under water, according to Theophrastus (*Hist. P.ant.* iv. 8) and Pliny (*H. N.* xiii. 50), who mention olive-trees in the Red Sea. The olive grows in Armenia, but only in the valleys on the south side of Ararat, not on the slopes of the mountain. It will not flourish at an elevation where even the mulberry, walnut, and apricot are found (Ritter, *Erdkunde*, x. 920).

only to his own locality. This sort of language is common enough in the Bible when only a small part of the globe is intended. Thus, for instance, it is said that " *all countries* came into Egypt to Joseph to buy corn;" and that " a decree went out from Cæsar Augustus that *all the world* should be taxed." In these and many similar passages the expressions of the writer are obviously not to be taken in an exactly literal sense. Even the apparently very distinct phrase " *all* the high hills that were *under the whole heaven* were covered " may be matched by another precisely similar, where it is said that God would put the fear and the dread of Israel upon *every nation under heaven.* It requires no effort to see that such language is framed with a kind of poetic breadth. The real difficulty lies in the connecting of this statement with the district in which Noah is supposed to have lived, and the assertion that the waters prevailed fifteen cubits upward. If the Ararat on which the ark rested be the present mountain of the same name, the highest peak of which is more than 17,000 feet above the sea [ARARAT], it would have been quite impossible for this to have been covered, the water reaching 15 cubits, *i. e.* 26 feet above it, unless the whole earth were submerged. The author of the *Genesis of the Earth*, etc., has endeavored to escape this difficulty by shifting the scene of the catastrophe to the low country on the banks of the Tigris and Euphrates (a miraculous overflow of these rivers being sufficient to account for the Deluge), and supposing that the " fifteen cubits upward " are to be reckoned, not from the top of the mountains, but from the surface of the plain. By " the high hills " he thinks may be meant only slight elevations, called " high " because they were the highest parts overflowed. But fifteen cubits is only a little more than twenty-six feet, and it seems absurd to suppose that such trifling elevations are described as " all the high hills under the whole heaven." At this rate the ark itself must have been twice the height of the highest mountain. The plain meaning of the narrative is, that far as the eye could sweep, not a solitary mountain reared its head above the waste of waters. On the other hand, there is no necessity for assuming that the ark stranded on the high peaks of the mountain now called Ararat, or even that that mountain was visible. A lower mountain-range, such as the Zagros range for instance, may be intended. And in the absence of all geographical certainty in the matter it is better to adopt some such explanation of the difficulty. Indeed it is out of the question to imagine that the ark rested on the top of a mountain which is covered for 4,000 feet from the summit with perpetual snow, and the descent from which would have been a very serious matter both to men and other animals. The local tradition, according to which fragments of the ark are still believed to remain on the summit, can weigh nothing when balanced against so extreme an improbability. Assuming, then, that the Ararat here mentioned is not the mountain of that name in Armenia, we may also assume the inundation to have been partial, and may suppose it to have extended over the whole valley of the Euphrates, and eastward as far as the range of mountains running down to the Persian Gulf, or further. As the

inundation is said to have been caused by the breaking up of the fountains of the great deep, as well as by the rain, some great and sudden subsidence of the land may have taken place, accompanied by an inrush of the waters of the Persian Gulf, similar to what occurred in the Runn of Cutch, on the eastern arm of the Indus, in 1819, when the sea flowed in, and in a few hours converted a tract of land, 2,000 square miles in area, into an inland sea or lagoon (see the account of this subsidence of the Delta of the Indus in Lyell's *Principles of Geology*, pp. 460–63).

It has sometimes been asserted that the facts of geology are conclusive against the possibility of a universal deluge. Formerly, indeed, the existence of shells and corals at the top of high mountains was taken to be no less conclusive evidence the other way. They were constantly appealed to as a proof of the literal truth of the Scripture narrative. And so troublesome and inconvenient a proof did it seem to Voltaire, that he attempted to account for the existence of fossil shells by arguing that either they were those of fresh-water lakes and rivers evaporated during dry seasons, or of land-snails developed in unusual abundance during wet ones; or that they were shells that had been dropped from the hats of pilgrims on their way from the Holy Land to their own homes; or in the case of the ammonites, that they were petrified reptiles. It speaks ill for the state of science that such arguments could be advanced, on the one side for, and on the other against, the universality of the Deluge. And this is the more extraordinary — and the fact shows how very slowly, where prejudices stand in the way, the soundest reasoning will be listened to — when we remember that so early as the year 1517 an Italian named Fracastoro had demonstrated the untenableness of the vulgar belief which associated these fossil remains with the Mosaic Deluge. " That inundation," he observed, " was too transient; it consisted principally of fluviatile waters; and if it had transported shells to great distances, must have strewed them over the surface, not buried them at vast depths in the interior of mountains. . . . But the clear and philosophical views of Fracastoro were disregarded, and the talent and argumentative powers of the learned were doomed for three centuries to be wasted in the discussion of these two simple and preliminary questions: first, whether fossil remains had ever belonged to living creatures; and secondly, whether, if this be admitted, all the phenomena could not be explained by the Deluge of Noah " Lyell, *Principles of Geology*, p. 20, 9th ed.). Even within the last thirty years geologists, like Cuvier and Buckland, have thought that the *superficial deposits* might be referred to the period of the Noachian Flood. Subsequent investigation, however, showed that if the received chronology were even approximately correct, this was out of the question, as these deposits must have taken place thousands of years before the time of Noah, and indeed before the creation of man. Hence the geologic diluvium is to be carefully distinguished from the historic. And although, singularly enough, the latest discoveries give some support to the opinion that man may have been in existence during the formation of the drift,[a] yet even then that formation could not have

---

: In a valuable paper by Mr. Joseph Prestwich (recently published in the *Philosophical Transactions*), it is suggested that in all probability the origin of man

will have to be thrown back into a greatly earlier antiquity than that usually assigned to it, but the pleistocene deposits to be brought down to a much more

resulted from a mere temporary submersion like that of the Mosaic Deluge, but must have been the effect of causes in operation for ages. So far then, it is clear, there is no evidence now on the earth's surface in favor of a universal Deluge.

But is there any positive geological evidence against it? Hugh Miller and other geologists have maintained that there is. They appeal to the fact that in various parts of the world, such as Auvergne in France, and along the flanks of Ætna, there are cones of loose scoriæ and ashes belonging to long extinct volcanoes, which must be at least triple the antiquity of the Noachian Deluge, and which yet exhibit no traces of abrasion by the action of water. These loose cones, they argue, must have been swept away had the water of the Deluge ever reached them. But this argument is by no means conclusive. The heaps of scoriæ are, we have been assured by careful scientific observers, not of that loose incoherent kind which they suppose. And it would have been quite possible for a gradually advancing inundation to have submerged these, and then gradually to have retired without leaving any mark of its action. Indeed, although there is no proof that the whole world ever was submerged at one time, and although, arguing from the observed facts of the geological cataclysms, we should be disposed to regard such an event as in the highest degree improbable, it cannot, on geological grounds alone, be pronounced impossible. The water of the globe is to the land in the proportion of three-fifths to two-fifths. There already existed therefore, in the different seas and lakes, water sufficient to cover the whole earth. And the whole earth might have been submerged for a twelvemonth, as stated in Genesis, or even for a much longer period, without any trace of such submersion being now discernible.

There is, however, other evidence conclusive against the hypothesis of a universal deluge, miracle apart. "The first effect of the covering of the whole globe with water would be a complete change in its climate, the general tendency being to lower and equalize the temperature of all parts of its surface. *Pari passu* with this process . . . would ensue the destruction of the great majority of marine animals. And this would take place, partly by reason of the entire change in climatal conditions, too sudden and general to be escaped by migration; and, in still greater measure, in consequence of the sudden change in the depth of the water. Great multitudes of marine animals can only live between tide-marks, or at depths less than fifty fathoms; and as by the hypothesis the land had to be depressed many thousands of feet in a few months, and to be raised again with equal celerity, it follows that the animals could not possibly have accommodated themselves to such vast and rapid changes. All the littoral animals, therefore, would have been killed. The race of acorn-shells and periwinkles would have been exterminated, and all the coral-reefs of the Pacific would at once have been converted into dead coral, never to grow again. But so far is this from being the case, that acorn-shells, periwinkles, and coral still survive, and there is good evidence that they have continued to exist and flourish for many thousands of years. On the other hand Noah was not directed to take marine animals of any kind into the ark, nor indeed is it easy to see how they could have been preserved.

recent period, geologically speaking, than geologists have hitherto allowed.

"Again, had the whole globe been submerged, the sea-water covering the land would at once have destroyed every fresh-water fish, mollusk, and worm; and as none of these were taken into the ark, the several species would have become extinct. Nothing of the kind has occurred.

"Lastly, such experiments as have been made with regard to the action of sea-water on terrestrial plants leave very little doubt that submergence in sea-water for ten or eleven months would have effectually destroyed not only the great majority of the plants, but their seeds as well. And yet it is not said that Noah took any stock of plants with him into the ark, or that the animals which issued from it had the slightest difficulty in obtaining pasture.

"There are, then, it must be confessed, very strong grounds for believing that no universal deluge ever occurred. Suppose the Flood, on the other hand, to have been local: suppose, for instance, the valley of the Euphrates to have been submerged; and then the necessity for preserving all the species of animals disappears. For, in the first place, there was nothing to prevent the birds and many of the large mammals from getting away; and in the next, the number of species peculiar to that geographical area, and which would be absolutely destroyed by its being flooded, supposing they could not escape, is insignificant."

All these consideration point with overwhelming force in the same direction, and compel us to believe, unless we suppose that a stupendous miracle was wrought, that the Flood of Noah (like other deluges of which we read) extended only over a limited area of the globe.

It now only remains to notice the later allusions to the catastrophe occurring in the Bible, and the traditions of it preserved in other nations besides the Jewish.

The word specially used to designate the Flood of Noah (הַמַּבּוּל *hammabbûl*) occurs in only one other passage of Scripture, Ps. xxix. 10. The poet there sings of the Majesty of God as seen in the storm. It is not improbable that the heavy rain accompanying the thunder and lightning had been such as to swell the torrents, and perhaps cause a partial inundation. This carried back his thoughts to the Great Flood of which he had often read, and he sang, "Jehovah sat as king at the Flood," and looking up at the clear face of the sky, and on the freshness and glory of nature around him, he added, "and Jehovah remaineth a king for ever." In Is. liv. 9, the Flood is spoken of as "the waters of Noah." God Himself appeals to his promise made after the Flood as a pledge of his faithfulness to Israel: "For this is as the waters of Noah unto Me: for as I have sworn that the waters of Noah should no more go over the earth; so have I sworn that I would not be wroth with thee nor rebuke thee."

In the N. T. our Lord gives the sanction of his own authority to the historical truth of the narrative, Matt. xxiv. 37 (cf. Luke xvii. 26), declaring that the state of the world at his Second Coming shall be such as it was in the days of Noah. St. Peter speaks of the "long suffering of God," which "waited in the days of Noah while the ark was a preparing, wherein few, that is, eight souls were saved by water," and sees in the waters of the Flood by which the ark was borne up a type of Baptism, by which the Church is separated

NOAH

from the world. And again, in his Second Epistle (ii. 5), he cites it as an instance of the righteous judgment of God who spared not the old world, etc.

The traditions of many nations have preserved the memory of a great and destructive flood from which but a small part of mankind escaped. It is not always very clear whether they point back to a common centre, whence they were carried by the different families of men as they wandered east and west, or whether they were of national growth, and embody merely records of catastrophes, such as especially in mountainous countries are of no rare occurrence. In some instances no doubt the resemblances between the heathen and the Jewish stories are so striking as to render it morally certain that the former were borrowed from the latter. We find, indeed, a mythological element, the absence of all moral purpose, and a national and local coloring, but, discernible amongst these, undoubted features of the primitive history. The traditions which come nearest to the Biblical account are those of the nations of Western Asia. Foremost amongst these is the Chaldæan. It is preserved in a Fragment of Berosus, and is as follows: "After the death of Ardates, his son Xisuthrus reigned eighteen sari. In his time happened a great Deluge: the history of which is thus described. The Deity Kronos appeared to him in a vision, and warned him that on the 15th day of the month Dæsius there would be a flood by which mankind would be destroyed. He therefore enjoined him to write a history of the beginning, course, and end of all things; and to bury it in the City of the Sun at Sippara: and to build a vessel (σκάφος), and to take with him into it his friends and relations; and to put on board food and drink, together with different animals, birds, and quadrupeds; and as soon as he had made all arrangements, to commit himself to the deep. Having asked the Deity whither he was to sail? he was answered, 'To the gods, after having offered a prayer for the good of mankind.' Whereupon, not being disobedient (to the heavenly vision), he built a vessel five stadia in length, and two in breadth. Into this he put everything which he had prepared, and embarked in it his wife, his children, and his personal friends. After the flood had been upon the earth and was in time abated, Xisuthrus sent out some birds from the vessel, which not finding any food, nor any place where they could rest, returned thither. After an interval of some days Xisuthrus sent out the birds a second time, and now they returned to the ship with mud on their feet. A third time he repeated the experiment and then they returned no more: whence Xisuthrus judged that the earth was visible above the waters; and accordingly he made an opening in the vessel (?), and seeing that it was stranded upon the site of a certain mountain, he quitted it with his wife and daughter, and the pilot. Having then paid his adoration to the earth, and having built an altar and offered sacrifices to the gods, he, together with those who had left the vessel with him, disappeared. Those who had remained behind, when they found that Xisuthrus and his companions did not return, in their turn left the vessel and began to look for him, calling him by his name. Him they saw no more, but a voice came to them from heaven, bidding them lead pious lives, and so join him who was gone to live with the gods; and further informing them that

his wife, his daughter, and the pilot had shared the same honor. It told them, moreover, that they should return to Babylon, and how it was ordained that they should take up the writings that had been buried in Sippara and impart them to mankind, and that the country where they then were was the land of Armenia. The rest having heard these words, offered sacrifices to the gods, and taking a circuit journeyed to Babylon. The vessel being thus stranded in Armenia, some part of it still remains in the mountains of the Corcyræans (or Cordyæans, i. e. the Kurds or Kurdistan) in Armenia: and the people scrape off the bitumen from the vessel and make use of it by way of charms. Now, when those of whom we have spoken returned to Babylon, they dug up the writings which had been buried at Sippara; they also founded many cities and built temples, and thus the country of Babylon became inhabited again" (Cory's *Ancient Fragments*,[a] pp. 26–29). Another version abridged, but substantially the same, is given from Abydenus (*Ibid.* pp. 33, 34). The version of Eupolemus (quoted by Eusebius, *Præp. Evang.* x. 9) is curious: "The city of Babylon," he says, "owes its foundation to those who were saved from the Deluge; they were giants, and they built the tower celebrated in history." Other notices of a Flood may be found (a) in the Phœnician mythology, where the victory of Pontus (the sea) over Demarous (the earth) is mentioned (see the quotation from Sanchoniathon in Cory, as above, p. 13): (b) in the Sibylline Oracles, partly borrowed no doubt from the Biblical narrative, and partly perhaps from some Babylonian story. In these mention is made of the Deluge, after which Kronos, Titan, and Japetus ruled the world, each taking a separate portion for himself, and remaining at peace till after the death of Noah, when Kronos and Titan engaged in war with one another (*Ib.* p. 52). To these must be added (c) the Phrygian story of king Annakos or Nannakos (Enoch) in Iconium, who reached an age of more than 300 years, foretold the Flood, and wept and prayed for his people, seeing the destruction that was coming upon them. Very curious, as showing what deep root this tradition must have taken in the country, is the fact that so late as the time of Septimius Severus, a medal was struck at Apamea,

Coin of Apamea in Phrygia, representing the Deluge.

on which the Flood is commemorated. "The city is known to have been formerly called 'Kibótos' or 'the Ark;' and it is also known that the coins of cities in that age exhibited some leading point in their mythological history. The medal in ques-

---

[a] We have here and there made an alteration, where the translator seemed to us not quite to have caught the meaning of the original.

tion represents a kind of square vessel floating in the water. Through an opening in it are seen two persons, a man and a woman. Upon the top of this chest or ark is perched a bird, whilst another flies toward it carrying a branch between its feet. Before the vessel are represented the same pair as having just quitted it, and got upon the dry land. Singularly enough, too, on some specimens of this medal the letters NΩ, or NΩE, have been found on the vessel, as in the annexed cut. (See Eckhel iii. 132, 133; Wiseman, *Lectures on Science and Revealed Religion*, ii. 126, 129.) This fact is no doubt remarkable, but too much stress must not be laid upon it; for, making full allowance for the local tradition as having occasioned it, we must not forget the influence which the Biblical account would have in modifying the native story.

As belonging to this cycle of tradition, must be reckoned also (1) the Syrian, related by Lucian (*De Deâ Syrâ*, c. 13), and connected with a huge chasm in the earth near Hieropolis into which the waters of the Flood are supposed to have drained: and (2) the Armenian, quoted by Josephus (*Ant.* i. 3) from Nicolaus Damascenus, who flourished about the age of Augustus. He says: "There is above Minyas in the land of Armenia, a great mountain, which is called Baris [i. e a ship], to which it is said that many persons fled at the time of the Deluge, and so were saved; and that one in particular was carried thither upon an ark (ἐπὶ λάρνακος), and was landed upon its summit; and that the remains of the vessel's planks and timbers were long preserved upon the mountain. Perhaps this was the same person of whom Moses the Legislator of the Jews wrote an account."

A second cycle of traditions is that of Eastern Asia. To this belong the Persian, Indian, and Chinese. The Persian is mixed up with its cosmogony, and hence loses anything like an historical aspect. "The world having been corrupted by Ahriman, it was necessary to bring over it a universal flood of water that all impurity might be washed away. The rain came down in drops as large as the head of a bull; the earth was under water to the height of a man, and the creatures of Ahriman were destroyed."

The Chinese story is, in many respects, singularly like the Biblical, according to the Jesuit M. Martinius, who says that the Chinese computed it to have taken place 4,000 years before the Christian era. Fáh-he, the reputed author of Chinese civilization, is said to have escaped from the waters of the Deluge. He reappears as the first man at the production of a renovated world, attended by seven companions — his wife, his three sons, and three daughters, by whose intermarriage the whole circle of the universe is finally completed (Hardwick, *Christ and other Masters*, iii. 16).[a]

The Indian tradition appears in various forms. Of these, the one which most remarkably agrees with the Biblical account is that contained in the Mahábhárata. We are there told that Brahma, having taken the form of a fish, appeared to the pious Manu (Satya, i. e. the righteous, as Noah is also called) on the banks of the river Wirini. Thence, at his request, Manu transferred him when he grew bigger to the Ganges, and finally, when he was too large even for the Ganges, to the ocean. Brahma now announces to Manu the approach of the Deluge, and bids him build a ship and put in it all kinds of seeds together with the seven Rishis, or holy beings. The Flood begins and covers the whole earth. Brahma himself appears in the form of a horned fish, and the vessel being made fast to him he draws it for many years, and finally lands on the loftiest summit of Mount Himarat (i. e. the Himalaya). Then, by the command of God, the ship is made fast, and in memory of the event the mountain called Naubandhana (i. e. *ship-binding*). By the favor of Brahma, Manu, after the Flood, creates the new race of mankind, which are hence termed Manudsha, i. e. born of Manu (Bopp, *die Sündfluth*). The Puránic or popular version is of much later date, and is, "according to its own admission, colored and disguised by allegorical imagery." Another and perhaps the most ancient version of all is that contained in the Çatapat'ha-Bráhmúna. The peculiarity of this is that its locality is manifestly *north* of the Himalaya range, over which Manu is supposed to have crossed into India. Both versions will be found at length in Hardwick's *Christ and other Masters*, ii. 145-152.

The account of the Flood in the Koran is drawn, apparently, partly from Biblical, and partly from Persian sources. In the main, no doubt, it follows the narrative in Genesis, but dwells at length on the testimony of Noah to the unbelieving (Sale's *Koran*, ch. xi. p. 181). He is said to have tarried among his people one thousand save fifty years (ch. xxix. p. 327). The people scoffed at and derided him; and "thus were they employed until our sentence was put in execution and the oven poured forth water." Different explanations have been given of this oven which may be seen in Sale's note. He suggests (after Hyde, *de Rel. Pers.*) that this idea was borrowed from the Persian Magi, who also fancied that the first waters of the Deluge gushed out of the oven of a certain old woman named Zala Cûfa. But the word *Tannûr* (oven), he observes, may mean only a receptacle in which waters are gathered, or the fissure from which they brake forth.[b] Another peculiarity of this version is, that Noah calls in vain to one of his sons to enter into the ark: he refuses, in the hope of escaping to a mountain, and is drowned before his father's eyes. The ark, moreover, is said to have rested on the mountain Al Jûdi, which Sale supposes should be written Jordi or Giordi, and connects with the Gordyæi, Cardu, etc., or Kurd Mountains on the borders of Armenia and Mesopotamia (ch. xi. pp. 181-183, and *notes*).

A third cycle of traditions is to be found among

a D. Gutzlaff, in a paper "On Buddhism in China," communicated to the Royal Asiatic Society (*Journal*, xvi. 79), says that he saw in one of the Buddhist temples, "in beautiful stucco, the scene where Kwan-yin, the Goddess of Mercy, looks down from heaven upon the lonely Noah in his ark, amidst the raging waves of the deluge, with the dolphins swimming around as his last means of safety, and the dove with an olive-branch in its beak flying toward the vessel. Nothing could have exceeded the beauty of the execution."

* It is stated, on good authority, that the Chinese attribute the origin of their famous cycle of 60 years to Ta-Nao, i. e. Nao the great, or divine Nao (Williams's *Middle Kingdom*, ii. 201, and Pauthier's *China*, ii. 28). H.

b The road from Salsburg to Bad-Gastein passes by some very singular fissures made in the limestone by the course of the stream, which are known by the name of "Die Ofen," or "The Ovens. '

the American nations. These, as might be expected, show occasionally some marks of resemblance to the Asiatic legends. The one in existence among the Cherokees reminds us of the story in the Mahábhárata, only that a dog here renders the same service to his master as the fish does there to Manu. " This dog was very pertinacious in visiting the banks of a river for several days, where he stood gazing at the water and howling piteously. Being sharply spoken to by his master and ordered home, he revealed the coming evil. He concluded his prediction by saying that the escape of his master and family from drowning depended upon their throwing *him* into the water; that to escape drowning himself he must take a boat and put in it all he wished to save: that it would then rain hard a long time, and a great overflowing of the land would take place. By obeying this prediction the man and his family were saved, and from them the earth was again peopled." (Schoolcraft, *Notes on the Iroquois*, pp. 358, 359.)

" Of the different nations that inhabit Mexico," says A. von Humboldt, " the' following had paintings resembling the deluge of Coxcox, namely, the Aztecs, the Mixtecs, the Zapotecs, the Tlascaltecs, and the Mechoacans. The Noah, Xisuthrus, or Manu of these nations is termed Coxcox, Teo-Cipactli, or Tezpi. He saved himself with his wife Xochiquetzatl in a bark, or, according to other traditions, on a raft. The painting represents Coxcox in the midst of the water waiting for a bark. The mountain, the summit of which rises above the waters, is the peak of Colhuacan, the Ararat of the Mexicans. At the foot of the mountain are the heads of Coxcox and his wife. The latter is known by two tresses in the form of horns, denoting the female sex. The men born after the Deluge were dumb: the dove from the top of a tree distributed among them tongues, represented under the form of small commas." Of the Mechoacan tradition he writes, " that Coxcox, whom they called Tezpi, embarked in a spacious *acalli* with his wife, his children, several animals, and grain. When the Great Spirit ordered the waters to withdraw, Tezpi sent out from his bark a vulture, the zopilote or *vultur aura*. This bird did not return on account of the carcases with which the earth was strewed. Tezpi sent out other birds, one of which, the humming-bird. alone returned, holding in its beak a branch clad with leaves. Tezpi, seeing that fresh verdure covered the soil, quitted his bark near the mountain of Colhuacan " (*Vues des Cordillères et Monumens de l'Amérique*, pp. 226, 227). A peculiarity of many of these American Indian traditions must be noted, and that is, that the Flood, according to them, usually took place in the time of the First Man, who, together with his family, escape. But Müller (*Americanische Urreligionen*) goes too far when he draws from this the conclusion that these traditions are consequently cosmogonic and have no historical

value. The fact seems rather to be that all memory of the age between the Creation and the Flood had perished, and that hence these two great events were brought into close juxtaposition. This is the less unlikely when we see how very meagre even the Biblical history of that age is.

It may not be amiss, before we go on to speak of the traditions of more cultivated races, to mention the legend still preserved among the inhabitants of the Fĳi islands, although not belonging to our last group. They say that, " after the islands had been peopled by the first man and woman, a great rain took place by which they were finally submerged; but before the highest places were covered by the waters, two large double canoes made their appearance. In one of these was Rokora the god of carpenters, in the other Rokola his head workman, who picked up some of the people and kept them on board until the waters had subsided, after which they were again landed on the island. It is reported that in former times canoes were always kept in readiness against another inundation. The persons thus saved, eight in number, were landed at Mbenga, where the highest of their gods is said to have made his first appearance. By virtue of this tradition, the chiefs of Mbenga take rank before all others and have always acted a conspicuous part among the Fĳis. They style themselves *Ngalidurn-ki-langi* — subject to heaven alone." (Wilkes, *Exploring Expedition*).[a]

One more cycle of traditions we shall notice — that, namely, of the Hellenic races.

Hellas has two versions of a flood, one associated with Ogyges (*Jul. Afric.* as quoted by Euseb. *Præp. Ev.* x. 10), and the other, in a far more elaborate form, with Deucalion. Both, however, are of late origin — they were unknown to Homer and Hesiod. Herodotus, though he mentions Deucalion as one of the first kings of the Hellenes, says not a word about the Flood (i. 56). Pindar is the first writer who mentions it (*Olymp.* ix. 37 ff.) In Apollodorus (*Biblio.* i. 7) and Ovid (*Metam.* i. 260), the story appears in a much more definite shape. Finally, Lucian gives a narrative (*De Dea Syr.* c. 12, 13), not very different from that of Ovid, except that he makes provision for the safety of the animals, which Ovid does not. He attributes the necessity for the Deluge to the exceeding wickedness of the existing race of men, and declares that the earth opened and sent forth waters to swallow them up, as well as that heavy rain fell upon them. Deucalion, as the one righteous man, escaped with his wives and children and the animals he had put into the chest (λάρνακα), and landed, after nine days and nine nights, on the top of Parnassus, whilst the chief part of Hellas was under water, and nearly all men perished, except a few who reached the tops of the highest mountains. Plutarch (*de Sollert. Anim.* § 13) mentions the dove which Deucalion made use of to ascertain whether the flood was abated.

a * Lücken, as quoted by Auberlen (*Die Göttl. Offenbarung*, i. 144), remarks, respecting these traditions among the American aborigines. that the form in which the natives relate them agrees in such a striking manner with the Bible history that we cannot blame the astonished Spaniards if on their first discovery of that continent, they believed, on account of these and similar traditions, that the Apostle Thomas must have preached Christianity there. Truly we must regard it as a work of Providence that this new world, which,

perhaps for centuries, unknown to the rest of mankind and separated from them, followed their own course of training, when suddenly discovered in the midst of the light of historical times, shows at once an agreement with the traditions of the old world, which must convince even the most incredulous that all mankind must originally have drunk from the same common source of intellectual life (*Die Traditionen des Menschengeschlechts . . . . unter den Heiden*).   B

Most of these accounts, it must be observed, localize the Flood, and confine it to Greece or some part of Greece. Aristotle speaks of a local inundation near Dodona only (*Meteorol.* i. 14).

It must also be confessed, that the later the narrative, the more definite the form it assumes, and the more nearly it resembles the Mosaic account.

It seems tolerably certain that the Egyptians had no records of the Deluge, at least if we are to credit Manetho. Nor has any such record been detected on the monuments, or preserved in the mythology of Egypt. They knew, however, of the flood of Deucalion, but seem to have been in doubt whether it was to be regarded as partial or universal, and they supposed it to have been preceded by several others.[a]

Everybody knows Ovid's story of Deucalion and Pyrrha. It may be mentioned, however, in reference to this as a very singular coincidence that, 'just as, according to Ovid, the earth was repeopled by Deucalion and Pyrrha throwing the bones of their mother (*i. e.* stones) behind their backs, so among the Tamanaki, a Carib tribe on the Orinoko, the story goes that a man and his wife escaping from the flood to the top of the high mountain Tapanacu, threw over their heads the fruit of the Mauritia-palm, whence sprung a new race of men and women. This curious coincidence between Hellenic and American traditions seems explicable only on the hypothesis of some common centre of tradition.[b]

After the Flood. — Noah's first act after he left the ark was to build an altar, and to offer sacrifices. This is the first altar of which we read in Scripture, and the first burnt sacrifice. Noah, it is said, took of every clean beast, and of every clean fowl, and offered burnt-offerings on the altar. And then the narrative adds with childlike simplicity: " And Jehovah smelled a smell of rest (or satisfaction), and Jehovah said in his heart, I will not again curse the ground any more for man's sake; for the imagination of man's heart is evil from his youth: neither will I again smite any more every living thing as I have done." Jehovah accepts the sacrifice of Noah as the acknowledgment on the part of man that he desires reconciliation and communion with God; and therefore the renewed earth shall no more be wasted with a plague of waters, but so long as the earth shall last, seed-time and harvest, cold and heat, summer and winter, day and night shall not cease.

Then follows the blessing of God (Elohim) upon Noah and his sons. They are to be fruitful and multiply: they are to have lordship over the inferior animals; not, however, as at the first by native right, but by terror is their rule to be established. All living creatures are now given to man for food; but express provision is made that the blood (in which is the life) should not be eaten. This does not seem necessarily to imply that animal food was not eaten before the flood, but only that now the use of it was sanctioned by divine permission. The prohibition with regard to blood reappears with fresh force in the Jewish ritual (Lev. iii. 17, vii. 26, 27, xvii. 10–14; Deut. xii. 16, 23, 24, xv. 23), and seemed to the Apostles so essentially human as well as Jewish that they thought it ought to be enforced upon Gentile converts. In later times the Greek Church urged it as a reproach against the Latin that they did not hesitate to eat things strangled (*suffocata in quibus sanguis tenetur*).

Next, God makes provision for the security of human life. The blood of man, which is his life, is yet more precious than the blood of beasts. When it has been shed God will require it, whether of beast or of man: and man himself is to be the appointed channel of Divine justice upon the homicide: " Whoso sheddeth man's blood, by man shall his blood be shed; for in the image of God made He man." Hence is laid the first foundation of the civil power. And just as the priesthood is declared to be the privilege of all Israel before it is made representative in certain individuals, so here the civil authority is declared to be a right of human nature itself, before it is delivered over into the hands of a particular executive.

Thus with the beginning of a new world God gives, on the one hand, a promise which secures the stability of the natural order of the universe, and, on the other hand, consecrates human life with a special sanctity as resting upon these two pillars — the brotherhood of men, and man's likeness to God.

Of the seven precepts of Noah, as they are called, the observance of which was required of all Jewish proselytes, three only are here expressly mentioned: the abstinence from blood; the prohibition of murder; and the recognition of the civil authority. The remaining four: the prohibition of idolatry, of blasphemy, of incest, and of

---

[a] * A friend conversant with the literature of this subject, Rev. E. Burgess, very properly suggests that this statement as to the ignorance of the Egyptians concerning a flood is too unqualified. Some Egyptologers maintain a different opinion. (1.) They allege that the name of Noah himself (*Nh, Nuh, Nou,* etc.) is found on the monuments, represented as " the god of water " (see Osburn's *Monumental Egypt,* i. 289). Osburn cites Champollion and Birch in favor of this interpretation, and has no doubt that the name is that of the patriarch through whom the race was perpetuated after the flood. (2.) The names of the first of the eight great gods of the Egyptians, as given by Wilkinson from the monuments, are believed to be different forms of the name Noah (*Manners and Customs of Ancient Egypt,* second series, i. 241). (3.) In the legend of Osiris, the chief primitive divinity of the Egyptians, incidents are stated which seem clearly to identify that deity with Noah of the Hebrew Scriptures (Bryant, *Mythology,* ii. 285 ff. [Lond. 1775] ; Kenrick's *Hist. of Egypt,* i. 355; Wilkinson's *Manners and Customs of Ancient Egypt,* i. 254 ff.). (4.) We have perhaps a reminiscence of the three sons of Noah in the occur-

rence of numerous localities in Egypt in which a triad of deities was worshipped. Wilkinson gives a list of a number of such places, among them Thebes, with the names of the deities (Wilkinson as above, i. 230). The knowledge of a flood ascribed by Plato to the Egyptians in the Timæus (p. 23 Steph.) is that they knew of several deluges, but affirmed that their own land had never been thus visited. Their national egotism may have led them to claim this exemption as the special favorites of heaven.   H.

[b] * " These primeval traditions of the human race," says Auberlen, " illustrate as much the historical credibility of the Mosaic writings, even in their minute recitals, as they do their essential purity and elevation, in contrast with the heathen myths. In this latter respect it will be seen especially how Israel only, together with the fact, maintains at the same time the innermost idea of the fact; while the heathen preserve the external forms remarkably enough, but clothe them with fantastic and national costumes. There is a difference here similar to that between the canonical and the apocryphal Gospels " (*Die Göttliche Offenbarung: ein apologetischer Versuch,* i. 147 b).   H.

theft, rested apparently on the general sense of mankind.

It is in the terms of the blessing and the covenant made with Noah after the Flood that we find the strongest evidence that in the sense of the writer it was universal, *i. e.* that it extended to *all the then known world.* The literal truth of the narrative obliges us to believe that *the whole human race,* except eight persons, perished by the waters of the flood. Noah is clearly the head of a new human family, the representative of the whole race. It is as such that God makes his covenant with him: and hence selects a *natural* phenomenon as the sign of tha: covenant, just as later in making a *national* covenant with Abraham, He made the seal of it to be an arbitrary sign in the flesh. The bow in the cloud, seen by every nation under heaven, is an unfailing witness to the truth of God. Was the rainbow, then, we ask, never seen before the Flood? Was this "sign in the heavens" beheld for the first time by the eight dwellers in the ark when, after their long imprisonment, they stood again upon the green earth, and saw the dark humid clouds spanned by its glorious arch? Such seems the meaning of the narrator. And yet this implies that there was no rain before the flood, and that the laws of nature were changed, at least in that part of the globe, by that event. There is no reason to suppose that in the world at large there has been such change in meteorological phenomena as here implied. That a certain portion of the earth should never have been visited by rain is quite conceivable. Egypt, though not absolutely without rain, very rarely sees it. But the country of Noah and the ark was a mountainous country; and the ordinary atmospherical conditions must have been suspended, or a new law must have come into operation after the Flood, if the rain then first fell, and if the rainbow had consequently never before been painted on the clouds. Hence, many writers have supposed that the meaning of the passage is, not that the rainbow now appeared for the first time, but that it was now for the first time invested with the sanctity of a sign; that not a new phenomenon was visible, but that a new meaning was given to a phenomenon already existing. It must be confessed, however, that this is not the *natural* interpretation of the words: "This is the sign of the covenant which I do set between me and you, and every living thing which is with you for everlasting generations: my bow have I set in the cloud, and it shall be for the sign of a covenant between me and the earth. And it shall come to pass that when I bring a cloud over the earth, then the bow shall be seen in the cloud, and I will remember my covenant which is between me and you and every living thing of all flesh," etc.

Noah now for the rest of his life betook himself to agricultural pursuits, following in this the tradition of his family. It is particularly noticed that he planted a vineyard, and some of the older Jewish writers, with a touch of poetic beauty, tell us that he took the shoots of a vine which had wandered out of paradise wherewith to plant his vineyard.[a] Whether in ignorance of its properties or otherwise, we are not informed, but he drank of the juice of the grape till he became intoxicated and shamefully exposed himself in his own tent. One of his sons, Ham, mocked openly at his father's disgrace. The others, with dutiful care and reverence, endeavored to hide it. Noah was not so drunk as to be unconscious of the indignity which his youngest son had put upon him; and when he recovered from the effects of his intoxication, he declared that in requital for this act of brutal unfeeling mockery, a curse should rest upon the sons of Ham, that *he* who knew not the duty of a child, should see his own son degraded to the condition of a slave. With the curse on his youngest son was joined a blessing on the other two. It ran thus, in the old poetic or rather rhythmical and alliterative form into which the more solemn utterances of antiquity commonly fell. And he said: —

> Cursed be Canaan,
> A slave of slaves shall he be to his brethren.

And he said: —

> Blessed be Jehovah, God of Shem,
> And let Canaan be their slave!
> May God enlarge Japhet,[b]
> And let him dwell in the tents of Shem,
> And let Canaan be their slave!

Of old, a father's solemn curse or blessing was held to have a mysterious power of fulfilling itself And in this case the words of the righteous man, though strictly the expression of a wish (Dr. Pye Smith is quite wrong in translating all the verbs as futures; they are optatives), did in fact amount to a prophecy. It has been asked why Noah did not curse Ham, instead of cursing Canaan. It might be sufficient to reply that at such times men are not left to themselves, and that a divine purpose as truly guided Noah's lips then, as it did the hands of Jacob afterwards. But, moreover, it was surely by a righteous retribution that he, who as youngest son had dishonored his father, should see the curse light on the head of his own youngest son. The blow was probably heavier than if it had lighted directly on himself. Thus early in the world's history was the lesson taught practically which the law afterwards expressly enunciated, that God visits the sins of the fathers upon the children. The subsequent history of Canaan shows in the clearest manner possible the fulfillment of the curse. When Israel took possession of his land, he became the slave of Shem: when Tyre fell before the arms of Alexander, and Carthage succumbed to her Roman conquerors, he became the slave of Japhet: and we almost hear the echo of Noah's curse in Hannibal's *Agnosco fortunam Carthaginis,* when the head of Hasdrubal his brother was thrown contemptuously into the Punic lines.[c]

It is uncertain whether in the words, "And let him dwell in the tents of Shem," "God," or "Japhet," is the subject of the verb. At first it seems more natural to suppose that Noah prays

---

[a] Armenia it has been observed, is still favorable to the growth of the vine. Xenophon (*Anab.* iv. 4, 9) speaks of the excellent wines of the country, and his account has been confirmed in more recent times (Ritter, *Erdk.* x. 819, 554, etc.). The Greek myth referred the discovery and cultivation of the vine to Dionysos, who according to one version brought it from India (Diod. Sic. iii. 32), according to another from Phrygia (Strabo x. 469). Asia at all events is the acknowledged home of the vine.

[b] There is an alliterative play upon words here which cannot be preserved in a translation.

[c] See Delitzsch, *Comm. in loc.*

th-t God would dwell there (the root of the verb is the same as that of the noun *Shechinah*). But the blessing of Shem has been spoken already. It is better therefore to take Japhet as the subject. What then is meant by his dwelling in the tents of Shem? Not of course that he should so occupy them as to thrust out the original possessors; nor even that they should melt into one people; but, as it would seem, that Japhet may enjoy the *religious privileges* of Shem. So Augustine: "Latificet Deus Japheth et habitet in tentoriis Sem, id est, in Ecclesiis quas filii Prophetarum Apostoli construxerunt." The Talmud sees this blessing fulfilled in the use of the Greek language in sacred things, such as the translation of the Scriptures. Thus Shem is blessed with the knowledge of Jehovah: and Japhet with temporal increase and dominion in the first instance, with the further hope of sharing afterwards in spiritual advantages. After this prophetic blessing we hear no more of the patriarch but the sum of his years. "And Noah lived after the flood three hundred and fifty years. And thus all the days of Noah were nine hundred and fifty years: and he died."

For the literature of this article the various commentaries on Genesis, especially those of modern date, may be consulted. Such are those of Tuch, 1838; of Baumgarten, 1843; Knobel, 1852; Schröder, 1846; Delitzsch, 3d ed. 1860. To the last of these especially the present writer is much indebted. Other works bearing on the subject more or less directly are Lyell's *Principles of Geology*, 1853; Pfaff's *Schöpfungs-Geschichte*, 1855; Wiseman's *Lectures on Science and Revealed Religion*; Hugh Miller's *Testimony of the Rocks*; Hardwick's *Christ and other Masters*, 1857; Müller's *Die Americanischen Urreligionen*; Bunsen's *Bibelwerk*, and Ewald's *Jahrbücher*, have also been consulted. The writer has further to express his obligations both to Professor Owen and to Professor Huxley, and especially to the latter gentleman, for much valuable information on the scientific questions touched upon in this article.

J. J. S. P.

* See especially Nägelsbach's article on Noah (Herzog's *Real-Encykl.* x. 394-403) for an admirable summary of the historical testimonies to the Mosaic account of the deluge. It is a satisfaction to observe that the author cites at every step the proper authority for his statements. On the question of the universality of the flood, may be mentioned, among American writers, Dr. Edward Hitchcock on the Historical and Geological Deluges in the *Bibl. Repository* (ix. 78 ff., x. 328 ff., and xi. 1 ff.), and his *Religion of Geology*, lect. xii. (Bost. 1861); Prof. C. H. Hitchcock on the Relations of Geology to Theology, *Bibl. Sacra*, xxiv. 463 ff.; and Prof. Tayler Lewis, who inserts an *excursus* on Gen. viii. 1-19, in his translation of Lange's *Commentary on Genesis*, pp. 314-322 (N. Y. 1868). These writers understand that the flood was limited locally, but was coextensive with the part of the earth inhabited at that time.

Dr. Edward Robinson has some good remarks on the philological or etymological proofs of the Biblical deluge under ARK, in his ed. of Calmet's *Dictionary of the Bible* (Bost. 1832). On that branch of the argument, see especially Philipp Buttmann's *Mythologus oder Die Sagen des Alterthums*, i. 180-234 (Berl. 1828). He finds evidence of the diffusion of the names of the Biblical Shemitic patriarchs, under analogous forms, in the languages of various ancient nations. Rawlinson mentions the Chaldæan legends of the flood (*Ancient Monarchies*, i. 184).   H.

NO'AH (נֹעָה [*motion, commotion*]: Νουά: *Noa*). One of the five daughters of Zelophehad (Num. xxvi. 33, xxvii. 1, xxxvi. 11; Josh. xvii. 3).

NO-A'MON, NO (נֹא אָמוֹן [see below]: μερὶς Ἀμμών: *Alexandria* (*populorum*), Nah. iii. 8: [a] נֹא: Διόσπολις: *Alexandria*, Jer. xlvi. 25; Ez. xxx. 14, 15, 16), a city of Egypt, Thebæ (Thebes), or Diospolis Magna. The second part of the first form is the name of AMEN, the chief divinity of Thebes, mentioned or alluded to in connection with this place in Jeremiah, "Behold, I will punish Amon [or 'the multitude,' with reference to Amen [b]] in No, and Pharaoh, and Egypt, with their gods, and their kings" (*l. c.*); and perhaps also alluded to in Ezekiel (xxx. 15). [AMON.] The second part of the Egyptian sacred name of the city, HA-AMEN, "the abode of Amen," is the same. There is a difficulty as to the meaning of No. It has been supposed, in accordance with the LXX. rendering of No-Amon by μερὶς Ἀμμών, that the Coptic ⲛⲟⲩⲃ, ⲛⲟⲩϩ, *funis, funiculus*, once *funis mensorius* (Mic. ii. 4), instead of ⲛⲟⲩⲃ ⲛⲣⲱⲙⲓ, might indicate that it signified "portion," so that the name would mean "the portion of Amon." But if so, how are we to explain the use of No alone? It thus occurs not only in Hebrew, but also in the language of the Assyrian inscriptions, in which it is written Ni'a, according to Sir Henry Rawlinson ("Illustrations of Egyptian History and Chronology," etc., *Trans. Roy. Soc. Lit.* 2d Ser. vii. 166).[c] The conjectures that Thebes was called Ⲡ ϩ Ⲁ ⲁⲙⲟⲩⲛ, "the abode of Amen," or, still nearer the Hebrew, Ⲛⲁ ⲁⲙⲟⲩⲛ, "the [city] of Amen," like ⲛⲁϩⲥⲓ, "the [city] of Isis," or, as Gesenius prefers, ⲙⲁ ⲁⲙⲟⲩⲛ, "the place of Amen" (*Thes.* s. v.), are all liable to two serious objections, that they neither represent the Egyptian name, nor afford an explanation of the use of No alone. It seems most reasonable to suppose that No is a Semitic name, and that Amon is added in Nahum (*l. c.*) to distinguish Thebes from some other place bearing the same name, or on account of the connection of Amen with that city. Thebes also bears in ancient Egyptian the common name, of doubt-

---

[a] * In Nah. iii. 8, the A. V. has incorrectly "populous No," instead of No-Amon.   H.

[b] The former is the more probable reading, as the gods of Egypt are mentioned almost immediately after.

[c] Sir Henry Rawlinson identifies Ni'a with No-Amon. The whole paper (pp. 137 ff.) is of great importance,

as illustrating the reference in Nahum to the capture of Thebes, by showing that Egypt was conquered by both Esarhaddon and Asshur-bani-pal, and that the latter twice took Thebes. If these wars were after the prophet's time, the narrative of them makes it more probable than it before seemed that there was a still earlier conquest of Egypt by the Assyrians.

NOB

ful signification, AP–T or T–AP, which the Greeks represented by Thebæ. The whole metropolis, on both banks of the river, was called TAM. (See Brugsch, *Geogr. Inschr.* i. 175 ff.)

Jerome supposes No to be either Alexandria or Egypt itself (*In Jesaiam*, lib. v. t. iii. col. 125, ed. Paris, 1704). Champollion takes it to be Diospolis in Lower Egypt (*L'Égypte sous les Pharaons*, ii. 131); but Gesenius (*l. c.*) well observes that it would not then be compared in Nahum to Nineveh. This and the evidence of the Assyrian record leave no doubt that it is Thebes. The description of No-Amon, as "situate among the rivers, the waters round about it" (Nah. *l. c.*), remarkably characterizes Thebes, the only town of ancient Egypt which we know to have been built on both sides of the Nile; and the prophecy that it should "be rent asunder" (Ez. xxx. 16) cannot fail to appear remarkably significant to the observer who stands amidst the vast ruins of its chief edifice, the great temple of Amen, which is rent and shattered as if by an earthquake, although it must be held to refer primarily, at least, rather to the breaking up or capture of the city (comp. 2 K. xxv. 4, Jer. lii. 7), than to its destruction. See THEBES.   R. S. P.

NOB (בֹּב [*elevation, height*]: Νομβά; [Vat. Νομμα, 1 Sam. xxii. 11 ;] Alex. Νοβα, exc. Νοβαθ, 1 Sam. xxii. 11; [FA.³] Νοβ, Neh. xi. 32 [where Rom. Vat. Alex. FA. omit]: *Nobe, Nob* in Neh.) was a sacerdotal city in the tribe of Benjamin, and situated on some eminence near Jerusalem. That it was on one of the roads which led from the north to the capital, and within sight of it, is certain from the illustrative passage in which Isaiah (x. 28–32) describes the approach of the Assyrian army: —

"He comes to Ai, passes through Migron,
At Michmash deposits his baggage ;
They cross the pass, Geba is our night-station ;
Terrified is Ramah, Gibeah of Saul flees.
Shriek with thy voice, daughter of Gallim ;
Listen, O Laish ! Ah, poor Anathoth !
Madmenah escapes, dwellers in Gebim take flight.*a*
Yet this day he halts at Nob :
He shakes his hand against the mount, daughter
    of Zion,
The hill of Jerusalem."

In this spirited sketch the poet sees the enemy pouring down from the north; they reach at length the neighborhood of the devoted city; they take possession of one village after another; while the inhabitants flee at their approach, and fill the country with cries of terror and distress. It is implied here clearly that Nob was the last station in their line of march, whence the invaders could see Jerusalem, and whence they could be seen, as they "shook the hand" in proud derision of their enemies. Lightfoot also mentions a Jewish tradition (*Opp.* ii. 203) that Jerusalem and Nob stood within sight of each other.

Nob was one of the places where the tabernacle, or ark of Jehovah, was kept for a time during the days of its wanderings before a home was provided for it on Mount Zion (2 Sam. vi. 1, &c.). A com-

pany of the Benjamites settled here after the return from the exile (Neh. xi. 32). But the event for which Nob was most noted in the Scripture annals, was a frightful massacre which occurred there in the reign of Saul (1 Sam. xxii. 17–19). David had fled thither from the court of the jealous king; and the circumstances under which he had escaped being unknown, Ahimelech, the high-priest at Nob, gave him some of the shew-bread from the golden table, and the sword of Goliath which he had in his charge as a sacred trophy. Doeg, an Edomite, the king's shepherd, who was present, reported the affair to his master. Saul was enraged on hearing that such favor had been shown to a man whom he hated as a rival; and nothing would appease him but the indiscriminate slaughter of all the inhabitants of Nob. The king's executioners having refused to perform the bloody deed (1 Sam. xxii. 17), he said to Doeg, the spy, who had betrayed the unsuspecting Ahimelech, "Turn thou, and fall upon the priests. And Doeg the Edomite turned, and he fell upon the priests, and slew on that day four-score and five persons that did wear a linen ephod. And Nob, the city of the priests, smote he with the edge of the sword, both men and women, children and sucklings, and oxen, and asses, and sheep, with the edge of the sword." Abiathar, a son of Ahimelech, was the only person who survived to recount the sad story.

It would be a long time, naturally, before the doomed city could recover from such a blow. It appears in fact never to have regained its ancient importance. The references in Is. x. 32 and Neh. xi. 32 are the only later allusions to Nob which we find in the O. T. All trace of the name has disappeared from the country long ago. Jerome states that nothing remained in his time to indicate where it had been. Geographers are not agreed as to the precise spot with which we are to identify the ancient locality. Some of the conjectures on this point may deserve to be mentioned. "It must have been situated," says Dr. Robinson (*Researches*, vol. i. p. 464), "somewhere upon the ridge of the Mount of Olives, northeast of the city. We sought all along this ridge from the Damascus road to the summit opposite the city, for some traces of an ancient site which might be regarded as the place of Nob; but without the slightest success." Kiepert's map places Nob at *el-Isâwîeh*, not far from *Anâtâ*, about a mile northwest of Jerusalem. Tobler (*Topographie von Jerus.* ii. § 719) describes this village as beautifully situated, and occupying unquestionably an ancient site. But it must be regarded as fatal to this identification that Jerusalem is not to be seen from that point.*b* *El-Isâwîeh* is in a valley, and the *dramatic* representation of the prophet would be unsuited to such a place. Mr. Porter (*Handb.* ii. 324) expresses the confident belief that Nob is to be sought on a low peaked tell, a little to the right of the northern road and opposite to *Shâfât*. He found there several cisterns hewn in the rock, large building stones, and various other indications of an ancient town. The top of this hill *c* affords an extensive view, and Mount Zion is distinctly seen, though

---

a "The full idea," says Gesenius (*Handw. s. v.*), "is that they hurry off to conceal their treasures."

b * Büetschi takes the same view of this difficulty and decides against the identification (Herzog's *Real-Encykl.* x. 404). The *gestus minantis* (Gesen.) has little

or no significance unless those menaced could see the invaders at the moment. Mr. Grove gives the preference to *el-Isâwîeh* (Clark's *Bible Atlas*, p. 204). H.

c * This hill, says Lieut. Warren (*Report*, Oct. 1st 1867), is called *Sŭmah*.   H

Moriah and Olivet are hid by an intervening ridge.

The Nob spoken of above is not to be confounded with another which Jerome mentions in the plain of Sharon, not far from Lydda. (See Von Raumer's *Palästina*, p. 196.) No allusion is made to this latter place in the Bible. The Jews after recovering the ark of Jehovah from the Philistines would be likely to keep it beyond the reach of a similar disaster; and the Nob which was the seat of the sanctuary in the time of Saul, must have been among the mountains. This Nob, or *Nobla* as Jerome writes, now *Beit Nûba*, could not be the village of that name near Jerusalem. The towns with which Isaiah associates the place put that view out of the question.   H. B. H.

NO′BAH (נֹבַח [*barking, a loud cry*]: Ναβώθ, Ναβαί; Alex. Ναβωθ, Ναβεθ: *Noba*, [*Nobe*]). The name conferred by the conqueror of KENATH and the villages in dependence on it on his new acquisition (Num. xxxii. 42). For a certain period after the establishment of the Israelite rule the new name remained, and is used to mark the course taken by Gideon in his chase after Zebah and Zalmunna (Judg. viii. 11). But it is not again heard of, and the original appellation, as is usual in such cases, appears to have recovered its hold, which it has since retained; for in the slightly modified form of *Kunâwat* it is the name of the place to the present day (see *Onomasticon*, Nabo).

Ewald (*Gesch.* ii. 268, *note* 2) identifies the Nobah of Gideon's pursuit with Nophah of Num. xxi. 30, and distinguishes them both from Nobah of Num. xxxii. 42, on the ground of their being mentioned with Dibon, Medeba, and Jogbehah. But if Jogbehah be, as he elsewhere (ii. 504, *note* 4) suggests, *el-Jebeibeh*, between *Ammân* and *es-Salt*, there is no necessity for the distinction. In truth the lists of Gad and Reuben in Num. xxxii. are so confused that it is difficult to apportion the towns of each in accordance with our present imperfect topographical knowledge of those regions. Ewald also (ii. 392, *note*) identifies Nobah of Num. xxxii. 42 with *Nawa* or *Nere*, a place 15 or 16 miles east of the north end of the Lake of Gennesaret (Ritter, *Jordan*, p. 356). But if Kenath and Nobah are the same, and *Kunâwat* be Kenath, the identification is both unnecessary and untenable.

Eusebius and Jerome, with that curious disregard of probability which is so puzzling in some of the articles in the *Onomasticon*, identify Nobah of Judg. viii. with Nob, "the city of the Priests, afterwards laid waste by Saul" (*Onom.* Νομβά and "Nabbe sive Nobba").

NO′BAH (נֹבַח [*barking, a loud cry*]: Ναβαῦ: *Nobi*). An Israelite warrior (Num. xxxii. 42 only), probably, like Jair, a Manassite, who during the conquest of the territory on the east of Jordan possessed himself of the town of Kenath and the villages or hamlets dependent upon it (Heb. "daughters"), and gave them his own name. According to the Jewish tradition (*Seder 'Olam Rabba*, ix.) Nobah was born in Egypt, died after the decease of Moses, and was buried during the passage of the Jordan.

It will be observed that the form of the name in the LXX. is the same as that given to Nebo.
                                        G.

*NOBLEMAN (βασιλικός), the title of a courtier or royal officer of Herod Antipas, who came to Jesus at Cana, to entreat him to heal his son, whom he had left at the point of death at his home, in Capernaum. On his return he found that the cure had been wrought at the very moment when Jesus said, "Thy son liveth" (John iv. 46, 47). Some critics (Ewald, DeWette with some hesitation, Baur) regard this miracle as identical with that of the healing of the centurion's servant (Matt. viii. 5; Luke vii. 1-10). But it is difficult to reconcile the differences in the two accounts with this supposition. Cana was the scene of the miracle related by John, and Capernaum that of the miracle related by Matthew and Luke. One of the men was a Jew (included at least among the Galileans, John iv. 48) in the service of the king or tetrarch, as his designation implies, the other a Roman and a centurion (Luke vii. 2). In one case it was a son of the petitioner who was sick, in the other his servant,[a] and, finally, the nobleman requested Jesus to come to his house, whereas the centurion felt that he was utterly unworthy to receive him under his roof. He is called βασιλικός with the same propriety that Herod Antipas is called βασιλεύς (Mark vi. 14), though the stricter title of the latter was τετράρχης (Matt. xiv. 1). It is a complimentary title rather than official as applied to both.   H.

NOD [נוד, *wandering*: Ναΐδ: *profugus*]. [CAIN.]

NO′DAB (נוֹדָב [*nobility*]: Ναδαβαῖοι: *Nodab*), the name of an Arab tribe mentioned only in 1 Chr. v. 19, in the account of the war of the Reubenites, the Gadites, and the half of the tribe of Manasseh, against the Hagarites (vv. 9-22); "and they made war with the Hagarites, with Jetur, and Nephish, and *Nodab*" (ver. 19). In Gen. xxv. 15 and 1 Chr. i. 31, Jetur, Naphish, and Kedemah are the last three sons of Ishmael, and it has been therefore supposed that Nodab also was one of his sons. But we have no other mention of Nodab, and it is probable, in the absence of additional evidence, that he was a grandson or other descendant of the patriarch, and that the name, in the time of the record, was that of a tribe sprung from such descendant. The Hagarites, and Jetur, Nephish, and Nodab, were pastoral people, for the Reubenites dwelt in their tents throughout all the east [land] of Gilead (1 Chr. v. 10), and in the war a great multitude of cattle — camels, sheep, and asses — were taken. A hundred thousand men were taken prisoners or slain, so that the tribes must have been very numerous and the Israelites "dwelt in their steads until the captivity." If the Hagarites (or Hagarenes) were, as is most probable, the people who afterwards inhabited Hejer [HAGARENES], they were driven southwards, into the northeastern province of Arabia, bordering the mouths of the Euphrates, and the low tracts surrounding them. [JETUR; ITUR.A; NAPHISH.]
                                        E. S. P.

NO′E (Νῶε: *Noē*). The patriarch Noah (Tob. iv. 12; Matt. xxiv. 37, 38; Luke iii. 36, xvii. 26, 27). [NOAH.]

NO′EBA (Νοεβά: *Nachoba*) = NEKODA 1 (1 Esdr. v. 31; comp. Ezr. ii. 48).

---

[a] Matthew, it is true, has ὁ παῖς μου, which signifies "servant" or "child" (viii. 6). Luke has the same (vii. 7); but the latter has also τὸν δοῦλον αὐτοῦ (ver. 3), and this resolves the ambiguity.   H.

NO'GAH (נֹגַהּ [*dawn, day-break*]: Ναγαί, Ναγέθ; [Alex. in 1 Chr. iii. 7, Ναγε, Comp. Νογε; FA. in xiv. 6, Ναγετ:] *Noge, Noga*). One of the thirteen sons of David who were born to him in Jerusalem (1 Chr. iii. 7, xiv. 6). His name is omitted from the list in 2 Sam. v.

NO'HAH (נוֹחָה [*rest*]: Νωδ; [Vat. Νοοα:] *Nohaa*). The fourth son of Benjamin (1 Chr. viii. 2).

* NOISOME (O. F. *noisir*, "to hurt," Lat. *nocere*) is used in its primitive sense of *noxious, baneful, destructive*, in Ps. xci. 3, Ez. xiv. 21, and Ex. viii. 21, Job xxxi. 40, marg.   A.

NON (נוֹן [in 1 Chr. vii. 27; but elsewhere, נוּן, *a fish*]: Νούν; [Vat. Alex. Νουμ:] *Nun*). Nun, the father of Joshua (1 Chr. vii. 27).

NOPH, MOPH (נֹף [see below]: Μέμφις: *Memphis*, Is. xix. 13, Jer. ii. 16, Ez. xxx. 13, 16; מֹף: Μέμφις: *Memphis*, Hos. ix. 6), a city of Egypt, Memphis. These forms are contracted from the ancient Egyptian common name, MEN-NUFR, or MEN-NEFRU, "the good abode," or perhaps "the abode of the good one:" also contracted in the Coptic forms ⲙⲉⲛϥⲓ, ⲙⲉⲙϥⲓ, ⲙⲉⲛⲃⲉ, ⲙⲉⲙⲃⲉ (M), ⲙⲉⲙϥⲉ (S); in the Greek Μέμφις; and in the Arabic *Menf*, مَنْف. The Hebrew forms are to be regarded as representing colloquial forms of the name, current with the Shemites, if not with the Egyptians also. As to the meaning of Memphis, Plutarch observes that it was interpreted to signify either the haven of good ones, or the sepulchre of Osiris (καὶ τὴν μὲν πόλιν οἱ μὲν ὁρμον ἀγαθῶν ἑρμηνεύουσιν, οἱ δ' [ἰδί] ως τάφον Ὀσίριδος, *De Iside et Osiride*, 20). It is probable that the epithet "good" refers to Osiris, whose sacred animal Apis was here worshipped, and here had its burial-place, the Serapeum, whence the name of the village Busiris (PA-HESAR? "the [abode?] of Osiris"), now represented in name, if not in exact site, by Aboo-Seer,[a] probably originally a quarter of Memphis. As the great Egyptian city is characterized in Nahum as "situate among the rivers" (iii. 8), so in Hosea the lower Egyptian one is distinguished by its Necropolis, in this passage as to the fugitive Israelites: "Mizraim shall gather them up, Noph shall bury them;" for its burial-ground, stretching for twenty miles along the edge of the Libyan desert, greatly exceeds that of any other Egyptian town. (See Brugsch, *Geogr. Inschr.* i. 234 ff., and MEMPHIS.)   R. S. P.

NO'PHAH (נֹפַח: *Nôphach*; the Samar. has the article, הנפח [*hill*, Fürst; Dietr.]: αl γυναῖκες, Alex. αl γ. αὐτῶν: *Nophe*), a place mentioned only in Num. xxi. 30, in the remarkable song apparently composed by the Amorites after their conquest of Heshbon from the Moabites, and therefore of an earlier date than the Israelite invasion. It is named with Dibon and Medeba, and was possibly in the neighborhood of Heshbon. A name very similar to Nophah is Nobah, which is twice mentioned; once as bestowed by the conqueror of the same name on Kenath (a place still existing more than 70 miles distant from the scene of the Amorite conflict), and again in connection with Jogbehah, which latter, from the mode of its occurrence in Num. xxxii. 36, would seem to have been in the neighborhood of Heshbon. Ewald (*Gesch.* ii. 268, *note*) decides (though without giving his grounds) that Nophah is identical with the latter of these. In this case the difference would be a dialectical one, Nophah being the Moabite or Amorite form. [NOBAH.]   G.

NOSE-JEWEL (נֶזֶם, pl. constr. נִזְמֵי: ἐνώτια: *inaures*: A. V., Gen. xxiv. 22; Ex. xxxv.

Arab woman with nose-ring.

22, "earring;" Is. iii. 21; Ez. xvi. 12, "jewel on the forehead:" rendered by Theod. and Symm. ἐπιρρίνιον, Ges. p. 870). A ring of metal, sometimes of gold or silver, passed usually through the right nostril, and worn by way of ornament by women in the East. Its diameter is usually 1 in. or 1¼ in., but sometimes as much as 3½ in. Upon it are strung beads, coral, or jewels. In Egypt it is now almost confined to the lower classes. It is mentioned in the Mishna, *Shabb.* vi. 1; *Celim*, xi. 8. Layard remarks that no specimen has been found in Assyrian remains. (Burckhardt, *Notes on Bed.* i. 51, 232; Niebuhr, *Descr. de l'Arab.* p. 57; *Voynges*, i. 133, ii. 56; Chardin, *Voy.* viii. 200; Lane, *Mod. Egypt.* i. 78; *App.* iii. 226; Saalschütz, *Hebr. Arch.* i. 3, p. 25; Layard, *Nin. and Bab.* pp. 262, 544.)   H. W. P.

* NOVICE, νεόφυτος, "neophyte," that which is newly born, or planted, is used in 1 Tim. iii. 6, figuratively, of one who had just embraced the Christian religion, "a new convert." Such a person was not a fit candidate for the office of bishop or overseer (ἐπίσκοπος, ver. 2); for the self-confidence of one who had just entered an untried course of life might lead him far astray.   R. D. C. R.

NUMBER.[b]   Like most oriental nations, it

---

a This Arabic name affords a curious instance of the use of Semitic names of similar sound but different signification in the place of names of other languages.

b 1. חֵקֶר, ἀριθμός, properly inquiry, investigation (Ges. p 515).

2. מִכְסָה, ἀριθμός, *numerus*.

3. מְנִי, Τύχη, *Fortuna*, probably a deity (Ges. p 798); rendered "number," Is. lxv. 11.

4. מִנְיָן, Chald. from same root as 3.

is probable that the Hebrews in their written calculations made use of the letters of the alphabet. That they did so in post-Babylonian times we have conclusive evidence in the Maccabæan coins; and it is highly probable that this was the case also in earlier times, both from internal evidence, of which we shall presently speak, and also from the practice of the Greeks, who borrowed it with their earliest alphabet from the Phœnicians, whose alphabet again was, with some slight variations, the same as that of the Samaritans and Jews (Chardin, *Voy.* ii. 421, iv. 288 and foll., Langlès; Thiersch, *Gr Gr.* §§ xii., lxxiii., pp. 23, 153; Jelf, *Gr. Gr.* i. 3; Müller, *Etrusker*, ii. 317, 321; *Eng. Cycl.* "Coins," "Numeral Characters;" Lane, *Mod. Egypt.* i. 91; Donaldson, *New Cratylus*, pp. 146, 151; Winer, *Zahlen*).

But though, on the one hand, it is certain that in all existing MSS. of the Hebrew text of the O. T. the numerical expressions are written at length (Lee, *Hebr. Gram.* §§ 19, 22), yet, on the other, the variations in the several versions between themselves and from the Hebrew text, added to the evident inconsistencies in numerical statement between certain passages of that text itself, seem to prove that some shorter mode of writing was originally in vogue, liable to be misunderstood, and in fact misunderstood by copyists and translators. The following may serve as specimens:—

1. In 2 K. xxiv. 8 Jehoiachin is said to have been 18 years old, but in 2 Chr. xxxvi. 9 the number given is 8.

2. In Is. vii. 8 Vitringa shows that for threescore and five one reading gives sixteen and five, the letter *jod* '(10) after *shesh* (6) having been mistaken for the Rabbinical abbreviation by omission of the *mem* from the plural *shishim*, which would stand for sixty. Six + 10 was thus converted into sixty + ten.

3. In 1 Sam. vi. 19 we have 50,070, but the Syriac and Arabic versions have 5,070.

4. In 1 K. iv. 26, we read that Solomon had 40,000 stalls for chariot-horses, but 4,000 only in 1 Chr. ix. 25.

5. The letters *vau* (6) and *zayin* (7) appear to have been interchanged in some readings of Gen. ii. 2.

These variations, which are selected from a copious list given by Glass (*De Caussis Corruptionis*, i. § 22, vol. ii. p. 188, ed. Dathe), appear to have proceeded from the alphabetic method of writing numbers, in which it is easy to see how, *e. g.* such letters as *vau* (ו) and *jod* (י), *nun* (נ) and *caph* (כ), may have been confounded and even sometimes omitted. The final letters, also, which were unknown to the early Phœnician or Samaritan alphabet, were used as early as the Alexandrian period to denote hundreds between 500 and 1,000.[a]

But whatever ground these variations may afford for reasonable conjecture, it is certain, from the fact mentioned above, that no positive rectification of them can at present be established, more especially as there is so little variation in the num-

bers quoted from the O. T., both in N. T. and in the Apocrypha, *e. g.* (1.) Num. xxv. 9, quoted 1 Cor. x. 8. (2.) Ex. xii. 40, quoted Gal. iii. 17. (3.) Ex. xvi. 35 and Ps. xcv. 10, quoted Acts xiii. 18. (4.) Gen. xvii. 1, quoted Rom. iv. 19. (5.) Num. i. 46, quoted Ecclus. xvi. 10.

Josephus also in the main agrees in his statements of numbers with our existing copies.

There can be little doubt, however, as was remarked by St. Augustine (*Civ. D.* x. 13, § 1), that some at least of the numbers mentioned in Scripture are intended to be representative rather than determinative. Certain numbers, as 7, 10, 40, 100, were regarded as giving the idea of completeness. Without entering into his theory of this usage, we may remark that the notion of representative numbers in certain cases is one extremely common among eastern nations, who have a prejudice against counting their possessions accurately; that it enters largely into many ancient systems of chronology, and that it is found in the philosophical and metaphysical speculations not only of the Pythagorean and other ancient schools of philosophy, both Greek and Roman, but also in those of the later Jewish writers, of the Gnostics, and also of such Christian writers as St. Augustine himself (August. *De Doctr. Christ.* ii. 16, 25; *Civ. D.* xv. 30; Philo, *De Mund. Opif.* i. 21; *De Abrah.* ii. 5; *De Sept. Num.* ii. 281, ed. Mangey; Joseph. *B. J.* vii. 5, § 5: Mishna, *Pirke Aboth*, v. 7, 8; Irenæus, i. 3, ii. 1, v. 29, 30; Hieronym. *Com. in Is.* iv. 1, vol. iv. p. 72, ed. Migne; Arist. *Metaphys.* i. 5, 6, xii. 6, 8; Ælian, *V. H.* iv. 17; Varro, *Hebdom.* fragm. i. 255, ed. Bipont.; Niebuhr, *Hist. of Rome*, ii. 72, ed. Hare; Burckhardt, *Trav. in Arabia*, i. 75; *Syria*, p. 560, comp. with Gen. xlii. 16 and xxii. 17; also see papers on Hindoo Chronology in Sir W. Jones's Works, Suppl. vol. ii. pp. 968, 1017).

We proceed to give some instances of numbers used (*a*) representatively, and thus probably by design indefinitely, or (*b*) definitely, but as we may say preferentially, *i. e.* because some meaning (which we do not in all cases understand) was attached to them.

1. *Seven*, as denoting either plurality or completeness, is so frequent as to make a selection only of instances necessary, *e. g. sevenfold*, Gen. iv. 24; *seven times, i. e.* completely, Lev. xxvi. 24; Ps. xii. 6; *seven* (*i. e.* many) *ways*, Deut. xxviii. 25. See also 1 Sam. ii. 5; Job v. 19, where six also is used; Prov. vi. 16, ix. 1; Eccl. xi. 2, where eight also is named; Is. iv. 1; Jer. xv. 9; Mic. v. 5; also Matt. xii. 45, *seven spirits*; Mark xvi. 9, *seven devils*; Rev. iv. 5, *seven Spirits*, xv. 1, *seven plagues*. Otho, *Lex. Rabb.* p. 411, says that Scripture uses seven to denote plurality. See also Christian authorities quoted by Suicer, *Thes. Eccl.* s. v. ἑβδόμος, Hofmann, *Lex.* s. v. "Septem," and the passages quoted above from Varro, Aristotle, and Ælian, in reference to the heathen value for the number 7.

2. *Ten* as a preferential number is exemplified in the Ten Commandments and the law of Tithe. It plays a conspicuous part in the later Jewish ritual code. See Otho, *Lex. Rabb.* p. 410.

---

5. מִסְפָּר.

6. סְפוֹרָה in plur. Ps. lxxi. 15, πραγματείας, literature.

7. מִנְיָן.

To number is (1) מָנָה, ἀριθμέω, *numero*. (2.) חָשַׁב, λογίζομαι, *i. e.* value, account, as in Is. xiii. 17. In Piel, count, or number, which is the primary notion of the word (Ges. p. 531).

[a] ר denotes 550, ם 600, ן 700, ף 800, ץ 900.

3. *Seventy*, as compounded of 7 X 10, appears frequently, e. g. *seventy-fold* (Gen. iv. 24; Matt. xviii. 22). Its definite use appears in the offerings of 70 shekels (Num. vii. 13, 19, and foll.); the 70 elders (xi. 16); 70 years of captivity (Jer. xxiv. 11). To these may be added the 70 descendants of Noah (Gen. x.), and the alleged Rabbinical qualification for election to the office of Judge among the 71 members of the Great Sanhedrim, of the knowledge of 70 languages (*Sanh.* ii. 6; and Carpzov, *App. Bibl.* p. 576). The number of 72 translators may perhaps also be connected with the same idea.

4. *Five* appears in the table of punishments, of legal requirements (Ex. xxii. 1; Lev. v. 16, xxii. 14, xxvii. 15; Num. v. 7, xviii. 16), and in the five empires of Daniel (Dan. ii.).

5. *Four* is used in reference to the 4 winds (Dan. vii. 2), and the so-called 4 corners of the earth; the 4 creatures, each with 4 wings and 4 faces, of Ezekiel (i. 5 and foll.); 4 rivers of Paradise (Gen. ii. 10); 4 beasts (Dan. vii. and Rev. iv. 6); the 4 equal-sided Temple-chamber (Ez. xl. 47).

6. *Three* was regarded, both by the Jews and other nations, as a specially complete and mystic number (Plato, *De Leg.* iv. 715; Dionys. Halic. iii. c. 12). It appears in many instances in Scripture as a definite number, e. g. 3 feasts (Ex. xxiii. 14, 17; Deut. xvi. 16), the triple offering of the Nazarite, and the triple blessing (Num. vi. 14, 24), the triple invocation (Is. vi. 3; Rev. i. 4), Daniel's 3 hours of prayer (Dan. vi. 10, comp. Ps. lv. 17), the third heaven (2 Cor. xii. 2), and the thrice-repeated vision, (Acts x. 16).

7. *Twelve* (3 X 4) appears in 12 tribes, 12 stones in the high-priest's breast-plate, 12 Apostles, 12 foundation-stones, and 12 gates (Rev. xxi. 19–21); 12,000 furlongs of the heavenly city (Rev. xxi. 16); 144,000 sealed (Rev. vii. 4).

8. *Forty* appears in many enumerations; 40 days of Moses (Ex. xxiv. 18); 40 years in the wilderness (Num. xiv. 34); 40 days and nights of Elijah (1 K. xix. 8); 40 days of Jonah's warning to Nineveh. (Jon. iii. 4); 40 days of temptation (Matt. iv. 2). Add to these the very frequent use of the number 40 in regnal years, and in political or other periods (Judg. iii. 11, xiii. 1; 1 Sam. iv. 18; 2 Sam. v. 4, xv. 7; 1 K. xi. 42; Ez. xxix. 11, 12; Acts xiii. 21).

9. *One hundred.* — 100 cubits' length of the Tabernacle-court (Ex. xxvii. 18); 100 men, i. e. a large number (Lev. xxvi. 8); Gideon's 300 men (Judg. vi. 6); the selection of 10 out of every 100, (xx. 10); 100 men (2 K. iv. 43); leader of 100 men (1 Chr. xii. 14); 100 stripes (Prov. xvii. 10); 100 times (Eccl. viii. 12); 100 children (vi. 3); 100 cubits' measurements in Ezekiel's Temple (Ez. xl., xli., xlii.); 100 sheep (Matt. xviii. 12); 100 pence (Matt. xviii. 28); 100 measures of oil or wheat (Luke xvi. 6, 7).

10. Lastly, the mystic number 666 (Rev. xiii. 18), of which the earliest attempted explanation is the conjecture of Irenæus, who of three words, Euanthas, Lateinos, and Teitan, prefers the last as fulfilling its conditions best. (For various other interpretations see Calmet, Whitby, and Irenæus, *De Antichrist.* v. c. 29, 30.)

It is evident, on the one hand, that whilst the representative, and also the typical character of certain numbers must be maintained (e. g. Matt. xix. 28), there is, on the other, the greatest danger of overstraining any particular theory on the subject, and thus degenerating into that subtle trifling, from which neither the Gnostics, nor some also of their orthodox opponents were exempt (see Clem Alex. *Strom.* vi. c. 11, p. 782, ed. Potter, and August. *l. c.*), and of which the Rabbinical writings present such striking instances. [CHRONOLOGY, CENSUS.]   H. W. P.

NUMBERING. [CENSUS.]

NUMBERS (וַיְדַבֵּר), from the first word; or בְּמִדְבַּר, from the words בְּמִדְבַּר סִינַי, in i. 1: 'Αριθμοί: *Numeri:* called also by the later Jews (הַפִּקּוּדִים), or סֵפֶר הַמִּסְפָּרִים, the fourth book of the Law or Pentateuch. It takes its name in the LXX. and Vulg. (whence our "Numbers") from the double numbering or census of the people; the first of which is given in cc. i.–iv., and the second in ch. xxvi.

A. *Contents.* — The book may be said to contain generally the history of the Israelites from the time of their leaving Sinai, in the second year after the Exodus, till their arrival at the borders of the Promised Land in the fortieth year of their journeyings. It consists of the following principal divisions: —

I. The preparations for the departure from Sinai (i. 1–x. 10).

II. The journey from Sinai to the borders of Canaan (x. 11–xiv. 45).

III. A brief notice of laws given, and events which transpired, during the thirty-seven years' wandering in the wilderness (xv. 1–xix. 22).

IV. The history of the last year, from the second arrival of the Israelites in Kadesh till they reach "the plains of Moab by Jordan near Jericho" (xx. 1–xxxvi. 13).

I. (*a.*) The object of the encampment at Sinai has been accomplished. The Covenant has been made, the Law given, the Sanctuary set up, the Priests consecrated, the service of God appointed, and Jehovah dwells in the midst of his chosen people. It is now time to depart in order that the object may be achieved for which Israel has been sanctified. That object is the occupation of the Promised Land. But this is not to be accomplished by peaceable means, but by the forcible expulsion of its present inhabitants; for "the iniquity of the Amorites is full," they are ripe for judgment, and this judgment Israel is to execute. Therefore Israel must be organized as Jehovah's army; and to this end a mustering of all who are capable of bearing arms is necessary. Hence the book opens with the numbering of the people,[a] chapters i.–iv. These contain, first, the census of all the tribes or clans, amounting in all to six hundred and three thousand, five hundred and fifty, with the exception of the Levites, who were not numbered with the rest (ch. i.); secondly, the arrangement of the camp, and the order of march (ch. ii.); thirdly, the special and separate census of the Levites, who are claimed by God instead of all the first-born, the three families of the tribe having their peculiar offices in the Tabernacle appointed them, both when it was at rest and when they were on the march (cc. iii., iv.).

(*b.*) Chapters v., vi. Certain laws apparently supplementary to the legislation in Leviticus; the removal of the unclean from the camp (v. 1 4); the law of restitution (v. 5–10); the trial of jeal-

---

[a] See Kurtz, *Gesch. des Alten Bundes*, ii. 383.

may (v 11–31); the law of the Nazarites (vi. 1–21); the form of the priestly blessing (vi. 22–27).

(c.) Chapters vii. 1–x. 10. Events occurring at this time, and regulations connected with them. Ch. vii. gives an account of the offerings of the princes of the different tribes at the dedication of the Tabernacle; ch. viii. of the consecration of the Levites (ver. 39 of ch. vii., and vv. 1–4 of ch. viii. seem to be out of place); ch. ix. 1–14, of the second observance of the Passover (the first in the wilderness) on the 14th day of the second month, and of certain provisions made to meet the case of those who by reason of defilement were unable to keep it. Lastly, ch. ix. 15–23 tells how the cloud and the fire regulated the march and the encampment; and x. 1–10, how two silver trumpets were employed to give the signal for public assemblies, for war, and for festal occasions.

II. March from Sinai to the borders of Canaan.

(a.) We have here, first, the order of march described (x. 14–28); the appeal of Moses to his father-in-law, Hobab, to accompany them in their journeys; a request urged probably because, from his desert life, he would be well acquainted with the best spots to encamp in, and also would have influence with the various wandering and predatory tribes who inhabited the peninsula (29–32): and the chant which accompanied the moving and the resting of the ark (vv. 35, 36).

(b.) An account of several of the stations and of the events which happened at them. The first was at Taberah, where, because of their impatient murmurings, several of the people were destroyed by lightning (these belonged chiefly, it would seem, to the motley multitude which came out of Egypt with the Israelites); the loathing of the people for the manna; the complaint of Moses that he cannot bear the burden thus laid upon him, and the appointment in consequence of seventy elders to serve and help him in his office (xi. 10–29); the quails sent, and the judgment following thereon, which gave its name to the next station, Kibroth-hattaavah (the graves of lust), xi. 31–35 (cf. Ps. lxxviii. 30, 31, cvi. 14, 15); arrival at Hazeroth, where Aaron and Miriam are jealous of Moses, and Miriam is in consequence smitten with leprosy (xii. 1–15); the sending of the spies from the wilderness of Paran (et-Tyh), their report, the refusal of the people to enter Canaan, their rejection in consequence, and their rash attack upon the Amalekites, which resulted in a defeat (xii. 16–xiv. 45).

III. What follows must be referred apparently to the thirty-seven years of wanderings; but we have no notices of time or place. We have laws respecting the meat and drink offerings, and other sacrifices (xv. 1–31); an account of the punishment of a Sabbath-breaker, perhaps as an example of the presumptuous sins mentioned in vv. 30, 31 (xv. 32–36); the direction to put fringes on their garments as mementos (xv. 37–41); the history of the rebellion of Korah, Dathan, and Abiram, and the murmuring of the people (xvi.); the budding of Aaron's rod as a witness that the tribe of Levi was chosen (xvii.); the direction that Aaron and his sons should bear the iniquity of the people, and the duties of the priests and Levites (xviii.); the law of the water of purification (xix.).

IV. (a.) The narrative returns abruptly to the second encampment of the Israelites in Kadesh. Here Miriam dies, and the people murmur for water, and Moses and Aaron, "speaking unadvisedly," are not allowed to enter the Promised Land (xx. 1–13). They intended perhaps, as before, to enter Canaan from the south. This, however, was not to be permitted. They therefore desired a passage through the country of Edom. Moses sent a conciliatory message to the king, asking permission to pass through, and promising carefully to abstain from all outrage, and to pay for the provisions which they might find necessary. The jealousy, however, of this fierce and warlike people was aroused. They refused the request, and turned out in arms to defend their border. And as those almost inaccessible mountain passes could have been held by a mere handful of men against a large and well-trained army, the Israelites abandoned the attempt as hopeless and turned southwards, keeping along the western borders of Idumæa till they reached Ezion-geber (xx. 14–21).

On their way southwards they stop at Mount Hor, or rather at Moserah, on the edge of the Edomite territory; and from this spot it would seem that Aaron, accompanied by his brother Moses and his son Eleazar, quitted the camp in order to ascend the mountain. Mount Hor lying itself within the Edomite territory, whilst it might have been perilous for a larger number to attempt to penetrate it, these unarmed wayfarers would not be molested, or might escape detection. Bunsen suggests that Aaron was taken to Mount Hor, in the hope that the fresh air of the mountain might be beneficial to his recovery; but the narrative does not justify such a supposition.

After Aaron's death, the march is continued southward; but when the Israelites approach the head of the Akabah at the southernmost point of the Edomite territory, they again murmur by reason of the roughness of the way, and many perish by the bite of venomous serpents (xx. 22–xxi. 9). The passage (xxi. 1–3) which speaks of the Canaanite king of Arad as coming out against the Israelites is clearly out of place, standing as it does after the mention of Aaron's death on Mount Hor. Arad is in the south of Palestine. The attack therefore must have been made whilst the people were yet in the neighborhood of Kadesh. The mention of Hormah also shows that this must have been the case (comp. xiv. 45). It is on this second occasion that the name of Hormah is said to have been given. Either therefore it is used proleptically in xiv. 45, or there is some confusion in the narrative. What "the way of Atharim" (A. V. "the way of the spies") was, we have no means now of ascertaining.

(b.) There is again a gap in the narrative. We are told nothing of the march along the eastern edge of Edom, but suddenly find ourselves transported to the borders of Moab. Here the Israelites successively encounter and defeat the kings of the Amorites and of Bashan, wresting from them their territory and permanently occupying it (xxi. 10–35). Their successes alarm the king of Moab, who, distrusting his superiority in the field, sends for a magician to curse his enemies; hence the episode of Balaam (xxiii. 1–xxv. 25). Other artifices are employed by the Moabites to weaken the Israelites, especially through the influence of the Moabitish women (xxv. 1), with whom the Midianites (ver. 6) are also joined; this evil is averted by the zeal of Phinehas (xxv. 7, 8); a second numbering of the Israelites takes place in the plains of Moab preparatory to their crossing the Jordan (xxvi.). A question arises as to the inheritance of daughters, and a decision is given thereon (xxvii. 1–11); Moses is warned of his death, and Joshua appointed to succeed him (xxvii. 12–23). Certain laws are given concerning the daily sacrifice, and the offerings for sabbaths and festivals (xxviii., xxix.); and the law respecting vows (xxx.); the conquest of the Midianites is narrated (xxxi.); and the partition of the country east of the Jordan among the tribes of Reuben and Gad, and the half-tribe of Manasseh (xxxii.). Then follows a recapitulation, though with some difference, of the various encampments of the Israelites in the desert (xxxiii. 1–49); the command to destroy the Canaanites (xxxiii. 50–56); the boundaries of the Promised Land, and the men appointed to divide it (xxxiv.); the appointment of the cities of the Levites and the cities of refuge (xxxv.); further directions respecting heiresses, with special reference to the case mentioned in ch. xxvii., and conclusion of the book (xxxvi.).

B. *Integrity.*— This, like the other books of the Pentateuch, is supposed by many critics to consist of a compilation from two or three, or more, earlier documents. According to De Wette, the following portions are the work of the Elohist [PENTATEUCH]: Ch. i. 1–x. 28; xiii. 2–16 (in its original, though not in its present form); xv.; xvi. 1, 2–11, 16–23, 24 (?); xvii.; xix.; xx. 1–13, 22–29; xxv.–xxxi. (except perhaps xxvi. 8–11); xxxii. 5, 28–42 (vv. 1–4 uncertain); xxxiii.–xxxvi. The rest of the book is, according to him, by the Jehovist or later editor. Von Lengerke (*Kenaan*, s. lxxxi.) and Stähelin (§ 2δ) make a similar division, though they differ as to some verses, and even whole chapters. Vaihinger (in Herzog's *Encyklopädie*, art. " Pentateuch ") finds traces of three distinct documents, which he ascribes severally to the pre-Elohist, the Elohist, and the Jehovist. To the first he assigns ch. x. 29–36; xi. 1–12, 16 (in its original form); xx. 14–21; xxi. 1–9, 13–35; xxxii. 33–42; xxxiii. 55, 56. To the Elohist belong ch. i. 1–x. 28; xi. 1–xii. 16; xiii. 1–xx. 13; xx. 22–29; xxi. 10–12; xxii. 1; xxv. 1–xxxi. 54; xxxii. 1–32; xxxii. 1–xxxvi. 19. To the Jehovist, xi. 1–xii. 16 (*überarbeitet*); xxii. 2–xxiv. 25; xxxi. 8, &c.

But the grounds on which this distinction of documents rests are in every respect most unsatisfactory. The use of the divine names, which was the starting-point of this criticism, ceases to be a criterion; and certain words and phrases, a particular manner or coloring, the narrative of miracles or prophecies, are supposed to decide whether a passage belongs to the earlier or the later documents. Thus, for instance, Stähelin alleges as reasons for assigning cc. xi., xii. to the Jehovist, the coming down of Jehovah to speak with Moses, xi. 17, 25; the pillar of a cloud, xii. 5; the relation between Joshua and Moses, xi. 28, as in Ex. xxxiii., xxxiv.; the seventy elders, xi. 16, as Ex. xxiv. 1, and so on. So again in the Jehovistic section, xiii., xiv., he finds traces of " the author of the First Legislation " in one passage (xiii. 2–17), because of the use of the word מַטֶּה, signifying " a tribe," and נָשִׂיא, as in Num. i. and vii. But נָשִׂיא is used also by the supposed supplementist, as in Ex. xxii. 27, xxxiv. 31; and that מַטֶּה is not peculiar to the older documents has been shown by Keil (*Comm. on Joshua*, s. xix.). Von Lengerke goes still further, and cuts off xiii. 2–16 altogether from what follows. He thus makes the story of the spies, as given by the Elohist, strangely maimed. We only hear of

their being sent to Canaan, but nothing of their return and their report. The chief reason for this separation is that in xiii. 27 occurs the Jehovistic phrase, " flowing with milk and honey," and some references to other earlier Jehovistic passages. De Wette again finds a repetition in xiv. 26–38 of xiv. 11–25, and accordingly gives these passages to the Elohist and Jehovist respectively. This has more color of probability about it, but has been answered by Ranke (*Untersuch.* ii. s. 197 ff.). Again, ch. xvi. is supposed to be a combination of two different accounts, the original or Elohistic document having contained only the story of the rebellion of Korah and his company, whilst the Jehovist mixed up with it the insurrection of Dathan and Abiram, which was directed rather against the temporal dignity than against the spiritual authority of Moses. But it is against this view, that, in order to justify it, vv. 12, 14, 27, and 32, are treated as interpolations. Besides, the discrepancies which it is alleged have arisen from the fusing of the two narratives disappear when fairly looked at. There is no contradiction, for instance, between xvi. 19, where Korah appears at the tabernacle of the congregation, and ver. 27, where Dathan and Abiram stand at the door of their tents. In the last passage Korah is not mentioned, and, even if we suppose him to be included, the narrative allows time for his having left the Tabernacle and returned to his own tent. Nor again, does the statement, ver. 35, that the 250 men who offered incense were destroyed by fire, and who had, as we learn from ver. 2, joined the leaders of the insurrection, Korah, Dathan, and Abiram, militate against the narrative in ver. 32, according to which Dathan and Abiram and all that appertained unto Korah were swallowed up alive by the opening of the earth. Further, it is clear, as Keil remarks (*Einleit.* p. 94), that the earlier document (*die Grundschrift*) implies that persons belonging to the other tribes were mixed up in Korah's rebellion, because they say to Moses and Aaron (ver. 3), " *All* the congregation is holy," which justifies the statement in vv. 1, 2, that, besides Korah the Levite, the Reubenites Dathan, Abiram, and On, were leaders of the insurrection.

In ch. xii. we have a remarkable instance of the jealousy with which the authority of Moses was regarded even in his own family. Considering the almost absolute nature of that authority, this is perhaps hardly to be wondered at. On the other hand, as we are expressly reminded, there was everything in his personal character to disarm jealousy. " Now the man Moses was very meek above all the men which were upon the face of the earth," says the historian (ver. 3). The pretext for the outburst of this feeling on the part of Miriam and Aaron was that Moses had married an Ethiopian woman (a woman of Cush). This was probably, as Ewald suggests, a second wife married after the death of Zipporah. But there is no reason for supposing, as he does (*Gesch.* ii. 229, *note*), that we have here a confusion of two accounts. He observes that the words of the brother and sister " Hath the Lord indeed spoken only by Moses, hath He not also spoken by us ? " show that the real ground of their jealousy was the apparent superiority of Moses in the prophetical office; whereas, according to the narrative, their dislike was occasioned by his marriage with a foreigner and a person of inferior rank. But nothing surely can be more natural than that the long pent-up feeling of jealousy should have fastened upon the marriage as a pretext to begin the quarrel, and then have shown itself in its true character in the words recorded by the historian.

It is not perhaps to be wondered at that the episode of Balaam (xxii. 2–xxiv. 25) should have been regarded as a later addition. The language is peculiar, as well as the general cast of the narrative. The prophecies are vivid and the diction of them highly finished: very different from the rugged, vigorous fragments of ancient poetry which meet us in ch. xxi. On these grounds, as well as on the score of the distinctly Messianic character of Balaam's prophecies, Ewald gives this episode to his Fifth Narrator, or the latest editor of the Pentateuch. This writer he supposes to have lived in the former half of the 8th century B. C., and hence he accounts for the reference to Assyria and the Cypriotes (the Kittim); the latter nation about that time probably infesting as pirates the coasts of Syria, whereas Assyria might be joined with Eber, because as yet the Assyrian power, though hostile to the southern nations, was rather friendly than otherwise to Judah. The allusions to Edom and Moab as vanquished enemies have reference, it is said, to the time of David (Ewald, *Gesch.* i. 143 ff., and compare ii. 277 ff.). The prophecies of Balaam, therefore, on this hypothesis, are *vaticinia ex eventu*, put into his mouth by a clever, but not very scrupulous writer of the time of Isaiah, who, finding some mention of Balaam as a prince of Midian in the older records, put the story into shape as we have it now. But this sort of criticism is so purely arbitrary that it scarcely merits a serious refutation, not to mention that it rests entirely on the assumption that in prophecy there is no such thing as prediction. We will only observe that, considering the peculiarity of the man and of the circumstances as given in the history, we might expect to find the narrative itself, and certainly the poetical portions of it, marked by some peculiarities of thought and diction. Even granting that this episode is not by the same writer as the rest of the book of Numbers, there seems no valid reason to doubt its antiquity, or its rightful claim to the place which it at present occupies. Nothing can be more improbable than that, as a later invention, it should have found its way into the Book of the Law.

At any rate, the picture of this great magician is wonderfully in keeping with the circumstances under which he appears and with the prophecies which he utters. This is not the place to enter into all the questions which are suggested by his appearance on the scene. How it was that a heathen became a prophet of Jehovah we are not informed; but such a fact seems to point to some remains of a primitive revelation, not yet extinct, in other nations besides that of Israel. It is evident that his knowledge of God was beyond that of most heathen, and he himself could utter the passionate wish to be found in his death among the true servants of Jehovah; but, because the soothsayer's craft promised to be gainful,. and the profession of it gave him an additional importance and influence in the eyes of men like Balak, he sought to combine it with his higher vocation. There is nothing more remarkable in the early history of Israel than Balaam's appearance. Summoned from his home by the Euphrates, he stands by his red altar-fires, weaving his dark and subtle sorceries, or goes to seek for enchantment, hoping, as he looked down

upon the tents of Israel among the acacia-groves of the valley, to wither them with his word, yet constrained to bless, and to foretell their future greatness.

The book of Numbers is rich in fragments of ancient poetry, some of them of great beauty, and all throwing an interesting light on the character of the times in which they were composed. Such, for instance, is the blessing of the high-priest (vi. 24–26): —

"Jehovah bless thee and keep thee :
  Jehovah make his countenance shine upon thee,
    And be gracious unto thee :
  Jehovah lift up his countenance upon thee,
    And give thee peace."

Such too are the chants which were the signal for the ark to move when the people journeyed, and for it to rest when they were about to encamp : —

"Arise, O Jehovah ! let thine enemies be scattered ;
  Let them also that hate thee flee before thee."

And, —

"Return, O Jehovah,
  To the ten thousands of the families of Israel."

In ch. xxi. we have a passage cited from a book called the "Book of the Wars of Jehovah." This was probably a collection of ballads and songs composed on different occasions by the watch-fires of the camp, and for the most part, though not perhaps exclusively, in commemoration of the victories of the Israelites over their enemies. The title shows us that these were written by men imbued with a deep sense of religion, and who were therefore foremost to acknowledge that not their own prowess, but Jehovah's right hand, had given them the victory when they went forth to battle. Hence it was called, not "The Book of the Wars of Israel," but "The Book of the Wars of Jehovah." Possibly this is the book referred to in Ex. xvii. 14, especially as we read (ver. 16) that when Moses built the altar which he called Jehovah-Nissi (Jehovah is my banner), he exclaimed "Jehovah will have war with Amalek from generation to generation." This expression may have given the name to the book.

The fragment quoted from this collection is difficult, because the allusions in it are obscure. The Israelites had reached the Arnon, "which," says the historian, "forms the border of Moab, and separates between the Moabites and Amorites." "Wherefore it is said," he continues, "in the Book of the Wars of Jehovah, —

"' Vaheb in Suphah and the torrent-beds ;
  Arnon and the slope of the torrent-beds
  Which turneth to where Ar lieth,
  And which leaneth upon the border of Moab.'"

The next is a song which was sung on the digging of a well at a spot where they encamped, and which from this circumstance was called Beër, or "The Well." It runs as follows : —

"Spring up, O well ! sing ye to it :
  Well, which the princes dug,
  Which the nobles of the people bored,
  With the sceptre of office, with their staves."

This song, first sung at the digging of the well, was afterwards no doubt commonly used by those who came to draw water. The maidens of Israel chanted it one to another, verse by verse, as they toiled at the bucket, and thus beguiled their labor. "Spring up, O well !" was the burden or refrain of the song, which would pass from one mouth to another at each fresh coil of the rope, till the full bucket reached the well's mouth. But the peculiar charm of the song lies not only in its antiquity, but in the characteristic touch which so manifestly connects it with the life of the time to which the narrative assigns it. The one point which is dwelt upon is, that the leaders of the people took their part in the work, that they themselves helped to dig the well. In the new generation, who were about to enter the Land of Promise, a strong feeling of sympathy between the people and their rulers had sprung up, which augured well for the future, and which left its stamp even on the ballads and songs of the time. This little carol is fresh and lusty with young life; it sparkles like the water of the well whose springing up first occasioned it; it is the expression, on the part of those who sung it, of lively confidence in the sympathy and coöperation of their leaders, which, manifested in this one instance, might be relied upon in all emergencies (Ewald, *Gesch.* ii. 264, 265).

Immediately following this "Song of the Well," comes a song of victory, composed after a defeat of the Moabites and the occupation of their territory. It is in a taunting, mocking strain; and is commonly considered to have been written by some *Israelitish* bard on the occupation of the Amorite territory. Yet the manner in which it is introduced would rather lead to the belief that we have here the translation of an old Amorite ballad. The history tells us that when Israel approached the country of Sihon they sent messengers to him, demanding permission to pass through his territory. The request was refused. Sihon came out against them, but was defeated in battle. "Israel," it is said, "smote him with the edge of the sword, and took his land in possession, from the Arnon to the Jabbok and as far as the children of Ammon; for the border of the children of Ammon was secure (*i. e.* they made too encroachments upon Ammonitish territory). Israel also took all these cities, and dwelt in all the cities of the Amorites in Heshbon, and all her daughters (*i. e.* lesser towns and villages)." Then follows a little scrap of Amorite history: "For Heshbon is the city of Sihon, king of the Amorites, and he had waged war with the former king of Moab, and had taken from him all his land as far as the Arnon. *Wherefore* the ballad-singers (הַמֹּשְׁלִים) say, —

" 'Come ye to Heshbon,
Let the city of Sihon be built and established!
For fire went forth from Heshbon,

A flame out of the stronghold (קִרְיַה) of Sihon,
Which devoured Ar of Moab,
The lords [a] of the high places of Arnon.
      Woe to thee, Moab!
Thou art undone, O people of Chemosh!
He (*i. e.* Chemosh thy god) hath given up his sons as fugitives,
And his daughters into captivity,
To Sihon king of the Amorites.
Then we cast them down ; [b] Heshbon perished even unto Dibon.
And we laid (it) waste unto Nophah, which (reacheth) unto Mèdebâ.' "

----

[a] Or "the possessors of, the men of, the high places," etc.
[b] So in Zunz's Bible, and this is the simplest ren-

If the song is of Hebrew origin, then the former part of it is a biting taunt, "Come, ye Amorites, into your city of Heshbon, and build it up again. Ye boasted that ye had burnt it with fire and driven out its Moabite inhabitants; but now *we* are come in our turn and have burnt Heshbon, and driven you out as ye once burnt it and drove out its Moabite possessors."

C. The alleged discrepancies between many statements in this and the other books of the Pentateuch, will be found discussed in other articles, DEUTERONOMY; EXODUS; PENTATEUCH.

J. J. S. P.

* *Recent exegetical works.* — Horsley, *Notes on Numbers* (*Bibl. Crit.* vol. i. 1820); Baumgarten-Crusius, *Theol. Com. zum Pent.* 1843; Bunsen, *Bibelwerk,* 1ter Th. *Das Gesetz,* 1858; Knobel, *Die Bücher Num. Deut. u. Jos. erklärt,* 1861 (*Exeget. Handb.* xiii.); Chr. Wordsworth, *Five Books of Moses,* 2d ed. 1861 (*Holy Bible with Notes,* vol. i.); Keil, *Num. u. Deut.* 1862 (Keil u. Delitzsch, *Bibl. Com.* 2ter Band); Lange, *Bibelwerk* (in press, 1868).

Special treatises on particular subjects of the book. On the brazen serpent: Moebius (*De serp. ær.,* 1686); Turretin, *Opera,* vol. iv.; Vitringa, *Obs. sacr.* ii. 15; Crusius, *De typ. serp. ær.*; Köhler (Herzog's *Real-Encyk.* art. *Schlange, eherne*). Michaelis, *De censibus Hebr.* (*Commentat.* Götting. 1774). Carpzov, *De stella ex Jacobo oriunda,* 1692. Moebius, *Balaami hist.* 1675; Deyling, *De Balaamo* (*Obs. sacr.* iii. 10); Waterland, *Hist. and Char. of Balaam* (*Works,* vol. ix.); De Geer, *De Bileamo, ejus hist. et ratic.* 1816; Horsley, *Balaam's Prophecies* (*Bibl. Crit.* vol. ii.); Hengstenberg, *Gesch. Bileams u. seine Weissag.* 1842; Vaihinger (Herzog's *Real-Encyk.* art. *Bileam*). [BALAAM, Amer. ed.]

T. J. C.

NUMENIUS (Νουμήνιος [*belonging to, or born at the time of, the new moon*]: *Numenius*), son of Antiochus, was sent by Jonathan on an embassy to Rome (1 Macc. xii. 16) and Sparta (xii. 17), to renew the friendly connections between these nations and the Jews, c. B. C. 144. It appears that he had not returned from his mission at the death of Jonathan (1 Macc. xiv. 22, 23). He was again dispatched to Rome by Simon, c. B. C. 141 (1 Macc. xiv. 24), where he was well received and obtained letters in favor of his countrymen, addressed to the various eastern powers dependent on the Republic, B. C. 139 (1 Macc. xv. 15 ff.). [LUCIUS.]

B. F. W.

NUN (נוּן, or נֹן, 1 Chr. vii. 27 [*fish*]: Ναυή: *Nun*). The father of the Jewish captain Joshua (Ex. xxxiii. 11, &c). His genealogical descent from Ephraim is recorded in 1 Chr. vii. Nothing is known of his life, which was doubtless spent in Egypt. The mode of spelling his name in the LXX. has not been satisfactorily accounted for. Gesenius asserts that it is a very early mistake of transcribers, who wrote NATH for NATN. But Ewald (*Gesch.* ii. 298) gives some good etymological reasons for the more probable opinion that the final N is omitted intentionally. [See also NON.]

W. T. B.

----

dering. Ewald and Bunsen: "We burned them ' Others: "We shot at them."

NURSE.[a] It is clear, both from Scripture and from Greek and Roman writers, that in ancient times the position of the nurse, wherever one was maintained, was one of much honor and importance. (See Gen. xxiv. 59, xxxv. 8; 2 Sam. iv. 4; 2 K. xi. 2; 3 Macc. i. 20; Hom. *Od.* ii. 361, xix. 15, 251, 466; Eurip. *Ion*, 1357; *Hippol.* 267 and fol.; Virg. *Æn.* vii. 1.) The same term is applied to a foster-father or mother, *e. g.* Num. xi. 12; Ruth iv. 16; Is. xlix. 23. In great families male servants, probably eunuchs in later times, were entrusted with the charge of the boys, 2 K. x. 1, 5. [CHILDREN.] See also *Karan*, iv. 63, Tegg's ed.; Mrs. Poole, *Englw. in Eg.* iii. 201.

H. W. P.

NUTS. The representative in the A. V. of the words *botnim* and *egôz.*

1. *Botnim* (בָּטְנִים : τερέβινθος: *terebinthus*). Among the good things of the land which the sons of Israel were to take as a present to Joseph in Egypt, mention is made of *botnim.* There can scarcely be a doubt that the *botnim* denote the fruit of the Pistachio-tree (*Pistacia vera*), though

Pistacia vera.

most modern versions are content with the general term *nuts.* (See Bochart, *Chanaan*, i. 10.) For other attempted explanations of the Hebrew term, comp. Celsius, *Hierob.* i. 24. The LXX. and Vulg. read *terebinth*, the Persian version has *pusteh*, from which it is believed the Arabic *fostak* is derived, whence the Greek πιστάκια, and the Latin *pistacia*;

the *Pistacia vera* is in form not unlike the *P. terebinthus*, another species of the same genus of plants; it is probable therefore that the *terebinthus* of the LXX. and Vulg. is used generically, and is here intended to denote the pistachio-tree, for the terebinth does not yield edible fruit.[b] Syria and Palestine have been long famous for pistachio-trees; see Dioscorides (i. 177), and Pliny (xiii. 5), who says " Syria has several trees that are peculiar to itself; among the nut-trees there is the well-known pistacia; " in another place (xv. 22) he states that Vitellius introduced this tree into Italy, and that Flaccus Pompeius brought it at the same time into Spain. The district around Aleppo is especially celebrated for the excellence of the pistachio-nuts, see Russell (*Hist. of Alep.* i. 82, 2d ed.) and Galen (*de Fac. Alim.* 2, p. 612), who mentions Berrhœa (Aleppo) as being rich in the production of these trees; the town of Batna in the same district is believed to derive its name from this circumstance Betonim, a town of the tribe of Gad (Josh. xiii. 26), has in all probability a similar etymology. [BETONIM.] Bochart draws attention to the fact that pistachio-nuts are mentioned together with almonds in Gen. xliii. 11, and observes that Dioscorides, Theophrastus, and others, speak of the pistachio-tree conjointly with the almond-tree. As there is no mention in early writers of the *Pistacia vera* growing in Egypt (see Celsius, *Hierob.* i. 27), it was doubtless not found there in Patriarchal times, wherefore Jacob's present to Joseph would have been most acceptable. There is scarcely any allusion to the occurrence of the *Pistacia vera* in Palestine amongst the writings of modern travellers; Kitto (*Phys. Hist. Pal.* p. 323) says " it is not much cultivated in Palestine, although found there growing wild in some very remarkable positions, as on Mount Tabor, and on the summit of Mount Attarous " (see Burckhardt, *Syria*, p. 334). Dr. Thomson (*Land and Book*, p. 267) says that the terebinth trees near *Mais el-Jebel* had been grafted with the pistachio from Aleppo by order of Ibrahim Pasha, but that " the peasants destroyed the grafts, lest their crop of oil from the berries of these trees should be diminished." Dr. Hooker saw only two or three pistachio-trees in Palestine. These were outside the north gate of Jerusalem. But he says the tree is cultivated at Beirut and elsewhere in Syria. The *Pistacia vera* is a small tree varying from 15 to 30 ft. in height; the male and female flowers grow on separate trees; the fruit, which is a green-colored oily kernel, not unlike an almond, is inclosed in a brittle shell. Pistachio-nuts are much esteemed as an article of diet both by Orientals and Europeans; the tree, which belongs to the natural order *Anacardiaceæ*, extends from Syria to Bokhara, and is naturalized over the south of Europe; the nuts are too well known to need mi nute description.

2. *Egôz* (אֱגוֹז : καρύα: *nux*) occurs only in Cant. vi. 11, " I went into the garden of nuts."

---

a 1. כֵּן, *m.*, τιθηνός, *nutrix*, *nutritius*; אֹמֶנֶת, *f.*, τιθηνός, *nutrix*, from אָמַן, to carry (see Is. lx. 4).

2. מֵינֶקֶת, part. f. Hiph., from יָנַק, " suck," with אִשָּׁה, γυνὴ τροφεύουσα (Ex. ii. 7). Connected with this is the doubtful verb נָהַק, θηλάζω, *nutrio* (Ges. p. 867).

3. In N. T. τροφός, *nutrix* (1 Thess. ii. 7)

b The Arabic بُطْم (*butm*) appears to be also used generically. It is more generally applied to the terebinth, but may comprehend the pistachio-tree, as Gesenius conjectures, and Dr. Royle (Kitto's *Cycl.*) has proved. He says the word is applied in some Arabic works to a tree which has green-colored kernels This must be the *Pistacia vera*.

The Hebrew word in all probability is here to be understood to refer to the *Walnut-tree*; the Greek καρύα is supposed to denote the tree, κάρυον the nut (see Soph. *Fr.* 892). Although κάρυον and *nux* may signify any kind of *nut*, yet the *walnut*, as the nut κατ' ἐξοχήν, is more especially that which is denoted by the Greek and Latin terms (see Casaubon *on Athenæus*, ii. 65; Ovid, *Nux Elegia;* Celsius, *Hierob.* i. 28). The Hebrew term is evidently allied to the Arabic *jawz*, which is from a Persian word of very similar form; whence Abu'l Fadli (in Celsius) says "the Arabs have borrowed the word *Gjaws* from the Persian; in Arabic the term is *Chusf*, which is a tall tree." The *Chusf* or *Chasf*, is translated by Freytag, "an esculent nut, the walnut." The Jewish Rabbis understand the walnut by *Egôz.*

According to Josephus (*B. J.* iii. 10, § 8) the walnut-tree was formerly common, and grew most luxuriantly around the lake of Gennesaret; Schulz, speaking of this same district, says he often saw walnut-trees growing there large enough to shelter four-and-twenty persons. See also Kitto (*Phys. Hist. Pal.* p. 250) and Burckhardt (*Syria*, p. 265). The walnut-tree (*Juglans regia*) belongs to the natural order *Juglandaceæ;* it is too well known to require any description.   W. H.

* The walnut is cultivated very extensively in Syria. At *Jebâa el-Halâny*, on the side of *Jebel Kishân*, inland about five hours from Sidon, there are large orchards of this tree, and the nuts are very cheap. I have bought them at a dollar and a quarter a thousand, including their transportation to a village two days distant. They are of the best quality. The common name for them in Syria is

جَوْز, which is undoubtedly the same as the

Hebrew (אֱגוֹז).   G. E. P.

NYM'PHAS (Νυμφᾶς [*spouse, bridegroom*]: *Nymphas*), a wealthy and zealous Christian in Laodicea (Col. iv. 15). His house was used as a place of assembly for the Christians; and hence Grotius, making an extraordinarily high estimate of the probable number of Christians in Laodicea, infers that he must have lived in a rural district.

In the Vatican MS. (B) this name is taken for that of a woman; and the reading appears in some Latin writers, as pseudo-Ambrose, pseudo-Anselm, and it has been adopted in Lachmann's N. T. The common reading, however, is found in the Alexandrian MS. and in that of Ephrem Syrus (A and C), and is the only one known to the Greek Fathers.   W. T. B.

O.

OAK. The following Hebrew words, which appear to be merely various forms of the same root,[a] occur in the O. T. as the names of some species of oak, namely, *él*, *élâh*, *élôn*, *ilân*, *alâh*, and *allôn*.

1. *El* (אֵיל: LXX. Vat. τερέβινθος; Alex. τερέμινθος; Aq., Sym., Theod., δρῦς: *campestria*) occurs only in the sing. number in Gen. xiv. 6

---

[a] From אָלַל, אֵיל or אֶל, "to be strong."

("El-paran"). It is uncertain whether *él* should be joined with Paran to form a proper name, or whether it is to be taken separately, as the "terebinth," or the "oak," or the "grove" of Paran. Onkelos and Saadias follow the Vulg., whence the "plain" of the A. V. (margin). (See Stanley, *S. & P.* pp. 519, 520, App.) Rosenmüller (*Schol.* ad l. c.) follows Jarchi (*Comment. in Pent.* ad Gen. xiv. 6), and is for retaining the proper name. Three plural forms of *él* occur: *êlim*, *élôth*, and *élath*. *Elim*, the second station where the Israelites halted after they had crossed the Red Sea, in all probability derived its name from the seventy palm-trees there; the name *él*, which more particularly signifies an "oak," being here put for any grove or plantation. Similarly the other plural form, *élôth* or *élath*, may refer, as Stanley (*S. & P.* p. 20) conjectures, to the palm-grove at Akaba. The plural *élim* occurs in Is. i. 29, where probably "oaks" are intended, in Is. lxi. 3, and Ez. xxxi. 14, any strong flourishing trees may be denoted.

2. *Elâh* (אֵלָה: τερέβινθος, δρῦς, Ἠλά, δένδρον, δένδρον συσκιάζον, Symm.; πλάτανος i. Hos. iv. 13; δένδοον σύσκιον: *terebinthus, quercus*. "oak," "elah," "teil-tree" in Is. vi. 13: "elms" in Hos. iv. 13). There is much difficulty in determining the exact meanings of the several varieties of the term mentioned above: the old versions are so inconsistent that they add but little by way of elucidation. Celsius (*Hierob.* i. 34) has endeavored to show that *él*, *élim*, *élôn*, *élâh*, and *allâh*, all stand for the terebinth-tree (*Pistacia terebinthus*), while *allôn* alone denotes an oak. Royle (in Kitto's *Cyc.* art. "Alah ") agrees with Celsius in identifying the *élâh* (אֵלָה) with the terebinth, and the *allôn* (אַלּוֹן) with the oak. Hiller (*Hierophyt.* i. 348) restricts the various forms of this word to different species of oak, and says no mention is made of the terebinth in the Hebrew Scriptures. Rosenmüller (*Bib. Not.* p. 237) gives the terebinth to *él* and *élâh*, and the oak to *allâh*, *allôn*, and *élôn* (אֵילוֹן).

For the various opinions upon the meaning of these kindred terms, see Ges. *Thes.* pp. 47, 51, 103, and Stanley, *S. & P.* p. 519.

That various species of oak may well have deserved the appellation of mighty trees is clear, from the fact that noble oaks are to this day occasionally seen in Palestine and Lebanon. On this subject we have been favored with some valuable remarks from Dr. Hooker, who says, "The forests have been so completely cleared off all Palestine, that we must not look for existing evidence of what the trees were in Biblical times and antecedently. In Syria proper there are only three common oaks. All form large trees in many countries, but very rarely now in Palestine; though that they do so occasionally is proof enough that they once did.' Abraham's oak, near Hebron, is a familiar example of a noble tree of one species. Dr. Robinson (*Bibl. Res.* ii. 81) has given a minute account of it: and "his description," says Dr. Hooker, "is good, and his measurements tally with mine." If we examine the claims of the terebinth to represent the *élâh*, as Celsius and others assert, we shall see that in point of size it cannot compete with some of the oaks of Palestine; and that therefore, if *élâh* ever denotes the terebinth, which

we by no means assert it does not, the term etymologically is applicable to it only in a second
degree; for the *Pistacia terebinthus*, although it
also occasionally grows to a great size, "spreading
its boughs," as Robinson (*Bibl. Res.* ii. 222) observes, "far and wide like a noble oak," yet it
does not form so conspicuously a good tree as
either the *Quercus pseudo-coccifera* or *Q. ægilops*.
Dr. Thomson (*Land and Book*, p. 243) remarks
on this point: "There are more mighty oaks here
in this immediate vicinity (*Mejdel es-Shems*) than
there are terebinths in all Syria and Palestine
together. I have travelled from end to end of
these countries, and across them in all directions,
and speak with absolute certainty." At p. 600, the
same writer remarks, "We have oaks in Lebanon
twice the size of this (Abraham's oak), and every
way more striking and majestic." Dr. Hooker
has no doubt that Thomson is correct in saying
there are far finer oaks in Lebanon; "though," he
observes, "I did not see any larger, and only one
or two at all near it. Cyril Graham told me there
were forests of noble oaks in Lebanon north of the

cedar valley" It is evident from these observations that two oaks (*Quercus pseudo-coccifera*
and *Q. ægilops*) are well worthy of the name of
mighty trees; though it is equally true that over
a greater part of the country the oaks of Palestine
are at present merely bushes.

3. *Elôn* (אֵילוֹן: ἡ δρῦς ἡ ὑψηλή, ἡ βάλανος,
'Ηλών: *convallis illustris, quercus*) occurs frequently in the O. T., and denotes, there can be
little doubt, some kind of oak. The A. V., following the Targum, translates *elôn* by "plain."
(See Stanley, *S. & P.* p. 520, App.)

4. *Ilân* (אִילָן: δένδρον: *arbor*) is found only
in Dan. iv. as the tree which Nebuchadnezzar saw
in his dream. The word appears to be used for
any "strong tree," the oak having the best claim
to the title, to which tree probably indirect allusion may be made.

5. *Allâh* (אַלָּה: ἡ τέρμινθος: Aq. and Symm.
ἡ δρῦς: *quercus*) occurs only in Josh. xxiv. 26,
and is correctly rendered "oak" by the A. V.

Abraham's Oak in the Plains of Mamre.

6. *Allôn* (אַלּוֹן: ἡ βάλανος, δένδρον βαλάνου,
δρῦς: *quercus*) is uniformly rendered "oak" by
the A. V., and has always been so understood by
commentators. It should be stated that *allôn*
occurs in Hos. iv. 13, as distinguished from the
other form *élâh*; consequently it is necessary to
suppose that two different trees are signified by
the terms. We believe, for reasons given above,
that the difference is specific, and not generic —
that two species of oaks are denoted by the Hebrew
terms: *allôn* may stand for an evergreen oak, as
the *Quercus pseudo-coccifera*, and *élâh* for one
of the deciduous kinds. The *Pistacia vera* could
never be mistaken for an oak. If, therefore,

specific allusion was ever made to this tree, we
cannot help believing that it would have been
under another name than any one of the numerous forms which are used to designate the different
species of the genus *Quercus*; perhaps under a
Hebrew form allied to the Arabic *butm*, "the terebinth." The oak-woods of Bashan are mentioned
in Is. ii. 13; Ez. xxvii. 6; Zech. xi. 2. The oaks
of Bashan belong in all probability to the species
known as *Quercus ægilops*, the Valonia oak, which
is said to be common in Gilead and Bashan.
Sacrifices were offered under oaks (Hos. iv. 13; Is
i. 29); of oak-timber the Tyrians manufacture
oars (Ez. xxvii 6), and idolaters their images (Is

xliv. 14); under the shade of oak-trees the dead were sometimes interred (Gen. xxxv. 8; see also 1 Sam. xxxi. 13).

Quercus pseudo-coccifera.

Another species of oak, besides those named above, is the *Quercus infectoria,* which is common in Galilee and Samaria. It is rather a small tree in Palestine, and seldom grows above 30 ft. high, though in ancient times it might have been a noble tree.

For a description of the oaks of Palestine, see Dr. Hooker's paper read before the Linnean Society, June, 1861, [and Tristram's *Nat. Hist. of the Bibl.,* pp. 367–371.]　　　　　W. H.

Quercus ægilops.

* The *Quercus pseudo-coccifera,* the evergreen oak of Syria, is the largest species. It is the one usually found near the Welies or tombs of the prophets.

Q. ægilops does not ordinarily attain as large a size, and, as its leaves are deciduous, it is not a favorite in the neighborhood of tombs. Nevertheless it is often found in groves, rarely by itself, in and around grave-yards. The number of forests of this and the preceding species is immense. The common name for *Q. pseudo-coccifera* is

سندیان, *Sindiân,* and of *Q. ægilops,* مَلُّول, *Mellûl.* There is another common species called

بلّوط, *Lik,* by the Arabs.　　　　　G. E. P.

OATH.[a] I. The principle on which an oath is held to be binding is incidentally laid down in Heb. vi. 16, namely, as an ultimate appeal to divine authority to ratify an assertion (see the principle stated and defended by Philo, *De Leg. Alleg.* iii. 73, i. 128, ed. Mang.). There the Almighty is represented as promising or denouncing with an oath, *i. e.* doing so in the most positive and solemn manner (see such passages as Gen. xxii. 16, xii. 7, compared with xxiv. 7; Ex. xvii. 16 and Lev. xxvi. 14 with Dan. ix. 11; 2 Sam. vii. 12, 13, with Acts ii. 30; Ps. cx. 4 with Heb. vii. 21, 28; Is. xlv. 23; Jer. xxii. 5, xxxii. 22). With this Divine asseveration we may compare the Stygian oath of Greek mythology (Hom. *Il.* xv. 37; Hes. *Theog.* 400, 805; see also the *Laws of Menu,* c. viii. 110; Sir W. Jones, *Works,* iii. 291).

II. On the same principle, that oath has always been held most binding which appealed to the highest authority, both as regards individuals and communities. (*a.*) Thus believers in Jehovah appealed to him, both judicially and extra-judicially, with such phrases as "The God of Abraham judge;" "As the Lord liveth;" "God do so to me and more also;" "God knoweth," and the like (see Gen. xxi. 23, xxxi. 53; Num. xiv. 2, xxx. 2; 1 Sam. xiv. 39, 44; 1 K. ii. 42; Is. xlviii. 1, lxv. 16; Hos. iv. 15). So also our Lord himself accepted the high-priest's adjuration (Matt. xxvi. 63), and St. Paul frequently appeals to God in confirmation of his statements (Acts xxvi. 29; Rom. i. 9, ix. 1; 2 Cor. i. 23, xi. 31; Phil. i. 8; see also Rev. x. 6). (*b.*) Appeals of this kind to authorities recognized respectively by adjuring parties were regarded as bonds of international security, and their infraction as being not only grounds of international complaint, but also offenses against divine justice. So Zedekiah, after swearing fidelity to the king of Babylon, was not only punished by him, but denounced by the prophet as a breaker of his oath (2 Chr. xxxvi. 13; Ez. xvii. 13, 18) Some, however, have supposed that the Law forbade any intercourse with heathen nations which involved the necessity of appeal by them to their own deities (Ex. xxiii. 32; Selden, *De Jur. Nat.* ii. 13; see Liv. i. 24; *Laws of Menu,* viii. 113; *Dict. of Antiq.* "Jus Jurandum").

III. As a consequence of this principle, (*a*) appeals to God's name on the one hand, and to heathen deities on the other, are treated in Scripture as tests of allegiance (Ex. xxiii. 13, xxxiv. 6; Deut. xxix. 12; Josh. xxiii. 7, xxiv. 16; 2 Chr. xv. 12 14; Is. xix. 18, xlv. 23; Jer. xii. 16; Am. viii.

---

a 1. אָלָה, *ἀρά, maledictio, juramentum,* with affinity to אֵל, the name of God (Ges. pp. 44, 99).

2. שְׁבֻעָה and שְׁבוּעָה, from שָׁבַע, "seven,' the sacred number (Ges. pp. 1354, 1366), ὅρκος, juramentum.

14, Zeph. i. 5). (b) So also the sovereign's name is sometimes used as a form of obligation, as was the case among the Romans with the name of the emperor; and Hofmann quotes a custom by which the kings of France used to appeal to themselves at their coronation (Gen. xlii. 15; 2 Sam. xi. 11, xiv. 19; Martyr. S. Polycarp. c. ix.; Tertull. Apol. c. 32; Suet. Calig. c. 27; Hofmann, Lex. art. "Juramentum"; Dict. of Antiq. u. s.; Michaelis, On Laws of Moses, art. 256, vol. iv. 102, ed. Smith).

IV. Other forms of oath, serious or frivolous, are mentioned; as, by the "blood of Abel" (Selden, De Jur. Nat. v. 8); by the "head;" by "Heaven," the "Temple," etc., some of which are condemned by our Lord (Matt. v. 33, xxiii. 16–22; and see Jam. v. 12). Yet He did not refuse the solemn adjuration of the high-priest (Matt. xxvi. 63, 64; see Juv. Sat. vi. 16; Mart. xi. 94; Mishna, Sanh. iii. 2, compared with Am. viii. 7; Spencer, De Leg. Hebr. ii. 1–4).

As to the subject-matter of oaths the following cases may be mentioned:—

1. Agreement or stipulation for performance of certain acts (Gen. xiv. 22, xxiv. 2, 8, 9; Ruth i. 17; 1 Sam. xiv. 24; 2 Sam. v. 3; Exr. x. 5; Neh. v. 12, x. 29, xiii. 25; Acts xxiii. 21; and see Joseph. Vit. c. 53).

2. Allegiance to a sovereign, or obedience from an inferior to a superior (Eccl. viii. 2; 2 Chr. xxxvi. 13; 1 K. xviii. 10). Josephus says the Essenes considered oaths unnecessary for the initiated, though they required them previously to initiation (B. J. ii. 8, §§ 6, 7; Ant. xv. 10, § 4; Philo, Quod omnis probus, I. 12, ii. 458, ed. Mangey.).

3. Promissory oath of a ruler (Josh. vi. 26; 1 Sam. xiv. 24, 28; 2 K. xxv. 24; Matt. xiv. 7). Priests took no oath of office (Heb. vii. 21).

4. Vow made in the form of an oath (Lev. v. 4).

5. Judicial oaths. (a.) A man receiving a pledge from a neighbor was required, in case of injury happening to the pledge, to clear himself by oath of the blame of damage (Ex. xxii. 10, 11; 1 K. viii. 31; 2 Chr. vi. 22). A willful breaker of trust. especially if he added perjury to his fraud, was to be severely punished (Lev. vi. 2–5; Deut. xix. 16–18). (b.) It appears that witnesses were examined on oath, and that a false witness, or one guilty of suppression of the truth, was to be severely punished (Lev. v. 1; Prov. xxix. 24; Michaelis, l. c. art. 256, iv. 109; Deut. xix. 16–19; Grotius, in Crit. Sacr. on Matt. xxvi. 63; Knobel on Lev. v. 1, in Kurzg. Exeg. Handb.). (c.) A wife suspected of incontinence was required to clear herself by oath (Num. v. 19–22).

It will be observed that a leading feature of Jewish criminal procedure was that the accused person was put upon his oath to clear himself (Ex. xxii. 11; Num. v. 19–22; 1 K. viii. 31; 2 Chr. vi. 22; Matt. xxvi. 63).

The forms of adjuration mentioned in Scripture are: 1. Lifting up the hand. Witnesses laid their hands on the head of the accused (Gen. xiv. 22; Lev. xxiv. 14; Deut. xxxii. 40; Is. iii. 7; Ex. xx. 5, 6; Sus. v. 35; Rev. x. 5: see Hom. Il. xix. 254; Virg. Æn. xii. 196; Carpzov, Apparatus, p. 652).

2. Putting the hand under the thigh of the person to whom the promise was made. As Josephus describes the usage, this ceremony was performed by each of the contracting parties to each other. It has been explained (a) as having reference to the covenant of circumcision (Godwyn, Moses and

Aaron, vi. 6, Carpzov, l. c. p. 653); (b) as containing a principle similar to that of phallic symbolism (Her. ii. 48; Plut. Is. et Osir. vii. 412, ed. Reiske; Knobel on Gen. xxiv. 2, in Kurzg. Exeg. Hdb.); (c) as referring to the promised Messiah (Aug. Qu. in Hept. 62; Civ. Dei, xvi. 33). It seems likely that the two first at least of these explanations may be considered as closely connected, if not identical with each other (Gen. xxiv. 2, xlvii. 29; Nicolaus, De Jur. xi. 6; Ges. p. 631, s. v. יָרֵךְ; Fagius and others in Crit. Sacr.; Joseph. Ant. i. 16, § 1).

3. Oaths were sometimes taken before the altar, or, as some understand the passage, if the persons were not in Jerusalem, in a position looking towards the Temple (1 K. viii. 31; 2 Chr. vi. 22; Godwyn, l. c. vi. 6; Carpzov, p. 654; see also Juv. Sat. xiv. 219; Hom. Il. xiv. 272).

4. Dividing a victim and passing between or distributing the pieces (Gen. xv. 10, 17; Jer. xxxiv. 18). This form was probably used to intensify the imprecation already ratified by sacrifice according to the custom described by classical writers under the phrases ὅρκια τέμνειν, foedus ferire, etc. We may perhaps regard in this view the acts recorded Judg. xix. 29, 1 Sam. xi. 7, and perhaps Herod. vii. 39.

As the sanctity of oaths was carefully inculcated by the Law, so the crime of perjury was strongly condemned; and to a false witness the same punishment was assigned which was due for the crime to which he testified (Ex. xx. 7; Lev. xix. 12; Deut. xix. 16–19; Ps. xv. 4; Jer. v. 2, vii. 9; Ex. xvi. 59; Hos. x. 4; Zech. viii. 17). Whether the "swearing" mentioned by Jeremiah (xxiii. 10) and by Hosea (iv. 2) was false swearing, or profane abuse of oaths, is not certain. If the latter, the crime is one which had been condemned by the Law (Lev. xxiv. 11, 16; Matt. xxvi. 74).

From the Law the Jews deduced many special cases of perjury, which are thus classified: 1. Jus jurandum promissorium, a rash inconsiderate promise for the future, or false assertion respecting the past (Lev. v. 4). 2. Vanum, an absurd self-contradictory assertion. 3. Depositi, breach of contract denied (Lev. xix. 11). 4. Testimonii, judicial perjury (Lev. v. 1; Nicolaus and Selden, De Juramentis, in Ugolini, Thesaurus, xxvi.: Lightfoot, Hor. Hebr. on Matt. v. 33, vol. ii. 292; Mishna, Sheb. iii. 7, iv. 1, v. 1, 2; Otho, Lex. Rabb., art. "Juramentum").

Women were forbidden to bear witness on oath, as was inferred from Deut. xix. 17 (Mishna, Sheb. iv. 1).

The Christian practice in the matter of oaths was founded in great measure on the Jewish. Thus the oath on the Gospels was an imitation of the Jewish practice of placing the hands on the Book of the Law (P. Fagius, on Onkel. ad Ex. xxiii. 1; Justinian, Nov. c. viii. Epil.: Matth. Paris, Hist. p. 916).

Our Lord's prohibition of swearing was clearly always understood by the Christian Church as directed against profane and careless swearing, not against the serious judicial form (Bingham, Antiq. Eccl. xvi. 7, §§ 4, 5; Aug. Ep. 157, c. v. 40); and thus we find the fourth Council of Carthage (c. 61) reproving clerical persons for swearing by created objects.

The most solemn Mohammedan oath is made on the open Koran. Mohammed himself used the form, "By the setting of the stars" (Chardin, Voy. vi. 87; Sale's Koran, lvi. p. 437).

Bedouin Arabs use various sorts of adjuration, one of which somewhat resembles the oath "by the Temple." The person takes hold of the middle tent-pole, and swears by the Life of the tent and its owners (Burckhardt, *Notes on Bed.* 1. 127, foll.; see also another case mentioned by Burckhardt, *Syria*, p. 398).

The stringent nature of the Roman military oath, and the penalties attached to infraction of it, are alluded to, more or less certainly, in several places in N. T., e. g. Matt. viii. 9, Acts xii. 19, xvi. 27, xxvii. 42; see also Dionys. Hal. xi. 43, and Aul. Gell. xvi. 4. [PERJURY.] H. W. P.

OBADI'AH (עֹבַדְיָה [*servant of Jehovah*]: Ἀβδία; [Vat. Ἀβδεια:] *Obdia*). The name of Obadiah was probably as common among the Hebrews as Abdallah among the Arabians, both of them having the same meaning and etymology.

1. The sons of Obadiah are enumerated in a corrupt passage of the genealogy of the tribe of Judah (1 Chr. iii. 21). The reading of the LXX. and Vulg. was בְּנוֹ, "his son," and of the Peshito Syriac בְּנֵי, "son of," for בְּנֵי, "sons of;" so that according to the two former versions Obadiah was the son of Arnan, and according to the last the son of Jesaiah.

2. (Ἀβδιού; [Vat. corrupt; Alex. Ὀβδια:] *Obadia*.) According to the received text, one of the five sons of Izrahiah, a descendant of Issachar and a chief man of his tribe (1 Chr. vii. 3). Four only, however, are mentioned, and the discrepancy is rectified in four of Kennicott's MSS., which omit the words "and the sons of Izrahiah" thus making Izrahiah brother and not father, of Obadiah, and both sons of Uzzi. The Syriac and Arabic versions follow the received text, but read "four" instead of "five."

3. (Ἀβδία; [Vat. Sin. Ἀβδεια:] *Obdia*.) One of the six sons of Azel, a descendant of Saul (1 Chr. viii. 38, ix. 44).

4. (Ἀβδία; Vat. Ἀβδεια; Alex. Ὀβδια.) A Levite, son of Shemaiah, and descended from Jeduthun (1 Chr. ix. 16). He appears to have been a principal musician in the Temple choir in the time of Nehemiah (Neh. xii. 25). It is evident, from a comparison of the last-quoted passage with 1 Chr. ix. 15-17 and Neh. xi. 17-19, that the first three names "Mattaniah, and Bakbukiah, Obadiah," belong to ver. 24, and the last three, "Meshullam, Talmon, Akkub," were the families of porters. The name is omitted in the Vat. MS. [so in Rom. Alex. FA.¹] in Neh. xii. 25, where the Codex Frid.-Aug. [FA.³] has Ὀβδιας and the Vulg. *Obedia*. In Neh. xi. 17, "Obadiah the son of Shemaiah, is called "ABDA the son of Shammua."

5. ([Vat. FA. Ἀβδεια:] *Obdias*.) The second in order of the lion-faced Gadites, captains of the host, who joined David's standard at Ziklag (1 Chr. xii. 9).

6. (Ἀβδία: Vat. Ἀβια.) One of the princes of Judah in the reign of Jehoshaphat, who were sent by the king to teach in the cities of Judah (2 Chr. xvii. 7).

7. (Ἀβαδία : [Vat. Ἀδεια :] *Obedia*.) The son of Jehiel, of the sons of Joab, who came up in the second caravan with Ezra, accompanied by 218 of his kinsmen (Ezr. viii. 9). [ABADIAS.]

8. (Ἀβδία; [Vat. FA. Ἀβδεια:] *Obdias*.) A

priest, or family of priests, who sealed the covenant with Nehemiah (Neh. x. 5).   W. A. W.

9. (Ὀβδιού; [Vat. Ὀβδειου; Alex. Ἀβδειου (Inser.), Ἀβδιου:] *Abdias*.) The prophet Obadiah. We know nothing of him except what we can gather from the short book which bears his name. The Hebrew tradition adopted by St. Jerome (*In Abd.*), and maintained by Abarbanel and Kimchi, that he is the same person as the Obadiah of Ahab's reign, is as destitute of foundation as another account, also suggested by Abarbanel, which makes him to have been a converted Idumæan, "the hatchet," according to the Hebrew proverb, "returning into the wood out of which it was itself taken" (Abarb. *In Obad. apud* Pfeifferi *Opera*, p. 1092, Ultraj. 1704). The question of his date must depend upon the interpretation of the 11th verse of his prophecy. He there speaks of the conquest of Jerusalem and the captivity of Jacob. If he is referring to the well-known captivity by Nebuchadnezzar he must have lived at the time of the Babylonish Captivity, and have prophesied subsequently to the year B. C. 588. If, further, his prophecy against Edom found its first fulfillment in the conquest of that country by Nebuchadnezzar in the year B. C. 583, we have its date fixed. It must have been uttered at some time in the five years which intervened between those two dates. Jæger argues at length for an earlier date. He admits that the 11th verse refers to a capture of Jerusalem, but maintains that it may apply to its capture by Shishak in the reign of Rehoboam (1 K. xiv. 25; 2 Chr. xii. 2); by the Philistines and Arabians in the reign of Jeboram (2 Chr. xxi. 16); by Joash in the reign of Amaziah (2 Chr. xxv. 23); or by the Chaldæans in the reign of Jehoiakim and of Jehoiachin (2 K. xxiv. 2 and 10). The Idumæans might, he argues, have joined the enemies of Judah on any of these occasions, as their inveterate hostility from an early date is proved by several passages of Scripture, e. g. Joel iii. 19; Am. i. 11. He thinks it probable that the occasion referred to by Obadiah is the capture of Jerusalem by the Ephraimites in the reign of Amaziah (2 Chr. xxv. 23). The utmost force of these statements is to prove a possibility. The only argument of any weight for the early date of Obadiah is his position in the list of the books of the minor prophets. Why should he have been inserted between Amos and Jonah if his date is about B. C. 585? Schnurrer seems to answer this question satisfactorily when he says that the prophecy of Obadiah is an amplification of the last five verses of Amos, and was therefore placed next after the book of Amos. Our conclusion is in favor of the later date assigned to him, agreeing herein with that of Pfeiffer, Schnurrer, Rosenmüller, De Wette, Hendewerk, and Maurer.

The book of Obadiah is a sustained denunciation of the Edomites, melting, as is the wont of the Hebrew prophets (cf. Joel iii., Am. ix.), into a vision of the future glories of Zion, when the arm of the Lord should have wrought her deliverance and have repaid double upon her enemies. Previous to the Captivity, the Edomites were in a similar relation to the Jews to that which the Samaritans afterwards held. They were near neighbors, and they were relatives. The result was that intensified hatred which such conditions are likely to produce, if they do not produce cordiality and good-will. The Edomites are the types of those who ought to be friends and are not — of those who ought to be helpers, but in the day of calamity are found "standing on the other side." The prophet first touches on their pride and self-confidence, and then denounces their "violence against their brother Jacob" at the time of the capture of Jerusalem. There is a sad tone of reproach in the form into which he throws his denunciation, which contrasts with the parallel denunciations of Ezekiel (xxv. and xxxv.), Jeremiah (Lam. iv. 21), and the author of the 137th Psalm, which seem to have been uttered on the same occasion and for the same cause. The psalmist's "Remember the children of Edom, O Lord, in the day of Jerusalem, how they said, Down with it, down with it, even to the ground!" coupled with the immediately succeeding imprecation on Babylon, is a sterner utterance, by the side of which the "Thou shouldest not" of Obadiah appears rather as the sad remonstrance of disappointment. He complains that they looked on and rejoiced in the destruction of Jerusalem; that they triumphed over her and plundered her; and that they cut off the fugitives who were probably making their way through Idumæa to Egypt.

The last six verses are the most important part of Obadiah's prophecy. The vision presented to the prophet is that of Zion triumphant over the Idumæans and all her enemies, restored to her ancient possessions, and extending her borders northward and southward and eastward and westward. He sees the house of Jacob and the house of Joseph (here probably denoting the ten tribes and the two) consuming the house of Esau as fire devours stubble (ver. 18). The inhabitants of the city of Jerusalem, now captive at Sepharad, are to return to Jerusalem, and to occupy not only the city itself, but the southern tract of Judæa (ver. 20). Those who had dwelt in the southern tract are to overrun and settle in Idumæa (ver. 19). The former inhabitants of the plain country are also to establish themselves in Philistia (ib.). To the north the tribe of Judah is to extend itself as far as the fields of Ephraim and Samaria, while Benjamin, thus displaced, takes possession of Gilead (ib.). The captives of the ten tribes are to occupy the northern region from the borders of the enlarged Judah as far as Sarepta near Sidon (ver. 20). What or where Sepharad is no one knows. The LXX., perhaps by an error of a copyist, read 'Ἐφραθά. St. Jerome's Hebrew tutor told him the Jews held it to be the Bosphorus. St. Jerome himself thinks it is derived from an Assyrian word meaning "bound" or "limit," and understands it as signifying "scattered abroad." So Maurer, who compares οἱ ἐν τῇ διασπορᾷ of Jam. i. 1. Hardt, who has devoted a volume to the consideration of the question, is in favor of Sipphara in Mesopotamia. The modern Jews pronounce for Spain. Schultz is probably right in saying that it is some town or district in Babylon, otherwise unknown.

The question is asked, Have the prophet's denunciations of the Edomites been fulfilled, and has his vision of Zion's glories been realized? Typically, partially, and imperfectly they have been fulfilled, but, as Rosenmüller justly says, they await a fuller accomplishment. The first fulfillment of the denunciation on Edom in all probability took place a few years after its utterance. For we read in Josephus (Ant. x. 9, § 7) that five years after the capture of Jerusalem Nebuchadnezzar reduced the Ammonites and Moabites, and

after their reduction made an expedition into Egypt. This he could hardly have done without at the same time reducing Idumæa. A more full, but still only partial and typical fulfillment would have taken place in the time of John Hyrcanus, who utterly reduced the Idumæans, and only allowed them to remain in their country on the condition of their being circumcised and accepting the Jewish rites, after which their nationality was lost for ever (Joseph. Ant. xiii. 9, § 1). Similarly the return from the Babylonish Captivity would typically and imperfectly fulfill the promise of the restoration of Zion and the extension of her borders. But "magnificentior sane est hæc promissio quàm ut ad Sorobabelica aut Maccabaica tempora referri possit," says Rosenmüller on ver. 21. And "necessitas cogit ut omnia ad prædicationem evangelii referamus," says Luther.

The full completion of the prophetical descriptions of the glories of Jerusalem — the future golden age towards which the seers stretched their hands with fond yearnings — is to be looked for in the Christian, not in the Jewish Zion — in the antitype rather than in the type. Just as the fate of Jerusalem and the destruction of the world are interwoven and interpenetrate each other in the prophecy uttered by our Lord on the mount, and his words are in part fulfilled in the one event, but only fully accomplished in the other; so in figure and in type the predictions of Obadiah may have been accomplished by Nebuchadnezzar, Zerubbabel, and Hyrcanus, but their complete fulfillment is reserved for the fortunes of the Christian Church and her adversaries. Whether that fulfillment has already occurred in the spread of the Gospel through the world, or whether it is yet to come (Rev. xx. 4), or whether, being conditional, it is not to be expected save in a limited and curtailed degree, is not to be determined here.

The book of Obadiah is a favorite study of the modern Jews. It is here especially that they read the future fate of their own nation and of the Christians. Those unversed in their literature may wonder where the Christians are found in the book of Obadiah. But it is a fixed principle of Rabbinical interpretation that by Edomites is prophetically meant Christians, and that by Edom is meant Rome. Thus Kimchi, on Obadiah, lays it down that "all that the prophets have said about the destruction of Edom in the last times has reference to Rome." So Rabbi Bechai, on Is. lxvi. 17; and Abarbanel has written a commentary on Obadiah resting on this hypothesis as its basis. Other examples are given by Buxtorf (Lex. Talm. in voc. אֱדוֹם, and Synagoga Judaica). The reasons of this Rabbinical dictum are as various and as ridiculous as might be imagined. Nachmanides, Bechai, and Abarbanel say that Janus, the first king of Latium, was grandson of Esau. Kimchi (on Joel iii. 19) says that Julius Cæsar was an Idumæan. Scaliger (ad Chron. Euseb. n. 2152) reports, "The Jews, both those who are comparatively ancient and those who are modern, believe that Titus was an Edomite, and when the prophets denounce Edom they frequently refer it to Titus." Aben Ezra says that there were no Christians except such as were Idumæans until the time of Constantine, and that Constantine having embraced their religion the whole Roman empire became entitled Idumæan. St. Jerome says that some of the Jews read רֻגְמָה, Rome, for דֻּמָה, Dumah, in Is. xxi. 11. Finally, some of the Rabbis, and with them Abarbanel, maintain that it was the soul of Esau which lived again in Christ.

The color given to the prophecies of Obadiah, when looked at from this point of view, is most curious. The following is a specimen from Abarbanel on ver. 1: " The true explanation, as I have said, is to be found in this: The Idumæans, by which, as I have shown, all the Christians are to be understood (for they took their origin from Rome), will go up to lay waste Jerusalem, which is the seat of holiness, and where the tomb of their God Jesus is, as indeed they have several times gone up already." Again, on ver. 2: " I have several times shown that from Edom proceeded the kings who reigned in Italy, and who built up Rome to be great among the nations and chief among the provinces; and in this way Italy and Greece and all the western provinces became filled with Idumæans. Thus it is that the prophets call the whole of that nation by the name of Edom." On ver. 8: " There shall not be found counsel or wisdom among the Edomite Christians when they go up to that war." On ver. 19: " Those who have gone as exiles into the Edomites', that is, into the Christians' land, and have there suffered affliction, will deserve to have the best part of their country and their metropolis as Mount Seir." On ver. 20 : " Sarepta " is "France;" "Sepharad" is "Spain." The "Mount of Esau," in ver. 21, is "the city of Rome," which is to be judged; and the Saviours are to be " the [Jewish] Messiah and his chieftains," who are to be " Judges."

The first nine verses of Obadiah are so similar to Jer. xlix. 7, &c., that it is evident that one of the two prophets must have had the prophecy of the other before him. Which of the two wrote first is doubtful. Those who give an early date to Obadiah thereby settle the question. Those who place him later leave the question open, as he would in that case be a contemporary of Jeremiah. Luther holds that Obadiah followed Jeremiah. Schnurrer makes it more probable that Jeremiah's prophecy is an altered form of Obadiah's. Eichhorn, Schulz, Rosenmüller, and Maurer agree with him.

See Ephrem Syrus, *Expl. in Abd.* v. 269, Rome, 1740; St. Jerome, *Comm. in Abd.* Op. iii. 1455, Paris, 1704; Luther, *Enarr. in Abd.* Op. iii. 538, Jenæ, 1612; Pfeiffer, *Tract. Phil. Antirrabbin.* Op. p. 1081, Ultraj. 1704; Schnurrer, *Dissertatio Philologica in Obadiam,* Tubing. 1787; Schulz, *Scholia in Vet. Test.* Norimb. 1793; Rosenmüller, *Scholia in Vet. Test.* Lips. 1813; Maurer, *Comm. in Vet. Test.* Lips. 1836; Jaeger, *Ueber das Zeitalter Obadja's,* Tübing. 1837.   F. M.

• For the commentators on the Minor Prophets see Amos: Habakkuk; Haggai (Amer. ed.). Dr. Pusey's unfinished work (*Minor Prophets, with a Commentary* (1861), and Dr. Paul Kleinert's Pt. xix. of Lange's *Bibelwerk des A. Test.* (1868), contain Obadiah. Other separate writers (see above) are Zeddel (*Annotatt. in Ob.* 1–4, 1830), Hendewerk (*Obadjæ oraculum in Idumæos* (1836), C. P. Caspari (*Der Prophet Obadjah,* 1842, an important work, pp. 1–145), Fr. Delitzsch (*Wann weissagte Obadjah?* in *Zeitschrift für lutherische Theologie,* 1851, pp. 91–102), and Nägelsbach (Herz. *Real-Encyk.* x. 506 ff.). The epitomized results in

the recent O. T. Introductions (Keil 1859 and Bleek 1860) show how wide a field of criticism this shortest book of the O. T. embraces.

Prof. Stuart (*Old Test. Canon,* p. 403) points out a use of this prophetic fragment which the history of nations shows to be not yet obsolete. " When Edom is held up before my eyes by Obadiah as having rushed upon the Jews, in the day of their humiliation by the power of Babylon; when the embittered enmity, the spirit of vengeance and of rapacity, and the unspeakable meanness of the Edomites, and their consequent punishment, are embodied and made palpable and held up to open view in this way; I am far more affected and even instructed by it, than I am by any abstract precept " which may inculcate the same lesson. H.

10. עֹבַדְיָהוּ: 'Αβδιού; [Vat. Αβδειου; Alex. Αδβιου, eight times, but Αβδιου, ver. 9:] *Abdias.*) An officer of high rank in the court of Ahab, who is described as "over the house," that is, apparently, lord high chamberlain, or mayor of the palace (1 K. xviii. 3). His influence with the king must have been great to enable him to retain his position, though a devout worshipper of Jehovah, during the fierce persecution of the prophets by Jezebel. At the peril of his life he concealed a hundred of them in caves, and fed them there with bread and water. But he himself does not seem to have been suspected (1 K. xviii. 4, 13). The occasion upon which Obadiah appears in the history shows the confidential nature of his office. In the third year of the terrible famine with which Samaria was visited, when the fountains and streams were dried up in consequence of the long-continued drought, and horses and mules were perishing for lack of water, Ahab and Obadiah divided the land between them and set forth, each unattended, to search for whatever remnants of herbage might still be left around the springs and in the fissures of the river beds. Their mission was of such importance that it could only be entrusted to the two principal persons in the kingdom. Obadiah was startled on his solitary journey by the abrupt apparition of Elijah, who had disappeared since the commencement of the famine, and now commanded him to announce to Ahab, "Behold Elijah! " He hesitated, apparently afraid that his long-concealed attachment to the worship of Jehovah should thus be disclosed and his life fall a sacrifice. At the same time he was anxious that the prophet should not doubt his sincerity, and appealed to what he had done in the persecution by Jezebel. But Elijah only asserted the more strongly his intention of encountering Ahab, and Obadiah had no choice but to obey (1 K. xviii. 7–16). The interview and its consequences belong to the history of Elijah [vol. i. p. 527]. According to the Jewish tradition preserved in Ephrem Syrus (Assemani, *Bibl. Or. Clem.* p. 70), Obadiah the chief officer of Ahab was the same with Obadiah the prophet. He was of Shechem in the land of Ephraim, and a disciple of Elijah, and was the third captain of fifty who was sent by Ahaziah (2 K. i. 13). After this he left the king's service, prophesied, died, and was buried with his father. The "certain woman of the wives of the sons of the prophets " who came to Elisha (2 K. iv. 1) was, according to the tradition in Rashi, his widow.

11. ('Αβδίας; [Vat. Αβδειας.]) The father of Ishmaiah, who was chief of the tribe of Zebulun in David's reign (1 Chr. xxvii. 19).

12. ['Aββίας; Vat. Aββεια-] A Merarite Levite in the reign of Josiah, and one of the overseers of the workmen in the restoration of the Temple (2 Chr. xxxiv. 12).   W. A. W.

O'BAL (עוֹבָל [bald, bare, as said of a country, Dietr.]: Εὐάλ; [Comp. Γέβαλ:] Ebal). A son of Joktan, and, like the rest of his family, apparently the founder of an Arab tribe (Gen. x. 28), which has not yet been identified. In 1 Chr. i. 22 the name is written EBAL (עֵיבָל: Alex. Γεμιαν: Hebal), which Knobel (Genesis) compares with the Gebanites of Pliny, a tribe of Southern Arabia. The similarity of the name with that of the Avalitæ, a troglodyte tribe of East Africa, induced Bochart (Phaleg, ii. 23) to conjecture that Obal migrated thither and gave his name to the Sinus Abalites or Avalites of Pliny (vi. 34).   W. A. W.

OBDI'A ('Οββία; [Vat. Οββεια:] Obia). Probably a corruption of Obaia, the form in which the name HABAIAH appears (comp. 1 Esdr. v. 38 with Ezr. ii. 61).

O'BED (עוֹבֵד [he who serves, sc. Jehovah, Ges., Fürst]: 'Ωβήδ; ['Ιωβήδ, Alex. in 1 Chr., and N. T. ed. Lachm. Tisch. Treg.:] Obed). 1. Son of Boaz and Ruth the Moabitess (Ruth iv. 17). The circumstances of his birth, which make up all that we know about him, are given with much beauty in the book of Ruth, and form a most interesting specimen of the religious and social life of the Israelites in the days of Eli, which a comparison of the genealogies of David, Samuel, and Abiathar shows to have been about the time of his birth. The famine which led to Elimelech and his sons migrating to the land of Moab may naturally be assigned to the time of the Philistine inroads in Eli's old age. Indeed there is a considerable resemblance between the circumstances described in Hannah's song (1 Sam. ii. 5), " They that were hungry ceased, so that the barren hath borne seven," and those of Obed's birth as pointed at, Ruth i. 6, and in the speech of the women to Naomi: " He shall be unto thee a restorer of thy life, and a nourisher of thine old age; for thy daughter-in-law which loveth thee, which is better to thee than seven sons, hath borne him: " as well as between the prophetic saying (1 Sam. ii. 7), " The Lord maketh poor, and maketh rich: he bringeth low, and lifteth up. He raiseth up the poor out of the dust, and lifteth up the beggar from the dunghill, to set them among princes, and to make them inherit the throne of glory: " and the actual history of the house of Elimelech, whose glory was prayed for by the people, who said, on the marriage of Ruth to Boaz, " The Lord make the woman that is come into thine house like Rachel and like Leah, which two did build the house of Israel, and do thou worthily in Ephratah, and be famous in Bethlehem." The direct mention of the Lord's Christ in 1 Sam. ii 10, also connects the passage remarkably with the birth of that child who was grandfather to King David, and the lineal ancestor of Jesus Christ.

The name of Obed occurs only in Ruth iv. 17, and in the four genealogies, Ruth iv. 21, 22; 1 Chr.

ii. 12; Matt. i. 5; Luke iii. 32. In all these five passages, and in the first with peculiar emphasis he is said to be the father of Jesse. It is incredible that in David's reign, when this genealogy was compiled, his own grandfather's name should have been forgotten, and therefore there is no escape from the conclusion that Obed was literally Jesse's father, and that we have all the generations recorded from Nahshon to David. [JESSE; NAHSHON.]
                                    A. C. H.

2. (Alex. [Ald.] 'Ιωβήδ.) A descendant of Jarha, the Egyptian slave of Sheshan in the line of Jerahmeel. He was grandson of Zabad, one of David's mighties (1 Chr. ii. 37, 38).

3. ('Ωβήθ; [Vat. Ιωβηθ; FA. Ιωβηλ; Comp. 'Ωβήδ;] Alex. Ιωβηδ.) One of David's mighty men (1 Chr. xi. 47).

4. ('Ωβήδ; Alex. Ιωβηδ.) One of the gatekeepers of the Temple: son of Shemaiah the firstborn of Obed-edom (1 Chr. xxvi. 7).

5. (Alex. Ιωβηδ.) Father of Azariah, one of the captains of hundreds who joined with Jehoiada in the revolution by which Athal'ah fell (2 Chr. xxiii. 1).   W. A. W.

O'BED-E'DOM (עֹבֵד אֱדוֹם [servant of Edom]: 'Αβεδδαρά in Sam. [and 1 Chr. xiii. 13, 14], 'Αβδεδόμ [Vat. FA. Αβδοδομ] in [1] Chr. [xv. 25]; Alex. Αβεδδαδομ in 2 Sam. vi. 11; [Vat. Αβεδδαραμ, FA. -αν, in 1 Chr. xiii. 14:] Obed-edom). 1. A Levite, apparently of the family of Kohath. He is described as a Gittite (2 Sam. vi. 10, 11), that is, probably, a native of the Levitical city of Gath-Rimmon in Manasseh,[a] which was assigned to the Kohathites (Josh. xxi. 25), and is thus distinguished from " Obed-edom the son of Jeduthun," who was a Merarite. After the death of Uzzah, the ark, which was being conducted from the house of Abinadab in Gibeah to the city of David, was carried aside into the house of Obed-edom, where it continued three months, and brought with its presence a blessing upon Obed-edom and his household. Hearing this, David, at the head of a large choir of singers and minstrels, clothed in fine linen, and attended by the elders of Israel and the chief captains, " went to bring up the ark of the covenant of Jehovah out of the house of Obed-edom with joy " (1 Chr. xv. 25; 2 Sam. vi. 12).

2. ['Αβδεδόμ; Vat. FA. in 1 Chr. xvi. 5, 38, Αβδοδομ; so Vat. xxvi. 4, 8. 15, and Alex. xvi. 38, xxvi. 4, 8, and 15 once; FA. 1 Chr. xv. 18, Αβδεδωμ; Vat.[1] 2 Chr. xxv. 24, Ιαβδεδωμ; Comp. generally 'Ωβήδ 'Εδώμ.] " Obed-edom the son of Jeduthun " (1 Chr. xvi. 38), a Merarite Levite, appears to be a different person from the last-mentioned. He was a Levite of the second degree and a gate-keeper for the ark (1 Chr. xv. 18, 24), appointed to sound " with harps on the Sheminith to excel " (1 Chr. xv. 21, xvi. 5). With his family of seven [eight] sons and their children, " mighty men of valor " (1 Chr. xxvi. 4–8), he kept the South Gate (1 Chr. xxvi. 15) and the house of Asuppim. There is one expression, however, which seems to imply that Obed-edom the gate-keeper and Obed-edom the Gittite may have been the same. After enumerating his seven [eight] sons the chronicler

_____

a * Not in Manasseh, says Rüetschl (Herzog's Real-Encyk. xx. 243), but in Dan (Josh. xiv. 45; xxi. 24). This writer recognizes only one Obed-edom, though he does not explain why the Levite is appar-

ently called a Kohathite and a son of Jeduthun at the same time. There is no reason except this for supposing two persons of this name to be meant.   H.

(1 Chr. xxvi. 5) adds, "for God blessed him," referring apparently to 2 Sam. vi. 11, "the Lord blessed Obed-edom and all his household." The family still remained at a much later time as keepers of the vessels of the Temple in the reign of Amaziah (2 Chr. xxv. 24).   W. A. W.

O'BETH ('Ωβήθ: [Vat. Ουβηρ:] om. in Vulg.). EBED the son of Jonathan is so called in 1 Esdr. viii. 32.

O'BIL (אֹובִיל [camel-driver]: 'Aβlas: Alex. [Ald.] Ούβlas; [Comp. 'Ωβίλ:] Ubil). An Ishmaelite who was appropriately appointed keeper of the herds of camels in the reign of David (1 Chr. xxvii. 30). Bochart (Hieroz. pt. i., ii. 2) conjectures that the name is that of the office, abál in Arabic denoting "a keeper of camels."

OBLATION. [SACRIFICE.]

O'BOTH (אֹבֹת [hollow passes, Fürst]: 'Ωβώθ; [Vat. in Num. xxxiii. Σωβωθ:] Oboth), one of the encampments of the Israelites, east of Moab (Num. xxi. 10, xxxiii. 43). Its exact site is unknown. [WILDERNESS OF THE WANDERING.]

* OCCUPY occurs in the sense of "to use," Exod. xxxviii. 24, Judg. xvi. 11, and especially, "to use in trade," as money, or "to deal in," as merchandise, Ez. xxvii. 9, 2 Esdr. xvi. 42; hence, intransitively, "to trade" or "traffic," Ez. xxvii. 16, "they occupied in thy fairs with emeralds, purple," etc.; so Ez. xxvii. 19, 21, 22; Luke xix. 13. These uses of the word were formerly common. So "the occupiers of thy merchandise," Ez. xxvii. 27, means "the traders in thy merchandise."
                           A.

* OCCURRENT = "occurrence," 1 K. v. 4.
                           A.

O'CHIEL ('Οχιῆλος; Alex.² Οζηλος: Oziel). The form in which the name JEIEL appears in 1 Esdr. i. 9 (comp. 2 Chr. xxxv. 9). The Geneva version has CHIELUS.

OCIDE'LUS (Ωκόδηλος; [Vat. Ωκαιληδος:] Alex. Ωκειδηλος: Jussio, Reddus). This name occupies, in 1 Esdr. ix. 22, the place of Jozabad in Ezr. x. 22, of which it is a manifest corruption. The original name is more clearly traced in the Vulgate.

OCI'NA ([Rom. 'Οκινd; Vat.] Οκεινα, and so Alex.; [Sin. and] Vulg. omit). "Sour and Ocina" are mentioned (Jud. ii. 28) among the places on the sea-coast of Palestine, which were terrified at the approach of Holofernes. The names seem to occur in a regular order from north to south; and as Ocina is mentioned between Sour (Tyre) and Jemnaan (Jabneh), its position agrees with that of the ancient ACCHO, now Akka, and in mediæval times sometimes called Acon (Brocardus; William of Tyre, etc.).   G.

OC'RAN (עָכְרָן [troubler or troubled]: 'Εχρdν: Ochran). The father of Pagiel, chief of

the tribe of Asher after the Exodus (Num. i. 12 ii. 27, vii. 72, 77, x. 26).

O'DED (עֹודֵד [erecting, confirming]. 'Ωδήδ; Alex. Aδαδ [and so Rom. Vat. in ver. 8:] Oded). 1. The father of Azariah the prophet in the reign of Asa (2 Chr. xv. 1). In 2 Chr. xv. 8, the prophecy in the preceding verses is attributed to him, and not to his son. The Alex. MS. and the Vulgate retain the reading which is probably the true one, "Azariah the son of Oded." These are supported by the Peah'to-Syriac, in which "Azur" is substituted for Oded.

· 2. ['Ωδήδ.] A prophet of Jehovah in Samaria, at the time of Pekah's invasion of Judah. Josephus (Ant. ix. 12, § 2) calls him 'Ωβηδάs. On the return of the victorious army with the 200,000 captives of Judah and Jerusalem, Oded met them and prevailed upon them to let the captives go free (2 Chr. xxviii. 9). He was supported by the chivalrous feelings of some of the chieftains of Ephraim; and the narrative of the restoration of the prisoners, fed, clothed, and anointed, to Jericho the city of palm-trees, is a pleasant episode of the last days of the northern kingdom.   W. A. W.

ODOL'LAM ('Οδολλάμ: Odollam). The Greek form of the name ADULLAM; found in 2 Macc. xii. 38 only. Adullam is stated by Eusebius and Jerome (Onomast. "Adollam") to have been in their day a large village, about 10 miles east of Eleutheropolis; and here (if Beit-jibrin be Eleutheropolis) a village with the name of Bet Dúla (Tobler, Bethlehem, p. 29; Dritte Wand. p. 151) or Beit Ula (Robinson, 1st ed. App. p. 117) now stands.

The obstacle to this identification is not that Adullam, a town of the Shefelah, should be found in the mountains, for that puzzling circumstance is not unfrequent (comp. KEILAH, etc., ii. 1529 a), so much as that in the catalogue of Joshua xv. it is mentioned with a group of towns (Zoreah, Socoh, etc.) which lay at the N. W. corner of Judah, while Bet Dúla is found with those (Nezib, Keilah, etc.) of a separate group, farther south.

Further investigation is requisite before we can positively say if there is any cavern in the neighborhood of Bet Dúla answering to the "cave of Adullam." The cavern at Khureitun,[a] 3 miles south of Bethlehem, usually shown to travellers as Adullam, is so far distant as to put it out of the question. It is more probable that this latter is the cavern in the wilderness of Engedi, in which the adventure[b] of Saul and David (1 Sam. xxiv.) occurred. Everything that can be said to identify it with the cave of Adullam has been said by Dr. Bonar (Land of Promise, pp. 248–50); but his strongest argument — an inference, from 1 Sam. xxii. 1, in favor of its proximity to Bethlehem — comes into direct collision with the statement of Jerome quoted above, which it should be observed is equally opposed to Dr. Robinson's proposal to place it at Deir-Dubbán. [See ADULLAM, Amer. ed.]

The name of Adullam appears to have been first

---

a Dr. Bonar has suggested to us that the name Khureitun represents the ancient Hareth (Khareth). This is ingenious, and may be correct; but Tobler (Umgebungen, etc., pp. 522, 523) has made out a strong case for the name being that of Chareitôn, or Kreton, a famous Essene hermit of the 3d or 4th century, who founded a Laura in the cavern in question. (See Acta Sanct. Sept. 28).

b Van de Velde (Syr. & Pal. ii. 88) illustrates this

charming narrative more forcibly than is his wont. The cave, he says, has still "the same narrow natural vaulting at the entrance, the same huge chamber in the rock, probably the place where Saul lay down to rest in the heat of the day; the same side vaults, too, where David and his men lay concealed, when, accustomed to the obscurity of the cavern, they saw Saul enter, while Saul, blinded by the glare of light outside, saw nothing of them."

applied to *Khureitun* at the time of the Crusades (Will. of Tyre, xv. 6). G.

ODONARKES (marg. Odomarra; [Rom. 'Οδοαρρήν; Sin. Alex. Comp. Ald.] 'Οδομηρά: *Odares*), the chief of a nomad tribe slain by Jonathan (1 Macc. ix. 66). The form in the A. V. does not appear to be supported by any authority. The Geneva version has " Odomeras."

          B. F. W.

* **OFFENCE** occurs in several passages of the A. V. as the rendering of the Heb. מִכְשׁוֹל, *micshôl*, " a stumbling-block," or of the Gr. σκάνδαλον, πρόσκομμα, προσκοπή, and is used in such a way as not to suggest the proper meaning to the common reader. Thus the declaration in Is. viii. 14, " he shall be for a stone of stumbling and a rock of *offence* (" a rock to strike against," Noyes) to both the houses of Israel," describes the ruinous consequences rather than the fact of the unbelief and disobedience of the Jews; comp. ver. 15, and Jer. vi. 21; Ex. iii. 20. In Matt. xvi. 23, " thou art an *offence* to me," is literally " thou art my stumbling-block " (so Noyes); " thou wouldst cause me to fall " (Norton). In Matt. xviii. 7, and Luke xvii. 1 " offence " (σκάνδαλον) means an occasion of sin, or a hindrance to the reception of Christ; see the context. To eat " with *offence* " (διὰ προσκόμματος, Rom. xiv. 20) is so to eat as to be an occasion of sin to the weaker brother. [OFFEND.] A.

* **OFFEND**, from the Latin *offendo*, " to strike against," like OFFENCE (which see) is used in the A. V. in senses which we do not now associate with the word, though they are naturally derived from its primitive meaning. " Great peace have they who love thy law, and nothing shall *offend* them (Ps. cxix. 165); lit. " there is no stumbling-block to them," *i. e.* their path shall be smooth, no evil shall befall them. In Matt. v. 29 (" if thy right eye *offend* thee "), 30, xviii. 6, 8, 9, Mark ix. 42, 43, 45, 47, " to offend " (σκανδαλί ζειν) means " to lead into sin," literally, " to be a stumbling-block to," " to cause to fall." Similarly, in Matt. xiii. 21, xxiv. 10, xxvi. 31, 33; Mark iv. 17, xiv. 27, 29; John xvi. 1, " to be offended " does not suggest to the common reader the meaning of σκανδαλίζεσθαι, which would in these passages be better translated " to fall away." In Rom. xiv. 21 and 2 Cor. xi. 29 the rendering of the A. V. is likewise misleading. A.

OFFERINGS. [SACRIFICE.]

OFFICER.[a] It is obvious that most, if not all, of the Hebrew words rendered " officer," are either of an indefinite character, or are synonymous terms for functionaries known under other and more specific names, as " scribe," " eunuch," etc.

The two words so rendered in the N. T. each bear in ordinary Greek a special sense. In the case of ὑπηρέτης this is of no very definite kind, but the word is used to denote an inferior officer of a court of justice, a messenger or bailiff, like the Roman *viator* or *lictor*. Πράκτορες at Athens were officers whose duty it was to register and collect fines imposed by courts of justice; and " deliver to the officer " [b] means, give the name of the debtor to the officer of the court (Demosthenes (or Dinarchus) *c. Theocr.* p. 1218, Reiske; *Dict. of Antiq.* " Practores," " Hyperetes;" Jul. Poll. viii. 114; Demosth. *c. Arist.* p. 778; Æsch. *c. Timarch.* p. 5. Grotius, on Luke xii. 58).[c]

Josephus says, that to each court of justice among the Jews, two Levites[d] were to be attached as clerks or secretaries, *Ant.* iv. 8, § 14. The Mishna also mentions the crier and other officials, but whether these answered to the officers of Josephus and the N. T. cannot be determined. Selden, from Maimonides, mentions the high estimation in which such officials were held. *Sanhedr.* iv. 3, vi. 1; Selden, *de Synedr.* ii. 13, 11. [PUNISHMENTS; SERJEANTS.]

The word "officers" is used to render the phrases οἱ ἀπὸ (or ἐπὶ) τῶν χρειῶν, 1 Macc. x. 41, xiii. 37, in speaking of the revenue officers of Demetrius.

It is also used to render λειτουργοί, Ecclus. x. 2, where the meaning is clearly the subordinates in a general sense to a supreme authority.

          H. W. P.

OG (עוֹג [*long-necked?*]: 'Ωγ: *Og*), an Amoritish king of Bashan, whose rule extended over sixty cities, of which the two chief were Ashtaroth-Karnaim and Edrei (Josh. xiii. 12). He was one of the last representatives of the giant race of Rephaim. According to eastern traditions, he escaped the deluge by wading beside the ark (Sale's *Koran*, ch. v. p. 83). He was supposed to be the largest of the sons of Anak, and a descendant of Ad. He is said to have lived no less than 3,000 years, and to have refused the warnings of Jethro (Shoaib), who was sent as a prophet to him and his people (D'Herbelot *s. vv.* " *Falastin*," " *Anak* "). Soiouthi wrote a long book about him and his race, chiefly taken from Rabbinic traditions, and called

---

a 1. נָצִיב, *Nasîb*, Vulg. *super omnia*, from נָצַב, to place."

2. From same, נָצַב, part. plur. in Niph. נִצָּבִים, *caðestamênoi*, *praefecti*, 1 K. iv. 7.

3. סָרִים, Gen. xl. 2, εὐνοῦχος. [EUNUCH.]

4. פָּקִיד, Esth. ii. 3, κωμάρχης; Gen. xli. 33, τοπάρχης; Neh. xi. 9, ἐπίσκοπος; *praepositus*; A. V. " overseer."

5. קְצִינָה, προστάτης, concr. for abstr.; properly, office, like " authority " in Eng. Both of these words (4) and (5) from פָּקַד, " visit."

6. רַב, εἰκούδμος, *princeps*, Esth. i. 8, joined with סָרִים, Dan. i. 3.

7. שֹׁמֵר, part. from שָׁמַר, " cut," or " inscribe," Ex. v. 6, γραμματεύς, *exactor*; Num. xi. 16, γραμματεύς, Deut. xvi. 18, γραμματοεισαγωγεύς, *magister*, Josh. i. 10, *princeps*.

8. The word " officer " is also used, Esth. ix. 3, to render מְלָאכָה, which is joined with עֹשֵׂי, marg. " those that did the business," γραμματεύς, *procuratores*.

In N. T. " officer " is used to render, (1) ὑπηρέτης, *minister*, (2) πράκτωρ, Luke xii. 58, *exactor*.

b Παραδοῦναι τῷ πράκτ.

c Πράκτωρ is used in LXX. to render נֹגֵשׂ, Is. III. 12; A. V. " oppressor," one who persecutes by exaction.

d Ὑπηρέται.

Aug fi khaber Aoug (Id. *s. v.* "*Aug*"). See, too, the *Journal Asiatique* for 1841, and *Chronique de Tabari trnd. du persan par Dubeux*, i. 48, f. (Ewald, *Gesch.* i. 306).

Passing over these idle fables, we find from Scripture that he was, with his children and his people, defeated and exterminated by the Israelites at Edrei, immediately after the conquest of Sihon, who is represented by Josephus as his friend and ally (Joseph. *Ant.* iv. 5, § 3). His sixty proud fenced cities were taken, and his kingdom assigned to the Reubenites, Gadites, and half the tribe of Manasseh (Deut. iii. 1-13; Num. xxxii. 33. Also Deut. i. 4, iv. 47, xxxi. 4; Josh. ii. 10, ix. 10, xiii. 12, 30). The giant stature of Og, and the power and bravery of his people, excited a dread which God himself alleviated by his encouragement to Moses before the battle; and the memory of this victory lingered long in the national memory (Ps. cxxxv. 11, cxxxvi. 20).

The belief in Og's enormous stature is corroborated by an appeal to a relic still existing in the time of the author of Deut. iii. 11. This was an iron bedstead, or bier, preserved in "Rabbath of the children of Ammon." How it got there we are not told; perhaps the Ammonites had taken it in some victory over Og. The verse itself has the air of a later addition (Dathe), although it is of course possible that the Hebrews may have heard of so curious a relic as this long before they conquered the city where it was treasured. Rabbath was first subdued in the reign of David (2 Sam. xii. 26); but it does not therefore follow that Deut. iii. 11 was not written till that time (Hävernick *ad loc.*). Some have supposed that this was one of the common flat beds [BEDS] used sometimes on the housetops of eastern cities, but made of iron instead of palm-branches, which would not have supported the giant's weight. It is more probable that the words עֶרֶשׂ בַּרְזֶל, *eres barzel*, mean a "sarcophagus of black basalt," a rendering of which they undoubtedly admit. The Arabs still regard black basalt as iron, because it is a stone "ferrei coloris atque duritiæ" (Plin. xxxvi. 11), and "contains a large percentage of iron." [IRON.] It is most abundant in the Hauran; and indeed is probably the cause of the name Argob (the stony) given to a part of Og's kingdom. This sarcophagus was 9 cubits long, and 4 cubits broad. It does not of course follow that Og was 15½ feet high. Maimonides (*More Nevochim*, ii. 48) sensibly remarks that a bed (supposing "a bed" to be intended) is usually one third [?] longer than the sleeper; and Sir J. Chardin, as well as other travellers, have observed the ancient tendency to make mummies and tombs far larger than the natural size of men, in order to leave an impression of wonder.

Other legends about Og may be found in Ben-Uzziel on Num. xxi. 33, Midrash Jalqût, fol. 13 (quoted by Ewald), and in Mohammedan writers; as that one of his bones long served for a bridge over a river; that he roasted at the sun a fish freshly caught, etc. An apocryphal Book of King Og, which probably contained these and other traditions, was condemned by Pope Gelasius (*Decret.* vi. 13, Sixt. Senensis, *Bibl. Sanct.* p. 86). The origin of the name is doubtful: some, but without any probability, would connect it with the Greek Ogyges (Ewald, *Gesch.* i. 306, ii. 269).   F. W. F.

* OFTEN in the expression "often infirmities," 1 Tim. v. 23, is an adjective, and not an improper use of the adverb, as some allege. Its restricted adverbial sense belongs to a later period than king James's time. See Trench, *Authorised Version*, p. 60 (1859).   H.

O'HAD (אֹהַד [*power*]: 'Aώδ; [Vat. Iωαδ and] Alex. Iαωαδι in Ex.: *Ahod*). One of the six sons of Simeon (Gen. xlvi. 10; Ex. vi. 15). His name is omitted from the lists in 1 Chr. iv. 24 and Num. xxvi. 14, though in the former passage the Syriac has אֹהֹר, *Ohor*, as in Gen. and Ex.

O'HEL (אֹהֶל [*tent*]: 'Oόλ: [Vat. Oσα:] *Ohol*). As the text now stands Ohel was one of the seven sons of Zerubbabel, though placed in a group of five who for some cause are separated from the rest (1 Chr. iii. 20). Whether they were by a different mother, or were born after the return from Babylon, can only be conjectured.

OIL.[a] (I.) Of the numerous substances, animal and vegetable, which were known to the ancients as yielding oil, the olive-berry is the one of which most frequent mention is made in the Scriptures. It is well-known that both the quality and the value of olive-oil differ according to the time of gathering the fruit, and the amount of pressure used in the course of preparation. These processes, which do not essentially differ from the modern, are described minutely by the Roman writers on agriculture, and to their descriptions the few notices occurring both in Scripture and the Rabbinical writings, which throw light on the ancient oriental method, nearly correspond. Of these descriptions the following may be taken as an abstract. The best oil is made from fruit gathered about November or December, when it has begun to change color, but before it has become black. The berry in the more advanced state yields more oil, but of an inferior quality. Oil was also made from unripe fruit by a special process as early as September or October, while the harder sorts of fruit were sometimes delayed till February or March (Virg. *Georg.* ii. 519; Palladius, *R. R.* xii. 4; Columella, *R. R.* xii. 47, 50; Cato, *R. R.* 65; Pliny, *N. H.* xv. 1-8; Varro, *R. R.* i. 55; Hor. 2 *Sat.* ii. 46.)

1. *Gathering.*— Great care is necessary in gathering, not to injure either the fruit itself or the boughs of the tree; and with this view it was either gathered by hand or shaken off carefully with a light reed or stick. The "boughing" of Deut. xxiv. 20 (marg.),[b] probably corresponds to the "shaking"[c] of Is. xvii. 6, xxiv. 13, *i. e.* a subsequent beating for the use of the poor. See Mishna,

a 1. יִצְהָר, from צָהַר, "shine" (Ges. pp. 1152-53), πιότης, ἔλαιον, *oleum*, clear olive-oil, as distinguished from —

2. שֶׁמֶן, "pressed juice," ἔλαιον, *oleum*, from שָׁמֵן, "become fat" (Ges. p. 1437); sometimes joined with זַיִת, ἔλαιον εξ ἐλαιῶν, *oleum de olivetis*, distin-

guishing olive-juice from oil produced from other sources. Also sometimes in A. V. "ointment" (Celsius, *Hierob.* ii. 279).

3. מִשְׁחָה, Chald., ἔλαιον, *oleum*, only in Ezr. vi. 9, vii. 22.

b פָּאַר.   c לְקַף, mislectionum.

Shebiith, iv. 2; *Peah*, vii. 2, viii. 3. After gather
ing and careful cleansing, the fruit was either at
once carried to the press, which is recommended as
the best course; or, if necessary, laid on tables with
hollow trays made sloping, so as to allow the first
juice (Amurca) to flow into other receptacles beneath; care being taken not to heap the fruit too
much, and so prevent the free escape of the juice,
which is injurious to the oil though itself useful in
other ways (Colum. u. s. xii. 50; Aug. *Civ. Dei*, i.
8, 2).

2. *Pressing.* — In order to make oil, the fruit
was either bruised in a mortar, crushed in a press
loaded with wood or stones, ground in a mill, or
trodden with the feet. Special buildings used for
grape-pressing were used also for the purpose of
olive-pressing, and contained both the press and the
receptacle for the pressed juice. Of these processes,
the one least expedient was the last (treading),
which perhaps answers to the " canalis et solea,"
mentioned by Columella, and was probably the one
usually adopted by the poor. The " beaten " oil of
Ex. xxvii. 20; Lev. xxiv. 2, and Ex. xxix. 40;
Num. xxviii. 5, was probably made by bruising in
a mortar. These processes, and also the place and
the machine for pressing, are mentioned in the
Mishna. Oil-mills are often made of stone, and
turned by hand. Others consist of cylinders inclosing a beam, which is turned by a camel or
other animal. An Egyptian olive-press is described by Niebuhr, in which the pressure exerted on
the fruit is given by means of weights of wood and
stone placed in a sort of box above. Besides the
above cited Scripture references, the following passages mention either the places, the processes, or
the machines used in olive-pressing: Mic. vi. 15;
Joel ii. 24, iii. 13; Is. lxiii. 3; Lam. i. 15; Hag.
ii. 16; *Menach.* viii. 4; *Shebiith*, iv. 9, vii. 6 (see

Ges. p. 179, s. v. חֵל) ; *Terum.* x. 7; *Shabb.* i.
9; *Baba Bathra*, iv. 5; Ges. pp. 351, 725, 848,
1096; Vitruvius, x. 1; Cato, *R. R.* 3; Celsius,
Hierob. ii. 346, 350; Niebuhr, *Voy.* i. 122, pl. xvii.;
Arundell, *Asia Minor*, ii. 196; Wellsted, *Trav.* ii.
420. [GETHSEMANE.]

3. *Keeping.* — Both olives and oil were kept in
jars carefully cleansed; and oil was drawn out for
use in horns or other small vessels (CRUSE). These
vessels for keeping oil were stored in cellars or
storehouses; special mention of such repositories is
made in the inventories of royal property and revenue (1 Sam. x. 1, xvi. 1, 13; 1 K. i. 39, xvii. 16;
2 K. iv. 2, 6, ix. 1, 3; 1 Chr. xxvii. 28; 2 Chr.
xi. 11, xxxii. 28; Prov. xxi. 20; *Shebiith*, v. 7;
Celim, ii. 5, xvii. 12; Columell. *l. c.*).

Oil of Tekoa was reckoned the best (*Menach.*
viii. 8). Trade in oil was carried on with the Tyrians, by whom it was probably often reëxported
to Egypt, whose olives do not for the most part
produce good oil. Oil to the amount of 20,000
baths (2 Chr. ii. 10; Joseph. *Ant.* viii. 2, § 9), or
20 measures (*cors*, 1 K. v. 11) was among the
supplies furnished by Solomon to Hiram. Direct
trade in oil was also carried on between Egypt and
Palestine (1 K. v. 11; 2 Chr. ii. 10, 15; Ezr. iii.
7; Is. xxx. 6, lvii. 9; Ez. xxvii. 17; Hos. xii. 1;
S. Hieronym. *Com. in Osee*, iii. 12; Joseph. *Ant.*
viii. 2, § 9; *B. J.* ii. 21, § 2; Strabo, xvii. p. 809;
Pliny, xv. 4, 13; Wilkinson, *Anc. Egypt.* ii. 28, sm.
ed.; Hasselquist, *Trav.* pp. 53, 117). [COM
MERCE; WEIGHTS AND MEASURES.]

(II.) Besides the use of olives themselves as food

common to all olive-producing countries (Hor. 1
Od. xxxi. 15; Martial, xiii. 36; Arvieux, *Trav.*
p. 209; *Terumoth*, i. 9, ii. 6), the principal uses
of olive-oil may be thus stated.

1. *As food.* — Dried wheat, boiled with either
butter or oil, but more commonly the former, is a
common dish for all classes in Syria. Hasselquist
speaks of bread baked in oil as being particularly
sustaining; and Faber, in his Pilgrimage, mentions
eggs fried in oil as Saracen and Arabian dishes. It
was probably on account of the common use of oil
in food that the " meat-offerings " prescribed by the
Law were so frequently mixed with oil (Lev. ii. 4,
7, 15, viii. 26, 31; Num. vii. 19, and foll.; Deut.
xii. 17, xxxii. 13; 1 K. xvii. 12, 15; 1 Chr. xii.
40; Ez. xvi. 13, 19; S. Hieronym. *Vit. S. Hilarion.*
c. 11, vol. ii. p. 32; Ibn Batuta, *Trav.* p. 60, ed.
Lee; Volney, *Trav.* i. 362, 406; Russell, *Aleppo*,
i. 80, 119; Harmer, *Obs.* i. 471, 474; Shaw, *Trav.*
p. 232; Bertrandon de la Brocquiere, *Early Trav.*
p. 332; Burckhardt, *Trav. in Arab.* i. 54; *Notes
on Bed.* i. 59; Arvieux, *l. c.*; Chardin, *Voy.* iv.
84; Niebuhr, *Voy.* ii. 302; Hasselquist, *Trav.* p.
132; Faber, *Evagatorium*, vol. i. p. 197, ii. 152,
415). [FOOD; OFFERING.]

2. *Cosmetic.* — As is the case generally in hot
climates, oil was used by the Jews for anointing
the body, *e. g.* after the bath, and giving to the
skin and hair a smooth and comely appearance,
e. g. before an entertainment. To be deprived of
the use of oil was thus a serious privation, assumed
voluntarily in the time of mourning or of calamity.
At Egyptian entertainments it was usual for a
servant to anoint the head of each guest, as he
took his seat [OINTMENT] (Deut. xxviii. 40; 2
Sam. xiv. 2; Ruth iii. 3; 2 Sam. xii. 20; Ps. ·
xxiii. 5, xcii. 10, civ. 15; Dan. x. 3; Is. lxi. 3;
Mic. vi. 15; Am. vi. 6; Sus. 17; Luke vii. 46).
Strabo mentions the Egyptian use of castor-oil for
this purpose, xviii. 824. The Greek and Roman
usage will be found mentioned in the following
passages: Hom. *Il.* x. 577, xviii. 596, xxiii. 281;
Od. vii. 107, vl. 96, x. 364; Hor. 3 *Od.* xiii. 6; 1
Sat. vi. 123; 2 *Sat.* i. 8; Pliny, xiv. 22; Aristoph.
Wasps, p. 608, *Clouds*, p. 816; Roberts, pl. 164.
Butter, as is noticed by Pliny, is used by the
negroes and the lower class of Arabs for the like
purposes (Pliny, xi. 41; Burckhardt, *Trav.* i. 53;
Nubia, p. 215; Lightfoot, *Hor. Hebr.* ii. 375; see
Deut. xxxiii. 24; Job xxix. 6; Ps. cix. 18).

The use of oil preparatory to athletic exercises,
customary among the Greeks and Romans, can
scarcely have had place to any extent among the
Jews, who in their earlier times had no such contests, though some are mentioned by Josephus with
censure as taking place at Jerusalem and Cæsarea
under Herod (Hor. 1 *Od.* viii. 8; Pliny, xv. 4;
Athenæus, xv. 34, p. 686: Hom. *Od.* vi. 79, 215;
Joseph. *Ant.* xv. 8, § 1, xvi. 5, § 1; *Dict. of Antiq.*,
" Aliptæ ").

3. *Funereal.* — The bodies of the dead were
anointed with oil by the Greeks and Romans,
probably as a partial antiseptic, and a similar
custom appears to have prevailed among the Jews
(*Il.* xxiv. 587; Virg. *Æn.* vi. 219). [ANOINT;
BURIAL.]

4. *Medicinal.* — As oil is in use in many cases
in modern medicine, so it is not surprising, that it
should have been much used among the Jews and
other nations of antiquity for medicinal purposes.
Celsus repeatedly speaks of the use of oil, especially
old oil, applied externally with friction in fevers,

and in many other cases. Pliny says that olive-oil is good to warm the body and fortify it against cold, and also to cool heat in the head, and for various other purposes. It was thus used previously to taking cold baths, and also mixed with water for bathing the body. Josephus mentions that among the remedies employed in the case of Herod, he was put into a sort of oil bath. Oil mixed with wine is also mentioned as a remedy used both inwardly and outwardly in the disease with which the soldiers of the army of Ælius Gallus were affected, a circumstance which recalls the use of a similar remedy in the parable of the good Samaritan. The prophet Isaiah alludes to the use of oil as ointment in medical treatment; and it thus furnished a fitting symbol, perhaps also an efficient remedy, when used by our Lord's disciples in the miraculous cures which they were enabled to perform. With a similar intention, no doubt, its use was enjoined by St. James, and, as it appears, practiced by the early Christian Church in general. An instance of cure through the medium of oil is mentioned by Tertullian. The medicinal use of oil is also mentioned in the Mishna, which thus exhibits the Jewish practice of that day. See, for the various instances above named, Is i. 6; Mark vi. 13; Luke x. 34; James v. 14; Josephus, *Ant.* xvii. 6, § 5; *B. J.* i. 33, § 5; *Shabb.* xiii. 4; Otho, *Lex. Rabb.* pp. 11, 526; Mosheim, *Eccl. Hist.* iv. 9; Corn. à Lap. on James v.; Tertull. *ad Scrp.* c. 4; Celsus, *De Med.* ii. 14, 17; iii. 6, 9, 18, 22, iv. 2; Hor. 2 *Sat.* i. 7; Pliny, xv. 4, 7, xxiii. 3, 4; Dio Cass. liii. 29; Lightfoot, *H. H.* ii. 304, 444; S. Hieronym. *l. c.*

5. *Oil for light.* — The oil for "the light" was expressly ordered to be olive-oil, beaten, *i. e.* made from olives bruised in a mortar (Ex. xxv. 6, xxvii. 20, 21, xxxv. 8; Lev. xxiv. 2; 2 Chr. xiii. 11; 1 Sam. iii. 3; Zech. iv. 3, 12; Mishna, *Demai,* i. 3; *Menuch.* viii. 4). The quantity required for the longest night is said to have been ½ log (13·79 cubic in. = ·4166 of a pint), *Menuch.* ix. 3; Otho, *Lex. Rabb.* p. 159. [CANDLESTICK.] In the same manner the great lamps used at the Feast of Tabernacles were fed (*Succah,* v. 2). Oil was used in general for lamps; it is used in Egypt with cotton wicks twisted round a piece of straw; the receptacle being a glass vessel, into which water is first poured (Matt. xxv. 1–8; Luke xii. 35; Lane, *Mod. Egypt.* i. 201).

6. *Ritual.* — (*a.*) Oil was poured on, or mixed with the flour or meal used in offerings.

(i.) The consecration offering of priests (Ex. xxix. 2, 23; Lev. vi. 15, 21).

(ii.) The offering of "beaten oil" with flour, which accompanied the daily sacrifice (Ex. xxix. 40).

(iii.) The leper's purification offering, Lev. xiv. 10–18, 21, 24, 28, where it is to be observed that the quantity of oil (1 log, = ·833 of a pint), was invariable, whilst the other objects varied in quantity according to the means of the person offering. The cleansed leper was also to be touched with oil on various parts of his body (Lev. xiv. 15–18).

(iv.) The Nazarite, on completion of his vow, was to offer unleavened bread anointed with oil, and cakes of fine bread mingled with oil (Num. vi. 15).

(v.) After the erection of the Tabernacle, the offerings of the "princes" included flour mingled with oil (Num. vii.).

(vi.) At the consecration of the Levites, fine flour mingled with oil was offered (Num. viii. 8).

(vii.) Meat-offerings in general were mingled or anointed with oil (Lev. vii. 10, 12).

On the other hand, certain offerings were to be devoid of oil; the sin-offering (Lev. v. 11), and the offering of jealousy (Num. v. 15).

The principle on which both the presence and the absence of oil were prescribed is clearly, that as oil is indicative of gladness, so its absence denoted sorrow or humiliation (Is. lxi. 3; Joel ii. 19; Rev. vi. 6). It is on this principle that oil is so often used in Scripture as symbolical of nourishment and comfort (Deut. xxxii. 13, xxxiii. 24; Job xxix. 6; Ps. xlv. 7, cix. 18; Is. lxi. 3).

(*b.*) Kings, priests, and prophets, were anointed with oil or ointment. [OINTMENT.]

7. (*a.*) As so important a necessary of life, the Jew was required to include oil among his first-fruit offerings (Ex. xxii. 29, xxiii. 16; Num. xviii. 12; Deut. xviii. 4; 2 Chr. xxxi. 5; *Terum.* xi. 3). In the Mishna various limitations are laid down; but they are of little importance except as illustrating the processes to which the olive-berry was subjected in the production of oil, and the degrees of estimation in which their results were held.

(*b.*) Tithes of oil were also required (Deut. xii. 17; 2 Chr. xxxi. 5; Neh. x. 37, 39, xiii. 12; Ez. xlv. 14).

8. Shields, if covered with hide, were anointed with oil or grease previous to use. [ANOINT.] Shields of metal were perhaps rubbed over in like manner to polish them. See Thenius on 2 Sam. i. 21; Virg. *Æn.* vii. 625; Plautus, *Mil.* i. 1, 2; and Ges. p. 825.

Oil of inferior quality was used in the composition of soap.

Of the substances which yield oil, besides the olive-tree, myrrh is the only one specially mentioned in Scripture. Oil of myrrh is the juice which exudes from the tree *Balsamodendron myrrha,* but olive-oil was an ingredient in many compounds which passed under the general name of oil (Esth. ii. 12; Celsus, *u. s.* iii. 10, 18, 19; Pliny, xii. 26, xiii. 1, 2, xv. 7; Wilkinson, *Anc. Egypt.* ii. 23; Balfour, *Plants of Bible,* p. 52; Winer, *Realw.* s. v. Myrrhe. [OINTMENT.]

H. W. P.

* **OIL-PRESS.** [OIL, 2.]

OIL-TREE (עֵץ שֶׁמֶן, *éts shemen:* κυπάρισσος, ξύλα κυπαρίσσινα: *lignum olivæ, frondes ligni pulcherrimi*). The Hebrew words occur in Neh. viii. 15; 1 K. vi. 23; and in Is. xli. 19. In this last passage the A. V. has "oil-tree;" but in Kings it has "olive-tree," and in Nehemiah "pine-branches." From the passage in Nehemiah, where the *éts shemen* is mentioned as distinct from the *zaïth* or "olive-tree," writers have sought to identify it with the *Elæagnus angustifolius,* Linn., sometimes called "the wild olive tree," or " narrow leaved oleaster," the *zackum-*tree of the Arabs. There is, however, some great mistake in this matter; for the *zackum-*tree cannot be referred to the *elæagnus,* the properties and characteristics of which tree do not accord with what travellers have related of the famed *zackum-*tree of Palestine. We are indebted to Dr. Hooker for the correction of this error. The *zackum* is the *Balanites Ægyptiaca,* a well-known and abundant shrub or small tree in the plain of Jordan. It is found all the way from the peninsula of India and the Ganges to Syria, Abyssinia, and the Niger. The zackum-oil is held in high repute by the Arabs for its medicinal properties. It is said to be very valuable against wounds and contusions. Comp. Maundrell (*Journ.* p. 86), Robinson (*Bibl. Res.* i. 560): see also BALM. It is quite probable that

Balanites Ægyptiaca.

the *zackum*, or *Balanites Ægyptiaca*, is the *êts shemen*, or oil-tree of Scripture. Celsius (*Hierob.* i. 309) understood by the Hebrew words any "fat or resinous tree:" but the passage in Nehemiah clearly points to some specific tree.   W. H.

* That the עֵץ שֶׁמֶן does not refer to the *zackum* seems to be evident, inasmuch as in Neh. viii. 15 it is spoken of as growing in the mountain, whereas *Balanites Ægyptiaca* is found only in the plain of Jordan. Then in 1 K. vi. 23 an image ten cubits high is spoken of as made of this tree. Can we suppose that the "shrub or small tree," *Balanites Ægyptiaca*, furnished the wood for this Cherub? Then again, in Is. xli. 19, this tree is

a sign of fertility, and of the blessing of God. Surely it is not such a tree as this, confined to a small district of Palestine, and of limited utility

nation of this tree are: (1.) A tree with wood of sufficient solidity and size and beauty to be

used in making a carved image ten cubits high, to be placed in the Holy of Holies.

(2.) A tree with branches so thick and leafy that they would be suitable to be associated with those of the olive, palm, myrtle, and other thick trees in the making of booths.

(3.) A tree fit to be associated with the cedar, the acacia, and the myrtle, as an emblem of the favor of God restored to a desolated land.

(4.) An oily, or oil-producing tree, growing in the mountains.

(5.) Not the olive itself, which would be excluded by Neh. viii. 15.

These conditions are not fulfilled in any tree so well as in the genus *Pinus*, of which there are several species in Syria. The *Pinus pinea* is the most celebrated of these. It is a tall and beautiful tree usually trimmed close to the trunk below, and allowed to expand in a broad top like a palm. It is one of the most picturesque trees of Syria. It often attains an immense size. Two or three specimens of it may be seen near Beirût, towering above the neighboring groves to a height of over 100 feet. The trunks are several feet in thickness. The wood is highly resinous and "*fat*," and the branches are commonly used to make *booths*. The wood is the most sought for for roofing purposes, and is often finely carved.[a] It is of a fine reddish hue in the older trees, and takes a high polish owing to the large amount of the resinous constituent contained in it. It is moreover usually *planted*, and does not occur in forests far distant from the haunts of men. Its abundance marks seasons of rest from war, and prosperity in the land. The reverse marks the occurrence of war and desolation, which always tend to destroy trees. Among the other species found in the East the *Pinus orientalis* is perhaps next in frequency. It is small, and does not answer the conditions so well as the first mentioned. (A description of these two species, with plates, may be found in Thomson's *Land and Book*, ii. 265–267.) The first named species is called by the Arabs *Snôbar*. The groves outside of Beirût are so dense in the shade which they afford, that, where they are planted thickly, scarce a ray of the powerful Syrian sunshine can penetrate even at noonday. How appropriate that this species should have been chosen for "booths," and how inappropriate that the straggling thorny branches of the *Balanites* should have been imagined to meet this requirement of the text (Neh. viii. 15). Among the other species of Syria may be noted also *Pinus maritimus* and *P. haleppensis*, both of which are common.

The תִּדְהָר at Is. xli. 19 and lx. 13 is probably not the *pine*, but the oak. This probability, which if established would exclude the mention of so common a tree as the pine from the Scripture, would of itself lead us to seek for an allusion to the pine under some other name.   G. E. P.

OINTMENT.[b] Besides the fact that olive-oil

---

[a] * If the olive be the wood intended at 1 K. vi. 23, it is singular that a wood of such hardness should have been chosen for a carving, when that carving was to be covered with gold, and thus the fine grain would be concealed.   G. E. P.

[b] 1. *Shemen.* See OIL (2).

2. רָקַח, μύρον, *unguentum*, from רָקַח, "anoint."

3. מִרְקַחַת or מֶרְקָחָה μύρον, *unguentum* (Ex. xxx. 25). Gesenius thinks it may be the vessel in which the ointment was compounded (p. 1309).

4. מִשְׁחָה, χρίσις, χρίσμα, *unguentum*, sometimes in A. V. "oil."

5. מְרוּקִים: in A. V. "things for purifying"

is itself a common ingredient in ointments, the purposes to which ointment, as mentioned in Scripture, is applied agree in so many respects with those which belong to oil, that we need not be surprised that the same words, especially 1 and 4, should be applied to both oil and ointment. The following list will point out the Scriptural uses of ointment: —

1. *Cosmetic.* — The Greek and Roman practice of anointing the head and clothes on festive occasions prevailed also among the Egyptians, and appears to have had place among the Jews (Ruth iii. 3; Eccl. vii. 1, ix. 8; Prov. xxvii. 9, 16; Cant. i. 3, iv. 10; Am. vi. 6; Ps. xlv. 7; Is. lvii. 9; Matt. xxvi. 7; Luke vii. 46; Rev. xviii. 13; *Yoma*, viii. 1; *Shabb.* ix. 4; Plato, *Symp.* i. 6, p. 193; see authorities in Hofmann, *Lex.* art. " Ungendi ritus "). Oil of myrrh, for like purposes, is mentioned Esth. ii. 12. Strabo says that the inhabitants of Mesopotamia use oil of sesamé, and the Egyptians castor-oil (kiki), both for burning, and the lower classes for anointing the body. Chardin and other travellers confirm this statement as regards the Persians, and show that they made little use of olive-oil, but used other oils, and among them oil of sesamé and castor-oil. Chardin also describes the Indian and Persian custom of presenting perfumes to guests at banquets (Strabo, xvi. 746, xvii. 824; Chardin, *Voy.* iv. 43, 84, 86; Marco Polo, *Trav.* (*Early Trav.*) p. 85; Olearius, *Trav.* p. 305). Egyptian paintings represent servants anointing guests on their arrival at their entertainer's house, and alabaster vases exist which retain the traces of the ointment which they were used to contain. Athenæus speaks of the extravagance of Antiochus Epiphanes in the article of ointments for guests, as well as of ointments of various kinds (Wilkinson, *Anc. Egypt.* i. 78, pl. 39, i. 157; Athenæus, x. 53, xv. 41). [ALABASTER; ANOINT.]

2. *Funereal.* — Ointments as well as oil were used to anoint dead bodies and the clothes in which they were wrapped. Our Lord thus spake of his own body being anointed by anticipation (Matt. xxvi. 12; Mark xiv. 3, 8; Luke xxiii. 56; John xii. 3, 7, xix. 40; see also Plutarch, *Consol.* p. 611, viii. 413, ed. Reiske). [BURIAL.]

3. *Medicinal.* — Ointment formed an important feature in ancient medical treatment (Celsus, *De Med.* iii. 19, v. 27; Plin. xxiv. 10, xxix. 3, 8, 9). The prophet Isaiah alludes to this in a figure of speech; and our Lord, in his cure of a blind man, adopted as the outward sign one which represented the usual method of cure. The mention of balm of Gilead and of eye-salve (*collyrium*) point to the same method (Is. i. 6; John ix. 6; Jer. viii. 22, xlvi. 11, li. 8; Rev. iii. 18; Tob. vi. 8, xi. 8, 13; Tertull. *De Idololatr.* 11).

4. *Ritual.* — Besides the oil used in many ceremonial observances, a special ointment was appointed to be used in consecration (Ex. xxx. 23, 33, xxix. 7, xxxvii. 29, xl. 9, 15). It was first compounded by Bezaleel, and its ingredients and proportions are precisely specified; namely of pure myrrh and cassia 500 shekels (250 ounces) each; sweet cinnamon and sweet calamus 250 shekels (125 ounces) each;

and of olive-oil 1 hin (about 5 quarts, 330·96 cubic inches). These were to be compounded according to the art of the apothecary [a] into an oil of holy ointment (Ex. xxx. 25). It was to be used for anointing — (1) the tabernacle itself; (2) the table and its vessels; (3) the candlestick and its furniture; (4) the altar of incense; (5) the altar of burnt-offering and its vessels; (6) the laver and its foot; (7) Aaron and his sons. Strict prohibition was issued against using this unguent for any secular purpose, or on the person of a foreigner, and against imitating it in any way whatsoever (Ex. xxx. 32, 33).

These ingredients, exclusive of the oil, must have amounted in weight to about 47 lbs. 8 oz. Now olive-oil weighs at the rate of 10 lbs. to the gallon. The weight therefore of the oil in the mixture would be 12 lbs. 8 oz. English. A question arises, in what form were the other ingredients, and what degree of solidity did the whole attain? Myrrh, "pure" (*dĕrŏr*),[b] free-flowing (Ges. p. 355), would seem to imply the juice which flows from the tree at the first incision, perhaps the " odorato sudantia ligno balsama " (*Georg.* ii. 118), which Pliny says is called " stacte," and is the best (xii. 15; Dioscorides, i. 73, 74, quoted by Celsus, L. 159; and Knobel on Exodus, *l. c.*).

This juice, which at its first flow is soft and oily, becomes harder on exposure to the air. According to Maimonides, Moses (not Bezaleel), having reduced the solid ingredients to powder, steeped them in water till all the aromatic qualities were drawn forth. He then poured in the oil, and boiled the whole till the water was evaporated. The residuum thus obtained was preserved in a vessel for use (Otho, *Lex. Rabb.* "Oleum"). This account is perhaps favored by the expression " powders of the merchant," in reference to myrrh (Cant. iii. 6; Keil, *Arch. Hebr.* p. 173). Another theory supposes all the ingredients to have been in the form of oil or ointment, and the measurement by weight of all, except the oil, seems to imply that they were in some solid form, but whether in an unctuous state or in that of powder cannot be ascertained. A process of making ointment, consisting, in part at least, in boiling, is alluded to in Job xli. 31. The ointment with which Aaron was anointed is said to have flowed down over his garments (Ex. xxix. 21; Ps. cxxxiii. 2: "skirts," in the latter passage, is literally " mouth," *i. e.* the opening of the robe at the neck; Ex. xxviii. 32).

The charge of preserving the anointing oil, as well as the oil for the light, was given to Eleazar (Num. iv. 16). The quantity of ointment made in the first instance seems to imply that it was intended to last a long time. The Rabbinical writers say that it lasted 900 years, *i. e.* till the Captivity, because it was said, " ye shall not make any like it " (Ex. xxx. 32); but it seems clear from 1 Chr. ix. 30 that the ointment was renewed from time to time (*Cheriith*, i. 1).

Kings, and also in some cases prophets, were, as well as priests, anointed with oil or ointment; but Scripture only mentions the fact as actually taking place in the cases of Saul, David, Solomon,

(Bath. ii. 12); LXX. σμύγματα; by Targum rendered " perfumed ointment," from מָרַק, " rub," " cleanse " (Ges. p. 820).

In N. T. and Apocrypha, "ointment" is the Δ. ¶ rendering for μύρον, *unguentum.*

[a] לָקַח, μυροψός, *unguentarius, pigmentarius.*

[b] דְּרוֹר, *δελεκτή, electa.*

Jehu, and Joash. The Rabbins say that Saul, Jehu, and Joash were only anointed with common oil, whilst for David and Solomon the holy oil was used (1 Sam. x. 1, xvi. 1, 13; 1 K. i. 39; 2 K. ix. 1, 3, 6, xi. 12; Godwyn, *Moses and Aaron*, i. 4; Carpzov, *Apparatus*, pp. 56, 57; Hofmann, *Lex.* art. "Ungendi ritus"; S. Hieron. *Com. in Osee*, iii. 134). It is evident that the sacred oil was used in the case of Solomon, and probably in the cases of Saul and David. In the case of Saul (1 Sam. x. 1) the article is used, "the oil," as it is also in the case of Jehu (2 K. ix. 1); and it seems unlikely that the anointing of Joash, performed by the high-priest, should have been defective in this respect.

A person whose business it was to compound ointments in general was called an "apothecary" (Neh. iii. 8 *a*; Eccl. x. 1; Ecclus. xlix. 1). [APOTHECARY.] The work was sometimes carried on by women "confectionaries" (1 Sam. viii. 13).

In the Christian Church the ancient usage of anointing the bodies of the dead was long retained, as is noticed by S. Chrysostom and other writers quoted by Suicer, *s. v.* ἔλαιον. The ceremony of chrism or anointing was also added to baptism. See authorities quoted by Suicer, *l. c.*, and under Βάπτισμα and Χρίσμα.   H. W. P.

OLA'MUS ('Ωλαμός: *Olamus*). MESHULLAM of the sons of Bani (1 Esdr. ix. 30; comp. Ezr. x. 29).

* OLD AGE. [AGE, OLD.]

OLD TESTAMENT. This article will treat (A) of the Text and (B) of the Interpretation of the Old Testament. Some observations will be subjoined respecting (C) the Quotations from the Old Testament in the New.

A. — TEXT OF THE OLD TESTAMENT.

1. *History of the Text.* — A history of the text of the O. T. should properly commence from the date of the completion of the Canon; from which time we must assume that no additions to any part of it could be legitimately made, the sole object of those who transmitted and watched over it being thenceforth to preserve that which was already written. Of the care, however, with which the text was transmitted we have to judge, almost entirely, by the phenomena which it and the versions derived from it now present, rather than by any recorded facts respecting it. That much scrupulous pains would be bestowed by Ezra, the "ready scribe in the law of Moses," and by his companions, on the correct transmission of those Scriptures which passed through their hands, is indeed antecedently probable. The best evidence of such pains, and of the respect with which the text of the sacred books was consequently regarded, is to be found in the jealous accuracy with which the discrepancies of various parallel passages have been preserved, notwithstanding the temptation which must have existed to assimilate them to each other. Such is the case with Psalms xiv. and liii., two recensions of the same hymn, both proceeding from David, where the reasons of the several variations may on examination be traced. Such also is the case with Psalm xviii. and 2 Sam. xxii. where the variations between the two copies are more than sixty in number, excluding those which merely consist in

a רָקַח, *pigmentarius*.

the use or absence of the *matres lectionis* ; and where, therefore, even though the design of all the variations be not perceived, the hypothesis of their having originated through accident would imply a carelessness in transcribing far beyond what even the rashest critics have in other passages contemplated.

As regards the form in which the sacred writings were preserved, there can be little doubt that the text was ordinarily written on skins, rolled up into volumes, like the modern synagogue-rolls (Ps. xl. 7; Jer. xxxvi. 14; Zech. v. 1; Ex. ii. 9). Josephus relates that the copy sent from Jerusalem as a present to Ptolemy in Egypt, was written with letters of gold on skins of admirable thinness, the joint of which could not be detected (*Ant.* xii. 2, § 11).

The original character in which the text was expressed is that still preserved to us, with the exception of four letters, on the Maccabæan coins, and having a strong affinity to the Samaritan character, which seems to have been treated by the later Jews as identical with it, being styled by them כתב

עברי. At what date this was exchanged for the present Aramaic or square character, כתב

אשורית, or כתב מרבע, is still as undetermined as it is at what date the use of the Aramaic language in Palestine superseded that of the Hebrew. The old Jewish tradition, repeated by Origen and Jerome, ascribed the change to Ezra. But the Maccabæan coins supply us with a date at which the older character was still in use; and even though we should allow that both may have been simultaneously employed, the one for sacred, the other for more ordinary purposes, we can hardly suppose that they existed side by side for any lengthened period. Hassencamp and Gesenius are at variance as to whether such errors of the Septuagint as arose from confusion of letters in the original text, are in favor of the Greek interpreters having had the older or the more modern character before them. It is sufficiently clear that the use of the square writing must have been well established before the time of those authors who attributed the introduction of it to Ezra. Nor could the allusion in Matt. v. 18 to the *yod* as the smallest letter have well been made except in reference to the more modern character. We forbear here all investigation of the manner in which this character was formed, or of the precise locality whence it was derived. Whatever modification it may have undergone in the hands of the Jewish scribes, it was in the first instance introduced from abroad; and this its name כתב אשורית, *i. e.* Assyrian writing, implies, though it may geographically require to be interpreted with some latitude. (The suggestion of Hupfeld that אשורית may be an appellative, denoting not *Assyrian*, but *firm*, writing, is improbable.) On the whole we may best suppose, with Ewald, that the adoption of the new character was coeval with the rise of the earliest Targums, which would naturally be written in the Aramaic style. It would thus be shortly anterior to the Christian era; and with this date all the evidence would well accord. It may be right, however, to mention, that while of late years Keil has striven anew to throw back the introduction of the square writing towards the time of Ezra Bleek, also, though not generally imbued with the conservative views of Keil, maintains not only that the use of the square writing for the sacred books owed its origin to Ezra, but also that the later books of the O. T. were never expressed in any other character.

No vowel points were attached to the text: they were, through all the early period of its history, entirely unknown. Convenience had indeed, at the time when the later books of the O. T. were written, suggested a larger use of the *matres lectionis*: it is thus that in those books we find them introduced into many words that had been previously spelt without them: קוֹדֶשׁ takes the place of קָדֶשׁ, דָוִיד of דָוִד. An elaborate endeavor has been recently made by Dr. Wall to prove that, up to the early part of the second century of the Christian era, the Hebrew text was free from vowel letters as well as from vowels. His theory is that they were then interpolated by the Jews, with a view of altering rather than of perpetuating the former pronunciation of the words: their object being, according to him, to pervert thereby the sense of the prophecies, as also to throw discredit on the Septuagint, and thereby weaken or evade the force of arguments drawn from that version in support of Christian doctrines. Improbable as such a theory is, it is yet more astonishing that its author should never have been deterred from prosecuting it by the palpable objections to it which he himself discerned. Who can believe, with him, that the Samaritans, notwithstanding the mutual hatred existing between them and the Jews, borrowed the interpolation from the Jews, and conspired with them to keep it a secret? Or that among other words to which by this interpolation the Jews ventured to impart a new sound, were some of the best known proper names; e. g. Isaiah, Jeremiah? Or that it was merely through a blunder that in Gen. i. 24, the substantive הַחַיְתוֹ in its construct state acquired its final ן, when the same anomaly occurs in no fewer than three passages of the Psalms? Such views and arguments refute themselves; and while the high position occupied by its author commends the book to notice, it can only be lamented that industry, learning, and ingenuity should have been so misspent in the vain attempt to give substance to a shadow.

There is reason to think that in the text of the O. T., as originally written, the words were generally, though not uniformly divided. Of the Phœnician inscriptions, though the majority proceed continuously, some have a point after every word, except when the words are closely connected. The same point is used in the Samaritan manuscripts; and it is observed by Gesenius (a high authority in respect of the Samaritan Pentateuch) that the Samaritan and Jewish divisions of the words generally coincide. The discrepancy between the Hebrew text and the Septuagint in this respect is sufficiently explained by the circumstance that the Jewish scribes did not separate the words which were closely connected: it is in the case of such that the discrepancy is almost exclusively found. The practice of separating words by spaces instead of points probably came in with the square writing. In the synagogue-rolls, which are written in conformity with the ancient rules, the words are regularly divided from each other; and indeed the Talmud minutely prescribes the space which should be left (Gesenius, *Gesch. der Heb. Sprache*, § 45).

Of ancient date, probably, are also the separations between the lesser Parshioth or sections; whether made, in the case of the more important divisions, by the commencement of a new line, or, in the case of the less important, by a blank space within the line [BIBLE]. The use of the letters פ and ס, however, to indicate these divisions is of more recent origin: they are not employed in the synagogue-rolls. These lesser and earlier Parshioth, of which there are in the Pentateuch 669, must not be confounded with the greater and later Parshioth, or Sabbath-lessons, which are first mentioned in the Masorah. The name Parshioth is in the Mishna (*Megill.* iv. 4) applied to the divisions in the Prophets as well as to those in the Pentateuch: e. g. to Isaiah lii. 3–5 (to the greater Parshioth here correspond the Haphtaroth). Even the separate psalms are in the Gemara called also Parshioth (*Berach. Bab.* fol. 9, 2; 10, 1). Some indication of the antiquity of the divisions between the Parshioth may be found in the circumstance that the Gemara holds them as old as Moses (*Berach.* fol. 12, 2). Of their real age we know but little. Hupfeld has found that they do not always coincide with the capitula of Jerome. That they are nevertheless more ancient than his time is shown by the mention of them in the Mishna. In the absence of evidence to the contrary, their disaccordance with the Kazin of the Samaritan Pentateuch, which are 966 in number, seems to indicate that they had a historical origin; and it is possible that they also may date from the period when the O. T. was first transcribed in the square character. Our present chapters, it may be remarked, spring from a Christian source.

Of any logical division, in the written text, of the prose of the O. T. into Pesukim, or verses, we find in the Talmud no mention; and even in the existing synagogue-rolls such division is generally ignored. While, therefore, we may admit the early currency of such a logical division, we must assume, with Hupfeld, that it was merely a traditional observance. It has indeed, on the other hand, been argued that such numerations of the verses as the Talmud records could not well have been made unless the written text distinguished them. But to this we may reply by observing that the verses of the numbering of which the Talmud speaks, could not have thoroughly accorded with those of modern times. Of the former there were in the Pentateuch 5,888 (or as some read, 8,888); it now contains but 5,845: the middle verse was computed to be Lev. xiii. 33; with our present verses it is Lev. viii. 5. Had the verses been distinguished in the written text at the time that the Talmudic enumeration was made, it is not easily explicable how they should since have been so much altered: whereas, were the logical division merely traditional, tradition would naturally preserve a more accurate knowledge of the places of the various logical breaks than of their relative importance, and thus, without any disturbance of the syntax, the number of computed verses would be liable to continual increase or diminution, by separation or aggregation. An uncertainty in the versual division is even now indicated by the doubtful accentuation and consequent vocalization of the Decalogue. In the poetical books, the Pesukim mentioned in the Talmud correspond to the poetical lines, not to our modern verses; and it is probable both from some expressions of Jerome, and from the analogous practice of other nations, that the poetical text was written stichometrically. It is still so written in our manuscripts in the poetical pieces in the Pentateuch and historical books; and even, generally, in our oldest manuscripts. Its partial discontinuance may be due, first to the desire to save space, and secondly to the diminution of the necessity for it by the introduction of the accents.

Of the documents which directly bear upon the history of the Hebrew text, the two earliest are the Samaritan copy of the Pentateuch, and the Greek translation of the LXX. For the latter we must refer to the article SEPTUAGINT: of the former some account will here be necessary. Mention had been made of the Samaritan Pentateuch, and, incidentally, of some of its peculiarities, by several of the Christian Fathers. Eusebius had taken note of its primeval chronology: Jerome had recorded its insertions in Gen. iv. 6; Deut. xxvii. 26: Procopius of Gaza had referred to its containing, at Num. x. 10 and Ex. xviii. 24, the words afterwards found in Deut. i. 6, v. 9: it had also been spoken of by Cyril of Alexandria, Diodore, and others. When in the 17th century Samaritan MSS. were imported into Europe by P. della Valle and Abp. Ussher, according with the representations that the Fathers had given, the very numerous variations between the Samaritan and the Jewish Pentateuch could not but excite attention; and it became thenceforward a matter of controversy among scholars which copy was entitled to the greater respect. The coördinate authority of both was advocated by Kennicott, who, however, in order to uphold the credit of the former, defended, in the celebrated passage Deut. xxvii. 4, the Samaritan reading Gerizim against the Jewish reading Ebal, charging corruption of the text upon the Jews rather than the Samaritans. A full examination of the readings of the Samaritan Pentateuch was at length made by Gesenius in 1815. His conclusions, fatal to its credit, have obtained general acceptance: nor have they been substantially shaken by the attack of a writer in the *Journal of Sacred Lit.* for July 1853; whose leading principle, that transcribers are more liable to omit than to add, is fundamentally unsound. Gesenius ranges the Samaritan variations from the Jewish Pentateuch under the following heads: grammatical corrections; glosses received into the text; conjectural emendations of difficult passages; corrections derived from parallel passages; larger interpolations derived from parallel passages; alterations made to remove what was offensive to Samaritan feelings; alterations to suit the Samaritan idiom; and alterations to suit the Samaritan theology, interpretation, and worship. It is doubtful whether even the grains of gold which he thought to find amongst the rubbish really exist; and the Samaritan readings which he was disposed to prefer in Gen. iv. 18, xiv. 14, xxii. 13, xlix. 14, will hardly approve themselves generally. The really remarkable feature respecting the Samaritan Pentateuch is its accordance with the Septuagint in more than a thousand places where it differs from the Jewish; being mostly those where either a gloss has been introduced into the text, or a difficult reading corrected for an easier, or the prefix ן added or removed. On the other hand, there are about as many places where the Septuagint supports the Jewish text

against the Samaritan; and some in which the Septuagint stands alone, the Samaritan either agreeing or disagreeing with the Jewish. Gesenius and others suppose that the Septuagint and the Samaritan text were derived from Jewish MSS. of a different recension to that which afterwards obtained public authority in Palestine, and that the Samaritan copy was itself subsequently further altered and interpolated. It is at least equally probable that both the Greek translators and the Samaritan copyists made use of MSS. with a large number of traditional marginal glosses and annotations, which they embodied in their own texts at discretion. As to the origin of the existence of the Pentateuch among the Samaritans, it was probably introduced thither when Manasseh and other Jewish priests passed over into Samaria, and contemporarily with the building of the temple on Mount Gerizim. Hengstenberg contends for this on the ground that the Samaritans were entirely of heathen origin, and that their subsequent religion was derived from Judæa (*Genuineness of Pent.* vol. i.): the same conclusion is reached also, though on very different grounds, by Gesenius, De Wette, and Bleek. To the hypothesis that the Pentateuch was perpetuated to the Samaritans from the Israelites of the kingdom of the ten tribes, and still more to another, that being of Israelitish origin they first became acquainted with it under Josiah, there is the objection, besides what has been urged by Hengstenberg. that no trace appears of the reception among them of the writings of the Israelitish prophets Hosea, Amos, and Jonah, which yet Josiah would so naturally circulate with the Pentateuch, in order to bring the remnant of his northern countrymen to repentance.

While such freedom in dealing with the sacred text was exercised at Samaria and Alexandria, there is every reason to believe that in Palestine the text was both carefully preserved and scrupulously respected. The boast of Josephus (*c. Apion,* i. 8), that through all the ages that had passed none had ventured to add to or to take away from, or to transpose aught of the sacred writings, may well represent the spirit in which in his day his own countrymen acted. In the translations of Aquila and the other Greek interpreters, the fragments of whose works remain to us in the Hexapla, we have evidence of the existence of a text differing but little from our own: so also in the Targums of Onkelos and Jonathan. A few centuries later we have, in the Hexapla, additional evidence to the same effect in Origen's transcriptions of the Hebrew text. And yet more important are the proofs of the firm establishment of the text, and of its substantial identity with our own, supplied by the translation of Jerome, who was instructed by the Palestinian Jews, and mainly relied upon their authority for acquaintance not only with the text itself, but also with the traditional unwritten vocalization of it.

This brings us to the middle of the Talmudic period. The learning of the schools which had been formed in Jerusalem about the time of our Saviour by Hillel and Shammai was preserved, after the destruction of the city, in the academies of Jabneh, Sepphoris, Cæsarea, and Tiberias. The great pillar of the Jewish literature of this period was R. Judah the Holy, to whom is ascribed the compilation of the Mishna, the text of the Talmud, and who died about A. D. 220. After his death there grew into repute the Jewish academies of

Sura, Nahardea, and Pum-Beditha, on the Euphrates. The twofold Gemara, or commentary, was now appended to the Mishna, thus completing the Talmud. The Jerusalem Gemara proceeded from the Jews of Tiberias, probably towards the end of the 4th century: the Babylonian from the academies on the Euphrates, perhaps by the end of the 5th. That along with the task of collecting and commenting on their various legal traditions, the Jews of these several academies would occupy themselves with the text of the sacred writings is in every way probable; and is indeed shown by various Talmudic notices.

In these the first thing to be remarked is the entire absence of allusion to any such glosses of interpretation as those which, from having been previously noted on the margins of MSS., had probably been loosely incorporated into the Samaritan Pentateuch and the Septuagint. Interpretation, properly so called, had become the province of the Targumist, not of the transcriber; and the result of the entire divorce of the task of interpretation from that of transcription had been to obtain greater security for the transmission of the text in its purity. In place, however, of such glosses of interpretation had crept in the more childish practice of reading some passages differently to the way in which they were written, in order to obtain a play of words, or to fix them artificially in the memory. Hence the formula אל תקרא כן אלא כן, "Read not so, but so." In other cases it was sought by arbitrary modifications of words to embody in them some casuistical rule. Hence the formula יש אם למקרא, יש אם למסרת, "There is ground for the traditional, there is ground for the textual reading" (Hupfeld, in Stud. und Kritiken, 1830, p. 55 ff.). But these traditional and confessedly apocryphal readings were not allowed to affect the written text. The care of the Talmudic doctors for the text is shown by the pains with which they counted up the number of verses in the different books, and computed which were the middle verses, words, and letters in the Pentateuch and in the Psalms. These last they distinguished by the employment of a larger letter, or by raising the letter above the rest of the text: see Lev. xi. 42; Ps. lxxx. 14 (Kiddushin, fol. 30, 1; Buxtorf's Tiberias, c. viii.). Such was the origin of these unusual letters: mystical meanings were, however, as we learn from the Talmud itself (Baba Bathra, fol. 109, 2), afterwards attached to them. These may have given rise to a multiplication of them, and we cannot therefore be certain that all had in the first instance a critical significance.

Another Talmudic notice relating to the sacred text furnishes the four following remarks (Nedarim, fol. 37, 2; Buxt. Tib. c. viii.):—

מקרא סופרים, "Reading of the scribes;" referring to the words מצרים, שמים, ארץ.

עיטור סופרים, "Rejection of the scribes;" referring to the omission of a ו prefix before the word אחר in Gen. xviii. 5, xxiv. 55; Num. xxxi. 2, and before certain other words in Ps. lxviii. 26, xxxvi. 6. It is worthy of notice that the two passages of Genesis are among those in which the

Septuagint and Samaritan agree in supplying ו against the authority of the present Hebrew text. In Num. xxxi. 2, the present Hebrew text, the Septuagint, and the Samaritan, all have it.

קריין ולא כתיבן, "Read but not written;" referring to something which ought to be read, although not in the text, in 2 Sam. viii. 3, xvi. 23; Jer. xxxi. 38, l. 29; Ruth ii. 11, iii. 5, 17. The omission is still indicated by the Masoretic notes in every place but Ruth ii. 11; and is supplied by the Septuagint in every place but 2 Sam. xvi. 23.

כתיבן ולא קריין, "Written but not read;" referring to something which ought in reading to be omitted from the text in 2 K. v. 18; Deut. vi. 1; Jer. li. 3; Ez. xlviii. 16; Ruth iii. 12. The Masoretic notes direct the omission in every place but Deut. vi. 1: the Septuagint preserves the word there, and in 2 K. v. 18, but omits it in the other three passages. In these last, an addition had apparently crept into the text from error of transcription. In Jer. li. 3, the word ידרך, in Ez. xlviii. 16, the word חמש had been accidentally repeated: in Ruth iii. 12, כי אם had been repeated from the preceding כי אמנם.

Of these four remarks, then, the last two,—there seems scarcely room for doubt, point to errors which the Jews had discovered, or believed to have discovered, in their copies of the text, but which they were yet generally unwilling to correct in their future copies, and which accordingly, although stigmatized, have descended to us. A like observation will apply to the Talmudic notices of the readings still indicated by the Masoretic Keris in Job xiii. 15; Hag. i. 8 (Sotah, v. 5; Yoma, fol. 21, 2). The scrupulousness with which the Talmudists thus noted what they deemed the truer readings, and yet abstained from introducing them into the text, indicates at once both the diligence with which they scrutinized the text, and also the care with which, even while acknowledging its occasional imperfections, they guarded it. Critical procedure is also evinced in a mention of their rejection of manuscripts which were found not to agree with others in their readings (Taanith Hierosol. fol. 68, 1); and the rules given with reference to the transcription and adoption of manuscripts attest the care bestowed upon them (Shabbath, fol. 103, 2; Gittin, fol. 45, 2). The "Rejection of the scribes" mentioned above, may perhaps relate to certain minute rectifications which the scribes had ventured, not necessarily without critical authority, to make in the actual written text. Wähner, however, who is followed by Hävernick and Keil, maintains that it relates to rectifications of the popular manner in which the text was read. And for this there is some ground in the circumstance that the "Reading of the scribes" bears apparently merely upon the vocalization, probably the pausal vocalization, with which the words ארץ, etc., were to be pronounced.

The Talmud further makes mention of the euphemistic Keris, which are still noted in our Bibles, e. g. at 2 K. vi. 25 (Megillah, fol. 25, 2). It also reckons six instances of extraordinary points placed over certain words, e. g. at Gen. xviii. 9 (Tr. Sopher. vi. 3); and of some of them it furnishes mystical explanations (Buxtorf, *Tib.* c. xvii.). The Masorah enumerates fifteen. They are noticed by Jerome, *Quæst. in Gen.* xviii. 35 [xix. 33]. They seem to have been originally designed as marks of the supposed spuriousness of certain words or letters. But in many cases the ancient versions uphold the genuineness of the words so stigmatized.

It is after the Talmudic period that Hupfeld places the introduction into the text of the two large points (in Hebrew סוֹף פָּסוּק, *Soph-pasuk*) to mark the end of each verse. They are manifestly of older date than the accents, by which they are, in effect, supplemented (*Stud. und Krit.* 1837, p. 857). Coeval, perhaps, with the use of the *Soph-pasuk* is that of the *Makkeph*, or hyphen, to unite words that are so closely conjoined as to have but one accent between them. It must be older than the accentual marks, the presence or absence of which is determined by it. It doubtless indicates the way in which the text was traditionally read, and therefore embodies traditional authority for the conjunction or separation of words. Internal evidence shows this to be the case in such passages as Ps. xlv. 5, וַעֲנָוָה־צֶדֶק. But the use of it cannot be relied on, as it often in the poetical books conflicts with the rhythm; *e. g.* in Ps. xix. 9. 10 (cf. Mason and Bernard's *Grammar*, ii. 187).

Such modifications of the text as these were the precursors of the new method of dealing with it which constitutes the work of the Masoretic period. It is evident from the notices of the Talmud that a number of oral traditions had been gradually accumulating respecting both the integrity of particular passages of the text itself, and also the manner in which it was to be read. The time at length arrived when it became desirable to secure the permanence of all such traditions by committing them to writing. The very process of collecting them would add greatly to their number; the traditions of various academies would be superadded the one upon the other; and with these would be gradually incorporated the various critical observations of the collectors themselves, and the results of their comparisons of different manuscripts. The vast heterogeneous mass of traditions and criticisms thus compiled and embodied in writing, forms what is known as the מָסֹרָה, *Masorah, i. e.* Tradition. A similar name had been applied in the Mishna to the oral tradition before it was committed to writing, where it had been described as the hedge or fence, סְיָג, of the Law (*Pirke Aboth,* iii. 13).

Buxtorf, in his *Tiberias,* which is devoted to an account of the Masorah, ranges its contents under the three heads of observations respecting the verses, words, and letters of the sacred text. In regard of the verses, the Masorets recorded how many there were in each book, and the middle verse in each: also how many verses began with particular letters, or began and ended with the same word, or contained a particular number of words and letters, or particular words a certain number of times, etc. In regard of the words, they recorded the Keris and Chethibs, where different words were to be read from those contained in the text, or where words were to be omitted or supplied. They noted that certain words were to

be found so many times in the beginning, middle, or end of a verse, or with a particular construction or meaning. They noted also of particular words, and this especially in cases where mistakes in transcription were likely to arise, whether they were to be written *plene* or *defective, i. e.* with or without the *matres lectionis:* also their vocalization and accentuation, and how many times they occurred so vocalized and accented. In regard of the letters, they computed how often each letter of the alphabet occurred in the O. T.: they noted fifteen instances of letters stigmatized with the extraordinary points: they commented also on all the unusual letters, namely, the *majusculæ,* which they variously computed; the *minusculæ,* of which they reckoned thirty-three; the *suspensæ,* four in number; and the *inversæ,* of which, the letter being in each case נ, there are eight or nine.

. The compilation of the Masorah did not meet with universal approval among the Jews, of whom some regretted the consequent cessation of oral traditions. Others condemned the frivolous character of many of its remarks. The formation of the written Masorah may have extended from the sixth or seventh to the tenth or eleventh century. It is essentially an incomplete work; and the labors of the Jewish doctors upon the sacred text might have unendingly furnished materials for the enlargement of the older traditions, the preservation of which had been the primary object in view. Nor must it be implicitly relied on. Its computations of the number of letters in the Bible are said to be far from correct; and its observations, as is remarked by Jacob ben Chaim, do not always agree with those of the Talmud, nor yet with each other; though we have no means of distinguishing between its earlier and its later portions.

The most valuable feature of the Masorah is undoubtedly its collection of Keris. The first rudiments of this collection meet us in the Talmud. Of those subsequently collected, it is probable that many were derived from the collation of MSS., others from the unsupported judgment of the Masorets themselves. They often rested on plausible but superficial grounds, originating in the desire to substitute an easier for a more difficult reading; and to us it is of little consequence whether it were a transcriber or a Masoretic doctor by whom the substitution was first suggested. It seems clear that the Keris in all cases represent the readings which the Masorets themselves approved as correct; but there would be the less hesitation in sanctioning them when it was assumed that they would be always preserved in documents separate from the text, and that the written text itself would remain intact. In effect, however, our MSS. often exhibit the text with the Keri readings incorporated. The number of Keris is, according to Elias Levita, who spent twenty years in the study of the Masorah, 848; but the Bomberg Bible contains 1,171, the Plantin Bible 793. Two lists of the Keris — the one exhibiting the variations of the printed Bibles with respect to them, the other distributing them into classes — are given in the beginning of Walton's Polyglot, vol. vi.

The Masorah furnishes also eighteen instances of what it calls תִּקּוּן סוֹפְרִים, "Correction of the scribes." The real import of this is doubtful; but the recent view of Bleek, that it relates to alterations made in the text by the scribes, because of something there offensive to them, and that therefore the rejected reading is in each case the true reading, is not borne out by the Septuagint, which in all the instances save one (Job vii. 20) confirms the present Masoretic text.

Furthermore the Masorah contains certain סבירין, "Conjectures," which it does not raise to the dignity of Keris, respecting the true reading in difficult passages. Thus at Gen. xix. 23, for יצא was conjectured יצאה, because the word שמש is usually feminine.

The Masorah was originally preserved in distinct books by itself. A plan then arose of transferring it to the margins of the MSS. of the Bible. For this purpose large curtailments were necessary; and various transcribers inserted in their margins only as much as they had room for, or strove to give it an ornamental character by reducing it into fanciful shapes. R. Jacob ben Chaim, editor of the Bomberg Bible, complains much of the confusion into which it had fallen; and the service which he rendered in bringing it into order is honorably acknowledged by Buxtorf. Further improvements in the arrangement of it were made by Buxtorf himself in his Rabbinical Bible. The Masorah is now distinguished into the *Masora magna* and the *Masora parva*, the latter being an abridgment of the former, and including all the Keris and other compendious observations, and being usually printed in Hebrew Bibles at the foot of the page. The *Masora magna*, when accompanying the Bible, is disposed partly at the side of the text, against the passages to which its several observations refer, partly at the end, where the observations are ranged in alphabetical order: it is thus divided into the *Masora textualis* and the *Masora finalis.*

The Masorah itself was but one of the fruits of the labors of the Jewish doctors in the Masoretic period. A far more important work was the furnishing of the text with vowel-marks, by which the traditional pronunciation of it was imperishably recorded. That the insertion of the Hebrew vowel-points was post-Talmudic is shown by the absence from the Talmud of all reference to them. Jerome also, in recording the true pronunciation of any word, speaks only of the way in which it was *read*; and occasionally mentions the ambiguity arising from the variety of words represented by the same letter (Hupfeld, *Stud. und Krit.* 1830, p. 549 ff.). The system was gradually elaborated, having been moulded in the first instance in imitation of the Arabian, which was itself the daughter of the Syrian. (So Hupfeld. Ewald maintains the Hebrew system to have been derived immediately from the Syrian.) The history of the Syrian and Arabian vocalization renders it probable that the elaboration of the system commenced not earlier than the seventh or eighth century. The vowel-marks are referred to in the Masorah; and as they are all mentioned by R. Judah Chiug, in the beginning of the eleventh century, they must have been perfected before that date. The Spanish Rabbis of the eleventh and twelfth centuries knew nought of their recent origin. That the system of punctuation with which we are familiar was

fashioned in Palestine is shown by its difference from the Assyrian or Persian system displayed in one of the eastern MSS. collated by Pinner at Odessa; of which more hereafter.

Contemporaneous with the written vocalization was the accentuation of the text. The import of the accents was, as Hupfeld has shown, essentially rhythmical (*Stud. und Krit.* 1837): hence they had from the first both a logical and musical significance. In respect of the former they were called מעמים, "senses;" in respect of the latter, נגינות, "tones." Like the vowel-marks, they are mentioned in the Masorah, but not in the Talmud.

The controversies of the sixteenth century respecting the late origin of the vowel-marks and accents are well known. Both are with the Jews the authoritative exponents of the manner in which the text is to be read: "Any interpretation," says Aben Ezra, "which is not in accordance with the arrangement of the accents, thou shalt not consent to it, nor listen to it." If in the books of Job, Psalms, and Proverbs, the accents are held by some Jewish scholars to be irregularly placed,[a] the explanation is probably that in those books the rhythm of the poetry has afforded the means of testing the value of the accentuation, and has consequently disclosed its occasional imperfections. Making allowance for these, we must yet on the whole admire the marvelous correctness, in the Hebrew Bible, of both the vocalization and accentuation. The difficulties which both occasionally present, and which a superficial criticism would, by overriding them, so easily remove, furnish the best evidence that both faithfully embody not the private judgments of the punctuators, but the traditions which had descended to them from previous generations.

Besides the evidences of various readings contained in the Keris of the Masorah, we have two lists of different readings purporting or presumed to be those adopted by the Palestinian and Babylonian Jews respectively. Both are given in Walton's Polyglot, vol. vi.

The first of these was printed by R. Jacob ben Chaim in the Bomberg Bible edited by him, without any mention of the source whence he had derived it. The different readings are 216 in number: all relate to the consonants, except two, which relate to the Mappik in the ה. They are generally of but little importance: many of the differences are orthographical, many identical with those indicated by the Keris and Chethibs. The list does not extend to the Pentateuch. It is supposed to be ancient, but post-Talmudic.

The other is the result of a collation of MSS. made in the eleventh century by two Jews, R. Aaron ben Asher, a Palestinian, and R. Jacob ben Naphtali, a Babylonian. The differences, 864 in number, relate to the vowels, the accents, the Makkeph, and in one instance (Cant. viii. 6) to the division of one word into two. The list helps to furnish evidence of the date by which the punctuation and accentuation of the text must have been completed. The readings of our MSS. commonly accord with those of Ben Asher.

It is possible that even the separate Jewish academies may in some instances have had their own

j Mason and Bernard's *Grammar*, ii. 235. The system of accentuation in these books is peculiar; but it will doubtless repay study no less than that in the

other books. The latest expositions of it are by Bär, a Jewish scholar, appended to vol. ii. of Delitzsch's *Comm. on the Psalter;* and by A. B. Davidson, 1861.

distinctive standard texts. Traces of minor variations between the standards of the two Babylonian academies of Sura and Nahardea are mentioned by De Rossi, *Prideg.* § 35.

From the end, however, of the Masoretic period onward, the Masorah became the great authority by which the text given in all the Jewish MSS. was settled. It may thus be said that all our MSS. are Masoretic: those of older date were either suffered to perish, or, as some think, were intentionally consigned to destruction as incorrect. Various standard copies are mentioned by the Jews, by which, in the subsequent transcriptions, their MSS. were tested and corrected, but of which none are now known. Such were the Codex Hillel in Spain; the Codex Ægyptius, or Hierosolymitanus, of Ben Asher; and the Codex Babylonius of Ben Naphtali. Of the Pentateuch there were the Codex Sinaiticus, of which the authority stood high in regard of its accentuation; and the Codex Hierichuntinus, which was valued in regard of its use of the *matres lectionis;* also the Codex Ezra, or Azarah, at Toledo, ransomed from the Black Prince for a large sum at his capture of the city in 1367, but destroyed in a subsequent siege (Scott Porter, *Princ. of Text. Crit.* p. 74).

2. *Manuscripts.* — We must now give an account of the O. T. MSS. known to us. They fall into two main classes: Synagogue-rolls and MSS. for private use. Of the latter, some are written in the square, others in the rabbinic or cursive character.

The synagogue-rolls contain, separate from each other, the Pentateuch, the Haphtaroth, or appointed sections of the Prophets, and the so-called Megilloth, namely, Canticles, Ruth, Lamentations, Ecclesiastes, and Esther. The text of the synagogue-rolls is written without vowels, accents, or sophpasuks: the greater parshioth are not distinguished, nor yet, strictly, the verses; these last are indeed often slightly separated, but the practice is against the ancient tradition. The prescribed rules respecting both the preparation of the skin or parchment for these rolls, and the ceremonies with which they are to be written, are exceedingly minute; and, though superstitious, have probably greatly contributed to the preservation of the text in its integrity. They are given in the Tract Sopherim, a later appendage to the Babylonian Talmud. The two modifications of the square character in which these rolls are written are distinguished by the Jews as the Tam and the Welsh, *i. e.* probably, the Perfect and the Foreign: the former is the older angular writing of the German and Polish, the latter the more modern round writing of the Spanish MSS. These rolls are not sold; and those in Christian possession are supposed by some to be mainly those rejected from synagogue use as vitiated.

Private MSS. in the square character are in the book-form, either on parchment or on paper, and of various sizes, from folio to 12mo. Some contain the Hebrew text alone; others add the Targum, or an Arabic or other translation, either interspersed with the text or in a separate column, occasionally in the margin. The upper and lower margins are generally occupied by the Masorah, sometimes by rabbinical commentaries, etc.; the outer margin, when not filled with a commentary, is used for corrections, miscellaneous observations, etc.; the inner margin for the Masora parva. The text marks all the distinctions of sections and verses which are wanting in the synagogue-rolls. These copies ordinarily passed through several hands in their prepa-

ration: one wrote the consonants; another supplied the vowels and accents, which are generally in a fainter ink; another revised the copy; another added the Masorah, etc. Even when the same person performed more than one of these tasks, the consonants and vowels were always written separately.

The date of a MS. is ordinarily given in the subscription; but as the subscriptions are often concealed in the Masorah or elsewhere, it is occasionally difficult to find them: occasionally also it is difficult to decipher them. Even when found and deciphered, they cannot always be relied on. Subscriptions were liable to be altered or supplied from the desire to impart to the MS. the value either of antiquity or of newness. For example, the subscription of the MS. Bible in the University Library at Cambridge (Kenn. No. 89), which greatly puzzled Kennicott, has now been shown by Zunz (*Zur Gesch. und Lit.* p. 214) to assign the MS. to the year A. D. 856; yet both Kennicott and Bruns agree that it is not older than the 13th century; and De Rossi too pronounces, from the form of the Masorah, against its antiquity. No satisfactory criteria have been yet established by which the ages of MSS. are to be determined. Those that have been relied on by some are by others deemed of little value. Few existing MSS. are supposed to be older than the 12th century. Kennicott and Bruns assigned one of their collation (No. 590) to the 10th century; De Rossi dates it A. D. 1018; on the other hand, one of his own (No. 634) he adjudges to the 8th century.

It is usual to distinguish in these MS. three modifications of the square character: namely, a Spanish writing, upright and regularly formed; a German, inclined and sharp-pointed; and a French and Italian, intermediate to the two preceding. Yet the character of the writing is not accounted a decisive criterion of the country to which a MS. belongs; nor indeed are the criteria of country much more definitely settled than those of age. One important distinction between the Spanish and German MSS. consists in the difference of order in which the books are generally arranged. The former follow the Masorah, placing the Chronicles before the rest of the Hagiographa; the latter conform to the Talmud, placing Jeremiah and Ezekiel before Isaiah, and Ruth, separate from the other Megilloth, before the Psalms. The other characteristics of Spanish MSS., which are accounted the most valuable, are thus given by Bruns: They are written with paler ink; their pages are seldom divided into three columns; the Psalms are arranged stichometrically; the Targum is not interspersed with the text, but assigned to a separate column; words are not divided between two lines; initial and unusual letters are eschewed, so also figures, ornaments, and flourishes; the parshioth are indicated in the margin rather than in the text; books are separated by a space of four lines, but do not end with a חזק; the letters are dressed to the upper guiding-line rather than the lower; Rapheh is employed frequently, Metheg and Mappik seldom.

Private MSS. in the rabbinic character. are mostly on paper, and are of comparatively late date. They are written with many abbreviations, and have no vowel-points or Masorah, but are occasionally accompanied by an Arabic version.

In computing the number of known MSS., it must be borne in mind that by far the greater part contain only portions of the Bible. Of the 581

Jewish MSS. collated by Kennicott, not more than 102 give the O. T. complete: with those of De Rossi the case is similar. In Kennicott's volumes the MSS. used for each book are distinctly enumerated at the end of the book. The number collated by Kennicott and De Rossi together were, for the book of Genesis 490; for the Megilloth, collectively, 549; for the Psalms, 495; for Ezra, and Nehemiah, 172; and for the Chronicles, 211. MS. authority is most plenteous for the book of Esther, least so for those of Ezra and Nehemiah.

Since the days of Kennicott and De Rossi modern research has discovered various MSS. beyond the limits of Europe. Of many of these there seems no reason to suppose that they will add much to our knowledge of the Hebrew text. Those found in China are not essentially different in character to the MSS. previously known in Europe: that brought by Buchanan from Malabar is now supposed to be a European roll. It is different with the MSS. examined by Pinner at Odessa, described by him in the *Prospectus der Odessaer Gesellschaft für Gesch. und Alt. gehörenden ältesten heb. und rabb. MSS.* One of these MSS. (A. No. 1), a Pentateuch roll, unpointed, brought from Derbend in Daghestan, appears by the subscription to have been written previously to the year A. D. 580; and, if so, is the oldest known Biblical Hebrew MS. in existence. It is written in accordance with the rules of the Masorah, but the number of the letters are remarkable. Another MS. (B. No. 3) containing the Prophets, on parchment, in small folio, although only dating, according to the inscription, from A. D. 916, and furnished with a Masorah, is a yet greater treasure. Its vowels and accents are wholly different from those now in use, both in form and in position, being all above the letters: they have accordingly been the theme of much discussion among Hebrew scholars. The form of the letters is here also remarkable. A fac-simile has been given by Pinner of the book of Habakkuk from this MS. The same peculiarities are wholly or partially repeated in some of the other Odessa MSS. Various readings from the texts of these MSS. are instanced by Pinner: those of B. No. 3 he has set forth at some length, and speaks of as of great importance, and as entitled to considerable attention on account of the correctness of the MS.: little use has however been made of them.

The Samaritan MSS. collated by Kennicott are all in the book-form, though the Samaritans, like the Jews, make use of rolls in their synagogues. They have no vowel-points or accents, and their diacritical signs and marks of division are peculiar to themselves. The unusual letters of the Jewish MSS. are also unknown in them. They are written on vellum or paper, and are not supposed to be of any great antiquity. This is, however, of little importance, as they sufficiently represent the Samaritan text.

3. *Printed Text.* — The history of the printed text of the Hebrew Bible commences with the early Jewish editions of the separate books. First appeared the Psalter, in 1477, probably at Bologna, in 4to, with Kimchi's commentary interspersed among the verses. Only the first four psalms had the vowel-points, and these but clumsily expressed. The text was far from correct, and the *matres lectionis* were inserted or omitted at pleasure. At Bologna there subsequently appeared, in 1482, the Pentateuch, in folio, pointed, with the Targum and the commentary of Jarchi, and the five Megilloth

(Ruth - Esther), in folio, with the commentaries of Jarchi and Aben Ezra. The text of the Pentateuch is reputed highly correct. From Soncino, near Cremona, issued in 1486 the Prophetæ Priores (Joshua - Kings), folio, unpointed, with Kimchi's commentary: of this the Prophetæ Posteriores (Isaiah - Malachi), also with Kimchi's commentary, was probably the continuation. The Megilloth were also printed, along with the prayers of the Italian Jews, at the same place and date, in 4to. Next year, 1487, the whole Hagiographa, pointed, but unaccentuated, with rabbinical commentaries, appeared at Naples, in either small fol. or large 4to, 2 vols. Thus every separate portion of the Bible was in print before any complete edition of the whole appeared.

The honor of printing the first entire Hebrew Bible belongs to the above-mentioned town of Soncino. The edition is in folio, pointed and accentuated. Nine copies only of it are now known, of which one belongs to Exeter College, Oxford. The earlier printed portions were perhaps the basis of the text. This was followed, in 1494, by the 4to or 8vo edition printed by Gersom at Brescia, remarkable as being the edition from which Luther's German translation was made. It has many peculiar readings, and instead of giving the Keris in the margin, incorporates them generally in the text, which is therefore not to be depended upon. The unusual letters also are not distinguished. This edition, along with the preceding, formed the basis of the first edition, with the Masorah, Targums, and rabbinical comments, printed by Bomberg at Venice in 1518, fol. under the editorship of the converted Jew Felix del Prato; though the "plurimis collatis exemplaribus" of the editor seems to imply that MSS. were also used in aid. This edition was the first to contain the Masora magna, and the various readings of Ben Asher and Ben Naphtali. On the Brescian text depended also, in greater or less degree, Bomberg's smaller Bibles, 4to, of 1518, 1521. From the same text, or from the equivalent text of Bomberg's first Rabbinical Bible, was, at a subsequent period, mainly derived that of Seb. Münster, printed by Froben at Basle, 4to, 1534–35: which is valued, however, as containing a list of various readings which must have been collected by a Jewish editor, and, in part, from MSS.

After the Brescian, the next primary edition was that contained in the Complutensian Polyglot, published at Complutum (Alcala) in Spain, at the expense of Cardinal Ximenes, dated 1514–17, but not issued till 1522. The whole work, 6 vols. fol., is said to have cost 50,000 ducats: its original price was 61 ducats, its present value about 40½. The Hebrew, Vulgate, and Greek texts of the O. T. (the latter with a Latin translation) appear in three parallel columns: the Targum of Onkelos, with a Latin translation, is in two columns below. The Hebrew is pointed, but unaccentuated: it was taken from seven MSS., which are still preserved in the University Library at Madrid.

To this succeeded an edition which has had more influence than any on the text of later times — the Second Rabbinical Bible, printed by Bomberg at Venice, 4 vols. fol. 1525–56. The editor was the learned Tunisian Jew, R. Jacob ben Chaim; a Latin translation of his preface will be found in Kennicott's Second Dissertation, p. 229 ff. The great feature of his work lay in the correction of the text by the precepts of the Masorah, in which he was profoundly skilled, and on which, as well as on the text itself, his labors were employed. Bomberg's Third Rabbinical Bible, 4 vols. fol. 1547-49, edited by Adelkind, was in the main a reprint of the preceding. Errors were, however, corrected, and some of the rabbinical commentaries were replaced by others. The same text substantially reappeared in the Rabbinical Bibles of John de Gara, Venice, 4 vols. fol. 1568, and of Bragadini, Venice, 4 vols. fol. 1617-18; also in the later 4to Bibles of Bomberg himself, 1528, 1533, 1544; and in those of R. Stephens, Paris, 4to, 1539-44 (so Opitz and Bleek: others represent this as following the Brescian text); R. Stephens, Paris, 16mo, 1544-46; Justiniani, Venice, 4to, 1551, 18mo, 1552, 4to, 1563, 4to, 1573; De la Rouviere, Geneva, various sizes, 1618; De Gara, Venice, various sizes, 1566, 1568, 1582; Bragadini, Venice, various sizes, 1614, 1615, 1619, 1628; Plantin, Antwerp, various sizes, 1566; Hartmann, Frankfort-on-Oder, various sizes, 1595, 1598; and Crato (Kraft), Wittemberg, 4to, 1586.

The Royal or Antwerp Polyglot, printed by Plantin, 8 vols. fol. 1569-72, at the expense of Philip II. of Spain, and edited by Arias Montanus and others, took the Complutensian as the basis of its Hebrew text, but compared this with one of Bomberg's, so as to produce a mixture of the two. This text was followed both in the Paris Polyglot of Le Jay, 9 vols. fol. 1645, and in Walton's Polyglot, London, 6 vols. fol. 1657. The printing of the text in the Paris Polyglot is said to be very incorrect. The same text appeared also in Plantin's later Bibles, with Latin translations, fol. 1571, 1584; and in various other Hebrew-Latin Bibles: Burgos, fol. 1581; Geneva, fol. 1609, 1618; Leyden, 8vo, 1613; Frankfort-on-Maine (by Knoch), fol. 1631; Vienna, 8vo, 1743; in the quadrilingual Polyglot of Reineccius, Leipsic, 3 vols. fol. 1750-51; and also in the same editor's earlier 8vo Bible, Leipsic, 1725, for which, however, he professes to have compared MSS.

A text compounded of several of the preceding was issued by the Leipsic professor, Elias Hutter, at Hamburg, fol. 1587: it was intended for students, the servile letters being distinguished from the radicals by hollow type. This was reprinted in his uncompleted Polyglot, Nuremberg, fol. 1591, and by Nissel, 8vo, 1662. A special mention is also due to the labors of the elder Buxtorf, who carefully revised the text after the Masorah, publishing it in 8vo at Basle, 1611, and again, after a fresh revision, in his valuable Rabbinical Bible, Basle, 2 vols. fol. 1618-19. This text was also reprinted at Amsterdam, 8vo, 1639, by R. Manasseh ben Israel, who had previously issued, in 1631, 1635. a text of his own with arbitrary grammatical alterations.

Neither the text of Hutter nor that of Buxtorf was without its permanent influence; but the Hebrew Bible which became the standard to subsequent generations was that of Joseph Athias, a learned rabbi and printer at Amsterdam. His text was based on a comparison of the previous editions with two MSS.; one bearing date 1299; the other a Spanish MS., boasting an antiquity of 900 years. It appeared at Amsterdam, 2 vols. 8vo, 1661, with a preface by Leusden, professor at Utrecht; and again, revised afresh, in 1667. These Bibles were much prized for their beauty and correctness; and a gold chain and medal were conferred on Athias, in token of their appreciation of them, by the States General of Holland. The progeny of the

text of Athias was as follows: (a.) That of Clodius, Frankfort-on-Maine, 8vo, 1677, reprinted, with alterations, 8vo, 1692, 4to, 1716. (b.) That of Jablonsky, Berlin, large 8vo or 4to, 1699; reprinted, but less correctly, 12mo, 1712. Jablonsky collated all the cardinal editions, together with several MSS., and bestowed particular care on the vowel-points and accents. (c.) That of Van der Hooght, Amsterdam and Utrecht, 2 vols. 8vo, 1705. This edition, of good reputation for its accuracy, but above all for the beauty and distinctness of its type, deserves special attention, as constituting our present textus receptus. The text was chiefly formed on that of Athias: no MSS. were used for it, but it has a collection of various readings from printed editions at the end. The Masoretic readings are in the margin. (d.) That of Opitz, Kiel, 4to, 1709, very accurate: the text of Athias was corrected by comparing seventeen printed editions and some MSS. (e.) That of J. H. Michaelis, Halle, 8vo and 4to, 1720. It was based on Jablonsky: twenty-four editions and five Erfurt MSS. were collated for it, but, as has been found, not thoroughly. Still the edition is much esteemed, partly for its correctness, and partly for its notes and parallel references. Davidson pronounces it superior to Van der Hooght's in every respect except legibility and beauty of type.

These editions show that on the whole the text was by this time firmly and permanently established. We may well regard it as a providential circumstance that, having been early conformed by Ben Chaim to the Masorah, the printed text should in the course of the next two hundred years have acquired in this its Masoretic form, a sacredness which the subsequent labors of a more extended criticism could not venture to contemn. Whatever errors, and those by no means unimportant, such wider criticism may lead us to detect in it, the grounds of the corrections which even the most cautious critics would adopt are often too precarious to enable us, in departing from the Masoretic, to obtain any other satisfactory standard; while in practice the mischief that would have ensued from the introduction into the text of the emendations of Houbigant and the critics of his school would have been the occasion of incalculable and irreparable harm. From all such it has been happily preserved free; and while we are far from deeming its authority absolute, we yet value it, because all experience has taught us that, in seeking to remodel it, we should be introducing into it worse imperfections than those which we desire to remove, while we should lose that which is, after all, no light advantage, a definite textual standard universally accepted by Christians and Jews alike. So essentially different is the treatment demanded by the text of the Old Testament and by that of the New.

The modern editions of the Hebrew Bible now in use are all based on Van der Hooght. The earliest of these was that of Simonis, Halle, 1752, and more correctly 1767; reprinted 1822, 1828. In England the most popular edition is the sterling one by Judah D'Allemand, 8vo, of high repute for correctness: there is also the pocket edition of Bagster, on which the same editor was employed. In Germany there are the 8vo edition of Hahn; the 12mo edition, based on the last, with preface by Rosenmüller (said by Keil to contain some conjectural alterations of the text by Landschreiber); and the 8vo edition of Theile.

4. *Critical Labors and Apparatus.* — The ne-

tory of the criticism of the text has already been brought down to the period of the labors of the Masorets and their immediate successors. It must be here resumed. In the early part of the 13th century, R. Meir Levita, a native of Burgos and inhabitant of Toledo, known by abbreviation as Haramah, by patronymic as Todrosius, wrote a critical work on the Pentateuch called *The Book of the Masorah the Hedge of the Law*, in which he endeavored, by a collation of MSS., to ascertain the true reading in various passages. This work was of high repute among the Jews, though it long remained in manuscript: it was eventually printed at Florence in 1750; again, incorrectly, at Berlin, 1761. At a later period R. Menahem de Lonzano collated ten MSS., chiefly Spanish, some of them five or six centuries old, with Bomberg's 4to Bible of 1544. The results were given in the work אוֹר תּוֹרָה, "Light of the Law," printed in the שְׁתֵּי יָדוֹת, Venice, 1618, afterwards by itself, but less accurately, Amsterdam, 1659. They relate only to the Pentateuch. A more important work was that of R. Solomon Norzi of Mantua, in the 17th century, גּוֹדֵר פֶּרֶץ, "Repairer of the Breach:" a copious critical commentary on the whole of the O. T., drawn up with the aid of MSS. and editions, of the Masorah, Talmud, and all other Jewish resources within his reach. In the Pentateuch he relied much on Todrosius: with R. Menahem he had had personal intercourse. His work was first printed, 116 years after its completion, by a rich Jewish physician, Raphael Chaim, Mantua, 4 vols. 4to, 1742, under the title מִנְחַת שַׁי: the emendations on Proverbs and Job alone had appeared in the margin of a Mantuan edition of those books in 1725. The whole was reprinted in a Vienna O. T., 4to, 1813-16.

Meanwhile various causes, such as the controversies awakened by the Samaritan text of the Pentateuch, and the advances which had been made in N. T. criticism, had contributed to direct the attention of Christian scholars to the importance of a more extended criticism of the Hebrew text of the O. T. In 1745 the expectations of the public were raised by the *Prolegomena* of Houbigant, of the Oratory at Paris; and in 1753 his edition appeared, splendidly printed, in 4 vols. fol. The text was that of Van der Hooght, divested of points, and of every vestige of the Masorah, which Houbigant, though he used it, rated at a very low value. In the notes copious emendations were introduced. They were derived — (a) from the Samaritan Pentateuch, which Houbigant preferred in many respects to the Jewish; (b) from twelve Hebrew MSS., which, however, do not appear to have been regularly collated, their readings being chiefly given in those passages where they supported the editor's emendations; (c) from the Septuagint and other ancient versions; and (d) from an extensive appliance of critical conjecture. An accompanying Latin translation embodied all the emendations adopted. The notes were reprinted at Frankfort-on-Maine, 2 vols. 4to, 1777: they constitute the cream of the original volumes, the splendor of which was disproportionate to their value, as they contained no materials besides those on which the editor directly rested. The whole work was indeed too ambitious: its canons of criticism were thoroughly unsound, and its ventures

rash. Yet its merits were also considerable: and the newness of the path which Houbigant was essaying may be pleaded in extenuation of its faults. It effectually broke the Masoretic coat of ice wherewith the Hebrew text had been incrusted; but it afforded also a severe warning of the difficulty of finding any sure standing-ground beneath.

In the same year, 1753, appeared at Oxford Kennicott's first Dissertation on the state of the Printed Text: the second followed in 1759. The result of these and of the author's subsequent annual reports was a subscription of nearly £10,000 to defray the expenses of a collation of Hebrew MSS. throughout Europe, which was performed from 1760 to 1769, partly by Kennicott himself, but chiefly, under his direction, by Professor Bruns of Helmstadt and others. The collation extended in all to 581 Jewish and 16 Samaritan MSS., and 40 printed editions, Jewish works, etc.; of which, however, only about half were collated throughout, the rest in select passages. The fruits appeared at Oxford in 2 vols. fol. 1776-80: the text is Van der Hooght's, unpointed; the various readings are given below; comparisons are also made of the Jewish and Samaritan texts of the Pentateuch, and of the parallel passages in Samuel and Chronicles, etc. They much disappointed the expectations that had been raised. It was found that a very large part of the various readings had reference simply to the omission or insertion of the *matres lectionis;* while of the rest many obviously represented no more than the mistakes of separate transcribers. Happily for the permanent interests of criticism this had not been anticipated. Kennicott's own weakness of judgment may also have made him less aware of the smallness of the immediate results to follow from his persevering toil; and thus a Herculean task, which in the present state of critical knowledge could scarcely be undertaken, was providentially, once for all, performed with a thoroughness for which, to the end of time, we may well be thankful.

The labors of Kennicott were supplemented by those of De Rossi, professor at Parma. His plan differed materially from Kennicott's: he confined himself to a specification of the various readings in select passages; but for these he supplied also the critical evidence to be obtained from the ancient versions, and from all the various Jewish authorities. In regard of manuscript resources, he collected in his own library 1,031 MSS., more than Kennicott had collated in all Europe: of these he collated 617, some being those which Kennicott had collated before: he collated also 134 extraneous MSS. that had escaped Kennicott's fellow-laborers; and he recapitulated Kennicott's own various readings. The readings of the various printed editions were also well examined. Thus, for the passages on which it treats, the evidence in De Rossi's work may be regarded as almost complete. It does not contain the text. It was published at Parma, 4 vols. 4to, 1784-88: an additional volume appeared in 1798.

A small Bible, with the text of Reineccius, and a selection of the more important readings of Kennicott and De Rossi, was issued by Doederlein and Meisner at Leipsic, 8vo, 1793. It is printed (except some copies) on bad paper, and is reputed very incorrect. A better critical edition is that of Jahn, Vienna, 4 vols. 8vo, 1806. The text is Van der Hooght's, corrected in nine or ten places: the more important various readings are subjoined.

with the authorities, and full information is given. But, with injudicious peculiarity, the books are arranged in a new order; those of Chronicles are split up into fragments, for the purpose of comparison with the parallel books; and only the principal accents are retained.

The first attempt to turn the new critical collations to public account was made by Boothroyd, in his unpointed Bible, with various readings and English notes, Pontefract, 4to, 1810–16, at a time when Houbigant's principles were still in the ascendant. This was followed in 1821 by Hamilton's *Codex Criticus*, modeled on the plan of the N. T. of Griesbach, which is, however, hardly adapted to the O. T., in the criticism of the text of which diplomatic evidence is of so much less weight than in the case of the N. T. The most important contribution towards the formation of a revised text that has yet appeared is unquestionably Dr. Dr. **son's** *Hebrew Text of the O. T., revised from critical Sources*, 1855. It presents a convenient epitome of the more important various readings of the MSS. and of the Masorah, with the authorities for them; and in the emendations of the text which he sanctions, when there is any Jewish authority for the emendation, he shows on the whole a fair judgment. But he ventures on few emendations for which there is no direct Jewish authority, and seems to have practically fallen into the error of disparaging the critical aid to be derived from the ancient versions, as much as it had by the critics of the last century been unduly exalted.

It must be confessed that little has yet been done for the systematic criticism of the Hebrew text from the ancient versions, in comparison of what might be accomplished. We have even yet to learn what critical treasures those versions really contain. They have, of course, at the cost of much private labor, been freely used by individual scholars, but the texts implied in them have never yet been fairly exhibited or analyzed, so as to enable the literary world generally to form any just estimate of their real value. The readings involved in their renderings are in Houbigant's volumes only adduced when they support the emendations which he desired to advance. By De Rossi they are treated merely as subsidiary to the MSS., and are therefore only adduced for the passages to which his manuscript collations refer. Nor have Boothroyd's or Davidson's treatment of them any pretensions whatever to completeness. Should it be alleged that they have given all the *important* version-readings, it may be at once replied that such is not the case, nor indeed does it seem possible to decide *primâ facie* of any version-reading whether it be important or not: many have doubtless been passed over again and again as unimportant, which yet either are genuine readings or contain the elements of them. Were the whole of the Septuagint variations from the Hebrew text lucidly exhibited in Hebrew, they would in all probability serve to suggest the true reading in many passages in which it has not yet been recovered; and no better service could be rendered to the cause of textual criticism by any scholar who would undertake the labor. Skill, scholarship, and patience would be required in deciphering many of the Hebrew readings which the Septuagint represents, and in cases of uncertainty that uncertainty should be noted. For the books of Samuel the task has been grappled with, appar-

ently with care, by Thenius in the *Exegetisches Handbuch;* but the readings are not conveniently exhibited, being given partly in the body of the commentary, partly at the end of the volume. For the Psalms we have Reinke's *Kurze Zusammenstellung aller Abweichungen vom heb. Texte in der Ps. übersetzung der LXX. und Vulg.*, etc.; but the criticism of the Hebrew text was not the author's direct object.

It might be well, too, if along with the version-readings were collected together all, or at least all the more important, conjectural emendations of the Hebrew text proposed by various scholars during the last hundred years, which at present lie buried in their several commentaries and other publications. For of these, also, it is only when they are so exhibited as to invite an extensive and simultaneous criticism that any true general estimate will be formed of their worth, or that the pearls among them, whether few or many, will become of any general service. That by far the greater number of them will be found beside the mark we may at once admit; but obscurity, or an unpopular name, or other cause, has probably withheld attention from many suggestions of real value.

5. *Principles of Criticism.* — The method of procedure required in the criticism of the O. T. is widely different from that practiced in the criticism of the N. T. Our O. T. textus receptus is a far more faithful representation of the genuine Scripture, nor could we on any account afford to part with it; but, on the other hand, the means of detecting and correcting the errors contained in it are more precarious, the results are more uncertain, and the ratio borne by the value of the diplomatic evidence of MSS. to that of a good critical judgment and sagacity is greatly diminished.

It is indeed to the direct testimony of the MSS. that, in endeavoring to establish the true text, we must first have recourse. Against the general consent of the MSS. a reading of the textus receptus, merely as such, can have no weight. Where the MSS. disagree, it has been laid down as a canon that we ought not to let the mere numerical majority preponderate, but should examine what is the reading of the earliest and best. This is no doubt theoretically correct, but it has not been generally carried out: nor, while so much remains to be done for the ancient versions, must we clamor too loudly for the expenditure, in the sifting of MSS., of the immense labor which the task would involve; for internal evidence can alone decide which MSS. are entitled to greatest authority, and the researches of any single critic into their relative value could not be relied on till checked by the corresponding researches of others, and in such researches few competent persons are likely to engage. While, however, we content ourselves with judging of the testimony of the MSS. to any particular reading by the number sanctioning that reading, we must remember to estimate not the absolute number, but the relative number to the whole number of MSS. collated for that passage. The circumstance that only half of Kennicott's MSS., and none of De Rossi's, were collated throughout, as also that the number of MSS. greatly varies for different books of the O. T., makes attention to this important. Davidson, in his *Revision of the Heb. Text*, has gone by the absolute number, which he should only have done when that number was very small.

The MSS. lead us for the most part only to our

first sure standing-ground, the Masoretic text; in other words, to the average written text of a period later by a thousand or fifteen hundred years than the latest book of the O. T. It is possible, however, that in particular MSS. pre-Masoretic readings may be incidentally preserved. Hence isolated MS. readings may serve to confirm those of the ancient versions.

In ascending upwards from the Masoretic text, our first critical materials are the Masoretic Keris, valuable as witnesses to the preservation of many authentic readings, but on which it is impossible to place any degree of reliance, because we can never be certain, in particular instances, that they represent more than mere unauthorized conjectures. A Keri therefore is not to be received in preference to a Chethib unless confirmed by other sufficient evidence, external or internal; and in reference to the Keris let the rule be borne in mind, "Proclivi scriptioni præstat ardua," many of them being but arbitrary softenings down of difficult readings in the genuine text. It is furthermore to be observed, that when the reading of any number of MSS. agrees, as is frequently the case, with a Masoretic Keri, the existence of such a Keri may be a damage rather than otherwise to the weight of the testimony of those MSS., for it may itself be the untrustworthy source whence their reading originated.

The express assertions of the Masorah, as also of the Targum, respecting the true reading in particular passages, are of course important: they indicate the views entertained by the Jews at a period prior to that at which our oldest MSS. were made.

From these we ascend to the version of Jerome, the most thoroughly trustworthy authority on which we have to rely in our endeavors to amend the Masoretic text. Dependent as Jerome was, for his knowledge of the Hebrew text and everything respecting it, on the Palestinian Jews, and accurate as are his renderings, it is not too much to say that a Hebrew reading which can be shown to have been received by Jerome, should, if sanctioned or countenanced by the Targum, be so far preferred to one upheld by the united testimony of all MSS. whatever. And in general we may definitely make out the reading which Jerome followed. There are, no doubt, exceptions. Few would think of placing much reliance on any translation as to the presence or absence of a simple ‎ו‎ copular in the original text. Again in Psalm cxliv. 2, where the authority of Jerome and of other translators is alleged for the reading ‎עַמִּים‎, "peoples," while the great majority of MSS. give ‎עַמִּי‎, "my people," we cannot be certain that he did not really read ‎עַמִּי‎, regarding it, although wrongly, as an apocopated plural. Hence the precaution necessary in bringing the evidence of a version to bear upon the text: when used with such precaution, the version of Jerome will be found of the very greatest service.

Of the other versions, although more ancient, none can on the whole be reckoned, in a critical point of view, so valuable as his. Of the Greek versions of Aquila, Symmachus, and Theodotion, we possess but mere fragments. The Syriac bears the impress of having been made too much under the influence of the Septuagint. The Targums are too often paraphrastic. For a detailed account of them the reader is referred to the various articles [VERSIONS, etc.]. Still they all furnish most important material for the correction of the Masoretic text; and their cumulative evidence, when they all concur in a reading different to that which it contains, is very strong.

The Septuagint itself, venerable for its antiquity, but on various accounts untrustworthy in the readings which it represents, must be treated for critical purposes in the same way as the Masoretic Keris. It doubtless contains many authentic readings of the Hebrew text not otherwise preserved to us; but, on the other hand, the presence of any Hebrew reading in it can pass for little, unless it can be independently shown to be probable that that reading is the true one. It may, however, suggest the true reading, and it may confirm it where supported by other considerations. Such, for example, is the case with the almost certain correction of ‎רַחֲמֵךְ‎, "shall keep holyday to thee," for ‎רַחֲבֵר‎, "thou shalt restrain," in Psalm lxxvi. 10. In the opposite direction of confirming a Masoretic reading against which later testimonies militate, the authority of the Septuagint, on account of its age, necessarily stands high.

Similar remarks would, à priori, seem to apply to the critical use of the Samaritan Pentateuch: it is, however, doubtful whether that document be of any real additional value.

In the case of the O. T., unlike that of the N. T., another source of emendations is generally allowed, namely, critical conjecture. Had we any reason for believing that, at the date of the first translation of the O. T. into Greek, the Hebrew text had been preserved immaculate, we might well abstain from venturing on any emendations for which no direct external warrant could be found; but the Septuagint version is nearly two centuries younger than the latest book of the O. T.; and as the history of the Hebrew text seems to show that the care with which its purity has been guarded has been continually on the increase, so we must infer that it is just in the earliest periods that the few corruptions which it has sustained would be most likely to accrue. Few enough they may be; but, if analogy may be trusted, they cannot be altogether imaginary. And thus arises the necessity of admitting, besides the emendations suggested by the MSS. and versions, those also which originate in the simple skill and honest ingenuity of the critic; of whom, however, while according him this license, we demand in return that he shall bear in mind the sole legitimate object of his investigations, and that he shall not obtrude upon us any conjectural reading, the genuineness of which he cannot fairly establish by circumstantial evidence. What that circumstantial evidence shall be it is impossible to define beforehand: it is enough that it be such as shall, when produced, bring some conviction to a reasoning mind.

There are cases in which the Septuagint will supply an indirect warrant for the reception of a reading which it nevertheless does not directly sanction: thus in Ez. xli. 11, where the present text has the meaningless word ‎מָקוֹם‎, "place," while the Septuagint inappropriately reads ‎מָאוֹר‎, "light," there arises a strong presumption that both readings are equally corruptions of ‎מָקוֹר‎, "fountain," referring to a water-gallery running along the walls of the Temple exactly in the position described in the Talmud. An indirect testimony of this kind may be even more conclusive than a direct testimony, inasmuch as no suspicion of design can attach to it. In Is. ix. 3, where the text, as emended by Professor Selwyn in his *Horæ Hebraicæ*, runs הרבית הגיל הגדלת השמחה, "Thou hast multiplied the gladness, thou hast increased the joy," one confirmation of the correctness of the proposed reading is well traced by him in the circumstance of the final ל of the second and the initial ה of the third word furnish the לה, "to it," implied in the פ of the Septuagint, and according with the assumed feminine noun הרבית, τὸ πλεῖστον, or with מרביה or הרבית which was substituted for it. (see this fully brought out, *Hor. Heb.* pp. 32 ff.).

It is frequently held that much may be drawn from parallel passages towards the correction of portions of the Hebrew text; and it may well be allowed that in the historical books, and especially in catalogues, etc., the texts of two parallel passages throw considerable light the one upon the other. Kennicott commenced his critical dissertations by a detailed comparison of the text of 1 Chr. xi. with that of 2 Sam. v., xxiii.; and the comparison brought to light some corruptions which cannot be gainsaid. On the other hand, in the poetical and prophetical books, and to a certain extent in the whole of the O. T., critical reliance on the texts of parallel passages is attended with much danger. It was the practice of the Hebrew writers, in revising former productions, or in borrowing the language to which others had given utterance, to make comparatively minute alterations, which seem at first sight to be due to mere carelessness, but which nevertheless, when exhibited together, cannot well be attributed to aught but design. We have a striking instance of this in the two recensions of the same hymn (both probably Davidic) in Ps. xviii. and 2 Sam. xxii. Again, Ps. lxxxvi. 14 is imitated from Ps. liv. 3, with the alteration of זרים, "strangers," into זדים, "proud." A headlong critic would naturally assimilate the two passages, yet the general purport of the two psalms makes it probable that each word is correct in its own place. Similarly Jer. xlviii. 45, is derived from Num. xxi. 28, xxiv. 17; the alterations throughout are curious, but especially at the end, where for וקרקר כל-בני-שת, "and destroy all the children of Sheth," we have וקדקד בני שאון, "and the crown of the head of the children of tumult;" yet no suspicion legitimately attaches to the text of either passage. From such instances, the caution needful in making use of parallels will be at once evident.

The comparative purity of the Hebrew text is probably different in different parts of the O. T. In the revision of Dr. Davidson, who has generally restricted himself to the admission of corrections warranted by MS., Masoretic, or Talmudic authority, those in the book of Genesis do not exceed 11; those in the Psalms are proportionately three times

as numerous: those in the historical books and the Prophets are proportionately more numerous than those in the Psalms. When our criticism takes a wider range, it is especially in the less familiar parts of Scripture that the indications of corruption present themselves before us. In some of these the Septuagint version has been made to render important service; in the genealogies, the errors which have been insisted on are for the most part found in the Septuagint as well as in the Hebrew, and are therefore of older date than the execution of the Septuagint. It has been maintained by Keil, and perhaps with truth (*Apol. Versuch über die Bücher der Chronik*, pp. 185, 295), that many of these are older than the sacred books themselves, and had crept into the documents which the authors incorporated, as they found them, into those books. This remark will not, however, apply to all; nor, as we have already observed, is there any ground for supposing that the period immediately succeeding the production of the last of the canonical writings was one during which those writings would be preserved perfectly immaculate. If Lord A. Hervey be right in his rectification of the genealogy in 1 Chr. iii. 19 ff. (*On the Geneal.* pp. 98–110), the interpolation at the beginning of ver. 22 must be due to some transcriber of the book of Chronicles; and a like observation will apply to the present text of 1 Chr. ii. 6, respecting which see Thrupp's *Introd. to the Psalms*, ii. 98, note.

In all emendations of the text, whether made with the aid of the critical materials which we possess, or by critical conjecture, it is essential that the proposed reading be one from which the existing reading may have been derived; hence the necessity of attention to the means by which corruptions were introduced into the text. One letter was accidentally exchanged by a transcriber for another: thus in Is. xxiv. 15, בארים may perhaps be a corruption for באיים (so Lowth). In the square alphabet the letters ד and ר, ו and י, were especially liable to be confused; there were also similarities between particular letters in the older alphabet. Words, or parts of words, were repeated (cf. the Talmudic detections of this, *supra*; similar is the mistake of "so no now" for "so now" in a modern English Bible); or they were dropped, and this especially when they ended like those that preceded, e. g. יואל after שמואל (1 Chr. vi. 13). A whole passage seems to have dropped out from the same cause in 1 Chr. xi. 13 (cf. Kennicott, *Diss.* i. 128 ff.). Occasionally a letter may have travelled from one word, or a word from one verse, to another; hence in Hos. vi. 5, ומשפטיך אור has been supposed by various critics (and so Selwyn, *Hor. Heb.* pp. 154 ff.), and that with the sanction of all the versions except Jerome's, to be a corruption for ומשפטי כאור. This is one of those cases where it is difficult to decide on the true reading; the emendation is highly probable, but at the same time too obvious not to excite suspicion; a scrupulous critic, like Maurer, rejects it. There can be little doubt that we ought to reject the proposed emendations of Ps. xlii. 5, 6, by the transference of אלהי into ver. 5, or by the supply of it in that verse, in order to assimilate it to ver. 11 and to Ps. xliii. 5. Had the verses in so familiar a psalm been originally alike, it is almost incredible that any transcriber should have rendered them different. With greater probability in Gen. xxvii. 33, Hitzig (*Begriff der Kritik*, p. 126) takes the final יהיה, and, altering it into והיה, transfers it into ver. 34, making the preceding word the infinitive. That glosses have occasionally found their way into the text we may well believe. The words הוא בידם in Is. x. 5 have much the appearance of being a gloss explanatory of מטה (Hitzig, *Begr*. pp. 157, 158), though the verse can be well construed without their removal; and that Deut. x. 6, 7, have crept into the text by some illegitimate means, seems, notwithstanding Hengstenberg's defense of them (*Gen. of Pent.* ii.), all but certain.

Willful corruption of the text on polemical grounds has also been occasionally charged upon the Jews; but the allegation has not been proved, and their known reverence for the text militates against it. More trustworthy is the negative bearing of that hostility of the Jews against the Christians, which, even in reference to the Scriptures, has certainly existed; and it may be fairly argued that if Aquila, who was employed by the Jews as a translator on polemical grounds, had ever heard of the modern reading כארי, "as a lion," in Ps. xxii. 17 (16), he would have been too glad to follow it, instead of translating כארו, "they pierced," by ὤρυξαν.

To the criticism of the vowel-marks the same general principles must be applied, *mutatis mutandis*, as to that of the consonants. Nothing can be more remote from the truth than the notion that we are at liberty to supply vowels to the text at our unfettered discretion. Even Hitzig, who does not generally err on the side of caution, holds that the vowel-marks have in general been rightly fixed by tradition, and that other than the Masoretic vowels are seldom required, except when the consonants have been first changed (*Begr*. p. 119).

In conclusion, let the reader of this or any article on the method of dealing with errors in the text beware of drawing from it the impression of a general corruptness of the text which does not really exist. The works of Biblical scholars have been on the whole more disfigured than adorned by the emendations of the Hebrew text which they have suggested; and the cautions by which the more prudent have endeavored to guard against the abuse of the license of emending, are, even when critically unsound, so far commendable, that they show a healthy respect for the Masoretic text which might with advantage have been more generally felt. It is difficult to reduce to formal rules the treatment which the text of the O. T. should receive, but the general spirit of it might thus be given: Deem the Masoretic text worthy of confidence, but do not refuse any emendations of it which can be fairly established: of such judge by the evidence adduced in their support, when advanced, not by any supposed previous necessity for them, respecting which the most erroneous views have been frequently entertained; and, lastly, remember that the judgment of the many will correct that of the few, the judgment of future generations that of the present, and that permanent neglect generally awaits emendations which approve

themselves by their brilliancy rather than by their soundness. (See generally Walton's *Prolegomena*, Kennicott's *Dissertatio Generalis*; De Rossi's *Prolegomena*; Bp. Marsh's *Lectures*; Davidson's *Bib. Criticism*, vol. i.; and the *Introductions* of Horne and Davidson, of De Wette, Hävernick, Keil, and Bleek.)

B. — INTERPRETATION OF THE OLD TESTAMENT.

1. History of the Interpretation. — We shall here endeavor to present a brief but comprehensive sketch of the treatment which the Scriptures of the O. T. have in different ages received.

At the period of the rise of Christianity two opposite tendencies had manifested themselves in the interpretation of them among the Jews; the one to an extreme literalism, the other to an arbitrary allegorism. The former of these was mainly developed in Palestine, where the Law of Moses was, from the nature of things, most completely observed. The Jewish teachers, acknowledging the obligation of that law in its minutest precepts, but overlooking the moral principles on which those precepts were founded and which they should have unfolded from them, there endeavored to supply by other means the imperfections inherent in every law in its mere literal acceptation. They added to the number of the existing precepts, they defined more minutely the method of their observance; and thus practically further obscured, and in many instances overthrew the inward spirit of the law by new outward traditions of their own (Matt. xv., xxiii.). On the other hand at Alexandria the allegorizing tendency prevailed. Germs of it had appeared in the apocryphal writings, as where in the book of Wisdom (xviii. 24) the priestly vestments of Aaron had been treated as symbolical of the universe. It had been fostered by Aristobulus, the author of the Ἐξηγήσεις τῆς Μωϋσέως γραφῆς, quoted by Clement and Eusebius; and at length, two centuries later, it culminated in Philo, from whose works we best gather the form which it assumed. For in the general principles of interpretation which Philo adopted, he was but following, as he himself assures us, in the track which had been previously marked out by those, probably the Therapeutæ, under whom he had studied. His expositions have chiefly reference to the writings of Moses, whom he regarded as the arch-prophet, the man initiated above all others into divine mysteries; and in the persons and things mentioned in these writings he traces, without denying the outward reality of the narrative, the mystical designations of different abstract qualities and aspects of the invisible. Thus the three angels who came to Abraham represent with him God in his essential being, in his beneficent power, and in his governing power. Abraham himself, in his dealings with Sarah and Hagar, represents the man who has an admiration for contemplation and knowledge: Sarah, the virtue which is such a man's legitimate partner: Hagar, the encyclical accomplishments of all kinds which serve as the handmaiden of virtue, the prerequisites for the attainment of the highest wisdom: her Egyptian origin sets forth that for the acquisition of this varied elementary knowledge the external senses of the body, of which Egypt is the symbol, are necessary. Such are Philo's interpretations. They are marked throughout by two fundamental defects. First, beautiful as are the moral lessons which he often unfolds, he yet shows no more appreciation than the Palestinian opponents of our Saviour of the moral teaching involved in the simpler acceptation of Scripture. And, secondly, his exposition is not the result of a legitimate drawing forth of the spiritual import which the Scripture contains, but of an endeavor to engraft the Gentile philosophy upon it. Of a Messiah, to whom the O. T. throughout spiritually pointed, Philo recked but little: the wisdom of Plato he contrives to find in every page. It was in fact his aim so to find it. The Alexandrian interpreters were striving to vindicate for the Hebrew Scriptures a new dignity in the eyes of the Gentile world, by showing that Moses had anticipated all the doctrines of the philosophers of Greece. Hence, with Aristobulus, Moses was an earlier Aristotle, with Philo, an earlier Plato. The Bible was with them a store-house of all the philosophy which they had really derived from other sources; and, in so treating it, they lost sight of the inspired theology, the revelation of God to man, which was its true and peculiar glory.

It must not be supposed that the Palestinian literalism and the Alexandrian allegorism ever remained entirely distinct. On the one hand, we find the Alexandrian Philo, in his treatise on the special laws, commending just such an observance of the letter and an infraction of the spirit of the prohibition to take God's name in vain, as our Saviour exposes and condemns in Matt. v. 33–37. On the other hand among the Palestinians, both the high-priest Eleazar (ap. Euseb. *Præp. Ev.* viii. 9), and at a later period the historian Josephus (*Ant. prooem.* 4), speak of the allegorical significance of the Mosaic writings in terms which lead us to suspect that their expositions of them, had they come down to us, would have been found to contain much that was arbitrary. And it is probable that traditional allegorical interpretations of the sacred writings were current among the Essenes. In fact the two extremes of literalism and arbitrary allegorism, in their neglect of the direct moral teaching and prophetical import of Scripture, had too much in common not to mingle readily the one with the other.

And thus we may trace the development of the two distinct yet coexistent spheres of Halachah and Hagadah, in which the Jewish interpretation of Scripture, as shown by the later Jewish writings, ranged. The former (הלכה, " repetition," "following") embraced the traditional legal determinations for practical observance: the latter (הגדה, " discourse ") the unrestrained interpretation, of no authentic force or immediate practical interest. Holding fast to the position for which, in theory, the Alexandrian allegorists had so strenuously contended, that all the treasures of wisdom and knowledge, including their own speculations, were virtually contained in the Sacred Law, the Jewish doctors proceeded to define the methods by which they were to be elicited from it. The meaning of Scripture was, according to them, either that openly expressed in the words (משמע, *sensus innatus*), or else that deduced from them (מדרש, דרשה, *sensus illatus*). The former was itself either literal, פשט, or figurative and mystical, סוד. The latter was partly obtained by simple logical inference; but partly also by the arbitrary detection of recondite meanings symbol-

ically indicated in the places, grammatical structure, or orthography of words taken apart from their logical context. This last was the cabalistic interpretation (קבלה, " reception," " received tradition "). Special mention is made of three processes by which it was pursued. By the process Gematria (גימטריא, *geometria*) a symbolical import was attached to the number of times that a word or letter occurred, or to the number which one or more letters of any word represented. By the process Notarjekon (נוטריקון, *notaricum*) new significant words were formed out of the initial or final words of the text, or else the letters of a word were constituted the initials of a new significant series of words. And in Temurah (תמורה, " change ") new significant words were obtained from the text either by anagram (e. g. משיח, " Messiah " from ישמח, Ps. xxi. 1), or by the alphabet Atbash, wherein the letters א, ב, etc., were replaced by ת, ש, etc. Of such artifices the sacred writers had possibly for special purposes made occasional use; but that they should have been ever applied by any school to the general exegesis of the O. T. shows only into what trifling even labors on Scripture may occasionally degenerate.

The earliest Christian non-apostolic treatment of the O. T. was necessarily much dependent on that which it had received from the Jews. The Alexandrian allegorism reappears the most fully in the fanciful epistle of Barnabas; but it influenced also the other writings of the sub-apostolic Fathers. Even the Jewish cabalism passed to some extent into the Christian Church, and is said to have been largely employed by the Gnostics (Iren. i. 3, 8, 16, ii. 24). But this was not to last. Irenæus, himself not altogether free from it, raised his voice against it; and Tertullian well laid it down as a canon that the words of Scripture were to be interpreted only in their logical connection, and with reference to the occasion on which they were uttered (*De Præscr. Hær.* 9). In another respect all was changed. The Christian interpreters by their belief in Christ stood on a vantage-ground for the comprehension of the whole burden of the O. T. to which the Jews had never reached; and thus however they may have erred in the details of their interpretations, they were generally conducted by them to the right conclusions in regard of Christian doctrine. It was through reading the O. T. prophecies that Justin had been converted to Christianity (*Dial. Tryph.* pp. 224, 225). The view held by the Christian Fathers that the whole doctrine of the N. T. had been virtually contained and foreshadowed in the Old, generally induced the search in the O. T. for such Christian doctrine rather than for the old philosophical dogmas. Thus we find Justin asserting his ability to prove by a careful enumeration that all the ordinances of Moses were types, symbols, and disclosures of those things which were to be realised in the Messiah (*Dial. Tryph.* p. 261). Their general convictions were doubtless here more correct than the details which they advanced; and it would be easy to multiply from the writings of either Justin, Tertullian, or Irenæus, typical interpretations that could no longer be defended. Yet even these were no unrestrained speculations: they were all designed to illustrate what was elsewhere unequivocally revealed, and were limited by the necessity of conforming in their results to the Catholic rule of faith, the tradition handed down in the Church from the Apostles (Tert. *De Præscr. Hær.* 13, 37; Iren. iv. 26). It was moreover laid down by Tertullian, that the language of the Prophets, although generally allegorical and figurative, was not always so (*De Res. Carnis,* 19); though we do not find in the early Fathers any canons of interpretation in this respect. A curious combination, as it must seem to us, of literal and spiritual interpretation meets us in Justin's exposition, in which he is not alone, of those prophecies which he explains of millennial blessings; for while he believes that it is the literal Jerusalem which will be restored in all her splendor for God's people to inhabit, he yet contends that it is the spiritual Israel, not the Jews, that will eventually dwell there (*Dial. Tryph.* pp. 306, 352). Both Justin and Irenæus upheld the historical reality of the events related in the O. T. narrative. Both also fell into the error of defending the less commendable proceedings of the patriarchs — as the polygamy of Jacob, and the incest of Lot — on the strength of the typical character assumedly attaching to them (Just. *Dial. Tryph.* pp. 364 ff.; Iren. v. 32 ff.).

It was at Alexandria, which through her previous learning had already exerted the deepest influence on the interpretation of the O. T., that definite principles of interpretation were by a new order of men, the most illustrious and influential teachers in the Christian Church, first laid down. Clement here led the way. He held that in the Jewish law a fourfold import was to be traced; literal, symbolical, moral, prophetical (*Strom.* i. c. 28). Of these the second, by which the persons and things mentioned in the law were treated as symbolical of the material and moral universe, was manifestly derived from no Christian source, but was rather the relic of the philosophical element that others had previously engrafted on the Hebrew Scriptures. The new gold had not yet shaken off the old alloy: and in practice it is to the symbolical class that the most objectionable of Clement's interpretations will be found to belong. Such are those which he repeats from the book of Wisdom and from Philo of the high-priest's garment, and of the relation of Sarah to Hagar; or that of the branches of the sacred candlestick, which he supposes to denote the sun and planets. Nor can we commend the proneness to allegorism which Clement everywhere displays, and which he would have defended by the mischievous distinction which he handed down to Origen between πίστις and γνῶσις, and by the doctrine that the literal sense leads only to a mere carnal faith, while for the higher Christian life the allegorical is necessary. Yet in Clement's recognition of a literal, a moral, and a prophetical import in the Law, we have the germs of the aspects in which the O. T. has been regarded by all subsequent ages; and his Christian treatment of the sacred oracles is shown by his acknowledging, equally with Tertullian and Irenæus, the rule of the tradition of the Lord as the key to their true interpretation (*Strom.* vii. c. 17).

Clement was succeeded by his scholar Origen. With him Biblical interpretation showed itself more decidedly Christian; and while the wisdom of the Egyptians, moulded anew, became the permanent inheritance of the Church, the distinctive symbolical meaning which philosophy had placed upon the O. T. disappeared. Origen's principles of interpretation are fully unfolded by him in the *De Princip.* iv. 11 ff. He recognises in Scripture, as it were, a body, soul, and spirit, answering to the body, soul, and spirit of man: the first serves for the edification of the simple, the second for that of the more advanced, the third for that of the perfect. The reality and the utility of the first, the letter of Scripture, he proves by the number of those whose faith is nurtured by it. The second, which is in fact the moral sense of Scripture, he illustrates by the interpretation of Deut. xxv. 4 in 1 Cor. ix. 9. The third, however, is that on which he principally dwells, showing how the Jewish Law, spiritually understood, contained a shadow of good things to come; and how the N. T. had recognized such a spiritual meaning not only in the narrative of Moses, and in his account of the tabernacle, but also in the historical narrative of the other books (1 Cor. x. 11; Gal. iv. 21–31; Heb. viii. 5; Rom. xi. 4, 5). In regard of what he calls the soul of Scripture, his views are, it must be owned, somewhat uncertain. His practice with reference to it seems to have been less commendable than his principles. It should have been the moral teaching of Scripture arising out of the literal sense applied in accordance with the rules of analogy; but the moral interpretations actually given by Origen are ordinarily little else than a series of allegorisms of moral tendency; and thus he is, unfortunately, more consistent with his own practice when he assigns to the moral exposition not the second but the third place, exalting it above the mystical or spiritual, and so removing it further from the literal (*Hom. in Gen.* ii. 6). Both the spiritual and (to use his own term) the psychical meaning be held to be always present in Scripture; the bodily not always. Alike in the history and the law, he found things inserted or expressions employed which could not be literally understood, and which were intended to direct us to the pursuit of a higher interpretation than the purely literal. Thus the immoral actions of the patriarchs were to him stumbling-blocks which he could only avoid by passing over the literal sense of the narrative, and tracing in it a spiritual sense distinct from the literal; though even here he seems to reject the latter not as untrue, but simply as profitless. For while he held the body of Scripture to be but the garment of its spirit, he yet acknowledged the things in Scripture which were literally true to be far more numerous than those which were not; and occasionally, where he found the latter tend to edifying, as for instance in the moral commandments of the Decalogue as distinguished from the ceremonial and therefore typical law, he deemed it needless to seek any allegorical meaning (*Hom. in Num.* xi. 1). Origen's own expositions of Scripture were, no doubt, less successful than his investigations of the principles on which it ought to be expounded. Yet as the appliances which he brought to the study of Scripture made him the father of Biblical criticism, so of all detailed Christian Scriptural commentaries his were the first; a fact not to be forgotten by those who would estimate aright their several merits and defects.

The labors of one genuine scholar became the inheritance of the next; and the value of Origen's researches was best appreciated, a century later, by Jerome. He adopted and repeated most of Origen's principles; but he exhibited more judgment in the practical application of them: he devoted more attention to the literal interpretation, the basis of the rest, and he brought also larger stores of learning to bear upon it. With Origen he held that Scripture was to be understood in a threefold manner, literally, tropologically,[a] mystically: the first meaning was the lowest, the last the highest (tom. v. p. 172, Vall.). But elsewhere he gave a new threefold division of Scriptural interpretation; identifying the ethical with the literal or first meaning, making the allegorical or spiritual meaning the second, and maintaining that, thirdly, Scripture was to be understood " secundum futurorum beatitudinem " (tom vi. p. 270). Interpretation of this last kind, vague and generally untenable as it is, was that denominated by succeeding writers the anagogical; a term which had been used by Origen as equivalent to spiritual (cf. De Princip. iv. 9), though the contrary has been maintained by writers familiar with the later distinction. Combining these two classifications given by Jerome of the various meanings of Scripture, we obtain the fourfold division which was current through the Middle Ages, and which has been perpetuated in the Romish Church down to recent times: —

" Littera gesta docet ; quid credas, Allegoria ;
Moralis quid agas ; quo tendas, Anagogia " —

and in which, it will be observed, in conformity with the practice rather than the precept of Origen, the moral or tropological interpretation is raised above the allegorical or spiritual.

The principles laid down by master-minds, notwithstanding the manifold lapses made in the application of them, necessarily exerted the deepest influence on all who were actually engaged in the work of interpretation. The influence of Origen's writings was supreme in the Greek Church for a hundred years after his death. Towards the end of the 4th century Diodore, bishop of Tarsus, previously a presbyter at Antioch, wrote an exposition of the whole of the O. T., attending only to the letter of Scripture, and rejecting the more spiritual interpretation known as θεωρία, the contemplation of things represented under an outward sign. He also wrote a work on the distinction between this last and allegory. Of the disciples of Diodore, Theodore of Mopsuestia pursued an exclusively grammatical interpretation into a decided rationalism, rejecting the greater part of the prophetical reference of the O. T., and maintaining it to be only applied to our Saviour by way of accommodation. Chrysostom, another disciple of Diodore, followed a sounder course, rejecting neither the literal nor the spiritual interpretation, but bringing out with much force from Scripture its moral lessons. He was followed by Theodoret, who interpreted both literally and historically, and also allegorically and prophetically. His commentaries display both diligence and soberness, and are uniformly instructive and pleasing: in some respects none are more valuable. Yet his mind was not of the highest order. He kept the historical and prophetical interpretations too widely apart, instead of making the one lean upon the other. Where historical illustration was abundant, he was content to rest in that, instead of finding in it larger help for pressing onward to the development of the

spiritus. seu. ve. So again wherever prophecy was literally fulfilled, he generally rested too much in the mere outward verification, not caring to inquire whether the literal fulfillment was not itself necessarily a type of something beyond. In the Canticles, however, where the language of Scripture is directly allegorical, he severely reprehends Theodore of Mopsuestia for imposing a historical interpretation upon it: even Diodore the literal interpreter, Theodore's master, had judged, as we learn from Theodoret, that that book was to be spiritually understood.

In the Western Church the influence of Origen, if not so unqualified at the first, was yet permanehtly greater than in the Eastern. Hilary of Poictiers is said by Jerome to have drawn largely from Origen in his Commentary on the Psalms. But in truth, as a practical interpreter, he greatly excelled Origen; carefully seeking out not what meaning the Scripture might bear, but what it really intended, and drawing forth the evangelical sense from the literal with cogency, terseness, and elegance. Here, too, Augustine stood somewhat in advance of Origen; carefully preserving in its integrity the literal sense of the historical narrative of Scripture as the substructure of the mystical, lest otherwise the latter should prove to be but a building in the air (Serm. 2, c. 6). It seems, therefore, to have been rather as a traditional maxim than as the expression of his own conviction, that he allowed that whatever in Scripture Had no proper or literal reference to honesty of manners, or to the truth of the faith, might by that be recognized as figurative (De Doctr. Chr. iii. 10). He fully acknowledges, however, that all, or nearly all, in the O. T. is to be taken not only literally but also figuratively (ibid. 22); and bids us earnestly beware of taking literally that which is figuratively spoken (ibid. 5). The fourfold classification of the interpretation of the O. T. which had been handed down to him, literal, aetiological, analogical, allegorical, is neither so definite nor so logical as Origen's (De Util. Cred. 2, 3; De Gen. ad Lit. lib. imp. 2): on the other hand neither are the rules of Tichonius, which he rejects, of much value. Still it is not so much by the accuracy of his principles of exposition as by what his expositions contain that he is had in honor. No more spiritually-minded interpreter ever lived. The main source of the blemishes by which his interpretations are disfigured, is his lack of acquaintance with Hebrew; a lack indeed far more painfully evident in the writings of the Latin Fathers than in those of the Greek. It was partly, no doubt, from a consciousness of his own shortcomings in this respect that Augustine urged the importance of such an acquaintance (De Doctr. Chr. ii. 11 ff.); rightly judging also that all the external scientific equipments of the interpreter of Scripture were not more important for the discovery of the literal than for that of the mystical meaning.

But whatever advances had been made in the treatment of O. T. Scripture by the Latins since the days of Origen were unhappily not perpetuated. We may see this in the Morals of Gregory on the Book of Job; the last great independent work of a Latin Father. Three senses of the sacred text are here recognized and pursued in separate threads;

---

[a] That is, morally. The term τροπολογία, which had in Justin and Origen denoted the doctrine of tropes, was perhaps first applied by Jerome to the

doctrine of manners ; in which sense it is also used by later Greek writers, as Andreas.

the historical and literal, the allegorical, and the moral. But the three have hardly any mutual connection: the very idea of such a connection is ignored. The allegorical interpretation is consequently entirely arbitrary; and the moral interpretation is, in conformity with the practice, not with the principles, of Origen, placed after the allegorical, so called, and is itself every whit as allegorical as the former. They differ only in their aims: that of the one is to set forth the history of Christ; that of the other to promote the edification of the Church by a reference of the language to the inward workings of the soul. No effort is made to apprehend the mutual relation of the different parts of the book, or the moral lessons which the course of the argument in that preëminently moral book was intended to bring out. Such was the general character of the interpretation which prevailed through the Middle Ages, during which Gregory's work stood in high repute. The mystical sense of Scripture was entirely divorced from the literal. Some guidance, however, in the paths of even the most arbitrary allegorism was found practically necessary; and this was obtained in the uniformity of the mystical sense attached to the several Scriptural terms. Hence the dictionary of the allegorical meanings — partly genuine, partly conventional — of Scriptural terms compiled in the 9th century by Rabanus Maurus. An exceptional value may attach to some of the mediæval comments on the O. T., as those of Rupert of Deutz († 1135); but in general even those which, like Gregory's Morals, are prized for their treasures of religious thought, have little worth as interpretations.

The first impulse to the new investigation of the literal meaning of the text of the O. T. came from the great Jewish commentators, mostly of Spanish origin, of the 11th and following centuries; Jarchi († 1105), Aben Ezra († 1167), Kimchi († 1240), and others. Following in the wake of these, the converted Jew Nicolaus of Lyra, near Evreux, in Normandy († 1341), produced his *Postillae Perpetuae* on the Bible, in which, without denying the deeper meanings of Scripture, he justly contended for the literal as that on which they all must rest. Exception was taken to these a century later by Paul of Burgos, also a converted Jew († 1435), who upheld, by the side of the literal, the traditional interpretations, to which he was probably at heart exclusively attached. But the very arguments by which he sought to vindicate them showed that the recognition of the value of the literal interpretation had taken firm root. The Restoration of Letters helped it forward. The Reformation contributed in many ways to unfold its importance; and the position of Luther with regard to it is embodied in his saying " Optimum grammaticum, eum etiam optimum theologum esse." That grammatical scholarship is not indeed the only qualification of a sound theologian, the German commentaries of the last hundred years have abundantly shown: yet where others have sown, the Church eventually reaps; and it would be ungrateful to close any historical sketch of the interpretation of the O. T. without acknowledging the immense service rendered to it by modern Germany, through the labors and learning alike of the disciples of the neologian school, and of those who have again reared aloft the banner of the faith.

In respect of the O. T. types, an important difference has prevailed among Protestant interpreters

between the adherents and opponents of that school which is usually, from one of the most eminent of its representatives, denominated the Coccian, and which practically, though perhaps unconsciously, trod much in the steps of the earlier Fathers, Justin, Irenæus, and Tertullian. Coccius, professor at Leyden († 1669), justly maintained that a typical meaning ran throughout the whole of the Jewish Scriptures; but his principle that Scripture signifies whatever it can signify (quicquid potest significare), as applied by him, opened the door for an almost boundless license of the interpreter's fancy. The arbitrariness of the Coccian interpretations provoked eventually a no less arbitrary reply; and, while the authority of the N. T. as to the existence of Scriptural types could not well be set aside, it became a common principle with the English theologians of the early part of the present century, that only those persons or things were to be admitted as typical which were so expressly interpreted in Scripture — or in the N. T. — itself. With sounder judgment, and not without considerable success, Fairbairn has of late years, in his Typology of Scripture, set the example of an investigation of the fundamental principles which govern the typical connection of the Old Testament with the New. See, for further information, J. G. Rosenmüller's contemptuous *Historia Interpretationis ab Apostolorum Ætate ad Literarum Instaurationem*, 5 vols. 1795–1814; Meyer's *Gesch. der Schrifterklärung seit der Wiederherstellung der Wissenschaften*, 5 vols. 1802–1809; Conybeare's *Bampton Lectures*, 1824; Olshausen's little tract, *Ein Wort über tiefern Schriftsinn*, 1824; Davidson's *Sacred Hermeneutics*, 1843, [and Diestel's *Gesch. d. A. T. in d. christl. Kirche*, 1869.]

2. *Principles of Interpretation.* — From the foregoing sketch it will have appeared that it has been very generally recognized that the interpretation of the O. T. embraces the discovery of its literal, moral, and spiritual meaning. It has given occasion to misrepresentation to speak of the existence in Scripture of more than a single sense: rather, then, let it be said that there are in it three elements, coexisting and coalescing with each other, and generally requiring each other's presence in order that they may be severally manifested. Correspondingly, too, there are three portions of the O. T. in which the respective elements, each in its turn, shine out with peculiar lustre. The literal (and historical) element is most obviously displayed in the historical narrative; the moral is specially honored in the Law, and in the hortatory addresses of the Prophets: the predictions of the Prophets bear emphatic witness to the prophetical or spiritual. Still, generally, in every portion of the O. T. the presence of all three elements may by the student of Scripture be traced. In perusing the story of the journey of the Israelites through the wilderness, he has the historical element in the actual occurrence of the facts narrated; the moral, in the warnings which God's dealings with the people and their own several disobediences convey; and the spiritual in the prefiguration by that journey, in its several features, of the Christian pilgrimage through the wilderness of life. In investigating the several ordinances of the Law relating to sacrifice, he has the historical element in the observances actually enjoined upon the Israelites; the moral in the personal unworthiness and self-surrender to God which those observances were designed to express, and which are themselves of universal interest; and the

spiritual in the prefiguration by those sacrifices of the one true sacrifice of Christ. In bending his eyes on the prophetical picture of the conqueror coming from Edom, with dyed garments from Bostrah, he has the historical element in the relations subsisting between the historical Edom and Israel, supplying the language through which the anticipations of triumph are expressed; the moral element in the assurance to all the persecuted of the condemnation of the unnatural malignity wherewith those nearest of kin to themselves may have exulted in their calamities; and the spiritual, in the prophecy of the loneliness of Christ's passion and of the gloriousness of his resurrection, in the strength of which, and with the signal of victory before her, the Church should trample down all spiritual foes beneath her feet. Yet again, in the greater number of the Psalms of David he has the historical element in those events of David's life which the language of the psalm reflects; the moral, in the moral connection between righteous faith and eventual deliverance by which it is pervaded; and the spiritual, in its fore-embodiment of the struggles of Christ, in whom it finds its essential and perfect fulfillment, and by her union with whom the Christian Church still claims and appropriates the psalm as her own. In all these cases it is requisite to the full interpretation of the O. T. that the so-called grammatico-historical,[a] the moral, and the spiritual interpretation should advance hand in hand: the moral interpretation presupposes the grammatico-historical, the spiritual rests on the two preceding. If the question be asked, Are the three several elements in the O. T. mutually coextensive? we reply, They are certainly coextensive in the O. T., taken as a whole, and in the several portions of it, largely viewed; yet not so as that they are all to be traced in each several section. The historical element may occasionally exist alone; for, however full a history may be of deeper meanings, there must also needs be found in it connecting links to hold the significant parts of it together: otherwise it sinks from a history into a mere succession of pictures. Not to cite doubtful instances, the genealogies, the details of the route through the wilderness and of the subsequent partition of the land of Canaan, the account of the war which was to furnish the occasion for God's providential dealings with Abraham and Lot (Gen. xiv. 1-12), are obvious and simple instances of such links. On the other hand there are passages of direct and simple moral exhortation, e. g. a considerable part of the book of Proverbs, into which the historical element hardly enters: the same is the case with Psalm i., which is, as it were, the moral preface to the psalms which follow, designed to call attention to the moral element which pervades them generally. Occcasionally also, as in Psalm ii., which is designed to bear witness of the prophetical import running through the Psalms, the prophetical element, though not altogether divorced from the historical and moral, yet completely overshadows them. It is moreover a maxim which cannot be too strongly enforced, that the historical, moral, or prophetical interest of a section of Scripture, or even of an entire book, may lie rather in the general tenor and result of the whole than in any number of separate passages: e. g. the

moral teaching of the book of Job lies preëminently not in the truths which the several speeches may contain, but in the great moral lesson to the unfolding of which they are all gradually working.

That we should use the New Testament as the key to the true meaning of the Old, and should seek to interpret the latter as it was interpreted by our Lord and his Apostles, is in accordance both with the spirit of what the earlier Fathers asserted respecting the value of the tradition received from them, and with the appeals to the N. T. by which Origen defended and fortified the threefold method of interpretation. But here it is the analogy of the N. T. interpretations that we must follow; for it were unreasonable to suppose that the whole of the Old Testament would be found completely interpreted in the New. Nor, provided only a spiritual meaning of the Old Testament be in the New sufficiently recognized, does it seem much more reasonable to expect every separate type to be there indicated or explained, or the fulfillment of every prophecy noted, than it would be to expect that the N. T. should unfold the historical importance or the moral lesson of every separate portion of the O. T. history. Why, indeed, should we assume that a full interpretation in any single respect of the older volume would be given in another of less than a quarter of its bulk, the primary design of which is not expository at all, and that when the use actually made of the former in the latter is in kind so manifold? The Apostles nowhere profess to give a systematic interpretation of the O. T. The nearest approach to any such is to be found in the explanation of the spiritual meaning of the Mosaic ritual in the Epistle to the Hebrews; and even here it is expressly declared that there are many things "of which we cannot now speak particularly" (ix. 5). We may well allow that the substance of all the O. T. shadows is in the N. T. contained, without holding that the several relations between the substance and the shadows are there in each case authoritatively traced.

With these preliminary observations we may glance at the several branches of the interpreter's task.

First, then, Scripture has its outward form or body, all the several details of which he will have to explore and to analyse. He must ascertain the thing outwardly asserted, commanded, foretold, prayed for, or the like; and this with reference, so far as is possible, to the historical occasion and circumstances, the time, the place, the political and social position, the manner of life, the surrounding influences, the distinctive character, and the object in view, alike of the writers, the persons addressed, and the persons who appear upon the scene. Taken in its wide sense, the outward form of Scripture will itself, no doubt, include much that is figurative. How should it indeed be otherwise, when all language is in its structure essentially figurative? Even, however, though we should define the literal sense of words to be that which they signify in their usual acceptation, and the figurative that which they intend in another than their usual acceptation, under some form or figure of speech, still when the terms literal and figurative simply belong (to use the words of Van Mildert) " to the verbal signification, which with respect to the sense may

---

[a] Convenience has introduced, and still sanctions the use of this somewhat barbarous word. The reader will pardon being reminded that the term grammatical

is the equivalent of *literal*; being derived from γράμμα, " letter," not from γραμματική, " grammar." [?]

be virtually the same, whether or not expressed by trope and figure," and when therefore it is impossible to conceive that by persons of moderate understanding any other than the figurative sense could ever have been deduced from the words employed, we rightfully account the investigation of such sense a necessary part of the most elementary Interpretation. To the outward form of Scripture thus belong all metonymies, in which one name is substituted for another, e. g. the cause for the effect, the mouth for the word; and metaphors, in which a word is transformed from its proper to a cognate signification, e. g. when hardness is predicated of the heart, clothing of the soul; so also all prosopopeias, or personifications; and even all anthropomorphic and anthropopathic descriptions of God, which could never have been understood in a purely literal sense, at least by any of the right-minded among God's people. Nor would even the exclusively grammatico-historical interpreter deem it no part of his task to explain such a continued metaphor as that in Ps. lxxx. 8 ff. or such a parable as that in Is. v. 1–7, or such a fable as that in Judg. ix. 8–15. The historical element in such passages only comes out when their allegorical character is perceived; nor can it be supposed that it was ever unperceived. Still the primary allegorical meaning in such passages may itself be an allegory of something beyond, with which latter the more rudimentary interpretation is not strictly concerned. An unexpectant Jewish reader of Is. v. 1–7 might have traced in the vineyard an image of the land of his inheritance, fenced off by its boundary heights, deserts, and sea from the surrounding territories; might have discerned in the stones the old heathen tribes that had been plucked up from off it, and in the choice vine the Israel that had been planted in their place; might have identified the tower with the city of David, as the symbol of the protecting Davidic sovereignty, and the wine-press with the Temple, where the blood of the sacrifices was poured forth, as the symbol of Israel's worship; and this without inquiring into or recking of the higher blessings of which all these things were but the shadows. Yet it is not to be denied that it is difficult, perhaps impossible, to draw the exact line where the province of spiritual interpretation begins and that of historical ends. On the one hand the spiritual significance of a passage may occasionally, perhaps often, throw light on the historical element involved in it: on the other hand the very large use of figurative language in the O. T., and more especially in the prophecies, prepares us for the recognition of the yet more deeply figurative and essentially allegorical import which runs, as a ὑπόνοια, through the whole.

Yet no unhallowed or unworthy task can it ever be to study, even for its own sake, the historical form in which the O. T. comes to us clothed. It was probably to most of us one of the earliest charms of our childhood, developing in us our sense of brotherhood with all that had gone before us, leading us to feel that we were not singular in that which befell us, and therefore, correspondingly, that we could not live for ourselves alone. Even by itself it proclaims to us the historical workings of God, and reveals the care wherewith He has ever watched over the interests of his Church. Above all the history of the O. T. is the indispensable preface to the historical advent of the Son of God in the flesh. We need hardly labor to prove that

the N. T. recognizes the general historical character of what the O. T. records. It is everywhere assumed. The gospel genealogies testify to it: so too our Lord when he spoke of the desires of the prophets and righteous men of old, or of all the righteous blood shed upon the earth which should be visited upon his own generation: so too Stephen and Paul in their speeches in the council-chamber and at Antioch; so, too, again, the latter, when he spoke of the things which "happened" unto the Israelites for examples. The testimonies borne by our Lord and his Apostles to the outward reality of particular circumstances could be easily drawn out in array, were it needful. Of course in reference to that which is not related as plain matter of history, there will always remain the question how far the descriptions are to be viewed as definitely historical, how far as drawn, for a specific purpose, from the imagination. Such a question presents itself, for example, in the book of Job. It is one which must plainly be in each case decided according to the particular circumstances. Scenes which could never have any outward reality may, as in the Canticles, be made the vehicle of spiritual allegory; and yet even here the historical element meets us in the historical person of the typical bridegroom, in the various local allusions which the allegorist has introduced into his description, and in the references to the manners and customs of the age. In examining the extent of the historical element in the prophecies, both of the prophets and the psalmists, we must distinguish between those which we either definitely know or may reasonably assume to have been fulfilled at a period not entirely distant from that at which they were uttered, and those which reached far beyond in their prospective reference. The former, once fulfilled, were thenceforth annexed to the domain of history (Is. xvii.; Ps. cvii. 33). It must be observed, however, that the prophet often beheld in a single vision, and therefore delineated as accomplished all at once, what was really, as in the case of the desolation of Babylon, the gradual work of a long period (Is. xiii.); or, as in Ezekiel's prophecy respecting the humiliation of Egypt, uttered his predictions in such ideal language as scarcely admitted of a literal fulfillment (Ez. xxix. 8–12; see Fairbairn in loco). With the prophecies of more distant scope the case stood thus. A picture was presented to the prophet's gaze, embodying an outward representation of certain future spiritual struggles, judgments, triumphs, or blessings: a picture suggested in general by the historical circumstances of the present (Zech. vi. 9–15; Ps. v., lxxii.), or of the past (Ez. xx. 35, 36; Is. xi. 15, xlviii. 21; Ps. xcix. 6 ff.), or of the near future, already anticipated and viewed as present (Is. xlix. 7–26; Ps. lvii. 6–11), or of all these, variously combined, altered, and heightened by the imagination. But it does not follow that that picture was ever outwardly brought to pass: the local had been exchanged for the spiritual, the outward type had merged in the inward reality before the fulfillment of the prophecy took effect. In some cases, more especially those in which the prophet had taken his stand upon the nearer future, there was a preliminary and typical fulfillment, or, rather, approach to it; for it seldom, if ever, corresponded to the full extent of the prophecy: the far-reaching import of the prophecy would have been obscured if it had. The measuring-line never outwardly went forth upon Gareb and compassed about to Goath (Jer. xxxi. 39) till the days of Herod Agrippa, after our Saviour's final doom upon the literal Jerusalem had been actually pronounced; and neither the temple of Zerubbabel nor that of Herod corresponded to that which had been beheld in vision by Ezekiel (xl. ff.). There are, moreover, as it would seem, exceptional cases in which even the outward form of the prophet's predictions was divinely drawn from the unknown future as much as from the historical circumstances with which he was familiar, and in which, consequently, the details of the imagery by means of which he concentrated all his conscious conceptions of the future were literally, or almost literally, verified in the events by which his prediction was fulfilled. Such is the case in Is. liii. The Holy Spirit presented to the prophet the actual death-scene of our Saviour as the form in which his prophecy of that event was to be embodied; and thus we trace in it an approach to a literal history of our Saviour's endurances before they came to pass.

(Respecting the rudiments of interpretation, let the following here suffice: The knowledge of the meanings of Hebrew words is gathered (a) from the context, (b) from parallel passages, (c) from the traditional interpretations preserved in Jewish commentaries and dictionaries, (d) from the ancient versions, (e) from the cognate languages, Chaldee, Syriac, and Arabic. The syntax must be almost wholly gathered from the O. T. itself; and for the special syntax of the poetical books, while the importance of a study of the Hebrew parallelism is now generally recognized, more attention needs to be bestowed than has been bestowed hitherto on the centralism and inversion by which the poetical structure and language is often marked. It may here too be in place to mention, that of the various systematic treatises which have by different generations been put forth on the interpretation of Scripture, the most standard work is the *Philologia Sacra* of Sol. Glassius (Prof. at Jena, † 1656), originally published in 1623, and often reprinted. A new edition of it, "accommodated to their times," and bearing the impress of the theological views of the new editors, was brought out by Dathe and Bauer, 1776–97. It is a vast store-house of materials; but the need of such treatises has been now much superseded by the special labors of more recent scholars in particular departments.)

From the outward form of the O. T. we proceed to its moral element or soul. It was with reference to this that St. Paul declared that all Scripture was given by inspiration of God, and was profitable for doctrine, for reproof, for correction, for instruction in righteousness (2 Tim. iii. 16); and it is in the implicit recognition of the essentially moral character of the whole, that our Lord and his Apostles not only appeal to its direct precepts (e. g. Matt. xv. 4, xix. 17–19), and set forth the fullness of their bearing (e. g. Matt. ix. 13), but also lay bare moral lessons in O. T. passages which lie rather beneath the surface than upon it (Matt. xix. 5, 6, xxii. 32; John x. 34, 35; Acts vii. 48, 49; 1 Cor. ix. 9, 10; 2 Cor. viii. 13–15). With regard more particularly to the Law, our Lord shows in his Sermon on the Mount how deep is the moral teaching implied in its letter; and in his denunciation of the Pharisees, upbraids them for their omission of its weightier matters — judgment, mercy, and faith. The history, too, of the O. T. finds frequent reference made in the N. T. to its moral teaching (Luke vi. 3; Rom. iv., ix. 17; 1 Cor. x. 6–11; Heb. iii. 7–11, xi.; 2 Pet. ii. 15–

16; 1 John iii. 12). No doubt it was with reference to the moral instruction to be drawn from them that that history had been made to dwell at greatest length on the events of greatest moral importance. The same reason explains also why it should be to so large an extent biographical. The interpreter of the O. T. will have, among his other tasks, to analyze in the lives set before him the various yet generally mingled workings of the spirit of holiness, and of the spirit of sin. He must not fall into the error of supposing that any of the lives are those of perfect men; Scripture nowhere asserts or implies it, and the sins of even the best testify against it. Nor must he expect to be expressly informed of each recorded action, any more than of each sentiment delivered by the several speakers in the book of Job, whether it were commendable or the contrary; nor must we assume, as some have done, that Scripture identifies itself with every action of a saintly man which, without openly condemning it, records. The moral errors by which the lives of even the greatest O. T. saints were disfigured are related, and that for our instruction, but not generally criticised: e. g. that of Abraham when, already once warned in Egypt, he suffered the king of Gerar to suppose that Sarah was merely his sister; or that of David, when, by feigning himself mad, he practiced deceit upon Achish. The interpreter of Scripture has no warrant for shutting his eyes to such errors; certainly not the warrant of David, who himself virtually confessed them in Ps. xxxiv. (see especially ver. 13). He must acknowledge and commend the holy faith which lay at the root of the earliest recorded deeds of Jacob, a faith rewarded by his becoming the heir of God's promises; but he must no less acknowledge and condemn Jacob's unbrotherly deceit and filial disobedience, offenses punished by the sorrows that attended him from his flight into Mesopotamia to the day of his death. And should he be tempted to desire that in such cases the O. T. had distinguished more directly and authoritatively the good from the evil, he will ask, Would it in that case have spoken as effectually? Are not our thoughts more drawn out, and our affections more engaged, by studying a man's character in the records of his life than in a summary of it ready prepared for us? Is it in a dried and labeled collection of specimens, or in a living garden where the flowers have all their several imperfections, that we best learn to appreciate the true beauties of floral nature? The true glory of the O. T. is here the choice richness of the garden into which it conducts us. It sets before us just those lives — the lives generally of religious men — which will best repay our study, and will most strongly suggest the moral lessons that God would have us learn; and herein it is that, in regard of the moral aspects of the O. T. history, we may most surely trace the overruling influence of the Holy Spirit by which the sacred historians wrote.

But the O. T. has further its spiritual and therefore prophetical element, the result of that organic unity of sacred history by means of which the same God who in his wisdom delayed, till the fullness of time should be come, the advent of his Son into the world, ordained that all the career and worship of his earlier people should outwardly anticipate the glories of the Redeemer and of his spiritually ransomed Church. Our attention is here first attracted to the avowedly predictive parts of the O. T., of the prospective reference of which, at the time that they were uttered, no question can exist, and the majority of which still awaited their fulfillment when the Redeemer of the world was born. No new covenant had up to that time been inaugurated (Jer. xxxi. 31–40); no temple built corresponding to that which Ezekiel had described (xl. ff.); nor had the new David ere that arisen to be a prince in Israel (ibid. xxxiv.). With Christ, then, the new era of the fulfillment of prophecy commenced. In Him were to be fulfilled all things that were written in the Law of Moses, and in the Prophets, and in the Psalms, concerning Him (Luke xxiv. 44; cf. Matt. xxvi. 54, &c.). A marvelous amount there was in his person of the verification of the very letter of prophecy — partly that it might be seen how definitely all had pointed to Him; partly because his outward mission, up to the time of his death, was but to the lost sheep of the house of Israel, and the letter had not yet been finally superseded by the spirit. Yet it would plainly be impossible to suppose that the significance of such prophecies as Zech. ix. 9 was exhausted by the mere outward verification; and with the delivery of Christ by his own people to the Gentiles, and the doom on the city of Jerusalem for rejecting Him, and the ratification of the new covenant by his death, and the subsequent mission of the Apostles to all nations, all consummated by the final blow which fell within forty years on the once chosen people of God, the outward blessings had merged forever in the spiritual, and the typical Israelitish nation in the Church Universal.

Hence the entire absence from the N. T. of any recognition, by either Christ or his Apostles, of such prospective outward glories as the prophecies, literally interpreted, would still have implied. No hope of outward restoration mingled with the sentence of outward doom which Christ uttered forth on the nation from which He himself had sprung (Matt. xxi. 43, xxiii. 38, xxiv. 2); no old outward deliverances with the spiritual salvation which He and his Apostles declared to be still in store for those of the race of Israel who should believe on Him (Matt. xxiii. 39; Acts iii. 19–21; Rom. xi.; 2 Cor. iii. 16). The language of the ancient prophecies is everywhere applied to the gathering together, the privileges, and the triumphs of the universal body of Christ (John x. 16, xi. 52; Acts ii. 39, xv. 15–17; Rom. ix. 25, 26, 32, 33, x. 11, 13, xi. 25, 26, 27; 2 Cor. vi. 16–18; Gal. iv. 27; 1 Pet. ii. 4–6, 10; Rev. iii. 7, 8, xx. 8, 9, xxi., xxii.); above all, in the crowning passage of the apostolic interpretation of O. T. prophecy (Heb. xii. 22), in which the Christian Church is distinctly marked out as the Zion of whose glory all the prophets had spoken. Even apart, however, from the authoritative interpretation thus placed upon them, the prophecies contain within themselves, in sufficient measure, the evidence of their spiritual import. It could not be that the literal Zion should be greatly raised in physical height (Is. ii. 2), or all the Holy Land leveled to a plain (Zech. xiv. 10), or portioned out by straight lines and in rectangles, without regard to its physical conformation (Ez. xlv.); or that the city of Jerusalem should lie to the south of the Temple (ibid. xl. 2), and at a distance of five miles from it (ibid. xlv. 6), and yet that it should occupy its old place (Jer. xxxi. 38, 39; Zech. xiv. 10); or that holy waters should issue from Jerusalem, increasing in depth as they roll on, not through the accession of any tributary streams, but simply because their source

is beneath the sanctuary (Ez. xlvii.). Nor could it well be that, after a long loss of genealogies and title-deeds, the Jews should be reorganized in their tribes and families (Zech. xii. 12–14; Mal. iii. 3; Ez. xliv. 15, xlviii.), and settled after their old estates (Ez. xxxvi. 11). Nor again, that all the inhabitants of the world should go up to Jerusalem to worship, not only to the festivals (Zech. xiv. 16), but even monthly and weekly (Is. lxvi. 23), and yet that while Jerusalem were thus the seat of worship for the whole world, there should also be altars everywhere (Is. xix. 19; Zeph. ii. 11; Mal. i. 11), both being really but different expressions of the same spiritual truth — the extension of God's pure worship to all nations. Nor can we suppose that Jews will ever again outwardly triumph over heathen nations that have long disappeared from the stage of history (Am. ix. 11, 12; Is. xi. 14; Mic. v. 5; Ob. 17–21). Nor will sacrifices be renewed (Ez. xliii. &c.) when Christ has by one offering perfected for ever them that are sanctified; nor will a special sanctity yet attach to Jerusalem, when the hour is come that " neither in this mountain nor yet at Jerusalem " shall men worship the Father; nor yet to the natural Israel (cf. Joel iii. 4), when in Christ there is neither Jew nor Greek, all believers being now alike the circumcision (Phil. iii. 3) and Abraham's seed (Gal. iii. 29), and the name Israel being frequently used in the N. T. of the whole Christian Church (Matt. xix. 28; Luke xxii. 30; Rom. xi. 26; Gal. vi. 16; cf. Rev. vii. 4, xxi. 12).

The substance, therefore, of these prophecies is the glory of the Redeemer's spiritual kingdom; it is but the form that is derived from the outward circumstances of the career of God's ancient people, which had passed, or all but passed away before the fulfillment of the promised blessings commenced. The one kingdom was indeed to merge into, rather than to be violently replaced by the other; the holy seed of old was to be the stock of the new generation; men of all nations were to take hold of the skirt of the Jew, and Israelitish Apostles were to become the patriarchs of the new Christian community. Nor was even the form in which the announcement of the new blessings had been clothed to be rudely cast aside: the imagery of the prophets is on every account justly dear to us, and from love, no less than from habit, we still speak the language of Canaan. But then arises the question, Must not this language have been divinely designed from the first as the language of God's Church? Is it easily to be supposed that the prophets, whose writings form so large a portion of the Bible, should have so extensively used the history of the old Israel as the garment wherein to enwrap their delineations of the blessings of the new, and yet that that history should not be in itself essentially an anticipation of what the promised Redeemer was to bring with him? Besides, the typical import of the Israelitish tabernacle and ritual worship is implied in Heb. ix. (" The Holy Ghost thus signifying "), and is almost universally allowed; and it is not easy to tear asunder the events of Israel's history from the ceremonies of Israel's worship; nor yet, again, the events of the preceding history of the patriarchs from those of the history of Israel. The N. T. itself implies the typical import of a large part of the O. T. narrative. The original dominion conferred upon man (1 Cor. xv. 27; Heb. ii. 8), the rest of God on the seventh day (Heb. iv. 4), the institution of martiage (Eph. v. 31), are in it all invested with a deeper and prospective meaning. So also the offering and martyrdom of Abel (Heb. xi. 4, xii. 24); the preservation of Noah and his family in the ark (1 Pet. 'iii. 21); the priesthood of Melchizedek (Heb. vii., following Ps. cx. 4); the mutual relation of Sarah and Hagar, and of their children (Gal. iv. 22 ff.); the offering and rescue of Isaac (Rom. viii. 32; Heb. xi. 19); the favor of God to Jacob rather than Esau (Rom. ix. 10–13, following Mal. i. 2, 3); the sojourn of Israel in Egypt (Matt. ii. 15); the passover feast (1 Cor. v. 7, 8); the shepherdship of Moses (Heb. xiii. 20, cf. Is. hiii. 11, Sept.); his veiling of his face at Sinai (2 Cor. iii. 13); the ratification of the covenant by blood (Heb. ix. 18 ff.); the priestly character of the chosen people (1 Pet. ii. 9); God's outward presence with them (2 Cor. vi. 16); the various events in their pilgrimage through the desert (1 Cor. x.), and specially the eating of manna from heaven (Matt. iv. 4; John vi. 48–51); the lifting up of the brazen serpent (John iii. 14); the promise of the divine presence with Israel after the removal of Moses, their shepherd, from them (Heb. xiii. 5, cf. Deut. xxxi. 6); the kingdom of David (Luke i. 32, 33); and the devouring of Jonah (Matt. xii. 40). If some of these instances be deemed doubtful, let at least the rest be duly weighed, and this not without regard to the cumulative force of the whole. In the O. T. itself we have, and this even in the latest times, events and persons expressly treated as typical: e. g. the making the once-rejected stone the headstone of the corner (probably an historical incident in the laying of the foundation of the second Temple (Ps. cxviii. 22); the arraying of Joshua the high-priest with fair garments (Zech. iii.), and the placing of crowns on his head to symbolize the union of royalty and priesthood (Zech. vi. 9 ff.). A further testimony to the typical character of the history of the Old Testament is furnished by the typical character of the events related even in the New. All our Lord's miracles were essentially typical, and are almost universally so acknowledged: the works of mercy which He wrought outwardly on the body betokening his corresponding operations within man's soul. So, too, the outward fulfillments of prophecy in the Redeemer's life were types of the deeper though less immediately striking fulfillment which it was to continue to receive ideally; and if this deeper and more spiritual significance underlie the literal narrative of the New Testament, how much more that of the Old, which was so essentially designed as a preparation for the good things to come! A remarkable and honorable testimony on this subject was borne in his later years by De Wette. "Long before Christ appeared," he says, " the world was prepared for his appearance; the entire O. T. is a great prophecy, a great type of Him who was to come, and did come. Who can deny that the holy seers of the O. T. saw, in spirit, the advent of Christ long beforehand, and in prophetic anticipations of greater or less clearness had presages of the new doctrine? The typological comparison, too, of the Old Testament with the New was no mere play of fancy; and it is scarcely altogether accidental that the evangelic history, in the most important particulars, runs parallel with the Mosaic " (cited by Tholuck, The Old Testament in the New).

It is not unlikely that there is in many quarters an unwillingness to recognize the spiritual element in the historical parts of the O. T., arising from the fear that the recognition of it may endanger that of the historical truth of the events recorded. Nor is such danger altogether visionary; for one-sided and prejudiced contemplation will be ever so abusing one element of Scripture as thereby to cast a slight upon the rest. But this does not affect its existence; and on the other hand there are certainly cases in which the spiritual element confirms the outward reality of the historical fact. So is it with the devouring of Jonah; which many would consign to the region of parable or myth, not apparently from any result of criticism, which is indeed at a loss to find an origin for the story save in fact, but simply from the unwillingness to give credit to an event the extraordinary character of which must have been patent from the first. But if the divine purpose were to prefigure in a striking and effective manner the passage of our Saviour through the darkness of the tomb, how could any ordinary event, akin to ordinary human experience, adequately represent that of which we have no experience? The utmost perils of the royal psalmist required, in Ps. xviii., to be heightened and compacted together by the aid of extraneous imagery in order that they might typify the horrors of death. Those same horrors were more definitely prefigured by the incarceration of Jonah: it was a marvelous type, but not more marvelous than the antitype which it foreshadowed; it testified by its very wondrousness that there are gloomy terrors beyond any of which this world supplies the experience, but over which Christ should triumph, as Jonah was delivered from the belly of the fish.

Of another danger besetting the path of the spiritual interpreter of the O. T., we have a warning in the unedifying puerilities into which some have fallen. Against such he will guard by foregoing too curious a search for mere external resemblances between the Old Testament and the New, though withal thankfully recognizing them wherever they present themselves. His true task will be rather to investigate the inward ideas involved in the O. T. narratives, institutions, and prophecies themselves, by the aid of the more perfect manifestation of those ideas in the transactions and events of gospel-times. The spiritual interpretation must rest upon both the literal and the moral; and there can be no spiritual analogy between things which have nought morally in common. One consequence of this principle will of course be, that we must never be content to rest in any mere outward fulfillment of prophecy. It can never, for example, be admitted that the ordinance respecting the entireness of the passover-lamb had reference merely to the preservation of our Saviour's legs unbroken on the cross, or that the concluding words of Zech. ix. 9, pointed merely to the animal on which our Saviour should outwardly ride into Jerusalem, or that the sojourn of Israel in Egypt, in its evangelic reference, had respect merely to the temporary sojourn of our Saviour in the same country. However remarkable the outward fulfillment be, it must always guide us to some deeper analogy, in which a moral element is involved. Another consequence of the foregoing principle of interpretation will be that that which was forbidden or sinful can, so far as it was sinful, not be regarded as typical of that which is free from sin. We may, for example, reject, as altogether groundless, the view, often propounded, but never proved, that Solomon's marriage with Pharaoh's daughter was a figure of the reception of the

Gentiles into the Church of the Gospel. On the other hand there is no more difficulty in supposing that that which was sinful may have originated the occasion for the exhibition of some striking type, than there is in believing that disobedience brought about the need of redemption. The Israelites sinned in demanding a king; yet the earthly kingdom of David was a type of the kingdom of Christ; and it was in consequence of Jonah's fleeing, like the first Adam, from the presence of the Lord, that he became so signal a type of the second Adam in his three days' removal from the light of heaven. So again that which was tolerated rather than approved may contain within itself the type of something imperfect, in contrast to that which is more perfect. Thus Hagar, as the concubine of Abraham, represented the covenant at Sinai; but it is only the bondage-aspect of that covenant which here comes directly under consideration, and the children of the covenant, symbolized by Ishmael, are those only who cleave to the element of bondage in it.

Yet withal, in laying down rules for the interpretation of the O. T., we must abstain from attempting to define the limits, or to measure the extent of its fullness. That fullness has certainly not yet been, nor will by us be exhausted. Search after truth, and reverence for the native worth of the written Word, authorize us indeed to reject past interpretations of it which cannot be shown to rest on any solid foundation. Still all interpretation is essentially progressive; and in no part of the O. T. can we tell the number of meanings and bearings, beyond those with which we are ourselves familiar, which may one day be brought out, and which then not only may approve themselves by their intrinsic reasonableness, but even may by their mutual harmony and practical interest furnish additional evidence of the divine source of that Scripture which cannot be broken.

C. — QUOTATIONS FROM THE OLD TESTAMENT IN THE NEW TESTAMENT.

The New Testament quotations from the Old form one of the outward bonds of connection between the two parts of the Bible. They are manifold in kind. Some of the passages quoted contain prophecies, or involve types of which the N. T. writers designed to indicate the fulfillment. Others are introduced as direct logical supports to the doctrines which they were enforcing. In all cases which can be clearly referred to either of these categories, we are fairly warranted in deeming the use which has been made of the older text authoritative; and from these, and especially from an analysis of the quotations which at first sight present difficulties, we may study the principles on which the sacred appreciation and exegesis of the older Scriptures has proceeded. Let it only be borne in mind that however just the interpretations virtually placed upon the passages quoted, they do not profess to be necessarily complete. The contrary is indeed manifest from the two opposite bearings of the same passage, Ps. xxiv. 1, brought out by St. Paul in the course of a few verses, 1 Cor. x. 26, 28. But in many instances, also, the N. T. writers have quoted the O. T. rather by way of illustration, than with the intention of leaning upon it; variously applying and adapting it, and making its language the vehicle of their own independent thoughts. It could hardly well be otherwise. The thoughts of all who have been deeply educated in the Scriptures

naturally move in Scriptural diction: it would have been strange had the writers of the N. T. formed exceptions to the general rule.

It may not be easy to distribute all the quotations into their distinctive classes. But among those in which a prophetical or typical force is ascribed in the N. T. to the passage quoted, may fairly be reckoned all that are introduced with an intimation that the Scripture was " fulfilled." And it may be observed that the word " fulfill," as applied to the accomplishment of what had been predicted or foreshadowed, is in the N. T. only used by our Lord himself and his companion-apostles: not by St. Mark nor St. Luke, except in their reports of our Lord's and Peter's sayings, nor yet by St. Paul (Mark xv. 28, is not genuine). It had grown familiar to the original Apostles from the continual verification of the O. T. which they had beheld in the events of their Master's career. These had testified to the deep connection between the utterances of the O. T. and the realities of the Gospel; and, through the general connection in turn casting down its radiance on the individual points of contact, the higher term was occasionally applied to express a relation for which, viewed merely in itself, weaker language might have sufficed. Three " fulfillments " of Scripture are traced by St. Matthew in the incidents of our Saviour's infancy (ii. 15, 18, 23). He beheld Him marked out as the true Israel, the beloved of God with high destiny before Him, by the outward correspondence between his and Israel's sojourn in Egypt. The sorrowing of the mothers of Bethlehem for their children was to him a renewal of the grief for the captives at Ramah, which grief Jeremiah had described in language suggested by the record of the patriarchal grief for the loss of Joseph: it was thus a present token (we need account it no more) of the spiritual captivity which all outward captivities recalled, and from which, since it had been declared that there was hope in the end, Christ was to prove the deliverer. And again, Christ's sojourn in despised Nazareth was an outward token of the lowliness of his condition; and if the prophets had rightly spoken, this lowliness was the necessary prelude, and therefore, in part, the pledge of his future glory. In the first and last of these cases the evangelist, in his wonted phrase, expressly declares that the events came to pass that that which was spoken " might be fulfilled: " language which must not be arbitrarily softened down. In the other case the phrase is less definitely strong: " Then was fulfilled," etc. The substitution of this phrase can, however, of itself decide nothing, for it is used of an acknowledged prophecy in xxvii. 9. And should any be disposed on other grounds to view the quotation from Jer. xxxi. 15 merely as an adornment of the narrative, let them first consider whether the evangelist, who was occupied with the history of Christ, would be likely formally to introduce a passage from the O. T. merely as an illustration of maternal grief.

In the quotations of all kinds from the Old Testament in the New, we find a continual variation from the letter of the older Scriptures. To this variation three causes may be specified as having contributed.

First, all the N. T. writers quoted from the Septuagint; correcting it indeed more or less by the Hebrew, especially when it was needful for their purpose: occasionally deserting it altogether; still abiding by it to so large an extent as to show that it was the primary source whence their quotations were drawn. Their use of it may be best illustrated by the corresponding use of our liturgical version of the Psalms; a use founded on love as well as on habit, but which nevertheless we forego when it becomes important that we should follow the more accurate rendering. Consequently, when the errors involved in the Septuagint version do not interfere with the purpose which the N. T. writer had in view, they are frequently allowed to remain in his quotation: see Matt. xv. 9 (a record of our Lord's words); Luke iv. 18; Acts xlii. 41, xv. 17; Rom. xv. 10; 2 Cor. iv. 13; Heb. viii. 9, x. 5, xi. 21. The current of apostolic thought, too, is frequently dictated by words of the Septuagint, which differ much from the Hebrew: see Rom. ii. 24; 1 Cor. xv. 55; 2 Cor. ix. 7; Heb. xiii. 15. Or even an absolute interpolation of the Septuagint is quoted, Heb. i. 6 (Deut. xxxii. 43). On the other hand, in Matt. xxi. 5; 1 Cor. iii. 19, the Septuagint is corrected by the Hebrew: so too in Matt. ix. 13; Luke xxii. 37, there is an effort to preserve an expressiveness of the Hebrew which the Septuagint had lost; and in Matt. iv. 15, 16; John xix. 37; 1 Cor. xv. 54, the Septuagint disappears altogether. In Rom. ix. 33, we have a quotation from the Septuagint combined with another from the Hebrew. In Mark xii. 30; Luke x. 27; Rom. xii. 19, the Septuagint and Hebrew are superadded the one upon the other. In the Epistle to the Hebrews, which in this respect stands alone, the Septuagint is uniformly followed; except in the one remarkable quotation, Heb. x. 30, which, according neither with the Hebrew nor the Septuagint, was probably derived from the last-named passage, Rom. xii. 19, wherewith it exactly coincides. The quotation in 1 Cor. ii. 9 seems to have been derived not directly from the O. T., but rather from a Christian liturgy or other document into which the language of Is. lxiv. 4 had been transferred.

Secondly, the N. T. writers must have frequently quoted from memory. The O. T. had been deeply instilled into their minds, ready for service, whenever needed; and the fulfillment of its predictions which they witnessed, made its utterances rise up in life before them: cf. John ii. 17, 22. It was of the very essence of such a living use of O. T. Scripture that their quotations of it should not of necessity be verbally exact.

Thirdly, combined with this there was an alteration of conscious or unconscious design. Sometimes the object of this was to obtain increased force: hence the variation from the original in the form of the divine oath, Rom. xiv. 11; or the result "I quake," substituted for the cause, Heb. xii. 21; or the insertion of rhetorical words to bring out the emphasis, Heb. xii. 26; or the change of person to show that what men perpetrated had its root in God's determinate counsel, Matt. xxvi. 31. Sometimes an O. T. passage is abridged, and in the abridgment so adjusted, by a little alteration, as to present an aspect of completeness, and yet omit what is foreign to the immediate purpose, Acts i. 20; 1 Cor. i. 31. At other times a passage is enlarged by the incorporation of a passage from another source: thus in Luke iv. 18, 19, although the contents are professedly those read by our Lord from Is. lxi., we have the words "to set at liberty them that are bruised," introduced from Is. lviii. 6 (Sept.): similarly in Rom. xi. 8, Deut. xxix. 4 is combined with Is. xxix. 10. In some cases still greater liberty of alteration is assumed. In Rom. x. 11, the word πᾶς is introduced into Is. xxviii. 16, to show that that is uttered of Jew and Gentile alike. In Rom. xi. 26, 27, the "to Zion" of Is. lix. 20 (Sept. ἕνεκεν Σιών) is replaced by "out of Sion" (suggested by Is. ii. 3): to Zion the Redeemer had already come; from Zion, the Christian Church, his law was to go forth; or even from the literal Jerusalem, cf. Luke xxiv. 47; Rom. xv. 19, for, till she was destroyed, the type was still in a measure kept up. In Matt. viii. 17, the words of Is. liii. 4 are adapted to the divine removal of disease, the outward token and witness of that sin which Christ was eventually to remove by his death, thereby fulfilling the prophecy more completely. For other, though less striking, instances of variation, see 1 Cor. xiv. 21; 1 Pet. iii. 15. In some places again, the actual words of the original are taken up, but employed with a new meaning: thus the ἐρχόμενος, which in Hab. ii. 3 merely qualified the verb, is in Heb. x. 37 made the subject to it.

Almost more remarkable than any alteration in the quotation itself, is the circumstance that in Matt. xxvii. 9, Jeremiah should be named as the author of a prophecy really delivered by Zechariah: the reason being, as has been well shown by Hengstenberg in his Christology, that the prophecy is based upon that in Jer. xviii., xix., and that without a reference to this original source the most essential features of the fulfillment of Zechariah's prophecy would be misunderstood.[a] The case is indeed not entirely unique; for in the Greek of Mark i. 2, 3, where Mal. iii. 1 is combined with Is. xl. 3, the name of Isaiah alone is mentioned: it was on his prophecy that that of Malachi partly depended. On the other hand in Matt. ii. 23; John vi. 45, the comprehensive mention of the prophets indicates a reference not only to the passages more particularly contemplated, Is. xi. 1, liv. 13, but also to the general tenor of what had been elsewhere prophetically uttered.

The above examples will sufficiently illustrate the freedom with which the Apostles and Evangelists interwove the older Scriptures into their writings. It could only result in failure were we to attempt any merely mechanical account of variations from the O. T. text which are essentially not mechanical. That which is still replete with life may not be dissected by the anatomist. There is a spiritual meaning in their employment of Scripture, even as there is a spiritual meaning in Scripture itself. And though it would be as idle to treat of their quotations without reference to the Septuagint, as it would be to treat of the inner meaning of the Bible without attending first to the literal interpretation, still it is only when we pay regard to the inner purpose for which each separate quotation was made, and the inner significance to the writer's mind of the passage quoted, that we can arrive at any true solution of the difficulties which the phenomena of these quotations frequently present. (Convenient tables of the quotations, ranged in the order of the N. T. passages, are given in the Introductions of Davidson and Horne. A much fuller table, embracing the informal verbal allusions, and ranged in the contrary order, but with a reverse index, has been compiled by Gough and published separately, 1855.)　　　J. F. T.

---

[a] • See the remarks on this passage, vol. i. p. 20 e and vol. ii. p. 1503 a.

* See on the mode of citing the Old Testament in the New, Tholuck's *Das A. Test. im Neuen Test.*, pp. 1–60 (3ᵗᵉ Aufl.), and transl. by Prof. C. A. Aiken, *Bibl. Sacra*, xi. 568–616; W. Lindsay Alexander's *Connexion and Harmony of the O. and N. Testaments*, lect. i. pt. ii. (Lond. 1841); Fairbairn's *Hermeneutical Manual*, pt. third, pp. 393–456 (Amer. repr. 1859); and Turpie's *The Old Test. in the New* (Lond. 1868).   H.

* OLEANDER. [WILLOWS, Amer. ed.]

OLIVE (זַיִת: ἐλαία). No tree is more closely associated with the history and civilization of man. Our concern with it here is in its sacred relations, and in its connection with Judæa and the Jewish people.

Many of the Scriptural associations of the olive-tree are singularly poetical. It has this remarkable interest, in the first place, that its foliage is the earliest that is mentioned by name, when the waters of the flood began to retire. "Lo! in the dove's mouth was an olive-leaf pluckt off: so Noah knew that the waters were abated from off the

Olive (Olea Europæa).

earth" (Gen. viii. 11). How far this early incident may have suggested the later emblematical meanings of the leaf, it is impossible to say; but now it is as difficult for us to disconnect the thought of peace from this scene of primitive patriarchal history, as from a multitude of allusions in the Greek and Roman poets. Next, we find it the most prominent tree in the earliest allegory. When the trees invited it to reign over them, its sagacious answer sets it before us in its characteristic relations to Divine worship and domestic life. "Should I leave my fatness, wherewith by me they honor God and man, and go to be promoted over the trees?" (Judg. ix. 8, 9). With David it is the emblem of prosperity and the divine blessing.

He compares himself to "a green olive tree in the house of God" (Ps. lii. 8); and he compares the children of a righteous man to the "olive-branches round about his table" (Ps. cxxviii. 3). So with the later prophets it is the symbol of beauty, luxuriance, and strength; and hence the symbol of religious privileges: "His branches shall spread, and his beauty shall be as the olive-tree," are the words in the concluding promise of Hosea (xiv. 6). "The Lord called thy name a green olive-tree, fair, and of goodly fruit," is the expostulation of Jeremiah when he foretells retribution for advantages abused (xi. 16). Here we may compare Ecclus. l. 10. We must bear in mind, in reading this imagery, that the olive was among the most abundant and characteristic vegetation of Judæa. Thus after the Captivity, when the Israelites kept the Feast of Tabernacles, we find them, among other branches for the booths, bringing "olive-branches" from the "mount" (Neh. viii. 15). "The mount" is doubtless the famous Olivet, or Mount of Olives, the "Olivetum" of the Vulgate. [OLIVES, MOUNT OF.] Here we cannot forget that the trees of this sacred hill witnessed not only the humiliation and sorrow of David in Absalom's rebellion (2 Sam. xv. 30), but also some of the most solemn scenes in the life of David's Lord and Son; the prophecy over Jerusalem, the agony in the garden (GETHSEMANE itself means "a press for olive-oil"), and the ascension to heaven. Turning now to the mystic imagery of Zechariah (iv. 3, 11–14), and of St. John in the Apocalypse (Rev. xi. 3, 4), we find the olive-tree used, in both cases, in a very remarkable way. We cannot enter into any explanation of "the two olive-trees . . . the two olive-branches . . . the two anointed ones that stand by the Lord of the whole earth" (Zech.); or of "the two witnesses . . . the two olive-trees standing before the God of the earth" (Rev.): but we may remark that we have here a very expressive link between the prophecies of the O. T. and the N. T. Finally, in the argumentation of St. Paul concerning the relative positions of the Jews and Gentiles in the counsels of God, this tree supplies the basis of one of his most forcible allegories (Rom. xi. 16–25). The Gentiles are the "wild olive" (ἀγριέλαιος), grafted in upon the "good olive" (καλλιέλαιος), to which once the Jews belonged, and with which they may again be incorporated. It must occur to any one that the natural process of grafting is here inverted, the custom being to engraft a good branch upon a bad stock. And it has been contended that in the case of the olive-tree the inverse process is sometimes practiced, a wild twig being engrafted to strengthen the cultivated olive. Thus Mr. Ewbank (*Comm. on Romans*, ii. 112) quotes from Palladius: —

"Fecundat sterilis pingues oleaster olivas,
Et quæ non novit munera ferre docet."

But whatever the fact may be, it is unnecessary to have recourse to this supposition: and indeed it confuses the allegory. Nor is it likely that St. Paul would hold himself tied by horticultural laws in using such an image as this. Perhaps the very stress of the allegory is in this, that the grafting is contrary to nature (παρὰ φύσιν ἐνεκεντρίσθης, v. 24).

This discussion of the passage in the Romans leads us naturally to speak of the cultivation of the olive-tree, its industrial applications, and general characteristics. It grows freely almost everywhere on the shores of the Mediterranean; but, as has been said above, it was peculiarly abundant in Palestine. See Deut. vi. 11, vii. 8, xxviii. 40. Olive-yards are a matter of course in descriptions of the country, like vineyards and corn-fields (Judg. xv. 5; 1 Sam. viii. 14). The kings had very extensive ones (1 Chr. xxvii. 28). Even now the tree is very abundant in the country. Almost every village has its olive-grove. Certain districts may be specified where at various times this tree has been very luxuriant. Of Asher, on the skirts of the Lebanon, it was prophesied that he should "dip his foot in oil" (Deut. xxxiii. 24). The immediate neighborhood of Jerusalem has already been mentioned. In the article on GAZA we have alluded to its large and productive olive-woods in the present day: and we may refer to Van de Velde's *Syria* (i. 386) for their extent and beauty in the vale of Shechem. The cultivation of the olive-tree had the closest connection with the domestic life of the Israelites, their trade, and even their public ceremonies and religious worship. A good illustration of the use of olive-oil for food is furnished by 2 Chr. ii. 10, where we are told that Solomon provided Hiram's men with "twenty thousand baths of oil." Compare Ezra iii. 7. Too much of this product was supplied for home consumption: hence we find the country sending it as an export to Tyre (Ez. xxvii. 17), and to Egypt (Hos. xii. 1). This oil was used in coronations. thus it was an emblem of sovereignty (1 Sam. x 1, xii. 3, 5). It was also mixed with the offerings in sacrifice (Lev. ii. 1, 2, 6, 15). Even in the wilderness very strict directions were given that, in the Tabernacle, the Israelites were to have "pure oil olive beaten for the light, to cause the lamp to

Old Olive-trees in the Garden of Gethsemane.

turn always" (Ex. xxvii. 20). For the burning of it in common lamps, see Matt. xxv. 3, 4, 8. The use of it on the hair and skin was customary, and indicative of cheerfulness (Ps. xxiii. 5; Matt. vi. 17). It was also employed medicinally in surgical cases (Luke x. 34).[a] See again Mark vi. 13; Jam. v. 14, for its use in combination with prayer on behalf of the sick. [OIL.; ANOINT.] Nor, in enumerating the useful applications of the olive-tree, must we forget the wood, which is hard and solid, with a fine grain, and a pleasing yellowish tint. In Solomon's Temple the cherubim were "of olive-tree" (1 K. vi. 23),[b] as also the doors

(vv. 31, 32) and the posts (ver. 33). As to the berries (Jam. iii. 12; 2 Esdr. xvi. 29), which produce the oil, they were sometimes gathered by shaking the tree (Is. xxiv. 13), sometimes by beating it (Deut. xxiv. 20). Then followed the treading of the fruit (Deut. xxxiii. 24; Mic. vi. 15). Hence the mention of "oil-fats" (Joel ii. 24). Nor must the flower be passed over without notice: —

"Si bene floruerint oleæ, nitidissimus annus."
                      Ov. *Fast.* v. 265.

The wind was dreaded by the cultivator of the

---

[a] All these subjects admit of very full illustration from Greek and Roman writers. And if this were not a Biblical article, we should dwell upon other classical associations of the tree which supplied the victor's wreath at the Olympic games, and a twig of which is the familiar mark on the coins of Athens. See Judith xv. 12.

[b] If the olive be the wood intended in 1 K. vi. 23, it is singular that a wood of such hardness should have been used for a carving, when the carving was to be covered with gold, and thus the fine grain would be concealed. Tristram (*Nat. Hist. of the Bible*, p. 371) thinks that the oleaster is meant here. See OIL TREE.   G. E. P.

olive; for the least ruffling of a breeze is apt to cause the flowers to fall: —

"Florebant oleæ: venti nocuere protervi."

Ov. Fast. v. 321.

Thus we see the force of the words of Eliphaz the Temanite: "He shall cast off his flower like the olive" (Job xv. 33). It is needless to add that the locust was a formidable enemy of the olive (Amos iv. 9). It happened not unfrequently that hopes were disappointed, and that "the labor of the olive failed" (Hab. iii. 17). As to the growth of the tree, it thrives best in warm and sunny situations. It is of a moderate height, with knotty gnarled trunks, and a smooth ash-colored bark. It grows slowly, but it lives to an immense age. Its look is singularly indicative of tenacious vigor: and this is the force of what is said in Scripture of its "greenness," as emblematic of strength and prosperity. The leaves, too, are not deciduous. Those who see olives for the first time are occasionally disappointed by the dusty color of their foliage; but those who are familiar with them find an inexpressible charm in the rippling changes of these slender gray-green leaves. Mr. Ruskin's pages in the *Stones of Venice* (iii. 175–177) are not at all extravagant.

The literature of this subject is very extensive. All who have written on the trees and plants of Scripture have devoted some space to the olive. One especially deserves to be mentioned, namely, Thomson, *Land and Book*, pp. 51–57. But, for Biblical illustration, no later work is so useful as the *Hierobotanicon* of Celsius, the friend and patron of Linnæus.   J. S. H.

* The noble olive-yards of Attica, which Paul must have seen whether he went from Athens to Corinth by the way of Megara or Piraeus (Acts xviii. 1), still preserve their ancient fame. Allusion is made above to the olive-press. Dr. W. M. Thomson found several such presses still well preserved from early Hebrew times, at *Um el-Awamin*, not far from Tyre, a little north of *Kânâh*. [KANAH.] "Two columns, about two feet square and eight feet high, stand on a stone base, and have a stone of the same length and size on the top. Sometimes there are two on the top, to make it more firm. These columns are about two feet apart, and in the inner sides, facing each other, are grooves cut from near the top to the bottom, about four inches deep and six wide, in which the plank which pressed on the olives moved up and down. . . . The plank was placed upon them and pressed down by a long beam acting as a lever, by the aid of the great stones on the top of the columns. . . . Close to the press, are two immense stone basins, in which the olives were ground. I measured one which had recently been uncovered. It was seven feet two inches in diameter, a foot deep, with a rim six inches thick; a huge bowl of polished stone, without a flaw or crack in it" (*Bibl. Sacra*, xii. 832 f.). The same writer (*Land and Book*, i. 72–76) explains in a striking manner the various

Scripture allusions to the olive (Job xv. 33; Hab. iii. 18; Is. xvii. 6; Deut. xxiv. 20). "The sites," says Mr. Tristram, "of many of the deserted towns of Judah bear witness to the former abundance of the olive, where it now no longer exists, by the oil-presses, with their gutters, troughs, and cisterns hewn out of the solid rock. I have seen many of them far south of Hebron, where not an olive has existed for centuries, and also many among deserted thickets of Carmel" (*Nat. Hist. of the Bible*, p. 376). Most of the passages which refer to the olive might have been written in our own day, so remarkably do the present customs accord with those of the oldest known inhabitants of the land. Løyrer (Herzog's *Real-Encyk.* x. 547) quotes Schulz (*Leitungen des Höchsten*, v. 86) as saying that the wild olive may be and is used in the East for grafting the cultivated olive when the latter becomes unfruitful; but it is generally allowed that Paul does not refer in Rom. xi. 17 to any actual process in nature, but assumes the case for the sake of illustration.   H.

* OLIVE-BERRIES (Jam. iii. 12). [OLIVE.]

OLIVES, MOUNT OF (הַר הַזֵּיתִים: τὸ ὅρος τῶν ἐλαιῶν : *Mons Olivarum*). The exact expression "the Mount of Olives" occurs in the O. T. in Zech. xiv. only; in the other places of the O. T. in which it is referred to, the form employed is the "ascent of the olives" (2 Sam. xv. 30; A. V. inaccurately "the ascent of *Mount* Olivet"), or simply "the mount" (Neh. viii. 15), "the mount facing Jerusalem" (1 K. xi. 7), or "the mountain which is on the east side of the city" (Ez. xi. 23).

In the N. T. three forms of the word occur: (1.) The usual one, "The Mount of Olives" (τὸ ὅρος τῶν ἐλαιῶν). (2.) By St. Luke twice (xix. 29, xxi. 37); "the mount called Elaiôn" (τὸ ὅ. τὸ καλ. ἐλαιῶν; Rec. Text, Ἐλαιῶν, which is followed by the A. V.). (3.) Also by St. Luke (Acts i. 12); the "mount called Olivet" (ὅρ. τὸ καλ. ἐλαιῶνος).

It is the well-known eminence on the east of Jerusalem, intimately and characteristically connected with some of the gravest and most significant events in the history of the Old Testament, the New Testament, and the intervening times, and one of the firmest links by which the two are united: the scene of the flight of David and the triumphal progress of the Son of David, of the idolatry of Solomon, and the agony and betrayal of Christ.

If anything were wanting to fix the position of the Mount of Olives, it would be amply settled by the account of the first of the events just named, as related in 2 Sam. xv., with the elucidations of the LXX. and Josephus (*Ant.* vii. 9). David's object was to place the Jordan between himself and Absalom. He therefore flies by the road called "the road of the wilderness" (xv. 23). This leads him across the Kidron, past the well-known olive-tree [b] which marked the path, up the toilsome ascent of

---

a מַעֲלֵה הַזֵּיתִים : ἀνάβασις τῶν ἐλαιῶν : *clivus olivarum*. The names applied to the mount in the Targums are as follows: טוּר זֵיתָא or זֵיתַיָּא (2 Sam. xv. 30, 2 K. xxiii. 13, Ez. xi. 23, Zech. xiv. 4), ט' מִשְׁחָא (Cant. viii. 3 ; and Gen. viii. 11, Pseudo jon. only). The latter is the name employed in the

Mishna (*Parah*, c. 3). Its meaning is "oil" or "ointment." The modern Arabic name for the whole ridge seems to be *Jebel es-Zeitûn*, i. e. Mount of Olives, or *Jebel Tûr*, the mount of the mount, meaning, the important mount.

b The allusion to this tree, which survives in the LXX. of ver. 18, has vanished from the present Hebrew text.

the mount — elsewhere exactly described as facing Jerusalem on the east (1 K. xi. 7; Ez. xi. 23; Mark xiii. 3) — to the summit,[a] where was a consecrated spot at which he was accustomed to worship God.[b] At this spot he again performed his devotions — it must have seemed for the last time — and took his farewell of the city, " with many tears, as one who had lost his kingdom." He then turned the summit, and after passing Bahurim, probably about where Bethany now stands, continued the descent through the " dry and thirsty[c] land " until he arrived " weary " at the bank of the river (Joseph. Ant. vii. 9, §§ 2–6: 2 Sam. xvi. 14, xvii. 21, 22).

This, which is the earliest mention[d] of the Mount of Olives, is also a complete introduction to it. It stands forth, with every feature complete, almost as if in a picture. Its nearness to Jerusalem; the ravine at its foot; the olive-tree at its base; the steep road through the trees[e] to the summit; the remarkable view from thence of Zion and the city, spread opposite and almost seeming

to rise towards the spectator ; the very " stones and dust "[f] of the rugged and sultry descent, — all are caught, nothing essential is omitted.

The remaining references to it in the Old Testament are but slight. The " high places " which Solomon constructed for the gods of his numerous wives, were in the mount " facing Jerusalem " (1 K. xi. 7) — an expression which applies to the Mount of Olives only, as indeed all commentators apply it. Modern tradition (see below) has, after some hesitation, fixed the site of these sanctuaries on the most southern of the four summits into which the whole range of the mount is divided, and therefore far removed from that principal summit over which David took his way. But there is nothing in the O. T. to countenance this, or to forbid our believing that Solomon adhered to the spot already consecrated in the time of his father. The reverence which in our days attaches to the spot on the very top of the principal summit, is probably only changed in its object from what it was in the time of the kingdom of Judah.

Mount of Olives. (From Bartlett's *Walks about Jerusalem*.)

During the next four hundred years we have only the brief notice of Josiah's iconoclasms at this spot. Ahaz and Manasseh had no doubt maintained and enlarged the original erections of Solomon. These Josiah demolished. He " defiled " the high places, broke to pieces the uncouth and obscene symbols

which deformed them, cut down the images, or possibly the actual groves, of Ashtaroth, and effectually disqualified them for worship by filling up the cavities with human bones (2 K. xxiii 13, 14). Another two hundred years and we find a further mention of it — this time in a thoroughly different connec-

---

[a] The mention of the summit marks the road to have been that over the present Mount of the Ascension. The southern road keeps below the summit the whole way.

[b] The expression of the text denotes that this was a known and frequented spot for devotion. The Talmudists say that it was the place at which the Ark and Tabernacle were first caught sight of in approaching Jerusalem over the Mount. Spots from which a sanctuary is visible are still considered in the East as themselves sacred. (See the citations in Lightfoot on Luke xxiv. 50 ; and compare MIZPEH, p. 1977 *note*.) It is worthy of remark that the expression is " where they worshipped God," not Jehovah ; as if it were one of the old sanctuaries of Elohim, like Bethel or Moreh.

[c] Ps. lxiii. — by its title and by constant tradition

— is referred to this day. The word rendered (" thirsty ' in ver. 1 is the same as that rendered " weary " in 2 Sam. xvi. 14 — עָיֵף.

[d] The author of the Targum Pseudojonathan introduces it still earlier. According to him, the olive-leaf which the dove brought back to Noah was plucked from it.

[e] It must be remembered that the mount had not yet acquired its now familiar name. All that is said is that David " ascended by the ascent of the olives."

[f] At Bahurim, while David and his men kept the road, Shimei scrambled along the slope of the overhanging hill above, even with him, and threw stones at him, and *covered him with dust* (2 Sam. xvi. 18) [in the Hebrew *dusted*].

tion. It is now the great repository for the vegetation of the district, planted thick with olive, and
the bushy myrtle, and the feathery palm. "Go
out" of the city "into the mount" — was the
command of Ezra for the celebration of the first
anniversary of the Feast of Tabernacles after the
Return from Babylon — " and fetch olive branches
and 'oil-tree' branches and myrtle-boughs, and
palm-leaves, and branches of thick trees to make
booths, as it is written" (Neh. viii. 15).

The cultivated and umbrageous character which
is implied in this description, as well as in the name
of the mount, it retained till the N. T. times.
Caphnatha, Bethphage, Bethany, all names of places
on the mount, and all derived from some fruit or
vegetation, are probably of late origin, certainly of
late mention. True, the " palm-branches " borne
by the crowd who flocked out of Jerusalem to welcome the "Prophet of Nazareth," were obtained
from the city (John xii. 13) — not impossibly
from the gardens of the Temple (Ps. xcii. 12, 13);
but the boughs which they strewed on the ground
before him, were cut or torn down from the fig or
olive trees which shadowed the road round the hill.

At this point in the history it will be convenient to describe the situation and appearance of the
Mount of Olives. It is not so much a "mount"
as a ridge, of rather more than a mile in length,
running in general direction north and south; covering the whole eastern side of the city, and screening it from the bare, waste, uncultivated country —
the " wilderness " — which lies beyond it, and fills
up the space between the Mount of Olives and the
Dead Sea. At its north end the ridge bends round
to the west so as to form an inclosure to the city
on that side also. But there is this difference, that
whereas on the north a space of nearly a mile of
tolerably level surface intervenes between the walls
of the city and the rising ground, on the east the
mount is close to the walls,[a] parted only by that
which from the city itself seems no parting at all —
the narrow ravine of the Kidron. You descend
from the Golden Gateway, or the Gate of St. Stephen, by a sudden and steep declivity, and no
sooner is the bed of the valley reached than you
again commence the ascent of Olivet. So great is
the effect of this proximity, that, partly from that,
and partly from the extreme clearness of the air,
a spectator from the western part of Jerusalem imagines Olivet to rise immediately from the side of
the Haram area (Porter, Handb. p. 103 a; also Stanley, S. & P. p. 186).

It is this portion which is the real Mount of
Olives of the history. The northern part — in all
probability Nob,[b] Mizpeh, and Scopus — is, though
geologically continuous, a distinct mountain; and
the so-called Mount of Evil Counsel, directly south
of the Coenaculum, is too distant and too completely isolated by the trench of the Kidron to
claim the name. We will therefore confine our-

selves to this portion. In general height it is not
very much above the city: 300 feet higher than
the Temple mount,[c] hardly more than 100 above
the so-called Zion. But this is to some extent
made up for by the close proximity which exagger-
ates its height, especially on the side next to it.

The word "ridge" has been used above as the
only one available for an eminence of some length
and even height, but that word is hardly accurate.
There is nothing "ridge like" in the appearance
of the Mount of Olives, or of any other of the limestone hills of this district of Palestine; all is
rounded, swelling, and regular in form. At a
distance its outline is almost horizontal, gradually
sloping away at its southern end; but when approached, and especially when seen from below the
eastern wall of Jerusalem, it divides itself into
three, or rather perhaps four, independent summits
or eminences. Proceeding from N. to S. these occur
in the following order: Galilee, or Viri Galilæi;
Mount of the Ascension; Prophets, subordinate to
the last, and almost a part of it; Mount of Offense.

1. Of these the central one, distinguished by the
minaret and domes of the Church of the Ascension,
is in every way the most important. The church,
and the tiny hamlet of wretched hovels which surround it, — the Kefr et-Tûr, — are planted slightly
on the Jordan side of the actual top, but not so far
as to hinder their being seen from all parts of the
western environs of the mountain, or, in their turn,
commanding the view of the deepest recesses of the
Kidron Valley (Porter, Handb. p. 103). Three paths
lead from the valley to the summit. The first
— a continuation of the path which descends from
the St. Stephen's Gate to the Tomb of the Virgin —
passes under the north wall of the inclosure of
Gethsemane, and follows the line of the depression
between the centre and the northern hill. The
second parts from the first about 50 yards beyond
Gethsemane, and striking off to the right up the
very breast of the hill, surmounts the projection on
which is the traditional spot of the Lamentation
over Jerusalem, and thence proceeds directly upwards to the village. This is rather shorter than
the former; but, on the other hand, it is much
steeper, and the ascent extremely toilsome and
difficult. The third leaves the other two at the
N. E. corner of Gethsemane, and making a considerable detour to the south, visits the so-called
" Tombs of the Prophets," and following a very
slight depression which occurs at that part of the
mount, arrives in its turn at the village.

Of these three paths the first, from the fact that
it follows the natural shape of the ground, is, unquestionably, older than the others, which deviate
in pursuit of certain artificial objects. Every consideration is in favor of its being the road taken
by David in his flight. It is, with equal probability,
that usually taken by our Lord and his disciples in
their morning and evening transit between Jeru-

---

a * This remark may mislead the reader. From
some positions the mount may appear to be " close to
the walls," but is actually one half or three fourth
of a mile distant, even in that part of the valley where
Olivet and Moriah approach nearest to each other.
                                        H.

b See MIZPEH, p. 1977.

c The following are the elevations of the neighbor-
hood (above the Mediterranean), according to Van de
Velde (Memoir, p. 179): —
Mount of Olives (Church of Ascension) 2,724 ft.

" Zion " (the Coenaculum) . . . . 2.537 ft.
" Moriah " (Haram area) . . . . 2.429 ft.
N. W. corner of city . . . . 2,610 ft.
Valley of Kidron (Gethsemane) . . . 2.351 ft.
Valley of Kidron (Bir Eyub) . . . . 1.896 ft.
Bethany . . . . 1.808 ft.
Jordan . . . . 1,209 ft.[1]

1 * Compare the table of elevations by Capt. Wilson, vol.
ii. p. 1278 (Amer. ed.).   H.

salem and Bethany, and that also by which the Apostles returned to Jerusalem after the Ascension. If the " Tombs of the Prophets " existed before the destruction of Jerusalem (and if they are the Peristereon of Josephus they did), then the third road is next in antiquity. The second — having probably been made for the convenience of reaching a spot the reputation of which is comparatively modern — must be the most recent.

The central hill, which we are now considering, purports to contain the sites of some of the most sacred and impressive events of Christian history. During the Middle Ages most of these were protected by an edifice of some sort; and to judge from the reports of the early travellers, the mount must at one time have been thickly covered with churches and convents. The following is a complete list of these, as far as the writer has been able to ascertain them.

(1.) Commencing at the western foot, and going gradually up the hill.[a]

[b] [*] Tomb of the Virgin: containing also those of Joseph, Joachim, and Anna.

Gethsemane: containing —

  Olive garden.

   [*] Cavern of Christ's Prayer and Agony. (A Church here in the time of Jerome and Willibald.)

   Rock on which the 3 disciples slept.

   [*] Place of the capture of Christ. (A Church in the time of Bernard the Wise.)

Spot from which the Virgin witnessed the stoning of St. Stephen.

Do. at which her girdle dropped during her Assumption.

Do. of our Lord's Lamentation over Jerusalem, Luke xix. 41. (A Church here formerly, called Dominus flevit; Surius, in Mislin, ii. 476.)

Do. on which He first said the Lord's Prayer, or wrote it on the stone with his finger (Sæwulf, Early Trav. p. 42). A splendid Church here formerly. Maundeville seems to give this as the spot where the Beatitudes were pronounced (E. Tr. p. 177).

Do. at which the woman taken in adultery was brought to Him (Bernard the Wise, E. Tr. p. 28).

[*] Tombs of the Prophets (Matt. xxiii. 29): containing, according to the Jews, those of Haggai and Zechariah.

Cave in which the Apostles composed the Creed: called also Church of St. Mark or of the 12 Apostles.

Spot at which Christ discoursed of the Judgment to come (Matt. xxiv. 3).

Cave of St. Pelagia: according to the Jews, sepulchre of Huldah the Prophetess.

[*] Place of the Ascension. (Church, with subsequently a large Augustine convent attached.)

Spot at which the Virgin was warned of her death by an angel. In the valley between

the Ascension and Viri Galilæi (Maundeville, p. 177, and so Doubdan); but Maundrell (E. Tr. p. 470) places it close to the cave of Pelagia.

Viri Galilæi. Spot from which the Apostles watched the Ascension: or at which Christ first appeared to the 3 Maries after his Resurrection (Tobler, p. 76, note e).

(2.) On the east side, descending from the Church of the Ascension to Bethany.

The field in which stood the fruitless fig-tree. Bethphage.

Bethany: House of Lazarus. (A Church there in Jerome's time; Lib. de Situ, etc. " Bethania.")

[*] Tomb of Lazarus.

[*] Stone on which Christ was sitting when Martha and Mary came to Him.

The majority of these sacred spots now command little or no attention; but three still remain, sufficiently sacred — if authentic — to consecrate any place. These are: (1.) Gethsemane, at the foot of the mount. (2.) The place of the Lamentation of our Saviour over Jerusalem, half-way up; and (3.) The spot from which He ascended, on the summit.

(1.) Of these, Gethsemane is the only one which has any claim to be authentic. Its claims, however, are considerable; they are spoken of elsewhere.

(2.) The first person who attached the Ascension of Christ to the Mount of Olives seems to have been the Empress Helena (A. D. 325). Eusebius (Vit. Const. iii. § 43) states that she erected as a memorial of that event a sacred house[c] of assembly on the highest part of the mount, where there was a cave which a sure tradition (λόγος ἀληθής) testified to be that in which the Saviour had imparted mysteries to his disciples. But neither this account, nor that of the same author (Euseb. Demonst. Evang. vi. 18) when the cave is again mentioned, do more than name the Mount of Olives, generally, as the place from which Christ ascended: they fix no definite spot thereon. Nor does the Bordeaux Pilgrim, who arrived shortly after the building of the church (A. D. 333), know anything of the exact spot. He names the Mount of Olives as the place where our Lord used to teach his disciples: mentions that a basilica of Constantine stood there . . . he carefully points out the Mount of Transfiguration in the neighborhood (!) but is silent on the Ascension. From this time to that of Arculf (A. D. 700) we have no information, except the casual reference of Jerome (A. D. 390), cited below. In that immense interval of 370 years, the basilica of Constantine or Helena had given way to the round church of Modestus (Tobler, p. 92, note), and the tradition had become firmly established. The church was open to the sky " because of the passage of the Lord's body," and on the ground in the centre were the prints of his feet in the dust (pulvere). The cave or spot hallowed by his preaching to his disciples appears to have been moved off to the north of Bethany (Early Trav. p. 6).

Since that day many changes in detail have oc-

<hr/>

[a] The above catalogue has been compiled from Quaresmius, Doubdan, and Mislin. The last of these works, with great pretension to accuracy, is very inaccurate. Collateral references to other works are occasionally given.

[b] Plenary Indulgence is accorded by the Church of Rome to those who recite the Lord's Prayer and the Ave Maria at the spots marked thus (*).

[c] Ἱερὸν οἶκον ἐκκλησίας. This church was surmounted by a conspicuous gilt cross, the glitter of which was visible far and wide. Jerome refers to it several times. See especially Epitaph. Paulæ, " crux rutilans," and his comment on Zeph. i. 15.

curred: the "dust" has given way to stone, in which the print of first one, then two feet, was recognized,[a] one of which by a strange fate is said now to rest in the Mosque of the Aksa.[b] The buildings too have gone through alterations, additions, and finally losses, which has reduced them to their present condition: a mosque with a paved and un-roofed court of irregular shape adjoining, round which are ranged the altars of various Christian churches In the centre is the miraculous stone surmounted by a cupola and screened by a Moslim Kibleh or praying-place,[c] with an altar attached, on which the Christians are permitted once a year to say mass (Williams, *Holy City*, ii. 445). But through all these changes the locality of the Ascension has remained constantly the same.

The tradition no doubt arose from the fact of Helena's having erected her memorial church on the summit of the hill. It has been pointed out that she does not appear to have had any intention of fixing on a precise spot; she desired to erect a memorial of the Ascension, and this she did on the summit of the Mount of Olives, partly no doubt because of its conspicuous situation, but mainly because of the existence there of the sacred cavern in which our Lord had taught.[d] It took nearly three centuries to harden and narrow this general recognition of the connection of the Mount of Olives with Christ, into a lying invention in contradiction of the Gospel narrative of the Ascension. For a contradiction it undoubtedly is. Two accounts of the Ascension exist, both by the same author — the one, Luke xxiv. 50, 51, the other, Acts i. 6–11. The former only of these names the place at which our Lord ascended. That place was not the summit of the mount, but Bethany — "He led them out as far as to Bethany" — on the eastern slopes of the mount nearly a mile beyond the traditional spot.[e] The narrative of the Acts does not name the scene of the occurrence, but it states that after it had taken place the Apostles "returned to Jerusalem from the mount called Olivet, which is from Jerusalem a sabbath day's journey." It was their natural, their only route: but St. Luke is writing for Gentiles ignorant of the localities, and therefore he not only names Olivet, but adds the general information that it — that is, the summit and main part of the mount — was a Sabbath-day's journey from Jerusalem. The specification of the distance no more applies to Bethany on the further

side of the mount than to Gethsemane on the nearer.

And if, leaving the evidence, we consider the relative fitness of the two spots for such an event, — and compare the retired and wooded slopes around Bethany, so intimately connected with the last period of his life and with the friends who relieved the dreadful pressure of that period, and to whom he was attached by such binding ties, with an open public spot visible from every part of the city, and indeed for miles in every direction — we shall have no difficulty in deciding which is the more appropriate scene for the last act in the earthly sojourn of One who always shunned publicity even before his death, and whose communications after his resurrection were confined to his disciples, and marked by a singular privacy and reserve.[f]

(3.) The third of the three traditionary spots mentioned — that of the Lamentation over Jerusalem (Luke xix. 41–44) — is not more happily chosen than that of the Ascension. It is on a mamelon or protuberance which projects from the slope of the breast of the hill, about 300 yards above Gethsemane. The sacred narrative requires a spot on the road from Bethany, at which the city or temple should suddenly come into view: but this is one which can only be reached by a walk of several hundred yards over the breast of the hill, *with the temple and city full in sight the whole time.* It is also pretty evident that the path which now passes the spot, is subsequent in date to the fixing of the spot. As already remarked, the natural road lies up the valley between this hill and that to the north, and no one, unless with the special object of a visit to this spot, would take this very inconvenient path. The inappropriateness of this place has been noticed by many; but Mr. Stanley was the first who gave it its death-blow, by pointing out the true spot to take its place. In a well-known passage of *Sinai and Palestine* (pp. 190–193), he shows that the road of our Lord's "Triumphal entry" must have been, not the short and steep path over the summit used by small parties of pedestrians, but the longer and easier route round the southern shoulder of the southern of the three divisions of the mount, which has the peculiarity of presenting two successive views of Jerusalem; the first its southwest portion — the modern Zion; the second, after an interval, the buildings on the Temple mount, answering to the two points in the nar-

a Even the toes were made out by some (Tobler, p. 108, *note*).

b The "Chapel at the foot of Isa" is at the south end of the main aisle of the Aksa, almost under the dome. Attached to its northern side is the Pulpit. At the time of Ali Bey's visit (ii. 218, and plate lxxi.) it was called *Sidna Aisa*, Lord Jesus; but he says nothing of the foot-mark.

c See the plan of the edifice, in its present condition, on the margin of Sig. Pierotti's map, 1861. Other plans are given in Quaresmius, ii. 318, and B Amico, No. 34. Arculf's sketch is in Tobler (*Siloah-quelle*, etc.).

d Since writing this, the writer has observed that Mr. Stanley has taken the same view, almost in the same words. (See *S. & P.* ch. xiv. p. 454.)

e The Mount of Olives seems to be used for Bethany also in Luke xxi. 37, compared with Matt. xxi. 17, xxvi. 6, Mark xiv. 3. The morning walk from Bethany did not at any rate terminate with the day after his arrival at Jerusalem. (See Mark xi. 20.) One mode of reconciling the two narratives — which do not need reconciling — is to say that the district of Beth-

any extended to the summit of the mount. But "Bethany" in the N. T. is not a district but a village; and it was "as far as" that well-known place that "He led them forth."

f * "Like the first appearance to the shepherds," says Dr. Howson, "as recorded by St. Luke, like the first miracle as described by St. John, like the whole biography, as given both by them and the other two Evangelists, was the simplicity and seclusion of his departure. At no time did the Kingdom of God 'come with observation.' Jesus never forced himself upon public notice. It was not the men high in station who knew Him best — not the men celebrated for learning — but the lonely sufferers, the penitent, the poor, the degraded, and the despised. The evidence was sufficient, but not irresistible" (*Lectures on the Character of St. Paul*, p. 280).

The passage in which this writer has grouped together the local and historical associations connected with the Mount of Olives, forms one of the most beautiful passages to be found in our English homiletic literature (*Lectures*, pp 227–232).   H.

rative — the Hosanna of the multitude, the weeping of Christ.

2. We have spoken of the central and principal portion of the mount. Next to it on the southern side, separated from it by a slight depression, up which the path mentioned above as the third takes its course, is a hill which appears neither to possess, nor to have possessed, any independent name. It is remarkable only for the fact that it contains the "singular catacomb" known as the "Tombs of the Prophets," probably in allusion to the words of Christ (Matt. xxiii. 29). Of the origin, and even of the history of this cavern, hardly anything is known. It is possible that it is the "rock called Peristereon," named by Josephus (B. J. v. 12, § 2) in describing the course of Titus's great wall [a] of circumvallation, though there is not much to be said for that view (see Rob. iii. 254, note). To the earlier pilgrims it does not appear to have been known; at least their descriptions hardly apply to its present size or condition. Mr. Stanley (S. & P. p. 453) is inclined to identify it with the cave mentioned by Eusebius as that in which our Lord taught his disciples, and also with that which is mentioned by Arculf and Bernard as containing "the four tables" of our Lord (Enr. Tr. pp. 4, 28). The first is not improbable, but the cave of Arculf and Bernard seems to have been down in the valley not far from the Tomb of the Virgin, and on the spot of the betrayal (E. Tr. p. 28), therefore close to Gethsemane.

3. The most southern portion of the Mount of Olives is that usually known as the "Mount of Offense," Mons Offensionis, though by the Arabs called Baten el-Hawa, "the bag of the wind." It rises next to that last mentioned; and in the hollow between the two, more marked than the depressions between the more northern portions, runs the road from Bethany, which was without doubt the road of Christ's entry to Jerusalem.

The title Mount of Offense, [b] or of Scandal, was bestowed on the supposition that it is the "Mount of Corruption," [c] on which Solomon erected the high places for the gods of his foreign wives (2 K. xxiii. 13; 1 K. xi. 7). This tradition appears to be of a recent date. It is not mentioned in the Jewish travellers, Benjamin, hap-Parchi, or Petachia, and the first appearance of the name or the tradition as attached to that locality among Christian writers, appears to be in John of Wirtzburg (Tobler, p. 80, note) and Brocardus (Descriptio Ter. S. cap. ix.), both of the 13th century. At that time the northern summit was believed to have been the site of the altar of Chemosh (Brocardus), the southern one that of Molech only (Thietmar, Peregr. xi. 2).

The southern summit is considerably lower than the centre one, and, as already remarked, it is much more definitely separated from the surrounding portions of the mountain than the others are. It is also sterner and more repulsive in its form. On the south it is bounded by the Wady en-Nar, the continuation of the Kidron, curving round eastward on its dreary course to S. Saba and the Dead Sea. From this barren ravine the Mount of Offense rears its rugged sides by acclivities barer and steeper than any in the northern portion of the mount, and its top presents a bald and desolate surface, contrasting greatly with the cultivation of the other summits, and which not improbably, as in the case of Mount Ebal, suggested the name which it now bears. On the steep ledges of its western face clings the ill-favored village of Silwân, a few dilapidated towers rather than houses, their gray bleared walls hardly to be distinguished from the rock to which they adhere, and inhabited by a tribe as mean and repulsive as their habitations. [SILOAM.]

Crossing to the back or eastern side of this mountain, on a half-isolated promontory or spur which overlooks the road of our Lord's progress from Bethany, are found tanks and foundations and other remains, which are maintained by Dr. Barclay (City, etc. p. 66) to be those of Bethphage (see also Stewart, Tent and Khan, p. 322).

4. The only one of the four summits remaining to be considered is that on the north of the "Mount of Ascension" — the Karem es-Seyad, or Vineyard of the Sportsman; or, as it is called by the modern Latin and Greek Christians, the Viri Galilæi. This is a hill of exactly the same character as the Mount of the Ascension, and so nearly its equal in height that few travellers agree as to which is the more lofty. The summits of the two are about 400 yards apart. It stands directly opposite the N. E. corner of Jerusalem, and is approached by the path between it and the Mount of Ascension, which strikes at the top into a cross path leading to el-Isawiyeh and Anata. The Arabic name well reflects the fruitful character of the hill, on which there are several vineyards, besides much cultivation of other kinds. The Christian name is due to the singular tradition, that here the two angels addressed the Apostles after our Lord's ascension — "Ye men of Galilee!" This idea, which is so incompatible, on account of the distance, even with the traditional spot of the Ascension, is of late existence and inexplicable origin. The first name by which we encounter this hill is simply "Galilee," ἡ Γαλιλαία (Perdiccas, cir. A. D. 1250, in Reland, Pal. cap. lii.). Brocardus (A. D. 1280) describes the moun

---

[a] The wall seems to have crossed the Kidron from about the present St. Stephen's Gate to the mount on the opposite side. It then "turned south and encompassed the mount as far as the rock called the Dovecot (ἄχρι τῆς Περιστερεῶνος καλουμένης πέτρας), and the other hill which lies next it, and is over the Valley of Siloam." Peristereon may be used as a synonym for columbarium, a late Latin word for an excavated cemetery; and there is perhaps some analogy between it and the Wady Hamâm, or Valley of Pigeons, in the neighborhood of Tiberias, the rocky sides of which abound in caves and perforations. Or it may be one of those half-Hebrew, half-Greek appellations, which there is reason to believe Josephus bestows on some of the localities of Palestine, and which have yet to be investigated. Tischendorf (Travels in the East, p. 176) is wrong in saying that Josephus "always calls it the Dovecot." He mentions it only this once.

[b] In German, Berg des Aergernisses.

[c] חַר הַמַּשְׁחִית. This seems to be connected etymologically in some way with the name by which the mount is occasionally rendered in the Targums — טוּר מַשְׁחִיתָא (Jonathan, Cant. viii. 9; Pseudojon Gen. viii. 11) One is probably a play on the other.

Mr. Stanley (S. & P. p. 188, note) argues that the Mount of Corruption was the northern hill (Viri Galilæi), because the three sanctuaries were south of it, and therefore on the other three summits.

tain as the site of Solomon's altar to Chemosh (*Descr.* cap. ix.), but evidently knows of no name for it, and connects it with no Christian event. This name may, as is conjectured (Quaresmius, ii. 319, and Reland, p. 341), have originated in its being the custom of the Apostles, or of the Galileans generally, when they came up to Jerusalem, to take up their quarters there; or it may be the echo or distortion of an ancient name of the spot, possibly the Geliloth of Josh. xviii. 17 — one of the landmarks of the south boundary of Benjamin, which has often puzzled the topographer. But, whatever its origin, it came at last to be considered as the actual Galilee of northern Palestine, the place at which our Lord appointed to meet his disciples after his resurrection (Matt. xxviii. 10), the scene of the miracle of Cana (Reland, p. 328). This transference, at once so extraordinary and so instructive, arose from the same desire, combined with the same astounding want of the critical faculty, which enabled the pilgrims of the Middle Ages to see without perplexity the scene of the Transfiguration (Bordeaux Pilgr.), of the Beatitudes (Maundeville, E. Tr. p. 177), and of the Ascension, all crowded together on the single summit of the central hill of Olivet. It testified to the same feeling which has brought together the scene of Jacob's vision at Bethel, of the sacrifice of Isaac on Moriah, and of David's offering in the threshing-floor of Araunah, on one hill; and which to this day has crowded within the walls of one church of moderate size all the events connected with the death and resurrection of Christ.

In the 8th century the place of the angels was represented by two columns [a] in the Church of the Ascension itself (Willibald, E. Tr. p. 19). So it remained with some trifling difference, at the time of Sæwulf's visit (A. D. 1102), but there was then also a chapel in existence — apparently on the northern summit — purporting to stand where Christ made his first appearance after the resurrection, and called "Galilee." So it continued at Maundeville's visit (1322). In 1580 the two pillars were still shown in the Church of the Ascension (Radzivil), but in the 16th century (Tobler, p. 75) the tradition had relinquished its ancient and more appropriate seat, and thenceforth became attached to the northern summit, where Maundrell (A. D. 1697) encountered it (E. Tr. p. 471), and where it even now retains some hold, the name Kalilea being occasionally applied to it by the Arabs. (See Pococke and Scholz, in Tobler, p. 72.) An ancient tower connected with the tradition was in course of demolition during Maundrell's visit, 'a Turk having bought the field in which it stood."

The presence of the crowd of churches and other edifices implied in the foregoing description must have rendered the Mount of Olives, during the early and middle ages of Christianity, entirely unlike what it was in the time of the Jewish kingdom, or of our Lord. Except the high places on the summit the only buildings then to be seen were probably the walls of the vineyards and gardens, and the towers and presses which were their invariable accompaniment. But though the churches are nearly all demolished there must be a consider-

able difference between the aspect of the mountain now and in those days when it received its name from the abundance of its olive-groves. It does not now stand so preëminent in this respect among the hills in the neighborhood of Jerusalem. "It is only in the deeper and more secluded slope leading up to the northernmost summit that these venerable trees spread into anything like a forest." The cedars commemorated by the Talmud (Lightfoot, ii. 305), and the date-palms implied in the name Bethany, have fared still worse: there is not one of either to be found within many miles. This change is no doubt due to natural causes, variations of climate, etc.; but the check was not improbably given by the ravages committed by the army of Titus, who are stated by Josephus to have stripped the country round Jerusalem for miles and miles of every stick or shrub for the banks constructed during the siege. No olive or cedar, however sacred to Jew or Christian, would at such a time escape the axes of the Roman sappers, and, remembering how under similar circumstances every root and fibre of the smallest shrubs were dug up for fuel by the camp-followers of our army at Sebastopol, it would be wrong to deceive ourselves by the belief that any of the trees now existing are likely to be the same or even descendants of those which were standing before that time.

Except at such rare occasions as the passage of the caravan of pilgrims to the Jordan, there must also be a great contrast between the silence and loneliness which now pervades the mount, and the busy scene which it presented in later Jewish times. Bethphage and Bethany are constantly referred to in the Jewish authors as places of much resort for business and pleasure. The two large cedars already mentioned had below them shops for the sale of pigeons and other necessaries for worshippers in the Temple, and appear to have driven an enormous trade (see the citations in Lightfoot, ii. 39, 305). Two religious ceremonies performed there must also have done much to increase the numbers who resorted to the mount. The appearance of the new moon was probably watched for, certainly proclaimed, from the summit — the long torches waving to and fro in the moonless night till answered from the peak of *Kurn Surtabeh*; and an occasion to which the Jews attached so much weight would be sure to attract a concourse. The second ceremony referred to was burning of the Red Heifer.[b] This solemn ceremonial was enacted on the central mount, and in a spot so carefully specified that it would seem not difficult to fix it. It was due east of the sanctuary, and at such an elevation on the mount that the officiating priest, as he slew the animal and sprinkled her blood, could see the façade of the sanctuary through the east gate of the Temple. To this spot a viaduct was constructed across the valley on a double row of arches, so as to raise it far above all possible proximity with graves or other defilements (see citations in Lightfoot, ii. 39). The depth of the valley is such at this place (about 350 feet from the line of the south wall of the present *Harem* area) that this viaduct must have been an important and conspicuous work. It was probably de-

---

[a] These columns appear to have been seen as late as A. D. 1580 by Radzivil (Williams, *Holy City*, ii. 127, note).

[b] There seems to be some doubt whether this was an annual ceremony. Jerome (*Epitaph. Paulæ*, § 12)

distinctly says so; but the Rabbis assert that from Moses to the Captivity it was performed but once; from the Captivity to the Destruction eight times (Lightfoot, ii. 305).

mofiabed by the Jews themselves on the approach of Titus, or even earlier, when Pompey led his army by Jericho and over the Mount of Olives. This would account satisfactorily for its not being alluded to by Josephus. During the siege the 10th legion had its fortified camp and batteries on the top of the mount, and the first, and some of the fiercest encounters of the siege took place here.

"The lasting glory of the Mount of Olives," it has been well said, "belongs not to the Old Dispensation, but to the New. Its very barrenness of interest in earlier times sets forth the abundance of those associations which it derives from the closing scenes of the sacred history. Nothing, perhaps, brings before us more strikingly the contrast of Jewish and Christian feeling, the abrupt and inharmonious termination of the Jewish dispensation — if we exclude the culminating point of the Gospel history — than to contrast the blank which Olivet presents to the Jewish pilgrims of the Middle Ages, only dignified by the sacrifice of 'the red heifer;' and the vision too great for words, which it offers to the Christian traveller of all times, as the most detailed and the most authentic abiding place of Jesus Christ. By one of those strange coincidences, whether accidental or borrowed, which occasionally appear in the Rabbinical writings, it is said in the Midrash,[a] that the Shechinah, or Presence of God, after having finally retired from Jerusalem, 'dwelt' three years and a half on the Mount of Olives, to see whether the Jewish people would not repent, calling, 'Return to me, O my sons, and I will return to you;' 'Seek ye the Lord while He may be found, call upon Him while He is near:' and then, when all was in vain, returned to its own place. W. ether or not this story has a direct allusion to the ministrations of Christ, it is a true expression of his relation respectively to Jerusalem and to Olivet. It is useless to seek for traces of his presence in the streets of the since ten times captured city. It is impossible not to find them in the free space of the Mount of Olives" (Stanley, S. & P. p 189).

A monograph on the Mount of Olives, exhausting every source of information, and giving the fullest references, will be found in Tobler's Siloahquelle und der Oelberg, St. Gallen, 1852. The ecclesiastical traditions are in Quaresmius, Elucidatio Terræ Sanctæ, ii. 277–340, &c. Doubdan's account (Le Voyage de la Terre Sainte, Paris, 1657) is excellent, and his plates very correct. The passages relating to the mount in Mr. Stanley's Sinai and Palestine (pp. 185-195, 452-454) are full of instruction and beauty, and in fixing the spot of our Lord's lamentation over Jerusalem he has certainly made one of the most important discoveries ever made in relation to this interesting locality. G.

OLIVET (2 Sam. xv. 30; Acts i. 12), probably derived from the Vulgate, mons quâ vocatur Oliveti in the latter of these two passages. [See OLIVES, MOUNT OF.]

● OLIVE-YARD. [OLIVE.]

● OLOFER'NES. [HOLOFERNES.]

OLYMPAS ('Ολυμπᾶς: Olympias), a Christan at Rome (Rom. xvi. 15), perhaps of the house-

hold of Philologus. It is stated by Pseudo-Hippolytus that he was one of the seventy disciples, and underwent martyrdom at Rome: and Baronius ventures to give A. D. 69 as the date of his death.
W. T. B.

OLYM'PIUS ('Ολύμπιος: Olympius). One of the chief epithets of the Greek deity Zeus, so called from Mount Olympus in Thessaly, the abode of the gods (2 Macc. vi. 2). [See JUPITER, vol. ii. p. 1518 b.]

OMAE'RUS ('Ισμαῆρος ; [Vat. Μανρος ; Ald. 'Ιωμάηρος:] Abranius). AMRAM of the sons of Bani (1 Esdr. ix. 34; comp. Ezr. x. 34). The Syriac seems to have read "Ishmael."

O'MAR (אוֹמָר [perh. eloquent, fluent]: 'Ωμάρ: Alex. Ωμαν in Gen. xxxvi. 11: Omar). Son of Eliphaz the first-born of Esau, and "duke" or phylarch of Edom (Gen. xxxvi. 11, 15; 1 Chr. i. 36). The name is supposed to survive in that of the tribe of Amir Arabs east of the Jordan. Bunsen asserts that Omar was the ancestor of the Bne 'Hammer in northern Edom (Bibelwerk, Gen. xxxvi. 11), but the names are essentially different.

O'MEGA (Ω). The last letter of the Greek alphabet, as Alpha is the first. It is used metaphorically to denote the end of anything: "I am Alpha and Omega, the beginning and the ending . . . . the first and the last" (Rev. i. 8, 11 [Rec. Text]). The symbol את, which contains the first and last letters of the Hebrew alphabet, is, according to Buxtorf (Lex. Talm. p. 244), "among the Cabalists often put mystically for the beginning and end, like Α and Ω in the Apocalypse." Schoettgen (Hor. Heb. p. 1086) quotes from the Jalkut Rubeni on Gen. i. 1, to the effect that in את are comprehended all letters, and that it is the name of the Shechinah. [ALPHA.]

OMER. [WEIGHTS AND MEASURES.]

OM'RI (עָמְרִי, i. e. עָמְרִיָה, probably "servant of Jehovah" (Gesenius): 'Αμβρι, [exc. Mic. vi. 16, Ζαμβρί; Vat. Ζαμβρει, exc. 2 K. viii. 26 (Vat.[1]), 2 Chr. xxii. 2, Αμβρει: Alex. Ζαμβρι, exc. 2 K. viii. 26, Αμβρι;] 'Αμαρῖνος, Joseph. Ant. viii. 12, § 5: Amri). 1. Originally a "captain of the host" to ELAH, was afterwards himself king of Israel, and founder of the third dynasty When Elah was murdered by Zimri at Tirzah, then capital of the northern kingdom, Omri was engaged in the siege of Gibbethon, situated in the tribe of Dan, which had been occupied by the Philistines, who had retained it, in spite of the efforts to take it made by Nadab, Jeroboam's son and successor. As soon as the army heard of Elah's death, they proclaimed Omri king. Thereupon he broke up the siege of Gibbethon, and attacked Tirzah, where Zimri was holding his court as king of Israel. The city was taken, and Zimri perished in the flames of the palace, after a reign of seven days. [ZIMRI.] Omri, however, was not allowed to establish his dynasty without a struggle against Tibni, whom "half the people" (1 K. xvi. 21) desired to raise to the throne, and who was bravely

---

assisted by his brother Joram.* The civil war lasted four years (cf. 1 K. xvi. 15, with 23). After the defeat and death of Tibni and Joram, Omri reigned for six years in Tirzah, although the palace there was destroyed; but at the end of that time, in spite of the proverbial beauty of the site (Cant. vi. 4), he transferred his residence, probably from the proved inability of Tirzah to stand a siege, to the mountain Shomron, better known by its Greek name Samaria, which he bought for two talents of silver from a rich man, otherwise unknown, called Shemer.* It is situated about six miles from Shechem, the most ancient of Hebrew capitals; and its position, according to Prof. Stanley (S. & P. p. 240), "combined, in a union not elsewhere found in Palestine, strength, fertility, and beauty." Bethel, however, remained the religious metropolis of the kingdom, and the calf worship of Jeroboam was maintained with increased determination and disregard of God's law (1 K. xvi. 26). At Samaria Omri reigned for six years more. He seems to have been a vigorous and unscrupulous ruler, anxious to strengthen his dynasty by intercourse and alliances with foreign states. Thus he made a treaty with Benhadad I., king of Damascus, though on very unfavorable conditions, surrendering to him some frontier cities (1 K. xx. 34), and among them probably Ramoth-gilead (1 K. xxii. 3), and admitting into Samaria a resident Syrian embassy, which is described by the expression "he made streets in Samaria" for Benhadad. (See the phrase more fully explained under AHAB.) As a part of the same system, he united his son in marriage to the daughter of a principal Phœnician prince, which led to the introduction into Israel of Baal worship, and all its attendant calamities and crimes. This worldly and irreligious policy is denounced by Micah (vi. 16) under the name of the "statutes of Omri," which appear to be contrasted with the Lord's precepts to his people, "to do justly, and to love mercy, and to walk humbly with thy God." It achieved, however, a temporary success, for Omri left his kingdom in peace to his son Ahab; and his family, unlike the ephemeral dynasties which had preceded him, gave four kings to Israel, and occupied the throne for about half a century, till it was overthrown by the great reaction against Baal-worship under Jehu. The probable date of Omri's accession (i. e. of the deaths of Elah and Zimri) was B. C. 935; of Tibni's defeat and the beginning of Omri's sole reign, B. C. 931, and of his death, B. C. 919.   G. E. L. C.

2. ('Αμαρίά; [Vat. Αμαρεια.]) One of the sons of Becher the son of Benjamin (1 Chr. vii. 8).

3. ('Αμρί; [Vat. Αμρει.]) A descendant of Pharez the son of Judah (1 Chr. ix. 4).

---

4. ('Αμβρί; [Vat. Αμβρει;] Alex. Αμρει.) Son of Michael, and chief of the tribe of Issachar in the reign of David (1 Chr. xxvii. 18).

ON (אוֹן: Αὔν; Alex. Αυναν: Ποη). The son of Peleth, and one of the chiefs of the tribe of Reuben who took part with Korah, Dathan, and Abiram in their revolt against Moses (Num. xvi. 1). His name does not again appear in the narrative of the conspiracy, nor is he alluded to when reference is made to the final catastrophe. Possibly he repented; and indeed there is a Rabbinical tradition to the effect that he was prevailed upon by his wife to withdraw from his associates. Abendana's note is, "behold On is not mentioned again, for he was separated from their company after Moses spake with them. And our Rabbis of blessed memory said that his wife saved him." Josephus (Ant. iv. 2, § 2) omits the name of On, but retains that of his father in the form Φαλαοῦς, thus apparently identifying Peleth with Phallu, the son of Reuben.   W. A. W.

ON (אוֹן, אֹן, אָוֶן, אוֹן [see below]: [Jer.] 'Ων, [Gen.] Ἡλιούπολις [Alex. Ἰλιουπολις]: Heliopolis), a town of lower Egypt, which is mentioned in the Bible under at least two names, BETH-SHEMESH, בֵּית שֶׁמֶשׁ (Jer. xliii. 13), corresponding to the ancient Egyptian sacred name HA-RA, "the abode of the sun," and that above, corresponding to the common name AN, and perhaps also spoken of as Ir-ha-heres, עִיר הַהֶרֶס, or הַהֶרֶס —, the second part being, in this case, either the Egyptian sacred name, or else the Hebrew חֶרֶס, but we prefer to read "a city of destruction." [IR-HA-HERES.] The two names were known to the translator or translators of Exodus in the LXX. where On is explained to be Heliopolis (Ων ἥ ἐστιν Ἡλιούπολις, i. 11); but in Jeremiah this version seems to treat Beth-shemesh as the name of a temple (τοὺς στύλους Ἡλιουπόλεως, τοὺς ἐν 'Ων, xliii. 13, LXX. l. 13). The Coptic version gives ⲰⲚ as the equivalent of the names in the LXX., but whether as an Egyptian word or such a word Hebraicized can scarcely be determined.*

The ancient Egyptian common name is written AN, or AN-T, and perhaps ANU; but the essential part of the word is AN, probably no more was pronounced. There were two towns called AN, Heliopolis, distinguished as the northern, AN-MEHEET, and Hermonthis, in Upper Egypt, as the southern, AN-RES (Brugsch, Geogr. Inschr.

. 254, 255, Nos. 1217 *a*, *b*, 1218, 870, 1225). As to the meaning, we can say nothing certain. Cyril, who, as bishop of Alexandria, should be listened to on such a question, says that On signified the sun (Ὤν δέ ἐστι κατ᾽ αὐτοὺς ὁ ἥλιος, ad *Hos.* p. 145), and the Coptic ΟΥⲰⲒⲚⲒ (M), ΟΥⲈⲒⲚ, ΟΥⲞⲈⲒⲚ (S), "light," has therefore been compared (see La Croze, *Lex.* pp. 71, 189), but the hieroglyphic form is UBEN, "shining," which has no connection with AN.

Heliopolis was situate on the east side of the Pelusiac branch of the Nile, just below the point of the Delta, and about twenty miles northeast of Memphis. It was before the Roman time the capital of the Heliopolite Nome, which was included in Lower Egypt. Now, its site is above the point of the Delta, which is the junction of the Phatmetic, or Damietta branch and the Bolbitine, or Rosetta, and about ten miles to the northeast of Cairo. The oldest monument of the town is the obelisk, which was set up late in the reign of Sesertesen I., head of the 12th dynasty, dating B. C. cir. 2050. According to Manetho, the bull Mnevis was first worshipped here in the reign of Kaiechôs, second king of the 2d dynasty (B. C. 2400). In the earliest times it must have been subject to the 1st dynasty so long as their sole rule lasted, which was perhaps for no more than the reigns of Menes (B. C. cir. 2717) and Athothis: it doubtless next came under the government of the Memphites, of the 3d (B. C. cir. 2640), 4th, and 6th dynasties: it then passed into the hands of the Diospolites of the 12th dynasty, and the Shepherds of the 15th; bu whether the former or the latter held it first, ot it was contested between them, we cannot as yet determine. During the long period of anarchy that followed the rule of the 12th dynasty, when Lower Egypt was subject to the Shepherd kings, Heliopolis must have been under the government of the strangers. With the accession of the 19th dynasty, it was probably recovered by the Egyp-

Plain and Obelisk of Heliopolis.

tians, during the war which Aähmes, or Amosis, head of that line, waged with the Shepherds, and thenceforward held by them, though perhaps more than once occupied by invaders (comp. Chabas, *Papyrus Magique Harris*), before the Assyrians conquered Egypt. Its position, near the eastern frontier, must have made it always a post of special importance. [NO-AMON.]

The chief object of worship at Heliopolis was the sun, under the forms RA, the sun simply, whence the sacred name of the place, HA-RA, "the abode of the sun," and ATUM, the setting sun, or sun of the nether world. Probably its chief temple was dedicated to both. SHU, the son of Atum, and TAFNET, his daughter, were also here worshipped, as well as the bull Mnevis, sacred to RA, Osiris, Isis, and the Phœnix, BENNU, probably represented by a living bird of the crane kind. (On the mythology see Brugsch, p. 254 ff.) The temple of the sun, described by Strabo (xvii. pp. 805, 806), is now only represented by the single

beautiful obelisk, which is of red granite, 68 feet 2 inches high above the pedestal, and bears a dedication, showing that it was sculptured in or after his 30th year (cir. 2050) by Sesertesen I., first king of the 12th dynasty (B. C. cir. 2080-2045). There were probably far more than a usual number of obelisks before the gates of this temple, on the evidence of ancient writers, and the inscriptions of some yet remaining elsewhere, and no doubt the reason was that these monuments were sacred to the sun. Heliopolis was anciently famous for its learning, and Eudoxus and Plato studied under its priests; but, from the extent of the mounds, it seems to have been always a small town.

The first mention of this place in the Bible is in the history of Joseph, to whom we read Pharaoh gave "to wife Asenath the daughter of Poti-pherah, priest of On" (Gen. xli. 45, comp. ver. 50, and xlvi. 20). Joseph was probably governor of Egypt under a king of the 15th dynasty, of which Memphis was, at least for a time, the capital. In this case he would doubtless have lived for part of the year at Memphis, and therefore near to Heliopolis. The name of Asenath's father was appropriate to a Heliopolite, and especially to a priest of that place (though according to some he may have been a prince), for it means "Belonging to Ra," or "the sun." The name of Joseph's master Potiphar is the same, but with a slight difference in the Hebrew orthography. According to the LXX. version, On was one of the cities built for Pharaoh by the oppressed Israelites, for it mentions three "strong cities" instead of the two "treasure cities" of the Heb., adding On to Pithom and Raamses (Καὶ ᾠκοδόμησαν πόλεις ὀχυρὰς τῷ Φαραῷ, τήν τε Πειθὼ, καὶ Ῥαμεσσῆ, καὶ Ὤν, ἥ ἐστιν Ἡλιούπολις, Ex. i. 11). If it be intended that these cities were founded by the labor of the people, the addition is probably a mistake, although Heliopolis may have been ruined and rebuilt; but it is possible that they were merely fortified, probably as places for keeping stores. Heliopolis lay at no great distance from the land of Goshen and from Raamses, and probably Pithom also.

Isaiah has been supposed to speak of On when he prophecies that one of the five cities in Egypt that should speak the language of Canaan, should be called Ir-ha-heres, which may mean the City of the Sun, whether we take "heres" to be a Hebrew or an Egyptian word; but the reading "a city of destruction" seems preferable, and we have no evidence that there was any large Jewish settlement at Heliopolis, although there may have been at one time from its nearness to the town of Onias. [IR-HA-HERES; ONIAS.] Jeremiah speaks of On under the name Beth-shemesh, "the house of the sun," where he predicts of Nebuchadnezzar, "He shall break also the pillars [? מצבות, but, perhaps, statues, comp. IDOL, ii. 1119] of Beth-shemesh, that [is] in the land of Egypt; and the houses of the gods of the Egyptians shall he burn with fire" (xliii. 13). By the word we have rendered "pillars," obelisks are reasonably supposed to be meant, for the number of which before the temple of the sun Heliopolis must have been famous, and perhaps by "the houses of the gods," the temples of this place are intended, as their being burnt would be a proof of the powerlessness of Ra and Atum, both forms of the sun, Shu the god of light, and Tafnet a fire-goddess, to save their dwellings from the very element over which they were supposed to rule. Perhaps it was on account of the many false gods of Heliopolis, that in Ezekiel, On is written Aven, by a change in the punctuation, if we can here depend on the Masoretic text, and so made to signify "vanity," and especially the vanity of idolatry. The prophet foretells, "The young men of Aven and of Pi-beseth shall fall by the sword: and these [cities] shall go into captivity" (xxx. 17). Pi-beseth or Bubastis is doubtless spoken of with Heliopolis as in the same part of Egypt, and so to be involved in a common calamity at the same time when the land should be invaded.

After the age of the prophets we hear no more in Scripture of Heliopolis. Local tradition however, points it out as a place where our Lord and the Virgin came, when Joseph brought them into Egypt, and a very ancient sycamore is shown as a tree beneath which they rested. The Jewish settlements in this part of Egypt, and especially the town of Onias, which was probably only twelve

miles distant from Heliopolis in a northerly direction, but a little to the eastward (*Modern Egypt and Thebes*, i. 297, 298), then flourished, and were nearer to Palestine than the heathen towns like Alexandria, in which there was any large Jewish population, so that there is much probability in this tradition. And, perhaps, Heliopolis itself may have had a Jewish quarter, although we do not know it to have been the Ir-ha-heres of Isaiah.

R. S. P.

O'NAM (אוֹנָם [*strong, vigorous*]: Ὠμάρ, Ὠνάν; Alex. Ωμαν, Ωναν: *Onam*). 1. One of the sons of Shobal the son of Seir (Gen. xxxvi. 23; 1 Chr. i. 40). Some Hebrew MSS. read "Onan."

2. (Ὀζόμ: Alex. Ουνομα.) The son of Jerahmeel by his wife Atarah (1 Chr. ii. 26, 28).

O'NAN (אוֹנָן [*strong, vigorous*]: Αὐνάν: *Onan*). The second son of Judah by the Canaanitess, "the daughter of Shua" (Gen. xxxviii. 4; 1 Chr. ii. 3). On the death of Er the first-born, it was the duty of Onan, according to the custom which then existed and was afterwards established by a definite law (Deut. xxv. 5–10), continuing to the latest period of Jewish history (Mark xii. 19), to marry his brother's widow and perpetuate his race. But he found means to prevent the consequences of marriage, "and what he did was evil in the eyes of Jehovah, and He slew him also," as He had slain his elder brother (Gen. xxxviii. 9). His death took place before the family of Jacob went down into Egypt (Gen. xlvi. 12; Num. xxvi. 19).

W. A. W.

ONES'IMUS (Ὀνήσιμος [*profitable or useful*]: *Onesimus*) is the name of the servant or slave in whose behalf Paul wrote the Epistle to Philemon. He was a native, or certainly an inhabitant of Colossae, since Paul in writing to the church there speaks of him (Col. iv. 9) as ὅς ἐστιν ἐξ ὑμῶν, "one of you." This expression confirms the presumption which his Greek name affords, that he was a Gentile, and not a Jew, as some have argued from μάλιστα ἐμοί in Phil. 16. Slaves were numerous in Phrygia, and the name itself of Phrygian was almost synonymous with that of slave. Hence it happened that in writing to the Colossians (iii. 22 –iv. 1) Paul had occasion to instruct them concerning the duties of masters and servants to each other. Onesimus was one of this unfortunate class of persons, as is evident both from the manifest implication in οὐκέτι ὡς δοῦλον in Phil. 16, and from the general tenor of the epistle. There appears to have been no difference of opinion on this point among the ancient commentators, and there is none of any critical weight among the modern. The man escaped from his master and fled to Rome, where in the midst of its vast population he could hope to be concealed, and to baffle the efforts which were so often made in such cases for retaking the fugitive. (Walter, *Die Geschichte des Röm. Rechts*, ii. 62 f.) It must have been to Rome that he directed his way, and not to Caesarea, as some contend; for the latter view stands connected with an indefensible opinion respecting the place whence the letter was written (see Neander's *Pflanzung*, ii. 506). Whether Onesimus had any other motive for the flight than the natural love of liberty we have not the means of deciding. It has been very generally supposed that he had committed some offense, as theft or embezzlement, and feared the punishment of his guilt. But as the ground of that opinion we must know the meaning of ἠδίκησε in Phil. 18, which is uncertain, not to say inconsistent with any such imputation (see notes in the *Epistle to Philemon*, by the American Bible Union, p. 60).[a] Commentators at all events go entirely beyond the evidence when they assert (as Conybeare, *Life and Epistles of Paul*, ii. 467) that he belonged to the dregs of society, that he robbed his master, and confessed the sin to Paul. Though it may be doubted whether Onesimus heard the Gospel for the first time at Rome, it is beyond question that he was led to embrace the Gospel there through the Apostle's instrumentality. The language in ver. 10 of the letter (ὃν ἐγέννησα ἐν τοῖς δεσμοῖς μου) is explicit on this point. As there were believers in Phrygia when the Apostle passed through that region on his third missionary tour (Acts xviii. 23), and as Onesimus belonged to a Christian household (Phil. 2), it is not improbable that he knew something of the Christian doctrine before he went to Rome. How long a time elapsed between his escape and conversion, we cannot decide; for πρὸς ὥραν in the 15th verse, to which appeal has been made, is purely a relative expression, and will not justify any inference as to the interval in question.

After his conversion, the most happy and friendly relations sprung up between the teacher and the disciple. The situation of the Apostle as a captive and an indefatigable laborer for the promotion of the Gospel (Acts xxviii. 30, 31) must have made him keenly alive to the sympathies of Christian friendship[b] and dependent upon others for various services of a personal nature, important to his efficiency as a minister of the word. Onesimus appears to have supplied this twofold want in an eminent degree. We see from the letter that he won entirely the Apostle's heart, and made himself so useful to him in various private ways, or evinced such a capacity to be so (for he may have gone back to Colossae soon after his conversion), that Paul wished to have him remain constantly with him. Whether he desired his presence as a personal attendant or as a minister of the Gospel, is not certain from ἵνα διακονῇ μοι in ver. 13 of the epistle. Be this as it may, Paul's attachment to him as a disciple, as a personal friend, and as a helper to him in his bonds, was such that he yielded him up only in obedience to that spirit of self-denial, and that sensitive regard for the feelings or the rights of others, of which his conduct on this occasion displayed so noble an example.

There is but little to add to this account, when we pass beyond the limits of the New Testament. The traditional notices which have come down to us are too few and too late to amount to much as historical testimony. Some of the later fathers assert that Onesimus was set free, and was subsequently ordained Bishop of Berœa in Macedonia (*Constit. Apost.* vii. 46). The person of the same

name mentioned as Bishop of Ephesus in the first epistle of Ignatius to the Ephesians (Hefele, *Patrum Apost. Opp.*, p. 152) was a different person (see Winer, *Realw.* ii. 175). It is related also that Onesimus finally made his way to Rome again, and ended his days there as a martyr during the persecution under Nero. H. B. H.

ONESIPH'ORUS (Ὀνησίφορος [*bringer of profit*]) is named twice only in the N. T., namely, 2 Tim. i. 16–18, and iv. 19. In the former passage Paul mentions him in terms of grateful love, as having a noble courage and generosity in his behalf, amid his trials as a prisoner at Rome, when others from whom he expected better things had deserted him (2 Tim. iv. 16); and in the latter passage he singles out "the household of Onesiphorus" as worthy of a special greeting. It has been made a question whether this friend of the Apostle was still living when the letter to Timothy was written, because in both instances Paul speaks of "the household" (in 2 Tim. i. 16, δῴη ἔλεος ὁ κύριος τῷ Ὀνησιφόρου οἴκῳ), and not separately of Onesiphorus himself. If we infer that he was *not* living, then we have in 2 Tim. i. 18, almost an instance of the apostolic sanction of the practice of praying for the dead. But the probability is that other members of the family were also active Christians; and as Paul wished to remember them at the same time, he grouped them together under the comprehensive τὸν Ὀν. οἶκον (2 Tim. iv. 19), and thus delicately recognized the common merit, as a sort of family distinction. The mention of Stephanas in 1 Cor. xvi. 17, shows that we need not exclude him from the Στεφανᾶ οἶκον in 1 Cor. i. 16. It is evident from 2 Tim. i. 18 (ὅσα ἐν Ἐφέσῳ διηκόνησε), that Onesiphorus had his home at Ephesus; though if we restrict the salutation near the close of the epistle (iv. 19) to his family, he himself may possibly have been with Paul at Rome when the latter wrote to Timothy. Nothing authentic is known of him beyond these notices. According to a tradition in Fabricius (*Lux Evang.* p. 117), quoted by Winer (*Realw.* ii. 175), he became bishop of Corone in Messenia. H. B. H.

ONI'ARES (Ὀνιάρης [Alex. -ρει-]), a name introduced into the Greek and Syriac texts of 1 Macc. xii. 19 by a very old corruption. The true reading is preserved in Josephus (*Ant.* xii. 4, § 10) and the Vulgate, (Ὀνίᾳ Ἀρείος, *Onia Arius*), and is given in the margin of the A. V.

ONI'AS (Ὀνίας: *Onias*), the name of five high-priests, of whom only two (1 and 3) are mentioned in the A. V., but an account of all is here given to prevent confusion. 1. [Vat.[1] Sin. Ἰωνίας.] The son and successor of Jaddua, who entered on the office about the time of the death of Alexander the Great, cir. B. C. 330–309, or, according to Eusebius, 300 (Joseph. *Ant.* xi. 7, § 7). According to

a * This milder view of the conduct of Onesimus has been generally overlooked or denied by interpreters. We are glad to be able to adduce for it so eminent a name as that of Dr. Bleek in his more recently published *Vorlesungen üb. die Briefe an die Kolosser, den Philemon*, etc. (Berl. 1865). His words are (p. 166 f.): "The clandestine escape of Onesimus might itself be regarded as a wrong against his master; and so also the loss of personal service which he had failed to render in his absence might be viewed as a debt which he had incurred. Whether it was known to the Apostle that he had committed some other offense, especially

embezzlement or theft, as many writers assume, we do not know. From this passage we by no means discover this; and, indeed, it is hardly probable that, if the Apostle had known or conjectured any such thing, he would have expressed himself in so half-sportive a manner as he has done." H.

b * This trait of Paul's character, which made the personal sympathy of others so important to him, Dr. Howson has illustrated with great beauty and effect in his *Lectures on the Character of St. Paul* (pp. 58–61). H.

Josephus he was father of Simon the Just (Joseph. *Ant.* xii. 2, § 4; Ecclus. l. 1). [ECCLESIASTICUS, vol. i. p. 651 *a*; SIMON.]

2. The son of Simon the Just (Joseph. *Ant.* xii. 4, § 1). He was a minor at the time of his father's death (cir. B. C. 290), and the high-priesthood was occupied in succession by his uncles Eleazar and Manasseh to his exclusion. He entered on the office at last cir. B. C. 240, and his conduct threatened to precipitate the rupture with Egypt, which afterwards opened the way for Syrian oppression. Onias, from avarice, it is said — a vice which was likely to be increased by his long exclusion from power — neglected for several years to remit to Ptol. Euergetes the customary annual tribute of 20 talents. The king claimed the arrears with threats of violence in case his demands were not satisfied. Onias still refused to discharge the debt, more, as it appears, from self-will than with any prospect of successful resistance. The evil consequences of this obstinacy were, however, averted by the policy of his nephew Joseph, the son of Tobias, who visited Ptolemy, urged the imbecility of Onias, won the favor of the king, and entered into a contract for farming the tribute, which he carried out with success. Onias retained the high-priesthood till his death cir. B. C. 226, when he was succeeded by his son Simon II. (Joseph. *Ant.* xii. 4).

3. The son of Simon II., who succeeded his father in the high-priesthood, cir. B. C. 198. In the interval which had elapsed since the government of his grandfather the Jews had transferred their allegiance to the Syrian monarchy (Dan. xi. 14), and for a time enjoyed tranquil prosperity. Internal dissensions furnished an occasion for the first act of oppression. Seleucus Philopator was informed by Simon, governor of the Temple, of the riches contained in the sacred treasury, and he made an attempt to seize them by force. At the prayer of Onias, according to the tradition (2 Macc. iii.), the sacrilege was averted; but the high-priest was obliged to appeal to the king himself for support against the machinations of Simon. Not long afterwards Seleucus died (B. C. 175), and Onias found himself supplanted in the favor of Antiochus Epiphanes by his brother Jason, who received the high-priesthood from the king. Jason, in turn, was displaced by his youngest brother Menelaus, who procured the murder of Onias (cir. B. C. 171), in anger at the reproof which he had received from him for his sacrilege (2 Macc. iv. 32–38). But though his righteous zeal was thus fervent, the punishment which Antiochus inflicted on his murderer was a tribute to his "sober and modest behavior" (2 Macc. iv. 37) after his deposition from his office. [ANDRONICUS, vol. i. p. 94.]

It was probably during the government of Onias III. that the communication between the Spartans and Jews took place (1 Macc. xii. 19–23; Joseph. *Ant.* xii. 4, § 10). [SPARTANS.] How powerful an impression he made upon his contemporaries is seen from the remarkable account of the dream of Judas Maccabæus before his great victory (2 Macc. xv. 12–16).

4. The youngest brother of Onias III., who bore the same name, which he afterwards exchanged for Menelaus (Joseph *Ant.* xii. 5, § 1). [MENELAUS.]

5. The son of Onias III., who sought a refuge in Egypt from the sedition and sacrilege which disgraced Jerusalem. The immediate occasion of his flight was the triumph of "the sons of Tobias," gained by the interference of Antiochus Epiphanes.

Onias, to whom the high-priesthood belonged by right, appears to have supported throughout the alliance with Egypt (Joseph. *B. J.* i. 1, § 1), and receiving the protection of Ptol. Philometor, he endeavored to give a unity to the Hellenistic Jews, which seemed impossible for the Jews in Palestine. With this object he founded the Temple at Leontopolis [ON], which occupies a position in the history of the development of Judaism of which the importance is commonly overlooked: but the discussion of this attempt to consolidate Hellenism belongs to another place, though the connection of the attempt itself with Jewish history could not be wholly overlooked (Joseph. *Ant.* xiii. 3; *B. J.* i. 1, § 1, vii. 10, § 2; Ewald, *Gesch.* iv. 405 ff.; Herzfeld, *Gesch.* ii. 460 ff., 557 ff.).   B. F. W.

THE CITY OF ONIAS, THE REGION OF ONIAS, the city in which stood the temple built by Onias, and the region of the Jewish settlements in Egypt. Ptolemy mentions the city as the capital of the Heliopolite nome: Ἡλιοπολίτης νομός, καὶ μητρόπολις Ὀνίον (iv. 5, § 53); where the reading Ἡλίου is not admissible, since Heliopolis is afterwards mentioned, and its different position distinctly laid down (§ 54). Josephus speaks of "the region of Onias," Ὀνίου χώρα (*Ant.* xiv. 8, § 1; *B. J.* i. 9, § 4; comp. vii. 10, § 2), and mentions a place there situate called "the Camp of the Jews," Ἰουδαίων στρατόπεδον (*Ant.* xiv. 8, § 2; *B. J.* l. c.). In the spurious letters given by him in the account of the foundation of the temple of Onias, it is made to have been at Leontopolis in the Heliopolite nome, and called a strong place of Bubastis (*Ant.* xiii. 3, §§ 1, 2); and when speaking of its closing by the Romans, he says that it was in a region 180 stadia from Memphis, in the Heliopolite nome, where Onias had founded a castle (lit. watch-post, φρούριον, *B. J.* vii. 10, §§ 2, 3, 4). Leontopolis was not in the Heliopolite nome, but in Ptolemy's time was the capital of the Leontopolite (iv. 5, § 51), and the mention of it is altogether a blunder. There is probably also a confusion as to the city Bubastis; unless, indeed, the temple which Onias adopted and restored were one of the Egyptian goddess of that name.

The site of the city of Onias is to be looked for in some one of those to the northward of Heliopolis which are called *Tel el-Yahood*, "the Mound of the Jews," or *Tel el-Yahoodeeyeh*, "the Jewish Mound." Sir Gardner Wilkinson thinks that there is little doubt that it is one which stands in the cultivated land near Shibbeen, to the northward of Heliopolis, in a direction a little to the east, at a distance of twelve miles. "Its mounds are of very great height." He remarks that the distance from Memphis (29 miles) is greater than that given by Josephus; but the inaccuracy is not extreme. Another mound of the same name, standing on the edge of the desert, a short distance to the south of Belbays, and 24 miles from Heliopolis, would, he thinks, correspond to the Vicus Judæorum of the *Itinerary of Antoninus.* (See *Modern Egypt and Thebes*, i. 297–300.)

During the writer's residence in Egypt, 1842–1849, excavations were made in the mound supposed by Sir Gardner Wilkinson to mark the site of the city of Onias. We believe, writing only from memory, that no result was obtained but the discovery of portions of pavement very much resembling the Assyrian pavements now in the British Museum.

From the account of Josephus, and the name

given to one of them, "the Camp of the Jews," these settlements appear to have been of a half-military nature. The chief of them seems to have been a strong place; and the same is apparently the case with another, that just mentioned, from the circumstances of the history even more than from its name. This name, though recalling the "Camp" where Psammetichus I. established his Greek mercenaries [MIGDOL], does not prove it was a military settlement, as the "Camp of the Tyrians" in Memphis (Her. ii. 112) was perhaps in its name a reminiscence of the Shepherd occupation, for there stood there a temple of "the Foreign Venus," of which the age seems to be shown by a tablet of Amenoph II. (B. C. cir. 1400) in the quarries opposite the city in which Ashtoreth is worshipped, or else it may have been a merchant-settlement. We may also compare the Coptic name of El-Geezeh, opposite Cairo, †ΠЄΡCΙΟΙ, which has been ingeniously conjectured to record the position of a Persian camp. The easternmost part of Lower Egypt, be it remembered, was always chosen for great military settlements, in order to protect the country from the incursions of her enemies beyond that frontier. Here the first Shepherd king Salatis placed an enormous garrison in the stronghold Avaris, the Zoan of the Bible (Manetho, ap. Jos. c. Ap. i. 14). Here foreign mercenaries of the Saïte kings of the 26th dynasty were settled; where also the greatest body of the Egyptian soldiers had the lands allotted to them, all being established in the Delta (Her. ii. 164-166). Probably the Jewish settlements were established for the same purpose, more especially as the hatred of their inhabitants towards the kings of Syria would promise their opposing the strongest resistance in case of an invasion.

The history of the Jewish cities of Egypt is a very obscure portion of that of the Hebrew nation. We know little more than the story of the foundation and overthrow of one of them, though we may infer that they were populous and politically important. It seems at first sight remarkable that we have no trace of any literature of these settlements; but as it would have been preserved to us by either the Jews of Palestine or those of Alexandria, both of whom must have looked upon the worshippers at the temple of Onias as schismatics, it could scarcely have been expected to have come down to us.   R. S. P.

ONIONS (בְּצָלִים, betsâlîm: τὰ κρόμμυα: cepe). There is no doubt as to the meaning of the Hebrew word, which occurs only in Num. xi. 5, as one of the good things of Egypt of which the Israelites regretted the loss. Onions have been from time immemorial a favorite article of food amongst the Egyptians. (See Her. ii. 125; Plin. xxxvi. 12.) The onions of Egypt are much milder in flavor and less pungent than those of this country. Hasselquist (Trav. p. 290) says, "Whoever has tasted onions in Egypt must allow that none can be had better in any other part in the universe: here they are sweet; in other countries they are nauseous and strong. . . . . They eat them roasted, cut into four pieces, with some bits of roasted meat which the Turks in Egypt call kebab; and with this dish they are so delighted that I have heard them wish they might enjoy it in Paradise. They likewise make a soup of them."   W. H.

* The Israelites might have spared their murmurings, in regard to the loss of Egyptian onions, as the onions of Palestine have the same sweet and delicious flavor that characterizes those of Egypt. They are still called بصل (busl) by the Arabs. They enter into almost every process of cookery in Palestine and Syria.   G. E. P.

ONO (אוֹנוֹ, and once אֹנוֹ [strong]: in Chr. ['Ωνάν,] Alex. [Ωνω]; elsewhere [Vat. Alex.] Ωνωνᵃ and Ωνω: Ono). One of the towns of Benjamin. It does not appear in the catalogues of the Book of Joshua, but is first found in 1 Chr. viii. 12, where Shamed or Shamer is said to have built Ono and Lod with their "daughter villages." It was therefore probably annexed by the Benjamites subsequently to their original settlement,[b] like Aijalon, which was allotted to Dan, but is found afterwards in the hands of the Benjamites (1 Chr. viii. 13). The men of Lod, Hadid, and Ono, to the number of 725 (or Neh. 721) returned from the Captivity with Zerubbabel (Ezr. ii. 33; Neh. vii. 37; see also 1 Esdr. v. 22). [ONUS.]

A plain was attached to the town, and bore its name — Bikath-Ono, "the plain of Ono" (Neh. vi. 2), perhaps identical with the "valley of craftsmen" (Neh. xi. 35). By Eusebius and Jerome it is not named. The Rabbis frequently mention it, but without any indication of its position further than that it was three miles from Lod. (See the citations from the Talmud in Lightfoot, Chor. Decad on S. Mark, ch. ix. § 3.) A village called Kefr 'Ana is enumerated by Robinson among the places in the districts of Ramleh and Lydd (Bibl. Res. 1st ed. App. 120, 121). This village, almost due N. of Lydd, is suggested by Van de Velde (Memoir, p. 337) as identical with Ono. Against the identification however are, the difference in the names — the modern one containing the Ain, — and the distance from Lydda, which instead of being 3 milliaria is fully 5, being more than 4 English miles according to Van de Velde's map. Winer remarks that Beit Unia is more suitable as far as its orthography is concerned; but on the other hand Beit Unia is much too far distant from Lûdd to meet the requirements of the passages quoted above.   G.

O'NUS ('Ωνούς: om. in Vulg.). The form in which the name ONO appears in 1 Esdr. v. 22.

ONYCHA (שְׁחֵלֶת,[c] shecheleth: ὄνυξ: onyx: according to many of the old versions denotes the operculum of some species of Strombus, a genus of gasteropodous Mollusca. The Hebrew word, which appears to be derived from a root which means "to shell or peel off," occurs only in Ex. xxx. 34, as one of the ingredients of the sacred perfume; in

---

a In Neh. vi. 2 the Vat. MS., according to Mai, reads ἐν πεδίῳ ἐν ᾧ . . .

b The tradition of the Talmudists is that it was left intact by Joshua, but burnt during the war of Gibeah (Judg. xx. 48), and that 1 Chr. viii. 12 describes its restoration (See Targum on this latter passage.)

c שָׁחַל, an unused root, i. q. كسل; whence probably our word "shell," "scale." (See Gesenius s. v.)

Ecclus. xxiv. 15, Wisdom is compared to the pleasant odor yielded by "galbanum, onyx, and sweet storax." There can be little doubt that the ὄνυξ of Dioscorides (ii. 10), and the *onyx* of Pliny (xxxii.) 10, are identical with the operculum of a *Strombus*, perhaps *S. lentiginosus*. There is frequent mention of the *onyx* in the writings of Arabian authors, and it would appear from them that the operculum of several kinds of strombus were prized as perfumes. The following is Dioscorides' description of the ὄνυξ: " The onyx is the operculum of a shell-fish resembling the *purpura*, which is found in India in the nard-producing lakes; it is odorous, because the shell-fish feed on the nard, and is collected after the heat has dried up the marshes: that is the best kind which comes from the Red Sea, and is whitish and shining; the Babylonian kind is dark and smaller than the other; both have a sweet odor when burnt, something like castoreum." It is not easy to see what Dioscorides can mean by "nard-producing lakes." The ὄνυξ, "nail," or "claw," seems to point to the operculum of the *Strombidæ*, which is of a claw shape and serrated, whence the Arabs call the mol-

A. *Strombus Dianæ*   B. *The Operculum.*

lusk "the devil's claw;" the *Unguis odoratus*, or *Blatta byzantina*, — for under both these terms apparently the devil claw (*Teufelsklau* of the Germans, see Winer, *Realw.* s. v.) is alluded to in old English writers on Materia Medica — has by some been supposed no longer to exist. Dr. Lister laments its loss, believing it to have been a good medicine " from its strong aromatic smell." Dr. Gray of the British Museum, who has favored us with some remarks on this subject, says that the opercula of the different kinds of *Strombidæ* agree with the figures of *Blatta byzantina* and *Unguis*

a Since the above was written, we have been favored with a communication from Mr. Daniel Hanbury, on the subject of the *Blatta byzantina* of old Pharmacological writers, as well as with specimens of the substance itself, which it appears is still found in the bazaars of the East, though not now in much demand. Mr. Hanbury procured some specimens in Damascus in October (1860), and a friend of his bought some in Alexandria a few months previously. The article appears to be always mixed with the opercula of some species of *Fusus*. As regards the perfume ascribed to this substance, it does not appear to us, from a specimen we burnt, to deserve the character of the excellent odor which has been ascribed to it, though it is not without an aromatic scent. See a figure of the true *B. byzant.* in Matthiolus' *Comment. in Dioscor.* (ii. 8), where there is a long discussion on the subject; also a figure of *Blatta byzantina* and the

odoratus in the old books; with regard to the odor he writes, — "The horny opercula when burnt al. emit an odor which some may call sweet according to their fancy." Bochart (*Hieroz.* iii. 797) believes some kind of bdellium is intended; but there can be no doubt that the ὄνυξ of the LXX. denotes the operculum of some one or more species of strombus. For further information on this subject see Rumph (*Amboinische Raritäten-Kammer*, cap. xvii. p. 48, the German ed. Vienna, 1766), and compare also Sprengel (*Comment. ad Dioscor.* ii. 10); Forskål (*Desc. Anim.* 143, 21, "Unguis odoratus"); *Philos. Transac.* (xvii. 641); Johnston (*Introduc. to Conchol.* p. 77); and Gesenius (*Thes.* s. v. שְׁחֵלֶת). a   W. H.

ONYX (שֹׁהַם, *shôham* : ὁ λίθος ὁ πράσινος, σμάραγδος, σάρδιος, σάπφειρος, βηρύλλιον, ὄνυξ; Aq. σαρδόνυξ; Symm. and Theod. ὄνυξ and ὄνυξ: *onychinus* (*lapis*), sardonychus, onyx). The A. V. uniformly renders the Hebrew *shôham* by "onyx;" the Vulgate too is consistent with itself, the *sardonyx* (Job xxviii. 16) being merely a variety of the *onyx*; but the testimonies of ancient interpreters generally are, as Gesenius has remarked, diverse and ambiguous. The *shôham* stone is mentioned (Gen. ii. 12) as a product of the land of Havilah. Two of these stones, upon which were engraven the names of the children of Israel, six on either stone, adorned the shoulders of the high-priest's ephod (Ex. xxviii. 9–12), and were to be worn as "stones of memorial" (see Kalisch on Ex. *l. c.*). A *shôham* was also the second stone in the fourth row of the sacerdotal breastplate (Ex. xxviii. 20). *Shôham* stones were collected by David for adorning the Temple (1 Chr. xxix. 2). In Job xxviii. 16, it is said that wisdom "cannot be valued with the gold of Ophir, with the b precious *shôham* or the sapphire." The *shôham* is mentioned as one of the treasures of the king of Tyre (Ex. xxviii. 13). There is nothing in the contexts of the several passages where the Hebrew term occurs to help us to determine its signification. Braun (*De Vest. sac. Heb.* p. 727) has endeavored to show that the sardonyx is the stone indicated, and his remarks are well worthy of careful perusal. Josephus (*Ant.* iii. 7, § 5, and *B. J.* v. 5, § 7) expressly states that the shoulder-stones of the high-priest were formed of two large sardonyxes, an onyx being, in his description, the second stone in the fourth row of the breastplate. Some writers believe that the "beryl" is intended, and the authority of the LXX. and other versions has been adduced in proof of this interpretation; but a

operculum of *Fusus* in Pomet's *Histoire des Drogues*, 1694, part 2, p. 97. "Mansfield Parkyns," writes Mr. Hanbury, "in his *Life in Abyssinia* (vol. I. p. 419), mentions among the exports from Massowah, a certain article called *Doofa*, which he states is the *operculum* of a shell, and that it is used in Nubia as a perfume, being burnt with sandal-wood. This bit of information is quite confirmatory of Forskål's statement concerning the *Doft el afrit* — (is not Parkyns's ' Doofa ' meant for *doft*, ضفت ?) — namely, ' e Mochha per Sués. Arabes etiam afferunt. Nigritis fumigatorium est.' "

b The Rev. C. W. King writes to us that " A large, perfect sardonyx is still precious. A dealer tells me he saw this summer (1861) in Paris one valued at £1,000, not engraved."

glance at the head of this article will show that the LXX. is most inconsistent, and that nothing can, a consequence, he learnt from it. Of those who identify the *shôham* with the beryl are Bellermann (*Die Urim und Thummim*, p. 64), Winer (*Bib. Realwört.* i. 313), and Rosenmüller (*The Mineralogy of the Bible*, p. 40, *Bib. Cab.*). Other interpretations of *shôham* have been proposed, but all are mere conjectures. Braun traces *shôham* to the Arabic *sachma*, "blackness": "Of such a color," says he, "are the Arabian sardonyxes, which have a black ground color." This agrees essentially with Mr. King's remarks (*Antique Gems*, p. 9): "The Arabian species," he says, "were formed of black or blue strata, covered by one of opaque white; over which again was a third of a vermilion color." But Gesenius and Fürst refer the Hebrew word to the Arabic *saham*, "to be pale." The different kinds of onyx and sardonyx,[a] however, are so variable in color, that either of these definitions is suitable. They all form excellent materials for the engraver's art. The balance of authority is, we think, in favor of some variety of the onyx. We are content to retain the rendering of the A. V., supported as it is by the Vulgate and the express statement of so high an authority as Josephus,[b] till better proofs in support of the claims of some other stone be forthcoming. As to the "Onyx" of Ecclus. xxiv. 15, see ONYCHA.

W. H.

OPHEL (הָעֹפֶל, always with the def. article [*swelling, hill*]: 'Οπέλ. ὁ 'Οφάλ, ['Οφλά: Vat. Οπλα, Ωφαλ, Οφεαλ:] Alex. ο Οφαλ, [Ωφαλ, Σοφλα:] *Ophel*). A part of ancient Jerusalem. The name is derived by the lexicographers from a root of similar sound, which has the force of a swelling or tumor (Gesenius, *Thes.*; Fürst, *Hdwb.* ii. 169 *b*). It does not come forward till a late period of Old Test. history. In 2 Chr. xxvii. 3, Jotham is said to have built much "on the wall of Ophel." Manasseh, amongst his other defensive works, "compassed about Ophel" (*Ibid.* xxxiii. 14). From the catalogue of Nehemiah's repairs to the wall of Jerusalem, it appears to have been near the "water gate" (Neh. iii. 26) and the "great tower that lieth out" (ver. 27). Lastly, the former of these two passages, and Neh. xi. 21, show that Ophel was the residence of the Levites. It is not again mentioned, though its omission in the account of the route round the walls at the sanctification of the second Temple, Neh. xii. 31-40, is singular.

In the passages of his history parallel to those quoted above, Josephus either passes it over altogether, or else refers to it in merely general terms — "very large towers" (*Ant.* ix. 11, § 2), "very high towers" (x. 3, § 2). But in his ac-

count of the last days of Jerusalem he mentions it four times as Ophla (ὁ 'Οφλά, accompanying it as in the Hebrew with the article). The first of these (*B. J.* ii. 17, § 9) tells nothing as to its position; but from the other three we can gather something. (1.) The old wall of Jerusalem ran above the spring of Siloam and the pool of Solomon, and on reaching the place called Ophla, joined the eastern porch of the Temple (*B. J.* v. 4, § 2). (2.) "John held the Temple and the places round it, not a little in extent, — both the Ophla and the valley called Kedron" (*Ibid.* v. 6, § 1). (3.) After the capture of the Temple, and before Titus had taken the upper city (the modern Zion) from the Jews, his soldiers burnt the whole of the lower city, lying in the valley between the two, "and the place called the Ophla" (*Ibid.* vi. 6, § 3).

From this it appears that Ophel was outside the south wall of the Temple, and that it lay between the central valley of the city, which debouches above the spring of Siloam, on the one hand, and the east portico of the Temple on the other. The east portico, it should be remembered, was not on the line of the east wall of the present *haram*, but 330 feet further west, on the line of the solid wall which forms the termination of the vaults in the eastern corner.[c] [See JERUSALEM, vol. ii. 1314; and the Plan, 1316.] This situation agrees with the mention of the "water-gate" in Neh. iii. 26, and the statement of xi. 21, that it was the residence of the Levites. Possibly the "great tower that lieth out," in the former of these, may be the "tower of Eder"—mentioned with "Ophel of the daughter of Zion," by Micah (iv. 8), or that named in an obscure passage of Isaiah—"Ophel and watchtower" (xxxii. 14; A. V. inaccurately "forts and towers").

Ophel, then, in accordance with the probable root of the name, was the swelling declivity by which the Mount of the Temple slopes off on its southern side into the Valley of Hinnom—a long, narrowish rounded spur or promontory, which intervenes between the mouth of the central valley of Jerusalem (the Tyropœon) and the Kidron, or Valley of Jehoshaphat.[d] Half-way down it on its eastern face is the "Fount of the Virgin," so called; and at its foot the lower outlet of the same spring—the Pool of Siloam. How much of this declivity was covered with the houses of the Levites, or with the suburb which would naturally gather round them, and where the "great tower" stood, we have not at present the means of ascertaining.[e]

Professor Stanley (*Sermons on the Apostolic Age*, pp. 329, 330) has ingeniously conjectured that the name Oblias ('Ωβλίας)—which was one of the titles by which St. James the Less was distinguished from other Jacobs of the time, and which is explained by Hegesippos (Euseb. *Hist. Eccl.* ii.

---

[a] The onyx has two strata, the sardonyx three.

[b] "Who speaks from actual observation: he expressly notices the fine quality of these two pieces of sardonyx." — [C. W. KING.]

[c] * The explorations of Lieut. Warren have demonstrated the incorrectness of the theory here named respecting the line of the east wall of the Temple-area, and confirmed the view given under JERUSALEM (§ iv. Amer. ed.).   S. W.

[d] * Later observations require us to modify this opinion. Mr. Grove inserts the following note on p. 50 of Clark's *Bible Atlas* (Lond. 1868): "There seems reason to suspect that the Hill of the Akra, the Hill of the Temple, and Ophel, were originally three sep-

arate heights. Lieutenant Warren has discovered what he conceives may have been either a deep ditch or a natural valley, now filled up with earth, running from east to west, just north of the platform of the Dome of the Rock (*Letter*, Nov. 12, 1867, p. 43); and the Tyropœon gully probably turned sharply round to the east, at the southwest corner of the Temple substruction, so as to cut off the Temple Mount from Ophel. (Dec. 12, 1867, p. 52.)"   H.

[e] Fürst (*Hdwb.* ii. 169) states, without a word that could lead a reader to suspect that there was any doubt on the point, that Ophel is identical with Millo. It may be so, only there is not a particle of evidence for or against it.

23) as meaning "bulwark (περιοχή) of the people," — was in its original form Ophli-am ^a (עָפְלִיָם). In this connection it is a singular coincidence that St. James was martyred by being thrown from the corner of the Temple, at, or close to, the very spot which is named by Josephus as the boundary of Ophel. [JAMES, vol. ii. 1207; EN-ROGEL, i. 741 *b*.] Ewald, however (*Geschichte*, vi. 204, *note*), restores the name as הֹכְלִיעֶם, as if from הֶכֶל, a fence or boundary. [CHEBEL.] This has in its favor the fact that it more closely agrees in signification with περιοχή than Ophel does.

The Ophel which appears to have been the residence of Elisha at the time of Naaman's visit to him (2 K. v. 24: A. V. "the tower") was of course a different place from that spoken of above. The narrative would seem to imply that it was not far from Samaria; but this is not certain. The LXX. and Vulg. must have read אֹפֶל, "darkness," for they give τὸ σκοτεινόν and *vesperi* respectively.   G.

O'PHIR (אוֹפִיר, אֹפִר [see below]: Ὀφείρ: *Ophir*). 1. The eleventh in order of the sons of Joktan, coming immediately after Sheba (Gen. x. 29; 1 Chr. i. 23). So many important names in the genealogical table in the 10th chapter of Genesis — such as Sidon, Canaan, Asshur, Aram (Syria), Mizraim (the two Egypts, Upper and Lower), Sheba, Caphtorim, and Philistim (the Philistines) — represent the name of some city, country, or people, that it is reasonable to infer that the same is the case with all the names in the table. It frequently happens that a father and his sons in the genealogy represent districts geographically contiguous to each other; yet this is not an invariable rule, for in the case of Tarshish the son of Javan (ver. 10), and of Nimrod the son of Cush, whose kingdom was Babel or Babylon (ver. 11), a son was conceived as a distant colony or offshoot. But there is one marked peculiarity in the sons of Joktan, which is common to them with the Canaanites alone, that precise geographical limits are assigned to their settlements. Thus it is said (ver. 19) that the border of the Canaanites was "from Sidon, as thou comest to Gerar, unto Gaza; as thou goest, unto Sodom and Gomorrah, and Admah, and Zeboim, even unto Lasha:" and in like manner (vv. 29, 30) that the dwelling of the sons of Joktan was "from Mesha, as thou goest unto Sephar a mountain of the east." The peculiar wording of these geographical limits, and the fact that the well-known towns which define the border of the Canaanites are mentioned so nearly in the same manner, forbid the supposition that Mesha and Sephar belonged to very distant countries, or were comparatively unknown: and as many of the sons of Joktan — such as Sheba, Hazarmaveth, Almodad, and others — are by common consent admitted to represent settlements in Arabia, it is an obvious inference that *all* the settlements corresponding to the names of the other sons are to be sought for in the same peninsula

^a Some of the MSS. of Eusebius have the name Ωὐλαεμ (Ὀφλαέμ), preserving the termination, though they corrupt the former part of the word.

alone. Hence, as Ophir is one of those sons, it may be regarded as a fixed point in discussions concerning the place Ophir mentioned in the book of Kings, that the author of the 10th chapter of Genesis regarded Ophir the son of Joktan as corresponding to some city, region, or tribe in Arabia.

Etymology. — There is, seemingly, no sufficient reason to doubt that the word Ophir is Semitic, although, as is the case with numerous proper names known to be of Hebrew origin, the precise word does not occur as a common name in the Bible. See the words from אאר and עבר in Gesenius's *Thesaurus*, and compare Ἀφάρ, the metropolis of the Sabæans in the Periplus, attributed to Arrian. Gesenius suggests that it means a "fruitful region," if it is Semitic. Baron von Wrede, who explored Hadhramaut in Arabia in 1843 (*Journal of the R. Geographical Society*, vol. xiv. p. 110), made a small vocabulary of Himyaritic words in the vernacular tongue, and amongst these he gives *ofir* as signifying *red*. He says that the Mahra people call themselves the tribes of the red country (*ofir*), and called the Red Sea, *bahr ofir*. If this were so, it might have some what of the same relation to *aphar*, "dust" or "dry ground" (א and ע being interchangeable), that *adom*, "red," has to *adamah*, "the ground." Still it is unsafe to accept the use of a word of this kind on the authority of any one traveller, however accurate; and the supposed existence and meaning of a word *ofir* is recommended for special inquiry to any future traveller in the same district.

2. (Σουφίρ, Σωφίρ, [and Ὠφείρ; Vat. Σουφειρ, Σωφειρ, Σωφειρα, Ὠφειρ; Alex. Σουφειρ, Σωφηρα, Ὠφειρδε, Ὠφειρ; Sin. in Job and Is., Σωφειρ, Σωφιρ, Σουφειρ:] *Ophira*, 1 K. ix. 28, the translation of the LXX. is εἰς Σωφιρά [Vat. Σωφηρα, Alex. Σωφαρα], though the ending in the original merely denotes motion towards Ophir, and is no part of the name.) A seaport or region from which the Hebrews in the time of Solomon obtained gold, in vessels which went thither in conjunction with Tyrian ships from Ezion-geber, near Elath, on that branch of the Red Sea which is now called the Gulf of Akabah. The gold was proverbial for its fineness, so that "gold of Ophir" is several times used as an expression for fine gold (Ps. xlv. 9; Job xxviii. 16; Is. xiii. 12; 1 Chr. xxix. 4); and in one passage (Job xxii. 24) the word "Ophir" by itself is used for gold of Ophir, and for gold generally. In Jer. x. 9 and Dan. x. 5 it is thought by Gesenius and others that Ophir is intended by the word "Uphaz" — there being a very trifling difference between the words in Hebrew when written without the vowel-points. In addition to gold, the vessels brought from Ophir almug-wood and precious stones.

The precise geographical situation of Ophir has long been a subject of doubt and discussion. Calmet (*Dictionary of the Bible*, s. v. "Ophir" regarded it as in Armenia; Sir Walter Raleigh (*History of the World*, book i. ch. 8) thought it was one of the Molucca Islands; and Arias Montanus (Bochart, *Phaleg*, Pref. and ch. 9), led by the similarity of the word Parvaim, supposed to be identical with Ophir (2 Chr. iii. 6), found it in

Peru.[a] But these countries, as well as Iberia and Phrygia, cannot now be viewed as affording matter for serious discussion on this point, and the three opinions which have found supporters in our own time were formerly represented, amongst other writers, by Huet (*Sur le Commerce et la Navigation des Anciens*, p. 59), by Bruce (*Travels*, book ii. c. 4), and by the historian Robertson (*Disquisition respecting Ancient India*, sect. 1), who placed Ophir in Africa; by Vitringa (*Geograph. Sacra*, p. 114) and Reland (*Dissertatio de Ophir*), who placed it in India; and by Michaelis (*Spicilegium*, ii. 184), Niebuhr, the traveller (*Description de l'Arabie*, p. 253), Gossellin (*Recherches sur la Géographie des Anciens*, ii. 99), and Vincent (*History of the Commerce and Navigation of the Ancients*, ii. 265–270), who placed it in Arabia. Of other distinguished geographical writers, Bochart (*Phaleg*, ii. 27) admitted two Ophirs, one in Arabia and one in India, i. e. at Ceylon; while D'Anville (*Dissertation sur le Pays d'Ophir, Mémoires de Littérature*, xxx. 83), equally admitting two, placed one in Arabia and one in Africa. In our own days the discussion has been continued by Gesenius, who in articles on Ophir in his *Thesaurus* (p. 141), and in Ersch and Gruber's *Encyklopädie* (s. v.) stated that the question lay between India and Arabia, assigned the reasons to be urged in favor of each of these countries, but declared the arguments for each to be so equally balanced that he refrained from expressing any opinion of his own on the subject. M. Quatremère, however, in a paper on Ophir which was printed in 1842 in the *Mémoires de l'Institut*, again insisted on the claims of Africa (*Académie des Inscriptions et Belles Lettres*, t. xv. ii. 362); and in his valuable work on Ceylon (part vii. chap. 1) Sir J. Emerson Tennent adopts the opinion, sanctioned by Josephus, that Malacca was Ophir. Otherwise the two countries which have divided the opinions of the learned have been India and Arabia — Lassen, Ritter, Bertheau (*Exeget. Handbuch*, 2 Chr. viii. 18), Thenius (*Exeget. Handbuch*, 1 K. x. 22), and Ewald (*Geschichte*, iii. 347, 2d ed.) being in favor of India, while Winer (*Realw. s. v.*), Fürst (*Hebr. und Chald. Handw. s. v.*), Knobel (*Völkertafel der Genesis*, p. 190), Forster (*Geogr. of Arabia*, i. 161–167), Crawfurd (*Descriptive Dictionary of the Indian Islands*, s. v.), and Kalisch (*Commentary on Genesis*, chap. "The Genealogy of Nations") are in favor of Arabia. The fullest treatise on the question is that of Ritter, who in his *Erdkunde*, vol. xiv., published in 1848, devoted 80 octavo pages to the discussion (pp. 351–431), and adopted the opinion of Lassen (*Ind. Alt.* i. 529) that Ophir was situated at the mouth of the Indus.

Some general idea of the arguments which may be advanced in favor of each of the three countries may be derived from the following statement In favor of Arabia, there are these considerations: 1st. The 10th chapter of Genesis, ver. 29, contains what is equivalent to an intimation of the author's opinion, that Ophir was in Arabia. [OPHIR 1.] 2dly. Three places in Arabia may be pointed out, the names of which agree sufficiently with the

word Ophir: namely, Aphar, called by Ptolemy Sapphara, now Zafár or Saphar, which, according to the Periplus ascribed to Arrian, was the metropolis of the Sabæans, and was distant twelve days' journey from the emporium Muza on the Red Sea: Doffir, a city mentioned by Niebuhr the traveller (*Description de l'Arabie*, p. 219), as a considerable town of Yemen, and capital of Bellad Hadaje, situated to the north of Loheia, and 15 leagues from the sea; and Zafar or Zafári [ARABIA, vol. i. p. 137 b] (Sepher, Dhafar), now Dofar, a city on the southern coast of Arabia, visited in the 14th century by Ibn Batuta, the Arabian traveller, and stated by him to be a month's journey by land from Aden, and a month's voyage, when the wind was fair, from the Indian shores (Lee's *Translation*, p. 57). 3dly. In antiquity, Arabia was represented as a country producing gold by four writers at least: namely, by the geographer Agatharchides, who lived in the 2d century before Christ (in Photius 250, and Hudson's *Geograph. Minores*, i. 60); by the geographer Artemidorus, who lived a little later, and whose account has been preserved, and, as it were, adopted by the geographer Strabo (xiv. 18); by Diodorus Siculus (ii. 50, iii. 44); and by Pliny the Elder (vi. 32). 4thly. Eupolemus, a Greek historian who lived before the Christian era, and who, besides other writings, wrote a work respecting the kings of Judæa, expressly states, as quoted by Eusebius (*Praep. Evang.* ix. 30), that Ophir was an island with gold mines in the Erythræan Sea (Οὐφρῆ, comp. Οὐφελρ, the LXX. Translation in Gen. x. 29), and that David sent miners thither in vessels which he caused to be built at Ælana = Elath. Now it is true that the name of the Erythræan Sea was deemed to include the Persian Gulf, as well as the Red Sea, but it was always regarded as closely connected with the shores of Arabia, and cannot be shown to have been extended to India. 5thly. On the supposition that, notwithstanding all the ancient authorities on the subject, gold really never existed either in Arabia, or in any island along its coasts, Ophir was an Arabian emporium, into which gold was brought as an article of commerce, and was exported into Judæa. There is not a single passage in the Bible inconsistent with this supposition; and there is something like a direct intimation that Ophir was in Arabia.

While such is a general view of the arguments for Arabia, the following considerations are urged in behalf of India. 1st. Sofir is the Coptic word for India; and Sophir, or Sophira is the word used for the place Ophir by the Septuagint translators, and likewise by Josephus. And Josephus positively states that it was a part of India (*Ant.* viii. 6, § 4), though he places it in the Golden Chersonese, which was the Malay peninsula, and belonged, geographically, not to India proper, but to India beyond the Ganges. Moreover, in three passages of the Bible, where the Septuagint has Σωφιρά or Σουφίρ, 1 K. ix. 28, x. 11; Is. xiii. 12, Arabian translators have used the word *India*. 2dly. All the three imports from Ophir, gold, precious stones,

---

and almug-wood, are essentially Indian. Gold is found in the sources of the Indus and the Cabool River before their juncture at Attock; in the Himalaya mountains, and in a portion of the Deccan, especially at Cochin. India has in all ages been celebrated for its precious stones of all kinds. And sandal-wood, which the best modern Hebrew scholars regard as the almug-wood of the Bible, is almost exclusively, or at any rate pre-eminently, a product of the coast of Malabar. 3dly. Assuming that the ivory, peacocks, and apes, which were brought to Ezion-geber once in three years by the navy of Tharshish in conjunction with the navy of Hiram (1 K. x. 22), were brought from Ophir, they also collectively point to India rather than Arabia. Moreover, etymologically, not one of these words in the Hebrew is of Hebrew or Semitic origin; one being connected with Sanskrit, another with the Tamil, and another with the Malay language. [TARSHISH.] 4thly. Two places in India may be specified, agreeing to a certain extent in name with Ophir; one at the mouths of the Indus, where Indian writers placed a people named the Abhira, agreeing with the name Ἀβήρια of the geographer Ptolemy; and the other, the Σουνάρα of Ptolemy, the Ὄππαρα of Arrian's Periplus, where the town of Goa is now situated, on the western coast of India.

Lastly, the following pleas have been urged in behalf of Africa. 1st. Of the three countries, Africa, Arabia, and India, Africa is the only one which can be seriously regarded as containing districts which have supplied gold in any great quantity. Although, as a statistical fact, gold has been found in parts of India, the quantity is so small, that India has never supplied gold to the commerce of the world; and in modern times no gold at all, nor any vestiges of exhausted mines have been found in Arabia. 2dly. On the western coast of Africa, near Mozambique, there is a port called by the Arabians Sofala, which, as the liquids *l* and *r* are easily interchanged, was probably the Ophir of the Ancients. When the Portuguese, in A. D. 1500, first reached it by the Cape of Good Hope, it was the emporium of the gold district in the interior; and two Arabian vessels laden with gold were actually off Sofala[a] at the time (see *Cadamosto*, cap. 58). 3dly. On the supposition that the passage (1 K. x. 22) applies to Ophir, Sofala has still stronger claims in preference to India. Peacocks, indeed, would not have been brought from it; but the peacock is too delicate a bird for a long voyage in small vessels, and the word *tukkiyim* probably signified "parrots." At the same time, ivory and apes might have been supplied in abundance from the district of which Sofala was the emporium. On the other hand, if Ophir had been in India, other Indian productions might have been expected in the list of imports; such as shawls, silk, rich tissues of cotton, perfumes, pepper, and cinnamon. 4thly. On the same supposition respecting 1 K. x. 22, it can, according to the traveller Bruce, be proved by the laws of the monsoons in the Indian Ocean, that Ophir was at Sofala; inasmuch as the voyage to Sofala from Ezion-geber would have been performed

exactly in three years; it could not have been accomplished in less time and it would not have required more (vol. i. p. 440).

From the above statement of the different views which have been held respecting the situation of Ophir, the suspicion will naturally suggest itself that no positive conclusion can be arrived at on the subject. And this seems to be true, in this sense, that the Bible in all its direct notices of Ophir as a place does not supply sufficient data for an independent opinion on this disputed point. At the same time, it is an inference in the highest degree probable, that the author of the 10th chapter of Genesis regarded Ophir as in Arabia; and, in the absence of conclusive proof that he was mistaken, it seems most reasonable to acquiesce in his opinion.

To illustrate this view of the question it is desirable to examine closely all the passages in the historical books which mention Ophir by name. These are only five in number: three in the books of Kings, and two in the books of Chronicles. The latter were probably copied from the former; and, at any rate, do not contain any additional information; so that it is sufficient to give a reference to them, 2 Chr. viii. 18, ix. 10. The three passages in the books of Kings, however, being short, will be set out at length. The first passage is as follows: it is in the history of the reign of Solomon. "And king Solomon made a navy of ships at Ezion-geber, which is beside Eloth, on the shore of the Red Sea, in the land of Edom. And Hiram sent in the navy his servants, shipmen that had knowledge of the sea, with the servants of Solomon. And they came to Ophir, and fetched from thence gold, four hundred and twenty talents, and brought it to king Solomon," 1 K. ix. 26-28. The next passage is in the succeeding chapter, and refers to the same reign. "And the navy also of Hiram that brought gold from Ophir, brought in from Ophir great plenty of almug-trees and precious stones," 1 K. x. 11. The third passage relates to the reign of Jehoshaphat king of Judah, and is as follows: "Jehoshaphat made ships of Tharshish to go to Ophir for gold; but they went not: for the ships were broken at Ezion-geber," 1 K. xxii. 48. In addition to these three passages, the following verse in the book of Kings has very frequently been referred to Ophir: "For the king (i. e. Solomon) had at sea a navy of Tharshish with the navy of Hiram: once in three years came the navy of Tharshish bringing gold and silver, ivory, and apes, and peacocks," 1 K. x. 22. But there is not sufficient evidence to show that the fleet mentioned in this verse was identical with the fleet mentioned in 1 K. ix. 26-28, and 1 K. x. 11, as bringing gold, almug-trees, and precious stones from Ophir; and if, notwithstanding, the identity of the two is admitted as a probable conjecture, there is not the slightest evidence that the fleet went only to Ophir, and that therefore the silver, ivory, apes, and peacocks must have come from Ophir. Indeed, the direct contrary might be inferred, even on the hypothesis of the identity of the two fleets, inasmuch as the actual mention of Ophir is distinctly confined to the imports of gold, almug-trees, and precious stones, and the compiler might seem carefully to have distinguished between

---

[a] Mr. Grove has pointed out a passage in Milton's *Paradise Lost*, xi. 399-401, favoring this Sofala: —

"Mombaza, and Quiloa, and Melind,
And Safala, thought Ophir, to the realm
Of Congo and Angola farthest south."

Milton followed a passage in Purchas's *Pilgrimes*, p. 1022 of the 2d volume, published in 1626; and all the modern geographical names in vv. 387-411 are in Purchas.

it and the country from which silver, ivory, apes, and peacocks were imported. Hence, without referring farther to the passage in 1 K. x. 22, we are thrown back, for the purpose of ascertaining the situation of Ophir, to the three passages from the book of Kings which were first set forth. And if those three passages are carefully examined, it will be seen that all the information given respecting Ophir is, that it was a place or region, accessible by sea from Ezion-geber on the Red Sea, from which imports of gold, almug-trees, and precious stones were brought back by the Tyrian and Hebrew sailors. No data whatever are given as to the distance of Ophir from Ezion-geber; no information direct or indirect, or even the slightest hint, is afforded for determining whether Ophir was the name of a town, or the name of a district; whether it was an emporium only, or the country which actually produced the three articles of traffic. Bearing in mind the possibility of its being an emporium, there is no reason why it may not have been either in Arabia, or on the Persian coast, or in India, or in Africa; but there is not sufficient evidence for deciding in favor of one of these suggestions rather than of the others.

Under these circumstances it is well to revert to the 10th chapter of Genesis. It has been shown [OPHIR 1] to be reasonably certain that the author of that chapter regarded Ophir as the name of some city, region, or tribe in Arabia. And it is almost equally certain that the Ophir of Genesis is the Ophir of the book of Kings. There is no mention, either in the Bible or elsewhere, of any other Ophir; and the idea of there having been *two* Ophirs, evidently arose from a perception of the obvious meaning of the 10th chapter of Genesis, on the one hand, coupled with the erroneous opinion on the other, that the Ophir of the book of Kings *could not* have been in Arabia. Now, whatever uncertainty may exist as to the time when the 10th chapter of Genesis was written (Knobel, *Völkertafel der Genesis*, p. 4, and Hartmann's *Forschungen über die 5 Bücher Moses*, p. 584), the author of it wrote while Hebrew was yet a living language; there is no statement in any part of the Bible inconsistent with his opinion; and the most ancient writer who can be opposed to him as an authority, lived, under any hypothesis, many centuries after his death. Hence the *burden of proof* lies on any one who denies Ophir to have been in Arabia.

But all that can be advanced against Arabia falls very short of such proof. In weighing the evidence on this point, the assumption that ivory, peacocks, and apes were imported from Ophir must be dismissed from consideration. In one view of the subject, and accepting the statement in 2 Chr. ix. 21, they might have connection with Tarshish [TARSHISH]; but they have a very slight bearing on the position of Ophir. Hence it is not here necessary to discuss the law of monsoons in the Indian Ocean; though it may be said in passing that the facts on which the supposed law is founded, which seemed so cogent that they induced the historian Robertson to place Ophir in Africa (*Disquisition on India*, § 2), have been pointedly denied by Mr. Salt in his *Voyage to Abyssinia* (p. 103). Moreover, the resemblance of names of places in India and Africa to Ophir, cannot reasonably be insisted on; for there is an equally great resemblance in the names of some places in Arabia. And in reference to Africa, especially, the place there imagined to be Ophir, namely, *Sofula*, has been

shown to be merely an Arabic word, corresponding to the Hebrew *Shefelah*, which signifies a plain or low country (Jer. xxxii. 44; Josh. xi. 16; the Σεφήλα of the Maccabees, 1 Macc. xii. 38; see Gesenius, *Lex.* s. v.). Again, the use of Sofir as the Coptic word for Ophir cannot be regarded as of much importance, it having been pointed out by Reland that there is no proof of its use except in late Coptic, and that thus its adoption may have been the mere consequence of the erroneous views which Josephus represented, instead of being a confirmation of them. Similar remarks apply to the Biblical versions by the Arabic translators. The opinion of Josephus himself would have been entitled to much consideration in the absence of all other evidence on the subject; but he lived about a thousand years after the only voyages to Ophir of which any record has been preserved, and his authority cannot be compared to that of the 10th chapter of Genesis. Again, he seems inconsistent with himself; for in *Ant.* ix. 1, § 4, he translates the Ophir of 1 K. xxii. 48, and the Tarshish of 2 Chr. xx. 36, as *Pontus* and Thrace. It is likewise some deduction from the weight of his opinion, that it is contrary to the opinion of Eupolemus, who was an earlier writer; though he too lived at so great a distance of time from the reign of Solomon that he is by no means a decisive authority. Moreover, imagination may have acted on Josephus to place Ophir in the Golden Chersonese, which to the ancients was, as it were, the extreme east; as it acted on Arias Montanus to place it in Peru, in the far more improbable and distant west. All the foregoing objections having been rejected from the discussion, it remains to notice those which are based on the assertion that sandal-wood (assumed to be the same as almug-wood), precious stones, and gold, are not productions of Arabia. And the following observations tend to show that such objections are not conclusive.

1st. In the Periplus attributed to Arrian, sandal-wood (ξύλα σαντάλινα) is mentioned as one of the imports into Omana, an emporium on the Persian Gulf; and it is thus proved, if any proof is requisite, that a sea-port would not necessarily be in India, because sandal-wood was obtained from it. But independently of this circumstance, the reasons advanced in favor of almug-wood being the same as sandal-wood, though admissible as a conjecture, seem too weak to justify the founding any argument on them. In 2 Chr. ii. 8, Solomon is represented as writing to Hiram, king of Tyre, in these words: "Send me also cedar-trees, fir-trees, and algum-trees, out of Lebanon; for I know that thy servants can skill to cut timber in Lebanon," a passage evidently written under the belief that almug-trees grew in Lebanon. It has been suggested that this was a mistake — but this is a point which cannot be assumed without distinct evidence to render it probable. The LXX. translator of the book of Kings, 1 K. x. 12, translates almug-wood by ξύλα πελεκητά, or ἀπελεκητά, which gives no information as to the nature of the wood; and the LXX. translator of the Chronicles renders it by ξύλα πεύκινα, which strictly means *fir-wood* (compare Ennius's translation of *Medea*, ver. 4), and which, at the utmost, can only be extended to any wood of resinous trees. The Vulgate translation is "thyina," i. e. wood made of thya (θύον, θυία), a tree which Theophrastus mentions as having supplied peculiarly durable timber for the roofs of temples; which he says is

like the wild cypress; and which is classed by him
as an evergreen with the pine, the fir, the juniper,
the yew-tree, and the cedar (*Histor'. Plant.* v. 3,
§ 7, i. 9, § 3). It is stated both by Buxtorf and
Gesenius (*s. v.*), that the Rabbins understood by
the word, *corals* — which is certainly a most improbable meaning — and that in the 3d century,
almug in the Mishnah (*Kelim* 13, 6) was used for
coral in the singular number. In the 13th
century, Kimchi, it is said, proposed the meaning
of Brazil wood. And it was not till last century
that, for the first time, the suggestion was made
that almug-wood was the same as sandal-wood.
This suggestion came from Celsius, the Swedish
botanist, in his *Hierobotanicon;* who at the same
time recounted thirteen meanings proposed by
others. Now, as all that has been handed down
of the uses of almug-wood is, that the king made
of it a prop a or support for the House of the Lord
and the king's house; and harps also and psalteries
for singers (1 K. x. 12), it is hard to conceive how
the greatest botanical genius that ever lived can
now do more than make a guess, more or less probable, at the meaning of the word.

Since the time of Celsius, the meaning of "sandal-wood" has been defended by Sanskrit etymologies. According to Gesenius (*Lexicon,* s. v.),
Bohlen proposed, as a derivation for *almuggim,*
the Arabic article *Al* and *micata,* from simple
mica, a name for red sandal-wood. Lassen, in
Indische Alterthumskunde (vol. i. pt. 1, p. 538),
adopting the form *algummim,* says that if the
plural ending is taken from it, there remains *valgu,*
as one of the Sanskrit names for sandal-wood,
which in the language of the Deccan is *valgum.*
Perhaps, however, these etymologies cannot lay
claim to much value until it is made probable,
independently, that almug-wood is sandal-wood.
It is to be observed that there is a difference of
opinion as to whether "al" in *algummim* is an
article or part of the noun, and it is not denied by
any one that *chandana* is the ordinary Sanskrit
word for sandal-wood. Moreover, Mr. Crawfurd,
who resided officially many years in the East and
is familiar with sandal-wood, says that it is never
— now, at least — used for musical instruments,
and that it is unfit for pillars, or stairs, balustrades
or banisters, or balconies. (See also his *Descriptive
Dictionary of the Indian Islands,* pp. 310–375.) It
is used for incense or perfume, or as fancy wood.

2. As to precious stones, they take up such
little room, and can be so easily concealed, if
necessary, and conveyed from place to place, that
there is no difficulty in supposing they came from
Ophir, simply as from an emporium, even admitting that there were no precious stones in Arabia.
But it has already been observed [ARABIA, i. 137 a]
that the Arabian peninsula produces the emerald
and onyx stone: and it has been well pointed out
by Mr. Crawfurd that it is impossible to identify
precious stones under so general a name with any

particular country. Certainly it cannot be shown
that the Jews of Solomon's time included under
that name the diamond, for which India is peculiarly renowned.

3. As to gold, far too great stress seems to have
been laid on the negative fact that no gold nor
trace of gold-mines has been discovered in Arabia.
Negative evidence of this kind, in which Ritter b
has placed so much reliance (vol. xiv. p. 408`, is by
no means conclusive. Sir Roderick Murchison and
Sir Charles Lyell concur in stating that, although no
rock is known to exist in Arabia from which gold
is obtained at the present day, yet the peninsula
has not undergone a sufficient geological examination to warrant the conclusion that gold did not
exist there formerly or that it may not yet be discovered there. Under these circumstances there is
no sufficient reason to reject the accounts of the
ancient writers who have been already adduced as
witnesses for the former existence of gold in Arabia.
It is true that Artemidorus and Diodorus Siculus
may merely have relied on the authority of Agatharchides, but it is important to remark that Agatharchides lived in Egypt and was guardian to one
of the young Ptolemies during his minority, so
that he must have been familiar with the general
nature of the commerce between Egypt and Arabia.
Although he may have been inaccurate in details,
it is not lightly to be admitted that he was altogether mistaken in supposing that Arabia produced
any gold at all. And it is in his favor that two of
his statements have unexpectedly received confirmation in our own time: 1st, respecting gold-mines
in Egypt, the position of which in the Bisharee
Desert was ascertained by Mr. Linant and Mr.
Bonomi (Wilkinson's *Ancient Egyptians,* ch. ix.);
and 2d, as to the existence of nuggets of pure
gold, some of the size of an olive-stone. some of a
medlar, and some of a chestnut. The latter statement was discredited by Michaelis (*Spicilegium,*
p. 287, " Nec credo ullibi massas auri non experti
castaneae nucis magnitudine reperiri "), but it has
been shown to be not incredible by the result of the
gold discoveries in California and Australia.

If, however, negative evidence is allowed to outweigh on this subject the authority of Agatharchides, Artemidorus, Diodorus Siculus, Pliny, and,
it may be added, Strabo, all of whom may possibly
have been mistaken, there is still nothing to prevent Ophir having been an Arabian emporium for
gold (Winer, *Realw.* s. v. "Ophir"). The Periplus, attributed to Arrian, gives an account of
several Arabian emporia. In the Red Sea, for example, was the Emporium Musa, only twelve
days distant from Aphar the metropolis of the
Sabaeans and the Homerites. It is expressly stated
that this port had commercial relations with Bary-
gaza, *i. e.* Beroach,. on the west coast of India, and
that it was always full of Arabs, either ship-
owners or sailors. Again, where the British town
of Aden is now situated, there was another em-

---

a The general meaning of מְסָעֵד, a prop or support, is certain. though its special meaning in 1 K. x.
12 seems irrecoverably lost. It is translated "pillars"
in the A. V., and ὑποστηρίγματα in the LXX. In the
corresponding passage of 2 Chr. ix. 11, the word is
מְסִלּוֹת, the usual meaning of which is *highways;*
and which is translated in the A. V. *terraces,* and in
the LXX ἀναβάσεις, *ascents,* or *stairs.* See Her. i.
181.

b Bearing this in mind, it is remarkable that Ritter
should have accepted Lassen's conjecture respecting
the position of Ophir at the mouths of the Indus.
Attock is distant from the sea 942 miles by the Indus,
and 648 in a straight line; and the upper part of the
Indus is about 860 miles long above Attock (Thorn-
ton's *Gazetteer of India*). Hence gold would be so
distant from the mouths of the Indus, that none
could be obtained thence, except from an emporium
situated there.

porium, with an excellent harbor, called Arabia Felix (to be carefully distinguished from the district so called), which received its name of Felix, according to the author of the Periplus, from its being the depot for the merchandise both of the Indians and Egyptians at a time when vessels did not sail direct from India to Egypt, and when merchants from Egypt did not dare to venture farther eastward towards India. At Zafár or Zafári, likewise, already referred to as a town in Hadramaút, there was an emporium in the Middle Ages, and there may have been one in the time of Solomon. And on the Arabian side of the Persian Gulf was the emporium of Gerrha, mentioned by Strabo (xvi. p. 766), which seems to have had commercial intercourse with Babylon both by caravans and by barges. Its exports and imports are not specified, but there is no reason why the articles of commerce to be obtained there should have been very different from those at Omana on the opposite side of the gulf, the exports from which were purple cloth, wine, dates, slaves, and *gold*, while the imports were brass, sandal-wood, horn, and ebony. In fact, whatever other difficulties may exist in relation to Ophir, no difficulty arises from any absence of emporia along the Arabian coast, suited to the size of vessels and the state of navigation in early times.

There do not, however, appear to be sufficient data for determining in favor of any one emporium or of any one locality rather than another in Arabia as having been the Ophir of Solomon. Mr. Forster (*Geography of Arabia*, i. 167) relies on an Ofor or Ofir, in Sale and D'Anville's maps, as the name of a city and district in the mountains of Omân; but he does not quote any ancient writer or modern traveller as an authority for the existence of such an Ofir, though this may perhaps be reasonably required before importance is attached, in a disputed point of this kind, to a name on a map. Niebuhr the traveller (*Description de l'Arabie*, p. 253) says that Ophir was probably the principal port of the kingdom of the Sabæans, that it was situated between Aden and Dafar (or Zafar), and that perhaps even it was Cane. Gosselin, on the other hand, thinks it was Doffir, the city of Yemen already adverted to; and in reference to the obvious objection (which applies equally to the metropolis Aphar) that it is at some distance from the sea, he says that during the long period which has elapsed since the time of Solomon, sands have encroached on the coast of Loheia, and that Ophir may have been regarded as a port, although vessels did not actually reach it (*Recherches sur la Géographie des Anciens*, l. c.). Dean Vincent agrees with Gosselin in confining Ophir to Sabæa, partly because in Gen. x. Ophir is mentioned in connection with sons of Joktan who have their residence in Arabia Felix, and partly because, in 1 K. ix., the voyage to Ophir seems related as if it were in consequence of the visit of the Queen of Sheba to Jerusalem (*History of the Commerce and Navigation of the Ancients*, l. c.). But the opinion that Jobab and Havilah represent parts of Arabia Felix would by no means command universal assent; and although the book of Kings certainly suggests the inference that there was some *connection* between the visit of the Queen of Sheba and the voyage to Ophir, this would be consistent with Ophir being either contiguous to Sabæa, or situated on any point of the southern or eastern coasts of Arabia; as in either of these cases it would have been politic

in Solomon to conciliate the good will of the Sabæans, who occupied a long tract of the eastern coast of the Red Sea, and who might possibly have commanded the Straits of Babelmandel. On the whole, though there is reason to believe that Ophir was in Arabia, there does not seem to be adequate information to enable us to point out the precise locality which once bore that name.

In conclusion it may be observed that objections against Ophir being in Arabia, grounded on the fact that no gold has been discovered in Arabia in the present day, seem decisively answered by the parallel case of Sheba. In the 72d Psalm, v. 15, " gold of Sheba," translated in the English Psalter " gold of Arabia," is spoken of just as " gold of Ophir " is spoken of in other passages of the O. T., and in Ezekiel's account of the trade with Tyre (xxvii. 22), it is stated, " the merchants of Sheba and Raamah, they were thy merchants: they occupied in thy fairs with chief of all spices and with *all precious stones, and gold*," just as in 1 K. x., precious stones and gold are said to have been brought from Ophir by the navy of Solomon and of Hiram. (Compare Plin. vi. 28; Horace, *Od.* i. 29, 1, ii. 12, 24, iii. 24, 2; *Epist.* i. 7, 36; and Judg. viii. 24.) Now, of two things one is true. Either the gold of Sheba and the precious stones sold to the Tyrians by the merchants of Sheba were the natural productions of Sheba, and in this case — as the Sheba here spoken of was confessedly in Arabia — the assertion that Arabia did not produce gold falls to the ground; or the merchants of Sheba obtained precious stones and gold in such quantities by trade, that they became noted for supplying them to the Tyrians and Jews, without curious inquiry by the Jews as to the precise locality whence these commodities were originally derived. And exactly similar remarks may apply to Ophir. The resemblance seems complete. In answer to objections against the obvious meaning of the tenth chapter of Genesis, the alternatives may be stated as follows. Either Ophir, although in Arabia, produced gold and precious stones; or, if it shall be hereafter proved in the progress of geological investigation that this could not have been the case, Ophir furnished gold and precious stones *as an emporium*, although the Jews were not careful to ascertain and record the fact.   E. T.

OPH'NI (הָעָפְנִי, with the def. article — " the Ophnite: " LXX. both MSS. omit; [Ald. Ἀφνί; Comp. Ἀφνή:] *Ophni*). A town of Benjamin, mentioned in Josh. xviii. 24 only, apparently in the northeastern portion of the tribe. Its name may perhaps imply that, like others of the towns of this region, it was originally founded by some non-Israelite tribe — the Ophnites — who in that case have left but this one slight trace of their existence. [See note *b* to vol. i. p. 277.] In the Biblical history of Palestine Ophni plays no part, but it is doubtless the Gophna of Josephus, a place which at the time of Vespasian's invasion was apparently so important as to be second only to Jerusalem (*B. J.* iii. 3, § 5). It was probably the Gufnith, Gufna, or Beth-gufnin of the Talmud (Schwarz, p. 126), which still survives in the modern *Jifna* or *Jufna*, 2½ miles northwest of Bethel (Reland, *Pal.*, p. 816; Rob. *Bibl. Res.* ii. 264). The change from the *Ain*, with which Ophni begins, to G, is common enough in the LXX. (Comp. Gomorrah, Athaliah, etc.)   G.

* This Ophni, the present *Jufna*, though not

named in the N. T., is probably connected with incidents mentioned there. Of the two military roads which led from Jerusalem to Antipatris, the more direct one (traces of the pavement of which still remain) was by the way of Gophna (Rob. *Bibl. Res.* ii. 138); and Paul, when sent thither on his night-journey to Cæsarea (Acts xxiii. 21), may be presumed to have followed that road. The escort in that case would arrive at Ophni or Gophna about midnight, and at daybreak would reach the last line of hills which overlook the plain of Sharon. See Howson's *Life and Letters of Paul*, ii. p. 331 (Amer. ed.). It is very possible also that when Saul went on his persecuting errand to Damascus he passed through Gophna to Neapolis (*Náblus*), and thence onward to the north. On the right of the road, just before coming to *Jufna* from the south, are some ruins of an ancient Greek church. The most important relic is a baptistery carved out of a single limestone block, in the form of a cross, two feet nine inches deep, and four feet four inches in diameter, or according to Dr. Robinson, five feet inside (*Bibl. Res.* iii. 78), which account appears to have included the width of the rim. Except a slight difference in the dimensions, this font is a *fac-simile* of one which the writer saw at *Tekü'a*, and has described under Tekoa. The present inhabitants of *Jufna*, about two hundred, are Christians. The appearance of the little village as approached from the south, surrounded by luxuriant vines and fruit-bearing trees, is uncommonly beautiful.   H.

OPH'RAH (עָפְרָה [*female fawn*]). The name of two places in the central part of Palestine

1. (In Josh., 'Εφραθ; Alex. Αφρα; in Sam. Γοφερα: *Ophra*, in Sam. *Aphra*.) In the tribe of Benjamin (Josh. xviii. 23). It is named between hap-Parah and Chephar ha-Ammonai, but as the position of neither of these places is known, we do not thereby obtain any clew to that of Ophrah. It appears to be mentioned again (1 Sam. xiii. 17) in describing the routes taken by the spoilers who issued from the Philistine camp at Michmash. One of these bands of ravagers went due west, on the road to Beth-horon; one towards the " ravine of Zeboim," that is in all probability one of the clefts which lead down to the Jordan Valley, and therefore due east; while the third took the road " to Ophrah and the land of Shual " — doubtless north, for south they could not go, owing to the position held by Saul and Jonathan. [GIBEAH, vol. ii. p. 915 *a*.] In accordance with this is the statement of Jerome (*Onomasticon*, " Aphra "), who places it 5 miles east of Bethel. Dr. Robinson (*Bibl. Res.* i. 447) suggests its identity with *et-Taiyibeh*, a small village on the crown of a conical and very conspicuous hill, 4 miles E. N. E. of *Beitin* (Bethel), on the ground that no other ancient place occurred to him as suitable, and that the situation accords with the notice of Jerome. In the absence of any similarity in the name, and of any more conclusive evidence, it is impossible absolutely to adopt this identification.

Ophrah is probably the same place with that which is mentioned under the slightly different form of EPHRAIN (or Ephron) and EPHRAIM. (See vol. i. p. 755 *a*.) It may also have given its name to the district or government of APHEREMA. (1 Macc. xi. 34.)

2. ('Εφραθ; and so Alex., excepting [viii. 27 and] in δ Εφραιμ, [Comp. in Josh. vi. 11, viii.

27, 32, 'Εφρά:] *Ephra*.) More fully OPHRAH OF THE ABI-EZRITES, the native place of Gideon (Judg. vi. 11); the scene of his exploits against Baal (ver. 24); his residence after his accession to power (ix. 5), and the place of his burial in the family sepulchre (viii. 32). In Ophrah also he deposited the ephod which he made or enriched with the ornaments taken from the Ishmaelite followers of Zebah and Zalmunna (viii. 27), and so great was the attraction of that object, that the town must then have been a place of great pilgrimage and resort. The indications in the narrative of the position of Ophrah are but slight. It was probably in Manasseh (vi. 15), and not far distant from Sheehem (ix. 1, 5). Van de Velde (*Memoir*) suggests a site called *Erfai*, a mile south of *Akrabeh*, about 8 miles from *Nablus*, and Schwarz (p. 156) " the village Erafa, north of Sanur," by which he probably intends *Amleh*. The former of them has the disadvantage of being altogether out of the territory of Manasseh. Of the latter, nothing either for or against can be said.

Ophrah possibly derives its name from Epher, who was one of the heads of the families of Manasseh in its Gileadite portion (1 Chr. v. 24), and who appears to have migrated to the west of Jordan with Abi-ezer and Shechem (Num. xxvi. 30; Josh. xvii. 2). [ABI-EZER; EPHER, vol. i. p. 744 *b*; MANASSEH, ii. 1170 *b*.]   G.

OPH'RAH (עָפְרָה [*female fawn*]: Γοφερά; Alex. Γοφορα; [Comp. 'Εφρά:] *Ophra*). The son of Meonothai (1 Chr. iv. 14). By the phrase "Meonothai begat Ophrah," it is uncertain whether we are to understand that they were father and son, or that Meonothai was the founder of Ophrah.

* OR in the phrase " or ever " represents the Anglo-Saxon *ær*, and is used in the A. V. in the sense of " ere," " before;" see I's. xc. 2; Prov. viii. 23; Song of Sol. vi. 12; Dan. vi. 24; Acts xxiii. 15. So " ere ever," Ecclus. xxiii. 20.   A.

* ORACLE. This word, in every case but one in which it occurs in the O. Testament stands for the Heb. דְּבִיר (LXX. δαβίρ), which is apparently employed, 1 K. viii. 6 (דְּבִיר הַבַּיִת), as equivalent to קֹדֶשׁ הַקֳּדָשִׁים (*Holy of Holies*). The translation " oracle " (Vulg. *oraculum*, comp. χρηματιστήριον, Aq. and Sym.) assumes the derivation of the Heb. word from דָּבַר, " to speak," as if to designate a place chosen for the special manifestation of the divine will. A more probable etymology, and that now generally received, connects it with דָּבַר, taken, like the Arab. دَبَرَ, in the sense of " to be behind," the name being thus supposed to be given to the most holy place, as the *hinder apartment* of the temple proper. The word is once employed (in the phrase " oracle of God," Heb. דְּבַר הָאֱלֹהִים) 2 Sam. xvi. 23, apparently in the general sense of any appointed means of obtaining a revelation from God.

In the N. T. only the plural form occurs (λόγια), always as a designation of truths supernaturally revealed, and once (Acts vii. 38) in connection with the epithet " lively " (rather "*living*," (ῶντα), expressive of their vital, quickening efficacy. [LIVELY, Amer. ed.]   D S. T.

ORATOR. 1. The A. V. rendering for *lach-ash*, a whisper, or incantation, joined with *nebòn*, skillful,[a] Is. iii. 3, A. V. "eloquent orator," marg. "skillful of speech." The phrase appears to refer to pretended skill in magic, comp. Ps. lviii. 5. [DIVINATION.]

2. The title[b] applied to Tertullus, who appeared as the advocate or *patronus* of the Jewish accusers of St. Paul before Felix, Acts xxiv. 1. The Latin language was used, and Roman forms observed in provincial judicial proceedings, as, to cite an obviously parallel case, Norman French was for so many ages the language of English law proceedings. The trial of St. Paul at Cæsarea was distinctly one of a Roman citizen; and thus the advocate spoke as a Roman lawyer, and probably in the Latin language (see Acts xxv. 9, 10 Val. Max. ii. 2, 2; Cic. *pro Cælio*, c. 30; *Brutus*, c. 37, 38, 41, where the qualifications of an advocate are described: Conybeare and Howson, *Life and Travels of St. Paul*, i. 3, ii. 348). [TERTULLUS.]

H. W. P.

ORCHARD. [GARDEN, vol. i. p. 868 *a*.]

O'REB (עֹרֵב; in its second occurrence only,

עוֹרֵב : 'Ωρήβ; [Vat. in Judg. vii. 25, Ωρηβ;] Alex. Ωρηβ: *Oreb*). The "raven" or "crow," the companion of Zeeb, the "wolf." One of the chieftains of the Midianite host which invaded Israel, and was defeated and driven back by Gideon.

The title given to them (שָׂרֵי, A. V. "princes") distinguishes them from Zebah and Zalmunna, the other two chieftains, who are called "kings" (מְלָכִי), and were evidently superior in rank to Oreb and Zeeb. They were killed, not by Gideon himself, or the people under his immediate conduct, but by the men of Ephraim, who rose at his entreaty and intercepted the flying horde at the fords of the Jordan. This was the second act of this great tragedy. It is but slightly touched upon in the narrative of Judges, but the terms in which Isaiah refers to it (x. 26) are such as to imply that it was a truly awful slaughter. He places it in the same rank with the two most tremendous disasters recorded in the whole of the history of Israel — the destruction of the Egyptians in the Red Sea, and of the army of Sennacherib. Nor is Isaiah alone among the poets of Israel in his reference to this great event. While it is the terrific slaughter of the Midianites which points his allusion, their discomfiture and flight are prominent in that of the author of Ps. lxxxiii. In imagery both obvious and vivid to every native of the gusty hills and plains of Palestine, though to us comparatively unintelligible, the Psalmist describes them as driven over the uplands of Gilead like the clouds of chaff blown from the threshing-floors; chased away like the spherical masses of dry weeds[c] which course over the plains of Esdraelon and Philistia — flying with the dreadful hurry and confusion of the flames, that rush and leap from tree to tree and hill to hill when the wooded mountains of a tropical country are by chance ignited (Ps. lxxxiii. 13, 14). The slaughter was concentrated round the rock at which Oreb fell, and which was long known by his name (Judg. vii. 25; Is. x. 26). This spot appears to have been on the east of Jordan, from whence the heads of the two chiefs were brought to Gideon to encourage him to further pursuit after the fugitive Zebah and Zalmunna.

This is a remarkable instance of the value of the incidental notices of the later books of the Bible in confirming or filling up the rapid and often necessarily slight outlines of the formal history. No reader of the relation in Judges would suppose that the death of Oreb and Zeeb had been accompanied by any slaughter of their followers. In the subsequent pursuit of Zebah and Zalmunna the "host" is especially mentioned, but in this case the chiefs alone are named. This the notices of Isaiah and the Psalmist, who evidently referred to facts with which their hearers were familiar, fortunately enable us to supply. Similarly in the narrative of the exodus of Israel from Egypt, as given in the Pentateuch, there is no mention whatever of the tempest, the thunder and lightning, and the earthquake, which from the incidental allusions of Ps. lxxvii. 16-18 we know accompanied that event, and which are also stated fully by Josephus (*Ant.* ii. 16, § 3). We are thus reminded of a truth perhaps too often overlooked, that the occurrences preserved in the Scriptures are not the only ones which happened in connection with the various events of the sacred history: a consideration which should dispose us not to reject too hastily the supplements to the Bible narrative furnished by Josephus, or by the additions and corrections of the Septuagint, and even those facts which are reflected, in a distorted form it is true, but still often with considerable remains of their original shape and character, in the legends of the Jewish, Mohammedan, and Christian East.

G.

O'REB (*Oreb*), *i. e.* Mount Horeb (2 Esdr. ii. 33). [HOREB.]

O'REB, THE ROCK (צוּר עֹרֵב: in Judges Σουρ [Ωρηβ], Alex. Σουρειν [only]; in Is. τόπος θλίψεως in both MSS.: *Petra Oreb*, and *Horeb*). The "raven's crag," the spot at which the Midianite chieftain Oreb, with thousands of his countrymen, fell by the hand of the Ephraimites, and which probably acquired its name therefrom. It is mentioned in Judg. vii. 25;[d] Is. x. 26. It seems plain from the terms of Judg. vii. 25 and viii. 1 that the rock Oreb and the winepress Zeeb were on the east side[e] of Jordan. Perhaps the place called 'Orbo (ערבו), which in the *Bereshith Rabba* (Reland, *Pal.* p. 913) is stated to have been in the neighborhood of Beth-shean, may have some connection with it. Rabbi

---

[a] נְבוֹן לָחַשׁ : συνετὸς ἀκροατής; Vulg. and Symm. *prudens eloquii mystici*; Aquila, συνετὸς φιθυρισμῷ; Theodot. συνετὸς ἐπωδῇ. See Ges. pp. 202, 754.

[b] Ῥήτωρ, *orator*.

[c] See a good passage on this by Thomson (*Land and Book*, ch. xxxvii.), describing the flight before the wind of the dry plants of the wild artichoke. He gives also a striking Arab imprecation in reference to it, which recalls in a remarkable way the words of the Psalm quoted above: "May you be whirled like the *'akkûb* before the wind, until you are caught in the thorns, or plunged into the sea!"

[d] The word "upon" in the Auth. version of this passage is not correct. The preposition is בְּ — "in" or "at."

[e] Such is the conclusion of Reland (*Pal.* p. 915, "Oreb").

Judah (*Ber. Rabba*, ibid.) was of opinion that the *Orebim* ("ravens') who ministered to Elijah were no ravens, but the people of this Orbo or of the rock Oreb,[a] an idea upon which even St. Jerome himself does not look with entire disfavor (*Comm. in Is.* xv. 7), and which has met in later times with some supporters. The present defective state of our knowledge of the regions east of the Jordan renders it impossible to pronounce whether the name is still surviving.   G.

O'REN (אֹרֶן [*pine-tree*, Ges.]: 'Αράμ; [Vat. Αμβραμ:] Alex. Αραν: *Aram*). One of the sons of Jerahmeel the firstborn of Hezron (1 Chr. ii. 25).

ORGAN (עוּגָב, Gen. iv. 21; Job xxi. 12; עֻגָּב, Job xxx. 31; Ps. cl. 4). The Hebrew word *'ûgâb* or *'uggâb*, thus rendered in our version, probably denotes a pipe or perforated wind-instrument, as the root of the word indicates.[b] In Gen. iv. 21 it appears to be a general term for all wind-instruments, opposed to *cinnôr* (A. V. "harp"), which denotes all stringed instruments. In Job xxi. 12 are enumerated the three kinds of musical instruments which are possible, under the general terms of the timbrel, harp, and *organ*. The *'ûgâb* is here distinguished from the timbrel and harp, as in Job xxx. 31, compared with Ps. cl. 4. Our translators adopted their rendering, "organ," from the Vulgate, which has uniformly *organum*, that is, the double or multiple pipe. The renderings of the LXX. are various: κιθάρα in Gen. iv. 21, ψαλμός in Job, and ὄργανον in Ps. cl. 4. The Chaldee in every case has אַבּוּבָא, *abbûbâ*, which signifies "a pipe," and is the rendering of the Hebrew word so translated in our version of Is. xxx. 29; Jer. xlviii. 36. Joel Bril, in his 2d preface to the Psalms in Mendelssohn's Bible, adopts the opinion of those who identify it with the Pandean pipes, or syrinx, an instrument of unquestionably ancient origin, and common in the East. It was a favorite with the shepherds in the time of Homer (*Il.* xviii. 526), and its invention was attributed to various deities: to Pallas Athene by Pindar (*Pyth.* xii. 12–14), to Pan by Pliny (vii. 57; cf. Virg. *Ecl.* ii. 32; Tibull. ii. 5, 30); by others to Marsyas or Silenus (Athen. iv. 184). In the last-quoted passage it is said that Hermes first made the syrinx with one reed, while Silenus, or, according to others, two Medes, Seuthes and Rhonakes, invented that with many reeds, and Marsyas fastened them with wax. The reeds were of unequal length but equal thickness, generally seven in number (Virg. *Ecl.* ii. 36), but sometimes nine (Theocr. *Id.* viii.). Those in use among the Turks sometimes numbered fourteen or fifteen (Calmet, *Diss. in Mus. Inst. Hebr.*, in Ugolini, *Thes.* xxxii. 790). Russell describes those he met with in Aleppo. "The syrinx, or Pan's pipe, is still a pastoral instrument in Syria; it is known also in the city, but very few of the performers can sound it tolerably well. The higher notes are clear and pleasing, but the longer reeds are apt, like the

dervis's flute, to make a hissing sound, though blown by a good player. The number of reeds of which the syrinx is composed varies in different instruments, from five to twenty three"[c] (*Aleppo*, b. ii. c. 2, vol. i. p. 155, 2d ed.).

If the root of the word *'ûgâb* above given be correct, a stringed instrument is out of the question, and it is therefore only necessary to mention the opinion of the author of *Shiltê Haggibbôrîm* (Ugol. vol. xxxii.), that it is the same as the Italian *viola da gamba*, which was somewhat similar in form to the modern violin, and was played upon with a bow of horsehair, the chief difference being that it had six strings of gut instead of four. Michaelis (*Suppl. ad Lex. Hebr.*, No. 1184) identifies the *'ûgâb* with the psaltery.

Winer (*Realw.* art. "Musikalische Instrumente") says that in the Hebrew version of the book of Daniel *'ûgâb* is used as the equivalent of סוּמְפֹּנְיָה, *sûmponyâh* (Gr. συμφωνία), rendered "dulcimer" in our version.   W. A. W.

ORI'ON (כְּסִיל: Ἕσπερος, Job ix. 9; Ὠρίων, Job xxxviii. 31: *Orium, Arcturus*, in Job xxxviii. 31). That the constellation known to the Hebrews by the name *cesîl* is the same as that which the Greeks called *Orion*, and the Arabs "the Giant," there seems little reason to doubt, though the ancient versions vary in their renderings. In Job ix. 9 the order of the words has evidently been transposed. In the LXX. it appears to have been thus, — *cîmâh, cesîl, 'âsh*: the Vulgate retains the words as they stand in the Hebrew; while the Peshito Syriac read *cîmâh, 'âsh, cesîl*, rendering the last-mentioned word ܓܢܒܪܐ *gaboro*, "the giant," as in Job xxxviii. 31. In Am. v. 8 there is again a difficulty in the Syriac version, which represents *cesîl* by ܟܣܝܠܐ, *'yâthô*, by which *'âsh* in Job ix. 9, and *'aish* in Job xxxviii. 32 (A. V. "Arcturus"), are translated. Again, in Job xxxviii. 32, *'aish* is represented by Ἕσπερος in the LXX., which raises a question whether the order of the words which the translators had before them in Job ix. 9 was not, as in the Syr., *cîmâh, 'âsh, cesîl*; in which case the last would be represented by Ἀρκτοῦρος, which was the rendering adopted by Jerome from his Hebrew teacher (*Comm. in Jes.* xiii. 10). But no known manuscript authority supports any such variation from the received Hebrew text.

The "giant" of oriental astronomy was Nimrod, the mighty hunter, who was fabled to have been bound in the sky for his impiety. The two dogs and the hare, which are among the constellations in the neighborhood of Orion, made his train complete. There is possibly an allusion to this belief in "the bands of *cesîl*" (Job xxxviii. 31), with which Gesenius (*Jes.* i. 458) compares Prov. vii. 22. In the *Chronicon Paschale* (p. 36) Nimrod is said to have been "a giant, the founder of Babylon, who, the Persians say, was deified and placed among the stars of heaven, whom they call Orion" (comp. Cedrenus, p. 14). The name *cesîl*, literally

is rude and simple. A common reed is taken, cut the required length, holes are burned in it, a mouth-piece is fitted on, and the instrument is complete." He supposes the Hebrew *'ûgâb* to have been a similar instrument. Dr. Conant renders the Hebrew word "pipe" in Job xxx. 31.   H.

---

[a] Manasseh ben-Israel, *Conciliator*, on Lev. xi. 15.

[b] עָגַב, to blow, or breathe.

[c] "The Arabs," says Mr. Porter (Kitto's *Bible Illustrations*, i. 106, Edinb. 1866), "have still the flute, and delight in its music. They make it themselves, and it

'a fool," and then "an impious, godless man," is supposed to be appropriate to Nimrod, who, according to tradition, was a rebel against God in building the tower of Babel, and is called by the Arab historians "the mocker." All this, however, is the invention of a later period, and is based upon a false etymology of Nimrod's name, and an attempt to adapt the word *cesil* to a Hebrew derivation. Some Jewish writers, the Rabbis Isaac Israel and Jonah among them, identified the Hebrew *cesil* with the Arabic *suhail*, by which was understood either Sirius or Canopus. The words of R. Jonah (Abulwalid), as quoted by Kimchi (*Lex. Heb.* s. v.), are — "*Cesil* is the large star called in Arabic *Sohail*, and the stars combined with it are called after its name, *cesilim*." The name *Suhail*, "foolish," was derived from the supposed influence of the star in causing folly in men, and was probably an additional reason for identifying it with *cesil*. These conjectures proceed, first, upon the supposition that the word is Hebrew in its origin, and, secondly, that, if this be the case, it is connected with the root of *cesil*, "a fool;" whereas it is more probably derived from a root signifying firmness or strength, and so would denote the "strong one," the giant of the Syrians and Arabs. A full account of the various theories which have been framed on the subject will be found in Michaelis, *Suppl. ad Lex. Hebr.*, No. 1192.   W. A. W.

ORNAMENTS, PERSONAL.

The number, variety, and weight of the ornaments ordinarily worn upon the person forms one of the characteristic features of oriental costume, both in ancient and modern times. The monuments of ancient Egypt exhibit the hands of ladies loaded with rings, ear-rings of very great size, anklets, armlets, bracelets of the most varied character, and frequently inlaid with precious stones or enamel, handsome and richly ornamented necklaces, either of gold or of beads, and chains of various kinds (Wilkinson, ii. 335–341). The modern Egyptians retain to the full the same taste, and vie with their progenitors in the number and beauty of their ornaments (Lane, vol. iii. Appendix A.). Nor is the display confined, as with us, to the upper classes: we are told that even "most of the women of the lower orders wear a variety of trumpery ornaments, such as earrings, necklaces, bracelets, etc., and sometimes a nose ring" (Lane, i. 78). There is sufficient evidence in the Bible that the inhabitants of Palestine were equally devoted to finery. In the Old Testament, Isaiah (iii. 18–23) supplies us with a detailed description of the articles with which the luxurious women of his day were decorated, and the picture is filled up by incidental notices in other places:

in the New Testament the Apostles lead us to infer the prevalence of the same habit when they recommend the women to adorn themselves, "not with broided hair, or gold, or pearls, or costly array, but with good works" (1 Tim. ii. 9, 10), even with "the ornament of a meek and quiet spirit, which is in the sight of God of great price" (1 Pet. iii. 4). Ornaments were most lavishly displayed at festivities, whether of a public (Hos. ii. 13) or a private character, particularly on the occasion of a wedding (Is. lxi. 10; Jer. ii. 32). In times of public mourning they were, on the other hand, laid aside (Ex. xxxiii. 4–6).

With regard to the particular articles noticed in the Old Testament, it is sometimes difficult to explain their form or use, as the name is the only source of information open to us. Much illustration may, however, be gleaned both from the monuments of Egypt and Assyria, and from the statements of modern travellers; and we are in all respects in a better position to explain the meaning of the Hebrew terms, than were the learned men of the Reformation era. We propose, therefore, to review the passages in which the personal ornaments are described, substituting, where necessary, for the readings of the A. V. the more correct sense in italics, and referring for more detailed descriptions of the articles to the various heads under which they may be found. The notices which occur in the early books of the Bible, imply the weight and abundance of the ornaments worn at that period. Eliezer decorated Rebekah with "a golden *nose-ring* [a] of half a shekel weight, and two bracelets [b] for her hands of ten shekels weight of gold" (Gen. xxiv. 22); and he afterwards added "*trinkets* [c] of silver and *trinkets* [c] of gold" (verse 53). Ear-rings [d] were worn by Jacob's wives, apparently as charms, for they are mentioned in connection with idols: "they gave unto Jacob all the strange gods, which were in their hand, and their ear-rings which were in their ears" (Gen. xxxv. 4). The ornaments worn by the patriarch Judah were a "signet," [e] which was suspended by a *string* [f] round the neck, and a "staff" (Gen. xxxviii. 18): the staff itself was probably ornamented, and thus the practice of the Israelites would be exactly similar to that of the Babylonians, who, according to Herodotus (i. 195), "each carried a seal, and a walking-stick, carved at the top into the form of an apple, a rose, an eagle, or something similar." The first notice of the ring occurs in reference to Joseph: when he was made ruler of Egypt, Pharaoh "took off his *signet*-ring [g] from his hand and put it upon Joseph's hand, and put a gold chain [h] about his neck" (Gen. xli. 42), the latter being probably a "simple gold chain in

---

[a] *Nezem* (נֶזֶם); A. V. "ear-ring." The term is used both for "ear-ring" and "nose-ring." That it was the former in the present case appears from ver. 47:

"I put the *nose-ring* upon her *face*" (עַל־אַפָּהּ). The term is etymologically more appropriate to the nose-ring than to the ear-ring. [EAR-RING; NOSE-RING.]

[b] *Tsâmîd* (צָמִיד), a particular kind of bracelet, named from a root signifying "to fasten." [BRACELET.]

[c] *Celî* (כְּלִי); A. V. "jewels." The word signifies generally "articles." They may have been either vessels or personal ornaments: we think the latter sense more adapted to this passage.

[d] The word *nezem* is again used, but with the addition of בְּאָזְנֵיהֶם, "in their ears."

[e] *Chôthâm* (חוֹתָם). [SEAL.]

[f] *Pâthîl* (פָּתִיל); A. V. "bracelets." The signet is still worn, suspended by a string, in parts of Arabia. (Robinson, i. 36.)

[g] *Tabba'ath* (טַבַּעַת). The signet-ring in this, as in other cases (Esth. iii. 10, viii. 2; 1 Macc. vi. 15), was not merely an ornament, but the symbol of authority.

[h] *Râbîd* (רָבִיד). The term is also applied to a chain worn by a woman (Ez. xvi. 11).

imitation of string, to which a stone scarabæus, set in the same precious metal, was appended " (Wilkinson, ii. 339). The number of personal ornaments worn by the Egyptians, particularly by the females, is incidentally noticed in Ex. iii. 22 : — " Every woman shall *ask* (A. V. " borrow ") of her neighbor *trinkets* *a* of silver and *trinkets* *a* of gold . . . and ye shall spoil the Egyptians: " in Ex. xi. 2 the order is extended to the males, and from this time we may perhaps date the more frequent use of trinkets among men; for, while it is said in the former passage: " ye shall put them upon your *sons* and upon your daughters," we find subsequent notices of ear-rings being worn at all events by young men (Ex. xxxii. 2), and again of offerings both from *men* and women of " *nose-rings,b* and ear-rings, and rings, and *necklaces,c* all articles of gold " (Ex. xxxv. 22). The profusion of those ornaments was such as to supply sufficient gold for making the sacred utensils for the Tabernacle, while the laver of brass was constructed out of the brazen *mirrors d* which the women carried about with them (Ex. xxxviii. 8). The Midianites appear to have been as prodigal as the Egyptians in the use of ornaments: for the Israelites are described as having captured " *trinkets* of gold, *armlets,e* and bracelets, rings, ear-rings,*f* and *necklaces,g* the value of which amounted to 16,750 shekels (Num. xxxi. 50, 52). Equally valuable were the ornaments obtained from the same people after their defeat by Gideon: " the weight of the golden *nose-rings h* was a thousand and seven hundred shekels of gold; beside *collars i* and *ear-pendants k* (Judg. viii. 26).

The poetical portions of the O. T. contain numerous references to the ornaments worn by the Israelites in the time of their highest prosperity. The appearance of the bride is thus described in the book of the Canticles: " Thy cheeks are comely with *beads,l* thy neck with *perforated=* (*pearls*); we will make thee *beads* of gold with studs of silver " (i. 10, 11). Her neck rising tall and stately " like the tower of David builded for an armoury," was decorated with various ornaments hanging like the " thousand bucklers, all shields of mighty men, on the walls of the armoury " (iv. 4): her hair falling gracefully over her neck is described figuratively as a " *chain* " *n* (iv. 9): and " the *roundings* " (not as in the A. V. " the joints ") of her thighs are likened to the *pendant o* of an ear-ring, which tapers gradually downwards (vii. 1). So again we read of the bridegroom: " his eyes are . . . fitly set," *p* as though they were gems filling the sockets of rings (v. 12): " his hands *are as* gold rings *q* set with the beryl," *i. e.* (as explained by Gesenius, *Thesaur.* p. 287) the fingers when curved are like gold rings, and the nails dyed with henna resemble gems. Lastly, the yearning after close affection is expressed thus: " Set me as a seal upon thine heart, as a seal upon thine arm," whether that the seal itself was the most valuable personal ornament worn by a man, as in Jer. xxii. 24; Hag. ii. 23, or whether perchance the close contiguity of the seal to the wax on which it is impressed may not rather be intended (Cant. viii. 6). We may further notice the imagery employed in the Proverbs to describe the effects of wisdom in beautify-

---

a *Cell.* See note *c,* p. 2267.

b *Chāch* (חָח); A. V. " bracelets." The meaning of the term is rather doubtful, some authorities preferring the sense " buckle." In other passages the same word signifies the ring placed through the nose of an animal, such as a bull, to lead him by.

c *Cūmāz* (כּוּמָז); A. V. " tablets." It means a necklace formed of perforated gold drops strung together. [NECKLACE.]

d *Marōth* (מַרְאוֹת); A. V. " looking-glasses." The use of polished mirrors is alluded to in Job xxxvii. 18. [MIRROR.]

e *Ets 'ādàh* (אֶצְעָדָה); A. V. " chains." A cognate term, used in Is. iii. 20, means " step-chain ; " but the word is used both here and in 2 Sam. i. 10 without reference to its etymological sense. [ARMLET.]

f *'Āgil* (עָגִיל); a *circular* ear-ring, of a solid character.

g *Cūmāz ;* A. V. " tablets." See note *c* above.

h *Nezem ;* A. V. " ear-rings." See note *a,* p. 2267. The term is here undefined ; but, as ear-rings are subsequently noticed in the verse, we think it probable that the nose-ring is intended.

i *Saharōnim* (שַׂהֲרֹנִים); A. V. " ornaments." The word specifies *moon-shaped* disks of metal, strung on a cord, and placed round the necks either of men or of camels. Compare ver. 21. [CHAIN.]

k *Netiphōth* (נְטִיפוֹת); A. V. " collars " or " sweet-jewels." The etymological sense of the word is *pendants,* which were no doubt attached to ear-rings.

l *Tōrim* (תֹּרִים); A. V. " rows." The term means, according to Gesenius (*Thes.* p. 1499), *rows* of pearls or beads ; but, as the etymological sense is connected with *circle,* it may rather mean the individual

beads, which might be strung together, and so make a row, encircling the cheeks. In the next verse the same word is rendered in the A. V. " borders." The sense must, however, be the same in both verses, and the point of contrast may perchance consist in the difference of the material, the beads in ver. 10 being of some ordinary metal, while those in ver. 11 were to be of gold.

m *Charūzim* (חֲרוּזִים); A. V. " chains." The word would apply to any perforated articles, such as beads, pearls, coral, etc.

n *'Anāk* (עֲנָק). In the A. V. it is supposed to mean literally a chain : and hence some critics explain the word attached to it, צַוָּארֵנָיִךְ, as meaning a " collar," instead of a " neck." The latter, which is the correct sense, may be retained by treating *'anāk* as metaphorically applied to a pendant lock of hair.

o *Chalāim* (חֲלָאִים); A. V. " jewels." Gesenius understands the term as referring to a necklace, and renders this passage, " the roundings of thy hips are like the knobs or bosses of a necklace." The two notions of *rounded* and *polished* may be combined in the word in this case. A cognate term is used in Hos. ii. 18, and is rendered in the A. V. " jewels."

p The words in the original literally mean *sitting in fullness;* and the previous reference to " rivers of waters ' would rather lead us to adopt a rendering in harmony with that image, as is done in the LXX. and the Vulgate, καθήμεναι ἐπὶ πληρώματα ὑδάτων, *juxta fluenta plenissima.*

q The term here rendered " rings," *gelīlim* (גְּלִילִים), is nowhere else found in this sense, at all events as a personal ornament. Its etymological sense implies something *rounded,* and therefore the word admits of being rendered " staffs ; " in which case a comparison would be instituted between the outstretched fingers and the handsomely decorated staff, of which we have already spoken (Hitzig, *in loc.*).

ing the character; in reference to the terms used we need only explain that the "ornament" of the A. V. in i. 9, iv. 9, is more specifically a *wreath* [a] or *garland*; the "chains" of i. 9, the *drops* [b] of which the necklace was formed; the "jewel of gold in a swine's snout" of xi. 22, a *nose-ring*; [c] the "jewel" of xx. 15, a *trinket*, and the "ornament" of xxv. 12, an *ear-pendant*. [d]

The passage of Isaiah (iii. 18-23), to which we have already referred, may be rendered as follows: (18) " In that day the Lord will take away the bravery of their *anklets*, [e] and their *lace caps* [f] and their *necklaces*; [g] (19) the *ear-pendants*, [h] and the *bracelets*, [i] and the *light veils*; [k] (20) the *turbans*, [l] and the *step-chains*, [m] and the *girdles*, [n] and the *scent-bottles*, [o] and the *amulets*; [p] (21) the rings and *nose-rings*; [q] (22) the *state-dresses* [r] and the *cloaks*, and the *shawls*, and the *purses*; [s] (23) the *mirrors*, [t] and the fine linen *shirts*, and the *turbans*, [u] and the *light dresses*." [v]

The following extracts from the Mishna (*Shabb.* cap. vi.) illustrate the subject of this article, it being premised that the object of the inquiry was to ascertain what constituted a proper article of dress, and what might be regarded by rabbinical refinement as a burden: " A woman must not go out (on the Sabbath) with linen or woollen laces, nor with the straps on her head: nor with a frontlet and pendants thereto, unless sewn to her cap: nor with a golden tower (*i. e.* an ornament in the shape of a tower): nor with a tight gold chain: nor with nose-rings: nor with finger-rings on which there is no seal: nor with a needle without any eye (§ 1): nor with a needle that has an eye: nor with a finger-ring that has a seal on it: nor with a diadem: nor with a smelling-bottle or balm-flask (§ 3).

A man is not to go out . . . with an amulet, unless it be by a distinguished sage (§ 2): knee-buckles are clean and a man may go out with them: step-chains are liable to become unclean, and a man must not go out with them " (§ 4).   W. L. B.

OR'NAN (אָרְנָן [*a strong one, a hero*]: 'Ορνά w: *Ornan*). The form in which the name of the Jebusite king, who in the older record of the book of Samuel is called Araunah, Aranyah, Haavarnah, or Haornah, is given in Chronicles (1 Chr. xxi. 15, 18, 20-25, 28; 2 Chr. iii. 1). This extraordinary variety of form is a strong corroboration to the statement that Ornan was a non-Israelite [ARAUNAH; JEBUSITE, vol. ii. p. 1223 *a*.]

In some of the Greek versions of Origen's Hexapla collected by Bahrdt, the threshing-floor of Ornan ('Ερνὰ τοῦ 'Ιεβουσαίου) is named for that of Nachon in 2 Sam. vi. 6.   G.

OR'PAH (עָרְפָּה [see below]: 'Ορφα: *Orpha*), [Ruth i. 4, 14.] A Moabite woman, wife of Chilion son of Naomi, and thereby sister-in-law to RUTH. On the death of their husbands Orpah accompanied her sister-in-law and her mother-in-law on the road to Bethlehem. But here her resolution failed her. The offer which Naomi made to the two younger women that they should return " each to their own mother's house," after a slight hesitation, she embraced. " Orpah kissed her mother-in-law," and went back " to her people and to her gods," leaving to the unconscious Ruth the glory, which she might have rivaled, of being the mother of the most illustrious house of that or any nation.   G.

* Simonis (p. 401) makes עָרְפָּה = עֹרֶף,

---

[a] *Livyih* (לִוְיָה).

[b] See note *a*, p. 2268.

[c] The word is *nezem*. See note *e*, p. 2267.

[d] *Chlî*. See note *o*, p. 2268.

[e] *'Achsim* (עֲכָסִים); A. V. " tinkling ornaments about their feet." The effect of the anklet is described in ver. 16, " making a tinkling with their feet." [ANKLET.]

[f] *Shbisim* (שְׁבִיסִים); A. V. " cauls " or " networks." The term has been otherwise explained as meaning ornaments *shaped like the sun*, and worn as a necklace. [HAIR.]

[g] *Saherânim*; A. V. " round tires like the moon." See note *i* p. 2268.

[h] *Netiphôth*; A. V. " chains " or " sweet balls." See note *k* p. 2268.

[i] *Shèrôth* (שֵׁרוֹת). The word refers to the construction of the bracelet by *intertwining* cords or metal rods.

[k] *Re'âlôth* (רְעָלוֹת); A. V. " mufflers " or " spangled ornaments." The word describes the *tremulous* motion of the veil. [VEIL.]

[l] *Peêrim* (פְּאֵרִים); A. V. " bonnets " The *peër* may mean more specifically the decoration in front of the turban. [HEAD-DRESS.]

[m] *Tsëâdôth* (צְעָדוֹת); A. V. " ornaments of the legs." See note *e* p. 2238. The effect of the step-chain is to give a " mincing " gait, as described in ver. 16.

[n] *Kishsurim* (קִשֻּׁרִים); A. V. " head-bands." It probably means a handsomely decorated girdle. [GIRDLE.] It formed part of a bride's attire (Jer. ii. 32).

[o] *Bottî hannephesh* (בָּתֵּי הַנֶּפֶשׁ); A. V. " tablets," or " houses of the soul," the latter being the literal rendering of the words. The scent-bottle was either attached to the girdle or suspended from the neck.

[p] *Lechâshim* (לְחָשִׁים); A. V. " ear-rings." The meaning of this term is extremely doubtful: it is derived from a root signifying " to whisper ; " and hence is applied to the mutterings of serpent charmers, and in a secondary sense to amulets. They may have been in the form of ear-rings, as already stated. The etymological meaning might otherwise make it applicable to describe light, *rustling* robes (Saalschütz, *Archaol.* i. 30).

[q] A. V. " nose-jewels."

[r] For this and the two following terms see DRESS.

[s] *Charîtim* (חֲרִיטִים); A. V. " crisping-pins." Compare 2 K. v. 23. According to Gesenius (*Thes.* p. 519), the purse is so named from its round, conical form.

[t] *Gilyônîm* (גִּלְיוֹנִים); A. V. " glasses." The term is not the same as was before used; nor is its sense well ascertained. It has been otherwise understood as describing a transparent material like gauze. See DRESS.

[u] A. V. " hoods." [HEAD-DRESS.]

[v] A. V. " vails." [DRESS.]

[w] Declined 'Ορνᾶ, 'Ορνᾶν, in the Vat. MS. (Mal); but in the Alex. MS. constantly Ορνα. In the Targum on Chronicles the name is given in four different forms: usually אֲרַוְנָן, but also אֶרְנֹון אֲרָנָן אֲרַוְנָן, and אֲרֹונָן. See the edition of Beck (*Aug. Vind.* 1680).

fawn (the letters being transposed); but Gesenius prefers *mane, forelock*, from חֶרֶד.   H.

ORTHO′SIAS ('Ορθωσίας; Alex. Ορθωσιαι Orthosius). Tryphon, when besieged by Antiochus Sidetes in Dora, fled by ship to Orthosias (1 Macc. xv. 37). Orthosia is described by Pliny (v. 17) as north of Tripolis, and south of the river Eleutherus, near which it was situated (Strabo, xvi. p. 753). It was the northern boundary of Phœnice, and distant 1130 stadia from the Orontes (id. p. 760). Shaw (*Trav.* pp 270, 271, 2d ed.) identifies the Eleutherus with the modern *Nahr el-Bárid* on the north bank of which, corresponding to the description of Strabo (p. 753), he found "ruins of a considerable city, whose adjacent district pays yearly to the bashaws of Tripoly a tax of fifty dollars by the name of *Or-tosa*. In Peutinger's Table, also, Orthosia is placed thirty miles to the south of Antaradus, and twelve miles to the north of Tripoly. The situation of it likewise is further illustrated by a medal of Antoninus Pius, struck at Orthosin; upon the reverse of which we have the goddess Astarte treading upon a river. For this city was built upon a rising ground on the northern banks of the river, within half a furlong of the sea, and, as the rugged eminences of Mount Libanus lie at a small distance in a parallel with the shore, Orthosia must have been a place of the greatest importance, as it would have hereby the entire command of the road (the only one there is) betwixt Phœnice and the maritime parts of Syria." On the other hand, Mr. Porter, who identifies the Eleutherus with the modern *Nahr el-Kebir*, describes the ruins of Orthosia as on the south bank of the *Nahr el-Bárid*, "the cold river" (*Handbk.* p. 593), thus agreeing with the accounts of Ptolemy and Pliny. The statement of Strabo is not sufficiently precise to allow the inference that he considered Orthosia north of the Eleutherus. But if the ruins on the south bank of the *Nahr el-Bárid* be really those of Orthosia, it seems an objection to the identification of the Eleutherus with the *Nahr el-Kebir*; for Strabo at one time makes Orthosia (xiv. p. 670), and at another the neighboring river Eleutherus (ὁ πλησίον ποταμός), the boundary of Phœnice on the north. This could hardly have been the case if the Eleutherus were 3½ hours, or nearly twelve miles, from Orthosia.

According to Josephus (*Ant.* x. 7, § 2), Tryphon fled to Apamea, while in a fragment of Charax, quoted by Grimm (*Kurzgef. Handb.*) from Müller's *Frag. Græc. Hist.* iii. p. 644, fr. 14, he is said to have taken refuge at Ptolemais. Grimm reconciles these statements by supposing that Tryphon fled first to Orthosia, then to Ptolemais, and lastly to Apamea where he was slain.   W. A. W.

OSA′IAS [3 syl.] ('Ωσαίας; [Vat. omits:] om. in Vulg.). A corruption of JESHAIAH (1 Esdr. viii. 48; comp. Ezr. viii. 19).

OSE′A (*Osee*). HOSHEA the son of Elah, king of Israel (2 Esdr. xiii. 40).

OSE′AS (*Osee*). The prophet HOSEA (2 Esdr. i. 39).

* OSE′E ('Ωσηέ; Tisch. Treg. 'Ωσηέ: *Osee*). The prophet HOSEA (Rom. ix. 25).   A.

OSHE′A (הוֹשֵׁעַ, i. e. Hoshea [see below]; Samar. יהושע: Αὐσή: *Osee*). The original name of Joshua the son of Nun (Num. xiii. 8), which on some occasion not stated — but which

we may with reason conjecture to have been his received from Moses (ver. 16) the addition of the great name of Jehovah, so lately revealed to the nation (Ex. vi. 3), and thus from "Help" became "Help of Jehovah." The Samaritan Codex has Jehoshua in both places, and therefore misses the point of the change.

The original form of the name recurs in Deut. xxxii. 44, though there the A. V. (with more accuracy than here) has Hoshea.

Probably no name in the whole Bible appears in so many forms as that of this great personage, in the original five, and in the A. V. no less than seven — Oshea, Hoshea, Jehoshua, Jehoshuah, Joshua, Jeshua, Jesus; and if we add Hosea (also identical with Oshea) and Osea, nine.   G.

OSPRAY (עָזְנִיָּה, *oznîyyáh* : ἁλιάετος: *haliæetus*). The Hebrew word occurs only in Lev. xi 13, and Deut. xiv. 12, as the name of some unclean bird which the law of Moses disallowed as food to the Israelites. The old versions and many

Pandion haliæetus.

commentators are in favor of this interpretation; but Bochart (*Hieroz.* ii. 774) has endeavored, though on no reasonable grounds, to prove that the bird denoted by the Hebrew term is identical with

Circaëtus gallicus.

the *melanaëtus* (μελανάετος) of Aristotle, the *Valeria aquila* of Pliny. There is, however, some difficulty in identifying the *haliæetus* of Aristotle and Pliny, on account of some statements these writers make with respect to the habits of this bird. The general description they give would suit either the ospray (*Pandion haliæetus*) or the white-tailed eagle (*Haliæetus albicilla*). The following passage, however, of Pliny (x. 3), points to the osprey: "The *haliæetus* poises itself aloft, and the moment it catches sight of a fish in the sea below pounces headlong upon it, and cleaving the water with its breast, carries off its booty." With this may be compared the description of a modern naturalist, Dr. Richardson: "When looking out for its prey it sails with great ease and elegance, in undulating lines at a considerable altitude above the water, from whence ,it precipitates itself upon its quarry, and bears it off in its claws." Again, both Aristotle and Pliny speak of the diving habits of the *haliæetus*. The osprey often plunges entirely under the water in pursuit of fish. The osprey belongs to the family *Falconidæ*, order *Raptatores*. It has a wide geographical range, and is occasionally seen in Egypt; but as it is rather a northern bird, the Hebrew word may refer, as Mr. Tristram suggests to us, either to the *Aquila nævia*, or *A. nævioïdes*, or more probably still to the very abundant *Circaëtus gallicus* which feeds upon reptilia.   W. H.

OSSIFRAGE (פֶּרֶס, *peres*: γρύψ: *gryps*). There is much to be said in favor of this translation of the A. V. The word occurs, as the name of an unclean bird, in Lev. xi. 13, and in the parallel passage of Deut. xiv. 12. (For other renderings of *peres* see Bochart, *Hieroz.* ii. 770.) The

Gypaëtus barbatus.

Arabic version has *okab*, which Bochart renders μελανάετος, "the black eagle." [ORPHAN.] This word, however, is in all probability generic, and is used to denote any bird of the eagle kind, 'or in the vernacular Arabic of Algeria *okab* is "the

generic name used by the Arabs to express any of the large kinds of the *Falconidæ*." (See Loche's *Catalogue des Oiseaux observés en Algérie*, p. 37.) There is nothing conclusive to be gathered from the γρύψ of the LXX. and the *gryps* of the Vulgate, which is the name of a fabulous animal. Etymologically the word points to some rapacious bird with an eminently "hooked beak;" and certainly the ossifrage has the hooked beak characteristic of the order *Raptatores* in a very marked degree. If much weight is to be allowed to etymology, the *peres* [a] of the Hebrew Scriptures may well be represented by the ossifrage, or bone-breaker; for *peres* in Hebrew means "the breaker." And the ossifrage (*Gypaëtus barbatus*) is well deserving of his name in a more literal manner, it will appear, than Col. H. Smith (Kitto's *Cyc.* art. "Peres") is willing to allow; for not only does he push kids and lambs, and even men, off the rocks, but he takes the bones of animals which other birds of prey have denuded of the flesh high up into the air, and lets them fall upon a stone in order to crack them, and render them more digestible even for his enormous powers of deglutition. (See Mr. Simpson's very interesting account of the *Lammergeyer* in *Ibis*, ii. 282.) The *lammergeyer*, or bearded vulture, as it is sometimes called, is one of the largest of the birds of prey. It is not uncommon in the East; and Mr. Tristram several times observed this bird "sailing over the high mountain-passes west of the Jordan" (*Ibis*, i. 23). The English word ossifrage has been applied to some of the *Falconidæ*; but the *ossifraga* of the Latins evidently points to the *lammergeyer*, one of the *Vulturidæ*.   W. H.

OSTRICH. There can be no doubt that the Hebrew words *bath haya'anâh, yâ'ên*, and *rânân*, denote this bird of the desert.

1. *Bath haya'anâh* (בַּת־הַיַּעֲנָה: στρουθός, στρουθίον, σειρήν: *struthio*) occurs in Lev. xi. 16, Deut. xiv. 15, in the list of unclean birds; and in other passages of Scripture. The A. V. erroneously renders the Hebrew expression, which signifies either "daughter of greediness" or "daughter of shouting," by "owl," or, as in the margin, "daughter of owl." In Job xxx. 29, Is. xxxiv. 13, and xliii. 20, the margin of the A. V. correctly reads "ostriches." Bochart considers that *bath haya'anâh* denotes the female ostrich only, and that *tachmâs*, the following word in the Hebrew text, is to be restricted to the male bird. In all probability, however, this latter word is intended to signify a bird of another genus. [NIGHT-HAWK.] There is considerable difference of opinion with regard to the etymology of the Hebrew word *ya'anâh*. Bochart (*Hieroz.* ii. 811) derives it from a root [b] meaning "to cry out" (see also Maurer, *Comment. in V. T. ad Thren.* iv. 3); and this is the interpretation of old commentators generally. Gesenius (*Thes. s. v.* יַעֲנָה) refers the word to a root which signifies "to be greedy or voracious;" [c] and demurs to the explanation given by Michaelis (*Suppl. ad Lex. Heb.* p. 1127), and by Rosenmüller (*Not. ad Hieroz.* ii. 829, and *Schol. ad Lev.* xi. 16), who trace the Hebrew word *ya'anâh* to one which in Arabic denotes "hard and sterile land:" [d] *bath haya'anâh* accordingly would

---

[a] פֶּרֶס, from פָּרַס, "to break," to "crash.'

[b] עָנָה, "to cry out."   [c] יַעַן.

[d] خَيَّق, *terra dura et sterilis.*

mean "daughter of the desert." Without entering into the merits of these various explanations, it will be enough to mention that any one of them is well suited to the habits of the ostrich. This bird, as is well known, will swallow almost any substance, pieces of iron, large stones, etc., etc.; this it does probably in order to assist the triturating action of the gizzard: so that the oriental expression of "daughter of voracity" is eminently characteristic of the ostrich.[a] With regard to the two other derivations of the Hebrew word, we may add that the cry of the ostrich is said sometimes to resemble the lion, so that the Hottentots of S. Africa are deceived by it; and that its particular haunts are the parched and desolate tracts of sandy deserts.

The loud crying of the ostrich seems to be referred to in Mic. i. 8: "I will wail and howl .... I will make a mourning as the ostriches" (see also Job xxx. 29). The other passages where *bath haya-'anâh* occurs point to the desolate places which are the natural habitat of these birds.

2. *Yâ'ên* (יָעֵן) occurs only in the plural number עֵנִים, *ye'ênim* (LXX. στρουθίον, *struthio*), in Lam. iv. 3, where the context shows that the ostrich is intended: "The daughter of my people is become cruel like the ostriches in the wilderness." This is important, as showing that the other word (1), which is merely the feminine form of this one, with the addition of *bath*, "daughter," clearly points to the ostrich as its correct translation, even if all the old versions were not agreed upon the matter. For remarks on Lam. iv. 3, see below.

3. *Rânân* (רְנָן). The plural form (רְנָנִים, *rendním*: LXX. τερπόμενοι: *struthio*) alone occurs in Job xxxix. 13; where, however, it is clear from the whole passage (13–18) that ostriches are intended by the word. The A. V. renders *rendním* by "peacocks," a translation which has not found favor with commentators; as "peacocks," for which there is a different Hebrew name,[b] were probably not known to the people of Arabia or Syria before the time of Solomon. [PEACOCKS.] The "ostrich" of the A. V. in Job xxxix. 13 is the representative of the Hebrew *nôtseh*, "feathers." The Hebrew *rendním* appears to be derived from the root *rânan*,[c] "to wail," or to "utter a stridulous sound," in allusion to this bird's nocturnal cries. Gesenius compares the Arabic *zimar*, "a female ostrich," from the root *zamar*, "to sing."

The following short account of the nidification of the ostrich (*Struthio camelus*) will perhaps elucidate those passages of Scripture which ascribe cruelty to this bird in neglecting her eggs or young. Ostriches are polygamous: the hens lay their eggs promiscuously in one nest, which is merely a hole scratched in the sand; the eggs are then covered over to the depth of about a foot, and are, in the case of those birds which are found within the tropics, generally left for the greater part of the day to the heat of the sun, the parent-birds taking their turns at incubation during the night. But in those countries which have not a tropical sun ostriches frequently incubate during the day, the male taking his turn at night, and watching over the eggs with great care and affection, as is evidenced by the fact that jackals and other of the smaller *carnivora* are occasionally found dead near the nest, having been killed by the ostrich in defense of the eggs or young. "As a further proof of the affection of the ostrich for its young" (we quote from Shaw's *Zoölogy*, xi. 426), "it is related by Thunberg that he once rode past a place where a female was sitting on her nest, when the bird sprang up and pursued him, evidently with a view to prevent his noticing her eggs or young." The habit of the ostrich leaving its eggs to be matured by the sun's heat is usually appealed to in order to confirm the Scriptural account, "she leaveth her eggs to the earth;" but, as has been remarked above, this is probably the case only with the tropical birds: the ostriches with which the Jews were acquainted were, it is likely, birds of Syria, Egypt, and North Africa; but, even if they were acquainted with the habits of the tropical ostriches, how can it be said that "she forgetteth that the foot may crush" the eggs, when they are covered a foot deep or more in sand?[d] We believe the true

Ostrich.

explanation of this passage is to be found in the fact that the ostrich deposits some of her eggs not in the nest, but around it; these lie about on the surface of the sand, to all appearance forsaken; they are, however, designed for the nourishment of the young birds, according to Levaillant and Bonjainville (Cuvier, *An. King.* by Griffiths and others, viii. 432). Are not these the eggs "that the foot may crush," and may not hence be traced the cruelty which Scripture attributes to the ostrich? We have had occasion to remark in a former article [ANT], that the language of Scripture is adapted to the opinions commonly held by the people of the East: for how otherwise can we explain, for instance, the passages which ascribe to

---

a Mr. Tristram, who has paid considerable attention to the habits of the ostrich, has kindly read over this article; he says, "The necessity for swallowing stones, etc., may be understood from the favorite food of the tame ostriches I have seen being the date-stone, the hardest of vegetable substances."

b תֻּכִּיִּים.

c רָנַן.

d See Tristram (*Ibis*, ii. 74); "Two Arabs began to dig with their hands, and presently brought up four fine fresh eggs from the depth of about a foot under the warm sand."

the hare or to the coney the habit of chewing the cud? And this remark will hold good in the passage of Job which speaks of the ostrich being without understanding. It is a general belief amongst the Arabs that the ostrich is a very stupid bird: indeed they have a proverb, "Stupid as an ostrich;" and Bochart (*Hieroz.* ii. 865) has given us five points on which this bird is supposed to deserve its character. They may be briefly stated thus: (1) Because it will swallow iron, stones, etc.; (2) Because when it is hunted it thrusts its head into a bush and imagines the hunter does not see it;[a] (3) Because it allows itself to be deceived and captured in the manner described by Strabo (xvi. 772, ed. Kramer): (4) Because it neglects its eggs;[b] (5) Because it has a small head and few brains. Such is the opinion the Arabs have expressed with regard to the ostrich; a bird, however, which by no means deserves such a character, as travellers have frequently testified. "So wary is the bird," says Mr. Tristram (*Ibis,* ii. 73), "and so open are the vast plains over which it roams, that no ambuscades or artifices can be employed, and the vulgar resource of dogged perseverance is the only mode of pursuit."

Dr. Shaw (*Travels,* ii. 345) relates as an instance of want of sagacity in the ostrich, that he "saw one swallow several leaden bullets, scorching hot from the mould." We may add that not unfrequently the stones and other substances which ostriches swallow prove fatal to them. In this one respect, perhaps, there is some foundation for the character of stupidity attributed to them.

The ostrich was forbidden to be used as food by the Levitical law, but the African Arabs, says Mr. Tristram, eat its flesh, which is good and sweet. Ostrich's brains were among the dainties that were placed on the supper-tables of the ancient Romans. The fat of the ostrich is sometimes used in medicine for the cure of palsy and rheumatism (Pocoke, *Travels,* i. 209). Burckhardt (*Syria,* Append. p. 664) says that ostriches breed in the Dhahy. They are found, and seem formerly to have been more abundant than now, in Arabia.

The ostrich is the largest of all known birds, and perhaps the swiftest of all cursorial animals. The capture of an ostrich is often made at the sacrifice of the lives of two horses (*Ibis,* ii. 73). Its strength is enormous. The wings are useless for flight, but when the bird is pursued they are extended and act as sails before the wind. The ostrich's feathers so much prized are the long white plumes of the wings. The best come to us from Barbary and the west coast of Africa. The ostrich belongs to the family *Struthionidæ,* order *Cursores.*
W. H.

* OTHER, in the A. V. Josh. viii. 22; 2 Chr. xxxii. 22; Job xxiv. 24; Phil. ii. 3, iv. 3, is used in the plural, for "others." In Luke xxiii. 32 the unfortunate rendering of the A. V., "two other malefactors," has been amended in some modern editions by inserting a comma after "other." The Greek is ἕτεροι δύο, κακοῦργοι, "two others, malefactors." A.

OTH'NI (עָתְנִי [prob. *lion of Jehovah*]: Ὀθνί; [Vat. Γοθνι;] Alex. Γοθνι: *Othni*). Son

of Shemaiah, the first-born of Obed-edom, one of the "able men for strength for the service" of the Tabernacle in the reign of David (1 Chr. xxvi. 7). The name is said by Gesenius to be derived from an obsolete word, '*Othen*, "a lion."

OTH'NIEL (עָתְנִיאֵל, *lion of God,* cf. Othni, 1 Chr. xxvi. 7: Γοθονιήλ: *Othoniel,* [*Gothoniel*]), son of Kenaz, and younger brother of Caleb (Josh. xv. 17; Judg. i. 13, iii. 9, 11; 1 Chr. iv. 13, xxvii. 15). But these passages all leave it doubtful whether Kenaz was his father, or, as is more probable, the more remote ancestor and head of the tribe, whose descendants were called Kenezites (Num. xxxii. 12, &c.), or sons of Kenaz. If Jephunneh was Caleb's father, then probably he was father of Othniel also. [CALEB.] The first mention of Othniel is on occasion of the taking of Kirjath-Sepher, or Debir, as it was afterwards called. Debir was included in the mountainous territory near Hebron, within the border of Judah, assigned to Caleb the Kenezite (Josh. xiv. 12-15); and in order to stimulate the valor of the assailants, Caleb promised to give his daughter Achsah to whosoever should assault and take the city. Othniel won the prize, and received with his wife in addition to her previous dowry the upper and nether springs in the immediate neighborhood. These springs are identified by Van de Velde, after Stewart, with a spring which rises on the summit of a hill on the north of Wady Dilbeh (2 hours S. W. from Hebron), and is brought down by an aqueduct to the foot of the hill. (For other views see DEBIR.) The next mention of Othniel is in Judg. iii. 9, where he appears as the first judge of Israel after the death of Joshua, and their deliverer from their first servitude. In consequence of their intermarriages with the Canaanites, and their frequent idolatries, the Israelites had been given into the hand of Chushan-Rishathaim, king of Mesopotamia, for eight years. From this oppressive servitude they were delivered by Othniel. "The Spirit of the Lord came upon him, and he judged Israel, and went out to war: and the Lord delivered Chushan-Rishathaim, king of Mesopotamia, into his hand; and his hand prevailed against Chushan-Rishathaim. And the land had rest forty years. And Othniel the son of Kenaz died."

This with his genealogy (1 Chr. iv. 13, 14), which assigns him a son, Hathath, whose posterity, according to Judith vi. 15, continued till the time of Holofernes, is all that we know of Othniel. But two questions of some interest arise concerning him, the one his exact relationship to Caleb; the other the time and duration of his judgeship.

(1.) As regards his relationship to Caleb, the doubt arises from the uncertainty whether the words in Judg. iii. 9, "Othniel the son of Kenaz, Caleb's younger brother," indicate that Othniel himself, or that Kenaz was the brother of Caleb. The most natural rendering, according to the canon of R. Moses ben Nachman, on Num. x. 29, that in constructions of this kind such designations belong to the principal person in the preceding sentence, makes Othniel to be Caleb's brother. And this is favored by the probability that Kenaz was not Othniel's father, but the father and head of the tribe, as we learn that Kenaz was, from the desig-

[a] This is an old conceit; see Pliny (x. 1), and the remark of Diodorus Siculus (ii. 50) thereon.
[b] Ostriches are very shy birds, and will, if their nest is discovered, frequently forsake the eggs. Surely this is a mark rather of sagacity than stupidity

nation of Caleb as "the Kenezite," or "son of Kenaz." Jerome also so translates it, "Othniel filius Cenez, frater Caleb junior;" and so did the LXX. originally, because even in those copies which now have ἀδελφοῦ, they still retain νεώτερον in the acc. case. Nor is the objection, which influences most of the Jewish commentators to understand that Kenaz was Caleb's brother, and Othniel his nephew, of any weight. For the marriage of an uncle with his niece is not expressly prohibited by the Levitical law (Lev. xviii. 12, xx. 19); and even if it had been, Caleb and Othniel as men of foreign extraction would have been less amenable to it, and more likely to follow the custom of their own tribe. On the other hand it must be acknowledged that the canon above quoted does not hold universally. Even in the very passage (Num. x. 29) on which the canon is adduced, it is extremely doubtful whether the designation "the Midianite, Moses' father-in-law," does not apply to Reuel, rather than to Hobab, seeing that Reuel, and not Hobab, was father to Moses' wife (Ex. ii. 18). In Jer. xxxii. 7, in the phrase "Hanameel the son of Shallum thine uncle," the words "thine uncle" certainly belong to Shallum, not to Hanameel, as appears from vv. 8, 9. And in 2 Chr. xxxv. 3, 4; Neh. xiii. 28, the designations "King of Israel," and "high-priest," belong respectively to David, and to Eliashib. The chronological difficulties as to Othniel's judgeship would also be mitigated considerably if he were nephew and not brother to Caleb, as in this case he might well be 25, whereas in the other he could not be under 40 years of age, at the time of his marriage with Achsah. Still the evidence, candidly weighed, preponderates strongly in favor of the opinion that Othniel was Caleb's brother.

(2.) And this leads to the second question suggested above, namely, the time of Othniel's judgeship. Supposing Caleb to be about the same age as Joshua, as Num. xiii. 6, 8; Josh. xiv. 10, suggest, we should have to reckon about 25 years from Othniel's marriage with Achsah till the death of Joshua at the age of 110 years (85 + 25 = 110). And if we take Africanus's allowance of 30 years for the elders after Joshua, in whose lifetime "the people served the Lord" (Judg. ii. 7), and then allow 8 years for Chushan-Rishathaim's dominion, and 40 years of rest under Othniel's judgeship, and suppose Othniel to have been 40 years old at his marriage, we obtain (40 + 25 + 30 + 8 + 40 =) 143 years as Othniel's age at his death. This we are quite sure cannot be right. Nor does any escape from the difficulty very readily offer itself. It is in fact a part of that larger chronological difficulty which affects the whole interval between the exodus and the building of Solomon's Temple, where the dates and formal notes of time indicate a period more than twice as long as that derived from the genealogies and other ordinary calculations from the length of human life, and general historical probability. In the case before us one would guess an interval of not more than 25 years between Othniel's marriage and his victory over Chushan-Rishathaim.

In endeavoring to bring these conflicting statements into harmony, the first thing that occurs to one is, that if Joshua lived to the age of 110 years, i. e. full 30 years after the entrance into Canaan, supposing him to have been 40 when he went as a spy, he must have outlived all the elder men of the generation which took possession of Canaan,

and that 10 or 12 years more must have seen the last of the survivors. Then again, it is not necessary to suppose that Othniel lived through the whole 80 years of rest, nor is it possible to avoid suspecting that these long periods of 40 and 80 years are due to some influences which have disturbed the true computation of time. If these dates are discarded, and we judge only by ordinary probabilities, we shall suppose Othniel to have survived Joshua not more than 20, or at the outside, 30 years. Nor, however unsatisfactory this may be, does it seem possible, with only our present materials, to arrive at any more definite result. It must suffice to know the difficulties and wait patiently for the solution, should it ever be vouchsafed to us.　　　　　　　A. C. H.

OTHONI'AS ('Οθονίας: Zochins). A corruption of the name MATTANIAH in Ezr. x. 27 (1 Esdr. ix. 28).

* OUCHES (Ex. xxviii. 11, 13, 14, 25, xxxix. 6, 13, 16, 18) denotes the bezels or sockets in which precious stones are set. In Old English it was also applied to the jewels themselves. The earlier form of the word is nouches or nowches, which occurs in Chaucer.　　　　　　　A.

* OUTROAD. To "make outroades" (1 Macc. xv. 41, A. V. ed. 1611) is to "make excursions." In some modern editions nonsense is made of the passage by printing it "make out roads."
　　　　　　　A.

OVEN (תַּנּוּר: κλίβανος). The eastern oven is of two kinds — fixed and portable. The former is found only in towns, where regular bakers are employed (Hos. vii. 4). The latter is adapted to the nomad state, and is the article generally intended by the Hebrew term tannûr. It consists of a large jar made of clay, about three feet high, and widening towards the bottom, with a hole for the extraction of the ashes (Niebuhr, Descr. de l'Arab. p. 46). Occasionally, however, it is not an actual jar, but an erection of clay in the form of a jar, built on the floor of the house (Wellsted, Travels, i. 350). Each household possessed such an article (Ex. viii. 3); and it was only in times of extreme dearth that the same oven sufficed for several families (Lev. xxvi. 26). It was heated with dry twigs and grass (Matt. vi. 30); and the loaves were placed both inside and outside of it. It was also used for roasting meat (Mishna, Taan. 3, § 8). The heat of the oven furnished Hebrew writers with an image of rapid and violent destruction (Ps. xxi. 9; Hos. vii. 7; Mal. iv. 1).
　　　　　　　W. L. B.

Egyptian Oven.

* OVERPASS (A. V. Jer. v. 28; Eccles. xiv 14) is "to pass by," "neglect."　　　　A.

* OVERRUN (A. V. 2 Sam. xviii. 23) means to "outrun." A.

* OVERSEERS, as a ministerial title, Acts xx. 28. [BISHOP.] H.

* OWE, in Lev. xiv. 35; Acts xxi. 11 (A. V. ed. 1611), is used in the sense of "to own," which has been substituted for it in modern editions. A.

OWL, the representative in the A. V. of the Hebrew words *bath haya'anâh, yanshûph, côs, kippôz,* and *lilith.*

1. *Bath haya'anâh* (בַּת־הַיַּעֲנָה). [Os-TRICH.]

2. *Yanshûph,* or *yanshôph* (יַנְשׁוֹף, יַנְשׁוּף: Ἴβις, γλαύξ:[a] *ibis*), occurs in Lev. xi. 17; Deut. xiv. 16, as the name of some unclean bird, and in Is. xxxiv. 11, in the description of desolate Edom, "the *yanshôph* and the raven shall dwell in it." The A. V. translates *yanshûph* by "owl," or "great owl." The Chaldee and Syriac are in favor of some kind of owl; and perhaps the etymology of the word points to a nocturnal bird. Bochart is satisfied that an "owl" is meant, and supposes the bird is so called from the Hebrew for "twilight" (*Hieroz.* iii. 23). For other conjectures see Bochart (*Hieroz.* iii. 24-29). The LXX. and Vulg. read Ἴβις (*ibis*), i. e. the *Ibis religiosa,* the sacred bird of Egypt. Col. H. Smith suggests that the night heron (*Ardea nycticorax,* Lin.) is perhaps intended, and objects to the ibis on the ground that so rare a bird, and one totally unknown in Palestine, could

Ibis religiosa.

not be the *yanshûph* of the Pentateuch; there is, however, no occasion to suppose that the *yanshûph* was ever seen in Palestine; the Levitical law was given soon after the Israelites left Egypt, and it is only natural to suppose that several of the unclean animals were Egyptian; some might never have been seen or heard of in Palestine: the *yanshûph* is mentioned as a bird of Edom (Is. *l. c.*), and the ibis might have formerly been seen there; the old Greek and Latin writers are in error when they state that this bird never leaves Egypt: Cuvier says it is found throughout the extent of Africa,

and latterly Dr. Heuglin met with it on the coast of Abyssinia (*List of Birds collected in the Red Sea;* "Ibis," i. 347). The Coptic version renders *yanshûph* by "Hippen," from which it is believed the Greek and Latin word *ibis* is derived (see Jablonski's *Opusc.* i. 93, ed. te Water). On the whole the evidence is inconclusive, though it is in favor of the *Ibis religiosa,* and probably the other Egyptian species (*Ibis falcinellus*) may be included under the term. See on the subject of the Ibis of the ancients, Savigny's *Histoire naturelle et mythologique de l'Ibis* (Paris, 180?, 8vo): and Cuvier's *Mémoire sur l'Ibis des Anciens Egyptiens* (*Ann. Mus.* iv. 116).

3. *Côs* (כּוֹס: νυκτικόραξ, ἐρωδιός: *bubo, herodius, nycticorax*), the name of an unclean bird (Lev. xi. 17; Deut. xiv. 16); it occurs again in Ps. cii. 6. There is good reason for believing that the A. V. is correct in its rendering of "owl" or "little owl." Most of the old versions and paraphrases are in favor of some species of "owl" as the proper translation of *côs:* Bochart is inclined to think that we should understand the pelican (*Hieroz.* iii. 17), the Hebrew *côs* meaning a "cup," or "pouch;" the pelican being so called from its membranous bill-pouch. He compares the Latin *truo,* "a pelican," from *trua,* "a scoop" or "ladle." But the ancient versions are against this theory, and there does not seem to be much doubt that *kaath* is the Hebrew name for the pelican. The passage in Ps. cii. 6, "I am like a pelican of the wilderness, I am like a *côs* of ruined places," points decidedly to some kind of owl. Michaelis, who has devoted great attention to the elucidation of this word, has aptly compared one of the Arabic names for the owl, *um elcharab* ("mother of ruins"), in reference to the expression

Otus ascalaphus.

in the psalm just quoted (comp. *Suppl. ad Lex. Heb.* p. 1236, and Rosenmüller, *Not. ad Hieroz.* l. c.). Thus the context of the passage in the Psalm where the Hebrew word occurs, as well as the authority of the old versions, goes far to prove that an *owl* is intended by it. The νυκτικόραξ of

<hr/>

[a] It is important to observe, in reference to the LXX. renderings of the Hebrew names of the different unclean birds, etc., that the verses of Deut. xiv. are

some of them evidently transposed (see Michaelis *Supp.* i. 1240, and *note*): the order as given in Lev. xi is, therefore, to be taken as the standard.

the LXX. is no doubt a general term to denote the different species of *horned owl* known in Egypt and Palestine; for Aristotle (*H. An.* viii. 14, § 6) tells us that *νυκτικόραξ* is identical with *ἄτος*, evidently, from his description, one of the horned owls, perhaps either the *Otus vulgaris*, or the *O. brachyotos*. The owl we figure is the *Otus ascalaphus*, the Egyptian and Asiatic representative of our great horned owl (*Bubo maximus*). Mr. Tristram says it swarms among the ruins of Thebes, and that he has been informed it is also very abundant at Petra and Baalbec; it is the great owl of all eastern ruins, and may well therefore be the "*ôbs* of ruined places."

4. *Kippôs* (קִפּוֹז: *ἐχῖνος*: *ericius*) occurs only in Is. xxxiv. 15: "There (*i. e.* in Edom) the *kippôs* shall make her nest, and lay and hatch and gather under her shadow." It is a hopeless affair to attempt to identify the animal denoted by this word; the LXX. and Vulg. give "hedgehog," reading no doubt *kippôd* instead of *kippôs*, which variation six Hebrew MSS. exhibit (Michaelis, *Supp.* p. 2199). Various conjectures have been made with respect to the bird which ought to represent the Hebrew word, most of which, however, may be passed over as unworthy of consideration. We cannot think with Bochart (*Hieroz.* iii. 194, &c.) that a darting serpent is intended (the *ἀκοντίας* of Nicander and Ælian, and the *jaculus* of Lucan), for the whole context (Is. xxxiv. 16) seems to point to some *bird*, and it is certainly stretching the words very far to apply them to any kind of serpent. Bochart's argument rests entirely on the fact that the cognate Arabic, *kipphaz*, is used by Avicenna to denote some darting tree-serpent; but this theory, although supported by Gesenius, Fürst, Rosenmüller, and other high authorities, must be rejected as entirely at variance with the plain and literal meaning of the prophet's words; though incubation by reptiles was denied by Cuvier, and does not obtain amongst the various orders and families of this class as a general rule, yet some few excepted instances are on record, but "the gathering under the shadow" clearly must be understood of the act of a bird fostering her young under her wings; the *kippôz*, moreover, is mentioned in the same verse with "vultures" (kites), so that there can be no doubt that some bird is intended.

Scops aldrovan.

Deodati, according to Bochart, conjectures the "Scops owl," being led apparently to this interpretation on somewhat strained etymological grounds.

See on this subject Bochart, *Hieroz.* iii. 197; and for the supposed connection of *σκώψ* with *σκώπτω*, see Ælian, *Nat. Anim.* xv. 28; Pliny, x. 49; Eustathius, on *Odys.* v. 66; and Jacobs' annotations to Ælian, *l. c.* We are content to believe that *kippôz* may denote some species of owl, and to retain the reading of the A. V. till other evidence be forthcoming. The wood-cut represents the *Athene meridionalis*, the commonest owl in Palestine. Mount Olivet is one of its favorite resorts (*Ibis,* i. 26). Another common species of owl is the *Scops zorca*; it is often to be seen inhabiting the mosque of Omar at Jerusalem (see Tristram, in *Ibis,* i. 26).

Athene meridionalis.

5. *Lilith* (לִילִית: *ὀνοκένταυροι*; Aq. Λιλίθ, Symm. λαμία: *lamia*). The A. V. renders this word by "screech-owl" in the text of Is. xxxiv. 14, and by "night-monster" in the margin. The *lilith* is mentioned in connection with the desolation that was to mark Edom. According to the Rabbins the *lilith* was a nocturnal spectre in the form of a beautiful woman that carried off children at night and destroyed them (see Bochart, *Hieroz.* iii. 829; Gesenius, *Thes. s. v.* לִילִית; Buxtorf, *Lex. Chald. et Talm.* p. 1140). With the *lilith* may be compared the *ghule* of the Arabian fables. The old versions support the opinion of Bochart that a spectre is intended. As to the *ὀνοκένταυροι* of the LXX., and the *lamia* of the Vulgate translations of Isaiah, see the *Hieroz.* iii. 822, and Gesenius (*Jesaia,* i. 915-920). Michaelis (*Suppl.* p. 1443) observes on this word, "in the poetical description of desolation we borrow images even from fables." If, however, some animal be denoted by the Hebrew term, the screech-owl (*strix flammea*) may well be supposed to represent it, for this bird is found in the Bible lands (see *Ibis,* i. 26, 46), and is, as is well known, a frequent inhabiter of ruined places. The statement of Irby and Mangles relative to Petra illustrates the passage in Isaiah under consideration: "The screaming of eagles, hawks, and owls, which were soaring above our heads in considerable numbers, seemingly annoyed at any one approaching their lonely habitation, added much to the singularity of the scene." (See also Stephens, *Incid. of Trav.* ii. 76.)   W. H

OX (צֹאן: *Idox*), an ancestor of Judith (Jud. viii. 1). B. F. W.

OX, the representative in the A. V. of several Hebrew words, the most important of which have been already noticed. [BULL; BULLOCK.]

We propose in this article to give a general review of what relates to the ox tribe (*Bovidæ*), so far as the subject has a Biblical interest. It will be convenient to consider (1) the ox in an economic point of view, and (2) its natural history.

1. There was no animal in the rural economy of the Israelites, or indeed in that of the ancient Orientals generally, that was held in higher esteem than the ox; and deservedly so, for the ox was *the* animal upon whose patient labors depended all the ordinary operations of farming. Ploughing with horses was a thing never thought of in those days Asses, indeed, were used for this purpose [ASS] ; but it was the ox upon whom devolved for the most part this important service. The preëminent value of the ox to "a nation of husbandmen like the Israelites," to use an expression of Michaelis in his article on this subject, will be at once evident from the Scriptural account of the various uses to which it was applied. Oxen were used for ploughing (Deut. xxii. 10; 1 Sam. xiv. 14; 1 K. xix. 19; Job i. 14; Am. vi. 12, &c.); for treading out corn (Deut. xxv. 4; Hos. x. 11; Mic. iv. 13; 1 Cor. ix. 9; 1 Tim. v. 18) [AGRICULTURE]; for draught purposes, when they were generally yoked in pairs (Num. vii. 3; 1 Sam. vi. 7; 2 Sam. vi. 6); as beasts of burden (1 Chr. xii. 40); their flesh was eaten (Deut. xiv. 4; 1 K. i. 9, iv. 23 xix. 21; Is. xxii. 13; Prov. xv. 17; Neh. v. 18); they were used in the sacrifices [SACRIFICES]; they supplied milk, butter, etc. (Deut. xxxii. 14; Is. vii. 22; 2 Sam. xvii. 23) [BUTTER; MILK].

Connected with the importance of oxen in the rural economy of the Jews is the strict code of laws which was mercifully enacted by God for their protection and preservation. The ox that threshed the corn was by no means to be muzzled; he was to enjoy rest on the Sabbath as well as his master (Ex. xxiii. 12; Deut. v. 14); nor was this only, as Michaelis has observed, on the people's account, because beasts can perform no work without man's assistance, but it was for the good of the beasts "that thine ox and thine ass may rest."

The law which prohibited the slaughter of any *clean* animal, excepting as "an offering unto the Lord before the tabernacle," during the time that the Israelites abode in the wilderness (Lev. xvii. 1–6), although expressly designed to keep the people from idolatry, no doubt contributed to the preservation of their oxen and sheep, which they were not allowed to kill excepting in public. There can be little doubt that during the forty years' wanderings oxen and sheep were rarely used as food, whence it was *flesh* that they so often lusted after. (See Michaelis, *Laws of Moses*, art. 169.)

It is not easy to determine whether the ancient Hebrews were in the habit of castrating their animals or not. The passage in Lev. xxii. 24 may be read two ways, either as the A. V. renders it, or thus, "Ye shall not offer to the Lord that which is bruised," etc., "neither shall ye make it so in your land." Le Clerc believed that it would have been impossible to have used an uncastrated ox for agricultural purposes on account of the danger. Michaelis, on the other hand, who cites the express testimony of Josephus (*Ant.* iv. 8, § 40), argues that

castration was wholly forbidden, and refers to the authority of Niebuhr (*Descr. de l'Arab.*, p. 81), who mentions the fact that Europeans use stallions for cavalry purposes. In the East, it is well known horses are as a rule not castrated. Michaelis observes (art. 168), with truth, that where people are accustomed to the management of uncastrated animals, it is far from being so dangerous as we from our experience are apt to imagine.

It seems clear from Prov. xv. 17, and 1 K. iv. 23, that cattle were sometimes stall-fed [FOOD], though as a general rule it is probable that they fed in the plains or on the hills of Palestine. That the Egyptians stall-fed oxen is evident from the representations on the monuments (see Wilkinson's *Anc. Egypt.* i. 27, ii. 49, ed. 1854). The cattle that grazed at large in the open country would no doubt often become fierce and wild, for it is to be remembered that in primitive times the lion and other wild beasts of prey roamed about Palestine. Hence. no doubt, the laws with regard to "goring," and the expression of "being wont to push with his horns" in time past (Ex. xxi. 28, &c.); hence the force of the Psalmist's complaint of his enemies, "Many bulls have compassed me, the mighty ones of Bashan have beset me round" (Ps. xxii. 13). The habit of surrounding objects which excite their suspicion is very characteristic of half-wild cattle. See Mr. Culley's observations on the Chillingham wild cattle, in Bell's *British Quadrupeds* (p. 424).

2. The monuments of Egypt exhibit representations of a long-horned breed of oxen, a short-horned, a polled, and what appears to be a variety of the zebu (*Bos Indicus*, Lin.). Some have identified this latter with the *Bos Dante* (the *Bos elegans et parcus Africanus* of Belon). The Abyssinian breed is depicted on the monuments at Thebes (see *Anc. Egypt.* i. 385), drawing a *ploustrum* or car. [CART.] These cattle are "white and black in clouds, low in the legs, with the horns hanging loose, forming small horny hooks nearly of equal thickness to the point, turning freely either way, and hanging against the cheeks" (see Hamilton Smith in Griffith's *Anim. King.* iv. 425). The drawings on Egyptian monuments shew that the cattle of ancient Egypt were fine handsome animals: doubtless these may be taken as a sample of the cattle of Palestine in ancient times. "The cattle of Egypt," says Col. H. Smith (Kitto's *Cyc.* art. "Ox"), a high authority on the *Ruminantia*, "continued to be remarkable for beauty for some ages after the Moslem conquest, for Abdollatiph the historian extols their bulk and proportions, and in particular mentions the Alchisiah breed for the abundance of the milk it furnished, and for the beauty of its curved horns." (See figures of Egyptian cattle under AGRICULTURE.) There are now fine cattle in Egypt; but the Palestine cattle appear to have deteriorated, in size at least, since Biblical times. "Herds of cattle," says Schubert (*Oriental Christian Spectator*, April, 1853), "are seldom to be seen; the bullock of the neighborhood of Jerusalem is small and insignificant; beef and veal are but rare dainties. Yet the bullock thrives better, and is more frequently seen, in the upper valley of the Jordan, also on Mount Tabor and near Nazareth, but particularly east of the Jordan on the road from Jacob's bridge to Damascus." See also Thomson (*Land and Book*, p. 322), who observes (p. 335) that danger from being gored has not ceased "among the half-wild droves that range

over the luxuriant pastures in certain parts of the country."

The buffalo (*Bubalus buffalus*) is not uncommon in Palestine; the Arabs call it *jámús*. Robinson (*Bibl. Res.* iii. 306) notices buffaloes "around the lake *el-Hûleh* as being mingled with the neat cattle, and applied in general to the same uses. They are a shy, ill-looking, ill tempered animal." These animals love to wallow and lie for hours in water or mud, with barely the nostrils above the surface. It is doubtful whether the domestic buffalo was known to the ancient people of Syria, Egypt, etc.; the animal under consideration is the *bhainsa*, or tame buffalo of India; and although now common in the West, Col. H. Smith is of opinion that it was not known in the Bible lands till after the Arabian conquest of Persia (A. D. 651). Robinson's remark, therefore, that the buffalo doubtless existed anciently in Palestine in a wild state, must be received with caution. [See further remarks on this subject under UNICORN.]

The A. V. gives "wild ox" in Deut. xiv. 5, and "wild bull" in Is. li. 20, as the representatives of the Hebrew word *teó* or *tó*.

Teó or *tó* (אוֹת, תֹּא : ὄρυξ, σευτλίον *a*; Aq., Symm., and Theod., ὄρυξ: *oryx*. Among the beasts that were to be eaten mention is made of the *teó* (Deut. *l. c.*); again, in Isaiah, "they lie at the head of all the streets like a *tó* in the nets." The most important ancient versions point to the oryx (*Oryx leucoryx*) as the animal denoted by the Hebrew words. Were it not for the fact that another Hebrew name (*yachmur*)*b* seems to stand for this animal,*b* we should have no hesitation in referring the *teó* to the antelope above named. Col. H. Smith suggests that the antelope he calls the Nubian Oryx (*Oryx tao*), may be the animal intended; this, however, is probably only a variety of the other. Oedmann (*Verm. Samm.* p. iv. 23) thinks the Bubule (*Alcephalus bubalis*) may be the *tó*; this is the *Bekker-el-wosh* of N. Africa mentioned by Shaw (*Trav.* i. 310, 8vo ed.). The point must be left undetermined. See FALLOW DEER.

W. H.

* The grain used for fodder in the East (see above) is principally barley; only the poorest of the people eat this grain, and they only when wheat fails them. Oats are not cultivated in the East for fodder. There is a wild species of *avena* which grows extensively as a weed in Syria, and is often plucked up with the *Hordeum bulbosum* and other *Gramineæ*, and fed as green fodder to the cattle, but it is never sown, and never threshed out. Its grain is small and lean, and would not be profitable as a crop. This species is called by the Arabs شَيفون (*shâphoon*). Barley is the universal fodder of the Orientals. It is given mixed with the fine-cut straw of its own stalk from the threshing-floors, also with the straw of wheat. This latter is called تِبْن (*tibn*). Barley is not used in the East for distilling purposes, as far as I know. I never saw native whiskey. The Arabic name for

barley شَعِير (*sha'ir*) is from the same root as the Hebrew, and undoubtedly refers to the long *hair-like* beards of the ripe ears.　　G. E. P.

OX-GOAD. [GOAD.]

O'ZEM (אֹצֶם, *i. e.* Otsem [*strength, power*]). The name of two persons of the tribe of Judah.

1. (['Ασάμ; Vat.]Alex. Ασομ: *Asom*.) The sixth son of Jesse, the next eldest above David (1 Chr. ii. 15). His name is not again mentioned in the Bible, nor do the Jewish traditions appear to contain anything concerning him.

2. ('Ασάν;*c* Alex. Ασομ: *Asom*.) Son of Jerahmeel, a chief man in the great family of Hezron (1 Chr. ii. 25).　　G.

OZI'AS ('Οζίας; [Vat. Sin. Οζειας, and so Alex. vi. 15, 21, viii. 28, 35, xv. 4:] *Ozias*). 1. The son of Micha of the tribe of Simeon, one of the "governors" of Bethulia, in the history of Judith (Jud. vi. 15 [16, 21], vii. 23 [30], viii. 10, 28, 35 [iv. 4]).　　B. F. W.

2. [Vat. Οζειας; Alex. Εζιας.] UZZI, one of the ancestors of Ezra (2 Esdr. i. 2); also called SAVIAS (1 Esdr. viii. 2).

3. [Lachm. Tisch. Treg. 'Οζείας.] UZZIAH, King of Judah (Matt. i. 8, 9).

O'ZIEL ('Οζιήλ; [Vat. Sin. Alex. Οζειηλ:] *Ozias*), an ancestor of Judith (Jud. viii. 1). The name occurs frequently in O. T. under the form UZZIEL.　　B. F. W.

OZ'NI (אָזְנִי [*having ears, attentive*]: 'Αζενί; [Vat. Αζενει:] Alex. Αζωνι: *Ozni*). One of the sons of Gad (Num. xxvi. 16), called EZBON in Gen. xlvi. 16, and founder of the family of the

OZ'NITES (אָזְנִי [as above]: δῆμος ὁ 'Αζενί [Vat. -νει]; Alex. ὁ Αζενι: *familia Oznitarum*), Num. xxvi. 16.

OZO'RA ('Εζωρά: [Ald. 'Οζωρά]). "The sons of Machnadebai," in Ezr. x. 40, is corrupted into "the sons of Ozora" (1 Esdr. ix. 34).

P.

PA'ARAI [3 syl.] (פַּעֲרַי [perh. *Jehovah reveals*, Fürst: Alex.] Φαραει: [Comp. Φααραί:] *Pharaï*). In the list of 2 Sam. xxiii. 35, "Paarai the Arbite" is one of David's mighty men. In 1 Chr. xi. 37, he is called "Naarai the son of Ezbai," and this in Kennicott's opinion is the true reading (*Diss.* p. 209-211). The Vat. MS. [Rom.] omits the first letter of the name, and reads the other three with the following word, thus, εὐραιοσερχί [Vat. -χει]. The Peshito-Syriac has "Gari of Arub," which makes it probable that "Naarai" is the true reading, and that the Syriac translators mistook ב for ג.

PA'DAN (פַּדָּן [*acre, field*]: Μεσοποταμία τῆς Συρίας: *Mesopotamia*). Padan-Aram (Gen. xlviii. 7).

---

a As to this word, see Schleusner, *Lex. in LXX.* s. v.

b *Yachmur*, in the vernacular Arabic of N. Africa, is one of the names for the oryx.

c The word following this — אֲחִיָּה — A. V. Ahijah, Vulg. *Achia*, is in the LXX. rendered ἀδελφὸς αὐτοῦ.

PA'DAN-A'RAM (פַּדַּן אֲרָם [see below]:
ἡ Μεσοποταμία Συρίας, Gen. xxv. 20, xxviii. 6, 7,
xxxiii. 18; ἡ M. Gen. xxviii. 2, 5, xxxi. 18; M. τῆς
Συρ· Gen. xxxv. 9, 26, xlvi. 15; Alex. η M. Gen. xxv.
20, xxviii. 5, 7, xxxi. 18; η M. Συρ· Gen. xxviii. 2,
xxxii. 18: *Mesopotamia*, Gen. xxv. 20, xxxi. 18;
M. Syria, Gen. xxviii. 2, 5, 6, xxxiii. 18, xxxv. 9,
26, xlvi. 15; *Syria*, Gen. xxvi. 15). By this name,
more properly *Puddan-Aram*, which signifies "the
table-land of Aram" according to Fürst and Gesenius, the Hebrews designated the tract of country
which they otherwise called Aram-naharaim,
"Aram of the two rivers," the Greek Mesopotamia
(Gen. xxiv. 10), and "the field (A. V. 'country')
of Aram" (Hos. xii. 12). The term was perhaps
more especially applied to that portion which bordered on the Euphrates, to distinguish it from the
mountainous districts in the N. and N. E. of Mesopotamia. Rashi's note on Gen. xxv. 20 is curious:
"Because there were two Arams, Aram-naharaim
and Aram Zobah, he (the writer) calls it Paddan-
Aram: the expression 'yoke of oxen' is in the
Targums פַּדָּן תּוֹרִין, *paddan tōrin*; and some
interpret Paddan-Aram as 'field of Aram,' because
in the language of the Ishmaelites they call a field
"*paddan*" (Ar فدان). In Syr. حقلا,
pidōnō, is used for a "plain" or "field;" and both
this and the Arabic word· are probably from the

root فد, *fadda*, "to plough," which seems akin
to *fid-* in *fidit*, from *findere*. If this etymology be
true *Paddan-Aram* is the arable land of Syria;
"either an upland tale in the hills, or a fertile district immediately at their feet" (Stanley, *S. & P.*
p. 129, *note*). *Padlan*, the ploughed land, would
thus correspond with the Lat. *arvum*, and is analogous to Eng. *field*, the *felled* land, from which the
trees have been cleared.

Padan-Aram plays an important part in the
early history of the Hebrews. The family of their
founder had settled there, and were long looked
upon as the aristocracy of the race, with whom
alone the legitimate descendants of Abraham might
intermarry, and thus preserve the purity of their
blood. Thither Abraham sent his faithful steward
(Gen. xxiv. 10), after the news had reached him in
his southern home at Beer-sheba that children had
been born to his brother Nahor. From this family
alone, the offspring of Nahor and Milcah, Abraham's brother and niece, could a wife be sought for
Isaac, the heir of promise (Gen. xxv. 20), and Jacob
the inheritor of his blessing (Gen. xxviii.).

It is elsewhere called PADAN simply (Gen.
xlviii. 7).   W. A. W.

* **PADDLE** is used in Deut. xxiii. 13 (A. V.)
in the sense of a "small spade" or "shovel."
The term is still applied in provincial English to
an instrument of this kind (also called *paddle-
staff*), used by ploughmen for freeing the share from
earth. "Thou shalt have a *paddle upon thy
weapon*," in the passage above referred to, would
be better translated, "Thou shalt have *a small
shovel among thy implements*" (*ein Schäuflein bei
deiner Geräthschaft*, Bunsen).   A.

PA'DON (פָּדוֹן ·[*deliverance*]: Φαδών:
Phadon). The ancestor of a family of Nethinim
who returned with Zerubbabel (Ezr. ii. 44; Neh
vii. 47). He is called PHALEAS in 1 Esdr. v. 29.

PAG'IEL (פַּגְעִיאֵל [*God allots*]: Φαγεήλ:
Alex. Φαγιηλ, [and so Vat. i. 13, ii. 27:] *Phe-
giel*). The son of Ocran, and chief of the tribe of
Asher at the time of the Exodus (Num. i. 13, ii
27, vii. 72, 77, x. 26).

PA'HATH-MO'AB (פַּחַת מוֹאָב : Φααθ
[Vat. also Φαλαβ, Φααδ, Φααβ (so FA. Neh. iii.
11, where Rom. Φαδτ)] Μααβ: *Phahath-Moab*,
"governor of Moab"). Head of one of the chief
houses of the tribe of Judah. Of the individual,
or the occasion of his receiving so singular a name,
nothing is known certainly, either as to the time
when he lived, or the particular family to which he
belonged. But as we read in 1 Chr. iv. 22, of a
family of Shilonites, of the tribe of Judah, who in
very early times "had dominion in Moab," it may
be conjectured that this was the origin of the name.
It is perhaps a slight corroboration of this conjecture that as we find in Ezr. ii. 6, that the sons of
Pahath-Moab had among their number "children
of Joab," so also in 1 Chr. iv. we find these families who had dominion in Moab very much mixed
with the sons of Caleb, among whom, in 1 Chr. ii.
54, iv. 14, we find the house of Joab.[a] It may
further be conjectured that this dominion of the
sons of Shelah in Moab, had some connection with
the migration of Elimelech and his sons into the
country of Moab, as mentioned in the book of Ruth;
nor should the close resemblance of the names
עָפְרָה (Ophrah), 1 Chr. iv. 14, and עָרְפָּה
(Orpah), Ruth i. 4, be overlooked. Jerome, indeed, following doubtless his Hebrew master, gives
a mystical interpretation to the names in 1 Chr.
iv. 22, and translates the strange word *Jashubi-
lehem*, "they returned to Leem" (Bethlehem).
And the author of *Quæst. Heb. in Lib. Paraleip.*
(printed in Jerome's works) follows up this opening, and makes JOKIM (qui stare fecit solem) to
mean ELIAKIM, and the men of Chozeba (viri
mendacii), Joash and Saraph (*securus et incendens*),
to mean Mahlon and Chilion, who took wives
(בְּעָלָה) in Moab, and returned (*i. e.* Ruth and
Naomi did) to the plentiful bread of Bethlehem
(*house of bread*); interpretations which are so far
worth noticing, as they point to ancient traditions
connecting the migration of Elimelech and his sons
with the Jewish dominion in Moab mentioned in
1 Chr. iv. 22.[b] However, as regards the name
Pahath-Moab, this early and obscure connection
of the families of Shelah the son of Judah with
Moab seems to supply a not improbable origin for
the name itself, and to throw some glimmering
upon the association of the children of Joshua and
Joab with the sons of Pahath-Moab. That this
family was of high rank in the tribe of Judah we
learn from their appearing *fourth* in order in the
two lists, Ezr. ii. 6; Neh. vii. 11, and from their
chief having signed *second*, among the lay princes,
in Neh. x. 14. It was also the most numerous
(2818) of all the families specified, except the

---

[a] The resemblance between *Laadah* (לַעְדָּה,
1 Chr. iv. 21), one of the sons of Shelah, and *Laadan*
(לַעְדָּן), an ancestor of Joshua (1 Chr. vii. 26), may

be noted in connection with the mention of Jeshua,
Ezr. ii. 6.

[b] 1 Sam. xxii. 3, may also be noticed in this con
nection.

Benjamite house of Senaah (Neh. vii. 38). The name of the chief of the house of Pahath-Moab, in Nehemiah's time, was Hashub; and, in exact accordance with the numbers of his family, we find him repairing *two* portions of the wall of Jerusalem (Neh. iii. 11, 23). It may also be noticed as slightly confirming the view of Pahath-Moab being a Shilonite family, that whereas in 1 Chr. ix. 5–7, Neh. xi. 5–7, we find the Benjamite families in close juxtaposition with the Shilonites, so in the building of the wall, where each family built the portion over against their own habitation, we find Benjamin and Hashub the Pahath-Moabite coupled together (Neh. iii. 23). The only other notices of the family are found in Ezr. viii. 4, where 200 of its males are said to have accompanied Eliboënai, the son of Zerahiah, when he came up with Ezra from Babylon; and in Ezr. x. 30, where eight of the sons of Pahath-Moab are named as having taken strange wives in the time of Ezra's government.   A. C. H.

* **PAI** (פָּעִי: Φογόρ: *Phau*), 1 Chr. i. 50, a town of Idumæa. [PAU.]   A.

PAINT (as a cosmetic). The use of cosmetic dyes has prevailed in all ages in eastern countries. We have abundant evidence of the practice of painting the eyes both in ancient Egypt (Wilkinson, ii. 342) and in Assyria (Layard's *Nineveh*, ii. 328); and in modern times no usage is more general. It does not appear, however, to have been by any means universal among the Hebrews. The notices of it are few; and in each instance it seems to have been used as a meretricious art, unworthy of a woman of high character. Thus Jezebel "put her eyes in painting" (2 K. ix. 30, margin); Jeremiah says of the harlot city, "Though thou rentest thy eyes with painting" (Jer. iv. 30); and Ezekiel again makes it a characteristic of a harlot (Ez. xxiii. 40; comp. Joseph. *B. J.* iv. 9, § 10). The expressions used in these passages are worthy of observation, as referring to the mode in which the process was effected. It is thus described by Chandler (*Travels*, ii. 140): "A girl, closing one of her

"Eye ornamented with Kohl, as represented in ancient paintings." (Lane, p. 37, new ed.)

eyes, took the two lashes between the forefinger and thumb of the left hand, pulled them forward, and then thrusting in at the external corner a bodkin which had been immersed in the soot, and extracting it again, the particles before adhering to it remained within, and were presently ranged round the organ." The eyes were thus literally "put in paint," and were "rent" open in the process. A broad line was also drawn round the eye, as represented in the accompanying cut. The effect was an apparent enlargement of the eye; and the expression in Jer. iv. 30 has been by some understood in this sense (Ges. *Thes.* p. 1239), which is without doubt admissible, and would harmonize

with the observations of other writers (Juv. ii. 94, "obliquâ *producit* acu;" Plin. *Ep.* vi. 2). The term used for the application of the dye was *kāchal,*[a] "to smear;" and Rabbinical writers described the paint itself under a cognate term (Mishn. *Shabb.* 8, § 3). These words still survive in *kohl,*[b] the modern oriental name for the powder used. [See note, vol. ii. p. 1391 (Amer. ed.).] The Bible gives no indication of the substance out of which the dye was formed. If any conclusion were deducible from the evident affinity between the Hebrew *pūk,*[c] the Greek φῦκος, and the Latin *fucus,* it would be to the effect that the dye was of a vegetable kind. Such a dye is at the present day produced from the henna plant (*Lawsonia inermis*), and is extensively applied to the hands and the hair (Russell's *Aleppo,* i. 109, 110). But the old versions (the LXX., Chaldee, Syriac, etc.) agree in pronouncing the dye to have been produced from antimony, the very name of which (στίβι, *stibium*) probably owed its currency in the ancient world to this circumstance, the name itself and the application of the substance having both emanated from Egypt.[d] Antimony is still used for the purpose in Arabia (Burckhardt's *Travels,* i. 376), and in Persia (Morier's *Second Journey,* p. 61), though lead is also used in the latter country (Russell, i. 366): but in Egypt the *kuhl* is a soot produced by burning either a kind of frankincense or the shells of almonds (Lane, i. 61). The dye-stuff was moistened with oil, and kept in a small jar, which we may infer to have been made of horn, from the proper name, Keren-happuch, "horn for paint"

Ancient Vessel and Probe for Kohl.

(Job xlii. 14). The probe with which it was applied was made either of wood, silver, or ivory, and had a blunted point. Both the probe and the jar have frequently been discovered in Egyptian tombs (Wilkinson, ii. 343). In addition to the passages referring to eye-paint already quoted from the Bible, we may notice probable allusions to the practice in Prov. vi. 25, Ecclus. xxvi. 9, and Is. iii. 16, the term rendered "wanton" in the last passage bearing the radical sense of painted. The contrast between the black paint and the white of the eye led to the transfer of the term *pūk* to describe the variegated stones used in the string courses of a handsome building (1 Chr. xxix. 2; A. V. "glistering stones," lit. *stones of eye-paint*); and again the dark cement in which marble or other bright stones were imbedded (Is. liv. 11; A. V. "I will lay thy stones with fair colors"). Whether the custom of staining the hands and feet, particularly the nails, now so prevalent in the East, was known to the Hebrews, is doubtful. The plant, *henna,* which is used for that purpose, was certainly known (Cant. i. 14; A. V. "camphire"), and the expressions in Cant. v. 14 may possibly refer to the custom.   W. L. B.

PALACE. There are few tasks more difficult or puzzling than the attempt to restore an ancient

---

[a] כָּחַל.

[b] The Hebrew verb has even been introduced into the Spanish version: "Alcoholaste tuos ojos" (Ges. *Thes.* p. 676).

[c] פּוּך.

[d] This mineral was imported into Egypt for the purpose. One of the pictures at *Beni Hassan* represents the arrival of a party of traders in stibium. The powder made from antimony has been always supposed to have a beneficial effect on the eyesight (Pin. xxxiii. 34; Russell, i. 111; Lane, i. 61).

building of which we possess nothing but two verbal descriptions, and these difficulties are very much enhanced when one account is written in a language like Hebrew, the scientific terms in which are, from our ignorance, capable of the widest latitude of interpretation; and the other, though written in a language of which we have a more definite knowledge, was composed by a person who never could have seen the buildings he was describing.

Notwithstanding this, the palace which Solomon occupied himself in erecting during the thirteen years after he had finished the Temple is a building of such world-wide notoriety, that it cannot

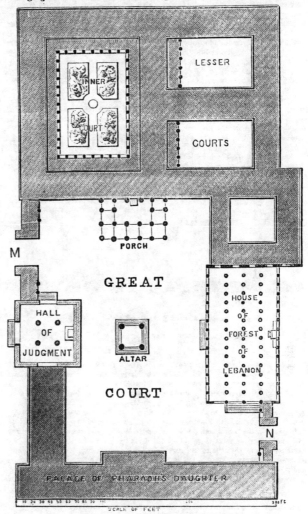

Fig. 1. Diagram Plan of Solomon's Palace.

be without interest to the Biblical student that those who have made a special study of the subject, and who are familiar with the arrangements of eastern palaces, should submit their ideas on the subject; and it is also important that our knowledge on this, as on all other matters connected with the Bible, should be brought down to the latest date. Almost all the restorations of this celebrated edifice which are found in earlier editions of the Bible are what may be called Vitruvian, namely, based on the principles of classical architecture, which were the only ones known to their authors. During the earlier part of this century attempts were made to introduce the principles of Egyptian design into these restorations, but with even less success. The Jews hated Egypt and all that it contained, and everything they did, or even thought, was antagonistic to the arts and feelings of that land of bondage. On the other hand, the exhumation of the palaces of Nineveh, and the more careful examination of those at Persepolis, have thrown a flood of light on the subject. Many expressions which before were entirely unintelligible are now clear and easily understood, and, if we cannot yet explain everything, we know at least where to look for analogies, and what was the character, even if we cannot predicate the exact form, of the buildings in question.

The site of the Palace of Solomon was almost certainly in the city itself, on the brow opposite to the Temple, and overlooking it and the whole city of David.[a] It is impossible, of course, to be at all certain what was either the form or the exact disposition of such a palace, but, as we have the dimensions of the three principal buildings given in the book of Kings, and confirmed by Josephus, we may, by taking these as a scale, ascertain pretty nearly that the building covered somewhere about 150,000 or 160,000 square feet. Less would not suffice for the accommodation specified, and more would not be justified, either from the accounts we have, or the dimensions of the city in which it was situated. Whether it was a square of 400 feet each way, or an oblong of about 550 feet by 300, as

represented in the annexed diagram, must always be more or less a matter of conjecture. The form here adopted seems to suit better not only the exigencies of the site, but the known disposition of the parts.

The principal building situated within the Palace was, as in all eastern palaces, the great hall of state and audience; here called the "House of the Forest of Lebanon." Its dimensions were 100 cubits, or 150 feet long, by half that, or 75 feet, in width. According to the Bible (1 K. vii. 2) it had "four rows of cedar pillars with cedar beams upon the pillars;" but it is added in the next verse that "it was covered with cedar above the beams that lay on 45 pillars, 15 in a row." This would be easily explicable if the description stopped there, and so Josephus took it. He evidently considered the hall, as he afterwards described the Stoa basilica of the Temple, as consisting of four rows of columns, three standing free, but the fourth built into the outer wall (Ant. xi. 5); and his expression, that the ceiling of the palace hall was in the Corinthian manner (Ant. vii. 5, § 2), does not mean that it was of that order, which was not then invented, but after the fashion of what was called in his day a Corinthian œcus, namely, a hall with

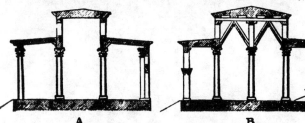

Fig. 2. Diagram Sections of the House of Cedars of Lebanon.

a clere-story. If we, like Josephus, are contented with these indications, the section of the hall was certainly as shown in fig. A. But the Bible goes on to say (ver. 4) that "there were windows in three rows, and light was against light in three ranks," and in the next verse it repeats, "and light was against light in three ranks." Josephus escapes the difficulty by saying it was lighted by "θυρώμασι τριγλύφοις," or by windows in three divisions, which might be taken as an extremely probable description if the Bible were not so very specific regarding it; and we must therefore adopt some such arrangement as that shown in figure B. Though other arrangements might be suggested, on the whole it appears probable that this is the one nearest the truth; as it admits of a clere-story, to which Josephus evidently refers, and shows the three rows of columns which the Bible description requires. Besides the clere-story there was probably a range of openings under the cornice of the walls, and then a range of open doorways, which would thus make the three openings required by the Bible description. In a hotter climate the first arrangement (fig. A) would be the more probable; but on a site so exposed and occasionally so cold

as Jerusalem, it is scarcely likely that the great hall of the palace was permanently open even on one side.

Another difficulty in attempting to restore this hall arises from the number of pillars being unequal ("15 in a row"), and if we adopt the last theory (fig. B), we have a row of columns in the centre both ways. The probability is that it was closed, as shown in the plan, by a wall at one end, which would give 15 spaces to the 15 pillars, and so provide a central space in the longer dimension of the hall in which the throne might have been placed. If the first theory be adopted, the throne may have stood either at the end, or in the centre of the longer side, but, judging from what we know of the arrangement of eastern palaces, we may be almost certain that the latter is the correct position.

Next in importance to the building just described is the hall or porch of judgment (ver. 7), which Josephus distinctly tells us (Ant. vii 5, § 1) was situated opposite to the centre of the longer side of the great hall: an indication which may be admitted with less hesitation, as such a position is identical with that of a similar hall at Persepolis,

a * This allusion to "the city of David" is based on the author's peculiar theory, which is set forth at length, and answered, in article JERUSALEM. Stanley suggests, with equal confidence, a different locality from the above. "The new Palace must have been apart from the castle of David, and considerably below the level of the Temple-mount." (History of the Jewish Church, ii. 215.)   S. W.

and with the probable position of one at Khorsabad.

Its dimensions were 50 cubits, or 75 feet square (Josephus says 30 in one direction at least), and its disposition can easily be understood by comparing the descriptions we have with the remains of the Assyrian and Persian examples. It must have been supported by four pillars in the centre, and had three entrances; the principal opening from the street and facing the judgment-seat, a second from the court-yard of the palace, by which the councillors and officers of state might come in, and a third from the palace, reserved for the king and his household as shown in the plan (fig. 1, N).

The third edifice is merely called "the Porch." Its dimensions were 50 by 30 cubits, or 75 feet by 45. Josephus does not describe its architecture; and we are unable to understand the description contained in the Bible, owing apparently to our ignorance of the synonyms of the Hebrew architectural terms. Its use, however, cannot be considered as doubtful, as it was an indispensable adjunct to an Eastern palace. It was the ordinary place of business of the palace, and the reception-room — the Guesten Hall — where the king received ordinary visitors, and sat, except on great state occasions, to transact the business of the kingdom.

Behind this, we are told, was the inner court, adorned with gardens and fountains, and surrounded by cloisters for shade; and besides this were other courts for the residence of the attendants and guards, and in Solomon's case, for the three hundred women of his harem: all of which are shown in the plan with more clearness than can be conveyed by a verbal description.

Apart from this palace, but attached, as Josephus tells us, to the Hall of Judgment, was the palace of Pharaoh's daughter — too proud and important a personage to be grouped with the ladies of the harem, and requiring a residence of her own.

There is still another building mentioned by Josephus, as a *naos* or temple, supported by massive columns, and situated opposite the Hall of Judgment. It may thus have been outside, in front of the palace in the city; but more probably was, as shown in the plan, in the centre of the great court. It could not have been a temple in the ordinary acceptation of the term, as the Jews had only one temple, and that was situated on the other side of the valley; but it may have been an altar covered by a baldachino. This would equally meet the exigencies of the description as well as the probabilities of the case; and so it has been represented in the plan (fig. 1).

If the site and disposition of the palace were as above indicated, it would require two great portals: one leading from the city to the great court, shown at M; the other to the Temple and the king's garden, at N. This last was probably situated where the stairs then were which led up to the City of David, and where the bridge afterwards joined the Temple to the city and palace.

The recent discoveries at Nineveh have enabled us to understand many of the architectural details of this palace, which before they were made were nearly wholly inexplicable. We are told, for instance, that the walls of the halls of the palace were wainscotted with three tiers of stone, apparently versi-colored marbles, hewn and polished, and surmounted by a fourth course, elaborately carved with representations of leafage and flowers. Above

this the walls were plastered and ornamented with colored arabesques. At Nineveh the walls were like these, wainscoted to a height of about eight feet, but with alabaster, a peculiar product of the country, and these were separated from the painted space above by an architectural band; the real difference being that the Assyrians reveled in sculptural representations of men and animals, as we now know from the sculptures brought home, as well as from the passage in Ezekiel (xxiii. 14) where he describes "men pourtrayed on the wall, the images of the Chaldeans pourtrayed with vermilion," etc. These modes of decoration were forbidden to the Jews by the second commandment, given to them in consequence of their residence in Egypt and their consequent tendency to that multiform idolatry. Some difference may also be due to the fact that the soft alabaster, though admirably suited to bassi-relievi, was not suited for sharp, deeply-cut foliage sculpture, like that described by Josephus; while, at the same time, the hard material used by the Jews might induce them to limit their ornamentation to one band only. It is probable, however, that a considerable amount of color was used in the decoration of these palaces, not only from the constant reference to gold and gilding in Solomon's buildings, and because that as a color could hardly be used alone, but also from such passages as the following: "Build me a wide house and large" — or through-aired — "chambers, and cutteth out windows; and it is ceiled with cedar, and painted with vermilion" (Jer. xxii. 14). It may also be added, that in the East all buildings, with scarcely an exception, are adorned with color internally, generally the three primitive colors used in all their intensity, but so balanced as to produce the most harmonious results.

Although incidental mention is made of other palaces at Jerusalem and elsewhere, they are all of subsequent ages, and built under the influence of Roman art, and therefore not so interesting to the Biblical student as this. Besides, none of them are anywhere so described as to' enable their disposition or details to be made out with the same degree of clearness, and no instruction would be conveyed by merely reiterating the rhetorical flourishes in which Josephus indulges when describing them; and no other palace is described in the Bible itself so as to render its elucidation indispensable in such an article as the present.   J. F.

* PALACE in A. V., singular and plural, is the rendering of several words of diverse meaning (בִּירָה, 1 Chr. xxix. 1 *al.*; הֵיכָל, Ezr. iv. 14 *al.*; אַרְמוֹן, 2 K. xv. 25 *al.*; הַרְמוֹן, Am. iv. 3; מִירָה, Ez. xxv. 4 *al.*; בַּיִת, 2 Chr. ix. 11 *al.*; אַפֶּדֶן, Dan. xi. 45; LXX. οἶκος, Isa. xxxii. 14 *al.*; πόλις, Esth. ii. 13 *al.*; ναός, Ps. xlv. 15 *al.*; βᾶρις, Lam ii. 5 *al.*; ἀβιρά. βιρά. Neh. i. 1, vii. 2; θεμέλια (pl.), Jer. vi. 5 *al.*; χώρα, Mic. v. 5 *al.*; ἄντρον, 1 K. xvi. 18; ἕλως, 1 K. xxi. 1; ἔπαυλις, †Ps. lxix. 25; πυργόβαρις, Ps. cxxii. 7; ἔπαλξις, Cant. viii. 9; γῆ, Jer. ix. 21; ἄμφοδα (pl.), Jer. xvii. 27 *al.*; Ἐφαδανὰ. Dan. xi. 45, Ῥομμὰ. Am. iv. 3; βασίλειον, Na. ii. 6; N. T., αὐλή, Matt. xxvi. 58 *al.*; πραιτώριον, Phil. i. 13).ᵃ

ᵃ * On "Palace" in Phil. i. 13 (A. V.), see JUDGMENT-SEAT [Amer. ed.], and PRAETORIUM at the end.   H.

It often designates the royal residence and usually suggests a fortress, or battlemented house — the citadel, as the most secure place, being commonly in eastern towns the abode of the ruler. The word occasionally (as in Esth. ix. 12) includes the whole city; and again (as in 1 K. xvi. 18) it is restricted to a part of the royal apartments. It is applied (as in 1 Chr. xxix. 1) to the Temple in Jerusalem. By "the palace which appertained to the house" (Nah. ii. 6) is probably meant the tower of Antonia adjacent to the Temple.

The Palace of Solomon, who "was building his own house thirteen years" (1 K. vii. 1), of which a conjectural restoration is attempted in the preceding article, must have stood on the high eastern brow of Zion, overlooking the Temple and the lower city. No site within the walls could have been more commanding, and the immense edifice, built of white stone and cedar-wood, must have been one of the most imposing. The Asmonean princes, according to Josephus, whose descriptions of the city have been mainly confirmed, erected a palace on the same site, adjoining the great bridge which spanned the Tyropœon. It was also occupied as a royal residence by the Herodian family, and was enlarged by king Agrippa. Magnificent private residences were probably embraced in the allusions found in the Psalms and the Prophets to the palaces of Zion. The massive foundations which have been uncovered, as the subterranean parts of the modern city have been explored, convey an impressive idea of the architectural solidity and grandeur of ancient Jerusalem.   S. W.

PA'LAL (פָּלָל [n judge]: Φαλάχ; [Vat. Φαλαλ; FA. Φαλαχ;] Alex. Φαλάξ: Phalel). The son of Uzai, who assisted in restoring the walls of Jerusalem in the time of Nehemiah (Neh. iii. 25).

PALESTI'NA and PAL'ESTINE. These two forms occur in the A. V. but four times in all, always in poetical passages: the first, in Ex. xv. 14, and Is. xiv. 29, 31; the second, Joel iii. 4. In each case the Hebrew is פְּלֶשֶׁת, Pelésheth, a word found, besides the above, only in Ps. lx. 8, lxxxiii. 7, lxxxvii. 4, and cviii. 9, in all which our translators have rendered it by "Philistia" or "Philistines." The LXX. has in Ex. Φυλιστιείμ, but in Is. and Joel ἀλλόφυλοι; the Vulg. in Ex. Philisthiim, in Is. Philisthœa, in Joel Palœsthini. The apparent ambiguity in the different renderings of the A. V. is in reality no ambiguity at all, for at the date of that translation "Palestine" was synonymous with "Philistia." Thus Milton, with

his usual accuracy in such points, mentions Dagon as

> "Dreaded through the coast
> Of Palestine, in Gath and Ascalon,
> And Accaron and Gaza's frontier bounds":
> (Par. Lost, i. 464.)

and again as

> "That twice-battered god of Palestine":
> (Hymn on Nat. 199)

— where if any proof be wanted that his meaning is restricted to Philistia, it will be found in the fact that he has previously connected other deities with the other parts of the Holy Land. See also, still more decisively, Samson Ag. 144, 1098.[a] But even without such evidence, the passages themselves show how our translators understood the word. Thus in Ex. xv. 14, "Palestine," Edom, Moab, and Canaan are mentioned as the nations alarmed at the approach of Israel. In Is. xiv. 29, 31, the prophet warns "Palestine" not to rejoice at the death of king Ahaz, who had subdued it. In Joel iii. 4, Phœnicia and "Palestine" are upbraided with cruelties practiced on Judah and Jerusalem.

Palestine, then, in the Authorized Version, really means nothing but Philistia. The original Hebrew word Pelésheth, which, as shown above, is elsewhere translated Philistia, to the Hebrews signified merely the long and broad strip of maritime plain inhabited by their encroaching neighbors. We shall see that they never applied the name to the whole country. An inscription of Iva-lush, king of Assyria (probably the Pul of Scripture), as deciphered by Sir H. Rawlinson, names "Palaztu on the Western Sea," and distinguishes it from Tyre, Damascus, Samaria, and Edom (Rawlinson's Herod. i. 467). In the same restricted sense it was probably employed — if employed at all — by the ancient Egyptians, in whose records at Karnak the Pulusatu has been deciphered in close connection with that of the Shairutana or Sharu, possibly the Sidonians or Syrians (Birch, doubtfully, in Layard, Nineveh, ii. 407, note). Nor does it appear that at first it signified more to the Greeks. As lying next the sea, and as being also the high-road from Egypt to Phœnicia and the richer regions north of it, the Philistine plain became sooner known to the western world than the country further inland, and was called by them Syria Palæstina — Συρίη Παλαιστίνη — Philistine Syria. This name is first found in Herodotus (i. 105; ii. 104; iii. 5; vii. 89); and there can be little doubt that on each occasion he is speaking of the coast, and the coast[b] only. (See also the testimony of Joseph. Ant. i. 6, § 2.) From thence it was

---

a Paradise Lost was written between 1660 and 1670. Shakespeare, on the other hand, uses the word in its modern sense in two passages, King John, act ii. scene 1, and Othello, act iv. scene 3: the date of the former of these plays is 1596, that of the latter 1602. But Shakespeare and Milton wrote for different audiences; and the language of the one would be as modern (for the time) as that of the other was classical and antique. That the name was changing its meaning from the restricted to the general sense just at the beginning of the 17th century, is curiously ascertainable from two Indexes "of the Hardest Wordes," appended to successive editions of Sylvester's Du Bartas (1606 and 1608), in one of which it is explained as "Judea, the Holy Land, first called Canaan," and in the other "the Land of the Philistines." Fuller, in his Pisgah-sight of Palestine (1650), of course uses it

in the largest sense; but it is somewhat remarkable that he says nothing whatever of the signification of the name. In France the original narrow signification has been retained. Thus ch. xxxi. of Volney's Travels treats of "Palestine, i. e. the plain which terminates the country of Syria on the west," and "comprehends the whole country between the Mediterranean on the west, the mountains on the east, and two lines, one drawn by Khan Younes, and the other between Kaisaria and the rivulet of Yafa." It is thus used repeatedly by Napoleon I. in his dispatches and correspondence. See Corresp. de Nap., Nos. 4020, 4035, &c.

b In the second of these passages, he seems to extend it as far north as Beirût — if the sculptures of the Nahr el-Kelb are the stelæ of Sesostris.

gradually extended to the country further inland, till in the Roman and later Greek authors, both heathen and Christian, it becomes the usual appellation for the whole country of the Jews, both west and east of Jordan. (See the citations of Reland, *Pal.* cc. vii. viii.) Nor was its use confined to heathen writers: it even obtained among the Jews themselves. Josephus generally uses the name for the country and nation of the Philistines (*Ant.* xiii. 5, § 10; vi. 1, § 1, &c.), but on one or two occasions he employs it in the wider sense (*Ant.* i. 6, § 4; viii. 10, § 3; *a. Ap.* i. 22). So does Philo, *De Abrah.* and *De Vitâ Mosis.* It is even found in such thoroughly Jewish works as the Talmudic treatises *Bereshith Rabba* and *Echa Rabbathi* (Reland, p. 39); and it is worthy of notice how much the feeling of the nation must have degenerated before they could apply to the Promised Land the name of its bitterest enemies — the "uncircumcised Philistines."

Jerome (cir. A. D. 400) adheres to the ancient meaning of *Palaestina*, which he restricts to Philistia (see *Ep. ad Dardanum,* § 4; *Comm. in Esaiam* xiv. 23; *in Amos* i. 6).[a] So also does Procopius of Gaza (cir. A. D. 510) in a curious passage on Gerar, in his comment on 2 Chr. xiv. 13.

The word is now so commonly employed in our more familiar language to designate the whole country of Israel, that, although Biblically a misnomer, it has been chosen here as the most convenient heading under which to give a general description of THE HOLY LAND, embracing those points which have not been treated under the separate headings of cities or tribes.

This description will most conveniently divide itself into two sections: —

I. The Names applied to the country of Israel in the Bible and elsewhere.

II. The Land: its situation, aspect, climate, physical characteristics, in connection with its history; its structure, botany, and natural history.[b]

The history of the country is so fully given under its various headings throughout the work, that it is unnecessary to recapitulate it here.

I. THE NAMES.

PALESTINE, then, is designated in the Bible by more than one name: —

1. During the Patriarchal period, the Conquest, and the age of the Judges, and also where those early periods are referred to in the later literature (as Ps. cv. 11; and Joseph. *Ant.* i. 7; 8; 20; v. 1, &c.), it is spoken of as "Canaan," or more frequently "the Land of Canaan," meaning thereby the country west of the Jordan, as opposed to "the Land of Gilead" on the east.[c] [CANAAN, LAND OF, vol. i. p. 351 f.] Other designations, during the same early period, are "the land of the Hebrews" (Gen. xl. 15 only — a natural phrase in the mouth of Joseph); the "land of the Hittites" (Josh. i. 4): a remarkable expression, occurring here only, in the Bible, though frequently used in the Egyptian records of Rameses II., in which *Cheta* or *Chita* appears to denote the whole country of Lower and Middle Syria. (Brugsch, *Geogr. Inschrift.* ii. 21, &c.) The name *Ta-ne-r* (i. e. Holy Land), which is found in the inscriptions of Rameses II. and Thothmes III., is believed by M. Brugsch to refer to Palestine (*Ibid.* 17). But this is contested by M. de Rougé (*Revue Archéologique,* Sept. 1861, p. 216). The Phoenicians appear to have applied the title Holy Land to their own country, and possibly also to Palestine at a very early date (Brugsch. p. 17). If this can be substantiated, it opens a new view to the Biblical student, inasmuch as it would seem to imply that the country had a reputation for sanctity before its connection with the Hebrews.

2. During the Monarchy the name usually, though not frequently, employed, is "Land of Israel" (אֶרֶץ יִשְׂרָאֵל; 1 Sam. xiii. 19; 2 K. v. 2, 4, vi. 23; 1 Chr. xxii. 2; 2 Chr. ii. 17). Of course this must not be confounded with the same appellation as applied to the northern kingdom only (2 Chr. xxx. 25; Ez. xxvii. 17). It is Ezekiel's favorite expression, though he commonly alters its form slightly, substituting אַדְמָה for אֶרֶץ. The pious and loyal aspirations of Hosea find vent in the expression "land of Jehovah" (Hos. ix. 3; comp. Is. lxii. 4, &c., and indeed Lev. xxv 23, &c.). In Zechariah it is "the holy land" (Zech. ii. 12); and in Daniel "the glorious land" (Dan. xi. 41). In Amos (ii. 10) alone it is "the land of the Amorite;" perhaps with a glance at Deut. i. 7. Occasionally it appears to be mentioned simply as "The Land;" as in Ruth i. 1; Jer. xxii. 27; 1 Macc. xiv. 4; Luke iv. 25, and perhaps even xxiii. 44. The later Jewish writers are fond of this title, of which several examples will be found in Reland, *Pal.* chap. v.

3. Between the Captivity and the time of our Lord, the name "Judaea" had extended itself from the southern portion to the whole of the country,[d] even that beyond Jordan (Matt. xix. 1; Mark x. 1; Joseph. *Ant.* ix. 14, § 1; xii. 4, § 11). In the book of Judith it is applied to the portion between the

---

[a] In his *Epit. Paulae* (§ 8) he extends the region of the Philistines as far north as Dor, close under Mount Carmel. We have seen above that Herodotus extends Palestine to Beirût. Caesarea was anciently entitled C. Palaestinae, to distinguish it from other towns of the same name, and it would seem to be even still called *Kaisariyet Felistin* by the Arabs (see note to Burckhardt, *Syria.* p. 337, July 15; also Schultens, *Index Geogr.* "Caesarea"). Ramleh, 10 miles east of Jaffa, retained in the time of hap-Parchi the same affix (see Asher's B. of Tudela, ii. 433). He identifies the latter with Gath.

[b] The reader will observe that the botany and natural history have been treated by Dr. Hooker and the Rev. W. Houghton. The paper of the former distinguished botanist derives a peculiar value from the fact that he has visited Palestine.

[c] For Mr. Grove's explanation of this apparently inappropriate name as applied to a land of valleys and plains like Palestine, see CANAAN, LAND OF. The generally received view, however, is that the name belonged originally to Phoenicia, which lay along the coast of the Mediterranean, where the Canaanites make their first appearance (Gen. x. 15-19), and that subsequently as they spread themselves into the interior they carried with them the old name into the new settlements. (See Kurtz, *Gesch. des Alten Bundes,* i. 104; Keil, *Bibl. Archäologie,* p. 175; Arnold, art. *Palastina* in Herzog's *Real-Encyk.* xi. 1; and others.) H.

[d] An indication of this is discovered by Reland (*Pal.* p. 82), as early as the time of Solomon, in the terms of 2 Chr. ix. 11; but there is nothing to imply that "Judah" in that passage means more than the actual territory of the tribe.

plain of Esdraelon and Samaria (xi. 19), as it is in
Luke xxiii. 5; though it is also used in the stricter
sense of Judæa proper (John iv. 3, vii. 1), that is,
the most southern of the three main divisions west
of Jordan. In this narrower sense it is employed
throughout 1 Macc. (see especially ix. 50, x. 30, 38,
xi. 34).

In the Epistle to the Hebrews (xi. 9) we find
Palestine spoken of as "the land of promise;"
and in 2 Esdr. xiv. 31, it is called "the land of
Sion."

4. The Roman division of the country hardly
coincided with the Biblical one, and it does not
appear that the Romans had any distinct name for
that which we understand by Palestine. The province of Syria, established by Pompey, of which
Scaurus was the first governor (quæstor proprætor)
in 62 B. C., seems to have embraced the whole seaboard from the Bay of Issus (*Iskunderûn*) to Egypt,
as far back as it was habitable, that is, up to the
desert which forms the background to the whole
district. "Judæa" in their phrase appears to have
signified so much of this country as intervened
between Idumæa on the south, and the territories
of the numerous free cities, on the north and west,
which were established with the establishment of
the province — such as Scythopolis, Sebaste, Joppa,
Azotus, etc. (*Dict. of Geogr.* ii. 1077). The district east of the Jordan, lying between it and the
desert — at least so much of it as was not covered
by the lands of Pella, Gadara, Canatha, Philadel-
pheia, and other free towns — was called Peræa.

5. Soon after the Christian era, we find the name
Palæstina in possession of the country. Ptolemy
(A. D. 161) thus applies it (*Geogr.* v. 16). "The
arbitrary divisions of Palæstina Prima, Secunda,
and Tertia, settled at the end of the 4th or beginning of the 5th cent. (see the quotations from the
Cod. Theodos. in Reland, p. 205), are still observed
in the documents of the Eastern Church" (*Dict.
of Geogr.* ii. 533 a). Palæstina Tertia, of which
Petra was the capital, was however out of the
Biblical limits; and the portions of Peræa not
comprised in Pal. Secunda were counted as in
Arabia.

6. Josephus usually employs the ancient name
"Canaan" in reference to the events of the earlier
history, but when speaking of the country in reference to his own time styles it Judæa (*Ant.* i. 6, §
2, &c.); though as that was the Roman name for
the southern province, it is sometimes (*e. g. B. J.*
i. 1, § 1; iii. 3, § 5 b) difficult to ascertain whether
he is using it in its wider or narrower [a] sense. In
the narrower sense he certainly does often employ
it (*e. g. Ant.* v. 1, § 22; *B. J.* iii. 3, § 4, 5 a).
Nicolaus of Damascus applies the name to the
whole country (Joseph. *Ant.* i. 7, § 2).

The Talmudists and other Jewish writers use
the title of the "Land of Israel." As the Greeks

styled all other nations but their own Barbarian,
so the Rabbis divide the whole world into two
parts — the Land of Israel, and the regions outside it.[b]

7. The name most frequently used throughout
the Middle Ages, and down to our own time, is
Terra Sancta — the Holy Land. In the long list
of Travels and Treatises given by Ritter (*Erdkunde*,
Jordan, 31–55), Robinson (*Bibl. Res.* ii. 534–555),
and Bonar (*Land of Promise*, pp. 517–535), it
predominates far beyond any other appellation.
Quaresmius, in his *Elucidatio Terræ Sanctæ* (I.
9, 10), after enumerating the various names above
mentioned, concludes by adducing seven reasons
why that which he has embodied in the title of
his own work, "though of later date than the rest,
yet in excellency and dignity surpasses them all;"
closing with the words of Pope Urban II. addressed
to the Council of Clermont: *Quam terram merito
Sanctam diximus, in qua non est etiam passus
pedis quem non illustraverit et sanctificaverit vel
corpus vel umbra Salvatoris, vel gloriosa præsentia
Sanctæ Dei genitricis, vel amplectendus Apostolorum commeatus, vel martyrum ebibendus sanguis
effusus.*

II. The Land.

The Holy Land is not in size or physical characteristics proportioned to its moral and historical
position, as the theatre of the most momentous
events in the world's history. It is but a strip of
country, about the size of Wales, less than 140
miles [c] in length, and barely 40 [d] in average breadth,
on the very frontier of the East, hemmed in between
the Mediterranean Sea on the one hand, and the
enormous trench of the Jordan Valley on the other,
by which it is effectually cut off from the mainland
of Asia behind it. On the north it is shut in by
the high ranges of Lebanon and anti-Lebanon, and
by the chasm of the *Litâny*,[e] which runs at their
feet and forms the main drain of their southern
slopes. On the south it is no less inclosed by the
arid and inhospitable deserts of the upper part of
the peninsula of Sinai, whose undulating wastes
melt imperceptibly into the southern hills of
Judæa.

1. Its position on the Map of the World — as
the world was when the Holy Land first made its
appearance in history — is a remarkable one.

(1.) It is on the very outpost — on the extremest
western edge of the East, pushed forward, as it
were, by the huge continent of Asia, which almost
seems to have rejected and cut off from communication with itself this tiny strip, by the broad and
impassable desert interposed between it and the
vast tracts of Mesopotamia and Arabia in its rear.
On the shore of the Mediterranean it stands, as if
it had advanced as far as possible toward the West
— toward that New World which in the fullness

---

[a] This very ambiguity is a sign (notwithstanding all
that Josephus says of the population and importance
of Galilee) that the southern province was by far the
most important part of the country. It conferred its
name on the whole.

[b] See the citations in Otho, *Lex. Rabb.* "Israelitæ
Regio;" and the Itineraries of Benjamin; Parchi;
Isaac ben Chelo, in Carmoly; etc.

[c] The latitude of *Banias*, the ancient Dan, is 33° 16′,
and that of Beer-sheba 31° 16′; thus the distance between these two points — the one at the north, the

other at the south — is 2 degrees, 120 geogr. or 139
English miles.

[d] The breadth of the country at Gaza, from the
shore of the Mediterranean to that of the Dead Sea, is
48 geogr. miles, while at the latitude of the *Litâny*
from the coast to the Jordan it is 20. The average
of the breadths between these two parallels, taken at
each half degree, gives 34 geogr. miles, or just 40 English miles.

[e] The latitude of the *Litâny* (or *Kasimiyeh*) differs
but slightly from that of *Banias*. Its mouth is given
by Van de Velde (*Memoir*, p. 59) at 33° 20′.

of time it was so mightily to affect; separated therefrom by that which, when the time arrived, proved to be no barrier, but the readiest medium of communication — the wide waters of the "Great Sea." Thus it was open to all the gradual influences of the rising communities of the West, while it was saved from the retrogression and decrepitude which have ultimately been the doom of all purely eastern states whose connections were limited to the East [a] only. And when at last its ruin was effected, and the nation of Israel driven from its home, it transferred without obstacle the result of its long training to those regions of the West with which by virtue of its position it was in ready communication.

(2.) There was, however, one channel, and but one, by which it could reach and be reached by the great oriental empires. The only road by which the two great rivals of the ancient world could approach one another — by which alone Egypt could get to Assyria, and Assyria to Egypt — lay along the broad flat strip of coast which formed the maritime portion of the Holy Land, and thence by the Plain of the Lebanon to the Euphrates. True, this road did not, as we shall see, lie actually through the country, but at the foot of the highlands which virtually composed the Holy Land; still the proximity was too close not to be full of danger; and though the catastrophe was postponed for many centuries, yet, when it actually arrived, it arrived through this channel.

(3.) After this the Holy Land became (like the Netherlands in Europe) the convenient arena on which in successive ages the hostile powers who contended for the empire of the East, fought their battles. Here the Seleucidae routed, or were routed by, the Ptolemies; here the Romans vanquished the Parthians, the Persians, and the Jews themselves; and here the armies of France, England, and Germany, fought the hosts of Saladin.

2. It is essentially a mountainous country. Not that it contains independent mountain chains, as in Greece, for example, dividing one region from another, with extensive valleys or plains between and among them — but that every part of the highland is in greater or less undulation. From its station in the north, the range of Lebanon pushes forth before it a multitude of hills and eminences, which crowd one another more or less thickly [b] over the face of the country to its extreme south limit. But it is not only a mountainous country. It contains in combination with its mountains a remarkable arrangement of plains, such as few other countries can show, which indeed form its chief peculiarity, and have had an equal, if not a more important bearing on its history than the mountains themselves. The mass of hills which occupies the centre of the country is bordered or framed on both sides, east and west, by a broad belt of lowland, sunk deep

below its own level. The slopes or cliffs which form, as it were, the retaining walls of this depression, are furrowed and cleft by the torrent beds which discharge the waters of the hills, and form the means of communication between the upper and lower level. On the west this lowland interposes between the mountains and the sea, and is the Plain of Philistia and of Sharon. On the east it is the broad bottom of the Jordan Valley deep down in which rushes the one river of Palestine to its grave in the Dead Sea.

3. Such is the first general impression of the physiognomy of the Holy Land. It is a physiognomy compounded of the three main features already named — the plains, the highland hills, and the torrent beds: features which are marked in the words of its earliest describers (Num. xiii. 29; Josh. xi. 16, xii. 8), and which must be comprehended by every one who wishes to understand the country, and the intimate connection existing between its structure and its history. In the accompanying sketch-map an attempt has been made to exhibit these features with greater distinctness than is usual, or perhaps possible, in maps containing more detail.

On a nearer view we shall discover some traits not observed at first, which add sensibly to the expression of this interesting countenance. About half-way up the coast the maritime plain is suddenly interrupted by a long ridge thrown out from the central mass, rising considerably [c] above the general level, and terminating in a bold promontory on the very edge of the Mediterranean. This ridge is Mount Carmel. On its upper side, the plain, as if to compensate for its temporary displacement, invades the centre of the country and forms an undulating hollow right across it from the Mediterranean to the Jordan Valley. This central lowland, which divides with its broad depression the mountains of Ephraim from the mountains of Galilee, is the plain of Esdraelon or Jezreel, the great battle-field of Palestine. North of Carmel the lowland resumes its position by the seaside till it is again interrupted and finally put an end to by the northern mountains which push their way out to the sea, ending in the white promontory of the *Ras Nakhûra*. Above this is the ancient Phoenicia — a succession of headlands sweeping down to the ocean, and leaving but few intervals of beach. Behind Phoenicia — north of Esdraelon, and inclosed between it, the *Litâny*, and the upper valley of the Jordan — is a continuation of the mountain district, not differing materially in structure or character from that to the south, but rising gradually in occasional elevation until it reaches the main ranges of Lebanon and anti-Lebanon (or Hermon), as from their lofty heights they overlook the whole land below them, of which they are indeed the parents.

---

[a] The contrast between East and West, and the position of the Holy Land as on the confines of each, is happily given in a passage in *Eōthen* (ch. 28).

[b] The district of the Surrey hills about Caterham, in its most regular portions, if denuded of most of its wood, turf, and soil, would be not unlike many parts of Palestine. So are (or were) the hills of Roxburghshire on the banks of the Tweed, as the following description of them by Washington Irving will show: "From a hill which" like Gerizim or Olivet "commanded an extensive prospect . . . I gazed about me for a time with surprise, I may almost say with disappointment. I beheld a succession of gray

waving hills, line beyond line, as far as my eye could reach, monotonous in their aspect, and entirely destitute of trees . . . . The far-famed Tweed appeared a naked stream flowing between bare hills. And yet" (what is even more applicable to the Holy Land) "such had been the magic web thrown over the whole, that it had a greater charm than the richest scenery in England."

[c] The main ridge of Carmel is between 1,700 and 1,800 feet high. The hills of Samaria immediately to the S. E. of it are only about 1,100 feet (Van de Velde, *Memoir*, 177, 178).

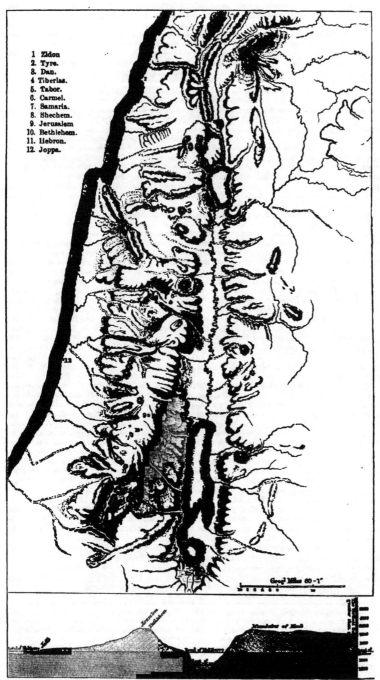

1 Zidon
2. Tyre.
8. Dan.
4 Tiberias.
5. Tabor.
6. Carmel.
7. Samaria.
8. Shechem.
9. Jerusalem
10. Bethlehem.
11. Hebron.
12. Joppa.

MAP OF PALESTINE, with section of the country from Jaffa to the mountains of Moab.

4. The country thus roughly portrayed, and which, as before stated, is less than 140 miles in length, and not more than 40 in average breadth, is to all intents and purposes the whole Land of Israel.[a] The northern portion is Galilee; the centre, Samaria; the south, Judæa. This is the Land of Canaan which was bestowed on Abraham; the covenanted home of his descendants. The two tribes and a half remained on the uplands beyond Jordan, instead of advancing to take their portion with the rest within its circumvallation of defense; but that act appears to have formed no part of the original plan. It arose out of an accidental circumstance, — the abundance of cattle which they had acquired during their stay in Egypt, or during the transit through the wilderness, — and its result was, that the tribes in question soon ceased to have any close connection with the others, or to form any virtual part of the nation. But even this definition might without impropriety be further circumscribed; for during the greater part of the O. T. times the chief events of the history were confined to the district south of Esdraelon, which contained the cities of Hebron, Jerusalem, Bethel, Shiloh, Shechem, and Samaria, the Mount of Olives, and the Mount Carmel. The battles of the Conquest and the early struggles of the era of the Judges once passed, Galilee subsided into obscurity and unimportance till the time of Christ.

5. Small as the Holy Land is on the map, and when contrasted either with modern states or with the two enormous ancient empires of Egypt and Assyria between which it lay, it seems even smaller to the traveller as he pursues his way through it. The long solid purple wall of the Moab and Gilead mountains, which is always in sight, and forms the background to almost every view to the eastward, is perpetually reminding him that the confines of the country in that direction are close at hand. There are numerous eminences in the highlands which command the view of both frontiers at the same time — the eastern mountains of Gilead with the Jordan at their feet on the one hand, on the other the Western Sea,[b] with its line of white sand and its blue expanse. Hermon, the apex of the country on the north, is said to have been seen from the southern end of the Dead Sea: it is certainly plain enough, from many a point nearer the centre. It is startling to find that from the top of the hills of Neby Samuel, Bethel, Tabor, Gerizim, or Safed, the eye can embrace at one glance, and almost without turning the head, such opposite points as the Lake of Galilee and the Bay of Akka, the farthest mountains of the Hauran and the long ridge of Carmel, the ravine of the Jabbok, or the green windings of Jordan, and the sand-hills of Jaffa.

The impression thus produced is materially assisted by the transparent clearness of the air and the exceeding brightness of the light, by which objects that in our duller atmosphere would be invisible from each other or thrown into dim distance are made distinctly visible, and thus appear to be much nearer together than they really are.

6. The highland district, thus surrounded and intersected by its broad lowland plains, preserves from north to south a remarkably even and horizontal profile. Its average height may be taken as 1,500 to 1,800 feet above the Mediterranean. It can hardly be denominated a plateau, yet so evenly is the general level preserved, and so thickly do the hills stand behind and between one another, that, when seen from the coast or the western part of the maritime plain, it has quite the appearance of a wall, standing in the background of the rich district between it and the observer — a district which from its gentle undulations, and its being so nearly on a level with the eye, appears almost immeasurable in extent. This general monotony of profile is, however, accentuated at intervals by certain centres of elevation. These occur in a line almost due north and south, but lying somewhat east of the axis of the country. Beginning from the south, they are Hebron,[c] 3,029 feet above the Mediterranean: Jerusalem, 2,610, and Mount of Olives, 2,724, with Neby Samuil on the north, 2,650; Bethel, 2,400; Sinjil, 2,685; Ebal and Gerizim, 2,700; "Little Hermon" and Tabor (on the north side of the Plain of Esdraelon), 1,900; Safed, 2,775; Jebel Jurmuk, 4,000. Between these elevated points runs the watershed[d] of the country, sending off on either hand — to the Jordan Valley on the east and the Mediterranean on the west, and be it remembered east and west[e] only — the long tortuous arms of its many torrent beds. But though keeping north and south as its general direction, the line of the watershed is, as might be expected from the prevalent equality of level of these highlands, and the absence of anything like ridge or saddle, very irregular, the heads of the valleys on the one side often passing and "overlapping" those of the other. Thus in the territory of the ancient Benjamin, the heads of the great wadies Fuwar (or Suweinit) and Mutyah (or Kelt) — the two main channels by which the torrents of the winter rains hurry down from the bald hills of this district into the valley of the Jordan — are at Bireh and Bei.in respectively, while the great Wady Belit, which enters the Mediterranean at Nahr Aujeh, a few miles above Jaffa, stretches its long arms as far as, and even farther than, Taiyibeh, nearly four miles to the east of either Bireh or Beitin. Thus also in the more northern district of Mount Ephraim

a "The whole area of the land of Palestine," says Dr. Robinson, "does not vary greatly from 12,000 geographical square miles, — about equal to the area of the two States of Massachusetts and Connecticut together. Of this whole area, more than one half, or about 7,000 square miles, being by far the most important portion, lies on the west of the Jordan. . . . . Only from that land has gone forth to other nations and to modern times all the true knowledge which exists of God, of his revelation of a future state, and of man's redemption through Jesus Christ. Compared with this distinction, the splendor and learning and fame of Egypt, Greece, and Rome fade away; and the traces of their influence upon the world become as the footprints of the traveller upon the sands of the desert." (Phys. Geogr. of the Holy Land, pp. 2, 18.)   H.

b The same word is used in Hebrew for "sea" and for "west."

c The altitudes are those given by Van de Velde, after much comparison and investigation, in his Memoir (pp. 170-188). [For the Lebanon summits, see Bibl. Sacra, xxxix. 552.]

d For the watershed see Ritter, Erdkunde, Jordan, pp. 474-488. His heights have been somewhat modified by more recent observations, for which see Van de Velde's Memoir.

e Except in the immediate neighborhood of the Plain of Esdraelon, and in the extreme north — where the drainage, instead of being to the Mediterranean

around *Nablus*, the ramifications of that extensive system of valleys which combine to form the *Wady Ferrah* — one of the main feeders of the central Jordan — interlace and cross by many miles those of the *Wady Shair*, whose principal arm is the Valley of *Nablus*, and which pours its waters into the Mediterranean at *Nahr Falaik*.

7. The valleys on the two sides of the watershed differ considerably in character. Those on the east — owing to the extraordinary depth of the Jordan Valley into which they plunge, and also to the fact already mentioned, that the watershed lies rather on that side of the highlands, thus making the fall more abrupt — are extremely steep and rugged. This is the case during the whole length of the southern and middle portions of the country. The precipitous descent between Olivet and Jericho, with which all travellers in the Holy Land are acquainted, is a type, and by no means an unfair type, of the eastern passes, from *Zuweirah* and *Ain-jidi* on the south to *Wady Bidan* on the north. It is only when the junction between the Plain of Esdraelon and the Jordan Valley is reached, that the slopes become gradual and the ground fit for the maneuvers of anything but detached bodies of foot soldiers. But, rugged and difficult as they are, they form the only access to the upper country from this side, and every man or body of men who reached the territory of Judah, Benjamin, or Ephraim from the Jordan Valley, must have climbed one or other of them.[a] The Ammonites and Moabites, who at some remote date left such lasting traces of their presence in the names of Chephar ha-Ammonai and Michmash, and the Israelites pressing forward to the relief of Gibeon and the slaughter of Beth-horon, doubtless entered alike through the great *Wady Fuwar* already spoken of. The Moabites, Edomites, and Mehunim swarmed up to their attack on Judah through the crevices of *Ain-jidi* (2 Chr. xx. 12, 16). The pass of Adummim was in the days of our Lord — what it still is — the regular route between Jericho and Jerusalem. By it Pompey advanced with his army when he took the city.

8. The western valleys are more gradual in their slope. The level of the external plain on this side is higher, and therefore the fall less, while at the same time the distance to be traversed is much greater. Thus the length of the *Wady Beldt* already mentioned, from its remotest head at *Taiyibeh* to the point at which it emerges on the Plain of Sharon, may be taken as 20 to 25 miles, with a total difference of level during that distance of perhaps 1,800 feet, while the *Wady el-Aujeh*, which falls from the other side of *Taiyibeh* into the Jordan, has a distance of barely 10 miles to reach the Jordan Valley, at the same time falling not less than 2,800 feet.

Here again the valleys are the only means of

communication between the lowland and the highland. From Jaffa and the central part of the plain there are two of these roads "going up to Jerusalem" : the one to the right by *Ramleh* and the *Wady Aly*; the other to the left by Lydda, and thence by the Beth-horons, or the *Wady Suleiman*, and Gibeon. The former of these is modern, but the latter is the scene of many a famous incident in the ancient history. Over its long acclivities the Canaanites were driven by Joshua to their native plains; the Philistines ascended to Michmash and Geba, and fled back past Ajalon; the Syrian force was stopped and hurled back by Judas; the Roman legions of Cestius Gallus were chased pell-mell to their strongholds at Antipatris.

9. Further south, the communications between the mountains of Judah and the lowland of Philistia are hitherto comparatively unexplored. They were doubtless the scene of many a foray and repulse during the lifetime of Samson and the struggles of the Danites, but there is no record of their having been used for the passage of any important force either in ancient or modern times.[b] North of Jaffa the passes are few. One of them, by the *Wady Beldt*, led from Antipatris to Gophna. By this route St. Paul was probably conveyed away from Jerusalem. [OPHNI, Amer. ed.] Another leads from the ancient sanctuary of Gilgal near *Kefr Saba*, to *Nablus*. These western valleys, though easier than those on the eastern side, are of such a nature as to present great difficulties to the passage of any large force encumbered by baggage. In fact these mountain passes really formed the security of Israel, and if she had been wise enough to settle her own intestinal quarrels without reference to foreigners, the nation might, humanly speaking, have stood to the present hour. The height, and consequent strength, which was the frequent boast of the prophets and psalmists in regard to Jerusalem, was no less true of the whole country, rising as it does on all sides from plains so much below it in level. The armies of Egypt and Assyria, as they traced and retraced their path between Pelusium and Carchemish, must have looked at the long wall of heights which closed in the broad level roadway they were pursuing, as belonging to a country with which they had no concern. It was to them a natural mountain fastness, the approach to which was beset with difficulties, while its bare and soilless hills were hardly worth the trouble of conquering, in comparison with the rich green plains of the Euphrates and the Nile, or even with the boundless cornfield through which they were marching. This may be fairly inferred from various notices in Scripture and in contemporary history. The Egyptian kings, from Rameses II. and Thothmes III. to Pharaoh Necho, were in the constant habit [c] of pursuing this route during their expeditions against the Chatti, or Hittites, in

or to the Jordan, is to the *Litâny*, — the statement in the text is strictly accurate.

a Nothing can afford so strong a testimony to the really unmilitary genius of the Canaanites, and subsequently, in their turn, of the Jews also, as the way in which they suffered their conquerors again and again to advance through these defiles, where their destruction might so easily have been effected. They always retired at once, and, shutting themselves up in their strongholds, awaited the attack there. From Jericho, Hebron, Jerusalem, to Silistria, the story is one and the same, — the dislike of Orientals to fight in the

open field, and their power of determined resistance when intrenched behind fortifications.

b Richard I., when intending to attack Jerusalem, moved from Ascalon to Blanche Garde (*Sajir*, or *Tell es-Safieh*), on the edge of the mountains of Judæa; and then, instead of taking a direct route to the Holy City through the passes of the mountains, turned northwards over the plain and took the road from Ramleh to Bettenuble (*Nuba*), that is, the ordinary approach from Jaffa to Jerusalem; a circuit of at least four days. (See Vinisauf, v. 48, in *Chron. of Crusades*, p. 294.)

c Rawlinson, note to Herod. ii. § 157.

the north of Syria; and the two last-named monarchs [a] fought battles at Megiddo, without, as far as [b] we know, having taken the trouble to penetrate into the interior of the country. The Pharaoh who was Solomon's contemporary came up the Philistine plain as far as Gezer (probably about *Ramleh*), and besieged and destroyed it, without leaving any impression of uneasiness in the annals of Israel. Later in the monarchy, Psammetichus besieged Ashdod in the Philistine plain for the extraordinary period of twenty-nine years (Herod. ii. 157); during a portion of that time an Assyrian army probably occupied part of the same [c] district, endeavoring to relieve the town. The battles must have been frequent; and yet the only reference to these events in the Bible is the mention of the Assyrian general by Isaiah (xx. 1), in so casual a manner as to lead irresistibly to the conclusion that neither Egyptians nor Assyrians had come up into the highland. This is illustrated by Napoleon's campaign in Palestine. He entered it from Egypt by *el-Arish*, and after overrunning the whole of the lowland, and taking Gaza, Jaffa, Ramleh, and the other places on the plain, he writes to the sheikhs of *Nablus* and Jerusalem, announcing that he has no intention of making war against them (*Corresp. de Nap.*, No. 4,020, " 19 Ventose, 1799 "). To use his own words, the highland country " did not lie within his base of operations; " and it would have been a waste of time, or worse, to ascend thither.

In the later days of the Jewish nation, and during the Crusades, Jerusalem became the great object of contest; and then the battle-field of the country, which had originally been Esdraelon, was transferred to the maritime plain at the foot of the passes communicating most directly with the capital. Here Judas Maccabæus achieved some of his greatest triumphs; and here some of Herod's most decisive actions were fought; and Blanchegarde, Ascalon, Jaffa, and Beitnuba (the Bettenuble of the Crusading historian), still shine with the brightest rays of the valor of Richard the First.

10. When the highlands of the country are more closely examined, a considerable difference will be found to exist in the natural condition and appearance of their different portions. The south, as being nearer the arid desert, and farther removed from the drainage of the mountains, is drier and less productive than the north. The tract below Hebron, which forms the link between the hills of Judah and the desert, was known to the ancient Hebrews by a term originally derived from its dryness (*Negeb*). This was THE SOUTH country. It contained the territory which Caleb bestowed on his daughter, and which he had afterwards to endow specially with the " upper and lower springs " of a less parched locality (Josh. xv. 19). Here

lived Nabal, so chary of his " water " (1 Sam. xxv. 11); and here may well have been the scene of the composition of the 63d Psalm [d] — the " dry and thirsty land where no water is." As the traveller advances north of this tract there is an improvement; but perhaps no country equally cultivated is more monotonous, bare, or uninviting in its aspect, than a great part of the highlands of Judah and Benjamin during the largest portion of the year. The spring covers even those bald gray rocks with verdure and color, and fills the ravines with torrents of rushing water; but in summer and autumn the look of the country from Hebron up to Bethel is very dreary and desolate. The flowers, which for a few weeks give so brilliant [e] and varied a hue to whole districts, wither and vanish before the first fierce rays of the sun of summer: they are " to-day in the field — to-morrow cast into the oven." Rounded [f] hills of moderate height fill up the view on every side, their coarse gray [g] stone continually discovering itself through the thin coating of soil, and hardly distinguishable from the remains of the ancient terraces which run round them with the regularity of contour lines, or from the confused heaps of ruin which occupy the site of former village or fortress. On some of the hills the terraces have been repaired or reconstructed, and these contain plantations of olives or figs, sometimes with and sometimes without vineyards, surrounded by rough stone walls, and with the watch-towers at the corners, so familiar to us from the parables of the Old and New Testaments. Others have a shaggy covering of oak bushes in clumps. There are traditions that in former times the road between Bethlehem and Hebron was lined with large trees; but all that now remains of them are the large oak-roots which are embedded in the rocky soil, and are dug up by the peasants for fuel (Miss Beaufort, ii. 124). The valleys of denudation which divide these monotonous hills are also planted with figs or olives, but oftener cultivated with corn or *dourra*, the long reed-like stalks of which remain on the stony ground till the next seed-time, and give a singularly dry and slovenly look to the fields. The general absence of fences in the valleys does not render them less desolate to an English eye, and where a fence is now and then encountered, it is either a stone wall trodden down and dilapidated, or a hedge of the prickly-pear cactus, gaunt, irregular, and ugly, without being picturesque. Often the track rises and falls for miles together over the edges of the white strata upturned into almost a vertical [h] position; or over sheets of bare rock spread out like flag-stones, [i] and marked with fissures which have all the regularity of artificial joints; or along narrow channels, through which the feet

---

[a] For Thothmes' engagement at Megiddo, see De Rougé's interpretation of his monuments recently discovered at Thebes, in the *Revue Archéologique*, 1861, p. 364, &c. For Pharaoh Necho, see 2 K. xxiii. 29.

[b] The identification of Megiddo, coinciding as it does with the statements of the Bible, is tolerably certain; but at present as much can hardly be said of the other names in these lists. Not only does the agreement of the names appear doubtful, but the lists, as now deciphered, present an amount of confusion — places in the north being jumbled up with those in the south, etc. — which raises a constant suspicion.

[c] Is. xx. 1, as explained by Gesenius, and by Rawlinson (ii. 242, *note*).

[d] This Psalm is also referred to the hot and water-

less road of the deep descent to Jericho and the Jordan. See OLIVES, MOUNT OF, p. 2243 a.

[e] Stanley (*S. & P.* p. 159) — not prone to exaggerate color (comp. 87, " Petra ") — speaks of it as " a blaze of scarlet."

[f] " Rounded swelling masses like huge bubbles," says Mr. Seldon the painter (p. 122). " Each one uglier than his neighbor " (Miss Beaufort, ii. 37). See also the description of Russegger the geologist, in Ritter, *Jordan*, p. 495.

[g] " Often looking as if burnt in the kiln " (Anderson, p. 173).

[h] As at *Beit-ur* (Beth-horon).

[i] As south of *Beitin* (Bethel), and many other places.

of centuries of travellers have with difficulty retained their hold on the steep declivities; or down flights of irregular steps hewn or worn in the solid rock of the ravine, and strewed thick with innumerable loose [a] stones. Even the gray villages — always on the top or near the top of the hills — do but add to the dreariness of the scene by the forlorn look which their flat roofs and absence of windows present to a European eye, and by the poverty and ruin so universal among them. At Jerusalem this reaches its climax, and in the leaden ashy hue which overspreads, for the major part of the year, much of the landscape immediately contiguous to the city, and which may well be owing to the débris [b] of its successive demolitions, there is something unspeakably affecting. The solitude which reigns throughout most of these hills and valleys is also very striking. "For miles and miles there is often no appearance of life except the occasional goat-herd on the hill-side, or gathering of women at the wells." [c]

To the west and northwest of the highlands, where the sea-breezes are felt, there is considerably more vegetation. The *Wady es-Sumt* derives its name from the acacias which line its sides. In the same neighborhood olives abound, and give the country "almost a wooded appearance" (Rob. ii. 21, 22). The dark grateful foliage of the *butm*, or terebinth, is frequent; and one of these trees, perhaps the largest in Palestine, stands a few minutes' ride from the ancient Socho (*ibid.* 222). About ten miles north of this, near the site of the ancient Kirjath-jearim, the "city of forests," are some thickets of pine (*snôber*) and laurel (*kebkûb*), which Tobler compares with European woods (*3te Wanderung*, p. 178).

11. Hitherto we have spoken of the central and northern portions of Judæa. Its eastern portion — a tract some 9 or 10 miles in width by about 35 in length — which intervenes between the centre and the abrupt descent to the Dead Sea, is far more wild and desolate, and that not for a portion of the year only, but throughout it.[d] This must have been always what it is now — an uninhabited desert, because uninhabitable; "a bare arid wilderness; an endless succession of shapeless yellow and ash-colored hills, without grass or shrubs, without water, and almost [e] without life," — even without ruins, with the rare exceptions of Masada, and a solitary watch-tower or two.

12. No descriptive sketch of this part of the country can be complete which does not allude to the caverns, characteristic of all limestone districts, but here existing in astonishing numbers. Every hill and ravine is pierced with them, some very large and of curious formation — perhaps partly natural, partly artificial — others mere grottoes. Many of them are connected with most important and interesting events of the ancient history of the

country. Especially is this true of the district now under consideration. Machpelah, Makkedah, Adullam, En-gedi, names inseparably connected with the lives, adventures, and deaths of Abraham, Joshua, David, and other Old Testament worthies, are all within the small circle of the territory of Judæa. Moreover, there is perhaps hardly one of these caverns, however small, which has not at some time or other furnished a hiding-place to some ancient Hebrew from the sweeping incursions of Philistine or Amalekite. For the bearing which the present treatment of many of the caverns has on the modern religious aspect of Palestine, and for the remarkable symbol which they furnish of the life of Israel, the reader must be referred to a striking passage in *Sinai and Palestine* (ch. ii. x. 3). [CAVE.]

13. The bareness and dryness which prevails more or less in Judæa is owing partly to the absence of wood (see below), partly to its proximity to the desert, and partly to a scarcity of water, arising from its distance from the Lebanon. The abundant springs which form so delightful a feature of the country further north, and many of which continue to flow even after the hottest summers, are here very rarely met with after the rainy season is over, and their place is but poorly supplied by the wells, themselves but few in number, bored down into the white rock of the universal substratum, and with mouths so narrow and so carefully closed that they may be easily passed without notice by travellers unaccustomed to the country.[f] [WELLS.]

14. But to this discouraging aspect there are happily some important exceptions. The valley of *Urtâs*, south of Bethlehem, contains springs which in abundance and excellence rival even those of *Nablus*; the huge "Pools of Solomon" are enough to supply a district for many miles round them; and the cultivation now going on in that neighborhood shows what might be done with a soil which requires only irrigation and a moderate amount of labor to evoke a boundless produce. At Bethlehem and *Mar Elyâs*, too, and in the neighborhood of the Convent of the Cross, and especially near Hebron, there are excellent examples of what can be done with vineyards, and plantations of olives and fig-trees. And it must not be forgotten that during the limited time when the plains and bottoms are covered with waving crops of green or golden corn, and when the naked rocks are shrouded in that brilliant covering of flowers to which allusion has already been made, the appearance of things must be far more inviting than it is during that greater portion of the year which elapses after the harvest, and which, as being the more habitual aspect of the scene, has been dwelt upon above.

15. It is obvious that in the ancient days of the nation, when Judah and Benjamin possessed the

---

[a] As in the *Wady Aly*, 7 miles west of Jerusalem. See Beaumont's description of this route in his *Diary of a Journey*, etc. i. 192.

[b] See JERUSALEM, vol. ii. p. 1280 b. The same remark will be found in Seddon's *Memoir*, p. 198.

[c] Stanley, *S. & P.* p. 117.

[d] Even on the 8th January, De Saulcy found no water.

[e] Van de Velde, *Syr. & Pal.* ii. 99; and see the same still more forcibly stated on p. 101; and a graphic description by Miss Beaufort, ii. 102, 103, 127, 128. The character of the upper part of the district, to the S. E. of the Mount of Olives, is well seized by

Mr. Seddon: "A wilderness of mountain-tops, in some places tossed up like waves of mud, in others wrinkled over with ravines, like models made of crumpled brown paper, the nearer ones whitish, strewed with rocks and bushes" (*Memoir*, p. 204).

[f] There is no adequate provision here or elsewhere in Palestine (except perhaps in Jerusalem) for catching and preserving the water which falls in the heavy rains of winter and spring — a provision easily made, and found to answer admirably in countries similarly circumstanced, such as Malta and Bermuda, where the rains furnish almost the whole water supply.

beeming population indicated in the Bible, the condition and aspect of the country must have been very different. Of this there are not wanting sure evidences. There is no country in which the ruined towns bear so large a proportion to those still existing. Hardly a hill-top of the many within sight, that is not covered with vestiges of some fortress or city.[a] That this numerous population knew how most effectually to cultivate their rocky territory, is shown by the remains of their ancient terraces, which constantly meet the eye, the only mode of husbanding so scanty a coating of soil, and preventing its being washed by the torrents into the valleys. These frequent remains enable the traveller to form an idea of the look of the landscape when they were kept up. But, besides this, forests appear to have stood in many parts of Judæa[b] until the repeated invasions and sieges caused their fall, and the wretched government of the Turks prevented their reinstatement; and all this vegetation must have reacted on the moisture of the climate, and, by preserving the water in many a ravine and natural reservoir, where now it is rapidly dried by the fierce sun of the early summer, must have influenced materially the look and the resources of the country.

16. Advancing northward from Judæa the country becomes gradually more open and pleasant. Plains of good soil occur between the hills, at first small,[c] but afterwards comparatively large. In some cases (such as the Mukhna, which stretches away from the feet of Gerizim for several miles to the south and east) these would be remarkable anywhere. The hills assume here a more varied aspect than in the southern districts, springs are more abundant and more permanent, until at last, when the district of the Jebel Nablús is reached — the ancient Mount Ephraim, — the traveller encounters an atmosphere and an amount of vegetation and water which, if not so transcendently lovely as the representations of enthusiastic travellers would make it, is yet greatly superior to anything he has met with in Judæa, and even sufficient to recall much of the scenery of the West.

17. Perhaps the Springs are the only objects which in themselves, and apart from their associations, really strike an English traveller with astonishment and admiration. Such glorious fountains as those of Ain-Jalúd or the Ras el-Mukátta, where a great body of the clearest water wells silently but swiftly out from deep blue recesses worn in the foot of a low cliff of limestone rock, and at once forms a considerable stream — or as that of Tell el-Kady, eddying forth from the base of a lovely, wooded mound into a wide, deep, and limpid pool — or those of Banias and Fijeh, where a large river leaps headlong, foaming and roaring, from its cave — or even as that of Jenín, bubbling upwards from the level ground — are very rarely to be met with out of irregular, rocky, mountainous countries, and being such unusual sights can hardly be looked on by the traveller without surprise and emotion. But, added to this their natural impressiveness, there is the consideration of the prominent part which so many of these springs have played in the history. Even the caverns are not more charac-

teristic of Palestine, or oftener mentioned in the accounts both of the great national crises and of more ordinary transactions. It is sufficient here to name En-hakkore, En-gedi, Gihon, and, in this particular district, the spring of Harod, the fountain of Jezreel, En-dor, and En-gannim, reserving a fuller treatment of the subject for the special head of SPRINGS. [See also FOUNTAINS.]

18. The valleys which lead down from the upper level in this district to the valley of the Jordan, and the mountains through which they descend, are also a great improvement on those which form the eastern portion of Judah, and even of Benjamin. The valleys are (as already remarked) less precipitous, because the level from which they start in their descent is lower, while that of the Jordan Valley is higher; and they have lost that savage character which distinguishes the naked clefts of the wadies Suweinit and Kelt, of the Ain-jidi or Zuweirah, and have become wider and shallower, swelling out here and there into basins, and containing much land under cultivation more or less regular. Fine streams run through many of these valleys, in which a considerable body of water is found even after the hottest and longest summers, their banks hidden by a thick shrubbery of oleanders and other flowering trees, — truly a delicious sight, and one most rarely seen to the south of Jerusalem, or within many miles to the north of it. The mountains, though bare of wood and but partially cultivated, have none of that arid, worn look which renders those east of Hebron, and even those between Mukhmas and Jericho, so repulsive. In fact, the eastern district of the Jebel Nablús contains some of the most fertile and valuable spots in Palestine.[d]

19. Hardly less rich is the extensive region which lies northwest of the city of Nablus, between it and Carmel, in which the mountains gradually break down into the Plain of Sharon. This has been very imperfectly explored, but it is spoken of as extremely fertile — huge fields of corn, with occasional tracts of wood, recalling the county of Kent[e] — but mostly a continued expanse of sloping downs.

20. But with all its richness, and all its advance on the southern part of the country, there is a strange dearth of natural wood about this central district. Olive-trees are indeed to be found everywhere, but they are artificially cultivated for their fruit, and the olive is not a tree which adds to the look of a landscape. A few carobs are also met with in such richer spots as the Valley of Nablus. But of all natural non-fruit-bearing trees there is a singular dearth. It is this which makes the wooded sides of Carmel and the park-like scenery of the adjacent slopes and plains so remarkable. True, when compared with European timber, the trees are but small, but their abundance is in strong contrast with the absolute dearth of wood in the neighboring mountains. Carmel is always mentioned by the ancient prophets and poets as remarkable for its luxuriance; and, as there is no reason to believe that it has changed its character, we have, in the expressions referred to, pretty conclusive evidence that the look of the adjoining dis-

[a] Stanley, S. & P. p. 117, where the lessons to be gathered from these ruins of so many successive nations and races are admirably drawn out.

[b] For a list of these, see FOREST.

[c] That at the northern foot of Neby Samwil, out of which rise the gentle hills which bear the ruins of Gibeon, Neballat, etc., is perhaps the first of these in the advance from south to north.

[d] Robinson, Bibl. Res. iii. 304.

[e] Lord Lindsay (Bohn's ed.), p. 256.

trict of Ephraim was not very different then from what it is now.

21. No sooner, however, is the Plain of Esdraelon passed, than a considerable improvement is perceptible. The low hills which spread down from the mountains of Galilee, and form the barrier between the plains of Akka and Esdraelon, are covered with timber, of moderate size, it is true, but of thick, vigorous growth, and pleasant to the eye. Eastward of these hills rises the round mass of Tabor, dark with its copses of oak, and set off by contrast with the bare slopes of *Jebel ed-Duhy* (the so called " Little Hermon ") and the white hills of Nazareth. North of Tabor and Nazareth is the plain of *el-Buttauf*, an upland tract hitherto very imperfectly described, but apparently of a similar nature to Esdraelon, though much more elevated. It runs from east to west, in which direction it is perhaps ten miles long, by two miles wide at its broadest part. It is described as extremely fertile, and abounding in vegetation. Beyond this the amount of natural growth increases at every step, until towards the north the country becomes what even in the West would be considered as well timbered. The centre part — the watershed between the upper end of the Jordan Valley on the one hand, and the Mediterranean on the other, is a succession of swelling hills, covered with oak and terebinth, its occasional ravines thickly clothed in addition with maple, arbutus, sumach, and other trees. So abundant is the timber that large quantities of it are regularly carried to the sea-coast at Tyre, and there shipped as fuel to the towns on the coast (Rob. ii. 450). The general level of the country is not quite equal to that of Judæa and Samaria, but on the other hand there are points which reach a greater elevation than anything in the south, such as the prominent group of *Jebel Jurmuk*, and perhaps *Tibnin* — and which have all the greater effect from the surrounding country being lower. *Tibnin* lies about the centre of the district, and as far north as this the valleys run east and west of the watershed, but above it they run northwards into the *Liâny*, which cleaves the country from east to west, and forms the northern border of the district, and indeed of the Holy Land itself.

22. The notices of this romantic district in the Bible are but scanty; in fact, till the date of the New Testament, when it had acquired the name of Galilee, it may be said, for all purposes of history, to be hardly mentioned. And even in the New Testament times the interest is confined to a very small portion — the south and southwest corner, containing Nazareth, Cana, and Nain, on the confines of Esdraelon, Capernaum, Tiberias, and Gennesaret, on the margin of the Lake.[a] In the great Roman conquest, or rather destruction, of Galilee, which preceded the fall of Jerusalem, the contest penetrated but a short distance into the interior. Jotapata and Giscala — neither of them more than 12 miles from the Lake — are the farthest points to which we know of the struggle extending in that wooded and impenetrable district. One of the earliest accounts we possess describes it as a land "quiet and secure" (Judg.

xviii. 27). There is no thoroughfare through it, nor any inducement to make one. May there not be, retired in the recesses of these woody hills and intricate valleys, many a village whose inhabitants have lived on from age to age, undisturbed by the invasions and depopulations with which Israelites, Assyrians, Romans, and Moslems have successively visited the more open and accessible parts of the country?

23. From the present appearance of this district we may, with some allowances, perhaps gain an idea of what the more southern portions of the central highlands were during the earlier periods in the history. There is little material difference in the natural conditions of the two regions. Galilee is slightly nearer the springs and the cool breezes of the snow-covered Lebanon, and further distant from the hot siroccos of the southern deserts, and the volcanic nature of a portion of its soil is more favorable to vegetation than the chalk of Judæa; but these circumstances, though they would tell to a certain degree, would not produce any very marked differences in the appearance of the country provided other conditions were alike. It therefore seems fair to believe that the hills of Shechem, Bethel, and Hebron, when Abram first wandered over them, were not very inferior to those of the *Belad Besharah* or the *Belad el-Buttauf*. The timber was probably smaller, but the oak-groves[b] of Moreh, Mamre, Tabor,[c] must have consisted of large trees; and the narrative implies that the "forests" or "woods" of Hareth, Ziph, and Bethel were more than mere scrub.

24. The causes of the present bareness of the face of the country are two, which indeed can hardly be separated. The first is the destruction of the timber in that long series of sieges and invasions which began with the invasion of Shishak (B. C. circa 970) and has not yet come to an end. This, by depriving the soil and the streams of shelter from the burning sun, at once made, as it invariably does, the climate more arid than before, and doubtless diminished the rainfall. The second is the decay of the terraces necessary to retain the soil on the steep slopes of the round hills. This decay is owing to the general unsettlement and insecurity which have been the lot of this poor little country almost ever since the Babylonian conquest. The terraces once gone, there was nothing to prevent the soil which they supported being washed away by the heavy rains of winter; and it is hopeless to look for a renewal of the wood, or for any real improvement in the general face of the country, until they have been first reëstablished. This cannot happen to any extent until a just and firm government shall give confidence to the inhabitants.

25. Few things are a more constant source of surprise to the stranger in the Holy Land than the manner in which the hill-tops are, throughout, selected for habitation. A town in a valley is a rare exception. On the other hand, scarce a single eminence of the multitude always in sight but is crowned with its city or village,[d] inhabited or in ruins, often so placed as if not accessibility but in-

---

[a] The associations of Mt. Tabor, dim as they are, belong to the Old Testament: for there can be very little doubt that it was no more the scene of the Transfiguration than the Mount of Olives was. [Hxxnox, Amer. ed. Tabor.

[b] In the Authorised Version rendered inaccurately "plain."

[c] Tabor (1 Sam. x. 3) has no connection with the mount of the same name.

[d] The same thing may be observed, though not with the same exclusive regularity, in Provence, a

accessibility had been the object of its builders.* And indeed such was their object. These groups of naked, forlorn structures, piled irregularly one over the other on the curve of the hill-top, their rectangular outline, flat roofs, and blank walls, suggestive to the western mind rather of fastness than of peaceful habitation, surrounded by filthy heaps of the rubbish of centuries, approached only by the narrow, winding path, worn white, on the gray or brown breast of the hill — are the lineal descendants, if indeed they do not sometimes contain the actual remains, of the "fenced cities, great and walled up to heaven," which are so frequently mentioned in the records of the Israelite conquest. They bear witness now, no less surely than they did even in that early age, and as they have done through all the ravages and conquests of thirty centuries, to the insecurity of the country — to the continual risk of sudden plunder and destruction incurred by those rash enough to take up their dwelling in the plain. Another and hardly less valid reason for the practice is furnished in the terms of our Lord's well-known apologue, — namely, the treacherous nature of the loose alluvial "sand" of the plain under the sudden rush of the winter torrents from the neighboring hills, as compared with the safety and firm foundation attainable by building on the naked "rock" of the hills themselves (Matt. vii. 24-27).

26. These hill-towns were not what gave the Israelites their main difficulty in the occupation of the country. Wherever strength of arm and fleetness of foot availed, there those hardy warriors, fierce as lions, sudden and swift as eagles, surefooted and fleet as the wild deer on the hills (1 Chr. xii. 8; 2 Sam. i. 23, ii. 18), easily conquered. It was in the plains, where the horses and chariots of the Canaanites and Philistines had space to manoeuvre, that they failed in dislodging the aborigines. "Judah drave out the inhabitants of the mountain, but could not drive out the inhabitants of the valley, because they had chariots of iron . . . . neither could Manasseh drive out the inhabitants of Beth-shean . . . . nor Megiddo," in the plain of Esdraelon . . . . "nor could Ephraim drive out the Canaanites that dwelt in Gezer," on the maritime plain near Ramleh . . . . "nor could Asher drive out the inhabitants of Accho . . . . and the Amorites forced the children of Dan into the mountain, for they would not suffer them to come down into the valley" (Judg. i. 19-35). Thus in this case the ordinary conditions of conquest were reversed — the conquerors took the hills, the conquered kept the plains. To a people so exclusive as the Jews there must have been a constant satisfaction in the elevation and inaccessibility of their highland regions. This is evident in every page of their literature, which is tinged throughout with a highland coloring. The "mountains" were to "bring peace," the "little hills, justice to the people:" when plenty came, the corn was to flourish on the "top of the moun-

tains" (Ps. lxxii. 3, 16). In like manner the mountains were to be joyful before Jehovah when He came to judge his people (xcviii. 8). What gave its keenest sting to the Babylonian conquest, was the consideration that the "mountains of Israel," the "ancient high places," were become a "prey and a derision;" while, on the other hand, one of the most joyful circumstances of the restoration is, that the mountains "shall yield their fruit as before, and be settled after their old estates" (Ez. xxxvi. 1, 8, 11). But it is needless to multiply instances of this, which pervades the writings of the psalmists and prophets in a truly remarkable manner, and must be familiar to every student of the Bible. (See the citations in S. & P. ch. ii. viii.) Nor was it unacknowledged by the surrounding heathen. We have their own testimony that in their estimation Jehovah was the "God of the mountains" (1 K. xx. 28), and they showed their appreciation of the fact by fighting (as already noticed), when possible, in the lowlands. The contrast is strongly brought out in the repeated expression of the psalmists. "Some," like the Canaanites and Philistines of the lowlands, "put their trust in chariots and some in horses; but we" — we mountaineers, from our "sanctuary" on the heights of "Zion" — "will remember the name of Jehovah our God," "the God of Jacob our father," the shepherd-warrior, whose only weapons were sword and bow — the God who is now a high fortress for us — "at whose command both chariot and horse are fallen," "who burneth the chariots in the fire" (Ps. xx. 1, 7, xlvi. 7-11, lxxvi. 2, 6).

27. But the hills were occupied by other edifices besides the "fenced cities." The tiny white domes which stand perched here and there on the summits of the eminences, and mark the holy ground in which some Mohammedan saint is resting — sometimes standing alone, sometimes near the village in either case surrounded with a rude inclosure, and overshadowed with the grateful shade and pleasant color of terebinth or carob — these are the successors of the "high places" or sanctuaries so constantly denounced by the prophets, and which were set up "on every high hill and under every green tree" (Jer. ii. 20; Ez. vi. 13).

28. From the mountainous structure of the Holy Land and the extraordinary variations in the level of its different districts, arises a further peculiarity most interesting and most characteristic — namely, the extensive views of the country which can be obtained from various commanding points. The number of panoramas which present themselves to the traveller in Palestine is truly remarkable. To speak of the west of Jordan only, for east of it all is at present more or less unknown — the prospects from the height of Beni naim,[b] near Hebron, from the Mount of Olives, from Neby Samwil, from Bethel, from Gerizim or Ebal, from Jenin, Carmel, Tabor, Safed, the Castle of Banias, the Kubbet en-Nasr above Damascus — are known to many travellers. Their peculiar charm resides in

---

country which, in its natural and artificial features, presents many a likeness to Palestine.

* Hence the Saviour's illustration from "a city set on a hill" (Matt. v. 14) was perfectly natural, without its being suggested by any particular place in sight at the time. Stanley writes incorrectly "the city" (S. & P. p. 121, Amer. ed.), and thinks that Safed was meant, so conspicuous from the traditional Mount of the Beatitudes (Kurûn Hattîn). The Greek has no article.   H.

a Two such may be named as types of the rest, — Kuriyet Jitt (perhaps an ancient Gath or Gitta), perched on one of the western spurs of the Jebel Nablus, and described high up beside the road from Jaffa to Nablus; and Wezr or Mzr, on the absolute top of the lofty peaked hill, at the foot of which the spring of Jalûd wells forth.

b Robinson, Bibl. Res. i. 490.

their wide extent, the number of spots historically remarkable which are visible at once, the limpid clearness of the air, which brings the most distant objects comparatively close, and the consideration that in many cases the feet must be standing on the same ground, and the eyes resting on the same spots which have been stood upon and gazed at by the most famous patriarchs, prophets, and heroes, of all the successive ages in the eventful history of the country. We can stand where Abraham and Lot stood looking down from Bethel into the Jordan Valley, when Lot chose to go to Sodom and the great destiny of the Hebrew people was fixed forever;[a] or with Abraham on the height near Hebron gazing over the gulf towards Sodom at the vast column of smoke as it towered aloft tinged with the rising sun, and wondering whether his kinsman had escaped; or with Gaal the son of Ebed on Gerizim when he watched the armed men steal along like the shadow of the mountains on the plain of the Nukhna; or with Deborah and Barak on Mount Tabor when they saw the hosts of the Canaanites marshalling to their doom on the undulations of Esdraelon; or with Elisha on Carmel looking across the same wide space towards Shunem, and recognizing the bereaved mother as she urged her course over the flat before him; or, in later times, with Mohammed on the heights above Damascus, when he put by an earthly for a heavenly paradise; or with Richard Cœur de Lion on *Neby Samwil* when he refused to look at the towers of the Holy City, in the deliverance of which he could take no part. These we can see; but the most famous and the most extensive of all we cannot see. The view of Balaam from Pisgah, and the view of Moses from the same spot, we cannot realize, because the locality of Pisgah is not yet accessible. [Yet see Addition to NEBO, Amer. ed.]

These views are a feature in which Palestine is perhaps approached by no other country, certainly by no country whose history is at all equal in importance to the world. Great as is their charm when viewed as mere landscapes, their deep and abiding interest lies in their intimate connection with the history and the remarkable manner in which they corroborate its statements. By its constant reference to localities — mountain, rock, plain, river, tree — the Bible seems to invite examination; and, indeed, it is only by such examination that we can appreciate its minute accuracy and realize how far its plain matter-of-fact statements of actual occurrences, to actual persons, in actual places — how far these raise its records above the unreal and unconnected rhapsodies, and the vain repetitions, of the sacred books of other religions.[b]

29. A few words must be said in general description of the maritime lowland, which it will be remembered intervenes between the sea and the highlands, and of which detailed accounts will be found under the heads of its great divisions.

This region, only slightly elevated above the level of the Mediterranean, extends without interruption from *el-Arish*, south of Gaza, to Mount Carmel. It naturally divides itself into two portions, each of about half its length: the lower one the wider; the upper one the narrower. The lower half is the Plain of the Philistines — Philistia, or, as the Hebrews called it, the *Shefelah* or lowland. [SEPHELA.] The upper half is the Sharon or Saron of the Old and New Testaments, the "Forest country" of Josephus and the LXX. (Joseph. *Ant.* xiv. 13, § 3; LXX. Is. lxv. 10). [SHARON.] Viewed from the sea this maritime region appears as a long, low coast of white or cream-colored sand, its slight undulations rising occasionally into mounds or cliffs, which in one or two places, such as *Jaffa* and *Um-khalid*, almost aspire to the dignity of headlands. Over these white undulations, in the farthest background, stretches the faint blue level line of the highlands of Judæa and Samaria.

30. Such is its appearance from without. But from within, when traversed, or overlooked from some point on those blue hills, such as *Beit-ur* or *Beit-nettif*, the prospect is very different.

The Philistine Plain is on an average fifteen or sixteen miles in width from the coast to the first beginning of the belt of hills, which forms the gradual approach to the highland of the mountains of Judah. This district of inferior hills contains many places which have been identified with those named in the lists of the Conquest as being in the plain, and it was therefore probably attached originally to the plain, and not to the highland. It is described by modern travellers as a beautiful open country, consisting of low calcareous hills rising from the alluvial soil of broad arable valleys, covered with inhabited villages and deserted ruins, and clothed with much natural shrubbery and with large plantations of olives in a high state of cultivation; the whole gradually broadening down into the wide expanse of the plain[c] itself. The plain is in many parts almost a dead level, in others gently undulating in long waves; here and there low mounds or hillocks, each crowned with its village, and more rarely still a hill overtopping the rest, like *Tell es-Safieh* or *Ajlûn*, the seat of some fortress of Jewish or Crusading times. The larger towns, as Gaza and Ashdod, which stand near the shore, are surrounded with huge groves of olive, sycamore, and palm, as in the days of King David (1 Chr. xxvii. 28) — some of them among the most extensive in the country. The whole plain appears to consist of a brown loamy soil, light, but rich, and almost without a stone. This is noted as its characteristic in a remarkable expression of one of the leaders in the Maccabæan wars, a great part of which were fought in this locality (1 Macc. x. 73). It is to this absence of stone that the disappearance of its ancient towns and villages — so much more complete than in other parts of the country — is to be traced. The common material is brick, made, after the Egyptian fashion, of the sandy loam of the plain mixed with stubble, and this has been washed away in almost all cases by the rains of successive centuries (Thomson, p. 563). It is now, as it was when the Philistines possessed

[a] Stanley, *S. & P* pp. 218, 219.

[b] Nothing can be more instructive than to compare (in regard to this one only of the many points in which they differ) the Bible with the Koran. So little ascertainable connection has the Koran with the life or career of Mohammed, that it seems impossible to arrange it with any certainty in the order, real or ostensible, of its composition. With the Bible, on the

other hand, each book belongs to a certain period. It describes the persons of that period; the places under the names which they then bore, and with many a note of identity by which they can often be still recognized; so that it may be said, almost without exaggeration, to be the best Handbook to Palestine.

[c] Robinson, *Bibl. Res.* ii. 15, 20, 29, 32–228.

It, one enormous cornfield; an ocean of wheat covers the wide expanse between the hills and the sand dunes of the sea-shore, without interruption of any kind — no break or hedge, hardly even a single olive-tree (Thomson, p. 552; Van de Velde, ii. 175). Its fertility is marvelous; for the prodigious crops which it raises are produced, and probably have been produced almost year by year for the last 40 centuries, without any of the appliances which we find necessary for success — with no manure beyond that naturally supplied by the washing down of the hill-torrents — without irrigation, without succession of crops, and with only the rudest method of husbandry. No wonder that the Jews struggled hard to get, and the Philistines to keep such a prize: no wonder that the hosts of Egypt and Assyria were content to traverse and re-traverse a region where their supplies of corn were so [a] abundant and so easily obtained.

The southern part of the Philistine Plain, in the neighborhood of *Beit Jibrin*, appears to have been covered, as late as the sixth century, with a forest, called the Forest of Gerar; but of this no traces are known now to exist (Procopius of Gaza, *Scholia* on 2 Chr. xiv.).

31. The Plain of Sharon is much narrower than Philistia. It is about ten miles wide from the sea to the foot of the mountains, which are here of a more abrupt character than those of Philistia, and without the intermediate hilly region there occurring. At the same time it is more undulating and irregular than the former, and crossed by streams from the central hills, some of them of considerable size, and containing water during the whole year. Owing to the general level of the surface and to the accumulation of sand on the shore, several of these streams spread out into wide marshes, which might without difficulty be turned to purposes of irrigation, but in their present neglected state form large boggy places. The soil is extremely rich, varying from bright red to deep black, and producing enormous crops of weeds or grain, as the case may be. Here and there, on the margins of the streams or the borders of the marshes, are large tracts of rank meadow, where many a herd of camels or cattle may be seen feeding, as the royal herds did in the time of David (1 Chr. xxvii. 29). At its northern end Sharon is narrowed by the low hills which gather round the western flanks of Carmel, and gradually encroach upon it until it terminates entirely against the shoulder of the mountain itself, leaving only a narrow beach at the foot of the promontory by which to communicate with the plain on the north.

32. The tract of white sand already mentioned as forming the shore line of the whole coast, is gradually encroaching on this magnificent region. In the south it has buried Askelon, and in the north between Cæsarea and Jaffa the dunes are said to be as much as three miles wide and 300 feet high. The obstruction which is thus caused to the outflow of the streams has been already noticed. All along the edge of Sharon there are pools and marshes due to it. In some places the sand is covered by a stunted growth of maritime pines, the descendants of the forests which at the Christian era gave its name to this portion of the Plain, and which seem to have existed as late as

the second Crusade (Vinisauf in *Chron. of Crus.*). It is probable, for the reasons already stated, that the Jews never permanently occupied more than a small portion of this rich and favored region. Its principal towns were, it is true, allotted to the different tribes (Josh. xv. 45–47; xvi. 3, Gezer xvii. 11, Dor, etc.); but this was in anticipation of the intended conquest (xiii. 3–6). The five cities of the Philistines remained in their possession (1 Sam. v., xxi. 10, xxvii.); and the district was regarded as one independent of and apart from Israel (xxvii. 2; 1 K. ii. 39; 2 K. viii. 2, 3). In like manner Dor remained in the hands of the Canaanites (Judg. i. 27), and Gezer in the hands of the Philistines till taken from them in Solomon's time by his father-in-law (1 K. ix. 16). We find that towards the end of the monarchy the tribe of Benjamin was in possession of Lydd, Jimzu, Ono, and other places in the plain (Neh. xi. 35; 2 Chr. xxviii. 18); but it was only by a gradual process of extension from their native hills, in the rough ground of which they were safe from the attack of cavalry and chariots. But, though the Jews never had any hold on the region, it had its own population, and towns probably not inferior to any in Syria. Both Gaza and Askelon had regular ports (*minjumas*): and there is evidence to show that they were very important and very large long before the fall of the Jewish monarchy (Kenrick, *Phœnicia*, pp. 27–29). Ashdod, though on the open plain, resisted for 29 years the attack of the whole Egyptian force: a similar attack to that which reduced Jerusalem without a blow (2 Chr. xii.), and was sufficient on another occasion to destroy it after a siege of a year and a half, even when fortified by the works of a score of successive monarchs (2 K. xxv. 1–3).

33. In the Roman times this region was considered the pride of the country (*B. J.* i. 29, § 9), and some of the most important cities of the province stood in it — Cæsarea, Antipatris, Diospolis. The one ancient port of the Jews, the "beautiful" city of Joppa, occupied a position central between the Shefelah and Sharon. Roads led from these various cities to each other, to Jerusalem, Neapolis, and Sebaste in the interior, and to Ptolemais and Gaza on the north and south. The commerce of Damascus, and, beyond Damascus, of Persia and India, passed this way to Egypt, Rome, and the infant colonies of the west; and that traffic and the constant movement of troops backwards and forwards must have made this plain one of the busiest and most populous regions of Syria at the time of Christ. *Now*, Cæsarea is a wave-washed ruin; Antipatris has vanished both in name and substance; Diospolis has shaken off the appellation which it bore in the days of its prosperity, and is a mere village, remarkable only for the ruin of its fine mediæval church, and for the palm-grove which shrouds it from view. Joppa alone maintains a dull life, surviving solely because it is the nearest point at which the sea-going travellers from the west can approach Jerusalem. For a few miles above Jaffa cultivation is still carried on, but the fear of the Bedouins who roam (as they always have [b] roamed) over parts of the plain, plundering all passers-by, and extorting black mail from the wretched peasants, has desolated a large district,

---

[a] *Le grenier de la Syrie* (Duc de Raguse, *Voyage*).
[b] The Bedouins from beyond Jordan, whom Gideon surprised, destroyed the earth "as far as Gaza;" *i. e.*

they filled the Plain of Esdraelon, and overflowed into Sharon, and thence southwards to the richest prize of the day.

and effectually prevents it being used any longer as the route for travellers from south to north; while in the portions which are free from this scourge, the teeming soil itself is doomed to unproductiveness through the folly and iniquity of its Turkish rulers, whose exactions have driven, and are driving, its industrious and patient inhabitants to remoter parts of the land.[a]

34. The characteristics already described are hardly peculiar to Palestine. Her hilly surface and general height, her rocky ground and thin soil, her torrent beds wide and dry for the greater part of the year, even her belt of maritime lowland — these she shares with other lands, though it would perhaps be difficult to find them united elsewhere. But there is one feature, as yet only alluded to, in which she stands alone. This feature is the Jordan — the one River of the country.

35. Properly to comprehend this, we must cast our eyes a few moments north and south, outside the narrow limits of the Holy Land. From top to bottom — from north to south — from Antioch to Akaba at the tip of the eastern horn of the Red Sea, Syria is cleft by a deep and narrow trench running parallel with the coast of the Mediterranean, and dividing, as if by a fosse or ditch, the central range of maritime highlands from those further east.[b] At two points only in its length is the trench interrupted: by the range of Lebanon and Hermon, and by the high ground south of the Dead Sea. Of the three compartments thus formed, the northern is the valley of the Orontes; the southern is the *Wady el-Arabah*, while the central one is the valley of the Jordan, the Arabah of the Hebrews, the Aulón of the Greeks, and the *Ghôr* of the Arabs. Whether this remarkable fissure in the surface of the earth originally ran without interruption from the Mediterranean to the Red Sea, and was afterwards (though still at a time long anterior to the historic period) broken by the protrusion or elevation of the two tracts just named, cannot be ascertained in the present state of our geological knowledge of this region. The central of its three divisions is the only one with which we have at present to do; it is also the most remarkable of the three. The river is elsewhere described in detail [JORDAN]: but it and the valley through which it rushes down its extraordinary

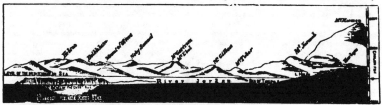

Profile-Section of the Holy Land from the Dead Sea to Mount Hermon, along the line of the Jordan.

descent — and which seems as it were to inclose and conceal it during the whole of its course — must be here briefly characterized as essential to a correct comprehension of the country of which they form the external barrier, dividing Galilee, Ephraim, and Judah from Bashan, Gilead, and Moab, respectively.

36. To speak first of the Valley. It begins with the river at its remotest springs of Hasbeiya on the N. W. side of Hermon, and accompanies it to the lower end of the Dead Sea, a length of about 150 miles. During the whole of this distance its course is straight, and its direction nearly due north and south. The springs of Hasbeiya are 1,700 feet above the level of the Mediterranean, and the northern end of the Dead Sea is 1,317 feet below it, so that between these two points the valley falls with more or less regularity through a height of more than 3,000 feet. But though the river disappears at this point, the *valley* still continues its descent below the waters of the Dead Sea till it reaches a further depth of 1,308 feet. So that the bottom of this extraordinary crevasse is actually more than 2,600 feet below the surface of the ocean.[c] Even that portion which extends down to the brink of the lake and is open to observation, is without a parallel in any other part of the world. It is obvious that the road by which these depths are reached from the Mount of Olives or Hebron must be very steep and abrupt. But this is not its real peculiarity. Equally great and sudden descents may be found in our own or other mountainous countries. That which distinguishes this from all others is the fact that it is made into the very bowels of the earth. The traveller who stands on the shore of the Dead Sea has reached a point nearly as far below the surface of the ocean as the miners in the lowest levels of the deepest mines of Cornwall.

37. In width the valley varies. In its upper and shallower portion, as between Banias and the lake of Hûleh, it is about five miles across; the inclosing mountains of moderate height, though tolerably vertical in character; the floor almost an absolute

---

[a] This district, called the *Sahel Athlit*, between the sea and the western flanks of Carmel, has been within a very few years reduced from being one of the most thriving and productive regions of the country, as well as one of the most profitable to the government, to desolation and desertion, by these wicked exactions. The taxes are paid in kind; and the officers who gather them demand so much grain for their own perquisites as to leave the peasant barely enough for the next sowing. In addition to this, as long as any people remain in a district they are liable for the whole of the tax at which the district is rated. No wonder that under such pressure the inhabitants of the *Sahel Athlit* have almost all emigrated to Egypt, where the system is better, and better administered.

[b] So remarkable is this depression, that it is adopted by the great geographer Ritter as the base of his description of Syria.

[c] Deep as it now is, the Dead Sea was once doubtless far deeper, for the sediment brought into it by the Jordan must be gradually accumulating. No data however, exist by which to judge of the rate of this accumulation.

flat, with the mysterious river hidden from sight in an impenetrable jungle of reeds and marsh vegetation.

Between the Hûleh and the Sea of Galilee, as far as we have any information, it contracts, and becomes more of an ordinary ravine or glen.

It is in its third and lower portion that the valley assumes its more definite and regular character. During the greater part of this portion, it is about seven miles wide from the one wall to the other. The eastern mountains preserve their straight line of direction, and their massive horizontal wall-like aspect, during almost the whole [a] distance. Here and there they are cloven by the vast mysterious rents, through which the Hieromax, the *Wady Zurka*, and other streams force their way down to the Jordan. The western mountains are more irregular in height, their slopes less vertical, and their general line is interrupted by projecting outposts such as *Tell Fasail*, and *Kurn Sürtubeh*. North of Jericho they recede in a kind of wide amphitheatre, and the valley becomes twelve miles broad, a breadth which it thenceforward retains to the southern extremity of the Dead Sea. What the real bottom of this cavity may be, or at what depth below the surface, is not yet known, but that which meets the eye is a level or gently undulating surface of light sandy soil, about Jericho brilliant white, about *Beisan* dark and reddish, crossed at intervals by the torrents of the western highlands which have ploughed their zigzag course deep down into its soft substance, and even in autumn betray the presence of moisture by the bright green of the thorn-bushes which flourish in and around their channels, and cluster in greater profusion round the spring-heads at the foot of the mountains. Formerly palms abounded on both sides [b] of the Jordan at its lower end, but none now exist there. Passing through this vegetation, such as it is, the traveller emerges on a plain of bare sand, furrowed out in innumerable channels by the rain-streams, all running eastward towards the river, which lies there in the distance, though invisible. Gradually these channels increase in number and depth till they form steep cones or mounds of sand of brilliant white, 50 to 100 feet high, their lower part loose but their upper portion indurated by the action of the rains and the tremendous heat of the sun.[c] Here and there these cones are marshaled in a tolerably regular line, like gigantic tents, and form the bank of a terrace overlooking a flat considerably lower in level than that already traversed. After crossing this lower flat for some distance, another descent, of a few feet only, is made into a thick growth of dwarf shrubs: and when this has been pursued until the traveller has well-nigh lost all patience, he suddenly arrives on the edge of a "hole" filled with thick trees and shrubs, whose tops rise to a level with his feet. Through the thicket comes the welcome sound of rushing waters. This is the Jordan.[d]

38. Buried as it is thus between such lofty ranges, and shielded from every breeze, the climate of the Jordan Valley is extremely hot and relaxing. Its enervating influence is shown by the inhabitants of Jericho, who are a small, feeble, exhausted race, dependent for the cultivation of their lands on the hardier peasants of the highland villages (Rob. i. 550), and to this day prone to the vices which are often developed by tropical climates, and which brought destruction on Sodom and Gomorrah. But the circumstances which are unfavorable to morals are most favorable to fertility. Whether there was any great amount of cultivation and habitation in this region in the times of the Israelites the Bible does not [e] say; but in post-biblical times there is no doubt on the point. The palms of Jericho, and of Abila (opposite Jericho on the other side of the river), and the extensive balsam and rose-gardens of the former place, are spoken of by Josephus, who calls the whole district a "divine spot" ($\theta\epsilon\tilde{\iota}o\nu$ $\chi\omega\rho\iota o\nu$, B. J. iv. 8, § 3; see vol. ii. 1265).[f] Bethshan was a proverb among the rabbis for its fertility. Succoth was the site of Jacob's first settlement west of the Jordan; and therefore was probably then, as it still is, an eligible spot. In later times indigo and sugar appear to have been grown near Jericho and elsewhere;[g] aqueducts are still partially standing, of Christian or Saracenic arches; and there are remains, all over the plain between Jericho and the river, of former residences or towns

---

[a] North of the *Wady Zurka* their character alters. They lose the vertical wall-like appearance, so striking at Jericho, and become more broken and sloping. The writer had an excellent view of the mountains behind *Beisan* from the Burj at Zerin in October, 1861. Zerin, though distant, is sufficiently high to command a prospect into the interior of the mountains. Thus viewed, their wall-like character had entirely vanished. There appeared, instead, an infinity of separate summits, fully as irregular and multitudinous as any district west of Jordan, rising gradually in height as they receded eastward. Is this the case with this locality only? or would the whole region east of the Jordan prove equally broken, if viewed sufficiently near? Prof. Stanley hints that such may be the case (S. & P. p. 320). Certainly the hills of Judah and Samaria appear as much a "wall" as those east of Jordan, when viewed from the sea-coast.

[b] Jericho was the city of palm-trees (2 Chr. xxviii. 15); and Josephus mentions the palms of Abila, on the eastern side of the river, as the scene of Moses' last address. "The whole shore of the Dead Sea," says Mr. Poole, "is strewed with palms" (*Geogr. Society's Journal*, 1856). Dr. Anderson (p. 192) describes a large grove as standing on the lower margin of the sea between *Wady Mojeb* (Arnon) and *Zurka Main* (Callirhoë).

[c] The writer is here speaking from his own observation of the lower part. A similar description is given by Lynch of the upper part (*Official Report*, April 13; Van de Velde, *Memoir*, p. 125).

[d] The lines which have given many a young mind its first and most lasting impression of the Jordan and its surrounding scenery, are not more accurate than many other versions of Scripture scenes and facts: —

"Sweet fields beyond the swelling flood
Stand dressed in living green :
So to the Jews old Canaan stood,
While Jordan rolled between."

[e] Besides Gilgal, the tribe of Benjamin had four cities or settlements in the neighborhood of Jericho (Josh. xviii. 21). The rebuilding of the last-named town in Ahab's reign probably indicates an increase in the prosperity of the district.

[f] This seems to have been the $\pi\epsilon\rho\iota\chi\omega\rho o\varsigma$, or "region round about" Jordan, mentioned in the Gospels, and possibly answering to the *Ciccar* of the ancient Hebrews. (See Stanley, S. & P. pp. 284, 488.)

[g] The word *suckkar* (sugar) is found in the names of places near Tiberias below Sebbeh (Masada), and near Gaza, as well as at Jericho. All these are in the depressed regions. For the indigo, see Poole (*Geogr. Journal*, xxvi. 57).

and of systems of irrigation (Ritter, *Jordan*, pp. 503, 512) Phasaelis, a few miles further north, was built by Herod the Great; and there were other towns either in or closely bordering on the plain. At present this part is almost entirely desert, and cultivation is confined to the upper portion, between *Sakut* and *Beisan*. There indeed it is conducted on a grand scale; and the traveller as he journeys along the road which leads over the foot of the western mountains, overlooks an immense extent of the richest land, abundantly watered, and covered with corn and other grain.[a] Here, too, as at Jericho, the cultivation is conducted principally by the inhabitants of the villages on the western mountains.

39. All the irrigation necessary for the towns, or for the cultivation which formerly existed, or still exists, in the *Ghôr*, is obtained from the torrents and springs of the western mountains. For all purposes to which a river is ordinarily applied, the Jordan is useless. So rapid that its course is one continued cataract; so crooked, that in the whole of its lower and main course, it has hardly half a mile straight; so broken with rapids and other impediments, that no boat can swim for more than the same distance continuously; so deep below the surface of the adjacent country that it is invisible, and can only with difficulty be approached; resolutely refusing all communication with the ocean, and, ending in a lake, the peculiar conditions of which render navigation impossible — with all these characteristics the Jordan, in any sense which we attach to the word "river," is no river at all: alike useless for irrigation and navigation, it is in fact, what its Arabic name signifies, nothing but a "great watering place" (*Sheriat el-Khebir*).

40. But though the Jordan is so unlike a river in the western sense of the term, it is far less so than the other streams of the Holy Land. It is at least perennial, while, with few exceptions, they are mere winter torrents, rushing and foaming during the continuance of the rain, and quickly drying up after the commencement of summer: "What time they wax warm they vanish; when it is hot they are consumed out of their place . . . . they go to nothing and perish " (Job vi. 17). For fully half the year, these "rivers " or "brooks," as our version of the Bible renders the special term (*nachal*) which designates them in the original, are often mere dry lanes of hot white or gray stones; or if their water still continues to run, it is a tiny rill, working its way through heaps of parched boulders in the centre of a broad flat tract of loose stones, often only traceable by the thin line of verdure which springs up along its course. Those who have travelled in Provence or Granada in the summer will have no difficulty in recognizing this description, and in comprehending how the use of such terms as "river " or "brook " must mislead those who can only read the exact and vivid narrative of the Bible through the medium of the Authorized Version.[b]

This subject will be more fully described, and a list of the few perennial streams of the Holy Land given under RIVER.

41. How far the valley of the Jordan was employed by the ancient inhabitants of the Holy Land as a medium of communication between the northern and southern parts of the country we can only conjecture. Though not the shortest route between Galilee and Judaea, it would yet, as far as the levels and form of the ground are concerned, be the most practicable for large bodies; though these advantages would be seriously counterbalanced by the sultry heat of its climate, as compared with the fresher air of the more difficult road over the highlands.

The ancient notices of this route are very scanty.

(1.) From 2 Chr. xxviii. 15, we find that the captives taken from Judah by the army of the northern kingdom were sent back from Samaria to Jerusalem by way of Jericho. The route pursued was probably by *Nablus* across the *Mukhna*, and by *Wady Farrah* or *Fasail* into the Jordan Valley. Why this road was taken is a mystery, since it is not stated or implied that the captives were accompanied by any heavy baggage which would make it difficult to travel over the central route. It would seem, however, to have been the usual road from the north to Jerusalem (comp. Luke xvii. 11 with xix. 1), as if there were some impediment to passing through the region immediately north of the city.

(2.) Pompey brought his army and siege-train from Damascus to Jerusalem (B. C. 40), past Scythopolis and Pella, and thence by Korea (possibly the present *Kerawa* at the foot of the *Wady Ferrah*) to Jericho (Joseph. *Ant.* xiv. 3, § 4; *B. J.* i. 6, § 5).

(3.) Vespasian marched from Emmaus, on the edge of the plain of Sharon, not far east of *Ramleh*, past Neapolis (*Nablus*), down the *Wady Ferrah* or *Fasail* to Korea, and thence to Jericho (*B. J.* iv. 8, § 1); the same route as that of the captive Judaeans in No. 1.

(4.) Antoninus Martyr (cir. A. D. 600), and possibly Willibald[c] (A. D. 722) followed this route to Jerusalem.

(5.) Baldwin I. is said to have journeyed from Jericho to Tiberias with a caravan of pilgrims.

(6.) In our own times the whole length of the valley has been traversed by De Bertou, and by Dr. Anderson, who accompanied the American Expedition as geologist, but apparently by few if any other travellers.

42. Monotonous and uninviting as much of the Holy Land will appear from the above description to English readers, accustomed to the constant verdure, the succession of flowers, lasting almost throughout the year, the ample streams and the varied surface of our own country — we must remember that its aspect to the Israelites after that weary march of forty years through the desert, and even by the side of the brightest recollections of Egypt that they could conjure up, must have been very different. After the "great and terrible wilderness " with its "fiery serpents," its "scorpions," "drought," and "rocks of flint " ; the slow and sultry march all day in the dust of that enormous procession; the eager looking forward to the well

---

[a] Robinson, iii. 314 ; and from the writer's own observation.

[b] * To prevent this confusion, some recent geographers (as Dr. Menke, on his map, Gotha, 1868) very properly distinguish the river and *Wady* from each other by different signs.   H.

[c] Willibald omits his route between Caesarea (? C. Philippi = *Banias*) and the monastery of St. John the Baptist near Jericho. He is always assumed to have come down the valley.

at which the encampment was to be pitched; the crowding, the fighting, the clamor, the bitter disappointment round the modicum of water when at last the desired spot was reached; the "light bread" [a] so long "loathed"; the rare treat of animal food when the quails descended, or an approach to the sea permitted the "fish" [b] to be caught; after this daily struggle for a painful existence, how grateful must have been the rest afforded by the Land of Promise! — how delicious the shade, scanty though it were, of the hills and ravines, the gushing springs and green plains, even the mere wells and cisterns, the vineyards and olive-yards and "fruit trees [c] in abundance," the cattle, sheep, and goats, covering the country with their long black lines, the bees swarming round their pendant combs [d] in rock or wood! Moreover they entered the country at the time of the Passover, [e] when it was arrayed in the full glory and freshness of its brief spring-tide, before the scorching sun of summer had had time to wither its flowers and embrown its verdure. Taking all these circumstances into account, and allowing for the bold metaphors [f] of oriental speech — so different from our cold depreciating expressions, — it is impossible not to feel that those wayworn travellers could have chosen no fitter words to express what their new country was to them than those which they so often employ in the accounts of the conquest — "a land flowing with milk and honey, the glory of all lands."

42. Again, the variations of the seasons may appear to us slight, and the atmosphere dry and hot; but after the monotonous climate of Egypt, where rain is a rare phenomenon, and where the difference between summer and winter is hardly perceptible, the "rain of heaven" must have been a most grateful novelty in its two seasons, the former and the latter — the occasional snow and ice of the winters of Palestine, and the burst of returning spring. must have had double the effect which they would produce on those accustomed to such changes. Nor is the change only a relative one; there is a real difference — due partly to the higher latitude of Palestine, partly to its proximity to the sea — between the sultry atmosphere of the Egyptian valley and the invigorating sea-breezes which blow over the hills of Ephraim and Judah.

44. The contrast with Egypt would tell also in another way. In place of the huge ever-flowing river whose only variation was from low to high, and from high to low again, and which lay at the lowest level of that level country, so that all irrigation had to be done by artificial labor — "a land

where thou sowedst thy seed and wateredst it with thy foot like a garden of herbs" [g] — in place of this, they were to find themselves in a land of constant and considerable undulation, where the water, either of gushing spring, or deep well, or flowing stream, could be procured at the most varied elevations, requiring only to be judiciously husbanded and skillfully conducted to find its own way through field or garden, whether terraced on the hill-sides or extended in the broad bottoms. [h] But such change was not compulsory. Those who preferred the climate and the mode of cultivation of Egypt could resort to the lowland plains of the Jordan Valley, where the temperature is more constant and many degrees higher than on the more elevated districts of the country, where the breezes never penetrate, where the light fertile soil recalls, as it did in the earliest [i] times, that of Egypt, and where the Jordan in its lowness of level presents at least one point of resemblance to the Nile.

45. In truth, on closer consideration, it will be seen that, beneath the apparent monotony, there is a variety in the Holy Land really remarkable. There is the variety due to the difference of level between the different parts of the country. There is the variety of climate and of natural appearances, proceeding, partly from those very differences of level, and partly from the proximity of the snow-capped Hermon and Lebanon on the north and of the torrid desert on the south; and which approximate the climate, in many respects, to that of regions much further north. There is also the variety which is inevitably produced by the presence of the sea — "the eternal freshness and liveliness of ocean."

46. Each of these is continually reflected in the Hebrew literature. The contrast between the highlands and lowlands is more than implied in the habitual forms of [k] expression, "going up" to Judah, Jerusalem, Hebron; "going down" to Jericho, Capernaum, Lydda, Cæsarea, Gaza, and Egypt. More than this, the difference is marked unmistakably in the topographical terms which so abound in, and are so peculiar to, this literature. "The mountain of Judah," "the mountain of Israel," "the mountain of Naphtali," are the names by which the three great divisions of the highlands are designated. The predominant names for the towns of the same district — Gibeah, Geba, Gaba, Gibeon (meaning "hill"); Ramah, Ramathaim (the "brow" of an eminence); Mizpeh, Zophim, Zephathah (all modifications of a root signifying a wide prospect) — all reflect the elevation of the region in which they were situated. On the other

---

[a] Num. xxi. 5.   [b] Num. xi. 22.
[c] Neh. ix. 25.   [d] 1 Sam. xiv. 26.
[e] Josh. v. 10, 11.

[f] See some useful remarks on the use of similar language by the natives of the East at the present day, in reference to spots inadequate to such expressions, in *The Jews in the East*, by Beaton and Frankl (ii. 359).

[g] * For the meaning of this expression, see FOOT, WATERING WITH THE (Amer. ed.).   H.

[h] The view taken above, that the beauty of the Promised Land was greatly enhanced to the Israelites by its contrast with the scenes they had previously passed through, is corroborated by the fact that such laudatory expressions as "the land flowing with milk and honey," "the glory of all lands," etc., occur, with rare exceptions, in those parts of the Bible only which purport to have been composed just before their

entrance, and that in the few cases of their employment by the Prophets (Jer. xi. 5, xxxii. 22; Ez. xx. 6, 15) there is always an allusion to "Egypt," "the iron furnace," the passing of the Red Sea, or the wilderness, to point the contrast.

[i] Gen. xiii. 10. Ali Bey (ii. 209) says that the maritime plain, from *Khan Younes*, to Jaffa, is "of rich soil, similar to the slime of the Nile." Other points of resemblance are mentioned by Robinson (*Bibl. Res.* ii. 22, 34, 35, 226), and Thomson (*Land and Book*, ch. 36). The plain of Gennesaret still "recalls the valley of the Nile" (Stanley, *S. & P.* p. 374). The papyrus is said to grow there (Buchanan, *Cler. Furlough*, p. 392).

[k] The same expressions are still used by the Arabs of the *Nejd*, with reference to Syria and their own country (Wallin, *Geogr. Soc. Journal*, xxiv. 174).

nand, the great lowland districts have each their peculiar name. The southern part of the maritime plain is "the Shefelah;" the northern, "Sharon;" the valley of the Jordan, "ha-Arâbah;" names which are never interchanged, and never confounded with the terms (such as *emek, nachal, gai*) employed for the ravines, torrent-beds, and small valleys of the highlands [a]

47. The differences in climate are no less often mentioned. The Psalmists, Prophets, and [b] historical books, are full of allusions to the fierce heat of the mid-day sun and the dryness of summer; no less than to the various accompaniments of winter — the rain, snow, frost, ice, and fogs, which are experienced at Jerusalem and other places in the upper country quite sufficiently to make every one familiar with them. Even the sharp alternations between the heat of the days and the coldness of the nights, which strike every traveller in Palestine, are mentioned.[c] The Israelites practiced no commerce by sea; and, with the single exception of Joppa, not only possessed no harbor along the whole length of their coast, but had no word by which to denote one. But that their poets knew and appreciated the phenomena of the sea is plain from such expressions as are constantly recurring in their works — "the great and wide sea," its "ships," its "monsters," its roaring and dashing "waves," its "depths," its "sand," its mariners, the perils of its navigation.

It is unnecessary here to show how materially the Bible has gained in its hold on western nations by these vivid reflections of a country so much more like those of the West than are most oriental regions: but of the fact there can be no doubt, and it has been admirably brought out by Professor Stanley in *Sinai and Palestine*, chap. ii. sect. vii.

48. In the preceding description allusion has been made to many of the characteristic features of the Holy Land. But it is impossible to close this account without mentioning a defect which is even more characteristic — its lack of monuments and personal relics of the nation who possessed it for so many centuries, and gave it its claim to our veneration and affection. When compared with other nations of equal antiquity — Egypt, Greece, Assyria, the contrast is truly remarkable. In Egypt and Greece, and also in Assyria, as far as our knowledge at present extends, we find a series of buildings, reaching down from the most remote and mysterious antiquity, a chain, of which hardly a link is wanting, and which records the progress of the people in civilization, art, and religion, as certainly as the buildings of the mediæval architects do that of the various nations of modern Europe. We possess also a multitude of objects of use and ornament, belonging to those nations, truly astonishing in number, and pertaining to every station, office, and fact in their official, religious, and domestic life. But in Palestine it is not too much to say that there does not exist a single edifice, or part of an edifice, of which we can be sure that it

is of a date anterior to the Christian era. Excavated tombs, cisterns, flights of stairs, which are encountered everywhere, are of course out of the question. They may be — some of them, such as the tombs of Hinnom and Shiloh, probably are — of very great age, older than anything else in the country. But there is no evidence either way, and as far as the history of art is concerned nothing would be gained if their age were ascertained. The only ancient buildings of which we can speak with certainty are those which were erected by the Greeks or Romans during their occupation of the country. Not that these buildings have not a certain individuality which separates them from any mere Greek or Roman building in Greece or Rome. But the fact is certain, that not one of them was built while the Israelites were masters of the country, and before the date at which western nations began to get a footing in Palestine. And as with the buildings so with other memorials. With one exception, the museums of Europe do not possess a single piece of pottery or metal work, a single weapon or household utensil, an ornament or a piece of armor, of Israelite make, which can give us the least conception of the manners or outward appliances of the nation before the date of the destruction of Jerusalem by Titus. The coins form the single exception. A few rare specimens still exist, the oldest of them attributed — though even that is matter of dispute — to the Maccabees, and their rudeness and insignificance furnish a stronger evidence than even their absence could imply, of the total want of art among the Israelites.

It may be said that Palestine is now only in the same condition with Assyria before the recent researches brought so much to light. But the two cases are not parallel. The soil of Babylonia is a loose loam or sand, of the description best fitted for covering up and preserving the relics of former ages. On the other hand, the greater part of the Holy Land is hard and rocky, and the soil lies in the valleys and lowlands, where the cities were only very rarely built. If any store of Jewish relics were remaining embedded or hidden in suitable ground — as for example, in the loose mass of debris which coats the slopes around Jerusalem — we should expect occasionally to find articles which might be recognized as Jewish. This was the case in Assyria. Long before the mounds were explored, Rich brought home many fragments of inscriptions, bricks, and engraved stones, which were picked up on the surface, and were evidently the productions of some nation whose art was not then known. But in Palestine the only objects hitherto discovered have all belonged to the West — coins or arms of the Greeks or Romans.

The buildings already mentioned as being Jewish in character, though carried out with foreign details, are the following: —

The tombs of the Kings and of the Judges: the buildings known as the tombs of Absalom, Zechariah, St. James, and Jehoshaphat: the monolith at Siloam, — all in the neighborhood of Jerusalem;

---

[a] It is impossible to trace these correspondences and distinctions in the English Bible, our translators not having always rendered the same Hebrew by the same English word. But the corrections will be found in the Appendix to Professor Stanley's *Sinai and Palestine*.

[b] Ps. xix. f xxxii. 4; Is. iv. 6, xxv. 5; Gen. xviii. 1; 1 Sam. xi. 9; Neh. vii. 8.

[c] Jer. xxxvi. 30. Gen. xxxi. 40 refers — unless the recent speculations of Mr. Beke should prove true — to Mesopotamia.

[*] Mr. Beke supposes a Haran in Syria near Damascus to be meant in Gen. xxxi. 40. For the grounds of that opinion and the insufficiency of them, see addition to HARAN, Amer. ed.   H.

the ruined synagogues at Meiron and *Kefr Birim*. But there are two edifices which seem to bear a character of their own, and do not so clearly betray the style of the West. These are, the inclosure round the sacred cave at Hebron; and portions of the western, southern, and eastern walls of the *Haram* at Jerusalem, with the vaulted passage below the *Aksa*. Of the former it is impossible to speak in the present state of our knowledge. The latter will be more fully noticed under the head of TEMPLE; it is sufficient here to name one or two considerations which seem to bear against their being of older date than Herod. (1.) Herod is distinctly said by Josephus to have removed the old foundations, and laid others in their stead, in-closing double the original area (*Ant.* xv. 11, § 3; *B. J.* i. 21, § 1). (2.) The part of the wall which all acknowledge to be the oldest contains the spring-ing of an arch. This and the vaulted passage can hardly be assigned to builders earlier than the time of the Romans. (3.) The masonry of these mag-nificent stones (absurdly called the "bevel"), on which so much stress has been laid, is not ex-clusively Jewish or even Eastern. It is found at Persepolis; it is also found at Cnidus and through-out Asia Minor, and at Athens; not on stones of such enormous size as those at Jerusalem, but similar in their workmanship.[a]

M. Renan, in his recent report of his proceedings in Phœnicia, has named two circumstances which must have had a great effect in suppressing art or architecture amongst the ancient Israelites, while their very existence proves that the people had no genius in that direction. These are (1) the pro-hibition of sculptured representations of living creatures, and (2) the command not to build a temple anywhere but at Jerusalem. The hewing or polishing of building-stones was even forbidden. "What," he asks, "would Greece have been, if it had been illegal to build any temples but at Delphi or Eleusis? In ten centuries the Jews had only three temples to build, and of these certainly two were erected under the guidance of foreigners. The existence of synagogues dates from the time of the Maccabees, and the Jews then naturally employed the Greek style of architecture, which at that time reigned universally."

In fact the Israelites never lost the feeling or the traditions of their early pastoral nomad life. Long after the nation had been settled in the country, the cry of those earlier days, "To your tents, O Israel!" was heard in periods of excitement [b] The prophets, sick of the luxury of the cities, are con-stantly recalling [c] the "tents" of that simpler, less artificial life; and the Temple of Solomon, nay even perhaps of Zerubbabel, was spoken of to the last as the "tent [d] of the Lord of hosts," the "place where David had pitched [e] his tent." It is a remarkable fact, that eminent as Jews have been in other de-partments of arts, science,[f] and affairs, no Jewish architect, painter, or sculptor has ever achieved any signal success.

THE GEOLOGY. — Of the geological structure of Palestine it has been said with truth that our information is but imperfect and indistinct, and that much time must elapse, and many a cherished hypothesis be sacrificed, before a satisfactory ex-planation can be arrived at of its more remarkable phenomena.

It is not intended to attempt here more than a very cursory sketch, addressed to the general and non-scientific reader. The geologist must be re-ferred to the original works from which these remarks have been compiled.

1. The main sources of our knowledge are (1) the observations contained in the Travels of Rus-segger, an Austrian geologist and mining engineer who visited this amongst other countries of the East in 1836-38 (*Reisen in Griechenland*, etc., 4 vols, Stuttgard, 1841-49, with *Atlas*); (2) the Report of H. J. Anderson, M. D., an American geologist, formerly Professor in Columbia College, New York, who accompanied Captain Lynch in his exploration of the Jordan and the Dead Sea (*Geol. Reconnaissance*, in Lynch's *Official Report*, 4to, 1852, pp. 75-207); and (3) the Diary of Mr. H Poole, who visited Palestine on a mission for the British government in 1836 (*Journal of Geogr. Society*, vol. xxvi. pp. 55-70). Neither of these contains anything approaching a complete investi-gation, either as to extent or to detail of observa-tions. Russegger travelled from Sinai to Hebron and Jerusalem. He explored carefully the route be-tween the latter place and the Dead Sea. He then

---

a * In the former of the passages here cited (*Ant.* xv. 11, § 3) Josephus limits Herod's work of recon-struction to the *Naos*, or body of the temple, and the adjacent porticoes. He expressly distinguishes be-tween the foundations of the Temple proper, which Herod relaid, and the solid walls of the outer inclosure, which were laid by Solomon. These outer walls he represents as composed of stones so vast and so firmly joined by bands of iron, as to be immovable for all time — ἀκινήτους τῷ παντὶ χρόνῳ. Some of the courses of the walls which he thus describes, evidently ex-isting in his day, are plainly recognizable now in the southern portion of the walls of *el-Haram*, including the immense layers which remain of the arch of the ancient bridge across the Tyropœon. His more minute description of the Temple and its area in another work (*B. J.* v. 5, §§ 1-6) correspond entirely with this state-ment. He also mentions (§ 8) the addition to this inclosure by Herod of the space occupied by the tower of Antonia. The original inclosure of the Temple measured four stadia in circumference; but he tells us (§ 2) that the area, "including the tower of An-tonia," measured six stadia.

When, now, in the latter passage quoted above (*B. J.*, i. 21, § 1), he tells us that Herod " inclosed double the original area," he clearly refers to this accession of the space of the tower of Antonia on the

north. He cannot refer to any dislocation of the "immovable" walls which Solomon had built above the valleys on the northeast and southwest, or to any enlargement by Herod of the area in those directions. "No mention is made of his having had anything to do with the massive walls of the exterior inclosure " (Robinson, *Bibl. Res.* i. 418). The portions of the walls referred to in the article above are almost indis-putably Jewish. In a previous article, " the masonry in the western wall near its southern extremity," is claimed by Mr. Fergusson as in the judgment of " al-most all topographers, a proof that the wall there formed part of the substructures of the Temple " (vol. ii. p. 1314, Amer. ed).

The recent excavations of Lieut. Warren appear to have fully convinced Mr. Grove that these sub-structions are " earlier than the times of the Romans," and clearly Jewish.   S. W.

b 2 Sam. xx. 1; 1 K. xii. 16 (that the words are not a mere formula of the historian is proved by their occurrence in 2 Chr. x. 16); 2 K. xiv. 12.

c Jer. xxx. 18; Zech. xii. 7; Ps. lxxviii. 55, &c

d Ps. lxxxiv. 1, xiiii. 3, lxxvi. 2; Judith ix. 8.

e Is. xxix. 1, xvi. 5.

f See the well-known passage in *Coningsby*, bk. iv. ch. 15.

proceeded to Jaffa by the ordinary road; and from
thence to Beyrût and the Lebanon by Nazareth,
Tiberias, Cana, Akka, Tyre, and Sidon. Thus he
left the Dead Sea in its most interesting portions,
the Jordan Valley, the central highlands, and the
important district of the upper Jordan, untouched.
His work is accompanied by two sections: from
the Mount of Olives to the Jordan, and from Tabor
to the Lake of Tiberias. His observations, though
clearly and attractively given, and evidently those
of a practiced observer, are too short and cursory
for the subject. The general notice of his journey
is in vol. iii. pp. 76–157; the scientific observations,
tables, etc., are contained between pp. 161 and 291.
Dr. Anderson visited the southwestern portion of
the Lebanon between Beyrût and Banias, Galilee.
the Lake of Tiberias, the Jordan; made the circuit
of the Dead Sea; and explored the district between
that lake and Jerusalem. His account is evidently
drawn up with great pains, and is far more elaborate than that of Russegger. He gives full analy-
ses of the different rocks which he examined, and
very good lithographs of fossils; but unfortunately
his work is deformed by a very unreadable style.
Mr. Poole's journey was confined to the western
and southeastern portions of the Dead Sea, the
Jordan, the country between the latter and Jerusalem, and the beaten track of the central highlands from Hebron to Nablus.

2. From the reports of these observers it appears
that the Holy Land is a much-disturbed mountainous tract of limestone of the secondary period
(jurassic and cretaceous); the southern offshoot of
the chain of Lebanon; elevated considerably above
the sea level; with partial interruptions from tertiary and basaltic deposits. It is part of a vast
mass of limestone, stretching in every direction
except west, far beyond the limits of the Holy
Land. The whole of Syria is cleft from north to
south by a straight crevasse of moderate width,
but extending in the southern portion of its centre
division to a truly remarkable depth (a 2,625 ft.)
below the sea level. This crevasse, which contains
the principal watercourse of the country, is also
the most exceptional feature of its geology. Such
fissures are not uncommon in limestone formations;
but no other is known of such a length and of so
extraordinary a depth, and so open throughout its
greatest extent. It may have been volcanic in its
origin; the result of an upheaval from beneath,
which has tilted the limestone back on each side,
leaving this huge split in the strata; the volcanic
force having stopped short at that point in the
operation, without intruding any volcanic rocks
into the fissure. This idea is supported by the
crater-like form of the basins of the Lake of Tiberias and of the Dead Sea (Russ. pp. 206, 207), and
by many other tokens of volcanic action, past and
present, which are encountered in and around those
lakes, and along the whole extent of the valley.
Or it may have been excavated by the gradual
action of the ocean during the immense periods of
geological operation. The latter appears to be the
opinion of Dr. Anderson (pp. 79, 140, 205); but
further examination is necessary before a positive
opinion can be pronounced. The ranges of the

hills of the surface take the direction nearly due
north and south, though frequently thrown from
their main bearing and much broken up into detached masses. The lesser watercourses run chiefly
east and west of the central highlands.

3. The limestone consists of two strata, or rather
groups of strata. The upper one, which usually
meets the eye, over the whole country from Hebron
to Hermon, is a tolerably solid stone, varying in
color from white to reddish brown, with very
few fossils, inclining to crystalline structure, and
abounding in caverns. Its general surface has been
formed into gently rounded hills, crowded more
or less thickly together, separated by narrow valleys
of denudation occasionally spreading into small
plains. The strata are not well defined, and although sometimes level b (in which case they lend
themselves to the formation of terraces), are more
often violently disarranged.c Remarkable instances
of such contortions are to be found on the road
from Jerusalem to Jericho, where the beds are
seen pressed and twisted into every variety of
form.

It is hardly necessary to say that these contortions, as well as the general form of the surface,
are due to forces not now in action, but are part of
the general configuration of the country, as it was
left after the last of that succession of immersions
below, and upheavals from, the ocean, by which
its present form was given it, long prior to the historic period. There is no ground for believing that
the broad geological features of this or any part of
the country are appreciably altered from what they
were at the earliest times of the Bible history.
The evidences of later action are, however, often
visible, as for instance where the atmosphere and
the rains have furrowed the face of the limestone
cliffs with long and deep vertical channels, often
causing the most fantastic forms (And. pp. 89, 111;
Poole, p. 56).

4. This limestone is often found crowned with
chalk, rich in flints, the remains of a deposit which
probably once covered a great portion of the country, but has only partially survived subsequent
immersions. In many districts the coarse flint or
chert which originally belonged to the chalk is
found in great profusion. It is called in the country chalcedony (Poole, p. 57).

On the heights which border the western side of
the Dead Sea, this chalk is found in greater abundance and more undisturbed, and contains numerous springs of salt and sulphurous water.

5. Near Jerusalem the mass of the ordinary
limestone is often mingled with large bodies of
dolomite (magnesian limestone), a hardish semi-
crystalline rock, reddish white or brown, with
glistening surface and pearly lustre, often containing pores and small cellular cavities lined with
oxide of iron or minute crystals of bitter spar.
It is not stratified; but it is a question whether it
has not been produced among the ordinary limestone by some subsequent chemical agency. Most
of the caverns near Jerusalem occur in this rock,
though in other parts of the country they are found
in the more friable chalky limestone.d So much
for the upper stratum.

---

a The surface of the Dead Sea is 1,317 feet below
the Mediterranean, and its depth 1,308 feet.

• The table of altitudes (vol. ii. p. 127, Amer. ed.)
makes the figures somewhat different.   H.

b As at the twin hills of el-Jib, the ancient Gibeon,
below Neby Samwil.

c As on the road between the upper and lower
Brit-ur about five miles from el-Jib.

d See the description of the caverns of Beit Jibrin

6. The lower stratum is in two divisions or series of beds — the upper, dusky in color, contorted and cavernous like that just described, but more ferruginous — the lower one dark gray, compact and solid, and characterized by abundant fossils of *cidaris*, an extinct echinus, the spines of which are the well-known "olives" of the convents. This last-named rock appears to form the substratum of the whole country, east as well as west of the Jordan.

The ravine by which the traveller descends from the summit of the Mount of Olives (2,700 feet above the Mediterranean) to Jericho (900 below it) cuts through the strata already mentioned, and affords an unrivaled opportunity for examining them. The lower formation differs entirely in character from the upper. Instead of smooth, commonplace, swelling outlines, everything here is rugged, pointed, and abrupt. Huge fissures, the work of the earthquakes of ages, cleave the rock in all directions — they are to be found as much as 1,000 feet deep by not more than 30 or 40 feet wide, and with almost vertical [a] sides. One of them, near the ruined khan at which travellers usually halt, presents a most interesting and characteristic section of the strata (Russegger, pp. 247-251, &c.).

7. After the limestone had received the general form which its surface still retains, but at a time far anterior to any historic period, it was pierced and broken by large eruptions of lava pushed up from beneath, which has broken up and overflowed the stratified beds, and now appears in the form of basalt or trap.

8. On the west of Jordan these volcanic rocks have been hitherto found only north of the mountains of Samaria. They are first encountered on the southwestern side of the Plain of Esdraelon (Russ. p. 258): then they are lost sight of till the opposite side of the plain is reached, being probably hidden below the deep rich soil, except a few pebbles here and there on the surface. Beyond this they abound over a district which may be said to be contained between *Delâta* on the north, Tiberias on the east, Tabor on the south, and Turan on the west. There seem to have been two centres of eruption: one, and that the most ancient (And. pp. 129, 134), at or about the *Kurn Hattin* (the traditional Mount of Beatitudes), whence the stream flowed over the declivities of the limestone towards the lake (Russ. pp. 259, 260). This mass of basalt forms the cliffs at the back of Tiberias, and to its disintegration is due the black soil, so extremely productive, of the *Ard el-Hamma* and the Plain of Gennesaret, which lie, the one on the south, the other on the north, of the ridge of *Hattin*. The other — the more recent — was more to the north, in the neighborhood of Safed, where three of the ancient craters still exist, converted into the reservoirs or lakes of *el-Jish, Taiteba*, and *Delâta* (And. pp. 128, 129; Calman, in Kitto's *Phys. Geog.* p. 119).

The basalt of Tiberias is fully described by Dr. Anderson. It is dark iron-gray in tint, cellular, but firm in texture, amygdaloidal, the cells filled with carbonate of lime, olivine and augite, with a specific gravity of 2·6 to 2·9. It is often columnar in its more developed portions, as, for instance, on the cliffs behind the town. Here the junctions of the two formations may be seen; the base of the cliffs being limestone, while the crown and brow are massive basalt (pp. 124, 135, 136).

The lava of *Delâta* and the northern centre differs considerably from that of Tiberias, and is pronounced by Dr. Anderson to be of later date. It is found of various colors, from black-brown to reddish-gray, very porous in texture, and contains much pumice and scoria: polygonal columns are seen at *el-Jish*, where the neighboring cretaceous beds are contorted in an unusual manner (And. pp. 128, 129, 130).

A third variety is found at a spur of the hills of Galilee, projecting into the *Ard el-Hûleh* below Kedes, and referred to by Dr. Anderson as *Tell el-Haiyeh*; but of this rock he gives no description, and declines to assign it any chronological position (p. 134).

9. The volcanic action which in pre-historic times projected this basalt, has left its later traces in the ancient records of the country, and is even still active in the form of earthquakes. Not to speak of passages [b] in the poetical books of the Bible, which can hardly have been suggested except by such awful catastrophes, there is at least one distinct allusion to them, namely, that of Zechariah (xiv. 5) to an earthquake in the reign of Uzziah, which is corroborated by Josephus, who adds that it injured the Temple, and brought down a large mass of rock from the Mount of Olives (*Ant.* ix. 10, § 4).

"Syria and Palestine," says Sir Charles Lyell (*Principles*, 8th ed. p. 340), "abound in volcanic appearances; and very extensive areas have been shaken at different periods, with great destruction of cities and loss of lives. Continued mention is made in history of the ravages committed by earthquakes in Sidon, Tyre, Beyrût, Laodicea, and Antioch." The same author (p. 342) mentions the remarkable fact that "from the 13th to the 17th centuries there was an almost entire cessation of earthquakes in Syria and Judæa; and that, during the interval of quiescence, the Archipelago, together with part of Asia Minor, Southern Italy, and Sicily, suffered greatly from earthquakes and volcanic eruptions." Since they have again begun to be active in Syria, the most remarkable earthquakes have been those which destroyed Aleppo in 1616 and 1822 (for this see Wolff, *Travels*, ch. 9), Antioch in 1737, and Tiberias and Safed in 1887 [c] (Thomson, ch. 19). A list of those which are known to have affected the Holy Land is given by Dr. Pusey in his *Commentary* on Amos iv. 11. See also the Index to Ritter, vol. viii. p. 1953.

The rocks between Jerusalem and Jericho show many an evidence of these convulsions, as we have already remarked. Two earthquakes only are recorded as having affected Jerusalem itself — that in the reign of Uzziah already mentioned, and that at the time of the crucifixion, when "the rocks were rent and the rocky tombs torn open" (Matt. xxvii. 51). Slight [d] shocks are still occasionally felt there

---

and *Deir Dubban* in Rob. ii. 23, 51-53; and Van de Velde, ii. 156.

[a] Similar rents were cleft in the rock of *el-Jish* by the earthquake of 1837 (Calman, in Kitto, *Ph. Geog.* p. 158).

[b] Is. xxiv. 17-20; Amos ix. 6, &c., &c.

[c] Four-fifths of the population of Safed, and one-fourth of that of Tiberias, were killed on this occasion.

[d] Even the tremendous earthquake of May 20, 1202, only did Jerusalem a very slight damage (Abdul-latif, in Kitto, *Phys. Geogr.* p. 148).

(*e. g.* Poole, p. 56), but the general exemption of that city from any injury by earthquakes, except in these two cases, is really remarkable. The ancient Jewish writers were aware of it, and appealed to the fact as a proof of the favor of Jehovah to his chosen city (Ps. xlvi. 1, 2).

10. But in addition to earthquakes, the hot salt and fetid springs which are found at Tiberias, Callirhoë, and other spots along the valley of the Jordan, and round the basins of its lakes,*a* and the rock-salt, nitre, and sulphur of the Dead Sea are all evidences of volcanic or plutonic action. Von Buch, in his letter to Robinson (*Bibl. Res.* i. 525), goes so far as to cite the bitumen of the Dead Sea as a further token of it. The hot springs of Tiberias were observed to flow more copiously, and to increase in temperature, at the time of the earthquake of 1837 (Thomson, ch. 19, 26).

11. In the Jordan Valley the basalt is frequently encountered. Here, as before, it is deposited on the limestone, which forms the substratum of the whole country. It is visible from time to time on the banks and in the bed of the river; but so covered with deposits of tufa, conglomerate, and alluvium, as not to be traceable without difficulty (And. pp. 136–152). On the western side of the lower Jordan and Dead Sea no volcanic formations have been found (And. pp. 81, 133; Russ. pp. 205, 251); nor do they appear on its eastern shore till the *Wady Zurka Main* is approached, and then only in erratic fragments (And. p. 191). At *Wady Hemârah*, north of the last-mentioned stream, the igneous rocks first make their appearance *in situ* near the level of the water (p. 194).

12. It is on the east of the Jordan that the most extensive and remarkable developments of igneous rocks are found. Over a large portion of the surface from Damascus to the latitude of the south of the Dead Sea, and even beyond that, they occur in the greatest abundance all over the surface. The limestone, however, still underlies the whole. These extraordinary formations render this region geologically the most remarkable part of all Syria. In some districts, such as the *Lejah* (the ancient Argob or Trachonitis), the *Sufd* and the *Harrâh*, it presents appearances and characteristics which are perhaps unique on the earth's surface. These regions are yet but very imperfectly known, but travellers are beginning to visit them, and we shall possibly be in possession ere long of the results of further investigation. A portion of them has been recently described in great detail *b* by Mr. Wetzstein, Prussian consul at Damascus. They lie, however, beyond the boundary of the Holy Land

proper, and the reader must therefore be referred for these discoveries to the head of TRACHONITIS.

13. The tertiary and alluvial beds remain to be noticed. These are chiefly remarkable in the neighborhood of the Jordan, as forming the floor of the valley, and as existing along the course, and accumulated at the mouths, of the torrents which deliver their tributary streams into the river, and into the still deeper cauldron of the Dead Sea. They appear to be all of later date than the igneous rocks described, though even this cannot be considered as certain.

14. The floor of the Jordan Valley is described by Dr. Anderson (p. 140) as exhibiting throughout more or less distinctly the traces of two independent *c* terraces. The upper one is much the broader of the two. It extends back to the face of the limestone mountains which form the walls of the valley on east and west. He regards this as older than the river, though of course formed after the removal of the material from between the walls. Its upper and accessible portions consist of a mass of detritus brought down by the ravines of the walls, always chalky, sometimes " an actual chalk; " usually bare of vegetation (And. p. 143), though not uniformly so (Rob. iii. 315).

Below this, varying in depth from 50 to 150 feet, is the second terrace, which reaches to the channel of the Jordan, and, in Dr. Anderson's opinion, has been excavated by the river itself before it had shrunk to its present limits, when it filled the whole space between the eastern and western faces of the upper terrace. The inner side of both upper and lower terraces is furrowed out into conical knolls, by the torrents of the rains descending to the lower level. These cones often attain the magnitude of hills, and are ranged along the edge of the terraces with curious regularity. They display convenient sections, which show sometimes a tertiary limestone or marl, sometimes quaternary deposits of sands, gravels, variegated clays, or unstratified detritus. The lower terrace bears a good deal of vegetation, oleander, agnus castus, etc. The alluvial deposits have in some places been swept entirely away, for Dr. Anderson speaks of crossing the upturned edges of nearly vertical strata of limestone, with neighboring beds contorted in a very violent manner (p. 148). This was a few miles N. of Jericho.

All along the channel of the river are found mounds and low cliffs of conglomerates, and breccias of various ages, and more various composition. Rolled boulders and pebbles of flinty sandstone or chert, which have descended from the upper hills,

---

a It may be convenient to give a list of the hot or brackish springs of Palestine, as far as they can be collected. It will be observed that they are all in or about the Jordan Valley. Beginning at the north : —

Ain Eyûb, and *Ain Tâbighah*, N. E. of Lake of Tiberias · slightly warm, too brackish to be drinkable. (Rob. ii. 405.)

Ain el-Bârideh, on shore of lake, S. of *Mejdel* : 80° Fahr., slightly brackish. (Rob. ii. 396.)

Tiberias : 144° Fahr.; salt, bitter, sulphureous.

Amaieh, in the *Wady Mandhur* : very hot, slightly sulphureous. (Burckhardt, May 6.)

Wady Malih (Salt Valley), in the Ghôr near *Sakût* : 98° Fahr. ; very salt, fetid. (Rob. iii. 308.)

Below *Ain-Feshkah* : fetid and brackish. (Lynch, Apr. 18.)

One day N. of *Ain-Jidy* : 80° Fahr. ; salt. (Poole, p. 67.)

Between *Wady Makras* and *W. Khusheibeh*, S. of *Ain-Jidy* : brackish. (Anderson, p. 177.)

Wady Mukariyat, 45/ E. of *Usdûm* : salt, containing small fish. (Ritter, *Jordan*, p. 736 ; Poole, p. 61.)

Wady el-Ahsy, S. E. end of Dead Sea : hot. (Burckhardt, Aug. 7.)

Wady Beni-Hamed, near Rabba, E. side of Dead Sea. (Ritter, *Syrien*, p. 1223.)

Wady Zerka Main (Callirhoë), E. side of Dead Sea : very hot, very slightly sulphureous. (Seetzen, Jan. 18; Irby, June 8.) [See, respecting these springs, Robinson's *Phys. Geogr. of Palestine*, pp. 250–254. — H.]

b Reisebericht über Hauran und die Trachonen, 1860 ; with map and woodcuts.

c Compare Robinson's diary of his journey across the Jordan near *Sakût* (iii. 313).

are found in the cross ravines; and tufas, both calcareous and siliceous, abound on the terraces (And.
p. 147).

15. Round the margin of the Dead Sea the tertiary beds assume larger and more important proportions than by the course of the river. The
marls, gypsites, and conglomerates continue along
the base of the western cliff as far as the *Wady
Sebbeh*, where they attain their greatest development. South of this they form a sterile waste of
brilliant white marl and bitter salt flakes, ploughed
by the rain torrents from the heights into pinna-
cles and obelisks (p. 180).

At the southeastern corner of the sea, sand-
stones begin to display themselves in great profusion, and extend northward beyond *Wady Zurka
Main* (p. 189). Their full development takes place
at the mouth of the *Wady Mojeb*, where the beds are
from 100 to 400 feet in height. They are deposited
on the limestone, and have been themselves gradually worn through by the waters of the ravine.
There are many varieties, differing in color, composition, and date. Dr. A. enumerates several of
these (pp. 190, 196), and states instances of the red
sandstone having been filled up, after excavation,
by non-conforming beds of yellow sandstone of a
much later date, which in its turn has been hollowed out, the hollows being now occupied by detritus of a stream long since extinct.

Russegger mentions having found a tertiary
breccia overlying the chalk on the south of Carmel,
composed of fragments of chalk and flint, cemented
by lime (p. 257).

16. The rich alluvial soil of the wide plains
which form the maritime portion of the Holy Land,
and also that of Esdraelon, Gennesaret, and other
similar plains, will complete our sketch of the
geology. The former of these districts is a region
of from eight to twelve miles in width, intervening
between the central highlands and the sea. It is
formed of washings from those highlands, brought
down by the heavy rains which fall in the winter
months, and which, though they rarely remain as
permanent streams, yet last long enough to spread
this fertilizing manure over the face of the country.
The soil is a light loamy sand, red in some places,
and deep black in others. The substratum is rarely
seen, but it appears to be the same limestone which
composes the central mountains. The actual coast
is formed of a very recent sandstone full of marine
shells, often those of existing species (Russ. pp.
256, 257), which is disintegrated by the waves and
thrown on the shore as sand,[a] where it forms a
tract of considerable width and height. This sand
in many places stops the outflow of the streams,
and sends them back on to the plain, where they
overflow and form marshes, which with proper
treatment might afford most important assistance
to the fertility of this already fertile district.

17. The Plain of Gennesaret is under similar
conditions, except that its outer edge is bounded by
the lake instead of the ocean. Its superiority in
fertility to the maritime land is probably due to
the abundance of running water which it contains
·ll the year round, and to the rich soil produced
from the decay of the volcanic rocks on the steep
aeights which immediately inclose it.

18. The Plain of Esdraelon lies between two
ranges of highland, with a third (the hills separating it from the Plain of Akka) at its northwest end. It is watered by some of the finest
springs of Palestine, the streams from which traverse it both east and west of the central watershed, and contain water or mud, moisture and
marsh, even during the hottest months of the year.
The soil of this plain is also volcanic, though not
so purely so as that of Gennesaret.

19. Bitumen or asphaltum, called by the Arabs
el hummar (the "slime" of Gen. xi. 3), is only met
with in the Valley of Jordan. At *Hasbeiya*, the
most remote of the sources of the river, it is obtained from pits or wells which are sunk through
a mass of bituminous earth to a depth of about 180
feet (And. pp. 115, 116). It is also found in small
fragments on the shore of the Dead Sea, and occasionally, though rarely, very large masses of it are
discovered floating in the water (Rob. i. 518).
This appears to have been more frequently the case
in ancient times (Joseph. *B. J.* iv. 8, § 4; Diod.
Sic. ii. 48). [SLIME.] The Arabs report that it
proceeds from a source in one of the precipices on
the eastern shore of the Dead Sea (Rob. i. 517)
opposite *Ain-Jidy* (Russ. p. 253); but this is not
corroborated by the observations of Lynch's party,
of Mr. Poole, or of Dr. Robinson, who examined
the eastern shore from the western side with special
reference thereto. It is more probable that the
bituminous limestone in the neighborhood of *Neby
Musa* exists in strata of great thickness, and
that the bitumen escapes from its lower beds into
the Dead Sea, and there accumulates until by
some accident it is detached, and rises to the surface.

20. Sulphur is found on the W. and S. and S. E.
portions of the shore of the Dead Sea (Rob. i. 512).
In many spots the air smells strongly of sulphurous
acid and sulphuretted hydrogen gas (And. p. 176;
Poole, p. 66; Beaufort, ii. 113), a sulphurous crust is
spread over the surface of the beach, and lumps of
sulphur are found in the sea (Rob. i. 512). Poole
(p. 63) speaks of "sulphur hills" on the peninsula
at the S. E. end of the sea (see And. p. 187).

Nitre is rare. Mr. Poole did not discover any,
though he made special search for it. Irby and
Mangles, Seetzen and Robinson, however, mention
having seen it (Rob. i. 513).

Rock-salt abounds in large masses. The salt
mound of *Kashm Usdum* at the southern end of
the Dead Sea is an enormous pile, 5 miles long by
2½ broad, and some hundred feet in height (And.
p. 181). Its inferior portion consists entirely of
rock-salt, and the upper part of sulphate of lime
and salt, often with a large admixture of alumina.

                                      G.

THE BOTANY. — The Botany of Syria and Palestine differs but little from that of Asia Minor,
which is one of the most rich and varied on the
globe. What differences it presents are due to a
slight admixture of Persian forms on the eastern
frontier, of Arabian and Egyptian on the southern,
and of Arabian and Indian tropical plants in the
low torrid depression of the Jordan and Dead Sea.
These latter, which number perhaps a hundred
different kinds, are anomalous features in the other-

---

[a] The statement in the text is from Thomson (*Land
and Book*, ch. 33). But the writer has learned that in
the opinion of Capt. Mansell, R. N. (than whom no one
has had more opportunity of judging), the sand of the
whole coast of Syria has been brought up from Egypt
by the S. S. W. wind. This is also stated by Josephus
(*Ant.* xv. 9, § 6).

wise Levantine landscape of Syria. On the other hand, Palestine forms the southern and eastern limit of the Asia-Minor flora, and contains a multitude of trees, shrubs, and herbs that advance no further south and east. Of these the pine, oak, elder, bramble, dog-rose, and hawthorn are conspicuous examples; their southern migration being checked by the drought and heat of the regions beyond the hilly country of Judæa. Owing, however, to the geographical position and the mountainous character of Asia Minor and Syria, the main features of their flora are essentially Mediterranean-European, and not Asiatic. A vast proportion of the commoner arboreous and frutescent plants are identical with those of Spain, Algeria, Italy, and Greece; and as they belong to the same genera as do British, Germanic, and Scandinavian plants, there are ample means of instituting such a comparison between the Syrian flora and that familiar to us as any intelligent non-botanical observer can follow and understand.

As elsewhere throughout the Mediterranean regions, Syria and Palestine were evidently once thickly covered with forests, which on the lower hills and plains have been either entirely removed, or else reduced to the condition of brushwood and copse; but which still abound on the mountains, and along certain parts of the sea-coast. The low grounds, plains, and rocky hills are carpeted with herbaceous plants, that appear in rapid succession from before Christmas till June, when they disappear; and the brown alluvial or white calcareous soil, being then exposed to the scorching rays of the sun, gives an aspect of forbidding sterility to the most productive regions. Lastly, the lofty regions of the mountains are stony, dry, swardless, and swampless, with few alpine or arctic plants, mosses, lichens, or ferns; thus presenting a most unfavorable contrast to the Swiss, Scandinavian, and British mountain floras at analogous elevations.

To a traveller from England, it is difficult to say whether the familiar or the foreign forms predominate. Of trees he recognizes the oak, pine, walnut, maple, juniper, alder, poplar, willow, ash, dwarf elder, plane, ivy, arbutus, rhamnus, almond, plum, pear, and hawthorn, all elements of his own forest scenery and plantations; but misses the beech, chestnut, lime, holly, birch, larch, and spruce; while he sees for the first time such southern forms as Pride of India (*Melia*), carob, sycamore, fig, jujube, pistachio, styrax, olive, phyllyræa, vitex, elæagnus, celtis, many new kinds of oak, the papyrus, castor oil, and various tall tropical grasses.

Of cultivated English fruits he sees the vine, apple, pear, apricot, quince, plum, mulberry, and fig; but misses the gooseberry, raspberry, strawberry, currant, cherry, and other northern kinds, which are as it were replaced by such southern and sub-tropical fruits as the date, pomegranate, cordia myxa (*sebastan* of the Arabs), orange, shaddock, lime, banana, almond, prickly pear, and pistachio-nut.

Amongst cereals and vegetables the English traveller finds wheat, barley, peas, potatoes, many varieties of cabbage, carrots, lettuces, endive, and mustard; and misses oats, rye, and the extensive fields of turnip, beet, mangold-wurzel, and fodder grasses, with which he is familiar in England. On the other hand, he sees for the first time the cotton, millet, rice, sorghum, sesamum, sugar-cane, maize, egg-apple, okra, or *Abelmoschus esculentus*, *Cor-*

chorus olitorius, various beans and lentils, as *Lablab vulgaris, Phaseolus mungos, and Cicer arietinum;* melons, gourds, pumpkins, cumin, coriander, fennel, anise, sweet potato, tobacco, yam, colocasia, and other sub-tropical and tropical field and garden crops.

The flora of Syria, so far as it is known, may be roughly classed under three principal Botanical regions, corresponding with the physical characters of the country. These are (1.), the western or seaboard half of Syria and Palestine, including the lower valleys of the Lebanon and Anti-Lebanon, the plain of Cœle-Syria, Galilee, Samaria, and Judæa. (2.) The desert or eastern half, which includes the east flanks of the Anti-Lebanon, the plain of Damascus, the Jordan and Dead Sea Valley. (3.) The middle and upper mountain regions of Mount Casius, and of Lebanon above 3,400 feet, and of the Anti-Lebanon above 4,000 feet. Nothing whatever is known botanically of the regions to the eastward, namely, the Hauran, Lejah, Gilead, Ammon. and Moab; countries extending eastward into Mesopotamia, the flora of which is Persian, and south to Idumea, where the purely Arabian flora begins.

These Botanical regions present no definite boundary line. A vast number of plants, and especially of herbs, are common to all except the loftiest parts of Lebanon and the driest spots of the eastern district, and in no latitude is there a sharp line of demarcation between them. But though the change is gradual from the dry and semi-tropical eastern flora to the moister and cooler western, or from the latter to the cold temperate one of the Lebanon, there is a great and decided difference between the floras of three such localities as the Lebanon at 5,000 feet, Jerusalem, and Jericho; or between the tops of Lel anon, of Carmel, and of any of the hills bounding the Jordan; for in the first locality we are most strongly reminded of northern Europe, in the second of Spain, and in the third of Western India or Persia.

I. *Western Syria and Palestine.* — The flora throughout this district is made up of such a multitude of different families and genera of plants, that it is not easy to characterize it by the mention of a few. Amongst trees, oaks are by far the most prevalent, and are the only ones that form continuous woods, except the *Pinus maritima* and *P. Halepensis* (Aleppo Pine); the former of which extends in forests here and there along the shore, and the latter crests the spurs of the Lebanon, Carmel, and a few other ranges as far south as Hebron. The most prevalent oak is the *Quercus pseudo-coccifera,* a plant scarcely different from the common *Q. coccifera* of the western Mediterranean, and which it strongly resembles in form, habit, and evergreen foliage. It is called holly by many travellers, and *Quercus ilex* by others, both very different trees. *Q. pseudo-coccifera* is perhaps the commonest plant in all Syria and Palestine, covering as a low dense bush many square miles of hilly country everywhere, but rarely or never growing in the plains. It seldom becomes a large tree, except in the valleys of the Lebanon, or where, as in the case of the famous oak of Mamre, it is allowed to attain its full size. It ascends about 5,000 feet on the mountains, but does not descend into the middle and lower valley of the Jordan; nor is it seen on the east slopes of the Anti-Lebanon, and scarcely to the eastward of Jerusalem; it may indeed have been removed by man from these regions, when the effect of its removal would be to dry the soil and climate, and prevent its reëstablishment. Even around Jerusalem it is rare, though its roots are said to exist in abundance in the soil. The only other oaks that are common are the *Q. infectoria* (a gall oak), and *Q. ægilops.* The *Q. infectoria* is a small deciduous-leaved tree, found here and there in Galilee, Samaria, and on the Lebanon; it is very conspicuous from the numbers of bright chestnut colored shining viscid galls which it bears, and which are sometimes exported to England, but which are a poor substitute for the true Aleppo galls. *Q. ægilops* again is the Valonia oak: a low, very stout-trunked sturdy tree, common in Galilee, and especially on Tabor and Carmel, where it grows in scattered groups, giving a park-like appearance to the landscape. It bears acorns of a very large size, whose cups, which are covered with long recurved spines, are exported to Europe as Valonia, and are used, like the galls of *Q. infectoria,* in the operation of dyeing. This, I am inclined to believe, is the oak of Bashan, both on account of its sturdy habit and thick trunk, and also because a fine piece of the wood of this tree was sent from Bashan to the Kew Museum by Mr. Cyril Graham. The other oaks of Syria are chiefly confined to the mountains, and will be noticed in their proper place.

The trees of the genus *Pistacia* rank next in abundance to the oak, — and of these there are three species in Syria, two wild and most abundant, but the third, *P. vera,* which yields the well-known pistachio-nut, very rare, and chiefly seen in cultivation about Aleppo, but also in Beyrût and near Jerusalem. The wild species are the *P. lentiscus* and *P. terebinthus,* both very common: the *P. lentiscus* rarely exceeds the size of a low bush, which is conspicuous for its dark evergreen leaves and numberless small red berries; the other grows larger, but seldom forms a fair-sized tree.

The Carob or Locust-tree, *Ceratonia siliqua,* ranks perhaps next in abundance to the foregoing trees. It never grows in clumps or forms woods, but appears as an isolated, rounded or oblong, very dense-foliaged tree, branching from near the base, of a bright lucid green hue, affording the best shade. Its singular flowers are produced from its thick branches in autumn, and are succeeded by the large pendulous pods, called St. John's Bread, and extensively exported from the Levant to England for feeding cattle. [HUSKS.]

The oriental Plane is far from uncommon, and though generally cultivated, it is to all appearance wild in the valleys of the Lebanon and Anti-Lebanon. The great plane of Damascus is a well-known object to travellers; the girth of its trunk was nearly 40 feet, but it is now a mere wreck.

The Sycamore-fig is common in the neighborhood of towns, and attains a large size; its wood is much used, especially in Egypt, where the mummy-cases were formerly made of it. Poplars, especially the aspen and white poplar, are extremely common by streams: the latter is generally trimmed for firewood, so as to resemble the Lombardy poplar. The Walnut is more common in Syria than in Palestine, and in both countries is generally confined to gardens and orchards. Of large native shrubs or small trees almost universally spread over this district, are *Arbutus Andrachne,* which is common in the hilly country from Hebron northward; *Cratægus Aronia,* which grows equally in dry rocky

exposures, as on the Mount of Olives, and in cool mountain valleys; it yields a large yellow or red haw that is abundantly sold in the markets. Cypresses are common about villages, and especially near all religious establishments, often attaining a considerable size, but I am not aware of their being indigenous to Syria. *Zizyphus Spina-Christi,* Christ's Thorn — often called jujube — the *Nubk* of the Arabs, is most common on dry open plains, as that of Jericho, where it is either a scrambling briar, a standard shrub, or rarely even a middling-sized tree with pendulous branches: it is familiar to the traveller from its sharp hooks, white undersides to the three-nerved leaves, and globular yellow sweetish fruit with a large woody stone. The *Paliurus aculeatus,* also called Christ's Thorn, resembles it a good deal, but is much less common; it abounds in the Anti-Lebanon, where it is used for hedges, and may be recognized by its curved prickles and curious dry fruit, with a broad flat wing at the top. *Styrax officinalis,* which used to yield the famous storax, abounds in all parts of the country where hilly; sometimes, as on the east end of Carmel and on Tabor, becoming a very large bush branching from the ground, but never assuming the form of a tree; it may be known by its small downy leaves, white flowers like orange blossoms, and round yellow fruit, pendulous from slender stalks, like cherries. The flesh of the berry, which is quite uneatable, is of a semi-transparent hue, and contains one or more large, chestnut-colored seeds. *Tamarisk* is common, but seldom attains a large size, and has nothing to recommend it to notice. *Oleander* claims a separate notice, from its great beauty and abundance; lining the banks of the streams and lakes in gravelly places, and bearing a profusion of blossoms. Other still smaller but familiar shrubs are *Phyllyrea, Rhamnus alaternus,* and others of that genus. *Rhus coriaria,* several leguminous shrubs, as *Anagyris fœtida, Calycotome* and *Genista; Cotoneaster,* the common bramble, dog-rose, and hawthorn, *Elæagnus,* wild olive, *Lycium Europæum, Vitex agnus-castus,* sweet-bay (*Laurus nobilis*), *Ephedra, Clematis,* Gum-Cistus, and the caper-plant: these nearly complete the list of the commoner shrubs and trees of the western district, which attain a height of four feet or more, and are almost universally met with, especially in the hilly country.

Of planted trees and large shrubs, the first in importance is the Vine, which is most abundantly cultivated all over the country, and produces, as in the time of the Canaanites, enormous bunches of grapes. This is especially the case in the southern districts; those of Eshcol being still particularly famous. Stephen Schultz states that at a village near Ptolemais (Acre) he supped under a large vine, the stem of which measured a foot and a half in diameter, its height being 30 feet; and that the whole plant, supported on a trellis, covered an area 50 feet either way. The bunches of grapes weighed 10–12 lbs., and the berries were like small plums. Mariti relates that no vines can vie for produce with those of Judæa, of which a bunch cannot be carried far without destroying the fruit; and we have ourselves heard that the bunches produced near Hebron are sometimes so long that, when attached to a stick which is supported on the shoulders of two men, the tip of the bunch trails on the ground.

Next to the vine, or even in some respects its superior in importance, ranks the Olive, which nowhere grows in greater luxuriance and abundance than in Palestine, where the olive orchards form a prominent feature throughout the landscape, and have done so from time immemorial. The olive-tree is in no respects a handsome or picturesque object; its bark is gray and rugged; its foliage is in color an ashy, or at best a dusky green, and affords little shade; its wood is useless as timber, its flowers are inconspicuous, and its fruit uninviting to the eye or palate; so that, even where most abundant and productive, the olive scarcely relieves the aspect of the dry soil, and deceives the superficial observer as to the fertility of Palestine. Indeed it is mainly owing to these peculiarities of the olive-tree, and to the deciduous character of the foliage of the fig and vine, that the impression is so prevalent amongst northern travellers, that the Holy Land is in point of productiveness not what it was in former times; for to the native of northern Europe especially, the idea of fertility is inseparable from that of verdure. The article OLIVE must be referred to for details of this tree, which is perhaps most skillfully and carefully cultivated in the neighborhood of Hebron, where for many miles the roads run between stone walls inclosing magnificent olive orchards, apparently tended with as much neatness, care, and skill as the best fruit gardens in England. The terraced olive-yards around Sebastieh must also strike the most casual observer, as admirable specimens of careful cultivation.

The Fig forms another most important crop in Syria and Palestine, and one which is apparently greatly increasing in extent. As with the olive and mulberry, the fig-trees, where best cultivated, are symmetrically planted in fields, whose soil is freed from stones, and kept as scrupulously clean of weeds as it can be in a semi-tropical climate. As is well known, the fig bears two or three crops in the year: Josephus says that it bears for ten months out of the twelve. The early figs, which ripen about June, are reckoned especially good. The summer figs again ripen in August, and a third crop appears still later when the leaves are shed; these are occasionally gathered as late as January. The figs are dried by the natives, and are chiefly purchased by the Arabs of the eastern deserts. The sycamore-fig, previously noticed, has much smaller and very inferior fruit.

The quince, apple,[a] almond, walnut, peach, and apricot, are all most abundant field or orchard crops, often planted in lines, rows, or quincunx order, with the olive, mulberry, or fig: but they are by no means so abundant as these latter. The pomegranate grows everywhere as a bush: but, like the orange, *Elæagnus*, and other less common plants, is more often seen in gardens than in fields. The fruit ripens in August, and is kept throughout the winter. Three kinds are cultivated — the acid, sweet, and insipid — and all are used in preparing sherbets: while the bark and fruit rind of all are used for dyeing and as medicine, owing to their astringent properties.

The Banana is only found near the Mediterranean; it ripens its fruit as far north as Beyrût, and occasionally even at Tripoli, but more constantly at Sidon and Jaffa; only one kind is commonly cultivated, but it is excellent. Dates are not frequent: they are most common at Caiffa and

Jaffa, where the fruit ripens, but there are now no groves of this tree anywhere but in Southern Palestine, such as once existed in the valley of the Jordan, near the assumed site of Jericho. Of that well-known grove no tree is standing; one log of date-palm, now lying in a stream near the locality, is perhaps the last remains of that ancient race, though that they were once abundant in the immediate neighborhood of the Dead Sea is obvious from the remark of Mr. Poole, that some part of the shore of that sea is strewn with their trunks. [See p. 2299, note *b*.] Wild dwarf dates, rarely producing fruit, grow by the shores of the Lake of Tiberias and near Caiffa; but whether they are truly indigenous. date-palms, or *crab-dates* produced from seedlings of the cultivated form, is not known.

The *Opuntia*, or Prickly Pear, is most abundant throughout Syria, and though a native of the New World, has here, as elsewhere throughout the dry, hot regions of the eastern hemisphere, established its claim to be regarded as a permanent and rapidly increasing denizen. It is in general use for bedding, and its well-known fruit is extensively eaten by all classes. I am not aware that the cochineal insect has ever been introduced into Syria, where there can, however, be little doubt but that it might be successfully cultivated.

Of dye-stuffs the *Carthamus* (Safflower) and Indigo are both cultivated; and of textiles, Flax, Hemp, and Cotton.

The Carob, or St. John's Bread (*Ceratonia siliqua*), has already been mentioned amongst the conspicuous trees: the sweetish pulp of the pods is used for sherbets, and abundantly eaten; the pods are used for cattle-feeding, and the leaves and bark for tanning.

The Cistus or Rock-rose, two or three species of which are abundant throughout the hilly districts of Palestine, is the shrub from which in former times gum-labdanum was collected in the islands of Candia and Cyprus.

With regard to the rich and varied herbaceous vegetation of West Syria and Palestine, it is difficult to afford any idea of its nature to the English non-botanical reader, except by comparing it with the British; which I shall first do, and then detail its most prominent botanical features.

The plants contained in this botanical region probably number not less than 2,000 or 2,500, of which perhaps 500 are British wild flowers; amongst the most conspicuous of these British ones are the *Ranunculus aquatilis, arvensis*, and *Ficaria*; the yellow water-lily, *Papaver Rhœas* and *hybridum*, and several Fumitories; fully 20 cruciferous plants, including *Draba verna*, water-cress, *Turritis glabra, Sisymbrium irio, Capsella bursa-pastoris, Cakile maritima, Lepidium draba*, charlock, mustard (often growing 8 to 9 feet high), two mignonnettes (*Reseda alba* and *lutea*), *Silene inflata*, various species of *Cerastium, Spergula, Stellaria*, and *Arenaria*, mallows, *Geranium molle, rotundifolium, lucidum, dissectum*, and *Robertianum, Erodium moschatum*, and *cicutarium*. Also many species of *Leguminosæ*, especially of *Medicago, Trifolium, Melilotus, Lotus, Ononis, Ervum, Vicia*, and *Lathyrus*. Of *Rosaceæ* the common bramble and dog-rose. *Lythrum Salicaria, Epilobium hirsutum, Bryonia dioica, Saxifraga tridactylites, Galium verum, Rubia peregrina, Asperula arvensis*. Various *Umbelliferæ* and *Compositæ*, including the daisy, wormwood, groundsel, dandelion, chicory, sowthistle, and many others. Blue and white pimpernel, *Cyclamen Europæum, Samolus Valerandi, Erica vagans,* borage, *Veronica anagallis, Beccabunga, agrestis, triphyllos,* and *Chamædrys, Lathræa squamaria,* vervain, *Lamium amplexicaule,* mint, horehound, *Prunella, Statice limonium,* many *Chenopodiaceæ, Polygonum,* and *Rumex,* Pellitory, *Mercurialis, Euphorbias,* nettles, box, elm, several willows and poplars, common duck-weed and pond weed, *Orchis morio, Crocus aureus,* butcher's-broom, black bryony, autumnal squill, and many rushes, sedges, and grasses.

The most abundant natural families of plants in West Syria and Palestine are: (1) *Leguminosæ,* (2) *Compositæ,* (3) *Labiatæ,* (4) *Cruciferæ;* after which come (5) *Umbelliferæ,* (6) *Caryophylleæ,* (7) *Boragineæ,* (8) *Scrophularineæ,* (9) *Gramineæ,* and (10) *Liliaceæ.*

(1.) *Leguminosæ* abound in all situations, especially the genera *Trifolium, Trigonella, Medicago, Lotus, Vicia,* and *Orobus,* in the richer soils, and *Astragalus* in enormous profusion in the drier and more barren districts. The latter genus is indeed the largest in the whole country, upwards of fifty species belonging to it being enumerated, either as confined to Syria, or common to it and the neighboring countries. Amongst them are the gum-bearing *Astragali,* which are, however, almost confined to the upper mountain regions. Of the shrubby *Leguminosæ* there are a few species of *Genista, Cytisus, Ononis, Retama, Anagyris, Calycotome, Coronilla,* and *Acacia.* One species, the *Ceratonia,* is arboreous.

(2.) *Compositæ.* — No family of plants more strikes the observer than the *Compositæ,* from the vast abundance of thistles and centauries, and other spring-plants of the same tribe, which swarm alike over the richest plains and most stony hills, often towering high above all other herbaceous vegetation. By the unobservant traveller these are often supposed to indicate sterility of soil, instead of the contrary, which they for the most part really do, for they are nowhere so tall, rank, or luxuriant as on the most productive soils. It is beyond the limits of this article to detail the botanical peculiarities of this vegetation, and we can only mention the genera *Centaurea, Echinops, Onopordum, Cirsium, Cynara,* and *Carduus,* as being eminently conspicuous for their numbers or size. The tribe *Cichoreæ* are scarcely less numerous, whilst those of *Gnaphaliæ, Asteroideæ,* and *Senecionideæ,* so common in more northern latitudes, are here comparatively rare.

(3.) *Labiatæ* form a prominent feature everywhere, and one all the more obtrusive from the fragrance of many of the genera. Thus the lovely hills of Galilee and Samaria are inseparably linked in the memory with the odoriferous herbage of marjoram, thymes, lavenders, calaminths, sages, and teucriums; of all which there are many species, as also there are of *Sideritis, Phlomis, Stachys, Ballota, Nepeta,* and *Mentha.*

(4.) Of *Cruciferæ* there is little to remark: its species are generally weed-like, and present no marked feature in the landscape. Among the most noticeable are the gigantic mustard, previously mentioned, which does not differ from the common mustard, *Sinapis nigra,* save in size, and the *Anastatica Hierochuntica,* or rose of Jericho, an Egyptian and Arabian plant, which is said to grow in the Jordan and Dead Sea valleys.

(5.) *Umbelliferæ* present little to remark on save the abundance of fennels and *Bupleurums:* the order is exceedingly numerous both in species and individuals, which often form a large proportion of the tall rank herbage at the edges of copsewood and in damp hollows. The gray and spiny *Eryngium,* so abundant on all the arid hills, belongs to this order.

(6.) *Caryophylleæ* also are not a very conspicuous order, though so numerous that the abundance of pinks, *Silene* and *Saponaria,* is a marked feature to the eye of the botanist.

(7.) The *Boragineæ* are for the most part annual weeds, but some notable exceptions are found in the *Echiums, Anchusas,* and *Onosmas,* which are among the most beautiful plants of the country.

(8.) Of *Scrophularineæ* the principal genera are *Scrophularia, Veronica, Linaria,* and *Verbascum* (Mulleins): the latter is by far the most abundant, and many of the species are quite gigantic.

(9.) *Grasses,* though very numerous in species, seldom afford a sward as in moister and colder regions; the pasture of England having for its oriental equivalent the herbs and herbaceous tips of the low shrubby plants which cover the country, and on which all herbivorous animals love to browse. The *Arundo Donax, Saccharum Ægyptiacum,* and *Erianthus Ravennæ,* are all conspicuous for their gigantic size and silky plumes of flowers of singular grace and beauty.

(10.) *Liliaceæ.* — The variety and beauty of this order in Syria is perhaps nowhere exceeded, and especially of the bulb-bearing genera, as tulips, fritillaries, squills, gageas, etc. The *Urginea scilla* (medicinal squill), abounds everywhere, throwing up a tall stalk beset with white flowers at its upper half; and the little purple autumnal squill is one of the commonest plants in the country, springing up in October and November in the most arid situations imaginable.

Of other natural orders worthy of notice, for one reason or another, are *Violaceæ,* for the paucity of its species; *Geraniaceæ,* which are very numerous and beautiful; *Rutaceæ,* which are common, and very strong-scented when bruised. *Rosaceæ* are not so abundant as in more northern climates, but are represented by one remarkable plant, *Poterium spinosum,* which covers whole tracts of arid, hilly country, much as the ling does in Britain. *Crassulaceæ* and *Saxifrageæ* are also not so plentiful as in cooler regions. *Dipsaceæ* are very abundant, especially the genera *Knautia, Scabiosa, Cephalaria,* and *Pterocephalus.* *Campanulaceæ* are common, and *Lobeliaceæ* rare. *Primulaceæ* and *Ericeæ* are both rare, though one or two species are not uncommon. There are very few *Gentianeæ,* but many *Convolvuli.* Of *Solaneæ, Mandragora, Solanum,* and *Hyoscyamus* are very common, also *Physalis, Capsicum,* and *Lycopersicum,* all probably escaped from cultivation. *Plumbagineæ* contain a good many *Statices,* and the blue-flowered *Plumbago Europæa* is a very common weed. *Chenopodiaceæ* are very numerous, especially the weedy *Atriplices* and *Chenopodia* and some shrubby *Salsolas.* *Polygona* are very common indeed, especially the smaller species of *Polygonum* itself. *Aristolochiæs* present several species. *Euphorbiaceæ.* The herbaceous genus *Euphorbia* is vastly abundant, especially in fields: upwards of fifty Syrian species are known. *Crozophora, Andrachne,* and *Ricinus,* all southern types, are also common

Urticeæ present the common European nettles, *Mercurialis*, and Pellitory. *Moreæ*, the common and sycamore figs, and the black and white mulberries. *Aroideæ* are very common, and many of them are handsome, having deep-purple lurid spathes, which rise out of the ground before the leaves.

Of *Balanophoræ*, the curious *Cynomorium coccineum*, or "Fungus Melitensis," used as a styptic during the Crusades by the knights of Malta, is found in the valleys of Lebanon near the sea. *Naiadeæ*, as in other dry countries, are scarce. *Orchideæ* contain about thirty to forty kinds, chiefly South European species of *Orchis*, *Ophrys*, *Spiranthes*, and *Serapias*.

Amaryllideæ present *Pancratium*, *Sternbergia*, *Ixiolirion*, and *Narcissus*. *Irideæ* has many species of *Iris* and *Crocus*, besides *Moræa*, *Gladiolus*, *Trichonema*, and *Romulea*. *Dioscoreæ*, *Tamus communis*. *Smilaceæ*, several *Asparagi*, *Smilax*, and *Ruscus aculeatus*. *Melanthaceæ* contain many *Colchicums*, besides *Merendera* and *Erythrostictus*. *Junceæ* contain none but the commoner British rushes and luzulas. *Cyperaceæ* are remarkably poor in species; the genus *Carex*, so abundant in Europe, is especially rare, not half a dozen species being enumerated.

Ferns are extremely scarce, owing to the dryness of the climate, and most of the species belong to the Lebanon flora. The common lowland ones are *Adiantum capillus-veneris*, *Cheilanthes fragrans*, *Gymnogramma leptophylla*, *Ceterach officinarum*, *Pteris lanceolata*, and *Asplenium Adiantum-nigrum*. *Selaginella denticulata* is also found.

One of the most memorable plants of this region, and indeed in the whole world, is the celebrated Papyrus of the ancients (*Papyrus antiquorum*), which is said once to have grown on the banks of the lower Nile, but which is nowhere found now in Africa north of the tropics. The only other known habitat beside Syria and tropical Africa is one spot in the island of Sicily. The papyrus is a noble plant, forming tufts of tall stout 3-angled green smooth stems, 6 to 10 feet high, each surmounted by a mop of pendulous threads: it abounds in some marshes by the Lake of Tiberias, and is also said to grow near Caiffa and elsewhere in Syria. It is certainly the most remarkable plant in the country.

Of other cryptogamic plants little is known. Mosses, lichens, and *Hepaticæ* are not generally common, though doubtless many species are to be found in the winter and spring months. The marine *Algæ* are supposed to be the same as in the rest of the Mediterranean, and of *Fungi* we have no knowledge at all.

Cucurbitaceæ, though not included under any of the above heads, are a very frequent order in Syria. Besides the immense crops of melons, gourds, and pumpkins, the colocynth apple, which yields the famous drug, is common in some parts, while even more so is the squirting cucumber (*Ecbalium elaterium*).

Of plants that contribute largely to that showy character for which the herbage of Palestine is famous, may be mentioned *Adonis*, *Ranunculus Asiaticus*, and others; *Anemone coronaria*, poppies, *Glaucium*, *Matthiola*, *Malcolmia*, *Alyssum*, *Biscutella*, *Helianthemum*, *Cistus*, the caper plant, many pinks, *Silene*, *Saponaria*, and *Gypsophila*; various *Phloxes*, mallows, *Lavatera*, *Hypericum*; many geraniums, *Erodiums*, and *Leguminosæ*, and *Labiatæ* far too numerous to individualize; *Sca-*

biosa, *Cephalaria*, chrysanthemums, *Pyrethrum*, *Inulas*, *Achilleas*, *Calendulas*, *Centaureas*, *Tragopogons*, *Scorzoneras*, and *Crepis*; many noble *Campanulas*, cyclamens, *Convolvuli*, *Anchusas*, *Onosmas*, and *Echiums*, *Acanthus*, *Verbascums* (most conspicuously), *Veronicas*, *Celsias*, *Hyoscyamus*; many *Arums* in autumn, orchis and *Ophrys* in spring; *Narcissus*, *Tazetta*, irises, *Pancratiums*, *Sternbergia*, *Gladiolus*; many beautiful crocuses and colchicums, squills, *Tulipa oculus-solis*, *Gageas*, fritillaries, *Alliums*, Star of Bethlehem, *Muscaris*, white lily, *Hyacinthus orientalis*, *Bellevalias*, and *Asphodeli*.

With such gay and delicate flowers as these, in numberless combinations, the ground is almost carpeted during spring and early summer; and as in similar hot and dry, but still temperate climates, as the Cape of Good Hope and Australia, they often color the whole landscape, from their lavish abundance.

II. *Botany of Eastern Syria and Palestine.* — Little or nothing being known of the flora of the range of mountains east of the Jordan and Syrian desert, we must confine our notice to the valley of the Jordan, that of the Dead Sea, and the country about Damascus.

Nowhere can a better locality be found for showing the contrast between the vegetation of the eastern and western districts of Syria than in the neighborhood of Jerusalem. To the west and south of that city the valleys are full of the dwarf oak, two kinds of *Pistacia*, besides *Smilax*, *Arbutus*, rose, Aleppo Pine, *Rhamnus*, *Phyllyræa*, bramble, and *Cratægus Aronia*. Of these the last alone is found on the Mount of Olives, beyond which, eastward to the Dead Sea, not one of these plants appears, nor are they replaced by any analogous ones. For the first few miles the olive groves continue, and here and there a carob and lentisk or sycamore recurs, but beyond Bethany these are scarcely seen. Naked rocks, or white chalky rounded hills, with bare open valleys, succeed, wholly destitute of copse, and sprinkled with sterile-looking shrubs of *Salsolas*, *Capparideæ*, *Zygophyllum*, rues, *Fagonia*, *Polygonum*, *Zizyphus*, tamarisks, alhagi, and *Artemisia*. Herbaceous plants are still abundant, but do not form the continuous sward that they do in Judæa. Amongst these, *Boragineæ*, *Alsineæ*, *Fagonia*, *Polygonum*, *Crozophora*, *Euphorbias*, and *Leguminosæ* are the most frequent.

On descending 1,000 feet below the level of the sea to the valley of the Jordan, the sub-tropical and desert vegetation of Arabia and West Asia is encountered in full force. Many plants wholly foreign to the western district suddenly appear, and the flora is that of the whole dry country as far east as the Panjab. The commonest plant is the *Zizyphus Spina-Christi*, or *nubk* of the Arabs, forming bushes or small trees. Scarcely less abundant, and as large, is the *Balanites Ægyptiaca*, whose fruit yields the oil called *zuk* by the Arabs, which is reputed to possess healing properties, and which may possibly be alluded to as Balm of Gilead. Tamarisks are most abundant, together with *Rhus* (*Syriaca?*), conspicuous for the bright green of its few small leaves, and its exact resemblance in foliage, bark, and habit to the true Balm of Gilead, the *Amyris Gileadensis* of Arabia. Other most abundant shrubs are *Ochradenus baccatus*, a tall, branching, almost leafless plant, with small white berries, and the twiggy, leafless broom called *Retama*. *Acacia Farnesiana* is very abundant, and celebrated for the delicious fragrance of its yellow flowers. It is chiefly upon it that the superb mistletoe, *Loranthus Acuciα*, grows, whose scarlet flowers are brilliant ornaments to the desert during winter, giving the appearance of flame to the bushes. *Capparis spinosa*, the common caper-plant, flourishes everywhere in the Jordan Valley, forming clumps in the very arid rocky bottoms, which are conspicuous for their pale-blue hue, when seen from a distance. *Alhagi Maurorum* is extremely common; as is the prickly *Solanum Sodomæum*, with purple flowers and globular yellow fruits, commonly known as the Dead Sea apple.

On the banks of the Jordan itself the arboreous and shrubby vegetation chiefly consists of *Populus Euphratica* (a plant found all over Central Asia, but not known west of the Jordan), tamarisk, *Osyris alba*, *Periploca*, *Acacia vera*, *Prosopis Stephaniana*, *Arundo Donax*, *Lycium*, and *Capparis spinosa*. As the ground becomes saline, *Atriplex Halimus* and large *Statices* (sea-pinks) appear in vast abundance, with very many succulent shrubby *Salsolas*, *Salicornias*, *Suædas*, and other allied plants to the number of at least a dozen, many of which are typical of the salt depressions of the Caspian and Central Asia.

Other very tropical plants of this region are *Zygophyllum coccineum*, *Boerhavia*, *Indigofera*; several *Astragali*, *Cassias*, *Gymnocarpum*, and *Nitraria*. At the same time thoroughly European forms are common, especially in wet places; as dock, mint, *Veronica anagallis*, and *Sium*. One remote and little-visited spot in this region is particularly celebrated for the tropical character of its vegetation. This is the small valley of En-gedi (*Ain-Jidy*), which is on the west shore of the Dead Sea, and where alone, it is said, the following tropical plants grow: *Sidi mutica* and *Asiatica*, *Calotropis procera* (whose bladdery fruits, full of the silky coma of the seeds, have even been assumed to be the Apple of Sodom), *Amberboa*, *Batatas littoralis*, *Aerva Javanica*, *Pluchea Dioscoridis*.

It is here that the *Salvadora Persica*, supposed by some to be the mustard-tree of Scripture, grows: it is a small tree, found as far south as Abyssinia or Aden, and eastward to the peninsula of India, but is unknown west or north of the Dead Sea. The late Dr. Royle — unaware, no doubt, how scarce and local it was, and arguing from the pungent taste of its bark, which is used as horse-radish in India — supposed that this tree was that alluded to in the parable of the mustard-tree; but not only is the pungent nature of the bark not generally known to the natives of Syria, but the plant itself is so scarce, local, and little known, that Jesus Christ could never have made it the subject of a parable that would reach the understanding of his hearers.

The shores immediately around the Dead Sea present abundance of vegetation, though almost wholly of a saline character. *Juncus maritimus* is very common in large clumps, and a yellow-flowered groundsel-like plant, *Inula crithmoides* (also common on the rocky shores of Tyre, Sidon, etc.). *Spergularia maritima*, *Atriplex Halimus*, *Balanites Ægyptiaca*, several shrubby *Suædas* and *Salicornias*, *Tamarix*, and a prickly-leaved grass (*Festuca*), all grow more or less close to the edge of the water; while of non-saline plants the *So-*

lanum Sodomæum, *Tamarix*, *Centaurea*, and immense brakes of *Arundo Donax* may be seen all around.

The most singular effect is, however, experienced in the re-ascent from the Dead Sea to the hills on its N. W. shore, which presents first a sudden steep rise, and then a series of vast water-worn terraces at the same level as the Mediterranean. During this ascent such familiar plants of the latter region are successively met with as *Poterium spinosum*, *Anchusa*, pink, *Hypericum*, *Inula viscosa*, etc.; but no trees are seen till the longitude of Jerusalem is approached.

III. *Flora of the Middle and Upper Mountain Regions of Syria.* — The oak forms the prevalent arboreous vegetation of this region below 5,000 feet. The *Quercus pseudo-coccifera* and *infectoria* is not seen much above 3,000 feet, nor the Valonia oak at so great an elevation; but above these heights some magnificent species occur, including the *Quercus Cerris* of the South of Europe, the *Q. Ehrenbergii*, or *castanæfolia*, *Q. Tæn*, *Q. Libani*, and *Q. Mannifera*, Lindl., which is perhaps not distinct from some of the forms of *Q. Robur*, or *sessiliflora*.[a]

At the same elevations junipers become common, but the species have not been satisfactorily made out. The *Juniperus communis* is found, but is not so common as the tall, straight, black kind (*J. excelsa*, or *fœtidissima*). On Mount Casius the *J. drupacea* grows, remarkable for its large plum-like fruit; and *J. Sabina*, *phœnicia*, and *oxycedrus*, are all said to inhabit Syria. But the most remarkable plant of the upper region is certainly the cedar; for which we must refer the reader to the article CEDAR.[b]

Lastly, the flora of the upper temperate and alpine Syrian mountains demands some notice. As before remarked, no part of the Lebanon presents a vegetation at all similar, or even analogous, to that of the Alps of Europe, India, or North America. This is partly owing to the heat and extreme dryness of the climate during a considerable part of the year, to the sudden desiccating influence of the desert winds, and to the sterile nature of the dry limestone soil on the highest summits of Lebanon, Hermon, and the Anti-Lebanon; but perhaps still more to a warm period having succeeded to that cold one during which the glaciers were formed (whose former presence is attested by the moraines in the cedar valley and elsewhere), and which may have obliterated almost every trace of the glacial flora. Hence it happens that far more boreal plants may be gathered on the Himalaya at 10–15,000 ft. elevation, than at the analogous heights on Lebanon of 8–10,000 ft.; and that whilst fully 300 plants belonging to the Arctic circle inhabit the ranges of North India, not half that number are found on the Lebanon, though those mountains are in a far higher latitude.

At the elevation of 4,000 feet on the Lebanon many plants of the middle and northern latitudes of Europe commence, amongst which the most conspicuous are hawthorn, dwarf elder, dog-rose, ivy, butcher's broom, a variety of the berberry, honeysuckle, maple, and jasmine. A little higher, at 5–7000 ft., occur *Cotoneaster*, *Rhododendron ponticum*, primrose, *Daphne oleoides*, several other roses,

---

a For some notices of the oaks of Syria, see *Transactions of the Linn. Society*, xxiii. 381, and plates 36–38.

b See also Dr. Hooker's paper "On the Cedars of Lebanon," etc., in the *Nat. Hist. Review*, No. 5; with 3 plates.

Poterium, Juniperus communis, fœtidissima (or *excelsa*), and cedar. Still higher, at 7–10,000 ft., there is no shrubby vegetation, properly so called. What shrubs there are form small, rounded, harsh, prickly bushes, and belong to genera, or forms of genera, that are almost peculiar to the dry mountain regions of the Levant and Persia, and West Asia generally. Of these *Astragali* are by far the most numerous, including the *A. Tragacantha*, which yields the famous gum in the greatest abundance; and next to them a curious tribe of *Statices* called *Acantholimon*, whose rigid, pungent leaves spread like stars over the whole surface of the plant; and, lastly, a small white chenopodiaceous plant called *Noæa*. These are the prevalent forms up to the very summit of Lebanon, growing in globular masses on the rounded flank of *Dhar el-Khodib* itself, 10,200 feet above the sea.

At the elevation of 8–9,000 feet the beautiful silvery *Vicia canescens* forms large tufts of pale blue, where scarcely anything else will grow.

The herbaceous plants of 7–10,000 feet altitude are still chiefly Levantine forms of *Campanula, Ranunculus, Corydalis, Draba, Silene, Arenaria, Saponaria, Geranium, Erodium,* several *Umbellifers, Galium, Erigeron, Scorzonera, Taraxacum, Androsace, Scrophularia, Nepeta, Sideritis, Asphodeline, Crocus, Ornithogalum;* and a few grasses and sedges. No gentians, heaths, *Primulas,* saxifrages, anemones, or other alpine favorites, are found.

The most boreal forms, which are confined to the clefts of rocks, or the vicinity of patches of snow above 9,000 feet, are *Drabas, Arenaria,* one small *Potentilla,* a *Festuca,* an *Arabis* like *alpina,* and the *Oxyria reniformis,* the only decidedly Arctic type in the whole country, and probably the only characteristic plant remaining of the flora which inhabited the Lebanon during the glacial period. It is, however, extremely rare, and only found nestling under stones, and in deep clefts of rocks, on the very summit, and near the patches of snow on *Dhar el-Khodib.*

No doubt Cryptogamic plants are sufficiently numerous in this region, but none have been collected, except ferns, amongst which are *Cystopteris fragilis, Polypodium vulgare, Nephrodium pallidum,* and *Polystichum angulare.*   J. D. H.

ZOÖLOGY. — Much information is still needed on this subject before we can possibly determine with any degree of certainty the fauna of Palestine; indeed, the complaint of Linnæus in 1747, that "we are less acquainted with the Natural History of Palestine than with that of the remotest parts of India," is almost as just now as it was when the remark was made. "There is perhaps," writes a recent visitor to the Holy Land, "no country frequented by travellers whose fauna is so little known as that of Palestine" (*Ibis,* i. 22); indeed, the complaint is general amongst zoölogists.

It will be sufficient in this article to give a general survey of the fauna of Palestine, as the reader will find more particular information in the several articles which treat of the various animals under their respective names.

Mammalia. — The *Cheiroptera* (bats) are probably represented in Palestine by the species which are known to occur in Egypt and Syria, but we want precise information on this point. [BAT.] Of the *Insectivora* we find hedgehogs (*Erinaceus Europæus*) and moles (*Talpa vulgaris, T. cæca* (?)) which are recorded to occur in great numbers and to commit much damage (Hasselquist, *Trav.* p. 120): doubtless the family of *Soricidæ* (shrews) is also represented, but we lack information. Of the *Carnivora* are still seen, in the Lebanon, the Syrian bear (*Ursus Syriacus*),[a] and the panther (*Leopardus varius*), which occupies the central mountains of the land. Jackals and foxes are common; the hyena and wolf are also occasionally observed; the badger (*Meles taxus*) is also said to occur in Palestine;[b] the lion is no longer a resident in Palestine or Syria, though in Biblical times this animal must have been by no means uncommon, being frequently mentioned in Scripture. [LION.] The late Dr. Roth informed Mr. Tristram that bones of the lion had recently been found among the gravel on the banks of the Jordan not far south of the Sea of Galilee. A species of squirrel (*Sciurus Syriacus*), which the Arabs term *Orkidaun,* "the leaper," has been noticed by Hemprich and Ehrenberg on the lower and middle parts of Lebanon; two kinds of hare, *Lepus Syriacus,* and *L. Ægyptius;* rats and mice, which are said to abound, but to be partly kept down by the tame Persian cats; the jerboa (*Dipus Ægyptius*); the porcupine (*Hystrix cristata*); the short-tailed field-mouse (*Arvicola agrestis*), a most injurious animal to the husbandman, and doubtless other species of *Castoridæ,* may be considered as the representatives of the *Rodentia.* Of the *Pachydermata,* the wild boar (*Sus scrofa*), which is frequently met with on Tabor and Little Hermon, appears to be the only living wild example. The Syrian hyrax appears to be now but rarely seen. [CONEY.]

There does not appear to be at present any wild ox in Palestine, though it is very probable that in Biblical times some kind of urus or bison roamed about the hills of Bashan and Lebanon. [UNICORN.] Dr. Thomson states that wild goats (Ibex?) are still (see 1 Sam. xxiv. 2) frequently seen in the rocks of En-gedi. Mr. Tristram possesses a specimen of *Capra ægagrus,* the Persian ibex, obtained by him a little to the south of Hebron. The gazelle (*Gazella dorcas*) occurs not unfrequently in the Holy Land; and is the antelope of the country. We want information as to other species of antelopes found in Palestine: probably the variety named, by Hemprich and Ehrenberg, *Antilope Arabica,* and perhaps the *Gazella Isabellina,* belong to the fauna. The Arabs hunt the gazelles with greyhound and falcon; the fallow-deer (*Dama vulgaris*) is said to be not unfrequently observed.

Of domestic animals we need only mention the Arabian or one-humped camel, asses,[c] and mules,

---

a There is some little doubt whether the brown bear (*U. arctos*) may not occasionally be found in Palestine. See Schubert (*Reise in das Morgenland*).

b Col. H. Smith, in Kitto's *Cyc.* art. "Badger," denies that the badger occurs in Palestine, and says it has not yet been found out of Europe. This animal, however, is certainly an inhabitant of certain

parts of Asia; and it is mentioned, together with wolves, jackals, porcupines, etc., by Mr. H. Poole, as abounding at Hebron (see *Geograph. Journal* for 1856, p. 58).

c * It may be well to add here that four of the five names for this animal used in the Hebrew Scriptures, are used by the Arabs of the present day in Syria

and houses, all which are in general use. The buffalo (*Bubalus buffalo*) is common, and is on account of its strength much used for ploughing and draught purposes. The ox of the country is small and unsightly in the neighborhood of Jerusalem, but in the richer pastures of the upper part of the country, the cattle, though small, are not unsightly, the head being very like that of an Alderney; the common sheep of Palestine is the broad-tail (*Ovis laticaudatus*), with its varieties [SHEEP]; goats are extremely common everywhere.

Aves. — Palestine abounds in numerous kinds of birds. Vultures, eagles, falcons, kites, owls of different kinds, represent the *Raptorial* order. Of the smaller birds may be mentioned, amongst others, the *Merops Persicus*, the *Upupa Epops*, the *Sitta Syriaca* or Dalmatian nuthatch, several kinds of *Sitrinda*, the *('anyris osea*, or Palestine sunbird, the *Ixos xanti.prygos*, Palestine nightingale — the finest songster in the country, which long before sunrise pours forth its sweet notes from the thick jungle which fringes the Jordan; the *Amydrus Tristramii*, or glossy starling, discovered by Mr. Tristram in the gorge of the Kedron not far from the Dead Sea, "the roll of whose music, something like that of the organ-bird of Australia, makes the rocks resound " — this is a bird of much interest, inasmuch as it belongs to a purely African group not before met with in Asia; the sly and wary *Crateropus chalybeus*, in the open wooded district near Jericho; the jay of Palestine (*Garrulus melanocephalus*); kingfishers (*Ceryle rudis*, and perhaps *Alcedo ispida*) abound about the Lake of Tiberias and in the streams above the Huleh; the raven, and carrion crow; the *Pastor roseus*, or locust-bird [see LOCUST]; the common cuckoo; several kinds of doves; sandgrouse (*Pterocles*), partridges, francolins, quails, the great bustard, storks, both the black and white kinds, seen often in flocks of some hundreds; herons, curlews, pelicans, sea-swallows (*Sterna*), gulls, etc., etc. For the ornithology of the Holy Land the reader is referred to Hemprich and Ehrenberg's *Symbolæ Physicæ* (Berlin, 1820–25), and to Mr. Tristram's paper in the *Ibis*, i. 22.

Reptilia. — Several kinds of lizards (*Saura*) occur. The *Lacerta stellio*, Lin., which the Arabs call *Hardun*, and the Turks kill, as they think it mimics them saying their prayers, is very common in ruined walls. The *Waran el hard* (*Psammosaurus scincus*) is very common in the deserts. The common Greek tortoise (*Testudo Græca*) Dr. Wilson observed at the sources of the Jordan; fresh-water tortoises (probably *Emus Caspica*) are found abundantly in the upper part of the country in the streams of Esdraelon and of the higher Jordan Valley, and in the lakes. The chameleon (*Chameleo vulgaris*) is common; the crocodile does not occur in Palestine; the *Monitor*

Niloticus has doubtless been confounded with it. In the south of Palestine especially reptiles of various kinds abound; besides those already mentioned, a large *Acanthodactylus* frequents old buildings; a large species of *Uromastix*, at least two species of Gecko (*Tarentola*), a *Gongylus* (*ocellatus ?*), several other *Acanthodactyli* and *Seps tridactylus* have been observed. Of *Ophidians*, there is more than one species of *Echidna*; a *Naia*, several *Tropidonoti*, a *Coronella*, a *Coluber* (*trivirgatus ?*) occur; and on the southern frontier of the land the desert form *Cerastes Hasselquistii* has been observed. Of the *Batrachia* we have little information beyond that supplied by Kitto, namely, that frogs (*Rana esculenta*) abound in the marshy pools of Palestine; that they are of a large size, but are not eaten by the inhabitants. The tree-frog (*Hyla*) and toad (*Bufo*) are also very common.

Pisces. — Fish were supplied to the inhabitants of Palestine both from the Mediterranean and from the inland lakes, especially from the Lake of Tiberias. The men of Tyre brought fish and sold on the Sabbath to the people of Jerusalem (Neh. xiii. 16). The principal kinds which are caught off the shores of the Mediterranean are supplied by the families *Sparidæ*, *Percidæ*, *Scomberidæ*, *Raindæ*, and *Pleuronectidæ*. The sea of Galilee has been always celebrated for its fish. Burckhardt (*Syria*, p. 332) says the most common species are the binny (*Cyprinus lepidotus*), frequent in all the fresh waters of Palestine and Syria, and a fish called *Mesht*, which he describes as being a foot long and five inches broad, with a flat body like the sole. The *Binny* is a species of barbel; it is the *Barbus Binni* of Cuv. and Valenc., and is said by Bruce to attain sometimes to a weight of 70 lbs.; it is common in the Nile, and is said to occur in all the fresh waters of Syria; the *Mesht* is undoubtedly a species of *Chromius*, one of the *Labridæ*, and is perhaps identical with the *C. Niloticus*, which is frequently represented on Egyptian monuments. The fish of this lake are, according to old tradition, nearly identical with the fish of the Nile; but we sadly want accurate information on this point. As to the fishes of Egypt and Syria, see Rüppell, E., *Neue Fische des Nils*, in *Verhandl. Senckenberg. Gesellsch.* Frankf., and Heckel, J., *Die Fische Syriens*, in Russegger, *Reise nach Egypten und Klein-Asien*. There does not appear to be any separate work published on the fishes of the Holy Land. [CAPERNAUM, i. 382.]

Concerning the other divisions of the animal kingdom we have little information. *Molluscs* are numerous; indeed in few areas of similar extent could so large a number of land molluscs be found; Mr. Tristram collected casually, and without search, upwards of 100 species in a few weeks. The land shells may be classified in four groups. In the north of the country the prevailing type is that of the Greek and Turkish mountain region, numerous species of the genus *Clausilia*, and of opaque *Bulimi* and *Pupæ* predominating. On the coast

---

(1.) حمار – חֲמוֹר, which is the generic name for the domestic ass. (2.) אתان – אָתוֹן, which is the name of the she-ass. (3.) עַיִר – عَيْر, a name used for the wild ass, indistinguishable from (4.) فراء – פֶּרֶא, which is without doubt the *Asinus hemippus* or *Asinus onager*.

---

and in the plains the common shells of the East Mediterranean basin abound, e. g. *Helix Pisana*, *H. Syriaca*, etc. In the south, in the hill country of Judæa, occurs a very interesting group, chiefly confined to the genus *Helix*, three subdivisions of which may be typified by *H. Boissieri*, *H. Seetzena*, *H. tuberculosa*, recalling by their thick, calcareous, lustreless coating, the prevalent types of Egypt, Arabia, and Sahara. In the valley of the Jordan the prevailing group is a subdivision of the genus *Bulimus*, rounded, semi-pellucid, and lustrous, very numerous in species, which are for the most part peculiar to this district. The reader will find a list of *Mollusca* found in the neighborhood of Jerusalem, in the *An. and Mag. of Nat. Hist.* vi. No. 34, p. 312. The following remark of a resident in Jerusalem may be mentioned. " No shells are found in the Dead Sea or on its margin except the bleached specimens of *Melanopsis*, *Neritina*, and various *Unionidæ*, which have been washed down by the Jordan, and afterwards drifted on shore. In fact, so intense is the bittersaline quality of its waters that no mollusc (nor, so far as I know, any other living creature) can exist in it.[a] These may be typified by *B. Jordani* and *B. Aleppensis*. Of the *Crustacea* we know scarcely anything. Lord Lindsay observed large numbers of a small crab in the sands near Akaba. Hasselquist (*Trav.* p. 238) speaks of a " running crab " seen by him on the coasts of Syria and Egypt. Dr. Baird has recently (*An. and Mag. N. H.* viii. No. 45, p. 209) described an interesting form of Entomostracous Crustacean, which he terms *Branchipus eximius*, reared from mud sent him from a pool near Jerusalem. Five other species of this group are described by Dr. Baird in the *An. and Mag. N. H.* for Oct. 1859. With regard to the *insects*, a number of beetles may be seen figured in the *Symbolæ Physicæ*.

The *Lepidoptera* of Palestine are as numerous and varied as might have been expected in a land of flowers. All the common butterflies of southern Europe, or nearly allied congeners, are plentiful in the cultivated plains and on the hill-sides. Numerous species of *Polyommatus* and *Lycæna*, *Thecla ilicis* and *acaciæ*; many kinds of *Pontia*; the lovely *Anthocaris eupheno* abounds on the lower hills in spring, as does *Parnassius Apollinus*; more than one species of *Thais* occurs; the genera *Argynnis* and *Melitæa* are abundantly represented, not so *Hipparchia*, owing probably to the comparative dryness of the soil. *Libythea* (*Celtis?*) is found, and the gorgeous genus *Vanessa* is very common in all suitable localities; the almost cosmopolitan *Cynthia Cardui* and *Vanessa Atalanta*, *V. L. album*, and *V. Antiopa*, may be mentioned; *Papilio Alexanor* and some others of the same species flit over the plains of Sharon, and the caterpillar

of the magnificent *Sphinx Nerii* feeds in swarms on the oleanders by the banks of the Jordan. Bees are common. [BEE.] At least three species of scorpions have been distinguished. Spiders are common. The *Abu Hanakein*, noticed as occurring at Sinai by Burckhardt, which appears to be some species of *Galeodes*, one of the Solpugidæ, probably may be found in Palestine. Locusts occasionally visit Palestine and do infinite damage. Ants are numerous; some species are described in the *Journal of the Linnean Society*, vi. No. 21, which were collected by Mr. Hanbury in the autumn of 1860. Of the *Annelida* we have no information; while of the whole sub-kingdoms of *Cœlenterata* and *Protozoa* we are completely ignorant.

It has been remarked that in its physical character Palestine presents on a small scale an epitome of the natural features of all regions, mountainous and desert, northern and tropical, maritime and inland, pastoral, arable, and volcanic. This fact, which has rendered the allusions in the Scriptures so varied as to afford familiar illustrations to the people of every climate, has had its natural effect on the zoölogy of the country. In no other district, not even on the southern slopes of the Himalayah, are the typical fauna of so many distinct regions and zones brought into such close juxtaposition. The bear of the snowy heights of Lebanon and the gazelle of the desert may be hunted within two days' journey of each other; sometimes even the ostrich approaches the southern borders of the land; the wolf of the north and the leopard of the tropics howl within hearing of the same bivouac; while the falcons, the linnets and buntings, recall the familiar inhabitants of our English fields, the sparkling little sun-bird (*Cinnyris osea*), and the grackle of the glen (*Amydrus Tristramii*) introduce us at once to the most brilliant types of the bird-life of Asia and S. Africa.

Within a walk of Bethlehem, the common frog of England, the chameleon, and the gecko of Africa, may be found almost in company; and descending to the lower forms of animal life, while the northern valleys are prolific in *Clausiliæ* and other genera of molluscs common to Europe, the valley of the Jordan presents types of its own, and the hill country of Judæa produces the same type of *Helices* as is found in Egypt and the African Sahara. So in insects, while the familiar forms of the butterflies of Southern Europe are represented on the plain of Sharon, the Apollo butterfly of the Alps is recalled on Mount Olivet by the exquisite *Parnassius Apollinus* hovering over the same plants as the sparkling *Thais medicaste* and the *Libythea* (*Celtis?*), northern representatives of sub-tropical lepidoptera.

If the many travellers who year by year visit the

---

[a] This statement with regard to the total absence of organic life in the Dead Sea is confirmed by almost every traveller, and there can be no doubt as to its general accuracy. It is, however, but right to state that Mr. Poole discovered some small fish in a brine-spring, about 100 yards distant from, and 80 feet above the level of the Dead Sea, which he was inclined to think had been produced from fish *in* the sea (see *Geograph. Journal* for 1856). These fish have been identified by Sir J. Richardson with *Cyprinodon Hammonis*, Cuv. et Val. xvii. 169; see *Proceed. of Zoölog. Soc.* for 1856, p. 371. Mr. Tristram observes that he found in the Sahara *Cyprinodon dispar* in hot salt-springs where the water was shallow, but that these

fish are never found in deep pools or lakes. Mr. Poole observed also a number of aquatic birds diving frequently in the Dead Sea, and thence concluded, justly, Sir J. Richardson thinks, " that they must have found something edible there." It would, moreover, be an interesting question to determine whether some species of *Artemia* (brine-shrimp) may not exist in the shallow pools at the extreme south end of the Salt Lake. In the open tanks at Lymington myriads of these transparent little brine-shrimps (they are about half an inch in length) are seen swimming actively about in water every pint of which contains as much as a quarter of a pound of salt!

Holy Land would pay some attention to its zoölogy, by bringing home collections and by investigations in the country, we should soon hope to have a fair knowledge of the fauna of a land which in this respect has been so much neglected, and should doubtless gain much towards the elucidation of many passages of Holy Scripture.

W. H. and H. B. TRISTRAM.

* Our most convenient manual on the *Natural History of the Bible* at present is that of Mr. Tristram, published by the Society for Promoting Christian Knowledge. (London, 1867.) The contributions of Dr. G. E. Post, in this edition of the *Dictionary*, will be found to be important to this branch of science.   H.

THE CLIMATE. — No materials exist for an accurate account of the climate of the very different regions of Palestine. Besides the casual notices of travellers (often unscientific persons), the following observations are all that we possess: —

(1.) Average monthly temperatures at Jerusalem, taken between June 1851, and Jan. 1855, inclusive, by Dr. R. G. Barclay, of Beyrût and Jerusalem, and published by him in a paper "On the State of Medical Science in Syria," in the *N. American Medico-Chirurgical Review* (Philadelphia), vol. i. 705-718.[a]

(2.) A set of observations of temperature, 206 in all, extending from Nov. 19, 1838, to Jan. 16, 1839, taken at Jerusalem, Jaffa, Nazareth, and Beyrût, by Russegger, and given in his work (*Reisen*, iii. 170-185).

(3.) The writer is indebted to his friend Mr. James Glaisher, F. R. S., for a table showing the mean temperature of the air at Jerusalem for each month, from May, 1843, to May, 1844;[b] and at Beyrût, from April, 1842, to May, 1845.

(4.) Register of the fall of rain at Jerusalem from 1846 to 1849, and 1850 to 1854, by Dr. R. G. Barclay (as above).

1. *Temperature.* — The results of these observa-

---

[a] These observations are inserted in Dr. Barclay's work (*City of the Great King*, p. 428), and are accompanied by his comments, the result of a residence of several years in Jerusalem (see also pp. 48-56).

[b] There is considerable variation in the above three sets of observations, as will be seen from the following comparative table of the mean temperatures of Jerusalem: —

Month.	(1.)	(2.)	(3.)
Jan.	49.4		47.7
Feb.	54.4		53.7
March	55.7		60.
April	61.4		54.7
May	73.8		66.8
June	75.2		71.7
July	79.1		77.8
Aug.	79.3		72.6
Sept.	77.	(Mean of 67 obs. from Nov. 19 to Dec. 5.)	72.2
Oct.	74.2		68.4
Nov.	63.8		58.9
Dec.	54.5	62.	47.4
Mean for the year.	66.5		62.6

---

tions at Jerusalem may be stated generally as follows. January is the coldest month, and July and August the hottest, though June and September are nearly as warm. In the first-named month the average temperature is 49.1° Fahr., and greatest cold 28°; in July and August the average is 78.4°; with greatest heat 92° in the shade and 143° in the sun. The extreme range in a single year was 52°; the mean annual temperature 65.6°. Though varying so much during the different seasons, the climate is on the whole pretty uniform from year to year. Thus the thermometric variation in the same latitude on the west coast of North America is nearly twice as great. The isothermal line of mean annual temperature of Jerusalem passes through California and Florida (to the north of Mobile), and Dr. Barclay remarks that in temperature and the periodicity of the seasons there is a close analogy between Palestine and the former state. The isothermal line also passes through Gibraltar, and near Madeira and the Bermudas. The heat, though extreme during the four midsummer months, is much alleviated by a sea-breeze from the N.W., which blows with great regularity from 10 A.M. till 10 P.M.; and from this and other unexplained causes the heat is rarely oppressive, except during the occasional presence of the Khamsin or sirocco, and is said to be much more bearable than even in many parts of the western world [e] which are deemed tropical. The Khamsin blows during February, March, and April (Wildenbruch). It is most oppressive when it comes from the east, bearing the heat and sand of the desert with it, and during its continuance darkening the air and filling everything with fine dust (Miss Beaufort, ii. 223).

During January and February snow often falls to the depth of a foot or more, though it may not make its appearance for several years together. In 1854-55 it remained on the ground for a fortnight.[d] Nor is this of late occurrence only, but is reported by Shaw in 1722. In 1818 it was between two and three feet deep.[e] In 1754 a heavy fall took place, and twenty-five persons are said to have been frozen to death at Nazareth.[f] Snow is repeatedly mentioned in the poetical books of the Bible, and must therefore have been known at that time (Ps. lxviii. 14, cxlvii. 16; Is. lv. 10, &c.). But in the narrative it only appears twice (1 Macc. xiii. 22; 2 Sam. xxiii. 20).

Thin ice is occasionally found on pools or sheets of water; and pieces of ground out of the reach of the sun's rays remain sometimes slightly frozen for several days. But this is a rare occurrence, and no injury is done to the vegetation by frost, nor do plants require shelter during winter (Barclay).

Observations made at Jerusalem are not applicable to the whole of the highland, as is obvious from Russegger's at Nazareth. These show us the result of fifty-five observations, extending from

---

It is understood that a regular series of observations, with standard barometer, thermometer, and rain-gauge, was made for 10 years by the late Dr. M'Gowan of the Hospital, Jerusalem, but the record of them has unfortunately been mislaid.

[c] Barclay, p. 48; Rob. *Bibl. Res.* i. 430; also Schwarz, p. 327.

[d] *Jewish Intelligencer*, 1856, p. 137, *note*.

[e] "1 *Ells hoch*," Scholz, quoted by Von Raumer, p. 79.

[f] S. Schulz, quoted by Von Raumer. Schwarz, p. 326.

Dec. 15 to 26: highest temp. 58.5°, lowest 46°, mean 53°, all considerably lower than those taken at Jerusalem a fortnight before.

2. *Rain.* — The result of Dr. Barclay's observations is to show that the greatest fall of rain at Jerusalem in a single year was 85 inches,[a] and the smallest 44, the mean being 61.6 inches. The greatest fall in any one month (Dec. 1850) was 33.8, and the greatest in three months (Dec. 1850, Jan. and Feb. 1851) 72.4. These figures will be best appreciated by recollecting that the average rain-fall of London during the whole year is only 25 inches, and that in the wettest parts of the country, such as Cumberland and Devon, it rarely exceeds 60 inches.

As in the time of our Saviour (Luke xii. 54), the rains come chiefly from the S. or S. W. They commence at the end of October or beginning of November, and continue with greater or less constancy till the end of February or middle of March, and occasionally, though rarely, till the end of April. It is not a heavy, continuous rain, so much as a succession of severe showers or storms with intervening periods of fine bright weather, permitting the grain crops to grow and ripen. And although the season is not divided by any entire cessation of rain for a lengthened interval, as some represent, yet there appears to be a diminution in the fall for a few weeks in December and January, after which it begins again, and continues during February and till the conclusion of the season. On the uplands the barley-harvest (which precedes the wheat) should begin about the last week of May, so that it is preceded by five or six weeks of summer weather. Any falling-off in the rain during the winter or spring is very prejudicial to the harvest; and, as in the days of the prophet Amos, nothing could so surely occasion the greatest distress or be so fearful a threat as a drought three months before harvest (Amos iv. 7).

There is much difference of opinion as to whether the former and the latter rain of Scripture are represented by the beginning and end of the present rainy season, separated by the slight interval mentioned above (*e. g.* Kenrick, *Phœnicia*, p. 33), or whether, as Dr. Barclay (*City, &c.* p. 54) and others affirm, the latter rain took place after the harvest, about midsummer, and has been withheld as a punishment for the sins of the nation. This will be best discussed under RAIN.

Between April and November there is, with the rarest exceptions, an uninterrupted succession of fine weather, and skies without a cloud. Thus the year divides itself into two, and only two, seasons — as indeed we see it constantly divided in the Bible — " winter and summer," " cold and heat," " seed-time and harvest."

During the summer the dews are very heavy, and often saturate the traveller's tent as if a shower had passed over it. The nights, especially towards sunrise, are very cold, and thick fogs or mists are common all over the country. Thunder-storms of great violence are frequent during the winter months.

3. So much for the climate of Jerusalem and the highland generally. In the lowland districts, on the other hand, the heat is much greater and more oppressive,[b] owing to the quantity of vapor in the atmosphere, the absence of any breeze, the sandy nature of the soil, and the manner in which the heat is confined and reflected by the inclosing heights; perhaps also to the internal heat of the earth, due to the depth below the sea level of the greater part of the Jordan Valley, and the remains of volcanic agency, which we have already shown to be still in existence in this very depressed region [p. 2305 *b*]. No indication of these conditions is discoverable in the Bible, but Josephus was aware of them (*B. J.* iv. 8, § 3), and states that the neighborhood of Jericho was so much warmer than the upper country that linen clothing was worn there even when Judæa was covered with snow. This is not quite confirmed by the experience of modern travellers, but it appears that when the winter is at its severest on the highlands, and both eastern and western mountains are white with snow, no frost visits the depths of the Jordan Valley, and the greatest cold experienced is produced by the driving rain of tempests (Seetzen, Jan. 9, ii. 300). The vegetation already mentioned as formerly or at present existing in the district — palms, indigo, sugar — testifies to its tropical heat. The harvest in the Ghor is fully a month in advance of that on the highlands, and the fields of wheat are still green on the latter when the grain is being threshed in the former (Rob. *Bibl. Res.* i. 431, 551, iii. 314). Thus Burckhardt on May 5 found the barley of the district between Tiberias and Beisan nearly all harvested, while on the upland plains of the Hauran, from which he had just descended, the harvest was not to commence for fifteen days. In this fervid and moist atmosphere irrigation alone is necessary to insure abundant crops of the finest grain (Rob. i. 550).

4. The climate of the maritime lowland exhibits many of the characteristics of that of the Jordan Valley,[c] but, being much more elevated, and exposed on its western side to the sea-breezes, is not so oppressively hot. Russegger's observations at Jaffa (Dec. 7 to 12) indicate only a slight advance in temperature on that of Jerusalem. But Mr. Glaisher's observations at Beyrût (mentioned above) show on the other hand that the temperature there is considerably higher, the Jan. being

---

[a] Here again there is a considerable discrepancy, since Mr. Poole (*Geogr. Journal*, xxvi. 57) states that Dr. M'Gowan had registered the greatest quantity in one year at 108 inches.

[b] At 5 P. M. on the 25th Nov. Russegger's thermometer at Jerusalem showed a temp. of 62.8°; but when he arrived at Jericho at 5.30 P. M. on the 27th it had risen to 72.5°. At 7.30 the following morning it was 63.5°, against 58° at Jerusalem on the 25th; and at noon, at the Jordan, it had risen to 81°. At Marsaba, at 11 A. M. of the 29th, it was 66°; and on returning to Jerusalem on the 1st Dec. it again fell to an average of 61°. An observation recorded by Dr. Robinson (iii. 210) at *Sakût* (Succoth), in the central part of the Jordan Valley, on May 14, 1852, in the shade, and close

to a spring, gives 92°, which is the very highest reading recorded at Jerusalem in July: later on the same day it was 98°, in a strong N. W. wind (p. 314). On May 12, 1838, at Jericho, it was 91° in the shade and the breeze. Dr. Anderson (p. 184) found it 106° Fahr. " through the first half of the night " at the S. E. corner of the Dead Sea. In a paper on the " Climate of Palestine," etc., in the *Edinburgh New Philos. Journal* for April, 1862, published while this sheet was passing through the press, the mean annual temperature of Jericho is stated as 72° Fahr., but without giving any authority.

[c] Robinson (ii. 223), on June 8, 1838, found the thermometer 88° Fahr. before sunrise, at *Brit Nettif*, on the lower hills overlooking the Plain of Philistia.

54°, July 82°, and the mean for the year 69.3°. The situation of Beyrût (which indeed is out of the confines of the Holy Land) is such as to render its climate very sultry. This district retains much tropical vegetation; all along the coast from Gaza to Beyrût, and inland as far as Ramleh and Lydd, the date-palm flourishes and fruits abundantly, and the orange, sycamore-fig, pomegranate, and banana grow luxuriantly at Jaffa and other places. Here also the harvest is in advance of that of the mountainous districts (Thomson, *Land and Book*, p. 543). In the lower portions of this extensive plain frost and snow are as little known as they are in the Ghor. But the heights, even in summer, are often very chilly,[a] and the sunrise is frequently obscured by a dense low fog (Thomson, pp. 490, 542; Rob. ii. 19). North of Carmel slight frosts are occasionally experienced.

In the winter months, however, the climate of these regions is very similar to that of the south of France or the maritime districts of the north of Italy. Napoleon, writing from Gaza on the "8th *Ventose* (26 Feb.), 1799," says, "Nous sommes ici dans l'eau et la boue jusqu'aux genoux. Il fait ici le même froid et le même temps qu'à Paris dans cette saison" (*Corr. de Napoléon*, No 3,993). Berthier to Marmont, from the same place (29 Dec. 1798), says, "Nous trouvons ici un pays qui ressemble à la Provence et le climat à celui d'Europe" (*Mém. du Duc de Raguse*, ii. 56).

A register of the weather and vegetation of the twelve months in Palestine, referring especially to the coast region, is given by Colonel von Wildenbruch in *Geogr. Society's Journal*, xx. 232. A good deal of similar information will be found in a tabular form on Petermann's *Physical Map of Palestine* in the *Biblical Atlas* of the Tract Society.

The permanence of the climate of Palestine, on the ground that the same vegetation which anciently flourished there still exists, is ingeniously maintained in a paper on *The Climate of Palestine in Modern compared to Ancient Times* in the *Edinburgh New Philosophical Journal* for April, 1862. Reference is therein made to a paper on the same subject by Schouw in vol. viii. of the same periodical. p. 311.

LITERATURE. — The list of works on the Holy Land is of prodigious extent. Dr. Robinson, in the Appendix to his *Biblical Researches*, enumerates no less than 183; to which Bonar (*Land of Promise*) adds a large number; and even then the list is far from complete.

* A unique work on this branch of bibliography is Dr. Tobler's *Bibliotheca Geographica Palestinæ*, pp. 265 (Leipzig, 1867). Beginning with A. D. 333, and coming down to 1866, he enumerates (if we have counted right) 1,066 writers in this field of exploration and study. They represent all the principal nationalities and languages. In most instances he characterizes the works mentioned with reference to their object and critical value. H.

Of course every traveller sees some things which none of his predecessors saw, and therefore none should be neglected by the student anxious thoroughly to investigate the nature and customs of

the Holy Land; but the following works will be found to contain nearly all necessary information:[b] —

1. Josephus. — Invaluable, both for its own sake, and as an accompaniment and elucidation of the Bible narrative. Josephus had a very intimate knowledge of the country. He possessed both the Hebrew Bible and the Septuagint, and knew them well; and there are many places in his works which show that he knew how to compare the various books together, and combine their scattered notices in one narrative, in a manner more like the processes of modern criticism than of ancient record. He possessed also the works of several ancient historians, who survive only through the fragments he has preserved. And it is evident that he had in addition other nameless sources of information, now lost to us, which often supplement the Scripture history in a very important manner. These and other things in the writings of Josephus have yet to be investigated. Two tracts by Tuch (*Quæstiones de F. Josephi libris*, etc., Leipzig, 1859), on geographical points, are worth attention.

2. The *Onomasticon* (usually so called) of Eusebius and Jerome. A tract of Eusebius (†340), "concerning the names of places in the Sacred Scriptures;" translated, freely and with many additions, by Jerome (†420), and included in his works as *Liber de Situ et Nominibus Locorum Hebraicorum*. The original arrangement is according to the Books of Scripture, but it was thrown into one general alphabetical order by Bonfrere (1631, &c.); and finally edited by J. Clericus, Amst. 1707, &c. [The best edition is that of Larsow and Parthey, Berlin, 1862. — A.] This tract contains notices (often very valuable, often absolutely absurd) of the situation of many ancient places of Palestine, as far as they were known to the two men who in their day were probably best acquainted with the subject. In connection with it, see Jerome's *Ep. ad Eustochium; Epit. Paula* — an itinerary through a large part of the Holy Land. Others of Jerome's Epistles, and his Commentaries, are full of information on the country.

3. The most important of the early travellers — from Arculf (A. D. 700) to Maundrell (1697) — are contained in *Early Travels in Palestine*, a volume published by Bohn. The shape is convenient, but the translation is not always to be implicitly relied on.

4. Reland. — *H. Relandi Palæstina ex Monumentis Veteribus illustrata*, 1714. A treatise on the Holy Land in three books: 1. The country; 2. The distances; 3. The places; with maps (excellent for their date), prints of coins and inscriptions. Reland exhausts all the information obtainable on his subject down to his own date (he often quotes Maundrell, 1703). His learning is immense, he is extremely accurate, always ingenious, and not wanting in humor. But honesty and strong sound sense are his characteristics. A sentence of his own might be his motto: "Conjecturæ, quibus non delectamur" (p. 139), or "Ego nil muto " (p. 671).

5. Benjamin of Tudela. — *Travels of Rabbi Benjamin* (in Europe, Asia, and Africa) from 1160-73. The best edition is that of A. Asher, 2 vols.

1840–41. The part relating to Palestine is contained in pp. 61–87. The editor's notes contain some curious information; but their most valuable part (ii. 397–445) is a translation of extracts from the work of Esthori B. Mose hap-Parchi on Palestine (A. D. 1314–22). These passages — notices of places and identifications — are very valuable, more so than those of Benjamin. The original work, *Caftor ra-Pherach*, "knop and flower," has been reprinted, in Hebrew, by Edelmann, Berlin, 1852. Other Itineraries of Jews have been translated and published by Carmoly (Brux. 1847), but they are of less value than the two already named.

6. Abulfeda. — The chief Moslem accounts of the Holy Land are those of Edrisi (cir. 1150), and Abulfeda (cir. 1300), translated under the titles of *Tabula Syriæ*, and *Descr. Arabiæ*. Extracts from these and from the great work of Yakoot are given by Schultens in an *Index Geographicus* appended to his edition of Bohaeddin's *Life of Saladin*, folio, 1755. Yakoot has yet to be explored, and no doubt he contains a mass of valuable information.

7. Quaresmius. — *Terræ Sanctæ Elucidatio*, etc. Ant. 1639, 2 vols. folio. The work of a Latin monk who lived in the Holy Land for more than twelve years, and rose to be Principal and Commissary Apostolic of the country. It is divided into eight books: the first three, general dissertations: the remainder "peregrinations" through the Holy Land, with historical accounts, and identifications (often incorrect), and elaborate accounts of the Latin traditions attaching to each spot, and of the ecclesiastical establishments, military orders, etc. of the time. It has a copious index. Similar information is given by the Abbé Mislin (*Les Saints Lieux*, Paris, 1858, 3 vols. 8vo); but with less elaboration than Quaresmius, and in too hostile a vein towards Lamartine and other travellers.

8. The great burst of modern travel in the Holy Land began with Seetzen and Burckhardt. Seetzen resided in Palestine from 1805 to 1807, during which time he travelled on both E. and W. of Jordan. He was the first to visit the Hauran, the Ghor, and the mountains of Ajlun: he travelled completely round the Dead Sea, besides exploring the east side a second time. As an experienced man of science, Seetzen was charged with collecting antiquities and natural objects for the Oriental Museum at Gotha; and his diaries contain inscriptions, and notices of flora and fauna, etc. They have been published in 3 vols., with a 4th vol. of notes (but without an index), by Kruse (Berlin, 1854–59). The Palestine journeys are contained in vols. 1 and 2. His Letters, founded on these diaries, and giving their results, are in Zach's *Monatl. Corresp.* vols. 17, 18, 26, 27.

9. Burckhardt. — *Travels in Syria and the Holy Land*, 4to, 1822. With the exception of an excursion of twelve days to Safed and Nazareth, Burckhardt's journeys S. of Damascus were confined to the east of the Jordan. These regions he explored and described more completely than Seetzen, or any later traveller till Wetzstein (1861), and even his researches do not extend over so wide an area. Burckhardt made two tours in the Hauran, in one of which he penetrated — first of Europeans — into the mysterious Leja. The southern portions of the Transjordanic country he traversed in his journey from Damascus to Petra and Sinai. The fullness of the notes which he contrived to keep under the very difficult circumstances in which he travelled is

astonishing. They contain a multitude of inscriptions, long catalogues of names, plans of sites, etc. The strength of his memory is shown not only by these notes but by his constant references to books, from which he was completely cut off. His diaries are interspersed with lengthened accounts of the various districts, and the manners and customs, commerce, etc., of their inhabitants. Burckhardt's accuracy is universally praised. No doubt justly. But it should be remembered that on the E. of Jordan no means of testing him as yet exist; while in other places his descriptions have been found imperfect or at variance *a* with facts. The volume contains an excellent preface by Colonel Leake, but is very defective from the want of an index. This is partially supplied in the German translation (Weimar, 1823–24, 2 vols. 8vo), which has the advantage of having been edited and annotated by Gesenius.

10. Irby and Mangles. — *Travels in Egypt and Nubia, Syria, and the Holy Land* (in 1817–18). Hardly worth special notice except for the portions which relate their route on the east of Jordan, especially about Kerek and the country of Moab and Ammon, which are very well told, and with an air of simple faithfulness. These portions are contained in chapters vi. and viii. The work is published in the *Home and Col. Library*, 1847.

11. Robinson. — (1.) *Biblical Researches in Palestine*, etc., in 1838: 1st ed. 1841, 3 vols. 8vo; 2d ed. 1856, 2 vols. 8vo. (2.) *Later Bib. Res. in* 1852, 8vo, 1856. Dr. Robinson's is the most important work on the Holy Land since Reland. His knowledge of the subject and its literature is very great, his common sense excellent, his qualifications as an investigator and a describer remarkable. He had the rare advantage of being accompanied on both occasions by Dr. Eli Smith, long resident in Syria, and perfectly versed in both classical and vernacular Arabic. Thus he was enabled to identify a host of ancient sites, which are mostly discussed at great length, and with full references to the authorities. The drawbacks to his work are a want of knowledge of architectural art, and a certain dogmatism, which occasionally passes into contempt for those who differ with him. He too uniformly disregards tradition, an extreme fully as bad as its opposite in a country like the East.

The first edition has a most valuable Appendix, containing lists of the Arabic names of modern places in the country, which in the second edition are omitted. Both series are furnished with indexes, but those of Geography and Antiquities might be extended with advantage.

* *Physical Geography of the Holy Land*, by Edward Robinson (Boston, 1865, pp. xvi., 394). This is a posthumous work, but eminently worthy of the author's reputation. At the outset he points out our best sources of a knowledge of sacred geography. The book seems not to have obtained the general recognition which it deserves.   H.

12. Wilson. — *The Lands of the Bible visited*, etc., 1847, 2 vols. 8vo. Dr. Wilson traversed the Holy Land twice, but without going out of the usual routes. He paid much attention to the topography, and keeps a constant eye on the reports of his predecessor Dr. Robinson. His book cannot be neglected with safety by any student of the coun-

---

a For examples of this see Robinson, *Bibl. Res.* iii. 823, 406, 478, 494. Stanley, *Sinai & Pal.* pp. 61, 72.

try; but it is chiefly valuable for its careful and detailed accounts of the religious bodies of the East, especially the Jews and Samaritans. His Indian labors having accustomed him to Arabic, he was able to converse freely with all the people he met, and his inquiries were generally made in the direction just named. His notice of the Samaritans is unusually full and accurate, and illustrated by copies and translations of documents and information not elsewhere given.

* Bonar and McCheyne's *Narrative of a Mission to the Jews in Palestine* (Edinb. 1852), often reprinted, continues to be one of the best sources of information on this subject.   H.

13. Schwarz. — *A Descriptive Geography, etc., of Palestine*, Philad. 1850, 8vo. A translation of a work originally published in Hebrew (*Sepher Tebuoth*, Jerusalem, 5605, A. D. 1845) by Rabbi Joseph Schwarz. Taking as his basis the catalogues of Joshua, Chronicles, etc., and the numerous topographical notices of the Rabbinical books, he proceeds systematically through the country, suggesting identifications, and often giving curious and valuable information. The American translation is almost useless for want of an index. This is in some measure supplied in the German version, *Das heilige Land*, etc., Frankfurt a. M. 1852.

14. De Saulcy. — *Voyage autour de la Mer Morte*, etc., 1853, 2 vols. 8vo, with *Atlas* of Maps and Plates, lists of Plants and Insects. Interesting rather from the unusual route taken by the author, the boldness of his theories, and the atlas of admirably engraved maps and plates which accompanies the text, than for its own merits. Like many French works, it has no index. Translated: *Narrative of a Journey*, etc., 2 vols. 8vo, 1854. See *The Dead Sea*, by Rev. A. A. Isaacs, 1857. Also a valuable Letter by "A Pilgrim," in the *Athenæum*, Sept. 9, 1854.

* De Saulcy has also published: *Voyage en Terre Sainte*, 2 vols., Paris, 1865, 8vo, with maps and wood-cuts. *Les derniers jours de Jérusalem*, Paris, 1866, 8vo, with views, plans, and a map of the Holy City. These works are regarded as more valuable than his earlier volumes.
                                                     A.

15. Lynch. — *Official Report of the United States Expedition to explore the Dead Sea and the Jordan*, 4to, Baltimore, 1852. Contains the daily Record of the Expedition, and separate Reports on the Ornithology, Botany, and Geology. The last of these Reports is more particularly described at pp. 2333, 2174.

* L. Vignes. — *Extrait des Notes d'un Voyage d'exploration à la Mer Morte, dans le Wady Arabah*, etc. (Paris, 1865).   H.

16. Stanley. — *Sinai and Palestine*, 1853 [6th ed. 1866], 8vo. Professor Stanley's work differs from those of his predecessors. Like them he made a lengthened journey in the country, is intimately acquainted with all the authorities, ancient and modern, and has himself made some of the most brilliant identifications of the historical sites. But his great object seems to have been not so much to make fresh discoveries, as to apply those already made, the structure of the country and the peculiarities of the scenery, to the elucidation of the history. This he has done with a power and a delicacy truly remarkable. To the sentiment and eloquence of Lamartine, the genial freshness of Miss Martineau, and the sound judgment of Robinson, he adds a reverent appreciation of the subject, and

a care for the smallest details of the picture, which no one else has yet displayed, and which render his descriptions a most valuable commentary on the Bible narrative. The work contains an Appendix on the Topographical Terms of the Bible, of importance to students of the English version of the Scriptures.

See also a paper on "Sacred Geography" by Professor Stanley in the *Quarterly Review*, No. clxxxviii.

* For valuable monographic sketches, see Rosen's art. *Das Thal u. die Umgegend Hebrons*, in *Zeitsch. der D. M. Gesellschaft*, xii. 477–513, and Pastor Valentiner's *Beitrag zur Topographie des Stammes Benjamin*, ibid. xii. 161 ff.

The *Bibliotheca Sacra* (vols. i.–xxvi., 1844–1869) is particularly rich in articles on Biblical geography from Dr. Robinson and various American missionaries in Palestine and other parts of the East. The July number for 1869 (pp. 541–71) contains a valuable paper on Mount Lebanon by Dr. Laurie, founded in part on his own personal observations.
                                                     H.

17. Tobler. — *Bethlehem*, 1849: *Topographie von Jerusalem u. seine Umgebungen*, 1854. These works are models of patient industry and research. They contain *everything* that has been said by everybody on the subject, and are truly valuable storehouses for those who are unable to refer to the originals. His *Dritte Wanderung*, 8vo, 1859, describes a district but little known, namely, part of Philistia and the country between Hebron and Ramleh, and thus possesses, in addition to the merits above named, that of novelty. It contains a sketch-map of the latter district, which corrects former maps in some important points.

* Dr. Tobler made a fourth journey to Palestine in 1865. His main object was to revisit Nazareth and collect materials for a special history of that place. But owing to cholera there, he was compelled to give up that purpose, and after a hurried visit to Jerusalem, returned to Europe. For the results of this journey see his *Nazareth in Palästina* (Berlin, 1866), described in note c, p. 2072 (Amer. ed.).   H.

18. Van de Velde. — *Syria and Palestine*, 2 vols. 8vo, 1854. Contains the narrative of the author's journeys while engaged in preparing his large *Map of the Holy Land* (1858), the best map yet published [Deutsche Ausgabe. nach d. 2. Aufl. d. "Map of the Holy Land," Gotha, 1868, considerably improved]. A condensed edition of this work, omitting the purely personal details too frequently introduced, would be useful. Van de Velde's *Memoir*, 8vo, 1858, gives elevations, latitudes and longitudes, routes, and much very excellent information. His *Pays d'Israel* [Paris, 1857–58], 100 colored lithographs from original sketches, are accurate and admirably executed, and many of the views are unique.

19. Ritter. — *Die Vergleichende Erdkunde*, etc. The six volumes of Ritter's great geographical work which relate to the peninsula of Sinai, the Holy Land, and Syria, and form together *Band viii*. They may be conveniently designated by the following names, which the writer has adopted in his other articles: 1. Sinai. 2. Jordan. 3. Syria (Index). 4. Palestine. 5. Lebanon. 6. Damascus (Index).

* The parts of this great work relating to the Sinaitic Peninsula and Palestine proper have been condensed and translated, with brief additions, by

William L. Gage, 4 vols. 8vo (London and New York, 1866).　　H.

20. Of more recent works the following may be noticed: Porter, *Five Years in Damascus, the Hauran*, etc., 2 vols. 8vo, 1855; *Handbook for Syria and Palestine*, 1858 [new ed., 2 vols., 1868]. Bonar, *The Land of Promise*, 1858. Thomson, *The Land and the Book*, 1859. The fruit of twenty-five years' residence in the Holy Land, by a shrewd and intelligent observer. Wetzstein, *Reisebericht über Hauran und die beiden Trachonen*, 1860, with wood-cuts, a plate of inscriptions, and a map of the district by Kiepert. The first attempt at a real exploration of those extraordinary regions east of the Jordan, which were partially visited by Burckhardt, and recently by Cyril Graham (*Cambridge Essays*, 1858; *Trans. R. S. Lit.* 1860, etc.). [Mr. Porter has given the results of his exploration of this region, in his *Giant Cities of Bashan* (1866). — H.] Drew, *Scripture Lands in Connection with their History*, 1860.

Two works by ladies claim especial notice. *Egyptian Sepulchres and Syrian Shrines*, by Miss E. A. Beaufort, 2 vols. 1861. The 2d vol. contains the record of six months' travel and residence in the Holy Land, and is full of keen and delicate observation, caught with the eye of an artist, and characteristically recorded. *Domestic Life in Palestine*, by Miss Rogers (1862), is, what its name purports, an account of a visit of several years to the Holy Land, during which, owing to her brother's position, the author had opportunities of seeing at leisure the interiors of many unsophisticated Arab and Jewish households, in places out of the ordinary track, such as few Englishwomen ever before enjoyed, and certainly none have recorded. These she has described with great skill and fidelity, and with an abstinence from descriptions of matters out of her proper path or at second-hand which is truly admirable.

It still remains, however, for some one to do for Syria what Mr. Lane has so faultlessly accomplished for Egypt, the more to be desired because the time is fast passing, and Syria is becoming every day more leavened by the West.

* Other recent works: — C. Furrer, *Wanderungen durch Palästina*, Zürich, 1863. ("Much that is new and fresh." — Tobler.) H. B. Tristram, *The Land of Israel; a Journal of Travels in Palestine, undertaken with special reference to its Physical Character*, Lond. 1865; 2d ed. 1866. (Valuable.) E. Arnaud, *La Palestine ancienne et moderne, ou géographie hist. et physique de la Terre Sainte. Avec 3 cart. chromo-lithogr.* Paris et Strasb. 1868. C. P. Caspari, *Chronol.-geogr. Einleitung in das Leben Jesu Christi. Nebst vier Karten u. Plänen*, Hamb. 1869. N. C. Burt, *The Land and its Story; or the Sacred Historical Geogr. of Palestine*, N. Y. 1869. In the two following important works by learned Jews, a comparatively untrodden field is explored: J. Derenbourg, *Essai sur l'hist. et la géog. de la Palestine, d'après les Thalmuds et les autres sources rabbiniques*, 1e partie, Paris, 1867; and A. Neubauer, *La géographie du Talmud; mémoire couronné par l'Acad. des Inscr. et Belles-Lettres*, Paris, 1868.　　A.

Views. — Two extensive collections of Views of the Holy Land exist — those of Bartlett and of Roberts. Pictorially beautiful as these plates are, they are not so useful to the student as the very accurate views of William Tipping, Esq. (published

in Traill's *Josephus*), some of which have been inserted in the article JERUSALEM. There are some instructive views taken from photographs, in the last edition of Keith's *Land of Israel*. Photographs have been published by Frith, Robertson, Rev. G. W. Bridges, and others. Photographs have also been taken by Salzmann, whose plates are accompanied by a treatise, *Jérusalem, Étude*, etc. (Paris, 1856).

* Those of Mr. Frith (see above) are sixty in number, and are superbly executed (on cards of 12 inches by 15). They embrace views of places and antiquities in Egypt and Idumæa, as well as in Palestine. A large and splendid collection of photographs accompanies the *Ordnance Survey of Jerusalem*. They furnish a panoramic view of the city and its environs (Olivet, Gethsemane, Valley of Jehoshaphat, etc.), a view of important sections of the city walls, and the walls of the Mosque of Omar, of the principal modern edifices, of numerous ancient monuments, etc., etc. The Palestine Exploration Fund has published numerous photographs of places, ruins, and scenery in the Holy Land (numbering 343).　　H.

Maps. — Mr. Van de Velde's map, already mentioned, has superseded all its predecessors; but much still remains to be done in districts out of the track usually pursued by travellers. On the east of Jordan, Kiepert's map (in Wetzstein's *Hauran*) is as yet the only trustworthy document. The new Admiralty surveys of the coast are understood to be rapidly approaching completion, and will leave nothing to be desired.

* The best collection of maps for the geography of Palestine, both ancient and modern, is no doubt the *Bible Atlas of Maps and Plans*, by Samuel Clark, M. A. (Lond. 1868), published by the Society for Promoting Christian Knowledge. It contains an Index compiled by Mr. Grove, representing all the instances of the occurrence " of any geographical name in the English version of the O. and N. Testaments and the Apocrypha, with its original in Hebrew or Greek, and the modern name of its site, whether known or only conjectured. In all cases, what may be regarded as certain is distinguished from what is uncertain." It contains also important dissertations and notes on questions relating to the identification of places and points of archæology, history, and exegesis.

Dr. Theodor Menke, *Bibel-Atlas in 8 Blättern* (Gotha, 1868). Similar to the preceding, but less complete. In addition to other points, it illustrates especially the topography of Jerusalem in the light of recent discoveries. Prominence is given to the ethnography of the ante-Hebrew nations or races. It is a great convenience that the author distinguishes rivers and *Wadies* from each other by different signs on the map.

The large wall *Map of Palestine and other parts of Syria*, by H. S. Osborn, LL. D. and Lyman Coleman, D. D., Philad. [1868?], 6 ft. by 9, is well adapted to its purpose. There is a good relief map of Palestine by H. W. Altmüller, *Das Heilige Land u. der Libanon in plastischer Darstellung nach den neuesten Forschungen*, Cassel, 1860. A *Reliefplan von Jerusalem* was also published by Altmüller in 1859; "improved and corrected by Conrad Schick," Cassel, 1865. H.

Of works on Jerusalem the following may be named: —

Williams. — *The Holy City*: 2d ed., 2 vols. 8vo, 1849. Contains a detailed history of Jerusalem.

an account of the modern town, and an essay on
the architectural history of the Church of the Sepulchre by Professor Willis. Mr. Williams in most
if not all cases supports tradition.

Barclay. — *The City of the Great King:* Philad.
1858. An account of Jerusalem as it was, is, and
will be. Dr. B. had some peculiar opportunities of
investigating the subterranean passages of the city
and the Haram area, and his book contains many
valuable notices. His large map of *Jerusalem and
Environs*, though badly engraved, is accurate and
useful, giving the form of the ground very well.

Fergusson. — *The Ancient Topography of Jerusalem*, etc., 1847, with 7 plates. Treats of the
Temple and the walls of ancient Jerusalem, and
the site of the Holy Sepulchre, and is full of the
most original and ingenious views, expressed in the
boldest language. From architectural arguments
the author maintains the so-called Mosque of Omar
to be the real Holy Sepulchre. He also shows that
the Temple, instead of occupying the whole of the
Haram area, was confined to its southwestern
corner. His arguments have never been answered
or even fairly discussed. The remarks of some of
his critics are, however, dealt with by Mr. F. in a
pamphlet, *Notes on the Site of the Holy Sepulchre*,
1861. See also vol. ii. of this Dictionary, pp. 1311-
1330.

* See especially Dr. Wolcott's elaborate examination of Mr. Fergusson's theory, under the head
"Topography of the City," vol. ii., pp. 1330-
1337, Amer. ed.   H.

Thrupp. — *Ancient Jerusalem, a new Investigation*, etc., 1855.

* We should recall the reader's attention here
to the *Ordnance Survey of Jerusalem* (Lond.
1865), and Lieut. Warren's *Reports*, etc., in the
service of the Exploration Fund, detailing his
labors and discoveries in and around the Holy
City.   H.

A good *résumé* of the controversy on the Holy
Sepulchre is given in the *Museum of Classical
Antiquities*, No. viii., and Suppl.

* *The Holy Sepulchre, and the Royal Temple at
Jerusalem*, two lectures before the Royal Institution, 1862 and 1865, by James Fergusson. He
maintains here, of course, his peculiar views on
the points in question.   H.

Maps. — Besides Dr. Barclay's, already mentioned, Mr. Van de Velde has published a very
clear and correct map (1858). So also has Signor
Pierotti (1861). The latter contains a great deal
of information, and shows plans of the churches,
etc., in the neighborhood of the city.   G.

PAL'LU (אַלֻּפ [*distinguished, eminent*] :
Φαλλούς; [in Num., Φαλλού :] *Phallu*). The
second son of Reuben, father of Eliab and founder
of the family of the PALLUITES (Ex. vi. 14; Num.
xxvi. 5, 8; 1 Chr. v. 3). In the A. V. of Gen.
xlvi. 9, he is called PHALLU, and Josephus appears
to identify him with Peleth in Num. xvi. 1, whom
he calls Φαλλούς. [See ON.]

PAL'LUITES, THE (הַפַּלֻּאִי [patr. see
above] : ὁ Φαλλουί; [Vat.] Alex. ὁ Φαλλουεί: *Phalluita*). The descendants of Pallu the
son of Reuben (Num. xxvi. 5).

* **PALM.** [HAND; PALM-TREE.]

* **PALMCRIST** (in the margin of Jon. iv. 6,
A. V.). [GOURD.]

PALMER-WORM (גָּזָם, *gāzām:* κάμπη:
eruca) occurs Joel i. 4, ii. 25; Am. iv. 9. Bochart
(*Hieroz.* iii. 253) has endeavored to show that
gāzām denotes some species of locust; it has already been shown that the ten Hebrew names to
which Bochart assigns the meaning of different
kinds of locusts cannot possibly apply to so many,
as not more than two or three destructive species
of locust are known in the Bible Lands. [LOCUST;
CATERPILLAR.] The derivation of the Hebrew
word from a root which means "to cut off," is as
applicable to several kinds of insects, whether in
their perfect or larva condition, as it is to a locust;
accordingly we prefer to follow the LXX. and
Vulg., which are consistent with each other in the
rendering of the Hebrew word in the three passages where it is found. The κάμπη of Aristotle
(*Anim. Hist.* ii. 17, 4, 5, 6) evidently denotes a caterpillar, so called from its "bending itself" up
(κάμπτω) to move, as the caterpillars called geometric, or else from the habit some caterpillars
have of "coiling" themselves up when handled.
The *Eruca* of the Vulg. is the κάμπη of the
Greeks, as is evident from the express assertion of
Columella (*De Re Rust.* xi. 3, 68, *Script. R. R.* ed.
Schneider). The Chaldee and Syriac understand
some locust larva by the Hebrew word. Oedmann
(*Verm. Samm.* fasc. ii. c. vi. p. 116) is of the
same opinion. Tychsen (*Comment. de locustis*, etc.,
p. 88) identifies the *gāzām* with the *Gryllus cristatus*, Lin., a South African species. Michaelis
(*Supp.* p. 220) follows the LXX. and Vulg. We
cannot agree with Mr. Denham (Kitto's *Cycl.* art.
"Locust") that the depredations ascribed to the
gāzām in Amos better agree with the characteristics of the locust than of a caterpillar, of which
various kinds are occasionally the cause of much
damage to fruit-trees, the fig and the olive, etc.
[JOEL.]   W. H.

PALM-TREE (תָּמָר : φοῖνιξ). Under this
generic term many species are botanically included;
but we have here only to do with the Date-palm,
the *Phœnix dactylifera* of Linnæus. It grew
very abundantly (more abundantly than now) in
many parts of the Levant. On this subject generally it is enough to refer to Ritter's monograph
("Ueber die geographische Verbreitung der Dattelpalme") in his *Erdkunde*, and also published
separately.

While this tree was abundant generally in the
Levant, it was regarded by the ancients as peculiarly characteristic of Palestine and the neighboring
regions. (Συρία, ὅπου φοίνικες οἱ καρποφόροι,
Xen. *Cyrop.* vi. 2, § 22. Judæa inclyta est palmis,
Plin. *H. N.* xiii. 4. Palmetis [Judæis] proceritas
et decor, Tac. *Hist.* v. 6. Compare Strabo xvii.
pp. 800, 818; Theophrast. *Hist. Plant.* ii. 8; Paus.
ix. 19, § 5). The following places may be enumerated from the Bible as having some connection
with the palm-tree, either in the derivation of the
name, or in the mention of the tree as growing on
the spot.

(1.) At ELIM, one of the stations of the Israelites between Egypt and Sinai, it is expressly stated
that there were "twelve wells (fountains) of water,
and threescore and ten palm-trees" (Ex. xv. 27;
Num. xxxiii. 9). The word "fountains" of the
latter passage is more correct than the "wells" of
the former: it is more in harmony, too, with the
habits of the tree; for, as Theophrastus says (*l. c.*),

the palm ἐπιζητεῖ μᾶλλον τὸ ναματιαῖον ὕδωρ. There are still palm-trees and fountains in *Wady Ghūrūndel*, which is generally identified with Elim (Rob. *Bibl. Res.* i. 69).

(2.) Next, it should be observed that ELATH (Deut. ii. 8; 1 K. ix. 26; 2 K. xiv. 22, xvi. 6; 2 Chr. viii. 17, xxvi. 2) is another plural form of the same word, and may likewise mean "the palm-trees." See Prof. Stanley's remarks (*S. & P.* pp. 20, 84, 519), and compare Reland (*Palæst.* p. 930). This place was in Edom (probably *Akṁba*); and we are reminded here of the "Idumææ palmæ" of Virgil (*Georg.* iii. 12) and Martial (x. 50).

(3.) No place in Scripture is so closely associated with the subject before us as JERICHO. Its rich palm-groves are connected with two very different periods — with that of Moses and Joshua on the one hand, and that of the Evangelists on the other. As to the former, the mention of "Jericho, the city of palm-trees" (Deut. xxxiv. 3), gives a peculiar vividness to the Lawgiver's last view from Pisgah: and even after the narrative of the conquest, we have the children of the Kenite, Moses' father-in-law, again associated with "the city of palm-trees" (Judg. i. 16). So Jericho is described in the account of the Moabite invasion after the death of Othniel (Judg. iii. 13); and, long after, we find the same phrase applied to it in the reign of Ahaz (2 Chr. xxviii. 15). What the extent of these palm-groves may have been in the desolate period of Jericho we cannot tell; but they were renowned in the time of the Gospels and Josephus. The Jewish historian mentions the luxuriance of these trees again and again; not only in allusion to the time of Moses (*Ant.* iv. 6, § 1), but in the account of the Roman campaign under Pompey (*Ant.* xiv. 4, § 1; *B. J.* i. 6, § 6), the proceedings of Antony and Cleopatra (*Ant.* xv. 4, § 2), and the war of Vespasian (*B. J.* iv. 8, §§ 2, 3). Herod the Great did much for Jericho, and took great interest in its palm-groves. Hence Horace's "Herodis palmeta pinguia" (*Ep.* ii. 2, 184), which seems almost to have been a proverbial expression. Nor is this the only heathen testimony to the same fact. Strabo describes this immediate neighborhood as πλεονάζον τῷ φοίνικι, ἐπὶ μῆκος σταδίων ἑκατόν (xvi. 763), and Pliny says, "Hiericuntem palmetis consitam" (*H. N.* v. 14), and adds elsewhere that, while palm-trees grow well in other parts in Judæa, "Hiericunte maxime" (xiii. 4). See also Galen, *De Aliment. facult.* ii., and Justin. xxxvi. 3. Shaw (*Trav.* p. 371, folio) speaks of several of these trees still remaining at Jericho in his time.

(4.) The name of HAZEZON-TAMAR, "the felling of the palm-tree," is clear in its derivation. This place is mentioned in the history both of Abraham (Gen. xiv. 7) and of Jehoshaphat (2 Chr. xx. 2). In the second of these passages it is expressly identified with En-gedi, which was on the western edge of the Dead Sea; and here we can adduce, as a valuable illustration of what is before us, the language of the Apocrypha, "I was exalted like a palm-tree in En-gaddi" (Ecclus. xxiv. 14). Here again, too, we can quote alike Josephus (γεννᾶται ἐν αὐτῇ φοῖνιξ ὁ κάλλιστος, *Ant.* ix. 1, § 2) and Pliny (Engadda oppidum secundum ab Hierosolymis, fertilitate palmetorumque nemoribus, *H. N.* v. 17).

(5.) Another place having the same element in its name, and doubtless the same characteristic in its scenery, was BAAL-TAMAR (Judg. xx. 33), the Βηθθαμῷρ of Eusebius. Its position was near Gibeah of Benjamin: and it could not be far from Deborah's famous palm-tree (Judg. iv. 5); if indeed it was not identical with it, as is suggested by Stanley (*S. & P.* p. 146).

(6.) We must next mention the TAMAR, "the palm," which is set before us in the vision of Ezekiel (xlvii. 19, xlviii. 28) as a point from which the southern border of the land is to be measured eastwards and westwards. Robinson identifies it with the Θαμαρά of Ptolemy (v. 16), and thinks its site may be at *el-Milh*, between Hebron and *Wady Musa* (*Bibl. Res.* ii. 198, 202). It seems from Jerome to have been in his day a Roman fortress.

(7.) There is little doubt that Solomon's TADMOR, afterwards the famous Palmyra, on another desert frontier far to the N. E. of Tamar, is primarily the same word; and that, as Gibbon says (*Decline and Fall*, ii. 38), "the name, by its signification in the Syriac as well as in the Latin language, denoted the multitude of palm-trees, which afforded shade and verdure to that temperate region." In fact, while the undoubted reading in 2 Chr. viii. 4 is תַּדְמוֹר, the best text in 1 K. ix. 18 is תָּמָר. See Joseph. *Ant.* viii. 6, § 1. The springs which he mentions there make the palm-trees almost a matter of course.

(8.) Nor again are the places of the N. T. without their associations with this characteristic tree of Palestine. BETHANY means "the house of dates;" and thus we are reminded that the palm grew in the neighborhood of the Mount of Olives. This helps our realization of our Saviour's entry into Jerusalem, when the people "took *branches of palm-trees* and went forth to meet Him" (John xii. 13). This again carries our thoughts backwards to the time when the Feast of Tabernacles was first kept after the Captivity, when the proclamation was given that they should "go forth unto the mount and fetch palm-branches" (Neh. viii. 15) — the only branches, it may be observed (those of the willow excepted), which are specified by name in the original institution of the festival (Lev. xxiii. 40). From this Gospel incident comes *Palm Sunday* (Dominica in Ramis Palmarum), which is observed with much ceremony in some countries where true palms can be had. Even in northern latitudes (in Yorkshire, for instance) the country people use a substitute which comes into flower just before Easter: —

"And willow branches hallow,
    That they palmes do use to call."

(9.) The word Phœnicia (Φοινίκη), which occurs twice in the N. T. (Acts xi. 19, xv. 3), is in all probability derived from the Greek word (φοῖν.ξ) for a palm. Sidonius mentions palms as a product of Phœnicia (*Paneg. Majorian.* p. 44). See also Plin. *H. N.* xiii. 4; Athen. i. 21. Thus we may imagine the same natural objects in connection with St. Paul's journeys along the coast to the north of Palestine, as with the wanderings of the Israelites through the desert on the south.

(10.) Lastly, Phœnix in the island of Crete, the harbor which St. Paul was prevented by the storm from reaching (Acts xxvii. 12), has doubtless the same derivation. Both Theophrastus and Pliny say that palm-trees are indigenous in this island. See Hoeck's *Kreta*, i. 38, 388. [PHENICE.]

From the passages where there is a literal reference to the palm-tree, we may pass to the emblematical uses of it in Scripture. Under this head may be classed the following: —

(1.) The striking appearance of the tree, its uprightness and beauty, would naturally suggest the giving of its name occasionally to women. As we find in the *Odyssey* (vi. 163) Nausicaa, the daughter of Alcinous, compared to a palm, so in Cant. vii. 7 we have the same comparison: " Thy stature is like to a palm-tree." In the O. T. three women named Tamar are mentioned : Judah's daughter-in-law (Gen. xxxviii. 6), Absalom's sister (2 Sam. xiii. 1), and Absalom's daughter (2 Sam. xiv. 27). The beauty of the two last is expressly mentioned.

(2.) We have notices of the employment of this form in decorative art, both in the real Temple of Solomon and in the visionary temple of Ezekiel. In the former case we are told (2 Chr. iii. 5) of this decoration in general terms, and elsewhere more specifically that it was applied to the walls (1 K. vi. 29), to the doors (vi. 32, 35), and to the " bases " (vii. 36) So in the prophet's vision we

Palm-Tree. (*Phœnix dactylifera.*)

find palm-trees on the posts of the gates (Ez. xl. 16, 22, 26, 31, 34, 37), and also on the walls and the doors (xli. 18–20, 25, 26). This work seems to have been in relief. We do not stay to inquire whether it had any symbolical meanings. It was a natural and doubtless customary kind of ornamentation in eastern architecture. Thus we are told by Herodotus (ii. 169) of the hall of a temple at Sais in Egypt, which was ἠσκημένη στύλοισι φοίνικας τὰ δένδρεα μεμιμημένοισι: and we are familiar now with the same sort of decoration in Assyrian buildings (Layard's *Nineveh and its Remains*, ii. 137, 396, 401). The image of such rigid and motionless forms may possibly have been before the mind of Jeremiah when he said of the idols of the heathen (x. 4, 5), " They fasten it with nails and with hammers, that it move not: they are upright as the palm-tree, but speak not."

(3.) With a tree so abundant in Judæa, and so

marked in its growth and appearance, as the palm, it seems rather remarkable that it does not appear more frequently in the imagery of the O. T. There is, however, in the Psalms (xcii. 12) the familiar comparison, " The righteous shall flourish like the palm-tree," which suggests a world of illustration, whether respect be had to the orderly and regular aspect of the tree, its fruitfulness, the perpetual greenness of its foliage, or the height at which the foliage grows, as far as possible from earth and as near as possible to heaven. Perhaps no point is more worthy of mention, if we wish to pursue the comparison, than the elasticity of the fibre of the palm, and its determined growth upwards, even when loaded with weights (" nititur in pondus palma "). Such particulars of resemblance to the righteous man were variously dwelt on by the early Christian writers. Some instances are given by Celsius in his *Hierobotanicon* (Upsal 1747), ii. 522–547. One, which he does not give, is worthy of quotation: " Well is the life of the righteous likened to a palm, in that the palm below is rough to the touch, and in a manner enveloped in dry bark, but above it is adorned with fruit, fair even to the eye; below, it is compressed by the enfoldings of its bark; above, it is spread out in amplitude of beautiful greenness. For so is the life of the elect, despised below, beautiful above. Down below it is, as it were, enfolded in many barks, in that it is straitened by innumerable afflictions; but on high it is expanded into a foliage, as it were, of beautiful greenness by the amplitude of the rewarding " (St. Gregory, *Mor. on Job* xix. 49).

(4.) The passage in Rev. vii. 9, where the glorified of all nations are described as " clothed with white robes and palms in their hands," might seem to us a purely classical image, drawn (like many of St. Paul's images) from the Greek games, the victors in which carried palms in their hands. But we seem to trace here a Jewish element also, when we consider three passages in the Apocrypha. In 1 Macc. xiii. 51, Simon Maccabæus, after the surrender of the tower at Jerusalem, is described as entering it with music and thanksgiving " and branches of palm-trees." In 2 Macc. x. 7, it is said that when Judas Maccabæus had recovered the Temple and the city " they bare branches and palms, and sang psalms also unto Him that had given them good success." In 2 Macc. xiv. 4, Demetrius is presented " with a crown of gold and a palm." Here we see the palm-branches used by Jews in token of victory and peace. (Such indeed is the case in the Gospel narrative, John xii. 13.)

There is a fourth passage in the Apocrypha, as commonly published in English, which approximates closely to the imagery of the Apocalypse. " I asked the angel, What are these? He answered and said unto me, These be they which have put off the mortal clothing, and now they are crowned and receive palms. Then said I unto the angel, What young person is it that crowneth them and giveth them palms in their hands? So he answered and said unto me, It is the Son of God, whom they have confessed in the world " (2 Esdr. ii. 44–47). This is clearly the approximation not of anticipation, but of an imitator. Whatever may be determined concerning the date of the rest of the book, this portion of it is clearly subsequent to the Christian era. [ESDRAS, THE SECOND BOOK OF.]

As to the industrial and domestic uses of the palm, it is well known that they are very numerous: but there is no clear allusion to them in the Bible. That the ancient Orientals, however, made use of wine and honey obtained from the palm-tree is evident from Herodotus (i. 193, ii. 86), Strabo (xvi. ch. 14, ed. Kram.), and Pliny (*H. N.* xiii. 4). It is indeed possible that the honey mentioned in some places may be palm-sugar. (In 2 Chr. xxxi. 5 the margin has "dates.") There may also in Cant. vii. 8, "I will go up to the palm-tree, I will take hold of the boughs thereof," be a reference to climbing for the fruit. The LXX. have ἀναβήσομαι ἐν τῷ φοίνικι, κρατήσω τῶν ὑψέων αὐτοῦ. So in ii. 3 and elsewhere (*c. g.* Ps. i. 3) the fruit of the palm may be intended: but this cannot be proved.[a] [SUGAR; WINE.]

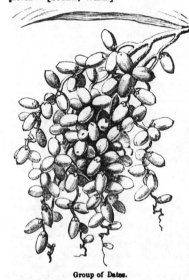

Group of Dates.

It is curious that this tree, once so abundant in Judæa, is now comparatively rare, except in the Philistine plain, and in the old Phoenicia about *Beyrout.* A few years ago there was just one palm-tree at Jericho: but that is now gone.[b] Old trunks are washed up in the Dead Sea. It would almost seem as though we might take the history of this tree in Palestine as emblematical of that of the people whose home was once in that land. The well-known coin of Vespasian representing the palm-tree with the legend "Judæa capta," is figured in vol. ii. p. 1308.   J. S. H.

---

[a] * The palm-tree being diœcious — that is to say, the stamens and pistils (male and female parts) being on different trees — it is evident that no edible fruit can be produced unless fertilization is effected either by insects or by some artificial means. That the mode of impregnating the female plant with the pollen of the male (ὀλυνθάζειν τὸν φοίνικα) was known to the ancients, is evident from Theophrastus (*H. P.* ii. 9), and Herodotus, who states that the Babylonians adopted a similar plan. The modern Arabs of Barbary, Persia, etc., take care to hang clusters of male flowers on female trees. The ancient Egyptians probably did the same. A cake of preserved dates was

PALSY. [MEDICINE, p. 1866 b.]

PALTI (פַּלְטִי [*deliverance of Jehovah*, Ges.]: Φαλτί [Vat. -τει]: *Phalti*). The son of Raphu; a Benjamite who was one of the twelve spies (Num. xiii. 9).

PALTIEL (פַּלְטִיאֵל [*deliverance of God*]: Φαλτιήλ [Vat. -τει-]: *Phaltiel*). The son of Azzan and prince of the tribe of Issachar (Num. xxxiv. 26). He was one of the twelve appointed to divide the land of Canaan among the tribes west of Jordan.

PALTITE, THE (הַפַּלְטִי [patr. from *Palti*]: ὁ Κελωθί [Vat. -θει]: Alex. ο φελλωνει: *de Phalti*). Helez "the Paltite" is named in 2 Sam. xxiii. 26 among David's mighty men. In 1 Chr. xi. 27, he is called "the Pelonite," and such seems to have been the reading followed by the Alex. MS. in 2 Sam. The Peshito-Syriac, however, supports the Hebrew, "Cholots of Pelat." But in 1 Chr. xxvii. 10, "Helez the Pelonite" of the tribe of Ephraim is again mentioned as captain of 24,000 men of David's army for the seventh month, and the balance of evidence therefore inclines to "Pelonite" as the true reading. The variation arose from a confusion between the letters ־ן and ־ט. In the Syriac of 1 Chr. both readings are combined, and Helez is described as "of Paltin."

PAMPHYLIA (Παμφυλία), one of the coast-regions in the south of Asia Minor, having CILICIA on the east, and LYCIA on the west. It seems in early times to have been less considerable than either of these contiguous districts; for in the Persian war, while Cilicia contributed a hundred ships and Lycia fifty, Pamphylia sent only thirty (Herod. vii. 91, 92). The name probably then embraced little more than the crescent of comparatively level ground between Taurus and the sea. To the north, along the heights of Taurus itself, was the region of PISIDIA. The Roman organization of the country, however, gave a wider range to the term Pamphylia. In St. Paul's time it was not only a regular province, but the Emperor Claudius had united Lycia with it (Dio Cass. lx. 17), and probably also a good part of Pisidia. However, in the N. T., the three terms are used as distinct. It was in Pamphylia that St. Paul first entered Asia Minor, after preaching the Gospel in Cyprus. He and Barnabas sailed up the river Cestrus to PERGA (Acts xiii. 13). Here they were abandoned by their subordinate companion John-Mark; a circumstance which is alluded to again with much feeling, and with a pointed mention of the place where the separation occurred (Acts xv. 38).[c] It might be the pain of this separation which induced Paul and Barnabas to leave Perga

---

found by Sir G. Wilkinson at Thebes (ii. 181, ed. 1854). It is certainly curious there is no distinct mention of dates in the Bible, though we cannot doubt that the ancient Hebrews used the fruit, and were probably acquainted with the art of fertilizing the flowers of the female plant.

[b] * Mr. Tristram now informs us that this is not strictly the case. "We discovered one wild palm of considerable size, with a clump of young ones round it, on the edge of the stream, a little below the modern village" (*Nat. Hist. of the Bible*, p. 382).   H.

[c] * The Greek (ἀποστάντα ἀπ᾽ αὐτῶν) as De Wette remarks on Acts xv. 38, implies that Mark was culpa-

without delay. They did however preach the Gospel there on their return from the interior (Acts xiv. 24, 25). We may conclude, from Acts ii. 10, that there were many Jews in the province; and possibly Perga had a synagogue. The two missionaries finally left Pamphylia by its chief seaport, ATTALIA. We do not know that St. Paul was ever in this district again: but many years afterwards he sailed near its coast, passing through "the sea of Cilicia and Pamphylia" on his way to a town of Lycia (Acts xxvii. 5). We notice here the accurate order of these geographical terms, as in the above-mentioned land journey we observe how Pisidia and Pamphylia occur in their true relations, both in going and returning (εἰς Πέργην τῆς Παμφυλίας . . . ἀπὸ τῆς Πέργης εἰς Ἀντιοχείαν τῆς Πισιδίας, xiii. 13, 14; διελθόντες τὴν Πισιδίαν ἦλθον εἰς Παμφυλίαν, xiv. 24).

J. S. H.

PAN. Of the six words *a* so rendered in A. V., two, *machbath* and *masréth*, seem to imply a shallow pan or plate, such as is used by Bedouins and Syrians for baking or dressing rapidly their cakes of meal, such as were used in legal oblations: the others, especially *sir*, a deeper vessel or cauldron for boiling meat, placed during the process on three stones (Burckhardt, *Notes on Bed.* i. 58; Niebuhr, *Descr. de l'Arab.* p. 46; Lane, *Mod. Egypt.* i. 181). [CALDRON.]   H. W. P.

PANNAG (פַּנַּג), an article of commerce exported from Palestine to Tyre (Ez. xxvii. 17), the nature of which is a pure matter of conjecture, as the term occurs nowhere else. In comparing the passage in Ezekiel with Gen. xliii. 11, where the most valued productions of Palestine are enumerated, the omission of tragacanth and ladanum (A. V. "spices and myrrh") in the former is very observable, and leads to the supposition that pannag represents some of the spices grown in that country. The LXX., in rendering it κασία, favors this opinion, though it is evident that cassia cannot be the particular spice intended (see ver. 19). Hitzig observes that a similar term occurs in Sanskrit (*pannaga*) for an aromatic plant. The Syriac version, on the other hand, understands by it "millet" (*panicum miliaceum*); and this view is favored by the expression in the book of Sohar, quoted by Gesenius (*s. v.*), which speaks of "bread of pannag:" though this again is not decisive, for the pannag may equally well have been some flavoring substance, as seems to be implied in the doubtful equivalent *b* given in the Targum.

W. L. B.

PAPER. [WRITING.]

* **PAPER-REEDS.** "The *paper-reeds* by

the *brooks*" (Is. xix. 7, A. V.) is probably a mistranslation for "the *meadows* by the *river*" (i. e. the Nile). So, substantially, Gesenius, Fürst, De Wette, Knobel, Ewald. [REED, 3.]   A.

PA′PHOS (Πάφος), a town at the west end of CYPRUS, connected by a road with SALAMIS at the east end. Paul and Barnabas travelled, on their first missionary expedition, "through the isle," from the latter place to the former (Acts xiii. 6).

What took place at Paphos was briefly as follows. The two missionaries found SERGIUS PAULUS, the proconsul of the island, residing here, and were enabled to produce a considerable effect on his intelligent and candid mind. This influence was resisted by ELYMAS (or Bar-Jesus), one of those oriental "sorcerers," whose mischievous power was so great at this period, even among the educated classes. Miraculous sanction was given to the Apostles, and Elymas was struck with blindness. The proconsul's faith having been thus confirmed, and doubtless a Christian Church having been founded in Paphos, Barnabas and Saul crossed over to the continent and landed in PAMPHYLIA (ver. 13). It is observable that it is at this point that the latter becomes the more prominent of the two, and that his name henceforward is Paul, and not Saul (Σαῦλος, ὁ καὶ Παῦλος, ver. 9). How far this was connected with the proconsul's name, must be discussed elsewhere.

The great characteristic of Paphos was the worship of Aphrodite or Venus, who was here fabled to have risen from the sea (Hom. *Od.* viii. 362). Her temple, however, was at "Old Paphos," now called *Kuklia*. The harbor and the chief town were at "New Paphos," at some little distance. The place is still called *Baffa*. The road between the two was often filled with gay and profligate processions (Strabo, xiv. p. 683); strangers came constantly to visit the shrine (Athen. xv. 18); and the hold which these local superstitions had upon the higher minds at this very period is well exemplified by the pilgrimage of Titus (Tac. *Hist.* ii. 2, 3) shortly before the Jewish war.

For notices of such scanty remains as are found at Paphos we must refer to Pococke (*Desc. of the East*, ii. 325–328), and especially Ross (*Reisen nach Kos, Halikarnassos, Rhodus u. Cyprus,* pp. 180–192). Extracts also are given in *Life and Epp. of St. Paul* (2d ed. i. 190, 191), from the MS. notes of Captain Graves, R. N., who recently surveyed the island of Cyprus. For all that relates to the harbor the Admiralty Chart should be consulted.   J. S. H.

PAPYRUS. [REED.]

PARABLE (מָשָׁל, *mâshâl*: παραβολή: pa-

---

ble in thus leaving his associates. Yet it is pleasing to know that the estrangement was only temporary; for Mark became subsequently Paul's fellow-traveller (Col. iv. 10), and is commended by him as eminently useful in the ministry (2 Tim. iv. 11).   H.

a 1. פָּיִר, or פּוּר; λέβης ὁ μέγας; *lebes* (1 Sam. ii. 14); elsewhere "laver" and "hearth," i. e. a brazier or pan for fire (Zech. xii. 6).

2. מַחֲבַת, from חָבַת, "bake" (Ges. p. 444); τήγανον; *sartago* (Lev. ii. 5), where it follows מַרְחֶשֶׁת, ἐσχάρα, *craticula*, "frying-pan," and is therefore distinct from it.

3. מַשְׂרֵת; τήγανον; "a baking-pan" (2 Sam. xiii. 9), Ges. p. 1342.

4. סִיר; λέβης; *olla*; from סִיר, "boil," joined (2 K. iv. 38) with גְּדוֹלָה, "great," i. e. the great kettle or cauldron.

5. פָּרוּר; χύτρα; *olla*.

6. צֶלָחוֹת, plur.; λέβητες; *olla* (2 Chr. xxxv 13). In Prov. xix. 24, "dish."

b קוּלְיָא.

rabola). The distinction between the Parable and one cognate form of teaching has been discussed under FABLE. Something remains to be said (1) as to the word, (2) as to the Parables of the Gospels, (3) as to the laws of their interpretation.

I. The word παραβολή does not of itself imply a narrative. The juxtaposition of two things, differing in most points, but agreeing in some, is sufficient to bring the comparison thus produced within the etymology of the word. The παραβολή of Greek rhetoric need not be more than the simplest argument from analogy. "You would not choose pilots or athletes by lot; why then should you choose statesmen?" (Aristot. *Rhet.* ii. 20). In Hellenistic Greek, however, it acquired a wider meaning, coextensive with that of the Hebrew *māshāl*, for which the LXX. writers, with hardly an exception, make it the equivalent.[a] That word (= *similitude*), as was natural in the language of a people who had never reduced rhetoric to an art, had a large range of application, and was applied sometimes to the shortest proverbs (1 Sam. x. 12, xxiv. 13; 2 Chr. vii. 20), sometimes to dark prophetic utterances (Num. xxiii. 7, 18, xxiv. 3; Ez. xx. 49), sometimes to enigmatic maxims (Ps. lxxviii. 2; Prov. i. 6), or metaphors expanded into a narrative (Ez. xii. 22). In Ecclesiasticus the word occurs with a striking frequency, and, as will be seen hereafter, its use by the son of Sirach throws light on the position occupied by parables in Our Lord's teaching. In the N. T. itself the word is used with a like latitude. While attached most frequently to the illustrations which have given it a special meaning, it is also applied to a short saying like, "Physician, heal thyself" (Luke iv. 23), to a mere comparison without a narrative (Matt. xxiv. 32), to the figurative character of the Levitical ordinances (Heb. ix. 9), or of single facts in patriarchal history (Heb. xi. 19).[b] The later history of the word is not without interest. Naturalized in Latin, chiefly through the Vulgate or earlier versions, it loses gradually the original idea of figurative speech, and is used for speech of any kind. Mediaeval Latin gives us the strange form of *parabolare*, and the descendants of the technical Greek word in the Romance languages are *parler*, *parole*, *parola*, *palabras* (Diez, *Roman. Wörterb. s. v.* "Parola").

II. As a form of teaching, the Parable, as has been shown, differs from the Fable, (1) in excluding brute or inanimate creatures passing out of the laws of their nature, and speaking or acting like men, (2) in its higher ethical significance. It differs, it may be added, from the Mythus, in being the result of a conscious deliberate choice, not the growth of an unconscious realism, personifying attributes, appearing, no one knows how, in popular belief. It differs from the Allegory, in that the latter, with its direct personification of ideas or attributes, and the names which designate them, involves really no comparison. The virtues and vices of mankind appear, as in a drama, in their own character and costume. The allegory is self-interpreting. The parable demands attention, insight, sometimes an actual explanation. It differs lastly from the Proverb, in that it must include a similitude of some kind, while the proverb may assert, without a similitude, some wide generalization of experience. So far as proverbs go beyond this, and state what they affirm in a figurative form, they may be described as condensed parables, and parables as expanded proverbs (comp. Trench *on Parables*, ch. i.; and Grotius *on Matt.* xiii.).

To understand the relation of the parables of the Gospels to our Lord's teaching, we must go back to the use made of them by previous or contemporary teachers. We have sufficient evidence that they were frequently employed by them. They appear frequently in the Gemara and Midrash (comp. Lightfoot, *Hor. Heb. in Matt.* xiii. 3; Jost, *Judenthum*, ii. 216), and are ascribed to Hillel, Shammai, and other great Rabbis of the two preceding centuries.[c] The panegyric passed upon the great Rabbi Meir, that after his death men ceased to speak parables, implies that, up to that time, there had been a succession of teachers more or less distinguished for them (*Sota*, fol. 49, in Jost, *Judenthum*, ii. 87; Lightfoot, *l. c.*). Later Jewish writers have seen in this employment of parables a condescension to the ignorance of the great mass of mankind, who cannot be taught otherwise. For them, as for women or children, parables are the natural and fit method of instruction (Maimonides, *Porta Mosis*, p. 84, in Wetstein, *on Matt.* xiii.), and the same view is taken by Jerome as accounting for the common use of parables in Syria and Palestine (Hieron. *in Matt.* xviii. 23). It may be questioned, however, whether this represents the use made of them by the Rabbis of our Lord's time. The language of the Son of Sirach confines them to the scribe who devotes himself to study. They are at once his glory and his reward (Ecclus. xxxix. 2, 3). Of all who eat bread by the sweat of their brow, of the great mass of men in cities and country, it is written that "they shall not be found where parables are spoken" (*Ibid.* xxxviii. 33). For these therefore it is probable that the scribes and teachers of the law had simply rules and precepts, often perhaps burdensome and oppressive (Matt. xxiii. 3, 4), formulae of prayer (Luke xi. 1), appointed times of fasting and hours of devotion (Mark ii. 18). They, with whom they would not even eat (comp. Wetstein and Lampe on *John* vii. 49), cared little to give even as much as this to the "people of the earth," whom they scorned as "knowing not the law," a brute herd for whom they could have no sympathy. For their own scholars they had, according to their individual character and power of thought, the casuistry with which the Mishna is for the most part filled, or the parables which here and there give tokens of some deeper insight. The parable was made the instrument for teaching the young disciple to discern the treasures of wisdom of which the "so-

---

[a] The word παροιμία is used by the LXX. in Prov. i. 1, xxv. 1, xxvi. 7; Ecclus. vi. 35, &c., and in some other passages by Symmachus. The same word, it will be remembered, is used throughout by St. John, instead of παραβολή.

[b] It should be mentioned that another meaning has been given by some interpreters to παραβολή in this passage, but, it is believed, on insufficient grounds.

[c] Some interesting examples of these may be seen in Trench's *Parables*, ch. iv. Others, presenting some striking superficial resemblances to those of the Pearl of Great Price, the Laborers, the Lost Piece of Money, the Wise and Foolish Virgins, may be seen in Wetstein's notes to those parables. The conclusion from them is, that there was at least a generic resemblance between the outward form of our Lord's teaching and that of the Rabbis of Jerusalem.

cused" multitude were ignorant. The teaching of our Lord at the commencement of his ministry was, in every way, the opposite of this. The Sermon on the Mount may be taken as the type of the "words of Grace" which he spake, "not as the scribes." Beatitudes, laws, promises were uttered distinctly, not indeed without similitudes, but with similitudes that explained themselves. So for some months He taught in the synagogues and on the sea-shore of Galilee, as He had before taught in Jerusalem, and as yet without a parable. But then there comes a change. The direct teaching was met with scorn, unbelief, hardness, and He seems for a time to abandon it for that which took the form of parables. The question of the disciples (Matt. xiii. 10) implies that they were astonished. Their Master was no longer proclaiming the Gospel of the kingdom as before. He was falling back into one at least of the forms of Rabbinic teaching (comp. Schoettgen's *Hor. Heb.* ii.. *Christus Rabbinorum Summus*). He was speaking to the multitude in the parables and dark sayings which the Rabbis reserved for their chosen disciples. Here for them were two grounds of wonder. Here, for us, is the key to the explanation which he gave, that He had chosen this form of teaching because the people were spiritually blind and deaf (Matt. xiii. 13), and in order that they might remain so (Mark. iv. 12). Two interpretations have been given of these words. (1.) Spiritual truths, it has been said, are in themselves hard and uninviting. Men needed to be won to them by that which was more attractive. The parable was an instrument of education for those who were children in age or character. For this reason it was chosen by the Divine teacher as fables and stories, "adminicula imbecillitatis" (Seneca, *Epist.* 59), have been chosen by human teachers (Chrysost. *Hom. in Johann.* 34). (2.) Others again have seen in this use of parables something of a penal character. Men have set themselves against the truth, and therefore it is hid from their eyes, presented to them in forms in which it is not easy for them to recognize it. To the inner circle of the chosen it is given to know the mysteries of the kingdom of God. To those who are without, all these things are done in parables. Neither view is wholly satisfactory. Each contains a partial truth. All experience shows (1) that parables do attract, and, when once understood, are sure to be remembered; (2) that men may listen to them and see that they have a meaning, and yet never care to ask what that meaning is. Their worth, as instruments of teaching, lies in their being at once a test of character, and in their presenting each form of character with that which, as a penalty or blessing, is adapted to it. They withdraw the light from those who love darkness. They protect the truth which they enshrine from the mockery of the scoffer. They leave something even with the careless which may be interpreted and understood afterwards. They reveal, on the other hand, the seekers after truth. These ask the meaning of the parable, will not rest till the teacher has explained it, are led step by step to the laws of interpretation, so that they can "understand all parables," and then pass on into the higher region in which parables are no longer necessary, but all

things are spoken plainly. In this way the parable did its work, found out the fit hearers and led them on. And it is to be remembered also that even after this self-imposed law of reserve and reticence, the teaching of Christ presented a marvelous contrast to the narrow exclusiveness of the scribes. The mode of education was changed, but the work of teaching or educating was not for a moment given up, and the aptest scholars were found in those whom the received system would have altogether shut out.

From the time indicated by Matt. xiii., accordingly, parables enter largely into our Lord's recorded teaching. Each parable of those which we read in the Gospels may have been repeated more than once with greater or less variation (as *e. g.* those of the Pounds and the Talents, Matt. xxv. 14; Luke xix. 12; of the Supper, in Matt. xxii. 2, and Luke xiv. 16). Everything leads us to believe that there were many others of which we have no record (Matt. xiii. 34; Mark iv. 33). In those which remain it is possible to trace something like an order.[a]

(A.) There is the group with which the new mode of teaching is ushered in, and which have for their subject the laws of the Divine Kingdom, in its growth, its nature, its consummation. Under this head we have —

1. The Sower (Matt. xiii.; Mark iv.; Luke viii.).
2. The Wheat and the Tares (Matt. xiii.).
3. The Mustard-Seed (Matt. xiii.; Mark iv.).
4. The Seed cast into the Ground (Mark iv.).
5. The Leaven (Matt. xiii.).
6. The Hid Treasure (Matt. xiii.).
7. The Pearl of Great Price (Matt. xiii.).
8. The Net cast into the Sea (Matt. xiii.).

(B.) After this there is an interval of some months of which we know comparatively little. Either there was a return to the more direct teaching, or else these were repeated, or others like them spoken. When the next parables meet us they are of a different type and occupy a different position. They occur chiefly in the interval between the mission of the seventy and the last approach to Jerusalem. They are drawn from the life of men rather than from the world of nature. Often they occur, not, as in Matt. xiii., in discourses to the multitude, but in answers to the questions of the disciples or other inquirers. They are such as these: —

9. The Two Debtors (Luke vii.).
10. The Merciless Servant (Matt. xviii.).
11. The Good Samaritan (Luke x.).
12. The Friend at Midnight (Luke xi.).
13. The Rich Fool (Luke xii.).
14. The Wedding-Feast (Luke xii.).
15. The Fig-Tree (Luke xiii.).
16. The Great Supper (Luke xiv.).
17. The Lost Sheep (Matt. xviii; Luke xv.).
18. The Lost Piece of Money (Luke xv.)
19. The Prodigal Son (Luke xv.).
20. The Unjust Steward (Luke xvi.).
21. The Rich Man and Lazarus (Luke xvi.).
22. The Unjust Judge (Luke xviii.).
23. The Pharisee and the Publican (Luke xviii.).
24. The Laborers in the Vineyard (Matt. xx.).

(C.) Towards the close of our Lord's ministry,

---

[a] The number of parables in the Gospels will of course depend on the range given to the application of the name. Thus Mr. Greswell reckons twenty-seven; Dean Trench, thirty. By others, the number has been extended to fifty.

Immediately before and after the entry into Jerusalem, the parables assume a new character. They are again theocratic, but the phase of the Divine Kingdom, on which they chiefly dwell, is that of its final consummation. They are prophetic, in part, of the rejection of Israel, in part of the great retribution of the coming of the Lord. They are to the earlier parables what the prophecy of Matt. xxiv. is to the Sermon on the Mount. To this class we may refer —

25. The Pounds (Luke xix.).
26. The Two Sons (Matt. xxi.).
27. The Vineyard let out to Husbandmen (Matt. xxi.; Mark xii.; Luke xx.).
28. The Marriage-Feast (Matt. xxii.).
29. The Wise and Foolish Virgins (Matt. xxv.).
30. The Talents (Matt. xxv.).
31. The Sheep and the Goats (Matt. xxv.).

It is characteristic of the several Gospels that the greater part of the parables of the first and third groups belong to St. Matthew, emphatically the Evangelist of the kingdom. Those of the second are found for the most part in St. Luke. They are such as we might expect to meet with in the Gospel which dwells most on the sympathy of Christ for all men. St. Mark, as giving vivid recollections of the acts rather than the teaching of Christ, is the scantiest of the three synoptic Gospels. It is not less characteristic that there are no parables properly so called in St. John. It is as if he, sooner than any other, had passed into the higher stage of knowledge in which parables were no longer necessary, and therefore dwelt less on them. That which his spirit appropriated most readily were the words of eternal life, figurative it might be in form, abounding in bold analogies, but not in any single instance taking the form of a narrative.[a]

Lastly it is to be noticed, partly as a witness to the truth of the four Gospels, partly as a line of demarcation between them and all counterfeits, that the apocryphal Gospels contain no parables. Human invention could imagine miracles (though these too in the spurious Gospels are stripped of all that gives them majesty and significance), but the parables of the Gospels were inimitable and unapproachable by any writers of that or the succeeding age. They possess a life and power which stamp them as with the "image and superscription" of the Son of Man. Even the total absence of any allusion to them in the written or spoken teaching of the Apostles shows how little their minds set afterwards in that direction, how little likely they were to do more than testify what they had actually heard.[b]

III. Lastly, there is the law of interpretation. It has been urged by some writers, by none with greater force or clearness than by Chrysostom (Hom. in Matt. 64), that there is a scope or purpose for each parable, and that our aim must be to discern this, not to find a special significance in each circumstance or incident. The rest, it is said, may be dealt with as the drapery which the parable needs for its grace and completeness, but which is not essential. It may be questioned, however, whether this canon of interpretation is likely to lead us to the full meaning of this portion of our Lord's teaching. True as it doubtless is, that there was in each parable a leading thought to be learnt partly from the parable itself, partly from the occasion of its utterance, and that all else gathers round that thought as a centre, it must be remembered that in the great patterns of interpretation which He himself has given us, there is more than this. Not only the sower and the seed and the several soils have their counterparts in the spiritual life, but the birds of the air, the thorns, the scorching heat, have each of them a significance. The explanation of the wheat and the tares, given with less fullness, an outline as it were, which the advancing scholars would be able to fill up, is equally specific. It may be inferred from these two instances that we are, at least, justified in looking for a meaning even in the seeming accessories of a parable. If the opposite mode of interpreting should seem likely to lead us, as it has led many, to strange and forced analogies, and an arbitrary dogmatism, the safeguard may be found in our recollecting that in assigning such meanings we are but as scholars guessing at the mind of a teacher whose words are higher than our thoughts, recognizing the analogies which may have been, but which were not necessarily those which he recognized. No such interpretation can claim anything like authority. The very form of the teaching makes it probable that there may be, in any case, more than one legitimate explanation. The outward fact in nature, or in social life, may correspond to spiritual facts at once in God's government of the world, and in the history of the individual soul. A parable may be at once ethical, and in the highest sense of the term prophetic. There is thus a wide field open to the discernment of the interpreter. There are also restraints upon the mere fertility of his imagination. (1.) The analogies must be real, not arbitrary. (2.) The parables are to be considered as parts of a whole, and the interpretation of one is not to override or encroach upon the lessons taught by others. (3.) The direct teaching of Christ presents the standard to which all our interpretations are to be referred, and by which they are to be measured. (Comp. Dean Trench On the Parables, Introductory Remarks; to which one who has once read it cannot but be more indebted than any mere references can indicate: Stier, Words of the Lord Jesus, on Matt. xiii. 11.)

                                        E. H. P.

* Literature. The following list embraces only a few of the more noticeable works on this subject. For fuller references see Hase's Leben Jesu, 5e Aufl. (1865), § 65, and Darling's Cyclop. Bibliographica (Subjects), col. 1873, ff. — Charles Bulkley, Discourses on the Parables of our Saviour, and on the Miracles, 4 vols. Lond. 1771. Andrew Gray, A Delineation of the Parables of our Saviour, with a Diss. on Parables and Allegorical Writing

---

[a] See an ingenious classification of the parables of each Gospel, according to their subject-matter, in Westcott, Introduction to the Study of the Gospels, ch. vii., and Appendix F.

[b] The existence of Rabbinic parables, presenting a superficial resemblance to those of the Gospel, is no real exception to this statement. Whether we believe them to have had an independent origin, and so to be fair specimens of the genus of this form of teaching among the Jews, or to have been (as chronologically they might have been) borrowed, consciously or unconsciously, from those of Christ, there is still in the latter a distinctive power, and purity, which place the others almost beyond the range of comparison, except as to outward form.

٭ *general,* Lond. 1777, 2d ed. 1814, German trans. 1783. Storr, *De Parab. Christi,* Tub. 1779, 4to, also in his *Opusc. Acad.* i. 89–143, Eng. trans. in *Essays and Diss. in Bibl. Lit.,* N. Y. 1829, vol. i., and in *Philol. Tracts* (vol. ix. of the Edinb. *Bibl. Cabinet*). F. A. Krummacher, *Über den Geist u. d. Form d. evang. Geschichte,* Leipz. 1805, §§ 197–225. J. F. R. Eylert, *Homilien üb. die Parab. Jesu,* Halle, 1806, 2° Aufl. 1819, with a prelim. essay *Ueber das Charakteristische d. Parab. Jesu.* J. J. Kromm, *Die sämmtl. Parab. Jesu, übersetzt, erläutert, u. prakt.-homilet. bearbeitet,* Fulda, 1823. W. Scholten, *Diatribe de Parab. Jesu Christi,* Delph. Bat. 1827. F. W. Rettberg, *De Parab. J. C.,* Gotting. 1827, 4to (prize essay). A. H. A. Schultze, *De Parab. J. C. Indole poetica,* Gotting. 1827, 4to (prize essay). A. F. Unger, *De Parab. Jesu Natura, Interpretatione, Usu,* Lips. 1828. (Highly commended.) B. Bailey, *Expos. of the Parables, with a Prelim. Diss. on the Parable,* Lond. 1828. F. G. Lisco, *Die Parabeln Jesu, exeget.-homilet. bearbeitet,* Berl. 1832, 5° Aufl. 1861, Eng. trans. by P. Fairbairn, Edin. 1840 (*Bibl. Cab.*). E. Greswell, *Expos. of the Parables and other Parts of the Gospel,* 5 vols. in 6, Oxf. 1834. R. C. Trench, *Notes on the Parables,* Lond. 1841, 9th ed. 1864, Amer. repr., 12th ed., N. Y. 1867, 8vo; condensed, N. Y. 1861, 12mo. (The best work on the subject.) Friedr. Arndt, *Die Gleichniss-Reden Jesu Christi.* [111] *Betrachtungen,* 6 Thle. Magd. 1842–47, 2° Aufl. 1846 -60. Neander, *Leben Jesu,* 4° Aufl. (1847), pp. 161–182, Amer. trans. p. 107 ff. (separately trans. by Prof. Hackett from an earlier ed., *Christian Review,* 1843, viii. 199 ff., 588 ff.). Lord Stanley (now Earl of Derby), *Conversations on the Parables,* new ed., Lond. 1849, 18mo. E. N. Kirk, *Lectures on the Parables,* N. Y. 1856. J. P. Lange, art. *Gleichniss* in Herzog's *Real-Encykl.* vol. v. Oxenden, *Parables of our Lord,* Lond. 1865.

On the later Jewish parables, see Trench's *Notes on the Parables,* Introd. Rem. ch. iv.; Hurwitz's *Hebrew Tales,* Lond. 1826, Amer. repr. N. Y. 1847; G. Levi, *Parabole, leggende e pensieri, raccolte dai libri talmudici,* Firenze, 1861.   A.

PARADISE (פַּרְדֵּס, *Pardês:* παράδεισος: *Paradisus*). Questions as to the nature and locality of Paradise as identical with the garden of Gen. ii. and iii. have been already discussed under EDEN. It remains to trace the history of the word and the associations connected with it, as it appears in the later books of the O. T. and in the language of Christ and His Apostles.

The word itself, though it appears in the above form in Cant. iv. 13, Eccl. ii. 5, Neh. ii. 8, may be classed, with hardly a doubt, as of Aryan rather than of Semitic origin. It first appears in Greek as coming straight from Persia (Xen. *ut inf.*). Greek lexicographers classify it as a Persian word (Julius Pollux, *Onomast.* ix. 3). Modern philologists accept the same conclusion with hardly a dissentient voice (Renan, *Langues Sémitiques,* ii. 1, p. 153). Gesenius (*s. v.*) traces it a step further, and connects it with the Sanskrit *para-dêça* = high, well-tilled land, and applied to an ornamental garden attached to a house. Other Sanskrit scholars, however, assert that the meaning of *para-deça* in classical Sanskrit is "foreign country," and although they admit that it may also mean "the best or most excellent country," they look on this as an instance of casual coincidence rather than derivation.٭ Other etymologies, more fanciful and far-fetched, have been suggested — (1) from παρά and δεύω, giving as a meaning, the "well-watered ground " (Suidas, *s. v.*); (2) from παρά and δείσα, a barbarous word, supposed to signify a plant, or collection of plants (Joann. Damasc. in Suidas, *l. c.*); (3) from פְּרֵה דָשֵׁא, to bring forth herbs; (4) פִּרְדַּה הַדַּס, to bring forth myrrh (Ludwig, *de raptu Pauli in Parad.* in Menthen's *Thesaur. Theolog.* p. 1702).

On the assumption that the Song of Solomon and Ecclesiastes were written in the time of Solomon, the occurrence of the foreign word may be accounted for either (1) on the hypothesis of later forms having crept into the text in the process of transcription, or (2) on that of the word having found its way into the language of Israel at the time when its civilization took a new flight under the Son of David, and the king borrowed from the customs of central Asia that which made the royal park or garden part of the glory of the kingdom. In Neh. ii. 8, as might be expected, the word is used in a connection which points it out as distinctly Persian. The account given of the hanging gardens of Babylon, in like manner, indicates Media as the original seat both of the word and of the thing. Nebuchadnezzar constructed them, terrace upon terrace, that he might reproduce in the plains of Mesopotamia the scenery with which the Median princess he had married had been familiar in her native country; and this was the origin of the κρεμαστὸς παράδεισος (Berosus, in Joseph. c. Ap. i. 19). In Xenophon the word occurs frequently, and we get vivid pictures of the scene which it implied. A wide open park, inclosed against injury, yet with its natural beauty unspoiled, with stately forest trees, many of them bearing fruit, watered by clear streams, on whose banks roved large herds of antelopes or sheep — this was the scenery which connected itself in the mind of the Greek traveller with the word παράδεισος, and for which his own language supplied no precise equivalent. (Comp. *Anab.* i. 2, § 7, 4, § 9; ii. 4, § 14; *Hellen.* iv. 1, § 15; *Cyrop.* i. 3, § 14; *Œconom.* 4, § 13.) Through the writings of Xenophon, and through the general admixture of orientalisms in the later Greek after the conquests of Alexander, the word gained a recognized place, and the LXX. writers chose it for a new use which gave it a higher worth and secured for it a more perennial life. The garden of Eden became ὁ παράδεισος τῆς τρυφῆς (Gen. ii. 15, iii. 23; Joel ii. 3). They used the same word whenever there was any allusion, however remote, to the fair region which had been the first blissful home of man. The valley of the Jordan, in their version, is the paradise of God (Gen. xiii. 10). There is no tree in the paradise of God equal to that which in the prophet's vision symbolizes the glory of Assyria (Ez. xxxi. 1-9). The imagery of this chapter furnishes a more vivid picture of the scenery of a παράδεισος than we find elsewhere. The prophet to whom "the word of the Lord came " by the river of Chebar may

---

٭ Professor Monier Williams allows the writer to say that he is of this opinion. Comp. also Busch-

mann, in Humboldt's *Cosmos,* ii. note 280, and Ersch u. Gruber, *Encyclop. s* v.

well have seen what he describes so clearly. Elsewhere, however, as in the translation of the three
passages in which *pardes* occurs in the Hebrew, it
is used in a more general sense. (Comp. Is. i. 30;
Num. xxiv. 6; Jer. xxix. 5; Susann. ver. 4.)

It was natural, however, that this higher meaning should become the exclusive one, and be associated with new thoughts. Paradise, with no other
word to qualify it, was the bright region which
man had lost, which was guarded by the flaming
sword. Soon a new hope sprang up. Over and
above all questions as to where the primeval garden
had been, there came the belief that it did not
belong entirely to the past. There was a paradise
still into which man might hope to enter. It is a
matter of some interest to ascertain with what associations the word was connected in the minds of
the Jews of Palestine and other countries at the
time of our Lord's teaching, what sense therefore
we may attach to it in the writings of the N. T.

In this as in other instances we may distinguish
three modes of thought, each with marked characteristics, yet often blended together in different
proportions, and melting one into the other by
hardly perceptible degrees. Each has its counterpart in the teaching of Christian theologians.
The language of the N. T. stands apart from and
above all. (1.) To the Idealist school of Alexandria, of which Philo is the representative, paradise
was nothing more than a symbol and an allegory.
Traces of this way of looking at it had appeared
previously in the teaching of the Son of Sirach.
The four rivers of Eden are figures of the wide
streams of Wisdom, and she is as the brook which
becomes a river and waters the Paradise of God
(Ecclus. xxiv. 25–30). This, however, was compatible with the recognition of Gen. ii. as speaking
of a fact. To Philo the thought of the fact was
unendurable. The primeval history spoke of no
garden such as men plant and water. Spiritual
perfection (ἀρετή) was the only paradise. The
trees that grew in it were the thoughts of the
spiritual man. The fruits which they bore were
life and knowledge and immortality. The four
rivers flowing from one source are the four virtues
of the later Platonists, each derived from the same
source of goodness (Philo, *de Alleg.* i.). It is obvious that a system of interpretation such as this
was not likely to become popular. It was confined
to a single school, possibly to a single teacher. It
has little or nothing corresponding to it in the N. T.

(2.) The Rabbinic schools of Palestine presented a phase of thought the very opposite of that of
the Alexandrian writer. They had their descriptions, definite and detailed, a complete topography
of the unseen world. Paradise, the garden of
Eden, existed still, and they discussed the question
of its locality. The answers were not always consistent with each other. It was far off in the distant East, further than the foot of man had trod.
It was a region of the world of the dead, of Sheol,
in the heart of the earth. Gehenna was on one
side, with its flames and torments. Paradise on
the other, the intermediate home of the blessed.
(Comp. Wetstein, Grotius, and Schoettgen on *Luc.*
xxiii.) The patriarchs were there, Abraham, and
Isaac, and Jacob, ready to receive their faithful
descendants into their bosoms (Joseph. *de Macc.*
c. 13). The highest place of honor at the feast
of the blessed souls was Abraham's bosom (Luke
xvi. 23). on which the new heir of immortality reclined as the favored and honored guest. Or,

again, paradise was neither on the earth, nor with
in it, but above it, in the third heaven, or in some
higher orb. [HEAVEN.] Or there were two paradises, the upper and the lower — one in heaven,
for those who had attained the heights of holiness
— one in earth, for those who had lived but de-
cently (Schoettgen, *Hor. Heb. in Apoc.* ii. 7), and
the heavenly paradise was sixty times as large as
the whole lower earth (Eisenmenger, *Entdeckt. Judenth.* ii. p. 297). Each had seven palaces, and in
each palace were its appropriate dwellers (*ibid.* p.
302). As the righteous dead entered paradise,
angels stripped them of their grave-clothes, arrayed
them in new robes of glory, and placed on their
heads diadems of gold and pearls (*ibid.* p. 310).
There was no night there. Its pavement was of
precious stones. Plants of healing power and
wondrous fragrance grew on the banks of its
streams (*ibid.* p. 313). From this lower paradise
the souls of the dead rose on sabbaths and on
feast-days to the higher (*ibid.* p. 318), where every
day there was the presence of Jehovah holding
council with His saints (*ibid.* p. 320). (Comp. also
Schoettgen, *Hor. Heb. in Luc.* xxiii.)

(3.) Out of the discussions and theories of the
Rabbis. there grew a broad popular belief, fixed in
the hearts of men, accepted without discussion,
blending with their best hopes. Their prayer for
the dying or the dead was that his soul might rest
in paradise, in the garden of Eden (Maimonides,
Porta Mosis, quoted by Wetstein in *Luc.* xxiii.;
Taylor, *Funeral Sermon on Sir G. Dalston*). The
belief of the Essenes, as reported by Josephus (*B
J.* ii. 8, § 11), may be accepted as a fair representation of the thoughts of those who, like them,
were not trained in the Rabbinical schools, living
in a simple and more childlike faith. To them
accordingly paradise was a far-off land, a region
where there was no scorching heat, no consuming
cold, where the soft west-wind from the ocean blew
forevermore. The visions of the 2d book of Esdras, though not without an admixture of Christian
thoughts and phrases, may be looked upon as representing this phase of feeling. There also we
have the picture of a fair garden, streams of milk
and honey, twelve trees laden with divers fruits,
mighty mountains whereon grow lilies and roses
(ii. 19) — a place into which the wicked shall not
enter.

It is with this popular belief, rather than with
that of either school of Jewish thought, that the
language of the N. T. connects itself. In this, as
in other instances, it is made the starting-point
for an education which leads men to rise from it to
higher thoughts. The old word is kept, and is
raised to a new dignity or power. It is significant,
indeed, that the word " paradise " nowhere occurs
in the public teaching of our Lord, or in his intercourse with his own disciples. Connected as it
had been with the thoughts of a sensuous happiness, it was not the fittest or the best word for
those whom He was training to rise out of sensuous
thoughts to the higher regions of the spiritual life.
For them, accordingly, the kingdom of Heaven,
the kingdom of God, are the words most dwelt on.
The blessedness of the pure in heart is that they
shall see God. If language borrowed from their
common speech is used at other times, if they hear
of the marriage-supper and the new wine, it is not
till they have been taught to understand parables
and to separate the figure from the reality. With
the thief dying on the cross the case was different

We can assume nothing in the robber-outlaw, but the most rudimentary forms of popular belief. We may well believe that the word used here, and here only, in the whole course of the Gospel history, had a special fitness for him. His reverence, sympathy, repentance, hope, uttered themselves in the prayer, "Lord, remember me when thou comest into thy kingdom!" What were the thoughts of the sufferer as to that kingdom we do not know. Unless they were supernaturally raised above the level which the disciples had reached by slow and painful steps, they must have been mingled with visions of an earthly glory, of pomp, and victory, and triumph. The answer to his prayer gave him what he needed most, the assurance of immediate rest and peace. The word paradise spoke to him, as to other Jews, of repose, shelter, joy — the greatest contrast possible to the thirst, and agony, and shame of the hours upon the cross. Rudimentary as his previous thoughts of it might be, this was the word fittest for the education of his spirit.

There is a like significance in the general absence of the word from the language of the Epistles. Here also it is found nowhere in the direct teaching. It occurs only in passages that are apocalyptic, and therefore almost of necessity symbolic. St. Paul speaks of one, apparently of himself, as having been "caught up into paradise," as having there heard things that might not be uttered (2 Cor. xii. 4).[a] In the message to the first of the Seven Churches of Asia, "the tree of life which is in the midst of the paradise of God," appears as the reward of him that overcometh, the symbol of an eternal blessedness. (Comp. Dean Trench, Comm. on the Epistles to the Seven Churches, in loc.) The thing, though not the word, appears in the closing visions of Rev. xxii.

(4.) The eager curiosity which prompts men to press on into the things behind the veil, has led them to construct hypotheses more or less definite as to the intermediate state, and these have affected the thoughts which Christian writers have connected with the word paradise. Patristic and later interpreters follow, as has been noticed, in the footsteps of the Jewish schools. To Origen and others of a like spiritual insight, paradise is but a synonym for a region of life and immortality — one and the same with the third heaven (Jerome, Ep. ad Joh. Hieros. in Wordsworth on 2 Cor. xii.). So far as it is a place, it is as a school in which the souls of men are trained and learn to judge rightly of the things they have done and seen on earth (Origen, de Princ. ii. 12). The sermon of Basil, de Paradiso, gives an eloquent representation of the common belief of Christians who were neither mystical nor speculative. Minds at once logical and sensuous ask questions as to the locality, and the answers are wildly conjectural. It is not in

Hades, and is therefore different from Abraham's bosom (Tertull. de Idol. c. 13). It is above and beyond the world, separated from it by a wall of fire (Tertull. Apol. c. 47). It is the "refrigerium" for all faithful souls, where they have the vision of saints, and angels, and of Christ himself (Just. M. Respons. ad Orthodox. 75 and 85), or for those only who are entitled, as martyrs, fresh from the baptism of blood, to a special reward above their fellows (Tertull. de Anim. c. 55).[b] It is in the fourth heaven (Clem. Alex. Fragm. § 51). It is in some unknown region of the earth, where the seas and skies meet, higher than any earthly mountain (Joann. Damasc. de Orthod. Fid. ii. 11), and had thus escaped the waters of the Flood (P. Lombard, Sentent. ii. 17, E.). It has been identified with the φυλακή of 1 Pet. iii. 19, and the spirits in it are those of the antediluvian races who repented before the great destruction overtook them (Bishop Horsley, Sermons, xx.). (Comp. an elaborate note in Thilo, Codex Apocryph. N. T. p. 754.) The word enters largely, as might be expected, into the apocryphal literature of the early Church. Where the true Gospels are most reticent, the mythical are most exuberant. The Gospel of Nicodemus, in narrating Christ's victory over Hades (the "harrowing of hell" of our early English mysteries), tells how, till then, Enoch and Elijah had been its sole inhabitants[c] — how the penitent robber was there with his cross on the night of the crucifixion — how the souls of the patriarchs were led thither by Christ, and were received by the archangel Michael, as he kept watch with the flaming swords at the gate. In the apocryphal Acta Philippi (Tischendorf, Act. Apost. p. 89), the Apostle is sentenced to remain for forty days outside the circle of paradise, because he had given way to anger and cursed the people of Hierapolis for their unbelief.

(5.) The later history of the word presents some facts of interest. Accepting in this, as in other instances, the mythical elements of eastern Christianity, the creed of Islam presented to its followers the hope of a sensuous paradise, and the Persian word was transplanted through it into the languages spoken by them.[d] In the West it passes through some strange transformations, and descends to baser uses. The thought that men on entering the Church of Christ returned to the blessedness which Adam had forfeited, was symbolized in the church architecture of the fourth century. The narthex, or atrium, in which were assembled those who, not being fideles in full communion, were not admitted into the interior of the building, was known as the "Paradise" of the church (Alt, Cultus, p. 591). Athanasius, it has been said, speaks scornfully of Arianism as creeping into this paradise,[e] implying that it addressed itself to the ignorant and untaught. In the West

---

[a] For the questions (1) whether the raptus of St. Paul was corporeal or incorporeal, (2) whether the third heaven is to be identified with or distinguished from paradise, (3) whether this was the upper or the lower paradise of the Jewish schools, comp. Meyer, Wordsworth, Alford, in loc.; August. de Gen. ad litt. xii.; Ludwig, Diss. de raptu Pauli, in Menthen's Thesaurus. Interpreted by the current Jewish belief of the period, we may refer the "third heaven" to a vision of the Divine Glory; "paradise," to a vision of the fellowship of the righteous dead, waiting in calmness and peace for their final resurrection.

[b] A special treatise by Tertullian, de Paradiso, is unfortunately lost.

[c] One trace of this belief is found in the Vulg. of Ecclus. xliv. 16, "translatus est in paradisum," in the absence of any corresponding word in the Greek text.

[d] Thus it occurs in the Koran in the form firdaus; and the name of the Persian poet Ferdusi is probably derived from it (Humboldt's Cosmos, ii. note 280).

[e] The passage quoted by Alt is from Orat. c. Arian. II. (vol. i. p. 307, Colon. 1686): Καὶ βιάζεται πᾶλιν εἰσελθεῖν εἰς τὸν παράδεισον τῆς ἐκκλησίας. Ingenious

we trace a change of form, and one singular change of application. Paradiso becomes in some Italian dialects Paraviso, and this passes into the French *parvis*,[a] denoting the western porch of a church, or the open space in front of it (Ducange, *s. v.* "Parvisus"; Diez, *Etymolog. Wörterb.* p. 703). In the church this space was occupied, as we have seen, by the lower classes of the people. The word was transferred from the place of worship to the place of amusement, and, though the position was entirely different, was applied to the highest and cheapest gallery of a French theatre (Alt, *Cultus*, l. c.). By some, however, this use of the word is connected only with the extreme height of the gallery, just as "chemin de Paradis" is a proverbial phrase for any specially arduous undertaking (Beschcrelle, *Dictionnaire Français*).   E. H. P.

* On this subject see W. A. Alger's *Critical History of the Doctrine of a Future Life*, 4th ed. N. Y. 1866, and for the literature, the bibliographical Appendix to that work (comp. references in the Index of Subjects).   A.

PARAH (הַפָּרָה, with the def. article [*the heifer*]: Φαρά; Alex. Αφαρ: *Aphphara*), one of the cities in the territory allotted to Benjamin, named only in the lists of the conquest (Josh. xviii. 23). It occurs in the first of the two groups into which the towns of Benjamin are divided, which seems to contain those of the northern and eastern portions of the tribe, between Jericho, Bethel, and Geba; the towns of the south, from Gibeon to Jerusalem, being enumerated in the second group.

In the *Onomasticon* ("Aphra") it is specified by Jerome only — the text of Eusebius being wanting, — as five miles east of Bethel. No traces of the name have yet been found in that position; but the name *Fârah* exists further to the S. E. attached to the *Wady Fârah*, one of the southern branches of the great *Wady Suweinit*, and to a site of ruins at the junction of the same with the main valley.

This identification, first suggested by Dr. Robinson (i. 439), is supported by Van de Velde (*Memoir*, p. 339) and Schwarz (p. 126). The drawback mentioned by Dr. R., namely, that the Arabic word (= "mouse") differs in signification from the Hebrew ("the cow") is not of much force, since it is the habit of modern names to cling to similarity of sound with the ancient names, rather than of signification. (Compare *Beit-ur*; *el Aal*, etc.)

A view of *Wady Fârah* is given by Barclay (*City*, etc. p. 558), who proposes it for Ænon. G.

* PARALYTIC, HEALING OF THE. [House, vol. ii. p. 1104.]

PARAN, EL-PARAN (פָּארָן, אֵל־

פָּארָן: Φαράν, LXX. and Joseph.; [1 Sam. xxv. 1, Rom. Μαών, Vat. Μααν: *Pharan*]).

1. It is shown under KADESH that the name Paran corresponds probably in general outline with the desert *et-Tîh*. The Sinaitic desert, including the wedge of metamorphic rocks, granite, syenite, and

porphyry, set, as it were, in a superficial margin of old red sandstone, forms nearly a scalene triangle with its apex southwards, and having its base or upper edge not a straight, but concave crescent line — the ridge, in short, of the *et-Tîh* range of mountains, extending about 120 miles from east to west, with a slight dip, the curve of the aforesaid crescent southwards. Speaking generally, the wilderness of Sinai (Num. x. 12, xii. 16), in which the march-stations of Taberah and Hazeroth, if the latter [HAZEROTH] be identical with *Hâdherâ*, are probably included towards its N. E. limit, may be said to lie S. of the *et-Tîh* range, the wilderness of Paran N. of it, and the one to end where the other begins. That of Paran is a stretch of chalky formation, the chalk being covered with coarse gravel, mixed with black flint and drifting sand. The surface of this extensive desert tract is a slope ascending towards the north, and in it appear to rise (by Russegger's map, from which most of the previous description is taken) three chalky ridges, as it were, terraces of mountainous formation, all to the W. of a line drawn from *Ras Mohammed* to *Kulat el-Arish* on the Mediterranean. The caravan-route from *Cairo* to *Akaba* crosses the *et-Tîh* desert in a line from W. to E., a little S. In this wide tract, which extends northwards to join the "wilderness of Beer-sheba" (Gen. xxi. 21, cf. 14), and eastward probably to the wilderness of Zin [KADESH] on the Edomitish border, Ishmael dwelt, and there probably his posterity originally multiplied. Ascending northwards from it on a meridian to the E. of Beer-sheba, we should reach Maon and Carmel, or that southern portion of the territory of Judah, W. of the Dead Sea, known as "the South," where the waste changes gradually into an uninhabited pasture-land, at least in spring and autumn, and in which, under the name of "Paran," Nabal fed his flocks (1 Sam. xxv. 1). Between the wilderness of Paran and that of Zin no strict demarcation exists in the narrative, nor do the natural features of the region, so far as yet ascertained, yield a well-defined boundary. The wilderness of Paran seems, as in the story of Ishmael, to have predominated towards the western extremity of the northern desert frontier of *et-Tîh*, and in Num. xxxiv. 4 the wilderness of Zin, not Paran, is spoken of as the southern border of the land or of the tribe of Judah (Josh. xv. 3). If by the Paran region we understand "that great and terrible wilderness" so emphatically described as the haunt of noxious creatures and the terror of the wayfarer (Deut. i. 19, viii. 15), then we might see how the adjacent tracts, which still must be called "wilderness," might, either as having less repulsive features, or because they lay near to some settled country, have a special nomenclature of their own. For the latter reason the wildernesses of Zin, eastward towards Edom and Mount Seir, and of Shur, westward towards Egypt, might be thus distinguished; for the former reason that of Sin and Sinai. It would not be inconsistent with the rules of Scriptural nomenclature, if we suppose these accessory wilds to be sometimes included

---

as his conjecture is, it may be questioned whether the sarcasm which he finds in the words is not the creation of his own imagination. There seems no ground for referring the word paradise to any section of the Church, but rather to the Church as a whole (comp. August. *de Gen.* ad litt. xii.). The Arians were to it what the serpent had been to the earlier paradise.

[a] This word will be familiar to many readers from the "Responsiones in *Parviso*" of the Oxford system of examination, however little they may previously have connected that place with their thoughts of paradise. By others, however, Parvisum (or *-sus*) is derived "a parvis pueris ibi edoctis" (*Ménage, Orig. de la Langue Franç. s. v.* "Parvis").

under the general name of "wilderness of Paran;" and to this extent we may perhaps modify the previous general statement that S. of the *et-Tih* range is the wilderness of Sinai, and N. of it that of Paran. St.II, construed strictly, the wildernesses of Paran and Zin would seem to lie as already approximately laid down. [KADESH.] If, however, as previously hinted, they may in another view be regarded as overlapping, we can more easily understand how Chedorlaomer, when he "smote" the peoples S. of the Dead Sea, returned round its southwestern curve to the el-Paran, or "terebinth-tree of Paran," viewed as indicating a locality in connection with the wilderness of Paran, and yet close, apparently, to that Dead Sea border (Gen. xiv. 6).

Was there, then, a Paran proper, or definite spot to which the name was applied? From Deut. i. 1 it should seem there must have been. This is con-

firmed by 1 K. xi. 18, from which we further learn the fact of its being an inhabited region; and the position required by the context here is one between Midian and Egypt. If we are to reconcile these passages by the aid of the personal history of Moses, it seems certain that the local Midian of the Sinaitic peninsula must have lain near the Mount Horeb itself (Ex. iii. 1, xviii. 1-5). The site of the "Paran" of Hadad the Edomite must then have lain to the N. W. or Egyptian side of Horeb. This brings us, if we assume any principal mountain, except *Serbál*,[a] of the whole Sinaitic group, to be "*the* Mount of God," so close to the *Wady Feiran* that the similarity of name,[b] supported by the recently expressed opinion of eminent geographers, may be taken as establishing substantial identity. Ritter (vol. xiv. p. 740, 741) and Stanley (pp. 39–41) both consider that Rephidim is to be found in *Wady Feiran*, and no

Ruins of Feirân in *Wady Feirân*.

other place in the whole peninsula seems, from its local advantages, to have been so likely to form an *entrepôt* in Solomon's time between Edom and Egypt. Burckhardt (*Syria*, etc. p. 602) describes this wady as narrowing in one spot to 100 paces, and adds that the high mountains adjacent, and the thick woods which clothe it, contribute with the bad water to make it unhealthy, but that it is, for productiveness, the finest valley[c] in the whole peninsula, containing four miles of gardens and date-groves. Yet he thinks it was *not* the Paran of Scripture. Professor Stanley, on the contrary, seems to speak on this point with greater confidence in the affirmative than perhaps on any other question connected with the Exodus. See especially his remarks (39–41) regarding the local term "hill" of Ex. xvii. 9, 10, which he considers to

be satisfied by an eminence adjacent to the *Wady Feiran*. The vegetable manna[d] of the tamarisk grows wild there (Seetzen, *Reisen*, iii. 75), as does the *colocynth*, etc. (Robinson, i. 121-124). What could have led Winer (*s. v.* "Paran") to place el-Paran near Elath, it is not easy to say, especially as he gives no authority.

2. "Mount" Paran occurs only in two poetic passages (Deut. xxxiii. 2; Hab. iii. 3), in one of which Sinai and Seir appear as local accessories, in the other Teman and (ver. 7) Cushan and Midian. We need hardly pause to inquire in what sense Seir can be brought into one local view with Sinai. It is clear from a third poetic passage, in which Paran does not appear (Judg. v. 4, 5), but which contains "Seir," more literally determined by "Edom," still in the same local connection with

---

[a] For the reasons why *Serbál* should not be accepted, see SINAI.

[b] Gesen *s. v.* פָּארָן, says the wilderness so called, "between Midian and Egypt, bears this name at the present day." No maps now in use give any closer approximation to the ancient name than *Feiran*.

[c] Compare, however, the same traveller's statement of the claims of a coast wady at *Tûr*, on the Gulf of Suez (Burckhardt, *Arab.* ii. 362; comp. Wellsted, ii. 9), "receiving all the waters which flow down from the higher range of Sinai to the sea." (Stanley, p. 19).

[d] The *Tamarix Gallica mannifera* of Ehrenberg, the *T'rfa* of the Arabs (Robinson, i. 115).

"Sinai," that the Hebrew found no difficulty in viewing the greater scenes of God's manifestation in the Exodus as historically and morally,[a] if not locally connected. At any rate Mount Paran here may with as good a right be claimed for the Sinaitic as for the Edomitish side of the difficulty. And the distance, after all, from Horeb to Mount Seir was probably one of ten days or less (Deut. i. 2). It is not unlikely that if the *Wady Feiran* be the Paran proper, the name "Mount" Paran may have been either assigned to the special member (the northwestern) of the Sinaitic mountain-group which lies adjacent to that wady,[b] or to the whole Sinaitic cluster. That special member is the five-peaked ridge of *Serbál.* If this view for the site of Paran is correct, the Israelites must have proceeded from their encampment by the sea (Num. xxxiii. 10), probably *Tayibéh* [WILDERNESS OF THE WANDERING], by the "middle" route of the three indicated by Stanley (pp. 38, 39).

H. H.

PAR'BAR (פַּרְבָּר), with the definite article [see below]: *διαδεχομένους: cellulæ*). A word occurring in Hebrew and A. V. only in 1 Chr. xxvi. 18, but there found twice: "At the Parbar westward four (Levites) at the causeway two at the Parbar." From this passage, and also from the context, it would seem that Parbar was some place on the west side of the Temple inclosure, the same side with the causeway and the gate Shallecheth. The latter was close to the causeway — perhaps on it as the *Bab Silsilis* now is — and we know from its remains that the causeway was at the extreme north of the western wall. Parbar therefore must have been south of Shallecheth.

As to the meaning of the name, the Rabbis generally agree[d] in translating it "the outside place;" while modern authorities take it as equivalent to the *parvárim*[e] in 2 K. xxiii. 11 (A. V. "suburbs"), a word almost identical with *parbar,* and used by the early Jewish interpreters as the equivalent of *migráshim,* the precincts (A. V. "suburbs") of the Levitical cities. Accepting this interpretation, there is no difficulty in identifying the Parbar with the suburb (τὸ προάστειον) mentioned by Josephus in describing Herod's Temple (*Ant.* xv. 11, § 5), as lying in the deep valley which separated the west wall of the Temple from the city opposite it; in other words, the southern end of the Tyropœon, which intervenes between the Wailing Place and the (so-called) Zion. The two gates in the original wall were in Herod's Temple increased to four.

It does not follow (as some have assumed) that Parbar was identical with the "suburbs" of 2 K. xxiii. 11, though the words denoting each may have the same signification. For it seems most consonant with probability to suppose that the "horses of the Sun" would be kept on the eastern side of the temple mount, in full view of the rising rays of the god as they shot over the Mount of Olives, and not in a deep valley on its western side.

Parbar is possibly an ancient Jebusite name, which perpetuated itself after the Israelite conquest of the city, as many a Danish and Saxon name has been perpetuated, and still exists, only slightly disguised, in the city of London.   G.

* PARCHED CORN. [RUTH, BOOK OF, Amer. ed.]

* PARCHED GROUND. The Hebrew term (שָׁרָב, *sháráb*) so rendered in Is. xxxv. 7 (A. V.) — "the parched ground shall become a pool" — is understood by the best scholars to denote the *mirage,* the Arabic name for which is *seráb.* So Gesenius, Fürst, De Wette, Hitzig, Knobel, Ewald, etc.; comp. Winer, *Bibl. Realwörterb.* art. "Sandmeer," and Thomson's *Land and Book,* ii. 287, 288. The phenomenon referred to is too well known to need description here. A.

PARCHMENT. [WRITING.]

PARLOR. A word in English usage meaning the common room of the family, and hence probably in A. V. denoting the king's audience-chamber, so used in reference to Eglon (Judg. iii. 20-25; Richardson, *Eng. Dict.*). [HOUSE, vol. ii. p. 1135.]   H. W. P.

PARMASHTA (פַּרְמַשְׁתָּא [*superior,* Sanskr., Ges.]: Μαρμασιμά; Alex. Μαρμασιμνα: [FA. Μαρμασιμ:] *Phermesta*). One of the ten sons of Haman slain by the Jews in Shushan (Esth. ix. 9).

PAR'MENAS (Παρμενᾶς [prob. a contraction of Parmenides, *steadfast*]). One of the seven deacons, "men of honest report, full of the Holy Ghost and wisdom," selected by the whole body of the disciples to superintend the ministration of their alms to the widows and necessitous poor. Parmenas is placed sixth on the list of those who were ordained by the laying on of the hands of the Apostles to this special function (Acts vi. 5). His name occurs but this once in Scripture; and ecclesiastical history records nothing of him save the tradition that he suffered martyrdom at Philippi in the reign of Trajan (Baron. ii. 55). In the

---

[a] The language in the three passages (Deut. xxxiii. 2; Hab. iii.; Judg. v. 4, 5) is as strikingly similar as is the purport and spirit of all the three. All describe a spiritual presence manifested by natural convulsions attendant; and all are confirmed by Ps. lxviii. 7, 8, in which Sinai alone is named. We may almost regard this lofty rhapsody as a commonplace of the inspired song of triumph, in which the seer seems to leave earth so far beneath him that the preciseness of geographic detail is lost to his view.

[b] Out of the *Wady Feiran,* in an easterly direction, runs the *Wady Skdikh,* which conducts the traveller directly to the "modern Horeb." See Kiepert's map.

[c] What Hebrew word the LXX. read here is not clear.

[d] See the Targum of the passage; also Buxtorf, *Lex.*

Talm. s. v. פרב; and the references in Lightfoot, *Prospect of Temple,* ch. v.

[e] Gesenius, *Thes.* p. 1123 a; Fürst, *Handwb.* ll. 235 b, etc. Gesenius connects *parvarim* with a similar Persian word, meaning a building open on all sides to the sun and air.

1. חֶדֶר; ἀποθήκη; *cubiculum;* once only "parlor" in 1 Chr. xxviii. 11; elsewhere usually "chamber," a withdrawing room (Ges. p. 448).

2. לִשְׁכָּה; κατάλυμα; *triclinium;* usually "chamber."

3. עֲלִיָּה, with art. in each instance where A. V has "parlor;" τὸ ὑπερῷον; *cænaculum;* usually "chamber." It denotes an upper chamber in 2 Sam xviii. 33, 2 K. xxiii. 12.

calendar of the Byzantine Church he and Prochorus are commemorated on July 28th.

E. H—s.

PAR'NACH (פַּרְנָךְ [*swift* or *delicate*, Ges.]: Φαρνάχ: *Pharnach*). Father or ancestor of Elizaphan prince of the tribe of Zebulun (Num. xxxiv. 25).

PA'ROSH (פַּרְעֹשׁ [*flea*]: Φαρές, Alex. Φορός in Exr. ii. 3; elsewhere Φόρος: *Pharos*). The descendants of Parosh, in number 2,172, returned from Babylon with Zerubbabel (Ezr. ii. 3; Neh. vii. 8). Another detachment of 150 males, with Zechariah at their head, accompanied Ezra (Ezr. viii. 3 [where A. V. reads PHAROSH]). Seven of the family had married foreign wives (Ezr. x. 25). They assisted in the building of the wall of Jerusalem (Neh. iii. 25), and signed the covenant with Nehemiah (Neh. x. 14). In the last-quoted passage the name Parosh is clearly that of a family, and not of an individual.

PARSHANDA'THA (פַּרְשַׁנְדָּתָא [see below]: Φαρσαννές; Alex. Φαρσανεσταν; [Comp. Φαρσανδαθά:] *Pharsandatha*). The eldest of Haman's ten sons who were slain by the Jews in Shushan (Esth. ix. 7). Fürst (*Handwb.*) renders it into old Persian *frashnadata*, "given by prayer," and compares the proper name Παρσόνδης, which occurs in Diod. ii. 33.

**PARTHIANS (Πάρθοι: *Parthi*) occurs only in Acts ii. 9, where it designates Jews settled in Parthia. Parthia Proper was the region stretching along the southern flank of the mountains which separate the great Persian desert from the desert of Kharesm. It lay south of Hyrcania, east of Media, and north of Sagartia. The country was pleasant, and fairly fertile, watered by a number of small streams flowing from the mountains, and absorbed after a longer or a shorter course by the sands. It is now known as the *Atak* or "skirt," and is still a valuable part of Persia, though supporting only a scanty population. In ancient times it seems to have been densely peopled; and the ruins of many large and apparently handsome cities attest its former prosperity. (See Fraser's *Khorassan*, p. 245.)

The ancient Parthians are called a "Scythic" race (Strab. xi. 9, § 2; Justin, xli. 1–4; Arrian, *Fr.* p. 1); and probably belonged to the great Turanian family. Various stories are told of their origin. Moses of Chorene calls them the descendants of Abraham by Keturah (*Hist. Armen.* ii. 65); while John of Malala relates that they were Scythians whom the Egyptian king Sesostris brought with him on his return from Scythia, and settled in a region of Persia (*Hist. Unio.* p. 26; compare Arrian, *l. s. c.*). Really, nothing is known of them till about the time of Darius Hystaspis, when they are found in the district which so long retained their name, and appear as faithful subjects of the Persian monarchs. We may fairly presume that they were added to the empire by Cyrus, about B. C. 550; for that monarch seems to have been the conqueror of all the northeastern provinces. Herodotus speaks of them as contained in the 16th satrapy of Darius, where they were joined with the Chorasmians, the Sogdians, and the Arians, or people of Herat (Herod. iii. 93). He also mentions that they served in the army which Xerxes led into Greece, under the same leader as the Chorasmians (vii. 66). They carried bows and

147

arrows, and short spears; but were not at this time held in much repute as soldiers. In the final struggle between the Greeks and Persians they remained faithful to the latter, serving at Arbela (Arr. *Exp. Alex.* iii. 8) but offering only a weak resistance to Alexander when, on his way to Bactria, he entered their country (*ibid.* 25). In the division of Alexander's dominions they fell to the share of Eumenes, and Parthia for some while was counted among the territories of the Seleucidæ. About B. C. 256, however, they ventured upon a revolt, and under Arsaces (whom Strabo calls "a king of the Dahæ," but who was more probably a native leader) they succeeded in establishing their independence. This was the beginning of the great Parthian empire, which may be regarded as rising out of the ruins of the Persian, and as taking its place during the centuries when the Roman power was at its height.

Parthia, in the mind of the writer of the Acts, would designate this empire, which extended from India to the Tigris, and from the Chorasmian desert to the shores of the Southern Ocean. Hence the prominent position of the name Parthians in the list of those present at Pentecost. Parthia was a power almost rivaling Rome — the only existing power which had tried its strength against Rome and not been worsted in the encounter. By the defeat and destruction of Crassus near Carrhæ (the Scriptural Harran) the Parthians acquired that character for military prowess which attaches to them in the best writers of the Roman classical period. (See Hor. *Od.* ii. 13; *Sat.* ii. 1, 15; Virg. *Georg.* iii. 31; Ov. *Art. Am.* i. 209, &c.) Their armies were composed of clouds of horsemen, who were all riders of extraordinary expertness; their chief weapon was the bow. They shot their arrows with wonderful precision while their horses were in full career, and were proverbially remarkable for the injury they inflicted with these weapons on an enemy who attempted to follow them in their flight. From the time of Crassus to that of Trajan they were an enemy whom Rome especially dreaded, and whose ravages she was content to repel without revenging. The warlike successor of Nerva had the boldness to attack them; and his expedition, which was well conceived and vigorously conducted, deprived them of a considerable portion of their territories. In the next reign, that of Hadrian, the Parthians recovered these losses; but their military strength was now upon the decline; and in A. D. 226, the last of the Arsacidæ was forced to yield his kingdom to the revolted Persians, who, under Artaxerxes, son of Sassan, succeeded in reëstablishing their empire. The Parthian dominion thus lasted for nearly five centuries, commencing in the third century before, and terminating in the third century after, our era.

It has already been stated that the Parthians were a Turanian race. Their success is to be regarded as the subversion of a tolerably advanced civilization by a comparative barbarism — the substitution of Tatar coarseness for Aryan polish and refinement. They aimed indeed at adopting the art and civilization of those whom they conquered; but their imitation was a poor travestie, and there is something ludicrously grotesque in most of their more ambitious efforts. At the same time, they occasionally exhibit a certain amount of skill and taste, more especially where they followed Greek models. Their architecture was better than their sculpture. The famous ruins of Ctesiphon have a grandeur of effect which strikes every traveller; and the Parthian constructions at Akkerkuf, El Hammam, etc., are among the most remarkable of oriental remains. Nor was grandeur of general

Figure of Fame, surmounting the Arch at *Tackt-i-Bostan.* (Sir R. K. Porter's *Travels,* vol. ii. fol. 62.)

effect the only merit of their buildings. There is sometimes a beauty and delicacy in their ornamentation which is almost worthy the Greeks. (For

Ornamentation of Arch at *Tackt-i-Bostan.*

specimens of Parthian sculpture and architecture, see the *Travels* of Sir R. K. Porter, vol. i. plates 19–24; vol. ii. plates 62–66 and 82, &c. For the general history of the nation, see Heeren's *Manual of Ancient History,* pp. 229–305, Eng. Tr.; and the article PARTHIA in *Dict. of Gr. and Rom. Geography.*) [See also Rawlinson's *Ancient Monarchies,* iii. 42, and iv. 19.]   G. R.

* **PARTITION, MIDDLE WALL OF,** Eph. ii. 14. The Greek is τὸ μεσότοιχον τοῦ φραγμοῦ, and in the figure the "middle wall" formed the "partition," or more strictly "fence" (φραγμός), which before the coming of Christ separated Jews and Gentiles from each other, but which his death abolished, so as to bring all nations together on the same common ground as regards their participation in the blessings of the Gospel. Many interpreters find here an allusion to the row of marble pillars or screen which in Herod's Temple fenced off the court of the Gentiles from that of the Jews, on which, as Philo and Josephus state, was written in Latin and Greek: "No foreigner may go further on penalty of death" (see Kuinoel, *Acta Apost.* p. 706: and Keil, *Bibl. Archäologie,* i. 142). Ellicott would admit a reference in this passage both to this middle wall and to the rending of the

veil at the moment when Christ died (Matt. xxii. 51; Eph. ii. 14). "The Temple was, as it were, a material embodiment of the law, and in its very outward structure was a symbol of spiritual distinctions." Yet we cannot insist on this view as certain, by any means, for the language may well be figurative without its having any such local origin. Some commentators (see Wordsworth *ad loc.*) regard the metaphor as that of a vineyard, in which the people of God were fenced off from other nations.

It was Paul's introducing Trophimus (as the Jews falsely alleged) into the part of the Temple (εἰς τὸ ἱερὸν) beyond the middle wall, between the courts of the Jews and of the Gentiles, which led to the tumult in which the Apostle came so near being killed by the mob (Acts xxi. 27–30).   H.

PARTRIDGE (קֹרֵא, *kôrê*: πέρδιξ, νυκτικόραξ: *perdix*) occurs only 1 Sam. xxvi. 20, where David compares himself to a hunted *kôrê* upon the mountains, and in Jer. xvii. 11, where it is said, "As a *kôrê* sitteth on eggs, and hatcheth them not; so he that getteth riches, and not by right, shall leave them in the midst of his days, and at his end shall be a fool." The translation of *kôrê* by "partridge" is supported by many of the old versions, the Hebrew name, as is generally supposed, having reference to the "call" of the cock bird; compare the German *Rebhuhn* from *rufen,* "to call." [a] Bochart (*Hieroz.* ii. 632) has attempted to show that *kôrê* denotes some species of "snipe," or "woodcock" (*rusticola* ?); he refers

Ammoperdix Heyii.

the Hebrew word to the Arabic *kariu,* which he believes, but upon very insufficient ground, to be the name of some one of these birds. Oedmann (*Verm. Samm.* ii. 57) identifies the *kariu* of Arabic writers with the *Merops apiaster* (the Bee-eater): this explanation has deservedly found favor with no commentators. What the *kariu* of the Arabs may be we have been unable to determine: but the *kôrê* there can be no doubt denotes a partridge. The "hunting this bird upon the mountains" [b] (1 Sam. xxvi. 20) entirely agrees with the habits of two well-known species of partridge, namely, *Cac-*

─────────────────────────────
a "Perdix enim nomen suum hebraicum קֹרֵא habet a *vocando,* quemadmodum eadem avis Germanis dicitur *Rephuhn* a *röpen,* i. e *rufen,* vocare" (Rosenmüll. *Schol. in Jer.* xvii. 11). Mr. Tristram says that *kore* would be an admirable imitation of the call-notes of *Caccabis saxatilis.*

b "The partridge of the mountains I suspect to be *Ammoperdix Heyii,* familiar as it must have been to David when he camped by the cave of Adullam — a bird more difficult by far to be induced to take wing than *C. saxatilis*" (H. B. Tristram).

cabis saxatilis (the Greek partridge) and *Ammoperdix Heyii.* The specific name of the former is partly indicative of the localities it frequents, namely, rocky and hilly ground covered with brushwood.

It will be seen by the marginal reading that the passage in Jeremiah may bear the following interpretation: As the *kôrê* "gathereth young which she hath not brought forth." This rendering is supported by the LXX. and Vulg., and is that which Maurer (*Comment. in Jer.* l. c.), Rosenmüller (*Sch. in Jer.* l. c.), Gesenius (*Thes.* s. v.), Winer (*Realxb.* "Rebhuhn"), and scholars generally, adopt. In order to meet the requirements of this latter interpretation, it has been asserted that the partridge is in the habit of stealing the eggs from the nests of its congeners and of sitting upon them, and that when the young are hatched they forsake their false parent; hence, it is said, the meaning of the simile: the man who has become rich by dishonest means loses his riches, as the fictitious partridge her stolen brood (see Jerome *in Jerem.* l. c.). It is perhaps almost needless to remark that this is a mere fable, in which, however, the ancient Orientals may have believed.

Caccabis saxatilis.

There is a passage in the Arabian naturalist Damir, quoted by Bochart (*Hieroz.* ii. 638), which shows that in his time this opinion was held with regard to some kind of partridge.[c] The explanation of the rendering of the text of the A. V. is obviously as follows. Partridges were often "hunted" in ancient times as they are at present, either by hawking or by being driven from place to place till they become fatigued, when they are knocked down by the clubs or *zerwattys* of the Arabs (see Shaw's *Trav.* i. 425, 8vo.). Thus, nests were no doubt constantly disturbed, and many destroyed: as, therefore, is a partridge which is driven from her eggs, so is he that enricheth himself by unjust means — "he shall leave them in the midst of his days."[b] The expression in Ecclus. xi. 30, "like as a partridge taken (and kept) in a cage," clearly refers, as Shaw (*Trav.* l. c.) has observed, to "a decoy partridge," and the Greek πέρδιξ θηρευτής

should have been so translated, as is evident both from the context and the Greek words;[c] compare Aristot. *Hist. Anim.* ix. 9, § 3 and 4. Besides the two species of partridge named above, the *Caccabis chukur* — the red-leg of India and Persia, which Mr. Tristram regards as distinct from the Greek partridge — is found about the Jordan. Our common partridge (*Perdix cinerea*), as well as the Barbary (*C. petrosa*) and red-leg (*C. rufa*), do not occur in Palestine. There are three or four species of the genus *Pterocles* (Sand-grouse) and *Francolinus* found in the Bible lands, but they do not appear to be noticed by any distinct term. [QUAIL.]

                              W. H.

* **PARTS, UPPER.** [UPPER COASTS, Amer. ed.]

PARU'AH (פָרוּחַ [blossoming, Ges.; increase, Fürst]: Φουασοϋδ; Alex. φαρρου: [Comp. Φαρουέ:] *Pharue*). The father of Jehoshaphat, Solomon's commissariat officer in Issachar (1 K. iv. 17).

PARVA'IM (פַּרְוָיִם [see below]: Φαρουίμ; [Vat. Alex. Φαρουαιμ: (aurum) *probatissimum*]), the name of a place or country whence the gold was procured for the decoration of Solomon's Temple (2 Chr. iii. 6). The name occurs but once in the Bible, and there without any particulars that assist to its identification. We may notice the conjectures of Hitzig (on Dan. x. 5), that the name is derived from the Sanskrit *paru,* "hill," and betokens the δίδυμα ὄρη in Arabia, mentioned by Ptolemy (vi. 7, § 11): of Knobel (*Völkert.* p. 191), that it is an abbreviated form of Sepharvaim, which stands in the Syriac version and the Targum of Jonathan for the Sephar of Gen. x. 30; and of Wilford (quoted by Gesenius, *Thes.* ii. 1125), that it is derived from the Sanskrit *pûrva,* "eastern," and is a general term for the East. Bochart's identification of it with Taprobane is etymologically incorrect.   W. L. B.

PA'SACH (פָּסַךְ [cut, incision, Ges.]: Φασέκ; [Vat. Βαισηχι:] Alex. Φεσηχι: *Phosech*). Son of Japhlet of the tribe of Asher (1 Chr. vii. 33), and one of the chiefs of his tribe.

PAS-DAM'MIM (פַּס דַּמִּים [the border of blood]: [Rom. Φασοδαμίν; Vat.] Φασοδομη; Alex. Φασοδομιν: *Phesdomim*). The form under which in 1 Chr. xi. 13 the name appears, which in 1 Sam. xvii. 1 is given more at length as EPHES-DAMMIM. The lexicographers do not decide which is the earlier or correcter of the two. Gesenius (*Thes.* p. 139) takes them to be identical in meaning. It will be observed that in the original of Pas-dammim, the definite article has taken the place of the first letter of the other form. In the parallel narrative of 2 Sam. xxiii., the name appears to be corrupted[d] to *charpham* (הַרְפָּם), in the A. V. rendered "there." The present text of Josephus (*Ant.* vii. 12, § 4) gives it as Arasamos (Ἀρόσαμος).

___

[a] Partridges, like gallinaceous birds generally, may occasionally lay their eggs in the nests of other birds of the same species: it is hardly likely, however, that this fact should have attracted the attention of the ancients; neither can it alone be sufficient to explain the simile.

[b] * Thomson (*Land and Book,* i. 300 f.) describes the mode of hunting partridges by the Syrians at the present time. See also Wood's *Bible Animals* (Lond. 1869), p. 427 f.   H.

[c] Mr. Tristram tells us the *Caccabis saxatilis* makes an admirable decoy, becoming very tame and clever. He brought one home with him from Cyprus.

[d] This is carefully examined by Kennicott (*Dissertation,* p. 137, &c.).

The chief interest attaching to the appearance of the name in this passage of Chronicles is the evidence it affords that the place was the scene of repeated encounters between Israel and the Philistines, unless indeed we treat 1 Chr. xi. 13 (and the parallel passage, 2 Sam. xxiii. 9) as an independent account of the occurrence related in 1 Sam. xvii. — which hardly seems possible.   [ELAH, VALLEY OF.]

A ruined site bearing the name of *Damún* or *Chirbet Damoun* lies near the road from Jerusalem to *Beit Jibrin* (Van de Velde, *Syr. & Pal.* ii. 193; Tobler, *3tte Wand.* 201), about three miles E. of *Shuweikeh* (Socho). This Van de Velde proposes to identify with Pas-dammim.   ·   G.

PASE´AH (פָּסֵחַ [*lame*]: Βεσσηέ; Alex. Φεσση: *Phesse*). 1. Son of Eshton, in an obscure fragment of the genealogies of Judah (1 Chr. iv. 12). He and his brethren are described as "the men of Rechah," which in the Targum of R. Joseph is rendered "the men of the great Sanhedrin."

2. (Φασή, Ezr. [Vat. Φισον]; Φασέκ, Neh.: *Phasea*.) The "sons of Paseah" were among the Nethinim who returned with Zerubbabel (Ezr. ii. 49). In the A. V. of Neh. vii. 51, the name is written PHASEAH. Jehoiada, a member of the family, assisted in rebuilding the old gate of the city under Nehemiah (Neh. iii. 6).

PA´SHUR (פַּשְׁחוּר [*freedom, redemption*, Fürst: in Jer. and 1 Chr.,] Πασχώρ; [1 Chr. ix. 12, Rom. Alex. Φασχώρ; Ezr. ii. 38, Φασσούρ, Alex. Φασσουρ; x. 22, Neh. x. 3, Φασούρ; Neh. vii. 41. Φασεούρ, Vat. Φασεδουρ:: xi. 12, Φασσούρ, Alex. FA. Φασεουρ:] *Phassur* [*Phesur, Phasur*]), of uncertain etymology, although Jer. xx. 3 seems to allude to the meaning of it: comp. Ruth i. 20; and see Gesen. *s. v.*

1. Name of one of the families of priests of the chief house of Malchijah (Jer. xxi. 1, xxxviii. 1; 1 Chr. ix. 12, xxiv. 9; Neh. xi. 12). In the time of Nehemiah this family appears to have become a chief house, and its head the head of a course (Ezr. ii. 38; Neh. vii. 41, x. 3); and, if the text can be relied upon, a comparison of Neh. x. 3 with xii. 2 would indicate that the time of their return from Babylon was subsequent to the days of Zerubbabel and Jeshua. The individual from whom the family was named was probably Pashur the son of Malchiah, who in the reign of Zedekiah was one of the chief princes of the court (Jer. xxxviii. 1). He was sent, with others, by Zedekiah to Jeremiah at the time when Nebuchadnezzar was preparing his attack upon Jerusalem, to inquire what would

be the issue, and received a reply full of forebodings of disaster (Jer. xxi.). Again somewhat later, when the temporary raising of the siege of Jerusalem by the advance of Pharaoh Hophra's army from Egypt had inspired hopes in king and people that Jeremiah's predictions would be falsified, Pashur joined with several other chief men in petitioning the king that Jeremiah might be put to death as a traitor, who weakened the hands of the patriotic party by his exhortations to surrender, and his prophecies of defeat, and he proceeded, with the other princes, actually to cast the prophet into the dry well where he nearly perished (Jer. xxxviii.). Nothing more is known of Pashur. His descendant Adaiah seems to have returned with Zerubbabel (1 Chr. ix. 12), or whenever the census then quoted was taken.

2. Another person of this name, also a priest, and "chief governor of the house of the Lord," is mentioned in Jer. xx. 1. He is described as "the son of Immer," who was the head of the 16th course of priests (1 Chr. xxiv. 14), and probably the same as Amariah, Neh. x. 3, xii. 2, &c. In the reign of Jehoiakim he showed himself as hostile to Jeremiah as his namesake the son of Malchiah did afterwards, and put him in the stocks by the gate of Benjamin, for prophesying evil against Jerusalem, and left him there all night. For this indignity to God's prophet, Pashur was told by Jeremiah that his name was changed to Magormissabib (*Terror on every side*), and that he and all his house should be carried captives to Babylon and there die (Jer. xx. 1–6). From the expression in v. 6, it should seem that Pashur the son of Immer acted the part of a prophet as well as that of priest.

3. Father of Gedaliah (Jer. xxxviii. 1).

A. C. H.

PASSAGE.[a] Used in plur. (Jer. xxii. 20), probably to denote the mountain region of Abarim, on the east side of Jordan [ABARIM] (Raumer, *Pal.* p. 62; Ges. p. 987; Stanley, *S. & P.* p. 204, and App. p. 503). It also denotes a river-ford or a mountain gorge or pass.   [MICHMASH.]

H. W. P.

* PASSION is used in Acts i. 3 in its etymological sense of "suffering," with reference to the death of our Lord. "To whom he showed himself alive after his *passion*" (lit. "after he suffered," μετὰ τὸ παθεῖν αὐτόν).   A.

PASSOVER (חַג הַפֶּסַח, פֶּסַח: τὸ πάσχα:[b] *phase, id est transitus*: also, חַג הַמַּצּוֹת

---

a 1. עָבַר; τὸ πέραν τῆς θαλάσσης.

2. מַעֲבָר; διάβασις; *vadum* (Gen. xxxii. 22); also a gorge (1 Sam. xiii. 23).

3. מַעֲבָרָה; φάραγξ; *transcensus* (Is. x. 29). * A ford " (Is. xvi. 2).

b This is evidently the word פֶּסְחָא, the Aramaean form of פֶּסַח, put into Greek letters. Some have taken the meaning of פֶּסַח, the root of חַג הַפֶּסַח, to be that of "a passing through," and have referred its application here to the passage of the Red Sea.

Hence the Vulgate has rendered פֶּסַח by *transitus*, Philo (*De Vit. Mosis*, lib. iii. c. 29) by διαβατήρια, and Gregory of Nazianzus by διάβασις. Augustine takes

the same view of the word; as do also Von Bohlen and a few other modern critics. Jerome applies *transitus* both to the *passing over* of the destroyer and the *passing through* the Red Sea (in Matt. xxvi.). But the true sense of the Hebrew substantive is plainly indicated in Ex. xii. 27; and the best authorities are agreed that פֶּסַח never expresses "passing through," but that its primary meaning is "leaping over." Hence the verb is regularly used with the preposition עַל. But since, when we jump or step over anything, we do not tread upon it, the word has a secondary meaning, " to spare," or " to show mercy " (comp. Is. xxxi. 5, with Ex. xii. 27). The LXX. have therefore used σκεπάζειν in Ex. xii. 13; and Onkelos has rendered פֶּסַח by חוּס, "the sacrifice of the Passover," by

הַמַּצּוֹר: τὰ ἄζυμα; in N. T. ἡ ἑορτὴ τῶν ἀζύμων, ἡμέραι τῶν ἀζύμων: azyma, festum azynorum), the first of the three great annual Festivals of the Israelites, celebrated in the month Nisan, from the 14th to the 21st.

The following are the principal passages in the Pentateuch relating to the Passover: Ex. xii. 1-51, in which there is a full account of its original institution and first observance in Egypt; Ex. xiii. 3-10, in which the unleavened bread is spoken of in connection with the sanctification of the firstborn, but there is no mention of the paschal lamb;[a] Ex. xxiii. 14-19, where, under the name of the feast of unleavened bread, it is first connected with the other two great annual festivals, and also with the sabbath, and in which the paschal lamb is styled "My sacrifice"; Ex. xxxiv. 18-26, in which the festival is brought into the same connection, with immediate reference to the redemption of the firstborn, and in which the words of Ex. xxiii. 18, regarding the paschal lamb, are repeated; Lev. xxiii. 4-14, where it is mentioned in the same connection, the days of holy convocation are especially noticed, and the enactment is prospectively given respecting the offering of the first sheaf of harvest, with the offerings which were to accompany it, when the Israelites possessed the promised land; Num. ix. 1-14, in which the Divine word repeats the command for the observance of the Passover at the commencement of the second year after the Exodus, and in which the observance of the Passover in the second month, for those who could not participate in it at the regular time, is instituted; Num. xxviii. 16-25, where directions are given for the offerings which were to be made on each of the seven days of the festival; Deut. xvi. 1-8, where the command is prospectively given that the Passover, and the other great festivals, should be observed in the place which the Lord might choose in the land of promise, and where there appears to be an allusion to the Chagigah, or voluntary peace-offerings (see p. 2346 a).

זֶבַח חַיִּים, "the sacrifice of mercy." Josephus rightly explains πάσχα by ὑπερβασία. In the same purport, agree Aquila, Theodotion, Symmachus, several of the Fathers, and the best modern critics. Our own translators, by using the word "Passover," have made clear Ex. xii. 12, 23, and other passages, which are not intelligible in the LXX. nor in several other versions. (See Bähr, Symbolik, ii. 627; Ewald, Alterthümer, p. 390; Gesenius, Thes. s. v.; Sulcer, sub πάσχα; Drusius, Notæ Majores, in Ex. xii. 27; Carpzov, App. Crit. p. 394.)

The explanation of πάσχα which hinges on the notion that it is derived from πάσχω needs no refutation, but is not without interest, as it appears to have given rise to the very common use of the word passion, as denoting the death of our Lord. It was held by Irenæus, Tertullian, and a few others. Chrysostom appears to avail himself of it for a paronomasia (Hom. V. ad 1 Tim.), as in another place he formally states the true meaning; ὑπέρβασίς ἐστι καθ' ἑρμηνείαν τὸ πάσχα. Gregory of Nazianzus seems to do the same (Orat. xlii.), since he elsewhere (as is stated above) explains πάσχα as = διάβασις. See Sulcer, sub voce. Augustine, who took this latter view, has a passage which is worth quoting: "Pascha, fratres, non sicut quidam existimant, Græcum nomen est, sed Hebræum: opportunissime tamen occurrit in hoc nomine quædam congruentia utrarumque linguarum. Quia enim pati Græce πάσχειν dicitur, ideo Pascha passio putata est, velut hoc nomen a passione sit appellatum; in sua

I. INSTITUTION AND FIRST CELEBRATION OF THE PASSOVER.

When the chosen people were about to be brought out of Egypt, the word of the Lord came to Moses and Aaron, commanding them to instruct all the congregation of Israel to prepare for their departure by a solemn religious ordinance. On the tenth day of the month Abib, which had then commenced, the head of each family was to select from the flock either a lamb or a kid, a male of the first year, without blemish. If his family was too small to eat the whole of the lamb, he was permitted to invite his nearest neighbor to join the party. On the fourteenth day of the month, he[b] was to kill his lamb while the sun was setting.[c] He was then to take the blood in a basin, and with a sprig of hyssop to sprinkle it on the two side-posts and the lintel of the door of the house. The lamb was then thoroughly roasted, whole. It was expressly forbidden that it should be boiled, or that a bone of it should be broken. Unleavened bread and bitter herbs were to be eaten with the flesh. No male who was uncircumcised was to join the company. Each one was to have his loins girt, to hold a staff in his hand, and to have shoes on his feet. He was to eat in haste, and it would seem that he was to stand during the meal. The number of the party was to be calculated as nearly as possible, so that all the flesh of the lamb might be eaten; but if any portion of it happened to remain, it was to be burned in the morning. No morsel of it was to be carried out of the house.

The legislator was further directed to inform the people of God's purpose to smite the first-born of the Egyptians, to declare that the Passover was to be to them an ordinance forever, to give them directions respecting the order and duration of the festival in future times, and to enjoin upon them to teach their children its meaning, from generation to generation.

When the message was delivered to the people, they bowed their heads in worship. The lambs were selected, on the fourteenth they were slain and the blood sprinkled, and in the following evening, after the fifteenth day of the month had commenced, the first paschal meal was eaten. At midnight the first-born of the Egyptians were smitten, from the first-born of Pharaoh that sat on his throne unto the first-born of the captive that was in

vero lingua, hoc est in Hebræa, Pascha transitus dicitur: propterea tunc primum Pascha celebravit populus Dei, quando ex Ægypto fugientes, rubrum mare transierunt. Nunc ergo figura illa prophetica in veritate completa est, cum sicut ovis ad immolandum ducitur Christus, cujus sanguine illitis postibus nostris, id est, cujus signo crucis signatis frontibus nostris, a perditione hujus seculi tanquam a captivitate vel interemptione Ægyptia liberamur; et agimus saluberrimum transitum, cum a diabolo transimus ad Christum, et ab isto instabili seculo ad ejus fundatissimum regnum, Col. i. 13" (In Joan. Tract. iv.).

[a] There are five distinct statutes on the Passover in the 12th and 13th chapters of Exodus (xii. 2-4, 5-20, 21-28, 42-51; xiii. 1-10).

[b] The words translated in A. V. "the whole assembly of the congregation" (Ex. xii. 6), evidently mean every man of the congregation. They are well rendered by Vitringa (Observat. Sac. ii. 3, § 9), "universa Israelitarum multitudo nemine excepto." The word קָהָל, though it primarily denotes an assembly, must here signify no more than a complete number of persons, not necessarily assembled together.

[c] See note e, p. 2342.

the dungeon, and all the firstlings of the cattle.[a] The king and his people were now urgent that the Israelites should start immediately, and readily bestowed on them supplies for the journey. In such haste did the Israelites depart, on that very day (Num. xxxiii. 3), that they packed up their kneading-troughs containing the dough prepared for the morrow's provision, which was not yet leavened.

Such were the occurrences connected with the institution of the Passover, as they are related in Ex. xii. It would seem that the law for the consecration of the first-born was passed in immediate connection with them (Ex. xiii. 1, 13, 15, 16).

II. OBSERVANCE OF THE PASSOVER IN LATER TIMES.

1. In the twelfth and thirteenth chapters of Exodus, there are not only distinct references to the observance of the festival in future ages (e. g. xii. 2, 14, 17, 24-27, 42, xiii. 2, 5, 8-10); but there are several injunctions which were evidently not intended for the first passover, and which indeed could not possibly have been observed. The Israelites, for example, could not have kept the next day, the 15th of Nisan, on which they commenced their march (Ex. xii. 51; Num. xxxiii. 3), as a day of holy convocation according to Ex. xii. 16. [FESTIVALS, vol. i. p. 818.]

In the later notices of the festival in the books of the Law, there are particulars added which appear as modifications of the original institution. Of this kind are the directions for offering the Omer, or first sheaf of harvest (Lev. xxiii. 10-14), the instructions respecting the special sacrifices which were to be offered each day of the festival week (Num. xxviii. 16-25), and the command that the paschal lambs should be slain at the national sanctuary, and that the blood should be sprinkled on the altar, instead of the lintels and door-posts of the houses (Deut. xvi. 1-6).

Hence it is not without reason that the Jewish writers have laid great stress on the distinction between the "Egyptian Passover" and "the perpetual Passover." The distinction is noticed in the Mishna (Pesachim, ix. 5). The peculiarities of the Egyptian passover which are there pointed out are, the selection of the lamb on the 10th day of the month, the sprinkling of the blood on the lintels and door-posts, the use of hyssop in sprinkling, the haste in which the meal was to be eaten, and the restriction of the abstinence from unleavened bread to a single day. Elias of Byzantium[b] adds, that there was no command to burn the fat on the altar, that the pure and impure all partook of the paschal meal contrary to the law afterwards given (Num. xviii. 11), that both men and women were then required to partake, but subsequently the command was given only to men (Ex. xxiii. 17; Deut. xvi. 16), that neither the Hallel nor any other hymn was sung, as was required in later times in accordance with Is. xxx. 29, that there were no days of holy convocation, and that the lambs were not slain in the consecrated place.[c]

2. The following was the general order of the observances of the Passover in later times according to the direct evidence of Scripture : On the 14th of Nisan, every trace of leaven was put away from the houses, and on the same day every male Israelite not laboring under any bodily infirmity or ceremonial impurity, was commanded to appear before the Lord at the national sanctuary with an offering of money in proportion to his means (Ex. xxiii. 15; Deut. xvi. 16, 17).[d] Devout women sometimes attended, as is proved by the instances of Hannah and Mary (1 Sam. i. 7; Luke ii. 41, 42). As the sun was setting,[e] the lambs were slain, and the fat

---

[a] Michaelis and Kurtz consider that this visitation was directed against the sacred animals, "the gods of Egypt," mentioned in Ex. xii. 12.

[b] Quoted by Carpzov, App. Crit p. 406. For other Jewish authorities, see Otho's Lexicon, s. v. "Pascha."

[c] Another Jewish authority (Tosiphta in Pesachim, quoted by Otho) adds that the rule that no one who partook of the lamb should go out of the house until the morning (Ex. xii. 22) was observed only on this one occasion ; a point of interest, as bearing on the question relating to our Lord's last supper. See p. 2347 b.

[d] This offering was common to all the feasts. According to the Mishna (Chagigah, i. 2), part of it was appropriated for burnt-offerings and the rest for the Chagigah.

[e] "Between the two evenings," בֵּין הָעַרְבָּיִם (Ex. xii. 6; Lev. xxiii. 5; Num. ix. 3, 5). The phrase also occurs in reference to the time of offering the evening sacrifice (Ex. xxix. 39, 41; Num. xxviii. 4), and in other connections (Ex. xvi. 12, xxx. 8). Its precise meaning is doubtful. The Karaites and Samaritans, with whom Aben Ezra (on Ex. xii. 6) agrees, consider it as the interval between sunset and dark. This appears to be in accordance with Deut. xvi. 6, where the paschal lamb is commanded to be slain "at the going down of the sun." But the Pharisees and Rabbinists held that the first evening commenced when the sun began to decline (δείλη πρωΐα), and that the second evening began with the setting sun (δείλη ὀψία). Josephus says that the lambs were slain from the ninth hour till the eleventh, i. e. between three and five o'clock (B. J. vi. 9, § 3); the Mishna seems to countenance this (Pesachim, v. 3); and Maimonides, who says they were killed immediately after the evening sacrifice. [The Mishna says, Pisach. v. 1, De Sola

and Raphall's translation : "The daily offering was slaughtered half an hour after the eighth hour (i. e. at 2.30 P. M.), and sacrificed half an hour after the ninth hour ; but on the day before Passover . . . it was slaughtered half an hour after the seventh hour, and sacrificed half an hour after the eighth hour. When the day before Passover happened on Friday, it was slaughtered half an hour after the sixth hour, sacrificed half an hour after the seventh hour, and the Passover sacrifice after it." Under certain circumstances the paschal lamb might be killed before the evening sacrifice ; but not before noon (ibid. § 3). — A.] A third notion has been held by Jarchi and Kimchi, that the two evenings are the time immediately before, and immediately after sunset, so that the point of time at which the sun sets divides them. Gesenius, Bähr, Winer, and most other critics, hold the first opinion, and regard the phrase as equivalent with בְּעֶרֶב (Deut. xvi. 6). See Gesenius, Thes. p. 1065; Bähr, Symbolik, ii. 614 ; Hupfeld, De Festis Hebraeorum, p. 15 ; Rosenmüller in Exod. xii. 6 ; Carpzov, App. Crit. p. 68.

[e] This account of the opinion of Jarchi (i. e. Rashi or Rabbi Solomon ben Isaac) and Kimchi has been shown by Ginsburg (art. "Passover" in the 3d ed. of Kitto's Cyclop. of Bibl. Lit. iii. 423) to be entirely erroneous. They agree with the opinion of the Pharisees and Rabbinists as stated above.

The interpretation of "the two evenings" given by the Pharisees and Rabbinists is supported also by Philo (De Septenario, c. 18, Opp. ii. 292, ed Mangey), who says that the paschal lamb is killed "from mid day till the evening" (ἐν ᾗ {ἑορτῇ} θύουσι πανδημεί, ἀρξάμενοι κατὰ μεσημβρίαν ἕως ἑσπέρας, or ἐσ μεσ.

and blood given to the priests (2 Chr. xxxv. 5, 6; comp. Joseph. *B. J.* vi. 9, § 3). In accordance with the original institution in Egypt, the lamb was then roasted whole, and eaten with unleavened bread and bitter herbs; no portion of it was to be left until the morning. The same night, after the 15th of Nisan had commenced, the fat was burned by the priest and the blood sprinkled on the altar (2 Chr. xxx. 16, xxxv. 11). On the 15th, the night being passed, there was a holy convocation, and during that day no work might be done, except the preparation of necessary food (Ex. xii. 16). On this and the six following days an offering in addition to the daily sacrifice was made of two young bullocks, a ram, and seven lambs of the first year, with meat-offerings, for a burnt-offering, and a goat for a sin-offering (Num. xxviii. 19-23). On the 16th of the month, " the morrow after the sabbath " (*i. e.* after the day of holy convocation), the first sheaf of harvest was offered and waved by the priest before the Lord, and a male lamb was offered as a burnt sacrifice with a meat and drink-offering. Nothing necessarily distinguished the four following days of the festival, except the additional burnt and sin-offerings, and the restraint from some kinds of labor. [FESTIVALS.] On the seventh day, the 21st of Nisan, there was a holy convocation, and the day appears to have been one of peculiar solemnity.[a] As at all the festivals, cheerfulness was to prevail during the whole week, and all care was to be laid aside (Deut. xxvii. 7; comp. Joseph. *Ant.* xi. 5; Michaelis, *Laws of Moses*, Art. 197). [PENTECOST.]

3. (*a.*) *The Paschal Lamb.* — After the first Passover in Egypt there is no trace of the lamb having been selected before it was wanted. In later times, we are certain that it was sometimes not provided before the 14th of the month (Luke xxii. 7-9; Mark xiv. 12-16). The law formally allowed the alternative of a kid (Ex. xii. 5), but a lamb was preferred,[b] and was probably nearly always chosen. It was to be faultless and a male, in accordance with the established estimate of ani-

mal perfection (see Mal. i. 14). Either the head of the family, or any other person who was not ceremonially unclean (2 Chr. xxx. 17), took it into the court of the Temple on his shoulders. According to some authorities, the lamb might, if circumstances should render it desirable, be slain at any time in the afternoon, even before the evening sacrifice, if the blood was kept stirred, so as to prevent it from coagulating, until the time came for sprinkling it (*Pesachim*, v. 3).

The Mishna gives a particular account of the arrangement which was made in the court of the Temple (*Pesachim*, v. 6-8). Those who were to kill the lamb entered successively in three divisions. When the first division had entered, the gates were closed and the trumpets were sounded three times. The priests stood in two rows, each row extending from the altar to the place where the people were assembled. The priests of one row held basins of silver, and those of the other basins of gold. Each Israelite[c] then slew his lamb in order, and the priest who was nearest to him received the blood in his basin, which he handed to the next priest, who gave his empty basin in return. A succession of full basins was thus passed towards the altar, and a succession of empty ones towards the people. The priest who stood next the altar threw the blood out towards the base in a single jet. When the first division had performed their work, the second came in, and then the third. The lambs were skinned, and the viscera taken out with the internal fat. The fat was carefully separated and collected in the large dish, and the viscera were washed and replaced in the body of the lamb, like those of the burnt sacrifices (Lev. i. 9, iii. 3-5; comp. *Pesachim*, vi. 1). Maimonides says that the tail was put with the fat (*Not. in Pes.* v. 10). While this was going on the Hallel was sung, and repeated a second, or even a third time, if the process was not finished. As it grew dark, the people went home to roast their lambs. The fat was burned on the altar, with incense, that same evening.[d] When the 14th of Nisan fell on the Sabbath, all these things were

---

ἄχρι ἑστ., Tischend. *Philonea* (Lips. 1868), p. 46). In the *Book of Jubilees* (supposed to belong to the 1st century) it is said that "the Passover is to be kept on the 14th of the 1st month ; it is to be killed before it is evening, and eaten at night, on the evening of the 15th, after sunset." Again, "The children of Israel shall keep the Passover on the 14th of the 1st month between the evenings, in the third part of the day till the third part of the night " (*i. e.* from about noon of the 14th of Nisan to the midnight following). " What remains of all its flesh after the third part of the night they shall burn with fire." (Cap. 49 of Dillmann's translation, in Ewald's *Jahrb. d. Bibl. wissensch.* iii. 63, 69.)   A.

[a] The seventh day of the Passover, and the eighth day of the Feast of Tabernacles (see John vii. 37), had a character of their own, distinguishing them from the first days of the feasts and from all other days of holy convocation, with the exception of the day of Pentecost. [PENTECOST.] This is indicated in regard to the Passover in Deut. xvi. 8. " Six days thou shalt eat unleavened bread ; and on the seventh day shall be a solemn assembly (עֲצֶרֶת) to the Lord." See also Ex. xiii. 6: " Seven days thou shalt eat unleavened bread, and in the seventh day shall be a feast to the Lord." The word עֲצֶרֶת is used in like manner for the last day of the Feast of Tabernacles (Lev. xxiii. 36, where it is associated with מִקְרָא־קֹדֶשׁ, "a holy

convocation;" Num. xxix. 35; 2 Chr. vii. 9; Neh. viii. 18). Our translators have in each case rendered it "solemn assembly," but have explained it in the margin by "restraint." The LXX. have ἐξόδιον. Michaelis and Iken imagined the primary idea of the word to be *restraint from labor*. Gesenius shows that this is a mistake, and proves the word to mean *assembly or congregation*. Its root is undoubtedly עָצַר, *to shut up*, or *constrain*. Hence Bähr (*Symbolik*, ii. 619) reasonably argues, from the occurrence of the word in the passages above referred to, that its strict meaning is that of *the closing assembly*; which is of course quite consistent with its being sometimes used for a solemn assembly in a more general sense, and with its application to the day of Pentecost.

[b] The Chaldee interpreters render שֶׂה, which means *one of the flock*, whether sheep or goat, by אִמַּר, *a lamb*; and Theodoret no doubt represents the Jewish traditional usage when he says, ἵνα ὁ μὲν πρόβατον ἔχων θύσῃ τοῦτο· ὁ δὲ σταυρίζων προβάτου τὸν ἔριφον (on Ex. xii.).

[c] Undoubtedly the usual practice was for the head of the family to slay his own lamb ; but on particular occasions (as in the great observances of the Passover by Hezekiah, Josiah, and Ezra) the slaughter of the lambs was committed to the Levites. See p. 2347.

[d] The remarkable passage in which this is commanded, which occurs Ex. xxiii. 17, 18, 19, and is

done in the same manner; but the court of the Temple, instead of being carefully cleansed as on other occasions, was merely flooded by opening a sluice.

A spit made of the wood of the pomegranate was thrust lengthwise through the lamb (*Pesachim*, vii. 1). According to Justin Martyr, a second spit, or skewer, was put transversely through the shoulders, so as to form the figure of a cross.[a] The oven was of earthenware, and appears to have been in shape something like a bee-hive with an opening in the side to admit fuel. The lamb was carefully so placed as not to touch the side of the oven, lest the cooking should be effected in part by hot earthenware, and not entirely by fire, according to Ex. xii. 9; 2 Chr. xxxv. 13. If any one concerned in the process broke a bone of the lamb so as to infringe the command in Ex. xii. 46, he was subject to the punishment of forty stripes. The flesh was to be roasted thoroughly [b] (Ex. xii. 9). No portion of it was allowed to be carried out of the house, and if any of it was not eaten at the meal, it was burned, along with the bones and tendons, in the morning of the 16th of Nisan; or, if that day happened to be the Sabbath, on the 17th.

As the paschal lamb could be legally slain, and the blood and fat offered, only in the national sanctuary (Deut. xvi. 2), it of course ceased to be

offered by the Jews after the destruction of Jerusalem. The spring festival of the modern Jews strictly consists only of the feast of unleavened bread.[c]

(*b.*) *The Unleavened Bread.* — There is no reason to doubt that the unleavened bread eaten in the Passover and that used on other religious occasions were of the same nature. It might be made of wheat, spelt, barley, oats, or rye, but not of rice or millet (*Pesachim*, ii. 5). It appears to have been usually made of the finest wheat flour [d] (Buxt. *Syn. Jud.* c. xviii. p. 397). The greatest care was taken that it should be made in perfectly clean vessels and with all possible expedition, lest the process of fermentation should be allowed to commence in the slightest degree (*Pesachim*, iii. 2–5). It was probably formed into dry, thin biscuits, not unlike those used by the modern Jews.

The command to eat unleavened bread during the seven days of the festival, under the penalty of being cut off from the people, is given with marked emphasis, as well as that to put away all leaven from the house during the festival (Ex. xii. 15, 19, 20, xiii. 7). But the Rabbinists say that the house was carefully cleansed and every corner searched for any fragment of leavened bread in the evening before the 14th of Nisan, though leavened bread might be eaten till the sixth hour of that day, when all that

---

repeated Ex. xxxiv. 25, 26, appears to be a sort of proverbial caution respecting the three great feasts. "Three times in the year all thy males shall appear before the Lord God. Thou shalt not offer the blood of my sacrifice with leavened bread; neither shall the fat of my sacrifice remain until the morning. The first of the first-fruits of thy land thou shalt bring into the house of the Lord thy God. Thou shalt not seethe a kid in his mother's milk." The references to the Passover and Pentecost are plain enough. That which is supposed to refer to Tabernacles (which is also found Deut. xiv. 21), "Thou shalt not seethe a kid in his mother's milk," is explained by Abarbanel, and in a Karaite MS. spoken of by Cudworth, as bearing on a custom of boiling a kid in the milk of its dam as a charm, and sprinkling fields and orchards with the milk to render them fertile (Cudworth, *True Notion of the Lord's Supper*, pp. 36, 37; Spencer, *Leg. Heb* ii. 8. For other interpretations of the passage, see Rosenmüller, in *Exod.* xxiii. 19). [IDOLATRY; vol. ii. p. 1129 *a*.]

a The statement is in the Dialogue with Trypho, c. 40: Καὶ τὸ κελευσθὲν πρόβατον ἐκεῖνο ὀπτὸν ὅλον γίνεσθαι, τοῦ πάθους τοῦ σταυροῦ, δι' οὗ πάσχειν ἔμελλεν ὁ Χριστός, σύμβολον ἦν. τὸ γὰρ ὀπτώμενον πρόβατον σχηματιζόμενον ὁμοίως τῷ σχήματι τοῦ σταυροῦ ὀπτᾶται. εἷς γὰρ ὄβελος ὀβελίσκος διαπεροῦται ἀπὸ τῶν κατωτάτω μηρῶν μέχρι τῆς κεφαλῆς, καὶ εἷς πάλιν κατὰ τὸ μετάφρενον, ᾧ προσαρτῶνται καὶ αἱ χεῖρες τοῦ προβάτου.

As Justin was a native of Flavia Neapolis, it is a striking fact that the modern Samaritans roast their paschal lambs in nearly the same manner at this day. Mr. George Grove, who visited *Nablous* in 1861, in a letter to the writer of this article, says, "The lambs (they require six for the community now) are roasted all together by stuffing them vertically, head downwards, into an oven which is like a small well, about three feet diameter, and four or five feet deep, roughly steaned, in which a fire has been kept up for several hours. After the lambs are thrust in, the top of the hole is covered with bushes and earth, to confine the heat till they are done. Each lamb has a stake or spit run through him to draw him up by; and, to prevent the spit from tearing away through the roast meat with the weight, a cross piece is put through the lower end of it." A similar account is

given in Miss Rogers's *Domestic Life in Palestine*. Vitringa, Bochart, and Hottinger have taken the statement of Justin as representing the ancient Jewish usage; and, with him, regard the crossed spits as a prophetic type of the cross of our Lord. But it would seem more probable that the transverse spit was a mere matter of convenience, and was perhaps never in use among the Jews. The rabbinical traditions relate that the lamb was called *Galeatus*, "qui quum totus assabatur, cum capite, cruribus, et intestinis, pedes autem et intestina ad latera ligabantur inter assandum, agnus ita quasi armatum repraesentaverit, qui galea in capite et ense in latere est munitus" (Otho, *Lex. Rab.* p. 508). [On the Samaritan Passover, see the addition to this article, p. 2857.]

b The word נָא, in A. V. "raw," is rendered "alive" by Onkelos and Jonathan. In 1 Sam. ii. 15, it plainly means *raw*. But Jarchi, Aben Ezra, and other Jewish authorities, understand it as *half-dressed* (Rosenmüller, *in loc.*).

c There are many curious particulars in the mode in which the modern Jews observe this festival, to be found in Buxt. *Syn. Jud.*, c. xviii. xix.; Picart, *Cérémonies Religieuses*, vol. i.; Mill, *The British Jews* (London, 1853); Stauben, *Scènes de la vie Juive en Alsace* (Paris, 1860); [Isaacs, *Ceremonies*, etc., *of the Jews*, p. 104 ff.; Allen's *Modern Judaism*, 2d ed., p. 394 ff.] The following appear to be the most interesting: A shoulder of lamb, thoroughly roasted, is placed on the table to take the place of the paschal lamb, with a hard-boiled egg as a symbol of wholeness. Besides the sweet sauce, to remind them of the sort of work carried on by their fathers in Egypt (see above, *c*), there is sometimes a vessel of salt and water, to represent the Red Sea, into which they dip the bitter herbs. But the most remarkable usages are those connected with the expectation of the coming of Elijah. A cup of wine is poured out for him, and stands all night upon the table. Just before the filling of the cups of the guests the fourth time, there is an interval of dead silence, and the door of the room is opened for some minutes to admit the prophet. [ELIJAH, i. 709, note *i.*]

d Ewald (*Alterthümer*, p. 881) and Hüllmann (quoted by Winer) conjecture the original unleavened bread of the Passover to have been of barley, in connection with the commencement of barley h.

remained was to be burned (*Pesachim*, i. 1, 4; [a] and citation in Lightfoot, *Temple Serv.*, xii. § 1).

(*c.*) *The Bitter Herbs and the Sauce.* — According to *Pesachim* (ii. 6) the bitter herbs (מְרֹרִים; πικρίδες; *lactucæ agrestes*, Ex. xii. 8), might be endive, chicory, wild lettuce, or nettles. These plants were important articles of food to the ancient Egyptians (as is noticed by Pliny), and they are said to constitute nearly half that of the modern Egyptians. According to Niebuhr they are still eaten at the Passover by the Jews in the East. They were used in former times either fresh or dried, and a portion of them is said to have been eaten before the unleavened bread (*Pesach.* x. 3).

The sauce into which the herbs, the bread, and the meat were dipped as they were eaten (John xiii. 26; Matt. xxvi. 23) is not mentioned in the Pentateuch. It is called in the Mishna חֲרוֹסֶת. According to Bartenora it consisted of only vinegar and water; but others describe it as a mixture of vinegar, figs, dates, almonds, and spice. The same sauce was used on ordinary occasions thickened with a little flour; but the rabbinists forbade this at the Passover, lest the flour should occasion a slight degree of fermentation. Some say that it was beaten up to the consistence of mortar or clay, in order to commemorate the toils of the Israelites in Egypt in laying bricks (Buxtorf, *Lex. Tal.* col. 831; *Pesachim*, ii. 8. x. 3, with the notes of Bartenora, Maimonides, and Surenhusius).

(*d.*) *The Four Cups of Wine.* — There is no mention of wine in connection with the Passover in the Pentateuch; but the Mishna strictly enjoins that there should never be less than four cups of it provided at the paschal meal even of the poorest Israelite (*Pes.* x. 1). The wine was usually red, and it was mixed with water as it was drunk (*Pes.* vii. 13, with Bartenora's note; and Otho's *Lex.* p. 507). The cups were handed round in succession at specified intervals in the meal (see below, *f*). Two of them appear to be distinctly mentioned Luke xxii. 17, 20. "The cup of blessing" (1 Cor. x. 16) was probably the latter one of these, and is generally considered to have been the third of the series, after which a grace was said; though a comparison of Luke xxii. 20 (where it is called the cup after supper") with *Pes.* x. 7, and the designation פּוֹס הַלֵּל, "cup of the Hallel," might rather suggest that it was the fourth and last cup. Schoettgen, however, is inclined to doubt whether there is any reference, in either of the passages of the N. T., to the formal ordering of the cups of the Passover, and proves that the name "cup of blessing" (פּוֹס שֶׁל בְּרָכָה) was applied in a general way to any cup which was drunk with thanksgiving, and that the expression was often used metaphorically, e. g. Ps. cxvi. 13 (*Hor. Heb.* in 1 Cor. x. 16. See also Carpzov, *App. Crit.* p. 380).

The wine drunk at the meal was not restricted to the four cups, but none could be taken during the interval between the third and fourth cups (*Pes.* x. 7).

(*e.*) *The Hallel.* — The service of praise sung at the Passover is not mentioned in the Law. The name is contracted from הַלְלוּ־יָהּ (*Hallelujah*). It consisted of the series of Psalms from cxiii. to cxviii. The first portion, comprising Ps. cxiii. and cxiv., was sung in the early part of the meal, and the second part after the fourth cup of wine. This is supposed to have been the "hymn" sung by our Lord and his Apostles (Matt. xxvi. 30; Mark xiv. 26; Buxtorf, *Lex. Tal.* s. v. הלל, and *Syn. Jud.* p. 48; Otho, *Lex.* p. 271; Carpzov, *App. Crit.* p. 374).

(*f.*) *Mode and Order of the Paschal Meal.* — Adopting as much from Jewish tradition as is not inconsistent or improbable, the following appears to have been the usual custom. All work, except that belonging to a few trades connected with daily life, was suspended for some hours before the evening of the 14th of Nisan. There was, however, a difference in this respect. The Galileans desisted from work the whole day; the Jews of the south only after the middle of the tenth hour, that is, half-past three o'clock. It was not lawful to eat any ordinary food after midday. The reason assigned for this was, that the paschal supper might be eaten with the enjoyment furnished by a good appetite. (*Pes.* iv. 1–3, x. 1, with Maimonides' note.) But it is also stated that this preliminary fasting was especially incumbent on the eldest son, and that it was intended to commemorate the deliverance of the first-born in Egypt. This was probably only a fancy of later times (Buxt. *Syn. Jud.* xviii. p. 401).

No male was admitted to the table unless he was circumcised, even if he was of the seed of Israel (Ex. xii. 48). Neither, according to the letter of the law, was any one of either sex admitted who was ceremonially unclean [b] (Num. ix. 6; Joseph. *B. J.* vi. 9, § 3). But this rule was on special occasions liberally applied. In the case of Hezekiah's Passover (2 Chr. xxx.) we find that a greater degree of legal purity was required to slaughter the lambs than to eat them, and that numbers partook "otherwise than it was written," who were not "cleansed according to the purification of the sanctuary." The Rabbinists expressly state that women were permitted, though not commanded, to partake (*Pes.* viii. 1; *Chagigah*, i. 1; comp. Joseph. *B. J.* vi. 9, § 3), in accordance with the instances in Scripture which have been mentioned of Hannah and Mary (p. 2342 *b*). But the Karaites, in more recent times, excluded all but full-grown men. It was customary for the number of a party to be not less than ten (Joseph. *B. J.* vi. 9, § 3). It was perhaps generally under twenty, but it might be as many as a hundred, if each one could have a piece of the lamb as large as an olive (*Pes.* viii. 7).

When the meal was prepared, the family was placed round the table, the paterfamilias taking a place of honor, probably somewhat raised above the rest. There is no reason to doubt that the ancient Hebrews sat, as they were accustomed to do at their ordinary meals (see Otho, *Lex.* p. 7). But when the custom of reclining at table had be-

---

[a] Other particulars of the precautions which were taken are given in *Pesachim*, and also by Maimonides, in his treatise *De Fermentato et Azymo*, a compendium of which is given by Carpzov, *App. Crit.* p. 404.

[b] Certain precautions to avoid pollution were taken a month before the Passover. Amongst these was the annual whitewashing of the sepulchres (cf. Matt. xxiii. 27) (Reland, *Ant.* iv. 2, 6). In John xi. 55, we find some Jews coming up to Jerusalem to purify themselves a week before the feast.

some general, that posture appears to have been enjoined, on the ground of its supposed significance. The Mishna says that the meanest Israelite should recline at the Passover "like a king, with the ease becoming a free man" (*Pes.* x. 1, with Maimonides' note). He was to keep in mind that when his ancestors stood at the feast in Egypt they took the posture of slaves (R. Levi, quoted by Otho, p. 504). Our Lord and his Apostles conformed to the usual custom of their time, and reclined (Luke xxii. 14, &c.). [MEALS, p. 1843 f.]

When the party was arranged, the first cup of wine was filled, and a blessing was asked by the head of the family on the feast, as well as a special one on the cup. The bitter herbs were then placed on the table, and a portion of them eaten, either with or without the sauce. The unleavened bread was handed round next, and afterwards the lamb was placed on the table in front of the head of the family (*Pes.* x. 3). Before the lamb was eaten, the second cup of wine was filled, and the son, in accordance with Ex. xii. 26, asked his father the meaning of the feast. In reply, an account was given of the sufferings of the Israelites in Egypt, and of their deliverance, with a particular explanation of Deut. xxvi. 5, and the first part of the Hallel (Ps. cxiii., cxiv.) was sung. This being gone through, the lamb was carved and eaten. The third cup of wine was poured out and drunk, and soon afterwards the fourth. The second part of the Hallel (Ps. cxv. to cxviii.) was then sung (*Pes.* x. 2-5). A fifth wine-cup appears to have been occasionally produced, but perhaps only in later times. What was termed the greater Hallel (Ps. cxx. to cxxxviii.) was sung on such occasions (Buxt. *Syn. Jud.* c. xviii.). The meal being ended, it was unlawful for anything to be introduced in the way of dessert.

The Israelites who lived in the country appear to have been accommodated at the feast by the inhabitants of Jerusalem in their houses, so far as there was room for them (Luke xxii. 10-12; Matt. xxvi. 18). It is said that the guests left in return for their entertainment the skin of the lamb, the oven, and other vessels which they had used. Those who could not be received into the city encamped without the walls in tents, as the pilgrims now do at Mecca. The number of these must have been very great, if we may trust the computation of Josephus that they who partook of the Passover amounted, in the reign of Nero, to above 2,700,000 (*B. J.* vi. 9, § 3 *a*). It is not wonderful that seditions were apt to break out in such a vast multitude so brought together (Jos. *Ant.* xvii. 9, § 2; *B. J.* i. 3, &c.; comp. Matt. xxvi. 5; Luke xiii. 1).

After the paschal meal, such of the Israelites from the country as were so disposed left Jerusalem, and observed the remainder of the festival at their respective homes (Deut. xvi. 7). But see Lightfoot, *on Luke* ii. 43.

(*g*.) *The first Sheaf of Harvest.* — The offering of the Omer, or sheaf (עֹמֶר; τὰ δράγματα; *manipulus spicarum*) is mentioned nowhere in the Law except Lev. xxiii. 10-14. It is there commanded that when the Israelites might reach the land of promise, they should bring, on the 16th of the month, " the morrow after the sabbath " (*i. e.* the day of holy convocation [PENTECOST, § 1, note]), the first sheaf of the harvest to the priest, to be waved by him before the Lord. A lamb, with a meat-offering and a drink-offering, was to be offered at the same time. Until this ceremony was performed, no bread, parched corn, or green ears, were to be eaten of the new crop (see Josh. v. 11, 12).[b] It was from the day of this offering that the fifty days began to be counted to the day of Pentecost (Lev. xxiii. 15). The sheaf was of barley, as being the grain which was first ripe (2 Kings iv. 42). Josephus relates (*Ant.* iii. 10, § 5) that the barley was ground, and that ten handfuls of the meal were brought to the altar, one handful being cast into the fire and the remainder given to the priests. The Mishna adds several particulars, and, amongst others, that men were formally sent by the Sanhedrim to cut the barley in some field near Jerusalem; and that, after the meal had been sifted thirteen times, it was mingled with oil and incense[c] (*Menachoth*, x. 2-6).

(*h*.) *The Chagigah.* — The daily sacrifices are enumerated in the Pentateuch only in Num. xxviii. 19-23, but reference is made to them Lev. xxiii. 8. Besides these public offerings (which are mentioned, p. 2343 *b*), there was another sort of sacrifice connected with the Passover, as well as with the other great festivals, called in the Talmud חֲגִיגָה (*Chagigah*, i. e. "festivity"). It was a voluntary peace-offering made by private individuals. The victim might be taken either from the flock or the herd. It might be either male or female, but it must be without blemish. The offerer laid his hand upon his head and slew it at the door of the sanctuary. The blood was sprinkled on the altar, and the fat of the inside, with the kidneys, was burned by the priest. The breast was given to the priest as a wave-offering, and the right shoulder as a heave-offering (Lev. iii. 1-5, vii. 29-34). What remained of the victim might be eaten by the offerer and his guests on the day on which it was slain, and on the day following, but if any portion was left till the third day, it was burned (Lev. vii. 16-18; *Pesach.* vi. 4). The connection of these free-will peace-offerings with the festivals appears to be indicated Num. x. 10; Deut. xiv. 26; 2 Chr. xxxi. 22, and they are included under the term Passover in Deut. xvi. 2 — "Thou shalt therefore sacrifice the passover unto the Lord thy God, of the flock and of the herd." Onkelos here understands the command to sacrifice from the flock, to refer to the paschal lamb; and that to sacrifice from the herd, to the Chagigah. But it seems more probable that both the flock and the herd refer to the Chagigah, as there is a specific command respecting the paschal lamb in vv. 5-7. (See De Muis' *note* in the *Crit. Sac.*; and Lightfoot, *Hor. Heb.* on John xviii. 28.) There are evidently similar references, 2 Chr. xxx. 22-24, and 2 Chr. xxxv. 7. Hezekiah and his princes gave away, at the great Passover which he celebrated, two thousand bullocks and seventeen thousand sheep; and Josiah, on a similar occasion, is said to have supplied the people at his own cost with lambs "for the Passover offerings," besides three thousand oxen. From these passages and others, it may be seen that the eating of the Chagigah

---

a He states that the number of lambs slain in a single Passover was 256,500. It is difficult to imagine how they could all have been slain, and their blood sprinkled, as described in the Mishna. See p. 2343.

b On this text, see PENTECOST.

c There is no mention of the Omer in *Pesachim*.

was an occasion of social festivity, connected with the festivals, and especially with the Passover. The principal day for sacrificing the Passover Chagigah was the 15th of Nisan, the first day of holy convocation, unless it happened to be the weekly Sabbath. The paschal lamb might be slain on the Sabbath, but not the Chagigah. With this exception, the Chagigah might be offered on any day of the festival, and on some occasions a Chagigah victim was slain on the 14th, especially when the paschal lamb was likely to prove too small to serve as meat for the party (*Pesach.* iv. 4, x. 8; Lightfoot, *Temple Service,* c. xii.; Reland, *Ant.* iv. c. ii. § 2).

That the Chagigah might be boiled, as well as roasted, is proved by 2 Chr. xxxv. 13, " And they roasted the passover with fire according to the ordinance: but the other holy offerings sod they in pots, and in caldrons, and in pans, and divided them speedily among the people."

(*i*) *Release of Prisoners.* — It is a question whether the release of a prisoner at the Passover (Matt. xxvii. 15; Mark xv. 6; Luke xxiii. 17; John xviii. 39) was a custom of Roman origin resembling what took place at the lectisternium (Liv. v. 13); and, in later times, on the birthday of an emperor; or whether it was an old Hebrew usage belonging to the festival, which Pilate allowed the Jews to retain. Grotius argues in favor of the former notion (*On Matt.* xxvii. 15). But others (Hottinger, Schoettgen, Winer) consider that the words of St John — ἔστι δὲ συνήθεια ὑμῖν — render it most probable that the custom was essentially Hebrew. Schoettgen thinks that there is an allusion to it in *Pesachim* (viii. 6), where it is permitted that a lamb should be slain on the 14th of Nisan for the special use of one in prison to whom a release had been promised. The subject is discussed at length by Hottinger, in his tract *De Ritu dimittendi Reum in Festo Paschatis,* in the *Thesaurus Novus Theologico-Philologicus.*

(*k.*) *The Second, or Little Passover.* — When the Passover was celebrated the second year, in the wilderness, certain men were prevented from keeping it, owing to their being defiled by contact with a dead body. Being thus prevented from obeying the Divine command, they came anxiously to Moses to inquire what they should do. He was accordingly instructed to institute a second Passover, to be observed on the 14th of the following month, for the benefit of any who had been hindered from keeping the regular one in Nisan (Num. ix. 11). The Talmudists called this the Little Passover (הַפֶּסַח הַקָּטֹן). It was distinguished, according to them, from the Greater Passover by the rites lasting only one day, instead of seven days, by it not being required that the Hallel should be sung during the meal, but only when the lamb was slaughtered, and by it not being necessary for leaven to be put out of the houses (*Pesach.* ix. 3; Buxt. *Lex. Tal.* col. 1766).

(*L*) *Observances of the Passover recorded in Scripture.* — Of these seven are of chief historical importance.

1. The first Passover in Egypt (Ex. xii.).

2. The first kept in the desert (Num. ix.).

There is no notice of the observance of any other Passover in the desert; and Hupfeld, Keil, and others have concluded that none took place between this one and that at Gilgal. The neglect of circumcision may render this probable. But Calvin imagines that a special commission was given to the people to continue the ordinance of the Passover. (See Keil on Joshua v. 10.)

3. That celebrated by Joshua at Gilgal immediately after the circumcision of the people, when the manna ceased (Josh. v.).

4. That which Hezekiah observed on the occasion of his restoring the national worship (2 Chr. xxx.). Owing to the impurity of a considerable proportion of the priests in the month Nisan, this Passover was not held till the second month, the proper time for the Little Passover. The postponement was determined by a decree of the congregation. By the same authority, the festival was repeated through a second seven days to serve the need of the vast multitude who wished to attend it. To meet the case of the probable impurity of a great number of the people, the Levites were commanded to slaughter the lambs, and the king prayed that the Lord would pardon every one who was penitent, though his legal pollution might be upon him.

5. The Passover of Josiah in the eighteenth year of his reign (2 Chr. xxxv.). On this occasion, as in the Passover of Hezekiah, the Levites appear to have slain the lambs (ver. 6), and it is expressly stated that they flayed them.

6. That celebrated by Ezra after the return from Babylon (Ezr. vi.). On this occasion, also, the Levites slew the lambs, and for the same reason as they did in Hezekiah's Passover.

7. The last Passover of our Lord's life.

III. THE LAST SUPPER.

1. Whether or not the meal at which our Lord instituted the sacrament of the Eucharist was the paschal supper according to the Law, is a question of great difficulty. No point in the Gospel history has been more disputed. If we had nothing to guide us but the three first Gospels, no doubt of the kind could well be raised, though the narratives may not be free from difficulties in themselves. We find them speaking, in accordance with Jewish usage, of the day of the supper as that on which " the Passover must be killed," and as " the first day of unleavened bread " [a] (Matt. xxvi. 17; Mark xiv. 12; Luke xxii. 7). Each relates that the use of the guest-chamber was secured in the manner usual with those who came from a distance to keep the festival. Each states that " they made ready the Passover," and that, when the evening was come, our Lord, taking the place at the head of the family, sat down with the twelve. He himself distinctly calls the meal " this Passover" (Luke xxii. 15, 16). After a thanksgiving, he passes round the first cup of wine (Luke xxii. 17), and, when the supper is ended, the usual " cup of blessing " (comp. Luke xxii. 20; 1 Cor. x. 16, xi. 25). A hymn is then sung (Matt. xxvi. 30; Mark xiv.

---

a Josephus in like manner calls the 14th of Nisan the first day of unleavened bread (*B. J.* v. 3, § 1): and he speaks of the festival of the Passover as lasting eight days (*Ant.* ii. 15, § 1). But he elsewhere calls the 15th of Nisan " the commencement of the feast of unleavened bread." (*Ant.* iii. 10, § 5.) Either mode of speaking was evidently allowable : in one case regarding it as a matter of fact that the eating of unleavened bread began on the 14th ; and in the other, distinguishing the feast of unleavened bread, lasting from the first day of holy convocation to the concluding one, from the paschal meal.

26), which it is reasonable to suppose was the last part of the Hallel.

If it be granted that the supper was eaten on the evening of the 14th of Nisan, the apprehension, trial, and crucifixion of our Lord must have occurred on Friday the 15th, the day of holy convocation, which was the first of the seven days of the Passover week. The weekly Sabbath on which He lay in the tomb was the 16th, and the Sunday of the resurrection was the 17th.

But, on the other hand, if we had no information but that which is to be gathered from St. John's Gospel, we could not hesitate to infer that the evening of the supper was that of the 13th of 'Nisan, the day preceding that of the paschal meal. It appears to be spoken of as occurring before the feast of the Passover (xiii. 1, 2). Some of the disciples suppose that Christ told Judas, while they were at supper, to buy what they "had need of against the feast" (xiii. 29). In the night which follows the supper, the Jews will not enter the prætorium lest they should be defiled and so not able to "eat the Passover" (xviii. 28). When our Lord is before Pilate, about to be led out to crucifixion, we are told that it was "the preparation of the Passover" (xix. 14). After the crucifixion, the Jews are solicitous, "because it was the preparation, that the bodies should not remain upon the cross on the Sabbath-day, for that Sabbath-day was a high day" (xix. 31).

If we admit, in accordance with the first view of these passages, that the Last Supper was on the 13th of Nisan, our Lord must have been crucified on the 14th, the day on which the paschal lamb was slain and eaten, He lay in the grave on the 15th (which was a "high day" or double Sabbath, because the weekly Sabbath coincided with the day of holy convocation), and the Sunday of the resurrection was the 16th.

It is alleged that this view of the case is strengthened by certain facts in the narratives of the synoptical Gospels, as well as that of St. John, compared with the Law and with what we know of Jewish customs in later times. If the meal was the paschal supper, the law of Ex. xii. 22, that none "shall go out of the door of his house until the morning," must have been broken, not only by Judas (John xiii. 30), but by our Lord and the other disciples (Luke xxii. 39).[a] In like manner it is said that the law for the observance of the 15th, the day of holy convocation with which the paschal week commenced (Ex. xii. 16; Lev. xxiii. 35, &c.), and some express enactments in the Talmud regarding legal proceedings and particular details, such as the carrying of spices, must have been infringed by the Jewish rulers in the apprehending of Christ, in his trials before the high-priest and the Sanhedrim, and in his crucifixion; and also by Simon of Cyrene, who was coming out of the country (Mark xv. 21; Luke xxiii. 26), by Joseph who bought fine linen (Mark xv. 46), by the women who bought spices (Mark xvi. 1; Luke xxiii. 56), and by Nicodemus who brought to the tomb a hundred pounds weight of a mixture of myrrh and aloes (John xix.

39). The same objection is considered to lie against the supposition that the disciples could have imagined, on the evening of the Passover, that our Lord was giving directions to Judas respecting the purchase of anything or the giving of alms to the poor. The latter act (except under very special conditions) would have been as much opposed to rabbinical maxims as the former.[b]

It is further urged that the expressions of our Lord, "My time is at hand" (Matt. xxvi. 18), and "this Passover" (Luke xxii. 15), as well as St. Paul's designating it as "the same night that He was betrayed," instead of the night of the Passover (1 Cor. xi. 23), and his identifying Christ as our slain paschal lamb (1 Cor. v. 7), seem to point to the time of the supper as being peculiar, and to the time of the crucifixion as being the same as that of the killing of the lamb (Neander and Lücke).

It is not surprising that some modern critics should have given up as hopeless the task of reconciling this difficulty. Several have rejected the narrative of St. John (Bretschneider, Weisse), but a greater number (especially De Wette, Usteri, Ewald, Meyer, and Theile) have taken an opposite course, and have been content with the notion that the three first Evangelists made a mistake and confounded the meal with the Passover.

2. The reconciliations which have been attempted fall under three principal heads:—

i. Those which regard the supper at which our Lord washed the feet of his disciples (John xiii.), as having been a distinct meal eaten one or more days before the regular Passover, of which our Lord partook in due course according to the synoptical narratives.

ii. Those in which it is endeavored to establish that the meal was eaten on the 13th, and that our Lord was crucified on the evening of the true paschal supper.

iii. Those in which the most obvious view of the first three narratives is defended, and in which it is attempted to explain the apparent contradictions in St. John, and the difficulties in reference to the law.

(i.) The first method has the advantage of furnishing the most ready way of accounting for St. John's silence on the institution of the Holy Communion. It has been adopted by Maldonat,[c] Lightfoot, and Bengel, and more recently by Kaiser.[d] Lightfoot identified the supper of John xiii. with the one in the house of Simon the leper at Bethany two days before the Passover, when Mary poured the ointment on the head of our Saviour (Matt. xxvi. 6; Mark xiv. 3); and quaintly remarks, "While they are grumbling at the anointing of his head, He does not scruple to wash their feet."[e] Bengel supposes that it was eaten only the evening before the Passover.[f]

But any explanation founded on the supposition of two meals, appears to be rendered untenable by the context. The fact that all four Evangelists introduce in the same connection the foretelling of the treachery of Judas with the dipping of the sop, and of the denials of St. Peter and the going out to

---

[a] It has been stated (p. 2342, note c) that, according to Jewish authorities, this law was disused in later times. But even if this were not the case, it does not seem that there can be much difficulty in adopting the arrangement of Greswell's Harmony, that the party did not leave the house to go over the brook till after midnight.

[b] Lightfoot, Hor. Heb. on Matt. xxvii. 1.
[c] On John xiii. 1.
[d] Chronologie und Harmonie der vier Ev. Mentioned by Tischendorf, Synop. Evang. p. xlv.
[e] Ex. Heb., on John xiii. 2, and Matt. xxvi. 6. Also, "Gleanings from Exodus," No. XIX.
[f] On Matt. xxvi. 17, and John xviii. 28.

the Mount of Olives, can hardly leave a doubt that they are speaking of the same meal. Besides this, the explanation does not touch the greatest difficulties, which are those connected with "the day of preparation."

(ii.) The current of opinion [a] in modern times has set in favor of taking the more obvious interpretation of the passages in St. John, that the supper was eaten on the 13th, and that our Lord was crucified on the 14th. It must, however, be admitted that most of those who advocate this view in some degree ignore the difficulties which it raises in any respectful interpretation of the synoptical narratives. Tittmann (*Meletemata*, p. 476) simply remarks that ἡ πρώτη τῶν ἀζύμων (Matt. xxvi. 17; Mark xiv. 12) should be explained as προτέρα τῶν ἀζύμων. Dean Alford, while he believes that the narrative of St. John "absolutely excludes such a supposition as that our Lord and his disciples ate the usual Passover," acknowledges the difficulty and dismisses it (on Matt. xxvi. 17).

Those who thus hold that the supper was eaten on the 13th day of the month have devised various ways of accounting for the circumstance, of which the following are the most important. It will be observed that in the first three the supper is regarded as a true paschal supper, eaten a day before the usual time; and in the other two, as a meal of a peculiar kind.

(*a.*) It is assumed that a party of the Jews, probably the Sadducees and those who inclined towards them, used to eat the Passover one day before the rest, and that our Lord approved of their practice. But there is not a shadow of historical evidence of the existence of any party which might have held such a notion until the controversy between the Rabbinists and the Karaites arose, which was not much before the eighth century.[b]

(*b.*) It has been conjectured that the great body of the Jews had gone wrong in calculating the true Passover-day, placing it a day too late, and that our Lord ate the Passover on what was really the 14th, but what commonly passed as the 13th. This was the opinion of Beza, Bucer, Calovius, and Scaliger. It is favored by Stier. But it is utterly unsupported by historical testimony.

(*c.*) Calvin supposed that on this occasion, though our Lord thought it right to adhere to the true legal time, the Jews ate the Passover on the 15th instead of the 14th, in order to escape from the burden of two days of strict observance (the day of holy convocation and the weekly Sabbath) coming

together.[c] But that no practice of this kind could have existed so early as our Lord's time is satisfactorily proved in Cocceius' note to *Sanhedrim*, i. § 2.[d]

(*d.*) Grotius[e] thought that the meal was a πάσχα μνημονευτικόν (like the paschal feast of the modern Jews, and such as might have been observed during the Babylonian captivity), not a πάσχα θύσιμον. But there is no reason to believe that such a mere commemorative rite was ever observed till after the destruction of the Temple.

(*e.*) A view which has been received with favor far more generally than either of the preceding is, that the Last Supper was instituted by Christ for the occasion, in order that He might himself suffer on the proper evening on which the paschal lamb was slain. Neander says, "He foresaw that He would have to leave his disciples before the Jewish Passover, and determined to give a peculiar meaning to his last meal with them, and to place it in a peculiar relation to the Passover of the Old Covenant, the place of which was to be taken by the meal of the New Covenant" (*Life of Christ*, § 265).[f] This view is substantially the same as that held by Clement, Origen, Erasmus, Calmet, Kuinoel, Winer, Alford.[g]

Erasmus (Paraphrase on John xiii. 1, xviii. 28, Luke xxii. 7) and others have called it an "anticipatory Passover," with the intention, no doubt, to help on a reconciliation between St. John and the other Evangelists. But if this view is to stand, it seems better, in a formal treatment of the subject, not to call it a Passover at all. The difference between it and the Hebrew rite must have been essential. Even if a lamb was eaten in the supper, it can hardly be imagined that the priests would have performed the essential acts of sprinkling the blood and offering the fat on any day besides the legal one (see Maimonides quoted by Otho, *Lex.* p. 501). It could not therefore have been a true paschal sacrifice.

(iii.) They who take the facts as they appear to lie on the surface of the synoptical narratives[h] start from a simpler point. They have nothing unexpected in the occurrences to account for, but they have to show that the passages in St. John may be fairly interpreted in such a manner as not to interfere with their own conclusion, and to meet the objections suggested by the laws relating to the observance of the festival. We shall give in succession, as briefly as we can, what appear to be their best explanations of the passages in question.

---

[a] Lücke, Ideler, Tittmann, Bleek, De Wette, Neander, Tischendorf, Winer [Meyer, Brückner, Ewald, Holtzmann, Godet, Caspari, Baur, Hilgenfeld, Scholten], Ebrard [formerly], Alford, Ellicott; of earlier critics, Erasmus, Grotius, Suicer, Carpzov.

[b] Iken (*Dissertationes*, vol. ii. diss. 10 and 12), forgetting the late date of the Karaite controversy, supposed that our Lord might have followed them in taking the day which, according to their custom, was calculated from the first appearance of the moon. Carpzov (*App. Crit.* p. 430) advocates the same notion, without naming the Karaites. Ebrard conjectures that some of the poorer Galilæans may have submitted to eat the Passover a day too early to suit the convenience of the priests, who were overdone with the labor of sprinkling the blood and (as he strangely imagines) of slaughtering the lambs. [Ebrard has since given up this hypothesis. — A.]

[c] *Harm.* in Matt. xxvi. 17. ii. 305, edit. Tholuck.

[d] *Surenhusius' Mishna*, iv. 209.

[e] On Matt. xxvi. 19, and John xiii. 1.

[f] Assuming this view to be correct, may not the change in the day made by our Lord have some analogy to the change of the weekly day of rest from the seventh to the first day?

[g] Dean Ellicott regards the meal as "a paschal supper" eaten twenty-four hours before that of the other Jews, "within what were popularly considered the limits of the festival," and would understand the expression in Ex. xii. 6, "between the two evenings," as denoting the time between the evenings of the 13th and 14th of the month. But see note [e], p. 2342. A somewhat similar explanation is given [by the Rev. Henry Constable] in the *Journal of Sacred Literature* for Oct. 1861.

[h] Lightfoot, Bochart, Reland, Schoettgen, Tholuck, Olshausen, Stier, Lange, Hengstenberg, Robinson, Davidson [formerly], Fairbairn, [Norton, Andrews, Wieseler, Lothardt, Bäumlein, Ebrard since 1842 Riggenbach.]

(a.) John xiii. 1, 2. Does πρὸ τῆς ἑορτῆς limit the time only of the proposition in the first verse, or is the limitation to be carried on to verse 2, so as to refer to the supper? In the latter case, for which De Wette and others say there is "a logical necessity," εἰς τέλος ἠγάπησεν αὐτούς must refer more directly to the manifestation of his love which He was about to give to his disciples in washing their feet; and the natural conclusion is, that the meal was one eaten before the paschal supper. Bochart, however, contends that πρὸ τῆς ἑορτῆς is equivalent to ἐν τῷ προεορτίῳ, "quod ita præcedit festum, ut tamen sit pars festi." Stier agrees with him. Others take πάσχα to mean the seven days of unleavened bread as not including the eating of the lamb, and justify this limitation by St. Luke xxii. 1 (ἡ ἑορτὴ τῶν ἀζύμων ἡ λεγομένη πάσχα). See note c, p. 2352. But not a few of those who take this side of the main question (Olshausen, Wieseler, Tholuck, and others) regard the first verse as complete in itself; understanding its purport to be that "Before the Passover, in the prospect of his departure, the Saviour's love was actively called forth towards his followers, and He gave proof of his love to the last." Tholuck remarks that the expression δείπνου γενομένου (Tischendorf reads γινομένου), "while supper was going on " (not as in the A. V., " supper being ended ") is very abrupt if we refer it to anything except the Passover. [See also Norton's note. — A.] The Evangelist would then rather have used some such expression as, καὶ ἐποίησαν αὐτῷ δεῖπνον; and he considers that this view is confirmed by John xxi. 20, where this supper is spoken of as if it was something familiarly known and not peculiar in its character — ὃς καὶ ἀνέπεσεν ἐν τῷ δείπνῳ. On the whole, Neander himself admits that nothing can be safely inferred from John xiii. 1, 2, in favor of the supper having taken place on the 13th.

(b.) John xiii. 29. It is urged that the things of which they had "need against the feast," might have been the provisions for the Chagigah, perhaps with what else was required for the seven days of unleavened bread. The usual day for sacrificing the Chagigah was the 15th, which was then commencing (see p 2347 a). But there is another difficulty, in the disciples thinking it likely either that purchases could be made, or that alms could be given to the poor, on a day of holy convocation. This is of course a difficulty of the same kind as that which meets us in the purchases actually made by the women, by Joseph, and Nicodemus. Now, it must be admitted, that we have no proof that the strict rabbinical maxims which have been appealed to on this point existed in the time of our Saviour, and that it is highly probable that the letter of the law in regard to trading was habitually relaxed in the case of what was required for religious rites, or for burials. There was plainly a distinction recognized between a day of holy convocation and the Sabbath in the Mosaic Law itself, in respect to the obtaining and preparation of food, under which head the Chagigah might come (Ex. xii. 16); and in the Mishna the same distinction is clearly maintained (Yom Tob, v. 2, and Megilla, i. 5). It also appears that the School of Hillel allowed more liberty in certain particulars on festivals and fasts in the night than in the day-time.[c] And it is expressly stated in the Mishna, that on the Sabbath itself, wine, oil, and bread could be obtained by leaving a cloak (חֲלוּק),[b] as a pledge, and when the 14th of Nisan fell on a Sabbath the paschal lamb could be obtained in like manner (Shabbath, xxiii. 1). Alms also could be given to the poor under certain conditions (Shabbath, i. 1).

(c.) John xviii. 28. The Jews refused to enter the prætorium, lest they should be defiled and so disqualified from eating the Passover. Neander and others deny that this passage can possibly refer to anything but the paschal supper. But it is alleged that the words ἵνα φάγωσι τὸ πάσχα, may either be taken in a general sense as meaning "that they might go on keeping the passover,"[c] or that τὸ πάσχα may be understood specifically to denote the Chagigah. That it might be so used is rendered probable by Luke xxii. 1; and the Hebrew word which it represents (פֶּסַח) evidently refers equally to the victims for the Chagigah and the paschal lamb (Deut. xvi. 2), where it is commanded that the Passover should be sacrificed " of the flock and the herd."[d] In the plural it is used in the same manner (2 Chr. xxxv. 7, 9). All is moreover to be kept in view that the Passover might be eaten by those who had incurred a degree of legal impurity, and that this was not the case in respect to the Chagigah.[e] Joseph appears not to have participated in the scruple of the other rulers, as he entered the prætorium to beg the body of Jesus (Mark xv. 43). Lightfoot (Ex. Heb. in loc.) goes so far as to draw an argument in favor of the 14th being the day of the supper from the very text in question. He says that the slight defilement incurred by entering a Gentile house, had the Jews merely intended to eat the supper in the evening, might have been done away in good time by mere ablution; but that as the festival had actually commenced, and they were probably just about to eat the Chagigah, they could not resort even to such a simple mode of purification.[f]

(d.) John xix. 14. " The preparation of the Passover " at first sight would seem as if it must be the preparation for the Passover on the 14th, a time set apart for making ready for the paschal week and for the paschal supper in particular. It is naturally so understood by those who advocate the notion that the Last Supper was eaten on the 13th. But they who take the opposite view affirm

---

[a] Pesachim, iv. 5. The special application of the license is rather obscure. See Bartenora's note. Comp. also Pesach. vi. 2.

[b] This word may mean an outer garment of any form. But it is more frequently used to denote the fringed scarf worn by every Jew in the service of the synagogue (Buxt. Lex. Talm. col 877).

[c] St. Augustine says, "O impia cæcitas! Habitaculo videlicet contaminarentur alieno, et non contaminarentur scelere proprio? Alienigenæ judicis prætorio contaminari timebant, et fratris innocentis sanguine non timebant. Dies enim agere cœperant axymorum: quibus diebus contaminatio illis erat in alienigenæ habitaculum intrare " (Tract. cxiv. in Joan. xviii. 2).

[d] See p. 2346 b, and Schoettgen on John xviii. 28.

[e] See 2 Chr. xxx. 17; also Pesachim, vii. 4, with Maimonides' note.

[f] Dr. Fairbairn takes the expression, " that they might eat the Passover," in its limited sense, and supposes that these Jews, in their determined hatred, were willing to put off the meal to the verge of, or even beyond, the legal time (Herm. Manual, p. 341)

that, though there was a regular "preparation" for the Sabbath, there is no mention of any "preparation" for the festivals (Bochart, Reland, Tholuck, Hengstenberg). The word παρασκευή is expressly explained by προσάββατον (Mark xv. 42: Lachmann reads πρὸς σάββατον). It seems to be essentially connected with the Sabbath itself (John xix. 31).[a] There is no mention whatever of the preparation for the Sabbath in the Old Testament, but it is mentioned by Josephus (Ant. xvi. 6, § 2), and it would seem from him that the time of preparation formally commenced at the ninth hour of the sixth day of the week. The προσάββατον is named in Judith viii. 6 as one of the times on which devout Jews suspended their fasts. It was called by the Rabbis עֲרוּבְתָּא‎, quia est עֶרֶב שַׁבָּת‎ (Buxt. Lex. Talm. col. 1659). The phrase in John xix. 14 may thus be understood as the preparation of the Sabbath which fell in the Passover week. This mode of taking the expression seems to be justified by Ignatius, who calls the Sabbath which occurred in the festival σάββατον τοῦ πάσχα (Ep. ad Phil. 13), and by Socrates, who calls it σάββατον τῆς ἑορτῆς (Hist. Eccl. v. 22). If these arguments are admitted, the day of the preparation mentioned in the Gospels might have fallen on the day of holy convocation, the 15th of Nisan.

(e.) John xix. 31. "That Sabbath-day was a high day" — ἡμέρα μεγάλη. Any Sabbath occurring in the Passover week might have been considered "a high day," as deriving an accession of dignity from the festival. But it is assumed by those who fix the supper on the 13th that the term was applied, owing to the 15th being "a double Sabbath," from the coincidence of the day of holy convocation with the weekly festival. Those, on the other hand, who identify the supper with the paschal meal, contend that the special dignity of the day resulted from its being that on which the Omer was offered, and from which were reckoned the fifty days to Pentecost. One explanation of the term seems to be as good as the other.

(f.) The difficulty of supposing that our Lord's apprehension, trial, and crucifixion took place on the day of holy convocation has been strongly urged.[b] If many of the rabbinical maxims for the observance of such days which have been handed down to us were then in force, these occurrences certainly could not have taken place. But the statements which refer to Jewish usage in regard to legal proceedings on sacred days are very inconsistent with each other. Some of them make the difficulty equally great whether we suppose the trial to have taken place on the 14th or the 15th. In others, there are exceptions permitted which seem to go far to meet the case before us. For example, the Mishna forbids that a capital offender should be examined in the night, or on the day, before the Sabbath or a feast-day (Sanhedrim, iv. 1). This law is modified by the glosses of the Gemara.[c] But if it had been recognized in its obvious meaning by the Jewish rulers, they would have outraged it in as great a degree on the preceding day (i. e. the 14th) as on the day of holy convocation before the Sabbath. It was also forbidden to administer justice on a high feast-day, or to carry arms (Yom Tob, v. 2). But these prohibitions are expressly distinguished from unconditional precepts, and are reckoned amongst those which may be set aside by circumstances. The members of the Sanhedrim were forbidden to eat any food on the same day after condemning a criminal.[d] Yet we find them intending to "eat the Passover" (John xviii. 28) after pronouncing the sentence (Matt. xxvi. 63, 66).

It was, however, expressly permitted that the Sanhedrim might assemble on the Sabbath as well as on feast-days, not indeed in their usual chamber, but in a place near the court of the women.[e] And there is a remarkable passage in the Mishna in which it is commanded that an elder not submitting to the voice of the Sanhedrim should be kept at Jerusalem till one of the three great festivals, and then executed, in accordance with Deut. xvii. 12, 13 (Sanhedrim, x. 4). Nothing is said to lead us to infer that the execution could not take place on one of the days of holy convocation. It is, however, hardly necessary to refer to this, or any similar authority, in respect to the crucifixion, which was carried out in conformity with the sentence of the Roman procurator, not that of the Sanhedrim.

But we have better proof than either the Mishna or the Gemara can afford that the Jews did not hesitate, in the time of the Roman domination, to carry arms and to apprehend a prisoner on a solemn feast-day. We find them at the feast of Tabernacles, on the "great day of the feast," sending out officers to take our Lord, and rebuking them for not bringing Him (John vii. 32–45). St. Peter also was seized during the Passover (Acts xii. 3, 4). And, again, the reason alleged by the rulers for not apprehending Jesus was, not the sanctity of the festival, but the fear of an uproar among the multitude which was assembled (Matt. xxvi. 5).

On the whole, notwithstanding the express declaration of the Law and of the Mishna that the days of holy convocation were to be observed precisely as the Sabbath, except in the preparation of food, it is highly probable that considerable license was allowed in regard to them, as we have already observed. It is very evident that the festival times were characterized by a free and jubilant character

---

which did not belong, in the same degree, to the Sabbath, and which was plainly not restricted to the days which fell between the days of holy convocation (Lev. xxiii. 40; Deut. xii. 7, xiv. 26: see p. 2343). It should also be observed that while the law of the Sabbath was enforced on strangers dwelling amongst the Israelites, such was not the case with the law of the Festivals. A greater freedom of action in cases of urgent need would naturally follow, and it is not difficult to suppose that the women who "rested on the Sabbath-day according to the commandment" had prepared the spices and linen for the intombment on the day of holy convocation. To say nothing of the way in which the question might be effected by the much greater license permitted by the school of Hillel than by the school of Shammai, in all matters of this kind, it is remarkable that we find, on the Sabbath-day itself, not only Joseph (Mark xv. 43), but the chief priests and Pharisees coming to Pilate, and, as it would seem, entering the prætorium (Matt. xxvii. 62).

3. There is a strange story preserved in the Gemara (*Sanhedrim*, vi. 2) that our Lord having vainly endeavored during forty days to find an advocate, was sentenced, and, on the 14th of Nisan, stoned, and afterwards hanged. As we know that the difficulty of the Gospel narratives had been perceived long before this statement could have been written, and as the two opposite opinions on the chief question were both current, the writer might easily have taken up one or the other. The statement cannot be regarded as worth anything in the way of evidence.[a]

Not much use can be made in the controversy of the testimonies of the Fathers. But few of them attempted to consider the question critically. Eusebius (*Hist. Ecc.* v. 23, 24) has recorded the traditions which were in favor of St. John having kept Easter on the 14th of the month. It has been thought that those traditions rather help the conclusion that the supper was on the 14th. But the question on which Eusebius brings them to bear is simply whether the Christian festival should be observed on the 14th, the day ἐν ᾗ θύειν τὸ πρόβατον 'Ιουδαίοις προηγόρευτο, on whatever day of the week it might fall, or on the Sunday of the resurrection. It seems that nothing whatever can be safely inferred from them respecting the day of the month of the supper or the crucifixion. Clement of Alexandria and Origen appeal to the Gospel of St. John as deciding in favor of the 13th. Chrysostom expresses himself doubtfully between the two. St. Augustine was in favor of the 14th.[b]

4. It must be admitted that the narrative of St. John, as far as the mere succession of events is concerned, bears consistent testimony in favor of the Last Supper having been eaten on the evening before the Passover. That testimony, however, does not appear to be so distinct, and so incapable of a second interpretation, as that of the synoptical Gospels, in favor of the meal having been the paschal supper itself, at the legal time (see especially Matt. xxvi. 17; Mark xiv. 1, 12; Luke xxii. 7). Whether the explanations of the passages in St. John, and of the difficulties resulting from the nature of the occurrences related, compared with the enactments of the Jewish law, be considered satisfactory or not, due weight should be given to the antecedent probability that the meal was no other than the regular Passover, and that the reasonableness of the contrary view cannot be maintained without some artificial theory, having no proper foundation either in Scripture or ancient testimony of any kind.

IV. MEANING OF THE PASSOVER.

1. Each of the three great festivals contained a reference to the annual course of nature. Two, at least, of them — the first and the last — also commemorated events in the history of the chosen people. The coincidence of the times of their observance with the most marked periods in the process of gathering in the fruits of the earth, has not unnaturally suggested the notion that their agricultural significance is the more ancient; that in fact they were originally harvest feasts observed by the patriarchs, and that their historical meaning was superadded in later times (Ewald, Hupfeld[c]).

It must be admitted that the relation to the natural year expressed in the Passover was less marked than that in Pentecost or Tabernacles, while its historical import was deeper and more pointed. It seems hardly possible to study the history of the Passover with candor and attention, as it stands in the Scriptures, without being driven to the conclusion that it was, at the very first, essentially the commemoration of a great historical fact. That

---

[a] Other Rabbinical authorities countenance the statement that Christ was executed on the 14th of the month (see Jost, *Judenth.* i. 404). But this seems to be a case in which, for the reason stated above, numbers do not add to the weight of the testimony.

[b] Numerous Patristic authorities are stated by Maldonat on Matt. xxvi.

[c] Hupfeld has devised an arrangement of the passages in the Pentateuch bearing on the Passover so as to show, according to this theory, their relative antiquity. The order is as follows: — (1) Ex. xxiii. 14–17; (2) Ex. xxxiv. 18–26; (3) Ex. xiii. 3–10; (4) Ex. xii. 15–20; (5) Ex. xii. 1–14; (6) Ex. xii. 43–50; (7) Num. ix. 10–14.

The view of Baur, that the Passover was an astronomical festival and the lamb a symbol of the sign Aries, and that of Von Bohlen, that it resembled the sun-feast of the Peruvians, are well exposed by Bähr (*Symbolik*). Our own Spencer has endeavored in his usual manner to show that many details of the festival were derived from heathen sources, though he admits the originality of the whole.

It may seem at first sight as if some countenance were given to the notion that the feast of unleavened bread was originally a distinct festival from the Passover, by such passages as Lev. xxiii. 5, 6: "In the fourteenth day of the first month at even is the Lord's Passover; and on the fifteenth day of the same month is the feast of unleavened bread unto the Lord: seven days ye must eat unleavened bread" (see also Num. xxviii. 16, 17). Josephus in like manner speaks of the feast of unleavened bread as "following the Passover" (*Ant.* iii. 10, § 5). But such language may mean no more than the distinction between the paschal supper and the seven days of unleavened bread, which is so obviously implied in the fact that the eating of unleavened bread was observed by the country Jews who were at home, though they could not partake of the paschal lamb without going to Jerusalem. Every member of the household had to abstain from leavened bread, but some only went up to the paschal meal. (See Maimon. *De Fermentato et Azymo*, vi. 1.) It is evident that the common usage, in later times at least, was to employ, as equivalent terms, *the feast of the Passover*, and *the feast of unleavened bread* (Matt. xxvi. 17; Mark xiv. 12; Luke xxii. 1; Joseph. *Ant* xiv. 2, § 1; *B. J.* ii. ii. 1, § 3). See note a, p. 2347.

part of its ceremonies which has a direct agricultural reference — the offering of the Omer — holds a very subordinate place.

But as regards the whole of the feasts, it is not very easy to imagine that the rites which belonged to them connected with the harvest, were of patriarchal origin. Such rites were adapted for the religion of an agricultural people, not for that of shepherds like the patriarchs. It would seem, therefore, that we gain but little by speculating on the simple impression contained in the Pentateuch, that the feasts were ordained by Moses in their integrity, and that they were arranged with a view to the religious wants of the people when they were to be settled in the Land of Promise.

2. The deliverance from Egypt was regarded as the starting-point of the Hebrew nation. The Israelites were then raised from the condition of bondmen under a foreign tyrant to that of a free people owing allegiance to no one but Jehovah. "Ye have seen," said the Lord, "what I did unto the Egyptians, and how I bare you on eagles' wings and brought you unto myself" (Ex. xix. 4). The prophet in a later age spoke of the event as *a creation* and *a redemption* of the nation. God declares himself to be "the creator of Israel," in immediate connection with evident allusions to his having brought them out of Egypt; such as his having made "a way in the sea, and a path in the mighty waters," and his having overthrown "the chariot and horse, the army and the power" (Is. xliii. 1, 15–17). The Exodus was thus looked upon as the birth of the nation; the Passover was its annual birthday feast. Nearly all the rites of the festival, if explained in the most natural manner, appear to point to this as its primary meaning. It was the yearly memorial of the dedication of the people to Him who had saved their first-born from the destroyer, in order that they might be made holy to Himself. This was the lesson which they were to teach to their children throughout all generations. When the young Hebrew asked his father regarding the paschal lamb, "What is this?" the answer prescribed was, "By strength of hand the Lord brought us out from Egypt, from the house of bondage: and it came to pass when Pharaoh would hardly let us go, that the Lord slew all the first-born in the land of Egypt, both the first-born of man and the first-born of beast; therefore I sacrifice to the Lord all that openeth the womb, being males; but all the first-born of my children I redeem" (Ex. xiii. 14, 15). Hence, in the periods of great national restoration in the times of Joshua, Hezekiah, Josiah, and Ezra, the Passover was observed in a special manner, to remind the people of their true position, and to mark their renewal of the covenant which their fathers had made.

3. (a.) The paschal lamb must of course be regarded as the leading feature in the ceremonial of the festival. Some Protestant divines during the last two centuries (Calov, Carpzov), laying great stress on the fact that nothing is said in the Law respecting either the imposition of the hands of the

priest on the head of the lamb, or the bestowing of any portion of the flesh on the priest, have denied that it was a sacrifice in the proper sense of the word. They appear to have been tempted to take this view, in order to deprive the Romanists of an analogical argument bearing on the Romish doctrine of the Lord's Supper. They affirmed that the lamb was *sacramentum*, not *sacrificium*. But most of their contemporaries (Cudworth, Bochart, Vitringa), and nearly all modern critics, have held that it was in the strictest sense a sacrifice. The chief characteristics of a sacrifice are all distinctly ascribed to it. It was offered in the holy place (Deut. xvi. 5, 6); the blood was sprinkled on the altar, and the fat was burned (2 Chr. xxx. 16, xxxv. 11). Philo and Josephus commonly call it θῦμα or θυσία. The language of Ex. xii. 27, xxiii. 18, Num. ix. 7, Deut. xvi. 2, 5, together with 1 Cor. v. 7, would seem to decide the question beyond the reach of doubt.

As the original institution of the Passover in Egypt preceded the establishment of the priesthood and the regulation of the service of the tabernacle, it necessarily fell short in several particulars of the observance of the festival according to the fully developed ceremonial law (see II. 1). The head of the family slew the lamb in his own house, not in the holy place: the blood was sprinkled on the doorway, not on the altar. But when the law was perfected, certain particulars were altered in order to assimilate the Passover to the accustomed order of religious service. It has been conjectured that the imposition of the hands of the priest was one of these particulars, though it is not recorded (Kurtz). But whether this was the case or not, the other changes which have been stated seem to be abundantly sufficient for the argument. It can hardly be doubted that the paschal lamb was regarded as the great annual peace offering of the family, a thank-offering for the existence and preservation of the nation (Ex. xiii. 14–16), the typical sacrifice of the elected and reconciled children of the promise. It was peculiarly the Lord's own sacrifice (Ex. xxiii. 18, xxxiv. 25). It was more ancient than the written Law, and called to mind that covenant on which the Law was based. It retained in a special manner the expression of the sacredness of the whole people, and of the divine mission of the head of every family,[a] according to the spirit of the old patriarchal priesthood. No part of the victim was given to the priest as in other peace-offerings, because the father was the priest himself. The custom, handed on from age to age, thus guarded from superstition the idea of a priesthood placed in the members of a single tribe, while it visibly set forth the promise which was connected with the deliverance of the people from Egypt 'Ye shall be unto me a kingdom of priests and a holy nation" (Ex. xix. 6).[b] In this way it became a testimony in favor of domestic worship. In the historical fact that the blood, in later times sprinkled on the altar, had at first had its divinely appointed place on the lintels and door-posts,[c] it was de-

a The fact which has been noticed, II. 3, (f), is remarkable in this connection, that those who had not incurred a degree of impurity sufficient to disqualify them from eating the paschal lamb, were yet not pure enough to take the priestly part in slaying it.

b Philo, speaking of the Passover, says, σύμπαν τὸ ἔθνος ἱεράται, τῶν κατὰ μέρος ἑκάστου τὰς ὑπὲρ αὐτοῦ θυσίας ἀναγόντων τότε καὶ χειρουργούντων. Ὁ μὲν οὖν ἄλλος ἅπας λεὼς ἐγεγήθει καὶ φαιδρὸς ἦν, ἑκάστου νομίζοντος ἱεροσύνῃ τετιμῆσθαι.—De Vit. Mosis, iii. 29, vol. iv. p. 250, ed. Tauch.

c As regards the mere place of sprinkling in the first Passover, on the reason of which there has been some speculation, Bähr reasonably supposes that the lintels and door-posts were selected as parts of the house most obvious to passers-by, and to which in

clared that the national altar itself represented the sanctity which belonged to the house of every Israelite, not that only which belonged to the nation as a whole.

A question, perhaps not a wise one, has been raised regarding the purpose of the sprinkling of the blood on the lintels and door-posts. Some have considered that it was meant as a mark to guide the destroying angel. Others suppose that it was merely a sign to confirm the faith of the Israelites in their safety and deliverance.[a] Surely neither of these views can stand alone. The sprinkling must have been an act of faith and obedience which God accepted with favor. " Through faith (we are told) Moses kept the Passover and the sprinkling of blood, lest he that destroyed the first-born should touch them " (Heb. xi. 28). Whatever else it may have been, it was certainly an essential part of a sacrament, of an " effectual sign of grace and of God's good will," expressing the mutual relation into which the covenant had brought the Creator and the creature. That it also denoted the purification of the children of Israel from the abominations of the Egyptians, and so had the accustomed significance of the sprinkling of blood under the Law (Heb. ix. 22), is evidently in entire consistency with this view.

No satisfactory reason has been assigned for the command to choose the lamb four days before the paschal supper. Kurtz (following Hofmann) fancies that the four days signified the four centuries of Egyptian bondage. As in later times, the rule appears not to have been observed (see p. 2342); the reason of it was probably of a temporary nature.

That the lamb was to be roasted and not boiled, has been supposed to commemorate the haste of the departure of the Israelites.[b] Spencer observes, on the other hand, that, as they had their cooking vessels with them, one mode would have been as expeditious as the other. Some think that, like the dress and the posture in which the first Passover was to be eaten, it was intended to remind the people that they were now no longer to regard themselves as settled down in a home, but as a host upon the march, roasting being the proper military mode of dressing meat. Kurtz conjectures that the lamb was to be roasted with fire, the purifying element, because the meat was thus left pure, without the mixture even of the water, which would have entered into it in boiling. The meat in its purity would thus correspond in signification with the unleavened bread (see II. 3, (b.)).

It is not difficult to determine the reason of the command, " not a bone of him shall be broken." The lamb was to be a symbol of unity; the unity of the family, the unity of the nation, the unity of God with his people whom He had taken into covenant with Himself. While the flesh was divided into portions, so that each member of the family could partake, the skeleton was left one and entire to remind them of the bonds which united

them. Thus the words of the Law are applied to the body of our Saviour, as the type of that still higher unity of which He was himself to be the author and centre (John xix. 36).

The same significance may evidently be attached to the prohibition that no part of the meat should be kept for another meal, or carried to another house. The paschal meal in each house was to be one, whole and entire.

(b.) The unleavened bread ranks next in importance to the paschal lamb. The notion has been very generally held, or taken for granted, both by Christian and Jewish writers of all ages, that it was intended to remind the Israelites of the unleavened cakes which they were obliged to eat in their hasty flight (Ex. xii. 34, 39). But there is not the least intimation to this effect in the sacred narrative. On the contrary, the command was given to Moses and Aaron that unleavened bread should be eaten with the lamb before the circumstance occurred upon which this explanation is based. Comp. Ex. xii. 8 with xii. 39.

It has been considered by some (Ewald, Winer, and the modern Jews) that the unleavened bread and the bitter herbs alike owe their meaning to their being regarded as unpalatable food. The expression " bread of affliction," לֶחֶם עֹנִי (Deut. xvi. 3), is regarded as equivalent to *fasting-bread*, and on this ground Ewald ascribes something of the character of a fast to the Passover. But this seems to be wholly inconsistent with the pervading joyous nature of the festival. The *bread of affliction* may mean bread which, in present gladness, commemorated, either in itself, or in common with the other elements of the feast, the past affliction of the people (Bähr, Kurtz, Hofmann). It should not be forgotten that unleavened bread was not peculiar to the Passover. The ordinary " meat-offering " was unleavened (Lev. ii. 4, 5, vii. 12, x. 12, &c.), and so was the shewbread (Lev. xxiv. 5–9). The use of unleavened bread in the consecration of the priests (Ex. xxix. 23), and in the offering of the Nazarite (Num. vi. 19), is interesting in relation to the Passover, as being apparently connected with the consecration of the person. On the whole, we are warranted in concluding that unleavened bread had a peculiar sacrificial character, according to the Law, and it can hardly be supposed that a particular kind of food should have been offered to the Lord because it was insipid or unpalatable.[c]

It seems more reasonable to accept St. Paul's reference to the subject (1 Cor. v. 6–8) as furnishing the true meaning of the symbol. Fermentation is decomposition, a dissolution of unity. This must be more obvious to ordinary eyes where the leaven in common use is a piece of sour dough, instead of the expedients at present employed in this country to make bread light. The pure dry biscuit, as distinguished from bread thus leavened, would be an apt emblem of unchanged duration, and, in its freedom from foreign mixture, of purity also.[d] If this was the accepted meaning among

---

scriptions of different kinds were often attached. Comp. Deut. vi. 9.

[a] Especially Bochart and Bähr. The former says, " Hoc signum Deo non datum sed Hebraeis ut eo confirmati de liberatione certi sint."

[b] So Bähr and most of the Jewish authorities.

[c] Hupfeld imagines that bread without leaven, being the simplest result of cooked grain, characterised the

old agricultural festival which existed before the sacrifice of the lamb was instituted.

[d] The root צָמַק signifies " to make dry." Kurtz thinks that *dryness* rather than *sweetness* is the idea in מַצּוֹת. But *sweet* in this connection has the sense of *uncorrupted*, or *incorruptible*, and hence is

the Jews, "the unleavened bread of sincerity and truth" must have been a clear and familiar expression to St. Paul's Jewish readers. Bähr conceives that as the blood of the lamb figured the act of purifying, the getting rid of the corruptions of Egypt, the unleavened bread signified the abiding state of consecrated holiness.

(c.) The bitter herbs are generally understood by the Jewish writers to signify the bitter sufferings which the Israelites had endured a (Ex. i. 14). But it has been remarked by Aben Ezra that these herbs are a good and wholesome accompaniment for meat, and are now, and appear to have been in ancient times, commonly so eaten (see p. 2345).

(d.) The offering of the Omer, though it is obviously that part of the festival which is immediately connected with the course of the seasons, bore a distinct analogy to its historical significance. It may have denoted a deliverance from winter, as the lamb signified deliverance from the bondage of Egypt, which might well be considered as a winter in the history of the nation.b Again, the consecration of the first-fruits, the first-born of the soil, is an easy type of the consecration of the first-born of the Israelites. This seems to be countenanced by Ex. xiii. 2–4, where the sanctification of the first-born, and the unleavened bread which figured it, seem to be emphatically connected with the time of year, Abib, *the month of green ears.*c

4. No other shadow of good things to come contained in the Law can vie with the festival of the Passover in expressiveness and completeness. Hence we are so often reminded of it, more or less distinctly, in the ritual and language of the Church. Its outline, considered in reference to the great deliverance of the Israelites which it commemorated, and many of its minute details, have been appropriated as current expressions of the truths which

God has revealed to us in the fullness of times in sending his Son upon earth.

It is not surprising that ecclesiastical writers should have pushed the comparison too far, and exercised their fancy in the application of trifling or accidental particulars either to the facts of our Lord's life or to truths connected with it.d But, keeping within the limits of sober interpretation indicated by Scripture itself, the application is singularly full and edifying. The deliverance of Israel according to the flesh from the bondage of Egypt was always so regarded and described by the prophets as to render it a most apt type of the deliverance of the spiritual Israel from the bondage of sin into the glorious liberty with which Christ has made us free (see IV. 2). The blood of the first paschal lambs sprinkled on the door-ways of the houses has ever been regarded as the best defined foreshadowing of that blood which has redeemed, saved, and sanctified us (Heb. xi. 28). The lamb itself, sacrificed by the worshipper without the intervention of a priest, and its flesh being eaten without reserve as a meal, exhibits the most perfect of peace-offerings, the closest type of the atoning Sacrifice who died for us and has made our peace with God (Is. liii. 7; John i. 29; cf. the expression "my sacrifice," Ex. xxxiv. 25, also Ex. xii. 27; Acts viii. 32; 1 Cor. v. 7; 1 Pet. i. 18, 19). The ceremonial law, and the functions of the priest in later times, were indeed recognized in the sacrificial rite of the Passover; but the previous existence of the rite showed that they were not essential for the personal approach of the worshipper to God (see IV. 3 (a.); Is. lxi. 6; 1 Pet. ii. 5, 9). The unleavened bread is recognized as the figure of the state of sanctification which is the true element of the believer in Christ e (1 Cor. v. 8). The haste with which the meal was eaten,

---

easily connected with dryness. Perhaps our Authorised Version has lost something in expressiveness by substituting the term "unleavened bread" for the "sweet bread" of the older versions, which still holds its place in 1 Esdr. i. 19.

a מְרֹרִים istud comedimus quia amaritudine affecerunt Ægyptii vitam patrum nostrorum in Ægypto. — Maimon. *in Pesachim*, viii. 4.

b This application of the rite perhaps derives some support from the form in which the ordinary first-fruit offering was presented in the Temple. [FIRST-FRUITS.] The call of Jacob ("a Syrian ready to perish"), and the deliverance of his children from Egypt, with their settlement in the land that flowed with milk and honey, were then related (Deut. xxvi. 5–10). It is worthy of notice that, according to *Pesachim*, an exposition of this passage was an important part of the reply which the father gave to his son's inquiry during the paschal supper.

The account of the procession in offering the first-fruits in the Mishna (*Biccurim*), with the probable reference to the subject in Is. xxx. 29, can hardly have anything to do with the Passover. The connection appears to have been suggested by the tradition mentioned by Aben Ezra, that the army of Sennacherib was smitten on the night of the Passover. Regarding this tradition, Vitringa says, "Non recipio, nec sperno" (*In Isaiam* xxx. 29).

c See Gesenius, *Thes.* In the LXX. it is called μὴν τῶν νέων, sc. καρπῶν. If *Nisan* is a Semitic word, Gesenius thinks that it means *the month of flowers*, in agreement with a passage in Macarius (*Hom.* xvii.) in which it is called μὴν τῶν ἀνθῶν. But he seems inclined to favor an explanation of the word suggested by a Zend root, according to which it would signify *the month of New Year's Day.*

d The crossed spits on which Justin Martyr laid stress are noticed, II. 3 (a). The subject is expanded by Vitringa, *Observat. Sac.* ii. 10. The time of the new moon, at which the festival was held, has been taken as a type of the brightness of the appearing of the Messiah; the lengthening of the days at that season of the year as figuring the ever-increasing light and warmth of the Redeemer's kingdom; the advanced hour of the day at which the supper was eaten, as a representation of the fullness of times; the roasting of the lamb, as the effect of God's wrath against sin; the thorough cooking of the lamb, as a lesson that Christian doctrine should be well arranged and digested; the prohibition that any part of the flesh should remain till the morning, as a foreshowing of the haste in which the body of Christ was removed from the cross; the unfermented bread, as the emblem of a humble spirit, while fermented bread was the figure of a heart puffed up with pride and vanity. (See Suicer, sub πάσχα.) In the like spirit, Justin Martyr and Lactantius take up the charge against the Jews of corrupting the O. T., with a view to deprive the Passover of its clearness as a witness for Christ. They specifically allege that the following passage has been omitted in the copies of the book of Ezra: "Et dixit Esdras ad populum: Hoc pascha salvator noster est, et refugium nostrum. Cogitate et ascendat in cor vestrum, quoniam habemus humiliare eum in signo: et post hæc sperabimus in eum, ne deseratur hic locus in æternum tempus." (Just. Mart. *Dialog. cum Tryph.*; Lact. *Inst.* iv. 18.) It has been conjectured that the words may have been inserted between vv. 20 and 21 in Ex. vi. But they have been all but universally regarded as spurious.

e The use which the Fathers made of this may be seen in Suicer, s. v. ἄζυμος.

and the girt-up loins, the staves and the sandals, are fit emblems of the life of the Christian pilgrim, ever hastening away from the world towards his heavenly destination [a] (Luke xii. 35; 1 Pet. i. 13, ii. 11; Eph. v. 15; Heb. xi. 13).

It has been well observed by Kurtz (on Ex. xii. 88), that, at the very crisis when the distinction between Israel and the nations of the world was most clearly brought out (Ex. xi. 7), a "mixed multitude" went out from Egypt with them (Ex. xii. 38), and that provision was then made for all who were willing to join the chosen seed and participate with them in their spiritual advantages (Ex. xii. 44). Thus, at the very starting-point of national separation, was foreshadowed the calling in of the Gentiles to that covenant in which all nations of the earth were to be blessed.

The offering of the Omer, in its higher signification as a symbol of the first-born, has been already noticed (IV. 3 (d.)). But its meaning found full expression only in that First-born of all creation, who, having died and risen again, became "the first-fruits of them that slept" (1 Cor. xv. 90). As the first of the first-fruits, no other offering of the sort seems so likely as the Omer to have immediately suggested the expressions used (Rom. viii. 23, xi. 16; Jam. i. 18; Rev. xiv. 4).

The crowning application of the paschal rites to the truths of which they were the shadowy promises appears to be that which is afforded by the fact that our Lord's death occurred during the festival. According to the Divine purpose, the true Lamb of God was slain at nearly the same time as "the Lord's Passover," in obedience to the letter of the Law. It does not seem needful that, in order to give point to this coincidence, we should (as some have done) draw from it an à priori argument in favor of our Lord's crucifixion having taken place on the 14th of Nisan (see III. 2, ii.). It is enough to know that our own Holy Week and Easter stand as the anniversary of the same great facts as were foreshown in those events of which the yearly Passover was a commemoration.

As compared with the other festivals, the Passover was remarkably distinguished by a single victim essentially its own, sacrificed in a very peculiar manner.[b] In this respect, as well as in the place it held in the ecclesiastical year, it had a formal dignity and character of its own. It was the representative festival of the year, and in this unique position it stood in a certain relation to circumcision as the second sacrament of the Hebrew Church (Ex. xii. 44). We may see this in what occurred at Gilgal, when Joshua, in renewing the Divine covenant, celebrated the Passover immediately after the circumcision of the people. But the nature of the relation in which these two rites stood to each other did not become fully developed until its types were fulfilled, and the Lord's Supper took its place as the sacramental feast of the elect people of God.[c] Hupfeld well observes: "En pul-

cherrima mysteriorum nostrorum exempla: circumcisio quidem baptismatis, scilicet signum gratiæ divinæ et fœderis cum Deo pacti, quo ad sanctitatem populi sacri vocamur; Paschalis vero agnus et ritus, continuatæ quippe gratiæ divinæ et servati fœderis cum Deo signum et pignus, quo sacra et cum Deo et cum cœteris populi sacri membris communio usque renovatur et alitur, cœnæ Christi sacræ typus aptissimus! "

LITERATURE. — Mishna, Pesachim, with the notes in Surenhusius [vol. ii.]; Bähr, Symbolik, b. iv. c. 3; Hupfeld, De Fest. Hebr.; Bochart, De Agno Paschali (vol. i. of the Hierozoicum); Ugolini, De Ritibus in Can. Dom. ex Pasch. illustr. (vol. xvii. of the Thesaurus); Maimonides, De Fermentato et Azymo; Rosenmüller, Scholia in Ex. xii., etc.; Otho, Lex. Rab. s. Pascha; Carpzov, App. Crit.; Lightfoot, Temple Service, and Hor. Hebr. on Matt. xxvi., John xiii., etc.; Vitringa, Obs. Sac. lib. ii. 3, 10; Reland, Antiq. iv. 3; Spencer, De Leg. Hebr. ii. 4; Kurtz, History of the Old Covenant, ii. 288 ff. (Clark's edit.); Hottinger, De Ritu dimittendi Reum in Fest. Pasch. (Thes. Noe. Theologico-Philolog. vol. ii.); Buxtorf, Synag. Jud. xviii.; Cudworth, True Notion of the Lord's Supper.

More especially on the question respecting the Lord's Supper, Robinson, Harmony of the Gospels, and Bibliotheca Sacra for Aug. 1845; Tholuck, on John xiii. [in 7th ed. of his Comm. (1857), Einl. pp. 38–52]; Stier, on John xii.; Kuinoel, on Matt. xxvi.; Neander, Life of Christ, § 265; Greswell, Harm. Evang. and Dissertations; Wieseler, Chronol. Synops. der vier Evang.; Tischendorf, Syn. Evang. p. xlv.; Bleek, Dissert. ueber den Monathstag des Todes Christi (Beiträge zur Evangelien-Kritik, 1846); Frischmuth, Dissertatio, etc. (Thes. Theol. Philolog.); Harenberg, Demonstratio, etc. (Thes. Novus Theol. Phil. vol. ii.). Tholuck praises Eude, Demonstratio quod Chr. in Can. σταυρωσίμφ ηgnum paschalem non comederit, Lips. 1742. Ellicott, Lectures on the Life of our Lord, p. 320; Fairbairn, Hermeneutical Manual, ii. 9; Davidson, Introduction to N. T. [1848] i. 102.   S. C.

[*] Additional Literature. The art. Passover by C. D. Ginsburg in the 3d edition of Kitto's Cyclop. of Bibl. Lit. deserves notice for its thoroughness, and for the minuteness of its account of the later Jewish usages. Winer's art. Pascha in his Bibl. Realwörterbuch is carefully elaborated. The subject is treated in Herzog's Real-Encykl. by Vaihinger; the art. on Easter (Pascha, christliches) and the early paschal controversies is, however, by Steits.

On the question respecting the Last Supper see the references to the literature under JOHN, GOSPEL OF, vol. ii. pp. 1437, 1438. Among the more recent writers on this subject the following are also worthy of notice: S. J. Andrews, Life of our Lord (N. Y. 1862), pp. 425–460. T. Lewin,

---

[a] See Theodoret, Interrog. XXIV. in Exod. There is an eloquent passage on the same subject in Greg. Naz. Orat. XLII.

[b] The only parallel case to this, in the whole range of the public religious observances of the Law, seems to be that of the scapegoat of the Day of Atonement.

[c] It is worthy of remark that the modern Jews distinguish these two rites above all others, as being immediately connected with the grand fulfillment of the promises made to their fathers. Though they refer

to the coming of Elijah in their ordinary grace at meals, it is only on these occasions that their expectation of the harbinger of the Messiah is expressed by the formal observances. When a child is circumcised, an empty chair is placed at hand for the prophet to occupy. At the paschal meal, a cup of wine is poured out for him; and at an appointed moment the door of the room is solemnly set open for him to enter. (See note c, p. 2344.)

Fasti Sacri (Lond. 1865), p. xxxi. ff. Prof. Wm. Milligan, arts. in the *Contemporary Review* for Aug. and Nov. 1868. Holtzmann, in Bunsen's *Bibelwerk*, viii. 305–322 (1868). Ebrard, *Wissensch. Krit. d. evang. Geschichte*, 3e Aufl. (1868), pp. 615–640. C. E. Caspari, *Chronol.-geogr. Einl. in das Leben Jesu Christi* (Hamb. 1869), pp. 164–186. Wieseler, *Beiträge zur richtigen Würdigung der Evangelien u. d. evang. Geschichte* (Goths, 1869), pp. 230–283. Of these writers, Andrews maintains that there is no real discrepancy between the Synoptists and John, — that they all place the crucifixion on the 15th of Nisan. Prof. Milligan holds the same opinion, contending that the paschal lamb might be eaten on *any part* of the day extending from the evening following the 14th of Nisan to the evening of the 15th, and thus finding no difficulty in John xviii. 28. But this view seems opposed to all our information respecting Jewish usage; see p. 2342, note c, and comp. Wieseler, *Beiträge*, p. 246, note. Holtzmann reviews the literature of the question, and finds the difference between the Synoptists and John irreconcilable. Ebrard, who in the 2d edition of his *Wissensch. Kritik d. ev. Geschichte* (1850) had been convinced by the arguments of Bleek that John places the crucifixion on the 14th of Nisan, has, in the 3d edition of this work, after a careful reëxamination of the subject, reversed his conclusion. Maintaining that John wrote for those who were acquainted with the Synoptic Gospels, he discusses the supposition that it was his intention to correct the chronology of the first three Evangelists in respect to the last day of our Saviour's life, and endeavors to show that it is quite untenable. But supposing John to assume on the part of his readers a knowledge of the facts recorded by the Synoptists, the controverted passages in his Gospel present, as Ebrard thinks, little difficulty. According to Caspari, the Synoptists place the death of Jesus, in agreement with John, on the 14th of Nisan. By the "eating the Passover" of which they speak, he understands not the eating of the paschal lamb, but of the *unleavened bread*, on the evening with which the 14th of Nisan began, i. e. after the sunset of the 13th. In most respects his view agrees with that of Westcott, *Introd. to the Study of the Gospels*, pp. 335–341, Amer. ed. But the difficulties, both archæological and exegetical, which beset this theory, appear overwhelming. The first day of unleavened bread could not have been regarded as beginning with the evening which followed the 13th of Nisan, when we learn from the Mishna (*Pesach.* 1, § 4), that leaven might be *eaten* on the 14th till 11 o'clock A. M. according to Rabbi Meir, or till 10 o'clock, according to Rabbi Jehudah, and it was not necessary to destroy it before 11 o'clock on that day. Wieseler defends with much learning and ability the view formerly presented by him in his *Chronol. Synopse der vier Evangelien* (1843), with which that of Robinson, Norton, Andrews, and Lewin essentially agree. See also his art. *Zeitrechnung, neutestamentliche*, in Herzog's *Real-Encykl.* xxi. 550 ff. Bleek's *Beiträge zur Evangelien-Kritik* (Berl. 1846) is still, perhaps, the ablest presentation of the opposite view: see also Meyer's *Komm., das Evang. des Johannes*, 5e Aufl. (1869).

A.

* The Samaritans still observe the Passover on Gerizim, their sacred mount (John iv. 20), and with some customs, especially the offering of sac-

rifices, which the Jews have discontinued since the destruction of the Temple at Jerusalem. Some account of the ceremony cannot fail to interest the reader. Various travellers who have been present on the occasion have described the scene. We abbreviate for our purpose Dean Stanley's narrative of the commemoration, as witnessed by him in company with the Prince of Wales and others, on the 13th of April, 1862. In that instance, for some reason, the Samaritans anticipated the 14th of Nisan by two days.

On coming to the top of Gerizim the party found the little community of about 152 persons encamped near the summit of the mount. The women were shut up in tents; and the men were assembled on the rocky terrace. Most of the men were in ordinary dress; only about fifteen of the elders and six youths having any distinguishing sacred costume. About half an hour before sunset the men all gathered about a long trough dug out for the occasion, and, assuming the oriental attitude of devotion, commenced (led by the priest) reciting in a loud chant prayers, chiefly devoted to praises of the patriarchs. In a short time the six young men before mentioned suddenly appeared driving along six sheep into the midst of the assembly. Meanwhile the sun had nearly set; the recitation became more vehement; and the entire history of the exodus was chanted with furious rapidity. As soon as the sun had touched the western horizon, the youths, pausing a moment to brandish their bright knives, suddenly threw the sheep on their backs and drew the knives across their throats. They then dipped their fingers in the blood of the victims, and stained slightly the noses and foreheads of the children. The animals were then fleeced and washed, two holes having been dug in the mountain side for that purpose.

After kindling a fire in one of the holes nearest to the place of sacrifice, and while two cauldrons of water hung over it were boiling, the recitation continued, and bitter herbs wrapped in a strip of unleavened bread were passed among the assembly. After a short prayer, the youths again appeared, poured the boiling water over the sheep, and fleeced them. The right fore-legs and entrails of the animals were burnt, the liver carefully put back, and the victims were then spitted on two transverse stakes suggesting slightly the crucial form. They were then carried to the other oven-like hole, in which a fire had been kindled. Into this they were thrust, and a hurdle covered with wet earth placed over the mouth to seal up the oven.

The sacrifice and preparations thus completed, the community retired. After about five hours, shortly after midnight, the feast began, to which the visitors found themselves admitted with reluctance. The hole being suddenly opened, a cloud of smoke and steam issued from it, and from the pit were dragged successively the blackened sheep, the outlines of their heads, ears, and legs yet visible. The bodies were then thrown upon mats, and wrapped in them were hurried to the first trench, already mentioned, and laid upon them between two lines of Samaritans. Those before distinguished by their sacred costume were now in addition to that garb provided with shoes and staffs and girded with ropes. The recitation of prayers was recommenced, and continued till they suddenly seated themselves, after the Arab fashion, and commenced eating. The flesh was torn away piecemeal with their fingers, and rapidly and all tently consumed. In ten minutes most of it was gone, separate morsels having been carried to the priest and to the women, and the remnants were gathered into the mats and burnt. Careful search was then made for the particles, which were thrown upon the fire. This finished the ceremony, and early the next morning the community returned to their habitations in the town.

In this ceremony the time, with a slight variation on this special occasion (Exod. xii. 63); the place chosen, outside their gates and on their ancient mountain sanctuary (Deut. xvi. 1); the exclusion of the women (Deut. xvi. 16); the time of day (Deut. xvi. 6); the recital of the circumstances attending the first inauguration of the Passover (Exod. xii. 26, 27); the bitter herbs and unleavened bread with which it was eaten (Exod. xii. 8); the mode of cooking it (Exod. xii. 8, 9); the careful exclusion of foreigners (Exod. xii. 43); the hasty manner in which the meal was eaten (Exod. xii. 11); the care taken to consume the remnants (Exod. xii. 10); and the return by early morning to their dwellings (Deut. xvi. 7), correspond exactly to the ancient Jewish law of the Passover.

The staining of the children's foreheads (2 Chr. xxx. 16); the fleecing of the animals (2 Chr. xxxv. 11); and the girding as if for a journey of only a few of the men (Ex. xii. 11), represent, without exactly imitating, the corresponding portions of the ancient Jewish ritual. (See Stanley's *Jewish Church*, i. 559–567, and his *Sermons in the East*, etc., pp. 175–181.)

The ceremony among the Samaritans is said to be gradually assuming this merely representative character. The number of this singular people is rapidly diminishing, and probably ere long the observance of the Passover will be associated with Gerizim only as a tradition.   H.

PAT'ARA (Πάταρα: [*Patara* (sing.)] the noun is plural), a Lycian city of some considerable note. One of its characteristics in the heathen world was that it was devoted to the worship of Apollo, and was the seat of a famous oracle (Hor. *Od.* iii. 4, 64). Fellows says that the coins of all the district around show the ascendency of this divinity. Patara was situated on the southwestern shore of Lycia, not far from the left bank of the river Xanthus. The coast here is very mountainous and bold. Immediately opposite is the island of RHODES. Patara was practically the seaport of the city of Xanthus, which was ten miles distant (Appian, *B. C.* iv. 81). These notices of its position and maritime importance introduce us to the single mention of the place in the Bible (Acts xxi. 1, 2). St. Paul was on his way to Jerusalem at the close of his third missionary journey. He had just come from Rhodes (v. 1); and at Patara he found a ship, which was on the point of going to Phœnicia (v. 2), and in which he completed his voyage (v. 3). This illustrates the mercantile connection of Patara with both the eastern and western parts of the Levant. A good parallel to the Apostle's voyage is to be found in Liv. xxxvii. 16. There was no time for him to preach the gospel here, but still Patara has a place in ecclesiastical history, having been the seat of a bishop (*Hierocl.* p. 684). The old name remains on the spot, and there are still considerable ruins, especially a theatre, some baths, and a triple arch which was one of the gates of the city. But sand-hills are grad-

ually concealing these ruins, and have blocked up the harbor. For fuller details we must refer to Beaufort's *Karamania*, the *Ionian Antiquities* published by the Dilettanti Society, Fellows' *Lycia and Asia Minor*, and the *Travels in Asia Minor* by Spratt and Forbes. [LYCIA; MYRA.]
                                        J. S. H.

PATHE'US [properly PATHÆ'US] (Παθαῖος: Alex. Φαθαῖος: *Facteas*). The same as PETHAHIAH the Levite (1 Esdr. ix. 23; comp. EZR. x. 23).

PATH'ROS (פַּתְרוֹס [see below]: Παθουρῆς [or ρῆ], [in Ezek., Rom. Vat.] Φαθωρῆς; [in Is. xi. 11, Βαβυλωνία :] *Phetros, Phathures, Phathures*), gent. noun PATHRUSIM (פַּתְרֻסִים : Πατροσωνιείμ: *Phetrusim*), a part of Egypt, and a Mizraite tribe. That Pathros was in Egypt admits of no question: we have to attempt to decide its position more nearly. In the list of the Mizraites, the Pathrusim occur after the Naphtuhim and before the Casluhim; the latter being followed by the notice of the Philistines, and by the Caphtorim (Gen. x. 13, 14; 1 Chr. i. 12). Isaiah prophesies the return of the Jews "from Mizraim, and from Pathros, and from Cush" (xi. 11). Jeremiah predicts their ruin *to* "all the Jews which dwell in the land of Egypt, which dwell at Migdol, and at Tahpanhes, and at Noph, and in the country of Pathros" (xliv. 1), and their reply is given, after this introduction, "Then all the men which knew that their wives had burned incense unto other gods, and all the women that stood by, a great multitude, even all the people that dwelt in the land of Egypt, in Pathros, answered Jeremiah" (15). Ezekiel speaks of the return of the captive Egyptians to "the land of Pathros, into the land of their birth " (xxix. 14), and mentions it with Egyptian cities, Noph preceding it, and Zoan, No, Sin, Noph again, Aven (On), Pi-beseth, and Tehaphnehes following it (xxx. 13–18). From the place of the Pathrusim in the list of the Mizraites, they might be supposed to have settled in Lower Egypt, or the more northern part of Upper Egypt. Four only of the Mizraite tribes or peoples can be probably assigned to Egypt, the last four, the Philistines being considered not to be one of these, but merely a colony: these are the Naphtuhim, Pathrusim, Casluhim, and Caphtorim. The first were either settled in Lower Egypt, or just beyond its western border; and the last in Upper Egypt, about Coptos. It seems, if the order be geographical, as there is reason to suppose, that it is to be inferred that the Pathrusim were seated in Lower Egypt, or not much above it, unless there be any transposition; but that some change has been made is probable from the parenthetic notice of the Philistines following the Casluhim, whereas it appears from other passages that it should rather follow the Caphtorim. If the original order were Pathrusim, Caphtorim, Casluhim, then the first might have settled in the highest part of Upper Egypt, and the other two below them. The mention in Isaiah would lead us to suppose that Pathros was Upper Egypt, if there were any sound reason for the idea that Mizraim or Mazor is ever used for Lower Egypt, which we think there is not. Rüdiger's conjecture that Pathros included part of Nubia is too daring to be followed (*Encyclop. Germ.* sect. iii. tom. xiii, p. 312), although there is some slender support for it. The occurrences in Jeremiah seem to favor the idea that Pathros was part of Lower Egypt, or the whole of that region for although it is mentioned in the prophecy against the Jews as a region where they dwelt after Migdol, Tahpanhes, and Noph, as though to the south, yet we are told that the prophet was answered by the Jews "that dwelt in the land of Egypt, in Pathros," as though Pathros were the region in which these cities were. We have, moreover, no distinct evidence that Jeremiah ever went into Upper Egypt. On the other hand, it may be replied that the cities mentioned are so far apart, that either the prophet must have preached to the Jews in them in succession, or else have addressed letters or messages to them (comp. xxix.). The notice by Ezekiel of Pathros as the land of the birth of the Egyptians seems to favor the idea that it was part of or all Upper Egypt, as the Thebais was probably inhabited before the rest of the country (comp. *Hdt.* ii. 15); an opinion supported by the tradition that the people of Egypt came from Ethiopia, and by the 1st dynasty's being of Thinite kings.

Pathros has been connected with the Pathyrite nome, the Phaturite of Pliny (*H. N.* v. 9, § 47),

in which Thebes was situate. The first form occurs in a Greek papyrus written in Egypt (Πα-θυρίτης τῆς Θηβαΐδος, Papyr. Anast. vid. Reuvens, *Lettres à M. Letronne*, 3 let. p. 4, 30, ap. Parthey, *Vocab.* s. v.). This identification may be as old as the LXX.; and the Coptic version, which reads ⲠⲀⲚⲒⲐⲞⲞⲨⲢⲎⲤ, ⲠⲀⲚⲒⲦⲞⲨⲢⲎⲤ, does not contradict it. The discovery of the Egyptian name of the town after which the nome was called puts the inquiry on a safer basis. It is written HA-HAT-HER, "The Abode of Hat-her," the Egyptian Venus. It may perhaps have sometimes been written P-HA-HAT-HER, in which case the P-H and T-H would have coalesced in the Hebrew form, as did T-H in Caphtor. [CAPH-TOR.] Such etymologies for the word Pathros as Ⲡ-ⲈⲦ-ⲢⲎⲤ, "that which is southern," and for the form in the LXX., ⲠⲀⲦⲞⲨⲢⲎⲤ, "the southern (region)" (Gesen. *Thes.* s. v.), must be abandoned.

On the evidence here brought forward, it seems

Patmos, Harbor, etc

reasonable to consider Pathros to be part of Upper Egypt, and to trace its name in that of the Pathyrite nome. But this is only a very conjectural identification, which future discoveries may overthrow. It is spoken of with cities in such a manner that we may suppose it was but a small district, and (if we have rightly identified it) that when it occurs Thebes is specially intended. This would account for its distinctive mention.

R. S. P.

PATHRU'SIM. [PATHROS.]

PATMOS (Πάτμος: [*Patmos*]), Rev. i. 9. Two recent and copious accounts, one by a German, the other by a French traveller, furnish us with very full information regarding this island. Ross visited it in 1841, and describes it at length (*Reisen auf den griechischen Inseln des ägäischen Meeres*, ii. 123-139). Guérin, some years later, spent a month there, and enters into more detail,

especially as regards ecclesiastical antiquities and traditions (*Description de l'Ile de Patmos et de l'Ile de Samos*, Paris, 1856, pp. 1-120). Among the older travellers who have visited Patmos we may especially mention Tournefort and Pococke. See also Walpole's *Turkey*, ii. 43.[a]

The aspect of the island is peculiarly rugged and bare. And such a scene of banishment for St. John in the reign of Domitian is quite in harmony with what we read of the custom of the period. It was the common practice to send exiles to the most rocky and desolate islands ("in asperrimas insularum"). See Suet. *Tit.* 8; Juv. *Sat.* i. 73. Such a scene too was suitable (if we may presume to say so) to the sublime and awful revelation which the Apostle received there. It is possible indeed that there was more greenness in Patmos formerly than now. Its name in the Middle Ages was *Palmosa*. But this has now almost entirely

---

a * Dean Stanley visited Patmos in returning from his second visit to Palestine (1862). See his account of the visit, *Sermons in the East*, etc., pp. 225-231.

The points on which he touches are the traditions of Patmos, and its connection with the Apocalypse.

H.

given place to the old classical name; and there is just one palm-tree in the island, in a valley which is called "the Saint's Garden" (ὁ κῆπος τοῦ 'Οσίου). Here and there are a few poor olives, about a score of cypresses, and other trees in the same scanty proportion.

Patmos is divided into two nearly equal parts, a northern and a southern, by a very narrow isthmus, where, on the east side, are the harbor and the town. On the hill to the south, crowning a commanding height, is the celebrated monastery, which bears the name of "John the Divine." Half-way up the ascent is the cave or grotto where tradition says that St. John received the Revelation, and which is still called τὸ σπήλαιον τῆς 'Αποκαλύψεως. A view of it (said by Ross to be not very accurate) will be found in Choiseul-Gouffier, i. pl. 57. Both Ross and Guérin give a very full, and a very melancholy account of the library of the monastery. There were in it formerly 600 MSS. There are now 240, of which Guérin gives a catalogue. Two ought to be mentioned here, which profess to furnish, under the title of αἱ περίοδοι τοῦ θεολόγου, an account of St. John after the ascension of our Lord. One of them is attributed to Prochorus, an alleged disciple of St. John; the other is an abridgment of the same by Nicetas, Archbishop of Thessalonica. Various places in the island are incorporated in the legend, and this is one of its chief points of interest. There is a published Latin translation in the Bibliotheca Maxima Patrum (1677, tom. ii.), but with curious modifications, one great object of which is to disengage St. John's martyrdom from Ephesus (where the legend places it), and to fix it in Rome.

We have only to add that Patmos is one of the Sporades, and is in that part of the Ægean which is called the Icarian Sea. It must have been conspicuous on the right when St. Paul was sailing (Acts xx. 15, xxi. 1) from Samos to Cos.

J. S. H.

PATRIARCHS. The name πατριάρχης is applied in the N. T. to Abraham (Heb. vii. 4), to the sons of Jacob (Acts vii. 8, 9), and to David (Acts ii. 29); and is apparently intended to be equivalent to the phrase רֹאשׁ בֵּית אָבוֹת, the "head" or "prince of a tribe," so often found in the O. T. It is used in this sense by the LXX. in 1 Chr. xxiv. 31, xxvii. 22; 2 Chr. xxiii. 20, xxvi. 12. In common usage the title of patriarch is assigned especially to those whose lives are recorded in Scripture previous to the time of Moses. By the "patriarchal system" is meant that state of society which developed itself naturally out of family relations, before the formation of nations properly so called, and the establishment of regular government; and by the "patriarchal dispensation" the communion into which God was pleased to enter with the families of Seth, Noah, and Abraham, before the call of the chosen people.

The patriarchal times are naturally divided into the ante-diluvian and post-diluvian periods.

1. In the former the Scripture record contains little except the list of the line from Seth, through

Enos, Cainan, Mahalaleel, Jared, Enoch, Methuselah, and Lamech, to Noah; with the ages of each at their periods of generation and at their deaths. [CHRONOLOGY.] To some extent parallel to this, is given the line of Cain; Enoch, Irad, Mehujael, Methusael, Lamech, and the sons of Lamech, Jabal, Jubal, and Tubal-Cain. To the latter line are attributed the first signs of material civilization, the building of cities, the division of classes, and the knowledge of mechanical arts; while the only moral record of their history obscurely speaks of violence and bloodshed. [LAMECH.] In the former line the one distinction is their knowledge of the true God (with the constant recollection of the promised "seed of the woman") which is seen in its fullest perfection in Enoch and Noah; and the only allusion to their occupation (Gen. v. 29) seems to show that they continued a pastoral and agricultural race. The entire corruption, even of the chosen family of Seth, is traced (in Gen. vi. 1–4) to the union between "the sons of God" and "the daughters of men" (Heb. "of Adam"). This union is generally explained by the ancient commentators of a contact with supernatural powers of evil in the persons of fallen angels; most modern interpretation refers it to intermarriage between the lines of Seth and Cain. The latter is intended to avoid the difficulties attaching to the comprehension of the former view, which nevertheless is undoubtedly far more accordant with the usage of the phrase "sons of God" in the O. T. (comp. Job i. 6, xxxviii. 7), and with the language of the passage in Genesis itself. (See Maitland's Eruvin, Essay vi.)

One of the main questions raised as to the antediluvian period turns on the longevity assigned to the patriarchs. With the single exception of Enoch (whose departure from the earth at 365 years of age is exceptional in every sense), their ages vary from 777 (Lamech) to 969 (Methuselah). It is to be observed that this longevity disappears gradually after the Flood. To Shem are assigned 600 years; and thence the ages diminish down to Terah (205 years), Abraham (175), Isaac (180), Jacob (147), and Joseph (110).[c]

This statement of ages is clear and definite. To suppose, with some, that the name of each patriarch denotes a clan or family, and his age its duration, or, with others, that the word שָׁנָה (because it properly signifies "iteration") may, in spite of its known and invariable usage for "year," denote a lunar revolution instead of a solar one (i. e. a month instead of a year) in this passage, appears to be a mere evasion of the difficulty.[b] It must either be accepted, as a plain statement of fact, or regarded as purely fabulous, like the legendary assignment of immense ages to the early Indian or Babylonian or Egyptian kings.

The latter alternative is adopted without scruple by many of the German commentators, some of whom attempt to find such significance in the patriarchal names as to make them personify natural powers or human qualities, like the gods and demigods of mythology. It belongs of course to the

---

a The Hebrew text is here taken throughout: for the variations in the LXX. and the Samaritan Pentateuch, see CHRONOLOGY.

b It is likely enough that the year (as in so many ancient calenders) may be a lunar year of 354 or 355 days, or even a year of 10 months; but this makes no

real difference. It is possible that there may be some corruption in the text, which may affect the numbers given; but the longevity of the patriarchs is noticed and commented upon, as a well-known fact, by Josephus (Ant. i. 3, § 9).

mythical view of Scripture, destroying its claim, in any sense, to authority and special inspiration.

In the acceptance of the literal meaning, it is not easy to say how much difficulty is involved. With our scanty knowledge of what is really meant by "dying of old age," with the certainty that very great effects are produced on the duration of life, both of men and animals, by even slight changes of habits and circumstances, it is impossible to say what might be *a priori* probable in this respect in the antediluvian period, or to determine under what conditions the process of continual decay and reconstruction, which sustains animal life, might be indefinitely prolonged. The constant attribution in all legends of great age to primeval men is at least as likely to be a distortion of fact, as a mere invention of fancy. But even if the difficulty were greater than it is, it seems impossible to conceive that a book, given by inspiration of God to be a treasure for all ages, could be permitted to contain a statement of plain facts, given undoubtingly, and with an elaborate show of accuracy, and yet purely and gratuitously fabulous, in no sense bearing on its great religious subject. If the Divine origin of Scripture be believed, its authority must be accepted in this, as in other cases; and the list of the ages of the patriarchs be held to be (what it certainly claims to be) a statement of real facts.

2. It is in the post-diluvian periods that more is gathered as to the nature of the patriarchal history.

It is at first general in its scope. The "Covenant" given to Noah is one free from all conditions, and fraught with natural blessings, extending to all alike; the one great command (against bloodshed) which marks it, is based on a deep and universal ground; the fulfillment of the blessing, "Be fruitful and multiply, and replenish the earth," is expressly connected, first with an attempt to set up an universal kingdom round a local centre, and then (in Gen. x.) with the formation of the various nations by conquest or settlement, and with the peopling of all the world. But the history soon narrows itself to that of a single tribe or family, and afterwards touches the general history of the ancient world and its empires, only so far as it bears upon this.

It is in this last stage that the principle of the patriarchal dispensation is most clearly seen. It is based on the sacredness of family ties and paternal authority. This authority, as the only one which is natural and original, is inevitably the foundation of the earliest form of society, and is probably seen most perfectly in wandering tribes, where it is not affected by local attachments and by the acquisition of wealth. It is one, from the nature of the case, limited in its scope, depending more on its sacredness than its power, and giving room for much exercise of freedom; and, as it extends from the family to the tribe, it must become less stringent and less concentrated, in proportion to its wider diffusion. In Scripture this authority is consecrated by an ultimate reference to God, as the God of the patriarch, the Father (that is) both of him and his children. Not, of course, that the idea of God's Fatherhood carried with it the knowledge of man's personal communion with his nature (which is revealed by the Incarnation); it rather implied faith in his protection, and a free and loving obedience to his authority, with the hope (more *r* less assured) of some greater blessing from Him

in the coming of the promised seed. At the same time, this faith was not allowed to degenerate, as it was prone to do, into an appropriation of God, as the mere tutelary God of the tribe. The Lord, it is true, suffers Himself to be called "the God of Shem, of Abraham, of Isaac, and of Jacob;" but He also reveals Himself (and that emphatically, as though it were his peculiar title) as the "God Almighty" (Gen. xvii. 1, xxviii. 3, xxxv. 11); He is addressed as the "Judge of all the earth" (xviii. 25), and as such is known to have intercourse with Pharaoh and Abimelech (xii. 17, xx. 3-8), to hallow the priesthood of Melchizedek (xiv. 18-20), and to execute wrath on Sodom and Gomorrah. All this would confirm what the generality of the covenant with Noah, and of the promise of blessing to "all nations" in Abraham's seed must have distinctly taught, that the chosen family were, not substitutes, but representatives, of all mankind, and that God's relation to them was only a clearer and more perfect type of that in which He stood to all.

Still the distinction and preservation of the chosen family, and the maintenance of the paternal authority, are the special purposes, which give a key to the meaning of the history, and of the institutions recorded. For this the birthright (probably carrying with it the priesthood) was reserved to the first-born, belonging to him by inheritance, yet not assured to him till he received his father's blessing; for this the sanctity of marriage was jealously and even cruelly guarded, as in Gen. xxxiv. 7, 13, 31 (Dinah), and in xxxviii. 24 (Tamar), from the license of the world without; and all intermarriage with idolaters was considered as treason to the family and the God of Abraham (Gen. xxvi. 34, 35, xxvii. 46, xxviii. 1, 6-9). Natural obedience and affection are the earthly virtues especially brought out in the history, and the sins dwelt upon (from the irreverence of Ham to the selling of Joseph) are all such as offend against these.

The type of character formed under it, is one imperfect in intellectual and spiritual growth, because not yet tried by the subtler temptations, or forced to contemplate the deeper questions of life; but it is one remarkably simple, affectionate, and free, such as would grow up under a natural authority, derived from God and centering in Him, yet allowing, under its unquestioned sacredness, a familiarity and freedom of intercourse with Him, which is strongly contrasted with the stern and awful character of the Mosaic dispensation. To contemplate it from a Christian point of view is like looking back on the unconscious freedom and innocence of childhood, with that deeper insight and strength of character which are gained by the experience of manhood. We see in it the germs of the future, of the future revelation of God, and the future trials and development of man.

It is on this fact that the typical interpretation of its history depends, an interpretation sanctioned directly by the example of St. Paul (Gal. iv. 21-31; Heb. vii. 1-17), indirectly supported by other passages of Scripture (Matt. xxiv. 37-39; Luke xvii. 28-32; Rom. ix. 10-13, etc.), and instinctively adopted by all who have studied the history itself.

Even in the brief outline of the antediluvian period, we may recognize the main features of the history of the world, the division of mankind into the two great classes, the struggle between the power of evil and good, the apparent triumph of the evil, and its destruction in the final judgment. In the post-diluvian history of the chosen family, is seen the distinction of the true believers, possessors of a special covenant, special revelation, and special privileges, from the world without. In it is therefore shadowed out the history of the Jewish nation and Christian Church, as regards the freedom of their covenant, the gradual unfolding of their revelation, and the peculiar blessings and temptations which belong to their distinctive position.

It is but natural that the unfolding of the characters of the patriarchs under this dispensation should have a typical interest. Abraham, as the type of a faith, both brave and patient, gradually and continuously growing under the education of various trials, stands contrasted with the lower character of Jacob, in whom the same faith is seen, tainted with deceit and selfishness, and needing therefore to be purged by disappointment and suffering. Isaac in the passive gentleness and submissiveness, which characterizes his whole life, and is seen especially in his willingness to be sacrificed by the hand of his father, and Joseph, in the more active spirit of love, in which he rejoiced to save his family and to forgive those who had persecuted and sold him, set forth the perfect spirit of sonship, and are seen to be types especially of Him, in whom alone that spirit dwelt in all fullness.

This typical character in the hands of the mythical school is, of course, made an argument against the historical reality of the whole; those who recognize a unity of principle in God's dispensations at all times, will be prepared to find, even in their earliest and simplest form, the same features which are more fully developed in their later periods.

A. B.

* With reference to the individual patriarchs, the reader will consult the articles which treat of them under their respective names in the Dictionary. See also Hess, *Gesch. der Patriarchen*, 2 vols. (1785); the art. *Patriarchen des A. Test.*, by J. P. Lange, in Herzog's *Real-Encykl.* xi. 192-200 ; Kurtz, *Geschichte des A. Bundes*, i. 139 - 344 (1853); Ewald, *Gesch. des Volkes Israel*, 3ᵉ Ausg., i. 412-519, or pp. 300-362, English translation; Stanley, *The Patriarchs* (Abraham, Isaac, Jacob, Joseph), in his *Jewish Church*, i. 3-108 (Lectt. i.-iv.); and Milman's *Hist. of the Jews*, i. 47-92 (N. Y. 1864). The interesting articles on *Heroes of Hebrew History* by the Bishop of Oxford (Samuel Wilberforce), in *Good Words* for 1869, include the patriarchs.   H.

PATROBAS (Πατροβᾶs : *Patrobas*). A Christian at Rome to whom St. Paul sends his salutation (Rom. xvi. 14). According to late and uncertain tradition, he was one of the 70 disciples, became bishop of Puteoli (Pseudo-Hippolytus, *De LXX. Apostolis*), and suffered martyrdom together with Philologus on Nov. 4th (Estius). Like many other names mentioned in Rom. xvi., this was borne by at least one member of the emperor's household (Suet. *Galba*, 20; Martial, *Ep.* ii. 32, 3). Probably the name is a contraction, like others of the same termination, and stands for Πατρόβιος (see Wolf, *Cur. Philolog.*).   W. T. B.

PATROCLUS or **PATRO′CLUS** (Πάτροκλος: *Patroclus*), the father of Nicanor, the famous adversary. of Judas Maccabæus (2 Macc. viii. 9).

* **PATTERNS**, as employed in Heb. ix. 23,

confuses the sense of the passage. The Greek term is ὑποδείγμα and may signify, indeed, pattern, or example (see John xiii. 15; Heb. iv. 11), but denotes also figure, outline, copy. The latter must be meant in the above passage; for the sacred writer there represents the "heavenly things" spoken of, which require no purification, as themselves "the patterns" or archetypes, of which the earthly tabernacle and its appurtenances were the copies, and not the reverse of this, as in the A. V., i. e. the earthly things, as "the patterns," at least, according to the present use of this expression. [TABERNACLE.] The older versions (Tyndale, Cranmer, the Genevan) have more correctly "similitudes." In Heb. viii. 5, "pattern" answers to τύπος, and occurs in its proper sense.   H.

PAU (פָּעוּ, but in 1 Chr. i. 50, PA′I, פָּעִי, though some copies agree with the reading in Gen.: Φογώρ: *Phau*), the capital of Hadar, king of Edom (Gen. xxxvi. 39). Its position is unknown. The only name that bears any resemblance to it is *Phauara*, a ruined place in Idumæa mentioned by Seetzen.   W. L. B.

PAUL (Παῦλος: *Paulus*), the Apostle of Jesus Christ to the Gentiles.

Original Authorities. — Nearly all the original materials for the Life of St. Paul are contained in the Acts of the Apostles, and in the Pauline Epistles. Out of a comparison of these authorities the biographer of St. Paul has to construct his account of the really important period of the Apostle's life. The early traditions of the Church appear to have left almost untouched the space of time for which we possess those sacred and abundant sources of knowledge; and they aim only at supplying a few particulars in the biography beyond the points at which the narrative of the Acts begins and terminates.

The history and the epistles lie side by side, and are to all appearance quite independent of one another. It was not the purpose of the historian to write a life of St. Paul, even as much as the received name of his book would seem to imply. The book called the Acts of the Apostles is an account of the beginnings of the kingdom of Christ on the earth. The large space which St. Paul occupies in it is due to the important part which he bore in spreading that kingdom. As to the epistles, nothing can be plainer than that they were written without reference to the history; and there is no attempt in the Canon to combine them with it so as to form what we should call in modern phrase the Apostle's "Life and Letters." What amount of agreement, and what amount of discrepancy, may be observed between these independent authorities, is a question of the greatest interest and importance, and one upon which various opinions are entertained. The most adverse and extreme criticism is ably represented by Dr. Baur of Tübingen,[a] who finds so much opposition between what he holds to be the few authentic Pauline epistles and the Acts of the Apostles, that he pronounces the history to be an interested fiction. But his criticism is the very caricature of captiousness. We have but to imagine it applied to any history and letters of acknowledged authenticity, and we feel irresistibly how arbitrary and unhistorical it is. Putting aside this extreme view, it is not to

---

a In his *Paulus der Apostel Jesu Christi*, Stuttgart, 1845 [2ᵉ Aufl., 1866-67].

be denied that difficulties are to be met with in reconciling completely the Acts and the received epistles of St. Paul. What the solutions of such difficulties may be, whether there are any direct contradictions, how far the apparent differences may be due to the purpose of the respective writers, by what arrangement all the facts presented to us may best be dove-tailed together, — these are the various questions which have given so much occupation to the critics and expositors of St. Paul, and upon some of which it seems to be yet impossible to arrive at a decisive conclusion.

We shall assume the Acts of the Apostles to be a genuine and authentic work of St. Luke, the companion of St. Paul, and shall speak of the epistles at the places which we believe them to occupy in the history.

Prominent Points in the Life. —It may be well to state beforehand a few of the principal occurrences upon which the great work done by St. Paul in the world is seen to depend, and which therefore serve as landmarks in his life. Foremost of all is his *Conversion*. This was the main root of his whole life, outward and inward. Next after this, we may specify his *Labors at Antioch*. From these we pass to the *First Missionary Journey*, in the eastern part of Asia Minor, in which St. Paul first assumed the character of the Apostle of Jesus Christ to the Gentiles. *The Visit to Jerusalem*, for the sake of settling the question of the relation of Gentile converts to the Jewish law, was a critical point, both in the history of the Church and of the Apostle. *The introduction of the Gospel into Europe,*[a] with the memorable visits to Philippi, Athens, and Corinth, was the boldest step in the carrying out of St. Paul's mission. A third great missionary journey, chiefly characterized by a long stay *at Ephesus*, is further interesting from its connection with four leading epistles. This was immediately followed by the *apprehension of St. Paul at Jerusalem*, and *his imprisonment at Cæsarea*. And the last event of which we have a full narrative is the *Voyage to Rome*.

The relation of these events to external chronology will be considered at the end of the article.

Saul of Tarsus, before his Conversion. — Up to the time of his going forth as an avowed preacher of Christ *to the Gentiles*, the Apostle was known by the name of Saul. This was the Jewish name which he received from his Jewish parents. But though a Hebrew of the Hebrews, he was born in a Gentile city. Of his parents we know nothing,[b] except that his father was of the tribe of Benjamin (Phil. iii. 5), and a Pharisee (Acts xxiii. 6), that he had acquired by some means the Roman fran-

chise ("I was free born," Acts xxii. 28', and that he was settled in Tarsus. "I am a Jew of Tarsus, a city in Cilicia, a citizen of no mean city " (Acts xxi. 39). Our attention seems to be specially called to this birthplace and early home of Saul by the repeated mention of it in connection with his name. Here he must have learnt to use the Greek language with freedom and mastery in both speaking and writing; and the general tone and atmosphere of a cultivated community cannot have been without their effect upon his highly susceptible nature. At Tarsus also he learnt that trade of σκηνοποιός (Acts xviii. 3), at which he afterwards occasionally wrought with his own hands. There was a goat's-hair cloth called *Cilicium*, manufactured in Cilicia, and largely used for tents. Saul's trade was probably that of making tents of this hair cloth. [TENTMAKER, Amer. ed.] It does not follow that the family were in the necessitous condition which such manual labor commonly implies; for it was a wholesome custom amongst the Jews, to teach every child some trade, though there might be little prospect of his depending upon it for his living.

When St. Paul makes his defense before his countrymen at Jerusalem (Acts xxii.), he tells them that though born in Tarsus, he had been "brought up" (ἀνατεθραμμένος) in Jerusalem. He must, therefore, have been yet a boy, when he was removed, in all probability for the sake of his education, to the Holy City of his fathers. We may imagine him arriving there perhaps at some age[c] between 10 and 15, already a Hellenist, speaking Greek and familiar with the Greek version of the Scriptures, possessing, besides the knowledge of his trade, the elements of Gentile learning, — to be taught at Jerusalem "according to the perfect manner of the law of the fathers." He learnt, he says, " at the feet of Gamaliel." He who was to resist so stoutly the usurpations of the Law, had for his teacher one of the most eminent of all the doctors of the law. [GAMALIEL.] It is singular, that on the occasion of his well-known intervention in the Apostolical history, the master's counsels of toleration are in marked contrast to the persecuting zeal so soon displayed by the pupil. The temper of Gamaliel himself was moderate and candid, and he was personally free from bigotry; but his teaching was that of the strictest of the Pharisees, and bore its natural fruit when lodged in the ardent and thorough-going nature of Saul. Other fruits, besides that of a zeal which persecuted the Church, may no doubt be referred to the time when Saul sat at the feet of Gamaliel. A thorough training in the Scriptures and in the traditions of the elders

---

[a] * It is by no means certain (if that be meant in the text above) that Paul first introduced the Gospel into Europe. Writers on the book of Acts often make this statement (see Baumgarten's *Apostelgeschichte*, i 495). Philippi was the first city in Europe where Paul himself preached; but in all probability Rome, at least, had received the Gospel at an earlier period. This result was the more inevitable, because in addition to the general intercourse between that capital of the world and the East, "strangers of Rome" (Acts ii. 10), i. e. Jews and Jewish proselytes, were present at Jerusalem on the day of Pentecost and heard the preaching of Peter. The Cretans too, who were present on this occasion, may have carried with them the seed of the word to Crete, from which sprung the churches of that island, of whose origin we have otherwise no information.   H.

[b] The story mentioned by Jerome (*Scrip. Eccl. Cat.* "Paulus ") that St. Paul's parents lived at Gischala in Galilee, and that, having been born there, the infant Saul emigrated with his parents to Tarsus upon the taking of that city by the Romans, is inconsistent with the fact that Gischala was not taken until a much later time, and with the Apostle's own statement that he was born at Tarsus (Acts xxii. 3).

[c] His words in the speech before Agrippa (Acts xxvi. 4, 5), according to the received text, refer exclusively to his life at Jerusalem. But if we read, with the better authorities, ἔν τε Ἱερ. for ἐν Ἱερ. he may be speaking of the life he led "amongst his own people" at Tarsus or elsewhere, *as well as* of his residence at Jerusalem.

ander an acute and accomplished master, must have done much to exercise the mind of Saul, and to make him feel at home in the subjects in which he was afterwards to be so intensely interested. And we are not at all bound to suppose that, because his zeal for the Law was strong enough to set him upon persecuting the believers in Jesus, he had therefore experienced none of the doubts and struggles which, according to his subsequent testimony, it was the nature of the Law to produce. On the contrary, we can scarcely imagine these as absent from the spiritual life of Saul as he passed from boyhood to manhood. Earnest persecutors are, oftener than not, men who have been tormented by inward struggles and perplexities. The pupil of Gamaliel may have been crushing a multitude of conflicts in his own mind when he threw himself into the holy work of extirpating the new heresy.

Saul was yet "a young man" (νεανίας, Acts vii. 58), when the Church experienced that sudden expansion which was connected with the ordaining of the Seven appointed to serve tables, and with the special power and inspiration of Stephen. Amongst those who disputed with Stephen were some "of them of Cilicia." We naturally think of Saul as having been one of these, when we find him afterwards keeping the clothes of those suborned witnesses who, according to the Law (Deut. xvii. 7), were the first to cast stones at Stephen. "Saul," says the sacred writer, significantly, "was consenting unto his death." The angelic glory that shone from Stephen's face, and the Divine truth of his words, failing to subdue the spirit of religious hatred now burning in Saul's breast, must have embittered and aggravated its rage. Saul was passing through a terrible crisis for a man of his nature. But he was not one to be moved from his stern purpose by the native refinement and tenderness which he must have been stifling within him. He was the most unwearied and unrelenting of persecutors. "As for Saul, he made havoc of the Church, entering into every house,[a] and haling men and women, committed them to prison" (Acts viii. 3).

Saul's Conversion. — The persecutor was to be converted. What the nature of that conversion was, we are now to observe. — Having undertaken to follow up the believers "unto strange cities," Saul naturally turned his thoughts to Damascus, expecting to find, amongst the numerous Jewish residents of that populous city, some adherents of "the way" (τῆς ὁδοῦ), and trusting, we must presume, to be allowed by the connivance of the governor to apprehend them. What befell him as he journeyed thither is related in detail three times in the Acts, first by the historian in his own person, then in the two addresses made by St. Paul at Jerusalem and before Agrippa. These three narratives are not repetitions of one another: there are differences between them which some critics choose to consider irreconcilable. Considering that the same author is responsible for all the accounts, we gain nothing, of course, for the authenticity of their statements by bringing them into agreement; but it seems pretty clear that the author himself could not have been conscious of any contradictions in the narratives. He can scarcely have had any motive for placing side by side inconsistent reports of St. Paul's conversion and that he should have admitted inconsistencies on such a matter through mere carelessness, is hardly credible. Of the three narratives, that of the historian himself must claim to be the most purely historical: St. Paul's subsequent accounts were likely to be affected by the purpose for which he introduced them. St. Luke's statement is to be read in Acts ix. 3-19, where, however, the words "It is hard for thee to kick against the pricks," included in the Vulgate and English version, ought to be omitted. The sudden light from heaven; the voice of Jesus speaking with authority to his persecutor; Saul struck to the ground, blinded, overcome; the three days' suspense; the coming of Ananias as a messenger of the Lord; and Saul's baptism; — these were the leading features, in the eyes of the historian, of the great event, and in these we must look for the chief significance of the conversion.

Let us now compare the historical relation with those which we have in St. Paul's speeches (Acts xxii. and xxvi.). The reader will do well to consider each in its place. But we have here to deal with the bare facts of agreement or difference. With regard to the light, the speeches add to what St. Luke tells us that the phenomenon occurred at mid-day, and that the light shone round, and was visible to Saul's companions as well as himself. The 2d speech says, that at the shining of this light, the whole company ("we all") fell to the ground. This is not *contradicted* by what is said, ix. 7, "the men which journeyed with him stood speechless," for there is no emphasis on "stood," nor is the standing antithetical to Saul's falling down. We have but to suppose the others rising before Saul, or standing still afterwards in greater perplexity through not seeing or hearing what Saul saw and heard, to reconcile the narratives without forcing either. After the question, "Why persecutest thou me?" the 2d speech adds, "It is hard for thee to kick against the goads." Then both the speeches supply a question and answer — "I answered, who art thou, Lord? And he said, I am Jesus (of Nazareth), whom thou persecutest." In the direction to go into Damascus and await orders there, the 1st speech agrees with Acts ix. But whereas according to that chapter the men with Saul "heard the voice," in the 1st speech it is said "they heard not the voice of him that spake to me." It seems reasonable to conclude from the two passages, that the men actually heard sounds, but not, like Saul, an articulate voice. With regard to the visit of Ananias, there is no collision between the 9th chapter and the 1st speech, the latter only attributing additional words to Ananias. The 2d speech ceases to give details of the conversion after the words, "I am Jesus, whom thou persecutest But rise and stand on thy feet." St. Paul adds, from the mouth of Jesus, an exposition of the purpose for which He had appeared to him. It is easy to say that in ascribing these words to Jesus, St. Paul or his professed reporter is violating the order and sequence of the earlier accounts. But, if we bear in mind the nature and purpose of St. Paul's address before Agrippa, we shall surely not suppose that he is violating the strict truth, when he adds to the words which Jesus spoke to him at the moment of the light and the sound, without interposing any reference to a later occasion, that fuller exposition of the meaning of the crisis through which he was passing, which he was not to receive

---

[a] * Not "every house," but strictly, *into the houses* (κατὰ τοὺς οἴκους), one after another, in which believers dwelt or had taken refuge.   H.

till afterwards. What Saul actually heard from Jesus on the way as he journeyed, was afterwards interpreted, to the mind of Saul, into those definite expressions.

For we must not forget that, whatever we hold as to the external nature of the phenomena we are considering, the whole transaction was essentially, in any case, a *spiritual* communication. That the Lord Jesus manifested Himself as a Living Person to the man Saul, and spoke to him so that his very words could be understood, is the substantial fact declared to us. The purport of the three narratives is that an actual conversation took place between Saul and the Lord Jesus. It is remarkable that in none of them is Saul said to have *seen* Jesus. The grounds for believing that he did are the two expressions of Ananias (Acts ix. 17), "The Lord Jesus, who appeared unto thee in the way," and (Acts xxii. 14), "That thou shouldest see the Just One," and the statement of St. Paul (1 Cor. xv. 8), "Last of all He was seen of me also." Comparing these passages with the narratives, we conclude, either that Saul had an instantaneous vision of Jesus as the flash of light blinded him, or that the "seeing" was that apprehension of his presence which would go with a real conversation. *How* it was that Saul "saw" and "heard" we are quite unable to determine. That the light, and the sound or voice, were both different from any ordinary phenomena with which Saul and his companions were familiar, is unquestionably implied in the narrative. It is also implied that they were specially significant to Saul, and not to those with him. We gather therefore that there were real outward phenomena, through which Saul was made inwardly sensible of a Presence revealed to him alone.

Externally there was a flash of light. Spiritually "the light of the gospel of the glory of the Christ, who is the image of God," shone upon Saul, and convicted the darkness of the heart which had shut out Love and knew not the glory of the Cross. Externally Saul fell to the ground. Spiritually he was prostrated by shame, when he knew whom he had been persecuting. Externally sounds issued out of heaven. Spiritually the Crucified said to Saul, with tender remonstrance, "I am Jesus, why persecutest thou me?" Whether audibly to his companions, or audibly to the Lord Jesus only, Saul confessed himself in the spirit the servant of Him whose name he had hated. He gave himself up, without being able to see his way, to the disposal of him whom he now knew to have vindicated his claim over him by the very sacrifice which formerly he had despised. The Pharisee was converted, once for all, into a disciple of Jesus the Crucified.

The only mention in the epistles of St. Paul of the outward phenomena attending his conversion is that in 1 Cor. xv. 8, "Last of all He was seen of me also." But there is one important passage in which he speaks distinctly of his conversion itself. Dr. Baur (*Paulus*, p. 64), with his readiness to find out discrepancies, insists that this passage represents quite a different process from that recorded in the Acts. It is manifestly not a repe-

tition of what we have been reading and considering, but it is in the most perfect harmony with it. In the Epistle to the Galatians (i. 15, 16) St. Paul has these words: "When it pleased God, who separated me from my mother's womb, and called me by His grace, *to reveal His Son in me*, that I might preach Him among the heathen . . ." (ἀποκαλύψαι τὸν υἱὸν αὑτοῦ ἐν ἐμοί). What words could express more exactly than these the spiritual experience which occurred to Saul on the way to Damascus? The manifestation of Jesus as the Son of God is clearly the main point in the narrative. This manifestation was brought about through a removal of the veils of prejudice and ignorance which blinded the eyes of Saul to a Crucified Deliverer, conquering through sacrifice. And, whatever part the senses may have played in the transaction, the essence of it in any case must have been Saul's inward vision of a spiritual Lord close to his spirit, from whom he could not escape, whose every command he was henceforth to obey in the Spirit.

It would be groundless to assume that the new convictions of that mid-day immediately cleared and settled themselves in Saul's mind. It is sufficient to say that he was then *converted*, or turned round. For a while, no doubt, his inward state was one of awe and expectation. He was being "led by the hand" spiritually by his Master, as well as bodily by his companions. Thus entering Damascus as a servant of the Lord Jesus, he sought the house of one whom he had, perhaps, intended to persecute. Judas may have been known to his guest as a disciple of the Lord.[a] Certainly the fame of Saul's coming had preceded him; and Ananias, "a devout man according to the law," but a believer in Jesus, when directed by the Lord to visit him, wonders at what he is told concerning the notorious persecutor. He obeys, however; and going to Saul in the name of "the Lord Jesus, who had appeared to him in the way," he puts his hands on him that he may receive his sight and be filled with the Holy Ghost. Thereupon Saul's eyes are immediately purged and his sight is restored. "The same hour," says St. Paul (Acts xxii. 13), "I looked up upon him. And he said, The God of our fathers hath chosen thee, that thou shouldest know His will, and see the Just One, and shouldest hear the voice of His mouth. For thou shalt be His witness unto all men of what thou hast seen and heard." Every word in this address strikes some chord which we hear sounded again and again in St. Paul's epistles. The new convert is not, as it is so common to say, converted from Judaism to Christianity — *the God of the Jewish fathers chooses* him. He is chosen *to know God's will*. That will is manifested *in the Righteous One*. Him Saul *sees and hears*, in order that he may be *a witness of Him* to all men. The eternal will of the God of Abraham, that will revealed in a Righteous Son of God; the testimony concerning Him, a Gospel to mankind: — these are the essentially Pauline principles which are declared in all the teaching of the Apostle, and illustrated in all his actions.

After the recovery of his sight, Saul received the

---

a "It seems improbable that this Judas was at that time a disciple. None of Saul's company were Christians, nor did they know that he had become a believer. Neither they, nor he, would probably know of a Christian family to which they could conduct him, nor would such a one have readily received him. He went, apparently, to his intended place of stopping, possibly, a public house. It is probable that the host and the guest were both personally strangers to him.   S. W.

washing away of his sins in baptism. He then broke his three days' fast, and was strengthened: an image, again, of the strengthening of his faint and hungering spirit through a participation in the Divine life of the Church of Damascus. He was at once received into the fellowship of the disciples, and began without delay the work to which Ananias had designated him; and to the astonishment of all his hearers he proclaimed Jesus in the synagogues, declaring him to be the Son of God. This was the actual sequel to his conversion: he was to proclaim Jesus the Crucified, first to the Jews as their own Christ, afterwards to the world as the Son of the Living God.

The narrative in the Acts tells us simply that he was occupied in this work, with increasing vigor, "for many days," up to the time when imminent danger drove him from Damascus. From the Epistle to the Galatians (i. 17, 18) we learn that the many days were at least a good part of "three years," and that Saul, not thinking it necessary to procure authority to preach from the Apostles that were before him, went after his conversion into Arabia, and returned from thence to Damascus. We know nothing whatever of this visit to Arabia: to what district Saul went, how long he stayed, or for what purpose he went there.[a] From the antithetical way in which it is opposed to a visit to the Apostles at Jerusalem, we infer that it took place before he deliberately committed himself to the task of proclaiming Jesus as the Christ; and also, with some probability, that he was seeking seclusion, in order that, by conferring "not with flesh and blood," but with the Lord in the Spirit, he might receive more deeply into his mind the commission given him at his conversion. That Saul did not spend the greater portion of the "three years" at Damascus seems probable, for these two reasons: (1) that the anger of the Jews was not likely to have borne with two or three years of such a life as Saul's now was without growing to a height; and (2) that the disciples at Jerusalem would not have been likely to mistrust Saul as they did, if they had heard of him as preaching Jesus at Damascus for the same considerable period. But it does not follow that Saul was in Arabia all the time he was not disputing at Damascus. For all that we know to the contrary he may have gone to Antioch or Tarsus or anywhere else, or he may have remained silent at Damascus for some time after returning from Arabia.

Now that we have arrived at Saul's departure from Damascus, we are again upon historical ground, and have the double evidence of St. Luke in the Acts, and of the Apostle in his 2d Epistle to the Corinthians. According to the former, the Jews lay in wait for Saul, intending to kill him, and watched the gates of the city that he might not escape from them. Knowing this, the disciples took him by night and let him down in a

basket from the wall. According to St. Paul (2 Cor. xi. 32) it was the ethnarch under Aretas the king who watched for him, desiring to apprehend him. There is no difficulty in reconciling the two statements. We might similarly say that our Lord was put to death either by the Jews or by the Roman governor. There is more difficulty in ascertaining how an officer of king Aretas should be governing in Damascus, and why he should lend himself to the designs of the Jews. But we learn from secular history that the affairs of Damascus were, at the time, in such an unsettled state as to make the narrative not improbable. [ARETAS.] Having escaped from Damascus, Saul betook himself to Jerusalem, and there "assayed to join himself to the disciples; but they were all afraid of him, and believed not that he was a disciple." In this natural but trying difficulty Saul was befriended by one whose name was henceforth closely associated with his. *Barnabas* became his sponsor to the Apostles and Church at Jerusalem, assuring them — from some personal knowledge, we must presume — of the facts of Saul's conversion and subsequent behavior at Damascus. It is noticeable that the *seeing* and *hearing* are still the leading features in the conversion, and the name of Jesus in the preaching. Barnabas declared how "Saul had seen the Lord in the way, and that he had spoken to him, and how that he had preached boldly at Damascus in the name of Jesus." Barnabas' introduction removed the fears of the Apostles, and Paul "was with them coming in and going out at Jerusalem." His Hellenistical education made him, like Stephen, a successful disputant against the "Grecians;" and it is not strange that the former persecutor was singled out from the other believers as the object of a murderous hostility. He was therefore again urged to flee; and by way of Caesarea betook himself to his native city Tarsus.

In the Epistle to the Galatians St. Paul adds certain particulars, in which only a perverse and captious criticism could see anything contradictory to the facts just related. He tells us that his motive for going up to Jerusalem rather than anywhere else was that he might see Peter; that he abode with him fifteen days; that the only Apostles he saw were Peter and James the Lord's brother; and that afterwards he came into the regions of Syria and Cilicia,[b] remaining unknown by face, though well-known for his conversion, to the churches in Judæa which were in Christ. St. Paul's object in referring to this connection of his with those who were Apostles before him, was to show that he had never accepted his apostleship as a commission from them. On this point the narrative in the Acts entirely agrees with St. Paul's own earnest asseverations in his epistles. He received his commission from the Lord Jesus, and also mediately through Ananias. This commission

---

[a] * Paul informs us, Gal. iv. 25, that one of the names of Sinai in Arabia was Hagar. No other writer mentions such a name, and the Apostle may be supposed to have learned the fact during his visit to that country (Gal. i. 17). This contact between the two passages is certainly remarkable. "It is difficult to resist the thought," says Stanley (*Sin. & Pal.* p. 50, Amer. ed.), "that Paul may have stood upon the rocks of Sinai, and heard from Arab lips the oft repeated 'Hagar,' — 'rock,' suggesting the double meaning" to which he alludes in the epistle. (See HAGAR, vol ii. p. 978, Amer. ed.) **H**

[b] * From Acts ix. 30 Paul appears to have gone by sea from Cæsarea to Tarsus; nor does the order "Syria and Cilicia" in Gal. i. 21 necessarily conflict with this. It appears to have been usual to associate the provinces in that order (see Acts xv. 23, 41), because that was the order of the land-route from Jerusalem to Cilicia, the one usually taken. Hence Paul, in the Epistle to the Galatians, as above, may have adhered to it from the force of association, though he went in fact first to Cilicia, and then made missionary excursions into Syria. **S**

included a special designation to preach Christ to the Gentiles. Upon the latter designation he did not act, until circumstances opened the way for it. But he at once began to proclaim Jesus as the Christ to his own countrymen. Barnabas introduced him to the Apostles, not as seeking their sanction, but as having seen and heard the Lord Jesus, and as having boldly spoken already in his name. Probably at first, Saul's independence as an Apostle of Christ was not distinctly thought of, either by himself or by the older Apostles. It was not till afterwards that it became so important; and then the reality of it appeared plainly from a reference to the beginning of his Apostolic work.

St. Paul at Antioch. — While Saul was at Tarsus, a movement was going on at Antioch, which raised that city to an importance second only to that of Jerusalem itself in the early history of the Church. In the life of the Apostle of the Gentiles Antioch claims a most conspicuous place. It was there that the preaching of the Gospel to the Gentiles first took root, and from thence that it was afterwards propagated. Its geographical position, its political and commercial importance, and the presence of a large and powerful Jewish element in its population, were the more obvious characteristics which adapted it for such a use. There came to Antioch, when the persecution which arose about Stephen scattered upon their different routes the disciples who had been assembled at Jerusalem, men of Cyprus and Cyrene, eager to tell all who would hear them the good news concerning the Lord Jesus. Until Antioch was reached, the word was spoken "to none but unto Jews only" (Acts xi. 19). But here the Gentiles also (*oi Ἕλληνες*) — not, as in the A. V., "the Grecians," — were amongst the hearers of the word. [See note *b*, vol. ii. p. 967.] A great number believed; and when this was reported at Jerusalem, Barnabas was sent on a special mission to Antioch.

As the work grew under his hands, and "much people was added unto the Lord," Barnabas felt the need of help, and went himself to Tarsus to seek Saul. Possibly at Damascus, certainly at Jerusalem, he had been a witness of Saul's energy and devotedness, and skill in disputation. He had been drawn to him by the bond of a most brotherly affection. He therefore longed for him as a helper, and succeeded in bringing him to Antioch. There they labored together unremittingly for "a whole year," mixing with the constant assemblies of the believers, and "teaching much people." All this time, as St. Luke would give us to understand, Saul was subordinate to Barnabas. Until "Saul" became "Paul," we read of "Barnabas and Saul" (Acts xi. 30, xii. 25, xiii. 2, 7). Afterwards the order changes to "Paul and Barnabas." It seems reasonable to conclude that there was no marked peculiarity in the teaching of Saul during the Antioch period. He held and taught, in common with the other Jewish believers, the simple faith in Jesus the Christ, crucified and raised from the dead. Nor did he ever afterwards depart from the simplicity of this faith. But new circumstances stirred up new questions; and then it was to Saul of Tarsus that it was given to see, more clearly than any others saw, those new applications of the old truth, those deep and world-wide relations of it, with which his work was to be permanently associated. In the mean time, according to the usual method of the Divine government, facts were

silently growing, which were to suggest and occasion the future developments of faith and practice, and of these facts the most conspicuous was the unprecedented accession of Gentile proselytes at Antioch.

An opportunity soon occurred, of which Barnabas and Saul joyfully availed themselves, for proving the affection of these new disciples towards their brethren at Jerusalem, and for knitting the two communities together in the bonds of practical fellowship. A manifest impulse from the Holy Spirit began this work. There came "prophets" from Jerusalem to Antioch: "and there stood up one of them, named Agabus, and signified by the Spirit that there should be great dearth throughout all the world." The "prophets" who now arrived may have been the Simeon and Lucius and Manaen, mentioned in xiii. 1, besides Agabus and others. The prediction of the dearth need not have been purposeless; it would naturally have a direct reference to the needs of the poorer brethren and the duty of the richer. It is obvious that the fulfillment followed closely upon the intimation of the coming famine. For the disciples at Antioch determined to send contributions immediately to Jerusalem; and the gift was conveyed to the elders of that church [at Jerusalem and perhaps of the churches in Judæa, Acts xi. 29] by the hands of Barnabas and Saul. The time of this dearth is vaguely designated in the Acts as the reign of Claudius. It is ascertained from Josephus's history, that a severe famine did actually prevail in Judæa, and especially at Jerusalem, at the very time fixed by the event recorded in Acts xii., the death of Herod Agrippa. This was in A. D. 44. [AGABUS.]

It could not have been necessary for the mere safe conduct of the contribution that Barnabas and Saul should go in person to Jerusalem. We are bound to see in the relations between the Mother-Church and that of Antioch, of which this visit is illustrative, examples of the deep feeling of the necessity of union which dwelt in the heart of the early Church. The Apostles did not go forth to teach a system, but to enlarge a body. The Spirit which directed and furthered their labors was essentially the Spirit of fellowship. By this Spirit Saul of Tarsus was being practically trained in strict coöperation with his elders in the Church. The habits which he learnt now were to aid in guarding him at a later time from supposing that the independence which he was bound to claim, should involve the slightest breach or loosening of the bonds of the universal brotherhood.

Having discharged their errand, Barnabas and Saul returned to Antioch, bringing with them another helper, John surnamed Mark, sister's son to Barnabas. [SISTER'S SON, Amer. ed.] The work of prophesying and teaching was resumed. Several of the oldest and most honored of the believers in Jesus were expounding the way of God and organizing the Church in that busy metropolis. Travellers were incessantly passing to and fro. Antioch was in constant communication with Cilicia, with Cyprus, with all the neighboring countries. The question must have forced itself upon hundreds of the "Christians" at Antioch, "What is the meaning of this faith of ours, of this baptism, of this incorporation, of this kingdom of the Son of God, *for the world?* The Gospel is not for Judæa alone: here are we called by it at Antioch. Is it meant to stop here?" The Church was pregnant with a great movement, and the time of her delivery was at hand. We forget the whole method of the Divine work in the nurture of the Church, if we ascribe to the impulses of the Holy Ghost any theatrical suddenness, and disconnect them from the thoughts which were brooding in the minds of the disciples. At every point we find both circumstances and inward reasonings preparing the crisis. Something of direct expectation seems to be implied in what is said of the leaders of the Church at Antioch, that they were " ministering to the Lord, and fasting," when the Holy Ghost spoke to them. Without doubt they knew it for a seal set upon previous surmises, when the voice came clearly to the general mind, " Separate me Barnabas and Saul for the work whereunto I have called them." That " work " was partially known already to the Christians of Antioch: who could be so fit for it as the two brothers in the faith and in mutual affection, the son of exhortation, and the highly accomplished and undaunted convert who had from the first been called " a chosen vessel, to bear the name of the Lord before the Gentiles, and kings, and the people of Israel " ?

When we look back, from the higher ground of St. Paul's apostolic activity, to the years that passed between his conversion and the first missionary journey, we cannot observe without reverence the patient humility with which Saul waited for his Master's time. He did not say for once only, " Lord, what wilt thou have me to do? " Obedience to Christ was thenceforth his ruling principle. Submitting, as he believed, to his Lord's direction, he was content to work for a long time as the subordinate colleague of his seniors in the faith. He was thus the better prepared, when the call came, to act with the authority which that call conferred upon him. He left Antioch, however, still the second to Barnabas. Everything was done with orderly gravity in the sending forth of the two missionaries. Their brethren, after fasting and prayer, laid their hands on them, and so they departed.

The first Missionary Journey. — Much must have been hid from Barnabas and Saul as to the issues of the journey on which they embarked. But one thing was clear to them, that *they were sent forth to speak the word of God.* They did not go in their own name or for their own purposes: they were instruments for uttering what the Eternal God Himself was saying to men. We shall find in the history a perfectly definite representation of what St. Paul announced and taught as he journeyed from city to city. But the first characteristic feature of his teaching was the absolute conviction that he was only the bearer of a heavenly message. It is idle to discuss St. Paul's character or views without recognizing this fact. We are compelled to think of him as of a man who was capable of cherishing such a conviction with perfect assurance. We are bound to bear in mind the unspeakable influence which that conviction must have exerted upon his nature. The writer of the Acts proceeds upon the same assumption. He tells us that as soon as Barnabas and Saul reached Cyprus, they began to "announce the word of God."

The second fact to be observed is, that for the present they delivered their message in the synagogues of the Jews only. [SYNAGOGUES, Amer. ed.] They trod the old path till they should be

drawn out of it. But when they had gone through the island, from Salamis to Paphos, they were called upon to explain their doctrine to an eminent Gentile, Sergius Paulus, the proconsul. This Roman officer, like so many of his countrymen, had already come under the influence of Jewish teaching; but it was in the corrupt form of magical pretensions, which throve so luxuriantly upon the godless credulity of that age. A Jew, named Barjesus, or Elymas, a *magus* and false prophet, had attached himself to the governor, and had no doubt interested his mind, for he was an intelligent man, with what he had told him of the history and hopes of the Jews. [ELYMAS.] Accordingly, when Sergius Paulus heard of the strange teachers who were announcing to the Jews the advent of their true Messiah, he wished to see them, and sent for them. The impostor, instinctively hating the Apostles, and seeing his influence over the proconsul in danger of perishing, did what he could to withstand them. Then Saul, "who is also called Paul," denouncing Elymas in remarkable terms, declared against him God's sentence of temporary blindness. The blindness immediately falls upon him; and the proconsul, moved by the scene and persuaded by the teaching of the Apostle, becomes a believer.

There is a singular parallelism in several points between the history of St. Paul and that of St. Peter in the Acts. Baur presents it in a highly effective form (*Paulus*, p. 91, &c.), to support his theory of the composition of this book; and this is one of the services which he has incidentally rendered to the full understanding of the early history of the Church. Thus St. Paul's discomfiture of Elymas reminds us of St. Peter's denunciation of Simon Magus. The two incidents bring strongly before us one of the great adverse elements with which the Gospel had to contend in that age. Everywhere there were counterfeits of the spiritual powers which the Apostles claimed and put forth. It was necessary for the preachers of Christ, not so much to prove themselves stronger than the magicians and soothsayers, as to guard against being confounded with them. One distinguishing mark of the true servants of the Spirit would be that of *not trading* upon their spiritual powers (Acts viii. 20). Another would be that of shunning every sort of concealment and artifice, and courting the daylight of open truth. St. Paul's language to Elymas is studiously directed to the reproof of the tricks of the religious impostor. The Apostle, full of the true Holy Ghost, looked steadily on the deceiver, spoke in the name of a God of light and righteousness and straightforward ways, and put forth the power of that God for the vindication of truth against delusion. The punishment of Elymas was itself symbolical, and conveyed "teaching of the Lord." He had chosen to create a spiritual darkness around him; and now there fell upon him a mist and a darkness, and he went about, seeking some one to lead him by the hand. If on reading this account we refer to St. Peter's reproof of Simon Magus, we shall be struck by the differences as well as the resemblance which we shall observe. But we shall undoubtedly gain a stronger impression of this part of the Apostolic work, namely, the conflict to be waged between the Spirit of Christ and of the Church, and the evil spirits of a dark superstition to which men were surrendering themselves as slaves. We shall feel the worth and power of that candid and open temper in which alone St. Paul would commend his cause; and in the conversion of Sergius Paulus we shall see an exemplary type of many victories to be won by the truth over falsehood.

This point is made a special crisis in the history of the Apostle by the writer of the Acts. Saul now becomes Paul, and begins to take precedence of Barnabas. Nothing is said to explain the change of name. No reader could resist the temptation of supposing that there must be some connection between Saul's new name and that of his distinguished Roman convert. But on reflection it does not seem probable that St. Paul would either have wished, or have consented to change his own name for that of a distinguished convert. If we put Sergius Paulus aside, we know that it was exceedingly common for Jews to bear, besides their own Jewish name, another borrowed from the country with which they had become connected. (See Conybeare and Howson, i. 163, for full illustrations.) Thus we have Simeon also named Niger, Barnabas also named Justus, John also named Marcus. There is no reason therefore why Saul should not have borne from infancy the other name of Paul. In that case he would be Saul amongst his own countrymen, Paulus amongst the Gentiles. And we must understand St. Luke as wishing to mark strongly the transition point between Saul's activity amongst his own countrymen, and his new labors as the Apostle of the Gentiles, by calling him Saul only, during the first, and Paul only afterwards.[a]

The conversion of Sergius Paulus may be said, perhaps, to mark the beginning of the work amongst the Gentiles; otherwise, it was not in Cyprus that any change took place in the method hitherto followed by Barnabas and Saul in preaching the Gospel. Their public addresses were as yet confined to the synagogues; but it was soon to be otherwise. From Paphos, "Paul and his company" set sail for the mainland, and arrived at Perga in Pamphylia, where the heart of their companion John failed him, and he returned to Jerusalem. [PERGA.] From Perga they travelled on to a place, obscure in secular history, but most memorable in the history of the kingdom of Christ,— Antioch in Pisidia. [ANTIOCH IN PISIDIA.] Here "they went into the synagogue on the sabbath day, and sat down." Small as the place was, it contained its colony of Jews, and with them proselytes who worshipped the God of the Jews. The degree to which the Jews had spread and settled themselves over the world, and the influence they had gained over the more respectable of their Gentile neighbors, and especially over the women of the better class, are facts difficult to appreciate justly, but proved by undoubted evidence, and very important for us to bear in mind. This Pisidian Antioch may have been more Jewish than most similar towns, but it was not more so than many of much

greater size and importance. What took place here in the synagogue and in the city is interesting to us not only on account of its bearing on the history, but also because it represents more or less exactly what afterwards occurred in many other places.

It cannot be without design that we have single but detailed examples given us in the Acts, of the various kinds of addresses which St. Paul used to deliver in appealing to his different audiences. He had to address himself, in the course of his missionary labors, to Jews, knowing and receiving the Scriptures; to ignorant barbarians: to cultivated Greeks; to mobs enraged against himself personally; to magistrates and kings. It is an inestimable help in studying the Apostle and his work, that we have specimens of the tone and the arguments he was accustomed to use in all these situations. These will be noticed in their places. In what he said at the synagogue in Antioch, we recognize the type of the addresses in which he would introduce his message to his Jewish fellow-countrymen.

The Apostles[b] of Christ sat still with the rest of the assembly, whilst the Law and the Prophets were read. They and their audience were united in reverence for the sacred books. Then the rulers of the synagogue sent to invite them, as strangers but brethren, to speak any word of exhortation which might be in them to the people. Paul stood up, and beckoning with his hand, he spoke. — The speech is given in Acts xiii. 16–41. The characteristics we observe in it are these. The speaker begins by acknowledging "the God of this people Israel." He ascribes to him the calling out of the nation and the conduct of its subsequent history. He touches on the chief points of that history up to the reign of David, whom he brings out into prominence. He then names Jesus as the promised Son of David. To convey some knowledge of Jesus to the minds of his hearers, he recounts the chief facts of the gospel history; the preparatory preaching and baptism of John (of which the rumor had spread perhaps to Antioch); the condemnation of Jesus by the rulers "who knew neither him nor the prophets," and his resurrection. That resurrection is declared to be the fulfillment of all God's promises of life, given to the fathers. Through Jesus, therefore, is now proclaimed by God Himself the forgiveness of sins and full justification. The Apostle concludes by drawing from the prophets a warning against unbelief. If this is an authentic example of Paul's preaching, it was impossible for Peter or John to start more exclusively from the Jewish covenant and promises than did the Apostle of the Gentiles. How entirely this discourse resembles those of St. Peter and of Stephen in the earlier chapters of the Acts! There is only one specially Pauline touch in the whole, — the words in ver. 39, " By Him all that believe are justified from all things, from which ye could not

[a] A little more prominence should probably be given here to the occurrence with which this change of name is associated, and to the communication of spiritual power which seems to have marked the transfer of precedence in the joint mission. The smiting of Elymas with blindness was the first miracle which the Apostle wrought; and miracles were the acknowledged credentials or "signs of an apostle" (2 Cor. xii. 12). At this juncture he appears to have received a special consecration to the apostleship to
149

which he had been called, "being filled with the Holy Ghost," not for the first time, but in a special sense. With the divine afflatus upon him, he addressed the sorcerer with the authority of an apostle of the Lord, and with a supernatural effect. This attestation of his apostolic commission would naturally be decisive with Barnabas, and may account for the quiet assumption, with the new name, by his associate, of the leadership from this point.   S. W.

[b] See APOSTLE on the use of this title.   H.

be justified by the law of Moses." "Evidently foisted in," says Baur (p. 103), who thinks we are dealing with a mere fiction, "to prevent the speech from appearing too Petrine, and to give it a slightly Pauline air." Certainly, it sounds like an echo of the epistles to the Romans and Galatians. But is there therefore the slightest incongruity between this and the other parts of the address? Does not that "forgiveness of sins" which St. Peter and St. Paul proclaimed with the most perfect agreement, connect itself naturally, in the thoughts of one exercised by the law as Saul of Tarsus had been, with justification not by the law but by grace? If we suppose that Saul had accepted just the faith which the older Apostles held in Jesus of Nazareth, the Messiah of the Jews, crucified and raised from the dead according to the teaching of the prophets, and in the remission of sins through him confirmed by the gift of the Holy Ghost; and that he had also had those experiences, not known to the older Apostles, of which we see the working in the epistles to the Romans and the Galatians; this speech, in all its parts, is precisely what we might expect; this is the very teaching which the Apostle of the Gentiles must have everywhere and always set forth, when he was speaking "God's word" for the first time to an assembly of his fellow-countrymen.

The discourse thus epitomized produced a strong impression; and the hearers (not "the Gentiles")[a] requested the Apostles to repeat their message on the next Sabbath. During the week so much interest was excited by the teaching of the Apostles, that on the Sabbath day "almost the whole city came together, to hear the word of God." It was this concern of the Gentiles which appears to have first alienated the minds of the Jews from what they had heard. They were filled with envy. They probably felt that there was a difference between those efforts to gain Gentile proselytes in which they had themselves been so successful, and this new preaching of a Messiah in whom a justification which the Law could not give was offered to men. The eagerness of the Gentiles to hear may have confirmed their instinctive apprehensions. The Jewish envy once roused became a power of deadly hostility to the Gospel; and these Jews at Antioch set themselves to oppose bitterly the words which Paul spoke. We have here, therefore, a new phase in the history of the Gospel. In these foreign countries it is not the Cross or Nazareth which is most immediately repulsive to the Jews in the proclaiming of Jesus. It is the wound given to Jewish importance in the association of Gentiles with Jews as the receivers of the good tidings. If the Gentiles had been asked to become Jews, no offense would have been taken. But the proclamation of the Christ could not be thus governed and restrained. It overleaped, by its own force, these narrowing methods. It was felt to be addressed not to one nation only, but to mankind.

The new opposition brought out new action on the part of the Apostles. Rejected by the Jews, they became bold and outspoken, and turned from them to the Gentiles. They remembered and declared what the prophets had foretold of the enlightening and deliverance of the whole world.

In speaking to the Gentiles, therefore, they were simply fulfilling the promise of the Covenant. The gift, we observe, of which the Jews were depriving themselves, and which the Gentiles who believed were accepting, is described as "eternal life" (ἡ αἰώνιος ζωή). It was the life of which the risen Jesus was the fountain, which Peter and John had declared at Jerusalem, and of which all acts of healing were set forth as signs. This was now poured out largely upon the Gentiles. The word of the Lord was published widely, and had much fruit. Henceforth, Paul and Barnabas knew it to be their commission, — not the less to present their message to Jews first; but in the absence of an adequate Jewish medium to deal directly with the Gentiles. But this expansion of the Gospel work brought with it new difficulties and dangers. At Antioch now, as in every city afterwards, the unbelieving Jews used their influence with their own adherents among the Gentiles, and especially the women of the higher class,[b] to persuade the authorities or the populace to persecute the Apostles, and to drive them from the place.

With their own spirits raised, and amidst much enthusiasm of their disciples, Paul and Barnabas now travelled on to Iconium, where the occurrences at Antioch were repeated, and from thence to the Lycaonian country which contained the cities Lystra and Derbe. Here they had to deal with uncivilized heathens. At Lystra the healing of a cripple took place, the narrative of which runs very parallel to the account of the similar act done by Peter and John at the gate of the Temple. The agreement becomes closer, if we insert here, with Lachmann, before "Stand upright on thy feet," the words "I say unto thee in the name of the Lord Jesus Christ." The parallel leads us to observe more distinctly that every messenger of Jesus Christ was a herald of life. The spiritual life — the ζωὴ αἰώνιος — which was of faith, is illustrated and expounded by the invigoration of impotent limbs. The same truth was to be conveyed to the inhabitants of Jerusalem and to the heathens of Lycaonia. The act was received naturally by these pagans. They took the Apostles for gods, calling Barnabas, who was of the more imposing presence, Zeus (Jupiter), and Paul, who was the chief speaker, Hermes (Mercurius). This mistake, followed up by the attempt to offer sacrifices to them, gives occasion to the recording of an address, in which we see a type of what the Apostles would say to an ignorant pagan audience. [LYSTRA, Amer. ed.] Appeals to the Scriptures, references to the God of Abraham and Isaac and Jacob, would have been out of place. The Apostles name the Living God, who made heaven and earth and the sea and all things therein, the God of the whole world and all the nations in it. They declare themselves to be his messengers. They expatiate upon the tokens of Himself which the Father of men had not withheld, in that He did them good, sending rain from heaven and fruitful seasons, the supporters of life and joy. They protest that in restoring the cripple they had only acted as instruments of the Living God. They themselves were not gods but human beings of like passions with the Lycaonians. The Living God was now mani-

a * The best copies omit τὰ ἔθνη after παρεκάλουν.   H.

b * These women of the higher class were Gentile women who had embraced Judaism, and could be easily excited against a sect who were represented to them by the crafty Jews as hostile to their faith. (See Acts xiii. 50, and xvii. 4.)   E.

festing Himself more clearly to men, desiring that henceforth the nations should not walk in their own ways, but his. They therefore call upon the people to give up the vanities of idol worship, and to turn to the Living God (comp. 1 Thess. i. 9, 10). In this address, the name of Jesus does not occur. It is easy to understand that the Apostles preached Him as the Son of that Living God to whom they bore witness, telling the people of his death and resurrection, and announcing his coming again.

Although the people of Lystra had been so ready to worship Paul and Barnabas, the repulse of their idolatrous instincts appears to have provoked them, and they allowed themselves to be persuaded into hostility by Jews who came from Antioch and Iconium, so that they attacked Paul with stones, and thought they had killed him. He recovered, however, as the disciples were standing round him, and went again into the city. The next day he left it with Barnabas, and went to Derbe, and thence they returned once more to Lystra, and so to Iconium and Antioch, renewing their exhortations to the disciples, bidding them not to think their trials strange, but to recognize them as the appointed door through which the kingdom of Heaven, into which they were called, was to be entered. In order to establish the churches after their departure, they solemnly appointed "elders" in every city. Then they came down to the coast, and from Attalia they sailed home to Antioch in Syria, where they related the successes which had been granted to them, and especially the "opening of the door of faith to the Gentiles." And so the First Missionary Journey ended.

The Council at Jerusalem. (Acts xv. Galatians ii.) — Upon that missionary journey follows most naturally the next important scene which the historian sets before us, — the council held at Jerusalem to determine the relations of Gentile believers to the Law of Moses. In following this portion of the history, we encounter two of the greater questions which the biographer of St. Paul has to consider. One of these is historical, What were the relations between the Apostle Paul and the Twelve? The other is critical, How is Galatians ii. to be connected with the narrative of the Acts?

The relations of St. Paul and the Twelve will best be set forth in the narrative. But we must explain here why we accept St. Paul's statements in the Galatian epistle as additional to the history in Acts xv. The *first* impression of any reader would be a supposition that the two writers might be referring to the same event. The one would at least bring the other to his mind. In both he reads of Paul and Barnabas going up to Jerusalem, reporting the Gospel preached to the uncircumcised, and discussing with the older Apostles the terms to be imposed upon Gentile believers. In both the conclusion is announced, that these believers should be entirely free from the necessity of circumcision. These are main points which the narratives have in common. On looking more closely into both, the *second* impression upon the reader's mind may possibly be that of a certain incompatibility between the two. Many joints and members of the transaction as given by St. Luke, do not appear in St. Paul. Others in one or two cases are substituted.

Further, the visit to Jerusalem is the 3d mentioned in the Acts, after Saul's conversion; in Galatians it is apparently mentioned as the 2d. Supposing this sense of incompatibility to remain, the reader will go on to inquire whether the visit to Jerusalem mentioned in Galatians coincides *better* with any other mentioned in the Acts, — as the 2d (xi. 30) or the 4th (xviii. 22). He will, in all probability, conclude without hesitation that it does *not.* Another view will remain, that St. Paul refers to a visit not recorded in the Acts at all. This is a perfectly legitimate hypothesis; and it is recommended by the vigorous sense of Paley. But where are we to place the visit? The only possible place for it is some short time before the visit of ch. xv. But it can scarcely be denied, that the language of ch. xv. decidedly implies that the visit there recorded was the first paid by Paul and Barnabas to Jerusalem, after their great success in preaching the Gospel amongst the Gentiles.

We suppose the reader, therefore, to recur to his first impression. He will then have to ask himself, "Granting the considerable differences, are there after all any plain *contradictions* between the two narratives, taken to refer to the same occurrences?" The answer must be, "There are *no plain contradictions.*" And this, he will perceive, is a very weighty fact. When it is recognized, the resemblances first observed will return with renewed force to the mind.

We proceed then to combine the two narratives. Whilst Paul and Barnabas were staying at Antioch, "certain men from Judæa" came there and taught the brethren that it was necessary for the Gentile converts to be circumcised. This doctrine was vigorously opposed by the two Apostles, and it was determined that the question should be referred to the Apostles and elders at Jerusalem. Paul and Barnabas themselves, and certain others, were selected for this mission. In Gal. ii. 2, St. Paul says that he went up "by revelation" (κατ᾽ ἀποκάλυψιν), so that we are to understand him as receiving a private intimation from the Divine Spirit, as well as a public commission from the Church at Antioch.[a] On their way to Jerusalem, they announced to the brethren in Phœnicia and Samaria the conversion of the Gentiles; and the news was received with great joy. "When they were come to Jerusalem, they were received by the Church, and by the Apostles and elders, and they declared all things that God had done with them" (Acts xv. 4). St. Paul adds that he communicated his views "privately to them which were of reputation," through anxiety as to the success of his work (Gal. ii. 2). The Apostles and the Church in general, it appears, would have raised no difficulties; but certain believers who had been Pharisees thought fit to maintain the same doctrine which had caused the disturbance at Antioch. In either place, St. Paul would not give way to such teaching for a single hour (Gal. ii. 5). It became necessary, therefore, that a formal decision should be come to upon the question. The Apostles and elders came together, and there was much disputing. Arguments would be used on both sides; but when the persons of highest authority spoke, they appealed to what was stronger than argu-

structed to propose the sending of delegates to Jerusalem; or the church may have proposed the measure and Paul have been directed to approve it, and go as one of the messengers.   B

ments, — the course of *facts*, through which the will of God had been manifestly shown. St. Peter, reminding his hearers that he himself had been first employed to open the door of faith to Gentiles, points out that God had himself bestowed on the uncircumcised that which was the seal of the highest calling and fellowship in Christ, the gift of the Holy Ghost. "Why do you not acquiesce in this token of God's will? Why impose upon Gentile believers ordinances which we ourselves have found a heavy burden? Have not we Jews left off trusting in our Law, to depend only on the grace of our Lord Jesus Christ?" — Then, carrying out the same appeal to the will of God as shown in facts, Barnabas and Paul relate to the silent multitude the wonders with which God had accompanied their preaching amongst the Gentiles. After they had done, St. James, with incomparable simplicity and wisdom, binds up the testimony of recent facts with the testimony of ancient prophecy, and gives a practical judgment upon the question.

The judgment was a decisive one. The injunction that the Gentiles should abstain from pollutions of idols and from fornication explained itself. The abstinence from things strangled and from blood is desired as a concession to the customs of the Jews, who were to be found in every city, and for whom it was still right, when they had believed 'n Jesus Christ, to observe the Law. St. Paul had completely gained his point. The older Apostles, James, Cephas, and John, perceiving the grace which had been given him (his effectual Apostleship), gave to him and Barnabas the right hand of fellowship. At this point it is very important to observe precisely what was the matter at stake between the contending parties (compare Prof. Jowett on "St. Paul and the Twelve," in *St. Paul's Epistles*, i. 417). St. Peter speaks of a heavy yoke; St. James of troubling the Gentile converts. But we are not to suppose that they mean merely the outward trouble of conforming to the Law of Moses. That was not what St. Paul was protesting against. The case stood thus: Circumcision and the ordinances of the Law were witnesses of a separation of the chosen race from other nations. The Jews were proud of that separation. But the Gospel of the Son of Man proclaimed that the time had come in which the separation was to be done away, and God's good-will manifested to all nations alike. It spoke of a union with God, through trust, which gave hope of a righteousness that the Law had been powerless to produce. Therefore to insist upon Gentiles being circumcised would have been to deny the Gospel of Christ. If there was to be simply an enlarging of the separated nation by the receiving of individuals into it, then the other nations of the world remained as much on the outside of God's covenant as ever. Then there was no Gospel to mankind; no justification given to men. The loss, in such a case, would have been as much to the Jew as to the Gentile. St. Paul felt this the most strongly; but St. Peter also saw that if the Jewish believers were thrown back on the Jewish law, and gave up the free and absolute grace of God, the Law became a mere burden, just as heavy to the Jew as it would be to the Gentile. The only hope for the

Jew was in a Saviour who *must be* the Saviour of mankind.

It implied therefore no difference of belief when it was agreed that Paul and Barnabas should go to the heathen, while James and Cephas and John undertook to be the Apostles of the Circumcision. St. Paul, wherever he went, was to preach "to the Jew first;" St. Peter was to preach to the Jews as free a Gospel, was to teach the admission of the Gentiles without circumcision as distinctly as St. Paul himself. The unity of the Church was to be preserved unbroken; and in order to nourish this unity the Gentiles were requested to remember their poorer brethren in Palestine (Gal. ii. 10). How zealously St. Paul cherished this beautiful witness of the common brotherhood we have seen in part already (Acts xi. 29, 30), but it is yet to appear more strikingly.

The judgment of the Church was immediately recorded in a letter addressed to the Gentile brethren in Antioch and Syria and Cilicia. That this letter might carry greater authority it was intrusted to "chosen men of the Jerusalem Church, Judas surnamed Barsabas, and Silas, chief men among the brethren." The letter speaks affectionately of Barnabas and Paul (with the elder Church Barnabas still retained the precedence, xv. 12, 25) as "men who have hazarded their lives for the name of our Lord Jesus Christ." So Judas and Silas come down with Paul and Barnabas to Antioch, and comfort the Church there with their message, and when Judas returned "it pleased Silas to abide there still."

/ It is usual to connect with this period of the history that rebuke of St. Peter which St. Paul records in Gal. ii. 11-14. The connection of subject makes it convenient to record the incident in this place, although it is possible that it took place before the meeting at Jerusalem, and perhaps most probable [a] that it did not occur till later, when St. Paul returned from his long tour in Greece to Antioch (Acts xviii. 22, 23). St. Peter was at Antioch, and had shown no scruple about "eating with the Gentiles," until "certain came from James." These Jerusalem Christians brought their Jewish exclusiveness with them, and St. Peter's weaker and more timid mood came upon him, and through fear of his stricter friends he too began to withdraw himself from his former free association with the Gentiles. Such an example had a dangerous weight, and Barnabas and the other Jews at Antioch were being seduced by it. It was an occasion for the intrepid faithfulness of St. Paul. He did not conceal his anger at such weak dissembling, and he publicly remonstrated with his elder fellow-Apostle. "If thou, being a Jew, livest after the manner of Gentiles, and not as do the Jews, why compellest thou the Gentiles to live as do the Jews?" (Gal. ii. 14). St. Peter had abandoned the Jewish exclusiveness, and deliberately claimed common ground with the Gentile: why should he, by separating himself from the uncircumcised, require the Gentiles to qualify themselves for full communion by accepting circumcision? This "withstanding" of St. Peter was no opposition of Pauline to Petrine views; it was a faithful rebuke of blamable moral weakness.[b]

---

[a] The presence of St. Peter, and the growth of Jewish prejudice, are more easily accounted for if we suppose St. Paul to have left Antioch for a long time.

[b] An interval of a year or a year and a half only could have elapsed between Paul's return to Antioch from the council at Jerusalem, and his departure on his second missionary tour, as the best chronologists

Second Missionary Journey. — The most resolute courage, indeed, was required for the work to which St. Paul was now publicly pledged. He would not associate with himself in that work one who had already shown a want of constancy. This was the occasion of what must have been a most painful difference between him and his comrade in the faith and in past perils, Barnabas. After remaining awhile at Antioch, Paul proposed to Barnabas to revisit the brethren in the countries of their former journey. Hereupon Barnabas desired that his nephew John Mark should go with them. But John had deserted them in Pamphylia, and St. Paul would not try him again. "And the contention was so sharp between them that they departed asunder one from the other; and so Barnabas took Mark, and sailed unto Cyprus; and Paul chose Silas, and departed." Silas, or Silvanus, becomes now a chief companion of the Apostle. The two went together through Syria and Cilicia, visiting the churches, and so came to Derbe and Lystra. Here they find Timotheus, who had become a disciple on the former visit of the Apostle, and who so attracted the esteem and love of St. Paul, that "he would have him go forth with him." Him St. Paul took and circumcised. If this fact had been omitted here and stated in another narrative, how utterly irreconcilable it would have been, in the eyes of some critics, with the history in the Acts! Paul and Silas were actually delivering the Jerusalem decree to all the churches they visited. They were no doubt triumphing in the freedom secured to the Gentiles. Yet at this very time our Apostle had the wisdom and largeness of heart to consult the feelings of the Jews by circumcising Timothy. There were many Jews in those parts, who knew that Timothy's father was a Greek, his mother a Jewess. That St. Paul should have had, as a chief companion, one who was uncircumcised, would of itself have been a hindrance to him in preaching to Jews; but it would have been a still greater stumbling block if that companion were half a Jew by birth, and had professed the Jewish faith. Therefore in this case St. Paul "became unto the Jews as a Jew that he might gain the Jews."

St. Luke now steps rapidly over a considerable space of the Apostle's life and labors. "They went throughout Phrygia and the region of Galatia" (xvi. 6). At this time St. Paul was founding "the churches of Galatia" (Gal. i. 2). He himself gives us hints of the circumstances of his preaching in that region, of the reception he met with, and of the ardent, though unstable, character of the people, in the following words: "Ye know how through infirmity of the flesh (ὅτι δι' ἀσθένειαν τῆς σαρκὸς) I preached the Gospel unto you at the first (τὸ πρότερον), and my temptation which was in my flesh ye despised not nor rejected, but received me as an angel of God, even as Christ Jesus. Where is then the blessedness ye spake of (ὁ μακαρισμὸς [a] ὑμῶν)? for I bear you record that, if it had been possible, ye would have plucked out your own eyes, and have given them to me" (iv. 13). It is not easy to decide as to the meaning

of the words δι' ἀσθένειαν τῆς σαρκός. Undoubtedly their grammatical sense implies that "weakness of the flesh" — an illness — was the *occasion* of St. Paul's preaching in Galatia; and De Wette and Alford adhere to this interpretation, understanding St. Paul to have been detained by illness, when otherwise he would have gone rapidly through the country. On the other hand, the form and order of the words are not what we should have expected if the Apostle meant to say this; and Professor Jowett prefers to assume an inaccuracy of grammar, and to understand St. Paul as saying that it was *in* weakness of the flesh that he preached to the Galatians. In either case St. Paul must be referring to a more than ordinary pressure of that bodily infirmity which he speaks of elsewhere as detracting from the influence of his personal address. It is hopeless to attempt to determine positively what this infirmity was. But we may observe here — (1) that St. Paul's sensitiveness may have led him to exaggerate this personal disadvantage; and (2) that, whatever it was, it allowed him to go through sufferings and hardships such as few ordinary men could bear. And it certainly did not repel the Galatians; it appears rather to have excited their sympathy and warmed their affection towards the Apostle.

St. Paul at this time had not indulged the ambition of preaching his Gospel in Europe. His views were limited to the peninsula of Asia Minor. Having gone through Phrygia and Galatia he intended to visit the western coast [ASIA]; but "they were forbidden by the Holy Ghost to preach the word" there. Then, being on the borders of Mysia, they thought of going back to the northeast into Bithynia; but again "the Spirit *of Jesus* suffered them not." [b] So they passed by Mysia, and came down to Troas. Here the Spirit of Jesus, having checked them on other sides, revealed to them in what direction they were to go. St. Paul saw in a vision a man of Macedonia, who besought him, saying, "Come over into Macedonia and help us." The vision was at once accepted as a heavenly intimation; the help wanted by the Macedonians was believed to be the preaching of the Gospel. It is at this point that the historian, speaking of St. Paul's company, substitutes "we" for "they." He says nothing of himself; we can only infer that St. Luke, to whatever country he belonged, became a companion of St. Paul at Troas. It is perhaps not too arbitrary a conjecture, that the Apostle, having recently suffered in health, derived benefit from the medical skill and attendance of "the beloved physician." The party, thus reinforced, immediately set sail from Troas, touched at Samothrace, then landed on the continent at Neapolis, and from thence journeyed to Philippi. They hastened to carry the "help" that had been asked to the first considerable city in Macedonia. Philippi was no inapt representative of the western world. A Greek city, it had received a body of Roman settlers, and was politically a Colonia. We must not assume that to Saul of Tarsus, the Roman citizen, there was anything very novel or strange in the world to which he had now come.

decide; and the statement in Acts xv. 31 certainly implies that the Judaistic question was essentially laid at rest for a season. Such a reaction therefore in favor of Judaism as the conduct of Peter at Antioch (Gal. ii. 11 ff.) shows to have taken place, must have arisen later, and belongs in all probability to Acts xviii. 23. H.

[a] May not this mean "your calling *me* blessed" making me as one of the μακάριοι θεοί.

[b] "The spirit of Jesus" is the reading of all the best MSS. and critical editions (Griesb., Lachm., Tisch. Tregelles, Alford) in Acts xvi. 7.   A.

But the name of Greece must have represented very imposing ideas to the Oriental and the Jew; and we may silently imagine what it must have been to St. Paul to know that he was called to be the herald of his Master, the Crucified Jesus, in the centre of the world's highest culture, and that he was now to begin his task. He began, however, with no flourish of trumpets, but as quietly as ever, and in the old way. There were a few Jews, if not many, at Philippi; and when the Sabbath came round, the Apostolic company joined their countrymen at the place by the river-side where prayer was wont to be made. The narrative in this part is very graphic: "We sat down," says the writer (xvi. 13). "and spoke to the women who had come together." Amongst these women was a proselyte from Thyatira (σεβομένη τὸν Θεόν), named Lydia, a dealer in purple. As she listened "the Lord opened her heart" to attend to what Paul was saying. The first convert in Macedonia was but an Asiatic woman who already worshipped the God of the Jews; but she was a very earnest believer, and besought the Apostle and his friends to honor her by staying in her house. They could not resist her urgency, and during their stay at Philippi they were the guests of Lydia (ver. 40).

But a proof was given before long that the preachers of Christ were come to grapple with the powers in the spiritual world to which heathenism was then doing homage. A female slave, who brought gain to her masters by her powers of prediction when she was in the possessed state, beset Paul and his company, following them as they went to the place of prayer, and crying out, "These men are servants of the Most High God, who publish to you (or to us) the way of salvation." Paul was vexed by her cries, and addressing the spirit in the girl, he said, "I command thee in the name of Jesus Christ to come out of her." Comparing the confession of this "spirit of divination" with the analogous confessions made by evil spirits to our Lord, we see the same singular character of a true acknowledgment extorted as if by force, and rendered with a certain insolence which implied that the spirits, though subject, were not willingly subject. The cries of the slave-girl may have sounded like sneers, mimicking what she had heard from the Apostles themselves, until St. Paul's exorcism, "in the name of Jesus Christ," was seen to be effectual. Then he might be recognized as in truth a servant of the Most High God, giving an example of the salvation which he brought, in the deliverance of this poor girl herself from the spirit which degraded her.

But the girl's masters saw that now the hope of their gains was gone. Here at Philippi, as afterwards at Ephesus, the local trade in religion began to suffer from the manifestation of the Spirit of Christ, and an interested appeal was made to local and national feelings against the dangerous innovations of the Jewish strangers. Paul and Silas were dragged before the magistrates, the multitude clamoring loudly against them, upon the vague charge of "troubling the city," and introducing observances which were unlawful for Romans. If the magistrates had desired to act justly they might

have doubted how they ought to deal with the charge. On the one hand Paul and Silas had abstained carefully, as the preachers of Christ always did, from disturbing public order, and had as yet violated no express law of the state. But on the other hand, the preaching of Jesus as King and Lord was unquestionably revolutionary, and aggressive upon the public religion, in its effects; and the Roman law was decided, in general terms, against such innovations (see reff. in Conyb. and Hows. i. 324). But the praetors or duumviri of Philippi were very unworthy representatives of the Roman magistracy. They yielded without inquiry to the clamor of the inhabitants, caused the clothes of Paul and Silas to be torn from them, and themselves to be beaten, and then committed them to prison. The jailer, having received their commands, "thrust them into the inner prison, and made their feet fast in the stocks." This cruel wrong was to be the occasion of a signal appearance of the God of righteousness and deliverance. It was to be seen which were the true servants of such a God, the magistrates or these strangers. In the night Paul and Silas, sore and sleepless, but putting their trust in God, prayed and sang praises so loudly that the other prisoners could hear them. Then suddenly the ground beneath them was shaken, the doors were opened, and every prisoner's bands were struck off (compare the similar openings of prison-doors in xii. 6–10, and v. 19). The jailer awoke and sprang up, saw with consternation that the prison-doors were open, and, concluding that the prisoners were all fled, drew his sword to kill himself. But Paul called to him loudly, "Do thyself no harm; we are all here." The jailer's fears were then changed to an overwhelming awe. What could this be? He called for lights, sprang in and fell trembling before the feet of Paul and Silas. Bringing them out from the inner dungeon, he exclaimed, "Sirs, what must I do to be saved?" (τί με δεῖ ποιεῖν ἵνα σωθῶ;). They answered, "Believe in the Lord Jesus Christ, and thou shalt be saved, and thy house." And they went on to speak to him and to all in his house "the word of the Lord." The kindness he now showed them reminds us of their miseries. He washed their wounds, took them into his own house, and spread a table before them. The same night he received baptism, "he and all his" (including slaves[a]), and rejoiced in his new-found faith in God.

In the morning the magistrates, either having heard of what had happened, or having repented of their injustice, or having done all they meant to do by way of pacifying the multitude, sent word to the prison that the men might be let go. But legal justice was to be more clearly vindicated in the persons of these men, who had been charged with subverting public order. St. Paul denounced plainly the unlawful acts of the magistrates, informing them moreover that those whom they had beaten and imprisoned without trial were Roman citizens. "And now do they thrust us out privily? Nay, verily, but let them come themselves and fetch us out." The magistrates, in great alarm, saw the necessity of humbling themselves ("Facinus est vinciri civem Romanum, scelus verberari," Cicero, in Verrem, v. 66). They came and begged

---

[a] * That is, if there were slaves in the family who believed. Luke's account limits the baptism to those in the jailer's household who, like the jailer, heard the word of the Lord spoken by Paul and Silas

(ἐλάλησαν αὐτῷ . . . σὺν πᾶσι τοῖς ἐν τῇ οἰκίᾳ αὐτοῦ), and like him received it and rejoiced in it (ἠγαλλιάσατο πανοικί). See especially Mayer and Lechler in loc.   H.

them to leave the city. Paul and Silas consented to do so, and, after paying a visit to "the brethren" in the house of Lydia, they departed.

The Church thus founded at Philippi, as the first-fruits of the Gospel in Europe, was called, as we have seen, in the name of a spiritual deliverer, of a God of justice, and of an equal Lord of freemen and slaves. That a warm and generous feeling distinguished it from the first, we learn from a testimony of St. Paul in the epistle written long after to this Church. "In the beginning of the Gospel," as soon as he left them, they began to send him gifts, some of which reached him at Thessalonica, others afterwards (Phil. iv. 15, 16). Their partnership in the Gospel (κοινωνία εἰς τὸ εὐαγγέλιον) had gladdened the Apostle from the first day (Phil. i. 5).

Leaving St. Luke, and perhaps Timothy for a short time, at Philippi, Paul and Silas travelled through Amphipolis and Apollonia, and stopped again at Thessalonica. At this important city there was a synagogue of the Jews. True to his custom, St. Paul went in to them, and for three Sabbath-days proclaimed Jesus to be the Christ, as he would have done in a city of Judæa. As usual, the proselytes were those who heard him most gladly, and among them were many women of station. Again, as in Pisidian Antioch, the envy of the Jews was excited. They contrived to stir up the lower class of the city to tumultuary violence by representing the preachers of Christ as revolutionary disturbers, who had come to proclaim one Jesus as king instead of Cæsar. The mob assaulted the house of Jason, with whom Paul and Silas were staying as guests, and, not finding them, dragged Jason himself and some other brethren before the magistrates. In this case the magistrates, we are told, and the people generally, were "troubled" by the rumors and accusations which they heard. But they seem to have acted wisely and justly, in taking security of Jason and the rest, and letting them go. After these signs of danger the brethren immediately sent away Paul and Silas by night.

The epistles to the Thessalonians were written very soon after the Apostle's visit, and contain more particulars of his work in founding that Church than we find in any other epistle. The whole of these letters ought to be read for the information they thus supply. St. Paul speaks to the Thessalonian Christians as being mostly Gentiles. He reminds them that they had turned from idols to serve the living and true God, and to wait for his Son from heaven, whom He raised from the dead, "Jesus who delivers us from the coming wrath" (1 Thess. i. 9, 10). The Apostle had evidently spoken much of the coming and presence of the Lord Jesus Christ, and of that wrath which was already descending upon the Jews (ii. 16, 19, &c.). His message had had a wonderful power amongst them, because they had known it to be really the word of a God who also wrought in them, having had helps towards this conviction in the zeal and disinterestedness and affection with which St. Paul (notwithstanding his recent shameful treatment at Philippi) proclaimed his Gospel amongst them (ii. 2, 8–13). He had purposely wrought with his own hands, even night and day, that his disinterestedness might be more apparent (1 Thess. ii. 9; 2 Thess. iii. 8). He exhorted them not to be drawn away from patient industry by the hopes of the kingdom into which

they were called, but to work quietly, and to cultivate purity and brotherly love (1 Thess. iv. 3, 9, 11). Connecting these allusions with the preaching in the synagogue (Acts xvii. 3), we see clearly how the teaching of St. Paul turned upon the person of Jesus Christ as the Son of the living God, prophesied of in the Scriptures, suffering and dying, raised up and exalted to a kingdom, and about to appear as the Giver of light and life, to the destruction of his enemies and the saving of those who trusted in him.

When Paul and Silas left Thessalonica they came to Berœa. Here they found the Jews more noble (εὐγενέστεροι) — more disposed to receive the news of a rejected and crucified Messiah, and to examine the Scriptures with candor — than those at Thessalonica had been. Accordingly they gained many converts, both Jews and Greeks; but the Jews of Thessalonica, hearing of it, sent emissaries to stir up the people, and it was thought best that St. Paul should himself leave the city, whilst Silas and Timothy remained behind. Some of "the brethren" went with St. Paul as far as Athens, where they left him, carrying back a request to Silas and Timothy that they would speedily join him. He apparently did not like to preach alone, and intended to rest from his apostolic labor until they should come up to him; but how could he refrain himself, with all that was going on at Athens round him? There he witnessed the most profuse idolatry side by side with the most pretentious philosophy. Either of these would have been enough to stimulate his spirit. To idolaters and philosophers he felt equally urged to proclaim his Master and the living God. So he went to his own countrymen and the proselytes in the synagogue and declared to them that the Messiah had come; but he also spoke, like another Socrates, with people in the market, and with the followers of the two great schools of philosophy, Epicureans and Stoics, naming to all Jesus and the Resurrection. The philosophers encountered him with a mixture of curiosity and contempt. The Epicurean, teaching himself to seek for tranquil enjoyment as the chief object of life, heard of One claiming to be the Lord of men, who had shown them the glory of dying to self, and had promised to those who fought the good fight bravely a nobler bliss than the comforts of life could yield. The Stoic, cultivating a stern and isolated moral independence, heard of One whose own righteousness was proved by submission to the Father in heaven, and who had promised to give his righteousness to those who trusted not in themselves but in Him. To all, the announcement of a Person was much stranger than the publishing of any theories would have been. So far as they thought the preacher anything but a silly trifler, he seemed to them, not a philosopher, but "a setter forth of strange gods" (ξένων δαιμονίων καταγγελεύς). But any one with a novelty was welcome to those who "spent their time in nothing else but either to hear or to tell some new thing." They brought him therefore to the Areopagus, that he might make a formal exposition of his doctrine to an assembled audience.

We are not to think here of the Council or Court, renowned in the oldest Athenian history, which took its name from Mars' Hill, but only of the elevated spot where the council met, not covered in, but arranged with benches and steps of stone so as to form a convenient place for a public address. Here the Apostle delivered that wonderful

PAUL

discourse, reported in Acts xvii. 22–31, which seems as fresh and instructive for the intellect of the 19th century as it was for the intellect of the first. In this we have the Pauline Gospel as it addressed itself to the speculative mind of the cultivated Greeks. How the "report" was obtained by the writer of the history we have no means of knowing. Possibly we have in it notes written down before or after the delivery of this address by St. Paul himself. Short as it is, the form is as perfect as the matter is rich. The loftiness and breadth of the theology, the dignity and delicacy of the argument, the absence of self, the straightforward and reverent nature of the testimony delivered — all the characteristics so strikingly displayed in this speech, — help us to understand what kind of a teacher had now appeared in the Grecian world. St. Paul, it is well understood, did not begin with calling the Athenians "too superstitious." "I perceive you," he said, "to be eminently religious." [a] He had observed an altar inscribed Ἀγνώστῳ Θεῷ, "To the unknown God." [b] It meant, no doubt, "To some unknown God." "I come," he said "as the messenger of that unknown God." And then he proceeds to speak of God in terms which were not altogether new to Grecian ears. They had heard of a God who had made the world and all things therein, and even of One who gave to all life, and breath, and all things. But they had never learnt the next lesson which was now taught them. It was a special truth of the new dispensation, that "God had made of one blood all nations of men, for to dwell on all the face of the earth, having determined the times assigned to them, and the bounds of their habitation, that they should seek the Lord, if haply they might feel after him and find him." [MARS' HILL, Amer. ed.]

Comparing it with the teaching given to other audiences, we perceive that it laid hold of the deepest convictions which had ever been given to Greeks, whilst at the same time it encountered the strongest prejudices of Greeks. We see, as at Lystra, that an apostle of Christ had no need to refer to the Jewish Scriptures, when he spoke to those who had not received them. He could speak to men as God's children, and subjects of God's educating discipline, and was only bringing them further tidings of Him whom they had been always feeling after. He presented to them the Son of Man as acting in the power of Him who had made all nations, and who was not far from any single man. He began to speak of Him as risen from the dead, and of the power of a new life which was in Him for men; but his audience would not hear of Him who thus claimed their personal allegiance. Some mocked, others more courteously, talked of hearing him again another time. The Apostle gained but few converts at Athens, and he soon took his departure and came to Corinth.

Athens still retained its old intellectual predominance; but Corinth was the political and commercial capital of Greece. It was in places of living activity that St. Paul labored longest and most

successfully, as formerly at Antioch, now at Corinth, and afterwards at Ephesus. The rapid spread of the Gospel was obviously promoted by the preaching of it in cities where men were continually coming and going; but besides this consideration, we may be sure that the Apostle escaped gladly from dull ignorance on the one side, and from philosophical dilettantism on the other, to places in which the real business of the world was being done. The Gospel, though unworldly, was yet a message to practical and inquiring men and it had more affinity to *work* of any kind than to torpor or to intellectual frivolity. One proof of the wholesome agreement between the following of Christ and ordinary labor was given by St. Paul himself during his stay at Corinth. Here, as at Thessalonica, he chose to earn his own subsistence by working at his trade of tent-making. This trade brought him into close connection with two persons who became distinguished as believers in Christ, Aquila and Priscilla. They were Jews, and had lately left Rome, in consequence of an edict of Claudius [see CLAUDIUS]; and as they also were tent-makers, St. Paul "abode with them and wrought." Laboring thus on the six days, the Apostle went to the synagogue on the Sabbath, and there by expounding the Scriptures sought to win both Jews and proselytes to the belief that Jesus was the Christ.

He was testifying with unusual effort and anxiety (συνείχετο τῷ λόγῳ), when Silas and Timothy came from Macedonia, and joined him. We are left in some uncertainty as to what the movements of Silas and Timothy had been, since they were with Paul at Beroea. From the statements in the Acts (xvii. 15, 16) that Paul, when he reached Athens, desired Silas and Timotheus to come to him *with all speed*, and *waited for them* there, compared with those in 1 Thess. (iii. 1, 2), "When we could no longer forbear, we thought it good to be left at Athens alone, and sent Timotheus, our brother, and minister of God, and our fellow-laborer in the Gospel of Christ, to establish you and to comfort you concerning your faith," — Paley (*Horæ Paulinæ*, 1 Thess. No. iv.) reasonably argues that Silas and Timothy had come to Athens, but had soon been dispatched thence, Timothy to Thessalonica, and Silas to Philippi, or elsewhere. From Macedonia they came together, or about the same time, to Corinth; and their arrival was the occasion of the writing of the First Epistle to the Thessalonians.

This is the first [c] extant example of that work by which the Apostle Paul has served the Church of all ages in as eminent a degree as he labored at the founding of it in his lifetime. All commentators upon the New Testament have been accustomed to notice the points of coincidence between the history in the Acts, and these Letters. Paley's *Horæ Paulinæ* is famous as a special work upon this subject. But more recently, important attempts have been made to estimate the Epistles of St. Paul more broadly, by considering them in their mutual order and relations, and in their bearing upon the question of the development of the writer's teach-

a See, in confirmation, passages quoted from ancient authors in Conybeare and Howson, i. 369, &c.

b • No doubt Θεῷ, as of the nature of a proper name, may be definite without the article; but it is more naturally indefinite here, the conception being that of a God dimly revealed to their consciousness, in addition to all the gods, so called, acknowledged by them.   H.

c Ewald believes, rather capriciously, that the Second Ep. to the Thess. was written *first*, and was sent from Beroea (*Die Sendschreiben des Apostels Paulus*, pp. 17, 18).

ing. Such attempts [a] must lead to a better understanding of the epistles themselves, and to a finer appreciation of the Apostle's nature and work. It is notorious that the order of the epistles in the book of the N. T. is not their real, or chronological order. The mere placing of them in their true sequence throws considerable light upon the history; and happily the time of composition of the more important epistles can be stated with sufficient certainty. The two epistles to the Thessalonians belong — and these alone — to the present Missionary Journey. The epistles to the Galatians, Romans, and Corinthians, were written during the next journey. Those to Philemon, the Colossians, the Ephesians, and the Philippians, belong to the captivity at Rome. With regard to the Pastoral Epistles, there are considerable difficulties, which require to be discussed separately.

Two general remarks relating to St. Paul's letters may find a place here. (1.) There is no reason to assume that the extant letters are all that the Apostle wrote. On the contrary, there is a strong presumption, and some slight positive evidence, that he wrote many which have not been preserved (Jowett, i. p. 195-201, 2d ed.). (2.) We must be on our guard against concluding too much from the contents and style of any epistle, as to the fixed bent of the Apostle's whole mind at the time when it was written. We must remember that the epistles to the Thessalonians were written whilst St. Paul was deeply absorbed in the peculiar circumstances of the Corinthian Church; and that the epistles to the Corinthians were written *between* those to the Galatians and the Romans. These facts are sufficient to remind us of the *versatility* of the Apostle's mind; — to show us how thoroughly the feelings and ideas suggested to him by the circumstances upon which he was dwelling had the power to mould his utterances.

The *First* Epistle to the Thessalonians was probably written soon after his arrival at Corinth, and before he turned from the Jews to the Gentiles. It was drawn from St. Paul by the arrival of Silas and Timothy. [THESSALONIANS, FIRST EPISTLE TO THE.] The largest portion of it consists of an impassioned recalling of the facts and feelings of the time when the Apostle was personally with them. But we perceive gradually that those expectations which he had taught them to entertain of the appearing and presence of the Lord Jesus Christ had undergone some corruption. There were symptoms in the Thessalonian church of a restlessness which speculated on the times and seasons of the future, and found present duties flat and unimportant. This evil tendency St. Paul seeks to correct, by reviving the first spirit of faith and hope and mutual fellowship, and by setting forth the appearing of Jesus Christ — not indeed as distant, but as the full shining of a day of which all believers in Christ were already children. The ethical characteristics apparent in this letter, the degree in which St. Paul identified himself with his friends, the entire surrender of his existence to his calling as a preacher of Christ, his anxiety for the good fame and wellbeing of his converts, are the same which will reappear continually. What interval of time separated the Second Letter to the Thessalonians from the First, we have no means of judging, except that the later one was certainly written before St.

Paul's departure from Corinth. [THESSALONIANS, SECOND EPISTLE TO THE.] The Thessalonians had been disturbed by announcements that those convulsions of the world which all Christians were taught to associate with the coming of Christ were immediately impending. To meet these assertions, St. Paul delivers express predictions in a manner not usual with him elsewhere; and whilst reaffirming all he had ever taught the Thessalonians to believe respecting the early coming of the Saviour and the blessedness of waiting patiently for it, he informs them that certain events, of which he had spoken to them, must run their course before the full manifestation of Jesus Christ could come to pass. At the end of this epistle St. Paul guards the Thessalonians against pretended letters from him, by telling them that every genuine letter, even if not written by his hand throughout, would have at least an autograph salutation at the close of it.

We return now to the Apostle's preaching at Corinth. When Silas and Timotheus came, he was testifying to the Jews with great earnestness, but with little success. So "when they opposed themselves and blasphemed, he shook out his raiment," and said to them, in words of warning taken from their own prophets (Ez. xxxiii. 4): "Your blood be upon your own heads; I am clean, and henceforth will go to the Gentiles." The experience of Pisidian Antioch was repeating itself. The Apostle went, as he threatened, to the Gentiles, and began to preach in the house of a proselyte named Justus. Already one distinguished Jew had become a believer, Crispus, the ruler of the synagogue, mentioned (1 Cor. i. 14) as baptized by the Apostle himself; and many of the Gentile inhabitants were receiving the Gospel and being baptized. The envy and rage of the Jews, therefore, were excited in an unusual degree, and seem to have pressed upon the spirit of St. Paul. He was therefore encouraged by a vision of the Lord, who appeared to him by night, and said, "Be not afraid, but speak, and hold not thy peace; for I am with thee, and no man shall set on thee, to hurt thee; for I have much people in this city." Corinth was to be an important seat of the Church of Christ, distinguished, not only by the number of believers, but also by the variety and the fruitfulness of the teaching to be given there. At this time St. Paul himself stayed there for a year and six months, "teaching the word of God amongst them."

Corinth was the chief city of the province of Achaia, and the residence of the proconsul. During St. Paul's stay, we find the proconsular office held by Gallio, a brother of the philosopher Seneca. [GALLIO.] Before him the Apostle was summoned by his Jewish enemies, who hoped to bring the Roman authority to bear upon him as an innovator in religion. But Gallio perceived at once, before Paul could "open his mouth" to defend himself, that the movement was due to Jewish prejudice, and refused to go into the question. "If it be a question of words and names and of your law," he said to the Jews, speaking with the tolerance of a Roman magistrate, "look ye to it; for I will be no judge of such matters." Then a singular scene occurred. The Corinthian spectators, either favoring St. Paul, or actuated only by anger against the Jews, seized on the principal person of those who

[a] Amongst these, the works of Prof. Jowett (*Epistles to the Thess., Gal., and Rom.*), of Ewald (*Die Sendschreiben*, etc.), and of Dr. Wordsworth (*Epistles of St. Paul*), may be named.

had brought the charge, and beat him before the judgment-seat. (See on the other hand Ewald, *Geschichte*, vi. 463-466.) Gallio left these religious quarrels to settle themselves. The Apostle therefore was not allowed to be "hurt," and remained some time longer at Corinth unmolested.

We do not gather from the subsequent epistles to the Corinthians many details of the founding of the Church at Corinth. The main body of the believers consisted of Gentiles, — (" Ye know that ye were Gentiles," 1 Cor. xii. 2). But, partly from the number who had been proselytes, partly from the mixture of Jews, it had so far a Jewish character, that St. Paul could speak of " *our* fathers " as having been under the cloud (1 Cor. x. 1). The tendency to intellectual display, and the traffic of sophists in philosophical theories, which prevailed at Corinth, made the Apostle more than usually anxious to be independent in his life and simple in bearing his witness. He wrought for his living that he might not appear to be taking *fees* of his pupils (1 Cor. ix. 18); and he put the Person of Jesus Christ, crucified and risen, in the place of all doctrines (1 Cor. ii. 1-5, xv. 3, 4). What gave infinite significance to his simple statements, was the nature of the Christ who had been crucified, and his relation to men. Concerning these mysteries St. Paul had uttered a wisdom, not of the world, but of God, which had commended itself chiefly to the humble and simple. Of these God had chosen and called not a few " into the fellowship of His Son Jesus Christ the Lord of men " (1 Cor. ii. 6, 7, i. 27, 9).

Having been the instrument of accomplishing this work, St. Paul took his departure for Jerusalem, wishing to attend a festival there. Before leaving Greece, he cut off his hair [a] at Cenchreæ, in fulfillment of a vow. We are not told where or why he had made the vow; and there is considerable difficulty in reconciling this act with the received customs of the Jews. [VOWS.] A passage in Josephus, if rightly understood (*B. J.* ii. 15, § 1), mentions a vow which included, besides a sacrifice, the cutting of the hair and the beginning of an abstinence from wine 30 days before the sacrifice. If St. Paul's was such a vow, he was going to offer up a sacrifice in the Temple at Jerusalem, and the " shearing of his head " was a preliminary to the sacrifice. The *principle* of the vow, whatever it was, must have been the same as that of the Nazarite vow, which St. Paul afterwards countenanced at Jerusalem. [NAZARITE, p. 2075 a.] There is therefore no difficulty in supposing him to have followed in this instance, for some reason not explained to us, a custom of his countrymen. — When he sailed from the Isthmus, Aquila and Priscilla went with him as far as Ephesus. Paul paid a visit to the synagogue at Ephesus, but would not stay. He was anxious to be at Jerusalem for the approaching feast, but he promised, God willing, to return to them again. Leaving Ephesus, he sailed to Cæsarea, and from thence went up to Jerusalem, and "saluted the Church." It is argued (Wieseler, pp. 48-50), from considerations founded on the suspension of navigation during the winter months, that the festival was probably the Pentecost. From Jerusalem, almost immediately, the Apostle went down to An-

tioch, thus returning to the same place from which he had started with Silas.

Third Missionary Journey, including the stay at Ephesus (Acts xviii. 23-xxi. 17). — Without inventing facts or discussions for which we have no authority, we may connect with this short visit of St. Paul to Jerusalem a very serious raising of the whole question, What was to be the relation of the new kingdom of Christ to the law and covenant of the Jews? Such a Church as that at Corinth, with its affiliated communities, composed chiefly of Gentile members, appeared likely to overshadow by its importance the Mother Church in Judæa. The jealousy of the more Judaical believers, not extinguished by the decision of the council at Jerusalem, began now to show itself everywhere in the form of an active and intriguing party-spirit. This disastrous movement could not indeed alienate the heart of St. Paul from the Law or the calling or the people of his fathers — his antagonism is never directed against these; but it drew him into the great conflict of the next period of his life, and must have been a sore trial to the intense loyalty of his nature. To vindicate the *freedom*, as regarded the Jewish Law, of believers in Christ; but to do this, for the very sake of maintaining *the unity of the Church*; — was to be the earnest labor of the Apostle for some years. In thus laboring he was carrying out completely the principles laid down by the elder Apostles at Jerusalem; and may we not believe that, in deep sorrow at appearing, even, to disparage the Law and the covenant, he was the more anxious to prove his fellowship in spirit with the Church in Judæa, by "remembering the poor," as " James, Cephas, and John " had desired that he would? (Gal. ii. 10). The prominence given, during the journeys upon which we are now entering, to the collection to be made amongst his churches for the benefit of the poor at Jerusalem, seems to indicate such an anxiety. The great epistles which belong to this period, those to the Galatians, Corinthians, and Romans, show how the " Judaizing " question exercised at this time the Apostle's mind.

St. Paul "spent some time " at Antioch, and during this stay, as we are inclined to believe, his collision with St. Peter (Gal. ii. 11-14), of which we have spoken above, took place. [See note b, vol. iii. p. 2372.] When he left Antioch, he "went over all the country of Galatia and Phrygia in order, strengthening all the disciples," and giving orders concerning the collection for the saints (1 Cor. xvi. 1). It is probable that *the Epistle to the Galatians* was written soon after this visit. [GALATIANS, EPISTLE TO THE.] When he was with them he had found the Christian communities infested by Judaizing teachers. He had "told them the truth " (Gal. iv. 16), he had warned them against the deadly tendencies of Jewish exclusiveness, and had re-affirmed the simple Gospel, concerning Jesus Christ the Son of God, which he had preached to them on his first visit (τὸ πρότερον, Gal. iv. 13). But after he left them the Judaizing doctrine raised its head again. The only course left to its advocates was to assail openly the authority of St. Paul; and this they did. They represented him as having derived his commission from the older Apostles, and as therefore acting disloyally if he opposed the views ascribed to Peter and James. The fickle minds of the Galatian Christians were influenced by these hardy assertions; and the Apostle heard, when he had come

---

[a] Acts xviii. 18. The act *may be* that of Aquila, but the historian certainly seems to be speaking not of him, but of St. Paul.

town to Ephesus, that his work in Galatia was being undone, and his converts were being seduced from the true faith in Christ. He therefore writes the epistle to remonstrate with them — an epistle full of indignation, of warning, of direct and impassioned teaching. He recalls to their minds the Gospel which he had preached amongst them, and asserts in solemn and even awful language its absolute truth (i. 8, 9). He declares that he had received it *directly from Jesus Christ the Lord*, and that his position towards the other Apostles had always been that, not of a pupil, but of an independent fellow-laborer. He sets before them Jesus the Crucified, the Son of God, as the fulfillment of the promise made to the fathers, and as the pledge and giver of freedom to men. He declares that in Him, and by the power of the Spirit of sonship sent down through Him, men have inherited the rights of adult sons of God; that the condition represented by the Law was the inferior and preparatory stage of boyhood. He then, most earnestly and tenderly, impresses upon the Galatians the responsibilities of their fellowship with Christ the Crucified, urging them to fruitfulness in all the graces of their spiritual calling, and especially to brotherly consideration and unity.

This letter was, in all probability, sent from Ephesus. This was the goal of the Apostle's journeyings through Asia Minor. He came down upon Ephesus from the upper districts (τὰ ἀνωτερικὰ μέρη) of Phrygia. What *Antioch* was for "the region of Syria and Cilicia," what *Corinth* was for Greece, what *Rome* was — we may add — for Italy and the West, that *Ephesus* was for the important province called Asia. Indeed, with reference to the spread of the Church Catholic, Ephesus occupied the central position of all. This was the meeting place of Jew, of Greek, of Roman, and of Oriental. Accordingly, the Apostle of the Gentiles was to stay a long time here, that he might found a strong Church, which should be a kind of mother-church to Christian communities in the neighboring cities of Asia.

A new element in the preparation of the world for the kingdom of Christ presents itself at the beginning of the Apostle's work at Ephesus. He finds there certain disciples (τινὰς μαθητάς) — about twelve in number, — of whom he is led to inquire, " Did ye receive the Holy Ghost when ye believed? They answered, No, we did not even hear of there being a Holy Ghost. Unto what then, asked Paul, were ye baptized? And they said, Unto John's baptism. Then said Paul, John baptized with the baptism of repentance, saying to the people that they should believe on him who was coming after him, that is, on Jesus. Hearing this, they were baptized into the name of the Lord Jesus, and when Paul had laid his hands upon them, the Holy Ghost came upon them, and they began to speak with tongues and to prophesy " (Acts, xix. 1-7). — It is obvious to compare this incident with the Apostolic act of Peter and John in Samaria, and to see in it an assertion of the full Apostolic dignity of Paul. But besides this bearing of it, we see in it indications which suggest more than they distinctly express, as to the spiritual movements of that age. These twelve disci-

ples are mentioned immediately after Apollos, who also had been at Ephesus just before St. Paul's arrival, and who had taught diligently concerning Jesus (τὰ περὶ τοῦ Ἰησοῦ), knowing only the baptism of John. But Apollos was of Alexandria, trained in the intelligent and inquiring study of the Hebrew Scriptures, which had been fostered by the Greek culture of that capital. We are led to suppose, therefore, that a knowledge of the baptism of John and of the ministry of Jesus had spread widely, and had been received with favor by some of those who knew the Scriptures most thoroughly, before the message concerning the exaltation of Jesus and the descent of the Holy Ghost had been received. What the exact belief of Apollos and these twelve " disciples " was concerning the character and work of Jesus, we have no means of knowing. But we gather that it was wanting in a recognition of the full lordship of Jesus and of the gift of the Holy Ghost. The Pentecostal faith was communicated to Apollos by Aquila and Priscilla, to the other disciples of the Baptist by St. Paul.

The Apostle now entered upon his usual work. He went into the synagogue, and for three months he spoke openly, disputing and persuading concerning " the kingdom of God." At the end of this time the obstinacy and opposition of some of the Jews led him to give up frequenting the synagogue, and he established the believers as a separate society, meeting " in the school of Tyrannus." This continued (though we may probably allow for an occasional absence of St. Paul) for two years. During this time many things occurred, of which the historian of the Acts chooses two examples, the triumph over magical arts, and the great disturbance raised by the silversmiths who made shrines for Artemis; and amongst which we are to note further the writing of the First Epistle to the Corinthians.

" God wrought special miracles," we are told (δυνάμεις οὐ τὰς τυχούσας), " by the hands of Paul." " It is evident that the arts of sorcery and magic — all those arts which betoken the belief in the presence of a spirit, but not of a Holy Spirit — were flourishing here in great luxuriance. Everything in the history of the Old or New Testament would suggest the thought that the exhibitions of *Divine* power took a more startling form where superstitions grounded mainly on the reverence for *diabolical* power were prevalent: that they were the proclamations of a beneficent and orderly government, which had been manifested to counteract and overcome one that was irregular and malevolent " (Maurice, *Unity of the New Testament*, p. 515). The powers of the new kingdom took a form more nearly resembling the wonders of the kingdom of darkness than was usually adopted, when handkerchiefs and aprons from the body of Paul (like the shadow of Peter, v. 15) were allowed to be used for the healing of the sick and the casting out of devils. But it was to be clearly seen that all was done by the healing power of the Lord Jesus Himself.[a] Certain Jews, and among them the seven sons of one Sceva (not unlike Simon Magus in Samaria), fancied that the effect was due to a magic formula, an ἐπῳδή. They therefore attempted to exorcise, by saying, " We adjure you by Jesus whom Paul preacheth." But the evil spirit, having a voice given to it, cried out, "Jesus I know, and Paul I know, but who are ye?" And the man who was possessed fell furiously upon the exorcists and drove them forth. The result of this testimony was that fear fell upon all the inhabitants of Ephesus, and the name of the Lord Jesus was magnified. And the impression produced bore striking practical fruits. The city was well known for its Ἐφέσια γράμματα, forms of incantation, which were sold at a high price. Many of those who had these books brought them together and burned them before all men, and when the cost of them was computed it was found to be 50,000 drachmæ = £1770. "So mightily grew the word of the Lord, and prevailed."

Whilst St. Paul was at Ephesus his communications with the Church in Achaia were not altogether suspended. There is strong reason to believe that a personal visit to Corinth was made by him, and a letter sent, neither of which is mentioned in the Acts. The visit is inferred from several allusions in the 2d Epistle to the Corinthians. "Behold, the third time I am ready to come to you" (2 Cor. xii. 14). "This is the third time I am coming to you" (2 Cor. xiii. 1). The visit he is contemplating is plainly that mentioned in Acts xx. 2, which took place when he finally left Ephesus. If that was the *third*, he must have paid a *second* during the time of his residence at Ephesus. It seems far-fetched, with Paley (*Horæ Paulinæ*, 2 Cor. No. xi.), to conclude that St. Paul is only affirming a *third intention*, and that the *second* intention had not been carried out. The context, in both cases, seems to refer plainly to *visits*, and not to intentions. Again, "I determined this with myself, that I would not come *again* to you *in heaviness*" (πάλιν ἐν λύπῃ): 2 Cor. ii. 1. Here St. Paul is apparently speaking of a previous visit which he had paid in sorrow of heart. He expresses an apprehension (2 Cor. xii. 21) lest "again when I come, my God should humble me among you" (μὴ πάλιν ἐλθόντος μου ταπεινώσει με — the πάλιν appearing certainly to refer to ταπεινώσει as much as to ἐλθόντος). The words in 2 Cor. xiii. 2, προείρηκα καὶ προλέγω, ὡς παρὼν τὸ δεύτερον καὶ ἀπὼν νῦν, may be translated, either "as *if* present the second time," or "as *when* present the second time." In the latter case we have here a distinct confirmation of the supposed visit. The former rendering seems at first sight to exclude it: but if we remember that the thought of his special *admonition* is occupying the Apostle's mind, we should naturally understand it, "I forewarn you now in my absence, as if I were present a second time to do it in person;" so that he would be speaking of the supposed visit as a *first*, with reference to the purpose which he has in his mind. The *primâ facie* sense of these passages implies a short visit, which we should place in the first half of the stay at Ephesus. And there are no strong reasons why we should not accept that *primâ facie* sense. St. Paul, we may imagine, heard of disorders which prevailed in the Corinthian Church. Apollos had returned to Ephesus some time before the 1st Epistle was written (1 Cor. xvi. 12), and it may have been from him that St. Paul learnt the tidings which distressed him. He was moved to go himself to see them. He stayed but a short time,

but warned them solemnly against the licentiousness which he perceived to be creeping in amongst them. If he went directly by sea to Corinth and back, this journey would not occupy much time. It was very natural, again, that this visit should be followed up by a letter. Either the Apostle's own reflections after his return, or some subsequent tidings which reached him, drew from him, it appears, a written communication in which he gave them some practical advice. "I wrote unto you in the Epistle not to keep company with fornicators" (ἔγραψα ὑμῖν ἐν τῇ ἐπιστολῇ: 1 Cor. v. 9). Then, at some point not defined in the course of the stay at Ephesus, St. Paul announced to his friends a plan of going through Macedonia and Achaia, and afterwards visiting Jerusalem; adding, "After I have been there, I must also see Rome." But he put off for a while his own departure, and sent before him Timothy and Erastus to the churches in Macedonia and Achaia, "to bring them into remembrance of his ways which were in Christ" (1 Cor. iv. 17).

Whether the First Epistle to the Corinthians was written before or after the tumult excited by Demetrius cannot be positively asserted. He makes an allusion, in that epistle, to a "battle with wild beasts" fought at Ephesus (ἐθηριομάχησα ἐν Ἐφέσῳ: 1 Cor. xv. 32), which it is usual to understand figuratively, and which is by many connected with that tumult. But this connection is arbitrary, and without much reason.[a] And as it would seem from Acts xx. 1 that St. Paul departed immediately after the tumult, it is probable that the epistle was written before, though not long before, the raising of this disturbance. Here then, while the Apostle is so earnestly occupied with the teaching of believers and inquirers at Ephesus and from the neighboring parts of "Asia," we find him throwing all his heart and soul into the concerns of the church at Corinth. [CORINTHIANS, FIRST EPISTLE TO THE.]

There were two external inducements for writing this epistle. (1.) St. Paul had received information from members of Chloe's household (ἐδηλώθη μοι ὑπὸ τῶν Χλόης, i. 11) concerning the state of the church at Corinth. (2.) That church had written him a letter, of which the bearers were Stephanas and Fortunatus and Achaicus, to ask his judgment upon various points which were submitted to him (vii. 1, xvi. 17). He had learnt that there were divisions in the church; that parties had been formed which took the names of Paul, of Apollos, of Cephas, and of Christ (i. 11, 12); and also that moral and social irregularities had begun to prevail, of which the most conspicuous and scandalous example was that a believer had taken his father's wife, without being publicly condemned by the church (v. 1, vi. 7, xi. 17-22, xiv. 33-40). To these evils we must add one doctrinal error, of those who said "that there was no resurrection of the dead" (xv. 12). It is probable that the teaching of Apollos the Alexandrian, which had been characteristic and highly successful (Acts xviii. 27, 28), had been the first occasion of the "divisions" in the church. We may take it for granted that his adherents did not form themselves into a party until he had left Corinth, and therefore that he had been some time with St. Paul at Ephesus. But after he was gone,

---

a The manner of the allusion, εἰ ἐθηριομάχησα ἐν Ἐφέσῳ, may imply, as Ewald (*Sendschreiben*, p. 214) suggests, that he had mentioned this conflict to the Corinthians in the previous non-extant letter.

the special *Alexandrian* features of his teaching were remembered by those who had delighted to hear him. Their Grecian intellect was captivated by his broader and more spiritual interpretation of the Jewish Scriptures. The connection which he taught them to perceive between the revelation made to Hebrew rulers and prophets and the wisdom by which other nations, and especially their own, had been enlightened, dwelt in their minds. That which especially occupied the Apollos school must have been *a philosophy of the Scriptures*. It was the tendency of this party which seemed to the Apostle particularly dangerous amongst the Greeks. He hardly seems to refer specially in his letter to the other parties, but we can scarcely doubt that in what he says about "the wisdom which the Greeks sought" (i. 22), he is referring not only to the general tendency of the Greek mind, but to that tendency as it had been caught and influenced by the teaching of Apollos. It gives him an occasion of delivering his most characteristic testimony. He recognizes wisdom, but it is the wisdom of God; and that wisdom was not only a Σοφία or a Λόγος through which God had always spoken to all men; it had been perfectly manifested in Jesus the crucified. Christ crucified was both the Power of God and the Wisdom of God. To receive Him required a spiritual discernment unlike the wisdom of the great men of the world; a discernment given by the Holy Spirit of God, and manifesting itself in sympathy with humiliation and in love.

For a detailed description of the epistles the reader is referred to the special articles upon each. But it belongs to the history of St. Paul to notice the personal characteristics which appear in them. We must not omit to observe therefore, in this epistle, how loyally the Apostle represents Jesus Christ the Crucified as the Lord of men, the Head of the body with many members, the Centre of Unity, the Bond of men to the Father. We should mark at the same time how invariably he connects the Power of the Spirit with the Name of the Lord Jesus. He meets all the evils of the Corinthian Church, the intellectual pride, the party spirit, the loose morality, the disregard of decency and order, the false belief about the Resurrection, by recalling their thoughts to the Person of Christ and to the Spirit of God as the breath of a common life to the whole body.

We observe also here, more than elsewhere, the *tact*, universally recognized and admired, with which the Apostle discusses the practical problems brought before him. The various questions relating to marriage (ch. vii.), the difficulty about meats offered to idols (cc. viii., x.), the behaviour proper for women (cc. xi., xiv.), the use of the gifts of prophesying and speaking with tongues (ch. xiv.), are made examples of a treatment which may be applied to all such questions. We see them all discussed with reference to first principles; the object, in every practical conclusion, being to guard and assert some permanent principle. We see St. Paul no less a lover of order and subordination than of freedom. We see him claiming for himself, and prescribing to others, great variety of conduct in varying circumstances, but under the strict obligation of being always true to Christ, and always seeking the highest good of men. Such a character, so steadfast in motive and aim, so versatile in action, it would be difficult indeed to find elsewhere in history.

What St. Paul here tells us of his own doings and movements refers chiefly to the nature of his preaching at Corinth (cc. i., ii.); to the hardships and dangers of the apostolic life (iv. 9–13); to his cherished custom of working for his own living (ch. ix.); to the direct revelations he had received (xi. 23, xv. 8); and to his present plans (ch. xvi.). He bids the Corinthians to raise a collection for the church at Jerusalem by laying by something on the first day of the week, as he had directed the churches in Galatia to do. He says that he shall tarry at Ephesus till Pentecost, and then set out on a journey towards Corinth through Macedonia, so as perhaps to spend the winter with them. He expresses his joy at the coming of Stephanas and his companions, and commends them to the respect of the church.

Having despatched this epistle he stayed on at Ephesus, where "a great door and effectual was opened to him, and there were many adversaries." The affairs of the church of Corinth continued to be an object of the gravest anxiety to him, and to give him occupation at Ephesus: but it may be most convenient to put off the further notice of these till we come to the time when the 2d Epistle was written. We have now no information as to the work of St. Paul at Ephesus, until that tumult occurred which is described in Acts xix. 24–41. The whole narrative may be read there. We learn that "this Paul" had been so successful, not only in Ephesus, but "almost throughout all Asia," in turning people from the worship of gods made with hands, that the craft of silversmiths, who made little shrines for Artemis, were alarmed for their manufacture. They raised a great tumult, and not being able, apparently, to find Paul, laid hands on two of his companions and dragged them into the theatre. Paul himself, not willing that his friends should suffer in his place, wished to go in amongst the people: but the disciples, supported by the urgent request of certain magistrates called Asiarchs, dissuaded him from his purpose. The account of the proceedings of the mob is highly graphic, and the address with which the town-clerk finally quiets the people is worthy of a discreet and experienced magistrate. His statement that "these men are neither robbers of churches, nor yet blasphemers of your goddess," is an incidental testimony to the temperance of the Apostle and his friends in their attacks on the popular idolatry. But St. Paul is only personally concerned in this tumult in so far as it proves the deep impression which his teaching had made at Ephesus, and the daily danger in which he lived.

He had been anxious to depart from Ephesus, and this interruption of the work which had kept him there determined him to stay no longer. He set out therefore for Macedonia, and proceeded first to Troas (2 Cor. ii. 12), where he might have preached the Gospel with good hope of success. But a restless anxiety to obtain tidings concerning the church at Corinth urged him on, and he advanced into Macedonia, where he met Titus, who brought him the news for which he was thirsting. The receipt of this intelligence drew from him a letter which reveals to us what manner of man St. Paul was when the fountains of his heart were stirred to their inmost depths. [CORINTHIANS, SECOND EPISTLE TO THE.] How the agitation which expresses itself in every sentence of this letter was excited, is one of the most interesting

questions we have to consider. Every reader may
perceive that, on passing from the First Epistle to
the Second, the scene is almost entirely changed.
In the *First*, the faults and difficulties of the
Corinthian Church are before us. The Apostle
writes of these, with spirit indeed and emotion, as
he always does, but without passion or disturbance. He calmly asserts his own authority over
the church, and threatens to deal severely with
offenders. In the *Second*, he writes as one whose
personal relations with those whom he addresses
have undergone a most painful shock. The acute
pain given by former tidings, the comfort yielded
by the account which Titus brought, the vexation
of a sensitive mind at the necessity of self-assertion, contend together for utterance. What had
occasioned this excitement?

We have seen that Timothy had been sent from
Ephesus to Macedonia and Corinth. He had rejoined St. Paul when he wrote this Second Epistle,
for he is associated with him in the salutation (2
Cor. i. 1). We have no account, either in the
Acts or in the epistles, of this journey of Timothy,
and some have thought it probable that he never
reached Corinth. Let us suppose, however, that
he arrived there soon after the First Epistle, conveyed by Stephanas and others, had been received
by the Corinthian Church. He found that a
movement had arisen in the heart of that Church
which threw (let us suppose) the case of the incestuous person (1 Cor. v. 1-5) into the shade.
This was a deliberate and sustained attack upon
the Apostolic authority and personal integrity of
the Apostle of the Gentiles. The party-spirit
which, before the writing of the First Epistle, had
been content with underrating the powers of Paul
compared with those of Apollos, and with protesting against the laxity of his doctrine of freedom,
had been fanned into a flame by the arrival of some
person or persons who came from the Judæan
Church, armed with letters of commendation, and
who openly questioned the commission of him
whom they proclaimed to be a self-constituted
Apostle (2 Cor. iii. 1, xi. 4, 12-15). As the spirit
of opposition and detraction grew strong, the tongue
of some member of the church (more probably a
Corinthian than the stranger himself) was loosed.
He scoffed at St. Paul's courage and constancy,
pointing to his delay in coming to Corinth, and
making light of his threats (i. 17, 23). He demanded proofs of his Apostleship (xii. 11, 12).
He derided the weakness of his personal presence,
and the simplicity of his speech (x. 10). He even
threw out insinuations touching the personal honesty and self-devotion of St. Paul (i. 12, xii. 17,
18). When some such attack was made openly
upon the Apostle, the church had not immediately
called the offender to account; the better spirit of
the believers being cowed, apparently, by the confidence and assumed authority of the assailants
of St. Paul. A report of this melancholy state
of things was brought to the Apostle by Timothy
or by others; and we can imagine how it must
have wounded his sensitive and most affectionate
nature, and also how critical the juncture must
have seemed to him for the whole Western Church.
He immediately sent off Titus to Corinth, with a
letter containing the sharpest rebukes, *using* the
authority which had been denied, and threatening
to enforce it speedily by his personal presence (ii.
2, 3, vii. 8). As soon as the letter was gone —
how natural a trait! — he began to repent of

having written it. He must have hated the appearance of claiming homage to himself; his heart
must have been sore at the requital of his love;
he must have felt the deepest anxiety as to the
issue of the struggle. We can well believe him
therefore when he speaks of what he had suffered:
"Out of much affliction and anguish of heart I
wrote to you with many tears" (ii. 4); "I had no
rest in my spirit (ii. 13); "Our flesh had no
rest, but we were troubled on every side; without
were fightings, within were fears" (vii. 5). It
appears that he could not bring himself to hasten
to Corinth so rapidly as he had intended (i. 15,
16): he would wait till he heard news which might
make his visit a happy instead of a painful one
(ii. 1). When he had reached Macedonia, Titus,
as we have seen, met him with such reassuring
tidings. The offender had been rebuked by the
church, and had made submission (ii. 6, 7); the
old spirit of love and reverence towards St. Paul
had been awakened, and had poured itself forth in
warm expressions of shame and grief and penitence.
The cloud was now dispelled; fear and pain gave
place to hope and tenderness and thankfulness.
But even now the Apostle would not start at once
for Corinth. He may have had important work to
do in Macedonia. But another letter would smooth
the way still more effectually for his personal visit;
and he accordingly wrote the Second Epistle, and
sent it by the hands of Titus and two other brethren
to Corinth.

When the epistle is read in the light of the
circumstances we have supposed, the symptoms it
displays of a highly wrought personal sensitiveness,
and of a kind of ebb and flow of emotion, are as
intelligible as they are noble and beautiful. Nothing but a temporary interruption of mutual regard
could have made the joy of sympathy so deep and
fresh. If he had been the object of a personal
attack, how natural for the Apostle to write as he
does in ii. 5-10. In vii. 12, "he that suffered
wrong" is Paul himself. All his protestations
relating to his Apostolic work, and his solemn
appeals to God and Christ, are in place; and we
enter into his feelings as he asserts his own sincerity and the openness of the truth which he
taught in the Gospel (cc. iii., iv.). We see what
sustained him in his self-assertion: he knew that
he did not preach himself, but Christ Jesus the
Lord. His own weakness became an argument to
him, which he can use to others also, of the power
of God working in him. Knowing his own fellowship with Christ, and that this fellowship was
the right of other men too, he would be persuasive
or severe, as the cause of Christ and the good of
men might require (cc. iv., v.). If he was appearing to set himself up against the churches in
Judæa, he was the more anxious that the collection
which he was making for the benefit of those
churches should prove his sympathy with them by
its largeness. Again he would recur to the maintenance of his own authority as an Apostle of
Christ, against those who impeached it. He would
make it understood that spiritual views, spiritual
powers, were *real*; that if he knew no man after
the flesh, and did not war after the flesh, he was
not the less able for the building up of the church
(ch. x.). He would ask them to excuse his anxious jealousy, his folly and excitement, whilst he
gloried in the practical proofs of his Apostolic
commission, and in the infirmities which made the
power of God more manifest; and he would plead

with them earnestly that they would give him no occasion to find fault or to correct them (cc. xi., xii., xiii.).

The hypothesis upon which we have interpreted this epistle is not that which is most commonly received. According to the more common view, the offender is the incestuous person of 1 Cor. v., and the letter which proved so sharp but wholesome a medicine, the First Epistle. But this view does not account so satisfactorily for the whole tone of the epistle, and for the particular expressions relating to the offender; nor does it find places so consistently for the missions of Timothy and Titus. It does not seem likely that St. Paul would have treated the sin of the man who took his father's wife as an offense against himself, nor that he would have spoken of it by preference as a *wrong* (ἀδικία) *done to another* (supposed to be the father). The view we have adopted is said, in De Wette's *Exegetisches Handbuch*, to have been held, in whole or in part, by Bleek, Credner, Olshausen, and Neander. More recently it has been advocated with great force by Ewald, in his *Sendschreiben des A. P.* pp. 223-232. The ordinary account is retained by Stanley, Alford, and Davidson, and with some hesitation by Conybeare and Howson.

The particular nature of this epistle, as an appeal to facts in favor of his own Apostolic authority, leads to the mention of many interesting features of St. Paul's life. His summary, in xi. 23-28, of the hardships and dangers through which he had gone, proves to us how little the history in the Acts is to be regarded as a complete account of what he did and suffered. Of the particular facts stated in the following words, "Of the Jews five times received I forty stripes save one; thrice was I beaten with rods, once was I stoned, thrice I suffered shipwreck, a night and a day I have been in the deep," — we know only of *one*, the beating by the magistrates at Philippi, from the Acts. The daily burden of "the care of all the churches" seems to imply a wide and constant range of communication, by visits, messengers, and letters, of which we have found it reasonable to assume examples in his intercourse with the Church of Corinth. The mention of "visions and revelations of the Lord," and of the "thorn (or rather *stake*) in the flesh," side by side, is peculiarly characteristic both of the mind and of the experiences of St. Paul. As an instance of the visions, he alludes to a trance which had befallen him fourteen years before, in which he had been caught up into paradise, and had heard unspeakable words. Whether this vision *may be* identified with any that is recorded in the Acts must depend on chronological considerations: but the very expressions of St. Paul in this place would rather lead us not to think of an occasion in which words *that could be reported* were spoken. We observe that he speaks with the deepest reverence of the privilege thus granted to him; but he distinctly declines to ground anything upon it as regards other men. Let them judge him, he says, not by any such pretensions, but by which were cognizable to them (xii. 1-6). facts he would not, even inwardly with himself, glory in visions and revelations without remembering how the Lord had guarded him from being puffed up by them. A stake in the flesh (σκόλοψ τῇ σαρκί) was given him, a messenger of Satan to buffet him, lest he should be exalted above measure. The different interpretations which have prevailed

of this σκόλοψ have a certain historical significance. (1.) Roman Catholic divines have inclined to understand by it strong *sensual temptation* (2.) Luther and his followers take it to mean temptations to *unbelief*. But neither of these would be "infirmities" in which St. Paul could "glory." (3.) It is almost the unanimous opinion of modern divines — and the authority of the ancient fathers on the whole is in favor of it — that the σκόλοψ represents some vexatious *bodily infirmity* (see especially Stanley *in loco*). It is plainly what St. Paul refers to in Gal. iv. 14: "My temptation in my flesh ye despised not nor rejected." This infirmity distressed him so much that he besought the Lord thrice that it might depart from him. But the Lord answered, "My grace is sufficient for thee; for my strength is made perfect in weakness." We are to understand therefore the affliction as remaining; but Paul is more than resigned under it, he even glories in it as a means of displaying more purely the power of Christ in him. That we are to understand the Apostle, in accordance with this passage, as laboring under some degree of ill-health, is clear enough. But we must remember that his constitution was at least strong enough, as a matter of fact, to carry him through the hardships and anxieties and toils which he himself describes to us, and to sustain the pressure of the long imprisonment at Cæsarea and in Rome.

After writing this epistle, St. Paul travelled through Macedonia, perhaps to the borders of ILLYRICUM (Rom. xv. 19), and then carried out the intention of which he had spoken so often, and arrived himself at Corinth. The narrative in the Acts tells us that "when he had gone over those parts (Macedonia), and had given them much exhortation, he came into Greece, and there abode three months" (xx. 2, 3). There is only one incident which we can connect with this visit to Greece, but that is a very important one — the writing of another great epistle, addressed to the Church at Rome. [ROMANS, EPISTLE TO THE.] That this was written at this time from Corinth appears from passages in the epistle itself, and has never been doubted.

It would be unreasonable to suppose that St. Paul was insensible to the mighty associations which connected themselves with the name of Rome. The seat of the imperial government to which Jerusalem itself, with the rest of the world, was then subject, must have been a grand object to the thoughts of the Apostle from his infancy upwards. He was himself a citizen of Rome; he had come repeatedly under the jurisdiction of Roman magistrates; he had enjoyed the benefits of the equity of the Roman law, and the justice of Roman administration. And, besides its universal supremacy, Rome was the natural head of the Gentile world, as Jerusalem was the head of the Jewish world. In this august city Paul had many friends and brethren. Romans who had travelled into Greece and Asia, strangers from Greece and Asia who had gone to settle at Rome, had heard of Jesus Christ and the kingdom of Heaven from Paul himself or from other preachers of Christ, and had formed themselves into a community, of which a good report had gone forth throughout the Christian world. We are not surprised therefore to hear that the Apostle was very anxious to visit Rome. It was his fixed intention to go to Rome, and from Rome to extend his journey as far as Spain (Rom. xv. 24, 28). He would thus bear his witness, both in the capital and to the extremities of the Western or Gentile world. For the present he could not go on from Corinth to Rome, because he was drawn by a special errand to Jerusalem — where indeed he was likely enough to meet with dangers and delays (xv. 25–32). But from Jerusalem he proposed to turn Romewards. In the mean while he would write them a letter from Corinth.

The letter is a substitute for the personal visit which he had longed "for many years" to pay; and, as he would have made the visit, so now he writes the letter, *because he is the Apostle of the Gentiles.* Of this office, to speak in common language, St. Paul was proud. All the labors and dangers of it he would willingly encounter; and he would also jealously maintain its dignity and its powers. He held it of Christ, and Christ's commission should not be dishonored. He represents himself grandly as a priest, appointed to offer up the faith of the Gentile world as a sacrifice to God (xv. 16). And he then proceeds to speak with pride of the extent and independence of his Apostolic labors. It is in harmony with this language that he should address the Roman Church as consisting mainly of Gentiles; but we find that he speaks to them as to persons deeply interested in Jewish questions (see Prof. Jowett's and Bp. Colenso's *Introductions* to the Epistle).

To the church thus composed, the Apostle of the Gentiles writes to declare and commend the Gospel which he everywhere preaches. That Gospel was invariably the announcement of Jesus Christ the Son of God, the Lord of men, who was made man, died, and was raised again, and whom his heralds present to the faith and obedience of mankind. Such a κήρυγμα might be variously commended to different bearers. In speaking to the Roman Church, St. Paul represents the chief value of it as consisting in the fact that, through it, the righteousness of God, as a righteousness not for God only, but also for men, was revealed. It is natural to ask what led him to choose and dwell upon this aspect of his proclamation of Jesus Christ. The following answers suggest themselves:— (1.) As he looked upon the condition of the Gentile world, with that *coup d' œil* which the writing of a letter to the Roman Church was likely to suggest, he was struck by the awful wickedness, the utter dissolution of moral ties, which has made that age infamous. His own terrible summary (i. 21–32) is well known to be confirmed by other contemporary evidence. The profligacy which we shudder to read of was constantly under St. Paul's eye. Along with the evil he saw also the beginnings of God's judgment upon it. He saw the miseries and disasters, begun and impending, which proved that God in heaven would not tolerate the unrighteousness of men. (2.) As he looked upon the condition of the Jewish people, he saw them claiming an exclusive righteousness, which, however, had manifestly no power to preserve them from being really unrighteous. (3.) Might not the thought also occur to him, as a Roman citizen, that the empire which was now falling to pieces through unrighteousness had been built up by righteousness, by that love of order and that acknowledgment of rights which were the great endowment of the Roman people? Whether we lay any stress upon this or not, it seems clear that to one contemplating the world from St.

Paul's point of view, no thought would be so naturally suggested as that of the need of the *true* Righteousness for the two divisions of mankind. How he expounds that God's own righteousness was shown, in Jesus Christ, to be a righteousness which men might trust in — sinners though they were, — and by trusting in it submit to it, and so receive it as to show forth the fruits of it in their own lives; how he declares the union of men with Christ as subsisting in the Divine idea and as realized by the power of the Spirit, — may be seen in the epistle itself. The remarkable exposition contained in ch. ix., x., xi., illustrates the personal character of St. Paul, by showing the intense love for his nation which he retained through all his struggles with unbelieving Jews and Judaizing Christians, and by what hopes he reconciled himself to the thought of their unbelief and their punishment. Having spoken of this subject, he goes on to exhibit in practical counsels the same love of Christian unity, moderation, and gentleness, the same respect for social order, the same tenderness for weak consciences, and the same expectation of the Lord's coming and confidence in the future, which appear more or less strongly in all his letters.

Before his departure from Corinth, St. Paul was joined again by St. Luke, as we infer from the change in the narrative from the third to the first person. We have seen already that he was bent on making a journey to Jerusalem, for a special purpose and within a limited time. With this view he was intending to go by sea to Syria. But he was made aware of some plot of the Jews for his destruction, to be carried out through this voyage; and he determined to evade their malice by changing his route. Several brethren were associated with him in this expedition, the bearers, no doubt, of the collections made in all the churches for the poor at Jerusalem. These were sent on by sea, and probably the money with them, to Troas, where they were to await St. Paul. He, accompanied by St. Luke, went northwards through Macedonia. The style of an eye-witness again becomes manifest. "From Philippi," says the writer, "we sailed away after the days of unleavened bread, and came unto them to Troas in five days, where we abode seven days." The marks of time throughout this journey have given occasion to much chronological and geographical discussion, which brings before the reader's mind the difficulties and uncertainties of travel in that age, and leaves the *precise* determination of the dates of this history a matter for reasonable conjecture rather than for positive statement. But no question is raised by the times mentioned which need detain us in the course of the narrative. During the stay at Troas there was a meeting on the first day of the week "to break bread," and Paul was discoursing earnestly and at length with the brethren. He was to depart the next morning, and midnight found them listening to his earnest speech, with many lights burning in the upper chamber in which they had met, and making the atmosphere oppressive. A youth named Eutychus was sitting in the window, and was gradually overpowered by sleep, so that at last he fell into the street or court from the third story, and was taken up dead. The meeting was interrupted by this accident, and Paul went down and fell upon him and embraced him, saying, "Be not disturbed, his life is in him." [EUTYCHUS, Amer. ed.] His friends then appear to have taken charge of him, whilst Paul went up again, first presided at the breaking of bread, afterwards took a meal, and continued conversing until day-break, and so departed.

Whilst the vessel which conveyed the rest of the party sailed from Troas to Assos, Paul gained some time by making the journey by land. At Assos he went on board again.[c] Coasting along by Mitylene, Chios, Samos, and Trogyllium, they arrived at Miletus. The Apostle was thus passing by the chief church in Asia; but if he had gone to Ephesus he might have arrived at Jerusalem too late for the Pentecost, at which festival he had set his heart upon being present. At Miletus, however, there was time to send to Ephesus; and the elders of the Church were invited to come down to him there. This meeting is made the occasion for recording another characteristic and *representative* address of St. Paul (Acts xx. 18–35).[b] This spoken address to the elders of the Ephesian Church may be ranked with the epistles, and throws the same kind of light upon St. Paul's Apostolical relations to the churches. Like several of the epistles, it is in great part an appeal to their memories of him and of his work. He refers to his labors in "serving the Lord" amongst them, and to the dangers he incurred from the plots of the Jews, and asserts emphatically the *unreserve* with which he had taught them. He then mentions a fact which will come before us again presently, that he was receiving inspired warnings, as he advanced from city to city, of the bonds and afflictions awaiting him at Jerusalem. It is interesting to observe that the Apostle felt it to be his duty to press on in spite of these warnings. Having formed his plan on good grounds and in the sight of God, he did not see, in dangers which might even touch his life, however clearly set before him, reasons for changing it. Other arguments might move him from a fixed purpose — not dangers. His one guiding principle was, to discharge the ministry which he had received of the Lord Jesus, to testify the Gospel of the grace of God. Speaking to his present audience as to those whom he was seeing for the last time, he proceeds to exhort them with unusual earnestness and tenderness, and expresses in conclusion that anxiety as to practical industry and liberality which has been increasingly occupying his mind. In terms strongly resembling the language

of the epistles to the Thessalonians and Corinthians, he pleads his own example, and entreats them to follow it, in "laboring for the support of the weak." "And when he had thus spoken he kneeled down and prayed with them all: and they all wept sore, and fell on Paul's neck, and kissed him, sorrowing most of all for the words which he spake, that they should see his face no more. And they accompanied him to the ship." . . . . This is the kind of narrative in which some learned men think they can detect the signs of a moderately clever fiction.

The course of the voyage from Miletus was by Coos and Rhodes to Patara, and from Patara in another vessel past Cyprus to Tyre. Here Paul and his company spent seven days; and there were disciples "who said to Paul through the Spirit, that he should not go up to Jerusalem."· Again there was a sorrowful parting: "They all brought us on our way, with wives and children, till we were out of the city; and we kneeled down on the shore and prayed." From Tyre they sailed to Ptolemais, where they spent one day, and from Ptolemais proceeded, apparently by land, to Cæsarea. In this place was settled Philip the Evangelist, one of the seven, and he became the host of Paul and his friends. Philip had four unmarried daughters, who "prophesied," and who repeated, no doubt, the warnings already heard. Cæsarea was within an easy journey of Jerusalem, and Paul may have thought it prudent not to be too long in Jerusalem before the festival; otherwise it might seem strange that, after the former haste, they now "tarried many days" at Cæsarea. During this interval the prophet Agabus (Acts xi. 28) came down from Jerusalem, and crowned the previous intimations of danger with a prediction expressively delivered. It would seem as if the approaching imprisonment were intended to be conspicuous in the eyes of the Church, as an agency for the accomplishment of God's designs. At this stage a final effort was made to dissuade Paul from going up to Jerusalem, by the Christians of Cæsarea, and by his travelling companions. But "Paul answered, What mean ye to weep and to break mine heart? for I am ready not to be bound only, but also to die at Jerusalem for the name of the Lord Jesus. And when he would not be persuaded, we ceased, saying, The will of the Lord be done." So, after a while, they went up to Jerusalem, and were

---

a * Assos, connected with Troas by a paved road, was about twenty miles distant. A Greek friend mentioned to me that he had travelled on foot between the places in five hours. The motive for Paul's foot-journey can only be conjectured. He may have wished to have the company of friends from Troas whom the crowded vessel could not accommodate, or to visit friends on the way, or (Howson) after the exciting scenes at Troas to gratify his desire for solitude and retirement.   H.

b * The memorable address at Miletus brings before us a characteristic of Paul, which enters essentially into a just conception of his personality, and is introduced in such a manner as to authenticate the speech. It will be noticed how strongly the Apostle asserts in this discourse his self-consciousness of entire rectitude in the eyes of men, and of his claim to be recognized as a true pattern of Christian fidelity "It appears," says Dr. Tholuck (*Reden des Apostels Paulus: Studien u. Kritiken* for 1839, p. 305 ff.) "to belong to the peculiarities of this Apostle that he in particular appeals so often to his blameless manner of life. The occasion for this lies sometimes in the calumnies of his enemies, as when he says in 2 Cor.

i. 12: 'For our boasting (καύχησις) is this, the testimony of our conscience, that in simplicity and godly sincerity, not with fleshly wisdom, but by the grace of God, we have had our conversation in the world, and more especially among you.' Ch. xi. shows what adversaries he had in view in this self-justification. But often those appeals spring only from that just confidence with which he can call upon others to imitate him, as he himself imitates the Saviour. Thus in 1 Cor. xi. 1, he cries : 'Be ye followers of me, even as I also am of Christ;' and in Phil. iii. 17: 'Brethren, be followers together of me, and mark them who walk so as ye have us for an ensample.' Such personal testimonies are not found in the other epistles of the N. T., nor are they frequent in the writings of other pious men ; and on that account we are authorized to consider their occurrence in this discourse (vv. 18–21) as a mark of its historical character." For examples of the linguistic affinity between this discourse and Paul's Epistles, see Lekebusch, *Composition der Apostelgeschichte*, p. 339. Dean Howson's remarks on this address (*Character of St. Paul*, p. 202 f.) are specially instructive.   H.

gladly received by the brethren. This is St. Paul's fifth and last visit to Jerusalem.

St. Paul's Imprisonment: Jerusalem and Cæsarea. — He who was thus conducted into Jerusalem by a company of anxious friends had become by this time a man of considerable fame amongst his countrymen. He was widely known as one who had taught with preëminent boldness that a way into God's favor was opened to the Gentiles, and that this way did not lie through the door of the Jewish Law. He had moreover actually founded numerous and important communities, composed of Jews and Gentiles together, which stood simply on the name of Jesus Christ, apart from circumcision and the observance of the Law. He had thus roused against himself the bitter enmity of that unfathomable Jewish pride which was almost as strong in some of those who had professed the faith of Jesus, as in their unconverted brethren. This enmity had for years been vexing both the body and the spirit of the Apostle. He had no rest from his persecutions; and his joy in proclaiming the free grace of God to the world was mixed with a constant sorrow that in so doing he was held to be disloyal to the calling of his fathers. He was now approaching a crisis in the long struggle, and the shadow of it had been made to rest upon his mind throughout his journey to Jerusalem. He came "ready to die for the name of the Lord Jesus," but he came expressly to prove himself a faithful Jew, and this purpose emerges at every point of the history.

St. Luke does not mention the contributions brought by Paul and his companions for the poor at Jerusalem.[a] But it is to be assumed that their first act was to deliver these funds into the proper hands. This might be done at the interview which took place on the following day with "James and all the elders." As on former occasions, the believers at Jerusalem could not but glorify God for what they heard; but they had been alarmed by the prevalent feeling concerning St. Paul. They said to him, "Thou seest, brother, how many thousands of Jews there are which believe; and they are all zealous of the Law; and they are informed of thee that thou teachest all the Jews which are among the Gentiles to forsake Moses, saying that they ought not to circumcise their children, neither to walk after the customs." This report, as James and the elders assume, was not a true one; it was a perversion of Paul's real teaching, which did not, in fact, differ from theirs. In order to dispel such rumors they ask him to do publicly an act of homage to the Law and its observances. They had four men who were under the Nazarite vow. The completion of this vow involved (Num. vi. 13–21) a considerable expense for the offerings to be presented in the Temple; and it was a meritorious act to provide these offerings for the poorer Nazarites. St. Paul was requested to put himself under the vow with those other four, and to supply the cost of their offerings. He at once accepted the proposal, and on the next day,

having performed some ceremony which implied the adoption of the vow, he went into the Temple, announcing that the due offerings for each Nazarite were about to be presented and the period of the vow terminated. It appears that the whole process undertaken by St. Paul required seven days to complete it. Towards the end of this time certain Jews from "Asia," who had come up for the Pentecostal feast, and who had a personal knowledge both of Paul himself and of his companion Trophimus, a Gentile from Ephesus, saw Paul in the Temple. They immediately set upon him, and stirred up the people against him, crying out, "Men of Israel, help: this is the man that teacheth all men everywhere against the people, and the Law, and this place; and further brought Greeks also into the Temple, and hath polluted this holy place." The latter charge had no more truth in it than the first: it was only suggested by their having seen Trophimus with him, not in the Temple, but in the city. They raised, however, a great commotion: Paul was dragged out of the Temple, of which the doors were immediately shut, and the people, having him in their hands, were proposing to kill him. But tidings were soon carried to the commander of the force which was serving as a garrison in Jerusalem, that "all Jerusalem was in an uproar;" and he, taking with him soldiers and centurions, hastened to the scene of the tumult. Paul was rescued from the violence of the multitude by the Roman officer, who made him his own prisoner, causing him to be chained to two soldiers, and then proceeded to inquire who he was and what he had done. The inquiry only elicited confused outcries, and the "chief captain" seems to have imagined that the Apostle might perhaps be a certain Egyptian pretender who had recently stirred up a considerable rising of the people. The account in the Acts (xxi. 34–40) tells us with graphic touches how St. Paul obtained leave and opportunity to address the people in a discourse which is related at length.

This discourse was spoken in Hebrew; that is, in the native dialect of the country, and was on that account listened to with the more attention. It is described by St. Paul himself, in his opening words, as his "defence," addressed to his brethren and fathers. It is in this light that it ought to be regarded. As we have seen, the desire which occupied the Apostle's mind at this time, was that of vindicating his message and work as those of a faithful Jew. The discourse spoken to the angry people at Jerusalem is his own justification of himself. He adopts the historical method, after which all the recorded appeals to Jewish audiences are framed. He is a servant of facts. He had been from the first a zealous Israelite like his hearers. He had changed his course because the God of his fathers had turned him from one path into another. It is thus that he is led into a narrative of his Conversion. We have already noticed the differences, in the statement of bare facts, between this narrative and that of the 9th chapter. The business of the

---

a • This remark is not correct, if understood to mean that Luke is altogether silent as to the alms which Paul had collected abroad, and had brought with him to Jerusalem. Luke represents the Apostle as saying in his speech before Felix (Acts xxiv. 17) that he was at Jerusalem on this business when he was apprehended by the Jews. This incidental notice, however, is, in fact, the only reference in the book of the Acts to these contributions which Paul had been taking up so extensively in the Gentile churches. (See Rom. xv. 25, 26; 1 Cor. xvi. 1-4; 2 Cor. viii. 1-4.) The manner in which the epistles supply this omission of Luke's history, as Paley so justly argues, furnishes a conclusive proof of the credibility of these writings.

H.

student, in this place, is to see how far the purpose of the Apostle will account for whatever is special to this address. That purpose explains the detailed reference to his rigorously Jewish education, and to his history before his conversion. It gives point to the announcement that it was by a direct operation from without upon his spirit, and not by the gradual influence of other minds upon his, that his course was changed. Incidentally, we may see a reason for the admission that his companions "heard not the voice of him that spake to me " in the fact that some of them, not believing in Jesus with their former leader, may have been living at Jerusalem, and possibly present amongst the audience. In this speech, the Apostle is glad to mention, what we were not told before, that the Ananias who interpreted the will of the Lord to him more fully at Damascus, was "a devout man according to the law, having a good report of all the Jews which dwelt there," and that he made his communication in the name of Jehovah, the God of Israel, saying, " The God of our fathers hath chosen thee, that thou shouldest know his will, and see the Righteous One, and hear a voice out of his mouth; for thou shalt be a witness for him unto all men of what thou hast seen and heard." Having thus claimed, according to his wont, the character of a simple instrument and witness, St. Paul goes on to describe another revelation of which we read nothing elsewhere. He had been accused of being an enemy to the Temple. He relates that after the visit to Damascus he went up again to Jerusalem, and was praying once in the Temple itself, till he fell into a trance. Then he saw the Lord, and was bidden to leave Jerusalem quickly, because the people there would not receive his testimony concerning Jesus. His own impulse was to stay at Jerusalem, and he pleaded with the Lord that there it was well known how he had persecuted those of whom he was now one, — implying, it would appear, that at Jerusalem his testimony was likely to be more impressive and irresistible than elsewhere; but the Lord answered with a simple command, "Depart: for I will send thee far hence unto the Gentiles."

Until this hated word, of a mission to the Gentiles, had been spoken, the Jews had listened to the speaker. They could bear the name of the Nazarene, though they despised it; but the thought of that free declaration of God's grace to the Gentiles, of which Paul was known to be the herald, stung them to fury. Jewish pride was in that generation becoming hardened and embittered to the utmost; and this was the enemy which St. Paul had come to encounter in its stronghold. "Away with such a fellow from the earth," the multitude now shouted: "it is not fit that he should live." [a] The Roman commander, seeing the tumult that arose, might well conclude that St. Paul had committed some heinous offense; and carrying him off, he gave orders that he should be forced by scourging to confess his crime. Again the Apostle took advantage of his Roman citizenship to protect himself from such an outrage. To the rights of that citizenship, he, a free-born Roman, had a better title than the chief captain himself; and if he had chosen to assert it before, he might have saved himself from the indignity of being manacled.

The Roman officer was bound to protect a citi-

zen, and to suppress tumult; but it was also a part of his policy to treat with deference the religion and the customs of the country. St. Paul's present history is the resultant of these two principles. The chief captain set him free from bonds, but on the next day called together the chief priests and the Sanhedrim, and brought Paul as a prisoner before them. We need not suppose that this was a regular legal proceeding: it was probably an experiment of policy and courtesy. If, on the one hand, the commandant of the garrison had no power to convoke the Sanhedrim; on the other hand he would not give up a Roman citizen to their judgment. As it was, the affair ended in confusion, and with no semblance of a judicial termination. The incidents selected by St. Luke from the history of this meeting form striking points in the biography of St. Paul, but they are not easy to understand. The difficulties arising here, not out of a comparison of two independent narratives, but out of a single narrative which must at least have appeared consistent and intelligible to the writer himself, are a warning to the student not to draw unfavorable inferences from all apparent discrepancies. St. Paul appears to have been put upon his defense, and with the peculiar habit, mentioned elsewhere also (Acts xiii. 9), of looking steadily when about to speak (ἀτενίσας), he began to say, " Men and brethren, I have lived in all good conscience (or, to give the force of πεπολίτευμαι, I have lived a conscientiously loyal life) unto God, until this day." [.] Here the high-priest Ananias commanded them that stood by him to smite him on the mouth. With a fearless indignation, Paul exclaimed: " God shall smite thee, thou whited wall; for sittest thou to judge me after the law, and commandest me to be smitten contrary to the law? " The bystanders said, " Revilest thou God's high-priest ? " Paul answered, " I knew not, brethren, that he was the high-priest; for it is written, Thou shalt not speak evil of the ruler of thy people." The evidence furnished by this apology, of St. Paul's respect both for the Law and for the high-priesthood, was probably the reason for relating the outburst which it followed. Whether the writer thought that outburst culpable or not, does not appear. St. Jerome (contra Pelag. iii., quoted by Baur) draws an unfavorable contrast between the vehemence of the Apostle and the meekness of his master; and he is followed by many critics, as amongst others De Wette and Alford. But it is to be remembered that He who was led as a lamb to the slaughter, was the same who spoke of " whited sepulchres," and exclaimed, " Ye serpents, ye generation of vipers, how shall ye escape the damnation of hell? " It is by no means certain, therefore, that St. Paul would have been a truer follower of Jesus if he had held his tongue under Ananias's lawless outrage. But what does his answer mean? How was it possible for him not to know that he who spoke was the high-priest? Why should he have been less willing to rebuke an iniquitous high-priest than any other member of the Sanhedrim, "sitting to judge him after the Law? " These are difficult questions to answer. It is not likely that Ananias was personally unknown to St. Paul; still less so, that the high-priest was not distinguished by dress or place from

---

a [*] The Greek is more energetic than this : " It was not fit (imperf. καθῆκεν) that he should live," i. e. he deserved to die long ago (Lechler, Der Apostel

Gesch. p. 358, 3 e Aufl.); or, as Meyer prefers (in loc.), should have been left to die instead of being rescued as he was (Acts xxi. 31).   H.

the other members of the Sanhedrim. The 'least objectionable solutions seem to be that for some reason or other — either because his sight was not good, or because he was looking another way, — he did not know whose voice it was that ordered him to be smitten; and that he wished to correct the impression which he saw was made upon some of the audience by his threatening protest, and therefore took advantage of the fact that he really did not know the speaker to be the high-priest, to explain the deference he felt to be due to the person holding that office.[a] The next incident which St. Luke records seems to some, who cannot think of the Apostle as remaining still a Jew, to cast a shadow upon his rectitude. He perceived, we are told, that the council was divided into two parties, the Sadducees and Pharisees, and therefore he cried out, "Men and brethren, I am a Pharisee, the son of a Pharisee; concerning the hope and resurrection of the dead I am called in question." This declaration, whether so intended or not, had the effect of stirring up the party spirit of the assembly to such a degree that a fierce dissension arose, and some of the Pharisees actually took Paul's side, saying, "We find no evil in this man; suppose a spirit or an angel has spoken to him?" — Those who impugn the authenticity of the Acts point triumphantly to this scene as an utterly impossible one; others consider that the Apostle is to be blamed for using a disingenuous artifice. But it is not so clear that St. Paul was using an artifice at all, at least for his own interest, in identifying himself as he did with the professions of the Pharisees. He had not come to Jerusalem to escape out of the way of danger, nor was the course he took on this occasion the safest he could have chosen. Two objects, we must remember, were dearer to him than his life: (1) to testify of him whom God had raised from the dead, and (2) to prove that in so doing he was a faithful Israelite. He may well have thought that both these objects might be promoted by an appeal to the nobler professions of the Pharisees. The creed of the Pharisee, as distinguished from that of the Sadducee, was unquestionably the creed of St. Paul. His belief in Jesus seemed to him to supply the ground and fulfillment of that creed. He wished to lead his brother Pharisees into a deeper and more living apprehension of their own faith.

Whether such a result was in any degree attained, we do not know: the immediate consequence of the dissension which occurred in the assembly was that Paul was like to be torn in pieces, and was carried off by the Roman soldiers. In the night he had a vision, as at Corinth (xviii. 9, 10) and on the voyage to Rome (xxvii. 23, 24), of the Lord standing by him, and encouraging him. "Be of good cheer, Paul," said his Master; "for as thou hast testified of me in Jerusalem, so must thou bear witness also at Rome." It was not safety that the Apostle longed for, but opportunity to bear witness of Christ.

Probably the factious support which Paul had gained by his manner of bearing witness in the council died away as soon as the meeting was dissolved. On the next day a conspiracy was formed, which the historian relates with a singular fullness of details. More than forty of the Jews bound themselves under a curse neither to eat nor to drink till they had killed Paul. Their plan was, to persuade the Roman commandant to send down Paul once more to the council, and then to set upon him by the way and kill him. This conspiracy became known in some way to a nephew of St. Paul's, his sister's son, who was allowed to see his uncle, and inform him of it, and by his desire was taken to the captain, who was thus put on his guard against the plot. This discovery baffled the conspirators; and it is to be feared that they obtained some dispensation from their vow. The consequence to St. Paul was that he was hurried away from Jerusalem. The chief captain, Claudius Lysias, determined to send him to Cæsarea, to Felix the governor, or procurator, of Judæa. He therefore put him in charge of a strong guard of soldiers, who took him by night as far as Antipatris. From thence a smaller detachment conveyed him to Cæsarea, where they delivered up their prisoner into the hands of the governor, together with a letter, in which Claudius Lysias had explained to Felix his reason for sending Paul, and had announced that his accusers would follow. Felix, St. Luke tells us with that particularity which marks this portion of his narrative, asked of what province the prisoner was: and being told that he was of Cilicia, he promised to give him a hearing when his accusers should come. In the mean-time he ordered him to be guarded, — chained, probably, to a soldier, — in the government house [or Prætorium], which had been the palace of Herod the Great.

Imprisonment at Cæsarea. — St. Paul was henceforth, to the end of the period embraced in the Acts, if not to the end of his life, in Roman custody. This custody was in fact a protection to him, without which he would have fallen a victim to the animosity of the Jews. He seems to have been treated throughout with humanity and consideration. His own attitude towards Roman magistrates was invariably that of a respectful but independent citizen; and whilst his franchise secured him from open injustice, his character and conduct could not fail to win him the good-will of those into whose hands he came. The governor before whom he was now to be tried, according to Tacitus and Josephus, was a mean and dissolute tyrant. [FELIX.] "Per omnem sævitiam ac libidinem jus regium servili ingenio exercuit" (Tacitus, Hist. v. 9). But these characteristics, except perhaps the servile ingenium, do not appear in our history. The orator or counsel retained by the Jews and brought down by Ananias and the elders, when they arrived in the course of five days at Cæsarea, begins the proceedings of the trial professionally by complimenting the governor. The charge he goes on to set forth against Paul shows precisely the light in which he was regarded by the fanatical Jews. He is a pestilent fellow (λοιμός); he stirs up divisions amongst the Jews throughout the world; he is a ringleader of the sect (αἱρέσεως) of the Nazarenes. His last offense had been an attempt to profane the Temple. [TERTULLUS.] St. Paul met the charge in his usual manner. He was glad that his judge had been for some years governor of a Jewish province; "because it is in thy power to ascertain that, not more than twelve days since, I came up to Jerusalem to worship." The emphasis is upon his coming up to worship. He denied positively the charges of stirring up strife and of profaning the Temple. But he admitted that "after the way (τὴν ὁδόν) which they call a sect, or a heresy," — so he worshipped the God of his fathers, believing all things written in the Law and in the Prophets. Again he gave prominence to the hope of a resurrection, which he held, as he said, in common with his accusers. His loyalty to the faith of his fathers he had shown by coming up to Jerusalem expressly to bring alms for his nation and offerings, and by undertaking the ceremonies of purification in the Temple. What fault then could any Jew possibly find in him? — The Apostle's answer was straightforward and complete. He had *not* violated the law of his fathers; he was still a true and loyal Israelite. Felix, it appears, knew a good deal about "the way" (τῆς ὁδοῦ), as well as about the customs of the Jews, and was probably satisfied that St. Paul's account was a true one. He made an excuse for putting off the matter, and gave orders that the prisoner should be treated with indulgence, and that his friends should be allowed free access to him. After a while, Felix heard him again. His wife Drusilla was a Jewess, and they were both curious to hear the eminent preacher of the new faith in Christ. But St. Paul was not a man to entertain an idle curiosity. He began to reason concerning righteousness, temperance,[a] and the coming judgment, in a manner which alarmed Felix and caused him to put an end to the conference. He frequently saw him afterwards, however, and allowed him to understand that a bribe would procure his release. But St. Paul would not resort to this method of escape, and he remained in custody until Felix left the province. The unprincipled governor had good reason to seek to ingratiate himself with the Jews; and to please them, he handed over Paul, as an untried prisoner, to his successor Festus.

At this point, as we shall see hereafter, the history of St. Paul comes into its closest contact with external chronology. Festus, like Felix, has a place in secular history, and he bears a much better char-

acter. Upon his arrival in the province, he went up without delay from Cæsarea to Jerusalem, and the leading Jews seized the opportunity of asking that Paul might be brought up there for trial, intending to assassinate him by the way. But Festus would not comply with their request. He invited them to follow him on his speedy return to Cæsarea, and a trial took place there, closely resembling that before Felix. Festus saw clearly enough that Paul had committed no offense against the law, but he was anxious at the same time, if he could, to please the Jews. "They had certain questions against him," Festus says to Agrippa, "of their own superstition (or religion), and of one Jesus, who was dead, whom Paul affirmed to be alive. And being puzzled for my part as to such inquiries, I asked him whether he would go to Jerusalem to be tried there." This proposal, not a very likely one to be accepted, was the occasion of St. Paul's appeal to Cæsar. In dignified and independent language he claimed his rights as a Roman citizen. We can scarcely doubt that the prospect of being forwarded by this means to Rome, the goal of all his desires, presented itself to him and drew him onwards, as he virtually protested against the indecision and impotence of the provincial governor, and exclaimed, "I appeal unto Cæsar." Having heard this appeal, Festus consulted with his assessors, found that there was no impediment in the way of its prosecution, and then replied, "Hast thou appealed to Cæsar? To Cæsar thou shalt go."

Properly speaking, an appeal was made *from the sentence* of an inferior court to the jurisdiction of a higher. But in St. Paul's case no sentence had been pronounced. We must understand, therefore, by his appeal, a demand to be tried by the imperial court, and we must suppose that a Roman citizen had the right of electing whether he would be tried in the province or at Rome. [APPEAL.]

The appeal having been allowed, Festus reflected that he must send with the prisoner a report of "the crimes laid against him." And he found that it was no easy matter to put the complaints of the Jews in a form which would be intelligible at Rome. He therefore took advantage of an opportunity which offered itself in a few days to seek some help in the matter. The Jewish prince Agrippa arrived with his sister Bernice on a visit to the new governor. To him Festus communicated his perplexity, together with an account of what had occurred before him in the case. Agrippa, who must have known something of the sect of the Nazarenes, and had probably heard of Paul himself, expressed a desire to hear him speak. The Apostle therefore was now called upon to bear the name of his Master "before Gentiles, and kings." The audience which assembled to hear him was the most dignified which he had yet addressed, and the state and ceremony of the scene proved that he was regarded as no vulgar criminal. Festus, when Paul had been brought into the council-chamber, explained to Agrippa and the rest of the company the difficulty in which he found himself, and then expressly referred the matter to the better knowledge of the Jewish king Paul therefore was to give an account of himself

<hr/>

[a] • Strictly "self-control" (ἐγκράτεια), especially chastity, so grossly violated by those to whom Paul was speaking. We have here a striking example of the Apostle's courage and fidelity. At the side of Felix was sitting a victim of his libertinism, an adulteress,

as Paul discoursed of immorality and a judgment to come. The woman's resentment was to be feared as well as that of the man. It was the implacable Herodias and not Herod, who demanded the head of John the Baptist.   H.

to Agrippa; and when he had received from him a courteous permission to begin, he stretched forth his hand and made his defense.

In this discourse (Acts xxvi.), we have the second explanation from St. Paul himself of the manner in which he had been led, through his conversion, to serve the Lord Jesus instead of persecuting his disciples; and the third narrative of the conversion itself. Speaking to Agrippa as to one thoroughly versed in the customs and questions prevailing amongst the Jews, Paul appeals to the well-known Jewish and even Pharisaical strictness of his youth and early manhood. He reminds the king of the great hope which sustained continually the worship of the Jewish nation, — the hope of a deliverer, promised by God Himself, who should be a conqueror of death. He had been led to see that this promise was fulfilled in Jesus of Nazareth; he proclaimed his resurrection to be the pledge of a new and immortal life. What was there in this of disloyalty to the traditions of his fathers? Did his countrymen disbelieve in this Jesus as the Messiah? So had he once disbelieved in Him; and had thought it his duty to be earnest in hostility against his name. But his eyes had been opened: he would tell how and when. The story of the conversion is modified in this address as we might fairly expect it to be. We have seen that there is no absolute contradiction between the statements of this and the other narratives. The main points, — the light, the prostration, the voice from heaven, the instructions from Jesus, — are found in all three. But in this account, the words, "I am Jesus whom thou persecutest," are followed by a fuller explanation, as if then spoken by the Lord, of what the work of the Apostle was to be. The other accounts defer this explanation to a subsequent occasion. But when we consider how fully the mysterious communication made at the moment of the conversion *included* what was afterwards conveyed, through Ananias and in other ways, to the mind of Paul; and how needless it was for Paul, in his present address before Agrippa, to mark the stages by which the whole lesson was taught, it seems merely captious to base upon the method of this account a charge of disagreement between the different parts of this history. They bear, on the contrary, a striking mark of genuineness in the degree in which they approach contradiction without reaching it. It is most natural that a story told on different occasions should be told differently; and if in such a case we find no contradiction as to the facts, we gain all the firmer impression of the substantial truth of the story. The particulars added to the former accounts by the present narrative are, that the words of Jesus were spoken in Hebrew, and that the first question to Saul was followed by the saying, "it is hard for thee to kick against the goads." (This saying is omitted by the best authorities in chapter ix.) The language of the commission which St. Paul says he received from Jesus deserves close study, and will be found to bear a striking resemblance to a passage in Colossians (i. 12–14). The ideas of light, redemption, forgiveness. inheritance, and faith in Christ, belong characteristically to the

Gospel which Paul preached amongst the Gentiles. Not less striking is it to observe the older terms in which he describes to Agrippa his obedience to the heavenly vision. He had made it his business, he says, to proclaim to all men "that they should repent and turn to God, and do works meet for repentance." Words such as John the Baptist uttered, but not less truly Pauline. And he finally reiterates that the testimony on account of which the Jews sought to kill him was in exact agreement with Moses and the prophets. They had taught men to expect that the Christ should suffer, and that He should be the first that should rise from the dead, and should show light unto the people and to the Gentiles. Of such a Messiah Saul was the servant and preacher.[a]

At this point Festus began to apprehend what seemed to him a manifest absurdity. He interrupted the Apostle discourteously, but with a compliment contained in his loud remonstrance. "Thou art mad, Paul; thy much learning is turning thee mad." The phrase τὰ πολλὰ γράμματα may possibly have been *suggested* by the allusion to Moses and the prophets; but it probably *refers* to the books with which St. Paul had been supplied, and which he was known to study, during his imprisonment. As a biographical hint, this phrase is not to be overlooked. "I am not mad," replied Paul, "most noble Festus: they are words of truth and soberness which I am uttering." Then, with an appeal of mingled dignity and solicitude, he turns to the king. He was sure the king understood him. "King Agrippa, believest thou the prophets ? — I know that thou believest." The answer of Agrippa can hardly have been the serious and encouraging remark of our English version. Literally rendered, it appears to be, You are briefly persuading me to become a Christian; and it is generally supposed to have been spoken ironically. "I would to God," is Paul's earnest answer, "that whether by a brief process or by a long one, not only thou but all who hear me to-day might become such as I am, with the exception of these bonds." He was wearing a chain upon the hand he held up in addressing them. With this prayer, it appears, the conference ended. Festus and the king, and their companions, consulted together and came to the conclusion that the accused was guilty of nothing that deserved death or imprisonment. And Agrippa's final answer to the inquiry of Festus was, "This man might have been set at liberty, if he had not appealed unto Cæsar."

The Voyage to Rome. — No formal trial of St. Paul had yet taken place. It appears from Acts xxviii. 18, that he knew how favorable the judgment of the provincial governor was likely to be. But the vehement opposition of the Jews, together with his desire to be conveyed to Rome, might well induce him to claim a trial before the imperial court. After a while arrangements were made to carry "Paul and certain other prisoners," in the custody of a centurion named Julius, into Italy; and amongst the company, whether by favor or from any other reason, we find the historian of the Acts. The narrative of this voyage is accordingly minute and circumstantial in a degree which has

<hr />

a "There never was any that understood the Old Testament so well as St. Paul, except John the Baptist, and John the Divine. . . . . O, he dearly loved Moses and Isaiah, for they, together with king David, were the chief prophets. The words and things of St. Paul are taken out of Moses and the prophets " (Luther's *Table Talk*, ccccxxviii., Engl. Trans.). Another striking remark of Luther's may be added here: "Whoso reads Paul may, with a safe conscience, build upon his words " (*Table Talk*, xxiii.).

excited much attention. The nautical and geographical details of St. Luke's account have been submitted to an apparently thorough investigation by several competent critics, especially by Mr. Smith of Jordanhill, in an important treatise devoted to this subject, and by Mr. Howson. The result of this investigation has been, that several errors in the received version have been corrected, that the course of the voyage has been laid down to a very minute degree with great certainty, and that the account in the Acts is shown to be written by an accurate eye-witness, not himself a professional seaman, but well acquainted with nautical matters. We shall hasten lightly over this voyage, referring the reader to the works above mentioned, and to the articles in this Dictionary on the names of places and the nautical terms which occur in the narrative.

The centurion and his prisoners, amongst whom Aristarchus (Col. iv. 10) is named, embarked at Cæsarea on board a ship of Adramyttium, and set sail for the coast of Asia. On the next day they touched at Sidon, and Julius began a course of kindly and respectful treatment by allowing Paul to go on shore to visit his friends. The westerly winds still usual at the time of year (late in the summer) compelled the vessel to run northwards under the lee of Cyprus. Off the coast of Cilicia and Pamphylia they would find northerly winds, which enabled them to reach Myra in Lycia. Here the voyagers were put on board another ship, which was come from Alexandria and was bound for Italy. In this vessel they worked slowly to windward, keeping near the coast of Asia Minor, till they came over against Cnidus. The wind being still contrary, the only course was now to run southwards, under the lee of Crete, passing the headland of Salmone. They then gained the advantage of a weather shore, and worked along the coast of Crete as far as Cape Matala, near which they took refuge in a harbor called Fair Havens, identified with one bearing the same name to this day.

It became now a serious question what course should be taken. It was late in the year for the navigation of those days. The fast of the day of expiation (Lev. xxiii. 27-29), answering to the autumnal equinox, was past, and St. Paul gave it as his advice that they should winter where they were. But the master and the owner of the ship were willing to run the risk of seeking a more commodious harbor, and the centurion followed their judgment. It was resolved, with the concurrence of the majority, to make for a harbor called Phœnix, sheltered from the S. W. winds, as well as from the N. W. (The phrase βλέποντα κατὰ λίβα is rendered either "looking down the S. W." [Smith and Alford], or "looking towards the S. W." when observed from the sea and towards the land inclosing it [Howson].) [PHENICE.] A change of wind occurred which favored the plan, and by the aid of a light breeze from the south they were sailing towards Phœnix (now Lutro), when a violent N. E. wind [EUROCLYDON] came

down from the land (κατ' αὐτῆς, scil. Κρήτης),[a] caught the vessel, and compelled them to let her drive before the wind. In this course they arrived under the lee of a small island called Clauda, about 20 miles from Crete, where they took advantage of comparatively smooth water to get the boat on board, and to undergird, or frap, the ship. Then was a fear lest they should be driven upon the Syrtis on the coast of Africa, and they therefore "lowered the gear," or sent down upon deck the gear connected with the fair-weather sails, and stood out to sea "with storm-sails set and on the starboard tack" (Smith). The bad weather continued, and the ship was lightened on the next day of her cargo, on the third of her loose furniture and tackling. For many days neither sun nor stars were visible to steer by, the storm was violent, and all began to despair of safety. The general discouragement was aggravated by the abstinence caused by the difficulty of preparing food, and the spoiling of it; and in order to raise the spirits of the whole company Paul stood forth one morning to relate a vision which had occurred to him in the night. An angel of the God "whose he was and whom he served" had appeared to him and said, "Fear not, Paul: thou must be brought before Cæsar; and behold, God hath given thee all them that sail with thee." At the same time he predicted that the vessel would be cast upon an island and be lost.

This shipwreck was to happen speedily. On the fourteenth night, as they were drifting through the sea [ADRIA], about midnight, the sailors perceived indications, probably the roar of breakers, that land was near. Their suspicion was confirmed by soundings. They therefore cast four anchors out of the stern, and waited anxiously for daylight. After a while the sailors lowered the boat with the professed purpose of laying out anchors from the bow, but intending to desert the ship, which was in imminent danger of being dashed to pieces. St. Paul, aware of their intention, informed the centurion and the soldiers of it, who took care, by cutting the ropes of the boat, to prevent its being carried out. He then addressed himself to the task of encouraging the whole company, assuring them that their lives would be preserved, and exhorting them to refresh themselves quietly after their long abstinence with a good meal. He set the example himself, taking bread, giving thanks to God, and beginning to eat in presence of them all. After a general meal, in which there were 276 persons to partake, they further lightened the ship by casting out what remained of the provisions on board (τὸν σῖτον is commonly understood to be the "wheat" which formed the cargo, but the other interpretation seems more probable).[b] When the light of the dawn revealed the land, they did not recognize it, but they discovered a creek with a smooth beach, and determined to run the ship aground in it. So they cut away the anchors, unloosed the rudder-paddles, raised the foresail to the wind, and made for the beach. When they came close to it they

a * On the question of the reference of αὐτῆς, see addition to CRETE (Amer. ed.). We think the pronoun refers to the vessel and not to the island.   H.

b * The objections to supposing the ship's provisions to be meant here are that "wheat" (σῖτος) has not this specific sense elsewhere in the N. T.; that the provisions still left, after so long a voyage, would have little or no effect on the ship's draft; and that the ship's cargo was undoubtedly wheat, since the vessel was a merchant-vessel bound from Alexandria to Italy. Prof. Blunt (Coincidences, p. 326 f., Amer. ed.) has drawn out a very striking confirmation of St. Luke's accuracy from the detached notices which reveal to us the nature of the ship's lading (comp. Acts xxvii. 6, 18, 38). See on this point Lechler's Der Apostel Geschichten in Lange's Bibelwerk, p. 408 (3te Aufl. 1869).   H.

found a narrow channel between the land on one side, which proved to be an islet, and the shore; and at this point, where the "two seas met," they succeeded in driving the fore part of the vessel fast into the clayey beach. The stern began at once to go to pieces under the action of the breakers; but escape was now within reach. The soldiers suggested to their commander that the prisoners should be effectually prevented from gaining their liberty by being killed; but the centurion, desiring to save Paul, stopped this proposition, and gave orders that those who could swim should cast themselves first into the sea and get to land, and that the rest should follow with the aid of such spars as might be available. By this creditable combination of humanity and discipline the deliverance was made as complete as St. Paul's assurances had predicted it would be.

The land on which they had been cast was found to belong to Malta. [MELITA.] The very point of the stranding is made out with great probability by Mr. Smith. The inhabitants of the island received the wet and exhausted voyagers with no ordinary kindness, and immediately lighted a fire to warm them. This particular kindness is recorded on account of a curious incident connected with it. The Apostle was helping to make the fire, and had gathered a bundle of sticks and laid them on the fire, when a viper came out of the heat, and fastened on his hand. When the natives saw the creature hanging from his hand they believed him to be poisoned by the bite, and said amongst themselves, "No doubt this man is a murderer, whom, though he has escaped from the sea, yet Vengeance suffers not to live." But when they saw no harm came of it they changed their minds and said that he was a god. This circumstance, as well as the honor in which he was held by Julius, would account for St. Paul being invited with some others to stay at the house of the chief man of the island, whose name was Publius. By him they were courteously entertained for three days. The father of Publius happened to be ill of fever and dysentery, and was healed by St. Paul: and when this was known many other sick persons were brought to him and were healed. So there was a pleasant interchange of kindness and benefits. The people of the island showed the Apostle and his company much honor, and when they were about to leave loaded them with such things as they would want. The Roman soldiers would carry with them to Rome a deepened impression of the character and the powers of the kingdom of which Paul was the herald.

After a three months' stay in Malta the soldiers and their prisoners left in an Alexandrian ship for Italy. They touched at Syracuse, where they stayed three days, and at Rhegium, from which place they were carried with a fair wind to Puteoli, where they left their ship and the sea. At Puteoli they found "brethren," for it was an important place, and especially a chief port for the traffic between Alexandria and Rome: and by these brethren they were exhorted to stay awhile with them. Permission seems to have been granted by the centurion: and whilst they were spending seven days at Puteoli news of the Apostle's arrival was sent on to Rome.

The Christians at Rome, on their part, sent forth some of their number, who met St. Paul at Appii Forum and Tres Tabernæ: and on this first introduction to the Church at Rome the Apostle felt that his long desire was fulfilled at last — "He thanked God and took courage."

St. Paul at Rome. — On their arrival at Rome the centurion delivered up his prisoners into the proper custody, that of the prætorian prefect.[a] Paul was at once treated with special consideration, and was allowed to dwell by himself with the soldier who guarded him. He was not released from this galling annoyance of being constantly chained to a keeper; but every indulgence compatible with this necessary restraint was readily allowed him. He was now therefore free "to preach the Gospel to them that were at Rome also;" and proceeded without delay to act upon his rule — "to the Jew first." He invited the chief persons amongst the Jews to come to him, and explained to them that though he was brought to Rome to answer charges made against him by the Jews in Palestine, he had really done nothing disloyal to his nation or the Law, nor desired to be considered as hostile to his fellow-countrymen. On the contrary, he was in custody for maintaining that "the hope of Israel" had been fulfilled. The Roman Jews replied that they had received no tidings to his prejudice. The sect of which he had implied he was a member they knew to be everywhere spoken against; but they were willing to hear what he had to say. It has been thought strange that such an attitude should be taken towards the faith of Christ by the Jews at Rome, where a flourishing branch of the Church had existed for some years; and an argument has been drawn from this representation against the authenticity of the Acts. But it may be accounted for without violence from what we know and may probably conjecture. (1.) The Church at Rome consisted mainly of Gentiles, though it must be supposed that they had been previously for the most part Jewish proselytes. (2.) The real Jews at Rome had been persecuted and sometimes entirely banished, and their unsettled state may have checked the contact and collision which would have been otherwise likely. (3.) St. Paul was possibly known by name to the Roman Jews, and curiosity may have persuaded them to listen to him. Even if he were not known to them, here, as in other places, his courteous bearing and strong expressions of adhesion to the faith of his fathers would win a hearing from them. A day was therefore appointed, on which a large number came expressly to hear him expound his belief; and from morning till evening he bore witness of the kingdom of God, persuading them concerning Jesus, both out of the Law of Moses and out of the prophets. So the Apostle of the Gentiles had not yet unlearnt the original Apostolic method. The hope of Israel was still his subject. But, as of old, the reception of his message by the Jews was not favorable. They were slow of heart to believe, at Rome as at Pisidian Antioch. The judgment pronounced by Isaiah was come, Paul testified, upon the people. They had made themselves blind and deaf and gross of heart. The Gospel must be proclaimed to the Gentiles, amongst whom it would

a * This was the usual course when prisoners were sent from the provinces to Rome, and may be supposed to have been taken in the case of Paul. The passage however in the common text, Acts xxviii. 16,
which states that this was done, cannot be relied on as certainly genuine. See note *a*, vol. i. p. 365 (Amer. ed.).   E.

find a better welcome. He turned therefore again to the Gentiles, and for two years he dwelt in his own hired house, and received all who came to him, proclaiming the kingdom of God and teaching concerning the Lord Jesus Christ, with all confidence, no man forbidding him.

These are the last words of the Acts. This history of the planting of the kingdom of Christ in the world brings us down to the time when the Gospel was openly proclaimed by the great Apostle in the Gentile capital, and stops short of the mighty convulsion which was shortly to pronounce that kingdom established as the Divine commonwealth for all men. The work of St. Paul belonged to the preparatory period. He was not to live through the time when the Son of Man came in the destruction of the Holy City and Temple, and in the throes of the New Age. The most significant part of his work was accomplished when in the Imperial City he had declared his Gospel " to the Jew first, and also to the Gentile." But his career is not abruptly closed. Before he himself fades out of our sight in the twilight of ecclesiastical tradition, we have letters written by himself, which contribute some particulars to his external biography, and give us a far more precious insight into his convictions and sympathies.

Period of the Later Epistles. — We might naturally expect that St. Paul, tied down to one spot at Rome, and yet free to speak and write to whom he pleased, would pour out in letters his love and anxiety for distant churches. It seems entirely reasonable to suppose that the author of the extant epistles wrote very many which are not extant. To suppose this, aids us perhaps a little in the difficult endeavor to contemplate St. Paul's epistles as living letters. It is difficult enough to connect in our minds the *writing* of these epistles with the external conditions of a human life; to think of Paul, with his incessant chain and soldier, sitting down to write or dictate, and producing for the world an inspired epistle. But it is almost more difficult to imagine the Christian communities of those days, samples of the population of Macedonia or Asia Minor, receiving and reading such letters. But the letters were actually written; and they must of necessity be accepted as representing the kind of communications which marked the intercourse of the Apostle and his fellow-Christians. When he wrote he wrote out of the fullness of his heart; and the ideas on which he dwelt were those of his daily and hourly thoughts. To that imprisonment to which St. Luke has introduced us, — the imprisonment which lasted for such a tedious time, though tempered by much indulgence, — belongs the noble group of letters to Philemon, to the Colossians, to the Ephesians, and to the Philippians. The three former of these were written at one time and sent by the same messengers. Whether that to the Philippians was written before or after these, we cannot determine; but the tone of it seems to imply that a crisis was approaching, and therefore it is commonly regarded as the latest of the four.

St. Paul had not himself founded the Church at Colossæ. But during his imprisonment at Rome he had for an associate — he calls him a " fellow-prisoner " (Philemon 23) — a chief teacher of the Colossian church named Epaphras. He had thus become deeply interested in the condition of that church. It happened that at the same time a slave named Onesimus came within the reach of St.

Paul's teaching, and was converted into a zealous and useful Christian. This Onesimus had run away from his master; and his master was a Christian of Colossæ. St. Paul determined to send back Onesimus to his master; and with him he determined also to send his old companion Tychicus (Acts xx. 4) as a messenger to the church at Colossæ, and to neighboring churches. This was the occasion of the letter to Philemon, which commended Onesimus, in language of singular tenderness and delicacy, as a faithful and beloved brother, to his injured master; and also of the two letters to the Colossians and Ephesians. [PHILEMON, EPISTLE TO.] That to the Colossians, being drawn forth by the most special circumstances, may be reasonably supposed to have been written first. It was intended to guard the church at Colossæ from false teaching, which the Apostle knew to be infesting it. For the characteristics of this epistle, we must refer to the special article. [COLOSSIANS, EPISTLE TO THE.] The end of it (iv. 7–18) names several friends who were with St. Paul at Rome, as Aristarchus, Marcus (St. Mark), Epaphras, Luke, and Demas. For the writing of the Epistle to the Ephesians, there seems to have been no more special occasion, than that Tychicus was passing through Ephesus. [EPHESIANS, EPISTLE TO THE.] The highest characteristic which these two epistles, to the Colossians and Ephesians, have in common, is that of a presentation of the Lord Jesus Christ, fuller and clearer than we find in previous writings, as the Head of creation and of mankind. All things created through Christ, all things coherent in Him, all things reconciled to the Father by Him, the eternal purpose to restore and complete all things in Him, — such are the ideas which grew richer and more distinct in the mind of the Apostle as he meditated on the Gospel which he had been preaching, and the truths implied in it. In the Epistle to the Colossians this divine headship of Christ is maintained as the safeguard against the fancies which filled the heavens with secondary divinities, and which laid down rules for an artificial sanctity of men upon the earth. In the Epistle to the Ephesians the eternity and universality of God's redeeming purpose in Christ, and the gathering of men unto Him as his members, are set forth as gloriously revealed in the Gospel. In both, the application of the truth concerning Christ as the image of God and the Head of men to the common relations of human life is dwelt upon in detail.

The Epistle to the Philippians resembles the Second to the Corinthians in the effusion of personal feeling, but differs from it in the absence of all soreness. The Christians at Philippi had regarded the Apostle with love and reverence from the beginning, and had given him many proofs of their affection. They had now sent him a contribution towards his maintenance at Rome, such as we must suppose him to have received from time to time for the expenses of " his own hired house." The bearer of this contribution was Epaphroditus, an ardent friend and fellow-laborer of St. Paul, who had fallen sick on the journey, or at Rome (Phil. ii. 27). The epistle was written to be conveyed by Epaphroditus on his return, and to express the joy with which St. Paul had received the kindness of the Philippians. He dwells, therefore, upon their fellowship in the work of spreading the Gospel, a work in which he was even now laboring, and scarcely with the less effect on account of his bonds. His imprisonment had made him known, and had given him fruitful opportunities of declaring his Gospel amongst the Imperial guard (i. 13), and even in the household of the Cæsar (iv. 22). He professes his undiminished sense of the glory of following Christ, and his expectation of an approaching time in which the Lord Jesus should be revealed from heaven as a deliverer. There is a *gracious* tone running through this epistle, expressive of humility, devotion, kindness, delight in all things fair and good, to which the favorable circumstances under which it was written gave a natural occasion, and which helps us to understand the kind of ripening which had taken place in the spirit of the writer. [PHILIPPIANS, EPISTLE TO THE.]

In this epistle St. Paul twice expresses a confident hope that before long he may be able to visit the Philippians in person (i. 25, οἶδα κ. τ. λ. ii. 24, πέποιθα κ. τ. λ.). Whether this hope was fulfilled or not, belongs to a question which now presents itself to us, and which has been the occasion of much controversy. According to the general opinion, the Apostle was liberated from his imprisonment and left Rome soon after the writing of the letter to the Philippians, spent some time in visits to Greece, Asia Minor, and Spain, returned again as a prisoner to Rome, and was put to death there. In opposition to this view it is maintained by some, that he was never liberated, but was put to death at Rome at an earlier period than is commonly supposed. The arguments adduced in favor of the common view are, (1) the hopes expressed by St. Paul of visiting Philippi (already named) and Colosse (Philemon 22); (2) a number of allusions in the Pastoral Epistles, and their general character; and (3) the testimony of ecclesiastical tradition. The arguments in favor of the single imprisonment appear to be wholly negative, and to aim simply at showing that there is no proof of a liberation, or departure from Rome. It is contended that St. Paul's expectations were not always realized, and that the passages from Philemon and Philippians are effectually neutralized by Acts xx. 25, "I know that ye all (at Ephesus) shall see my face no more;" inasmuch as the supporters of the ordinary view hold that St. Paul went again to Ephesus. This is a fair answer. The argument from the Pastoral Epistles is met most simply by a denial of their genuineness. The tradition of ecclesiastical antiquity is affirmed to have no real weight.

The decision must turn mainly upon the view taken of the Pastoral Epistles. It is true that there are many critics, including Wieseler and Dr. Davidson, who admit the genuineness of these epistles, and yet by referring 1 Timothy and Titus to an earlier period, and by strained explanations of the allusions in 2 Timothy, get rid of the evidence they are generally understood to give in favor of a second imprisonment. The voyages required by the two former epistles, and the writing of them, are placed within the three years spent chiefly at Ephesus (Acts xx. 31). But the hypothesis of voyages during that period not recorded by St. Luke is just as arbitrary as that of a release from Rome, which is objected to expressly because it is arbitrary; and such a distribution of the Pas-

toral Epistles is shown by overwhelming evidence to be untenable. The whole question is discussed in a masterly and decisive manner by Alford in his Prolegomena to the Pastoral Epistles. If, however, these epistles are not accepted as genuine, the main ground for the belief in a second imprisonment is cut away. For a special consideration of the epistles, let the reader refer to the articles on TIMOTHY and TITUS.

The difficulties which have induced such critics as De Wette and Ewald to reject these epistles, are not inconsiderable, and will force themselves upon the attention of the careful student of St. Paul. But they are overpowered by the much greater difficulties attending any hypothesis which assumes these epistles to be spurious. We are obliged, therefore, to recognize the modifications of St. Paul's style, the developments in the history of the church, and the movements of various persons, which have appeared suspicious in the epistles to Timothy and Titus, as nevertheless historically true. And then without encroaching on the domain of conjecture, we draw the following conclusions: (1.) St. Paul must have left Rome, and visited Asia Minor and Greece; for he says to Timothy (1 Tim. i. 3.), "I besought thee to abide still at Ephesus, when I was setting out for Macedonia." After being once at Ephesus, he was purposing to go there again (1 Tim. iv. 13), and he spent a considerable time at Ephesus (2 Tim. i. 18). (2.) He paid a visit to Crete, and left Titus to organize churches there (Titus i. 5). He was intending to spend a winter at one of the places named NICOPOLIS (Tit. iii. 12). (3.) He travelled by Miletus (2 Tim. iv. 20), Troas (2 Tim. iv. 13), where he left a cloak or case,[a] and some books, and Corinth (2 Tim. iv. 20). (4.) He is a prisoner at Rome, "suffering unto bonds as an evil-doer" (2 Tim. ii. 9), and expecting to be soon condemned to death (2 Tim. iv. 6). At this time he felt deserted and solitary, having only Luke, of his old associates, to keep him company; and he was very anxious that Timothy should come to him without delay from Ephesus, and bring Mark with him (2 Tim. i. 15, iv. 16, 9–12.).

These facts may be amplified by probable additions from conjecture and tradition. There are strong reasons for placing the three epistles at an advanced a date as possible, and not far from one another. The peculiarities of style and diction by which these are distinguished from all his former epistles, the affectionate anxieties of an old man, and the glances frequently thrown back on earlier times and scenes, the disposition to be hortatory rather than speculative, the references to a more complete and settled organization of the Church, the signs of a condition tending to moral corruption, and resembling that described in the apocalyptic letters to the Seven Churches — would incline us to adopt the latest date which has been suggested for the death of St. Paul, so as to interpose as much time as possible between the Pastoral Epistles and the former group. Now the earliest authorities for the date of St. Paul's death are Eusebius and Jerome, who place it, the one (*Chronic. Ann.* 2083) in the 13th, the other (*Cat. Script. Eccl.* "Paulus") in the 14th year of Nero. These dates would allow some four or five years between the

---

first imprisonment and the second. During these years, according to the general belief of the early church, St. Paul accomplished his old design (Rom. xv. 28) and visited Spain. Ewald, who denies the genuineness of the Pastoral Epistles, and with it the journeyings in Greece and Asia Minor, believes that St. Paul was liberated and paid this visit to Spain (*Geschichte*, vi. pp. 621, 631, 632); yielding upon this point to the testimony of tradition. The first writer quoted in support of the journey to Spain is one whose evidence would indeed be irresistible if the language in which it is expressed were less obscure. Clement of Rome, in a hortatory and rather rhetorical passage (*Ep.* 1 *ad Cor.* c. 5) refers to St. Paul as an example of patience, and mentions that he preached ἔν τε τῇ ἀνατολῇ καὶ ἐν τῇ δύσει, and that before his martyrdom he went ἐπὶ τὸ τέρμα τῆς δύσεως. It is probable, but can hardly be said to be certain, that by this expression, "the goal of the west," Clement was describing Spain, or some country yet more to the west. The next testimony labors under a somewhat similar difficulty from the imperfection of the text, but it at least names unambiguously a "profectionem Pauli ab urbe ad Spaniam proficiscentis." This is from Muratori's Fragment on the Canon (Routh, *Rel. Sac.* iv. p. 1-12). (See the passage quoted and discussed in Wieseler, *Chron. Apost. Zeit.* p. 536, &c , or Alford, iii. p. 93.) Afterwards Chrysostom says simply, Μετὰ τὸ γενέσθαι ἐν Ῥώμῃ, πάλιν εἰς τὴν Σπανίαν ἀπῆλθεν (on 2 Tim. iv. 20); and Jerome speaks of St. Paul as set free by Nero, that he might preach the Gospel of Christ "in Occidentis quoque partibus" (*Cat. Script. Eccl.* "Paulus"). Against these assertions nothing is produced, except the absence of allusions to a journey to Spain in passages from some of the fathers where such allusions might more or less be expected. Dr. Davidson (*Introd. New Test.* iii. 15, 84) gives a long list of critics who believe in St. Paul's release from the first imprisonment. Wieseler (p. 521) mentions some of these, with references, and adds some of the more eminent German critics who believe with him in but one imprisonment. These include Schrader, Hemsen, Winer, and Baur. The only English name of any weight to be added to this list is that of Dr. Davidson.

We conclude then, that after a wearing imprisonment of two years or more at Rome, St. Paul was set free, and spent some years in various journeyings eastwards and westwards. Towards the close of this time he pours out the warnings of his less vigorous but still brave and faithful spirit in the letters to Timothy and Titus. The first to Timothy and that to Titus were evidently written at very nearly the same time. After these were written, he was apprehended again and sent to Rome. As an eminent Christian teacher St. Paul was now in a far more dangerous position than when he was first brought to Rome. The Christians had been exposed to popular odium by the false charge of being concerned in the great Neronian conflagration of the city, and had been subjected to a most cruel persecution. The Apostle appears now to have been treated, not as an honorable state-prisoner, but as a felon (2 Tim. ii. 9). But he was at least allowed to write this Second

Letter to his "dearly beloved son" Timothy: and though he expresses a confident expectation of his speedy death, he yet thought it sufficiently probable that it might be delayed for some time, to warrant him in urging Timothy to come to him from Ephesus. Meanwhile, though he felt his isolation, he was not in the least daunted by his danger. He was more than ready to die (iv. 6), and had a sustaining experience of not being deserted by his Lord. Once already, in this second imprisonment, he had appeared before the authorities; and "th Lord then stood by him and strengthened him," and gave him a favorable opportunity for the one thing always nearest to his heart, the public declaration of his Gospel.

This epistle,[a] surely no unworthy utterance at such an age and in such an hour even of a St. Paul, brings us, it may well be presumed, close to the end of his life. For what remains, we have the concurrent testimony of ecclesiastical antiquity, that he was beheaded at Rome, about the same time that St. Peter was crucified there. The earliest allusion to the death of St. Paul is in that sentence from Clemens Romanus, already quoted, ἐπὶ τὸ τέρμα τῆς δύσεως ἐλθὼν καὶ μαρτυρήσας ἐπὶ τῶν ἡγουμένων, οὕτως ἀπηλλάγη τοῦ κόσμου, which just fails of giving us any particulars upon which we can conclusively rely. The next authorities are those quoted by Eusebius in his *H. E.* ii. 25. Dionysius, bishop of Corinth (A. D. 170), says that Peter and Paul went to Italy and taught there together, and suffered martyrdom about the same time. This, like most of the statements relating to the death of St. Paul, is mixed up with the tradition, with which we are not here immediately concerned, of the work of St. Peter at Rome. Caius of Rome, supposed to be writing within the 2d century, names the grave of St. Peter on the Vatican, and that of St. Paul on the Ostian way. Eusebius himself entirely adopts the tradition that St. Paul was beheaded under Nero at Rome. Amongst other early testimonies, we have that of Tertullian, who says (*De Praescr. Haeret.* 36) that at Rome "Petrus passioni Dominicæ adæquatur, Paulus Johannis [the Baptist] exitu coronatur;" and that of Jerome (*Cat. Sc. Paulus*), "Hic ergo 14to Neronis anno (eodem die quo Petrus) Romæ pro Christo capite truncatus sepultusque est, in via Ostiensi." It would be useless to enumerate further testimonies of what is undisputed.

It would also be beyond the scope of this article to attempt to exhibit the traces of St. Paul's Apostolic work in the history of the Church. But there is one indication, so exceptional as to deserve special mention, which shows that the difficulty of understanding the Gospel of St. Paul and of reconciling it with a true Judaism was very early felt. This is in the Apocryphal work called the Clementines (τὰ Κλημέντια), supposed to be written before the end of the 2d century. These curious compositions contain direct assaults (for though the name is not given, the references are plain and undisguised) upon the authority and the character of St. Paul. St. Peter is represented as the true Apostle, of the Gentiles as well as of the Jews, and St. Paul as ὁ ἐχθρὸς ἄνθρωπος, who opposes St. Peter and St. James. The portions of the Clementines which illustrate the writer's view of St. Paul will be

the thoughts and beliefs of that epistle, to whomsoever the composition of it be attributed, are by no means alien to the Apostle's habits of mind.

found in Stanley's *Corinthians* (Introd. to 2 Cor.); and an account of the whole work, with references to the treatises of Schliemann and Baur, in Giesseler, *Eccl. Hist.* i. § 58.

Chronology of St. Paul's Life. — It is usual to distinguish between the internal or absolute, and the external or relative, chronology of St. Paul's life. The former is that which we have hitherto followed. It remains to mention the points at which the N. T. history of the Apostle comes into contact with the outer history of the world. There are *two* principal events which serve as fixed dates for determining the Pauline chronology — the death of Herod Agrippa, and the accession of Festus; and of these the latter is by far the more important. The time of this being ascertained, the particulars given in the Acts enable us to date a considerable portion of St. Paul's life. Now it has been proved almost to certainty that Felix was recalled from Judæa and succeeded by Festus in the year 60 (Wieseler, pp. 66, &c.; Conybeare and Howson, ii. note C). In the autumn, then, of A. D. 60 St. Paul left Cæsarea. In the spring of 61 he arrived at Rome. There he lived two years, that is, till the spring of 63, with much freedom in his own hired house. After this we depend upon conjecture; but the Pastoral Epistles give us reasons, as we have seen, for deferring the Apostle's death until 67, with Eusebius. or 68, with Jerome. Similarly we can go *backwards* from A. D. 60. St. Paul was two years at Cæsarea (Acts xxiv. 27); therefore he arrived at Jerusalem on his last visit by the Pentecost of 58. Before this he had wintered at Corinth (Acts xx. 2, 3), having gone from Ephesus to Greece. He left Ephesus, then, in the latter part of 57, and as he stayed 3 years at Ephesus (Acts xx. 31), he must have come thither in 54. Previously to this journey he had spent " some time " at Antioch (Acts xviii. 23), and our chronology becomes indeterminate. We can only add together the time of a hasty visit to Jerusalem, the travels of the great second missionary journey, which included 1½ year at Corinth, another indeterminate stay at Antioch, the important third visit to Jerusalem, another " long " residence at Antioch (Acts xiv. 28), the first missionary journey, again an indeterminate stay at Antioch (Acts xii. 25) — until we come to the second visit to Jerusalem, which nearly synchronized with the death of Herod Agrippa, in A. D. 44 (Wieseler, p. 130). Within this interval of some 10 years the most important date to fix is that of the third visit to Jerusalem; and there is a great concurrence of the best authorities in placing this visit in either 50 or 51. St. Paul himself (Gal. ii. 1) places this visit " 14 years after " either his conversion or the first visit. In the former case we have 37 or 38 for the date of the conversion. The conversion was followed by 3 years (Gal. i. 18) spent in Arabia and Damascus, and ending with the first visit to Jerusalem; and the space between the first visit (40 or 41) and the second (44 or 45) is filled up by an indeterminate time, presumably 2 or 3 years, at Tarsus (Acts ix. 30), and 1 year at Antioch (Acts xi. 26). The date of the martyrdom of Stephen can only be conjectured, and is very variously placed between A. D. 30 and the year of St. Paul's conversion. In the account of the death of Stephen St. Paul is called " a young man " (Acts vii. 58). It is not improbable therefore that he was born between A. D. 0 and A. D. 5, so that he might be past 60 years of age when he calls himself " Paul

the aged " in Philemon 9. More detailed conjectures will be found in almost every writer on St. Paul. *Comparative* chronological tables (showing the opinions of 30 and 34 critics) are given by Wieseler and Davidson; tables of events only, by Conybeare and Howson, Alford, Jowett, and many others.

Personal Appearance and Character of St. Paul — We have no very trustworthy sources of information as to the personal appearance of St. Paul. Those which we have are referred to and quoted in Conybeare and Howson (i. ch. 7, end). They are the early pictures and mosaics described by Mrs. Jameson, and passages from Malalas, Nicephorus, and the apocryphal *Acta Pauli et Theclæ* (concerning which see also Conybeare and Howson, i. 197). They all agree in ascribing to the Apostle a short stature, a long face with high forehead, an aquiline nose, close and prominent eyebrows. Other characteristics mentioned are baldness, gray eyes, a clear complexion, and a winning expression. Of his temperament and character St. Paul is himself the best painter. His speeches and letters convey to us, as we read them, the truest impressions of those qualities which helped to make him The great Apostle. We perceive the warmth and ardor of his nature, his deeply affectionate disposition, the tenderness of his sense of honor, the courtesy and personal dignity of his bearing, his perfect fearlessness, his heroic endurance; we perceive the rare combination of subtlety, tenacity, and versatility in his intellect; we perceive also a practical wisdom which we should have associated with a cooler temperament, and a tolerance which is seldom united with such impetuous convictions. And the principle which harmonized all these endowments and directed them to a practical end was, beyond dispute, a knowledge of Jesus Christ in the Divine Spirit. Personal allegiance to Christ as to a living Master, with a growing insight into the relation of Christ to each man and to the world, carried the Apostle forwards on a straight course through every vicissitude of personal fortunes and amidst the various habits of thought which he had to encounter. The conviction that he had been entrusted with a Gospel concerning a Lord and Deliverer of men was what sustained and purified his love for his own people, whilst it created in him such a love for mankind that he only knew himself as the servant of others for Christ's sake.

A remarkable attempt has recently been made by Professor Jowett, in his Commentary on some of the epistles, to qualify what he considers to be the blind and undiscriminating admiration of St. Paul, by representing him as having been, with all his excellences, a man " whose appearance and discourse made an impression of feebleness," " out of harmony with life and nature," a confused thinker, uttering himself " in broken words and hesitating forms of speech, with no beauty or comeliness of style," and so undecided in his Christian belief that he was preaching, in the 14th year after his conversion, a Gospel concerning Christ which he himself, in four years more, confessed to have been carnal. In these paradoxical views, however, Professor Jowett stands almost alone: the result of the freest, as of the most reverent, of the numerous recent studies of St. Paul and his works (amongst which Professor Jowett's own Commentary is one of the most interesting) having been only to add an independent tribute to the ancient admiration of Christendom. Those who judge St. Paul as they would judge any other remarkable man confess him unanimously to have been "one of the greatest spirits of all time;" whilst those who believe him to have been appointed by the Lord of mankind, and inspired by the Holy Ghost, to do a work in the world of almost unequalled importance, are lost in wonder as they study the gifts with which he was endowed for that work, and the sustained devotion with which he gave himself to it.

Modern Authorities. — It has not been thought necessary to load the pages of this article with references to the authors about to be mentioned, because in each of them it is easy for the student to turn at once to any part of St. Paul's life or writings with regard to which he may desire to consult them. A very long catalogue might be made of authors who have written on St. Paul; amongst whom the following may be recommended as of some independent value. In English, the work of Messrs. Conybeare and Howson, on the *Life and Epistles of St. Paul*, is at once the most comprehensive and the most popular. Amongst Commentaries, those of Professor Jowett on the Epistles to the Thessalonians, Galatians, and Romans, and of Professor Stanley on the Epistles to the Corinthians, are expressly designed to throw light on the Apostle's character and work. The general Commentaries of Dean Alford and Dr. Wordsworth include abundant matter upon everything relating to St. Paul. So does Dr. Davidson's *Introduction to the New Testament*, which gives also in great profusion the opinions of all former critics, English and foreign. Paley's well-known *Horæ Paulinæ*; Mr. Smith's work on the *Voyage and Shipwreck of St. Paul* [3d ed. 1866]; Mr. Tate's *Continuous History of St. Paul*; and Mr. Lewin's *St. Paul*, are exclusively devoted to Pauline subjects. Of the older works by commentators and others, which are thoroughly sifted by more recent writers, it may be sufficient to mention a book which had a great reputation in the last century, that of Lord Lyttelton on the *Conversion of St. Paul*. Amongst German critics and historians the following may be named: Ewald, in his *Geschichte des Volkes Israel*, vol. vi. and his *Sendschreiben des Apostels Paulus*; Wieseler, *Chronologie des Apostolischen Zeitalters*, which is universally accepted as the best work on the chronology of St. Paul's life and times; De Wette, in his *Einleitung* and his *Exegetisches Handbuch*; Neander, *Pflanzung und Leitung der Christl. Kirche*; works on *Paulus*, by Baur, Hemsen, Schrader, Schneckenburger; and the Commentaries of Olshausen, Meyer, etc. In French, the work of Salvador on *Jésus Christ et sa Doctrine*, in the chapter "St. Paul et l'Église," gives the view of a modern Jew; and the *Discourses on St. Paul*, by M. de Pressensé, are able and eloquent.   J. Ll. D.

* The *literature* under ACTS (see especially Amer. ed.) pertains largely to the history of Paul. Luke's narrative in the Acts may be read with new interest in the later and more accurate translations (Bible Union, Noyes, Alford). Stier's *Reden der Apostel* is now translated by G. H. Venables, *The Words of the Apostles*, etc. (Edinb. 1869), one of the series of Clark's Foreign Theol. Library. For extended sketches of the life and teachings of Paul the reader may see Dr. Schaff's *History of the Apostolic Church*, ch. iii. pp. 226–348; Pressensé's *Histoire des trois premiers Siècles*, i. 425 ff. and ii. 1–104; and Dr. William Smith's *New Test. His-

tory*, pp. 340–536, Amer. ed. Among the recent treatises or works may be mentioned *Paulus der Apostel*, by J. P. Lange, in Herzog's *Real-Encykl.* xi. 238–243; *Paulus*, by H. Besser, author of *Die Bibelstunden*, in Zeller's *Bibl. Wörterb.* ii. 234–242; Lewin's *Fasti Sacri* (Lond. 1865), important for the chronology; Ch. J. Trip, *Paulus nach der Apostelgesch.* (Leiden, 1866), a prize essay; J. R. Oertel, *Paulus in der Apostelgesch.* etc. (Halle a. S. 1868), showing the historical character of the Pauline portions; Howson, *Hulsean Lectures for 1862 on The Character of St. Paul* (2d ed. Lond. 1864); *Scenes from the Life of St. Paul* (Bost. 1867); *The Metaphors of St. Paul* (Lond. 1868), reprinted in the *Theological Eclectic*, vols. iv. & v.; *Die Apostelgeschichte in Bibelstunden* (i.–lxxxiii.) *ausgelegt* von Karl Gerok, 2 vols. (1868); Th. Binney, *Lectures on St. Paul: his Life and Ministry* (Lond. 1866), popular and practical; A. Hausrath, *Der Apostel Paulus* (Heidelb. 1865); F. Bungener, *Saint Paul, sa vie, son œuvre et ses épîtres* (Paris, 1865); Renan, *Saint Paul* (Paris, 1869); Paulus Cassel, *Die Inschrift des Altars zu Athen* (Berlin, 1867), able, but incorrectly assumes Paul's object to be anti-pantheistic not anti-polytheistic.

On the *doctrine* of St. Paul, see L. Usteri, *Entwickelung d. paulin. Lehrbegriffs* (Zürich, 1824, 6e Aufl. 1851); A. F. Dähne, *Entwickl. d. paulin. Lehrbegriffs* (Halle, 1835); J. F. Rübiger, *De Christologia Paulina, contra Baurium* (Vratisl. 1852); R. A. Lipsius, *Die paulinische Rechtfertigungslehre* (Leipz. 1853); Abp. Whately, *Essays on some of the Difficulties in the Writings of St. Paul, from the 8th London ed.*, Andover, 1865; and the biblico-theological works of Neander, Reuss, Lutterbeck, Baur, Messner, Lechler, C. F. Schmid, and Beyschlag, referred to under JOHN, GOSPEL OF, vol. ii. p. 1439 a. — For copious references to the literature relating to the Apostle, see particularly Reuss's *Gesch. der Heiligen Schriften N. T.* 4e Aufl. § 58 ff.   H.

* *Paul's peculiar Mission as an Apostle.* — Saint Paul is generally regarded as one of the apostolic college, perhaps, indeed, as *primus inter pares*, yet as distinguished from the others only by his late and abnormal admission into their ranks, — a distinction which in some quarters essentially impaired his authority and influence. In our apprehension, he was specifically and officially separated from the twelve, and was intrusted with a mission, to which no one of them was equally adequate, and for which his nativity, culture, and antecedent life had trained and qualified him.

The seeds of Christianity were planted at the outset in the decaying trunk of Judaism, as those of the mistletoe are lodged in the ancient oak The earliest Christians not only were regarded, but regarded themselves, as a reformed sect of Jews. The original disciples were punctilious Hebrews, and held Christianity as a code supplementary to that of Moses. They were scandalized and horror-stricken at the thought of abjuring the ceremonial law. When, after the divine monition in the case of Cornelius, they reluctantly began to admit Gentile converts, they stretched the yoke of Judaism before the gate of the church, and sought to compel their proselytes to stoop under it, as the essential, or at least the most hopeful condition of Christian citizenship. This narrowness of vision was the necessary result of their humble origin, obscure condition, scanty culture, and provincial associations, and it was among their special fitnesses for the apostleship. Had they been more catholic in their tolerance, and broader in their sympathies, they would have hopelessly alienated their fellow-countrymen, and would thus have been left without any point of support for propagandism among the Gentiles. It was their continued devotion to the law and ritual of their fathers, that won for them a not impatient hearing, even from the very Pharisees, that enabled them to preach Christ in the synagogues, and that obtained for the new religion in Gentile cities the liberty of profession, which, restricted as it was and nowhere inviolable, had cost Judaism several generations of untempered contumely and persecution. Thus was it ordained that the heavenly exotic should gain richness and strength, should reach forth boughs of ample shade and sufficing fruitfulness, before it should be severed from the parent trunk, and left without support to the winds and storms of a hostile world.

But the hour had arrived when the more vigorous vitality of the younger plant could no longer find nourishment in its parasitic condition; and Paul was the appointed agent for the essential and pre-determined separation. In his mind, and under his administration, Christianity was first required and treated as independent and sovereign. Under him grew up the organization, by which it was thenceforth to assume its unshared place, to discharge its undivided office, and to overshadow and supplant the growths of uncounted ages. This bold and delicate mission demanded not alone devotion and zeal, not alone intimate conversance with the mind of Christ. He to whom it was intrusted needed a profound acquaintance with Judaism as it then was, its traditions and its philosophy, in order that the separation might be effected, on the one hand, without leaving the least radicle or fibre of the transplanted scion in the ancient stock, and on the other, without marring the venerable, though effete majesty of the tree which God had in the earlier ages planted for the healing of the nations, and whose " branches he had made strong for himself." For this work there was also requisite a thorough knowledge of those extra-Judaic religions and philosophies, which were to vanish with the growth of Christianity, but each of which, by the germs of truth which it embodied, might offer special vantage-ground for the tilth of the spiritual husbandman. It was fitting, too, that the chief agent in this divine enterprise should have become familiar with the customs, prejudices, needs, and susceptibilities of the so many and diverse nations that were to be sheltered and fed by the same " tree of life." Above all, there were required for this movement a weight of character and a cogency of influence which could command respect and constrain attention, a sanctity of life beyond the shadow of reproach, and dialectic and rhetorical faculties which needed not to shrink from the encounter with the subtilty of the schools or the eloquence of the popular assembly.

If, then, Paul has had no superior, hardly an equal among men, he was no more than level with his work. We cannot but regard him as the first man of his age, and we can name no man of any age who seems to us greater than he. Indeed, apart from the intrinsic character of Christianity and the internal evidence of its records, there seems to us no stronger proof of the authenticity of those records and the divine origin of their contents, than the simple fact that Paul — who lived so near the birth-time of the religion, when imposture could have been laid bare and delusion rent away, and who of all men was the least likely to have been deceived by false shows or borne headlong by baseless enthusiasm — was a Christian.

His training for his Work. — Let us pass in review his providential training for his great life-work; for God always " makes up his jewels," and those that are to glow with the purest lustre in his coronet are always ground, polished, and set by the special agencies of nature, experience, and association best adapted to develop in each the peculiar traits of the divine beauty and glory which it is designed to mirror to the world. At the Christian era there was not a spot on earth so well fitted as Tarsus, for the nurture of him to whom that once world-renowned city now owes the survivance of its very name in the popular memory. Its site and surroundings must have taken an early and strong hold on a mind like his, and have helped to generate the fervor, the glow, the torrent-like rush of thought, the vivid imagination, the overcharged intensity of emotion manifested in his writings. The city lay on a richly variegated plain of unsurpassed fertility. In its rear rose the lofty, bold, snow-crowned cliffs of Mount Taurus, piled against the northern sky, summit against summit, crag upon crag, rolling up their mist-wreaths to meet the ascending sun, and arresting midway his declining path. From these cliffs, clear as crystal, made deathly cold even in midsummer by the melting snow, tumbled rather than flowed the Cydnus, over perpetual rapids, and frequent waterfalls of unsurpassed beauty and of grandeur hardly paralleled on the Eastern Continent, till only as it approached the city it became tractable to the oar, and navigable thence to the great sea. In full sight of the city lay the vast Mediterranean, the ocean of the Old World, whitened with the sails of a multitudinous commerce, now serene as a land-locked lake, and then lashed into commotion wild and grand as that with which the Atlantic breaks upon its shores. This discipline of valley, mountain, river, and sea, was well adapted to make the perceptive powers keen and vivid, to inspire gorgeous fancies, to stretch to their utmost capacity the extensor muscles of the inner man, to form habits of rapid thought and sightlike intuition.

Then, as regarded Paul's training for the cosmopolitan life for which he was destined, Tarsus was the metropolis of eastern travel and commerce. Nowhere else except in Rome was there so free a commingling of people from every quarter of the civilized world, or so favorable a position for acquiring an intimacy with a broad diversity of languages, habits, customs, and opinions. The city was a microcosm in its population. The native barbarian stock was depressed, yet little changed by immigration. The descendants of an early Greek colony held the foremost places of wealth and social influence, rivalled by a horde of officials and mercantile residents from Rome; while, separated from both by faith and ancestral customs, but mingling with them in all the departments of active life, were large numbers of the Hebrew race, whose migratory instincts were already fulfilling the ancient prophecy of their dispersion among all nations. Tarsus was also celebrated as a seat of learning, taking precedence, at that epoch, of Athens which was then losing, and of Alexandria which had not yet attained the supremacy in mental culture. [TARSUS.] That Paul had enjoyed a liberal culture under Grecian auspices is evident from the freedom and fluency of his style, from his repeated classical allusions and quotations, and from his dialectic acumen and skill.

From Tarsus Paul was probably removed at an early age to Jerusalem; and that on the Jewish side his education was thorough and perfect, his teacher's name alone is ample warrant. Gamaliel was the most learned Jew of his age, and was reckoned among the seven in the long series of Rabbis, who were honored with the title of *Rabban*, equivalent to "*Most Excellent Master*." It is a saying of the Talmud, that "the glory of the Law ceased" at his death. He was, of course, a Pharisee, and as such, not only held in reverence the entire canon of the Old Testament, but attached even greater importance to oral tradition, and to the (so-called) religious writings in the then vernacular dialect; so that through him Paul gained access to the distinctive opinions and mental habits of the sect with which he was afterwards brought into so frequent collision, and from whose members he knew how to gain a favorable hearing. Undoubtedly Paul may have learnt from Gamaliel the lessons that made him a persecutor of the infant church. The Rabbi's prudent counsel in the case of Peter does not show that he was tolerant of reputed error. That counsel savored as much of the fox as of the dove, and, taken by itself, it only indicates a deep insight into the springs of human action, and a shrewd perception of what would have been the surest way of exterminating Christianity, had it been indeed, as he supposed it, a base-born superstition. There is extant a prayer of Gamaliel against misbelievers, which shows that he relied implicitly on the divine vengeance for the work of destruction from which he dissuaded his fellow-countrymen. We attach no little importance to Paul's education and experience as a persecutor. It must have taught him tolerance, generosity, magnanimity toward his opponents. We accordingly find him using the language, not of harsh condemnation, but of conciliation, tenderness, pity toward the unconverted Jews, evidently maintaining a strong fellow-feeling with them, never forgetting that he had been honestly and fervently what they still were. Under the same influence we see him more than just towards rival Christian teachers, rejoicing in whatever good work they wrought for the common cause, and acknowledging the loyalty to their master, and the successful propagandism of those who "added affliction to his bonds" (Philip. i. 16).

His social Position. — There is reason to believe that St. Paul's social position in early life was above mediocrity. He inherited from his father the citizenship of Rome. A Jew, or a native of Tarsus, could have obtained this only by purchase, or in reward of distinguished services. If in the former way, the cost was larger than a poor man could have paid, or one in an obscure position would have cared to offer; if in the latter, the implication of a prominent and influential social standing is still more direct and certain. A similar inference might be drawn from the high, though cruel official eminence and trust confided to him by his fellow-countrymen before his conversion. It is worthy of remark, also, that alike in Judæa, before Festus, Felix, and Agrippa, on his voyage to Rome, and while permitted to live in his own hired house during his detention in Rome,

he was uniformly treated as a prisoner of distinction. Nor is our conclusion from these facts invalidated by his trade as a tent-maker; for it was customary for Jewish youth, of whatever condition in life, to learn some form of handicraft. We do not allude to this point because the mere accident of birth attaches to him the slightest preëminence above his colleagues from the fishing-boats on the Galilean Lake. But he lived at a period when the lines of social distinction were sharply drawn, and had not begun to be blended by the Gospel of human brotherhood, and whatever advantage of position he possessed must have opened to him avenues of influence which were closed against the original Apostles, and must have won for him larger freedom of access to the persons of exalted station, and even royal dignity, before whom he was often permitted to plead the cause of Christ. Then too, the higher his position, the larger was his sacrifice in joining the company of unlettered rustics and fishermen, and bearing with them the reproach of the despised Nazarene. Yet more, the farther he was removed from the condition of those who had little to lose by becoming Christians, the more improbable is his conversion on any theory of naturalism; the stronger the certainty that he had a vision of the Saviour on the way to Damascus, and was miraculously called to the apostleship.

However this may be, we cannot be mistaken in assigning a prominent place among his qualifications to his high-bred courtesy, — to his possession in an eminent degree of the traits belonging to that much abused, yet choice designation, a *gentleman*, — "the highest style of man;" for even the Christian is but half-regenerated, when the grace of God has not its outblooming in gentleness, courtesy, and kindness in the whole intercourse of life. These traits are everywhere manifest in him. His style of address before high official personages is free equally from sycophancy and from rudeness, betraying alike the tact of a highly accomplished man, and the dignity of a Christian. In his epistles there is a pervading grace of manner, indicating at once the politeness of a loving heart, and familiarity with the most becoming modes of expressing that politeness. His very rebukes are conciliatory. He prepares the way for needed censure by merited praise. He conveys unpalatable truth at once with considerate gentleness and with unmistakable explicitness. He shows equal delicacy in the reluctant asking and the grateful acknowledgment of favors. His numerous salutations are gracefully diversified in form, and sometimes strikingly beautiful. His epistle to Philemon grows upon our admiration, when we compare it with the most courtly models of epistolary composition, ancient and modern. It was by this perfect urbanity that he became all things to all men, studying the *mollia tempora fandi*, the fit opportunities and methods of access, and presenting the great truths of religion in the form best suited to disarm opposition and conciliate respect.

Paul as an Orator. — Let us now consider some of St. Paul's qualities as an orator and a writer. In estimating his genius as an orator, we cannot forget what he tells us of the impediments in the way of his success. He cites those who speak of his bodily presence as mean and his voice as contemptible; and there are traditions, undoubtedly authentic, of his having been a little, bald-headed man, with nothing in his outward aspect to inspire especial regard. This may have been the case. and his oratory have had for this only the more winning and commanding efficacy. The lack of physical gifts is often a source of added power to a soul full of great, burning, energizing thoughts. We have seen a deformed dwarf rise before a vast audience, in which at the outset the prestige of a distinguished reputation could not suppress the blended feeling of pity and aversion, and in a few moments he has obtained a purchase upon that audience which would have been denied to manly strength or beauty; for to their apprehension that curved spine has become a huge mass of brain, and of brain on fire, and that puny body seems a human frame no longer, but a conductor of successive thunder-strokes of fervid emotion from soul to soul. So too, have we heard a slender, harsh, shrill, or unmanageable voice, when the vehicle of brilliant thought or profound feeling, rise into an eloquence as far above all rhetorical rules as it was wide of them, so that we have almost forgotten that there were uttered words, and have felt as if it were that silent infusion of sentiment which we can imagine as superseding the need and use of language between unembodied spirits. We can conceive of Paul's person as paltry and unattractive, yet as irradiated in countenance, mien, and gesture, transfigured, glorified by the vividness of his conceptions, the intensity of his zeal, the ecstasy of his devotion. His voice, too, may have been such as no artificial training could have made melodious or effective; yet it must have surged and swelled, grown majestic in intonation and rhythm, trembled with deep emotion, risen into grandeur, as he spoke of Christ and of heaven, and have struck the sweetest chords under the inspiration of the cross. A soul like his could have assimilated the meanest apparatus of bodily organs to its own intense and noble vitality, could have become transparent through the most opaque medium, and have made itself profoundly felt even with a stammering tongue or in a barbarous dialect.

The prime element of an orator's efficiency is his character. His own soul is his chief instrument. What he can accomplish can never transcend the measure of what he is. His words and gestures are but small multiplicands, of which his mass of mind and heart is the multiplier. Paul was the greatest and most efficient orator of his age, because he was the greatest and best man of his age, — because the question that mounted to his lips when he rose from the lightning-flash that closed his outward vision to open the inward eye to the realm of spiritual truth, " Lord, what wilt thou have me to do ? " was thenceforward the question of his life, — because from that moment he " conferred not with flesh and blood," but only with the spirit of the living God, — because his whole vast nature was consecrated by an ineffaceable Corban to the service of Christ and the salvation of man.

Next to the power of personal character, the orator needs complete mastery of his subject and his position. We need not say how thoroughly Paul was master of his subject, — how his treasures heaped up from schools of philosophy, from travels in many lands, from vast and varied experience, were all so transmuted into spiritual truth, that, though one of the most learned men upon earth, he literally " knew nothing but Jesus Christ, and Him crucified." At the same time, no man can ever have been more entirely the master of his position. He analyzes an assembly at first sight,

discerns at once where and how to strike, what there is in the condition of his hearers that may be made subservient to his purpose, how favor may be conciliated without a sacrifice of integrity, how the false believer or the sinner may be refuted or condemned on his own ground. He understands the rare art of so dividing an indifferent or unfriendly audience, as to draw over to his own side those who have any points of affinity with himself, however remote. Thus, in a mixed assembly in Jerusalem, he wins a patient hearing from the Pharisees, by putting foremost in his speech what always held the first place in his heart, the resurrection of the dead (Acts xxiii. 6 ff.). The most noteworthy instance of his skill in the management of a specific audience is to be found in his discourse at Athens. We need not enlarge on this topic here. It may suffice to refer the reader to Luke's report of the speech itself (Acts xvii. 22–31), and to the account of the circumstances of its delivery and of its wise adaptation to the Apostle's object, which has been given in a previous article (MARS' HILL, Amer. ed.).

Paul as a Writer. — We pass to notice some of this Apostle's characteristics as a writer. Among these we would name as most prominent the singular union, throughout the greater part of his epistles, of strong reasoning and vivid emotion. He is severely logical, and at the same time full of intense feeling. The keenest shafts of his logic are forged in the red heat of fervent devotion: his most glowing utterances of piety are often argumentative in their form; and some of those rapturous doxologies that break the continuity of his discourse occur in the midst of polemic discussions on mooted and abstruse points of Christian doctrine and duty.

St. Paul is often charged with obscurity. Much of this alleged obscurity results from the indifference of readers to the occasion on which each separate epistle was written, and the purpose which the writer had in view. Any letters, read as his generally are, would be obscure; for epistles are always to be interpreted in great part by the circumstances to which they owe their origin. In the case of Paul's writings, these circumstances are in every instance to be determined, or conjectured with the strongest show of probability, from the comparison of their text with the parallel history of the Acts of the Apostles and with other sources of information concerning the communities and persons to whom the epistles were severally addressed.

Another source of obscurity in these writings, obviated, however, by careful study, consists in St. Paul's use of Greek particles. No author makes more profuse and at the same time more discriminating use of particles than he; and whether a reader shall trace the continuity of his discourse, or shall see only abrupt transitions and trackless involutions of thought, depends very much on the degree of his conversance with the Pauline use of illatives, connectives, and that whole delicately organized network of conjunctions, prepositions, and adverbs which confuses and bewilders where it does not guide. Moreover, the mere classical scholar is at fault as to these epistles; for Paul often uses particles (as well as other words) in accordance, not with Greek, but with Hebrew idioms, — in the acceptation in which they are employed by the writers of the Septuagint.

There is, however, a sense in which St. Paul's

writings are involved and desultory. His sentences are absolutely loaded down with meaning. He condenses in a single period exceptions, qualifications, subsidiary thoughts, cognate ideas, which an ordinary writer would spin out into a long paragraph. His digressions are, indeed, frequent; but they are always forays into a rich country which he lays under a heavy tribute; and he uniformly returns to his starting point, resumes the thread of his discourse, and never drops a discussion till he has brought it to a satisfactory close. He always has a definite purpose in view, and advances steadily in its pursuit, with a vast profusion of argument and illustration indeed, but all of it pertinent, all of it tending to raise the reader to his own lofty point of vision, and to inspire him with his own profound feeling of the infinite truths and immortal hopes which are the life-tide of his being.

St. Paul's rhetoric is as perfect as his logic. He never forgets the proportion which style should bear to the subject of discourse. He fills out more completely than any other writer extant Cicero's definition of the eloquent man, — *is, qui poterit parva summisse, modica temperate, magna graviter, dicere.* How many are the passages in his writings, which in their blended beauty and majesty transcend the power of imitation, and distance all efforts of human genius hardly more in the divine inspiration that flooded his soul than in the mere instrumentalities of phrase and diction, — in the burning words that clothe the God-breathed thoughts! Was there ever a moral portraiture that could be compared with his delineation of charity? As trait after trait drops from his pen, the grace of love grows and spreads till it takes into its substance the whole of life, the whole of character, all relations, all obligations, — till, like the child in the apocalyptic vision, the earth-born virtue is "caught up unto God and to his throne," and we feel that it must indeed outlast faith and hope, constituting the very essence of the heavenly life, — superseding the doubtful reasonings and lame philosophy of this world, so that knowledge in its wonted processes shall cease, — becoming its own interpreter from spirit to spirit, so that tongues shall fail, and ransomed man shall be love as God is love. Or we might refer to that sublime chapter on the resurrection, in which the Apostle takes his stand by the broken sepulchre of the Redeemer, at the foot of the rock which the angel rolled away plants the ladder reaching from earth to heaven, and on rungs that are massive day-beams of the resurrection-morning, leads up his tried and persecuted converts to those celestial heights where the corruptible is clothed in incorruption, — where goes forth forever the shout of triumph, "O death, where is thy sting? O grave, where is thy victory?"

Value of Paul's Epistles. — It remains for us to speak of the importance of the epistles of St. Paul as a portion of the Christian canon. But in entering on this subject we cannot deny that they have been a most copious fountain of false doctrine. There has never been a heresy so absurd, or a vagary so wild, as not to resort for its prooftexts, chiefly, to this portion of the sacred volume. This, however, has been due to two fundamental errors as to the interpretation of the Pauline epistles. The first is a misapprehension of their nature and uses. They have been regarded as primary and independent treatises on Christian theology, rather than as writings of specific purpose and limited application. The phraseology by

which St. Paul characterized and refuted ephemeral crudities and follies, and which is closely circumscribed in meaning by the history of the times, has been generalized into universal propositions. His contemptuous estimate of the heartless routine of an effete ritual has been extended to the fundamental laws of personal and social duty, and Antinomians of the foulest type have justified their abominations by the very terms in which he inculcated a faith which makes men virtuous, in opposition to a ceremonial law which left them to unrebuked iniquity. In fine, his epistles have been treated, not as the commentaries of a divinely inspired man on the original and complete revelation through Christ, but as a supplementary revelation of paramount magnitude and moment. Thus, instead of tracing principles in their authoritative applications, men have transmuted the applications into principles. Even where no grave falsity or error has resulted from this source, it has tended to render the terminology of religion harmfully technical and complex, and to obscure the simple beauty of the truth as it fell from the Saviour's lips, by incorporating with it words and phrases which derived their origin and their sole fitness from conditions of the Jewish and Pagan mind that have long since passed into oblivion.

Another source of error from these epistles has been the habit of aphoristical interpretation, — the treatment of separate sentences, and fragments of sentences, as if they were complete in themselves, without needing to be modified by the context. No writings extant are so little adapted as St. Paul's to this mode of interpretation. They contain comparatively few independent sentences, isolated sentiments, statements not contingent for a portion of their meaning on what precedes or follows them. A sentence taken by itself is more likely to denote the opposite of what the writer meant by it, than it is to present his meaning with any good degree of definiteness and accuracy. He often traces out his adversary's line of argument, or assumes his postulates, in order to demonstrate the falsity of his inferences from them. He sometimes holds an imaginary colloquy with an objector and states the fallacy which he is aiming to expose, without indicating to the careless reader that he is not giving utterance to his own thoughts; and in some instances he regards the statement of a falsity as its sufficient refutation, — as virtually a *reductio ad absurdum.*

In treating of the uses of St. Paul's epistles, we would first refer to the essential place they hold among the evidences of Christianity. They at once establish their own genuineness, and furnish ample confirmation of the authenticity of the historical books of the New Testament. They bear unmistakable tokens of their having been written by the very Paul who appears as the chief historical personage in the Acts of the Apostles; and our conclusion in favor of their genuineness is constantly confirmed by the disinterring of minute, latent, manifestly undesigned coincidences in the epistles with statements in the Acts, and with the results of historical and archæological research. Indeed, the Pauline origin of the greater part of these epistles is generally acknowledged even by the most skeptical of critics, and, when called in question, is disputed on grounds unappreciable to a mind of ordinary perspicacity. Now, these epistles imply, at the time when they were written, the existence of precisely the condition of things that must have

existed, if Jesus Christ lived and taught, died and
rose from the dead, when, where, and as he is said
to have done in the Gospels. They discuss just
such questions as must needs have arisen in the
course of Christian experience, — cases of casuistry,
scruples of the morbidly conscientious, terms of
toleration and fellowship, tests of religious character and progress, — in fine, questions parallel with
those which converts from heathenism might, and
no doubt do, ask at the present day. They are,
for the most part, questions which could have been
asked only by mere novices. Such discussions we
do not find in the Gospels, which contain simply
the form in which Christian truth is said to have
fallen from the Master's lips, not the record of its
workings on men's anterior beliefs and habits.
This could have been the case only if the Gospels
are genuine and authentic. If they were written
by other than apostolic men, and at a later than
the apostolic age, it is impossible that they should
not have borne numerous marks of the then condition of Christian experience, — that they should
not have adapted the Saviour's words to the then
existing exigencies of the Church. That they contain only the rudiments, not the diversified applications, of Christian doctrine, can be accounted for
only by the theory that they are literal history,
written by men who had direct access to the historical fountains.

Not only do these epistles attest the primeval
antiquity of our Gospels, but even were that denied, they are themselves a luculent record of the
very historical Christianity which is maintained by
critics of the various skeptical schools to have been
wholly post-apostolic and of very gradual growth.
St. Paul's epistles were, all of them, written (we
have positive proof that most of them were) before
the close of the first century of the Christian era.
They recognize a Christianity founded on the expressly divine sonship and mission, the sacrificial
death and the resurrection of Jesus Christ. As to
the latter event, St. Paul evidently had been at
pains carefully to investigate the evidence. He
states his belief of it, not on *a priori* or transcendental grounds, but on the testimony of numerous
eye-witnesses, some of whose names he specifies,
while we infer that he knew the names of many
more, as he says that most of them were still
living, though some had died; and he makes this
salient fact in the Christian narrative the basis of
all satisfying faith and efficient propagandism. In
fine, historical Christianity had as clear and definite and undisputed a place in the faith of Paul
and his contemporary Christians in the very generation that had seen the face and heard the voice
of Jesus Christ, as it has in the belief of the most
rigid adherent to the letter of Scripture in our own
day. These epistles are thus fatal to the "development theory," according to which Christianity
could not have attained its definite shape and consistency, or the person of Christ from that of a
wise and virtuous Jewish peasant have towered by
mythical accretions into the figure of the world's
Redeemer and the heaven-born Son of God, until
his contemporaries had all passed away and yielded
place to a new generation.

Finally, these epistles are invaluable to us, and
to Christians of every age, as embodying decisions,
guided by the inspiration of God, on momentous
questions of Christian ethics, and thus as a collateral interpretation of the mind of Christ as conveyed to us in the Gospels. They bear toward the
Gospels very much the same relation that is borne
to the Constitution of the United States by the
recorded decisions of those judges who were intimately conversant with the views, aims, and purposes of its founders. To the Christian Church
Jesus gave its constitution in his teachings and his
life. But from the very nature of the case there
were few or no decisions of mooted points under
that constitution prior to his ascension; for the
Church cannot be said to have existed before the
day of Pentecost. In Paul we have a judge on
whom the spirit of the Master rested, and who
held for many years the foremost place in the
ecclesiastical administration. To him were brought
for adjudication numerous subjects of doubt and
controversy, and his decisions remain on record in
his epistles. The questions of those earlier ages
have indeed long since passed away; but strictly
analogous questions, depending on the very same
principles for their solution, are constantly recurring. The heart's inmost experiences, needs, and
cravings are the same in America in the nineteenth
century that they were in Europe and Asia in the
first; and in Paul's epistles we have an inexhaustible repertory of instruction, admonition, edification,
and comfort for our several conditions and emergencies as the called of Christ and the heirs of
heaven.   A. P. P.

PAVEMENT. [GABBATHA.]

PAVILION. 1. *Sôc,*[a] properly an inclosed
place, also rendered "tabernacle," "covert," and
"den," once only "pavilion" (Ps. xxvii. 5).

2. *Succâh,*[b] usually "tabernacle" and "booth."
[SUCCOTH.]

3. *Shaphrûr,*[c] and *Shaphrîr,* a word used once
only in Jer. xliii. 10, to signify glory or splendor,
and hence probably to be understood of the splendid covering of the royal throne. It is explained
by Jarchi and others "a tent." [TENT.]
                                      H. W. P.

● **PEACE.** [SALUTATION.]

PEACOCKS (תֻּכִּיִּים and הַתֻּכִּיִּים, *tuccig-
yîm: ταῶνες: pati*). Amongst the natural products of the land of Tarshish which Solomon's fleet
brought home to Jerusalem mention is made of
"peacocks:" for there can, we think, be no doubt
at all that the A. V. is correct in thus rendering
tucciyyîm, which word occurs only in 1 K. x. 22,
and 2 Chr. ix. 21; most of the old versions, with
several of the Jewish Rabbis being in favor of this
translation. Some writers have, however, been
dissatisfied with the rendering of "peacocks," and
have proposed "parrots," as Huet (*Diss. de Nav.
Sal.* 7, § 6) and one or two others. Keil (*Diss. de
Ophir,* p. 104, and *Comment. on* 1 K. x. 22), with
a view to support his theory that Tarshish is the
old Phœnician Tartessus in Spain, derives the Hebrew name from Tucca, a town of Mauritania and

---

a כֹּן, from סָכַךְ, "enclose" (Ges. 952); σκηνή;
tabernaculum.

b סֻכָּה, from same root; σκηνή; tabernaculum;

also 2 Sam. xxii. 12, *latibulum.* In 1 K. xx. 16,
Σοκχώ, *umbraculum.*

c שַׁפְרוּר and Keri שַׁפְרִיר (Ges. 1469).

Numidia, and concludes that the "Aves Numidicæ" (Guinea Fowls) are meant: which birds, however, in spite of their name, never existed in Numidia, nor within a thousand miles of that country!

There can be no doubt that the Hebrew word is of foreign origin. Gesenius (*Thes.* p. 1502) cites many authorities to prove that the *tucci* is to be traced to the Tamul or Malabaric *togei*, "peacock;" which opinion has recently been confirmed by Sir E. Tennent (*Ceylon*, ii. 102, and i. p. xx. 3d ed.), who says, "It is very remarkable that the terms by which these articles (ivory, apes, and peacocks) are designated in the Hebrew Scriptures are identical with the Tamil names, by which some of them are called in Ceylon to the present day, — *takeyim* may be recognized in *tukei*, the modern name for these birds." Thus Keil's objection, "that this supposed *togei* is not yet itself sufficiently ascertained" (*Comment. on* 1 K. x. 22), is satisfactorily met.[a]

Peacocks are called "Persian birds" by Aristophanes, *Aves*, 484; see also *Acharn.* 63; Diod. Sic. ii. 53.

Peacocks were doubtless introduced into Persia from India or Ceylon; perhaps their first introduction dates from the time of Solomon; and they gradually extended into Greece, Rome, and Europe generally. The ascription of the quality of vanity to the peacock is as old as the time of Aristotle, who says (*Hist. An.* i. 1, § 15), "Some animals are jealous and vain like the peacock." The A. V. in Job xxxix. 13 speaks of "the goodly wings of the peacocks;" but this is a different Hebrew word and has undoubted reference to the "ostrich."　　　　　W. H.

PEARL (גָּבִישׁ, *gábísh*: γαβίς: *eminentia*). The Heb. word occurs, in this form, only in Job xxviii. 18, where the price of wisdom is contrasted with that of *rámóth* ("coral") and *gábísh*; and the same word, with the addition of the syllable *al* (אֶל), is found in Ez. xiii. 11, 13, xxxviii. 22, with *aíné*, "stones," i. e. "stones of ice." The ancient versions contribute nothing by way of explanation. Schultens (*Comment. in Job*, l. c.) leaves the word untranslated: he gives the signification of "pearls" to the Hebrew term *penintim* (A. V. "rubies") which occurs in the same verse. Gesenius, Fürst, Rosenmüller, Maurer, and commentators generally, understand "crystal" by the term, on account of its resemblance to ice. Lee (*Comment. on Job*, l. c.) translates *rámóth vegábísh* "things high and massive." Carey renders *gábísh* by "mother-of-pearl," though he is by no means content with this explanation. On the whole the balance of probability is in favor of "crystal," since *gábísh* denotes "ice" (not "hailstones," as Carey supposes, without the addition of *abné*, "stones") in the passages of Ezekiel where the word occurs. There is nothing to which ice can be so well compared as to crystal. The objection to this interpretation is that crystal is not an article of much value; but perhaps reference may here be made to the beauty and pure lustre of rock crystal, or this substance may by the ancient Orientals have been held in high esteem.

Pearls (μαργαρῖται), however, are frequently mentioned in the N. T.: comp. Matt. xiii. 45, 46, where the kingdom of heaven is likened unto "a merchant-man seeking goodly pearls." Pearls formed part of women's attire (1 Tim. ii. 9; Rev. xvii. 4). "The twelve gates" of the heavenly Jerusalem were twelve pearls (Rev. xxi. 21); perhaps "mother-of-pearl" is here more especially intended.

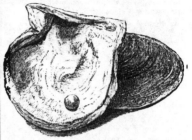

Pearl Oyster.

Pearls are found inside the shells of various species of *Mollusca*. They are formed by the deposit of the nacreous substance around some foreign body as a nucleus. The *Unio margaritiferus*, *Mytilus edulis*, *Ostrea edulis*, of our own country, occasionally furnish pearls; but "the pearl of great price" is doubtless a fine specimen yielded by the pearl oyster (*Avicula margaritifera*) still found in abundance in the Persian Gulf, which has long been celebrated for its pearl fisheries. In Matt. vii. 6 pearls are used metaphorically for anything of value; or perhaps more especially for "wise sayings," which in Arabic, according to Schultens (*Hariri Consess.* i. 12, ii. 102), are called pearls. (See Parkhurst, *Gr. Lex.* s. v. *Μαργαρίτης*. As to פְּנִינִים, see RUBIES.)　　　　　W. H.

PED'AHEL (פְּדַהְאֵל [*whom God delivers*]: Φαδαήλ: *Phedaël*). The son of Ammihud, and prince of the tribe of Naphtali (Num. xxxiv. 28); one of the twelve appointed to divide the land west of Jordan among the nine and a half tribes.

PEDAH'ZUR (פְּדָהצוּר [*the rock*, i. e. *God delivers*]: Φαδασσούρ; [Vat. in i. 10, Φαδασουρ, and so Alex. in vii. 54:] *Phadassur*). Father of Gamaliel, the chief of the tribe of Manasseh at the time of the Exodus (Num. i. 10, ii. 20, vii. 54, 59, x. 23).

PEDA'IAH [3 syl.] (פְּדָיָה: [*whom Jehovah delivers*]: Φαδαΐά; [Vat. Εδεειλ;] Alex. Ειεδδιλα; [Comp. Φαδαΐα:] *Phadaia*). 1. The father of Zebudah, mother of king Jehoiakim (2 K. xxiii. 36). He is described as "of Rumah," which has not with certainty been identified.

2. (Φαδαΐας; [Vat. Φαλδαιας; in ver. 19, Vat. Alex. Σαλαθιηλ.]) The brother of Salathiel, or Shealtiel, and father of Zerubbabel, who is usually called the "son of Shealtiel," being, as Lord A. Hervey (*Genealogies*, p. 100) conjectures, in reality, his uncle's successor and heir, in consequence

---

[a] The Hebrew names for apes and ivory are clearly traceable to the Sanskrit; but though *togei* does not appear in Sanskrit, it has been derived from the Sanskrit word *sikhin*, meaning furnished with a crest (Max Müller, *Science of Language*, p. 190).

of the failure of issue in the direct line (1 Chr. iii. 17-19).

3. (Φαδαΐα.) Son of Parosh, that is, one of the family of that name, who assisted Nehemiah in repairing the walls of Jerusalem (Neh. iii. 25).

4. (Φαδαΐας.) Apparently a priest; one of those who stood on the left hand of Ezra, when he read the Law to the people (Neh. viii. 4). In 1 Esdr. ix. 44, he is called PHALDAIUS.

5. (Φαδαΐα; [Vat.] FA. Φαλαια.) A Benjamite, ancestor of Sallu (Neh. xi. 7).

6. Φαδαΐα; [Vat. Φαλαια.] A Levite in the time of Nehemiah, appointed by him one of the "treasurers over the treasury," whose office it was "to distribute unto their brethren" (Neh. xiii. 13).

7. (פְּדָיָהוּ: Φαδαΐα [Vat. Φαλαια]; Alex. Φαλδιι.) The father of Joel, prince of the half tribe of Manasseh in the reign of David (1 Chr. xxvii. 20).

* PEEP in Is. viii. 19, x. 14 (A. V.), is used in the sense of to *chirp*, or to utter a feeble, shrill sound, like that made by young birds on breaking from the shell (Lat. *pipio*, Germ. *pipen*). The wizards or necromancers that pretended to evoke the shades of the departed spoke in the low shrill tones which, according to the popular superstition, belonged to the inhabitants of the underworld; see Gesenius or Rosenmüller on Is. viii. 19, and comp. Is. xxix. 4, where the word translated "whisper" (marg. "peep, *or* chirp") is the same which is rendered "peep" in the two passages referred to above.   A.

PE'KAH (פֶּקַח [*opening or open-eyed*, Ges.; *oversight*, Fürst]: Φακεέ; Φακέας, Joseph.: *Phacee*), son of Remaliah, originally a captain of Pekahiah king of Israel, murdered his master, seized the throne, and became the 18th sovereign (and last but one) of the northern kingdom. His native country was probably Gilead, as fifty Gileadites joined him in the conspiracy against Pekahiah; and if so, he furnishes an instance of the same undaunted energy which distinguished, for good or evil, so many of the Israelites who sprang from that country, of which Jephthah and Elijah were the most famous examples (Stanley, *S. & P.* 327). [ELIJAH.] Under his predecessors Israel had been much weakened through the payment of enormous tribute to the Assyrians (see especially 2 K. xv. 20), and by internal wars and conspiracies. Pekah seems steadily to have applied himself to the restoration of its power. For this purpose he sought for the support of a foreign alliance, and fixed his mind on the plunder of the sister kingdom of Judah. He must have made the treaty by which he proposed to share its spoil with Rezin king of Damascus, when Jotham was still on the throne of Jerusalem (2 K. xv. 37); but its execution was long delayed, probably in consequence of that prince's righteous and vigorous administration (2 Chr. xxvii.). When, however, his weak son Ahaz succeeded to the crown of David, the allies no longer hesitated, and formed the siege of Jerusalem. The history of the war, which is sketched under AHAZ, is found in 2 K. xvi. and 2 Chr. xxviii.; and in the latter (ver. 6) we read that Pekah "slew in Judah one hundred and twenty thousand in one day, which were all valiant men," a statement which, even if we should be obliged to diminish the number now read in the text, from

the uncertainty as to numbers attaching to our present MSS. of the books of Chronicles (ABIJAH, CHRONICLES; Kennicott, *Hebrew Text of the Old Testament Considered*, p. 532), proves that the character of his warfare was in full accordance with Gileadite precedents (Judg. xi. 33, xii. 6). The war is famous as the occasion of the great prophecies in Isaiah vii.-ix. Its chief result was the capture of the Jewish port of Elath on the Red Sea; but the unnatural alliance of Damascus and Samaria was punished through the final overthrow of the ferocious confederates by Tiglath-pileser, king of Assyria, whom Ahaz called to his assistance, and who seized the opportunity of adding to his own dominions and crushing a union which might have been dangerous. The kingdom of Damascus was finally suppressed, and Rezin put to death, while Pekah was deprived of at least half of his kingdom, including all the northern portion, and the whole district to the east of Jordan. For though the writer in 2 K. xv. 29 tells us that Tiglath-pileser "took Ijon, and Abel-beth-maachah, and Janoah, and Kedesh, and Hazor, and Gilead, and Galilee, all the land of Naphtali," yet from comparing 1 Chr. v. 26, we find that Gilead must include "the Reubenites, and the Gadites, and half the tribe of Manasseh." The inhabitants were carried off, according to the usual practice, and settled in remote districts of Assyria. Pekah himself, now fallen into the position of an Assyrian vassal, was of course compelled to abstain from further attacks on Judah. Whether his continued tyranny exhausted the patience of his subjects, or whether his weakness emboldened them to attack him, we do not know; but, from one or the other cause, Hoshea the son of Elah conspired against him and put him to death. Josephus says that Hoshea was his friend (φίλου τινὸς ἐπιβουλεύσαντος αὐτῷ, Ant. ix. 13, § 1). Comp. Is. vii. 16, which prophecy Hoshea was instrumental in fulfilling. [HOSHEA.] Pekah ascended the throne B. C. 757. He must have begun to war against Judah B. C. 740, and was killed B. C. 737. The order of events above given is according to the scheme of Ewald's *Geschichte des Volkes Israel*, vol. iii. p. 602. Mr. Rawlinson (*Bampton Lectures for 1859*, Lect. iv.) seems wrong in assuming two invasions of Israel by the Assyrians in Pekah's time, the one corresponding to 2 K. xv. 29, the other to 2 K. xvi. 7-9. Both these narratives refer to the same event, which in the first place is mentioned briefly in the short sketch of Pekah's reign, while, in the second passage, additional details are given in the longer biography of Ahaz. It would have been scarcely possible for Pekah, when deprived of half his kingdom, to make an alliance with Rezin, and to attack Ahaz. We learn further from Mr. Rawlinson that the conquests of Tiglath-pileser are mentioned in an Assyrian fragment, though there is a difficulty, from the occurrence of the name *Menahem* in the inscription, which may have proceeded from a mistake of the engraver. Comp. the title, *son of Khumri* (Omri), assigned to Jehu in another inscription; and see Rawlinson, note 35 on Lect. iv. As may be inferred from Pekah's alliance with Rezin, his government was no improvement, morally and religiously, on that of his predecessors. G. E. L. C.

PEKAHI'AH (פְּקַחְיָה [*Jehovah watches*, Fürst: or, *opens his eyes*, Ges.]: Φακεσίας; Alex. Φακειας: *Phaceia*), son and successor of Menahem, was the 17th king of the separate kingdom of Israel. After a brief reign of scarcely two years, a conspiracy was organized against him by "one of his captains" (probably of his body guard), Pekah, son of Remaliah, and who, at the head of fifty Gileadites, attacked him in his palace, murdered him and his friends Argob and Arieh, and seized the throne. The date of his accession is B. C. 759, of his death 757. This reign was no better than those which had gone before; and the calf-worship was retained (2 K. xv. 22–26).

G. E. L. C.

PE′KOD (פְּקוֹד), [see below] an appellative applied to the Chaldæans. It occurs only twice, namely, in Jer. l. 21, and Ez. xxiii. 23, in the latter of which it is connected with Shoa and Koa, as though these three were in some way subdivisions of "the Babylonians and all the Chaldæans." Authorities are undecided as to the meaning of the term. It is apparently connected with the root *pākad*, "to visit," and in its secondary senses "to punish," and "to appoint a ruler:" hence Pekod may be applied to Babylon in Jer. l. as significant of its impending punishment, as in the margin of the A. V. "visitation." But this sense will not suit the other passage, and hence Gesenius here assigns to it the meaning of "prefect" (*Thes.* p. 1121, as though it were but another form of *pākid*). It certainly is unlikely that the same word would be applied to the same object in two totally different senses. Hitzig seeks for the origin of the word in the Sanskrit *bhacān*, "noble" — Shoa and Koa being respectively "prince" and "lord;" and he explains its use in Jer. l. as a part for the whole. The LXX. treats it as the name of a district (Φακουκ; Alex. Φουδ) in Ezekiel, and as a verb (ἐκδικήσον) in Jeremiah.

W. L. B.

PELA′IAH [3 syl.] (פְּלָאיָה) [*whom Jehovah distinguishes*]). 1. ([Φαδαΐα; Vat. Φαρα; Alex. Φαλαια: *Phelein*]). A son of Elioёnai, one of the last members of the royal line of Judah (1 Chr. iii. 24).

2. (LXX. om. in Neh. viii.; Φελία; [Vat. FA.[1] omit;] Alex. [FA.[3]] Φελεία: *Phalīz*.) One of the Levites who assisted Ezra in expounding the law (Neh. viii. 7). He afterwards sealed the covenant with Nehemiah (Neh. x. 10). He is called BIATAS in 1 Esdr. ix. 48.

PELALI′AH (פְּלַלְיָה) [*Jehovah judges*]: Φαλαλία; [Vat. FA.[1] omit:] *Phelelia*). The son of Amzi, and ancestor of Adaiah a priest at Jerusalem after the return from Babylon (Neh. xi. 12).

PELATI′AH (פְּלַטְיָה) [*Jehovah delivers*]: Φαλεττία; [Vat. Φαλλετι; Alex. Φαλλετια:] *Phaltias*). 1. Son of Hananiah the son of Zerubbabel (1 Chr. iii. 21). In the LXX. and Vulg. he is further described as the father of Jesaiah.

2. (Φαλαεττία [Vat. -τει-]; Alex. Φαλεττια). One of the captains of the marauding band of five hundred Simeonites, who in the reign of Hezekiah made an expedition to Mount Seir and smote the fugitive Amalekites (1 Chr. iv. 42).

3. (Φαλτία; [FA.[1] Φαλδεια. corr. Φαλτεια:] *Pheltia*) One of the heads of the people, and probably the name of a family, who sealed the covenant with Nehemiah (Neh. x. 22).

4. (פְּלַטְיָהוּ) Φαλτίας; [Vat.[1] in ver. 1, Φαλτιο-:] *Pheltias*). The son of Benaiah, and one of the princes of the people against whom Ezekiel

was directed to utter the words of doom recorded in Ez. xi. 5–12. The prophet in spirit saw him stand at the east gate of the Temple, and, as he spoke, the same vision showed him Pelatiah's sudden death (Ez. xi. 1, 13).

PE′LEG (פֶּלֶג) [*stream, division*]: Φαλέγ, [Alex.] Φαλεχ; [in 1 Chr. i. 25, Vat. Φαλεχ:] *Phaleg*), a son of Eber, and brother of Joktan (Gen. x. 25, xi. 16). The only incident connected with his history is the statement that "in his days was the earth divided" — an event which was embodied in his name, Peleg meaning "division." This notice refers, not to the general dispersion of the human family subsequently to the Deluge, but to a division of the family of Eber himself, the younger branch of whom (the Joktanids) migrated into southern Arabia, while the elder remained in Mesopotamia. The occurrence of the name *Phaliga* for a town at the junction of the Chaboras with the Euphrates is observable in consequence of the remark of Winer (*Realwb.*) that there is no geographical name corresponding to Peleg. At the same time the late date of the author who mentions the name (Isidorus of Charax) prevents any great stress being laid upon it. The separation of the Joktanids from the stock whence the Hebrews sprang, finds a place in the Mosaic table, as marking an epoch in the age immediately succeeding the Deluge.

W. L. B.

PE′LET (פֶּלֶט) [*deliverance*]: Φαλέκ; Alex. Φαλετ: *Phalet*). 1. A son of Jahdai in an obscure genealogy (1 Chr. ii. 47).

2. (Ἰωφαλήτ; Alex. Φαλλητ: *Phallet*). The son of Azmaveth, that is, either a native of the place of that name, or the son of one of David's heroes. He was among the Benjamites who joined David in Ziglag (1 Chr. xii. 3).

PE′LETH (פֶּלֶת) [*swiftness*]: Φαλέθ; *Pheleth*). 1. The father of On the Reubenite, who joined Dathan and Abiram in their rebellion (Num. xvi. 1). Josephus (*Ant.* iv. 2, § 2), omitting all mention of On, calls Peleth Φαλαούς, apparently identifying him with PHALLU the son of Reuben. In the LXX. Peleth is made the son of Reuben, as in the Sam. text and version, and one Heb. MS. supports this rendering.

2. ([Vat. Θαλεθ:] *Phaleth*). Son of Jonathan and a descendant of Jerahmeel through Onam, his son by Atarah (1 Chr. ii. 33).

PEL′ETHITES (פְּלֵתִי): [Φελετί,] Φελεθί; [Vat. Φελεττει, Φελεθθει, Φαλτεια; Alex. Φελεθθει, Οφελεθθει, Φαλλεθθι; FA. in 1 Chr., Φαλτια:] *Phelethi*), mentioned only in the phrase הַכְּרֵתִי וְהַפְּלֵתִי, rendered in the A. V. "the Cherethites and the Pelethites." These two collectives designate a force that was evidently David's body-guard. Their names have been supposed either to indicate their duties, or to be gentile nouns. Gesenius renders them "executioners and runners," comparing the הַכָּרִי וְהָרָצִים, "executioners and runners" of a later time (2 K. xi. 4, 19); and the unused roots כָּרַת and פָּלַט, as to both of which we shall speak later, admit this sense. In favor of this view, the supposed parallel phrase, and the duties in which these guards were employed, may be cited. On the other hand, the LXX. and Vulg. retain their names untranslated, and the Syriac and Targ. Jon. translate them differently from the rendering above and from each other. In one place, moreover, the Gittites are mentioned with the Cherethites and Pelethites among David's troops (2 Sam. xv. 18); and elsewhere we read of the Cherethim, who bear the same name in the plural, either as a Philistine tribe or as Philistines themselves (1 Sam. xxx. 14; Ez. xxv. 16; Zeph. ii. 5). Gesenius objects that David's body-guard would scarcely have been chosen from a nation so hateful to the Israelites as the Philistines. But it must be remembered that David in his later years may have mistrusted his Israelite soldiers, and relied on the Philistine troops, some of whom, with Ittai the Gittite, who was evidently a Philistine, and not an Israelite from Gath [ITTAI], were faithful to him at the time of Absalom's rebellion. He also argues that it is improbable that two synonymous appellations should be thus used together; but this is on the assumption that both names signify Philistines, whereas they may designate Philistine tribes. (See *Thes.* pp. 719, 1107.)

The Egyptian monuments throw a fresh light upon this subject. From them we find that kings of the XIXth and XXth dynasties had in their service mercenaries of a nation called SHAYRETANA, which Rameses III. conquered, under the name "SHAYRETANA of the Sea." This king fought a naval battle with the SHAYRETANA of the Sea, in alliance with the TOKKAREE, who were evidently, from their physical characteristics, a kindred people to them, and to the PELESATU, or Philistines, also conquered by him. The TOKKAREE and the PELESATU both wear a peculiar dress. We thus learn that there were two peoples of the Mediterranean kindred to the Philistines, one of which supplied mercenaries to the Egyptian kings of the XIXth and XXth dynasties. The name SHAYRETANA, of which the first letter was also pronounced KH, is almost letter for letter the same as the Hebrew Cherethim; and since the SHAYRETANA were evidently cognate to the Philistines, their identity with the Cherethim cannot be doubted. But if the Cherethim supplied mercenaries to the Egyptian kings in the thirteenth century B. C., according to our reckoning, it cannot be doubted that the same name in the designation of David's body-guard denotes the same people or tribe. The Egyptian SHAYRETANA of the sea are probably the Cretans. The Pelethites, who, as already remarked, are not mentioned except with the Cherethites, have not yet been similarly traced in Egyptian geography, and it is rash to suppose their name to be the same as that of the Philistines, פְּלֵתִי, for פְּלִשְׁתִּי; for, as Gesenius remarks, this contraction is not possible in the Semitic languages. The similarity, however, of the two names would favor the idea which is suggested by the mention together of the Cherethites and Pelethites, that the latter were of the Philistine stock as well as the former. As to the etymology of the names, both may be connected with the migration of the Philistines. As already noticed, the former has

been derived from the root פָּרַת, "be cut, cut off, destroyed," in Niphal "be was cut off from his country, driven into exile, or expelled," so that we might as well read "exiles"[a] as "executioners." The latter, from פלת, an unused root, the Arab. فَلَتَ, "he escaped, fled," both being cognate to פָּלַט, "he was smooth," thence "he slipped away, escaped, and caused to escape," where the rendering "the fugitives" is at least as admissible as "the runners." If we compare these two names so rendered with the gentile name of the Philistine nation itself, פְּלִשְׁתִּי, "a wanderer, stranger," from the unused root פָּלַשׁ, "he wandered or emigrated," these previous inferences seem to become irresistible. The appropriateness of the names of these tribes to the duties of David's body-guard would then be accidental, though it does not seem unlikely that they should have given rise to the adoption in later times of other appellations for the royal body-guard, definitely signifying "executioners and runners." If, however, הַכְּרֵתִי וְהַפְּלֵתִי meant nothing but executioners and runners, it is difficult to explain the change to הַכָּרִי וְהָרָצִים.   R. S. P.

PELI'AS (Πεδίας; Alex. Παιδειας: *Pelias*). A corruption of BEDEIAH (1 Esdr. ix. 34; comp. Ezr. x. 35). Our translators followed the Vulgate.

PELICAN (קָאַת, *kâath*: πελεκάν, ὄρνεον, χαμαιλέων, καταρράκτης: *onocrotalus, pelican*). Amongst the unclean birds mention is made of the *kâath* (Lev. xi. 18; Deut. xiv. 17). The suppliant psalmist compares his condition to "a *kâath* in the wilderness" (Ps. cii. 6). As a mark of the desolation that was to come upon Edom, it is said that "the *kâath* and the bittern should possess it " (Is. xxxiv. 11). The same words are spoken of Nineveh (Zeph. ii. 14). In these two last places the A. V. has "cormorant " in the text, and "pelican " in the margin. The best authorities are in favor of the pelican being the bird denoted by *kâath*. The etymology of the name, from a word meaning "to vomit," leads also to the same conclusion, for it doubtless has reference to the habit which this bird has of pressing its under mandible against its breast, in order to assist it to disgorge the contents of its capacious pouch for its young. This is, with good reason, supposed to be the origin of the fable about the pelican feeding its young with its own blood, the red nail on the upper mandible serving to complete the delusion.[b]

The expression "pelican of the wilderness " has, with no good reason, been supposed by some to prove that the *kâath* cannot be denoted by this bird. Shaw (*Trav.* ii. 303, 8vo ed.) says "the pelican must of necessity starve in the desert," as it is essentially a water bird. In answer to this objection, it will be enough to observe that the term

---

[a] Michaelis Philistæos פְּרֵתִי, dictos esse censet, utpote *exsules* (v. rad. Niph. no. 3) ut idem valeat quod Ἀλλόφυλοι (*Thes.* p. 719).

[b] The reader is referred to a curious work by a Scotch divine, Archibald Simson by name, entitled

[a] Hieroglyphica Animalium, Vegetabilium et Metallorum, quæ in Scripturis sacris reperiuntur," Edinb. 1622, 4to. In this work are some wild fancies about the pelican, which serve to show the state of zoölogy, etc., at the period in which the author lived.

midbar ("wilderness ") is by no means restricted to barren sandy spots destitute of water. " The idea," says Prof. Stanley, " is that of a wide open space, with or without actual pasture; the country of the nomads, as distinguished from that of the agricultural and settled people " (*S. & P.* p. 486, 5th ed.).[a] Pelicans (*Pelecanus onocrotalus*) are often seen associated in large flocks; at other times single individuals may be observed sitting in lonely and pensive silence on the ledge of some rock a few feet above the surface of the water. (See Kitto, *Pict. Bib.* on Ps. cii. 6.) It is not quite clear what is the particular point in the nature or character of the pelican with which the psalmist compares his pitiable condition. Some have supposed that it consists in the loud cry of the bird: compare " the voice of my sighing " (ver. 5). We are inclined to believe that reference is made to its general aspect as it sits in apparent melancholy mood, with its bill resting on its breast. There is, we think, little doubt but that the pelican is the *káath* of the Hebrew Scriptures. Oedmann's opinion that the *Pelecanus graculus*, the shag cormorant (*Verm. Samm.* iii. 57), and Bochart's, that the " bittern " is intended, are unsupported by any good evidence. The *P. onocrotalus* (common pel-

Pelecanus onocrotalus.

lean) and the *P. crispus* are often observed in Palestine, Egypt, etc Of the latter Mr. Tristram observed an immense flock swimming out to sea within sight of Mount Carmel (*Ibis,* i. 37).[b]

W. H.

PEL'ONITE, THE (הַפְּלוֹנִי) [see below]: ὁ Φελωνί [Vat. -νει], Alex. ο Φαλλωνί, 1 Chr. xi. 27; ὁ Φελλωνί, [Vat. FA. ο Φεδωνει,] 1 Chr. xi. 36; ὁ ἐκ Φαλλούς, [Comp. ὁ Φαλλωνί,] 1 Chr. xxvii. 10 : *Phalonites, Phelonites, Phallonites*). Two of David's mighty men, Helez and Ahijah, are called Pelonites (1 Chr. xi. 27, 36). From 1 Chr. xxvii. 10, it appears that the former was of the tribe of Ephraim, and " Pelonite " would there-

fore be an appellation derived from his place of birth or residence. But in the Targum of R Joseph it is evidently regarded as a patronymic, and is rendered in the last mentioned passage " of the seed of Pelan." In the list of 2 Sam. xxiii. Helez is called (ver. 26) " the Paltite," that is, as Bertheau (on 1 Chr. xi.) conjectures, of Beth-Palet, or Beth-Phelet, in the south of Judah. But it seems probable that " Pelonite " is the correct reading. [See PALTITE.] " Ahijah the Pelonite " appears in 2 Sam. xxiii. 34 as " Eliam the son of Ahithophel the Gilonite," of which the former is a corruption; " Ahijah " forming the first part of " Ah.thophel," and " Pelonite " and " Gilonite " differing only by פ and ג. If we follow the LXX. of 1 Chr. xxvii. the place from which Helez took his name would be of the form Phallu, but there is no trace of it elsewhere, and the LXX. must have had a differently pointed text. In Heb. *pelóni* corresponds to the Greek ὁ δεῖνα, "such a one: " it still exists in Arabic and in the Spanish *Don Fulano*, " Mr. So-and-so."

W. A. W.

PEN. [WRITING.]

PEN'IEL (פְּנִיאֵל; Samar. פנו אל [see below]: εἶδος θεοῦ: *Phanuel*, and so also Peshito). The name which Jacob gave to the place in which he had wrestled with God: " He called the name of the place ' Face of El,' for I have seen Elohim face to face " (Gen. xxxii. 30). With that singular correspondence between the two parts of this narrative which has been already noticed under MAHANAIM, there is apparently an allusion to the bestowal of the name in xxxiii. 10, where Jacob says to Esau, " I have seen thy face as one sees the face of Elohim." In xxxii. 31, and the other passages in which the name occurs, its form is changed to PENUEL. On this change the lexicographers throw no light. It is perhaps not impossible that Penuel was the original form of the name, and that the slight change to Peniel was made by Jacob or by the historian to suit his allusion to the circumstance under which the patriarch first saw it. The Samaritan Pentateuch has Penu-el in all. The promontory of the *Ras es-Shukah*, on the coast of Syria above *Beirút*, was formerly called *Theouprosópon*, probably a translation of Peniel, or its Phœnician equivalent.

G.

PENIN'NAH (פְּנִנָּה [*coral*] : Φεννάνα: *Phenenna*), one of the two wives of Elkanah, the other being Hannah, the mother of Samuel (1 Sam. i. 2).

• PENKNIFE (Jer. xxxvi. 23). [KNIFE.]

PENNY, PENNYWORTH. In the A. V., in several passages of the N. T., "penny," either alone or in the compound "pennyworth," occurs as the rendering of the Greek δηνάριον, the name of the Roman *denarius* (Matt. xx. 2, xxii. 19; Mark vi. 37, xii. 15; Luke xx. 24; John vi. 7; Rev. vi. 6). The denarius was the chief Roman silver coin, from the beginning of the coinage of the city to the early part of the third century. Its name continued to be applied to a silver piece as late as the time of the earlier Byzantines. The states that arose from the ruins of the Roman

---

a As a matter of fact, however, the pelican, after having filled its pouch with fish and mollusks, often does retire miles inland away from water, to some spot where it consumes the contents of its pouch.

b " *P crispus* breeds in vast numbers in the flat plain of the Dobrudscha. (in European Turkey); its habits there bear out your remark of the pelican retiring inland to digest its food. — H. B. TRISTRAM.

empire imitated the coinage of the imperial mints, and in general called their principal silver coin the denarius, whence the French name *denier* and the Italian *denaro*. The chief Anglo-Saxon coin, and for a long period the only one, corresponded to the denarius of the Continent. It continued to be current under the Normans, Plantagenets, and Tudors, though latterly little used. It is called peuny, denarius, or denier, which explains the employment of the first word in the A. V. [In Udal's version of the Paraphrase of Erasmus (1549) the word is Anglicized by "denarie."] R. S. P.

PENTATEUCH, THE. The Greek name given to the five books commonly called the Five Books of Moses (ἡ πεντάτευχος sc. βίβλος; Pentateuchus sc. liber; the fivefold book; from τεῦχος, which meaning originally "vessel, instrument," etc., came in Alexandrine Greek to mean "book"). In the time of Ezra and Nehemiah it was called "the Law of Moses" (Ezr. vii. 6); or "the book of the Law of Moses" (Neh. viii. 1); or simply "the Book of Moses" (Ezr. vi. 18; Neh. xiii. 1; 2 Chr. xxv. 4, xxxv. 12). This was beyond all reasonable doubt our existing Pentateuch. The book which was discovered in the Temple in the reign of Josiah, and which is entitled (2 Chr. xxxiv. 14) "the book of the Law of Jehovah by the hand of Moses," was substantially, it would seem, the same volume, though it may have undergone some revision by Ezra. In 2 Chr. xxxiv. 30, it is styled "the book of the Covenant," and so also in 2 K. xxiii. 2, 21, whilst in 2 K. xxii. 8 Hilkiah says, I have found "the book of the Law." Still earlier n the reign of Jehoshaphat we find a "book of the Law of Jehovah" in use (2 Chr. xvii. 9). And this was probably the earliest designation, for a "book of the Law" is mentioned in Deuteronomy (xxxi. 26), though it is questionable whether the name as there used refers to the whole Pentateuch, or only to Deuteronomy; probably, as we shall see, it applies only to the latter. The present Jews usually call the whole by the name of *Torah*, i. e. "the Law," or *Torath Mosheh*, "the Law of Moses." The Rabbinical title is חֲמִשָּׁה

דָאגְמִשֵׁי הַתִּרָה, "the five-fifths of the Law." In the preface to the Wisdom of Jesus the son of Sirach, it is called "the Law," which is also a usual name for it in the New Testament (Matt. xii. 5, xxii. 36, 40; Luke x. 26; John viii. 5, 17). Sometimes the name of Moses stands briefly for the whole work ascribed to him (Luke xxiv. 27). Finally, the whole Old Testament is sometimes called *a potiori parte*, "the Law" (Matt. v. 18; Luke xvi. 17; John vii. 49, x. 34, xii. 34). In John xv. 25; Rom. iii. 19, words from the Psalms, and in 1 Cor. xiv. 21 from Isaiah, are quoted as words of the Law.

The division of the whole work into five parts has by some writers been supposed to be original. Others (as Leusden, Hävernick, and Lengerke), with more probability, think that the division was made by the Greek translators. For the titles of the several books are not of Hebrew but of Greek origin. The Hebrew names are merely taken from the first words of each book, and in the first instance only designated particular *sections* and not whole books. The MSS. of the Pentateuch form a single roll or volume, and are divided not into books, but into the larger and smaller sections called *Parshiyoth* and *Sedarim*. Besides this, the Jews

distribute all the laws in the Pentateuch under the two heads of affirmative and negative precepts. Of the former they reckon 248; because, according to the anatomy of the Rabbins, so many are the parts of the human body: of the latter they make 365, which is the number of days in the year, and also the number of veins in the human body. Accordingly the Jews are bound to the observance of 613 precepts: and in order that these precepts may be perpetually kept in mind, they are wont to carry a piece of cloth foursquare, at the four corners of which they have fringes consisting of 8 threads a-piece, fastened in 5 knots. These fringes are called צִיצִית, a word which in numbers denotes 600: add to this the 8 threads and the 5 knots, and we get the 613 precepts. The five knots denote the five books of Moses. (See Bab. Talmud, *Maccoth*, sect. 3; Maimon. *Pref. to Jad Hachazakah*; Leusden, *Philol.* p. 33.) Both Philo (*de Abraham., ad init.*) and Josephus (c. *Apion.* i. 8) recognize the division now current. As no reason for this division can satisfactorily be found in the structure of the work itself, Vaihinger supposes that the symbolical meaning of the number five led to its adoption. For ten is the symbol of completion or perfection, as we see in the ten commandments [and so in Genesis we have ten "generations"], and therefore five is a number which as it were confesses imperfection and prophesies completion. The Law is not perfect without the Prophets, for the Prophets are in a special sense the bearers of the Promise; and it is the Promise which completes the Law. This is questionable. There can be no doubt, however, that this division of the Pentateuch influenced the arrangement of the Psalter in five books. The same may be said of the five Megilloth cf the Hagiographa (Canticles, Ruth, Lamentations, Ecclesiastes, and Esther), which in many Hebrew Bibles are placed immediately after the Pentateuch.

For the several names and contents of the Five Books we refer to the articles on each Book, where questions affecting their integrity and genuineness are also discussed. In the article on Genesis the scope and design of the whole work is pointed out. We need only briefly observe here that this work, beginning with the record of Creation and the history of the primitive world, passes on to deal more especially with the early history of the Jewish family. It gives at length the personal history of the three great Fathers of the family: it then describes how the family grew into a nation in Egypt, tells us of its oppression and deliverance, of its forty years' wandering in the wilderness, of the giving of the Law, with all its enactments both civil and religious, of the construction of the Tabernacle, of the numbering of the people, of the rights and duties of the priesthood, as well as of many important events which befell them before their entrance into the Land of Canaan, and finally concludes with Moses' last discourses and his death. The unity of the work in its existing form is now generally recognized. It is not a mere collection of loose fragments carelessly put together at different times, but bears evident traces of design and purpose in its composition. Even those who discover different authors in the earlier books, and who deny that Deuteronomy was written by Moses, are still of opinion that the work in its present form is a connected whole, and was at least relaeed to its present shape by a single reviser or editor.[a]

The question has also been raised, whether the Book of Joshua does not, properly speaking, constitute an integral portion of this work. To this question Ewald (*Gesch.* l. 175), Knobel (*Genesis*, Vorbem. § 1, 2), Lengerke (*Kenaan*, lxxxiii.), and Stähelin (*Krit. Unters.* p. 91) give a reply in the affirmative. They seem to have been led to do so, partly because they imagine that the two documents, the Elohistic and Jehovistic, which characterize the earlier books of the Pentateuch, may still be traced, like two streams, the waters of which never wholly mingle though they flow in the same channel, running on through the book of Joshua; and partly because the same work which contains the promise of the land (Gen. xv.) must contain also — so they argue — the fulfillment of the promise. But such grounds are far too arbitrary and uncertain to support the hypothesis which rests upon them. All that seems probable is, that the book of Joshua received a final revision at the hands of Ezra, or some earlier prophet, at the same time with the books of the Law.

The fact that the Samaritans, who it is well known did not possess the other books of Scripture, have besides the Pentateuch a book of Joshua (see *Chronicon Samaritanum*, etc., ed. Juynboll, Lugd. Bat. 1848), indicates no doubt an early association of the one with the other; but is no proof that they originally constituted one work, but rather the contrary. Otherwise the Samaritans would naturally have adopted the canonical recension of Joshua. We may therefore regard the Five Books of Moses as one separate and complete work. For a detailed view of the several books we must refer, as we have said, to the Articles where they are severally discussed. The questions which we have left for this article are those connected with the authorship and date of the Pentateuch as a whole.

It is necessary here at the outset to state the exact nature of the investigation which lies before us. Many English readers are alarmed when they are told, for the first time, that critical investigation renders it doubtful whether the whole Pentateuch in its present form was the work of Moses. On this subject there is a strange confusion in many minds. They suppose that to surrender the recognized authorship of a sacred book is to surrender the truth of the book itself. Yet a little reflection should suffice to correct such an error. For who can say now who wrote the books of Samuel, or Ruth, or Job, or to what authorship many of the Psalms are to be ascribed? We are quite sure that these books were not written by the persons whose names they bear. We are scarcely less sure that many of the Psalms ascribed to David were not written by him, and our own translators have signified the doubtfulness of the inscriptions by separating them from the Psalms, of which in the Hebrew text they were made to form a constituent

part. These books of Scripture, however, and these divine poems, lose not a whit of their value or of their authority because the names of their authors have perished. Truth is not a thing dependent on names. So likewise, if it should turn out that portions of the Pentateuch were not written by Moses, neither their inspiration nor their trustworthiness is thereby diminished. All will admit that one portion at least of the Pentateuch — the 34th chapter of Deuteronomy, which gives the account of Moses' death — was not written by him. But in making this admission the principle for which we contend is conceded. Common sense compels us to regard this chapter as a later addition. Why then may not other later additions have been made to the work? If common sense leads us to such a conclusion in one instance, critical examination may do so on sufficient grounds in another.[b]

At different times suspicions have been entertained that the Pentateuch as we now have it is not the Pentateuch of the earliest age, and that the work must have undergone various modifications and additions before it assumed its present shape.

So early as the second century we find the author of the Clementine Homilies calling in question the authenticity of the Mosaic writings. According to him the Law was only given orally by Moses to the seventy elders, and not consigned to writing till after his death; it subsequently underwent many changes, was corrupted more and more by means of the false prophets, and was especially filled with erroneous anthropomorphic conceptions of God, and unworthy representations of the characters of the Patriarchs (*Hom.* ii. 38, 43, iii. 4, 47; Neander, *Gnost. Systeme*, 380). A statement of this kind, unsupported, and coming from an heretical, and therefore suspicious source, may seem of little moment: it is however remarkable, so far as it indicates an early tendency to cast off the received traditions respecting the books of Scripture; whilst at the same time it is evident that this was done cautiously, because such an opinion respecting the Pentateuch was said to be for the advanced Christian only, and not for the simple and unlearned.

Jerome, there can be little doubt, had seen the difficulty of supposing the Pentateuch to be altogether, in its present form, the work of Moses; for he observes (*contra Helcid.*): " Sive Mosen dicere volueris auctorem Pentateuchi sive Esram ejusdem instauratorem operis," with reference apparently to the Jewish tradition on the subject. Aben Ezra (†1167), in his *Comm.* on Deut. i. 1, threw out some doubts as to the Mosaic authorship of certain passages, such as Gen. xii. 6, Deut. iii. 10, 11, xxxi. 9, which he either explained as later interpolations, or left as mysteries which it was beyond his power to unravel. For centuries, however, the Pentateuch was generally received in the Church without question as written by Moses. The age

---

[a] See Ewald, *Geschichte*, i. 175; and Stähelin, *Kritisch. Unters.* p. 1.

[b] It is strange to see how widely the misconception which we are anxious to obviate extends. A learned writer, in a recent publication, says, in reference to the alleged existence of different documents in the Pentateuch : " This exclusive use of the one Divine Name in some portions, and of the other in other portions, it is said, characterizes two different authors living at different times ; and consequently Genesis is

composed of two different documents, the one Elohistic the other Jehovistic, which moreover differ in statement ; and consequently this book was not written by Moses, and is neither inspired nor trustworthy " (*Aids to Faith*, p. 190). How it follows that a book is neither inspired nor trustworthy because its authorship is unknown we are at a loss to conceive. A large part of the canon must be sacrificed, if we are only to receive books whose authorship is satisfactorily ascertained.

2410 PENTATEUCH, THE

of criticism had not yet come. The first signs of its approach were seen in the 17th century. In the year 1651 we find Hobbes writing: "Videtur Pentateuchus potius *de* Mose quam *a* Mose scriptus" (*Leviathan*, c. 33). Spinoza (*Tract. Theol.-Polit.* c. 8, 9, published in 1679) set himself boldly to controvert the received authorship of the Pentateuch. He alleged against it (1) later names of places, as Gen. xiv. 14 comp. with Judg. xviii. 29; (2) the continuation of the history beyond the days of Moses, Ex. xvi. 35 comp. with Josh. v. 12; (3) the statement in Gen. xxxvi. 31, "before there reigned any king over the children of Israel." Spinoza maintained that Moses issued his commands to the elders, that by them they were written down and communicated to the people, and that later they were collected and assigned to suitable passages in Moses' life. He considered that the Pentateuch was indebted to Ezra for the form in which it now appears. Other writers began to suspect that the book of Genesis was composed of written documents earlier than the time of Moses. So Vitringa (*Observ. Sacr.* i. 3); Le Clerc (*de Script. Pentateuchi*, § 11), and R. Simon (*Hist. Critique du V. T.* lib. i. c. 7, Rotterdam, 1685). According to the last of these writers, Genesis was composed of earlier documents, the Laws of the Pentateuch were the work of Moses, and the greater portion of the history was written by the public scribe who is mentioned in the book. Le Clerc supposed that the priest who, according to 2 K. xvii. 27, was sent to instruct the Samaritan colonists, was the author of the Pentateuch.

But it was not till the middle of the last century that the question as to the authorship of the Pentateuch was handled with anything like a discerning criticism. The first attempt was made by a layman, whose studies we might have supposed would scarcely have led him to such an investigation. In the year 1753, there appeared at Brussels a work, entitled: "Conjectures sur les Mémoires originaux, dont il paroît que Moyse s'est servi pour composer le Livre de Genèse." It was written in his 69th year by Astruc, Doctor and Professor of Medicine in the Royal College at Paris, and Court Physician to Louis XIV. His critical eye had observed that throughout the book of Genesis, and as far as the 6th chapter of Exodus, traces were to be found of two original documents, each characterized by a distinct use of the names of God; the one by the name Elohim, and the other by the name Jehovah. Besides these two principal documents, he supposed Moses to have made use of ten others in the composition of the earlier part of his work. Astruc was followed by several German writers on the path which he had traced; by Jerusalem in his *Letters on the Mosaic Writings and Philosophy*; by Schultens, in his *Dissertatio quâ disquiritur, unde Moses res in libro Geneseos descriptas didicerit;* and with considerable learning and critical acumen by Ilgen (*Urkunden der Jerusalemischen Tempelarchivs*, 1er Theil, Halle, 1798), and Eichhorn (*Einleitung in d. A. T.*).

But this "documentary hypothesis," as it is called, was too conservative and too rational for some critics. Vater, in his *Commentar üb. den Pentateuch*, 1815, and A. T. Hartmann, in his *Linguist. Einl. in d. Stud. der Bücher des A. Test.* 1818, maintained that the Pentateuch consisted merely of a number of fragments loosely strung together without order or design. The former supposed a collection of laws, made in the times of

PENTATEUCH, THE

David and Solomon, to have been the foundation of the whole: that this was the book discovered in the reign of Josiah, and that its fragments were afterwards incorporated in Deuteronomy. All the rest, consisting of fragments of history and of laws written at different periods up to this time, were, according to him, collected and shaped into their present form between the times of Josiah and the Babylonish Exile. Hartmann also brings down the date of the existing Pentateuch as late as the Exile. This has been called the "Fragmentary hypothesis." Both of these have now been superseded by the "Supplementary hypothesis," which has been adopted with various modifications by De Wette, Bleek, Stähelin, Tuch, Lengerke, Hupfeld, Knobel, Bunsen, Kurtz, Delitzsch, Schultz, Vaihinger, and others. They all alike recognize two documents in the Pentateuch. They suppose the narrative of the Elohist, the more ancient writer, to have been the foundation of the work, and that the Jehovist or later writer making use of this document, added to and commented upon it, sometimes transcribing portions of it intact, and sometimes incorporating the substance of it into his own work.

But though thus agreeing in the main, they differ widely in the application of the theory. Thus, for instance, De Wette distinguishes between the Elohist and the Jehovist in the first four Books, and attributes Deuteronomy to a different writer altogether (*Einl. ins A. T.* § 150 ff.). So also Lengerke, though with some differences of detail in the portions he assigns to the two editors. The last places the Elohist in the time of Solomon, and the Jehovistic editor in that of Hezekiah; whereas Tuch puts the first under Saul, and the second under Solomon. Stähelin, on the other hand, declares for the identity of the Deuteronomist and the Jehovist; and supposes the last to have written in the reign of Saul, and the Elohist in the time of the Judges. Hupfeld (*die Quellen der Genesis*) finds, in Genesis at least, traces of three authors, an earlier and a later Elohist, as well as the Jehovist. He is peculiar in regarding the Jehovistic portion as an altogether original document, written in entire independence, and without the knowledge even of the Elohistic record. A later editor or compiler, he thinks, found the two books, and threw them into one. Vaihinger (in Herzog's *Encyklopädie*) is also of opinion that portions of three original documents are to be found in the first four books, to which he adds some fragments of the 32d and 34th chapters of Deuteronomy. The Fifth Book, according to him, is by a different and much later writer. The Pre-elohist he supposes to have flourished about 1200 B. C., the Elohist some 200 years later, the Jehovist in the first half of the 8th century B. C., and the Deuteronomist in the reign of Hezekiah.

Delitzsch agrees with the writers above mentioned in recognizing two distinct documents as the basis of the Pentateuch, especially in its earlier portions; but he entirely severs himself from them in maintaining that Deuteronomy is the work of Moses. His theory is this: the kernel or first foundation of the Pentateuch is to be found in the Book of the Covenant (Ex. xix.-xxiv.), which was written by Moses himself, and afterwards incorporated into the body of the Pentateuch, where it at present stands. The rest of the Laws given in the wilderness, till the people reached the plains of Moab, were communicated orally by Moses and taken down by the priests, whose business it was thus to provide for their preservation (Deut. xvii. 11, comp. xxiv. 8, xxx'ii. 10; Lev. x. 11, comp. xv. 31). Inasmuch as Deuteronomy does not presuppose the existence in writing of the entire earlier legislation, but on the contrary recapitulates it with the greatest freedom, we are not obliged to assume that the proper codification of the Law took place during the forty years' wandering in the desert. This was done, however, shortly after the occupation of the land of Canaan. On that sacred soil was the first definite portion of the history of Israel written; and the writing of the history itself necessitated a full and complete account of the Mosaic legislation. A man, such as Eleazar the son of Aaron, the priest (see Num. xxvi. 1, xxxi. 21), wrote the great work beginning with the first words of Genesis, including in it the Book of the Covenant, and perhaps gave only a short notice of the last discourses of Moses, because Moses had written them down with his own hand. A second — who may have been Joshua (see especially Deut. xxxii. 44; Josh. xxiv. 26, and comp. on the other hand 1 Sam. x. 25), who was a prophet, and spake as a prophet, or one of the elders ^ whom Moses' spirit rested (Num. xi. 25), and many of whom survived Joshua (Josh. xxiv. 31) — completed the work, taking Deuteronomy, which Moses had written, for his model, and incorporating it into his own Look. Somewhat in this manner arose the *Torah* (or Pentateuch), each narrator further availing himself when he thought proper of other written documents.

Such is the theory of Delitzsch, which is in many respects worthy of consideration, and which has been adopted in the main by Kurtz (*Gesch. d. A. B.* i. § 20, and ii. § 99, 6), who formerly was opposed to the theory of different documents, and sided rather with Hengstenberg and the critics of the extreme conservative school. There is this difference, however, that Kurtz objects to the view that Deuteronomy existed before the other books, and believes that the rest of the Pentateuch was committed to writing before, not after, the occupation of the Holy Land. Finally, Schultz, in his recent work on Deuteronomy, recognizes two original documents in the Pentateuch, the Elohistic being the base and groundwork of the whole, but contends that the Jehovistic portions of the first four books, as well as Deuteronomy, except the concluding portion, were written by Moses. Thus he agrees with Delitzsch and Kurtz in admitting two documents and the Mosaic authorship of Deuteronomy, and with Stähelin in identifying the Deuteronomist with the Jehovist. That these three writers more nearly approach the truth than any others who have attempted to account for the phenomena of the existing Pentateuch, we are convinced. Which of the three hypotheses is best supported by facts and by a careful examination of the record, we shall see hereafter.

One other theory has, however, to be stated before we pass on.

The author of it stands quite alone, and it is not likely that he will ever find any disciple bold enough to adopt his theory: even his great admirer Bunsen forsakes him here. But it is due to Ewald's great and deserved reputation as a scholar, and to his uncommon critical sagacity, briefly to state what that theory is. He distinguishes, then, seven different authors in the great Book of Origines or Primitive History (comprising the Pentateuch and Joshua). The oldest histor-

ical work, of which but a very few fragments remain, is the Book of the Wars of Jehovah. Then follows a biography of Moses, of which also but small portions have been preserved. The third and fourth documents are much more perfect: these consist of the Book of the Covenant, which was written in the time of Samson, and the Book of Origines, which was written by a priest in the time of Solomon. Then comes, in the fifth place, the third historian of the primitive times, or the first prophetic narrator, a subject of the northern kingdom in the days of Elijah or Joel. The sixth document is the work of the fourth historian of primitive times, or the second prophetic narrator, who lived between 800 and 750. Lastly comes the fifth historian, or third prophetic narrator, who flourished not long after Joel, and who collected and reduced into one corpus the various works of his predecessors. The real purposes of the history, both in its prophetical and its legal aspects, began now to be discerned. Some steps were taken in this direction by an unknown writer at the beginning of the 7th century, B. C.; and then in a far more comprehensive manner by the Deuteronomist, who flourished in the time of Manasseh, and lived in Egypt. In the time of Jeremiah appeared the poet who wrote the Blessing of Moses, as it is given in Deuteronomy. A somewhat later editor incorporated the originally independent work of the Deuteronomist, and the lesser additions of his two colleagues, with the history as left by the fifth narrator, and thus the whole was finally completed. "Such," says Ewald (and his words, seriously meant, read like delicate irony), "were the strange fortunes which this great work underwent before it reached its present form."

Such is a brief summary of the views which have been entertained by a large number of critics, many of them men of undoubted piety as well as learning, who have found themselves compelled, after careful investigation, to abandon the older doctrine of the Mosaic authorship of the Pentateuch, and to adopt, in some form or other, the theory of a compilation from earlier documents.

On the other side, however, stands an array of names scarcely less distinguished for learning, who maintain not only that there is a unity of design in the Pentateuch — which is granted by many of those before mentioned — but who contend that this unity of design can only be explained on the supposition of a single author, and that this author could have been none other than Moses. This is the ground taken by Hengstenberg, Hävernick, Drechsler, Ranke, Welte, and Keil. The first mentioned of these writers has no doubt done admirable service in reconciling and removing very many of the alleged discrepancies and contradictions in the Pentateuch: but his zeal carries him in some instances to attempt a defense the very ingenuity of which betrays how unsatisfactory it is; and his attempt to explain the use of the Divine Names, by showing that the writer had a special design in the use of the one or the other, is often in the last degree arbitrary. Drechsler, in his work on the *Unity and Genuineness of Genesis* (1838), fares no better, though his remarks are the more valuable because in many cases they coincide, quite independently, with those of Hengstenberg. Later, however, Drechsler modified his view, and supposed that the several uses of the Divine Names were owing to a didactic purpose on the part of the writer according as his object was to show a particular relation of God to the world, whether as Elohim or as Jehovah. Hence he argued that, whilst different streams flowed through the Pentateuch, they were not from two different fountain-heads, but varied according to the motive which influenced the writer, and according to the fundamental thought in particular sections; and on this ground, too, he explained the characteristic phraseology which distinguishes such sections. Ranke's work (*Untersuchungen über den Pentateuch*) is a valuable contribution to the exegesis of the Pentateuch. He is especially successful in establishing the inward unity of the work, and in showing how inseparably the several portions, legal, genealogical, and historical, are interwoven together. Kurtz (in his *Einheit der Genesis*, 1846, and in the first edition of his first volume of the *Geschichte des Alten Bundes*) followed on the same side; but he has since abandoned the attempt to explain the use of the Divine Names on the principle of the different meanings which they bear, and has espoused the theory of two distinct documents. Keil, also, though he does not despair of the solution of the problem, confesses (*Luther. Zeitschr.* 1851–52, p. 235) that "all attempts as yet made, notwithstanding the acumen which has been brought to bear to explain the interchange of the Divine Names in Genesis on the ground of the different meanings which they possess, must be pronounced a failure." Ebrard (*Das Alter des Jehova-Namens*) and Tiele (*Stud. und Krit.* 1852) make nearly the same admission. This manifest doubtfulness in some cases, and desertion in others from the ranks of the more conservative school, is significant. And it is certainly unfair to claim consistency and unanimity of opinion for one side to the prejudice of the other. The truth is, that diversities of opinion are to be found among those who are opposed to the theory of different documents, as well as amongst those who advocate it. Nor can a theory which has been adopted by Delitzsch, and to which Kurtz has become a convert, be considered as either irrational or irreligious. It may not be established beyond doubt, but the presumptions in its favor are strong; nor, when properly stated, will it be found open to any serious objection.

II. We ask in the next place what is the testimony of the Pentateuch itself with regard to its authorship?

1. We find on reference to Ex. xxiv. 3, 4, that "Moses came and told the people all the words of Jehovah and all the judgments," and that he subsequently "wrote down all the words of Jehovah." These were written on a roll called "the book of the covenant" (ver. 7), and "read in the audience of the people." These "words" and "judgments" were no doubt the Sinaitic legislation so far as it had as yet been given, and which constituted in fact the covenant between Jehovah and the people. Upon the renewal of this covenant after the idolatry of the Israelites, Moses was again commanded by Jehovah to "write these words" (xxxiv. 27).

"And," it is added, "he wrote upon the tables the words of the covenant, the ten commandments." Leaving Deuteronomy aside for the present, there are only two other passages in which mention is made of the writing of any part of the Law, and those are Ex. xvii. 14, where Moses is commanded to write the defeat of Amalek in a book (or rather in *the* book, one already in use for the purpose [a]); and Num. xxxiii. 2, where we are informed that Moses wrote the journeyings of the children of Israel in the desert and the various stations at which they encamped. It obviously does not follow from these statements that Moses wrote all the rest of the first four books which bear his name. Nor on the other hand does this specific testimony with regard to certain portions justify us in coming to an opposite conclusion. So far nothing can be determined positively one way or the other. But it may be said that we have an express testimony to the Mosaic authorship of the Law in Deut. xxxi. 9–12, where we are told that "Moses wrote this Law" (הַתּוֹרָה הַזֹּאת), and delivered it to the custody of the priests with a command that it should be read before all the people at the end of every seven years, on the Feast of Tabernacles. In ver. 24 it is further said, that when he "had made an end of writing the words of this Law in a book till they were finished," he delivered it to the Levites to be placed in the side of the ark of the covenant of Jehovah, that it might be preserved as a witness against the people. Such a statement is no doubt decisive, but the question is, How far does it extend? Do the words "this Law" comprise all the Mosaic legislation as contained in the last four books of the Pentateuch, or must they be confined only to Deuteronomy? The last is apparently the only tenable view. In Deut. xvii. 18, the direction is given that the king on his accession "shall write him a copy of this Law in a book out of that which is before the priests the Levites." The words "copy of this Law," are literally "repetition of this Law" (מִשְׁנֵה תֹרַת הַזֹּאת), which is another name for the book of Deuteronomy, and hence the LXX. render here τὸ δευτερονόμιον τοῦτο, and Philo τὴν ἐπινομίδα, and although it is true that Onkelos uses מִשְׁנֶה (Mishneh) in the sense of "copy," and the Talmud in the sense of "duplicate" (Carpzov on Schickard's *Jus reg. Hebræor.* pp. 82–84), yet as regards the passage already referred to in xxxi. 9, &c., it was in the time of the second Temple received as an unquestionable tradition that Deuteronomy only, and not the whole Law was read at the end of every seven years, in the year of release. The words are מִתְּחִלַּת חוּמַשׁ אֵלֶּה הַדְּבָרִים, "from the beginning of Deuteronomy" (*Sota*, c. 7; Maimon. *Jad hachazakah* in Hilchoth Chagiga, c. 3; Reland, *Antiq. Sac.* p. iv. § 11).[b]

Besides, it is on the face of it very improbable

---

[a] Delitzsch, however, will not allow that בַּסֵּפֶר means in the already existing book, but in one which was to be taken for the occasion; and he refers to Num. v. 23, 1 Sam. x. 25, 2 Sam. xi. 15, for a similar use of the article. סֵפֶר he takes here, as in Is. xxx. 8, to mean a separate leaf or plate on which the record was to be made. But the three passages to which he refers do not help him. In the first two

[b] "The passage of the *Sifri*," says Delitzsch on Genesis, p. 68, "one of the oldest Midrashim of the school of Rab (1247), on Deut. xvii. 18, to which Rashi refers on Sota 41ᵃ, is as clear as it is important: 'Let him (the king) copy אֵת מִשְׁנֵה תֹרַת הַזֹּאת in a

a particular book kept for the purpose is probably intended; and in 2 Sam. xi. 15, *the* book or leaf is meant which had already been mentioned in the previous verse. Hence the article is indispensable.

that the whole Pentateuch should have been read at a national feast, whereas that Deuteronomy, summing up, spiritualizing, and at the same time enforcing the Law should so have been read, is in the highest degree probable and natural. It is in confirmation of this view that all the later literature, and especially the writings of the prophets, are full of references to Deuteronomy as the book with which they might expect the most intimate acquaintance on the part of their hearers. So in other passages in which a written law is spoken of we are driven to conclude that only some part and not the whole of the Pentateuch is meant. Thus in chap. xxvii. 3, 8, Moses commands the people to write "all the words of this Law very plainly" on the stones set up on Mount Ebal. Some have supposed that only the Decalogue, others, that the blessings and curses which immediately follow, were so to be inscribed. Others again (as Schulz, *Deuteron.* p. 87) think that some summary of the Law may have been intended; but it is at any rate quite clear that the expression "all the words of this Law" does not refer to the whole Pentateuch. This is confirmed by Josh. viii. 32. There the history tells us that Joshua wrote upon the stones of the altar which he had built on Mount Ebal "a copy of the Law of Moses (*mishneh torath Mosheh* — the same expression which we have in Deut. xvii. 18), which he wrote in the presence of the children of Israel. . . . And afterward he read all the words of the Law, the blessings and cursings, according to all that is written in the book of the Law." On this we observe, first, that "the blessings and the cursings" here specified as having been engraven on the plaster with which the stones were covered, are those recorded in Deut. xxvii., xxviii, and, next, that the language of the writer renders it probable that other portions of the Law were added. If any reliance is to be placed on what is apparently the oldest Jewish tradition (see p. 2412, note *b*), and if the words rendered in our version "copy of the Law" mean "repetition of the Law," *i. e.* the book of Deuteronomy, then it was this which was engraven upon the stones and read in the hearing of Israel. It seems clear that the whole of the existing Pentateuch cannot be meant, but either the book of Deuteronomy only, or some summary of the Mosaic legislation. In any case nothing can be argued from any of the passages to which we have referred as to the authorship of the first four books. Schultz, indeed, contends that with chap. xxx. the discourses of Moses end, and that therefore whilst the phrase "this law," whenever it occurs in chaps. i.–xxx., means only Deuteronomy, yet in chap. xxxi., where the narrative is resumed and the history of Moses brought to a conclusion, "this law" would naturally refer to the whole previous legislation. Chapter xxxi. brings, as he says, to a termination, not Deuteronomy only, but the previous books as well; for without it they would be incomplete. In a section, therefore, which concludes the whole, it is reasonable to suppose that the words "this law" designate the whole. He appeals, moreover (against Delitzsch), to the Jewish tradition, and to the words of Josephus, ὁ ἀρχιερεὺς ἐπὶ βήματος ὑψηλοῦ

σταθεὶς . . . . ἀναγιγνωσκέτω τοὺς νόμους πᾶσι, and also to the absence of the article in xxxi 24, where Moses is said to have made an end of writing the Law in *a* Book (עַל סֵפֶר), whereas when different portions are spoken of, they are said to have been written in *the* Book already existing (Ex. xvii. 14; 1 Sam. x. 25; Josh. xxiv. 26). It is scarcely conceivable, he says, that Moses should have provided so carefully for the safe custody and transmission of his own sermons on the Law, and have made no like provision for the Law itself, though given by the mouth of Jehovah. Even therefore if "this Law" in xxxi. 9, 24, applies in the first instance to Deuteronomy, it must indirectly include, if not the whole Pentateuch, at any rate the whole Mosaic legislation. Deuteronomy everywhere supposes the existence of the earlier books, and it is not credible that at the end of his life the great Legislator should have been utterly regardless of the Law which was the text, and solicitous only about the discourses which were the comment. The one would have been unintelligible apart from the other. There is, no doubt, some force in these arguments; but as yet they only render it probable that if Moses were the author of Deuteronomy, he was the author of a great part at least of the three previous books.

So far, then, the direct evidence from the Pentateuch itself is not sufficient to establish the Mosaic authorship of every portion of the Five Books. Certain parts of Exodus, Leviticus, and Numbers, and the whole of Deuteronomy to the end of chap. xxx., is all that is expressly said to have been written by Moses.

Two questions are yet to be answered. Is there evidence that parts of the work were not written by Moses? Is there evidence that parts of the work are later than his time?

2. The next question we ask is this: Is there any evidence to show that he did *not* write portions of the work which goes by his name? We have already referred to the last chapter of Deuteronomy which gives an account of his death. Is it probable that Moses wrote the words in Ex. xi. 3, "Moreover the man Moses was very great in the land of Egypt, in the sight of Pharaoh's servants, and in the sight of the people;" — or those in Num. xii. 3, "Now the man Moses was very meek above all the men which were upon the face of the earth?" On the other hand, are not such words of praise just what we might expect from the friend and disciple — for such perhaps he was — who pronounced his eulogium after his death — "And there arose not a prophet since in Israel like unto Moses, whom Jehovah knew face to face" (Deut. xxxiv. 10)?

3. But there is other evidence, to a critical eye not a whit less convincing, which points in the same direction. If, without any theory casting its shadow upon us, and without any fear of consequences before our eyes, we read thoughtfully only the Book of Genesis, we can hardly escape the conviction that it partakes of the nature of a compilation. It has, indeed, a unity of plan, a coherence of parts, a shapeliness and an order, which satisfy

---

book for himself in particular, and let him not be satisfied with one that he has inherited from his ancestors. משנה means nothing else but מִשְׁנֶה תּוֹרָה (Deuteronomy). Not this exclusively, how-

ever, because in ver. 19 is said, to observe *all* the words of this Law. If so, then why is Deuteronomy only mentioned? Because on the day of assembly Deuteronomy only was read.' "

ns that as it stands it is the creation of a single mind. But it bears, also, manifest traces of having been based upon an earlier work; and that earlier work itself seems to have had imbedded in it fragments of still more ancient documents. Before proceeding to prove this, it may not be unnecessary to state, in order to avoid misconstruction, that such a theory does not in the least militate against the divine authority of the book. The history contained in Genesis could not have been narrated by Moses from personal knowledge; but whether he was taught it by immediate divine suggestion, or was directed by the Holy Spirit to the use of earlier documents, is immaterial in reference to the inspiration of the work. The question may therefore be safely discussed on critical grounds alone.

We begin, then, by pointing out some of the phenomena which the book of Genesis presents. At the very opening of the book, peculiarities of style and manner are discernible, which can scarcely escape the notice of a careful reader even of a translation, which certainly are no sooner pointed out than we are compelled to admit their existence.

The language of chapter i. 1–ii. 3 (where the first chapter ought to have been made to end) is totally unlike that of the section which follows, ii. 4–iii. 23. This last is not only distinguished by a peculiar use of the divine names — for here, and nowhere else in the whole Pentateuch, except Ex. ix. 30, have we the combination of the two, Jehovah Elohim — but also by a mode of expression peculiar to itself. It is also remarkable for preserving an account of the creation distinct from that contained in the first chapter. It may be said, indeed, that this account does not contradict the former, and might therefore have proceeded from the same pen. But, fully admitting that there is no contradiction, the representation is so different that it is far more natural to conclude that it was derived from some other, though not antagonistic, source. It may be argued that here we have, not as in the first instance the Divine idea and method of creation, but the actual relation of man to the world around him, and especially to the vegetable and animal kingdoms: that this is therefore only a resumption and explanation of some things which had been mentioned more broadly and generally before. Still in any case it cannot be denied that this second account has the character of a supplement; that it is designed, if not to correct, at least to explain the other. And this fact, taken in connection with the peculiarities of the phraseology and the use of the divine names in the same section, is quite sufficient to justify the supposition that we have here an instance, not of independent narrative, but of compilation from different sources.

To take another instance. Chapter xiv. is beyond all doubt an ancient monument — papyrus-roll it may have been, or inscription on stone, which has been copied and transplanted in its original form into our present book of Genesis. Archaic it is in its whole character: distinct, too, again, from the rest of the book in its use of the name of God. Here we have El 'Elyon, " the Most High God," used by Melchizedec first, and then by Abraham, who adopts it and applies it to Jehovah, as if to show that it was one God whom he worshipped and whom Melchizedec acknowledged, though they knew Him under different appellations.

We believe, then, that at least these two portions of Genesis — chap. ii. 4–iii. 24. and chap. xiv. — are original documents, preserved, it may have been, like the genealogies, which are also a very prominent feature of the book, in the tents of the patriarchs, and made use of either by the Elohist or the Jehovist for his history. Indeed, Eichhorn seems to be not far from the truth when he observes, " The early portion of the history was composed merely of separate small notices; whilst the family history of the Hebrews, on the contrary, runs on in two continuous narratives: these, however, again have not only here and there some passages inserted from other sources, as chap. xiv., xxxiii. 18–xxxiv. 31, xxxvi. 1–43, xlix. 1–27, but, even where the authors wrote more independently, they often bring together traditions which in the course of time had taken a different form, and merely give them as they had received them, without intimating which is to be preferred " (*Einl. in A. T.* iii. 91, § 412).

We come now to a more ample examination of the question as to the distinctive use of the divine names. Is it the fact, as Astruc was the first to surmise, that this early portion of the Pentateuch, extending from Gen. i. to Ex. vi., does contain two original documents characterized by their separate use of the divine names and by other peculiarities of style? Of this there can be no reasonable doubt. We do find, not only scattered verses, but whole sections thus characterized. Throughout this portion of the Pentateuch the name יהוה (Jehovah) prevails in some sections, and אלהים (Elohim) in others. There are a few sections where both are employed indifferently; and there are, finally, sections of some length in which neither the one nor the other occurs. A list of these has been given in another article. [GENESIS.] And we find, moreover, that in connection with this use of the divine names there is also a distinctive and characteristic phraseology. The style and idiom of the Jehovah sections is not the same as the style and idiom of the Elohim sections. After Ex. vi. 2–vii. 7, the name Elohim almost ceases to be characteristic of whole sections: the only exceptions to this rule being Ex. xiii. 17–19 and chap. xviii. Such a phenomenon as this cannot be without significance. If, as Hengstenberg and those who agree with him would persuade us, the use of the divine names is to be accounted for throughout by a reference to their etymology — if the author uses the one when his design is to speak of God as the Creator and the Judge, and the other when his object is to set forth God as the Redeemer — then it still cannot but appear remarkable that only up to a particular point do these names stamp separate sections of the narrative, whereas afterwards all such distinctive criterion fails. How is this fact to be accounted for? Why is it that up to Ex. vi. each name has its own province in the narrative, broad and clearly defined, whereas in the subsequent portions the name Jehovah prevails, and Elohim is only interchanged with it here and there? But the alleged design in the use of the divine names will not bear a close examination. It is no doubt true that throughout the story of creation in i. 1–ii. 3 we have Elohim — and this squares with the hypothesis. There is some plausibility also in the attempt to explain the compound use of the divine names in the next section, by the fact that here we have the transition from the History of Creation to the

History of Redemption; that here consequently we should expect to find God exhibited in both characters, as the God who made and the God who redeems the world. That after the Fall it should be Jehovah who speaks in the history of Cain and Abel is on the same principle intelligible, namely, that this name harmonizes best with the features of the narrative. But when we come to the history of Noah the criterion fails us. Why, for instance, should it be said that "Noah found grace in the eyes of Jehovah" (vi. 8), and that "Noah walked with Elohim" (vi. 9)? Surely on the hypothesis it should have been, "Noah walked with Jehovah," for Jehovah, not Elohim, is His Name as the God of covenant, and grace, and self-revelation. Hengstenberg's attempt to explain this phrase by an opposition between "walking with God" and "walking with the world" is remarkable only for its ingenuity. Why should it be more natural or more forcible even then to imply an opposition between the world and its Creator, than between the world and its Redeemer? The reverse is what we should expect. To walk with the world does not mean with the created things of the world, but with the *spirit* of the world; and the emphatic opposition to that spirit is to be found in the spirit which confesses its need and lays hold of the promise of Redemption. Hence to walk with *Jehovah* (not Elohim) would be the natural antithesis to walking with the world. So, again, how on the hypothesis of Hengstenberg, can we satisfactorily account for its being said in vi. 22, "Thus did Noah; according to all that God (*Elohim*) commanded him, so did he;" and in vii. 5, "And Noah did according unto all that *Jehovah* commanded him;" while again in vii. 9 *Elohim* occurs in the same phrase? The elaborate ingenuity by means of which Hengstenberg, Drechsler, and others attempt to account for the specific use of the several names in these instances is in fact its own refutation. The stern constraint of a theory could, alone have suggested it.

The fact to which we have referred that there is this distinct use of the names Jehovah and Elohim in the earlier portion of the Pentateuch, is no doubt to be explained by what we are told in Ex. vi. 2, "And Elohim spake unto Moses, and said unto him, I am Jehovah: and I appeared unto Abraham, unto Isaac, and unto Jacob as El-Shaddai, but by my name Jehovah was I not known to them." Does this mean that the name Jehovah was literally unknown to the Patriarchs? that the first revelation of it was that made to Moses in ch. iii. 13, 14? where we read: "And Moses said unto God, Behold, when I come unto the children of Israel, and shall say unto them, The God of your fathers hath sent me unto you: and they shall say to me, What is His Name? what shall I say unto them? And God said unto Moses, I AM THAT I AM: and He said, Thus shalt thou say unto the children of Israel, I AM hath sent me unto you"

This is undoubtedly the first *explanation* of the name. It is now, and now first, that Israel is to be made to understand the full import of that Name. This they are to learn by the redemption out of Egypt. By means of the deliverance they are to recognize the character of their deliverer. The God of their fathers is not a God of power only, but a God of faithfulness and of love, the God who has made a covenant with his chosen, and who therefore will not forsake them. This

seems to be the meaning of the "I AM THAT I AM" (אֶהְיֶה אֲשֶׁר אֶהְיֶה), or as it may perhaps be better rendered, "I am He whom I prove myself to be." The abstract idea of self-existence can hardly be conveyed by this name; but rather the idea that God is what He is *in relation to his people.* Now, in this sense it is clear God had not fully made Himself known before.

The name Jehovah may have existed, though we have only two instances of this in the history, — the one in the name Moriah (Gen. xxii. 2), and the other in the name of the mother of Moses (Ex. vi. 20), who was called Jochebed; both names formed by composition from the divine name Jehovah. It is certainly remarkable that during the patriarchal times we find no other instance of a proper name so compounded. Names of persons compounded with El and Shaddai we do find, but not with Jehovah. This fact abundantly shows that the name Jehovah was, if not altogether unknown, at any rate not understood. And thus we have "an undesigned coincidence" in support of the accuracy of the narrative. God says in Exodus, He was not known by that name to the patriarchs. The Jehovistic writer of the patriarchal history, whether Moses or one of his friends, uses the name freely as one with which he himself was familiar, but it never appears *in the history* and life of the Patriarchs as one which was familiar to them. On the other hand, passages like Gen. iv. 26, and ix. 23, seem to show that the name was not altogether unknown. Hence Astruc remarks: "Le passage de l'Exode bien entendu ne prouve point que le nom de Jehova fut un nom de Dieu inconnu aux Patriarches et révelé à Moyse le premier, mais prouve seulement que Dieu n' avoit pas fait connoître aux Patriarches toute l'étendue de la signification de ce nom, au lieu qu'il l'a manifestée à Moyse." The expression in Ex. vi. 3, "I was not known, or did not make myself known," is in fact to be understood with the same limitation as when (John i. 17) it is said, that "Grace and truth came by Jesus Christ" as in opposition to the Law of Moses, which does not mean that there was no Grace or Truth in the Old Covenant; or as when (John vii. 39) it is said, "The Holy Ghost was not yet, because Jesus was not yet glorified," which does not of course exclude all operation of the Spirit before. [JEHOVAH, Amer. ed.]

Still this phenomenon of the distinct use of the divine names would scarcely of itself prove the point, that there are two documents which form the groundwork of the existing Pentateuch. But there is other evidence pointing the same way. We find, for instance, the same story told by the two writers, and their two accounts manifestly interwoven; and we find also certain favorite words and phrases which distinguish the one writer from the other.

(1.) In proof of the first, it is sufficient to read the history of Noah.

In order to make this more clear, we will separate the two documents, and arrange them in parallel columns: —

JEHOVAH.	ELOHIM.
Gen. vi. 5. And Jehovah saw that the wickedness of man was great in the earth, and that every imagination of the thoughts of his heart was	Gen. vi. 12. And Elohim saw the earth, and behold it was corrupt; for all flesh had corrupted his way upon the earth.

JEHOVAH.

only evil continually. And it repented Jehovah, etc.

7. And Jehovah said, I will blot out man whom I have created from off the face of the ground.

vii. 1. And Jehovah said to Noah . . . . Thee have I seen righteous before me in this generation.

vii. 2. Of all cattle which is clean thou shalt take to thee by sevens, male and his female, and of all cattle which is not clean, two, male and his female.

3. Also of fowl of the air by sevens, male and female, to preserve seed alive on the face of all the earth.

vii. 4. For in yet seven days I will send rain upon the earth forty days and forty nights, and I will blot out all the substance which I have made from off the face of the ground.

vii. 5. And Noah did according to all that Jehovah commanded him.

ELOHIM.

13. And Elohim said to Noah, The end of all flesh is come before me, for the earth is filled with violence because of them, and behold I will destroy them with the earth.

vi. 9. Noah a righteous man was perfect in his generation. With Elohim did Noah walk.

vi. 19. And of every living thing of all flesh, two of all shalt thou bring into the ark to preserve alive with thee: male and female shall they be.

20. Of fowl after their kind, and of cattle after their kind, of every thing that creepeth on the ground after his kind, two of all shall come unto thee: that thou mayest preserve (them) alive.

vi. 17. And I, behold I do bring the flood, waters upon the earth, to destroy all flesh wherein is the breath of life, from under heaven, all that is in the earth shall perish.

vi. 22. And Noah did according to all that Elohim commanded him; so did he.

Without carrying this parallelism further at length, we will merely indicate by references the traces of the two documents in the rest of the narrative of the Flood: vii. 1, 6, on the Jehovah side, answer to vi. 18, vii. 11, on the Elohim side; vii. 7, 8, 9, 17, 23, to vii. 13, 14, 15, 16, 18, 21, 22; viii. 21, 22, to ix. 8, 9, 10, 11.

It is quite true that we find both in earlier and later writers repetitions, which may arise either from accident or from want of skill on the part of the author or compiler; but neither the one nor the other would account for the *constant* repetition which here runs through *all parts* of the narrative.

(2.) But again we find that these duplicate narratives are characterized by peculiar modes of expression; and that, generally, the Elohistic and Jehovistic sections have their own distinct and individual coloring.

We find certain favorite phrases peculiar to the Elohistic passages. Such, for instance, are אֲחֻזָּה, "possession;" אֶרֶץ מְגֻרִים, "land of sojournings;" לְדֹרֹתָם or לְדֹרֹתֵיכֶם, "after your, or their, generations;" לְמִינוֹ, or לְמִינָה, "after his, or her, kind;" בְּעֶצֶם הַיּוֹם הַזֶּה, "on the self-same day;" פַּדָּן אֲרָם, "Padan Aram"—for which in the Jehovistic portions we always find אֲרַם נַהֲרַיִם

"Aram Naharaim," or simply אֲרָם, "Aram;" פָּרָה וְרָבָה, "be fruitful and multiply;" בְּרִית, "establish a covenant"—the Jehovistic phrase being כָּרַת בְּרִית, "to make (lit. 'cut') a covenant." So again we find אוֹת בְּרִית "sign of the covenant;" בְּרִית עוֹלָם, "everlasting covenant;" זָכָר וּנְקֵבָה, "male and female" (instead of the Jehovistic (אִישׁ וְאִשְׁתּוֹ; שֶׁרֶץ, "swarming or creeping thing;" and שָׁרַץ: and the common superscription of the genealogical portions, אֵלֶּה תּוֹלְדוֹת, "these are the generations of," etc., are, if not exclusively, yet almost exclusively, characteristic of those sections in which the name Elohim occurs.

There is therefore, it seems, good ground for concluding that, besides some smaller independent documents, traces may be discovered of two original historical works, which form the basis of the present book of Genesis and of the earlier chapters of Exodus.

Of these there can be no doubt that the Elohistic is the earlier. The passage in Ex. vi. establishes this, as well as the matter and style of the document itself. Whether Moses himself was the author of either of these works is a different question. Both are probably in the main as old as his time; the Elohistic certainly is, and perhaps older. But other questions must be considered before we can pronounce with certainty on this head.

4. But we may now advance a step further. There are certain references of time and place which prove clearly that the work, *in its present form*, is later than the time of Moses. Notices there are scattered here and there which can only be accounted for fairly on one of two suppositions, namely, either a later composition of the whole, or the revision of an editor who found it necessary to introduce occasionally a few words by way of explanation or correction. When, for instance, it is said (Gen. xii. 6, comp. xiii. 7), "And the Canaanite was then (אָז) in the land," the obvious meaning of such a remark seems to be that the state of things was different in the time of the writer; that now the Canaanite was there no longer; and the conclusion is that the words must have been written after the occupation of the land by the Israelites. In any other book, as Vaihinger justly remarks, we should certainly draw this inference.

The principal notices of time and place which have been alleged as bespeaking for the Pentateuch a later date are the following:—

(a.) References of *time*. Ex. vi. 26, 27, need not be regarded as a later addition, for it obviously sums up the genealogical register given just before, and refers back to ver. 13. But it is more naturally reconcilable with some other authorship than that of Moses. Again, Ex. xvi. 33-36, though it must have been introduced after the rest of the book was written, may have been added by Moses himself, supposing him to have composed the rest of the book. Moses there directs Aaron to lay up the manna before Jehovah, and then we read: "As Jehovah commanded Moses, so Aaron laid it up before the Testimony (i. e. the Ark) to be kept.

And the children of Israel did eat manna forty years, until they came to a land inhabited; they did eat manna until they came unto the borders of the land of Canaan." Then follows the remark, "Now an omer is the tenth part of an ephah." It is clear then that this passage was written not only after the ark was made, but after the Israelites had entered the Promised Land. The plain and obvious intention of the writer is to tell us when the manna *ceased*, not, as Hengstenberg contends, merely how long it *continued*. So it is said (Josh. v. 12), "And the manna ceased on the morrow after they had eaten of the old corn of the land," etc. The observation, too, about the omer could only have been made when the omer as a measure had fallen into disuse, which it is hardly supposable could have taken place in the lifetime of Moses. Still these passages are not absolutely irreconcilable with the Mosaic authorship of the book. Verse 35 may be a later gloss only, as Le Clerc and Rosenmüller believed.

The difficulty is greater with a passage in the book of Genesis. The genealogical table of Esau's family (ch. xxxvi.) can scarcely be regarded as a later interpolation. It does not interrupt the order and connection of the book; on the contrary, it is a most essential part of its structure; it is one of the ten "generations" or genealogical registers which form, so to speak, the backbone of the whole. Here we find the remark (ver. 31), "And these are the kings that reigned in the land of Edom, before there reigned any king over the children of Israel" Le Clerc supposed this to be a later addition, and Hengstenberg confesses the difficulty of the passage (*Auth. d. Pentat.* ii. 202). But the difficulty is not set aside by Hengstenberg's remark that the reference is to the prophecy already delivered in xxxv. 11, "Kings shall come out of thy loins." No unprejudiced person can read the words, "before there reigned any king over the children of Israel," without feeling that, when they were written, kings had already begun to reign over Israel. It is a simple historical fact that for centuries after the death of Moses no attempt was made to establish a monarchy amongst the Jews. Gideon indeed (Judg. viii. 22, 23) might have become king, or perhaps rather military dictator, but was wise enough to decline with firmness the dangerous honor. His son Abimelech, less scrupulous and more ambitious, prevailed upon the Shechemites to make him king, and was acknowledged, it would seem, by other cities, but he perished after a turbulent reign of three years, without being able to perpetuate his dynasty. Such facts are not indicative of any desire on the part of the Israelites at that time to be ruled by kings. There was no deep-rooted national tendency to monarchy which could account for the observation in Gen. xxxvi. on the part of a writer who lived centuries before a monarchy was established. It is impossible not to feel in the words, as Ewald observes, that the narrator almost envies Edom because she had enjoyed the blessings of a regular well-ordered kingdom so long before Israel. An historical remark of this kind, it must be remembered, is widely different from the provision made in Deuteronomy for the possible case that at some later time a monarchy

would be established. It is one thing for a writer framing laws, which are to be the heritage of his people and the basis of their constitution for all time, to prescribe what shall be done when they shall elect a king to reign over them. It is another thing for a writer comparing the condition of another country with his own to say that the one had a monarchical form of government long before the other. The one might be the dictate of a wise sagacity forecasting the future; the other could only be said at a time when both nations alike were governed by kings. In the former case we might even recognize a spirit of prophecy: in the latter this is out of the question. Either then we must admit that the book of Genesis did not exist as a whole till the times of David and Solomon, or we must regard this particular verse as the interpolation of a later editor. And this last is not so improbable a supposition as Vaihinger would represent it. Perfectly true it is that the whole genealogical table could have been no later addition: it is manifestly an integral part of the book. But the words in question, ver. 31, may have been inserted later from the genealogical table in 1 Chr. i. 43; and if so, it may have been introduced by Ezra in his revision of the Law.[a]

Similar remarks may perhaps apply to Lev. xviii. 28: "That the land spue not you out also when ye defile it, as it *spued out the nation that was before you*." This undoubtedly assumes the occupation of the Land of Canaan by the Israelites. The great difficulty connected with this passage, however, is that it is not a supplementary remark of the writer's, but that the words are the words of God directing Moses what he is to say to the children of Israel (ver. 1). And this is not set aside even if we suppose the book to have been written, not by Moses, but by one of the elders after the entrance into Canaan.

(b.) In several instances older *names of places* give place to those which came later into use in Canaan. In Gen. xiv. 14, and in Deut. xxxiv. 1, occurs the name of the well-known city of Dan. But in Josh. xix. 47 we are distinctly told that this name was given to what was originally called Leshem (or Laish) by the children of Dan after they had wrested it from the Canaanites. The same account is repeated still more circumstantially in Judg. xviii. 27–29, where it is positively asserted that "the name of the city was Laish at the first." It is natural that the city should be called Dan in Deut. xxxiv., as that is a passage written beyond all doubt after the occupation of the Land of Canaan by the Israelites. But in Genesis we can only fairly account for its appearance by supposing that the old name Laish originally stood in the MS., and that Dan was substituted for it on some later revision. [DAN.]

In Josh. xiv. 15 (comp. xv. 13, 54) and Judg. i. 10 we are told that the original name of Hebron before the conquest of Canaan was Kirjath-Arba. In Gen. xxiii. 2 the older name occurs, and the explanation is added (evidently by some one who wrote later than the occupation of Canaan), "the same is Hebron." In Gen. xiii. 18 we find the name of Hebron standing alone and without any explanation. Hence Keil supposes that this was

<hr/>

a Psalm xiv. furnishes a curious instance of the way in which a passage may be introduced into an earlier book. St. Paul, quoting this psalm in Rom. iii. 10, subjoins other passages of Scripture to his quota-

tion. Hence the LXX. have transferred these passages from the Epistle into the Psalm, and have been followed by the Vulg. and Arab.

the original name, that the place came to be called Kirjath-Arba in the interval between Abraham and Moses, and that in the time of Joshua it was customary to speak of it by its ancient instead of its more modern name. This is not an impossible supposition; but it is more obvious to explain the apparent anachronism as the correction of a later editor, especially as the correction is actually given in so many words in the other passage (xxiii. 2).

Another instance of a similar kind is the occurrence of Hormah in Num. xiv. 45, xxi. 1–3, compared with Judg. i. 17. It may be accounted for, however, thus: In Num. xxi. 3 we have the origin of the name explained. The book of Numbers was written later than this, and consequently, even in speaking of an earlier event which took place at the same spot, the writer might apply the name, though at that point of the history it had not been given. Then in Judg. i. 17 we have the *Canaanite* name Zephath (for the Canaanites naturally would not have adopted the Hebrew name given in token of their victory), and are reminded at the same time of the original Hebrew designation given in the Wilderness.

So far, then, judging the work simply by what we find in it, there is abundant evidence to show that, though the main bulk of it is Mosaic, certain detached portions of it are of later growth. We are not obliged, because of the late date of these portions, to bring down the rest of the book to later times. This is contrary to the express claim advanced by large portions at least to be from Moses, and to other evidence, both literary and historical, in favor of a Mosaic origin. On the other hand, when we remember how entirely during some periods of Jewish history the Law seems to have been forgotten, and again how necessary it would be after the seventy years of exile to explain some of its archaisms and to add here and there short notes to make it more intelligible to the people, nothing can be more natural than to suppose that such later additions were made by Ezra and Nehemiah.

III. We are now to consider the evidence lying outside of the Pentateuch itself, which bears upon its authorship and the probable date of its composition. This evidence is of three kinds: first, direct mention of the work as already existing in the later books of the Bible; secondly, the existence of a book substantially the same as the present Pentateuch amongst the Samaritans; and, lastly, allusions less direct, such as historical references, quotations, and the like, which presuppose its existence.

1. We have direct evidence for the authorship of the Law in Josh. i. 7, 8, "according to all the Law which Moses my servant commanded thee," — "this book of the Law shall not depart out of thy mouth," — and viii. 31, 34, xxiii. 6 (in xxiv. 26, "the book of the Law of God"), in all which places Moses is said to have written it. This agrees with what we have already seen respecting Deuteronomy and certain other portions of the Pentateuch which are ascribed in the Pentateuch itself to Moses. They cannot, however, be cited as proving that the Pentateuch in its present form and in all its parts is Mosaic.

The book of Judges does not speak of the book of the Law. A reason may be alleged for this difference between the books of Joshua and Judges. In the eyes of Joshua, the friend and immediate successor of Moses, the Law would possess unspeakable value. It was to be his guide as the Captain of the people, and on the basis of the Law was to rest all the life of the people both civil and religious, in the land of Canaan. He had received, moreover, from God Himself, an express charge to observe and do according to all that was written in the Law. Hence we are not surprised at the prominent position which it occupies in the book which tells us of the exploits of Joshua. In the book of Judges on the other hand, where we see the nation departing widely from the Mosaic institutions, lapsing into idolatry, and falling under the power of foreign oppressors, the absence of all mention of the Book of the Law is easily to be accounted for.

It is a little remarkable, however, that no direct mention of it occurs in the books of Samuel. Considering the express provision made for a monarchy in Deuteronomy, we should have expected that on the first appointment of a king some reference would have been made to the requirements of the Law. A prophet like Samuel, we might have thought, could not fail to direct the attention of the newly made king to the Book in accordance with which he was to govern. But if he did this, the history does not tell us so; though there are, it is true, allusions which can only be interpreted on the supposition that the Law was known. The first mention of the Law of Moses after the establishment of the monarchy is in David's charge to his son Solomon, on his death-bed (1 K. ii. 3). From that passage there can be no doubt that David had himself framed his rule in accordance with it, and was desirous that his son should do the same. The words "as it is written in the Law of Moses," show that some portion, at any rate, of our present Pentateuch is referred to, and that the Law was received as the Law of Moses. The allusion, too, seems to be to parts of Deuteronomy, and therefore favors the Mosaic authorship of that book. In viii. 9, we are told that "there was nothing in the ark save the two tables of stone which Moses put there at Horeb." In viii. 53, Solomon uses the words, "As thou spakest by the hand of Moses thy servant;" but the reference is too general to prove anything as to the authorship of the Pentateuch. The reference may be either to Ex. xix. 5, 6, or to Deut. xiv. 2.

In 2 K. xi. 12, "the testimony" is put into the hands of Joash at his coronation. This must have been a book containing either the whole of the Mosaic Law, or at least the Book of Deuteronomy, a copy of which, as we have seen, the king was expected to make with his own hand at the time of his accession.

In the Books of Chronicles far more frequent mention is made of "the Law of Jehovah," or "the book of the Law of Moses:" — a fact which may be accounted for partly by the priestly character of those books. Thus we find David's preparation for the worship of God is "according to the Law of Jehovah" (1 Chr. xvi. 40). In his charge to Solomon occur the words "the Law of Jehovah thy God, the statutes and the judgments which Jehovah charged Moses with concerning Israel" (xxii. 12, 13). In 2 Chr. xii. it is said that Rehoboam "forsook the Law of Jehovah;" in xiv. 4, that Asa commanded Judah "to seek Jehovah the God of their fathers, and to do the Law and the commandment." In xv. 3, the prophet Azariah reminds Asa that "now for a long season Israel hath been without the true God, and without a *teaching priest*, and without *Law*;" and in xvii. 9, we find Jehoshaphat appointing certain princes together with priests and Levites, to teach: "they taught in Judah, and had the book of the Law of Jehovah with them." In xxv. 4, Amaziah is said to have acted in a particular instance "as it is written in the Law in the book of Moses." In xxxi. 3, 4, 21, Hezekiah's regulations are expressly said to have been in accordance with "the Law of Jehovah." In xxxiii. 8, the writer is quoting the word of God in reference to the Temple — "so that they will take heed to do all that I have commanded them, according to the whole Law and the statutes, and the ordinances by the hand of Moses." In xxxiv. 14, occurs the memorable passage in which Hilkiah the priest is said to have "found a book of the Law of Jehovah (given) by Moses." This happened in the eighteenth year of the reign of Josiah. And accordingly we are told in xxxv. 26, that Josiah's life had been regulated in accordance with that which was "written in the Law of Jehovah."

In Ezra and Nehemiah we have mention several times made of the Law of Moses, and here there can be no doubt that our present Pentateuch is meant; for we have no reason to suppose that any later revision of it took place. At this time, then, the existing Pentateuch was regarded as the work of Moses. Ezra iii. 2, "as it is written in the Law of Moses the man of God;" vi. 18, "as it is written in the book of Moses;" vii. 6, Ezra, it is said, "was a ready scribe in the Law of Moses." In Neh. i. 7, &c., "the commandments, judgments, etc., which Thou commandedst Thy servant Moses," viii. 1, &c., we have the remarkable account of the reading of "the book of the Law of Moses." See also ix. 3, 14, xiii. 1–3.

The books of Chronicles, though undoubtedly based upon ancient records, are probably in their present form as late as the time of Ezra. Hence it might be supposed that if the reference is to the present Pentateuch in Ezra, the present Pentateuch must also be referred to in Chronicles. But this does not follow. The book of Ezra speaks of the Law as it existed in the time of the writer; the books of Chronicles speak of it as it existed long before. Hence the author of the latter (who may have been Ezra) in making mention of the Law of Moses refers of course to that recension of it which existed at the particular periods over which his history travels. Substantially, no doubt, it was the same book; and there was no special reason why the Chronicler should tell us of any corrections and additions which in the course of time had been introduced into it.

In Dan. ix. 11, 13, the Law of Moses is mentioned, and here again, a book differing in nothing from our present Pentateuch is probably meant.

These are all the passages of the Old Testament Canon in which "the Law of Moses," "the book of the Law," or such like expressions occur, denoting the existence of a particular book, the authorship of which was ascribed to Moses. In the Prophets and in the Psalms, though there are many allusions to the Law, evidently as a written document, there are none as to its authorship. But the evidence hitherto adduced from the historical books is unquestionably strong; first in favor of an early existence of the main body of the Pentateuch — more particularly of Genesis and the legal portions of the remaining books; and next, as showing a universal belief amongst the Jews that the work was written by Moses.

2. Conclusive proof of the early composition of the Pentateuch, it has been argued, exists in the fact that the Samaritans had their own copies of it, not differing very materially from those possessed by the Jews, except in a few passages which had probably been purposely tampered with and altered; such for instance as Ex. xii. 40; Deut. xxvii. 4. The Samaritans, it is said, must have derived their Book of the Law from the Ten Tribes, whose land they occupied; on the other hand, it is out of the question to suppose that the Ten Tribes would be willing to accept religious books from the Two. Hence the conclusion seems to be irresistible that the Pentateuch must have existed in its present form before the separation of Israel from Judah: the only part of the O. T. which was the common heritage of both.

If this point could be satisfactorily established, we should have a limit of time in one direction for the composition of the Pentateuch. It could not have been later than the times of the earliest kings. It must have been earlier than the reign of Solomon, and indeed than that of Saul. The history becomes at this point so full, that it is scarcely credible that a measure so important as the codification of the Law, if it had taken place, could have been passed over in silence. Let us, then, examine the evidence. What proof is there that the Samaritans received the Pentateuch from the Ten Tribes? According to 2 K. xvii. 24–41, the Samaritans were originally heathen colonists belonging to different Assyrian and Arabian [a] tribes, who were transplanted by Shalmaneser to occupy the room of the Israelites whom he had carried away captive. It is evident, however, that a considerable portion of the original Israelitish population must still have remained in the cities of Samaria. For we find (2 Chr. xxx. 1-20) that Hezekiah invited the remnant of the Ten Tribes who were in the land of Israel to come to the great Passover which he celebrated, and the different tribes are mentioned (vv. 10, 11) who did, or did not respond to the invitation. Later, Esarhaddon adopted the policy of Shalmaneser and a still further deportation took place (Ezr. iv. 2). But even after this, though the heathen element in all probability preponderated, the land was not swept clean of its original inhabitants. Josiah, it is true, did not, like Hezekiah, invite the Samaritans to take part in the worship at Jerusalem. But finding himself strong enough to disregard the power of Assyria, now on the decline, he virtually claimed the land of Israel as the rightful apanage of David's throne, adopted energetic measures for the suppression of idolatry, and even exterminated the Samaritan priests. But what is of more importance as showing that some portion of the Ten Tribes was still left in the land, is the fact, that when the collection was made for the repairs of the Temple, we are told that the Levites gathered the money "of the hand of *Manasseh and Ephraim, and of all the remnant of Israel*," as well as "of Judah and Benjamin"

---

a It is a curious and interesting fact, for the knowledge of which we are indebted to Sir H. Rawlinson, that Sargon penetrated far into the interior of Arabia, and carrying off several Arabian tribes, settled them in Samaria. This explains how Geshem the Arabian came to be associated with Sanballat in the government of Judæa, as well as the mention of Arabians in the army of Samaria ("Illustrations of Egyptian History," etc., in the *Trans. of Roy. Soc. Lit.*, 1860, part i. pp 148, 149).

(2 Chr. xxxiv. 9). And so also, after the discovery of the Book of the Law. Josiah bound not only "all who were present in Judah and Benjamin" to stand to the covenant contained in it, but he "took away all the abominations out of all the countries that pertained to the *children of Israel*, and made all that were present *in Israel* to serve, even to serve Jehovah their God. And all his days they departed not from serving Jehovah *the God of their fathers*" (2 Chr. xxxiv. 32, 33).

Later yet, during the vice-royalty of Gedaliah, we find still the same feeling manifested on the part of the Ten Tribes which had shown itself under Hezekiah and Josiah. Eighty devotees from Shechem, from Shiloh, and from Samaria, came with all the signs of mourning, and bearing offerings in their hand, to the Temple at Jerusalem. They thus testified both their sorrow for the desolation that had come upon it, and their readiness to take a part in the worship there, now that order was restored. And this, it may be reasonably presumed, was only one party out of many who came on a like errand. All these facts prove that, so far was the intercourse between Judah and the remnant of Israel from being embittered by religious animosities, that it was the religious bond that bound them together. Hence it would have been quite possible during any portion of this period for the mixed Samaritan population to have received the Law from the Jews.

This is far more probable than that copies of the Pentateuch should have been preserved amongst those families of the Ten Tribes who had either escaped when the land was shaven by the razor of the king of Assyria, or who had straggled back thither from their exile. If even in Jerusalem itself the Book of the Law was so scarce, and had been so forgotten, that the pious king Josiah knew nothing of its contents till it was accidentally discovered; still less probable is it that in Israel, given up to idolatry and wasted by invasions, any copies of it should have survived.

On the whole, we should be led to infer that there had been a gradual fusion of the heathen settlers with the original inhabitants. At first the former, who regarded Jehovah as only a local and national deity like one of their own false gods, endeavored to appease Him by adopting in part the religious worship of the nation whose land they occupied. They did this in the first instance, not by mixing with the resident population, but by sending to the king of Assyria for one of the Israelitish priests who had been carried captive. But in process of time, the amalgamation of races became complete, and the worship of Jehovah superseded the worship of idols, as is evident both from the wish of the Samaritans to join in the Temple worship after the Captivity, and from the absence of all idolatrous symbols on Gerizim. So far, then, the history leaves us altogether in doubt as to the time at which the Pentateuch was received by the Samaritans. Copies of it *might* have been left in the northern kingdom after Shalmaneser's invasion, though this is hardly probable; or they might have been introduced thither during the religious reforms of Hezekiah or Josiah.

But the actual condition of the Samaritan Pentateuch is against any such supposition. It agrees so remarkably with the existing Hebrew Pentateuch, and that, too, in those passages which are manifestly interpolations and corrections as late as the time of Ezra, that we must look for some other period to which to refer the adoption of the Books

of Moses by the Samaritans. This we find after the Babylonish exile, at the time of the institution of the rival worship on Gerizim. Till the return from Babylon there is no evidence that the Samaritans regarded the Jews with any extraordinary dislike or hostility. But the manifest distrust and suspicion with which Nehemiah met their advances when he was rebuilding the walls of Jerusalem provoked their wrath. From this time forward, they were declared and open enemies. The quarrel between the two nations was further aggravated by the determination of Nehemiah to break off all marriages which had been contracted between Jews and Samaritans. Manasseh the brother of the highpriest (so Josephus calls him, *Ant.* xi. 7, § 2), and himself acting high-priest, was one of the offenders. He refused to divorce his wife, and took refuge with his father-in-law Sanballat, who consoled him for the loss of his priestly privilege in Jerusalem by making him high-priest of the new Samaritan temple on Gerizim. With Manasseh many other apostate Jews who refused to divorce their wives, fled to Samaria. It seems highly probable that these men took the Pentateuch with them, and adopted it as the basis of the new religious system which they inaugurated. A full discussion of this question would be out of place here. It is sufficient merely to show how far the existence of a Samaritan Pentateuch, not materially differing from the Hebrew Pentateuch, bears upon the question of the antiquity of the latter. And we incline to the view of Prideaux (*Connect.* book vi. chap. iii.), that the Samaritan Pentateuch was in fact a transcript of Ezra's revised copy. The same view is virtually adopted by Gesenius (*De Pent. Sam.* pp. 8, 9).

3. We are now to consider evidence of a more indirect kind, which bears not so much on the Mosaic authorship as on the early existence of the work as a whole. This last circumstance, however, if satisfactorily made out, is, indirectly at least, an argument that Moses wrote the Pentateuch. Hengstenberg has tried to show that all the later books, by their allusions and quotations, presuppose the existence of the Books of the Law. He traces, moreover, the influence of the Law upon the whole life, civil and religious, of the nation after their settlement in the land of Canaan. He sees its spirit transfused into all the national literature, historical, poetic, and prophetical: he argues that except on the basis of the Pentateuch as already existing before the entrance of the Israelites into Canaan, the whole of their history after the occupation of the land becomes an inexplicable enigma. It is impossible not to feel that this line of proof is, if established, peculiarly convincing, just in proportion as it is indirect and informal, and beyond the reach of the ordinary weapons of criticism.

Now, beyond all doubt, there are numerous most striking references both in the Prophets and in the books of Kings to passages which are found in our present Pentateuch. One thing at least is certain, that the theory of men like Von Bohlen, Vatke, and others, who suppose the Pentateuch to have been written in the times of the latest kings, is utterly absurd. It is established in the most convincing manner that the legal portions of the Pentateuch already existed in writing before the separation of the two kingdoms. Even as regards the historical portions, there are often in the later books almost verbal coincidences of expression, which render it more than probable that these also existed in writing. All this has been argued with much learning, the most indefatigable research, and in some instances with great success by Hengstenberg in his *Authentie des Pentateuchs*. We will satisfy ourselves with pointing out some of the most striking passages in which the coincidences between the later books and the Pentateuch (omitting Deuteronomy for the present) appear.

In Joel, who prophesied only in the kingdom of Judah; in Amos, who prophesied in both kingdoms; and in Hosea, whose ministry was confined to Israel, we find references which imply the existence of a written code of laws. The following comparison of passages may satisfy us on this point: Joel ii. 2 with Ex. x. 14; ii. 3 with Gen. ii. 8, 9 (comp. xiii. 10); ii. 17 with Num. xiv. 13; ii. 20 with Ex. x. 19; iii. 1 [ii. 28, E. V.] with Gen. vi. 12; ii. 13 with Ex. xxxiv. 6; iv. [iii.] 18 with Num. xxv. 1. — Again, Amos ii. 2 with Num. xxi. 28; ii. 7 with Ex. xxiii. 6, Lev. xx. 3; ii. 8 with Ex. xxii. 25, &c.; ii. 9 with Num. xiii. 32, &c.; iii. 7 with Gen. xviii. 17; iv. 4 with Lev. xxiv. 3, and Deut. xiv. 28, xxvi. 12; v. 12 with Num. xxxv. 31 (comp. Ex. xxiii. 6 and Am. ii. 7); v. 17 with Ex. xii. 12; v. 21, &c. with Num. xxix. 35, Lev. xxiii. 36; vi. 1 with Num. i. 17; vi. 6 with Gen. xxxvii. 25 (this is probably the reference: Hengstenberg's is wrong); vi. 8 with Lev. xxvi. 19; vi. 14 with Num. xxxiv. 8; viii. 6 with Ex. xxi. 2, Lev. xxv. 39; ix. 13 with Lev. xxvi. 3–5 (comp. Ex. iii. 8). — Again, Hosea i. 2 with Lev. xx. 5–7; ii. 1 [i. 10] with Gen. xxii. 17, xxxii. 12; ii. 2 [i. 11] with Ex. i. 10; iii. 2 with Ex. xxi. 32; iv. 8 with Lev. vi. 17, &c., and vii. 1, &c.; iv. 10 with Lev. xxvi. 26; iv. 17 with Lev. xxxii. 9, 10; v. 6 with Ex. x. 9; vi. 2 with Gen. xvii. 18; vii. 8 with Ex. xxxiv. 12–16; xii. 6 [A. V. 5] with Ex. iii. 15; xii. 10 [9] with Lev. xxiii. 43; xii. 15 [14] with Gen. ix. 5.

In the books of Kings we have also references as follows: 1 K. xx. 42 to Lev. xxvii. 29; xxi. 3 to Lev. xxv. 23, Num. xxxvi. 8; xxi. 10 to Num. xxxv. 30, comp. Deut. xvii. 6, 7, xix. 15; xxii. 17 to Num. xxvii. 16, 17. — 2 K. iii. 20 to Ex. xxix. 38, &c.; iv. 1 to Lev. xxv. 39, &c.; v. 27 to Ex. iv. 6, Num. xii. 10; vi. 18 to Gen. xix. 11; vi. 28 to Lev. xxvi. 29; vii. 2, 19 to Gen. vii. 11; vii. 3 to Lev. xiii. 46 (comp. Num. v. 3).

But now if, as appears from the examination of all the extant Jewish literature, the Pentateuch existed as a canonical book; if, moreover, it was a book so well known that its words had become household words among the people; and if the prophets could appeal to it as a recognized and well-known document, — how comes it to pass that in the reign of Josiah, one of the latest kings, its existence as a canonical book seems to have been almost forgotten? Yet such was evidently the fact. The circumstances, as narrated in 2 Chr. xxxiv. 14, &c., were these: In the eighteenth year of his reign, the king, who had already taken active measures for the suppression of idolatry, determined to execute the necessary repairs of the Temple, which had become seriously dilapitated, and to restore the worship of Jehovah in its purity. He accordingly directed Hilkiah the high priest to take charge of the moneys that were contributed for the

purpose. During the progress of the work, Hilkiah, who was busy in the Temple, came upon copy of the Book of the Law — which must have long lain neglected and forgotten — and told Shaphan the scribe of his discovery. The effect produced by this was very remarkable. The king, to whom Shaphan read the words of the book, was filled with consternation when he learnt for the first time how far the nation had departed from the Law of Jehovah. He sent Hilkiah and others to consult the prophetess Huldah, who only confirmed his fears. The consequence was that he held a solemn assembly in the house of the Lord, and "read in their ears all the words of the book of the covenant that was found in the house of the Lord."

How are we to explain this surprise and alarm in the mind of Josiah, betraying as it does such utter ignorance of the Book of the Law, and of the severity of its threatenings — except on the supposition that as a written document it had well-nigh perished? This must have been the case, and it is not so extraordinary a fact perhaps as it appears at first sight. It is quite true that in the reign of Jehoshaphat pains had been taken to make the nation at large acquainted with the Law. That monarch not only instituted "teaching priests," but we are told that as they went about the country they had the Book of the Law with them. But that was 300 years before, a period equal to that between the days of Luther and our own; and in such an interval great changes must have taken place. It is true that in the reign of Ahas the prophet Isaiah directed the people, who in their hopeless infatuation were seeking counsel of ventriloquists and necromancers, to turn "to the Law and to the Testimony;" and Hezekiah, who succeeded Ahaz, had no doubt reigned in the spirit of the prophet's advice. But the next monarch was guilty of outrageous wickedness, and filled Jerusalem with idols. How great a desolation might one wicked prince effect, especially during a lengthened reign! To this we must add, that at no time, in all probability, were there many copies of the Law existing in writing. It was probably then the custom, as it still is in the East, to trust largely to the memory for its transmission. Just as at this day in Egypt, persons are to be found, even illiterate in other respects, who can repeat the whole Kurán by heart, and as some modern Jews are able to recite the whole of the Five Books of Moses,[a] so it probably was then: the Law, for the great bulk of the nation, was orally preserved and inculcated. The ritual would easily be perpetuated by the mere force of observance, though much of it doubtless became perverted, and some part of it perhaps obsolete, through the neglect of the priests. Still it is against the perfunctory and lifeless manner of their worship, not against their total neglect, that the burning words of the prophets are directed. The command of Moses, which laid upon the king the obligation of making a copy of the Law for himself, had of course long been disregarded. Here and there perhaps only some prophet or righteous man possessed a copy of the sacred book. The bulk of the nation were without it. Nor was there any

---

[a] See Mr. Grove's very interesting paper on Nablus and the Samaritans in *Vacation Tourists*, 1861. Speaking of the service of the *yom kippūr* in the Samaritan synagogue, he says that the recitation of the Pentateuch was continued through the night, "without

even the feeble lamp which on every other night of the year but this burns in front of the holy books. The two priests and a few of the people know the whole of the Torah by heart" (p. 346).

reason why copies should be brought under the notice of the king. We may understand this by a parallel case. How easy it would have been in our own country, before the invention of printing, for a similar circumstance to have happened. How many copies, do we suppose, of the Scriptures were made? Such as did exist would be in the hands of a few learned men, or more probably in the libraries of monasteries.[a] Even after a translation, like Wycliffe's, had been made, the people as a whole would know nothing whatever of the Bible; and yet they were a Christian people, and were in some measure at least instructed out of the Scriptures, though the volume itself could scarcely ever have been seen. Even the monarch, unless he happened to be a man of learning or piety, would remain in the same ignorance as his subjects. Whatever knowledge there was of the Bible and of religion would be kept alive chiefly by means of the Liturgies used in public worship. So it was in Judah. The oral transmission of the Law and the living witness of the prophets had superseded the written document, till at last it had become so scarce as to be almost unknown. But the hand of God so ordered it that when king and people were both zealous for reformation, and ripest for the reception of the truth, the written document itself was brought to light.

On carefully weighing all the evidence hitherto adduced, we can hardly question, without a literary skepticism which would be most unreasonable, that the Pentateuch is to a very considerable extent as early as the time of Moses, though it may have undergone many later revisions and corrections, the last of these being certainly as late as the time of Ezra. But as regards any direct and unimpeachable testimony to the composition of the whole work by Moses we have it not. Only one book out of the five — that of Deuteronomy — claims in express terms to be from his hand. And yet, strange to say, this is the very book in which modern criticism refuses most peremptorily to admit the claim. It is of importance therefore to consider this question separately.

All allow that the Book of the Covenant in Exodus, perhaps a great part of Leviticus, and some part of Numbers, were written by Israel's greatest leader and prophet. But Deuteronomy, it is alleged, is in style and purpose so utterly unlike the genuine writings of Moses that it is quite impossible to believe that he is the author. But how then set aside the express testimony of the book itself? How explain the fact that Moses is there said to have written all the words of this Law, to have consigned it to the custody of the priests, and to have charged the Levites sedulously to preserve it by the side of the ark? Only by the bold assertion that the fiction was invented by a later writer, who chose to personate the great Lawgiver in order to give the more color of consistency to his work! The author first feigns the name of Moses that he may gain the greater consideration under the shadow of his name, and then proceeds to reënact, but in a broader and more spiritual manner, and with true prophetic inspiration, the chief portions of the earlier legislation.

But such an hypothesis is devoid of all probability. For what writer in later times would ever have presumed, unless he were equal to Moses, to correct or supplement the Law of Moses? And if he were equal to Moses, why borrow his name (as Ewald supposes the Deuteronomist to have done) in order to lend greater weight and sanction to his book? The truth is, those who make such a supposition import modern ideas into ancient writings. They forget that what might be allowable in a modern writer of fiction would not have been tolerated in one who claimed to have a Divine Commission, who came forward as a prophet to rebuke and to reform the people. Which would be more weighty to win their obedience, "Thus saith Jehovah," or "Moses wrote all these words"?

It has been argued indeed that in thus assuming a feigned character the writer does no more than is done by the author of Ecclesiastes. He in like manner takes the name of Solomon that he may gain a better hearing for his words of wisdom. But the cases are not parallel. The Preacher only pretends to give an old man's view of life, as seen by one who had had a large experience and no common reputation for wisdom. Deuteronomy claims to be a Law imposed on the highest authority, and demanding implicit obedience. The first is a record of the struggles, disappointments, and victory of a human heart. The last is an absolute rule of life, to which nothing may be added, and from which nothing may be taken (iv. 2, xxxi. 1).

But, besides the fact that Deuteronomy claims to have been written by Moses, there is other evidence which establishes the great antiquity of the book.

1. It is remarkable for its allusions to Egypt,[b] which are just what would be expected supposing Moses to have been the author. Without insisting upon it that in such passages as iv. 15–18, or vi. 8, xi. 18–20 (comp. Ex. xiii. 16), where the command is given to wear the Law after the fashion of an amulet, or xxvii. 1–8, where writing on stones covered with plaster is mentioned, are probable references to Egyptian customs, we may point to more certain examples. In xx. 5 there is an allusion to Egyptian regulations in time of war; in xxv. 2 to the Egyptian bastinado; in xi. 10 to the Egyptian mode of irrigation. The references which Delitzsch sees in xxii. 5 to the custom of the Egyptian priests to hold solemn processions in the masks of different deities, and in viii. 9 to Egyptian mining operations, are by no means so certain. Again, among the curses threatened are the sicknesses of Egypt, xxviii. 60 (comp. vii. 15). According to xxviii. 68, Egypt is the type of all the oppressors of Israel: "Remember that thou wast a slave in the land of Egypt," is an expression which is several times made use of as a motive in enforcing the obligations of the book (v. 15, xxiv. 18, 22; see the same appeal in Lev. xix. 34, a passage occurring in the remarkable section Lev. xvii.–xx., which has so much affinity with Deuteronomy). Lastly, references to the sojourning in Egypt are numerous: "We were Pharaoh's bondmen in Egypt," etc. (vi. 21–23; see also vii. 8, 18, xi. 3); and these occur even in the laws, as in the law of the king

a That even in monasteries the Bible was a neglected and almost unknown book, is clear from the story of Luther's conversion.

b It is a significant fact that Ewald, who will have it that Deuteronomy was written in the reign of Manasseh, is obliged to make his supposed author live in Egypt, in order to account plausibly for the acquaintance with Egyptian customs which is discernible in the book.

(xvii. 16), which would be very extraordinary if the book had only been written in the time of Manasseh.

The phraseology of the book, and the archaisms found in it, stamp it as of the same age with the rest of the Pentateuch. The form הוּא, instead of הִיא, for the feminine of the pronoun (which occurs in all 195 times in the Pentateuch), is found 36 times in Deuteronomy. Nowhere do we meet with הִיא in this book, though in the rest of the Pentateuch it occurs 11 times. In the same way, like the other books, Deuteronomy has נַעַר of a maiden, instead of the feminine נַעֲרָה, which is only used once (xxii. 19). It has also the third pers. pret. חַי, which in prose occurs only in the Pentateuch (Ewald, *Lehrbuch*, § 142 b). The demonstrative pronoun הָאֵל, which (according to Ewald, § 183 a, is characteristic of the Pentateuch) occurs in Deut. iv. 42, vii. 22, xix. 11, and nowhere else out of the books of Moses, except in the late book, 1 Chr. xx. 8, and the Aramaic Ezra, v. 15. The use of the ה *locale*, which is comparatively rare in later writings, is common to Deuteronomy with the other books of the Pentateuch; and so is the old and rare form of writing תִּמְצָאן, and the termination of the future in יִדָן. The last, according to König (*A. T. Stud.* 2 Heft), is more common in the Pentateuch than in any other book: it occurs 58 times in Deuteronomy. Twice even in the preterite, viii. 3, 16, a like termination presents itself; on the peculiarity of which Ewald (§ 190 b, note) remarks, as being the original and fuller form. Other archaisms which are common to the whole five books are: the shortening of the Hiphil, לִרְאֹת, i. 33; לַעְשֹׁר, xxvi. 12, &c.; the use of קָרָה=קָרָא, "to meet;" the construction of the passive with אֵת of the object (for instance, xx. 8); the interchange of the older יָשֹׁב (xix. 4) with the more usual כֶּבֶשׂ; the use of זָכוּר (instead of זָכָר), xvi. 16, xx. 13, a form which disappears altogether after the Pentateuch; many ancient words, such as שֶׁגַר, יְקוּם, אָבִיב (Ex. xiii. 12). Amongst these are some which occur besides only in the book of Joshua, or else in very late writers, like Ezekiel, who, as is always the case in the decay of a language, studiously imitated the oldest forms; some which are found afterwards only in poetry, as אֲלָפִים (vii. 13, xxviii. 4, &c.), and מָתִים, so common in Deuteronomy. Again, this book has a number of words which have an archaic character. Such are, חֶרֶם (for the later מֶגֶל), שֶׂה (instead of סֶל); the old Canaanite עַשְׁתָּרֹת הַצֹּאן, "offspring of the flocks;" יְשֻׁרוּן, which as a name of Israel is borrowed, Is. xliv. 2; הֵהִין, i. 41, "to act rashly;" הֶחֱזִיק, "to be silent;" הַסְכִּית, xv.

14, "to give," lit. "to put like a collar on the neck;" הִתְעַמֵּר, "to play the lord;" מַדְוֶה, "sickness."

2. A fondness for the use of figures is another peculiarity of Deuteronomy. See xxix. 17, 18; xxviii. 13, 44; i. 31, 44; viii. 5; xxviii. 29, 49. Of similar comparisons there are but few (Delitzsch says but three) in the other books. The results are most surprising when we compare Deuteronomy with the Book of the Covenant (Ex. xix.–xxiv.) on the one hand, and with Ps. xc. (which is said to be Mosaic) on the other. To cite but one example: the images of devouring fire and of the bearing on eagles' wings occur only in the Book of the Covenant and in Deuteronomy. Comp. Ex. xxiv. 17, with Deut. iv. 24, ix. 3; and Ex. xix. 4, with Deut. xxxii. 11. So again, not to mention numberless undesigned coincidences between Ps. xc. and the book of Deuteronomy, especially chap. xxxii., we need only here cite the phrase מַעֲשֵׂה יָדָיִם (Ps. xc. 17), "work of the hands," as descriptive of human action generally, which runs through the whole of Deut. ii. 7, xiv. 29, xvi. 15, xxiv. 19, xxviii. 12, xxx. 9. The same close affinity, both as to matter and style, exists between the section to which we have already referred in Leviticus (ch. xvii.–xx., so manifestly different from the rest of that book), the Book of the Covenant (Ex. xix.–xxiv.), and Deuteronomy.

In addition to all this, and very much more might be said — for a whole harvest has been gleaned on this field by Schultz in the Introduction to his work on Deuteronomy — in addition to all these peculiarities which are arguments for the Mosaic authorship of the book, we have here, too, the evidence strong and clear of post-Mosaic times and writings. The attempt by a wrong interpretation of 2 K. xxii. and 2 Chr. xxxiv. to bring down Deuteronomy as low as the time of Manasseh fails utterly. A century earlier the Jewish prophets borrow their words and their thoughts from Deuteronomy. Amos shows how intimate his acquaintance was with Deuteronomy by such passages as ii. 9, iv. 11, ix. 7, whose matter and form are both colored by those of that book. Hosea, who is richer than Amos in these references to the past, whilst, as we have seen, full of allusions to the whole Law (vi. 7, xii. 4, &c., xiii. 9, 10), in one passage, viii. 12, using the remarkable expression, "I have written to him the ten thousand things of my Law," manifestly includes Deuteronomy (comp. xi. 8 with Deut. xxix. 22), and in many places shows that that book was in his mind. Comp. iv. 13 with Deut. xii. 2; viii. 13 with Deut. xxviii. 68; xi. 3 with Deut. i. 31; xiii. 6 with Deut. viii. 11–14. Isaiah begins his prophecy with the words, "Hear, O heavens, and give ear, O earth," taken from the mouth of Moses in Deut. xxxii. 1. In fact, echoes of the tones of Deuteronomy are heard throughout the solemn and majestic discourse with which his prophecy opens. (See Caspari, *Beiträge zur Einl. in d. Buch Jesaia*, p. 203–210.) The same may be said of Micah. In his protest against the apostasy of the nation from the Covenant with Jehovah, he appeals to the mountains as the sure foundations of the earth, in like manner as Moses, Deut. xxxii. 1. to the heavens and the earth. The controversy of Jehovah with his people (Mic. vi. 3–5) is a compendium, as it were, of the history of the Pentateuch from Exodus onwards, whilst the expression בֵּית עֲבָדִים, "Slave-house" of Egypt,

Is taken from Deut. vii. 8, xiii. 5. In vi. 8, there
is, no doubt, an allusion to Deut. x. 12, and the
threatenings of vi. 13–16 remind us of Deut. xxviii.
as well as of Lev. xxvi.

Since, then, not only Jeremiah and Ezekiel, but
Amos and Hosea, Isaiah and Micah, speak in the
words of Deuteronomy, as well as in words borrowed from other portions of the Pentateuch, we
see at once how untenable is the theory of those
who, like Ewald, maintain that Deuteronomy was
composed during the reign of Manasseh, or, as Vaihinger does, during that of Hezekiah.

But, in truth, the book speaks for itself. No
imitator could have written in such a strain. We
scarcely need the express testimony of the work to
its own authorship. But, having it, we find all the
internal evidence conspiring to show that it came
from Moses. Those magnificent discourses, the
grand roll of which can be heard and felt even in a
translation, came warm from the heart and fresh from
the lips of Israel's Lawgiver. They are the out-
pourings of a solicitude which is nothing less than
parental. It is the father uttering his dying advice
to his children, no less than the prophet counseling
and admonishing his people. What book can vie
with it either in majesty or in tenderness? What
words ever bore more surely the stamp of genuineness? If Deuteronomy be only the production of
some timorous reformer, who, conscious of his own
weakness, tried to borrow dignity and weight from
the name of Moses, then assuredly all arguments
drawn from internal evidence for the composition
of any work are utterly useless. We can never tell
whether an author is wearing the mask of another,
or whether it is he himself who speaks to us.

In spite, therefore, of the dogmatism of modern
critics, we declare unhesitatingly for the Mosaic
authorship of Deuteronomy.

Briefly, then, to sum up the results of our inquiry.

1. The book of Genesis rests chiefly on documents much earlier than the time of Moses, though
it was probably brought to very nearly its present
shape either by Moses himself, or by one of the
elders who acted under him.

2. The books of Exodus, Leviticus, and Numbers,
are to a great extent Mosaic. Besides those portions which are expressly declared to have been
written by him (see above), other portions, and
especially the legal sections, were, if not actually
written, in all probability dictated by him.

3. Deuteronomy, excepting the concluding part,
is entirely the work of Moses, as it professes to be.

4. It is not probable that this was written before
the three preceding books, because the legislation
in Exodus and Leviticus as being the more formal
is manifestly the earlier, whilst Deuteronomy is
the spiritual interpretation and application of the
Law. But the letter is always before the spirit;
the thing before its interpretation.

5. The first composition of the Pentateuch as a
whole could not have taken place till after the
Israelites entered Canaan. It is probable that
Joshua, and the elders who were associated with
him, would provide for its formal arrangement, custody, and transmission.

6. The whole work did not finally assume its
present shape till its revision was undertaken by
Ezra after the return from the Babylonish Captivity.

IV. *Literature.*

1. Amongst the earlier Patristic expositors may
be mentioned —

Augustine, *De Genesi contra Manich.; De
Genesi ad litteram; Locutiones* (Gen. — Jud.);
and *Quæstiones in Heptateuchum.*

Jerome, *Liber Quæstionum Hebraicarum in
Genesin.*

Chrysostom, *In Genesim, Homiliæ et Sermones.*
(Opp. Montfaucon, vol. vi. With these will also be
found those of Severian of Gabala.)

Theodoret, *Quæstiones in Gen., Ex., Lev.,
Numer., Deut.,* etc.

Ephraem Syrus, *Explanat. in Genesin.*

Cyril of Alexandria, *Glaphyra in libros Mosis.*

2. In the Middle Ages we have the Jewish commentators — Isaaki or Rashi (an abbreviation of his
name Rabbi Solomon Isaaki, sometimes wrongly
called Jarchi) of Troyes, in the 11th century;
Aben-Ezra of Toledo in the 12th; David Kimchi
of Narbonne in the 13th.

3. Of the Reformation period: —

The commentary of Calvin on the Five Books is
a masterpiece of exposition.

Luther wrote, both in German and in Latin,
commentaries on Genesis, the last being finished
but a short time before his death.

4. Later we have the commentaries of Calovius
in his *Biblia Illustrata,* and Mercerus, *in Genesin;*
Rivetus, *Exercitationes in Genesin,* and *Commentarii in Exodum,* in his *Opp. Theolog.* vol. i. Roter.
1865; Grotius, *Annot. ad Vet. Test.* in *Opp.* vol. i.;
Le Clerc (Clericus), *Mosis Prophetæ Lib. V.;* in
the 1st vol. of his work on the Old Testament
Amst. 1710, with a special dissertation, *De Scriptore Pentateuchi Mose;* Spencer, *De Legibus Hebræorum.*

5. The number of books written on this subject
in Germany alone during the last century, is very
considerable. Reference may be made to the General
Introductions of Michaelis, Eichhorn (5 vols. 1823),
Jahn (1814), De Wette (7th ed. 1852), Keil (1st
ed. 1853), Hävernick (1856), Bleek (1861), Stähelin (1862). Further, on the one hand, to Hengstenberg's *Authentie des Pentateuchs* (1836, 1839);
Ranke's *Untersuchungen* (1834); Drechsler, *Eis-
heit,* etc., *der Genesis* (1838); König, *Alt. Stud.*
(2 Heft, 1839); Kurtz, *Gesch. des Alten Bundes*
(2d ed. 1853); and on the other to Ewald, *Geschichte des Volkes Israels;* Von Lengerke, Kenaan (1844); Stähelin, *Krit. Untersuchungen*
(1843); Bertheau, *Die Sieben Gruppen,* etc.

As Commentaries on the whole or parts of the
Pentateuch may be consulted —

(1) Critical: — Rosenmüller, *Scholia,* vol. i. 3d
ed. (1821); Knobel (on all the books), in the
Kurzgef. Exeget. Handbuch; Tuch, *Die Genesis*
(1838); Schumann, *Genesis* (1829); Bunsen, *Bibelwerk.*

(2) Exegetical: — Baumgarten, *Theol. Comment.*
(1843); Schröder, *Das Erste Buch Mose* (1846);
Delitzsch, *Genesis* (3d ed. 1861); Schultz, *Deu-
teronomium* (1859). Much will be found bearing
on the general question of the authorship and date
of the Pentateuch in the Introductions to the last
two of these works.

In England may be mentioned Graves's *Lectures
on the last four Books of the Pentateuch,* who
argues strenuously for the Mosaic authorship. So
also do Rawlinson on *The Pentateuch,* in *Aids to
Faith,* 1862; and M'Caul on the *Mosaic Cosmogony,*
in the same volume; though the former admits that
Moses made free use of ancient documents in com-
piling Genesis.

Davidson, on the other hand, in Horne's *Intro-*

duction, vol. ii. (10th ed. 1856), argues for two documents, and supposes the Jehovist to have written in the time of the Judges, and the Elohist in that of Joshua, and the two to have been incorporated in one work in the reign of Saul or David. He maintains, however, the Mosaic authorship of Deuteronomy. [In his *Introd. to the Old Test.*, vol. i. (Lond. 1862), Davidson has abandoned this view of Deuteronomy. — A.]

The chief American writers who have treated of the Pentateuch are Stuart, *Crit. Hist. and Defence of the O. T. Canon;* and Bush, *Commentaries on the Five Books.*   J. J. S. P.

* The foregoing able discussion certainly makes all needful concessions to the modern critics of the Pentateuch, and its concluding propositions might be still more conservatively stated. It is, perhaps, enough to say that Genesis apparently rests to a considerable extent (rather than "chiefly") on earlier documents. The second, third, and fourth of the closing propositions may be quite firmly held. It is too much to concede (5thly) that the composition of the Pentateuch as a whole "*could* not have taken place till after the Israelites entered Canaan." For, the revision admitted in the sixth proposition needed to be but slight, in order to produce all the present marks of later date. After half a century of debate, we are in a position to see that, notwithstanding all the scholarship and acuteness that have been brought to attack the authorship and authenticity of the Pentateuch, few movements in the history of criticism have comprised a greater amount of arbitrary and extravagant assertion, irrelevant reasoning, mutual contradiction, and unwarranted conclusion. Meanwhile the style and structure of these books has undergone a searching investigation, many interesting features have been brought to light, several untenable positions abandoned, and some important concessions made. The most unsparing criticism is now compelled to admit: (1.) The essential and systematic unity of the present Pentateuch (Ewald, *Geschichte*, i. 92; Tuch, *Genesis*, Vorr. xxi.; Knobel, *Genesis*, § 16; Hupfeld, *Die Quellen*, p. 196). (2.) The general historic truthfulness of the narrative, from the dispersion of the nations onward, excepting its miraculous portions (Knobel, *Genesis*, p. 23; *Exodus*, p. 22; Tuch, *Genesis*, p. 11, &c.). (3.) The extraordinary character, career, and influence of Moses; even Ewald recognizing that age (*Geschichte*, ii. 239, &c.) as "a wonderfully elevated period, a focus of most surprising power, resolution, and activity;" the deliverance of the nation as an event of "unparalleled importance;" the victory at the Red Sea as a far brighter day than Marathon or Salamis; and Moses himself as "the mighty originator and leader of this entire new national movement," its "law-giver and prophet." So also Knobel to the same effect (*Ex.* p 22), and Bunsen (*Bibelwerk, Die Mosaische Geschichte*). (4.) The important fact that portions of the Mosaic narrative certainly are as old as the time of Moses, and even older. Thus De Wette declares of the odes in Num. xxi. 17, 18, 27-30, that they may with certainty be referred to the time of Moses (*Einleit.* § 149); Knobel, that Moses published his laws in writing, "though it is uncertain to what extent" (*Komm. Numb.* p. 592). Davidson, following Bleek chiefly, specifies more than twenty chapters which must have come from Moses with very slight change (*Introd.* i. 109), among which the passage Ex. xxv. - xxxi.

was "probably written down by him in its present state." Ewald pronounces Lamech's song to be very ancient, belonging to a time anterior to Moses (i. 75, note); the fourteenth of Genesis of the highest antiquity, also coming down from " before the age of Moses" (i. 80, 146). He admits the preservation of actual laws, sayings, and songs of Moses and his contemporaries (ii. 29-32), among which are the Decalogue, and Num. vi. 24-26, x. 35, 36, xxi. 17, 18, 27-30; Ex. iii. 15, xvii. 16, xv. 1-21. Such admissions, however grudging and scanty, from the ablest, wildest, and most captious of scholarly critics, show the necessities of the case; and they carry with them consequences which are more easily blinked than faced. It remained for one whose scholarship was extemporized like that of the Bishop of Natal, to deem it "quite possible, and indeed as far as our present inquiries have gone, highly probable, that Moses may be an historical character," although, "this is merely conjectural" (Colenso, *Pent.* ii. 70).

The most objectionable features of the modern German criticism of the Pentateuch have been its constant dogmatism, its frequent extravagance, the steady rationalistic bias under which it has been conducted, and, quite commonly, the hiatus between its premises and its conclusions. The following observations may cast further light on the subject.

(i.) It is proper to admit that the question of the authorship of the Pentateuch has been so presented as to affect its historic value and its authority. Ewald and others ask us to accept it as containing traditions originating at a period remote from the events, vouched for by no responsible authority, and, though containing a basis of truth, yet uncertain and unsatisfactory in detail, and of course destitute of proper value even as history. Whereas, if it comes from Moses, it carries not only the historic weight of a narrative by an actor in the events, but the extraordinary weight of Moses's character and circumstances. The attempt at disintegration has been made also an attempt at invalidation. Dr. Colenso openly avows this issue (*Pent.* ii. 62). Anonymous books of the Canon are indeed received with entire confidence and reverence. But an important difference is, that in the present instance there are claims of authorship positively put forth by the writer, and as positively denied by the critics. Not only do Kurtz and Delitzsch, but De Wette, Knobel, and Davidson, affirm that the book of Deuteronomy (as a whole) claims to have been written by Moses. Davidson coolly remarks, that "this was a bold step for the unknown author" (*Introd.* i. 375), and De Wette, that "the obscurity and unfitness of these claims deprive them of all value as proofs" (*Introd.* § 162). Consequently when these writers openly deny the fact, they impeach the veracity of the book. This aspect of the case it is not necessary nor wise to overlook.

(ii.) At the same time the extravagances and the mutual divergences and conflicts of the critics are a legitimate subject of consideration, in estimating the force of their conclusions. Many able scholars seem to have lost sobriety and fairness on this subject. They adduce arguments which would have no weight in any other discussion, — which they are themselves obliged to admit are not conclusive. What is more preposterous than the theory of Vater and Hartmann, that the Pentateuch consists only of a series of fragments strung together without order or design? What wilder than the claim of the learned Ewald to a critical sagacity which can detect some seven principal documents and writers, followed by the Deuteronomist (also drawing largely on "many documents"), and several other editors? Meanwhile the advocates of the "supplement" theory are by no means agreed in any one aspect of the case — whether it be the number, the dates, or the respective portions of the writers. It is hardly an adequate statement to say of De Wette, Bleek, Stähelin, Tuch, Lengerke, Hupfeld, Knobel, Bunsen, Kurtz, Delitzsch, Schultz, Vaihinger, that "they all alike recognise two documents." They hold this, and more also. Tuch, indeed, recognizes in the first four books but two main documents, together with various sections from independent sources; and De Wette, after two or three changes, adopted the same opinion. He however makes the Deuteronomist to be a third distinct writer; while Stähelin identifies the Deuteronomist with the Jehovist. Vaihinger finds in Genesis alone three writers, a pre-Elohist, an Elohist, and a Jehovist; also a separate writer for Deuteronomy. Hupfeld finds four persons concerned in the composition of Genesis: two Elohists, a Jehovist, and a compiler. He differs also from most of his compeers in supposing that the Jehovist knew nothing of the Elohistic work; while he holds to a separate Deuteronomist. Knobel finds four writers besides the Deuteronomist: a ground-work, a law-book, a war-book, and a Jehovist. Bleek thinks that an Elohistic document, whose limits he wisely declines to specify, lay at the foundation of the earlier parts of the Pentateuch, but that the supplementer or Jehovist of David's time had before him various other documents, longer or shorter, including a second account of creation, the song of Lamech, the narrative of Abram's expedition (Gen. xiv.), the sketch of Nimrod (Gen. x. 8–12), the section concerning the Sons of God (vi. 1–4), Jacob's blessing (xlix. 1–27), and other passages; together with whole chapters and smaller fragments in the central books from the hand of Moses, e. g. Lev. i. - vii., xi. - xvi., xvii., xxv.; Num. i., ii., iv., v. 1–3, vi. 22–27, x. 1–3, xix., xxi. 14, 15, 17, 18, 27–30; Ex. xx. 2–14, xxv. - xxxi. 17. Deuteronomy he refers to a later writer in the time of Hezekiah or Josiah. Bunsen, in his *Bibelwerk*, is also very indefinite. He, indeed, holds that the first four books were put into their present shape by a narrator of Hezekiah's time; but simply says that this writer had before him "writings from the hand of Moses, and other ancient documents which had survived the desolations of the Judges' times, and of which he found collections already made, consisting of prose-epic narratives, poetic utterances, and songs (Bd. v. Abth. ii. pp. 108, 258, 261). He, however, expressly declares that the name Jehovah was a name of patriarchal times, which had gone into disuse and lost its significance till renewed under Moses; and he asserts that the Jehovistic narrative of Gen. ii. 5 f., is "neither an appendage nor supplement, much less a repetition of the previous narrative." Yet these writers, thus widely differing, agree on one point, — the late origin of the Pentateuch. But here Kurtz, Delitzsch, and Schultz part company with them. While they recognize two distinct sources in the *historical* parts of the Pentateuch, they agree in ascribing to Moses himself the book of Deuter-

onomy as a whole, and the "book of the Covenant" together with various smaller sections, and in referring the whole Pentateuch to Moses or to persons appointed and instructed by him. It will be seen that the unity of view among these writers is therefore somewhat nominal. And when we examine their analysis of particular passages we meet with great diversities. The two names of God, indeed, furnish a general ground of agreement until Ex. vi. 3. But even prior to that point no little diversity is found (e. g. Gen. vii.), and often very direct collisions. Gen. xx. contains the name Elohim five times and Jehovah but twice; yet Knobel makes the entire passage Jehovistic, against Tuch and Delitzsch, the former of whom pronounces the whole tone of the language and mode of view Elohistic. Again, the *connected* narrative (Gen. xxviii. 10 – xxxiii.) contains both the divine names quite abundantly, Elohim largely preponderating, with certain characteristics of style, which, as Tuch maintains, mark the Elohist. To this writer accordingly he refers it, after deducting some troublesome portions. But Knobel assigns only eleven and a half verses in detached sections to the Elohist, and thirty-four verses in six fragments to the Jehovist, twelve detached passages to a "law-book," and thirteen other sections, verses, and half verses, to a "war-book" used by the Jehovist. Such instances, which might be multiplied indefinitely, show alike the unlimited license which these theorists assume, and the general uncertainty and confusion that spreads through their speculations. The chief point of agreement is the easy proposition that these were documents used in the composition.

(iii.) Our attention is naturally arrested by the great liberties which these theorists take with the narrative. There is neither law nor limit to the disintegration. Each writer is for the most part a law unto himself, and the limits of the dismemberment are the exigencies of his theory. Knobel dissects the forty-first chapter of Genesis into some twenty fragments, from three different writers; and Davidson (following Boehmer) into forty; while Tuch refers the whole chapter, and Hupfeld, Stähelin, and Delitzsch none of it, to the Elohist, or groundwork. Gen. xxxv. is divided by Knobel into ten distinct sections, by Davidson into fifteen. Davidson dissects Gen. xxi. into twelve fragments from four writers, and ch. xxxi. into thirty-five fractions from the same writers; Knobel into nine and six fragments, respectively. The other analysts widely differ from them here and elsewhere. Again, the excision of verses, clauses, and even single words is resorted to without the slightest hesitation, when the theory requires. Thus in Gen. v. the single verse 29, and in ch. vii. the last clause of ver. 16 is by all these critics remanded from the midst of Elohistic passages to the Jehovist. Hupfeld removes an intermediate half-verse in Gen. xii. 4, xxxv. 16, 21; Tuch drops out Gen. xii. 7; Knobel, xvi. 2, xxv. 21–23, xxix. 3, vii. 5, and parts of x. 25, xii. 8, xiii. 10, 18, xxxix. 2. Tuch, Knobel, and Delitzsch, leave to the Elohist only ver. 29 of ch. xix. In ch. xxi. Knobel cuts off from the Elohist the first clause of ver. 1, and the word "Jehovah" of the last clause; and of ch. xvii. he remarks that the whole chapter, "except ' Jehovah' of the first verse, is an unchanged portion of the groundwriting." Similar methods are abundantly employed to sustain the allegation of a difference of phraseology in the respective writers. Knobel declares that נָשִׂיא קָיל occurs only in the Jehovist; and having found two cases (Gen. xxvii. 38, xxix. 11), he simply forces the third by cutting away the last half of xxi. 16, and referring it also to the Jehovist. In ver. 14 of the same chapter he also removes the single phrase " putting on his shoulder," to sustain his theory that the Jehovist is more minute in description than the Elohist. Davidson declares that the expression "angel of God," or "angel of Jehovah," never occurs in the Elohist; and, to escape the force of Gen. xxi. 17, and xxxi. 11, he ascribes the first, notwithstanding the invariable Elohim before and after, to the redactor, and the second, similarly situated and twice containing Elohim, to a *second* Elohist. He finally surrenders his position on this subject of diverse phraseology, by declaring that his "argument is based on the prevailing, not the exclusive usage in each" (*Introd. to the O. T.* p. 30). For other specimens of this arbitrary and inconsistent method, see EXODUS. Surely it is a cheap process to build theories of such materials.

(iv.) It is instructive to observe the somewhat steady retrogression of these theories in the land of their birth. The "fragment hypothesis" of Vater and Hartmann was long ago exploded by the doctrine of an elaborate editorship. The "supplement hypothesis" that followed was unable to sustain itself in any one form; but relief was sought by various enlargements of the number of documents. Thus Dr. Davidson in 1862, after accepting a theory of four principal writers in Genesis, still finds it necessary to add, that "probably the Elohist used several brief documents besides oral tradition. So, too, the Jehovist may have done." Bunsen and Bleek, who are among the latest of these speculators, are extremely vague and cautious in details. And in regard to the supposed date of the Elohist and the Jehovist, we have the following remarkable scale of approach to the time of Moses, not quite in chronological order: Lengerke (1844) refers the Elohist to the time of Solomon, and the supplementer to that of Hezekiah; Tuch (1838) to the times of Saul and Solomon; Bleek to the times of Saul or the Judges and of David; Stähelin, of the Judges and of Saul; Delitzsch (1852), of Moses and of Joshua, or one of the elders who survived him; Kurtz (1853, 2d ed.) supposes Deuteronomy and sections of the other books written by Moses in the Desert, and the Pentateuch completed, perhaps by one of Aaron's sons, immediately after the occupation of the promised land; and Schultz (1859) makes the later writer or Jehovist to be also the author of Deuteronomy, and none other than Moses himself. This movement is both hopeful and significant, notwithstanding that the later dates still find abundant advocates.

(v.) It is well to mark the obvious inconclusiveness of much of the reasoning of these hypotheses. The most elaborate showing of documents does not, . as seems often to be assumed, disprove Mosaic authorship. Moses may have used them — unless they can be positively shown to be of later date. He may be, as Schultz holds, the very Jehovist. A modern historian, like Bancroft, incorporates directly into his narrative large quotations from other accounts. He is glad to avail himself of the very words of actors and eye-witnesses. But he is no less the author of the history, when he employs,

and as it were vouches for, these original accounts. Accordingly, we may freely recognize the use of older documents and firmly hold Moses to be the historian, — as do Rosenmüller, Jahn, Bush, Stuart, Lewis, Rawlinson, Murphy, and even Keil. Why should not the account of Creation, Paradise, and the Fall, have been handed down? And of so stupendous an event as the Flood, that has imprinted itself on the memory of almost all nations, even the most degraded, why should not the careful narrative, reading in the original like the minute record of an eye-witness, have descended down the chosen line of Shem from the scene itself? Why reject the striking indications that Gen. xiv. is a narrative older than the time of Moses, slightly modernized? On the other hand, a few external marks of a later period — a name or two, here and there an explanatory remark or interpolated comment, such as the lapse of several hundred years might naturally occasion, and which a modern editor would attach in the form of foot-notes, — by no means prove the later composition of the book, more especially if there are valid reasons on other grounds to believe the contrary. Still more hollow is the attempt to argue a later date by accumulated references to passages which cannot themselves be shown to have had a later origin, e. g. Gen. xiii. 18 (Hebron), xl. 15 (the Hebrews), Deut. xvii. 14–20 (the future monarchy). Dr. Davidson, who has gathered up a large array of reasons for believing the later date of Deuteronomy, is obliged repeatedly to admit the inconclusiveness of several portions of his argument. He devotes ten pages to a showing of the differences between its legislation and that of the other books; and yet concedes that the changes and modifications "are not radical ones," and are "only a development of the first"; and that it is "possible indeed to conceive of Moses" making these very modifications (*Introd.* i. 353, 363). Again after presenting a catalogue of historic deviations from the other books, he closes by granting that "there is no positive contradiction between them" (p. 367). And yet these utterly inconclusive considerations are steadily paraded as proofs. In order to show a difference in the tone of thought, Davidson is not ashamed to cite the injunction, "circumcise the foreskin of your heart," in evidence that "the ceremonial law was less valued" then (p. 369). The scholarly Knobel does not hesitate to swell his catalogue of diversities of style by instancing long lists of words limited in their use by the very nature of the subject, such as the technical words concerning the sacrifices. Nor should we overlook the cool assumption which has prevailed from De Wette to Davidson, and which begs the whole question of a revelation, by taking for granted that a narrative of miracles disproves a contemporaneous origin; or the equally vicious assumption which invalidates much of Bleek's arguing, that not only any prophetic utterance or allusion, but anything which can be construed as an anticipative transaction, must have been written after the event so anticipated. It is in such modes that no little of this reasoning is carried on.

(vi.) We cannot fail to observe how very few are the *clear* marks of a later hand, whether anachronisms or seeming interpolations. Considering the labor expended, the undoubted results are small. The fact of glosses or interpolations upon the original narrative has long been admitted. The Rabbins noticed eighteen passages of this kind, not all

equally clear. Sixty years ago Jahn specified nine
or ten short passages (Ex. vi. 14–29, vii. 7, xi. 3;
Deut. ii. 10–12, 20–24, iii. 9–11, 13, 14, x. 6–9;
Num. xxxii. 41), as undoubtedly not belonging to
the text, and Num. xii. 3 as doubtful. Modern
writers have cited others, often on unsatisfactory
grounds. Of clear anachronisms, the number is
exceedingly slight. Of course the account of
Moses's death was by a later hand; and a sufficient
intimation is given in the book itself, in the declaration (Deut. xxxi. 24 ff.) that when Moses finished
the Book of the Law, he handed it over to the Levites to keep. In modern books the account of the
author usually precedes the work, though in some
cases it is otherwise, as in Sleidan's work on the
reign of Charles V., of which all the complete editions proceed without a break, to give an account
of the death and burial of the author. The word
" Dan" (Gen. xiv. 14) we incline to regard as
later, though reasons can be given to the contrary;
" Hebron" and " Hormah" we do not. [DAN,
HEBRON, HORMAH.] The Gilgal of Deut. xi. 30
is clearly a different place from that which was
first named in Josh. v. 9. See Keil on Joshua.
" The Canaanite was then in the land" (Gen. xii.
6, xiii. 7), admits of three explanations, maintained
respectively by Knobel, Delitzsch, and Kalisch, either
of which removes all implication of a later date;
" already in the land," says Kalisch, " for they were
never entirely extirpated." " Before there reigned
any king over Israel" (Gen. xxxvi. 31), might
spring from the time of the kings; or (Delitzsch)
it might be written from the stand-point of the
previous promise, v. 11. " I was stolen from the
land of the Hebrews" (Gen. xl. 1, 5), is a natural
expression to the Egyptians, who had known
" Abram the Hebrew," and who knew the people
of that land as Hebrews (Gen. xxxix. 14, xli. 12).
" As the land spued out the nations before you"
(Levit. xviii. 28) ceases to carry any weight when
we translate, as the Hebrew equally admits, and as
ver. 20 implies, " will have spued out." The
phrase "unto this day," sometimes cited, is so
indefinite, in one instance denoting merely a part
of Jacob's lifetime (Gen. xlviii. 15) and in another
(Josh. vi. 25) a part of Rahab's life, that even
Davidson does not insist on it. "Seaward,"
meaning westward (Gen. xii. 8, &c.), and " beyond
Jordan" (Gen. l. 11), meaning east of Jordan, are
cited as indications of a Palestinian writer. But
if Gesenius is right in declaring the Hebrew to
have had its early home in Palestine, both phrases
would be simply old and settled terms of the language, with a fixed geographical meaning. Ex.
xvi. 35, 36 certainly has the aspect of a later origin, notwithstanding the defense of Hengstenberg,
Keil, Hävernick, and Murphy. These are the
strongest cases of supposed anachronisms; of which
but one is absolutely certain, and only two or three
others present any considerable claims; while all
together, if admitted, would make but a small show.
Other cases are instanced, but with less plausibility. For we cannot for a moment admit the
principle by which Bleek cites prospective laws, like
Deut. xvii. 14–20, xix. 14, xx. 5, 6, as proofs of
later composition.

The attempt of Colenso and others to show that
the use of the word Jehovah itself indicates a late
origin, and to sustain this position by reference to
the Jehovistic and Elohistic Psalms is destitute of
any solid basis. Too many questions concerning
the date, authorship, and arrangement of the

Psalms are unsettled, to make the argument of any
account. But (1) in order to make a great contrast between the earlier and later psalms in the
use of the word Jehovah, Colenso parts company
with the men of his school, and accepts the historic
assertions of early date in the titles — when it will
serve his turn; and he rejects them, when they will
not answer his purpose, as in Ps. xxxiv. and cxlii.
the former of which is exclusively Jehovistic, —
rejects them for the circular reason that these
psalms do "contain the name of Jehovah so often."
(2.) Of the six psalms accepted by him as early
psalms, one half contain the name Jehovah. (3.) It
is questionable whether the Davidic psalms of the
three later books are by David or his royal successors. [PSALMS]. (4.) Some have held that the
arrangement of the Psalms was governed by the
preponderant use of the Divine names. (5.) The
attempt is futile in the face of the historic statement in Ex. vi. 3, that God had made Himself emphatically known to Moses as Jehovah, while the
earlier names Jochebed and probably Moriah, are
proofs that this was not the first disclosure of the
name itself; a fact which further appears in a large
number of other names found in 1 Chron. ii. 8, 25,
32, iv. 2, vii. 2, 3, 8, xxiii. 8, 17, 19, 20 — although
Colenso remarks that the chronicler "simply invented the names," and Davidson observes that
"little weight attaches to these, because the
Hebrews often altered older names for later
ones!"

The apparent number of explanatory glosses is
greater than that of the seeming anachronisms;
but the clear cases are not numerous. Here opinions will differ. Some passages so clearly break
the connection as to be commonly admitted. It is
perhaps conceded by sober critics that Deut. x. 6,
7 (probably 6–9) is an interpolation (or, certainly a
misplacement); also most or all of iii. 9–14 and ii.
10–12, 20–23. (Rosenmüller, however. ascribes the
last mentioned to Moses at the end of his life, and
Hengstenberg and Keil refer all three to him.)
Jahn would add Num. xxxii. 41, and, with no very
obvious necessity, such historic supplements as the
titles Deut. i. 1–4, iv. 44–49, and others not specified. Many would include (Rosenmüller, Eichhorn,
Jahn) the assertion of Moses' meekness (Num. xii.
3), and (with Jahn) other remarks concerning him,
Ex. vi. 26, 27, vii. 7, xi. 3; while some writers still
maintain that these remarks are demanded by the
connection and occasion, and that Moses could be
divinely guided thus to speak the truth concerning
himself. These are the strongest cases that are
adduced. Others are cited, of which the most that
can be said is that they might be interpolations;
and also that they might not. It is of no avail for
Bleek to allege Num. xv. 32, " while the children
of Israel were in the wilderness": for they had left
the wilderness before the death of Moses. On the
whole there is almost reason for surprise that so
very few passages can be found in the Pentateuch
which could not have come from the hand of Moses
himself. In a composition so ancient we should
naturally look for more, rather than fewer marks
of editorial revision.

(vii.) We can now look at the strength of the
evidence that Moses was the author of the book as
a whole. Hardly any thing is lacking to the completeness of the concurrent testimony. We can
merely call attention to it in the most meagre of
outlines. 1. The supposition is rendered entirely
admissible by all the circumstances of the case.

(a.) The art of writing was in abundant use, and the Israelites in Egypt had lived in the midst of it. (b.) The requisite impulse for a written composition had arrived, in the completion of a great national and religious epoch, and the permanent establishment of laws and institutions founded on a great deliverance. (c.) The occasion had come for such a book as the Pentateuch, incorporating the institutions with the history. (d.) The requisite person had appeared in Moses, — the man whom even Ewald names "the mighty originator and leader of this entire new national movement," a "master-mind" "putting forth the highest energies and sublimest efforts of the spirit" with "clear insight and self-possession," "the greatest and most original of prophets," with endowments so remarkable that the same spirit "has in no other prophet produced results so important in the history of the world as in Moses." Such a work became such a man; and such a man might be supposed to possess the requisite "insight" for such a work.

2. The fact of his authorship is sustained by positive and concurrent evidence, in great variety and abundance. It is easier for objectors to overlook than to meet it. (a.) The Pentateuch itself declares of Moses, and of him only, that he was concerned in its composition. Nearly the whole of Deuteronomy, as even De Wette, Knobel, and Davidson concede, claims to have been written by him. Statements are explicitly made concerning portions of Exodus and Numbers to the same effect: Ex. xxiv. 7, xxxiv. 27, 28, xvii. 14; Num. xxxiii. 1–3. In one of these passages (Ex. xvii. 14) the direction is given to write "it in the book" (not a book, as E. V.). Similar allusions to such a book, and to the Law as a written law, are found in Deut. xvii. 18, 19, xxxi. 9–11, 24, xxviii. 58, 61, xxix. 20, 21, 27, xxx. 10. Meanwhile we find God giving explicit directions (Ex. xxv. 16–21, 22) to deposit his communications to Moses in the ark; corresponding to this direction is the claim, repeated over and over, that such utterances are the precise utterances of Jehovah, e. g. Lev. xxvii. 34; Num. xxxvi. 13; while the expressions, "the Lord spake unto Moses, saying," and "the Lord said unto Moses," occur in connection with various groups of commandments in Exodus, Leviticus, and Numbers more than 100 times — besides other similar forms; and some fifty times in announcing the performance of many of these commandments, we are told that it took place "as the Lord commanded Moses," or, "according to the commandment of the Lord by the hand of Moses." These constant claims to be exact statements of God's commandments by Moses, placed beside the direction to deposit in the ark, constitute the clearest and most pervading assertion of the Mosaic authorship of the main portion of the three central books. (b.) Deuteronomy, confessedly asserting its own Mosaic origin, everywhere presupposes the earlier books; and it re-asserts and vouches for all the main portions of their history from the dispersion of the race to the death of Aaron and the arrangements for Moses' successor, while its comments include directly and implicitly all the leading features of their legislation. As Schultz remarks, it is incredible that at the end of his life the great legislator should have been regardless of the text of his law, and solicitous only about the discourses which were the comment. (c.) The subsequent books of the O. T. abundantly presuppose the Pentateuch, and in every instance in which they allude to the authorship, they refer it to Moses. This topic has been sufficiently developed in the original article. (d.) It was the undisputed testimony of the Jewish nation at and before the time of Christ that Moses wrote the Pentateuch. Such is the testimony of Philo from Alexandria, and of Josephus from Jerusalem. (Philo, Mangey, II. 141, 149, Josephus, Bekker, III. ii. 5, xii. etc.) So also the Talmud from Babylon, in a passage apparently of great antiquity. Their statements are supported by the occasional references of the N. T., which at the lowest estimate show the current view by referring a passage from Exodus, Leviticus, or Deuteronomy alike to "Moses," and by recognizing the whole O. T. as consisting, according to the then prevailing classification, of "the law of Moses, the prophets and the Psalms," or hagiographa (Luke xxiv. 44). (e.) The Lord Jesus Christ and the writers of the N. T. add their testimony. The Law is the law of Moses (John vii. 23; Acts xv. 5; Heb. x. 28), or simply Moses (Acts xxi. 21). Moses gave the Law (John i. 17, vii. 19). Statements found in the several books are statements of Moses (Luke xx. 37, Rom. x. 5, Acts iii. 22; Matt. xix. 8). The entire utterances of the Pentateuch concerning the priesthood are what "Moses spake concerning the priesthood" (Heb. vii. 14). The Saviour directly declares (John vi. 46, 47), that Moses "wrote of me," and that he left "writings" then in the hands of the Jews. See also Luke xxiv. 27, 44, Acts xxvi. 22, xxviii. 23, xv. 21; 2 Cor. iii. 15, Luke xvi. 23, 31. Those only who hold the views of Colenso and Davidson will deem it sufficient to say that the Saviour only shared the ignorance of his age. Nor will it satisfy the conditions of the case to say that He simply accommodated himself to the prevalent view by the argumentum ad hominem; for Christ's declaration in John v. 46, 47, is too direct and self-originated to be easily disposed of otherwise than (in Alford's words) as "a testimony to the fact of Moses having written those books which were then and are still known by his name." (f.) The force of all these testimonies is increased by the fact that they are absolutely uncontradicted. While the Pentateuch itself, the subsequent books of the O. T., the Jewish nation. the Saviour and the Apostles, point to Moses with such entire unanimity that the echo comes back from foreign nations, in Manetho, Hecatæus, Strabo, Tacitus, referring the Jewish laws and institutions to Moses alone, not one hint is to be found in the whole range of history or literature that any person later or other than Moses composed either the volume or any integral portion of it. Never was testimony more unbroken.

3. The direct testimony is confirmed by various collateral indications, which we can only suggest. (a.) Traces of the Pentateuch in the other books of the O. T. extending almost up to the time of Moses, — except as the authenticity and early date of those books also are denied. (b.) Various archaisms characteristic of the five books, and of those almost or quite alone: e. g. הִוא as a feminine 195 times (36 in Deuteronomy), and in no certain instance elsewhere; נַעַר as a feminine; the demonstrative הָאֵל, found but twice elsewhere; the Kal future ending וּן for וּ; the far greater predominance of the full future וֹ; the

abundant use of ה local; for עָשָׂב for בְּעָשָׂב here only, fifteen times: זָכָר for זְכוּר; חָזָה, רָקָב, בּוֹצֵל, שֶׁגֶר, אָסִין, יְהוּם, אָבִיב, שָׂעִיר, and others, only here. The word מְתִים disappears afterwards, except in poetry; מִין occurs 29 times, afterwards but once; מֶרְכָּבָה 21 times, and but once afterwards. There is a prevalence of rough consonants; thus צָהַק, 13 times in the Pentateuch, and twice only elsewhere, while the softer form שָׂחַק, is found 38 times in the later books (c.) Egyptian words and traces of Egyptian residence. Among the Hebrew words corresponding to Egyptian ones, as given by Gesenius, Bunsen, and Seyffarth, are אֵיפָה, הִין, שׁוֹטֵר, רָאָם, כּוּס, אַחוּ, תֵּבָה, גֹּמֶא, מַפֵּחַ, זֶרֶת, and many others. The word הִין, occurring twenty-one times in the Pentateuch, afterwards disappears, except twice in Ezekiel. The word חֹמֶר, which had Ethiopic and apparently Egyptian affinities, went gradually into disuse, and was replaced, except in poetry, by כֹּר. (d.) Marks of the wilderness. Constant reference to tents and camps (Ex. xix. 17, &c.); regulations for marching and halting (Num. ii. etc.); and the absence of allusions to permanent dwellings except prospectively. The minute and elaborate directions for constructing and transporting the tabernacle for the ark, would never have been committed to writing except at the time. The wood of the Tabernacle and its furniture (shittim) was the product of the desert; while the cypress of Palestine never appears in the Pentateuch. The cedar, which is the growth of Palestine and Syria, is mentioned, but in a very remarkable manner, — never as a building-material, but in slight quantities, on two occasions, in cleansing from the leprosy (Lev. xiv.), and in forming water of purification for the unclean (Num. xix. 6). Now we learn elsewhere that cedar was imported from Syria into Egypt for furniture, small boxes, coffins, and various objects connected with the dead, and was also used in ointments for elephantiasis, ulcers, and some other complaints. The uses designated thus remind us of Egypt, the quantities employed conform to the circumstances of a journey which restricted it to small amounts. Yet the later books of the Bible abound in allusions to the cedar as the noblest of trees and building materials. Certain regulations were made for the wilderness and afterwards relaxed, Lev. xvii. 34; Deut. xii. 15, 20, 21. The law for leprosy contemplates both the condition of the people in the wilderness and in their future home. Some regulations concerning uncleanness suppose all the people in the vicinity of the Tabernacle. Some instances of supplementary legislation are founded on occurrences or laws of the wilderness; thus in regard to the Passover, the regulation, Num. ix. 8–11, grows out of Num. v. 2. Laws in regard to Sabbath-breaking and blasphemy, Levit. xxiv., Num. xv. 32–36, originated in like manner. Stanley shows (*Jewish Church*, i. 189) that the regulations concerning clean and unclean animals, in several of their specifications, include

what was peculiarly "the game of the wilderness.' The consecration of the whole tribe of Levi, as the same writer remarks (i. 188), is a clear memorial of that early period, since at no later time was there furnished any such occasion; and the provision of cities of refuge (i. 191) points back to a nomadic life and the morals of the desert. (e.) Delitzsch shows that there was no subsequent period of the nation from which the Law as a whole could have sprung: neither the barbarous times of the Judges, nor the insignificant time of Saul; whereas the reigns of David and Solomon, rich as they are in historic materials, give no indication whatever that the Law then first assumed written form. It did not originate after the division of the kingdoms, for Israel and Judah alike acknowledged its sway. Nor in the exile; for the people in returning from the exile return also to the *thorah* as the original divine basis of their long shattered commonwealth. And as to Ezra, both history and tradition disclose him only as a restorer and never as an originator. (f.) Finally, those who deny the authorship by Moses, cannot suggest, much less agree upon any plausible substitute.

(viii.) Let us now summarily notice the invalidity of all the objections raised, as against this evidence. The "higher criticism" has failed to shake the testimony. Von Bohlen's attempt to show errors in the allusions to Egyptian customs notably recoiled. The arithmetical objections marshaled by Colenso have been superabundantly demolished. The alleged errors and false implications concerning the wilderness have been largely addressed to our ignorance; and many of the objections have been shown also to have sprung from ignorance; whereas every new research brings to light new correspondences between the narrative and the circumstances. The cited anachronisms shrink into the smallest compass; and, so far as they exist, can be legitimately accounted for as revisions. The apparent interpolations are themselves indications of the antiquity of the text. The assertion, that "the mythological, traditional, and exaggerated element" (Davidson) — that is, the miraculous — shows that Moses could not have been the author, is a mere begging of the whole question of the supernatural. The argument that there is not difference enough between the language of the Pentateuch and of the later books, breaks down in several ways: It is conceded by the objectors (e. g. Davidson, i. 104) that there are differences, but they are alleged to be insufficient, — a matter of degree and a question of opinion. That the diversities should not be great is explicable from the isolation, the consolidation, and complete intercommunication of the nation, as well as from the uniformity of their mode of life, and the fixedness of their institutions and their civilization. It is paralleled by the fact that the Syriac of the Peshito in the second century is substantially the same as that of Syriac writers of the 13th century. And furthermore, it is admitted on all hands, by De Wette, Knobel, Bleek, Ewald, that portions of the Pentateuch are actually as old as Moses; and Knobel even admits the difficulty of deciding what is Mosaic and what is not; while the difference between the admitted psalms of David and the language of Ezra's time — though a period far more eventful in historic changes — are not such as to have made the Psalms difficult of apprehension at the latter period. Again, "repetitions, duplicate and diverse narratives " — if all the cited instances were real — do not bear upon this question. No more does the alleged composite character of the book; for, to whatever extent a compilation, unless there be positive proof of later date, nothing prevents Moses from having been the "redactor" or the "Jehovist." Without here going further into that question, we will only say that while Hengstenberg has too vehemently repelled the idea of a composite character, and has gone to extremes in the endeavor to find always a special reason for the use of Elohim and Jehovah respectively, on the other hand, the opposite school have gone to a still greater extreme in the attempt to dissect and precisely to determine the sources of each part of the composition. It is a well-considered remark of Kurtz at the close of his *History of the Old Covenant:* "We venture to express it as our confident persuasion that the question as to the origin and composition of the Pentateuch is far from having been settled, either by Hävernick, Hengstenberg, or Keil, on the one hand, or by Tuch, Stähelin, and Delitzsch on the other, and still less by Ewald or Hupfeld."

There is nothing then to invalidate the clear evidence that Moses was the author, unless it be the few detached words and passages seemingly of later growth. But it has been well said by the writer of the preceding article, "we are not obliged because of the later date of these portions to bring down the rest of the book to later times." Indeed no procedure is, under the circumstances, more unreasonable, provided they can be satisfactorily explained otherwise. But they can be thus explained. The succession of prophets continued till Ezra and Nehemiah, more than a thousand years after Moses. In view of the lapse of time and of the effects of the exile, (1) it is a perfectly natural supposition that explanatory additions should have been made by some of these later prophets. (2.) The Scriptures render the supposition probable by their notices of Ezra. He is not only in general "the scribe" (Neh. viii. 4), but he is "a ready scribe in the Law of Moses" (Ez. vii. 6), "a scribe of the words of the commandments of the Lord and of his statutes to Israel" (vii 11), who "had prepared his heart to seek the Law of the Lord and to do it, and to teach in Israel statutes and judgments" (ver. 10). He is also declared not only to have brought the Law of Moses before the people, and to have read it publicly in their hearing through a succession of days (Ez. viii. 1–5, 18), but he and his coadjutors "read in the Law of God distinctly, and gave the sense, and caused them to understand the reading" (viii. 8). Now let Ezra but have done for the Scriptures permanently and in view of the permanent necessity, that which he did orally and transiently on this occasion, and we have the phenomena fully explained. (3.) Accordingly there are traditional indications that this kind of supplementary work was actually performed. The Babylonian Talmud, in a well-known passage apparently of great antiquity (see Westcott, *The Bible in the Church*, pp. 35–37), ascribes eight verses of the Pentateuch [the last eight] to Joshua; and the same passage declares that several of the books of the O. T. were "written" (or reduced to their

present form) by others than their proper authors, among them "the men of the Great Synagogue"; while Ezra and Nehemiah end the list with writing their own books and completing the books of Chronicles. Concurrent with this is the tradition of 2 Esdras (xiv. 20–40), handed down also by the early fathers, fabulously embellished indeed, and ascribing to Ezra the reproduction of the lost Scriptures by immediate inspiration. But, as Dr. Davidson well said in his *Biblical Criticism* (i. 103), "the historic basis of the view that Ezra bore a leading part in collecting and revising the sacred books is not shaken by the fabulous circumstances in the writings of the early fathers, in passages of the Talmud, and in later Jewish authors." We may well accept this method of explaining the phenomenon.

We accordingly reach the conclusion that nothing adduced by recent discussions need shake our belief that Moses was the author of the Pentateuch. We may accept the traces of earlier narratives, as having been employed and authenticated by him; and we may admit the marks of later date as indications of a surface revision by authorized persons not later than Ezra and Nehemiah.

Among the later publications are Murphy on *Genesis* (1864) and *Exodus* (1866); Kalisch on *Genesis, Exodus*, and *Leviticus* (1858–1867); Lange on *Genesis*; Jacobus on *Genesis*; Macdonald's *Introduction to the Pentateuch* (1861); Davidson's *Introduction to the Old Testament* (1862–63); and *The Book of Genesis; the Common Version revised for the Amer. Bible Union, with Explanatory Notes*, by T. J. Conant (N. Y. 1868). See also a discussion of the historic character and authorship of the Pentateuch, in the *Bibl. Sacra* for April and July, 1863, and July and October, 1864, by the present writer.   S. C. B.

חַג הַקָּצִיר בִּכּוּרֵי מַעֲשֶׂיךָ **PENTECOST**
(Ex. xxiii. 16) : ἑορτὴ θερισμοῦ πρωτογεννημάτων : *solemnitas messis primitivorum;* "the feast of harvest, the first fruits of thy labors;"

חַג שָׁבֻעֹת (Ex. xxxiv. 22; Deut. xvi. 10): ἑορτὴ ἑβδομάδων : *solemnitas hebdomadarum* "the feast of weeks:" יוֹם הַבִּכּוּרִים (Num. xxviii. 26, cf. Lev. xxiii. 17): ἡμέρα τῶν νέων: *dies primitivorum;* "the day of first fruits"). In later times it appears to have been called יוֹם חֲמִשִּׁים (see Joseph. *B. J.* ii. 3, § 1); and hence, ἡμέρα τῆς Πεντηκοστῆς (Tob. ii. 1; 2 Macc. xii. 32; Acts ii. 1, xx. 16; 1 Cor. xvi. 8). But the more common Jewish name was עֲצֶרֶת[a] (in Chaldee; עֲצַרְתָּא ; 'Ασαρθά, in Joseph. *Ant.* iii. 10, § 6). The second of the great festivals of the Hebrews. It fell in due course on the sixth day of Sivan, and its rites, according to the Law, were restricted to a single day. The most important passages relating to it are, Ex. xxiii. 16, Lev. xxiii. 15–22, Num. xxviii. 26–31, Deut. xvi 9–12.

I. The time of the festival was calculated from the second day of the Passover, the 16th of Nisan. The Law prescribes that a reckoning should be kept from "the morrow after the Sabbath"[b] (Lev.

---

[a] This word in the O. T. is applied to the seventh day of the Passover and the eighth day of Tabernacles, but not to the day of Pentecost. [PASSOVER, note a, p. 2343.] On its application to Pentecost, which is found

in the Mishna (*Rosh hash.* i. 2, and *Chagigah*, ii. 4, &c.), in the Targum (Num. xxviii. 26), in Josephus, and elsewhere, see § 5.

[b] There has been from early times some difference

xxiii. 11, 15) [PASSOVER, II. 3] to the morrow after the completion of the seventh week, which would of course be the fiftieth day (Lev. xxiii. 15, 16; Deut. xvi. 9). The fifty days formally included the period of grain-harvest, commencing with the offering of the first sheaf of the barley-harvest in the Passover, and ending with that of the two first loaves which were made from the wheat-harvest, at this festival.

It was the offering of these two loaves which was the distinguishing rite of the day of Pentecost. They were to be leavened. Each loaf was to contain the tenth of an ephah *a* (*i. e.* about 3½ quarts) of the finest wheat flour of the new crop (Lev. xxiii. 17). The flour was to be the produce of the land.*b* The loaves, along with a peace-offering of two lambs of the first year, were to be waved before the Lord and given to the priests. At the same time a special sacrifice was to be made of seven lambs of the first year, one young bullock and two rams, as a burnt-offering (accompanied by the proper meat and drink offerings), and a kid for a sin-offering (Lev. xxiii. 18, 19). Besides these offerings, if we adopt the interpretation of the Rabbinical writers, it appears that an addition was made to the daily sacrifice of two bullocks, one ram, and seven lambs, as a burnt-offering (Num. xxviii. 27).*c* At this, as well as the other festivals, a free-will offering was

to be made by each person who came to the sanctuary, according to his circumstances (Deut. xvi. 10). [PASSOVER, p. 2342, note *d.*] It would seem that its festive character partook of a more free and hospitable liberality than that of the Passover, which was rather of the kind which belongs to the mere family gathering. In this respect it resembled the Feast of Tabernacles. The Levite, the stranger, the fatherless, and the widow, were to be brought within its influence (Deut. xvi. 11, 14). The mention of the gleanings to be left in the fields at harvest for "the poor and the stranger," in connection with Pentecost, may perhaps have a bearing on the liberality which belonged to the festival (Lev. xxiii. 22). At Pentecost (as at the Passover) the people were to be reminded of their bondage in Egypt, and they were especially admonished of their obligation to keep the Divine law (Deut. xvi. 12).

II. Of the information to be gathered from Jewish writers respecting the observance of Pentecost, the following particulars appear to be the best worthy of notice. The flour for the loaves was sifted with peculiar care twelve times over. They were made either the day before, or, in the event of a Sabbath preceding the day of Pentecost, two days before the occasion (*Menachoth*, vi. 7, xi. 9). They are said to have been made in a particular form. They were seven palms in length and four in breadth

---

of opinion as to the meaning of the words מָחֳרַת הַשַּׁבָּת. It has however been generally held, by both Jewish and Christian writers of all ages, that the Sabbath here spoken of is the first day of holy convocation of the Passover, the 15th of Nisan, mentioned Lev. xxiii. 7. In like manner the word שַׁבָּת is evidently used as a designation of the day of atonement (Lev. xxiii. 32); and שַׁבָּתוֹן (*sabbati observatio*) is applied to the first and eighth days of Tabernacles and to the Feast of Trumpets. That the LXX. so understood the passage in question can hardly be doubted from their calling it "the morrow after the first day" (*i. e.* of the festival): ἡ ἐπαύριον τῆς πρώτης. The word in vv. 15 and 16 has also been understood as "week," used in the same manner as σάββατα in the N. T. (Matt. xxviii. 1; Luke xviii. 12; John xx. 1. &c.). But some have insisted on taking the Sabbath to mean nothing but the seventh day of the week, or "the sabbath of creation," as the Jewish writers have called it; and they see a difficulty in understanding the same word in the general sense of *week* as a period of seven days, contending that it can only mean a regular week, beginning with the first day, and ending with the Sabbath. Hence the Baithusian (or Sadducean) party, and in later times the Karaites, supposed that the omer was offered on the day following the weekly Sabbath which might happen to fall within the seven days of the Passover. The day of Pentecost would thus always fall on the first day of the week. Hitzig (*Ostern und Pfingsten*, Heidelberg, 1837) has put forth the notion that the Hebrews regularly began a new week at the commencement of the year, so that the 7th, 14th, and 21st of Nisan were always Sabbath days. He imagines that "the morrow after the Sabbath" from which Pentecost was reckoned, was the 22d day of the month, the day after the proper termination of the Passover. He is well answered by Bähr (*Symbolik,* ii. 620), who refers especially to Josh. v. 11, as proving, in connection with the law in Lev. xxiii. 14, that the omer was offered on the 16th of the month. It should be observed that the words in that passage, עֲבוּר הָאָרֶץ, mean merely *corn of the land*, not a in A. V "the old corn of the land." "The morrow

after the Passover" (מָחֳרַת הַפֶּסַח), might at first sight seem to express the 15th of Nisan; but the expression may, on the whole, with more probability, be taken as equivalent with "the morrow after the Sabbath," that is, the 16th day. See Keil on Josh. 11; Masius and Drusius, on the same text, in the *Crit. Sac.*; Bähr, *Symb.* ii. 621; Selden, *De Anno Civili,* ch. 7; Bartenora, in *Chagigah,* ii. 4; Buxt. *Syn. Jud.* xx.; Fagius, *in Lev.* xxiii. 15; Drusius, *Notæ Majores in Lev.* xxiii. 16. It is worthy of remark that the LXX. omit τῇ ἐπαύριον τοῦ πάσχα, according to the texts of Tischendorf and Theile.

a The עִשָּׂרוֹן, or *tenth* (in A. V. "tenth deal"), is explained in Num. v. 15, עֲשִׂירִית הָאֵיפָה, "the tenth part of an ephah." It is sometimes called עֹמֶר, *omer,* literally, *a handful* (Ex. xvi. 36), the same word which is applied to the first sheaf of the Passover. (See Joseph. *Ant.* viii. 2, § 9.) [WEIGHTS AND MEASURES]

b This is what is meant by the words in Lev. xxiii. 17, which stand in the A. V. "out of your habitations," and in the Vulgate, "ex omnibus habitaculis vestris." The Hebrew word is not בַּיִת, *a house,* as *the home of a family,* but מוֹשָׁב, *a place of abode,* as *the territory of a nation.* The LXX. has, ἀπὸ τῆς κατοικίας ὑμῶν; Jonathan, "e loco habitationum vestrum." See Drusius, in *Crit. Sac.*

c The differing statements respecting the proper sacrifices for the day in Lev. xxiii. 18, and Num. xxviii. 27. are thus reconciled by the Jewish writers (Mishna, *Menachoth,* iv. 2, with the notes of Bartenora and Maimonides). Josephus appears to add the two statements together, not quite accurately, and does not treat them as relating to two distinct sacrifices (*Ant.* iii. 10, § 6). He enumerates, as the whole of the offerings for the day, a single loaf, two lambs for a peace-offering, three bullocks, two rams and fourteen lambs for a burnt-offering, and two kids for a sin-offering. Bähr, Winer, and other modern critics, regard the statements as discordant, and prefer that of Num. xxviii. as being most in harmony with the sacrifices which belong to the other festivals.

(*Menachoth*, xi. 4, with Maimonides' note). The two hanks for a peace-offering were to be waved by the priest, before they were slaughtered, along with the loaves, and afterwards the loaves were waved a second time along with the shoulders of the lambs. One loaf was given to the high-priest and the other to the ordinary priests who officiated [a] (Maimon. *in Tamid*, c. 8, quoted by Otho). The bread was eaten that same night in the Temple, and no fragment of it was suffered to remain till the morning (Joseph. *B. J.* vi. 5, § 3; *Ant.* iii. 10, § 6).

Although, according to the Law, the observance of Pentecost lasted but a single day, the Jews in foreign countries, since the Captivity, have prolonged it to two days. They have treated the Feast of Trumpets in the same way. The alteration appears to have been made to meet the possibility of an error in calculating the true day.[b] It is said by Bartenora and Maimonides that, while the Temple was standing, though the religious rites were confined to the day, the festivities, and the bringing in of gifts, continued through seven days (Notes to *Chagigah*, ii. 4). The Hallel is said to have been sung at Pentecost as well as at the Passover (Lightfoot, *Temple Service*, § 3). The concourse of Jews who attended Pentecost in later times appears to have been very great (Acts ii.; Joseph. *Ant.* xiv. 13, § 14, xvii. 10, § 2; *B. J.* ii. 3, § 1).

No occasional offering of first-fruits could be made in the Temple before Pentecost (*Biccurim*, i. 3, 6). Hence probably the two loaves were designated " the first of the first-fruits " (Ex. xxiii. 19) [PASSOVER, p. 2343, note *d*], although the offering of the omer had preceded them. The proper time for offering first-fruits was the interval between Pentecost and Tabernacles (*Bicc.* i. 6, 10; comp. Ex. xxiii. 16). [FIRST-FRUITS.]

The connection between the omer and the two loaves of Pentecost appears never to have been lost sight of. The former was called by Philo, προεόρτιος ἑτέρας ἑορτῆς μείζονος [c] (*De Sept.* § 21, v. 25; comp. *De Decem Orac.* iv. 302, ed. Taueh.). The interval between the Passover and Pentecost was evidently regarded as a religious season.[d] The custom has probably been handed down from ancient times, which is observed by the modern Jews, of keeping a regular computation of the fifty days by a formal observance, beginning with a short prayer on the evening of the day of the omer, and continued on each succeeding day by a solemn declaration of its number in the succession, at evening

prayer, while the members of the family are standing with respectful attention [e] (Buxt. *Syn. Jud.* xx. 440).

III. Doubts have been cast on the common interpretation of Acts ii. 1, according to which the Holy Ghost was given to the Apostles on the day of Pentecost. Lightfoot contends that the passage, ἐν τῷ συμπληροῦσθαι τὴν ἡμέραν τῆς Πεντηκοστῆς, means *when the day of Pentecost had passed*, and considers that this rendering is countenanced by the words of the Vulgate, " cum complerentur dies Pentecostes." He supposes that Pentecost fell that year on the Sabbath, and that it was on the ensuing Lord's Day that ἦσαν ἅπαντες ὁμοθυμαδὸν ἐπὶ τὸ αὐτό (*Exercit. in Act.* ii. 1). Hitzig, on the other hand (*Ostern und Pfingsten*, Heidelberg, 1837), would render the words, " As the day of Pentecost was approaching its fulfillment." Neander has replied to the latter, and has maintained the common interpretation (*Planting of the Christian Church*, i. 5, Bohn's ed.).

The question on what day of the week this Pentecost fell must of course be determined by the mode in which the doubt is solved regarding the day on which the Last Supper was eaten. [PASSOVER, III.] If it was the legal paschal supper, on the 14th of Nisan, and the Sabbath during which our Lord lay in the grave was the day of the omer, Pentecost must have followed on the Sabbath. But if the Supper was eaten on the 13th, and He was crucified on the 14th, the Sunday of the Resurrection must have been the day of the omer, and Pentecost must have occurred on the first day of the week.

IV. There is no clear notice in the Scriptures of any historical significance belonging to Pentecost. But most of the Jews of later times have regarded the day as the commemoration of the giving of the Law on Mount Sinai. It is made out from Ex. xix. that the Law was delivered on the fiftieth day after the deliverance from Egypt (Selden, *De Jur. Nat. et Gent.* iii. 11). It has been conjectured that a connection between the event and the festival may possibly be hinted at in the reference to the observance of the Law in Deut. xvi. 12. But neither Philo[f] nor Josephus has a word on the subject. There is, however, a tradition of a custom which Schöttgen supposes to be at least as ancient as the Apostolic times, that the night before Pentecost was a time especially appropriated for thanking God for the gift of the Law.[g] Several of the Fathers noticed

<hr>

[a] In like manner, the leavened bread which was offered with the ordinary peace-offering was waved and given to the priest who sprinkled the blood (Lev. vii. 13, 14).

[b] Lightfoot, *Exercit. Heb.* Acts ii. 1; Reland, *Ant.* iv. 4, 5; Seiden, *De Ann. Civ.* c. vii.

[c] He elsewhere mentions the festival of Pentecost with the same marked respect. He speaks of a peculiar feast kept by the Therapeutæ as προεόρτιος μείζονος ἑορτῆς κ. Πεντηκοστῆς (*De Vit. Contemp.* v. 334).

[d] According to the most generally received interpretation of the word δευτερόπρωτος (Luke vi. 1), the period was marked by a regularly designated succession of Sabbaths, similar to the several successions of Sundays in our own calendar. It is assumed that the day of the omer was called δεύτερα (in the LXX., Lev. xxiii. 11, ἡ ἐπαύριον τῆς πρώτης). The Sabbath which came next after it was termed δευτερόπρωτον; the second, δευτεροδεύτερον; the third, δευτερότριτον; and so onwards, till Pentecost. This explanation was first proposed by Scaliger (*De Emend. Temp.* lib. vi. p. 557), and has been adopted by Frischmuth, Petavius,

Casaubon, Lightfoot, Godwyn, Carpzov, and many others.

[e] The less educated of the modern Jews regard the fifty days with strange superstition, and. it would seem, are always impatient for them to come to an end. During their continuance, they have a dread of sudden death, of the effect of malaria, and of the influence of evil spirits over children. They relate with gross exaggeration the case of a great mortality which, during the first twenty-three days of the period, befell the pupils of Akiba, the great Mishnical doctor of the second century. at Jaffa. They do not ride, or drive, or go on the water, unless they are impelled by absolute necessity. They are careful not to whistle in the evening, lest it should bring ill luck. They scrupulously put off marriages till Pentecost. (Stanben, *La Vie Juive en Alsace* (Paris, 1860), p. 124; Mills, *British Jews*, p. 207.)

[f] Philo expressly states that it was at the Feast of Trumpets that the giving of the Law was commemorated (*De Sept.* c. 22). [TRUMPETS. FEAST OF.]

[g] Hor. Heb. in Act. ii. 1. Schöttgen conjectures

the coincidence of the day of the giving of the Law with that of the festival, and made use of it. Thus Jerome says, "Supputemus numerum, et invenimus quinquagesimo die egressionis Israël ex Ægypto in vertice montis Sinai legem datam. Unde et Pentecostes celebratur solemnitas, et postea Evangelii sacramentum Spiritus Sancti descensione completur" (*Epist. ad Fabiolam, Mansio XII.*). St. Augustin speaks in a similar manner: "Pentecosten etiam, id est, a passione et resurrectione Domini, quinquagesimum diem celebramus, quo nobis Sanctum Spiritum Paracletum quem promiserat misit: quod futurum etiam per Judæorum pascha significatum est, cum quinquagesimo die post celebrationem ovis occisæ, Moyses digito Dei scriptam legem accepit in monte" (*Contra Faustum*, lib. xxxii. c. 12). The later Rabbis spoke with confidence of the commemoration of the Law as a prime object in the institution of the feast. Maimonides says, "Festum septimanarum est dies ille, quo lex data fuit. Ad hujus diei honorem pertinet quod dies a præcedenti solenni festo (Pascha) ad illum usque diem numerantur" (*More Nevochim*, iii. 41). Abarbanel recognizes the fact, but denies that it had anything to do with the institution of the feast, observing, "lex divina non opus habet sanctificatione diei, quo ejus memoria recolatur." He adds, "causa festi septimanarum est initium messis tritici" (*in Leg.* 262). But in general the Jewish writers of modern times have expressed themselves on the subject without hesitation, and, in the rites of the day, as it is now observed, the gift of the Law is kept prominently in view.[a]

V. If the feast of Pentecost stood without an organic connection with any other rites, we should have no certain warrant in the Old Testament for regarding it as more than the divinely appointed solemn thanksgiving for the yearly supply of the most useful sort of food. Every reference to its meaning seems to bear immediately upon the completion of the grain-harvest. It might have been a Gentile festival, having no proper reference to the election of the chosen race. It might have taken a place in the religion of any people who merely felt that it is God who gives rain from heaven and fruitful seasons, and who fills our hearts with food and gladness (Acts xiv. 17). But it was, as we have seen, essentially linked on to the Passover, that festival, which, above all others, expressed the fact of a race chosen and separated from other nations.

It was not an insulated day. It stood as the culminating point of the Pentecostal season. If the offering of the omer was a supplication for the Divine blessing on the harvest which was just commencing, and the offering of the two loaves was a thanksgiving for its completion, each rite was brought into a higher significance in consequence of the omer forming an integral part of the Passover. It was thus set forth that He who had delivered his people from Egypt, who had raised

them from the condition of slaves to that of free men in immediate covenant with Himself, was the same that was sustaining them with bread from year to year. The inspired teacher declared to God's chosen one, "He maketh peace in thy borders, He filleth thee with the finest of the wheat" (Ps. cxlvii. 14). If we thus regard the day of Pentecost as the solemn termination of the consecrated period, intended, as the seasons came round, to teach this lesson to the people, we may see the fitness of the name by which the Jews have mostly called it, עֲצֶרֶת, *the concluding assembly.*[b] [PASSOVER, p. 2343, note a.]

As the two loaves were leavened, they could not be offered on the altar, like the unleavened sacrificial bread. [PASSOVER, IV. 3 (b).] Abarbanel (in *Lev.* xxiii.) has proposed a reason for their not being leavened which seems hardly to admit of a doubt. He thinks that they were intended to represent the best produce of the earth in the actual condition in which it ministers to the support of human life. Thus they express, in the most significant manner, what is evidently the idea of the festival.

We need not suppose that the grain-harvest in the Holy Land was in all years precisely completed between the Passover and Pentecost. The period of seven weeks was evidently appointed in conformity with the Sabbatical number, which so frequently recurs in the arrangements of the Mosaic Law. [FEASTS; JUBILEE.] Hence, probably. the prevailing use of the name, "The Feast of Weeks," which might always have suggested the close religious connection in which the festival stood to the Passover.

It is not surprising that, without any direct authority in the O. T., the coincidence of the day on which the festival was observed with that on which the Law appears to have been given to Moses, should have strongly impressed the minds of Christians in the early ages of the Church. The Divine Providence had ordained that the Holy Spirit should come down in a special manner, to give spiritual life and unity to the Church, on that very same day in the year on which the Law had been bestowed on the children of Israel which gave to them national life and unity. They must have seen that, as the possession of the Law had completed the deliverance of the Hebrew race wrought by the hand of Moses, so the gift of the Spirit perfected the work of Christ in the establishment of his kingdom upon earth.

It may have been on this account that Pentecost was the last Jewish festival (as far as we know) which St. Paul was anxious to observe (Acts xx. 16, 1 Cor. xvi. 8), and that Whitsuntide came to be the first annual festival instituted in the Christian Church (Hessey's *Bampton Lectures*, pp. 88, 96). It was rightly regarded as the Church's birthday, and the Pentecostal season, the period between it and Easter, bearing as it does such a clear analogy

---

that the Apostles on the occasion there spoken of were assembled together for this purpose, in accordance with Jewish custom.

• *a* Some of the Jews adorn their houses with flowers, and wear wreaths on their heads, with the declared purpose of testifying their joy in the possession of the Law. They also eat such food as is prepared with milk, because the purity of the divine law is likened to milk. (Compare the expression, "the sincere milk of the word," 1 Pet. ii. 2.)

It is a fact of some interest, though in nowise connected with the present argument, that, in the service

of the synagogue, the book of Ruth is read through at Pentecost, from the connection of its subject with harvest (Buxt. *Syn. Jud.* xx. ; [Stauben,] *La Vie Juive en Alsace*, pp. 129, 142.)

b So Godwyn, Lightfoot, Reland, Bähr. The full name appears to have been עֲצֶרֶת שֶׁל פֶּסַח, *the concluding assembly of the Passover.* The designation of the offering of the omer used by Philo, προσφορὰς ἑτέρας ἑορτῆς μείζονος, strikingly tends for the same purpose.

to the fifty days of the old Law, thus became the ordinary time for the baptism of converts (Tertullian, *De Bapt.* c. 19; Jerome, *in Zech.* xiv. 8).

(Carpzov, *App. Crit.* iii. 5; Reland, *Ant.* iv. 4; Lightfoot, *Temple Service,* § 3; *Exercit. in Act.* ii. 1; Bähr, *Symbolik,* iv. 3; Spencer, *De Leg. Heb.* L ix. 2, iii. viii. 2; Meyer, *De Fest. Heb.* ii. 13; Hupfeld, *De Fest. Heb.* ii.; Iken, *De Duobus Panibus Pentecost.* Brem. 1729; Mishna, *Menachoth* and *Biccurim,* with the Notes in Surenhusius; Drusius, *Notæ Majores in Lev.* xxiii. 15, 21 (*Crit. Sac.*); Otho, *Lex. Rab. s. Festa;* Buxtorf, *Syn. Jud.* c. xx.)   S. C.

PENU'EL (פְּנוּאֵל [*face of God*] : in Gen. εἶδος θεοῦ, elsewhere Φανουήλ : *Phanuel*). The usual, and possibly the original, form of the name of a place which first appears under the slightly different form of PENIEL (Gen. xxxii. 30, 31). From this narrative it is evident that it lay somewhere between the torrent Jabbok and Succoth (comp. xxxii. 22 with xxxiii. 17). This is in exact agreement with the terms of its next occurrence, when Gideon, pursuing the hosts of the Midianites across the Jordan into the uplands of Gilead, arrives first at Succoth, and from thence mounts to Penuel (Judg. viii. 5, 8). It had then a tower, which Gideon destroyed on his return, at the same time slaying the men of the place because they had refused him help before (ver. 17). Penuel was rebuilt or fortified by Jeroboam at the commencement of his reign (1 K. xii. 25), no doubt on account of its commanding the fords of Succoth and the road from the east of Jordan to his capital city of Shechem, and also perhaps as being an ancient sanctuary. Succoth has been identified with tolerable certainty at *Sakût,* but no trace has yet been found of Penuel.   G.

* PENU'EL (פְּנוּאֵל, see above: Φανουήλ : *Phanuel*).

1. A descendant of Judah the "father" or founder of Gedor (1 Chr. iv. 4).

2. A son of Shashak, and one of the chiefs of the tribe of Benjamin. He dwelt at Jerusalem (1 Chr. viii. 25, 28).   A.

PE'OR (פְּעוֹר, "the Peor," with the def. article [*opening, cleft*] : τοῦ [a] Φογόρ : *mons Phohor* [*Phogor*]). A mountain in Moab, from whence, after having without effect ascended the lower or less sacred summits of Bamoth-Baal and Pisgah, the prophet Balaam was conducted by Balak for his final conjurations (Num. xxiii. 28 only).

Peor — or more accurately "the Peor" — was "facing Jeshimon." The same thing is said of Pisgah. But unfortunately we are as yet ignorant of the position of all three, so that nothing can be inferred from this specification. [NEBO.]

In the *Onomasticon* ("Fogor;" "Bethphogor;" "Danaba") it is stated to be above the town of Libias (the ancient Beth-aram), and opposite Jericho. The towns of Beth peor and Dinhaba were on the mountain, six miles from Libias, and seven from Heshbon, respectively. A place named *Fâkhûrah* is mentioned in the list of towns south of *Es-Salt* in the appendix to the 1st edit. of Dr. Robinson's *Bibl. Res.* (iii. App. 169), and this is placed by Van de Velde at the head of the *Wady Eshteh,* 8 miles N. E. of *Hesbân.* But in our present igno-

rance of these regions all this must be mere conjecture.

Gesenius (*Thes.* 1119 a) gives it as his opinion that Baal-Peor derived his name from the mountain, not the mountain from him.

A Peor, under its Greek garb of Phagor, appears among the eleven names added by the LXX. [Josh xv. 59] to the list of the allotment of Judah, between Bethlehem and Aitan (Etham). It was known to Eusebius and Jerome, and is mentioned by the latter in his translation of the *Onomasticon* as Phaora. It probably still exists under the name of *Beit Fâghûr* or *Kirbet Fâghûr,* 5 miles S. W. of Bethlehem, barely a mile to the left of the road from Hebron (Tobler, *3te Wanderung*). It is somewhat singular that both Peor and Pisgah, names so prominently connected with the East of Jordan, should be found also on the West.

The LXX. also read the name, which in the Hebrew text is PAU and PAI, as Peor; since in both cases they have *Phogór.*

2. (פְּעוֹר), without the article: Φογόρ : *idolum Phehor* [*Phogor*], *Phohor* [*Phogor*], *Beel Phegor.*) In four passages (Num. xxv. 18, twice; xxxi. 16; Josh. xxii. 17) Peor occurs as a contraction for Baal-peor; always in reference to the licentious rites of Shittim which brought such destruction on Israel. In the three first cases the expression is, the "matter," or "for the sake" (literally "word" in each) "of Peor;" in the fourth, "iniquity, or crime, of Peor."   G.

PER'AZIM, MOUNT (הַר־פְּרָצִים [*mount of breaches*] : ὄρος ἀσεβῶν [a] : *mons divisiorum*). A name which occurs in Is. xxviii. 21 only, — unless the place which it designates be identical with the BAAL-PERAZIM mentioned as the scene of one of David's victories over the Philistines. Isaiah, as his manner was (comp. x. 26), is referring to some ancient triumphs of the arms of Israel as symbolical of an event shortly to happen —

> Jehovah shall rise up as at Mount Perazim,
> He shall be wroth as in the valley of Gibeon.

The commentators almost unanimously take his reference to be to David's victories, above alluded to, at Baal Perazim, and Gibeon (Gesenius; Strachey), or to the former of these on the one hand, and Joshua's slaughter of the Canaanites at Gibeon and Beth-horon on the other (Eichhorn; Rosenmüller; Michaelis). Ewald alone — perhaps with greater critical sagacity than the rest — doubts that David's victory is intended, "because the prophets of this period are not in the habit of choosing such examples from his history " (*Propheten,* i. 261).

If David's victory is alluded to in this passage of the prophet, it furnishes an example, similar to that noticed under OREB, of the slight and casual manner in which events of the gravest importance are sometimes passed over in the Bible narrative. But for this later reference no one would infer that the events reported in 2 Sam. v. 18-25, and 1 Chr. xiv. 8-17, had been important enough to serve as a parallel to one of Jehovah's most tremendous judgments. In the account of Josephus (*Ant.* vii. 4, § 1), David's victory assumes much larger proportions than in Samuel and Chronicles. The attack is made not by the Philistines only, but by "all

---

[a] The LXX. have here represented the Hebrew letter *Ain* by *g,* as they have also in Raguel, Gomorrah, Athaliah, etc.

[b] Perhaps considering the word as derived from פָּרַע, which the LXX. usually render by ἀσεβής.

Syria and Phœnicia, with many other warlike nations besides." This is a good instance of the manner in which Josephus, apparently from records now lost to us, supplements and completes the scanty narratives of the Bible, in agreement with the casual references of the Prophets or Psalmists. He places the scene of the encounter in the "groves of weeping," as if alluding to the Baca of Ps. lxxxiv.

The title *Mount* Perazim, when taken in connection with the *Baal* Perazim of 2 Sam. v., seems to imply that it was an eminence with a heathen sanctuary of Baal upon it. [BAAL, vol. i. p. 209 a.]   G.

PE'RESH (פֶּרֶשׁ [*excrement, dung*]: Φαρές; [Vat. omits:] *Phares*). The son of Machir by his wife Maachah (1 Chr. vii. 16).

PE'REZ (פֶּרֶץ [*a breach, rent*]: Φαρές; [Vat. Neh. xi. 6, Ζεφες:] *Phares*). The "children of Perez," or Pharez, the son of Judah, appear to have been a family of importance for many centuries. In the reign of David one of them was chief of all the captains of the host for the first month (1 Chr. xxvii. 3); and of those who returned from Babylon, to the number of 468, some occupied a prominent position in the tribe of Judah, and are mentioned by name as living in Jerusalem (Neh. xi. 4, 6). [PHAREZ.]

PE'REZ-UZ'ZA (פֶּרֶץ עֻזָּא: Διακοπὴ Ο(ά: *divisio Ozæ*), 1 Chr. xiii. 11; and

PE'REZ-UZ'ZAH (פֶּ עֻזָּה [*breach of Uzzah*]: [Διακοπὴ Ο(ᾶ:] *percussio Ozæ*), 2 Sam. vi. 8. The title which David conferred on the threshing-floor of Nachon, or Cidon, in com-

memoration of the sudden death of Uzzah: "*Ant.* David was wroth because Jehovah had broken this breach on Uzzah, and he *a* called the place ' Uzzah's breaking' unto this day." The word *perez* was a favorite with David on such occasions. He employs it to commemorate his having "broken up' the Philistine force in the valley of Rephaim (2 Sam. v. 20). [BAAL PERAZIM.] He also uses it in a subsequent reference to Uzzah's destruction in 1 Chr. xv. 13.

It is remarkable that the statement of the continued existence of the name should be found not only in Samuel and Chronicles, but also in Josephus, who says (*Ant.* vii. 4, § 2), as if from his own observation, "the place where he died is even now (ἔτι νῦν) called 'the cleaving of Oza.'"

The situation of the spot is not known. [NACHON.] If this statement of Josephus may be taken literally, it would however be worth while to make some search for traces of the name between Jerusalem and Kirjath-jearim.   G.

PERFUMES (קְטֹרָה). The free use of perfumes was peculiarly grateful to the Orientals (Prov xxvii. 9), whose olfactory nerves are more than usually sensitive to the offensive smells engendered by the heat of their climate (Burckhardt's *Travels* ii. 85). The Hebrews manufactured their perfumes chiefly from spices imported from Arabia, though to a certain extent also from aromatic plants growing in their own country. [SPICES.] The modes in which they applied them were various occasionally a bunch of the plant itself was worn about the person as a nosegay, or inclosed in a bag (Cant. i. 13); or the plant was reduced to a powder and used in the way of fumigation (Cant. iii. 6);

Perga.

or, again, the aromatic qualities were extracted by some process of boiling, and were then mixed with oil, so as to be applied to the person in the way of ointment (John xii. 3); or, lastly, the scent was carried about in smelling-bottles *b* suspended from the girdle (Is. iii. 20). Perfumes entered largely into the Temple service, in the two forms of incense and ointment (Ex. xxx. 22–38). Nor were they less used in private life: not only were they applied to the person, but to garments (Ps. xlv. 8; Cant.

iv. 11), and to articles of furniture, such as beds (Prov. vii. 17). On the arrival of a guest the same compliments were probably paid in ancient as in modern times; the rooms were fumigated; the person of the guest was sprinkled with rose-water; and then the incense was applied to his face and beard (Dan. ii. 46; Lane's *Mod. Egypt.* ii. 14). When a royal personage went abroad in his litter, attendants threw up "pillars of smoke" *c* about his path (Cant. iii. 6). Nor is it improbable that

---

a Or, with equal accuracy, and perhaps more convenience, "one called it,' that is, "it was called"— as in 2 K. xviii. 4. [NEHUSHTAN.]

b בָּתֵּי הַנֶּפֶשׁ; lit. "houses of the soul."

c A similar usage is recorded of the Indian princes: "Quum rex semet in publico conspici patitur, turibula argentea ministri ferunt, totumque iter per quod ferri destinavit odoribus complent" (Curtius, viii. 9, § 23).

other practices, such as scenting the breath by chewing frankincense (Lane, i. 246), and the skin by washing in rose-water (Burckhardt's *Arab.* i. 58), and fumigating drinkables (Lane, i. 185; Burckhardt, i. 52), were also adopted in early times. The use of perfumes was omitted in times of mourning, whence the allusion in Is. iii. 24, " instead of sweet smell there shall be stink." The preparation of perfumes in the form either of ointment or incense was a recognized profession *a* among the Jews (Ex. xxx. 25, 35; Eccl. x. 1). [Incense; Ointment.] W. L. B.

PER'GA (Πέργη: [*Perge*]), an ancient and important city of Pamphylia, situated on the river Cestius, at a distance of 60 stadia from its mouth, and celebrated in antiquity for the worship of Artemis (Diana), whose temple stood on a hill outside the town (Strab. xiv. p. 667; Cic. *Verr.* i. 20; Plin. v. 26; Mela, i. 14; Ptol. v. 5, § 7). The goddess and the Temple are represented in the coins of Perga. The Cestius was navigable to Perga; and St. Paul landed here on his voyage from Paphos (Acts xiii. 13). He visited the city a second time on his return from the interior of Pamphylia, and preached the Gospel there (Acts xiv. 25). For further details see PAMPHYLIA. There are still extensive remains of Perga at a spot called by the Turks *Eski-Kálesi* (Leake, *Asia Minor*, p. 132; Fellows, *Asia Minor*, p. 190).

PER'GAMOS [b] (ἡ Πέργαμος, or τὸ Πέργαμον). A city of Mysia, about three miles to the N. of the river *Bakyr-tchai*, the Caicus of antiquity, and twenty miles from its present mouth The name was originally given to a remarkable hill, presenting a conical appearance when viewed from the plain. The local legends attached a sacred character to this place. Upon it the Cabiri were said to have been witnesses of the birth of Zeus, and the whole of the land belonging to the city of the same name which afterwards grew up around the original Pergamos, to have belonged to these. The sacred character of the locality, combined with its natural strength, seems to have made it, like some others of the ancient temples, a bank for chiefs who desired to accumulate a large amount of specie; and Lysimachus, one of Alexander's successors, deposited there an enormous sum — no less than 9,000 talents — in the care of an Asiatic eunuch named Philetærus. In the troublous times which followed the break up of the Macedonian conquests, this officer betrayed his trust, and by successful temporizing, and perhaps judicious employment of the funds at his command, succeeded in retaining the treasure and transmitting it at the end of twenty years to his nephew Eumenes, a petty dynast in the neighborhood. Eumenes was succeeded by his cousin Attalus, the founder of the Attalic dynasty of Pergamene kings, who by allying himself with the rising Roman power laid the foundation of the future greatness of his house. His successor, Eumenes II., was rewarded for his fidelity to the Romans in their wars with Antiochus and Perseus by a gift of all the territory which the former had possessed to the north of the Taurus range. The great wealth which accrued to him from this source he employed in laying out a magnificent residential

city, and adorning it with temples and other public buildings. His passion, and that of his successor, for literature and the fine arts, led them to form a library which rivaled that of Alexandria; and the impulse given to the art of preparing sheepskins for the purpose of transcription, to gratify the taste of the royal *dilettanti*, has left its record in the name *parchment* (charta pergamena). Eumenes's successor, Attalus II., is said to have bid 600,000 sesterces for a picture by the painter Aristides, at the sale of the plunder of Corinth; and by so doing to have attracted the attention of the Roman general Mummius to it, who sent it off at once to Rome, where no foreign artist's work had then been seen. For another picture by the same artist he paid 100 talents. But the great glory of the city was the so-called Nicephorium, a grove of extreme beauty, laid out as a thank-offering for a victory over Antiochus, in which was an assemblage of temples, probably of all the deities, Zeus, Athenè, Apollo, Æsculapius, Dionysus, and Aphroditè. The Temple of the last was of a most elaborate character. Its façade was perhaps inlaid after the manner of *pietra dura* work; for Philip V. of Macedonia, who was repulsed in an attempt to surprise Pergamos during the reign of Attalus II., vented his spite in cutting down the trees of the grove, and not only destroying the Aphrodisium, but injuring the stones in such a way as to prevent their being used again. At the conclusion of peace it was made a special stipulation that this damage should be made good.

The Attalic dynasty terminated B. C. 133, when Attalus III., dying at an early age, made the Romans his heirs. His dominions formed the province of *Asia propria*, and the immense wealth which was directly or indirectly derived from this legacy, contributed perhaps even more than the spoils of Carthage and Corinth to the demoralization of Roman statesmen.

The sumptuousness of the Attalic princes had raised Pergamos to the rank of the first city in Asia as regards splendor, and Pliny speaks of it as without a rival in the province. Its prominence, however, was not that of a commercial town, like Ephesus or Corinth, but arose from its peculiar features. It was a sort of union of a pagan cathedral city, an university town, and a royal residence, embellished during a succession of years by kings who all had a passion for expenditure and ample means of gratifying it. Two smaller streams, which flowed from the north, embracing the town between them, and then fell into the Caicus, afforded ample means of storing water, without which, in those latitudes, ornamental cultivation (or indeed cultivation of any kind) is out of the question. The larger of those streams — the *Bergama-tchai*, or Cetius of antiquity — has a fall of more than 150 feet between the hills to the north of Pergamos and its junction with the Caicus, and it brings down a very considerable body of water. Both the Nicephorium, which has been spoken of above, and the Grove of Æsculapius, which became yet more celebrated in the time of the Roman empire, doubtless owed their existence to the means of irrigation thus available; and furnished the appliances for those licentious rituals

---

a לִקַח; A. V. "apothecary."

b [*] The name should have been written Pergamus
[r*] Pergamum in the A. V. The translators usually

adopted the Latin termination of the names of such places. A similar exception to the rule occurs in the use of Assos for Assus (Acts xx. 18, 14). (See Trench, *Authorized Version*, etc., p. 78, 2d ed.) H.

of pagan antiquity which flourished wherever there were groves and hill-altars. Under the Attalic kings, Pergamos became a city of temples, devoted to a sensuous worship; and being in its origin, according to pagan notions, a sacred place, might not unnaturally be viewed by Jews and Jewish Christians, as one "where was the throne of Satan" (ὅπου ὁ θρόνος τοῦ Σατανᾶ, Rev. ii. 13).

After the extinction of its independence, the sacred character of Pergamos seems to have been put even more prominently forward. Coins and inscriptions constantly describe the Pergamenes as νεωκόροι or νεωκόροι πρῶτοι τῆς Ἀσίας. This title always indicates the duty of maintaining a religious worship of some kind (which indeed naturally goes together with the usufruct of religious property). What the deities were to which this title has reference especially, it is difficult to say. In the time of Martial, however, Æsculapius had acquired so much prominence that he is called Pergameus deus. His grove was recognized by the Roman senate in the reign of Tiberius as possessing the rights of sanctuary. Pausanias, too, in the course of his work, refers more than once to the Æsculapian ritual at Pergamus as a sort of standard. From the circumstance of this notoriety of the Pergamene Æsculapius, from the title Σωτήρ being given to him, from the serpent (which Judaical Christians would regard as a symbol of evil) being his characteristic emblem, and from the fact that the medical practice of antiquity included charms and incantations among its agencies, it has been supposed that the expressions ὁ θρόνος τοῦ Σατανᾶ and ὅπου ὁ Σατανᾶς κατοικεῖ have an especial reference to this one pagan deity, and not to the whole city as a sort of focus of idolatrous worship. But although undoubtedly the Æsculapius worship of Pergamos was the most famous, and in later times became continually more predominant from the fact of its being combined with an excellent medical school (which among others produced the celebrated Galen), yet an inscription of the time of Marcus Antoninus distinctly puts Zeus, Athenè, Dionysus, and Asclepius in a coördinate rank, as all being special tutelary deities of Pergamos. It seems unlikely, therefore, that the expressions above quoted should be so interpreted as to isolate one of them from the rest.

It may be added, that the charge against a portion of the Pergamene Church that some among them were of the school of Balaam, whose policy was "to put a stumbling-block before the children of Israel, by inducing them φαγεῖν εἰδωλόθυτα καὶ πορνεῦσαι" (Rev. ii. 14), is in both its particulars very inappropriate to the Æsculapian ritual. It points rather to the Dionysus and Aphroditè worship; and the sin of the Nicolaitans, which is condemned, seems to have consisted in a participation in this, arising out of a social amalgamation of themselves with the native population. Now, from the time of the war with Antiochus at least, it is certain that there was a considerable Jewish population in Pergamene territory. The decree of the Pergamenes quoted by Josephus (Ant. xiv. 10, § 22) seems to indicate that the Jews had farmed the tolls in some of the harbors of their territory, and likewise were holders of land. They are — in accordance with the expressed desire of the Roman senate — allowed to levy port-dues upon all vessels except those belonging to king Ptolemy. The growth of a large and wealthy class naturally leads to its obtaining a share in political rights, and the

only bar to the admission of Jews to privileges of citizenship in Pergamos would be their unwillingness to take any part in the religious ceremonies, which were an essential part of every relation of life in pagan times. The more lax, however, might regard such a proceeding as a purely formal act of civil obedience, and reconcile themselves to it as Naaman did to "bowing himself in the house of Rimmon" when in attendance upon his sovereign. It is perhaps worth noticing, with reference to this point, that a Pergamene inscription published by Boeckh, mentions by two names (Nicostratus, who is also called Trypho) an individual who served the office of gymnasiarch. Of these two names the latter, a foreign one, is likely to have been borne by him among some special body to which he belonged, and the former to have been adopted when, by accepting the position of an official, he merged himself in the general Greek population.

(Strab. xiii. 4; Joseph. Ant. xiv.; Martial, ix. 17; Plin. H. N. xxxv. 4, 10; Liv. xxxii. 33, 4; Polyb. xvi. 1, xxxii. 23; Boeckh, Inscript. Nos. 3538, 3550, 3553; Philostratus, De Vit. Soph. p. 45, 106; Tchihatcheff, Asie Mineure, p. 230; Arundell, Discoveries in Asia Minor, ii. 304.)   J. W. B.

PERIDA (פְּרִידָא [kernel]: Φεριδά; [Vat. FA. Φερειδα;] Alex. Φαρειδα: Pharida). The children of Perida returned from Babylon with Zerubbabel (Neh. vii. 57). In Ezr. ii. 55 the name appears as PERUDA, and in 1 Esdr. v. 33 as PHARIRA. One of Kennicott's MSS. has "Peruda" in Nehemiah.

PER'IZZITE, THE, and PER'IZZITES (הַפְּרִזִּי, in all cases in the Heb. singular [see below]: οἱ Φερεζαῖοι; in Ezr. only ὁ Φερεσθεί [Vat.; Rom. Alex. ὁ Φερε(ζ]: Pherezæus). One of the nations inhabiting the Land of Promise before and at the time of its conquest by Israel. They are not named in the catalogue of Gen. x.; so that their origin, like that of other small tribes, such as the Avites, and the similarly named Gerizites, is left in obscurity. They are continually mentioned in the formula so frequently occurring to express the Promised Land (Gen. xv. 20; Ex. iii. 8, 17, xxiii. 23, xxxiii. 2, xxxiv. 11; Deut. vii. 1, xx. 17; Josh. iii. 10, ix. 1, xxiv. 11; Judg. iii. 5; Ezr. ix. 1; Neh. ix. 8). They appear, however, with somewhat greater distinctness on several occasions. On Abram's first entrance into the land it is said to have been occupied by "the Canaanite and the Perizzite" (Gen. xiii. 7). Jacob also, after the massacre of the Shechemites, uses the same expression, complaining that his sons had "made him to stink among the inhabitants of the land, among the Canaanite and the Perizzite" (xxxiv. 30). So also in the detailed records of the conquest given in the opening of the book of Judges (evidently from a distinct source to those in Joshua), Judah and Simeon are said to have found their territory occupied by "the Canaanite and the Perizzite" (Judg. i. 4, 5), with Bezek (a place not yet discovered) as their stronghold, and Adoni-bezek their most noted chief. And thus too a late tradition, preserved in 2 Esdr. i. 21, mentions only "the Canaanites, the Pheresites, and the Philistines," as the original tenants of the country. The notice just cited from the book of Judges locates them in the southern part of the Holy Land. Another independent and equally remarkable fragment of the history of the conquest seems to speak of them as occupying, with the Rephaim, or giants, the "forest country" on the western flanks of Mount " Carmel (Josh. xvii. 15-18). Here again the Canaanites only are named with them. As a tribe of mountaineers, they are enumerated in company with Amorite, Hittite, and Jebusite in Josh. xi. 3, xii. 8; and they are catalogued among the remnants of the old population whom Solomon reduced to bondage, both in 1 K. ix. 20, and 2 Chr. viii. 7. By Josephus the Perizzites do not appear to be mentioned.

The signification of the name is not by any means clear. It possibly meant rustics, dwellers in open, unwalled villages, which are denoted by a similar word.[b] Ewald (Geschichte, i. 317) inclines to believe that they were the same people with the Hittites. But against this there is the fact that both they and the Hittites appear in the same lists; and that not only in mere general formulas, but in the records of the conquest as above. Redslob has examined the whole of these names with some care (in his Alttestam. Namen der Israelitenstaats, 1846), and his conclusion (p. 103) is that, while

the Chavvoth were villages of tribes engaged in the care of cattle, the Perazoth were inhabited by peasants engaged in agriculture, like the Fellahs of the Arabs.   G.

PERSEP'OLIS (Περσέπολις: Persepolis) is mentioned only in 2 Macc. ix. 2, where we hear of Antiochus Epiphanes attempting to burn its temples, but provoking a resistance which forced him to fly ignominiously from the place. It was the capital of Persia Proper, and the occasional residence of the Persian court from the time of Darius Hystaspis, who seems to have been its founder, to the invasion of Alexander. Its wanton destruction by that conqueror is well known. According to Q. Curtius the destruction was complete, as the chief building material employed was cedar-wood, which caused the conflagration to be rapid and general (De Rebus Alex. Magn. v. 7). Perhaps the temples, which were of stone, escaped. At any rate, if ruined, they must have been shortly afterwards restored, since they were still the depositories of treasure in the time of Epiphanes.

Persepolis has been regarded by many as iden-

Persepolis.

tical with Pasargadæ, the famous capital of Cyrus (see Niebuhr's Lectures on Ancient History, i. 115; Ouseley, Travels, ii. 316-318). But the positions are carefully distinguished by a number of ancient writers (Strab. xv. 3, § 6, 7; Plin. H. N. vi. 26; Arrian, Exp. Alex. vii. 1; Ptolem. vi. 4); and the ruins, which are identified beyond any reasonable doubt, show that the two places were more than 40 miles apart. Pasargadæ was at Murgaub, where the tomb of Cyrus may still be seen; Persepolis was 42 miles to the south of this, near Istakher, on the site now called the Chehl-Minar, or Forty Pillars. Here, on a platform hewn out of the solid rock, the sides of which face the four cardinal points, are the remains of two great palaces, built respectively by Darius Hystaspis and his son Xerxes, besides a number of other edifices, chiefly temples. These ruins have been so frequently described that it is unnecessary to do more than refer

the reader to the best accounts which have been given of them (Niebuhr, Reise, ii. 121; Chardin, Voyages, ii. 245; Ker Porter, Travels, i. 576; Heeren, Asiatic Nations, i. 143-196; Rich, Residence in Kurdistan, vol. ii. pp. 218-222; Fergusson, Palaces of Nineveh and Persepolis Restored, pp. 89-124, &c.). They are of great extent and magnificence, covering an area of many acres. At the foot of the rock on which they are placed, in the plain now called Merdusht, stood probably the ancient town, built chiefly of wood, and now altogether effaced.

Persepolis may be regarded as having taken the place of Pasargadæ, the more ancient capital of Persia Proper, from the time of Darius Hystaspis. No exact reason can be given for this change, which perhaps arose from mere royal caprice, Darius having taken a fancy to the locality, near which he erected his tomb. According to Athenæus the

---

a See MANASSEH, vol. ii. p. 1770 b.

b Cophir hap-perazi. A. V. "country villages" (1 Sam. vi. 18): Arri hap-perazi, "unwalled towns" (Deut. iii. 5). In both these passages the LXX. un-

derstand the Perizzites to be alluded to, and translate accordingly. In Josh. xvi. 10 they add the Perizzites to the Canaanites as inhabitants of Gezer.

court resided at Persepolis during three months of each year (*Deipnosoph.* xii. 513, F), but the conflicting statements of other writers (Xen. *Cyrop.* viii. 6, § 22, Plut. *de Exil.* ii. 604; Zonar. iii. 26, &c.) make this uncertain. We cannot doubt, however, that it was one of the royal residences; and we may well believe the statement of Strabo, that, in the later times of the empire, it was, next to Susa, the richest of all the Persian cities (*Geograph.* xv. 3, § 6). It does not seem to have long survived the blow inflicted upon it by Alexander; for after the time of Antiochus Epiphanes it disappears altogether from history as an inhabited place. [For fuller information see Rawlinson's *Ancient Monarchies*, iv. 11, 237–267.—H.]　　　G. R.

PER′SEUS [2 syl.] (Περσεύς: *Perses*), the eldest (illegitimate or supposititious?) son of Philip V. and last king of Macedonia. After his father's death (B. C. 179) he continued the preparations for the renewal of the war with Rome, which was seen to be inevitable. The war, which broke out in B. C. 171, was at first ably sustained by Perseus; but in 168 he was defeated by L. Æmilius Paullus at Pydna, and shortly afterwards surrendered with

Perseus, King of Macedonia.
Tetradrachm of Perseus (Attic talent). Obv. Head of King, r. bound with fillet. Rev. ΒΑΣΙΛΕΩΣ ΠΕΡΣΕΩΣ, Eagle on thunderbolt; all within wreath.

his family to his conquerors. He graced the triumph of Paullus, and died in honorable retirement at Alba. The defeat of Perseus put an end to the independence of Macedonia, and extended even to Syria the terror of the Roman name (1 Macc. viii. 5).　　　B. F. W.

PER′SIA (פָּרַס, *i. e. Pâras*: Περσίς: *Persis*) was strictly the name of a tract of no very large dimensions on the Persian Gulf, which is still known as *Fars* or *Farsistan*, a corruption of the ancient appellation. This tract was bounded on the west by Susiana or Elam, on the north by Media, on the south by the Persian Gulf, and on the east by Carmania, the modern *Kerman*. It was, speaking generally, an arid and unproductive region (Herod. ix. 122; Arr. *Exp. Alex.* v. 4; Plat. *Leg.* iii. 695, A); but contained some districts of considerable fertility. The worst part of the country was that towards the south, on the borders of the Gulf, which has a climate and soil like Arabia, being sandy and almost without streams, subject to pestilential winds, and in many places covered with particles of salt. Above this miserable region is a tract very far superior to it, consisting of rocky mountains — the continuation of Zagros, among which are found a good many fertile valleys and plains, especially towards the north, in the vicinity of Shiraz. Here is an important stream, the *Bendamir*, which flowing through the beautiful valley of

Merdasht, and by the ruins of Persepolis, is then separated into numerous channels for the purpose of irrigation, and, after fertilizing a large tract of country (the district of *Kurjan*), ends its course in the salt lake of *Baktigan*. Vines, oranges, and lemons, are produced abundantly in this region; and the wine of *Shiraz* is celebrated throughout Asia. Further north an arid country again succeeds, the outskirts of the Great Desert, which extends from Kerman to Mazenderan, and from Kashan to Lake Zerrah.

Ptolemy (*Geograph.* vi. 4) divides Persia into a number of provinces, among which the most important are Parætacene on the north, which was sometimes reckoned to Media (Herod. i. 101; Steph. Byz. *ad voc.* (Παραίτακα), and Mardyene on the south coast, the country of the Mardi. The chief towns were Pasargadæ, the ancient, and Persepolis, the later capital. Pasargadæ was situated near the modern village of *Murgaub*, 42 miles nearly due north of Persepolis, and appears to have been the capital till the time of Darius, who chose the far more beautiful site in the valley of the Bendamir, where the *Chehl Minar* or "Forty Pillars" still stand. [See PERSEPOLIS.] Among other cities of less importance were Parætaca and Gabæ in the mountain country, and Taoce upon the coast. (See Strab. xv. 3, § 1–8; Plin. *H. N.* vi. 25, 26; Ptolem. *Geog.* vi. 4; Kinneir's *Persian Empire*, pp. 54–80; Malcolm, *History of Persia*, i. 2; Ker Porter, *Travels*, i. 458, &c.; Rich, *Journey from Bushire to Persepolis*, etc.)

While the district of *Fars* is the true original Persia, the name is more commonly applied, both in Scripture and by profane authors, to the entire tract which came by degrees to be included within the limits of the Persian Empire. This empire extended at one time from India on the east to Egypt and Thrace upon the west, and included, besides portions of Europe and Africa, the whole of Western Asia between the Black Sea, the Caucasus, the Caspian, and the Jaxartes, upon the north, the Arabian desert, the Persian Gulf, and the Indian Ocean upon the south. According to Herodotus (iii. 89), it was divided into twenty governments, or satrapies; but from the inscriptions it would rather appear that the number varied at different times, and, when the empire was most flourishing, considerably exceeded twenty. In the inscription upon his tomb at *Nakhsh-i-Rustam* Darius mentions no fewer than thirty countries as subject to him besides Persia Proper. These are Media, Susiana, Parthia, Aria, Bactria, Sogdiana, Chorasmia, Zarangia, Arachosia, Sattagydia, Gandaria, India, Scythia, Babylonia, Assyria, Arabia, Egypt, Armenia, Cappadocia, Saparda, Ionia, (European) Scythia, the islands (of the Ægean), the country of the Scodræ, (European) Ionia, the lands of the Tacabri, the Budians, the Cushites or Ethiopians, the Mardians, and the Colchians.

The only passage in Scripture where Persia designates the tract which has been called above "Persia Proper" is Ez. xxxviii. 5. Elsewhere the Empire is intended.　　　G. R.

PER′SIANS (פָּרַס: Πέρσαι: *Persæ*). The name of the people who inhabited the country called above "Persia Proper," and who thence conquered a mighty empire. There is reason to believe that the Persians were of the same race as the Medes, both being branches of the great Aryan stock, which under various names established their sway over the whole tract between Mesopotamia and Burmah.ᵃ The native form of the name is *Parsa*, which the Hebrew פָּרַס fairly represents, and which remains but little changed in the modern "Parsee." It is conjectured to signify "the Tigers."

1. *Character of the Nation.* — The Persians were a people of lively and impressible minds, brave and impetuous in war, witty, passionate, for Orientals truthful, not without some spirit of generosity, and of more intellectual capacity than the generality of Asiatics. Their faults were vanity, impulsiveness, a want of perseverance and solidity, and an almost slavish spirit of sycophancy and servility towards their lords. In the times anterior to Cyrus they were noted for the simplicity of their habits, which offered a strong contrast to the luxuriousness of the Medes; but from the date of the Median overthrow, this simplicity began to decline; and it was not very long before their manners became as soft and effeminate as those of any of the conquered peoples. They adopted the flowing Median robe (Fig. 1) which was probably of silk, in lieu of the old national costume (Fig. 2) — a close-fitting tunic and trousers of leather (Herod. i. 71; compare i. 135); beginning at the same time the practice of wearing on their persons chains, bracelets, and collars of gold, with which precious metal they also adorned their horses. Polygamy was commonly practiced among them; and besides legitimate wives a Persian was allowed any number of concubines. They were fond of the pleasures of the table, indulging in a great variety of food, and spending a long time over their meals, at which they were accustomed to swallow large quantities of wine. In war they fought bravely, but without discipline, generally gaining their victories by the vigor of their first attack; if they were strenuously resisted, they soon flagged; and if they suffered a repulse, all order was at once lost, and the retreat speedily became a rout.

2. *Religion.* — The religion which the Persians brought with them into Persia Proper seems to have been of a very simple character, differing from natural religion in little, except that it was deeply tainted with Dualism. Like the other Aryans, the Persians worshipped one Supreme God, whom they called *Aura-mazda* [or Ahura-mazda] (Oromasdes) — a term signifying (as is believed) "the Great Giver of Life." From Oromasdes came all blessings — "he gave the earth, he gave the heavens, he gave mankind, he gave life to mankind" (Inscriptions, *passim*) — he settled the Persian kings upon their thrones, strengthened them, established them, and granted them victory over all their enemies. The royal inscriptions rarely mention any other god. Occasionally, however, they indicate a slight and modified polytheism. Oromasdes is "the chief of the gods," so that there are other gods besides

him; and the highest of these is evidently *Mithra*, who is sometimes invoked to protect the monarch, and is beyond a doubt identical with "the sun." To the worship of the sun as Mithra was probably attached, as in India, the worship of the moon, under the name of Homa, as the third greatest god. Entirely separate from these — their active resister and antagonist — was *Ahriman* (Arimanius) "the Death-dealing" — the powerful, and (probably) self-existing Evil Spirit, from whom war, disease, frost, hail, poverty, sin, death, and all other evils had their origin. *Ahriman* was Satan, carried to an extreme — believed to have an existence of his own, and a real power of resisting and defying God. *Ahriman* could create spirits, and as the beneficent *Auramazda* had surrounded himself with good angels, who were the ministers of his mercies towards mankind, so *Ahriman* had surrounded himself with evil spirits, to carry out his malevolent purposes. Worship was confined to Au-

Fig. 1.   Median dress.   Fig. 2.   Old Persian dress.

ramazda, and his good spirits; Ahriman and his demons were not worshipped, but only hated and feared.

The character of the original Persian worship was simple. They were not destitute of temples, as Herodotus asserts (Herod. i. 131; compare *Beh. Inscr.* col. i. par. 14, § 5); but they had probably no altars, and certainly no images. Neither do they appear to have had any priests. Processions were formed, and religious chants were sung in the temples, consisting of prayer and praise intermixed, whereby the favor of *Auramazda* and his good spirits was supposed to be secured to the worshippers. Beyond this it does not appear that they had any religious ceremonies. Sacrifices, apparently, were unknown;ᵇ though thank-offerings may have been made in the temples.

ᵃ * For a fuller account of the origin of the Persians and of other topics discussed in the article, see Rawlinson's *Ancient Monarchies*, iv. 348 ff.   H.

ᵇ * In his *Ancient Monarchies*, iv. 334, Prof. Rawlinson admits that the Persians sacrificed certain animals, and may have sacrificed human victims in extreme cases, in some periods of their history.   —.

From the first entrance of the Persians, as immigrants, into their new territory, they were probably brought into contact with a form of religion very different from their own. Magianism, the religion of the Scythic or Turanian population of Western Asia, had long been dominant over the greater portion of the region lying between Mesopotamia and India. The essence of this religion was worship of the elements — more especially, of the subtlest of all, fire. It was an ancient and imposing system, guarded by the venerable hierarchy of the Magi, boasting its fire-altars where from time immemorial the sacred flame had burnt without intermission, and claiming to some extent mysterious and miraculous powers. The simplicity of the Aryan religion was speedily corrupted by its contact with this powerful rival, which presented special attractions to a rude and credulous people. There was a short struggle for preëminence, after which the rival systems came to terms. Dualism was retained, together with the names of Auramazda and Ahriman, and the special worship of the sun and moon under the appellations of Mithra and Homa; but to this was superadded the worship of the elements and the whole ceremonial of Magianism, including the divination to which the Magian priesthood made pretense. The worship of other deities, as Tanata or Anaitis, was a still later addition to

Persian Warriors.   (From Persepolis.)

the religion, which grew more complicated as time went on. but which always maintained as its leading and most essential element that Dualistic principle whereon it was originally based.

3. *Language.* — The language of the ancient Persians was closely akin to the Sanskrit, or ancient language of India. We find it in its earliest stage in the Zendavesta [more properly called " Avesta," simply] — the sacred book of the whole Aryan race, where, however, it is corrupted by a large admixture of later forms. The inscriptions of the Achæmenian kings give us the language in its second stage, and, being free from these later additions, are of the greatest importance towards determining what was primitive, and what more recent in this type of speech. Modern Persian is its degenerate representative, being, as it is. a motley idiom, largely impregnated with Arabic; still, however, both in its grammar and its vocabulary, it is mainly Aryan: and historically, it must be regarded as the continuation of the ancient tongue, just as Italian is of Latin, and modern of ancient Greek.

4 *Division into Tribes, etc.* — Herodotus tells us that the Persians were divided into ten tribes, of which three were noble, three agricultural, and four nomadic. The noble tribes were the Pasargadæ, who dwelt, probably, in the capital and its immediate neighborhood; the Maraphians, who are per-

haps represented by the modern *Mdfee*, a Persian tribe which prides itself on its antiquity; and the Maspians, of whom nothing more is known. The three tribes engaged in agriculture were called the Panthialæans, the Derusiæans, and the Germanians, or (according to the true orthography) the Carmanians. These last were either the actual inhabitants of *Kerman*, or settlers of the same race, who remained in Persia while their fellow-tribesmen occupied the adjoining region. The nomadic tribes are said to have been the Dahi, who appear in Scripture as the " Dehavites " (Ezr. iv. 9), the Mardi, mountaineers famous for their thievish habits (Steph. Byz.), together with the Sagartians and the Derbices or Dropici, colonists from the regions east of the Caspian. The royal race of the Achæmenidæ was a phratry or clan of the Pasargadæ (Herod. i. 126); to which it is probable that most of the noble houses likewise belonged. Little is heard of the Maraphians, and nothing of the Maspians, in history; it is therefore evident that their nobility was very inferior to that of the leading tribe.

5. *History.* — In remote antiquity it would appear that the Persians dwelt in the region east of the Caspian, or possibly in a tract still nearer India. The first Fargard of the Vendidad seems to describe their wanderings in these countries, and shows the general line of their progress to have been from east to west, down the course of the Oxus, and then, along the southern shores of the Caspian Sea, to Rhages, and Media. It is impossible to determine the period of these movements; but there can be no doubt that they were anterior to B. C. 880. at which time the Assyrian kings seem for the first time to have come in contact with Aryan tribes east of Mount Zagros. Probably the Persians accompanied the Medes in their migration from Khorassan, and, after the latter people took possession of the tract extending from the river *Kur* to Ispahan, proceeded still further south, and occupied the region between Media and the Persian Gulf. It is uncertain whether they are to be identified with the *Bartsu* or *Partsu* of the Assyrian monuments. If so, we may say that from the middle of the 9th to the middle of the 8th century B. C. they occupied southeastern Armenia, but by the end of the 8th century had removed into the country which thenceforth went by their name. The leader of this last migration would seem to have been a certain Achæmenes, who was recognized as king of the newly-occupied territory, and founded the famous dynasty of the Achæmenidæ, about B. C. 700. Very little is known of the history of Persia between this date and the accession of Cyrus the Great, near a century and a half later. The crown appears to have descended in a right line through four princes — Teïspes, Cambyses I., Cyrus I., and Cambyses II., who was the father of Cyrus the Conqueror. Teïspes must have been a prince of some repute, for his daughter, Atossa, married Pharnaces, king of the distant Cappadocians (Diod. Sic. ap. Phot. *Bibliothec.* p. 1158). Later, however, the Persians found themselves unable to resist the growing strength of Media, and became tributary to that power about B. C. 630, or a little earlier. The line of native kings was continued on the throne, and the internal administration was probably untouched; but external independence was altogether lost until the revolt under Cyrus.

Of the circumstances under which this revolt took place we have no certain knowledge. The stories told by Herodotus (i. 108–129) and Nicolas of Damascus (*Fr.* 66) are internally improbable; and they are also at variance with the monuments, which prove Cyrus to have been the son of a Persian king. [See CYRUS.] We must therefore discard them, and be content to know that after about seventy or eighty years of subjection, the Persians revolted from the Medes, engaged in a bloody struggle with them, and finally succeeded, not only in establishing their independence, but in changing places with their masters, and becoming the ruling people. The probable date of the revolt is B. C. 558. Its success, by transferring to Persia the dominion previously in the possession of the Medes, placed her at the head of an empire, the bounds of which were the Halys upon the west, the Euxine upon the north, Babylonia upon the south, and upon the east the salt desert of Iran. As usual in the East, this success led on to others. Crœsus the Lydian monarch, who had united most of Asia Minor under his sway, venturing to attack the newly-risen power, in the hope that it was not yet firmly established, was first repulsed, and afterwards defeated and made prisoner by Cyrus, who took his capital, and added the Lydian empire to his dominions. This conquest was followed closely by the submission of the Greek settlements on the Asiatic coast, and by the reduction of Caria, Caunus, and Lycia. The empire was soon afterwards extended greatly towards the northeast and east. Cyrus rapidly overran the flat countries beyond the Caspian, planting a city, which he called after himself (Arr. *Exp. Alex.* iv. 3), on the Jaxartes (*Jyhun*); after which he seems to have pushed his conquests still further to the east, adding to his dominions the districts of Herat, Cabul, Candahar, Seistan, and Beloochistan, which were thenceforth included in the empire. (See Ctes. *Pers. Exc.* § 5, *et seq.*; and compare Plin. *H. N.* vi. 23.) In B. C. 539 or 538, Babylon was attacked, and after a stout defense fell before his irresistible bands. [BABYLON.] This victory first brought the Persians into contact with the Jews. The conquerors found in Babylon an oppressed race, — like themselves abhorrers of idols, — and professors of a religion in which to a great extent they could sympathize. This race, which the Babylonian monarchs had torn violently from their native land and settled in the vicinity of Babylon, Cyrus determined to restore to their own country; which he did by the remarkable edict recorded in the first chapter of Ezra (Ez. i. 2–4). Thus commenced that friendly connection between the Jews and Persians, which prophecy had already foreshadowed (Is. xliv. 28, xlv. 1–4), and which forms so remarkable a feature in the Jewish history. After the conquest of Babylon, and the consequent extension of his empire to the borders of Egypt, Cyrus might have been expected to carry out the design, which he is said to have entertained (Herod. i. 153), of an expedition against Egypt. Some danger, however, seems to have threatened the northeastern provinces, in consequence of which his purpose was changed; and he proceeded against the Massagetæ or the Derbices, engaged them, but was defeated and slain. He reigned, according to Herodotus, twenty-nine years.

Under his son and successor, Cambyses III., the conquest of Egypt took place (B. C. 525), and the Persian dominions were extended southward to Elephantiné and westward to Euesperidæ on the North-African coast. This prince appears to be the Ahasuerus of Ezra (iv. 6), who was asked to alter Cyrus's policy towards the Jews, but (apparently) declined all interference. We have in Herodotus (book iii.) a very complete account of his warlike expeditions, which at first resulted in the successes above mentioned, but were afterwards unsuccessful, and even disastrous. One army perished in an attempt to reach the temple of Ammon, while another was reduced to the last straits in an expedition against Ethiopia. Perhaps it was in consequence of these misfortunes that, in the absence of Cambyses with the army, a conspiracy was formed against him at court, and a Magian priest, Gomates (*Gaumata*) by name, professing to be Smerdis (*Bardiya*), the son of Cyrus, whom his brother, Cambyses, had put to death secretly, obtained quiet possession of the throne. Cambyses was in Syria when news reached him of this bold attempt; and there is reason to believe that, seized with a sudden disgust, and despairing of the recovery of his crown, he fled to the last resort of the unfortunate, and ended his life by suicide (*Behistun Inscription*, col. i. par. 11, § 10). His reign had lasted seven years and five months.

Gomates the Magian found himself thus, without a struggle, master of Persia (B. C. 522). His situation, however, was one of great danger and delicacy. There is reason to believe that he owed his elevation to his fellow-religionists, whose object in placing him upon the throne was to secure the triumph of Magianism over the Dualism of the Persians. It was necessary for him therefore to accomplish a religious revolution, which was sure to be distasteful to the Persians, while at the same time he had to keep up the deception on which his claim to the crown was professedly based, and to prevent any suspicion arising that he was not Smerdis, the son of Cyrus. To combine these two aims was difficult; and it would seem that Gomates soon discarded the latter, and entered on a course which must have soon caused his subjects to feel that their ruler was not only no Achæmenian, but no Persian. He destroyed the national temples, substituting for them the fire-altars, and abolished the religious chants and other sacred ceremonies of the Oromasdians. He reversed the policy of Cyrus with respect to the Jews, and forbade by an edict the further building of the Temple (Ez. iv. 17–22). [ARTAXERXES.] He courted the favor of the subject-nations generally by a remission of tribute for three years, and an exemption during the same space from forced military service (Herod. iii. 67). Towards the Persians he was haughty and distant, keeping them as much as possible aloof from his person, and seldom showing himself beyond the walls of his palace. Such conduct made him very unpopular with the proud people which held the first place among his subjects, and, the suspicion that he was a mere pretender having after some months ripened into certainty, a revolt broke out, headed by Darius, the son of Hystaspes, a prince of the blood-royal, which in a short time was crowned with complete success. Gomates quitted his capital, and, having thrown himself into a fort in Media, was pursued, attacked and slain. Darius, then, as the chief of the conspiracy, and after his father the next heir to the throne, was at once acknowledged king. The reign of Gomates lasted seven months.

The first efforts of Darius were directed to the reëstablishment of the Oromasdian religion in all its purity. He "rebuilt the temples which Gomates the Magian had destroyed, and restored to the people the religious chants and the worship of which Gomates the Magian had deprived them" (*Beh. Inscr.* col. i. par. 14). Appealed to, in his second year, by the Jews, who wished to resume the construction of their Temple, he not only allowed them, confirming the decree of Cyrus, but assisted the work by grants from his own revenues, whereby the Jews were able to complete the Temple as early as his sixth year (Ez. vi. 1–15). During the first part of the reign of Darius, the tranquillity of the empire was disturbed by numerous revolts. The provinces regretted the loss of those exemptions which they had obtained from the weakness of the pseudo-Smerdis, and hoped to shake off the yoke of the new prince before he could grasp firmly the reins of government. The first revolt was that of Babylon, where a native, claiming to be Nebuchadnezzar, the son of Nabonadius, was made king; but Darius speedily crushed this revolt and executed the pretender. Shortly afterwards a far more extensive rebellion broke out. A Mede, named Phraortes, came forward and, announcing himself to be "Xathrites, of the race of Cyaxares," assumed the royal title. Media, Armenia, and Assyria immediately acknowledged him; the Median soldiers at the Persian court revolted to him; Parthia and Hyrcania after a little while declared in his favor; while in Sagartia another pretender, making a similar claim of descent from Cyaxares, induced the Sagartians to revolt; and in Margiana, Arachotia, and even Persia Proper, there were insurrections against the authority of the new king. His courage and activity, however, seconded by the valor of his Persian troops and the fidelity of some satraps, carried him successfully through these and other similar difficulties; and the result was, that, after five or six years of struggle, he became as firmly seated on his throne as any previous monarch. His talents as an administrator were, upon this, brought into play. He divided the whole empire into satrapies, and organized that somewhat complicated system of government on which they were henceforth administered (Rawlinson's *Herodotus*, ii. 555–568). He built himself a magnificent palace at Persepolis, and another at Susa [PERSEPOLIS, SHUSHAN]. He also applied himself, like his predecessors, to the extension of the empire; conducted an expedition into European Scythia, from which he returned without disgrace; conquered Thrace, Pæonia, and Macedonia towards the west, and a large portion of India on the east, besides (apparently) bringing into subjection a number of petty nations (see the *Nakhsh-i-Rustam* Inscription). On the whole he must be pronounced, next to Cyrus, the greatest of the Persian monarchs. The latter part of his reign was, however, clouded by reverses. The disaster of Mardonius at Mount Athos was followed shortly by the defeat of Datis at Marathon; and, before any attempt could be made to avenge that blow, Egypt rose in revolt (B. C. 486), massacred its Persian garrison, and declared itself independent. In the palace at the same time there was dissension; and when, after a reign of thirty-six years, the fourth Persian monarch died (B. C. 485), leaving his throne to a young prince of strong and ungoverned passions, it was evident that the empire had reached its highest point of greatness, and was already verging towards its decline.

Xerxes, the eldest son of Darius by Atossa, daughter of Cyrus, and the first son born to Darius after he mounted the throne, seems to have obtained the crown, in part by the favor of his father, over whom Atossa exercised a strong influence, in part by right, as the eldest male descendant of Cyrus, the founder of the empire. His first act was to reduce Egypt to subjection (B. C. 484), after which he began at once to make preparations for his invasion of Greece. It is probable that he was the Ahasuerus of Esther. [AHASUERUS.] The great feast held in Shushan the palace in the third year of his reign, and the repudiation of Vashti, fall into the period preceding the Grecian expedition, while it is probable that he kept open house for the "princes of the provinces," who would from time to time visit the court, in order to report the state of their preparations for the war. The marriage with Esther, in the seventh year of his reign, falls into the year immediately following his flight from Greece, when he undoubtedly returned to Susa, relinquishing warlike enterprises, and henceforth devoting himself to the pleasures of the seraglio. It is unnecessary to give an account of the well-known expedition against Greece, which ended so disastrously for the invaders. Persia was taught by the defeats of Salamis and Platæa the danger of encountering the Greeks on their side of the Ægean, while she learned at Mycalé the retaliation which she had to expect on her own shores at the hands of her infuriated enemies. For a while some vague idea of another invasion seems to have been entertained by the court;[a] but discreeter counsels prevailed, and relinquishing all aggressive designs, Persia from this point in her history stood upon the defensive, and only sought to maintain her own territories intact, without anywhere trenching upon her neighbors. During the rest of the reign of Xerxes, and during part of that of his son and successor, Artaxerxes, she continued at war with the Greeks, who destroyed her fleets, plundered her coasts, and stirred up revolt in her provinces: but at last, in B. C. 449, a peace was concluded between the two powers, who then continued on terms of amity for half a century.

A conspiracy in the seraglio having carried off Xerxes (B. C. 465), Artaxerxes his son, called by the Greeks Μακρόχειρ, or "the Long-Handed," succeeded him, after an interval of seven months, during which the conspirator Artabanus occupied the throne. This Artaxerxes, who reigned forty years, is beyond a doubt the king of that name who stood in such a friendly relation towards Ezra (Ezr. vii. 11–28) and Nehemiah (Neh. ii. 1–9, &c.). [ARTAXERXES.] His character, as drawn by Ctesias, is mild but weak; and under his rule the disorders of the empire seem to have increased rapidly. An insurrection in Bactria, headed by his brother Hystaspes, was with difficulty put down in the first year of his reign (B. C. 464), after which a revolt broke out in Egypt, headed by Inarus the Libyan and Amyrtæus the Egyptian, who, receiving the support of an Athenian fleet, maintained themselves for six years (B. C. 460–455) against the whole power of Persia, but were at last overcome by Megabyzus, satrap of Syria. This powerful and haughty noble soon afterwards (B. C. 447), on

---

[a] The force collected in Pamphylia, which Cimon defeated and dispersed (B. C. 466), seems to have been intended for aggressive purposes.

occasion of a difference with the court, himself became a rebel, and entered into a contest with his sovereign, which at once betrayed and increased the weakness of the empire. Artaxerxes is the last of the Persian kings who had any special connection with the Jews, and the last but one mentioned in Scripture. His successors were Xerxes II., Sogdianus, Darius Nothus, Artaxerxes Mnemon, Artaxerxes Ochus, and Darius Codomanus, who is probably the "Darius the Persian" of Nehemiah (xii. 22). These monarchs reigned from B. C. 424 to B. C. 330. None were of much capacity; and during their reigns the decline of the empire was scarcely arrested for a day, unless it were by Ochus, who reconquered Egypt, and gave some other signs of vigor. Had the younger Cyrus succeeded in his attempt, the regeneration of Persia was, perhaps, possible. After his failure the seraglio grew at once more powerful and more cruel. Eunuchs and women governed the kings, and dispensed the favors of the crown, or wielded its terrors, as their interests or passions moved them. Patriotism and loyalty were alike dead, and the empire must have fallen many years before it did, had not the Persians early learnt to turn the swords of the Greeks against one another, and at the same time raised the character of their own armies by the employment, on a large scale, of Greek mercenaries. The collapse of the empire under the attack of Alexander is well known, and requires no description here. On the division of Alexander's dominions among his generals Persia fell to the Seleucidæ, under whom it continued till after the death of Antiochus Epiphanes, when the conquering Parthians advanced their frontier to the Euphrates, and the Persians came to be included among their subject-tribes (B. C. 164). Still their nationality was not obliterated. In A. D. 226, three hundred and ninety years after their subjection to the Parthians, and five hundred and fifty-six years after the loss of their independence, the Persians shook off the yoke of their oppressors, and once more became a nation. The kingdom of the Sassanidæ, though not so brilliant as that of Cyrus, still had its glories; but its history belongs to a time which scarcely comes within the scope of the present work.

(See, for the history of Persia, besides Herodotus, Ctesias, *Excerpta Persica*; Plutarch, *Vit. Artaxerx.*; Xenophon, *Anabasis*; Heeren, *Asiatic Nations*, vol. i.; Malcolm, *History of Persia from the Earliest Ages to the Present Times*, 2 vols., 4to , London, 1816; and Sir H. Rawlinson's *Memoir on the Cuneiform Inscriptions of Ancient Persia*, published in the *Journal of the Asiatic Society*, vols. x. and xi. For the religion see Hyde, *De Religione Veterum Persarum*; Brockhaus, *Vendidad-Sadé*; Bunsen, *Egypt's Place in Universal History*, iii. 472–506; and Rawlinson's *Herodotus*, i. 426–431. For the system of government, see Rawlinson's *Herodotus*, ii. 555–568.)　　　　　G. R.

* Among the more recent works on the *religion* of the ancient Persians, the following deserve notice: — AVESTA, *die heiligen Schriften der Parsen, aus dem Grundtexte übersetzt von F. Spiegel*, 3 Bde. Leipz. 1852–63; AVESTA: *the Religious Books of the Parsees, from Spiegel's German Translation, by A. H. Bleeck*, 3 vols. in one, Hertford, 1864; F. Spiegel, *Commentar üb. das Avesta*, 2 Bde., Leipz. 1865–69; W. D. Whitney, *On the Avesta*, in the *Journ. of the Amer. Orient. Soc.*, 1856, v. 337–383; DER BUNDEHESH, *zum ersten Male herausgegeben, übersetzt*, etc. *von Ferd. Justi*,

Leipz. 1868; Spiegel, art. *Parsismus* in Herzog's *Real-Encykl.* xi. 115–128 (1859); id. *Die traditionelle Literatur der Parsen*, Wien, 1860; id. *Erân*, Berl. 1863; M. Haug, *Essays on the Sacred Language, Writings, and Religion of the Parsees*, Bombay, 1862 (a new edition is promised), comp. *Amer. Presb. and Theol. Rev.* for April, 1863; F. Windischmann, *Zoroastrische Studien*, Berl 1863; Miss F. P. Cobbe, *The Sacred Books of the Zoroastrians*, in her *Studies New and Old*, etc. (Lond. 1865), pp. 89–143; A. Kohut, *Ueber die jüd. Angelologie u. Dæmonologie in ihrer Abhängigkeit vom Parsismus*, Leipz. 1866 (*Abhandll. d. Deutschen Morgenl. Gesellschaft*, Bd. iv. No. 3); id. *Was hat die talmudische Eschatologie aus dem Parsismus aufgenommen?* in the *Zeitschr. d. D. M. Gesellschaft*, 1867, xx. 552–591; A. Rapp, *Die Religion u. Sitte der Perser . . . nach d. griech. u. römischen Quellen*, in the *Zeitschr. d. D. M. Gesellschaft*, 1866 and 1867, xix. 1–89, xx. 49–140; M. Duncker, *Gesch. der Arier in der Alten Zeit*, pp. 393–582 (Bd. ii. of his *Gesch. des Alterthums*) 3e Aufl. (much enlarged) Leipz. 1867; Max Müller, arts. No. 3, 5, 6, 7, in his *Chips from a German Workshop*, vol. i. (Amer. ed., N. Y., 1869); O. Pfleiderer, *Die Religion* (Leipz. 1869), ii. 246–267; and J. F. Clarke, *Zoroaster and the Zend-Avesta*, in the *Atlantic Monthly* for Aug. 1869. For the earlier literature relating to this interesting subject, see the bibliographical Appendix to Alger's *History of the Doctrine of a Future Life* (N. Y., 1864), Nos. 1366–1404. See also in that work the essay on the "Persian Doctrine of a Future Life," pp 127–144.　　　　　A.

PER'SIS (Περσίς, ["a Persian woman:" *Persis*]). A Christian woman at Rome (Rom. xvi. 12) whom St. Paul salutes, and commends with special affection on account of some work which she had performed with singular diligence (see Origen *in loco*).　　　　　W. T. B.

PERU'DA (פְרוּדָא [*kernel*, Ges.]: Φαδουρά; [Comp. Φαρουδά :] *Pharuda*). The same as PERIDA (Ezr. ii. 55). The LXX. reading is supported by one of Kennicott's MSS.

PESTILENCE. [PLAGUE.]

PETER (Πέτρος, the Greek for כֵּיפָא: Κηφᾶς, *Cephas, i. e.* "a stone" or "rock," on which name see note at the end of this article: [*Petrus*]). His original name was Simon, שִׁמְעוֹן, *i. e.* "hearer." The two names are commonly combined, Simon Peter, but in the early part of his history, and in the interval between our Lord's death and resurrection, he is more frequently named Simon; after that event he bears almost exclusively the more honorable designation Peter, or, as St. Paul sometimes writes, Cephas. The notices of this Apostle's early life are few, but not unimportant, and enable us to form some estimate of the circumstances under which his character was formed, and prepared for his great work. He was the son of a man named Jonas (Matt. xvi. 17: John i. 42, xxi. 16), and was brought up in his father's occupation, a fisherman on the sea of Tiberias.[a] The occupation was of course a humble one, but not, as is often assumed, mean or servile, or incompatible with some degree of mental culture.

---

[a] There is a tradition that his mother's name was Johanna (Cotelier, *Patres Apost.* ii. 68).

His family were probably in easy circumstances. He and his brother Andrew were partners of John and James, the sons of Zebedee, who had hired servants; and from various indications in the sacred narrative we are led to the conclusion that their social position brought them into contact with men of education. In fact the trade of fishermen, supplying some of the important cities on the coasts of that inland lake, may have been tolerably remunerative, while all the necessaries of life were cheap and abundant in the singularly rich and fertile district where the Apostle resided. He did not live, as a mere laboring man, in a hut by the sea-side, but first at Bethsaida, and afterwards in a house at Capernaum, belonging to himself or his mother-in-law, which must have been rather a large one, since he received in it not only our Lord and his fellow-disciples, but multitudes who were attracted by the miracles and preaching of Jesus. It is certain that when he left all to follow Christ, he made what he regarded, and what seems to have been admitted by his Master, to have been a considerable sacrifice. The habits of such a life were by no means unfavorable to the development of a vigorous, earnest, and practical character, such as he displayed in after years. The labors, the privations, and the perils of an existence passed in great part upon the waters of that beautiful but stormy lake, the long and anxious watching through the nights, were calculated to test and increase his natural powers, his fortitude, energy, and perseverance. In the city he must have been brought into contact with men engaged in traffic, with soldiers, and foreigners, and may have thus acquired somewhat of the flexibility and geniality of temperament all but indispensable to the attainment of such personal influence as he exercised in after-life. It is not probable that he and his brother were wholly uneducated. The Jews regarded instruction as a necessity, and legal enactments enforced the attendance of youths in schools maintained by the community.[a] The statement in Acts iv. 13, that " the council perceived they (i. e. Peter and John) were unlearned and ignorant men," is not incompatible with this assumption. The translation of the passage in the A. V. is rather exaggerated, the word rendered " unlearned " (ἰδιῶται) being nearly equivalent to " laymen," i. e. men of ordinary education, as contrasted with those who were specially trained in the schools of the Rabbis. A man might be thoroughly conversant with the Scriptures, and yet be considered ignorant and unlearned by the Rabbis, among whom the opinion was already prevalent that " the letter of Scripture was the mere shell, an earthen vessel containing heavenly treasures, which could only be discovered by those who had been taught to search for the hidden cabalistic meaning." Peter and his kinsmen were probably taught to read the Scriptures in childhood. The history of their country, especially of the great events of early days, must have been familiar to them as attendants at the synagogue,

and their attention was there directed to those portions of Holy Writ from which the Jews derived their anticipations of the Messiah.

The language of the Apostles was of course the form of Aramaic spoken in northern Palestine, a sort of patois, partly Hebrew, but more nearly allied to the Syriac.[b] Hebrew, even in its debased form, was then spoken only by men of learning, the leaders of the pharisees and scribes.[c] The men of Galilee were, however, noted for rough and inaccurate language, and especially for vulgarities of pronunciation.[d] It is doubtful whether our Apostle was acquainted with Greek in early life. It is certain that there was more intercourse with foreigners in Galilee than in any district of Palestine, and Greek appears to have been a common, if not the principal, medium of communication. Within a few years after his call St. Peter seems to have conversed fluently in Greek with Cornelius, at least there is no intimation that an interpreter was employed, while it is highly improbable that Cornelius, a Roman soldier, should have used the language of Palestine. The style of both of St. Peter's epistles indicates a considerable knowledge of Greek — it is pure and accurate, and in grammatical structure equal to that of St. Paul. That may, however, be accounted for by the fact, for which there is very ancient authority, that St. Peter employed an interpreter in the composition of his epistles, if not in his ordinary intercourse with foreigners.[e] There are no traces of acquaintance with Greek authors, or of the influence of Greek literature upon his mind, such as we find in St. Paul, nor could we expect it in a person of his station even had Greek been his mother-tongue. It is on the whole probable that he had some rudimental knowledge of Greek in early life,[f] which may have been afterwards extended when the need was felt, but not more than would enable him to discourse intelligibly on practical and devotional subjects. That he was an affectionate husband, married in early life to a wife who accompanied him in his apostolic journeys, are facts inferred from Scripture, while very ancient traditions, recorded by Clement of Alexandria (whose connection with the church founded by St. Mark gives a peculiar value to his testimony), and by other early but less trustworthy writers, inform us that her name was Perpetua, that she bore a daughter, or perhaps other children, and suffered martyrdom. It is uncertain at what age he was called by our Lord. The general impression of the Fathers is that he was an old man at the date of his death, A. D. 64, but this need not imply that he was much older than our Lord. He was probably between thirty and forty years of age at the date of his call.

That call was preceded by a special preparation. He and his brother Andrew, together with their partners James and John, the sons of Zebedee, were disciples of John the Baptist (John i. 35). They were in attendance upon him when they were first

a A law to this effect was enacted by Simon ben-Shelach, one of the great leaders of the Pharisaic party under the Asmonean princes. See Jost, Geschichte des Judenthums, i. 246.

b See E. Renan, Histoire des Langues Sémitiques, p. 294. The only extant specimen of that patois is the Book of Adam or " Codex Nasirœus," edited by Norberg, Lond. Goth. 1815-16. [See especially LANGUAGE OF THE N. TEST., Amer. ed.]

c See Buxtorf, s. v. בְּלִילָא.

d See Reuss, Geschichte der H. S. § 41.

e Reuss (l. c. § 49) rejects this as a mere hypothesis, but gives no reason. The tradition rests on the authority of Clement of Alexandria, Irenæus, and Tertullian. See the notes on Euseb. H. E. iii. 39, v. 8, and vi. 25.

f Even highly educated Jews, like Josephus, spoke Greek imperfectly (see Ant. xx. 11, § 2). On the antagonism to Greek influence, see Jost, l. c. i. 198, and M. Nicolas, Les Doctrines religieuses des Juifs, l. c. 2

called to the service of Christ. From the circumstances of that call, which are recorded with graphic minuteness by St. John, we learn some important facts touching their state of mind and the personal character of our Apostle. Two disciples, one named by the Evangelist St. Andrew, the other in all probability St. John himself, were standing with the Baptist at Bethany on the Jordan, when he pointed out Jesus as He walked, and said, Behold the Lamb of God! That is, the antitype of the victims whose blood (as all true Israelites, and they more distinctly under the teaching of John,[a] believed) prefigured the atonement for sin. The two at once followed Jesus, and upon his invitation abode with Him that day. Andrew then went to his brother Simon, and saith unto him, We have found the Messias, the anointed One, of whom they had read in the prophets. Simon went at once, and when Jesus looked on him He said, Thou art Simon the son of Jona; thou shalt be called Cephas. The change of name is of course deeply significant. As son of Jona (a name of doubtful meaning, according to Lampe equivalent to Johanan or John, i. e. grace of the Lord; according to Lange, who has some striking but fanciful observations, signifying dove) he bore as a disciple the name Simon, i. e. bearer, but as an Apostle, one of the twelve on whom the Church was to be erected, he was hereafter (κληθήσῃ) to be called Rock or Stone. It seems a natural impression that the words refer primarily to the original character of Simon: that our Lord saw in him a man firm, steadfast, not to be overthrown, though severely tried; and such was generally the view taken by the Fathers: but it is perhaps a deeper and truer inference that Jesus thus describes Simon, not as what he was, but as what he would become under his influence — a man with predispositions and capabilities not unfitted for the office he was to hold, but one whose permanence and stability would depend upon union with the living Rock. Thus we may expect to find Simon, as the natural man, at once rough, stubborn, and mutable, whereas Peter, identified with the Rock, will remain firm and unmovable unto the end.[b]

This first call led to no immediate change in St. Peter's external position. He and his fellow disciples looked henceforth upon our Lord as their teacher, but were not commanded to follow him as regular disciples. There were several grades of disciples among the Jews, from the occasional hearer, to the follower who gave up all other pursuits in order to serve a master. At the time a recognition of his Person and office sufficed. They returned to Capernaum, where they pursued their usual business, waiting for a further intimation of his will.

The second call is recorded by the other three Evangelists; the narrative of St. Luke being apparently supplementary[c] to the brief, and so to speak, official accounts given by Matthew and Mark. It took place on the sea of Galilee near Capernaum — where the four disciples, Peter and Andrew James and John, were fishing. Peter and Andrew were first called. Our Lord then entered Simon Peter's boat, and addressed the multitude on the shore; after the conclusion of the discourse He wrought the miracle by which He foreshadowed the success of the Apostles in the new, but analogous, occupation which was to be theirs, that of fishers of men. The call of James and John followed. From that time the four were certainly enrolled formally among his disciples, and although as yet invested with no official character, accompanied Him in his journeys, those especially in the north of Palestine.

Immediately after that call our Lord went to the house of Peter, where He wrought the miracle of healing on Peter's wife's mother, a miracle succeeded by other manifestations of divine power which produced a deep impression upon the people. Some time was passed afterwards in attendance upon our Lord's public ministrations in Galilee, Decapolis, Peræa, and Judæa: though at intervals the disciples returned to their own city, and were witnesses of many miracles, of the call of Levi, and of their Master's reception of outcasts, whom they in common with their zealous but prejudiced countrymen had despised and shunned. It was a period of training, of mental and spiritual discipline preparatory to their admission to the higher office to which they were destined. Even then Peter received some marks of distinction. He was selected, together with the two sons of Zebedee, to witness the raising of Jairus' daughter.

The special designation of Peter and his eleven fellow disciples took place some time afterwards, when they were set apart as our Lord's immediate attendants, and as his delegates to go forth wherever He might send them, as apostles, announcers of his kingdom, gifted with supernatural powers as credentials of their supernatural mission (see Matt. x. 2–4; Mark iii. 13–19, the most detailed account — Luke vi. 13). They appear then first to have received formally the name of Apostles, and from that time Simon bore publicly, and as it would seem all but exclusively, the name Peter, which had hitherto been used rather as a characteristic appellation than as a proper name.

From this time there can be no doubt that St. Peter held the first place among the Apostles, to whatever cause his precedence is to be attributed. There was certainly much in his character which marked him as a representative man; both in his strength and in his weakness, in his excellences and his defects he exemplifies the changes which the natural man undergoes in the gradual transformation into the spiritual man under the personal influence of the Saviour. The precedence did not depend upon priority of call, or it would have devolved upon his brother Andrew, or that other disciple who first followed Jesus. It seems scarcely probable that it depended upon seniority, even sup-

---

[a] See Lücke, Tholuck, and Lange, on the Gospel of St. John.

[b] Lücke describes this character well, as that firmness or rather hardness of power, which, if not purified, easily becomes violence. The deepest and most beautiful observations are those of Origen on John, tom. ii. c. 20.

[c] This is a point of great difficulty, and hotly contested. Many writers of great weight hold the occurrences to be altogether distinct; but the generality of commentators, including some of the most earnest and devout in Germany and England, appear now to concur in the view which I have here taken. Thus Trench On the Parables, Neander, Lücke, Lange, and Ebrard. The object of Strauss, who denies the identity, is to make out that St. Luke's account is a mere myth. The most satisfactory attempt to account for the variations is that of Spanheim, Dubia Evangelica, ii. 341.

posing, which is a mere conjecture,[a] that he was older than his fellow disciples. The special designation by Christ, alone accounts in a satisfactory way for the facts that he is named first in every list of the Apostles, is generally addressed by our Lord as their representative, and on the most solemn occasions speaks in their name. Thus when the first great secession took place in consequence of the offense given by our Lord's mystic discourse at Capernaum (see John vi. 66–69), " Jesus said unto the twelve, Will ye also go away? Then Simon Peter answered Him, Lord, to whom shall we go? Thou hast the words of eternal life: and we believe and are sure that Thou art that Christ, the Son of the living God." Thus again at Cæsarea Philippi, soon after the return of the twelve from their first missionary tour, St. Peter (speaking as before in the name of the twelve, though, as appears from our Lord's words, with a peculiar distinctness of personal conviction) repeated that declaration, " Thou art the Christ, the Son of the living God." The confirmation of our Apostle in his special position in the Church, his identification with the rock on which that Church is founded, the ratification of the powers and duties attached to the apostolic office,[b] and the promise of permanence to the Church, followed as a reward of that confession. The early Church regarded St. Peter generally, and most especially on this occasion, as the representative of the apostolic body, a very distinct theory from that which makes him their head, or governor in Christ's stead. Even in the time of Cyprian, when communion with the Bishop of Rome as St. Peter's successor for the first time was held to be indispensable, no powers of jurisdiction, or supremacy, were supposed to be attached

to the admitted precedency of rank.[c] Primus inter pares, Peter held no distinct office, and certainly never claimed any powers which did not belong equally to all his fellow Apostles.

This great triumph of Peter, however, brought other points of his character into strong relief The distinction which he then received, and it may be his consciousness of ability, energy, zeal, and absolute devotion to Christ's person, seem to have developed a natural tendency to rashness and forwardness bordering upon presumption. On this occasion the exhibition of such feelings brought upon him the strongest reproof ever addressed to a disciple by our Lord. In his affection and self-confidence Peter ventured to reject as impossible the announcement of the sufferings and humiliation which Jesus predicted, and heard the sharp words, " Get thee behind me, Satan, thou art an offense unto me; for thou savourest not the things that be of God, but those that be of men." That was Peter's first fall; a very ominous one: not a rock, but a stumbling-stone,[d] not a defender, but an antagonist and deadly enemy of the faith, when the spiritual should give place to the lower nature in dealing with the things of God. It is remarkable that on other occasions when St. Peter signalized his faith and devotion, he displayed at the time, or immediately afterwards, a more than usual deficiency in spiritual discernment and consistency. Thus a few days after that fall he was selected together with John and James to witness the transfiguration of Christ, but the words which he then uttered prove that he was completely bewildered, and unable at the time to comprehend the meaning of the transaction.[e] Thus again, when his zeal

a * This conjecture is chiefly founded on his being the only one of the apostles who is mentioned as married (Matt. viii. 14; Mark i. 30; Luke iv. 38, and comp. 1 Cor. ix. 5). The representation of Peter with a bald head by artists has no doubt the same origin, though said also to follow a distinct tradition.   H.

b The accounts which have been given of the precise import of this declaration may be summed up under these heads: 1. That our Lord spoke of Himself, and not of St. Peter, as the rock on which the Church was to be founded. This interpretation expresses a great truth, but it is irreconcilable with the context, and could scarcely have occurred to an unbiassed reader, and certainly does not give the primary and literal meaning of our Lord's words. It has been defended, however, by candid and learned critics, as Glass and Dathe. 2. That our Lord addresses Peter as the type or representative of the Church, in his capacity of chief disciple. This is Augustine's view, and it was widely adopted in the early Church. It is hardly borne out by the context, and seems to involve a false metaphor. The Church would in that case be founded on itself in its type. 3. That the rock was not the person of Peter, but his confession of faith. This rests on much better authority, and is supported by stronger arguments. The authorities for it are given by Suicer. v. Πέτρος, § 1, note 3. Yet it seems to have been originally suggested as an explanation, rather than an interpretation, which it certainly is not in a literal sense. 4. That St. Peter himself was the rock on which the Church would be built; as the representative of the Apostles, as professing in their name the true faith, and as entrusted specially with the duty of preaching it, and thereby laying the foundation of the Church. Many learned and candid Protestant divines have acquiesced in this view (e. g. Pearson, Hammond, Bengel, Rosenmüller, Schleusner, Kuinoel, Bloomfield, etc.). It is borne out by the facts that St. Peter on

the day of Pentecost, and during the whole period of the establishment of the Church, was the chief agent in all the work of the ministry, in preaching, in admitting both Jews and Gentiles, and laying down the terms of communion. This view is wholly incompatible with the Roman theory, which makes him the representative of Christ, not personally, but in virtue of an office essential to the permanent existence and authority of the Church. Passaglia, the latest and ablest controversialist, takes more pains to refute this than any other view; but wholly without success: it being clear that St. Peter did not retain, even admitting that he did at first hold, any primacy of rank after completing his own special work ; that he never exercised any authority over or independently of the other Apostles ; that he certainly did not transmit whatever position he ever held to any of his colleagues after his decease. At Jerusalem, even during his residence there, the chief authority rested with St. James; nor is there any trace of a central power or jurisdiction for centuries after the foundation of the Church. The same arguments, mutatis mutandis, apply to the keys. The promise was literally fulfilled when St. Peter preached at Pentecost, admitted the first converts to baptism, confirmed the Samaritans, and received Cornelius, the representative of the Gentiles, into the Church. Whatever privileges may have belonged to him personally, died with him. The authority required for the permanent government of the Church was believed by the Fathers to be deposited in the episcopate, as representing the apostolic body, and succeeding to its claims.

c See an admirable discussion of this question in Rothe's Anfänge der Christlichen Kirche.

d Lightfoot suggests that such may have been the real meaning of the term "rock." An amusing instance of the blindness of party feeling. See Hors Heb. on John, vol. xii. p. 287.

e As usual, the least favorable view of St. Peter's

and courage prompted him to leave the ship and walk on the water to go to Jesus (Matt. xiv. 29), a sudden failure of faith withdrew the sustaining power; he was about to sink when he was at once reproved and saved by his Master. Such traits, which occur not unfrequently, prepare us for his last great fall, as well as for his conduct after the Resurrection, when his natural gifts were perfected and his deficiencies supplied by "the power from on High." We find a mixture of zeal and weakness in his conduct when called upon to pay tribute-money for himself and his Lord, but faith had the upper hand, and was rewarded by a significant miracle (Matt. xvii. 24–27). The question which about the same time Peter asked our Lord as to the extent to which forgiveness of sins should be carried, indicated a great advance in spirituality from the Jewish standing-point, while it showed how far as yet he and his fellow disciples were from understanding the true principle of Christian love (Matt. xviii. 21). We find a similar blending of opposite qualities in the declaration recorded by the synoptical evangelists (Matt. xix. 27; Mark x. 28; Luke xviii. 28), " Lo, we have left all and followed Thee." It certainly bespeaks a consciousness of sincerity, a spirit of self-devotion and self-sacrifice, though it conveys an impression of something like ambition; but in that instance the good undoubtedly predominated, as is shown by our Lord's answer. He does not reprove Peter, who spoke, as usual, in the name of the twelve, but takes that opportunity of uttering the strongest prediction touching the future dignity and paramount authority of the Apostles, a prediction recorded by St. Matthew only.

Towards the close of our Lord's ministry St. Peter's characteristics become especially prominent. Together with his brother, and the two sons of Zebedee, he listened to the last awful predictions and warnings delivered to the disciples in reference to the second advent (Matt. xxiv. 3; Mark xiii. 3, who alone mentions these names; Luke xxi. 7). At the last supper Peter seems to have been particularly earnest in the request that the traitor might be pointed out, expressing of course a general feeling, to which some inward consciousness of infirmity may have added force. After the supper his words drew out the meaning of the significant, almost sacramental act of our Lord in washing his disciples' feet, an occasion on which we find the same mixture of goodness and frailty, humility and deep affection, with a certain taint of self-will, which was at once hushed into submissive reverence by the voice of Jesus. Then, too, it was that he made those repeated protestations of unalterable fidelity, so soon to be falsified by his miserable fall. That event is, however, of such critical import in its bearings upon the character and position of the Apostle, that it cannot be dismissed without a careful, if not an exhaustive discussion.

Judas had left the guest-chamber when St. Peter put the question, Lord, whither goest Thou? words

which modern theologians generally represent as savoring of idle curiosity, or presumption, but in which the early fathers (as Chrysostom and Augustine) recognized the utterance of love and devotion. The answer was a promise that Peter should follow his Master, but accompanied with an intimation of present unfitness in the disciple. Then came the first protestation, which elicited the sharp and stern rebuke, and distinct prediction of Peter's denial (John xiii. 36–38). From comparing this account with those of the other evangelists (Matt. xxvi. 33 35; Mark xiv. 90–31; Luke xxii. 00, 04), it seems evident that with some diversity of circumstances both the protestation and warning were thrice repeated. The tempter was to sift all the disciples, our Apostle's faith was to be preserved from failing by the special intercession of Christ, he being thus singled out either as the representative of the whole body, or as seems more probable, because his character was one which had special need of supernatural aid. St. Mark, as usual, records two points which enhance the force of the warning and the guilt of Peter, namely, that the cock would crow twice, and that after such warning he repeated his protestation with greater vehemence. Chrysostom, who judges the Apostle with fairness and candor, attributes this vehemence to his great love, and more particularly to the delight which he felt when assured that he was not the traitor, yet not without a certain admixture of forwardness and ambition, such as had previously been shown in the dispute for preëminence. The fiery trial soon came. After the agony of Gethsemane, when the three, Peter, James, and John were, as on former occasions, selected to be with our Lord, the only witnesses of his passion, where also all three had alike failed to prepare themselves by prayer and watching, the arrest of Jesus took place. Peter did not shrink from the danger. In the same spirit which had dictated his promise he drew his sword, alone against the armed throng, and wounded the servant (τὸν δοῦλον, not a servant) of the high-priest, probably the leader of the band.[a] When this bold but unauthorized attempt at rescue was reproved, he did not yet forsake his Master, but followed Him with St. John into the focus of danger, the house of the high-priest.[b] There he sat in the outer hall. He must have been in a state of utter confusion: his faith, which from first to last was bound up with hope, his special characteristic, was for the time powerless against temptation. The danger found him unarmed. Thrice, each time with greater vehemence, the last time with blasphemous asseveration, he denied his Master. The triumph of Satan seemed complete. Yet it is evident that it was an obscuration of faith, not an extinction. It needed but a glance of his Lord's eye to bring him to himself. His repentance was instantaneous, and effectual. The light in which he himself regarded his conduct, is clearly shown by the terms in which it is related by St Mark. The inferences are weighty as regards his

conduct and feelings is given by St. Mark, i. e. by himself.

a * The leader of the band would naturally be the chiliarch mentioned by John (xviii. 12); and at all events a slave (δοῦλον) would not be likely to be placed over the " servants " or apparitors (ὑπηρέται) of the Jewish council. The man whom Peter struck may have been specially officious in laying hold of Jesus [MALCHUS].   H

b * The Saviour foretold that all the disciples would forsake him (Matt. xxvi. 31; Mark xiv. 27); and this took place, according to every intimation, at the time of the apprehension in the garden, and hence before the entrance into the hall. Peter and John, however, were no doubt the first of the disciples to recover from this panic.   H personal character, which represents more completely perhaps than any in the New Testament, the weakness of the natural and the strength of the spiritual man: still more weighty as bearing upon his relations to the apostolic body, and the claims resting upon the assumption that he stood to them in the place of Christ.

On the morning of the resurrection we have proof that St. Peter, though humbled, was not crushed by his fall. He and St. John were the first to visit the sepulchre; he was the first who entered it. We are told by Luke (in words still used by the Eastern Church as the first salutation on Easter Sunday) and by St. Paul,[a] that Christ appeared to him first among the Apostles — he who most needed the comfort was the first who received it, and with it, as may be assumed, an assurance of forgiveness. It is observable, however, that on that occasion he is called by his original name, Simon, not Peter; the higher designation was not restored until he had been publicly reinstituted, so to speak, by his Master. That reinstitution took place at the sea of Galilee (John xxi.), an event of the very highest import. We have there indications of his best natural qualities, practical good sense, promptness and energy; slower than St. John to recognize his Lord, Peter was the first to reach Him; he brought the net to land. The thrice repeated question of Christ, referring doubtless to the three protestations and denials, were thrice met by answers full of love and faith, and utterly devoid of his hitherto characteristic failing, presumption, of which not a trace is to be discerned in his later history. He then received the formal commission to feed Christ's sheep; not certainly as one endued with exclusive or paramount authority, or as distinguished from his fellow-disciples, whose fall had been marked by far less aggravating circumstances; rather as one who had forfeited his place, and could not resume it without such an authorization. Then followed the prediction of his martyrdom, in which he was to find the fulfillment of his request to be permitted to follow the Lord.[b]

With this event closes the first part of St. Peter's history. It has been a period of transition, during which the fisherman of Galilee had been trained first by the Baptist, then by our Lord, for the great work of his life. He had learned to know the Person and appreciate the offices of Christ: while his own character had been chastened and elevated by special privileges and humiliations, both reaching their climax in the last recorded transactions. Henceforth, he with his colleagues were to establish and govern the Church founded by their Lord, without the support of his presence.

The first part of the Acts of the Apostles is occupied by the record of transactions, in nearly all of which Peter stands forth as the recognized leader of the Apostles; it being, however, equally

clear that he neither exercises nor claims any authority apart from them, much less over them. In the first chapter it is Peter who points out to the disciples (as in all his discourses and writings drawing his arguments from prophecy) the necessity of supplying the place of Judas. He states the qualifications of an Apostle, but takes no special part in the election. The candidates are selected by the disciples, while the decision is left to the searcher of hearts. The extent and limits of Peter's primacy might be inferred with tolerable accuracy from this transaction alone. To have one spokesman, or foreman, seems to accord with the spirit of order and humility which ruled the Church, while the assumption of power or supremacy would be incompatible with the express command of Christ (see Matt. xxiii. 10). In the 2d chapter again, St. Peter is the most prominent person in the greatest event after the resurrection, when on the day of Pentecost the Church was first invested with the plenitude of gifts and powers. Then Peter, not speaking in his own name, but with the eleven (see ver. 14), explained the meaning of the miraculous gifts, and showed the fulfillment of prophecies (accepted at that time by all Hebrews as Messianic), both in the outpouring of the Holy Ghost and in the resurrection and death of our Lord. This discourse, which bears all the marks of Peter's individuality, both of character and doctrinal views,[c] ends with an appeal of remarkable boldness.

It is the model upon which the apologetic discourses of the primitive Christians were generally constructed. The conversion and baptism of three thousand persons, who continued steadfastly in the Apostle's doctrine and fellowship, attested the power of the Spirit which spake by Peter on that occasion.

The first miracle after Pentecost was wrought by St. Peter (Acts iii.); and St. John was joined with him in that, as in most important acts of his ministry: but it was Peter who took the cripple by the hand, and bade him "in the name of Jesus of Nazareth rise up and walk," and when the people ran together to Solomon's porch, where the Apostles, following their Master's example, were wont to teach, Peter was the speaker; he convinces the people of their sin, warns them of their danger, points out the fulfillment of prophecy, and the special objects for which God sent his Son first to the children of the old covenant.[d]

The boldness of the two Apostles, of Peter more especially as the spokesman, when, "filled with the Holy Ghost," he confronted the full assembly, headed by Annas and Caiaphas, produced a deep impression upon those cruel and unscrupulous hypocrites; an impression enhanced by the fact that the words came from ignorant and unlearned men. The words spoken by both Apostles, when commanded not to speak at all nor teach in the

---

[a] A fact very perplexing to the Tübingen school, being utterly irreconcilable with their theory of antagonism between the Apostles at first.

[b] * Peter's inquiry, on this occasion, respecting the fate of John after his own martyrdom had been foretold (John xxi. 18-22), seems to have arisen from a feeling of jealousy towards John. The severity of Christ's answer to his question ("If I will that he tarry till I come, what is that to thee?"), and the evangelist's recital of the special marks of favor which the Saviour had conferred on himself (ver. 20), admit otherwise of no easy explanation. (For a fuller ex-

position of this view see "Biblical Notes," *Bibl. Sacra* for 1868, xxv. 783.)   H.

[c] See Schmid, *Biblische Theologie*, ii 153; and Weiss, *Der petrinische Lehrbegriff*, p. 19.

[d] This speech is at once strikingly characteristic of St. Peter, and a proof of the fundamental harmony between his teaching and the more developed and systematic doctrines of St. Paul: differing in form, to an extent utterly incompatible with the theory of Baur and Schwegler touching the object of the writer of the Acts; identical in spirit, as issuing from the same source.

name of Jesus, have ever since been the watch-words of martyrs (iv. 19, 20).

This first miracle of healing was soon followed by the first miracle of judgment. The first open and deliberate sin against the Holy Ghost, a sin combining ambition, fraud, hypocrisy, and blasphemy, was visited by death, sudden and awful as under the old dispensation. St. Peter was the minister in that transaction. As he had first opened the gate to penitents (Acts ii. 37, 38), he now closed it to hypocrites. The act stands alone, without a precedent or parallel in the Gospel; but Peter acted simply as an instrument, not pronouncing the sentence, but denouncing the sin, and that in the name of his fellow Apostles and of the Holy Ghost. Penalties similar in kind, though far different in degree, were inflicted, or commanded on various occasions by St. Paul. St. Peter appears, perhaps in consequence of that act, to have become the object of a reverence bordering, as it would seem, on superstition (Acts v. 15), while the numerous miracles of healing wrought about the same time, showing the true character of the power dwelling in the Apostles, gave occasion to the second persecution. Peter then came into contact with the noblest and most interesting character among the Jews, the learned and liberal tutor of St. Paul, Gamaliel, whose caution, gentleness, and dispassionate candor, stand out in strong relief contrasted with his colleagues, but make a faint impression compared with the steadfast and uncompromising principles of the Apostles, who after undergoing an illegal scourging, went forth rejoicing that they were counted worthy to suffer shame for the name of Jesus. Peter is not specially named in connection with the appointment of deacons, an important step in the organization of the church; but when the Gospel was first preached beyond the precincts of Judæa, he and St. John were at once sent by the Apostles to confirm the converts at Samaria, a very important statement at this critical point, proving clearly his subordination to the whole body, of which he was the most active and able member.

Up to that time it may be said that the Apostles had one great work, namely, to convince the Jews that Jesus was the Messiah; in that work St. Peter was the master builder, the whole structure rested upon the doctrines of which he was the principal teacher: hitherto no words but his are specially recorded by the writer of the Acts. Henceforth he remains prominent, but not exclusively prominent, among the propagators of the Gospel. At Samaria he and John established the precedent for the most important rite not expressly enjoined in Holy Writ, namely, confirmation, which the Western Church [a] has always held to belong exclusively to the functions of bishops as successors to the ordinary powers of the Apostolate. Then also St. Peter was confronted with Simon Magus, the first teacher of heresy. [SIMON MAGUS.] As in the case of Ananias he had denounced the first sin against holiness, so in this case he first declared the penalty due to the sin called after Simon's name. About three years later (compare Acts ix. 26, and Gal. i. 17, 18) we have two accounts of the first meeting of St. Peter and St. Paul. In the Acts it is stated generally that Saul was at first distrusted by the disciples, and received by the Apostles upon the recommendation of Barnabas. From the Galatians we learn that St. Paul went to Jerusalem specially to see Peter; that he abode with him fifteen days, and that James was the only other Apostle present at the time. It is important to note that this account — which, while it establishes the independence of St. Paul, marks the position of St. Peter as the most eminent of the Apostles — rests not on the authority of the writer of the Acts, but on that of St. Paul; as though it were intended to obviate all possible misconceptions touching the mutual relations of the Apostles of the Hebrews and the Gentiles. This interview was followed by other events marking Peter's position — a general apostolical tour of visitation to the churches hitherto established (διερχόμενον διὰ πάντων, Acts ix. 32), in the course of which two great miracles were wrought on Æneas and Tabitha, and in connection with which the most signal transaction after the day of Pentecost is recorded, the baptism of Cornelius. That was the crown and consummation of Peter's ministry. Peter who had first preached the resurrection to the Jews, baptized the first converts, confirmed the first Samaritans, now, without the advice or coöperation of any of his colleagues, under direct communication from heaven, first threw down the barrier which separated proselytes of the gate [b] from Israelites, first establishing principles which in their gradual application and full development issued in the complete fusion of the Gentile and Hebrew elements in the Church. The narrative of this event, which stands alone in minute circumstantiality of incidents, and accumulation of supernatural agency, is twice recorded by St. Luke. The chief points to be noted are, first, the peculiar fitness of Cornelius, both as a representative of Roman force and nationality, and as a devout and liberal worshipper, to be a recipient of such privileges; and secondly, the state of the Apostle's own mind. Whatever may have been his hopes or fears touching the heathen, the idea had certainly not yet crossed him that they could become Christians without first becoming Jews. As a loyal and believing Hebrew he could not contemplate the removal of Gentile disqualifications, without a distinct assurance that the enactments of the law which concerned them were abrogated by the divine legislator. The vision could not therefore have been the product of a subjective impression. It was, strictly speaking, objective, presented to his mind by an external influence. Yet the will of the Apostle was not controlled, it was simply enlightened. The intimation in the state of trance did not at once overcome his reluctance. It was not until his consciousness was fully restored, and he had well considered the meaning of the vision, that he learned that the distinction of cleanness and uncleanness in outward things belonged to a temporary dispensation. It was no mere acquiescence in a positive command, but the development of a spirit full of generous impulses, which found utterance in the words spoken by Peter on that occasion, — both in the presence of Cornelius, and afterwards at Jerusalem. His conduct gave great offense to all his countrymen (Acts xi. 2), and it needed all his authority, corroborated

---

[a] Not so the Eastern, which combines the act with baptism, and leaves it to the officiating priest. It is one of the points upon which Photius and other eastern controversialists lay special stress.

[b] A term to which objection has been made, but shown by Jost to be strictly correct.

by a special manifestation of the Holy Ghost, to
induce his fellow-Apostles to recognize the propriety of this great act, in which both he and they
saw an earnest of the admission of Gentiles into
the Church on the single condition of spiritual
repentance. The establishment of a church in
great part of Gentile origin at Antioch, and the
mission of Barnabas, between whose family and
Peter there were the bonds of near intimacy, set
the seal upon the work thus inaugurated by St.
Peter.

This transaction was soon followed by the imprisonment of our Apostle. Herod Agrippa having
first tested the state of feeling at Jerusalem by the
execution of James, one of the most eminent Apostles, arrested Peter. The hatred, which at that
time first showed itself as a popular feeling, may
most probably be attributed chiefly to the offense
given by Peter's conduct towards Cornelius. His
miraculous deliverance marks the close of this second great period of his ministry. The special work
assigned to him was completed. He had founded
the Church, opened its gates to Jews and Gentiles,
and distinctly laid down the conditions of admission.
From that time we have no continuous history of
Peter. It is quite clear that he retained his rank
as the chief Apostle, equally so, that he neither exercised nor claimed any right to control their proceedings. At Jerusalem the government of the
Church devolved upon James the brother of our
Lord. In other places Peter seems to have confined his ministrations to his countrymen — as
Apostle of the circumcision. He left Jerusalem,
but it is not said where he went. Certainly not to
Rome, where there are no traces of his presence
before the last years of his life; he probably remained in Judæa, visiting and confirming the
churches; some old but not trustworthy traditions represent him as preaching in Cæsarea and
other cities on the western coast of Palestine; six
years later we find him once more at Jerusalem,
when the Apostles and elders came together to
consider the question whether converts should be
circumcised. Peter took the lead in that discussion, and urged with remarkable cogency the principles settled in the case of Cornelius. Purifying
faith and saving grace (xv. 9 and 11) remove all
distinctions between believers. His arguments,
adopted and enforced by James, decided that question at once and forever. It is, however, to be remarked, that on that occasion he exercised no one
power which Romanists hold to be inalienably attached to the chair of Peter. He did not preside
at the meeting; he neither summoned nor dismissed it; he neither collected the suffrages nor
pronounced the decision.[a]

It is a disputed point whether the meeting between St. Paul and St. Peter, of which we have an
account in the Galatians (ii. 1-10), took place at
this time. The great majority of critics believe
that it did, and this hypothesis, though not without difficulties, seems more probable than any other
which has been suggested.[b] The only point of real
importance was certainly determined before the
Apostles separated, the work of converting the Gentiles being henceforth specially intrusted to Paul
and Barnabas, while the charge of preaching to the
circumcision was assigned to the elder Apostles,
and more particularly to Peter (Gal. ii. 7-9). This
arrangement cannot, however, have been an exclusive one. St. Paul always addressed himself first
to the Jews in every city: Peter and his old colleagues undoubtedly admitted and sought to make
converts among the Gentiles It may have been
in full force only when the old and new Apostles
resided in the same city. Such at least was the
case at Antioch, where St. Peter went soon afterwards. There the painful collision took place between the two Apostles; the most remarkable, and,
in its bearings upon controversies at critical periods,
one of the most important events in the history of
the Church. St. Peter at first applied the principles which he had lately defended, carrying with
him the whole Apostolic body, and on his arrival
at Antioch ate with the Gentiles, thus showing
that he believed all ceremonial distinctions to be
abolished by the Gospel: in that he went far beyond the strict letter of the injunctions issued by
the Council.[c] That step was marked and condemned by certain members of the Church of Jerusalem sent by James. It appeared to them one
thing to recognize Gentiles as fellow-Christians,
another to admit them to social intercourse,
whereby ceremonial defilement would be contracted
under the law to which all the Apostles, Barnabas
and Paul included, acknowledged allegiance.[d] Peter, as the Apostle of the circumcision, fearing to
give offense to those who were his special charge,
at once gave up the point, suppressed or disguised
his feelings,[e] and separated himself not from communion, but from social intercourse with the Gentiles. St. Paul, as the Apostle of the Gentiles, saw
clearly the consequences likely to ensue, and could
ill brook the misapplication of a rule often laid
down in his own writings concerning compliance
with the prejudices of weak brethren. He held
that Peter was infringing a great principle, withstood him to the face, and using the same arguments which Peter had urged at the Council, pronounced his conduct to be indefensible. The statement that Peter compelled the Gentiles to Judaize,
probably means, not that he enjoined circumcision,
but that his conduct, if persevered in, would have
that effect, since they would naturally take any
steps which might remove the barriers to familiar
intercourse with the first Apostles of Christ. Pe-

---

a In accordance with this representation, St. Paul
names James before Cephas and John (Gal. ii. 9).

b Lange (Das Apostolische Zeitalter, ii. 878) fixes the
date about three years after the Council. Wieseler
has a long excursus to show that it must have occurred after St. Paul's second apostolic journey. He
gives some weighty reasons, but wholly fails in the attempt to account for the presence of Barnabas, a fatal
objection to his theory See Der Brief an die Gala-
ter, Excursus, p. 579. On the other side are Theodoret, Pearson, Eichhorn, Olshausen, Meyer, Neander,
Howson, Schaff, etc. [See note b, p. 2372. The history of Barnabas is too imperfectly known to render
the objection above of any decisive weight. — H.]

c This decisively overthrows the whole system of
Baur, which rests upon a supposed antagonism between St. Paul and the elder Apostles, especially St.
Peter. St. Paul grounds his reproof upon the inconsistency of Peter, not upon his Judaizing tendencies.

d See Acts xviii. 18-21, xx. 16, xxi. 18-24. passages
borne out by numerous statements in St. Paul's
epistles.

e Ὑπέστελλεν, συνυπεκρίθησαν. ὑπόκρισις, must be
understood in this sense. It was not hypocrisy in the
sense of an affectation of holiness, but in that of an
outward deference to prejudices which certainly neither Peter nor Barnabas any longer shared.

ter was wrong, but it was an error of judgment; an act contrary to his own feelings and wishes, in deference to those whom he looked upon as representing the mind of the Church; that he was actuated by selfishness, national pride, or any remains of superstition, is neither asserted nor implied in the strong censure of St. Paul: nor,·much as we must admire the earnestness and wisdom of St. Paul, whose clear and vigorous intellect was in this case stimulated by anxiety for his own special charge, the Gentile Church, should we overlook Peter's singular humility in submitting to public reproof from one so much his junior, or his magnanimity both in adopting St. Paul's conclusions (as we must infer that he did from the absence of all trace of continued resistance), and in remaining on terms of brotherly communion (as is testified by his own written words), to the end of his life (1 Pet. v. 10; 2 Pet. iii. 15, 16).

From this time until the date of his epistles, we have no distinct notices in Scripture of Peter's abode or work. The silence may be accounted for by the fact that from that time the great work of propagating the Gospel was committed to the marvelous energies of St. Paul. Peter was probably employed for the most part in building up and completing the organization of Christian communities in Palestine and the adjoining districts. There is, however, strong reason to believe that he visited Corinth at an early period; this seems to be implied in several passages of St. Paul's first epistle to that church,[a] and it is a natural inference from the statements of Clement of Rome (1 *Epistle to the Corinthians*, c. 4). The fact is positively asserted by Dionysius, Bishop of Corinth (A. D. 180 at the latest), a man of excellent judgment, who was not likely to be misinformed, nor to make such an assertion lightly in an epistle addressed to the Bishop and Church of Rome.[b] The reference to collision between parties who claimed Peter, Apollos, Paul, and even Christ for their chiefs, involves no opposition between the Apostles themselves, such as the fabulous Clementines and modern infidelity assume. The name of Peter as founder, or joint founder, is not associated with any local church save those of Corinth, Antioch,[c] or Rome, by early ecclesiastical tradition. That of Alexandria may have been established by St. Mark after Peter's death. That Peter preached the Gospel in the countries of Asia, mentioned in his first epistle, appears from Origen's own words[d] (κεκηρυκέναι ἔοικεν) to be a mere conjecture, not in itself improbable, but of little weight in the absence of all positive evidence, and of all personal reminiscences in the epistle itself. From that epistle,

however, it is to be inferred that towards the end of his life, St. Peter either visited, or resided for some time at Babylon, which at that time, and for some hundreds of years afterwards, was a chief seat of Jewish culture. This of course depends upon the assumption, which on the whole seems[e] most probable, that the word Babylon is not used as a mystic designation of Rome, but as a proper name, and that not of an obscure city in Egypt, but of the ancient capital of the East. There were many inducements for such a choice of abode. The Jewish families formed there a separate community,[f] they were rich, prosperous, and had established settlements in many districts of Asia Minor. Their language, probably a mixture of Hebrew and Nabatean, must have borne a near affinity to the Galilean dialect. They were on far more familiar terms than in other countries with their heathen neighbors, while their intercourse with Judæa was carried on without intermission. Christianity certainly made considerable progress at an early time in that and the adjoining districts, the great Christian schools at Edessa and Nisibis probably owed their origin to the influence of Peter, the general tone of the writers of that school is what is now commonly designated as Petrine. It is no unreasonable supposition that the establishment of Christianity in those districts may have been specially connected with the residence of Peter at Babylon. At that time there must have been some communications between the two great Apostles, Peter and Paul, thus stationed at the two extremities of the Christian world. St. Mark, who was certainly employed about that time by St. Paul, was with St. Peter when he wrote the epistle. Silvanus, St. Paul's chosen companion, was the bearer, probably the amanuensis of St. Peter's epistle: not improbably sent to Peter from Rome, and charged by him to deliver that epistle, written to support Paul's authority, to the churches founded by that Apostle on his return.

More important in its bearings upon later controversies is the question of St. Peter's connection with Rome.

It may be considered as a settled point that he did not visit Rome before the last year of his life. Too much stress may perhaps be laid on the fact that there is no notice of St. Peter's labors or presence in that city in the Epistle to the Romans; but that negative evidence is not counterbalanced by any statement of undoubted antiquity. The date given by Eusebius[g] rests upon a miscalculation, and is irreconcilable with the notices of St. Peter in the Acts of the Apostles. Protestant critics, with scarcely one exception,[h] are unanimous upon this point, and Roman controversialists are

a See Routh, *Rell. Sacræ*, i. 179.

b The attempt to set aside the evidence of Dionysius, on the ground that he makes an evident mistake in attributing the foundation of the Corinthian Church to Peter and Paul, is futile. If Peter took any part in organizing the Church, he would be spoken of as a joint founder. Schaff supposes that Peter may have first visited Corinth on his way to Rome towards the end of his life.

c It is to be observed that even St. Leo represents the relation of St. Peter to Antioch as precisely the same with that in which he stands to Rome (Ep. 92).

d Origen, ap. Euseb. iii. 1, adopted by Epiphanius *Hær*. xxvii.) and Jerome (*Catal.* c. 1).

e On the other hand, the all but unanimous opinion of ancient commentators that Rome is designated has been adopted, and maintained with great ingenu-

ity and some very strong arguments, by Schaff (*Geschichte der Christlichen Kirche*, p. 800), Neander, Steiger, De Wette, and Wieseler. Among ourselves, Pearson takes the name Babylon literally, though with some difference as to the place so named.

f For many interesting and valuable notices see Jost, *Geschichte des Judenthums*, i. 337, ii. 127.

g He gives A. D. 42 in the *Chronicon* (i. e. in the Armenian text), and says that Peter remained at Rome twenty years. In this he is followed by Jerome, *Catal.* c. 1 (who gives twenty-five years), and by most Roman Catholic writers.

h Thiersch is the only exception. He belongs to the Irvingite sect, which can scarcely be called Protestant. See *Versuch*, p. 104. His ingenious arguments are answered by Lange, *Das apostolische Zeitalter*, p. 381, and by Schaff, *Kirchengeschichte*, p. 806.

far from being agreed in their attempts [a] to remove the difficulty.

The fact, however, of St. Peter's martyrdom at Rome rests upon very different grounds. The evidence for it is complete, while there is a total absence of any contrary statement in the writings of the early Fathers. We have in the first place the certainty of his martyrdom, in our Lord's own prediction (John xxi. 18, 19). Clement of Rome, writing before the end of the first century, speaks of it,[b] but does not mention the place, that being of course well known to his readers. Ignatius, in the undoubtedly genuine Epistle to the Romans (ch. iv.), speaks of St. Peter in terms which imply a special connection with their church. Other early notices of less weight coincide with this, as that of Papias (Euseb. ii. 15), and the apocryphal Praedicatio Petri, quoted by Cyprian. In the second century, Dionysius of Corinth, in the Epistle to Soter, Bishop of Rome (ap. Euseb. H. E. ii. 25), states, as a fact universally known, and accounting for the intimate relations between Corinth and Rome, that Peter and Paul both taught in Italy, and suffered martyrdom about the same time.[c] Irenaeus, who was connected with St. John, being a disciple of Polycarp, a hearer of that Apostle, and thoroughly conversant with Roman matters, bears distinct witness to St. Peter's presence at Rome (Adv. Haer. iii. 1 and 3). It is incredible that he should have been misinformed. In the next century there is the testimony of Caius, the liberal and learned Roman presbyter (who speaks of St. Peter's tomb in the Vatican), that of Origen, Tertullian, and of the ante and post-Nicene Fathers, without a single exception. In short, the churches most nearly connected with Rome, and those least affected by its influence, which was as yet but inconsiderable in the East, concur in the statement that Peter was a joint founder of that church, and suffered death in that city. What the early Fathers do not assert, and indeed implicitly deny, is that Peter was the sole founder or resident head of that Church, or that the See of Rome derived from him any claim to supremacy: at the utmost they place him on a footing of equality with St. Paul.[d] That fact is sufficient for all purposes of fair controversy. The denial of the statements resting on such evidence seems almost to indicate an uneasy consciousness, truly remarkable in those who believe that they have, and who in fact really have, irrefragable grounds for rejecting the pretensions of the Papacy.

The time and manner of the Apostle's martyrdom are less certain. The early writers imply, or distinctly state, that he suffered at, or about the same time (Dionysius, κατὰ τὸν αὐτὸν καιρόν) with St. Paul, and in the Neronian persecution. All agree that he was crucified, a point sufficiently determined by our Lord's prophecy. Origen (ap. Eus. iii. 1), who could easily ascertain the fact, and though fanciful in speculation, is not inaccurate in historical matters, says that at his own request he was crucified with his head downwards. This statement was generally received by Christian antiquity: nor does it seem inconsistent with the fervent temperament and deep humility of the Apostle to have chosen such a death: one, moreover, not unlikely to have been inflicted in mockery by the instruments of Nero's wanton and ingenious cruelty.

The legend found in St. Ambrose is interesting, and may have some foundation in fact. When the persecution began, the Christians at Rome, anxious to preserve their great teacher, persuaded him to flee, a course which they had Scriptural warrant to recommend, and he to follow; but at the gate he met our Lord. "Lord, whither goest thou?" asked the Apostle. "I go to Rome," was the answer, "there once more to be crucified." St. Peter well understood the meaning of those words, returned at once and was crucified.[e]

Thus closes the Apostle's life. Some additional facts, not perhaps unimportant, may be accepted on early testimony. From St. Paul's words it may be inferred with certainty that he did not give up the ties of family life when he forsook his temporal calling. His wife accompanied him in his wanderings. Clement of Alexandria, a writer well informed in matters of ecclesiastical interest, and thoroughly trustworthy, says (Strom. iii. p. 448) that "Peter and Philip had children, and that both took about their wives, who acted as their coadjutors in ministering to women at their own homes; by their means the doctrine of the Lord penetrated without scandal into the privacy of women's apartments." Peter's wife is believed, on the same authority, to have suffered martyrdom, and to have been supported in the hour of trial by her husband's exhortation. Some critics believe that she is referred to in the salutation at the end of the First Epistle of St. Peter. The Apostle is said to have employed interpreters. Basilides, an early Gnostic, professed to derive his system from Glaucias, one of these interpreters. This shows at least the impression, that the Apostle did not understand Greek, or did not speak it with fluency. Of far more importance is the statement that St. Mark wrote his Gospel under the teaching of Peter, or that he embodied in that Gospel the substance of our Apostle's oral instructions. This statement

[a] The most ingenious attempt is that of Windischmann, Vindiciae Petrinae, p. 112 f. He assumes that Peter went to Rome immediately after his deliverance from prison (Acts xii.), i. e. A. D. 44, and left in consequence of the Claudian persecution between A. D. 49 and 51.

[b] Μαρτυρήσας ἐπορεύθη εἰς τὸν ὀφειλόμενον τόπον τῆς δόξης (1 Cor v.). The first word might simply mean "bore public witness;" but the last are conclusive.

[c] One of the most striking instances of the hypercritical skepticism of the Tübingen school is Baur's attempt to prove that this distinct and positive statement was a mere inference from the epistle of Clement. The intercourse between the two churches was unbroken from the Apostles' times.

[d] Coteiler has collected a large number of passages from the early Fathers, in which the name of Paul precedes that of Peter (Pat. Apost. i. 414: see also Valesius, Eus. H. E. iii. 21). Fabricius observes that this is the general usage of the Greek Fathers. It is also to be remarked that when the Fathers of the 4th and 5th centuries — for instance, Chrysostom and Augustine — use the words ὁ Ἀπόστολος, or Apostolus, they mean Paul, not Peter. A very weighty fact.

[e] See Tillemont, Mém. i. p. 187, and 555. He shows that the account of Ambrose (which is not to be found in the Bened. edit.) is contrary to the apocryphal legend. Later writers rather value it as reflecting upon St. Peter's want of courage or constancy. That St. Peter, like all good men, valued his life, and suffered reluctantly, may be inferred from our Lord's words (John xxi.); but his flight is more in harmony with the principles of a Christian than willful exposure to persecution. Origen refers to the words then said to have been spoken by our Lord, but quotes an apocryphal work (On St. John, tom. ii.).

vets upon such an amount of external evidence,[a] and is corroborated by so many internal indications, that they would scarcely be questioned in the absence of a strong theological bias. The fact is doubly important in its bearings upon the Gospel, and upon the character of our Apostle. Chrysostom, who is followed by the most judicious commentators, seems first to have drawn attention to the fact, that in St. Mark's Gospel every defect in Peter's character and conduct is brought out clearly, without the slightest extenuation, while many noble acts and peculiar marks of favor are either omitted, or stated with far less force than by any other Evangelist. Indications of St. Peter's influence, even in St. Mark's style, much less pure than that of St. Luke, are traced by modern criticism:[b]

The only written documents which St. Peter has left, are the First Epistle, about which no doubt has ever been entertained in the Church; and the Second, which has both in early times, and in our own, been a subject of earnest controversy.

FIRST EPISTLE. — The external evidence of authenticity is of the strongest kind. Referred to in the Second Epistle (iii. 1); known to Polycarp, and frequently alluded to in his Epistle to the Philippians; recognized by Papias (ap. Euseb. *H. E.* iii. 39); repeatedly quoted by Irenæus, Clemens of Alexandria, Tertullian, and Origen; it was accepted without hesitation by the universal Church.[c] The internal evidence is equally strong. Schwegler the most reckless, and De Wette the most vacillating of modern critics, stand almost alone in their denial of its authenticity.

It was addressed to the churches of Asia Minor, which had for the most part been founded by St. Paul and his companions. Supposing it to have been written at Babylon (see above), it is a probable conjecture that Silvanus, by whom it was transmitted to those churches, had joined St. Peter after a tour of visitation, either in pursuance of instructions from St. Paul, then a prisoner at Rome, or in the capacity of a minister of high authority in the Church, and that his account of the condition of the Christians in those districts determined the Apostle to write the epistle. From the absence of personal salutations, and other indications, it may perhaps be inferred that St. Peter had not hitherto visited the churches; but it is certain that he was thoroughly acquainted both with their external circumstances and spiritual state. It is clear that Silvanus is not regarded by St. Peter as one of his own coadjutors, but as one whose personal character he had sufficient opportunity of appreciating (v. 12). Such a testimonial

as the Apostle gives to the soundness of his faith, would of course have the greatest weight with th Hebrew Christians, to whom the epistle appears to have been specially, though not exclusively addressed.[d] The assumption that Silvanus was employed in the composition of the epistle is not borne out by the expression, " by Silvanus, I have written unto you," such words according to ancient usage applying rather to the bearer than to the writer or amanuensis. Still it is highly probable that Silvanus, considering his rank, character, and special connection with those churches, and with their great Apostle and founder, would be consulted by St. Peter throughout, and that they would together read the epistles of St. Paul, especially those addressed to the churches in those districts: thus, partly with direct intention, partly it may be unconsciously, a Pauline coloring, amounting in passages to something like a studied imitation of St. Paul's representations of Christian truth, may have been introduced into the epistle. It has been observed above that there is good reason to suppose that St. Peter was in the habit of employing an interpreter; nor is there anything inconsistent with his position or character in the supposition that Silvanus, perhaps also St. Mark, may have assisted him in giving expression to the thoughts suggested to him by the Holy Spirit. We have thus at any rate, a not unsatisfactory solution of the difficulty arising from correspondences both of style and modes of thought in the writings of two Apostles who differed so widely in gifts and acquirements.[e]

The objects of the epistle, as deduced from its contents, coincide with these assumptions. They were: 1. To comfort and strengthen the Christians in a season of severe trial. 2. To enforce the practical and spiritual duties involved in their calling. 3. To warn them against special temptations attached to their position. 4. To remove all doubt as to the soundness and completeness of the religious system which they had already received. Such an attestation was especially needed by the Hebrew Christians, who were wont to appeal from St. Paul's authority to that of the elder Apostles, and above all to that of Peter. The last, which is perhaps the very principal object, is kept in view throughout the epistle, and is distinctly stated, ch. v. ver. 12.

These objects may come out more clearly in a brief analysis.

The epistle begins with salutations and general description of Christians (i. 1, 2), followed by a statement of their present privileges and future inheritance (3–5); the bearings of that statement upon their conduct under persecution (6–9); reference, according to the Apostle's wont, to proph-

---

a Papias and Clem. Alex., referred to by Eusebius, *H. E.* ii. 15; Tertullian, *c. Marc.* iv. c. 5; Irenæus, iii. 1, and iv. 9. Petavius (on Epiphanius, p. 428) observes that Papias derived his information from John the Presbyter. For other passages see Fabricius (*Bibl. Gr.* tom. iii. 182). The slight discrepancy between Eusebius and Papias indicates independent sources of information.

b Giessler, quoted by Davidson.

c No importance can be attached to the omission n the mutilated fragment on the Canon, published by Muratori. See Routh, *Rell. Sac.* i. 396, and the note of Freindaller, which Routh quotes, p. 424. Theodorus of Mopsuestia, a shrewd but rash critic, is said to have rejected all, or some, of the Catholic epistles; but the statement is ambiguous. See Davidson (*Int.* iii. 391), whose translation is incorrect.

d This is the general opinion of the ablest commentators. The ancients were nearly unanimous in holding that it was written for Hebrew converts. But several passages are evidently meant for Gentiles: *e. g.* i. 14, 18; ii. 9, 10; iii. 6; iv. 3. Reuss an original and able writer, is almost alone in the opinion that it was addressed chiefly to Gentile converts (p. 133). He takes πάροικοι and παρεπίδημοι as = גֵּ֣ר‎, Israelites by faith, not by ceremonial observance (*nicht nach dem Cultus*). See also Weiss, *Der petrinische Lehrbegriff*, p. 28, n. 2

e The question has been thoroughly discussed by Hug, Ewald, Bertholdt, Weiss, and other critics. The most striking resemblances are perhaps 1 Pet. i. 3, with Eph. i. 3; ii. 18, with Eph. vi. 5; iii. 1, with Eph. v. 22; and v. 5, with v. 21: but allusions nearly as distinct are found to the Romans, Corinthians, Colossians, Thessalonians, and Philemon.

ecies concerning both the sufferings of Christ and the salvation of his people (10–12); exhortations based upon those promises to earnestness, sobriety, hope, obedience, and holiness, as results of knowledge of redemption, of atonement by the blood of Jesus, and of the resurrection, and as proofs of spiritual regeneration by the word of God. Peculiar stress is laid upon the cardinal graces of faith, hope, and brotherly love, each connected with and resting upon the fundamental doctrines of the Gospel (13–25). Abstinence from the spiritual sins most directly opposed to those graces is then enforced (ii. 1); spiritual growth is represented as dependent upon the nourishment supplied by the same Word which was the instrument of regeneration (2, 3); and then, by a change of metaphor, Christians are represented as a spiritual house, collectively and individually as living stones, and royal priests elect, and brought out of darkness into light (4–10). This portion of the epistle is singularly rich in thought and expression, and bears the peculiar impress of the Apostle's mind, in which Judaism is spiritualized, and finds its full development in Christ. From this condition of Christians, and more directly from the fact that they are thus separated from the world, pilgrims and sojourners, St. Peter deduces an entire system of practical and relative duties, self-control, care of reputation, especially for the sake of Gentiles; submission to all constituted authorities; obligations of slaves, urged with remarkable earnestness, and founded upon the example of Christ and his atoning death (11–25); and duties of wives and husbands (iii. 1–7). Then generally all Christian graces are commended, those which pertain to Christian brotherhood, and those which are especially needed in times of persecution, gentleness, forbearance, and submission to injury (8–17): all the precepts being based on imitation of Christ, with warnings from the history of the deluge, and with special reference to the baptismal covenant.

In the following chapter (iv. 1, 2) the analogy between the death of Christ and spiritual mortification, a topic much dwelt on by St. Paul, is urged with special reference to the sins committed by Christians before conversion, and habitual to the Gentiles. The doctrine of a future judgment is inculcated, both with reference to their heathen persecutors as a motive for endurance, and to their own conduct as an incentive to sobriety, watchfulness, fervent charity, liberality in all external acts of kindness, and diligent discharge of all spiritual duties, with a view to the glory of God through Jesus Christ (3–11).

This epistle appears at the first draught to have terminated here with the doxology, but the thought of the fiery trial to which the Christians were exposed stirs the Apostle's heart, and suggests additional exhortations. Christians are taught to rejoice in partaking of Christ's sufferings, being thereby assured of sharing his glory, which even in this life rests upon them, and is especially manifested in their innocence and endurance of persecution: judgment must come first to cleanse the house of God, then to reach the disobedient: suffering according to the will of God, they may commit their souls to Him in well doing as unto a faithful Creator. Faith and hope are equally conspicuous in these exhortations. The Apostle then (v. 1–4) addresses the presbyters of the churches, warning them as one of their own body, as a witness (μάρτυς) of Christ's sufferings, and partaker of future glory, against negligence, covetousness, and love of power: the younger members he exhorts to submission and humility, and concludes this part with a warning against their spiritual enemy, and a solemn and most beautiful prayer to the God of all grace. Lastly, he mentions Silvanus with special commendation, and states very distinctly what we have seen reason to believe was a principal object of the epistle, namely, that the principles inculcated by their former teachers were sound, the true grace of God, to which they are exhorted to adhere.[a] A salutation from the church in Babylon and from St. Mark, with a parting benediction, closes the epistle.

The harmony of such teaching with that of St. Paul is sufficiently obvious, nor is the general arrangement or mode of discussing the topics unlike that of the Apostle of the Gentiles; still the indications of originality and independence of thought are at least equally conspicuous, and the epistle is full of what the Gospel narrative and the discourses in the Acts prove to have been characteristic peculiarities of St. Peter. He dwells more frequently than St. Paul upon the future manifestation of Christ, upon which he bases nearly all his exhortations to patience, self-control, and the discharge of all Christian duties. There is not a shadow of opposition here, the topic is not neglected by St. Paul, nor does St. Peter omit the Pauline argument from Christ's sufferings; still what the Germans call the eschatological element predominates over all others. The Apostle's mind is full of one thought, the realization of Messianic hopes. While St. Paul dwells with most earnestness upon justification by our Lord's death and merits, and concentrates his energies upon the Christian's present struggles, St. Peter fixes his eyes constantly upon the future coming of Christ, the fulfillment of prophecy, the manifestation of the promised kingdom. In this he is the true representative of Israel, moved by those feelings which were best calculated to enable him to do his work as the Apostle of the circumcision. Of the three Christian graces hope is his special theme. He dwells much on good works, but not so much because he sees in them necessary results of faith, or the complement of faith, or outward manifestations of the spirit of love, aspects most prominent in St. Paul, St. James, and St. John, as because he holds them to be tests of the soundness and stability of a faith which rests on the fact of the resurrection, and is directed to the future in the developed form of hope.

But while St. Peter thus shows himself a genuine Israelite, his teaching is directly opposed to Judaizing tendencies. He belongs to the school, or, to speak more correctly, is the leader of the school, which at once vindicates the unity of the Law and the Gospel, and puts the superiority of the latter on its true basis, that of spiritual development. All his practical injunctions are drawn from Christian, not Jewish principles, from the precepts, example, life, death, resurrection, and future coming of Christ. The Apostle of the Circumcision says not a word in this epistle of the perpetual obligation, the dignity, or even the bearings of the Mosaic Law. He is full of the Old Testament; his style and thoughts are charged with its imagery, but he contemplates and applies its teaching in the light of the Gospel; he regards the privileges and glory of the ancient people of God entirely in their spiritual

a The reading ἐστήτε is in all points preferable to that of the textus receptus, ἑστήκατε.

development in the Church of Christ. Only one who had been brought up as a Jew could have had his spirit so impregnated with these thoughts; only one who had been thoroughly emancipated by the Spirit of Christ could have risen so completely above the prejudices of his age and country. This is a point of great importance, showing how utterly opposed the teaching of the original Apostles, whom St. Peter certainly represents, was to that Judaistic narrowness which speculative rationalism has imputed to all the early followers of Christ, with the exception of St. Paul. There are in fact more traces of what are called Judaizing views, more of sympathy with national hopes, not to say prejudices, in the epistles to the Romans and Galatians, than in this work. In this we see the Jew who has been born again, and exchanged what St. Peter himself calls the unbearable yoke of the Law for the liberty which is in Christ. At the same time it must be admitted that our Apostle is far from tracing his principles to their origin, and from drawing out their consequences with the vigor, spiritual discernment, internal sequence of reasoning, and systematic completeness which are characteristic of St. Paul.[a] A few great facts, broad solid principles on which faith and hope may rest securely, with a spirit of patience, confidence, and love, suffice for his unspeculative mind. To him objective truth was the main thing; subjective struggles between the intellect and spiritual consciousness, such as we find in St. Paul, and the intuitions of a spirit absorbed in contemplation like that of St. John, though not by any means alien to St. Peter, were in him wholly subordinated to the practical tendencies of a simple and energetic character. It has been observed with truth, that both in tone and in form the teaching of St. Peter bears a peculiarly strong resemblance to that of our Lord, in discourses bearing directly upon practical duties. The great value of the epistle to believers consists in this resemblance; they feel themselves in the hands of a safe guide, of one who will help them to trace the hand of their Master in both dispensations, and to confirm and expand their faith.

SECOND EPISTLE. — The Second Epistle of St. Peter presents questions of far greater difficulty than the former. There can be no doubt that, whether we consider the external or the internal evidence, it is by no means easy to demonstrate its genuineness. We have few references, and none of a very positive character, in the writings of the early Fathers; the style differs materially from that of the First Epistle, and the resemblance, amounting to a studied imitation, between this epistle and that of St. Jude, seems scarcely reconcilable with the position of St. Peter. Doubts as to its genuineness were entertained by the greatest critics of the early Church; in the time of Eusebius it was reckoned among the disputed books, and was not formally admitted into the Canon until the year 393, at the Council of Hippo. The opinion of critics of what is called the liberal school, including all shades from Lücke to Baur, has been decidedly

unfavorable, and that opinion has been adopted by some able writers in England. There are, however, very strong reasons why this verdict should be reconsidered. No one ground on which it rests is unassailable. The rejection of this book affects the authority of the whole Canon, which, in the opinion of one of the keenest and least scrupulous critics (Reuss, of modern Germany, is free from any other error. It is not a question as to the possible authorship of a work like that of the Hebrews, which does not bear the writer's name: this epistle must either be dismissed as a deliberate forgery, or accepted as the last production of the first among the Apostles of Christ. The Church, which for more than fourteen centuries has received it, has either been imposed upon by what must in that case be regarded as a Satanic device, or derived from it spiritual instruction of the highest importance. If received, it bears attestation to some of the most important facts in our Lord's history, casts light upon the feelings of the Apostolic body in relation to the elder church and to each other, and, while it confirms many doctrines generally inculcated, is the chief, if not the only, voucher for eschatological views touching the destruction of the framework of creation, which from an early period have been prevalent in the Church.

The contents of the epistle seem quite in accordance with its asserted origin.

The customary opening salutation is followed by an enumeration of Christian blessings and exhortation to Christian duties, with special reference to the maintenance of the truth which had been already communicated to the Church (i. 1–13). Referring then to his approaching death, the Apostle assigns as grounds of assurance for believers his own personal testimony as eye-witness of the transfiguration, and the sure word of prophecy, that is the testimony of the Holy Ghost (14–21). The danger of being misled by false prophets is dwelt upon with great earnestness throughout the second chapter, their covetousness and gross sensuality combined with pretences to spiritualism, in short all the permanent and fundamental characteristics of Antinomianism, are described, while the overthrow of all opponents of Christian truth is predicted (ii. 1–29) in connection with prophecies touching the second advent of Christ, the destruction of the world by fire, and the promise of new heavens and a new earth wherein dwelleth righteousness. After an exhortation to attend to St. Paul's teaching, in accordance with the less explicit admonition in the previous epistle and an emphatic warning, the epistle closes with the customary ascription of glory to our Lord and Saviour Jesus Christ.

We may now state briefly the answers to the objections above stated.

1. With regard to its recognition by the early church, we observe that it was not likely to be quoted frequently; it was addressed to a portion of the church not at that time much in intercourse with the rest of Christendom: [b] the documents of the primitive church are far too scanty to give weight to the argument (generally a questionable

a Thus Reuss, *Pierre n'a pas de système*. See also Brückner and Weiss, pp. 14, 17.

[b] Ritschl's observations on the Epistle of St. James are at least equally applicable to this. It would be, comparatively speaking, little known to Gentile converts, while the Jewish party gradually died out, and was not at any time mixed up with the general move-

ment of the church. The only literary documents of the Hebrew Christians were written by Ebionites, to whom this epistle would be most distasteful. Had the book not been supported by *strong external credentials*, its general reception or circulation seem unaccountable.

one) from omission. Although it cannot be proved to have been referred to by any author earlier than Origen, yet passages from Clement of Rome, Hermas, Justin Martyr, Theophilus of Antioch, and Irenæus, suggest an acquaintance with this epistle:[a] to these may be added a probable reference in the Martyrdom of Ignatius, quoted by Westcott (*On the Canon*, p. 87), and another in the Apology of Melito, published in Syriac by Dr. Cureton. It is also distinctly stated by Eusebius, *H. E.* vi. 14, and by Photius, cod. 109, that Clement of Alexandria wrote a commentary on all the disputed epistles, in which this was certainly included. It is quoted twice by Origen, but unfortunately in the translation of Ruffinus, which cannot be relied upon. Didymus refers to it very frequently in his great work on the Trinity. It was certainly included in the collection of Catholic Epistles known to Eusebius and Origen, a very important point made out by Olshausen (*Opuscula Theol.* p. 29). It was probably known in the third century in different parts of the Christian world: in Cappadocia to Firmilian, in Africa to Cyprian, in Italy to Hippolytus, in Phœnicia to Methodius. A large number of passages has been collected by Dietlein, which, though quite insufficient to prove its reception, add somewhat to the probability that it was read by most of the early Fathers. The historical evidence is certainly inconclusive, but not such as to require or to warrant the rejection of the epistle. The silence of the Fathers is accounted for more easily than its admission into the Canon after the question as to its genuineness had been raised. It is not conceivable that it should have been received without positive attestation from the churches to which it was first addressed. We know that the autographs of Apostolic writings were preserved with care. It must also be observed that all motive for forgery is absent. This epistle does not support any hierarchical pretensions, nor does it bear upon any controversies of a later age.

2. The difference of style may be admitted. The only question is, whether it is greater than can be satisfactorily accounted for, supposing that the Apostle employed a different person as his amanuensis. That the two epistles could not have been composed and written by the same person is a point scarcely open to doubt. Olshausen, one of the fairest and least prejudiced of critics, points out eight discrepancies of style, some perhaps unimportant, but others almost conclusive, the most important being the appellations given to our Saviour, and the comparative absence of references to the Old Testament in this epistle. If, however, we admit that some time intervened between the composition of the two works, that in writing the first the Apostle was aided by Silvanus, and in the second by another, perhaps St. Mark, that the circumstances of the churches addressed by him were considerably changed, and that the second was written in greater haste, not to speak of a possible

decay of faculties, the differences may be regarded as insufficient to justify more than hesitation in admitting its genuineness. The resemblance to the Epistle of St. Jude may be admitted without affecting our judgment unfavorably. Supposing, as some eminent critics have believed, that this epistle was copied by St. Jude, we should have the strongest possible testimony to its authenticity;[b] but if, on the other hand, we accept the more general opinion of modern critics, that the writer of this epistle copied St. Jude, the following considerations have great weight. It seems quite incredible that a forger, personating the chief among the Apostles, should select the least important of all the Apostolical writings for imitation; whereas it is probable that St. Peter might choose to give the stamp of his personal authority to a document bearing so powerfully upon practical and doctrinal errors in the churches which he addressed. Considering, too, the characteristics of our Apostle, his humility, his impressionable mind, so open to personal influences, and his utter forgetfulness of self when doing his Master's work, we should hardly be surprised to find that part of the epistle which treats of the same subjects colored by St. Jude's style. Thus in the First Epistle we find everywhere, especially in dealing with kindred topics, distinct traces of St. Paul's influence. This hypothesis has moreover the advantage of accounting for the most striking, if not all the discrepancies of style between the two epistles.

3. The doubts as to its genuineness appear to have originated with the critics of Alexandria, where, however, the epistle itself was formally recognized at a very early period. Those doubts, however, were not quite so strong as they are now generally represented. The three greatest names of that school may be quoted on either side. On the one hand there were evidently external credentials, without which it could never have obtained circulation; on the other, strong subjective impressions, to which these critics attached scarcely less weight than some modern inquirers. They rested entirely, so far as can be ascertained, on the difference of style. The opinions of modern commentators may be summed up under three heads. Many, as we have seen, reject the epistle altogether as spurious, supposing it to have been directed against forms of Gnosticism prevalent in the early part of the second century. A few[c] consider that the first and last chapters were written by St. Peter or under his dictation, but that the second chapter was interpolated. So far, however, is either of these views from representing the general results of the latest investigations, that a majority of names,[d] including nearly all the writers of Germany opposed to Rationalism, who in point of learning and ability are at least upon a par with their opponents, may be quoted in support of the genuineness and authenticity of this epistle. The statement that all critics of eminence and impar-

[a] The passages are quoted by Guerike, *Einleitung*, p. 482.

[b] See Dr. Wordsworth's Commentary on 2 Peter. His chief ground is that St. Peter predicts a state of affairs which St. Jude describes as actually existing. A very strong ground, admitting the authenticity of both epistles.

[c] E. g. Bunsen, Ullmann, and Lange.

[e] This account is not accurate. Bunsen regards as genuine only 2 Pet. i. 1–11, with the doxology at the end of the epistle. He supposes this very short letter

to be really the *first* Epistle of Peter, and to be referred to in 1 Pet. v 12 (*Bibelwerk*, viii. 531–534; *Hippolytus and his Age*, 2d ed., i. 24 f.). Ullmann considers only the first chapter genuine (*Der 2e Brief Petri kritisch untersucht*, Heidelb. 1821). Lange supposes the interpolation to extend from 2 Pet. i. 20 to iii. 2, inclusive (art. *Petrus, der Apostel*, in Herzog's *Real-Encykl.* xi. 487).

[d] Nitzsche, Flatt, Dahlman [Huhl?], Windischmann, Heydenreich, Guerike, Pott, Augusti, Olshausen, Thiersch, Stier, and Dietlein.

A.

tiality concur in rejecting it is simply untrue, unless it be admitted that a belief in the reality of objective revelation is incompatible with critical impartiality, that belief being the only common point between the numerous defenders of the canonicity of this document. If it were a question now to be decided for the first time upon the external or internal evidences still accessible, it may be admitted that it would be far more difficult to maintain this than any other document in the New Testament; but the judgment of the early church is not to be reversed without far stronger arguments than have been adduced, more especially as the epistle is entirely free from objections which might be brought, with more show of reason, against others now all but universally received: inculcating no new doctrine, bearing on no controversies of post-apostolical origin, supporting no hierarchical innovations, but simple, earnest, devout, and eminently practical, full of the characteristic graces of the Apostle, who, as we believe, bequeathed this last proof of faith and hope to the Church.

Some Apocryphal writings of very early date obtained currency in the Church as containing the substance of the Apostle's teaching. The fragments which remain are not of much importance, nor could they be conveniently discussed in this notice. The preaching (κήρυγμα) or doctrine (διδαχή) of Peter,[a] probably identical with a work called the Preaching of Paul, or of Paul and Peter, quoted by Lactantius, may have contained some traces of the Apostle's teaching, if, as Grabe, Ziegler, and others supposed, it was published soon after his death. The passages, however, quoted by Clement of Alexandria are for the most part wholly unlike St. Peter's mode of treating doctrinal or practical subjects.[b] Another work, called the Revelation of Peter (ἀποκάλυψις Πέτρου), was held in much esteem for centuries. It was commented on by Clement of Alexandria, quoted by Theodotus in the Eclogæ, named together with the Revelation of St. John in the Fragment on the Canon published by Muratori (but with the remark, "quam quidam ex nostris legi in Ecclesia nolunt "), and according to Sozomen (E. H. vii. 19) was read once a year in some churches of Palestine. It is said, but not on good authority, to have been preserved among the Coptic Christians. Eusebius looked on it as spurious, but not of heretic origin. From the fragments and notices it appears to have consisted chiefly of denunciations against the Jews, and predictions of the fall of Jerusalem, and to have been of a wild fanatical character. The most complete account of this curious work is given by Lücke in his general introduction to the Revelation of St. John, p. 47.

The legends of the Clementines are wholly devoid of historical worth; but from those fictions originating with an obscure and heretical sect, have been derived some of the most mischievous speculations of modern rationalists, especially as regards

the assumed antagonism between St. Paul and the earlier Apostles. It is important to observe, however, that in none of these spurious documents, which belong undoubtedly to the two first centuries, are there any indications that our Apostle was regarded as in any peculiar sense connected with the church or see of Rome, or that he exercised or claimed any authority over the apostolic body, of which he was the recognized leader or representative.   F. C. C.

[CEPHAS (Κηφᾶς) occurs in the following passages: John i. 42; 1 Cor. i. 12, iii. 22, ix. 5, xv. 5; Gal. ii. 9, i. 18, ii. 11, 14 (the last three according to the text of Lachmann and Tischendorf).

Cephas is the Chaldee word Cepha, כֵּיפָא, itself a corruption of, or derivation from, the Hebrew Ceph, כֵּף, "a rock," a rare word, found only in Job xxx. 6, and Jer. iv. 29. It must have been the word actually pronounced by our Lord in Matt. xvi. 18, and on subsequent occasions when the Apostle was addressed by Him or other Hebrews by his new name. By it he was known to the Corinthian Christians. In the ancient Syriac version of the N. T. (Peshito), it is uniformly found where the Greek has Petros. When we consider that our Lord and the Apostles spoke Chaldee, and that therefore (as already remarked) the Apostle must have been always addressed as Cephas, it is certainly remarkable that throughout the Gospels, no less than 97 times, with one exception only, the name should be given in the Greek form, which was of later introduction, and unintelligible to Hebrews, though intelligible to the far wider Gentile world among which the Gospel was about to begin its course. Even in St. Mark, where more Chaldee words and phrases are retained than in all the other Gospels put together, this is the case. It is as if in our English Bibles the name were uniformly given, not Peter, but Rock; and it suggests that the meaning contained in the appellation is of more vital importance, and intended to be more carefully seized at each recurrence, than we are apt to recollect. The commencement of the change from the Chaldee name to its Greek synonym is well marked in the interchange of the two in Gal. ii. 7, 8, 9 (Stanley, Apostolic Age, pp 116, 117).]

* Literature. — On the much debated question of St. Peter's residence in Rome, it may be sufficient to name the work of Ellendorf, Ist Petrus in Rom u. Bischof d. röm. Kirche gewesen? Darmstadt, 1841, trans. in the Bibl. Sacra for July, 1858, and Jan. 1859; and, on the other side, Das alte Gespenst . . . neu aufgeführt von J. Ellendorf . . . beschworen durch einen römischen Exorcisten [A. J. Binterim], Düsseldorf, 1842. On this question, and on the life of Peter in general, one may also consult Schaff's Hist. of the Apostolic Church (N. Y. 1854), pp. 348-374

a The two names are believed by critics — i, e. Cave, Grabe, Ittig, Mill, etc. — to belong to the same work. (See Schliemann, Die Clementinen, p. 253.)

b Ruffinus and Jerome allude to a work which they call "judicium Petri:" for which Cave (Grabe) accounts by a happy conjecture, adopted by Nitzsche, Mayerhoff, Reuss, and Schliemann, that Ruffinus found ερμα for κήρυγμα, and read κρίμα.

c Hilgenfeld supposes that the book referred to by Ruffinus as "Duæ Viæ vel Judicium Petri" is iden-

tical with one which has been repeatedly published (e. g. by Bickell in his Gesch. des Kirchenrechts, Giessen, 1843) as Αἱ διαταγαὶ αἱ Κλήμεντος καὶ κανόνες ἐκκλησιαστικοὶ τῶν ἁγίων ἀποστόλων, and has edited it as such in his Nov. Test. extra Canonem receptum, Fasc. iv. (Lips. 1866), pp. 93-106. This document has much in common with Book vii. co. 1-20 of the Apostolical Constitutions and the last 4 chapters of the epistle ascribed to Barnabas.   A.

For the literature of the subject, see Gieseler's *Eccl. Hist.* vol. i. § 27, and Winer's *Realwörterb.* art. *Petrus*.

On the critical questions concerning the epistles of Peter, the following works may be mentioned, in addition to the various Introductions to the New Test. (De Wette, Credner, Reuss, Bleek, Davidson, Guericke, etc.), works on the history of the Apostolic and post-Apostolic Church (Neander, Baur. Schwegler, Thiersch, Lange, Schaff, etc.), and the Commentaries: E. T. Mayerhoff, *Hist. crit. Einleitung in die petrinischen Schriften*, Hamb. 1835. F. Windischmann (Cath.), *Vindiciæ Petrinæ*, Ratisb. 1836. Arts. in the *Theol. Stud. u. Krit.* by Seyler (1832, pp. 44–70) and Bleek (1836, pp. 1021–1072). Baur, *Der erste petrinische Brief*, in the *Theol. Jahrb.* 1856, pp. 193–240. "J. Q." *On the Epistles of Peter*, two elaborate arts. in Kitto's *Journal of Sacred Literature* for Jan. and July, 1861, the latter relating to the 2d Epistle, and the apocryphal writings ascribed to Peter. B. Weiss, *Die petrinische Frage*, in the *Theol. Stud. u. Krit.* for 1865, pp. 619–657 (1st Epist.), and 1866, pp. 255–308 (2d Epist.). E. R. Rauch, *Rettung der Originalität des ersten Briefes des Ap. Petrus*, in Winer's *Neues krit. Journ. d. theol. Lit.* (1828), viii. 385–442. E. Lecoultre, *Sur la prem. ép. de Pierre*, Gen. 1839.

On the Second Epistle of Peter in particular, see F. A. L. Nietzsche, *Ep. Petri posterior Auctori suo vindicata*, Lips. 1785. C. C. Flatt, *Genuina secundæ Ep. Petri origo denuo defenditur*, Tub. 1806. J. C. W. Dahl, *De αὐθεντίᾳ Ep. Petr. posterioris atque Judæ*, Rost. 1807, 4to. (*Pro.*) E. A. Richter, *De Origine poster. Ep. Petri ex Ep. Judæ repetenda*, Vit. 1810, 4to. Ullmann, see note *b*, p. 2459. H. Olshausen, *De Integ. et Authent. posterioris Petri Epist.*, Regiom. 1822–23, 4to, reprinted in his *Opusc. Acad.*, and translated, with an introduction, by B. B. Edwards, in the *Bibl. Repository* for July and Oct. 1836 (vol. viii.). E. Moutier, *La 2e ép. de P. et celle de Jude sont authentiques*, Strasb. 1829. P. E. Picot, *Recherches sur la 2e ép. de Pierre*, Gen. 1829. (*Pro.*) J. A. Delille, *Authentie de la 2e ép. de Pierre*, Strasb. 1835. (*Pro.*) H. Magnus, *Exam. de l'authent. de la 2e ép. de Pierre*, Strasb. 1835. (*Con.*) A. L. C. Heydenreich, *Ein Wort zur Vertheidigung d. Aechtheit des 2en Br. Petri*, Herborn, 1837. L. Audemars, *La 2e ép. de Pierre*, Gen. 1838. (*Con.*) A. L. Daumas, *Introd. crit. à la 2e ép. de P.* Strasb. 1845. (*Con.*)

For references to the more important general commentaries which include the Epistles of Peter, see the article JOHN, FIRST EPISTLE OF, vol. ii. p. 1441 *a*. Among the special commentaries, passing by earlier works, we may notice those of Semler, *Paraphrasis*, etc. in *Ep. I. Petri*, Hal. 1783; in *Ep. II. Petri et Ep. Judae*, ibid. 1784. Morus, *Prælectt. in Jac. et Petri Epp.*, Lips. 1794. C. G. Hensler, *Der 1e Br. Petri übers., mit einem Kommentar*, Sulzb. 1813. J. J. Hottinger, *Epp. Jacobi et Petri I. cum Vers. Germ. et Comm. Lat.*, Lips. 1815. W. Steiger, *Der erste Brief Petri . . . ausgelegt*, Berl. 1832, trans. by P. Fairbairn, 2 vols. Edinb. 1836 (*Bibl. Cab.* vols. xiii., xiv.). Wiesinger, *Der 1e Br. d. Ap. Petrus erklärt*, Königsb. 1856, and *Der 2e Br. d. Petrus u. d. Br. d. Judas*, ibid. 1862 (Bd. vi. Abth. 2 and 3 of Olshausen's *Bibl. Comm.*). T. Schott, *Der 1e Brief Petri erklärt*, Erlang. 1861, and *Der 2e Br. P. u. d. Br. Judä erklärt*, ibid. 1863. De

Wette, *Kurze Erkl. der Briefe des 1'etrus, Judas u. Jacobus, 3e Ausg. bearb. von B Brückner*, Leipz. 1865 (Bd. iii. Abth. i. of his *Exeg. Handbuch*). J. E. Huther, *Krit. exeg. Handb. üb. d. 1. Brief des Petrus, den Br. d. Judas, u. d. 2. Br. d. Petrus*, 3d ed. Götting. 1867 (Abth. xii. of Meyer's *Kommentar*). Fronmüller, *Die Briefe Petri u. d. Br. Judä, theol.-homilet. bearbeitet*, 2e Aufl. Bielefeld, 1861 (Theil xiv. of Lange's *Bibelwerk*); translated, with additions, by J. I. Mombert, N. Y. 1867, as part of vol. ix. of Lange's *Commentary*, edited by Dr. Schaff. W. O. Dietlein, *Der 2e Br. Petri*, Berl. 1851. (Uncritical.) F. Steinfass, *Der 2e Br. d. Ap. Petrus*, Rost. 1863. In English, we also have Abp. Leighton's *Practical Commentary on the First Ep. of Peter*, in numerous editions (highly esteemed); Barnes's *Notes (Epistles of James, Peter, John, and Jude*, N. Y. 1847); John Brown, *Expos. Discourses on the First Epistle of St. Peter*, 2d ed. 2 vols. Edinb. 1849, 8vo (reprinted in 1 vol., N. Y.); J. F. Demarest, *Trans. and Exposition of the First Ep. of Peter*, N. Y. 1851; *Comm. on the Second Ep. of Peter*, N. Y. 1865; and Dr. John Lillie, *Lectures on the First and Second Epistles of Peter*, N. Y. 1869, embracing a new translation of the epistles, and a commentary both critical and practical. Of the commentaries named above the most valuable are those of De Wette, Huther, and Wiesinger. See further the literature referred to under JUDE, EPISTLE OF.

On the doctrine of the epistles of Peter, in addition to the works on Biblical theology by Neander, Reuss, Lutterbeck, Messner, Schmid, Lechler, and Baur, referred to under JOHN, GOSPEL OF, vol. ii. p. 1439 *a*, see B. Weiss, *Der petrinische Lehrbegriff*, Berl. 1855, 8vo, and the review by Baur in the *Theol. Jahrb.* 1856: also G. F. Simon, *Étude dogm. sur S. Pierre*, Strasb. 1858.

On the apocryphal writings ascribed to Peter one may consult Fabricius, *Cod. apocr. Nori Testamenti* (ed. 2da, 1719); Grabe's *Spicilegium*, vol. i. (ed. alt. 1714); Tischendorf's *Acta Apostolorum Apocrypha* (1851); and Hilgenfeld's *Novum Test. extra Canonem receptum*, Fasc. iv. (1866). Credner's speculations about the Gospel of Peter in his *Beiträge zur Einl. in die bibl. Schriften*, Bd. i. (1832), are completely demolished by Mr. Norton, in a Note to vol. i. of his *Genuineness of the Gospels*, 1st ed. (Bost. 1837), pp. ccxxxii.–cclv. (not reprinted in the 2d ed. of that work).   A.

PETHAHI′AH (פְּתַחְיָה: Φεταλά; Alex. Φεθεΐα: *Phetaia*). 1. A priest, over the 19th course in the reign of David (1 Chr. xxiv. 16).

2. (Φεθεΐα; [Vat. Φαθαια; Alex. Φεθεια; FA. Φααια:] *Phataia, Phathahia*.) A Levite in the time of Ezra, who had married a foreign wife (Ezr. x. 23). He is probably the same who, with others of his tribe, conducted the solemn service on the occasion of the fast, when "the seed of Israel separated themselves from all strangers" (Neh. ix. 5), though his name does not appear among those who sealed the covenant (Neh. x.).

3. (Φαθαΐα; [Vat. Παθαια; FA. Παθεΐα:] *Phathahia.*) The son of Meshezabeel and descendant of Zerah the son of Judah (Neh. xi. 24), who was "at the king's hand in all matters concerning the people." The "king" here is explained by Rashi to be Darius: "he was an associate in the counsel of the king Darius for all matters affecting the people, to speak to the king concerning them."

PE'THOR (פְּתוֹר): Φαθουρά; [Alex. Βα-
θουρα: *ariolum*; in Deut., LXX. and Vulg. om.]),
a town of Mesopotamia where Balaam resided (Num.
xxii. 5; Deut. xxiii. 4). Its position is wholly unknown.   W. L. B.

PETHU'EL (פְּתוּאֵל: Βαθουήλ: *Phatuel*).
The father of the prophet Joel (Joel i. 1).

* The prophet's name was not uncommon (JOEL),
and the addition of the father's name distinguished
him from others who bore it. The name is probably = מְרִתּיאֵל, *man of God* (Fürst, Ges.).   H.

PEUL'THAI [3 syl.] פְּעֻלְּתַי [*wages of
Jehovah*]: Φελαθί; Alex. Φολλαθι : *Phollathi*).
Properly "Peullethai;" the eighth son of Obed-
edom (1 Chr. xxvi. 5).

PHA'ATH MO'AB ([Vat.] Φθαλει Μωαβεις;
[Rom.] Alex. Φααθ Μωαβ: *Phocmo*), 1 Esdr. v.
11=PAHATH MOAB. In this passage the number
(2812) agrees with that in Ezra and disagrees with
Nehemiah.

PHACA'RETH (Φαχαρέθ; Alex. Φακαρεθ:
Sachareth)=POCHERETH of Zebaim (1 Esdr. v.
34).

PHAI'SUR [2 syl.] (Φαισούρ; Alex. Φαισου:
Fosere). PASHUR, the priestly family (1 Esdr.
ix. 22).

PHALDAI'US [3 syl.] (Φαλδαῖος; [Vat.
Φαλαδαιος:] *Faldeus*)=PEDAIAH 4 (1 Esdr. ix.
44).

PHALE'AS [properly PHALÆ'AS] (Φαλαῖος:
Hellu) = PADON (1 Esdr. v. 29).

PHA'LEC (Φάλεκ [or Φαλέκ, Elz., Tisch.] :
Phaleg). PELEG the son of Eber (Luke iii. 35).

PHAL'LU (פַלּוּא [*distinguished*]: Φαλλός;
Alex. Φαλλουδ: *Phallu*). Pallu the son of Reuben
is so called in the A. V. of Gen. xlvi. 9.

PHAL'TI (פַלְטִי [*deliverance of Jehovah*]:
Φαλτί; [Vat. Φαλτει:] *Phalti*). The son of
Laish of Gallim, to whom Saul gave Michal in marriage after his mad jealousy had driven David forth
as an outlaw (1 Sam. xxv. 44). In 2 Sam. iii. 15
he is called PHALTIEL. Ewald (*Gesch.* iii. 129)
suggests that this forced marriage was a piece of
policy on the part of Saul to attach Phalti to his
house. With the exception of this brief mention
of his name, and the touching little episode in
2 Sam. iii. 16, nothing more is heard of Phalti.
Michal is there restored to David. "Her husband
went with her along weeping behind her to Bahurim," and there, in obedience to Abner's abrupt
command, "Go, return," he turns and disappears
from the scene.

PHAL'TIEL (פַלְטִיאֵל [*deliverance of Jehovah*]: Φαλτιήλ; *Phaltiel*). The same as PHALTI
(2 Sam. iii. 15).

PHANU'EL (Φανουήλ: *Phanuel*). The
father of Anna, the prophetess of the tribe of Aser
(Luke ii. 36).

PHAR'ACIM (Φαρακίμ; Alex. Φαρακειμ:
Fanon). The "sons of Pharacim" were among
the servants of the Temple who returned with Zerubbabel, according to the list in 1 Esdr. v. 31.
No corresponding name is found in the parallel
narratives of Ezra and Nehemiah.

PHA'RAOH [pron. *fā'ro*] פַּרְעֹה: Φα-
paó: Pharao), the common title of the native
kings of Egypt in the Bible, corresponding to
P-RA or PH-RA, "the Sun," of the hieroglyphics. This identification, respecting which there
can be no doubt, is due to the Duke of Northum-
berland and General Felix (Rawlinson's *Herod.* ii.
293). It has been supposed that the original was
the same as the Coptic ΟΤΡΟ "the king," with
the article, ΠΙΟΤΡΟ, ΦΟΤΡΟ ; but this
word appears not to have been written, judging
from the evidence of the Egyptian inscriptions and
writings, in the times to which the Scriptures refer. The conjecture arose from the idea that Pharaoh must signify, instead of merely implying,
"king," a mistake occasioned by a too implicit
confidence in the exactness of ancient writers (Joseph. *Ant.* viii. 6, § 2; Euseb. ed. Scal. p. 20,
v. 1).

By the ancient Egyptians the king was called
"the Sun," as the representative on earth of the
god RA, or "the Sun." It was probably on this
account that more than one of the Pharaohs bear
in the nomen, in the second royal ring, the title
"ruler of Heliopolis," the city of Ra, HAK-AN,
as in the case of Rameses III., a distinction shared,
though in an inferior degree, if we may judge from
the frequency of the corresponding title, by Thebes,
but by scarcely any other city.a One of the most
common regal titles, that which almost always precedes the nomen, is "Son of the Sun," SA-RA.
The prenomen, in the first royal ring, regularly
commences with a disc, the character which represents the sun, and this name which the king took
on his accession, thus comprises the title Pharaoh:
for instance, the prenomen of Psammitichus II., the
successor of Necho, is RA-NUFR-HAT, "Pharaoh" or "Ra of the good heart." In the period
before the VIth dynasty, when there was but a
single ring, the use of the word RA was not invariable, many names not commencing with it, as
SHUFU or KHUFU, the king of the IVth dynasty who built the Great Pyramid. It is difficult
to determine, in rendering these names, whether
the king or the divinity be meant: perhaps in royal
names no distinction is intended, both Pharaoh
and Ra being meant.

The word Pharaoh occurs generally in the Bible,
and always in the Pentateuch, with no addition,
for the king of Egypt. Sometimes the title "king
of Egypt" follows it, and in the cases of the last
two native kings mentioned, the proper name is
added, Pharaoh-Necho, Pharaoh-Hophra, with
sometimes the further addition "king (or the king)
of Egypt." It is remarkable that Shishak and
Zerah (if, as we believe, the second were a king of
Egypt), and the Ethiopians So and Tirhakah, are
never distinctly called Pharaoh (the mention of a
Pharaoh during the time of the Ethiopians probably referring to the Egyptian Sethos), and that
the latter were foreigners and the former of foreign
extraction.

As several kings are only mentioned by the title
"Pharaoh" in the Bible, it is important to endeavor to discriminate them. We shall therefore
here state what is known respecting them in order,

---

a The kings who bear the former title are chiefly of
the name Rameses, "Born of Ra," the god of Heliopolis, which renders the title especially appropriate.

adding an account of the two Pharaohs whose proper names follow the title.

1. *The Pharaoh of Abraham.* — The Scripture narrative does not afford us any clear indications for the identification of the Pharaoh of Abraham. At the time at which the patriarch went into Egypt, according to Hales's as well as Ussher's chronology, it is generally held that the country, or at least Lower Egypt, was ruled by the Shepherd kings, of whom the first and most powerful line was the XVth dynasty, the undoubted territories of which would be first entered by one coming from the east. Manetho relates that Salatis, the head of this line, established at Avaris, the Zoan of the Bible, on the eastern frontier, what appears to have been a great permanent camp, at which he resided for part of each year. [ZOAN.] It is noticeable that Sarah seems to have been taken to Pharaoh's house immediately after the coming of Abraham; and if this were not so, yet, on account of his flocks and herds, the patriarch could scarcely have gone beyond the part of the country which was always more or less occupied by nomad tribes. It is also probable that Pharaoh gave Abraham camels, for we read, that Pharaoh "entreated Abram well for Sarah's sake: and he had sheep, and oxen, and he asses, and menservants, and maidservants, and she asses, and camels" (Gen. xii. 16), where it appears that this property was the gift of Pharaoh, and the circumstance that the patriarch afterwards held an Egyptian bondwoman, Hagar, confirms the inference. If so, the present of camels would argue that this Pharaoh was a Shepherd king, for no evidence has been found in the sculptures, paintings, and inscriptions of Egypt, that in the Pharaonic ages the camel was used, or even known there,[a] and this omission can be best explained by the supposition that the animal was hateful to the Egyptians as of great value to their enemies the Shepherds.

The date at which Abraham visited Egypt (according to the chronology we hold most probable), was about B. C. 2081, which would accord with the time of Salatis, the head of the XVth dynasty, according to our reckoning.

2. *The Pharaoh of Joseph.* — The history of Joseph contains many particulars as to the Pharaoh whose minister he became. We first hear of him as the arbitrary master who imprisoned his two servants, and then, on his birthday-feast, reinstated the one and hanged the other. We next read of his dreams, how he consulted the magicians and wise men of Egypt, and on their failing to interpret them, by the advice of the chief of the cupbearers, sent for Joseph from the prison, and after he had heard his interpretation and counsel, chose him as governor of the country, taking, as it seems, the advice of his servants. The sudden advancement of a despised stranger to the highest place under the king is important as showing his absolute power and manner of governing. From this time we read more of Joseph than of Pharaoh. We are told, however, that Pharaoh liberally received Joseph's kindred, allowing them to dwell in the land of Goshen, where he had cattle. The last mention of a Pharaoh in Joseph's history is in the account of the death and burial of Jacob. It has been supposed from the following passage that the position of Joseph had then become changed. "Joseph spake unto the house of Pharaoh, saying, If now I have found grace in your eyes, speak, I pray you, in the ears of Pharaoh, saying, My father made me swear, saying, Lo, I die: in my grave which I have digged for me in the land of Canaan, there shalt thou bury me. Now therefore let me go up, I pray thee, and bury my father, and I will come again. And Pharaoh said, Go up and bury thy father, according as he made thee swear" (Gen. l. 4–6). The account of the embalming of Jacob, in which we are told that "Joseph commanded his servants the physicians to embalm his father" (ver. 2), shows the position of Joseph, which is more distinctly proved by the narrative of the subsequent journey into Palestine. "And Joseph went up to bury his father: and with him went up all the servants of Pharaoh, the elders of his house, and all the elders of the land of Egypt, and all the house of Joseph, and his brethren, and his father's house: only their little ones, and their flocks, and their herds, they left in the land of Goshen. And there went up with him both chariots and horsemen: and it was a very great company" (7–9). To make such an expedition as this, with perhaps risk of a hostile encounter, would no doubt require special permission, and from Joseph's whole history we can understand that he would have hesitated to ask a favor for himself, while it is most natural that he should have explained that he had no further motive in the journey. The fear of his brethren that after their father's death he would take vengeance on them for their former cruelty, and his declaration that he would nourish them and their little ones, prove he still held a high position. His dying charge does not indicate that the persecution had then commenced, and that it had not seems quite clear from the narrative at the beginning of Exodus. It thus appears that Joseph retained his position until Jacob's death; and it is therefore probable, nothing being stated to the contrary, that the Pharaoh who made Joseph governor was on the throne during the time that he seems to have held office, twenty-six years. We may suppose that the "new king" "which knew not Joseph" (Ex. i. 8) was head of a new dynasty. It is very unlikely that he was the immediate successor of this Pharaoh, as the interval from the appointment of the governor to the beginning of the oppression was not less than eighty years, and probably much more.

The chief points for the identification of the line to which this Pharaoh belonged, are that he was a despotic monarch, ruling all Egypt, who followed Egyptian customs, but did not hesitate to set them aside when he thought fit; that he seems to have desired to gain complete power over the Egyptians; and that he favored strangers. These particulars certainly appear to lend support to the idea that he was an Egyptianized foreigner rather than an Egyptian; and M. Mariette's recent discoveries at Zoan, or Avaris, have positively settled what was the great difficulty to most scholars in the way of this view, for it has been ascertained that the Shepherds, of at least one dynasty, were so thoroughly Egyptianized that they executed monuments of an Egyptian character, differing alone in a peculiarity of style. Before, however, we state the main heads of argument in favor of the idea that the Pharaoh of Joseph was a Shepherd, it will be well to mention the grounds of the theories that make him an Egyptian. Baron Bunsen supposed that he was

---

[a] It has been erroneously asserted that a hieroglyphic representing the head and neck of the camel is found on the Egyptian monuments.

Sesertesen I., the head of the XIIth dynasty, on account of the mention in a hieroglyphic inscription of a famine in that king's reign. This identification, although receiving some support from the statement of Herodotus, that Sesostris, a name reasonably traceable to Sesertesen, divided the land and raised his chief revenue from the rent paid by the holders, must be abandoned, since the calamity recorded does not approach Joseph's famine in character, and as the age is almost certainly too remote. According to our reckoning this king began to reign about B. C. 2080, and Baron Bunsen places him much earlier, so that this idea is not tenable, unless we take the long chronology of the Judges, and hold the sojourn in Egypt to have lasted 430 years. If we take the Rabbinical date of the Exodus, Joseph's Pharaoh would have been a king of the XVIIIth dynasty, unless, with Bunsen, we lengthen the Hebrew chronology before the Exodus as arbitrarily as, in adopting that date, we shorten it after the Exodus. To the idea that this king was of the XVIIIth dynasty there is this objection, which we hold to be fatal, that the monuments of that line, often recording the events of almost every year, present no trace of the remarkable circumstances of Joseph's rule. Whether we take Ussher's or Hales's date of the Exodus, Joseph's government would fall before the XVIIIth dynasty, and during the Shepherd period. (By the Shepherd period is generally understood the period after the XIIth dynasty and before the XVIIIth, during which the foreigners were dominant over Egypt, although it is possible that they already held part of the country at an earlier time.) If, discarding the idea that Joseph's Pharaoh was an Egyptian, we turn to the old view that he was one of the Shepherd kings, a view almost inevitable if we infer that he ruled during the Shepherd period, we are struck with the fitness of all the circumstances of the Biblical narrative. These foreign rulers, or at least some of them, were Egyptianized, yet the account of Manetho, if we somewhat lessen the coloring that we may suppose national hatred gave it, is now shown to be correct in making them disregard the laws and religion of the country they had subdued. They were evidently powerful military despots. As foreigners ruling what was treated as a conquered country, if not actually won by force of arms, they would have encouraged foreign settlers, particularly in their own especial region in the east of Lower Egypt, where the Pharaoh of Joseph seems to have had cattle (Gen. xlvii. 5, 6). It is very unlikely, unless we suppose a special interposition of Providence, that an Egyptian Pharaoh, with the acquiescence of his counselors, should have chosen a Hebrew slave as his chief officer of state. It is stated by Eusebius that the Pharaoh to whom Jacob came was the Shepherd Apophis; and although it may be replied that this identification was simply a result of the adjustment of the dynasties to his view of Hebrew chronology, it should be observed that he seems to have altered the very dynasty of Apophis, both in its number (making it the XVIIth instead of the XVth), and in its duration, as though he were convinced that this king was really the Pharaoh of Joseph, and must therefore be brought to his time. Apophis belonged to the XVth dynasty, which was certainly of Shepherds, and the most powerful foreign line. for it seems clear that there was at least one if not two more. This dynasty, according to our view of Egyptian chronology, ruled for either 284 years

(Africanus), or 259 years 10 months (Josephus), from about B. C. 2080. If Hales's chronology, which we would slightly modify, be correct, the government of Joseph fell under this dynasty, [and,] commencing about B. C. 1876, which would be during the reign of the last but one or perhaps the last king of the dynasty, was possibly in the time of Apophis, who ended the line according to Africanus. It is to be remarked that this dynasty is said to have been of Phœnicians, and if so was probably of a stock predominantly Shemite, a circumstance in perfect accordance with what we know of the government and character of Joseph's Pharaoh, whose act in making Joseph his chief minister finds its parallels in Shemite history, and in that of nations which derived their customs from Shemites. An Egyptian king would scarcely give so high a place to any but a native, and that of the military or priestly class; but, as already remarked, this may have been due to divine interposition.

This king appears, as has been already shown, to have reigned from Joseph's appointment (or, perhaps, somewhat earlier, since he was already on the throne when he imprisoned his servants), until Jacob's death, a period of at least twenty-six years, from B. C. cir. 1876 to 1850, and to have been the fifth or sixth king of the XVth dynasty.

3. *The Pharaoh of the Oppression.* — The first persecutor of the Israelites may be distinguished as the Pharaoh of the Oppression, from the second, the Pharaoh of the Exodus, especially as he commenced, and probably long carried on, the persecution. Here, as in the case of Joseph's Pharaoh, there has been difference of opinion as to the line to which the oppressor belonged. The general view is that he was an Egyptian, and this at first sight is a probable inference from the narrative, if the line under which the Israelites were protected be supposed to have been one of Shepherds. The Biblical history here seems to justify clearer deductions than before. We read that Joseph and his brethren and that generation died, and that the Israelites multiplied and became very mighty and filled the land. Of the events of the interval between Jacob's death and the oppression we know almost nothing; but the calamity to Ephraim's house, in the slaughter of his sons by the men of Gath, born as it seems in Egypt [BERIAH], renders it probable that the Israelites had become a tributary tribe, settled in Goshen, and beginning to show that warlike vigor that is so strong a feature in the character of Abraham, that is not wanting in Jacob's, and that fitted their posterity for the conquest of Canaan. The beginning of the oppression is thus narrated: " Now there arose a new king over Egypt, which knew not Joseph" (Ex. i. 8). The expression, "a new king " (comp. "another king," Acts vii. 18), does not necessitate the idea of a change of dynasty, but favors it. The next two verses are extremely important: " And he said unto his people, Behold, the people of the children of Israel [are] more and mightier than we: come on, let us deal wisely with them; lest they multiply, and it come to pass that, when there falleth out any war, they join also unto our enemies, and fight against us, and [so] get them up out of the land " (9, 10). Here it is stated that Pharaoh ruled a people of smaller numbers and less strength than the Israelites, whom he feared lest they should join with some enemies in a possible war in Egypt, and so leave the country. In order to weaken the Is

raelites he adopted a subtle policy which is next related. "Therefore they did set over them task-masters to afflict them with their burdens. And they built for Pharaoh treasure cities, Pithom and Raamses" (11). The name of the second of these cities has been considered a most important point of evidence. They multiplied notwithstanding, and the persecution apparently increased. They were employed in brickmaking and other labor connected with building, and perhaps also in making pottery (Ps. lxxxi. 6). This bondage producing no effect, Pharaoh commanded the two Hebrew midwives to kill every male child as it was born; but they deceived him, and the people continued to increase. He then made a fresh attempt to enfeeble them. "And Pharaoh charged all his people, saying, Every son that is born ye shall cast into the river, and every daughter ye shall save alive" (22). How long this last infamous command was in force we do not know, probably but for a short time, unless it was constantly evaded, otherwise the number of the Israelites would have been checked. It may be remarked that Aaron was three years older than Moses, so that we might suppose that the command was issued after his birth; but it must also be observed that the fear of the mother of Moses, at his birth, may have been because she lived near a royal residence, as appears from the finding of the child by Pharaoh's daughter. The story of his exposure and rescue shows that even the oppressor's daughter could feel pity, and disobey her father's command; while in her saving Moses, who was to ruin her house, is seen the retributive justice that so often makes the tyrant pass by and even protect, as Pharaoh must have done, the instrument of his future punishment. The etymology of the name of Moses does not aid us: if Egyptian, it may have been given by a foreigner; if foreign, it may have been given by an Egyptian to a foreign child. It is important that Pharaoh's daughter adopted Moses as her son, and that he was taught in all the wisdom of Egypt. The persecution continued, "And it came to pass in those days, when Moses was grown, that he went out unto his brethren, and looked on their burdens: and he spied an Egyptian smiting an Hebrew, one of his brethren. And he looked this way and that way, and when he saw that [there was] no man, he slew the Egyptian, and hid him in the sand" (ii. 11, 12). When Pharaoh attempted to slay Moses, he fled into the land of Midian. From the statement in Hebrews that he "refused to be called the son of Pharaoh's daughter; choosing rather to suffer affliction with the people of God, than to enjoy the pleasures of sin for a season; esteeming the reproach of Christ greater riches than the treasures in Egypt" (xi. 24–26), it is evident that the adoption was no mere form, and this is a point of evidence not to be slighted. While Moses was in Midian Pharaoh died, and the narrative implies that this was shortly before the events preceding the Exodus.

This Pharaoh has been generally supposed to have been a king of the XVIIIth or XIXth dynasty; we believe that he was of a line earlier than either. The chief points in the evidence in favor of the former opinion are the name of the city Raamses, whence it has been argued that one of the oppressors was a king Rameses, and the probable

change of line. The first king of this name known was head of the XIXth dynasty, or last king of the XVIIIth. According to Manetho's story of the Exodus, a story so contradictory to historical truth as scarcely to be worthy of mention, the Israelites left Egypt in the reign of Menptah, who was great grandson of the first Rameses, and son and successor of the second. This king is held by some Egyptologists to have reigned about the time of the Rabbinical date of the Exodus, which is virtually the same as that which has been supposed to be obtainable from the genealogies. There is however good reason to place these kings much later; in which case Rameses I. would be the oppressor; but then the building of Raamses could not be placed in his reign without a disregard of Hebrew chronology. But the argument that there is no earlier known king Rameses loses much of its weight when we bear in mind that one of the sons of Aähmes, head of the XVIIIth dynasty, who reigned about two hundred years before Rameses I., bore the same name, besides that very many names of kings of the Shepherd period, perhaps of two whole dynasties, are unknown. Against this one fact, which is certainly not to be disregarded, we must weigh the general evidence of the history, which shows us a king apparently governing a part of Egypt, with subjects inferior to the Israelites, and fearing a war in the country. Like the Pharaoh of the Exodus, he seems to have dwelt in Lower Egypt, probably at Avaris.[a] Compare this condition with the power of the kings of the later part of the XVIIIth and of the XIXth dynasties; rulers of an empire, governing a united country from which the head of their line had driven the Shepherds. The view that this Pharaoh was of the beginning or middle of the XVIIIth dynasty seems at first sight extremely probable, especially if it be supposed that the Pharaoh of Joseph was a Shepherd king. The expulsion of the Shepherds at the commencement of this dynasty would have naturally caused an immediate or gradual oppression of the Israelites. But it must be remembered that what we have just said of the power of some kings of this dynasty is almost as true of their predecessors. The silence of the historical monuments is also to be weighed, when we bear in mind how numerous they are, and that we might expect many of the events of the oppression to be recorded if the Exodus were not noticed. If we assign this Pharaoh to the age before the XVIIIth dynasty, which our view of Hebrew chronology would probably oblige us to do, we have still to determine whether he were a Shepherd or an Egyptian. If a Shepherd, he must have been of the XVIth or the XVIIth dynasty; and that he was Egyptianized does not afford any argument against this supposition, since it appears that foreign kings, who can only be assigned to one of these two lines, had Egyptian names. In corroboration of this view we quote a remarkable passage that does not seem otherwise explicable: "My people went down aforetime into Egypt to sojourn there; and the Assyrian oppressed them without cause" (Is. lii. 4): which may be compared with the allusions to the Exodus in a prediction of the same prophet respecting Assyria (x. 24, 26). Our inference is strengthened by the discovery that kings bearing

a When Moses went to see his people and slew the Egyptian, he does not seem to have made any journey, and the burying in sand shows that the place was in

a part of Egypt like Goshen, encompassed by sandy deserts.

a name almost certainly an Egyptian translation of an Assyrian or Babylonian regal title, are among those apparently of the Shepherd age in the Turin Papyrus (Lepsius, *Königsbuch*, taf. xviii. xix. 275, 285).

The reign of this king probably commenced a little before the birth of Moses, which we place B. c. 1732, and seems to have lasted upwards of forty years, perhaps much more.

4. *The Pharaoh of the Exodus.* — What is known of the Pharaoh of the Exodus is rather biographical than historical. It does not add much to our means of identifying the line of the oppressors excepting by the indications of race his character affords. His life is spoken of in other articles. [PLAGUES, etc.] His acts show us a man at once impious and superstitious, alternately rebelling and submitting. At first he seems to have thought that his magicians could work the same wonders as Moses and Aaron, yet even then he begged that the frogs might be taken away, and to the end he prayed that a plague might be removed, promising a concession to the Israelites, and as soon as he was respited failed to keep his word. This is not strange in a character principally influenced by fear, and history abounds in parallels to Pharaoh. His vacillation only ended when he lost his army in the Red Sea, and the Israelites were finally delivered out of his hand. Whether he himself was drowned has been considered matter of uncertainty, as it is not so stated in the account of the Exodus. Another passage, however, appears to affirm it (Ps. cxxxvi. 15). It seems to be too great a latitude of criticism either to argue that the expression in this passage indicates the overthrow but not the death of the king, especially as the Hebrew expression "shaked off" or "threw in" is very literal, or that it is only a strong Semitic expression. Besides, throughout the preceding history his end is foreshadowed, and is, perhaps, positively foretold in Ex. ix. 15; though this passage may be rendered "For now I might have stretched out my hand, and might have smitten thee and thy people with pestilence; and thou wouldest have been cut off from the earth," as by Kalisch (*Commentary* in loc.), instead of as in the A. V.

Although we have already stated our reasons for abandoning the theory that places the Exodus under the XIXth dynasty, it may be well to notice an additional and conclusive argument for rejecting as unhistorical the tale preserved by Manetho, which makes Menptah, the son of Rameses II., the Pharaoh in whose reign the Israelites left Egypt. This tale was commonly current in Egypt, but it must be remarked that the historian gives it only on the authority of tradition. M. Mariette's recent discoveries have added to the evidence we already had on the subject. In this story the secret of the success of the rebels was that they had allotted to them by Amenophis, or Menptah, the city of Avaris formerly held by the Shepherds, but then in ruins. That the people to whom this place was given were working in the quarries east of the Nile is enough of itself to throw a doubt on the narrative, for there appear to have been no quarries north of those opposite Memphis, from which Avaris was distant nearly the whole length of the Delta; but when it is found that this very king, as well as his father, adorned the great temple of Avaris, the story is seen to be essentially false. Yet it is not improbable that some calamity occurred about this time, with which the Egyptians willfully or igno-

rantly confounded the Exodus: if they did so ignorantly, there would be an argument that this event took place during the Shepherd period, which was probably in after times an obscure part of the annals of Egypt.

The character of this Pharaoh finds its parallel among the Assyrians rather than the Egyptians. The impiety of the oppressor and that of Sennacherib are remarkably similar, though Sennacherib seems to have been more resolute in his resistance than Pharaoh. This resemblance is not to be overlooked, especially as it seems to indicate an idiosyncrasy of the Assyrians and kindred nations, for national character was more marked in antiquity than it is now in most peoples, doubtless because isolation was then general and is now special. Thus, the Egyptian monuments show us a people highly reverencing their gods and even those of other nations, the most powerful kings appearing as suppliants in the representations of the temples and tombs; in the Assyrian sculptures, on the contrary, the kings are seen rather as protected by the gods than as worshipping them, so that we understand how in such a country the famous decree of Darius, which Daniel disobeyed, could be enacted. Again the Egyptians do not seem to have supposed that their enemies were supported by gods hostile to those of Egypt, whereas the Assyrians considered their gods as more powerful than those of the nations they subdued. This is important in connection with the idea that at least one of the Pharaohs of the oppression was an Assyrian.

Respecting the time of this king we can only say that he was reigning for about a year or more before the Exodus, which we place B. c. 1652.

Before speaking of the later Pharaohs we may mention a point of weight in reference to the identification of these earlier ones. The accounts of the campaigns of the Pharaohs of the XVIIIth, XIXth, and XXth dynasties have not been found to contain any reference to the Israelites. Hence it might be supposed that in their days, or at least during the greater part of their time, the Israelites were not yet in the Promised Land. There is, however, an almost equal silence as to the Canaanite nations. The land itself, KANANA or KANAAN, is indeed mentioned as invaded, as well as those of KHETA and AMAR, referring to the Hittites and Amorites; but the latter two must have been branches of those nations seated in the valley of the Orontes. A recently discovered record of Thothmes III. published by M. de Rougé, in the *Revue Archéologique* (Nov. 1861, pp. 344 ff.), contains many names of Canaanite towns conquered by that king, but not one recognized as Israelite. These Canaanite names are, moreover, on the Israelite borders, not in the heart of the country. It is interesting that a great battle is shown to have been won by this king at Megiddo. It seems probable that the Egyptians either abstained from attacking the Israelites from a recollection of the calamities of the Exodus, or that they were on friendly terms. It is very remarkable that the Egyptians were granted privileges in the Law (Deut. xxiii. 7), and that Shishak, the first king of Egypt after the Exodus whom we know to have invaded the Hebrew territories, was of foreign extraction, if not actually a foreigner.

5. *Pharaoh, father-in-law of Mered.* — In the genealogies of the tribe of Judah, mention is made

of the daughter of Pharaoh, married to an Israelite; "Bithiah the daughter of a Pharaoh, which Mered took" (1 Chr. iv. 18). That the name Pharaoh here probably designates an Egyptian king we have already shown, and observed that the date of Mered is doubtful, although it is likely that he lived before, or not much after, the Exodus. [BITHIAH.] It may be added that the name Miriam, of one of the family of Mered (17), apparently his sister, or perhaps a daughter by Bithiah, suggests that this part of the genealogies may refer to about the time of the Exodus. This marriage may tend to aid us in determining the age of the sojourn in Egypt. It is perhaps less probable that an Egyptian Pharaoh would have given his daughter in marriage to an Israelite, than that a Shepherd king would have done so, before the oppression. But Bithiah may have been taken in war after the Exodus, by the surprise of a caravan, or in a foray.

6. *Pharaoh, father-in-law of Hadad the Edomite.* — Among the enemies who were raised up against Solomon was Hadad, an Edomite of the blood royal, who had escaped as a child from the slaughter of his nation by Joab. We read of him and his servants, "And they arose out of Midian, and came to Paran: and they took men with them out of Paran, and they came to Egypt, unto Pharaoh king of Egypt; who gave him an house, and appointed him victuals, and gave him land. And Hadad found great favor in the sight of Pharaoh, so that he gave him to wife the sister of his own wife, the sister of Tahpenes the queen. And the sister of Tahpenes bare him Genubath his son, whom Tahpenes weaned in Pharaoh's house: and Genubath was in Pharaoh's household among the sons of Pharaoh" (1 K. xi. 18-20). When, however, Hadad heard that David and Joab were both dead, he asked Pharaoh to let him return to his country, and was unwillingly allowed to go (21, 22). Probably the fugitives took refuge in an Egyptian mining-station in the peninsula of Sinai, and so obtained guides to conduct them into Egypt. There they were received in accordance with the Egyptian policy, but with the especial favor that seems to have been shown about this time towards the eastern neighbors of the Pharaohs, which may reasonably be supposed to have led to the establishment of the XXIId dynasty of foreign extraction. For the identification of this Pharaoh we have chronological indications, and the name of his wife. Unfortunately, however, the history of Egypt at this time is extremely obscure, neither the monuments nor Manetho giving us clear information as to the kings. It appears that towards the latter part of the XXth dynasty the high-priests of Amen, the god of Thebes, gained great power, and at last supplanted the Rameses family, at least in Upper Egypt. At the same time a line of Tanite kings, Manetho's XXIst dynasty, seems to have ruled in Lower Egypt. From the latest part of the XXth dynasty three houses appear to have reigned at the same time. The feeble XXth dynasty was probably soon extinguished, but the priest-rulers and the Tanites appear to have reigned contemporaneously, until they were both succeeded by the Bubastites of the XXIId dynasty, of whom Sheshonk I., the Shishak of the Bible, was the first. The monuments have preserved the names of several of the high-priests, perhaps all, and probably of some of the Tanites; but it is a question whether Mane-

tho's Tanite line does not include some of the former, and we have no means of testing the accuracy of its numbers. It may be reasonably supposed that the Pharaoh or Pharaohs spoken of in the Bible as ruling in the time of David and Solomon were Tanites, as Tanis was nearest to the Israelite territory. We have therefore to compare the chronological indications of Scripture with the list of this dynasty. Shishak, as we have shewn elsewhere, must have begun to reign in about the 24th or 25th year of Solomon (B. C. cir. 990-989). [CHRONOLOGY.] The conquest of Edom probably took place some 50 years earlier. It may therefore be inferred that Hadad fled to a king of Egypt who may have ruled at least 25 years, probably ceasing to govern before Solomon married the daughter of a Pharaoh early in his reign; for it seems unlikely that the protector of David's enemy would have given his daughter to Solomon, unless he were a powerless king, which appears was not the case with Solomon's father-in-law. This would give a reign of 25 years, or 25 + *x* separated from the close of the dynasty by a period of 24 or 25 years. According to Africanus, the list of the XXIst dynasty is as follows: Smendes, 26 years; Psusennes, 46; Nephelcheres, 4; Amenothis, 9; Osochor, 6; Psinaches, 9; Psusennes, 14; but Eusebius gives the second king 41, and the last, 35 years, and his numbers make up the sum of 130 years, which Africanus and he agree in assigning to the dynasty. If we take the numbers of Eusebius, Osochor would probably be the Pharaoh to whom Hadad fled, and Psusennes II. the father-in-law of Solomon; but the numbers of Africanus would substitute Psusennes I., and probably Psinaches. We cannot, however, be sure that the reigns did not overlap, or were not separated by intervals, and the numbers are not to be considered reliable until tested by the monuments. The royal names of the period have been searched in vain for any one resembling Tahpenes. If the Egyptian equivalent to the similar geographical name Tahpanhes, etc., were known, we might have some clew to that of this queen. [TAHPENES; TAHPANHES.]

7. *Pharaoh, father-in-law of Solomon.* — In the narrative of the beginning of Solomon's reign, after the account of the deaths of Adonijah, Joab, and Shimei, and the deprivation of Abiathar, we read: "And the kingdom was established in the hand of Solomon. And Solomon made affinity with Pharaoh king of Egypt, and took Pharaoh's daughter, and brought her into the city of David, until he had made an end of building his own house, and the house of the LORD, and the wall of Jerusalem round about" (1 K. ii. 46, iii. 1). The events mentioned before the marriage belong altogether to the very commencement of Solomon's reign, excepting the matter of Shimei, which extending through three years is carried on to its completion. The mention that the queen was brought into the city of David, while Solomon's house, and the Temple, and the city-wall, were building, shows that the marriage took place not later than the eleventh year of the king, when the Temple was finished, having been commenced in the fourth year (vi. 1, 37, 38). It is also evident that this alliance was before Solomon's falling away into idolatry (iii. 3), of which the Egyptian queen does not seem to have been one of the causes. From this chronological indication it appears that the marriage must have taken place between about 24

and 11 years before Shishak's accession. It must be recollected that it seems certain that Solomon's father-in-law was not the Pharaoh who was reigning when Hadad left Egypt. Both Pharaohs, as already shown, cannot yet be identified in Manetho's list. [PHARAOH'S DAUGHTER.]

This Pharaoh led an expedition into Palestine, which is thus incidentally mentioned, where the building of Gezer by Solomon is recorded: "Pharaoh king of Egypt had gone up, and taken Gezer, and burnt it with fire, and slain the Canaanites that dwelt in the city, and given it [for] a present unto his daughter, Solomon's wife" (ix. 16). This is a very curious historical circumstance, for it shows that in the reign of David or Solomon, more probably the latter, an Egyptian king, apparently on terms of friendship with the Israelite monarch, conducted an expedition into Palestine, and besieged and captured a Canaanite city. This occurrence warns us against the supposition that similar expeditions could not have occurred in earlier times without a war with the Israelites. Its incidental mention also shows the danger of inferring, from the silence of Scripture as to any such earlier expedition, that nothing of the kind took place. [PAL-ESTINE, p. 2291, a.]

This Egyptian alliance is the first indication, after the days of Moses, of that leaning to Egypt which was distinctly forbidden in the Law, and produced the most disastrous consequences in later times. The native kings of Egypt and the Ethiopians readily supported the Hebrews, and were unwilling to make war upon them, but they rendered them mere tributaries, and exposed them to the enmity of the kings of Assyria. If the Hebrews did not incur a direct punishment for their leaning to Egypt, it must have weakened their trust in the Divine favor, and paralysed their efforts to defend the country against the Assyrians and their party.

The next kings of Egypt mentioned in the Bible are Shishak, probably Zerah, and So. The first and second of these were of the XXIId dynasty, if the identification of Zerah with Userken be accepted, and the third was doubtless one of the two Shebeks of the XXVth dynasty, which was of Ethiopians. The XXIId dynasty was a line of kings of foreign origin, who retained foreign names, and it is noticeable that Zerah is called a Cushite in the Bible (2 Chr. xiv. 9; comp. xvi. 8). Shebek was probably also a foreign name. The title "Pharaoh" is probably not once given to these kings in the Bible, because they were not Egyptians, and did not bear Egyptian names. The Shepherd kings, it must be remarked, adopted Egyptian names, and therefore some of the earlier sovereigns called Pharaohs in the Bible may be conjectured to have been Shepherds notwithstanding that they bear this title. [SHISHAK; ZERAH; SO.]

8. *Pharaoh, the Opponent of Sennacherib.* — In the narrative of Sennacherib's war with Hezekiah, mention is made not only of "Tirhakah king of Cush," but also of "Pharaoh king of Mizraim." Rabshakeh thus taunted the king of Judah for having sought the aid of Pharaoh: "Lo, thou trustest in the staff of this broken reed, on Egypt;

whereon if a man lean, it will go into his hand, and pierce it: so [is] Pharaoh king of Egypt to all that trust in him" (Is. xxxvi. 6). The comparison of Pharaoh to a broken reed is remarkable, as the common hieroglyphics for "king," restricted to Egyptian sovereigns, SU-TEN, strictly a title of the ruler of Upper Egypt, commence with a bent reed, which is an ideographic symbolical sign proper to this word, and is sometimes used alone without any phonetic complement. This Pharaoh can only be the Sethos whom Herodotus mentions as the opponent of Sennacherib, and who may be reasonably supposed to be the Zet of Manetho, the last king of his XXIIId dynasty. Tirhakah, as an Ethiopian, whether then ruling in Egypt or not, is, like So, apparently not called Pharaoh. [TIRHA-KAH.]

9. *Pharaoh Necho.* — The first mention in the Bible of a proper name with the title Pharaoh is in the case of Pharaoh Necho, who is also called Necho simply. His name is written Necho, נְכוֹ, and Nechoh, נְכֹה, and in hieroglyphics NEKU. This king was of the Salte XXVIth dynasty, of which Manetho makes him either the fifth ruler (Africanus) or the sixth (Eusebius). Herodotus calls him Nekôs, and assigns to him a reign of sixteen years, which is confirmed by the monuments.[a] He seems to have been an enterprising king, as he is related to have attempted to complete the canal connecting the Red Sea with the Nile, and to have sent an expedition of Phœnicians to circumnavigate Africa, which was successfully accomplished. At the commencement of his reign (B. C. 610) he made war against the king of Assyria, and, being encountered on his way by Josiah, defeated and slew the king of Judah at Megiddo. The empire of Assyria was then drawing to a close, and it is not unlikely that Necho's expedition tended to hasten its fall. He was marching against Carchemish on the Euphrates, a place already of importance in the annals of the Egyptian wars of the XIXth dynasty (*Sel. Pap. Sallier*, 2). As he passed along the coast of Palestine, Josiah disputed his passage, probably in consequence of a treaty with Assyria. The king of Egypt remonstrated, sending ambassadors to assure him that he did not make war upon him, and that God was on his side. "Nevertheless Josiah would not turn his face from him, but disguised himself, that he might fight with him, and hearkened not unto the words of Necho from the mouth of God, and came to fight in the valley of Megiddo." Here he was wounded by the archers of the king of Egypt, and died (comp. 2 Chr. xxxv. 20-24; 2 K. xxiii. 29, 30). Necho's assertion, that he was obeying God's command in warring with the Assyrians, seems here to be confirmed. Yet it can scarcely be understood as more than a conviction that the war was predestined, for it ended in the destruction of Necho's army and the curtailment of his empire. Josiah seems from the narrative to have known he was wrong in opposing the king of Egypt; otherwise an act so contrary to the Egyptianizing policy of his house would scarcely have led to his destruction and be condemned in the

---

a According to this historian, he was the son of ?sammetichus I. : this the monuments do not corroborate. Dr. Brugsch says that he married NEET-AKERT, Nitocris, daughter of Psammetichus I. and queen SHEPUN-TEPET, who appears, like her mother, o have been the heiress of an Egyptian royal line,

and supposes that he was the son of Psammetichus by another wife (see *Histoire d' Égypte*, p. 252; comp 248). If he married Nitocris, he may have been called by Herodotus by mistake the son of Psammet lchus.

history. Herodotus mentions this battle, relating that Necho made war against the Syrians, and defeated them at Magdolus, after which he took Cadytis, "a large city of Syria" (ii. 159). There can be no reasonable doubt that Magdolus is Megiddo, and not the Egyptian town of that name [MIGDOL], but the identification of Cadytis is difficult. It has been conjectured to be Jerusalem, and its name has been supposed to correspond to the ancient title "the Holy," הקדושה, but it is elsewhere mentioned by Herodotus as a great coast-town of Palestine near Egypt (iii. 5), and it has therefore been supposed to be Gaza. The difficulty that Gaza is not beyond Megiddo would perhaps be removed if Herodotus be thought to have confounded Megiddo with the Egyptian Magdolus, but this is not certain. (See Sir Gardner Wilkinson's note to *Her.* ii. 159, ed. Rawlinson.) It seems possible that Kadytis is the Hittite city KETESH, on the Orontes, which was the chief stronghold in Syria of those captured by the kings of the XVIIIth and XIXth dynasties. The Greek historian adds that Necho dedicated the dress he wore on these occasions to Apollo at the temple of Branchidae (*l. c.*). On Josiah's death his son Jehoahaz was set up by the people, but dethroned three months afterwards by Pharaoh, who imposed on the land the moderate tribute of a hundred talents of silver and a talent of gold, and put in his place another son of Josiah, Eliakim, whose name he changed to Jehoiakim, conveying Jehoahaz to Egypt, where he died (2 K. xxiii. 30–34; 2 Chr. xxxvi. 1–4). Jehoiakim appears to have been the elder son, so that the deposing of his brother may not have been merely because he was made king without the permission of the conqueror. Necho seems to have soon returned to Egypt: perhaps he was on his way thither when he deposed Jehoahaz. The army was probably posted at Carchemish, and was there defeated by Nebuchadnezzar in the fourth year of Necho (B. C. 607), that king not being, as it seems, then at its head (Jer. xlvi. 1, 2, 6, 10). This battle led to the loss of all the Asiatic dominions of Egypt; and it is related, after the mention of the death of Jehoiakim, that "the king of Egypt came not again any more out of his land: for the king of Babylon had taken from the river of Egypt unto the river Euphrates all that pertained to the king of Egypt" (2 K. xxiv. 7). Jeremiah's prophecy of this great defeat by Euphrates is followed by another, of its consequence, the invasion of Egypt itself; but the latter calamity did not occur in the reign of Necho, nor in that of his immediate successor, Psammetichus II., but in that of Hophra, and it was yet future in the last king's reign when Jeremiah had been carried into Egypt after the destruction of Jerusalem.

10. *Pharaoh Hophra.* — The next king of Egypt mentioned in the Bible is Pharaoh Hophra, the second successor of Necho, from whom he was separated by the six years' reign of Psammetichus II. The name Hophra is in hieroglyphics WAH-(P)RAHAT, and the last syllable is equally omitted by Herodotus, who writes Apries, and by Manetho, who writes Uaphris. He came to the throne about B. C. 58, and ruled nineteen years. Herodotus makes him son of Psammetichus II., whom he calls Psammis, and great-grandson of Psammetichus I. The historian relates his great prosperity, how he attacked Sidon, and fought a battle at sea with the king of Tyre, until at length

an army which he had dispatched to conquer Cyrene was routed, and the Egyptians, thinking he had purposely caused its overthrow to gain entire power, no doubt by substituting mercenaries for native troops, revolted, and set up Amasis as king. Apries, only supported by the Carian and Ionian mercenaries, was routed in a pitched battle. Herodotus remarks in narrating this, "It is said that Apries believed that there was not a god who could cast him down from his eminence, so firmly did he think that he had established himself in his kingdom." He was taken prisoner, and Amasis for awhile treated him with kindness, but when the Egyptians blamed him, "he gave Apries over into the hands of his former subjects, to deal with as they chose. Then the Egyptians took him and strangled him" (ii. 161–169). In the Bible it is related that Zedekiah, the last king of Judah, was aided by a Pharaoh against Nebuchadnezzar, in fulfillment of a treaty, and that an army came out of Egypt, so that the Chaldæans were obliged to raise the siege of Jerusalem. The city was first besieged in the ninth year of Zedekiah, B. C. 590, and was captured in his eleventh year, B. C. 588. It was evidently continuously invested for a length of time before it was taken, so that it is most probable that Pharaoh's expedition took place during 590 or 589. There may, therefore, be some doubt whether Psammetichus II. be not the king here spoken of; but it must be remembered that the siege may be supposed to have lasted some time before the Egyptians could have heard of it and marched to relieve the city, and also that Hophra may have come to the throne as early as B. C. 590. The Egyptian army returned without effecting its purpose (Jer. xxxvii. 5–8; Ez. xvii. 11–18; comp. 2 K. xxv. 1–4). Afterwards a remnant of the Jews fled to Egypt, and seem to have been kindly received. From the prophecies against Egypt and against these fugitives we learn more of the history of Hophra; and here the narrative of Herodotus, of which we have given the chief heads, is a valuable commentary. Ezekiel speaks of the arrogance of this king in words which strikingly recall those of the Greek historian. The prophet describes him as a great crocodile lying in his rivers, and saying "My river [is] mine own, and I have made [it] for myself" (xxix. 3). Pharaoh was to be overthrown and his country invaded by Nebuchadnezzar (xxix., xxx., xxxi., xxxii.). This prophecy was yet unfulfilled in B. C. 572 (xxix. 17–20). Jeremiah, in Egypt, yet more distinctly prophesied the end of Pharaoh, warning the Jews, — "Thus saith the LORD; Behold, I will give Pharaoh-hophra king of Egypt into the hand of his enemies, and into the hand of them that seek his life; as I gave Zedekiah king of Judah into the hand of Nebuchadrezzar king of Babylon, his enemy, and that sought his life" (xliv. 30). In another place, when foretelling the defeat of Necho's army, the same prophet says, — "Behold, I will punish Amon in No, and Pharaoh, and Egypt, with their gods, and their kings; even Pharaoh, and [all] them that trust in him; and I will deliver them into the hand of those that seek their lives, and into the hand of Nebuchadrezzar king of Babylon, and into the hand of his servants" (xlvi. 25, 26). These passages, which entirely agree with the account Herodotus gives of the death of Apries, make it not improbable that the invasion of Nebuchadnezzar was the cause of that disaffection of his subjects which ended in the overthrow and death of this Pharaoh. The invasion is not spoken of by any reliable profane historian, excepting Berosus (Cory, *Anc. Frag.* 2d ed. pp. 37, 38), but the silence of Herodotus and others can no longer be a matter of surprise, as we now know from the Assyrian records in cuneiform of conquests of Egypt either unrecorded elsewhere or only mentioned by second-rate annalists. No subsequent Pharaoh is mentioned in Scripture, but there are predictions doubtless referring to the misfortunes of later princes until the second Persian conquest, when the prophecy, " there shall be no more a prince of the land of Egypt " (Es. xxx. 13), was fulfilled.   R. S. P.

PHARAOH'S DAUGHTER; PHARAOH, THE DAUGHTER OF. Three Egyptian princesses, daughters of Pharaohs, are mentioned in the Bible.

1. The preserver of Moses, daughter of the Pharaoh who first oppressed the Israelites. She appears from her conduct towards Moses to have been heiress to the throne, something more than ordinary adoption seeming to be indicated in the passage in Hebrews respecting the faith of Moses (xi. 23-26), and the designation " Pharaoh's daughter," perhaps here indicating that she was the only daughter. She probably lived for at least forty years after she saved Moses, for it seems to be implied in Hebrews (*l. c.*) that she was living when he fled to Midian. Artapanus, or Artabanus, a historian of uncertain date, who appears to have preserved traditions current among the Egyptian Jews, calls this princess Merrhis, and her father, the oppressor, Palmanothes, and relates that she was married to Chenephres, who ruled in the country above Memphis, for that at that time there were many kings of Egypt, but that this one, as it seems, became sovereign of the whole country (*Frag. Hist. Grœc.* iii. pp. 220 ff.). Palmanothes may be supposed to be a corruption of Amenophis, the equivalent of Amen-hept the Egyptian name of four kings of the XVIIIth dynasty, and also, but incorrectly, applied to one of the XIXth, whose Egyptian name, Menptah, is wholly different from that of the others. No one of these however had, as far as we know, a daughter with a name resembling Merrhis, nor is there any king with a name like Chenephres of this time. These kings Amenophis, moreover, do not belong to the period of contemporary dynasties. The tradition is apparently of little value excepting as showing that one quite different from that given by Manetho and others was anciently current.   [See PHARAOH, 3.]

2. Bithiah, wife of Mered an Israelite, daughter of a Pharaoh of an uncertain age, probably of about the time of the Exodus.   [See BITHIAH; PHARAOH, 5.]

3. A wife of Solomon, most probably daughter of a king of the XXIst dynasty. She was married to Solomon early in his reign, and apparently treated with distinction. It has been supposed that the Song of Solomon was written on the occasion of this marriage; but the idea is, we think, repugnant to sound criticism. She was at first wrought into the city of David (1 K. iii. 1), and afterwards a house was built for her (vii. 8, ix. 24), because Solomon would not have her dwell in the house of David, which had been rendered holy by the ark having been there (2 Chr. viii. 11).   [See PHARAOH, 7.]   R. S. P.

PHARAOH, THE WIFE OF. The wife of one Pharaoh, the king who received Hadad the Edomite, is mentioned in Scripture. She is called " queen," and her name, Tahpenes, is given. Her husband was most probably of the XXIst dynasty [TAHPENES; PHARAOH, 6.]   R. S. P.

PHARATHO'NI [a] ([Rom. Ald. Comp. Φαραθωνί; Alex.] Φαραθων; [Sin.¹ omits;] Joseph. Φαραθώ: Peshito, *Pherath:* Vulg. *Phara*). One of the cities of Judæa fortified by Bacchides during his contests with Jonathan Maccabæus (1 Macc ix. 50). In both MSS. [see note below] of the LXX. the name is joined to the preceding—Thamnatha-Pharathon; but in Josephus, the Syriac, and Vulgate, the two are separated. Ewald (*Geschichte*, iv. 373) adheres to the former. Pharathon doubtless represents an ancient Pirathon, though hardly that of the Judges, since that was in Mt. Ephraim, probably at *Ferata*, a few miles west of *Nablus*, too far north to be included in Judæa properly so called.   G.

PHA'RES (Φαρές: *Phares*), PHAREZ or PEREZ, the son of Judah (Matt. i. 3; Luke iii. 33).

PHA'REZ. 1. (PEREZ, 1 Chr. xxvii. 3; PHARES, Matt. i. 3, Luke iii. 33, 1 Esdr. v. 5), (פֶּרֶץ: Φαρές: *Phares*, " a breach," Gen. xxxviii. 29), twin son, with Zarah, or Zerah, of Judah and Tamar his daughter-in-law. The circumstances of his birth are detailed in Gen. xxxviii. Pharez seems to have kept the right of primogeniture over his brother, as, in the genealogical lists, his name comes first. The house also which he founded was far more numerous and illustrious than that of the Zarhites. Its remarkable fertility is alluded to in Ruth iv. 12, " Let thy house be like the house of Pharez, whom Tamar bare unto Judah." [b] Of Pharez's personal history or character nothing is known. We can only speak of him therefore as a demarch, and exhibit his genealogical relations. At the time of the sojourn in the wilderness the families of the tribe of Judah were: of Shelah, the family of the Shelanites, or Shilonites; of Pharez, the family of the Pharzites; of Zerah, the family of the Zarhites. And the sons of Pharez were, of Hezron the family of the Hezronites, of Hamul the family of the Hamulites (Num. xxvi. 20, 21). After the death, therefore, of Er and Onan without children, Pharez occupied the rank of Judah's second son, and moreover, from two of his sons sprang two new chief houses, those of the Hezronites and Hamulites. From Hezron's second son Ram, or Aram, sprang David and the kings of Judah, and eventually Jesus Christ. [GENEALOGY OF JESUS CHRIST.] The house of Caleb was also incorporated into the house of Hezron [CALEB], and so were reckoned among the descendants of Pharez. Another line of Pha-

---

a Whence our translators borrowed the final i of this name does not appear: there is nothing in either of the originals to suggest it. The Geneva Vers. has it too. [The readings given above sufficiently account for the form of the word in the common English version. Mr. Grove does not seem to be aware that the

Vatican manuscript (B) does not contain the Books of Maccabees. — A.]

b • Pharez is named there and in ver. 18 for the additional reason that he was the progenitor of Boaz and perhaps of the Bethlehemites as a distinct clan. H.

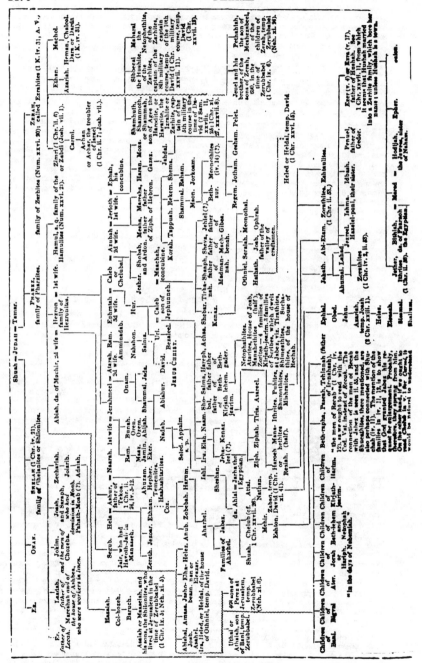

rez's descendants were reckoned as sons of Manasseh by the second marriage of Hezron with the
daughter of Machir (1 Chr. ii. 21–23). In the
census of the house of Judah contained in 1 Chr.
iv., drawn up apparently in the reign of Hezekiah
(iv. 41), the houses enumerated in ver. 1 are Pharez, Hezron, Carmi, Hur, and Shobal. Of these
all but Carmi (who was a Zarhite, Josh. vii. 1)
were descendants of Pharez. Hence it is not unlikely that, as is suggested in the margin of A. V.,
Carmi is an error for *Chelubai*. Some of the sons
of Shelah are mentioned separately at vv. 21, 22.
[PAHATH-MOAB.] In the reign of David the
house of Pharez seems to have been eminently distinguished. The chief of all the captains of the
host for the first month, Jashobeam, the son of
Zabdiel (1 Chr. xxvii. 2, 3), so famous for his
prowess (1 Chr. xi. 11), and called "the chief
among the captains" (*ib.* and 2 Sam. xxiii. 8), was
of the sons of Perez, or Pharez. A considerable
number of the other mighty men seem also, from
their patronymic or gentile names, to have been of
the same house, those namely who are called Bethlehemites, Paltites (1 Chr. ii. 33–47), Tekoites,
Netophathites,[a] and Ithrites (1 Chr. ii. 53, iv. 7).
Zabad the son of Ahlai, and Joab, and his brothers, Abishai and Asahel, we know were Pharzites
(1 Chr. ii. 31, 36, 54, xi. 41). And the royal
house itself was the head of the family. We have
no means of assigning to their respective families
those members of the tribe of Judah who are incidentally mentioned after David's reign, as Adnah,
the chief captain of Judah in Jehoshaphat's reign,
and Jehohanan and Amasiah, his companions (2
Chr. xvii. 14–16); but that the family of Pharez
continued to thrive and multiply, we may conclude
from the numbers who returned from captivity.
At Jerusalem alone 468 of the sons of Perez, with
Athaiah, or Uthai, at their head, were dwelling in
the days of Zerubbabel (1 Chr. ix. 4; Neh. xi.
4–6), Zerubbabel himself of course being of the
family (1 Esdr. v. 5). Of the lists of returned
captives in Ezr. ii., Neh. vii., in Nehemiah's time,
the following seem to have been of the sons of
Pharez, judging as before from the names of their
ancestors, or the towns to which they belonged:
the children of Bani (Ezr. ii. 10; comp. 1 Chr. ix.
4); of Bigvai (ii. 14; comp. Ezr. viii. 14); of Ater
(ii. 16; comp. 1 Chr. ii. 26, 54); of Jorah, or Har-
iph (ii. 18; Neh. vii. 24; comp. 1 Chr. ii. 51); of
Beth-lehem and Netophah (ii. 21, 22; comp. 1 Chr.
ii. 54); of Kirjath-arim (ii. 25; comp. 1 Chr. ii.
50, 53); of Harim (ii. 32; comp. 1 Chr. iv. 8); and,
judging from their position, many of the intermediate ones also (comp. also the lists in Ezr. x. 25–
43; Neh. x. 14–27). Of the builders of the wall
named in Neh. iii. the following were of the house
of Pharez: Zaccur the son of Imri (v. 2, by comparison with 1 Chr. ix. 4, and Ezr. viii. 14, where
we ought, with many MSS., to read *Zaccur* for
Zabbud); Zadok the son of Baana (v. 4, by comparison with 2 Sam. xxiii. 29, where we find that
Baanah was a Netophathite, which agrees with
Zadok's place here next to the Tekoites, since
Beth-lehem, Netophah, and Tekoa, are often in close
juxtaposition, comp. 1 Chr. ii. 54, iv. 4, 5, Ezr. ii.
21, 22, Neh. vii. 26, and the situation of the Netophathites close to Jerusalem, among the Benja-

mites, Neh. xii. 28, 29, compared with the mixture
of Benjamites with Pharzites and Zarhites in Neh.
iii. 2–7); the Tekoites (vv. 5 and 27, compared with
1 Chr. ii. 24, iv. 5); Jehoiada, the son of Paseah
(v. 6, compared with 1 Chr. iv. 12, where Paseah,
a Chelubite, is apparently descended from Ashur,
the father of Tekoa); Rephaiah, the son of Hur (v.
9, compared with 1 Chr. ii. 20, 50, iv. 4,12, Beth-
Raphah); Hanun (v. 13 and 30), with the inhabitants of Zanoah (compared with 1 Chr. iv. 18);
perhaps Malchiah the son of Rechab (v. 14, compared with 1 Chr. ii. 55); Nehemiah, son of Azbuk,
ruler of Beth-zur (v. 16, compared with 1 Chr. ii.
45); and perhaps Baruch, son of Zabba, or Zaccai
(v. 20), if for Zaccai we read Zaccur as the mention of "the *other*, or second, *piece*" makes probable, as well as his proximity to Meremoth in this
record piece, as Zaccur was to Meremoth in their
first pieces (vv. 2, 4).

The table on the opposite page displays the chief
descents of the house of Pharez, and shows its
relative greatness, as compared with the other
houses of the tribe of Judah. It will be observed
that many of the details are more topographical
than genealogical, and that several towns in Dan,
Simeon, and Benjamin, as Eshtaol, Zorah, Etam,
and Gibea, seem to have been peopled with Pharez's
descendants. The confusion between the elder and
younger Caleb is inextricable, and suggests the
suspicion that the elder Caleb or Chelubai may
have had no real, but only a genealogical existence, intended to embrace all those families who
on the settlement in Canaan were reckoned to
the house of Caleb, the son of Jephunneh, the
Kenezite.

2. (Φόρος; [Vat. Φαρες:] *Phares*) = PAROSH
(1 Esdr. viii. 30; comp. Ezr. viii. 3).

                                        A. C. H.

PHARI′RA (Φαριρά; [Vat. Φαρειδα;] Alex.
Φαριδα: *Phasida*) = PERIDA or PERUDA (1 Esdr.
v. 33).

PHAR′ISEES (Φαρισαῖοι: *Pharisæi*), a religious party or school amongst the Jews at the time
of Christ, so called from *Perishin*, the Aramaic
form of the Hebrew word *Perúshim*, "separated."
The name does not occur either in the Old Testament or in the Apocrypha; but it is usually considered that the Pharisees were essentially the same
with the Assideans (i. e. *chasidim* = godly men,
saints) mentioned in the 1st Book of Maccabees ii.
42, vii. 13–17, and in the 2d Book xiv. 6. And
those who admit the existence of Maccabean Psalms
find allusions to the Assideans in Psalms lxxix. 2,
xcvii. 10, cxxxii. 9, 16, cxlix. 9, where *chasidim* is
translated "saints" in the A. V. (See Fürst's
Handwörterbuch, i. 420 *b*.) In the 2d Book of
Maccabees, supposed by Geiger to have been written by a Pharisee (*Urschrift und Uebersetzungen
der Bibel*, p. 226), there are two passages which
tend to illustrate the meaning of the word "separated;" one in xiv. 3, where Alcimus, who had
been high-priest, is described as having defiled
himself willfully "in the times of the mingling"
— ἐν τοῖς τῆς ἐπιμιξίας χρόνοις, — and
another in xiv. 38, where the zealous Razis is said
to have been accused of Judaism, "in the former
times when there was no mingling," ἐν τοῖς
ἔμπροσθεν χρόνοις τῆς ἀμιξίας. In both cases
the expression "mingling" refers to the time when
Antiochus Epiphanes had partially succeeded in
breaking down the barrier which divided the Jews

---

[a] Maharai the Netophathite was however a Zarhite
(1 Chr. xxvii. 14), while Heldai, or Heled, the descendant of Othniel, was a Pharzite (1 Chr. xxvii. 15).

from his other subjects; and it was in the resolute determination to resist the adoption of Grecian customs, and the slightest departure from the requirements of their own Law, that the "Separated" took their rise as a party. Compare 1 Macc. i. 13–15, 41–49, 62, 63. Subsequently, however (and perhaps not wholly at first), this by no means exhausted the meaning of the word "Pharisees."

A knowledge of the opinions and practices of this party at the time of Christ is of great importance for entering deeply into the genius of the Christian religion. A cursory perusal of the Gospels is sufficient to show that Christ's teaching was in some respects thoroughly antagonistic to theirs. He denounced them in the bitterest language; and in the sweeping charges of hypocrisy which He made against them as a class, He might even, at first sight, seem to have departed from that spirit of meekness,[a] of gentleness in judging others, and of abstinence from the imputation of improper motives, which is one of the most characteristic and original charms of his own precepts. See Matt. xv. 7, 8, xxiii. 5, 13, 14, 15, 23; Mark vii. 6; Luke xi. 42–44, and compare Matt. vii. 1–5, xi. 29, xii. 19, 20; Luke vi. 28, 37–42. Indeed it is difficult to avoid the conclusion that his repeated denunciations of the Pharisees mainly exasperated them into taking measures for causing his death; so that in one sense He may be said to have shed his blood, and to have laid down his life in protesting against their practice and spirit. (See especially verses 53, 54 in the 11th chapter of Luke, which follow immediately upon the narration of what he said while dining with a Pharisee.) Hence to understand the Pharisees is, by contrast, an aid towards understanding the spirit of uncorrupted Christianity.

Authorities. — The sources of information respecting the Pharisees are mainly threefold. 1st. The writings of Josephus, who was himself a Pharisee (*Vit.* p. 2), and who in each of his great works professes to give a direct account of their opinions (*B. J.* ii. 8, § 2–14; *Ant.* xviii. 1, § 2, and compare xiii. 10, § 5–6, xvii. 2, § 4, xiii. 16, § 2, and *Vit.* p. 38). The value of Josephus's accounts

would be much greater, if he had not accommodated them, more or less, to Greek ideas, so that in order to arrive at the exact truth, not only much must be added, but likewise much of what he has written must be retranslated, as it were, into Hebrew conceptions. 2dly. The New Testament, including St. Paul's epistles, in addition to the Gospels and the Acts of the Apostles. St. Paul had been instructed by an illustrious Rabbi (Acts xxii. 3); he had been a rigid Pharisee (xxiii 6, xxvi. 5), and the remembrance of the galling bondage from which he had escaped (Gal. iv. 9, 10, v. 1) was probably a human element in that deep spirituality, and that uncompromising opposition to Jewish ceremonial observances, by which he preëminently contributed to make Christianity the religion of the civilized world. 3dly. The first portion of the Talmud, called the Mishna, or "second law." This is by far the most important source of information respecting the Pharisees; and it may safely be asserted that it is nearly impossible to have adequate conceptions respecting them, without consulting that work. It is a digest of the Jewish traditions, and a compendium of the whole ritual law, reduced to writing in its present form by Rabbi Jehudah the Holy, a Jew of great wealth and influence, who flourished in the 2d century. He succeeded his father Simeon as patriarch of Tiberias, and held that office at least thirty years. The precise date of his death is disputed; some placing it in a year somewhat antecedent to 194, A. D. (see Graetz, *Geschichte der Juden*, iv. 251), while others place it as late as 220 A. D., when he would have been about 81 years old (Jost's *Geschichte des Judenthums und seiner Sekten*, ii. 118). The Mishna is very concisely written, and requires notes. This circumstance led to the Commentaries called Gemara [b] (*i. e.* Supplement, Completion, according to Buxtorf), which form the second part of the Talmud, and which are very commonly meant when the word "Talmud" is used by itself. The language of the Mishna is that of the later Hebrew, purely written on the whole, though with a few grammatical Aramaisms, and interspersed with Greek, Latin, and Aramaic words which had become naturalized. The work

---

[a] This is thus noticed by Milton, from the point of view of his own peculiar ecclesiastical opinions: "The invincible warrior Zeal, shaking loosely the slack reins, drives over the heads of scarlet prelates, and such as are insolent to maintain traditions, bruising their stiff necks under his flaming wheels. Thus did the true prophets of old combat with the false. *Thus Christ Himself, the fountain of meekness, found acrimony enough to be still galling and vexing the prelatical Pharisees.*" — Apology for Smectymnuus.

[b] There are two Gemaras: one of Jerusalem, in which there is said to be no passage which can be proved to be later than the first half of the 4th century; and the other of Babylon, completed about 500 A. D. The latter is the most important, and by far the longest. It was estimated by Chiarini to be fifteen times as long as the Mishna. The *whole* of the Gemaras has never been translated; though a proposal to make such a translation was brought before the public by Chiarini (*Théorie du Judaïsme appliquée à la Réforme des israélites*, A. D. 1830). But Chiarini died in 1832. Fifteen treatises of the Jerusalem Gemara, and two of the Babylonian, are given, accompanied by a Latin translation, in Ugolino's *Thesaurus*, vols. xvii.–xx. Some interpret Gemara to be identical in meaning with Talmud, signifying "doctrine."

* Ugolini's *Thesaurus* contains *twenty* treatises of

the Jerusalem Gemara with a Latin translation, and *three* of the Babylonian; see, in addition to the vols referred to above, vols. xxv. and xxx. Chiarini (*Le Talmud de Babylone trad. en langue française*, vols. i., ii., Leips. 1831) has translated both the Mishna and Gemara of the first treatise in the Talmud (*Berachoth*, "Blessings"), and prefixed to it a full account of the Talmud by way of introduction. The treatise *Berachoth* has also been published in the original with a German translation, notes, etc., by E. M. Pinner, Berlin, 1842, fol., who has likewise prefixed to it an Introduction to the Talmud. For an account of the various books of the Talmud in English one may see the art. *Talmud* by S. Davidson in Kitto's *Cyclopædia of Bibl. Lit.*, 3d ed. (1866). iii. 963–945; the appendix to Robt. Young's translation of *The Ethics of the Fathers* (Pirke Aboth), Edinb. 1862; or Dr. I. Nordheimer's article, *The Talmud and the Rabbies*, in the *Amer. Bibl. Repository* for Oct. 1839. For fuller information about the Talmud, see Wolf, *Bibl. Hebraea*, ii. 657–998, and Pressel's art. *Talmud* in Herzog's *Real-Encykl.* xv. 615–665; also the famous art. on the Talmud by E. Deutsch in the *Quarterly Review* for Oct. 1867, and an art. by M. Grünbaum in the *North Amer. Review* for April, 1868. There is a brief, popular account of the Talmud, by Dr. C. E. Stowe, in the *Atlantic Monthly* for June, 1868.   A.

is distributed into six great divisions or orders. The first (*Zeraim*) relates to "seeds," or productions of the land, and it embraces all matters connected with the cultivation of the soil, and the disposal of its produce in offerings or tithes. It is preceded by a treatise on "Blessings" (*Beracoth*). The 2d (*Moed*) relates to festivals and their observances. The 3d (*Nashim*) to women, and includes regulations respecting betrothals, marriages, and divorces. The 4th (*Nezikin*) relates to damages sustained by means of man, beasts, or things; with decisions on points at issue between man and man in commercial dealings and compacts. The 5th (*Kodashim*) treats of holy things, of offerings, and of the temple-service. The 6th (*Tohoróth*) treats of what is clean and unclean. These 6 Orders are subdivided into 61 Treatises, as reckoned by Maimonides; but want of space precludes describing their contents; and the mention of the titles would give little information without such description. For obtaining accurate knowledge on these points, the reader is referred to Surenhusius's admirable edition of the *Mishna* in 6 vols. folio, Amsterdam, 1698–1703, which contains not only a Latin translation of the text, but likewise ample prefaces and explanatory notes, including those of the celebrated Maimonides. Others may prefer the German translation of Jost, in an edition of the Mishna wherein the Hebrew text is pointed; but the German is in Hebrew letters, 3 vols. 4to, Berlin. [1832–34. There is also a German translation, with notes, by J. J. Rabe, in 6 vols. 4to, Onolzb. 1760–63, a copy of which is in the library of Yale College. — A.] And an English reader may obtain an excellent idea of the whole work from an English translation of 18 of its Treatises by De Sola and Raphall, London, 1843. There is no reasonable doubt, that although it may include a few passages of a later date, the Mishna was composed, as a whole, in the 2d century, and represents the traditions which were current amongst the Pharisees at the time of Christ. This may be shown in the following way. 1st. Josephus, whose autobiography was apparently not written later than A. D. 100, the third year of the reign of Trajan, is an authority to show that up to that period no important change had been introduced since Christ's death; and the general facts of Jewish history render it morally impossible that there should have been any essential alteration either in the reign of Trajan, the epoch of the great Jewish revolts in Egypt, Cyrene, and Cyprus; or in the reign of Hadrian, during which there was the disastrous second rebellion in Judæa. And it was at the time of the suppression of this rebellion that Rabbi Jehudah was born; the tradition being that his birth was on the very same day that Rabbi Akiba was flayed alive and put to death, A. D. 136–137. 2dly. There is frequent reference in the Mishna to the sayings and decisions of Hillel and Shammai, the celebrated leaders of two schools among the Pharisees, differing from each other on what would seem to Christians to be comparatively unimportant points. But Hillel and Shammai flourished somewhat before the birth of Christ; and, except on the incredible supposition of forgeries or mistakes on a very large scale, their decisions conclusively furnish particulars of the general system in force among the Pharisees during the period of Christ's teaching. There is likewise occasional reference to the opinion of Rabbi Gamaliel, the grandson of Hillel, and the teacher of St. Paul. 3dly. The Mishna contains numerous ceremonial regulations, especially in the 5th Order, which presuppose that the Temple-service is still subsisting, and it cannot be supposed that these were invented after the destruction of the Temple by Titus. But these breathe the same general spirit as the other traditions, and there is no sufficient reason for assuming any difference of date between the one kind and the other. Hence for *facts* concerning the system of the Pharisees, as distinguished from an appreciation of its merits or defects, the value of the Mishna as an authority is greater than that of all other sources of information put together.

Referring to the Mishna for details, it is proposed in this article to give a general view of the peculiarities of the Pharisees; afterwards to notice their opinions on a future life and on free-will; and finally, to make some remarks on the proselytizing spirit attributed to them at the time of Christ. Points noticed elsewhere in this Dictionary will be as far as possible avoided. Hence information respecting Corban and Phylacteries, which in the New Testament are peculiarly associated with the Pharisees, must be sought for under the appropriate titles. See CORBAN and FRONTLETS.

I. The fundamental principle of the Pharisees common to them with all orthodox modern Jews is, that by the side of the written Law regarded as a summary of the principles and general laws of the Hebrew people, there was an oral law to complete and to explain the written Law. It was an article of faith that in the Pentateuch there was no precept, and no regulation, ceremonial, doctrinal, or legal, of which God had not given to Moses all explanations necessary for their application, with the order to transmit them by word of mouth (Klein's *Vérité sur le Talmud*, p. 9). The classical passage in the Mishna on this subject is the following: "Moses received the (oral) law from Sinai, and delivered it to Joshua, and Joshua to the elders, and the elders to the prophets, and the prophets to the men of the Great Synagogue" (*Pirke Abóth*, i.). This remarkable statement is so destitute of what would at the present day be deemed historical evidence, and would, it might be supposed, have been rendered so incredible to a Jew by the absence of any distinct allusion[a] to the fact in the Old Testament, that it is interesting to consider by what process of argument the principle could ever have won acceptance. It may be conceived in the following way. The Pentateuch, according to the Rabbins, contains 613 laws, including 248 commands, and 365 prohibitions; but whatever may be the number of the laws, however minutely they may be anatomized, or into whatever form they may be thrown, there is nowhere an

---

[a] A passage in Deuteronomy (xvii. 8–11) has been interpreted so as to serve as a basis for an oral law. But that passage seems merely to prescribe obedience to the priests, the Levites, and to the judges in civil and criminal matters of controversy between man and man. A fanciful application of the words עַל־פִּי in ver. 11 has favored the rabbinical interpretation. In the "Festival Prayers" of the English Jews, p. 69, for Pentecost, it is stated, of God, in a prayer, "He explained it (the Law) to his people *face to face*, and on every point are ninety-eight explanations."

allusion to the duty of prayer, or to the doctrine of a future life. The absence of the doctrine of a future life has been made familiar to English theologians by the author of "The Divine Legation of Moses;" and the fact is so undeniable, that it is needless to dwell upon it farther. The absence of any injunction to pray has not attracted equal attention, but seems to be almost equally certain. The only passage which by any ingenuity has ever been interpreted to enjoin prayer is in Ex. xxiii. 25, where the words are used, "And ye shall *serve* Jehovah your God." But as the Pentateuch abounds with specific injunctions as to the *mode* of serving Jehovah; by sacrifices, by meat-offerings, by drink-offerings, by the rite of circumcision, by observing festivals, such as the Sabbath, the Passover, the feast of weeks, and the feast of tabernacles, by obeying all his ceremonial and moral commands, and by loving him, it is contrary to sound rules of construction to import into the general word "serve" Jehovah the specific meaning "pray to" Jehovah, when that particular mode of service is nowhere distinctly commanded in the Law. There being then thus no mention either of a future life, or of prayer as a duty,[a] it would be easy for the Pharisees at a time when prayer was universally practiced, and a future life was generally believed in or desired, to argue from the supposed inconceivability of a true revelation not commanding prayer, or not asserting a future life, to the necessity of Moses having treated of both orally. And when the principle of an oral tradition in two such important points was once admitted, it was easy for a skillful controversialist to carry the application of the principle much farther by insisting that there was precisely the same evidence for numerous other traditions having come from Moses as for those two; and that it was illogical, as well as presumptuous, to admit the two only, and to exercise the right of selection and private 'udgment respecting the rest.

It is not to be supposed that all the traditions which bound the Pharisees were believed to be direct revelations to Moses on Mount Sinai. In addition to such revelations, which were not disputed, although there was no proof from the written Law to support them, and in addition to interpretations received from Moses, which were either implied in the written Law or to be elicited from them by reasoning, there were three other classes of traditions. 1st. Opinions on disputed points, which were the result of a majority of votes. To this class belonged the secondary questions on which there was a difference between the schools of Hillel and Shammai. 2dly. Decrees made by prophets and wise men in different ages, in conformity with a saying attributed to the men of the Great Synagogue, "Be deliberate in judgment; train up many disciples: and *make a fence for the Law.*" These carried prohibitions farther than the written Law or oral law of Moses, in order to protect the Jewish people from temptations to sin or pollution. For example, the injunction, "Thou shalt not seethe a

kid in his ..oth.r's milk,"[b] Ex. xxiii. 19, xxxiv. 26; Deut. xiv. 21; was interpreted by the oral law to mean that the flesh of quadrupeds might not be cooked, or in any way mixed with milk for food; so that even now amongst the orthodox Jews milk may not be eaten for some hours after meat. But this was extended by the wise men to the flesh of birds; and now, owing to this "fence to the Law," the admixture of *poultry* with any milk, or its preparations, is rigorously forbidden. When once a decree of this kind has been passed, it could not be reversed; and it was subsequently said that not even Elijah himself could take away anything from the 18 points which had been determined on by the school of Shammai and the school of Hillel. 3dly. Legal decisions of proper ecclesiastical authorities on disputed questions. Some of these were attributed to Moses, some to Joshua, and some to Ezra. Some likewise to Rabbis of later date, such as Hillel and Gamaliel. However, although in these several ways, *all* the traditions of the Pharisees were not deemed direct revelations from Jehovah, there is no doubt that all became invested, more or less, with a peculiar sanctity; so that, regarded collectively, the study of them and the observance of them became as imperative as the study and observance of the precepts in the Bible.

Viewed as a whole, they treated men like children, formalizing and defining the minutest particulars of ritual observances. The expressions of "bondage," of "weak and beggarly elements," and of "burdens too heavy for men to bear," faithfully represent the impression produced by their multiplicity. An elaborate argument might be advanced for many of them individually, but the sting of them consisted in their aggregate number, which would have a tendency to quench the fervor and the freshness of a spiritual religion. They varied in character, and the following instances may be given of three different classes: 1st, of those which, admitting certain principles, were points reasonable to define; 2dly, of points defined which were superfluously particularized; and 3dly, of points defined where the discussion of them at all was superstitious and puerile. Of the first class the very first decision in the Mishna is a specimen. It defines the period up to which a Jew is bound, as his evening service, to repeat the Shema. The Shema is the celebrated passage in Deut. vi. 4-9, commencing, "Hear, O Israel: the Lord our God is one Lord, and thou shalt love the Lord thy God with all thine heart, and with all thy soul, and with all thy might." It is a tradition that every Israelite is bound to recite this passage twice in the twenty-four hours, morning and evening — for which authority is supposed to be found in verse 7, where it is said of these words, "Thou shalt talk of them . . . . when thou liest down and when thou risest up." The compulsory recitation of even these words twice a day might be objected to as leading to formalism; but, accepting the recitation as a religious duty, it might not be unreasonable that the range of time permitted for the recitation should be

---

[a] Mohammed was preceded both by Christianity and by the latest developments of Judaism: from both of which he borrowed much. See, as to Judaism, Geiger's essay, *Was hat Mohammed aus dem Judenthum aufgenommen?* Still, one of the most marked characteristics of the Korân is the unwearied reiteration of the duty of prayer, and of the certainty of a future state of retribution.

[b] Although this prohibition occurs three times, no light is thrown upon its meaning by the context. The most probable conjecture is that given under the head of IDOLATRY (ii. 1129 a), that it was aimed against some practice of idolaters. Mr. Laing gives a similar explanation of the Christian prohibition in Scandinavia against eating horse-flesh.

defined. The following is the decision on this point in the Mishna, *Beracoth* i.: "From what time do they recite the Shema in the evening? From the time that the priests are admitted to eat their oblations till the end of the first watch. The words of Rabbi Eliezer: but the wise men say, up to midnight. Rabban Gamaliel says, until the column of dawn has arisen. Case: His sons returning from a house of entertainment said, We have not yet recited the Shema; to whom he said, If the column of dawn has not yet arisen, you are bound to recite it. But not this alone; but wherever the wise men have said 'to midnight,' their injunction is in force until the column of dawn has arisen. . . . . If so, why did the wise men say till midnight? In order to keep men far from transgression." The following is an instance of the second class. It relates to the lighting candles on the eve of the Sabbath, which is the duty of every Jew: it is found in the Mishna, in the treatise *Shabbath*, c. ii., and is printed in the Hebrew and English Prayer-Book, according to the form of the German and Polish Jews, p. 66, from which to avoid objections, this translation, and others, where it is possible, are taken. "With what sort of wick and oil are the candles of the Sabbath to be lighted, and with what are they not to be lighted? They are not to be lighted with the woolly substance that grows upon cedars, nor with undressed flax, nor with silk, nor with rushes, nor with leaves out of the wilderness, nor with moss that grows on the surface of water, nor with pitch, nor with wax, nor with oil made of cotton-seed, nor with the fat of the tail or the entrails of beasts. Nathan Hamody saith it may be lighted with boiled suet; but the wise men say, be it boiled or not boiled, it may not be lighted with it. It may not be lighted with burnt oil on festival-days. Rabbi Ishmael says it may not be lighted with train-oil because of honor to the Sabbath; but the wise men allow of all sorts of oil: with mixed oil, with oil of nuts, oil of radish-seed, oil of fish, oil of gourd-seed, of resin and gum. Rabbi Tarphun saith they are not to be lighted but with oil of olives. Nothing that grows out of the woods is used for lighting but flax, and nothing that grows out of woods doth not pollute by the pollution of a tent but flax: the wick of cloth that is doubled, and has not been singed, Rabbi Eleazar saith it is unclean, and may not be lighted withal; Rabbi Akibah saith it is clean, and may be lighted withal. A man may not split a shell of an egg and fill it with oil and put it in the socket of a candlestick, because it shall blaze, though the candlestick be of earthenware; but Rabbi Jehudah permits it: if the potter made it with a hole through at first, it is allowed, because it is the same vessel. No man shall fill a platter with oil, and give it place next to the lamp, and put the head of the wick in a platter to make it drop the oil; but Rabbi Jehudah permits it." Now in regard to details of this kind, admitting it was not unreasonable to make some regulations concerning lighting candles, it certainly seems that the above particulars are too minute, and that all which was really essential could have been brought within a much smaller compass. 3dly. A specimen of the 3d class may be pointed out in the beginning of the treatise on festivals (*Moed*), entitled *Beitzah*, an *Egg*, from the following case of the egg being the first point discussed in it. We are gravely informed that "an egg laid on a festival may be eaten, according to the school of Shammai; but the school of

Hillel says it must not be eaten." In order to understand this important controversy, which reminds us of the two parties in a well-known work who took their names from the end on which each held that an egg ought to be broken, it must be observed that, for a reason into which it is unnecessary to enter at present, it was admitted on all hands, both by the school of Hillel and the school of Shammai, that if a bird which was neither to be eaten nor killed laid an egg on a festival, the egg was not to be eaten. The only point of controversy was respecting an egg laid by a hen that would be afterwards eaten. Now the school of Hillel interdicted the eating of such an egg, on account of a passage in the 5th verse of the 16th chapter of Exodus, wherein Jehovah said to Moses respecting the people who gathered manna, " on the sixth day they shall prepare that which they bring in." For it was inferred from these words that on a common day of the week a man might "prepare" for the Sabbath, or prepare for a feast-day, but that he might not prepare for the Sabbath on a feast-day, nor for a feast-day on the Sabbath. Now, as an egg laid on any particular day was deemed to have been "prepared" the day before, an egg laid on a feast-day following a Sabbath might not be eaten, because it was *prepared* on the Sabbath, and the eating of it would involve a breach of the Sabbath. And although *all* feast-days did not fall on a day following the Sabbath, yet as many did, it was deemed better, *ex majori cautelâ*, "as a fence to the Law," to interdict the eating of an egg which had been laid on any feast-day, whether such day was or was not the day after the Sabbath (see Surenhusius's *Mishna*, ii. 282). In a world wherein the objects of human interest and wonder are nearly endless, it certainly does seem a degradation of human intelligence to exercise it on matters so trifling and petty.

In order, however, to observe regulations on points of this kind, mixed with others less objectionable, and with some which, regarded from a certain point of view, were in themselves individually not unreasonable, the Pharisees formed a kind of society. A member was called a *châbêr* (חָבֵר), and those among the middle and lower classes who were not members were called "the people of the land," or the vulgar. Each member undertook, in the presence of three other members, that he would remain true to the laws of the association. The conditions were various. One of transcendent importance was that a member should refrain from everything that was not tithed (comp. Matt. xxiii. 23, and Luke xviii. 12). The Mishna says, "He who undertakes to be *trustworthy* (a word with a technical Pharisaical meaning) tithes whatever he eats, and whatever he sells, and whatever he buys, and *does not eat and drink with the people of the land.*" This was a point of peculiar delicacy, for the portion of produce reserved as tithes for the priests and Levites was *holy*, and the enjoyment of what was holy was a deadly sin. Hence a Pharisee was bound, not only to ascertain as a buyer whether the articles which he purchased had been duly tithed, but to have the same certainty in regard to what he eat in his own house and when taking his meals with others. And thus Christ, in eating with publicans and sinners, ran counter to the first principles, and shocked the most deeply-rooted prejudices, of Pharisaism; for, independently of other obvious considerations, He ate and

drank with "the people of the land," and it would
have been assumed as undoubted that He partook
on such occasions of food which had not been duly
uthed.

Perhaps some of the most characteristic laws of
the Pharisees related to what was clean (*táhôr*) and
unclean (*tâmé*). Among all oriental nations there
has been a certain tendency to symbolism in religion; and if any symbolism is admitted on such a
subject, nothing is more natural than to symbolize
purity and cleanliness of thought by cleanliness of
person, dress, and actions. Again, in all climates,
but especially in warm climates, the sanitary advantages of such cleanliness would tend to confirm
and perpetuate this kind of symbolism; and when
once the principle was conceded, superstition would
be certain to attach an intrinsic moral value to the
rigid observance of the symbol. In addition to
what might be explained in this manner, there arose
among the Jews — partly from opposition to idolatrous practices, or to what savored of idolatry,
partly from causes which it is difficult at the present day even to conjecture, possibly from mere
prejudice, individual antipathy, or strained fanciful
analogies — peculiar ideas concerning what was
clean and unclean, which at first sight might appear purely conventional. But, whether their origin was symbolical, sanitary, religious, fanciful, or
conventional, it was a matter of vital importance to
a Pharisee that he should be well acquainted with
the Pharisaical regulations concerning what was
clean and what was unclean; for, as among the
modern Hindoos (some of whose customs are very
similar to those of the Pharisees), every one tech-
nically unclean is cut off from almost every religious ceremony, so, according to the Levitical Law,
every unclean person was cut off from all religious
privileges, and was regarded as defiling the sanctuary of Jehovah (Num. xix. 20: compare Ward's
Hindoo History, Literature, and Religion, ii. 147).
On principles precisely similar to those of the
Levitical laws (Lev. xx. 25, xxii. 4-7), it was possible to incur these awful religious penalties either
by *eating* or by *touching* what was unclean in the
Pharisaical sense. In reference to *eating*, independently of the slaughtering of holy sacrifices, which is
the subject of two other treatises, the Mishna contains one treatise called *Cholin,* which is specially
devoted to the slaughtering of fowls and cattle for
domestic use (see Surenhusius, v. 114; and De Sola
and Raphall, p. 325). One point in its very first
section is by itself vitally distinctive; and if the
treatise had contained no other regulation, it would
still have raised an insuperable barrier between the
free social intercourse of Jews and other nations.
This point is, "that *any thing* slaughtered by a
heathen should be deemed unfit to be eaten, like the

carcase of an animal that had died of itself, and like
such carcase should pollute the person who carried
it." [a] On the reasonable assumption that under
such circumstances animals used for food would be
killed by Jewish slaughterers, regulations the most
minute are laid down for their guidance. In reference likewise to *touching* what is unclean, the
Mishna abounds with prohibitions and distinctions
no less minute; and by far the greatest portion of
the 6th and last "Order" relates to impurities contracted in this manner. Referring to that "Order"
for details, it may be observed that to any one fresh
from the perusal of them, and of others already adverted to, the words "Touch not, taste not, handle
not," seem a correct but almost a pale summary of
their drift and purpose (Col. ii. 21); and the stern
antagonism becomes vividly visible between them
and Him who proclaimed boldly that a man was
defiled not by anything he ate, but by the bad
thoughts of the heart alone (Matt. xv. 11); and who,
even when the guest of a Pharisee, pointedly abstained from washing his hands before a meal, in
order to rebuke the superstition which attached a
moral value to such a ceremonial act. (See Luke
xi. 37-40; and compare the Mishna vi. 480, where
there is a distinct treatise, *Yadaim,* on the washing of hands.) [b]

It is proper to add that it would be a great mistake to suppose that the Pharisees were wealthy
and luxurious, much more that they had degenerated into the vices which were imputed to some of
the Roman popes and cardinals during the 200
years preceding the Reformation. Josephus compared the Pharisees to the sect of the Stoics. He
says that they lived frugally, in no respect giving in to luxury, but that they followed the leadership of reason in what it had selected and transmitted as a good (*Ant.* xviii. 1, § 3). With this
agrees what he states in another passage, that the
Pharisees had so much weight with the multitude,
that if they said anything against a king or a high-
priest they were at once believed (xiii. 10, § 5); for
this kind of influence is more likely to be obtained
by a religious body over the people, through austerity and self-denial, than through wealth, luxury,
and self-indulgence. Although there would be
hypocrites among them, it would be unreasonable
to charge all the Pharisees as a body with hypocrisy, in the sense wherein we at the present day
use the word. A learned Jew, now living, charges
against them rather the holiness of works than hyp-
ocritical holiness — *Werkheiligkeit, nicht Schein-
heiligkeit* (Herzfeld, *Geschichte des Voltes Israel,*
iii. 359). At any rate they must be regarded as
having been some of the most intense *formalists*
whom the world has ever seen; and looking at the
average standard of excellence among mankind, it

---

[a] At the present day a strict orthodox Jew may not
eat meat of any animal, unless it has been killed by a
Jewish butcher. According to Mr. I. Disraeli (*The
Genius of Judaism,* p. 154), the butcher searches the
animal for any blemish, and, on his approval, causes
a leaden seal, stamped with the Hebrew word *cáshér*
(lawful), to be attached to the meat, attesting its
"cleanness." Mr. Disraeli likewise points out that in
Herodotus (ii. 38) a seal is recorded to have been used
for a similar purpose by Egyptian priests, to attest
that a bull about to be sacrificed was "clean," καθαρός. The Greek and Hebrew words are perhaps akin
in origin, *s* and *th* being frequently interchanged in
language.

[b] The Egyptians appear to have had ideas of "un-

cleanness" through tasting, touching, and handling,
precisely analogous to those of the Levitical Law and
of the Pharisees. The priests would not endure even
to look at beans, deeming them not *clean,* καθάρους
οὐ καθαρόν μιν εἶναι ὀσπριον (καθαρός is the Greek
word in the LXX. for *táhôr*). "No Egyptian," says
Herodotus, "would salute a Greek with a kiss, nor
use a Greek knife, or spits, or cauldron; or taste the
meat of an ox which had been cut by a Greek knife.
They drank out of bronze vessels, *rinsing them perpetually.* And if any one accidentally touched a pig, he
would plunge into the Nile, without stopping to un-
dress" (*Herodot.* ii. 37, 41, 47). Just as the Jews regarded all other nations, the Egyptians regarded all
other nations, including the Jews: namely, as unclean.

is nearly certain that men whose lives were spent in the ceremonial observances of the Mishna, would cherish feelings of self-complacency and spiritual pride not justified by intrinsic moral excellence. The supercilious contempt towards the poor publican, and towards the tender penitent love that bathed Christ's feet with tears, would be the natural result of such a system of life.

It was alleged against them, on the highest spiritual authority, that they "made the word of God of none effect by their traditions." This would be true in the largest sense, from the purest form of religion in the Old Testament being almost incompatible with such endless forms (Mic. vi. 8); but it was true in another sense, from some of the traditions being decidedly at variance with genuine religion. The evasions connected with Corban are well known. To this may be added thefollowing instances: It is a plain precept of morality and religion that a man shall pay his debts (Ps. xxxvii. 21); but, according to the treatise of the Mishna called *Avodah sarah*, i. 1, a Jew was prohibited from paying money to a heathen three days before any heathen festival, just as if a debtor had any business to meddle with the question of how his creditor might spend his own money. In this way, Cato or Cicero might have been kept for a while out of his legal rights by an ignoble Jewish money-dealer in the Transtiberine district. In some instances, such a delay in the payment of debts might have ruined a heathen merchant. Again, it was an injunction of the Pentateuch that an Israelite should "love his neighbor as himself" (Lev. xix. 18); and although in this particular passage it might be argued that by "neighbor" was meant a brother Israelite, it is evident that the spirit of the precept went much farther (Luke x. 27-29, &c.). In plain violation of it, however, a Jewish midwife is forbidden, in the *Avodah sarah*, ii. 1, to assist a heathen mother in the labors of childbirth, so that through this prohibition a heathen mother and child might have been left to perish for want of a Pharisee's professional assistance. A great Roman satirist, in holding up to view the unsocial customs of the Roman Jews, specifies as two of their traditions that they were not to show the way, or point out springs of water to any but the circumcised.

> " Tradidit arcano quodcunque volumine Moses,
> Non monstrare vias eadem nisi sacra colenti,
> Quæsitum ad fontem solos deducere verpos." ·
>   JUVENAL, xiv. 102-4.

Now the truth of this statement has in our times been formally denied, and it seems certain that neither of these particular prohibitions is found in the Mishna; but the regulation respecting the Jewish midwives was more unsocial and cruel than the two practices referred to in the satirist's lines; and individual Pharisees, while the spirit of antagonism to the Romans was at its height, may have supplied instances of the imputed churlishness, al-

though not justified by the letter of their traditions. In fact, Juvenal did really somewhat *understate* what was true in principle, not of the Jews universally, but of the most important religious party among the Jews, at the time when he wrote.

An analogy has been pointed out by Geiger (p. 104) between the Pharisees and our own Puritans; and in some points there are undoubted features of similarity, beginning even with their names. Both were innovators: the one against the legal orthodoxy of the Sadducees, the others against Episcopacy. Both of them had republican tendencies: the Pharisees glorifying the office of rabbi, which depended on learning and personal merit, rather than that of priest, which, being hereditary, depended on the accident of birth; while the Puritans in England abolished monarchy and the right of hereditary legislation. Even in their zeal for religious education there was some resemblance: the Pharisees exerting themselves to instruct disciples in their schools with an earnestness never equaled in Rome or Greece; while in Scotland the Puritans set the most brilliant example to modern Europe of parochial schools for the common people. But here comparison ceases. In the most essential points of religion they were not only not alike, but they were directly antagonistic. The Pharisees were under the bondage of forms in the manner already described; while, except in the strict observance of the Sabbath, the religion of the Puritans was in theory purely spiritual, and they assailed even the ordinary forms of Popery and Prelacy with a bitterness of language copied from the denunciations of Christ against the Pharisees.

II. In regard to a future state, Josephus presents the ideas of the Pharisees in such a light to his Greek readers, that whatever interpretation his ambiguous language might possibly admit, he obviously would have produced the impression on Greeks that the Pharisees believed in the transmigration of souls. Thus his statement respecting them is, "They say that every soul is imperishable, but that the soul of good men only passes over (or transmigrates) into another body — $\mu\epsilon\tau\alpha\beta\alpha\iota\nu\epsilon\iota\nu$ $\epsilon\iota\varsigma$ $\epsilon\tau\epsilon\rho\rho\nu$ $\sigma\hat{\omega}\mu\alpha$ — while the soul of bad men is chastised by eternal punishment" (*B. J.* ii. 8, § 14; compare iii. 8, § 5, and *Ant.* xviii. 1, § 3, and Boettcher, *De Inferis*, pp. 519, 552). And there are two passages in the Gospels which might countenance this idea: one in Matt. xiv. 2, where Herod the tetrarch is represented as thinking that Jesus was John the Baptist risen from the dead (though a different color is given to Herod's thoughts in the corresponding passage, Luke ix. 7-9); and another in John ix. 2, where the question is put to Jesus whether the blind man himself[a] had sinned, or his parents, that he was born blind? Notwithstanding these passages, however, there does not appear to be sufficient reason for doubting that the Pharisees believed in a resurrection of the dead very much in the same sense as the early

---

[a] At least five different explanations have been suggested of the passage John ix. 2. 1st. That it alludes to a Jewish doctrine of the transmigration of souls. 2dly. That it refers to an Alexandrine doctrine of the preëxistence of souls, but not to their transmigration. 3dly. That the words mean, "Did this man sin, *as the Greeks say*, or did his parents sin, *as we say*, that he was born blind?" 4thly. That it involves the Rabbinical idea of the possibility of an infant's sinning in his mother's womb. 5thly. That it is founded on the

predestinarian notion that the blindness from birth was a *preceding* punishment for sins which the blind man afterwards committed : just as it has been suggested, in a remarkable passage, that the death before 1688 of the Princess Anne's infant children (three in number) was a preceding punishment for her subsequent abandonment of her father, James II. See Stewart's *Philosophy*, vol. ii. App. vi., and the Commentaries of De Wette and Lücke, *ad locum*.

Christians. This is most in accordance with St.
Paul's statement to the chief priests and council
(Acts xxiii. 6), that he was a Pharisee, the son of
a Pharisee, and that he was called in question for
the hope and resurrection of the dead — a statement which would have been peculiarly disingenuous, if the Pharisees had merely believed in
the transmigration of souls; and it is likewise
almost implied in Christ's teaching, which does
not insist on the doctrine of a future life as anything new, but assumes it as already adopted by
his hearers, except by the Sadducees, although he
condemns some unspiritual conceptions of its nature
as erroneous (Matt. xxii. 30; Mark xii. 25; Luke
xx. 34–36). On this head the Mishna is an illustration of the ideas in the Gospels, as distinguished
from any mere transmigration of souls; and the
peculiar phrase, "the world to come," of which ὁ
αἰὼν ὁ ἐρχόμενος was undoubtedly only the translation, frequently occurs in it (הָעוֹלָם הַבָּא,
Avoth, ii. 7, iv. 16; comp. Mark x. 30; Luke xviii.
30). This phrase of Christians, which is anterior
to Christianity, but which does not occur in the
O. T., though fully justified by certain passages to
be found in some of its latest books,[a] is essentially
different from Greek conceptions on the same subject; and generally, in contradistinction to the
purely temporal blessings of the Mosaic legislation,
the Christian ideas that this world is a state of
probation, and that every one after death will have
to render a strict account of his actions, were expressed by Pharisees in language which it is impossible to misunderstand: "This world may be
likened to a court-yard in comparison of the world
tó come; therefore prepare thyself in the ante-
chamber that thou mayest enter into the dining-
room" (Avoth, iv. 16). "Everything is given to
man on security, and a net is spread over every
living creature; the shop is open, and the merchant credits; the book is open, and the hand
records; and whosoever chooses to borrow may
come and borrow: for the collectors are continually
going round daily, and obtain payment of man,
whether with his consent or without it; and the
judgment is true justice; and all are prepared for
the feast" (Avoth, iii. 16). "Those who are born
are doomed to die, the dead to live, and the quick
to be judged; to make us know, understand, and
be informed that He is God: He is the Former,
Creator, Intelligent Being, Judge, Witness, and
suing Party, and will judge thee hereafter. Blessed
be He; for in his presence there is no unrighteousness, forgetfulness, respect of persons, nor acceptance of a bribe; for everything is his. Know also
that everything is done according to the account,
and let not thine evil imagination persuade thee
that the grave is a place of refuge for thee: for
against thy will wast thou formed, and against
thy will wast thou born; and against thy will dost
thou live, and against thy will wilt thou die; and
against thy will must thou hereafter render an
account, and receive judgment in the presence of
the Supreme King of kings, the Holy God, blessed
is He" (Avoth, iv. 22). Still it must be borne in
mind that the actions of which such a strict
account was to be rendered were not merely those
referred to by the spiritual prophets Isaiah and
Micah (Is. i. 16, 17; Mic. vi. 8), nor even those

enjoined in the Pentateuch, but included those
fabulously supposed to have been orally transmitted
by Moses on Mount Sinai, and the whole body of
the traditions of the elders. They included, in
fact, all those ceremonial "works," against the
efficacy of which, in the deliverance of the human
soul, St. Paul so emphatically protested.

III. In reference to the opinions of the Pharisees concerning the freedom of the will, a difficulty
arises from the very prominent position which they
occupy in the accounts of Josephus, whereas nothing vitally essential to the peculiar doctrines of
the Pharisees seems to depend on those opinions,
and some of his expressions are Greek, rather than
Hebrew. "There were three sects of the Jews,"
he says, "which had different conceptions respecting human affairs, of which one was called Pharisees, the second Sadducees, and the third Essenes.
The Pharisees say that some things, and not all
things, are the work of fate; but that some things
are in our own power to be and not to be. But
the Essenes declare that Fate rules all things, and
that nothing happens to man except by its decree.
The Sadducees, on the other hand, take away
Fate, holding that 'it is a thing of nought, and
that human affairs do not depend upon it; but in
their estimate all things are in the power of ourselves, as being ourselves the causes of our good
things, and meeting with evils through our own
inconsiderateness" (comp. xviii. 1, § 3, and B. J.
ii. 8, § 14). On reading this passage, and the
others which bear on the same subject in Josephus's works, the suspicion naturally arises that
he was biassed by a desire to make the Greeks
believe that, like the Greeks, the Jews had philosophical sects amongst themselves. At any rate
his words do not represent the opinions as they
were really held by the three religious parties.
We may feel certain, that the influence of fate
was not the point on which discussions respecting
free-will turned, though there may have been differences as to the way in which the interposition
of God in human affairs was to be regarded. Thus
the ideas of the Essenes are likely to have been
expressed in language approaching to the words of
Christ (Matt. x. 29, 30, vi. 25–34), and it is very
difficult to believe that the Sadducees, who accepted
the authority of the Pentateuch and other books
of the Old Testament, excluded God, in their conceptions, from all influence on human action.
On the whole, in reference to this point, the opinion of Graetz (Geschichte der Juden, iii. 509) seems
not improbable, that the real difference between
the Pharisees and Sadducees was at first practical
and political. He conjectures that the wealthy
and aristocratical Sadducees in their wars and
negotiations with the Syrians entered into matters
of policy and calculations of prudence, while the
zealous Pharisees, disdaining worldly wisdom, laid
stress on doing what seemed right, and on leaving
the event to God: and that this led to differences
in formal theories and metaphysical statements.
The precise nature of those differences we do not
certainly know, as no writing of a Sadducee on
the subject has been preserved by the Jews, and
on matters of this kind it is unsafe to trust un-
reservedly the statements of an adversary. [SAD-
DUCEES.]

---

a The earliest text in support of the expression is
perhaps "the new heavens and the new earth" promised by Isaiah (Is. lx. 17–22). Compare Dan. vii. 27
ii. 44; Is. xxvi. 19.

IV. In reference to the spirit of proselytism among the Pharisees, there is undisputable authority for the statement that it prevailed to a very great extent at the time of Christ (Matt. xxiii. 15); and attention is now called to it on account of its probable importance in having paved the way for the early diffusion of Christianity. The district of Palestine, which was long in proportion to its breadth, and which yet, from Dan to Beer-sheba, was only 160 Roman miles, or not quite 148 English miles long, and which is represented as having been civilized, wealthy, and populous 1,000 years before Christ, would under any circumstances have been too small to continue maintaining the whole growing population of its children. But, through kidnapping (Joel iii. 6), through leading into captivity by military incursions and victorious enemies (2 K. xvii. 6, xviii. 11, xxiv. 15; Am. i. 6, 9), through flight (Jer. xliii. 4–7), through commerce (Joseph. *Ant.* xx. 2, § 3), and probably through ordinary emigration, Jews at the time of Christ had become scattered over the fairest portions of the civilized world. On the day of Pentecost, that great festival on which the Jews suppose Moses to have brought the perfect Law down from heaven (*Festival Prayers for Pentecost*, p. 6), Jews are said to have been assembled with one accord in one place at Jerusalem, " from every region under heaven." Admitting that this was an oriental hyperbole (comp. John xxi. 25), there must have been some foundation for it in fact; and the enumeration of the various countries from which Jews are said to have been present gives a vivid idea of the widely-spread existence of Jewish communities. Now it is not unlikely, though it cannot be *proved* from Josephus (*Ant.* xx. 2, § 3), that missions and organized attempts to produce conversions, although unknown to Greek philosophers, existed among the Pharisees (De Wette, *Exegetisches Handbuch*, Matt. xxiii. 15). But, at any rate, the then existing regulations or customs of synagogues afforded facilities which do not exist now either in synagogues or Christian churches for presenting new views to a congregation (Acts xvii. 2; Luke iv. 16). Under such auspices the proselytizing spirit of the Pharisees inevitably stimulated a thirst for inquiry, and accustomed the Jews to theological controversies. Thus there existed precedents and favoring circumstances for efforts to make proselytes, when the greatest of all missionaries, a Jew by race, a Pharisee by education, a Greek by language, and a Roman citizen by birth, preaching the resurrection of Jesus to those who for the most part already believed in the resurrection of the dead, confronted the elaborate ritual-system of the written and oral law by a pure spiritual religion: and thus obtained the coöperation of many Jews themselves in breaking down every barrier between Jew, Pharisee, Greek, and Roman, and in endeavoring to unite all mankind by the brotherhood of a common Christianity.

Literature. — In addition to the New Testament, Josephus, and the Mishna, it is proper to read Epiphanius *Adversus Hæreses*, lib. I. xvi.; and the notes of Jerome to Matt. xxii. 23, xxiii. 5, &c., though the information given by both these writers is very imperfect.

In modern literature, see several treatises in Ugolino's *Thesaurus*, vol. xxii.; and Lightfoot's *Horæ Hebraicæ* on Matt. iii. 7, where a curious rabbinical description is given of seven sects of Pharisees, which, from its being destitute of any intrinsic value, is not inserted in this article. See likewise Brucker's *Historia Critica Philosophiæ*, ii. 744–759; Milman's *History of the Jews*, ii. 71; Ewald's *Geschichte des Volkes Israel*, iv. 415–419; and the *Jahrhundert des Heils*, p. 5, &c. of Gfrörer, who has insisted strongly on the importance of the Mishna, and has made great use of the Talmud generally. See also the following works by modern learned Jews: Jost, *Geschichte des Judenthums und seiner Sekten*, i. 196; Grætz, *Geschichte der Juden*, iii. 508–518; Herzfeld, *Geschichte des Volkes Israel*, iii. 358–362; and Geiger, *Urschrift und Uebersetzungen der Bibel*, p. 103, &c.   E. T.

* *Additional Literature.* — See Grossmann, *De Judæorum Disciplina Arcani*, Part. 1, 2, Lips. 1833–34; *De Pharisaismo Judæorum Alexandrino Commentatio*, Part. 1–3, ibid. 1846–50; *De Collegio Pharisæorum*, ibid. 1851. Biedermann, *Pharisäer u. Sadducäer*, Zürich, 1854. Reuss, art. *Pharisäer*, in Herzog's *Real-Encykl.* xi. 496–509. Geiger, *Sadducäer u. Pharisäer*, from the *Jüd. Zeitschr. f. Wiss. u. Leben*, Breslau, 1863; see also his *Das Judenthum u. seine Geschichte*, 2e Aufl. ibid. 1865. Delitzsch, *Jesus u. Hillel* (against Renan and Geiger), Erlangen, 1866. Ginsburg, art. *Pharisees* in Kitto's *Cycl. of Bibl. Lit.*, 3d ed., 1866. T. Keim, *Gesch. Jesu von Nazara*, Zürich, 1867, i. 251–272. J. Derenbourg, *Essai sur l'hist. et la geogr. de la Palestine*, Paris, 1867, i. 119–144, 452 ff. A. Hausrath, *Neutest. Zeitgeschichte*, Heidelb. 1868, i. 117–133.   A.

PHA'ROSH (שׁעְרַפּ [*a flea*]: Φόρος: *Pharos*). Elsewhere PAROSH. The same variation is found in the Geneva Version (Ezr. viii. 3).

PHAR'PAR (רַפְּרַפ [*swift, rapid*, Ges., Fürst], *i. e.* Parpar: [Rom. Φαρφάρ; Vat.] Ἀφαρφά; Alex. Φαρφαρα: *Pharphar*). The second of the two "rivers of Damascus" — Abana and Pharpar — alluded to by Naaman (2 K. v. 12).

The two principal streams in the district of Damascus are the *Barada* and the *Awaj*: in fact, there are no others worthy of the name of "river." There are good grounds for identifying the Barada with the Abana, and there seems therefore to be no alternative but to consider the Awaj as being the Pharpar. But though in the region of Damascus, the Awaj has not, like the Barada, any connection with the city itself. It does not approach it nearer than 8 miles, and is divided from it by the ridge of the *Jebel Aswad*. It takes its rise on the S. E. slopes of Hermon, some 5 or 6 miles from *Beit Jenn*, close to a village called *Arny*, the name of which it bears during the first part of its course. It then runs S. E. by *Kefr Hawwar* and *Sasa*, but soon recovering itself by a turn northwards, ultimately ends in the *Bahret Hijaneh*, the most southerly of the three lakes or swamps of Damascus, nearly due east of, and about 40 miles from, the point at which it started. The *Awaj* has been investigated by Dr. Thomson, and is described by him in the *Bibliotheca Sacra* for May, 1849; see also Robinson (*Bibl. Res.* iii. 447, 448). It is evidently much inferior to the Barada, for while that is extraordinarily copious, and also perennial in the

---

a The A at the commencement of this name suggests the Hebrew definite article; but no trace of it appears in the Hebrew MSS.

nottest seasons, this is described as a small lively[a] stream, not unfrequently dry in the lower part of its course. On the maps of Kiepert (1856) and Van de Velde (1858) the name of *Wady Barbar* is found, apparently that of a valley parallel to the *Arny* near *Kefr Hawowr;* but what the authority for this is the writer has not succeeded in discovering. Nor has he found any name on the maps or in the lists of Dr. Robinson answering to *Taúrah,* ٿوری, by which Pharpar is rendered in the Arabic version of 2 K. v. 12.

The tradition of the Jews of Damascus, as reported by Schwarz (54, also 20, 27), is curiously subversive of our ordinary ideas regarding these streams. They call the river *Fijeh* (that is the Barada) the Pharpar, and give the name Amana or Karmion (an old Talmudic name, see vol. i. p. 2 b) to a stream which Schwarz describes as running from a fountain called *el-Barady,* 1½ miles from *Beth Djana (Beit Jenn),* in a N. E. direction, to Damascus (see also the reference to the Nubian geographer by Gesenius, *Thes.* 1132 a). What is intended by this the writer is at a loss to know.

                          G.

PHAR'ZITES, THE (הַפַּרְצִי [patr., see Pharez]: ὁ Φαρεσί: [Vat.] Alex. Φαρες: *Pharesitæ*). The descendants of Pharez, the son of Judah (Num. xxvi. 20). They were divided into two branches, the Hezronites and the Hamulites.

PHASE'AH (פָּסֵחַ [*lame,* Ges.; *born at the Passover,* Fürst]: Φεσή; Alex. [Φεσση; FA.] φαιση: *Phasea*). PASEAH 2 (Neh. vii. 51).

PHASE'LIS (Φασηλίς: *Phaselis*). A town on the coast of Asia Minor, on the confines of Lycia and Pamphylia, and consequently ascribed by the ancient writers sometimes to one and sometimes to the other. Its commerce was considerable in the sixth century B. C., for in the reign of Amasis it was one of a number of Greek towns which carried on trade somewhat in the manner of the Hanseatic confederacy in the Middle Ages. They had a common temple, the Hellenium, at Naucratis in Egypt, and nominated προστάται for the regulation of commercial questions and the decision of disputes arising out of contracts, like the *preud'hommes* of the Middle Ages, who presided over the courts of pie powder (*pieds poudrés,* pedlars) at the different staples. In later times Phaselis was distinguished as a resort of the Pamphylian and Cilician pirates. Its port was a convenient one to make, for the lofty mountain of Solyma (now *Takhtalu*), which backed it at a distance of only five miles, is nearly 8,000 feet in height, and constitutes an admirable landmark from a great distance. Phaselis itself stood on a rock of 50 or 100 feet elevation above the sea, and was joined to the main by a low isthmus, in the middle of which was a lake, now a pestiferous marsh. On the eastern side of this were a closed port and a roadstead, and on the western a larger artificial harbor, formed by a mole run out into the sea. The remains of this may still be traced to a considerable extent below the surface of the water. The masonry of the pier which protected the small eastern port is nearly perfect. In this sheltered position the pirates could lie safely while they sold their

booty, and also refit, the whole region having been anciently so thickly covered with wood as to give the name of Pityusa to the town. For a time the Phaselites confined their relations with the Pamphylians to the purposes just mentioned; but they subsequently joined the piratical league, and suffered in consequence the loss of their independence and their town lands in the war which was waged by the Roman consul Publius Servilius Isauricus in the years 77–75 B. C. But at the outset the Romans had to a great extent fostered the pirates, by the demand which sprang up for domestic slaves upon the change of manners brought about by the spoliation of Carthage and Corinth. It is said that at this time many thousand slaves were passed through Delos — which was the mart between Asia and Europe — in a single day; and the proverb grew up there, Ἔμπορε, κατάπλευσον ἐξελοῦ πάντα πέπραται. But when the Cilicians had acquired such power and audacity as to sweep the seas as far as the Italian coast, and interrupt the supplies of corn, it became time to interfere, and the expedition of Servilius commenced the work which was afterwards completed by Pompey the Great.

It is in the interval between the growth of the Cilician piracy and the Servilian expedition that the incidents related in the First Book of Maccabees occurred. The Romans are represented as requiring all their allies to render up to Simon the high-priest any Jewish exiles who may have taken refuge among them. After naming Ptolemy, Demetrius (king of Syria), Attalus (king of Pergamus), Ariarathes (of Pontus), and Arsaces (of Parthia), as recipients of these missives, the author adds that the consul also wrote εἰς πάσας τὰς χώρας καὶ Σαμψάμῃ (Grotius conjectures Λαμψάκῳ, and one MS. has Μεσανίσσῃ) καὶ Σπαρτιάταις καὶ εἰς Δῆλον καὶ εἰς Μύνδον καὶ εἰς Σικυῶνα καὶ εἰς τὴν Καρίαν καὶ εἰς Σάμον καὶ εἰς τὴν Παμφυλίαν καὶ εἰς τὴν Λυκίαν καὶ εἰς Ἀλικαρνασσὸν, καὶ εἰς Ῥόδον καὶ εἰς Φασηλίδα καὶ εἰς Κῶ καὶ εἰς Σίδην καὶ εἰς Ἄραδον καὶ εἰς Γόρτυναν καὶ Κνίδον, καὶ Κύπρον καὶ Κυρήνην (1 Macc. xv. 23). It will be observed that all the places named, with the exception of Cyprus and Cyrene, lie on the highway of marine traffic between Syria and Italy. The Jewish slaves, whether kidnapped by their own countrymen (Ex. xxi. 16) or obtained by raids (2 K. v. 2), appear in early times to have been transmitted to the west coast of Asia Minor by this route (see Ez. xxvii. 13; Joel iii. 6).

The existence of the mountain Solyma, and a town of the same name, in the immediate neighborhood of Phaselis, renders it probable that the descendants of some of these Israelites formed a population of some importance in the time of Strabo (Herod. ii. 178; Strab. xiv. c. 3; Liv. xxxvii. 23; Mela, i. 14; Beaufort, *Karamania,* pp. 53–56).   J. W. B.

PHAS'TRON (Φασιρόν; [Sin. Φασεφων:] *Phaseron; Pasiron*), the name of the head of an Arab tribe, "the children of Phasiron" (1 Macc. ix. 66), defeated by Jonathan, but of whom nothing more is known.   B. F. W.

PHAS'SARON (Φασσοῦρος; [Vat. Φασ-

---

[a] Such is the meaning of the word *Pharpar,* treated as Hebrew, according to Gesenius and Fürst. Dr. Pusey, however (*Comm. on Amos* i. 5), renders it "crooked."

σσσσ; Ald. Φασσαρὸι:] *Phasuriss*). PASHUR (1 Esdr. v. 25).

PHE'BE. [PHŒBE.]

PHE'NICE. 1. See PHŒNICE, PHŒNICIA. 2. More properly PHŒNIX (Φοῖνιξ, Acts xxvii. 12), though probably our translators meant it to be pronounced *Phénice* in two syllables, as opposed to *Phenicè* (Φοινίκη, Acts xi. 19) in three.

The place under our present consideration was a town and harbor on the south coast of CRETE: and the name was doubtless derived from the Greek word for the palm-tree, which Theophrastus says was indigenous in the island. [PALM-TREE.] The ancient notices of Phœnix converge remarkably to establish its identity with the modern *Lutro*. Besides Ptolemy's longitudes, we have Pliny's statement that it was (as Lutro is) in the narrowest part of the island. Moreover, we find applied to this locality, by the modern Greeks, not only the word *Phinika*, which is clearly *Phœnix*, but also the words *Anopolis* and *Aradena*. Now Stephanus Byzantinus says that Anopolis is the same with Aradena, and Hierocles says that Aradena is the same with Phœnix. The last authority adds also that the island of CLAUDA is very near. We see further that all these indications correspond exactly with what we read in the Acts. St. Paul's ship was at FAIR HAVENS, which is some miles to the E. of Lutro; but she was bound to the westward, and the sailors wished to reach Phœnix (xxvii. 8–12); and it was in making the attempt that they were caught by the gale and driven to Clauda (*ibid.* 13–16).

Still there were till lately two difficulties in the matter: and the recent and complete removal of them is so satisfactory, that they deserve to be mentioned. First, it used to be asserted, by persons well acquainted with this coast, that there is no such harbor hereabouts at all affording a safe anchorage. This is simply an error of fact. The matter is set at rest by abundant evidence, and especially by the late survey of our own officers, an extract from whose drawing, showing the excellent soundings of the harbor, was first published (1852) in the first edition of the *Life and Epistles of St. Paul*, ii. 332. An account by recent travellers will be found in the second edition of Smith's *Voyage and Shipwreck of St. Paul*, p. 256. The other difficulty is a verbal one. The sailors in the Acts describe Phœnix as λιμένα τῆς Κρητῆς βλέποντα κατὰ λίβα καὶ κατὰ χῶρον, whereas *Lutro* is precisely sheltered from these winds. But it ought to have been remembered that seamen do not recommend a harbor because of its exposure to certain winds; and the perplexity is at once removed either by taking κατὰ as expressing the direction in which the wind blows, or by bearing in mind that a sailor speaks of everything from his own point of view. The harbor of Phœnix or *Lutro* does "look" *from the water toward the land which incloses it* — in the direction of "southwest and northwest."   J. S. H.

* Mr. Twistleton's article on Phenice, in some earlier copies of the *Dictionary*, was superseded (except a few sentences) by that of Dr. Howson (as would seem) on account of his different interpretation of βλέποντα κατὰ λίβα, etc. (see above). Mr. T. maintains that the words can mean only that "the harbor looked to the southwest and northwest," and will not bear any other explanation. Scholars generally have heretofore held this opinion, which seems to exclude the supposition that *Lutro* and Phenice are the same.

Mr. Smith (*Voyage and Shipwreck of Paul*, p. 87 ff., 3d ed.) and Dean Alford (on Acts xxvii. 12) understand κατά of the direction *whither* and not *whence*, and thus identify Phenice with the modern *Lutro*. Captain Spratt of the Royal Navy (*Travels and Researches in Crete*, ii. 249, Lond. 1865) assigns good reasons for this identification, though, strangely enough, he separates κατὰ λίβα, etc., altogether from the question. He urges that the name *Phineka* (from Φοῖνιξ) is still current as applied to Lutro, and also that a Latin inscription found at Lutro, dating from the emperor Nerva (A. D. 96–98), shows that ships from Alexandria (see Acts xxvii. 6) resorted to this harbor. It is the only one, says this navigator, on the south of Crete which affords a safe winter refuge. Instead, however, of referring βλέποντα . . . χῶρον to the opening of the harbor, he understands it of the course of the voyage from Fair Havens to Phenice, namely, first southwest and then beyond Cape Littinus for the rest of the way northwest. According to that view we learn absolutely nothing from the text respecting the situation of the harbor. But βλέποντα agreeing with λιμένα shows that the point of observation must be the port, and not the vessel.

It will be noticed that the above writers (Howson, Smith, Alford, Spratt), who assume Lutro and Phenice to be the same, by no means agree in their mode of reconciling Luke's language with that conclusion. The argument on this side of the question would be stronger if that disagreement did not exist. Dr. Lechler represents in part a still different opinion. He accords with those who understand κατὰ λίβα and the like (correctly we think) of the quarter whence the winds blow; but suggests that Luke may be stating here only the common opinion or report in regard to Phenice, and not his own testimony; for Paul's ship did not reach Phenice, and the historian had no personal knowledge on the subject (see his *Der Apostel Geschichten*, p. 400, 3te Aufl., 1869). For a fuller criticism on this topic, see the writer's *Commentary on Acts*, pp. 420–422 (2d ed.).

The case is certainly not without its difficulty. Among the possibilities are that Lutro and Phenice may *not* be the same; or, that Luke deviates here somewhat from the ordinary usage in speaking of winds; or, that the coast-line of the harbor may have changed in the course of time. The statements both of Pashley (*Travels in Crete*, Lond. 1837) and of Spratt show that upheavals and submergences have been frequent in Crete. We do not presume at present to decide the question.   H.

PHER'ESITES (Φερεζαῖοι: *Pherezssi*), 1 Esdr. viii. 69; = PERIZZITES; comp. Ezr. ix. 1.

PHER'EZITE; PHER'EZITES (ὁ Φερεζαῖος: *Pherexæus; Pherezzi*), Jud. v. 16; 2 Esdr. i. 21. The latter of these passages contains a statement in accordance with those of Gen. xiii. 7, xxxiv. 30; Judg. i. 4, &c., noticed under PERIZZITE.

* PHI-BE'SETH, Ezek. xxx. 17. [PI-BESETH.]

PHI'CHOL (פִּיכֹל [*strong, mighty*, Fürst]; Samar. פי כל: Φιχόλ; Alex. Φικολ; Joseph. Φίκολος: *Phichol*), chief captain of the army of Abimelech, king of the Philistines of Gerar in the days of both Abraham (Gen. xxi. 22, 32) and Isaac (xxvi. 26). Josephus mentions him on the second occasion only. On the other hand the LXX. introduce Ahuzzath, Abimelech's other companion, on the first also. By Gesenius the name is treated as Hebrew, and as meaning the "mouth of all." By Fürst (*Handwb.* ii. 215 *a*), it is derived from a root פָּכַל, to be strong. But Hitzig (*Philistäer*, § 57) refers it to the Sanskrit *pitschula*, a tamarisk, pointing out that Abraham had planted a tamarisk in Beer-sheba, and comparing the name with Elah, Berosus, Tappuach, and other names of persons and places signifying different kinds of trees; and with the name Φίγαλος, a village of Palestine (Joseph. *Ant.* xii. 4, § 2), and Φιγαλία in Greece. Stark (*Gaza*, etc., p. 96) more cautiously avoids such speculations. The natural conclusion from these mere conjectures is that Phichol is a Philistine name, the meaning and derivation of which are lost to us.   G.

* Phichol (whatever its origin) was no doubt a military title (like *mudir* or *mushir* in the East at present), and hence would be expected to recur in the history again and again. In speaking of Turkish officers now the name is very seldom heard, and they are known to the public almost exclusively by their titles (Thomson's *Land and Book*, ii. 352).
H.

PHILADELPHIA (ἡ Φιλαδέλφεια [*brotherly lore*]: *Philadelphia*), Rev. iii. 7.

A town on the confines of Lydia and Phrygia Catacecaumene, built by Attalus II., king of Pergamus. It was situated on the lower slopes of Tmolus, on the southern side of the valley of the *Ain-e-ghinl Son*,

Philadelphia (Macfarlane's *Apocalyptic Churches*).

a river which is probably the Cogamus of antiquity, and falls into the *Wadis-tchai* (the Hermus) in the neighborhood of *Sart-Kalesi* (Sardis), about 25 miles to the west of the site of Philadelphia. This latter is still represented by a town called *Allah-shehr* (city of God). Its elevation is 952 feet above the sea. The region around is highly volcanic, and geologically speaking belongs to the district of Phrygia Catacecaumene, on the western edge of which it lies. The soil was extremely favorable to the growth of vines, celebrated by Virgil for the soundness of the wine they produced; and in all probability Philadelphia was built by Attalus as a mart for the great wine-producing region, extending for 500 stades in length by 400 in breadth; for its coins have on them the head of Bacchus or a female Bacchant. Strabo compares the soil with that in the neighborhood of Catana in Sicily; and modern travellers describe the appearance of the country as resembling a billowy sea of disintegrated lava, with here and there vast trap-dykes protruding. The original population of Philadelphia seems to have been Macedonian, and the national character to have been retained even in the time of Pliny. There was, however, as appears from Rev. iii. 9, a synagogue of Hellenizing Jews there, as well as a Christian Church. The locality continued to be subject to constant earthquakes, which in the times of Strabo rendered even the town-walls of Philadelphia unsafe; but its inhabitants held pertinaciously to the spot, perhaps from the profit which naturally accrued to them from their city being the staple of the great wine-district. But the expense of reparation was constant, and hence perhaps the poverty of the members of the Christian Church (οἶδα . . . ὅτι μικρὰν ἔχεις δύναμιν, Rev. iii. 8), who no doubt were a portion of the urban population, and heavily taxed for public purposes, as well as subject to private loss by the destruction of their own property. Philadelphia was not of sufficient importance in the Roman times to have law-courts of its own, but belonged to a jurisdiction of which Sardis was the centre.

It has been supposed by some that Philadelphia occupied the site of another town named Callatebus, of which Herodotus speaks, in his account of Xerxes's march, as famous for the production of a sugar from the *holcus sorghum* and sweetwort (ἐν τῇ ἄνδρες δημιοεργοὶ μέλι ἐκ μυρίκης τε καὶ συροῦ ποιεῦσι, vii. 31). But by the way in which he mentions Callatebus (of which the name is only known from him) it would seem to have been not far from the Maeander, from which the ruins of *Allah-shehr* cannot be less distant than from 30 to 40 miles, while they are very near the Cogamus. The enormous plane tree, too, which struck Xerxes's attention, and the abundance of the μυρίκη, point to a region well furnished with springs of water, which is the case with the northern side of the Mæander, where Xerxes crossed it, and not so with the vicinity of *Allah-shehr*. At the same time the Persian king, in his two days' march from Cydrara to Sardis, must have passed very near the site of the future Philadelphia. (Strab. xii. c. 8, xiii. c. 4; Virg. *Georg.* ii. 98; Herod. vii. 31; Plin. *H. N.* v. 29; Arundell, *Discoveries in Asia Minor*, i. 34, &c.; Tchihatcheff, *Asie Mineure*, p. 237, &c.)

J. W. B.

PHILAR'CHES. This word occurs as a proper name in A. V. in 2 Macc. viii. 32, where it is really the name of an office (ὁ φυλάρχης = ὁ φύλαρχος, "the commander of the cavalry"). The Greek text seems to be decisive as to the true rendering; but the Latin version (" et Philarchen qui cum Timotheo erat . . . ") might easily give rise to the error, which is very strangely supported by Grimm, *ad loc.*

B. F. W.

PHILE'MON (Φιλήμων [*loving, affectionate*]: *Philemon*), the name of the Christian to whom Paul addressed his epistle in behalf of Onesimus. He was a native probably of Colossæ, or at all events lived in that city when the Apostle wrote to him; first, because Onesimus was a Colossian (Col. iv. 9); and secondly, because Archippus was a Colossian (Col. iv. 17), whom Paul associates with Philemon at the beginning of his letter (Philem. 1, 2). Wieseler (*Chronologie*, p. 452) argues, indeed, from Col. iv. 17, that Archippus was a Laodicean, but the εἴπατε in that passage, on which the point turns, refers evidently to the Colossians (of whom Archippus was one therefore), and not to the church at Laodicea spoken of in the previous verse, as Wieseler without reason assumes. [LAODICEA, Amer. ed.] Theodoret (*Proœm. in Epist. ad Phil.*) states the ancient opinion in saying that Philemon was a citizen of Colossæ, and that his house was pointed out there as late as the fifth century. The legendary history supplies nothing on which we can rely. It is related that Philemon became bishop of Colossæ (*Constit. Apost.* vii. 46), and died as a martyr under Nero.

It is evident from the letter to him that Philemon was a man of property and influence, since he is represented as the head of a numerous household, and as exercising an expensive liberality towards his friends and the poor in general. He was indebted to the Apostle Paul as the medium of his personal participation in the Gospel. All interpreters agree in assigning that significance to σεαυτόν μοι προσοφείλεις in Philem. 19. It is not certain under what circumstances they became known to each other. If Paul visited Colossæ when he passed through Phrygia on his second missionary journey (Acts xvi. 6), it was undoubtedly there, and at that time, that Philemon heard the Gospel and attached himself to the Christian party. On the contrary, if Paul never visited that city in person, as many critics infer from Col. ii. 1, then the best view is, that he was converted during Paul's protracted stay at Ephesus (Acts xix. 10), about A. D. 54-57. That city was the religious and commercial capital of Western Asia Minor. The Apostle labored there with such success that "all they who dwelt in Asia heard the word of the Lord Jesus." Phrygia was a neighboring province, and among the strangers who repaired to Ephesus and had an opportunity to hear the preaching of Paul, may have been the Colossian Philemon.

Paul terms Philemon συνεργός (ver. 1), which may denote a preacher of the word (2 Cor. viii. 23; Phil. ii. 25, etc.); but as nothing in the letter indicates that he performed this service, and as the appellation may designate other modes of labor (applied to Priscilla, Rom. xvi. 3), it probably has not the official sense in this instance. Meyer thinks that Philemon may have been an elder. It is evident that, on becoming a disciple, he gave no common proof of the sincerity and power of his faith. His character, as shadowed forth in the epistle to him, is one of the noblest which the sacred record makes known to us. He was full of faith and good works, was docile, confiding, grateful, was forgiving, sympathizing, charitable, and a man who on a question of simple justice needed only a hint of his duty to prompt him to go even beyond it (ὑπὲρ ὃ λέγω ποιήσεις). Any one who studied the epistle will perceive that it ascribes to him these varied qualities; it bestows on him a measure of commendation, which forms a striking contrast with the ordinary reserve of the sacred writers. It was through such believers that the primitive Christianity evinced its divine origin, and spread so rapidly among the nations.

H. B. H.

PHILE'MON, THE EPISTLE OF PAUL TO, is one of the letters (the others are Ephesians, Colossians, Philippians) which the Apostle wrote during his first captivity at Rome. The arguments which show that he wrote the Epistle to the Colossians in *that city* and at *that period*, involve the same conclusion in regard to this; for it is evident from Col. iv. 7, 9, as compared with the contents of this epistle, that Paul wrote the two letters at the same time, and forwarded them to their destination by the hands of Tychicus and Onesimus, who accompanied each other to Colossæ. A few modern critics, as Schulz, Schott, Böttger, Meyer, maintain that this letter and the others assigned usually to the first Roman captivity, were written during the two years that Paul was imprisoned at Cæsarea (Acts xxiii. 35, xxiv. 27). But this opinion, though supported by some plausible arguments, can be demonstrated with reasonable certainty to be incorrect. [COLOSSIANS, EPISTLE TO THE.]

The *time* when Paul wrote may be fixed with much precision. The Apostle at the close of the letter expresses a hope of his speedy liberation. He speaks in like manner of his approaching deliverance, in his Epistle to the Philippians (ii. 23, 24), which was written during the same imprisonment. Presuming, therefore, that he had good reasons for such an expectation, and that he was not disappointed in the result, we may conclude that this letter was written by him about the year A. D. 63, or early in A. D. 64; for it was in the latter year, according to the best chronologists, that he was freed from his first Roman imprisonment.

Nothing is wanting to confirm the *genuineness* of this epistle. The external testimony is unimpeachable. It is not quoted so often by the earlier Christian fathers as some of the other letters; its brevity, and the fact that its contents are not didactic or polemic, account for that omission. We need not urge the expressions in Ignatius, cited as evidence of that apostolic Father's knowledge and use of the epistle; though it is difficult to regard the similarity between them and the language in ver. 20 as altogether accidental. See Kirchhofer's *Quellensammlung*, p. 205. The Canon of Muratori which comes to us from the second century (Credner, *Geschichte des Kanons*, p. 69), enumerates this as one of Paul's epistles. Tertullian mentions it, and says that Marcion admitted it into his collection. Sinope in Pontus, the birthplace of Marcion, was not far from Colossæ where Philemon lived, and the letter would find its way to the neighboring churches at an early period. Origen and Eusebius include it among the universally acknowledged writings (ὁμολογούμενα) of the early Christian times. It is so well attested historically, that, as De Wette says (*Einleitung ins Neue Testament*, p. 278), its genuineness on that ground is beyond doubt.

Nor does the epistle itself offer anything to conflict with this decision. It is impossible to conceive of a composition more strongly marked within the same limits by those unstudied assonances of thought, sentiment, and expression, which indicate an author's hand, than this short epistle as compared with Paul's other productions. Paley has a paragraph in his *Horæ Paulinæ*, which illustrates this feature of the letter in a very just and forcible manner. It will be found also that all the historical allusions which the Apostle makes to events in his own life, or to other persons with whom he was connected, harmonize perfectly with the statements or incidental intimations contained in the Acts of the Apostles or the other epistles of Paul. It belongs to a commentary to point out the instances of such agreement.

Baur (*Paulus*, p. 475) would divest the epistle of its historical character, and make it the personified illustration from some later writer, of the idea that Christianity unites and equalizes in a higher sense those whom outward circumstances have separated. He does not impugn the external evidence. But, not to leave his theory wholly unsupported, he suggests some linguistic objections to Paul's authorship of the letter, which must be pronounced unfounded and frivolous. He finds, for example, certain words in the epistle, which are alleged to be not Pauline; but to justify that assertion, he must deny the genuineness of such other letters of Paul as happen to contain these words. He admits that the Apostle could have said σπλάγχνα twice, but thinks it suspicious that he should say it three times. A few terms he adduces, which are not used elsewhere in the epistles; but to argue from these that they disprove the apostolic origin of the epistle, is to assume the absurd principle that a writer, after having produced two or three compositions, must for the future confine himself to an unvarying circle of words, whatever may be the subject he discusses, or whatever the interval of time between his different writings.

The arbitrary and purely subjective character of such criticisms can have no weight against the varied testimony admitted as decisive by Christian scholars for so many ages, upon which the canonical authority of the Epistle to Philemon is founded. They are worth repeating only as illustrating Baur's own remark, that modern criticism in assailing this particular book runs a greater risk of exposing itself to the imputation of an excessive distrust, a morbid sensibility to doubt and denial, than in questioning the claims of any other epistle ascribed to Paul.

Our knowledge respecting the *occasion and object* of the letter we must derive from declarations or inferences furnished by the letter itself. For the relation of Philemon and Onesimus to each other, the reader will see the articles on those names. Paul, so intimately connected with the master and the servant, was anxious naturally to effect a reconciliation between them. He wished also (waiving the ἀνῆκον, the matter of duty or right) to give Philemon an opportunity of manifesting his Christian love in the treatment of Onesimus, and his regard, at the same time, for the personal convenience and wishes, not to say official authority, of his spiritual teacher and guide. Paul used his influence with Onesimus (ἀνέπεμψα, in ver. 12) to induce him to return to Colossæ, and place himself again at the disposal of his master. Whether Onesimus assented merely to the proposal of the Apostle, or had a desire at the same time to revisit his former home, the epistle does not enable us to determine. On his departure, Paul put into his hand this letter as evidence that Onesimus was a true and approved disciple of Christ, and entitled as such to be received not as a servant, but above a servant, as a brother in the faith, as the representative and equal in that respect of the Apostle himself, and worthy of the same consideration and love. It is instructive to observe how entirely Paul identifies himself with Onesimus, and pleads his cause as if it were his own. He intercedes for him as his own child, promises reparation if he had done any wrong, demands for him not only a remission of all penalties, but the reception of sympathy, affection, Christian brotherhood; and while he solicits these favors for another, consents to receive them with the same gratitude and sense of obligation as if they were bestowed on himself. Such was the purpose and such the argument of the epistle.

The *result* of the appeal cannot be doubted. It may be assumed from the character of Philemon that the Apostle's intercession for Onesimus was not unavailing. There can be no doubt that, agreeably to the express instructions of the letter, the past was forgiven; the master and the servant were reconciled to each other; and, if the liberty which Onesimus had asserted in a spirit of independence was not conceded as a boon or right, it was enjoyed at all events under a form of servitude which henceforth was such in name only. So much must be regarded as certain; or it follows that the Apostle was mistaken in his opinion of Philemon's character, and his efforts for the welfare of Onesimus were frustrated. Chrysostom declares, in his impassioned style, that Philemon must have been less than a man, must have been alike destitute of sensibility and reason (ποῖος λίθος, ποῖος θηρίον), not to be moved by the arguments and spirit of such a letter to fulfil every wish and intimation of the Apostle. Surely no fitting response to his pleadings for Onesimus could involve less than a cessation of everything oppressive and harsh in his civil condition, as far as it depended on Philemon to mitigate or neutralize the evils of a legalized system of bondage, as well as a cessation of everything violative of his rights as a Christian. How much further than this an impartial explanation of the epistle obliges us or authorizes us to go, has not yet been settled by any very general consent of interpreters. Many of the best critics construe certain expressions (τὸ ἀγαθόν in ver. 14, and ὑπὲρ ὃ λέγω in ver. 21) as conveying a distinct expectation on the part of Paul that Philemon would liberate Onesimus. Nearly all agree that he could hardly have failed to confer on him that favor, even if it was not requested in so many words, after such an appeal to his sentiments of humanity and justice. Thus it was, as Dr. Wordsworth remarks (*St. Paul's Epistles*, p. 328), "by Christianizing the master that the Gospel enfranchised the slave. It did not legislate about mere names and forms, but it went to the root of the evil, it spoke to the heart of man. When the heart of the master was filled with divine grace and was warmed with the love of Christ, the rest would soon follow. The lips would speak kind words, the hands would do liberal things. Every Onesimus would be treated by every Philemon as a beloved brother in Christ."

The Epistle to Philemon has one peculiar feature — its *æsthetical character* it may be termed — which distinguishes it from all the other epistles, and demands a special notice at our hands. It has been admired deservedly as a model of delicacy and skill in the department of composition to which it belongs. The writer had peculiar difficulties to overcome. He was the common friend of the parties at variance. He must conciliate a man who supposed that he had good reason to be offended. He must commend the offender, and yet neither deny nor aggravate the imputed fault. He must assert the new ideas of Christian equality in the face of a system which hardly recognized the humanity of the enslaved. He could have placed the question on the ground of his own personal rights, and yet must waive them in order to secure an act of spontaneous kindness. His success must be a triumph of love, and nothing be demanded for the sake of the justice which could have claimed everything. He limits his request to a forgiveness of the alleged wrong, and a restoration to favor and the enjoyment of future sympathy and affection, and yet would so guard his words as to leave scope for all the generosity which benevolence might prompt toward one whose condition admitted of so much alleviation. These are contrarieties not easy to harmonize; but Paul, it is considered, has shown a degree of self denial and a tact in dealing with them, which in being equal to the occasion could hardly be greater.

There is a letter extant of the younger Pliny (*Epist.* ix. 21) which he wrote to a friend whose servant had deserted him, in which he intercedes for the fugitive, who was anxious to return to his master, but dreaded the effects of his anger. Thus the occasion of the correspondence was similar to that between the Apostle and Philemon. It has occurred to scholars to compare this celebrated letter with that of Paul in behalf of Onesimus; and as the result they hesitate not to say, that not only in the spirit of Christian love, of which Pliny was ignorant, but in dignity of thought, argument, pathos, beauty of style, eloquence, the communication of the Apostle is vastly superior to that of the polished Roman writer.

Among the later Commentaries on this epistle may be mentioned those of Rothe (*Interpretatio Historico-Exegetica*, Bremæ, 1844), Hagenbach (one of his early efforts, Basel, 1829), Koch (Zürich, 1846, excellent), Wiesinger (1851), one of the continuators of Olshausen's work, Meyer (1859), De Wette, Ewald (brief notes with a translation, Göttingen (1857). Alford, Wordsworth, Ellicott, and the Amer. Bible Union (N. Y. 1860). The celebrated Lavater preached thirty-nine sermons on the contents of this brief composition, and published them in two volumes.   H. B. H.

* Among the patristic commentators Chrysostom excels in bringing out the delicate touches of the letter. In tom. v. of the *Critici Sacri* (Francf. 1695) the jurist, Scipio Gentilis, devotes eighty folio pages to Philemon. D. H. Wildschut treats *De vi dictionis et sermonis elegantia, in Epistola Pauli ad Philemonem* (Traj. ad Rhen., 1809). Rev. J. S. Buckminster has a sermon on the entire letter as a text (*Sermons*, pp. 78–92, Bost. 1815). Still later helps are, F. Kühne, *Der Epistel Pauli an Philemon, in Bibelstunden* (Leips. 1856); Bleek, *Vorlesungen üb. die Briefe an die Colosser, den Philemon*, etc. 1865); and J. J. Van Oosterzee, *Der Brief an Philemon*, in pt. xi. of Lange's *Bibelwerk des N. Test.* (1862), translated with additions by H. B. Hackett in Dr. Schaff's *Commentary* (N. Y. 1868). On the relation of the epistle to the subject of slavery see the opinions of eminent writers as quoted at the end of the above translation (pp. 29–31).   H.

PHILE'TUS (Φίλητος [*beloved, or worthy of love*]: *Philetus*) was possibly a disciple of Hymenæus, with whom he is associated in 2 Tim. ii. 17 and who is named without him in an earlier epistle (1 Tim. i. 20). Waterland (*Importance of the Doctrine of the Holy Trinity*, ch. iv., *Works*, iii. 459) condenses in a few lines the substance of many dissertations which have been written concerning their opinions, and the sentence which was inflicted upon at least one of them: "They appear to have been persons who believed the Scriptures of the O. T., but misinterpreted them, allegorizing away the doctrine of the Resurrection, and resolving it all into figure and metaphor. The delivering over unto Satan seems to have been a form of excommunication declaring the person reduced to the state of a heathen; and in the Apostolical age it was accompanied with supernatural or miraculous effects upon the bodies of the persons so delivered." Walchius is of opinion that they were of Jewish origin; Hammond connects them with the Gnostics; Vitringa (with less probability) with the Sadducees. They understood resurrection to signify the knowledge and profession of the Christian religion, or regeneration and conversion, according to J. G. Walchius, whose lengthy dissertation, *De Hymenæo et Phileto*, in his *Miscellanea Sacra*, 1744, pp. 81–121, seems to exhaust the subject. Amongst writers who preceded him may be named Vitringa, *Observ. Sacr.* iv. 9, 922–930; Buddeus, *Ecclesia Apostolica*, v. 297–305. See also, on the heresy, Burton, *Bampton Lectures*, and Dean Ellicott's notes on the Pastoral Epistles; and Potter on *Church Government*, ch. v., with reference to the sentence. The names of Philetus and Hymenæus occur separately among those of Cæsar's household whose relics have been found in the Columbaria at Rome.   W. T. B.

PHILIP (Φίλιππος [*lover of horses*]: *Philippus*). 1. The father of Alexander the Great (1 Macc i. 1; v. i. 2), king of Macedonia, B. C. 359–336.

2. A Phrygian, left by Antiochus Epiph. as governor at Jerusalem (c. B. C. 170), where he behaved with great cruelty (2 Macc. v. 22), burning the fugitive Jews in caves (2 Macc. vi. 11), and taking the earliest measures to check the growing power of Judas Macc. (2 Macc. viii. 9). He is commonly identified with,

3. The foster brother (σύντροφος, 2 Macc. ix.

29) of Antiochus Epiph., whom the king upon his death-bed appointed regent of Syria and guardian of his son Antiochus V., to the exclusion of Lysias (B. C. 164, 1 Macc. vi. 14, 15, 55). He returned with the royal forces from Persia (1 Macc. vi. 56) to assume the government, and occupied Antioch. But Lysias, who was at the time besieging "the Sanctuary" at Jerusalem, hastily made terms with Judas, and marched against him. Lysias stormed Antioch, and, according to Josephus (*Ant.* xii. 9, § 7), put Philip to death. In 2 Macc., Philip is said to have fled to Ptol. Philometor on the death of Antiochus (2 Macc. ix. 29), though the book contains traces of the other account (xiii. 23). The attempts to reconcile the narratives (Winer, *s. v.*) have no probability.

Philip V. of Macedon.

Didrachm of Philip V. (Attic talent). Obv.: Head of king, r, bound with fillet. Rev.: ΒΑΣΙΛΕΩΣ ΦΙΛΙΠΠΟΥ; club of Hercules : all within wreath.

4. Philip V., king of Macedonia, B. C. 220–179. His wide and successful endeavors to strengthen and enlarge the Macedonian dominion brought him into conflict with the Romans, when they were engaged in the critical war with Carthage. Desultory warfare followed by hollow peace lasted till the victory of Zama left the Romans free for more vigorous measures. Meanwhile Philip had consolidated his power, though he had degenerated into an unscrupulous tyrant. The first campaign of the Romans on the declaration of war (B. C. 200) were not attended by any decisive result, but the arrival of Flamininus (B. C. 198) changed the aspect of affairs. Philip was driven from his commanding position, and made unsuccessful overtures for peace. In the next year he lost the fatal battle of Cynoscephalæ, and was obliged to accede to the terms dictated by his conquerors. The remainder of his life was spent in vain endeavors to regain something of his former power; and was embittered by cruelty and remorse. In 1 Macc. viii. 5, the defeat of Philip is coupled with that of Perseus as one of the noblest triumphs of the Romans.   B. F. W.

PHILIP THE APOSTLE (Φίλιππος: *Philippus*). The Gospels contain comparatively scanty notices of this disciple. He is mentioned as being of Bethsaida, the city of Andrew and Peter [a] (John i. 44), and apparently was among the Galilæan peasants of that district who flocked to hear the preaching of the Baptist. The manner in which St. John speaks of him, the repetition by him of the self-same words with which Andrew had brought to Peter the good news that the Christ had at last appeared, all indicate a previous friendship with the sons of Jonah and of Zebedee, and a consequent participation in their Messianic hopes. The close union of the two in John vi.

and xii. suggests that he may have owed to Andrew the first tidings that the hope had been fulfilled. The statement that Jesus *found* him (John i. 43) implies a previous seeking. To him first in the whole circle of the disciples [b] were spoken the words so full of meaning, "Follow me" (Ibid.). As soon as he has learnt to know his Master, he is eager to communicate his discovery to another who had also shared the same expectations. He speaks to Nathanael, probably on his arrival in Cana (comp. John xxi. 2, Ewald, *Gesch.* v. p. 251), as though they had not seldom communed together of the intimations of a better time, of a divine kingdom, which they found in their sacred books. We may well believe that he, like his friend, was an "Israelite indeed in whom there was no guile." In the lists of the twelve Apostles, in the Synoptic Gospels, his name is as uniformly at the head of the second group of four, as the name of Peter is at that of the first (Matt. x. 3; Mark iii. 18; Luke vi. 14); and the facts recorded by St. John give the reason of this priority. In those lists again we find his name uniformly coupled with that of Bartholomew, and this has led to the hypothesis that the latter is identical with the Nathanael of John i. 45, the one being the personal name, the other, like Barjonah or Bartimæus, a patronymic. Donaldson (*Jashar*, p. 9) looks on the two as brothers, but the precise mention of τὸν ἴδιον ἀδελφὸν in ver. 41, and its omission here, is, as Alford remarks (on Matt. x. 3), against this hypothesis.

Philip apparently was among the first company of disciples who were with the Lord at the commencement of his ministry, at the marriage of Cana, on his first appearance as a prophet in Jerusalem (John ii.). When John was cast into prison, and the work of declaring the glad tidings of the kingdom required a new company of preachers, we may believe that he, like his companions and friends, received a new call to a more constant discipleship (Matt. iv. 18–22). When the Twelve were specially set apart for their office, he was numbered among them. The first three Gospels tell us nothing more of him individually. St. John, with his characteristic fullness of personal reminiscences, records a few significant utterances. The earnest, simple-hearted faith which showed itself in his first conversion, required, it would seem, an education; one stage of this may be traced, according to Clement of Alexandria (*Strom.* iii. 25), in the history of Matt. viii. 21. He assumes, as a recognized fact, that Philip was the disciple who urged the plea, "Suffer me first to go and bury my father," and who was reminded of a higher duty, perhaps also of the command previously given, by the command, "Let the dead bury their dead; follow thou me." When the Galilæan crowds had halted on their way to Jerusalem to hear the preaching of Jesus (John vi. 5–9), and were faint with hunger, it was to Philip that the question was put, "Whence shall we buy bread that these may eat?" "And this he said," St. John adds, "to prove him, for He himself knew what He would do." The answer, "Two hundred pennyworth of bread is not sufficient for them that every one may take a little," shows how little he was prepared for the work of

---

[a] Greswell's suggestion (*Dissert. on Harmony*, xxxii.) that the Apostle was an inhabitant (ἀπὸ) of Bethsaida, but a native (ἐκ) of Capernaum, is to be noticed, but hardly to be received.

[b] It has been assumed, on the authority of patristic tradition (*infr.*), that his call to the apostleship involved the abandonment, for a time, of his wife and daughter.

divine power that followed.[a] It is noticeable that here, as in John i., he appears in close connection with Andrew.

Another incident is brought before us in John xii. 20–22. Among the pilgrims who had come to keep the passover at Jerusalem were some Gentile proselytes (Hellenes) who had heard of Jesus, and desired to see Him. The Greek name of Philip may have attracted them. The zealous love which he had shown in the case of Nathanael may have made him prompt to offer himself as their guide. But it is characteristic of him that he does not take them at once to the presence of his Master. "Philip cometh and telleth Andrew, and again Andrew and Philip tell Jesus." The friend and fellow-townsman to whom probably he owed his own introduction to Jesus of Nazareth, is to introduce these strangers also.[b]

There is a connection not difficult to be traced between this fact and that which follows on the last recurrence of Philip's name in the history of the Gospels. The desire to see Jesus gave occasion to the utterance of words in which the Lord spoke more distinctly than ever of the presence of his Father with Him, to the voice from heaven which manifested the Father's will (John xii. 28). The words appear to have sunk into the heart of at least one of the disciples, and he brooded over them. The strong cravings of a passionate but unenlightened faith led him to feel that one thing was yet wanting. They heard their Lord speak of his Father and of their Father. He was going to his Father's house. They were to follow Him there. But why should they not have even now a vision of the Divine glory? It was part of the childlike simplicity of his nature that no reserve should hinder the expression of the craving. "Lord, shew us the Father, and it sufficeth us" (John xiv. 8). And the answer to that desire belonged also specially to him. He had all along been eager to lead others to see Jesus. He had been with Him, looking on Him from the very commencement of his ministry, and yet he had not known Him. He had thought of the glory of the Father as consisting in something else than the Truth, Righteousness, Love that he had witnessed in the Son. "Have I been so long time with you, and yet hast thou not known me, Philip? He that hath seen me hath seen the Father. How sayest thou, Shew us the Father?" No other fact connected with the name of Philip is recorded in the Gospels. The close relation in which we have seen him standing to the sons of Zebedee and Nathanael might lead us to think of him as one of the two unnamed disciples in the list of fishermen on the Sea of Tiberias who meet us in John xxi. He is among the company of disciples at Jerusalem after the Ascension (Acts i. 13), and on the day of Pentecost.

After this all is uncertain and apocryphal. He is mentioned by Clement of Alexandria as having had a wife and children, and as having sanctioned the marriage of his daughters instead of binding them to vows of chastity (Strom. iii. 52; Euseb. H. E. iii. 30), and is included in the list of those who had borne witness of Christ in their lives, but

had not died what was commonly looked on as a martyr's death (Strom. iv. 73). Polycrates (Euseb. H. E. iii. 31), Bishop of Ephesus, speaks of him as having fallen asleep in the Phrygian Hierapolis, as having had two daughters who had grown old unmarried, and a third, with special gifts of inspiration (ἐν Ἁγίῳ Πνεύματι πολιτευσαμένη), who had died at Ephesus. There seems, however, in this mention of the daughters of Philip, to be some confusion between the Apostle and the Evangelist. Eusebius in the same chapter quotes a passage from Caius, in which the four daughters of Philip, prophetesses, are mentioned as living with their father at Hierapolis and as buried there with him, and himself connects this fact with Acts xxi. 8, as though they referred to one and the same person. Polycrates in like manner refers to him in the Easter Controversy, as an authority for the Quartodeciman practice (Euseb. H. E. v. 24). It is noticeable that even Augustine (Serm. 266) speaks with some uncertainty as to the distinctness of the two Philips. The apocryphal "Acts Philippi" are utterly wild and fantastic, and if there is any grain of truth in them, it is probably the bare fact that the Apostle or the Evangelist labored in Phrygia, and died at Hierapolis. He arrives in that city with his sister Mariamne and his friend Bartholomew.[c] The wife of the proconsul is converted. The people are drawn away from the worship of a great serpent. The priests and the proconsul seize on the Apostles and put them to the torture. St. John suddenly appears with words of counsel and encouragement. Philip, in spite of the warning of the Apostle of Love reminding him that he should return good for evil, curses the city, and the earth opens and swallows it up. Then his Lord appears and reproves him for his vindictive anger, and those who had descended to the abyss are raised out of it again. The tortures which Philip had suffered end in his death, but, as a punishment for his offense, he is to remain for forty days excluded from Paradise. After his death a vine springs up on the spot where his blood had fallen, and the juice of the grapes is used for the Eucharistic cup (Tischendorf, Acta Apocrypha, pp. 75–94). The book which contains this narrative is apparently only the last chapter of a larger history, and it fixes the journey and the death as after the eighth year of Trajan. It is uncertain whether the other apocryphal fragment professing to give an account of his labors in Greece is part of the same work, but it is at least equally legendary. He arrives in Athens clothed like the other Apostles, as Christ had commanded, in an outer cloak and a linen tunic. Three hundred philosophers dispute with him. They find themselves baffled, and send for assistance to Ananias the high-priest at Jerusalem. He puts on his pontifical robes, and goes to Athens at the head of five hundred warriors. They attempt to seize on the Apostle, and are all smitten with blindness. The heavens open; the form of the Son of Man appears, and all the idols of Athens fall to the ground; and so on through a succession of marvels, ending with his remaining two years in the city, establishing a church there,

---

[a] Bengel draws from this narrative the inference that it was part of Philip's work to provide for the daily sustenance of the company of the Twelve.

[b] The national pride of some Spanish theologians has led them to claim these inquirers as their countrymen, and so to explain the reverence which places the

patron saint of so many of their kings on a level with Saint Iago as the patron saint of the people (Acta Sanctorum, May 1).

[c] The union of the two names is significant, and points to the Apostle.

and then going to preach the Gospel in Parthia (Tischendorf, *Acta Apocr.* pp. 95–104). Another tradition represents Scythia as the scene of his labors (Abdias, *Hist. Apost.* in Fabricius, *Cod. Apoc. N. T.* i. 739), and throws the guilt of his death upon the Ebionites (*Acta Sanctorum*, May 1).

E. H. P.

PHILIP THE EVANGELIST. The first mention of this name occurs in the account of the dispute between the Hebrew and Hellenistic disciples in Acts vi. He is one of the Seven appointed to superintend the daily distribution of food and alms, and so to remove all suspicion of partiality. The fact that all the seven names are Greek, makes it at least very probable that they were chosen as belonging to the Hellenistic section of the Church, representatives of the class which had appeared before the Apostles in the attitude of complaint. The name of Philip stands next to that of Stephen; and this, together with the fact that these are the only two names (unless Nicolas be an exception; comp. NICOLAS) of which we hear again, tends to the conclusion that he was among the most prominent of those so chosen. He was, at any rate, well reported of as "full of the Holy Ghost, and wisdom," and had so won the affections of the great body of believers as to be among the objects of their free election, possibly (assuming the votes of the congregation to have been taken for the different candidates) gaining all but the highest number of suffrages. Whether the office to which he was thus appointed gave him the position and the title of a Deacon of the Church, or was special and extraordinary in its character, must remain uncertain (comp. DEACON).

The after-history of Philip warrants the belief, in any case, that his office was not simply that of the later Diaconate. It is no great presumption to think of him as contributing hardly less than Stephen to the great increase of disciples which followed on this fresh organization, as sharing in that wider, more expansive teaching which shows itself for the first time in the oration of the proto-martyr, and in which he was the forerunner of St. Paul. We should expect the man who had been his companion and fellow-worker to go on with the work which he left unfinished, and to break through the barriers of a simply national Judaism. And so accordingly we find him in the next stage of his history. The persecution of which Saul was the leader must have stopped the "daily ministrations" of the Church. The teachers who had been most prominent were compelled to take to flight, and Philip was among them. The cessation of one form of activity, however, only threw him forward into another. It is noticeable that the city of Samaria is the first scene of his activity (Acts viii.). He is the precursor of St. Paul in his work, as Stephen had been in his teaching. It falls to his lot, rather than to that of an Apostle, to take that first step in the victory over Jewish prejudice and the expansion of the Church, according to its Lord's command. As a preparation for that work there may have been the Messianic hopes which were cherished by the Samaritans no less than by the Jews (John iv. 25), the recollection of the two days which had witnessed

the presence there of Christ and his disciples (John iv. 40), even perhaps the craving for spiritual powers which had been roused by the strange influence of Simon the Sorcerer. The scene which brings the two into contact with each other, in which the magician has to acknowledge a power over nature greater than his own, is interesting, rather as belonging to the life of the heresiarch than to that of the Evangelist. [SIMON MAGUS.] It suggests the inquiry whether we can trace through the distortions and perversions of the "hero of the romance of heresy," the influence of that phase of Christian truth which was likely to be presented by the preaching of the Hellenistic Evangelist.

This step is followed by another. He is directed by an angel of the Lord to take the road that led down from Jerusalem to Gaza on the way to Egypt. (For the topographical questions connected with this history, see GAZA.) A chariot passes by in which there is a man of another race, whose complexion or whose dress showed him to be a native of Ethiopia. From the time of Psammeticus [comp. MANASSEH] there had been a large body of Jews settled in that region, and the eunuch or chamberlain at the court of Candace might easily have come across them and their sacred books, might have embraced their faith, and become by circumcision a proselyte of righteousness. He had been on a pilgrimage to Jerusalem. He may have heard there of the new sect. The history that follows is interesting as one of the few records in the N. T. of the process of individual conversion, and one which we may believe St. Luke obtained, during his residence at Cæsarea, from the Evangelist himself. The devout proselyte reciting the prophecy which he does not understand, the Evangelist-preacher running at full speed till he overtakes the chariot, the abrupt question, the simple-hearted answer, the unfolding, from the starting-point of the prophecy, of the glad tidings of Jesus, the craving for the means of admission to the blessing of fellowship with the new society, the simple baptism in the first stream or spring,[a] the instantaneous, abrupt departure of the missionary-preacher, as of one carried away by a Divine impulse, these help us to represent to ourselves much of the life and work of that remote past. On the hypothesis which has just been suggested, we may think of it as being the incident to which the mind of Philip himself recurred with most satisfaction.

A brief sentence tells us that he continued his work as a preacher at Azotus (Ashdod) and among the other cities that had formerly belonged to the Philistines, and, following the coast-line, came to Cæsarea. Here for a long period, not less than eighteen or nineteen years, we lose sight of him. He may have been there when the new[b] convert Saul passed through on his way to Tarsus (Acts ix. 30). He may have contributed by his labors to the eager desire to be guided further into the Truth which led to the conversion of Cornelius. We can hardly think of him as giving up all at once the missionary habits of his life. Cæsarea, however, appears to have been the centre of his activity. The last glimpse of him in the N. T. is

---

[a] The verse which inserts the requirement of a confession of faith as the condition of baptism appears to have been the work of a transcriber anxious to bring the narrative into harmony with ecclesiastical usage. (Comp. Alford, Meyer, Tischendorf, *in loc.*)

[b] Three years at least had passed since the Apostle's conversion (comp. Acts ix. 30, Gal i. 18). H.

In the account of St. Paul's journey to Jerusalem. It is to his house, as to one well known to them, that St. Paul and his companions turn for shelter. He is still known as "one of the Seven." His work has gained for him the yet higher title of Evangelist (comp. EVANGELIST). He has four daughters, who possess the gift of prophetic utterance, and who apparently give themselves to the work of teaching instead of entering on the life of home (Acts xxi. 8, 9). He is visited by the prophets and elders of Jerusalem. At such a place as Cæsarea the work of such a man must have helped to bridge over the ever-widening gap which threatened to separate the Jewish and the Gentile Churches. One who had preached Christ to the hated Samaritan, the swarthy African, the despised Philistine, the men of all nations who passed through the seaport of Palestine, might well welcome the arrival of the Apostle of the Gentiles (comp. J. P. Lange, in Herzog's Real-Encyklopäd. s. v. "Philippus").

The traditions in which the Evangelist and the Apostle who bore the same name are more or less confounded have been given under PHILIP THE APOSTLE. According to another, relating more distinctly to him, he died Bishop of Tralles (Acta Sanct. June 6). The house in which he and his daughters had lived was pointed out to travellers in the time of Jerome (Epit. Paulæ, § 8). (Comp. Ewald, Geschichte, vi. 175, 208–214; Baumgarten, Apostel Geschichte, §§ 15, 16.)   E. H. P.

PHILIP HEROD I., II. [HEROD; vol ii. pp. 1052, 1853.]

PHILIPPI (Φιλιπποι: Philippi).

A city of Macedonia, about nine miles from the sea, to the N. W. of the island of Thasos, which is twelve miles distant from its port Neapolis, the modern Kavalla. It is situated in a plain between the ranges of Pangæus and Hæmus. St. Paul, when, on his first visit to Macedonia in company with Silas, he embarked at Troas, made a straight run to Samothrace, and from thence to Neapolis, which he reached on the second day (Acts xvi. 11). This was built on a rocky promontory, on the western side of which is a roadstead, furnishing a safe refuge from the Etesian winds. The town is cut off from the interior by a steep line of hills,

Ruins at Philippi.

anciently called Symbolum, connected towards the N. E. with the western extremity of Hæmus, and towards the S. W., less continuously, with the eastern extremity of Pangæus. A steep track, following the course of an ancient paved road, leads over Symbolum to Philippi, the solitary pass being about 1,600 feet above the sea-level. At this point the traveller arrives in little more than half an hour's riding, and almost immediately begi-s to descend by a yet steeper path into the plain. From a point near the watershed, a simultaneous view is obtained both of Kavalla and of the ruins of Philippi. Between Pangæus and the nearest part of Symbolum the plain is very low, and there are large accumulations of water. Between the foot of Symbolum and the site of Philippi, two Turkish cemeteries are passed, the gravestones of which are all derived from the ruins of the ancient city, and in the immediate[a] neighborhood of the one first reached is the modern Turkish village Beretli. This is the nearest village to the ancient ruins, which are not at the present time inhabited at all. Near the second cemetery are some ruins on a slight eminence, and also a khan, kept by a Greek family. Here is a large monumental block of marble, 12 feet high and 7 feet square, apparently the pedestal of a statue, as on the top a hole exists, which was obviously intended for its reception. This hole is pointed out by local tradition as the crib out of which Alexander's horse, Bucephalus, was accustomed to eat his oats. On two sides of the block is a mutilated Latin inscription, in which the names of Caius Vibius and Cornelius Quartus may be deciphered. A stream employed in turning a mill bursts out from a sedgy pool in the neighborhood, and probably finds its way to the marshy ground mentioned as existing in the S. W. portion of the plain.

After about twenty minutes' ride from the khan, over ground thickly strewed with fragments of marble columns, and slabs that have been employed in building, a river-bed 66 feet wide is crossed,

---

[a] It appears to be some miles distant, but is distinctly seen from that point.   5

through which the stream rushes with great force,[a] and immediately on the other side the walls of the ancient Philippi may be traced. Their direction is adjusted to the course of the stream; and at only 350 feet from its margin there appears a gap in their circuit indicating the former existence of a gate. This is, no doubt, the gate[b] out of which the Apostle and his companion passed to the "prayer meeting" on the banks of a river, where they made the acquaintance of Lydia, the Thyatiran seller of purple. The locality, just outside the walls, and with a plentiful supply of water for their animals, is exactly the one which would be appropriated as a market for itinerant traders, "quorum cophinus fœnumque supellex," as will appear from the parallel case of the Egerian fountain near Rome, of whose desecration Juvenal complains (Sat. iii. 13). Lydia had an establishment in Philippi for the reception of the dyed goods which were imported from Thyatira and the neighboring towns of Asia; and were dispersed by means of pack-animals among the mountain clans of the Hæmus and Pangæus, the agents being doubtless in many instances her own co-religionists. High up in Hæmus lay the tribe of the Satræ, where was the oracle of Dionysus, — not the rustic deity of the Attic vine-dressers, but the prophet-god of the Thracians (ὁ Θρηξὶ μάντις, Eurip. Hecub. 1267). The "damsel with the spirit of divination" (παιδίσκη ἔχουσα πνεῦμα πύθωνα) may probably be regarded as one of the hierodules of this establishment, hired by Philippian citizens, and frequenting the country-market to practice her art upon the villagers who brought produce for the consumption of the town. The fierce character of the mountaineers would render it imprudent to admit them within the walls of the city; just as in some of the towns of North Africa, the Kabyles are not allowed to enter, but have a market allotted to them outside the walls for the sale of the produce they bring. Over such an assemblage only a summary jurisdiction can be exercised; and hence the proprietors of the slave, when they considered themselves injured, and hurried Paul and Silas into the town, to the agora, — the civic market where the magistrates (ἄρχοντες) sat, — were at once turned over to the military authorities (στρατηγοί), and these, naturally assuming that a stranger frequenting the extra-mural market must be a Thracian mountaineer or an itinerant trader, proceeded to inflict upon the ostensible cause of a riot (the merits of which they would not attempt to understand) the usual treatment in such cases. The idea of the Apostle possessing the Roman franchise, and consequently an exemption from corporal outrage, never occurred to the rough soldier who ordered him to be scourged; and the whole transaction seems to have passed so rapidly that he had no time to plead his citizenship, of which the military authorities first heard the next day. But the illegal treatment (ὕβρις) obviously

made a deep impression on the mind of its victim, as is evident, not only from his refusal to take his discharge from prison the next morning (Acts xvi. 37), but from a passage in the Epistle to the Church at Thessalonica (1 Thess. ii. 2), in which he reminds them of the circumstances under which he first preached the Gospel to them (προπαθόντες καὶ ὑβρισθέντες, καθὼς οἴδατε, ἐν Φιλίπποις). And subsequently at Jerusalem, under parallel circumstances of tumult, he warns the officer (to the great surprise of the latter) of his privilege (Acts xxii. 25).

The Philippi which St. Paul visited, the site of which has been described above, was a Roman colony[a] founded by Augustus, and the remains which strew the ground are no doubt derived from that city. [COLONY, Amer. ed.] The establishment of Philip of Macedonia was probably not exactly on the same site; for it is described by Appian as being on a hill, and it may perhaps be looked for upon the elevation near the second cemetery. Philip is said to have occupied it and fortified the position by way of a defense against the neighboring Thracians, so that the nucleus of his town, at any rate, would have been of the nature of an acropolis. Nothing would be more natural than that the Roman town should have been built in the immediate neighborhood of the existing Greek one, on a site more suitable for architectural display.

Philip, when he acquired possession of the site, found there a town named Datus or Datum, which was in all probability in its origin a factory of the Phœnicians, who were the first that worked the gold-mines in the mountains here, as in the neighboring Thasos. Appian says that these were in a hill (λόφος) not far from Philippi, that the hill was sacred to Dionysus, and that the mines went by the name of "the sanctuary" (τὰ ἄσυλα). But he shows himself quite ignorant of the locality, to the extent of believing the plain of Philippi to lie open to the river Strymon, whereas the massive wall of Pangæus is really interposed between them. In all probability the "hill of Dionysus" and the "sanctuary" are "the temple of Dionysus" high up the mountains among the Satræ, who preserved their independence against all invaders down to the time of Herodotus at least. It is more likely that the gold-mines coveted by Philip were the same as those at Scaptè Hyle, which was certainly in this immediate neighborhood. Before the great expedition of Xerxes, the Thasians had a number of settlements on the main, and this among the number, which produced them 80 talents a year as rent to the state. In the year 463 B. C., they ceded their possessions on the continent to the Athenians; but the colonists, 10,000 in number, who had settled on the Strymon and pushed their encroachments eastward as far as this point, were crushed by a simultaneous effort of the Thracian tribes (Thucydides, i. 100, iv. 102; Herodotus, ix.

---

a * The deep water-course is always there; but whether it contains water or not depends on the season of the year. On the 13th of December, 1859, it was a rapid torrent, varying in depth at different points from one and two feet to four and five feet, and covering a bed of about thirty feet in width. It is said to be still known as Angkista. Some others who were there a few weeks earlier than this reported that the channel at that time was entirely dry. H.

b * The A. V. has "city" (πόλεως) there, but the

best copies read "gate" (πύλης). Thus Luke's narrative accords precisely with the topography, in regard to the implied vicinity of the place of worship to the city-gate.   H.

c * Luke terms it also "the first city (chief city, A. V.) of that part of Macedonia." (Acts xvi. 12), but in what sense it was first (πρώτη) has been controverted. See on this point the addition to MACEDONIA, Amer. ed.   M.

75; Pausanias, i. 29, 4). From that time until the rise of the Macedonian power, the mines seem to have remained in the hands of native chiefs; but when the affairs of Southern Greece became thoroughly embroiled by the policy of Philip, the Thasians made an attempt to repossess themselves of this valuable territory, and sent a colony to the site — then going by the name of "the Springs" (Κρηνίδες). Philip, however, aware of the importance of the position, expelled them and founded Philippi, the last of all his creations. The mines at that time, as was not wonderful under the circumstances, had become almost insignificant in their produce; but their new owner contrived to extract more than 1,000 talents a year from them, with which he minted the gold coinage called by his name.

The proximity of the gold-mines was of course the origin of so large a city as Philippi, but the plain in which it lies is of extraordinary fertility. The position, too, was on the main road from Rome to Asia, the Via Egnatia, which from Thessalonica to Constantinople followed the same course as the existing post-road. The usual course was to take ship at Brundisium and land at Dyrrachium, from whence a route led across Epirus to Thessalonica. Ignatius was carried to Italy by this route, when sent to Rome to be cast to wild beasts. ·

The ruins of Philippi are very extensive, but present no striking feature except two gateways, which are considered to belong to the time of Claudius. Traces of an amphitheatre, theatre, or stadium — for it does not clearly appear which — are also visible in the direction of the hills on the N. E. side. Inscriptions both in the Latin and Greek languages, but more generally in the former, are found.

St. Paul visited Philippi twice more, once immediately after the disturbances which arose at Ephesus out of the jealousy of the manufacturers of silver shrines for Artemis. By this time the hostile relation in which the Christian doctrine necessarily stood to all purely ceremonial religions was perfectly manifest: and wherever its teachers appeared, popular tumults were to be expected, and the jealousy of the Roman authorities, who dreaded civil disorder above everything else, to be feared. It seems not unlikely that the second visit of the Apostle to Philippi was made specially with the view of counteracting this particular danger. The Epistle to the Philippians, which was written to them from Rome, indicates that at that time some of the Christians there were in the custody of the military authorities as seditious persons, through some proceedings or other connected with their faith (ὑμῖν ἐχαρίσθη τὸ ὑπὲρ Χριστοῦ, οὐ μόνον τὸ εἰς αὐτὸν πιστεύειν ἀλλὰ καὶ τὸ ὑπὲρ αὐτοῦ πάσχειν· τὸν αὐτὸν ἀγῶνα ἔχοντες οἷον εἴδετε ἐν ἐμοὶ καὶ νῦν ἀκούετε ἐν ἐμοί: Phil. i. 29). The reports of the provincial magistrates to Rome would of course describe St. Paul's first visit to Philippi as the origin of the troubles there; and if this were believed, it would be put together with the charge against him by the Jews at Jerusalem which induced him to appeal to Cæsar, and with the disturbances at Ephesus and elsewhere; and the general conclusion at which the government would arrive, might not improbably be that he was a dangerous person and should be got rid of. This will explain the strong exhortation in the first eighteen verses of chapter ii., and the peculiar way in which it winds

up. The Philippian Christians, who are at the same time suffering for their profession, are exhorted in the most earnest manner, not to firmness (as one might have expected), but to moderation, to abstinence from all provocation and ostentation of their own sentiments (μηδὲν κατὰ ἐριθείαν μηδὲ κενοδοξίαν, ver. 3), to humility, and consideration for the interests of others. They are to achieve their salvation with fear and trembling, and without quarreling and disputing, in order to escape all blame — from such charges, that is, as the Roman colonists would bring against them. If with all this prudence and temperance in the profession of their faith, their faith is still made a penal offence, the Apostle is well content to take the consequences, — to precede them in martyrdom for it, — to be the libation poured out upon them the victims (εἰ καὶ σπένδομαι ἐπὶ τῇ θυσίᾳ καὶ λειτουργίᾳ τῆς πίστεως ὑμῶν, χαίρω καὶ συγχαίρω πᾶσιν ὑμῖν, ver. 17). Of course the Jewish formalists in Philippi were the parties most likely to misrepresent the conduct of the new converts; and hence (after a digression on the subject of Epaphroditus) the Apostle reverts to cautions against them, such precisely as he had given before, consequently by word of mouth. "Beware of those dogs" — (for they will not be children at the table, but eat the crumbs underneath) — "those doers (and bad doers too) of the Law — those flesh-manglers (for circumcised I won't call them, we being the true circumcision") etc. (iii. 2, 3). Some of these enemies St. Paul found at Rome, who "told the story of Christ insincerely" (κατήγγειλαν οὐχ ἁγνῶς, i. 17) in the hope to increase the severity of his imprisonment by exciting the jealousy of the court. These he opposes to such as "preached Christ" (ἐκήρυξαν) loyally, and consoles himself with the reflection that, at all events, the story circulated, whatever the motives of those who circulated it.

The Christian community at Philippi distinguished itself in liberality. On the Apostle's first visit he was hospitably entertained by Lydia, and when he afterwards went to Thessalonica, where his reception appears to have been of a very mixed character, the Philippians sent him supplies more than once, and were the only Christian community that did so (Phil. iv. 15). They also contributed readily to the collection made for the relief of the poor at Jerusalem, which St. Paul conveyed to them at his last visit (2 Cor. viii. 1–6). And it would seem as if they sent further supplies to the Apostle after his arrival at Rome. The necessity for these seems to have been urgent, and some delay to have taken place in collecting the requisite funds; so that Epaphroditus, who carried them, risked his life in the endeavor to make up for lost time (μέχρι θανάτου ἤγγισεν παραβουλευσάμενος τῇ ψυχῇ, ἵνα ἀναπληρώσῃ τὸ ὑμῶν ὑστέρημα τῆς πρὸς μέ λειτουργίας, Phil. ii. 30). The delay, however, seems to have somewhat stung the Apostle at the time, who fancied his beloved flock had forgotten him (see iv. 10–17). Epaphroditus fell ill with fever from his efforts, and nearly died. On recovering he became homesick, and wandering in mind (ἀδημονῶν) from the weakness which is the sequel of fever; and St. Paul, although intending soon to send Timothy to the Philippian Church, thought it desirable to let Epaphroditus go without delay to them, who had already heard of his sickness, and carry with him the letter which is included in the Canon — one which was written after the Apostle's imprisonment at Rome had lasted a considerable time. Some domestic troubles connected with religion had already broken out in the community. Euodia (the name of a female, not Euodias, as in A. V.: see EUODIAS) and Syntyche, perhaps deaconesses, are exhorted to agree with one another in the matter of their common faith; and St. Paul entreats some one, whom he calls "true yoke-fellow," to "help" these women,[a] that is, in the work of their reconciliation, since they had done good service to the Apostle in his trials at Philippi. Possibly a claim on the part of these females to superior insight in spiritual matters may have caused some irritation; for the Apostle immediately goes on to remind his readers, that the peace of God is something superior to the highest intelligence (ὑπερέχουσα πάντα νοῦν).

When St. Paul passed through Philippi a third time he does not appear to have made any considerable stay there (Acts xx. 6). He and his companion are somewhat loosely spoken of as sailing from Philippi; but this is because in the common apprehension of travellers the city and its port were regarded as one. Whoever embarked at the Piraeus might in the same way be said to set out on a voyage from Athens. On this occasion the voyage to Troas took the Apostle five days, the vessel being probably obliged to coast in order to avoid the contrary wind, until coming off the headland of Sarpedon, whence she would be able to stand across to Troas with an E. or E. N. E. breeze, which at that time of year (after Easter) might be looked for. (Strab. Fragment. lib. vii.; Thucyd. i. 100, iv. 102; Herod. ix. 75; Diod. Sic. xvi. 3 ff.; Appian. Bell. Civ. iv. 101 ff.; Pausan. i. 28, § 4; Hackett's Journey to Philippi in the Bible Union Quarterly for August, 1860) [and Bibl. Sacra for 1860, vol. xvii. pp. 866–898. For other sources see MACEDONIA, at the end.]   J. W. B.

* PHILIP'PIANS (Φιλιππήσιοι: Philippenses), inhabitants of Philippi, but limited (Phil. iv. 14) to those whom Paul addressed in his letter as Christians. See the next article.   H.

PHILIP'PIANS, EPISTLE TO THE.
1. The canonical authority, Pauline authorship and integrity of this epistle were unanimously acknowledged up to the end of the 18th century. Marcion (A. D. 140) in the earliest known Canon held common ground with the Church touching the authority of this epistle (Tertullian, Adv. Marcion. iv. 5, v. 20): it appears in the Muratorian Fragment (Routh, Reliquiæ Sacræ, i. 395); among the "acknowledged" books in Eusebius (H. E. iii. 25); in the lists of the Council of Laodicea, A. D. 365, and the Synod of Hippo, 393; and in all subsequent lists, as well as in the Peshito and later versions. Even contemporary evidence may be claimed for it. Philippian Christians who had contributed to the collections for St. Paul's support at Rome, who had been eye and ear witnesses of the return of Epaphroditus and the first reading of St. Paul's epistle, may have been still alive at Philippi when Polycarp wrote (A. D. 107) his letter to them, in which (cc. 2, 3) he refers[b] to St. Paul's epistle

as a well known distinction belonging to the Philippian Church. It is quoted as St. Paul's by Irenæus, iv. 18, § 4; Clem. Alex. Pædag. i. 6, § 52, and elsewhere; Tertullian, Adv. Mar. v. 20, De Res. Carn. ch. 23. A quotation from it (Phil. ii. 6) is found in the Epistle of the Churches of Lyons and Vienne, A. D. 177 (Eusebius, H. E. v. 2). The testimonies of later writers are innumerable. But F. C. Baur (1845), followed by Schwegler (1846), has argued from the phraseology of the epistle and other internal marks, that it is the work not of St. Paul, but of some Gnostic forger in the 2d century. He has been answered by Lünemann (1847), Brückner (1848), and Resch (1850). Even if his inference were a fair consequence from Baur's premises, it would still be neutralized by the strong evidence in favor of Pauline authorship, which Paley, Horæ Paulinæ, ch. 7, has drawn from the epistle as it stands. The arguments of the Tübingen school are briefly stated in Reuss, Gesch. N. T. §§ 130–133, and at greater length in Wiesinger's Commentary. Most persons who read them will be disposed to concur in the opinion of Dean Alford (N. T. vol. iii. p. 27, ed. 1856), who regards them as an instance of the insanity of hyper-criticism. The canonical authority and the authorship of the epistle may be considered as unshaken.

There is a break in the sense at the end of the second chapter of the epistle, which every careful reader must have observed. It is indeed quite natural that an epistle written amid exciting circumstances, personal dangers, and various distractions should bear in one place at least a mark of interruption. Le Moyne (1685) thought it was anciently divided into two parts. Heinrichs (1810) followed by Paulus (1818) has conjectured from this abrupt recommencement that the two parts are two distinct epistles, of which the first, together with the conclusion of the Ep. (iv. 21–23) was intended for public use in the church, and the second exclusively for the Apostle's special friends in Philippi. It is not easy to see what sufficient foundation exists for this theory, or what illustration of the meaning of the epistle could be derived from it. It has met with a distinct reply from Krause (1811 and 1818) and the integrity of the epistle has not been questioned by recent critics. Ewald (Sendschreiben des A. Paulus, p. 431) is of opinion that St. Paul sent several epistles to the Philippians: and he refers to the texts ii. 12 and iii. 18, as partly proving this. But some additional confirmation or explanation of his conjecture is requisite before it can be admitted as either probable or necessary.

2. Where written. — The constant tradition that this epistle was written at Rome by St. Paul in his captivity, was impugned first by Oeder (1731), who, disregarding the fact that the Apostle was in prison, i. 7, 13, 14, when he wrote, imagined that he was at Corinth (see Wolf's Curæ Philologicæ, iv. 168, 270); and then by Paulus (1799), Schulz (1829), Böttger (1837), and Rilliet (1841), in whose opinion the epistle was written during the Apostle's confinement at Cæsarea (Acts xxiv. 23);

tione, xxxvi., naming Philippi as one of those Apostolic churches "in which at this day [A. D. 200] the very seats of the Apostles preside over their regions, in which the authentic epistles themselves of the Apostles are read, speaking with the voice and representing the face of each."

sent the references to the "palace" (prætorium, i. 13), and to "Cæsar's household," iv. 22, seem to point to Rome rather than to Cæsarea; and there is no reason whatever for supposing that the Apostle felt in Cæsarea that extreme uncertainty of life connected with the approaching decision of his cause, which he must have felt towards the end of his captivity at Rome, and which he expresses in this epistle, i. 19, 20, ii. 17, iii. 10; and further, the dissemination of the Gospel described in Phil. i. 12–18, is not even hinted at in St. Luke's account of the Cæsarean captivity, but is described by him as taking place at Rome: compare Acts xxiv. 23 with xxviii. 30, 31. Even Reuss (*Gesch. N. T.* 1860), who assigns to Cæsarea three of St. Paul's epistles, which are generally considered to have been written at Rome, is decided in his conviction that the Epistle to the Philippians was written at Rome.

3. *When written.* — Assuming then that the epistle was written at Rome during the imprisonment mentioned in the last chapter of the Acts, it may be shown from a single fact that it could not have been written long before the end of the two years. The distress of the Philippians on account of Epaphroditus' sickness was known at Rome when the epistle was written; this implies four journeys, separated by some indefinite intervals, to or from Philippi and Rome, between the commencement of St. Paul's captivity and the writing of the epistle. The Philippians were informed of his imprisonment, sent Epaphroditus, were informed of their messenger's sickness, sent their message of condolence. Further, the absence of St. Luke's name from the salutations to a church where he was well known, implies that he was absent from Rome [a] when the epistle was written: so does St. Paul's declaration, ii. 20, that no one who remained with him felt an equal interest with Timothy in the welfare of the Philippians. And by comparing the mention of St. Luke in Col. iv. 14, and Philem. 24 with the abrupt conclusion of his narrative in the Acts, we are led to the inference that he left Rome after those two epistles were written and before the end of the two years' captivity. Lastly, it is obvious from Phil. i. 20, that St. Paul, when he wrote, felt his position to be very critical, and we know that it became more precarious as the two years drew to a close. In A. D. 62 the infamous Tigellinus succeeded Burrus the upright Prætorian præfect in the charge of St. Paul's person; and the marriage of Poppæa brought his imperial judge under an influence, which if exerted, was hostile to St. Paul. Assuming that St. Paul's acquittal and release took place in 63, we may date the Epistle to the Philippians early in that year.

4. *The writer's acquaintance with the Philippians.* — St. Paul's connection with Philippi was of a peculiar character, which gave rise to the writing of this epistle. That city, important as a mart for the produce of the neighboring gold mines, and as a Roman stronghold to check the rude Thracian mountaineers, was distinguished as the scene of the great battle fatal to Brutus and Cassius, B. C. 42 [PHILIPPI]. In A. D. 51 St. Paul entered its walls, accompanied by Silas, who had been with him since he started from Antioch, and by Timothy and Luke, whom he had afterwards attached to himself; the former at Derbe, the latter

quite recently at Troas. It may well be imagined that the patience of the zealous Apostle had been tried by his mysterious repulse, first from Asia, then from Bithynia and Mysia, and that his expectations had been stirred up by the vision which hastened his departure with his new found associate, Luke, from Troas. A swift passage brought him to the European shore at Neapolis, whence he took the road about ten miles [b] long across the mountain ridge called Symbolum to Philippi (Acts xvi. 12). There, at a greater distance from Jerusalem than any Apostle had yet penetrated, the long restrained energy of St. Paul was again employed in laying the foundation of a Christian church. Seeking first the lost sheep of the house of Israel, he went on a Sabbath day with the few Jews who resided in Philippi, to their small proseucha on the bank of the river Gangitas. The missionaries sat down and spoke to the assembled women. One of them, Lydia, not born of the seed of Abraham, but a proselyte, whose name and occupation, as well as her birth, connect her with Asia, gave heed unto St. Paul, and she and her household were baptized, perhaps on the same Sabbath day. Her house became the residence of the missionaries. Many days they resorted to the proseucha, and the result of their short sojourn in Philippi was the conversion of many persons (xvi. 40), including at last their jailer and his household. Philippi was endeared to St. Paul, not only by the hospitality of Lydia, the deep sympathy of the converts, and the remarkable miracle which set a seal on his preaching, but also by the successful exercise of his missionary activity after a long suspense, and by the happy consequences of his undaunted endurance of ignominies, which remained in his memory (Phil. i. 30) after a long interval of eleven years. Leaving Timothy and Luke to watch over the infant church, Paul and Silas went to Thessalonica (1 Thess. ii. 2), whither they were followed by the alms of the Philippians (Phil. iv. 16), and thence southwards. Timothy having probably carried out similar directions to those which were given to Titus (i. 5) in Crete, soon rejoined St. Paul. We know not whether Luke remained at Philippi. The next six years of his life are a blank in our records. At the end of that period he is found again (Acts xx. 6) at Philippi.

After the lapse of five years, spent chiefly at Corinth and Ephesus, St. Paul, escaping from the incensed worshippers of the Ephesian Diana, passed through Macedonia, A. D. 57, on his way to Greece, accompanied by the Ephesians Tychicus and Trophimus, and probably visited Philippi for the second time, and was there joined by Timothy. His beloved Philippians, free, it seems, from the controversies which agitated other Christian churches, became still dearer to St. Paul on account of the solace which they afforded him when, emerging from a season of dejection (2 Cor. vii. 5), oppressed by weak bodily health, and anxious for the steadfastness of the churches which he had planted in Asia and Achaia, he wrote at Philippi his Second Epistle to the Corinthians.

On returning from Greece, unable to take ship there on account of the Jewish plots against his life, he went through Macedonia, seeking a favorable port for embarking. After parting from his

---

[a] Was St. Luke at Philippi? — the "true yoke-fellow" mentioned in iv. 3? [YOKE-FELLOW, Amer. ed.]

[b] * Nearer *nine*, as stated in note *c*, vol. iii. p 2078.

H.

companions (Acts xx. 4), he again found a refuge among his faithful Philippians, where he spent some days at Easter, A. D. 58, with St. Luke, who accompanied him when he sailed from Neapolis.

Once more, in his Roman captivity (A. D. 62) their care of him revived again. They sent Epaphroditus, bearing their alms for the Apostle's support, and ready also to tender his personal service (Phil. ii. 25). He stayed some time at Rome, and while employed as the organ of communication between the imprisoned Apostle and the Christians, and inquirers in and about Rome, he fell dangerously ill. When he was sufficiently recovered, St. Paul sent him back to the Philippians, to whom he was very dear, and with him our epistle.

5. *Scope and contents of the Epistle.* — St Paul's aim in writing is plainly this: while acknowledging the alms of the Philippians and the personal services of their messenger, to give them some information respecting his own condition, and some advice respecting theirs. Perhaps the intensity of his feelings and the distraction of his prison prevented the following out his plan with undeviating closeness, for the preparations for the departure of Epaphroditus, and the thought that he would soon arrive among the warm-hearted Philippians, filled St. Paul with recollections of them, and revived his old feelings towards those fellow-heirs of his hope of glory who were so deep in his heart (i. 7), and so often in his prayers (i. 4).

After the inscription (i. 1, 2) in which Timothy as the second father of the church is joined with Paul, he sets forth his own condition (i. 3–26), his prayers, care, and wishes for his Philippians, with the troubles and uncertainty of his imprisonment, and his hope of eventually seeing them again. Then (i. 27–ii. 18) he exhorts them to those particular virtues which he would rejoice to see them practicing at the present time — fearless endurance of persecution from the outward heathen: unity among themselves, built on Christ-like humility and love; and an exemplary life in the face of unbelievers. He hopes soon to hear a good report of them (ii. 19–30), either by sending Timothy, or by going himself to them, as he now sends Epaphroditus, whose diligent service is highly commended. Reverting (iii. 1–21) to the tone of joy which runs through the preceding descriptions and exhortations — as in i. 4, 18, 25, ii. 2, 16, 17, 18, 28 — he bids them take heed that their joy be *in the Lord*, and warns them, as he had often previously warned them (probably in his last two visits), against admitting itinerant Judaizing teachers, the tendency of whose doctrine was towards a vain confidence in mere earthly things; in contrast to this, he exhorts them to follow him in placing their trust humbly but entirely in Christ, and in pressing forward in their Christian course, with the Resurrection day [a] constantly before their minds. Again (iv. 1–9), adverting to their position in the midst of unbelievers, he beseeches them, even with personal appeals, to be firm, united, joyful in the Lord; to be full of prayer and peace, and to lead such a life as must approve itself to the moral sense of all men. Lastly (iv. 10–23), he thanks them for the contribution sent by Epaphroditus for his support, and concludes with salutations and a benediction.

6. *Effect of the Epistle.* — We have no account

of the reception of this epistle by the Philippians. Except doubtful traditions that Erastus was their first bishop, and with Lydia and Parmenas was martyred in their city, nothing is recorded of them for the next forty-four years. But, about A. D. 107, Philippi was visited by Ignatius, who was conducted through Neapolis and Philippi, and across Macedonia in his way to martyrdom at Rome. And his visit was speedily followed by the arrival of a letter from Polycarp of Smyrna, which accompanied, in compliance with a characteristic request of the warm-hearted Philippians, a copy of all the letters of Ignatius which were in the possession of the church of Smyrna. It is interesting to compare the Philippians of A. D. 63, as drawn by St. Paul, with their successors in A. D. 107 as drawn by the disciple of St. John. Steadfastness in the faith, and a joyful sympathy with sufferers for Christ's sake, seem to have distinguished them at both periods (Phil. i. 5, and Polyc. Ep. i.). The character of their religion was the same throughout, practical and emotional rather than speculative: in both epistles there are many practical suggestions, much interchange of feeling, and an absence of doctrinal discussion. The Old Testament is scarcely, if at all, quoted: as if the Philippian Christians had been gathered for the most part directly from the heathen. At each period false teachers were seeking, apparently in vain, an entrance into the Philippian Church, first Judaizing Christians, seemingly putting out of sight the Resurrection and the Judgment which afterwards the Gnosticizing Christians openly denied (Phil. iii., and Polyc. vi., vii.). At both periods the same tendency to petty internal quarrels seems to prevail (Phil. i. 27, ii. 14, iv. 2, and Polyc. ii., iv., v., xii.). The student of ecclesiastical history will observe the faintly-marked organization of bishops, deacons, and female coadjutors to which St. Paul refers (Phil. i. 1, iv. 3), developed afterwards into broadly-distinguished priests, deacons, widows, and virgins (Polyc. iv., v., vi.). Though the Macedonian churches in general were poor, at least as compared with commercial Corinth (2 Cor. viii. 2), yet their gold mines probably exempted the Philippians from the common lot of their neighbors, and at first enabled them to be conspicuously liberal in alms-giving, and afterwards laid them open to strong warnings against the love of money (Phil. iv. 15; 2 Cor. viii. 3; and Polyc. iv., vi., xi.).

Now, though we cannot trace the immediate effect of St. Paul's epistle on the Philippians, yet no one can doubt that it contributed to form the character of their church, as it was in the time of Polycarp. It is evident from Polycarp's epistle that the church, by the grace of God and the guidance of the Apostle, had passed through those trials of which St. Paul warned it, and had not gone back from the high degree of Christian attainments which it reached under St. Paul's oral and written teaching (Polyc. i., iii., ix., xi.). If it had made no great advance in knowledge, still unsound teachers were kept at a distance from its members. Their sympathy with martyrs and confessors glowed with as warm a flame as ever, whether it was claimed by Ignatius or by Paul. And they maintained their ground with meek firmness among the

---

[a] The denial of an actual Resurrection was one of the earliest errors in the Christian Church. (See 1 Cor. xv. 12; 2 Tim. ii. 18; Polycarp, vii.; Irenæus,

ii. 31; and the other passages quoted by Dean Ellicott on 2 Tim. ii. 18.)

heathen, and still held forth the light of an exemplary, though not a perfect Christian life.ᵃ

7. *The Church at Rome.* — The state of the church at Rome should be considered before entering on the study of the Epistle to the Philippians. Something is to be learned of its condition about A. D. 58 from the Epistle to the Romans, about A. D. 61 from Acts xxviii. Possibly the Gospel was planted there by some who themselves received the seed on the day of Pentecost (Acts ii. 10). The converts were drawn chiefly from Gentile proselytes to Judaism, partly also from Jews who were such by birth, with possibly a few converts direct from heathenism. In A. D. 58, this church was already eminent for its faith and obedience: it was exposed to the machinations of schismatical teachers; and it included two conflicting parties, the one insisting more or less on observing the Jewish law in addition to faith in Christ as necessary to salvation, the other repudiating outward observances even to the extent of depriving their weak brethren of such as to them might be really edifying. We cannot gather from the Acts whether the whole church of Rome had then accepted the teaching of St. Paul as conveyed in his epistle to them. But it is certain that when he had been two years in Rome, his oral teaching was partly rejected by a party which perhaps may have been connected with the former of those above mentioned. St. Paul's presence in Rome, the freedom of speech allowed to him, and the personal freedom of his fellow-laborers were the means of infusing fresh missionary activity into the church (Phil. i. 12-14). It was in the work of Christ that Epaphroditus was worn out (ii. 30). Messages and letters passed between the Apostle and distant churches; and doubtless churches near to Rome, and both members of the church and inquirers into the new faith at Rome addressed themselves to the Apostle, and to those who were known to be in constant personal communication with him. And thus in his bondage he was a cause of the advancement of the Gospel. From his prison, as from a centre, light streamed into Cæsar's household and far beyond (iv. 22, i. 12-19).

8. *Characteristic Features of the Epistle.* — Strangely full of joy and thanksgiving amidst adversity, like the Apostle's midnight hymn from the depth of his Philippian dungeon, this epistle went forth from his prison at Rome. In most other epistles he writes with a sustained effort to instruct, or with sorrow, or with indignation; he is striving to supply imperfect, or to correct erroneous teaching, or to put down scandalous impurity, or to heal schism in the church which he addresses. But in this epistle, though he knew the Philippians intimately, and was not blind to the faults and tendencies to fault of some of them, yet he mentions no evil so characteristic of the whole church as to call for general censure on his part, or amendment on theirs. Of all his epistles to churches, none has so little of an official character as this. He withholds his title of "Apostle" in the Inscrip-

tion. We lose sight of his high authority, and of the subordinate position of the worshippers by the river side; and we are admitted to see the free action of a heart glowing with inspired Christian love, and to hear the utterance of the highest friendship addressed to equal friends conscious of a connection which is not earthly and temporal, but in Christ, for eternity. Who that bears in mind the condition of St. Paul in his Roman prison, can read unmoved of his continual prayers for his distant friends, his constant sense of their fellowship with him, his joyful remembrance of their past Christian course, his confidence in their future, his tender yearning after them all in Christ, his eagerness to communicate to them his own circumstances and feelings, his carefulness to prepare them to repel any evil from within or from without which might dim the brightness of their spiritual graces? Love, at once tender and watchful, that love which "is of God," is the key-note of this epistle: and in this epistle only we hear no undertone of any different feeling. Just enough, and no more, is shown of his own harassing trials to let us see how deep in his heart was the spring of that feeling, and how he was refreshed by its sweet and soothing flow.

9. *Text, Translation, and Commentaries.* — The Epistle to the Philippians is found in all the principal uncial manuscripts, namely in A, B, C, D, E, F, G, J, K. In C, however, the verses preceding i. 22, and those following iii. 5, are wanting.

Our A. V. of the epistle, published in 1611, was the work of that company of King James' translators who sat at Westminster, consisting of seven persons, of whom Dr. Barlow, afterwards Bishop of Rochester, was one. It is, however, substantially the same as the translation made by some unknown person for Archbishop Parker, published in the Bishops' Bible, 1568. See Bagster's *Hexapla*, preface. A revised edition of the A. V. by Four Clergymen, is published (1861) by Parker and Bourn.

A complete list of works connected with this epistle may be found in the Commentary of Rheinwald. Of Patristic commentaries, those of Chrysostom (translated in the Oxford *Library of the Fathers*, 1843), Theodoret, and Theophylact, are still extant; perhaps also that of Theodore of Mopsuestia in an old Latin translation (see *Journ. of Class. and Sac. Phil.* iv. 302). Among later works may be mentioned those of Calvin, 1539; Estius, 1614; Daillé, 1659 (translated by Sherman, 1843); Ridley, 1548; Airay's *Sermons*, 1618; I. Ferguson, 1656; the annotated English New Testaments of Hammond, Fell, Whitby, and Macknight; the Commentaries of Peirce, 1733; Storr, 1783 (translated in the *Edinburg Biblical Cabinet*); Am Ende, 1798; Rheinwald, 1827; T. Passavant, 1834; St. Matthies, 1835; Van Hengel, 1838, Hölemann, 1839; Rilliet, 1841; De Wette, 1847; Meyer, 1847 [3d ed. 1865]; Neander, 1849 (translated into English, 1851 [by Mrs. H. C. Conant, published in N. Y.]); Wiesinger, 1850 (translated

---

ᵃ It is not easy to suppose that Polycarp was without a copy of St. Paul's epistle. Yet it is singular that though he mentions it twice, it is almost the only epistle of St. Paul which he does not quote. This fact may at least be regarded as additional evidence of the genuineness of Polycarp's epistle. No forger would have been guilty of such an omission. Its authenticity was first questioned by the Magdeburg Centuriators,

and by Daillé, whom Pearson answered (*Vindiciæ Ignat.* i. 5); also by Semler; and more recently by Zeller, Schliemann, Bunsen, and others: of whose criticism Ewald says, that it is the greatest injustice to Polycarp that men in the present age should deny that this epistle proceeded from him (*Gesch. Isr.* vii. 277, ed. 1859). [Bunsen regards the epistle as in the main genuine. — A.]

into English, 1850); Kähler, 1855; Professor Eadie [1859]; Dean Ellicott, 1861, and those included in the recent editions of the Greek N. T. by Dean Alford and Canon Wordsworth.　　　　W. T. B.

* *Additional Literature.* — In German: George Fr. Jatho, *Pauli Brief an die Philipper* (1857). Bernhard Weiss, *Der Philipper-Brief ausgelegt u. die Gesch. seiner Auslegung,* etc. (Berl. 1859); one of its objects is to illustrate the relations of the epistle to dogmatic theology. D. Schenkel, *Die Briefe an die Epheser, Philipper u. Kolosser* (1862). Karl Braune, *Die Briefe an die Epheser, Kolosser, Philipper* in pt. ix. of Lange's *Bibelwerk des N. T.* (1867), transl. with additions by H. B. Hackett and J. B. G. Pidge for Dr. Schaff's Commentary (N. Y. 1869). Gottfried Menken, *Predigten* xxii. - xxix. in his *Schriften,* v. 408–471 (Bremen, 1858). In English: Webster and Wilkinson, *The Greek Testament with Notes,* etc., ii. 506–528 (Lond. 1861). J. Trapp, *Commentary upon the Epistle of St. Paul to the Philippians,* in his Commentary on the N. T. (Webster's ed. Lond. 1865). Robert Hall, *Practical Exposition of the Epistle to the Philippians* (twelve discourses delivered at Cambridge, 1801 and 1802); they are good specimens of pulpit exposition by one of the great masters of sacred eloquence. F. D. Maurice, *Epistle to the Philippians,* pp. 549–558, in his *Unity of the N. T.* (1854). J. B. Lightfoot, *St. Paul's Epistle to the Philippians* (Lond. 1868); it contains a revised text, with Introduction, Notes, and Dissertations. On the important passage ii. 6–9, may be mentioned Tholuck's *Disputatio Christologica* (1847); and the remarks of Prof. Stuart, *Miscellanies,* pp. 112–115 (Andover, 1846). Dr. Howson has drawn out some of the finest illustrations of his theme (*Lectures on the Character of St. Paul,* Lond. 2d ed. 1864) from this epistle. He fully justifies Neander's remark that we look deeper into the Apostle's heart, have his distinctively personal traits more fully disclosed to us here, than in any one of his other writings.　　　　H.

PHILISTIA (פְּלֶשֶׁת, *Peléshéth* [perh. *wandering, migration*]: ἀλλόφυλοι: *alienigenae*). The word thus translated (in Ps. lx. 8; lxxxvii. 4; cviii. 9) is in the original identical with that elsewhere rendered PALESTINE. [See that article, p. 2284.] "Palestine" originally meant nothing but the district inhabited by the "Philistines," who are called by Josephus Παλαιστῖνοι, "Palestines." In fact the two words are the same, and the difference in their present form is but the result of gradual corruption. The form Philistia does not occur anywhere in LXX. or Vulgate. The nearest approach to it is Luther's *Philistäa.*　　　　G.

* **PHILISTIM** (פְּלִשְׁתִּים), only in Gen. x. 14, the Hebrew plural instead of Philistines as elsewhere. The A. V. retains this Hebrew form

also of the other names, in the same verse, and incorrectly omits the article which belongs to them all in the original.　　　　H.

PHILISTINES (פְּלִשְׁתִּי [perh. *wanderer, emigrant*]: Φυλιστιείμ, ἀλλόφυλοι: *Philistiim*). The origin of the Philistines is nowhere expressly stated in the Bible; but as the prophets describe them as "the Philistines from Caphtor" (Am. ix. 7), and "the remnant of the maritime district of Caphtor" (Jer. xlvii. 4), it is *primâ facie* probable that they were the "Caphtorims which came out of Caphtor" who expelled the Avim from their territory and occupied it in their place (Deut. ii. 23), and that these again were the Caphtorim mentioned in the Mosaic genealogical table among the descendants of Mizraim (Gen. x. 14). But in establishing this conclusion certain difficulties present themselves. In the first place, it is observable that in Gen. x. 14 the Philistines are connected with the Casluhim rather than the Caphtorim. It has generally been assumed that the text has suffered a transposition, and that the parenthetical clause " out of whom came Philistim " ought to follow the words " and Caphtorim." This explanation is, however, inadmissible: for (1) there is no external evidence whatever of any variation in the text, either here or in the parallel passage in 1 Chr. i. 12; and (2) if the transposition were effected, the desired sense would not be gained; for the words rendered in the A. V. " out of whom " a really mean " whence," and denote a local movement rather than a genealogical descent, so that, as applied to the Caphtorim, they would merely indicate a sojourn of the Philistines in their land, and not the identity of the two races. The clause seems to have an appropriate meaning in its present position: it looks like an interpolation into the original document with the view of explaining when and where the name Philistine was first applied to the people whose proper appellation was Caphtorim. It is an etymological as well as an historical memorandum; for it is based on the meaning of the name Philistine,[b] namely, "emigrant," and is designed to account for the application of that name. But a second and more serious difficulty arises out of the language of the Philistines; for while the Caphtorim were Hamitic, the Philistine language is held to have been Semitic.[c] It has hence been inferred that the Philistines were in reality a Semitic race, and that they derived the title of Caphtorim simply from a residence in Caphtor (Ewald, i. 331; Movers, *Phœniz.* iii. 258), and it has been noticed in confirmation of this, that their land is termed Canaan (Zeph. ii. 5). But this is inconsistent with the express assertion of the Bible that they were Caphtorim (Deut. ii. 23), and not simply that they came from Caphtor; and the term Canaan is applied to their country, not ethnologically but etymologically, to describe the trading habits of the

---

[a] אֲשֶׁר מִשָּׁם.

[b] The name is derived from the root פָּלַשׁ and the Æthiopic *falasa,* " to migrate ; " a term which is said to be still current in Abyssinia (Knobel, *Völkert.* p. 281). In Egyptian monuments it appears under the form of *Poulost* (Brugsch, *Hist. d'Égypte,* p. 187). The rendering of the name in the LXX., Ἀλλόφυλοι, "strangers," is probably in reference to the etymological meaning of the name, though it may otherwise be regarded as having originated with the Israelites,

to whom the Philistines were ἀλλόφυλοι, as opposed to ὁμόφυλοι (Stark's *Gaza,* p. 67 ff.). Other derivations of the name Philistine have been proposed, as that it originated in a transposition of the word *shephêlâh* (שְׁפֵלָה), applied to the Philistine plain ; or, again, that it is connected with Pelasgi, as Hitzig supposes.

[c] Hitzig, in his *Urgeschichte d. Phil.,* however, maintains that the language is Indo-European, with a view to prove the Philistines to be Pelasgi. He is, we believe, singular in his view.

Philistines. The difficulty arising out of the question of language may be met by assuming either that the Caphtorim adopted the language of the conquered Avim (a not unusual circumstance where the conquered form the bulk of the population), or that they diverged from the Hamitic stock at a period when the distinctive features of Hamitism and Semitism were yet in embryo. A third objection to their Egyptian origin is raised from the application of the term "uncircumcised" to them (1 Sam. xvii. 26; 2 Sam. i. 20), whereas the Egyptians were circumcised (Herod. ii. 36). But this objection is answered by Jer. ix. 25, 26, where the same term is in some sense applied to the Egyptians, however it may be reconciled with the statement of Herodotus.

The next question that arises relates to the early movements of the Philistines. It has been very generally assumed of late years that Caphtor represents Crete, and that the Philistines migrated from that island, either directly or through Egypt, into Palestine. This hypothesis presupposes the Semitic origin of the Philistines; for we believe that there are no traces of Hamitic settlements in Crete, and consequently the Biblical statement that Caphtorim was descended from Mizraim forms an *a priori* objection to the view. Moreover, the name Caphtor can only be identified with the Egyptian Coptos. [CAPHTOR.] But the Cretan origin of the Philistines has been defended, not so much from the name Caphtor,[a] as from that of the Cherethites. This name in its Hebrew form[b] bears a close resemblance to Crete, and is rendered Cretans in the LXX. A further link between the two terms has been apparently discovered in the term *câri*,[c] which is applied to the royal guard (2 K. xi. 4, 19), and which sounds like Carians. The latter of these arguments assumes that the Cherethites of David's guard were identical with the Cherethites of the Philistine plain, which appears in the highest degree improbable.[d] With regard to the former argument, the mere coincidence of the names cannot pass for much without some corroborative testimony. The Bible furnishes none, for the name occurs but thrice (1 Sam. xxx. 14; Ez. xxv. 16; Zeph. ii. 5), and apparently applies to the occupants of the southern district; the testimony of the LXX. is invalidated by the fact that it is based upon the mere sound of the word (see Zeph. ii. 6,

where *cerôth* is also rendered Crete): and lastly, we have to account for the introduction of the classical name of the island side by side with the Hebrew term Caphtor. A certain amount of testimony is indeed adduced in favor of a connection between Crete and Philistia; but, with the exception of the vague rumor, recorded but not adopted by Tacitus[e] (*Hist.* v. 3), the evidence is confined to the town of Gaza, and even in this case is not wholly satisfactory.[f] The town, according to Stephanus Byzantinus (*s. v.* Γάζα), was termed Minoa, as having been founded by Minos, and this tradition may be traced back to, and was perhaps founded on an inscription on the coins of that city, containing the letters MEINΩ; but these coins are of no higher date than the first century B. C., and belong to a period when Gaza had attained a decided Greek character (Joseph. *B. J.* ii. 6, § 3). Again, the worship of the god Marna, and its identity with the Cretan Jove, are frequently mentioned by early writers (Movers, *Phœniz.* i. 662); but the name is Phœnician, being the *maran*, "lord" of 1 Cor. xvi. 22, and it seems more probable that Gaza and Crete derived the worship from a common source, Phœnicia. Without therefore asserting that migrations may not have taken place from Crete to Philistia, we hold that the evidence adduced to prove that they did is insufficient.

The last point to be decided in connection with the early history of the Philistines is, the time when they settled in the land of Canaan. If we were to restrict ourselves to the statements of the Bible, we should conclude that this took place before the time of Abraham: for they are noticed in his day as a pastoral tribe in the neighborhood of Gerar (Gen. xxi. 32, 34, xxvi. 1, 8): and this position accords well with the statement in Deut. ii. 23, that the Avim dwelt in Hazerim, *i. e.* in nomad encampments; for Gerar lay in the south country, which was just adapted to such a life. At the time of the Exodus they were still in the same neighborhood, but grown sufficiently powerful to inspire the Israelites with fear (Ex. xiii. 17, xv. 14). When the Israelites arrived, they were in full possession of the Shefelah from the "river of Egypt" (*el-Arish*) in the south, to Ekron in the north (Josh. xv. 4, 47), and had formed a confederacy of five powerful cities[g] — Gaza, Ashdod, Ashkelon, Gath, and Ekron (Josh. xiii. 3). The interval that

---

[a] The only ground furnished by the Bible for this view is the application of the term rendered "island" to Caphtor in Jer. xlvii. 4. But the term also means *maritime district;* and "the maritime district of Caphtor" is but another term for Philistia itself.

[b] כְּרֵתִים.   [c] כָּרִי.

[d] It has been held by Ewald (i. 330) and others, that the Cherethites and Pelethites (2 Sam. xx. 23) were Cherethites and Philistines. The objections to this view are: (1) that it is highly improbable that David would select his officers from the hereditary foes of his country, particularly so immediately after he had enforced their submission; (2) that there seems no reason why an undue prominence should have been given to the Cherethites by placing that name first, and altering Philistines into Pelethites, so as to produce a paronomasia; (3) that the names subsequently applied to the same body (2 K. xi. 19) are appellatives; and (4) that the terms admit of a probable explanation from Hebrew roots.

[e] Among other accounts of the origin of the Jews, he gives this: "Judæos, Creta insula profugos, novissima Libyæ insedisse " and, as part of the same tra-

dition, adds that the name Judæus was derived from Ida — a circumstance which suggests a foundation for the story. The statement seems to have no more real weight than the reported connection between Hierosolyma and the Solymi of Lycia. Yet it is accepted as evidence that the Philistines, whom Tacitus is supposed to describe as Jews, came from Crete.

[f] The resemblance between the names Aptera and Caphtor (Keil, *Einleit.* ii. 236), Phalasarna and Philistine (Ewald, i. 330), is too slight to be of any weight. Added to which, those places lie in the part of Crete most remote from Palestine.

[g] At what period these cities were originally founded, we know not; but there are good grounds for believing that they were of Canaanitish origin, and had previously been occupied by the Avim. The name Gath is certainly Canaanitish: so most probably are Gaza, Ashdod, and Ekron. Askelon is doubtful; and the terminations both of this and Ekron may be Philistine. Gaza is mentioned as early as in Gen. x. 19 as a city of the Canaanites; and this as well as Ashdod and Ekron were in Joshua's time the asylum of the Canaanitish Anakim (Josh. xi. 22).

elapsed between Abraham and the Exodus seems sufficient to allow for the alteration that took place in the position of the Philistines, and their transformation from a pastoral tribe to a settled and powerful nation. But such a view has not met with acceptance among modern critics, partly because it leaves the migrations of the Philistines wholly unconnected with any known historical event, and partly because it does not serve to explain the great increase of their power in the time of the judges. To meet these two requirements a double migration on the part of the Philistines, or of the two branches of that nation, has been suggested. Knobel, for instance, regards the Philistines proper as a branch of the same stock as that to which the Hyksos belonged, and he discovers the name Philistine in the opprobrious name Philition, or Philitis, bestowed on the shepherd kings (Herod. ii. 128): their first entrance into Canaan from the Casluhim would thus be subsequent to the patriarchal age, and coincident with the expulsion of the Hyksos. The Cherethites he identifies with the Caphtorim who displaced the Avim; and these he regards as Cretans who did not enter Canaan before the period of the judges. The former part of his theory is inconsistent with the notices of the Philistines in the book of Genesis; these, therefore, he regards as additions of a later date[a] (Völkert. p. 218 ff.). The view adopted by Movers is, that the Philistines were carried westward from Palestine into Lower Egypt by the stream of the Hyksos movement at a period subsequent to Abraham; from Egypt they passed to Crete, and returned to Palestine in the early period of the judges (Phœniz. iii. 258). This is inconsistent with the notices in Joshua.[b] Ewald, in the second edition of his Geschichte, propounds the hypothesis of a double immigration from Crete, the first of which took place in the ante-patriarchal period, as a consequence either of the Canaanitish settlement or of the Hyksos movement, the second in the time of the judges (Gesch. i. 329-331). We cannot regard the above views in any other light than as speculations, built up on very slight data, and unsatisfactory, inasmuch as they fail to reconcile the statements of Scripture. For they all imply (1) that the notice of the Caphtorim in Gen. x. 14 applies to an entirely distinct tribe from the Philistines, as Ewald (i. 331, note) himself allows; (2) that either the notices in Gen. xx., xxvi., or those in Josh. xv. 45-47. or perchance both, are interpolations; and (3) that the notice in Deut. ii. 23, which certainly bears marks of high antiquity, belongs to a late date, and refers solely to the Cherethites. But, beyond these inconsistencies, there are two points which appear to militate against the theory of the second immigration in the time of the judges; (1) that the national title of the nation always remained Philistine, whereas, according to these theories, it was the Cretan or Cherethite element which led to the

great development of power in the time of the judges; and (2) that it remains to be shown why a seafaring race like the Cretans, coming direct from Caphtor in their ships (as Knobel, p. 234, understands "Caphtorim from Caphtor" to imply) would seek to occupy the quarters of a nomad race living in encampments, in the wilderness region of the south.[c] We hesitate, therefore, to indorse any of the proffered explanations, and, while we allow that the Biblical statements are remarkable for their fragmentary and parenthetical nature, we are not prepared to fill up the gaps. If those statements cannot be received as they stand, it is questionable whether any amount of criticism will supply the connecting links. One point can, we think, be satisfactorily shown, namely, that the hypothesis of a second immigration is not needed in order to account for the growth of the Philistine power. Their geographical position and their relations to neighboring nations will account for it. Between the times of Abraham and Joshua, the Philistines had changed their quarters, and had advanced northwards into the Shefelah or plain of Philistia. This plain has been in all ages remarkable for the extreme richness of its soil; its fields of standing corn, its vineyards and oliveyards, are incidentally mentioned in Scripture (Judg. xv. 5); and in time of famine the land of the Philistines was the hope of Palestine (2 K. viii. 2). We should, however, fail to form a just idea of its capacities from the scanty notices in the Bible. The crops which it yielded were alone sufficient to insure national wealth. It was also adapted to the growth of military power; for while the plain itself permitted the use of war chariots, which were the chief arm of offense, the occasional elevations which rise out of it offered secure sites for towns and strongholds. It was, moreover, a commercial country; from its position it must have been at all times the great thoroughfare between Phœnicia and Syria in the north, and Egypt and Arabia in the south. Ashdod and Gaza were the keys of Egypt, and commanded the transit trade, and the stores of frankincense and myrrh which Alexander captured in the latter place prove it to have been a depôt of Arabian produce (Plut. Alex. cap. 25). We have evidence in the Bible that the Philistines traded in slaves with Edom and southern Arabia (Am. i. 6; Joel iii. 3, 5), and their commercial character is indicated by the application of the name Canaan to their land (Zeph. ii. 5). They probably possessed a navy; for they had ports attached to Gaza and Ashkelon; the LXX. speaks of their ships in its version of Is. xi 14; and they are represented as attacking the Egyptians out of ships. The Philistines had at an early period attained proficiency in the arts of peace; they were skillful as smiths (1 Sam. xiii. 20), as armorers (1 Sam. xvii. 5, 6), and as builders, if we may judge from the prolonged sieges which several of their towns sustained. Their images and the golden mice and emerods (1 Sam. vi. 11) imply an acquaintance with the founder's and goldsmith's arts. Their wealth was abundant (Judg. xvi. 5, 18), and they appear in all respects to have been a prosperous people.

Possessed of such elements of power, the Philistines had attained in the time of the judges an important position among eastern nations. Their history is, indeed, almost a blank; yet the few particulars preserved to us are suggestive. About B. C. 1209 we find them engaged in successful war with the Sidonians, the effect of which was so serious to the latter power that it involved the transference of the capital of Phœnicia to a more secure position on the island of Tyre (Justin, xviii. 3). About the same period, but whether before or after is uncertain, they were engaged in a naval war with Rameses III. of Egypt, in conjunction with other Mediterranean nations: in these wars they were unsuccessful (Brugsch, *Hist. d'Égypte*, pp. 185, 187), but the notice of them proves their importance, and we cannot therefore be surprised that they were able to extend their authority over the Israelites, devoid as these were of internal union, and harassed by external foes. With regard to their tactics and the objects that they had in view in their attacks on the Israelites, we may form a fair idea from the scattered notices in the books of Judges and Samuel. The warfare was of a guerilla character, and consisted of a series of *raids* into the enemy's country. Sometimes these extended only just over the border, with the view of plundering the threshing-floors of the agricultural produce (1 Sam. xxiii. 1); but more generally they penetrated into the heart of the country and seized a commanding position on the edge of the Jordan Valley, whence they could secure themselves against a combination of the trans- and cis-Jordanite divisions of the Israelites, or prevent a return of the fugitives who had hurried across the river on the alarm of their approach. Thus at one time we find them crossing the central district of Benjamin and posting themselves at Michmash (1 Sam. xiii. 16), at another time following the coast road to the plain of Esdraelon and reaching the edge of the Jordan Valley by Jezreel (1 Sam. xxix. 11). From such posts as their head-quarters, they sent out detached bands to plunder the surrounding country (1 Sam. xiii. 17), and, having obtained all they could, they erected a column *a* as a token of their supremacy (1 Sam. x. 5, xiii. 3), and retreated to their own country. This system of incursions

kept the Israelites in a state of perpetual disquietude: all commerce was suspended, from the insecurity of the roads (Judg. v. 6); and at the approach of the foe the people either betook themselves to the natural hiding-places of the country, or fled across the Jordan (1 Sam. xiii. 6, 7). By degrees the ascendency became complete, and a virtual disarmament of the population was effected by the suppression of the smiths (1 Sam. xiii. 19). The profits of the Philistines were not confined to the goods and chattels they carried off with them. They seized the persons of the Israelites and sold them for slaves; the earliest notice of this occurs in 1 Sam. xiv. 21, where, according to the probably correct reading *b* followed by the LXX., we find that there were numerous slaves in the camp at Michmash: at a later period the prophets inveigh against them for their traffic in human flesh (Joel iii. 6; Am. i. 6): at a still later period we hear that "the merchants of the country" followed the army of Gorgias into Judæa for the purpose of buying the children of Israel for slaves (1 Macc. iii. 41), and that these merchants were Philistines is a fair inference from the subsequent notice that Nicanor sold the captive Jews to the "cities upon the sea-coast" (2 Macc. viii. 11). There can be little doubt, too, that tribute was exacted from the Israelites, but the notices of it are confined to passages of questionable authority, such as the rendering of 1 Sam. xiii. 21 in the LXX., which represents the Philistines as making a charge of three shekels a tool for sharpening them; and again the expression "Methegammah" in 2 Sam. viii. 1, which is rendered in the Vulg. *frenum tributi*, and by Symmachus τὴν ἐξουσίαν τοῦ φόρου. *c* In each of the passages quoted, the versions presuppose a text which yields a better sense than the existing one.

And now to recur to the Biblical narrative: The territory of the Philistines, having been once occupied by the Canaanites, formed a portion of the promised land, and was assigned to the tribe of Judah (Josh. xv. 2, 12, 45-47). No portion, however, of it was conquered in the life-time of Joshua (Josh. xiii. 2), and even after his death no permanent conquest was effected (Judg. iii. 3), though, on the authority of a somewhat doubtful passage, *d* we are informed that the three cities of Gaza, Ashkelon, and Ekron were taken (Judg. i. 18). The Philistines, at all events, soon recovered these, and commenced an aggressive policy against the Israelites, by which they gained a complete ascendency over them. We are unable to say at

---

a The Hebrew term *netzib*, which implies this practice, is rendered "garrison" in the A. V., which neither agrees with the context nor gives a true idea of the Philistine tactics. Stark, however, dissents from this view, and explains the term of military officers (*Gaza*, p. 164).

b עֲבָדִים, and not עִבְרִים.

c The true text may have been הַמֵּצָדָה, instead of הָאַמָּה.

d The apparent discrepancy between Judg. i. 18, iii. 3, has led to suspicions as to the text of the former, which are strengthened by the rendering in the LXX., al οὐκ ἐκληρονόμησεν, presupposing in the Hebrew the reading וְלֹא לָכַד, instead of וַיִּלְכֹּד. The testimony of the LXX. is weakened by the circumstances (1) that it interpolates a notice of Ashdod and its suburbs (Ἀσσεδώθ, a peculiar term in lieu of the

ὅρια applied to the three other towns); and (2) that the term ἐκληρονόμησεν is given as the equivalent for לָכַד, which occurs in no other instance. Of the two, therefore, the Greek text is more open to suspicion. Stark (*Gaza*, p. 129) regards the passage as an interpolation.

* The alleged discrepancy (see above) does not exist if וַיִּלְכֹּד means that they took the cities by storm, but did not retain them or drive out the inhabitants (Judg. iii. 3). See Cassel's *Bücher der Richter u. Ruth*, p. 12. The same verb occurs with regard to the capture of Jerusalem (Judg. i. 8), though we read expressly (2 Sam. v. 6 ff.) that the Hebrews did not entirely drive out the inhabitants till long after that time. [JEBUS, Amer ed.] With the idea of permanent possession, the strict term would have been הוֹרִישׁ (see Bachmann, *Buch der Richter*, p. 128).   H.

what intervals their incursions took place, as nothing is recorded of them in the early period of the judges. But they must have been frequent, inasmuch as the national spirit of the Israelites was so entirely broken that they even reprobated any attempt at deliverance (Judg. xv. 12). Individual heroes were raised up from time to time whose achievements might well kindle patriotism, such as Shamgar the son of Anath (Judg. iii. 31), and still more Samson (Judg. xiii. - xvi.): but neither of these men succeeded in permanently throwing off the yoke.[a] Of the former only a single daring feat is recorded the effect of which appears, from Judg. v. 6, 7, to have been very short-lived. The true series of deliverances commenced with the latter, of whom it was predicted that "he shall begin to deliver" (Judg. xiii. 5), and were carried on by Samuel, Saul, and David. The history of Samson furnishes us with some idea of the relations which existed between the two nations. As a "borderer" of the tribe of Dan, he was thrown into frequent contact with the Philistines, whose supremacy was so established that no bar appears to have been placed to free intercourse with their country. His early life was spent on the verge of the *Shefelah* between Zorah and Eshtaol, but when his actions had aroused the active hostility of the Philistines he withdrew into the central district and found a secure post on the rock of Etam, to the S. W. of Bethlehem. Thither the Philistines followed him without opposition from the inhabitants. His achievements belong to his personal history: it is clear that they were the isolated acts of an individual, and altogether unconnected with any national movement; for the revenge of the Philistines was throughout directed against Samson personally. Under Eli there was an organized but unsuccessful resistance to the encroachments of the Philistines, who had penetrated into the central district and were met at Aphek (1 Sam. iv. 1). The production of the ark on this occasion demonstrates the greatness of the emergency, and its loss marked the lowest depth of Israel's degradation. The next action took place under Samuel's leadership, and the tide of success turned in Israel's favor: the Philistines had again penetrated into the mountainous country near Jerusalem: at Mizpeh they met the cowed host of the Israelites, who, encouraged by the signs of Divine favor, and availing themselves of the panic produced by a thunderstorm, inflicted on them a total defeat. For the first time, the Israelites erected their pillar or "*stele*" at Eben-ezer as the token of victory. The results were the recovery of the border towns and their territories "from Ekron even unto Gath," i. e. in the northern district. The success of Israel may be partly attributed to their peaceful relations at this time with the Amorites (1 Sam. vii. 9-14). The Israelites now attributed their past weakness to their want of unity, and they desired a king, with the special object

of leading them against the foe (1 Sam. viii. 20). It is a significant fact that Saul first felt inspiration in the presence of a pillar (A. V. "garrison") erected by the Philistines in commemoration of a victory (1 Sam. x. 5, 10). As soon as he was prepared to throw off the yoke, he occupied with his army a position at Michmash, commanding the defiles leading to the Jordan Valley, and his heroic general Jonathan gave the signal for a rising by overthrowing the pillar which the Philistines had placed there. The challenge was accepted; the Philistines invaded the central district with an immense force,[b] and, having dislodged Saul from Michmash, occupied it themselves, and sent forth predatory bands into the surrounding country. The Israelites shortly after took up a position on the other side of the ravine at Geba, and, availing themselves of the confusion consequent upon Jonathan's daring feat, inflicted a tremendous slaughter upon the enemy (1 Sam. xiii., xiv.). No attempt was made by the Philistines to regain their supremacy for about twenty-five years, and the scene of the next contest shows the altered strength of the two parties: it was no longer in the central country, but in a ravine leading down to the Philistine plain, the Valley of Elah, the position of which is about 14 miles S. W. of Jerusalem: on this occasion the prowess of young David secured success to Israel, and the foe was pursued to the gates of Gath and Ekron (1 Sam. xvii.). The power of the Philistines was, however, still intact on their own territory, as proved by the flight of David to the court of Achish (1 Sam. xxi. 10–15), and his subsequent abode at Ziklag (1 Sam. xxvii.), where he was secured from the attacks of Saul. The border warfare was continued; captures and reprisals, such as are described as occurring at Keilah (1 Sam. xxiii. 1–5) being probably frequent. The scene of the next conflict was far to the north, in the valley of Esdraelon, whither the Philistines may have made a plundering incursion similar to that of the Midianites in the days of Gideon. The battle on this occasion proved disastrous to the Israelites: Saul himself perished, and the Philistines penetrated across the Jordan, and occupied the forsaken cities (1 Sam. xxxi. 1–7). The dissensions which followed the death of Saul were naturally favorable to the Philistines: and no sooner were these brought to a close by the appointment of David to be king over the united tribes, than the Philistines attempted to counterbalance the advantage by an attack on the person of the king: they therefore penetrated into the Valley of Rephaim, S. W. of Jerusalem, and even pushed forward an advanced post as far as Bethlehem (1 Chr. xi. 16). David twice attacked them at the former spot, and on each occasion with signal success, in the first case capturing their images, in the second pursuing them "from Geba until thou come to Gazer"[c] (2 Sam. v. 17–25; 1 Chr. xiv. 8–16).

---

[a] A brief notice occurs in Judg. x. 7 of invasions by the Philistines and Ammonites, followed by particulars which apply exclusively to the latter people. It has been hence supposed that the brief reference to the Philistines is in anticipation of Samson's history. In Herzog's *Real-Encyk.* (s. v. "Philister") it is rather unnecessarily assumed that the text is imperfect, and that the words "that year" refer to the Philistines, and the "eighteen years" to the Ammonites.

* The difference may be simply that the particulars

are mentioned in one case, but omitted in the other. It is unnecessary to call in question the fact of "invasions" by both tribes.   H.

[b] The text states the force at 30,000 chariots and 6,000 horsemen (1 Sam. xiii. 5): these numbers are, however, quite out of proportion. The chariots were probably 1,000, the present reading being a mistake of a copyist who repeated the final ל of Israel, and thus converted the number into 30,000.

[c] There is some difficulty in reconciling the geo-

Henceforth the Israelites appear as the aggressors: about seven years after the defeat at Rephaim, David, who had now consolidated his power, attacked them on their own soil, and took Gath with its dependencies (1 Chr. xviii. 1), and thus (according to one interpretation of the obscure expression " Metheg-ammah " in 2 Sam. viii. 1) " he took the arm-bridle out of the hand of the Philistines " (Bertheau, Comm. on 1 Chr. in loc.), or (according to another) " he took the bridle of the metropolis out of the hand of the Philistines " (Gesen. Thes. p. 113)—meaning in either case that their ascendency was utterly broken. This indeed was the case: for the minor engagements in David's life-time probably all took place within the borders of Philistia: Gob, which is given as the scene of the second and third combats, being probably identical with Gath, where the fourth took place (2 Sam. xxi. 15–22; comp. LXX., some of the copies of which read Γέθ instead of Γόβ). The whole of Philistia was included in Solomon's empire, the extent of which is described as being "from the river unto the land of the Philistines, unto the border of Egypt " a (1 K. iv. 21; 2 Chr. ix. 26), and again "from Tiphsah even unto Gaza " (1 K. iv. 24; A. V. " Azzah ") [though the Hebrew form is the same]. The several towns probably remained under their former governors, as in the case of Gath (1 K. ii. 39), and the sovereignty of Solomon was acknowledged by the payment of tribute (1 K. iv. 21). There are indications, however, that his hold on the Philistine country was by no means established: for we find him securing the passes that led up from the plain to the central district by the fortification of Gezer and Beth-horon (1 K. ix. 17), while no mention is made either of Gaza or Ashdod, which fully commanded the coast-road. Indeed the expedition of Pharaoh against Gezer, which stood at the head of the Philistine plain, and which was quite independent of Solomon until the time of his marriage with Pharaoh's daughter, would lead to the inference that Egyptian influence was paramount in Philistia at this period (1 K. ix. 16). The division of the empire at Solomon's death was favorable to the Philistine cause: Rehoboam secured himself against them by fortifying Gath and other cities bordering on the plain (2 Chr. xi. 8): the Israelite monarchs were either not so prudent or not so powerful, for they allowed the Philistines to get hold of Gibbethon, commanding one of the defiles leading up from the plain of Sharon to Samaria, the recovery of which involved them in a protracted struggle in the reigns of Nadab and Zimri (1 K. xv. 27, xvi. 15). Judah meanwhile had lost the tribute; for it is recorded as an occurrence that marked Jehoshaphat's suc-

cess, that " some of the Philistines brought presents " (2 Chr. xvii. 11). But this subjection was of brief duration: in the reign of his son Jehoram they avenged themselves by invading Judah in conjunction with the Arabians, and sacking the royal palace (2 Chr. xxi. 16, 17). The increasing weakness of the Jewish monarchy under the attacks of Hazael led to the recovery of Gath, which had been captured by that monarch in his advance on Jerusalem from the western plain in the reign of Jehoash (2 K. xii. 17), and was probably occupied by the Philistines after his departure as an advanced post against Judah: at all events it was in their hands in the time of Uzziah, who dismantled (2 Chr. xxvi. 6) and probably destroyed it: for it is adduced by Amos as an example of Divine vengeance (Am. vi. 2), and then disappears from history. Uzziah at the same time dismantled Jabneh (Jamnia) in the northern part of the plain, and Ashdod, and further erected forts in different parts of the country to intimidate the inhabitants b (2 Chr. xxvi. 6). The prophecies of Joel and Amos prove that these measures were provoked by the aggressions of the Philistines, who appear to have formed leagues both with the Edomites and Phœnicians, and had reduced many of the Jews to slavery (Joel iii. 4–6; Am. i. 6–10). How far the means adopted by Uzziah were effectual we are not informed; but we have reason to suppose that the Philistines were kept in subjection until the time of Ahaz, when, relying upon the difficulties produced by the Syrian attacks, they attacked the border cities in the Shefelah, and " the south " of Judah (2 Chr. xxviii. 18). Isaiah's declarations (xiv. 29–32) throw light upon the events subsequent to this: from them we learn that the Assyrians, whom Ahaz summoned to his aid, proved themselves to be the " cockatrice that should come out of the serpent's (Judah's) root," by ravaging the Philistine plain. A few years later the Philistines, in conjunction with the Syrians and Assyrians (" the adversaries of Rezin "), and perhaps as the subject-allies of the latter, carried on a series of attacks on the kingdom of Israel (Is. ix. 11, 12). Hezekiah's reign inaugurated a new policy, in which the Philistines were deeply interested: that monarch formed an alliance with the Egyptians, as a counterpoise to the Assyrians, and the possession of Philistia became henceforth the turning-point of the struggle between the two great empires of the East. Hezekiah, in the early part of his reign, re-established his authority over the whole of it, "even unto Gaza " (2 K. xviii. 8). This movement was evidently connected with his rebellion against the king of Assyria, and was undertaken in conjunction with the Egyptians; for we find the latter

---

graphical statements in the narrative of this campaign. Instead of the " Geba " of Samuel, we have " Gibeon " in Chronicles. The latter lies N. W. of Jerusalem; and there is a Geba in the same neighborhood, lying more to the E. But the Valley of Rephaim is placed S. W. of Jerusalem, near to neither of these places. Thenius (on 2 Sam. v. 18) transplants the valley to the N. W. of Jerusalem; while Bertheau (on 1 Chr. xiv. 16) identifies Geba with the Gibeah of Josh. xv. 57, and the Jeba'h noticed by Robinson (ii. 6, 16) as lying W. of Bethlehem. Neither of these explanations can be accepted. We must assume that the direct retreat from the valley to the plain was cut off, and that the Philistines were compelled to flee northwards, and regained the plain by the pass of Beth-horon, which lay between Gibeon (as well as between Geba) and Gazer.

a The Hebrew text, as it at present stands, in 1 K.

iv. 21, will not bear the sense here put upon it; but a comparison with the parallel passage in 2 Chr. shows that the word עַד has dropped out before the " land of the P."

b The passage in Zech. ix. 5–7 refers, in the opinion of those who assign an earlier date to the concluding chapters of the book, to the successful campaign of Uzziah. Internal evidence is in favor of this view. The alliance with Tyre is described as " the expectation " of Ekron: Gaza was to lose her king, i. e. her independence: Ashkelon should be depopulated: a " bastard," i. e. one who was excluded from the congregation of Israel on the score of impure blood, should dwell in Ashdod, holding it as a dependency of Judah; and Ekron should become " as a Jebusite," subject to Judah.

people shortly after in possession of the five Philistine cities, to which alone are we able to refer the
prediction in Is. xix. 18, when coupled with the
fact that both Gaza and Ashkelon are termed
Egyptian cities in the annals of Sargon (Bunsen's
Egypt, iv. 603). The Assyrians under Tartan, the
general of Sargon, make an expedition against
Egypt, and took Ashdod, as the key of that country (Is. xx. 1, 4, 5). Under Sennacherib Philistia
was again the scene of important operations: in
his first campaign against Egypt Ashkelon was
taken and its dependencies were plundered; Ashdod, Ekron, and Gaza submitted, and received
as a reward a portion of Hezekiah's territory
(Rawlinson, i. 477): in his second campaign other
towns on the verge of the plain, such as Libnah
and Lachish, were also taken (2 K. xviii. 14, xix.
8). The Assyrian supremacy, though shaken by
the failure of this second expedition, was restored
by Esar-haddon, who claims to have conquered
Egypt (Rawlinson, i. 481); and it seems probable
that the Assyrians retained their hold on Ashdod
until its capture, after a long siege, by the Egyptian
monarch Psammetichus (Herod. ii. 157), the effect
of which was to reduce the population of that important place to a mere "remnant" (Jer. xxv. 20).
It was about this time, and probably while Psammetichus was engaged in the siege of Ashdod, that
Philistia was traversed by a vast Scythian horde
on their way to Egypt: they were, however, diverted from their purpose by the king, and retraced
their steps, plundering on their retreat the rich
temple of Venus at Ashkelon (Herod. i. 105). The
description of Zephaniah (ii. 4–7), who was contemporary with this event, may well apply to this terrible scourge, though more generally referred to a
Chaldæan invasion. The Egyptian ascendency was
not as yet reëstablished, for we find the next king,
Neco, compelled to besiege Gaza (the Cadytis of
Herodotus, ii. 159) on his return from the battle of
Megiddo. After the death of Neco, the contest was
renewed between the Egyptians and the Chaldæans
under Nebuchadnezzar, and the result was specially
disastrous to the Philistines: Gaza was again taken
by the former, and the population of the whole plain
was reduced to a mere "remnant" by the invading
armies (Jer. xlvii.). The "old hatred" that the
Philistines bore to the Jews was exhibited in acts
of hostility at the time of the Babylonish captivity
(Ez. xxv. 15–17): but on the return this was somewhat abated, for some of the Jews married Philistine women, to the great scandal of their rulers
(Neh. xiii. 23, 24). From this time the history of
Philistia is absorbed in the struggles of the neighboring kingdoms. In B. C. 332, Alexander the
Great traversed it on his way to Egypt, and captured Gaza, then held by the Persians under Betis,
after a two months' siege. In 312 the armies of
Demetrius Polioreetes and Ptolemy fought in the
neighborhood of Gaza. In 198 Antiochus the
Great, in his war against Ptolemy Epiphanes, invaded Philistia and took Gaza. In 166 the Phili-
tines joined the Syrian army under Gorgias in its
attack on Judæa (1 Macc. iii. 41). In 148 the
adherents of the rival kings Demetrius II. and Alexander Balas, under Apollonius and Jonathan respectively, contended in the Philistine plain: Jona-

than took Ashdod, triumphantly entered Ashkelon,
and received Ekron as his reward (1 Macc. x. 69–
89). A few years later Jonathan again descended
into the plain in the interests of Antiochus VI.,
and captured Gaza (1 Macc. xi. 60–62). No further notice of the country occurs until the capture
of Gaza in 97 by the Jewish king Alexander Jannæus in his contest with Lathyrus (Joseph. *Ant.*
xiii. 13, § 3; *B. J.* i. 4, § 2). In 63 Pompey annexed Philistia to the province of Syria (*Ant.* xiv.
4, § 4), with the exception of Gaza, which was assigned to Herod (xv. 7, § 3). together with Jamnia,
Ashdod, and Ashkelon, as appears from xvii. 11, § 5.
The three last fell to Salome after Herod's death,
but Gaza was reannexed to Syria (xvii. 11, §§ 4, 5).
The latest notices of the Philistines as a nation,
under their title of ἀλλόφυλοι, occur in 1 Macc.
iii.–v. The extension of the name from the district occupied by them to the whole country, under
the familiar form of PALESTINE, has already been
noticed under that head.

With regard to the institutions of the Philistines
our information is very scanty. The five chief
cities had, as early as the days of Joshua, constituted themselves into a confederacy, restricted, however, in all probability, to matters of offense and defense. Each was under the government of a prince
whose official title was *seren* [a] (Josh. xiii. 3; Judg.
iii. 3, &c.), and occasionally *sâr* [b] (1 Sam. xviii. 30,
xxix. 6). Gaza may be regarded as having exercised a hegemony over the others, for in the lists of
the towns it is mentioned the first (Josh. xiii. 3;
Am. i. 7, 8), except where there is an especial
ground for giving prominence to another, as in the
case of Ashdod (1 Sam. vi. 17). Ekron always
stands last, while Ashdod, Ashkelon, and Gath interchange places. Each town possessed its own
territory, as instanced in the case of Gath (1 Chr.
xviii. 1), Ashdod (1 Sam. v. 6), and others, and
each possessed its dependent towns or "daughters"
(Josh. xv. 45–47; 1 Chr. xviii. 1; 2 Sam. i. 20;
Ez. xvi. 27, 57), and its villages (Josh. *l. c.*). In
later times Gaza had a senate of five hundred (Joseph. *Ant.* xiii. 13, § 3). The Philistines appear to
have been deeply imbued with superstition: they
carried their idols with them on their campaigns
(2 Sam. v. 21), and proclaimed their victories in
their presence (1 Sam. xxxi. 9). They also carried
about their persons charms of some kind that had
been presented before the idols (2 Macc. xii. 40).
The gods whom they chiefly worshipped were Dagon, who possessed temples both at Gaza (Judg.
xvi. 23) and at Ashdod (1 Sam. v. 3–5; 1 Chr. x.
10; 1 Macc. x. 83); Ashtaroth, whose temple at
Ashkelon was far-famed (1 Sam. xxxi. 10; Herod.
i. 105); Baal-zebub, whose fane at Ekron was consulted by Ahaziah (2 K. i. 2–6); and Derceto, who
was honored at Ashkelon (Diod. Sic. ii. 4), though
unnoticed in the Bible. Priests and diviners (1
Sam. vi. 2) were attached to the various seats of
worship. (The special authorities for the history
of the Philistines are Stark's *Gaza*; Knobel's
Völkertafel; Movers' *Phönizier*; and Hitzig's
Urgeschichte.)   W. L. B.

PHILOL'OGUS (Φιλόλογος [*fond of talk,
talkative*, and also *learned*]: *Philologus*). A Christian at Rome to whom St. Paul sends his salutation

---

[a] סֶרֶן. Two derivations have been proposed for
this word, namely, שָׂר by Ewald (i. 332), סֶרֶן,
"axle," by Gesenius (*Thes.* p. 972) and Keil in Josh.

xiii. 3, the latter being supported by the analogy of
an Arabic expression.

[b] שַׂר.

(Rom. xvi. 15). Origen conjectures that he was the master of a Christian household which included the other persons named with him. Pseudo-Hippolytus (*De LXX. Apostolis*) makes him one of the 70 disciples, and bishop of Sinope. His name is found in the Columbarium " of the freedmen of Livia Augusta " at Rome; which shows that there was a Philologus connected with the imperial household at the time when it included many Julias.
W. T. B.

* **PHILOMETOR** (Φιλομήτωρ, *mother-loving: Philometor*), a surname of PTOLEMÆUS or Ptolemy VI., king of Egypt, 2 Macc. iv. 21.
A.

PHILOSOPHY. It is the object of the following article to give some account (I.) of that development of thought among the Jews which answered to the philosophy of the West; (II.) of the recognition of the preparatory (propædeutic) office of Greek philosophy in relation to Christianity: (III.) of the systematic progress of Greek philosophy as forming a complete whole; and (IV.) of the contact of Christianity with philosophy. The limits of the article necessarily exclude everything but broad statements. Many points of great interest must be passed over unnoticed; and in a fuller treatment there would be need of continual exceptions and explanations of detail, which would only create confusion in an outline. The history of ancient philosophy in its religious aspect has been strangely neglected. Nothing, as far as we are aware, has been written on the pre-Christian era answering to the clear and elegant essay of Matter on post-Christian philosophy (*Histoire de la Philosophie dans ses rapports avec la Religion depuis l'ère Chrétienne*, Paris, 1854). There are useful hints in Carové's *Vorhalle des Christenthums* (Jena, 1851), and Ackermann's *Das Christliche im Plato* (Hamb. 1835). The treatise of Denis, *Histoire des Théories et des Idées morales dans l'Antiquité* (Paris, 1856), is limited in range and hardly satisfactory. Döllinger's [*Heidenthum u. Judenthum*] *Vorhalle zur Gesch. d. Christenthums* (Regensbg. 1857 [Eng. trans., *The Gentile and the Jew*, etc. Lond. 1862]) is comprehensive, but covers too large a field. The brief survey in De Pressensé's *Hist. des trois premiers Siècles de l'Eglise Chrétienne* (Paris, 1858) [translated under the title *The Religions before Christ*, Edin. 1862] is much more vigorous, and on the whole just. But no one seems to have apprehended the real character and growth of Greek philosophy so well as Zeller (though with no special attention to its relations to religion) in his history (*Die Philosophie der Griechen*, 2te Aufl. [3 Theile in 5 Abth.] Tüb. 1856–68), which for subtlety and completeness is unrivaled. [See also the literature at the end of the article.]

I. THE PHILOSOPHIC DISCIPLINE OF THE JEWS.

Philosophy, if we limit the word strictly to describe the free pursuit of knowledge of which truth is the one complete end, is essentially of western growth. In the East the search after wisdom has always been connected with practice: it has remained there, what it was in Greece at first, a part of religion. The history of the Jews offers no exception to this remark: there is no Jewish philosophy properly so called. Yet on the other hand speculation and action meet in truth; and perhaps the most obvious lesson of the Old Testament lies in the gradual construction of a divine philosophy

by fact, and not by speculation. The method of Greece was to proceed from life to God; the method of Israel (so to speak) was to proceed from God to life. The axioms of one system are the conclusions of the other. The one led to the successive abandonment of the noblest domains of science which man had claimed originally as his own, till it left bare systems of morality; the other, in the fullness of time, prepared many to welcome the Christ — the Truth.

From what has been said, it follows that the philosophy of the Jews, using the word in a large sense, is to be sought for rather in the progress of the national life than in special books. These, indeed, furnish important illustrations of the growth of speculation, but the history is written more in acts than in thoughts. Step by step the idea of the family was raised into that of the people; and the kingdom furnished the basis of those wider promises which included all nations in one kingdom of heaven. The social, the political, the cosmical relations of man were traced out gradually in relation to God.

The philosophy of the Jews is thus essentially a moral philosophy, resting on a definite connection with God. The doctrines of Creation and Providence, of an Infinite Divine Person and of a responsible human will, which elsewhere form the ultimate limits of speculation, are here assumed at the outset. The difficulties which they involve are but rarely noticed. Even when they are canvassed most deeply, a moral answer drawn from the great duties of life is that in which the questioner finds repose. The earlier chapters of Genesis contain an introduction to the direct training of the people which follows. Premature and partial developments, kingdoms based on godless might, stand in contrast with the slow foundation of the Divine polity To distinguish rightly the moral principles which were successively called out in this latter work, would be to write a history of Israel; but the philosophical significance of the great crises through which the people passed, lies upon the surface. The call of Abraham set forth at once the central lesson of faith in the Unseen, on which all others were raised. The father of the nation was first isolated from all natural ties before he received the promise: his heir was the son of his extreme age: his inheritance was to him "as a strange land." The history of the patriarchs brought out into yet clearer light the sovereignty of God: the younger was preferred before the elder: suffering prepared the way for safety and triumph. God was seen to make a covenant with man, and his action was written in the records of a chosen family. A new era followed. A nation grew up in the presence of Egyptian culture. Persecution united elements which seem otherwise to have been on the point of being absorbed by foreign powers. God revealed Himself now to the people in the wider relations of Lawgiver and Judge. The solitary discipline of the desert familiarized them with his majesty and his mercy. The wisdom of Egypt was hallowed to new uses. The promised land was gained by the open working of a divine Sovereign. The outlines of national faith were written in defeat and victory; and the work of the theocracy closed. Human passion then claimed a dominant influence. The people required a king. A fixed Temple was substituted for the shifting Tabernacle. Times of disruption and disaster followed; and the voice of the prophets declared the spiritual meaning of the kingdom. In the midst of sorrow and defeat and desolation, the horizon of hope was extended. The kingdom which man had prematurely founded was seen to be the image of a nobler "kingdom of God." The nation learned its connection with "all the kindred of the earth." The Captivity confirmed the lesson, and after it the Dispersion. The moral effects of these, and the influence which Persian, Greek, and Roman, the inheritors of all the wisdom of the East and West, exercised upon the Jews, have been elsewhere noticed. [CYRUS; DISPERSION.] The divine discipline closed before the special human discipline began. The personal relations of God to the individual, the family, the nation, mankind, were established in ineffaceable history, and then other truths were brought into harmony with these in the long period of silence which separates the two Testaments. But the harmony was not always perfect. Two partial forms of religious philosophy arose. On the one side the predominance of the Persian element gave rise to the Kabbala: on the other the predominance of the Greek element issued in Alexandrine theosophy.

Before these one sided developments of the truth were made, the fundamental ideas of the Divine government found expression in words as well as in life. The Psalms, which, among the other infinite lessons which they convey, give a deep insight into the need of a personal apprehension of truth, everywhere declare the absolute sovereignty of God over the material and moral worlds. The classical scholar cannot fail to be struck with the frequency of natural imagery, and with the close connection which is assumed to exist between man and nature as parts of one vast Order. The control of all the elements by One All-wise Governor, standing out in clear contrast with the deification of isolated objects, is no less essentially characteristic of Hebrew as distinguished from Greek thought. In the world of action Providence stands over against fate, the universal kingdom against the individual state, the true and the right against the beautiful. Pure speculation may find little scope, but speculation guided by these great laws will never cease to affect most deeply the intellectual culture of men. (Compare especially Ps. viii., xix., xxix.; l., lxv., lxviii.; lxxvii., lxxviii., lxxxix.; xcv., xcvii., civ.: cvi., cxxxvi., cxlvii., etc. It will be seen that the same character is found in Psalms of every date.) For a late and very remarkable development of this philosophy of Nature see the article BOOK OF ENOCH [vol. i. p. 738 ff.]; Dillmann, Das B. Henoch, xiv. xv.

One man above all is distinguished among the Jews as "the wise man." The description which is given of his writings serves as a commentary on the national view of philosophy. "And Solomon's wisdom excelled the wisdom of all the children of the east country and all the wisdom of Egypt. . . . And he spake three thousand proverbs; and his songs were a thousand and five. And he spake of trees, from the cedar that is in Lebanon even unto the hyssop that springeth out of the wall: he spake also of beasts, and of fowl, and of creeping things, and of fishes" (1 K. iv. 30–33). The lesson of practical duty, the full utterance of "a large heart" (ibid. 29), the careful study of God's creatures: this is the sum of wisdom. Yet in fact the very practical aim of this philosophy leads to the revelation of the most sublime truth. Wisdom was gradually felt to be a Person, throned by God, and holding converse with men (Prov. viii.). She was

seen to stand in open enmity with "the strange woman," who sought to draw them aside by sensuous attractions; and thus a new step was made towards the central doctrine of Christianity — the Incarnation of the Word.

Two books of the Bible, Job and Ecclesiastes, of which the latter at any rate belongs to the period of the close of the kingdom, approach more nearly than any others to the type of philosophical discussions. But in both the problem is moral and not metaphysical. The one deals with the evils which afflict "the perfect and upright; " the other with the vanity of all the pursuits and pleasures of earth. In the one we are led for an answer to a vision of "the enemy" to whom a partial and temporary power over man is conceded (Job i. 6–12); in the other to that great future when "God shall bring every work to judgment" (Eccl xii. 14). The method of inquiry is in both cases abrupt and irregular. One clew after another is followed out, and at length abandoned: and the final solution is obtained, not by a consecutive process of reason, but by an authoritative utterance, which faith welcomes as the truth, towards which all partial efforts had tended. (Compare Maurice, Moral and Metaphysical Philosophy, first edition.)

The Captivity necessarily exercised a profound influence upon Jewish thought. [Comp. CYRUS, vol. i. p. 527.] The teaching of Persia seems to have been designed to supply important elements in the education of the chosen people. But it did yet more than this. The imagery of Ezekiel (chap. i.) gave an apparent sanction to a new form of mystical speculation. It is uncertain at what date this earliest Kabbala (i. e. Tradition) received a definite form; but there can be no doubt that the two great divisions of which it is composed, "the chariot" (Mercabah, Ex. i.) and "the Creation" (Bereshith, Gen. i.), found a wide development before the Christian era. The first dealt with the manifestation of God in Himself; the second with his manifestation in Nature; and as the doctrine was handed down orally, it received naturally, both from its extent and form, great additions from foreign sources. On the one side it was open to the Persian doctrine of emanation, on the other to the Christian doctrine of the Incarnation; and the tradition was deeply impressed by both before it was first committed to writing in the seventh or eighth century. At present the original sources for the teaching of the Kabbala are the Sepher Jetzirah, or Book of Creation, and the Sepher ka-Zohar, or Book of Splendor. The former of these dates in its present form from the eighth, and the latter from the thirteenth century (Zunz, Gottesd. Vortr. d. Juden, p. 165; Jellinek, Moses ben Schemtob de Leon, Leipsic, 1851). Both are based upon a system of Pantheism. In the Book of Creation the Cabbalistic ideas are given in their simplest form, and offer some points of comparison with the system of the Pythagoreans. The book begins with an enumeration of the thirty-two ways of wisdom seen in the constitution of the world; and the analysis of this number is supposed to contain the key to the mysteries of nature. The primary division is into $10 + 22$. The number 10 represents the ten Sephiroth (figures), which answer to the ideal world; 22, on the other hand, the number of the Hebrew alphabet, answers to the world of objects; the object being related to the idea as a word, formed of letters, to a number.

Twenty-two again is equal to $3 + 7 + 12$; and each of these numbers, which constantly recur in the O. T. Scriptures, is invested with a peculiar meaning. Generally the fundamental conceptions of the book may be thus represented. The ultimate Being is Divine Wisdom (*Chocmah*, Σοφία). The universe is originally a harmonious thought of Wisdom (Number, *Sephiroth*): and the thought is afterwards expressed in letters, which form, as words, the germ of things. Man, with his twofold nature, thus represents in some sense the whole universe. He is the Microcosm, in which the body clothes and veils the soul, as the phenomenal world veils the spirit of God. It is impossible to follow out here the details of this system, and its development in Zohar; but it is obvious how great an influence it must have exercised on the interpretation of Scripture. The calculation of the numerical worth of words (comp. Rev. xiii. 18; *Gematria*, Buxtorf, *Lex. Rabb.* p. 446), the resolution of words into initial letters of new words (*Notaricon*, Buxtorf, 1339). and the transposition or interchange of letters (*Temurah*), were used to obtain the inner meaning of the text; and these practices have continued to affect modern exegesis (Lutterbeck, *Neutest. Lehrbegriff*, i. 223–254; Reuss, *Kabbala*, in Herzog's *Encyklop.* ; Joel, *Die Relig.-Phil. d. Zohar*, 1849; Jellinek, as above; Westcott, *Introd. to Gospels*, pp. 131–134; Franck, *La Kabbale*, 1843; OLD TESTAMENT, B § 1).

The contact of the Jews with Persia thus gave rise to a traditional mysticism. Their contact with Greece was marked by the rise of distinct sects. In the third century B. C. the great doctor Antigonus of Socho bears a Greek name, and popular belief pointed to him as the teacher of Sadoc and Boethus, the supposed founders of Jewish rationalism. At any rate, we may date from this time the twofold division of Jewish speculation which corresponds to the chief tendencies of practical philosophy. The Sadducees appear as the supporters of human freedom in its widest scope; the Pharisees of a religious Stoicism. At a later time the cycle of doctrine was completed, when by a natural reaction the Essenes established a mystic Asceticism. The characteristics of these sects are noticed elsewhere. It is enough now to point out the position which they occupy in the history of Judaism (comp. *Introd. to Gospels*, pp. 60–66). At a later period the FOURTH BOOK OF MACCABEES (q. v.) is a very interesting example of Jewish moral (Stoic) teaching.

The conception of wisdom which appears in the Book of Proverbs was elaborated with greater detail afterwards [WISDOM OF SOLOMON], both in Palestine [ECCLESIASTICUS] and in Egypt; but the doctrine of *the Word* is of greater speculative interest. Both doctrines, indeed, sprang from the same cause, and indicate the desire to find some mediating power between God and the world, and to remove the direct appearance and action of God from a material sphere. The personification of Wisdom represents only a secondary power in relation to God; the Logos, in the double sense of Reason (λόγος ἐνδιάθετος) and Word (λόγος προφορικός), both in relation to God and in relation to the universe. The first use of the term Word (*Memra*), based upon the common formula of the prophets, is 'n the Targum of Onkelos (first cent. B. C.), in which "the Word of God" is commonly substituted for God in his immediate, personal relations with man (*Introd. to Gospels*, p. 137);

and it is probable that round this traditional rendering a fuller doctrine grew up. But there is a clear difference between the idea of the Word then prevalent in Palestine and that current at Alexandria. In Palestine the Word appears as the outward mediator between God and man, like the Angel of the Covenant; at Alexandria it appears as the spiritual connection which opens the way to revelation. The preface to St. John's Gospel includes the element of truth in both. In the Greek apocryphal books there is no mention of the Word (yet comp. Wisd. xviii. 15). For the Alexandrine teaching it is necessary to look alone to Philo (cir. B. C. 20 — A. D. 50); and the ambiguity in the meaning of the Greek term, which has been already noticed, produces the greatest confusion in his treatment of the subject. In Philo language domineers over thought. He has no one clear and consistent view of the Logos. At times he assigns to it divine attributes and personal action; and then again he affirms decidedly the absolute indivisibility of the divine nature. The tendency of his teaching is to lead to the conception of a twofold personality in the Godhead, though he shrinks from the recognition of such a doctrine (*De Monarch.* § 5; *De Somn.* § 37; *Quod. det. pot. ins.* § 24; *De Somn.* § 39, &c.). Above all, his idea of the Logos was wholly disconnected from all Messianic hopes, and was rather the philosophic substitute for them. (*Introd. to Gospels*, pp. 138–141; Dähne, *Jüd.-Alex. Relig.-Philos.* 1834; Gfrörer, *Philo*, etc. 1835; Dorner, *Die Lehre v. d. Person Christi*, i. 23 ff., Lücke, *Comm.* i. 207 [272, 3ᵃ Aufl.], who gives an account of the earlier literature.) [WORD, THE. Amer. ed.]

* On Philo's idea of the Logos see also Keferstein, *Philo's Lehre von dem göttl. Mittelwesen*, Leipz. 1846; Niedner, *De Subsistentia τῷ θείῳ λόγῳ apud Philonem Judaeum et Joannem Apost. tributa*, in his *Zeitschr f. d. hist. Theol.*, 1849, Heft 3; Norton's *Statement of Reasons*, etc., 3d ed. (Bost. 1856), pp. 307–349; Jowett, *St. Paul and Philo*, in his *Epistles of St. Paul*, etc. 2d ed., Lond. 1859, i. 448 ff.; Zeller, *Philos. der Griechen*, Bd. iii. Abth. 2.   A.

II. THE PATRISTIC RECOGNITION OF THE PROPÆDEUTIC OFFICE OF GREEK PHILOSOPHY.

The divine discipline of the Jews was, as has been seen, in nature essentially moral. The lessons which it was designed to teach were embodied in the family and the nation. Yet this was not in itself a complete discipline of our nature. The reason, no less than the will and the affections, had an office to discharge in preparing man for the Incarnation. The process and the issue in the two cases were widely different, but they were in some sense complementary. Even in time this relation holds good. The divine kingdom of the Jews was just overthrown when free speculation arose in the Ionian colonies of Asia. The teaching of the last prophet nearly synchronized with the death of Socrates. All other differences between the discipline of reason and that of revelation are implicitly included in their fundamental difference of method. In the one, man boldly aspired at once to God, in the other, God disclosed Himself gradually to man. Philosophy failed as a religious teacher practically (Rom. i. 21, 22), but it bore noble witness to an inward law (Rom. ii. 14, 15). It laid open instinctive wants which it could not satisfy. It cleared away error, when it could not found truth.

It swayed the foremost minds of a nation, when it left the mass without hope. In its purest and grandest forms it was "a schoolmaster to bring men to Christ" (Clem. Alex. *Strom.* i. § 28).

This function of ancient philosophy is distinctly recognized by many of the greatest of the fathers. The principle which is involved in the doctrine of Justin Martyr on "the Seminal Word" finds a clear and systematic expression in Clement of Alexandria. (Comp. Redepenning, *Origenes*, i. 437–439.) "Every race of men participated in the Word. And they who lived with the Word were Christians, even if they were held to be godless (ἄθεοι), as for example, among the Greeks, Socrates and Heraclitus, and those like them" (Just. Mart. *Ap.* i. 46; comp. *Ap.* i. 5, 28; and ii. 10, 13). "Philosophy," says Clement, "before the coming of the Lord, was necessary to Greeks for righteousness; and now it proves useful for godliness, being in some sort a preliminary discipline (προπαιδεία τις οὖσα) for those who reap the fruits of the faith through demonstration. . . . . Perhaps we may say that it was given to the Greeks with this special object (προηγουμένως), for it brought (ἐπαιδαγώγει) the Greek nation to Christ, as the Law brought the Hebrews" (Clem. Alex. *Strom.* i. 5, § 28; comp. 9, § 43, and 16, § 80). In this sense he does not scruple to say that "Philosophy was given as a peculiar testament (διαθήκην) to the Greeks, as forming the basis of the Christian philosophy" (*Strom.* vi. 8, § 67; comp. 5, § 41). Origen, himself a pupil of Ammonius Saccas, speaks with less precision as to the educational power of philosophy, but his whole works bear witness to its influence. The truths which philosophers taught, he says, referring to the words of St. Paul, were from God, for "God manifested these to them, and all things that have been nobly said" (*c. Cels.* vi. 3; *Philoc.* p. 15). Augustine, while depreciating the claims of the great Gentile teachers, allows that "some of them made great discoveries, so far as they received help from Heaven, while they erred as far as they were hindered by human frailty" (Aug. *De Civ.* ii. 7; comp. *De Doctr. Chr.* ii. 18). They had, as he elsewhere says, a distant vision of the truth, and learnt from the teaching of nature what prophets learnt from the Spirit (*Serm.* lxviii. 3, cxl. etc.).

But while many thus recognized in philosophy the free witness of the Word speaking among men, the same writers in other places sought to explain the partial harmony of philosophy and revelation by an original connection of the two. This attempt, which in the light of a clearer criticism is seen to be essentially fruitless and even suicidal, was at least more plausible in the first centuries. A multitude of writings were then current bearing the names of the Sibyl or Hystaspes, which were obviously based on the O. T. Scriptures, and as long as they were received as genuine it was impossible to doubt that Jewish doctrines were spread in the West before the rise of philosophy. And on the other hand, when the Fathers ridicule with the bitterest scorn the contradictions and errors of philosophers, it must be remembered that they spoke often fresh from a conflict with degenerate professors of systems which had long lost all real life. Some, indeed, there were, chiefly among the Latins, who consistently inveighed against philosophy. But even Tertullian, who is among its fiercest adversaries, allows that at times the philosophers hit upon truth by a happy chance or

blind good fortune, and yet more by that "general feeling with which God was pleased to endow the soul" (Tert. *De An.* c. 2). The use which was made of heathen speculation by heretical writers was one great cause of its disparagement by their catholic antagonists. Irenæus endeavors to reduce the Gnostic teachers to a dilemma: either the philosophers with whom they argued knew the truth or they did not; if they did, the Incarnation was superfluous; if they did not, whence comes the agreement of the true and the false? (*Adv. Hær.* ii. 14, 7). Hippolytus follows out the connection of different sects with earlier teachers in elaborate detail. Tertullian, with characteristic energy, declares that "Philosophy furnishes the arms and the subjects of heresy. What (he asks) has Athens in common with Jerusalem? the Academy with the Church? heretics with Christians? Our training is from the Porch of Solomon. . . Let those look to it who bring forward a Stoic, a Platonic, a dialectic Christianity. We have no need of curious inquiries after the coming of Christ Jesus, nor of investigation after the Gospel" (Tert. *De Præscr. Hær.* c. 7).

This variety of judgment in the heat of controversy was inevitable. The full importance of the history of ancient philosophy was then first seen when all rivalry was over, and it became possible to contemplate it as a whole, animated by a great law, often trembling on the verge of Truth, and sometimes by a "bold venture" claiming the heritage of faith. Yet even now the relations of the "two old covenants"—Philosophy and the Hebrew Scriptures—to use the language of Clement—have been traced only imperfectly. What has been done may encourage labor, but it does not supersede it. In the porticoes of eastern churches Pythagoras and Plato are pictured among those who prepared the way for Christianity (Stanley, p. 41); but in the West, Sibyls and not philosophers are the chosen representatives of the divine element in Gentile teaching.

III. The Development of Greek Philosophy.

The complete fitness of Greek philosophy to perform this propaedeutic office for Christianity, as an exhaustive effort of reason to solve the great problems of being, must be apparent after a detailed study of its progress and consummation; and even the simplest outline of its history cannot fail to preserve the leading traits of the natural (or even necessary) law by which its development was governed.

The various attempts which have been made to derive western philosophy from eastern sources have signally failed. The external evidence in favor of this opinion is wholly insufficient to establish it (Ritter, *Gesch. d. Phil.* i. 159, &c.; Thirlwall, *Hist. of Gr.* ii. 130; Zeller, *Gesch. d. Phil. d. Griechen*, i. 18–34; Max Müller, *On Language*, 84 *note*), and on internal grounds it is most improbable. It is true that in some degree the character of Greek speculation may have been influenced, at least in its earliest stages, by religious ideas which were originally introduced from the East; but this indirect influence does not affect the real originality of the great Greek teachers. The spirit of pure philosophy is (as has been already seen) wholly alien from eastern thought; and it was comparatively late when even a Greek ventured to separate philosophy from religion. But in Greece the separation, when it was once effected, remained essentially complete. The opinions of the ancient philosophers might or might not be outwardly reconcilable with the popular faith; but philosophy and faith were independent. The very value of Greek teaching lies in the fact that it was, as far as is possible, a result of simple reason, or, if faith asserts its prerogative, the distinction is sharply marked. In this we have a record of the power and weakness of the human mind written at once on the grandest scale and in the fairest characters.

Of the various classifications of the Greek schools which have been proposed, the simplest and truest seems to be that which divides the history of philosophy into three great periods, the first reaching to the era of the Sophists, the next to the death of Aristotle, the third to the Christian era. In the first period the world objectively is the great centre of inquiry; in the second, the "ideas" of things, truth, and being; in the third, the chief interest of philosophy falls back upon the practical conduct of life. Successive systems overlap each other, both in time and subjects of speculation, but broadly the sequence which has been indicated will hold good (Zeller, *Die Philosophie der Griechen*, i. 111, &c.). After the Christian era philosophy ceased to have any true vitality in Greece, but it made fresh efforts to meet the changed conditions of life at Alexandria and Rome. At Alexandria Platonism was vivified by the spirit of oriental mysticism, and afterwards of Christianity; at Rome Stoicism was united with the vigorous virtues of active life. Each of these great divisions must be passed in rapid review.

1. *The pre-Socratic Schools.* — The first Greek philosophy was little more than an attempt to follow out in thought the mythic cosmogonies of earlier poets. Gradually the depth and variety of the problems included in the idea of a cosmogony became apparent, and, after each clew had been followed out, the period ended in the negative teaching of the Sophists. The questions of creation, of the immediate relation of mind and matter, were pronounced in fact, if not in word, insoluble, and speculation was turned into a new direction.

What is the one permanent element which underlies the changing forms of things? this was the primary inquiry to which the *Ionic* school endeavored to find an answer. THALES (cir. B. C. 610–625), following, as it seems, the genealogy of Hesiod, pointed to moisture (water) as the one source and supporter of life. ANAXIMENES (cir. B. C. 520–480) substituted air for water, as the more subtle and all-pervading element; but equally with Thales he neglected all consideration of the force which might be supposed to modify the one primal substance. At a much later date (cir. B. C. 450) DIOGENES of Apollonia, to meet this difficulty, represented this elementary "air" as endowed with intelligence (νόησις), but even he makes no distinction between the material and the intelligent. The atomic theory of DEMOCRITUS (cir. B. C. 460–357), which stands in close connection with this form of Ionic teaching, offered another and more plausible solution. The motion of his atoms included the action of force, but he wholly omitted to account for its source. Meanwhile another mode of speculation had arisen in the same school. In place of one definite element ANAXIMANDER (B. C. 610–547) suggested the unlimited (τὸ ἄπειρον) as the adequate origin of all special existen-

ces. And somewhat more than a century later ANAXAGORAS summed up the result of such a line of speculation: "All things were together; then mind (νοῦς) came and disposed them in order" (Diog. Laert. ii. 6). Thus we are left face to face with an ultimate dualism.

The *Eleatic* school started from an opposite point of view. Thales saw moisture present in material things, and pronounced this to be their fundamental principle: XENOPHANES (cir. B. C. 530–50) "looked up to the whole heaven and said that the One is God" (Arist. *Met.* i. b, τὸ ἓν εἶναί φησι τὸν θεόν). "Thales saw gods in all things: Xenophanes saw all things in God" (Thirlwall, *Hist. of Gr.* ii. 136). That which *is*, according to Xenophanes, must be one, eternal, infinite, immovable, unchangeable. PARMENIDES of Elea (B. C. 500) substituted abstract "being" for "God" in the system of Xenophanes, and distinguished with precision the functions of sense and reason. Sense teaches us of "the many," the false (phenomena): Reason of "the one," the true (the absolute). ZENO of Elea (cir. B. C. 450) developed with logical ingenuity the contradictions involved in our perceptions of things (in the idea of *motion*, for instance), and thus formally prepared the way for skepticism. If the one alone *is*, the phenomenal world is an illusion. The sublime aspiration of Xenophanes, when followed out legitimately to its consequences, ended in blank negation.

The teaching of HERACLITUS (B. C. 500) offers a complete contrast to that of the Eleatics, and stands far in advance of the earlier Ionic school, with which he is historically connected. So far from contrasting the existent and the phenomenal, he boldly identified being with change. "There ever was, and is, and shall be, an ever-living fire, unceasingly kindled and extinguished in due measure" (ἀπτόμενον μέτρα καὶ ἀποσβεννύμενον μέτρα, Clem. Alex. *Strom.* v. 14, § 105). Rest and continuance is death. That which is is the instantaneous balance of contending powers (Diog. Laert. ix. 7, διὰ τῆς ἐναντιοτροπῆς ἡρμόσθαι τὰ ὄντα). Creation is the *play* of the Creator. Everywhere, as far as his opinions can be grasped, Heraclitus makes noble "guesses at truth;" yet he leaves "fate" (εἱμαρμένη) as the supreme creator (Stob. *Ecl.* i. p. 59, ap. Ritter & Preller, § 42). The cycles of life and death run on by its law. It may have been by a natural reaction that from these wider speculations he turned his thoughts inwards. "I investigated myself," he says, with conscious pride (Plut. *adv. Col.* 1118, c.); and in this respect he foreshadows the teaching of Socrates, as Zeno did that of the Sophists.

The philosophy of PYTHAGORAS (cir. B. C. 840–510) is subordinate in interest to his social and political theories, though it supplies a link in the course of speculation; others had labored to trace a unity in the world in the presence of one underlying element or in the idea of a whole: he sought to combine the separate harmony of parts with total unity. Numerical unity includes the finite and the infinite; and in the relations of number there is a perfect symmetry, as all spring out of the fundamental unit. Thus numbers seemed to Pythagoras to be not only "patterns" of things (τῶν ὄντων), but causes of their being (τῆς οὐσίας). How he connected numbers with concrete being it is impossible to determine; but it may not be wholly fanciful to see in the doctrine of transmigration of souls an attempt to trace in the successive forms of life an outward expression of a harmonious law in the moral as well as in the physical world. (The remains of the pre-Socratic philosophers have been collected in a very convenient form by F. Mullach in Didot's *Biblioth. Gr.*, Paris, 1860.)

The first cycle of philosophy was thus completed. All the great primary problems of thought had been stated, and typical answers rendered. The relation of spirit and matter was still unsolved. Speculation issued in dualism (Anaxagoras), materialism (Democritus), or pantheism (Xenophanes). On one side reason was made the sole criterion of truth (Parmenides); on the other, experience (Heraclitus). As yet there was no rest, and the Sophists prepared the way for a new method.

Whatever may be the moral estimate which is formed of the Sophists, there can be little doubt as to the importance of their teaching as preparatory to that of Socrates. All attempts to arrive at certainty by a study of the world had failed: might it not seem, then, that truth is subjective? "Man is the measure of all things." Sensations are modified by the individual; and may not this hold good universally? The conclusion was applied to morals and politics with fearless skill. The belief in absolute truth and right was well-nigh banished; but meanwhile the Sophists were perfecting the instrument which was to be turned against them. Language, in their hands, acquired a precision unknown before, when words assumed the place of things. Plato might ridicule the pedantry of Protagoras, but Socrates reaped a rich harvest from it.

2. *The Socratic Schools.* — In the second period of Greek philosophy the scene and subject were both changed. Athens became the centre of speculations which had hitherto chiefly found a home among the more mixed populations of the colonies. And at the same time inquiry was turned from the outward world to the inward, from theories of the origin and relation of things to theories of our knowledge of them. A philosophy of ideas, using the term in its widest sense, succeeded a philosophy of nature. In three generations Greek speculation reached its greatest glory in the teaching of Socrates, Plato, and Aristotle. When the sovereignty of Greece ceased, all higher philosophy ceased with it. In the hopeless turmoil of civil disturbances which followed, men's thoughts were chiefly directed to questions of personal duty.

The famous sentence in which Aristotle (*Met. M.* 4) characterizes the teaching of SOCRATES (B. C. 468–399) places his scientific position in the clearest light. There are two things, he says, which we may rightly attribute to Socrates, inductive reasoning, and general definition (τοὺς τ' ἐπακτικοὺς λόγους καὶ τὸ ὁρίζεσθαι καθόλου). By the first he endeavored to discover the permanent element which underlies the changing forms of appearances and the varieties of opinion; by the second he fixed the truth which he had thus gained. But, besides this, Socrates rendered another service to truth. He changed not only the method but also the subject of philosophy (Cic. *Acad. Post.* i. 4). Ethics occupied in his investigations the primary place which had hitherto been held by Physics. The great aim of his induction was to establish the sovereignty of Virtue; and before entering on other speculations he determined to obey the Delphian maxim and "know himself" (Plat. *Phædr.* 229). It was a necessary consequence

of a first effort in this direction that Socrates regarded all the results which he derived as like in kind. Knowledge (ἐπιστήμη) was equally absolute and authoritative, whether it referred to the laws of intellectual operations or to questions of morality. A conclusion in geometry and a conclusion on conduct were set forth as true in the same sense. Thus vice was only another name for ignorance (Xen. *Mem.* iii. 9, 4; Arist. *Eth. Eud.* i. 5). Every one was supposed to have within him a faculty absolutely leading to right action, just as the mind necessarily decides rightly as to relations of space and number, when each step in the proposition is clearly stated. Socrates practically neglected the determinative power of the will. His great glory was, however, clearly connected with this fundamental error in his system. He affirmed the existence of a universal law of right and wrong. He connected philosophy with action, both in detail and in general. On the one side he upheld the supremacy of Conscience, on the other the working of Providence. Not the least fruitful characteristic of his teaching was what may be called its desultoriness. He formed no complete system. He wrote nothing. He attracted and impressed his readers by his many-sided nature. He helped others to give birth to thoughts, to use his favorite image, but he was barren himself (Plat. *Theæt.* p. 150). As a result of this, the most conflicting opinions were maintained by some of his professed followers, who carried out isolated fragments of his teaching to extreme conclusions. Some adopted his method (Euclides, cir. B. C. 400, the *Megarians*); others his subject. Of the latter, one section, following out his proposition of the identity of self-command (ἐγκράτεια) with virtue, professed an utter disregard of everything material (Antisthenes, cir. B. c. 366, the *Cynics*), while the other (Aristippus, cir. B. c. 366, the *Cyrenaics*), inverting the maxim that virtue is necessarily accompanied by pleasure, took immediate pleasure as the rule of action.

These "minor Socratic schools" were, however, premature and imperfect developments. The truths which they distorted were embodied at a later time in more reasonable forms. PLATO alone (B. c. 430–347), by the breadth and nobleness of his teaching, was the true successor of Socrates: with fuller detail and greater elaborateness of parts, his philosophy was as manysided as that of his master. Thus it is impossible to construct a consistent Platonic system, though many Platonic doctrines are sufficiently marked. Plato, indeed, possessed two commanding powers, which, though apparently incompatible, are in the highest sense complementary: a matchless destructive dialectic, and a creative imagination. By the first he refuted the great fallacies of the Sophists on the uncertainty of knowledge and right, carrying out in this the attacks of Socrates; by the other he endeavored to bridge over the interval between appearance and reality, and gain an approach to the eternal. His famous doctrines of ideas and recollection (ἀνάμνησις) are a solution by imagination of a logical difficulty. Socrates had shown the existence of general notions; Plato felt constrained to attribute to them a substantive existence (Arist. *Met. M.* 4). A glorious vision gave completeness to his view. The unembodied spirits were exhibited in immediate presence of the "ideas" of things (*Phædr.* p. 247); the law of their embodiment was sensibly portrayed; and the more or less vivid remembrance of supramundane realities in this life was traced to antecedent facts. All men were thus supposed to have been face to face with Truth: the object of teaching was to bring back impressions latent but uneffaced.

The "myths" of Plato, to one of the most famous of which reference has just been made, play a most important part in his system. They answer in the philosopher to faith in the Christian. In dealing with immortality and judgment he leaves the way of reason, and ventures, as he says, on a rude raft to brave the dangers of the ocean (*Phæd.* 85 D; *Gorg.* 523 A). "The peril and the prize are noble and the hope is great" (*Phæd.* 114, C, D). Such tales, he admits, may seem puerile and ridiculous; and if there were other surer and clearer means of gaining the desired end, the judgment would be just (*Gorg.* 527 A). But, as it is, thus only can he connect the seen and the unseen. The myths, then, mark the limit of his dialectics. They are not merely a poetical picture of truth already gained, or a popular illustration of his teaching, but real efforts to penetrate beyond the depths of argument. They show that his method was not commensurate with his instinctive desires; and point out in intelligible outlines the subjects on which man looks for revelation. Such are the relations of the human mind to truth (*Phædr.* pp. 246–249); the preëxistence and immortality of the soul (*Meno*, pp. 81–83; *Phædr.* pp. 110–112; *Tim.* p. 41); the state of future retribution (*Gorg.* pp. 523–525; *Rep.* x. 614–616); the revolutions of the world (*Polit.* p. 269. Compare also *Sympos.* pp. 189–191, 203–205; Zeller, *Philos. d. Griech.* pp. 361–363, who gives the literature of the subject).

The great difference between Plato and ARISTOTLE (B. C. 384–322) lies in the use which Plato thus made of imagination as the exponent of instinct. The dialectic of Plato is not inferior to that of Aristotle, and Aristotle exhibits traces of poetic power not unworthy of Plato; but Aristotle never allows imagination to influence his final decision. He elaborated a perfect method, and he used it with perfect fairness. His writings, if any, contain the highest utterance of pure reason. Looking back on all the earlier efforts of philosophy, he pronounced a calm and final judgment. For him many of the conclusions which others had maintained were valueless, because he showed that they rested on feeling, and not on argument. This stern severity of logic gives an indescribable pathos to those passages in which he touches on the highest hopes of men; and perhaps there is no more truly affecting chapter in ancient literature than that in which he states in a few unimpassioned sentences the issue of his inquiry into the immortality of the soul. Part of it may be immortal, but that part is impersonal (*De An.* iii. 5). This was the sentence of reason, and he gives expression to it without a word of protest, and yet as one who knew the extent of the sacrifice which it involved. The conclusion is, as it were, the epitaph of free speculation. Laws of observation and argument, rules of action, principles of government remain, but there is no hope beyond the grave.

It follows necessarily that the Platonic doctrine of ideas was emphatically rejected by Aristotle, who gave, however, the final development to the original conception of Socrates. With Socrates "ideas" (general definitions) were mere abstractions; with Plato they had an absolute existence;

with Aristotle they had no existence separate from things in which they were realized, though the form (μορφή), which answers to the Platonic idea, was held to be the essence of the thing itself (comp. Zeller, *Philos. d. Griech.* i. 119, 120).

There is one feature common in essence to the systems of Plato and Aristotle which has not yet been noticed. In both, Ethics is a part of Politics. The citizen is prior to the man. In Plato this doctrine finds its most extravagant development in theory, though his life, and, in some places, his teaching, were directly opposed to it (e. g. *Gorg.* p. 527 D). This practical inconsequence was due, it may be supposed, to the condition of Athens at the time, for the idea was in complete harmony with the national feeling; and, in fact, the absolute subordination of the individual to the body includes one of the chief lessons of the ancient world. In Aristotle the "political" character of man is defined with greater precision, and brought within narrower limits. The breaking-up of the small Greek states had prepared the way for more comprehensive views of human fellowship, without destroying the fundamental truth of the necessity of social union for perfect life. But in the next generation this was lost. The wars of the Succession obliterated the idea of society, and philosophy was content with aiming at individual happiness.

The coming change was indicated by the rise of a school of skeptics. The skepticism of the Sophists marked the close of the first period, and in like manner the skepticism of the Pyrrhonists marks the close of the second (STILPO, cir. B. C. 290; PYRRHON, cir. B. C. 290). But the Pyrrhonists rendered no positive service to the cause of philosophy, as the Sophists did by the refinement of language. Their immediate influence was limited in its range, and it is only as a symptom that the rise of the school is important. But in this respect it foreshows the character of after-philosophy by denying the foundation of all higher speculations. Thus all interest was turned to questions of practical morality. Hitherto morality had been based as a science upon mental analysis, but by the Pyrrhonists it was made subservient to law and custom. Immediate experience was held to be the rule of life (comp. Ritter and Preller, § 350).

3. The post-Socratic Schools. — After Aristotle, philosophy, as has been already noticed, took a new direction. The Socratic schools were, as has been shown, connected by a common pursuit of the permanent element which underlies phenomena. Socrates placed Virtue, truth in action, in a knowledge of the ideas of things. Plato went further, and maintained that these ideas are alone truly existent. Aristotle, though differing in terms, yet only followed in the same direction, when he attributed to Form, not an independent existence, but a fashioning, vivifying power in all individual objects. But from this point speculation took a mainly personal direction. Philosophy, in the strict sense of the word, ceased to exist. This was due both to the circumstances of the time and to the exhaustion consequent on the failure of the Socratic method to solve the deep mysteries of being. Aristotle had, indeed, laid the wide foundations of an inductive system of physics, but few were inclined to continue his work. The physical theories which were brought forward were merely adaptations from earlier philosophers.

In dealing with moral questions two opposite systems are possible, and have found advocates in

all ages. On the one side it may be said that
the character of actions is to be judged by their
results; on the other, that it is to be sought only
in the actions themselves. Pleasure is the test
of right in one case; an assumed, or discovered,
law of our nature in the other. If the world were
perfect and the balance of human faculties undisturbed, it is evident that both systems would give
identical results. As it is, there is a tendency
to error on each side, which is clearly seen in the
rival schools of the Epicureans and Stoics, who
practically divided the suffrages of the mass of
educated men in the centuries before and after the
Christian era.

EPICURUS (B. C. 352–270) defined the object of
philosophy to be the attainment of a happy life.
The pursuit of truth for its own sake he regarded
as superfluous. He rejected dialectics as a useless
study, and accepted the senses, in the widest acceptation of the term [EPICUREANS, i. 570], as
the criterion of truth. Physics he subordinated
entirely to ethics (Cic. de Fin. i. 7). But he
differed widely from the Cyrenaics in his view of
happiness. The happiness at which the wise man
aims is to be found, he said, not in momentary
gratification, but in lifelong pleasure. It does not
consist necessarily in excitement or motion, but
often in absolute tranquillity (ἀταραξία). "The
wise man is happy even on the rack" (Diog. Laert.
x. 118), for "virtue alone is inseparable from
pleasure" (id. 138). To live happily and to
live wisely, nobly, and justly, are convertible
phrases (id. 140). But it followed as a corollary
from his view of happiness, that the Gods, who
were assumed to be supremely happy and eternal,
were absolutely free from the distractions and emotions consequent on any care for the world or man
(id. 139; comp. Lucr. ii. 645–647). All things
were supposed to come into being by chance, and
so pass away; and the study of Nature was chiefly
useful as dispelling the superstitious fears of the
Gods and death by which the multitude are tormented. It is obvious how such teaching would
degenerate in practice. The individual was left
master of his own life, free from all regard to any
higher law than a refined selfishness.

While Epicurus asserted in this manner the
claims of one part of man's nature in the conduct
of life, ZENO of Citium (cir. B. C. 280), with equal
partiality, advocated a purely spiritual (intellectual)
morality. The opposition between the two was
complete. The infinite, chance-formed worlds of
the one stand over against the one harmonious
world of the other On the one side are Gods
regardless of material things, on the other a Being
permeating and vivifying all creation. This difference necessarily found its chief expression in ethics.
For when the Stoics taught that there were only
two principles of things, Matter (τὸ πάσχον), and
God, Fate, Reason — for the names were many by
which it was fashioned and quickened (τὸ ποιοῦν)
— it followed that the active principle in man is
of Divine origin, and that his duty is to live con-
formably to nature (τὸ ὁμολογουμένως [τῇ φύσει]
ζῆν). By "Nature" some understood the nature
of man, others the nature of the universe; but both
agreed in regarding it as a general law of the whole,
and not particular passions or impulses. Good,
therefore, was but one. All external things were

indifferent. Reason was the absolute sovereign of
man. Thus the doctrine of the Stoics, like that
of Epicurus, practically left man to himself. But
it was worse in its final results than Epicurism, for
it made him his own god.[a]

In one point the Epicureans and Stoics were
agreed. They both regarded the happiness and
culture of the individual as the highest good. Both
systems belonged to a period of corruption and
decay. They were the efforts of the man to support himself in the ruin of the state. But at the
same time this assertion of individual independence
and breaking down of local connections performed
an important work in preparation for Christianity.
It was for the Gentile world an influence corresponding to the Dispersion for the Jews. Men,
as men, owned their fellowship as they had not done
before. Isolating superstitions were shattered by
the arguments of the Epicureans. The unity of the
human conscience was vigorously affirmed by the
Stoics (comp. Antoninus, iv. 4, 33, with Gataker's
notes).

Meanwhile in the New Academy Platonism degenerated into skepticism. Epicurus found an authoritative rule in the senses. The Stoics took refuge
in what seems to answer to the modern doctrine
of "common sense," and maintained that the
senses give a direct knowledge of the object. CAR-
NEADES (B. C. 213–129) combated these views,
and showed that sensation cannot be proved to declare the real nature, but only some of the effects,
of things. Thus the slight philosophical basis of
the later schools was undermined. Skepticism
remained as the last issue of speculation; and, if
we may believe the declaration of Seneca (Quaest.
Nat. vii. 32), skepticism itself soon ceased to be
taught as a system. The great teachers had sought
rest, and in the end they found unrest. No science
of life could be established. The reason of the few
failed to create an esoteric rule of virtue and happiness. For in this they all agreed, that the blessings of philosophy were not for the mass. A
"Gospel preached to the poor" was as yet unknown.

But though the Greek philosophers fell short of
their highest aim, it needs no words to show the
work which they did as pioneers of a universal
Church. They revealed the wants and the instincts
of men with a clearness and vigor elsewhere unattainable, for their sight was dazzled by no reflections from a purer faith. Step by step great
questions were proposed — Fate, Providence — Conscience, Law — the State, the Man — and answers
were given, which are the more instructive because
they are generally one-sided. The discussions,
which were primarily restricted to a few, in time
influenced the opinions of the many. The preacher
who spoke of "an unknown God" had an audience
who could understand him, not at Athens only or
Rome, but throughout the civilized world.

The complete course of philosophy was run before the Christian era, but there were yet two mixed
systems afterwards which offered some novel features.
At Alexandria Platonism was united with various
elements of eastern speculation, and for several
centuries exercised an important influence on
Christian doctrine. At Rome Stoicism was vivified
by the spirit of the old republic, and exhibited the
extreme western type of philosophy. Of the first

<hr>

a This statement, which is true generally, is open to
many exceptions. The famous hymn of Cleanthes is

one of the noblest expressions of belief in Divine
Power (Mullach, Fragm. Philos. p. 151).

nothing can be said here. It arose only when Christianity was a recognized spiritual power, and was influenced both positively and negatively by the Gospel. The same remark applies to the efforts to quicken afresh the forms of Paganism, which found their climax in the reign of Julian. These have no independent value as an expression of original thought; but the Roman Stoicism calls for brief notice from its supposed connection with Christian morality (SENECA, † A. D. 65; EPIC- TETUS, † cir. A. D. 115; M. AURELIUS ANTONINUS, 121–180). The belief in this connection found a singular expression in the apocryphal correspond- ence of St. Paul and Seneca, which was widely received in the early Church (Jerome, *De Vir. ill.* xii.). And lately a distinguished writer (Mill, *On Liberty*, p. 58, quoted by Stanley, *Eastern Ch. Lect.* VI., apparently with approbation) has specu- lated on the " tragical fact " that Constantine, and not Marcus Aurelius, was the first Christian em- peror. The superficial coincidences of Stoicism with the N. T. are certainly numerous. Coinci- dences of thought, and even of language, might easily be multiplied (Gataker, *Antoninus*, Præf. pp. xi. etc.), and in considering these it is impossible not to remember that Semitic thought and phrase- ology must have exercised great influence on Stoic teaching (Grant, *Oxford Essays*, 1858, p. 82).[a] But beneath this external resemblance of Stoicism to Christianity, the later Stoics were fundament- ally opposed to it. For good and for evil they were the Pharisees of the Gentile world. Their highest aspirations are mixed with the thanksgiv- ing " that they were not as other men are " (comp. *Anton.* i.). Their worship was a sublime egotism.[b] The conduct of life was regarded as an art, guided in individual actions by a conscious reference to reason (*Anton.* iv. 2, 3, v. 32), and not a sponta- neous process rising naturally out of one vital prin- ciple.[c] The wise man, " wrapt in himself " (vii. 28), was supposed to look with perfect indifference on the changes of time (iv. 49); and yet beneath this show of independence he was a prey to a hope- less sadness. In words he appealed to the great law of fate which rapidly sweeps all things into oblivion as a source of consolation (iv. 2, 14, vi. 15); but there is no confidence in any future retribution. In a certain sense the elements of which we are composed are eternal (v. 13), for they are incorpo- rated in other parts of the universe, but *we* shall cease to exist (iv. 14, 21, vi. 24, vii. 10). Not only is there no recognition of communion between an immortal man and a personal God, but the idea is excluded. Man is but an atom in a vast universe, and his actions and sufferings are meas- ured solely by their relation to the whole (*Anton.* x. 5, 6, 20, xii. 26, vi. 45, v. 22, vii. 9). God is

but another name for " the mind of the universe " (ὁ τοῦ ὅλου νοῦς, v. 30), " the soul of the world " (iv. 40), " the reason that ordereth matter " (vi. 1), " universal nature " (ἡ τῶν ὅλων φύσις, vii. 33, ix. 1; comp. x. 1), and is even identified with the world itself (τοῦ γεννήσαντος κόσμου, xii. 1; comp. Gataker on iv. 23). Thus the Stoicism of M. Aurelius gives many of the moral precepts of the Gospel (Gataker, *Præf.* p. xviii.), but without their foundation, which can find no place in his system. It is impossible to read his reflections without emotion, but they have no creative energy. They are the last strain of a dying creed, and in themselves have no special affinity to the new faith. Christianity necessarily includes whatever is noblest in them, but they affect to supply the place of Christianity, and do not lead to it. The real elements of greatness in M. Aurelius are many, and truly Roman; but the study of his *Meditations* by the side of the N. T. can leave little doubt that he could not have helped to give a national stand ing place to a Catholic Church.[d]

IV. CHRISTIANITY IN CONTACT WITH ANCIENT PHILOSOPHY.

The only direct trace of the contact of Chris- tianity with western philosophy in the N. T. is in the account of St. Paul's visit to Athens, where " certain philosophers of the Epicureans and of the Stoics " (Acts xvii. 18) — the representatives, that is, of the two great moral schools which divided the West — " encountered him; " and there is nothing in the apostolic writings to show that it exercised any important influence upon the early church (comp. 1 Cor. i. 22–4). But it was oth- erwise with eastern speculation, which, as it was less scientific in form, penetrated more deeply through the mass of the people. The " philosophy " against which the Colossians were warned (Col. ii. 8) seems undoubtedly to have been of eastern origin, containing elements similar to those which were afterwards embodied in various shapes of Gnosticism, as a selfish asceticism and a supersti- tious reverence for angels (Col. ii. 16–23); and in the Epistles to Timothy, addressed to Ephesus, in which city St. Paul anticipated the rise of false teaching (Acts xx. 30), two distinct forms of error may be traced in addition to Judaism, due more or less to the same influence. One of these was a vain spiritualism, insisting on ascetic observances and interpreting the resurrection as a moral change (1 Tim. iv. 1–7; 2 Tim. ii. 16–18); the other a materialism allied to sorcery (2 Tim. iii. 13, γόητες). The former is that which is peculiarly " false-styled gnosis " (1 Tim. vi. 20), abounding in " profane and old wives' fables " (1 Tim. iv. 7) and empty discussions (i. 6, vi. 20); the latter has

---

a Citium, the birthplace of Zeno, was a Phœnician colony; Herillus, his pupil, was a Carthaginian; Chrysippus was born at Soli or Tarsus; of his schol- ars and successors, Zeno and Antipater were natives of Tarsus, and Diogenes of Babylonia. In the next generation, Posidonius was a native of Apamea in Syria; and Epictetus, the noblest of Stoics, was born at Hierapolis in Phrygia.

b Seneca, *Ep.* 53, 11: " Est aliquid quo sapiens antecedat Deum; ille beneficio naturæ non timet, suo sapiens." Comp. *Ep.* 41. Anton. xii. 26, ὁ ἐκάστου νοῦς θεὸς καὶ ἐκεῖθεν ἐπερρύηκε. Comp. v. 10.

c This explains the well-known reference of Marcus Aurelius to the Christians. They were ready to die of mere obstinacy " (κατὰ ψιλὴν παράταξιν, i. e.

faith), whereas, he says, this readiness ought to come " from personal judgment after due calculation " (ἀπὸ ἰδικῆς κρίσεως . . . . λελογισμένως . . . . xi. 3). So also Epictetus (*Diss.* ix. 7, k) contrasts the fortitude gained by " habit," by the Galilæans, with the true fortitude based on " reason and demonstra- tion."

d The writings of Epictetus contain in the main the same system, but with somewhat less arrogance. It may be remarked that the silence of Epictetus and M. Aurelius on the teaching of Christianity can hardly be explained by ignorance. It seems that the philoso- pher would not notice (in word) the believer. Comp Lardner, *Works*, vii. 356–57.

a close connection with earlier tendencies at Ephesus (Acts xix. 19), and with the traditional accounts of Simon Magus (comp. Acts viii. 9), whose working on the early church, however obscure, was unquestionably most important. These antagonistic and yet complementary forms of heresy found a wide development in later times; but it is remarkable that no trace of dualism, of the distinction of the Creator and the Redeemer, the Demiurge and the true God, which formed so essential a tenet of the Gnostic schools, occurs in the N. T. (comp. Thiersch, *Versuch zur Herst. d. hist. Standp.* etc., 231–304).

The writings of the sub-apostolic age, with the exception of the famous anecdote of Justin Martyr (*Dial.* 2–4), throw little light upon the relations of Christianity and philosophy. The heretical systems again are too obscure and complicated to illustrate more than the general admixture of foreign (especially eastern) tenets with the apostolic teaching. One book, however, has been preserved in various shapes, which, though still unaccountably neglected in church histories, contains a vivid delineation of the speculative struggle which Christianity had to maintain with Judaism and Heathenism. The Clementine *Homilies* (ed. Dressel, 1853) and *Recognitions* (ed. Gersdorf, 1838) are a kind of Philosophy of Religion, and in subtlety and richness of thought yield to no early Christian writings. The picture which the supposed author draws of his early religious doubts is evidently taken from life (Clem. *Recogn.* i. 1–3; Neander, *Ch. Hist.* i. 43, E. T.); and in the discussions which follow there are clear traces of western as well as eastern philosophy (Uhlborn, *Die Hom. u. Recogn. d. Clem. Rom.* pp. 404, &c.).

At the close of the second century, when the Church of Alexandria came into marked intellectual preëminence, the mutual influence of Christianity and Neo-Platonism opened a new field of speculation, or rather the two systems were presented in forms designed to meet the acknowledged wants of the time. According to the commonly received report, Origen was the scholar of Ammonius Saccas, who first gave consistency to the later Platonism, and for a long time he was the contemporary of Plotinus (A. D. 205–270), who was its noblest expositor. Neo-Platonism was, in fact, an attempt to seize the spirit of Christianity apart from its historic basis and human elements. The separation between the two was absolute; and yet the splendor of the one-sided spiritualism of the Neo-Platonists attracted in some cases the admiration of the Christian Fathers (Basil, Theodoret), and the wide circulation of the writings of the pseudo-Dionysius the Areopagite served to propagate many of their doctrines under an orthodox name among the schoolmen and mystics of the Middle Ages (Vogt, *Neu-Platonismus u. Christenthum*, 1836; Herzog, *Encyklop.* s. v. *Neu-Platonismus*).

The want which the Alexandrine Fathers endeavored to satisfy is in a great measure the want of our own time. If Christianity be truth, it must have points of special connection with all nations and all periods. The difference of character in the constituent writings of the N. T. are evidently typical, and present the Gospel in a form (if technical language may be used) now ethical, now logical, now mystical. The varieties of aspect thus indicated combine to give the idea of a harmonious whole. Clement rightly maintained that

there is a "gnosis" in Christianity distinct from the errors of Gnosticism. The latter was a premature attempt to connect the Gospel with earlier systems; the former a result of conflict grounded on faith (Möhler, *Patrologie*, 424, &c.). Christian philosophy may be in one sense a contradiction in terms, for Christianity confessedly derives its first principles from revelation, and not from simple reason; but there is no less a true philosophy of Christianity, which aims to show how completely these, by their form, their substance, and their consequences, meet the instincts and aspirations of all ages. The exposition of such a philosophy would be the work of a modern Origen.   B. F. W.

* It may be worth while to mention some of the more recent works which illustrate points touched upon in the preceding article. See J. F. Bruch, *Weisheits-Lehre der Hebräer*, Strassb. 1851. M. Nicolas, *Des doctrines religieuses des Juifs pendant les deux siècles antérieurs à l'ère chrétienne*, Paris, 1860. C. G. Ginsburg, *The Kabbalah*, London, 1865. — C. A. Brandis, *Handb. der Gesch. d. griech.-römischen Philosophie*, 3 Theile in 5 Abth., Berl. 1835–66. A. B. Krische, *Forschungen*, etc. or, *Die theol. Lehren der griech. Denker, eine Prüfung der Darstellung Cicero's*, Götting. 1840. Norton's *Evid. of the Genuineness of the Gospels*, 2d ed. vol. iii. (Bost. 1848). L. F. A. Maury, *Hist. des religions de la Grèce antique*, 3 tom. Paris, 1857–59. Sir Alex. Grant, *The Ancient Stoics*, in *Oxford Essays* for 1858, pp. 80–123. Id. *The Ethics of Aristotle, illustrated with Essays and Notes*, 2d ed., 2 vols. Lond. 1866. Zeller, *Die Entwickelung der Monotheismus bei den Griechen*, in his *Vorträge u. Abhandlungen*, Leips. 1865. W. A. Butler, *Lectures on the Hist. of Anc. Philosophy*, 2 vols. Lond. 1866. G. H. Lewes, *Hist. of Philos. from Thales to the Present Day*, 3d ed., vol. i. (Lond. 1866). Grote, *Plato and the other Companions of Sokrates*, 2d ed., 3 vols. Lond. 1867. — J. Huber, *Die Philosophie der Kirchenväter*, München, 1859. A. Stoeckl, *Gesch. d. Philos. d. patristischen Zeit*, Würzb. 1859. E. W. Möller, *Gesch. d. Kosmologie in der griech. Kirche, bis auf Origenes*, Halle, 1860. — Ueberweg's *Grundriss d. Gesch. d. Philos. von Thales bis auf d. Gegenwart*, 3e Aufl. 3 Theile, Berl. 1867–68, is not only an excellent compendium, but is very full in its references to the literature of the subject.   A.

PHIN′EES [3 syl.] (Φινεές; [1 Esdr. viii. 2, Vat. Φεινεες; 1 Macc., Alex. Φινεως:] *Phineas*). 1. The son of Eleazar son of Aaron, the great hero of the Jewish priesthood (1 Esdr. v. 5, viii. 2, 29: [a] 2 Esdr. i. 2b; Ecclus. xlv. 23; 1 Macc. ii. 26).

2. Phinehas the son of Eli, 2 Esdr. i. 2a: but the insertion of the name in the genealogy of Ezra (in this place only) is evidently an error, since Ezra belonged to the line of Eleazar, and Eli to that of Ithamar. It probably arose from a confusion of the name with that of the great Phinehas, who was Ezra's forefather.

3. [Vat. Φεινεες.] A priest or Levite of the time of Ezra, father of Eleazar (1 Esdr. viii. 63).

4. (Φινοί: *Sinone*.) 1 Esdr. v. 31.   [PASEAH, 2.]   G.

PHIN′EHAS (פִּינְחָס, *i. e.* Pinechas [*oracle-mouth, utterance*, Fürst; *brazen mouth*, Ges.]:

---

[a] Here the LXX. [Vat.] has Φορος [but Rom. Alex Φινεές].

[Rom. Alex.] Φινεές; but [Vat.] once in Pent. and uniformly elsewhere, Φεινεές; Jos. Φινεέσης: *Phinees*). Son of Eleazar and grandson of Aaron (Ex. vi. 25). His mother is recorded as one of the daughters of Putiel, an unknown person, who is identified by the Rabbis with Jethro the Midianite (*Targ. Pseudojon.* on Ex. vi. 25; Wagenseil's *Sota*, viii. 6). Phinehas is memorable for having while quite a youth, by his zeal and energy at the critical moment of the licentious idolatry of Shittim, appeased the divine wrath and put a stop to the plague which was destroying the nation (Num. xxv. 7). For this he was rewarded by the special approbation of Jehovah, and by a promise that the priesthood should remain in his family forever (10–13). This seems to have raised him at once to a very high position in the nation, and he was appointed to accompany as priest the expedition by which the Midianites were destroyed (xxxi. 6). Many years later he also headed the party who were despatched from Shiloh to remonstrate against the Altar which the trans-Jordanic tribes were reported to have built near Jordan (Josh. xxii. 13–32). In the partition of the country he received an allotment of his own — a hill on Mount Ephraim which bore his name — Gibeath-Pinechas. Here his father was buried (Josh. xxiv. 33).

During the life of Phinehas he appears to have been the chief of the great family of the Korahites or Korhites who guarded the entrances to the sacred tent and the whole of the sacred camp (1 Chr. ix. 20). After Eleazar's death he became high-priest — the third of the series. In this capacity he is introduced as giving the oracle to the nation during the struggle with the Benjamites on the matter of Gibeah (Judg. xx. 28). Where the Ark and Tabernacle were stationed at that time is not clear. From ver. 1 we should infer that they were at Mizpeh, while from vv. 18, 26, it seems equally probable that they were at Bethel (which is also the statement of Josephus, *Ant.* v. 2, § 11). Or the Hebrew words in these latter verses may mean, not Bethel the town, but, as they are rendered in the A. V., "house of God," and refer to the Tabernacle at Shiloh. But wherever the Ark may have been, there was the aged priest "standing before it," and the oracle which he delivered was one which must have been fully in accordance with his own vehement temper, "Shall we go out to battle . . . or shall we cease?" And the answer was, "Go up: for to-morrow I will deliver them into your hand."

The memory of this champion of Jehovah was very dear to the Jews. The narrative of the Pentateuch presents him as the type of an ardent and devoted priest. The numerous references to him in the later literature all adopt the same tone. He is commemorated in one of the Psalms (cvi. 30, 31) in the identical phrase which is consecrated forever by its use in reference to the great act of faith of Abraham; a phrase which perhaps more than any other in the Bible binds together the old and new dispensations — "that was *counted to him for righteousness* unto all generations for-evermore" (comp. Gen. xv. 6; Rom. iv. 3). The "covenant" made with him is put into the same rank for dignity and certainty with that by which the throne was assured to King David (Ecclus. xlv. 25). The zeal of Mattathias the Maccabee is sufficiently praised by a comparison with that of "Phinees against Zambri the son of Salom" (1 Macc. ii. 26). The priests who returned from the

Captivity are enrolled in the official lists as the sons of Phinehas (Ezr. viii. 2; 1 Esdr. v. 5). In the *Seder Olam* (ch. xx.) he is identified with "the Prophet" of Judg. vi. 8.

Josephus (*Ant.* iv. 6, § 12), out of the venerable traditions which he uses with such excellent effect, adds to the narrative of the Pentateuch a statement that "so great was his courage and so remarkable his bodily strength, that he would never relinquish any undertaking, however difficult and dangerous, without gaining a complete victory." The later Jews are fond of comparing him to Elijah, if indeed they do not regard them as one and the same individual (see the quotations in Meyer, *Chron. Hebr.* p. 845; Fabricius, *Codex pseudepig.* p. 894, *note*). In the Targum Pseudo-jonathan of Num. xxv. the slaughter of Zimri and Cozbi is accompanied by twelve miracles, and the covenant made with Phinehas is expanded into a promise, that he shall be "the angel of the covenant, shall live forever, and shall proclaim redemption at the end of the world." His Midianite origin (already noticed) is brought forward as adding greater lustre to his zeal against Midian, and enhancing his glorious destiny.

The verse which closes the book of Joshua is ascribed to Phinehas, as the description of the death of Moses at the end of Deuteronomy is to Joshua (*Baba Bathra*, in Fabricius, p. 893). He is also reported to be the author of a work on sacred names (*ibid.*), which however is so rare that Fabricius had never seen it.

The succession of the posterity of Phinehas in the high-priesthood was interrupted when Eli, of the race of Ithamar, was priest; but it was resumed in the person of Zadok, and continued in the same line to the destruction of Jerusalem. [HIGH-PRIEST, vol. ii. p. 1070 ff.] One of the members of the family — Manasseh son of Johanan, and brother of Jaddua — went over to the Samaritans, and they still boast that they preserve the succession (see their Letter to Scaliger, in Eichhorn's *Repertorium*, xiii. 262).

The tomb of Phinehas, a place of great resort to both Jews and Samaritans, is shown at *Awertah*, four miles S. E. of *Nablus*. It stands in the centre of the village, inclosed within a little area or compound, which is overshadowed by the thickly-trellised foliage of an ancient vine. A small mosque joins the wall of the compound. Outside the village, on the next hill, is a larger inclosure, containing the tomb of Eleazar, and a cave ascribed to Elijah, overshadowed by two venerable terebinth trees, surrounded by arcades, and forming a retired and truly charming spot. The local tradition asserts that *Awertah* and its neighborhood are the "Hill of Phinehas."

In the Apocryphal Books his name is given as PHINEES.

2. [Vat. Φεινεες.] Second son of Eli (1 Sam. i. 3, ii. 34, iv. 4, 11, 17, 19, xiv. 3). He was not of the same line as his illustrious and devoted namesake, but of the family of Ithamar. [ELI.] Phinehas was killed with his brother by the Philistines when the ark was captured. He had two sons, Ahitub, the eldest — whose sons Ahijah and Ahimelech were high-priests at Shiloh and Nob in the time of Saul (xiv. 3) — and Ichabod. He is introduced, apparently by mistake, in the genealogy of Ezra in 2 Esdr. i. 2 a. [PHINEES, 2.]

3. [Vat. Φεινεες.] A Levite of Ezra's time (Ezr. viii. 33), unless the meaning be that Eleazar was of the family of the great Phinehas. In the parallel passage of 1 Esdr. he is called PHINEES.

G.

PHI'SON (Φεισῶν; Alex. Φισων: Phison). The Greek form of the name PISON (Ecclus. xxiv. 25).

PHLE'GON (Φλέγων [burning]: Phlegon). A Christian at Rome whom St. Paul salutes (Rom. xvi. 14). Pseudo-Hippolytus (De LXX. Apostolis) makes him one of the seventy disciples and bishop of Marathon. He is said to have suffered martyrdom on April 8th (Martyrologium Romanum, apud Estium), on which day he is commemorated in the calendar of the Byzantine Church.

W. T. B.

PHŒ'BE [A. V. PHEBE] (Φοίβη [shining, bright]: Phœbe), the first, and one of the most important, of the Christian persons the detailed mention of whom fills nearly all the last chapter of the Epistle to the Romans. What is said of her (Rom. xvi. 1, 2) is worthy of especial notice, because of its bearing on the question of the deaconesses of the Apostolic Church. On this point we have to observe, (1) that the term διάκονος, here applied to her, though not in itself necessarily an official term, is the term which would be applied to her, if it were meant to be official; (2) that this term is applied in the Apostolical Constitutions to women who ministered officially, the deaconess being called ἡ διάκονος, as the deacon is called ὁ διάκονος; (3) that it is now generally admitted that in 1 Tim. iii. 11, St. Paul applies it so himself; (4) that in the passage before us Phœbe is called the διάκονος of a particular church, which seems to imply a specific appointment; (5) that the Church of CENCHREÆ, to which she belonged, could only have been a small church: whence we may draw a fair conclusion as to what was customary, in the matter of such female ministration, in the larger churches; (6) that, whatever her errand to Rome might be, the independent manner of her going there seems to imply (especially when we consider the secluded habits of Greek women) not only that she was a widow or a woman of mature age, but that she was acting officially; (7) that she had already been of great service to St. Paul and others (προστάτις πολλῶν, καὶ ἐμοῦ αὐτοῦ), either by her wealth or her energy, or both; a statement which closely corresponds with the description of the qualifications of the enrolled widows in 1 Tim. v. 10; (8) that the duty which we here see Phœbe discharging implies a personal character worthy of confidence and respect. [DEACONESS.]

J. S. H.

PHŒNI'CE, PHŒNICIA (Φοινίκη [see below]: Phœnice: rarely in Latin, Phœnicia: see Facciolati's Lexicon, s. v.), a tract of country, of which Tyre and Sidon were the principal cities, to the north of Palestine, along the coast of the Mediterranean Sea; bounded by that sea on the west, and by the mountain range of Lebanon on the east. The name was not the one by which its native inhabitants called it, but was given to it by the Greeks; probably from the palm-tree, φοῖνιξ, with which it may then have abounded; just as the name Brazil was given by Europeans to a large

territory in South America, from the Brazil-wood which a part of it supplied to Europe. The palm-tree is seen, as an emblem, on some coins of Aradus, Tyre, and Sidon; and there are now several palm-trees within the circuit of modern Tyre, and along the coast at various points; but the tree is not at the present day one of the characteristic features of the country. The native name of Phœnicia was Kenaan (Canaan) or Knâ, signifying lowland, so named in contrast to the adjoining Aram, i. e. Highland; the Hebrew name of Syria. The name Kenaan is preserved on a coin of Laodicea, of the time of Antiochus Epiphanes, whereon Laodicea is styled "a mother city in Canaan," לאדכא בכנען אם. And Knâ or Chnâ (Χνᾶ) is mentioned distinctly by Herodian [a] the grammarian, as the old name of Phœnicia. (See Περὶ μονήρους λέξεως, under the word 'Αθηρᾶ.) Hence, as Phœnicians or Canaanites were the most powerful of all tribes in Palestine at the time of its invasion by Joshua, the Israelites, in speaking of their own territory as it was before the conquest, called it "the land of Canaan."

The length of coast to which the name Phœnicia was applied varied at different times, and may be regarded under different aspects before and after the loss of its independence. 1. What may be termed Phœnicia Proper was a narrow undulating plain, extending from the pass of Rás el-Beyád or Abyad, the "Promontorium Album" of the ancients, about six miles south of Tyre, to the Nahr el-Auly, the ancient Bostrenus, two miles north of Sidon (Robinson's Bibl. Res. ii. 473). The plain is only 28 miles in length, and, considering the great importance of Phœnicia in the world's history, this may well be added to other instances in Greece, Italy, and Palestine, which show how little the intellectual influence of a city or state has depended on the extent of its territory. Its average breadth is about a mile (Porter's Handbook for Syria, ii. 396); but near Sidon, the mountains retreat to a distance of two miles, and near Tyre to a distance of five miles (Kenrick's Phœnicia, p. 19). The whole of Phœnicia, thus understood, is called by Josephus (Ant. v. 3, § 1) the great plain of the city of Sidon, τὸ μέγα πεδίον Σιδῶνος πόλεως. In it, near its northern extremity, was situated Sidon, in the north latitude of 33° 34' 05''; and scarcely more than 17 geographical miles to the south was Tyre, in the latitude of 33° 17' (Admiral Smyth's Mediterranean, p. 469): so that in a straight line those two renowned cities were less than 20 English miles distant from each other. Zarephath, the Sarepta of the New Testament, was situated between them, eight miles south of Sidon, to which it belonged (1 K. xvii. 9; Obad. 20; Luke iv. 26). 2. A still longer district, which afterwards became fairly entitled to the name of Phœnicia, extended up the coast to a point marked by the island of Aradus, and by Antaradus towards the north; the southern boundary remaining the same as in Phœnicia Proper. Phœnicia, thus defined, is estimated by Mr. Grote (History of Greece, iii. 354) to have been about 190 miles in length; while its breadth, between Lebanon and the sea,

---

[a] Through mistake, a sentence of Herodian, τὸ Χνᾶ, οὕτω γὰρ πρότερον ἡ Φοινίκη ἐκαλεῖτο, is printed in the Fragmenta Historicorum Græcorum, p. 17 (Paris, 1841), as an extract from Hecatæus of Miletus, and is usually quoted as from Hecatæus. It is, however, in fact, merely the assertion of the grammarian himself; though it is most probable that he had in his mind the usage of Hecatæus.

never exceeded 20 miles, and was generally much less. This estimate is most reasonable, allowing for the bends of the coast; as the direct difference in latitude between Tyre and Antaradus (Tortosa) is equivalent to 106 English miles; and six miles to the south of Tyre, as already mentioned, intervene before the beginning of the pass of *Rás el-Abyàd.* The claim of the whole of this district to the name of Phœnicia rests on the probable fact, that the whole of it, to the north of the great plain of Sidon, was occupied by Phœnician colonists; not to mention that there seems to have been some kind of political connection, however loose, between all the inhabitants (Diodorus, xvi. 41). Scarcely 16 geographical miles farther north than Sidon was Berytus; with a roadstead so well suited for the purposes of modern navigation that, under the modern name of *Beirût,* it has eclipsed both Sidon and Tyre as an emporium for Syria. Whether this Berytus was identical with the Beróthah and Berothai of Ezekiel xlvii. 16, and of 2 Sam. viii. 8, is a disputed point. [BEROTHAH.] Still farther north was Byblus, the Gebal of the Bible (Ez. xxvii. 9), inhabited by seamen and calkers. Its inhabitants are supposed to be alluded to in the word *Giblim,* translated "stone-squarers" in the authorized version of 1 K. v. 18 (32). It still retains in Arabic the kindred name of *Jebeil.* Then came Tripolis (now *Tárábulus*), said to have been founded by colonists from Tyre, Sidon, and Aradus, with three distinct towns, each a furlong apart from one another, each with its own walls, and each named from the city which supplied its colonists. General meetings of the Phœnicians seem to have been held at Tripolis (Diod. xvi. 41), as if a certain local jealousy had prevented the selection for this purpose of Tyre, Sidon, or Aradus. And lastly, towards the extreme point north was Aradus itself, the Arvad of Gen. x. 18, and Ez. xxvii. 8; situated, like Tyre, on a small island near the mainland, and founded by exiles from Sidon. The whole of Phœnicia Proper is well watered by various streams from the adjoining hills: of these the two largest are the *Khàsimiyeh,* a few miles north of Tyre — the ancient name of which, strange to say, is not certain, though it is conjectured to have been the Leontes — and the Bostrenus, already mentioned, north of Sidon. The soil is fertile, although now generally ill-cultivated; but in the neighborhood of Sidon there are rich gardens and orchards; "and here," says Mr. Porter, "are oranges, lemons, figs, almonds, plums, apricots, peaches, pomegranates, pears, and bananas, all growing luxuriantly, and forming a forest of finely-tinted foliage" (*Handbook for Syria,* ii. 398). The havens of Tyre and Sidon afforded water of sufficient depth for all the requirements of ancient navigation, and the neighboring range of the Lebanon, in its extensive forests, furnished what then seemed a nearly inexhaustible supply of timber for ship-building. To the north of Bostrenus, between that river and *Beirût,* lies the only bleak and barren part of Phœnicia. It is crossed by the ancient Tamyras or Damuras, the modern *Nahr ed-Dàmûr.* From *Beirût,* the plains are again fertile. The principal streams[a] are the Lycus, now the *Nahr el-Kelb,* not far north from *Beirût;* the Adonis, now the

Nahr Ibrahim, about five miles south of Gebal; and the Eleutherus, now the *Nahr el-Kebir,* in the bend between Tripolis and Antaradus.

In reference to the period when the Phœnicians had lost their independence, scarcely any two Greek and Roman writers give precisely the same geographical boundaries to Phœnicia. Herodotus uses an expression which seems to imply that he regarded its northern extremity as corresponding with the Myriandrian Bay, or Bay of Issus (iv. 38). It is doubtful where exactly he conceived it to terminate at the south (iii. 5). Ptolemy is distinct in making the river Eleutherus the boundary, on the north, and the river Chorseus, on the south. The Chorseus is a small stream or torrent, south of Mount Carmel and of the small Canaanitish city Dor, the inhabitants of which the tribe of Manasseh was confessedly unable to drive out (Judg. i. 27). This southern line of Ptolemy coincides very closely with the southern boundary of Pliny the Elder, who includes Dor in Phœnicia, though the southern boundary specified by him is a stream called Crocodilôn, now *Nahr Zurka,* about two miles to the north of Cæsarea. Pliny's northern boundary, however, is different, as he makes it include Antaradus. Again, the geographer Strabo, who was contemporary with the beginning of the Christian era, differs from Herodotus, Ptolemy, and Pliny, by representing Phœnicia as the district between Orthosia and Pelusium (xvi. 21), which would make it include not only Mount Carmel, but likewise Cæsarea, Joppa, and the whole coast of the Philistines.

In the Old Testament, the word Phœnicia does not occur, as might be expected from its being a Greek name. In the Apocrypha, it is not defined, though spoken of as being, with Cœle-Syria, under one military commander (2 Macc. iii. 5, 8, viii. 8, x. 11; 3 Macc. iii. 15). In the New Testament, the word occurs only in three passages, Acts xi. 19, xv. 3, xxi. 2;[b] and not one of these affords a clew as to how far the writer deemed Phœnicia to extend. On the other hand, Josephus possibly agreed with Strabo; for he expressly says that Cæsarea is situated in Phœnicia (*Ant.* xv. 9, § 6); and although he never makes a similar statement respecting Joppa, yet he speaks, in one passage, of the coast of Syria, Phœnicia, and Egypt, as if Syria and Phœnicia exhausted the line of coast on the Mediterranean Sea to the north of Egypt (*B. J.* iii. 9, § 2).   E. T.

PHŒNICIANS. The name of the race who in earliest recorded history inhabited Phœnicia, and who were the great maritime and commercial people of the ancient world. For many centuries they bore somewhat of the same relation to other nations which the Dutch bore, though less exclusively, to the rest of Europe in the 17th century. They were, moreover, preëminent in colonization as well as in trade; and in their settlement of Carthage, producing the greatest general of antiquity, they proved the most formidable of all antagonists to Rome in its progress to universal empire. A complete history, therefore, of the Phœnicians would occupy a large extent of ground which would be foreign to the objects of this Dictionary. Still some notice is desirable of such an important people, who were in one quarter the

---

a • See notices of these streams by Dr. T. Laurie, formerly a missionary in Syria, *Bibl. Sacra* for July, 1869, p. 568 ff.   H.

b • Our Lord in the course of his Peræan ministry

(Matt. xv. 21; Mark vii. 24) on one occasion, at least entered Phœnicia and probably passed through Sidon itself (Mark, vii. 31, where the approved reading is διὰ Σιδῶνος).   H

nearest neighbors of the Israelites, and indirectly influenced their history in various ways. Without dwelling on matters which belong more strictly to the articles TYRE and SIDON, it may be proper to touch on certain points connected with the language, race, trade, and religion of the Phœnicians, which may tend to throw light on Biblical history and literature. The communication of letters by the Phœnicians to the European nations will likewise deserve notice.

I. The Phœnician language belonged to that family of languages which, by a name not altogether free from objection, but now generally adopted, is called " Semitic." *a* Under this name are included three distinct branches: 1st. Arabic, to which belongs Æthiopian as an offshoot of the Southern Arabic or Himyaritic. 2dly. Aramaic, the vernacular language of Palestine at the time of Christ, in which the few original words of Christ which have been preserved in writing appear to have been spoken (Matt. xxvii. 46; Mark v. 41; and mark especially Matt. xvi. 18, which is not fully significant either in Greek or Hebrew). Aramaic, as used in Christian literature, is called Syriac, and as used in the writings of the Jews, has been very generally called Chaldee. 3dly. Hebrew, in which by far the greatest part of the Old Testament was composed. Now one of the most interesting points to the Biblical student, connected with Phœnician, is, that it does not belong to either of the two first branches, but to the third; and that it is in fact so closely allied to Hebrew, that Phœnician and Hebrew, though different dialects, may practically be regarded as the same language. This may be shown in the following way: 1st, in passages which have been frequently quoted (see especially Gesenius's *Monumenta Scripturæ Linguæque Phœnicia*, p. 231), testimony is borne to the kinship of the two languages by Augustine and Jerome, in whose time Phœnician or Carthaginian was still a living language. Jerome, who was a good Hebrew scholar, after mentioning, in his Commentaries on Jeremiah, lib. v. c. 25, that Carthage was a Phœnician colony, proceeds to state — " Unde et Pœni sermone corrupto quasi Phœni appellantur, quorum lingua Hebrææ linguæ magnâ ex parte confinis est." And Augustine, who was a native of Africa, and a bishop there, of Hippo, a Tyrian colony, has left on record a similar statement several times. In one passage he says of the two languages, " Istæ linguæ non multum inter se differunt " (*Quæstiones in Heptateuchum*, vii. 16). In another passage he says, " Cognatæ sunt istæ linguæ et vicinæ, Hebræa, et Punica, et Syra " (*In Joann. Tract.* 15). Again, on Gen. xviii. 9, he says of a certain mode of speaking (Gen. viii. 9), " Locutio est, quam propterea Hebræam puto, quia et Punicæ linguæ familiarissima est, in quâ multa invenimus Hebræis verbis consonantia " (lib. i. locut. 24). And on another occasion, remarking on the word Messias, he says, " quod verbum Pun-

icæ linguæ consonum est, *sicut alia Hebræa multa et pæne omnia* " (*Contra literas Petiliani*, ii. c. 104). 2dly. These statements are fully confirmed by a passage of Carthaginian preserved in the *Pœnulus* of Plautus, act v. scene 1, and accompanied by a Latin translation as part of the play. There is no doubt that the Carthaginians and the Phœnicians were the same race: and the Carthaginian extract is undeniably intelligible through Hebrew to Hebrew scholars (see Bochart's *Canaan*; and especially Gesenius's *Monumenta Phœnicia*, pp. 357–382, where the passage is translated with notes, and full justice is done to the previous translation of Bochart). 3dly. The close kinship of the two languages is, moreover, strikingly confirmed by very many Phœnician and Carthaginian names of places and persons, which, destitute of meaning in Greek and Latin, through which languages they have become widely known, and having sometimes in those languages occasioned false etymologies, become really significant in Hebrew. Thus through Hebrew it is known that Tyre, as *Tsôr*, signifies " a rock," referring doubtless to the rocky island on which the city was situated: that Sidon, as *Tzidôn*, means " Fishing " or " Fishery," which was probably the occupation of its first settlers: that Carthage, or, as it was originally called, " Carthada," means " New Town," or " Newton: " and that Byrsa, which, as a Greek name, suggested the etymological mythus of the Bull's Hide (*Æneid*, i. 366–67), was simply the citadel of Carthage — *Carthaginis arcem*, as Virgil accurately termed it: the Carthaginian name of it, softened by the Greeks into Βύρσα, being merely the Hebrew word Botsrah, " citadel; " identical with the word called Bozrah in the English Version of Isaiah lxiii. 1. Again, through Hebrew, the names of celebrated Carthaginians, though sometimes disfigured by Greek and Roman writers, acquire a meaning. Thus Dido is found to belong to the same root as David,*b* " beloved; " meaning " his love," or " delight;" *i. e.* the love or delight either of Baal or of her husband: Hasdrubal is the man " whose help Baal is: " Hamilcar the man whom the god " Milcar graciously granted " (comp. Hananeel; Θεόδωρος): and, with the substitution of Baal for El or God, the name of the renowned Hannibal is found to be identical in form and meaning with the name of Hanniel, who is mentioned in Num. xxxiv. 23 as the prince of the tribe of Manasseh: Hanniel meaning the grace of God, and Hannibal the grace of Baal. 4thly. The same conclusion arises from the examination of Phœnician inscriptions, preserved to the present day: all of which can be interpreted, with more or less certainty, through Hebrew. Such inscriptions are of three kinds: 1st, on gems and seals; 2dly, on coins of the Phœnicians and of their colonies; 3dly, on stone. The first class are few, unimportant, and for the most part of uncertain origin. The oldest known coins with Phœnician words belong to Tar-

---

a So called from the descendants of Shem (Gen. x. 21–29); nearly all of whom, as represented by nations, are known to have spoken cognate languages. There have been hitherto two objections to the name: 1st. That the language of the Elamites and Assyrians (see ver. 22) belonged to a different family. 2dly. That the Phœnicians, as Canaanites, are derived from Ham (Gen. x. 6). If the recent interpretations of Assyrian inscriptions are admitted to prove the identity of Assyrian with Aramaic or Syrian, the objection to the word "Semitic" nearly disappears. Mr. Max Müller,

a high authority on such a point, regards it as certain, that the inscriptions of Nineveh, as well as of Babylon, are Semitic. — *Lectures on the Science of Language*, p. 265.

b Movers and Fürst, supported by the *Etymologicum Magnum*, adopt " nedîdâ," or " nedîdâh," as the etymology of Dido, in the sense of " travel-tost," or " wanderer." Although a possible derivation, this seems less probable in itself, and less countenanced by Hebrew analogies.

was and other Cilician cities, and were struck in the period of the Persian domination. But coins are likewise in existence of Tyre, Sidon, and other cities of Phœnicia; though all such are of later date, and belong to the period either of the Seleucidæ, or of the Romans. Moreover, other coins have been found belonging to cities in Sicily, Sardinia, Africa, and Spain. The inscriptions on stone are either of a public or a private character. The former are comparatively few in number, but relate to various subjects: such, for example, as the dedication of a temple, or the commemoration of a Numidian victory over the Romans. The private inscriptions were either in the nature of votive tablets erected as testimonials of gratitude to some deity, or were sepulchral memorials engraven on tombstones. Phœnician inscriptions on stone have been found not only in all the countries last mentioned, except Spain, but likewise in the island of Cyprus near Citium, in Malta, at Athens, at Marseilles, and at Sidon.ᵃ

II. Concerning the original race to which the Phœnicians belonged, nothing can be known with certainty, because they are found already established along the Mediterranean Sea at the earliest dawn of authentic history, and for centuries afterwards there is no record of their origin. According to Herodotus (vii. 89), they said of themselves in his time that they came in days of old from the shores of the Red Sea — and in this there would be nothing in the slightest degree improbable, as they spoke a language cognate to that of the Arabians, who inhabited the east coast of that sea; and both Hebrew and Arabic, as well as Aramaic, are seemingly derived from some one Semitic language now lost. Still neither the truth nor the falsehood of the tradition can now be proved; for language, although affording strong presumptions of race, is not conclusive on the point, as is shown by the language at present spoken by the descendants of the Normans in France. But there is one point respecting their race which can be proved to be in the highest degree probable, and which has peculiar interest as bearing on the Jews, namely, that the Phœnicians were of the same race as the Canaanites. This remarkable fact, which, taken in connection with the language of the Phœnicians, leads to some interesting results, is rendered probable by the following circumstances: 1st. The native name of Phœnicia, as already pointed out, was Canaan, a name signifying "lowland" [PHŒNICIA]. This was well given to the narrow slip of plain between the Lebanon and the Mediterranean Sea, in contrast to the elevated mountain range adjoining; but it would have been inappropriate to that part of Palestine conquered by the Israelites, which was undoubtedly a hill-country (see Movers, Das Phönizische Alterthum, Theil 1, p. 5); so that, when it is known that the Israelites at the time of their invasion found in Palestine a powerful tribe called the Canaanites, and from them called Palestine the land of Canaan, it is obviously suggested that the Canaanites came originally from the neighboring plain, called Canaan, along the sea-coast. 2dly. This is further confirmed through the name in Africa whereby the Carthaginian Phœnicians called themselves, as attested by Augustine, who

states that the peasants in his part of Africa, if asked of what race they were, would answer, in Punic or Phœnician, "Canaanites." "Interrogati rustici nostri quid sint, Punicé respondentes, Canani, corruptâ scilicet sicut in talibus unâ litterâ (accurate enim dicere debebant Chanani) quid aliud respondent quam Chananæi" (Opera Omnia, iv. 1235; Exposit. Epist. ad Rom. § 13). 3dly. The conclusion thus suggested is strongly supported by the tradition that the names of persons and places in the land of Canaan — not only when the Israelites invaded it, but likewise previously, when "there were yet but a few of them," and Abraham is said to have visited it — were Phœnician or Hebrew: such, for example, as Abimelek, "Father of the king" (Gen. xx. 2); Melchizedek, "King of righteousness" (xiv. 18); Kirjath-sepher, "city of the book" (Josh. xv. 15).

As this obviously leads to the conclusion that the Hebrews adopted Phœnician as their own language, or, in other words, that what is called the Hebrew language was in fact "the language of Canaan," as a prophet called it (Is. xix. 18), and this not merely poetically, but literally and in philological truth; and as this is repugnant to some preconceived notions respecting the peculiar people, the question arises whether the Israelites might not have translated Canaanitish names into Hebrew. On this hypothesis the names now existing in the Bible for persons and places in the land of Canaan would not be the original names, but merely the translations of those names. The answer to this question is, 1st. That there is not the slightest direct mention, nor any indirect trace, in the Bible, of any such translation. 2dly. That it is contrary to the analogy of the ordinary Hebrew practice in other cases; as, for example, in reference to the names of the Assyrian monarchs (perhaps of a foreign dynasty) Pul, Tiglath-Pileser, Sennacherib, or of the Persian monarchs Darius, Ahasuerus, Artaxerxes, which remain unintelligible in Hebrew, and can only be understood through other Oriental languages. 3dly. That there is an absolute silence in the Bible as to there having been any difference whatever in language between the Israelites and the Canaanites, although in other cases where a difference existed, that difference is somewhere alluded to, as in the case of the Egyptians (Ps. lxxxi. 5, cxiv. 1), the Assyrians (Is. xxxvi. 11), and the Chaldees (Jer. v. 15). Yet in the case of the Canaanites there was stronger reason for alluding to it; and without some allusion to it, if it had existed, the narration of the conquest of Canaan under the leadership of Joshua would have been singularly imperfect.

It remains to be added on this point, that although the previous language of the Hebrews must be mainly a matter for conjecture only, yet it is most in accordance with the Pentateuch to suppose that they spoke originally Aramaic. They came through Abraham, according to their traditions, from Ur of the Chaldees in Mesopotamia, where Aramaic at a later period is known to have been spoken; they are instructed in Deuteronomy to say that an Aramæan (Syrian) ready to perish was their father (xxvi. 5); and the two earliest words of Aramaic contained in the Bible, Yegar sahadû-

---

has done more than any one scholar since Buxtorf to facilitate the study of Hebrew. His opinion on the relation of Phœnician to Hebrew is: "Omnino hoc tenendum est, pleræque et pene omn'a cum Hebræis

thō, are, in the Book of Genesis, put into the mouth of Laban, the son of Abraham's brother, and first cousin of Isaac (xxxi. 47).[a]

III. In regard to Phœnician trade, as connected with the Israelites, the following points are worthy of notice. 1. Up to the time of David, not one of the twelve tribes seems to have possessed a single harbor on the sea-coast: it was impossible therefore that they could become a commercial people. It is true that according to Judg. i. 31, combined with Josh. xix. 26, Accho or Acre, with its excellent harbor, had been assigned to the tribe of Asher; but from the same passage in Judges it seems certain that the tribe of Asher did not really obtain possession of Acre, which continued to be held by the Canaanites. However wistfully, therefore, the Israelites might regard the wealth accruing to their neighbors the Phœnicians from trade, to vie with them in this respect was out of the question. But from the time that David had conquered Edom, an opening for trade was afforded to the Israelites. The command of Ezion-geber near Elath, in the land of Edom, enabled them to engage in the navigation of the Red Sea. As they were novices, however, at sailing, as the navigation of the Red Sea, owing to its currents, winds, and rocks, is dangerous even to modern sailors, and as the Phœnicians, during the period of the independence of Edom, were probably allowed to trade from Ezion-geber, it was politic in Solomon to permit the Phœnicians of Tyre to have docks, and build ships at Ezion-geber on condition that his sailors and vessels might have the benefit of their experience. The results seem to have been strikingly successful. The Jews and Phœnicians made profitable voyages to Ophir in Arabia, whence gold was imported into Judæa in large quantities; and once in three years still longer voyages were made, by vessels which may possibly have touched at Ophir, though their imports were not only gold, but likewise silver, ivory, apes, and peacocks, 1 K. x. 22. [TARSHISH.] There seems at the same time to have been a great direct trade with the Phœnicians for cedar-wood (ver. 27), and generally the wealth of the kingdom reached an unprecedented point. If the union of the tribes had been maintained, the whole sea-coast of Palestine would have afforded additional sources of revenue through trade; and perhaps even ultimately the "great plain of Sidon" itself might have formed part of the united empire. But if any possibilities of this kind existed, they were destroyed by the disastrous secession of the ten tribes; a heavy blow from which the Hebrew race has never yet recovered during a period of nearly 3000 years.[b]

2. After the division into two kingdoms, the curtain falls on any commercial relation between the Israelites and Phœnicians until a relation is brought

to notice, by no means brotherly, as in the fleets which navigated the Red Sea, nor friendly, as between buyers and sellers, but humiliating and exasperating, as between the buyers and the bought. The relation is meant which existed between the two nations when Israelites were sold as slaves by Phœnicians. It was a custom in antiquity, when one nation went to war against another, for merchants to be present in one or other of the hostile camps, in order to purchase prisoners of war as slaves. Thus at the time of the Maccabees, when a large army was sent by Lysias to invade and subdue the land of Judah, it is related that "the merchants of the country, hearing the fame of them, took silver and gold very much with servants, and came into the camp to buy the children of Israel for slaves" (1 Macc. iii. 41), and when it is related that, at the capture of Jerusalem by Antiochus Epiphanes, the enormous number of 40,000 men were slain in battle, it is added that there were "no fewer sold than slain" (2 Macc. v. 14; Credner's Joel, p. 240). Now this practice, which is thus illustrated by details at a much later period, undoubtedly prevailed in earlier times (Odyssey, xv. 427; Herod. i. 1), and is alluded to in a threatening manner against the Phœnicians by the prophets (Joel iii. 4, and Am. i. 9, 10), about 800 years before Christ.[c] The circumstances which led to this state of things may be thus explained. After the division of the two kingdoms, there is no trace of any friendly relation between the kingdom of Judah and the Phœnicians: the interest of the latter rather led them to cultivate the friendship of the kingdom of Israel; and the Israelitish king, Ahab, had a Sidonian princess as his wife (1 K. xvi. 31). Now, not improbably in consequence of these relations, when Jehoshaphat king of Judah endeavored to restore the trade of the Jews in the Red Sea, and for this purpose built large ships at Ezion-geber to go to Ophir for gold, he did not admit the Phœnicians to any participation in the venture, and when king Ahaziah, Ahab's son, asked to have a share in it, his request was distinctly refused (1 K. xxii. 48, 49). That attempt to renew the trade of the Jews in the Red Sea failed, and in the reign of Jehoram, Jehoshaphat's son, Edom revolted from Judah and established its independence; so that if the Phœnicians wished to despatch trading-vessels from Ezion-geber, Edom was the power which it was mainly their interest to conciliate, and not Judah. Under these circumstances the Phœnicians seem, not only to have purchased and to have sold again as slaves, and probably in some instances to have kidnapped inhabitants of Judah, but even to have sold them to their enemies the Edomites (Joel, Amos, as above). This was regarded with reason as a departure from the old brotherly covenant, when Hiram was a great lover

---

convenire, sive radices spectas sive verborum et formandorum et flectendorum rationem " (Mon. Phœn. p 335).

[a] It seems to be admitted by philologers that neither Hebrew, Aramaic, nor Arabic, is derived the one from the other; just as the same may be said of Italian, Spanish, and Portuguese. (See Lewis, On the Romance Languages, p. 42). It is a question, however, which of the three languages, Hebrew, Aramaic, and Arabic, is likely to resemble most the original Semitic language. Fürst, one of the best Aramaic scholars now living, is in favor of Aramaic (Lehrgebäude der Aramäischen Idiome, p. 2). But his opinion has been strongly impugned in favor of Hebrew (Bleek's Einleitung in das A. T. p. 76).

[b] After the disruption, the period of union was looked back to with endless longing.

[c] In Joel iii. 6 (Heb. iv. 6), "sons of the Ionians," i. e. of the Greeks, is the most natural translation of Benê-Yavanim. But there is a Yawan mentioned in Arabia Felix, and there is still a Yavan in Yemen: and both Cr-dner and Fürst think that, looking to Am. i. 9, an Arabian people, and not Grecians, are here alluded to. The threat, however, of selling the Phœnicians in turn to the Sabæans, "a people far off," which seems to imply that the Yawanim were not "far off," tends to make it improbable that the Yawanim were near the Sabæans, as they would have been in Arabia Felix. [See JAVAN, SONS OF, Amer. ed.]

of David, and subsequently had the most friendly commercial relations with David's son: and this may be regarded as the original foundation of the hostility of the Hebrew prophets towards Phœnician Tyre. (Is. xxiii.; Ez. xxviii.)

3. The only other notice in the Old Testament of trade between the Phœnicians and the Israelites is in the account given by the prophet Ezekiel of the trade of Tyre (xxvii. 17). While this account supplies valuable information respecting the various commercial dealings of the most illustrious of Phœnician cities [TYRE], it likewise makes direct mention of the exports to it from Palestine. These were wheat, honey (i. e. sirup of grapes), oil, and balm. The export of wheat deserves attention (concerning the other exports, see HONEY, OIL, BALM), because it shows how important it must have been to the Phœnicians to maintain friendly relations with their Hebrew neighbors, and especially with the adjoining kingdom of Israel. The wheat is called wheat of Minnith,[a] which was a town of the Ammonites, on the other side of Jordan, only once mentioned elsewhere in the Bible: and it is not certain whether Minnith was a great inland emporium, where large purchases of corn were made, or whether the wheat in its neighborhood was peculiarly good, and gave its name to all wheat of a certain fineness in quality. Still, whatever may be the correct explanation respecting Minnith, the only countries specified for exports of wheat are Judah and Israel, and it was through the territory of Israel that the wheat would be imported into Phœnicia. It is suggested by Heeren in his *Historical Researches*, ii. 117, that the fact of Palestine being thus, as it were, the granary of Phœnicia, explains in the clearest manner the lasting peace that prevailed between the two countries. He observes that with many of the other adjoining nations the Jews lived in a state of almost continual warfare; but that they never once engaged in hostilities with their nearest neighbors the Phœnicians. The fact itself is certainly worthy of special notice; and is the more remarkable as there were not wanting tempting occasions for the interference of the Phœnicians in Palestine if they had desired it. When Elijah at the brook Kishon, at the distance of not more than thirty miles in a straight line from Tyre, put to death 450 prophets of Baal (1 K. xviii. 40), we can well conceive the agitation and anger which such a deed must have produced at Tyre. And at Sidon, more especially, which was only twenty miles farther distant from the scene of slaughter, the first impulse of the inhabitants must have been to march forth at once in battle array to strengthen the hands of Jezebel, their own princess, in behalf of Baal, their Phœnician god. When again afterwards, by means of falsehood and treachery, Jehu was enabled to massacre the worshippers of Baal in the land of Israel, we cannot doubt that the intelligence was received in Tyre, Sidon, and the other cities of Phœnicia, with a similar burst of horror and indignation to that with which the news of the Massacre on St. Bartholomew's day was received in all Protestant countries: and there must have been an intense desire in the Phœnicians, if they had the power, to invade the territories of Israel without delay and inflict signal chastisement on

Jehu (2 K. x. 18–28). The fact that Israel was their granary would undoubtedly have been an element in restraining the Phœnicians, even on occasions such as these; but probably still deeper motives were likewise at work. It seems to have been part of the settled policy of the Phœnician cities to avoid attempts to make conquests on the continent of Asia. For this there were excellent reasons in the position of their small territory, which with the range of Lebanon on one side as a barrier, and the sea on the other, was easily defensible by a wealthy power having command of the sea, against second or third rate powers, but for the same reason was not well situated for offensive war on the land side. It may be added that a pacific policy was their manifest interest as a commercial nation, unless by war they were morally certain to obtain an important accession of territory, or unless a warlike policy was an absolute necessity to prevent the formidable preponderance of any one great neighbor. At last, indeed, they even carried their system of non-intervention in continental wars too far, if it would have been possible for them by any alliances in Syria and Cœle-Syria to prevent the establishment on the other side of the Lebanon of one great empire. For from that moment their ultimate doom was certain, and it was merely a question of *time* as to the arrival of the fatal hour when they would lose their independence. But too little is known of the details of their history to warrant an opinion as to whether they might at any time by any course of policy have raised up a barrier against the empire of the Assyrians or Chaldees.

IV. The religion of the Phœnicians is a subject of vast extent and considerable perplexity in details, but of its general features as bearing upon the religion of the Hebrews there can be no doubt. As opposed to Monotheism, it was a Pantheistical personification of the forces of nature, and in its most philosophical shadowing forth of the Supreme powers, it may be said to have represented the male and female principles of production. In its popular form, it was especially a worship of the sun, moon, and five planets, or, as it might have been expressed according to ancient notions, of the seven planets — the most beautiful, and perhaps the most natural, form of idolatry ever presented to the human imagination. These planets, however, were not regarded as lifeless globes of matter, obedient to physical laws, but as intelligent animated powers, influencing the human will, and controlling human destinies. An account of the different Phœnician gods named in the Bible will be found elsewhere [see BAAL, ASHTAROTH, ASHERAH, etc.]; but it will be proper here to point out certain effects which the circumstance of their being worshipped in Phœnicia produced upon the Hebrews.

1. In the first place, their worship was a constant temptation to Polytheism and idolatry. It is the general tendency of trade, by making merchants acquainted with different countries and various modes of thought, to enlarge the mind, to promote the increase of knowledge, and, in addition, by the wealth which it diffuses, to afford opportunities in various ways for intellectual culture. It can scarcely be doubted that, owing to these circumstances, the Phœnicians, as a great commercial

---

[a] In ver. 17 the word "Pannag" occurs, which is not found elsewhere. Opinions are divided as to whether it is the name of a place, like Minnith, or the name of an article of food; "sweet cake," for example.

Perhaps no one can really do more than to make a guess on the point. The evidence for each meaning is inconclusive.

people, were more generally intelligent, and, as we should now say, civilized, than the inland agricultural population of Palestine. When the simple-minded Jews, therefore, came in contact with a people more versatile and, apparently, more enlightened than themselves, but who nevertheless, either in a philosophical or in a popular form, admitted a system of Polytheism, an influence would be exerted on Jewish minds, tending to make them regard their exclusive devotion to their own one God, Jehovah, however transcendant his attributes, as unsocial and morose. It is in some such way that we must account for the astonishing fact that Solomon himself, the wisest of the Hebrew race, to whom Jehovah is expressly stated to have appeared twice — once, not long after his marriage with an Egyptian princess, on the night after his sacrificing 1,000 burnt offerings on the high place of Gibeon, and the second time, after the consecration of the Temple — should have been so far beguiled by his wives in his old age as to become a Polytheist, worshipping, among other deities, the Phœnician or Sidonian goddess Ashtaroth (1 K. iii. 1–5, ix. 2, xi. 1–5). This is not for a moment to be so interpreted, as if he ever ceased to worship Jehovah, to whom he had erected the magnificent Temple, which in history is so generally connected with Solomon's name. Probably, according to his own erroneous conceptions, he never ceased to regard himself as a loyal worshipper of Jehovah, but he at the same time deemed this not incompatible with sacrificing at the altars of other gods likewise. Still the fact remains, that Solomon, who by his Temple in its ultimate results did so much for establishing the doctrine of one only God, died himself a practical Polytheist. And if this was the case with him, Polytheism in other sovereigns of inferior excellence can excite no surprise. With such an example before him, it is no wonder that Ahab, an essentially bad man, should after his marriage with a Sidonian princess not only openly tolerate, but encourage, the worship of Baal; though it is to be remembered even in him, that he did not disavow the authority of Jehovah, but, when rebuked by his great antagonist Elijah, he rent his clothes, and put sackcloth on his flesh, and showed other signs of contrition evidently deemed sincere (1 K. xvi. 31, xxi. 27–29). And it is to be observed generally that although, before the reformation of Josiah (2 K. xxiii.), Polytheism prevailed in Judah as well as Israel, yet it seems to have been more intense and universal in Israel, as might have been expected from its greater proximity to Phœnicia: and Israel is sometimes spoken of as if it had set the bad example to Judah (2 K. xvii. 19; Jer. iii. 8): though, considering the example of Solomon, this cannot be accepted as a strict historical statement.

2. The Phœnician religion was likewise in other respects deleterious to the inhabitants of Palestine, being in some points essentially demoralizing. For example, it sanctioned the dreadful superstition of burning children as sacrifices to a Phœnician god. "They have built also," says Jeremiah, in the name of Jehovah (xix. 5), "the high places of Baal, to burn their sons with fire for burnt offerings unto Baal, which I commanded not, nor spake it, neither

came it into my mind" (comp. Jer. xxxii. 35). This horrible custom was probably in its origin founded on the idea of sacrificing to a god what was best and most valuable in the eyes of the suppliant; [a] but it could not exist without having a tendency to stifle natural feelings of affection, and to harden the heart. It could scarcely have been first adopted otherwise than in the infancy of the Phœnician race; but grown-up men and grown-up nations, with their moral feelings in other respects cultivated, are often the slaves in particular points of an early-implanted superstition, and it is worthy of note that, more than 250 years after the death of Jeremiah, the Carthaginians, when their city was besieged by Agathocles, offered as burnt sacrifices to the planet Saturn, at the public expense, 200 boys of the highest aristocracy; and, subsequently, when they had obtained a victory, sacrificed the most beautiful captives in the like manner (Diod. xx. 14, 65). If such things were possible among the Carthaginians at a period so much later, it is easily conceivable how common the practice of sacrificing children may have been at the time of Jeremiah among the Phœnicians generally: and if this were so, it would have been certain to prevail among the Israelites who worshipped the same Phœnician gods; especially as, owing to the intermarriages of their forefathers with Canaanites, there were probably few Israelites who may not have had some Phœnician blood in their veins (Judg. iii. 5). Again, parts of the Phœnician religion, especially the worship of Astarte, tended to encourage dissoluteness in the relations of the sexes, and even to sanctify impurities of the most abominable description. Connected with her temples and images there were male and female prostitutes, whose polluted gains formed part of the sacred fund appropriated to the service of the goddess. And, to complete the deification of immorality, they were even known by the name of the "consecrated." Nothing can show more clearly how deeply this baneful example had eaten into the hearts and habits of the people, notwithstanding positive prohibitions and the repeated denunciations of the Hebrew prophets, than the almost incredible fact that, previous to the reformation of Josiah, this class of persons was allowed to have houses or tents close to the Temple of Jehovah, whose treasury was perhaps even replenished by their gains. (2 K. xxiii. 7; Deut. xxiii. 17, 18; 1 K. xiv. 24, xv. 12, xxii. 46; Hos. iv. 14; Job xxxvi. 14; Lucian, Lucius, c. 35; De Deâ Syrâ, cc. 27, 51; Gesenius, Thesaurus, s. v. קָדֵשׁ, p. 1196; Movers, Phönizier, i. 678, &c.; Spencer, De Legibus Hebraorum, i. 561.)

V. The most important intellectual invention of man, that of letters, was universally asserted by the Greeks and Romans to have been communicated by the Phœnicians to the Greeks. The earliest written statement on the subject is in Herodotus, v. 57, 58, who incidentally, in giving an account of Harmodius and Aristogeiton, says that they were by race Gephyræans; and that he had ascertained by inquiry that the Gephyræans were Phœnicians, amongst those Phœnicians who came over with Cadmus [b] into Bœotia, and instructing the

---

[a] Whatever else the arrested sacrifice of Isaac symbolizes (Gen. xxii. 13), it likewise symbolizes the substitution in sacrifices of the inferior animals for children. Faith, if commanded, was ready to sacrifice even children; but the Hebrews were spared this dreadful trial, and were permitted to substitute sheep, and goats, and bulls.

[b] In Hebrew there is a root Kadesh, from which is

Greeks in many other arts and sciences, taught them likewise letters. It was an easy step from this to believe, as many of the ancients believed, that the Phœnicians *invented* letters.

"Phœnices primi, famæ si creditur, ausi
Mansuram rudibus vocem signare figuris."
LUCAN's *Pharsal.* iii. 220, 221.

This belief, however, was not universal; and Pliny the elder expresses his own opinion that they were of Assyrian origin, while he relates the opinion of Gellius that they were invented by the Egyptians, and of others that they were invented by the Syrians (*Nat. Hist.* vii. 57). Now, as Phœnician has been shown to be nearly the same language as Hebrew, the question arises whether Hebrew throws any light on the time or the mode of the invention of letters, on the question of who invented them, or on the universal belief of antiquity that the knowledge of them was communicated to the Greeks by the Phœnicians. The answer is as follows: Hebrew literature is as silent as Greek literature respecting the precise date of the invention of letters, and the name of the inventor or inventors; but the names of the letters in the Hebrew alphabet are in accordance with the belief that the Phœnicians communicated the knowledge of letters to the Greeks: for many of the names of letters in the Greek alphabet, though without meaning in Greek, have a meaning in the corresponding letters of Hebrew. For example: the four first letters of the Greek alphabet, Alpha, Beta, Gamma, Delta, are not to be explained through the Greek language; but the corresponding four first letters of the Hebrew alphabet, namely, Aleph, Beth, Gimel, Daleth, being essentially the same words, are to be explained in Hebrew. Thus in Hebrew Aleph or Eleph means an ox; Beth or Bayith a house; Gamal a camel; and Deleth a door. And the same is essentially, though not always so clearly, the case with almost all the sixteen earliest Greek letters said to have been brought over from Phœnicia by Cadmus, ΑΒΓΔΕϜΙΚΛΜΝΟΠΡΣΤ;[a] and called on this account Phœnician or Cadmeian letters (*Herodot.* l. c.; Pliny, *Hist. Nat.* vii. 57; Jelf's *Greek Gram.* i. 2). Moreover, as to writing, the ancient Hebrew letters, substantially the same as Phœnician, agree closely with ancient Greek letters — a fact which, taken by itself, would not prove that the Greeks received them from the Phœnicians, as the Phœnicians might possibly have received them from the Greeks; but which, viewed in connection with Greek traditions on the subject, and with the significance of the letters in Hebrew, seems reasonably conclusive that the letters were transported from Phœnicia into Greece. It is true that modern Hebrew writing and the later Greek writing of antiquity have not much resemblance to each other; but this is owing partly to gradual changes in the writing of Greek letters, and partly to the fact that the character in which Hebrew Bibles are now printed, called the Assyrian or square character, was not the one originally in use among the Jews, but seems to have been learnt in the Babylonian Captivity, and afterwards gradually adopted by them on their return to Palestine. (Gesenius, *Geschichte der Hebräischen Sprache und Schrift*, p. 156.)

As to the mode in which letters were invented, some clew is afforded by some of the early Hebrew and the Phœnician characters, which evidently aimed, although very rudely, like the drawing of very young children, to represent the object which the name of the letter signified. Thus the earliest Alpha has some vague resemblance to an ox's head, Gimel to a camel's back, Daleth to the door of a tent, Vau to a hook or peg. Again, the written letters, called respectively, Lamed (an ox goad), Ayin (an eye), Qoph (the back of the head), Reish or Roash (the head), and Tav (a cross), are all efforts, more or less successful, to portray the things signified by the names. It is said that this is equally true of Egyptian phonetic hieroglyphics; but, however this may be, there is no difficulty in understanding in this way the formation of an alphabet, when the idea of representing the component sounds or half-sounds of a word by figures was once conceived. But the original idea of thus representing sounds, though peculiarly felicitous, was by no means obvious, and millions of men lived and died without its occurring to any one of them.

In conclusion, it may not be unimportant to observe that, although so many letters of the Greek alphabet have a meaning in Hebrew or Phœnician, yet their Greek names are not in the Hebrew or Phœnician, but in the Aramaic form. There is a peculiar form of the noun in Aramaic, called by grammarians the *status emphaticus*, in which the termination *á* ($\aleph$) is added, to a noun, modifying it according to certain laws. Originally this termination was probably identical with the definite article "ha"; which, instead of being prefixed, was subjoined to the noun, as is the case now with the definite article in the Scandinavian languages. This form in *á* is found to exist in the oldest specimen of Aramaic in the Bible, *Yegar sahadûthâ*, in Genesis xxxi. 47, where *sahadûth*, testimony, is used by Laban in the *status emphaticus*. Now it is worthy of note that the names of a considerable proportion of the "Cadmeian letters" in the Greek alphabet are in this Aramaic form, such as Alpha, Beta, Gamma, Delta, Eta, Theta, Iota, Kappa, Lambda; and although this fact by itself is not sufficient to support an elaborate theory on the subject, it seems in favor, as far as it goes, of the conjecture that when the Greeks originally received the knowledge of letters, the names by which the several letters were taught to them were Aramaic. It has been suggested, indeed, by Gesenius, that the Greeks themselves made the addition in all these cases, in order to give the words a Greek termination, as "they did with other Phœnician words as melet, μάλθα, nevel, νάβλα." If, however, a list is examined of Phœnician words naturalized in Greek, it will not be found that the

---

Kedem, a noun with the double meaning of the "East" and "ancient time." With the former sense, Cadmus might mean "Eastern," or one from the East, like the name "Norman," or "Fleming," or, still more closely, the "Western," or "Southern," in English. With the latter sense for *Kedem*, the name would mean "Olden" r "Antient," and an etymological significance might

be given to a line of Sophocles, in which Cadmus is mentioned; —

Ὦ τέκνα Κάδμου τοῦ πάλαι νέα τροφή.
Œdip. Tyr. 1.

[a] The sixth letter, afterwards disused, and now generally known by the name of Digamma (from Dionysius, i. 20), was unquestionably the same as the Hebrew letter Vau (a hook).

ending in *d* has been the favorite mode of accommodating them to the Greek language. For example, the following sixteen words are specified by Bleek (*Einleitung in das A. T.*, p. 69), as having been communicated through the Phœnicians to the Greeks: νάρδος = nêrd; κιννάμωμον = kinnamôn; σάπφειρος = sappir; μύῤῥα, μύρον = mor; κασία, κασσία = ketziah; ὕσσωπος = ézôr; λίβανος, λιβανωτός = levonâh; βύσσος = bûts; κύμινον = kammôn; μάννα = mân; φῦκος = pûk; συκάμινος = shikmâh; νάβλα = nével; κιννύρα = kinnôr; κάμηλος = gâmâl; ἀῤῥαβόν = eravôn. Now it is remarkable that, of these sixteen, only four end in *a* in Greek which have not a similar termination in Hebrew; and, of these four, one is a late Alexandrine translation, and two are names of musical instruments, which, very probably, may first have been communicated to Greeks, through Syrians, in Asia Minor. And, under any circumstances, the proportion of the Phœnician words which end in *a* in Greek is too small to warrant the inference that any common practice of the Greeks in this respect will account for the seeming fact that nine out of the sixteen Cadmeian letters are in the Aramaic *status emphaticus*. The inference, therefore, from their endings in *a* remains unshaken. Still this must not be regarded in any way as proving that the alphabet was invented by those who spoke the Aramaic language. This is a wholly distinct question, and far more obscure; though much deference on the point is due to the opinion of Gesenius, who, from the internal *a* evidence of the names of the Semitic letters, has arrived at the conclusion that they were invented by the Phœnicians (*Paläographie*, p. 294).

Literature. — In English, see Kenrick's *Phœnicia*, London, 1855: in Latin, the second part of Bochart's *Geographia Sacra*, under the title "Canaan," and Gesenius' work, *Scripturæ Linguæque Phœniciæ Monumenta quotquot supersunt*, Lipsiæ, 1837: in German, the exhaustive work of Movers, *Die Phönizier*, and *Das Phönizische Alterthum*, 5 vols., Berlin, 1841–1856; an article on the same subject by Movers, in Ersch and Gruber's *Encyclopädie*, and an article in the same work by Gesenius on *Paläographie*. See likewise, Gesenius' *Geschichte der Hebräischen Sprache und Schrift*, Leipzig, 1815; Bleek's *Einleitung in das Alte Testament*, Berlin, 1860. Phœnician inscriptions discovered since the time of Gesenius have been published by Judas, *Étude démonstrative de la langue Phénicienne et de la langue Libyque*, Paris, 1847, and forty-five other inscriptions have been published by the Abbé Bourgade, Paris, 1852, fol. In 1845 a votive tablet was discovered at Marseilles, respecting which see Movers' *Phœnizische Texte*, 1847. In 1855, an inscription was discovered at Sidon on the sarcophagus of a Sidonian king named Eshmunazar, respecting which see Dietrich's *Zwei Sidonische Inschriften, und eine alte Phönizische Königsinschrift*, Marburg, 1855, and Ewald's *Erklärung der grossen Phönizischen Inschrift von Sidon*, Göttingen, 1856, 4to; from the

seventh volume of the *Abhandlungen der Königlicher Gesellschaft zu Göttingen*. Information respecting these works, and others on Phœnician inscriptions, is given by Bleek, pp. 64, 65.

E. T.

PHO'ROS (Φόρος: *Phares, Foro*) = PAROSH (1 Esdr. v. 9, ix. 26).

PHRYG'IA (Φρυγία: *Phrygia*). Perhaps there is no geographical term in the New Testament which is less capable of an exact definition. Many maps convey the impression that it was co-ordinate with such terms as Bithynia, Cilicia, or Galatia. But in fact there was no Roman province of Phrygia till considerably after the first establishment of Christianity in the peninsula of Asia Minor. The word was rather ethnological than political, and denoted, in a vague manner, the western part of the central region of that peninsula. Accordingly, in two of the three places where it is used, it is mentioned in a manner not intended to be precise (διελθόντες τὴν Φρυγίαν καὶ τὴν Γαλατικὴν χώραν, Acts xvi. 6; διερχόμενος καθεξῆς τὴν Γαλατικὴν χώραν καὶ Φρυγίαν, Acts xviii. 23), the former having reference to the second missionary journey of St. Paul, the latter to the third. Nor is the remaining passage (Acts ii. 10) inconsistent with this view, the enumeration of those foreign Jews who came to Jerusalem at Pentecost (though it does follow, in some degree, a geographical order) having no reference to political boundaries. By Phrygia we must understand an extensive district, which contributed portions to several Roman provinces, and varying portions at different times. As to its physical characteristics, it was generally a table-land, but with considerable variety of appearance and soil. Several towns mentioned in the New Testament were Phrygian towns; such, for instance, as Iconium and Colossæ: but it is better to class them with the provinces to which they politically belonged. All over this district the Jews were probably numerous. They were first introduced there by Antiochus the Great (Joseph. *Ant.* xii. 3, § 4): and we have abundant proof of their presence there from Acts xiii. 14, xiv. 1, 19, as well as from Acts ii. 10. [See PHILIP, p. 2485 *b*.]

J. S. H.

PHUD (Φούδ) = PHUT (Jud. ii. 23; comp. Ezr. xxvii. 10).

PHU'RAH (פֻּרָה [*bough, branch*]: Φαρά: *Phara*). Gideon's servant (lit. "lad," or "boy "), probably his armor-bearer (comp. 1 Sam. xiv. 1), who accompanied him in his midnight visit to the camp of the Midianites (Judg. vii. 10, 11).

PHU'RIM (τῶν Φουραί; [Alex. Φουραιμ; FA.³ Φουρυμ:] *Phurim*), Esth. xi. 1. [PURIM.]

PHUT, PUT (פּוּט [see below]: Φούδ, [Alex. in 1 Chr. Φουτ; in Jer., Ezek., Nah.] Λίβυες: *Phuth, Phut, Libyes, Libya, Africa* [?]), the third name in the list of the sons of Ham (Gen. x. 6; 1 Chr. i. 8), elsewhere applied to an African country or people. In the list it follows Cush and Mizraim, and precedes Canaan. The settlements of Cush

---

a The strongest argument of Gesenius against the Aramaic invention of the letters is, that although doubtless many of the names are both Aramaic and Hebrew, some of them are not Aramaic; at least, not in the Hebrew signification: while the Syrians use other words to express the same ideas. Thus אֵלֶף

in Aramaic means only 1000, and not an ox ; the word for "door" in Aramaic is not דלת, but תרע: while the six following names of Cadmeian letters are not Aramaic : הֹף (םהם (Syr.), פָּא, מֵים, יוֹד, וֹן, תֹּר.

extended from Babylonia to Ethiopia above Egypt, those of Mizraim stretched from the Philistine territory through Egypt and along the northern coast of Africa to the west; and the Canaanites were established at first in the land of Canaan, but afterwards were spread abroad. The order seems to be ascending towards the north: the Cushite chain of settlements being the most southern, the Mizraite chain extending above them, though perhaps through a smaller region, at least at the first, and the Canaanites holding the most northern position. We cannot place the tract of Phut out of Africa, and it would thus seem that it was almost parallel to that of the Mizraites, as it could not be further to the north: this position would well agree with Libya. But it must be recollected that the order of the nations or tribes of the stocks of Cush, Mizraim, and Canaan, is not the same as that we have inferred to be that of the principal names, and that it is also possible that Phut may be mentioned in a supplementary manner, perhaps as a nation or country dependent on Egypt.

The few mentions of Phut in the Bible clearly indicate, as already remarked, a country or people of Africa, and, it must be added, probably not far from Egypt. It is noticeable that they occur only in the list of Noah's descendants and in the prophetical Scriptures. Isaiah probably makes mention of Phut as a remote nation or country, where the A. V. has PUL, as in the Masoretic text (Is. lxvi. 19). Nahum, warning Nineveh by the fall of No-Amon, speaks of Cush and Mizraim as the strength of the Egyptian city, and Phut and Lubim as its helpers (iii. 9). Jeremiah tells of Phut in Necho's army with Cush and the Ludim (xlvi. 9). Ezekiel speaks of Phut with Persia and Lud as supplying mercenaries to Tyre (xxvii. 10), and as sharing with Cush, Lud, and other helpers of Egypt, in her fall (xxx. 5); and again, with Persia, and Cush, perhaps in the sense of mercenaries, as warriors of the army of Gog (xxxviii. 5).[a]

From these passages we cannot infer anything as to the exact position of this country or people; unless indeed in Nahum, Cush and Phut, Mizraim and Lubim are respectively connected, which might indicate a position south of Egypt. The serving in the Egyptian army, and importance of Phut to Egypt, make it reasonable to suppose that its position was very near.

In the ancient Egyptian inscriptions we find two names that may be compared to the Biblical Phut. The tribes or peoples called the Nine Bows, IX PETU or IX NA-PETU, might partly or wholly represent Phut. Their situation is doubtful, and they are never found in a geographical list, but only in the general statements of the power and prowess of the kings. If one people be indicated by them, we may compare the Naphtuhim of the Bible. [NAPHTUHIM.] It seems unlikely that the Nine Bows should correspond to Phut, as their name does not occur as a geographical term in use in the directly historical inscriptions, though it may be supposed that several well-known names there take its place as those of individual tribes; but this is an improbable explanation. The second name is that of Nubia, TO-PET, "the region of the Bow," also called TO-MERU-PET, "the region, the island

of the Bow," whence we conjecture the name of Meroë to come. In the geographical lists the latter form occurs in that of a people, ANU-MERU-PET, found, unlike all others, in the lists of the southern peoples and countries as well as the northern. The character we read PET is an unstrung bow, which until lately was read KENS, as a strung bow is found following, as if a determinative, the latter word, which is a name of Nubia, perhaps, however, not including so large a territory as the names before mentioned. The reading KENS is extremely doubtful, because the word does not signify bow in Egyptian, as far as we are aware, and still more because the bow is used as the determinative of its name PET, which from the Egyptian usage as to determinatives makes it almost impossible that it should be employed as a determinative of KENS. The name KENS would therefore be followed by the bow to indicate that it was a part of Nubia. This subject may be illustrated by a passage of Herodotus, explained by Mr. Harris of Alexandria, if we premise that the unstrung bow is the common sign, and, like the strung bow, is so used as to be the symbol of Nubia. The historian relates that the king of the Ethiopians unstrung a bow, and gave it to the messengers of Cambyses, telling them to say that when the king of the Persians could pull so strong a bow so easily, he might come against the Ethiopians with an army stronger than their forces (iii. 21, 22, ed. Rawlinson: Sir G. Wilkinson's note). For the hieroglyphic names see Brugsch's *Geogr. Inschr.*

The Coptic **ⲚⲓⲪⲀⲒⲀⲦ** must also be compared with Phut. The first syllable being the article, the word nearly resembles the Hebrew name. It is applied to the western part of Lower Egypt beyond the Delta; and Champollion conjectures it to mean the Libyan part of Egypt, so called by the Greeks, comparing the Coptic name of the similar eastern portion, **ⲦⲀⲢⲀⲂⲒⲀ**, **ⲦⲀⲢⲀⲂⲒⲀ**, the older Arabian part of Egypt and Arabian Nome (*L'Égypte sous les Pharaons*, ii. pp. 28–31, 243). Be this as it may, the name seems nearer to NAPHTUHIM than to Phut. To take a broad view of the question, all the names which we have mentioned may be reasonably connected with the Hebrew Phut; and it may be supposed that the Naphtuhim were Mizraites in the territory of Phut; perhaps intermixed with peoples of the latter stock. It is, however, reasonable to suppose that the PET of the ancient Egyptians, as a geographical designation, corresponds to the Phut of the Bible, which would therefore denote Nubia or the Nubians, the former, if we are strictly to follow Egyptian usage. This identification would account for the position of Phut after Mizraim in the list in Genesis, notwithstanding the order of the other names; for Nubia has been from remote times a dependency of Egypt, excepting in the short period of Ethiopian supremacy, and the longer time of Ethiopian independence. The Egyptian name of Cush, KEESH, is applied to a wider region well corresponding to Ethiopia. The governor of Nubia in the time of the Pharaohs was called Prince of KEESH, perhaps because his authority extended beyond Nubia. The identification of Phut with Nubia is not repugnant to the mention in the prophets: on the contrary, the great importance of Nubia in their time, which comprehended that of the Ethiopian supremacy, would account for their speaking of Phut as a support of Egypt, and as furnishing it with warriors.

The identification with Libya has given rise to attempts to find the name in African geography, which we shall not here examine, as such mere similarity of sound is a most unsafe guide.

R. S. P.

* Some Egyptologers identify the *Put* with the *Punt* of the Egyptian monuments. Thus Bunsen, (*Egypt's Place*, vol. ii. p. 304) says, "the *Put* of Scripture is analogous with *Punt*, just as *Moph* is with *Menf*, *Sheshak* with *Sheshonk*." Accordingly he regards the *Put* as Mauritanians. Ebers (*Ægypten und die Bücher Mose's*, i. 64) says, "the name *Punt* is identical with *Put*, for the Egyptians, to whom a medial T sound was so difficult, always prefixed to this a nasal *n*, when it occurred in a foreign name. For a like reason they wrote Ndarius for Darius." If this identification with the *Punt* is admitted, then the home of the *Put* could not have been either Nubia or Lydia. The *Punt* were Arabians, and their country lay to the east of Egypt (Brugsch, *Geog. Inschrift.* ii. 15). This is evident from monumental inscriptions which represent a commerce with the land of Phut by means of ships, that brought incense, spices, precious stones, and other well-known products of Arabia. This commerce was probably by way of the Arabian Gulf. The view here suggested is maintained at length by Ebers, but the identification is still doubtful. J. P. T.

PHU'VAH (פֻּוָה [perh. *mouth*]: Φουέ: *Phua*). One of the sons of Issachar (Gen. xlvi. 13), and founder of the family of the PUNITES. In the A. V. of Num. xxvi. 23 he is called PUA, though the Heb. is the same; and in 1 Chr. vii. 1, PUAH is another form of the name.

PHYGEL'LUS (Φύγελλος, or Φύγελος [Lachm. Tisch.]: *Phigelus*), 2 Tim. i. 15. A Christian connected with those in Asia of whom St. Paul speaks as turned away from himself. It is open to question whether their repudiation of the Apostle was joined with a declension from the faith (see Buddeus, *Eccl. Apostol.* ii. 310), and whether the open display of the feeling of Asia took place — at least so far as Phygellus and Hermogenes were concerned — at Rome. It was at Rome that Onesiphorus, named in the next verse, showed the kindness for which the Apostle invokes a blessing on his household in Asia: so perhaps it was at Rome that Phygellus displayed that change of feeling toward St. Paul which the Apostle's former followers in Asia avowed. It seems unlikely that St. Paul would write so forcibly if Phygellus had merely neglected to visit him in his captivity at Rome. He may have forsaken (see 2 Tim. iv. 16) the Apostle at some critical time when his support was expected; or he may have been a leader of some party of nominal Christians at Rome, such as the Apostle describes at an earlier period (Phil. i. 15, 16) opposing him there.

Dean Ellicott, on 2 Tim. i. 15, who is at variance with the ancient Greek commentators as to the exact force of the phrase "they which are in Asia," states various opinions concerning their aversion from St. Paul. The Apostle himself seems to have foreseen it (Acts xx. 30); and there is nothing in the fact inconsistent with the general picture of the state of Asia at a later period which we have in the first three chapters of the Revelation.

W. T. B.

PHYLACTERY. [FRONTLETS.]

* PHYSICIAN. [MEDICINE.]

PI-BE'SETH [A. V. ed. 1611, PHI-BESETH] (פִּי־בֶסֶת [see below]: Βούβαστος: *Bubastus*), a town of Lower Egypt, mentioned but once in the Bible (Ez. xxx. 17). In hieroglyphics its name is written BAHEST, BAST, and HA-BAHEST, followed by the determinative sign for an Egyptian city, which was probably not pronounced. The Coptic forms are ⲂⲀⲤⲦ, with the article ⲚⲒ prefixed, ⲠⲞⲨⲂⲀⲤⲦⲈ. ⲠⲞⲨⲂⲀⲤⲦ, ⲪⲞⲨⲂⲀⲤⲞⲒ, ⲂⲞⲨⲀⲤⲦⲒ, ⲠⲞⲨⲀⲤⲦ, and the Greek, Βούβαστις, Βούβαστος. The first and second hieroglyphic names are the same as those of the goddess of the place, and the third signifies the abode of BAHEST, that goddess. It is probable that BAHEST is an archaic mode of writing, and that the word was always pronounced, as it was sometimes written, BAST. It seems as if the civil name was BAHEST, and the sacred, HA-BAHEST. It is difficult to trace the first syllable of the Hebrew and of the Coptic and Greek forms in the hieroglyphic equivalents. There is a similar case in the names HAHESAR, ⲂⲞⲨⲤⲒⲢⲒ, ⲠⲞⲨⲤⲒⲢⲒ, Βούσιρις, *Busiris*. Dr. Brugsch and M. Devéria read PE or PA, instead of HA; but this is not proved. It may be conjectured that in pronunciation the masculine definite article PEPA or PEE was prefixed to HA, as could be done in Coptic: in the ancient language the word appears to be common, whereas it is masculine in the later. Or it may be suggested that the first syllable or first letter was a prefix of the vulgar dialect, for it is frequent in Coptic. The name of Philæ may perhaps afford a third explanation, for it is written EELEK-T, EELEK, and P-EELEK (Brugsch, *Geogr. Inschr.* i. 156, Nos. 626, 627); whence it would seem that the sign city (not abode) was common, as in the first form the feminine article, and in the last the masculine one, is used, and this would admit of the reading PA-BAST, "the [city] of Bubastis [the goddess]."

Bubastis was situate on the west bank of the Pelusiac or Bubastite branch of the Nile, in the Bubastite nome, about 40 miles from the central part of Memphis. Herodotus speaks of its site as having been raised by those who dug the canals for Sesostris, and afterwards by the labor of criminals under Sabacôs the Ethiopian, or, rather the Ethiopian dominion. He mentions the temple of the goddess Bubastis as well worthy of description, being more beautiful than any other known to him. It lay in the midst of the city, which, having been raised on mounds, overlooked it on every side. An artificial canal encompassed it with the waters of the Nile, and was beautified by trees on its bank. There was only a narrow approach leading to a lofty gateway. The enclosure thus formed was surrounded by a low wall, bearing sculptures; within was the temple, surrounded by a grove of fine trees (ii. 137, 138). Sir Gardner Wilkinson observes that the ruins of the city and temple confirm this account. The height of the mounds and the site of the temple are very remarkable, as well as the beauty of the latter, which was "of the finest red granite." It "was surrounded by a sacred enclosure, about 600 feet square . . . beyond which was a larger circuit, measuring 940 feet by 1200, containing the minor one and the canal." The temple is entirely ruined, but the names of Rameses II. of the XIXth dynasty, Userken I. (Osorchon I.) of the XXIId, and Nekht-har-heb (Necta-nebo I.) of the XXXth, have been found here, as well as that of the eponymous goddess BAST. There are also remains of the ancient houses of the town, and, "amidst the houses on the N. W. side are the thick walls of a fort, which protected the temple below" (Notes by Sir G. Wilkinson in Rawlinson's *Herodotus*, vol. ii. pp. 219, plan, and 102). Bubastis thus had a fort, besides being strong from its height.

The goddess BAST, who was here the chief object of worship, was the same as PESHT, the goddess of fire. Both names accompany · a lion-headed figure, and the cat was sacred to them. Herodotus considers the goddess Bubastis to be the same as Artemis (ii. 137), and that this was the current opinion in Egypt in the Greek period is · evident from the name Speos Artemidos of a rock temple dedicated to PESHT, and probably of a neighboring town or village. The historian speaks of the annual festival of the goddess held at Bubastis as the chief and most largely attended of the Egyptian festivals. It was evidently the most popular, and a scene of great license, like the great Muslim festival of the Seyyid el-Bedawee celebrated at Tanteh in the Delta (ii. 59, 60).

There are scarcely any historical notices of Bubastis in the Egyptian annals. In Manetho's list it is related that in the time of Boethos, or Bochos, first king of the IId dynasty (B. C. cir. 2470), a chasm of the earth opened at Bubastis, and many perished (Cory's *Ancient Fragments*, 2d ed. pp. 98, 99). This is remarkable, since, though shocks of earthquakes are frequent in Egypt, the actual earthquake is of very rare occurrence. The next event in the list connected with Bubastis is the accession of the XXIId dynasty (B. C. cir. 990), a line of Bubastite kings (*Ibid.* pp. 124, 125). These were either foreigners or partly of foreign extraction, and it is probable that they chose Bubastis as their capital, or as an occasional residence, on account of its nearness to the military settlements. [MIGDOL.] Thus it must have been a city of great importance when Ezekiel thus foretold its doom: "The young men of Aven and of Pi-beseth shall fall by the sword: and these [cities] shall go into captivity" (xxx. 17). Heliopolis and Bubastis are near together, and both in the route of an invader from the east marching against Memphis.   R. S. P.

* In Egyptian mythology, the goddess *Pesht*, the divinity of Bubastis, is described as the best-beloved of Ptah. To her was attributed the creation of the Asiatic race, which immediately succeeded the creation of the Egyptians by Ra, the Sun-god. She appears also as the avenger of crimes, and in this character is depicted with the head of a lioness. Perhaps under these two forms of creating and punishing, she represented the solar ray as both vivifying and destructive. But she was also presented under a gracious aspect

toward men, and then, as at Bubastis, the cat's-head was her symbol. Some good examples of this are to be seen in the Museums of Berlin, Leyden, and the Louvre at Paris.

Diodorus (i. 27) has an inscription concerning *Isis*, which says: "I am queen of the whole country, brought up by Hermes: I am the eldest daughter of the youngest god, Chronos. For me *Bubastis* was built." But Isis personated various divinities, and sometimes Pesht, appearing with the cat's-head, and the usual symbols of that goddess (Bunsen, i. 420).   J. P. T.

PICTURE.[a] In two of the three passages in which "picture" is used in A. V. it denotes idolatrous representations, either independent images or more usually stones "portrayed," *i. e.* sculptured in low relief, or engraved and colored (Ez. xxiii. 14; Layard, *Nin. & Bab.* ii. 306, 308). Movable pictures, in the modern sense, were doubtless unknown to the Jews; but colored sculptures and drawings on walls or on wood, as mummy-cases, must have been familiar to them in Egypt (see Wilkinson, *Anc. Egypt.* ii. 277). In later times we read of portraits (εἰκόνας), perhaps busts or intagli sent by Alexandra to Antony (Joseph. *Ant.* xv. 2, § 6). The "pictures of silver" of Prov. xxv. 11, were probably wall-surfaces or cornices with carvings, and the "apples of gold" representations of fruit or foliage, like Solomon's flowers and pomegranates (1 K. vi., vii.). The walls of Babylon were ornamented with pictures on enameled brick.   [BRICKS.]   H. W. P.

PIECE OF GOLD. The A. V., in rendering the elliptical expression "six thousand of gold," in a passage respecting Naaman, relating that he "took with him ten talents of silver, and six thousand of gold, and ten changes of raiment" (2 K. v. 5), supplies "pieces" as the word understood. The similar expression respecting silver, in which the word understood appears to be shekels, probably justifies the insertion of that definite word. [PIECE OF SILVER.] The same expression, if a weight of gold be here meant, is also found in the following passage: "And king Solomon made two hundred targets [of] beaten gold: six hundred of gold went to one target" (1 K. x. 16). Here the A. V. supplies the word "shekels," and there seems no doubt that it is right, considering the number mentioned, and that a common weight must be intended. That a weight of gold is meant in Naaman's case may be inferred, because it is extremely unlikely that coined money was already invented at the time referred to, and indeed that it was known in Palestine before the Persian period. [MONEY; DARIC.] Rings or ingots of gold may have been in use, but we are scarcely warranted in supposing that any of them bore the name of shekels, since the practice was to weigh money. The rendering "pieces of gold" is therefore very doubtful; and "shekels of gold," as designating the value of the whole quantity, not individual pieces, is preferable.   R. S. P.

* **PIECE OF MONEY.**   [STATER.]

PIECE OF SILVER. The passages in the O. T. and those in the N. T. in which the

a 1. מַשְׂכִּית, from שָׂכָה, "behold," with

אֶבֶן: λίθος σκοπός: *insignislapis* (Lev. xxvi. 1.), A. V. "image of stone"; Num. xxxiii. 52, σκοπιά: *titulus*.

In Ez. viii. 12. · th חֶדֶר: κοιτῶν κρυπτός: *abscond-*

itum cubiculi: A. V. "chamber of imagery:" Luther *schönsten kammer*. [IMAGERY, CHAMBERS OF, Amer. ed.]

2. שְׂכִיָּה, from same root (Is. ii. 16): θεά (πλοίων) κάλλους: *quod visu pulchrum est*: Prov. xxv. 11. "Apples of gold in pictures of silver": LXX. ἐν ὁρμίσκῳ σαρδίου: *in lectis argenteis*: Luther, Schelen.

A. V. uses this term must be separately considered.

I. In the O. T. the word "pieces" is used in the A. V. for a word understood in the Hebrew, if we except one case to be afterwards noticed. The phrase is always "a thousand" or the like "of silver" (Gen. xx. 16, xxxvii. 28, xlv. 22; Judg. ix. 4, xvi. 5; 2 K. vi. 25; Hos. iii. 2; Zech. xi. 12, 13). In similar passages the word "shekels" occurs in the Hebrew, and it must be observed that these are either in the Law, or relate to purchases, some of an important legal character, as that of the cave and field of Machpelah, that of the threshing-floor and oxen of Araunah, or to taxes, and the like (Gen. xxiii. 15, 16; Ex. xxi. 32; Lev. xxvii. 3, 6, 16; Josh. vii. 21; 2 Sam. xxiv. 24; 1 Chr. xxi. 25, where, however, shekels of gold are spoken of; 2 K. xv. 20; Neh. v. 15; Jer. xxxii. 9). There are other passages in which the A. V. supplies the word "shekels" instead of "pieces" (Deut. xxii. 19, 29; Judg. xvii. 2, 3, 4, 10; 2 Sam. xviii. 11, 12), and of these the first two require this to be done. It becomes then a question whether there is any ground for the adoption of the word "pieces," which is vague if actual coins be meant, and inaccurate if weights. The shekel, be it remembered, was the common weight for money, and therefore most likely to be understood in an elliptical phrase. When we find good reason for concluding that in two passages (Deut. xxii. 19, 20) this is the word understood, it seems incredible that any other should be in the other places. The exceptional case in which a word corresponding to "pieces" is found in the Hebrew is in the Psalms, where presents of submission are prophesied to be made of "pieces of silver," רַצֵּי־כָסֶף (lxviii. 30, Heb. 31). The word רַץ, which occurs nowhere else, if it preserve its radical meaning, from רָצַץ, must signify a piece broken off, or a fragment: there is no reason to suppose that a coin is meant.

II. In the N. T. two words are rendered by the phrase "piece of silver," drachma, δραχμή, and ἀργύριον. (1.) The first (Luke xv. 8, 9) should be represented by drachma. It was a Greek silver coin, equivalent, at the time of St. Luke, to the Roman denarius, which is probably intended by the Evangelist, as it had then wholly or almost superseded the former. [DRACHMA.] (2.) The second word is very properly thus rendered. It occurs in the account of the betrayal of our Lord for "thirty pieces of silver" (Matt. xxvi. 15, xxvii. 3, 5, 6, 9). It is difficult to ascertain what coins are here intended. If the most common silver pieces be meant, they would be denarii. The parallel passage in Zechariah (xi. 12, 13) must, however, be taken into consideration, where, if our view be correct, shekels must be understood. It may, however, be suggested that the two thirties may correspond, not as of exactly the same coin, but of the chief current coin. Some light may be thrown on our difficulty by the number of pieces. It can scarcely be a coincidence that thirty shekels of silver was the price of blood in the case of a slave accidentally killed (Ex. xxi. 32). It may be objected that there is no reason to suppose that shekels were current in our Lord's time; but it must be replied that the tetradrachms of depreciated Attic weight of the Greek cities of Syria of that time were of the same weight as the shekels which we believe to be of Simon the Maccabee [MONEY], so that Josephus speaks of the

shekel as equal to four Attic drachmæ (*Ant.* iii. 8, § 2). These tetradrachms were common at the time of our Lord, and the piece of money found by St. Peter in the fish must, from its name, have been of this kind. [STATER.] It is therefore more probable that the thirty pieces of silver were tetradrachms than that they were denarii. There is no difficulty in the use of two terms, a name designating the denomination and "piece of silver," whether the latter mean the tetradrachm or the denarius, as it is a vague appellation that implies a more distinctive name. In the received text of St. Matthew the prophecy as to the thirty pieces of silver is ascribed to Jeremiah, and not to Zechariah, and much controversy has thus been occasioned. The true explanation seems to be suggested by the absence of any prophet's name in the Syriac version, and the likelihood that similarity of style would have caused a copyist inadvertently to insert the name of Jeremiah instead of that of Zechariah. [ACELDAMA, Amer. ed.]   R. S. P.

PIETY. This word occurs but once in A. V.: "Let them learn first to show *piety* at home" (τὸν ἴδιον οἶκον εὐσεβεῖν, better, "towards their own household," 1 Tim. v. 4). The choice of this word here instead of the more usual equivalents of "godliness," "reverence," and the like, was probably determined by the special sense of *pietas*, as "erga parentes" (Cic. *Partit.* 22, *Rep.* vi. 15, *Inv.* ii. 22). It does not appear in the earlier English versions, and we may recognize in its application in this passage a special felicity. A word was wanted for εὐσεβεῖν which, unlike "showing godliness," would admit of a human as well as a divine object, and this *piety* supplied.   E. H. P.

PIGEON. [TURTLE-DOVE.]

PI-HAHI'ROTH (פִּי הַחִירֹת, הַחִירֹת [see below]: ἡ ἔπαυλις, τὸ στόμα Εἰρώθ, Εἰρώθ: *Phihahiroth*), a place before or at which the Israelites encamped, at the close of the third march from Rameses, when they went out of Egypt. Pi-hahiroth was before Migdol, and on the other hand were Baal-zephon and the sea (Ex. xiv. 2, 9; Num. xxxiii. 7, 8). The name is probably that of a natural locality, from the unlikelihood that there should have been a town or village in both parts of the country where it is placed in addition to Migdol and Baal-zephon, which seem to have been, if not towns, at least military stations, and its name is susceptible of an Egyptian etymology giving a sense apposite to this idea. The first part of the word is apparently treated by its omission as a separate prefix (Num. xxxiii. 8), and it would therefore appear to be the masculine definite article PE, PA, or PEE. Jablonsky proposed the Coptic ⲠⲒ-Ⲁ-ⲬⲒ-ⲢⲰⲦ, "the place where sedge grows," and this, or a similar name, the late M. Fulgence Fresnel recognised in the modern *Ghuweybet-el-boos*, "the bed of reeds." It is remarkable that this name occurs near where we suppose the passage of the Red Sea to have taken place, as well as near Suez, in the neighborhood usually chosen as that of this miracle; but nothing could be inferred as to place from such a name being now found, as the vegetation it describes is fluctuating. [EXODUS, THE.]   R. S. P.

PI'LATE, PON'TIUS (Πόντιος Πιλάτος [Πειλᾶτος, Tisch., 8th ed.]: *Pontius Pilatus*, his prænomen being unknown). The name indicates that he was connected, by descent or adoption, with the *gens* of the Pontii, first conspicuous in Roman history in the person of C. Pontius Telesinus, the great Samnite general.[a] He was the sixth Roman procurator of Judæa, and under him our Lord worked, suffered, and died, as we learn, not only from the obvious Scriptural authorities, but from Tacitus (*Ann.* xv. 44, " Christus Tiberio imperitante, per procuratorem Pontium Pilatum supplicio adfectus erat ").[b] A *procurator* (ἐπίτροπος, Philo, *Leg. ad Caium*, and Joseph. *B. J.* ii. 9, § 2; but less correctly ἡγεμών, Matt. xxvii. 2; and Joseph. *Ant.* xviii. 3, § 1) was generally a Roman knight, appointed to act under the governor of a province as collector of the revenue, and judge in causes connected with it. Strictly speaking, *procuratores Cæsaris* were only required in the imperial provinces, i. e. those which, according to the constitution of Augustus, were reserved for the special administration of the emperor, without the intervention of the senate and people, and governed by his legate. In the senatorian provinces, governed by proconsuls, the corresponding duties were discharged by quæstors. Yet it appears that sometimes *procuratores* were appointed in those provinces also, to collect certain dues of the *fiscus* (the emperor's special revenue), as distinguished from those of the *ærarium* (the revenue administered by the senate). Sometimes in a small territory, especially in one contiguous to a larger province, and dependent upon it, the procurator was head of the administration, and had full military and judicial authority, though he was responsible to the governor of the neighboring province. Thus Judæa was attached to Syria upon the deposition of Archelaus (A. D. 6), and a procurator appointed to govern it, with Cæsarea for its capital. Already, during a temporary absence of Archelaus, it had been in charge of the procurator Sabinus; then, after the ethnarch's banishment, came Coponius; the third procurator was M. Ambivius; the fourth, Annius Rufus; the fifth Valerius Gratus; and the sixth Pontius Pilate (Joseph. *Ant.* xviii. 2, § 2), who was appointed A. D. 25–26, in the twelfth year of Tiberius. One of his first acts was to remove the headquarters of the army from Cæsarea to Jerusalem. The soldiers of course took with them their standards, bearing the image of the emperor, into the Holy City. No previous governor had ventured on such an outrage.[c] Pilate had been obliged

to send them in by night, and there were no bounds to the rage of the people on discovering what had thus been done. They poured down in crowds to Cæsarea where the procurator was then residing, and besought him to remove the images. After five days of discussion, he gave the signal to some concealed soldiers to surround the petitioners, and put them to death unless they ceased to trouble him; but this only strengthened their determination, and they declared themselves ready rather to submit to death than forego their resistance to an idolatrous innovation. Pilate then yielded, and the standards were by his orders brought down to Cæsarea (Joseph. *Ant.* xviii. 3, §§ 1, 2, *B. J.* ii. 9, §§ 2–4). On two other occasions he nearly drove the Jews to insurrection; the first when, in spite of this warning about the images, he hung up in his palace at Jerusalem some gilt shields inscribed with the names of deities, which were only removed by an order from Tiberius (Philo, *ad Caium*, § 38, ii. 589); the second when he appropriated the revenue arising from the redemption of vows (Corban; comp. Mark vii. 11) to the construction of an aqueduct. This order led to a riot, which he suppressed by sending among the crowd soldiers with concealed daggers, who massacred a great number, not only of rioters, but of casual spectators [d] (Joseph. *B. J.* ii. 9, § 4). To these specimens of his administration, which rest on the testimony of profane authors, we must add the slaughter of certain Galileans, which was told to our Lord as a piece of news (ἀπαγγέλλοντες, Luke xiii. 1), and on which He founded some remarks on the connection between sin and calamity. It must have occurred at some feast at Jerusalem, in the outer court of the Temple, since the blood of the worshippers was *mingled with their sacrifices*; but the silence of Josephus about it seems to show that riots and massacres on such occasions were so frequent that it was needless to recount them all.

It was the custom for the procurators to reside at Jerusalem during the great feasts, to preserve order, and accordingly, at the time of our Lord's last passover, Pilate was occupying his official residence in Herod's palace; and to the gates of this palace Jesus, condemned on the charge of blasphemy, was brought early in the morning by the chief priests and officers of the Sanhedrim, who were unable to enter the residence of a Gentile, lest

---

[a] The cognomen Pilatus has received two explanations. (1.) As armed with the *pilum* or javelin; comp. " pilata agmina," Virg. *Æn.* xii. 121. (2.) As contracted from *pileatus*. The fact that the *pileus* or cap was the badge of manumitted slaves (comp. Suetonius, *Nero*, c. 57, *Tiber.* c. 4) makes it probable that the epithet marked him out as a *libertus*, or as descended from one.   E. H. P.

[b] Of the early history of Pilate we know nothing; but a German legend fills up the gap strangely enough. Pilate is the bastard son of Tyrus, king of Mayence. His father sends him to Rome as a hostage. There he is guilty of a murder; but being sent to Pontus, rises into notice as subduing the barbarous tribes there, receives in consequence the new name of Pontius, and is sent to Judæa. It has been suggested that the twenty-second legion, which was in Palestine at the time of the destruction of Jerusalem, and was afterwards stationed at Mayence, may have been in this case either the bearers of the tradition or the inventors of the fable. (Comp. Vilmar's *Deutsch. Nation. Liter.* i. 217.)   E. H. P.

[c] Herod the Great, it is true, had placed the Roman eagle on one of his new buildings; but this had been

followed by a violent outbreak, and the attempt had not been repeated (Ewald, *Geschichte*, iv. 509). The extent to which the scruples of the Jews on this point were respected by the Roman governors, is shown by the fact that no effigy of either god or emperor is found on the money coined by them in Judæa before the war under Nero (*Ibid.* v. 83, referring to De Sauley *Recherches sur la Numismatique Judaique*, pl. viii., ix.) Assuming this, the denarius with Cæsar's image and superscription of Matt. xxiii. must have been a coin from the Roman mint, or that of some other province. The latter was probably current for the common purposes of life. The shekel alone was received as a Temple-offering.   E. H. P.

[d] Ewald suggests that the Tower of Siloam may have been part of the same works, and that this was the reason why its fall was looked on as a judgment (*Geschichte*, vi. 40; Luke xiii. 4). The Pharisaic reverence for whatever was set apart for the Corban (Mark vii. 11), and their scruples as to admitting into it anything that had an impure origin (Matt. xxvii. 6), may be regarded, perhaps, as outgrowths of the same feeling.   E. H. P.

they should be defiled, and unfit to eat the passover (John xviii. 28). Pilate therefore came out to learn their purpose, and demanded the nature of the charge. At first they seem to have expected that he would have carried out their wishes without further inquiry, and therefore merely described our Lord as a κακοποιός (disturber of the public peace), but as a Roman procurator had too much respect for justice, or at least understood his business too well to consent to such a condemnation, and as they knew that he would not enter into theological questions, any more than Gallio afterwards did on a somewhat similar occasion (Acts xviii. 14), they were obliged to devise a new charge, and therefore interpreted our Lord's claims in a political sense, accusing him of assuming the royal title, perverting the nation, and forbidding the payment of tribute to Rome (Luke xxiii. 3; an account plainly presupposed in John xviii. 33). It is plain that from this moment Pilate was distracted between two conflicting feelings; a fear of offending the Jews, who had already grounds of accusation against him, which would be greatly strengthened by any show of lukewarmness in punishing an offense against the imperial government, and a conscious conviction that Jesus was innocent, since it was absurd to suppose that a desire to free the nation from Roman authority was criminal in the eyes of the Sanhedrim. Moreover, this last feeling was strengthened by his own hatred of the Jews, whose religious scruples had caused him frequent trouble, and by a growing respect for the calm dignity and meekness of the sufferer. First he examined our Lord privately, and asked Him whether He was a king? The question which He in return put to his judge, " *Sayest thou this of thyself, or did others tell it thee of me?* " seems to imply that there was in Pilate's own mind a suspicion that the prisoner really was what He was charged with being; a suspicion which shows itself again in the later question, " *Whence art thou?* " (John xix. 9), in the increasing desire to release Him (12), and in the refusal to alter the inscription on the cross (22). In any case Pilate accepted as satisfactory Christ's assurance that his *kingdom was not of this world,* that is, not worldly in its nature or objects, and therefore not to be founded by this world's weapons, though he could not understand the assertion that it was to be established by bearing witness to the truth. His famous reply, " *What is truth?* " was the question of a worldly-minded politician, skeptical because he was indifferent; one who thought truth an empty name, or at least could not see " any connection between ἀλήθεια and βασιλεία, truth and policy " (Dr. C. Wordsworth, *Comm.* in loco). With this question he brought the interview to a close, and came out to the Jews and declared the prisoner innocent. To this they replied that his teaching had stirred up all the people from Galilee to Jerusalem. The mention of Galilee suggested to Pilate a new way of escaping from his dilemma, by sending on the case to Herod Antipas, tetrarch of that country, who had come up to Jerusalem to the feast, while at the same time this gave him an opportunity for making overtures of reconciliation to Herod,

with whose jurisdiction he had probably in some recent instance interfered. But Herod, though propitiated by this act of courtesy, declined to enter into the matter, and merely sent Jesus back to Pilate dressed in a shining kingly robe (ἐσθῆτα λαμπράν, Luke xxiii. 11), to express his ridicule of such pretensions, and contempt for the whole business. So Pilate was compelled to come to a decision, and first, having assembled the chief priests and also the people, whom he probably summoned in the expectation that they would be favorable to Jesus, he announced to them that the accused had done nothing worthy of death, but at the same time, in hopes of pacifying the Sanhedrim, he proposed to scourge Him before he released Him. But as the accusers were resolved to have his blood, they rejected this concession, and therefore Pilate had recourse to a fresh expedient. It was the custom for the Roman governor to grant every year, in honor of the Passover, pardon to one condemned criminal. The origin of the practice is unknown, though we may connect it with the fact mentioned by Livy (v. 13) that at a Lectisternium " vinctis quoque dempta vincula." Pilate therefore offered the people their choice between two, the murderer Barabbas,[a] and the prophet whom a few days before they had hailed as the Messiah. To receive their decision he ascended the βῆμα, a portable tribunal which was carried about with a Roman magistrate to be placed wherever he might direct, and which in the present case was erected on a tessellated pavement (λιθόστρωτον) in front of the palace, and called in Hebrew *Gabbatha,* probably from being laid down on a slight elevation (גַּב, " to be high "). As soon as Pilate had taken his seat, he received a mysterious message from his wife, according to tradition a proselyte of the gate (θεοσεβής), named Procla or Claudia Procula (*Evang. Nicod.* ii.), who had " suffered many things in a dream," which impelled her to intreat her husband not to condemn the Just One. But he had no longer any choice in the matter, for the rabble, instigated of course by the priests, chose Barabbas for pardon, and clamored for the death of Jesus; insurrection seemed imminent, and Pilate reluctantly yielded. But, before issuing the fatal order, he washed his hands before the multitude, as a sign that he was innocent of the crime, in imitation probably of the ceremony enjoined in Deut. xxi., where it is ordered that when the perpetrator of a murder is not discovered, the elders of the city in which it occurs shall wash their hands, with the declaration, " Our hands have not shed this blood, neither have our eyes seen it." Such a practice might naturally be adopted even by a Roman, as intelligible to the Jewish multitude around him. As in the present case it produced no effect, Pilate ordered his soldiers to inflict the scourging preparatory to execution; but the sight of unjust suffering so patiently borne seems again to have troubled his conscience, and prompted a new effort in favor of the victim. He brought Him out bleeding from the savage punishment, and decked in the scarlet robe and crown of thorns which the soldiers had put on Him in derision,

---

[a] Comp. BARABBAS. Ewald suggests that the insurrection of which St. Mark speaks must have been that connected with the appropriation of the Corban (*supra*), and that this explains the eagerness with which the people demanded his release. He infers further, from

his name, that he was the son of a Rabbi (Abba was a Rabbinic title of honor) and thus accounts for the part taken in his favor by the members of the Sanhedrim

E. H. P

and said to the people, "Behold the man!" hoping that such a spectacle would rouse them to shame and compassion. But the priests only renewed their clamors for his death, and, fearing that the political charge of treason might be considered insufficient, returned to their first accusation of blasphemy, and quoting the law of Moses (Lev. xxiv. 16), which punished blasphemy with stoning, declared that He must die "because He made himself the Son of God." But this title υἱὸς θεοῦ augmented Pilate's superstitious fears, already aroused by his wife's dream (μᾶλλον ἐφοβήθη, John xix. 7); he feared that Jesus might be one of the heroes or demigods of his own mythology; he took Him again into the palace, and inquired anxiously into his descent ("Whence art thou?") and his claims, but, as the question was only prompted by fear or curiosity, Jesus made no reply. When Pilate reminded Him of his own absolute power over Him, He closed this last conversation with the irresolute governor by the mournful remark, "Thou couldst have no power at all against me, except it were given thee from above; therefore be that delivered me unto thee hath the greater sin." God had given to Pilate power over Him, and power only, but to those who delivered Him up God had given the means of judging of His claims; and therefore Pilate's sin, in merely exercising this power, was less than theirs who, being God's own priests, with the Scriptures before them, and the word of prophecy still alive among them (John xi. 50, xviii. 14), had deliberately conspired for his death. The result of this interview was one last effort to save Jesus by a fresh appeal to the multitude; but now arose the formidable cry, "If thou let this man go, thou art not Cæsar's friend," and Pilate, to whom political success was as the breath of life, again ascended the tribunal, and finally pronounced the desired condemnation.[a]

So ended Pilate's share in the greatest crime which has been committed since the world began. That he did not immediately lose his feelings of anger against the Jews who had thus compelled his acquiescence, and of compassion and awe for the sufferer whom he had unrighteously sentenced, is plain from his curt and angry refusal to alter the inscription which he had prepared for the cross (ὃ γέγραφα, γέγραφα), his ready acquiescence in the request made by Joseph of Arimathæa that the Lord's body might be given up to him rather than consigned to the common sepulchre reserved for those who had suffered capital punishment, and his

sullen answer to the demand of the Sanhedrim that the sepulchre should be guarded.[b] And here, as far as Scripture is concerned, our knowledge of Pilate's life ends. But we learn from Josephus (Ant. xviii. 4, § 1) that his anxiety to avoid giving offense to Cæsar did not save him from political disaster. The Samaritans were unquiet and rebellious. A leader of their own race had promised to disclose to them the sacred treasures which Moses was reported to have concealed in Mount Gerizim.[c] Pilate led his troops against them, and defeated them easily enough. The Samaritans complained to Vitellius, now president of Syria, and he sent Pilate to Rome to answer their accusations before the emperor (Ibid. § 2). When he reached it, he found Tiberius dead and Caius (Caligula) on the throne, A. D. 36. Eusebius adds (H. E. ii. 7) that soon afterwards, "wearied with misfortunes," he killed himself. As to the scene of his death there are various traditions. One is, that he was banished to Vienna Allobrogum (Vienne on the Rhone), where a singular monument, a pyramid on a quadrangular base, 52 feet high, is called Pontius Pilate's tomb (Dictionary of Geography, art. "Vienna). Another is, that he sought to hide his sorrows on the mountain by the lake of Lucerne, now called Mount Pilatus; and there, after spending years in its recesses, in remorse and despair rather than penitence, plunged into the dismal lake which occupies its summit. According to the popular belief, "a form is often seen to emerge from the gloomy waters, and go through the action of one washing his hands; and when he does so, dark clouds of mist gather first round the bosom of the Infernal Lake (such it has been styled of old), and then, wrapping the whole upper part of the mountain in darkness, presage a tempest or hurricane, which is sure to follow in a short space." (Scott, Anne of Geierstein, ch. i.) (See below.)

We learn from Justin Martyr (Apol. i. pp. 76, 84), Tertullian (Apol. c. 21), Eusebius (H. E. ii. 2), and others, that Pilate made an official report to Tiberius of our Lord's trial and condemnation; and in a homily ascribed to Chrysostom, though marked as spurious by his Benedictine editors (Hom. viii. in Pasch. vol. viii. p. 968, D), certain ὑπομνήματα (Acta, or Commentarii Pilati) are spoken of as well-known documents in common circulation. That he made such a report is highly probable, and it may have been in existence in Chrysostom's time; but the Acta Pilati now extant in Greek, and two Latin epistles from him to

---

[a] The proceedings of Pilate in our Lord's trial supply many interesting illustrations of the accuracy of the Evangelists, from the accordance of their narrative with the known customs of the time. Thus Pilate, being only a procurator, had no quæstor to conduct the trial, and therefore examined the prisoner himself. Again, in early times Roman magistrates had not been allowed to take their wives with them into the provinces, but this prohibition had fallen into neglect, and latterly a proposal made by Cæcina to enforce it had been rejected (Tac. Ann. iii. 33, 34). Grotius points out that the word ἀνέπεμψεν, used when Pilate sends our Lord to Herod (Luke xxiii. 7) is "propria Romani juris vox: nam remittitur reus qui alicubi comprehensus mittitur ad judicem aut originis aut habitationis" (see Alford, in loco). The tessellated pavement (Λιθόστρωτον) was so necessary to the forms of justice, as well as the βῆμα, that Julius Cæsar carried one about with him on his expeditions (Suet. Jul c. 46). The

power of life and death was taken from the Jews when Judæa became a province (Joseph. Ant. xx. 9, § 1). Scourging before execution was a well-known Roman practice.

[b] Matt. xxvii. 65, ἔχετε κουστωδίαν ὑπάγετε, ἀσφαλίσασθε ὡς οἴδατε. Ellicott would translate this, "Take a guard," on the ground that the watchers were Roman soldiers, who were not under the command of the priests. But some might have been placed at their disposal during the feast, and we should rather expect λάβετε if the sentence were imperative.

[c] Ewald (Geschichte, v. 43) ventures on the conjecture that this Samaritan leader may have been Simon Magus. The description fits in well enough; but the class of such impostors was so large, that there are but slight grounds for fixing on him in particular. E. H. P.

the emperor (Fabric. *Cod. Apocr. N. T.* i. 237, 298, iii. 456), are certainly spurious.   (For further particulars see below.)

The character of Pilate may be sufficiently inferred from the sketch given above of his conduct at our Lord's trial. He was a type of the rich and corrupt Romans of his age; a worldly-minded statesman, conscious of no higher wants than those of this life, yet by no means unmoved by feelings of justice and mercy. His conduct to the Jews, in the instances quoted from Josephus, though severe, was not thoughtlessly cruel or tyrannical, considering the general practice of Roman governors, and the difficulties of dealing with a nation so arrogant and perverse. Certainly there is nothing in the facts recorded by profane authors inconsistent with his desire, obvious from the Gospel narrative, to save our Lord. But all his better feelings were overpowered by a selfish regard for his own security. He would not encounter the least hazard of personal annoyance in behalf of innocence and justice; the unrighteous condemnation of a good man was a trifle in comparison with the fear of the emperor's frown and the loss of place and power. While we do not differ from Chrysostom's opinion that he was παράνομος (Chrys. i. 802, *adv. Judæos,* vi.), or that recorded in the Apostolical Constitutions (v. 14), that he was ἄνανδρος, we yet see abundant reason for our Lord's merciful judgment, "He that delivered me unto thee hath the greater sin." At the same time his history furnishes a proof that worldliness and want of principle are sources of crimes no less awful than those which spring from deliberate and reckless wickedness. The unhappy notoriety given to his name by its place in the two universal creeds of Christendom is due, not to any desire of singling him out for shame, but to the need of fixing the date of our Lord's death, and so bearing witness to the claims of Christianity to rest on a historical basis (August. *De Fide et Symb.* c. v. vol. vi. p. 156; Pearson, *On the Creed,* pp. 239, 240, ed. Burt, and the authorities quoted in note c). The number of dissertations on Pilate's character and all the circumstances connected with him, his "facinora," his "Christum servandi studium," his wife's dream, his supposed letters to Tiberius, which have been published during the last and present centuries, is quite overwhelming. The student may consult with advantage Dean Alford's *Commentary*; Ellicott, *Historical Lectures on the Life of our Lord,* sect. vii.; Neander's *Life of Christ,* § 285 (Bohn); Winer, *Realwörterbuch,* art. "Pilatus;" Ewald, *Geschichte,* v. 30, &c.

                                                    G. E. L. C.

ACTA PILATI. — The number of extant Acta Pilati, in various forms, is so large as to show that very early the demand created a supply of documents manifestly spurious, and we have no reason for looking on any one of those that remain as more authentic than the others. The taunt of Celsus that the Christians circulated spurious or distorted narratives under this title (Orig. *c. Cels.*),[a] and the complaint of Eusebius (*H. E.* ix. 5) that the heathens made them the vehicle of blasphemous calumnies, show how largely the machinery of falsification was used on either side. Such of these documents as are extant are found in the collections

of Fabricius, Thilo, and Tischendorf. Some of them are but weak paraphrases of the Gospel history. The most extravagant are perhaps the most interesting, as indicating the existence of modes of thought at variance with the prevalent traditions. Of these anomalies the most striking is that known as the *Paradosis Pilati* (Tischendorf, *Evang. Apoc.* p. 426). The emperor Tiberius, startled at the universal darkness that had fallen on the Roman Empire on the day of the Crucifixion, summons Pilate to answer for having caused it. He is condemned to death, but before his execution he prays to the Lord Jesus that he may not be destroyed with the wicked Hebrews, and pleads his ignorance as an excuse. The prayer is answered by a voice from heaven, assuring him that all generations shall call him blessed, and that he shall be a witness for Christ at his second coming to judge the twelve tribes of Israel. An angel receives his head, and his wife dies filled with joy, and is buried with him. Startling as this imaginary history may be, it has its counterpart in the traditional customs of the Abyssinian Church, in which Pilate is recognized as a saint and martyr, and takes his place in the calendar on the 25th of June (Stanley, *Eastern Church,* p. 13; Neale, *Eastern Church,* i. 806). The words of Tertullian, describing him as "jam pro suâ conscientiâ Christianus" (*Apol.* c. 21), indicate a like feeling, and we find traces of it also in the Apocryphal Gospel, which speaks of him as "uncircumcised in flesh, but circumcised in heart" (*Evang. Nicod.* i. 12, in Tischendorf, *Evang. Apoc.* p. 236).

According to another legend (*Mors Pilati,* in Tischendorf's *Evang. Apoc.* p. 432), Tiberius, hearing of the wonderful works of healing that had been wrought in Judæa, writes to Pilate, bidding him to send to Rome the man that had this divine power. Pilate has to confess that he has crucified him; but the messenger meets Veronica, who gives him the cloth which had received the impress of the divine features, and by this the emperor is healed. Pilate is summoned to take his trial, and presents himself wearing the holy and seamless tunic. This acts as a spell upon the emperor, and he forgets his wonted severity. After a time Pilate is thrown into prison, and there commits suicide. His body is cast into the Tiber, but as storms and tempest followed, the Romans take it up and send it to Vienne. It is thrown into the Rhone; but the same disasters follow, and it is sent on to Losania (Lucerne or Lausanne?). There it is sunk in a pool, fenced round by mountains, and even there the waters boil or bubble strangely. The interest of this story obviously lies in its presenting an early form (the existing text is of the 14th century) of the local traditions which connect the name of the procurator of Judæa with the Mount Pilatus that overlooks the Lake of Lucerne. The received explanation (Ruskin, *Modern Painters,* v. 128) of the legend, as originating in a distortion of the descriptive name Mons Pileatus (the "cloud-capped"), supplies a curious instance of the *genesis* of a mythus from a false etymology; but it may be questioned whether it rests on sufficient grounds, and is not rather the product of a pseudo-criticism, finding in a name the starting-point, not the embodiment of a legend. Have we any evidence that

assertion that no judgment fell on Pilate for his alleged crime (ii. 28).

the mountain was known as "Pileatus" before the legend? Have we not, in the apocryphal story just cited, the legend independently of the name?[a] (comp. Vilmar, *Deutsch. Nation. Liter.* i. 217).

Pilate's wife is also, as might be expected, prominent in these traditions. Her name is given as Claudia Procula (Niceph. *H. E.* i. 30).[b] She had been a proselyte to Judaism before the Crucifixion (*Evang. Nicod.* c. 2). Nothing certain is known as to her history, but the tradition that she became a Christian is as old as the time of Origen (*Hom. in Matt.* xxxv.). The system of administration under the Republic forbade the governors of provinces to take their wives with them, but the practice had gained ground under the Empire, and Tacitus (*Ann.* iii. 33) records the failure of an attempt to reinforce the old regulation. (See p. 2529, note *a*.)

E. H. P.

PIL'DASH (פִּלְדָּשׁ [*flame of fire*, Fürst]: Φαλδές; Alex. Φαλδας: *Pheldas*). One of the eight sons of Nahor, Abraham's brother, by his wife and niece, Milcah (Gen. xxii. 22). The settlement of his descendants has not been identified with any degree of probability. Bunsen (*Bibelwerk*, Gen. xxii. 22) compares *Ripalthas*, a place in the northeast of Mesopotamia: but the resemblance of the two names is probably accidental.

PIL'EHA (פִּלְחָא [*incision, slice*]: Φαλαί; [Vat. Φαδα, -ει· joined with the following; FA. Φαδ, -αει joined with the following; Alex. Φαλαει·] *Phalea*). The name of one of the chief of the people, probably a family, who signed the covenant with Nehemiah (Neh. x. 24).

* **PILGRIMS.** [STRANGERS.]

PILLAR.[c] The notion of a pillar is of a shaft or isolated pile, either supporting or not supporting a roof. Pillars form an important feature in oriental architecture, partly perhaps as a reminiscence of the tent with its supporting poles, and partly also from the use of flat roofs, in consequence of which the chambers were either narrower or divided into portions by columns. The tent-principle is exemplified in the open halls of Persian and other eastern buildings, of which the fronts, supported by pillars, are shaded by curtains or awnings fastened to the ground outside by pegs, or to trees in the garden-court (Esth. i. 6; Chardin, *Voy.* vii. 387, ix. 469, 470, and plates 39, 81; Layard, *Nin. & Bab.* pp. 530, 648; Burckhardt, *Notes on Bed.* i. 37). Thus also a figurative mode of describing

heaven is as a tent or canopy supported by pillars (Ps. civ. 2; Is. xl. 22), and the earth as a flat surface resting on pillars (1 Sam. ii. 8; Ps. lxxv 3). [TENTS, Amer. ed.]

It may be remarked that the word "place," in 1 Sam. xv. 12, is in Hebrew "hand."[d] In the Arab tent two of the posts are called *yed* or "hand" (Burckhardt, *Bed.* i. 37).

The general practice in oriental buildings of supporting flat roofs by pillars, or of covering open spaces by awnings stretched from pillars, led to an extensive use of them in construction. In Indian architecture an enormous number of pillars, sometimes amounting to 1,000, is found. A similar principle appears to have been carried out at Persepolis. At Nineveh the pillars were probably of wood [CEDAR], and it is very likely that the same construction prevailed in the "house of the forest of Lebanon," with its hall and porch of pillars (1 K. vii. 2, 6). The "chapiters" of the two pillars Jachin and Boaz resembled the tall capitals of the Persepolitan columns (Layard, *Nin. & Bab.* pp. 252, 650; *Nineveh*, ii. 274; Fergusson, *Handbk.* pp. 8, 174, 178, 188, 190, 196, 198, 231-233; Roberts, *Sketches*, Nos. 182, 184, 190, 198; Euseb. *Vit. Const.* iii. 34, 38; Burckhardt, *Trav. in Arabia*, i. 244, 245).

But perhaps the earliest application of the pillar was the votive or monumental. This in early times consisted of nothing but a single stone or pile of stones. Instances are seen in Jacob's pillars (Gen. xxviii. 18, xxxi. 46, 51, 52, xxxv. 14); in the twelve pillars set up by Moses at Mount Sinai (Ex. xxiv 4); the twenty-four stones erected by Joshua (Josh. iv. 8, 9; see also Is. xix. 19, and Josh. xxiv. 27). The trace of a similar notion may probably be found in the holy stone of Mecca (Burckhardt, *Trav.* i. 297). Monumental pillars have also been common in many countries and in various styles of architecture. Such were perhaps the obelisks of Egypt (Fergusson, 6, 8, 115, 246, 340; Ibn Batuta, *Trav.* p. 111; Strabo, iii. 171, 172; Herod. ii. 106; Amm. Marc. xvii. 4; Joseph. *Ant.* i. 2, § 3, the pillars of Seth).

The stone Ezel (1 Sam. xx. 19) was probably a terminal stone or a waymark.

The "place" set up by Saul (1 Sam. xv. 12) is explained by St. Jerome to be a trophy, Vulg. *fornicem triumphalem* (Jerome, *Quæst. Hebr. in lib. i. Reg.* iii. 1339). The word used is the same as that for Absalom's pillar, *Matstsēbāh*, called by Josephus χεῖρα (*Ant.* vii. 10, § 3), which was clearly of a monumental or memorial character, but not

---

a The extent to which the terror connected with the belief formerly prevailed is somewhat startling. If a stone were thrown into the lake, a violent storm would follow. No one was allowed to visit it without a special permission from the authorities of Lucerne. The neighboring shepherds were bound by a solemn oath, renewed annually, never to guide a stranger to it (Gessner, *Descript. Mont. Pilat.* p. 40, Zurich. 1555). The spell was broken in 1584 by Johannes Müller, curé of Lucerne, who was bold enough to throw stones and abide the consequences. (Golbery, *Univers Pittoresque de Suisse*, p. 327.) It is striking that traditions of Pilate attach themselves to several localities in the South of France (comp. Murray's *Handbook of France*, Route 125).

b If it were possible to attach any value to the Codex of St. Matthew's Gospel, of which portions have been published by Simonides, as belonging to the 1st century, the name of Pempele might claim precedence.

c 1. מַצֵּב (1 K. x. 12): ὑποστηρίγματα : *fulcra*, from סָעַד, "support;" marg. "rails."

2. מַצֵּבָה; the same, or nearly so.

3. מַצֶּבֶת, from נָצַב, "place:" στήλη : *titulus*; a pile of stones, or monumental pillar.

4. נְצִיב: στήλη : *statua* (Gen. xix. 26), of Lot's wife; from same root as 2 and 3.

5. מָצוֹר: πέτρα: *munitio*: "tower;" only in Hab. ii. 1; elsewhere "strong city," *i. e.* a place of defense, from צוּר, "press," "confine."

6. עַמּוּד: στύλος: *columna*: from עָמַד "stand."

d יָד: χεῖρα: *fornicem triumphalem*.

necessarily carrying any representation of a hand in its structure, as has been supposed to be the case. So also Jacob set up a pillar over Rachel's grave (Gen. xxxv. 20, and Robinson, i. 218). The monolithic tombs and obelisks of Petra are instances of similar usage (Burckhardt, *Syria*, p. 422; Roberts, *Sketches*, p. 105; Irby and Mangles, *Travels*, p. 125).

But the word *Matstsêbâh*, "pillar," is more often rendered "statue" or "image" (*e. g.* Deut. vii. 5, xii. 3, xvi. 22; Lev. xxvi. 1; Ex. xxiii. 24, xxxiv. 13; 2 Chr. xiv. 3, xxxi. 1; Jer. xliii. 13; Hos. iii. 4, x. 1; Mic. v. 13). This agrees with the usage of heathen nations, and practiced, as we have seen, by the patriarch Jacob, of erecting blocks or piles of wood or stone, which in later times grew into ornamented pillars in honor of the deity (Clem. Alex. *Coh. ad Gent.* c. iv.; *Strom.* i. 24 [a]). Instances of this are seen in the Attic Hermæ (Paus. iv. 33, 4), seven pillars significant of the planets (iii. 21, 9, also vii. 17, 4, and 22, 2, viii. 37); and Arnobius mentions the practice of pouring libations of oil upon them, which again recalls the case of Jacob (*Adv. Gent.* i. 335, ed. Gauthier).

The termini or boundary marks were originally, perhaps always, rough stones or posts of wood, which received divine honors (Ov. *Fast.* ii. 641, 684). [IDOL, ii. 1120 *a.*]

Lastly, the figurative use of the term "pillar," in reference to the cloud and fire accompanying the Israelites on their march, or as in Cant. iii. 6 and Rev. x. 1, is plainly derived from the notion of an isolated column not supporting a roof.

H. W. P.

PILLAR, PLAIN OF THE (אֵלוֹן)

מֻצָּב : τῇ βαλάνῳ τῇ εὑρετῇ[b] τῆς στάσεως; Alex. omits τῇ εὑρετῇ: *quercum quæ stabat*), or rather "oak[c] of the pillar" — that being the real signification of the Hebrew word *elôn*. A tree which stood near Shechem, and at which the men of Shechem and the house of Millo assembled, to crown Abimelech son of Gideon (Judg. ix. 6). There is nothing said by which its position can be ascertained. It possibly derived its name of *Muttsâb* from a stone or pillar set up under it; and reasons have already been adduced for believing that this tree may have been the same with that under which Jacob buried the idols and idolatrous trinkets of his household, and under which Joshua erected a stone as a testimony of the covenant there reëxecuted between the people and Jehovah. [ME-ONENIM.] There was both time and opportunity during the period of commotion which followed the death of Joshua for this sanctuary to return into the hands of the Canaanites, and the stone left standing there by Joshua to become appropriated to idolatrous purposes as one of the *Mattsêbâhs* in which the religion of the aborigines of the Holy Land delighted. [IDOL, ii. 1119 *b.*] The terms in which Joshua speaks of this very stone (Josh. xxiv. 27) almost seem to overstep the bounds of mere imagery, and would suggest and warrant its being afterwards regarded as endowed with miraculous qualities, and therefore a fit object for veneration.

---

[a] Σημαίνει ὁ στύλος τὸ ἀνεικονιστὸν τοῦ Θεοῦ.

[b] A double translation of the Hebrew word: εὑρετῇ originated in the erroneous idea that the word is connected with מצא, "to find."

[c] This is given in the margin of the A. V.

Especially would this be the case if the singular expression, "it hath heard all the words of Jehovah our God *which He spake to us*," were intended to indicate that this stone had been brought from Sinai, Jordan, or some other scene of the communications of Jehovah with the people. The Samaritans still show a range of stones on the summit of Gerizim as those brought from the bed of Jordan by the twelve tribes.

G.

PILLED (Gen. xxx. 37, 38): PEELED (Is. xviii. 2; Ex. xxix. 18) [Tob. xi. 13]. The verb "to pill" appears in old Eng. as identical in meaning with "to peel = to strip," and in this sense is used in the above passages from Genesis. Of the next stage in its meaning as = plunder, we have traces in the word "pillage," pilfer. If the difference between the two forms be more than accidental, it would seem as if in the English of the 17th century "peel" was used for the latter signification. The "people scattered and peeled," are those that have been plundered of all they have.[d] The soldiers of Nebuchadnezzar's army (Ex. xxix. 18), however, have their shoulder *peeled* in the literal sense. The skin is worn off with carrying earth to pile up the mounds during the protracted siege of Tyre. ["Pilled" has the sense of "bald" in Lev. xiii. 40 *marg.*]

E. H. P.

* PILLOW (προσκεφάλαιον), a cushion for the head.. Pillows were used on the divans or couches, on which the Orientals recline for rest and sleep. So our Saviour had laid himself down for repose after a day of fatigue, on a pillow in the hinder part of the ship, when the storm arose, as recorded in Mark iv. 38. The article in Greek indicates that the pillow belonged to the furniture of the boat. The pillow [מְרַאֲשׁוֹת = at the head] on which the head of the image that was made to represent David in 1 Sam. xix. 13, was placed, was made of goat's hair; or, as some conjecture, a texture of goat's hair was placed at the head of the image, so as by its resemblance to David's hair to make the deception more complete (see Ges. *Hebr. Handw.* p. 17, 6te Aufl.). Jacob used stones for his pillow, or, more literally, placed them at his head, when overtaken by night he slept at Luz (Gen. xxviii. 11, 18). In Ez. xiii. 18, 20, cushions ("pillows," A. V.) were used as especial appliances of luxury and effeminacy; whilst generally those sitting upon a couch only had pillows for the elbow to rest upon, these women made (sewed) them (together) even for all the joints of the hand. The word does not occur further in the A. V.

R. D. C. R.

PIL'TAI [2 syl.] (פִּלְטָי [*whom Jehovah delivers*]: Φελετί; [Vat. Alex. FA.¹ omit; FA.ᵃ Φελτ-τει:] *Phelti*). The representative of the priestly house of Moadiah, or Maadiah, in the time of Joiakim the son of Jeshua (Neh. xii. 17).

PINE-TREE. 1. *Tidhâr*,[e] from a root signifying *to revolve*. What tree is intended is not certain. Gesenius inclines to think the oak, as implying duration. It has been variously explained

---

[d] Comp. "peeling their prisoners," Milton, *P. R.* iv

"To peel the chiefs, the people to devour."

Dryden, *Homer, Iliad* (Richardson).

[e] תִּדְהָר : πεύκη: *pinus* (Is. lx. 13); from דּוּר, "revolve" (Ges. p. 323). In Is. xli. 19, *σπενδάμνῳ*: *ulmus.*

to be the Indian plane, the larch and the elm (Celsius, *Hierob.* ii. 271). But the rendering "pine" seems least probable of any, as the root implies either curvature or duration, of which the latter is not particularly applicable to the pine, and the former remarkably otherwise. The LXX. rendering in Is. xli. 19, βραθυδαρῳ, appears to have arisen from a confused amalgamation of the words *berôsh* and *tidhâr*, which follow each other in that passage. Of these *berôsh* is sometimes rendered "cypress," and might stand for "juniper." That species of juniper which is called *savin*, is in Greek βραθύ. The word δαδρ is merely an expression in Greek letters for *tidhâr*. (Pliny, xxiv. 11, 61; Schleusner, s. v.; Celsius, *Hierob.* i. 78.) [FIR.]

2. *Shemen* ª (Neh. viii. 15) is probably the wild olive. The cultivated olive was mentioned just before (Ges. p. 1437). H. W. P.

PINNACLE (τὸ πτερύγιον: *pinna, pinnaculum*: only in Matt. iv. 5, and Luke iv. 9). The word is used in O. T. to render, 1. *Cânâph*,ᵇ a wing or border, *e. g.* of a garment (Num. xv. 38; 1 Sam. xv. 27, xxiv. 4). 2. *Snappir*, fin of a fish (Lev. xi. 9. So Arist. *Anim.* i. 5, 14). 3. *Kâtsâh*, edge; A. V. end (Ex. xxviii. 26). Hesychius explains πτ. as ἀκρωτήριον.

It is plain, 1. that τὸ πτερ. is not *a* pinnacle, but *the* pinnacle. 2. That by the word itself we should understand an edge or border, like a feather or a fin. The only part of the Temple which answered to the modern sense of pinnacle was the golden spikes erected on the roof, to prevent birds from settling there (Joseph. *B. J.* v. 5, § 6). To meet the sense, therefore, of "wing," or to use our modern word founded on the same notion, "aisle," Lightfoot suggests the porch or vestibule which projected, like shoulders on each side of the Temple (Joseph. *B. J.* v. 5, § 4; Vitruv. iii. 2).

Another opinion fixes on the royal porch adjoining the Temple, which rose to a total height of 400 cubits above the Valley of Jehoshaphat (Joseph. *Ant.* xv. 11, § 5, xx. 9, § 7).

Eusebius tells us that it was from "the pinnacle" (τὸ πτερ.) that St. James was precipitated, and it is said to have remained until the 4th century (Euseb. *H. E.* ii. 23; Williams, *Holy City*, ii. 338).

Perhaps in any case τὸ πτερ. means the battlement ordered by law to be added to every roof. It is in favor of this that the word *Canaph* is used to indicate the top of the Temple (Dan. ix. 37; Hammond, Grotius, Calmet, De Wette, Lightfoot, *H. Hebr. on Matt.* iv.). H. W. P.

PI'NON (פִּינֹן [*darkness, obscurity*?]: Φινών; [Alex. in Gen. Φινες; Vat. in 1 Chr. Φεινων:] *Phinon*). One of the "dukes" of Edom; that is, head or founder of a tribe of that nation (Gen. xxxvi. 41; 1 Chr. i. 52). By Eusebius and Jerome (*Onomasticon*, Φινὼν, and "Fenon") the seat of the tribe is said to have been at PUNON, one of the stations of the Israelites in the Wilderness; which again they identify with Phæno, "between Petra and Zoar," the site of the famous Roman copper mines. No name answering to Pinon appears to have been yet discovered in Arabic literature, or amongst the existing tribes.

* PINS. [CRISPING PINS, Amer. ed., and TENT.]

PIPE (חָלִיל, *châlîl*). The Hebrew word so rendered is derived from a root signifying "to bore, perforate," and is represented with sufficient correctness by the English "pipe" or "flute," as in the margin of 1 K. i. 40. It is one of the simplest and therefore, probably, one of the oldest of musical instruments, and in consequence of its simplicity of form there is reason to suppose that the "pipe" of the Hebrews did not differ materially from that of the ancient Egyptians and Greeks. It is associated with the tabret (*tôph*) as an instrument of a peaceful and social character, just as in Shakespeare (*Much Ado*, ii. 3), "I have known when there was no music with him but the drum and fife, and now had he rather hear the *tabor and the pipe*" — the constant accompaniment of merriment and festivity (Luke vii. 32), and especially characteristic of "the *piping* time of peace." The pipe and tabret were used at the banquets of the Hebrews (Is. v. 12), and their bridal processions (Mishna, *Baba metsia*, vi. 1), and accompanied the simpler religious services, when the young prophets, returning from the high-place, caught their inspiration from the harmony (1 Sam. x. 5); or the pilgrims, on their way to the great festivals of their ritual, beguiled the weariness of the march with psalms sung to the simple music of the pipe (Is. xxx. 29). When Solomon was proclaimed king the whole people went up after him to Gihon, piping with pipes (1 K. i. 40). The sound of the pipe was apparently a soft wailing note, which made it appropriate to be used in mourning and at funerals (Matt. ix. 23), and in the lament of the prophet over the destruction of Moab (Jer. xlviii. 36). The pipe was the type of perforated wind instruments, as the harp was of stringed instruments (1 Macc. iii. 45),and was even used in the Temple-choir, as appears from Ps. lxxxvii. 7, where "the players on instruments" are properly "pipers." Twelve days in the year, according to the Mishna (*Arach.* ii. 3), the pipes sounded before the altar: at the slaying of the First Passover, the slaying of the Second Passover, the first feast-day of the Passover, the first feast-day of the Feast of Weeks, and the eight days of the Feast of Tabernacles. On the last-mentioned occasion the playing on pipes accompanied the drawing of water from the fountain of Siloah (*Succah*, iv. 1, v. 1) for five and six days. The pipes which were played before the altar were of reed, and not of copper or bronze, because the former gave a softer sound. Of these there were not less than two nor more than twelve. In later times the office of mourning at funerals became a profession, and the funeral and death-bed were never without the professional pipers or flute-players (αὐληταί, Matt. ix. 23), a custom which still exists (comp. Ovid, *Fast.* vi. 660, "cantabat mœstis tibia funeribus"). It was incumbent on even the poorest Israelite, at the death of his wife, to provide at least two pipers and one woman to make lamentation. [MUSIC, vol. iii. p. 2039 b.]

In the social and festive life of the Egyptians the pipe played as prominent a part as among the Hebrews. "While dinner was preparing, the party

---

ª שֶׁמֶן: ξύλον κυπαρίσσινον: *lignum pulcherrimum.*

ᵇ 1. כָּנָף: πτερύγιον: *angulus.*

2. סְנַפִּיר: πτερ.: *pinnula.*

3. קָצָה: πτερ.: *summitas.*

was enlivened by the sound of music; and a band, consisting of the harp, lyre, guitar, tambourine, double and single pipe, flute and other instruments, played the favorite airs and songs of the country" (Wilkinson, *Anc. Eg.* ii. 222). In the different combinations of instruments used in Egyptian bands, we generally find either the double pipe or the flute, and sometimes both; the former being played both by men and women, the latter exclusively by women. The Egyptian single pipe, as described by Wilkinson (*Anc. Eg.* ii. 308), was "a straight tube, without any increase at the mouth; and, when played, was held with both hands. It was of moderate length, apparently not exceeding a foot and a half, and many have been found much smaller; but these may have belonged to the peasants, without meriting a place among the instruments of the Egyptian band. . . . . Some have three, others four holes. . . . and some were furnished with a small mouthpiece" of reed or thick straw. This instrument must have been something like the *Náy*, or dervish's flute, which is described by Mr. Lane (*Mod. Eg.* ii. chap. v.) as "a simple reed, about 18 inches in length, seven-eighths of an inch in diameter at the upper extremity, and three-quarters of an inch at the lower. It is pierced with six holes in front, and generally with another hole at the back. . . . . In the hands of a good performer the *náy* yields fine, mellow tones; but it requires much practice to sound it well." The double pipe, which is found as frequently in Egyptian paintings as the single one, "consisted of two pipes, perhaps occasionally united together by a common mouthpiece, and played each with the corresponding hand. It was common to the Greeks and other people, and, from the mode of holding it, received the name of right and left pipe, the *tibia dextra* and *sinistra* of the Romans: the latter had but few holes, and, emitting a deep sound, served as a bass. The other had more holes, and gave a sharp tone" (Wilkinson, *Anc. Eg.* ii. 309, 310). It was played on chiefly by women, who danced as they played, and is imitated by the modern Egyptians, in their *zummára*, or double reed, a rude instrument, used principally by peasants and camel drivers out of doors (*ibid.* pp. 311, 312). In addition to these is also found in the earliest sculptures a kind of flute, held with both hands, and sometimes so long that the player was obliged to stretch his arms to their full length while playing.

Any of the instruments above described would have been called by the Hebrews by the general term *chálil,* and it is not improbable that they might have derived their knowledge of them from Egypt. The single pipe is said to have been the invention of the Egyptians alone, who attribute it to Osiris (Jul. Poll. *Onomast.* iv. 10), and as the material of which it was made was the lotus-wood (Ovid, *Fas.* iv. 190, "horrendo lotos adunca sono") there may be some foundation for the conjecture. Other materials mentioned by Julius Pollax are reed, brass, boxwood, and horn. Pliny (xvi. 66) adds silver, and the bones of asses. Bartenora, in his note on *Arachim,* ii. 3, above quoted, identifies the *chálil* with the French *chalumeau,* which is the German *schalmeie* and our *shawm* or *shalm,* of which the clarionet is a modern improvement. The shawm, says Mr. Chappell (*Pop. Mus.* i. 35, note *b*), "was played with a reed like the wayte, or hautboy, but being a bass instrument, with about the compass of an octave, had probably more the

tone of a bassoon." This can scarcely be correct, or Drayton's expression, "the *shrillest shawm*" (*Polyol.* iv. 366), would be inappropriate.

W. A. W.

* PIPER, Rev. xviii. 22. [MINSTREL; PIPE.]

PI'RA (οἱ ἐκ Πειρᾶς [Vat., οἱ ἐκ Πίρας, Ald.; Rom. Alex. omit]), 1 Esdr. v. 19. Apparently a repetition of the name CAPHIRA in the former part of the verse.

PI'RAM (פִּרְאָם [perh. *fleet as the wild ass*]: Φιδών; [Vat. Φειδών;] Alex. Φερααμ; [Comp. Φεραμ:] *Pharam*). The Amorite king of Jarmuth at the time of Joshua's conquest of Canaan (Josh. x. 3). With his four confederates he was defeated in the great battle before Gibeon, and fled for refuge to the cave at Makkedah, the entrance to which was closed by Joshua's command. At the close of the long day's slaughter and pursuit, the five kings were brought from their hiding-place, and hanged upon five trees till sunset, when their bodies were taken down and cast into the cave "wherein they had been hid" (Josh. x. 27).

PIR'ATHON (פִּרְעָתוֹן [*princely*, Ges.]: [Vat.] Φαραθωμ; [Rom. Φαραθών;] Alex. Φραθων: *Pharathon*), "in the land of Ephraim in the mount of the Amalekite;" a place named nowhere but in Judg. xii. 15, and there recorded only as the burial-place of Abdon ben-Hillel the Pirathonite, one of the Judges. Its site was not known to Eusebius or Jerome; but it is mentioned by the accurate old traveller hap-Parchi as lying about two hours west of Shechem, and called *Ferata* (Asher's *Benjamin of Tud.* ii. 426). Where it stood in the 14th century it stands still, and is called by the same name. It was reserved for Dr. Robinson to rediscover it on an eminence about a mile and a half south of the road from *Jaffa* by *Hableh* to *Nablús,* and just six miles, or two hours, from the last (Robinson, iii. 134).

Of the remarkable expression, "the mount (or mountain district) of the Amalekite," no explanation has yet been discovered beyond the probable fact that it commemorates a very early settlement of that roving people in the highlands of the country.

Another place of the same name probably existed near the south. But beyond the mention of PHARATHONI in 1 Macc. ix. 50, no trace has been found of it. G.

PIR'ATHONITE (פִּרְעָתֹנִי and פִּרְעָתוֹנִי [patr. see above]: Φαραθωνείτης, Φαραθωνεί, ἐκ Φαραθών: *Pharathonites*), the native of, or dweller in, PIRATHON. Two such are named in the Bible. 1. [Φαραθωνίτης (Vat. -νει-).] Abdon ben-Hillel (Judg. xii. 13, 15), one of the minor judges of Israel. In the original the definite article is present, and it should be rendered "*the* Pirathonite."

2. [Φαραθωνί (Vat. -νει), ἐκ Φαραθων: *Pharathonites, Pharatomites.*] From the same place came "Benaiah the Pirathonite of the children of Ephraim," captain of the eleventh monthly course of David's army (1 Chr. xxvii. 14) and one of the king's guard (2 Sam. xxiii. 30; 1 Chr. xi. 31) G.

PIS'GAH (הַפִּסְגָּה, with the def. article [*the part, piece*]: Φασγά, in Deut. iii. 17, xxxiv

1, and in Joshua; elsewhere τὸ λελαξευμένον [a] or ἡ λαξευτή: Phasga). An ancient topographical name which is found, in the Pentateuch and Joshua only, in two connections.

1. The top, or head, of the Pisgah (רֹאשׁ הַפִּ), Num. xxi. 20, xxiii. 14; Deut. iii. 27, xxxiv. 1.

2. Ashdoth hap-Pisgah, perhaps the springs, or roots, of the Pisgah, Deut. iii. 17, iv. 49; Josh. xii. 3, xiii. 20.

The latter has already been noticed under its own head. [ASHDOTH-PISGAH.] Of the former but little can be said. "The Pisgah" must have been a mountain range or district, the same as, or a part of that called the mountains of Abarim (comp. Deut. xxxii. 49 with xxxiv. 1). It lay on the east of Jordan, contiguous to the field of Moab, and immediately opposite Jericho. The field of Zophim was situated on it, and its highest point or summit — its "head" — was the Mount Nebo. If it was a proper name we can only conjecture that it denoted the whole or part of the range of the highlands on the east of the lower Jordan. In the late Targums of Jerusalem and Pseudojonathan, Pisgah is invariably rendered by ramatha,[b] a term in common use for a hill. It will be observed that the LXX. also do not treat it as a proper name. On the other hand Eusebius and Jerome (Onomasticon, "Abarim," "Fasga") report the name as existing in their day in its ancient locality. Mount Abarim and Mount Nabau were pointed out on the road leading from Livias to Hesbbon (i. e. the Wady Hesban), still bearing their old names, and close to Mount Phogor (Peor), which also retained its name, whence, says Jerome (à quo), the contiguous region was even then called Phasgo. This connection between Phogor and Phasgo is puzzling, and suggests a possible error of copyists.

No traces of the name Pisgah have been met with in later times on the east of Jordan, but in the Arabic garb of Ras el-Feshkah (almost identical with the Hebrew Rosh hap-Pisgah) it is attached to a well-known headland on the northwestern end of the Dead Sea, a mass of mountain bounded on the south by the Wady en-Nar, and on the north by the Wady Sidr, and on the northern part of which is situated the great Mussulman sanctuary of Neby Mûsa (Moses). This association of the names of Moses and Pisgah on the west side of the Dead Sea — where to suppose that Moses ever set foot would be to stultify the whole narrative of his decease — is extremely startling. No explanation of it has yet been offered. Certainly that of M. De Saulcy and of his translator,[c] that the Ras el-Feshkah is identical with Pisgah, cannot be entertained. Against this the words of Deut. iii. 27, "Thou shalt not go over this Jordan," are decisive.

Had the name of Moses alone existed here, it might with some plausibility be conceived that the reputation for sanctity had been at some time, during the long struggles of the country, transferred from east to west, when the original spot was out of the reach of the pilgrims. But the existence of the name Feshkah — and, what is equally curious, its non-existence on the east of Jordan — seems to preclude this suggestion. [NEBO, MOUNT, Amer. ed.]   G.

PISIDIA (Πισιδία: Pisidia) was a district of Asia Minor, which cannot be very exactly defined. But it may be described sufficiently by saying that it was to the north of PAMPHYLIA, and stretched along the range of Taurus. Northwards it reached to, and was partly included in, PHRYGIA, which was similarly an indefinite district, though far more extensive. Thus ANTIOCH IN PISIDIA was sometimes called a Phrygian town. The occurrences which took place at this town give a great interest to St. Paul's first visit to the district. He passed through Pisidia twice, with Barnabas, on the first missionary journey, i. e. both in going from PERGA to ICONIUM (Acts xiii. 13, 14, 51), and in returning (xiv. 21, 24, 25; compare 2 Tim. iii. 11). It is probable also that he traversed the northern part of the district, with Silas and Timotheus, on the second missionary journey (xvi. 6): but the word Pisidia does not occur except in reference to the former journey. The characteristics both of the country and its inhabitants were wild and rugged; and it is very likely that the Apostle encountered here some of those "perils of robbers" and "perils of rivers" which he mentions afterwards. His routes through this region are considered in detail in Life and Epp. of St. Paul (2d ed. vol. i. pp. 197-207, 240, 241), where extracts from various travellers are given.   J. S. H.

PI'SON (פִּישׁוֹן [streaming, current, Ges.]: [Rom. Φισών; Alex.] Φεισων: Phison). One of the four "heads" into which the stream flowing through Eden was divided (Gen. ii. 11). Nothing is known of it; the principal conjectures will be found under EDEN [vol. i. p. 656 f.].

PIS'PAH (פִּסְפָּה [expansion]: Φασφά; [Vat. Φασφαι:] Phaspha). An Asherite: one of the sons of Jether, or Ithran (1 Chr. vii. 38).

PIT. In the A. V. this word appears with a figurative as well as a literal meaning. It passes from the facts that belong to the outward aspect of Palestine and its cities to states or regions of the spiritual world. With this power it is used to represent several Hebrew words, and the starting point which the literal meaning presents for the spiritual is, in each case, a subject of some interest.

1. Shĕôl (שְׁאוֹל), in Num. xvi. 30, 33; Job xvii. 16. Here the word is one which is used only of the hollow, shadowy world, the dwelling of the dead, and as such it has been treated of under HELL.

2. Shachath (שַׁחַת). Here, as the root שׁוּחַ shows, the sinking of the pit is the primary thought (Gesen. Thes. s. v.). It is dug into the earth (Ps. ix. 15, cxix. 85). A pit thus made and then covered lightly over, served as a trap by which animals or men might be ensnared (Ps. xxxv. 7). It

---

[a] The singular manner in which the LXX. translators of the Pentateuch have fluctuated in their renderings of Pisgah between the proper name and the appellative, leads to the inference that their Hebrew text was different in some of the passages to ours. Mr. W. A. Wright has suggested that in the latter cases they may have read פסלה for פסגה,

from פסל, a word which they actually translate by λαξεύειν in Ex. xxxiv. 1, 4, Deut. x. 1.

[b] Probably the origin of the marginal reading of the A. V. "the hill."

[c] See De Saulcy's Voyage, etc., and the notes to ll. 60-66 of the English edition.

thus became a type of sorrow and confusion, from which a man could not extricate himself, of the great doom which comes to all men, of the dreariness of death (Job xxxiii. 18, 24, 28, 30). To "go down to the pit," is to die without hope. It is the penalty of evil-doers, that from which the righteous are delivered by the hand of God.

3. *Bôr* (בּוֹר). In this word, as in the cognate *Bêêr*, the special thought is that of a pit or well dug for water (Gesen. *Thes.* s. v.). The process of desynonymizing which goes on in all languages, seems to have confined the former to the state of the well or cistern, dug into the rock, but no longer filled with water. Thus, where the sense in both cases is figurative, and the same English word is used, we have pit (*beer*) connected with the "deep water," "the waterflood," "the deep" (Ps. lxix. 15), while in pit (=בּוֹר), there is nothing but the "miry clay" (Ps. xl. 2). Its dreariest feature is that there is "no water" in it (Zech. ix. 11). So far the idea involved has been rather that of misery and despair than of death. But in the phrase "they that go down to the *pit*" (בּוֹר), it becomes even more constantly than the synonyms already noticed (*Sheol, Shachath*), the representative of the world of the dead (Ez. xxxi. 14, 16, xxxii. 18, 24; Ps. xxviii. 1, cxliii. 7). There may have been two reasons for this transfer. 1. The wide, deep excavation became the place of burial. The "graves were set in the sides of the pit" (*bôr*) (Ez. xxxii. 24). To one looking into it it was visibly the home of the dead, while the vaguer, more mysterious Sheol carried the thoughts further to an invisible home. 2. The *pit*, however, in this sense, was never simply equivalent to burial-place. There is always implied in it a thought of scorn and condemnation. This too had its origin apparently in the use made of the excavations, which had either never been wells, or had lost the supply of water. The prisoner in the land of his enemies, was left to perish in the pit (*bôr*) (Zech. ix. 11). The greatest of all deliverances is that the captive exile is released from the slow death of starvation in it (*shachath*, Is. li. 14). The history of Jeremiah, cast into the dungeon, or pit (*bôr*) (Jer. xxxviii. 6, 9), let down into its depths with cords, sinking into the filth at the bottom (here also there is no water), with death by hunger staring him in the face, shows how terrible an instrument of punishment was such a pit. The condition of the Athenian prisoners in the stone quarries of Syracuse (Thuc. vii. 87), the Persian punishment of the σπόδος (Ctesias, *Pers.* 48), the oubliettes of mediæval prisons present instances of cruelty, more or less analogous. It is not strange that with these associations of material horror clustering round, it should have involved more of the idea of a place of punishment for the haughty or unjust, than did the *sheol*, the grave.

In Rev. ix. 1, 2, and elsewhere, the "bottomless pit," is the translation of τὸ φρέαρ τῆς ἀβύσσου. The A. V. has rightly taken φρέαρ here as the equivalent of *bôr* rather than *beer*. The pit of the abyss is as a dungeon. It is opened with a key (Rev. ix. 1, xx. 1). Satan is cast into it, as a prisoner (xx. 3).   E. H. P.

PITCH (זֶפֶת, חֵמָר, כֹּפֶר : πίσσα: *pix*). The three Hebrew terms above given all represent the same object, namely, mineral pitch or asphalt, in its different aspects: *zepheth* (the *zift* of the modern Arabs, Wilkinson, *Anc. Eg.* ii. 120) in its liquid state, from a root signifying "to flow;" *chêmâr*, in its solid state, from its red color, though also explained in reference to the manner in which it boils up (the former, however, being more consistent with the appearance of the two terms in juxtaposition in Ex. ii. 3; A. V. "pitch and slime"); and *copher*, in reference to its use in overlaying wood-work (Gen. vi. 14). Asphalt is an opaque, inflammable substance, which bubbles up from subterranean fountains in a liquid state, and hardens by exposure to the air, but readily melts under the influence of heat. In the latter state it is very tenacious, and was used as a cement in lieu of mortar in Babylonia (Gen. xi. 3; Strab. xvi. p. 743; Herod. i. 179), as well as for coating the outsides of vessels (Gen. vi. 14; Joseph. *B. J.* iv. 8, § 4), and particularly for making the papyrus boats of the Egyptians water-tight (Ex. ii. 3; Wilkinson, ii. 120). The Babylonians obtained their chief supply from springs at Is (the modern *Hit*), which are still in existence (Herod. i. 179). The Jews and Arabians got theirs in large quantities from the Dead Sea, which hence received its classical name of *Lacus Asphaltites*. The latter was particularly prized for its purple hue (Plin. xxviii. 23). In the early ages of the Bible the slime-pits (Gen. xiv. 10), or springs of asphalt, were apparent in the Vale of Siddim, at the southern end of the sea. They are now concealed through the submergence of the plain, and the asphalt probably forms itself into a crust on the bed of the lake, whence it is dislodged by earthquakes or other causes. Early writers describe the masses thus thrown up on the surface of the lake as of very considerable size (Joseph. *B. J.* iv. 8, § 4; Tac. *Hist.* v. 6; Diod. Sic. ii. 48). This is now a rare occurrence (Robinson, *Res.* i. 517), though small pieces may constantly be picked up on the shores. The inflammable nature of pitch is noticed in Is. xxxiv. 9.   W. L. B.

PITCHER.[c] The word "pitcher" is used in A. V. to denote the water-jars or pitchers with one or two handles, used chiefly by women for carrying water, as in the story of Rebecca (Gen. xxiv. 15–20; but see Mark xiv. 13; Luke xxii. 10).[b] This practice has been and is still usual both in the East and elsewhere. The vessels used for the purpose are generally carried on the head or the shoulder. The Bedouin women commonly use skin-bottles. Such was the "bottle" carried by Hagar (Gen. xxi. 14; Harmer, *Obs.* iv. 246; Layard, *Nin. & Bab.* p. 578; Roberts, *Sketches*, pl. 164; Arvieux, *Trav.* p. 203; Burckhardt, *Notes on Bed.* i. 351).

---

a 1. כַּד : ὑδρία : *hydria, lagena*; akin to Sanskrit *kut* and κάδος. Also "barrel" (1 K. xvii. 12, xviii. 33). (Ges. p. 660 ; Eichhoff, *Vergleich. der Sprachen*, p. 219.)

2 נֵבֶל and נָבֶל : ἀγγεῖον : *vas* ; A. V. "bottle,"

only once a "pitcher" (Lam. iv. 2), where it is joined with חֶרֶשׂ, an earthen vessel (Ges. 522).

3. In N. T. κεράμιον, twice only : Mark xiv. 12, *infra*; Luke xxii. 10, *amphora*.

b * Hence the owner of the guest-chamber was the more readily known, as pointed out in note *a*, vol. 2 p. 1375.   H.

The same word *cad* is used of the pitchers employed by Gideon's 300 men (Judg. vii. 16), where the use made of them marks the material. Also the vessel (A. V. "barrel") in which the meal of the Sareptan widow was contained (1 K. xvii. 12), and the "barrels" of water used by Elijah at Mount Carmel (xviii. 33). [BARREL, Amer. ed.] It is also used figuratively of the life of man (Eccl. xii. 6). [FOUNTAIN; MEDICINE.] It is thus probable that earthen vessels were used by the Jews as they were by the Egyptians for containing both liquids and dry provisions (Birch, *Anc. Pottery*, i. 43). In the view of the Fountain of Nazareth [vol. i. p. 838], may be seen men and women with pitchers which scarcely differ from those in use in Egypt and Nubia (Roberts, *Sketches*, plates 29, 164). The water-pot of the woman of Samaria was probably one of this kind, to be distinguished from the much larger amphoræ of the marriage-feast at Cana. [FOUNTAIN; CRUSE; BOTTLE; FLAGON; POT.]   H. W. P.

PI'THOM (פִּתֹם [see below]: Πειθώ; [Alex. Πιθωμ:] *Phithom*), one of the store-cities built by the Israelites for the first oppressor, the Pharaoh "which knew not Joseph" (Ex. i. 11). In the Heb. these cities are two, Pithom and Raamses: the LXX. adds On, as a third. It is probable that Pithom lay in the most eastern part of Lower Egypt, like Raamses, if, as is reasonable, we suppose the latter to be the Rameses mentioned elsewhere, and that the Israelites were occupied in public works within or near to the land of Goshen. Herodotus mentions a town called Patumus, Πάτουμος, which seems to be the same as the Thoum or Thou of the *Itinerary* of Antoninus, probably the military station Thohu of the *Notitia*. Whether or not Patumus be the Pithom of Scripture, there can be little doubt that the name is identical. The first part is the same as in Bubastis and Bu-siris, either the definite article masculine, or a possessive pronoun, unless indeed, with Brugsch, we read the Egyptian word "abode" PA, and suppose that it commences these names. [PI-BESETH.] The second part appears to be the name of ATUM or TUM, a divinity worshipped at On, or Heliopolis, as well as Ra, both being forms of the sun [ON], and it is noticeable that Thoum or Thou was very near the Heliopolite nome, and perhaps more anciently within it, and that a monument at *Aboo-Kesheyd* shows that the worship of Heliopolis extended along the valley of the Canal of the Red Sea. As we find Thoum and Patumus and Rameses in or near to the land of Goshen, there can be no reasonable doubt that we have here a correspondence to Pithom and Raamses, and the probable connection in both cases with Heliopolis confirms the conclusion. It is remarkable that the Coptic version of Gen. xlvi. 28 mentions Pithom for, or instead of, the Heroöpolis of the LXX. The Hebrew reads, "And he sent Judah before him unto Joseph, to direct his face unto Goshen; and they came into the land of Goshen." Here the LXX. has, καθ' Ἡρώων πόλιν, εἰς γῆν Ῥαμεσσῆ, but the Coptic, Ⲉ̄ ⲓⲟⲩ︦ⲗ︦ ⲧⲃⲁⲕⲓ ⲇⲉⲛ ⲡⲕⲁϩⲓ ⲛ̄ⲣⲁⲙⲙⲥⲥⲏ. Whether Patumus and Thoum be the same, and the position of one or both, have yet to be determined, before we can speak positively as to the Pithom of Exodus. Herodotus places Patumus

in the Arabian nome upon the Canal of the Red Sea (ii. 48). The *Itinerary* of Antoninus puts Thou 50 Roman miles from Heliopolis, and 48 from Pelusium; but this seems too far north for Patumus, and also for Pithom, if that place were near Heliopolis, as its name and connection with Raamses seem to indicate. Under Raamses is a discussion of the character of these cities, and of their importance in Egyptian history. [RAMESES.]
           R. S. P.

* Chabas (*Voyage d'un Égyptien*, p. 286) suggests the probable identity of *Pithom* and the *Etham* of Ex. xiii. 20: the initial *p* being simply the masculine singular of the article in Egyptian. But this seems to call for two cities or towers of the same name, in the same general locality, since there is good reason for placing the Pithom of Ex. i. 11, to the west of Raamses. The children of Israel would naturally assemble for the exodus at the point nearest the eastern desert; and their place of rendezvous was Raamses; nor would they be likely to encamp near a fortified city such as Pithom was. In his *Mélanges Égypt.* ii. 154, M. Chabas gives at length the arguments for the identification of Pithom with the Patumus of Herodotus, and with the ruins of *Aboo-Kesheyd*. A thorough archæological exploration of the Delta alone could determine these localities with certainty. This we may hope for when M. Mariette shall have finished his most rewarding work in the Nile valley. The Patamus of Herodotus lay upon the canal that joined the Nile to the Bitter Lakes, and the sweet-water canal of Lesseps, by restoring fertility to the ancient Goshen, and inviting thither a permanent population, may give occasion for discoveries that shall illustrate and confirm the history of Israel in Egypt.
           J. P. T.

PI'THON (פִּיתוֹן [*harmless*, Fürst]: Φιθών; [in ix. 41, Vat. Sin. Φαιθων:] *Phithon*). One of the four sons of Micah, the son of Meribbaal, or Mephibosheth (1 Chr. viii. 35, ix. 41).

PLAGUE, THE. The disease now called the Plague, which has ravaged Egypt and neighboring countries in modern times, is supposed to have prevailed there in former ages. Manetho, the Egyptian historian, speaks of "a very great plague" in the reign of Semempses, the seventh king of the first dynasty, B. C. cir. 2500. The difficulty of determining the character of the pestilences of ancient and mediæval times, even when carefully described, warns us not to conclude that every such mention refers to the Plague, especially as the cholera has, since its modern appearance, been almost as severe a scourge to Egypt as the more famous disease, which, indeed, as an epidemic seems there to have been succeeded by it. Moreover, if we admit, as we must, that there have been anciently pestilences very nearly resembling the modern Plague, we must still hesitate to pronounce any recorded pestilence to be of this class unless it be described with some distinguishing particulars.

The Plague in recent times has not extended far beyond the Turkish Empire and the kingdom of Persia. It has been asserted that Egypt is its cradle, but this does not seem to be corroborated by the later history of the disease. It is there both sporadic and epidemic; in the first form it has appeared almost annually, in the second at rarer intervals. As an epidemic it takes the character of a pestilence, sometimes of the greatest severity. Our subsequent remarks apply to it in this form.

It is a much-vexed question whether it is ever endemic: that such is the case is favored by its rareness since sanitary measures have been enforced.

The Plague when most severe usually appears first on the northern coast of Egypt, having previously broken out in Turkey or North Africa west of Egypt. It ascends the river to Cairo, rarely going much further. Thus Mr. Lane has observed that the great plague of 1835 "was certainly introduced from Turkey" (*Modern Egyptians*, 5th ed. p. 3, note 1). It was first noticed at Alexandria, ascended to Cairo, and further to the southern part of Egypt, a few cases having occurred at Thebes; and it "extended throughout the whole of Egypt, though its ravages were not great in the southern parts" (*Ibid.*). The mortality is often enormous, and Mr. Lane remarks of the plague just mentioned: "It destroyed not less than eighty thousand persons in Cairo, that is, one-third of the population; and far more, I believe, than two hundred thousand in all Egypt" (*Ibid.*).[a] The writer was in Cairo on the last occasion when this pestilence visited Egypt, in the summer of 1843, when the deaths were not numerous, although, owing to the Government's posting a sentry at each house in which any one had died of the disease, to enforce quarantine, there was much concealment, and the number was not accurately known (Mrs. Poole, *Englishwoman in Egypt*, ii. 32–35). Although since then Egypt has been free from this scourge, Benghàzee (Hesperides), in the pashalic of Tripoli, was almost depopulated by it during part of the years 1860 and 1861. It generally appears in Egypt in midwinter, and lasts at most for about six months.

The Plague is considered to be a severe kind of typhus, accompanied by buboes. Like the cholera it is most violent at the first outbreak, causing almost instant death; later it may last three days, and even longer, but usually it is fatal in a few hours. It has never been successfully treated except in isolated cases or when the epidemic has seemed to have worn itself out. Depletion and stimulants have been tried, as with cholera, and stimulants with far better results. Great difference of opinion has obtained as to whether it is contagious or not. Instances have, however, occurred in which no known cause except contagion could have conveyed the disease.

In noticing the places in the Bible which might be supposed to refer to the Plague we must bear in mind that, unless some of its distinctive characteristics are mentioned, it is not safe to infer that this disease is intended.

In the narrative of the Ten Plagues there is, as we point out below [p. 2542, a], none corresponding to the modern Plague. The plague of boils has indeed some resemblance, and it might be urged that, as in other cases known scourges were sent (their miraculous nature being shown by their opportune occurrence and their intense character), so in this case a disease of the country, if indeed the Plague anciently prevailed in Egypt, might have been employed. Yet the ordinary Plague would rather exceed in severity this infliction than the contrary, which seems fatal to this supposition. [PLAGUES, THE TEN.]

a A curious story connected with this plague is given in the notes [of Mr. Lane] to the *Thousand and One Nights*, ch. lii.

Several Hebrew words are translated "pestilence" or "plague." (1.) דֶּבֶר, properly "destruction," hence "a plague;" in LXX. commonly θάνατος. It is used with a wide signification for different pestilences, being employed even for murrain in the account of the plague of murrain (Ex. ix. 3). (2.) מָוֶת, properly "death," hence "a deadly disease, pestilence." Gesenius compares the *Schwarzer Tod*, or Black Death, of the middle ages. (3.) נֶגֶף and מַגֵּפָה, properly anything with which people are smitten, especially by God, therefore a plague or pestilence sent by Him. (4.) קֶטֶב, "pestilence" (Deut. xxxii. 24, A. V. "destruction"; Ps. xci. 6, "the pestilence [that] walketh in darkness"), and perhaps also הֶבֶל, if we follow Gesenius, instead of reading with the A. V. "destruction," in Hos. xiii. 14. (5.) רֶשֶׁף, properly "a flame," hence "a burning fever," "a plague" (Deut. xxxii. 24; Hab. iii. 5, where it occurs with דֶּבֶר). It is evident that not one of these words can be considered as designating by its signification the Plague. Whether the disease be mentioned must be judged from the sense of passages, not from the sense of words.

Those pestilences which were sent as special judgments, and were either supernaturally rapid in their effects, or in addition directed against particular culprits, are beyond the reach of human inquiry. But we also read of pestilences which, although sent as judgments, have the characteristics of modern epidemics, not being rapid beyond nature, nor directed against individuals. Thus in the remarkable threatenings in Leviticus and Deuteronomy, pestilence is spoken of as one of the enduring judgments that were gradually to destroy the disobedient. This passage in Leviticus evidently refers to pestilence in besieged cities: "And I will bring a sword upon you, that shall avenge the quarrel of [my] covenant: and when ye are gathered together within your cities, I will send the pestilence among you; and ye shall be delivered into the hand of the enemy" (xxvi. 25). Famine in a besieged city would occasion pestilence. A special disease may be indicated in the parallel portion of Deuteronomy (xxviii. 21): "The LORD shall make the pestilence cleave unto thee, until he [or "it"] have consumed thee from off the land whither thou goest to possess it." The word rendered "pestilence" may, however, have a general signification, and comprise calamities mentioned afterwards, for there follows an enumeration of several other diseases and similar scourges (xxviii. 21, 22). The first disease here mentioned, has been supposed to be the Plague (Bunsen, *Bibelwerk*). It is to be remembered that "the botch of Egypt" is afterwards spoken of (27), by which it is probable that ordinary boils are intended, which are especially severe in Egypt in the present day, and that later still "all the diseases of Egypt" are mentioned (60). It therefore seems unlikely that so grave a disease as the Plague, if then known, should not be spoken of in either of these two passages. In neither place does it seem certain that the Plague is specified, though, in the one, if it were to be in the land it would fasten upon the population of besieged cities, and in the other, if then known, it would probably be alluded to as a terrible judgment in an enumeration of dis-cases. The notices in the prophets present the same difficulty; for they do not seem to afford sufficiently positive evidence that the Plague was known in those times. With the prophets, as in the Pentateuch, we must suppose that the diseases threatened or prophesied as judgments must have been known, or at least called by the names used for those that were known. Two passages might seem to be explicit. In Amos we read, " I have sent among you the pestilence after the manner of Egypt: your young men have I slain with the sword, and have taken away your horses; and I have made the stink of your camps to come up unto your nostrils " (Am. iv. 10). Here the reference is perhaps to the death of the firstborn, for the same phrase, "after the manner of Egypt," is used by Isaiah (x. 24, 26), with a reference to the Exodus, and perhaps to the oppression preceding it; and an allusion to past history seems probable, as a comparison with the overthrow of the cities of the plain immediately follows (Am. iv. 11). The prophet Zechariah also speaks of a plague with which the Egyptians, if refusing to serve God, should be smitten (xiv. 18), but the name, and the description which appears to apply to this scourge, seem to show that it cannot be the Plague (12).

Hezekiah's disease has been thought to have been the plague, and its fatal nature, as well as the mention of a boil, makes this not improbable. On the other hand, there is no mention of a pestilence among his people at the time.

There does not seem, therefore, to be any distinct notice of the Plague in the Bible, and it is most probable that this can be accounted for by supposing either that no pestilence of antiquity in the East was as marked in character as the modern Plague, or that the latter disease then frequently broke out there as an epidemic in crowded cities, instead of following a regular course.

(See Russell's *Natural History of Aleppo*; Clot-Bey, *De la Peste*, and *Aperçu Général sur l'Égypte*, ii. 348–350.)   R. S. P.

PLAGUES, THE TEN. In considering the history of the Ten Plagues we have to notice the place where they occurred, and the occasion on which they were sent, and to examine the narrative of each judgment, with a view to ascertain what it was, and in what manner Pharaoh and the Egyptians were punished by it, as well as to see if we can trace any general connection between the several judgments.

I. *The Place.* — Although it is distinctly stated that the plagues prevailed throughout Egypt, save, in the case of Goshen, the Israelite territory, the land of Goshen, yet the descriptions seem principally to apply to that part of Egypt which lay nearest to Goshen, and more especially to " the field of Zoan," or the tract about that city, since it seems almost certain that Pharaoh dwelt in Zoan, and that territory is especially indicated in Ps. lxxviii. 43. That the capital at this time was not more distant from Rameses than Zoan is evident from the time in which a message could be sent from Pharaoh to Moses on the occasion of the Exodus. The descriptions of the first and second plagues seem especially to refer to a land abounding in streams and lakes, and so rather to the lower than to the upper country. We must therefore look especially to Lower Egypt for our illustrations, while bearing in mind the evident prevalence of the plagues throughout the land.

II. *The Occasion.* — When that Pharaoh who seems to have been the first oppressor was dead, God sent Moses to deliver Israel, commanding him to gather the elders of his people together, and to tell them his commission. It is added, " And they shall hearken to thy voice: and thou shalt come, thou and the elders of Israel, unto the king of Egypt, and ye shall say unto him, The LORD God of the Hebrews hath met with us: and now let us go, we beseech thee, three days' journey into the wilderness, that we may sacrifice to the LORD our God. And I am sure that the king of Egypt will not let you go, no, not by a mighty hand. And I will stretch out my hand, and smite Egypt with all my wonders which I will do in the midst thereof: and after that he will let you go " (Ex. iii. 18–20). From what follows, that the Israelites should borrow jewels and raiment, and " spoil Egypt " (21, 22), it seems evident that they were to leave as if only for the purpose of sacrificing; but it will be seen that if they did so, Pharaoh, by his armed pursuit and overtaking them when they had encamped at the close of the third day's journey, released Moses from his engagement.

When Moses went to Pharaoh, Aaron went with him, because Moses, not judging himself to be eloquent, was diffident of speaking to Pharaoh. " And Moses said before the LORD, Behold, I [am] of uncircumcised lips, and how shall Pharaoh hearken unto me? And the LORD said unto Moses, See, I have made thee a god to Pharaoh: and Aaron thy brother shall be thy prophet " (Ex. vi. 30, vii. 1; comp. iv. 10–16). We are therefore to understand that even when Moses speaks it is rather by Aaron than himself. It is perhaps worthy of note that in the tradition of the Exodus which Manetho gives, the calamities preceding the event are said to have been caused by the king's consulting an Egyptian prophet; for this suggests a course which Pharaoh is likely to have adopted, rendering it probable that the magicians were sent for as the priests of the gods of the country, so that Moses was exalted by contrast with these vain objects of worship. We may now examine the narrative of each plague.

III. *The Plagues.* — 1. *The Plague of Blood.* When Moses and Aaron came before Pharaoh, a miracle was required of them. Then Aaron's rod became " a serpent " (A. V.), or rather " a crocodile " (רַפֹּין). Its being changed into an animal reverenced by all the Egyptians, or by some of them, would have been an especial warning to Pharaoh. The Egyptian magicians called by the king produced what seemed to be the same wonder, yet Aaron's rod swallowed up the others (vii. 3–12). This passage, taken alone, would appear to indicate that the magicians succeeded in working wonders, but, if it is compared with those others relating their opposition on the occasions of the first three plagues, a contrary inference seems more reasonable. In this case the expression, " they also did in like manner with their enchantments " (11) is used, and it is repeated in the cases of their seeming success on the occasions of the first plague (22), and the second (viii. 7), as well as when they failed on the occasion of the third plague (18). A comparison with other passages strengthens us in the inference that the magicians succeeded merely by juggling. [MAGIC.] Yet, even if they were able to produce any real effects by magic, a broad distinction should be drawn between the general and powerful nature of the wonders wrought by the hand of Moses and Aaron and their partial and weak imitations. When Pharaoh had refused to let the Israelites go, Moses was sent again, and, on the second refusal, was commanded to smite upon the waters of the river and to turn them and all the waters of Egypt into blood. The miracle was to be wrought when Pharaoh went forth in the morning to the river. Its general character is very remarkable, for not only was the water of the Nile smitten, but all the water, even that in vessels, throughout the country. The fish died, and the river stank. The Egyptians could not drink of it, and digged around it for water. This plague appears to have lasted seven days, for the account of it ends, "And seven days were fulfilled, after that the LORD had smitten the river " (vii. 13–25), and the narrative of the second plague immediately follows, as though the other had then ceased. Some difficulty has been occasioned by the mention that the Egyptians digged for water, but it is not stated that they so gained what they sought, although it may be conjectured that only the water that was seen was smitten, in order that the nation should not perish. This plague was doubly humiliating to the religion of the country, as the Nile was held sacred, as well as some kinds of its fish, not to speak of the crocodiles, which probably were destroyed. It may have been a marked reproof for the cruel edict that the Israelite children should be drowned, and could scarcely have failed to strike guilty consciences as such, though Pharaoh does not seem to have been alarmed by it. He saw what was probably an imitation wrought by the magicians, who accompanied him, as if he were engaged in some sacred rites, perhaps connected with the worship of the Nile. Events having some resemblance to this are mentioned by ancient writers: the most remarkable is related by Manetho, according to whom it was said that, in the reign of Nephercheres, seventh king of the IId dynasty, the Nile flowed mixed with honey for eleven days. Some of the historical notices of the earliest dynasties seem to be of very doubtful authenticity, and Manetho seems to treat this one as a fable, or, perhaps as a tradition. Nephercheres, it must be remarked, reigned several hundred years before the Exodus. Those who have endeavored to explain this plague by natural causes, have referred to the changes of color to which the Nile is subject, the appearance of the Red Sea, and the so-called rain and dew of blood of the Middle Ages; the last two occasioned by small fungi of very rapid growth. But such theories do not explain why the wonder happened at a time of year when the Nile is most clear, nor why it killed the fish and made the water unfit to be drunk. These are the really weighty points, rather than the change into blood, which seems to mean a change into the semblance of blood. The employment of natural means in effecting a miracle is equally seen in the passage of the Red Sea; but the Divine power is proved by the intensifying or extending that means, and the opportune occurrence of the result, and its fitness for a great moral purpose.

2. *The Plague of Frogs.* — When seven days had passed after the smiting of the river, Pharaoh was threatened with another judgment, and, on his refusing to let the Israelites go, the second plague was sent. The river and all the open waters of Egypt brought forth countless frogs, which not only covered the land, but filled the houses, even in their driest parts and vessels, for the ovens and kneading-troughs are specified. The magicians again had a seeming success in their opposition; yet Pharaoh, whose very palaces were filled by the reptiles, entreated Moses to pray that they might be removed, promising to let the Israelites go; but, on the removal of the plague, again hardened his heart (vii. 25, viii. 1–15). This must have been an especially trying judgment to the Egyptians, as frogs were included among the sacred animals, probably not among those which were reverenced throughout Egypt, like the cat, but in the second class of local objects of worship, like the crocodile. The frog was sacred to the goddess HEKT, who is represented with the head of this reptile. In hieroglyphics the frog signifies "very many," "millions," doubtless from its abundance. In the present day frogs abound in Egypt, and in the summer and autumn their loud and incessant croaking in all the waters of the country gives some idea of this plague. They are not, however, heard in the spring, nor is there any record, excepting the Biblical one, of their having been injurious to the inhabitants. It must be added that the supposed cases of the same kind elsewhere, quoted from ancient authors, are of very doubtful authenticity.

3. *The Plague of Lice.* — The account of the third plague is not preceded by the mention of any warning to Pharaoh. We read that Aaron was commanded to stretch out his rod and smite the dust, which became, as the A. V. reads the word, "lice" in man and beast. The magicians again attempted opposition; but, failing, confessed that the wonder was of God (viii. 16–19). There is much difficulty as to the animals meant by the term כִּנָּם. The Masoretic punctuation is כֵּן, which would probably make it a collective noun with ־ם formative; but the plural form כִּנִּים also occurs (ver. 16 [Heb. 12]; Ps. cv. 31), of which we once find the singular כֵּן in Isaiah (li. 6). It is therefore reasonable to conjecture that the first form should be punctuated כִּנָּם, as the defective writing of כִּנִּים; and it should also be observed that the Samaritan has כנים. The LXX. has σκνῖφες, and the Vulg. *sciniphes*, mosquitoes, mentioned by Herodotus (ii. 95), and Philo (*De Vita Mosis*, i. 20, p. 97, ed. Mang.), as troublesome in Egypt. Josephus, however, makes the כנים lice (*Ant.* ii. 14, § 3), with which Bochart agrees (*Hieroz.* ii. 572 ff.). The etymology is doubtful, and perhaps the word is Egyptian. The narrative does not enable us to decide which is the more probable of the two renderings, excepting, indeed, that if it be meant that exactly the same kind of animal attacked man and beast, mosquitoes would be the more likely translation. In this case the plague does not seem to be especially directed against the superstitions of the Egyptians: if, however, it were of lice, it would have been most distressing to their priests, who were very cleanly, apparently, like the Muslims, as a religious duty. In the present day both mosquitoes and lice are abundant in Egypt: the latter may be avoided, but there is no escape from the former, which are so distressing an annoyance that an increase of

them would render life almost insupportable to beasts as well as men.

4. *The Plague of Flies.* — In the case of the fourth plague, as in that of the first, Moses was commanded to meet Pharaoh in the morning as he came forth to the water, and to threaten him with a judgment if he still refused to give the Israelites leave to go and worship. He was to be punished by עָרֹב, which the A. V. renders "swarms [of flies]," "a swarm [of flies]," or, in the margin, "a mixture [of noisome beasts]." These creatures were to cover the people, and fill both the houses and the ground. Here, for the first time, we read that the land of Goshen, where the Israelites dwelt, was to be exempt from the plague. So terrible was it that Pharaoh granted permission for the Israelites to sacrifice in the land, which Moses refused to do, as the Egyptians would stone his people for sacrificing their "abomination." Then Pharaoh gave them leave to sacrifice in the wilderness, provided they did not go far; but, on the plague being removed, broke his agreement (viii. 20–32). The proper meaning of the word עָרֹב, is a question of extreme difficulty. The explanation of Josephus (*Ant.* ii. 14, § 3), and almost all the Hebrew commentators, is that it means "a mixture," and here designates a mixture of wild animals, in accordance with the derivation from the root עָרַב, "he mixed." Similarly, Jerome renders it *omne genus muscarum*, and Aquila πάμμυια. The LXX., however, and Philo (*De Vita Mosis,* i. 23, ii. 101, ed. Mang.) suppose it to be a dog-fly, κυνόμυια. The second of these explanations seems to be a compromise between the first and the third. It is almost certain, from two passages (Ex. viii. 29, 31; Hebrew, 25, 27), that a single creature is intended. If so, what reason is there in favor of the LXX. rendering? Oedmann (*Verm. Sammlungen,* ii. 150, ap. Ges. *Thes.* s. v.) proposes the *blatta orientalis,* a kind of beetle, instead of a dog-fly; but Gesenius objects that this creature devours things rather than stings men, whereas it is evident that the animal of this plague attacked or at least annoyed men, besides apparently injuring the land. From Ps. lxxviii. 45, where we read, "He sent the עָרֹב, which devoured them," it must have been a creature of devouring habits, as is observed by Kalisch (*Comment. on Exod.* p. 138), who supports the theory that a beetle is intended. The Egyptian language might be hoped to give us a clew to the rendering of the LXX. and Philo. In hieroglyphics a fly is AF, and a bee SHEB, or KHEB, SH and KH being interchangeable, in different dialects; and in Coptic these two words are confounded in ⲁⲁϥ, ⲁϥ, ⲁⲃ, ϩⲁϥ, *musca, apis, scarabæus.* We can therefore only judge from the description of the plague; and here Gesenius seems to have too hastily decided against the rendering "beetle," since the beetle sometimes attacks men. Yet our experience does not bear out the idea that any kind of beetle is injurious to man in Egypt; but there is a kind of gad-fly found in that country which sometimes stings men, though usually attacking beasts. The difficulty, however, in the way of the supposition that a stinging fly is meant is that all such flies are, like 'his one, plagues to beasts rather than men; and 'f we conjecture that a fly is intended, perhaps it is more reasonable to infer that it was the common

fly, which in the present day is probably the most troublesome insect in Egypt. That this was a more severe plague than those preceding it, appears from its effect on Pharaoh, rather than from the mention of the exemption of the Israelites, for it can scarcely be supposed that the earlier plagues affected them. As we do not know what creature is here intended, we cannot say if there were any reference in this case to the Egyptian religion. Those who suppose it to have been a beetle might draw attention to the great reverence in which that insect was held among the sacred animals, and the consequent distress that the Egyptians would have felt at destroying it, even if they did so unintentionally. As already noticed, no insect is now so troublesome in Egypt as the common fly, and this is not the case with any kind of beetle, which fact, from our general conclusions, will be seen to favor the evidence for the former. In the hot season the flies not only cover the food and drink, but they torment the people by settling on their faces, and especially round their eyes, thus promoting ophthalmia.

5. *The Plague of the Murrain of Beasts.* — Pharaoh was next warned that, if he did not let the people go, there should be on the day following "a very grievous murrain," upon the horses, asses, camels, oxen, and sheep of Egypt, whereas those of the children of Israel should not die. This came to pass, and we read that "all the cattle of Egypt died: but of the cattle of the children of Israel died not one." Yet Pharaoh still continued obstinate (Ex. ix. 1–7). It is to be observed that the expression "all the cattle" cannot be understood to be universal, but only general, for the narrative of the plague of hail shows that there were still at a later time some cattle left, and that the want of universal terms in Hebrew explains this seeming difficulty. The mention of camels is important, since it appears to favor our opinion that the Pharaoh of the Exodus was a foreigner, camels apparently not having been kept by the Egyptians of the time of the Pharaohs. This plague would have been a heavy punishment to the Egyptians as falling upon their sacred animals of two of the kinds specified, the oxen and the sheep; but it would have been most felt in the destruction of the greatest part of their useful beasts. In modern times murrain is not an unfrequent visitation in Egypt, and is supposed to precede the plague. The writer witnessed a very severe murrain in that country in 1842, which lasted nine months, during the latter half of that year and the spring of the following one, and was succeeded by the plague, as had been anticipated (Mrs. Poole, *Englishwoman in Egypt,* ii. 32, i. 59, 114). " 'A very grievous murrain,' forcibly reminding us of that which visited this same country in the days of Moses, has prevailed during the last three months " — the letter is dated October 18th, 1842 —, " and the already distressed peasants feel the calamity severely, or rather (I should say) the few who possess cattle. Among the rich men of the country, the loss has been enormous. During our voyage up the Nile " in the July preceding, " we observed several dead cows and buffaloes lying in the river, as I mentioned in a former letter; and some friends who followed us, two months after, saw many on the banks; indeed, up to this time, great numbers of cattle are dying in every part of the country " (*Id.* i. 114, 115). The similarity of the calamity in character is remarkably in contrast with its difference in dura-

tion: the miraculous murrain seems to have been as sudden and nearly as brief as the destruction of the first-born (though far less terrible), and to have therefore produced, on ceasing, less effect than other plagues upon Pharaoh, nothing remaining to be removed.

6. *The Plague of Boils.* — The next judgment appears to have been preceded by no warning, excepting indeed that, when Moses publicly sent it abroad in Egypt, Pharaoh might no doubt have repented at the last moment. We read that Moses and Aaron were to take ashes of the furnace, and Moses was to " sprinkle it toward the heaven in the sight of Pharaoh." It was to become " small dust " throughout Egypt, and " be a boil breaking forth [with] blains upon man, and upon beast." This accordingly came to pass. The magicians now once more seem to have attempted opposition, for it is related that they " could not stand before Moses because of the boil: for the boil was upon the magicians, and upon all the Egyptians." Notwithstanding, Pharaoh still refused to let the Israelites go (ix. 8-12). This plague may be supposed to have been either an infliction of boils, or a pestilence like the plague of modern times, which is an extremely severe kind of typhus fever, accompanied by swellings. [PLAGUE.] The former is, however, the more likely explanation, since, if the plague had been of the latter nature, it probably would have been less severe than the ordinary pestilence of Egypt has been in this nineteenth century, whereas with other plagues which can be illustrated from the present phenomena of Egypt, the reverse is the case. That this plague followed that of the murrain seems, however, an argument on the other side, and it may be asked whether it is not likely that the great pestilence of the country, probably known in antiquity, would have been one of the ten plagues; but to this it may be replied that it is more probable, and in accordance with the whole narrative, that extraordinary and unexpected wonders should be effected than what could be paralleled in the history of Egypt. The tenth plague, moreover, is so much like the great Egyptian disease in its suddenness, that it might rather be compared to it if it were not so wholly miraculous in every respect as to be beyond the reach of human inquiry. The position of the magicians must be noticed as indicative of the gradation of the plagues: at first they succeeded, as we suppose, by deception, in imitating what was wrought by Moses, then they failed, and acknowledged the finger of God in the wonders of the Hebrew prophet, and at last they could not even stand before him, being themselves smitten by the plague he was commissioned to send.

7. *The Plague of Hail.* — The account of the seventh plague is preceded by a warning, which Moses was commanded to deliver to Pharaoh, respecting the terrible nature of the plagues that were to ensue if he remained obstinate. And first of all of them it is said, " Behold, to-morrow about this time, I will cause it to rain a very grievous hail, such as hath not been in Egypt since the foundation thereof even until now." He was then told to collect his cattle and men into shelter, for that everything hailed upon should die. Accordingly, such of Pharaoh's servants as " feared the LORD," brought in their servants and cattle from the field. We read that " Moses stretched forth his rod toward heaven: and the LORD sent thunder and hail, and the fire ran along upon the ground." Thus man and beast were smitten, and the herbs and every tree broken, save in the land of Goshen. Upon this Pharaoh acknowledged his wickedness and that of his people, and the righteousness of God, and promised if the plague were withdrawn to let the Israelites go. Then Moses went forth from the city, and spread out his hands, and the plague ceased, when Pharaoh, supported by his servants, again broke his promise (ix. 13-35). The character of this and the following plagues must be carefully examined, as the warning seems to indicate an important turning-point. The ruin caused by the hail was evidently far greater than that effected by any of the earlier plagues; it destroyed men, which those others seem not to have done, and not only men but beasts and the produce of the earth. In this case Moses, while addressing Pharaoh, openly warns his servants how to save something from the calamity. Pharaoh for the first time acknowledges his wickedness. We also learn that his people joined with him in the oppression, and that at this time he dwelt in a city. Hail is now extremely rare, but not unknown, in Egypt, and it is interesting that the narrative seems to imply that it sometimes falls there. Thunder-storms occur, but, though very loud and accompanied by rain and wind, they rarely do serious injury. We do not remember to have heard while in Egypt of a person struck by lightning, nor of any ruin excepting that of decayed buildings washed down by rain.

8. *The Plague of Locusts.* — Pharaoh was now threatened with a plague of locusts, to begin the next day, by which everything the hail had left was to be devoured. This was to exceed any like visitations that had happened in the time of the king's ancestors. At last Pharaoh's own servants, who had before supported him, remonstrated, for we read: " And Pharaoh's servants said unto him, How long shall this man be a snare unto us? let the men go, that they may serve the LORD their God: knowest thou not yet that Egypt is destroyed ? " Then Pharaoh sent for Moses and Aaron, and offered to let the people go, but refused when they required that all should go, even with their flocks and herds: " And Moses stretched forth his rod over the land of Egypt, and the LORD brought an east wind upon the land all that day, and all [that] night; [and] when it was morning, the east wind brought the locusts. And the locusts went up over all the land of Egypt, and rested in all the coasts of Egypt: very grievous [were they]; before them there were no such locusts as they, neither after them shall be such. For they covered the face of the whole earth, so that the land was darkened; and they did eat every herb of the land, and all the fruit of the trees which the hail had left: and there remained not any green thing in the trees, or in the herbs of the field, through all the land of Egypt." Then Pharaoh hastily sent for Moses and Aaron and confessed his sin against God and the Israelites, and begged them to forgive him. " Now therefore forgive, I pray thee, my sin only this once, and intreat the LORD your God, that He may take away from me this death only." Moses accordingly prayed. " And the LORD turned a mighty strong west wind, which took away the locusts, and cast them into the Red Sea; there remained not one locust in all the coasts of Egypt." The plague being removed, Pharaoh again would not let the people go (x. 1-

20). This plague has not the unusual nature of the one that preceded it, but it even exceeds it in severity, and so occupies its place in the gradation of the more terrible judgments that form the later part of the series. Its severity can be well understood by those who, like the writer, have been in Egypt in a part of the country where a flight of locusts has alighted. In this case the plague was greater than an ordinary visitation, since it extended over a far wider space, rather than because it was more intense; for it is impossible to imagine any more complete destruction than that always caused by a swarm of locusts. So well did the people of Egypt know what these creatures effected, that, when their coming was threatened, Pharaoh's servants at once remonstrated. In the present day locusts suddenly appear in the cultivated land, coming from the desert in a column of great length. They fly rapidly across the country, darkening the air with their compact ranks, which are undisturbed by the constant attacks of kites, crows, and vultures, and making a strange whizzing sound like that of fire, or many distant wheels. Where they alight they devour every green thing, even stripping the trees of their leaves. Rewards are offered for their destruction, but no labor can seriously reduce their numbers. Soon their continue their course, and disappear gradually in a short time, leaving the place where they have been a desert. We speak from recollection, but we are permitted to extract a careful description of the effects of a flight of locusts from Mr. Lane's manuscript notes. He writes of Nubia: "Locusts not unfrequently commit dreadful havoc in this country. In my second voyage up the Nile, when before the village of Boostán, a little above Ibreem, many locusts pitched upon the boat. They were beautifully variegated, yellow and blue. In the following night a southerly wind brought other locusts, in immense swarms. Next morning the air was darkened by them, as by a heavy fall of snow; and the surface of the river was thickly scattered over by those which had fallen and were unable to rise again. Great numbers came upon and within the boat, and alighted upon our persons. They were different from those of the preceding day; being of a bright yellow color, with brown marks. The desolation they made was dreadful. In four hours a field of young durah [millet] was cropped to the ground. In another field of durah more advanced only the stalks were left. Nowhere was there space on the ground to set the foot without treading on many. A field of cotton-plants was quite stripped. Even the acacias along the banks were made bare, and palm-trees were stripped of the fruit and leaves. Last night we heard the creaking of the sákiyehs [water-wheels], and the singing of women driving the cows which turned them: to-day not one sákiyeh was in motion, and the women were going about howling, and vainly attempting to frighten away the locusts. On the preceding day I had preserved two of the more beautiful kind of these creatures with a solution of arsenic: on the next day some of the other locusts ate them almost entirely, poisoned as they were, unseen by me till they had nearly finished their meal. On the third day they were less numerous, and gradually disappeared. Locusts are eaten by most of the Bedawees of Arabia, and by some of the Nubians. We ate a few, dressed in the most approved manner, being stripped of the legs, wings, and head, and fried in butter. They had a flavor somewhat like that of the woodcock, owing to their food. The Arabs preserve them as a common article of provision by parboiling them in salt and water, and then drying them in the sun."

The parallel passages in the prophecy of Joel form a remarkable commentary on the description of the plague in Exodus, and a few must be here quoted, for they describe with wonderful exactness and vigor the devastations of a swarm of locusts. "Blow ye the trumpet in Zion, and sound an alarm in my holy mountain: let all the inhabitants of the land tremble: for the day of the LORD cometh, for [it is] nigh at hand; a day of darkness and of gloominess, a day of clouds and of thick darkness, as the morning spread upon the mountains: a great people and a strong; there hath not been ever the like, neither shall be any more after it, [even] to the years of many generations. A fire devoureth before them; and behind them a flame burneth: the land [is] as the garden of Eden before them, and behind, a desolate wilderness; yea, and nothing shall escape them. The appearance of them [is] as the appearance of horses; and as horsemen, so shall they run. Like the noise of chariots on the tops of the mountains shall they leap, like the noise of a flame of fire that devoureth the stubble, as a strong people set in battle array. . . . . They shall run like mighty men; they shall climb the wall like men of war, and they shall march every one on his ways, and they shall not break their ranks. . . . . The earth shall quake before them; the heavens shall tremble: the sun and the moon shall be dark, and the stars shall withdraw their shining " (ii. 1–5, 7, 10; see also 6, 8, 9, 11–25; Rev. ix. 1–12). Here, and probably also in the parallel passage of Rev., locusts are taken as a type of a destroying army or horde, since they are more terrible in the devastation they cause than any other creatures.

9. *The Plague of Darkness.* — After the plague of locusts we read at once of a fresh judgment. "And the LORD said unto Moses, Stretch out thine hand toward heaven, that there be darkness over the land of Egypt, that [one] may feel darkness. And Moses stretched forth his hand toward heaven; and there was a thick darkness in all the land of Egypt three days: they saw not one another, neither rose any from his place for three days: but all the children of Israel had light in their dwellings." Pharaoh then gave the Israelites leave to go if only they left their cattle, but when Moses required that they should take these also, he again refused (x. 21–29). The expression we have rendered, "that [one] may feel darkness," according to the A. V. in the margin, where in the text the freer translation "darkness [which] may be felt" is given, has occasioned much difficulty. The LXX. and Vulg. give this rendering, and the moderns generally follow them. It has been proposed to read "and they shall grope in darkness," by a slight change of rendering and the supposition that the particle בְ is understood (Kalisch, *Comm. on Ex.* p. 171). It is unreasonable to argue that the forcible words of the A. V. are too strong for Semitic phraseology. The difficulty is, however, rather to be solved by a consideration of the nature of the plague. It has been illustrated by reference to the Samoom and the hot wind of the Khamáseen. The former is a sand-storm which occurs in the desert, seldom lasting

according to Mr. Lane, more than a quarter of an hour or twenty minutes (*Mod. Eg.* 5th ed. p. 2); but for the time often causing the darkness of twilight, and affecting man and beast. Mrs. Poole, on Mr. Lane's authority, has described the Samoom as follows: "The 'Samoom,' which is a very violent, hot, and almost suffocating wind, is of more rare occurrence than the Khamáseen winds, and of shorter duration: its continuance being more brief in proportion to the intensity of its parching heat, and the impetuosity of its course. Its direction is generally from the southeast, or south-southeast. It is commonly preceded by a fearful calm. As it approaches, the atmosphere assumes a yellowish hue, tinged with red; the sun appears of a deep blood color, and gradually becomes quite concealed before the hot blast is felt in its full violence. The sand and dust raised by the wind add to the gloom, and increase the painful effects of the heat and rarity of the air. Respiration becomes uneasy, perspiration seems to be entirely stopped; the tongue is dry, the skin parched, and a prickling sensation is experienced, as if caused by electric sparks. It is sometimes impossible for a person to remain erect, on account of the force of the wind; and the sand and dust oblige all who are exposed to it to keep their eyes closed. It is, however, most distressing when it overtakes travellers in the desert. My brother encountered at Koos, in Upper Egypt, a samoom which was said to be one of the most violent ever witnessed. It lasted less than half an hour, and a very violent samoom seldom continues longer. My brother is of opinion that, although it is extremely distressing, it can never prove fatal, unless to persons already brought almost to the point of death by disease, fatigue, thirst, or some other cause. The poor camel seems to suffer from it equally with his master: and will often lie down with his back to the wind, close his eyes, stretch out his long neck upon the ground, and so remain until the storm has passed over " (*Englishwoman in Egypt*, i. 96, 97). The hot wind of the Khamáseen usually blows for three days and nights, and carries so much sand with it, that it produces the appearance of a yellow fog. It thus resembles the Samoom, though far less powerful and far less distressing in its effects. It is not known to cause actual darkness; at least the writer's residence in Egypt afforded no example either on experience or hearsay evidence. By a confusion of the Samoom and the Khamáseen wind it has even been supposed that a Samoom in its utmost violence usually lasts three days (Kalisch, *Com. Ex.* p. 170), but this is an error. The plague may, however, have been an extremely severe sandstorm, miraculous in its violence and its duration, for the length of three days does not make it natural, since the severe storms are always very brief. Perhaps the three days was the imit, as about the longest period that the people could exist without leaving their houses. It has been supposed that this plague rather caused a supernatural terror than actual suffering and loss, but this is by no means certain. The impossibility of moving about, and the natural fear of darkness which affects beasts and birds as well as men, as in a total eclipse, would have caused suffering, and if the plague were a sandstorm of unequaled severity, it would have produced the conditions of terror by its parching heat, besides causing much distress of other kinds. An evidence in favor of the wholly supernatural character of this plague is its preceding the last judgment of all, the death of the first-

born, as though it were a terrible foreshadowing of that great calamity.

10. *The Death of the Firstborn.* — Before the tenth plague Moses went to warn Pharaoh. "And Moses said, Thus saith the LORD, About midnight will I go out into the midst of Egypt: and all the firstborn in the land of Egypt shall die, from the firstborn of Pharaoh that sitteth upon his throne, even unto the firstborn of the maidservant that [is] behind the mill; and all the firstborn of beasts. And there shall be a great cry throughout all the land of Egypt, such as there was none like it, nor shall be like it any more." He then foretells that Pharaoh's servants would pray him to go forth. Positive as is this declaration, it seems to have been a conditional warning, for we read, "And he went out from Pharaoh in heat of anger," and it is added, that God said that Pharaoh would not hearken to Moses, and that the king of Egypt still refused to let Israel go (xi. 4–10). The Passover was then instituted, and the houses of the Israelites sprinkled with the blood of the victims. The firstborn of the Egyptians were smitten at midnight, as Moses had forewarned Pharaoh. "And Pharaoh rose up in the night, he, and all his servants, and all the Egyptians; and there was a great cry in Egypt; for [there was] not a house where [there was] not one dead " (xii. 30). The clearly miraculous nature of this plague, in its severity, its falling upon man and beast, and the singling out of the firstborn, puts it wholly beyond comparison with any natural pestilence, even the severest recorded in history, whether of the peculiar Egyptian Plague, or other like epidemics. The Bible affords a parallel in the smiting of Sennacherib's army, and still more closely in some of the punishments of murmurers in the wilderness. The prevailing customs of Egypt furnished a curious illustration of the narrative of this plague to the writer. "It is well known that many ancient Egyptian customs are yet observed. Among these one of the most prominent is the wailing for the dead by the women of the household, as well as those hired to mourn. In the great cholera of 1848 I was at Cairo. This pestilence, as we all know, frequently follows the course of rivers. Thus, on that occasion, it ascended the Nile and showed itself in great strength at Boolák, the port of Cairo, distant from the city a mile and a half to the westward. For some days it did not traverse this space. Every evening at sunset, it was our custom to go up to the terrace on the roof of our house. There, in that calm, still time, I heard each night the wail of the women of Boolák for their dead borne along in a great wave of sound a distance of two miles, the lamentation of a city stricken with pestilence. So, when the firstborn were smitten, 'there was a great cry in Egypt.' "

The history of the ten plagues strictly ends with the death of the firstborn. The pursuit and the passage of the Red Sea are discussed elsew' re. [EXODUS, THE; RED SEA, PASSAGE OF.] ..ere it is only necessary to notice that with the event last mentioned the recital of the wonders wrought in Egypt concludes, and the history of Israel as a separate people begins.

Having examined the narrative of the ten p   ues, we can now speak of their general character.

In the first place, we have constantly kept in view the arguments of those who hold that the plagues were not miraculous, and, while fully admitting all the illustration that the physical history of Egypt has afforded us, both in our own observation and the observation of others, we have found no reason for the naturalistic view in a single instance, while in many instances the illustrations from known phenomena have been so different as to bring out the miraculous element in the narrative with the greatest force, and in every case that element has been necessary, unless the narrative be deprived of its rights as historical evidence. Yet more, we have found that the advocates of a naturalistic explanation have been forced by their bias into a distortion and exaggeration of natural phenomena in their endeavor to find in them an explanation of the wonders recorded in the Bible.

In the examination we have made it will have been seen that the Biblical narrative has been illustrated by reference to the phenomena of Egypt and the manners of the inhabitants, and that, throughout, its accuracy in minute particulars has been remarkably shown, to a degree that is sufficient of itself to prove its historical truth. This in a narrative of wonders is of no small importance.

Respecting the character of the plagues, they were evidently nearly all miraculous in time of occurrence and degree rather than essentially, in accordance with the theory that God generally employs natural means in producing miraculous effects. They seem to have been sent as a series of warnings, each being somewhat more severe than its predecessor, to which we see an analogy in the warnings which the providential government of the world often puts before the sinner. The first plague corrupted the sweet water of the Nile and slew the fish. The second filled the land with frogs, which corrupted the whole country. The third covered man and beast with vermin or other annoying insects. The fourth was of the same kind and probably a yet severer judgment. With the fifth plague, the murrain of beasts, a loss of property began. The sixth, the plague of boils, was worse than the earlier plagues that had affected man and beast. The seventh plague, that of hail, exceeded those that went before it, since it destroyed everything in the field, man and beast and herb. The eighth plague was evidently still more grievous, since the devastation by locusts must have been far more thorough than that by the hail, and since at that time no greater calamity of the kind could have happened than the destruction of all remaining vegetable food. The ninth plague we do not sufficiently understand to be sure that it exceeded this in actual injury, but it is clear from the narrative that it must have caused great terror. The last plague is the only one that was general in the destruction of human life, for the effects of the hail cannot have been comparable to those it produced, and it completes the climax, unless indeed it be held that the passage of the Red Sea was the crowning point of the whole series of wonders, rather than a separate miracle. In this case its magnitude, as publicly destroying the king and his whole army, might even surpass that of the tenth plague.

The gradual increase in severity of the plagues is perhaps the best key to their meaning. They seem to have been sent as warnings to the oppressor, to afford him a means of seeing God's will and an opportunity of repenting before Egypt was ruined. It is true that the hardening of Pharaoh's heart is a mystery which St. Paul leaves unexplained, answering the objector, "Nay but, O man, who art thou that repliest against God?" (Rom.

ix. 20). Yet the Apostle is arguing that we have no right to question God's righteousness for not having mercy on all, and speaks of his long-suffering towards the wicked. The lesson that Pharaoh's career teaches us seems to be, that there are men whom the most signal judgments do not affect so as to cause any lasting repentance. In this respect the after-history of the Jewish people is a commentary upon that of their oppressor. R. S. P.

* In studying the ten plagues of Egypt two points must be kept distinctly in view: (1) their reality, and (2) their judicial character. Were these plagues actual occurrences? Were they divine judgments? Ewald, who admits a general foundation of fact for the story as given in Exodus, nevertheless regards it as the growth of successive traditions, finally redacted many centuries after the event. "Everything in this story is on a coherent and sublime plan, is grand and instructive, excites and satisfies the mind. It is like a divine drama, exhibited on earth in the midst of real history; to be regarded in this light, and to be treasured accordingly. Not that we hereby assert, that this story does not on the whole exhibit the essence of the event as it actually happened. For the sequel of the narrative shows that Pharaoh did not voluntarily allow the people to go; and we cannot form too exalted an idea of Moses. But we do insist that the story as it now is cannot have been drawn up before the era of the great Prophets" (*History of Israel*, Martineau's trans., i. 488). In answer to this theory of a late composition of the story, Mr. Poole (*supra*) has aptly remarked that the minute accuracy of the Biblical narrative in its references to Egypt is a signal proof of its historical truth. Admitting the general analogy of the plagues with the phenomena of the country, the knowledge of the physical features of Egypt, its soil, climate, productions, natural history, and meteorology, which the author of this narrative exhibits, is such as could have been gained only by a personal residence in Egypt, and argues a personal observation of the events described. Moreover this narrative occurs in a book which exhibits throughout the personal familiarity of its author with the customs of Egypt, religious, social, and domestic, with its cities and forts, its laws and institutions, its superstitions and modes of worship, its arts and manufactures; and this knowledge, revealing itself in a merely incidental way, is so much the stronger evidence of the genuineness and authenticity of the account given by Moses.

But Ewald's theory finds also a positive refutation in the institution of the Passover. He himself traces this observance back to the time of Joshua. "About this time, many customs certainly first received proper legal sanction, which, though closely connected with the existing religion, possessed more popular importance for the fully established community; as the Feast of the Passover, in commemoration of the deliverance out of Egypt; and circumcision, as marking every male member of the community. Not without reason does the earliest narrator make Gilgal the scene of the first general circumcision, and likewise of the first Passover. At Gilgal near the Jordan, doubtless, many in still later days loved to keep the Passover; being more forcibly reminded by the sight of the Jordan of the triumphant entry into Canaan, of the previous adventures in the desert, and of the deliverance out of Egypt" (Ewald,

Hist. of Israel, ii. 34). Thus Ewald distinctly admits that, as far back as the time of Joshua, the Passover was observed, to commemorate the deliverance out of Egypt. The Passover is a perpetual witness for the Exodus. But the Passover contains features so unnatural, so remote in themselves from mere imagination or invention, that one cannot conceive of their origin except in some fact of actual occurrence. This is true especially of the time and manner of killing the lamb, and the sprinkling of the blood on the side posts and the upper door-post of the houses. As the observance itself witnesses for the departure out of Egypt, so do these unique features of it witness for the facts which are recorded as having attended its own institution. But the tenth decisive plague was only the culmination of a series, and the whole narrative must stand or fall together. The plagues were actual occurrences.

Were they also divine judgments? Upon this point Ewald again says (vol. i. p. 484), "Among the ten plagues by which Pharaoh is ultimately coerced into compliance, eight are nothing more than extraordinary calamities of such a kind as may occur in any country, but most frequently and easily in the swampy northern portion of Egypt (only that, in connection with this history, they are to be viewed in that terrible light in which the locusts are regarded by Joel), and are arranged in an appropriate advance in severity: frogs out of the water, mosquitoes as if swarming from the dust, dogflies, murrain among the cattle, a kind of blains, hail, locusts, darkness . . . . The whole constitutes a very Egyptian picture, indeed more so than the separate details; in no nation was the observation and the fear of extraordinary atmospheric and other natural phenomena so early and carefully developed as in Egypt. The Egyptians are beaten by the true God in and through their own faith — that is the fundamental thought of the whole." Now it is this fundamental thought, sustained by certain special features of phenomena in other respects natural, that gives to these calamities the character of divine judgments. They came in rapid succession, apparently at unusual seasons, and all point toward one end. They come and go at the word or prayer of Moses, and are even announced by him beforehand in terms of warning. At first they are feebly imitated or simulated by the magicians, but their resources soon come to an end. In several instances the Israelites are exempted from the plague that smites everything around them. These peculiarities cannot be accounted for by the operation of natural causes: and, "where natural power is pushed beyond natural limits, the event is just as miraculous as where the power is wholly unknown to nature." The manifestation of supernatural power within the sphere of phenomena peculiar to Egypt was the more impressive as a proof that the God of the Hebrews had supreme dominion over all natural and spiritual powers in Egypt also. This Pharaoh himself at last acknowledged.

The hardening of his heart was due to his own willfulness. He is said again and again to have hardened it; and the divine agency in that result was simply that of multiplying appeals and wonders fitted to convert him, though it was foreseen that he would resist them all. The Hebrew Scriptures, overlooking secondary agencies, ascribe to Jehovah whatever He in any wise causes or suffers to come to pass.   J. P. T.

PLAINS. This one term does duty in the Authorized Version for no less than seven distinct Hebrew words, each of which had its own independent and individual meaning, and could not be — at least *is not* — interchanged with any other; some of them are proper names exclusively attached to one spot, and one has not the meaning of plain at all.

1. *Abél* (אָבֵל). This word perhaps answers more nearly to our word "meadow" than any other, its root having, according to Gesenius, the force of moisture like that of grass. It occurs in the names of ABEL-MAIM, ABEL-MEHOLAH, ABEL-SHITTIM, and is rendered "plain" in Judg. xi. 33, "plain of vineyards."

2. *Bik'áh* (בִּקְעָה). From a root signifying "to cleave or rend" (Gesen. *Thes.* p. 232; Fürst, *Handwb.* i. 212). Fortunately we are able to identify the most remarkable of the *Bikahs* of the Bible, and thus to ascertain the force of the term. The great Plain or Valley of Cœle-Syria, the "hollow land" of the Greeks, which separates the two ranges of Lebanon and Antilebanon, is the most remarkable of them all. It is called in the Bible the Bika'ath Aven (Am. i. 5), and also probably the Bika'ath Lebanon (Josh. xi. 17, xii. 7) and Bika'ath-Mizpeh (xi. 8), and is still known throughout Syria by its old name, as *el-Beka'a*, or *Ard el-Beka'a*. "A long valley, though broad," says Dr. Pusey (*Comment.* on Am. i. 5), "if seen from a height looks like a cleft;" and this is eminently the case with the "Valley of Lebanon" when approached by the ordinary roads from north or south.[b] It is of great extent, more than 60 miles long by about 5 in average breadth, and the two great ranges shut it in on either hand, Lebanon especially, with a very wall-like appearance [LEBANON.] Not unlike it in this effect is the Jordan Valley at Jericho, which appears to be once mentioned under the same title in Deut. xxxiv. 3 (A. V. "the Valley of Jericho"). This, however, is part of the Arabah, the proper name of the Jordan Valley. Besides these the "plain of Megiddo" (2 Chr. xxxv. 22; Zech. xii. 11, A. V. "valley of M.") and "the plain of Ono" (Neh. vi. 2) have not been identified.[c]

Out of Palestine we find denoted by the word *Bik'áh* "the plain in the land of Shinar" (Gen. xi. 2), the "plain of Mesopotamia" (Ex. iii. 22, 23, viii. 4, xxxvii. 2), and the "plain in the province of Dura" (Dan. iii. 1). 🖝

Bik'áh perhaps appears, with other Arabic[d]

---

[a] An entirely different word in Hebrew (though identical in English) from the name of the son of Adam, which is *Hebel.*

[b] For instance, from the mountain between Zebdany and Baalbec, half an hour past the Roman bridge.

[c] * For the situation of "the plain of Ono" see Robinson's *Phys. Geogr. of Palestine,* pp. 118, 126. It was no doubt near LOD or LYDDA.   H.

[d] For instance, the farm-houses which "sparkle amid the eternal verdure of the Vega of Granada" are called *carmenes,* a term derived through the Arabic from the Hebrew *cerem,* a vineyard, a rich spot — a Carmel. Another Semitic word naturalised in Spain is Seville (see further down, No. 6). But indeed they are most numerous. For other examples see *Glossaire des mots espagnols dérivés de l'Arabe,* par Engelmann, Leyden, 1861.

worus, in Spanish as *Vega*, a term applied to well-watered valleys, between hills (Ford, *Handbk.* sect. iii.), and especially to the Valley of Granada, the most extensive and most fruitful of them all, of which the Moors were accustomed to boast that it was larger and richer than the *Ghûttah*, the Oasis of Damascus.

3. *Hac-Ciccâr* (הַכִּכָּר). This, though applied to a plain, has not (if the lexicographers are right) the force of flatness or extent, but rather seems to be derived from a root signifying roundness. In its topographical sense (for it has other meanings, such as a coin, a cake, or flat loaf) it is confined to the Jordan Valley. This sense it bears in Gen. xiii. 10, 11, 12, xix. 17, 25-29; Deut. xxxiv. 3; 2 Sam. xviii. 23; 1 K. vii. 46; 2 Chr. iv. 17; Neh. iii. 22, xii. 28. The LXX. translate it by περίχωρος and περίοικος, the former of which is often found in the N. T., where the English reader is familiar with it as "the region round about." It must be confessed that it is not easy to trace any connection between a "circular form" and the nature or aspect of the Jordan Valley, and it is difficult not to suspect that *Ciccar* is an archaic term which existed before the advent of the Hebrews, and was afterwards adopted into their language. [REGION-ROUND-ABOUT.]

4. *Ham-Mîshôr* (הַמִּישׁוֹר). This is by the lexicographers explained as meaning "straightforward," "plain," as if from the root *yâshar*, to be just or upright; but this seems far-fetched, and it is more probable that in this case also we have an archaic term existing from a pre-historic date. It occurs in the Bible in the following passages: Deut. iii. 10, iv. 43; Josh. xiii. 9, 16, 17, 21, xx. 8; 1 K. xx. 23, 25; 2 Chr. xxvi. 10; Jer. xlviii. 8, 21. In each of these, with one exception, it is used for the district in the neighborhood of Heshbon and Dibon — the *Belka* of the modern Arabs, their most noted pasture-ground; a district which, from the scanty descriptions we possess of it, seems to resemble the "Downs" of our own country in the regularity of its undulations, the excellence of its turf, and its fitness for the growth of flocks. There is no difficulty in recognizing the same district in the statement of 2 Chr. xxvi. 10. It is evident from several circumstances that Uzziah had been a great conqueror on the east of Jordan, as well as on the shore of the Mediterranean (see Ewald's remarks, *Geschichte*, iii. 588, *note*), and he kept his cattle on the rich pastures of Philistines on the one hand, and Ammonites on the other. Thus in all the passages quoted above the word *Mishor* seems to be restricted to one special district, and to belong to it as exclusively as *Shefelah* did to the lowland of Philistia, or *Arabah* to the sunken district of the Jordan Valley. And therefore it is puzzling to find it used in one passage (1 K. xx. 23, 25) apparently with the mere general sense of low land, or rather flat land, in which chariots could be manœuvred — as opposed to uneven mountainous ground. There is some reason to believe that the scene of the battle in question was on the east side of the Sea of Gennesaret in the plain of *Jaulan*; but this is no explanation of the difficulty, because we are not

warranted in extending the *Mishor* further than the mountains which bounded it on the north, and where the districts began which bore, like it, their own distinctive names of Gilead, Bashan, Argob, Golan, Hauran, etc. Perhaps the most feasible explanation is that the word was used by the Syrians of Damascus without any knowledge of its strict signification, in the same manner indeed that it was employed in the later Syro-Chaldee dialect, in which *meshra* is the favorite term to express several natural features which in the older and stricter language were denominated each by its own special name.

5. *Ha-Arâbâh* (הָעֲרָבָה). This again had an absolutely definite meaning — being restricted to the valley of the Jordan, and to its continuation south of the Dead Sea. [See ARABAH, vol. i. pp. 133, 134; and for a description of the aspect of the region, PALESTINE, vol. iii. pp. 2298, 2299.] No doubt the *Arabah* was the most remarkable plain of the Holy Land — but to render it by so general and common a term (as our translators have done in the majority of cases) is materially to diminish its force and significance in the narrative. This is equally the case with

6. *Ha-Shefêlâh* (הַשְּׁפֵלָה), the invariable designation of the depressed, flat, or gently undulating region which intervened between the highlands of Judah and the Mediterranean, and was commonly in possession of the Philistines. [PALESTINE, p. 2296; SEPHELA.] To the Hebrews this, and this only, was The Shefelah; and to have spoken of it by any more general term would have been as impossible as for natives of the Carse of Stirling or the Weald of Kent to designate them differently. *Shefelah* has some claims of its own to notice. It was one of the most tenacious of these old Hebrew terms. It appears in the Greek text and in the Authorized Version of the Book of Maccabees (1 Macc. xii. 38), and is preserved on each of its other occurrences, even in such corrupt dialects as the Samaritan Version of the Pentateuch, and the Targums of Pseudo-jonathan, and of Rabbi Joseph. And although it would appear to be no longer known in its original seat, it has transferred itself to other countries, and appears in Spain as *Seville*, and on the east coast of Africa as *Sofala*.

7. *Êlôn* (אֵלוֹן). Our translators have uniformly rendered this word "plain," doubtless following the Vulgate,[a] which in about half the passages has *convallis*. But this is not the verdict of the majority or the most trustworthy of the ancient versions. They regard the word as meaning an "oak" or "grove of oaks," a rendering supported by all, or nearly all, the commentators and lexicographers of the present day. It has the advantage also of being much more picturesque, and throws a new light (to the English reader) over many an incident in the lives of the Patriarchs and early heroes of the Bible. The passages in which the word occurs erroneously translated "plain," are as follows: Plain of Moreh (Gen. xii. 6; Deut. xi. 30), Plain of Mamre (Gen. xiii. 18, xiv. 13, xviii. 1), Plain of Zaanaim (Judg. iv. 11), Plain of the

---

a Jerome, again, probably followed the Targum or other Jewish authorities, and they usually employ the rendering above mentioned. Fürst alone endeavors to find a reason for it — not a satisfactory one: "be cause trees frequent plains or meadows" (*Handwt* i. 90 b).

Pillar (Judg. ix. 6), Plain of Meonenim (ix. 37), Plain of Tabor (1 Sam. x. 3)

8. The Plain of Esdraelon which to the modern traveller in the Holy Land forms the third of its three most remarkable depressions, is designated in the original by neither of the above terms, but by *emek*, an appellative noun frequently employed in the Bible for the smaller valleys of the country — "the valley of Jezreel." Perhaps Esdraelon may anciently have been considered as consisting of two portions; the Valley of Jezreel the eastern and smaller, the Plain of Megiddo the western and more extensive of the two. G.

* PLAINS OF JERICHO. [Jericho.]

* PLANE-TREE, Ecclus. xxiv. 14. [Chest-nut-Tree.]

PLASTER.[a] The mode of making plaster-cement has been described above. [Morter.] Plaster is mentioned thrice in Scripture: 1. (Lev. xiv. 42, 48), where when a house was infected with "leprosy," the priest was ordered to take away the portion of infected wall and re-plaster it (Michaelis, *Laws of Moses*, § 211, iii. 297-305, ed. Smith). [House; Leprosy.]

2. The words of the Law were ordered to be en-graved on Mount Ebal on stones which had been previously coated with plaster (Deut. xxvii. 2, 4; Josh. viii. 32). The process here mentioned was probably of a similar kind to that adopted in Egypt for receiving bas-reliefs. The wall was first made smooth, and its interstices, if necessary, filled up with plaster. When the figures had been drawn, and the stone adjacent cut away so as to leave them in relief, a coat of lime whitewash was laid on, and followed by one of varnish after the painting of the figures was complete. In the case of the natural rock the process was nearly the same. The ground was covered with a thick layer of fine plaster, con-sisting of lime and gypsum carefully smoothed and polished. Upon this a coat of lime whitewash was laid, and on it the colors were painted, and set by means of glue or wax. The whitewash appears in most instances to have been made of shell-limestone not much burnt, which of itself is tenacious enough without glue or other binding material (Long, quoting from Belzoni, *Eg. Ant.* ii. 49-50).

At Behistun in Persia, the surface of the in-scribed rock-tablet was covered with a varnish to preserve it from weather; but it seems likely that in the case of the Ebal tablets the inscription was cut while the plaster was still moist (Layard, *Nin-ereh*, ii. 188; Vaux, *Nin. & Persep.* p. 172).

3. It was probably a similar coating of cement, on which the fatal letters were traced by the mystic hand "on the plaster of the wall" of Belshazzar's palace at Babylon (Dan. v. 5). We here obtain an incidental confirmation of the Biblical narrative. For while at Nineveh the walls are paneled with alabaster slabs, at Babylon, where no such mate-rial is found, the builders were content to cover their tiles or bricks with enamel or stucco, fitly termed plaster, fit for receiving ornamental designs (Layard, *Nin. and Bab.* p. 529; Diod. ii. 8). [Bricks.] H. W. P.

* PLATES. [Laver, 2 (d).]

---

a 1. בִּר, בִּיר, Ch. בִּירָא : κονία : calx. In Is. xxvii. 9, "chalk-stone."

2. שִׂיד : κονία : calx.

PLEIADES. The Hebrew word (כִּימָה, *cîmâh*) so rendered occurs in Job ix. 9, xxxviii. 31, and Am. v. 8. In the last passage our A. V. has "the seven stars," although the Geneva version translates the word "Pleiades" as in the other cases. In Job the LXX. has Πλειάς, the order of the Hebrew words having been altered [see Orion], while in Amos there is no trace of the original, and it is difficult to imagine what the translators had before them. The Vulgate in each passage has a different rendering: *Hyades* in Job ix. 9, *Pleiades* in Job xxxviii. 31, and *Arcturus* in Am. v. 8. Of the other versions the Peshito-Syriac and Chaldee merely adopt the Hebrew word; Aquila in Job xxxviii., Symmachus in Job xxxviii. and Amos, and Theodotion in Amos give "Pleiades," while with remarkable inconsistency Aquila in Amos has "Arcturus." The Jewish commentators are no less at variance. R. David Kimchi in his Lexicon says: "R. Jonah wrote that it was a collection of stars called in Arabic *Al Thuraiyâ*. And the wise Rabbi Abraham Aben Ezra, of blessed memory, wrote that the ancients said *Cîmâh* is seven stars, and they are at the end of the constellation Aries, and those which are seen are six. And he wrote that what was right in his eyes was that it was a single star, and that a great one, which is called the left eye of Taurus; and *Cesil* is a great star, the heart of the constellation Scorpio." On Job xxxviii. 31, Kimchi continues: "Our Rabbis of blessed mem-ory have said (*Beracoth*, 58, 2), *Cîmâh* hath great cold and bindeth up the fruits, and *Cesil* hath great heat and ripeneth the fruits: therefore He said, 'or loosen the bands of *Cesil*,' for it openeth the fruits and bringeth them forth." In addition to the evi-dence of R. Jonah, who identifies the Hebrew *cîmâh* with the Arabic *Al Thuraiyâ*, we have the testimony of R. Isaac Israel, quoted by Hyde in his notes on the Tables of Ulugh Beigh (pp. 31-32, ed. 1665) to the same effect. That *Al Thuraiyâ* and the Pleiades are the same is proved by the words of Aben Ragel (quoted by Hyde, p. 33): "Al Thuraiyâ is the mansion of the moon, in the sign Taurus, and it is called the celestial hen with her chickens." With this Hyde compares the Fr. *pulsinière*, and Eng. *Hen and chickens*, which are old names for the same stars: and Niebuhr (*Descr. de l'Arabie*, p. 101) gives as the result of his in-quiry of the Jew at Sanâ, "Kimeh, Pleiades, qu'on appelle aussi en Allemagne la poule qui glousse." The "Ancients," whom Aben Ezra quotes (on Job xxxviii. 31), evidently understood by the seven small stars at the end of the constellation Aries the Pleiades, which are indeed in the left shoulder of the Bull, but so near the Ram's tail, that their position might properly be defined with reference to it. With the statement that "those which are seen are six" may be compared the words of Didy-mus on Homer, τῶν δὲ Πλειάδων οὐσῶν ἑπτὰ πάνυ ἀμαυρὸς ὁ ἕβδομος ἀστήρ, and of Ovid (*Fast.* iv. 170) —

"Quæ septem dici, sex tamen esse solent."

The opinion of Aben Ezra himself has been fre-quently misrepresented. He held that *Cîmâh* was a single large star, *Aldebaran* the brightest of the Hyades, while *Cesil* [A. V. "Orion"] was *Anta-res* the heart of Scorpio. "When these rise in the east," he continues, "the effects which are recorded appear." He describes them as *opposite* each other, and the difference in Right Ascension between Aldebaran and Antares is as nearly as possible twelve hours. The belief of Aben Ezra had probably the same origin as the rendering of the Vulgate, *Hyades*.

One other point is deserving of notice. The Rabbis, as quoted by Kimchi, attribute to *Cîmâh* great cold and the property of checking vegetation, while *Cesîl* works the contrary effects. But the words of R. Isaac Israel on Job xxxviii. 31 (quoted by Hyde, p. 72), are just the reverse. He says, "The stars have operations in the ripening of the fruits, and such is the operation of *Cîmâh*. And some of them retard and delay the fruits from ripening, and this is the operation of *Cesîl*. The interpretation is, 'Wilt thou bind the fruits which the constellation *Cîmâh* ripeneth and openeth; or wilt thou open the fruits which the constellation *Cesîl* contracteth and bindeth up?'"

On the whole, then, though it is impossible to arrive at any certain conclusion, it appears that our translators were perfectly justified in rendering *Cîmâh* by "Pleiades." The "seven stars" in Amos clearly denoted the same cluster in the language of the 17th century, for Cotgrave in his French Dictionary gives "Pleiade, f., one of the *seven stars*."

Hyde maintained that the Pleiades were again mentioned in Scripture by the name Succoth Benoth. The discussion of this question must be reserved to the Article on that name.

The etymology of *Cîmâh* is referred to the Arab.

كومَة, "a heap," as being a heap or cluster of stars. The full Arabic name given by Gesenius is

عَقْل الثُّرَيَا, "the knot of the Pleiades;" and, in accordance with this, most modern commentators render Job xxxviii. 31, "Is it thou that bindest the knots of the Pleiades, or loosenest the bands of Orion?" Simonis (*Lex. Hebr.*) quotes the Greenland name for this cluster of stars, "*Killukterset*, i. e. *stellas colligatas*," as an instance of the existence of the same idea in a widely different language. The rendering "sweet influences" of the A. V. is a relic of the lingering belief in the power which the stars exerted over human destiny. The marginal note on the word "Pleiades" in the Geneva Version is, "which starres arise when the sunne is in Taurus, which is the spring tyme, and bring flowers," thus agreeing with the explanation of R. Isaac Israel quoted above.

For authorities, in addition to those already referred to, see Michaelis (*Suppl. ad Lex. Hebr.* No. 1136), Simonis (*Lex. Hebr.*), and Gesenius (*Thesaurus*).   W. A. W.

* PLEDGE. The words so translated in the A. V. are עֲרֻבָּה, עֵרָבוֹן, עֲבוֹט, חֲבֹלָה, חֲבֹל. All these, except the last, designate something given as security for the payment of a debt or the fulfillment of a promise. The passage 1 Sam. xvii. 18, where alone עֲרֻבָּה is rendered *pledge* by our translators (it occurs but once elsewhere, Prov. xvii. 18: עֹרֵב עֲרֻבָּה, rendered *becometh surety*), is of doubtful import. See Thenius *in loc.*

The practice of taking pledges for the payment of debt, common from time immemorial throughout the East (Job xxii. 6, xxiv. 3, 9; for the present usage see *Land and Book*, i. 499), was regulated in the Mosaic Law as follows: (1.) The creditor was not allowed to enter the house of his debtor, in order to take a pledge, but it must be brought out to him, Deut. xxiv. 10, 11. (2.) A handmill was not allowed to be taken in pledge (Deut. xxiv. 6), nor the raiment (בֶּגֶד) of a widow (Deut. xxiv. 17). (3.) An outer garment (שַׂלְמָה i. q. שִׂמְלָה, used also as a night-covering) taken in pledge must be delivered to the owner at sunset (Ex. xxii. 26; Deut. xxiv. 13). For allusions to the disregard of these enactments, see Ezek. xviii. 7, 12, 16, xxxiii. 15; Am. ii. 8.

One of the Hebrew words given above, עֵרָבוֹן, occurs in the N. T. in the form of ἀρῥαβών (A. V. "earnest"), 2 Cor. i. 22, v. 5; Eph. i. 14; most probably, however, in the sense not simply of a pledge of something to be bestowed in future, but of such a pledge as, being, like earnest-money, of the same or a kindred nature with the ultimate gift or payment, should be also thus a partial anticipation of it. [See EARNEST.] Another cognate form is found in the expression בְּנֵי הַתַּעֲרֻבוֹת (A. V. "hostages"), 2 K. xiv. 14; 2 Chr. xxv. 24, employed to designate persons given to be held in pledge for the performance of treaty obligations.   D. S. T.

PLOUGH. [AGRICULTURE.]

* PLUMB-LINE. [LINE, Amer. ed.]

* PLUMMET, 2 K. xxviii. 13; Is. xxi. 18. [HANDICRAFT; LINE.]

POCHE'RETH (פֹּכֶרֶת [*snaring, catching*]. Φαχερά θ [Vat. Φααραθ]; Alex. Φακεραθ, in Ezr.; Φακαρθ, Alex. Φαχαραθ [FA. Φαχαρατ], in Neh.: *Phochereth*). The children of Pochereth of Zebaim were among the children of Solomon's servants who returned with Zerubbabel (Ezr. ii. 57; Neh. vii. 59). He is called in 1 Esdr. v. 34, PHACARETH. [ZEBAIM.]

POETRY, HEBREW. The subject of Hebrew Poetry has been treated at great length by many writers of the last three centuries, but the results of their speculations have been, in most instances, in an inverse ratio to their length. That such would be the case might have been foretold as a natural consequence of their method of investigation. In the 16th and 17th centuries the influence of classical studies upon the minds of the learned was so great as to imbue them with the belief that the writers of Greece and Rome were the models of all excellence, and consequently, when their learning and critical acumen were directed to the records of another literature, they were unable to divest themselves of the prejudices of early education and habits, and sought for the same excellences which they admired in their favorite models. That this has been the case with regard to most of the speculations on the poetry of the Hebrews, and that the failure of those speculations is mainly due to this cause, will be abundantly manifest to any one who is acquainted with the literature of the subject. But, however barren of results, the history of the various theories which have been framed with regard to the external form of Hebrew poetry is a necessary part of the present article, and will serve in some measure as a warning, to any who may hereafter attempt the solution of the problem, what to avoid. The attributes which are common to all poetry, and which the poetry of the Hebrews pos senses in a higher degree perhaps than the literature of any other people, it is unnecessary here to describe. But the points of contrast are so numerous, and the peculiarities which distinguish Hebrew poetry so remarkable, that these alone require a full and careful consideration. It is a phenomenon which is universally observed in the literatures of all nations, that the earliest form in which the thoughts and feelings of a people find utterance is the poetic. Prose is an aftergrowth, the vehicle of less spontaneous, because more formal, expression. And so it is in the literature of the Hebrews. We find in the sober narrative which tells us of the fortunes of Cain and his descendants the earliest known specimen of poetry on record, the song of Lamech to his wives, "the sword song," as Herder terms it, supposing it to commemorate the discovery of weapons of war by his son Tubal-Cain. But whether it be a song of triumph for the impunity which the wild old chief might now enjoy for his son's discovery, or a lament for some deed of violence of his own, this chant of Lamech has of itself an especial interest as connected with the oldest genealogical document, and as possessing the characteristics of Hebrew poetry at the earliest period with which we are acquainted. Its origin is admitted by Ewald to be pre-Mosaic, and its antiquity the most remote. Its lyrical character is consistent with its early date, for lyrical poetry is of all forms the earliest, being, as Ewald (*Dicht. des A. B.* 1 Th. i. § 2, p. 11) admirably describes it, "the daughter of the moment, of swift-rising powerful feelings, of deep stirrings and fiery emotions of the soul." This first fragment which has come down to us possesses thus the eminently lyrical character which distinguishes the poetry of the Hebrew nation from its earliest existence to its decay and fall. It has besides the further characteristic of parallelism, to which reference will be hereafter made.

Of the three kinds of poetry which are illustrated by the Hebrew literature, the *lyric* occupies the foremost place. The Shemitic nations have nothing approaching to an *epic* poem, and in proportion to this defect the lyric element prevailed more greatly, commencing, as we have seen, in the pre-Mosaic times, flourishing in rude vigor during the earlier periods of the Judges, the heroic age of the Hebrews, growing with the nation's growth and strengthening with its strength, till it reached its highest excellence in David, the warrior-poet, and from thenceforth began slowly to decline. *Gnomic* poetry is the product of a more advanced age. It arises from the desire felt by the poet to express the results of the accumulated experiences of life in a form of beauty and permanence. Its thoughtful character requires for its development a time of peacefulness and leisure; for it gives expression, not like the lyric to the sudden and impassioned feelings of the moment, but to calm and philosophic reflection. Being less spontaneous in its origin, its form is of necessity more artificial. The gnomic poetry of the Hebrews has not its measured flow disturbed by the shock of arms or the tumult of camps; it rises silently, like the Temple of old, without the sound of a weapon, and its groundwork is the home life of the nation. The period during which it flourished corresponds to its domestic and settled character. From the time of David onwards through the reigns of the earlier kings, when the nation was quiet and at peace, or, if not at peace, at least so firmly fixed in its acquired terri-

tory that its wars were no struggle for existence gnomic poetry blossomed and bare fruit. We meet with it at intervals up to the time of the Captivity, and, as it is chiefly characteristic of the age of the monarchy, Ewald has appropriately designated this era the "artificial period" of Hebrew poetry. From the end of the 8th century B. C. the decline of the nation was rapid, and with its glory departed the chief glories of its literature. The poems of this period are distinguished by a smoothness of diction and an external polish which betray tokens of labor and art; the style is less flowing and easy, and, except in rare instances, there is no dash of the ancient vigor. After the Captivity we have nothing but the poems which formed part of the liturgical services of the Temple. Whether *dramatic* poetry, properly so called, ever existed among the Hebrews, is, to say the least, extremely doubtful. In the opinion of some writers the Song of Songs, in its external form, is a rude drama, designed for a simple stage. But the evidence for this view is extremely slight, and no good and sufficient reasons have been adduced which would lead us to conclude that the amount of dramatic action exhibited in that poem is more than would be involved in an animated poetic dialogue in which more than two persons take part. Philosophy and the drama appear alike to have been peculiar to the Indo-Germanic nations, and to have manifested themselves among the Shemitic tribes only in their crudest and most simple form.

1. *Lyrical Poetry.* — The literature of the Hebrews abounds with illustrations of all forms of lyrical poetry, in its most manifold and wide-embracing compass, from such short ejaculations as the songs of the two Lamechs, and Pss. xv., cxviii., and others, to the longer chants of victory and thanksgiving, like the songs of Deborah and David (Judg. v., Ps. xviii.). The thoroughly national character of all lyrical poetry has been already alluded to. It is the utterance of the people's life in all its varied phases, and expresses all its most earnest strivings and impulses. In proportion as this expression is vigorous and animated, the idea embodied in lyric song is in most cases narrowed or rather concentrated. One truth, and even one side of a truth, is for the time invested with the greatest prominence. All those characteristics will be found in perfection in the lyric poetry of the Hebrews. One other feature which distinguishes it is its form and its capability for being set to a musical accompaniment. The names by which the various kinds of songs were known among the Hebrews will supply some illustration of this.

1. שִׁיר, *shír,* a song in general, adapted for the voice alone.

2. מִזְמוֹר, *mizmôr,* which Ewald considers a lyric song, properly so called, but which rather seems to correspond with the Greek ψαλμός, a psalm, or song to be sung with any instrumental accompaniment.

3. נְגִינָה, *négínáh,* which Ewald is of opinion is equivalent to the Greek ψαλμός, is more probably a melody expressly adapted for stringed instruments.

4. מַשְׂכִּיל, *mascíl,* of which it may be said that, if Ewald's suggestion be not correct, that it denotes a lyrical song requiring nice musical skill, it is difficult to give any more probable explanation. [MASCHIL.]

5. מִכְתָּם, *mictâm*, a term of extremely doubtful meaning. [MICHTAM.]

6. שִׁגָּיוֹן, *shiggâyôn* (Ps. vii. 1), a wild, irregular, dithyrambic song, as the word appears to denote; or, according to some, a song to be sung with variations. The former is the more probable meaning. [SHIGGAION.] The plural occurs in Hab. iii. 1.

But, besides these, there are other divisions of lyrical poetry of great importance, which have regard rather to the subject of the poems than to their form or adaptation for musical accompaniments. Of these we notice: —

1. תְּהִלָּה, *tĕhillâh*, a hymn of praise. The plural *tĕhillîm* is the title of the Book of Psalms in Hebrew. The 145th Psalm is entitled "David's (Psalm) of praise;" and the subject of the psalm is in accordance with its title, which is apparently suggested by the concluding verse, "the *praise* of Jehovah my mouth shall speak, and let all flesh bless his holy name for ever and ever." To this class belong the songs which relate to extraordinary deliverances, such as the songs of Moses (Ex. xv.) and of Deborah (Judg. v.), and the Psalms xviii. and lxviii., which have all the air of chants to be sung in triumphal processions. Such were the hymns sung in the Temple services, and by a bold figure the Almighty is apostrophized as "Thou that inhabitest the *praises* of Israel," which rose in the holy place with the fragrant clouds of incense (Ps. xxii. 3). To the same class also Ewald refers the shorter poems of the like kind with those already quoted, such as Pss. xxx., xxxii., cxxxviii., and Is. xxxviii., which relate to less general occasions, and commemorate more special deliverances. The songs of victory sung by the congregation in the Temple, as Pss. xlvi., xlviii., xxiv. 7-10, which is a short triumphal ode, and Ps. xxix., which praises Jehovah on the occasion of a great natural phenomenon, are likewise all to be classed in this division of lyric poetry. Next to the hymn of praise may be noticed, —

2. קִינָה, *kînâh*, the lament, or dirge, of which there are many examples, whether uttered over an individual or as an outburst of grief for the calamities of the land. The most touchingly pathetic of all is perhaps the lament of David for the death of Saul and Jonathan (2 Sam. i. 19-27), in which passionate emotion is blended with touches of tenderness of which only a strong nature is capable. Compare with this the lament for Abner (2 Sam. iii. 33, 34) and for Absalom (2 Sam. xviii. 33). Of the same character also, doubtless, were the songs which the singing men and singing women spake over Josiah at his death (2 Chr. xxxv. 25), and the songs of mourning for the disasters which befell the hapless land of Judah, of which Psalms xlix., lx., lxxiii., cxxxvii., are examples (comp. Jer. vii. 29, ix. 10 [9]), and the Lamentations of Jeremiah the most memorable instances.

3. שִׁיר יְדִידֹת, *shîr yĕdîdôth*, a love-song (Ps. xlv. 1), in its external form at least. Other kinds of poetry there are which occupy the middle ground between the lyric and gnomic, being lyric

in form and spirit, but gnomic in subject. These may be classed as —

4. מָשָׁל, *mâshâl*, properly a similitude, and then a parable, or sententious saying couched in poetic language.[a] Such are the songs of Balaam (Num. xxiii. 7, 18; xxiv. 3, 15, 20, 21, 23), which are eminently lyrical in character; the mocking ballad in Num. xxi. 27-30, which has been conjectured to be a fragment of an old Amorite war-song [NUMBERS, p. 2197 *b*]; and the apologue of Jotham (Judg. ix. 7-20), both which last are strongly satirical in tone. But the finest of all is the magnificent prophetic song of triumph over the fall of Babylon (Is. xiv. 4-27). חִידָה, *chîdah*, an enigma (like the riddle of Samson, Judg. xiv. 14), or "dark saying," as the A. V. has it in Ps. xlix. 4, lxxviii. 2. The former passage illustrates the musical, and therefore lyric character of these "dark sayings: "I will incline mine ear to a parable, I will open my dark saying upon the harp." *Mâshâl* and *chîdah* are used as convertible terms in Ez. xvii. 2. Lastly, to this class belongs מְלִיצָה, *mĕlîtsâh*, a mocking, ironical poem (Hab. ii. 6).

5. תְּפִלָּה, *tĕphillâh*, prayer, is the title of Pss. xvii., lxxxvi., xc., cii., cxlii., and Hab. iii. All these are strictly lyrical compositions, and the title may have been assigned to them either as denoting the object with which they were written, or the use to which they were applied. As Ewald justly observes, all lyric poetry of an elevated kind, in so far as it reveals the soul of the poet in a pure, swift outpouring of itself, is of the nature of a prayer; and hence the term "prayer" was applied to a collection of David's songs, of which Ps. lxxii. formed the conclusion.

II. *Gnomic Poetry.* — The second grand division of Hebrew poetry is occupied by a class of poems which are peculiarly Shemitic, and which represent the nearest approaches made by the people of that race to anything like philosophic thought. Reasoning there is none: we have only results, and those rather the product of observation and reflection than of induction or argumentation. As lyric poetry is the expression of the poet's own feelings and impulses, so gnomic poetry is the form in which the desire of communicating knowledge to others finds vent. There might possibly be an intermediate stage in which the poets gave out their experiences for their own pleasure merely, and afterwards applied them to the instruction of others, but this could scarcely have been of long continuance. The impulse to teach makes the teacher, and the teacher must have an audience. It has been already remarked that gnomic poetry, as a whole, requires for its development a period of national tranquillity. Its germs are the floating proverbs which pass current in the mouths of the people, and embody the experiences of many with the wit of one. From this small beginning it arises, at a time when the experience of the nation has become matured, and the mass of truths which are the result of such experience have passed into circulation. The fame of Solomon's wisdom was so great that no less than three thousand proverbs are attributed to him, this being the form in which the Hebrew mind found its most

___

[a] Lowth (Is. xiv. 4) understands *mâshâl* to be "the general name for poetic style among the Hebrews, including every sort of it, as ranging under one, or other,

of all the characters, of sententious, figurative, and sublime."

congenial utterance. The sayer of sententious sayings was to the Hebrews the wise man, the philosopher. Of the earlier isolated proverbs but few examples remain. One of the earliest occurs in the mouth of David, and in his time it was the proverb of the ancients: "from the wicked cometh wickedness" (1 Sam. xxiv. 13 [14]). Later on, when the fortunes of the nation were obscured, their experience was embodied in terms of sadness and despondency: "The days are prolonged, and every vision faileth," became a saying and a by-word (Ez. xii. 22); and the feeling that the people were suffering for the sins of their fathers took the form of a sentence, "The fathers have eaten sour grapes, and the children's teeth are set on edge" (Ez. xviii. 2). Such were the models which the gnomic poet had before him for imitation. These detached sentences may be fairly assumed to be the earliest form, of which the fuller apophthegm is the expansion, swelling into sustained exhortations, and even dramatic dialogue.

III. *Dramatic Poetry.* — It is impossible to assert that no form of the drama existed among the Hebrew people; the most that can be done is to examine such portions of their literature as have come down to us, for the purpose of ascertaining how far any traces of the drama proper are discernible, and what inferences may be made from them. It is unquestionably true, as Ewald observes, that the Arab reciters of romances will many times in their own persons act out a complete drama in recitation, changing their voice and gestures with the change of person and subject. Something of this kind may possibly have existed among the Hebrews; but there is no evidence that it did exist, nor any grounds for making even a probable conjecture with regard to it. A rude kind of farce is described by Mr. Lane (*Mod. Eg.* ii. chap. vii.), the players of which "are called *Mohhabbazee'n.* These frequently perform at the festivals prior to weddings and circumcisions, at the houses of the great; and sometimes attract rings of auditors and spectators in the public places in Cairo. Their performances are scarcely worthy of description: it is chiefly by vulgar gestures and indecent actions that they amuse and obtain applause. The actors are only men and boys: the part of a woman being always performed by a man or boy in female attire." Then follows a description of one of these plays, the plot of which was extremely simple. But the mere fact of the existence of these rude exhibitions among the Arabs and Egyptians of the present day is of no weight when the question to be decided is, whether the Song of Songs was designed to be so represented, as a simple pastoral drama. Of course, in considering such a question, reference is made only to the external form of the poem, and, in order to prove it, it must be shown that the dramatic is the only form of representation which it could assume, and not that, by the help of two actors and a chorus, it is capable of being exhibited in a dramatic form. All that has been done, in our opinion, is the latter. It is but fair, however, to give the views of those who hold the opposite. Ewald maintains that the Song of Songs is designed for a simple stage, because it develops a complete action and admits of definite pauses in the action, which are only suited to the drama. He distinguishes it in this respect from the Book of Job, which is dramatic in form only, though, as it is occupied with a sublime subject, he compares it with *tragedy*, while the Song of Songs, being taken from the common life of the nation, may be

compared to *comedy.* The one comparison is probably as appropriate as the other. In Ewald's division the poem falls into 13 cantos of tolerably equal length, which have a certain beginning and ending, with a pause after each. The whole forms four acts for which three actors are sufficient: a hero, a maiden, and a chorus of women, these being all who would be on the stage at once. The following are the divisions of the acts: —

First Act, i. 2 – ii. 7 . . .	1st canto,	i. 2 – 8.
	2d "	i. 9 – ii. 7.
Second Act, ii. 8 – iii. 5	3d "	ii. 8 – 17.
	4th "	iii. 1 – 5.
	5th "	iii. 6 – 11.
	6th "	iv. 1 – 7.
	7th "	iv. 8 – v. 1.
	8th "	v. 2 – 8.
Third Act, iii. 6 – viii. 4	9th "	v. 9 – vi. 3.
	10th "	vi. 4 – vii. 1.
	11th "	vii. 2 – 10.
	12th "	vii. 10 – viii. 4.
Fourth Act, viii. 5–14. .	13th canto.	

The latest work on the subject is that of M. Renan (*Le Cantique des Cantiques*), who has given a spirited translation of the poem, and arranged it in acts and scenes, according to his own theory of the manner in which it was intended to be represented. He divides the whole into 16 cantos, which form five acts and an epilogue. The acts and scenes are thus arranged: —

First Act, i. 2 – ii. 7 . . .	Scene 1.	i. 2 – 6.
	" 2.	i. 7 – 11.
	" 3.	i. 12 – ii. 7.
Second Act, ii. 8 – iii. 5 . .	Scene 1.	ii. 8 – 17.
	" 2.	iii. 1 – 5.
Third Act, iii. 6 – v. 1 . . .	Scene 1.	iii. 6 – 11.
	" 2.	iv. 1 – 6.
	" 3.	iv. 7 – v. 1
Fourth Act, v. 2 – vi. 3	. of a single scene.	
Fifth Act, vi. 4 – viii. 7 . .	Scene 1	vi. 4 – 9.
	" 2.	vi. 10 – vii. 11.
	" 3.	vii. 12 – viii. 4.
	" 4.	viii. 5–7.
Epilogue, viii. 8–14.		

But M. Renan, who is compelled, in accordance with his own theory of the mission of the Shemitic races, to admit that no trace of anything approaching to the regular drama is found among them, does not regard the Song of Songs as a drama in the same sense as the products of the Greek and Roman theatres, but as dramatic poetry in the widest application of the term, to designate any composition conducted in dialogue and corresponding to an action. The absence of the regular drama he attributes to the want of a complicated mythology, analogous to that possessed by the Indo-European peoples. Monotheism, the characteristic religious belief of the Shemitic races, stifled the growth of a mythology and checked the development of the drama. Be this as it may, dramatic representation appears to have been alien to the feelings of the Hebrews. At no period of their history before the age of Herod is there the least trace of a theatre at Jerusalem, whatever other foreign innovations may have been adopted, and the burst of indignation which the high-priest Jason incurred for attempting to establish a gymnasium and to introduce the Greek games is a significant symptom of the repugnance which the people felt for such spectacles. The same antipathy remains to the present day among the Arabs, and the attempts to introduce theatres at Beyrout and in Algeria have signally failed. But, says M.

Renan, the Song of Songs is a dramatic poem: there were no public performances in Palestine, therefore it must have been represented in private; and he is compelled to frame the following hypothesis concerning it: that it is a *libretto* intended to be completed by the play of the actors and by music, and represented in private families, probably at marriage-feasts, the representation being extended over the several days of the feast. The last supposition removes a difficulty which has been felt to be almost fatal to the idea that the poem is a continuously developed drama. Each act is complete in itself; there is no suspended interest, and the structure of the poem is obvious and natural if we regard each act as a separate drama intended for one of the days of the feast. We must look for a parallel to it in the Middle Ages, when, besides the mystery plays, there were scenic representations sufficiently developed. The Song of Songs occupies the middle place between the regular drama and the eclogue or pastoral dialogue, and finds a perfect analogue, both as regards subject and scenic arrangement, in the most celebrated of the plays of Arras, *Le Jeu de Robin et Marion*. Such is M. Renan's explanation of the outward form of the Song of Songs, regarded as a portion of Hebrew literature. It has been due to his great learning and reputation to give his opinion somewhat at length; but his arguments in support of it are so little convincing that it must be regarded at best but as an ingenious hypothesis, the groundwork of which is taken away by M. Renan's own admission that dramatic representations are alien to the spirit of the Shemitic races. The simple corollary to this proposition must be that the Song of Songs is not a drama, but in its external form partakes more of the nature of an eclogue or pastoral dialogue.

It is scarcely necessary after this to discuss the question whether the Book of Job is a dramatic poem or not. Inasmuch as it represents an action and a progress, it is a drama as truly and really as any poem can be which develops the working of passion, and the alternations of faith, hope, distrust, triumphant confidence, and black despair, in the struggle which it depicts the human mind as engaged in, while attempting to solve one of the most intricate problems it can be called upon to regard. It is a drama as life is a drama, the most powerful of all tragedies; but that it is a dramatic poem, intended to be represented upon a stage, or capable of being so represented, may be confidently denied.

One characteristic of Hebrew poetry, not indeed peculiar to it, but shared by it in common with the literature of other nations, is its intensely national and local coloring. The writers were Hebrews of the Hebrews, drawing their inspiration from the mountains and rivers of Palestine, which they have immortalized in their poetic figures, and even while uttering the sublimest and most universal truths never forgetting their own nationality in its narrowest and intensest form. Their images and metaphors, says Munk (*Palestine*, p. 444 *a*), "are taken chiefly from nature and the phenomena of Palestine and the surrounding countries, from the pastoral life, from agriculture and the national history. The stars of heaven, the sand of the seashore, are the image of a great multitude. Would they speak of a mighty host of enemies invading the country, they are the swift torrents or the roaring waves of the sea, or the clouds that bring on a tempest; the war-chariots advance swiftly like lightning or the whirlwinds. Happiness rises as the dawn and shines like the daylight; the blessing of God descends like the dew or the bountiful rain; the anger of Heaven is a devouring fire that annihilates the wicked as the flame which devours the stubble. Unhappiness is likened to days of clouds and darkness; at times of great catastrophes the sun sets in broad day, the heavens are shaken, the earth trembles, the stars disappear, the sun is changed into darkness and the moon into blood, and so on. The cedars of Lebanon, the oaks of Bashan, are the image of the mighty man, the palm and the reed of the great and the humble, briers and thorns of the wicked; the pious man is an olive ever green, or a tree planted by the water-side. The animal kingdom furnished equally a large number of images: the lion, the image of power, is also, like the wolf, bear, etc., that of tyrants and violent and rapacious men; and the pious who suffers is a feeble sheep led to the slaughter. The strong and powerful man is compared to the he-goat or the bull of Bashan; the kine of Bashan figure, in the discourses of Amos, as the image of rich and voluptuous women; the people who rebel against the Divine will are a refractory heifer. Other images are borrowed from the country life and from the life domestic and social: the chastisement of God weighs upon Israel like a wagon laden with sheaves; the dead cover the earth as the dung which covers the surface of the fields. The impious man sows crime and reaps misery, or he sows the wind and reaps the tempest. The people yielding to the blows of their enemies are like the corn crushed beneath the threshing instrument. God tramples the wine in the wine-press when He chastises the impious and sheds their blood. The wrath of Jehovah is often represented as an intoxicating cup, which He causes those to empty who have merited his chastisement: terrors and anguish are often compared to the pangs of childbirth. Peoples, towns, and states are represented by the Hebrew poets under the image of daughters or wives; in their impiety they are courtesans or adulteresses. The historical allusions of most frequent occurrence are taken from the catastrophe of Sodom and Gomorrha, the miracles of the departure from Egypt, and the appearance of Jehovah on Sinai." Examples might easily be multiplied in illustration of this remarkable characteristic of the Hebrew poets: they stand thick upon every page of their writings, and in striking contrast to the vague generalizations of the Indian philosophic poetry.

In Hebrew, as in other languages, there is a peculiarity about the diction used in poetry — a kind of poetical dialect, characterized by archaic and irregular forms of words, abrupt constructions, and unusual inflexions, which distinguish it from the contemporary prose or historical style. It is universally observed that archaic forms and usages of words linger in the poetry of a language after they have fallen out of ordinary use. A few of these forms and usages are here given from Gesenius's *Lehrgebäude*. The Piel and Hiphil voices are used intransitively (Jer. li. 56; Ex. x. 7; Job xxix. 24): the apocopated future is used as a present (Job xv. 33; Ps. xi. 6; Is. xlii. 6). The termination הָ‎ is found for the ordinary feminine הָ‎ (Ex. xv. 2; Gen. xlix. 22; Ps. cxxxii. 4); and for the plural יםִ‎ we have יןִ‎ (Job xv. 13; Ex.

xxvi. 18) and יְ־ (Jer. xxii. 14; Am. vii. 1). The verbal suffixes, מוֹ, ־מוֹ, and יְ־מוֹ (Ex. xv. 9), and the pronominal suffixes to nouns ־מוֹ for יְם, and יְדהוּ for יְו (Hab. iii. 10), are peculiar to the poetical books; as are וְדהִי (Ps. cxvi. 12), יְ־מוֹ (Deut. xxxii. 37; Ps. xi. 7), and the more unusual forms, יִחֲמָה (Ex. xl. 16), יִכְבָּה (Ex. i. 11), יִכְבָּה (Ex. xiii. 20). In poetical language also we find לָמוֹ for לוֹ or לָהֶם, לְמוֹ for בְּמוֹ, בְּ for כְּמוֹ, כְּ for פְּ; the plural forms of the prepositions, אֱלֵי for אֶל, עֲדֵי for עַד, עֲלֵי; and the peculiar forms of the nouns, הַרְרֵי for עֲמָמִים for עַמִּים, חָרֵי for חֲרִי, הַרְרֵי חֲרִי, and so on.

But the form of Hebrew poetry is its distinguishing characteristic, and what this form is, has been a vexed question for many ages. The Therapeutæ, as described by Philo (de Vitâ Contempl. § 3, vol. ii. p. 475, ed. Mang.), sang hymns and psalms of thanksgiving to God, in divers measures and strains; and these were either new or ancient ones composed by the old poets, who had left behind them measures and melodies of trimeter verses, of processional songs, of hymns, of songs sung at the offering of libations, or before the altar, and continuous choral songs, beautifully measured out in strophes of intricate character (§ 10, p. 484). The value of Philo's testimony on this point may be estimated by another passage in his works, in which he claims for Moses a knowledge of numbers and geometry, the theory of rhythm, harmony, and metre, and the whole science of music, practical and theoretical (de Vitâ Mosis, i. 5, vol. ii. p. 84). The evidence of Josephus is as little to be relied upon. Both these writers labored to magnify the greatness of their own nation, and to show that in literature and philosophy the Greeks had been anticipated by the Hebrew barbarians. This idea pervades all their writings, and it must always be borne in mind as the key-note of their testimony on this as on other points. According to Josephus (Ant. ii. 16, § 4), the Song of Moses at the Red Sea (Ex. xv.) was composed in the hexameter measure (ἐν ἑξαμέτρῳ τόνῳ); and again (Ant. iv. 8, § 44), the song in Deut. xxxii. is described as a hexameter poem. The Psalms of David were in various metres, some trimeters and some pentameters (Ant. vii. 12, § 3). Eusebius (de Præp. Evang. xi. 3, 514, ed. Col. 1688) characterizes the great Song of Moses and the 118th (119th) Psalm as metrical compositions in what the Greeks call the heroic metre. They are said to be hexameters of sixteen syllables. The other verse compositions of the Hebrews are said to be in trimeters. This saying of Eusebius is attacked by Julian (Cyrill. contr. Jul. vii. 2), who on his part endeavored to prove the Hebrews devoid of all culture. Jerome (Præf. in Hiob) appeals to Philo, Josephus, Origen, and Eusebius, for proof that the Psalter, the Lamentations of Jeremiah, and almost all the songs of Scripture, are composed in metre, like the odes of Horace, Pindar, Alcæus, and Sappho. Again, he says that the Book of Job, from

iii. 3 to xlii. 6, is in hexameters, with dactyls and spondees, and frequently, on account of the peculiarity of the Hebrew language, other feet which have not the same syllables but the same time. In Epist. ad Paulam (Opp. ii. 709, ed. Martianay) occurs a passage which shows in some measure how far we are to understand literally the terms which Jerome has borrowed from the verse literature of Greece and Rome, and applied to the poetry of the Hebrews. The conclusion seems inevitable that these terms are employed simply to denote a general external resemblance, and by no means to indicate the existence, among the poets of the Old Testament, of a knowledge of the laws of metre, as we are accustomed to understand the term. There are, says Jerome, four alphabetical Psalms, the 110th (111th), 111th (112th), 118th (119th), and the 144th (145th). In the first two, one letter corresponds to each clause or versicle, which is written in trimeter iambics. The others are in tetrameter iambics, like the song in Deuteronomy. In Ps. 118 (119), eight verses follow each letter: in Ps. 144 (145), a letter corresponds to a verse. In Lamentations we have four alphabetical acrostics, the first two of which are written in a kind of Sapphic metre; for three clauses which are connected together and begin with one letter (i. e. in the first clause) close with a period in heroic measure (Heroici comma). The third is written in trimeter, and the verses in threes each begin with the same letter. The fourth is like the first and second. The Proverbs end with an alphabetical poem in tetrameter iambics, beginning, " A virtuous woman who can find?" In the Præf. in Chron. Euseb. Jerome compares the metres of the Psalms to those of Horace and Pindar, now running in Iambics, now ringing with Alcaics, now swelling with Sapphics, now beginning with a half foot. What, he asks, is more beautiful than the song of Deuteronomy and Isaiah? What more weighty than Solomon? What more perfect than Job? All which, as Josephus and Origen testify, are composed in hexameters and pentameters. There can be little doubt that these terms are mere generalities, and express no more than a certain rough resemblance, so that the songs of Moses and Isaiah may be designated hexameters and pentameters, with as much propriety as the first and second chapters of Lamentations may be compared to Sapphic odes. The resemblance of the Hebrew verse composition to the classic metres, is expressly denied by Gregory of Nyssa (1 Tract. in Psalm. cap. iv.). Augustine (Ep. 131 ad Numerium) confesses his ignorance of Hebrew, but adds that those skilled in the language believed the Psalms of David to be written in metre. Isidore of Seville (Orig. i. 18) claims for the heroic metre the highest antiquity, inasmuch as the Song of Moses was composed in it, and the Book of Job, who was contemporary with Moses, long before the times of Pherecydes and Homer, is written in dactyls and spondees. Joseph Scaliger (Animadv. ad Eus. Chron. p. 6 b, etc.) was one of the first to point out the fallacy of Jerome's statement with regard to the metres of the Psalter and the Lamentations, and to assert that these books contained no verse bound by metrical laws, but that their language was merely prose, animated by a poetic spirit. He admitted the Song of Moses in Deuteronomy, the Proverbs, and Job, to be the only books in which there was necessarily any trace of rhythm, and this rhythm he compares to that of two dimeter iambles, sometimes of more, sometimes of fewer sylla-bles as the sense required. Gerhard Vossius (de Nat. et Const. Artis Poët. lib. 1, c. 13, § 2) says, that in Job and the Proverbs there is rhythm but no metre; that is, regard is had to the number of syllables but not to their quantity. In the Psalms and Lamentations not even rhythm is observed.

But, in spite of the opinions pronounced by these high authorities, there were still many who believed in the existence of a Hebrew metre, and in the possibility of recovering it. The theories pro-posed for this purpose were various. Gomarus, professor at Groningen (Davidis Lyra, Lugd. Bat. 1637), advocated both rhymes and metre; for the latter he laid down the following rules. The vowel alone, as it is long or short, determines the length of a syllable. Shēva forms no syllable. The periods or versicles of the Hebrew poems never contain less than a distich, or two verses, but in proportion as the periods are longer they contain more verses. The last syllable of a verse is indif-ferently long or short. This system, if system it may be called (for it is equally adapted for prose), was supported by many men of note; among others by the younger Buxtorf, Heinsius, L. de Dieu, Constantin l'Empereur, and Hottinger. On the other hand it was vigorously attacked by L. Cappellus, Calovius, Danhauer, Pfeiffer, and Solo-mon Van Til. Towards the close of the 17th cen-tury Marcus Meibomius announced to the world, with an amount of pompous assurance which is charming, that he had discovered the lost metrical system of the Hebrews. By the help of this mys-terious secret, which he attributed to divine revela-tion, he proposed to restore not only the Psalms but the whole Hebrew Scriptures, to their pristine condition, and thus confer upon the world a knowl-edge of Hebrew greater than any which had existed since the ages which preceded the Alexandrine translators. But Meibomius did not allow his en-thusiasm to get the better of his prudence, and the condition on which this portentous secret was to be made public was, that six thousand curious men should contribute 5l. sterling a-piece for a copy of his book, which was to be printed in two volumes folio. It is almost needless to add that his scheme fell to the ground. He published some specimens of his restoration of ten psalms, and six entire chap-ters of the Old Testament in 1690. The glimpses which he gives of his grand secret are not such as would make us regret that the knowledge of it perished with him. The whole Book of Psalms, he says, is written in distichs, except the first psalm, which is in a different metre, and serves as an in-troduction to the rest. They were therefore in-tended to be sung, not by one priest, or by one chorus, but by two. Meibomius "was severely chastised by J. H. Maius, B. H. Gebhardus, and J. G. Zentgravius" (Jebb, Sacr. Lit. p. 11). In the last century the learned Francis Hare, bishop of Chichester, published an edition of the Hebrew Psalms, metrically divided, to which he prefixed a dissertation on the ancient poetry of the Hebrews (Psalm. lib. in versiculos metrice divisus, etc., Lond. 1736). Bishop Hare maintained that in Hebrew poetry no regard was had to the quantity of sylla-bles. He regarded Shēvas as long vowels, and long vowels as short at his pleasure. The rules which he laid down are the following. In Hebrew poetry all the feet are dissyllables, and no regard is had to the quantity of a syllable. Clauses consist of an

equal or unequal number of syllables. If the number of syllables be equal, the verses are tro-chaic; if unequal, iambic. Periods for the most part consist of two verses, often three or four, sometimes more. Clauses of the same periods are of the same kind, that is, either iambic or trochaic, with very few exceptions. Trochaic clauses generally agree in the number of the feet, which are sometimes three, as in Pss. xciv. 1, cvi. 1, and this is the most frequent; sometimes five, as in Ps. ix. 5. In iam-bic clauses the number of feet is sometimes the same, but they generally differ. Both kinds of verse are mixed in the same poem. In order to carry out these rules they are supplemented by one which gives to the versifier the widest license. Words and verses are contracted or lengthened at will, by syncope, elision, etc. In addition to this, the bishop was under the necessity of maintaining that all grammarians had hitherto erred in laying down the rules of ordinary punctuation. His system, if it may be so called, carries its own refutation with it, but was considered by Lowth to be worthy a reply under the title of Metricæ Harianæ Brevis Confutatio, printed at the end of his De Sacra Poes. Heb. Prælectiones, etc.

Anton (Conject. de Metro Heb. Ant. Lips. 1770), admitting the metre to be regulated by the accents, endeavored to prove that in the Hebrew poems was a highly artistic and regular system, like that of the Greeks and Romans, consisting of strophes, antistrophes, epodes, and the like; but his method is as arbitrary as Hare's. The theory of Lautwein (Versuch einer richtigen Theorie von der bibl. Verskunst, Tüb. 1775) is an improvement upon those of his predecessors, inasmuch as he re-jects the measurement of verse by long and short syllables, and marks the scansion by the tone ac-cent. He assumes little more than a free rhythm: the verses are distinguished by a certain relation in their contents, and connected by a poetic euphony. Sir W. Jones (Comment. Poes. Asiat. 1774) attempted to apply the rules of Arabic metre to Hebrew. He regarded as a long syllable one which terminated in a consonant or quiescent letter (א, ה, י); but he did not develope any system. The present Arabic prosody, however, is of com-paratively modern invention; and it is not consistent with probability that there could be any system of versification among the Hebrews like that imagined by Sir W. Jones, when in the example he quotes of Cant. i. 5, he refers the first clause of the verse to the second, and the last to the fifteenth kind of Arabic metre. Greve (Ultima Capita Jobi, etc. 1791) believed that in Hebrew, as in Arabic and Syriac, there was a metre, but that it was obscured by the false orthography of the Masorets. He therefore assumed for the Hebrew an Arabic vo-calization, and with this modification he found iambic trimeters, dimeters, and tetrameters, to be the most common forms of verse, and lays down the laws of versification accordingly. Bellermann (Versuch über die Metrik der Hebräer, 1813) was the last who attempted to set forth the old Hebrew metres. He adopted the Masoretic orthography and vocalization, and determined the quantity of syllables by the accentuation, and what he termed the "Morensystem," denoting by moren the com-pass of a single syllable. Each syllable which has not the tone accent must have three moren; every syllable which has the tone accent may have either four or two, but generally three. The moren are reckoned as follows: a long vowel has two; a short vowel, one; every consonant, whether single or double, has one *more*. *Sheva* simple or composite is not reckoned. The quiescent letters have no *more*. *Dagesh forte* compensative has one; so has *metheg*. The majority of dissyllable and trisyllable words, having the accent on the last syllable, will thus form iambics and anapæsts. But as many have the accent on the penultimate, these will form trochees. The most common kinds of feet are iambics and anapæsts, interchanging with trochees and tribrachs. Of verses composed of these feet, though not uniform as regards the numbers of the feet, consist, according to Bellermann, the poems of the Hebrew Scriptures.

Among those who believed in the existence of a Hebrew metre, but in the impossibility of recovering it, were Carpzov, Lowth, Pfeiffer, Herder to a certain extent, Jahn, Bauer, and Buxtorf. The opinions of Lowth, with regard to Hebrew metre, are summed up by Jebb (*Sacr. Lit.* p. 16) as follows: "He begins by asserting, that certain of the Hebrew writings are not only animated with the true poetic spirit, but, in some degree, couched in poetic numbers; yet, he allows, that the quantity, the rhythm, or modulation of Hebrew poetry, not only is unknown, but admits of no investigation by human art or industry; he states, after Abarbanel, that the Jews themselves disclaim the very memory of metrical composition; he acknowledges, that the artificial conformation of the sentences, is the sole indication of metre in these poems; he barely maintains the *credibility* of attention having been paid to numbers or feet in their compositions; and, at the same time, he confesses the utter impossibility of determining, whether Hebrew poetry was modulated by the ear alone, or according to any definite and settled rules of prosody." The opinions of Scaliger and Vossius have been already referred to. Vitringa allows to Isaiah a kind of oratorial measure, but adds that it could not on this account be rightly termed poetry. Michaelis (*Not.* 4 *in Præl.* iii.) in his notes on Lowth, held that there never was metre in Hebrew, but only a free rhythm, as in recitative, though even less trammeled. He declared himself against the Masoretic distinction of long and short vowels, and made the rhythm to depend upon the tone syllable; adding, with regard to fixed and regular metre, that what has evaded such diligent search he thought had no existence. On the subject of the rhythmical character of Hebrew poetry, as opposed to metrical, the remarks of Jebb are remarkably appropriate. "Hebrew poetry," he says (*Sacr. Lit.* p. 20), "is universal poetry: the poetry of all languages, and of all peoples: the collocation of words (whatever may have been the sound, for of this we are quite ignorant) is primarily directed to secure the best possible announcement and discrimination of the sense: let, then, a translator only be literal, and, so far as the genius of his language will permit, let him preserve the original order of the words, and he will infallibly put the reader in possession of all, or nearly all, that the Hebrew text can give to the best Hebrew scholar of the present day. Now, had there been originally metre, the case, it is presumed, could hardly have been such; somewhat must have been sacrificed to the importunities of metrical necessity; the sense could not have invariably predominated over the sound; and the poetry could not have been, as it unquestionably and emphatically is, a poetry, not of sounds, or of words, but of things. Let

not this last assertion, however, be misinterpreted; I would be understood merely to assert that sound, and words in subordination to sound, do not in Hebrew, as in classical poetry, enter into the essence of the thing; but it is happily undeniable, that the words of the poetical Scriptures are exquisitely fitted to convey the sense; and it is highly probable, that, in the lifetime of the language, the sounds were sufficiently harmonious: when I say sufficiently harmonious, I mean so harmonious as to render the poetry grateful to the ear in recitation, and suitable to musical accompaniment; for which purpose, the cadence of well-modulated prose would fully answer; a fact which will not be controverted by any person with a moderately good ear, that has ever heard a chapter of Isaiah skillfully read from our authorized translation, that has ever listened to one of Kent's Anthems well performed, or to a song from the Messiah of Handel."

Abarbanel (on Is. v.) makes three divisions of Hebrew poetry, including in the first the modern poems which, in imitation of the Arabic, are constructed according to modern principles of versification. Among the second class he arranges such as have no metre, but are adapted to melodies. In these occur the poetical forms of words, lengthened and abbreviated, and the like. To this class belong the songs of Moses in Ex. xv., Deut. xxxii., the song of Deborah, and the song of David. The third class includes those compositions which are distinguished not by their form but by the figurative character of their descriptions, as the Song of Songs, and the Song of Isaiah.

Among those who maintain the absence of any regularity perceptible to the ear in the composition of Hebrew poetry, may be mentioned Richard Simon (*Hist. Crit. du V. T.* i. c. 8, p. 57), Wasmuth (*Inst. Acc. Hebr.* p. 14), Alstedius (*Enc. Bibl.* c. 27, p. 257), the author of the book Cozri, and R. Azariah de' Rossi, in his book entitled *Meor Enayim*. The author of the book Cozri held that the Hebrews had no metre bound by the laws of diction, because their poetry being intended to be sung was therefore independent of metrical laws. R. Azariah expresses his approbation of the opinions of Cozri and Abarbanel, who deny the existence of songs in Scripture composed after the manner of modern Hebrew poems, but he adds nevertheless, that beyond doubt there are other measures which depend upon the sense. Mendelssohn (on Ex. xv.) also rejects the system of ירֵהדית וּרֵנוּעִרֵת (literally, pegs and vowels).[a] Rabbi Azariah appears to have anticipated Bishop Lowth in his theory of parallelism: at any rate his treatise contains the germ which Lowth developed, and may be considered, as Jebb calls it, the technical basis of his system. But it also contains other elements, which will be alluded to hereafter. His conclusion, in Lowth's words (*Isaiah*, prel. diss.), was as follows: "That the sacred songs have undoubtedly certain measures and proportions; which, however, do not consist in the number of syllables, perfect or imperfect, according to the form of the modern verse which the Jews make use of, and which is borrowed from the Arabians (though the Arabic prosody, he observes, is too

---

[a] רֵד is a syllable, simple or compound, beginning with a consonant bearing moving *Shĕva* (Masc. and Barnard's *Heb. Gr.* ii. 203).

complicated to be applied to the Hebrew language); but in the number of things, and of the parts of things, — that is, the subject, and the predicate, and their adjuncts, in every sentence and proposition. Thus a phrase, containing two parts of a proposition, consists of two measures; add another containing two more, and they become four measures; another again, containing three parts of a proposition, consists of three measures; add to it another of the like, and you have six measures."

The following example will serve for an illustration:—

Thy-right-hand, O-Jehovah, is-glorious in-power,
Thy-right-hand, O-Jehovah, hath-crushed the-enemy.

The words connected by a hyphen form a term, and the two lines, forming four measures each, may be called tetrameters. "Upon the whole, the author concludes, that the poetical parts of the Hebrew Scriptures are not composed according to the rules and measures of certain feet, dissyllables, trisyllables, or the like, as the poems of the modern Jews are; but nevertheless have undoubtedly other measures which depend on things, as above explained. For which reason they are more excellent than those which consist of certain feet, according to the number and quantity of syllables. Of this, says he, you may judge yourself in the Songs of the Prophets. For do you not see, if you translate some of them into another language, that they still keep and retain their measure, if not wholly, at least in part? which cannot be the case in those verses, the measures of which arise from a certain quantity and number of syllables." Lowth expresses his general agreement with R. Azariah's exposition of the rhythmus of things; but instead of regarding terms, or phrases, or senses, in single lines, as measures, he considered "only that relation and proportion of one verse to another, which arises from the correspondence of terms, and from the form of construction; from whence results a rhythmus of propositions, and a harmony of sentences." But Lowth's system of parallelism was more completely anticipated by Schoettgen in a treatise, of the existence of which the bishop does not appear to have been aware. It is found in his *Horæ Hebraicæ*, vol. i. pp. 1249-1263, diss. vi., "de Exergasia Sacra." This *exergasia* he defines to be, the conjunction of entire sentences signifying the same thing: so that *exergasia* bears the same relation to sentences that synonymy does to words. It is only found in those Hebrew writings which rise above the level of historical narrative and the ordinary kind of speech. Ten canons are then laid down, each illustrated by three examples, from which it will be seen how far Schoettgen's system corresponded with Lowth's. (1.) Perfect *exergasia* is when the members of the two clauses correspond, each to each; as in Ps. xxxiii. 7; Num. xxiv. 17; Luke i. 47. (2.) Sometimes in the second clause the subject is omitted, as in Is. i. 18; Prov. vii. 19; Ps. cxxix. 3. (3.) Sometimes part of the subject is omitted, as in Ps. xxxvii. 30, cii. 28; Is. liii. 5. (4.) The predicate is sometimes omitted in the second clause, as in Num. xxiv. 5; Ps. xxxiii. 12. (5.) Sometimes part only of the predicate is omitted, as in Ps. lvii. 9, ciii. 1, cxxix. 7. (6.) Words are added in one member which are omitted in the other, as in Num. xxiii. 18; Ps. cii. 28; Dan. xii. 3. (7.) Sometimes two propositions will occur, treating of different things, but referring to one general proposition, as

in Ps. xciv. 9, cxxviii. 3; Wisd. iii. 16. (8.) Cases occur, in which the second proposition is the contrary of the first, as in Prov. xv. 8, xiv. 1, 11. (9.) Entire propositions answer each to each, although the subject and predicate are not the same, as in Ps. li. 7, cxix. 168; Jer. viii. 22. (10.) *Exergasia* is found with three members, as in Ps. i. 1, cxxx. 5, lii. 9. These canons Schoettgen applied to the interpretation of Scripture, of which he gives examples in the remainder of this and the following dissertation.

But whatever may have been achieved by his predecessors, there can be no question that the delivery of Lowth's lectures on Hebrew Poetry, and the subsequent publication of his translation of Isaiah, formed an era in the literature of the subject, more marked than any that had preceded it. Of his system it will be necessary to give a somewhat detailed account; for whatever may have been done since his time, and whatever modifications of his arrangement may have been introduced, all subsequent writers have confessed their obligations to the two works above mentioned, and have drawn their inspiration from them. Starting with the alphabetical poems as the basis of his investigation, because that in them the verses or stanzas were more distinctly marked, Lowth came to the conclusion that they consist of verses properly so called, " of verses regulated by some observation of harmony or cadence; of measure, numbers, or rhythms," and that this harmony does not arise from rhyme, but from what he denominates parallelism. Parallelism he defines to be the correspondence of one verse or line with another, and divides it into three classes, synonymous, antithetic, and synthetic.

1. Parallel lines *synonymous* correspond to each other by expressing the same sense in different but equivalent terms, as in the following examples, which are only two of the many given by Lowth:

" O-Jehovah. in-thy-strength the-king shall-rejoice;
And-in-thy-salvation how greatly shall-he-exult!
The-desire of-his-heart thou-hast-granted unto-him;
And-the-request of-his-lips thou-hast-not denied."
Ps. xxi. 1, 2.

" For the-moth shall-consume-them like-a-garment;
And-the-worm shall-eat-them like wool;
But-my-righteousness shall-endure for-ever;
And-my-salvation to-the-age of-ages." — Is. li. 8.

It will be observed from the examples which Lowth gives that the parallel lines sometimes consist of three or more synonymous terms, sometimes of two, sometimes only of one. Sometimes the lines consist each of a double member, or two propositions, as Ps. cxliv. 5, 6; Is. lxv. 21, 22. Parallels are formed also by a repetition of part of the first sentence (Ps. lxxvii. 1, 11, 16; Is. xxvi. 5, 6; Hos. vi. 4); and sometimes a part has to be supplied from the former to complete the sentence (2 Sam. xxii. 41; Job xxvi. 5; Is. xli. 28). Parallel triplets occur in Job iii. 4, 6, 9; Ps. cxii. 10; Is. ix. 20; Joel iii. 13. Examples of parallels of four lines, in which two distichs form one stanza, are Ps. xxxvii. 1, 2; Is. i. 3, xlix. 4; Am. i. 2. In periods of five lines the odd line sometimes comes in between two distichs, as in Job viii. 5, 6; Is. xlvi. 7; Hos. xiv. 9; Joel iii. 16: or after two distichs closes the stanza, as in Is. xliv. 26. Alternate parallelism in stanzas of four lines is found in Ps. ciii. 11, 12; Is. xxx. 16 but the most striking examples of the alternate quatrain are Deut. xxxii. 25, 42, the first line forming a continuous sense with the third, and the second with the fourth (comp. Is. xxxiv. 6; Gen.

xlix. 6). In Is. l. 10 we find an alternate quatrain
followed by a fifth line. To this first division of
Lowth's Jebb objects that the name *synonymous* is
inappropriate, for the second clause, with few exceptions, "*diversifies* the preceding clause, and
generally so as to rise above it, forming a sort of
climax in the sense." This peculiarity was recognized by Lowth himself in his 4th Prælection, where
he says, "idem iterant, variant, augent," thus
marking a cumulative force in this kind of parallelism. The same was observed by Abp. Newcome
in his Preface to Ezekiel, where examples are given
in which "the following clauses so diversify the
preceding ones as to rise above them" (Is. xlii. 7,
xliii. 16; Ps. xcv. 2, civ. 1). Jebb, in support of his
own opinion, appeals to the passages quoted by
Lowth (Ps. xxi. 12, cvii. 38; Is. lv. 6, 7), and suggests as a more appropriate name for parallelism of
this kind, *cognate parallelism* (*Sacr. Lit.* p. 38).

2. Lowth's second division is *antithetic parallelism;* when two lines correspond with each other
by an opposition of terms and sentiments; when
the second is contrasted with the first, sometimes in
expressions, sometimes in sense only, so that the
degrees of antithesis are various. As for example —

"A wise son rejoiceth his father;
But a foolish son is the grief of his mother."
                                        Prov. x. 1.
"The memory of the just is a blessing;
But the name of the wicked shall rot."
                                        Prov. x. 7.
The gnomic poetry of the Hebrews abounds with
illustrations of antithetic parallelism. Other ex-
amples are Ps. xx. 7, 8: —

"These in chariots, and those in horses,
But we in the name of Jehovah our God will be
    strong.
They are bowed down, and fallen;
But we are risen, and maintain ourselves firm"
Compare also Ps. xxx. 5, xxxvii. 10, 11; Is. liv.
10, ix. 10. On these two kinds of parallelism Jebb
appropriately remarks: "The *Antithetic Parallelism* serves to mark the broad distinctions between
truth and falsehood, and good and evil: the *Cognate Parallelism* discharges the more difficult and
more critical function of discriminating between
different degrees of truth and good on the one hand,
of falsehood and evil on the other" (*Sacr. Lit.*
p. 39).

3. *Synthetic* or *constructive parallelism*, where
the parallel "consists only in the similar form of
construction; in which word does not answer to
word, and sentence to sentence, as equivalent or
opposite; but there is a correspondence and equality
between different propositions, in respect of the
shape and turn of the whole sentence, and of the
constructive parts — such as noun answering to
noun, verb to verb, member to member, negative
to negative, interrogative to interrogative." One
of the examples of constructive parallels given by
Lowth is, Is. l. 5, 6: —

"The Lord Jehovah hath opened mine ear,
And I was not rebellious;
Neither did I withdraw myself backward —
I gave my back to the smiters,
And my cheeks to them that plucked off the hair;
My face I hid not from shame and spitting."
Jebb gives as an illustration Ps. xix. 7-10: —

"The law of Jehovah is perfect, converting the soul,
The testimony of Jehovah is sure, making wise the
    simple," etc.

It is instructive, as showing how difficult, if not
impossible, it is to make any strict classification of
Hebrew poetry, to observe that this very passage is
given by Gesenius as an example of synonymous
parallelism, while De Wette calls it synthetic. The
illustration of synthetic parallelism quoted by Gesenius is Ps. xxvii. 4: —

"One thing I ask from Jehovah.
    It will I seek after —
My dwelling in the house of Jehovah all the days
    of my life,
To behold the beauty of Jehovah,
    And to inquire in his temple."

In this kind of parallelism, as Nordheimer (*Gram.
Anal.* p. 87) observes, "an idea is neither repeated
nor followed by its opposite, but is kept in view
by the writer, while he proceeds to develop and
enforce his meaning by accessory ideas and modifications."

4. To the three kinds of parallelism above described Jebb adds a fourth, which seems rather to be
an unnecessary refinement upon than distinct from
the others. He denominates it *introverted parallelism*, in which he says, "there are stanzas so constructed that, whatever be the number of lines, the
first line shall be parallel with the last: the second with the penultimate; and so throughout in an
order that looks inward, or, to borrow a military
phrase, from flanks to centre" (*Sacr. Lit.* p. 53).
Thus —

"My son, if thine heart be wise,
    My heart also shall rejoice;
    Yea, my reins shall rejoice
When thy lips speak right things."
                                        Prov. xxiii. 15, 16.
"Unto Thee do I lift up mine eyes, O Thou that dwell-
    est in the heavens;
Behold as the eyes of servants to the hand of their
    masters;
As the eyes of a maiden to the hands of her mis-
    tress:
Even so look our eyes to Jehovah our God, until he
    have mercy upon us." — Ps. cxxiii. 1, 2.

Upon examining these and the other examples
quoted by Bishop Jebb in support of his new division, to which he attaches great importance, it will
be seen that the peculiarity consists in the structure of the stanza, and not in the nature of the
parallelism; and any one who reads Ewald's elaborate treatise on this part of the subject will rise
from the reading with the conviction that to attempt
to classify Hebrew poetry according to the character of the stanzas employed will be labor lost and
in vain, resulting only in a system which is no system, and in rules to which the exceptions are more
numerous than the examples.

A few words may now be added with respect to
the classification proposed by De Wette, in which
more regard was had to the rhythm. The four
kinds of parallelism are — 1. That which consists
in an equal number of words in each member, as in
Gen. iv. 23. This he calls the original and perfect
kind of parallelism of members, which corresponds
with metre and rhyme, without being identical with
them (*Die Psalmen, Einl.* §7). Under this head
are many minor divisions. — 2. Unequal parallelism,
in which the number of words in the members is
not the same. This again is divided into — a. The
simple, as Ps. lxviii. 33. b. The composite, consisting of the synonymous (Job x. 1; Ps. xxxvi. 6), the
antithetic (Ps. xv. 4), and the synthetic (Ps. xv. 5).
c. That in which the simple member is dispropor-

tionately small (Ps. xl. 10). *d.* Where the composite member grows up into three and more sentences (Ps. i. 3, lxv. 10). *e.* Instead of the close parallelism there sometimes occurs a short additional clause, as in Ps. xxiii. 3. — 3. Out of the parallelism which is unequal in consequence of the composite character of one member, another is developed, so that both members are composite (Ps. xxxi. 11). This kind of parallelism again admits of three subdivisions. — 4. Rhythmical parallelism, which lies merely in the external form of the diction. Thus in Ps. xix. 11 there is nearly an equal number of words: —

> "Moreover by them was thy servant warned,
> In keeping of them there is great reward."

In Ps. xxx. 3 the inequality is remarkable. In Ps. xiv. 7 is found a double and a single member, and in Ps. xxxi. 23 two double members. De Wette also held that there were in Hebrew poetry the beginnings of a composite rhythmical structure like our strophes. Thus in Ps. xlii., xliii., a refrain marks the conclusion of a larger rhythmical period. Something similar is observable in Ps. cvii. This artificial structure appears to belong to a late period of Hebrew literature, and to the same period may probably be assigned the remarkable gradational rhythm which appears in the Songs of Degrees, *e. g.* Ps. cxxi. It must be observed that this gradational rhythm is very different from the cumulative parallelism of the Song of Deborah, which is of a much earlier date, and bears traces of less effort in the composition. Strophes of a certain kind are found in the alphabetical pieces in which several Masoretic clauses belong to one letter (Ps ix., x., xxxvii., cxix.; Lam. iii.), but the nearest approach to anything like a strophical character is found in poems which are divided into smaller portions by a refrain, and have the initial or final verse the same or similar (Ps. xxxix., xlii., xliii.). In the opinion of some the occurrence of the word Selah is supposed to mark the divisions of the strophes.

It is impossible here to do more than refer to the essay of Koester (*Theol. Stud. und Krit.* 1831, pp. 40–114) on the strophes, or the parallelism of verses in Hebrew poetry; in which he endeavors to show that the verses are subject to the same laws of symmetry as the verse members; and that consequently Hebrew poetry is essentially strophical in character. Ewald's treatise requires more careful consideration; but it must be read itself, and a slight sketch only can here be given. Briefly thus: — Verses are divided into verse-members in which the number of syllables is less restricted, as there is no syllabic metre. A verse-member generally contains from seven to eight syllables. Two members, the rise and fall, are the fundamental constituents: thus (Judg. v. 3): —

> "Hear, ye kings! give ear, ye princes!
> I to Jahve, I will sing."

To this all other modifications must be capable of being reduced. The variations which may take place may be either amplifications or continuations of the rhythm, or compositions in which a complete rhythm is made the half of a new compound, or we may have a diminution or enfeeblement of the original. To the two members correspond two thoughts which constitute the life of the verse, and each of these again may distribute itself. Gradations of symmetry are formed — 1. By the echo of the whole sentence, where the same sense which is given in the first member rises again in the second,

in order to exhaust itself more thoroughly (Gen. iv. 23; Prov. i. 8). An important word of the first member often reserves its force for the second, as in Ps. xx. 8; and sometimes in the second member a principal part of the sense of the first is further developed, as Ps. xlix. 5 [6]. — 2. When the thought trails through two members of a verse, as in Ps. cx. 5, it gives rise to a less animated rhythm (comp. also Ps. cxli. 10). — 3. Two sentences may be brought together as protasis and apodosis, or simply to form one complex thought; the external harmony may be dispensed with, but the harmony of thought remains. This may be called the intermediate rhythm. The forms of structure assumed by the verse are many. First, there is the single member, which occurs at the commencement of a series in Ps. xviii. 2, xxiii. 1; at the end of a series in Ex. xv. 18, Ps. xcii. 8; and in the middle, after a short pause, in Ps. xxix. 7. The bimembral verse is most frequently found, consisting of two members of nearly equal weight. Verses of more than two members are formed either by increasing the number of members from two to three, so that the complete fall may be reserved for the third, all three possessing the same power; or by combining four members two and two, as in Ps. xviii. 7, xxviii. 1.

The varieties of this structure of verse are too numerous to be recounted, and the laws of rhythm in Hebrew poetry are so free, that of necessity the varieties of verse structure must be manifold. The gnomic or sententious rhythm, Ewald remarks, is the one which is perfectly symmetrical. Two members of seven or eight syllables, corresponding to each other as rise and fall, contain a thesis and antithesis, a subject and its image. This is the constant form of genuine gnomic sentences of the best period. Those of a later date have many members or trail themselves through many verses. The animation of the lyrical rhythm makes it break through all such restraints, and leads to an amplification or reduplication of the normal form; or the passionate rapidity of the thoughts may disturb the simple concord of the members, so that the unequal structure of verse intrudes with all its varieties. To show how impossible it is to attempt a classification of verse uttered under such circumstances, it will be only necessary to quote Ewald's own words. "All these varieties of rhythm, however, exert a perfectly free influence upon every lyrical song, just according as it suits the mood of the moment to vary the simple rhythm. The most beautiful songs of the flourishing period of poetry allow, in fact, the verse of many members to predominate whenever the diction rises with any sublimity; nevertheless, the standard rhythm still returns in each when the diction flags, and the different kinds of the more complex rhythm are employed with equal freedom and ease of variation, just as they severally accord with the fluctuating hues of the mood of emotion, and of the sense of the diction. The late alphabetical songs are the first in which the fixed choice of a particular versification, a choice, too, made with designed art, establishes itself firmly, and maintains itself symmetrically throughout all the verses" (*Dichter des A. B.* i. 83; trans. in Kitto's *Journal,* i. 318). It may, however, be generally observed, that the older rhythms are the most animated, as if accompanied by the hands and feet of the singer (Num. xxi.; Ex. xv.; Judg. v.), and that in the time of David the rhythm had attained its most perfect development. By the end of the 8th century B. C.

the decay of versification begins, and to this period belong the artificial forms of verse.

It remains now only to notice the rules of Hebrew poetry as laid down by the Jewish grammarians, to which reference was made in remarking upon the system of R. Azariah. They have the merit of being extremely simple, and are to be found at length, illustrated by many examples, in Mason and Bernard's *Heb. Gram.* vol. ii. let. 57, and accompanied by an interesting account of modern Hebrew versification. The rules are briefly these: 1. That a sentence may be divided into members, some of which contain *two, three*, or even *four* words, and are accordingly termed *Binary, Ternary*, and *Quaternary* members respectively. 2. The sentences are composed either of *Binary, Ternary*, or *Quaternary* members entirely, or of these different members intermixed. 3. That in two consecutive members it is an elegance to express the same idea in different words. 4. That a word expressed in either of these parallel members is often not expressed in the alternate member. 5. That a word without an accent, being joined to another word by *Makkiph*, is generally (though not always) reckoned with that second word as one. It will be seen that these rules are essentially the same with those of Lowth, De Wette, and other writers on parallelism, and from their simplicity are less open to objection than any that have been given.

In conclusion, after reviewing the various theories which have been framed with regard to the structure of Hebrew poetry, it must be confessed that beyond the discovery of very broad general laws, little has been done towards elaborating a satisfactory system. Probably this want of success is due to the fact that there is no system to discover, and that Hebrew poetry, while possessed, in the highest degree, of all sweetness and variety of rhythm and melody, is not fettered by laws of versification as we understand the term.

For the literature of the subject, in addition to the works already quoted, reference may be made to the following: Carpzov, *Intr. ad Libr. Can. Bibl.* pt. 2, c. 1; Lowth, *De Sacra Poesi Hebræorum Prælectiones*, with notes by J. D. Michaelis and Rosenmüller (Oxon. 1828) [translated, with notes, by Calvin E. Stowe, Andover, 1829]; the Preliminary Dissertation in his translation of Isaiah; Herder, *Geist der Hebr. Poesie* [transl. by President James Marsh, 2 vols., Burlington, 1833]; Jebb, *Sacred Literature*; Saalschütz, *Von der Form der Hebr. Poesie*, Königsberg, 1825, which contains the most complete account of all the various theories; De Wette, *Ueber die Psalmen* [transl. by Prof. J. Torrey, *Bibl. Repos.* iii. 445–518]; Meier, *Gesch. der Poet. National-Literatur der Hebräer;* Delitzsch, *Commentar über den Psalter;* und Hupfeld, *Die Psalmen.* W. A. W.

 * Other and in part later writers: F. Gomarus, *Davidis Lyra* (1637); J. C. Schramm, *De Poesi Hebræorum* (1723). (The two essays just named, with others on the same subject by Ebert, the Abbé Fleury, Dannhawer, Pfeiffer, Leyser, Le Clerc, Hare, and Lowth, are reprinted in vol. xxxi. of Ugolini's *Thesaurus.*) Herder, *Briefe das Studium d. Theol. betreffend*, the first twelve of which letters he devotes to the poetry of the Hebrews, pointing out its characteristics and illustrating them by translations from the Pentateuch (Jacob's blessings, the farewell of Moses), from Judges (the Song of Deborah and Barak), and from the Psalms and the Prophets. A. von Humboldt, *Cosmos* (Eng.

transl. ii. 57 f.), according to whom "nature to the Hebrew poet is not a self-dependent object — but a work of creation and order, the living expression of the omnipresence of the Divinity in the visible world." A single Psalm (the 104th) almost "represents the image of the whole *Cosmos.*" A. G. Hoffmann, art. *Hebräische Literatur* (Ersch and Gruber's *Allgem. Encykl.*, 2e Sect. iii. 337 ff. (1828). Prof. S. H. Turner, D. D., *Claims of the Hebrew Language and Literature* (Five Lectures), especially as founded on the character of its Poetry, *Bibl. Repository*, i. 508 ff. (1831). M. Nicolas, *Forme de la poesie hébraïque* (1833). Franz Delitzsch, *Zur Geschichte der jüdischen Poesie*, extending from the close of the O. T. collection to modern times (Leipz. 1836). Prof. B. B. Edwards, *Reasons for the Study of the Hebr. Language*, an Inaugural Address, in which he urges this study among other arguments on account of its opening to us the treasures of so rich a poetic literature (*Amer. Bibl. Repository* for July, 1838, pp. 113–132). The thoughts are suggestive and beautifully expressed. J. G. Sommer, *Von Reime in der hebr. Volkspoesie*, in his *Bibl. Abhandlungen*, pp. 85–92 (Bonn, 1846). Ed. Reuss, *Hebräische Poesie*, in Herzog's *Real-Encykl.* v. 598–608 (1856). Isaac Taylor, *The Spirit of Hebrew Poetry* (Amer. reprint, 1862). The author's point of view is "that not less in relation to the most highly cultivated minds than to the most rude — not less to minds disciplined in abstract thought, than to such as are unused to generalization of any kind — the Hebrew Scriptures, in their metaphoric style and their poetic diction, are the fullest medium for conveying what it is their purpose to convey, concerning the Divine Nature, and concerning the spiritual life, and concerning the correspondence of man — the finite, with God — the Infinite." In its sphere as an able exposition of this train of thought, there is no better treatise than this. Heinrich Ewald, *Allgemeines üb. die hebräische Dichtung*, etc. (re-wrought, Götting. 1866; half of vol. i. of his *Dichter des A. Bundes*). Leyrer, art. *Dichtkunst* in Zeller's *Bibl. Wörterb.* i. 232–242 (1866). Prof. Hupfeld, *Rhythm and Accentuation in Hebrew Poetry* (we adopt the briefer title), translated by Professor Charles M. Mead, *Bibl. Sacra*, xxiv. 1–40 (1867). Dr. Diestel, art. *Dichtkunst* in Schenkel's *Bibel-Lexikon*, i. 607–615 (1868), valuable.

For information on this subject see also the Introductions to the Old Testament (Eichhorn, Hävernick, De Wette, Keil, Bleek), as well as the Commentaries on the O. T. poetic books (mentioned in the *Dictionary* under these books).

As regards the examples of poetry in the N. T. Schenkel's art. *Dichtkunst, urchristliche im N. T.*, (in his *Bibel-Lexikon*, i. 615–618) deserves attention. The songs (as they may be termed) of Elizabeth (Luke i. 42–45), of Mary (46–55) and of Zacharias (78–69), breathe the spirit of the Hebrew poets, and are largely expressed in language derived from them. See also Acts iv. 24 ff., xvi. 25; Rev. iv. 11, xv. 3, 4. In Col. iii. 16 and Eph. v. 19, Paul recognizes the use of "psalms, hymns, and spiritual songs" as forming a part of the social worship of the first Christians. With this intimation agrees Pliny's statement (*Epist.* x. 97) that those in Bithynia who professed this faith assembled at early dawn and sung praises to Christ (*carmen Christo quasi deo dicere secum invicem*). It is generally allowed that we have a fragment of such a hymn in 1 Tim. iii. 16. Not a few of Paul's sentences which we are accustomed to read as prose, bring back to the ear the cadence of Hebrew verse. The following is an example of this (2 Tim. ii. 11): —

" For if we died with him,
  We shall also live with him ;
If we endure, we shall also reign with him ;
  If we shall deny him,
  He also will deny us ;
If we are faithless, he remains faithful ;
  For he cannot deny himself."

It may be well to remark that although "hymn" and " hymning " do not occur in our English translation of the O. T., the correspondent Greek terms often occur in the Septuagint. The verb "to hymn " (ὑμνέω) has sometimes the general sense of "to praise," but when applied to any particular composition refers to the use of the Psalms for that purpose. In the titles of the Psalms, the Greek phrase for " hymns of David " is generally found, in the place of "psalms of David " in the A. V. See Biel's *Lexicon in LXX. Interpretes*, s. vv. ὑμνέω and ὕμνος. The usage of the LXX. no doubt influenced the N. T. phraseology in this respect. Comp. Matt. xxvi. 30; Mark xiv. 26; Acts xvi. 25; Heb. ii. 12.

On the hymnology of the early Church the reader may see Daniel's *Thesaurus Hymnologicus* (1841), and the art. *Hymnologie*, by Christ. Palmer in Herzog's *Real-Encyk*. vi. 305 ff., where a list of other writers will be found, as also under HYMN in this *Dictionary*.   H.

POISON. Two Hebrew words are thus rendered in the A. V. but they are so general as to throw little light upon the knowledge and practice of poisons among the Hebrews. 1. The first of these, חֵמָה, *chêmâh*, from a root signifying "to be hot," is used of the heat produced by wine (Hos. vii. 5), and the hot passion of anger (Deut. xxix. 27, &c.), as well as of the burning venom of poisonous serpents (Deut. xxxii. 24, 33; Ps. lviii. 4, cxl. 3). It in all cases denotes animal poison, and not vegetable or mineral. The only allusion to its application is in Job vi. 4, where reference seems to be made to the custom of anointing arrows with the venom of a snake, a practice the origin of which is of very remote antiquity (comp. Hom. *Od.* i. 261, 262; Ovid, *Trist.* iii. 10, 64, *Fast.* v. 397, &c.; Plin. xviii. 1). The Soanes, a Caucasian race mentioned by Strabo (xi. 499), were especially skilled in the art. Pliny (vi. 34) mentions a tribe of Arab pirates who infested the Red Sea, and were armed with poisoned arrows like the Malays of the coast of Borneo. For this purpose the berries of the yew-tree (Plin. xvi. 20) were employed. The Gauls (Plin. xxvii. 76) used a poisonous herb, *limeum*, supposed by some to be the " leopard's bane," and the Scythians dipped their arrow-points in viper's venom mixed with human blood. These were so deadly that a slight scratch inflicted by them was fatal (Plin. xi. 115). The practice was so common that the name τοξικόν, originally a poison in which arrows were dipped, was applied to poison generally.

2. רֹאשׁ (once רוֹשׁ, Deut. xxxii. 32 *a*), *rôsh*, if a poison at all, denotes a vegetable poison primarily, and is only twice (Deut. xxix. 33; Job xx. 16)

---

a In some MSS. this reading occurs in other passages, of which a list is given by Michaelis (*Suppl.* p. 2225).

161

---

used of the venom of a serpent. In other passages where it occurs, it is translated " gall " in the A. V., except in Hos. x. 4, where it is rendered "hemlock." In the margin of Deut. xxix. 18, our translators, feeling the uncertainty of the word, give as an alternative " rosh, or, *a poisonful herb*." Beyond the fact that, whether poisonous or not, it was a plant of bitter taste, nothing can be inferred. That bitterness was its prevailing characteristic is evident from its being associated with wormwood (Deut. xxix. 18 [17]; Lam. iii. 19; Am. vi. 12), and from the allusions to " water of rosh " in Jer. viii. 14, ix. 15, xxiii. 15. It was not a juice or liquid (Ps. lxix. 21 [22]; comp. Mark xv. 23), but probably a bitter berry, in which case the expression in Deut. xxxii. 32, " grapes of rosh," may be taken literally. Gesenius, on the ground that the word in Hebrew also signifies "head," rejects the hemlock, colocynth, and darnel of other writers, and proposes the "poppy" instead; from the "heads" in which its seeds are contained. " Water of rosh " is then "opium," but it must be admitted that there appears in none of the above passages to be any allusion to the characteristic effects of opium. The effects of the rosh are simply nausea and loathing. It was probably a general term for any bitter or nauseous plant, whether poisonous or not, and became afterwards applied to the venom of snakes, as the corresponding word in Chaldee is frequently so used. [GALL.]

There is a clear case of suicide by poison related in 2 Macc. x. 13, where Ptolemæus Macron is said to have destroyed himself by this means. But we do not find a trace of it among the Jews, and certainly poisoning in any form was not in favor with them. Nor is there any reference to it in the N. T., though the practice was fatally common at that time in Rome (Suet. *Nero*, cc. 33, 34, 35; *Tib.* c. 73; *Claud.* c. 1). It has been suggested, indeed, that the φαρμακεία of Gal. v. 20 (A. V. " witchcraft "), signifies poisoning, but this is by no means consistent with the usage of the word in the LXX. (comp. Ex. vii. 11, viii. 7, 18, &c.), and with its occurrence in Rev. ix. 21, where it denotes a crime clearly distinguished from murder (see Rev. xxi. 8, xxii. 15). It more probably refers to the concoction of magical potions and love philtres.

On the question of the wine mingled with myrrh, see GALL.   W. A. W

POLLUX. [CASTOR AND POLLUX.]

POLYGAMY. [MARRIAGE.]

POMEGRANATE (רִמּוֹן, *rimmôn*: ῥόα, ῥοά, ῥοΐσκος, κώδων: *malum punicum, malum granatum, malogranatum*) by universal consent is acknowledged to denote the Heb. *rimmôn*, a word which occurs frequently in the O. T., and is used to designate either the pomegranate-tree or its fruit. The pomegranate was doubtless early cultivated in Egypt: hence the complaint of the Israelites in the wilderness of Zin (Num. xx. 5), this " is no place of figs, or of vines, or of pomegranates." The tree, with its characteristic calyx-crowned fruit, is easily recognized on the Egyptian sculptures (*Anc. Egypt.* i. 36, ed. 1854). The spies brought to Joshua " of the pomegranates " of the land of Canaan (Num. xiii. 23; comp. also Deut. viii. 8). The villages or towns of Rimmon (Josh. xv. 32), Gath-rimmon (xxi. 25), En-rimmon (Neh. xi. 29), possibly derived their names from pomegranate-trees which grew in their vicinity. These trees suffered occasionally from the devastations of locusts (Joel i. 12; see also Hag. ii. 19). Mention is made of "an orchard of pomegranates" in Cant. iv. 13; and in iv. 3, the cheeks (A. V. "temples") of the Beloved are compared to a section of "pomegranate within the locks," in allusion to the beautiful rosy color of the fruit. Carved figures of the pomegranate adorned the tops of the pillars in Solomon's Temple (1 K. vii. 18, 20, &c.); and worked representations of this fruit, in blue, purple, and scarlet, ornamented the hem of the robe of the ephod (Ex. xxviii. 33, 34). Mention is made of "spiced wine of the juice of the pomegranate" in Cant. viii. 2; with this may be compared the pomegranate-wine (βοίτης οἶνος) of which Dioscorides (v. 34) speaks, and which is still used in the East. Chardin says that great quantities of it were made in Persia, both for home consumption

Punica granatum.

and for exportation, in his time (*Script. Herb.* p. 399; Harmer's *Obs.* i. 377). Russell (*Nat. Hist. of Aleppo*, i. 85, 2d ed.) states "that the pomegranate" (*rummân* in Arabic, the same word as the Heb.) "is common in all the gardens." He speaks of three varieties, "one sweet, another very acid, and a third that partakes of both qualities equally blended. The juice of the sour sort is used instead of vinegar: the others are cut open when served up to table; or the grains taken out, and, besprinkled with sugar and rose-water, are brought to table in saucers." He adds that the trees are apt to suffer much in severe winters from extraordinary cold.

The pomegranate-tree (*Punica granatum*) derives its name from the Latin *pomum granatum*, "grained apple." The Romans gave it the name of *Punica*, as the tree was introduced from Carthage; it belongs to the natural order *Myrtaceæ*, being, however, rather a bush than a tree. The foliage is dark green, the flowers are crimson; the fruit is red when ripe, which in Palestine is about the middle of October, and contains a quantity of juice. The rind is used in the manufacture of morocco leather, and, together with the bark, is sometimes used medicinally to expel the tape-worm. Pomegranates without seeds are said to grow near the river Cabul. Dr. Royle (Kitto's *Cyc.* art. "Rimmon") states that this tree is a native of Asia, and is to be traced from Syria through Persia even to the mountains of Northern India.

W. H.

POMMELS, only in 2 Chr. iv. 12, 13. In 1 K. vii. 41, "bowls." The word signifies convex projections belonging to the capitals of pillars. [BOWL; CHAPITER.]   H. W. P.

POND. *Agâm.*[a] The ponds of Egypt (Ex. vii. 19, viii. 5) were doubtless water left by the inundation of the Nile. In Is. xix. 10, where Vulg. has *qui faciebant lacunas ad capiendos pisces*, LXX. has οἱ τὸν ζῦθον ποιοῦντες, *they who make the beer*. This rendering, so characteristic of Egypt (Her. ii. 77; Diod. i. 34; Strabo, p. 799), arises from regarding *ágám* as denoting a result indicated by its root, *i. e.* a fermented liquor. St. Jerome, who alludes to beer called by the name of Sabaius, explains *dgâm* to mean water fermenting from stagnation (Hieron. *Com. on Is.* lib. vii. vol. iv. p. 292; Calmet; Stanley, *S. & P.* App. § 57).   H. W. P.

PON′TIUS PI′LATE.   [PILATE.]

PONTUS (Πόντος), a large district in the north of Asia Minor, extending along the coast of the Pontus Euxinus, from which circumstance the name was derived. It is three times mentioned in the N. T. It is spoken of along with Asia, Cappadocia, Phrygia, and Pamphylia (Acts ii. 9, 10), as one of the regions whence worshippers came to Jerusalem at Pentecost: it is specified (Acts xviii. 2) as the native country of Aquila; and its "scattered strangers" are addressed by St. Peter (1 Pet. i. 1), along with those of Galatia, Cappadocia, Asia, and Bithynia. All these passages agree in showing that there were many Jewish residents in the district. As to the annals of Pontus, the one brilliant passage of its history is the life of the great Mithridates; but this is also the period of its coming under the sway of Rome. Mithridates was defeated by Pompey, and the western part of his dominions was incorporated with the province of Bithynia, while the rest was divided, for a considerable time, among various chieftains. Under Nero the whole region was made a Roman province, bearing the name of Pontus. The last of the petty monarchs of the district was Polemo II., who married Berenice, the great-grand-daughter of Herod the Great. She was probably with Polemo when St. Paul was travelling in this neighborhood about the year 52. He saw her afterwards at Cæsarea, about the year 60, with her brother, Agrippa II.   J. S. H.

POOL. (1.) *Agâm,* see POND. (2.) *Berécàh*[b] in pl. once only, *pools* (Ps. lxxxiv. 6). (3.) The usual word is *Berécàh,* closely connected with the Arabic *Birkeh,* and the derived Spanish with the Arabic article, Al-berca. A reservoir for water. These pools, like the tanks of India, are in many

---

a אֲגַם: ἕλος: *palus:* plur. in Jer. li. 32; A. V. "reeds," *i. e.* reedy places; συστήματα: *paludes:* also "pool."

b 2 בְּרֵכָה: κοιλάς: *vallis.*

3. בְּרֵכָה: κρήνη: *piscina, aquæductus* (Cant. vii. 4); κολυμβήθρα, λίμνη; from בָּרַךְ, "fall on the knees" (see Judg. vii. 5, 6).— In N. T. κολυμβήθρα, only in John v. 2, ix. 7.

parts of Palestine and Syria the only resource for water during the dry season, and the failure of them involves drought and calamity (Is. xlii. 15). Some are supplied by springs, and some are merely receptacles for rain-water (Burckhardt, *Syria*, p. 314). Of the various pools mentioned in Scripture, as of Hebron, Samaria, etc. (for which see the articles on those places), perhaps the most celebrated are the pools of Solomon near Bethlehem, called by the Arabs *el-Burak*, from which an aqueduct was carried which still supplies Jerusalem with water (Eccl. ii. 6; Ecclus. xxiv. 30, 31).

They are three in number, partly hewn out of the rock, and partly built with masonry, but all lined with cement, and formed on successive levels with conduits leading from the upper to the lower, and flights of steps from the top to the bottom of each (Sandys, *Trav.* p. 150). They are all formed in the sides of the valley of Etham, with a dam across its opening, which forms the E. side of the lowest pool. Their dimensions are thus given by Dr. Robinson: (1.) Upper pool, length 380 feet: breadth at E. 236, at W. 229; depth at E. 25 feet; distance above middle pool, 160 feet. (2.)

Pools of Solomon, and Hill Country of Judah, from S. W

Middle pool, length 423 feet; breadth at E. 250, at W. 160; depth 39; distance above lower pool 248 feet. (3.) Lower pool, length 582 feet; breadth at E. 207, at W. 148; depth 50 feet. They appear to be supplied mainly from a spring in the ground above (FOUNTAIN; CISTERN; JERUSALEM, vol. ii. pp. 1287 a, 1323; CONDUIT; Robinson, *Res.* i. 348, 474).   H. W. P.

* POOL OF BETHESDA. [BETHESDA.]

POOR.ᵃ The general kindly spirit of the law towards the poor is sufficiently shown by such passages as Deut. xv. 7 for the reason that (ver.

11), " the poor shall never cease out of the land," and a remarkable agreement with some of its directions is expressed in Job xx. 19, xxiv. 3, foll., where among acts of oppression are particularly mentioned " taking (away) a pledge," and withholding the sheaf from the poor, vv. 9, 10 [LOAN], xxix. 12, 16, xxxi. 17, " eating with " the poor (comp. Deut. xxvi. 12, &c.). See also such passages as Ex. xviii. 12, 16, 17, xxii. 29; Jer. xxii. 13, 16, v 28; Is. x. 2; Am. ii. 7; Zech. vii. 10, and Ecclus. iv. 1, 4, vii. 32; Tob. xii. 8, 9. [ALMS.]

Among the special enactments in their favor the following must be mentioned. 1. The right of

---

ᵃ 1. אֶבְיוֹן: πτωχός: *pauper.*

2. דַּל: πένης: *pauper.*

3. חֵלְכָה: πτωχός: *pauper.*

4. מִסְכֵּן: πένης: *pauper;* a word of later usage, connected with مِسْكِين, probably the original of *meschino, masquin,* etc. (Ges. p. 954).

5. עָנָה, Chald. (Dan. iv. 27): πένης: *pauper;* from same root as,

6. עָנִי, the word most usually " poor " in A. V.: πτωχός, πτωχός, πένης: *indigens, pauper.* Also Zech. ix. 9, and Is. xxvi. 6, πραΰς: *pauper.*

7. רָשׁ, part. of רוּשׁ: ταπεινός: *pauper.* In 2 Sam. xii. 1, רָאשׁ: πένης, πτωχός.

8. Poverty: מַחְסוֹר: ἐνδεία: *egestas.* In N. T., πτωχός, *pauper.* and πένης: *egenus,* once only, 2 Cor. ix. 9. " Poor " is also used in the sense of " afflicted," " humble," etc.; *e. g.* Matt. v. 3

gleaning. The "corners" of the field were not to be reaped, nor all the grapes of the vineyard to be gathered, the olive-trees not to be beaten a second time, but the stranger, fatherless, and widow to be allowed to gather what was left. So too if a sheaf forgotten was left in the field, the owner was not to return for it, but leave it for them (Lev. xix. 9, 10; Deut. xxiv. 19, 21). Of the practice in such cases in the times of the Judges, the story of Ruth is a striking illustration (Ruth ii. 2, &c.). [CORNER; GLEANING; RUTH, BOOK OF (Amer. ed.)]

2. From the produce of the land in sabbatical years, the poor and the stranger were to have their portion (Lev. xxiii. 11; Lev. xxv. 6).

3. Reëntry upon land in the jubilee year, with the limitation as to town homes (Lev. xxv. 25–30). [JUBILEE.]

4. Prohibition of usury, and of retention of pledges, i. e. loans without interest enjoined (Lev. xxv. 35, 37: Ex. xxii. 25–27; Deut. xv. 7, 8, xxiv. 10–13). [LOAN.]

5. Permanent bondage forbidden, and manumission of Hebrew bondsmen or bondswomen enjoined in the sabbatical and jubilee years, even when bound to a foreigner, and redemption of such previous to those years (Deut. xv. 12–15; Lev. xxv. 39–42, 47–54).

6. Portions from the tithes to be shared by the poor after the Levites (Deut. xiv. 28, xxvi. 12, 13). [TITHES.]

7. The poor to partake in entertainments at the feasts of Weeks and Tabernacles (Deut. xvi. 11, 14; see Neh. viii. 10).

8. Daily payment of wages (Lev. xix. 13).

On the other hand, while equal justice was commanded to be done to the poor man, he was not allowed to take advantage of his position to obstruct the administration of justice (Ex. xxiii. 3; Lev. xix. 15).

On the law of gleaning the Rabbinical writers founded a variety of definitions and refinements, which notwithstanding their minute and frivolous character, were on the whole strongly in favor of the poor. They are collected in the treatise of Maimonides *Mithnoth Ainim*, de jure pauperis, translated by Prideaux (Ugolini, viii. 721), and specimens of their character will appear in the following titles.

There are, he says, 13 precepts, 7 affirmative and 6 negative, gathered from Lev. xix., xxiii.; Deut. xiv., xv., xxiv. On these the following questions are raised and answered, What is a "corner," a "handful?" What is to "forget" a sheaf? What is a "stranger?" What is to be done when a field or a single tree belongs to two persons; and further, when one of them is a Gentile, or when it is divided by a road, or by water; — when insects or enemies destroy the crop? How much grain must a man give by way of alms? Among prohibitions is one forbidding any proprietor to frighten away the poor by a savage beast. An Israelite is forbidden to take alms openly from a Gentile. Unwilling almsgiving is condemned, on the principle expressed in Job xxx. 25. Those who gave less than their due proportion, to be punished. Mendicants are divided into two classes, settled poor and vagrants. The former were to be relieved

by the authorized collectors, but all are enjoined to maintain themselves if possible. [ALMS.] Lastly, the claim of the poor to the portions prescribed is laid down as a positive right.

Principles similar to those laid down by Moses are inculcated in N. T., as Luke iii. 11, xiv. 13; Acts vi. 1; Gal. ii. 10; Jas. ii. 15. In later times, mendicancy, which does not appear to have been contemplated by Moses, became frequent. Instances actual or hypothetical may be seen in the following passages: Luke xvi. 20, 21, xviii. 35; Mark x. 46; John ix. 8; Acts iii. 2. On the whole subject, besides the treatise above named, see Mishna, *Peah*, i. 2, 3, 4, 5; ii. 7; *Pesach.* iv. 8; Selden, *de Jure Natur.* vi. 6, p. 735, &c.; Saalschütz, *Arch. Heb.* ii. p. 256; Michaelis, § 142, vol. ii. p. 248; Otho, *Lex. Rabb.* p. 308.   H. W. P.

POPLAR (לִבְנֶה‎, *libneh*: στυράκινος, in Gen. xxx. 37; λεύκη, in Hos. iv. 13: *populus*), the rendering of the above named Hebrew word, which occurs only in the two places cited. Peeled rods of the *libneh* were put by Jacob before Laban's ring-streaked sheep. This tree is mentioned with the oak and the terebinth, by Hosea, as one under which idolatrous Israel used to sacrifice.

Several authorities, Celsius amongst the number (*Hierob.* i. 292), are in favor of the rendering of the A. V., and think the "white poplar" (*Populus alba*) is the tree denoted; others understand the "storax tree" (*Styrax officinale*, Linn.). This opinion is confirmed by the LXX. translator of Genesis, and by the Arabic version of Saadias

which has the term *lubna* (لُبْنَى), i. e. the "Styrax tree." [a]

Both poplars [b] and styrax or storax trees are common in Palestine, and either would suit the passages where the Heb. term occurs. Dioscorides (i. 79) and Pliny (*N. H.* xii. 17 and 25) both speak of the *Styrax officinale*, and mention several kinds of exudation. Pliny says, "that part of Syria which adjoins Judæa above Phœnicia produces storax, which is found in the neighborhood of Gabala (*Jebeil*) and Marathus, as also of Casius, a mountain of Seleucia. . . . . That which comes from the mountain of Amanus in Syria is highly esteemed for medicinal purposes, and even more so by the perfumers."

Storax (στόραξ) is mentioned in Ecclus. xxiv. 15, together with other aromatic substances. The modern Greek name of the tree, as we learn from Sibthorpe (*Flor. Græc.* i. 275) is στουρακι, and is a common wild shrub in Greece and in most parts of the Levant. The resin exudes either spontaneously or after incision. This property, however, it would seem, is only for the most part possessed by trees which grow in a warm country; for English specimens, though they flower profusely, do not produce the drug. Mr. Dan. Hanbury, who has discussed the whole subject of the storax plants with much care (see the *Pharmaceutical Journal and Transactions* for Feb. 1857), tells us that a friend of his quite failed to obtain any exudation from *Styrax officinale*, by incisions made in the hottest part of the summer of 1856, on specimens growing in the botanic garden at Montpellier.

---

a Arbor lac emittens mellis instar, quo et suffitus fit: videtur esse Styracis arbor. Kâm Dj. See Freytag, *Lex. Arab.* s. v.

b "*Populus alba* and *P. Euphratica* I saw. *P. dilatata* and *nigra* are also said to grow in Syria" (J. D. Hooker).

" The experiment was quite unsuccessful; neither aqueous sap nor resinous juice flowed from the incisions." Still Mr. Hanbury quotes two authorities to show that under certain favorable circumstances the tree may exude a fragrant resin even in France and Italy.

Styrax officinale.

The *Styrax officinale* is a shrub from nine to twelve feet high, with ovate leaves, which are white underneath; the flowers are in racemes, and are white or cream-colored. This *white* appearance agrees with the etymology of the Heb. *libneh.* The *liquid storax* of commerce is the product of the *Liquidambar Orientale*, Mill. (see a fig. in Mr. Hanbury's communication), an entirely different plant, whose resin was probably unknown to the ancients.

                         W. H.

PORA'THA (פּוֹרָתָא [Pers. = perh. *favored by fate*]: Φαραδαθά; Alex. Βαρδαθα; [FA. Φαραθα:] *Phoratha*). One of the ten sons of Haman slain by the Jews in Shushan the palace (Esth. ix. 8). Perhaps " Poradatha " was the full form of the name, which the LXX. appear to have had before them (compare Aridatha, Parshandatha).

PORCH. 1. *Ûlam,*[a] or *ûlam.* 2. *Misderôn ûlâm,* strictly a vestibule (Ges. p. 43), was probably a sort of verandah chamber in the works of Solomon, open in front and at the sides, but capable of being inclosed with awnings or curtains, like that of the royal palace at Ispahan described by Chardin (vii. 386, and pl. 39). The word is used in the Talmud (*Middoth,* iii. 7).

Misd'rôn was probably a corridor or colonnade connecting the principal rooms of the house (Wilkinson, *A. E.* i. 11). The porch[b] (Matt. xxvi.

[a] 1. אֻלָם, or אֻלָּם: αἰλάμ: *porticus* (1 Chr. xxviii. 11); ναός: *porticus.*

2. מִסְדְּרוֹן: παραστάς: *porticus*; only once used Judg. iii. 23.

[b] πυλών.

71) was probably the passage from the street into the first court of the house, in which, in eastern houses, is the *mastâbah* or stone-bench for the porter or persons waiting, and where also the master of the house often receives visitors and transacts business (Lane, *Mod. Eg.* i. 32; Shaw, *Trav.* p. 207). [HOUSE.] The word in the parallel passage (Mark xiv. 68) is προαύλιον, the outer court. The scene therefore of the [second?] denial of our Lord took place, either in that court, or in the passage from it to the house-door. The term στοά is used for the colonnade or portico of Bethesda, and also for that of the Temple called Solomon's porch (John v. 2, x. 23; Acts iii. 11, v. 12).

Josephus describes the porticoes or cloisters which surrounded the Temple of Solomon, and also the royal portico These porticoes are described by Tacitus as forming an important line of defense during the siege (Joseph. *Ant.* viii. 3, § 9, xv. 11, §§ 3, 5; *B. J.* v. 5, § 2; Tac. *Hist.* v. 12). [TEMPLE; SOLOMON'S PORCH.]   H. W. P.

* The "porch" between which and the altar the priests were directed to pray and weep (Joel ii. 17), was on the east side of the Temple, leading from the court of the priests into the sanctuary or outer apartment of the fane of the Temple. The priests standing here had the altar behind them with their faces towards the sanctuary, which was the proper position when they offered prayer. It is mentioned (Ezek. viii. 16) as an insult to Jehovah, a heathenish act, that the priests stood with their backs towards the sanctuary and their faces towards the east.   H.

POR'CIUS FESTUS. [FESTUS.]

* **PORT**, Neh. ii. 13, is used in the Latin sense of "gate," from *porta,* whence "porter," a gate-keeper. Port = seaport, is from *portus,* a harbor. On the "Dung Port" or Dung Gate, see JERUSALEM, vol. ii. p. 1322.   H.

PORTER. This word when used in the A. V. does not bear its modern signification of a carrier of burdens,[c] but denotes in every case a gate-keeper, from the Latin *portarius,* the man who attended to the *porta.* In the original the word is שׁוֹעֵר, *shôêr,* from שַׁעַר, *sha'ar,* a gate: θυρωρός, and πυλωρός: *portarius* and *janitor.* This meaning is evidently implied in 1 Chr. ix. 21; 2 Chr. xxiii. 19, xxxv. 15; John x. 3. It is generally employed in reference to the Levites who had charge of the entrances to the sanctuary, but is used also in other connections in 2 Sam. xviii. 26; 2 K. vii. 10, 11; Mark xiii. 34; John x. 3, xviii. 16, 17. In two passages (1 Chr. xv. 23, 24) the Hebrew word is rendered "doorkeepers," and in John xviii. 16, 17, ἡ θυρωρός is "she that kept the door."   G.

* Rhoda was portress in the house of the mother of John Mark, at Jerusalem (Acts xii. 13). Luke employs in that passage the classical term (ὑπακοῦσαι) signifying to answer a call or knock at the door (Kypke, *Observv. Sacræ,* ii. 60). Women often performed that office among the Greeks and Romans as well as the Jews. The "porter" (John

[c] The two words are in fact quite distinct, being derived from different roots. "Porter" in the modern sense is from the French *porteur.* The similarity between the two is alluded to in a passage quoted from Watts by Dr. Johnson.

x. 3) was the gate-keeper of one of the larger sheep-folds jointly occupied by several shepherds: they had a right to be admitted at the door, but thieves sought to enter by another way. See Wahl, *Clavis N. T.* s. v. θυρωρός. [GATE.]   H.

* PORTION, DOUBLE, *i. e.* "the portion" (more literally *mouthful*) "of two" (פִּי שְׁנַיִם). So in Deut. xxi. 17, of the treatment of the first-born son, who is to be distinguished from those later born, by receiving a larger portion of the father's estate. In 2 Kings ii. 9, Elisha asks Elijah as he is about to ascend to heaven that a *double* portion, *i. e.* an abundant supply, of his spirit may fall upon himself.   R. D. C. R.

POSIDO′NIUS (Ποσιδώνιος: *Posidonius*), an envoy sent by Nicanor to Judas (2 Macc. xiv. 19).

POSSESSION.   [DEMONIACS.]

POST. I. 1. *Ayil,*[a] a word indefinitely rendered by LXX. and Vulg. Probably, as Gesenius argues, the door-case of a door, including the lintel and side-posts (Ges. *Thes.* p. 43). Akin to this is *ailâm,*[b] only used in plur. (Ez. xl. 16, &c.), probably a portico, and so rendered by Symm. and Syr. Vers. (Ges. p. 48).

2. *Ammâh,*[c] usually "cubit," once only "post" (Is. vi. 4).

3. *Mezuzah,*[d] from a root signifying to shine, *i. e.* implying motion (on a centre).

4. *Saph,*[e] usually "threshold."

The ceremony of boring the ear of a voluntary bondsman was performed by placing the ear against the door-post of the house (Ex. xxi. 6; see Juv. *Sat.* i. 103, and Plaut. *Pœn.* v. 2, 21). [SLAVE; PILLAR.]

The posts of the doors of the Temple were of olive-wood (1 K. vi. 33).

II. *Râts,*[f] A. V. "post" (Esth. iii. 13), else-where "runner," and also "guard." A courier or carrier of messages, used among other places in Job ix. 25. [ANGAREUO.]   H. W. P.

* Our English "post" (in French *poste* and Italian *posta*) is from *positum*, a fixed place, as a military *post*, then a station for travellers and relays of horses, and thence transferred to the traveller himself, especially on expeditious journeys. (See Eastwood and Wright's *Bible Word-Book*, p. 378.)   H.

POT. The term "pot"[g] is applicable to so many sorts of vessels, that it can scarcely be restricted to any one in particular. [BOWL; CALDRON; BASIN; CUP, etc.]

[a] אֵיל: τὸ αἴθριον: *frons.*

[b] אֵילָם: τὰ αἰλάμ: *vestibulum.*

[c] אַמָּה: ὑπέρθυρον: *superliminare.*

[d] מְזוּזָה: σταθμός, φλιά: *postis*, from זוז, *mico.*

[e] סַף: φλιά: *limen*; in plur. τὰ πρόπυλα: *superliminaria* (Am. ix. 1).

[f] רָץ, part. of רוץ, "run"; βιβλιαφόρος: *cursor.*

[g] 1. אָסוּךְ: ἀγγεῖον (2 K. iv. 2), applied to oil.

2. נָבִיעַ: κεράμιον: *scyphus* (Jer. xxxv. 5; Ges. p. 260); usually "bowl" or "cup."

But from the places where the word is used we may collect the uses, and also in part the materials of the utensils implied.

1. *Asúc,* an earthen jar, deep and narrow, without handles, probably, like the Roman and Egyptian amphora, inserted in a stand of wood or stone (Wilkinson, *Anc. Eg.* i. 47; Sandys, *Trav.* p. 150).

2. *Cheres,* an earthen vessel for stewing or seething. Such a vessel was used for baking (Ez. iv. 9). It is contrasted in the same passage (Lev. vi. 28) with a metal vessel for the same purpose. [VESSEL.]

3. *Dúd,* a vessel for culinary purposes, mentioned (1 Sam. ii. 14) in conjunction with "caldron" and "kettle," and so perhaps of smaller size.

4. *Sir* is combined with other words to denote special uses, as *basher,* "flesh" (Ex. xvi. 3); *rachatz,* "washing" (Ps. lx. 8; LXX. has λέβης τῆς ἐλπίδος); *matseph,* "fining-pot" (Prov. xxvii. 21).

The blackness which such vessels would contract is alluded to in Joel ii. 6.

The "pots," *gebiyim,* set before the Rechabites (Jer. xxxv. 5), were probably bulging jars or bowls.

The water-pots of Cana appear to have been large amphoræ, such as are in use at the present day in Syria (Fisher, *Views,* p. 56; Jolliffe, i. 33). These were of stone or hard earthenware; but gold, silver, brass, or copper, were also used for vessels both for domestic and also, with marked preference, for ritual use (1 K. vii. 45, x. 21; 2 Chr. iv. 16, ix. 20; Mark vii. 4; Heb. ix. 4; John ii. 6; Michaelis, *Laws of Moses,* § 217, iii. 335, ed. Smith).

Crucibles for refining metal are mentioned (Prov. xxvi. 23, xxvii. 21).

The water-pot of the Samaritan woman may have been a leathern bucket, such as Bedouin women use (Burckhardt, *Notes,* i. 45).

The shapes of these vessels we can only conjecture, as very few remains have yet been discovered, but it is certain that pottery formed a branch of native Jewish manufacture. [POTTERY.]   H. W. P.

POT′IPHAR (פּוֹטִיפַר) [see below]: Πετεφρής; [Alex. in xxxvii. 36, Πετρεφης:] *Putiphar*), an Egyptian pr. n., also written פּוֹטִי פֶרַע, POTIPHERAH. That these are but two forms of one name is shown by the ancient Egyptian equivalent, PET-P-RA, which may have been pronounced, at least in Lower Egypt, PET-PH-RA It signifies "Belonging to the Sun." Rosellini

3. דּוּד: κόφινος: *cophinus*; also "basket."

4. כְּלִי: σκεῦος: *vas*; usually "vessel," once only "pot" (Lev. vi. 28).

5. סִיר: λέβης: *olla*; used with בָּשָׂר (Jer. i. 13), "a seething-pot."

6. פָרוּר: χαλκεῖον: *cacabus.*

7. צִנְצֶנֶת: στάμνος: *vas* (Ex. xvi. 33; Heb. ix. 4).

8. שְׁפַתַּיִם: κλῆροι: *cleri*; "allotments of land."

9. חֶרֶשׂ: σκεῦος ὀστράκινον: *vas fictile* (Lev. vi. 21 [28]).

remarks that it is of very frequent occurrence on the Egyptian monuments (*Monumenti Storici*, i. 117, 118). The fuller form is clearly nearer to the Egyptian.

Potiphar is described as "an officer of Pharaoh, chief of the executioners (סָרִים פַּרְעֹה שַׂר), (הַטַּבָּחִים), an Egyptian". (Gen. xxxix. 1; comp. xxxvii. 36). The word we render "officer," as in the A. V.,[a] is literally "eunuch," and the LXX. and Vulg. so translate it here (σπάδων, *eunuchus*); but it is also used for an officer of the court, and this is almost certainly the meaning here, as Potiphar was married, which is seldom the case with eunuchs, though some, as those which have the custody of the Ka'abeh at Mekkeh are exceptions, and his office was one which would not usually be held by persons of a class ordinarily wanting in courage, although here again we must except the occasional usage of Muslim sovereigns, whose executioners were sometimes eunuchs, as Haroon er-Rasheed's Mesroor, in order that they might be able to carry out the royal commands even in the hareems of the subjects. Potiphar's office was "chief of the executioners," not, as the LXX. makes it, "of the cooks" (ἀρχιμάγειρος), for the prison was in his house, or, at least, in that of the chief of the executioners, probably a successor of Potiphar, who committed the disgraced servants of Pharaoh to Joseph's charge (xl. 2-4). He is called an Egyptian, though his master was probably a Shepherd-king of the XVth dynasty; and it is to be noticed that his name contains that of an Egyptian divinity, which does not seem to be the case with the names of the kings of that line, though there is probably an instance in that of a prince. [CHRONOLOGY, vol. i. p. 443.] He appears to have been a wealthy man, having property in the field as well as in the house, over which Joseph was put, evidently in an important post (xxxix. 4-6). In this position Joseph was tempted by his master's wife. The view we have of Potiphar's household is exactly in accordance with the representations on the monuments, in which we see how carefully the produce of the land was registered and stored up in the house by overseers, as well as the liberty that the women of all ranks enjoyed. When Joseph was accused, his master contented himself with casting him into prison (19, 20), probably being a merciful man, although he may have been restrained by God from acting more severely. After this we hear no more of Potiphar, unless, which is unlikely, the chief of the executioners afterwards mentioned be he. [See JOSEPH.]

R. S. P.

POTIPHE′RAH (פּוֹטִי פֶרַע [see below]: Πετεφρῆς; [Alex. Πετρεφης:] *Putiphare*), an Egyptian pr. n., also written פּוֹטִיפַר, POTIPHAR, corresponding to the PET-P-RA, "Belonging to the Sun," of the hieroglyphics.

Potipherah was priest or prince of On (פֹּהֶן אֹן), and his daughter Asenath was given Joseph to wife by Pharaoh (xli. 45, 50, xlvi. 20). His name, implying devotion to the sun, is very appropriate to

a Heliopolite, especially to a priest of Heliopolis, and therefore the rendering "priest" is preferable in his case, though the other can scarcely be asserted to be untenable. [ON; ASENATH; JOSEPH.]

R. S. P.

POTSHERD (חֶרֶשׂ: ὄστρακον: *testa, vas fictile*): also in A. V. "sherd" (*i. e.* anything divided or separated, from *share*, Richardson's *Dict.*), a piece of earthenware, broken either by the heat of the furnace in the manufacture, by fire when used as a crucible (Prov. xxvi. 23), or otherwise. [POTTERY.] [For illustrations, see Thomson's *Land and Book*, ii. 284.] H. W. P.

* POTTAGE. [LENTILES.]

POTTER'S FIELD, THE (ὁ ἀγρὸς τοῦ κεραμέως: *ager figuli*). A piece of ground which, according to the statement of St. Matthew (xxvii. 7), was purchased by the priests with the thirty pieces of silver rejected by Judas, and converted into a burial-place for Jews not belonging to the city (see Alford, *ad loc.*). In the narrative of the Acts the purchase is made by Judas himself, and neither the potter's field, its connection with the priests, nor its ultimate application are mentioned. [ACELDAMA.]

That St. Matthew was well assured of the accuracy of his version of the occurrence is evident from his adducing it (ver. 9) as a fulfillment of an ancient prediction. What that prediction was, and who made it, is not, however, at all clear. St. Matthew names Jeremiah: but there is no passage in the Book of Jeremiah, as we possess it (either in the Hebrew or LXX.), resembling that which he gives; and that in Zechariah, which is usually supposed to be alluded to, has only a very imperfect likeness to it. This will be readily seen:—

St. Matt. xxvii. 9, 10.	Zech. xi. 12, 13.
Then was fulfilled that which was spoken by Jeremy the prophet, saying, "And they took the thirty pieces of silver, the price of him that was valued, whom they of the children of Israel did value, and gave them for the potter's field, as the Lord appointed me."	And I said unto them, "If ye think good, give my price; and if not, forbear." So they weighed for my price thirty pieces of silver. And Jehovah said unto me, "Cast it unto the potter; a goodly price that I was prised at by them!" And I took the thirty pieces of silver, and cast them to the potter in the house of Jehovah.

And even this is doubtful; for the word above translated "potter" is in the LXX. rendered "furnace," and by modern scholars (Gesenius, Fürst, Ewald, De Wette, Herxheimer — following the Targum, Peshito-Syriac, and Kimchi) "treasury" [b] or "treasurer." Supposing, however, this passage to be that which St. Matthew refers to, three explanations suggest themselves:—

1. That the Evangelist unintentionally substituted the name of Jeremiah for that of Zechariah, at the same time altering the passage to suit his immediate object, in the same way that St. Paul has done in Rom. x. 6-9 (compared with Deut. viii. 17, xxx. 11-14), 1 Cor. xv. 45 (comp. with Gen. ii. 7). See Jowett's *St. Paul's Epistles* (*Essay on Quotations, etc.*)

---

a * In Gen. xxxix. 1 the A. V. has "captain of the guard."   H.

b הַיּוֹצֵר. If this be the right translation, the

passage, instead of being in agreement, is directly at variance with the statement of Matt. xxvii. 6, that the silver was not put into the treasury.

2. That this portion of the Book of Zechariah — a book the different portions of which there is reason to believe are in different styles and by different authors — was in the time of St. Matthew attributed to Jeremiah.

3. That the reference is to some passage of Jeremiah which has been lost from its place in his book, and exists only in the Evangelist. Some slight support is afforded to this view by the fact that potters and the localities occupied by them are twice alluded to by Jeremiah. Its partial correspondence with Zech. xi. 12, 13, is no argument against its having at one time formed a part of the prophecy of Jeremiah: for it is well known to every student of the Bible that similar correspondences are continually found in the prophets. See, for instance, Jer. xlviii. 45, comp. with Num. xxi. 27, 28, xxiv. 17; Jer. xlix. 27, comp. with Am. i.

4. For other examples, see Dr. Pusey's *Commentary* on Amos and Micah. [On this question see vol. i. p. 20 *a*, and vol. ii. p. 1503 *a*, Amer. ed.]

The position of ACELDAMA has been treated of under that head. But there is not now any pottery in Jerusalem, nor within several miles of the city.[a]   G.

* **POTTER'S VESSEL.** [POTTERY.]

POTTERY. The art of pottery is one of the most common and most ancient of all manufactures. The modern Arab culinary vessels are chiefly of wood or copper (Niebuhr, *Voy.* i. 183): but it is abundantly evident, both that the Hebrews used earthenware vessels in the wilderness, where there would be little facility for making them, and that the potters' trade was afterwards carried on in Palestine. They had themselves

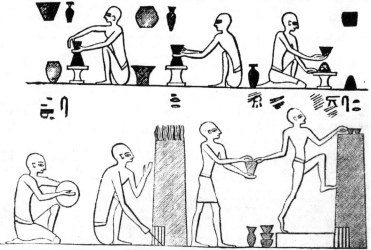

Egyptian Pottery. (Wilkinson.)

been concerned in the potters' trade in Egypt (Ps. lxxxi. 6), and the wall-paintings minutely illustrate the Egyptian process, which agrees with such notices of the Jewish practice as are found in the Prophets, and also in many respects with the process as pursued in the present day. The clay, when dug, was trodden by men's feet so as to form a paste (Is. xli. 25; Wisd. xv. 7) [BRICKS]; then placed by the potter[b] on the wheel beside which he sat, and shaped by him with his hands. How early the wheel came into use in Palestine we know not, but it seems likely that it was adopted from Egypt. It consisted of a wooden disk[c] placed on another larger one, and turned by the hand by an attendant, or worked by a treadle (Is. xlv. 9; Jer. xviii. 3; Ecclus. xxxviii. 29, 30; see Tennent, *Ceylon,* i. 452). The vessel was then smoothed and coated with a glaze,[d] and finally burnt in a furnace (Wilkinson, *Anc. Eg.* ii. 108). We find allusions to the potsherds, *i. e.* broken pieces[e] of vessels used as crucibles, or burst by the furnace, and to the necessity of keeping the latter clean (Is. xxx. 14, xlv. 9; Job ii. 8; Ps. xxii. 15; Prov. xxvi. 23; Ecclus. x. s.).

Earthen vessels were used, both by Egyptians and Jews, for various purposes besides culinary.

---

a * The writer visited a pottery at Jerusalem, in company with Dr. Barclay, author of *The City of the Great King.* It was "in the nave of the ruins of a church of the Crusaders, near St. Stephen's gate, on Bezetha" (*MS. notes,* April 17, 1852). This pottery is also mentioned in the *Ordnance Survey of Jerusalem,* p. 59, where it is said that the clay used there is brought from *El-Jib,* Gibeon. Dr. Tobler speaks of three potteries on Bezetha, and describes the process of making various kinds of earthenware (*Denkblätter aus Jerusalem,* p. 267). Mr. Williams mentions an illustration of Jer. xviii. 1-10, which he saw in one of these potteries (*Holy City,* vol. i., *Mem.* p. 24).

Both of these writers speak of potters' clay as found near Jerusalem.   H.

b 1. יוֹצֵר, part. of יָצַר "press:" κεραμεὺς *figulus.*

2. פֶּחָר, only in Dan. ii. 41: *figulus.*

c אָבְנַיִם lit. "two stones:" λίθοι: *rota* (see Ges. p. 16).

d Χοῖσυα (Ecclus. l. c.).

e חֶרֶשׂ: ὄστρακον: *testa.* See Pot, 9 (note)

Deeds were kept in them (Jer. xxxii. 14). Tiles with patterns and writing were common both in Egypt and Assyria, and were also in use in Palestine (Ez. iv. 1). There was at Jerusalem a royal establishment of potters (1 Chr. iv. 23), from whose employment, and from the fragments cast away in the process, the Potter's Field perhaps received its name (Is. xxx. 14). Whether the term "potter" (Zech. xi. 13) is to be so interpreted may be doubted, as it may be taken for "artificer" in general, and also "treasurer," as if the coin mentioned were to be weighed, and perhaps melted down to be recoined (Ges. p. 619; Grotius, Calmet, St. Jerome, Hitzig, Birch, *Hist. of Pottery*, i. 152; Saalschütz, *Hebr. Arch.* i. 14, 11).

                             H. W. P.

POUND. 1. A weight. See WEIGHTS AND MEASURES.

2. (Μνᾶ.) A money of account, mentioned in the parable of the Ten Pounds (Luke xix. 12–27), as the talent is in the parable of the Talents (Matt. xxv. 14–30), the comparison of the Saviour to a master who intrusted money to his servants wherewith to trade in his absence being probably a frequent lesson in our Lord's teaching (comp. Mark xiii. 32–37). The reference appears to be to a Greek pound, a weight used as a money of account, of which sixty went to the talent, the weight depending upon the weight of the talent. At this time the Attic talent, reduced to the weight of the earlier Phœnician, which was the same as the Hebrew, prevailed in Palestine, though other systems must have been occasionally used. The Greek name doubtless came either from the Hebrew *maneh* or from a common origin; but it must be remembered that the Hebrew talent contained but fifty manehs, and that we have no authority for supposing that the maneh was called in Palestine by the Greek name, so that it is most reasonable to consider the Greek weight to be meant. [TALENT; WEIGHTS AND MEASURES.]   R. S. P.

* POWER is used in 2 Chr. xxxii. 9 (A. V.) to denote a military force, an army. The abstract is similarly used for the concrete in Eph. ii. 2, where "the prince of the power of the air" (τὸν ἄρχοντα τῆς ἐξουσίας τοῦ ἀέρος) denotes the ruler of the powers (evil spirits) that dwell in the air. [AIR, Amer. ed.; PRINCIPALITY, do.]   A.

PRÆTO'RIUM (πραιτώριον). The headquarters of the Roman military governor, wherever he happened to be. In time of peace some one of the best buildings of the city which was the residence of the proconsul or prætor was selected for this purpose. Thus Verres appropriated the palace of king Hiero at Syracuse; at Cæsarea that of Herod the Great was occupied by Felix (Acts xxiii. 35); and at Jerusalem the new palace erected by the same prince was the residence of Pilate. This last was situated on the western, or more elevated hill of Jerusalem, and was connected with a system of fortifications, the aggregate of which constituted the παρεμβολή, or fortified barrack. It was the dominant position on the western hill, and — at any rate on one side, probably the eastern — was mounted by a flight of steps (the same from which St. Paul made his speech in Hebrew to the angry crowd of Jews, Acts xxii. 1 ff.). From the level below the barrack, a terrace led eastward to a gate opening into the western side of the cloister surrounding the Temple, the road being carried across the Valley of Tyropœon (separating the West-

ern from the Temple hill) on a causeway built up of enormous stone blocks. At the angle of the Temple cloister just above this entrance, *i. e.* the N. W. corner [see JERUSALEM, vol. ii. pp. 1300, 1318] stood the old citadel of the Temple hill, the βᾶρις, or Byrsa, which Herod rebuilt and called by the name *Antonia*, after his friend and patron the triumvir. After the Roman power was established in Judæa, a Roman guard was always maintained in the Antonia, the commander of which for the time being seems to be the official termed στρατηγὸς τοῦ ἱεροῦ in the Gospels and Acts. The guard in the Antonia was probably relieved regularly from the cohort quartered in the παρεμβολή, and hence the plural form στρατηγοί is sometimes used, the officers, like the privates, being changed every watch; although it is very conceivable that a certain number of them should have been selected for the service from possessing a superior knowledge of the Jewish customs, or skill in the Hebrew language. Besides the cohort of regular legionaries there was probably an equal number of local troops, who when on service acted as the "supports" (δεξιολάβοι, *coverers of the right flank*, Acts xxiii. 23) of the former, and there were also a few squadrons of cavalry; although it seems likely that both these and the local troops had separate barracks at Jerusalem, and that the παρεμβολή, or prætorian camp, was appropriated to the Roman cohort. The ordinary police of the Temple and the city seems to have been in the hands of the Jewish officials, whose attendants (ὑπηρέται) were provided with dirks and clubs, but without the regular armor and the discipline of the legionaries. When the latter were required to assist this *gendarmerie*, either from the apprehension of serious tumult, or because the service was one of great importance, the Jews would apply to the officer in command at the Antonia, who would act so far under their orders as the commander of a detachment in a manufacturing town does under the orders of the civil magistrate at the time of a riot (Acts iv. 1, v. 24). But the power of life and death, or of regular scourging, rested only with the prætor, or the person representing him and commissioned by him. This power, and that which would always go with it, — the right to press whatever men or things were required for the public exigencies, — appears to be denoted by the term ἐξουσία, a term perhaps the translation of the Latin *imperium*, and certainly its equivalent. It was inherent in the prætor or his representatives — hence themselves popularly called ἐξουσίαι, or ἐξουσίαι ὑπέρτεραι (Rom. xiii. 1, 3) — and would be communicated to all military officers in command of detached posts, such as the centurion at Capernaum, who describes himself as possessing summary powers of this kind because he was ὑπ' ἐξουσίᾳ, covered by the privilege of the *imperium* (Matt. viii. 9). The forced purveyances (Matt. v. 40), the requisitions for baggage animals (Matt. v. 41), the summary punishments following transgression of orders (Matt. v. 39) incident to a military occupation of the country, of course must have been a perpetual source of irritation to the peasantry along the lines of the military roads, even when the despotic authority of the Roman officers might be exercised with moderation. But such a state of things also afforded constant opportunities to an unprincipled soldier to extort money under the pretense of a loan, as the price of exemption from personal services which he was competent to insist upon, or as a bribe to buy off the prosecution of some vexatious charge before a military tribunal (Matt. v. 42; Luke iii. 14).

The relations of the military to the civil authorities in Jerusalem come out very clearly from the history of the Crucifixion. When Judas first makes his proposition to betray Jesus to the chief priests, a conference is held between them and the στρατηγοί as to the mode of effecting the object (Luke xxii. 4). The plan involved the assemblage of a large number of the Jews by night, and Roman jealousy forbade such a thing, except under the surveillance of a military officer. An arrangement was accordingly made for a military force, which would naturally be drawn from the Antonia. At the appointed hour Judas comes and takes with him "the troops" a together with a number of police (ὑπηρέτας) under the orders of the high-priests and Pharisees (John xviii. 3). When the apprehension of Jesus takes place, however, there is scarcely any reference to the presence of the military. Matthew and Mark altogether ignore their taking any part in the proceeding. From St. Luke's account one is led to suppose that the military commander posted his men outside the garden, and entered himself with the Jewish authorities (xxii. 52). This is exactly what might be expected under the circumstances. It was the business of the Jewish authorities to apprehend a Jewish offender, and of the Roman officer to take care that the proceeding led to no breach of the public peace. But when apprehended, the Roman officer became responsible for the custody of the offender, and accordingly he would at once chain him by the wrists to two soldiers (Acts xxi. 33) and carry him off. Here St. John accordingly gives another glimpse of the presence of the military: "the troops then, and the chiliarch and the officers of the Jews apprehended Jesus, and put him in bonds and led him away, first of all to Annas" (xviii. 12). The insults which St. Luke mentions (xxii. 63), are apparently the barbarous sport of the ruffianly soldiers and police while waiting with their prisoner for the assembling of the Sanhedrim in the hall of Caiaphas; but the blows inflicted are those with the vine-stick, which the centurions carried, and with which they struck the soldiers on the head and face (Juvenal, Sat. viii. 247), not a flagellation by the hands of lictors.

When Jesus was condemned by the Sanhedrim and accordingly sent to Pilate, the Jewish officials certainly expected that no inquiry would be made into the merits of the case, but that Jesus would be simply received as a convict on the authority of his own countrymen's tribunal, thrown into a dungeon, and on the first convenient opportunity executed. They are obviously surprised at the question, "What accusation bring ye against this man?" and at the apparition of the governor himself outside the precinct of the prætorium. The cheapness in which he had held the life of the native population on a former occasion (Luke xiii. 1), must have led them to expect a totally different course from him. His scrupulosity, most extraordinary in any Roman, stands in striking contrast with the recklessness of the commander who proceeded at once to put St. Paul to torture, simply to ascertain why it was that so violent an attack

was made on him by the crowd (Acts xxii. 24). Yet this latter is undoubtedly a typical specimen of the feeling which prevailed among the conquerors of Judæa in reference to the conquered. The ordering the execution of a native criminal would, in ninety-nine instances out of a hundred, have been regarded by a Roman magnate as a simply ministerial act, — one which indeed only he was competent to perform, but of which the performance was unworthy of a second thought. It is probable that the hesitation of Pilate was due rather to a superstitious fear of his wife's dream, than to a sense of justice or a feeling of humanity towards an individual of a despised race; at any rate such an explanation is more in accordance with what we know of the feeling prevalent among his class in that age.

When at last Pilate's effort to save Jesus was defeated by the determination of the Jews to claim Barabbas, and he had testified, by washing his hands in the presence of the people, that he did not consent to the judgment passed on the prisoner by the Sanhedrim, but must be regarded as performing a merely ministerial act, — he proceeds at once to the formal infliction of the appropriate penalty. His lictors take Jesus and inflict the punishment of scourging upon Him in the presence of all (Matt. xxvii. 26). This, in the Roman idea, was the necessary preliminary to capital punishment, and had Jesus not been an alien, his head would have been struck off by the lictors immediately afterwards. But crucifixion being the customary punishment in that case, a different course becomes necessary. The execution must take place by the hands of the military, and Jesus is handed over from the lictors to these. They take Him into the prætorium, and muster the whole cohort — not merely that portion which is on duty at the time (Matt. xxvii. 27; Mark xv. 16). While a centurion's guard is being told off for the purpose of executing Jesus and the two criminals, the rest of the soldiers divert themselves in mocking the reputed King of the Jews (Matt. xxvii. 28–30; Mark xv. 17–19; John xix. 2–3), Pilate, who in the mean time has gone in, being probably a witness of the pitiable spectacle. His wife's dream still haunts him, and although he has already delivered Jesus over to execution, and what is taking place is merely the ordinary course,b he comes out again to the people to protest that he is passive in the matter, and that they must take the prisoner, there before their eyes in the garb of mockery, and crucify Him (John xix. 4–6). On their reply that Jesus had asserted Himself to be the Son of God, Pilate's fears are still more roused, and at last he is only induced to go on with the military execution, for which he is himself responsible, by the threat of a charge of treason against Cæsar in the event of his not doing so (John xix. 7–13). Sitting then solemnly on the bema, and producing Jesus, who in the mean time has had his own clothes put upon Him, he formally delivers Him up to be crucified in such a manner as to make it appear that he is acting solely in the discharge of his duty to the emperor (John xix. 13–16).

The centurion's guard now proceed with the prisoners to Golgotha, Jesus himself carrying the cross-piece of wood to which his hands were to be nailed.

---

a Called τὴν σπεῖραν, although of course only a detachment from the cohort.

b Herod's guard had pursued precisely the same brutal conduct just before.

Weak from loss of blood, the result of the scourging, He is unable to proceed; but just as they are leaving the gate they meet Simon the Cyrenian, and at once use the military right of pressing (ἀγγαρεύειν) him for the public service. Arrived at the spot, four soldiers are told off for the business of the executioner, the remainder keeping the ground. Two would be required to hold the hands, and a third the feet, while the fourth drove in the nails. Hence the distribution of the garments into *four* parts. The centurion in command, the principal Jewish officials and their acquaintance (hence probably St. John xviii. 15), and the nearest relations of Jesus (John xix. 26, 27), might naturally be admitted within the cordon — a square of perhaps 100 yards. The people would be kept outside of this, but the distance would not be too great to read the title, "Jesus the Nazarene, the King of the Jews," or at any rate to gather its general meaning.*a* The whole acquaintance of Jesus, and the women who had followed Him from Galilee — too much afflicted to mix with the crowd in the immediate vicinity, and too numerous to obtain admission inside the cordon — looked on from a distance (ἀπὸ μακρόθεν), doubtless from the hill on the other side of the Valley of Kedron *b* — a distance of not more than 600 or 700 yards, according to Mr. Fergusson's view of the site of Golgotha.*c* The vessel containing vinegar (John xix. 29) was set within the cordon for the benefit of the soldiers, whose duty it was to remain under arms (Matt. xxvii. 36) until the death of the prisoners, the centurion in command being responsible for their not being taken down alive. Had the Jews not been anxious for the removal of the bodies, in order not to shock the eyes of the people coming in from the country on the following day, the troops would have been relieved at the end of their watch, and their place supplied by others until death took place. The jealousy with which any interference with the regular course of a military execution was regarded appears from the application of the Jews to Pilate — not to the centurion — to have the prisoners dispatched by breaking their legs. For the performance of this duty other soldiers were dispatched (xix. 32), not merely permission given to the Jews to have the operation performed. Even for the watching of the sepulchre recourse is had to Pilate, who bids the applicants "take a guard" (Matt. xxvii. 65), which they do, and put a seal on the stone in the presence of the soldiers, in a way exactly analogous to that practiced in the custody of the sacred robes of the high-priest in the Antonia (Joseph. *Ant.* xv. 11, § 4).

The Prætorian camp at Rome, to which St. Paul refers (Phil. i. 13), was erected by the emperor Tiberius, acting under the advice of Sejanus. Before that time the guards were billeted in different parts of the city. It stood outside the walls, at some distance short of the fourth milestone, and so near either to the Salarian or the Nomentane road, that Nero, in his flight by one or the other of them

to the house of his freedman Phaon, which was situated between the two, heard the cheers of the soldiers within for Galba. In the time of Vespasian the houses seem to have extended so far as to reach it (Tacitus, *Annal.* iv. 2; Suetonius, *Tib.* 37, *Nero.* 48; Plin. *H. N.* iii. 5). From the first, buildings must have sprung up near it for sutlers and others. St. Paul appears to have been permitted for the space of two years to lodge, so to speak, "within the rules" of the Prætorium (Acts xxviii. 30), although still under the custody of a soldier.

J. W. B.

PRAYER. The words generally used in the O. T. are תְּחִנָּה (from root חָנַן, "to incline," "to be gracious," whence in Hithp. "to entreat grace or mercy"): LXX. (generally), δέησις: Vulg. *deprecatio*: and תְּפִלָּה (from root פָּלַל, "to judge," whence in Hithp. "to seek judgment"): LXX. προσευχή: Vulg. *oratio*. The latter is used to express intercessory prayer. The two words point to the two chief objects sought in prayer, namely, the prevalence of right and truth, and the gift of mercy.

The object of this article will be to touch briefly on (1.) the doctrine of Scripture as to the nature and efficacy of prayer; (2.) its directions as to time, place, and manner of prayer; (3.) its types and examples of prayer.

(1.) Scripture does not give any theoretical explanation of the mystery which attaches to prayer. The difficulty of understanding its real efficacy arises chiefly from two sources: from the belief that man lives under general laws, which in all cases must be fulfilled unalterably; and the opposing belief that he is master of his own destiny, and need pray for no external blessing. The first difficulty is even increased when we substitute the belief in a Personal God for the sense of an Impersonal Destiny; since not only does the predestination of God seem to render prayer useless, but his wisdom and love, giving freely to man all that is good for him, appear to make it needless.

The difficulty is familiar to all philosophy, the former element being far the more important: the logical inference from it is the belief in the absolute uselessness of prayer.*d* But the universal instinct of prayer, being too strong for such reasoning, generally exacted as a compromise the use of prayer for good in the abstract (the "mens sana in corpore sano"); a compromise theoretically liable to the same difficulties, but wholesome in its practical effect. A far more dangerous compromise was that adopted by some philosophers, rather than by mankind at large, which separated internal spiritual growth from the external circumstances which give scope thereto, and claimed the former as belonging entirely to man, while allowing the latter to be gifts of the gods, and therefore to be fit objects of prayer.*e*

---

a The latter supposition is perhaps the more correct, as the four Evangelists give four different forms.

b * It is impossible to be so precise in our ignorance of the place of the crucifixion.　H.

c The two first Evangelists name Mary Magdalene among these women (Matt. xxvii. 56; Mark xv. 40). St. John names her, together with the Lord's mother, and Mary Clopas, as at the side of the cross.

d See the well-known lines: —

"Permittes ipsis exper iere Numinibus, quid

Conveniat nobis, rebusque sit utile nostris.
Carior est illis homo quam sibi."
JUV. *Sat.* x. 346–349.

And the older quotation, referred to by Plato (*Alc.* ii. 154): —

Ζεῦ βασιλεῦ, τὰ μὲν ἐσθλὰ καὶ εὐχομένοις καὶ ἀνεύκτοις

Ἄμμι δίδου· τὰ δὲ δειλὰ καὶ εὐχομένοις ἀπάλεξε.

e "Sed satis est orare Jovem, quæ donat et aufert Det vitam, det opes; æquum mi animum ipse parabo."
Hor. *Ep.* i. xviii. 111; comp.
Cic. *De Nat. Deor.* iii. 36.

The most obvious escape from these difficulties is to fall back on the mere subjective effect of prayer, and to suppose that its only object is to produce on the mind that consciousness of dependence which leads to faith, and that sense of God's protection and mercy which fosters love. These being the conditions of receiving, or at least of rightly entering into, God's blessings, it is thought that in its encouragement of them all the use and efficacy of prayer consist.

Now Scripture, while, by the doctrine of spiritual influence, it entirely disposes of the latter difficulty, does not so entirely solve that part of the mystery which depends on the nature of God. It places it clearly before us, and emphasizes most strongly those doctrines on which the difficulty turns. The reference of all events and actions to the will or permission of God, and of all blessings to his free grace, is indeed the leading idea of all its parts, historical, prophetic, and doctrinal; and this general idea is expressly dwelt upon in its application to the subject of prayer. The principle that our "Heavenly Father knoweth what things we have need of before we ask Him," is not only enunciated in plain terms by our Lord, but is at all times implied in the very form and nature of all Scriptural prayers; and moreover, the ignorance of man, who "knows not what to pray for as he ought," and his consequent need of the Divine guidance in prayer, are dwelt upon with equal earnestness. Yet, while this is so, on the other hand the instinct of prayer is solemnly sanctioned and enforced in every page. Not only is its subjective effect asserted, but its real objective efficacy, as a means appointed by God for obtaining blessing, is both implied and expressed in the plainest terms. As we are bidden to pray for general spiritual blessings, in which instance it might seem as if prayer were simply a means of preparing the heart, and so making it capable of receiving them; so also are we encouraged to ask special blessings, both spiritual and temporal, in hope that thus (and thus only) we may obtain them, and to use intercession for others, equally special and confident, in trust that an effect, which in this case cannot possibly be subjective to ourselves, will be granted to our prayers. The command is enforced by direct promises, such as that in the Sermon on the Mount (Matt. vii. 7, 8), of the clearest and most comprehensive character; by the example of all saints and of our Lord Himself; and by historical records of such effect as granted to prayer again and again.

Thus, as usual in the case of such mysteries, the two apparently opposite truths are emphasized, because they are needful to man's conception of his relation to God; their reconcilement is not, perhaps cannot be, fully revealed. For, in fact, it is involved in that inscrutable mystery which attends on the conception of any free action of man as necessary for the working out of the general laws of God's unchangeable will.

At the same time it is clearly implied that such a reconcilement exists, and that all the apparently isolated and independent exertions of man's spirit in prayer are in some way perfectly subordinated to he One supreme will of God, so as to form a part of his scheme of Providence. This follows from the condition, expressed or understood in every prayer, "Not my will, but Thine, be done." It is seen in the distinction between the granting of our petitions (which is not absolutely promised), and the

certain answer of blessing to all faithful prayer; a distinction exemplified in the case of St. Paul's prayer against the "thorn in the flesh," and of our Lord's own agony in Gethsemane. It is distinctly enunciated by St. John (1 John v. 14, 15): "If we ask any thing *according to his will*, He heareth us: and if we know that He hear us, whatsoever we ask, we know that we have the petitions that we desired of Him."

It is also implied that the key to the mystery lies in the fact of man's spiritual unity with God in Christ, and of the consequent gift of the Holy Spirit. All true and prevailing prayer is to be offered "in the name of Christ" (John xiv. 13, xv. 16, xvi. 23-27), that is, not only for the sake of his Atonement, but also in dependence on his intercession; which is therefore as a central influence, acting on all prayers offered, to throw off whatever in them is evil, and give efficacy to all that is in accordance with the Divine will. So also is it said of the spiritual influence of the Holy Ghost on each individual mind, that while "we know not what to pray for," the indwelling "Spirit makes intercession for the saints, *according to the will of God*" (Rom. viii. 26, 27). Here, as probably in all other cases, the action of the Holy Spirit on the soul is to free agents, what the laws of nature are to things inanimate, and is the power which harmonizes free individual action with the universal will of God. The mystery of prayer, therefore, like all others, is seen to be resolved into that great central mystery of the Gospel, the communion of man with God in the Incarnation of Christ. Beyond this we cannot go.

(2.) There are no directions as to prayer given in the Mosaic Law: the duty is rather taken for granted, as an adjunct to sacrifice, than enforced or elaborated. The Temple is emphatically designated as "the House of Prayer" (Is. lvi. 7); it could not be otherwise, if "He who hears prayer" (Ps. lxv. 2) there manifested his special presence; and the prayer of Solomon offered at its consecration (1 K. viii. 30, 35, 38) implies that in it were offered, both the private prayers of each single man, and the public prayers of all Israel.

It is hardly conceivable that, even from the beginning, public prayer did not follow every public sacrifice, whether propitiatory or eucharistie, as regularly as the incense, which was the symbol of prayer (see Ps. cxli. 2; Rev. vii. 3, 4). Such a practice is alluded to as common, in Luke i. 10; and in one instance, at the offering of the first-fruits, it was ordained in a striking form (Deut. xxvi. 12-15). In later times it certainly grew into a regular service, both in the Temple and in the Synagogue.

But, besides this public prayer, it was the custom of all at Jerusalem to go up to the Temple, at regular hours if possible, for private prayer (see Luke xviii. 10; Acts iii. 1); and those who were absent were wont to "open their windows towards Jerusalem," and pray "towards" the place of God's Presence (1 K. viii. 46-49; Dan. vi. 10; Ps. v. 7, xxviii. 2; cxxxviii. 2). The desire to do this was possibly one reason, independently of other and more obvious ones, why the house-top or the mountain-top were chosen places of private prayer.

The regular hours of prayer seem to have been three (see Ps. lv. 17; Dan. vi. 10), "the evening," that is, the ninth hour (Acts iii. 1, x. 3) the hour of the evening sacrifice (Dan. ix. 21); the "morning," that is, the third hour (Acts ii. 15), that of the morning sacrifice; and the sixth hour, or "noonday." To these would naturally be added some prayer at rising and lying down to sleep; and thence might easily be developed (by the love of the mystic number seven), the "seven times a day" of Ps. cxix. 164, if this is to be literally understood, and the seven hours of prayer of the ancient church. Some at least of these hours seem to have been generally observed by religious men in private prayer at home, or in the midst of their occupation and in the streets (Matt. vi. 5). Grace before meat would seem to have been an equally common practice (see Matt. xv. 36; Acts xxvii. 35).

The posture of prayer among the Jews seems to have been most often standing (1 Sam. i. 26; Matt. vi. 5; Mark xi. 25; Luke xviii. 11); unless the prayer were offered with especial solemnity, and humiliation, which was naturally expressed by kneeling (1 K. viii. 54; comp. 2 Chr. vi. 13; Ezr. ix. 5; Ps. xcv. 6; Dan. vi. 10); or prostration (Josh. vii. 6; 1 K. xviii. 42; Neh. viii. 6). The hands were "lifted up," or "spread out" before the Lord (Ps. xxviii. 2, cxxxiv. 2; Ex. ix. 33, &c., &c.). In the Christian Church no posture is mentioned in the N. T. excepting that of kneeling; see Acts vii. 60 (St. Stephen); ix. 40 (St. Peter); xx. 36, xxi. 5 (St. Paul); perhaps from imitation of the example of our Lord in Gethsemane (on which occasion alone his posture in prayer is recorded). In after-times, as is well known, this posture was varied by the custom of standing in prayer on the Lord's-day, and during the period from Easter to Whit-Sunday, in order to commemorate his resurrection, and our spiritual resurrection in Him.

(3.) The only form of prayer given for perpetual use in the O. T. is the one in Deut. xxvi. 5-15, connected with the offering of tithes and first-fruits, and containing in simple form the important elements of prayer, acknowledgment of God's mercy, self-dedication, and prayer for future blessing. To this may perhaps be added the threefold blessing of Num. vi. 24-26, couched as it is in a precatory form; and the short prayers of Moses (Num. x. 35, 36) at the moving and resting of the cloud, the former of which was the germ of the 68th Psalm.

Indeed the forms given, evidently with a view to preservation and constant use, are rather hymns or songs than prayers properly so called, although they often contain supplication. Scattered through the historical books, we have the Song of Moses, *taught* to the children of Israel (Deut. xxxii. 1-43); his less important songs after the passage of the Red Sea (Ex. xv. 1-19) and at the springing out of the water (Num. xxi. 17, 18); the Song of Deborah and Barak (Judg. v.); the Song of Hannah in 1 Sam. ii. 1-10 (the effect of which is seen by reference to the Magnificat); and the Song of David (Ps. xviii.) singled out in 2 Sam. xxii. But after David's time, the existence and use of the Psalms, and the poetical form of the Prophetic books, and of the prayers which they contain, must have tended to fix this Psalmic character on all Jewish prayer. The effect is seen plainly in the form of Hezekiah's prayers in 2 K. xix. 15-19; Is. xxxviii. 9-20.

But of the prayers recorded in the O. T., the two most remarkable are those of Solomon at the dedication of the Temple (1 K. viii. 23-53), and

of Joshua the high-priest, and his colleagues, after the Captivity (Neh. ix. 5-38).[a] The former is a prayer for God's presence with his people in time of national defeat (vv. 33, 34), famine or pestilence (35-37), war (44, 45), and captivity (46-50), and with each individual Jew and stranger (41-43) who may worship in the Temple. The latter contains a recital of all God's blessings to the children of Israel from Abraham to the Captivity, a confession of their continual sins, and a fresh dedication of themselves to the Covenant. It is clear that both are likely to have exercised a strong liturgical influence, and accordingly we find that the public prayer in the Temple, already referred to, had in our Lord's time grown into a kind of liturgy. Before and during the sacrifice there was a prayer that God would put it into their hearts to love and fear Him; then a repeating of the Ten Commandments, and of the passages written on their phylacteries [FRONTLETS]; next three or four prayers, and ascriptions of glory to God; and the blessing from Num. vi. 24-26, "The Lord bless thee," etc., closed this service. Afterwards, at the offering of the meat-offering, there followed the singing of psalms, regularly fixed for each day of the week, or specially appointed for the great festivals (see Bingham, b. xiii. ch. v. sect. 4). A somewhat similar liturgy formed a regular part of the Synagogue worship, in which there was a regular minister, as the leader of prayer (שְׁלִיחַ הַצָּבוּר, "legatus ecclesiæ"); and public prayer, as well as private, was the special object of the Proseuchæ. It appears also, from the question of the disciples in Luke xi. 1, and from Jewish tradition, that the chief teachers of the day gave special forms of prayer to their disciples, as the badge of their discipleship and the best fruits of their learning.

All Christian prayer is, of course, based on the Lord's Prayer: but its spirit is also guided by that of his prayer in Gethsemane, and of the prayer recorded by St. John (ch. xvii.), the beginning of his great work of intercession. The first is the comprehensive type of the simplest and most universal prayer; the second justifies prayers for special blessings of this life, while it limits them by perfect resignation to God's will; the last, dwelling as it does on the knowledge and glorification of God, and the communion of man with Him, as the one object of prayer and life, is the type of the highest and most spiritual devotion. The Lord's Prayer has given the form and tone of all ordinary Christian prayer; it has fixed, as its leading principles, simplicity and confidence in Our Father, community of sympathy with all men, and practical reference to our own life; it has shown, as its true objects, first the glory of God, and next the needs of man. To the intercessory prayer, we may trace up its transcendental element, its desire of that communion through love with the nature of God, which is the secret of all individual holiness, and of all community with men.

The influence of these prayers is more distinctly traced in the prayers contained in the Epistles (see Eph. iii. 14-21; Rom. xvi. 25-27; Phil. i. 3-11; Col. i. 9-15; Heb. xiii. 20, 21; 1 Pet. v. 10, 11, &c.), than in those recorded in the Acts. The public prayer, which from the beginning became the principle of life and unity in the Church (see

---

[a] To these may be added Dan. ix. 4-19.

Acts ii. 42; and comp. i. 24, 25, iv. 24–30, vi. 6, xii. 5, xiii. 2, 3, xvi. 25, xx. 36, xxi. 5), although doubtless always including the Lord's Prayer, probably in the first instance took much of its form and style from the prayers of the synagogues. The only form given (besides the very short one of Acts i. 24, 25), dwelling as it does (Acts iv. 24–30) on the Scriptures of the O. T. in their application to our Lord, seems to mark this connection. It was probably by degrees that they assumed the distinctively Christian character.

In the record of prayers accepted and granted by God, we observe, as always, a special adaptation to the period of his dispensation to which they belong. In the patriarchal period, they have the simple and childlike tone of domestic supplication for the simple and apparently trivial incidents of domestic life. Such are the prayers of Abraham for children (Gen. xv. 2, 3); for Ishmael (xvii. 18); of Isaac for Rebekah (xxv. 21); of Abraham's servant in Mesopotamia (xxiv. 12–14); although sometimes they take a wider range in intercession, as with Abraham for Sodom (Gen. xviii. 23–32), and for Abimelech (xx. 7, 17). In the Mosaic period they assume a more solemn tone and a national bearing; chiefly that of direct intercession for the chosen people; as by Moses (Num. xi. 2, xii. 13, xxi. 7); by Samuel (1 Sam. vii. 5, xii. 19, 23); by David (2 Sam. xxiv. 17, 18); by Hezekiah (2 K. xix. 15–19); by Isaiah (2 K. xix. 4; 2 Chr. xxxii. 20); by Daniel (Dan. ix. 20, 21); or of prayer for national victory, as by Asa (2 Chr. xiv. 11); Jehoshaphat (2 Chr. xx. 6–12). More rarely are they for individuals, as in the prayer of Hannah (1 Sam. i. 12); in that of Hezekiah in his sickness (2 K. xx. 2); the intercession of Samuel for Saul (1 Sam. xv. 11, 35), &c. A special class are those which precede and refer to the exercise of miraculous power; as by Moses (Ex. viii. 12, 30, xv. 25); by Elijah at Zarephath (1 K. xvii. 20) and Carmel (1 K. xviii. 36, 37); by Elisha at Shunem (2 K. iv. 33) and Dothan (vi. 17, 18); by Isaiah (2 K. xx. 11); by St. Peter for Tabitha (Acts ix. 40); by the elders of the Church (James v. 14, 15, 16). In the New Testament they have a more directly spiritual bearing; such as the prayer of the Church for protection and grace (Acts iv. 24–30); of the Apostles for their Samaritan converts (viii. 15); of Cornelius for guidance (x. 4, 31); of the Church for St. Peter (xii. 5); of St. Paul at Philippi (xvi. 25); of St. Paul against the thorn in the flesh, answered, although not granted (2 Cor. xii. 7–9), &c. It would seem the intention of Holy Scripture to encourage all prayer, more especially intercession, in all relations, and for all righteous objects.   A. B.

* **PREACHING.** The word "preach" is derived through the French *prêcher* from the Latin *prædicare.* As such it means primarily to publish or proclaim by public authority, as a herald or crier (*præco*), and answers to the Greek κηρύσσω, properly, *to proclaim as a herald* (κῆρυξ), and then in general simply *to proclaim, publish,* as one acting by authority. This latter, the common classical meaning of κηρύσσω, is its frequent meaning in the New Testament. In the Gospels it rarely, if at all, appears in any other than its simple classical signification, and such, therefore, in the Gospels at least, is the uniform meaning of its corresponding "preach." Thus (Matt. iii. 1), "John the Baptist, preaching," i. e. making proclama-

tion, in the wilderness of Judæa (iv. 23); "preaching the Gospel," i. e., proclaiming the glad news "of the kingdom;" (x. 27) "that preach ye," i. e. proclaim, "on the house-tops." Gradually, however, the word κηρύσσω, from its frequent special use, came to take, like many other New Testament words (as εὐαγγέλιον, ἀπόστολος, ἐπίσκοπος, διάκονος), a specific and half technical religious sense. Hence in the Epistles it appears partly in its proper sense, as (Rom. x. 14), "How shall they hear without one to make proclamation (τοῦ κηρύσσοντος)?" and partly as a half technical term denotes the proclaiming of salvation without the added substantive. Thus the "foolishness of preaching" is the foolishness (in the judgment of human wisdom) of proclaiming salvation through the cross, and (1 Pet. iii. 19) the preaching to the spirits in prison, whatever the form and locality of the preaching, is undoubtedly the proclaiming of salvation and not of judgment. In this sense the word approximates in the New Testament to the idea of the English "preach," though it is by no means so strictly a religious word, and never perhaps carries with it the idea of a set formal discourse, which is so commonly implied in the English word.

"Preach," however, is employed in the New Testament to translate other words besides κηρύσσω. It is sometimes used as a rendering of λαλέω, *to speak;* once of διαγγέλλω, *to announce abroad, to spread news* (Luke ix. 60); twice of διαλέγομαι, *to discourse* (Acts xx. 7, 9); three or four times of καταγγέλλω, *to announce thoroughly* (as Acts iv. 2); and frequently of εὐαγγελίζομαι, *to bring good news,* or *glad tidings,* but translated, in this case, *to preach the Gospel.* Of this word, "preach the Gospel" is often a sufficiently accurate translation, though in many cases it is not. Thus (Matt. xi. 5), "the poor have the Gospel preached to them," would be more properly rendered "the poor have glad tidings brought to them." Still more unfortunate is the rendering "preach the Gospel" in the following passages: Rom. x. 15, "How beautiful are the feet of them that preach the Gospel of peace," where all the force of the imagery is lost (the feet of them that bring us as from afar the glad tidings of peace): Gal. iii. 8, "The Scripture . . . preached before the Gospel unto Abraham," i. e. brought before, or formerly, the joyful message to Abraham; Heb. iv. 2, "For unto us was the Gospel preached as well as unto them," i. e. for we have had the glad announcement (of a rest) just as did they.

As a rendering of εὐαγγελίζομαι, "preach the Gospel" refers simply to the annunciation of the Gospel under the character of glad tidings; as a rendering of κηρύσσω, it refers to it simply as a public and authorized proclamation. In both cases it refers rather to the first announcement of the Gospel to the ignorant and estranged, rather than to the instructions given to the historic body by pastors and teachers. These would naturally be designated by some other word. Of that extension of the word "preach," by which it comes to denote the ordinary religious discourses of a pastor to his people, the New Testament knows nothing; although this is undoubtedly a very natural extension of the term. The words originally employed to denote the announcement of the Gospel to the heathen, might very easily slide over into an application to all public and established utterances of religious truth.

It is obvious that the oral preaching of the Gospel is divinely enjoined in the New Testament, and is that which the departing Saviour instituted as the grand means of evangelizing the world. Something might, indeed, be due to the great imperfection then attendant on any other means of propagating the Gospel, and the almost complete dependence of the mass of men upon oral communication, for instruction on any subject. Still the Saviour consulted not only the necessity of the times, but the constitution of human nature. Nothing reaches the human mind and heart so quickly as the fresh and living utterances from kindred hearts and lips, and we may well believe, therefore, that the office of preaching and the divine credentials of the preacher have their source equally in the authority and the wisdom of God. "Preaching," the oral proclamation of the Gospel, is divinely enjoined. The New Testament heralds of the cross do not make their proclamation except as they are sent forth (Rom. x. 15). The Christian preacher is the "legate of the skies, his office sacred, his credentials clear;" and his function is to endure in undiminished sacredness and importance, until the Gospel has achieved its last triumph, and the Church is ready for the coming of her Lord.   A. C. K.

* PRECIPITATION.   [PUNISHMENTS, (5).]

* PREPARATION OF THE PASS-OVER (John xix. 14).   [PASSOVER, p. 2350 f.]

* PRESENTLY = immediately (1 Sam. ii. 16 ; Matt. xxvi. 53). The difference between "now" and "soon" is important to the sense in those passages.   H.

PRESENTS. [GIFTS.]

PRESIDENT. Sárac,[a] or Sárĕcá, only used Dan. vi., the Chaldee equivalent for Hebrew Shôtêr, probably from Sara, Zend, a "head" (see Strabo, xi. 331). Σαραπδραι = κεφαλοτόμος is connected with the Sanskrit siras or çirʒs, and is traced in Sargon and other words (Eichhoff, Vergl. Spr. pp. 129, 415; see Her. iii. 89, where he calls Satrap a Persian word).   H. W. P.

* PREVENT (from prœvenio, "to come before,") is never used in the A. V. in its present sense of to hinder, but occurs in other senses, now obsolete, which are likely to perplex the common reader. In the O. T. it is the rendering of the Piel and Hiphil forms of the Heb. קָדַם, kâdam, signifying, primarily, "to go or come before;" in the Apocrypha and the N. T., of φθάνω, and once, προφθάνω, "to anticipate." It is used, accordingly, (1) in the literal sense of "to come before," e. g. Ps. lxxxviii. 13, "in the morning shall my prayer prevent thee;" so Ps. xcv. 2, marg.; (2) "to anticipate," Ps. cxix. 147, "I prevented the dawning of the morning" (more strictly. "I rise early in the dawn "); so ver. 148; Wisd. vi. 13, xvi. 28; Matt. xvii. 25; 1 Thess. iv. 15, "shall not prevent them which are asleep;" (3) "to meet" as a friend, Ps. xxi. 3, "Thou preventest him with the blessings of goodness;" so Ps. lix. 10, lxxix. 8; Is. xxi. 14: Job iii. 12 (receive); (4) "to meet" as an enemy, "come upon," "fall upon," e. g. Job xxx. 27, "the days of affliction prevented me;" similarly 2 Sam. xxii. 6 (seized upon), 19; Ps.

xviii. 5, 18; Am. ix. 10; Ps. xvii. 13 marg. Job xli. 11, "Who hath prevented me, that I should repay him?" (A. V.) is well rendered by Dr. Noyes, "Who hath done me a favor," etc.   A.

* PRICE is used in the A. V. (ed. 1611) in 1 Cor. ix. 24; Phil. iii. 14, for prize, which is substituted in modern editions.   A.

* PRICKS.   [GOAD.]

PRIEST (כּוֹהֵן, cóhén: ἱερεύς: sacerdos).

Name. — It is unfortunate that there is nothing like a consensus of interpreters as to the etymology of this word. Its root-meaning, uncertain as far as Hebrew itself is concerned, is referred by Gesenius (Thesaurus, s. v.) to the idea of prophecy. The Cóhén delivers a divine message, stands as a mediator between God and man, represents each to the other. This meaning, however, belongs to the Arabic, not to the Hebrew form, and Ewald connects the latter with the verb הֵכִין (hêcîn), to array, put in order (so in Is. lxi. 10), seeing in it a reference to the primary office of the priests as arranging the sacrifice on the altar (Alterthüm. p. 272). According to Saalschütz (Archäol. der Hebr. c. 78), the primary meaning of the word = minister, and he thus accounts for the wider application of the name (infra). Bähr (Symbolik, ii. 15) connects it with an Arabic root = קָרַב, to draw near. Of these etymologies, the last has the merit of answering most closely to the received usage of the word. In the precise terminology of the Law, it is used of one who may "draw near" to the Divine Presence (Ex. xix. 22, xxx 20) while others remain afar off, and is applied accordingly, for the most part, to the sons of Aaron, as those who were alone authorized to offer sacrifices. In some remarkable passages it takes a wider range. It is applied to the priests of other nations or religions, to Melchizedek (Gen. xiv. 18), Potipherah (Gen. xli. 45), Jethro (Ex. ii. 16), to those who discharged priestly functions in Israel before the appointment of Aaron and his sons (Ex. xix. 22). A case of greater difficulty presents itself in 2 Sam. viii. 18, where the sons of David are described as priests (Cóhănîm), and this immediately after the name had been applied in its usual sense to the sons of Aaron. The writer of 1 Chr. xviii. 17, as if reluctant to adopt this use of the title, or anxious to guard against mistake, gives a paraphrase, "the sons of David were first at the king's hand" (A. V. "chief about the king"). The LXX. and A. V. suppress the difficulty, by translating Cóhănîm into αὐλάρχαι, and "chief officers." The Vulgate more honestly gives "sacerdotes." Luther and Coverdale follow the Hebrew strictly, and give "priests." The received explanation is, that the word is used here in what is assumed to be its earlier and wider meaning, as equivalent to rulers, or, giving it a more restricted sense, that the sons of David were Vicarii Regis as the sons of Aaron were Vicarii Dei (comp. Patrick, Michaelis, Rosenmüller, in loc., Keil on 1 Chr. xviii. 17). It can hardly be said, however, that this accounts satisfactorily for the use of the same title in two successive verses in two entirely different senses. Ewald accordingly (Alterthüm. p. 276) sees in it an actual suspension of the usual law in favor of members of the royal house, and finds a parallel instance in the acts of David (2 Sam. vi. 14) and Solomon (1 K. iii. 15). De Wette and Gesenius,

* שָׂרָה, or שָׂרְכָא: ταπτικός: princeps.

in like manner, look on it as a revival of the old household priesthoods. These theories are in their turn unsatisfactory, as contradicting the whole spirit and policy of David's reign, which was throughout that of reverence for the Law of Jehovah, and the priestly order which it established. A conjecture midway between these two extremes is perhaps permissible. David and his sons may have been admitted, not to distinctively priestly acts, such as burning incense (Num. xvi. 40; 2 Chr. xxvi. 18), but to an honorary, titular priesthood. To wear the ephod in processions (2 Sam. vi. 14), at the time when this was the special badge of the order (1 Sam. xxii. 18), to join the priests and Levites in their songs and dances, might have been conceded, with no deviation from the Law, to the members of the royal house.a There are some indications that these functions (possibly this liturgical retirement from public life) were the lot of the members of the royal house who did not come into the line of succession, and who belonged, by descent or incorporation, to the house of Nathan as distinct from that of David (Zech. xii. 12). The very name Nathan, connected, as it is, with Nethinim, suggests the idea of dedication. [NETHINIM.] The title *Cohen* is given to Zabud, the son of Nathan (1 K. iv. 5). The genealogy of the line of Nathan in Luke iii. includes many names — Levi, Eliezer, Malchi, Jochanan, Mattathias, Heli — which appear elsewhere as belonging to the priesthood. The mention in 1 Esdr. v. 5 of Joiakim as the son of Zerubbabel, while in Neh. xii. 10 he appears as the son of Jeshua, the son of Josedek, indicates, either a strange confusion or a connection, as yet imperfectly understood, between the two families.b The same explanation applies to the parallel cases of Ira the Jairite (2 Sam. xx. 26), where the LXX. gives ἱερεύς. It is noticeable that this use of the title is confined to the reigns of David and Solomon, and that the synonym "at the king's hand" of 1 Chr. xviii. 17 is used in 1 Chr. xxv. 2 of the sons of Asaph as "prophesying" under their head or father, and of the relation of Asaph himself to David in the choral service of the Temple.

Origin. — The idea of a priesthood connects itself, in all its forms, pure or corrupted, with the consciousness, more or less distinct, of sin. Men feel that they have broken a law. The power above them is holier than they are, and they dare not approach it. They crave for the intervention of some one of whom they can think as likely to be more acceptable than themselves. He must offer up their prayers, thanksgivings, sacrifices. He becomes their representative in "things pertaining unto God." c He may become also (though this does not always follow) the representative of God to man. The functions of the priest and prophet may exist in the same person. The reverence which men pay to one who bears this consecrated character may lead them to acknowledge the priest as being also their king. The claim to fill the office may rest on characteristics belonging only to the individual man, or confined to a single family or tribe. The conditions of the priesthood, the office and influence of the priests, as they are among the most conspicuous facts of all religions of the ancient world, so do they occupy a like position in the history of the religion of Israel.

No trace of an hereditary or caste-priesthood meets us in the worship of the patriarchal age. Abraham, Isaac, and Jacob perform priestly acts, offer sacrifices, "draw near" to the Lord (Gen. xii. 8, xviii. 23, xxvi. 25, xxxiii. 20). To the eldest son, or to the favored son exalted to the place of the eldest, belongs the "goodly raiment" (Gen. xxvii. 15), the "coat of many colors" (Gen. xxxvii. 3), in which we find perhaps the earliest trace of a sacerdotal vestment d (comp. Blunt, *Scriptural Coincid.* i. 1; Ugolini, xiii. 188). Once, and once only does the word *Cóhén* meet us as belonging to a ritual earlier than the time of Abraham. Melchizedek is "the priest of the most high God" (Gen. xiv. 18). The argument of the Epistle to the Hebrews has an historical foundation in the fact that there are no indications in the narrative of Gen. xiv. of any one preceding or following him in that office. The special Divine names which are connected with him as the priest of " the most

---

a The apocryphal literature of the N. T., worthless as a witness to a fact, may perhaps be received as an indication of the feeling which saw in the house and lineage of David a kind of quasi-sacerdotal character. Joseph, though of the tribe of Judah, is a priest living in the Temple (*Hist. Joseph.* c. 2, in Tischendorf, *Evang. Apoc.*). The kindred of Jesus are recognized as taking tithes of the people (*Evang. Nicod.* i. 16, *ibid.*). In what approaches more nearly to history, James the Just, the brother of the Lord, is admitted (partly, it is true, as a Nazarite) into the Holy Place, and wears the linen dress of the priests (Hegesipp. ap. Euseb. H. E. ii. 23). The extraordinary story found in Suidas, s. v. Ἰησοῦς, represents the priests of Jerusalem as electing the "Son of Joseph" to a vacant office in the priesthood, on the ground that the two families had been so closely connected, that there was no great deviation from usage in admitting one of the lineage of David to the privileges of the sons of Aaron. Augustine was inclined to see in this intermingling of the royal and priestly lines a possible explanation of he apocryphal traditions that the Mother of the Lord was of the tribe of Levi (c. *Faust.* xxiii. 9). The marriage of Aaron himself with the sister of the prince of Judah (Ex. vi. 23), that of Jehoiada with Jehoshabeath (2 Chr. xxii. 11), and of Joseph with one who was "cousin" to a daughter of Aaron (Luke i. 36), are historical instances of this connection. The state-

ment of Eutychius (= Sayd ibn Batrik), patriarch of Alexandria (Selden, *De Success. Pont.* i. 13), that Aristobulus was a priest of the house of David, suggests a like explanation.

b Comp. the remarkable passage in Augustine, *De divers. Quæst.* lxi.: "A David enim in duas familias, regiam et sacerdotalem, origo illa distributa est, quarum duarum familiarum, sicut dictum est, regiam descendens Matthæus, sacerdotalem adscendens Lucas secutus est, ut Dominus noster Jesus Christus, rex et sacerdos noster, et cognationem duceret de stirpe sacerdotali, et non esset tamen de tribu sacerdotali." The *cognatio* he supposes to have been the marriage of Nathan with one of the daughters of Aaron.

c The true idea of the priesthood, as distinct from all other ministerial functions like those of the Levites, is nowhere given more distinctly than in Num. xvi. 5. The priest is Jehovah's, is "holy," is "chosen," "draws near" to the Lord In all these points he represents the ideal life of the people (Ex. xix. 3-6). His highest act, that which is exclusively sacerdotal (Num. xvi. 40; 2 Chr. xxvi. 18), is to offer the incense which is the symbol of the prayers of the worshippers (Ps. cxli. 2; Rev. viii. 3).

d In this sacerdotal, dedicated character of Joseph's youth, we find the simplest explanation of the words which speak of him as "the separated one" "the Nazarite" (*Nazir*), among his brethren (Gen. xlix. 26; Deut. xxxiii. 16).

high God, the possessor of heaven and earth," render it probable that he rose, in the strength of those great thoughts of God, above the level of the other inhabitants of Canaan. In him Abraham recognized a faith like his own, a life more entirely consecrated, the priestly character in its perfection [comp. MELCHIZEDEK]. In the worship of the patriarchs themselves, the chief of the family, as such, acted as the priest. The office descended with the birthright, and might apparently be transferred with it. As the family expanded, the head of each section probably stood in the same relation to it. The thought of the special consecration of the firstborn was recognized at the time of the Exodus (*infra*). A priesthood of a like kind continued to exist in other Semitic tribes. The Book of Job, whatever may be its date, ignores altogether the institutions of Israel, and represents the man of Uz as himself " sanctifying " his sons, and offering burnt-offerings (Job i. 5). Jethro is a " priest of Midian " (Ex. ii. 16, iii. 1), Balak himself offers a bullock and a ram upon the seven altars on Pisgah (Num. xxiii. 2, &c.).

In Egypt the Israelites came into contact with a priesthood of another kind, and that contact must have been for a time a very close one. The marriage of Joseph with the daughter of the priest of On — a priest, as we may infer from her name, of the goddess Neith — (Gen. xli. 45) [ASENATH], the special favor which he showed to the priestly caste in the years of famine (Gen. xlvii. 26), the training of Moses in the palace of the Pharaohs, probably in the colleges and temples of the priests (Acts vii. 22), — all this must have impressed the constitution, the dress, the outward form of life upon the minds of the lawgiver and his contemporaries. Little as we know directly of the life of Egypt at this remote period, the stereotyped fixedness of the customs of that country warrants us in referring to a tolerably distant past the facts which belong historically to a later period, and in doing so, we find coincidences with the ritual of the Israelites too numerous to be looked on as accidental, or as the result of forces which were at work, independent of each other, but taking parallel directions. As circumcision was common to the two nations (Herod. ii. 37), so the shaving of the whole body (*ibid.*) was with both part of the symbolic purity of the priesthood, once for all with the Levites of Israel (Num. viii. 7), every third day with those of Egypt. Both are restricted to garments of linen (Herod. ii. 37, 81; Plutarch, *De Isid.* c. 4; Juven. vi. 533; Ex. xxviii. 39; Ez. xliv. 18). The sandals of byblus worn by the Egyptian priests were but little removed from the bare feet with which the sons of Aaron went into the sanctuary (Herod. ii. 37). For both there were multiplied ablutions. Both had a public maintenance assigned, and had besides a large share in the flesh of the victims offered (Herod. *l. c.*). Over both there was one high-priest. In both the law of succession was hereditary (*ibid.*; comp. also Spencer, *De Leg. Hebr.* c. iii. 1, 5, 11; Wilkinson, *Ancient Egyptians*, iii. p. 116).

Facts such as these leave scarcely any room for

doubt that there was a connection of some kind between the Egyptian priesthood and that of Israel. The latter was not, indeed, an outgrowth or imitation of the former. The faith of Israel in Jehovah, the one Lord, the living God, of whom there was no form or similitude, presented the strongest possible contrast to the multitudinous idols of the polytheism of Egypt. The symbolism of the one was cosmic, " of the earth, earthy," that of the other, chiefly, if not altogether, ethical and spiritual. But looking, as we must look, at the law and ritual of the Israelites as designed for the education of a people who were in danger of sinking into such a polytheism, we may readily admit that the education must have started from some point which the subjects of it had already reached, must have employed the language of symbolic acts and rites with which they were already familiar. The same alphabet had to be used, the same root-forms employed as the elements of speech, though the thoughts which they were to be the instruments of uttering were widely different. The details of the religion of Egypt might well be used to make the protest against the religion itself at once less startling and more attractive.[a]

At the time of the Exodus there was as yet no priestly caste. The continuance of solemn sacrifices (Ex. v. 1, 3) implied, of course, a priesthood of some kind, and priests appear as a recognized body before the promulgation of the Law on Sinai (Ex. xix. 22). It has been supposed that these were identical with the " young men of the children of Israel '] who offered burnt-offerings and peace-offerings (Ex. xxiv. 5) either as the first-born,[b] or as representing in the freshness of their youth the purity of acceptable worship (comp. the analogous case of " the young man the Levite " in Judg. xvii. and Ewald, *Alterthüm.* p. 273). On the principle, however, that difference of title implies in most cases difference of functions, it appears more probable that the " young men ' were not those who had before performed priestly acts, but were chosen by the lawgiver to be his ministers in the solemn work of the covenant, representing, in their youth, the stage in the nation's life on which the people were then entering (Keil, *in loc.*). There are signs that the priests of the older ritual were already dealt with as belonging to an obsolescent system. Though they were known as those that " come near " to the Lord (Ex. xix. 22), yet they are not permitted to approach the Divine Presence on Sinai. They cannot " sanctify " themselves enough to endure that trial. Aaron alone, the future high-priest, but as yet not known as such, enters with Moses into the thick darkness. It is noticeable also that at this transition-stage, when the old order was passing away, and the new was not yet established, there is the proclamation of the truth, wider and higher than both, that the whole people was to be " a kingdom of priests " (Ex. xix. 6). The idea of the life of the nation was, that it was to be as a priest and a prophet to the rest of mankind. They were called to a universal priesthood (comp. Keil, *in loc.*). As a people, however,

---

a For a temperate discussion of the connection between the *cultus* of Israel and that of Egypt, on views opposed to Spencer, see Bähr's *Symbolik* (Einleit. § 4, B. c. i. § 3); and Fairbairn's *Typology of Scripture* (b. III. c. 3, § 3).

b The Targums both of Babylon and Jerusalem give " first-born " as an equivalent (Saubert, *De Sacerd.*

Hebr. in Ugolini, *Thes.* xii. 2; comp. also xiii. 126). Jewish interpreters (Saadias, Rashi, Aben-Ezra) take the same view; and the Talmud (*Sevach.* xiv. 4) expressly asserts the priesthood of the first-born in the pre-Mosaic times. It has, however, been denied by Vitringa and others. (Comp. Bähr's *Symbolik*, ii. 4; Selden, *De Synedr.* i. 16, *De Success. Pont.* c. i.)

they needed a long dis●line before they could make the idea a reality. They drew back from their high vocation (Ex. xx. 18–21). As for other reasons so also for this, that the central truth required a rigid, unbending form for its outward expression, a distinctive priesthood was to be to the nation what the nation was to mankind. The position given to the ordinances of the priesthood indicated with sufficient clearness, that it was subordinate, not primary, a means and not an end. Not in the first proclamation of the great laws of duty in the Decalogue (Ex. xx. 1–17), nor in the applications of those laws to the chief contingencies of the people's life in the wilderness, does it find a place. It appears together with the Ark and the Tabernacle, as taking its position in the education by which the people were to be led toward the mark of their high calling. As such we have to consider it.

Consecration. — The functions of the HIGH-PRIEST, the position and history of the LEVITES as the consecrated tribe, have been discussed fully under those heads. It remains to notice the characteristic facts connected with "the priests, the sons of Aaron," as standing between the two. Solemn as was the subsequent dedication of the LEVITES, that of the priests involved a yet higher consecration. A special word (שׁדָּק, *kâdash*) was appropriated to it. Their old garments were laid aside. Their bodies were washed with clean water (Ex. xxix. 4; Lev. viii. 6) and anointed with the perfumed oil, prepared after a prescribed formula, and to be used for no lower purpose [a] (Ex. xxix. 7, xxx. 22–33). The new garments belonging to their office were then put on them (*infra*). The truth that those who intercede for others must themselves have been reconciled, was indicated by the sacrifice of a bullock as a sin-offering, on which they solemnly laid their hands, as transferring to it the guilt which had attached to them (Ex. xxix. 10; Lev. viii. 18). The total surrender of their lives was represented by the ram slain as a burnt-offering, a "sweet savour" to Jehovah (Ex. xxix. 18; Lev. viii. 21). The blood of these two was sprinkled on the altar, offered to the Lord. The blood of a third victim, the ram of consecration, was used for another purpose. With it Moses sprinkled the right ear that was to be open to the Divine voice, the right hand and the right foot that were to be active in divine ministrations (Ex. xxix. 20; Lev. viii. 23, 4). Lastly, as they were to be the exponents, not only of the nation's sense of guilt, but of its praise and thanksgiving, Moses was to "fill their hands" [b] with cakes of unleavened bread and portions of the sacrifices, which they were to present before the Lord as a wave-offering. The whole of this mysterious ritual was to be repeated for seven days, during which they remained within the Tabernacle, separated from the people, and not till then was the consecration perfect (comp. on the meaning of all these acts Bähr, *Symbolik*, ii. c. v. § 2).

Moses himself, as the representative of the Unseen King, is the consecrator, the sacrificer throughout these ceremonies; as the channel through which the others receive their office, he has for the time a higher priesthood than that of Aaron (Selden, *De Synedr.* i. 16; Ugolini, xii. 3). In accordance with the principle which runs through the history of Israel, he, the ruler, solemnly divests himself of the priestly office and transfers it to another. The fact that he had been a priest, was merged in his work as a lawgiver. Only once in the language of a later period was the word *Côhên* applied to him (Ps. xcix. 6).

The consecrated character thus imparted did not need renewing. It was a perpetual inheritance transmitted from father to son through all the centuries that followed. We do not read of its being renewed in the case of any individual priest of the sons of Aaron.[c] Only when the line of succession was broken, and the impiety of Jeroboam intruded the lowest of the people into the sacred office, do we find the reappearance of a like form (2 Chr. xiii. 9) of the same technical word. The previous history of Jeroboam and the character of the worship which he introduced make it probable that, in that case also, the ceremonial was, to some extent, Egyptian in its origin.

High-priest.

Dress. — The "sons of Aaron" thus dedicated were to wear during their ministrations a special apparel — at other times apparently they wore the common dress of the people. The material was linen, but that word included probably, as in the case of the Egyptian priests, the byssus, and the cotton stuff of that country (Ex. xxviii. 42; comp. COTTON).[d]

[a] The sons of Aaron, it may be noticed, were simply sprinkled with the precious oil (Lev. viii. 30). Over Aaron himself it was poured till it went down to the skirts of his clothing (*Ibid.* 12; Ps. cxxxiii. 2).

[b] This appears to have been regarded as the *essential* part of the consecration; and the Hebrew, "to fill the hand," is accordingly used as a synonym for "to consecrate" (Ex. xxix. 9; 2 Chr. xiii. 9).

[c] Ewald (*Alterthüm.* p. 289–291) writes as if the ceremonies of consecration were repeated on the ad-

mission of every priest to the performance of his functions; but this is on the assumption, apparently, that Ex. xxix. and Lev. viii. are not historical, but embody the customs of a later period. Bähr (*Symbolik*, l. c.) leaves it as an open question, and treats it as of no moment.

[d] The reason for fixing on this material is given in Ex. xliv. 18; but the feeling that there was something unclean in clothes made from the skin or wool of an animal was common to other nations. Egypt has been

Linen drawers ["breeches," A. V.] from the loins to the thighs were "to cover their nakedness." The *verecundia* of the Hebrew ritual in this and in other places (Ex. xx. 26, xxviii. 42) was probably a protest against some of the fouler forms of nature-worship, as *e. g.* in the worship of Peor (Maimonides, *More Nevochim*, iii. 45, in Ugolini, xiii. p. 385), and possibly also, in some Egyptian rites (Herod. ii. 60). Over the drawers was worn the *cetoneth*, or close-fitting cassock, also of fine linen,

Dress of Egyptian Priests. (Wilkinson.)

white, but with a diamond or chess-board pattern on it (Bähr, *Symb.* ii. c. iii. § 2). This came nearly to the feet (ποδήρης χιτών, Joseph. *Ant.* iii. 7, § 1), and was to be woven in its garment-shape (not cut out and then sewed together), like the χιτὼν ἄρραφος of John xix. 23, in which some interpreters have even seen a token of the priesthood of him who wore it (Ewald, *Gesch.* v. 177; Ugolini, xiii. p. 218).[a] The white cassock was gathered round the body with a girdle of needle-work, into which, as in the more gorgeous belt of the high-priest, blue, purple, and scarlet were intermingled with white, and worked in the form of flowers (Ex. xxviii. 39, 40, xxxix. 2; Ez. xliv. 17–19). Upon their heads they were to wear caps or bonnets (in the English of the A. V. the two words are synonymous) in the form of a cup-shaped flower, also of fine linen. These garments they might wear at any time in the Temple, whether on duty or not, but they were not to sleep in them (Joseph. *B. J.* v. 5, § 7). When they became soiled, they were not washed or used again, but torn up to make wicks for the lamps in the Tabernacle (Selden, *De Synedr.* xiii. 11). They had besides them other "clothes of service," which were probably simpler, but are not described (Ex. xxxi. 10; Ez. xlii. 14). In all their acts of ministration they were to be barefooted.[b] Then, as now, this was the strongest recognition of the sanctity of a holy place which the Oriental mind could think of (Ex. iii. 5; Josh. v. 15), and throughout the whole existence of the Temple service, even though it drew upon them the scorn of the heathen (Juven. *Sat.* vi. 159), and

Dress of Egyptian High-priests.

seriously affected the health of the priests (Ugolini, viii. p. 976, xiii. p. 405), it was scrupulously adhered to.[c] In the earlier liturgical costume, the

already mentioned. The Arab priests in the time of Mohammed wore linen only (Ewald, *Alterth.* p. 289).

a Here also modern Eastern customs present an analogy in the woven, seamless *ihram* worn by the Mecca pilgrims (Ewald, *Alterth.* p. 289).

b This is inferred (1) from the absence of any direc-tion as to a covering for the feet; (2) from the later custom; (3) from the universal feeling of the East. Shoes were worn as a protection against defilement. In a sanctuary there was nothing that could defile.

c Bähr (*Symbolik*, ii. c. iii. § 1, 2) finds a mystic meaning in the number, material, color, shape, of the

ephod is mentioned as belonging to the high-priest only (Ex. xxviii. 6–12, xxxix. 2–5). At a later period it is used apparently by all the priests (1 Sam. xxii. 18), and even by others, not of the tribe of Levi, engaged in religious ceremonial (2 Sam. vi. 14). [EPHOD.]

Regulations. — The idea of a consecrated life, which was thus asserted at the outset, was carried through a multitude of details. Each probably had a symbolic meaning of its own. Collectively they formed an education by which the power of distinguishing between things holy and profane, between the clean and the unclean, and so ultimately between moral good and evil, was awakened and developed (Ez. xliv. 23). Before they entered the Tabernacle they were to wash their hands and their feet (Ex. xxx. 17–21, xl. 30–32). During the time of their ministration they were to drink no wine or strong drink (Lev. x. 9; Ez. xliv. 21). Their function was to be more to them than the ties of friendship or of blood, and, except in the case of the nearest relationships (six degrees are specified, Lev. xxi. 1–5; Ez. xliv. 25), they were to make no mourning for the dead. The high-priest, as carrying the consecrated life to its highest point, was to be above the disturbing power of human sorrow even in these instances. Customs which appear to have been common in other priesthoods were (probably for that reason) forbidden them. They were not to shave their heads. They were to go through their ministrations with the serenity of a reverential awe, not with the orgiastic wildness which led the priests of Baal in their despair to make cuttings in their flesh (Lev. xix. 28; 1 K. xviii. 28), and carried those of whom Atys was a type to a more terrible mutilation (Deut. xxiii. 1). The same thought found expression in two other forms affecting the priests of Israel. The priest was to be one who, as the representative of other men, was to be physically as well as liturgically perfect.[a] As the victim was to be without blemish so also was the sacrificer (comp. Bähr, *Symbol.* ii. c. ii. § 3). The law specified in broad outlines the excluding defects (Lev. xxi. 17–21), and these were such as impaired the purity, or at least the dignity, of the ministrant. The morbid casuistry of the later rabbis drew up a list of not less than 142 faults or infirmities which involved permanent, of 22 which involved temporary deprivation from the priestly office (Carpzov. *App. Critic.* pp. 92, 93; Ugolini, xii. 54, xiii. 903); and the original symbolism of the principle (Philo, *De Vict.* and *De Monarch.* ii. 5) was lost in the prurient minuteness which, here as elsewhere, often makes the study of rabbinic literature a somewhat repulsive task. If the Christian Church has sometimes seemed to approximate, in the conditions it laid down for the priestly character, to the rules of Judaism, it was yet careful to reject the Jewish principles, and to rest its regulations simply on the grounds of expediency (*Constt. Apost.* 77, 78). The marriages of the sons of Aaron were, in like manner, hedged round with special rules. There is, indeed, no evidence for what has sometimes been asserted, that either the high-priest (Philo, *De Monarch.* ii. 11, ii. 229, ed. Mang.; Ewald, *Alterth.* p. 302) or the other sons of Aaron (Ugolini, xii. 52)

were limited in their choice to the women of their own tribe, and we have some distinct instances to the contrary. It is probable, however, that the priestly families frequently intermarried, and it is certain that they were forbidden to marry an unchaste woman, or one who had been divorced, or the widow of any but a priest (Lev. xxi. 7, 14; Ez. xliv. 22). The prohibition of marriage with one of an alien race was assumed, though not enacted in the law; and hence the reforming zeal of a later time compelled all who had contracted such marriages to put away their strange wives (Ezr. x. 18), and counted the offspring of a priest and a woman taken captive in war as illegitimate (Joseph. *Ant.* iii. 10, xi. 4; c. *Apion,* i. 7), even though the priest himself did not thereby lose his function (Ugolini, xii. 924). The high-priest was to carry the same idea to a yet higher point, and was to marry none but a virgin in the first freshness of her youth (Lev. xxi. 13). Later casuistry fixed the age within the narrow limits of twelve and twelve and a half (Carpzov. *App. Crit.* p. 88). It followed as a matter of necessity from these regulations, that the legitimacy of every priest depended on his genealogy. A single missing or faulty link would vitiate the whole succession. To those genealogies, accordingly, extending back unbroken for 2000 years, the priests could point, up to the time of the destruction of the Temple (Joseph. c. *Apion.* i. 7). In later times, wherever the priest might live — Egypt, Babylon, Greece — he was to send the register of all marriages in his family to Jerusalem (*ibid.*). They could be referred to in any doubtful or disputed case (Ezr. ii. 62; Neh. vii. 64). In them was registered the name of every mother as well as of every father (*ibid.*; comp. also the story already referred to in Suidas, *s. v.* Ἰησοῦς). It was the distinguishing mark of a priest, not of the Aaronic line, that he was ἀπάτωρ, ἀμήτωρ, ἀγενεαλόγητος (Heb. vii. 3), with no father or mother named as the ground of his title.

The age at which the sons of Aaron might enter upon their duties was not defined by the Law, as that of the Levites was. Their office did not call for the same degree of physical strength; and if twenty-five in the ritual of the Tabernacle (Num. viii. 24) and twenty in that of the Temple (1 Chr. xxiii. 27) was the appointed age for the latter, the former were not likely to be kept waiting till a later period. In one remarkable instance, indeed, we have an example of a yet earlier age. The boy Aristobulus at the age of seventeen ministered in the Temple in his pontifical robes, the admired of all observers, and thus stirred the treacherous jealousy of Herod to remove so dangerous a rival (Joseph. *Ant.* xv. 3, § 3). This may have been exceptional, but the language of the rabbis indicates that the special consecration of the priest's life began with the opening years of manhood. As soon as the down appeared on his cheek the young candidate presented himself before the Council of the Sanhedrim, and his genealogy was carefully inspected. If it failed to satisfy his judges, he left the Temple clad in black, and had to seek another calling; if all was right so far, another ordeal awaited him. A careful inspection was to determine whether he was subject to any one of the 141

priestly vestments, discusses each point elaborately, and dwells in § 3 on the *differences* between them and those of the Egyptian priesthood.

  [a] The idea of the perfect body, as symbolizing the

holy soul, was, as might be expected, wide-spread among the religions of heathenism. "Sacerdos non integri corporis quasi mali ominis res vitanda est" (Seneca, *Controv.* iv. 2).

defects which would invalidate his priestly acts. If he was found free from all blemish, he was clad in the white linen tunic of the priests, and entered on his ministrations. If the result of the examination was not satisfactory, he was relegated to the half-menial office of separating the sound wood for the altar from that which was decayed and worm-eaten, but was not deprived of the emoluments of his office (Lightfoot, *Temple Service*, c. 6).

Functions. — The work of the priesthood of Israel was, from its very nature, more stereotyped by the Mosaic institutions than any other element of the national life. The functions of the Levites — less defined, and therefore more capable of expansion — altered, as has been shown [LEVITES], from age to age; but those of the priests continued throughout substantially the same, whatever changes might be brought about in their social position and organization. The duties described in Exodus and Leviticus are the same as those recognised in the Books of Chronicles, as those which the prophet-priest Ezekiel sees in his vision of the Temple of the future. They, assisting the high-priest, were to watch over the fire on the altar of burnt-offerings and to keep it burning evermore both by day and night (Lev. vi. 12; 2 Chr. xiii. 11), to feed the golden lamp outside the veil with oil (Ex. xxvii. 20, 21; Lev. xxiv. 2), to offer the morning and evening sacrifices, each accompanied with a meat-offering and a drink-offering, at the door of the Tabernacle (Ex. xxix. 38–44). These were the fixed, invariable duties; but their chief function was that of being always at hand to do the priest's office for any guilty, or penitent, or rejoicing Israelite. The worshipper might come at any time. If he were rich and brought a bullock, it was the priest's duty to slay the victim, to place the wood upon the altar, to light the fire, to sprinkle the altar with the blood (Lev. i. 5). If he were poor and brought a pigeon, the priest was to wring its neck (Lev. i. 15). In either case he was to burn the meat-offering and the peace-offering which accompanied the sacrifice (Lev. ii. 2, 9, iii. 11). After the birth of every child, the mother was to come with her sacrifice of turtle-doves or pigeons (Lev. xii. 6; Luke ii. 22–24), and was thus to be purified from her uncleanness. A husband who suspected his wife of unfaithfulness might bring her to the priest, and it belonged to him to give her the water of jealousy as an ordeal, and to pronounce the formula of execration (Num. v. 11–31). Lepers were to come, day by day, to submit themselves to the priest's inspection, that he might judge whether they were clean or unclean, and when they were healed perform for them the ritual of purification (Lev. xiii., xiv., and comp. Mark i. 44). All the numerous accidents which the Law looked on as defilements or sins of ignorance had to be expiated by a sacrifice, which the priest, of course, had to offer (Lev. xv. 1–33). As they thus acted as mediators for those who were laboring under the sense of guilt, so they were to help others who were striving to attain, if only for a season, the higher standard of a consecrated life. The Nazarite was to, come to them with his sacrifice and his wave-offering (Num. vi. 1–21).

Other duties of a higher and more ethical character were hinted at, but were not, and probably could not be, the subject of a special regulation. They were to teach the children of Israel the statutes of the Lord (Lev. x. 11; Deut. xxxiii. 10; 2 Chr. xv. 3; Ezek. xliv. 23, 24). The "priest's lips" (in the language of the last prophet looking back upon the ideal of the order) were to "keep knowledge" (Mal. ii. 7). Through the whole history, with the exception of the periods of national apostasy, these acts, and others like them, formed the daily life of the priests who were on duty. The three great festivals of the year were, however, their seasons of busiest employment. The pilgrims who came up by tens of thousands to keep the feast, came each with his sacrifices and oblations. The work at such times was, on some occasions at least, beyond the strength of the priests in attendance, and the Levites had to be called in to help them (2 Chr. xxix. 34, xxxv. 14). Other acts of the priests of Israel, significant as they were, were less distinctively sacerdotal. They were to bless the people at every solemn meeting; and that this part of their office might never fall into disuse, a special formula of benediction was provided (Num. vi. 22–27). During the journeys in the wilderness it belonged to them to cover the ark and all the vessels of the sanctuary with a purple or scarlet cloth before the Levites might approach them (Num. iv. 5–15). As the people started on each day's march they were to blow "an alarm" with long silver trumpets (Num. x. 1–8), — with two if the whole multitude were to be assembled, with one if there was to be a special council of the elders and princes of Israel. With the same instruments they were to proclaim the commencement of all the solemn days, and days of gladness (Num. x. 10); and throughout all the changes in the religious history of Israel this adhered to them as a characteristic mark. Other instruments of music might be used by the more highly trained Levites and the schools of the Prophets, but the trumpets belonged only to the priests. They blew them in the solemn march round Jericho[a] (Josh. vi. 4), in the religious war which Judah waged against Jeroboam (2 Chr. xiii. 12), when they summoned the people to a solemn penitential fast (Joel ii. 1, 15). In the service of the second temple there were never to be less than 21 or more than 84 blowers of trumpets present in the Temple daily (Ugolini, xiii. 1011). The presence of the priests on the field of battle for this purpose, often in large numbers, armed for war, and sharing in the actual contest (1 Chr. xii. 23. 27; 2 Chr. xx. 21, 22), led, in the later periods of Jewish history, to the special appointment at such times of a war-priest, deputed by the Sanhedrim to be the representative of the high-priest, and standing next but one to him in the order of precedence (comp. Ugolini, xii. 1031, *De Sacerdote Castrensi*; and xiii. 871).[b]

Other functions were hinted at in Deuteronomy which might have given them greater influence as the educators and civilizers of the people. They

---

[a] In this case, however, the trumpets were of rams' horns, not of silver.

[b] Jost (*Judenth.* i. 153) regards the war-priest as belonging to the ideal system of the later Rabbis, not to the historical constitution of Israel. Deut. xx. 2 however, supplies the germ out of which such an office might naturally grow. Judas Maccabæus, in his wars, does what the war-priest was said to do (1 Macc. iii. 56).

were to act (whether individually or collectively does not distinctly appear) as a court of appeal in the more difficult controversies in criminal or civil cases (Deut. xvii. 8–13). A special reference was to be made to them in cases of undetected murder, and they were thus to check the vindictive blood-feuds which it would otherwise have been likely to occasion (Deut. xxi. 5). It must remain doubtful, however, how far this order kept its ground during the storms and changes that followed. The judicial and the teaching functions of the priesthood remained probably for the most part in abeyance through the ignorance and vices of the priests. Zealous reformers kept this before them as an ideal (2 Chr. xvii. 7–9, xix. 8–10; Ez. xliv. 24), but the special stress laid on the attempts to realize it shows that they were exceptional.[a]

Maintenance. — Functions such as these were clearly incompatible with the common activities of men. At first the small number of the priests must have made the work almost unintermittent, and even when the system of rotation had been adopted, the periodical absences from home could not fail to be disturbing and injurious, had they been dependent on their own labors. The serenity of the priestly character would have been disturbed had they had to look for support to the lower industries. It may have been intended (*supra*) that their time, when not liturgically employed, should be given to the study of the Law, or to instructing others in it. On these grounds therefore a distinct provision was made for them. This consisted [b] — (1) of one tenth of the tithes which the people paid to the Levites, one per cent. *i. e.* on the whole produce of the country (Num. xviii. 26–28). (2) Of a special tithe every third year (Deut. xiv. 28, xxvi. 12). (3) Of the redemption-money, paid at the fixed rate of five shekels a head, for the first-born of man or beast (Num. xviii. 14–19).[c] (4) Of the redemption-money paid in like manner for men or things specially dedicated to the Lord (Lev. xxvii.). (5) Of spoil, captives, cattle, and the like, taken in war (Num. xxxi. 25–47). (6) Of what may be described as the perquisites of their sacrificial functions, the shew-bread, the flesh of the burnt-offerings, peace-offerings, trespass-offerings (Num. xviii. 8–14; Lev. vi. 26, 29, vii. 6–10), and, in particular, the heave-shoulder and the wave-breast (Lev. x. 12–15). (7) Of an undefined amount of the first-fruits of corn, wine, and oil (Ex. xxiii. 19; Lev. ii. 14; Deut. xxvi. 1–10). Of some of these, as "most holy," none but the priests were to partake (Lev. vi. 29). It was lawful for their sons and daughters (Lev. x. 14), and even in some cases for their home-born slaves, to eat of others (Lev. xxii. 11). The stranger and the hired servant were in all cases excluded (Lev. xxii. 10). (8) On their settlement in Canaan the priestly families had thirteen cities assigned them, with "suburbs" or pasture-grounds for their flocks (Josh. xxi. 13–19). While the Levites were scattered over all the conquered country, the cities of the priests were within the tribes of Judah, Simeon, and Benjamin, and this concentra-

tion was not without its influence on their subsequent history. [Comp. LEVITES.] These provisions were obviously intended to secure the religion of Israel against the dangers of a caste of pauper-priests, needy and dependent, and unable to bear their witness to the true faith. They were, on the other hand, as far as possible removed from the condition of a wealthy order. Even in the ideal state contemplated by the Book of Deuteronomy, the Levite (here probably used generically, so as to include the priests) is repeatedly marked out as an object of charity, along with the stranger and the widow (Deut. xii. 12, 19, xiv. 27–29). During the long periods of national apostasy, tithes were probably paid with even less regularity than they were in the more orthodox period that followed the return from the Captivity (Neh. xiii. 10; Mal. iii. 8–10). The standard of a priest's income, even in the earliest days after the settlement in Canaan, was miserably low (Judg. xvii. 10). Large portions of the priesthood fell, under the kingdom, into a state of abject poverty (comp. 1 Sam. ii. 36). The clinging evil throughout their history was not that they were too powerful and rich, but that they sank into the state from which the Law was intended to preserve them, and so came to "teach for hire" (Mic. iii. 11; comp. Saalschütz, *Archäologie der Hebräer*, ii. 344–355).

Classification and Statistics. — The earliest historical trace of any division of the priesthood, and corresponding cycle of services, belongs to the time of David. Jewish tradition indeed recognizes an earlier division, even during the life of Aaron, into eight houses (Gem. Hieros. *Taanith*, in Ugolini, xiii. 873), augmented during the period of the Shiloh-worship to sixteen, the two families of Eleazar and Ithamar standing in both cases on an equality. It is hardly conceivable, however, that there could have been any rotation of service while the number of priests was so small as it must have been during the forty years of sojourn in the wilderness, if we believe Aaron and his lineal descendants to have been the only priests officiating. The difficulty of realizing in what way the single family of Aaron were able to sustain all the burden of the worship of the Tabernacle and the sacrifices of individual Israelites, may, it is true, suggest the thought that possibly in this, as in other instances, the Hebrew idea of sonship by adoption may have extended the title of the "Sons of Aaron" beyond the limits of lineal descent, and, in this case, there may be some foundation for the Jewish tradition. Nowhere in the later history do we find any disproportion like that of three priests to 22,000 Levites. The office of supervision over those that "kept the charge of the sanctuary," entrusted to Eleazar (Num. iii. 32), implies that some others were subject to it besides Ithamar and his children, while these very keepers of the sanctuary are identified in ver. 38 with the sons of Aaron who are encamped with Moses and Aaron on the east side of the Tabernacle. The allotment of not less than thirteen cities to those

a The teaching functions of the priest have probably been unduly magnified by writers like Michaelis, who aim at bringing the institutions of Israel to the standard of modern expediency (*Comm. on Laws of Moses*, i. 35–52), as they have been unduly depreciated by Saalschütz and Jahn.

b The later Rabbis enumerate no less than twenty-

four sources of emolument. Of these the chief only are given here (Ugolini, xiii. 1124).

c It is to be noticed that the Law, by recognizing the substitution of the Levites for the first-born, and ordering payment only for the small number of the latter in excess of the former, deprived Aaron and his sons of a large sum which would otherwise have accrued to them (Num. iii. 44–51).

who bore the name, within little more than forty years from the Exodus, tends to the same conclusion, and at any rate indicates that the priesthood were not intended to be always in attendance at the Tabernacle, but were to have homes of their own, and therefore, as a necessary consequence, fixed periods only of service. Some notion may be formed of the number on the accession of David from the facts (1) that not less than 3700 tendered their allegiance to him while he was as yet reigning at Hebron over Judah only (1 Chr. xii. 27), and (2) that one-twenty fourth part were sufficient for all the services of the statelier and more frequented worship which he established. To this reign belonged accordingly the division of the priesthood into the four-and-twenty "courses" or orders (מַחְלְקוֹת, διαιρέσεις, ἐφημερίαι, 1 Chr. xxiv. 1-19; 2 Chr. xxiii. 8; Luke i. 5), each of which was to serve in rotation for one week, while the further assignment of special services during the week was determined by lot (Luke i. 9). Each course appears to have commenced its work on the Sabbath, the outgoing priests taking the morning sacrifice, and leaving that of the evening to their successors (2 Chr. xxiii. 8; Ugolini, xiii. 319). In this division, however, the two great priestly houses did not stand on an equality. The descendants of Ithamar were found to have fewer representatives than those of Eleazar,[a] and sixteen courses accordingly were assigned to the latter, eight only to the former (1 Chr. xxiv. 4; comp. Carpzov. App. Crit. p. 98). The division thus instituted was confirmed by Solomon, and continued to be recognized as the typical number of the priesthood. It is to be noted, however, that this arrangement was to some extent elastic. Any priest might be present at any time, and even perform priestly acts, so long as he did not interfere with the functions of those who were officiating in their course (Ugolini, xiii. 881), and at the great solemnities of the year, as well as on special occasions like the opening of the Temple, they were present in great numbers. On the return from the Captivity there were found but four courses out of the twenty-four, each containing, in round numbers, about a thousand [b] (Ezr. ii. 36-39). Out of these, however, to revive, at least, the idea of the old organization, the four-and-twenty courses were reconstituted, bearing the same names as before, and so continued till the destruction of Jerusalem. If we may accept the numbers given by Jewish writers as at all trustworthy, the proportion of the priesthood to the population of Palestine during the last century of their existence as an order must have been far greater than that of the clergy has ever been in any Christian nation. Over and above those that were scattered in the country and took their turn, there were not fewer than 24,000 stationed permanently at Jerusalem, and 12,000 at Jericho (Gemar. Hieros. Taanith, fol. 67, in Carpzov. App. Crit. p. 100). It was a Jewish tradition that it had never fallen to the lot of any priest to offer incense twice (Ugolini, xii. 18). Oriental statistics are, however, always open to some suspicion, those of the Talmud not least so; and there is, probably, more

truth in the computation of Josephus, who estimates the total number of the four houses of the priesthood, referring apparently to Ezr. ii. 36, at about 20,000 (c. Apion. ii. 7). Another indication of number is found in the fact that a "great multitude" could attach themselves to the "sect of the Nazarenes" (Acts vi. 7), and so have cut themselves off, sooner or later, from the Temple services, without any perceptible effect upon its ritual. It was almost inevitable that the great mass of the order, under such circumstances, should sink in character and reputation. Poor and ignorant, despised and oppressed by the more powerful members of their own body, often robbed of their scanty maintenance by the rapacity of the high-priests, they must have been to Palestine what the clergy of a later period have been to Southern Italy, a dead weight on its industry and strength, not compensating for their unproductive lives by any services rendered to the higher interests of the people. The Rabbinic classification of the priesthood, though belonging to a somewhat later date, reflects the contempt into which the order had fallen. There were — (1) the heads of the twenty-four courses, known sometimes as ἀρχιερεῖς; (2) the large number of reputable officiating but inferior priests; (3) the plebeii, or (to use the extremest formula of Rabbinic scorn) the "priests of the people of the earth," ignorant and unlettered; (4) those that, through physical disqualifications or other causes, were non-efficient members of the order, though entitled to receive their tithes (Ugolini, xii. 18; Jost, Judenthum, i. 156).

History. — The new priesthood did not establish itself without a struggle. The rebellion of Korah, at the head of a portion of the Levites as representatives of the first-born, with Dathan and Abiram as leaders of the tribe of the first-born son of Jacob (Num. xvi. 1), showed that some looked back to the old patriarchal order rather than forward to the new, and it needed the witness of "Aaron's rod that budded" to teach the people that the latter had in it a vitality and strength which had departed from the former. It may be that the exclusion of all but the sons of Aaron from the service of the Tabernacle drove those who would not resign their claim to priestly functions of some kind to the worship (possibly with a rival tabernacle) of Moloch and Chiun (Am. v. 25, 26; Ez. xx. 16). Prominent as was the part taken by the priests in the daily march of the host of Israel (Num. x. 8), in the passage of the Jordan (Josh. iii. 14, 15), in the destruction of Jericho (Josh. vi. 12-16), the history of Micah shows that within that century there was a strong tendency to relapse into the system of a household instead of an hereditary priesthood (Judg. xvii.). The frequent invasions and conquests during the period of the Judges must have interfered (as stated above) with the payment of tithes, with the maintenance of worship, with the observance of all festivals, and with this the influence of the priesthood must have been kept in the background. If the descendants of Aaron, at some unrecorded crisis in the history of Israel, rose, under Eli, into the position of national defenders, it was only to sink in his

---

[a] This diminution may have been caused partly by the slaughter of the priests who accompanied Hophni and Phinehas (Ps. lxxviii. 34), partly by the massacre at Nob

[b] The causes of this great reduction are not stated, but large numbers must have perished in the siege and storm of Jerusalem (Lam. iv. 16), and many may have preferred remaining in Babylon.

sons into the lowest depth of sacerdotal corruption. For a time the prerogative of the line of Aaron was in abeyance. The capture of the Ark, the removal of the Tabernacle from Shiloh, threw everything into confusion, and Samuel, a Levite, but not within the priestly family [SAMUEL], sacrifices, and "comes near" to the Lord: his training under Eli, his Nazarite life,[a] his prophetic office, being regarded apparently as a special consecration (comp. August. c. Faust. xii. 33; De Civ. Dei, xvii. 4). For the priesthood, as for the people generally, the time of Samuel must have been one of a great moral reformation, while the expansion, if not the foundation, of the Schools of the Prophets, at once gave to it the support of an independent order, and acted as a check on its corruptions and excesses, a perpetual safeguard against the development from it of any Egyptian or Brahminic caste-system (Ewald, Gesch. Isr. ii. 185), standing to it in much the same relation as the monastic and mendicant orders stood, each in its turn, to the secular clergy of the Christian Church. Though Shiloh had become a deserted sanctuary, Nob (1 Sam. xxi. 1) was made for a time the centre of national worship, and the symbolic ritual of Israel was thus kept from being forgotten. The reverence which the people feel for them, and which compels Saul to have recourse to one of alien blood (Doeg the Edomite) to carry his murderous counsel into act, shows that there must have been a great step upwards since the time when the sons of Eli "made men to abhor the offerings of the Lord" (1 Sam. xxii. 17, 18). The reign of Saul was, however, a time of suffering for them. He had manifested a disposition to usurp the priest's office (1 Sam. xiii. 9). The massacre of the priests at Nob showed how insecure their lives were against any unguarded or savage impulse.[b] They could but wait in silence for the coming of a deliverer in David. One at least among them shared his exile, and, so far as it was possible, lived in his priestly character, performing priestly acts, among the wild company of Adullam (1 Sam. xxiii. 6, 9). Others probably were sheltered by their remoteness, or found shelter in Hebron as the largest and strongest of the priestly cities. When the death of Saul set them free they came in large numbers to the camp of David, prepared apparently not only to testify their allegiance, but also to support him, armed for battle, against all rivals (1 Chr. xii. 27). They were summoned from their cities to the great restoration of the worship of Israel, when the Ark was brought up to the new capital of the kingdom (1 Chr. xv. 4). For a time, however (another proof

of the strange confusion into which the religious life of the people had fallen), the Ark was not the chief centre of worship; and while the newer ritual of psalms and minstrelsy gathered round it under the ministration of the Levites, headed by Benaiah and Jahaziel as priests (1 Chr. xvi. 5, 6), the older order of sacrifices was carried on by the priests in the Tabernacle on the high-place at Gibeon (1 Chr. xvi. 37–39, xxi. 29; 2 Chr. i. 3). We cannot wonder that first David and then Solomon should have sought to guard against the evils incidental to this separation of the two orders, and to unite in one great Temple priests and Levites, the symbolic worship of sacrifice and the spiritual offering of praise.

The reigns of these two kings were naturally the culminating period of the glory of the Jewish priesthood. They had a king whose heart was with them, and who joined in their services dressed as they were (1 Chr. xv. 27), while he yet scrupulously abstained from all interference with their functions. The name which they bore was accepted (whatever explanation may be given of the fact) as the highest title of honor that could be borne by the king's sons (2 Sam. viii. 18, supra). They occupied high places in the king's council (1 K. iv. 2, 4), and might even take their places, as in the case of Benaiah, at the head of his armies (1 Chr. xii. 27, xxvii. 5), or be recognized, as Zabud the son of Nathan was, as the "king's friends," the keepers of the king's conscience (1 K. iv. 5; Ewald, Gesch. iii. 334).

The position of the priests under the monarchy of Judah deserves a closer examination than it has yet received. The system which has been described above gave them for every week of service in the Temple twenty-three weeks in which they had no appointed work. Was it intended that they should be idle during this period? Were they actually idle? They had no territorial possessions to cultivate. The cities assigned to them and to the Levites gave but scanty pasturage to their flocks. To what employment could they turn? (1.) The more devout and thoughtful found, probably, in the schools of the prophets that which satisfied them. The history of the Jews presents numerous instances of the union of the two offices. [Comp. LEVITES.] They became teaching-priests (2 Chr. xv. 3), students, and interpreters of the Divine Law. From such as these, men might be chosen by the more zealous kings to instruct the people (2 Chr. xvii. 8), or to administer justice (2 Chr. xix. 8). (2.) Some, perhaps, as stated above, served in the king's army. We have no ground for transferring our modern conceptions of the peacefulness of the

---

[a] Another remarkable instance of the connection between the Nazarite vow, when extended over the whole life, and a liturgical, quasi-priestly character, is found in the history of the Rechabites. They, or others like them, are named by Amos (ii. 11) as having a vocation like that of the prophets. They are received by Jeremiah into the house of the Lord, into the chamber of a prophet-priest (Jer. xxxv. 4). The solemn blessing which the prophet pronounces (xxxv. 19) goes beyond the mere perpetuation of the name.

The term he uses, "to stand before me" (מֵד)

(לְפָנַי), is one of special significance. It is used emphatically of ministerial functions, like those of the prophet (1 K. xvii. 1, xviii. 15; Jer. xv. 19), or the priest (Deut. x. 8, xviii. 5–7; Judg. xx. 28). The

Targum of Jonathan accordingly gives this meaning to it here. Strangely enough, we have in the history of the death of James the Just (Hegesipp. in Eus. H. E. ii. 23) an indication of the fulfillment of the blessing in this sense. Among the priests who are present, there is one "belonging to the Rechabim of whom Jeremiah had spoken." The mention of the house of Rechab among the "families of the scribes," in 1 Chr. ii. 55, points to something of the same nature. The title prefixed in the LXX. and Vulg. to Ps. lxxi. connects it with the "sons of Jonadab, the first that went into captivity." Augustine takes this as the starting-point for his interpretation (Enarr. in Psalm lxx.).

[b] It is to be noticed that while the Heb. text gives 85 as the number of priests slain, the LXX. increases it to 305, Josephus (Ant. vi. 12, 6) to 385.

priestly life to the remote past of the Jewish people. Priests, as we have seen, were with David at Hebron as men of war. They were the trumpeters of Abijah's army (2 Chr. xiii. 12). The Temple itself was a great armory (2 Chr. xxiii. 9). The heroic struggles of the Maccabees were sustained chiefly by their kindred of the same family (2 Macc. viii. 1). (3.) A few chosen ones might enter more deeply into the divine life, and so receive, like Zechariah, Jeremiah, Ezekiel, a special call to the office of a prophet. (4.) We can hardly escape the conclusion that many did their work in the Temple of Jehovah with a divided allegiance, and acted at other times as priests of the high-places (Ewald, Gesch. iii. 704). Not only do we read of no protests against the sins of the idolatrous kings, except from prophets who stood forth, alone and unsupported, to bear their witness, but the priests themselves were sharers in the worship of Baal (Jer. ii. 8), of the sun and moon, and of the host of heaven (Jer. viii. 1, 2). In the very Temple itself they "ministered before their idols" (Ez. xliv. 12), and allowed others, "uncircumcised in heart, and uncircumcised in flesh," to join them (ibid. 7). They ate of unclean things and polluted the Sabbaths. There could be no other result of this departure from the true idea of the priesthood than a general degradation. Those who ceased to be true shepherds of the people found nothing in their ritual to sustain or elevate them. They became as sensual, covetous, tyrannical, as ever the clergy of the Christian Church became in its darkest periods; conspicuous as drunkards and adulterers (Is. xxviii. 7, 8, lvi. 10–12). The prophetic order, instead of acting as a check, became sharers in their corruption (Jer. v. 31; Lam. iv. 13; Zeph. iii. 4). For the most part the few efforts after better things are not the result of a spontaneous reformation, but of conformity to the wishes of a reforming king. In the one instance in which they do act spontaneously — their resistance to the usurpation of the priest's functions by Uzziah — their protest, however right in itself, was yet only too compatible with a wrong use of the office which they claimed as belonging exclusively to themselves (2 Chr. xxvi. 17). The discipline of the Captivity, however, was not without its fruits. A large proportion of the priests had either perished or were content to remain in the land of their exile; but those who did return were active in the work of restoration. Under Ezra they submitted to the stern duty of repudiating their heathen wives (Ez. x. 18, 19). They took part — though here the Levites were the more prominent — in the instruction of the people (Ez. iii. 2; Neh. viii. 9–13). The root-evils, however, soon reappeared. The work of the priesthood was made the instrument of covetousness. The priests of the time of Malachi required payment for every ministerial act, and would not even "shut the doors" or "kindle fire" for nought (Mal. i. 10). They "corrupted the covenant of Levi" (Mal. ii. 8). The idea of the priest as the angel, the messenger, of the Lord of Hosts, was forgotten (Mal. ii. 7; comp. Eccl. v. 6). The inevitable result was that they again lost their influence. They became "base and contemptible before all the people" (Mal. ii. 9). The office of the scribe rose in repute as that of the priest de-

clined (Jost, Judenth. i. 37, 148). The sects that multiplied during the last three centuries of the national life of Judaism were proofs that the established order had failed to do its work in maintaining the religious life of the people. No great changes affected the outward position of the priests under the Persian government. When that monarchy fell before the power of Alexander, they were ready enough to transfer their allegiance.[a] Both the Persian government and Alexander had, however, respected the religion of their subjects; and the former had conferred on the priests immunities from taxation (Ez. vi. 8, 9, vii. 24; Joseph. Ant. xi. 8). The degree to which this recognition was carried by the immediate successors of Alexander is shown by the work of restoration accomplished by Simon the son of Onias (Ecclus. l. 12–20); and the position which they thus occupied in the eyes of the people, not less than the devotion with which his zeal inspired them, prepared them doubtless for the great struggle which was coming, and in which, under the priestly Maccabees, they were the chief defenders of their country's freedom. Some, indeed, at that crisis, were found among the apostates. Under the guidance of Jason (the heathenized form of Joshua) they forsook the customs of their fathers; and they who, as priests, were to be patterns of a self-respecting purity, left their work in the Temple to run naked in the circus which the Syrian king had opened in Jerusalem (2 Macc. iv. 13, 14). Some, at an earlier period, had joined the schismatic Onias in establishing a rival worship (Joseph. Ant. xii. 3, § 4). The majority, however, were true-hearted; and the Maccabean struggle which left the government of the country in the hands of their own order, and, until the Roman conquest, with a certain measure of independence, must have given to the higher members of the order a position of security and influence. The martyr-spirit showed itself again in the calmness with which they carried on the ministrations in the Temple, when Jerusalem was besieged by Pompey, till they were slain even in the act of sacrificing (Jos. Ant. xiv. 4, § 3; B. J. i. 7, § 5). The reign of Herod, on the other hand, in which the high-priesthood was kept in abeyance, or transferred from one to another at the will of one who was an alien by birth and half a heathen in character, must have tended to depress them.

It will be interesting to bring together the few facts that indicate their position in the N. T. period of their history. The division into four-and-twenty courses is still maintained (Luke i. 5; Joseph. Vit. 1), and the heads of these courses, together with those who have held the high-priesthood (the office no longer lasting for life), are "chief priests" (ἀρχιερεῖς) by courtesy (Carpzov. App. Crit. p. 102), and take their place in the Sanhedrim. The number scattered throughout Palestine was, as has been stated, very large. Of these the greater number were poor and ignorant, despised by the more powerful members of their own order, not gaining the respect or affection of the people. The picture of cowardly selfishness in the priest of the parable of Luke x. 31. can hardly be thought of as other than a representative one, indicating the estimate commonly and truly formed

---

a A real submission is hardly concealed by the narrative of the Jewish historian. The account of the effect produced on the mind of the Macedonian king by the solemn procession of priests in their linen ephods (Joseph. Ant. xi. 8) stands probably on the same footing as Livy's account of the retreat of Porsena from the walls of unconquered Rome.

of the character of the class. The priestly order, like the nation, was divided between contending sects. The influence of Hyrcanus, himself in the latter part of his life a Sadducee (Joseph. *Ant.* xiii. 10, § 6), had probably made the tenets of that party popular among the wealthier and more powerful members, and the chief priests of the Gospels and the Acts, the whole ἀρχιερατικὸν γένος (Acts iv. 1, 6, v. 17), were apparently consistent Sadducees, sometimes combining with the Pharisees in the Sanhedrim, sometimes thwarted by them, persecuting the followers of Jesus because they preached the resurrection of the dead. The great multitude (ὄχλος), on the other hand, who received that testimony [a] (Acts vi. 7) must have been free from, or must have overcome Sadducean prejudices. It was not strange that those who did not welcome the truth which would have raised them to a higher life, should sink lower and lower into an ignorant and ferocious fanaticism. Few stranger contrasts meet us in the history of religion than that presented in the life of the priesthood in the last half-century of the Temple, now going through the solemn sacrificial rites, and joining in the noblest hymns, now raising a fierce clamor at anything which seemed to them a profanation of the sanctuary, and rushing to dash out the brains of the bold or incautious intruder,[b] or of one of their own order who might enter while under some ceremonial defilement, or with a half-humorous cruelty setting fire to the clothes of the Levites who were found sleeping when they ought to have been watching at their posts (Lightfoot, *Temple Service*, c. 1). The rivalry which led the Levites to claim privileges which had hitherto belonged to the priests has been already noticed. [LEVITES.] In the scenes of the last tragedy of Jewish history the order passes away, without honor, "dying as a fool dieth." The high-priesthood is given to the lowest and vilest of the adherents of the frenzied Zealots (Joseph. *B. J.* iv. 3, § 6). Other priests appear as deserting to the enemy (*Ibid.* vi. 6, § 1). It is from a priest that Titus receives the lamps, and gems, and costly raiment of the sanctuary (*Ibid.* vi. 8, § 3). Priests report to their conquerors the terrible utterance "Let us depart," on the last Pentecost ever celebrated in the Temple (*Ibid.* vi. 5, § 3). It is a priest who fills up the degradation of his order by dwelling on the fall of his country with a cold-blooded satisfaction, and finding in Titus the fulfillment of the Messianic prophecies of the O. T. (*Ibid.* vi. 5, § 4). The destruction of Jerusalem deprived the order at one blow of all but an honorary distinction. Their occupation was gone. Many families must have altogether lost their genealogies. Those who still prided themselves on their descent, were no longer safe against the claims of pretenders. The jealousies of the lettered class, which had been kept under some restraint as long as the Temple stood, now had full play, and the influence of the Rabbis increased with

the fall of the priesthood. Their position in mediæval and modern Judaism has never risen above that of complimentary recognition. Those who claim to take their place among the sons of Aaron, are entitled to receive the redemption money of the first-born, to take the Law from its chest, to pronounce the benediction in the synagogues (Ugolini, xii. 48).

The language of the N. T. writers in relation to the priesthood ought not to be passed over. They recognize in Christ, the first-born, the king, the Anointed, the representative of the true primeval priesthood after the order of Melchizedek (Heb. vii., viii.), from which that of Aaron, however necessary for the time, is now seen to have been a deflection. But there is no trace of an order in the new Christian society, bearing the name, and exercising functions like those of the priests of the older Covenant. The Synagogue and not the Temple furnishes the pattern for the organization of the Church. The idea which pervades the teaching of the Epistles is that of an universal priesthood. All true believers are made kings and priests (Rev. i. 6; 1 Pet. ii. 9), offer spiritual sacrifices (Rom. xii. 1), may *draw near*, may enter into the holiest (Heb. x. 19–22) as having received a true priestly consecration. They too have been washed and sprinkled as the sons of Aaron were (Heb. x. 22). It was the thought of a succeeding age that the old classification of the high-priest, priests, and Levites was reproduced in the bishops, priests, and deacons of the Christian Church.[c] The idea which was thus expressed rested, it is true, on the broad analogy of a threefold gradation, and the terms, "priest," "altar," "sacrifice," might be used without involving more than a legitimate symbolism, but they brought with them the inevitable danger of reproducing and perpetuating in the history of the Christian Church many of the feelings which belonged to Judaism, and ought to have been left behind with it. If the evil has not proved so fatal to the life of Christendom as it might have done, it is because no bishop or pope, however much he might exaggerate the harmony of the two systems, has ever dreamt of making the Christian priesthood hereditary. We have perhaps reason to be thankful that two errors tend to neutralise each other, and that the age which witnessed the most extravagant sacerdotalism was one in which the celibacy of the clergy was first exalted, then urged, and at last enforced.

The account here given has been based on the belief that the books of the O. T. give a trustworthy account of the origin and history of the priesthood of Israel. Those who question their authority have done so, for the most part, on the strength of some preconceived theory. Such a hierarchy as the Pentateuch prescribes, is thought impossible in the earlier stages of national life, and therefore the reigns of David and Solomon are looked on, not as the restoration, but as the starting-point of the

---

[a] It deserves notice that from these priests may have come the statements as to what passed within the Temple at the time of the Crucifixion (Matt. xxvii. 51), and that these facts may have had some influence in determining their belief. They, at any rate, would be brought into frequent contact with the teachers who continued daily in the Temple and taught in Solomon's porch (Acts v. 12).

[b] It belonged to the priests to act as sentinels over the Holy Place, as to the Levites to guard the wider

area of the precincts of the Temple (Ugolini, xiii. 1052).

[c] The history of language presents few stranger facts than those connected with these words. Priest, our only equivalent for ἱερεύς, comes to us from the word which was chosen because it excluded the idea of a sacerdotal character. *Bishop* has narrowly escaped a like perversion, occurring, as it does constantly, in Wykliffe's version as the translation of ἀρχιερεύς (e. g. John xviii. 15. Heb. viii. 1).

order (Von Bohlen, *Die Genesis*, Einl. § 16). It is alleged that there could have been no tribe like that of Levi, for the consecration of a whole tribe is without a parallel in history (Vatke, *Bibl. Theol.* i. p. 222). Deuteronomy, assumed for once to be older than the three books which precede it, represents the titles of the priest and Levite as standing on the same footing, and the distinction between them is therefore the work of a later period (George, *Die älteren Jüd. Feste*, pp. 45, 51; comp. Bähr, *Symbolik*, b. ii. c. i. § 1, whence these references are taken). It is hardly necessary here to do more than state these theories. E. H. P.

* In addition to the writers named in the preceding article (Saubert, Krumbholtz, etc. in Ugolini's *Thesaur.* vols. xii. and xiii., Michaelis, Spencer, Bähr, Ewald, Saalschütz, Jost), a few others should be mentioned. Lightfoot, *The Temple Service as it stood in the Days of our Saviour*, Lond. 1649, or *Works*, Pitman's ed., vol. ix. J. Braun, *De Vestitu sacerdotum Hebraeorum* (1680). J. Buxtorf, *Dissert. de pontifice maximo Hebr.* (1685). A. Tholuck, *Ueber den Opfer- und Priester-Begriff im A. und N. Test.* (5th ed.), appended to his *Das Alte Test. im Neuen Test.* Winer, *Priester*, in his *Bibl. Realw.* ii. 269–275 (an elaborate summary both of sources and results). Oehler, *Priesterthum im Altem Testament*, in Herzog's *Real-Encyk.* xii. 174–187; and *ibid.* art. *Leviten*, viii. 347 ff. Merz, *Priester*, in Zeller's *Bibl. Wörterb.* ii. 279–283. C. R. Küper, *Das Priesterthum des A. Bundes* (Berl. 1865), mainly archaeological, together with a history of the Hebrew priesthood. K. F. Keil, *Bibl. Archäologie*, i. 154–187 (1858). J. P. Smith, *Discourses on the Sacrifice and Priesthood of Christ* (Lond. 1842). Stanley, *The Jewish Priesthood*, in his *Lectures on Jewish History*, ii. 448–477 (Amer. ed.). On the priesthood of Melchizedek see the literature under that name. For the number and situation of the Levitical cities, see Clark's *Bible Atlas of Maps and Plans*, p. 27 f. (Lond. 1868). The related articles in the *Dictionary* on LEVITES, SACRIFICES, TABERNACLE, TEMPLE, and VOWS may be consulted. H.

PRINCE. ᵃ **PRINCESS.** The only special uses of the word "prince" are — 1. "Princes of provinces" ᵇ (1 K. xx. 14), who were probably local governors or magistrates, who took refuge in Samaria during the invasion of Benhadad, and

their "young men" were their attendants, παιδάρια, pedissequi (Thenius, Ewald, *Gesch.* iii. 495). Josephus says, υἱοὶ τῶν ἡγεμόνων (*Ant.* viii. 14, § 2). 2. The "princes" mentioned in Dan. vi. 1 (see Esth. i. 1) were the predecessors, either in fact or in place, of the satraps of Darius Hystaspis (Her. iii. 89). H. W. P.

* The "prince of Persia," "prince of Grecia," and "Michael your prince" (Dan. x. 13, 20, 21, xii. 1), are apparently the patron or guardian angels of the nations referred to. [ANGELS, vol. i. p. 97.] See Rosenm. and Hitzig on Dan. x. 13, the LXX., Deut. xxxii 8; Ecclus. xvii. 17; and Eisenmenger's *Entdecktes Judenthum*, i. 803 ff. A.

* **PRINCE OF DEMONS.** [DEMON, iii.]

* **PRINCE OF THE POWER OF THE AIR**, Eph. ii. 2. [AIR, Amer. ed.]

* **PRINCIPALITY.** The word translated "principalities" in Jer. xiii. 18 (A. V.), — "For your *principalities* shall come down, even the crown of your glory," — is understood by Gesenius, Ewald, Hitzig, De Wette, and others, to mean "heads," and they render, "from your heads shall come down the crown of your glory." Some, as Rosenmüller and Fürst, with the margin of the A. V. ("head-tires"), take the word to denote an ornament worn on the head = crown. In 2 Macc. iv. 27, "principality" is used in reference to the office of high-priest. In several passages of the N. T. the terms ἀρχαὶ καὶ ἐξουσίαι, "principalities and powers," appear to denote different orders of angels, good or bad. See Eph. vi. 12, "For we wrestle not against flesh and blood, but against principalities, against powers," etc. (Comp. the art. AIR, i. 57 a.) In Col. ii. 14, 15, God (not Christ, see ver. 13) is spoken of as "blotting out the handwriting in ordinances that was against us," and taking it out of the way, "nailing it to the cross" (τῷ σταυρῷ, not his cross, A. V.); "and having despoiled (or, perhaps, "having disarmed") *principalities and powers*, he made a show of them openly, triumphing over them in it" (or perhaps, "in him," *i. e.* Christ). Here, in boldly figurative language, the image being that of a conqueror leading in triumph his captives in war, is described the victory over the powers of evil won by the death and resurrection of Christ. Compare John xii. 31, 32; Heb. ii. 14, 15; 1 Cor. xv. 24–26. In other passages, as

ᵃ 1. פַחַן, only in a few places; commonly "priest."

2. נָגִיד: ἄρχων, ὁ ἡγούμενος: dux: applied to Messiah (Dan. ix. 25).

3. נָדִיב, properly "willing," chiefly in poet. (Ges. p. 858): ἄρχων: princeps.

4. נָסִיךְ, from נָסַךְ, "prince," an anointed One: ἄρχων: princeps: also in A. V. "duke" (Josh. xiii. 21).

5. נָשִׂיא, verb adj. from נָשָׂא, "raise:" ἄρχων, ἡγούμενος, ἡγεμών, βασιλεύς: princeps, dux: also in A. V. "ruler," "chief," "captain." This word appears on the coins of Simon Maccabaeus (Ges. 917).

6. קָצִין: ἀρχηγός, ἄρχων: princeps: also "captain," and "ruler."

7. רַב, an adj. "great," also as a subst. "captain," and used in composition, as Rab-saris: ἄρχων, ἡγεμών: optimus.

8. רָזֹן, part. of רָזַן, "bear," a poet. word: σατράπης, δυνάστης: princeps, legum conditor.

9. שַׂר: ἄρχων: princeps: also in A. V. "captain," "ruler," prefixed to words of office, as "chief-baker," etc. שָׂרָה: ἄρχουσα: regina.

10. שַׁלִּים, "ruler," "captain;" שָׁלִישׁ, "captain," "prince:" τριστάτης: dux.

11. In plur. only, פַּרְתְּמִים: akin to Sanskr. prathama, primus: ἔνδοξοι: inclyti (Esth. i. 3).

12. סְגָנִים: ἄρχοντες: magistratus: usually "rulers."

13. חַשְׁמַנִּים: πρέσβεις: legati: only in Ps lxviii. 31.

14. אֲחַשְׁדַּרְפְּנִים and אֲחַשְׁדַּרְפְנַיָּא: σατραπ: διοικηταί: satrapa: a Persian word.

ᵇ מְדִינוֹת: χώραι: provincia.

Eph. iii. 10, Col. i. 16, the terms "principalities" and "powers" are applied to good angels, and so probably in Eph. i. 21, Col. ii. 10, at least inclusively; comp. 1 Pet. iii. 21. The reference in Rom. viii. 38 is more doubtful. That the terms θρόνοι, κυριότητες, ἀρχαί, ἐξουσίαι in Col i. 16 (comp. Milton's "Thrones, Dominations, Princedoms, Virtues, Powers") denote different orders of angels is probable, but there is little ground for speculation about their relative dignity. "Thrones" may naturally be taken as denoting the highest, and Fritzsche (on Rom. viii. 38) observes that in the various enumerations "principalities" (ἀρχαί) always precedes "powers" (ἐξουσίαι), from which he infers the superior rank of the former. In the account of the seven heavens given in the *Testaments of the Twelve Patriarchs*, a work of the second century (*Levi*, c. 3), the angels designated as δυνάμεις τῶν παρεμβολῶν, literally "powers of the armies," are placed in the *third* heaven, and the θρόνοι καὶ ἐξουσίαι, "thrones and authorities," in the *fourth* or *fifth* (not the *seventh*, as Meyer represents). In the *Ascension of Isaiah* (c. vii.), translated by Laurence from the Ethiopic (Oxon. 1819), an angel surpassing others in splendor is represented as enthroned in each of the first six heavens, and these angels are themselves called "thrones." This part of the work however only represents the notions of some Gnostic Christian in the second half of the third century (Dillmann, in Herzog's *Real-Encykl.* xii. 313). The passages in respect to different orders of angels cited from the Rabbinical writings by Bartolocci (*Bibl. magna Rabbin.* i. 267 ff.), J. H. Maius (*Synopsis Theol. Jud.* p. 76 f.), Eisenmenger (*Entdecktes Judenth.* ii. 374, and Gfrörer (*Jahrhundert des Heils*, i. 358 ff.), throw no light on the phraseology of Paul. The notions of the Christian Fathers on this subject are set forth with great fullness by Petavius, *Theol. Dogm.* vol. iii. p. 55 ff. (Antwerp edition, 1700). [ANGELS; POWER.]   A.

* PRINTED, A. V. Job xix. 23, should be "inscribed" or "marked down" (Noyes).   A.

PRIS'CA (Πρίσκα [*ancient*]: *Prisca*), 2 Tim. iv. 19. [PRISCILLA.]

PRISCIL'LA (Πρισκίλλα [dimin. of Prisca]: *Priscilla*). To what has been said elsewhere under the head of AQUILA the following may be added. The name is Prisca (Πρίσκα) in 2 Tim. iv. 19. and (according to the true reading) in Rom. xvi. 3, and also (according to some of the best MSS.) in 1 Cor. xvi. 19. Such variation in a Roman name is by no means unusual. We find that the

name of the wife is placed before that of the husband in Rom. xvi. 3, 2 Tim. iv. 19, and (according to some of the best MSS.) in Acts xviii. 26. It is only in Acts xviii. 2 and 1 Cor. xvi. 19 that Aquila has unequivocally the first place. Hence we should be disposed to conclude that Priscilla was the more energetic character of the two; and it is particularly to be noticed that she took part, not only in her husband's exercise of hospitality, but likewise in the theological instruction of APOLLOS. Yet we observe that the husband and the wife are always mentioned together. In fact we may say that Priscilla is the example of what the married woman may do, for the general service of the Church, in conjunction with home duties, as PHŒBE is the type of the unmarried servant of the Church, or deaconess. Such female ministration was of essential importance in the state of society in the midst of which the early Christian communities were formed. [DEACONESS, Amer. ed.] The remarks of Archdeacon Evans on the position of Timothy at Ephesus are very just: "In his dealings with the female part of his flock, which, in that time and country, required peculiar delicacy and discretion, the counsel of the experienced Priscilla would be invaluable. Where, for instance, could he obtain more prudent and faithful advice than hers, in the selection of widows to be placed upon the eleemosynary list of the Church, and of deaconesses for the ministry?" (*Script. Biog.* ii. 298). It seems more to our purpose to lay stress on this than on the theological learning of Priscilla. Yet Winer mentions a monograph *de Priscilla, Aquila uxore, tanquam feminarum e gente Judaicâ eruditarum specimine*, by G. G. Zeltner (Altorf, 1709).   J. S. H.

PRISON.[a] For imprisonment as a punishment, see PUNISHMENTS. The present article will only treat of prisons as places of confinement.

In Egypt it is plain both that special places were used as prisons, and that they were under the custody of a military officer (Gen. xl. 3, xli. 17).

During the wandering in the desert we read on two occasions of confinement "in ward" (Lev. xxiv. 12; Num. xv. 34); but as imprisonment was not directed by the Law, so we hear of none till the time of the kings, when the prison appears as an appendage to the palace, or a special part of it (1 K. xxii. 27). Later still it is distinctly described as being in the king's house (Jer. xxxii. 2, xxxvii. 21; Neh. iii. 25). This was the case also at Babylon (2 K. xxv. 27). But private

---

a 1. אֵסוּר, Aramaic for בֵּ...ם...ס, "a chain," is joined with בֵּית, and rendered a prison: οἶκος δεσμῶν: *carcer.*

2. כֶּלֶא, כְּלוּא, and כְּלִיא, with בֵּית: οἶκος φυλακῆς (Jer. xxxvii. 15).

3. מַהְפֶּכֶת, from הָפַךְ, "turn," or "twist," the stocks (Jer. xx. 2).

4. מִשְׁמָרָה and מִשְׁמְרָא: φυλακή: *carcer* (Gen. p. 879).

5. מַסְגֵּר: δεσμωτήριον: *carcer.*

6. מִשְׁמָר: φυλακή: *custodia*; also plur. מִשְׁמֶרֶת: A. V. "hard."

7. עֹצֶר: *angustia*: ταπείνωσις (Ges. 1059).

8. פְּקַהְ־קוֹחַ (Is. lxi. 1), more properly written in one word: ἀνάβλεψις: *apertio* (Ges. 1121).

9. סֹהַר: ὀχύρωμα: *carcer*; properly a tower.

10. בֵּית־הַפְּקֻדֹּת: οἰκία μύλωνος: *domus carceris.* בֵּית is also sometimes "prison" in A. V., as Gen. xxxix. 20.

11. צִינֹק: καταρράκτης: *carcer*; probably "the stocks" (as A. V.) or some such instrument of confinement; perhaps understood by LXX. as a sewer or underground passage.

houses were sometimes used as places of confinement (Jer. xxxvii. 15), probably much as Chardin describes Persian prisons in his day, namely, houses kept by private speculators for prisoners to be maintained there at their own cost (*Voy.* vi. 100). Public prisons other than these, though in use by the Canaanitish nations (Judg. xvi. 21, 25), were unknown in Judæa previous to the Captivity. Under the Herods we hear again of royal prisons attached to the palace, or in royal fortresses (Luke iii. 20; Acts xii. 4, 10; Joseph. *Ant.* xviii. 5, § 2; Machærus). By the Romans Antonia was used as a prison at Jerusalem (Acts xxiii. 10), and at Cæsarea the prætorium of Herod (*ib.* 35). The sacerdotal authorities also had a prison under the superintendence of special officers, δεσμοφύλακες (Acts v. 18-23, viii. 3, xxvi. 10). The royal prisons in those days were doubtless managed after the Roman fashion, and chains, fetters, and stocks used as means of confinement (see Acts xvi. 24, and Job xiii. 27).

One of the readiest places for confinement was a dry or partially dry well or pit (see Gen. xxxvii. 24 and Jer. xxxviii. 6-11); but the usual place appears, in the time of Jeremiah, and in general, to have been accessible to visitors (Jer. xxxvi. 5; Matt. xi. 2, xiv. 36, 39; Acts xxiv. 23).   H. W. P.

* **PRISON-GATE.** [JERUSALEM, vol. ii. p. 1322.]

* **PRIZE.** [GAMES; PRICE.]

PROCH'ORUS (Πρόχορος [*leader of a dance or chorus: Prochorus*]). One of the seven deacons, being the third on the list, and named next after Stephen and Philip (Acts vi. 5). No further mention of him is made in the N. T. There is a tradition that he was consecrated by St. Peter bishop of Nicomedia (Baron. i. 292). In the *Magna Bibliotheca Patrum*, Colon. Agripp. 1618, i. 49-69, will be found a fabulous "Historia Prochori, Christi Discipuli, de vita B. Joannis apostoli."   E. H—s.

PROCONSUL. The Greek ἀνθύπατος, for which this is the true equivalent, is rendered uniformly "deputy" in the A. V. of Acts xiii. 7, 8, 12, xix. 38, and the derived verb ἀνθυπατεύω, in Acts xviii. 12, is translated "to be deputy." At the division of the Roman provinces by Augustus in the year B. C. 27, into Senatorial and Imperial, the emperor assigned to the senate such portions of territory as were peaceable and could be held without force of arms (Suet. *Oct.* 47; Strabo, xvii. p. 840; Dio Cass. liii. 12), an arrangement which remained with frequent alterations till the 3d century. Over these senatorial provinces the senate appointed by lot yearly an officer, who was called "proconsul" (Dio Cass. liii. 13), who exercised purely civil functions, had no power over life and death, and was attended by one or more legates (Dio Cass. liii. 14). He was neither girt with the sword nor wore the military dress (Dio Cass. liii. 13). The provinces were in consequence called "proconsular." With the exception of Africa and Asia, which were assigned to men who had passed the office of consul, the senatorial provinces were given to those who had been prætors, and were divided by lot each year among those who had held this office five years previously. Their term of office was one year.

Among the senatorial provinces in the first arrangement by Augustus, were Cyprus, Achaia, and Asia within the Halys and Taurus (Strabo, xvii. p. 840). The first and last of these are alluded to in Acts xiii. 7, 8, 12, xix. 38, as under the government of proconsuls. Achaia became an imperial province in the second year of Tiberius, A. D. 16, and was governed by a procurator (Tac. *Ann.* i. 76), but was restored to the senate by Claudius (Suet. *Claud.* 25), and therefore Gallio, before whom St. Paul was brought, is rightly termed "proconsul" in Acts xviii. 12. Cyprus also, after the battle of Actium, was first made an imperial province (Dio Cass. liii. 12), but five years afterwards (B. C. 22) it was given to the senate, and is reckoned by Strabo (xvii. p. 840) ninth among the provinces of the people governed by στρατηγοί, as Achaia is the seventh. These στρατηγοί, or proprætors, had the title of proconsul. Cyprus and Narbonese Gaul were given to the senate in exchange for Dalmatia, and thus, says Dio Cassius (liv. 4), proconsuls (ἀνθύπατοι) began to be sent to those nations. In Boeckh's *Corpus Inscriptionum*, No. 2631, is the following relating to Cyprus: ἡ πόλις Κόϊντον Ἰούλιον Κόρδον ἀνθύπατον ἀγγελας. This Quintus Julius Cordus appears to have been proconsul of Cyprus before the 12th year of Claudius. He is mentioned in the next inscription (No. 2632) as the predecessor of another proconsul, Lucius Annius Bassus. The date of this last inscription is the 12th year of Claudius, A. D. 52. The name of another proconsul of Cyprus in the time of Claudius occurs on a copper coin, of which an engraving is given in vol. i. p. 524. A coin of Ephesus [see vol. i. p. 749] illustrates the usage of the word ἀνθύπατος in Acts xix. 38.   W. A. W.

PROCURATOR. The Greek ἡγεμών,[a] rendered "governor" in the A. V., is applied in the N. T. to the officer who presided over the imperial province of Judæa. It is used of Pontius Pilate (Matt. xxvii.), of Felix (Acts xxiii., xxiv.), and of Festus (Acts xxvi. 30). In all these cases the Vulgate equivalent is *præses.* The office of procurator (ἡγεμονία) is mentioned in Luke iii. 1, and in this passage the rendering of the Vulgate is more close (*procurante Pontio Pilato Judæam*). It is explained, under the head of PROCONSUL, that after the battle of Actium, B C. 27, the provinces of the Roman empire were divided by Augustus into two portions, giving some to the senate, and reserving to himself the rest. The imperial provinces were administered by legates, called *legati Augusti pro prætore,* sometimes with the addition of *consulari potestate,* and sometimes *legati consulares,* or *legati* or *consulares* alone. They were selected from among men who had been consuls or prætors, and sometimes from the inferior senators (Dio Cass. liii. 13, 15). Their term of office was indefinite, and subject only to the will of the emperor (Dio Cass. liii. 13). These officers were also called *præsides,* a term which in later times was applied indifferently to the governors both of the senatorial and of the imperial provinces (Suet. *Claud.* 17). They were attended by six lictors, used the military dress, and wore the sword (Dio Cass. liii. 13). No quæstor came into the emperor's provinces, but the property and revenues of

---

[a] Ἡγεμών is the general term, which is applied also to the governor (*præses*) of the imperial province of Syria (Luke ii. 2); the Greek equivalent of *procurator* is strictly ἐπίτροπος (Jos. *Ant.* xx. 6, § 2, 8, § 5; comp. xx. 5, § 1), and his office is called ἐπιτροπή (Jos. *Ant.* xx. 5, § 1).

the imperial treasury were administered by the *Rationales*, *Procuratores*, and *Actores* of the emperor, who were chosen from among his freedmen, or from among the knights (Tac. *Hist.* v. 9; Dio Cass. liii. 15). These procurators were sent both to the imperial and to the senatorial provinces (Dio Cass. liii. 15 [a]). Sometimes a province was governed by a procurator with the functions of a praeses. This was especially the case with the smaller provinces and the outlying districts of a larger province; and such is the relation in which Judæa stood to Syria. After the deposition of Archelaus, Judæa was annexed to Syria, and the first procurator was Coponius, who was sent out with Quirinus to take a census of the property of the Jews and to confiscate that of Archelaus (Jos. *Ant.* xviii. 1, § 1). His successor was Marcus Ambivius, then Annius Rufus, in whose time the emperor Augustus died. Tiberius sent Valerius Gratus, who was procurator for eleven years, and was succeeded by Pontius Pilate (Jos. *Ant.* xviii. 2, § 2), who is called by Josephus (*Ant.* xviii. 3, § 1) ἡγεμών, as he is in the N. T. He was subject to the governor (*praeses*) of Syria, for the council of the Samaritans denounced Pilate to Vitellius, who sent him to Rome and put one of his own friends, Marcellus, in his place (Jos. *Ant.* xviii. 4, § 2). The head-quarters of the procurator were at Cæsarea (Jos. *B. J.* ii. 9, § 2; Acts xxiii. 23), where he had a judgment-seat (Acts xxv. 6) in the audience chamber (Acts xxv. 23 [b]), and was assisted by a council (Acts xxv. 12) whom he consulted in cases of difficulty, the *assessores* (Suet. *Galb.* 14), or ἡγεμόνες, who are mentioned by Josephus (*B. J.* ii. 16, § 1) as having been consulted by Cestius, the governor of Syria, when certain charges were made against Florus, the procurator of Judæa. More important cases were laid before the emperor (Acts xxv. 12; comp. Jos. *Ant.* xx. 6, § 2). The procurator, as the representative of the emperor, had the power of life and death over his subjects (Dio Cass. liii. 14; Matt. xxvii. 26), which was denied to the proconsul. In the N. T. we see the procurator only in his judicial capacity. Thus Christ is brought before Pontius Pilate as a political offender (Matt. xxvii. 2, 11), and the accusation is heard by the procurator, who is seated on the judgment-seat (Matt. xxvii. 19). Felix heard St. Paul's accusation and defense from the judgment-seat at Cæsarea (Acts xxiv.), which was in the open air in the great stadium (Jos. *B. J.* ii. 9, § 2), and St. Paul calls him "judge" (Acts xxiv. 10), as if this term described his chief functions. The procurator (ἡγεμών) is again alluded to in his judicial capacity in 1 Pet. ii. 14. He was attended by a cohort as body-guard (Matt. xxvii. 27), and apparently went up to Jerusalem at the time of the high festivals, and there resided in the palace of Herod (Jos. *B. J.* ii. 14, § 3; Philo, *De Leg. ad Caium*, § 37, ii. 589, ed Mang.), in which was the *prætorium*, or "judgment-hall," as it is rendered in the A. V. (Matt. xxvii. 27; Mark xv. 16; comp. Acts xxiii. 35). Sometimes it appears Jerusalem was made his winter quarters (Jos. *Ant.* xviii. 3, § 1). The High-Priest was appointed and removed at the will of the procurator (Jos. *Ant.*

xviii. 2, § 2). Of the oppression and extortion practiced by one of these officers, Gessius Florus, which resulted in open rebellion, we have an account in Josephus (*Ant.* xx. 11, § 1; *B. J.* ii. 14, § 2). The same laws held both for the governors of the imperial and senatorial provinces, that they could not raise a levy or exact more than an appointed sum of money from their subjects, and that when their successors came they were to return to Rome within three months (Dio Cass. liii. 15). For further information see Walter, *Gesch. des Röm. Rechts.* W. A. W.

* **PROPER** is used in the A. V. in Heb. xi. 23 ("because they saw he was a *proper* child") in the sense of "handsome," "fair" (Gr. ἀστεῖος). So often in Shakespeare. A.

PROPHET (נָבִיא: προφήτης: *propheta*). I. THE NAME. — The ordinary Hebrew word for prophet is *nâbî* (נָבִיא), derived from the verb נָבָא, connected by Gesenius with נָבַע, "to bubble forth," like a fountain. If this etymology is correct, the substantive would signify either a person who, as it were, involuntarily bursts forth with spiritual utterances under the divine influence (cf. Ps. xlv. 1, "My heart is *bubbling up* of a good matter"), or simply one who pours forth words. The analogy of the word נָטַף (*nâtaph*), which has the force of "dropping" as honey, and is used by Micah (ii. 6, 11), Ezekiel (xxi. 2), and Amos (vii. 16), in the sense of prophesying, points to the last signification. The verb נָבָא is found only in the *niphal* and *hithpael*, a peculiarity which it shares with many other words expressive of speech (cf. loqui, fari, vociferari, concionari, φθέγγομαι, as well as μαντεύομαι and vaticinari). Bunsen (*Gott in d. Geschichte*, p. 141) and Davidson (*Intr. Old Test.* ii. 430) suppose *nâbî* to signify the man *to whom announcements are made* by God, i. e. inspired. But it is more in accordance with the etymology and usage of the word to regard it as signifying (actively) one *who announces* or *pours forth* the declarations of God. The latter signification is preferred by Ewald, Hävernick, Oehler, Heugstenberg, Bleek, Lee, Pusey, M'Caul, and the great majority of Biblical critics.

Two other Hebrew words are used to designate a prophet, רֹאֶה, *roêh*, and חֹזֶה, *chozeh*, both signifying *one who sees*. They are rendered in the A. V. by "seer;" in the LXX. usually by βλέπων or ὁρῶν, sometimes by προφήτης (1 Chr. xxvi. 28; 2 Chr. xvi. 7, 10). The three words seem to be contrasted with each other in 1 Chr. xxix. 29. "The acts of David the king, first and last, behold they are written in the book of Samuel the seer (*roêh*), and in the book of Nathan the prophet (*nâbî*), and in the book of Gad the seer (*chozeh*)." *Roêh* is a title almost appropriated to Samuel. It is only used ten times, and in seven of these it is applied to Samuel (1 Sam. ix. 9, 11, 18, 19; 1 Chr. ix. 22; xxvi. 28; xxix. 29). On two other occasions it is applied to Hanani (2 Chr. xvi. 7, 10). Once it is used by Isaiah (Is. xxx. 10) with no reference

---

[a] A curious illustration of this is given by Tacitus (*Ann.* xiii. 1), where he describes the poisoning of Junius Silanus, proconsul of Asia, by P. Celer, a Roman knight, and Helius, a freedman, who had the

care of the imperial revenues in Asia (rei familiaris principis in Asia impositi).

[b] Unless the ἀκροατήριον (A. V. "place of hearing") was the great stadium mentioned by Josephus (*B. J.* ii. 9, § 2).

to any particular person. It was superseded in general use by the word *nábi*, which Samuel (himself entitled *nábi* as well as *roëh*, 1 Sam. iii. 20; 2 Chr. xxxv. 18) appears to have revived after a period of desuetude (1 Sam. ix. 9), and to have applied to the prophets organized by him.[a] The verb רָאָה, from which it is derived, is the common prose word signifying "to see:" רֹאֶה — whence the substantive רֹאֶה, *chozeh*, is derived — is more poetical. *Chozeh* is rarely found except in the books of the Chronicles, but חָזוֹן is the word constantly used for the prophetical vision. It is found in the Pentateuch, in Samuel, in the Chronicles, in Job, and in most of the prophets.

Whether there is any difference in the usage of these three words, and, if any, what that difference is, has been much debated (see Witsius, *Miscell. Sacra*, i. 1, § 19; Carpzovius, *Introd. ad Libros Canon. V. T.* iii. 1, § 2; Winer, *Real-Wörterbuch*, art. "Propheten"). Hävernick (*Einleitung*, Th. i.; *Abth.* v. s. 56) considers *nábi* to express the title of those who officially belonged to the prophetic order, while *roëh* and *chozeh* denote those who received a prophetical revelation. Dr. Lee (*Inspiration of Holy Scripture*, p. 543), agrees with Hävernick in his explanation of *nábi*, but he identifies *roëh* in meaning rather with *nábi* than with *chozeh*. He further throws out a suggestion that *chozeh* is the special designation of the prophet attached to the royal household. In 2 Sam. xxiv. 11, Gad is described as "the prophet (*nábi*) Gad, David's seer (*chozeh*);" and elsewhere he is called "David's seer (*chozeh*)" (1 Chr. xxi. 9), "the king's seer (*chozeh*)" (2 Chr. xxix. 25). "The case of Gad," Dr. Lee thinks, "affords the clew to the difficulty, as it clearly indicates that attached to the royal establishment there was usually an individual styled 'the king's seer,' who might at the same time be a *nábi*." The suggestion is ingenious (see, in addition to places quoted above, 1 Chr. xxv. 5, xxix. 29; 2 Chr. xxix. 30, xxxv. 15), but it was only David (possibly also Manasseh, 2 Chr. xxxiii. 18) who, so far as we read, had this seer attached to his person; and in any case there is nothing in the word *chozeh* to denote the relation of the prophet to the king, but only in the connection in which it stands with the word king. On the whole it would seem that the same persons are designated by the three words *nábi*, *roëh*, and *chozeh*; the last two titles being derived from the prophets' power of seeing the visions presented to them by

God, the first from their function of revealing and proclaiming God's truth to men. When Gregory Naz. (*Or.* 28) calls Ezekiel ὁ τῶν μεγάλων ἐπόπτης καὶ ἐξηγητὴς μυστηρίων, he gives a sufficiently exact translation of the two titles *chozeh* or *roëh*, and *nábi*.

The word *Nábi* is uniformly translated in the LXX. by προφήτης, and in the A. V. by "prophet." In classical Greek προφήτης signifies *one who speaks for another*, specially *one who speaks for a god* and so interprets his will to man (Liddell & Scott, *s. v.*). Hence its essential meaning is "an interpreter." Thus Apollo is a προφήτης as being the interpreter of Zeus (Æsch. *Eum.* 19). Poets are the Prophets of the Muses, as being their interpreters (Plat. *Phædr.* 262 D). The προφῆται attached to heathen temples are so named from their interpreting the oracles delivered by the inspired and unconscious μάντεις (Plat. *Tim.* 72 B; Herod. vii. 111, *note*, ed. Bæhr). We have Plato's authority for deriving μάντις from μαίνομαι (*l. c.*). The use of the word προφήτης in its modern sense is post-classical, and is derived from the LXX.

From the mediæval use of the word προφητεία, *prophecy* passed into the English language in the sense of *prediction*, and this sense it has retained as its popular meaning (see Richardson, *s. v.*). The larger sense of *interpretation* has not, however, been lost. Thus we find in Bacon, "An exercise commonly called *prophesying*, which was this: that the ministers within a precinct did meet upon a week day in some principal town, where there was some ancient grave minister that was president, and an auditory admitted of gentlemen or other persons of leisure. Then every minister successively, beginning with the youngest, did handle one and the same part of Scripture, spending severally some quarter of an hour or better, and in the whole some two hours. And so the exercise being begun and concluded with prayer, and the president giving a text for the next meeting, the assembly was dissolved" (*Pacification of the Church*). This meaning of the word is made further familiar to us by the title of Jeremy Taylor's treatise "On Liberty of Prophesying." Nor was there any risk of the title of a book published in our own days, "On the Prophetical Office of the Church" (Oxf. 1838), being misunderstood. In fact the English word prophet, like the word inspiration, has always been used in a larger and in a closer sense. In the larger sense our Lord Jesus Christ is a "prophet," Moses is a "prophet," Mahomet is a "prophet." The expression means that they proclaimed and

<hr>

[a] In 1 Sam. ix. 9 we read, "He that is now called a prophet (*nábi*) was beforetime called a seer (*roëh*);" from whence Dr. Stanley (*Lect. on Jewish Church*) has concluded that *roëh* was "the oldest designation of the prophetic office," "superseded by *nábi* shortly after Samuel's time, when *nábi first came into use*" (*Lect.* xviii., xix.). This seems opposed to the fact that *nábi* is the word commonly used in the Pentateuch, whereas *roëh* does not appear until the days of Samuel. The passage in the book of Samuel is clearly a parenthetical insertion, perhaps made by the *nábi* Nathan (or whoever was the original author of the book), perhaps added at a later date, with the view of explaining how it was that Samuel bore the title of *roëh*, instead of the now usual appellation of *nábi*. To the writer the days of Samuel were "beforetime," and he explains that in those ancient days, that is the days of Samuel, the word used for prophet was *roëh*, not *nábi*. But that does not imply that *roëh* was

the primitive word, and that *nábi* first came into use subsequently to Samuel (see Hengstenberg, *Beitrage zur Einleitung ins A. T.* iii. 835). Dr. Stanley represents *chozeh* as "another *antique* title." But on no sufficient grounds. *Chozeh* is first found in 2 Sam. xxiv. 11; so that it does not seem to have come into use until *roëh* had almost disappeared. It is also found in the books of Kings (2 K. xvii. 13) and Chronicles (frequently), in Amos (vii. 12), Isaiah (xxix. 10), Micah (iii. 7), and the derivatives of the verb *cházáh* are used by the prophets to designate their visions down to the Captivity (cf Is. i. 1; Dan. viii. 1; Zech. xiii 4). The derivatives of *rá'áh* are rarer, and, as being prose words, are chiefly used by Daniel (cf. Ez. i. 1; Dan. x. 7) On examination we find that *nábi* existed before and after and alongside of both *roëh* and *chozeh*, but that *chozeh* was somewhat more modern than *roëh*.

published a new religious dispensation. In a similar though not identical sense, the Church is said to have a "prophetical," *i. e.* an expository and interpretative office. But in its closer sense the word, according to usage though not according to etymology, involves the idea of foresight. And this is and always has been its more usual acceptation.[a] The different meanings, or shades of meaning, in which the abstract noun is employed in Scripture, have been drawn out by Locke as follows: "Prophecy comprehends three things: prediction; singing by the dictate of the Spirit; and understanding and explaining the mysterious, hidden sense of Scripture, by an immediate illumination and motion of the Spirit" (*Paraphrase of 1 Cor.* xii. note, p. 121, Lond. 1742). It is in virtue of this last signification of the word, that the prophets of the N. T. are so called (1 Cor. xii.): by virtue of the second, that the sons of Asaph, etc. are said to have "prophesied with a harp" (1 Chr. xxv. 3), and Miriam and Deborah are termed "prophetesses." That the idea of potential if not actual prediction enters into the conception expressed by the word prophecy, when that word is used to designate the function of the Hebrew prophets, seems to be proved by the following passages of Scripture, Deut. xviii. 22; Jer. xxviii. 9; Acts ii. 30, iii. 18, 21; 1 Pet. i. 10; 2 Pet. i. 19, 20, iii. 2. Etymologically, however, it is certain that neither prescience nor prediction are implied by the term used in the Hebrew, Greek, or English language.

II. Prophetical Order. — The sacerdotal order was originally the instrument by which the members of the Jewish Theocracy were taught and governed in things spiritual. Feast and fast, sacrifice and offering, rite and ceremony, constituted a varied and ever-recurring system of training and teaching by type and symbol. To the priests, too, was intrusted the work of "teaching the children of Israel all the statutes which the Lord hath spoken unto them by the hand of Moses" (Lev. x. 11). Teaching by act and teaching by word were alike their task. This task they adequately fulfilled for some hundred or more years after the giving of the Law at Mount Sinai. But during the time of the Judges, the priesthood sank into a state of degeneracy, and the people were no longer affected by the acted lessons of the ceremonial service. They required less enigmatic warnings and exhortations. Under these circumstances a new moral power was evoked — the Prophetic Order. Samuel, himself a Levite, of the family of Kohath (1 Chr. vi. 28), and

almost certainly a priest,[b] was the instrument used at once for effecting a reform in the sacerdotal order (1 Chr. ix. 22), and for giving to the prophets a position of importance which they had never before held. So important was the work wrought by him, that he is classed in Holy Scripture with Moses (Jer. xv. 1; Ps. xcix. 6; Acts iii. 24), Samuel being the great religious reformer and organiser of the prophetical order, as Moses was the great legislator and founder of the priestly rule. Nevertheless, it is not to be supposed that Samuel created the prophetic order as a new thing before unknown. The germs both of the prophetic and of the regal order are found in the Law as given to the Israelites by Moses (Deut. xiii. 1, xviii. 20, xvii. 18), but they were not yet developed, because there was not yet the demand for them. Samuel, who evolved the one, himself saw the evolution of the other. The title of prophet is found before the legislation of Mount Sinai. When Abraham is called a prophet (Gen. xx. 7), it is probably in the sense of a friend of God, to whom He makes known His will; and in the same sense the name seems to be applied to the patriarchs in general (Ps. cv. 15).[c] Moses is more specifically a prophet, as being a proclaimer of a new dispensation, a revealer of God's will, and in virtue of his divinely inspired songs (Ex. xv.; Deut. xxxii., xxxiii.; Ps. xc.), but his main work was not prophetical, and he is therefore formally distinguished from prophets (Num. xii. 6) as well as classed with them (Deut. xviii. 15, xxxiv. 10). Aaron is the prophet of Moses (Ex. vii. 1); Miriam (Ex. xv. 20) is a prophetess; and we find the prophetic gift in the elders who "prophesied" when "the Spirit of the Lord rested upon them," and in Eldad and Medad, who "prophesied in the camp" (Num. xi. 27). At the time of the sedition of Miriam, the possible existence of prophets is recognized (Num. xii. 6). In the days of the Judges we find that Deborah (Judg. iv. 4) is a prophetess; a prophet (Judg. vi. 8) rebukes and exhorts the Israelites when oppressed by the Midianites; and, in Samuel's childhood, "a man of God" predicts to Eli the death of his two sons, and the curse that was to fall on his descendants (1 Sam. ii. 27).

Samuel took measures to make his work of restoration permanent as well as effective for the moment. For this purpose he instituted Companies, or Colleges of Prophets. One we find in his lifetime at Ramah (1 Sam. xix. 19, 20); others afterwards at Bethel (2 K. ii. 3), Jericho (2 K. ii. 5), Gilgal (2 K. iv. 38), and elsewhere (2 K. vi. 1).

---

[a] It seems to be incorrect to say that the English word was "originally" used in the wider sense of "preaching," and that it became "limited" to the meaning of "predicting," in the seventeenth century, in consequence of "an etymological mistake" (Stanley, *Lect.* xix., xx.). The word entered into the English language in its sense of predicting. It could not have been otherwise, for at the time of the formation of the English language, the word προφητεία had, by usage, assumed popularly the meaning of prediction. And we find it ordinarily employed, by early as well as by late writers, in this sense (see Polydore Virgil, *History of England*, iv. 161, Camden. ed. 1846; *Coventry Mysteries*, p. 65, Shakespeare Soc. ed., 1841, and Richardson, *s. v.*). It is probable that the meaning was "limited" to "prediction" as much and as little before the seventeenth century as it has been since.

[b] Dr. Stanley (*Lect.* xviii.) declares it to be "doubtful if he was of Levitical descent, and certain that he

was not a priest." If the record of 1 Chr. vi. 28 is correct, it is certain that he was a Levite by descent though an Ephrathite by habitation (1 Sam. i. 1). There is every probability that he was a priest (cf. 1 Sam. i. 22, ii. 11, 18, vii. 5, 17, x. 1, xiii. 11) and no presumption to the contrary. The fact on which Dr. Stanley relies, that Samuel lived "not at Gibeon or at Nob but at Ramah," and that "the prophetic schools were at Ramah, and at Bethel, and at Gilgal, not at Hebron and Anathoth," does not suffice to raise a presumption. As judge, Samuel would have lived where it was most suitable for the judge to dwell. Of the three colleges, that at Ramah was alone founded by Samuel, of course where he lived himself, and even where Ramah was we do not know: one of the latest hypotheses places it two miles from Hebron.

[c] According to Hengstenberg's view of prophecy, Abraham was a prophet because he received revelations *by the means of dream and vision* (Gen. xv. 12).

Their constitution and object were similar to those of Theological Colleges. Into them were gathered promising students, and here they were trained for the office which they were afterwards destined to fulfill. So successful were these institutions, that from the time of Samuel to the closing of the Canon of the Old Testament, there seems never to have been wanting a due supply of men to keep up the line of official prophets.[a] The apocryphal books of the Maccabees (I. iv. 46, ix. 27, xiv. 41) and of Ecclesiasticus (xxxvi. 15) represent them as extinct. The colleges appear to have consisted of students differing in number. Sometimes they were very numerous (1 K. xviii. 4, xxii. 6; 2 K. ii. 16). One elderly, or leading prophet, presided over them (1 Sam. xix. 20), called their Father (1 Sam. x. 12), or Master (2 K. ii. 3), who was apparently admitted to his office by the ceremony of anointing (1 K. xix. 16; Is. lxi. 1; Ps. cv. 15). They were called his sons. Their chief subject of study was, no doubt, the Law and its interpretation; oral, as distinct from symbolical, teaching being henceforward tacitly transferred from the priestly to the prophetical order.[b] Subsidiary subjects of instruction were music and sacred poetry, both of which had been connected with prophecy from the time of Moses (Ex. xv. 20) and the Judges (Judg. iv. 4, v. 1). The prophets that meet Saul "came down from the high place with a psaltery and a tabret, and a pipe and a harp before them" (1 Sam. x. 5). Elisha calls a minstrel to evoke the prophetic gift in himself (2 K. iii. 15). David "separates to the service of the sons of Asaph and of Heman and of Jeduthun, who should prophesy with harps and with psalteries and with cymbals. . . . All these were under the hands of their father for song in the house of the Lord with cymbals, psalteries, and harps for the service of the house of God " (1 Chr. xxv. 6). Hymns, or sacred songs, are found in the books of Jonah (ii. 2), Isaiah (xii. 1, xxvi. 1), Habakkuk (iii. 2). And it was probably the duty of the prophetical students to compose verses to be sung in the Temple. (See Lowth, Sacred Poetry of the Hebrews, Lect. xviii.) Having been themselves trained and taught, the prophets, whether still residing within their college, or having left its precincts, had the task of teaching others. From the question addressed to the Shunammite by her husband, " Wherefore wilt thou go to him to-day? It is neither new moon nor Sabbath " (2 K. iv. 23), it appears that weekly and monthly religious meetings were held as an ordinary practice by the prophets (see Patrick, Comm. in loc.). Thus we find that "Elisha sat in his house," engaged in his official occupation (cf. Ex. viii. 1, xiv. 1, xx. 1), "and the elders sat with him" (2 K. vi. 32), when the King of Israel sent to slay him. It was at these meetings, probably, that many of the warnings and exhortations on morality and spiritual

religion were addressed by the prophets to their countrymen. The general appearance and life of the prophet were very similar to those of the Eastern dervish at the present day. His dress was a hairy garment, girt with a leathern girdle (Is. xx. 2; Zech. xiii. 4; Matt. iii. 4). He was married or unmarried as he chose; but his manner of life and diet were stern and austere (2 K. iv. 10, 38; 1 K. xix. 6; Matt. iii. 4).

III. THE PROPHETIC GIFT. — We have been speaking of the Prophetic Order. To belong to the prophetic order and to possess the prophetic gift are not convertible terms. There might be members of the prophetic order to whom the gift of prophecy was not vouchsafed. There might be inspired prophets, who did not belong to the prophetic order. Generally, the inspired prophet came from the College of the Prophets, and belonged to the prophetic order; but this was not always the case. In the instance of the Prophet Amos, the rule and the exception are both manifested. When Amaziah, the idolatrous Israelitish priest, threatens the prophet, and desires him to "flee away into the land of Judah, and there eat bread and prophesy there, but not to prophesy again any more at Bethel," Amos in reply says, "I was no prophet, neither was I a prophet's son; but I was an herdsman, and a gatherer of sycamore fruit; and the Lord took me as I followed the flock, and the Lord said unto me, Go prophesy unto my people Israel " (vii. 14). That is, though called to the prophetic office, he did not belong to the prophetic order, and had not been trained in the prophetical colleges; and this, he indicates, was an unusual occurrence. (See J. Smith on Prophecy, c. ix.).

The sixteen prophets whose books are in the Canon have therefore that place of honor, because they were endowed with the prophetic gift as well as ordinarily (so far as we know) belonging to the prophetic order. There were hundreds of prophets contemporary with each of these sixteen prophets; and no doubt numberless compositions in sacred poetry and numberless moral exhortations were issued from the several schools, but only sixteen books find their place in the Canon. Why is this? Because these sixteen had what their brother-collegians had not, the Divine call to the office of prophet, and the Divine illumination to enlighten them. It was not sufficient to have been taught and trained in preparation for a future call. Teaching and training served as a preparation only. When the schoolmaster's work was done, then, if the instrument was worthy, God's work began. Moses had an external call at the burning bush (Ex. iii. 2). The Lord called Samuel, so that Eli perceived, and Samuel learned, that it was the Lord who called him (1 Sam. iii. 10). Isaiah (vi. 8). Jeremiah (i. 5), Ezekiel (ii. 4), Amos (vii. 15),

a There seems no sufficient ground for the common statement that, after the schism, the colleges existed only in the Israelitish kingdom, or for Knobel's supposition that they ceased with Elisha (Prophetismus, ii. 39), nor again for Bishop Lowth's statement that "they existed from the earliest times of the Hebrew republic " (Sacred Poetry, Lect. xviii.), or for M. Nicolas' assertion that their previous establishment can be inferred from 1 Sam. viii., ix., x. (Études critiques sur la Bible, p. 365). We have, however, no actual proof of their existence except in the days of Samuel and of Elijah and Elisha.

b It is a vulgar error respecting Jewish history to suppose that there was an antagonism between the prophets and the priests. There is not a trace of such antagonism. Isaiah may denounce a wicked hierarchy (i. 10), but it is because it is wicked, not because it is a hierarchy. Malachi "sharply reproves " the priests (ii. 1), but it is in order to support the priesthood (cf. i. 14). Mr. F. W. Newman even designates Ezekiel's writings as "hard sacerdotalism," "tedious and unedifying as Leviticus itself" (Hebr. Monarch. p. 390). The Prophetical Order was, in truth, supplemental, not antagonistic to the Sacerdotal.

declare their special mission. Nor was it sufficient for this call to have been made once for all. Each prophetical utterance is the result of a communication of the Divine to the human spirit, received either by " vision " (Is. vi. 1) or by " the word of the Lord " (Jer. ii. 1). (See *Aids to Faith*, Essay iii., " On Prophecy.") What then are the characteristics of the sixteen prophets, thus called and commissioned, and entrusted with the messages of God to his people?

(1.) They were the national poets of Judæa. We have already shown that music and poetry, chants and hymns, were a main part of the studies of the class from which, generally speaking, they were derived. As is natural, we find not only the songs previously specified, but the rest of their compositions, poetical or breathing the spirit of poetry.[a]

(2.) They were annalists and historians. A great portion of Isaiah, of Jeremiah, of Daniel, of Jonah, of Haggai, is direct or indirect history.

(3.) They were preachers of patriotism; their patriotism being founded on the religious motive. To the subject of the Theocracy, the enemy of his nation was the enemy of God, the traitor to the public weal was a traitor to his God; a denunciation of an enemy was a denunciation of a representative of evil, an exhortation in behalf of Jerusalem was an exhortation in behalf of God's Kingdom on earth, " the city of our God, the mountain of holiness, beautiful for situation, the joy of the whole earth, the city of the great King " (Ps. xlviii. 1, 2).

(4.) They were preachers of morals and of spiritual religion. The symbolical teaching of the Law had lost much of its effect. Instead of learning the necessity of purity by the legal washings, the majority came to rest in the outward act as in itself sufficient. It was the work, then, of the prophets to hold up before the eyes of their countrymen a high and pure morality, not veiled in symbols and acts, but such as none could profess to misunderstand. Thus, in his first chapter, Isaiah contrasts ceremonial observances with spiritual morality: " Your new moons and your appointed feasts my soul hateth: they are a trouble to me; I am weary to bear them. . . . . Wash you, make you clean; put away the evil of your doings from before mine eyes; cease to do evil; learn to do well; seek judgment; relieve the oppressed, judge the fatherless, plead for the widow " (i. 14–17). He proceeds to denounce God's judgments on the oppression and covetous-

ness of the rulers, the pride of the women (c. iii.) on grasping, profligacy, iniquity, injustice (e. v.), and so on throughout. The system of morals put forward by the prophets, if not higher, or sterner, or purer than that of the Law, is more plainly declared, and with greater, because now more needed, vehemence of diction.[b]

(5.) They were extraordinary, but yet authorized, exponents of the Law. As an instance of this, we may take Isaiah's description of a true fast (lviii. 3–7); Ezekiel's explanation of the sins of the father being visited on the children (c. xviii.); Micah's preference of " doing justly, loving mercy, and walking humbly with God," to " thousands of rams and ten thousands of rivers of oil " (vi. 6–8). In these as in other similar cases (cf. Hos. vi. 6; Amos v. 21), it was the task of the prophets to restore the balance which had been overthrown by the Jews and their teachers dwelling on one side or on the outer covering of a truth or of a duty, and leaving the other side or the inner meaning out of sight.

(6.) They held, as we have shown above, a pastoral or quasi-pastoral office.

(7.) They were a political power in the state. Strong in the safeguard of their religious character, they were able to serve as a counterpoise to the royal authority when wielded even by an Ahab.

(8.) But the prophets were something more than national poets and annalists, preachers of patriotism, moral teachers, exponents of the Law, pastors, and politicians. We have not yet touched upon their most essential characteristic, which is, that they were instruments of revealing God's will to man, as in other ways, so, specially, by predicting future events, and, in particular, by foretelling the incarnation of the Lord Jesus Christ, and the redemption effected by Him.[c] There are two chief ways of exhibiting this fact: one is suitable when discoursing with Christians, the other when arguing with unbelievers. To the Christian it is enough to show that the truth of the New Testament and the truthfulness of its authors, and of the Lord Himself, are bound up with the truth of the existence of this predictive element in the prophets. To the unbeliever it is necessary to show that facts have verified their predictions.

(a.) In St. Matthew's Gospel, the first chapter, we find a quotation from the prophet Isaiah, " Behold a virgin shall be with child, and shall bring forth a son, and they shall call his name Em-

---

[a] Bishop Lowth " esteems the whole book of Isaiah poetical, a few passages exempted, which, if brought together, would not at most exceed the bulk of five or six chapters," " half of the book of Jeremiah," " the greater part of Ezekiel." The rest of the prophets are mainly poetical, but Haggai is " prosaic," and Jonah and Daniel are plain prose (*Sacred Poetry*, Lect. xxi.).

[b] "Magna fides et grandis audacia Prophetarum," says St. Jerome (*in Ezek.*). This was their general characteristic, but that gifts and graces might be dis severed, is proved by the cases of Balaam, Jonah, Caiaphas, and the disobedient prophet of Judah.

[c] Dr. Davidson pronounces it as " now commonly admitted that the essential part of Biblical prophecy does not lie in predicting contingent events, but in divining the essentially religious in the course of history. . . . In no prophecy can it be shown that the literal predicting of distant historical events is contained. . . . In conformity with the analogy

of prophecy generally, special predictions concerning Christ do not appear in the Old Testament." Dr. Davidson must mean that this is " now commonly admitted " by writers like himself, who, following Eichhorn, resolve " the prophet's delineations of the future " into " in essence *nothing but forebodings* — efforts *of the spiritual eye* to bring up before itself the distinct form of the future. The prevision of the prophet is intensified presentiment." Of course, if the powers of the prophets were simply " forebodings " and " presentiments " of the human spirit in " its preconscious region," they could not do more than make indefinite guesses about the future. But this is not the Jewish nor the Christian theory of prophecy. See S. Basil (*in Esai.* iii.), S. Chrys. (*Hom.* xxii. t. v. 137, ed. 1612), Clem. Alex. (*Strom.* l. h.), Euseb. (*Dem. Evang.* v. 132, ed. 1544), and Justin Martyr (*Dial cum Tryph.* p. 234, ed. 1686). (See *Suicer, s. v.* προφήτης.)

manuel;" and, at the same time, we find a statement that the birth of Christ took place as it did "that it might be fulfilled which was spoken of the Lord by the prophet," in those words (i. 22, 23). This means that the prophecy was the declaration of God's purpose, and that the circumstances of the birth of Christ were the fulfillment of that purpose. Then, either the predictive element exists in the book of the Prophet Isaiah, or the authority of the Evangelist St. Matthew must be given up. The same evangelist testifies to the same prophet having "spoken of" John the Baptist (iii. 3) in words which he quotes from Is. xl. 3. He says (iv. 13-15) that Jesus came and dwelt in Capernaum, "that" other words "spoken by" the same prophet (ix. 1) "might be fulfilled." He says (viii. 17) that Jesus did certain acts, "that it might be fulfilled which was spoken by Esaias the prophet" (Is. liii. 4). He says (xii. 17) that Jesus acted in a particular manner, "that it might be fulfilled which was spoken by Esaias the prophet" in words quoted from chap. xlii. 1. Then, if we believe St. Matthew, we must believe that in the pages of the Prophet Isaiah there was predicted that which Jesus some seven hundred years afterwards fulfilled.[a] But, further, we have not only the evidence of the Evangelist; we have the evidence of the Lord Himself. He declares (Matt. xiii. 14) that in the Jews of his age "is fulfilled the prophecy of Esaias, which saith —" (Is. vi. 9). He says (Matt. xv. 7) "Esaias well prophesied of them" (Is. xxix. 13). Then, if we believe our Lord's sayings and the record of them, we must believe in prediction as existing in the Prophet Isaiah. This prophet, who is cited between fifty and sixty times, may be taken as a sample; but the same argument might be brought forward with respect to Jeremiah (Matt. ii. 18; Heb. viii. 8), Daniel (Matt. xxiv. 15), Hosea (Matt. ii. 15; Rom. ix. 25), Joel (Acts ii. 17), Amos (Acts vii. 42; xv. 16), Jonah (Matt. xii. 40), Micah (Matt. xii. 7), Habakkuk (Acts xiii. 41), Haggai (Heb. xli. 26), Zechariah (Matt. xxi. 5; Mark xiv. 27; John xix. 37), Malachi (Matt. xi. 10; Mark i. 2; Luke vii. 27). With this evidence for so many of the prophets, it would be idle to cavil with respect to Ezekiel, Obadiah, Nahum, Zephaniah; the more, as "the prophets" are frequently spoken of together (Matt. ii. 23; Acts xiii. 40, xv. 15) as authoritative. The Psalms are quoted no less than seventy times, and very frequently as being predictive.

(β.) The argument with the unbeliever does not admit of being brought to an issue so concisely. Here it is necessary (1) to point out the existence of certain declarations as to future events, the probability of which was not discernible by human sagacity at the time that the declarations were made; (2) to show that certain events did afterwards take place corresponding with these declarations; (3) to show that a chance coincidence is not an adequate hypothesis on which to account for that correspondence.

Davison, in his valuable *Discourses on Prophecy* fixes a "Criterion of Prophecy," and in accordance with it he describes "the conditions which would confer cogency of evidence on single examples of prophecy," in the following manner first, "the known promulgation of the prophecy prior to the event; secondly, the clear and palpable fulfillment of it; lastly, the nature of the event itself, if, when the prediction of it was given, it lay remote from human view, and was such as could not be foreseen by any supposable effort of reason, or be deduced upon principles of calculation derived from probability and experience" (*Disc.* viii. 378). Applying his test, the learned writer finds that the establishment of the Christian Religion and the person of its Founder were predicted when neither reason nor experience could have anticipated them; and that the predictions respecting them have been clearly fulfilled in history. Here, then, is an adequate proof of an inspired prescience in the prophets who predicted these things. He applies his test to the prophecies recorded of the Jewish people, and their actual state, to the prediction of the great apostasy and to the actual state of corrupted Christianity, and finally to the prophecies relating to Nineveh, Babylon, Tyre, Egypt, the Ishmaelites, and the Four Empires, and to the events which have befallen them; and in each of these cases he finds proof of the existence of the predictive element in the prophets.

In the book of Kings we find Micaiah the son of Imlah uttering a challenge, by which his predictive powers were to be judged. He had pronounced, by the word of the Lord, that Ahab should fall at Ramoth-Gilead. Ahab, in return, commanded him to be shut up in prison until he came back in peace. "And Micaiah said, If thou return at all in peace" (that is, if the event does not verify my words), "the Lord hath not spoken by me" (that is, I am no prophet capable of predicting the future) (1 K. xxii. 28). The test is sound as a negative test, and so it is laid down in the Law (Deut. xviii. 22); but as a positive test it would not be sufficient. Ahab's death at Ramoth-Gilead did not prove Micaiah's predictive powers, though his escape would have disproved them. But here we must notice a very important difference between single prophecies and a series of prophecy. The fulfillment of a single prophecy does not prove the prophetical power of the prophet, but the fulfillment of a long series of prophecies by a series or number of events does in itself constitute a proof that the prophecies were intended to predict the events, and, consequently, that predictive power resided in the prophet or prophets. We may see this in the so far parallel cases of satirical writings. We know for certain that Aristophanes refers to Cleon, Pericles, Nicias (and we should be equally sure of it were his satire more concealed than it is) simply from the fact of a number of satirical hits converging together on

---

a This conclusion cannot be escaped by pressing the words ἵνα πληρωθῇ, for if they do not mean that certain things were done in order that the Divine predestination might be accomplished, which predestination was already declared by the prophet, they must mean that Jesus Christ knowingly moulded his acts so as to be in accordance with what was said in an ancient book which in reality had no reference to him, a thing which is entirely at variance with the character drawn of him by St. Matthew, and which would make him a conscious impostor, inasmuch as he himself appeals to the prophecies. Further, it would imply (as in Matt. i. 22) that God Himself contrived certain events (as those connected with the birth of Christ), not in order that they might be in accordance with his will, but in order that they might be agreeable to the declarations of a certain book — than which nothing could well be more absurd.

the object of his satire. One, two, or three strokes might be intended for more persons than one, but the addition of each stroke makes the aim more apparent, and when we have a sufficient number before us we can no longer possibly doubt his design. The same may be said of fables, and still more of allegories. The fact of a *complicated* lock being opened by a key shows that the lock and key were meant for each other. Now the Messianic picture drawn by the prophets as a body contains at least as many traits as these: — That salvation should come through the family of Abraham, Isaac, Jacob, Judah, David: that at the time of the final absorption of the Jewish power, Shiloh (the tranquillizer) should gather the nations under his rule: that there should be a great Prophet, typified by Moses; a King descended from David ; a Priest forever, typified by Melchisedek: that there should be born into the world a child to be called Mighty God, Eternal Father, Prince of Peace: that there should be a Righteous Servant of God on whom the Lord would lay the iniquity of all: that Messiah the Prince should be cut off, but not for himself: that an everlasting kingdom should be given by the Ancient of Days to one like the Son of Man. It seems impossible to harmonize so many apparent contradictions. Nevertheless it is an undoubted fact that, at the time seemingly pointed out by one or more of these predictions, there was born into the world a child of the house of David, and therefore of the family of Abraham, Isaac, Jacob, and Judah, who claimed to be the object of these and other predictions; who is acknowledged as Prophet, Priest, and King, as Mighty God, and yet as God's Righteous Servant who bears the iniquity of all; who was cut off, and whose death is acknowledged not to have been for his own, but for others' good; who has instituted a spiritual kingdom on earth, which kingdom is of a nature to continue forever, if there is any continuance beyond this world and this life; and in whose doings and sufferings on earth a number of specific predictions were minutely fulfilled. Then we may say that we have here a series of prophecies which are so applicable to the person and earthly life of Jesus Christ as to be thereby shown to have been designed to apply to Him. And if they were designed to apply to Him, prophetical prediction is proved.

Objections have been urged: — 1. *Vagueness.* — It has been said that the prophecies are too darkly and vaguely worded to be proved predictive by the events which they are alleged to foretell. This objection is stated with clearness and force by Ammon. He says, " Such simple sentences as the following: Israel has not to expect a king, but a teacher; this teacher will be born at Bethlehem during the reign of Herod; he will lay down his life under Tiberius, in attestation of the truth of his religion; through the destruction of Jerusalem, and the complete extinction of the Jewish state, he will spread his doctrine in every quarter of the world — a few sentences like these, expressed in plain historical prose, would not only bear the character of true predictions, but, when once their genuineness was proved, they would be of incomparably greater worth to us than all the oracles of the Old Testament taken together " (*Christology*, p. 12). But to this it might be answered, and has been in effect answered by Hengstenberg — 1. That God never forces men to believe, but that there is such an union of definiteness and vague-

ness in the prophecies as to enable those who are willing to discover the truth, while the willfully blind are not forcibly constrained to see it. 2. That, had the prophecies been couched in the form of direct declarations, their fulfillment would have thereby been rendered impossible, or, at least, capable of frustration. 3. That the effect of prophecy (e. g. with reference to the time of the Messiah's coming) would have been far less beneficial to believers, as being less adapted to keep them in a state of constant expectation. 4. That the Messiah of Revelation could not be so clearly portrayed in his varied character as God and Man, as Prophet, Priest, and King, if he had been the mere " teacher" which is all that Ammon acknowledges him to be. 5. That the state of the Prophets, at the time of receiving the Divine revelation, was (as we shall presently show) such as necessarily to make their predictions fragmentary, figurative, and abstracted from the relations of time. 6. That some portions of the prophecies were intended to be of double application, and some portions to be understood only on their fulfillment (cf. John xiv. 29; Ex. xxxvi. 33).

2. *Obscurity of a part or parts of a prophecy otherwise clear.* — The objection drawn from " the unintelligibleness of one part of a prophecy, as invalidating the proof of foresight arising from the evident completion of those parts which are understood " is akin to that drawn from the vagueness of the whole of it. And it may be answered with the same arguments, to which we may add the consideration urged by Butler that it is, for the argument in hand, the same as if the parts not understood were written in cipher or not written at all: " Suppose a writing, partly in cipher and partly in plain words at length; and that in the part one understood there appeared mention of several known facts — it would never come into any man's thought to imagine that if he understood the whole, perhaps he might find that these facts were not in reality known by the writer " (*Analogy*, pt. ii. c. vii.). Furthermore, if it be true that prophecies relating to the first coming of the Messiah refer also to his second coming, some part of those prophecies must *necessarily* be as yet not fully understood.

It would appear from these considerations that Davison's second " condition," above quoted, " the clear and *palpable* fulfillment of the prophecy," should be so far modified as to take into account the necessary difficulty, more or less great, in recognizing the fulfillment of a prophecy which results from the necessary vagueness and obscurity of the prophecy itself.

3. *Application of the several prophecies to a more immediate subject.* — It has been the task of many Biblical critics to examine the different passages which are alleged to be predictions of Christ, and to show that they were delivered in reference to some person or thing contemporary with, or shortly subsequent to, the time of the writer. The conclusion is then drawn, sometimes scornfully, sometimes as an inference not to be resisted, that the passages in question have nothing to do with the Messiah. We have here to distinguish carefully between the conclusion proved, and the corollary drawn from it. Let it be granted that it may be proved of all the predictions of the Messiah — it certainly may be proved of many — that they primarily apply to some historical and present fact: in that case a certain law, under which God

vouchsafe, his prophetical revelations, is discovered; but there is no semblance of disproof of the further Messianic interpretation of the passages under consideration. That some such law does exist has been argued at length by Mr. Davison. He believes, however, that "it obtains only in some of the more distinguished monuments of prophecy," such as the prophecies founded on, and having primary reference to, the kingdom of David, the restoration of the Jews, the destruction of Jerusalem (*On Prophecy*, Disc. v.). Dr. Lee thinks that Davison "exhibits too great reserve in the application of this important principle" (*On Inspiration*, Lect. iv.). He considers it to be of universal application; and upon it he founds the doctrine of the "double sense of prophecy," according to which a prediction is fulfilled in two or even more distinct but analogous subjects: first in type, then in antitype; and after that perhaps awaits a still further and more complete fulfillment. This view of the fulfillment of prophecy seems necessary for the explanation of our Lord's prediction on the mount, relating at once to the fall of Jerusalem and to the end of the Christian dispensation. It is on this principle that Pearson writes: "Many are the prophecies which concern Him, many the promises which are made of Him; but yet some of them very obscure. . . . . Wheresoever He is spoken of as the Anointed, it may well be *first* understood of some other person: except one place in Daniel, where Messiah is foretold 'to be cut off'" (*On the Creed*, Art. II.).

Whether it can be proved by an investigation of Holy Scripture, that this relation between Divine announcements for the future and certain present events does so exist as to constitute a law, and whether, if the law is proved to exist, it is of universal, or only of partial application, we do not pause to determine. But it is manifest that the existence of a primary sense cannot exclude the possibility of a secondary sense. The question, therefore, really is, whether the prophecies are applicable to Christ: if they are so applicable, the previous application of each of them to some historical event would not invalidate the proof that they were designed as a whole to find their full completion in Him. Nay, even if it could be shown that the prophets had in their thoughts nothing beyond the primary completion of their words (a thing which we at present leave undetermined), no inference could thence be drawn against their secondary application; for such an inference would assume, what no believer in Inspiration will grant, viz., that the prophets are the sole authors of their prophecies. The rule, *Nihil in scripto quod non prius in scriptore*, is sound; but, the question is, who is to be regarded as the true author of the prophecies — the human instrument or the Divine Author? (See Hengstenberg, *Christology*, Appendix VI., p. 433.)

4. *Miraculous character.* — It is probable that this lies at the root of the many and various efforts made to disprove the predictive power of the prophets. There is no question that if miracles are, either physically or morally, impossible, then prediction is impossible; and those passages which have ever been accounted predictive, must be explained away as being vague, as being obscure, as applying only to something in the writer's lifetime, or on some other hypothesis. This is only saying that belief in prediction is not compatible with the theory of Atheism, or with the philosophy which rejects the overruling Providence of a personal God. And this is not to be denied.

IV. THE PROPHETIC STATE. — We learn from Holy Scripture that it was by the agency of the Spirit of God that the prophets received the Divine communication. Thus, on the appointment of the seventy elders, "The Lord said, I will take of the Spirit which is upon thee, and will put it upon them. . . . . And the Lord . . . took of the Spirit that was upon him, and gave it unto the seventy elders; and it came to pass that when the Spirit rested upon them, they prophesied and did not cease. . . . . And Moses said, Would God that all the Lord's people were prophets, and that the Lord would put his Spirit upon them" (Num. xi. 17, 25. 29). Here we see that what made the seventy prophesy, was their being endued with the Lord's Spirit by the Lord Himself. So it is the Spirit of the Lord which made Saul (1 Sam. x. 6) and his messengers (1 Sam. xix. 20) prophesy. And thus St. Peter assures us that "prophecy came not in old time by the will of man, but holy men of God spake, moved (φερόμενοι) by the Holy Ghost" (2 Pet. i. 21), while false prophets are described as those "who speak a vision of their own heart. and not out of the mouth of the Lord" (Jer. xxiii. 16), "who prophesy out of their own hearts, . . who follow their own spirit, and have seen nothing" (Ez. xiii. 2, 3).[a] The prophet held an intermediate position in communication between God and man. God communicated with him by his Spirit, and he, having received this communication, was "the spokesman" of God to man (cf. Ex. vii. 1 and iv. 16). But the means by which the Divine Spirit communicated with the human spirit, and the conditions of the human spirit under which the Divine communications were received, have not been clearly declared to us. They are, however, indicated. On the occasion of the sedition of Miriam and Aaron, we read, "And the Lord said, Hear now my words: If there be a prophet among you, I the Lord will make myself known unto him in a vision, and will speak unto him in a dream. My servant Moses is not so, who is faithful in all mine house: with him will I speak mouth to mouth, even apparently, and not in dark speeches, and the similitude of the Lord shall he behold" (Num. xii. 6–8). Here we have an exhaustive division of the different ways in which the revelations of God are made to man. 1. Direct declaration and manifestation, "I will speak mouth to mouth, apparently, and the similitude of the Lord shall he behold." 2. Vision. 3. Dream. It is indicated that, at least at this time, the vision and the dream were the special means of conveying a revelation to a prophet, while the higher form of direct declaration and manifestation was reserved for the more highly favored Moses.[b] Joel's prophecy ap-

---

a Hence the emphatic declarations of the Great Prophet of the Church that he did not speak of Himself (John vii. 17, &c.).

b Maimonides has drawn out the points in which Moses is considered superior to all other prophets as follows: "1. All the other prophets saw the prophecy in a dream or in a vision, but our Rabbi Moses saw it whilst awake. 2. To all the other prophets it was revealed through the medium of an angel, and therefore they saw that which they saw in an alle-

years to make the same division, "Your old men shall dream dreams, and your young men shall see visions," these being the two methods in which the promise, "your sons and your daughters shall prophesy," are to be carried out (ii. 28). And of Daniel we are told that "he had understanding in all visions and dreams" (Dan. i. 17). Can these phases of the prophetic state be distinguished from each other? and in what did they consist?

According to the theory of Philo and the Alexandrian school, the prophet was in a state of entire unconsciousness at the time that he was under the influence of Divine inspiration, "for the human understanding," says Philo, "takes its departure on the arrival of the Divine Spirit, and, on the removal of the latter, again returns to its home, for the mortal must not dwell with the immortal" (*Quis Rer. Div. Hær.* t. i. p. 511). Balaam is described by him as an unconscious instrument through whom God spoke (*De Vitâ Mosis*, lib. I. t. ii. p. 124). Josephus makes Balaam excuse himself to Balak on the same principle: "When the Spirit of God seizes us, It utters whatsoever sounds and words It pleases, without any knowledge on our part, ... for when It has come into us, there is nothing in us which remains our own" (*Antiq.* iv. 6, § 5, t. i. p. 216). This theory identifies Jewish prophecy in all essential points with the heathen μαντική, or divination, as distinct from προφητεία, or interpretation. Montanism adopted the same view: "Defendimus, in causa novæ prophetiæ, gratiæ exstasin, id est amentiam, convenire. In spiritu enim homo constitutus, præsertim cum gloriam Dei conspicit, vel cum per ipsum Deus loquitur, necesse est excidat sensu, obumbratus scilicet virtute divina, de quo inter nos et Psychicos (catholicos) quæstio est" (Tertullian, *Adv. Marcion.* iv. 22). According to the belief, then, of the heathen, of the Alexandrian Jews, and of the Montanists, the vision of the prophet was seen while he was in a state of ecstatic unconsciousness, and the enunciation of the vision was made by him in the same state. The Fathers of the Church opposed the Montanist theory with great unanimity. In Eusebius's History (v. 17) we read that Miltiades wrote a book περὶ τοῦ μὴ δεῖν προφήτην ἐν ἐκστάσει λαλεῖν. St. Jerome writes: "Non loquitur propheta ἐν ἐκστάσει, ut Montanus et Prisca Maximillaque delirant, sed quod prophetat liber est visionis intelligentis universa quæ loquitur" (*Prolog. in Nahum*). And again: "Neque vero ut Montanus cum insanis fœminis somniat, prophetæ in ecstasi locuti sunt ut nescierint quid loquerentur, et cum alios erudirent ipsi ignorarent quid dicerent" (*Prolog. in Esai.*). Origen (*Contr. Celsum,* vii. 4), and St. Basil (*Commentary on Isaiah,* Prooem. c. 5), contrast the prophet with the soothsayer, on the ground of the latter being deprived of his senses. St. Chrysostom draws out the contrast: Τοῦτο γὰρ μάντεως ἴδιον, τὸ ἐξεστηκέναι, τὸ ἀνάγχην ὑπομένειν, τὸ ὠθεῖσθαι, τὸ ἕλκεσθαι, τὸ σύρεσθαι ὥσπερ μαινόμενον. Ὁ δὲ προφήτης οὐχ οὕτως, ἀλλὰ μετὰ διανοίας νηφούσης καὶ σωφρονούσης καταστάσεως, καὶ εἰδὼς ἃ φθέγ-

γεται, φησὶν ἅπαντα· ὥστε καὶ πρὸ τῆς ἐκβάσεως κάντεύθεν γνώριζε τὸν μάντιν καὶ τὸν προφήτην (*Hom.* xxix. *in Epist. ad Corinth.*). At the same time, while drawing the distinction sharply between heathen soothsaying and Montanist prophesying on the one side, and Hebrew prophecy on the other, the Fathers use expressions so strong as almost to represent the Prophets to be passive instruments acted on by the Spirit of God. Thus it is that they describe them as musical instruments, — the pipe (Athenagoras, *Leg. pro Christianis,* c. ix.; Clem. Alex. *Cohort. ad Gent.* c. i.), the lyre (Justin Martyr, *Cohort. ad Græc.* c. viii.; Ephraem Syr. *Rhythm.* xxix.; Chrysostom, *Ad Pop. Antioch.* Hom. i. t. ii.); or as pens (St. Greg. Magn. *Præf. in Mor. in Job*). Expressions such as these (many of which are quoted by Dr. Lee, Appendix G.) must be set against the passages which were directed against the Montanists. Nevertheless, there is a very appreciable difference between their view and that of Tertullian and Philo. Which is most in accordance with the indications of Holy Scripture?

It does not seem possible to draw any very precise distinction between the prophetic "dream" and the prophetic "vision." In the case of Abraham (Gen. xv. 1) and of Daniel (Dan. vii. 1), they seem to melt into each other. In both, the external senses are at rest, reflection is quiescent, and intuition energizes. The action of the ordinary faculties is suspended in the one case by natural, in the other supernatural or extraordinary causes. (See Lee, *Inspiration,* p. 173.) The state into which the prophet was, occasionally, at least, thrown by the ecstacy, or vision, or trance, is described poetically in the Book of Job (iv. 13–16, xxxiii. 15), and more plainly in the Book of Daniel. In the case of Daniel, we find first a deep sleep (viii. 18, x. 9) accompanied by terror (viii. 17, x. 8). Then he is raised upright (viii. 18) on his hands and knees, and then on his feet (x. 10, 11). He then receives the Divine revelation (viii. 19, x. 12). After which he falls to the ground in a swoon (x. 15, 17); he is faint, sick, and astonished (viii. 27). Here, then, is an instance of the ecstatic state; nor is it confined to the Old Testament, though we do not find it in the New Testament accompanied by such violent effects upon the body. At the Transfiguration, the disciples fell on their face, being overpowered by the Divine glory, and were restored, like Daniel, by the touch of Jesus's hand. St. Peter fell into a trance (ἔκστασις) before he received his vision, instructing him as to the admission of the Gentiles (Acts x. 10, xi. 5). St. Paul was in a trance (ἐν ἐκστάσει) when he was commanded to devote himself to the conversion of the Gentiles (Acts xxii. 17), and when he was caught up into the third heaven (2 Cor. xii. 1). St. John was probably in the same state (ἐν πνεύματι) when he received the message to the seven churches (Rev. i. 10). The prophetic trance, then, must be acknowledged as a Scriptural account of the state in which the prophets and other inspired persons, sometimes, at least, received Divine revela-

gory or enigma, but to Moses it is said: With him will I speak mouth to mouth (Num. xii. 8) and face to face (Ex. xxxiii. 11). 3 All the other prophets were terrified, but with Moses it was not so; and this is what the Scripture says: As a man speaketh unto his friend (Ex. xxxiii. 11). 4. All the other prophets could not prophesy at any time that they wished, but with Moses it was not so, but at any time that he wished for it, the Holy Spirit came upon him; so that it was not necessary for him to prepare his mind, for he was always ready for it, like the ministering angels" (*Yad Hachazakah,* c. vii., Bernard's transl. p 116, quoted by Lee, p. 457).

tions. It would seem to have been of the following nature.

(1.) The bodily senses were closed to external objects as in deep sleep. (2.) The reflective and discursive faculty was still and inactive. (3.) The spiritual faculty ($\pi\nu\epsilon\hat{v}\mu\alpha$) was awakened to the highest state of energy. Hence it is that revelations in trances are described by the prophets as "seen" or "heard" by them, for the spiritual faculty energizes by immediate perception on the part of the inward sense, not by inference and thought. Thus Isaiah "*saw* the Lord sitting" (Is. vi. 1). Zechariah "lifted up his eyes and *saw*" (Zech. ii. 1); "the word of the Lord which Micah *saw*" (Mic. i. 1); "the wonder which Habakkuk did *see*" (Hab. i. 1). "Peter *saw* heaven opened . . . and there came a *voice* to him" (Acts x. 11). Paul was "in a trance, and *saw* Him *saying*" (Acts xxii. 18). John "*heard* a great voice . . . and *saw* seven golden candlesticks" (Rev. i. 12). Hence it is, too, that the prophets' visions are unconnected and fragmentary, inasmuch as they are not the subject of the reflective but of the perceptive faculty. They described what they saw and heard, not what they had themselves thought out and systematized. Hence, too, succession in time is disregarded or unnoticed. The subjects of the vision being, to the prophets' sight, in juxtaposition or enfolding each other, some in the foreground, some in the background, are necessarily abstracted from the relations of time. Hence, too, the imagery with which the prophetic writings are colored, and the dramatic cast in which they are moulded; these peculiarities resulting, as we have already said, in a necessary obscurity and difficulty of interpretation.

But though it must be allowed that Scripture language seems to point out the state of dream and of trance, or ecstasy, as a condition in which the human instrument received the Divine communications, it does not follow that all the prophetic revelations were thus made. We must acknowledge the state of trance in such passages as Is. vi. (called ordinarily the vision of Isaiah), as Ex. i. (called the vision of Ezekiel), as Dan. vii., viii., x., xi., xii. (called the visions of Daniel), as Zech. i., iv., v., vi. (called the visions of Zechariah), as Acts x. (called the vision of St. Peter), as 2 Cor. xii. (called the vision of St. Paul), and similar instances, which are indicated by the language used. But it does not seem true to say, with Hengstenberg, that "the difference between these prophecies and the rest is a vanishing one, and if we but possess the power and the ability to look more deeply into them, the marks of the vision may be discerned" (*Christology*, vol. iv. p. 417).[a] St. Paul distinguishes "revelations" from "visions" (2 Cor. xii. 1). In the books of Moses "speaking mouth to mouth" is contrasted with "visions and dreams" (Num. xii. 8). It is true that in this last-quoted passage, "visions and dreams" alone appear to be attributed to the prophet, while "speaking mouth to mouth" is reserved for Moses. But when Moses was dead, the cause of this difference would cease. During the era of prophecy there were none nearer to God, none with whom He would, we may suppose, communicate more openly than the prophets. We should expect, then, that they would be the recipients, not only of visions

in the state of dream or ecstasy, but also of the direct revelations which are called speaking mouth to mouth. The greater part of the Divine communications we may suppose to have been thus made to the prophets in their waking and ordinary state, while the visions were exhibited to them either in the state of sleep, or in the state of ecstasy. "The more ordinary mode through which the word of the Lord, as far as we can trace, came, was through a divine impulse given to the prophet's own thoughts" (Stanley, p. 426). Hence it follows that, while the Fathers in their opposition to Montanism and $\mu\alpha\nu\acute{\iota}\alpha$ were pushed somewhat too far in their denial of the ecstatic state, they were yet perfectly exact in their descriptions of the condition under which the greater part of the prophetic revelations were received and promulgated. No truer description has been given of them than that of Hippolytus, and that of St. Basil: Οὐ γὰρ ἐξ ἰδίας δυνάμεως ἐφθέγγοντο, οὐδὲ ἅπερ αὐτοὶ ἐβούλοντο ταῦτα ἐκήρυττον, ἀλλὰ πρῶτον μὲν διὰ τοῦ Λόγου ἐσοφίζοντο ὀρθῶς, ἔπειτα δι' ὁραμάτων προεδιδάσκοντο τὰ μέλλοντα καλῶς· εἶθ' οὕτω πεπεισμένοι ἔλεγον ταῦτα ἅπερ αὐτοῖς ἦν μόνοις ἀπὸ τοῦ Θεοῦ ἀποκεκρυμμένα (Hippol. *De Antichristo*, c. ii.). Πῶς προεφήτευον αἱ καθαραὶ καὶ διαυγεῖς ψυχαί; οἱονεὶ κάτοπτρα γινόμενα τῆς θείας ἐνεργείας, τὴν ἔμφασιν ῥανὴν καὶ ἀσύγχυτον καὶ οὐδὲν ἐπιθολουμένην ἐκ τῶν παθῶν τῆς σαρκὸς ἐπεδείκνυντο· πᾶσι μὲν γὰρ πάρεστι τὸ Ἅγιον Πνεῦμα (St. Basil, *Comm. in Esai.* Procem.).

Had the prophets a full knowledge of that which they predicted? It follows from what we have already said that they had not, and could not have. They were the "spokesmen" of God (Ex. vii. 1), the "mouth" by which his words were uttered, or they were enabled to view, and empowered to describe, pictures presented to their spiritual intuition; but there are no grounds for believing that, contemporaneously with this miracle, there was wrought another miracle enlarging the understanding of the prophet so as to grasp the whole of the Divine counsels which he was gazing into, or which he was the instrument of enunciating. We should not expect it beforehand; and we have the testimony of the prophets themselves (Dan. xii. 8; Zech. iv. 5), and of St. Peter (1 Pet. i. 10), to the fact that they frequently did not comprehend them. The passage in St. Peter's Epistle is very instructive: "Of which salvation the prophets have inquired and searched diligently. who prophesied of the grace that should come unto you: searching what, or what manner of time the Spirit of Christ which was in them did signify, when it testified beforehand the sufferings of Christ, and the glory that should follow. Unto whom it was revealed, that not unto themselves, but unto us they did minister the things, which are now reported unto you by them that have preached the gospel unto you with the Holy Ghost sent down from heaven." It is here declared (1) that the Holy Ghost through the prophet, or the prophet by the Holy Ghost, testified of Christ's sufferings and ascension, and of the institution of Christianity; (2) that after having uttered predictions on those subjects, the minds of the prophets occupied themselves in searching into the full meaning of the words that they had uttered; (3) that they were then divinely in-

---

[a] This view is advocated also by Velthusen (*De optica rerum futurarum descriptione*), Jahn (*Einleit. in die göttlichen Bücher des A. B*), Tholuck (*Die Propheten und ihre Weissagungen*).

PROPHET

formed that their predictions were not to find their completion until the last days, and that they themselves were instruments for declaring good things that should come not to their own but to a future generation. This is exactly what the prophetic state above described would lead us to expect. While the Divine communication is being received, the human instrument is simply passive. He sees or hears by his spiritual intuition or perception, and declares what he has seen or heard. Then the reflective faculty which had been quiescent but never so overpowered as to be destroyed, awakens to the consideration of the message or vision received, and it strives earnestly to understand it, and more especially to look at the revelation as in instead of *out of* time. The result is failure; but this failure is softened by the Divine intimation that the time is not yet.[a] The two questions, What did the prophet understand by this prophecy? and, What was the meaning of this prophecy? are totally different in the estimation of every one who believes that "the Holy Ghost spake by the Prophets," or who considers it possible that he did so speak.[b]

V. INTERPRETATION OF PREDICTIVE PROPHECY. — We have only space for a few rules, deduced from the account which we have given of the nature of prophecy. They are, (1.) Interpose distances of time according as history may show them to be necessary with respect to the past, or inference may show them to be likely in respect to the future, because, as we have seen, the prophetic visions are abstracted from relations in time. (2.) Distinguish the *form* from the *idea*. Thus Isaiah (xi. 15) represents the *idea* of the removal of all obstacles from before God's people in the *form* of the Lord's destroying the tongue of the Egyptian sea, and smiting the river into seven streams. (3.) Distinguish in like manner figure from what is represented by it, e. g., in the verse previous to that quoted, do not understand literally, "They shall *fly upon the shoulders* of the Philistines " (Is. xi. 14). (4.) Make allowance for the imagery of the prophetic visions, and for the poetical diction in which they are expressed. (5.) In respect to things past, interpret by the apparent meaning, checked by reference to events; in respect to things future, interpret by the apparent meaning, checked by reference to the analogy of the faith. (6.) Interpret according to the principle which may be deduced from the examples of visions explained in the Old Testament. (7.) Interpret according to the principle which may be deduced from the examples of prophecies interpreted in the New Testament.

VI. USE OF PROPHECY. — Predictive prophecy is at once a part and an evidence of revelation: at

the time that it is delivered, and until its fulfilment, a part; after it has been fulfilled, an evidence. St. Peter (Ep. 2, i. 19) describes it as "a light shining in a dark place," or "a taper glimmering where there is nothing to reflect its rays," that is, throwing some light, but only a feeble light as compared with what is shed from the Gospel history. To this light, feeble as it is, "you do well," says the Apostle, "to take heed." And he warns them not to be offended at the feebleness of the light, because it is of the nature of prophecy until its fulfilment — (in the case of Messianic predictions, of which he is speaking, described as "until the day dawn, and the day-star arise in your hearts") — to shed only a feeble light. Nay, he continues, even the prophets could not themselves interpret its meaning,[c] "for the prophecy came not in old time by the will of man," i. e. the prophets were not the authors of their predictions, "but holy men of old spake by the impulse (φερόμενοι) of the Holy Ghost." This, then, was the use of prophecy before its fulfilment, — to act as a feeble light in the midst of darkness, which it did not dispel, but through which it threw its rays in such a way as to enable a true-hearted believer to direct his steps and guide his anticipations (cf. Acts xiii. 27). But after fulfilment, St. Peter says, "the word of prophecy " becomes "more sure" than it was before, that is, it is no longer merely a feeble light to guide, but it is a firm ground of confidence, and, combined with the apostolic testimony, serves as a trustworthy evidence of the faith; so trustworthy, that even after he and his brother Apostles are dead, those whom he addressed will feel secure that they "had not followed cunningly devised fables," but the truth.

As an evidence, fulfilled prophecy is as satisfactory as anything can be, for who can know the future except the Ruler who disposes future events; and from whom can come prediction except from Him who knows the future? After all that has been said and unsaid, prophecy and miracles, each resting on their own evidence, must always be the chief and direct evidences of the truth of the Divine character of a religion. Where they exist, a Divine power is proved. Nevertheless, they should never be rested on alone, but in combination with the general character of the whole scheme to which they belong. Its miracles, its prophecies, its morals, its propagation, and its adaptation to human needs, are the chief evidences of Christianity. None of these must be taken separately. The fact of their conspiring together is the strongest evidence of all. That one object with which predictions are delivered is to serve in an after age as an evidence on which faith may reasonably rest, is stated by our Lord

---

a See Keble, *Christian Year*, 18th S. aft. Trin., and Lee, *Inspiration*, p. 210.

b It is on this principle rather than as it is explained by Dr. M'Caul (*Aids to Faith*) that the prophecy of Hosea xi. 1 is to be interpreted. Hosea, we may well believe, understood in his own words no more than a reference to the historical fact that the children of Israel came out of Egypt. But Hosea was not the author of the prophecy — he was the instrument by which it was promulgated. The Holy Spirit intended something further — and what this something was He informs us by the Evangelist St. Matthew (Matt. ii 15). The two facts of the Israelites being called out of Egypt and of Christ's return from Egypt appear to Professor Jowett so distinct that the refer-

ence by St. Matthew to the Prophet is to him inexplicable except on the hypothesis of a mistake on the part of the Evangelist (see Jowett's *Essay on the Interpretation of Scripture*). A deeper insight into Scripture shows that "the Jewish people themselves, their history, their ritual, their government, all present one grand prophecy of the future Redeemer " (Lee, p. 107). Consequently "Israel" is one of the *forms* naturally taken in the prophetic vision by the *idea* "*Messiah.*"

c This is a more probable meaning of the words ἰδίας ἐπιλύσεως οὐ γίνεται than that given by Pearson (*On the Creed*, art. i. p. 17, ed. Burton), "that no prophecy did so proceed from the prophet that he of himself or by his own instinct did open his mouth to prophesy."

Himself: " And now I have told you before it come to pass, *that when it is come to pass ye might believe*" (John xiv. 29).

VII. DEVELOPMENT OF MESSIANIC PROPHECY. — Prediction, in the shape of promise and threatening, begins with the Book of Genesis. Immediately upon the Fall, hopes of recovery and salvation are held out, but the manner in which this salvation is to be effected is left altogether indefinite. All that is at first declared is that it shall come through a child of woman (Gen. iii. 15). By degrees the area is limited. It is to come through the family of Shem (Gen. ix. 26), through the family of Abraham (Gen. xii. 3), of Isaac (Gen. xxii. 18), of Jacob (Gen. xxviii. 14), of Judah (Genesis xlix. 10). Balaam seems to say that it will be wrought by a warlike Israelitish King (Num. xxiv. 17); Jacob, by a peaceful Ruler of the earth (Gen. xlix. 10); Moses, by a Prophet like himself, *i. e.* a revealer of a new religious dispensation (Deut. xviii. 15). Nathan's announcement (2 Sam. vii. 16) determines further that the salvation is to come through the house of David, and through a descendant of David who shall be himself a king. This promise is developed by David himself in the Messianic Psalms. Pss. xviii. and lxi. are founded on the promise communicated by Nathan, and do not go beyond the announcement made by Nathan. The same may be said of Ps. lxxxix., which was composed by a later writer. Pss. ii. and cx. rest upon the same promise as their foundation, but add new features to it. The Son of David is to be the Son of God (ii. 7), the anointed of the Lord (ii. 2), not only the King of Zion (ii. 6, cx. 1), but the inheritor and lord of the whole earth (ii. 8, cx. 6), and, besides this, a Priest forever after the order of Melchisedek (cx. 4). At the same time he is, as typified by his progenitor, to be full of suffering and affliction (Pss. xxii., lxxi., cii., cix.): brought down to the grave, yet raised to life without seeing corruption (Ps. xvi.). In Pss. xlv., lxxii., the sons of Korah and Solomon describe his peaceful reign. Between Solomon and Hezekiah intervened some 200 years, during which the voice of prophecy was silent. The Messianic conception entertained at this time by the Jews might have been that of a King of the royal house of David who would arise, and gather under his peaceful sceptre his own people and strangers. Sufficient allusion to his prophetical and priestly offices had been made to create thoughtful consideration, but as yet there was no clear delineation of him in these characters. It was reserved for the Prophets to bring out these features more distinctly. The sixteen Prophets may be divided into four groups: the Prophets of the Northern Kingdom, — Hosea, Amos, Joel,

Jonah; the Prophets of the Southern Kingdom, — Isaiah, Jeremiah, Obadiah, Micah, Nahum, Habakkuk, Zephaniah; the Prophets of the Captivity, — Ezekiel and Daniel; the Prophets of the Return, — Haggai, Zechariah, Malachi. In this great period of prophetism there is no longer any chronological development of Messianic Prophecy, as in the earlier period previous to Solomon. Each prophet adds a feature, one more, another less clearly: combine the features, and we have the portrait; but it does not grow gradually and perceptibly under the hands of the several artists. Here, therefore, the task of tracing the chronological *progress* of the revelation of the Messiah comes to an end: its *culminating* point is found in the prophecy contained in Is. lii. 13–15, and liii. We here read that there should be a Servant of God, lowly and despised, full of grief and suffering, oppressed, condemned as a malefactor, and put to death. But his sufferings, it is said, are not for his own sake, for he had never been guilty of fraud or violence; they are spontaneously taken, patiently borne, vicarious in their character; and, by God's appointment, they have an atoning, reconciling, and justifying efficacy. The result of his sacrificial offering is to be his exaltation and triumph. By the path of humiliation and expiatory suffering he is to reach that state of glory foreshown by David and Solomon. The prophetic character of the Messiah is drawn out by Isaiah in other parts of his book as the atoning work here. By the time of Hezekiah therefore (for Hengstenberg, *Christology*, vol. ii., has satisfactorily disproved the theory of a Deutero-Isaiah of the days of the Captivity) the portrait of the Θεάνθρωπος — at once King, Priest, Prophet, and Redeemer — was drawn in all its essential features.[a] The contemporary and later Prophets (cf. Mic. v. 2; Dan. vii. 9; Zech. vi. 13; Mal. iv. 2) added some particulars and details, and so the conception was left to await its realization after an interval of some 400 years from the date of the last Hebrew Prophet.

It is the opinion of Hengstenberg (*Christology*, i. 235) and of Pusey (*Minor Prophets*, Part i. Introd.) that the writings of the Minor Prophets are chronologically placed. Accordingly, the former arranges the list of the Prophets as follows: Hosea, Joel, Amos, Obadiah, Jonah, Micah, Isaiah (" the principal prophetical figure in the first or Assyrian period of canonical prophetism "), Nahum, Habakkuk, Zephaniah, Jeremiah (" the principal prophetical figure in the second or Babylonian period of canonical prophetism "), Ezekiel, Daniel, Haggai, Zechariah, Malachi. Calmet (*Dict. Bibl.* s. v. " Prophet ") as follows: Hosea, Amos, Isaiah, Jonah, Micah, Nahum, Jeremiah, Zephaniah, Joel, Daniel, Ezekiel, Habakkuk, Obadiah,[b] Haggai,

---

[a] The modern Jews, in opposition to their ancient exposition, have been driven to a non-Messianic interpretation of Is. liii. Among Christians the non-Messianic interpretation commenced with Grotius. He applies the chapter to Jeremiah. According to Doederlein, Schuster, Stephani, Eichhorn, Rosenmüller, Hitzig, Hendewerk, Köster (after the Jewish expositors, Jarchi, Aben-Ezra, Kimchi, Abarbanel, Lipmann), the subject of the prophecy is the Israelitish people. According to Eckermann, Ewald, Bleek, it is the ideal Israelitish people. According to Paulus, Ammon, Maurer, Thenius, Knobel, it is the godly portion of the Israelitish people. According to De Wette, Gesenius, Schenkel, Umbreit, Hofmann, it is the prophetical body. Augusti refers it to king Uzziah; Konynenburg and Bahrdt to Hezekiah; Stäudlin to Isaiah himself; Bolten to the house of David. Ewald thinks that no

historical person was intended, but that the author of the chapter has misled his readers by inserting a passage from an older book, in which a martyr was spoken of. " This," he says, " quite spontaneously suggested itself, and has impressed itself on his mind more and more; " and he thinks that " controversy on chap. liii. will never cease until this truth is acknowledged " (*Propheten*, ii. 8. 407). Hengstenberg gives the following list of German commentators who have maintained the Messianic explanation: Dathe, Hensler, Kocher, Koppe, Michaelis, Schmieder, Storr, Hansi, Krüger, Jahn, Steudel, Sack, Reinke, Tholuck, Hävernick, Stier. Hengstenberg's own exposition, and criticism of the expositions of others, is well worth consultation (*Christology*, vol. ii.).

[b] Obadiah is generally considered to have lived at a later date than is compatible with a chronological ar

Zechariah, Malachi. Dr. Stanley (*Lect.* xix.) in the following order: Joel, Jonah, Hosea, Amos, Isaiah, Micah, Nahum, Zechariah, Zephaniah, Habakkuk, Obadiah, Jeremiah, Ezekiel, Isaiah, Daniel, Haggai, Zechariah, Malachi. Whence it appears that Dr. Stanley recognizes two Isaiahs and two Zechariahs, unless "the author of Is. xl.-lxvi. is regarded as the older Isaiah transported into a style and position later than his own time" (p. 423).

VIII. PROPHETS OF THE NEW TESTAMENT. — So far as their predictive powers are concerned, the Old Testament prophets find their New Testament counterpart in the writer of the Apocalypse [REVELATION OF ST. JOHN; ANTICHRIST]; but in their general character, as specially illumined revealers of God's will, their counterpart will rather be found, first in the Great Prophet of the Church, and his forerunner John the Baptist, and next in all those persons who were endowed with the extraordinary gifts of the Spirit in the Apostolic age, the speakers with tongues and the interpreters of tongues, the prophets and the discerners of spirits, the teachers and workers of miracles (1 Cor. xii. 10, 28). The connecting link between the O. T. prophet and the speaker with tongues is the state of ecstasy in which the former at times received his visions and in which the latter uttered his words. The O. T. prophet, however, was his own interpreter: he did not speak in the state of ecstasy: he saw his visions in the ecstatic and declared them in the ordinary state. The N. T. discerner of spirits has his prototype in such as Micaiah the son of Imlah (1 K. xxii. 22), the worker of miracles in Elijah and Elisha, the teacher in each and all of the prophets. The prophets of the N. T. represented their namesakes of the O. T. as being expounders of Divine truth and interpreters of the Divine will to their auditors.

That predictive powers did occasionally exist in the N. T. prophets is proved by the case of Agabus (Acts xi. 28), but this was not their characteristic. They were not an order, like apostles, bishops or presbyters, and deacons, but they were men or women (Acts xxi. 9) who had the χάρισμα προφητείας vouchsafed them. If men, they might at the same time be apostles (1 Cor. xiv.); and there was nothing to hinder the different χαρίσματα of wisdom, knowledge, faith, teaching, miracles, prophecy, discernment, tongues, and interpretation (1 Cor. xii.) being all accumulated on one person, and this person might or might not be a presbyter. St. Paul describes prophecy as being effective for the conversion, apparently the sudden and immediate conversion, of unbelievers (1 Cor. xiv. 24), and for the instruction and consolation of believers (*Ibid.* 31). This shows its nature. It was a spiritual gift which enabled men to understand and to teach the truths of Christianity, especially as veiled in the Old Testament, and to exhort and warn with authority and effect greater than human (see Locke, *Paraphrase*, note on 1 Cor. xii., and Conybeare and Howson, i. 461). The prophets of the N. T. were supernaturally-illuminated expounders and preachers.

S. Augustinus, *De Civitate Dei*, lib. xviii. c. xxvii. *et seq.*, *Op.* tom. vii. p. 508, Paris, 1685. J. G. Carpzovius, *Introd. ad Libros Canonicos*,

Lips. 1757. John Smith, *Select Discourses: On Prophecy*, p. 179, Lond. 1821, and prefixed in Latin to Le Clerc's *Commentary*, Amst. 1731. Lowth, *De Sacra Poesi Hebraeorum*, Oxon. 1821, and translated by Gregory, Lond. 1835. Davison, *Discourses on Prophecy*, Oxf. 1839. Butler, *Analogy of Religion*, Oxf. 1849. Horsley, *Biblical Criticism*, Lond. 1820. Horne, *Introduction to Holy Scripture*, c. iv. § 3, Lond. 1828. Van Mildert, *Boyle Lectures*, S. xxii., Lond. 1831. Eichhorn, *Die Hebräischen Propheten*, Gütting. 1816. Knobel, *Der Prophetismus der Hebräer*, Bresl. 1837. Köster, *Die Propheten des A. und N. T.*, Leipz. 1838. Ewald, *Die Propheten des Alten Bundes*, Stuttg. 1840. Hofmann, *Weissagung und Erfüllung im A. und N. T.*, Nördl. 1841. Hengstenberg, *Christology of the Old Testament*, in T. T. Clark's Translation, Edinb. 1854. Fairbairn, *Prophecy, its Nature, Functions, and Interpretation*, Edinb. 1856. Lee, *Inspiration of Holy Scripture*, Lond. 1857. Oehler, art. *Prophetenthum des A. T.* in Herzog's *Real-Encyklopädie*, Goth. 1860. Pusey, *The Minor Prophets*, Oxf. 1861. *Aids to Faith*, art. "Prophecy" and "Inspiration," Lond. 1861. R. Payne Smith, *Messianic Interpretation of the Prophecies of Isaiah*, Oxf. 1862. Davidson, *Introduction to the Old Testament*, ii. 422, "On Prophecy," Lond. 1862. Stanley, *Lectures on the Jewish Church*, Lond. 1863.   F. M.

* A few other works may be added to the preceding list. Umbreit, *Die Propheten des A. Test. die ältesten u. würdigsten Volksredner*, in the *Studien u. Kritiken* for 1833, pp. 1043-1056. Hävernick, *Vorlesungen üb. die Theol. des A. Test.* (1848), pp. 145-175. J. L. Saalschütz, *Das Mosaische Recht*, i. 128 ff. A. Tholuck, *Die Propheten u. ihre Weissagungen* (1861), and *Theol. Encyklopädia*, transl. by Prof. E. A. Park in the *Bibl. Sacra*, i. 361 ff. F. R. Hasse, *Geschichte des A. Bundes*, especially pp. 93-211. K. F. Keil, *Lehrbuch der Einl. in das A. Test.*, pp. 138-316 (1859). Fr. Bleek, *Einleitung in das A. Test.*, pp. 409-611 (1860). Fronmüller, *Propheten*, in Zeller's *Bibl. Wörterbuch*, ii. 284-292 (an excellent summary). F. D. Maurice, *Prophets and Kings of the Old Test.* (2d ed. Bost. 1853). M. Stuart, *Hints on the Interpretation of Prophecy* (Andover, 1844). Prof. E. P. Barrows, *The Element of Time in Prophecy*, in the *Bibl. Sacra*, xii. 789-821. Isaac Taylor, *The Spirit of Hebrew Poetry*, pp. 239-354 (N. Y. 1862). Dr. Thomas Arnold, *Two Sermons on the Interpretation of Prophecy*, with Notes and two Appendices, in his *Works*, i. 373-456 (Lond. 1845).

For works more especially on the Messianic Prophecies, see the literature under MESSIAH (Amer. ed.). For Commentaries on particular prophets see their names in the *Dictionary*.   H.

* PROPHETS, SCHOOLS OF THE. [PROPHETS, p. 2592 f.]

PROSELYTES (גֵּרִים: προσήλυτοι, 1 Chr. xxii. 2, &c.; γειόραι, Ex. xii. 19: *Proselyti*). The Hebrew word thus translated is in the A. V. commonly rendered "stranger" (Gen. xv. 13, Ex. ii. 22, Is. v. 17, &c.). The LXX., as above, commonly gives the equivalent in meaning (προσήλυ-

---

rangement of the canon, in consequence of his reference to the capture of Jerusalem. But such an inference is not necessary, for the prophet might have thrown himself in imagination forward to the date of

his prophecy (Hengstenberg), or the words which, as translated by the A. V., are a remonstrance as to the past, may be really but an imperative as to the future (Pusey).

τοι ἀπὸ τοῦ προσεληλυθέναι καιν; καὶ φιλοθέῳ πολιτείᾳ, Philo and Suidas, s. v.), but sometimes substitutes a Hellenized form (γειώρας) of the Aramaic form גִּיּוֹרָא. In the N. T. the A. V. has taken the word in a more restricted meaning, and translated it accordingly (Matt. xxiii. 15, Acts ii. 10, vi. 5).

The existence, through all stages of the history of the Israelites, of a body of men, not of the same race, but holding the same faith and adopting the same ritual, is a fact which, from its very nature, requires to be dealt with historically. To start with the technical distinctions and regulations of the later Rabbis is to invert the natural order, and leads to inevitable confusion. It is proposed accordingly to consider the condition of the proselytes of Israel in the five great periods into which the history of the people divides itself, namely, (I.) the age of the patriarchs; (II.) from the Exodus to the commencement of the monarchy; (III.) the period of the monarchy; (IV.) from the Babylonian captivity to the destruction of Jerusalem; (V.) from the destruction of Jerusalem downwards.

I. The position of the family of Israel as a distinct nation, with a special religious character, appears at a very early period to have exercised a power of attraction over neighboring races. The slaves and soldiers of the tribe of which Abraham was the head (Gen. xvii. 27), who were included with him in the covenant of circumcision, can hardly perhaps be classed as proselytes in the later sense. The case of the Shechemites, however (Gen. xxxiv.), presents a more distinct instance. The converts are swayed partly by passion, partly by interest. The sons of Jacob then, as afterwards, require circumcision as an indispensable condition (Gen. xxxiv. 14). This, and apparently this only, was required of proselytes in the pre-Mosaic period.

II. The life of Israel under the Law, from the very first, presupposes and provides for the incorporation of men of other races. The "mixed multitude" of Ex. xii. 38 implies the presence of proselytes more or less complete. It is recognized in the earliest rules for the celebration of the Passover (Ex. xii. 19). The "stranger" of this and other laws in the A. V. answers to the word which distinctly means "proselyte," and is so translated in the LXX., and the prominence of the class may be estimated by the frequency with which the word recurs: 9 times in Exodus, 20 in Leviticus, 11 in Numbers, 19 in Deuteronomy. The laws clearly point to the position of a convert. The "stranger" is bound by the law of the Sabbath (Ex. xx. 10, xxiii. 12; Deut. v. 14). Circumcision is the condition of any fellowship with him (Ex. xii. 48; Num. ix. 14). He is to be present at the Passover (Ex. xii. 19), the Feast of Weeks (Deut. xvi. 11), the Feast of Tabernacles (Deut. xvi. 14), the Day of Atonement (Lev. xvi. 29). The laws of prohibited marriages (Lev. xviii. 26) and abstinence from blood (Lev. xvii. 10) are binding upon him. He is liable to the same punishment for Molech-worship (Lev. xx. 2), and for blasphemy (Lev. xxiv. 16) may claim the same right of asylum as the Israelites in the cities of refuge (Num. xxxv. 15; Josh. xx. 9). On the other side he is subjected to some drawbacks. He cannot hold land (Lev. xix. 10). He has no jus connubii with the descendants of Aaron (Lev. xxi. 14). His condition is assumed to be, for the most part, one of poverty (Lev. xxiii. 22), often of servitude (Deut. xxix. 11). For this reason he is

placed under the special protection of the Law (Deut. x. 18). He is to share in the right of gleaning (Lev. xix. 10), is placed in the same category as the fatherless and the widow (Deut. xxiv. 17, 19, xxvi. 12, xxvii. 19), is joined with the Levite as entitled to the tithe of every third year's produce (Deut. xiv. 29, xxvi. 12). Among the proselytes of this period the KENITES, who under HOBAB accompanied the Israelites in their wanderings, and ultimately settled in Canaan, were probably the most conspicuous (Judg. i. 16). The presence of the class was recognized in the solemn declaration of blessings and curses from Ebal and Gerizim (Josh. viii. 33).

The period after the conquest of Canaan was not favorable to the admission of proselytes. The people had no strong faith, no commanding position. The Gibeonites (Josh. ix.) furnish the only instance of a conversion, and their condition is rather that of slaves compelled to conform than of free proselytes. [NETHINIM.]

III. With the monarchy, and the consequent fame and influence of the people, there was more to attract stragglers from the neighboring nations, and we meet accordingly with many names which suggest the presence of men of another race conforming to the faith of Israel. Doeg the Edomite (1 Sam. xxi. 7), Uriah the Hittite (2 Sam. xi. 3), Araunah the Jebusite (2 Sam. xxiv. 23), Zelek the Ammonite (2 Sam. xxiii. 37), Ithmah the Moabite (1 Chr. xi. 46) — these two, in spite of an express law to the contrary (Deut. xxiii. 3) — and at a later period Shebna the scribe (probably, comp. Alexander on Is. xxii. 15), and Ebed-Melech the Ethiopian (Jer. xxxviii. 7), are examples that such proselytes might rise even to high offices about the person of the king. The CHERETHITES and PELETHITES consisted probably of foreigners who had been attracted to the service of David, and were content for it to adopt the religion of their master (Ewald, Gesch. i. 330, iii. 183). The vision in Ps lxxxvii. of a time in which men of Tyre, Egypt, Ethiopia, Philistia, should all be registered among the citizens of Zion, can hardly fail to have had its starting-point in some admission of proselytes within the memory of the writer (Ewald and De Wette, in loc.). A convert of another kind, the type, as it has been thought, of the later proselytes of the gate (see below), is found in Naaman the Syrian (2 K. v. 15, 18) recognizing Jehovah as his God, yet not binding himself to any rigorous observance of the Law.

The position of the proselytes during this period appears to have undergone considerable changes. On the one hand men rose, as we have seen, to power and fortune. The case for which the Law provided (Lev. xxv. 47) might actually occur, and they might be the creditors of Israelite debtors, the masters of Israelite slaves. It might well be a sign of the times in the later days of the monarchy that they became "very high," the "head" and not the "tail" of the people (Deut. xxviii. 43, 44). The picture had, however, another side. They were treated by David and Solomon as a subjectclass, brought (like Pericœci, almost like Helots) under a system of compulsory labor from which others were exempted (1 Chr. xxii. 2; 2 Chr. ii. 17, 18). The statistics of this period, taken probably for that purpose, give their number (probably, i. e. the number of adult working males) at 153,600 (ibid.). They were subject at other times to wanton insolence and outrage (Ps. xciv. 6). As some compensation for their sufferings they became the special objects of the care and sympathy of the prophets. One after another of the "goodly fellowship" pleads the cause of the proselytes as warmly as that of the widow and the fatherless (Jer. vii. 6, xxii. 3; Ez. xxii. 7, 29; Zech. vii. 10; Mal. iii. 5). A large accession of converts enters into all their hopes of the Divine Kingdom (Is. ii. 2, xi. 10, lvi. 3–6; Mic. iv. 1). The sympathy of one of them goes still further. He sees, in the far future, the vision of a time when the last remnant of inferiority shall be removed, and the proselytes, completely emancipated, shall be able to hold and inherit land even as the Israelites (Ez. xlvii. 22).[a]

IV. The proselytism of the period after the Captivity assumed a different character. It was for the most part the conformity, not of a subject race, but of willing adherents. Even as early as the return from Babylon we have traces of those who were drawn to a faith which they recognized as holier than their own, and had "separated themselves" unto the law of Jehovah (Neh. x. 28). The presence of many foreign names among the NETHINIM (Neh. vii. 46–59) leads us to believe that many of the new converts dedicated themselves specially to the service of the new Temple. With the conquests of Alexander, the wars between Egypt and Syria, the struggle under the Maccabees, the expansion of the Roman empire, the Jews became more widely known and their power to proselytize increased. They had suffered for their religion in the persecution of Antiochus, and the spirit of martyrdom was followed naturally by propagandism. Their monotheism was rigid and unbending. Scattered through the east and west, a marvel and a portent, wondered at and scorned, attracting and repelling, they presented, in an age of shattered creeds, and corroding doubts, the spectacle of a faith, or at least a dogma, which remained unshaken. The influence was sometimes obtained well, and exercised for good. In most of the great cities of the empire, there were men who had been rescued from idolatry and its attendant debasements, and brought under the power of a higher moral law. It is possible that in some cases the purity of Jewish life may have contributed to this result, and attracted men or women who shrank from the unutterable contamination, in the midst of which they lived.[b] The converts who were thus attracted, joined; with varying strictness (infra) in the worship of the Jews. They were present in their synagogues (Acts xiii. 42, 43, 50, xvii. 4, xviii. 7). They came up as pilgrims to the great feasts at Jerusalem (Acts ii. 10). In Palestine itself the influence was often stronger and better. Even Roman centurions learnt to love the conquered nation, built synagogues for them (Luke vii. 5), fasted and prayed, and gave alms, after the pattern of the strictest Jews (Acts x. 2, 30), and became preachers of the new faith to the soldiers under them (ibid. v. 7). Such men, drawn by what was best in Judaism, were naturally among

the readiest receivers of the new truth which rose out of it, and became, in many cases, the nucleus of a Gentile Church.

Proselytism had, however, its darker side. The Jews of Palestine were eager to spread their faith by the same weapons as those with which they had defended it. Had not the power of the Empire stood in the way, the religion of Moses, stripped of its higher elements, might have been propagated far and wide, by force, as was afterwards the religion of Mohammed. As it was, the Idumæans had the alternative offered them by John Hyrcanus of death, exile, or circumcision (Joseph. Ant. xiii. 9, § 3). The Ituræans were converted in the same way by Aristobulus (ibid. xiii. 11, § 3). In the more frenzied fanaticism of a later period, the Jews under Josephus could hardly be restrained from seizing and circumcising two chiefs of Trachonitis who had come as envoys (Joseph. Vit. p. 23). They compelled a Roman centurion, whom they had taken prisoner, to purchase his life by accepting the sign of the covenant (Joseph. B. J. ii. 11, § 10). Where force was not in their power (the "veluti Judæi, cogemus" of Hor. Sat. i. 4, 142, implies that they sometimes ventured on it even at Rome), they obtained their ends by the most unscrupulous fraud. They appeared as soothsayers, diviners, exorcists, and addressed themselves especially to the fears and superstitions of women. Their influence over these became the subject of indignant satire (Juv. Sat. vi. 543–547). They persuaded noble matrons to send money and purple to the Temple (Joseph. Ant. xviii. 3, § 5). At Damascus the wives of nearly half the population were supposed to be tainted with Judaism (Joseph. B. J. ii. 10, § 2). At Rome they numbered in their ranks, in the person of Poppæa, even an imperial concubine (Joseph. Ant. xx. 7, § 11). The converts thus made, cast off all ties of kindred and affection (Tac. Hist. v. 9). Those who were most active in proselytizing were precisely those from whose teaching all that was most true and living had departed. The vices of the Jew were engrafted on the vices of the heathen. A repulsive casuistry released the convert from obligations which he had before recognized,[c] while in other things he was bound, hand and foot, to an unhealthy superstition. It was no wonder that he became "twofold more the child of Gehenna" (Matt. xxiii. 15) than the Pharisees themselves.

The position of such proselytes was indeed every way pitiable. At Rome, and in other large cities, they became the butts of popular scurrility. The words "curtus," "verpes," met them at every corner (Hor. Sat. i. 4, 142; Mart. vii. 29, 34, 81, xi. 95, xii. 37). They had to share the fortunes of the people with whom they had cast in their lot, might be banished from Italy (Acts xviii. 2; Suet. Claud. p. 25), or sent to die of malaria in the most unhealthy stations of the empire (Tac. Ann. ii. 85). At a later time, they were bound to make a public profession of their conversion, and to pay a special tax (Suet. Domit. xii.). If they failed to do this and were suspected, they might

a The significance of this passage in its historical connection with Ps. lxxxvii , already referred to, and its spiritual fulfillment in the language of St. Paul (Eph. ii. 19), deserve a fuller notice than they have yet received.

b This influence is not perhaps to be altogether excluded, but it has sometimes been enormously exaggerated. Comp. Dr. Temple's "Essay on the Education of the World" (Essays and Reviews, p. 12).

c The Law of the Corban may serve as one instance (Matt. xv. 4–6). Another is found in the Rabbinic teaching as to marriage. Circumcision, like a new birth, canceled all previous relationships, and unions within the nearest degrees of blood were therefore no longer incestuous (Maimon. ex Jebam. p. 982; Selden, de Jure Nat. et Gent. ii. 4; Uxor Hebr. ii. 18).

be subject to the most degrading examination to ascertain the fact of their being proselytes (*ibid.*). Among the Jews themselves their case was not much better. For the most part the convert gained but little honor even from those who gloried in having brought him over to their sect and party. The popular Jewish feeling about them was like the popular Christian feeling about a converted Jew. They were regarded (by a strange Rabbinic perversion of Is. xiv. 1) as the leprosy of Israel, " cleaving " to the house of Jacob (*Jebam.* 47, 4; *Kiddush.* 70, 6). An opprobrious proverb coupled them with the vilest profligates (" proselyti et pæderastæ ") as hindering the coming of the Messiah (Lightfoot, *Hor. Heb.* in Matt. xxiii. 5). It became a recognized maxim that no wise man would trust a proselyte even to the twenty-fourth generation (*Jalkuth Ruth*, f. 163 a).

The better Rabbis did their best to guard against these evils. Anxious to exclude all unworthy converts, they grouped them, according to their motives, with a somewhat quaint classification.

(1.) Love-proselytes, where they were drawn by the hope of gaining the beloved one. (The story of Syllæus and Salome, Joseph. *Ant.* xvi. 7, § 6, is an example of a half-finished conversion of this kind.)

(2.) Man-for-Woman, or Woman-for-Man proselytes, where the husband followed the religion of the wife, or conversely.

(3.) Esther-proselytes, where conformity was assumed to escape danger, as in the original Purim (Esth. viii. 17).

(4.) King's-table-proselytes, who were led by the hope of court favor and promotion, like the converts under David and Solomon.

(5.) Lion-proselytes, where the conversion originated in a superstitious dread of a divine judgment, as with the Samaritans of 2 K. xvii. 26.

(Gem. Hieros. *Kiddush.* 65, 6; Jost, *Judenth.* i. p. 448.) None of these were regarded as fit for admission within the covenant. When they met with one with whose motives they were satisfied, he was put to a yet further ordeal. He was warned that in becoming a Jew he was attaching himself to a persecuted people, that in this life he was to expect only suffering, and to look for his reward in the next. Sometimes these cautions were in their turn carried to an extreme, and amounted to a policy of exclusion. A protest against them on the part of a disciple of the Great Hillel is recorded, which throws across the dreary rubbish of Rabbinism the momentary gleam of a noble thought. " Our wise men teach," said Simon ben Gamaliel, " that when a heathen comes to enter into the covenant, our part is to stretch out our hand to him and to bring him under the wings of God " (Jost, *Judenth.* i. 447).

Another mode of meeting the difficulties of the case was characteristic of the period. Whether we may transfer to it the full formal distinction between Proselytes of the Gate and Proselytes of Righteousness (*infra*) may be doubtful enough, but we find two distinct modes of thought, two distinct policies in dealing with converts. The history of Helena, queen of Adiabene, and her son Izates, presents the two in collision with each other. They had been converted by a Jewish merchant, Ananias, but the queen feared lest the circumcision of her son should disquiet and alarm her subjects.

Ananias assured her that it was not necessary. Her son might worship God, study the Law, keep the commandments, without it. Soon, however, a stricter teacher came, Eleazar of Galilee. Finding Izates reading the Law, he told him sternly that it was of little use to study that which he disobeyed, and so worked upon his fears, that the young devotee was eager to secure the safety of which his uncircumcision had deprived him (Joseph. *Ant.* xx. 2, § 5; Jost, *Judenth.* i. 341). On the part of some, therefore, there was a disposition to dispense with what others looked on as indispensable. The centurions of Luke vii. (probably) and Acts x., possibly the Hellenes of John xii. 20 and Acts xiii. 42, are instances of men admitted on the former footing. The phrases οἱ σεβόμενοι προσήλυτοι (Acts xiii. 43), οἱ σεβόμενοι (xvii. 4, 17; Joseph. *Ant.* xiv. 7, § 2), ἄνδρες εὐλαβεῖς (Acts ii. 5, vii. 2) are often, but inaccurately, supposed to describe the same class — the Proselytes of the Gate. The probability is, either that the terms were used generally of all converts, or, if with a specific meaning, were applied to the full Proselytes of Righteousness (comp. a full examination of the passages in question by N. Lardner, *On the Decree of Acts* xv.; Works xi. 305). The two tendencies were, at all events, at work, and the battle between them was renewed afterwards on holier ground and on a wider scale. Ananias and Eleazar were represented in the two parties of the Council of Jerusalem. The germ of truth had been quickened into a new life, and was emancipating itself from the old thraldom. The decrees of the Council were the solemn assertion of the principle that believers in Christ were to stand on the footing of Proselytes of the Gate, not of Proselytes of Righteousness. The teaching of St. Paul as to righteousness and its conditions, its dependence on faith, its independence of circumcision, stands out in sharp clear contrast with the teachers who taught that that rite was necessary to salvation, and confined the term "righteousness" to the circumcised convert.

V. The teachers who carried on the Rabbinical succession consoled themselves, as they saw the new order waxing and their own glory waning, by developing the decaying system with an almost microscopic minuteness. They would at least transmit to future generations the full measure of the religion of their fathers. In proportion as they ceased to have any power to proselytize, they dwelt with exhaustive fullness on the question how proselytes were to be made. To this period accordingly belong the rules and decisions which are often carried back to an earlier age, and which may now be conveniently discussed. The precepts of the Talmud may indicate the practices and opinions of the Jews from the 2d to the 5th century. They are very untrustworthy as to any earlier time. The points of interest which present themselves for inquiry are, (1.) The classification of Proselytes. (2.) The ceremonies of their admission.

The division which has been in part anticipated, was recognized by the Talmudic Rabbis, but received its full expansion at the hands of Maimonides (*Hilc. Mel.* i. 6). They claimed for it a remote antiquity, a divine authority. The term Proselytes of the Gate (בְּרֵי הַשַׁעַר), was derived from the frequently occurring description in the Law, "the stranger (גֵּר) that is within thy gates" (Ex. xx. 10, &c.). They were known also as the sojourners (גֵּרֵי תוֹשָׁב), with a reference to Lev. xxv. 47, &c. To them were referred the greater part of the precepts of the Law as to the "stranger." The Targums of Onkelos and Jonathan give this as the equivalent in Deut. xxiv. 21. Converts of this class were not bound by circumcision and the other special laws of the Mosaic code. It was enough for them to observe the seven precepts of Noah (Otho, *Lex. Rabb.* "Noachida;" Selden, *De Jur. Nat. et Gent.* i. 10), *i. e.* the six supposed to have been given to Adam, (1) against idolatry, (2) against blaspheming, (3) against bloodshed, (4) against uncleanness, (5) against theft, (6) of obedience, with (7) the prohibition of "flesh with the blood thereof" given to Noah. The proselyte was not to claim the privileges of an Israelite, might not redeem his first-born, or pay the half-shekel (Leyrer, *ut inf.*). He was forbidden to study the Law under pain of death (Otho, *l. c.*). The later Rabbis, when Jerusalem had passed into other hands, held that it was unlawful for him to reside within the holy city (Maimon. *Beth-haccher.* vii. 14). In return they allowed him to offer whole burnt-offerings for the priest to sacrifice, and to contribute money to the Corban of the Temple. They held out to him the hope of a place in the paradise of the world to come (Leyrer). They insisted that the profession of his faith should be made solemnly in the presence of three witnesses (Maimon. *Hilc. Mel.* viii. 10). The Jubilee was the proper season for his admission (Müller, *De Pros.* in Ugolini xxii. 841).

All this seems so full and precise, that we cannot wonder that it has led many writers to look on it as representing a reality, and most commentators accordingly have seen these Proselytes of the Gate in the σεβόμενοι, εὐλαβεῖς, φοβούμενοι τὸν Θεόν of the Acts. It remains doubtful, however, whether it was ever more than a paper scheme of what ought to be, disguising itself as having actually been. The writers who are most full, who claim for the distinction the highest antiquity, confess that there had been no Proselytes of the Gate since the Two Tribes and a half had been carried away into captivity (Maimon. *Hilc. Melc.* i. 6). They could only be admitted at the jubilee, and there had since then been no jubilee celebrated (Müller, *l. c.*). All that can be said, therefore, is, that in the time of the N. T. we have independent evidence (*ut supra*) of the existence of converts of two degrees, and that the Talmudic division is the formal systematizing of an earlier fact. The words "proselytes," and οἱ σεβόμενοι τὸν Θεόν, were, however, in all probability limited to the circumcised.

In contrast with these were the Proselytes of Righteousness (גֵּרֵי הַצֶּדֶק), known also as Proselytes of the Covenant, perfect Israelites. By some writers the Talmudic phrase *proselyti tracti* (גְּרוּרִים) is applied to them as *drawn* to the covenant by spontaneous conviction (Buxtorf, *Lexic.* s. v.), while others (Kimchi) refer it to those who were constrained to conformity, like the Gibeonites. Here also we must receive what we find with the same limitation as before. All seems at

first clear and definite enough. The proselyte was first catechised as to his motives (Maimon. *ut supra*). If these were satisfactory, he was first instructed as to the Divine protection of the Jewish people, and then circumcised. In the case of a convert already circumcised (a Midianite, *e. g.* or an Egyptian), it was still necessary to draw a few drops of "the blood of the covenant" (Gem. Bab. *Shabb.* f. 135 *a*). A special prayer was appointed to accompany the act of circumcision. Often the proselyte took a new name, opening the Hebrew Bible and accepting the first that came (Leyrer, *ut infr.*).

All this, however, was not enough. The convert was still "a stranger." His children would be counted as bastards, *i. e.* aliens. Baptism was required to complete his admission. When the wound was healed, he was stripped of all his clothes, in the presence of the three witnesses who had acted as his teachers, and who now acted as his sponsors, the "fathers" of the proselyte (*Ketubh.* xi., *Erubh.* xv. 1), and led into the tank or pool. As he stood there, up to his neck in water, they repeated the great commandments of the Law. These he promised and vowed to keep, and then, with an accompanying benediction, he plunged under the water. To leave one hand-breadth of his body unsubmerged would have vitiated the whole rite (Otho, *Lex. Rabb.* "Baptismus;" Reisk. *De Bapt. Pros.* in Ugolini xxii.). Strange as it seems, this part of the ceremony occupied, in the eyes of the later Rabbis, a coördinate place with circumcision. The latter was incomplete without it, for baptism also was of the fathers (Gem. Bab. *Jebam.* f. 461, 2). One Rabbi appears to have been bold enough to declare baptism to have been sufficient by itself (*ibid.*); but for the most part, both were reckoned as alike indispensable. They carried back the origin of the baptism to a remote antiquity, finding it in the command of Jacob (Gen. xxxv. 2) and of Moses (Ex. xix. 10). The Targum of the Pseudo-Jonathan inserts the word "Thou shalt circumcise and *baptize*" in Ex. xii. 44. Even in the Ethiopic version of Matt. xxiii. 1*b*, we find "compass sea and land to *baptise* one proselyte" (Winer, *Rwb.* s. v.). Language foreshadowing, or caricaturing, a higher truth was used of this baptism. It was a new birth[a] (*Jebam.* f. 62, 1; 92, 1; Maimon. *Issur. Bich.* c. 14; Lightfoot, *Harm. of Gospels*, iii. 14; *Exerc. on John* iii.). The proselyte became a little child. He received the Holy Spirit (*Jebam.* f. 22 *a*, 48 *b*.). All natural relationships, as we have seen, were canceled.

The baptism was followed, as long as the Temple stood, by the offering or Corban. It consisted, like the offerings after a birth (the analogy apparently being carried on), of two turtle-doves or pigeons (Lev. xii. 8). When the destruction of Jerusalem made the sacrifice impossible, a vow to offer it as soon as the Temple should be rebuilt was substituted. For women-proselytes, there were only baptism[b] and the Corban, or, in later times, baptism by itself.

It is obvious that this account suggests many questions of grave interest. Was this ritual observed as early as the commencement of the first century? If so, was the baptism of John, or that

---

[a] This thought probably had its starting-point in the language of Ps. lxxxvii. There also the proselytes of Babylon and Egypt are registered as "born" in Zion.

[b] The Galilean female proselytes were said to have objected to this, as causing barrenness (Winer, *Realwb.*).

of the Christian Church in any way derived from, or connected with the baptism of proselytes? If not, was the latter in any way borrowed from the former?

It would be impossible here, to enter at all into the literature of this controversy. The list of works named by Leyrer occupies nearly a page of Herzog's *Real-Encyclopädie*. It will be enough to sum up the conclusions which seem fairly to be drawn from them.

(1.) There is no *direct* evidence of the practice being in use before the destruction of Jerusalem. The statements of the Talmud as to its having come from the fathers, and their exegesis of the O. T. in connection with it, are alike destitute of authority.

(2.) The negative argument drawn from the silence of the O. T., of the Apocrypha, of Philo, and of Josephus, is almost decisive against the belief that there was in their time a baptism of proselytes, with *as much* importance attached to it as we find in the Talmudists.

(3.) It remains probable, however, that there was a baptism in use at a period considerably earlier than that for which we have direct evidence. The symbol was in itself natural and fit. It fell in with the disposition of the Pharisees and others to multiply and discuss "washings" (βαπτισμοί, Mark vii. 4) of all kinds. The tendency of the later Rabbis was rather to heap together the customs and traditions of the past than to invent new ones. If there had not been a baptism, there would have been no initiatory rite at all for female proselytes.

(4.) The history of the N. T. itself suggests the existence of such a custom. A sign is seldom chosen unless it already has a meaning for those to whom it is addressed. The fitness of the sign in this case would be in proportion to the associations already connected with it. It would bear witness, on the assumption of the previous existence of the proselyte-baptism, that the change from the then condition of Judaism to the kingdom of God was as great as that from idolatry to Judaism. The question of the Priests and Levites, "Why baptizest thou then?" (John i. 25), implies that they wondered, not at the thing itself, but at its being done for Israelites by one who disclaimed the names which, in their eyes, would have justified the introduction of a new order. In like manner the words of our Lord to Nicodemus (John iii. 10) imply the existence of a teaching as to baptism like that above referred to. He, "the teacher of Israel," had been familiar with "these things" — the new birth, the gift of the Spirit — as words and phrases applied to heathen proselytes. He failed to grasp the deeper truth which lay beneath them, and to see that they had a wider, an universal application.

(5.) It is, however, not improbable that there may have been a reflex action in this matter, from the Christian upon the Jewish Church. The Rabbis saw the new society, in proportion as the Gentile element in it became predominant, throwing off circumcision, relying on baptism only. They could not ignore the reverence which men had for the outward sign, their belief that it was all but identical with the thing signified. There was everything to lead them to give a fresh prominence to what had been before subordinate. If the Nazarenes attracted men by their baptism, they would show that they had baptism as well as circum-

cision. The necessary absence of the Corban after the destruction of the Temple would also tend to give more importance to the remaining rite.

Two facts of some interest remain to be noticed. (1.) It formed part of the Rabbinic hopes of the kingdom of the Messiah that then there should be no more proselytes. The distinctive name, with its brand of inferiority, should be laid aside, and all, even the Nethinim and the Manzerim (children of mixed marriages) should be counted pure (Schoettgen, *Hor. Heb.* ii. p. 614). (2.) Partly, perhaps, as connected with this feeling, partly in consequence of the ill-repute into which the word had fallen, there is, throughout the N. T., a sedulous avoidance of it. The Christian convert from heathenism is not a proselyte, but a νεόφυτος (1 Tim. iii. 6).

Literature. — Information more or less accurate is to be found in the Archæologies of Jahn, Carpzov, Saalschütz, Lewis, Leusden. The treatises cited above in Ugolini's *Thesaurus*, xxii.; Slevogt. *de Proselytis*; Müller, *de Proselytis*; Reisk. *de Bapt. Judæorum*; Danz. *Bapt. Proselyt.*, are all of them copious and interesting. The article by Leyrer in Herzog's *Real-Encyklop.* s. v. "Proselyten," contains the fullest and most satisfying discussion of the whole matter at present accessible. The writer is indebted to it for much of the materials of the present article, and for most of the Talmudic references.   E. H. P.

* For "religious" applied to "proselytes," (A. V.) Acts xiii. 43, the Greek has σεβόμενοι, "worshipping," sc. God and not idols as formerly. The English reader might suppose that some of the proselytes were meant to be distinguished as more religious than others. The same Greek term (ver. 50) describes "the women" at Antioch (called "devout" in the A. V.) as Jewish converts, and thus explains why the Jews could so easily instigate them (being at the same time wives of "the chief men") to persecute Paul and Barnabas, and drive them from the city. The same Greek term in Acts xvii. 4 and 17 ("devout," A. V.) states simply that the Greeks spoken of at Thessalonica and at Athens had been Jewish proselytes before their conversion to Christianity. On this use of σέβεσθαι as thus definite without an object, see Cremer's *Wörterb. der Neutest. Grācität*, ii. 476 (1868). The Jewish proselytes who embraced the gospel formed the principal medium through which Christianity passed to the Gentile races. See the addition to SYNAGOGUES (Amer. ed.).   H.

PROVERBS, BOOK OF. 1. *Title.* — The title of this book in Hebrew is, as usual, taken from the first word, מִשְׁלֵי, *mishlê*, or, more fully, מִשְׁלֵי שְׁלֹמֹה, *mishlê Shĕlômôh*, and is in this case appropriate to the contents. By this name it is commonly known in the Talmud; but among the later Jews, and even among the Talmudists themselves, the title סֵפֶר חָכְמָה, *sêpher chocmâh*, "book of wisdom," is said to have been given to it. It does not appear, however, from the passages of the *Tosephoth* to the *Baba Bathra* (fol. 14 b), that this is necessarily the case. All that is there said is that the books of Proverbs and Ecclesiastes are both "books of wisdom," with a reference rather to their contents than to the titles by which they were known. In the early Christian Church the title παροιμίαι Σολομῶντος was adopted from the translation of the LXX.; and the book is also quoted as σοφία, " wisdom," or ἡ πανάρετος σοφία, " wisdom that is the sum of all virtues." This last title is given to it by Clement in the *Ep. ad Cor.* i. 57, where Prov. i. 23–31 is quoted with the introduction οὕτως γὰρ λέγει ἡ πανάρετος σοφία; and Eusebius (*H. E.* iv. 22) says that not only Hegesippus, but Irenæus and the whole band of ancient writers, following the Jewish unwritten tradition, called the Proverbs of Solomon πανάρετον σοφίαν. According to Melito of Sardes (Euseb. *H. E.* iv. 26), the Proverbs were also called σοφία, " wisdom," simply; and Gregory of Nazianzus refers to them (*Orat.* xi.) as παιδαγωγικὴ σοφία. The title in the Vulgate is *Liber Proverbiorum, quem Hebræi Misle appellant.*

The significance of the Hebrew title may here be appropriately discussed. מָשָׁל, *mâshâl,* rendered in the A. V. " by-word," " parable," " proverb," expresses all and even more than is conveyed by these its English representatives. It is derived from a root, מָשַׁל, *mâshal,* " to be like," a and the primary idea involved in it is that of likeness, comparison. This form of comparison would very naturally be taken by the short pithy sentences which passed into use as popular sayings and proverbs, especially when employed in mockery and sarcasm, as in Mic. ii. 4, Hab. ii. 6, and even in the more developed taunting song of triumph for the fall of Babylon in Is. xiv. 4. Probably all proverbial sayings were at first of the nature of similes, but the term *mâshâl* soon acquired a more extended significance. It was applied to denote such short, pointed sayings, as do not involve a comparison directly, but still convey their meaning by the help of a figure, as in 1 Sam. x. 12, Ez. xii. 22, 23, xvii. 2, 3 (comp. παραβολή, Luke iv. 23). From this stage of its application it passed to that of sententious maxims generally, as in Prov. i. 1, x. 1, xxv. 1, xxvi. 7, 9, Eccl. xii. 9, Job xiii. 12, many of which, however, still involve a comparison (Prov. xxv. 3, 11, 12, 13, 14, &c., xxvi. 1, 2, 3, &c.). Such comparisons are either expressed, or the things compared are placed side by side, and the comparison left for the hearer or reader to supply. Next we find it used of those longer pieces in which a single idea is no longer exhausted in a sentence, but forms the germ of the whole, and is worked out into a didactic poem. Many instances of this kind occur in the first section of the Book of Proverbs: others are found in Job xxvii., xxix., in both which chapters Job takes up his *mâshâl,* or " parables," as it is rendered in the A. V. The " parable " of Balaam, in Num. xxiii. 7-10, xxiv. 3-9, 15-19, 20, 21-22, 23-24, are prophecies conveyed in figures; but *mâshâl* also denotes the " parable " proper, as in Ez. xvii. 2, xx. 49 (xxi. 5), xxiv. 3. Lowth, in his notes on Is. xiv. 4, speaking of *mâshâl,* says: " I take this to be the general name for poetic style among the Hebrews, including every sort of it, as ranging under one, or other, or all of the characters, of sententious, figurative, and sublime; which are all contained in the original notion, or in the use and application of the word

---

a Compare Arab. مَثَلَ, *mathala,* " to be like; " مِثْل, *mithl,* " likeness; " and the adj. مَثَل, *mathal,* " like." The cognate Æthiopic and Syriac roots have the same meaning.

mashal. Parables or proverbs, such as those of Solomon, are always expressed in short, pointed sentences; frequently figurative, being formed on some comparison, both in the matter and the form. And such in general is the style of the Hebrew poetry. The verb *mashal* signifies to rule, to exercise authority; to make equal, to compare one thing with another; to utter parables, or acute, weighty, and powerful speeches, in the form and manner of parables, though not properly such. Thus Balaam's first prophecy, Num. xxiii. 7-10, is called his *mashal;* though it has hardly anything figurative in it: but it is beautifully sententious, and, from the very form and manner of it, has great spirit, force, and energy. Thus Job's last speeches, in answer to the three friends, chaps. xxvii.-xxxi., are called *mashals,* from no one particular character which discriminates them from the rest of the poem, but from the sublime, the figurative, the sententious manner, which equally prevails through the whole poem, and makes it one of the first and most eminent examples extant of the truly great and beautiful in poetic style." But the Book of Proverbs, according to the introductory verses which describe its character, contains, besides several varieties of the *mâshâl,* sententious sayings of other kinds, mentioned in i. 6. The first of these is the חִידָה, *chîdâh,* rendered in the A. V. " dark saying," " dark speech," " hard question," " riddle," and once (Hab. ii. 6) " proverb." It is applied to Samson's riddle in Judg. xiv., to the hard questions with which the queen of Sheba plied Solomon (1 K. x. 1; 2 Chr. ix. 1), and is used almost synonymously with *mâshâl* in Ez. xvii. 2, and in Ps. xlix. 4 (5), lxxviii. 2, in which last passages the poetical character of both is indicated. The word appears to denote a knotty, intricate saying, the solution of which demanded experience and skill: that it was obscure is evident from Num. xii. 8. In addition to the *chîdâh* was the מְלִיצָה, *mêlîtzâh* (Prov. i. 6, A. V. " the interpretation," marg. " an eloquent speech "), which occurs in Hab. ii. 6 in connection both with *chîdâh* and *mâshâl.* It has been variously explained as a mocking, taunting speech (Ewald); or a speech dark and involved, such as needed a *mêlîts,* or interpreter (cf. Gen. xlii. 23; 2 Chr. xxxii. 31; Job xxxiii. 23; Is. xliii. 27); or again, as by Delitzsch (*Der prophet Habakuk,* p. 59), a brilliant or splendid saying (" Glanz- oder Wohlrede, *oratio splendida, elegans, luminibus ornata* "). This last interpretation is based upon the usage of the word in modern Hebrew, but it certainly does not appear appropriate to the Proverbs; and the first explanation, which Ewald adopts, is as little to the point. It is better to understand it as a dark enigmatical saying, which, like the *mâshâl,* might assume the character of sarcasm and irony, though not essential to it.

2. *Canonicity of the book and its place in the Canon.* — The canonicity of the Book of Proverbs has never been disputed except by the Jews themselves. It appears to have been one of the points urged by the school of Shammai, that the contradictions in the Book of Proverbs rendered it apocryphal. In the Talmud (*Shabbath,* fol. 30 b) it is said: " And even the Book of Proverbs they sought to make apocryphal, because its words were contradictory the one to the other. And wherefore did they not make it apocryphal? The words of the book Koheleth [are] not [apocryphal] we have

looked and found the sense; here also we must look." That is, the book Koheleth, in spite of the apparent contradictions which it contains, is allowed to be canonical, and therefore the existence of similar contradictions in the Book of Proverbs forms no ground for refusing to acknowledge its canonicity. It occurs in all the Jewish lists of canonical books, and is reckoned among what are called the "writings" (*Cethúbim*) or Hagiographa, which form the third great division of the Hebrew Scriptures. Their order in the Talmud (*Baba Bathra,* fol. 14 *b*) is thus given: Ruth, Psalms, Job, Proverbs, Ecclesiastes, Song of Songs, Lamentations, Daniel, Esther, Ezra (including Nehemiah), and Chronicles. It is in the *Tosephoth* on this passage that Proverbs and Ecclesiastes are styled "books of wisdom." In the German MSS. of the Hebrew O. T. the Proverbs are placed between the Psalms and Job, while in the Spanish MSS., which follow the Masorah, the order is, Psalms, Job, Proverbs. This latter is the order observed in the Alexandrian MS. of the LXX. Melito, following another Greek MS., arranges the Hagiographa thus : Psalms, Proverbs, Ecclesiastes, Song of Songs, Job, as in the list made out by the Council of Laodicea; and the same order is given by Origen, except that the Book of Job is separated from the others by the prophets Isaiah, Jeremiah, Daniel, and Ezekiel. But our present arrangement existed in the time of Jerome (see *Præf. in libr. Regum* iii.; "Tertius ordo ἁγιόγραφα possidet. Et primus liber incipit ab Job. Secundus a David. . . . . Tertius est Salomon, tres libros habens: Proverbia, quæ illi parabolas, id est Masaloth appellant: Ecclesiastes, id est, Coeleth: Canticum Canticorum, quem titulo Sir Asirim prænotant"). In the Peshito Syriac, Job is placed before Joshua, while Proverbs and Ecclesiastes follow the Psalms, and are separated from the Song of Songs by the Book of Ruth. Gregory of Nazianzus, apparently from the exigencies of his verse, arranges the writings of Solomon in this order, Ecclesiastes, Song of Songs, Proverbs. Pseudo-Epiphanius places Proverbs, Ecclesiastes, and Song of Songs between the 1st and 2d Books of Kings and the minor prophets. The Proverbs are frequently quoted or alluded to in the New Testament, and the canonicity of the book thereby confirmed. The following is a list of the principal passages : —

Prov. i. 16	compare	Rom. iii. 10, 15.
iii. 7	"	Rom. xii. 16.
iii. 11, 12	"	Heb. xii. 5, 6 ; see also Rev. iii. 19.
iii. 34	"	Jam. iv. 6.
x. 12	"	1 Pet. iv. 8.
xi. 31	"	1 Pet. iv. 18.
xvii. 13	"	Rom. xii. 17 ; 1 Thess. v. 15 ; 1 Pet. iii. 9.
xvii. 27	"	Jam. i. 19.
xx. 9	"	1 John i. 8.
xx. 20	"	Matt. xv. 4 ; Mark vii. 10.
xxii. 8 (LXX.)	"	2 Cor. ix. 7.
xxv. 21, 22	"	Rom. xii. 20.
xxvi. 11	"	2 Pet. ii. 22.
xxvii. 1	"	Jam. iv. 13, 14.

3. *Authorship and date.* — The superscriptions which are affixed to several portions of the Book of Proverbs, in i. 1, x. 1, xxv. 1, attribute the authorship of those portions to Solomon, the son of David, king of Israel. With the exception of the last two chapters, which are distinctly assigned to other authors, it is probable that the statement of the superscriptions is in the main correct, and

that the majority of the proverbs contained in the book were uttered or collected by Solomon. It was natural, and quite in accordance with the practice of other nations, that the Hebrews should connect Solomon's name with a collection of maxims and precepts which form a part of their literature to which he is known to have contributed most largely (1 K. iv. 32). In the same way the Greeks attributed most of their maxims to Pythagoras; the Arabs to Lokman, Abu Obeid, Al Mofaddel, Meidani, and Zamakhshari; the Persians to Ferid Attar; and the northern people to Odin. But there can be no question that the Hebrews were much more justified in assigning the Proverbs to Solomon, than the nations which have just been enumerated were in attributing the collections of national maxims to the traditional authors above mentioned. The parallel may serve as an illustration, but must not be carried too far. According to Bartolocci (*Bibl. Rabb.* iv. 373 *b*), quoted by Carpzov (*Introd.* pt. ii. c. 4, § 4), the Jews ascribe the composition of the Song of Songs to Solomon's youth, the Proverbs to his mature manhood, and the Ecclesiastes to his old age. But in the *Seder Olam Rabba* (ch. xv. p. 41, ed. Meyer) they are all assigned to the end of his life. There is nothing unreasonable in the supposition that many, or most of the proverbs in the first twenty-nine chapters may have originated with Solomon. Whether they were left by him in their present form is a distinct question, and may now be considered. Before doing so, however, it will be necessary to examine the different parts into which the book is naturally divided. Speaking roughly, it consists of three main divisions, with two appendices. 1. Chaps. i. - ix. form a connected *mâshâl,* in which Wisdom is praised and the youth exhorted to devote themselves to her. This portion is preceded by an introduction and title describing the character and general aim of the book. 2. Chaps. x. 1–xxiv., with the title, "the Proverbs of Solomon," consist of three parts: x. 1–xxii. 16, a collection of single proverbs, and detached sentences out of the region of moral teaching and worldly prudence; xxii. 17–xxiv. 21, a more connected *mâshâl,* with an introduction, xxii. 17–22, which contains precepts of righteousness and prudence: xxiv. 23–34, with the inscription, "these also belong to the wise," a collection of unconnected maxims, which serve as an appendix to the preceding. Then follows the third division, xxv.–xxix., which, according to the superscription, professes to be a collection of Solomon's proverbs, consisting of single sentences, which the men of the court of Hezekiah copied out. The first appendix, ch. xxx., "the words of Agur," is a collection of partly proverbial and partly enigmatical sayings; the second, ch. xxxi., is divided into two parts, "the words of king Lemuel" (1–6), and an alphabetical acrostic in praise of a virtuous woman, which occupies the rest of the chapter. Rejecting, therefore, for the present, the two last chapters, which do not even profess to be by Solomon, or to contain any of his teaching, we may examine the other divisions for the purpose of ascertaining whether any conclusion as to their origin and authorship can be arrived at. At first sight it is evident that there is a marked difference between the collections of single maxims and the longer didactic pieces, which both come under the general head *mâshâl.* The collection of Solomon's proverbs made by the men of Hezekiah (xxv.–xxix.) belongs to the former class of detached sentences, and in this respect corresponds with those in the second main division (x. 1-xxii. 16). The expression in xxv. 1, "these also are the proverbs of Solomon," implies that the collection was made as an appendix to another already in existence, which we may not unreasonably presume to have been that which stands immediately before it in the present arrangement of the book. Upon one point most modern critics are agreed, that the germ of the book in its present shape is the portion x. 1-xxii. 16, to which is prefixed the title, "the Proverbs of Solomon." At what time it was put into the form in which we have it, cannot be exactly determined. Ewald suggests as a probable date about two centuries after Solomon. The collector gathered many of that king's genuine sayings, but must have mixed with them many by other authors and from other times, earlier and later. It seems clear that he must have lived before the time of Hezekiah, from the expression in xxv. 1, to which reference has already been made. In this portion many proverbs are repeated in the same, or a similar form, a fact which of itself militates against the supposition that all the proverbs contained in it proceeded from one author. Compare xiv. 12 with xvi. 25 and xxi. 2ᵃ; xxi. 9 with xxi. 19; x. 1ᵃ with xv. 20ᵃ; x. 2ᵇ with xi. 4ᵇ; x. 15ᵃ with xviii. 11ᵃ; xv. 33ᵇ with xviii. 12ᵇ; xi. 21ᵃ with xvi. 5ᵇ; xiv. 31ᵃ with xvii. 5ᵃ; xix. 12ᵃ with xx 2ᵃ. Such repetitions, as Bertheau remarks, we do not expect to find in a work which proceeds immediately from the hands of its author. But if we suppose the contents of this portion of the book to have been collected by one man out of divers sources, oral as well as written, the repetitions become intelligible. Bertholdt argues that many of the proverbs could not have proceeded from Solomon, because they presuppose an author in different circumstances of life. His arguments are extremely weak, and will scarcely bear examination. For example, he asserts that the author of x. 5, xii. 10, 11, xiv. 4, xx. 4, must have been a landowner or husbandman; that x. 15 points to a man living in want; xi. 14, xiv. 20, to a private man living under a well-regulated government; xi. 26, to a tradesman without wealth; xii. 4, to a man not living in polygamy; xii. 9, to one living in the country; xiii. 7, 8, xvi. 8, to a man in a middle station of life; xiv. 1. xv. 25, xvi. 11, xvii. 2, xix. 13, 14, xx. 10, 14, 23, to a man of the rank of a citizen; xiv. 21, xvi. 19, xviii. 23, to a man of low station; xvi. 10, 12-15, xix. 12, xx. 2, 26, 28, to a man who was not a king; xxi. 5, to one who was acquainted with the course of circumstances in the common citizen life; xxi. 17, to one who was an enemy to luxury and festivities. It must be confessed, however, that an examination of these passages is by no means convincing to one who reads them without having a theory to maintain. That all the proverbs in this collection are not Solomon's is extremely probable; that the majority of them are his there seems no reason to doubt, and this fact would account for the general title in which they are all attributed to him. It is obvious that between the proverbs in this collection and those that precede and follow it, there is a marked difference, which is sufficiently apparent even in the English Version. The poetical style, says Ewald, is the simplest and most antique imaginable. Most of the proverbs are examples of antithetic parallelism, the second clause containing the contrast to the first. Each verse consists of two members, with generally three or four, but

seldom five words in each. The only exception to the first law is xix. 7, which Ewald accounts for by supposing a clause omitted. This supposition may be necessary to his theory, but cannot be admitted on any true principle of criticism. Furthermore, the proverbs in this collection have the peculiarity of being contained in a single verse. Each verse is complete in itself, and embodies a perfectly intelligible sentiment; but a thought in all its breadth and definiteness is not necessarily exhausted in a single verse, though each verse must be a perfect sentence, a proverb, a lesson. There is one point of great importance to which Ewald draws attention in connection with this portion of the book; that it is not to be regarded, like the collections of proverbs which exist among other nations, as an accumulation of the popular maxims of lower life which passed current among the people and were gathered thence by a learned man; but rather as the efforts of poets, artistically and scientifically arranged, to comprehend in short sharp sayings the truths of religion as applied to the infinite cases and possibilities of life. While admitting, however, this artistic and scientific arrangement, it is difficult to assent to Ewald's further theory, that the collection in its original shape had running through it a continuous thread, binding together what was manifold and scattered, and that in this respect it differed entirely from the form in which it appears at present. Here and there, it is true, we meet with verses grouped together apparently with a common object, but these are the exceptions, and a rule so general cannot be derived from them. No doubt the original collection of Solomon's proverbs, if such there were, from which the present was made, underwent many changes, by abbreviation, transposition, and interpolation, in the two centuries which, according to Ewald's theory, must have elapsed before the compiler of the present collection put them in the shape in which they have come down to us; but evidence is altogether wanting to show what that original collection may have been, or how many of the three thousand proverbs which Solomon is said to have spoken, have been preserved. There is less difficulty in another proposition of Ewald's, to which a ready assent will be yielded: that Solomon was the founder of this species of poetry: and that in fact many of the proverbs here collected may be traced back to him, while all are inspired with his spirit. The peace and internal tranquillity of his reign were favorable to the growth of a contemplative spirit, and it is just at such a time that we should expect to find gnomic poetry developing itself and forming an epoch in literature.

In addition to the distinctive form assumed by the proverbs of this earliest collection, may be noticed the occurrence of favorite and peculiar words and phrases. "Fountain of life" occurs in Prov. x. 11, xiii. 14, xiv. 27, xvi. 22 (comp. Ps. xxxvi. 9 [10]); "tree of life," Prov. xi. 30, xiii. 12, xv. 4 (comp. iii. 18); "snares of death," Prov. xiii. 14, xiv. 27 (comp. Ps. xviii. 5 [6]); מַרְפֵּא, marpé, "healing, health," Prov. xii. 18, xiii. 17, xvi. 24 (comp. xiv. 30, xv. 4), but this expression also occurs in iv. 22, vi. 15 (comp. iii. 8), and is hardly to be regarded as peculiar to the older portion of the book; nor is it fair to say that the passages in the early chapters in which it occurs are imitations; מְחִתָּה, mĕchittâh, "destruction," Prov. x. 14, 15, 29, xiii. 3, xiv. 28, xviii. 7, xxi. 15, and nowhere else in the book; יָפִיחַ, *yáphīdch*, which Ewald calls a participle, but which may be regarded as a future with the relative omitted, Prov. xii. 17, xiv. 5, 25, xix. 5, 9 (comp. vi. 19); סֶלֶף, *seleph*, "perverseness," Prov. xi. 3, xv. 4; סִלֵּף, *silléph*, the verb from the preceding, Prov. xiii. 6, xix. 3, xxii. 12; לֹא יִנָּקֶה, *lō yinnákeh*, "shall not be acquitted," Prov. xi. 21, xvi. 5, xvii. 5, xix. 5, 9 (comp. vi. 29, xxviii. 20); רָדַף, *rúdéph*, "pursued," Prov. xi. 19, xii. 11, xiii. 21, xv. 9, xix. 7 (comp. xxviii. 19). The antique expressions עַד אַרְגִּיעָה, '*ad argī́dh*, A. V., "but for a moment," Prov. xii. 19; יָד לְיָד, *yād lěyād*, lit. "hand to hand," Prov. xi. 21, xvi. 5; הִתְגַּלַּע, *hithgalla'*, "meddled with," Prov. xvii. 14, xviii. 1, xx. 3; נִרְגָּן, *nirgán*, "whisperer, talebearer," Prov. xvi. 28, xviii. 8 (comp. xxvi. 20, 22), are almost confined to this portion of the Proverbs. There is also the peculiar usage of יֵשׁ, *yēsh*, "there is," in Prov. xi. 24, xii. 18, xiii. 7, 23, xiv. 12, xvi. 25, xviii. 24, xx. 15. It will be observed that the use of these words and phrases by no means assists in determining the authorship of this section, but gives it a distinctive character.

With regard to the other collections, opinions differ widely both as to their date and authorship. Ewald places next in order chaps xxv.–xxix., the superscription to which fixes their date about the end of the 8th century B. C. "These also are the proverbs of Solomon, which the men of Hezekiah copied out," or compiled. The memory of these learned men of Hezekiah's court is perpetuated in Jewish tradition. In the Talmud (*Baba Buthra*, fol. 15 *a*) they are called the סִיעָה, *si'áh*, "society" or "academy" of Hezekiah, and it is there said, "Hezekiah and his academy wrote Isaiah, Proverbs, Song of Songs, Ecclesiastes." R. Gedaliah (*Shalsheleth Hakkabbakah*, fol. 66 *b*), quoted by Carpzov (*Introd.* part. ii. c. 4, § 4), says, "Isaiah wrote his own book and the Proverbs, and the Song of Songs, and Ecclesiastes." Many of the proverbs in this collection are mere repetitions, with slight variations, of some which occur in the previous section. Compare, for example, xxv. 24 with xxi. 9; xxvi. 13 with xxii. 13; xxvi. 15 with xix. 24; xxvi. 22 with xviii. 8; xxvii. 13 with xx. 16; xxvii. 15 with xix. 13; xxvii. 21 with xvii. 3; xxviii. 6 with xix. 1; xxviii. 19 with xii. 11; xxix. 22 with xv. 18, &c. We may infer from this, with Bertheau, that the compilers of this section made use of the same sources from which the earlier collection was derived. Hitzig (*Die Sprüche Slomo's*, p. 258) suggests that there is a probability that a great, or the greatest part of these proverbs were of Ephraimitic origin, and that after the destruction of the northern kingdom, Hezekiah sent his learned men through the land to gather together the fragments of literature which remained current among the people and had survived the general wreck. There does not appear to be the slightest ground, linguistic or otherwise, for this hypothesis, and it is therefore properly rejected by Bertheau. The question now arises, in this as in the former section: were all these proverbs Solomon's? Jahn says Yes; Bertholdt, No; for xxv. 2–7 could not have been

by Solomon or any king, but by a man who had lived for a long time at a court. In xxvii. 11, it is no monarch who speaks, but an instructor of youth; xxviii. 16 censures the very errors which stained the reign of Solomon, and the effect of which deprived his son and successor of the ten tribes; xxvii. 23–27 must have been written by a sage who led a nomad life. There is more force in these objections of Bertholdt than in those which he advanced against the previous section. Hensler (quoted by Bertholdt) finds two or three sections in this division of the book, which he regards as extracts from as many different writings of Solomon. But Bertholdt confesses that his arguments are not convincing.

The peculiarities of this section distinguish it from the older proverbs in x.–xxii. 16. Some of these may be briefly noted. The use of the interrogation "seest thou?" in xxvi. 12, xxix. 20 (comp. xxii. 29), the manner of comparing two things by simply placing them side by side and connecting them with the simple copula "and," as in xxv. 3, 20, xxvi. 3, 7, 9, 21, xxvii. 15, 20. We miss the pointed antithesis by which the first collection was distinguished. The verses are no longer of two equal members; one member is frequently shorter than the other, and sometimes even the verse is extended to three members in order fully to exhaust the thought. Sometimes, again, the same sense is extended over two or more verses, as in xxv. 4, 5, 6, 7, 8–10; and in a few cases a series of connected verses contains longer exhortations to morality and rectitude, as in xxvi. 23–28, xxvii. 23–27. The character of the proverbs is clearly distinct. Their construction is looser and weaker, and there is no longer that sententious brevity which gives weight and point to the proverbs in the preceding section. Ewald thinks that in the contents of this portion of the book there are traceable the marks of a later date; pointing to a state of society which had become more dangerous and hostile, in which the quiet domestic life had reached greater perfection, but the state and public security and confidence had sunk deeper. There is, he says, a cautious and mournful tone in the language when the rulers are spoken of; the breath of that untroubled joy for the king and the high reverence paid to him, which marked the former collection, does not animate these proverbs. The state of society at the end of the 8th century B. C., with which we are thoroughly acquainted from the writings of the prophets, corresponds with the condition of things hinted at in the proverbs of this section, and this may therefore, in accordance with the superscription, be accepted as the date at which the collection was made. Such is Ewald's conclusion. It is true we know much of the later times of the monarchy, and that the condition of those times was such as to call forth many of the proverbs of this section as the result of the observation and experience of their authors, but it by no means follows that the whole section partakes of this later tone; or that many or most of the proverbs may not reach back as far as the time of Solomon, and so justify the general title which is given to the section, "These also are the proverbs of Solomon." But of the state of society in the age of Solomon himself we know so little, everything belonging to that period is encircled with such a halo of dazzling splendor, in which the people almost disappear, that it is impossible to assert that the circumstances of the times might not have given birth to many of the maxims which apparently carry with them the marks of a later period. At best such reasoning from internal evidence is uncertain and hypothetical, and the inferences drawn vary with each commentator who examines it. Ewald discovers traces of a later age in chapters xxviii., xxix., though he retains them in this section, while Hitzig regards xxviii. 17-xxix. 27 as a continuation of xxii. 16, to which they were added probably after the year 750 B. C.[a] This apparent precision in the assignment of the dates of the several sections, it must be confessed, has very little foundation, and the dates are at best but conjectural. All that we know about the section xxv.-xxix., is that in the time of Hezekiah, that is, in the last quarter of the 8th century B. C. it was supposed to contain what tradition had handed down as the proverbs of Solomon, and that the majority of the proverbs were believed to be his there seems no good reason to doubt. Beyond this we know nothing. Ewald, we have seen, assigns the whole of this section to the close of the 8th century B. C., long before which time, he says, most of the proverbs were certainly not written. But he is then compelled to account for the fact that in the superscription they are called "the proverbs of Solomon." He does so in this way. Some of the proverbs actually reach back into the age of Solomon, and those which are not immediately traceable to Solomon or his time, are composed with similar artistic flow and impulse. If the earlier collection rightly bears the name of "the proverbs of Solomon" after the mass which are his, this may claim to bear such a title of honor after some important elements. The argument is certainly not sound, that, because a collection of proverbs, the majority of which are Solomon's, is distinguished by the general title "the proverbs of Solomon," therefore a collection, in which at most but a few belong to Solomon or his time, is appropriately distinguished by the same superscription. It will be seen afterwards that Ewald attributes the superscription in xxv. 1 to the compiler of xxii. 17-xxv. 1.

The date of the sections i.-ix., xxii. 17-xxv. 1, has been variously assigned. That they were added about the same period Ewald infers from the occurrence of favorite words and constructions, and that that period was a late one he concludes from the traces which are manifest of a degeneracy from the purity of the Hebrew. It will be interesting to examine the evidence upon this point, for it is a remarkable fact, and one which is deeply instructive as showing the extreme difficulty of arguing from internal evidence, that the same details lead Ewald and Hitzig to precisely opposite conclusions; the former placing the date of i.-ix. in the first half of the 7th century, while the latter regards it as the oldest portion of the book, and assigns it to the 9th century. To be sure those points on which Ewald relies as indicating a late date for the section, Hitzig summarily disposes of as interpolations. Among the favorite words which occur in these chapters are חָכְמוֹת, chocmôth, "wisdoms," for "wisdom" in the abstract, which is found only in i. 20, ix. 1,

xxiv. 7; זָרָה, zârâh, "the strange woman," and נָכְרִיָּה, nocryyâh, "the foreigner," the adulteress who seduces youth, the antithesis of the virtuous wife or true wisdom, only occur in the first collection in xxii. 14, but are frequently found in this, ii. 16, v. 3, 20, vi. 24, vii. 5, xxiii. 27. Traces of the decay of Hebrew are seen in such passages as v. 2, where שְׂפָתַיִם, a dual fem., is constructed with a verb masc. pl., though in v. 3 it has properly the feminine. The unusual plural אִישִׁים (viii. 4), says Ewald, would hardly be found in writings before the 7th century. These difficulties are avoided by Hitzig, who regards the passages in which they occur as interpolations. When we come to the internal historical evidence these two authorities are no less at issue with regard to their conclusions from it. There are many passages which point to a condition of things in the highest degree confused, in which robbers and lawless men roamed at large through the land and endeavored to draw aside their younger contemporaries to the like dissolute life (i. 11-19, ii. 12-15, iv. 14-17, xxiv. 15). In this Ewald sees traces of a late date. But Hitzig avoids this conclusion by asserting that at all times there are individuals who are reckless and at war with society and who attach themselves to bands of robbers and freebooters (comp. Judg. ix. 4, xi. 3; 1 Sam. xxii. 2; Jer. vii. 11), and to such allusion is made in Prov. i. 10; but there is nowhere in these chapters (i.-ix.) a complaint of the general depravity of society. So far he is unquestionably correct, and no inference with regard to the date of the section can be drawn from these references. Further evidence of a late date Ewald finds in the warnings against lightly rising to oppose the public order of things (xxiv. 21), and in the beautiful exhortation (xxiv. 11) to rescue with the sacrifice of one's self the innocent who is being dragged to death, which points to a confusion of right pervading the whole state, of which we nowhere see traces in the older proverbs. With these conclusions Hitzig would not disagree, for he himself assigns a late date to the section xxii. 17-xxiv. 34. We now come to evidence of another kind, and the conclusions drawn from it depend mainly upon the date assigned to the Book of Job. In this collection, says Ewald, there is a new danger of the heart warned against, which is not once thought of in the older collections, envy at the evident prosperity of the wicked (iii. 31, xxiii. 17, xxiv. 1, 19), a subject which for the first time is brought into the region of reflection and poetry in the Book of Job. Other parallels with this book are found in the teaching that man, even in the chastisement of God, should see his love, which is the subject of Prov. iii., and is the highest argument in the Book of Job; the general apprehension of Wisdom as the Creator and Disposer of the world (Prov. iii., viii.) appears as a further conclusion from Job xxviii.; and though the author of the first nine chapters of the Proverbs does not adopt the language of the Book of Job, but only in some measure its spirit and teaching, yet some images and words appear to be reech-

---

a Hitzig's theory about the Book of Proverbs in its present shape is this: that the oldest portion consists of chaps. i.-ix., to which was added, probably after the year 750 B. C., the second part, x.-xxii. 16, xxviii. 17-xxix.: that in the last quarter of the same century the anthology, xxv.-xxvii., was formed, and coming into the hands of a man who already possessed the

other two parts, inspired him with the composition of xxii. 17-xxiv. 34, which he placed before the anthology, and inserted the two before the last sheet of the second part. Then, finding that xxviii. 17 was left without a beginning, being separated from xxii. 1-16. he wrote xxviii. 1-16 on his last blank leaf. This was after the exile.

ced here from that book (comp. Prov. viii. 25 with Job xxxviii. 6; Prov. ii. 4, iii. 14, viii. 11, 19, with Job xxviii. 12-19; Prov. vii. 23 with Job xvi. 13, xx. 25; Prov. iii. 23, &c., with Job v. 22, &c.). Consequently the writer of this section must have been acquainted with the Book of Job, and wrote at a later date, about the middle of the 7th century B. C. Similar resemblances between passages in the early chapters of the Proverbs and the Book of Job are observed by Hitzig (comp. Prov. iii. 25 with Job v. 21; Prov. ii. 4, 14 with Job iii. 21, 22; Prov. iv. 12 with Job xviii. 7; Prov. iii. 11, 13 with Job v. 17; Prov. viii. 25 with Job xv. 7), but the conclusion which he derives is that the writer of Job had already read the Book of Proverbs, and that the latter is the more ancient. Reasoning from evidence of the like kind he places this section (i.-ix.) later than the Song of Songs, but earlier than the second collection (x. 1-xxii. 16, xxviii. 17-xxix.), which existed before the time of Hezekiah, and therefore assigns it to the 9th century B. C. Other arguments in support of this early date are the fact that idolatry is nowhere mentioned, that the offerings had not ceased (vii. 14), nor the congregations (v. 14). The two last would agree as well with a late as with an early date, and no argument from the silence with respect to idolatry can be allowed any weight, for it would equally apply to the 9th century as to the 7th. To all appearances, Hitzig continues, there was peace in the land, and commerce was kept up with Egypt (vii. 16). The author may have lived in Jerusalem (i. 20, 21, vii. 12, viii. 3); vii. 16, 17 points to the luxury of a large city, and the educated language belongs to a citizen of the capital. After a careful consideration of all the arguments which have been adduced, by Ewald for the late, and by Hitzig for the early date of this section, it must be confessed that they are by no means conclusive, and that we must ask for further evidence before pronouncing so positively as they have done upon a point so doubtful and obscure. In one respect they are agreed, namely, with regard to the unity of the section, which Ewald considers as an original whole, perfectly connected and flowing as it were from one outpouring. It would be a well-ordered whole, says Hitzig, if the interpolations, especially vi. 1-19, iii. 22-26, viii. 4-12, 14-16, ix. 7-10, &c., are rejected. It never appears to strike him that such a proceeding is arbitrary and uncritical in the highest degree, though he clearly plumes himself on his critical sagacity. Ewald finds in these chapters a certain development which shows that they must be regarded as a whole and the work of one author. The poet intended them as a general introduction to the Proverbs of Solomon, to recommend wisdom in general. The blessings of wisdom as the reward of him who boldly strives after her are repeatedly set forth in the most charming manner, as on the other hand folly is represented with its disappointment and enduring misery. There are three main divisions after the title, l. 1-7. (a.) i. 8-iii. 35; a general exhortation to the youth to follow wisdom, in which all, even the higher arguments, are touched upon, but nothing fully completed. (b.) iv. 1-vi. 19 exhausts whatever is individual and particular; while in (c.) the language rises gradually with ever-increasing power to the most universal and loftiest themes, to conclude in the sublimest and almost lyrical strain (vi. 20-ix. 18). But, as Bertheau remarks, there appears nowhere-throughout this section to be any reference to what follows, which must have been the case had it been intended

for an introduction. The development and progress which Ewald observes in it are by no means so striking as he would have us believe. The unity of plan is no more than would be found in a collection of admonitions by different authors referring to the same subject, and is not such as to necessitate the conclusion that the whole is the work of one. There is observable throughout the section, when compared with what is called the earlier collection, a complete change in the form of the proverb. The single proverb is seldom met with, and is rather the exception, while the characteristics of this collection are connected descriptions, continuous elucidations of a truth, and longer speeches and exhortations. The style is more highly poetical, the parallelism is synonymous and not antithetic or synthetic, as in x. 1-xxii. 16; and another distinction is the usage of Elohim in ii. 5, 17, iii. 4, which does not occur in x. 1-xxii. 16. Amidst this general likeness, however, there is considerable diversity. It is not necessary to lay so much stress as Bertheau appears to do upon the fact that certain paragraphs are distinguished from those with which they are placed, not merely by their contents, but by their external form; nor to argue from this that they are therefore the work of different authors. Some paragraphs, it is true, are completed in ten verses, as i. 10-19, iii. 1-10, 11-20, iv. 10-19, viii. 12-21, 22-31; but it is too much to assert that an author because he sometimes wrote paragraphs of ten verses, should always do so, or to say with Bertheau, if the whole were the work of one author it would be very remarkable if he only now and then bound himself by the strict law of numbers. The argument assumes the strictness of the law, and then attempts to bind the writer to observe it. There is more force in the appeal to the difference in the formation of sentences and the whole manner of the language as indicating diversity of authorship. Compare ch. ii with vii. 4-27, where the same subject is treated of. In the former, one sentence is wearily dragged through 22 verses, while in the latter the language is easy, flowing, and appropriate. Again the connection is interrupted by the insertion of vi. 1-19. In the previous chapter the 'exhortation to listen to the doctrine of the speaker is followed by the warning against intercourse with the adulteress. In vi. 1-19 the subject is abruptly changed, and a series of proverbs applicable to different relations of life is introduced. From all this Bertheau concludes against Ewald that these introductory chapters could not have been the product of a single author, forming a gradually developed and consistent whole, but that they are a collection of admonitions by different poets, which all aim at rendering the youth capable of receiving good instruction, and inspiring him to strive after the possession of wisdom. This supposition is somewhat favored by the frequent repetitions of favorite figures or impersonations: the strange woman and wisdom occur many times over in this section, which would hardly have been the case if it had been the work of one author. But the occurrence of these repetitions, if it is against the unity of authorship, indicates that the different portions of the section must have been contemporaneous, and were written at a time when such vivid impersonations of wisdom and its opposite were current and familiar. The tone of thought is the same, and the question therefore to be considered is whether it is more probable that a writer would repeat himself, or that fragments of a number of writers should be found, distinguished by the same way of thinking, and by the use of the same striking figures and personifications. If the proverbs spoken by one man were circulated orally for a time, and after his death collected and arranged, there would almost of necessity be a recurrence of the same expressions and illustrations, and from this point of view the argument from repetitions loses much of its force. With regard to the date as well as the authorship of this section it is impossible to pronounce with certainty. In its present form it did not exist till probably some long time after the proverbs which it contains were composed. There is positively no evidence which would lead us to a conclusion upon this point, and consequently the most opposite results have been arrived at: Ewald, as we have seen, placing it in the 7th century, while Hitzig refers it to the 9th. At whatever time it may have reached its present shape, there appears no sufficient reason to conclude that Solomon may not have uttered many or most of the proverbs which are here collected, although Ewald positively asserts that we here find no proverb of the Solomonian period. He assumes, and it is a mere assumption, that the form of the true Solomonian proverb is that which distinguishes the section x. 1–xxii. 16, and has already been remarked. Bleek regards cc i.–ix. as a connected *mâshâl*, the work of the last editor, written by him as an introduction to the Proverbs of Solomon which follow, while i. 1–6 was intended by him as a superscription to indicate the aim of the book, less with reference to his own *mâshâl* than to the whole book, and especially to the proverbs of Solomon contained in it. Bertholdt argues against Solomon being the author of these early chapters, that it was impossible for him, with his large harem, to have given so forcibly the precept about the blessings of a single wife (v. 18, &c.); nor, with the knowledge that his mother became the wife of David through an act of adultery, to warn so strongly against intercourse with the wife of another (vi. 24, &c., iii. 5–23). These arguments do not appear to us so strong as Bertholdt regarded them. Eichhorn, on the contrary, maintains that Solomon wrote the introduction in the first nine chapters. From this diversity of opinion, which be it remarked is entirely the result of an examination of internal evidence, it seems to follow naturally that the evidence which leads to such varying conclusions is of itself insufficient to decide the question at issue.

We now pass on to another section, xxii. 17–xxiv., which contains a collection of proverbs marked by certain peculiarities. These are, 1. The structure of the verses, which is not so regular as in the preceding section, x. 1–xxii. 16. We find verses of eight, seven, or six words, mixed with others of eleven (xxii. 29, xxiii. 31, 35), fourteen (xxiii. 29) and eighteen words (xxiv. 12). The equality of the verse members is very much disturbed, and there is frequently no trace of parallelism. 2. A sentence is seldom completed in one verse, but most frequently in two; three verses are often closely connected (xxiii. 1–3, 6–8, 19–21); and sometimes as many as five (xxiv. 30–34). 3. The form of address "my son," which is so frequent in the first nine chapters, occurs also here in xxiii. 19, 26, xxiv. 13; and the appeal to the hearer is often made in the second person. Ewald regards this section as a kind of appendix to the earliest collection of the proverbs of Solomon, added not long after the introduction in the first nine chapters, though not by the same author. He thinks it probable that the compiler of this section added

also the collection of proverbs which was made by the learned men of the court of Hezekiah, to which he wrote the superscription in xxv. 1. This theory of course only affects the date of the section in its present form. When the proverbs were written there is nothing to determine. Bertheau maintains that they in great part proceeded from one poet, in consequence of a peculiar construction which he employs to give emphasis to his presentation of a subject or object by repeating the pronoun (xxii. 19; xxiii. 14, 15, 19, 20, 28; xxiv. 6, 27, 32). The compiler himself appears to have added xxii. 17–21 as a kind of introduction. Another addition (xxiv. 23–34) is introduced with "these also belonged to the wise," and contains apparently some of "the words of the wise" to which reference is made in i. 6. Jahn regards it as a collection of proverbs not by Solomon. Hensler says it is an appendix to a collection of doctrines which is entirely lost and unknown; and with regard to the previous part of the section xxii. 17–xxiv. 22, he leaves it uncertain whether or not the author was a teacher to whom the son of a distinguished man was sent for instruction. Hitzig's theory has already been given.

After what has been said, the reader must be left to judge for himself whether Keil is justified in asserting so positively as he does the single authorship of cc. i.–xxix., and in maintaining that "the contents in all parts of the collection show one and the same historical background, corresponding only to the relations, ideas, and circumstances, as well as to the progress of the culture and experiences of life, acquired by the political development of the people in the time of Solomon."

The concluding chapters (xxx., xxxi.) are in every way distinct from the rest and from each other. The former, according to the superscription, contains "the words of Agur the son of Jakeh." Who was Agur, and who was Jakeh, are questions which have been often asked, and never satisfactorily answered. The Rabbins, according to Rashi, and Jerome after them, interpreted the name symbolically of Solomon, who "collected understanding" (from אָגֻר, *âgur*, "to collect," "gather,"), and is elsewhere called "Koheleth." All that can be said of him is that he is an unknown Hebrew sage, the son of an equally unknown Jakeh, and that he lived after the time of Hezekiah. Ewald attributes to him the authorship of xxx. 1–xxxi. 9, and places him not earlier than the end of the 7th or beginning of the 6th cent. B. C. Hitzig, as usual, has a strange theory: that Agur and Lemuel were brothers, both sons of the queen of Massa, a district in Arabia, and that the father was the reigning king. [See JAKEH.] Bunsen (*Bibelwerk*, i. p. clxxviii.), following Hitzig, contends that Agur was an inhabitant of Massa, and a descendant of one of the five hundred Simeonites who in the reign of Hezekiah drove out the Amalekites from Mount Seir. All this is mere conjecture. Agur, whoever he was, appears to have had for his pupils Ithiel and Ucal, whom he addresses in xxx. 1–6, which is followed by single proverbs of Agur's. Ch. xxxi. 1–9 contains "the words of king Lemuel, the prophecy that his mother taught him." Lemuel, like Agur, is unknown. It is even uncertain whether he is to be regarded as a real personage, or whether the name is merely symbolical, as Eichhorn and Ewald maintain. If the present text be retained it is difficult to see what other conclution can be arrived at. If Lemuel were a real personage he must have been a foreign neighbor-king or the chief of a nomad tribe, and in this case the proverbs attributed to him must have come to the Hebrews from a foreign source, which is highly improbable and contrary to all we know of the people. Dr. Davidson indeed is in favor of altering the punctuation of xxx. 1, with Hitzig and Bertheau, by which means Agur and Lemuel became brothers, and both sons of a queen of Massa. Reasons against this alteration of the text are given under the article JAKEH. Eichhorn maintains that Lemuel is a figurative name appropriate to the subject. [LEMUEL.]

The last section of all, xxxi. 10-31, is an alphabetical acrostic in praise of a virtuous woman. Its artificial form stamps it as the production of a late period of Hebrew literature, perhaps about the 7th century B. C. The coloring and language point to a different author from the previous section, xxx. 1-xxxi. 9.

To conclude, it appears, from a consideration of the whole question of the manner in which the Book of Proverbs arrived at its present shape, that the nucleus of the whole was the collection of Solomon's proverbs in x. 1-xxii. 16; that to this was added the further collection made by the learned men of the court of Hezekiah, xxv.-xxix.; that these two were put together and united with xxii. 17-xxiv., and that to this as a whole the introduction i.-ix. was affixed, but that whether it was compiled by the same writer who added xxii. 16-xxiv. cannot be determined. Nor is it possible to assert that this same compiler may not have added the concluding chapters of the book to his previous collection. With regard to the date at which the several portions of the book were collected and put in their present shape, the conclusions of various critics are uncertain and contradictory. The chief of these have already been given.

The nature of the contents of the Book of Proverbs precludes the possibility of giving an outline of its plan and object. Such would be more appropriate to the pages of a commentary. The chief authorities which have been consulted in the preceding pages are the introductions of Carpzov, Eichhorn, Bertholdt, Jahn, De Wette, Keil, Davidson, and Bleek; Rosenmüller, Scholia; Ewald, Die Dicht. des A. B. 4 Th.; Bertheau, Die Sprüche Salomo's; Hitzig, Die Sprüche Salomo's; Elster, Die Salomonischen Sprüche. To these may be added, as useful aids in reading the Proverbs, the commentaries of Albert Schultens, of Eichel in Mendelssohn's Bible (perhaps the best of all), of Loewenstein, Umbreit, and Moses Stuart. There is also a new translation by Dr. Noyes, of Harvard University, of the three books of Proverbs, Ecclesiastes, and Canticles, which may be consulted, as well as the older works of Hodgson and Holden.

W. A. W.

* The preceding discussion leaves room for a more particular analysis of the contents of this remarkable book. After a brief introduction (ch. i.

1-6), setting forth its design and uses, the ground-thought of the whole is expressed in ver. 7; namely, that all true knowledge has its beginning in the fear of God, the seminal principle of which the whole moral life is the growth, and the central law of our moral relations; that only fools despise this heavenly wisdom, and the means of acquiring it. This is the key to the instructions of the book. The following are very distinctly marked divisions.

1. Chapters i.-ix. First division, consisting of short continuous discourses, on various topics of religion and morality. Vv. 10-19. Against enticements to crime and criminal gains, and the fatal influences of a covetous spirit. Vv. 20-23. Wisdom's expostulations with those who refuse her warnings. Chap. ii. Rewards of those who seek wisdom.[a] Chap. iii. A discourse in several parts, commending kindness and truth, as foundation principles in all social relations (vv. 1-4): trust in Jehovah, and conscious reference to Him in all things (vv. 5-8); recognition of Him in the use of his gifts (vv. 9, 10), and filial submission to his chastisements (vv. 11, 12); blessedness of attaining the true wisdom (vv. 13-26); practical precepts for direction in the relations of social life (vv. 27-35). Chap. iv. Admonition to seek wisdom (vv. 1-9); to heed instruction and avoid the way of the wicked (vv. 10-19); to keep the heart, from which the outward life proceeds (Matt. xv. 19), and shun every deviation from the right (vv. 20-27). Chap. v. Admonition to shun the fatal snare of the strange woman (vv. 1-14); to regard the divinely instituted law of the marriage relation, and be satisfied with its pure and chaste enjoyments (vv. 15-23). Chap. vi. Against being surety for another (vv. 1-5); against slothfulness (vv. 6-11); against the false and insidious mischief-maker (vv. 12-15); seven abominations of Jehovah (vv. 16-19); value of parental instruction and of its restraints in the conduct of life (vv. 20-35). Chap. vii. Warning against the allurements of the strange woman. Chap. viii. WISDOM'S DISCOURSE. Her appeal to the sons of men (vv. 1-11); her claim to be their true and proper guide in the affairs of life (vv. 12-21); her relation to Jehovah as his companion and delight before the worlds were, and his associate in founding the heavens and the earth (vv. 22-31); blessedness of those who hearken to her voice (vv. 32-36).[b] Chap. ix. Wisdom's invitation to her feast (vv. 1-6); the scoffer scorns reproof, which the wise gratefully accepts (vv. 7-9); contrast of the foolish woman, and of the fate of her victim (vv. 13-18).

2. Chapters x.-xxii. 16. Second division, consisting of single unconnected sayings, or maxims, expressing in few words the accumulated treasures of practical wisdom.

3. Chapters xxii. 17- xxiv. 22. Third division, consisting of brief moral lessons, in very short, continuous discourses, less extended than those of the first division. An introductory paragraph admonishes to a diligent and heedful consideration of the words of the wise (vv. 17-21); against robbery and oppression of the weak and poor (vv. 22, 23); against companionship with the passionate man,

---

[a] * In this beautifully constructed discourse, the statement of the conditions (vv. 1-4) is followed by a twofold expression of the reward of compliance; namely, one in ver. 5. and another in ver. 9, each confirmed and illustrated by the verses following it. Vv. 12, 16, 20, all stand in the same relation; each expressing an end or object to be attained, of which the principal, and the sum of all, is given in ver. 20.   T. J. C.

---

[b] * WISDOM here personates a divine principle, established as the law of the universe, to which all created things are subjected. The delight of Jehovah, and the guide of his creative work, she here claims to be the guide and friend of his creature man.

T. J. C

and the influence of his evil example (vv. 24, 25); against being surety for another's indebtedness (vv. 26, 27); against the perfidious removal of landmarks (v. 28); caution against indulgence of appetite at the table of a ruler (ch. xxiii. 1-3); folly of a craving for riches (vv. 4-5); accept no favors from the grudging and envious (vv. 6-8); leave the fool to his folly (v. 9); removal of landmarks, and violation of the orphan's domain, will surely be avenged (vv. 10, 11); correction needful and salutary for the child (vv. 13, 14); a parent's joy in a wise and discreet son (vv. 15-18); against companionship with the dissolute (vv. 19-21); regard due to parents (vv. 22-25); a parent's plea for the love and obedience of a son, especially as a security from the most fatal snare of the young (vv. 26-28); description of the victim of the intoxicating cup, and warning against its seductions (vv. 29-35).[a] Chap. xxix. consists, for the most part, of brief practical directions for the conduct of life, closing with the spirited description of the neglected fields of the sluggard.

4. Chapters xxv.-xxix. Fourth division, being another collection of the Proverbs of Solomon.

5. Chapters xxx. - xxxi.　An appendix, containing the words of Agur, and the words of king Lemuel, and closing with the beautiful portraiture of a capable woman [b] (xxxi. 10-31).

From this brief and necessarily partial analysis of the book, something may be inferred of the extent and variety of its topics. Of the richness of its teachings, the trains of thought suggested by single pregnant expressions, an analysis can give no conception. The gnomic poetry of the most enlightened of other ancient nations will not bear comparison with it, in the depth and certainty of its foundation principles, or in the comprehensiveness and the moral grandeur of its conceptions of human duty and responsibility. There is no relation in life which has not its appropriate instruction, no good or evil tendency without its proper incentive or correction. The human consciousness is everywhere brought into immediate relation with the Divine, with the All-seeing Eye, from which no act of the outward life or thought of the heart can be concealed, and man walks as in the presence of his Maker and Judge. But he is taught to know Him also as the loving Father and Guide, seeking to succor the tempted, to win the wayward, to restrain the lawless, to restore the penitent.

The knowledge of human nature, in its various developments, is also worthy of note. Every type of humanity is found in this ancient book; and though sketched three thousand years ago, is still as true to nature as if now drawn from its living representative.

In the beautiful description of the chaste relations of husband and wife (ch. v. 15-23), the writer's meaning is lost in the A. V., and his statements made contradictory, by rendering ver. 16 affirmatively. It should be rendered as an interrogative expostulation, thus: —

Shall thy fountains spread abroad,
Streams of water in the streets?

The book is not wanting in strokes of wit and humor, by which the gravest moral lesson is often most effectively pointed. One example has been given above, from ch. xxiii. 35.　In ch. xv. 33, it is said, with sarcastic humor: —

Wisdom dwells in the heart of the discerning;
But in fools it shall be taught.

The "heart of the discerning" is Wisdom's home, her proper dwelling-place, and there she abides. Fools are sometimes "taught" a lesson in wisdom; but it is after the manner described in Judges viii. 16, "he took thorns of the wilderness, and briers, and with them he taught the men of Succoth." In ch. xix. 7, it is said —

All the poor man's brethren hate him;
Much more do his friends keep far from him;
He follows after words — them he has!

A polished irony points the concluding member. The favors he is encouraged to hope for he finds to be empty talk, and that in seeking them he has "followed after words" — which he gets!

The older commentaries are given by Rosenmüller. The later critical works are : Holden, Improved trans. of Prov. with notes crit. and expl., 1819. Dereser (Die h. Schrift, von Brentano), 1825. Umbreit, Comm. über die Sprüche Salomo's, 1826. Gramberg, Das Buch der Sprüche Salomo's, 1828. Rosenmüller, Proverbia Salomonis, 1829. Böckel, Die Denksprüche Salomo's, 1829. French and Skinner, New trans. of the Prov. with expl. notes, 1831. Ewald, Sprüche Salomo's (poet. Bücher des A. T. 1837), 2te Aug. 1867. Maurer, Comm. Crit. vol. iii., 1838. Löwenstein, Proverbien Salomo's (aus Handschriften edirt), 1838. Noyes, New trans. of Prov. Eccl. and Cant. with notes, Boston, 1846 (3d ed. 1867). Bertheau, Die Sprüche Salomo's (Exeget. Handbuch, Lief. vii.), 1847. Stuart, Comm. on the Book of Prov., New York, 1852. Vaihinger, Sprüche u. Klayl. übers. u. erkl., 1857. Hitzig, Die Sprüche Salomo's, 1858. Elster, Comm. über die Salomon. Sprüche, 1858. Diedrich, Die Salomon. Schriften, 1865. Muenscher, The Book of Prov., amended vers. with Int. and expl. notes, Gambier, Ohio, 1866. Zöckler, Die Sprüche Salomo's (Lange's Bibelwerk, 12ter Th.), 1867. Kamphausen (in Bunsen's Bibelwerk). Conant, T. J., The Book of Proverbs: Part first, Heb. text, with revised Eng. version, and crit. and phil. notes; Part second, revised Eng. version, with expl. notes (in press, 1869). Delitzsch, art. Sprüche Salomo's, Herzog's Real-Encykl. vol. xiv. pp. 691-718.　　　　　　　　　　T. J. C.

* PROVOKE (from provocare, "to call forth") is used in a few passages of the A. V. in the sense of to "excite," "incite," "stimulate," as in Heb. x. 24, "to provoke to love and good works." So 1 Chr. xxi. 1; Rom. x. 19, xi. 11, 14; 2 Cor. ix. 2.　　　　　　　　　　　　　　H.

PROVINCE (מְדִינָה : ἐπαρχία, N.T. χώρα, LXX.: provincia). It is not intended here to do

---

[a] * The grave humor of the inebriate's helpless unconsciousness, in vv. 34, 35, is but partially expressed in the A. V., through the defective rendering of the latter verse. It should be translated thus: —

They smite me, I feel no pain;
They beat me, I know it not.

When shall I awake?
I will seek it yet again.

All his senses are locked up. If there is any dreamy consciousness, it is of a longing to awake, and take another draught; he will seek it yet again!
　　　　　　　　　　　　　　T. J. C.

[b] * Not a "virtuous woman" (as in the A. V., "a virtuous woman who can find"), but one competent to the duties of her station.　　T. J. C.

more than indicate the points of contact which this word presents with Biblical history and literature.

(1.) In the O. T. it appears in connection with the wars between Ahab and Benhadad (1 K. xx. 14, 15, 19). The victory of the former is gained chiefly "by the young men of the princes of the provinces," i. e. probably, of the chiefs of tribes in the Gilead country, recognizing the supremacy of Ahab, and having a common interest with the Israelites in resisting the attacks of Syria. They are specially distinguished in ver. 15 from "the children of Israel." Not the hosts of Ahab, but the youngest warriors ("armor-bearers," Keil, in loc.) of the land of Jephthah and Elijah, fighting with a fearless faith, are to carry off the glory of the battle (comp. Ewald, Gesch. iii. 492).

(2.) More commonly the word is used of the divisions of the Chaldæan (Dan. ii. 49, iii. 1, 30) and the Persian kingdoms (Exr. ii. 1; Neh. vii. 6; Esth. i. 1, 22, ii. 3, etc.). The occurrence of the word in Eccl. ii. 8, v. 8, may possibly be noted as an indication of the later date now commonly ascribed to that book.

The facts as to the administration of the Persian provinces which come within our view in these passages are chiefly these: Each province has its own governor, who communicates more or less regularly with the central authority for instructions (Exr. iv. and v.). Thus Tatnai, governor of the provinces on the right bank of the Euphrates, applies to Darius to know how he is to act as to the conflicting claims of the Apharsachites and the Jews (Exr. v.). Each province has its own system of finance, subject to the king's direction (Herod. iii. 89). The "treasurer" is ordered to spend a given amount upon the Israelites (Exr. vii. 22), and to exempt them from all taxes (vii. 24). [TAXES.] The total number of the provinces is given at 127 (Esth. i. 1, viii. 9). Through the whole extent of the kingdom there is carried something like a postal system. The king's couriers (βιβλιοφόροι, the ἄγγαροι of Herod. viii. 98) convey his letters or decrees (Esth. i. 22, iii. 13). From all provinces concubines are collected for his harem (ii. 3). Horses, mules or dromedaries, are employed on this service (viii. 10). (Comp. Herod. viii. 98; Xen. Cyrop. viii. 6; Heeren's Persians, ch. ii.)

The word is used, it must be remembered, of the smaller sections of a satrapy rather than of the satrapy itself. While the provinces are 127, the satrapies are only 20 (Herod. iii. 89). The Jews who returned from Babylon are described as "children of the province" (Exr. ii. 1; Neh. vii. 6), and have a separate governor [TIRSHATHA] of their own race (Exr. ii. 63; Neh. v. 14, viii. 9); while they are subject to the satrap (פֶּחָר) of the whole province west of the Euphrates (Exr. v. 6, vi. 6).

(3.) In the N. T. we are brought into contact with the administration of the provinces of the Roman empire. The classification given by Strabo (xvii. p. 840) of provinces (ἐπαρχίαι) supposed to need military control, and therefore placed under the immediate government of the Cæsar, and those still belonging theoretically to the republic, and administered by the senate; and of the latter

again into proconsular (ὑπατικαί) and prætorian (στρατηγικαί), is recognized, more or less distinctly, in the Gospels and the Acts. Cyrenius (Quirinius) is the ἡγεμών of Syria (Luke ii. 2), the word being in this case used for præses or proconsul. Pilate was the ἡγεμών of the sub-province of Judæa (Luke iii. 1, Matt. xxvii. 2, etc.), as procurator with the power of a legatus; and the same title is given to his successors, Felix and Festus (Acts xxiii. 24, xxv. 1, xxvi. 30). The governors of the senatorial provinces of Cyprus, Achaia, and Asia, on the other hand, are rightly described as ἀνθύπατοι, proconsuls (Acts xiii. 7, xviii. 12, xix. 38).[a] In the two former cases the province had been originally an imperial one, but had been transferred, Cyprus by Augustus (Dio Cass. liv. 4), Achaia by Claudius (Sueton. Claud. 25), to the senate. The στρατηγοί of Acts xvi. 22 ("magistrates," A. V.), on the other hand, were the duumviri, or prætors of a Roman colony. The duty of the legati and other provincial governors to report special cases to the emperor is recognized in Acts xxv. 26, and furnished the groundwork for the spurious Acta Pilati. [PILATE.] The right of any Roman citizen to appeal from a provincial governor to the emperor meets us as asserted by St. Paul (Acts xxv. 11). In the council (συμβούλιον) of Acts xxv. 12 we recognize the assessors who were appointed to take part in the judicial functions of the governor. The authority of the legatus, proconsul, or procurator, extended, it need hardly be said, to capital punishment (subject in the case of Roman citizens, to the right of appeal), and in most cases the power of inflicting it belonged to him exclusively. It was necessary for the Sanhedrim to gain Pilate's consent to the execution of our Lord (John xviii. 31). The strict letter of the law forbade governors of provinces to take their wives with them, but the cases of Pilate's wife (Matt. xxvii. 19) and Drusilla (Acts xxiv. 24) show that it had fallen into disuse. Tacitus (Ann. iii. 33, 34) records an unsuccessful attempt to revive the old practice.

The financial administration of the Roman provinces is discussed under PUBLICANS and TAXES.   E. H. P.

* **PRUNING-HOOK.** [KNIFE, 5.]

PSALMS, BOOK OF. 1. *The Collection as a Whole.* — It does not appear how the Psalms were, as a whole, anciently designated. Their present Hebrew appellation is תהלים, "Praises." But in the actual superscriptions of the psalms the word תהלה is applied only to one, Ps. cxlv., which is indeed emphatically a praise-hymn. The LXX. entitled them Ψαλμοί, or "Psalms," using the word ψαλμός at the same time as the translation of מזמור, which signifies strictly a rhythmical composition (Lowth, Prælect. III.), and which was probably applied in practice to any poem specially intended, by reason of its rhythm, for musical performance with instrumental accompaniment. But the Hebrew word is, in the O. T., never used in the plural: and in the superscriptions of even the Davidic psalms it is applied only to some, not to all; probably to those which had been composed most expressly for the harp. The notice at the end of Ps. lxxii. has suggested that the Psalms may in the earliest times have been known as תפלות, "Prayers;" and in fact "Prayer" is the title prefixed to the most ancient of all the psalms, that of Moses, Ps. xc. But the same designation is in the superscriptions applied to only three besides, Pss. xvii., lxxxvi., cii.; nor have all the psalms the character of prayers. The other special designations applied to particular psalms are the following: שיר, "Song," the outpouring of the soul in thanksgiving, used in the first instance of a hymn of private gratitude, Ps. xxx., afterwards of hymns of great national thanksgiving, Pss. xlvi., xlviii., lxv., etc.; משכיל, maschil, "Instruction" or "Homily," Pss xxxii., xlii., xliv., etc. (comp. the אשכילך, "I will instruct thee," in Ps. xxxii. 8); מכתם, michtam, "Private Memorial," from the root כתם (perhaps also with an anagrammatical allusion to the root תמך, "to support," "maintain," comp. Ps. xvi. 5), Pss. xvi., lvi.-lix.; עדות, eduth, "Testimony," Pss. lx., lxxx.; and שגיון, shiggaion, "Irregular or Dithyrambic Ode," Ps. vii. The strict meaning of these terms is in general to be gathered from the earlier superscriptions. Once made familiar to the psalmists, they were afterwards employed by them more loosely.

The Christian Church obviously received the Psalter from the Jews not only as a constituent portion of the sacred volume of Holy Scripture, but also as the liturgical hymn-book which the Jewish Church had regularly used in the Temple. The number of separate psalms contained in it is, by the concordant testimony of all ancient authorities, one hundred and fifty; the avowedly "supernumerary" psalm which appears at the end of the Greek and Syriac Psalters being manifestly apocryphal. This total number commends itself by its internal probability as having proceeded from the last sacred collector and editor of the Psalter. In the details, however, of the numbering, both the Greek and Syriac Psalters differ from the Hebrew. The Greek translators joined together Pss. ix., x., and Pss. cxiv., cxv., and then divided Ps. cxvi. and Ps. cxlvii.; this was perpetuated in the versions derived from the Greek, and amongst others in the Latin Vulgate. The Syriac so far followed the Greek as to join together Pss. cxiv., cxv., and to divide Ps. cxlvii. Of the three divergent systems of numbering, the Hebrew (as followed in our A. V.) is, even on internal grounds, to be preferred. It is decisive against the Greek numbering that Ps. cxvi., being symmetrical in its construction, will not bear to be divided; and against the Syriac, that it destroys the outward correspondence in numerical place between the three great triumphal psalms, Pss. xviii., lxviii., cxviii., as also between the two psalms containing the praise of 'he Law, Pss. xix., cxix. There are also some discrepancies in the versual numberings. That of our A. V. frequently differs from that of the Hebrew in consequence of the Jewish practice of reckoning the superscription as the first verse.

2. *Component Parts of the Collection.* — An-

cient tradition and internal evidence concur in parting the Psalter into five great divisions or books. The ancient Jewish tradition is preserved to us by the abundant testimonies of the Christian Fathers. And of the indications which the sacred text itself contains of this division the most obvious are the doxologies which we find at the ends of Pss xli., lxxii., lxxxix., cvi., and which, having for the most part no special connection with the psalms to which they are attached, mark the several ends of the first four of the five Books. It suggests itself at once that these books must have been originally formed at different periods. This is by various further considerations rendered all but certain, while the few difficulties which stand in the way of admitting it vanish when closely examined.

Thus, there is a remarkable difference between the several books in their use of the divine names Jehovah and Elohim, to designate Almighty God. In Book I. the former name prevails: it is found 272 times, while Elohim occurs but 15 times. (We here take no account of the superscriptions or doxology, nor yet of the occurrences of Elohim when inflected with a possessive suffix.) On the other hand, in Book II. Elohim is found more than five times as often as Jehovah. In Book III. the preponderance of Elohim in the earlier is balanced by that of Jehovah in the later psalms of the book. In Book IV. the name Jehovah is exclusively employed; and so also, virtually, in Book V., Elohim being there found only in two passages incorporated from earlier psalms. Those who maintain, therefore, that the psalms were all collected and arranged at once, contend that the collector distributed the psalms according to the divine names which they severally exhibited. But to this theory the existence of Book III., in which the preferential use of the Elohim gradually yields to that of the Jehovah, is fatal. The large appearance, in fact, of the name Elohim in Books II. and III. depends in great measure on the period to which many of the psalms of those Books belong; the period from the reign of Solomon to that of Hezekiah, when through certain causes the name Jehovah was exceptionally disused. The preference for the name Elohim in most of the Davidic psalms which are included in Book II., is closely allied with that character of those psalms which induced David himself to exclude them from his own collection, Book I.; while, lastly, the sparing use of the Jehovah in Ps. lxviii., and the three introductory psalms which precede it, is designed to cause the name, when it occurs, and above all JAH, which is emphatic for Jehovah, to shine out with greater force and splendor.

This, however, brings us to the observance of the superscriptions which mark the authorship of the several psalms; and here again we find the several groups of psalms which form the respective five books distinguished, in great measure, by their superscriptions from each other. Book I. is exclusively Davidic. Of the forty-one psalms of which it consists, thirty-seven have David's name prefixed; and of the remaining four, Pss. i., ii. are probably outwardly anonymous only by reason of their prefatory character, Pss. x., xxxiii., by reason of their close connection with those which they immediately succeed.[a] Book II. (in which the apparent anonymousness of Pss. xliii., lxvi., lxvii.,

a An old Jewish canon, which may be deemed to hold good for the earlier but not for the later Books, enacts that all anonymous psalms be accounted the compositions of the authors named in the superscriptions last preceding.

lxxi., may be similarly explained) falls, by the superscriptions of its psalms, into two distinct subdivisions, a Lævitic and a Davidic. The former consists of Pss. xlii. - xlix., ascribed to the Sons of Korah, and Ps. l., "A Psalm of Asaph:" the latter comprises Pss. li. - lxxi., bearing the name of David, and supplemented by Ps. lxxii., the psalm of Solomon. In Book III. (Pss. lxxiii. - lxxxix.), where the Asaphic psalms precede those of the Sons of Korah, the psalms are all ascribed, explicitly or virtually, to the various Levite singers, except only Ps. lxxxvi., which bears the name of David: this, however, is not set by itself, but stands in the midst of the rest. In Books IV., V., we have, in all, seventeen psalms marked with David's name. They are to a certain extent, as in Book III., mixed with the rest, sometimes singly, sometimes in groups. But these books differ from Book III. in that the non-Davidic psalms, instead of being assigned by superscriptions to the Levite singers, are left anonymous. Special attention, in respect to authorship, is drawn by the superscriptions only to Ps. xc., "A Prayer of Moses," etc.; Ps. cii., "A Prayer of the Afflicted," etc.; and Ps. cxxvii., marked with the name of Solomon.

In reasoning from the phenomena of the superscriptions, which indicate in many instances not only the authors, but also the occasions of the several psalms, as well as the mode of their musical performance, we have to meet the preliminary inquiry which has been raised, Are the superscriptions authentic? For the affirmative it is contended that they form an integral, and till modern times almost undisputed, portion of the Hebrew text of Scripture;[a] that they are in analogy with other Biblical super- or subscriptions, Davidic or otherwise (comp. 2 Sam. i. 18, probably based on an old superscription; *ib.* xxiii. 1; Is. xxxviii. 9; Hab. iii. 1, 19); and that their diversified, unsystematic, and often obscure and enigmatical character is inconsistent with the theory of their having originated at a later period. On the other hand is urged their analogy with the untrustworthy subscriptions of the N. T. epistles: as also the fact that many arbitrary superscriptions are added in the Greek version of the Psalter. The above represents, however, but the outside of the controversy. The real pith of it lies in this: Do they, when individually sifted, approve themselves as so generally correct, and as so free from any single fatal objection to their credit, as to claim our universal confidence? This can evidently not be discussed here. We must simply avow our conviction, founded on thorough examination, that they are, when rightly interpreted, fully trustworthy, and that every separate objection that has been made to the correctness of any one of them can be fairly met. Moreover, some of the arguments of their assailants obviously recoil upon themselves. Thus when it is alleged that the contents of Ps. xxxiv. have no connection with the occasion indicated in the superscription, we reply that the fact of the connection not being readily apparent renders it improbable that the superscription should have been prefixed by any but David himself.

Let us now then trace the bearing of the superscriptions upon the date and method of compilation of the several books. Book I. is, by the superscriptions, entirely Davidic; nor do we find in it a trace of any but David's authorship. No such trace exists in the mention of the "Temple" (v. 7), for that word is even in 1 Sam. i. 9, iii. 3 applied to the Tabernacle; nor yet in the phrase "bringeth back the captivity" (xiv. 7), which is elsewhere used, idiomatically, with great latitude of meaning (Job xlii. 10; Hos. vi. 11; Ez. xvi. 53); nor yet in the acrosticism of Pss. xxv., etc., for that all acrostic psalms are of late date is a purely gratuitous assumption, and some even of the most skeptical critics admit the Davidic authorship of the partially acrostic Pss. ix., x. All the psalms of Book I. being thus Davidic, we may well believe that the compilation of the book was also David's work. In favor of this is the circumstance that it does not comprise all David's psalms, nor his latest, which yet would have been all included in it by any subsequent collector; also the circumstance that its two prefatory psalms, although not superscribed, are yet shown by internal evidence to have proceeded from David himself; and furthermore, that of the two recensions of the same hymn, Pss. xiv., liii., it prefers that which seems to have been more specially adapted by its royal author to the temple-service. Book II. appears by the date of its latest psalm, Ps. xlvi., to have been compiled in the reign of King Hezekiah. It would naturally comprise, 1st, several or most of the Levitical psalms anterior to that date; and 2dly, the remainder of the psalms of David, previously uncompiled. To these latter the collector, after properly appending the single psalm of Solomon, has affixed the notice that "the prayers of David the son of Jesse are ended" (Ps. lxxii. 20); evidently implying, at least on the *primâ facie* view, that no more compositions of the royal psalmist remained. How then do we find, in the later Books III., IV., V., further psalms yet marked with David's name? Another question shall help us to reply. How do we find, in Book III. rather than Book II.. eleven psalms, Pss. lxxiii. - lxxxiii., bearing the name of David's contemporary musician Asaph? Clearly because they proceeded not from Asaph himself. No critic whatever contends that *all* these eleven belong to the age of David; and, in real truth, internal evidence is in every single instance in favor of a later origin. They were composed then by the "sons of Asaph" (2 Chr. xxix. 13, xxxv. 15, &c.), the members, by hereditary descent, of the choir which Asaph founded. It was to be expected that these psalmists would, in superscribing their psalms, prefer honoring and perpetuating the memory of their ancestor to obtruding their own personal names on the Church: a consideration which both explains the present superscriptions, and also renders it improbable that the person intended in them could, according to a frequent but now waning hypothesis, be any second Asaph, of younger generation and of inferior fame. The superscriptions of Pss. lxxxviii., lxxxix., "Maschil of Heman," "Maschil of Ethan," have doubtless a like purport; the one psalm having been written, as in fact the rest of its superscription states, by the Sons of Korah, the choir of which Heman was the founder; and the other correspondingly proceeding from the third Levitical choir, which owed its origin to Ethan or Jeduthun. If now in the times posterior to those of David the

---

Levite choirs prefixed to the psalms which they composed the names of Asaph, Heman, and Ethan, out of a feeling of veneration for their memories; how much more might the name of David be prefixed to the utterances of those who were not merely his descendants, but also the representatives for the time being, and so in some sort the pledges, of the perpetual royalty of his lineage! The name David is used to denote, in other parts of Scripture, after the original David's death, the then head of the Davidic family; and so, in prophecy, the Messiah of the seed of David, who was to sit on David's throne (1 K. xii. 16; Hos. iii. 5; Is. lv. 3; Jer. xxx. 9; Ez. xxxiv. 23, 24). And thus then we may explain the meaning of the later Davidic superscriptions in the Psalter. The psalms to which they belong were written by Hezekiah, by Josiah, by Zerubbabel, or others of David's posterity. And this view is confirmed by various considerations. It is confirmed by the circumstance that in the later books, and even in Book V. taken alone, the psalms marked with David's name are not grouped all together. It is confirmed in some instances by the internal evidence of occasion: thus Psalm ci. can ill be reconciled with the historical circumstances of any period of David's life, but suits exactly with those of the opening of the reign of Josiah. It is confirmed by the extent to which some of these psalms — Pss. lxxxv., cviii., cxliv. — are compacted of passages from previous psalms of David. And it is confirmed lastly by the fact that the Hebrew text of many (see, above all Ps. cxxxix.), is marked by grammatical Chaldaisms, which are entirely unparalleled in Pss. i. – lxxii., and which thus afford sure evidence of a comparatively recent date. They cannot therefore be David's own: yet that the superscriptions are not on that account to be rejected, as false, but must rather be properly interpreted, is shown by the improbability that any would, carelessly or presumptuously, have prefixed David's name to various psalms *scattered* through a collection, while yet leaving the rest — at least in Books IV., V. — altogether unsuperscribed.

The above explanation removes all serious difficulty respecting the history of the later books of the Psalter. Book III., the interest of which centres in the times of Hezekiah, stretches out, by its last two psalms, to the reign of Manasseh: it was probably compiled in the reign of Josiah. Book IV. contains the remainder of the psalms up to the date of the Captivity; Book V. the psalms of the Return. There is nothing to distinguish these two books from each other in respect of outward decoration or arrangement, and they may have been compiled together in the days of Nehemiah.

The superscriptions, and the places which the psalms themselves severally occupy in the Psalter, are thus the two guiding clews by which, in conjunction with the internal evidence, their various authors, dates, and occasions, are to be determined. In the critical results obtained on these points by those scholars who have recognized and used these helps there is, not indeed uniformity, but at least a visible tendency towards it. The same cannot be said for the results of the judgments of those, of whatever school, who have neglected or rejected them; nor indeed is it easily to be imagined that internal evidence alone should suffice to assign one hundred and fifty devotional hymns, even approximately, to their several epochs.

It would manifestly be impossible, in the compass of an article like the present, to exhibit in detail the divergent views which have been taken of the dates of particular psalms. There is, however, one matter which must not be altogether passed over in silence: the assignment of various psalms, by a large number of critics, to the age of the Maccabees. Two preliminary difficulties fatally beset such procedure: the hypothesis of a Maccabean authorship of any portion of the Psalter can ill be reconciled either with the history of the O. T. canon, or with that of the translation of the LXX. But the difficulties do not end here. How — for we shall not here discuss the theories of Hitzig and his followers Lengerke and Justus Olshausen, who would represent the greater part of the Psalter as Maccabean, — how is it that the psalms which one would most naturally assign to the Maccabean period meet us not in the close but in the middle, *i. e.* in the Second and Third Books of the Psalter? The three named by De Wette (*Einl. in das A. T.* § 270) as bearing, apparently, a Maccabean impress, are Pss. xliv., lx., lxxix.; and in fact these, together with Ps. lxxiii., are perhaps all that would, when taken alone, seriously suggest the hypothesis of a Maccabean date. Whence then arise the early places in the Psalter which these occupy? But even in the case of these, the internal evidence, when more narrowly examined, proves to be in favor of an earlier date. In the first place the superscription of Ps. lx. cannot possibly have been invented from the historical books, inasmuch as it disagrees with them in its details. Then the mention by name in that psalm of the Israelitish tribes, and of Moab, and Philistia, is unsuited to the Maccabean epoch. In Ps. xliv. the complaint is made that the tree of the nation of Israel was no longer spreading over the territory that God had assigned it. Is it conceivable that a Maccabean psalmist should have held this language without making the slightest allusion to the Babylonish Captivity; as though the tree's growth were now first being seriously impeded by the wild stocks around, notwithstanding that it had once been entirely transplanted, and that, though restored to its place, it had been weakly ever since? In Ps. lxxiv. it is complained that "there is no more any prophet." Would that be a natural complaint at a time when Jewish prophecy had ceased for more than two centuries? Lastly, in Ps. lxxix. the mention of "kingdoms" in ver. 6 ill suits the Maccabean time; while the way in which the psalm is cited by the author of the First Book of Maccabees (vii. 16, 17), who omits those words which are foreign to his purpose, is such as would have hardly been adopted in reference to a contemporary composition.

3. *Connection of the Psalms with the Israelitish history.* — In tracing this we shall, of course, assume the truth of the conclusions at which in the previous section we have arrived.

The psalms grew, essentially and gradually, out of the personal and national career of David and of Israel. That of Moses, Psalm xc., which, though it contributed little to the production of the rest, is yet, in point of actual date, the earliest, faithfully reflects the long, weary wanderings, the multiplied provocations, and the consequent punishments of the wilderness; and it is well that the Psalter should contain at least one memorial of those forty years of toil. It is, however, with David that Israelitish psalmody may be said virtually to commence. Previous mastery over his harp had probably already prepared the way for his future strains, when the anointing oil of Samuel descended upon him, and he began to drink in special measure from that day forward, of the Spirit of the Lord. It was then that, victorious at home over the mysterious melancholy of Saul and in the field over the vaunting champion of the Philistine hosts, he sang how from even babes and sucklings God had ordained strength because of his enemies (Ps. viii.). His next psalms are of a different character: his persecutions at the hands of Saul had commenced. Ps. lviii. was probably written after Jonathan's disclosures of the murderous designs of the court: Ps. lix. when his house was being watched by Saul's emissaries. The inhospitality of the court of Achish at Gath, gave rise to Ps. lvi.: Ps. xxxiv. was David's thanksgiving for deliverance from that court, not unmingled with shame for the unworthy stratagem to which he had there temporarily had recourse. The associations connected with the cave of Adullam are embodied in Ps. lvii.; the feelings excited by the tidings of Doeg's servility in Ps. lii. The escape from Keilah, in consequence of a divine warning, suggested Ps. xxxi. Ps. liv. was written when the Ziphites officiously informed Saul of David's movements. Pss. xxxv., xxxvi., recall the colloquy at Engedi. Nabal of Carmel was probably the original of the fool of Ps. liii.; though in this case the closing verse of that psalm must have been added when it was further altered, by David himself, into Ps. xlv. The most thoroughly idealized picture suggested by a retrospect of all the dangers of his outlaw-life is that presented to us by David in Ps. xxii. But in Ps. xxiii., which forms a side-piece to it, and the imagery of which is drawn from his earlier shepherd-days, David acknowledges that his past career had had its brighter as well as its darker side; nor had the goodness and mercy which were to follow him all the days of his life been ever really absent from him. Two more psalms, at least, must be referred to the period before David ascended the throne, namely, xxxviii. and xxxix., which naturally associate themselves with the distressing scene at Ziklag after the inroad of the Amalekites. Ps. xl. may perhaps be the thanksgiving for the retrieval of the disaster that had there befallen.

When David's reign has commenced, it is still with the most exciting incidents of his history, private or public, that his psalms are mainly associated. There are none to which the period of his reign at Hebron can lay exclusive claim. But after the conquest of Jerusalem his psalmody opened afresh with the solemn removal of the ark to Mount Zion; and in Pss. xxiv.–xxix., which belong together, we have the earliest definite instance of David's systematic composition or arrangement of psalms for public use. Ps. xxx. is of the same date: it was composed for the dedication of David's new palace, which took place on the same day with the establishment of the ark in its new tabernacle. Other psalms (and in these first do we trace any allusions to the promise of perpetual royalty now conveyed through Nathan) show the feelings of David in the midst of his foreign wars. The imagery of Ps. ii. is perhaps drawn from the events of this period; Pss. lx., lxi. belong to the campaign against Edom; Ps. xx. to .he second campaign, conducted by David in person, of the war against the allied Ammonites and Syrians; and Ps. xxi. to the termination of that war by the capture of Rabbah. Intermediate in date to the last-mentioned two psalms is Ps. li.; connected with the dark episode which made David tremble not only for himself, but also for the city whereon he had labored, and which he had partly

named by his own name, lest God should in displeasure not permit the future Temple to be reared on Mount Zion, nor the yet imperfect walls of Jerusalem to be completed. But rich above all, in the psalms to which it gave rise, is the period of David's flight from Absalom. To this we may refer Pss. iii.–vii. (the "Cush" of Ps. vii. being Shimei); also Ps. lv., which reflects the treachery of Ahithophel, Ps. lxii., which possibly alludes to the falsehood of both Ziba and Mephibosheth, and Ps. lxiii., written in the wilderness between Jerusalem and the Jordan.

Even of those psalms which cannot be referred to any definite occasion, several reflect the general historical circumstances of the times. Thus Ps. ix. is a thanksgiving for the deliverance of the land of Israel from its former heathen oppressors. Ps. x. is a prayer for the deliverance of the Church from the high-handed oppression exercised from within. The succeeding psalms dwell on the same theme, the virtual internal heathenism by which the Church of God was weighed down. So that there remain very few, e. g. Pss. xv.–xvii., xix., xxxii. (with its choral appendage xxxiii.), xxxvi., of which some historical account may not be given; and even of these some are manifestly connected with psalms of historical origin, e. g. Ps. xv. with Ps. xxiv.; and of others the historical reference may be more reasonably doubted than denied.

A season of repose near the close of his reign induced David to compose his grand personal thanksgiving for the deliverances of his whole life, Ps. xviii.; the date of which is approximately determined by the place at which it is inserted in the history (2 Sam. xxii.). It was probably at this period that he finally arranged for the sanctuary-service that collection of his psalms which now constitutes the First Book of the Psalter. From this he designedly excluded all (Pss. li.–lxiv.) that, from manifest private reference, or other cause, were unfitted for immediate public use; except only where he so fitted them by slightly generalizing the language, and by mostly substituting for the divine name Elohim the more theocratic name Jehovah; as we see by the instance of Ps. xiv. = liii., where both the altered and original copies of the hymn happen to be preserved. To the collection thus formed be prefixed by way of preface Ps. i., a simple moral contrast between the ways of the godly and the ungodly, and Ps. ii., a prophetical picture of the reign of that promised Ruler of whom he knew himself to be but the type. The concluding psalm of the collection, Ps. xli., seems to be a sort of ideal summary of the whole.

The course of David's reign was not, however, as yet complete. The solemn assembly convened by him for the dedication of the materials of the future Temple (1 Chr. xxviii., xxix.) would naturally call forth a renewal of his best efforts to glorify the God of Israel in psalms; and to this occasion we doubtless owe the great festal hymns Pss. lxv.–lxvii., lxviii., containing a large review of the past history, present position, and prospective glories of God's chosen people. The supplications of Ps. lxix. suit best with the renewed distress occasioned by the sedition of Adonijah. Ps. lxxi., to which Ps. lxx., a fragment of a former psalm, is introductory, forms David's parting strain. Yet that the psalmody of Israel may not seem finally to terminate with him, the glories of the future are forthwith anticipated by his son in Ps. lxxii. And so closes the first great blaze of the lyrical devotions of Israel. David is not merely the soul of it; he stands in it absolutely alone. It is from the events of his own career that the greater part of the psalms have sprung; he is their author, and on his harp are they first sung; to him too is due the design of the establishment of regular choirs for their future sacred performance; his are all the arrangements by which that design is carried out; and even the improvement of the musical instruments needed for the performance is traced up to him (Amos vi. 5).

For a time the single psalm of Solomon remained the only addition to those of David. Solomon's own gifts lay mainly in a different direction; and no sufficiently quickening religious impulses mingled with the generally depressing events of the reigns of Rehoboam and Abijah to raise up to David any lyrical successor. If, however, religious psalmody were to revive, somewhat might be not unreasonably anticipated from the great assembly of King Asa (2 Chr. xv.); and Ps. l. suits so exactly with the circumstances of that occasion, that it may well be assigned to it. Internal evidence renders it more likely that this " Psalm of Asaph" proceeded from a descendant of Asaph than from Asaph himself; and possibly its author may be the Azariah the son of Oded, who had been moved by the Spirit of God to kindle Asa's zeal. Another revival of psalmody more certainly occurred under Jehoshaphat at the time of the Moabite and Ammonite invasion (2 Chr. xx.). Of this, Pss. xlvii., xlviii. were the fruits; and we may suspect that the Levite singer Jahaziel, who foretold the Jewish deliverance, was their author. The great prophetical ode (Ps. xlv.) connects itself most readily with the splendors of Jehoshaphat's reign. And after that psalmody had thus definitely revived, there would be no reason why it should not thenceforward manifest itself in seasons of anxiety, as well as of festivity and thanksgiving. Hence Ps. xlix. Yet the psalms of this period flow but sparingly. Pss. xlii. - xliv., lxiv., are best assigned to the reign of Ahaz; they delineate that monarch's desecration of the sanctuary, the sighings of the faithful who had exiled themselves in consequence from Jerusalem, and the political humiliation to which the kingdom of Judah was, through the proceedings of Ahaz, reduced. The reign of Hezekiah is naturally rich in psalmody. Pss. xlvi., lxxiii., lxxv.,, lxxvi., connect themselves with the resistance to the supremacy of the Assyrians and the divine destruction of their host. The first of these psalms indeed would by its place in the Psalter more naturally belong to the deliverance in the days of Jehoshaphat, to which some, as Delitzsch, actually refer it; but if internal evidence be deemed to establish sufficiently its later date, it may have been exceptionally permitted to appear in Book II. on account of its similarity in style to Pss. xlvii., xlviii. We are now brought to a series of psalms of peculiar interest, springing out of the political and religious history of the separated ten tribes. In date of actual composition they commence before the times of Hezekiah. The earliest is probably Ps. lxxx., a supplication for the Israelitish people at the time of the Syrian oppression. Ps. lxxxi. is an earnest appeal to them, indicative of what God would yet do for them if they would hearken to his voice: Ps. lxxxii. a stern reproof of the internal oppression prevalent, by the testimony of Amos, in the realm of Israel. In Ps. lxxxiii. we have a prayer for deliverance from that extensive confederacy of ene-

mies from all quarters, of which the traces meet us in Joel iii., Amos i., and which probably was eventually crushed by the contemporaneous victories of Jeroboam II. of Israel and Uzziah of Judah. All these psalms are referred by their superscriptions to the Levite singers, and thus bear witness to the efforts of the Levites to reconcile the two branches of the chosen nation. In Ps. lxxviii, belonging, probably, to the opening of Hezekiah's reign, the psalmist assumes a bolder tone, and, reproving the disobedience of the Israelites by the parable of the nation's earlier rebellions, sets forth to them the Temple at Jerusalem as the appointed centre of religious worship, and the heir of the house of David as the sovereign of the Lord's choice. This remonstrance may have contributed to the partial success of Hezekiah's messages of invitation to the ten tribes of Israel. Ps. lxxxiv. represents the thanks and prayers of the northern pilgrims, coming up, for the first time in two hundred and fifty years, to celebrate the passover in Jerusalem: Ps. lxxxv. may well be the thanksgiving for the happy restoration of religion, of which the advent of those pilgrims formed part. Ps. lxxvii., on the other hand, is the lamentation of the Jewish Church for the terrible political calamity which speedily followed, whereby the inhabitants of the northern kingdom were carried into Captivity, and Joseph lost, the second time, to Jacob. The prosperity of Hezekiah's own reign outweighed the sense of this heavy blow, and nursed the holy faith whereby the king himself in Ps. lxxxvi., and the Levites in Ps. lxxxvii., anticipated the future welcome of all the Gentiles into the Church of God. Ps. lxxix. (an Asaphic psalm, and therefore placed with the others of like authorship) may best be viewed as a picture of the evil days that followed through the transgressions of Manasseh. And in Pss. lxxxviii., lxxxix. we have the pleadings of the nation with God under the severest trial that it had yet experienced, the captivity of its anointed sovereign, and the apparent failure of the promise made to David and his house.

The captivity of Manasseh himself proved to be but temporary; but the sentence which his sins had provoked upon Judah and Jerusalem still remained to be executed, and precluded the hope that God's salvation could be revealed till after such an outpouring of his judgments as the nation never yet had known. Labor and sorrow must be the lot of the present generation; through these mercy might occasionally gleam, but the glory which was eventually to be manifested must be for posterity alone. The psalms of Book IV. bear generally the impress of this feeling. The Mosaic Psalm xc., from whatever cause here placed, harmonizes with it. Pss. xci., xcii. are of a peaceful, simple, liturgical character; but in the series of psalms Pss. xciii. - c., which foretell the future advent of God's kingdom, the days of adversity of the Chaldæan oppression loom in the foreground. Pss. ci., ciii., "of David," readily refer themselves to Josiah as their author; the former embodies his early resolutions of piety; the latter belongs to the period of the solemn renewal of the covenant after the discovery of the book of the Law, and after the assurance to Josiah that for his tenderness of heart he should be graciously spared from beholding the approaching evil. Intermediate to these in place, and perhaps in date, is Ps. cii., "A Prayer of the afflicted," written by one who is almost entirely wrapped up in the prospect of the

Impending desolation, though he recognises withal the divine favor which should remotely but eventually be manifested. Ps. civ., a meditation on the providence of God, is itself a preparation for that "hiding of God's face" which should ensue are the Church were, like the face of the earth, renewed; and in the historical Pss. cv., cvi., the one the story of God's faithfulness, the other of the people's transgressions, we have the immediate prelude to the Captivity, together with a prayer for eventual deliverance from it.

We pass to Book V. Ps. cvii. is the opening psalm of the return, sung probably at the first Feast of Tabernacles (Ezr. iii.) The ensuing Davidic psalms may well be ascribed to Zerubbabel; Ps. cviii. (drawn from Pss. lvii., lx.) being in anticipation of the returning prosperity of the Church; Ps. cix., a prayer against the efforts of the Samaritans to hinder the rebuilding of the Temple; Ps. cx., a picture of the triumphs of the Church in the days of the future Messiah, whose union of royalty and priesthood had been at this time set forth in the type and prophecy of Zech. vi. 11–13.[a] Ps. cxviii., with which Pss. cxiv.–cxvii. certainly, and in the estimation of some Ps. cxiii., and even Pss. cxi., cxii., stand connected, is the festal hymn sung at the laying of the foundations of the second Temple. We here pass over the questions connected with Ps. cxix.; but a directly historical character belongs to Pss. cxx.–cxxxiv., styled in our A. V. "Songs of Degrees." [DEGREES, SONGS OF, where the different interpretations of the Hebrew title are given.] Internal evidence refers these to the period when the Jews under Nehemiah were, in the very face of the enemy, repairing the walls of Jerusalem; and the title may well signify "Songs of goings up (as the Hebrew phrase is) upon the walls," the psalms being, from their brevity, well adapted to be sung by the workmen and guards while engaged in their respective duties. As David cannot well be the author of Pss. cxxii., cxxiv., cxxxi., cxxxiii., marked with his name, so neither, by analogy, can Solomon well be the actual author of Ps. cxxvii. Theodoret thinks that by "Solomon" Zerubbabel is intended, both as deriving his descent from Solomon, and as renewing Solomon's work: with yet greater probability we might ascribe the psalm to Nehemiah. Pss. cxxxv., cxxxvi., by their parallelism with the confession of sins in Neh. ix., connect themselves with the national fast of which that chapter speaks. Of somewhat earlier date, it may be, are Ps. cxxxvii. and the ensuing Davidic psalms. Of these, Ps. cxxxix. is a psalm of the new birth of Israel, from the womb of the Babylonish Captivity, to a life of righteousness: Pss. cxl.–cxliii. may be a picture of the trials to which the unrestored exiles were still exposed in the realms of the Gentiles. Henceforward, as we approach the close of the Psalter, its strains rise in cheerfulness; and it fittingly terminates with Pss. cxlvii.–cl., which were probably sung on the occasion of the thanksgiving procession of Neh. xii., after the rebuilding of the walls of Jerusalem had been completed.

4. *Moral Characteristics of the Psalms.* — Foremost among these meets us, undoubtedly, the universal recourse to communion with God. "My voice is unto God, and I will cry " (Ps. lxxvii. 1), might well stand as a motto to the whole of the Psalter; for, whether immersed in the depths, or whether blessed with greatness and comfort on every side, it is to God that the psalmist's voice seems ever to soar spontaneously aloft. Alike in the welcome of present deliverance or in the contemplation of past mercies, he addresses himself straight to God as the object of his praise. Alike in the persecutions of his enemies and the desertions of his friends, in wretchedness of body and in the agonies of inward repentance, in the hour of impending danger and in the hour of apparent despair, it is direct to God that he utters forth his supplications. Despair, we say; for such, as far as the description goes, is the psalmist's state in Ps. lxxxviii. But meanwhile he is praying; the apparent impossibility of deliverance cannot restrain his God-ward voice; and so the very force of communion with God carries him, almost unawares to himself, through the trial.

Connected with this is the faith by which he everywhere lives in God rather than in himself. God's mercies, God's greatness form the sphere in which his thoughts are ever moving: even when through excess of affliction reason is rendered powerless, the naked contemplation of God's wonders of old forms his effectual support (Ps. lxxvii.).

It is of the essence of such faith that the psalmist's view of the perfections of God should be true and vivid. The Psalter describes God as He is: it glows with testimonies to his power and providence, his love and faithfulness, his holiness and righteousness. Correspondingly it testifies against every form of idol which men would substitute in the living God's place: whether it be the outward image, the work of men's hands (Ps. cxv.), or whether it be the inward vanity of earthly comfort or prosperity, to be purchased at the cost of the honor which cometh from God alone (Ps. iv.).

The solemn "See that there is no idol-way (דֶרֶךְ עֹצֶב) in me" of Ps. cxxxix., the striving of the heart after the very truth and nought beside, is the exact anticipation of the "Little children, keep yourselves from idols," of the loved Apostle in the N. T.

The Psalms not only set forth the perfections of God: they proclaim also the duty of worshipping Him by the acknowledgment and adoration of his perfections. They encourage all outward rites and means of worship: new songs, use of musical instruments of all kinds, appearance in God's courts, lifting up of hands, prostration at his footstool, holy apparel (A. V. "beauty of holiness"). Among these they recognize the ordinance of sacrifice (Pss. iv., v., xxvii., li.) as an expression of the worshipper's consecration of himself to God's service. But not the less do they repudiate the outward rite when separated from that which it was designed to express (Pss. xl., lxix.): a broken and contrite heart is, from erring man, the genuine sacrifice which God requires (Ps. li.).

Similar depth is observable in the view taken by the psalmist of human sin. It is to be traced not only in its outward manifestations, but also in

---

a A very strong feeling exists that Mark xii. 36, &c., show Ps. cx. to have been composed by David himself. To the writer of this article it appears, that as our Saviour's argument remains the same from whichever of his ancestors the psalm proceeded, so his words do not necessarily imply more than is intended in the superscription of the psalm.

the inward workings of the heart (Ps. xxxvi.), and is to be primarily ascribed to man's innate corruption (Pss. li., lviii.). It shows itself alike in deeds, in words (Pss. xvii., cxli.), and in thoughts (Ps. cxxxix.); nor is even the believer able to discern all its various ramifications (Ps. xix.). Connected with this view of sin is, on the one hand, the picture of the utter corruption of the ungodly world (Ps. xiv.); on the other, the encouragement to genuine repentance, the assurance of divine forgiveness (Ps. xxxii.), and the trust in God as the source of complete redemption (Ps. cxxx.).

In regard of the Law, the psalmist, while warmly acknowledging its excellence, feels yet that it cannot so effectually guide his own unassisted exertions as to preserve him from error (Ps. xix.). He needs an additional grace from above, the grace of God's Holy Spirit (Ps. li.). But God's Spirit is also a free spirit (ib.): led by this he will discern the Law, with all its precepts, to be no arbitrary rule of bondage, but rather a charter and instrument of liberty (Ps. cxix.).

The Psalms bear repeated testimony to the duty of instructing others in the ways of holiness (Pss. xxxii., xxxiv., li.). They also indirectly enforce the duty of love, even to our enemies (Ps. vii. 4, xxxv. 13, cix. 4). On the other hand they imprecate, in ·the strongest terms, the judgments of God on transgressors. Such imprecations are levelled at transgressors as a body, and are uniformly uttered on the hypothesis of their willful persistence in evil, in which case the overthrow of the sinner becomes a necessary part of the uprooting of sin. They are in nowise inconsistent with any efforts to lead sinners individually to repentance. [PSALMS IMPRECATORY, Amer. ed.]

This brings us to notice, lastly, the faith of the psalmists in a righteous recompense to all men according to their deeds (Ps. xxxvii., &c.). They generally expected that men would receive such recompense in great measure during their own lifetime. Yet they felt withal that it was not then complete: it perpetuated itself to their children (Ps. xxxvii. 25, cix. 12, &c.); and thus we find set forth in the Psalms, with sufficient distinctness, though in an unmatured and consequently imperfect form, the doctrine of a retribution after death.

5. *Prophetical Character of the Psalms.* — The moral struggle between godliness and ungodliness, so vividly depicted in the Psalms, culminates, in Holy Scripture, in the life of the Incarnate Son of God upon earth. It only remains to show that the Psalms themselves definitely anticipated this culmination. Now there are in the Psalter at least three psalms of which the interest evidently centres in a person distinct from the speaker, and which, since they cannot without violence to the language be interpreted of any but the Messiah, may be termed directly and exclusively Messianic. We refer to Pss. ii., xlv., cx.; to which may perhaps be added Ps. lxxii.

It would be strange if these few psalms stood, in their prophetical significance, absolutely alone among the rest: the more so, inasmuch as Ps. ii. forms part of the preface to the First Book of the Psalter, and would, as such, be entirely out of place, did not its general theme virtually extend itself over those which follow, in which the interest generally centres in the figure of the suppliant or worshipper himself. And hence the impossibility of viewing the psalms generally, notwithstanding the historical drapery in which they are

outwardly clothed, as simply the past devotions of the historical David or the historical Israel. Other arguments to the same effect are furnished by the idealized representations which many of them present; by the outward points of contact between their language and the actual earthly career of our Saviour; by the frequent references made to them both by our Saviour Himself and by the Evangelists; and by the view taken of them by the Jews, as evidenced in several passages of the Targum. There is yet another circumstance well worthy of note in its bearing upon this subject. Alike in the earlier and in the later portions of the Psalter, all those psalms which are of a personal rather than of a national character are marked in the superscriptions with the name of David, as proceeding either from David himself or from one of his descendants. It results from this, that while the Davidic psalms are partly personal, partly national, the Levitic psalms are uniformly national. Exceptions to this rule exist only in appearance: thus Ps. lxxiii., although couched in the first person singular, is really a prayer of the Jewish faithful against the Assyrian invaders; and in Pss. xlii., xliii., it is the feelings of an exiled company rather than of a single individual to which utterance is given. It thus follows that it was only those psalmists who were types of Christ by external office and lineage as well as by inward piety, that were charged by the Holy Spirit to set forth beforehand, in Christ's own name and person, the sufferings that awaited him and the glory that should follow. The national hymns of Israel are indeed also prospective; but in general they anticipate rather the struggles and the triumphs of the Christian Church than those of Christ Himself.

We annex a list of the chief passages in the Psalms which are in anywise quoted or embodied in the N. T.: Ps. ii. 1, 2, 7, 8, 9, iv. 4, v. 9, vi. 3, 8, viii. 2, 4–6, x. 7, xiv. 1–3, xvi. 8–11, xviii. 4, 49, xix. 4, xxii. 1, 8, 18, 22, xxiii. 6, xxiv. 1, xxxi. 5, xxxii. 1, 2, xxxiv. 8, 12–16, 20, xxxv. 9, xxxvi. 1, xxxvii. 11, xl. 6–8, xli. 9, xliv. 22, xlv. 6, 7, xlviii. 2, li. 4, lv. 22, lxviii. 18, lxix. 4, 9, 22, 23, 25, lxxv. 8, lxxviii. 2, 24, lxxxii. 6, lxxxvi. 9, lxxxix. 20, xc. 4, xci. 11, 12, xcii. 7, xciv. 11, xcv 7–11, cii. 25–27, civ. 4, cix. 8, cx. 1, 4, cxii. 9, cxvi. 10, cxvii. 1, cxviii. 6, 22, 23, 25, 26, cxxv. 5, cxl. 3.

6. *Literature.* — The list of Jewish commentators on the Psalter includes the names of Saadiah (who wrote in Arabic), Jarchi, Aben Ezra, and Kimchi. Among later performances that of Sforno († 1550) is highly spoken of (reprinted in a Furth Psalter of 1804); and special mention is also due to the modern German translation of Mendelssohn († 1786), to which again is appended a comment by Joel Bril. In the Christian Church devotional familiarity with the Psalter has rendered the number of commentators on it immense; and in modern times even the number of private translations of it has been so large as to preclude enumeration here. Among the Greek Fathers, Theodoret is the best commentator, Chrysostom the best homilist, on the Psalms: for the rest, a catena of the Greek comments was formed by the Jesuit Corderius. In the West the pithy expositions of Hilary and the sermons of Augustine are the main patristic helps. A list of the chief mediæval comments, which are of a devotional and mystical rather than of a critical character, will be found in Neale's *Commentary* (vol. i. 1860), which is mainly derived from them, and favorably introduces them to modern English

readers. Later Roman Catholic laborers on the Psalms are Genebrard (1587), Agellius (1606), Bellarmine (1617), Lorinus (1619), and De Muis (1650): the valuable critical commentary of the last named has been reprinted, accompanied by the able preface and terse annotations of Bossuet. Among the Reformers, of whom Luther, Zwingle, Bucer, and Calvin all applied themselves to the Psalms, Calvin naturally stands, as a commentator, preëminent. Of subsequent works those of Geier (1668) and Venema (1762, &c.) are still held in some repute; while Rosenmüller's *Scholia* give, of course, the substance of others. The modern German laborers on the Psalms, commencing with De Wette, are very numerous. Maurer shines as an elegant grammatical critic: Ewald (*Dichter des A. B.* i. and ii.) as a translator. Hengstenberg's Commentary holds a high place. The two latest Commentaries are that of Hupfeld (in progress), a work of high philological merit, but written in strong opposition to Hengstenberg, and from an unsatisfactory point of theological view; and that of Delitzsch (1859–60), the diligent work of a sober-minded theologian, whose previous *Symbolæ ad Pss. illustr. isagogicæ* had been a valuable contribution to the external criticism of the Psalms. Of English works we may mention the Paraphrase of Hammond; the devotional Commentary of Bishop Horne, and along with this the unpretending but useful *Plain Commentary* recently published; Merrick's *Annotations*; Bishop Horsley's Translation and Notes (1815, posthumous); Dr. Mason Good's *Historical Outline*, and also his Translation with Notes (both posthumous; distinguished by taste and originality rather than by sound judgment or accurate scholarship); Phillips's Text, with Commentary, for Hebrew students; J. Jebb's *Literal Translation and Dissertations* (1846); and lastly Thrupp's *Introduction to the Psalms* (1860), to which the reader is referred for a fuller discussion of the various matters treated of in this article. In the press, a new translation, etc., by Perowne, of which specimens have appeared. A catalogue of commentaries, treatises, and sermons on the Psalms is given in Darling's *Cyclop. Bibliographica* (subjects), p. 374–514.

7. *Psalter of Solomon.* — Under this title is extant, in a Greek translation, a collection of eighteen hymns, evidently modeled on the canonical psalms, breathing Messianic hopes, and forming a favorable specimen of the later popular Jewish literature. They have been variously assigned by critics to the times of the persecution of Antiochus Epiphanes (Ewald, Dillmann), or to those of the rule of Herod (Movers, Delitzsch). They may be found in the *Codex Pseudepigraphus V. T.* of Fabricius. J. F. T.

* On the *Psalter of Solomon* see art. MACCABEES, vol. ii. p. 1713 f., and note a, p. 1714. It is best edited in Hilgenfeld's *Messias Judæorum*, Lips. 1869. A.

* *Additional Literature.* — The following are the latest critical works on the Psalms: De Wette, *Commentar über die Psalmen*, 1811; 5te Aufl. von G. Baur, 1856. Rosenmüller, *Scholia in Psalmos*, 1831. Claus, *Beiträge zur Krit. und Exeg. der Psalmen*, 1831. Noyes, *A new Translation of the Book of Psalms, with an Introduction*, 1831; 3d ed. 1867. Keil, *Siebzig ausgew. Psalmen ausgelegt*, 1834–5. Hitzig, *Die Psalmen, hist. krit. Commentar*, 1835–6; *Die Psalmen, uebersetzt u. ausgelegt*, 1863–5 (a new work). Maurer, *Psalmi* (comment.

crit. vol. iii.), 1838. Ewald, *Die Psalmen erklärt*, 1839; 3te Ausg. 1866. Dursch, *Ein allgem. Comment. über die Psalmen des A. T.*, 1842. Hengstenberg, *Commentar über die Psalmen*, 1842–7; 2te Aufl. 1849–52; Eng. trans., 3 vols. Edinb. 1857. Tholuck, *Uebersetzung und Auslegung der Psalmen*, 1843; Eng. trans., Phila. 1858. Vaihinger, *Die Psalmen metr. übersetzt und erklärt*, 1845. Delitzsch, *Symbolæ ad Psalmos illustrandos isagogicæ*, 1846. Phillips, *The Psalms in Hebrew, with crit. exeget. and phil. commentary*, 1846. Lengerke, *Die fünf Bücher der Psalmen*, 1847. Alexander, *The Psalms translated and explained*, 1850. Olshausen, *Die Psalmen erklärt* (Exeget. Handb. 14ter Th.), 1853. Hupfeld, *Die Psalmen übersetzt und ausgelegt*, 1855–62; 2te Aufl. von Riehm, 1867–9. Reinke (Cath.), *Die messian. Psalmen, Einl., Grundtext u. Uebers., nebst einem phil.-krit. u. hist. Comm.*, 1857–9. Delitzsch, *Commentar über den Psalter*, 1859–60; *Die Psalmen, neue Ausarbeitung* (Bibl. Com. 4ter Th.), 1867. Thrupp, *Emendations on the Psalms* (Journal of Class. and Sacr. Phil.), 1860. Van Ortenberg, *Zur Textkritik der Psalmen*, 1861. Böhl, *Zwölf Messianische Psalmen*, 1862. Kamphausen, *Die Psalmen* (Bunsen's Bibelwerk), 1863. Perowne, *The Book of Psalms, a new Translation, with Introductions and Notes expl. and crit.*, 1864–8; 2d ed. (in press, 1869). Wordsworth, *The Book of Psalms*, 1867. *The Psalms chronologically arranged; an amended version, with hist. introductions and explan. notes, by Four Friends*, Lond. 1867. Ehrt, *Abfassungszeit und Abschluss des Psalters*, 1869. Moll, *Die Psalter*, 1te Hälfte (Lange's Bibelwerk, 11ter Th.), 1869. Barnes, *Notes crit. expl. and pract. on the book of Psalms*, 3 vols. 1869. Didham, *A new Translation of the Psalms*; Part I., Pss. i.–xxv., 1869. Conant, *The Psalms, revised version, with an Introduction and occasional notes* (in press, 1869).

T. J. C.

* PSALMS, IMPRECATORY. The psalms designated under this title are those in which the author is supposed to invoke curses upon his enemies, and for the gratification of a vindictive spirit to delight in their sufferings. Entire psalms usually classed as imprecatory in this sense are xxxv., lviii., lix., lxix., and cix., all of which bear strong marks of the authorship of David. Parts of other psalms have also been classed as imprecatory: Ps. iii. 3, 7, ix. 2–4, xviii. 37–43, xvi. 7–11, xxxvii. 12–15, lii. 5–7, lv. 9, 15, and 23, lxiii. 9–11, lxiv. 7–9, cxxxv. 8–12, cxxxvii. 7–9. Among the strongest passages in which this maledictory spirit is said to appear are the following: —

"Set thou a wicked man over him,
And let Satan stand at his right hand.
When he shall be judged, let him be condemned,
And let his prayer become sin " (cix. 6, 7).

" Let his children be fatherless, and his wife a widow,
Let his children be continually vagabonds and beg.
Let the extortioner catch all that he hath,
And let strangers spoil his labor " (cix. 9–11).

(Of a later date) —

" O daughter of Babylon, who art to be destroyed,
Happy shall he be that rewardeth thee
As thou hast served us.
Happy shall he be that taketh
And dasheth thy little ones against the stones "
(cxxxvii. 8, 9).

It is undeniable that these and such expressions in the Psalms have been a source of grief and perplexity to the Christian, while they have furnished occasion for cavil and scoffing to the skeptical. Various theories have been proposed for explaining the language so as to remove this ground of complaint against the Scriptures. It has been suggested that the so called imprecations are simply predictions of the evil which is likely to befall the wicked. But the study of the Hebrew original does not warrant such a view: the imprecation is expressed by the forms of the verb (imperative as well as future) employed in Hebrew for uttering a wish or prayer. This, moreover, is a timid way of dealing with the difficulty. It is better at once to admit the apparent inconsistency between this spirit of the Psalms and that of the teachings and example of Christ, and then inquire what explanation can be given of it. Within the limits to which we are restricted, we can only glance at some of the leading considerations.

(i.) In the first place it has been said that the duty of forgiving and loving our enemies is not distinctly taught in the O. T., and that David therefore is not to be expected to rise above the standard of duty and character of the dispensation to which he belonged. But we must reply to this that David was not ignorant of this requisition; for the Jewish Scriptures condemned a spirit of revenge, and enjoined the requiting of evil with good. In Ex. xxiii. 4, 5, we read (as correctly translated): "If thou seest thine enemy's ox or his ass going astray, thou shalt surely bring it back to him. When thou seest the ass of him that hateth thee lying under its burden, thou shalt forbear to leave him: thou shalt surely help him loose it." So in Lev. xix. 18: "Thou shalt not avenge nor bear any grudge against the children of thy people; but thou shalt love thy neighbor as thyself;" Prov. xxiv. 17, 18: "Rejoice not when thine enemy falleth; and let not thine heart be glad when he stumbleth; lest the Lord see it, and it displease Him" (see also ver. 29); and xxv. 21, 22: "If thine enemy be hungry, give him bread to eat; and if he be thirsty, give him water to drink: for thou shalt heap coals of fire upon his head, and the Lord shall reward thee." Not only so, but David himself recognized this obligation, and, as all admit, was certainly in his general conduct a remarkable example of patience under multiplied wrongs and of magnanimity to his foes when he had them in his power (see *infra*).

(ii.) Some would regard the psalms here under consideration as historical in their character, and not strictly preceptive or didactic. That is, they are the records of facts, and hence express the actual feelings of the writers, just as the biography of good men in the Bible and elsewhere relates other acts of such men, of the character of which the reader is left to judge according to his own standard of piety and morality. If inspired men may do things which are wrong, they may utter words which are selfish, or passionate, or resentful, and yet not forfeit their character for general uprightness or their claim in other respects to confidence as religious teachers. It is precisely this fidelity with which the Scriptures record the acts and feelings of men who usually were eminent servants of God, suppressing nothing, palliating nothing, that, more than any ingenious defense of apologists, has given to the Bible its hold on the confidence of the world. This perfect truthfulness makes an irresistible appeal. With wonderful wisdom the Bible does not present to us for a model, the piety of the saint or angel, but piety in its human development, struggling with sins, temptations, difficulties: not the highest form of religion, but the highest form which man can understand. The failings of David, Moses, and Peter have benefited the Church as well as the unblemished correctness of Joseph and Daniel. The experience of any one takes hold of us, when his real feelings, good and bad, are honestly told. They are so much like our own that we sympathize with him. They interest intensely each successive generation of mankind, for "one touch of nature makes us all akin." The wonder and beauty of these compositions is that they are a glass through which we see nature exactly: they give a Shakespearian picture of all the moral workings of the heart. The Psalmist does not select his best feelings for exhibition and hold his bad ones in the shade, but all ideas and emotions are given just as they are. Rev. Albert Barnes admits an element of truth in this explanation, and Dr. Tholuck distinctly holds that a personal feeling has occasionally mixed itself with David's denunciations of the wicked. Hengstenberg objects to such a view that it invalidates the character of the Psalms as a normal expression of only such acts and feelings as God must approve.

(iii.) In the third place, it is undeniable that some critics have greatly exaggerated this charge of vindictiveness on the part of David. In reality very few of the Psalms have with any appearance of truth incurred this censure. Of the one hundred and fifty psalms, Stanley (*Lectures on the Jewish Church*, ii. 170) singles out only four as marked illustrations of this spirit. With reference to these, or others which may be classed with these, we are to make due allowance for the *vehemence of oriental expression* as compared with our own habits of thought and language. It is a maxim in literature that an author is to be judged by the standard of his own age and time, not by the standard of our own. This is a simple principle of justice readily granted to all authors, and due certainly to the Biblical authors as well as others. An honest effort to understand the imprecatory psalms requires that we study the genius of Hebrew poetry, the spirit of the age in which David lived, and the circumstances of David at the moment when he uttered the imprecations. To understand an author, we must with pains and study reach the author's exact point of view. We must distinguish between the real meaning of the man and the color given to that meaning by his education and habits of thought. A very little study shows us that Hebrew poetry partakes of the intenseness of oriental temperament. The Oriental expresses in the language of strong passion the same meaning which to the European appears to be the dictate of reason and common sense. If the European says that God loves men, the Asiatic prophet expresses the same idea by a phrase which is almost amatory; "Thy Maker is thine husband;" "As the bridegroom rejoiceth over the bride, so shall thy God rejoice over thee." Now the sentiments of indignation are expressed with the same hyperbole. If the European merely says that justice will be done to the wicked the Oriental means the same thing, but expresses it by saying: —

"The righteous shall rejoice when he seeth the vengeance,

He shall wash his feet in the blood of the wicked

When the Psalmist utters a denunciation which to us seems terrific, he may have intended only to express a plain thought with ordinary vigor. A generous and certainly a thorough examiner will take the genius of the age and of the man for the background of his criticism upon the man's production; he will criticise poetry as poetry, and Oriental Poetry as a department of the art, distinct and separate in itself: he will not complain because in the poetry of Isaiah there are found some expressions which would not be pertinent to a demonstration of Euclid, nor will he expect to find in Homer the same style of expression which he looks for in Sir William Hamilton.

(iv.) Another consideration which, if not rightly understood, will confuse the reader of these psalms, is that their author identifies the enemies of God with his own enemies. The spirit of David is well expressed in his own words: " Do I not hate them, O Lord, that hate thee? I hate them with perfect hatred; I count them mine enemies;" or, in the colder language of Solomon: " The fear of the Lord is to hate evil: pride, and arrogancy, and the evil way, and the froward mouth do I hate." Even Catiline had insight enough to say, " An identity of wishes and aversions, this alone is true friendship;"*a* and such was the friendship between David and Jehovah. So close was the union between David and his Master that intuitively David assailed the Lord's enemies as his own. The truth is that David's personal attitude towards his enemies was different from that of any other warrior in history. The cause of God was placed in his hands obviously and directly. He was called upon to uphold the cause of Jehovah against the heathen without and the house of Saul within the Jewish kingdom. He had the wrongs of Jehovah as well as his own to requite, and in requiting the wrongs of Jehovah he probably lost sight of his own altogether. During his youth, spies in the employ of Saul were around him continually, and often was he pursued by a band of furious and blood-thirsty men, who, by exterminating him, hoped to extinguish the cause of God altogether. He was situated like the English statesman who in an attack upon himself sees the crown and government to be really aimed at. Hence the terrible strength of David's retort. He replied not for himself, but for those whom he represented. His zeal for God spent itself in a tempest of fury upon God's enemies. It was when he felt God's honor to be insulted that he rose to a loftiness of vengeance all his own, and prayed: —

" That thy foot may be dipped in the blood of thine enemies,
And the tongue of thy dogs in the same."

Unless we rise to this view, we are left to suppose that David left the vast responsibility of defending God's earthly honor, for the little work of redressing his personal wrongs. The elevation of his character above such a motive is evident from his sparing the chief of his enemies when he had him in his power, and from the generous eloquence of his lamentation when that enemy fell. David's real feeling towards his enemies he expresses thus (Ps. xxxv. 12, 13): —

" They rewarded me evil for good ;
My soul is made desolate (orphaned) ;

---

a " Nam idem velle atque idem nolle, ea demum firma amicitia est " (Sallust, *Catiline*, 20, 4).

But as for me, when they were sick,
My clothing was sackcloth.
I afflicted my soul with fasting,
And my prayer returned into mine own bosom."

David also wrote (Ps. lxix. 24): —

" Pour out thine indignation upon them,
And let thy wrathful anger take hold of them."

But in the one case he spoke of his own enemies, and in the other case of the enemies of God, as he shows in the very next verse: —

" For they persecute him whom thou hast smitten,
And they talk to the grief of those whom thou hast wounded."

(v.) These considerations prepare the way for the main explanation of the Imprecatory Psalms. They express the sense of outraged justice. In the nature of things, the sense of wrong and injustice must have its rebound. There are times when forbearance ceases to be a virtue, when Heaven encourages men to express the pent-up indignation of their hearts. It is not to be supposed God intends that the saints shall bear all the Inquisitions, Saint Bartholomews, Smithfield fires of the enemy in total silence. If man is liable to oppression, he is also gifted with resistive powers, and of those powers the spirit of God only invigorates the proper use. The grace which makes men free from sin, makes them free from the earthly tyrant, and the spirit of God is the real force which inspires men to resist oppression with the pen and the sword. David was the Milton and the Cromwell of his time. With dauntless courage and determination he fought the earthly battles of the Lord, and the English poet caught the echo of his lyre, when he sang, —

" Avenge, O Lord, thy slaughtered saints, whose bones
Lie scattered on the Alpine mountains cold."

The wicked man is not merely the foe of the one whom he injures; he is the common enemy of all mankind. While the judge and the executioner are engaged in punishing him, they may be cheered in their work by the prayer of the Christian and the song of the poet. Any government would be justly derided which showed itself unable or unwilling to punish at the proper time. Based upon this irrepressible instinct of human nature, we rise to survey the vast field of revealed doctrine, and see that the spirit of the Imprecatory Psalms is no morbid or inconsistent sentiment of the Bible; but if that spirit is necessary to a natural government, it is equally necessary to a perfect revelation. From a low moral standpoint these psalms seem to be an irregular part of the Bible; they take their place with poise and beauty in the great scheme when we rise sufficiently high to see the whole of it. If the main purpose of God's mind is love to the universal good, its alternate expression is denunciation of evil. It is but a narrow spirit which condemns, in a small portion of the Psalms, that resistance to evil, which goes forth from the throne of God to form all that is manly in human nature, and around which every other sentiment of the Bible is adjusted.

(vi.) Nearly every book of the Scriptures has a form of denouncing sin, which is peculiar to itself. The Pentateuch denounces by the severity of its laws against the wicked man: it gives that view of sin which is peculiar to the lawgiver's mind. The historical books of the Bible do not denounce sin, but they quietly show its effects. In the individual case they show that a bad character is naturally connected with the loss of all resources, and, generally speaking, with a miserable end. In the case of a nation, they show that its guilt is closely connected with its enslavement; for after sin has mastered the national character, the government soon loses all vigor and cohesion, and the sword of the tyrant rapidly presses through the breach which sin has made in the rampart of public virtue. This part of the Bible pictures sin as it is seen from the historic standpoint. The prophets denounce sin in a manner more rhetorical and direct, and the imprecations of David are gentle, compared with the anathemas of Isaiah, Ezekiel, Amos, and Hosea. If our Saviour had uttered no imprecations, those of David could certainly be questioned; but He did utter them with a scope, duration, and intensity of meaning which David never knew, for the greater the being the greater is his power to destroy. The very gentleness of the Saviour's character prevents any suspicion that He could have been influenced by private resentment, and gives an indescribable air of truth and justice to his threatenings. Now why is it that in a few songs of David the same spirit is so much condemned? We answer that, as far as we can judge, there is an ambiguity in the object of David's imprecation. In his case, the enemies of God and his own enemies were the same persons, and the Psalmist is accused of attacking those as his own enemies, while there is overwhelming reason to believe he attacked them only as the enemies of God. It is probably this circumstance alone which has confused the mind of the good, and exposed the Psalmist to the charge of vindictiveness.

(vii.) The revealed word is reflected in man's experience, and we remark finally that the events of history continually give the Imprecatory Psalms new meaning. Experience is their best interpreter. When the cause of truth is borne down for the moment, when the wicked oppose, and the good man is anxious, and the time-server is silent and afraid, then the soul, heated by persecution, is prepared to grasp the spirit of the Imprecatory Psalms. In the palace of God's truth these psalms hang like a sword upon the wall: in times of peace we make idle criticisms upon its workmanship and idle theories as to its use; sound the trumpet of danger, and we instinctively grasp it — it is all that we have between us and death. In the day of prosperity these psalms seem useless, in the darkness of affliction they are luminous; as a piece of fireworks has no prominence in the day-time, but it is the splendor and illumination of the night. There are times when the Christian is not to blame for having the spirit of these psalms, but he would deserve the contempt of mankind if he failed to have it. Resentment becomes the holiest of instincts when it resents the proper object. The spirit of the prophet is not dead, who was asked, "Doest thou well to be angry?" and he answered, "I do well." With wonderful wisdom the Bible provides, not only for man's present, but for his future emergencies, as the earth is stored with mine after mine which successive ages shall open. These psalms have a "springing and germinant fulfillment;" every throe and struggle of humanity comments upon them, and each generation of mankind penetrates further into their meaning. Think not that any truth is useless; the rolling wheel of time shall at length come upon it.

Such is a brief view of these celebrated compositions. Truthful in delineating the human heart, Asiatic in the exuberance of their diction, marking the unity of their author's mind with God, they furnish an expression of that majestic spirit of resistance to evil, which, planted by God in the human bosom, is expressed with increasing clearness as God's revelation is disclosed, and, deriving new power from every crisis of human experience, looks forward with augmented confidence to a day of the triumph of truth and justice over all enemies.

The following writers on this subject may be mentioned: Hengstenberg, Die Psalmen, iv. 299–305. Tholuck, Uebersetzung u. Auslegung der Psalmen, § 4 (transl. by J. I. Mombert). Hupfeld, Die Psalmen, iv. 431 f. The article Psalmen by Delitzsch in Herzog's Real-Encyk. xii. 230, and id., by Wunderlich in Zeller's Bibl. Wörterb. ii. 295 f. Perowne, The Psalms of David, Introd. lxxii., and on Ps. lxix. Isaac Taylor, Spirit of Hebrew Poetry, pp. 210–217 (N. Y., 1862). B. B. Edwards, Imprecations in the Scriptures, in his Life and Writings, by E. A. Park, ii. 364 ff. Prof. J. J. Owen, Imprecatory Psalms, in the Bibl. Sacra, xiii. 551–563. Prof. E. A. Park, Imprecatory Psalms, in the Bibl. Sacra, xix. 165–210. Rev. Albert Barnes, Commentary on the Psalms, Introd. § 6 (1869).   W. E. P.

PSALTERY. The psaltery was a stringed instrument of music to accompany the voice. The Hebrew נֵבֶל, nébel, or נֶבֶל, nebel, is so rendered in the A. V. in all passages where it occurs, except in Is. v. 12, xiv. 11, xxii. 24 marg.: Am. v. 23, vi. 5, where it is translated viol, following the Geneva Version, which has riole in all cases, except 2 Sam. vi. 5; 1 K. x. 12 ("psaltery"); 2 Esdr. x. 22; Ecclus. xl. 21 ("psalterion"); Is. xxii. 24 ("musicke"); and Wisd. xix. 18 ("instrument of musike"). The ancient viol was a six-stringed guitar. "Viols had six strings, and the position of the fingers was marked on the fingerboard by frets, as in the guitars of the present day" (Chappell, Pop. Mus. i. 246). In the Prayer Book version of the Psalms, the Hebrew word is rendered "lute." This instrument resembled the guitar, but was superior in tone, "being larger, and having a convex back, somewhat like the vertical section of a gourd, or more nearly resembling that of a pear. . . . It had virtually six strings, because, although the number was eleven or twelve, five, at least, were doubled; the first or treble, being sometimes a single string. The head in which the pegs to turn the strings were inserted, receded almost at a right angle" (Chappell, i. 102). These three instruments, the psaltery or sautry, the viol, and the lute, are frequently associated in the old English poets, and were clearly instruments resembling each other, though still different. Thus in Chaucer's Flower and Leaf, 337, —

> "And before hem went minstreles many one,
> As harpes, pipes, lutes, and sautry;"

and again in Drayton's Polyolbion, iv. 356: —

> "The trembling lute some touch, some strain the viol best."

The word psaltery in its present form appears to have been introduced about the end of the 16th century, for it occurs in the unmodified form psalterion in two passages of the Gen. Version (1560). Again, in North's Plutarch (Them. p. 124, ed. 1595) we read that Themistocles, "being mocked

. . . by some that had studied humanitie, and other liberall sciences, he was driuen for reuenge and his owne defence, to aunswer with greate and stoute words, saying, that in deed he could no skill to tune a harpe, nor a violl, nor to play of a *psalterion;* but if they did put a citie into his hands that was of small name, weake, and litle, he knew wayes enough how to make it noble, strong, and great." The Greek ψαλτήριον, from which our word is derived, denotes an instrument played with the fingers instead of a plectrum or quill, the verb ψάλλειν being used (Eur. *Bacch.* 784), of twanging the bowstring (comp. ψαλμοὶ τόξων, Eur. *Ion,* 173). But it only occurs in the LXX. as the rendering of the Heb. *nébel* or *nebel* in Neh. xii. 27, and Is. v. 12, and in all the passages of the Psalms, except Ps. lxxi. 22 (ψαλμός), and Ps. lxxxi. 2 (κιθάρα), while in Am. v. 23, vi. 5, the general term ὄργανον is employed. In all other cases νάβλα represents *nébel* or *nebel.* These various renderings are sufficient to show that at the time the translation of the LXX. was made, there was no certain identification of the Hebrew instrument with any known to the translators. The rendering νάβλα commends itself on account of the similarity of the Greek word with the Hebrew. Josephus appears to have regarded them as equivalent, and his is the only direct evidence upon the point. He tells us (*Ant.* vii. 12, § 3) that the difference between the κινύρα (Heb. כִּנּוֹר, *cinnôr*) and the νάβλα was, that the former had ten strings and was played with the plectrum, the latter had twelve notes and was played with the hand. Forty thousand of these instruments, he adds (*Ant.* viii. 3, § 8), were made by Solomon of electrum for the Temple choir. Rashi (on Is. v. 12) says that the *nebel* had more strings and pegs than the *cinnôr.* That *nabla* was a foreign name is evident from Strabo (x. 471), and from Athenæus (iv. 175), where its origin is said to be Sidonian. Beyond this, and that it was a stringed instrument (Ath. iv. 175), played by the hand (Ovid, *Art. Am.* iii. 327), we know nothing of it, but in these facts we have strong presumptive evidence that *nabla* and *nebel* are the same; and that the *nabla* and *psalterion* are identical appears from the Glossary of Philoxenus, where *nablio* = ψάλτης, and *nablieo* = ψάλλω, and from Suidas, who makes *psalterion* and *naula,* or *nabla,* synonymous. Of the psaltery among the Greeks there appear to have been two kinds. The τηκτίς, which was of Persian (Athen. xiv. 636) or Lydian (*ibid.* 635) origin, and the μαγάδις. The former had only two (Athen. iv. 183) or three (*ibid.*) strings; the latter as many as twenty (Athen. xiv. 634), though sometimes only five (*ibid.* 637). They are sometimes said to be the same, and were evidently of the same kind. Both Isidorus (*de Origg.* iii. 21) and Cassiodorus (*Præf. in Psal.* c. iv.) describe the psaltery as triangular in shape, like the Greek Δ, with the sounding-board above the strings, which were struck downwards. The latter adds that it was played with a plectrum, so that he contradicts Josephus if the psaltéry and *nebel* are really the same. In this case Josephus is the rather to be trusted. St. Augustine (on Ps. xxxii. [xxxiii.]) makes the position of the sounding-board

the point in which the cithara and psaltery differ, in the former it is below, in the latter above the strings. His language implies that both were played with the plectrum. The distinction between the cithara and psaltery is observed by Jerome (*Prol. in Psal.*). From these conflicting accounts it is impossible to say positively with what instrument the *nebel* of the Hebrew exactly corresponded. It was probably of various kinds, as Kimchi says in his note on Is. xxii. 24, differing from each other both with regard to the position of the pegs and the number of the strings. In illustration of the descriptions of Isidorus and Cassiodorus reference may be made to the drawings from Egyptian musical instruments given by Sir Gard. Wilkinson (*Anc. Eg.* ii. 280, 287), some one of which may correspond to the Hebrew *nebel.*[a] Munk (*Palestine,* plate 16, figs. 12, 13) gives an engraving of an instrument which Niebuhr saw. Its form is that of an inverted delta placed upon a round box of wood covered with skin.

The *nebel 'âsôr* (Ps. xxxiii. 2, xcii. 3 [4], cxliv. 9) appears to have been an instrument of the psaltery kind which had ten strings, and was of a trapezium shape, according to some accounts (Forkel, *Gesch. d. Mus.* i. 133). Aben Ezra (on Ps. cl. 3) says the *nebel* had ten holes. So that he must have considered it to be a kind of pipe.

From the fact that *nebel* in Hebrew also signifies a wine-bottle or skin, it has been conjectured that the term, when applied to a musical instrument, denotes a kind of bagpipe, the old English *cornamute,* Fr. *cornemuse;* but it seems clear, whatever else may be obscure concerning it, that the *nebel* was a stringed instrument. In the Mishna (*Célim,* xvi. 7) mention is made of a case (רִיק = θήκη) in which it was kept.

Its first appearance in the history of the O. T. is in connection with the "string" of prophets who met Saul as they came down from the high place (1 Sam. x. 5). Here it is clearly used in a religious service, as again (2 Sam. vi. 5; 1 Chr. xiii. 8), when David brought the ark from Kirjath-jearim. In the Temple band organized by David were the players on psalteries (1 Chr. xv. 16, 20), who accompanied the ark from the house of Obededom (1 Chr. xv. 28). They played when the ark was brought into the Temple (2 Chr. v. 12); at the thanksgiving for Jehoshaphat's victory (2 Chr. xx. 28); at the restoration of the Temple under Hezekiah (2 Chr. xxix. 25), and the dedication of the walls of Jerusalem after they were rebuilt by Nehemiah (Neh. xii. 27). In all these cases, and in the passages in the Psalms where allusion is made to it, the psaltery is associated with religious services (comp. Am. v. 23; 2 Esdr. x. 22). But it had its part also in private festivities, as is evident from Is. v. 12, xiv. 11, xxii. 24; Am. vi. 5, where it is associated with banquets and luxurious indulgence. It appears (Is. xiv. 11) to have had a soft plaintive note.

The psalteries of David were made of cypress (2 Sam. vi 5), those of Solomon of algum or almug-trees (2 Chr. ix. 11). Among the instruments of the band which played before Nebuchadnezzar's golden image on the plains of Dura, we again meet with the psaltery (פְּסַנְתֵּרִין), Dan. iii.

---

[a] Abraham de Porté-Leone, the author of *Shilte Haggibborim* (c. 5), identifies the *nebel* with the Italian *liuto,* the lute, or rather with the particular kind called *liuto chitarronato* (the Germ. *mandoline*), the thirteen strings of which were of gut or sinew, and were struck with a quill.

5, 10, 15; פְּסַנְתֵּרִין, *pĕsantêrîn*). The Chaldee word appears to be merely a modification of the Greek χαλτήριον. Attention is called to the fact that the word is singular in Gesenius (*Thes.* p. 1116), the termination יִן corresponding to the Greek -*ιον*.   W. A. W.

[PTOLEMÆUS, in A. V.] PTOLEMEE and PTOLEME'US (Πτολεμαῖος: *Ptolemæus*). 1. "The son of Dorymenes" (1 Macc. iii. 38; 2 Macc. iv. 45; comp. Polyb. v. 61), a courtier who possessed great influence with Antiochus Epiphanes. He was induced by a bribe to support the cause of Menelaus (2 Macc. iv. 45–50); and afterwards took an active part in forcing the Jews to apostatize (2 Macc. vi. 8, according to the true reading) When Judas had successfully resisted the first assaults of the Syrians, Ptolemy took part in the great expedition which Lysias organized against him, which ended in the defeat at Emmaus (B. C. 166), but nothing is said of his personal fortunes in the campaign (1 Macc. iii. 38).

2. The son of Agesarchus (Ath. vi. 246 C), a Megalopolitan, surnamed Macron (2 Macc. x. 12), who was governor of Cyprus during the minority of Ptol. Philometor. This office he discharged with singular fidelity (Polyb. xxvii. 12); but afterwards he deserted the Egyptian service to join Antiochus Epiphanes. He stood high in the favor of Antiochus, and received from him the government of Phœnicia and Cœle-Syria (2 Macc. viii. 8, x. 11, 12). On the accession of Ant. Eupator, his conciliatory policy toward the Jews brought him into suspicion at court. He was deprived of his government, and in consequence of his disgrace he poisoned himself c. B. C. 164 (2 Macc. x. 13).

Ptol. Macron is commonly identified with Ptol. "the son of Dorymenes," and it seems likely from a comparison of 1 Macc. iii. 38 with 2 Macc. viii. 8, 9, that they were confused in the popular account of the war. But the testimony of Athenæus distinctly separates the governor of Cyprus from "the son of Dorymenes" by his parentage. It is also doubtful whether Ptol. Macron had left Cyprus as early as B. C. 170, when "the son of Dorymenes" was at Tyre (2 Macc. iv. 45), though there is no authority for the common statement that he

gave up the island into the hands of Antiochus, who did not gain it till B. C. 168.

. 3. The son of Abubus, who married the daughter of Simon the Maccabee. He was a man of great wealth, and, being invested with the government of the district of Jericho, formed the design of usurping the sovereignty of Judæa. With this view he treacherously murdered Simon and two of his sons (1 Macc. xvi. 11–16; Joseph. *Ant.* xii. 7, § 4; 8, § 1, with some variations); but Johannes Hyrcanus received timely intimation of his design, and escaped. Hyrcanus afterwards besieged him in his stronghold of Dôk, but in consequence of the occurrence of the Sabbatical year, he was enabled to make his escape to Zeno Cotylas, prince of Philadelphia (Joseph. *Ant.* xiii. 8, § 1).

4. A citizen of Jerusalem, father of Lysimachus, the Greek translator of Esther (Esth. xi.). [LYSIMACHUS 1.]   B. F. W.

PTOLEMÆUS (in A. V. PTOL'OMEE and PTOLEME'US — Πτολεμαῖος, "the war-like," πτόλεμος = πόλεμος), the dynastic name of the Greek kings of Egypt. The name, which occurs in the early legends (Il. iv. 228; Paus. x. 5), appears first in the historic period in the time of Alexander the Great, and became afterwards very frequent among the states which arose out of his conquests.

For the civil history of the Ptolemies the student will find ample references to the original authorities in the articles in the *Dictionary of Biography*, ii. 581, etc. and in Pauly's *Real-Encyclopädie*.

The literature of the subject in its religious aspects has been already noticed. [ALEXANDRIA; DISPERSION.] A curious account of the literary activity of Ptol. Philadelphus is given — by Simon de Magistris — in the *Apologia sent. Pat. de LXX. Vers.*, appended to *Daniel sec. LXX.* (Roma, 1772), but this is not always trustworthy. More complete details of the history of the Alexandrine Libraries are given by Ritschl, *Die Alexandrinischen Bibliotheken*, Breslau, 1838; and Parthey, *Das Alexandr. Museum*, Berlin, 1838.

The following table gives the descent of the royal line as far as it is connected with Biblical history.   B. F. W.

GENEALOGICAL TABLE OF THE PTOLEMIES.

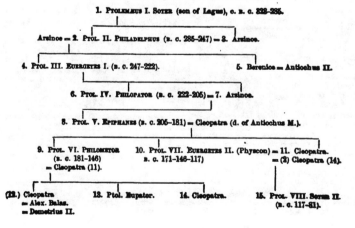

1. PTOLEMÆUS I. SOTER (son of Lagus), c. B. C. 323–285.

Arsinoe = 2. PTOL. II. PHILADELPHUS (B. C. 285–247) = 3. Arsinoe.

4. PTOL. III. EUERGETES I. (B. C. 247–222).   5. Berenice = Antiochus II.

6. PTOL. IV. PHILOPATOR (B. C. 222–205) = 7. Arsinoe.

8. PTOL. V. EPIPHANES (B. C. 205–181) = Cleopatra (d. of Antiochus M.).

9. PTOL. VI. PHILOMETOR   10. PTOL. VII. EUERGETES II. (Physcon) = 11. Cleopatra.
(B. C. 181–146)   B. C. 171–146–117)   = (2) Cleopatra (14).
= Cleopatra (11).

(12.) Cleopatra   13. Ptol. Nupator.   14. Cleopatra.   15. PTOL. VIII. Soter II.
= Alex. Balas.   (B. C. 117–81).
= Demetrius II.

PTOLEMÆUS I. SOTER, known as the son of Lagus, a Macedonian of low rank, was generally supposed to have been an illegitimate son of Philip. He distinguished himself greatly during the campaigns of Alexander; at whose death, foreseeing the necessary subdivision of the empire, he secured for himself the government of Egypt, where he proceeded at once to lay the foundations of a kingdom (B. C. 323). His policy during the wars of the succession was mainly directed towards the consolidation of his power, and not to wide conquests. He maintained himself against the attacks of Perdiccas (B. C. 321), and Demetrius (B. C. 312), and gained a precarious footing in Syria and Phœnicia. In B. C. 307 he suffered a very severe defeat at sea off Cyprus from Antigonus, but successfully defended Egypt against invasion. After the final defeat of Antigonus, B. C. 301, he was obliged to concede the debatable provinces of Phœnicia and Cœle-Syria to Seleucus; and during the remainder of his reign his only important achievement abroad was the recovery of Cyprus, which he permanently attached to the Egyptian monarchy (B. C. 295). He abdicated in favor of his youngest son Ptol. II. Philadelphus, two years before his death, which took place in B. C. 283.

Ptol. Soter is described very briefly in Daniel (xi. 5) as one of those who should receive part of the empire of Alexander when it was "divided toward the four winds of heaven." "*The king of the south* [Egypt in respect of Judæa] *shall be strong; and one of his princes* [Seleucus Nicator, *shall be strong*]; *and he* [Seleucus] *shall be strong above him* [Ptolemy], *and have dominion.*" Seleucus, who is here mentioned, fled from Babylon, where Antigonus sought his life, to Egypt in B. C. 316, and attached himself to Ptolemy. At last the decisive victory of Ipsus (B. C. 301), which was mainly gained by his services, gave him the command of an empire which was greater than any other held by Alexander's successors; and "*his dominion was a great dominion*" (Dan. *l. c.*).[a]

Ptolemy I., King of Egypt.

Pentadrachm of Ptolemy I. (Alexandrian talent). Obv. Head of king, r. f., bound with fillet. Rev. ΠΤΟΛΕΜΑΙΟΥ ΣΩΤΗΡΟΣ. Eagle, l., on thunderbolt. (Struck at Tyre.)

In one of his expeditions into Syria, probably B. C. 320, Ptolemy treacherously occupied Jerusalem on the Sabbath, a fact which arrested the attention of the heathen historian Agatharcides (*ap.* Joseph. *c. Ap.* i. 22; *Ant.* xii. 1). He carried away many Jews and Samaritans captive to Alexandria; but, aware probably of the great importance of the good will of the inhabitants of Palestine in the event of a Syrian war, he gave them the full privileges of citizenship in the new city. In the campaign of Gaza (B. C. 312) he reaped the fruits of his liberal policy; and many Jews voluntarily emigrated to Egypt, though the colony was from the first disturbed by internal dissensions (Joseph. *as above; Hecat. ap.* Joseph. *c. Ap.* l. c.).

                               B. F. W.

PTOLEMÆUS II. PHILADEL'-PHUS, the youngest son of Ptol. I., was made king two years before his death, to confirm the irregular succession. The conflict between Egypt and Syria was renewed during his reign in consequence of the intrigue of his half-brother Magas. "*But in the end of years they* [the kings of Syria and Egypt] *joined themselves together* [in friendship]. *For the king's daughter of the south* [Berenice, the daughter of Ptol. Philadelphus] *came* [as bride] *to the king of the north* [Antiochus II.], *to make an agreement*" (Dan. xi. 6). The unhappy issue of this marriage has been noticed already [Antiochus II., vol. i. p. 115]; and the political events of the reign of Ptolemy, who, however, retained possession of the disputed provinces of Phœnicia and Cœle-Syria, offer no further points of interest in connection with Jewish history.

In other respects, however, this reign was a critical epoch for the development of Judaism, as it was for the intellectual history of the ancient world. The liberal encouragement which Ptolemy bestowed on literature and science (following out in this the designs of his father) gave birth to a new school of writers and thinkers. The critical faculty was called forth in place of the creative, and learning in some sense supplied the place of original speculation. Eclecticism was the necessary result of the concurrence and comparison of dogmas; and it was impossible that the Jew, who was now become as true a citizen of the world as the Greek, should remain passive in the conflict of opinions. The origin and influence of the translation of the LXX. will be considered in another place. [Septuagint.] It is enough now to observe the greatness of the consequences involved in the union of Greek language with Jewish thought. From this time the Jew was familiarized with the great types of Western literature, and in some degree aimed at imitating them. Ezechiel (ὁ τῶν Ἰουδαϊκῶν τραγῳδιῶν ποιητής, Clem. Alex. *Str.* i. 23, § 155) wrote a drama on the subject of the Exodus, of which considerable fragments, in fair iambic verse, remain (Euseb. *Præp. Ev.* ix. 28, 29; Clem. Alex. *l. c.*), though he does not appear to have adhered strictly to the laws of classical composition. An elder Philo celebrated Jerusalem in a long hexameter poem — Eusebius quotes the 14th book — of which the few corrupt lines still preserved (Euseb. *Præp. Ev.* ix. 20, 24, 28) convey no satisfactory notion. Another epic poem, "on the Jews," was written by Theodotus; and as the extant passages (Euseb. *Præp. Ev.* ix. 22) treat of the history of Sichem, it has been conjectured that he was a Samaritan. The work of Aristobulus on the interpretation of the Law was a still more important result of the combination of the old faith with Greek culture, as forming the groundwork of later allegories. And while the Jews appropriated the fruits of Western science, the Greeks looked towards

---

[a] Jerome (*ad Dan.* l. c.) very strangely refers the latter clauses of the verse to Ptol. Philadelphus, whose empire surpassed that of his father." The whole tenor of the passage requires the contrast of the two kingdoms on which the fortunes of Judæa hung.

the East with a new curiosity. The histories of Berosus and Manetho and Hecatæus opened a world as wide and novel as the conquests of Alexander. The legendary sibyls were taught to speak in the language of the prophets. The name of Orpheus, which was connected with the first rise of Greek polytheism, gave sanction to verses which set forth nobler views of the Godhead (Euseb. *Præp. Ev.* xiii. 12, &c.). Even the most famous poets were not free from interpolation (Ewald, *Gesch.* iv. 297, *note*). Everywhere the intellectual approximation of Jew and Gentile was growing closer, or at least more possible. The later specific forms of teaching to which this syncretism of East and West gave rise have been already noticed. [ALEXANDRIA, vol. i. pp. 64, 65.] A second time and in a new fashion Egypt disciplined a people of God. It first impressed upon a nation the firm unity of a family, and then in due time reconnected a matured people with the world from which it had been called out.   **B. F. W.**

Ptolemy II.

Octodrachm of Ptolemy II. Obv. ΑΔΕΛΦΩΝ. Busts of Ptolemy II. and Arsinoe, r. Rev. ΘΕΩΝ. Busts of Ptolemy I. and Berenice, r.

PTOLEMÆUS III. EUER'GETES

was the eldest son of Ptol. Philad. and brother of Berenice, the wife of Antiochus II. The repudiation and murder of his sister furnished him with an occasion for invading Syria (c. B. C. 246). He " *stood up, a branch out of her stock* [sprung from the same parents] *in his* [father's] *estate ; and set himself at* [the head of] *his army, and came against the fortresses of the king of the north* [Antiochus], *and dealt against them and prevailed* " (Dan. xi. 7). He extended his conquests as far as Antioch, and then eastwards to Babylon, but was recalled to Egypt by tidings of seditions which had broken out there. His success was brilliant and complete. " *He carried captive into Egypt the gods* [of the conquered nations] *with their molten images, and with their precious vessels of silver and gold* " (Dan. xi. 8). This capture of sacred trophies, which included the recovery of images taken from Egypt by Cambyses (Jerome, *ad loc.*), earned for the king the name *Euergetes* — " Benefactor " — from the superstitious Egyptians, and was specially recorded in the inscriptions which he set up at Adule in memory of his achievements (Cosmas Ind. *ap.* Clint. *F. H.* 382 *note*). After his return to Egypt (cir. B. C. 743) he suffered a great part of the conquered provinces to fall again under the power of Seleucus. But the attempts which Seleucus made to attack Egypt terminated disastrously to himself. He first collected a fleet which was almost totally destroyed by a storm : and then, " as if by some judicial infatuation," " *he came against the realm of the king of the south and* [being defeated] *returned to his own land* [to Antioch] " (Dan. xi. 9; Justin. xxvii. 2). After this Ptolemy " *desisted*

some years from [attacking] *the king of the north* " (Dan. xi. 8), since the civil war between Seleucus and Antiochus Hierax, which he fomented, secured him from any further Syrian invasion. The remainder of the reign of Ptolemy seems to have been spent chiefly in developing the resources of the empire, which he raised to the highest pitch of its prosperity. His policy towards the Jews was similar to that of his predecessors, and on his occupation of Syria he " offered sacrifices, after the custom of the Law, in acknowledgment of his success, in the Temple at Jerusalem, and added gifts worthy of his victory " (Joseph. *c. Ap.* ii. 5). The famous story of the manner in which Joseph the son of Tobias obtained from him the lease of the revenues of Judæa is a striking illustration both of the condition of the country and of the influence of individual Jews (Joseph. *Ant.* xii. 4). [OXIAS.]   **B. F. W.**

Ptolemy III.

Octodrachm of Ptolemy III. (Egyptian talent). Obv. Bust of king, r., wearing radiate diadem, and carrying trident. Rev. ΒΑΣΙΛΕΩΣ ΠΤΟΛΕΜΑΙΟΥ. Radiate cornucopia.

PTOLEMÆ'US IV. PHILOP'ATOR.

After the death of Ptol. Euergetes the line of the Ptolemies rapidly degenerated (Strabo, xvi. 12, 13, p. 798). Ptol. Philopator, his eldest son, who succeeded him, was to the last degree sensual, effeminate, and debased. But externally his kingdom retained its power and splendor ; and when circumstances forced him to action, Ptolemy himself showed ability not unworthy of his race. The description of the campaign of Raphia (B. C. 217) in the Book of Daniel gives a vivid description of his character. " The sons of Seleucus [Seleucus Ceraunus and Antiochus the Great] were *stirred up and assembled a multitude of great forces ; and one of them* [Antiochus] *came and overflowed and passed through* [even to Pelusium, Polyb. v. 62]; *and he returned* [from Seleucia, to which he had retired during a faithless truce, Polyb. v. 66] ; *and they* [Antiochus and Ptolemy] *were stirred up* [in war] *even to his* [Antiochus'] *fortress. And the king of the south* [Ptol. Philopator] *was moved with choler, and came forth and fought with him* [at Raphia] ; *and he set forth a great multitude ; and the multitude was given into his hand* [to lead to battle]. *And the multitude raised itself* [proudly for the conflict], *and his heart was lifted up, and he cast down ten thousands* (cf. Polyb. v. 86); *but he was not vigorous* " [to reap the fruits of his victory] (Dan. xi. 10-12 ; cf. 3 Macc. I. 1-5). After this decisive success Ptol. Philopator visited the neighboring cities of Syria, and among others Jerusalem. After offering sacrifices of thanksgiving in the Temple he attempted to enter the sanctuary. A sudden paralysis hindered his design ; but when he returned to Alexandria, he determined to inflict on the Alexandrine Jews the vengeance for his disappointment. In this, however, he was again hindered; and eventually he confirmed to them the full privileges which they had enjoyed before. [3 MACCABEES.] The recklessness of his reign was further marked by the first insurrection of the native Egyptians against their Greek rulers (Polyb. v. 107). This was put down, and Ptolemy, during the remainder of his life, gave himself up to unbridled excesses. He died B. C. 205, and was succeeded by his only child, Ptol. V. Epiphanes, who was at the time only four or five years old (Jerome, *ad Dan.* xi. 10–12).   B. F. W.

gave him [Ptolemy, his daughter Cleopatra] *a young maiden* " [as his betrothed wife] (Dan. xi. 18). But in the end his policy only partially succeeded. After the marriage of Ptolemy and Cleopatra was consummated (B. C. 193), Cleopatra did "*not stand on his side*," but supported her husband in maintaining the alliance with Rome. The disputed provinces, however, remained in the possession of Antiochus; and Ptolemy was poisoned at the time when he was preparing an expedition to recover them from Seleucus, the unworthy successor of Antiochus, B. C. 181.   B. F. W.

Ptolemy IV.

Tetradrachm of Ptolemy IV. (Egyptian talent). Obv. Bust of king, r., bound with fillet. Rev. ΠΤΟΛΕΜΑΙΟΥ ΦΙΛΟΠΑΤΟΡΟΣ Eagle, l., on thunderbolt. (Struck at Tyre.)

Ptolemy V.

Tetradrachm of Ptolemy V. (Egyptian talent). Obv. Bust of king, r., bound with fillet adorned with ears of wheat. Rev. ΒΑΣΙΛΕΩΣ ΠΤΟΛΕΜΑΙΟΥ. Eagle, l., on thunderbolt.

PTOLEMÆ US V. EPIPH′ANES.

The reign of Ptol. Epiphanes was a critical epoch in the history of the Jews. The rivalry between the Syrian and Egyptian parties, which had for some time divided the people, came to an open rupture in the struggles which marked his minority. The Syrian faction openly declared for Antiochus the Great, when he advanced on his second expedition against Egypt; and the Jews, who remained faithful to the old alliance, fled to Egypt in great numbers, where Onias, the rightful successor to the high-priesthood, not long afterwards established the temple at Leontopolis.[a] [ONIAS.] In the strong language of Daniel, "*The robbers of the people exalted themselves to establish the vision*" (Dan. xi. 14) — to confirm by the issue of their attempt the truth of the prophetic word, and at the same time to forward unconsciously the establishment of the heavenly kingdom which they sought to anticipate. The accession of Ptolemy and the confusion of a disputed regency furnished a favorable opportunity for foreign invasion. "*Many stood up against the king of the south*," under Antiochus the Great and Philip III. of Macedonia, who formed a league for the dismemberment of his kingdom. "*So the king of the north* [Antiochus] *came, and cast up a mount, and took the most fenced city* [Sidon, to which Scopas, the general of Ptolemy, had fled: Jerome, *ad loc.*], *and the arms of the south did not withstand*" [at Paneas, B. C. 198, where Antiochus gained a decisive victory] (Dan. xi. 14, 15). The interference of the Romans, to whom the regents had turned for help, checked Antiochus in his career; but in order to retain the provinces of Coele-Syria, Phœnicia, and Judæa, which he had reconquered, really under his power, while he seemed to comply with the demands of the Romans, who required them to be surrendered to Ptolemy, "*he*

PTOLEMÆ′US VI. PHILOMETOR.

On the death of Ptol. Epiphanes, his wife Cleopatra held the regency for her young son, Ptol. Philometor, and preserved peace with Syria till she died, B. C. 173. The government then fell into unworthy hands, and an attempt was made to recover Syria (comp. 2 Macc. iv. 21). Antiochus Epiphanes seems to have made the claim a pretext for invading Egypt. The generals of Ptolemy were defeated near Pelusium, probably at the close of B. C. 171 (Clinton, *F. H.* iii. 319; 1 Macc. i. 16 ff.); and in the next year Antiochus, having secured the person of the young king, reduced almost the whole of Egypt (comp. 2 Macc. v. 1). Meanwhile Ptol. Euergetes II., the younger brother of Ptol. Philometor, assumed the supreme power at Alexandria; and Antiochus, under the pretext of recovering the crown for Philometor, besieged Alexandria in B. C. 169. By this time, however, his selfish designs were apparent: the brothers were reconciled, and Antiochus was obliged to acquiesce for the time in the arrangement which they made. But while doing so, he prepared for another invasion of Egypt, and was already approaching Alexandria, when he was met by the Roman embassy led by C. Popillius Lænas, who, in the name of the Roman senate, insisted on his immediate retreat (B. C. 168), a command which the late victory at Pydna made it impossible to disobey.[b]

These campaigns, which are intimately connected with the visits of Antiochus to Jerusalem in B. C. 170, 168, are briefly described in Dan. xi. 25–30: "*He* [Antiochus] *shall stir up his power and his courage against the king of the south with a great army; and the king of the south* [Ptol. Philometor] *shall be stirred up to battle with a very great and mighty army; but he shall not stand: for they* [the ministers, as it appears, in whom he trusted]

---

[a] Jerome (*ad Dan.* xi. 14) places the flight of Onias to Egypt and the foundation of the temple of Leontopolis in the reign of Ptol. Epiphanes. But Onias was still a youth at the time of his father's death, cir. B. C. 171.

[b] Others reckon only three campaigns of Antiochus

against Egypt in 171, 170, 168 (Grimm on 1 Macc. i. 18). Yet the campaign of 169 seems clearly distinguished from those in the years before and after; though in the description of Daniel the campaigns of 170 and 169 are not noticed separately.

shall forecast devices against him. Yea, they that feed of the portion of his meat shall destroy him, and his army shall melt away, and many shall fall down slain. And both these kings' hearts shall be to do mischief, and they shall speak lies at one table [Antiochus shall profess falsely to maintain the cause of Philometor against his brother, and Philometor to trust in his good faith]; *but it shall not prosper* [the resistance of Alexandria shall preserve the independence of Egypt]; *for the end shall be at the time appointed. Then shall he* [Antiochus] *return into his land, and his heart shall be against the holy covenant; and he shall do exploits, and return to his own land. At the time appointed he shall return and come towards the south; but it shall not be as the former so also the latter time.* [His career shall be checked at once] *for the ships of Chittim* [comp. Num. xxiv. 24: the Roman fleet] *shall come against him: therefore he shall be dismayed and return and have indignation against the holy covenant.*"

Ptolemy VI.

Tetradrachm of Ptolemy VI. (Egyptian talent). Obv. Head of king, r., bound with fillet. Rev. ΠΤΟΛΕΜΑΙΟΥ ΦΙΛΟΜΗΤΟΡΟΣ. Eagle, l., with palm-branch, on thunderbolt.

After the discomfiture of Antiochus, Philometor was for some time occupied in resisting the ambitious designs of his brother, who made two attempts to add Cyprus to the kingdom of Cyrene, which was allotted to him. Having effectually put down these attempts, he turned his attention again to Syria. During the brief reign of Antiochus Eupator he seems to have supported Philip against the regent Lysias (comp. 2 Macc. ix. 29). After the murder of Eupator by Demetrius I., Philometor espoused the cause of Alexander Balas, the rival claimant to the throne, because Demetrius had made an attempt on Cyprus; and when Alexander had defeated and slain his rival, he accepted the overtures which he made, and gave him his daughter Cleopatra in marriage (B. C. 150 : 1 Macc. x. 51-58). But, according to 1 Macc. xi. 1, 10, &c., the alliance was not made in good faith, but only as a means towards securing possession of Syria. According to others, Alexander himself made a treacherous attempt on the life of Ptolemy (comp. 1 Macc. xi. 10), which caused him to transfer his support to Demetrius II., to whom also he gave his daughter, whom he had taken from Alexander. The whole of Syria was quickly subdued, and he was crowned at Antioch king of Egypt and Asia (1 Macc. xi. 13). Alexander made an effort to recover his crown, but was defeated by the forces of Ptolemy and Demetrius, and shortly afterwards put to death in Arabia. But Ptolemy did not long enjoy his success. He

fell from his horse in the battle, and died within a few days (1 Macc. xi. 18), B. C. 145.

Ptolemæus Philometor is the last king of Egypt who is noticed in sacred history, and his reign was marked also by the erection of the temple at Leontopolis. The coincidence is worthy of notice, for the consecration of a new centre of worship placed a religious as well as a political barrier between the Alexandrine and Palestinian Jews. Henceforth the nation was again divided. The history of the temple itself is extremely obscure, but even in its origin it was a monument of civil strife. Onias, the son of Onias III.,[a] who was murdered at Antioch, B. C. 171, when he saw that he was excluded from the succession to the high-priesthood by mercenary intrigues, fled to Egypt, either shortly after his father's death or upon the transference of the office to Alcimus, B. C. 162 (Joseph. *Ant.* xii. 9, § 7). It is probable that his retirement must be placed at the later date, for he was a child (παῖς, Joseph. *Ant.* xii. 5, § 1) at the time of his father's death, and he is elsewhere mentioned as one of those who actively opposed the Syrian party in Jerusalem (Joseph. *B. J.* i. 1). In Egypt he entered the service of the king, and rose, with another Jew, Dositheus, to the supreme command. In this office he rendered important services during the war which Ptol. Physcon waged against his brother; and he pleaded these to induce the king to grant him a ruined temple of Diana (τῆς ἀγρίας Βουβάστεως) at Leontopolis, as the site of a temple, which he proposed to build "after the pattern of that at Jerusalem, and of the same dimensions." His alleged object was to unite the Jews in one body, who were at the time "divided into hostile factions, even as the Egyptians were, from their differences in religious services" (Joseph. *Ant.* xiii. 3, § 1). In defense of the locality which he chose, he quoted the words of Isaiah (Is. xix. 18, 19), who spoke of "an altar to the Lord in the midst of the land of Egypt," and according to one interpretation mentioned "the city of the Sun" (עִיר הַחֶרֶס), by name. The site was granted and the temple built; but the original plan was not exactly carried out. The *Naos* rose "like a tower to the height of sixty cubits" (Joseph. *B. J.* vii. 10, § 3, πύργῳ παραπλήσιον . . . εἰς ἑξήκοντα πήχεις ἀνεστηκότα). The altar and the offerings were similar to those at Jerusalem; but in place of the seven-branched candlestick, was "a single lamp of gold suspended by a golden chain." The service was performed by priests and Levites of pure descent; and the temple possessed considerable revenues, which were devoted to their support and to the adequate celebration of the divine ritual (Joseph. *B. J.* vii. 10, § 3; *Ant.* xiii. 3, § 3). The object of Ptol. Philometor in furthering the design of Onias, was doubtless the same as that which led to the erection of the "golden calves" in Israel. The Jewish residents in Egypt were numerous and powerful; and when Jerusalem was in the hands of the Syrians, it became of the utmost importance to weaken their connection with their mother city. In this respect the position of the temple on the eastern border of the kingdom was peculiarly important (Jost, *Gesch. d. Judenthums*, i. 117). On the other hand, it is probable that Onias saw no hope in the Hellenized Judaism of a Syrian province; and the triumph of the Maccabees was still unachieved when the temple at Leontopolis was founded. The date of this event cannot indeed be exactly determined. Josephus says (*B. J.* vii. 10, § 4) that the temple had existed "343 years" at the time of its destruction, *cir.* A. D. 71; but the text is manifestly corrupt. Eusebius (*ap.* Hieron. viii. p. 507, ed. Migne) notices the flight of Onias and the building of the temple under the same year (B. C. 162), possibly from the natural connection of the events without regard to the exact date of the latter. Some time at least must be allowed for the military service of Onias, and the building of the temple may perhaps be placed after the conclusion of the last war with Ptol. Physcon (c. B. C. 154), when Jonathan "began to judge the people at Machmas" (1 Macc. ix. 73). In Palestine the erection of this second temple was not condemned so strongly as might have been expected. A question indeed was raised in later times whether the service was not idolatrous (*Jerus. Joma* 43 d, *ap.* Jost, *Gesch. d. Judenth.* i. 119), but the Mishna, embodying without doubt the old decisions, determines the point more favorably. "Priests who had served at Leontopolis were forbidden to serve at Jerusalem; but were not excluded from attending the public services." "A vow might be discharged rightly at Leontopolis as well as at Jerusalem, but it was not enough to discharge it at the former place only" (*Menach.* 109, a, *ap.* Jost, *as above*). The circumstances under which the new temple was erected were evidently accepted as in some degree an excuse for the irregular worship. The connection with Jerusalem, though weakened in popular estimation, was not broken; and the spiritual significance of the one Temple remained unchanged for the devout believer (Philo, *de Monarch.* ii. § 1, &c.). [ALEXANDRIA, vol. i. p. 63.]

The Jewish colony in Egypt, of which Leontopolis was the immediate religious centre, was formed of various elements and at different times. The settlements which were made under the Greek sovereigns, though the most important, were by no means the first. In the later times of the kingdom of Judah many "trusted in Egypt," and took refuge there (Jer xliii. 6, 7); and when Jeremiah was taken to Tahpanhes, he spoke to "all the Jews which dwell in the land of Egypt, which dwell at Migdol and Tahpanhes, and at Noph, and in the country of Pathros" (Jer. xliv. 1). This colony, formed against the command of God, was devoted to complete destruction (Jer. xliv. 27), but when the connection was once formed, it is probable that the Persians, acting on the same policy as the Ptolemies, encouraged the settlement of Jews in Egypt to keep in check the native population. After the Return the spirit of commerce must have contributed to increase the number of emigrants: but the history of the Egyptian Jews is involved in the same deep obscurity as that of the Jews of Palestine till the invasion of Alexander. There cannot, however, be any reasonable doubt as to the power and influence of the colony; and the mere fact of its existence is an important consideration

in estimating the possibility of Jewish ideas finding their way to the west. Judaism had secured in old times all the treasures of Egypt, and thus the first installment of the debt was repaid. A preparation was already made for a great work when the founding of Alexandria opened a new era in the history of the Jews. Alexander, according to the policy of all great conquerors, incorporated the conquered in his armies. Samaritans (Joseph. *Ant.* xi. 8, § 6) and Jews (Joseph. *Ant.* xi. 8, § 5; Hecat. *ap.* Joseph. *c. Ap.* i. 22) are mentioned among his troops; and the tradition is probably true which reckons them among the first settlers at Alexandria (Joseph. *B. J.* ii. 18, § 7; *c. Ap.* ii. 4). Ptolemy Soter increased the colony of the Jews in Egypt both by force and by policy; and their numbers in the next reign may be estimated by the statement (Joseph. *Ant.* xii. 2, § 1) that Ptol. Philadelphus gave freedom to 120,000. The position occupied by Joseph (Joseph. *Ant.* xii. 4) at the court of Ptol. Euergetes I., implies that the Jews were not only numerous, but influential. As we go onwards, the legendary accounts of the persecution of Ptol. Philopator bear witness at least to the great number of Jewish residents in Egypt (3 Macc. iv. 15, 17), and to their dispersion throughout the Delta. In the next reign many of the inhabitants of Palestine who remained faithful to the Egyptian alliance fled to Egypt to escape from the Syrian rule (comp. Jerome *ad Dan.* xl. 14, who is, however, confused in his account). The consideration which their leaders must have thus gained, accounts for the rank which a Jew, Aristobulus, is said to have held under Ptol. Philometor, as "tutor of the king" (διδάσκαλος, 2 Macc. i. 10). The later history of the Alexandrine Jews has been noticed before (vol. i. p. 63). They retained their privileges under the Romans, though they were exposed to the illegal oppression of individual governors, and quietly acquiesced in the foreign dominion (Joseph. *B. J.* vii. 10, § 1). An attempt which was made by some of the fugitives from Palestine to create a rising in Alexandria after the destruction of Jerusalem, entirely failed; but the attempt gave the Romans an excuse for plundering, and afterwards (B. C. 71) for closing entirely the temple at Leontopolis (Joseph. *B. J.* vii. 10).

B. F. W.

PTOLEMAÏS (Πτολεμαΐς : *Ptolemais*). This article is merely supplementary to that on ACCHO. The name is in fact an interpolation in the history of the place. The city which was called Accho in the earliest Jewish annals, and which is again the *Akka* or *St. Jean d'Acre* of crusading and modern times, was named Ptolemais in the Macedonian and Roman periods. In the former of these periods it was the most important town upon the coast, and it is prominently mentioned in the first book of Maccabees, v. 15, 55, x. 1, 58, 60, xii. 48. In the latter its eminence was far outdone by Herod's new city of CÆSAREA.[a] Still in the N. T. Ptolemais is a marked point in St. Paul's travels both by land and sea. He must have passed through it on all his journeys along the great coast-road which connected Cæsarea and Antioch[b] (Acts xi. 30, xii. 25, xv. 2, 30, xviii. 22);

---

[a] It is worthy of notice that Herod, on his return from Italy to Syria, landed at Ptolemais (Joseph. *Ant.* xiv. 15, § 1).

[b] On the journey from Antioch to Jerusalem Acts xv. 3 ff.) Paul, instead of following the coast-road to Cæsarea, appears to have turned inland from Ptolemais, across the Plain of Esdraelon, since he passed on that occasion through Phœnicia and Samaria to Jerusalem.

H.

and the distances are given both in the Antonine and Jerusalem itineraries (Wesseling, *Itin.* pp. 158, 584). But it is specifically mentioned in Acts xxi. 7, as containing a Christian community, visited for one day by St. Paul. On this occasion he came to Ptolemais by sea. He was then on his return voyage from the third missionary journey. The last harbor at which he had touched was Tyre (ver. 3). From Ptolemais he proceeded, apparently by land, to Cæsarea (ver. 8) and thence to Jerusalem (ver. 17).   J. S. H.

* PTOL'EMEE, PTOLEME'US, PTOL'-OMEE, PTOLOME'US, A. V. in Esther (Apoc.) and 1 and 2 Maccabees.   [PTOLEMÆUS.]

PU'A (פֻּאָה [= פּוּאָה]: Φουά: *Phua*), properly Puvvah. PHUVAH the son of Issachar (Num. xxvi. 23).

PU'AH (פֻּאָה [*utterance*, Fürst; *mouth*, Ges.]: Φουά: *Phua*). 1. The father of Tola, a man of the tribe of Issachar, and judge of Israel after Abimelech (Judg. x. 1). In the Vulgate, instead of "the son of Dodo," he is called "the uncle of Abimelech;" and in the LXX. Tola is said to be "the son of Phua, the son (υἱός) of his father's brother;" both versions endeavoring to render "Dodo" as an appellative, while the latter introduces a remarkable genealogical difficulty.

2. [Vat. Φουε.] The son of Issachar (1 Chr. vii. 1), elsewhere called PHUVAH and PUA.

3. (פֻּעָה [*gracefulness, beauty*, Ges., Fürst]). One of the two midwives to whom Pharaoh gave instructions to kill the Hebrew male children at their birth (Ex. i. 15). In the A. V. they are called "Hebrew midwives," a rendering which is not required by the original, and which is doubtful, both from the improbability that the king would have intrusted the execution of such a task to the women of the nation he was endeavoring to destroy, as well as from the answer of the women themselves in ver. 19, "for the Hebrew women are not like the Egyptian women;" from which we may infer that they were accustomed to attend upon the latter, and were themselves, in all probability, Egyptians. If we translate Ex. i. 18 in this way, "And the king of Egypt said to the women who acted as midwives to the Hebrew women," this difficulty is removed. The two, Shiphrah and Puah, are supposed to have been the chief and representatives of their profession; as Aben Ezra says, "They were chiefs over all the midwives: for no doubt there were more than five hundred midwives, but these two were chiefs over them to give tribute to the king of the hire." According to Jewish tradition, Shiphrah was Jochebed, and Puah, Miriam: "because," says Rashi, "she *cried* and talked and murmured to the child, after the manner of the women that lull a weeping infant." The origin of all this is a play upon the name Puah, which is derived from a root signifying "to cry out," as in Is. xlii. 14 and used in Rabbinical writers of the bleating of sheep.

W. A. W.

* There are some reasons for the other opinion with regard to Puah's nationality. It not being said that Pharaoh appointed the midwives, the more obvious supposition is that those who acted in this capacity among the Hebrews were women of their own race, and so much the more, as the Hebrews at this time lived apart from the Egyptians in their own separate province (see Ex. ix. 26). The fear of God ascribed to the midwives as the motive for their humanity (Ex. i. 19) leads us to think of them as Hebrews and not Egyptians; and, further, according to the best view, the names of the women (Puah, Shiphrah) are Shemitic and not Egyptian. The rendering of the A. V. is the more obvious one (the construction like that in ver. 19), and is generally adopted.   H.

PUBLICAN (τελώνης: *publicanus*). The word thus translated belongs only, in the N. T., to the three Synoptic Gospels. The class designated by the Greek word were employed as collectors of the Roman revenue. The Latin word from which the English of the A. V. has been taken was applied to a higher order of men. It will be necessary to glance at the financial administration of the Roman provinces in order to understand the relation of the two classes to each other, and the grounds of the hatred and scorn which appear in the N. T. to have fallen on the former.

The Roman senate had found it convenient, at a period as early as, if not earlier than, the second Punic war, to farm the *vectigalia* (direct taxes) and the *portoria* (customs, including the *octroi* on goods carried into or out of cities) to capitalists who undertook to pay a given sum into the treasury (*in publicum*), and so received the name of *publicani* (Liv. xxxii. 7). Contracts of this kind fell naturally into the hands of the *equites*, as the richest class of Romans. Not unfrequently they went beyond the means of any individual capitalist, and a joint-stock company (*societas*) was formed, with one of the partners, or an agent appointed by them, acting as managing director (*magister*; Cic. *ad Div.* xiii. 9). Under this officer, who resided commonly at Rome, transacting the business of the company, paying profits to the partners and the like, were the *sub-magistri*, living in the provinces. Under them, in like manner, were the *portitores*, the actual custom-house officers (douaniers), who examined each bale of goods exported or imported, assessed its value more or less arbitrarily, wrote out the ticket, and enforced payment. The latter were commonly natives of the province in which they were stationed, as being brought daily into contact with all classes of the population. The word τελῶναι, which etymologically might have been used of the *publicani* properly so called (τέλη, ὠνέομαι), was used popularly, and in the N. T. exclusively, of the *portitores*.

The *publicani* were thus an important section of the equestrian order. An orator wishing, for political purposes, to court that order, might describe them as "flos equitum Romanorum, ornamentum civitatis, firmamentum Reipublicæ" (Cic. *pro Planc.* p. 9). The system was, however, essentially a vicious one, the most detestable, perhaps, of all modes of managing a revenue (comp. Adam Smith, *Wealth of Nations*, v. 2), and it bore its natural fruits. The *publicani* were banded together to support each other's interest, and at once resented and defied all interference (Liv. xxv. 3). They demanded severe laws, and put every such law into execution. Their agents, the *portitores*, were encouraged in the most vexations or fraudulent exactions, and a remedy was all but impossible. The popular feeling ran strong even against the equestrian capitalists. The Macedonians complained, as soon as they were brought under Roman government, that, "ubi publicanus est, ibi aut jus publicum vanum, aut libertas sociis *salis*." (Liv. xlv. 18). Cicero, in writing to his brother (*ad Quint.* i. 1, 11), speaks of the difficulty of keeping the *publicani* within bounds, and yet not offending them, as the hardest task of the governor of a province. Tacitus counted it as one bright feature of the ideal life of a people unlike his own, that there "nec publicanus atterit" (*Germ.* p. 29). For a moment the capricious liberalism of Nero led him to entertain the thought of sweeping away the whole system of *portoria*, but the conservatism of the senate, servile as it was in all things else, rose in arms against it, and the scheme was dropped (Tac. *Ann.* xiii. 50): and the "immodestia publicanorum" (*ibid.*) remained unchecked.

If this was the case with the directors of the company, we may imagine how it stood with the underlings. They overcharged whenever they had an opportunity (Luke iii. 13). They brought false charges of smuggling in the hope of extorting hush-money (Luke xix. 8). They detained and opened letters on mere suspicion (Terent. *Phorm.* i. 2, 99; Plaut. *Trinumm.* iii. 3, 64). The *injuriæ portitorum*, rather than the *portoria* themselves, were in most cases the subject of complaint (Cic. *ad Quint.* i. 1, 11). It was the basest of all livelihoods (Cic. *do Offic.* i. 42). They were the wolves and bears of human society (Stobæus, *Serm.* ii. 34). "Πάντες τελῶναι, πάντες ἅρπαγες" had become a proverb, even under an earlier régime, and it was truer than ever now (Xeno. Comic. *ap.* Dicæarch. Meineke, *Frag. Com.* iv. 596).[a]

All this was enough to bring the class into ill-favor everywhere. In Judæa and Galilee there were special circumstances of aggravation. The employment brought out all the besetting vices of the Jewish character. The strong feeling of many Jews as to the absolute unlawfulness of paying tribute at all made matters worse. The Scribes who discussed the question (Matt. xxii. 15) for the most part answered it in the negative. The followers of JUDAS of GALILEE had made this the special grievance against which they rose. In addition to their other faults, accordingly, the Publicans of the N. T. were regarded as traitors and apostates, defiled by their frequent intercourse with the heathen, willing tools of the oppressor. They were classed with sinners (Matt. ix. 11, xi. 19), with harlots (Matt. xxi. 31, 32), with the heathen (Matt. xviii. 17). In Galilee they consisted probably of the least reputable members of the fisherman and peasant class. Left to themselves, men of decent lives holding aloof from them, their only friends or companions were found among those who like themselves were outcasts from the world's law. Scribes and people alike hated them as priests and peasants in Ireland have hated a Roman Catholic who took service in collecting tithes or evicting tenants.

The Gospels present us with some instances of this feeling. To eat and drink "with publicans" seems to the Pharisaic mind incompatible with the character of a recognised Rabbi (Matt. ix. 11).

They spoke in their scorn of our Lord as the friend of publicans (Matt. xi. 19). Rabbinic writings furnish some curious illustrations of the same feeling. The Chaldee Targum and R. Solomon find in "the archers who sit by the waters" of Judg. v. 11, a description of the τελῶναι sitting on the banks of rivers or seas in ambush for the wayfarer. The casuistry of the Talmud enumerates three classes of men with whom promises need not be kept, and the three are murderers, thieves, and publicans (*Nedar.* iii. 4). No money known to come from them was received into the alms-box of the synagogue or the Corban of the Temple (*Baba kama*, x. 1). To write a publican's ticket, or even to carry the ink for it on the Sabbath-day was a distinct breach of the commandment (*Shabb.* viii. 2). They were not fit to sit in judgment, or even to give testimony (*Sanhedr.* f. 25, 2). Sometimes there is an exceptional notice in their favor. It was recorded as a special excellence in the father of a Rabbi that, having been a publican for thirteen years, he had lessened instead of increasing the pressure of taxation (*ibid.*).[b] (The references are taken, for the most part, from Lightfoot.)

The class thus practically excommunicated furnished some of the earliest disciples both of the Baptist and of our Lord. Like the outlying, so-called "dangerous classes" of other times, they were at least free from hypocrisy. Whatever morality they had, was real and not conventional. We may think of the Baptist's preaching as having been to them what Wesley's was to the colliers of Kingswood or the Cornish miners. The publican who cried in the bitterness of his spirit, "God be merciful to me a sinner" (Luke xviii. 13), may be taken as the representative of those who had come under this influence (Matt. xxi. 32). The Galilean fishermen had probably learnt, even before their Master taught them, to overcome their repugnance to the publicans who with them had been sharers in the same baptism. The publicans (Matthew perhaps among them) had probably gone back to their work learning to exact no more than what was appointed them (Luke iii. 13). However startling the choice of Matthew the publican to be of the number of the Twelve may have seemed to the Pharises, we have no trace of any perplexity or offense on the part of the disciples.

The position of ZACCHÆUS as an ἀρχιτελώνης (Luke xix. 2) implies a gradation of some kind among the persons thus employed. Possibly the balsam trade, of which Jericho was the centre, may have brought larger profits, possibly he was one of the *sub-magistri* in immediate communication with the Bureau at Rome. That it was possible for even a Jewish publican to attain considerable wealth, we find from the history of John the τελώνης (Joseph. *B. J.* ii. 14, § 4), who acts with the leading Jews and offers a bribe of eight talents to the Procurator, Gessius Florus. The fact that Jericho was at this time a city of the priests — 12,000 are said to have lived there — gives, it need hardly be said, a special significance to our Lord's preference of the house of Zacchæus.   E. H. P.

---

[a] Amusing instances of the continuance of this feeling may be seen in the extracts from Chrysostom and other writers, quoted by Suicer, *s. v.* τελώνης. In part these are perhaps rhetorical amplifications of what they found in the Gospels; but it can hardly be doubted that they testify also to the never-dying dislike of the tax-payer to the tax-collector.

Their vehement denunciations stand almost on a footing with Johnson's definition of an exciseman [or rather of excise].

[b] We have a singular parallel to this in the statues τῷ καλῶς τελωνήσαντι, mentioned by Suetonius as erected by the cities of Asia to Sabinus, the father of Vespasian (Suet. *Vesp.* 1).

PUBLIUS (Πόπλιος: *Publius*). The chief man — probably the governor — of Melita, who received and lodged St. Paul and his companions on the occasion of their being shipwrecked off that island (Acts xxviii. 7). It soon appeared that he was entertaining an angel unawares, for St. Paul gave proof of his divine commission by miraculously healing the father of Publius of a fever, and afterwards working other cures on the sick who were brought unto him. Publius possessed property in Melita; the distinctive title given to him is " the first of the island; " and two inscriptions, one in Greek, the other in Latin, have been found at Città Vecchia, in which that apparently official title occurs (Alford). Publius may perhaps have been the delegate of the Roman prætor of Sicily to whose jurisdiction Melita or Malta belonged. The Roman martyrologies assert that he was the first bishop of the island, and that he was afterwards appointed to succeed Dionysius as bishop of Athens. St. Jerome records a tradition that he was crowned with martyrdom (*De Viris Illust.* xix.; Baron. i. 554).   E. H—s.

* The best information which we can obtain respecting the situation of Malta at the time of Paul's visit, renders it doubtful, to say the least, whether the interpreters are in the right as it regards the station of Publius. In a Greek inscription of an earlier date we find mention made of two persons holding the office of *archon* or magistrate in the island. A later inscription of the times of the Emperors may be translated as follows : " Lucius Pudens, son of Claudius, of the tribe Quirina, a Roman eques, first [πρῶτος, as in Acts] and patron of the Melitæans, after being magistrate and having held the post of flamen to Augustus, erected this." Here it appears that the person named was still chief man of the island, although his magistracy had expired. From this inscription and others in Latin found at Gozzo, it is probable that the inhabitants of both islands had received the privilege of Roman citizenship, and were enrolled in the tribe *Quirina*. The magistracy was, no doubt, that of the *Duumvirs*, the usual municipal chief officers. The other titles correspond with titles to be met with on marbles relating to towns in Italy. Thus the title of *chief* corresponds to that of *princeps* in the colony of Pisa, and is probably no more a name of office than the title of *patron*. For no such officer is known to have existed in the colonies or in the *municipia*, and the *princeps coloniæ* of Pisa is mentioned at a time when it is said that owing to a contention between candidates there were no magistrates.   T. D. W.

PUDENS (Πούδης: *Pudens*), a Christian friend of Timothy at Rome. St. Paul, writing about A. D. 68, says, " Eubulus greeteth thee, and Pudens, and Linus, and Claudia " (2 Tim. iv. 21). He is commemorated in the Byzantine Church on April 14; in the Roman Church on May 19. He is included in the list of the seventy disciples given by Pseudo-Hippolytus. Papebroch; the Bollandist editor (*Acta Sanctorum*, Maii, tom. iv. p. 296), while printing the legendary histories, distinguishes between two saints of this name, both Roman senators; one the host of St. Peter and

friend of St. Paul, martyred under Nero; the other, the grandson of the former, living about A. D. 150, the father of Novatus, Timothy,* Praxedis, and Pudentiana, whose house, in the valley between the Viminal hill and the Esquiline, served in his lifetime for the assembly of Roman Christians, and afterwards gave place to a church, now the Church of S. Pudenziana, a short distance at the back of the Basilica of Sta. Maria Maggiore. Earlier writers (as Baronius, *Ann.* 44, § 61; *Ann.* 59, § 18; *Ann.* 162) are disposed to believe in the existence of one Pudens only.

About the end of the 16th century it was observed (F. de Monceaux, *Eccl. Christianæ veteris Britannicæ incunabula*, Tournay, 1614; Estius, or his editor; Abp. Parker, *De Antiquit. Britann. Eccl.* 1605; M. Alford, *Annales Ecc. Brit.* 1663; Camden, *Britannia*, 1586) that Martial, the Spanish poet, who went to Rome A. D. 66, or earlier, in his 23d year, and dwelt there for nearly forty years, mentions two contemporaries, Pudens and Claudia, as husband and wife (*Epig.* iv. 13); that he mentions Pudens or Aulus Pudens in i. 32, iv. 29, v. 48, vi. 58, vii. 11, 97; Claudia or Claudia Rufina in viii. 60, xi. 53; and, it might be added, Linus, in i. 76, ii. 54, iv. 66, xi. 25, xii. 49. That Timothy and Martial should have each three friends bearing the same names at the same time and place, is at least a very singular coincidence. The poet's Pudens was his intimate acquaintance, an admiring critic of his epigrams, an immoral man if judged by the Christian rule. He was an Umbrian and a soldier: first he appears as a centurion aspiring to become a primipilus; afterwards he is on military duty in the remote north; and the poet hopes that on his return thence he may be raised to equestrian rank. His wife Claudia is described as of British birth, of remarkable beauty and wit, and the mother of a flourishing family.

A Latin inscription b found in 1723 at Chichester connects a [Pud]ens with Britain and with the Claudian name. It commemorates the erection of a temple by a guild of carpenters, with the sanction of King Tiberius Claudius Cogidubnus, the site being the gift of [Pud]ens the son of Pudentinus. Cogidubnus was a native king appointed and supported by Rome (Tac. *Agricola*, 14). He reigned with delegated power probably from A. D. 52 to A. D. 76. If he had a daughter she would inherit the name Claudia and might, perhaps as a hostage, be educated at Rome.

Another link seems to connect the Romanizing Britons of that time with Claudia Rufina and with Christianity (see Musgrave, quoted by Fabricius, *Lux Evangelii*, p. 702). The wife of Aulus Plautius, who commanded in Britain from A. D. 43 to A. D. 52, was Pomponia Græcina, and the Rufi were a branch of her house. She was accused at Rome, A. D. 57, on a capital charge of " foreign superstition; " was acquitted, and lived for nearly forty years in a state of austere and mysterious melancholy (Tac. *Ann.* xiii. 32). We know from the Epistle to the Romans (xvi. 13) that the Rufi were well represented among the Roman Christians in A. D. 58.

Modern researches among the Columbaria at

---

a This Timothy is said to have preached the Gospel in Britain.

b "(N]eptuno et Minervæ templum [pr]o salute domus divinæ, auctoritate Tiberii Claudii [Co]gidubni ·gis legati augusti in Brit., [colle]gium fabrorum et

qui in eo [a sacris sunt] de suo dedicaverunt, donante aream [Pud]ente, Pudentini filio." A corner of the stone was broken off, and the letters within brackets have been inserted on conjecture.

Rome appropriated to members of the Imperial household have brought to light an inscription in which the name of Pudens occurs as that of a servant of Tiberius or Claudius (*Journal of Classical and Sacred Philology*, iv. 76).

On the whole, although the identity of St. Paul's Pudens with any legendary or heathen namesake is not absolutely proved, yet it is difficult to believe that these facts add nothing to our knowledge of the friend of Paul and Timothy. Future discoveries may go beyond them, and decide the question. They are treated at great length in a pamphlet entitled *Claudia and Pudens*, by Archdeacon Williams, Llandovery, 1848, p. 58 ; and more briefly by Dean Alford, *Greek Testament*, iii. 104, ed. 1856; and by Conybeare and Howson, *Life of St. Paul*, ii. 594, ed. 1858. They are ingeniously woven into a pleasing romance by a writer in the *Quarterly Review*, vol. xcvii. pp. 100–105. See also Ussher, *Eccl. Brit. Antiquitates*, § 3, and Stillingfleet's *Antiquities*. [CLAUDIA, Amer. ed.]   W. T. B.

PU'HITES, THE (הַפּוּתִי) [patr.]: Μιφ- ιθίμ : [Vat. Μειφειθειμι;] Alex. Ηφιθειν : *Aphuthii*). According to 1 Chr. ii. 53, the "Puhites" or "Puthites" belonged to the families of Kirjath-jearim. There is a Jewish tradition, embodied in the Targum of R. Joseph, that these families of Kirjath-jearim were the sons of Moses whom Zipporah bare him, and that from them were descended the disciples of the prophets of Zorah and Eshtaol.

PUL (פּוּל) [see below] Φούδ; some codd. Φουθ: *Africa*, a country or nation once mentioned, if the Masoretic text be here correct, in the Bible (Is. lxvi. 19). The name is the same as that of Pul, king of Assyria. It is spoken of with distant nations; "the nations (הַגּוֹיִם), [to] Tarshish, Pul, and Lud, that draw the bow, [to] Tubal, and Javan, [to] the isles afar off." If a Mizraite Lud be intended [LUD, LUDIM] Pul may be African. It has accordingly been compared by Bochart (*Phaleg*, iv. 26) and J. D. Michaelis (*Spicileg*. i. 256; ii. 114) with the island Philæ, called in Coptic ⲡⲉⲗⲁⲕ, ⲡⲓⲗⲁⲕ, ⲡⲓⲗⲁⲕⲣ ; the hieroglyphic name being EELEK, P-EELEK, EELEK-T. If it be not African, the identity with the king's name is to be noted, as we find Shishak (שִׁישַׁק) as the name of a king of Egypt of Babylonian or Assyrian race, and Sheshak (שֵׁשַׁךְ), which some rashly take to be artificially formed after the cabbalistic manner from Babel (בָּבֶל) for Babylon itself, the difference in the final letter probably arising from the former name being taken from the Egyptian SHESHENK. In the line of Shishak, the name TAKELAT has been compared by Birch with forms of that of the Tigris תִּדְקֵל, Chald. דִּגְלָה (دِجْلَة ,دِجْلَة ,دَجْلَة), which Gesenius has thought to be identical with the first part of the name of Tiglath-Pileser (*Thes.* s. v.).

The common LXX. reading suggests that the Heb. had originally Phut (Put) in this place, although we must remember, as Gesenius observes (*Thes.* s. v. פּוּט), that Φωτ could be easily changed to Φωτ by the error of a copyist. Yet in three other places Put and Lud occur together (Jer. xlvi. 9; Ez. xxvii. 10, xxx. 5). [LUDIM.] The circumstance that this name is mentioned with names or designations of importance, makes it nearly certain that some great and well-known country or people is intended. The balance of evidence is therefore almost decisive in favor of the African Phut or Put. [PHUT.]   R. S. P.

PUL (פּוּל) [see above] : Φούλ, Φαλόχ; [a] [Alex. in Chr. Φαλως:] *Phul*) was an Assyrian king, and is the first of those monarchs mentioned in Scripture. He made an expedition against Menahem, king of Israel, about B. C. 770. Menahem appears to have inherited a kingdom which was already included among the dependencies of Assyria; for as early as B. C. 884, Jehu gave tribute to Shalmaneser, the Black-Obelisk king (see vol. i. p. 188 *a*), and if Judæa was, as she seems to have been, a regular tributary from the beginning of the reign of[b] Amaziah (B. C. 838), Samaria, which lay between Judæa and Assyria, can scarcely have been independent. Under the Assyrian system the monarchs of tributary kingdoms, on ascending the throne, applied for "confirmation in their kingdoms" to the Lord Paramount, and only became established on receiving it. We may gather from 2 K. xv. 19, 20, that Menahem neglected to make any such application to his liege lord, Pul — a neglect which would have been regarded as a plain act of rebellion. Possibly, he was guilty of more overt and flagrant hostility. "Menahem smote Tiphsah" (2 K. xv. 16), we are told. Now if this Tiphsah is the same with the Tiphsah of 1 K. iv. 24, which is certainly Thapsacus, — and it is quite a gratuitous supposition to hold that there were two Tiphsahs (Winer, *Realwb*. ii. 613), — we must regard Menahem as having attacked the Assyrians, and deprived them for a while of their dominion west of the Euphrates, recovering in this direction the boundary fixed for his kingdom by Solomon (1 K. iv. 24). However this may have been, it is evident that Pul looked upon Menahem as a rebel. He consequently marched an army into Palestine for the purpose of punishing his revolt, when Menahem hastened to make his submission, and having collected by means of a poll-tax, the large sum of a thousand talents of gold, he paid it over to the Assyrian monarch, who consented thereupon to "confirm" him as king. This is all that Scripture tells us of Pul. The Assyrian monuments have a king, whose name is read very doubtfully as *Vul-lush* or *Iva-lush*, at about the period when Pul must have reigned. This monarch is the grandson of Shalmaneser (the Black-Obelisk king, who warred with Ben-hadad and Hazael, and took tribute from Jehu), while he is certainly anterior to the whole line of monarchs forming the lower dynasty — Tiglath-Pileser, Shalmaneser, Sargon, etc. His probable date therefore is B. C. 800–750, while Pul, as we have seen, ruled over Assyria in B. C. 770. The Hebrew name Pul is undoubtedly curtailed; for no Assyrian name con-

---

[a] Other readings of this name are Φουά, Φουλά, and Φαλώς.

[b] This is perhaps implied in the words " the king-

dom *was confirmed* in his hand " (2 K. xiv 5; comp xv. 19).

sists of a single element. If we take the "Phalos" for "Phaloch" of the Septuagint as probably nearer to the original type, we have a form not very different from *Vul-lush* or *Iva-lush*. If, on these grounds, the identification of the Scriptural Pul with the monumental *Vul-lush* be regarded as established, we may give some further particulars of him which possess considerable interest. *Vul-lush* reigned at Calah (*Nimrud*) from about b. c. 800 to b. c. 750. He states that he made an expedition into Syria, wherein he took Damascus; and that he received tribute from the Medes, Armenians, Phœnicians, Samaritans, Damascenes, Philistines, and Edomites. He also tells us that he invaded Babylonia and received the submission of the Chaldæans. His wife, who appears to have occupied a position of more eminence than any other wife of an Assyrian monarch, bore the name of Semiramis, and is thought to be at once the Babylonian queen of Herodotus (i. 184), who lived six generations before Cyrus, and the prototype of that earlier sovereign of whom Ctesias told such wonderful stories (Diod. Sic. ii. 4–20), and who long maintained a great local reputation in Western Asia (Strab. xvi. 1, § 2). It is not improbable that the real Semiramis was a Babylonian princess whom *Vul-lush* married on his reduction of the country, and whose son Nabonassar (according to a further conjecture) he placed upon the Babylonian throne. He calls himself in one inscription "the monarch to whose son Asshur, the chief of the gods, has granted the kingdom of Babylon." He was probably the last Assyrian monarch of his race. The list of Assyrian monumental kings, which is traceable without a break and in a direct line to him from his seventh ancestor, here comes to a stand; no son of *Vul-lush* is found; and Tiglath-Pileser, who seems to have been *Vul-lush's* successor, is evidently a usurper, since he makes no mention of his father or ancestors. The circumstances of *Vul-lush's* death, and of the revolution which established the lower Assyrian dynasty, are almost wholly unknown; no account of them having come down to us upon any good authority. Not much value can be attached to the statement in Agathias (ii. 25, p. 119) that the last king of the upper dynasty was succeeded by his own gardener.   G. R.

* PULPIT, only in Neh. viii. 4, the rendering of מִגְדָּל, (generally "tower" in the A. V.), a high stage or platform erected in the open space (less correctly "street," A. V.) before one of the gates at Jerusalem, from which Ezra and other Levites read and explained the Law of Moses (the Pentateuch) to the assembled people. This was after the return from the Babylonian captivity, during which the language of the Jews had changed so much that many words in the Hebrew Scriptures required interpretation and explanation. The Targums or Chaldee translations which formed so important a part of the later Jewish literature, grew out of this necessity. [VERSIONS, ANCIENT (TARGUM).] Yet another object of Ezra's public recitals no doubt was to promote among the Jews a better knowledge of the Scriptures which they had too much neglected in their exile, and to reassert the authority of the Law. We may add that the word "pulpit" has come to us from the Latin *pulpitum*, which among the Romans was the part of the stage (as distinguished from the orchestra) on which the actors performed their parts. The word, as thus applied, forms an exception to the general rule, for most of our ecclesiastical terms are derived from the Greek.   H.

PULSE (זֵרֹעִים, *zērō'im*, and זֵרְעֹנִים, *zēr'ōnim*: ὄσπρια; Theod. σπέρματα: *legumina*) occurs only in the A. V. in Dan. i. 12, 16. as the translation of the above plural nouns, the literal meaning of which is "seeds" of any kind. The *zērō'im* on which "the four children" thrived for ten days is perhaps not to be restricted to what we now understand as "pulse," i. e. the grains of leguminous vegetables: the term probably includes edible seeds in general. Gesenius translates the words "vegetables, herbs, such as are eaten in half-fast, as opposed to flesh and more delicate food." Probably the term denotes uncooked grains of any kind, whether barley, wheat, millet, vetches, etc.

                         W. H.

PUNISHMENTS. The earliest theory of punishment current among mankind is doubtless the one of simple retaliation, "blood for blood" [BLOOD, REVENGER OF], a view which in a limited form appears even in the Mosaic law. Viewed historically, the first case of punishment for crime mentioned in Scripture, next to the Fall itself, is that of Cain the first murderer. His punishment, however, was a substitute for the retaliation which might have been looked for from the hand of man, and the mark set on him, whatever it was, served at once to designate, protect, and perhaps correct the criminal. That death was regarded as the fitting punishment for murder appears plain from the remark of Lamech (Gen. iv. 24). In the post-diluvian code, if we may so call it, retribution by the hand of man, even in the case of an offending animal, for blood shed, is clearly laid down (Gen. ix. 5, 6); but its terms give no sanction to that "wild justice" executed even to the present day by individuals and families on their own behalf by so many of the uncivilized races of mankind. The prevalence of a feeling of retribution due for bloodshed may be remarked as arising among the brethren of Joseph in reference to their virtual fratricide (Gen. xlii. 21).

Passing onwards to Mosaic times, we find the sentence of capital punishment in the case of murder, plainly laid down in the law. The murderer was to be put to death, even if he should have taken refuge at God's altar or in a refuge city, and the same principle was to be carried out even in the case of an animal (Ex. xxi. 12, 14, 28, 36; Lev. xxiv. 17, 21; Num. xxxv. 31; Deut. xix. 11, 12; and see 1 K. ii. 28, 34).

I. The following offenses also are mentioned in the Law as liable to the punishment of death:

1. Striking, or even reviling, a parent (Ex. xxi. 15, 17).

2. Blasphemy (Lev. xxiv. 14, 16, 23; see Philo, V. M. iii. 25; 1 K. xxi. 10; Matt. xxvi. 65, 66).

3. Sabbath-breaking (Num. xv. 32–36; Ex. xxxi. 14, xxxv. 2).

4. Witchcraft, and false pretension to prophecy (Ex. xxii. 18; Lev. xx. 27; Deut. xiii. 5, xviii. 20; 1 Sam. xxviii. 9).

5. Adultery (Lev. xx. 10; Deut. xxii. 22; see John viii. 5, and Joseph. Ant. iii. 12, § 1).

6. Unchastity, (a.) previous to marriage, but detected afterwards (Deut. xxii. 21). (b.) In a betrothed woman with some one not affianced to her (ib. ver. 23). (c.) In a priest's daughter (Lev. xxi. 9).

7. Rape (Deut. xxii. 25).

8. Incestuous and unnatural connections (Lev. xx. 11, 14, 15; Ex. xxii. 19).

9. Man-stealing (Ex. xxi. 16; Deut. xxiv. 7).

10. Idolatry, actual or virtual, in any shape (Lev. xx. 2; Deut. xiii. 6, 10, 15, xvii. 2–7; see Josh. vii. and xxii. 20, and Num. xxv. 8).

11. False witness in certain cases (Deut. xix. 16, 19).

Some of the foregoing are mentioned as being in earlier times liable to capital or severe punishment by the hand either of God or of man, as (6.) Gen. xxxviii. 24; (1.) Gen. ix. 25; (8.) Gen. xix., xxxviii. 10; (5.) Gen. xii. 17, xx. 7, xxxix. 19.

II. But there is a large number of offenses, some of them included in this list, which are named in the Law as involving the penalty of "cutting a off from the people." On the meaning of this expression some controversy has arisen. There are altogether thirty-six or thirty-seven cases in the Pentateuch in which this formula is used, which may be thus classified: (a.) Breach of Morals. (b.) Breach of Covenant. (c.) Breach of Ritual.

1. Willful sin in general (Num. xv. 30, 31).
   *15 cases of incestuous or unclean connection (Lev. xviii. 29, and xx. 9–21).

2. *†Uncircumcision (Gen. xvii. 14; Ex. iv. 24).
   Neglect of Passover (Num. ix. 13).
   *Sabbath-breaking (Ex. xxxi. 14).
   Neglect of Atonement-day (Lev. xxiii. 29).
   †Work done on that day (Lev. xxiii. 30).
   *†Children offered to Molech (Lev. xx. 3).
   *†Witchcraft (Lev. xx. 6).
   Anointing a stranger with holy oil (Ex. xxx. 33).

3. Eating leavened bread during Passover (Ex. xii. 15, 19).
   Eating fat of sacrifices (Lev. vii. 25).
   Eating blood (Lev. vii. 27, xvii. 14).
   *Eating sacrifice in an unclean condition (Lev. vii. 20, 21, xxii. 3, 4, 9).
   Offering too late (Lev. xix. 8).
   Making holy ointment for private use (Ex. xxx. 32, 33).
   Making perfume for private use (Ex. xxx. 38).
   Neglect of purification in general (Num. xix. 13, 20).
   Not bringing offering after slaying a beast for food (Lev. xvii. 9).
   Not slaying the animal at the tabernacle-door (Lev. xvii. 4).
   *†Touching holy things illegally (Num. iv. 15, 18, 20: and see 2 Sam. vi. 7; 2 Chr. xxvi. 21).

In the foregoing list, which, it will be seen, is classified according to the view supposed to be taken by the Law of the principle of condemnation, the cases marked with * are (a) those which are expressly threatened or actually visited with death, as well as with cutting off. In those (b) marked † the hand of God is expressly named as the instrument of execution. We thus find that of (a) there are in class 1, 7 cases, all named in Lev. xx. 9–16.
   class 2, 4 cases,
   class 3, 2 cases,
while of (b) we find in class 2, 4 cases, of which 3 belong also to (a), and in class 3, 1 case. The question to be determined is, whether the phrase

---

a רַרַכ: ἐξολεθρεύω.

"cut off" be likely to mean death in all cases, and to avoid that conclusion Le Clerc, Michaelis, and others, have suggested that in some of them, the ceremonial ones, it was intended to be commuted for banishment or privation of civil rights (Mich. Laws of Moses, § 237, vol. iii. p. 436, trans.). Rabbinical writers explained "cutting off" to mean excommunication, and laid down three degrees of severity as belonging to it (Selden, de Syn. i. 6). [ANATHEMA.] But most commentators agree, that, in accordance with the prima facie meaning of Heb. x. 28, the sentence of "cutting off" must be understood to be death-punishment of some sort. Saalschütz explains it to be premature death by God's hand, as if God took into his own hand such cases of ceremonial defilement as would create difficulty for human judges to decide. Knobel thinks death-punishment absolutely is meant. So Corn. à Lapide and Ewald. Jahn explains, that when God is said to cut off, an act of divine Providence is meant, which in the end destroys the family, but that "cutting off" in general means stoning to death as the usual capital punishment of the Law. Calmet thinks it means privation of all rights belonging to the Covenant. It may be remarked (a), that two instances are recorded, in which violation of a ritual command took place without the actual infliction of a death-punishment: (1.) that of the people eating with the blood (1 Sam. xiv. 32); (2.) that of Uzziah (2 Chr. xxvi. 19, 21)—and that in the latter case the offender was in fact excommunicated for life; (b), that there are also instances of the directly contrary course, namely, in which the offenders were punished with death for similar offenses, — Nadab and Abihu (Lev. x. 1, 2), Korah and his company (Num. xvi. 10, 33), who "perished from the congregation," Uzzah (2 Sam. vi. 7), — and further, that the leprosy inflicted on Uzziah might be regarded as a virtual death (Num. xii. 12). To whichever side of the question this case may be thought to incline, we may perhaps conclude that the primary meaning of "cutting off" is a sentence of death to be executed in some cases without remission, but in others voidable: (1) by immediate atonement on the offender's part; (2) by direct interposition of the Almighty, i. e. a sentence of death always "recorded," but not always executed. And it is also probable that the severity of the sentence produced in practice an immediate recourse to the prescribed means of propitiation in almost every actual case of ceremonial defilement (Num. xv. 27, 28; Saalschütz, Arch. Hebr. x. 74, 75, vol. ii. 299; Knobel, Calmet, Corn. à Lapide on Gen. xvii. 13, 14; Keil, Bibl. Arch. vol. ii. 264, § 153; Ewald, Gesch. App. to vol. iii. p. 158; Jahn, Arch. Bibl. § 257).

III. Punishments in themselves are twofold, Capital and Secondary.

(a.) Of the former kind, the following only are prescribed by the Law. (1.) Stoning, which was the ordinary mode of execution (Ex. xvii. 4; Luke xx. 6; John x. 31; Acts xiv. 5). We find it ordered in the cases which are marked in the lists above as punishable with death; and we may remark further, that it is ordered also in the case of an offending animal (Ex. xxi. 29, and xix. 13). The false witness also, in a capital case, would by the law of retaliation become liable to death (Deut. xix. 19; Maccoth, i. 1, 6). In the case of idolatry, and it may be presumed in other cases also, the witnesses, of whom there were to be at least two, were required to cast the first stone (Deut.

xiii. 9, xvii. 7; John viii. 7; Acts vii. 58). The Rabbinical writers add, that the first stone was cast by one of them on the chest of the convict, and if this failed to cause death, the bystanders proceeded to complete the sentence. (*Sanhedr.* vi. 1, 3, 4; Godwyn, *Moses and Aaron*, p. 121.) The body was then to be suspended till sunset (Deut. xxi. 23; Josh. x. 26; Joseph. *Ant.* iv. 8, § 24), and not buried in the family grave (*Sanhedr.* vi. 5).

(2.) *Hanging* is mentioned as a distinct punishment (Num. xxv. 4; 2 Sam. xxi. 6, 9); but is generally, in the case of Jews, spoken of as following death by some other means.

(3.) *Burning*, in pre-Mosaic times, was the punishment for unchastity (Gen. xxxviii. 24). Under the Law it is ordered in the case of a priest's daughter (Lev. xxi. 9), of which an instance is mentioned (*Sanhedr.* vii. 2). Also in case of incest (Lev. xx. 14); but it is also mentioned as following death by other means (Josh. vii. 25), and some have thought it was never used excepting after death. A tower of burning embers is mentioned in 2 Macc. xiii. 4–8. The Rabbinical account of burning by means of molten lead poured down the throat has no authority in Scripture.

(4.) *Death by the sword or spear* is named in the Law (Ex. xix. 13, xxxii. 27; Num. xxv. 7); but two of the cases may be regarded as exceptional; but it occurs frequently in regal and post-Babylonian times (1 K. ii. 25, 34, xix. 1; 2 Chr. xxi. 4; Jer. xxvi. 23; 2 Sam. i. 15, iv. 12, xx. 22; 1 Sam. xv. 33, xxii. 18; Judg. ix. 5; 2 K. x. 7; Matt. xiv. 8, 10), a list in which more than one case of assassination, either with or without legal forms, is included.

(5.) *Strangling* is said by the Rabbins to have been regarded as the most common but least severe of the capital punishments, and to have been performed by immersing the convict in clay or mud, and then strangling him by a cloth twisted round the neck (Godwyn, *Moses and Aaron*, p. 122; Otho, *Lex. Rab.* s. v. " Supplicia ; " Sanhedr. vii. 3 ; Ker Porter, *Trav.* ii. 177; C. B. Michaelis, *De Judiciis*, ap. Pott, *Syll. Comm.* iv. §§ 10, 12).

This Rabbinical opinion, founded, it is said, on oral tradition from Moses, has no Scripture authority.

(b.) Besides these ordinary capital punishments, we read of others, either of foreign introduction or of an irregular kind. Among the former (1.) CRUCIFIXION is treated alone (vol. i. p. 513), to which article the following remark may be added, that the Jewish tradition of capital punishment, independent of the Roman governor, being interdicted for forty years previous to the Destruction, appears in fact, if not in time, to be justified (John xviii. 31, with De Wette's *Comment.* ; Godwyn, p. 121; Keil, ii. 264; Joseph. *Ant.* xx. 9, § 1).

(2.) *Drowning*, though not ordered under the Law, was practiced at Rome, and is said by St. Jerome to have been in use among the Jews (Cic. pro. *Sext. Rosc. Am.* 25; Jerome, *Com. on Matth.* lib. iii. p. 138; Matt. xviii. 6; Mark ix. 42). [MILL, Amer. ed.]

(3.) *Sawing asunder* or crushing beneath iron instruments. The former is said to have been practiced on Isaiah. The latter may perhaps not have always caused death, and thus have been a torture rather than a capital punishment (2 Sam. xii. 31, and perhaps Prov. xx. 26; Heb. xi. 37; Just. Mart. *Tryph.* 120). The process of sawing

asunder, as practiced in Barbary, is described by Shaw (*Trav.* p. 254).

(4.) *Pounding in a mortar, or beating to death*, is alluded to in Prov. xxvii. 22, but not as a legal punishment, and cases are described (2 Macc. vi. 28, 30). Pounding in a mortar is mentioned as a Cingalese punishment by Sir E. Tennent (*Ceylon*, ii. 88).

(5.) *Precipitation*, attempted in the case of our Lord at Nazareth, and carried out in that of captives from the Edomites, and of St. James, who is said to have been cast from " the pinnacle " of the Temple. Also it is said to have been executed on some Jewish women by the Syrians (2 Macc. vi. 10; Luke iv. 29; Euseb. *H. E.* ii. 23; 2 Chr. xxv. 12).

Criminals executed by law were buried outside the city gates, and heaps of stones were flung upon their graves (Josh. vii. 25, 26; 2 Sam. xviii. 17; Jer. xxii. 19). Mohammedans to this day cast stones, in passing, at the supposed tomb of Absalom (Fabri, *Evagatorium*, i. 409; Sandys, *Trav.* p. 189; Raumer, *Palä st.* p. 272).

(c.) *Of secondary punishments* among the Jews the original principles were, (1.) *retaliation*, " eye for eye," etc. (Ex. xxi. 24, 25; see Gell. *Noct. Att.* xx. 1).

(2.) *Compensation*, identical (restitution) or analogous; payment for loss of time or of power (Ex. xxi. 18–36; Lev. xxiv. 18–21; Deut. xix. 21). The man who stole a sheep or an ox was required to restore four sheep for a sheep and five oxen for an ox thus stolen (Ex. xxii. 1). The thief caught in the fact in a dwelling might even be killed or sold, or if a stolen animal were found alive, he might be compelled to restore double (Ex. xxii. 2–4). Damage done by an *animal* was to be fully compensated (*ib.* ver. 5). *Fire* caused to a neighbor's corn was to be compensated (ver. 6). A *pledge* stolen, and found in the thief's possession, was to be compensated by double (ver. 7). All *trespass* was to pay double (ver. 9). A *pledge* lost or damaged was to be compensated (vv. 12, 13). A *pledge* withheld, to be restored with 20 per cent. of the value (Lev. vi. 4, 5). The " seven-fold " of Prov. vi. 31, by its notion of completeness, probably indicates servitude in default of full restitution (Ex. xxii. 2–4). *Slander* against a wife's honor was to be compensated to her parents by a fine of 100 shekels, and the traducer himself to be punished with stripes (Deut. xxii. 18, 19).

(3.) *Stripes*, whose number was not to exceed forty (Deut. xxv. 3); whence the Jews took care not to exceed thirty-nine (2 Cor. xi. 24; Joseph. *Ant.* iv. 8, § 21). The convict was stripped to the waist and tied in a bent position to a low pillar, and the stripes, with a whip of three thongs, were inflicted on the back between the shoulders [Acts xxii. 25]. A single stripe in excess subjected the executioner to punishment (*Maccoth*, iii. 1, 2, 3, 13, 14). It is remarkable that the Abyssinians use the same number (Wolff, *Trav.* ii. 276).

(4.) *Scourging* with thorns is mentioned Judg. viii. 16. The *stocks* are mentioned Jer. xx. 2 [Acts xvi. 24]; *passing through fire*, 2 Sam. xii. 31; *mutilation*, Judg. i. 6, 2 Macc. vii. 4, and see 2 Sam. iv. 12; *plucking out hair*, Is. l. 6; in later times, *imprisonment*, and *confiscation or exile*, Ezr. vii. 26; Jer. xxxvii. 15, xxxviii. 6; Acts iv. 3, v. 18, xii. 4. As in earlier times imprisonment formed no part of the Jewish system, the sentences were executed at once (see Esth vii. 8–10; Selden. *De*

Syn. ii. c. 13, p. 888). Before death a grain of frankincense in a cup of wine was given to the criminal to intoxicate him (*ib.* 889). The command for witnesses to cast the first stone shows that the duty of execution did not belong to any special officer (Deut. xvii. 7).

Of punishments inflicted by other nations we have the following notices: In Egypt the power of life and death and imprisonment rested with the king, and to some extent also with officers of high rank (Gen. xl. 3, 22, xlii. 20). Death might be commuted for slavery (xlii. 19, xliv. 9, 33). The law of retaliation was also in use in Egypt, and the punishment of the bastinado, as represented in the paintings, agrees better with the Mosaic directions than with the Rabbinical (Wilkinson, *A. E.* ii. 214, 215, 217). In Egypt, and also in Babylon, the chief of the executioners, *Rab-Tabbachim*, was a great officer of state (Gen. xxxvii. 36, xxxix., xl.; Dan. ii. 14; Jer. xxxix. 13, xli. 10, xliii. 6, lii. 15, 16; Michaelis, iii. 412; Joseph. *Ant.* x. 8, § 5 [CHERETHIM]; Mark vi. 27). He was sometimes a eunuch (Joseph. *Ant.* vii. 5, § 4).

Putting out the eyes of captives, and other cruelties, as flaying alive, burning, tearing out the tongue, etc., were practiced by Assyrian and Babylonian conquerors; and parallel instances of despotic cruelty are found in abundance in both ancient and modern times in Persian and other history. The execution of Haman and the story of Daniel are

King putting out the Eyes of a Captive, who, with Others, is held Prisoner by a Hook in the Lips. Botta's *Ninive.*

pictures of summary Oriental procedure (2 K. xxv. 7; Esth. vii. 9, 10; Jer. xxix. 22; Dan. iii. 6, vi. 7, 24; Her. vii. 39, ix. 112, 113; Chardin, *Voy.* vi. 21, 118; Layard, *Nineveh,* ii. 369, 374, 377, *Nin. & Bab.* pp. 456, 457). And the duty of counting the numbers of the victims, which is there represented, agrees with the story of Jehu (2 K. x. 7) and with one recorded of Shah Abbas Mirza, by Ker Porter (*Travels,* ii. 524, 525; see also Burckhardt, *Syria,* p. 57; and Malcolm, *Sketches of Persia,* p. 47).

With the Romans, stripes and the stocks, πεντε-σύργγον ξύλον, *nervus* and *columbar,* were in use, and imprisonment, with a chain attached to a sol-

dier. There were also the *libera cust dia* in private houses [PRISON] (Acts xvi. 23, xxii. 24, xxviii. 16; Xen. *Hell.* iii. 3, 11; Herod. ix. 37; Plautus, *Rud.* iii. 6, 30, 34, 38, 50; Arist. *Eq.* 1044 (ed. Bekker); Joseph. *Ant.* xviii. 6, § 7, xix. 6, § 1; Sall. *Cat.* 47; *Dict. of Antiq.* "Flagrum").

Exposure to wild beasts appears to be mentioned by St. Paul (1 Cor. xv. 32; 2 Tim. iv. 17), but not with any precision.   H. W. P.

* *Striking on the mouth* (as inflicted on Paul, Acts xxiii. 2), was a punishment for speaking with undue liberty or insolence. It signified that the mouth must be shut which uttered such speech. Travellers report instances of this practice still in the East. "As soon as the ambassador came," says Morier (*Second Journey through Persia,* p. 8), "he punished the principal offenders by causing them to be beaten before him; and those who had spoken their minds too freely, he smote upon the mouth with a shoe." For another illustration see p. 94 of the same work.   H.

PU'NITES, THE (הַפּוּנִי: ὁ Φουεί: *Phunitae*). The descendants of Pua, or Phuvah, the son of Issachar (Num. xxvi. 23).

PU'NON (פִּינֹן, *i. e.* Phunon [*ore-pit,* Fürst; *darkness* (?), Ges.]: Samarit. פינם: [Vat.] Φεινώ; [Rom.] Alex. Φινω; [Ald. Φινών:] *Phunon*). One of the halting-places of the Israelite host during the last portion of the Wandering (Num. xxxiii. 42, 43). It lay next beyond Zalmonah, between it and Oboth, and three days' journey from the mountains of Abarim, which formed the boundary of Moab.

By Eusebius and Jerome (*Onomasticon,* Φινών, "Fenon") it is identified with Pinon, the seat of the Edomite tribe of that name, and, further, with Phæno, which contained the copper-mines so notorious at that period, and was situated between Petra and Zoar. This identification is supported by the form of the name in the LXX. and Samaritan; and the situation falls in with the requirements of the Wanderings. No trace of such a name appears to have been met with by modern explorers.   G.

* Among the ruined places on the caravan road east of Mt. Seir, Seetzen's Arab guide mentioned to him a certain *Kalaat* (*i. e.* Castle) *Phendu* (Zach's *Monatl. Corr.* xvii. 137). This is conjectured by L. Vülter (Zeller's *Bibl. Wörterb.* ii. 267) and others to be the Punon or Phunon referred to in Numbers, as above.   A.

PURIFICATION. The term "purification," in its legal and technical sense, is applied to the ritual observances whereby an Israelite was formally absolved from the taint of uncleanness, whether evidenced by any overt act or state, or whether connected with man's natural depravity. The cases that demanded it in the former instance are defined in the Levitical law [UNCLEANNESS]: with regard to the latter, it is only possible to lay down the general rule that it was a fitting prelude to any nearer approach to the Deity: as, for instance, in the admission of a proselyte to the congregation [PROSELYTE], in the baptism (καθαρισμός, John iii. 25) of the Jews as a sign of repentance [BAPTISM], in the consecration of priests and Levites [PRIEST; LEVITE], or in the performance of special religious acts (Lev. xvi. 4; 2 Chr. xxx. 19). In the present article we are concerned solely with the former class, inasmuch as in this alone were the ritual observances of a special character

The essence of purification, indeed, in all cases, consisted in the use of water, whether by way of ablution or aspersion; but in the *mejora delicta* of legal uncleanness, sacrifices of various kinds were added, and the ceremonies throughout bore an expiatory character. Simple ablution of the person was required after sexual intercourse (Lev. xv. 18; 2 Sam. xi. 4): ablution of the clothes, after touching the carcass of an unclean beast, or eating or carrying the carcass of a clean beast that had died a natural death (Lev. xi. 25, 40): ablution both of the person and of the defiled garments in cases of *gonorrhea dormientium* (Lev. xv. 16, 17) — the ceremony in each of the above instances to take place on the day on which the uncleanness was contracted. A higher degree of uncleanness resulted from prolonged *gonorrhea* in males, and menstruation in women: in these cases a probationary interval of seven days was to be allowed after the cessation of the symptoms; on the evening of the seventh day the candidate for purification performed an ablution both of the person and of the garments, and on the eighth offered two turtle-doves or two young pigeons, one for a sin-offering, the other for a burnt-offering (Lev. xv. 1-15, 19-30). Contact with persons in the above states, or even with clothing or furniture that had been used by them while in those states, involved uncleanness in a minor degree, to be absolved by ablution on the day of infection generally (Lev. xv. 5-11, 21-23), but in one particular case after an interval of seven days (Lev. xv. 24). In cases of childbirth the sacrifice was increased to a lamb of the first year with a pigeon or turtle-dove (Lev. xii. 6), an exception being made in favor of the poor who might present the same offering as in the preceding case (Lev. xii. 8; Luke ii. 22-24). The purification took place forty days after the birth of a son, and eighty after that of a daughter, the difference in the interval being based on physical considerations. The uncleannesses already specified were comparatively of a mild character: the more severe were connected with death, which, viewed as the penalty of sin, was in the highest degree contaminating. To this head we refer the two cases of (1) touching a corpse, or a grave (Num. xix. 16), or even killing a man in war (Num. xxxi. 19); and (2) leprosy, which was regarded by the Hebrews as nothing less than a living death. The ceremonies of purification in the first of these two cases are detailed in Num. xix. A peculiar kind of water, termed the *water of uncleanness*[a] (A. V. "water of separation"), was prepared in the following manner: An unblemished red heifer, on which the yoke had not passed, was slain by the eldest son of the high-priest outside the camp. A portion of its blood was sprinkled seven times towards[b] the sanctuary; the rest of it, and the whole of the carcass, including even its dung, were then burnt in the sight of the officiating priest, together with cedar-wood, hyssop, and scarlet. The ashes were collected by a clean man and deposited in a clean place outside the camp. Whenever occasion required, a portion of the ashes was mixed with spring water in a jar, and the unclean person was

sprinkled with it on the third, and again on the seventh day after the contraction of the uncleanness. That the water had an expiatory efficacy, is implied in the term *sin-offering*[c] (A. V. "purification for sin") applied to it (Num. xix. 9), and all the particulars connected with its preparation had a symbolical significance appropriate to the object sought. The sex of the victim (female, and hence life-giving), its red color (the color of blood, the seat of life), its unimpaired vigor (never having borne the yoke), its youth, and the absence in it of spot or blemish, the cedar and the hyssop (possessing the qualities, the former of incorruption, the latter of purity), and the scarlet (again the color of blood) — all these symbolized life in its fullness and freshness as the antidote of death. At the same time the extreme virulence of the uncleanness is taught by the regulations that the victim should be wholly consumed outside the camp, whereas generally certain parts were consumed on the altar, and the offal only outside the camp (comp. Lev. iv. 11, 12); that the blood was sprinkled *towards*, and not *before* the sanctuary; that the officiating minister should be neither the high-priest, nor yet simply a priest, but the *presumptive* high-priest, the office being too impure for the first, and too important for the second; that even the priest and the person that burnt the heifer were rendered unclean by reason of their contact with the victim; and, lastly, that the purification should be effected, not simply by the use of water, but of water mixed with ashes which served as a lye, and would therefore have peculiarly cleansing qualities.

The purification of the leper was a yet more formal proceeding, and indicated the highest pitch of uncleanness. The rites are thus described in Lev. xiv. 4-32: The priest having examined the leper and pronounced him clear of his disease, took for him two birds "alive and clean," with cedar, scarlet, and hyssop. One of the birds was killed under the priest's directions over a vessel filled with spring water, into which its blood fell; the other, with the adjuncts, cedar, etc., was dipped by the priest into the mixed blood and water, and, after the unclean person had been seven times sprinkled with the same liquid, was permitted to fly away "into the open field." The leper then washed himself and his clothes, and shaved his head. The above proceedings took place outside the camp, and formed the first stage of purification. A probationary interval of seven days was then allowed, which period the leper was to pass "abroad out of his tent:"[d] on the last of these days the washing was repeated, and the shaving was more rigidly performed, even to the eyebrows and all his hair. The second stage of the purification took place on the eighth day, and was performed "before the LORD at the door of the tabernacle of the congregation." The leper brought thither an offering consisting of two he-lambs, a yearling ewe-lamb, fine flour mingled with oil, and a log of oil: in cases of poverty the offering was reduced to one lamb, and two turtle-doves, or two young pigeons, with a less quantity of fine flour, and a log of oil. The priest slew one of the he-lambs as a trespass-offering, and applied

---

[a] מֵי הַנִּדָּה.

[b] אֶל־נֹכַח פְּנֵי   The A. V incorrectly renders t "directly before."

[c] חַטָּאת.

[d] The Rabbinical explanation of this was in conformity with the addition in the Chaldee version, "et non accedet ad latus uxoris suae." The words cannot, however, be thus restricted: they are designed to mark the partial restoration of the leper — inside the camp, but outside his tent.

a portion of its blood to the right ear, right thumb, and great toe of the right foot of the leper: he next sprinkled a portion of the oil seven times before the Lord, applied another portion of it to the parts of the body already specified, and poured the remainder over the leper's head. The other he-lamb and the ewe-lamb, or the two birds, as the case might be, were then offered as a sin-offering, and a burnt-offering, together with the meat-offering. The significance of the cedar, the scarlet, and the hyssop, of the running water, and of the "alive (full of life) and clean" condition of the birds, is the same as in the case previously described. The two stages of the proceedings indicated, the first, which took place outside the camp, the re-admission of the leper to the community of men; the second, before the sanctuary, his re-admission to communion with God. In the first stage, the slaughter of the one bird and the dismissal of the other, symbolised the punishment of death deserved and fully remitted. In the second, the use of oil and its application to the same parts of the body as in the consecration of priests (Lev. viii. 23, 24) symbolized the re-dedication of the leper to the service of Jehovah.

The ceremonies to be observed in the purification of a house or a garment infected with leprosy, were identical with the first stage of the proceedings used for the leper (Lev. xiv. 33–53).

The necessity of purification was extended in the post-Babylonian period to a variety of unauthorized cases. Cups and pots, brazen vessels and couches, were washed as a matter of ritual observance (Mark vii. 4). The washing of the hands before meals was conducted in a formal manner [a] (Mark vii. 3), and minute regulations are laid down on this subject in a treatise of the Mishna, entitled *Yadaim*. These ablutions required a large supply of water, and hence we find at a marriage feast no less than six jars containing two or three firkins apiece, prepared for the purpose (John ii. 6). We meet with references to purification after childbirth (Luke ii. 22), and after the cure of leprosy (Matt. viii. 4; Luke xvii. 14), the sprinkling of the water mixed with ashes being still retained in the latter case (Heb. ix. 13). What may have been the specific causes of uncleanness in those who came up to purify themselves before the Passover (John xi. 55), or in those who had taken upon themselves the Nazarite's vow (Acts xxi. 24, 26), we are not informed; in either case it may have been contact with a corpse, though in the latter it would rather appear to have been a general purification preparatory to the accomplishment of the vow.

In conclusion it may be observed, that the distinctive feature in the Mosaic rites of purification is their expiatory character. The idea of uncleanness was not peculiar to the Jew: it was attached by the Greeks to the events of childbirth and death

(Thucyd. iii. 104; Eurip. *Iph. in Taur.* 383), and by various nations to the case of sexual intercourse (Herod. i. 198, ii. 64; Pers. ii. 16). But with all these nations simple ablution sufficed: no sacrifices were demanded. The Jew alone was taught by the use of expiatory offerings to discern to its full extent the connection between the outward sign and the inward fount of impurity.   W. L. B.

PURIM (פּוּרִים:[b] Φουραί;[c] [in ver. 26, FA.[g] Φρουριμ, Φουρ; ver. 31, Alex. τῶν Φρουραια, FA.[1] τῶν Φρουραν, FA.[6] τ. Φρουριμ:] *Phurim*: also, יְמֵי הַפֻּרִים (Esth. ix. 26, 31): *dies sortium*), the annual festival instituted to commemorate the preservation of the Jews in Persia from the massacre with which they were threatened through the machinations of Haman (Esth. ix.; Joseph. *Ant.* xi. 6, § 13). [ESTHER.] It was probably called Purim by the Jews in irony. Their great enemy Haman appears to have been very superstitious and much given to casting lots (Esth. iii. 7). They gave the name Purim, or Lots, to the commemorative festival, because he had thrown lots to ascertain what day would be auspicious for him to carry into effect the bloody decree which the king had issued at his instance (Esth. ix. 24).

The festival lasted two days, and was regularly observed on the 14th and 15th of Adar. But if the 14th happened to fall on the Sabbath, or on the second or fourth day of the week, the commencement of the festival was deferred till the next day. It is not easy to conjecture what may have been the ancient mode of observance, so as to have given the occasion something of the dignity of a national religious festival. The traditions of the Jews, and their modern usage respecting it are curious. It is stated that eighty-five of the Jewish elders objected at first to the institution of the feast, when it was proposed by Mordecai (Jerus. Gem. *Megillah* — Lightfoot on John x. 21). A preliminary fast was appointed, called "the fast of Esther," to be observed on the 13th of Adar, in memory of the fast which Esther and her maids observed, and which she enjoined, through Mordecai, on the Jews of Shushan (Esth. iv. 16). If the 13th was a Sabbath, the fast was put back to the fifth day of the week; it could not be held on the sixth day, because those who might be engaged in preparing food for the Sabbath would necessarily have to taste the dishes to prove them. According to modern custom, as soon as the stars begin to appear, when the 14th of the month has commenced, candles are lighted up in token of rejoicing, and the people assemble in the synagogue.[d] After a short prayer and thanksgiving, the reading of the Book of Esther commences. The book is written in a peculiar manner, on a roll called κατ' ἐξοχήν, "the Roll" (מְגִלָּה, *Megillah*).[e] The reader translates the text,

---

[a] Various opinions are held with regard to the term συγμῷ. The meaning "with the fist" is in accordance with the general tenor of the Rabbinical usages, the hand used in washing the other being closed lest the palm should contract uncleanness in the act.

[b] The word פּוּר (*pur*) is Persian. In the modern language, it takes the form *pâreh*, and it is cognate with *pars* and *part* (Gesen. *Thes.*). It is explained, Esth. iii. 7, and ix. 24, by the Hebrew גּוֹרָל: κλῆροι: *sortes*.

[c] It can hardly be doubted then the conjecture of

the editor of the Complutensian Polyglot (approved by Grotius, in *Esth.* iii. 7, and by Schleusner, *Lex. in LXX.* s. Φρουραί) is correct, and that the reading should be Φουραί. In like manner, the modern editors of Josephus have changed Φρουραίοι into Φουραίοι (*Ant.* xi. 6, § 13). The old editors imagined that Josephus connected the word with Φρουρεῖν.

[d] This service is said to have taken place in former times on the 15th in walled towns, but on the 14th in the country and unwalled towns, according to Esth. ix. 18, 19.

[e] Five books of the O. T. (Ruth, Esther, Ecclesias-

as he goes on, into the vernacular tongue of the place, and makes comments on particular passages. He reads in a histrionic manner, suiting his tones and gestures to the changes in the subject matter. When he comes to the name of Haman the whole congregation cry out, "May his name be blotted out," or "Let the name of the ungodly perish." At the same time, in some places, the boys who are present make a great noise with their hands, with mallets, and with pieces of wood or stone on which they have written the name of Haman, and which they rub together so as to obliterate the writing. When the names of the sons of Haman are read (ix. 7, 8, 9) the reader utters them with a continuous enunciation, so as to make them into one word, to signify that they were hanged all at once. When the Megillah is read through, the whole congregation exclaim, "Cursed be Haman; blessed be Mordecai; cursed be Zoresh (the wife of Haman); blessed be Esther; cursed be all idolators; blessed be all Israelites, and blessed be Harbonah who hanged Haman." The volume is then solemnly rolled up. All go home and partake of a repast said to consist mainly of milk and eggs. In the morning service in the synagogue, on the 14th, after the prayers, the passage is read from the Law (Ex. xvii. 8–16) which relates the destruction of the Amalekites, the people of Agag (1 Sam. xv. 8), the supposed ancestor of Haman (Esth. iii. 1). The Megillah is then read again in the same manner, and with the same responses from the congregation, as on the preceding evening. All who possibly can are bound to hear the reading of the Megillah — men, women, children, cripples, invalids, and even idiots — though they may, if they please, listen to it outside the synagogue (Mishna, *Rosh. Hash.* iii. 7).

The 14th of Adar,[a] as the very day of the deliverance of the Jews, is more solemnly kept than the 13th. But when the service in the synagogue is over, all give themselves up to merrymaking. Games of all sorts, with dancing and music, commence. In the evening a quaint dramatic entertainment, the subject of which is connected with the occasion, sometimes takes place, and men frequently put on female attire, declaring that the festivities of Purim, according to Esth. ix. 22, suspend the law of Deut. xxii. 5, which forbids one sex to wear the dress of the other. A dainty meal then follows, sometimes with a free indulgence of wine, both unmixed and mulled. According to the Gemara (*Megillah,* vii. 2), "tenetur homo in festo Purim eo usque inebriari, ut nullum discrimen norit, inter maledictionem Hamanis et benedictionem Mardochæi."[b]

On the 15th the rejoicing is continued, and gifts consisting chiefly of sweetmeats and other eatables, are interchanged. Offerings for the poor are also made by all who can afford to do so, in proportion to their means (Esth. ix. 19, 22).

When the month Adar used to be doubled, in the Jewish leap-year, the festival was repeated on the 14th and 15th of the second Adar.

It would seem that the Jews were tempted to associate the Christians with the Persians and Amalekites in the curses of the synagogue.[c] Hence probably arose the popularity of the feast of Purim in those ages in which the feeling of enmity was so strongly manifested between Jews and Christians. Several Jewish proverbs are preserved which strikingly show the way in which Purim was regarded, such as, "The Temple may fail, but Purim never;" "The Prophets may fail, but not the Megillah." It was said that no books would survive in the Messiah's kingdom except the Law and the Megillah. This affection for the book and the festival connected with it is the more remarkable because the events on which they are founded affected only an exiled portion of the Hebrew race, and because there was so much in them to shock the principles and prejudices of the Jewish mind.

Ewald, in support of his theory that there was in patriarchal times a religious festival at every new and full moon, conjectures that Purim was originally the full moon feast of Adar, as the Passover was that of Nisan, and Tabernacles that of Tiari.

It was suggested first by Kepler that the ἑορτὴ τῶν Ἰουδαίων of John v. 1 was the feast of Purim. The notion has been confidently espoused by Petavius, Olshausen, Stier, Wieseler, Winer, and Anger (who, according to Winer, has proved the point beyond contradiction), and is favored by Alford and Ellicott. The question is a difficult one. It seems to be generally allowed that the opinion of Chrysostom, Cyril, and most of the Fathers, which was taken up by Erasmus, Calvin, Beza, and Bengel, that the feast was Pentecost, and that of Cocceius, that it was Tabernacles (which is countenanced by the reading of one inferior MS.), are precluded by the general course of the narrative, and especially by John iv. 35 (assuming that the words of our Lord which are there given were spoken in seed-time)[d] compared with v. 1. The interval indicated by a comparison of these texts could scarcely have extended beyond Nisan. The choice is thus left between Purim and the Passover.

The principal objections to Purim are, (a) that it was not necessary to go up to Jerusalem to keep

tes, Canticles, and Lamentations) are designated by the Rabbinical writers "the Five Rolls," because, as it would seem, they used to be written in separate volumes for the use of the synagogue (Gesen. *Thes.* s. בָּלַל). [ESTHER, BOOK OF.]

a It is called ἡ Μαρδοχαϊκὴ ἡμέρα, 2 Macc. xv. 36.

b Buxtorf remarks on this passage: "Hoc est, nesciat supputare numerum qui ex singularum vocum literis exstruitur: nam literæ בָּרוּךְ מָרְדְּכַי et אָרוּר הָמָן in Gematria eundem numerum conficiunt. Perinde est ac si diceretur, posse illos in tantum bibere, ut quinque manus digitos numerare amplius non possint."

c See Cod. Theodos. lib. xvi. tit. viii. 18: "Judæos,

quodam festivitatis suæ solemni, Aman, ad pœnæ quondam recordationem incendere, et crucis adsimulatam speciem in contemptu Christianæ fidei sacrilega mente exurere, Provinciarum Rectores prohibeant: ne locis suis fidei nostræ signum immisceant, sed ritus suos infra contemptum Christianæ legis retineant, amissuri sine dubio permissa hactenus, nisi ab illicitis temperaverint."

d This supposition does not appear to be materially weakened by our taking as a proverb τετράμηνός ἐστιν καὶ ὁ θερισμὸς ἔρχεται. Whether the expression was such or not, it surely adds point to our Lord's words, if we suppose the figurative language to have been suggested by what was actually going on in the fields before the eyes of Himself and his hearers

the festival; (b) that it is not very likely that our Lord would have made a point of paying especial honor to a festival which appears to have had but a very small religious element in it, and which seems rather to have been the means of keeping alive a feeling of national revenge and hatred. It is alleged on the other hand that our Lord's attending the feast would be in harmony with his deep sympathy with the feelings of the Jewish people, which went further than his merely "fulfilling all righteousness" in carrying out the precepts of the Mosaic Law. It is further urged that the narrative of St. John is best made out by supposing that the incident at the pool of Bethesda occurred at the festival which was characterized by showing kindness to the poor, and that our Lord was induced, by the enmity of the Jews then evinced, not to remain at Jerusalem till the Passover, mentioned John vi. 4 (Stier).

The identity of the Passover with the feast in question has been maintained by Irenæus, Eusebius, and Theodoret, and, in modern times, by Luther, Scaliger, Grotius, Hengstenberg, Greswell, Neander, Tholuck, Robinson, and the majority of commentators. The principal difficulties in the way are, (a) the omission of the article, involving the improbability that the great festival of the year should be spoken of as "a feast of the Jews;" (b) that as our Lord did not go up to the Passover mentioned John vi. 4, He must have absented himself from Jerusalem for a year and a half, that is, till the feast of Tabernacles (John vii. 2). Against these points it is contended, that the application of ἑορτή without the article to the Passover is countenanced by Matt. xxvii. 15; Luke xxiii. 17 (comp. John xviii. 39); that it is assigned as a reason for his staying away from Jerusalem for a longer period than usual, that "the Jews sought to kill him" (John vii. 1; cf. v. 18); that this long period satisfactorily accounts for the surprise expressed by his brethren (John vii. 3), and that, as it was evidently his custom to visit Jerusalem once a year, He went up to the feast of Tabernacles (vii. 2) instead of going to the Passover.

On the whole, the only real objection to the Passover seems to be the want of the article before ἑορτή.[a] That the language of the New Testament will not justify our regarding the omission as expressing emphasis on any general ground of usage, is proved by Winer (Grammar of the N. T. dialect, lii. 19). It must be admitted that the difficulty is no small one, though it does not seem to be sufficient to outweigh the grave objections which lie against the feast of Purim.

The arguments on one side are best set forth by Stier and Olshausen on John v. 1, by Kepler (Eclogae Chronicae, Francfort, 1615), and by Anger (de temp. in Act. Apost. i. 24); those on the other side, by Robinson (Harmony, note on the Second Passover), and Neander, Life of Christ, § 143. See also Lightfoot, Kuinoel, and Tholuck, on John v. 1; and Greswell, Diss. viii. vol. ii.; Ellicott, Lect. p. 135.

---

[a] Tischendorf inserts the article in his text, and Winer allows that there is much authority in its favor. But the nature of the case seems to be such, that the insertion of the article in later MSS. may be more easily accounted for than its omission in the older ones.

* The article is inserted in the Sinaitic and Ephrem MSS., and apparently in I, of the sixth century, which

See Carpzov, App. Crit. iii. 11; Reland, Ant. iv. 9; Schickart, Purim sive Bacchanalia Judaeorum (Crit. Sac. iii. col. 1184); Buxtorf, Syn. Jud. xxix. The Mishnical treatise, Megilla, contains directions respecting the mode in which the scroll should be written out and in which it should be read, with other matters, not much to the point in hand, connected with the service of the synagogue. Stauben, La Vie Juive en Alsace; Mills, British Jews, p. 188.   S. C.

* PURPLE. [COLORS, 1.]

PURSE. The Hebrews, when on a journey, were provided with a bag (variously termed cis,[b] tserôr, and chârît), in which they carried their money (Gen. xlii. 35; Prov. i. 14, vii. 20; Is. xlvi. 6); and, if they were merchants, also their weights Deut. xxv. 13; Mic. vi. 11). This bag is described in the N. T. by the terms βαλάντιον (Tisch. βαλλάντιον) (peculiar to St. Luke, x. 4, xii. 33, xxii. 35, 36), and γλωσσόκομον (peculiar to St. John, xii. 6, xiii. 29). The former is a classical term (Plat. Conviv. p. 190, E, σύσπαστα βαλάντια): the latter is connected with the classical γλωσσόκομείον, which originally meant the bag in which musicians carried the mouthpieces of their instruments. In the LXX. the term is applied to the chest for the offerings at the Temple (2 Chr. xxiv. 8, 10, 11), and was hence adopted by St. John to describe the common purse carried by the disciples. The girdle also served as a purse, and hence the term ζώνη occurs in Matt. x. 9; Mark vi. 8. [GIRDLE.] Ladies wore ornamental purses (Is. iii. 23). The Rabbinists forbade any one passing through the Temple with stick, shoes, and purse, these three being the indications of travelling (Mishn. Berach. 9, § 5). [SCRIP.]
       W. L. B.

PUT, 1 Chr. i. 8; Nah. iii. 9. [PHUT.]

PUTE'OLI (Ποτίολοι: [Puteoli]) appears alike in Josephus (Vit. c. 3; Ant. xvii. 12, § 1, xviii. 7, § 2) and in the Acts of the Apostles (xxviii. 13) in its characteristic position under the early Roman emperors, namely, as the great landing-place of travellers to Italy from the Levant, and as the harbor to which the Alexandrian cornships brought their cargoes. These two features of the place in fact coincided; for in that day the movements of travellers by sea depended on merchant-vessels. Puteoli was at that period a place of very great importance. We cannot elucidate this better than by saying that the celebrated bay which is now "the bay of Naples," and in early times was "the bay of Cumæ," was then called "Sinus Puteolanus." The city was at the northeastern angle of the bay. Close to it was Baiæ, one of the most fashionable of the Roman watering-places. The emperor Caligula once built a ridiculous bridge between the two towns; and the remains of it must have been conspicuous when St. Paul landed at Puteoli in the Alexandrian ship which brought him from Malta. [CASTOR AND

may be regarded as a fair offset to A B D. The uncial MSS. are about equally divided both in respect to authority and number, there being 10 on each side. The article is also added in the Sahidic and Coptic (or Thebaic and Memphitic) versions.   A.

[b] צְרוֹר, פִּיס, and חָרִים. The last occurs only in 2 K. v. 23 ("bags;" Is. iii. 22, A. V. "crisping-pins." The latter is supposed to refer to the long round form of the purse.

POLLUX; MELITA; RHEGIUM; SYRACUSE.] In illustration of the arrival here of the corn-ships we may refer to Seneca (*Ep.* 77) and Suetonius (*Octav.* 98).

The earlier name of Puteoli, when the lower part of Italy was Greek, was Dicæarchia; and this name continued to be used to a late period. Josephus uses it in two of the passages above referred to: in the third (*Vit.* c. 3) he speaks of himself (after the shipwreck which, like St. Paul, he had recently gone through) as διασωθεὶς εἰς τὴν Δικαιαρχίαν, ἣν Ποτιόλους Ἰταλοὶ καλοῦσιν. So Philo, in describing the curious interview which he and his fellow Jewish ambassadors had here with Caligula, uses the old name (*Legat. ad Caium,* ii. 521). The word Puteoli was a true Roman name, and arose (whether *a puteis* or *a putendo*) from the strong mineral springs which are characteristic of the place. Its Roman history may be said to have begun with the Second Punic War. It rose continually into greater importance, from the causes above mentioned. No part of the Campanian shore was more frequented. The associations of Puteoli with historical personages are very numerous. Scipio sailed from hence to Spain. Cicero had a villa (his "Puteolanum") in the neighborhood. Here Nero planned the murder of his mother. Vespasian gave to this city peculiar privileges, and here Hadrian was buried. In the 5th century Puteoli was ravaged both by Alaric and Genseric, and it never afterwards recovered its former eminence. It is now a fourth-rate Italian town, still retaining the name of *Pozzuoli.*

In connection with St. Paul's movements, we must notice its communications in Nero's reign along the mainland with Rome. The coast-road leading northwards to Sinuessa was not made till the reign of Domitian; but there was a cross-road leading to Capua, and there joining the Appian Way. [APPII FORUM; THREE TAVERNS.] The remains of this road may be traced at intervals; and thus the Apostle's route can be followed almost step by step. We should also notice the fact that there were Jewish residents at Puteoli. We might be sure of this from its mercantile importance; but we are positively informed of it by Josephus (*Ant.* xvii. 12, § 1) in his account of the visit of the pretended Herod-Alexander to Augustus; and the circumstance shows how natural it was that the Apostle should find Christian "brethren" there immediately on landing.

The remains of Puteoli are considerable. The aqueduct, the reservoirs, portions (probably) of baths, the great amphitheatre, the building called the Temple of Serapis, which affords very curious indications of changes of level in the soil, are all well worthy of notice. But our chief interest here is concentrated on the ruins of the ancient mole, which is formed of the concrete called *Pozzolana,* and sixteen of the piers of which still remain. No Roman harbor has left so solid a memorial of itself as this one at which St. Paul landed in Italy.

J. S. H.

PUTIEL (פּוּטִיאֵל [*afflicted of God*, Ges.]: Φουτιήλ: *Phutiel*). One of the daughters of Putiel was wife of Eleazar the son of Aaron, and mother of Phinehas (Ex. vi. 25). Though he does not appear again in the Bible records, Putiel has some celebrity in more modern Jewish traditions. They identify him with Jethro the Midianite, "who fatted the calves for idolatrous worship" (Targum

Pseudojon. on Ex. vi. 25; *Gemara of Sota* by Wagenseil, viii. § 6). What are the grounds for the tradition or for such an accusation against Jethro is not obvious. G.

PYGARG (יַחְמוּר, *dishôn*: πύγαργος: *pygargus*) occurs only (Deut. xiv. 5) in the list of clean animals as the rendering of the Heb. *dishôn*, the name apparently of some species of antelope, though it is by no means easy to identify it. The Greek πύγαργος denotes an animal with a "white rump," and is used by Herodotus (iv. 192) as the name of some Libyan deer or antelope. Ælian (vii. 19) also mentions the πύγαργος, but gives no more than the name; comp. also Juvenal (*Sat.* xi. 138). It is usual to identify the *pygarg* of the Greek and Latin writers with the *addax* of North Africa, Nubia, etc. (*Addax nasomaculatus*); but we cannot regard this point as satisfactorily settled. In the first place, this antelope does not present at all the required characteristic implied by its name; and, in the second, there is much reason for believing, with Rüppell (*Atlas zu der Reise im Nörd. Afrik,* p. 21), and Hamilton Smith (Griffith's *Cuvier's Anim. King.* iv. 193), that the *Addax* is identical with the *Strepsiceros* of Pliny (*N. H.* xi. 37), which animal, it must be observed, the Roman naturalist distinguishes from the *pygargus* (viii. 53). Indeed we may regard the identity of the *Addax* and Pliny's *Strepsiceros* as established; for when this species was, after many years, at length rediscovered by Hemprich and Rüppell, it was found to be called by the Arabic name of *akas* or *adas,* the very name which Pliny gives as the local one of his *Strepsiceros.* The *pygargus,* therefore, must be sought for in some animal different from the *addax.* There are several antelopes which have the characteristic white croup required; many of which, however, are inhabitants of South Africa, such as the Spring-bok (*Antidorcas euchore*) and the Bonte-bok (*Damalis pygarga*). We are inclined to consider the πύγαργος, or *pygargus,* as a generic name to denote any of the white-rumped antelopes of North Africa, Syria, etc., such as the Ariel gazelle (*Antilope Arabica,* Hemprich), the Isabella gazelle (*Gazella Isabellina*); perhaps too the mohr, both of Abyssinia (*G. Soemmeringii*) and of Western Africa (*G. Mohr*), may be included under the term. Whether, however, the LXX. and Vulg. are correct in their interpretation of *dishôn* is another question: but there is no collateral evidence of any kind beyond the authority of the two most important versions to aid us in our investigation of this word, of which various etymologies have been given from which nothing definite can be learnt. W. H.

* **PYR'RHUS** (Πύρρος, *red-haired: Pyrrhus*), father of Sopater, one of Paul's company on his journey from Greece to Asia (Acts xx. 4). The name in that passage is undoubtedly genuine, being found in the best copies of the text, though omitted in the *textus receptus,* and hence also in the A. V. The father was no doubt a Berean as well as the son, but whether he was a Christian or not is uncertain, unless, as some suppose. Sopater and Sosipater (Rom. xvi. 21) were forms of the same name, and belonged in this history to the same person. In the latter case he was at Corinth when Paul wrote to the Church at Rome. The mention of the father serves to distinguish this Sopater from others of the same name. The same usage exists in modern Greek. H.

Q.

QUAILS (שְׂלָו, *sělâv*; but in *Keri* שַׂלְוִיו, *sělâv*: ὀρτυγομήτρα: *coturnix*). Various opinions have been held as to the nature of the food denoted by the Heb. *sělâv*, which on two distinct occasions was supplied to the Israelites in the wilderness; see Ex. xvi. 13, on which occasion the people were between Sin and Sinai; and Num. xi. 31, 32, when at the station named, in consequence of the judgment which befell them, Kibroth-hattaavah. That the Hebrew word is correctly rendered "quails," is we think beyond a shadow of doubt, notwithstanding the different interpretations which have been assigned to it by several writers of eminence. Ludolf, for instance, an author of high repute, has endeavored to show that the *sělâv* were locusts; see his *Dissertatio de Locustis, cum Diatriba*, etc., Franc. ad Moen. 1694. His opinion has been fully advocated and adopted by Patrick (*Comment. on Num.* xi. 31, 32); the Jews in Arabia also, as we learn from Niebuhr (*Beschreib. von Arab.* p. 172), "are convinced that the birds which the Israelites ate in such numbers were only clouds of locusts, and they laugh at those translators who suppose that they found quails where quails were never seen." Rudbeck (*Ichthyol. Bibl. Spec.* i.) has argued in favor of the *sělâv* meaning "flying-fish," some species of the genus *Exocetus*; Michaelis at one time held the same opinion, but afterwards properly abandoned it (see Rosenmüller, *Not. ad* Bochart. *Hieroz.* ii. 549). A late writer, Ehrenberg (*Geograph. Zeit.* ix. 86), from having observed a number of "flying fish" (gurnards, of the genus *Trigla* of Oken, *Dactylopterus* of modern icthyologists) lying dead on the shore near Elim, believed that *this* was the food of the Israelites in the wilderness, and named the fish "Trigla Israelitarum." Hermann von der Hardt supposed that the locust bird (*Pastor Roseus*), was intended by *sělâv*; and recently Mr. Forster (*Voice of Israel*, p. 98) has advanced an opinion that "red geese" of the genus *Casarca* are to be understood by the Hebrew term; a similar explanation has been suggested by Stanley (*S. & P.* p. 82) and adopted by Tennent (*Ceylon*, i. 487, *note*): this is apparently an old conceit, for Patrick (*Numb.* xxi. 31) alludes to such an explanation, but we have been unable to trace it to its origin. Some writers, while they hold that the original word denotes "quails," are of opinion that a species of sand-grouse (*Pterocles alchata*), frequent in the Bible-lands, is also included under the term; see Winer (*Bibl. Realwört.* ii. 772): Rosenmüller (*Not. ad Hieroz.* ii. 649); Faber (*ad Harmer*, ii. 442); Gesenius (*Thes.* s. v. שְׂלָו). It is usual to refer to Hasselquist as the authority for believing that the *Kata* (sand-grouse) is denoted: this traveller, however, was rather inclined to believe, with some of the writers named above, that "locusts," and not birds, are to be understood (p. 443); and it is difficult to make out what he means by *Tetrao Israelitarum*. Linnæus supposed he intended by it the common "quail:" in one paragraph he states that the Arabians call a bird "of a grayish color and less than our partridge," by the name of *Katta*. He adds "An Selaw?" This cannot be the *Pterocles alchata*.

The view taken by Ludolf may be dismissed with a very few words. The expression in Ps. lxxviii. 27 of "feathered fowl" (עוֹף כָּנָף), which is used in reference to the *sělâv*, clearly denotes some bird, and Ludolf quite fails to prove that it may include winged insects; again there is not a shadow of evidence to support the opinion that *sělâv* can signify any "locust," this term being used in the Arabic and the cognate languages to denote a "quail." As to any species of "flying-fish," whether belonging to the genus *Dactylopterus*, or to that of *Exocetus*, being intended, it will be enough to state that "flying-fish" are quite unable to sustain their flight above a few hundred yards at the most, and never could have been taken in the Red Sea in numbers sufficient to supply the Israelitish host. The interpretation of *sělâv* by "wild geese," or "wild cranes," or any "wild fowl," is a gratuitous assumption, without a particle of evidence in its favor. The *Casarca*, with which Mr. Forster identifies the *sělâv*, is the *C. rutilla*, a bird about the size of a mallard, which can by no means answer the supposed requisite of standing three feet high from the ground. "The large red-legged cranes," of which Professor Stanley speaks, are evidently white storks (*Ciconia alba*), and would fulfill the condition as to height; but the flesh is so nauseous that no Israelite could have done more than have tasted it. With respect

Pterocles alchata.

to the *Pterocles alchata*, neither it nor indeed any other species of the genus can square with the Scriptural account of the *sělâv*; the sand-grouse are birds of strong wing and of unwearied flight, and never could have been captured in any numbers by the Israelitish multitudes. We much question, moreover, whether the people would have eaten to excess — for so much the expression translated "fully satisfied" (Ps. lxxviii. 29) implies — of the flesh of this bird, for according to the testimony of travellers, from Dr. Russell (*Hist. of Aleppo*, ii. 194, 2d ed.) down to observers of to-day, the flesh of sand-grouse is hard and tasteless. It is clear, however, that the *sělâv* of the Pentateuch and the 105th Psalm denotes the common "quail" (*Coturnix dactylisonans*) and no bird. In the first place, the Hebrew word שְׂלָו is unquestionably identical with the Arabic *salwá* (سلوى), a "quail." According to Schultens (*Orig. Heb.* i. 231) the Heb. שְׂלָו is derived from an Arabic root "to be fat;" the round, plump form of a quail is eminently suitable to this etymology; indeed, its fatness is proverbial. The objections which have been urged by Patrick and others against "quails" being intended are very easily refuted. The expression, "as if it were two cubits (high) upon the face of the earth" (Num xi. 31) is explained by the LXX., by the Vulg., and by Josephus (*Ant.* iii. 1, § 5), to refer to the height at which quails flew above the ground, in their exhausted condition from their long flight. As to the enormous quantities which the least successful Israelite is said to have taken, namely, "ten homers," in the space of a night and two days, there is every reason for believing that the "homers" here spoken of do not denote strictly the measure of that name, but simply "a heap:" this is the explanation given by Onkelos and the Arabic versions of Saadias and Erpenius, in Num. xi. 31.

Coturnix vulgaris.

The quail migrates in immense numbers; see Pliny (*H. N.* x. 23), and Tournefort (*Voyage*, i. 329), who says that all the islands of the Archipelago at certain seasons of the year are covered with these birds. Col. Sykes states that such quantities were once caught in Capri, near Naples, as to have afforded the bishop no small share of his revenue, and that in consequence he has been called Bishop of Quails. The same writer mentions also (*Trans. Zoöl. Soc.* ii.) that 160,000 quails have been netted in one season on this little island; according to Temminck 100,000 have been taken near Nettuno, in one day. The Israelites would have had little difficulty in capturing large quantities of these birds, as they are known to arrive at places sometimes so completely exhausted by their flight as to be readily taken, not in nets only, but by the hand. See Diod. Sic. (i. 82, ed. Dindorf); Prosper Alpinus (*Rerum Ægypt.* iv. 1); Josephus (*Ant.* iii. 1, § 5). Sykes (*l. c.*) says "they arrive in spring on the shores of Prov-

ence so fatigued that for the first few days they allow themselves to be taken by the hand." [a] The Israelites "spread the quails round about the camp;" this was for the purpose of drying them. The Egyptians similarly prepared these birds; see Herodotus (ii. 77), and Maillet (*Lettres sur l'Égypte*, ix. 21, iv. 130). The expression "quails from the sea," Num. xi. 31, must not be restricted to denote that the birds came from the sea as their starting-point, but it must be taken to show the direction from which they were coming: the quails were, at the time of the event narrated in the sacred writings, on their spring journey of migration northwards, an interesting proof, as Col. Sykes has remarked, of the perpetuation of an instinct through some 3300 years; the flight which fed the multitudes at Kibroth-hattaavah might have started from Southern Egypt and crossed the Red Sea near Ras Mohammed, and so up the Gulf of Akabah into Arabia Petræa. It is interesting to note the time specified; "it was at even" that they began to arrive; and they no doubt continued to come all the night. Many observers have recorded that the quail migrates by night, though this is denied by Col. Montagu (*Ornithol. Dict.* art. "Quail").[b] The flesh of the quail, though of an agreeable quality, is said by some writers to be heating, and it is supposed by some that the deaths that occurred from eating the food in the wilderness resulted partly from these birds feeding on hellebore (Pliny, *H. N.* x. 23) and other poisonous plants; see Winer, *Bib. Realwb.* ii. 773; but this is exceedingly improbable, although the immoderate gratification of the appetite for the space of a whole month (Num. xi. 20) on such food, in a hot climate, and in the case of a people who at the time of the wanderings rarely tasted flesh, might have induced dangerous symptoms. "The plague" seems to have been directly sent upon the people by God as a punishment for their murmurings, and perhaps is not, even in a subordinate sense to be attributed to natural causes.

The quail (*Coturnix dactylisonans*), the only species of the genus known to migrate, has a very wide geographical range, being found in China, India, the Cape of Good Hope and England, and, according to Temminck, in Japan. See Col. Sykes's paper on "The Quails and Hemipodii of India" (*Trans. of Zoöl. Soc.* ii.).

The ὀρτυγομήτρα of the LXX. should not be passed over without a brief notice. It is not easy to determine what bird is intended by this term as used by Aristotle and Pliny (*ortygometra*): according to the account given of this bird by the Greek and Latin writers on Natural History just mentioned, the *ortygometra* precedes the quail in its migrations, and acts as a sort of leader to the flight. Some ornithologists, as Belon and Fleming (*Brit. Anim.* p. 98) have assigned this term to the "Landrail" (*Crex pratensis*), the Roi des

---

[a] * In the northern parts of Persia and Armenia, according to Morier, quails are taken in great abundance, and with great ease, with the simplest possible machinery. The men stick two poles in their girdles, on which poles they so stretch a coat or pair of trousers, that the sleeves or the legs shall project like the horns of a beast. Thus disguised, they prowl about the fields with a hand-net, and the quails, simply supposing the strange object to be a horned beast, and therefore harmless to them, allow him to approach till he throws the net over them. Rude as such a contrivance seems, the Persians catch them

thus with astonishing rapidity (*Second Journey*, p. 343, as quoted by P. H. Gosse in Fairbairn's *Imperial Bible Dict.* ii. 741). For other modes of capturing these birds still practiced in the East, see Wood's *Bible Animals* (Lond. 1869), pp. 485, 436.   A.

[b] "On two successive years I observed enormous flights of quails on the N. coast of Algeria, which arrived from the South *in the night*, and were at daybreak in such numbers through the plains, that scores of sportsmen had only to shoot as fast as they could reload" (H. B. Tristram).

Cailles of the French, Re di Quaglie of the Italians, and the Wachtel-König of the Germans, but with what reason we are unable to say; probably the LXX. use the term as a synonym of ὄρτυξ, or to express the good condition in which the birds were, for Hesychius explains ὀρτυγομήτρα by ὄρτυξ ὑπερμεγέθης. i. e. "a quail of large size."

Thus, in point of etymology, zoölogy, history, and the authority of almost all the important old versions, we have as complete a chain of evidence in proof of the quail being the true representative of the *sĕlâv* as can possibly be required.   W. H.

* **QUARRIES, THE** (פְּסִילִים: ἀπὸ τῶν γλυπτῶν: *ubi erant idola*) are mentioned in Judg. iii. 19, 26 (A. V.), as a place well known near Gilgal. Ehud, after having brought his present to Eglon, king of Moab, went with his attendants on their return as far as these "quarries" (A. V.), and then "turned again from them," and went back to execute the meditated murder alone. Instead of "quarries," or "quarry," the A. V. renders *pesilim* or *pesel* elsewhere (31 times in the singular and 21 times in the plural, and also, Judg. iii. 19, in the margin) by "graven" or "carved images." It is certainly unsafe, in view of such a usage, to admit an exceptional meaning in this place. See against that supposition especially Bachmann, *Das Buch der Richter*, p. 208 ff. (1868). A few make the word a proper name, *Pesilim*, with reference to some ancient idolatry there, though no longer practiced in Ehud's time.

Professor Cassel, *Richter u. Ruth*, p. 37, in Lange's *Bibelwerk* (1865), suggests another explanation. He understands that the פְּסִילִים were landmarks (consisting of pillars or heaps of stone, στῆλαι) which marked the boundary between the territory of the Moabites on the west of the Jordan (held by them as conquerors at that time) and that of the Hebrews; and that it was from these stone heaps or pillars that Ehud turned back after parting with his servants. *Pesilim*, in this sense, would be nearly allied to that of "images," idol-gods (comp. Deut. vii. 25 and Isa. xlii. 8), since boundaries (*lapides sacri, termini*) were regarded as properly inviolate, consecrated. To the heathen they were hardly less than objects of religious veneration. The Hebrews would naturally speak of them with reference to the feelings of their foreign oppressors, though we need not altogether acquit the Hebrews of a similar superstition. Fürst sanctions "quarries," but as Targumic rather than Hebrew.   H.

QUARTUS (Κούαρτος [Lat. *fourth*]: *Quartus*), a Christian of Corinth, whose salutations St. Paul sends to the brethren at Rome (Rom. xvi. 23). There is the usual tradition that he was one of the Seventy disciples; and it is also said that he ultimately became Bishop of Berytus (Tillemont, i. 334).[a]   E. H—s.

QUATERNION (τετράδιον: *quaternio*), a military term, signifying a guard of four soldiers, two of whom were attached to the person of a prisoner, while the other two kept watch outside the door of his cell (Vegetius, *De Re mil.* iii. 8; Polyb. vi. 33, § 7). Peter was delivered over to four such

---

[a] * In the Greek it is Quartus — "the brother" (not indefinite, A. V.), which implies that he was well known to the Roman Christians.   H.

bodies of four (Acts xii. 4), each of which took charge of him for a single watch of the night.   W. L. B.

* Of the quaternion on guard at a given time, two may have watched at the door of the cell, and two at the gate which opened into the city. Peter, in making his escape, "passed through" (διελθεῖν) a first and a second watch (φυλακή), which suggests the idea of more than one sentinel at each post. Walch thinks that the two soldiers to whom Peter was bound in the prison (ver. 6) did not belong to the quaternion, inasmuch as the security of Peter might not require them to be changed during the night like the others. On these details, and the archæology of the subject generally, see especially Walch, *De vinculis Petri*, in his *Dissert. ad Acta Apost.* pp. 147–190.   H.

QUEEN (גְּבִירָה; שֵׁגָל; מַלְכָּה). Of the three Hebrew terms cited as the equivalents of "queen" in the A. V., the first alone is applied to a queen-*reynant*; the first and second equally to a queen-*consort*, without, however, implying the dignity which in European nations attaches to that position; and the third to the queen-*mother*, to whom that dignity is transferred in oriental courts. The etymological force of the words accords with their application. *Malcâh* is the feminine of *melech*, "king;" it is applied in its first sense to the queen of Sheba (1 K. x. 1), and in its second to the wives of the first rank, as distinguished from the concubines, in a royal harem (Esth. i. 9 ff., vii. 1 ff.; Cant. vi. 8): the term "princesses" is similarly used in 1 K. xi. 3. *Shêgâl* simply means "wife;" it is applied to Solomon's bride (Ps. xlv. 9), and to the wives of the first rank in the harems of the Chaldee and Persian monarchs (Dan. v. 2, 3; Neh. ii. 6). *Gĕbîrâh*, on the other hand, is expressive of authority; it means "powerful" or "mistress." It would therefore be applied to the female who exercised the highest authority, and this, in an oriental household, is not the wife but the mother of the master. Strange as such an arrangement at first sight appears, it is one of the inevitable results of polygamy: the number of the wives, their social position previous to marriage, and the precariousness of their hold on the affections of their lord, combine to annihilate their influence, which is transferred to the mother as being the only female who occupies a fixed and dignified position. Hence the application of the term *gĕbîrâh* to the queen-*mother*, the extent of whose influence is well illustrated by the narrative of the interview of Solomon and Bathsheba, as given in 1 K. ii. 19 ff. The term is applied to Maachah, Asa's mother, who was deposed from her dignity in consequence of her idolatry (1 K. xv. 13; 2 Chr. xv. 16); to Jezebel as contrasted with Joram (2 K. x. 13, "the children of the king, and the children of the queen "); and to the mother of Jehoiachin or Jeconiah (Jer. xiii. 18; comp. 2 K. xxiv. 12; Jer. xxix. 2). In 1 K. xi. 19, the text probably requires emendation, the reading followed in the LXX., הַגְּדוֹלָה, "the elder," according better with the context.   W. L. B.

QUEEN OF HEAVEN. In Jer. vii. 18, xliv. 17, 18, 19, 25, the Heb. מְלֶכֶת הַשָּׁמַיִם *mĕleceth hashshâmayim*, is thus rendered in the A. V. In the margin is given "frame or workmanship of heaven," for in twenty of Kennicott's MSS. the reading is מְלֶאכֶת, *mĕleceth*, of which this is the translation, and the same is the case in fourteen MSS. of Jer. xliv. 18, and in thirteen of Jer. xliv. 19. The latter reading is followed by the LXX. and Peshito Syriac in Jer. vii. 18, but in all the other passages the received text is adopted, as by the Vulgate in every instance. Kimchi says:

"אֵ is wanting, and it is as if מְלֶאכֶת, 'workmanship of heaven,' i. e. the stars; and some interpret 'the queen of heaven,' i. e. a great star which is in the heavens." Rashi is in favor of the latter; and the Targum renders throughout "the star of heaven." Kircher was in favor of some constellation, the Pleiades or Hyades. It is generally believed that the "queen of heaven" is the moon (comp. "siderum regina," Hor. Carm. Sec. 35, and "regina cœli," Apul. Met. xi. 657), worshipped as Ashtaroth or Astarte, to whom the Hebrew women offered cakes in the streets of Jerusalem. Hitzig (Der Proph. Jeremja, p. 64) says the Hebrews gave this title to the Egyptian Neith, whose name in the form Ta-nith, with the Egyptian article, appears with that of Baal Hammân, on four Carthaginian inscriptions. It is little to the purpose to inquire by what other names this goddess was known among the Phœnician colonists: the Hebrews, in the time of Jeremiah, appear not to have given her any special title. The Babylonian Venus, according to Harpocration (quoted by Selden, de Dis Syris, synt. 2, cap. 6, p. 220, ed. 1617), was also styled "the queen of heaven." Mr. Layard identifies Hera, "the second deity mentioned by Diodorus, with Astarte, Mylitta, or Venus," and with the "'queen of heaven,' frequently mentioned in the sacred volumes. . . . . The planet which bore her name was sacred to her, and in the Assyrian sculptures a star is placed upon her head. She was called Beltis, because she was the female form of the great divinity, or Baal; the two, there is reason to conjecture, having been originally but one, and androgyne. Her worship penetrated from Assyria into Asia Minor, where its Assyrian origin was recognized. In the rock tablets of Pterium she is represented, as in those of Assyria, standing erect on a lion, and crowned with a tower or mural coronet; which, we learn from Lucian, was peculiar to the Semitic figure of the goddess. This may have been a modification of the high cap of the Assyrian bas-reliefs. To the Shemites she was known under the names of Astarte, Ashtaroth, Mylitta, and Alitta, according to the various dialects of the nations amongst which her worship prevailed" (Nineveh, ii. 454, 456, 457). It is so difficult to separate the worship of the moon-goddess from that of the planet Venus in the Assyrian mythology when introduced among the western nations, that the two are frequently confused. Movers believes that Ashtoreth was originally the moon-goddess, while according to Rawlinson (Herod. i. 521) Ishtar is the Babylonian Venus, one of whose titles in the Sardanapalus inscriptions is "the mistress of heaven and earth."

With the cakes (כַּוָּנִים, cavvānīm: χαυῶνες) which were offered in her honor, with incense and libations, Selden compares the πίτυρα (A. V. "bran") of Ep. of Jer. 43, which were burnt by the women who sat by the wayside near the idolatrous temples for the purposes of prostitution. These πίτυρα were offered in sacrifice to Hecate, while invoking her aid for success in love (Theocr.

Λ. 33). The Targum gives כַּרְדּוּטִין, cardūtīn,

which elsewhere appears to be the Greek χειριδωτός, a sleeved tunic. Rashi says the cakes had the image of the god stamped upon them, and Theodoret that they contained pine-cones and raisins.

W. A. W.

* **QUEEN OF THE SOUTH** (Luke xi. 31). [SHEBA.]

* **QUICK** (from A.-S. cwic or cwoc) = living, alive, Lev. xiii. 10; Num. xvi. 30; Ps. lv. 15, cxxiv. 3; Acts x. 42; 2 Tim. iv. 1; Heb. iv. 12; 1 Pet. iv. 5. H.

* **QUICKEN** = to make alive (A.-S. cwician), Ps. cxix. 50; 1 Cor. xv. 36; Eph. ii. 1, etc. [QUICK.] H.

QUICKSANDS, THE (ἡ Σύρτις: Syrtis), more properly THE SYRTIS (Acts xxvii. 17), the broad and deep bight on the North African coast between Carthage and Cyrene. The name is derived from Sert, an Arabic word for a desert. For two reasons this region was an object of peculiar dread to the ancient navigators of the Mediterranean, partly because of the drifting sands and the heat along the shore itself, but chiefly because of the shallows and the uncertain currents of water in the bay. Josephus, who was himself once wrecked in this part of the Mediterranean, makes Agrippa say (B. J. ii. 16, § 4), φοβεραὶ καὶ τοῖς ἀκούουσι Σύρτεις. So notorious were these dangers, that they became a commonplace with the poets (see Hor. Od. i. 22, 5; Ov. Fast. iv. 499; Virgil, Æn. i. 111; Tibull. iii. 4, 91; Lucan, Phars. ix. 431). It is most to our purpose here, however, to refer to Apollonius Rhodius, who was familiar with all the notions of the Alexandrian sailors. In the 4th book of his Argonaut. 1232-1237, he supplies illustrations of the passage before us, in more respects than one — in the sudden violence (ἀναρπάγδην) of the terrible north wind (ὀλοὴ Βορέαο θύελλα), in its long duration (ἐννέα πάσας Νύκτας ὁμῶς καὶ τόσσα φέρ' ἤματα), and in the terror which the sailors felt of being driven into the Syrtis (Προτρὸ μάλ' ἔνδοθι Σύρτιν, δθ' οὐκέτι νόστος ὀπίσσω Νηυσὶ πέλει). [See CLAUDA and EUBOCLYDON.] There were properly two Syrtes, the eastern or larger, now called the Gulf of Sidra, and the western or smaller, now the Gulf of Cabes. It is the former to which our attention is directed in this passage of the Acts. The ship was caught by a northeasterly gale on the south coast of CRETE, near Mount Ida, and was driven to the island of Clauda. This line of drift, continued, would strike the greater Syrtis: whence the natural apprehension of the sailors. [SHIP.] The best modern account of this part of the African coast is that which is given (in his Memoir on the Mediterranean, pp. 87-91, 186-190) by Admiral Smyth, who was himself the first to survey this bay thoroughly, and to divest it of many of its terrors.

J. S. H.

QUIN'TUS MEMM'IUS, 2 Macc. xi. 34. [See MANLIUS, T. vol. ii. p. 1779 b.]

* **QUIRIN'IUS.** [CYRENIUS.]

* **QUIT**, in the sense of acquit: "Quit yourselves like men" (1 Sam. iv. 9); and, 'Quit you like men" (1 Cor. xvi. 13). H.

QUIVER. Two distinct Hebrew terms are represented by this word in the A. V.

(1) תְּלִי, thĕlî. This occurs only in Gen. xxvii. 3: "Take thy weapons (lit. "thy things"), thy

quiver and thy bow." It is derived (by Gesenius, *Thes.* p. 1504, and Fürst, *Handwb.* ii. 528) from a root which has the force of hanging. The passage itself affords no clew to its meaning. It may therefore signify either a quiver, or a suspended weapon

Assyrian Warrior with Quiver.

— for instance, such a sword as in our own language was formerly called a "hanger." Between these two significations the interpreters are divided. The LXX., Vulgate, and Targum Pseudojon. adhere to the former; Onkelos, the Peshito and Arabic Versions, to the latter.

(2.) אַשְׁפָּה, *ashpâh.* The root of this word is uncertain (Gesenius, *Thes.* p. 161). From two of its

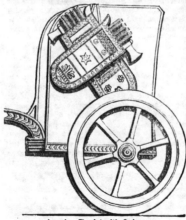

Assyrian Chariot with Quiver.

occurrences its force would seem to be that of containing or concealing (Ps. cxxvii. 5; Is. xlix. 2). It is connected with arrows only in Lam. iii. 13. Its other occurrences are Job xxxix. 23, Is. xxii. 6, and Jer. v. 16. In each of these the LXX. trans-

late it by "quiver" (φαρέτρα), with two exceptions, Job xxxix. 23, and Ps. cxxvii. 5, in the former of which they render it by "bow," in the latter by ἐπιθυμία.

As to the thing itself, there is nothing in the Bible to indicate either its form or material, or in what way it was carried. The quivers of the Assyrians are rarely shown in the sculptures. When they do appear they are worn at the back, with the top between the shoulders of the wearer, or hung at the side of the chariot.

The Egyptian warriors, on the other hand, wore them slung nearly horizontal, drawing out the arrows from beneath the arm (Wilkinson, *Popular Account,* i. 354). The quiver was about 4 inches diameter, supported by a belt passing over the shoulder and across the breast to the opposite side. When not in actual use, it was shifted behind.

The English word "quiver" is a variation of "cover" — from the French *couvrir;* and therefore answers to the second of the two Hebrew words.   G.

* QUOTATIONS FROM THE O. T. IN THE NEW. [OLD TESTAMENT, iii.]

R.

RA′AMAH (רַעְמָה [*trembling,* and *mane of a horse*]: Ῥεγμά, [Alex. Ῥεγχμα,] Gen. x. 7; Ραμμά, [Vat. Ραμα, Alex. Ραγμα,] Ez. xxvii. 22: [רַעְמָא: Ῥεγμά, 1 Chr. i. 9:] *Regma, Reema*). A son of Cush, and father of the Cushite Sheba and Dedan. The tribe of Raamah became afterwards renowned as traders; in Ezekiel's lamentation for Tyre it is written, "The merchants of Sheba and Raamah, they [were] thy merchants; they occupied in thy fairs with chief of all the spices, and with all precious stones and gold " (xxvii. 22). The general question of the identity, by intermarriage, etc., of the Cushite Sheba and Dedan with the Keturahites of the same names is discussed, and the 27th chapter of Ezekiel examined, in art. DEDAN. Of the settlement of Raamah on the shores of the Persian Gulf there are several indications. Traces of Dedan are very faint; but Raamah seems to be recovered, through the LXX. reading of Gen. x. 7, in the Ῥεγμά of Ptol. vi. 7, and Ῥῆγμα of Steph. Byzant. Of Sheba, the other son of Raamah, the writer has

found a trace in a ruined city so named (شِبَا, *Shebà*) on the island of Awál (Marásid, *s. v.*), belonging to the province of Arabia called El-Bahreyn on the shores of the gulf. [SHEBA.] This identification strengthens that of Raamah with Ῥεγμά, and the establishment of these Cushite settlements on the Persian Gulf is of course important to the theory of the identity of these Cushite and Keturahite tribes: but, besides etymological grounds there are the strong reasons stated in DEDAN for holding that the Cushites colonized that region, and for connecting them commercially with Palestine by the great desert route.

The town mentioned by Niebuhr called Reymeh (ﺭﻳﻤﺔ, *Descr. de l'Arabie*) cannot, on etymological grounds, be connected with Raamah, as it wants an equivalent for the ע; nor can we suppose that it is to be probably traced three days' journey from San'à [UZAL], the capital of the Yemen.   E. S. P.

RAAMI'AH (רַעַמְיָה: 'Peeλμά; [Vat. Naaμια, 2. m. Naεμια;] FA. δαεμια: Raamins). One of the chiefs who returned with Zerubbabel (Neh. vii. 7). In Ezr. ii. 2 he is called REELAIAH, and the Greek equivalent of the name in the LXX. of Nehemiah appears to have arisen from a confusion of the two readings, unless, as Burrington (Geneal. ii. 68) suggests, 'Peeλμά is an error of the copyist for Peeλαία, the uncial letters AI having been mistaken for M. In 1 Esdr. v. 8 the name appears as REESAIAS.

RAAM'SES, Ex. i. 11.   [RAMESES.]

RAB'BAH. The name of several ancient places, both east and west of the Jordan. The root is rab, meaning " multitude," and thence "greatness," of size or importance [a] (Gesenius, Thes. p. 1254; Fürst, Handwb. ii. 347). The word survives in Arabic as a common appellative, and is also in use as the name of places — e. gr. Rabba on the east of the Dead Sea; Rabbah, a temple in the tribe of Medshidj (Freytag, ii. 107 a); and perhaps also Rabat in Morocco.

1. (רַבָּה: [b] 'Paββάθ, 'Paββθ, ἡ 'Paββά; [Rom. 'Apάδ, Josh. xiii. 25 (so Vat.); 'Paββά, 1 Chr. xx. 1; ἡ πόλις τοῦ 'Aμμών, Ez. xxv. δ (so Vat. Alex.); elsewhere 'Paββάθ: — Vat. in 1 Chr. xvii. 27, Paβαθ ; 1 Chr. xx. 1, Paββαν, Paββα; Am. i. 14, Paββα (so Alex.); Josh. and Ez. as above; elsewhere Paββαθ; — Alex. in Josh. xiii. 25, Am. i. 14, Paββα; 2 Sam. xii. 26, Paβαθ; Ez. as above; elsewhere Paββαθ; — FA.[1] Jer. xlix. 2, Paβαθ, ver. 3, FA. Peββαθ:] Rabba, Rabbath.) A very strong place on the east of Jordan, which, when its name is first introduced in the sacred records, was the chief city of the Ammonites. In five passages (Deut. iii. 11; 2 Sam. xii. 26, xvii. 27; Jer. xlix. 2; Ez. xxi. 20) it is styled at length Rabbath bene-Ammón, A. V. [in Deut. iii. 11, Ez. xxi. 20] Rabbath [elsewhere Rabbah] of the Ammonites, or, children of Ammon; but elsewhere (Josh. xxiii. 25; 2 Sam. xi. 1, xii. 27, 29; 1 Chr. xx. 1; Jer. xlix. 8; Ez. xxv. 5; Amos i. 14) simply RABBAH.

It appears in the sacred records as the single city of the Ammonites, at least no other bears any distinctive name, a fact which, as has been already remarked (vol. i. p. 84 b), contrasts strongly with the abundant details of the city life of the Moabites.

Whether it was originally, as some conjecture, the HAM of which the Zuzim were dispossessed by Chedorlaomer (Gen. xiv. 5), will probably remain forever a conjecture.[c] When first named, it is in the hands of the Ammonites, and is mentioned as containing the bed or sarcophagus of the giant Og (Deut. iii. 11), possibly the trophy of some successful war of the younger nation of Lot, and more recent settler in the country, against the more ancient Rephaim. With the people of Lot, their kinsmen the Israelites had no quarrel, and Rabbath-of-the-children-of-Ammon remained to all appearance unmolested during the first period of the Israelite occupation. It was not included in the territory of the tribes east of Jordan; the border of Gad stops at " Aroer, which faces Rabbah" (Josh. xiii. 25). The attacks of the Bene-Ammon on Israel, however, brought these peaceful relations to an end. Saul must have had occupation enough on the west of Jordan in attacking and repelling the attacks of the Philistines and in pursuing David through the woods and ravines of Judah to prevent his crossing the river, unless on such special occasions as the relief of Jabesh. At any rate we never hear of his having penetrated so far in that direction as Rabbah. But David's armies were often engaged against both Moab and Ammon.

His first Ammonite campaign appears to have occurred early in his reign. A part of the army, under Abishai, was sent as far as Rabbah to keep the Ammonites in check (2 Sam. x. 10, 14), but the main force under Joab remained at Medeba (1 Chr. xix. 7). The following year was occupied in the great expedition by David in person against the Syrians at Helam, wherever that may have been (2 Sam. x. 15-19). After their defeat the Ammonite war was resumed, and this time Rabbah was made the main point of attack (xi. 1). Joab took the command, and was followed by the whole of the army. The expedition included Ephraim and Benjamin, as well as the king's own tribe (ver. 11): the "king's slaves" (vv. 1, 17, 24); probably David's immediate body-guard, and the thirty-seven chief captains. Uriah was certainly there, and, if a not improbable Jewish tradition may be adopted, Ittai the Gittite was there also. [ITTAI.] The ark accompanied the camp (ver. 11), the only time [d] that we hear of its doing so, except that memorable battle with the Philistines, when its capture caused the death of the high-priest. David alone, to his cost, remained in Jerusalem. The country was wasted, and the roving Ammonites were driven with all their property (xii. 30) into their single stronghold, as the Bedouin Kenites were driven from their tents inside the walls of Jerusalem when Judah was overrun by the Chaldæans. [RECHABITES.] The 'siege must have lasted nearly, if not quite, two years; since during its progress David formed his connection with Bathsheba, and the two children, that which died and Solomon, were successively born. The sallies of the Ammonites appear to have formed a main feature of the siege (2 Sam. xi. 17, &c.). At the end of that time Joab succeeded in capturing a portion of the place — the "city of waters," that is, the lower town, so called from its containing the perennial stream which rises in and still flows through it. The fact (which seems undoubted) that the source of the stream was within the lower city, explains its having held out for so long. It was also called the "royal city" (עִיר הַמְּלוּכָה), perhaps from its connection with Molech or Milcom

a It is hardly necessary to point out that the title Rabbi is directly derived from the same root.

b In Deut. iii. 11 it is τῇ ἄκρᾳ τῶν υἱῶν 'Aμμών in both MSS. In Josh. xiii. 25 the Vat. has 'Apαβα ἡ ἐστιν κατὰ πρόσωπον 'Apάδ, where the first and last words of the sentence seem to have changed places.

c The statement of Eusebius (Onom. " Amman ") that it was originally a city of the Rephaim, implies that it was the Ashteroth Karnaim of Gen. xiv. In

agreement with this is the fact that it was in later times known as Astarte (Steph. Byz., quoted by Ritter, p. 1155). In this case the dual ending of Karnaim may point, as some have conjectured in Jerushalaim, to the double nature of the city — a lower town and a citadel.

d On a former occasion (Num. xxxi. 6) the "holy things" only are specified; an expression which hardly seems to include the ark.

— the "king"— more probably from its containing the palace of Hanun and Nahash. But the citadel, which rises abruptly on the north side of the lower town, a place of very great strength, still remained to be taken, and the honor of this capture, Joab (with that devotion to David which runs like a bright thread through the dark web of his character) insists on reserving for the king. "I have fought," writes he to his uncle, then living at ease in the harem at Jerusalem, in all the satisfaction of the birth of Solomon — "I have fought against Rabbah, and have taken *a* the city of waters: but the citadel still remains: now therefore gather the rest of the people together and come; put yourself at the head of the whole army, renew the assault against the citadel, take it, and thus finish the siege which I have carried so far," and then he ends with a rough banter *b* — half jest, half earnest — "lest I take the city and in future it go under my name." The waters of the lower city once in the hands of the besiegers, the fate of the citadel was certain, for that fortress possessed in itself (as we learn from the invaluable notice of Josephus, *Ant.* vii. 7, § 5) but one well of limited supply, quite inadequate to the throng which crowded its walls. The provisions also were at last exhausted, and shortly after David's arrival the fortress was taken, and its inmates, with a very great booty, and the idol of Molech, with all its costly adornments, fell into the hands of David. [ITTAI; MOLECH.]

We are not told whether the city was demolished or whether David was satisfied with the slaughter of its inmates. In the time of Amos, two centuries and a half later, it had again a "wall" and "palaces," and was still the sanctuary of Molech — "the king" (Am. i. 14). So it was also at the date of the invasion of Nebuchadnezzar (Jer. xlix. 2, 3), when its dependent towns ("daughters") are mentioned, and when it is named in such terms as imply that it was of equal importance with Jerusalem (Ez. xxi. 20). At Rabbah, no doubt, Baalis, king of the Bene-Ammon (Jer. xl. 14), held such court as he could muster, and within its walls was plotted the attack of Ishmael which cost Gedaliah his life, and drove Jeremiah into Egypt. [ISHMAEL 6, vol. ii. p. 1172 *b*.] The denunciations of the prophets just named may have been fulfilled, either at the time of the destruction of Jerusalem, or five years afterwards, when the Assyrian armies overran the country east of Jordan on their road to Egypt (Joseph. *Ant.* x. 9, § 7). See Jerome, on *Amos* i. 41.

In the period between the Old and New Testaments, Rabbath-Ammon appears to have been a place of much importance, and the scene of many contests. The natural advantages of position and water supply which had always distinguished it, still made it an important citadel by turns to each side, during the contentions which raged for so long over the whole of the district. It lay on the road between Heshbon and Bosra, and was the last place at which a stock of water could be obtained for the journey across the desert, while as it stood on the confines of the richer and more civilized country, it formed an important garrison station, for repelling the incursions of the wild tribes of the desert.

From Ptolemy Philadelphus (B. C. 285–247) it received the name of Philadelphia (Jerome on Ez. xxv. 1), and the district either then or subsequently was called Philadelphene (Joseph. *B. J.* iii. 3, § 3), or Arabia Philadelphensis (Epiphanius, in Ritter, *Syrien*, p. 1155). In B. C. 218 it was taken from the then Ptolemy (Philopator) by Antiochus the Great, after a long and obstinate resistance from the besieged in the citadel. A communication with the spring in the lower town had been made since (possibly in consequence of) David's siege, by a long secret subterranean passage, and had not this been discovered to Antiochus by a prisoner, the citadel might have been enabled to hold out (Polybius, v. 17, in Ritter, *Syrien*, p. 1155). During the struggle between Antiochus the Pious (Sidetes), and Ptolemy the son-in-law of Simon Maccabæus (cir. B. C. 134), it is mentioned as being governed by a tyrant named Cotylas (*Ant.* xiii. 8, § 1). Its ancient name, though under a cloud, was still used; it is mentioned by Polybius (v. 71) under the hardly altered form of Rabbatámana ('Ραββατάμανα). About the year 65 we hear of it as in the hands of Aretas (one of the Arab chiefs of that name), who retired thither from Judæa when menaced by Scaurus, Pompey's general (Joseph. *B. J.* i. 6, § 3). The Arabs probably held it till the year B. C. 30, when they were attacked there by Herod the Great. But the account of Josephus (*B. J.* i. 19, §§ 5, 6) seems to imply that the city was not then inhabited, and that although the citadel formed the main point of the combat, yet that it was only occupied on the instant. The water communication above alluded to also appears not to have been then in existence, for the people who occupied the citadel quickly surrendered from thirst, and the whole affair was over in six days.

At the Christian era Philadelphia formed the eastern limit of the region of Peræa (*B. J.* iii. 3, § 3). It was one of the cities of the Decapolis, and as far down as the 4th century was esteemed one of the most remarkable and strongest cities of the whole of Cœle-Syria (Eusebius, *Onom.* "Amman;" Ammianus Marc. in Ritter, p. 1157). Its magnificent theatre (said to be the largest *c* in Syria), temples, odeon, mausoleum, and other public buildings were probably erected during the 2d and 3d centuries, like those of *Jerash*, which they resemble in style, though their scale and design are grander (Lindsay). Amongst the ruins of an "immense temple" on the citadel hill, Mr. Tipping saw some prostrate columns 5 ft. diameter. Its coins are extant, some bearing the figure of Astarte, some the word Herakleion, implying a worship of Hercules; probably the continuation of that of Molech or Milcom. From Stephanus of Byzantium we learn that it was also called Astarte, doubtless from its containing a temple of that goddess. Justin Martyr, a native of Shechem, writing about A. D. 140, speaks of the city as containing a multitude of Ammonites (*Dial. with Trypho*), though it would probably not be safe to interpret this too strictly.

Philadelphia became the seat of a Christian bishop, and was one of the nineteen sees of "Palestina tertia," which were subordinate to Bostra

---

a The Vulgate alters the force of the whole passage by rendering this *et capienda est urbs aquarum*, "the city of waters is about to be taken." But neither Hebrew nor LXX. will bear this interpretation.

b Very characteristic of Joab. See a similar strain, 2 Sam. xix. 6.

c Mr. Tipping gives the following dimensions in his journal. Breadth 240 ft.; height 42 steps; namely first row 10, second 14, third 18.

(Reland, *Pal.* p. 228.) The church still remains "in excellent preservation" with its lofty steeple (Lord Lindsay). Some of the bishops appear to have signed under the title of Bakatha; which Bakatha is by Epiphanius (himself a native of Palestine) mentioned in such a manner as to imply that it was but another name for Philadelphia, derived from an Arab tribe in whose possession it was at that time (A. D. cir. 400). But this is doubtful. (See Reland, *Pal.* p. 612; Ritter, p. 1157.)

Amman [a] lies about 22 miles from the Jordan at the eastern apex of a triangle, of which Hesbbon and *es-Salt* form respectively the southern and northern points It is about 14 miles from the former, and 12 from the latter. Jerash is due north more than 20 miles distant in a straight line, and 35 by the usual road (Lindsay, p. 278). It lies in a valley which is a branch, or perhaps the main course, of the *Wady Zerka*,[b] usually identi-

fied with the Jabbok. The *Moiet-Amman*, or water of Amman, a mere streamlet, rises within the basin which contains the ruins of the town. The main valley is a mere winter torrent, but appears to be perennial, and contains a quantity of fish, by one observer said to be trout (see Burckhardt, p. 358; G. Robinson ii. 174; " a perfect fishpond," Tipping). The stream runs from west to east, and north of it is the citadel on its isolated hill.

When the Moslems conquered Syria they found the city in ruins (Abulfeda in Ritter, p. 1158; and in note to Lord Lindsay); and in ruins remarkable for their extent and desolation even for Syria, the " Land of ruins," it still remains. The public buildings are said to be Roman, in general character like those at *Jerash*, except the citadel, which is described as of large square stones put together without cement, and which is probably more

Amman, from the East: showing the perennial stream and part of the citadel-hill. From a sketch by Wm. Tipping, Esq.

ancient than the rest. The remains of private houses scattered on both sides of the stream are very extensive. They have been visited, and described in more or less detail, by Burckhardt (*Syria*, pp. 357 –360), who gives a plan; Seetzen (*Reisen*, i. 396, iv. 212-214); Irby (June 14); Buckingham, *E. Syria*, pp. 68–82; Lord Lindsay (5th ed. pp. 278–284); G. Robinson (ii. 172–178); Lord Claud Hamilton (in Keith, *Evid. of Proph.* ch. vi.). Burckhardt's plan gives a general idea of the disposition of the place, but a comparison with Mr. Tipping's sketch (on the accuracy of which every dependence may be placed) seems to show that it is not correct as to the proportions of the different parts. Two views are given by Laborde (*Vues en Syrie*), one of a tomb, the other of the theatre; but neither of these embraces the characteristic features of the place — the streamlet and the citadel. The ac-

companying view has been engraved (for the first time) from one of several careful sketches made in 1840 by William Tipping, Esq., and by him kindly placed, with some valuable information, at the disposal of the author. It is taken looking towards the east. On the right is the beginning of the citadel hill. In front is an arch (also mentioned by Burckhardt) which spans the stream. Below and in front of the arch is masonry, showing how the stream was formerly embanked or quayed in.

No inscriptions have been yet discovered. A lengthened and excellent summary of all the information respecting this city will be found in Ritter's *Erdkunde, Syrien* (pp. 1145–1159).

* These ruins, among the most impressive in Syria, are not, with the exception of the citadel, those of the Rabbath of the Ammonites. That has vanished with the iron bedstead of the last

---

[a] عمان, essentially the same word as the Hebrew *Ammôn*.

[b] This is distinctly stated by Abulfeda (Ritter, p. 1158, Lindsay, note 37).

giant king of Bashan. The remains of the Roman Philadelphia appear in the elaborate but mutilated Grecian sculpture with which the site is now strewed. (Tristram, *Land of Israel*, pp. 548–055, 2d ed.)   S. W.

2. Although there is no trace of the fact in the Bible, there can be little doubt that the name of Rabbah was also attached in Biblical times to the chief city of Moab. Its Biblical name is AR, but we have the testimony of Eusebius (*Onomast.* "Moab") that in the 4th century it possessed the special title of Rabbath Moab, or as it appears in the corrupted orthography of Stephanus of Byzantium, the coins, and the Ecclesiastical Lists, *Rabathmoba*, *Rabbathmoma*, and *Ratba* or *Robba Moabitis* (Reland, pp. 957, 226; Seetzen, *Reisen*, iv. 227; Ritter, p. 1290). This name was for a time displaced by Areopolis, in the same manner that Rab-

bath-Ammon had been by Philadelphia: these, however, were but the names imposed by the temporary masters of the country, and employed by them in their official documents, and when they passed away, the original names, which had never lost their place in the mouths of the common people, reappeared, and *Rabba* and *Ammân* still remain to testify to the ancient appellations. *Rabba* lies on the highlands at the S. E. quarter of the Dead Sea, between *Kerak* and *Jibel Shihân*. Its ruins, which are unimportant, are described by Burckhardt (July 15), Seetzen (*Reisen*, i. 411), and De Saulcy (Jan. 18).

3. (הָרַבָּה, with the definite article: Σωθηβά; Alex. ΑρεΒΒα: *Arebba*.) A city of Judah, named with Kirjath-jearim, in Josh. xv. 60 only. No trace of its existence has yet been discovered.

Coin of Philadelphia, showing the Tent or Shrine of Herakles, the Greek equivalent to Molech. Obv.. AVT·KAICM·AVP·ANTⲰNINV, Bust of M. Aurelius, r. Rev.: ΦΙΑΚΟϹΥΡΗΡΑΚΛΕϹΙΟΝ ΡΜΑ [A. ▼ C. 690]. Shrine in quadriga, r. [ΦΙΛΛΔΕΛΦΕΩΝ ΚΟΙΑΗϹ ϹΥΡΙΑϹ ΗΡΑΚΛΕϹΙΟΝ].

4. In one passage (Josh. xi. 8) ZIDON is mentioned with the affix Rabbah — Zidon-rabbah. This is preserved in the margin of the A. V., though in the text it is translated "great Zidon."   G.

RAB'BATH OF THE CHILDREN OF AMMON, and R. OF THE AMMONITES.

(The former is the more accurate, the Hebrew being in both cases רַבַּת בְּנֵי עַמּוֹן: ἡ ἄκρα τῶν υἱῶν Ἀμμών [Ἀμμάν, Vat.¹], 'Ραββὰθ υἱῶν Ἀμμών: *Rabbath filiorum Ammon*). This is the full appellation of the place commonly given as RABBAH. It occurs only in Deut. iii. 11 and Ez. xxi. 20. The *th* is merely the Hebrew mode of connecting a word ending in *ah* with one following it. (Comp. RAMATH, GIBEATH, KIRJATH, etc.)   G.

RAB'BI (רַבִּי: 'Ραββί).

A title of respect given by the Jews to their doctors and teachers, and often addressed to our Lord (Matt. xxiii. 7, 8, xxvi. 25, 49; Mark ix. 5, xi. 21, xiv. 45; John i. 38, 49, iii. 2, 26, iv. 31, vi. 25, ix. 2, xi. 8). The meaning of the title is interpreted in express words by St. John, and by implication in St. Matthew, to mean Master, Teacher; Διδάσκαλε, John i. 38 (compare xi. 28, xiii. 13), and Matt. xxiii. 8. where recent editors (Tischendorf, Wordsworth, Alford), on the authority of MSS., read ὁ διδάσκαλος, instead of ὁ καθηγητής of the Textus Receptus. The same interpretation is given by St. John of the kindred title RABBONI, 'Ραββουνί (John xx. 16), which also occurs in Mark x. 35, where the Textus Receptus, with less authority, spells the word 'Ραββονί. The reading in John xx. 16, which has perhaps the greatest weight of authority,

makes an addition to the common text: "She turned herself and said unto Him, in the Hebrew tongue (Ἑβραϊστί), Rabboni; which is to say, Master." The ־ which is added to these titles, רַב (*rab*) and רַבּוֹן (*rabbôn*) or רַבָּן (*rabbân*), has been thought to be the pronominal affix "My;" but it is to be noted that St. John does not translate either of these by "My Master," but simply "Master," so that the ־ would seem to have lost any especial significance as a possessive pronoun intimating appropriation or endearment, and, like the "my" in titles of respect among ourselves, or in such terms as *Monseigneur*, *Monsieur*, to be merely part of the formal address. Information on these titles may be found in Lightfoot, *Harmony of the Four Evangelists*, John i. 38; *Horæ Hebraicæ et Talmudicæ*, Matt. xxiii. 7.

The Latin translation. Magister (connected with *magnus*, *magis*), is a title formed on the same principle as Rabbi, from *rab*, "great." Rab enters into the composition of many names of dignity and office. [RABSHAKEH; RAB-SARIS; RAB-MAG.]

The title Rabbi is not known to have been used before the reign of Herod the Great, and is thought to have taken its rise about the time of the disputes between the rival schools of Hillel and Shammai. Before that period the prophets and the men of the great synagogue were simply called by their proper names, and the first who had a title is said to be Simeon the son of Hillel, who is supposed by some to be the Simeon who took our Saviour in his arms in the Temple: he was called Rabban, and from his time such titles came to be in fashion. Rabbi was considered a higher title than Rab, and Rabban higher than Rabbi;

yet it was said in the Jewish books that greater was he who was called by his own name than even he who was called Rabban. Some account of the Rabbis and the Mishnical and Talmudical writings may be found in Prideaux, *Connection*, part i. book 5, under the year B. C. 446; part ii. book 8, under the year B. C. 37; and a sketch of the history of the school of rabbinical learning at Tiberias, founded by Rabbi Judah Hakkodesh, the compiler of the Mishnah, in the second century after Christ, is given in Robinson's *Biblical Researches*, ii. 391. See also note 14 to Burton's *Bampton Lectures*, and the authorities there quoted, for instance, Brucker, vol. ii. p. 820, and Basnage, *Hist. des Juifs*, iii. 6, p. 138. E. P. E.

RAB'BITH (חָרַבִּית [*the multitude*], with the def. article; [Rom. Δαβιρόν; Vat.] Δαβειρων; Alex. Ραββωθ: *Rabboth*). A town in the territory, perhaps on the boundary, of Issachar (Josh. xix. 20 only). It is not again mentioned, nor is anything yet known of it, or of the places named in company with it. G.

RABBO'NI, John xx. 16. [RABBI.]

RAB-MAG' (רַב־מָג [see below]: 'Ραβ-μάγ, 'Ραβαμάχ: *a Rebmag*) is found only in Jer. xxxix. 3 and 13. In both places it is a title borne by a certain Nergal-sharezer, who is mentioned among the "princes" that accompanied Nebuchadnezzar to the last siege of Jerusalem. It has already been shown that Nergal-sharezer is probably identical with the king, called by the Greeks Neriglissar, who ascended the throne of Babylon two years after the death of Nebuchadnezzar. [NERGAL-SHAREZER.] This king, as well as certain other important personages, is found to bear the title in the Babylonian inscriptions. It is written indeed with a somewhat different vocalization, being read as *Rabu-Emga* by Sir H. Rawlinson. The signification is somewhat doubtful. *Rabu* is most certainly "great," or "chief," an exact equivalent of the Hebrew רַב, whence Rabbi, "a great one, a doctor:" but *Mag*, or *Emga*, is an obscure term. It has been commonly identified with the word "Magus" (Gesenius, *ad voc.* מָג; Calmet, *Commentaire littéral*, vi. 203, &c.); but this identification is very uncertain, since an entirely different word — one which is read as *Magusu* — is used in that sense throughout the Behistun inscription (Oppert, *Expédition Scientifique en Mesopotamie*, ii. 209). Sir H. Rawlinson inclines to translate *emga* by "priest," but does not connect it with the Magi, who in the time of Neriglissar had no footing in Babylon. He regards this rendering, however, as purely conjectural, and thinks we can only say at present that the office was one of great power and dignity at the Babylonian court, and probably gave its possessor special facilities for obtaining the throne. G. R.

RAB'SACES ('Ραψάκης: *Rabsaces*). RAB-SHAKEH (Ecclus. xlviii. 18).

RAB'-SARIS (רַב־סָרִים [see below]: 'Ραφίς; Vat. Ραφεις; Alex. Ραβσαρεις: *Rabsaris*). 1. An officer of the king of Assyria sent up with Tartan and Rabshakeh against Jerusalem in the time of Hezekiah (2 K. xviii. 17).

2. (Ναβουσαρείς; Alex. Ναβουζαρις: *Rab-*

sares.) One of the princes of Nebuchadnezzar, who was present at the capture of Jerusalem, B. C. 588, when Zedekiah, after endeavoring to escape, was taken and blinded and sent in chains to Babylon (Jer. xxxix. 3). Rab-saris is mentioned afterwards (ver. 13) among the other princes who at the command of the king were sent to deliver Jeremiah out of the prison.

Rab-saris is probably rather the name of an office than of an individual, the word signifying chief eunuch; in Dan. i. 3, Ashpenaz is called the master of the eunuchs (Rab-sarisim). Luther translates the word, in the three places where it occurs, as a name of office, the arch-chamberlain (der Erzkämmerer, der oberste Kämmerer). Josephus, *Ant. x.* 8, § 2, takes them as the A. V. does, as proper names. The chief officers of the court were present attending on the king; and the instance of the eunuch Narses would show that it was not impossible for Rab-saris to possess some of the qualities fitting him for a military command. In 2 K. xxv. 19, an eunuch (סָרִיס, *Sáris*, in the text of the A. V. "officer," in the margin "eunuch") is spoken of as set over the men of war; and in the sculptures at Nineveh "eunuchs are represented as commanding in war; fighting both on chariots and on horseback, and receiving the prisoners and the heads of the slain after battle" (Layard's *Nineveh*, vol. ii. p. 325).

It is not improbable that in Jeremiah xxxix. we have not only the title of the Rab-saris given, but his name also, either Sarsechim (ver. 3) or (ver. 13) Nebu-shasban (worshipper of Nebo, Is. xlvi. 1), in the same way as Nergal-sharezer is given in the same passages as the name of the Rab-mag. E. P. E.

RAB'SHAKEH (רַב־שָׁקֵה [see below]: 'Ραψάκης, 2 K. xviii., xix.; 'Ραβσάκης, [Sin. Alex. Ραψακης,] Is. xxxvi., xxxvii.: *Rabsaces*). One of the officers of the king of Assyria sent against Jerusalem in the reign of Hezekiah. Sennacherib, having taken other cities of Judah, was now besieging Lachish, and Hezekiah, terrified at his progress, and losing for a time his firm faith in God, sends to Lachish with an offer of submission and tribute. This he strains himself to the utmost to pay, giving for the purpose not only all the treasures of the Temple and palace, but stripping off the gold plates with which he himself in the beginning of his reign had overlaid the doors and pillars of the house of the Lord (2 K. xviii. 16; 2 Chr. xxix. 3; see Rawlinson's *Bampton Lectures*, iv. 141; Layard's *Nineveh and Babylon*, p. 145). But Sennacherib, not content with this, his cupidity being excited rather than appeased, sends a great host against Jerusalem under Tartan, Rab-saris, and Rabshakeh; not so much, apparently, with the object of at present engaging in the siege of the city, as with the idea that, in its present disheartened state, the sight of an army, combined with the threats and specious promises of Rabshakeh, might induce a surrender at once.

In Is. xxxvi., xxxvii., Rabshakeh alone is mentioned, the reason of which would seem to be, that he acted as ambassador and spokesman, and came so much more prominently before the people than the others. Keil thinks that Tartan had the supreme command, inasmuch as in 2 K. he is

Ραμαβακ; Comp. 'Ραβαμάγ; the source of the form given above is not apparent. A.

mentioned first, and, according to Is. xx. 1, conducted the siege of Ashdod. In 2 Chr. xxxii., where, with the addition of some not unimportant circumstances, there is given an extract of these events, it is simply said that (ver. 9) "Sennacherib king of Assyria sent his servants to Jerusalem." Rabshakeh seems to have discharged his mission with much zeal, addressing himself not only to the officers of Hezekiah, but to the people on the wall of the city, setting forth the hopelessness of trusting to any power, human or divine, to deliver them out of the hand of "the great king, the king of Assyria," and dwelling on the many advantages to be gained by submission. Many have imagined, from the familiarity of Rabshakeh with Hebrew,[a] that he either was a Jewish deserter or an apostate captive of Israel. Whether this be so or not, it is not impossible that the assertion which he makes on the part of his master, that Sennacherib had even the sanction and command of the Lord Jehovah for his expedition against Jerusalem ("Am I now come up without the Lord to destroy it? The Lord said to me, Go up against this land to destroy it") may have reference to the prophecies of Isaiah (viii. 7, 8, x. 5, 6) concerning the desolation of Judah and Israel by the Assyrians, of which, in some form more or less correct, he had received information. Being unable to obtain any promise of submission from Hezekiah, who, in the extremity of his peril returning to trust in the help of the Lord, is encouraged by the words and predictions of Isaiah, Rabshakeh goes back to the king of Assyria, who had now departed from Lachish.

The English version takes Rabshakeh as the name of a person; it may, however, be questioned whether it be not rather the name of the office which he held at the court, that of chief cupbearer, in the same way as RAB-SARIS denotes the chief eunuch, and RAB-MAG possibly the chief priest.

Luther in his version is not quite consistent, sometimes (2 K. xviii. 17; Is. xxxvi. 2) giving Rabshakeh as a proper name, but ordinarily translating it as a title of office, arch-cupbearer (der Erzschenke).

The word Rab may be found translated in many places of the English version, for instance, 2 K. xxv. 8, 20; Jer. xxxix. 11; Dan. ii. 14 (רַב־טַבָּחִים), Rab-tabbâchîm, "captain of the guard," in the margin "chief marshal," "chief of the execu-

tioners." Dan. i. 3, Rab-sarisin, 'master of the eunuchs;" ii. 48 (רַב־סָגְנִין), Rab-signin, "chief of the governors;" iv. 9, v. 11 (רַב־חַרְטֻמִּין), Rab-chartummin, "master of the magicians;" Jonah i. 6 (רַב הַחֹבֵל), Rab-hachobêl, "shipmaster." It enters into the titles Rabbi, Rabboni, and the name Rabbah. [On this name see also Rawlinson's Ancient Monarchies, ii. 440 f.]

E. P. E.

RA'CA (Ῥακά), a term of reproach used by the Jews of our Saviour's age (Matt. v. 22). Critics are agreed in deriving it from the Chaldee term רֵיקָא with the sense of "worthless," but they differ as to whether this term should be connected with the root רוּק, conveying the notion of emptiness (Gesen. Thes. p. 1279), or with one of the cognate roots רָקַק (Tholuck), or רָקַע (Ewald), conveying the notion of thinness (Olshausen, De Wette, on Matt. v. 22). The first of these views is probably correct. We may compare the use of רִיק, "vain," in Judg. ix. 4, xi. 3, al., and of kerê in Jam. ii. 20.   W. L. B.

RACE.   [GAMES, vol. i. p. 864.]

RA'CHAB (Ῥαχάβ: Rahab). RAHAB the harlot (Matt. i. 5).

RA'CHAL[b] רָכָל [traffic]: [Alex. Ραχηλ; Comp. Ῥαχάλ:] Rachal). One of the places which David and his followers used to haunt during the period of his freebooting life, and to the people of which he sent a portion of the plunder taken from the Amalekites. It is named in 1 Sam. xxx. 29 only. The Vatican LXX. inserts five names in this passage between "Eshtemoa" and "the Jerahmeelites." The only one of these which has any similarity to Racal is Carmel, which would suit very well as far as position goes; but it is impossible to consider the two as identical without further evidence.[c] No name like Racal has been found in the south of Judah.   G.

RA'CHEL (רָחֵל,[d] a ewe; the word rahel occurs in Gen. xxxi. 38, xxxii. 14; Cant. vi. 6; Is. liii. 7: A. V. rendered "ewe" and "sheep:" Ῥαχήλ: Rachel). The younger of the daughters of Laban, the wife of Jacob, the mother of Joseph and Benjamin. The incidents of her life may be

---

a The difference between speaking in the Hebrew and the Aramaean, "in the Jews' language" (יְהוּדִית, J'hudith), and in the "Syrian language" (אֲרָמִית, Aramith), would be rather a matter of pronunciation and dialect than of essential difference of language. See for the "Syrian tongue," Ezr. iv. 7; Dan ii. 4.

b In this name ch is sounded like hard c, as the representative of the Hebrew caph. In Rachel, on the other hand, it represents cheth, and should properly be pronounced like a guttural h (see A. V. of Jer. xxxi. 15).

c Thenius, with his usual rashness, says "Racal is a residuum of Carmel."

d It is not obvious how our translators came to spell the name רָחֵל as they do in their final revision of 1611. namely, Rachel. Their practice — almost, if not quite, invariable — throughout the Old Test. of that edition, is to represent ח, the hard guttural aspirate, by h (e. g. Halah for חֲלָח) : the ch (hard, of course) they reserve with equal consistency for כ. On this principle Rachel should have been given throughout "Rahel," as indeed it is in one case, retained in the most modern editions — Jer. xxxi 15 And in the earlier editions of the English Bible (e. g. 1540, 1551, 1566) we find Rahel throughout. It is difficult not to suspect that Rachel (however originating) was a favorite woman's name in the latter part of the 16th and beginning of the 17th centuries, and that it was substituted for the less familiar though more accurate Rahel in deference to that fact, and in obedience to the rule laid down for the guidance of the translators, that "the names in the text are to be retained as near as may be, accordingly as they are vulgarly used."

Rachael (so common in the literature of a century ago) is a corruption as Rebecca of Rebekah.   G.

found in Gen. xxix.-xxxiii., xxxv. The story of Jacob and Rachel has always had a peculiar interest; there is that in it which appeals to some of the deepest feelings of the human heart. The beauty of Rachel, the deep love with which she was loved by Jacob from their first meeting by the well of Haran, when he showed to her the simple courtesies of the desert life, and kissed her and told her he was Rebekah's son; the long servitude with which he patiently served for her, in which the seven years "seemed to him but a few days, for the love he had to her;" their marriage at last, after the cruel disappointment through the fraud which substituted the elder sister in the place of the younger; and the death of Rachel at the very time when in giving birth to another son her own long-delayed hopes were accomplished, and she had become still more endeared to her husband; his deep grief and ever-living regrets for her loss (Gen. xlviii. 7): these things make up a touching tale of personal and domestic history which has kept alive the memory of Rachel — the beautiful, the beloved, the untimely taken away — and has preserved to this day a reverence for her tomb; the very infidel invaders of t̲ ̲ Holy Land having respected the traditions of the site, and erected over the spot a small rude shrine, which conceals whatever remains may have once been found of the pillar first set up by her mourning husband over her grave.

Yet from what is related to us concerning Rachel's character there does not seem much to claim any high degree of admiration and esteem. The discontented and fretful impatience shown in her grief at being for a time childless, moved even her fond husband to anger (Gen. xxx. 1, 2). She appears, moreover, to have shared all the duplicity and falsehood of her family, of which we have such painful instances in Rebekah, in Laban, and not least in her sister Leah, who consented to bear her part in the deception practiced upon Jacob. See, for instance, Rachel's stealing her father's images, and the ready dexterity and presence of mind with which she concealed her theft (Gen. xxxi.): we seem to detect here an apt scholar in her father's school of untruth. From this incident we may also infer (though this is rather the misfortune of her position and circumstances) that she was not altogether free from the superstitions and idolatry which prevailed in the land whence Abraham had been called (Josh. xxiv. 2, 14), and which still to some degree infected even those families among whom the true God was known.

The events which preceded the death of Rachel are of much interest and worthy of a brief consideration. The presence in his household of these idolatrous images, which Rachel and probably others also had brought from the East, seems to have been either unknown to or connived at by Jacob for some years after his return from Haran; till, on being reminded by the Lord of the vow which he had made at Bethel when he fled from the face of Esau, and being bidden by Him to erect an altar to the God who appeared to him there,

Jacob felt the glaring impiety of thus so'emnly appearing before God with the taint of imj iety cleaving to him or his, and "said to his household and all that were with him, Put away the strange gods from among you" (Gen. xxxv. 2). After thus casting out the polluting thing from his house, Jacob journeyed to Bethel, where, amidst the associations of a spot consecrated by the memories of the past, he received from God an emphatic promise and blessing, and, the name of the Supplanter being laid aside, he had given to him instead the holy name of Israel. Then it was, after his spirit had been there purified and strengthened by communion with God, by the assurance of the Divine love and favor, by the consciousness of evil put away and duties performed, then it was, as he journeyed away from Bethel, that the chastening blow fell and Rachel died. These circumstances are alluded to here not so much for their bearing upon the spiritual discipline of Jacob, but rather with reference to Rachel herself, as suggesting the hope that they may have had their effect in bringing her to a higher sense of her relations to that Great Jehovah in whom her husband, with all his faults of character, so firmly believed.

Rachel's Tomb. — "Rachel died and was buried in the way to Ephrath, which is Bethlehem. And Jacob set a pillar upon her grave: that is the pillar of Rachel's grave unto this day" (Gen. xxxv. 19, 20). As Rachel is the first related instance of death in childbearing, so this pillar over her grave is the first recorded example of the setting up of a sepulchral monument; caves having been up to this time spoken of as the usual places of burial. The spot was well known in the time of Samuel and Saul (1 Sam. x. 2); and the prophet Jeremiah, by a poetic figure of great force and beauty, represents the buried Rachel weeping for the loss and captivity of her children, as the bands of the exiles, led away on their road to Babylon, passed near her tomb (Jer. xxxi. 15–17). St. Matthew (ii. 17, 18) applies this to the slaughter by Herod of the infants at Bethlehem.

The position of the Ramah here spoken of is one of the disputed questions in the topography of Palestine; but the site of Rachel's tomb, "on the way to Bethlehem," "a little way[a] to come to Ephrath," "in the border of Benjamin," has never been questioned. It is about 2 miles S. of Jerusalem, and one mile N. of Bethlehem.[b] "It is one of the shrines which Muslims, Jews, and Christians agree in honoring, and concerning which their traditions are identical." It was visited by Maundrell, 1697. The description given by Dr. Robinson (i. 218) may serve as the representative of the many accounts, all agreeing with each other, which may be read in almost every book of eastern travel. It is "merely an ordinary Muslim Wely, or tomb of a holy person, a small square building of stone with a dome, and within it a tomb in the ordinary Mohammedan form, the whole plastered over with mortar. Of course the building is not ancient: in the seventh century there was here only a pyramid of stones. It is now neglected and falling to decay,[c]

---

a Hebrew *Cibrâh;* in the LXX. here, xlviii. 7, and 2 K. v. 19, Χαβραθά. This seems to have been accepted as the name of the spot (Demetrius in Eus. *Pr. Ev.* ix. 21), and to have been actually encountered here by a traveller in the 12th cent. (Burchard de Strasburg, by Saint Genois, p. 85), who gives the Arabic name of Rachel's tomb as *Cabrata* or *Carbata.*

b * The distance of Rachel's tomb is at least 5 miles from Jerusalem, and not more than half a mile from Bethlehem.   H.

c Since Robinson's last visit, it has been enlarged by the addition of a square court on the east side, with high walls and arches (*Later Researches,* 232).

though pilgrimages are still made to it by the Jews. The naked walls are covered with names in several languages, many of them in Hebrew. The general correctness of the tradition which has fixed upon

this spot for the tomb of Rachel cannot well be drawn in question, since it is fully supported by the circumstances of the Scriptural narrative. It is also mentioned by the *Itin. Hieros.*, A. D. 333;

Rachel's Tomb.

and by Jerome (Ep. lxxxvi. *ad Eustoch., Epitaph. Paulæ*) in the same century." [a]

Those who take an interest in such interpretations may find the whole story of Rachel and Leah allegorized by St. Augustine (*contra Faustum Manichæum*, xxii., li.-lviii. vol. viii. 432, etc., ed. Migne), and Justin Martyr (*Dialogue with Trypho*, c. 134, p. 360).   E. P. E.

RAD'DAI (רַדַּי [*treading down*, Ges.] : [Vat.] Zaβδαι; [Rom.] Zαββαί; [Alex. Pαββαί:] Joseph. Pίηλος: *Raddai*). One of David's brothers, fifth son of Jesse (1 Chr. ii. 14). He does not appear in the Bible elsewhere than in this list, unless he be, as Ewald conjectures (*Geschichte*, iii. 266 *note*), identical with REI. But this does not seem probable. Fürst (*Handwb.* ii. 355 *b*) considers the final i of the name to be a remnant of Jah or Jehovah [= *J. is freedom*].   G.

RA'GAU (Pαγαῦ: *Ragau*). 1. A place named only in Jud. i. 5, 15. In the latter passage the "mountains of Ragau" are mentioned. It is probably identical with RAGES.

2. One of the ancestors of our Lord, the son of Phalec (Luke iii. 35). He is the same person with REU son of Peleg; and the difference in the name arises from our translators having followed the Greek form, in which the Hebrew ע was frequently expressed by γ, as is the case in Raguel

(which once occurs for Reuel), Gomorrha, Guni, liah (for Atholiah), Phogor (for Peor), etc.   G.

RA'GES (Pάγη, Pάγοι: *Rages*) was an important city in northeastern Media, where that country bordered upon Parthia. It is not mentioned in the Hebrew Scriptures, but occurs frequently in the Book of Tobit (i. 14, v. 5, vi. 9, 12, &c.), and twice in Judith [in the form of RAGAU] (i. 5, 15). According to Tobit, it was a place to which some of the Israelitish captives taken by Shalmaneser (Enemessar) had been transported, and thither the angel Raphael conducted the young Tobiah. In the Book of Judith it is made the scene of the great battle between Nabuchodonosor and Arphaxad, wherein the latter is said to have been defeated and taken prisoner. Neither of these accounts can be regarded as historic; but the latter may conceal a fact of some importance in the history of the city.

Rages is a place mentioned by a great number of profane writers. It appears as Ragha in the Zendavesta, in Isidore, and in Stephen; as Raga in the inscriptions of Darius; Rhagæ in Duris of Samos (Fr. 25), Strabo (xi. 9, § 1), and Arrian (*Exp. Alex.* iii. 20); and Rhagæ in Ptolemy (vi. 5). Properly speaking, Rages is a town, but the town gave name to a province, which is sometimes called Rages or Rhagæ, sometimes Rhagiana. It appears from the Zendavesta that here was one of the earliest settlements of the Aryans, who were mingled, in Rhagiana, with two other races, and were thus brought into contact with heretics (Bunsen, *Philosophy of Universal History*, iii. 485). Isidore calls Rages "the greatest city in Media' (p. 6), which may have been true in his day; but other writers commonly regard it as much inferior to Ecbatana. It was the place to which *Frawartish* (Phraortes), the Median rebel, fled, when defeated by Darius Hystaspis, and at which he was made prisoner by one of Darius' generals (*Beh. Inscr.* col. ii. par. 13). [MEDIA.] This is probably the fact which the apocryphal writer of Judith had in his mind when he spoke of Arphaxad as having been captured at Ragau. When Darius Codomannus fled from Alexander, intending to make a final stand in Bactria, he must have passed through Rages on his way to the Caspian Gates; and so we find that Alexander arrived there in pursuit of his enemy, on the eleventh day after he quitted Ecbatana (Arrian, *Exp. Alex.* iii. 20). In the troubles which followed the death of Alexander, Rages appears to have gone to decay, but it was soon after rebuilt by Seleucus I. (Nicator), who gave it the name of Europus (Strab. xi. 13, § 6; Steph. Byz. *ad voc.*). When the Parthians took it, they called it Arsacia, after the Arsaces of the day; but it soon afterwards recovered its ancient appellation, as we see by Strabo and Isidore. That appellation it has ever since retained, with only a slight corruption, the ruins being still known by the name of *Rhey*. These ruins lie about five miles southeast of Teheran, and cover a space 4,500 yards long by 3,500 yards broad. The walls are well marked, and are of prodigious thickness; they appear to have been flanked by strong towers, and are connected with a lofty citadel at their northeastern angle. The importance of the place consisted in its vicinity to the Caspian Gates, which, in a certain sense, it guarded. Owing to the barren and desolate character of the great salt desert of Iran, every army which seeks to pass from Bactria, India, and Afghanistan to Media and Mesopotamia, or *vice versâ*, must skirt the range of mountains which runs along the southern shore of the Caspian. These mountains send out a rugged and precipitous spur in about long. 52° 25′ E. from Greenwich, which runs far into the desert, and can only be rounded with the extremest difficulty. Across this spur is a single pass, — the Pylæ Caspiæ of the ancients, — and of this pass the possessors of Rhages must have at all times held the keys. The modern Teheran, built out of its ruins, has now superseded *Rhey;* and it is perhaps mainly from the importance of its position that it has become the Persian capital. (For an account of the ruins of *Rhey*, see Ker Porter's *Travels*, i. 357-364; and compare Fraser's *Khorassan*, p. 286.)

                                    G. R.

RAGU'EL, or REU'EL (רְעוּאֵל [*friend of God*]: Ῥαγουήλ: *Raguel*). 1. A prince-priest of Midian, the father of Zipporah according to Ex. ii. 21, and of Hobab according to Num. x. 29. As the father-in-law of Moses is named Jethro in Ex. iii. 1, and Hobab in Judg. iv. 11, and perhaps in Num. x. 29 (though the latter passage admits of another sense), the *primâ facie* view would be that Raguel, Jethro, and Hobab were different names for the same individual. Such is probably the case with regard to the two first at all events, if not with the third. [HOBAB.] One of the names may represent an official title, but whether Jethro or Raguel, is uncertain, both being appropriately

significant:[a] Josephus was in favor of the former (τοῦτο, i. e. Ἰοθεγλαῖος, ἦν ἐπίκλημα τῷ Ῥαγουήλῳ, *Ant.* ii. 12, § 1), and this is not unlikely, as the name Reuel was not an uncommon one. The identity of Jethro and Reuel is supported by the indiscriminate use of the names in the LXX. (Ex. ii. 16, 18); and the application of more than one name to the same individual was a usage familiar to the Hebrews, as instanced in Jacob and Israel, Solomon and Jedidiah, and other similar cases. Another solution of the difficulty has been sought in the loose use of terms of relationship among the Hebrews; as that *chôthên*,[b] in Ex. iii. 1, xviii. 1; Num. x. 29, may signify any relation by marriage, and consequently that Jethro and Hobab were brothers-in-law of Moses; or that the terms *ab*[c] and *bath*,[d] in Ex. ii. 16, 21, mean *grandfather* and *granddaughter*. Neither of these assumptions is satisfactory, the former in the absence of any corroborative evidence, the latter because the omission of Jethro the father's name in so circumstantial a narrative as in Ex. ii. is inexplicable, nor can we conceive the indiscriminate use of the terms father and grandfather without good cause. Nevertheless this view has a strong weight of authority in its favor, being supported by the Targum Jonathan, Aben Ezra, Michaelis, Winer, and others.

                             W. L. B.

2. Another transcription of the name REUEL, occurring in Tobit, where Raguel, a pious Jew of " Ecbatane, a city of Media," is father of Sara the wife of Tobias (Tob. iii. 7, 17, &c.). The name was not uncommon, and in the book of Enoch it is applied to one of the great guardian angels of the universe, who was charged with the execution of the Divine judgments on the (material) world and the stars (cc. xx. 4, xxiii. 4, ed. Dillmann).

                             B. F. W.

RA'HAB, or RA'CHAB (רָחָב [*broad, large*]: Ῥαχάβ, and Ῥαάβ: *Rahab*, and *Raab*), a celebrated woman of Jericho, who received the spies sent by Joshua to spy out the land, hid them in her house from the pursuit of her countrymen, was saved with all her family when the Israelites sacked the city, and became the wife of Salmon, and the ancestress of the Messiah.

Her history may be told in a few words. At the time of the arrival of the Israelites in Canaan she was a young unmarried woman, dwelling in a house of her own alone, though she had a father and mother, and brothers and sisters, living in Jericho. She was a "harlot," and probably combined the trade of lodging-keeper for wayfaring men. She seems also to have been engaged in the manufacture of linen and the art of dyeing, for which the Phoenicians were early famous; since we find the flat roof of her house covered with stalks of flax put there to dry, and a stock of scarlet or crimson (שָׁנִי) line in her house: a circumstance which, coupled with the mention of Babylonish garments at Josh. vii. 21, as among the spoils of Jericho, indicates the existence of a trade in such articles between Phoenicia and Mesopotamia. Her house was situated on the wall, probably near the town gate, so as to be convenient for persons coming in and going out of the city. Traders coming from Mesopotamia or Egypt to Phoenicia would frequently

---

[a] Jethro = "preëminent," from יֶתֶר, " to excel,"

and Raguel = "friend of God," from רֵעַ אֵל.

[b] חֹתֵן.   [c] אָב.   [d] בַּת.

pass through Jericho, situated as it was near the fords of the Jordan; and of these many would resort to the house of Rahab. Rahab therefore had been well informed with regard to the events of the Exodus. She had heard of the passage through the Red Sea, of the utter destruction of Sihon and Og, and of the irresistible progress of the Israelitish host. The effect upon her mind had been what one would not have expected in a person of her way of life. It led her to a firm faith in Jehovah as the true God, and to the conviction that He purposed to give the land of Canaan to the Israelites. When therefore the two spies sent by Joshua came to her house, they found themselves under the roof of one who, alone probably of the whole population, was friendly to their nation. Their coming, however, was quickly known; and the king of Jericho, having received information of it while at supper, according to Josephus, sent that very evening to require her to deliver them up. It is very likely that, her house being a public one, some one who resorted there may have seen and recognized the spies, and gone off at once to report the matter to the authorities. But not without awakening Rahab's suspicions; for she immediately hid the men among the flax-stalks which were piled on the flat roof of her house, and, on the arrival of the officers sent to search her house, was ready with the story that two men, of what country she knew not, had, it was true, been to her house, but had left it just before the gates were shut for the night. If they pursued them at once, she added, they would be sure to overtake them. Misled by the false information, the men started in pursuit to the fords of the Jordan, the gates having been opened to let them out, and immediately closed again. When all was quiet, and the people were gone to bed, Rahab stole up to the house-top, told the spies what had happened, and assured them of her faith in the God of Israel, and her confident expectation of the capture of the whole land by them; an expectation, she added, which was shared by her countrymen, and had produced a great panic amongst them. She then told them her plan for their escape. It was to let them down by a cord from the window of her house which looked over the city wall, and that they should flee into the mountains which bounded the plains of Jericho, and lie hid there for three days, by which time the pursuers would have returned, and the fords of the Jordan be open to them again. She asked, in return for her kindness to them, that they should swear by Jehovah, that when their countrymen had taken the city they would spare her life, and the lives of her father and mother, brothers and sisters, and all that belonged to them. The men readily consented, and it was agreed between them that she should hang out her scarlet line at the window from which they had escaped, and bring all her family under her roof. If any of her kindred went out of doors into the street, his blood would be upon his own head, and the Israelites in that case would be guiltless. The event proved the wisdom of her precautions. The pursuers returned to Jericho after a fruitless search, and the spies got safe back to the Israelitish camp. The news they brought of the terror of the Canaanites doubtless inspired Israel with fresh courage, and, within three days of their return,

the passage of the Jordan was effected. In the utter destruction of Jericho which ensued, Joshua gave the strictest orders for the preservation of Rahab and her family; and accordingly, before the city was burnt, the two spies were sent to her house, and they brought out her, her father and mother, and brothers, and kindred, and all that she had, and placed them in safety in the Israelitish camp. The narrator adds, "and she dwelleth in Israel unto this day;" not necessarily implying that she was alive at the time he wrote, but that the family of strangers of which she was reckoned the head, continued to dwell among the children of Israel. May not the 345 "children of Jericho," mentioned in Ezr. ii. 34, Neh. vii. 36, and "the men of Jericho" who assisted Nehemiah in rebuilding the walls of Jerusalem (Neh. iii. 2), have been their posterity? Their continued sojourn among the Israelites, as a distinct family, would be exactly analogous to the cases of the Kenites, the house of Rechab, the Gibeonites, the house of Caleb, and perhaps others.

As regards Rahab herself, we learn from Matt. i. 5, that she became the wife of Salmon the son of Naasson, and the mother of Boaz, Jesse's grandfather. The suspicion naturally arises that Salmon may have been one of the spies whose life she saved, and that gratitude for so great a benefit led in his case to a more tender passion, and obliterated the memory of any past disgrace attaching to her name. We are expressly told that the spies were "young men" (Josh. vi. 23), νεανίσκους, ii. 1, LXX.; and the example of the former spies who were sent from Kadesh-Barnea, who were all "heads of Israel" (Num. xiii. 3), as well as the importance of the service to be performed, would lead one to expect that they were persons of high station. But, however this may be, it is certain, on the authority of St. Matthew, that Rahab became the mother of the line from which sprung David, and eventually Christ; and there can be little doubt that it was so stated in the public archives from which the Evangelist extracted our Lord's genealogy, in which only four women are named, namely, Thamar, Rachab, Ruth, and Bathsheba, who were all apparently foreigners, and named for that reason. [BATH-SHUA.] For that the Rachab mentioned by St. Matthew is Rahab the harlot, is as certain as that David in the genealogy is the same person as David in the books of Samuel. The attempts that have been made to prove Rachab different from Rahab,[a] in order to get out of the chronological difficulty, are singularly absurd, and all the more so, because, even if successful, they would not diminish the difficulty, as long as Salmon remains as the son of Naasson and the father of Boaz. However, as there are still found[b] those who follow Outhov in his opinion, or at least speak doubtfully, it may be as well to call attention, with Dr. Mill (p. 131), to the exact coincidence in the age of Salmon, as the son of Nahshon, who was prince of the children of Judah in the wilderness, and Rahab the harlot; and to observe that the only conceivable reason for the mention of Rachab in St. Matthew's genealogy is, that she was a remarkable and well-known person, as Tamar, Ruth, and Bathsheba were.[c] The mention of an utterly un-

a Chiefly by Outhov, a Dutch professor, in the Biblioth. Bremens. The earliest expression of any doubt is by Theoph:lact in the 11th century.

b Valpy's Greek Test. with Eng. notes, on Matt. i. 5; Burrington, On the Genealogies, i. 192-4, &c.: Kuinoel on Matt. i. 5; Olshausen, ib.

c There does not seem to be any force in Bengel's

known Rahab in the line would be absurd. The allusions to "Rahab the harlot" in Heb. xi. 31, Jam. ii. 25, by classing her among those illustrious for their faith, make it still more impossible to suppose that St. Matthew was speaking of any one else. The four successive generations, Nahshon, Salmon, Boaz, Obed, are consequently as certain as words can make them.

The character of Rahab has much and deep interest. Dismissing as inconsistent with truth, and with the meaning of זוֹנָה and πόρνη, the attempt to clear her character of stain by saying that she was only an innkeeper, and not a harlot (πανδοκεντρία, Chrysostom and Chald. Vers.), we may yet notice that it is very possible that to a woman of her country and religion such a calling may have implied a far less deviation from the standard of morality than it does with us ("vitæ genus vile magis quàm flagitiosum" Grotius), and, moreover, that with a purer faith she seems to have entered upon a pure life.

As a case of casuistry, her conduct in deceiving the king of Jericho's messengers with a false tale, and, above all, in taking part against her own countrymen, has been much discussed. With regard to the first, strict truth, either in Jew or heathen, was a virtue so utterly unknown before the promulgation of the Gospel, that, as far as Rahab is concerned, the discussion is quite superfluous. The question as regards ourselves, whether in any case a falsehood is allowable, say to save our own life or that of another, is different, but need not be argued here.[a] With regard to her taking part against her own countrymen, it can only be justified, but is fully justified, by the circumstance that fidelity to her country would in her case have been infidelity to God, and that the higher duty to her Maker eclipsed the lower duty to her native land. Her anxious provision for the safety of her father's house shows how alive she was to natural affections, and seems to prove that she was not influenced by a selfish insensibility, but by an enlightened preference for the service of the true God over the abominable pollutions of Canaanite idolatry. If her own life of shame was in any way connected with that idolatry, one can readily understand what a further stimulus this would give, now that her heart was purified by faith, to her desire for the overthrow of the nation to which she belonged by birth, and the establishment of that to which she wished to belong by a community of faith and hope. Anyhow, allowing for the difference of circumstances, her feelings and conduct were analogous to those of a Christian Jew in St. Paul's time, who should have preferred the triumph of the Gospel to the triumph of the old Judaism; or to those of a converted Hindoo in our own days, who should side with Christian Englishmen against the attempts of his own countrymen to establish the supremacy either of Brahma or Mohammed.

This view of Rahab's conduct is fully borne out by the references to her in the N. T. The author of the Epistle to the Hebrews tells us that "by faith the harlot Rahab perished not with them that believed not, when she had received the spies with peace" (Heb. xi. 31); and St. James fortifies his doctrine of justification by works, by asking, "Was not Rahab the harlot justified by works, when she had received the messengers, and had sent them out another way?" (Jam. ii. 25.) And in like manner Clement of Rome says, "Rahab the harlot was saved for her faith and hospitality" (ad Corinth. xii.).

The Fathers generally (miro consensu, Jacobson) consider the deliverance of Rahab as typical of salvation, and the scarlet line hung out at her window as typical of the blood of Jesus, in the same way as the ark of Noah and the blood of the paschal lamb were; a view which is borne out by the analogy of the deliverances, and by the language of Heb. xi. 31 (τοῖς ἀπειθήσασιν, "the disobedient"), compared with 1 Pet. iii. 20 (ἀπειθήσασίν ποτε). Clement (ad Corinth. xii.) is the first to do so. He says that by the symbol of the scarlet line it was "made manifest that there shall be redemption through the blood of the Lord to all who believe and trust in God;" and adds, that Rahab in this was a prophetess as well as a believer, a sentiment in which he is followed by Origen (in lib. Jes., Hom. iii.). Justin Martyr in like manner calls the scarlet line "the symbol of the blood of Christ, by which those of all nations, who once were harlots and unrighteous, are saved;" and in a like spirit Irenæus draws from the story of Rahab the conversion of the Gentiles, and the admission of publicans and harlots into the kingdom of heaven through the symbol of the scarlet line, which he compares with the Passover and the Exodus. Ambrose, Jerome, Augustine (who, like Jerome and Cyril, takes Ps. lxxxvii. 4 to refer to Rahab the harlot), and Theodoret, all follow in the same track; but Origen, as usual, carries the allegory still further. Irenæus makes the singular mistake of calling the spies three, and makes them symbolical of the Trinity! The comparison of the scarlet line with the scarlet thread which was bound round the hand of Zarah is a favorite one with them.[b]

The Jews, as might perhaps be expected, are embarrassed as to what to say concerning Rahab. They praise her highly for her conduct; but some Rabbis give out that she was not a Canaanite, but of some other Gentile race, and was only a sojourner in Jericho. The Gemara of Babylon mentions a tradition that she became the wife of Joshua, a tradition unknown to Jerome (adv. Jovin.), and eight persons who were both priests and prophets sprung from her, and also Huldah the prophetess, mentioned 2 K. xxii. 14 (see Patrick, ad loc.). Josephus describes her as an innkeeper, and her house as an inn (καταγώγιον), and never applies to her the epithet πόρνη, which is the term used by the LXX.

Rahab is one of the not very numerous cases of the calling of Gentiles before the coming of Christ; and her deliverance from the utter destruction which fell upon her countrymen is so beautifully illustrative of the salvation revealed in the Gospel,

---

remark, adopted by Olshausen, that the article (ἐκ τῆς 'Ραχάβ) proves that Rahab of Jericho is meant, seeing that all the proper names in the genealogy, which are in the oblique case, have the article, though many of them occur nowhere else; and that it is omitted before Μαρίας in ver. 16.

[a] The question, in reference both to Rahab and to Christians, is well discussed by Augustine contr. Mendacium (Opp. vi. 33, 34: comp. Bullinger, 3d De Serm. iv.).

[b] Bullinger (5th Dec. Serm. vi.) views the line as a sign and seal of the covenant between the Israelites and Rahab.

that it is impossible not to believe that it was in the fullest sense a type of the redemption of the world by Jesus Christ.

See the articles JERICHO; JOSHUA. Also Bengel, Lightfoot, Alford, Wordsworth, and Olshausen on Matt. i. 5; Patrick, Grotius, and Hitzig on Josh. ii.; Dr. Mill, *Descent and Parentage of the Saviour*; Ewald, *Geschichte*, ii. 390, etc.; Josephus, *Ant.* v. 1; Clemens Rom. *ad Corinth.* cap. xli.; Irenæus, *c. Hær.* iv. 20, § 12; Just. Mart. *contr. Tryph.* p. 11; Jerome, *adv. Jovin.* lib. i.; *Epist.* xxxiv. *ad Nepot.*; *Breviar.* in *Ps.* lxxxvi.; Origen, *Hom. in Jesum Nave*, iii. and vi.; *Comm. in Math.* xxvii.; Chrysost. *Hom.* 3 *in Matth.*, also 3 *in Ep. ad Rom.*; Ephr. Syr. *Rhythm* 1 and 7 *on Nativ.*, *Rhythm* 7 *on the Faith*; Cyril of Jerus., *Catechet.* Lect. ii. 9, x. 11; Bullinger, *l. c.*; Tyndale, *Doctr. Treat.* x. 11; (Parker Soc.), pp. 119, 120; Schleusner, *Lexic. N. T.* s. v. πόρνη.

A. C. H.

RA'HAB (רָחָב: [in Ps. lxxxvii. 4] 'Ραάβ: *Rahab* [Job xxvi. 12, τὸ κῆτος, Ps. lxxxix. 10, ὑπερήφανος; Is. li. 9, LXX. omit: *superbus*]), a poetical name of Egypt. The name signifies "fierceness, insolence, pride;" if Hebrew, when applied to Egypt, it would indicate the national character of the inhabitants. Gesenius thinks it was probably of Egyptian origin, but accommodated to Hebrew, although no likely equivalent has been found in Coptic, or, we may add, in ancient Egyptian (*Thes.* s. v.). That the Hebrew meaning is alluded to in connection with the proper name, does not seem to prove that the latter is Hebrew, but this is rendered very probable by its apposite character, and its sole use in poetical books.

This word occurs in a passage in Job, where it is usually translated, as in the A. V., instead of being treated as a proper name. Yet if the passage be compared with parallel ones, there can scarcely be a doubt that it refers to the Exodus, "He divideth the sea with His power, and by His understanding He smiteth through the proud" [or "Rahab"] (xxvi. 12). The prophet Isaiah calls on the arm of the Lord, "[Art] not thou it that hath cut Rahab [and] wounded the dragon? [Art] not thou it which hath dried the sea, the waters of the great deep; that hath made the depths of the sea a way for the ransomed to pass over?" (li. 9, 10; comp. 15). In Ps. lxxiv. the division of the sea is mentioned in connection with breaking the heads of the dragons and the heads of the leviathan (13, 14). So too in Ps. lxxxix. God's power to subdue the sea is spoken of immediately before a mention of his having "broken Rahab in pieces" (9, 10). Rahab, as a name of Egypt, occurs once only without reference to the Exodus: this is in Psalm lxxxvii., where Rahab, Babylon, Philistia, Tyre, and Cush are compared with Zion (4, 5). In one other passage the name is alluded to, with reference to its Hebrew signification, where it is prophesied that the aid of the Egyptians should not avail those who sought it, and this sentence follows: רַהַב הֵם שָׁבֶת, *Insolence* [i. e. 'the insolent'], they sit still" (Is. xxx. 7), as Gesenius reads, considering it to be undoubtedly a proverbial expression.

R. S. P.

RA'HAM (רַחַם [*womb, maiden*] : 'Ραέμ: [Vat. Ραα,-] *Raham*). In the genealogy of the descendants of Caleb the son of Hezron (1 Chr. ii. 44), Raham is described as the son of Shema and father of Jorkoam. Rashi and the author of the *Quæst. in Paral.*, attributed to Jerome, regard Jorkoam as a place, of which Raham was founder and prince.

RA'HEL (רָחֵל [*ewe, sheep*] : 'Ραχήλ : *Rachel*). The more accurate form of the familiar name elsewhere rendered RACHEL. In the older English versions it is employed throughout, but survives in the Authorized Version of 1611, and in our present Bibles, in Jer. xxxi. 15 only.

G.

RAIN. מָטָר (*mâtâr*), and also גֶּשֶׁם (*geshem*), which, when it differs from the common word מָטָר, signifies a more violent rain; it is also used as a generic term, including the early and latter rain (Jer. v. 24; Joel ii. 23).

EARLY RAIN, the rains of the autumn, יוֹרֶה (*yôreh*), part. subst. from יָרָה, "he scattered" (Deut. xi. 14; Jer. v. 24); also the hiphil part. מוֹרֶה (Joel ii. 23): ὑετὸς πρόϊμος, LXX.

LATTER RAIN, the rain of spring, מַלְקוֹשׁ (*malkôsh*) (Prov. xvi. 15; Job xxix. 23; Jer. iii. 3 Hos. vi. 3; Joel ii. 23; Zech. x. 1); ὑετὸς ὄψιμος. The early and latter rains are mentioned together (Deut. xi. 14; Jer. v. 24; Joel ii. 23; Hos. vi. 3; James v. 7).

Another word, of a more poetical character, is רְבִיבִים (*rebîbîm*, a plural form, connected with *rab*, "many," from the multitude of the drops), translated in our version "showers" (Deut. xxxii. 2; Jer. iii. 3, xiv. 22; Mic. v. 7 (Heb. 6); Ps. lxv. 10 (Heb. 11), lxxii. 6). The Hebrews have also the word זֶרֶם (*zerem*), expressing violent rain, storm, tempest, accompanied with hail — in Job xxiv. 8, the heavy rain which comes down on mountains; and the word שָׂגְרִיר (*sagrir*), which occurs only in Prov. xxvii. 15, continuous and heavy rain, ἐν ἡμέρᾳ χειμερινῇ.

In a country comprising so many varieties of elevation as Palestine, there must of necessity occur corresponding varieties of climate; an account that might correctly describe the peculiarities of the district of Lebanon, would be in many respects inaccurate when applied to the deep depression and almost tropical climate of Jericho. In any general statement, therefore, allowance must be made for not inconsiderable local variations. Compared with England, Palestine would be a country in which rain would be much less frequent than with ourselves; contrasted with the districts most familiar to the children of Israel before their settlement in the land of promise, Egypt and the Desert, rain might be spoken of as one of its distinguishing characteristics (Deut. xi. 10, 11; Herodotus iii. 10). For six months in the year no rain falls, and the harvests are gathered in without any of the anxiety with which we are so familiar lest the work be interrupted by unseasonable storms. In this respect at least the climate has remained unchanged since the time when Boaz slept by his heap of corn; and the sending thunder and rain in wheat harvest was a miracle which filled the people with fear and wonder (1 Sam. xii. 16–18); and Solomon could speak of "rain in harvest" as the most forcible expression for conveying the idea of something utterly out of place and unnatural (Prov. xxvi. 1). There are, however, very considerable, and perhaps more than compensating, disadvantages occasioned by this long absence of rain: the whole land becomes dry, parched, and brown, the cisterns are empty, the springs and fountains fail, and the autumnal rains are eagerly looked for to prepare the earth for the reception of the seed. These, the early rains, commence about the latter end of October or beginning of November, in Lebanon a month earlier: not suddenly but by degrees; the husbandman has thus the opportunity of sowing his fields of wheat and barley. The rains come mostly from the west or southwest (Luke xii. 54), continuing for two or three days at a time, and falling chiefly during the night; the wind then shifts round to the north or east, and several days of fine weather succeed (Prov. xxv. 23). During the months of November and December the rains continue to fall heavily, but at intervals; afterwards they return, only at longer intervals, and are less heavy; but at no period during the winter do they entirely cease. January and February are the coldest months, and snow falls sometimes to the depth of a foot or more, at Jerusalem, but it does not lie long; it is very seldom seen along the coast and in the low plains. Thin ice occasionally covers the pools for a few days, and while Porter was writing his Handbook, the snow was eight inches deep at Damascus, and the ice a quarter of an inch thick. Rain continues to fall more or less during the month of March; it is very rare in April, and even in Lebanon the showers that occur are generally light. In the valley of the Jordan the barley harvest begins as early as the middle of April, and the wheat a fortnight later; in Lebanon the grain is seldom ripe before the middle of June. (See Robinson, *Biblical Researches*, i. 429: and Porter, *Handbook*, p. xlviii.) [PALESTINE, p. 2318.]

With respect to the distinction between the early and the latter rains, Robinson observes that there are not at the present day "any particular periods of rain or succession of showers, which might be regarded as distinct rainy seasons. The whole period from October to March now constitutes only one continued season of rain without any regularly intervening term of prolonged fine weather. Unless, therefore, there has been some change in the climate, the early and the latter rains for which the husbandman waited with longing, seem rather to have implied the first showers of autumn which revived the parched and thirsty soil and prepared it for the seed; and the latter showers of spring which continued to refresh and forward both the ripening crops and the vernal products of the fields" (James v. 7; Prov. xvi. 15).

In April and May the sky is usually serene; showers occur occasionally, but they are mild and refreshing. On the 1st of May Robinson experienced showers at Jerusalem, and "at evening there was thunder and lightning (which are frequent in winter), with pleasant and reviving rain. The 6th of May was also remarkable for thunder and for several showers, some of which were quite heavy. The rains of both these days extended far to the north, ... but the occurrence of rain so late in the season was regarded as a very unusual circum-

stance." (*Bibl. Res.* i. 430: he is speaking of the year 1838.)

In 1856, however, "there was very heavy rain accompanied with thunder all over the region of Lebanon, extending to Beirut and Damascus, on the 28th and 29th of May; but the oldest inhabitant had never seen the like before, and it created, says Porter (*Handbook*, xlviii.), almost as much astonishment as the thunder and rain which Samuel brought upon the Israelites during the time of wheat harvest."

During Dr. Robinson's stay at Beirut on his second visit to Palestine, in 1852, there were heavy rains in March, once for five days continuously, and the weather continued variable, with occasional heavy rain, till the close of the first week in April. The "latter rains" thus continued this season for nearly a month later than usual, and the result was afterwards seen in the very abundant crops of winter grain (Robinson, *Bibl. Res.* iii. 9).[a]

These details will, it is thought, better than any generalized statement, enable the reader to form his judgment on the "former" and "latter" rains of Scripture, and may serve to introduce a remark or two on the question, about which some interest has been felt, whether there has been any change in the frequency and abundance of the rain in Palestine, or in the periods of its supply. It is asked whether "these stony hills, these deserted valleys," can be the land flowing with milk and honey; the land which God cared for; the land upon which were always the eyes of the Lord, from the beginning of the year to the end of the year (Deut. xi. 12). As far as relates to the other considerations which may account for diminished fertility, such as the decrease of population and industry, the neglect of terrace-culture and irrigation, and husbanding the supply of water, it may suffice to refer to the article on AGRICULTURE, and to Stanley (*Sinai and Palestine*, pp. 120-123). With respect to our more immediate subject, it is urged that the very expression "flowing with milk and honey" implies abundant rains to keep alive the grass for the pasture of the numerous herds supplying the milk, and to nourish the flowers clothing the now bare hill-sides, from whence the bees might gather their stores of honey. It is urged that the supply of rain in its due season seems to be promised as contingent upon the fidelity of the people (Deut. xi. 13-15; Lev. xxvi. 3-5) and that as from time to time, to punish the people for their transgressions, "the showers have been withholden, and there hath been no latter rain" (Jer. iii. 3; 1 K. xvii., xviii.), so now, in the great and long-continued apostasy of the children of Israel, there has come upon even the land of their forfeited inheritance a like long-continued withdrawal of the favor of God, who claims the sending of rain as one of His special prerogatives (Jer. xiv. 22).

The early rains, it is urged, are by comparison scanty and interrupted, the latter rains have altogether ceased, and hence, it is maintained, the curse has been fulfilled, "Thy heaven that is over thy head shall be brass, and the earth that is under

a * For a diary of the weather at Beirut from April, 1842, to May, 1843, by Dr. De Forest, see *Climatology of Palestine* in the *Bibl. Sacra*, i. 221-224. The months of greatest rain were November, December, and January, and of least, June, July, August, and September. Of the climate of Nazareth in this and other

respects, Tobler gives full information in his *Nazareth in Palästina*, pp. 6-11. Thomson mentions (*Land and Book*, ii. 66) that in Palestine the rain frequently falls very unequally, so as to water one city or field and pass over the next (comp. Am. iv. 7, 8).   E.

thee shall be iron. The Lord shall make the rain of thy land powder and dust " (Deut. xxviii. 23, 24; Lev. xxvi. 19). Without entering here into the consideration of the justness of the interpretation which would assume these predictions of the withholding of rain to be altogether different in the manner of their infliction from the other calamities denounced in these chapters of threatening, it would appear that, as far as the question of fact is concerned, there is scarcely sufficient reason to imagine that any great and marked changes with respect to the rains have taken place in Palestine. In early days, as now, rain was unknown for half the year; and if we may judge from the allusions in Prov. xvi. 15, Job xxix. 23, the latter rain was even then, while greatly desired and longed for, that which was somewhat precarious, by no means to be absolutely counted on as a matter of course. If we are to take as correct our translation of Joel ii. 23, " the latter rain in the first (month a)," i. e. Nisan or Abib, answering to the latter part of March and the early part of April, the times of the latter rain in the days of the prophets would coincide with those in which it falls now. The same conclusion would be arrived at from Amos iv. 7, " I have withholden the rain from you when there were yet three months to the harvest." The rain here spoken of is the latter rain, and an interval of three months between the ending of the rain and the beginning of harvest would seem to be in an average year as exceptional now as it was when Amos noted it as a judgment of God. We may infer also from the Song of Solomon ii. 11–13, where is given a poetical description of the bursting forth of vegetation in the spring, that when the " winter " was past, the rain also was over and gone: we can hardly, by any extension of the term " winter," bring it down to a later period than that during which the rains still fall. [See PALESTINE, p. 2318.]

It may be added that travellers have, perhaps unconsciously, exaggerated the barrenness of the land, from confining themselves too closely to the southern portion of Palestine; the northern portion, Galilee, of such peculiar interest to the readers of the Gospels, is fertile and beautiful (see Stanley, *Sinai and Palestine*, chap. x., and Van de Velde, there quoted), and in his description of the valley of *Nablus*, the ancient Shechem, Robinson (*Bibl. Res.* ii. 275) becomes almost enthusiastic: " Here a scene of luxuriant and almost unparalleled verdure burst upon our view. The whole valley was filled with gardens of vegetables and orchards of all kinds of fruits, watered by several fountains, which burst forth in various parts and flow westward in refreshing streams. It came upon us suddenly, like a scene of fairy enchantment. We saw nothing like it in all Palestine." The account given by a recent lady traveller (*Egyptian Sepulchres and Syrian Shrines*, by Miss Beaufort) of the luxuriant fruit-trees and vegetables which she saw at Meshullam's farm in the valley of Urtas, a little south of Bethlehem (possibly the site of Solomon's gardens, Eccl. ii. 4–6),

may serve to prove how much now, as ever, may be effected by irrigation.[b]

Rain frequently furnishes the writers of the Old Testament with forcible and appropriate metaphors, varying in their character according as they regard it as the beneficent and fertilizing shower, or the destructive storm pouring down the mountain-side and sweeping away the labor of years. Thus Prov. xxviii. 3, of the poor that oppresseth the poor; Ex. xxxviii. 22, of the just punishments and righteous vengeance of God (compare Ps. xl. 6; Job xx. 23). On the other hand, we have it used of speech wise and fitting, refreshing the souls of men; of words earnestly waited for and heedfully listened to (Deut. xxxii. 2; Job xxix. 23); of the cheering favor of the Lord coming down once more upon the penitent soul; of the gracious presence and influence for good of the righteous king among his people; of the blessings, gifts, and graces of the reign of the Messiah (Hos. vi. 3; 2 Sam. xxiii. 4; Ps. lxxii. 6).   E. P. E.

RAINBOW (קֶשֶׁת (i. e. a bow with which to shoot arrows), Gen. ix. 13–16; Ez. i. 28: τόξον, so Ecclus. xliii. 11: *arcus*. In N. T., Rev. iv. 3, x. 1, ἶρις). The token of the covenant which God made with Noah when he came forth from the ark, that the waters should no more become a flood to destroy all flesh. With respect to the covenant itself, as a charter of *natural* blessings and mercies (" the World's covenant, not the Church's "), re-establishing the peace and order of Physical Nature, which in the flood had undergone so great a convulsion, see Davison *On Prophecy*, lect. iii. pp. 76–80. With respect to the token of the covenant, the right interpretation of Gen. ix. 13 seems to be that God took the rainbow, which had hitherto been but a beautiful object shining in the heavens when the sun's rays fell on falling rain, and consecrated it as the sign of His love and the witness of His promise.

The following passages, Num. xiv. 4; 1 Sam. xii. 13; 1 K. ii. 35, are instances in which נָתַן (*nâthan*, lit. " give "), the word used in Gen. ix. 13, " I do *set* my bow in the cloud," is employed in the sense of " constitute," " appoint." Accordingly there is no reason for concluding that ignorance of the natural cause of the rainbow occasioned the account given of its institution in the Book of Genesis. [SIGNS, Amer. ed.]

The figurative and symbolical use of the rainbow as an emblem of God's mercy and faithfulness must not be passed over. In the wondrous vision shown to St. John in the Apocalypse (Rev. iv. 3), it is said that " there was a rainbow round about the throne, in sight like unto an emerald:" amidst the awful vision of surpassing glory is seen the symbol of Hope, the bright emblem of Mercy and of Love. " Look upon the rainbow," saith the son of Sirach (Ecclus. xliii. 11, 12), " and praise Him that made it: very beautiful it is in the brightness thereof; it compasseth the heaven about with a glorious circle, and the hands of the Most High have bended it."   E. P. E.

---

a The word " month " is supplied by our translators, and their rendering is not supported by either the LXX. (καθὼς ἔμπροσθεν) or the Vulg. (*sicut in principio*) Another interpretation is indeed equally probable ; but the following passages, Gen. viii. 13, Num. ix. 5, Ex. xxix. 17, xlv. 18, 21, justify the rendering בָּרִאשׁוֹן " in the first (month)."

b * The discovery of a single fountain, and the removal of rubbish which had choked up the soil, effected the transformation. The writer was told on the ground, that five different crops of vegetables may be raised there one after another in a single season (see *Illustr. of Scripture*, p. 155 f.).   H.

RAISINS. [VINE.]

RA'KEM (רָקֶם, in pause רָקֶם [*flower garden*]: 'Ροκόμ; om. in [Vat. and] Alex.; [Comp. Ald. Ρακάμ:] *Recen*). Among the descendants of Machir the son of Manasseh, by his wife Maachah, are mentioned Ulam and Rakem, who are apparently the sons of Sheresh (1 Chr. vii. 16). Nothing is known of them. [In Hebrew this name and Rekem (which see) are the same, out of pause. — H.]

RAK'KATH (רַקַּת [*shore*]: ['Ωμαθα]δακέθ: Alex. Ρεκκαθ: *Reccath*). One of the fortified towns of Naphtali, named between HAMMATH and CHINNERETH (Josh. xix. 35). Hammath was probably at the hot springs of Tiberias: but no trace of the name of Rakkath has been found in that or any other neighborhood. [See Rob. *Bibl. Res.* iii. 266.] The nearest approach is *Kerak*, formerly Tarichææ, three miles further down the shore of the lake, close to the embouchure of the Jordan.   G.

RAK'KON (הָרַקּוֹן, with the def. article [*the temple* (of the head), Ges.; a *well watered place*, Fürst]: 'Ιερακων; [Comp. ('Ιερακων και) 'Ηρακκων:] *Arecon*). One of the towns in the inheritance of Dan (Josh. xix 46), apparently not far distant from Joppa. The LXX. (both MSS.) give only one name (that quoted above) for this and Mejarkon, which in the Hebrew text precedes it. This fact, when coupled with the similarity of the two names in Hebrew, suggests that the one may be merely a repetition of the other. Neither has been yet discovered.   G.

RAM (רָם [*high, exalted*]: 'Αράμ; [Vat.] Alex. Αρραν in Ruth; [Vat. Οραμ and Αρραν, Alex.] Οραμ and Αραμ in 1 Chr.: *Aram*). 1. Son of Hezron and father of Amminadab. He was born in Egypt after Jacob's migration there, as his name is not mentioned in Gen. xlvi. 4. He first appears in Ruth iv. 19. The genealogy in 1 Chr. ii 9, 10, 25, adds no further information concerning him, except that he was the *second* son of Hezron, Jerahmeel being the first-born. He appears in the N. T. only in the two lists of the ancestry of Christ (Matt. i. 3, 4; Luke iii. 33), where he is called ARAM, after the LXX. and Vulgate. [AMMINADAB; NAHSHON.]   A. C. H.

2. ('Ράμ; [Vat. Ραν, Αραμ; Alex. in ver. 25, Αραν:] *Ram*.) The first-born of Jerahmeel, and therefore nephew of the preceding (1 Chr. ii. 25, 27). He had three sons, Maaz, Jamin, and Eker.

3. [Rom. Vat. Sin. 'Ράμ; Alex. Ραμα: *Ram*.] Elihu, the son of Barachel the Buzite, is described as "of the kindred of Ram" (Job xxxii. 2) Rashi's note on the passage is curious: "'of the family of Ram:' Abraham, for it is said, 'the greatest man among the Anakim' (Josh. xiv.); this

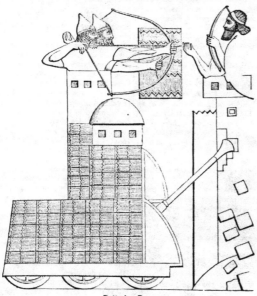

Battering Ram.

[is] Abraham." Ewald identifies Ram with Aram, mentioned in Gen. xxii. 21 in connection with Huz and Buz (*Gesch.* i. 414). Elihu would thus be a collateral descendant of Abraham, and this may have suggested the extraordinary explanation given by Rashi.   W. A. W.

RAM. [SHEEP; SACRIFICES.]

RAM, BATTERING (כַּר: βελόστασις, χάραξ: *aries*). This instrument of ancient siege operations is twice mentioned in the O. T. (Ez. iv 2, xxi. 22 [27]); and as both references are to the battering-rams in use among the Assyrians and Babylonians, it will only be necessary to describe those which are known from the monuments to have been employed in their sieges. With regard to the meaning of the Hebrew word there is but little doubt. It denotes an engine of war which was called a ram, either because it had an iron head shaped like that of a ram, or because, when used for battering down a wall, the movement was like the butting action of a ram.

In attacking the walls of a fort or city, the first step appears to have been to form an inclined plane or bank of earth (comp. Ex. iv. 2, " cast a mount against it "), by which the besiegers could bring their battering-rams and other engines to the foot of the walls. " The battering-rams," says Mr. Layard, " were of several kinds. Some were joined to movable towers which held warriors and armed men. The whole then formed one great temporary building, the top of which is represented in sculptures as on a level with the walls, and even turrets, of the besieged city. In some bas-reliefs the battering-ram is without wheels; it was then perhaps constructed upon the spot, and was not intended to be moved. The movable tower was probably sometimes unprovided with the ram, but I have not met with it so represented in the sculptures. . . . . When the machine containing the battering-ram was a simple framework, and did not form an artificial tower, a cloth or some kind of drapery, edged with fringes and otherwise ornamented, appears to have been occasionally thrown over it. Sometimes it may have been covered with hides. It moved either on four or on six wheels, and was provided with one ram or with two. The mode of working the rams cannot be determined from the Assyrian sculptures. It may be presumed from the representations in the bas-reliefs that they were partly suspended by a rope fastened to the outside of the machine, and that men directed and impelled them from within. Such was the plan adopted by the Egyptians, in whose paintings the warriors working the ram may be seen through the frame. Sometimes this engine was ornamented by a carved or painted figure of the presiding divinity, kneeling on one knee and drawing a bow. The artificial tower was usually occupied by two warriors; one discharged his arrows against the besieged, whom he was able, from his lofty position, to harass more effectually than if he had been below; the other held up a shield for his companion's defense. Warriors are not unfrequently represented as stepping from the machine to the battlements. . .

. . Archers on the walls hurled stones from slings, and discharged their arrows against the warriors in the artificial towers; whilst the rest of the besieged were no less active in endeavoring to frustrate the attempts of the assailants to make breaches in their walls. By dropping a doubled chain or rope from the battlements, they caught the ram, and could either destroy its efficacy altogether, or break the force of its blows. Those below, however, by placing hooks over the engine, and throwing their whole weight upon them, struggled to retain it in its place. The besieged, if unable to displace the battering-ram, sought to destroy it by fire, and threw lighted torches or firebrands upon it; but water was poured upon the flames through pipes attached to the artificial tower " (*Nineveh and its Remains*, ii. 367–370).

W. A. W.

RA'MA ('Ραμᾶ: *Rama*), Matt. ii. 18, referring to Jer. xxxi. 15. The original passage alludes to a massacre of Benjamites or Ephraimites (comp. ver. 9, 18), at the Ramah in Benjamin or in Mount Ephraim. This is seized by the Evangelist and turned into a touching reference to the slaughter of the Innocents at Bethlehem, near to which was (and is) the sepulchre of Rachel. The name of Rama is alleged to have been lately discovered attached to a spot close to the sepulchre. If it existed there in St. Matthew's day, it may have prompted his allusion, though it is not necessary to suppose this, since the point of the quotation does not lie in the name Ramah, but in the lamentation of Rachel for the children, as is shown by the change of the υἱοῖς of the original to τέκνα.

G.

RA'MAH (הָרָמָה, with the definite article [*the height*], excepting a few cases named below). A word which in its simple or compound shape forms the name of several places in the Holy Land; one of those which, like Gibeah, Geba, Gibeon, or Mizpeh, betrays the aspect of the country. The lexicographers with unanimous consent derive it from a root which has the general sense of elevation — a root which produced the name of Aram,[a] " the high lands," and the various modifications of Ram, Ramah, Ramath, Ramoth, Remeth, Ramathaim, Arimathæa, in the Biblical records. As an appellative it is found only in one passage (Ez. xvi. 24–39), in which it occurs four times, each time rendered in the A. V. " high place." But in later Hebrew *ramtha* is a recognized word for a hill, and as such is employed in the Jewish versions of the Pentateuch for the rendering of Pisgah.

1. ('Ραμά; [Neh. vii. 30, 'Αραμά; Vat. also Αραμ,] Ρααμα, Βαμα, etc.; [Jer. xl. 1, Vat. FA. Δαμαν;] Alex. Ιαμα, Ραμμαν, [Ραμμα,] Ραμα: *Rama*.) One of the cities of the allotment of Benjamin (Josh. xviii. 25), a member of the group which contained Gibeon and Jerusalem. Its place in the list is between Gibeon and Beeroth. There is a more precise specification of its position in the invaluable catalogue of the places north of Jerusalem which are enumerated by Isaiah as disturbed by the gradual approach of the king of Assyria (Is. x. 28–32). At Michmash he crosses the ravine; and then successively dislodges or alarms Geba, Ramah, and Gibeah of Saul. Each of these may be recognized with almost absolute certainty at the present day. Geba is *Jeba*, on the south brink of the great valley; and a mile and a half beyond it, directly between it and the main road to the city, is *er-Râm* (its name the exact equivalent of ha-Râmah) on the elevation which its ancient name implies.[b] Its distance from the city is two hours, *i. e.* five English or six Roman miles, in perfect accordance with the notice of Eusebius and Jerome in the *Onomasticon* (" Rama "),[c] and nearly agreeing with that of Josephus (*Ant.* viii. 12, § 3), who places it 40 stadia north of Jerusalem.

Its position is also in close agreement with the notices of the Bible. The palm-tree of Deborah (Judg. iv. 5) was " between Ramah[d] and Bethel,"

---

a So Sir H. C. Rawlinson, in *Athenæum*, No. 1799, p. 580.

b Its place in the list of Joshua (mentioned above), namely, between Gibeon and Beeroth, suits the present *Ram-Allah*; but the considerations named in the text make it very difficult to identify any other site with t than *er-Râm*.

c In his commentary on Hos. v. 8, Jerome mentions Rama as "juxta Gabaa in septimo lapide a Ierosolymis sita."

d The Targum on this passage substitutes for the Palm of Deborah, Ataroth-Deborah, no doubt referring to the town of Ataroth. This has everything in its favor, since '*Atâra* is still found on the left hand of

in one of the sultry valleys inclosed in the lime
stone hills which compose this district. The Levite
and his concubine in their journey from Bethlehem
to Ephraim passed Jerusalem, and pressed on to
Gibeah, or even if possible beyond it to Ramah
(Judg. xix. 13). In the struggles between north
and south, which followed the disruption of the
kingdom, Ramah, as a frontier town, the possession
of which gave absolute command of the north road
from Jerusalem (1 K. xv. 17), was taken, fortified,
and retaken (ibid. 21, 22; 2 Chr. xvi. 1, 5, 6).

After the destruction of Jerusalem it appears to
have been used as the depot for the prisoners (Jer.
xl. 1); and, if the well-known passage of Jeremiah
(xxxi. 15), in which he introduces the mother of
the tribe of Benjamin weeping over the loss of her
children, alludes to this Ramah, and not to one
nearer to her sepulchre at Bethlehem, it was probably also the scene of the slaughter of such of the
captives as from age, weakness, or poverty, were
not worth the long transport across the desert to
Babylon [RAMA.] Its proximity to Gibeah is implied in 1 Sam. xxii. 6[a]; Hos. v. 8; Ezr. ii. 26;
Neh. vii. 30: the last two of which passages show
also that its people returned after the Captivity.
The Ramah in Neh. xi. 33 occupies a different
position in the list, and may be a distinct place
situated further west, nearer the plain. (This and
Jer. xxxi. 15 are the only passages in which the
name appears without the article.) The LXX.
find an allusion to Ramah in Zech. xiv. 10. where
they render the words which are translated in the
A. V. " and shall be lifted up (רָאֲמָה), and inhabited in her place," by " Ramah shall remain
upon her place."

Er-Rām was not unknown to the mediæval
travellers, by some of whom (e. g. Brocardus,
Descr. ch. vii.) it is recognized as Ramah; but it
was reserved for Dr. Robinson to make the identification certain and complete (Bibl. Res. i. 576).
He describes it as lying on a high hill, commanding a wide prospect — a miserable village of a few
half-deserted houses, but with remains of columns,
squared stones, and perhaps a church, all indicating
former importance.

In the catalogue of 1 Esdr. v. (20) the name
appears as CIRAMA.

2 ('Αρμαθαίμ in both MSS., except only 1 Sam.
xxv. 1, xxviii. 3, where the Alex. has 'Ραμα [and
1 Sam. xix. 19, 22, 23. xx. 1, where Rom. Vat.
Alex. have the same: Ramatha].) The home of
Elkanah, Samuel's father (1 Sam. i. 19, ii. 11),
the birth-place of Samuel himself, his home and
official residence, the site of his altar (vii. 17, viii.
4, xv. 34, xvi. 13, xix. 18), and finally his burial-
place (xxv. 1, xxviii. 3). In the present instance
it is a contracted form of RAMATHAIM-ZOPHIM,
which in the existing Hebrew text is given at length
but once, although the LXX. exhibit Armathaim
on every occasion.

All that is directly said as to its situation is

that it was in Mount Ephraim (1 Sam. i. 1), and
this would naturally lead us to seek it in the
neighborhood of Shechem. But the whole tenor
of the narrative of the public life of Samuel (in
connection with which alone this Ramah is mentioned) is so restricted to the region of the tribe of
Benjamin, and to the neighborhood of Gibeah the
residence of Saul, that it seems impossible not to
look for Samuel's city in the same locality. It
appears from 1 Sam. vii. 17 that his annual functions as prophet and judge were confined to the
narrow round of Bethel, Gilgal, and Mizpeh — the
first the north boundary of Benjamin, the second
near Jericho at its eastern end, and the third on
the ridge in more modern times known as Scopas,
overlooking Jerusalem, and therefore near the southern confines of Benjamin. In the centre of these
was Gibeah of Saul, the royal residence during the
reign of the first king, and the centre of his operations. It would be doing a violence to the whole
of this part of the history to look for Samuel's
residence outside these narrow limits.

On the other hand, the boundaries of Mount
Ephraim are nowhere distinctly set forth. In the
mouth of an ancient Hebrew the expression would
mean that portion of the mountainous district
which was at the time of speaking in the possession
of the tribe of Ephraim. " Little Benjamin " was
for so long in close alliance with and dependence on
its more powerful kinsman, that nothing is more
probable than that the name of Ephraim may have
been extended over the mountainous region which
was allotted to the younger son of Rachel. Of this
there are not wanting indications. The palm-tree
of Deborah was " in Mount Ephraim," between
Bethel and Ramah, and is identified with great
plausibility by the author of the Targum on
Judg. iv. 5 with Ataroth, one of the landmarks on
the south boundary of Ephraim, which still survives
in 'Atâra, 2½ miles north of Ramah of Benjamin
(er-Râm). Bethel itself, though in the catalogue
of the cities of Benjamin (Josh. xviii. 22), was
appropriated by Jeroboam as one of his idol
sanctuaries, and is one of the "cities of Mount
Ephraim" which were taken from him by Baasha
and restored by Asa (2 Chr. xiii. 19, xv. 8). Jeremiah (ch. xxxi.) connects Ramah of Benjamin with
Mount Ephraim (vv. 6, 9. 15, 18).

In this district, tradition, with a truer instinct
than it sometimes displays, has placed the residence
of Samuel. The earliest attempt to identify it is
in the Onomasticon of Eusebius, and was not so
happy. His words are, " Armathem Seipha: the city
of Helkana and Samuel; it lies near[b] (πλησίον)
Diospolis: thence came Joseph, in the Gospels said
to be from Arimathæa." Diospolis is Lydda, the
modern Lûdd, and the reference of Eusebius is no
doubt to Ramleh, the well-known modern town
two miles from Lûdd. But there is a fatal obstacle
to this identification, in the fact that Ramleh ("the
sandy") lies on the open face of the maritime plain,
and cannot in any sense be said to be in Mount

---

the north road, very nearly midway between er-Râm
and Beitîn.

[a] This passage may either be translated (with Junius, Michaelis, De Wette, and Bunsen), "Saul abode
in Gibeah under the tamarisk on the height" (in which
case it will add one to the scanty number of cases in
which the word is used otherwise than as a proper
name), or it may imply that Ramah was included
within the precincts of the king's city. The LXX.

read Bama for Ramah, and render the words " on the
hill under the field in Bama." Eusebius, in the
Onomasticon (Ραμά), characterises Ramah as the
"city of Saul."

[b] Jerome agrees with Eusebius in his translation
of this passage; but in the Epitaphium Paulæ (Epist.
cviii.) he connects Ramleh with Arimathæa only, and
places it haud procul a Lydda.

Ephraim, or any other mountain district. Eusebius possibly refers to another Ramah named in Neh. xi. 33 (see below, No. 6).

But there is another tradition, that just alluded to, common to Moslems, Jews, and Christians, up to the present day, which places the residence of Samuel on the lofty and remarkable eminence of *Neby Samwil*, which rises four miles to the N. W. of Jerusalem, and which its height (greater than that of Jerusalem itself), its commanding position, and its peculiar shape, render the most conspicuous object in all the landscapes of that district, and make the names of Ramah and Zophim exceedingly appropriate to it. The name first appears in the travels of Arculf (A. D. cir. 700), who calls it Saint Samuel. Before that date the relics of the Prophet had been transported from the Holy Land to Thrace by the emperor Arcadius (see Jerome *contr. Vigilantium*, § 5), and Justinian had enlarged or completed " a well and a wall " for the sanctuary (Procopius, *de Ædif.* v. cap. 9). True, neither of these notices names the spot, but they imply that it was well known, and so far support the placing it at *Neby Samwil*. Since the days of Arculf the tradition appears to have been continuous (see the quotations in Robinson, *Bibl. Res.* i. 459; Tobler, p. 881, &c.). The modern village, though miserable even among the wretched collections of hovels which crown the hills in this neighborhood, bears marks of antiquity in cisterns and other traces of former habitation. The mosque is said to stand on the foundations of a Christian church, probably that which Justinian built or added to. The ostensible tomb is a mere wooden box; but below it is a cave or chamber, apparently excavated, like that of the patriarchs at Hebron, from the solid rock of the hill, and, like that, closed against all access except by a narrow aperture in the top, through which devotees are occasionally allowed to transmit their lamps and petitions to the sacred vault below.

Here, then, we are inclined, in the present state of the evidence, to place the Ramah of Samuel.[a] And there probably would never have been any resistance to the traditional identification if it had not been thought necessary to make the position of Ramah square with a passage with which it does not seem to the writer to have necessarily any connection. It is usually assumed that the city in which Saul was anointed by Samuel (1 Sam. ix., x.) was Samuel's own city Ramah. Josephus certainly (*Ant.* vi. 4, § 1) does give the name of the city as Armathem, and in his version of the occurrence implies that the Prophet was at the time in his own house; but neither the Hebrew nor the LXX. contains any statement which confirms this, if we except the slender fact that the " land of Zuph " (ix. 5) may be connected with the Zophim of Ramathaim-zophim. The words of the maidens (ver. 12) may equally imply either that Samuel had just entered one of his cities of circuit, or that he had just returned to his own house. But, however this may be, it follows from the minute specification

of Saul's route in 1 Sam. x. 2, that the city in which the interview took place was near the sepulchre of Rachel, which, by Gen. xxxv. 16, 19, and other reasons, appears to be fixed with certainty as close to Bethlehem. And this supplies a strong argument against its being Ramathaim-zophim, since, while Mount Ephraim, as we have endeavored already to show, extended to within a few miles north of Jerusalem, there is nothing to warrant the supposition that it ever reached so far south as the neighborhood of Bethlehem. Saul's route will be most conveniently discussed under the head of SAUL; but the question of both his outward and his homeward journey, minutely as they are detailed, is beset with difficulties, which have been increased by the assumptions of the commentators. For instance, it is usually taken for granted that his father's house, and therefore the starting-point of his wanderings, was Gibeah. True, Saul himself, after he was king, lived at Gibeah; but the residence of Kish would appear to have been at ZELA [b] where his family sepulchre was (2 Sam. xxi. 14), and of Zela no trace has yet been found. The Authorized Version has added to the difficulty by introducing the word " meet " in x. 3 as the translation of the term which they have more accurately rendered " find " in the preceding verse. Again, where was the " hill of God," the *gibeath-Elohim*, with the *netsib* [c] of the Philistines? A *netsib* of the Philistines is mentioned later in Saul's history (1 Sam. xiii. 3) as at Geba opposite Michmash. But this is three miles north of Gibeah of Saul, and does not at all agree with a situation near Bethlehem for the anointing of Saul. The Targum interprets the " hill of God " as " the place where the ark of God was," meaning Kirjathjearim.

On the assumption that Ramathaim-zophim was the city of Saul's anointing, various attempts have been made to find a site for it in the neighborhood of Bethlehem. (*a.*) Gesenius (*Thes.* p. 1276 *a*) suggests the *Jebel Fureidis*, four miles southeast of Bethlehem, the ancient Herodium, the " Frank mountain " of more modern times. The drawback to this suggestion is that it is not supported by any hint or inference either in the Bible, Josephus (who was well acquainted with the Herodion), or more recent authority. (*b.*) Dr. Robinson (*Bibl. Res.* ii. 8) proposes *Sôba*, in the mountains six miles west of Jerusalem, as the possible representative of Zophim: but the hypothesis has little besides its ingenuity to recommend it, and is virtually given up by its author in a foot-note to the passage. (*c.*) Van de Velde (*Syr. & Pal.* ii. 50), following the lead of Wolcott, argues for *Rameh* (or *Ramet el-Khalil*, Rob. i. 216), a well-known site of ruins about two and a half miles north of Hebron. His main argument is that a castle of S. Samuel is mentioned by F. Fabri in 1483 [d] (apparently) as north of Hebron; that the name *Rameh* is identical with Ramah; and that its position suits the requirements of 1 Sam. x. 2–5. This is also supported by Stewart (*Tent and Khan*, p. 247). (*d.*)

---

[a] " Beth-horon and her suburbs " were allotted to the Kohathite Levites, of whom Samuel was one by descent. Perhaps the village on the top of *Neby Samwil* may have been dependent on the more regularly fortified Beth-horon (1 K. ix. 17).

[b] Zela (צֵלַע) is quite a distinct name from Zelzach (צֶלְצַח), with which some would identify it (*s. g.*

Stewart, *Tent and Khan*, p. 247; Van de Velde, *Memoir*, etc., etc.).

[c] The meaning of this word is uncertain. It may signify a garrison, an officer, or a commemoration column — a trophy.

[d] In the time of Benjamin of Tudela it was known as the " house of Abraham " (*B. of T.*, ed. Asher, B 96).

Dr. Bonar (*Land of Promise*, pp. 178, 554) adopts *er-Ram*, which he places a short distance north of Bethlehem, east of Rachel's sepulchre. Eusebius (*Onom.* 'Ραβεδέ) says that "Rama of Benjamin" is near (περὶ) Bethlehem, where the "voice in Rama was heard;" and in our times the name is mentioned, besides Dr. Bonar, by Prokesch and Salzbacher (cited in Rob. *Bibl. Res.* ii. 8 *note*), but this cannot be regarded as certain, and Dr. Stewart has pointed out that it is too close to Rachel's monument to suit the case.

Two suggestions in an opposite direction must be noticed : —

(*a.*) That of Ewald (*Geschichte*, ii. 550), who places Ramathaim-zophim at *Ram-Allah*, a mile west of *el-Bireh*, and nearly five north of *Neby Samuil*. The chief ground for the suggestion appears to be the affix *Allah*, as denoting that a certain sanctity attaches to the place. This would be more certainly within the limits of Mount Ephraim, and merits investigation. It is mentioned by Mr. Williams (*Dict. of Geogr.* "Ramatha") who, however, gives his decision in favor of *Neby Samuil*.

(*b.*) That of Schwarz (pp. 152-158), who, starting from Gibeah-of-Saul as the home of Kish, fixes upon *Rameh*, north of Samaria and west of *Sanur*, which he supposes also to be Ramoth or Jarmuth, the Levitical [a] city of Issachar. Schwarz's arguments must be read to be appreciated.

* The site of this Ramah, Dean Stanley pronounces "without exception the most complicated and disputed problem of sacred topography." The writer, with others, has devoted many fruitless hours to its solution; and the difficulties of the case, inherent and apparently ineradicable, may be briefly stated. (1.) The Ramah of Samuel's birth was in Mount Ephraim (see above). (2.) The Ramah of his residence and burial was the Ramah of his birth (see above). "The inference is direct and stringent, that the two were identical." Robinson's *Bibl. Sacra*, p. 506 (1843). (3.) The Ramah of his interview with Saul was the Ramah of his residence (see above). "It is hardly possible to avoid identifying them. This, which is not stated expressly in the Old Testament [though fairly implied], is taken for granted by Josephus " (Dr. Stanley, *S. & P.* p. 220). Josephus, without doubt, was familiar with all the localities, and would know whether his statement was compatible with the sacred narrative. (4.) The Ramah in which Saul was anointed by Samuel was so situated that, in

passing from it to his home in Benjamin, he would pass by the tomb of Rachel (see above).

Neither of these four points can yet be disproved, and on every proposed site of the Ramah of the prophet, some one of them directly impinges; and the prospect now is, that the question will remain inexplicable.[b]   S. W.

3. ('Αραήλ; [c] Alex. Ραμα: *Arama*.) One of the nineteen fortified places of Naphtali (Josh. xix. 36) named between Adamah and Hazor. It would appear, if the order of the list may be accepted, to have been in the mountainous country N. W. of the Lake of Gennesaret. In this district a place bearing the name of *Rameh* has been discovered by Dr. Robinson (*Bibl. Res.* iii. 78), which is not improbably the modern representative of the Ramah in question. It lies on the main track between *Akka* and the north end of the Sea of Galilee, and about eight miles E. S. E. of *Safed*. It is, perhaps, worth notice that, though the spot is distinguished by a very lofty brow, commanding one of the most extensive views in all Palestine (Rob. *Bibl. Res.* iii. 78), and answering perfectly to the name of Ramah, yet that the village of *Rameh* itself is on the lower slope of the hill.

4. ('Ραμά: *Horma*.) One of the landmarks on the boundary (A. V. "coast") of Asher (Josh. xix. 29), apparently between Tyre and Zidon. It does not appear to be mentioned by the ancient geographers or travellers, but two places of the same name have been discovered in the district allotted to Asher: the one east of Tyre, and within about three miles of it (Van de Velde, *Map*, *Memoir*) the other more than ten miles off, and southeast of the same city (Van de Velde, *Map*; Robinson, *Bibl. Res.* iii. 64). The specification of the boundary of Asher is very obscure, and nothing can yet be gathered from it; but, if either of these places represent the Ramah in question, it certainly seems safer to identify it with that nearest to Tyre and the sea-coast.

5. ('Ρεμμώθ, Alex. Ραμωθ; [in 2 Chr. xxii. 6, Rom. Vat. Ραμωθ, Alex. Ραμα:] *Ramoth*.) By this name in 2 K. viii. 29 and 2 Chr. xxii. 6, only, is designated RAMOTH-GILEAD. The abbreviation is singular, since, in both cases, the full name occurs in the preceding verse.

6. [Rom. Vat. Alex. FA.[1] omit; FA.[3] Comp. *Ραμά: Rama*.] A place mentioned in the catalogue of those reinhabited by the Benjamites after their return from the Captivity (Neh. xi. 33). It may be the Ramah of Benjamin (above, No. 1) or the

---

[a] But Ramoth was allotted to the Gershonites, while Samuel was a Kohathite.

[b] * The German missionary, Pastor Valentiner, regards the Ramah in Isaiah's vision (No. 1 above) and the Ramah of Samuel (No. 2) as the same, namely, the present *Er-Ram*, about 6 miles north of Jerusalem on the traveller's right in going to Bethel and Shechem. Samuel's father, Elkanah (as he maintains), is said to be "a man of Ramathaim-sophim, of Mount Ephraim " (1 Sam. i. 1, &c.), not because he lived there at the time of Samuel's birth, but because he dwelt there originally, and afterwards migrated to Ramah in Benjamin. Further, he considers it unnecessary (so also Stanley, *Jewish Church*, i 464, Keil on 1 Sam. ix. 6 ff. and others) to identify the Ramah of Samuel with the nameless city of Saul's interview with Samuel as related 1 Sam. ix. 1 ff. Among his positive reasons for this identification of Ramah with *Er-Ram* are that it lies fairly within the territory of Benjamin; that it forms the central point of Samuel's judicial

circuit (Gilgal on the east, Bethel on the north, and Mizpeh (= *Neby Samuil*) on the west, 1 Sam. vii. 16); and that the vicinity of Saul's Gibeah to this Ramah (= *Er-Ram*) tallies well with the local relations of Gibeah and Ramah to each other in the narrative, 1 Sam. co. xix. and xx. It follows from this view that Ramah No. 1 and Ramah No. 2 may be the same place. The difficulties, whatever they may be, as to ZUPH and the course of Saul's journey in search of the lost asses encumber any one hypothesis of the Ramah question as well as another. See Valentiner's art. *Beitrag zur Topographie des Stammes Benjamin*, in the *Zeitschr. der deutsch. M. Gesellsch.* xii. 161-170.

[c] Prof. Graf in like manner (*Lage von Bethel, Rama u. Gilgal*, in the *Stud. u. Krit.* 1854, pp. 851-902, recognizes only one Ramah, which he identifies with *Er-Ram*, but he distinguishes Ramathaim-sophim and Ramah from each other.   H.

[c] For the preceding name — Adamah — they give 'Αρμαίθ.

Ramah of Samuel, but its position in the list (remote from Geba, Michmash, Bethel, ver. 31, comp. Ezr. ii. 26, 28) seems to remove it further west, to the neighborhood of Lod, Hadid, and Ono. There is no further notice in the Bible of a Ramah in this direction, but Eusebius and Jerome allude to one, though they may be at fault in identifying it with Ramathaim and Arimathæa (*Onom.* " Armatha Sophim; " and the remarks of Robinson, *Bibl. Res.* ii. 239). The situation of the modern *Ramleh* agrees very well with this, a town too important and too well placed not to have existed in the ancient times.[a] The consideration that *Ramleh* signifies " sand," and Ramah " a height," is not a valid argument against the one being the legitimate successor of the other. If so, half the identifications of modern travellers must be reversed. *Beit-ûr* zan no longer be the representative of Beth-horon, because *ûr* means " eye," while *horon* means " caves; " ûr*-* *Beit-lahm*, of Bethlehem, because *lahm* is " flesh," and *lehem* " bread; " nor *el-Aul*, of Elealeh, because *el* is in Arabic the article, and in Hebrew the name of God. In these cases the tendency of language is to retain the sound at the expense of the meaning.   G.

RA'MATH-LE'HI (רָמַת לֶחִי [see below]: 'Αναίρεσις σιαγόνος: *Ramathlechi, quod interpretatur elevatio maxillæ*). The name which purports to have been bestowed by Samson on the scene of his slaughter of the thousand Philistines with the jaw-bone (Judg. xv. 17). " He cast away the jaw-bone out of his hand, and called that place ' Ramath-lehi,' " — as if " heaving of the jaw-bone." In this sense the name (wisely left untranslated in the A. V.) is rendered by the LXX. and Vulgate (as above). But Gesenius has pointed out (*Thes.* p. 752 a) that to be consistent with this the vowel points should be altered, and the words become רָמַת לֶחִי; and that as they at present stand they are exactly parallel to Ramath-mizpeh and Ramath-negeb, and mean the " height of Lechi." If we met with a similar account in ordinary history we should say that the name had already been Ramath-lehi, and that the writer of the narrative, with that fondness for *paronomasia* which distinguishes these ancient records, had indulged himself in connecting the name with a possible exclamation of his hero. But the fact of the positive statement in this case may make us hesitate in coming to such a conclusion in less authoritative records. [See LEHI, note *c*, vol. ii. p. 1627.]   G.

RA'MATH-MIZ'PEH (רָמַת הַמִּצְפֶּה)
with def. article [*height of the watch-tower*]: 'Αραβὼθ κατὰ τὴν Μασσηφά; Alex. Ραμωθ[b] κ. τ. Μασφα: *Ramath, Masphe*). A place mentioned, in Josh. xiii. 26 only, in the specification of the territory of Gad, apparently as one of its northern landmarks, Heshbon being the limit on the south. But of this our ignorance of the topography east of the Jordan forbids us to speak at present with any certainty.

There is no reason to doubt that it is the same

place with that early sanctuary at which Jacob and Laban set up their cairn of stones, and which received the names of MIZPEH, Galeed, and Jegar Sahadutha: and it seems very probable that all these are identical with Ramoth-Gilead, so notorious in the later history of the nation. In the Books of Maccabees it probably appears in the garb of Maspha (1 Macc. v. 35), but no information is afforded us in either Old Test. or Apocrypha as to its position. The lists of places in the districts north of *es-Salt*, collected by Dr. Eli Smith, and given by Dr. Robinson (*Bibl. Res.* 1st edit. App. to vol. iii.), contain several names which may retain a trace of Ramath, namely, *Rumeimin* (167 *b*), *Reimûn* (166 *a*), *Rumrâna* (165 *a*), but the situation of these places is not accurately known, and it is impossible to say whether they are appropriate to Ramath-Mizpeh or not.   G.

RA'MATH OF THE SOUTH (רָמַת נֶגֶב: Βαμὲθ κατὰ λίβα; Alex. by double transl. θερηγραμμωθ . . . ιαμεθ κ. λ.: *Ramath contra australem plagam*), more accurately Ramah of the South. One of the towns in the allotment of Simeon (Josh. xix. 8), apparently at its extreme south limit. It appears from this passage to have been another name for BAALATH-BEER. Ramah is not mentioned in the list of Judah (comp. Josh. xv. 21-32), nor in that of Simeon in 1 Chr. iv. 28-33, nor is it mentioned by Eusebius and Jerome. Van de Velde (*Memoir*, p. 342) takes it as identical with Ramath-Lehi, which he finds at *Tell el-Lekiyeh*; but this appears to be so far south as to be out of the circle of Samson's adventures, and at any rate must wait for further evidence.

It is in all probability the same place as SOUTH RAMOTH (1 Sam. xxx. 27), and the towns in company with which we find it in this passage confirm the opinion given above that it lay very much to the south.   G.

RAMATHA'IM-ZO'PHIM (הָרָמָתַיִם צוֹפִים [see below]: 'Αρμαθαὶμ [Σιφά, Vat.] Σειφα; Alex. A. Σωφιμ: *Ramathaim Sophim*). The full form of the name of the town in which Elkanah, the father of the prophet Samuel, resided. It is given in its complete shape in the Hebrew text and A. V. but once (1 Sam. i. 1). Elsewhere (i. 19, ii. 11, vii. 17, viii. 4, xv. 34, xvi. 13, xix. 18, 19, 22, 23, xx. 1, xxv. 1, xxvii. 1, xxviii. 3) it occurs in the shorter form of Ramah. [RAMAH, 2.] The LXX., however (in both MSS.), give it throughout as Armathaim, and insert it in i. 3 after the words " his city," where it is wanting in the Hebrew and A. V.

Ramathaim, if interpreted as a Hebrew word, is dual — " the double eminence." This may point to a peculiarity in the shape or nature of the place, or may be an instance of the tendency, familiar to all students, which exists in language to force an archaic or foreign name into an intelligible form. This has been already remarked in the case of Jerusalem (vol. ii. p. 1272 *a*); and, like that, the present name appears in the form of RAMATHEM, as as well as that of Ramathaim.

---

[a] This is evidenced by the attempts of Benjamin of Tudela and others to make out Ramleh to be Gath, Gezer, etc.

[b] This reading of Ramoth for Ramath is countenanced by one Hebrew MS. collated by Kennicott. It is also followed by the Vulgate, which gives *Ramoth*,

Masphe (the reading in the text is from the Benedictine Edition of the *Bibliotheca Divina*). On the other hand, there is no warrant whatever for separating the two words, as if belonging to distinct places, as is done in both the Latin texts.

Of the force of "Zophim" no feasible explanation has been given. It was an ancient name on the east of Jordan (Num. xliii. 14), and there, as here, was attached to an eminence. In the Targum of Jonathan, Ramathaim-zophim is rendered "Ramatha of the scholars of the prophets;" but this is evidently a late interpretation, arrived at by regarding the prophets as watchmen (the root of *zophim*, also that of *mizpeh*, having the force of looking out afar), coupled with the fact that at Naioth in Ramah there was a school of prophets. It will not escape observation that one of the ancestors of Elkanah was named Zophai or Zuph (1 Chr. vi. 26, 35), and that when Saul approached the city in which he encountered Samuel he entered the land of Zuph; but no connection between these names and that of Ramathaim-zophim has yet been established.

Even without the testimony of the LXX. there is no doubt, from the narrative itself, that the Ramah of Samuel — where he lived, built an altar, died, and was buried — was the same place as the Ramah or Ramathaim-Zophim in which he was born. It is implied by Josephus, and affirmed by Eusebius and Jerome in the *Onomasticon* ("Armathem Seipha "), nor would it ever have been questioned had there not been other Ramahs mentioned in the sacred history.

Of its position nothing, or next to nothing, can be gathered from the narrative. It was in Mount Ephraim (1 Sam. i. 1). It had apparently attached to it a place called NAIOTH, at which the "company" (or "school," as it is called in modern times) of the sons of the prophets was maintained (xix. 18, &c., xx. 1); and it had also in its neighborhood (probably between it and Gibeah-of-Saul) a great well known as the well of Has-Sechu (xix. 22). [SECHU.] But unfortunately these scanty particulars throw no light on its situation. Naioth and Sechu have disappeared, and the limits of Mount Ephraim are uncertain. In the 4th century Ramathaim-Zophim (*Onomasticon*, "Armatha-sophim ") was located near Diospolis (Lydda), probably at Ramleh; but that is quite untenable, and quickly disappeared in favor of another, probably older, certainly more feasible tradition, which placed it on the lofty and remarkable hill four miles N.W. of Jerusalem, known to the early pilgrims and Crusaders as Saint Samuel and Mont Joye. It is now universally designated *Neby Samwil* — the "Prophet Samuel;" and in the mosque which crowns its long ridge (itself the successor of a Christian church), his sepulchre is still reverenced alike by Jews, Moslems, and Christians.

There is no trace of the name of Ramah or Zophim having ever been attached to this hill since the Christian era, but it has borne the name of the great prophet certainly since the 7th century, and not improbably from a still earlier date. It is not too far south to have been within the limits of Mount Ephraim. It is in the heart of the district where Saul resided, and where the events in which Samuel took so large a share occurred. It completes the circle of the sacred cities to which the prophet was in the habit of making his annual circuit, and which lay — Bethel on the north, Mizpeh [a] on the south, Gilgal on the east, and (if we accept this identification) Ramathaim-zophim on

the west — round the royal city of Gibeah, in which the king resided who had been anointed to his office by the prophet amid such universal expectation and good augury. Lastly, as already remarked, it has a tradition in its favor of early date and of great persistence. It is true that even these grounds are but slight and shifting, but they are more than can be brought in support of any other site; and the task of proving them fallacious must be undertaken by those who would disturb a tradition so old, and which has the whole of the evidence, slight as that is, in its favor.

This subject is examined in greater detail, and in connection with the reasons commonly alleged against the identification, under RAMAH, No. 2.

G.

RAM′ATHEM ('Ραθαμείν, Mai [Sin.] and Alex.; [Rom. 'Ραμαθέμ;] Joseph. 'Ραμαθά: *Ramathan*). One of the three "governments" (νομοί and τοπαρχίαι) which were added to Judæa by king Demetrius Nicator, out of the country of Samaria (1 Macc. xi. 34); the others were Apherema and Lydda. It no doubt derived its name from a town of the name of RAMATHAIM, probably that renowned as the birthplace of Samuel the Prophet, though this cannot be stated with certainty.

G.

RA′MATHITE, THE (הָרָמָתִי [patr.]: ὁ ἐκ 'Ραήλ; Alex. ὁ Ραμαθαιος: *Ramathites*). Shimei the Ramathite had charge of the royal vineyards of king David (1 Chr. xxvii. 27). The name implies that he was native of a place called Ramah, but of the various Ramahs mentioned none is said to have been remarkable for vines, nor is there any tradition or other clew by which the particular Ramah to which this worthy belonged can be identified.

G.

RAM′ESES (רַעְמְסֵס [see below]: 'Ραμεσσῆ; [Vat. in Num., Ραμεσσων, Ραμεσσης:] *Ramesses*), or **RAAM′SES** (רַעְמְסֵס: 'Ραμεσσῆ: *Ramesses*), a city and district of Lower Egypt. There can be no reasonable doubt that the same city is designated by the Rameses and Raamses of the Hebrew text, and that this was the chief place of the land of Rameses, all the passages referring to the same region. The name is Egyptian, the same as that of several kings of the empire, of the XVIIIth, XIXth, and XXth dynasties. In Egyptian it is written RA-MESES or RA-MSES, it being doubtful whether the short vowel understood occurs twice or once: the first vowel is represented by a sign which usually corresponds to the Heb. ע, in Egyptian transcriptions of Hebrew names, and Hebrew, of Egyptian.

The first mention of Rameses is in the narrative of the settling by Joseph of his father and brethren in Egypt, where it is related that a possession was given them "in the land of Rameses" (Gen. xlvii. 11). This land of Rameses, אֶרֶץ רַעְמְסֵס either corresponds to the land of Goshen, or was a district of it, more probably the former, as appears from a comparison with a parallel passage (6). The name next occurs as that of one of the two cities built for the Pharaoh who first oppressed the children of Israel. "And they built for Pharaoh treasure cities (עָרֵי מִסְכְּנוֹת), Pithom and Raamses" (Ex. i. 11). So in the A. V. The LXX.

however, reads πόλεις ὀχυράς, and the Vulg. urbes tabernaculorum, as if the root had been שֻׂכֹּן.

The signification of the word מִסְכְּנוֹת is decided by its use for storehouses of corn, wine, and oil, which Hezekiah had (2 Chr. xxxii 28). We should therefore here read store-cities, which may have been the meaning of our translators. The name of PITHOM indicates the region near Heliopolis, and therefore the neighborhood of Goshen or that tract itself, and there can therefore be no doubt that Raamses is Rameses in the land of Goshen. In the narrative of the Exodus we read of Rameses as the starting-point of the journey (Ex. xii. 37; see also Num. xxxiii. 3, 5).

If then we suppose Rameses or Raamses to have been the chief town of the land of Rameses, either Goshen itself or a district of it, we have to endeavor to determine its situation. Lepsius supposes that Aboo-Kesheyd is on the site of Rameses (see Map, vol. i. p. 794). His reasons are, that in the LXX. Heroöpolis is placed in the land of Rameses (καθ' Ἡρώων πόλιν, ἐν γῇ Ῥαμεσσῇ, or εἰς γῆν Ῥαμεσσῇ), in a passage where the Hebrew only mentions "the land of Goshen" (Gen. xlvi. 28), and that there is a monolithic group at Aboo-Kesheyd representing Tum, and Ra, and, between them, Rameses II., who was probably there worshipped. There would seem therefore to be an indication of the situation of the district and city from this mention of Heroöpolis, and the statue of Rameses might mark a place named after that king. It must, however, be remembered (a) that the situation of Heroöpolis is a matter in great doubt, and that therefore we can scarcely take any proposed situation as an indication of that of Rameses; (b) that the land of Rameses may be that of Goshen, as already remarked, in which case the passage would not afford any more precise indication of the position of the city Rameses than that it was in Goshen, as is evident from the account of the Exodus; and (c) that the mention of Heroöpolis in the LXX. would seem to be a gloss. It is also necessary to consider the evidence in the Biblical narrative of the position of Rameses, which seems to point to the western part of the land of Goshen, since two full marches, and part at least of a third, brought the Israelites from this town to the Red Sea: and the narrative appears to indicate a route for the chief part directly towards the sea. After the second day's journey they "encamped in Etham, in the edge of the wilderness" (Ex. xiii. 20), and on the third day they appear to have turned. If, however, Rameses was where Lepsius places it, the route would have been almost wholly through the wilderness, and mainly along the tract bordering the Red Sea in a southerly direction, so that they would have turned almost at once. If these difficulties are not thought insuperable, it must be allowed that they render Lepsius's theory extremely doubtful, and the one fact that Aboo-Kesheyd is within about eight miles of the ancient head of the gulf, seems to us fatal to his identification. Even could it be proved that it was anciently called Rameses, the case would not be made out, for there is good reason to suppose that many cities in Egypt bore this name. Apart from the ancient evidence, we may mention that there is now a place called "Remsees" or "Ramses" in the Boheyreh (the great province on the west of the Rosetta branch of the Nile), mentioned in the list of towns and villages of Egypt in De Sacy's "Abd-allatif," p. 664. It gave to its district the name of "Hôf-Remsees" or "Ramsees." This "Hôf" must not be confounded with the "Hof" commonly known, which was in the district of Bilbeys.

An argument for determining under what dynasty the Exodus happened has been founded on the name Rameses, which has been supposed to indicate a royal builder. This argument has been stated elsewhere: here we need only repeat that the highest date to which Rameses I. can be reasonably assigned is consistent alone with the Rabbinical date of the Exodus, and that we find a prince of the same name two centuries earlier, and therefore at a time perhaps consistent with Ussher's date, so that the place might have taken its name either from this prince, or a yet earlier king or prince Rameses. [CHRONOLOGY; EGYPT; PHARAOH.]   R. S. P.

RAMES'SE (Ῥαμεσσῆ: om. in Vulg.) = RAMESES (Jud. i. 9).

RAMI'AH (רַמְיָה [Jehovah exalted]: 'Ῥαμία: Remeia). A layman of Israel, one of the sons of Parosh, who put away his foreign wife at Ezra's command (Ezr. x. 25). He is called HIERMAS in 1 Esdr. ix. 26.

RA'MOTH (רָאמוֹת [heights]: ἡ 'Ῥαμώθ; [Vat. Alex.² omit:] Ramoth). One of the four Levitical cities of Issachar according to the catalogue in 1 Chr. (vi. 73). In the parallel list in Joshua (xxi. 28, 29), amongst other variations, Jarmuth appears in place of Ramoth. It appears impossible to decide which is the correct reading; or whether again REMETH, a town of Issachar, is distinct from them, or one and the same. No place has yet been discovered which can be plausibly identified with either.   G.

RA'MOTH (רָמוֹת [heights]: [Vat.] Μημων; [FA. Μηνων; Rom.] Alex. Ρημωθ: Ramoth). An Israelite layman, of the sons of Bani, who had taken a strange wife, and at Ezra's instigation agreed to separate from her (Ezr. x. 29). In the parallel passage of 1 Esdras (ix. 30) the name is given as HIEREMOTH.   G.

RA'MOTH GIL'EAD (רָמֹת גִּלְעָד [see below]: 'Ῥεμμάθ, 'Ῥεμμόθ, and 'Ῥαμώθ, [also 1 Chr. vi. 80, 'Ῥαμμώθ (Vat. Ραμμων), 1 K. iv. 13, 'Ῥαβάθ,] Γαλαάδ: [2 Chr. xviii. 2, 3, 'Ῥαμώθ τῆς Γαλααδίτιδος (Vat. -δειτ-); Vat. in 1 K. iv. 13,] Ἐρεμαθγαλααθ: [in 2 Chr. xxii. 5, Ραμαγαλααθ:] Alex. Ραμμωθ, [and several other forms;] Joseph. 'Αραμαθά: Ramoth Galaad), the "heights of Gilead." One of the great fastnesses on the east of Jordan, and the key to an important district, as is evident not only from the direct statement of 1 K. iv. 13, that it commanded the regions of Argob and of the towns of Jair, but also from the obstinacy with which it was attacked and defended by the Syrians and Jews in the reigns of Ahab, Ahaziah, and Joram.

It seems probable that it was identical with Ramath-Mizpeh, a name which occurs but once (Josh. xiii. 26), and which again there is every reason to believe occupied the spot on which Jacob had made his covenant with Laban by the simple rite of piling up a heap of stones, which heap is expressly stated to have borne the names of both GILEAD and MIZPEH, and became the great sanctuary of the regions east of Jordan. The variation of Ramoth and Ramath is quite feasible. Indeed, it occurs in the case of a town of Judah. Probably from its commanding position in the territory of Gad, as well as its sanctity and strength, it was chosen by Moses as the City of Refuge for that tribe. It is in this capacity that its name is first introduced (Deut. iv. 43; Josh. xx. 8, xxi. 38). We next encounter it as the residence of one of Solomon's commissariat officers, Ben-geber, whose authority extended over the important region of Argob, and the no less important district occupied by the towns of Jair (1 K. iv. 13).

In the second Syrian war Ramoth-Gilead played a conspicuous part. During the invasion related in 1 K. xv. 20, or some subsequent incursion, this important place had been seized by Benhadad I. from Omri (Joseph. *Ant.* viii. 15, § 3). Ahab had been too much occupied in repelling the attacks of Syria on his interior to attempt the recovery of a place so distant, but as soon as these were at an end and he could secure the assistance of Jehoshaphat, the great and prosperous king of Judah, he planned an attack (1 K. xxii.; 2 Chr. xviii.). The incidents of the expedition are well known: the attempt failed, and Ahab lost his life. [JEZREEL; MICAIAH; NAAMAN: ZEDEKIAH.]

During Ahaziah's short reign we hear nothing of Ramoth, and it probably remained in possession of the Syrians till the suppression of the Moabite rebellion gave Joram time to renew the siege. He allied himself for the purpose as his father had done, and as he himself had done on his late campaign, with his relative the king of Judah. He was more fortunate than Ahab. The town was taken by Israel (Joseph. *Ant.* ix. 6, § 1), and held in spite of all the efforts of Hazael (who was now on the throne of Damascus) to regain it (2 K. ix. 14). During the encounter Joram himself narrowly escaped the fate of his father, being (as we learn from the LXX. version of 2 Chr. xxii. 6, and from Josephus) wounded by one of the Syrian arrows, and that so severely as to necessitate his leaving the army and retiring to his palace at Jezreel (2 K. viii. 28, ix. 15; 2 Chr. xxii. 6). The fortress was left in charge of Jehu. But he was quickly called away to the more important and congenial task of rebelling against his master. He drove off from Ramoth-Gilead as if on some errand of daily occurrence, but he did not return, and does not appear to have revisited the place to which he must mainly have owed his reputation and his advancement.

Henceforward Ramoth-Gilead disappears from our view. In the account of the Gileadite campaign of the Maccabees it is not recognizable, unless it be under the name of Maspha (Mizpeh). Carnaim appears to have been the great sanctuary of the district at that time, and contained the sacred close (τέμενος) of Ashtaroth, in which fugitives took refuge (1 Macc. v. 43).

Eusebius and Jerome specify the position of Ramoth as 15 miles from Philadelphia (*Ammân*).

Their knowledge of the country on that side of the Jordan was, however, very imperfect, and in this case they are at variance with each other, Eusebius placing it west, and Jerome east of Philadelphia. The latter position is obviously untenable. The former is nearly that of the modern town of *es-Salt*,[a] which Gesenius (notes to Burckhardt, p. 1061) proposes to identify with Ramoth-Gilead. Ewald (*Gesch.* iii. 500, *note*), indeed, proposes a site further north as more probable. He suggests *Reimun*, on the northern slopes of the *Jebel Ajlûn*, a few miles west of *Jerash*, and between it and the well-known fortress of *Kulât er-Rubud*. The position assigned to it by Eusebius answers tolerably well for a site bearing the name of *Jel'âd* (جلعاد), exactly identical with the ancient Hebrew *Gilead*, which is mentioned by Seetzen (*Reisen*, March 11, 1806), and marked on his map (*Ibid.*, iv.) and that of Van de Velde (1858) as four or five miles north of *es-Salt*. And probably this situation is not very far from the truth. If Ramoth-Gilead and Ramath-Mizpeh are identical, a more northern position than *es-Salt* would seem inevitable, since Ramath-Mizpeh was in the northern portion of the tribe of Gad (Josh. xiii. 26). This view is supported also by the Arabic version of the Book of Joshua, which gives *Ramah el-Jerash*, i. e. the Gerasa of the classical geographers, the modern *Jerash*; with which the statement of the careful Jewish traveller Parchi agrees, who says that "Gilead is at present [b] Djerash" (Zunz in Asher's *Benjamin*, p. 405). Still the fact remains that the name of *Jebel Jil'ad*, or Mount Gilead, is attached to the mass of mountain between the *Wady Sho'eib* on the south, and *Wady Zerka* on the north, the highest part, the Ramoth, of which, is the *Jebel Osha*.   G.

* Tristram assumes the identity of the site of Ramoth-Gilead with *es-Salt*, about six hours N. E. of *Ammân*. He found there a flourishing modern town with few traces of antiquity (*Land of Israel*, pp. 552–555, 2d ed.).   S. W.

RA'MOTH IN GIL'EAD (רָאמֹת בַּגִּלְעָד) [*heights in Gilead*]: ἡ Ῥαμὼθ ἐν Γαλαάδ, Ἀρμὼθ [ἐν τῇ Γ.], Ῥεμμὼθ Γαλαάδ; Alex. Ῥαμμὼθ, Ῥαμωθ: *Ramoth in Galaad*), Deut. iv. 43; Josh. xx. 8, xxi. 38; 1 K. xxii 3.[c] Elsewhere the shorter form, RAMOTH GILEAD, is used.

RAMS' HORNS. [CORNET; JUBILEE.]

RAMS' SKINS DYED RED (עֹרֹת), אֵילִים מְאָדָּמִים, 'oroth elim meoddamim: δέρματα κριῶν ἠρυθροδανωμένα: pelles arietum rubricatae) formed part of the materials that the Israelites were ordered to present as offerings for the making of the Tabernacle (Ex. xxv. 5): of which they served as one of the inner coverings, there being above the rams' skins an outer covering of badgers' skins. [See BADGER.]

There is no doubt that the A. V., following the

---

[a] *Es-Salt* appears to be an Arabic appropriation of the ecclesiastical name *Salton hieraticon* — the sacred forest — which occurs in lists of the episcopal cities on the east of Jordan (Reland, *Pal.* pp. 315, 317). It has now, as is usual in such cases, acquired a new meaning of its own — "the broad Star." (Compare ELEALEH.)

[b] In this connection it is curious that the Jews should derive Jerash (which they write בְּרַשׁ), by

---

contraction, from יַגְרשַׂהֲדוּתָא, *Jegar Sahadutha*, one of the names conferred on Mizpeh (Zunz, as above).

[c] The "in" in this last passage (though not distinguished by *italics*) is a mere interpolation of the translator; the Hebrew words do not contain the preposition, as they do in the three other passages, but are exactly those which elsewhere are rendered "Ramoth-Gilead."

LXX. and Vulgate, and the Jewish interpreters, is correct. The original words, it is true, admit of being rendered thus — "skins of red rams," in which case *méodddmim* agrees with *êlîm* instead of *'ôrôth* (see Ewald, *Gr.* § 570). The red ram is by Ham. Smith (Kitto, *Cycl.* s. v.) identified with the Aoudad sheep (*Ammotragus Tragelaphus*; see a figure in vol. i. p. 411), "whose normal color is red, from bright chestnut to rufous chocolate." It is much more probable, however, that the skins were those of the domestic breed of rams, which, as Rashi says, "were dyed red after they were prepared."   W. H.

* **RANGES.** The rendering of כִּירַיִם in Lev. vi. 35, explained by Keil (*in loc.*) as a pot or pan with its cover (hence the dual); but by Fürst as a cooking furnace, consisting of two ranges of stones so laid as to form an angle. [POT.] It is the rendering also of שְׂדֵרָה in 2 K. xi. 8, 15, and 2 Chr. xxiii. 14. As applied there it refers to the long array of armed soldiers through whose ranks Jehoiada ordered Athaliah the queen to be dragged out of the Temple, and, according to Josephus (*Ant. ix.* 7, § 4) out of the city, so as not to pollute the holy places with blood, before putting her to death. For a graphic picture of the scene, see Stanley's *Lectures on the Jewish Church,* ii. 437 ff. [ATHALIAH.]   H.

* **RANSOM.** [PUNISHMENTS; SAVIOUR; SLAVE.]

RA'PHA (רָפָא [*quiet, silent;* or perh. *high, tall*]: Ῥαφαία; [Vat. Ῥαφαι; Comp. Ῥαφά:] *Rapha*). Son of Binea, among the descendants of Saul and Jonathan (1 Chr. viii. 37). He is called REPHAIAH in 1 Chr. ix. 43.

RA'PHAEL (Ῥαφαήλ = רָפָאֵל, "*the divine healer:*" [*Raphael*]). "One of the seven holy angels which . . . . go in and out before the glory of the Holy One" (Tob. xii. 15). According to another Jewish tradition, Raphael was one of the *four* angels which stood round the throne of God (Michael, Uriel, Gabriel, Raphael). His place is said to have been behind the throne, by the standard of Ephraim (comp. Num. ii. 18), and his name was interpreted as foreshadowing the healing of the schism of Jeroboam, who arose from that tribe (1 K. xi. 26; Buxtorf, *Lex. Rabb.* p. 47). In Tobit he appears as the guide and counsellor of Tobias. By his help Sara was delivered from her plague (vi. 16, 17), and Tobit from his blindness (xi. 7, 8). In the book of Enoch he appears as "the angel of the spirits of men" (xx. 3; comp. Dillmann, *ad loc.*). His symbolic character in the apocryphal narrative is clearly indicated when he describes himself as "Azarias the son of Ananias" (Tob. v. 12), the messenger of the Lord's help, springing from the Lord's mercy. [TOBIT.] The name occurs in 1 Chr. xxvi. 7 as a simple proper name. [REPHAEL.]   B. F. W.

RAPHA'IM ([Rom. omits; Alex.] Ῥαφαιν [Sin. Ῥαφαειν] = רְפָאִים, *Raphaim*). The name of an ancestor of Judith (Jud. viii. 1). In some MSS. this name, with three others, is omitted.   B. F. W.

RA'PHON ([Mai] Ῥαφειόν; [Rom. Sin.] Alex. and Joseph. Ῥαφόν: Pesh. : *Raphon*).

A city of Gilead, under the walls of which Judas Maccabæus defeated Timotheus (1 Macc. v. 37 only). It appears to have stood on the eastern side of an important wady, and at no great distance from Carnaim — probably Ashteroth-Karnaim. It may have been identical with Raphana, which is mentioned by Pliny (*H. N.* v. 16) as one of the cities of the Decapolis, but with no specification of its position. Nor is there anything in the narrative of 1 Macc., of 2 Macc. (xii.), or of Josephus (*Ant.* xii. 8, § 3), to enable us to decide whether the torrent in question is the *Hieromax,* the *Zurka,* or any other.

In Kiepert's map accompanying Wetzstein's *Hauran,* etc. (1860), a place named *Er-Râfe* is marked, on the east of *Wady Hrêr,* one of the branches of the *Wady Mandhur,* and close to the great road leading to *Sanamein,* which last has some claims to be identified with Ashteroth Carnaim. But in our present ignorance of the district this can only be taken as mere conjecture. If *Er-Râfe* be Raphana we should expect to find large ruins.   G.

RA'PHU (רָפוּא [*healed*]: Ῥαφοῦ: *Raphu*). The father of Palti, the spy selected from the tribe of Benjamin (Num. xiii. 9).

RAS'SES, CHILDREN OF (viol Ῥασσίς; [Vat. Sin. Ald. Ῥασσεὶς:] *filii Tharsis*). One of the nations whose country was ravaged by Holofernes in his approach to Judæa (Jud. ii. 23 only). They are named next to Lud (Lydia), and apparently south thereof. The old Latin version reads *Thirus et Rasis,* with which the Peshito was probably in agreement before the present corruption of its text. Wolff (*Das Buch Judith,* 1861, pp. 95, 96) restores the original Chaldee text of the passage as Thars and Rosos, and compares the latter name with Rhosus, a place on the Gulf of Issus, between the *Ras el-Khanzir* (Rhossicus scopulus) and *Iskenderûn,* or Alexandretta. If the above restoration of the original text is correct, the interchange of Meshech and Rosos, as connected with Thar or Thiras (see Gen. x. 2), is very remarkable; since if Meshech be the original of Muscovy, Rosos can hardly be other than that of Russia. [ROSH.]   G.

RATH'UMUS [or RATHU'MUS] (Ῥάθυμος: Alex. [in ver. 16] Ῥαθυος: *Rathimus*). "Rathumus the story writer" of 1 Esdr. ii. 16, 17, 25, 30, is the same as "REHUM the chancellor" of Ezr. iv. 8, 9, 17, 23.

RAVEN (עֹרֵב, *'ôrêb:* κόραξ: *corvus*), the well-known bird of that name which is mentioned in various passages in the Bible. There is no doubt that the Heb. *'ôrêb* is correctly translated, the old versions agreeing on the point, and the etymology, from a root signifying "to be black," favoring this rendering. A raven was sent out by Noah from the ark to see whether the waters were abated (Gen. viii. 7). This bird was not allowed as food by the Mosaic law (Lev. xi. 15): the word *'ôrêb* is doubtless used in a generic sense, and includes other species of the genus *Corvus,* such as the crow (*C. corone*), and the hooded crow (*C. cornix*). Ravens were the means, under the Divine command, of supporting the prophet Elijah at the brook Cherith (1 K. xvii. 4, 6). They are expressly mentioned as instances of God's protecting love and goodness (Job xxxviii. 41; Luke xii. 24; Ps. cxlvii. 9). They are enumerated with the owl, the bittern, etc., as marking the desolation of Edom (Is. xxxiv. 11). "The locks of the beloved" are compared to the glossy blackness of the raven's plumage (Cant. v. 11). The raven's carnivorous habits, and especially his readiness to attack the eye, are alluded to in Prov. xxx. 17.

The LXX. and Vulg. differ materially from the Hebrew and our Authorized Version in Gen. viii. 7, for whereas in the Hebrew we read "that the raven went forth to and fro [from the ark] until the waters were dried up," in the two old versions named above, together with the Syriac, the raven is represented as "not returning until the water was dried from off the earth." On this subject the reader may refer to Houbigant (*Not. Crit.* i. 12), Bochart (*Hieroz.* ii. 801), Rosenmüller (*Schol. in V. T.*), Kalisch (*Genesis*), and Patrick (*Commentary*), who shows the manifest incorrectness of the LXX. in representing the raven as keeping away from the ark while the waters lasted, but as returning to it when they were dried up. The expression "to and fro" clearly proves that the raven must have returned to the ark at intervals. The bird would doubtless have found food in the floating carcasses of the deluge, but would require a more solid resting-ground than they could afford.

The subject of Elijah's sustenance at Cherith by means of ravens has given occasion to much fanciful speculation. It has been attempted to show that the *'örebim* ("ravens") were the people of Orbo, a small town near Cherith; this theory has been well answered by Reland (*Palaest.* ii. 913). Others have found in the ravens merely merchants; while Michaelis has attempted to show that Elijah merely plundered the ravens' nests of hares and other game! Keil (*Comment in K.* xvii.) makes the following just observation: "The text knows nothing of bird-catching and nest-robbing, but acknowledges the Lord and Creator of the creatures, who *commanded* the ravens to provide his servant with bread and flesh." [CHERITH, Amer. ed.]

Jewish and Arabian writers tell strange stories of this bird and its cruelty to its young; hence, say some, the Lord's express care for the young ravens, after they had been driven out of the nests by the parent birds; but this belief in the raven's want of affection to its young is entirely without foundation. To the fact of the raven being a common bird in Palestine, and to its habit of flying restlessly about in constant search for food to satisfy its voracious appetite, may perhaps be traced the reason for its being selected by our Lord and the inspired writers as the especial object of God's providing care. The raven belongs to the order *Insessores,* family *Corvidae.* W. H.

RA'ZIS ([Rom. 'Ραζίς: Alex.] Ραζείς: *Rasias*). "One of the elders of Jerusalem," who killed himself under peculiarly terrible circumstances, that he might not fall "into the hands of the wicked" (2 Macc. xiv. 37–46). In dying he is reported to have expressed his faith in a resurrection (ver. 46) — a belief elsewhere characteristic of the Maccabaean conflict. This act of suicide,

which was wholly alien to the spirit of the Jewish law and people (Ewald, *Alterth.* 198; John vii. 22; comp. Grot. *De Jure Belli,* II. xix. 5), has been the subject of considerable discussion. It was quoted by the Donatists as the single fact in Scripture which supported their fanatical contempt of life (Aug. *Ep.* 104, 6). Augustine denies the fitness of the model, and condemns the deed as that of a man "non eligendæ mortis sapiens, sed ferendæ humilitatis impatiens" (Aug. *l. c.*; comp. *c. Gaud.* i. 36–39). At a later time the favor with which the writer of 2 Macc. views the conduct of Razis — a fact which Augustine vainly denies — was urged rightly by Protestant writers as an argument against the inspiration of the book. Indeed, the whole narrative breathes the spirit of pagan heroism, or of the later zealots (comp. Jos. *B. J.* iii. 7, iv. 1, § 10), and the deaths of Samson and Saul offer no satisfactory parallel (comp. Grimm, *ad loc.*). B. F. W.

RAZOR.[a] Besides other usages, the practise of shaving the head after the completion of a vow must have created among the Jews a necessity for the special trade of a barber (Num. vi. 9, 18, viii. 7; Lev. xiv. 8; Judg. xiii. 5; Is. vii. 20; Ez. v. 1; Acts xviii. 18). The instruments of his work were probably, as in modern times, the razor, the basin, the mirror, and perhaps also the scissors, such as are described by Lucian (*Adv. Indoct.* p. 395, vol. ii. ed. Amst.; see 2 Sam. xiv. 26). The process of oriental shaving, and especially of the head, is minutely described by Chardin (*Voy.* iv. 144). It may be remarked that, like the Levites, the Egyptian priests were accustomed to shave their whole bodies (Her. ii. 36, 37). H. W. P.

REAI'A (רְאָיָה [*whom Jehovah sees*]: *Ρηχά:* *Reia*). A Reubenite, son of Micah, and apparently prince of his tribe (1 Chr. v. 5). The name is identical with

REAI'AH (רְאָיָה [*as above*]: *Ρεδά;* Alex. *Ρεια: Raia*). 1. A descendant of Shobal, the son of Judah (1 Chr. iv. 2).

2. ('Ραιά, [Vat. Ρεηα,] Ezr.; *Ρααιά,* [Vat. FA. Ρααα,] Neh.: *Raaia.*) The children of Reaiah were a family of Nethinim who returned from Babylon with Zerubbabel (Ezr. ii. 47; Neh. vii. 50). The name appears as AIRUS in 1 Esdr. v. 31.

* REAPING. [AGRICULTURE; RUTH, BOOK OF.]

RE'BA (רֶבַע [*four*]: 'Ροβόκ in Num., 'Ροβέ in Josh.: *Rebe*). One of the five kings of the Midianites slain by the children of Israel in their avenging expedition, when Balaam fell (Num. xxxi. 8; Josh. xiii. 21). The different equivalents for the name in the LXX. of Numbers and Joshua seem to indicate that these books were not translated by the same hand.

REBEC'CA ('Ρεβέκκα: *Rebecca*). The Greek form of the name REBEKAH (Rom. ix. 10 only).

REBEK'AH (רִבְקָה, *i. e. Ribkah* [*cord with a noose,* then *ensnarer*]: 'Ρεβέκκα: *Rebecca*), daughter of Bethuel (Gen. xxii. 23) and sister of Laban, married to Isaac, who stood in the relation

---

a 1. מוֹרָה: σίδηρος, ξυρόν: *novacula, ferrum*: from מָרָה, "scrape," or "sweep." Gesenius connects it with the root יָרֵא, "to fear" (*Thes.* p. 819).

2. תַּעַר: ρομφαία: *gladius*.

2. גָּלַב: κουρεύς: *tonsor* (2 Sam. xx. 8). In the Syriac Vers. of 2 Sam. xx. 8, *galabo* is "a razor" (*Ges.* p. 288).

of a first cousin to her father and to Lot. She is first presented to us in the account of the mission of Elieser to Padan-aram (Gen. xxiv.), in which his interview with Rebekah, her consent and marriage, are related. The whole chapter has been pointed out as uniting most of the circumstances of a pattern-marriage. The sanction of parents, the guidance of God, the domestic occupation of Rebekah, her beauty, courteous kindness, willing consent and modesty, and success in retaining her husband's love. For nineteen years she was childless: then, after the prayers of Isaac and her journey to inquire of the Lord, Esau and Jacob were born, and while the younger was more particularly the companion and favorite of his mother (xxv. 19–28) the elder became a grief of mind to her (xxvi. 35). When Isaac was driven by a famine into the lawless country of the Philistines, Rebekah's beauty became, as was apprehended, a source of danger to her husband. But Abimelech was restrained by a sense of justice such as the conduct of his predecessor (xx.) in the case of Sarah would not lead Isaac to expect. It was probably a considerable time afterwards when Rebekah suggested the deceit that was practiced by Jacob on his blind father. She directed and aided him in carrying it out, foresaw the probable consequence of Esau's anger, and prevented it by moving Isaac to send Jacob away to Padan-aram (xxvii.) to her own kindred (xxix. 12). The Targum Pseudojon. states (Gen. xxxv. 8) that the news of her death was brought to Jacob at Allon-bachuth. It has been conjectured that she died during his sojourn in Padan-aram; for her nurse appears to have left Isaac's dwelling and gone back to Padan-aram before that period (compare xxiv. 59 and xxxv. 8), and Rebekah is not mentioned when Jacob returns to his father, nor do we hear of her burial till it is incidentally mentioned by Jacob on his deathbed (xlix. 31).

St. Paul (Rom. ix. 10) refers to her as being made acquainted with the purpose of God regarding her children before they were born.

For comments on the whole history of Rebekah, see Origen, Hom. in Gen. x. and xii.; Chrysostom, Hom. in Genesin, pp. 48–54. Rebekah's inquiry of God, and the answer given to her, are discussed by Deyling, Obser. Sac. i. 12, p. 53 seq., and in an essay by J. A. Schmid in Nov. Thes. Theol.-Philolog. i. 188.　　　W. T. B.

* RECEIPT OF CUSTOM (τελώνιον) denotes not so directly the act as the place of collecting customs. It is mentioned in the accounts of Matthew's call (Matt. ix. 9, Mark ii. 14, and Luke v. 27). Matthew was a tax-collector on the shore of the lake of Galilee, probably near Capernaum. The toll-house may have been a building or a booth merely with a seat and table. [PUBLICAN; TAXES.]　　　H.

RE'CHAB (רֵכָב = horseman, from רָכַב, rācab, "to ride ': 'Ρηχάβ: Rechab). Three persons bearing this name are mentioned in the O. T.

1. [Vat. in 1 Chr. Ρηχα.] The father or ancestor of Jehonadab (2 K. x. 15, 23; 1 Chr. ii. 55; Jer. xxxv. 6–19), identified by some writers, but conjecturally only, with Hobab (Arias Monta-

nus on Judg. i.; Sanctius, quoted by Calmet, Diss. sur les Rechabites). [RECHABITES.]

2. One of the two "captains of bands" (ἡγούμενοι συστρεμμάτων, principes latronum), whose Ish-bosheth took into his service, and who, when his cause was failing, conspired to murder him (2 Sam. iv. 2). Josephus (Ant. vii. 2, § 1) calls him Θάννος. [BAANAH; ISH-BOSHETH, vol. ii. p. 1168.]

3. The father of Malchiah, ruler of part of Beth-haccerem (Neh. iii. 14), named as repairing the Dung Gate in the fortifications of Jerusalem under Nehemiah.　　　E. H. P.

RE'CHABITES (רֵכָבִים [horsemen]: Ἀρχαβείν; [Alex.] Αλχαβειν, [χαραβειν: Comp. 'Ρηχαβείν, 'Ρηχαβείμ:] Rechabitæ). The tribe thus named appears before us in one memorable scene. Their history before and after it lies in some obscurity. We are left to search out and combine some scattered notices, and to get from them what light we can.

(I.) In 1 Chr. ii. 55, the house of Rechab is identified with a section of the Kenites, who came into Canaan with the Israelites and retained their nomadic habits, and the name of Hammath is mentioned as the patriarch of the whole tribe. [KENITES: HEMATH.] It has been inferred from this passage that the descendants of Rechab belonged to a branch of the Kenites settled from the first at Jabez in Judah. [JEHONADAB.] The fact, however, that Jehonadab took an active part in the revolution which placed Jehu on the throne, seems to indicate that he and his tribe belonged to Israel rather than to Judah, and the late date of 1 Chr., taken together with other facts (infra), makes it more probable that this passage refers to the locality occupied by the Rechabites after their return from the Captivity.[a] Of Rechab himself nothing is known. He may have been the father, he may have been the remote ancestor of Jehonadab. The meaning of the word makes it probable enough that it was an epithet passing into a proper name. It may have pointed, as in the robber-chief of 2 Sam. iv. 2, to a conspicuous form of the wild Bedouin life, and Jehonadab, the son of the Rider, may have been, in part at least, for that reason, the companion and friend of the fierce captain of Israel who drives as with the fury of madness (2 K. ix. 20).

Another conjecture as to the meaning of the name is ingenious enough to merit a disinterment from the forgotten learning of the sixteenth century. Boulduc (De Eccles. ante Leg. iii. 10) infers from 2 K. ii. 12, xiii. 14, that the two great prophets Elijah and Elisha were known, each of them in his time, as the chariot (רֶכֶב, Recheb) of Israel, i. e. its strength and protection. He infers from this that the special disciples of the prophets, who followed them in all their austerity, were known as the "sons of the chariot," B'né Receb, and that afterwards, when the original meaning had been lost sight of, this was taken as a patronymic, and referred to an unknown Rechab. At present, of course, the different vowel-points of the two words are sufficiently distinctive; but the strange reading of the LXX. in Judg. i. 19 (ὅτι 'Ρηχὰβ διεστείλατο αὐτοῖς, where the A. V. has

---

[a] In confirmation of this view, it may be noticed that the "shearing-house" of 2 K. x. 14 was probably the known rendezvous of the nomad tribe of the Kenites, with their flocks of sheep. [SHEARING-HOUSE.]

"because they had *chariots* of iron ") shows that one word might easily enough be taken for the other. Apart from the evidence of the name, and the obvious probability of the fact, we have the statement (*valeat quantum*) of John of Jerusalem that Jehonadab was a disciple of Elisha (*De Instit. Monach.* c. 25).

(II.) The personal history of JEHONADAB has been dealt with elsewhere. Here we have to notice the new character which he impressed on the tribe, of which he was the head. As his name, his descent, and the part which he played indicate, he and his people had all along been worshippers of Jehovah, circumcised, and so within the covenant of Abraham, though not reckoned as belonging to Israel, and probably therefore not considering themselves bound by the Mosaic law and ritual. The worship of Baal introduced by Jezebel and Ahab was accordingly not less offensive to them than to the Israelites. The luxury and license of Phoenician cities threatened the destruction of the simplicity of their nomadic life (Amos ii. 7, 8, vi. 3-6). A protest was needed against both evils, and as in the case of Elijah, and of the Nazarites of Amos ii. 11, it took the form of asceticism. There was to be a more rigid adherence than ever to the old Arab life. What had been a traditional habit, was enforced by a solemn command from the sheikh and prophet of the tribe, the destroyer of idolatry, which no one dared to transgress. They were to drink no wine, nor build house, nor sow seed, nor plant vineyard, nor have any. All their days they were to dwell in tents, as remembering that they were strangers in the land (Jer. xxxv. 6, 7). This was to be the condition of their retaining a distinct tribal existence. For two centuries and a half they adhered faithfully to this rule; but we have no record of any part taken by them in the history of the period. We may think of them as presenting the same picture which other tribes, uniting the nomad life with religious austerity, have presented in later periods.

The Nabathæans, of whom Diodorus Siculus speaks (xix. 94) as neither sowing seed, nor planting fruit tree, nor using nor building house, and enforcing these transmitted customs under pain of death, give us one striking instance.[a] Another is found in the prohibition of wine by Mohammed (Sale's *Koran, Prelim. Diss.* § 5). A yet more interesting parallel is found in the rapid growth of the sect of the Wahabys during the last and present centuries. Abd-ul-Wahab, from whom the sect takes its name, reproduces the old type of character in all its completeness. Anxious to protect his countrymen from the revolting vices of the Turks, as Jehonadab had been to protect the Kenites from the like vices of the Phoenicians, the Bedouin reformer felt the necessity of returning to the old austerity of Arab life. What wine had

been to the earlier preacher of righteousness, the outward sign and incentive of a fatal corruption, opium and tobacco were to the later prophet, and, as such, were rigidly proscribed. The rapidity with which the Wahabys became a formidable party, the Puritans of Islam, presents a striking analogy to the strong political influence of Jehonadab in 2 K. x. 15, 23 (com; . Burckhar-t, *Bedouins and Wahabys,* p. 283, &c.).

(III.) The invasion of Judah by Nebuchadnezzar in B. C. 607, drove the Rechabites from their tents. Possibly some of the previous periods of danger may have led to their settling within the limits of the territory of Judah. Some inferences may be safely drawn from the facts of Jer. xxxv. The names of the Rechabites show that they continued to be worshippers of Jehovah. They are already known to the prophet. One of them (ver. 3) bears the same name. Their rigid Nazarite life gained for them admission into the house of the Lord, into one of the chambers assigned to priests and Levites, within its precincts. They were received by the sons or followers of a "man of God," a prophet or devotee of special sanctity (ver. 4). Here they are tempted and are proof against the temptation, and their steadfastness is turned into a reproof for the unfaithfulness of Judah and Jerusalem. [JEREMIAH.] The history of this trial ends with a special blessing, the full import of which has, for the most part, not been adequately apprehended: "Jonadab, the son of Rechab, shall not want a man to stand before me forever" (ver. 19). Whether we look on this as the utterance of a true prophet, or as a *vaticinium ex eventu,* we should hardly expect at this precise point to lose sight altogether of those of whom they were spoken, even if the words pointed only to the perpetuation of the name and tribe. They have however, a higher meaning. The words "to stand before me" (לֹמֶר לְפָנַי) are essentially liturgical. The tribe of Levi is chosen to "stand before" the Lord (Deut. x. 8, xvii. 5, 7). In Gen. xviii. 22; Judg. xx. 28; Ps. cxxxiv. 1; Jer. xv. 19, the liturgical meaning is equally prominent and unmistakable (comp. Gesen. *Thes.* s. v.; Grotius *in loc.*). The fact that this meaning is given ("ministering before me") in the Targum of Jonathan, is evidence (1) as to the received meaning of the phrase; (2) that this rendering did not shock the feelings of studious and devout Rabbis in our Lord's time; (3) that it was at least probable that there existed representatives of the Rechabites connected with the Temple services in the time of Jonathan. This then, was the extent of the new blessing. The Rechabites were solemnly adopted into the families of Israel, and were recognized as incorporated into the tribe of Levi.[b] Their purity, their faithfulness, their con-

---

[a] The fact that the Nabathæans habitually drank "wild honey" (μέλι ἄγριον) mixed with water (Diod. Sic. xix. 94), and that the Bedouins as habitually still make locusts an article of food (Burckhardt, *Bedouins,* p. 270), shows very strongly that the Baptist's life was fashioned after the Rechabite as well as the Nazarite type.

[b] It may be worth while to refer to a few authorities agreeing in the general interpretation here given, though differing as to details. Vatablus (*Crit. Sac.* in loc.) mentions a Jewish tradition (R. Judah, as cited by Kimchi; comp. Scaliger, *Elench. Trihæres. Serrar.*

p. 26) that the daughters of the Rechabites married Levites, and that thus their children came to minister in the Temple. Clarius (*Ibid.*) conjectures that the Rechabites themselves were chosen to sit in the great Council. Sanctius and Calmet suppose them to have ministered in the same way as the Nethinim (Calmet *Diss. sur les Rechab.* in Com. vi. p. xviii. 1726). Serrarius (*Trihæres.*) identifies them with the Essenes; Scaliger (*l. c.*) with the Chasidim, in whose name the priests offered special daily sacrifices, and who, in this way, were "standing before the Lord" continually.

secrated life gained for them, as it gained for other Nazarites, that honor (comp. PRIESTS). In Lam. iv. 7, we may perhaps trace a reference to the Rechabites, who had been the most conspicuous examples of the Nazarite life in the prophet's time, and most the object of his admiration.

(IV.) It remains for us to see whether there are any traces of their after-history in the Biblical or later writers. It is believed that there are such traces, and that they confirm the statements made in the previous paragraph.

(1.) We have the singular heading of the Ps. lxxi. in the LXX. version (τῷ Δαυίδ, υἱῶν Ἰωναδάβ, καὶ τῶν πρώτων αἰχμαλωτισθέντων), evidence, of course, of a corresponding Hebrew title in the 3d century B. C., and indicating that the "sons of Jonadab" shared the captivity of Israel, and took their place among the Levite psalmists who gave expression to the sorrows of the people.[a]

(2.) There is the significant mention of a son of Rechab in Neh. iii. 14, as coöperating with the priests, Levites and princes in the restoration of the wall of Jerusalem.

(3.) The mention of the house of Rechab in 1 Chr. ii. 55, though not without difficulty, points, there can be little doubt, to the same conclusion.

The Rechabites have become scribes (סֹפְרִים, Sôpherim). They give themselves to a calling which, at the time of the return from Babylon, was chiefly if not exclusively in the hands of Levites. The other names (TIRATHITES, SHIMEATHITES, and SUCHATHITES in A. V.) seem to add nothing to our knowledge. The Vulg. rendering, however (evidence of a traditional Jewish interpretation in the time of Jerome) gives a translation based on etymologies, more or less accurate, of the proper names, which strikingly confirms the view now taken. "Cognationes quoque Scribarum habitantium in Jabes, canentes atque resonantes, et in tabernaculis commorantes."[b] Thus interpreted, the passage points to a resumption of the outward form of their old life and its union with their new functions. It deserves notice also that while in 1 Chr. ii. 54, 55, the Rechabites and Netophathites are mentioned in close connection, the "sons of the singers" in Neh. xii. 28 appear as coming in large numbers from the villages of the same Netophathites. The close juxtaposition of the Rechabites with the descendants of David in 1 Chr. iii. 1 shows also in how honorable an esteem they were held at the time when that book was compiled.

(4.) The account of the martyrdom of James the Just, given by Hegesippus (Eus. H. E. ii. 23), brings the name of the Rechabites once more before us, and in a very strange connection. While the Scribes and Pharisees were stoning him, "one of the priests of the sons of Rachab, the son of Rechabim, who are mentioned by Jeremiah the prophet," cried out, protesting against the crime. Dr. Stanley (Sermons and Essays on the Apostolic Age, p. 333), struck with the seeming anomaly of a

priest "not only not of Levitical, but not even of Jewish descent," supposes the name to have been used loosely as indicating the abstemious life of James and other Nazarites, and points to the fact that Epiphanius (Hær. lxxviii. 14) ascribes to Symeon the brother of James the words which Hegesippus puts into the mouth of the Rechabite, as a proof that it denoted merely the Nazarite form of life. Calmet (Diss. sur les Rechab. l. c.) supposes the man to have been one of the Rechabite Nethinim, whom the informant of Hegesippus took, in his ignorance, for a priest. The view which has been here taken presents, it is believed, a more satisfactory solution. It was hardly possible that a writer like Hegesippus, living at a time when the details of the Temple-services were fresh in the memories of men, should have thus spoken of the Rechabim unless there had been a body of men to whom the name was commonly applied. He uses it as a man would do to whom it was familiar, without being struck by any apparent or real anomaly. The Targum of Jonathan on Jer. xxxv. 19 indicates, as has been noticed, the same fact. We may accept Hegesippus therefore as an additional witness to the existence of the Rechabites as a recognized body up to the destruction of Jerusalem, sharing in the ritual of the Temple, partly descended from the old "sons of Jonadab," partly recruited by the incorporation into their ranks of men devoting themselves, as did James and Symeon, to the same consecrated life. The form of austere holiness presented in the life of Jonadab, and the blessing pronounced on his descendants, found their highest representatives in the two Brothers of The Lord.

(5) Some later notices are not without interest. Benjamin of Tudela, in the 12th century (Edit. Asher, 1840, i. 112–114), mentions that near El-Jubar (= Pumbenitha) he found Jews who were named Rechabites. They tilled the ground, kept flocks and herds, abstained from wine and flesh, and gave tithes to teachers who devoted themselves to studying the Law, and weeping for Jerusalem. They were 100,000 in number, and were governed by a prince, Salomon ban-Nasi, who traced his genealogy up to the house of David, and ruled over the city of Thema and Telmas. A later traveller, Dr. Wolff, gives a yet stranger and more detailed report. The Jews of Jerusalem and Yemen told him that he would find the Rechabites of Jer. xxxv. living near Mecca (Journal, 1829, ii. 334). When he came near Senaa he came in contact with a tribe, the Beni-Khabr, who identified themselves with the sons of Jonadab. With one of them, Mousa, Wolff conversed, and reports the dialogue as follows: "I asked him, 'Whose descendants are you?' Mousa answered, 'Come, and I will show you,' and read from an Arabic Bible the words of Jer. xxxv. 5–11. He then went on. 'Come, and you will find us 60,000 in number. You see the words of the Prophet have been fulfilled, Jonadab the son of Rechab shall not want a man to stand before me forever'" (ibid. p. 335). In a later

a Neither Ewald nor Hengstenberg nor De Wette notices this inscription. Ewald, however, refers the Psalm to the time of the Captivity. Hengstenberg, who asserts its Davidic authorship, indicates an alphabetic relation between it and Ps. lxx., which is at least presumptive evidence of a later origin, and points, with some fair probability, to Jeremiah as the writer. (Comp. LAMENTATIONS.) It is noticed, however, by Augustine (Enarr. in Ps. lxx. § 2), and is referred by him to the Rechabites of Jer. xxxv.

b The etymologies on which this version rests are, it must be confessed, somewhat doubtful. Scaliger (Elench. Trihær. Serrar. c. 28) rejects them with scorn. Pellican and Calmet, on the other hand, defend the Vulg. rendering, and Gill (in loc.) does not dispute it. Most modern interpreters follow the A. V. in taking the words as proper names.

journal (*Journ.* 1839, p. 389) he mentions a second interview with Moussa, describes them as keeping strictly to the old rule, calls them now by the name of the B'nê-Arbab, and says that B'nê Israel of the tribe of Dan live with them.[a]   E. H. P.

RE'CHAH (רֵכָה [*hinder part, recess*]: Ῥηχάβ; Alex. Ῥηφα; [Comp. Ῥηχά]: *Recha*). In 1 Chr. iv. 12, Beth-Rapha, Paseah, and Tehinnah the father, or founder, of Ir-nahash, are said to have been the "men of Rechah." In the Targum of R. Joseph the are called "the men of the great Sanhedrin," the Targumist apparently reading רֵכָה.

RECORDER (מַזְכִּיר), an officer of high rank in the Jewish state, exercising the functions, not simply of an annalist, but of chancellor or president of the privy council. The title itself may perhaps have reference to his office as adviser of the king: at all events the notices prove that he was more than an annalist, though the superintendence of the records was without doubt entrusted to him. In David's court the recorder appears among the high officers of his household (2 Sam. viii. 16, xx. 24; 1 Chr. xviii. 15). In Solomon's, he is coupled with the three secretaries, and is mentioned last, probably as being their president (1 K. iv. 3). Under Hezekiah, the recorder, in conjunction with the prefect of the palace and the secretary, represented the king (2 K. xviii. 18, 37): the patronymic of the recorder at this time, Joah the son of Asaph, makes it probable that he was a Levite. Under Josiah, the recorder, the secretary, and the governor of the city were entrusted with the superintendence of the repairs of the Temple (2 Chr. xxxiv. 8). These notices are sufficient to prove the high position held by him.   [TOWN CLERK.]
                                                        W. L. B.

* RED. [COLORS, 3.]

RED-HEIFER. [SIN-OFFERING.]

RED SEA. The sea known to us as the Red Sea was by the Israelites called "the sea," הַיָּם, Ex. xiv. 2, 9, 16, 21, 28: xv. 1, 4, 8, 10, 19; Josh. xxiv. 6, 7; and many other passages); and specially "the sea of sûph" (יַם־סוּף), Ex. x. 19, xiii. 18, xv. 4, 22, xxiii. 31; Num. xiv. 25, xxi. 4, xxxiii. 10, 11; Deut. xi. 4; Josh. ii. 10, iv. 23, xxiv. 6; Judg. xi. 16; 1 K. ix. 26; Neh. ix. 9; Ps. cvi. 7, 9, 22, cxxxvi. 13, 15; Jer. xlix. 21). It is also perhaps written סוּפָה (Ζωόβ, LXX.) in Num. xxi. 14, rendered "Red Sea" in A. V.; and in like manner, in Deut. i. 1, סוּף, without יָם. The LXX. always render it ἡ ἐρυθρὰ θάλασσα

(except in Judg. xi. 16, where סוֹף, Σίφ, is preserved). So too in N. T. (Acts vii. 36; Heb. xi. 29); and this name is found in 1 Macc. iv. 9. By the classical geographers this appellation, like its Latin equivalent *Mare Rubrum* or *M. Erythraeum*, was extended to all the seas washing the shores of the Arabian peninsula, and even the Indian Ocean: the Red Sea itself, or Arabian Gulf, was ὁ Ἀράβιος κόλπος, or Ἀραβικὸς κ., or *Sinus Arabicus*, and its eastern branch, or the Gulf of the 'Akabeh, Αἰλανίτης, Ἐλανίτης, Ἐλανιτικὸς κόλπος, *Sinus Ælanites*, or *S. Ælaniticus*. The Gulf of Suez was specially the Heroöpolite Gulf, Ἡρωοπολίτης κόλπος, *Sinus Heroöpolites*, or *S. Heroöpoliticus*. Among the peoples of the East, the Red Sea has for many centuries lost its old names: it is now called generally by the Arabs, as it was in mediæval times, Bahr El-Kulzum, "the sea of El-Kulzum," after the ancient Clysma, "the sea beach," the site of which is near, or at, the modern Suez.[b] In the Kur-án, part of its old name is preserved, the rare Arabic word *yamm* being used in the account of the passage of the Red Sea (see also foot-note to p. 1012, *infra*, and El-Beydáwee's *Comment.* on *the Kur-án*, vii. 132, p. 341; and xx. 81, p. 602).[c]

Of the *names* of this sea (1.) יָם (Syr. ܝܰܡܳܐ and ܝܰܡܳܐ — the latter generally "a lake:" Hierog. YUMA; Copt. ⲓⲟⲙ; Arabic, يَمّ signifies "the sea," or any sea. It is also applied to the Nile (exactly as the Arabic *bahr* is so applied) in Nah. iii. 8, "Art thou better than populous No, that was situate among the rivers (*yeórim*), [that had] the waters round about it, whose rampart [was] the sea (*yám*), and her wall was from the sea (*yám*)?"[d]

(2.) יַם־סוּף; in the Coptic version, ⲫⲓⲟⲙ ⲛ̄ϣⲁⲣⲓ. The meaning of *sûph*, and the reason of its being applied to the sea, have given rise to much learned controversy. Gesenius renders it *rush, reed, sea-weed*. It is mentioned in the O. T. almost always in connection with the sea of the Exodus. It also occurs in the narrative of the exposure of Moses in the יְאֹר (*yeór*); for he was laid in *sûph*, on the brink of the *yeór* (Ex. ii. 3), where (in the *sûph*) he was found by Pharaoh's daughter (5); and in the "burden of Egypt" (Is. xix.), with the drying up of the waters of Egypt: "And the waters shall fail from the sea (*yám*), and the river (*náhár*) shall be wasted and dried up. And they shall turn the rivers (*náhár*, constr. pl.) far away; [and] the brooks (*yeór*) of defense (or

[a] A paper "On Recent Notices of the Rechabites," by Signor Pierotti, has been read, since the above was in type, at the Cambridge Meeting of the British Association (October, 1862). He met with a tribe calling themselves by that name near the Dead Sea, about two miles S. E. from it. They had a Hebrew Bible, and said their prayers at the tomb of a Jewish Rabbi. They told him precisely the same stories as had been told to Wolff thirty years before.

[b] Or, as some Arab authors say, the sea is so named from the drowning of Pharaoh's host; Kulsum being a derivative of قُلْزُم, with this signification: or, according to others, from its being hemmed in by moun-

tains, from the same root (El-Makreeze's *Khitat*, descr. of the Sea of El-Kulzum).

[c] Its general name is "the Sea of El-Kulzum;" but in different parts it is also called after the nearest coast, as "the sea of the Hijáz," etc. (Yákoot, in the *Moajam*).

[d] *Yamm* signifies a *bahr* of which the bottom is not reached. *Bahr* applies to a "sea" or a "great river."

[e] Gesenius adds Is. xix. 5, quoted below: but it is not easy to see why this should be the Nile (except from preconceived notions), instead of the ancient extension of the Red Sea. He allows the "tongue of the Egyptian sea (*yám*)" in Is. xi. 15, where the river [Nile] is *náhár*.

of Egypt?) shall be emptied and dried up: the reeds and flags (súph) shall wither. The paper reeds[a] by the brooks (yeór), by the mouth of the brooks (yeór), and everything sown by the brooks (yeór), shall wither, be driven away, and be no [more]. The fishers also shall mourn, and all they that cast angle into the brooks (yeór) shall lament, and they that spread nets upon the waters shall languish. Moreover they that work in fine flax, and they that weave net works (white linen?) shall be confounded. And they shall be broken in the purposes thereof, all that makes sluices [and] ponds for fish" (xix. 5–10). Súph only occurs in one place besides those already referred to: in Jon. ii. 5, it is written, "The waters compassed me about, [even] to the soul; the depth closed me round about, the weeds (súph) were wrapped about my head." With this single exception, which shows that this product was also found in the Mediterranean, súph is Egyptian, either in the Red Sea, or in the yeór, and this yeór in Ex. ii. was in the land of Goshen. What yeór signifies here, in Is. xix, and generally, we shall examine presently. But first of súph.

The signification of סוּף, súph, must be gathered from the foregoing passages. In Arabic, the word, with this signification (which commonly is "wool"), is found only in one passage in a rare lexicon (the Mohkam MS.). The author says, "Soof-el-bahr (the soof of the sea) is like the wool of sheep. And the Arabs have a proverb: 'I will come to thee when the sea ceases to wet the soof,'" i. e. never. The סוּף of the יָם, it seems quite certain, is a sea-weed resembling wool. Such sea-weed is thrown up abundantly on the shores of the Red Sea. Fürst says, s. v. סוּף, "Ab Æthiopibus herba quædam supho appellabatur, quæ in profundo maris rubri crescit, quæ rubra est, rubrumque colorem continet, pannis tingendis inservientem, teste Hieronymo de qualitate maris rubri" (p. 47, &c.). Diodorus (iii. ch. 19), Artemidorus (ap. Strabo, p. 770), and Agatharchides (ed. Müller, p. 136–37), speak of the weed of the Arabian Gulf. Ehrenberg (in Winer) enumerates Fucus latifolius on the shores of this sea, and at Suez Fucus crispus, F. trinodis, F. turbinatus, F. papillosus, F. diaphanus, etc., and the specially red weed Trichodesmium erythræum. The Coptic version renders súph by shari (see above), supposed to be the hieroglyphic "SHER" (sea?). If this be the same as the sari of Pliny (see next paragraph), we must conclude that shari, like súph, was both marine and fluvial. The passage in Jonah proves it to be a marine product; and that it was found in the Red Sea, the numerous passages in which that sea is called the sea of súph leave no doubt.

But סוּף may have been also applied to any substance resembling wool, produced by a fluvial rush, such as the papyrus, and hence by a synecdoche to such rush itself. Golius says, s. v.

بَرْدِى, on the authority of Ibn-Maaroof (after explaining بَرْدِى by "papyrus herba"), "Hinc قطن البردى [the cotton of the papyrus] gossipplum papyri, quod lanæ simile ex thyrso colligitur, et permixtum calci efficit tenacissimum cæmenti genus." This is curious; and it may also be observed that the papyrus, which included more than one kind of cyperus, grew in the marshes, and in lands on which about two feet in depth of the waters of the inundation remained (Wilkinson's Ancient Egyptians, iii. 61, 149, citing Pliny, xiii. 11; Strab. xvii. 550); and that this is agreeable to the position of the ancient head of the gulf, with its canals and channels for irrigation (yeórim?) connecting it with the Nile and with Lake Mareotis; and we may suppose that in this and other similar districts, the papyrus was cultivated in the yeórim: the marshes of Egypt are now in the north of the Delta and are salt lands. — As a fluvial rush, súph would be found in marsh-lands as well as streams, and in brackish water as well as in sweet. It is worthy of note that a low marshy place near the ancient head of the gulf is to this day called Ghuweybet el-Boos, "the bed of reeds," and another place near Suez has the same name; traces perhaps of the great fields of reeds, rushes, and papyrus, which flourished here of old. See also PI-HAHIROTH, "the place where sedge grows" (?). Fresnel (Dissertatium sur le schari des Égyptiens et le souf des Hebreux, Journ. Asiat. 4e série, xi. pp. 274, &c.) enumerates some of the reeds found in Egypt. There is no sound reason for identifying any one of these with súph. Fresnel, in this curious paper, endeavors to prove that the Coptic "shari" (in the yam shari) was the Arundo Ægyp iaca of Desfontaines (in modern Arabic boos Fârisee, or Persian cane): but there appear to be no special grounds for selecting this variety for identification with the fluvial shari; and we must entirely dissent from his suggestion that the shari of the Red Sea was the same, and not sea-weed: apart from the evidence which controverts his arguments, they are in themselves quite inconclusive. Sir Gardiner Wilkinson's catalogue of reeds, etc., is fuller than Fresnel's, and he suggests the Cyprus Dives or fastigiatus (Arabic, Dees) to be the sari of Pliny. The latter says, "Fructicosi est genus sari, circa Nilum nascens, duorum fere cubitorum altitudine, pollicari crassitudine, coma papyri, simileque manditur modo" (H. N. xiii. 23; see also Theophr. iv. 9).

The occurrence of súph in the yeór (Ex ii., Isa. xix.) in the land of Goshen (Ex. ii.), brings us to a consideration of the meaning of the latter, which in other respects is closely connected with the subject of this article.

(3.) יְאֹר (Hierog. ATUR, AUR; Copt. ⲉⲓⲉⲣⲟ,

---

of trees. . . . . .; here used of the grassy places on the banks of the Nile:" but this is unsatisfactory. Boothroyd says, "Our translators, after others, supposed this word to signify the papyrus; but without any just authority. Kimchi explains, 'Aroth est nomen appellativum olerum et herbarum virentium.' Hence we may render. 'The marshy [sic] medows [sic] at the mouth of the river,'" etc.

ϫⲁⲣⲟ, ϫⲁⲣⲱ, Memphitic dialect, ⲓⲉⲣⲟ, Sahidic) signifies "a river." It seems to apply to "a great river," or the like, and also to "an arm of the sea;" and perhaps to "a sea" absolutely; like the Arabic *bahr*. Gesenius says it is almost exclusively used of the Nile: but the passages in which it occurs do not necessarily bear out this conclusion. By far the greater number refer to the sojourn in Egypt: these are Gen. xli. 1, 2. 3, 17, 18, Pharaoh's dream; Ex. i. 22, the exposure of the male children; Ex. ii. 3, 5, the exposure of Moses; Ex. vii. 15 ff., and xvii. 5, Moses before Pharaoh and the plague of blood; and Ex. viii. 5, 7, the plague of frogs. The next most important instance is the prophecy of Isaiah, already quoted in full. Then, that of Amos (viii. 8, comp. ix. 5), where the land ·shall rise up wholly as a flood (yeór); and shall be cast out and drowned as [by] the flood (yeór) of Egypt. The great prophecy of Ezekiel against Pharaoh and against all Egypt, where Pharaoh is "the great dragon that lieth in the midst of his rivers (יְאֹרָיו) which hath said, My river (יְאֹרִי) is mine own, and I have made [it] for myself" (xxix. 3), uses the pl. throughout, with the above exception and verse 9, "because he hath said, The river (יְאֹר) [is] mine, and I have made it." It cannot be supposed that Pharaoh would have said of the *Nile* that he had made it, and the passage seems to refer to a great canal. As Ezekiel was contemporary with Pharaoh Necho, may he not here have referred to the reëxcavation of the canal of the Red Sea by that Pharaoh? That canal may have at least received the name of the canal of Pharaoh, just as the same canal when reëxcavated for the last time was "the canal of the Prince of the Faithful," and continued to be so called. *Yeór* occurs elsewhere only in Jer. xlvi. 7, 8, in the prophecy against Necho; in Isa. xxiii. 10, where its application is doubtful; and in Dan. xii. 5, 6, where it is held to be the Euphrates, but may be the great canal of Babylon. The pl. *yeórim*, seems to be often used interchangeably with *yeór* (as in Ez. xxix., and Nah. iii. 8); it is used for "rivers," or "channels of water;" and, while it is not restricted to Egypt, especially of those of the Nile.

From a comparison of all the passages in which it occurs there appears to be no conclusive reason for supposing that *yeór* applies generally, if ever, to the Nile. In the passages relating to the exposure of Moses it appears to apply to the ancient extension of the Red Sea towards Tanis (ZOAN, Avaris), or to the ancient canal (see below) through which the water of the Nile passed to the "tongue of the Egyptian Sea." The water was potable (Ex. vii. 18), but so is that of the Lake of the Feiyoom to its own fishermen, though generally very brackish: and the canal must have received water from the Nile during every inundation, and then must have been sweet. During the height of the inundation, ·the sweet water would flow into the Red Sea. The passage of the canal was regulated by sluices, which

excluded the waters of the Red Sea and sweetened by the water of the canal the salt lakes. Strabo (xvii. 1, § 25) says that they were thus rendered sweet, and in his time contained good fish and abounded with water fowl: the position of these lakes is more conveniently discussed in another part of this article, on the ancient geography of the head of the gulf. It must not be forgotten that the Pharaoh of Moses was of a dynasty residing at Tanis, and that the extension of the Red Sea, "the tongue of the Egyptian Sea," stretched in ancient times into the borders of the land of Goshen, about 50 miles north of its present head, and half-way towards Tanis. There is abundant proof of the former cultivation of this country, which must have been effected by the canal from the Nile just mentioned, and by numerous canals and channels for irrigation, the *yeórim*, so often mentioned with the *yeór*. There appears to be no difficulty in Isa. xix. 6 (comp. xi. 15), for, if the Red Sea became closed at Suez or thereabout, the *súph* left on the beaches of the *yeór* must have dried up and rotted. The ancient beaches in the tract here spoken of, which demonstrate successive elevations, are well known.[a]

(4.) Ἡ ἐρυθρὰ θάλασσα. The origin of this appellation has been the source of more speculation even than the obscure *súph*; for it lies more within the range of general scholarship. The theories advanced to account for it have been often puerile, and generally unworthy of acceptance. Their authors may be divided into two schools. The first have ascribed it to some natural phenomenon; such as the singularly red appearance of the mountains of the western coast, looking as if they were sprinkled with Havannah or Brazil snuff, or brickdust (Bruce), or of which the redness was reflected in the waters of the sea (Gosselin, ii. 78–84); the red color of the water sometimes caused by the presence of zoöphytes (Salt; Ehrenberg); the red coral of the sea; the red sea-weed; and the red storks that have been seen in great numbers, etc. Reland (*De Mare Rubro*, *Diss. Miscell.* i. 59–117) argues that the epithet red was applied to this and the neighboring seas on account of their tropical heat; as indeed was said by Artemidorus (*ap.* Strabo, xvi. 4, 20), that the sea was called red because of the reflection of the sun. The second have endeavored to find an etymological derivation. Of these the earliest (European) writers proposed a derivation from Edom, "red," by the Greeks translated literally. Among them were N. Fuller (*Miscell. Sacr.* iv. c. 20); before him, Scaliger, in his notes to *Festus*; voce *Ægyptinos*, ed. 1574; and still earlier Genebrard, *Comment. ad Ps.* 106; Bochart (*Phaleg*, iv. c. 34) adopted this theory (see Reland, *Diss. Miscell.* i. 85, ed. 1706). The Greeks and Romans tell us that the sea received its name from a great king, Erythras, who reigned in the adjacent country (Strab. xvi. 4, § 20; Pliny, *H. N.* vi. cap. 23, § 28; Agatharch. i. § 5; Philostr. iii. 15, and others):[b] the stories that have come down to us appear to be distortions of the tra-

---

[a] The Mohammedan account of the exposure of Moses is curious. Moses, we read, was laid in the *yamm* (which is explained to be the Nile, though that river is not elsewhere so called), and the ark was carried by the current along a canal or small river (*nahr*) to a lake, at the further end of which was Pharaoh's pavilion (El-Beydáwee's *Comment. on the Kur-án*, xx. 39, p. 595, and Ez-Zamakhsheree's *Comment.*, entitled the *Keshsháf*). While we place no dependance on Mo-

hammedan relations of Biblical events, there may be here a glimmer of truth.

[b] Reland (*Diss. Miscell.* i. 87, &c.) is pleasantly severe on the story of king Erythras; but, with all his rare learning, he was ignorant of Arab history, which is here of the utmost value, and of the various proofs of a connection between this Erythras and Himyar, and the Phœnicians in language, race, and religion. Besides, Reland had a theory of his own to support.

dition that Himyer was the name of apparently the chief family of Arabia Felix, the great South-Arabian kingdom, whence the Himyerites, and Homerites. Himyer appears to be derived from the Arabic "ahmar," red (Himyer was so called because of the red color of his clothing, *En-Nuweyree in Caussin*, i. 54): "aafar" also signifies "red," and is the root of the names of several places in the peninsula so called on account of their redness (see *Murásid*, 263, &c.); this may point to Ophir: φοῖνιξ is red, and the Phœnicians came from the Erythræan Sea (Herod. vii. 89). We can scarcely doubt, on these etymological grounds,[a] the connection between the Phœnicians and the Himyerites, or that in this is the true origin of the appellation of the Red Sea. But when the ethnological side of the question is considered, the evidence is much strengthened. The South-Arabian kingdom was a Joktanite (or Shemite) nation mixed with a Cushite. This admixture of races produced two results (as in the somewhat similar cases of Egypt, Assyria, etc.): a genius for massive architecture, and rare seafaring ability. The Southern-Arabians carried on all the commerce of Egypt, Palestine, and Arabia, with India, until shortly before our own era. It is unnecessary to insist on this Phœnician characteristic, nor on that which made Solomon call for the assistance of Hiram to build the Temple of Jerusalem. The Philistine, and early Cretan and Carian, colonists may have been connected with the South-Arabian race. If the Assyrian school would trace the Phœnicians to a Chaldæan or an Assyrian origin, it might be replied that the Cushites, whence came Nimrod, passed along the south coast of Arabia, and that Berosus (in Cory, 2d ed. p. 60) tells of an early Arab domination of Chaldæa before the Assyrian dynasty, a story also preserved by the Arabian historians (El-Mes'oodee, *Golden Meadows*, MS.). The Red Sea, therefore, was most probably the Sea of the Red men. It adds a link to the curious chain of emigration of the Phœnicians from the Yemen to Syria, Tyre, and Sidon, the shores and islands of the Mediterranean, especially the African coasts of that sea, and to Spain and the far-distant northerly ports of their commerce; as distant, and across oceans as terrible, as those reached by their Himyerite brethren in the Indian and Chinese Seas.

Ancient Limits. — The most important change in the Red Sea has been the drying up of its northern extremity, "the tongue of the Egyptian Sea." The land about the head of the gulf has risen, and that near the Mediterranean become depressed. The head of the gulf has consequently retired gradually since the Christian era. Thus the prophecy of Isaiah has been fulfilled: "And the Lord shall utterly destroy the tongue of the Egyptian sea " (xi. 15); "the waters shall fail from the sea " (xix. 5): the tongue of the Red Sea has dried up for a distance of at least 50 miles from its ancient head, and a cultivated and well-peopled province has been changed into a desolate wilderness. An ancient canal conveyed the waters of the Nile to the Red Sea, flowing through the *Wádi-t-Tumeylát* and irrigating with its system of water-channels a large extent of country; it also provided a means for conveying all the commerce of the Red Sea, once so important, by water to the Nile, avoiding the risks of the desert journey, and securing water-carriage from the Red Sea to the Mediterranean. The drying up of the head of the gulf appears to have been one of the chief causes of the neglect and ruin of this canal.

The country, for the distance above indicated, is now a desert of gravelly sand, with wide patches about the old sea-bottom, of rank marsh land, now called the "Bitter Lakes" (not those of Strabo). At the northern extremity of this salt waste is a small lake sometimes called the Lake of Heroöpolis (the city after which the Gulf of Suez was called the Heroöpolite Gulf): the lake is now *Birket et-Timsáh*, "the lake of the Crocodile," and is supposed to mark the ancient head of the gulf. The canal that connected this with the Nile was of Pharaonic origin.[b] It was anciently known as the "Fossa Regum," and the "canal of Hero." Pliny, Diodorus, and Strabo, state that (up to their time) it reached only to the bitter springs (which appear to be not the present bitter lakes, but lakes west of Heroöpolis), the extension being abandoned on account of the supposed greater height of the waters of the Red Sea. According to Herod. (ii. cap. 158) it left the Nile (the Tanitic branch, now the canal of *El-Mo'izz*) at Bubastis (Pi-beseth), and a canal exists at this day in this neighborhood, which appears to be the ancient channel. The canal was four days' voyage in length, and sufficiently broad for two *triremes* to row abreast (Herod. ii. 158 or 100 cubits, Strab. xvii. 1, § 26; and 100 feet, Pliny, vi. cap. 29, § 33). The time at which the canal was extended, after the drying up of the head of the gulf, to the present head is uncertain, but it must have been late, and probably since the Mohammedan conquest. Traces of the ancient channel throughout its entire length to the vicinity of Bubastis, exist at intervals in the present day (*Descr. de l'Égypte*, E. M. xi. 37–381, and v. 135–158, 8vo ed.). The *Amnis Trajanus* (Τραϊανὸς ποτ. pt. iv. 5, § 54), now the canal of Cairo, was probably of Pharaonic origin; it was at any rate repaired by the emperor Adrian; and it joined the ancient canal of the Red Sea between Bubastis and Heroöpolis. At the Arab conquest of Egypt, this was found to be closed, and was reopened by 'Amr by command of 'Omar, after whom it was called the "canal of the Prince of the Faithful." Country-boats sailed down it (and passed into the Red Sea to Yembo' — see " Shems ed-Deen " in *Descr. de l'Égypte*, 8vo ed. xi. 359), and the water of the Nile ran into the sea at *El-Kulzum*; but the former commerce of Egypt was not in any degree restored; the canal was opened with the intention of securing supplies of grain from Egypt in case of famine in Arabia; a feeble intercourse with the newly-important holy cities of Arabia, to provide for the wants of the pilgrims, was its principal use.

---

a If we concede the derivation, it cannot be held that the Greeks mistranslated the name of Himyer. (See Reland. *Diss. Miscell.* i. 101.) It is worthy of mention that the Arabs often call themselves "the red men," as distinguished from the black or negro, and the yellow or Turanian, races; though they call themselves "the black," as distinguished from the more northern races, whom they term "the red;" as this epithet is used by them, when thus applied, as meaning both "red" and "white."

b Commenced by Sesóstris (Aristot. *Meteor.* i. 14; Strab. i. and xvii.; Plin. *Hist. Nat.* vi. 29 ; Herod. ii. 158 ; Diod. i. 33) or by Necho II., most probably the former; continued by Darius Hystaspis, and by Ptol. Philadelphus. See *Encyc. Brit.* art "Egypt."

In A. H. 105, El-Mansoor ordered it to be filled up (the *Khitat*, Descr. of the Canals), in order to cut off supplies to the Shiya'ee heretics in *El-Medee-neh*. Now it does not flow many miles beyond Cairo, but its channel is easily traceable.

The land north of the ancient head of the gulf is a plain of heavy sand, merging into marsh-land near the Mediterranean coast, and extending to Palestine. We learn from El-Makreezee that a tradition existed of this plain having been formerly well cultivated with saffron, safflower, and sugar-cane, and peopled throughout, from the frontier-town of *El-'Areesh* to *El-'Abbáseh* in *Wádi-t-Tumeylát* (see EXODUS, THE, *Map*; The *Khitat*, s. v. *Jifár*; comp. *Marásid*, ib.). Doubtless the dry-ing up of the gulf with its canal in the south, and the depression of the land in the north, have con-verted this once (if we may believe the tradition, though we cannot extend this fertility as far as El-'Areesh) notoriously fertile tract into a proverbially sandy and parched desert. This region, including *Wádi-t-Tumeylát*, was probably the frontier land occupied in part by the Israelites, and open to the incursions of the wild tribes of the Arabian desert; and the *yeór*, as we have given good reason for be lieving, in this application, was apparently the an-cient head of the gulf or the canal of the Red Sea, with its *yeórim* or water-channels, on which Goshen and much of the plain north of it depended for their fertility.

Physical Description.—In extreme length, the Red Sea stretches from the *Straits of Báb el-Mendeb* (or rather *Rás Báb el-Mendeb*) in lat. 12° 40′ N., to the modern head of the Gulf of Suez, lat. 30′ N. Its greatest width may be stated roughly at about 200 geographical miles; this is about lat. 16° 30′, but the navigable channel is here really narrower than in some other portions, groups of islands and rocks stretching out into the sea, between 30 and 40 miles from the Arabian coast, and 50 miles from the African coast. From shore to shore, its narrowest part is at *Rás Benás* lat. 24°, on the African coast, to *Rás Bereedee* opposite, a little north of *Yembo'*, the port of *El-Medeeneh* and thence northwards to *Rás Mo-hammad* (i. e. exclusive of the Gulfs of Suez and the 'Akabeh), the sea maintains about the same average width of 100 geographical miles. South-wards from *Rás Benás*, it opens out in a broad reach; contracts again to nearly the above narrow-ness at *Jeddah* (correctly *Juddah*), lat. 21° 30′, the port of *Mekkeh*; and opens to its extreme width south of the last-named port.

At *Rás Mohammed*, the Red Sea is split by the gigantic peninsula of Sinai into two gulfs: the westernmost, or Gulf of Suez, is now about 130 geographical miles in length, with an average width of about 18, though it contracts to less than 10 miles: the easternmost, or Gulf of *El-'Akabeh*, is only about 90 miles long, from the Straits of *Tirán*, to the 'Akabeh [ELATH], and of propor-tionate narrowness. The navigation of the Red Sea and Gulf of Suez, near the shores, is very difficult from the abundance of shoals, coral reefs, rocks, and small islands which render the channel intricate, and cause strong currents, often of un-known force and direction; but in mid-channel, exclusive of the Gulf of Suez, there is generally a width of 100 miles clear, except the Dædalus reef (Wellsted, ii. 300). — The bottom in deep sound-ings is in most places sand and stones, from Suez as far as *Juddah*; and thence to the Straits it is

commonly mud. The deepest sounding in the excellent Admiralty chart is 1054 fathoms, in lat. 22° 30′.

Journeying southwards from Suez, on our left is the peninsula of Sinai [SINAI]: on the right, is the desert coast of Egypt, of limestone formation like the greater part of the Nile valley in Egypt, the cliffs on the sea-margin stretching landwards in a great rocky plateau, while more inland a chain of volcanic mountains (beginning about lat. 28° 4′ and running south) rear their lofty peaks at in-tervals above the limestone, generally about 15 miles distant. Of the most important is *Gebel Ghárib*, 6,000 feet high; and as the Straits of Jubal are passed, the peaks of the primitive range attain a height of about 4,500 to 6,900 ft., until the " Elba " group rises in a huge mass about lat. 22°. Further inland is the *Gebel-ed-Dukhkhán*, the " porphyry mountain " of Ptolemy (iv. 5, § 27; M. Claudianus, see Müller, *Geogr. Min.* Atlas vii.), 6,000 ft. high, about 27 miles from the coast, where the porphyry quarries formerly supplied Rome, and where are some remains of the time of Trajan (Wilkinson's *Modern Egypt and Thebes*, ii. 383); and besides these, along this desert south-wards are " quarries of various granites, serpen-tines, Breccia Verde, slates, and micaceous, talcose, and other schists " (*id.* 382). *Gebel-ez-Zeyt*, " the mountain of oil," close to the sea, abounds in pe-troleum (*id.* 385). This coast is especially inter-esting in a Biblical point of view, for here were some of the earliest monasteries of the Eastern Church, and in those secluded and barren moun-tains lived very early Christian hermits. The convent of St. Anthony (of the Thebais), " Deyr Már Antooniyoos," and that of St. Paul, " Deyr Már Búlus," are of great renown, and were once important. They are now, like all Eastern monas-teries, decayed; but that of St. Anthony gives, from its monks, the Patriarch of the Coptic church, formerly chosen from the Nitrian monas-teries (*id.* 381). — South of the " Elba " chain, the country gradually sinks to a plain, until it rises to the highland of *Geedán*, lat. 15°, and thence to the straits extend a chain of low mountains. The greater part of the African coast of the Red Sea is sterile, sandy, and thinly peopled; first beyond Suez by Bedawees chiefly of the Ma'azee tribe. South of the Kuseyr road, are the 'Abáb'deh; and beyond, the Bishárees, the southern branch of which are called by Arab writers " Bejá," whose cus-toms, language, and ethnology, demand a careful investigation, which would undoubtedly be repaid by curious results (see El-Makreezee's *Khitat*, *Descr. of the Bejá*, and *Descr. of the Desert of Eydháb*; Quatremère's *Essays* on these subjects, in his *Mémoires Hist. et Géogr. sur l'Égypte*, ii. pp. 134, 162; and *The Genesis of the Earth and of Man*, 2d ed. p. 109); and then, coast-tribes of Abyssinia.

The Gulf of *El-'Akabeh* (i. e. " of the Moun-tain-road ") is the termination of the long valley of the Ghór or '*Arabah* that runs northwards to the Dead Sea. It is itself a narrow valley; the sides are lofty and precipitous mountains, of en-tire barrenness; the bottom is a river-like sea, running nearly straight for its whole length of about 90 miles. The northerly winds rush down this gorge with uncommon fury, and render its navigation extremely perilous, causing at the same time strong counter-currents; while most of the few anchorages are open to the southerly gake. It "has the appearance of a narrow, deep ravine, extending nearly a hundred miles in a straight direction, and the circumjacent hills rise in some places two thousand feet perpendicularly from the shore" (Wellsted, ii. 108). The western shore is the peninsula of SINAI. The Arabian chain of mountains, the continuation of the southern spurs of the Lebanon, skirt the eastern coast, and rise to about 3,500 ft., while *Gebel Teybet-'Alee* near the Straits is 6,000 ft. There is no pasturage, and little fertility, except near the '*Akabeh*, where are date-groves and other plantations, etc. In earlier days, this last-named place was (it is said) famous for its fertility. The Island of Grain, *Jezeeret Fara'oon*, once fortified and held by the Crusaders, is near its northern extremity, on the Sinaitic side. The sea, from its dangers, and sterile shores, is entirely destitute of boats.

The Arabian coast outside the Gulf of the '*Akabeh* is skirted by the range of Arabian mountains, which in some few places approach the sea, but generally leave a belt of coast country, called *Tihámeh*, or the Ghór, like the Sheelah of Palestine. This tract is generally a sandy, parched plain, thinly inhabited; these characteristics being especially strong in the north. (Niebuhr, *Descr.* 305; Wellsted.) The mountains of the Hejáz consist of ridges running parallel towards the interior, and increasing in height as they recede (Wellsted, ii. 242). Burckhardt remarks that the descent on the eastern side of these mountains, like the Lebanon and the whole Syrian range east of the Dead Sea, is much less than that on the western; and that the peaks, seen from the east or sand side, appear mere hills (*Arabia*, p. 321 *seq.*). In clear weather they are visible at a distance of 40 to 70 miles (Wellsted, ii. 242). The distant ranges have a rugged, pointed outline, and are granitic; at *Wejh*, with horizontal veins of quartz; nearer the sea many of the hills are fossiliferous limestone, while the beach hills "consist of light-colored sandstone, fronted by and containing large quantities of shells and masses of coral" (Wellsted, ii. 243). Coral also "enters largely into the composition of some of the most elevated hills." The more remarkable mountains are *Jabel 'Eyn-Unná* (or "Eynuwunná," *Marásid, s. v.* "Eyn," "Oyyn" of Ptol.), 6,090 ft. high near the Straits; a little further south, and close to *Mo'eyleh*, are mountains rising from 6,330 to 7,700 ft., of which Wellsted says, "The coast . . . is low, gradually ascending with a moderate elevation to the distance of six or seven miles, when it rises abruptly to hills of great height, those near *Mowilahh* terminating in sharp and singularly-shaped peaks . . . Mr. Irwin [1777] . . . has styled them Bullock's Horns. To me the whole group seemed to bear a great resemblance to representations which I have seen of enormous icebergs" (ii. 176; see also the Admiralty Chart, and Müller's *Geogr. Min.*). A little north of *Yembo'* is a remarkable group, the pyramidal mountains of Agatharchides; and beyond, about 25 miles distant, rises *J. Radwá*. Further south, *J. Subh* is remarkable for its magnitude and elevation, which is greater than any other between *Yembo'* and *Jiddah*; and still further, but about 80 miles distant from the coast, *J. Rás-el-Kurà* rises behind the Holy city, Mekkeh. It is of this mountain that Burckhardt writes so enthusiastically — how rarely is he enthusiastic — contrasting its verdure and cool breezes with the sandy waste of *Tihá-*

meh (*Arabia*, p. 65 *seqq.*). The chain continues the whole length of the sea, terminating in the highlands of the Yemen. The Arabian mountains are generally fertile, agreeably different from the parched plains below, and their own bare granite peaks above. The highlands and mountain summits of the Yemen. "Arabia the Happy," the Jebel as distinguished from the plain, are precipitous, lofty, and fertile (Niebuhr, *Descr.* 161); with many towns and villages in their valleys and on their sides. — The coast-line itself, or *Tihámeh*, "north of *Yembo*', is of moderate elevation, varying from 50 to 100 feet, with no beach. To the southward [to *Juddah*] it is more sandy and less elevated; the inlets and harbors of the former tract may be styled coves; in the latter they are lagoons" (Wellsted, ii. 244). — The coral of the Red Sea is remarkably abundant, and beautifully colored and variegated. It is often red, but the more common kind is white; and of hewn blocks of this many of the Arabian towns are built.

The earliest navigation of the Red Sea (passing by the pre-historical Phoenicians) is mentioned by Herodotus. "Sesostris (Rameses II.) was the first who, passing the Arabian Gulf in a fleet of long vessels, reduced under his authority the inhabitants of the coast bordering the Erythræan Sea; proceeding still further, he came to a sea which, from the great number of its shoals, was not navigable;" and after another war against Ethiopia he set up a stela on the promontory of Dira, near the straits of the Arabian Gulf. Three centuries later Solomon's navy was built "in Ezion-geber which is beside Eloth, on the shore of the Red Sea (*Yam Súph*), in the land of Edom" (1 K. ix. 26). In the description of the Gulf of *El-'Akabeh*, it will be seen that this narrow sea is almost without any safe anchorage, except at the island of Grain near the '*Akabeh*, and about 50 miles southward, the harbor of *Edh-Dhahab*. It is possible that the sea has retired here as at Suez, and that Ezion-geber is now dry land. [See EZION-GEBER; ELATH.] Solomon's navy was evidently constructed by Phoenician workmen of Hiram, for he "sent in the navy his servants, shipmen that had knowledge of the sea, with the servants of Solomon." This was the navy that sailed to Ophir. We may conclude that it was necessary to transport wood as well as men to build and man these ships on the shores of the Gulf of the '*Akabeh*, which from their natural formation cannot be supposed to have much altered, and which were besides part of the wilderness of the wandering; and the Edomites were pastoral Arabs, unlike the seafaring Himyerites. Jehoshaphat also "made ships of Tarshish to go to Ophir for gold; but they went not, for the ships were broken at Ezion-geber" (1 K. xxii. 48). The scene of this wreck has been supposed to be *Edh-Dhahab*, where is a reef of rocks like a "giant's backbone " (= Ezion-geber) (Wellsted, ii. 153), and this may strengthen an identification with that place. These ships of Jehoshaphat were manned by "his servants," who from their ignorance of the sea may have caused the wreck. Pharaoh-Necho constructed a number of ships in the Arabian gulf, and the remains of his works existed in the time of Herodotus (ii. 159), who also tells us that these ships were manned by Phoenician sailors.

The fashion of the ancient ships of the Red Sea,

or of the Phœnician ships of Solomon, is unknown. From Pliny we learn that the ships were of papyrus and like the boats of the Nile; and this statement was no doubt in some measure correct. But the coasting craft must have been very different from those employed in the Indian trade. More precise and curious is El-Makreezee's description, written in the first half of the 15th century, of the ships that sailed from *Eydháb* on the Egyptian coast to *Juddah*. "Their 'jelebehs' (P. Lobo, *ap.* Quatremère *Mémoires*, ii. 164, calls them 'gelves'), which carry the pilgrims on the coast, have not a nail used in them, but their planks are sewed together with fibre, which is taken from the cocoanut-tree, and they caulk them with the fibres of the wood of the date-palm; then they 'pay' them with butter, or the oil of the palma Christi, or with the fat of the kirsh (squalus carcharias; Forskål, *Descr. Animalium*, p. viii. No. 19) . . . The sails of these jelebehs are of mats made of the dôm-palm" (the *Khitat*, "Desert of Eydháb"). One of the sea-going ships of the Arabs is shown

in the view of *El-Basrah*, from a sketch by Colonel Chesney, (from Lane's '1001 Nights'). The crews of the latter, when not exceptionally Phœnicians, as were Solomon's and Pharaoh Necho's, were without doubt generally Arabians, rather than Egyptians—those Himyerite Arabs whose ships carried all the wealth of the East either to the Red Sea or the Persian Gulf. The people of 'Omán, the southeast province of Arabia, were among the foremost of these navigators (El-Mes'oodee's *Golden Meadows*, MS., and *The Accounts of Two Mohammedan Travellers of the Ninth Century*). It was customary, to avoid probably the dangers and delays of the narrow seas, for the ships engaged in the Indian trade to transship their cargoes at the straits of *Báb el-Mendeb* to Egyptian and other vessels of the Red Sea (Agath. § 103, p. 190; *anon. Peripl.* § 26, p. 277, ed. Müller). The fleets appear to have sailed about the autumnal equinox, and returned in December or the middle of January (Pliny, *H. N.* vi. cap. xxiii. § 26; comp. *Peripl.* passim). St.

El-Basrah. From a Drawing by Colonel Chesney.

Jerome says that the navigation was extremely tedious. At the present day the voyages are periodical, and guided by the seasons; but the old skill of the seamen has nearly departed, and they are extremely timid, and rarely venture far from the coast.

The Red Sea, as it possessed for many centuries the most important sea-trade of the East, contained ports of celebrity. Of these, Elath and Ezion-geber alone appear to be mentioned in the Bible. The Heroöpolite Gulf is of the chief interest: it was near to Goshen; it was the scene of the passage of the Red Sea; and it was the "tongue of the Egyptian Sea." It was also the seat of the Egyptian trade in this sea and to the Indian Ocean. Heroopolis is doubtless the same as Hero, and its site has been probably identified with the modern *Aboo-Kesheyd*, at the head of the old gulf. By the consent of the classics, it stood on or near the head of the gulf, and was 68 miles (according to the *Itinerary* of Antoninus) from Clysma, by the Arabs called *El-Kulzum*, near the modern Suez, which is close to the *present* head. Suez is a poor town,

and has only an unsafe anchorage, with very shoal water. On the shore of the Heroöpolite gulf was also Arsinoë, founded by Ptolemy Philadelphus: its site has not been settled. Berenice, founded by the same, on the southern frontier of Egypt, rose to importance under the Ptolemies and the Romans; it is now of no note. On the western coast was also the anchorage of Myos Hormos, a little north of the modern town *El-Kuseyr*, which now forms the point of communication with the old route to Coptos. On the Arabian coast the principal ports are *Mu'eyleh, Yembo'* (the port of *El-Medeeneh*), *Juddah* (the port of *Mekkeh*), and *Mukhá*, by us commonly written *Mocha*. The Red Sea in most parts affords anchorage for country-vessels well acquainted with its intricacies, and able to creep along the coast among the reefs and islands that girt the shore. Numerous creeks on the Arabian shore (called "shuroom," sing. "sharm,") indent the land. Of these the anchorage called *Esh-Sharm*, at the southern extremity of the peninsula of Sinai, is much frequented.

The commerce of the Red Sea was, in very an-ent times, unquestionably great. The earliest records tell of the ships of the Egyptians, the Phœnicians, and the Arabs. Although the ports of the Persian gulf received a part of the Indian traffic [DEDAN], and the Himyerite maritime cities in the south of Arabia supplied the kingdom of SHEBA, the trade with Egypt was, we must believe, the most important of the ancient world. That all this traffic found its way to the head of the Heroöpolite gulf seems proved by the absence of any important Pharaonic remains further south on the Egyptian coast. But the shoaling of the head of the gulf rendered the navigation, always dangerous, more difficult; it destroyed the former anchorages, and made it necessary to carry merchandise across the desert to the Nile. This change appears to have been one of the main causes of the decay of the commerce of Egypt. We have seen that the long-voyaging ships shifted their cargoes to Red Sea craft at the Straits; and Ptolemy Philadelphus, after founding Arsinoë and endeavoring to re-open the old canal of the Red Sea, abandoned the upper route and established the southern road from his new city Berenice on the frontier of Egypt and Nubia to Coptos on the Nile. Strabo tells us that this was done to avoid the dangers encountered in navigating the sea (xvii. 1, § 45). Though the stream of commerce was diverted, sufficient seems to have remained to keep in existence the former ports, though they have long since utterly disappeared. Under the Ptolemies and the Romans the commerce of the Red Sea varied greatly, influenced by the decaying state of Egypt and the route to Palmyra (until the fall of the latter). But even its best state at this time cannot have been such as to make us believe that the 120 ships sailing from Myos Hormos, mentioned by Strabo (ii. 5, § 12), was other than an annual convoy. The wars of Heraclius and Khosroes affected the trade of Egypt as they influenced that of the Persian gulf. Egypt had fallen low at the time of the Arab occupation, and yet it is curious to note that Alexandria even then retained the shadow of its former glory. Since the time of Mohammed the Red Sea trade has been insignificant.   E. S. P.

* *Recent explorations.* In 1857 Th. v. Heuglin made a scientific exploration of the Red Sea, the results of which were published in Petermann's *Mittheilungen* for 1860. These researches cover the physical features of the sea and its coast, the Fauna and Flora, the meteorological and hypsometrical phenomena, etc., all which are given with much minuteness of detail. Valuable contributions to the same purport, from Th. Kinzelbach and Dr. Steudner, appear in the same geographical journal for 1864. The *Mittheilungen* for September 1860 contains the journal of Th. v. Heuglin's travels along the western coast of the Sea, from Cairo to *Qosseïr*, from *Qosseïr* to *Sawakin*, from *Sawakin* to *Massawa*, thence along the *Samher* coast and in the adjacent Archipelago of *Dahlak*, and thence down the *Danakil* coast to *Bab-el-Mandeb*. This journal is accompanied with an excellent map, the most minute and accurate yet published, of the Red Sea and the principal harbors on its western side. These are *Qosseïr* in lat. 26° 7′ N. *Sawakin*, lat. 19° 8′, and *Massawa*, lat. 15° 33′. *Qosseïr* was much used by the ancient Egyptians in their commerce with Arabia, serving as a port to the Theban capital, as Suez now answers to Cairo. Mention is made of this route of traffic in ancient monuments and papyri. (See in Chabas, *Voyage*

169

d'un Égyptien, p. 62.) *Qosseïr* is to-day a city of 3,000 inhabitants, cleanly and well built, with a good mole and harbor. It is a port of entry, and sometimes maintains a lively traffic with pilgrims on their way to and from Mecca. Fishing and handicrafts are its principal support. The pearl-fisheries of the Red Sea are less profitable than in former times. *Sawakin*, the capital of a province of the same name, is a city of 8,000 inhabitants, with a small but well-sheltered harbor. *Massawa*, situated on an island in the Gulf of *Harkiko*, is an important avenue of trade for Abyssinia. Its climate is hot, and the inhabitants sometimes suffer for want of water — their supply being collected in cisterns, in the rainy season. The highest mountains along the western coast range from 4,000 to 7,000 feet English, and the coast line is generally abrupt, though indented with numerous little bays. The opening of the Suez canal will more than restore the Red Sea to its ancient importance in the commerce of the world.   J. P. T.

RED SEA, PASSAGE OF.

The passage of the Red Sea was the crisis of the Exodus. It was the miracle by which the Israelites left Egypt and were delivered from the oppressor. Probably on this account St. Paul takes it as a type of Christian baptism. All the particulars relating to this event, and especially those which show its miraculous character, require careful examination. The points that arise are the place of the passage, the narrative, and the importance of the event in Biblical history.

1. It is usual to suppose that the most northern place at which the Red Sea could have been crossed is the present head of the Gulf of Suez. This supposition depends upon the erroneous idea that in the time of Moses the gulf did not extend further to the northward than at present. An examination of the country north of Suez has shown, however, that the sea has receded many miles, and there can be no doubt that this change has taken place within the historical period, doubtless in fulfillment of the prophecy of Isaiah (xi. 15, xix. 5: comp. Zech. x. 11). The old bed is indicated by the *Birket-et-Timsâh*, or "Lake of the Crocodile," and the more southern Bitter Lakes, the northernmost part of the former probably corresponding to the head of the gulf at the time of the Exodus. In previous centuries, it is probable that the gulf did not extend further north, but that it was deeper in its northernmost part.

It is necessary to endeavor to ascertain the route of the Israelites before we can attempt to discover where they crossed the sea. The point from which they started was Rameses, a place certainly in the Land of Goshen, which we identify with the *Wâdí-t-Tumeilât*. [RAMESES: GOSHEN.] After the mention that the people journeyed from Rameses to Succoth, and before that of their departure from Succoth, a passage occurs which appears to show the first direction of the journey, and not a change in the route. This we may reason ably infer from its tenor, and from its being followed by the statement that Joseph's bones were taken by Moses with him, which must refer to the commencement of the journey. "And it came to pass, when Pharaoh had let the people go, that God led them not [by] the way of the land of the Philistines, although that [was] near; for God said, Lest peradventure the people repent when they see war, and they return to Egypt: but God caused the people to turn

[by] the way of the wilderness of the Red Sea" (Ex. xiii. 17, 18). It will be seen by reference to the map already given [vol. i. p. 794] that, from the *Wádi-t-Tumeylát*, whether from its eastern end or from any other part, the route to Palestine by way of Gaza through the Philistine territory is near at hand. In the Roman time the route to Gaza from Memphis and Heliopolis passed the western end of the *Wádi-t-Tumeylát*, as may be seen by the *Itinerary* of Antoninus (Parthey, *Zur Erdkunde d. Alt. Ægyptens*, map vi.), and the chief modern route from Cairo to Syria passes along the *Wádi-t-Tumeylát* and leads to Gaza (Wilkinson, *Handbook*, new ed. p. 209).

At the end of the second day's journey the camping-place was at Etham "in the edge of the wilderness" (Ex. xiii. 20; Num. xxxiii. 6). Here the *Wádi-t-Tumeylát* was probably left, as it is cultivable and terminates in the desert. After leaving this place the direction seems to have changed. The first passage relating to the journey, after the mention of the encamping at Etham, is this, stating a command given to Moses: "Speak unto the children of Israel, that they turn [or 'return'] and encamp [or 'that they encamp again,' וְיָשֻׁבוּ וְיַחֲנוּ] before Pi-hahiroth, between Migdol and the sea, over against Baal-zephon" (Ex. xiv. 2). This explanation is added: "And Pharaoh will say of the children of Israel, They [are] entangled in the land, the wilderness hath shut them in" (3). The rendering of the A. V., "that they turn and encamp," seems to us the most probable of those we have given: "return" is the closer translation, but appears to be difficult to reconcile with the narrative of the route: for the more likely inference is that the direction was changed, not that the people returned: the third rendering does not appear probable, as it does not explain the entanglement. The geography of the country does not assist us in conjecturing the direction of the last part of the journey. If we knew that the highest part of the gulf at the time of the Exodus extended to the west, it would be probable that, if the Israelites turned, they took a northerly direction, as then the sea would oppose an obstacle to their further progress. If, however, they left the *Wádi-t-Tumeylát* at Etham "in the edge of the wilderness," they could not have turned far to the northward, unless they had previously turned somewhat to the south. It must be borne in mind that Pharaoh's object was to cut off the retreat of the Israelites: he therefore probably encamped between them and the head of the sea.

At the end of the third day's march, for each camping-place seems to mark the close of a day's journey, the Israelites encamped by the sea. The place of this last encampment, and that of the passage, on the supposition that our views as to the most probable route are correct, would be not very far from the Persepolitan monument. [See map, vol. i. p. 794.] The monument is about thirty miles to the northward of the present head of the Gulf of Suez, and not far south of the position where we suppose the head of the gulf to have been at the time of the Exodus. It is here neces-

sary to mention the arguments for and against the common opinion that the Israelites passed near the present head of the gulf. Local tradition is in its favor, but it must be remembered that local tradition in Egypt and the neighboring countries, judging from the evidence of history, is of very little value. The Muslims suppose Memphis to have been the city at which the Pharaoh of the Exodus resided before that event occurred. From opposite Memphis a broad valley leads to the Red Sea. It is in part called the *Wádi-t-Teeh*, or "Valley of the Wandering." From it the traveller reaches the sea beneath the lofty *Gebel-et-Tákah*,[a] which rises on the north and shuts off all escape in that direction, excepting by a narrow way along the sea-shore, which Pharaoh might have occupied. The sea here is broad and deep, as the narrative is generally held to imply. All the local features seem suited for a great event; but it may well be asked whether there is any reason to expect that suitableness that human nature seeks for and modern imagination takes for granted, since it would have been useless for the objects for which the miracle appears to have been intended. The desert-way from Memphis is equally poetical, but how is it possible to recognize in it a route which seems to have had two days' journey of cultivation, the wilderness being reached only at the end of the second day's march? The supposition that the Israelites took an upper route, now that of the Mekkeh caravan, along the desert to the north of the elevated tract between Cairo and Suez, must be mentioned, although it is less probable than that just noticed, and offers the same difficulties. It is, however, possible to suppose that the Israelites crossed the sea near Suez without holding to the traditional idea that they attained it by the *Wádi-t-Teeh*. If they went through the *Wádi-t-Tumeylát* they might have turned southward from its eastern end, and so reached the neighborhood of Suez; but this would make the third day's journey more than thirty miles at the least, which, if we bear in mind the composition of the Israelite caravan, seems quite incredible. We therefore think that the only opinion warranted by the narrative is that already stated, which supposes the passage of the sea to have taken place near the northernmost part of its ancient extension. The conjecture that the Israelites advanced to the north, then crossed a shallow part of the Mediterranean, where Pharaoh and his army were lost in the quicksands, and afterwards turned southwards towards Sinai, is so repugnant to the Scripture narrative as to amount to a denial of the occurrence of the event, and indeed is scarcely worth mentioning.

The last camping-place was before Pi-hahiroth. It appears that Migdol was behind Pi-hahiroth, and, on the other hand, Baal-zephon and the sea. These neighboring places have not been identified, and the name of Pi-hahiroth (if, as we believe, rightly supposed to designate a reedy tract, and to be still preserved in the Arabic name *Ghuweybet el-boos*, "the bed of reeds"), is now found in the neighborhood of the two supposed sites of the passage, and therefore cannot be said to be identified, besides that we must not expect a natural locality still to

---

[a] In order to favor the opinion that the Israelites took the route by the *Wadi-t-Teeh*, this name, *Gebel-et-Tákah* (to which it is difficult to assign a probable meaning), has been changed to *Gebel-'Atákah*, as if signifying "the Mountain of Deliverance;" though,

to have this signification, it should rather be *Gebel-el-'Atákah*, the other form deviating from general usage *El-Tákah* and *'Atákah* in the mouth of an Arab are widely different.

retain its name. It must be remembered that the name Pi-hahiroth, since it describes a natural locality, probably does not indicate a town or other inhabited place named after such a locality, and this seems almost certain from the circumstance that it is unlikely that there would have been more than two inhabited places, even if they were only forts, in this region. The other names do not describe natural localities. The nearness of Pi-hahiroth to the sea is therefore the only sure indication of its position, and, if we are right in our supposition as to the place of the passage, our uncertainty as to the exact extent of the sea at the time is an additional difficulty. [EXODUS, THE; PI-HA-HIROTH.]

From Pi-hahiroth the Israelites crossed the sea. The only points bearing on geography in the account of this event are that the sea was divided by an east [a] wind, whence we may reasonably infer that it was crossed from west to east, and that the whole Egyptian army perished, which shows that it must have been some miles broad. Pharaoh took at least six hundred chariots, which, three abreast, would have occupied about half a mile, and the rest of the army cannot be supposed to have taken up less than several times that space. Even if in a broad formation, some miles would have been required.[b] It is more difficult to calculate the space taken up by the Israelite multitude, but probably it was even greater. On the whole we may reasonably suppose about twelve miles as the smallest breadth of the sea.

2. A careful examination of the narrative of the passage of the Red Sea is necessary to a right understanding of the event. When the Israelites had departed, Pharaoh repented that he had let them go. It might be conjectured, from one part of the narrative (Ex. xiv. 1–4), that he determined to pursue them when he knew that they had encamped before Pi-hahiroth, did not what follows this imply that he set out soon after they had gone, and also indicate that the place in question refers to the pursuit through the sea, not to that from the city whence he started (5–10). This city was most probably Zoan, and could scarcely have been much nearer to Pi-hahiroth, and the distance is therefore too great to have been twice traversed, first by those who told Pharaoh, then by Pharaoh's army, within a few hours. The strength of Pharaoh's army is not further specified than by the statement that "he took six hundred chosen chariots, and [or ' even '] all the chariots of Egypt, and captains over every one of them " (7). The war-chariots of the Egyptians held each but two men, an archer and a charioteer.

The former must be intended by the word שָׁלִשִׁם, rendered in the A. V. "captains." Throughout the narrative the chariots and horsemen of Pharaoh are mentioned, and " the horse and his rider," xv. 21, are spoken of in Miriam's song, but we can scarcely hence infer that there was in Pharaoh's army a body of horsemen as well as of men in chariots, as in ancient Egyptian the chariot-force is always called HTAR or HETRA, " the horse," and these expressions may therefore be respectively ple-

onastic and poetical. There is no evidence in the records of the ancient Egyptians that they used cavalry. and, therefore, had the Biblical narrative expressly mentioned a force of this kind, it, might have been thought to support the theory that the Pharaoh of the Exodus was a Shepherd-king. With this army, which, even if a small one, was mighty in comparison to the Israelite multitude, encumbered with women, children, and cattle, Pharaoh overtook the people " encamping by the sea " (9). When the Israelites saw the oppressor's army they were terrified, and murmured against Moses. " Because [there were] no graves in Egypt, hast thou taken us away to die in the wilderness ? " (11). Along the bare mountains that skirt the valley of Upper Egypt are abundant sepulchral grottoes, of which the entrances are conspicuously seen from the river and the fields it waters: in the sandy slopes at the foot of the mountains are pits without number and many built tombs, all of ancient times. No doubt the plain of Lower Egypt, to which Memphis, with part of its far-extending necropolis, belonged politically though not geographically, was throughout as well provided with places of sepulture. The Israelites recalled these cities of the dead, and looked with Egyptian horror at the prospect that their carcasses should be left on the face of the wilderness. Better, they said, to have continued to serve the Egyptians than thus to perish (12). Then Moses encouraged them, bidding them see how God would save them, and telling them that they should behold their enemies no more. There are few cases in the Bible in which those for whom a miracle is wrought are commanded merely to stand by and see it. Generally the Divine support is promised to those who use their utmost exertions. It seems from the narrative that Moses did not know at this time how the people would be saved, and spoke only from a heart full of faith, for we read, " And the Lord said unto Moses, Wherefore criest thou unto me ? speak unto the children of Israel that they go forward: but lift thou up thy rod, and stretch out thine hand over the sea, and divide it: and the children of Israel shall go on dry [ground] through the midst of the sea " (15, 16). That night the two armies, the fugitives and the pursuers, were encamped near together. Between them was the pillar of the cloud, darkness to the Egyptians and a light to the Israelites. The monuments of Egypt portray an encampment of an army of Rameses II., during a campaign in Syria; it is well planned and carefully guarded: the rude modern Arab encampments bring before us that of Israel on this memorable night. Perhaps in the camp of Israel the sounds of the hostile camp might be heard on the one hand, and on the other the roaring of the sea. But the pillar was a barrier and a sign of deliverance. The time was now come for the great decisive miracle of the Exodus. "And Moses stretched out his hand over the sea: and the Lord caused the sea to go [back] by a strong east wind all that night, and made the sea dry [land], and the waters were divided. And the children of Israel went through the midst of the sea upon the dry [ground]: and the waters [were] a wall unto them on their

---

a The LXX. has " south," instead of " east." The Heb. קָדִים, lit. " in front," may, however, indicate the whole distance between the two extreme points of sunrise, those of the two solstices, and hence it is not limited to absolute east, agreeably with the use of the

Arabs in every case like the narrative under consideration.

b It has been calculated, that if Napoleon I. had advanced by one road into Belgium, in the Waterloo campaign, his column would have been sixty miles in length.

right hand and on their left " (21, 22, comp. 29). The narrative distinctly states that a path was made through the sea, and that the waters were a wall on either hand. The term "wall" does not appear to oblige us to suppose, as many have done, that the sea stood up like a cliff on either side, but should rather be considered to mean a barrier, as the former idea implies a seemingly needless addition to the miracle, while the latter seems to be not discordant with the language of the narrative. It was during the night that the Israelites crossed, and the Egyptians followed. In the morning watch, the last third or fourth of the night, or the period before sunrise, Pharaoh's army was in full pursuit in the divided sea, and was there miraculously troubled, so that the Egyptians sought to flee (23–25). Then was Moses commanded again to stretch out his hand, and the sea returned to its strength, and overwhelmed the Egyptians, of whom not one remained alive (26–28). The statement is so explicit that there could be no reasonable doubt that Pharaoh himself, the great offender, was at last made an example, and perished with his army, did it not seem to be distinctly stated in Psalm cxxxvi. that he was included in the same destruction (15). The sea cast up the dead Egyptians, whose bodies the Israelites saw upon the shore.

In a later passage some particulars are mentioned which are not distinctly stated in the narrative in Exodus. The place is indeed a poetical one, but its meaning is clear, and we learn from it that at the time of the passage of the sea there was a storm of rain with thunder and lightning, perhaps accompanied by an earthquake (Ps. lxxvii. 15–20). To this St. Paul may allude where he says that the fathers "were all baptized unto Moses in the cloud and in the sea" (1 Cor. x. 2); for the idea of baptism seems to involve either immersion or sprinkling, and the latter could have here occurred: the reference is evidently to the pillar of the cloud: it would, however, be impious to attempt an explanation of what is manifestly miraculous. These additional particulars may illustrate the troubling of the Egyptians, for their chariots may have been thus overthrown.

Here, at the end of their long oppression, delivered finally from the Egyptians, the Israelites glorified God. In what words they sang his praise we know from the Song of Moses, which, in its vigorous brevity, represents the events of that memorable night, scarcely of less moment than the night of the Passover (Ex. xv. 1–18: ver. 19 is probably a kind of comment, not part of the song). Moses seems to have sung this song with the men, Miriam with the women also singing and dancing, or perhaps there were two choruses (20, 21). Such a picture does not recur in the history of the nation. Neither the triumphal Song of Deborah, nor the rejoicing when the Temple was recovered from the Syrians, celebrated so great a deliverance, or was joined in by the whole people. In leaving Goshen, Israel became a nation; after crossing the sea, it was free. There is evidently great significance, as we have suggested, in St. Paul's use of this mira-

cle as a type of baptism; for, to make the analogy complete, it must have been the beginning of a new period of the life of the Israelites.

3. The importance of this event in Biblical history is shown by the manner in which it is spoken of in the books of the O. T. written in later times. In them it is the chief fact of Jewish history. Not the call of Abraham, not the rule of Joseph, not the first Passover, not the conquest of Canaan, are referred to in such a manner as this great deliverance. In the Book of Job it is mentioned with the acts of creation (xxvi. 10–13). In the Psalms it is related as foremost among the deeds that God had wrought for his people. The prophet Isaiah recalls it as the great manifestation of God's interference for Israel, and an encouragement for the descendants of those who witnessed that great sight. There are events so striking that they are remembered in the life of a nation, and that, like great heights, increasing distance only gives them more majesty. So no doubt was this remembered long after those were dead who saw the sea return to its strength and the warriors of Pharaoh dead upon the shore.

It may be inquired how it is that there seems to have been no record or tradition of this miracle among the Egyptians. This question involves that of the time in Egyptian history to which this event should be assigned. The date of the Exodus according to different chronologers varies more than three hundred years; the dates of the Egyptian dynasties ruling during this period of three hundred years vary full one hundred. The period to which the Exodus may be assigned therefore virtually corresponds to four hundred years of Egyptian history. If the lowest date of the beginning of the XVIIIth dynasty be taken and the highest date of the Exodus, both which we consider the most probable of those which have been conjectured in the two cases, the Israelites must have left Egypt in a period of which monuments or other records are almost wanting. Of the XVIIIth and subsequent dynasties we have as yet no continuous history, and rarely records of events which occurred in a succession of years. We know much of many reigns, and of some we can be almost sure that they could not correspond to that of the Pharaoh of the Exodus. We can in no case expect a distinct Egyptian monumental record of so great a calamity, for the monuments only record success; but it might be related in a papyrus. There would doubtless have long remained a popular tradition of the Exodus, but if the king who perished was one of the Shepherd strangers, this tradition would probably have been local, and perhaps indistinct.[a]

Endeavors have been made to explain away the miraculous character of the passage of the Red Sea. It has been argued that Moses might have carried the Israelites over by a ford, and that an unusual tide might have overwhelmed the Egyptians. But no real diminution of the wonder is thus effected. How was it that the sea admitted the passing of the Israelites, and drowned Pharaoh and his army? How was it that it was shallow at

---

a While this article is going through the press, M. Chabas has published a curious paper, in which he conjectures that certain laborers employed by the Pharaohs of the XIXth and XXth dynasties in the quarries and elsewhere are the Hebrews. Their name reads APERIU or APERUI, which might correspond to

"Hebrews" עִבְרִים ; but his finding them still in Egypt under Rameses IV., about B. C. 1200, certainly after the latest date of the Exodus, is a fatal objection to an identification with the Israelites.

the right time, and deep at the right time? This attempted explanation would never have been put forward were it not that the fact of the passage is so well attested that it would be uncritical to doubt it were it recorded on mere human authority. Since the fact is undeniable, an attempt is made to explain it away. Thus the school that pretends to the severest criticism is compelled to deviate from its usual course; and when we see that in this case it must do so, we may well doubt its ? ?ndness in other cases, which, being differ-n..y stated, are more easily attacked.   R. S. P.

* The opening of the Suez Canal may contribute to the solution of the problem of the route of the Israelites from Raamses to the Red Sea. The sweet-water canal, which flows from the Nile eastward through *Wadi-t-Tumeylat*, has already restored to a region of the ancient Goshen, a degree of fertility which suggests that this may truly have been " the best of the land " in the time of the Israelites, when, under the ancient system of irrigation, it was watered with " streams, rivers, ponds, and pools," Ex. vii. 19. This canal runs from the Nile to *Ismaila*, a new town on Lake Timsah, and thence southward to Suez. It is twenty-six feet wide with an average depth of four feet, and by means of lateral sluices is made to irrigate a large area. So valuable is it for this purpose, that the Egyptian government purchased it of the Canal Company at a cost of four hundred thousand pounds, expecting to reimburse itself by the enhanced value of lands.

Unruh (*Der Zug den Israeliten aus Ägypten nach Canaan*) places the Land of Goshen in the northeastern portion of the Delta, with a sea-coast on the Mediterranean from Tanis to Avaris, and Raamses in the vicinity of the latter city. He first carries the Israelites around the head of the gulf, which then extended as a reedy marsh far above the modern Suez; then leads them down upon the *east* side of the gulf to a point opposite Suez, where he finds a small bay or arm of the gulf projecting into the Arabian peninsula, — a little above *Ayun Musa*, — and thus he makes the scene of the crossing narrated in Exodus. At the opposite extreme, Schleiden (*Die Landenge von Sues*) places Raamses in the line of the ancient canal, and near the Bitter Lakes, but first turns the course of the Israelites northward toward the Mediterranean, as the direct route to Palestine. They are overtaken on the coast of the Mediterranean, in a marshy region, lying east of Avaris upon the borders of the wilderness: having *here* escaped from Pharaoh, they turn southward and enter the desert of Sinai, keeping always to the east of the Gulf of Suez. But these theories equally violate the requirements of the narrative of the Exodus in respect of the successive days' marches of the Israelites. The distance from Raamses to the head of the gulf was about thirty miles, and so great a caravan as the Israelites with their cattle and attendants made, would require three days for such a march. The second day would bring them to about the line between the head of the gulf and the Bitter Lakes on the edge of the great eastern desert. From this " Etham " they turned backward, and went down the western side of the gulf to the vicinity of Suez, — and at this point, probably, the crossing took place. " The miracle was wrought by natural means supernaturally applied. A strong N. E. wind acting here upon the ebb tide, would necessarily have the effect to drive out the waters from

the small arm of the sea which runs up by Suez, and also from the end of the gulf itself, leaving the shallower portions dry; while the more northern part of the arm, which was anciently broader and deeper than at present, would still remain covered with water. Thus the waters would be divided, and be a wall to the Israelites on the right hand and on the left." No better theory of the place of the crossing and the manner of the miracle has been presented than this of Dr. E. Robinson (*Researches*, i. 54–59). It harmonizes well all the details of the narrative. The arm of the gulf stretching north of Suez thus becomes a condition of the fulfillment of the miracle.   J. P. T.

REED. Under this name we propose noticing the following Hebrew words: *agmón, góme, 'aróth,* and *kaneh.*

1. *Agmón* (אַגְמוֹן: κρίκος, ἔνθραξ, μικρός, τέλος: *circulus, fervens, refrenans*) occurs Job xl. 26 (A. V. xli. 2), "Canst thou put *agmón*" (A. V. " hook ") into the nose of the crocodile? Again, in xl. 12 (A. V. xli. 20), " out of his nostrils goeth smoke, as out of a seething-pot or *agmón*" (A. V. " caldron "). In Is. ix. 14, it is said Jehovah " will cut off from Israel head and tail, branch and *agmón*" (A. V. " rush "). The *agmón* is mentioned also as an Egyptian plant, in a sentence similar to the last, in Is. xix. 15; while from lviii. 5 we learn that the *agmón* had a pendulous panicle. There can be no doubt that the *agmón* denotes some aquatic reed-like plant, whether of the Nat. order *Cyperaceæ* or that of *Gramineæ*. The term is allied closely to the Hebrew *ágám* (אֲגַם), which, like the corresponding Arabic *ajam*

(أَجِمْ), denotes a marshy pool or reed-bed.[a] (See Jer. li. 32, for this latter signification.) There is some doubt as to the specific identity of the *agmón*, some believing that the word denotes " a rush " as well as a " reed." See Rosenmüller (*Bibl Bot.* p. 184) and Winer (*Realwörterb.* ii. 484). Celsius has argued in favor of the *Arundo phragmitis* (*Hierob.* i. 465); we are inclined to adopt his opinion. That the *agmón* denotes some specific plant is probable both from the passages where it occurs as well as from the fact that *kaneh* (קָנֶה) is the generic term for reeds in general. The *Arundo phragmitis* (now the *Phragmitis communis*), if it does not occur in Palestine and Egypt, is represented by a very closely allied species, namely, the *A. isiaca* of Delisle. The drooping panicle of this plant will answer well to the " bowing down the head " of which Isaiah speaks; but, as there are other kinds of reed-like plants to which this character also belongs, it is impossible to do more than give a probable conjecture. The expression " Canst thou put an *agmón*" into the crocodile's nose? has been variously explained. The most probable interpretation is that which supposes allusion is made to the mode of passing a reed or a rush through the gills of fish in order to carry them home; but see the Commentaries and Notes of

---

[a] أَجِمْ. " Densi frutices, arundinetum, palus." (Freytag.)

Rosenmüller, Schultens, Lee, Cary, Mason Good, etc. The *agmôn* of Job xli. 20 seems to be derived from an Arabic root signifying to " be burning: " hence the *ferrens* of the Vulg. The *Phragmitis* belongs to the Nat. order *Graminaceæ*.

2. *Gôme*, (גֹּמֶא : πάπειρος, βίβλινος, ἕλος: *scirpeus, scirpus, papyrus, iuncus*), translated " rush " and " bulrush " by the A. V., without doubt denotes the celebrated paper-reed of the ancients (*Papyrus Antiquorum*), a plant of the Sedge family, *Cyperaceæ*, which formerly was common in some parts of Egypt. The Hebrew word is found four times in the Bible. Moses was hid in a vessel

Papyrus antiquorum.

made of the papyrus (Ex. ii. 3). Transit boats were made out of the same material by the Ethiopians (Is. xviii. 2); the paper-reed is mentioned together with *Káneh*, the usual generic term for a " reed," in Is. xxxv. 7, and in Job viii. 11, where it is asked, " Can the papyrus plant grow without mire? " The modern Arabic name of this plant is *Berdî* (بَرْدِي). According to Bruce the modern Abyssinians use boats made of the papyrus reed; Ludolf (*Hist. Æthiop.* i. 8) speaks of the Tzamic lake being navigated " monoxylis lintribus ex typha præcrassa confertis," a kind of sailing, he

says, which is attended with considerable danger to the navigators. Wilkinson (*Anc. Ægypt.* ii. 96, ed. 1854) says that the right of growing and selling the papyrus plants belonged to the government, who made a profit by its monopoly, and thinks other species of the *Cyperaceæ* must be understood as affording all the various articles, such as baskets, canoes, sails, sandals, etc., which have been said to have been made from the real papyrus. Considering that Egypt abounds in *Cyperaceæ*, many kinds of which might have served for forming canoes, etc., it is improbable that the papyrus alone should have been used for such a purpose: but that the true *papyrus* was used for boats there can be no doubt, if the testimony of Theophrastus (*Hist. Pl.* iv. 8, § 4), Pliny (*H. N.* xiii. 11), Plutarch, and other ancient writers, is to be believed.

From the soft cellular portion of the stem the ancient material called papyrus was made. " Papyri," says Sir G. Wilkinson, " are of the most remote Pharaonic periods. The mode of making them was as follows: the interior of the stalks of the plant, after the rind had been removed, was cut into thin slices in the direction of their length, and these being laid on a flat board in succession, similar slices were placed over them at right angles, and their surfaces being cemented together by a sort of glue, and subjected to a proper degree of pressure and well dried, the papyrus was completed; the length of the slices depend, of course on the breadth of the intended sheet, as that of the sheet on the number of slices placed in succession beside each other, so that though the breadth was limited the papyrus might be extended to an indefinite length." [WRITING.] The papyrus reed is not now found in Egypt: it grows, however, in Syria. Dr. Hooker saw it on the banks of Lake Tiberias, a few miles north of the town: it appears to have existed there since the days of Theophrastus and Pliny, who give a very accurate description of this interesting plant. Theophrastus (*Hist. Plant.* iv. 8, § 4) says, " The papyrus grows also in Syria around the lake in which the sweet-scented reed is found, from which Antigonus used to make cordage for his ships." [a] (See also Pliny, *H. N.* xiii. 11.) This plant has been found also in a small stream two miles N. of Jaffa. Dr. Hooker believes it is common in some parts of Syria: it does not occur anywhere else in Asia: it was seen by Lady Callcott on the banks of the Anapus, near Syracuse, and Sir Joseph Banks possessed paper made of papyrus from the Lake of Thrasymene (*Script. Herb.* p. 379). The Hebrew name of this plant is derived from a root which means " to absorb," compare Lucan (*Phars.* iv. 136).[b] The lower part of the papyrus reed was used as food by the ancient Egyptians; " those who wish to eat the byblus dressed in the most delicate way, stew it in a hot pan and then eat it " (Herod ii. 92: see also Theophr. *Hist. Plant.* iv. 9). The statement of Theophrastus with regard to the sweetness and flavor of the sap has been confirmed by some writers; the Chevalier Landolina made papyrus from the pith of the plant, which, says Heeren (*Histor. Res. Afric. Nat.*, ii. 350, *note*), " is rather clearer than the Egyptian;" but other writers say the

---

a * The papyrus is very abundant in a swamp at the north end of the Plain of Gennesaret, and also covers many acres on the marshy shores of *Huleh*, the ancient Merom. These two places and Jaffa (see above) are said to be the only places in Asia where this plant is known to exist at the present day (Tristram, *Nat. Hist. of the Bible*, p. 433).   H.

b " Conseritur bibula Memphitis cymba papyro "

stem is neither juicy nor agreeable. The papyrus plant (*Papyrus antiquorum*) has an angular stem from 3 to 6 feet high, though occasionally it grows to the height of 14 feet; it has no leaves; the flowers are in very small spikelets, which grow on the threadlike flowering branchlets which form a bushy crown to each stem: it is found in stagnant pools as well as in running streams, in which latter case, according to Bruce, one of its angles is always opposed to the current of the stream.

3. 'Ardth (עָרוֹה: τὸ ἄχι τὸ χλωρὸν πᾶν[a]) is translated " paper-reed " in Is. xix. 7, the only passage where the pl. noun occurs; there is not the slightest authority for this rendering of the A. V., nor is it at all probable, as Celsius (*Hierob.* ii. 230) has remarked, that the prophet who speaks of the paper-reed under the name *góme* in the preceding chapter (xviii. 2), should in this one mention the same plant under a totally different name. "*Aroth*," says Kimchi, " is the name to designate pot-herbs and green plants." The LXX. translate it by " all the green herbage " (comp. אוֹרֹת, Gen. xli. 2, and see FLAG). The word is derived from '*áráh*, " to be bare," or " destitute of trees;" it probably denotes the open grassy land on the banks of the Nile; and seems to be allied to the Arabic '*ará*

(عَرَاء), *locus apertus*, *spatiosus.* Michaelis (*Suppl.* No. 1973), Rosenmüller (*Schol. in Jes.* xix. 7), Gesenius (*Thes.* s. v.), Maurer (*Comment.* s. v.), and Simonis (*Lex. Heb.* s. v.), are all in favor of this or a similar explanation. Vitringa (*Comment. in Isaiam*) was of opinion that the Hebrew term denoted the papyrus, and he has been followed by J. G. Unger, who has published a dissertation on this subject (*De* עָרוֹת, *hoc est de Papyro frutice, von der Papier-Staude, ad* Is. xiv. 7; Lips. 1731, 4to).

4. *Káneh* (קָנֶה: κάλαμος, καλαμίσκος, καλάμινος, πῆχος, ἀγκών, ζυγός, πυθμήν: *culmus, calamus, arundo, fistula, statera*), the generic name of a reed of any kind; it occurs in numerous passages of the O. T., and sometimes denotes the " stalk " of wheat (Gen. xli. 5, 22), or the " branches " of the candlestick (Ex. xxv. and xxxvii.); in Job xxxi. 22, *káneh* denotes the bone of the arm between the elbow and the shoulder (*os humeri*); it was also the name of a measure of length equal to six cubits (Ez. xli. 8, xl. 5). The word is variously rendered in the A. V. by " stalk," " branch," " bone," " calamus," " reed." In the N. T. κάλαμος may signify the " stalk " of plants (Mark xv. 36; Matt. xxvii. 48, that of the hyssop, but this is doubtful), or " a reed " (Matt. xi. 7, xii. 20; Luke vii. 24; Mark xv. 19); or " a measuring rod " (Rev. xi. 1, xxi. 15, 16); or a " pen " (3 John 13). Strand (*Flor. Palæst.* pp. 28–30) gives the following names of the reed plants of Palestine: *Saccharum officinale, Cyperus papyrus (Papyrus antiquorum), C. rotundus*, and *C. esculentus*, and *Arundo scriptoria*; but no doubt the species are numerous. See Bové (*Voyage en Palest., Annal. des Scienc. Nat.* 1834, p. 165), " Dans les déserts qui environnent ces montagnes j'ai trouvé plusieurs

Saccharum, Milium arundinaceum et plusieurs Cypéracé." The *Arundo donax*, the *A. Ægyptiaca* (?) of Bové (*Ibid.* p. 72), is common on the banks of the Nile, and may perhaps be " the staff " of the bruised reed " to which Sennacherib compared the power of Egypt (2 K. xviii. 21; Ez. xxix. 6, 7). See also Is. xlii. 3. The thick stem of this reed may have been used as walking-staves by the ancient Orientals; perhaps the measuring-reed was this plant; at present the dry culms of this huge grass are in much demand for fishing-rods, etc.

Some kind of fragrant reed is denoted by the word *kéneh* (Is. xliii. 24; Ez. xxvii. 19; Cant. iv. 14), or more fully by *kéneh bósem* (קְנֵה בֹשֶׂם), see Ex. xxx. 23, or by *káneh hattób* (קָנֶה הַטּוֹב), Jer. vi 20; which the A. V. renders " sweet cane," and " calamus." Whatever may be the substance denoted, it is certain that it was one of foreign importation, " from a far country " (Jer. vi. 20). Some writers (see Sprengel, *Com. in Dioscor.* i., xvii.) have sought to identify the *káneh bósem* with the *Acorus calamus*, the " sweet sedge," to which

Arundo donax.

they refer the κάλαμος ἀρωματικός of Dioscorides (i. 17), the κάλαμος εὐώδης of Theophrastus (*Hist. Plant.* iv. 8 § 4), which, according to this lastnamed writer and Pliny (*H. N.* xii. 22), formerly grew about a lake " between Libanus and another mountain of no note; " Strabo identifies this with the Lake of Gennesaret (*Geog.* xvi. p. 755, ed. Kramer). Burckhardt was unable to discover any sweet-scented reed or rush near the lake, though he saw many tall reeds there. " High reeds grow along the shore, but I found none of the aromatic reeds and rushes mentioned by Strabo " (*Syria*, p. 319); but whatever may be the " fragrant reed " intended, it is certain that it did not grow in Syria, otherwise we cannot suppose it should be spoken of as a valuable product from a far country. Dr. Royle refers the κάλαμος ἀ ρωματικός of Dioscorides to a

---

[a] It is difficult to see how the Vulg. understood the term

species of *Andropogon*, which he calls *A. calamus aromaticus*, a plant of remarkable fragrance, and a native of Central India, where it is used to mix with ointments on account of the delicacy of its odor (see Kitto's *Cycl.* Art. " *Kaneh bosem;* " and a fig. of this plant in Royle's *Illustrations of Himalayan Botany*, p. 425. t. 97). It is possible this may be the "reed of fragrance; " but it is hardly likely that Dioscorides, who, under the term σχοῖνος gives a description of the *Andropogon Schœnanthus*, should speak of a closely allied species under a totally different name. Still there is no necessity to refer the *Kĕnĕh bósem* or *hattôb* to the κάλαμος ἀρωματικός of Dioscorides; it may be

Andropogon Schœnanthus.

represented by Dr. Royle's plant or by the *Andropogon Schœnanthus*, the lemon grass of India and Arabia.   W. H.

REËLAIAH [4 syl.] (רְעֵלָיָה [*who trembles before Jehovah*, Ges.]: Ῥεελίας; [Vat. Πεελαια:] *Raheïña*). One of the children of the province who went up with Zerubbabel (Ezr. ii. 2). In Neh. vii. 7 he is called RAAMIAH, and in 1 Esdr. v. 8 REESAIAS.

REËLIUS (Ῥεελίας; [Vat. Βοραλειας]).

This name occupies the place of BIGVAI in Esr. ii. 2 (1 Esdr. v. 8). The list in the Vulgate is so corrupt that it is difficult to trace either.

REËSAIAS [4 syl.] (Ῥησαίας; [Ald. Ῥεεσαίας:] *Elimeus*). The same as REELAIAH or RAAMIAH (1 Esdr. v. 8).

REFINER (צָרַף; מְצָרֵף). The refiner's art was essential to the working of the precious metals. It consisted in the separation of the dross from the pure ore, which was effected by reducing the metal to a fluid state by the application of heat, and by the aid of solvents, such as alkali [a] (Is. i. 25) or lead (Jer. vi. 29), which, amalgamating with the dross, permitted the extraction of the unadulterated metal. The term [b] usually applied to refining had reference to the process of melting: occasionally, however, the effect of the process is described by a term [c] borrowed from the filtering of wine. The instruments required by the refiner were a crucible or furnace,[d] and a bellows or blowpipe.[e] The workman sat at his work (Mal. iii. 3, " He shall sit as a refiner "), as represented in the cut of an Egyptian refiner already given (see vol. ii. p. 992): he was thus better enabled to watch the process, and let the metal run off at the proper moment. [MINES, p. 1939.] The notices of refining are chiefly of a figurative character, and describe moral purification as the result of chastisement (Is. i. 25; Zech. xiii. 9; Mal. iii. 2, 3). The failure of the means to effect the result is graphically depicted in Jer. vi. 29: " The bellows glow with the fire (become quite hot from exposure to the heat): the lead (used as a solvent) is expended :[f] the refiner melts in vain, for the refuse will not be separated." The refiner appears, from the passage whence this is quoted, to have combined with his proper business that of assaying metals: " I have set thee for an assayer " [g] (*lb.* ver. 27).   W. L. B.

* **REFRAIN** formerly signified to bridle, or hold in check (as in Latin *refrœnare*). So in Prov. x. 19: " He that refraineth his lips is wise."   H.

REFUGE, CITIES OF. [CITIES OF REFUGE.]

RE'GEM (רֶגֶם [*friend, i. e. of God*, Ges.]: Ῥαγέμ: Alex. Ῥεγεμ: *Regom*). A son of Jahdai, whose name unaccountably appears in a list of the descendants of Caleb by his concubine Ephah (1 Chr. ii. 47). Rashi considers Jahdai as the son of Ephah, but there appear no grounds for this assumption.

---

[a] צֶבֶר; A. V. " purely," but more properly " as with alkali."

[b] צָרַף.   [c] זָקַק.

[d] כּוּר. The term מְצָרֵף occurs twice only (Prov. xvii. 3, xxvii. 21; A. V. " fining-pot "). The expression in Ps. xii. 6, rendered in the A. V. " furnace of earth," is of doubtful signification, but certainly cannot signify that. The passage may be rendered, " as silver, melted in a workshop, flowing down to the earth."

[e] מַפֻּחַ.   [f] Keri, תַּם תֵּאָשׁ.

[g] בָּחוֹן. The A. V. adopts an incorrect punctuation, בָּחוּן, and renders it " a tower."